Big Book of Colleges

Edited By
Amy Campbell, Matt Hamman,
Bridget Daley, and Jen Vella

Additional Contributions By
Mark Benvenuto, Omid Gohari,
and Luke Skurman

ISBN: 978-1-4274-0008-6
© Copyright 2009 College Prowler
All Rights Reserved
Printed in the U.S.A.
www.collegeprowler.com

Special Thanks To: Roland Allen, Chris Babyak, Adam Burns, Babs Carryer, Jared Cohon, The Donald H. Jones Center for Entrepreneurship, Meghan Dowdell, Bill Ecenberger, Thomas Emerson, Mark Exler, Daniel Fayock, Andy Hannah, David Koegler, Christina Koshzow, LaunchCyte, Dave Lehman, Christopher Mason, Jerry McGinnis, Idie McGinty, Glen Meakem, Kimberly Moore, Jaime Myers, Abu Noaman, Gabriela Oates, Tim O'Brien, Carrie Petersen, Alyson Pope, Joey Rahimi, Jesse Rapsack, Jon Reider, Kyle Russell, Bob Sehlinger, Jon Skindzier, Terry Slease, Daniel Steinmeyer, Meryl Sustarsic, Team Evankovich, Lauren Varacalli, Larry Winderbaum, Jacque Zaremba, and the College Prowler student authors.

College Prowler®
5001 Baum Blvd.
Suite 750
Pittsburgh, PA 15213

Phone:	1(800) 290-2682
Fax:	1(800) 772-4972
E-mail:	info@collegeprowler.com
Web:	collegeprowler.com

Welcome to College Prowler

During the writing of College Prowler's guidebooks, we felt it was critical that our content was unbiased and unaffiliated with any college or university. We think it's important that our readers get honest information and a realistic impression of the student opinions on any campus—that's why if any aspect of a particular school is terrible, we (unlike a campus brochure) intend to publish it. While we do keep an eye out for the occasional extremist—the cheerleader or the cynic—we take pride in letting the students tell it like it is. We strive to create a book that's as representative as possible of each particular campus. Our books cover both the good and the bad, and whether the survey responses point to recurring trends or a variation in opinion, these sentiments are directly and proportionally expressed through our guides.

College Prowler guidebooks are in the hands of students throughout the entire process of their creation. Because you can't make student-written guides without the students, we have students at each campus who help write, randomly survey their peers, edit, layout, and perform accuracy checks on every book that we publish. From the very beginning, student writers gather the most up-to-date stats, facts, and inside information on their colleges. They fill each section with student quotes and summarize the findings in editorial reviews. In addition, each school receives a collection of letter grades (A through F) that reflect student opinion and help to represent contentment, prominence, or satisfaction for each of our specific categories. Just as in grade school, the higher the mark, the more content, more prominent, or more satisfied the students are with the particular category.

Once a book is written, additional students serve as editors and check for accuracy even more extensively. Our bounce-back team—a group of randomly selected students who have no involvement with the project—are asked to read over the material in order to help ensure that the book accurately expresses every aspect of the university and its students.

This same process is applied to the 200-plus schools College Prowler currently covers. Each book is the result of endless student contributions, hundreds of pages of research and writing, and countless hours of hard work. All of this has led to the creation of a student information network that stretches across the nation to every school that we cover. It's no easy accomplishment, but it's the reason that our guides are such a great resource.

When reading our books and looking at our grades, keep in mind that every college is different and that the students who make up each school are not uniform—as a result, it is important to assess schools on a case-by-case basis. Because it's impossible to summarize an entire school with a single number or description, each book provides a dialogue, not a decision, that's made up of different topics and hundreds of student quotes. In the end, we hope that this guide will serve as a valuable tool in your college selection process. Enjoy!

What's in This Book?

Rankings & Grades

Picking a college is hard, but we're here to help. The lists at the beginning of this book group each school in a variety of categories. Interested in location, size, or selectivity? Check the lists. Curious about which schools have the best dining, dorms, or local atmosphere? We rank those, too. Cross-compare between the different lists to find the schools that match all of your needs.

TIP: First, decide what's important to you. Are you a party animal or straight-laced? A sports nut or a bookworm? A city kid or a nature-lover? Numbers and rankings can never provide the final answer; this is why we cover everything from academics to dining. It might be helpful to make some notes that detail what each category means to you. It's your four years—make the most of it.

Individual School Profiles

Dive into our school-specific sections and find out why those colleges you have your eye on scored well in one category and poor in another. Just like the original College Prowler guidebooks, each school's section is student-written and provides its own unique dialogue to help you discover if the college is right for you.

Each in-depth section dedicates four complete pages to a specific school and provides stats, reviews, and student quotes on a sampling of our categories of consideration. There's also a report card for each school that lists student satisfaction grades for all of the 20 areas we cover.

Verbal Outtakes

We come across a lot of crazy student quotes, so we figured we'd share. Flip through these pages if you need a good laugh. Choosing a college doesn't have to be so stressful.

Words to Know

Learn a few new words to stay in the know.

About the Authors

Each college's section was written by its own student author. Read this for more information about each writer and check out their advice. Good luck with your college search—maybe you'll be the next student to write a College Prowler guidebook!

Need More?

Once you've narrowed down your choices, check out College Prowler's expanded single-school guides—160 pages of inside information on each school with even more student quotes, admissions statistics, and categories. Great for campus visits, making your final decision, and preparing for your first year, Off the Record guidebooks are your last stop in the college search process.

For more help, visit collegeprowler.com.

BIG BOOK OF COLLEGES
Table of Contents

Region

North

Alfred University
Allegheny College
American University
Amherst College
Babson College
Bard College
Barnard College
Baruch College
Bates College
Bentley College
Binghamton University
Boston College
Boston University
Bowdoin College
Brandeis University
Brown University
Bryn Mawr College
Bucknell University
Carnegie Mellon University
Catholic University of America
Clark University (MA)
Colby College
Colgate University
College of the Holy Cross
Columbia University
Connecticut College
Cornell University
Dartmouth College
Dickinson College
Drexel University
Duquesne University
Emerson College
Fashion Institute of Technology
Fordham University
Franklin & Marshall College
Geneva College
George Washington University
Georgetown University
Gettysburg College
Goucher College
Grove City College
Hamilton College
Hampshire College
Harvard University
Haverford College
Hofstra University
Howard University
Hunter College
Ithaca College
Johns Hopkins University
Juniata College
La Roche College
Lafayette College
Lehigh University
Loyola College in Maryland
Manhattan College
Manhattanville College
Marlboro College
McGill University
Middlebury College
MIT
Mount Holyoke College
Muhlenberg College
New York University
Northeastern University
Penn State University
Princeton University
Providence College
Rensselaer Polytechnic Institute
Rhode Island School of Design
Rochester Institute of Technology
Rutgers New Brunswick
Saint Joseph's University
Sarah Lawrence College
Seton Hall University
Simmons College

Skidmore College
Slippery Rock University
Smith College
St. John's University
Stony Brook University
Susquehanna University
Swarthmore College
Syracuse University
Temple University
Towson University
Trinity College (CT)
Tufts University
Union College
University at Albany
University at Buffalo
University of Connecticut
University of Delaware
University of Maine
University of Maryland
University of Massachusetts
University of New Hampshire
University of Pennsylvania
University of Pittsburgh
University of Rhode Island
University of Rochester
University of Vermont
Ursinus College
Vassar College
Villanova University
Washington & Jefferson College
Wellesley College
Wesleyan University
West Point Military Academy
Wheaton College (MA)
Wilkes University
Williams College
Yale University

South

Auburn University
Birmingham-Southern College
Centenary College of Louisiana
Centre College
Clark Atlanta University
Clemson University
College of Charleston
College of William & Mary
Davidson College
Duke University
East Carolina University
Elon University
Emory University
Florida State University
Furman University
Georgia Institute of Technology
Guilford College
Hampton University
Hollins University
James Madison University
Louisiana State University
Middle Tennessee State University
Millsaps College
New College of Florida
North Carolina State University
Old Dominion University
Radford University
Rhodes College
Rollins College
Spelman College
Stetson University
Tennessee State University
Tulane University
University of Alabama
University of Central Florida
University of Florida
University of Georgia
University of Kentucky

University of Louisville
University of Miami
University of Mississippi
University of North Carolina
Univ. of North Carolina – Greensboro
University of Richmond
University of South Carolina
University of South Florida
University of Tennessee
University of Virginia
Vanderbilt University
Virginia Commonwealth University
Virginia Tech
Wake Forest University
Warren Wilson College
Washington and Lee University
West Virginia University

West

Arizona State University
Baylor University
Brigham Young University
Cal Poly
Cal Poly Pomona
Cal State Northridge
Caltech
Claremont McKenna College
Colorado College
Gonzaga University
Harvey Mudd College
Idaho State University
Lewis & Clark College
Loyola Marymount University
Montana State University
Northern Arizona University
Occidental College
Pepperdine University
Pitzer College
Pomona College
Reed College
Rice University
Sacramento State
San Diego State University
Santa Clara University
Scripps College
Seattle University
Southern Methodist University
Southwestern University
Stanford University
Texas A&M University
Texas Christian University
Texas Tech University
Trinity University (TX)
UC Berkeley
UC Davis
UC Irvine
UC Riverside
UC San Diego
UC Santa Barbara
UC Santa Cruz
UCLA
University of Arizona
University of Colorado
University of Denver
University of Montana
University of Oklahoma
University of Oregon
University of Puget Sound
University of San Diego
University of San Francisco
University of South Dakota
University of Southern California
University of Texas
University of Utah
University of Washington
UNLV
Whitman College
Willamette University

Midwest

Albion College
Alverno College
Ball State University
Beloit College
Bradley University
Carleton College
Case Western Reserve University
College of Wooster
Creighton University
Denison University
DePaul University
DePauw University
Earlham College
Grinnell College
Gustavus Adolphus College
Hanover College
Hastings College
Illinois State University
Illinois Wesleyan University
Indiana University
Iowa State University
IUPUI
Kansas State University
Kent State University
Kenyon College
Lawrence University
Loyola University Chicago
Luther College
Macalester College
Marquette University
Miami University
Michigan State University
Northern Illinois University
Northwestern University
Oberlin College
Ohio State University
Ohio University
Ohio Wesleyan University
Purdue University
St. Louis University
St. Olaf College
Truman State University
University of Chicago
University of Cincinnati
University of Illinois
University of Iowa
University of Kansas
University of Michigan
University of Minnesota
University of Missouri
University of Nebraska
University of Notre Dame
University of Wisconsin
University of Wisconsin – Stout
Valparaiso University
Washington University in St. Louis
Wheaton College (IL)
Wright State University
Xavier University

Note: *Northern schools are located in Connecticut, Delaware, District of Columbia, Maine, Maryland, Massachusetts, New Hampshire, New Jersey, New York, Pennsylvania, Rhode Island, and Vermont.*

Southern schools are located in Alabama, Florida, Georgia, Kentucky, Louisiana, Mississippi, North Carolina, South Carolina, Tennessee, Virginia, and West Virginia.

Western schools are located in Arizona, California, Colorado, Idaho, Montana, Nevada, Oklahoma, Oregon, South Dakota, Texas, Utah, and Washington.

Midwestern schools are located in Illinois, Indiana, Iowa, Kansas, Michigan, Minnesota, Missouri, Nebraska, Ohio, and Wisconsin.

Environment

Urban

Alverno College
American University
Barnard College
Baruch College
Birmingham-Southern College
Boston University
Bradley University
Brown University
Carnegie Mellon University
Case Western Reserve University
Catholic University of America
Centenary College of Louisiana
Clark Atlanta University
Colorado College
Columbia University
Creighton University
DePaul University
Drexel University
Duke University
Duquesne University
Emerson College
Fashion Institute of Technology
Fordham University
George Washington University
Georgetown University
Georgia Institute of Technology
Gonzaga University
Guilford College
Harvard University
Howard University
Hunter College
IUPUI
Johns Hopkins University
Lewis & Clark College
Louisiana State University
Loyola College in Maryland
Loyola University Chicago
Macalester College
Manhattan College
Marquette University
McGill University
MIT
New College of Florida
New York University
North Carolina State University
Northeastern University
Occidental College
Ohio State University
Old Dominion University
Providence College
Reed College
Rhode Island School of Design
Rhodes College
Rice University
Rochester Institute of Technology
Sacramento State
Saint Joseph's University
San Diego State University
Seattle University
Simmons College
Southern Methodist University
Spelman College
St. John's University
St. Louis University
Temple University
Tennessee State University
Texas Christian University
Trinity University
Tulane University
UC Irvine
UC Riverside
UCLA
University at Buffalo
University of Arizona
University of Central Florida
University of Chicago
University of Cincinnati
University of Denver
University of Kentucky
University of Louisville
University of Miami
University of Minnesota
University of Nebraska
Univ. of North Carolina–Greensboro
University of Pennsylvania
University of Pittsburgh
University of Richmond
University of Rochester
University of San Diego
University of San Francisco
University of South Florida
University of Southern California
University of Texas
University of Washington
University of Wisconsin
UNLV
Vanderbilt University
Washington University in St. Louis
Xavier University
Yale University

Suburban

Babson College
Bates College
Bentley College
Boston College
Bowdoin College
Brandeis University
Brigham Young University
Bryn Mawr College
Cal State Northridge
Caltech
Claremont McKenna College
College of Wooster
Connecticut College
Davidson College
Denison University
Emory University
Geneva College
Goucher College
Harvey Mudd College
Haverford College
Hofstra University
Kansas State University
Kent State University
La Roche College
Loyola Marymount University
Manhattanville College
Michigan State University
Middle Tennessee State University
Northwestern University
Ohio Wesleyan University
Pepperdine University
Pitzer College
Pomona College
Princeton University
Rollins College
Sarah Lawrence College
Scripps College
Seton Hall University
Skidmore College
Southwestern University
Stanford University
Stetson University
Stony Brook University
Towson University
Tufts University
UC Davis
UC San Diego
University of Delaware
University of Maryland
University of North Carolina
Ursinus College

Valparaiso University
Vassar College
Villanova University
Washington & Jefferson College
Wellesley College
West Point Military Academy
Wheaton College (IL)
Wheaton College (MA)
Wright State University

Mid-sized City

Arizona State University
Baylor University
Cal Poly Pomona
Clark University
College of Charleston
College of the Holy Cross
Florida State University
Hampton University
Millsaps College
Muhlenberg College
Rensselaer Polytechnic Institute
Santa Clara University
Syracuse University
Texas Tech University
Trinity College
UC Berkeley
University of Georgia
University of Michigan
University of Notre Dame
University of Oklahoma
University of Oregon
University of Puget Sound
University of South Carolina
University of Tennessee
University of Utah
Virginia Commonwealth University
Wake Forest University
Willamette University

Small City

Ball State University
Binghamton University
Cal Poly
East Carolina University
Franklin & Marshall College
Furman University
Hollins University
Idaho State University
Illinois State University
Illinois Wesleyan University
Indiana University
Iowa State University
Lawrence University
Lehigh University
Northern Arizona University
Northern Illinois University
Rutgers New Brunswick
Texas A&M University
UC Santa Barbara
UC Santa Cruz
Union College
University at Albany
University of Alabama
University of Colorado
University of Florida
University of Illinois
University of Iowa
University of Kansas
University of Missouri
Wesleyan University
Wilkes University

Rural

Albion College
Alfred University
Allegheny College
Amherst College
Auburn University
Bard College
Beloit College
Bucknell University
Carleton College
Centre College
Clemson University
Colby College
Colgate University
College of William & Mary
Cornell University
Dartmouth College
DePauw University
Dickinson College
Earlham College
Elon University
Gettysburg College
Grinnell College
Grove City College
Gustavus Adolphus College
Hamilton College
Hampshire College
Hanover College
Hastings College
Ithaca College
James Madison University
Juniata College
Kenyon College
Lafayette College
Luther College
Marlboro College
Miami University
Middlebury College
Montana State University
Mount Holyoke College
Oberlin College
Ohio University
Penn State University
Purdue University
Radford University
Slippery Rock University
Smith College
St. Olaf College
Susquehanna University
Swarthmore College
Truman State University
University of Connecticut
University of Maine
University of Massachusetts
University of Mississippi
University of Montana
University of New Hampshire
University of Rhode Island
University of South Dakota
University of Vermont
University of Virginia
University of Wisconsin–Stout
Virginia Tech
Warren Wilson College
Washington and Lee University
West Virginia University
Whitman College
Williams College

Note: Urban schools are located in cities
with populations greater than 200,000.

Suburban schools are located in suburbs of
large cities.

Mid-size city schools are located in cities
with populations of 100,000–199,999.

Small city schools are located in cities with
populations of 50,000–99,999.

Rural schools are located in small college
towns or in the middle of nowhere.

Size

Super-Small

Albion College
Alfred University
Amherst College
Babson College
Bard College
Bates College
Beloit College
Birmingham-Southern College
Bowdoin College
Bryn Mawr College
Caltech
Carleton College
Centenary College of Louisiana
Centre College
Claremont McKenna College
Colby College
College of Wooster
Connecticut College
Davidson College
Earlham College
Geneva College
Goucher College
Grinnell College
Hamilton College
Hampshire College
Hanover College
Harvey Mudd College
Hastings College
Haverford College
Hollins University
Juniata College
Kenyon College
La Roche College
Lawrence University
Lewis & Clark College
Macalester College
Manhattanville College
Marlboro College
Millsaps College
New College of Florida
Occidental College
Ohio Wesleyan University
Pitzer College
Pomona College
Reed College
Rhode Island School of Design
Rhodes College
Rollins College
Sarah Lawrence College
Scripps College
Simmons College
Southwestern University
Susquehanna University
Swarthmore College
Ursinus College
Warren Wilson College
Washington & Jefferson College
Washington and Lee University
Wheaton College (MA)
Whitman College
Willamette University
Williams College

Small

Allegheny College
Alverno College
Barnard College
Brandeis University
Bucknell University
Case Western Reserve University
Catholic University of America
Clark Atlanta University
Clark University (MA)
Colgate University

College of the Holy Cross
Colorado College
Creighton University
Denison University
DePauw University
Dickinson College
Emerson College
Franklin & Marshall College
Furman University
Gettysburg College
Grove City College
Guilford College
Gustavus Adolphus College
Illinois Wesleyan University
Lafayette College
Loyola College in Maryland
Luther College
Manhattan College
Middlebury College
Mount Holyoke College
Muhlenberg College
Oberlin College
Pepperdine University
Providence College
Rice University
Seattle University
Skidmore College
Smith College
Spelman College
St. Olaf College
Stetson University
Trinity College
Trinity University
Union College
University of Puget Sound
University of Richmond
Valparaiso University
Vassar College
Wellesley College
Wesleyan University
Wheaton College (IL)
Wilkes University
Xavier University

Mid-Sized

American University
Baruch College
Bentley College
Boston College
Bradley University
Brown University
Carnegie Mellon University
College of Charleston
College of William & Mary
Columbia University
Dartmouth College
Duke University
Duquesne University
Elon University
Emory University
Fashion Institute of Technology
Fordham University
George Washington University
Georgetown University
Gonzaga University
Hampton University
Harvard University
Hofstra University
Howard University
Ithaca College
Johns Hopkins University
Lehigh University
Loyola Marymount University
Loyola University Chicago
Marquette University
MIT
Montana State University

Northwestern University
Princeton University
Radford University
Rensselaer Polytechnic Institute
Saint Joseph's University
Santa Clara University
Seton Hall University
Slippery Rock University
Southern Methodist University
St. Louis University
Stanford University
Tennessee State University
Texas Christian University
Truman State University
Tufts University
Tulane University
University of Chicago
University of Denver
University of Maine
University of Miami
University of Montana
University of Notre Dame
University of Rochester
University of San Diego
University of San Francisco
University of South Dakota
University of Vermont
University of Wisconsin–Stout
Vanderbilt University
Villanova University
Wake Forest University
Washington University in St. Louis
West Point Military Academy
Yale University

Large

Auburn University
Ball State University
Baylor University
Binghamton University
Boston University
Cal Poly
Cal Poly Pomona
Clemson University
Cornell University
DePaul University
Drexel University
East Carolina University
Georgia Institute of Technology
Hunter College
Idaho State University
Illinois State University
IUPUI
James Madison University
Kansas State University
Kent State University
Miami University
Middle Tennessee State University
New York University
Northeastern University
Northern Arizona University
Northern Illinois University
Ohio University
Old Dominion University
Rochester Institute of Technology
Sacramento State
St. John's University
Stony Brook University
Syracuse University
Towson University
UC Riverside
UC Santa Barbara
UC Santa Cruz
University at Albany
University at Buffalo
University of Alabama
University of Cincinnati

University of Connecticut
University of Delaware
University of Iowa
University of Kansas
University of Kentucky
University of Louisville
University of Massachusetts
University of Mississippi
University of Nebraska
University of New Hampshire
University of North Carolina
Univ. of North Carolina–Greensboro
University of Oklahoma
University of Oregon
University of Pennsylvania
University of Pittsburgh
University of Rhode Island
University of Southern California
University of Utah
University of Virginia
UNLV
Virginia Commonwealth University
West Virginia University
Wright State University

Huge

Arizona State University
Brigham Young University
Cal State Northridge
Florida State University
Indiana University
Iowa State University
Louisiana State University
McGill University
Michigan State University
North Carolina State University
Ohio State University
Penn State University
Purdue University
Rutgers New Brunswick
San Diego State University
Temple University
Texas A&M University
Texas Tech University
UC Berkeley
UC Davis
UC Irvine
UC San Diego
UCLA
University of Arizona
University of Central Florida
University of Colorado
University of Florida
University of Georgia
University of Illinois
University of Maryland
University of Michigan
University of Minnesota
University of Missouri
University of South Carolina
University of South Florida
University of Tennessee
University of Texas
University of Washington
University of Wisconsin
Virginia Tech

Note: *Super-small schools have a total student body size of fewer than 2,000 students.*
Small schools have 2,000–4,000 students.
Mid-sized schools have 4,000–10,000 students.
Large schools have 10,000–20,000 students.
Huge schools have more than 20,000 students.

Selectivity

Less Selective

Albion College
Alfred University
Allegheny College
Alverno College
Arizona State University
Auburn University
Ball State University
Beloit College
Birmingham-Southern College
Bradley University
Brigham Young University
Cal State Northridge
Case Western Reserve University
Catholic University of America
Centenary College of Louisiana
Centre College
College of Charleston
College of Wooster
Creighton University
DePaul University
DePauw University
Drexel University
Duquesne University
Earlham College
East Carolina University
Geneva College
Georgia Institute of Technology
Gonzaga University
Goucher College
Gustavus Adolphus College
Hanover College
Hastings College
Hollins University
Idaho State University
Illinois State University
Indiana University
Iowa State University
Ithaca College
IUPUI
James Madison University
Juniata College
Kansas State University
Kent State University
Louisiana State University
Loyola College in Maryland
Loyola University Chicago
Luther College
Marquette University
Miami University
Michigan State University
Middle Tennessee State University
Millsaps College
Montana State University
North Carolina State University
Northern Arizona University
Northern Illinois University
Ohio University
Ohio Wesleyan University
Old Dominion University
Purdue University
Radford University
Rochester Institute of Technology
Sacramento State
Saint Joseph's University
Seattle University
Seton Hall University
Southern Methodist University
Southwestern University
St. Louis University
Stetson University
Susquehanna University
Temple University
Tennessee State University
Texas A&M University
Texas Tech University
Towson University

Truman State University
UC Davis
UC Riverside
UC Santa Cruz
University of Alabama
University of Arizona
University of Cincinnati
University of Colorado
University of Delaware
University of Denver
University of Illinois
University of Iowa
University of Kansas
University of Kentucky
University of Louisville
University of Maine
University of Massachusetts
University of Mississippi
University of Missouri
University of Montana
University of Nebraska
Univ. of North Carolina–Greensboro
University of Oklahoma
University of Oregon
University of Puget Sound
University of Rhode Island
University of San Francisco
University of South Dakota
University of Tennessee
University of Utah
University of Vermont
University of Washington
University of Wisconsin–Stout
UNLV
Valparaiso University
Virginia Tech
Warren Wilson College
West Virginia University
Wheaton College (IL)
Wilkes University
Willamette University
Wright State University
Xavier University

Mid-Range

American University
Baylor University
Boston University
Bryn Mawr College
Cal Poly
Cal Poly Pomona
Clark Atlanta University
Clark University
Clemson University
Dickinson College
Elon University
Fashion Institute of Technology
Florida State University
Fordham University
Furman University
Grinnell College
Grove City College
Guilford College
Hampshire College
Hampton University
Hofstra University
Howard University
Illinois Wesleyan University
La Roche College
Lawrence University
Lewis & Clark College
Loyola Marymount University
Macalester College
Manhattan College
Manhattanville College
Marlboro College
McGill University

Mount Holyoke College
Muhlenberg College
New College of Florida
Occidental College
Ohio State University
Penn State University
Providence College
Rensselaer Polytechnic Institute
Rhodes College
Rollins College
Rutgers New Brunswick
San Diego State University
Santa Clara University
Sarah Lawrence College
Scripps College
Simmons College
Slippery Rock University
Smith College
St. John's University
St. Olaf College
Stony Brook University
Syracuse University
Texas Christian University
Trinity College
Trinity University
UC Irvine
UC San Diego
UC Santa Barbara
Union College
University at Albany
University at Buffalo
University of Central Florida
University of Connecticut
University of Florida
University of Georgia
University of Maryland
University of Michigan
University of Minnesota
University of New Hampshire
University of Pittsburgh
University of Richmond
University of Rochester
University of San Diego
University of South Carolina
University of South Florida
University of Texas
University of Wisconsin
Ursinus College
Virginia Commonwealth University
Wake Forest University
Wheaton College (MA)
Whitman College

Selective

Babson College
Bard College
Barnard College
Baruch College
Bates College
Bentley University
Binghamton University
Boston College
Brandeis University
Bucknell University
Carleton College
Carnegie Mellon University
Colby College
Colgate University
College of the Holy Cross
College of William & Mary
Colorado College
Connecticut College
Davidson College
Denison University
Emerson College
Franklin & Marshall College

George Washington University
Gettysburg College
Hamilton College
Harvey Mudd College
Haverford College
Hunter College
Johns Hopkins University
Kenyon College
Lafayette College
Lehigh University
New York University
Northeastern University
Northwestern University
Oberlin College
Pepperdine University
Reed College
Rhode Island School of Design
Skidmore College
Spelman College
Tufts University
Tulane University
University of Chicago
University of Miami
University of North Carolina
University of Southern California
University of Virginia
Vanderbilt University
Vassar College
Villanova University
Washington & Jefferson College
Washington and Lee University
Wellesley College
Wesleyan University

Ultra Selective

Amherst College
Bowdoin College
Brown University
Caltech
Claremont McKenna College
Columbia University
Cornell University
Dartmouth College
Duke University
Emory University
Georgetown University
Harvard University
Middlebury College
MIT
Pitzer College
Pomona College
Princeton University
Rice University
Stanford University
Swarthmore College
UC Berkeley
UCLA
University of Notre Dame
University of Pennsylvania
Washington University in St. Louis
West Point Military Academy
Williams College
Yale University

Note: Less selective schools have acceptance rates of 60 percent and up.

Mid-range schools have acceptance rates between 40–59 percent.

Selective schools have acceptance rates between 25–39 percent.

Ultra selective schools have acceptance rates below 25 percent.

Academics

A+

Bowdoin College
Caltech
Dartmouth College
Harvey Mudd College
MIT
Princeton University
Stanford University
University of Chicago
Williams College

A

Amherst College
Bard College
Barnard College
Brown University
Bryn Mawr College
Carleton College
Carnegie Mellon University
Claremont McKenna College
College of William & Mary
Columbia University
Davidson College
Duke University
Harvard University
Macalester College
Middlebury College
New College of Florida
Northwestern University
Oberlin College
Pomona College
Reed College
Rice University
Scripps College
Smith College
St. Olaf College
Swarthmore College
Tufts University
University of Pennsylvania
University of Rochester
Ursinus College
Vanderbilt University
Vassar College
Washington and Lee University
Wellesley College
Yale University

A-

Alverno College
Bates College
Brandeis University
Case Western Reserve University
Clark University (MA)
Colby College
Colgate University
Colorado College
Connecticut College
Cornell University
Emory University
Fashion Institute of Technology
Georgetown University
Georgia Institute of Technology
Grinnell College
Hamilton College
Hanover College
Hastings College
Haverford College
Johns Hopkins University
Kenyon College
Lawrence University
McGill University
Rhode Island School of Design
Trinity College
Tulane University
UC Berkeley
UCLA
University of Michigan
University of Notre Dame
University of Southern California
University of Virginia
Washington University in
    St. Louis
Wesleyan University
Willamette University

B+

Albion College
American University
Babson College
Baruch College
Birmingham-Southern College
Boston College
Boston University
Bradley University
Brigham Young University
Bucknell University

Centre College
College of the Holy Cross
College of Wooster
DePauw University
Dickinson College
Earlham College
Emerson College
Franklin & Marshall College
George Washington University
Grove City College
Hampshire College
Howard University
Illinois Wesleyan University
Indiana University
Lafayette College
Lehigh University
Mount Holyoke College
Muhlenberg College
New York University
Occidental College
Pennsylvania State University
Pitzer College
Purdue University
Rensselaer Polytechnic Institute
Rhodes College
Rochester Institute of Technology
Saint Joseph's University
Sarah Lawrence College
Southern Methodist University
Susquehanna University
UC San Diego
UC Santa Barbara
University of Illinois
University of Maryland
University of Miami
University of North Carolina
University of Pittsburgh
University of Puget Sound
University of Richmond
University of Texas
University of Wisconsin
Valparaiso University
Villanova University
Virginia Tech
Wake Forest University
Wheaton College (IL)
Wheaton College (MA)
Whitman College

A high Academics grade generally indicates that professors are knowledgeable, accessible, and genuinely interested in their students' welfare. Other determining factors include class size, how well professors communicate, and whether or not classes are engaging.

B

Alfred University
Allegheny College
Ball State University
Beloit College
Bentley College
Cal Poly
Catholic University of America
Centenary College of Louisiana
College of Charleston
Creighton University
Denison University
DePaul University
Duquesne University
Elon University
Furman University
Geneva College
Gettysburg College
Gonzaga University
Goucher College
Guilford College
Gustavus Adolphus College
Hollins University
Illinois State University
Ithaca College
James Madison University
Juniata College
La Roche College
Lewis & Clark College
Loyola College in Maryland
Loyola Marymount University
Luther College
Manhattan College
Manhattanville College
Marlboro College
Marquette University
Miami University
Millsaps College
North Carolina State University
Northeastern University
Ohio State University
Ohio University
Ohio Wesleyan University
Pepperdine University
Providence College
Rollins College
Rutgers New Brunswick
Santa Clara University
Seattle University
Seton Hall University
Simmons College
Skidmore College
Southwestern University

Spelman College
Stetson University
Syracuse University
Texas Christian University
Texas Tech University
Trinity University
Truman State University
UC Davis
UC Irvine
UC Riverside
UC Santa Cruz
Union College
University at Buffalo
University of Arizona
University of Cincinnati
University of Connecticut
University of Delaware
University of Denver
University of Florida
University of Georgia
University of Iowa
University of Kansas
University of Massachusetts
University of Minnesota
University of Montana
University of Nebraska
University of North Carolina–
   Greensboro
University of Oklahoma
University of Rhode Island
University of San Diego
University of South Carolina
University of South Dakota
University of Vermont
University of Washington
University of Wisconsin–Stout
Virginia Commonwealth
   University
Warren Wilson College
Washington & Jefferson College
West Point Military Academy
Xavier University

B-

Arizona State University
Auburn University
Baylor University
Binghamton University

Cal Poly Pomona
Cal State Northridge
Clark Atlanta University
Clemson University
Drexel University
East Carolina University
Florida State University
Fordham University
Hampton University
Hofstra University
Hunter College
Idaho State University
Iowa State University
IUPUI
Kansas State University
Kent State University
Louisiana State University
Loyola University Chicago
Michigan State University
Middle Tennessee State
   University
Montana State University
Northern Arizona University
Northern Illinois University
Old Dominion University
Radford University
Sacramento State
San Diego State University
Slippery Rock University
St. John's University
St. Louis University
Stony Brook University
Temple University
Tennessee State University
Texas A&M University
Towson University
University at Albany
University of Alabama
University of Central Florida
University of Colorado
University of Kentucky
University of Louisville
University of Maine
University of Mississippi
University of Missouri
University of New Hampshire
University of Oregon
University of San Francisco
University of South Florida
University of Tennessee
University of Utah
UNLV
West Virginia University
Wilkes University
Wright State University

Local Atmosphere

A+

Boston University
Emerson College
Georgetown University
Harvard University
McGill University
MIT
New York University
Northeastern University
UCLA
University of Texas

A

American University
Barnard College
Baruch College
Boston College
Columbia University
Fashion Institute of Technology
George Washington University
Hofstra University
Howard University
Hunter College
Manhattan College
Northern Arizona University
Ohio State University
San Diego State University
Simmons College
UC San Diego
University of Central Florida
University of Miami
University of North Carolina–
    Greensboro
University of San Francisco

A-

Alverno College
Arizona State University
Bradley University
Brown University
Clark Atlanta University
DePaul University
Drexel University
Emory University
Georgia Institute of Technology
Loyola Marymount University
Loyola University Chicago
Macalester College

Occidental College
Reed College
Rhode Island School of Design
Rollins College
Saint Joseph's University
Seattle University
Southern Methodist University
Spelman College
Temple University
Tufts University
Tulane University
UC Berkeley
University of Chicago
University of Colorado
University of Georgia
University of Minnesota
University of Pennsylvania
University of San Diego
University of South Florida
University of Southern California
University of Vermont
University of Washington
UNLV

B+

Bard College
Bentley College
Brandeis University
Caltech
Carnegie Mellon University
Duquesne University
East Carolina University
Fordham University
Goucher College
IUPUI
Johns Hopkins University
La Roche College
Lewis & Clark College
Louisiana State University
Loyola College in Maryland
Manhattanville College
Montana State University
North Carolina State University
Providence College
Rhodes College
Rice University
Rutgers New Brunswick
St. John's University
St. Louis University
Tennessee State University
Texas Christian University
Towson University
Trinity University
UC Santa Barbara
UC Santa Cruz

University at Buffalo
University of Florida
University of Kansas
University of Louisville
University of Maine
University of Maryland
University of Michigan
University of Mississippi
University of Missouri
University of North Carolina
University of Oklahoma
University of Oregon
University of Pittsburgh
University of South Carolina
University of Wisconsin
Vanderbilt University
Virginia Commonwealth
    University
Washington University in
    St. Louis
West Virginia University
Wheaton College (IL)

B

Beloit College
Cal Poly
Case Western Reserve University
Catholic University of America
College of Charleston
Florida State University
Furman University
Idaho State University
Iowa State University
Marquette University
Middle Tennessee State
    University
Pennsylvania State University
Pepperdine University
Sacramento State
St. Olaf College
Syracuse University
UC Davis
University at Albany
University of Alabama
University of Arizona
University of Cincinnati
University of Denver
University of Kentucky
University of Nebraska
University of New Hampshire
University of Rhode Island
University of Tennessee
University of Utah
University of Virginia

B-

Babson College
Birmingham-Southern College
Brigham Young University
Bryn Mawr College
Cal Poly Pomona
Clemson University
Creighton University
Gonzaga University
Guilford College
Hanover College
Hastings College
Haverford College
Hollins University
Illinois State University
Illinois Wesleyan University
Indiana University
James Madison University
Juniata College
Marlboro College
Michigan State University
New College of Florida
Ohio University
Old Dominion University
Radford University
Seton Hall University
Stanford University
Stetson University
Swarthmore College
UC Irvine
University of Illinois
University of Iowa
University of Puget Sound
University of Richmond
University of South Dakota
University of Wisconsin–Stout
Villanova University
Virginia Tech
Wellesley College
Yale University

C+

Albion College
Auburn University
Ball State University
Binghamton University
Bowdoin College
Bucknell University
Cal State Northridge
Centenary College of Louisiana
Claremont McKenna College
Colgate University
College of William & Mary
Cornell University
Davidson College

Hamilton College
Hampton University
Harvey Mudd College
Ithaca College
Kent State University
Kenyon College
Lawrence University
Miami University
Middlebury College
Mount Holyoke College
Muhlenberg College
Northwestern University
Pitzer College
Pomona College
Princeton University
Purdue University
Rochester Institute of Technology
Santa Clara University
Scripps College
Southwestern University
Stony Brook University
Susquehanna University
Texas A&M University
Texas Tech University
Truman State University
UC Riverside
University of Delaware
University of Montana
University of Rochester
Valparaiso University
Vassar College
Wake Forest University
West Point Military Academy
Whitman College
Williams College
Wright State University
Xavier University

C

Alfred University
Amherst College
Carleton College
College of Wooster
Colorado College
Dickinson College
Duke University
Earlham College
Gettysburg College
Grinnell College
Grove City College
Hampshire College
Kansas State University
Lehigh University
Millsaps College
Ohio Wesleyan University
Sarah Lawrence College
Smith College
University of Massachusetts

Ursinus College
Warren Wilson College
Willamette University

C-

Bates College
Centre College
Clark University (MA)
Colby College
College of the Holy Cross
Connecticut College
Dartmouth College
DePauw University
Franklin & Marshall College
Geneva College
Gustavus Adolphus College
Lafayette College
Luther College
Skidmore College
Slippery Rock University
Trinity College
Union College
Washington & Jefferson College
Washington and Lee University
Wesleyan University
Wheaton College (MA)

D+

Baylor University
Denison University
Oberlin College
University of Connecticut

D

Elon University
Rensselaer Polytechnic Institute
Wilkes University

D-

Allegheny College
University of Notre Dame

A high Local Atmosphere grade indicates that the area surrounding campus is safe and scenic. Other factors include nearby attractions, proximity to other schools, and the town's attitude toward students.

Facilities

A+

University of Florida
University of Oregon

A

Amherst College
Arizona State University
DePaul University
Duke University
Emory University
Florida State University
Indiana University
Iowa State University
James Madison University
Marquette University
Middlebury College
Ohio State University
Purdue University
St. Olaf College
Susquehanna University
Texas A&M University
Texas Tech University
University of Arizona
University of Central Florida
University of Cincinnati
University of Delaware
University of North Carolina
University of North Carolina –
    Greensboro
University of Oklahoma
University of Texas
Vanderbilt University
Wake Forest University

A-

Baylor University
Bucknell University
Centre College
Clemson University
Colgate University
Cornell University
Davidson College
Franklin & Marshall College
George Washington University
Gustavus Adolphus College
Harvard University
Idaho State University
Kansas State University
Loyola College in Maryland

Loyola Marymount University
Manhattanville College
Middle Tennessee State
    University
Muhlenberg College
Northeastern University
Northern Arizona University
Ohio University
Rollins College
Rutgers New Brunswick
Santa Clara University
Smith College
UC Davis
UC Irvine
UC Riverside
UCLA
University at Buffalo
University of Alabama
University of Connecticut
University of Denver
University of Georgia
University of Illinois
University of Maryland
University of Michigan
University of Montana
University of Nebraska
University of Notre Dame
University of Pittsburgh
University of Rhode Island
University of Rochester
University of San Diego
University of South Carolina
University of Southern California
University of Washington
University of Wisconsin
West Virginia University
Williams College
Yale University

B+

Albion College
Auburn University
Babson College
Bentley College
Binghamton University
Birmingham-Southern College
Boston College
Boston University
Brigham Young University
Cal Poly
Cal State Northridge
Carleton College
Case Western Reserve
    University
Claremont McKenna College

Dickinson College
Earlham College
East Carolina University
Elon University
Furman University
Hanover College
Harvey Mudd College
Hastings College
Hollins University
Illinois Wesleyan University
Ithaca College
Johns Hopkins University
Juniata College
La Roche College
Lafayette College
Lehigh University
Miami University
Michigan State University
MIT
Oberlin College
Pennsylvania State University
Pepperdine University
Pitzer College
Pomona College
Princeton University
Reed College
Rensselaer Polytechnic Institute
Rice University
San Diego State University
Scripps College
St. Louis University
Stanford University
Syracuse University
Temple University
Texas Christian University
Truman State University
Tulane University
UC Berkeley
UC San Diego
UC Santa Barbara
UC Santa Cruz
University of Chicago
University of Kansas
University of Maine
University of Miami
University of Minnesota
University of Missouri
University of New Hampshire
University of Pennsylvania
University of South Florida
University of Tennessee
University of Vermont
Ursinus College
Vassar College
Virginia Tech
Washington and Lee University
Wellesley College
West Point Military Academy
Xavier University

B

Alfred University
Allegheny College
Alverno College
American University
Ball State University
Bard College
Bowdoin College
Brandeis University
Brown University
Bryn Mawr College
Cal Poly Pomona
Caltech
Colby College
College of Charleston
College of the Holy Cross
College of William & Mary
College of Wooster
Connecticut College
Creighton University
Dartmouth College
Denison University
DePauw University
Duquesne University
Emerson College
Fashion Institute of Technology
Georgia Institute of Technology
Gettysburg College
Gonzaga University
Grinnell College
Guilford College
Hampton University
Haverford College
Hofstra University
Louisiana State University
Luther College
Montana State University
Mount Holyoke College
Northern Illinois University
Northwestern University
Ohio Wesleyan University
Providence College
Radford University
Rhodes College
Rochester Institute of Technology
Saint Joseph's University
Seattle University
Simmons College
Skidmore College
Southwestern University
Stetson University
Stony Brook University
Swarthmore College
Tennessee State University
Towson University
Trinity College
Trinity University

Tufts University
Union College
University of Colorado
University of Iowa
University of Kentucky
University of Mississippi
University of Puget Sound
University of Richmond
University of San Francisco
University of Utah
University of Virginia
University of Wisconsin–Stout
UNLV
Villanova University
Virginia Commonwealth University
Washington & Jefferson College
Wesleyan University
Wheaton College (IL)
Wheaton College (MA)
Wilkes University
Willamette University
Wright State University

B-

Barnard College
Baruch College
Bates College
Beloit College
Carnegie Mellon University
Centenary College of Louisiana
Columbia University
Georgetown University
Grove City College
Howard University
Kent State University
Kenyon College
Lawrence University
Lewis & Clark College
Loyola University Chicago
Macalester College
Manhattan College
Marlboro College
North Carolina State University
Old Dominion University
Rhode Island School of Design
Seton Hall University
Slippery Rock University
Spelman College
University of Massachusetts
University of South Dakota
Washington University in St. Louis
Whitman College

C+

Catholic University of America
Colorado College
Drexel University
Fordham University
Goucher College
Hamilton College
Illinois State University
IUPUI
McGill University
Millsaps College
New College of Florida
Sacramento State
Sarah Lawrence College
University at Albany
University of Louisville
Valparaiso University
Warren Wilson College

C

Bradley University
Clark Atlanta University
Clark University (MA)
Geneva College
Hampshire College
Hunter College
Occidental College
Southern Methodist University
St. John's University

C-

New York University

A high Facilities grade indicates that the campus is aesthetically pleasing and well-maintained; facilities are state-of-the-art, and libraries are exceptional. Other determining factors include the quality of both athletic and student centers and an abundance of things to do on campus.

For more lists and rankings, check out our *Off the Record* guides or visit us online!
www.collegeprowler.com

Campus Dining

A+

Boston University
Bowdoin College
Cornell University
Dartmouth College
University of Notre Dame

A

American University
Boston College
Bryn Mawr College
Claremont McKenna College
Colby College
Harvey Mudd College
Middlebury College
Northeastern University
Pomona College
Scripps College
St. Olaf College
University of Arizona
University of Central Florida
University of Montana
Virginia Tech
Wheaton College (MA)

A-

Arizona State University
Bates College
Brandeis University
Cal Poly Pomona
Connecticut College
Duke University
George Washington University
Gustavus Adolphus College
James Madison University
Macalester College
Mount Holyoke College
Pepperdine University
Pitzer College
Princeton University
Trinity University
Tufts University
UCLA
University of Oklahoma
University of Puget Sound
University of South Carolina
Willamette University

B+

Auburn University
Brigham Young University
Cal State Northridge
Clark Atlanta University
Colgate University
College of the Holy Cross
College of Wooster
DePauw University
Dickinson College
Elon University
Emerson College
Furman University
Hamilton College
Harvard University
Hofstra University
Ithaca College
Kansas State University
Loyola College in Maryland
Miami University
Muhlenberg College
North Carolina State University
Northern Illinois University
Ohio Wesleyan University
Rensselaer Polytechnic Institute
Sacramento State
Santa Clara University
Smith College
Stanford University
Texas A&M University
Texas Tech
UC Davis
University of Alabama
University of Chicago
University of New Hampshire
University of San Diego
University of Vermont
University of Washington
University of Wisconsin–Stout
Villanova University
Washington University in
    St. Louis
Whitman College
Wilkes University
Williams College

B

Alverno College
Amherst College
Babson College
Ball State University
Binghamton University

Bucknell University
Caltech
Catholic University of America
Clemson University
Creighton University
Davidson College
Duquesne University
East Carolina University
Franklin & Marshall College
Gettysburg College
Goucher College
Hanover College
Hollins University
Howard University
Idaho State University
Illinois State University
Illinois Wesleyan University
Iowa State University
Kenyon College
Lehigh University
Louisiana State University
Manhattanville College
McGill University
Michigan State University
New York University
Ohio University
Pennsylvania State University
Purdue University
Rice University
Rollins College
Rutgers New Brunswick
Seattle University
Simmons College
Susquehanna University
Towson University
UC Irvine
UC Riverside
UC San Diego
UC Santa Cruz
Union College
University at Albany
University of Connecticut
University of Georgia
University of Kentucky
University of Missouri
University of Oregon
University of San Francisco
University of Southern California
University of Tennessee
University of Texas
Washington and Lee University
Wellesley College
Wesleyan University
Yale University

B-

Albion College
Baylor University
Beloit College
Brown University
College of William & Mary
Colorado College
Hampshire College
Kent State University
Lewis & Clark College
Loyola Marymount University
Luther College
Northwestern University
Occidental College
Radford University
Rhode Island School of Design
San Diego State University
Southern Methodist University
Southwestern University
St. Louis University
Swarthmore College
Tulane University
UC Berkeley
UC Santa Barbara
University of Maryland
University of Mississippi
University of Nebraska
University of North Carolina –
    Greensboro
University of Pittsburgh
University of Richmond
University of South Dakota
University of South Florida
University of Utah
Vanderbilt University
Wright State University

Johns Hopkins University
Juniata College
Lawrence University
Manhattan College
Marlboro College
Millsaps College
MIT
New College of Florida
Oberlin College
Providence College
Reed College
Rochester Institute of Technology
Seton Hall University
Skidmore College
Slippery Rock University
Syracuse University
Texas Christian University
Trinity College
University of Colorado
University of Delaware
University of Denver
University of Kansas
University of Massachusetts
University of Miami
University of North Carolina
UNLV
Ursinus College
Valparaiso University
Virginia Commonwealth
    University
Wake Forest University
Warren Wilson College
Washington &Jefferson College
Wheaton College (IL)
Xavier University

Sarah Lawrence College
Spelman College
St. John's University
Temple University
Tennessee State University
Truman State University
University at Buffalo
University of Cincinnati
University of Florida
University of Iowa
University of Louisville
University of Maine
University of Michigan
University of Minnesota
University of Pennsylvania
University of Rhode Island
University of Virginia
University of Wisconsin
West Point Military Academy
West Virginia University

C-

Centenary College of Louisiana
Fashion Institute of Technology
Gonzaga University
Hampton University
Hunter College
Marquette University
Ohio State University
Old Dominion University
Stetson University
Stony Brook University
University of Rochester
Vassar College

C+

Alfred University
Barnard College
Bentley College
Birmingham-Southern College
Cal Poly
Carleton College
College of Charleston
Columbia University
Denison University
DePaul University
Earlham College
Florida State University
Geneva College
Georgetown University
Grove City College
Haverford College
IUPUI

C

Allegheny College
Baruch College
Bradley University
Carnegie Mellon University
Case Western Reserve
    University
Centre College
Clark University (MA)
Drexel University
Emory University
Georgia Institute of Technology
Hastings College
Indiana University
Lafayette College
Loyola University Chicago
Middle Tennessee State
    University
Montana State University
Northern Arizona University
Rhodes College
Saint Joseph's University

D+

Bard College
Grinnell College

D

Fordham University
Guilford College
La Roche College
University of Illinois

*Our grade on Campus Dining
addresses the quality of both school-
owned dining halls and independent
on-campus restaurants as well as the price,
availability, and variety of food.*

Dorms

A+

Bowdoin College
Harvard University
Loyola College in Maryland
Pepperdine University
Scripps College

A

Bryn Mawr College
Claremont McKenna College
Elon University
George Washington University
Harvey Mudd College
Haverford College
Hollins University
Lawrence University
Middlebury College
Mount Holyoke College
Skidmore College
Smith College
Trinity University
Wilkes University
Yale University

A-

Alverno College
American University
Bentley College
Brown University
Colgate University
Cornell University
Dartmouth College
Emerson College
Grinnell College
Hastings College
La Roche College
Occidental College
Ohio University
Reed College
Rice University
Sarah Lawrence College
University of Puget Sound
University of Utah
Vassar College
Wheaton College (IL)
Wright State University

B+

Beloit College
Case Western Reserve University
College of Wooster
Connecticut College
Davidson College
DePaul University
Georgetown University
Hampshire College
James Madison University
Lafayette College
Loyola University Chicago
Muhlenberg College
New College of Florida
New York University
Northeastern University
Providence College
Seattle University
St. Olaf College
Towson University
Truman State University
UC Irvine
UC Santa Barbara
Union College
University of Colorado
University of Montana
University of San Diego
Vanderbilt University
Washington & Jefferson College
Washington University in St. Louis
Willamette University
Xavier University

B

Albion College
Amherst College
Babson College
Binghamton University
Boston College
Bucknell University
Cal State Northridge
Caltech
Carleton College
Carnegie Mellon University
Catholic University of America
Centenary College of Louisiana
Centre College
Clark University (MA)
College of Charleston
Colorado College
DePauw University
Earlham College
Emory University

Fordham University
Furman University
Geneva College
Gettysburg College
Grove City College
Gustavus Adolphus College
Indiana University
Ithaca College
Johns Hopkins University
Juniata College
Kenyon College
Lewis & Clark College
Loyola Marymount University
Manhattan College
Manhattanville College
Marlboro College
McGill University
Miami University
Michigan State University
Montana State University
Northwestern University
Ohio Wesleyan University
Pitzer College
Purdue University
Radford University
Rensselaer Polytechnic Institute
Rhodes College
Rutgers New Brunswick
Santa Clara University
Seton Hall University
Slippery Rock University
Southern Methodist University
Southwestern University
Spelman College
Susquehanna University
Syracuse University
Texas Tech
UC Berkeley
UC Riverside
University of Chicago
University of Iowa
University of Miami
University of Minnesota
University of Nebraska
University of North Carolina
University of North Carolina – Greensboro
University of Notre Dame
University of Oklahoma
University of Rochester
University of Southern California
University of Wisconsin–Stout
Ursinus College
Villanova University
Wake Forest University
Washington and Lee University
Wellesley College
Wesleyan University
West Virginia University
Whitman College

B-

Alfred University
Allegheny College
Baylor University
Brandeis University
Brigham Young University
Clemson University
College of the Holy Cross
College of William & Mary
Creighton University
Denison University
Dickinson College
Duke University
East Carolina University
Fashion Institute of Technology
Gonzaga University
Guilford College
Hamilton College
Hanover College
Howard University
Illinois State University
Illinois Wesleyan University
Iowa State University
Kansas State University
Lehigh University
Luther College
MIT
North Carolina State University
Northern Arizona University
Oberlin College
Pomona College
Princeton University
Rochester Institute of Technology
Rollins College
Simmons College
St. Louis University
Stanford University
Stetson University
Swarthmore College
Texas A&M University
Texas Christian University
Trinity College
Tufts University
UC Davis
UC Santa Cruz
University at Albany
University at Buffalo
University of Alabama
University of Arizona
University of Cincinnati
University of Georgia
University of Illinois
University of Kansas
University of Massachusetts
University of New Hampshire
University of Oregon
University of Pennsylvania
University of Rhode Island

University of Richmond
University of San Francisco
University of South Carolina
University of Tennessee
University of Texas
University of Wisconsin
Virginia Commonwealth
    University
Warren Wilson College
Wheaton College (MA)
Williams College

C+

Arizona State University
Ball State University
Bates College
Birmingham-Southern College
Bradley University
Cal Poly
Cal Poly Pomona
Colby College
Columbia University
Duquesne University
Goucher College
Hunter College
Idaho State University
Kent State University
Louisiana State University
Macalester College
Marquette University
Saint Joseph's University
Temple University
Tennessee State University
Tulane University
UC San Diego
University of Connecticut
University of Denver
University of Maryland
University of Michigan
University of Pittsburgh
University of Virginia
Valparaiso University

C

Bard College
Barnard College
Clark Atlanta University
Florida State University
Georgia Institute of Technology
Hofstra University
Middle Tennessee State
    University
Millsaps College
Northern Illinois University

Ohio State University
Old Dominion University
Pennsylvania State University
UCLA
University of Central Florida
University of Delaware
University of Florida
University of Kentucky
University of Maine
University of Mississippi
University of Missouri
University of Vermont
Virginia Tech

C-

Auburn University
Drexel University
Rhode Island School of Design
San Diego State University
Stony Brook University
University of Louisville
University of South Dakota
University of South Florida
University of Washington

D+

Boston University
Franklin & Marshall College
IUPUI
Sacramento State

D

St. John's University
UNLV
West Point Military Academy

D-

Hampton University

A high Dorms (Campus Housing) grade indicates that dorms are clean, well-maintained, and spacious. Other determining factors include variety of dorms, proximity to classes, and social atmosphere.

Girls

A+

Arizona State University
Florida State University
Hampton University
Howard University
Loyola College in Maryland
Loyola Marymount University
Pepperdine University
San Diego State University
St. Olaf College
Texas Tech University
UC Santa Barbara
University of Arizona
University of Georgia
University of San Diego
University of Texas
Vanderbilt University

A

Auburn University
Boston College
Brigham Young University
Clark Atlanta University
Clemson University
Colgate University
College of Charleston
DePauw University
Duquesne University
Fashion Institute of Technology
Illinois State University
James Madison University
Kansas State University
Louisiana State University
Miami University
Muhlenberg College
Ohio State University
Ohio University
Rollins College
Southern Methodist University
Syracuse University
Texas A&M University
UCLA
University of Alabama
University of Central Florida
University of Colorado
University of Florida
University of Maryland
University of Miami
University of Mississippi
University of North Carolina
University of South Carolina
University of South Florida
University of Southern California
University of Tennessee
University of Virginia
University of Wisconsin
UNLV
Villanova University
Wake Forest University

A-

Bentley College
Birmingham-Southern College
Bucknell University
Cal Poly
Dickinson College
Elon University
Emerson College
Georgetown University
Gustavus Adolphus College
Indiana University
McGill University
Michigan State University
Middlebury College
New York University
Northern Illinois University
Providence College
Scripps College
Seattle University
Seton Hall University
St. Louis University
Susquehanna University
Tennessee State University
Texas Christian University
Trinity College
Trinity University
University of Illinois
University of Iowa
University of Kentucky
University of Michigan
University of Missouri
University of Oklahoma
University of Richmond
Wheaton College (IL)

B+

Albion College
Alverno College
Bates College
Baylor University
Boston University
Bradley University
Cal State Northridge
Catholic University of America
Claremont McKenna College
Colby College
College of the Holy Cross
Connecticut College
Denison University
East Carolina University
Furman University
Hamilton College
Hanover College
Hastings College
Idaho State University
Ithaca College
Kent State University
Lafayette College
Manhattan College
Manhattanville College
Middle Tennessee State
    University
Montana State University
Northeastern University
Northern Arizona University
Occidental College
Ohio Wesleyan University
Old Dominion University
Pennsylvania State University
Purdue University
Radford University
Rhode Island School of Design
Saint Joseph's University
Santa Clara University
Simmons College
Skidmore College
Slippery Rock University
Southwestern University
Spelman College
Stetson University
Towson University
Tulane University
UC Davis
Union College
University of Delaware
University of Kansas
University of Massachusetts
University of North Carolina –
    Greensboro
University of Rhode Island
University of San Francisco
University of Washington
Ursinus College
Vassar College
Virginia Commonwealth
    University
Warren Wilson College
Washington and Lee University
West Virginia University
Whitman College
Yale University

B

Amherst College
Ball State University
Barnard College
Baruch College
Binghamton University
Brown University
Centre College
College of William & Mary
College of Wooster
Colorado College
Creighton University
Davidson College
DePaul University
Duke University
Earlham College
Fordham University
Franklin & Marshall College
George Washington University
Gettysburg College
Gonzaga University
Guilford College
Hofstra University
Hollins University
Hunter College
Illinois Wesleyan University
Iowa State University
La Roche College
Loyola University Chicago
Marlboro College
Millsaps College
Mount Holyoke College
North Carolina State University
Northwestern University
Pitzer College
Princeton University
Rhodes College
Rutgers New Brunswick
Sacramento State
Sarah Lawrence College
Smith College
Temple University
UC Riverside
UC San Diego
University at Albany
University at Buffalo
University of Cincinnati
University of Connecticut
University of Denver
University of Louisville
University of Maine
University of Minnesota
University of Montana
University of New Hampshire
University of Oregon
University of Pittsburgh
University of Utah
University of Vermont

University of Wisconsin–Stout
Virginia Tech
Wellesley College
Wheaton College (MA)
Wilkes University
Willamette University
Wright State University

B-

Bowdoin College
Cal Poly Pomona
Centenary College of Louisiana
Geneva College
Goucher College
Harvard University
IUPUI
Juniata College
Lehigh University
Luther College
Macalester College
Marquette University
Reed College
Rice University
Stony Brook University
UC Irvine
UC Santa Cruz
University of Nebraska
University of Rochester
University of South Dakota
Xavier University

C+

Alfred University
American University
Babson College
Brandeis University
Bryn Mawr College
Clark University (MA)
Columbia University
Cornell University
Dartmouth College
Grove City College
Hampshire College
Haverford College
Johns Hopkins University
Kenyon College
Lewis & Clark College
New College of Florida
Oberlin College
Pomona College
Rochester Institute of Technology

St. John's University
Stanford University
Tufts University
UC Berkeley
University of Notre Dame
University of Pennsylvania
University of Puget Sound
Valparaiso University

C

Allegheny College
Bard College
Drexel University
Emory University
Grinnell College
Harvey Mudd College
Lawrence University
Rensselaer Polytechnic Institute
Swarthmore College
Truman State University
University of Chicago
Washington University in
   St. Louis
Wesleyan University
West Point Military Academy
Williams College

C-

Beloit College
Caltech
Carleton College
Carnegie Mellon University
Case Western Reserve
   University
Georgia Institute of Technology
MIT
Washington & Jefferson College

A high grade for Girls not only implies that the women on campus are attractive, smart, friendly, and engaging, but also that there is a fair ratio of girls to guys.

For more lists
and rankings,
check out our *Off the
Record* guides or visit
us online!

www.collegeprowler.com

Guys

A+

Texas A&M University
University of Arizona

A

Arizona State University
Auburn University
Brigham Young University
Clemson University
Florida State University
Illinois State University
Loyola Marymount University
Montana State University
Ohio University
Pepperdine University
Purdue University
San Diego State University
Texas Tech University
UC Santa Barbara
University of Colorado
University of Florida
University of Oklahoma
University of Tennessee
University of Texas
University of Virginia

A-

Baylor University
Bowdoin College
Bucknell University
Catholic University
Colgate University
DePauw University
Howard University
Indiana University
Kansas State University
Louisiana State University
Loyola College in Maryland
Miami University
Michigan State University
Middlebury College
Muhlenberg College
Ohio State University
Seton Hall University
Southern Methodist University
Susquehanna University
Syracuse University
Trinity College
UCLA
Union College

University of Alabama
University of Georgia
University of Kentucky
University of Maryland
University of Missouri
University of North Carolina
University of Richmond
University of San Diego
University of South Florida
University of Southern California
University of Wisconsin
Villanova University
Wake Forest University
Wheaton College (IL)

B+

American University
Bentley College
Birmingham-Southern College
Boston College
Cal Poly
Claremont McKenna College
Davidson College
Duke University
Duquesne University
Elon University
Gustavus Adolphus College
Hamilton College
Hanover College
Hastings College
Iowa State University
Ithaca College
James Madison University
Johns Hopkins University
Lafayette College
La Roche College
Lehigh University
Manhattan College
Marquette University
Millsaps College
Northeastern University
Ohio Wesleyan University
Providence College
Rollins College
St. Louis University
St. Olaf College
Stetson University
Texas Christian University
Trinity University
University at Buffalo
University of Central Florida
University of Denver
University of Illinois
University of Iowa
University of Kansas
University of Massachusetts

University of Minnesota
University of Mississippi
University of Notre Dame
University of Utah
University of Washington
Ursinus College
Vanderbilt University
Virginia Commonwealth University
Yale University

B

Albion College
Amherst College
Ball State University
Baruch College
Bates College
Binghamton University
Bradley University
Brown University
Cal Poly Pomona
Cal State Northridge
Centre College
Clark Atlanta University
Colby College
College of the Holy Cross
College of Wooster
Colorado College
Cornell University
Denison University
East Carolina University
Franklin & Marshall College
Furman University
Georgetown University
Gettysburg College
Hampton University
Harvard University
Hofstra University
Kent State University
Manhattanville College
Middle Tennessee State University
North Carolina State University
Occidental College
Old Dominion University
Pennsylvania State University
Princeton University
Radford University
Rutgers New Brunswick
Saint Joseph's University
Santa Clara University
Slippery Rock University
Stanford University
Stony Brook University
Tennessee State University
Tulane University
UC Davis

(B Guys Continued)
University at Albany
University of Cincinnati
University of Connecticut
University of Delaware
University of Maine
University of Miami
University of Michigan
University of Montana
University of Pittsburgh
University of Rhode Island
University of Rochester
University of South Carolina
University of South Dakota
University of Wisconsin–Stout
UNLV
Vassar College
Virginia Tech
Warren Wilson College
Washington and Lee University
West Point Military Academy
West Virginia University
Whitman College
Wilkes University
Wright State University

B-

Babson College
College of Charleston
College of William & Mary
Connecticut College
Dartmouth College
Dickinson College
Earlham College
Emerson College
Emory University
George Washington University
Georgia Institute of Technology
Gonzaga University
Grove City College
Guilford College
Hampshire College
Idaho State University
Illinois Wesleyan University
IUPUI
Juniata College
Kenyon College
Loyola University Chicago
Macalester College
Marlboro College
McGill University
New York University
Northern Arizona University
Northern Illinois University
Pitzer College
Rhodes College
Rice University
Rochester Institute of Technology

Sacramento State
Seattle University
Skidmore College
Southwestern University
Temple University
Truman State University
UC Berkeley
UC Riverside
UC San Diego
University of Louisville
University of Nebraska
University of New Hampshire
University of North Carolina – Greensboro
University of Oregon
University of Pennsylvania
University of San Francisco
University of Vermont
Valparaiso University
Willamette University

C+

Alfred University
Boston University
Case Western Reserve University
Centenary College of Louisiana
Columbia University
DePaul University
Drexel University
Fordham University
Geneva College
Harvey Mudd College
Haverford College
Hunter College
Luther College
Pomona College
Reed College
Rensselaer Polytechnic Institute
Rhode Island School of Design
Sarah Lawrence College
Towson University
UC Irvine
University of Chicago
Washington & Jefferson College
Washington University in St. Louis
Wheaton College (MA)
Xavier University

C

Allegheny College
Bard College
Beloit College

Brandeis University
Caltech
Carnegie Mellon University
Creighton University
Goucher College
Grinnell College
Lawrence University
Lewis & Clark College
MIT
New College of Florida
Northwestern University
Oberlin College
St. John's University
Swarthmore College
Tufts University
UC Santa Cruz
University of Puget Sound
Wesleyan University

C-

Carleton College
Clark University (MA)
Williams College

D+

Fashion Institute of Technology

N/A

Alverno College
Barnard College
Bryn Mawr College
Hollins University
Mount Holyoke College
Scripps College
Simmons College
Smith College
Spelman College
Wellesley College

A high grade for Guys indicates that the male population on campus is attractive, smart, friendly, and engaging, and that the school has a decent ratio of guys to girls.

Athletics

A+

Louisiana State University
Ohio State University
University of Florida
University of Southern California
University of Tennessee
University of Texas

A

Auburn University
Boston College
Brigham Young University
Clemson University
Florida State University
Georgia Institute of Technology
Hanover College
Indiana University
Iowa State University
Kansas State University
Michigan State University
Pennsylvania State University
Purdue University
Stanford University
Syracuse University
Texas A&M University
Texas Tech University
University of Alabama
University of Arizona
University of Georgia
University of Illinois
University of Iowa
University of Miami
University of Michigan
University of North Carolina
University of Notre Dame
University of Oklahoma
University of Oregon
University of Virginia
University of Washington
University of Wisconsin
Virginia Tech

A-

Arizona State University
Bradley University
Colgate University
Davidson College
Duke University
Hastings College
Marquette University

North Carolina State University
UCLA
University of Cincinnati
University of Colorado
University of Connecticut
University of Kansas
University of Kentucky
University of Louisville
University of Maine
University of Maryland
University of Minnesota
University of Mississippi
University of Missouri
University of Montana
University of Nebraska
University of Pittsburgh
Villanova University
Wake Forest University
West Virginia University
Xavier University

B+

Albion College
Baylor University
Bentley College
Bowdoin College
College of Wooster
Gonzaga University
Gustavus Adolphus College
Lehigh University
Middlebury College
Northern Illinois University
Providence College
Rutgers New Brunswick
Saint Joseph's University
Seton Hall University
UC Berkeley
UC Davis
Union College
University of Delaware
University of New Hampshire
University of Pennsylvania
University of Rhode Island
University of South Carolina
University of South Dakota
University of Utah
Ursinus College
Valparaiso University
Virginia Commonwealth
  University
Washington & Jefferson College
West Point Military Academy
Wheaton College (IL)
Wilkes University

B

Amherst College
Birmingham-Southern College
Bucknell University
Carleton College
Claremont McKenna College
Colby College
College of the Holy Cross
Colorado College
Connecticut College
Creighton University
Dartmouth College
Georgetown University
Hamilton College
Idaho State University
Illinois State University
Juniata College
Manhattan College
Miami University
Northwestern University
Ohio University
Princeton University
St. John's University
Temple University
Tennessee State University
Texas Christian University
University of Massachusetts
University of Richmond
University of South Florida
UNLV
Vanderbilt University

B-

Babson College
Binghamton University
Boston University
College of Charleston
Cornell University
DePaul University
Dickinson College
East Carolina University
Elon University
Furman University
Hampton University
Harvard University
Haverford College
Illinois Wesleyan University
James Madison University
Johns Hopkins University
Lafayette College
Luther College
Manhattanville College
Montana State University
Northeastern University
Northern Arizona University

(B- Athletics Continued)
Occidental College
Ohio Wesleyan University
Old Dominion University
Rensselaer Polytechnic Institute
Rice University
Rochester Institute of Technology
Rollins College
San Diego State University
Skidmore College
Stetson University
Towson University
Tulane University
UC Santa Barbara
University of Central Florida
University of Denver
University of San Diego
University of Vermont
University of Wisconsin–Stout
Washington University in
    St. Louis
Williams College

Baruch College
Bates College
Brown University
Cal Poly Pomona
Carnegie Mellon University
Case Western Reserve
    University
Centenary College of Louisiana
Centre College
DePauw University
Drexel University
Duquesne University
Geneva College
Gettysburg College
Grinnell College
Hofstra University
Howard University
Kent State University
Lawrence University
Loyola College in Maryland
Loyola Marymount University
Loyola University Chicago
Macalester College
MIT
Pepperdine University
Santa Clara University
Seattle University
Southern Methodist University
St. Louis University
Susquehanna University
Trinity College
Trinity University
UC Riverside
UC Santa Cruz
University at Buffalo
University of Chicago

University of North Carolina –
    Greensboro
University of Puget Sound
University of Rochester
University of San Francisco
Vassar College
Warren Wilson College
Washington and Lee University
Wheaton College (MA)
Whitman College
Wright State University
Yale University

Allegheny College
American University
Beloit College
Brandeis University
Cal Poly
Cal State Northridge
College of William & Mary
Denison University
Earlham College
Fordham University
Franklin & Marshall College
George Washington University
Grove City College
Guilford College
Harvey Mudd College
Hollins University
Ithaca College
IUPUI
Kenyon College
Middle Tennessee State
    University
Millsaps College
Mount Holyoke College
Muhlenberg College
Pitzer College
Pomona College
Simmons College
Slippery Rock University
Smith College
St. Olaf College
Stony Brook University
Truman State University
Wellesley College
Willamette University

Alfred University
Ball State University
Bard College
Bryn Mawr College
Catholic University of America

Emory University
Goucher College
Hampshire College
McGill University
Oberlin College
Radford University
Rhodes College
Sacramento State
Scripps College
Southwestern University
Swarthmore College
Tufts University
UC Irvine
University at Albany
Wesleyan University

Alverno College
Caltech
Clark Atlanta University
La Roche College
Lewis & Clark College
Reed College
Sarah Lawrence College
UC San Diego

Barnard College
Clark University (MA)
Columbia University
Hunter College
New York University
Rhode Island School of Design
Spelman College

Emerson College
Fashion Institute of Technology

Marlboro College
New College of Florida

*A high grade in Athletics indicates that
students have school spirit, that sports
programs are respected, that games are
well-attended, and that intramurals are a
prominent part of student life.*

Drug Scene

A+

Brigham Young University
West Point Military Academy

A

Alverno College
Caltech
College of William & Mary
Creighton University
Furman University
Geneva College
Grove City College
Hanover College
Idaho State University
UC Davis
Wheaton College (IL)

A-

Barnard College
Baruch College
Bentley College
Bryn Mawr College
Cal State Northridge
Case Western Reserve
   University
Claremont McKenna College
Davidson College
Duquesne University
Elon University
Georgetown University
Harvey Mudd College
Howard University
IUPUI
Johns Hopkins University
Juniata College
La Roche College
Luther College
Mount Holyoke College
Northeastern University
Rensselaer Polytechnic Institute
Simmons College
Spelman College
Texas A&M University
UC Irvine
University of Notre Dame
University of Richmond
University of Utah
Ursinus College
Wake Forest University
Wheaton College (MA)

Whitman College
Williams College

B+

Alfred University
American University
Auburn University
Babson College
Baylor University
Birmingham-Southern College
Bowdoin College
Bucknell University
Cal Poly
Carnegie Mellon University
Catholic University of America
Centre College
Clemson University
Colby College
Colgate University
College of Wooster
Cornell University
Dartmouth College
East Carolina University
Emerson College
Fashion Institute of Technology
Gettysburg College
Harvard University
Haverford College
Hollins University
Hunter College
Illinois Wesleyan University
Iowa State University
Kansas State University
Lawrence University
Loyola Marymount University
Marquette University
Miami University
Michigan State University
Millsaps College
MIT
North Carolina State University
Ohio University
Pepperdine University
Providence College
Rice University
Rutgers New Brunswick
Southwestern University
St. Louis University
St. Olaf College
Stanford University
Susquehanna University
Swarthmore College
Tennessee State University
Texas Christian University
Trinity University
Truman State University
Tufts University

UC Riverside
University of Chicago
University of Kansas
University of North Carolina
University of Puget Sound
UNLV
Valparaiso University
Vanderbilt University
Villanova University
Wellesley College
Xavier University

B

Allegheny College
Amherst College
Beloit College
Binghamton University
Brandeis University
Cal Poly Pomona
Centenary College of Louisiana
Clark University (MA)
College of the Holy Cross
Connecticut College
Dickinson College
Drexel University
Earlham College
George Washington University
Gonzaga University
Gustavus Adolphus College
Hastings College
Indiana University
Kent State University
Lehigh University
Lewis & Clark College
Manhattanville College
McGill University
Middlebury College
Montana State University
Muhlenberg College
Northwestern University
Occidental College
Ohio State University
Ohio Wesleyan University
Pennsylvania State University
Pitzer College
Pomona College
Princeton University
Purdue University
Rochester Institute of Technology
Saint Joseph's University
Scripps College
Seattle University
Stetson University
Texas Tech University
Towson University
UC San Diego
University at Buffalo

(B Drug Scene Continued)

University of Cincinnati
University of Connecticut
University of Florida
University of Louisville
University of Maine
University of Maryland
University of Minnesota
University of Mississippi
University of Missouri
University of North Carolina – Greensboro
University of Oklahoma
University of Pittsburgh
University of Rhode Island
University of Rochester
University of South Carolina
University of Virginia
University of Washington
Virginia Tech
Virginia Commonwealth University
Washington and Lee University
West Virginia University
Willamette University
Wright State University
Yale University

B-

Albion College
Arizona State University
Boston College
Bradley University
Brown University
Carleton College
College of Charleston
Columbia University
Denison University
DePaul University
DePauw University
Duke University
Fordham University
Franklin & Marshall College
Georgia Institute of Technology
Goucher College
Hampton University
Illinois State University
James Madison University
Kenyon College
Lafayette College
Loyola College in Maryland
Manhattan College
Middle Tennessee State University
Northern Illinois University
Old Dominion University
Radford University
Rhode Island School of Design

Rhodes College
San Diego State University
Santa Clara University
Slippery Rock University
Stony Brook University
Trinity College
Union College
University of Alabama
University of Arizona
University of Denver
University of Illinois
University of Kentucky
University of Massachusetts
University of Nebraska
University of Pennsylvania
University of South Dakota
University of South Florida
University of Southern California
University of Tennessee
University of Wisconsin–Stout
Washington University in St. Louis
Washington & Jefferson College

C+

Ball State University
Boston University
Colorado College
Florida State University
Guilford College
Louisiana State University
Loyola University Chicago
Macalester College
New College of Florida
Northern Arizona University
Oberlin College
Sacramento State
Skidmore College
St. John's University
Temple University
Tulane University
UC Berkeley
UC Santa Barbara
UC Santa Cruz
University of Central Florida
University of Delaware
University of Georgia
University of Iowa
University of Miami
University of Michigan
University of Montana
University of Oregon
University of San Diego
University of San Francisco
University of Texas
University of Vermont
Warren Wilson College
Wesleyan University
Wilkes University

C

Bates College
Clark Atlanta University
Emory University
Reed College
Seton Hall University
Smith College
Syracuse University
UCLA
University of Colorado
University of Wisconsin

C-

Bard College
Grinnell College
Hampshire College
Ithaca College
Marlboro College
New York University
Rollins College
Southern Methodist University
University at Albany
University of New Hampshire
Vassar College

D+

Hofstra University
Sarah Lawrence College

D-

Hamilton College

A high grade in Drug Scene indicates that drugs are not a noticeable part of campus life; drug use is not visible, and no pressure to use them seems to exist.

For more lists and rankings, check out our *Off the Record* guides or visit us online!
www.collegeprowler.com

Safety & Security

A+

Bard College
Boston College
Bowdoin College
Brigham Young University
Bucknell University
Colgate University
Dartmouth College
Davidson College
Grove City College
Hollins University
Southwestern University
Truman State University
West Point Military Academy

A

Alfred University
Alverno College
American University
Bryn Mawr College
DePauw University
Dickinson College
Elon University
Furman University
Hanover College
Haverford College
Idaho State University
James Madison University
Juniata College
Kenyon College
Lawrence University
Luther College
Manhattanville College
Middlebury College
Muhlenberg College
Pepperdine University
Princeton University
Purdue University
Radford University
Santa Clara University
Stanford University
Susquehanna University
UC Davis
UC Irvine
University of Florida
University of Maine
University of Nebraska
University of Oklahoma
University of Richmond
Villanova University
Wake Forest University
Washington and Lee University
Wheaton College (IL)
Whitman College

A-

Albion College
Allegheny College
Babson College
Baruch College
Beloit College
Bentley College
Binghamton University
Brandeis University
Carleton College
Centre College
Claremont McKenna College
Clemson University
College of the Holy Cross
Connecticut College
Earlham College
Emory University
Grinnell College
Harvey Mudd College
Illinois State University
Iowa State University
Ithaca College
Kansas State University
Kent State University
Lewis & Clark College
Macalester College
Mount Holyoke College
New College of Florida
Oberlin College
Ohio University
Pitzer College
Pomona College
Reed College
Scripps College
Simmons College
Slippery Rock University
Spelman College
St. Olaf College
Stetson University
Swarthmore College
Texas Tech
Trinity University
UC San Diego
UC Santa Barbara
University of Central Florida
University of Denver
University of Kansas
University of Mississippi
University of Missouri
University of New Hampshire
University of North Carolina
University of Notre Dame
University of Puget Sound
University of Rhode Island
University of San Diego
University of South Dakota
University of Utah
University of Vermont
University of Wisconsin

Valparaiso University
Warren Wilson College
Washington & Jefferson
Washington University in
    St. Louis
Wellesley College
Willamette University
Williams College

B+

Amherst College
Bates College
Baylor University
Boston University
Colby College
College of William & Mary
Denison University
DePaul University
Duquesne University
Fashion Institute of Technology
Florida State University
Geneva College
Goucher College
Guilford College
Hamilton College
Hampshire College
Hampton University
Hastings College
Illinois Wesleyan University
Indiana University
Lafayette College
Manhattan College
Marlboro College
Miami University
Michigan State University
Occidental College
Pennsylvania State University
Rice University
Saint Joseph's University
Skidmore College
Smith College
Tufts University
UCLA
University of Alabama
University of Connecticut
University of Illinois
University of Miami
University of Michigan
University of Minnesota
University of Montana
University of Rochester
University of South Florida
University of Virginia
University of Wisconsin–Stout
Ursinus College
Vanderbilt University
Vassar College

(B+ Safety Continued)
Virginia Tech
West Virginia University

B

Arizona State University
Auburn University
Caltech
Carnegie Mellon University
Centenary College of Louisiana
College of Charleston
Cornell University
East Carolina University
Emerson College
Franklin & Marshall College
Georgetown University
Gettysburg College
Harvard University
Hunter College
IUPUI
Loyola Marymount University
McGill University
MIT
Montana State University
North Carolina State University
Northern Arizona University
Ohio Wesleyan University
Rensselaer Polytechnic Institute
Rhode Island School of Design
Rochester Institute of
    Technology
San Diego State University
Seattle University
Seton Hall University
Stony Brook University
Temple University
Texas A&M University
Texas Christian University
Towson University
UC Santa Cruz
Union College
University at Albany
University of Iowa
University of Maryland
University of Massachusetts
University of San Francisco
University of South Carolina
University of Texas
UNLV
Virginia Commonwealth
    University
Wheaton College (MA)
Xavier University

B-

Barnard College
Birmingham-Southern College
Bradley University
Cal Poly Pomona
Cal State Northridge
Case Western Reserve
    University
College of Wooster
Colorado College
Columbia University
Fordham University
Georgia Institute of Technology
Gustavus Adolphus College
Johns Hopkins University
La Roche College
Louisiana State University
Loyola College in Maryland
Marquette University
New York University
Northern Illinois University
Ohio State University
Providence College
Rhodes College
Rollins College
Southern Methodist University
UC Riverside
University of Arizona
University of Chicago
University of Colorado
University of Georgia
University of Louisville
University of North Carolina –
    Greensboro
University of Oregon
University of Pittsburgh
University of Tennessee
Yale University

C+

Ball State University
Brown University
Cal Poly
George Washington University
Gonzaga University
Lehigh University
Northwestern University
Sacramento State
Sarah Lawrence College
St. John's University
St. Louis University
Syracuse University
UC Berkeley

University of Cincinnati
University of Delaware
University of Kentucky
University of Pennsylvania
University of Southern California
Wesleyan University
Wilkes University
Wright State University

C

Catholic University of America
Clark Atlanta University
Clark University (MA)
Drexel University
Duke University
Hofstra University
Howard University
Loyola University Chicago
Middle Tennessee State
University
Millsaps College
Northeastern University
Tennessee State University
Tulane University
University at Buffalo
University of Washington

C-

Creighton University
Old Dominion University
Rutgers New Brunswick
Trinity College

*A high grade in Safety & Security means
that students generally feel safe, campus
police are visible, blue-light phones and
escort services are readily available, and
safety precautions are not overly necessary.*

For more lists
and rankings,
check out our *Off
the Record* guides
or visit us online!
www.collegeprowler.com

Did You Know?

Every school showcased in this compendium is also available as a complete Off the Record single-school guide with 160 pages of student-authored content. So after you narrow down your college choice with the Big Book, you can pick up some single-school guides for a more in-depth look.

And now you can gain access to our entire library of single-school guides online when you visit **collegeprowler.com**.

INDIVIDUAL SCHOOL PROFILES

Use these student-created profiles to get an honest, inside look at each college. There are tons of factors that can determine whether or not a school is a good fit. Be sure to consider all of them.

Albion College

611 East Porter Street; Albion, MI 49224
(517) 629-1000; www.albion.edu

THE BASICS:

Acceptance Rate: 83%
Setting: Rural
F-T Undergrads: 1,842

SAT Range: 1560–1910*
Control: Private
Tuition: $28,380

Most Popular Majors: Social Sciences, Biological/Life Sciences, Psychology, English, Business/Marketing

*of 2400

Academics	B+	Guys	B
Local Atmosphere	C+	Girls	B+
Safety & Security	A-	Athletics	B+
Computers	A+	Nightlife	C
Facilities	B+	Greek Life	A-
Campus Dining	B-	Drug Scene	B-
Off-Campus Dining	D	Campus Strictness	B-
Campus Housing	B	Parking	B+
Off-Campus Housing	D	Transportation	C
Diversity	D	Weather	C-

Students Speak Out
ON ACADEMICS

Q "I have been very pleased overall with the professors at Albion. **They seem to really care about the students** and are eager to help everyone understand. They are very knowledgeable and find ways to make the material interesting."

Q "**Academically, I don't find Albion to be competitive**. In fact, many students seem very disinterested in the academic part of college. Many students are just plain lazy and would rather spend all of their time drinking and partying instead of getting an education."

Q "**The professors are one of my favorite things about Albion**. They are, for the most part, very nice individuals willing to lend a helping hand whenever they can. Also, professors are often very accessible and easy to talk to."

Q "Some believe that teachers are difficult at Albion while I'd say much to the opposite. A great deal of professors make you work, and if you do, you'll be better off in the long run. However, **some professors are also known for being notoriously easy**. While their courses may be a breeze, you'll get nothing out of them."

STUDENT AUTHOR: **Academics at Albion are a large part of why the retention rate is 87 percent. On a small campus and with such small class sizes, it is easy to get to know the faculty on a personal level. Most of them are incredibly approachable and will often go to extremes to make sure you're getting the best out of your education at Albion.**

Students Speak Out
ON LOCAL ATMOSPHERE

Q "Albion is a **typical small town**. At first, it's sort of a shock, but eventually it becomes homey."

Q "The town is pretty small and not used by students as much as it should be. A lot of students don't realize all of the great things about the town, like going for a drive through the country and discovering a one-room schoolhouse from the 1850s or finding a family cemetery from the turn of the century. **There's a lot of history here that's fun to discover**."

Q "In the first few weeks of school, you should be able to figure out what you like and dislike. From there, **you can figure out what it is that you'll do for fun on campus**."

Q "Albion doesn't really have many sights and sounds worth traveling to, though there is Victory Park and a quaint downtown that are at least fun to walk through every now and then. **Albion is regarded as a 'suitcase college'** by some. Fulfilling that name, Albion is located close to other colleges that you may get a greater kick out of visiting."

STUDENT AUTHOR: **The main deterrent to prospective students may be the size and state of the town of Albion. There's not much to look at as the downtown area is pretty much limited to one street. However, once you've been at Albion for a while, you will start to see its charm. Plus, a lot of good friendships are made through the common boredom of living in the town of Albion.**

Students Speak Out
ON FACILITIES

Q "Most of the buildings on campus are aesthetically pleasing. **Buildings are constantly being renovated** and repainted to keep them in good shape. However, the library is a bit dingy, and the theater could stand some renovation."

Q "The athletic facilities are adequate for the type of school we are. **There are enough athletic fields and equipment for athletes and non-athletes**."

Q "**Our library is very small**, but that makes sense considering how small our school is. We can rent quite a few films from the library, and they take recommendations for orders, which is cool."

Q "The facilities are extremely nice. Much of the College's **budget goes into maintaining and building structures around campus**, so much so that our professors are underpaid."

Q "I didn't really start to use the Dow until my sophomore year, but I've really enjoyed it since then. There are all sorts of things to do, from an elliptical machine to racquetball to swimming. **There's even a hot tub**! If you spend a decent amount of time in the Kellogg Center, you will run into tons of people you know. It's a good place to meet in groups."

STUDENT AUTHOR: **The facilities on campus range from functional to life-saving. The Stockwell-Mudd Library falls into the latter category. Offering an abundance of places to study, the library is the place to be most weeknights. If you're looking to kill some time or hang out with friends outside of the dorms, then you may want to check out the Dow, Albion's athletic center.**

Famous Alumni

Carolyn Aishton, Prentiss Marsh Brown, David L. Camp, Sherry Hood Penney Livingston, John S. Ludington, Richard M. Smith, William K. Stoffer, Robert M. Teeter

Students Speak Out
ON CAMPUS DINING

Q "The food is one of the best parts about Albion. **There's so much variety and so much food at Baldwin**. Even if you don't like the 'meal of the day,' you can make a sandwich, stir-fry, Belgian waffle, pasta creation, pizza, or anything else you can come up with. Plus, the cafeteria has really good desserts."

Q "The cafeteria food consists largely of fried foods, lots of chicken, and lots of potatoes. We do have salad, pizza, Mexican, and pasta bars, as well as ice cream and deserts, but the **vegetarian or vegan options are sparse**."

Q "**Baldwin is mediocre**, as the food gets repetitive. The Eat Shop makes me almost believe there is a God and that he occasional descends to make me a triple grilled cheese."

Q "The fact that Baldwin has an **unlimited meal plan is very convenient** and works well for the school."

Q "The food is not very pleasant. **It is cafeteria food, and that is that**."

STUDENT AUTHOR: **Students love to complain about Baldwin Hall, but after a while it just becomes comfortable, if not comforting. Although the food can get redundant, it's nice to have an unlimited meal plan. When Baldwin closes, the only dining option on campus is the Eat Shop. Open until midnight, the Eat Shop specializes in short-order food. Each semester, every student is given $25 to use there. Some say the money goes too fast, but it's good while it lasts.**

Students Speak Out
ON DORMS

Q "All the dorms are pretty nice. **You'll pretty much only have community bathrooms as a freshman** and maybe as a sophomore. The community bathrooms are nice, though, because they're cleaned every day."

Q "The dorms all have their ups and downs. **Wesley is full of freshmen, which is a lot more fun if you are a freshman**. But even then, it can get a little irritating with all the unnecessary fire alarms and other such ruckus. Overall, living in the dorms is a good experience."

Q "Mitchell is really nice. It's a lot less dingy than Whitehouse or Wesley. My advice to freshmen is to **tough out Wesley for a year—you'll probably meet your best friends there**."

STUDENT AUTHOR: **Albion's living situations can be pretty dismal at first. Freshmen are limited to Wesley and Seaton. Some say that Seaton is better because the rooms seem bigger due to newer, stackable furniture and it's closer to everything on campus. With Wesley, you're farther away from everything, but you will be living with almost all first-years. After sophomore year, you pretty much have your pick of where you want to live.**

? Did You Know?
90% of undergrads live on campus.

Students Speak Out
ON GUYS & GIRLS

Q "I would say that there are more attractive girls on campus than guys, and most attractive guys join fraternities. **Albion is a very preppy campus**, and **most students are usually well-dressed**."

Q "**There isn't much of a gay population, but it's growing**. Physically speaking, the stereotypical Albion male and female students are blonde, tan, and fit."

Q "It kind of feels like a lot of **all-American guys and girls congregate at Albion**."

Q "My initial reaction is to say that the vast majority of students at Albion are **rich white kids from the suburbs of Detroit**, and in many respects that is a true statement. However, there are all kinds of different-looking guys and girls."

STUDENT AUTHOR: **The students at Albion are not unattractive. There is a good mix of people, and you eventually may be able to find what you're looking for here. Just try not to stereotype people because of who they hang out with or what they look like. You could really miss out. If you go to a frat party looking to find a meaningful relationship, you're probably looking in the wrong place. It's better to meet people in class, Baldwin, the library, or simply put, when you are sober.**

Traditions

Drive-In Movie
Every fall, the Union Board sets up a drive-in movie in the Quad, complete with a giant screen and speakers.

The Rock
The Rock, at the northeast corner of the Quad, gets painted almost daily. Painting of the Rock usually is done in the dark of night, and it is a huge tradition.

Overall School Spirit
At Albion, it sometimes seems like students are prouder of what fraternity or sorority they belong to than the school itself.

Students Speak Out
ON ATHLETICS

Q "Varsity sports are fairly big on campus. **Lots of students participate**, but there are also a great deal of students who do not. IM sports are huge, and they tend to draw in a variety of different people, which is pretty cool."

Q "**I think it is a lot like watching really good high school sports** because of the smaller size and lower competition level. They are still fun to watch, though."

Q "There are a lot of athletes here, but the sports themselves aren't that big of an event. **Football and basketball games are the most attended**, though I don't go to either very often."

Q "About a third of students are involved in at least one sport. **IM sports are also very popular**."

STUDENT AUTHOR: **Albion may only be a Division III school, but a large number of students come here because they want to play sports. With a wide variety of teams, almost everyone has opportunity to compete. There are 18 varsity sports offered and plenty of intramural sports available. Spectators are sometimes few and far between, but those who do attend have some serious Briton pride.**

Students Speak Out
ON DRUG SCENE

Q "**I'm not aware of any particular drug problems on campus**. I'm sure there are a few students using drugs here or there, but it's nothing I've heard about."

Q "There is a brisk trade in prescription medication for ADHD, like Ritalin and Adderall. **Smoking pot is common among students**, but it isn't very visible."

Q "There are drugs, probably about the same amount of marijuana as in my high school, which is a decent amount. A lot of people will smoke it in a group at a party, but not as many people possess it on campus. There are also harder drugs—like coke, for instance—but it's kept more hush-hush than marijuana. **And, I know a lot of people like to abuse Adderall and painkillers.**"

STUDENT AUTHOR: **The drug scene on campus is hardly overwhelming. Drugs are definitely present, but they don't often find you if you aren't looking for them. The most recent craze of drugs, as with many American campuses, has been the use of amphetamines, mainly to help with studying.**

12:1	Student-to-Faculty Ratio
86%	Freshman Retention Rate
63%	Four-Year Graduation Rate
87%	Financial Aid Applicants Receiving Aid

Students Speak Out
SAFETY & SECURITY

Q "Campus Safety is always around, which can be a good or bad thing depending on your perspective. The campus is pretty safe overall. **Sure, there have been a few incidents, but none of them were serious**, and they all could have been prevented if the students had requested rides from Campus Safety."

Q "A few late-night muggings are not that big of a deal. **We are so hung up on the crime rate being zero** that we freak out when something happens."

Q "Campus Safety is always willing to walk students from late-night study spots to their dorms. Safety is something I believe the school is concerned about, and **they manage to take care of pretty much everything**."

STUDENT AUTHOR: **With Campus Safety officers constantly roaming Albion's well-lit campus, it is rare that a student feels unsafe. There have been a few incidents of violence and crime in the past, but as long as you care about and are aware of your safety, you shouldn't have a problem.**

Questions?
For more inside information and survival tips, pick up College Prowler's full-length book on this school, written by an actual student! Check it out at *www.collegeprowler.com*.

Students Speak Out
ON OVERALL EXPERIENCE

Q "I really like Albion. **I think a smaller school was the way to go** because having my professors know my name and not getting a nose bleed from sitting so far back in the classroom was something really important to me. Sure, the city is kind of lifeless, especially after dark, and the campus isn't all that diverse despite the school's attempts to make it otherwise, but college is whatever you make of it."

Q "I often feel very isolated and cut off from the rest of the world at Albion because I hardly venture outside of the school. On the other hand, I love the professors that I have had, and I would not trade the friends I've made for anything. Albion **students love to complain, but there are plenty of great things about this school**."

Q "I've had a great experience, **met the best friends of my life here**, and learned so much—and not just inside the classroom."

Q "Despite all the negatives, **I have come to really enjoy Albion**. It's true that there isn't a lot to do on campus or in town, but relying on yourself and your friends to make the fun is a good skill to have. Overall, I've been satisfied."

STUDENT AUTHOR: **Overall, Albion College is great for a number of reasons. The small campus makes it easy to make friends immediately and meet new people. While living in Albion can be boring at times, making the most of it is sometimes what will leave you with the most memories. There is a sense of community on Albion's campus that is hard to duplicate anywhere else. This isn't to say that everyone gets along, but there is a certain bond between all Albion students.**

Alfred University

1 Saxon Drive; Alfred, NY 14802-1205
(607) 871-2111; www.alfred.edu

THE BASICS:

Acceptance Rate: 74% **SAT Range:** 1490–1830*
Setting: Rural **Control:** Private
F-T Undergrads: 1,943 **Tuition:** $23,428

Most Popular Majors: Art, Engineering, Business Management and Marketing, Psychology, Education

*of 2400

Academics	B	Guys	C+
Local Atmosphere	C	Girls	C+
Safety & Security	A	Athletics	C-
Computers	B+	Nightlife	C
Facilities	B	Greek Life	N/A
Campus Dining	C+	Drug Scene	B+
Off-Campus Dining	B	Campus Strictness	B+
Campus Housing	B-	Parking	C-
Off-Campus Housing	B-	Transportation	D
Diversity	C-	Weather	D

Students Speak Out
ON ACADEMICS

Q "**The teachers are kind of a toss-up**. There are a lot of really cool, interesting professors, but then a lot of average or below average professors, too. But you can usually figure out pretty quickly which professors to take classes from by asking the upperclassmen."

Q "I think the professors that I liked **were very dedicated to the students** and were not afraid to tell you something sucked or that it was horrible, so they understood."

Q "They're **very available to everybody**. And you could always meet up with them for lunch or stay late and talk. They're just very personable."

Q "All of the teachers at Alfred are **down-to-earth and approachable**. I never felt like I couldn't ask to meet with a professor to discuss something. They were even open to discussing projects that were not class related. The classes in my field of study were interesting. It was kind of hard getting through some of the courses that you had absolutely no interest in but had to take to fill some requirement."

STUDENT AUTHOR: **If you think of your professors as professionals, mentors, or even baby-sitters, you might like Alfred. Departments and classes tend to be small, even intimate. While professors at some other universities may leave the teaching to a few bewildered TAs, faculty at Alfred are actively involved with their students. It's also not uncommon to be invited to a professor's home for tea or a cookout.**

Students Speak Out
ON LOCAL ATMOSPHERE

Q "It's pretty quiet. It's nice because I like being alone in a learning environment. **It could also be sort of isolating**. I would say it's very friendly, but that goes with any small town. It's the same every day, so you get really cozy."

Q "The atmosphere in Alfred is very friendly and calm. SUNY Alfred State is right across the street from us. Stay away from skunks and deer unless you want to be on one of those *Animals Gone Wild* tapes. **I would say visit and explore everything**. Especially the observatory—it's great!"

Q "I've never been in the South, but I almost felt like it was a small, Southern town. **Slow and friendly**, and everybody knows your business; just kind of quaint."

Q "**We're basically in the middle of nowhere**. Though 'middle' makes it sound too central. It's more like off on the far edge of nowhere. There's the state college across the road, but that's generally to be avoided. There's not really anything around except trees and cows."

STUDENT AUTHOR: **The town of Alfred is comprised of professors, blue-collar families, and a ghetto of graduate students. Despite a tepid but ongoing rivalry with Alfred State College, which lies across the valley, the general feeling in town is calm and friendly. Although the nearby cities of Buffalo and Rochester offer a hint of something urban, the general feeling is overwhelmingly rural.**

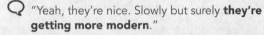

5 Best Things	5 Worst Things
1 Your friends	1 Sporadic weather
2 Financial aid	2 Isolation
3 Cool teachers	3 Boredom
4 Nature	4 Finding a parking spot
5 Senior shows	5 Ade Dining Hall

Students Speak Out
ON FACILITIES

"Yeah, they're nice. Slowly but surely **they're getting more modern**."

"**The facilities on campus are mediocre**; they are not bad, but not anything to write home about by any means. The school is small, so keep in mind the lack of funding and resources for larger and better facilities. Externally, the buildings are pretty nice looking, but don't let it fool you!"

"Most facilities are up to par, especially in the art building. **The gym, however, is definitely not up to par**. Recently, it has become very apparent that our school is just lacking in funds."

"Everything is kept up well. I guess I could say it's **done well enough for a college campus**, because I know how hard it can be to keep up a place with 2,000 college kids. For the way that it's treated, I think they're good facilities."

"Alfred has **some of the best facilities for students that you will ever see on a campus**. The campus center is always accessible for students, and the meeting rooms and activity rooms are amazing."

STUDENT AUTHOR: The facilities on campus seem to be similar to that of many other campuses. We have new and old buildings. The best part about the old buildings is that they are reminiscent of times long past. There is even a castle on campus. There are two libraries on campus, and if you're looking for something to do on the weekend, there is always a movie to catch in the Nevins Theatre. Some of the newest movies are shown every Friday and Saturday night for a mere $3.

Famous Alumni

Robert Littell, Mary Newton Bruder, Robert Klein, Peter Jenkins

Students Speak Out
ON CAMPUS DINING

"**The dining hall food is bad**. You know, poor quality, presentation, and taste. Li'l Alf is okay."

"People will complain about dining hall food just like every other college. However, **the staff really does try very hard** to expand their menu and bring in restaurants for special meals."

"The food on campus **isn't bad as school food goes**, and the dining services are constantly looking for (and responding to) feedback from students to make it even better. Most people prefer the Powell Dining Hall to Ade, mostly because it's cozier and feels less like a cafeteria. And the new library being built will have a café."

"**The food on campus is awful**. Three years ago, when we had a different food provider, it was pretty good, but now I refuse to go to both of the two dining halls because the food is unbearable."

"It was half good. It was decent for a university of that size. **Nothing too outrageous, but pretty accessible for everybody**. Although, I think it was funny that they tried to have Kosher food for Passover, and then they served quiche!"

STUDENT AUTHOR: At both Ade and Powell Dining Hall, students have the option of burgers and fries, pizza, a soup and salad bar, deli, or roast. There's also a feature entrée daily. We even host guest chefs and caterers from nearby restaurants. The only hitch is that the same menu every week can be monotonous. Also, the dismal offering of vegetarian/vegan choices is inexcusable.

Student Body

African American:	4%	Male/Female:	50/50%
Asian American:	2%	Out-of-State:	33%
Hispanic:	3%	International:	1%
Native American:	<1%	Unknown:	25%
White:	65%		

Popular Faiths: The two main religious groups on campus are BASIC and Varsity Interfaith.

Gay Pride: GLBT students have a great support system at Alfred. Spectrum, the GLBT group, is a force to be reckoned with on campus.

Economic Status: There certainly is economic diversity at Alfred. Ninety percent of all students at Alfred University receive some form of financial aid.

Students Speak Out
ON DORMS

Q "Your freshman year really won't matter. **All the dorms tend to be similar**. You want the party crowd? Go to Openhym (yes, I know this sounds a bit like false advertising, but believe me, it's the biggest dorm). Like studying? Go to Baressi, or go live in the library!"

Q "The dorms are okay—**nothing fancy**. Freshman halls are pretty standard—double rooms, alternating floors of men and women. There are four halls together in the 'freshman quad,' and then Openhym, which is much larger and noisier on the other side of campus."

Q "The dorms are good. I never had a problem with the dorms—**I like the setup**. I like where they were located on campus. Each had its own kind of character."

STUDENT AUTHOR: **Your residential experience at Alfred will vary greatly according to where you live. Openhym is the largest and the most social. The rest of the freshman dorms are smaller with larger doubles. Although most students are pleased to leave the freshman dorms behind, many miss the sense of community they provided.**

Did You Know?
67% of undergrads live on campus.

Students Speak Out
ON GUYS & GIRLS

Q "The people in Alfred are **not hot at all**. The guys and girls are mostly overweight or are all plain janes/johns. When I first came to Alfred, I was surprised to find such ugly people."

Q "**All the cute boys sleep around**, and if they're not sleeping around, they're stupid. But if you are ugly, it is a great place to meet another ugly person and fall in love, and have the possibility to have good-looking children."

Q "Because it's such a small school, **there tends to be a cliquey atmosphere**. Engineers will hang out together and so forth. It doesn't make it hard to approach them, it just makes them kind of inaccessible. For instance, if you don't go to their kind of parties, you have to go find them."

STUDENT AUTHOR: **Guys? They're pretty sloppy and a touch androgynous (even the jocks). Girls? They're pretty sloppy and a touch androgynous. What can I say? We've got a huge art department. It's rumored that *Playboy* magazine once rated Alfred University as having the ugliest girls. It's a rumor, of course. We're all just up here doing our thing and trying to keep warm; and nothing keeps you warmer than, well, doing your thing!**

Traditions

AIDS Charity Basketball Game
Every year, teams from AU and Alfred State compete against each other to raise money for victims of HIV.

The Alfies
Each year in Harder Hall, the University gives out awards specially tailored to the Alfred Community.

Hot Dog Day
Every spring, the town comes out for an entire weekend of drinking, games, and pork products. Hot Dog Day is also the premiere weekend for poor decision making and random hookups.

Students Speak Out
ON ATHLETICS

Q "Considering that we were Division III, sports are not very big, but **we definitely had teams that stand out**, like swimming and equestrian. I don't think the football team ever won a game."

Q "Varsity sports don't seem big to me, and **I don't know what IM sports are**."

Q "**Sports are really not that big at all**. A big problem on campus is low attendance at sporting events, and the teams are, for the most part, not that great. But every year is different! Intramural sports are there, and there's participation, but it's not huge."

Q "Sports are not big on campus, though **most people play them**. The teams are bad to mediocre."

STUDENT AUTHOR: **Team sports take on an interesting dimension here at school, one that emphasizes the individual. Here sports seem to be more about participation than competition. Attendance at sporting events varies depending on the day. As the University sees increased and more diverse enrollment, however, team sports are improving.**

Students Speak Out
ON DRUG SCENE

Q "My friends and I pretty much are the drug scene. It's an art school. **If you want drugs, they won't be hard to find**, unless we're having a dry spell because we live on the far edge of nowhere."

Q "I guess, **like on any college campus, pot is a definite**. I personally think it's pretty easily accessible. Alcohol is definitely easily accessible—it's a big part."

Q "A lot of kids drink. A lot of kids smoke pot, but **I think a lot less do it regularly**. I've known people who do pills, but as far as I know, it's not a huge issue."

STUDENT AUTHOR: **One might think that a campus like Alfred would be driven to drug use simply for the lack of activities. On the contrary, Alfred students seem much more interested in innovating new and dangerous winter sports than getting high. The great thing about Alfred is that there's very little peer pressure to get into, well, anything, drugs included.**

11:1	Student-to-Faculty Ratio
80%	Freshman Retention Rate
49%	Four-Year Graduation Rate
86%	Financial Aid Applicants Receiving Aid

Students Speak Out
SAFETY & SECURITY

Q "It's **pretty safe**, and there are Alfred cops riding around. It's an open campus where anyone could come in, though, so be wary of unknown faces."

Q "I always felt extremely safe on campus. **Our security guards were students**, so in that respect, it was a little daunting. I wouldn't have minded if there were a few more professionals."

Q "I personally felt very safe because I knew the whole campus, since it was so small. Plus, I guess I have common sense not to be in the middle of the woods by myself on a Friday night. On the other hand, because everybody just flocks into the town, **it could be sketchy on campus because nobody's around**. The only time I ever had campus security drive me home was once when I was drunk, and it was quite nice."

STUDENT AUTHOR: **It's a small campus, so you're never too far from safety. There are emergency phones strategically placed around campus, and campus police are constantly patrolling on foot or on horseback. They'll even escort you the whole five feet to your dorm.**

> **Questions?**
> For more inside information and survival tips, pick up College Prowler's full-length book on this school, written by an actual student! Check it out at *www.collegeprowler.com.*

Students Speak Out
ON OVERALL EXPERIENCE

Q "Alfred has given me everything it could since I was a sophomore. By the end of my second year, I was seriously thinking about transferring, but never did. Entering my senior year, I deeply regret my decision. Despite what people tell you, school name recognition is important, and **no one in Rochester even knows about Alfred**. Going to school in a bigger city will allow easier networking and internship opportunities."

Q "If only for the people that i've met, I'm glad I'm at Alfred. **I probably could have gotten a better education somewhere else**, but I'm not paying anything here, and I wouldn't trade my friends from here for anything."

Q "I think it is **very typical of a college experience**. You grow anywhere you go, and in four years, I've learned a lot about myself, about belonging, and about my friends. I think Alfred helped me when I needed it to, and now that I'm done, I'm ready to experience somewhere else."

Q "I've enjoyed my time at Alfred. I don't think I really could have ended up anyplace else. I've learned a lot, and I've made amazing lifetime friends, and **I wouldn't change it at all**. There is no place in the world like Alfred, New York."

STUDENT AUTHOR: **Students at AU make threats to transfer at least twice daily. Still, very few actually do. AU students will disparage their time at AU with venom. When asked to appraise their experience honestly, however, they'll shrug their shoulders and admit that Alfred has helped them to learn and grow as an individual. While some individuals transfer, the majority of students who chose Alfred know deep down that they couldn't be anywhere else.**

Allegheny College

520 North Main Street; Meadville PA 16335
(814) 332-3100; www.allegheny.edu

THE BASICS:

Acceptance Rate: 63%
Setting: Rural
F-T Undergrads: 2,048

SAT Range: 1110–1310*
Control: Private
Tuition: $31,680

Most Popular Majors: Biology, Psychology, English, Political Science

*of 1600

Academics	B	Guys	C
Local Atmosphere	D-	Girls	C
Safety & Security	A-	Athletics	C
Computers	D+	Nightlife	C+
Facilities	B	Greek Life	A
Campus Dining	C	Drug Scene	B
Off-Campus Dining	C+	Campus Strictness	B
Campus Housing	B-	Parking	B-
Off-Campus Housing	B-	Transportation	D+
Diversity	D-	Weather	C-

Students Speak Out
ON ACADEMICS

Q "The **professors work alongside students** rather than simply lecturing them. They have so much time for their students outside of class because they love to teach as much as they love the topic they're teaching."

Q "The professors are very helpful, but the **informality sometimes dumbs down classes**."

Q "The professors are accessible, always professional, **very willing to help students**, and are eager to share their research interests with those who ask about them. They require a lot of hard work from their students, which may at times seem like too much, but afterwards, students realize how much they have learned and how much they have improved as a result."

Q "There are two married English professors here who open their home to students and faculty for receptions after poetry readings and other departmental events. I feel like **I have really gotten to know many of my teachers** as mentors and friends."

STUDENT AUTHOR: At Allegheny College, academics are first priority. Classes can become quite competitive, but that doesn't keep students from working together. School work often becomes a social event where people get together to study, work on homework, or proofread papers. Also, since the different areas of study aren't divided into separate colleges, students' majors and minors are required to be from two different areas, making students well-rounded in their interests.

Students Speak Out
ON LOCAL ATMOSPHERE

Q "Allegheny is in Meadville, a rather dead city in rural Pennsylvania. I think **it's absolutely beautiful around here**—the four seasons, farmland, trees. Woodcock dam is a nice place to go walking on the trails or around the dam. Edinboro University is about 30 minutes north of here."

Q "**Meadville is a hole**. There isn't much around and anything that is closes at 4 p.m. The Penny Bar is a fun place to be after hours, though."

Q "For a while, there was a surprisingly decent punk and hardcore scene in town. That has been waning with the breakup of a pretty established local band, but the underground is still very much alive. If you're into that sort of thing, definitely keep your eyes open for shows. But keep in mind, the punk underground is sort of **a backlash against the conservative culture of the town**."

Q "I think **Meadville is quaint and cute**. I've never felt so safe in my life, and I probably never will again. There is a lot to do on campus, and the community is great, as well, due to the large number of locally-owned businesses in town."

STUDENT AUTHOR: Meadville is a small town in a cluster of smaller towns. It certainly doesn't have the entertainment or cultural attractions of a city. There are many little, independently-owned restaurants and shops that make up for our lack of big-name corporate businesses and give Meadville a small-town charm. There are also several parks for bike riding, hiking, swimming, or camping.

Students Speak Out
ON FACILITIES

Q "Most facilities are **well kept and fairly new**. Some departments have better facilities than others, and the computers are all outdated and old."

Q "The indoor athletic facility is very nice with lots of resources available for use, but the **outdoor facilities need to be updated**. The computers are older, and it is hard to guarantee that they will function properly. The student center has just been renovated and is very nice, but it's hard to adjust to the new layout."

Q "The **natural science facilities are excellent**. It seems that the art and music departments have sufficient, but not by any means excellent, facilities. Practice rooms and enough studio space are available."

Q "The Wise Center is well funded and generally looks nice. They **recently expanded** the weight room, though, which meant setting up an assortment of machines in the lobby. The Student Center was remodeled in the spring of 2004, so it's still in nice shape. With comfortable plush furniture everywhere, an elevator, the a la carte dining facility, a really attractive bookstore, and post office, anyone could be comfortable there."

STUDENT AUTHOR: **Facilities at Allegheny range from the modern, state-of-the-art Campus Center to Bentley Hall, built in 1820, which is still very attractive on the outside but rather lopsided in some places on the inside. Though our newer buildings seem to be the future of Allegheny, the other, less commonly used buildings do not seem as well maintained.**

Famous Alumni

Benjamin Burtt, Ida Tarbell, Lewis Walker

Students Speak Out
ON CAMPUS DINING

Q "The dining halls are like any college dining hall. The food is mass-produced, and that's a fact. I do think that the food services spend a lot of time getting the students' opinions and fixing things so that the **majority can be appeased**."

Q "The food is abysmal. It is slowly and poorly prepared, and criminally overpriced. ($3.50 for a cheeseburger, anyone?) **Shortages of main course items** occur all the time. The taste of different items varies, but most of it is pretty disgusting. Also, the food itself has the disturbing habit of leaving the body all too quickly."

Q "My favorite meal plan is the one that gives you about $900 worth of flexible spending money for over $1,000. Obviously, it would just be **cheaper to pay with cash**. Bravo, Allegheny College, bravo."

Q "For mass-produced food, ours is pretty good. It's not Mom's cooking, and it's often not restaurant quality, but it's a hell of a lot **better than anything you got in high school**. Salads, cereal, vegetarian, and vegan meals are offered, as well as the classic pizza and grill stuff."

STUDENT AUTHOR: **Most Allegheny students seem to think the food on campus is good. There are only two dining halls on campus and nowhere to use your meal plan off campus, so the school tries to customize our food as much as possible. The real problem students seem to have with the food on campus is the cost of the meal plan, which students are required to have while they live on campus.**

Student Body

African American:	2%	Male/Female:	44/56%
Asian American:	3%	Out-of-State:	44%
Hispanic:	1%	International:	1%
Native American:	<1%	Unknown:	0%
White:	93%		

Popular Faiths: Most students are Christian, although there are a variety of religions practiced on campus.

Gay Pride: There is a special interest house on campus, as well as organizations like Allegheny Gay Pride and Pride Alliance to support the small gay community at Allegheny.

Economic Status: Though it ranges, the college seems to be predominantly upper-middle class.

Students Speak Out
ON DORMS

Q "**Schultz is awesome**. It's definitely the best place freshmen can get into. There's good sized rooms and new furniture."

Q "Avoid Baldwin. The **biggest rooms are in Ravine**. College Court is nice for seniors who still want on campus housing."

Q "**Buildings on campus are all pretty old** and sometimes you can tell. (In Brooks and Caflisch, they have steam heaters that can be loud.)"

Q "The thing to worry about is their proximity to the academic buildings and dining halls. Because of this, **Schultz and Baldwin are favorites**. Avoid Ravine, South Highland, and Crawford. Rooms seem to be the same everywhere."

STUDENT AUTHOR: **With the three-year residency requirement, you had better like the on-campus housing. Luckily, the school allows students a lot of freedom with their rooms. Students can paint them as long as they repaint them white at the end of the year. They can also have any kind of pet that lives in an aquarium, although lots of people secretively have furry pets. The college is pretty lenient, so you can make it as homey as you want.**

Did You Know?
78% of undergrads live on campus.

Students Speak Out
ON GUYS & GIRLS

Q "We are known for our personality and character. **We are good-looking**, I hope, but there is more to people than just looks. You learn that here. Clothes also do not matter. Get over it!"

Q "There are **definitely some hot chicks out there**, like most colleges, and some are nice. After all, what's the point of a chick being hot if you're going to be a complete witch?"

Q "**There's an Allegheny 'Rule of Thirds'** about guys: 1/3 are jerks, 1/3 are taken, and 1/3 are gay."

Q "People at other schools are much better looking. I don't know what bizarre social phenomenon accounts for this, but **we at Allegheny are seriously ugly**."

STUDENT AUTHOR: **Most of the students are just plain average when it comes to looks. We like to party and have fun, and we would like to date attractive people, but intelligence and success are what most Alleghenians find most attractive. Another great aspect of Allegheny is the mix of lifestyles. There are hippies, jocks, preppy people, nerds, punks, and every other possible type of person you could think of.**

Traditions

Burning of the Comps
During senior week, seniors get together to burn their comps as a sign that they are free from all the work.

Hut-a-thon
Habitat for Humanity builds a hut every year and camps out there for a weekend to raise money and awareness about homelessness.

Overall School Spirit
Most students don't have school spirit in the "sports nut" sense of the word, but many are proud that they go to Allegheny for its academic reputation.

Students Speak Out
ON ATHLETICS

Q "Don't come here just for the sports; come here for good professors and a small-college atmosphere, or **you will be disappointed**."

Q "Sports? We have varsity sports teams? **Sure we have them**, but they're not nearly as 'on top of the world' as they were in high school. Sure, the athletic department's budget is nearing 100 times my father's salary, but if academics don't come first here, you won't cut it. Rugby seems to be as popular as football."

Q "There are a lot of people playing sports on both the varsity and intramural levels. Allegheny is not a school-spirit type of school where people get all fired up and go to the games. **Tailgating properly is against the rules**."

Q "Varsity isn't so big. Intramural is pretty popular. It's a nice **stress reliever**."

STUDENT AUTHOR: **Most of the varsity sports teams at Allegheny are competitive in their division. Much of the student body, however, isn't even aware of that. Intramural sports are a little more popular, and there's always the recreation center, but as a whole, Allegheny is just not a big sports college.**

Students Speak Out
ON DRUG SCENE

Q "Apparently, **there is hard drug use here**, like cocaine, but I personally don't know anyone who uses anything besides marijuana and alcohol."

Q "**People get high** everywhere."

Q "I have **never encountered drugs** on campus and have never heard stories of them being on campus."

Q "To say there isn't one is a lie, but it really isn't that bad. **I don't feel unsafe or insecure**."

Q "Pot is pretty prevalent in a lot of circles. You'll find the **occasional harder drugs as well** (coke, acid, 'shrooms)."

STUDENT AUTHOR: Majority of the time, the most people do at Allegheny is get drunk. You would never have to worry about being pressured to do drugs since most people don't, and even those who do are well aware that everyone has different likes and dislikes. Drugs tend to travel only in certain circles, so if you stay out of those circles, you won't see them.

14:1	Student-to-Faculty Ratio
87%	Freshman Retention Rate
70%	Four-Year Graduation Rate
86%	Financial Aid Applicants Receiving Aid

Students Speak Out
SAFETY & SECURITY

Q "I have discovered that campus isn't as safe as the school claims it is. For example, more **domestic violence happens** than is reported. Generally, I feel safer here than I would in a big city, though."

Q "I love when security stops you after a night of hard partying and then **lets you right off** the hook. Also, I love the unlit call boxes."

Q "If you take a tour of the campus, your tour guide will likely point out the security call boxes on the route. Unfortunately, that's pretty much the only place you'll find them. However, I have made hundreds of trips across campus alone at night and **have never felt threatened**. But if you're not comfortable with that, there are security escorts available."

STUDENT AUTHOR: There isn't much crime on campus, so students generally feel safe. However, there is little effort to prevent crimes from happening. Several of the dorms are left unlocked all day, and buildings with computer labs are left open until late at night with no security cameras.

Questions?
For more inside information and survival tips, pick up College Prowler's full-length book on this school, written by an actual student! Check it out at *www.collegeprowler.com*.

Students Speak Out
ON OVERALL EXPERIENCE

Q "I would have transferred if it weren't for the professors. The education you get here is **worth all the trouble**."

Q "**I absolutely love it here** and wouldn't change my decision for anything in the world. Allegheny gives you a great education, excellent opportunities, and lots of fun along with the stress."

Q "My overall Allegheny experience was bittersweet. While at Allegheny, I met people and had experiences that I will remember for the rest of my life, but **the academic rigors branded me with a number of stress-related neuroses**. Allegheny is for those with incentive and great reserves of emotional stamina. If you can make it here, it's a wonderful education."

Q "I love the school, but it's a ton of work. **I get stressed out a lot** and often think that it would be easier at a different school."

Q "Allegheny is great. The education is wonderful. **Meadville isn't the most exciting place**, but it's relaxed and you don't have to worry about safety issues you would in a more metropolitan area."

STUDENT AUTHOR: There are students that have regrets or were in some way disappointed with their Allegheny education. Allegheny isn't perfect, but for the majority of people, they wouldn't trade their time at Allegheny for anything. Even the people that came to Allegheny because they didn't get into their first-choice university usually find that, in the end, Allegheny was the right college for them. Most students are thankful for the education they received and all the great people they met.

Alverno College

3400 South 43rd Street; Milwaukee, WI 53234-3922
(414) 382-6000; www.alverno.edu

THE BASICS:

Acceptance Rate: 89%
Setting: Urban
F-T Undergrads: 2,371

ACT Range: 17–22
Control: Private
Tuition: $18,624

Most Popular Majors: Health Professions, Business, Communications, Psychology, Education

Academics	A-	Guys	N/A
Local Atmosphere	A-	Girls	B+
Safety & Security	A	Athletics	D+
Computers	B+	Nightlife	A-
Facilities	B	Greek Life	D
Campus Dining	B	Drug Scene	A
Off-Campus Dining	A-	Campus Strictness	C
Campus Housing	A-	Parking	A
Off-Campus Housing	A	Transportation	B
Diversity	D	Weather	C

Students Speak Out
ON ACADEMICS

Q "The teachers are basically amazing. I know when I walk into each and every class that the only agenda my teachers have is to benefit my development as a student. **I know so many of my teachers, and they know me**. There are relationships and connections being made—we are like an awesome, super-functioning community of learners."

Q "**The teachers range from really good to horrific**. It really depends on the department and how/why you're interacting with the teacher. Some teachers tend to be nicer toward students with whom they are more familiar, and teachers are definitely nicer and more understanding when you apply yourself."

Q "**The instructors at Alverno are all very unique and worldly**. Many of the instructors I have had know a lot of current events and are up on their information."

Q "The teachers are an interesting bunch. Being a smaller college, **you can really get to know the professors in your major quite well**, not only their teaching style but also as real people."

STUDENT AUTHOR: Here at Alverno, everyone wants you to succeed. Professors want you to call them by their first names and will often give you their personal e-mails or home phone numbers. Truly, countless professors feel they are learning from their students just as much as their students learn from the professor.

Students Speak Out
ON LOCAL ATMOSPHERE

Q "I am originally from Chicago, so Milwaukee seems rather small and drab by comparison. I am very politically active, and **Milwaukee has proven to be a very good size for activism**. There are seedy bars and dangerous neighborhoods just like in any other city, and there are some things to do, but I'm homesick most of the time."

Q "Alverno is located in a metropolitan city, but we are in the middle of a residential neighborhood. **We are about five minutes from the lake as well as downtown,** and there are stores within walking distance."

Q "**I really like Milwaukee**. There are various museums to visit, a lively nightlife, and many other things to do, especially in the summer and warmer months. I don't think that there is anything that I would necessarily stay away from. Other universities close by are Marquette, UW-Milwaukee, and MATC."

Q "Alverno is wonderful because you are at a small school but are still **only minutes away from a large city**."

STUDENT AUTHOR: Alverno College is in the middle of a quiet residential area, which is has its pros and its cons. It is easy to forget Alverno is even in Milwaukee because it is not downtown between the skyscrapers or next to Lake Michigan, but being removed from the urban hustle is nice as well. Milwaukee is a student-friendly city, and everything seems to be within a 15-minute drive.

Students Speak Out
ON FACILITIES

Q "The workout facility is nice but a little small. **My favorite place on campus is The Mug**, our coffeehouse. Great coffee! Great sofas/couches! Great people! Wonderful atmosphere!"

Q "The facilities are pretty nice. There are some outdated areas of the school, but **the recent remodel really gave the campus a facelift**. The grounds are beautiful and serene, and the parking garage is so nice to have."

Q "Alverno offers new and clean facilities. **The gym was recently built** and has comfortable bleachers and a beautiful wooden floor to practice basketball or dance on. The computers are really easy to type on and offer clear graphics and easy-to-use icons."

Q "**Alverno is always ridiculously clean** and much of the school is new. The fitness center is new, and the computer labs are new."

Q "The facilities overall are well-kept, but **they are rather small**."

STUDENT AUTHOR: The facilities on campus are small but clean, and students are often asked for their input on how to make areas such as the commons or the fitness center more student-friendly. As the number of students increases at Alverno, the larger the facilities become. Weekends can get really boring if you are stuck on campus, but the fitness center and library have weekend hours. Also, the green space and flowers on campus throughout spring, summer, and autumn are gorgeous and well kept.

Famous Alumni

Stephanie Arenda, Barbara Kluka, Carol Meils, Sister Joel Read, Sister Catherine Ryan, Kiyoko Toyama

Students Speak Out
ON CAMPUS DINING

Q "Food is good on campus. **With only one cafeteria, lunch can seem monotonous** day after day, and the lunchroom is often crowded. Often I opt to grab lunch and eat it somewhere else on campus."

Q "Incoming students don't seem to mind the food, but if you live on campus for more than a year, the menu doesn't really change, and it gets repetitive. There's a little bit of variety with a salad and sandwich bar, but **the hot items are like cafeterias in high school**. A lot of it is deep fried so it can be difficult to eat healthy without eating a salad or sandwich."

Q "From what I have had on campus, **the food isn't that bad**. I have had better, and I have had worse. I usually get a club sandwich or a sub— both are really good. The Commons/lunchroom is clean, and you can usually find a place to sit."

Q "**It can be pricey** to eat on campus unless you are a resident or have a meal account set up, which is not hard to do."

Q "**The sandwiches tend to be the freshest** and most healthy option for vegetarians."

STUDENT AUTHOR: Alverno recently switched from doing its own food to having a company come in to handle dining services. This has made a drastic change in the food and atmosphere on campus. They are trying new, healthier food options, including a variety of vegetarian dishes. The food on campus is far from five-star gourmet, but they do have a lot of options for everyone.

Student Body

African American:	16%	Male/Female:	0/100%
Asian American:	4%	Out-of-State:	2%
Hispanic:	12%	International:	1%
Native American:	1%	Unknown:	0%
White:	65%		

Popular Faiths: Catholic, although everyone's religion or lack of religion is respected.

Gay Pride: The Alverno chapter of the Gay-Straight Alliance (GSA) goes in and out of activity, depending on the leadership.

Economic Status: Since Alverno is a private college, there is a solid percentage of students who have parents who pay for their education because they can afford it.

Students Speak Out
ON DORMS

Q "The dorms are great. The rooms are fairly large compared to other campuses in the area, and all rooms have a sink. **There are only two dorms**. Clare is for the more studious, quiet types, and Austin houses all incoming students and the general population."

Q "**Alverno is mostly a commuter college, so less than half the students live on campus**. The residence hall has a lot of fun programs that the RAs put on, and it is very social and active."

Q "**I would definitely recommend that freshmen and sophomores live on campus** because the experience is great and the social aspect is important when creating that firm foundation to strive for success as a college student."

STUDENT AUTHOR: **The dorms at Alverno are extremely spacious and include high ceilings and large windows. The rooms in Austin Hall all have built-in shelving units, drawers, spacious closets, and a sink accompanied by shelves and cupboards. Clare Hall is currently going through renovations, which will make living at Clare awesome. Students will have their own fitness center, computers labs, and laundry facilities on each floor.**

Did You Know?
9% of undergrads live on campus.

Students Speak Out
ON GUYS & GIRLS

Q "**Considering Alverno is a women's college, the men are few and far between**. I haven't had any issues with other students. If I did, it's nothing that cannot be worked out before or in class."

Q "Although we are a single-sex college, I believe this aspect is conducive to learning and that there are **many outlets within the community to network with possible relationship partners**."

Q "**No guys**. Sorry, girls."

Q "Alverno is an all-girls college, so there aren't any guys in the student body. As for the girls, **it's diverse, so you have your choice no matter your taste**."

STUDENT AUTHOR: **Being that Alverno is a women's college, there are girls of every shape, size, and walk of life. The girls here are incredible listeners, engaging conversationalists, and well-rounded individuals. A large portion of the students are also non-traditional (meaning they have children or are married). There are a few males, but these are few and far between because they are part of a master's or licensure program.**

Traditions

Rotunda Ball
The Rotunda Ball is an annual December winter dance that is put on by Page Board. It is essentially a glorified prom.

Wing Wars
The biggest event during Homecoming Week is Wing Wars. Students are given a theme and have to decorate their hallway accordingly. The most creative interpretation wins a prize party.

Overall School Spirit
The community felt on campus is not exactly school spirit, but there is definitely a feeling of that we're all here together and we're all Alverno women.

Students Speak Out
ON ATHLETICS

Q "Alverno does have sports, but the young program is not established enough to be the draw for the College. **There is a strong focus on academics, and sports come second**. This is not to say that the athletic department is overlooked, though."

Q "Sports are not very big on campus because there are so many non-traditional commuter students. **Alverno students are more focused on their academics**, which is what the school is known for."

Q "One of the great things about sports on campus is that **all the sporting events are free**. Being able to go to sporting events makes me feel more involved and a part of the community here."

Q "I feel **we kind of lack the excitement of college sports**. There are no big rallies."

STUDENT AUTHOR: **Athletics could honestly be better. There is very little following for the students who actually play sports. The majority of students who try out for teams make it because there is such a small pool of athletes to choose from. The athletics program is becoming bigger, but it is quite slow.**

Students Speak Out
ON DRUG SCENE

Q "Aside from sometimes randomly smelling pot in the dorms, which is hardly ever, there isn't really a drug scene. There's not a group of people who hover around doing drugs. If anyone does, they tend to keep to themselves. **It's a pretty clean campus**."

Q "I know girls who live on campus who smoke weed, but they don't do it on campus. **Drugs just aren't prevalent on campus**. I think Alverno has done a good job of banishing drugs. They even got rid of tobacco on campus."

Q "**It's really hidden**. I know there are drugs on campus, but most people are at least respectful enough to not do them here."

STUDENT AUTHOR: **There really is not a drug scene on campus because when there are drugs on campus and the administration or residence life staff find out, they lay the smack down. The campus is also tobacco-free because it wants students to learn to have healthier lifestyles. Even though there are mentions of pot being on campus, this is seldom to hardly ever.**

21:1	Student-to-Faculty Ratio
73%	Freshman Retention Rate
21%	Four-Year Graduation Rate
99%	Financial Aid Applicants Receiving Aid

Students Speak Out
SAFETY & SECURITY

Q "Security is definitely present and supportive on campus. It's nice to get updates on security alerts during the rare times that there are problems. **Things are not swept under the rug**."

Q "Not once have I ever felt unsafe on campus at Alverno. **It's like this little oasis in the middle of Milwaukee**."

Q "**I have never felt unsafe at Alverno**—not by myself, late at night, or any other time. Maybe it's because there aren't boys crawling all over the place, or maybe it's because everything is pretty well lit. However, it seems like security is more preoccupied by other "more serious" threats like catching the smokers than anything else."

STUDENT AUTHOR: **The Alverno campus is quite compact and extremely well lit, so there really aren't many unsafe, hidden, or dark places. However, if students feel uncomfortable walking anywhere on campus, security officers do offer escorts. Security also has quite a presence on campus and make rounds through each building during their shifts.**

> **Questions?**
> For more inside information and survival tips, pick up College Prowler's full-length book on this school, written by an actual student! Check it out at *www.collegeprowler.com*.

Students Speak Out
ON OVERALL EXPERIENCE

Q "I love Alverno, and **I am glad that I made the choice to overcome my boy-crazy mind**. You never really realize there aren't guys in your classes and that, for the most part, the only men you see are the faculty and staff. It is a great school, and the personal relationships that you gain with your instructors are amazing because you get the help you need and you are more than just a number."

Q "Alverno's alternative ability-based curriculum and small classes were the reason I chose to attend school here, and **the kind professors and challenging education are the reasons I stay**. I am so glad I chose to live on campus, as the convenience of living five minutes from class is unbeatable, and the programs and friends I've met here are absolutely phenomenal."

Q "I actually transferred out after my second year at Alverno, but I really hated the school I was attending. **I didn't realize how good of a school Alverno was until I left**. Now I'm back, and I love it."

Q "**The grading system is really nice because you get to show what you know in many ways** and you aren't simply taking in information and spitting it back out through multiple-choice tests."

STUDENT AUTHOR: **Alverno teaches women (and some men) to think outside the box and to understand themselves. Graduates from Alverno go on to be important women in their workplaces, their communities, their churches, and their homes. Most people say going to college is an investment in your future, but coming to Alverno is an investment in your future as well as your community's future.**

American University

4400 Massachusetts Avenue; Washington, DC 20016
(202) 885-1000; www.american.edu

THE BASICS:

Acceptance Rate: 53% **SAT Range:** 1750–2050*
Setting: Urban **Control:** Private
F-T Undergrads: 5,781 **Tuition:** $32,816

Most Popular Majors: Business, Int'l Service, CLEG (Communication, Law, Economics, and Government)

*of 2400

Academics	B+	Guys	B+
Local Atmosphere	A	Girls	C+
Safety & Security	A	Athletics	C
Computers	B+	Nightlife	A-
Facilities	B	Greek Life	B
Campus Dining	A	Drug Scene	B+
Off-Campus Dining	A-	Campus Strictness	C
Campus Housing	A-	Parking	D-
Off-Campus Housing	C	Transportation	A
Diversity	C-	Weather	B-

Students Speak Out
ON ACADEMICS

Q "The academics are not as impressive as you would think. AU often tries to **hire professors for their names rather than for their quality**. But opportunities in the city make up for shortfalls in the faculty. There are lots of good professors. Nonetheless, you just have to search for some of them."

Q "For some reason, **AU has some of the best faculty in the United States**. I've been exceedingly satisfied with 90 percent of the faculty I've had here. Most of the resident faculty have doctorates while those who are adjunct (meaning they have another job outside of teaching), have really great backgrounds, and have worked all over the map in top positions."

Q "**Some you will love; some you will hate**. The great thing about DC is that you have teachers who also do other stuff while teaching, like being ambassadors to other countries."

Q "My classes were all small. My largest was a 60-person biology lecture; my smallest class had seven. **The average was probably 12 students**, so there was a lot of personal attention, and I always felt free to go to my professors' office hours for help."

STUDENT AUTHOR: The school has a varied curriculum, and many agree that politics and business are the strongest areas of study. AU's location provides hands-on opportunities, especially to international service, political science, and communications majors.

Students Speak Out
ON LOCAL ATMOSPHERE

Q "DC is great. It's a small city and it's split into the northwest, northeast, southeast, and southwest. You pretty much want to stay in northwest, but that is easy because it is the biggest section. Obviously, **you have to go see the monuments**, go walk in Georgetown, and of course, you have to take a train up to Baltimore's South Harbor and see a baseball game."

Q "American's neighborhood is pretty rich. There are tons of stores and restaurants, but some **locals might act a little snooty** to the college kids. For the most part, though, it's a really nice area."

Q "**Washington is uptight**, a tad on the conservative side, behavior-wise, political, and ethnically diverse, (though, largely segregated like many big cities). The city itself is small, but has a lot to offer. Make the Smithsonians and the monuments a priority. Also, see some free performances at the Kennedy Center. Go to the festivals (Taste of DC especially), go shopping in Georgetown, and experience Eastern Market and Adams Morgan."

STUDENT AUTHOR: DC is considered one of the best college towns in the country, and there is no shortage of young people out to have a great time (or climb the social ladder in hopes of political success). At the same time, AU offers a haven from the intensity in its quiet suburban-type setting, with easy access to I-95 and quainter towns in Maryland and Virginia.

Students Speak Out
ON FACILITIES

Q "The facilities are really nice. The classrooms are great; a lot recently got redone. The student center is nice—it's small, but it's good. There are **Internet hookups everywhere**. The gym is great. It's all pretty new and really nice!"

Q "The fitness center, cafeteria, and the student center are very nice and have all been recently modernized. The library, several classroom buildings, and some of the dorms are antiquated, but the campus architecture and **facilities all blend the old classical-style characteristic of Washington** with a modern academic look."

Q "The student center is a collection of food vendors, including Einstein Brothers Bagels. There are no games (there is a television and lots of seating), but there's a big city out there. **There's really no point in having an enormous student center**, so we don't have one."

Q "The facilities are fine. **I'm not blown away by any of them**, but they all certainly meet my needs. AU doesn't have tons of money, so they don't have flashy facilities, but like I said, they always get the job done for me."

STUDENT AUTHOR: **AU has taken great pains in the past to update and modernize their facilities, but students remain underwhelmed due to the facilities' small sizes. However, most agree that they are good enough with Internet access and a decent choice in food. Students generally approve of the dorms, and the fitness center is a popular spot and usually crowded. Facilities at AU may not be thrilling, but they are always clean and up-to-date.**

Famous Alumni

David Aldridge, Robert Byrd, Robert Engel, Goldie Hawn, Al Koken, Mike Mills, Star Jones, Judith Sheindlin "Judge Judy"

Students Speak Out
ON CAMPUS DINING

Q "On campus, **there's a tavern, a deli, and a minor buffet-style dining hall**—all housed in the same building as the Main Hall. There is a McDonald's, a convenience store, and several coffee shops where you can eat."

Q "Dining Services are now **contracted through Bon Appetit**. There's one main dining hall that has an outstanding selection. AU has a diverse ethnic population, and therefore offers diverse cuisine and vegetarian food, as well as the usual things like pizza and burgers."

Q "The **food quality went down a little** during my four years (or I just got sick of it), but there are a lot of options. TDR is the main dining hall, and it has a lot of options, like a salad bar, 'make your own pizza,' and a sandwich bar. You can always find something. There are also smaller specialty places that do sandwiches, soups, burgers."

Q "TDR is okay: lots of variety, mediocre execution. There are food vendors all over campus, two of which, **Jamba Juice and Chick-fil-A**, take meal plans."

STUDENT AUTHOR: **AU's cafeteria is considered much better than typical college fare, featuring unusual multiethnic cuisine and vegetarian and vegan options that are usually very tasty. Students complain more about getting bored with food from the same source throughout their semesters, rather than the quality of the food. AU has several fast food options, as well as an on-campus convenience store (Eagle's Nest).**

Student Body

African American:	7%	Male/Female:	38/62%
Asian American:	5%	Out-of-State:	89%
Hispanic:	5%	International:	8%
Native American:	<1%	Unknown:	18%
White:	56%		

Popular Faiths: The school is affiliated with the United Methodist church.

Gay Pride: Two words: very tolerant. The GLBTA Resource center takes an active role in helping AU students find GLBTA related volunteer, internship, and study abroad opportunities.

Economic Status: Mostly middle- to upper-middle class, although 47 percent of student receive aid.

Students Speak Out
ON DORMS

Q "Dorms on the south side are Anderson, Letts, and Centennial. They are known to be big, loud, and fun. Dorms on the north side of campus are McDowell, Hughes, and an international dorm. They are smaller and quieter but still fun. In general, **dorms aren't that small, and many have cool wall units**, two beds, and two desks."

Q "The dorms are very nice. **There are north and south sides of campus**, both with a different atmosphere. The north side is quieter—no Greeks, but more athletes and international students. These dorms are Hughes, Leonard, and McDowell. The south side is more outgoing and fun with people always outside hanging out. There are more Greeks and more parties. These dorms are Letts, Anderson, and Centennial, which is for upperclassmen only."

STUDENT AUTHOR: **Leonard is an international dorm, and there are specialized floors elsewhere, including all-women floors and community service floors. Many freshmen live on campus and say it makes meeting people easier, but by junior year, some students start moving off campus.**

 Did You Know?
75% of undergrads live on campus.

Students Speak Out
ON GUYS & GIRLS

Q "My overall take on the student body is that they are diverse (in terms of interests, culture, where they come from, and goals), smart, politically and socially aware, and nice. Lots of AU people go into the Peace Corps or other service programs after college. Lots work on Capitol Hill or for other government agencies. **I am constantly impressed with the people I meet**."

Q "Oh, dear, didn't anyone tell you? AU is overwhelmingly female. Of the small male population, a near majority are gay. However, don't be too discouraged. They're all nice, and the **town is crawling with undergrads**, Congressional staffers, interns, and law students. There is no shortage of eligible men, and they are indeed hot—East Coast style, though. Be forewarned."

STUDENT AUTHOR: **Fear not: you don't have to look like a supermodel to** find a mate at AU. The cosmopolitan and ambitious student body tends to place a greater emphasis on individuality, motivation, and intelligence than on appearance, but a fresh, clean-cut look doesn't hurt either. Straight women at AU complain that satisfactory boyfriends are hard to find, as girls vastly outnumber the guys on campus.

Traditions

Primal Scream
Around finals time, students gather in the courtyard between Hughes and McDowell Halls to yell their heads off and watch other students flash them from the overlooking dorms. It's a stress reliever.

Overall School Spirit
The Screaming Eagles are a club that actively supports the sports teams (think customized T-shirts, face paint, and wild and crazy cheers).

Students Speak Out
ON ATHLETICS

Q "There is lacrosse, soccer, swimming, diving, and rugby as varsity-type sports, and then there are club teams for roller-hockey, hockey, and the like. Personally, I think that fraternity flag football is **more exhilarating than any actual University sport**."

Q "Both varsity and IM sports are big on campus. **AU is Division I, so we are totally into our basketball team**. However, we don't have a football team at all."

Q "**Sports are largely ignored**, which is surprising for a Division I school."

Q "**AU is not an athletically-oriented campus** like Notre Dame or Penn State, but the varsity teams are Division I, and for the meager funding and publicity they get, they are quite good, especially women's volleyball, the soccer teams, and the men's basketball team. IM sports are not big, and they are poorly run by the athletics department, but they are mostly fun, nonetheless."

STUDENT AUTHOR: **A recently-founded club, the Screaming Eagles, go all out at the games, painting their faces and coming up with their own cheers. Basketball and volleyball are popular sports, and in the rare instance where are game is being televised, the turnout is better than usual.**

Students Speak Out
ON DRUG SCENE

Q "Our campus is very strict. **There is no drinking or pot (obviously) allowed on campus**. If you get caught, you must do community service. If you get caught a second time, you have to do even more community service and also go to an educational mediation session. The best bet is to go off campus for that. People still get away with it on campus, but you just have to be careful."

Q "Pot is probably the most heavily-used drug, but even that is not all that prevalent. I've heard of other things being used—acid, E, and coke—but I've never actually seen anyone use them. If you don't want to do drugs, you don't have to. Don't try stuff on campus; they are strict about it. **Drinking is this school's stronghold**."

STUDENT AUTHOR: AU is known to be a strict campus that has recently cracked down on the drug scene by confiscating drugs and severely punishing the student drug dealers involved. Despite its presence, it's quite possible to not even see one drug during your entire four years of college at AU.

14:1	Student-to-Faculty Ratio
86%	Freshman Retention Rate
73%	Four-Year Graduation Rate
72%	Financial Aid Applicants Receiving Aid

Students Speak Out
SAFETY & SECURITY

Q "I always felt perfectly safe, even by myself at night. The campus is fairly small and compact, so getting from one side to the other only takes a few minutes. It's well lit, and the surrounding neighborhood is very nice. It is right near a lot of embassies, so there's a lot of security off campus as well. **The area is patrolled by campus security**, DC Metro police, and embassy security. I left my dorm room door unlocked all the time for the two years I lived in the dorms and never had a problem."

Q "I can tell you that AU's Public Safety department is highly trained (through the police academy) and capable. **They take serious infractions seriously**—hate crimes, sexual assaults, and the like."

STUDENT AUTHOR: Being in a more affluent neighborhood means a lower risk for crime at AU. The campus police are visible and effective, providing students with a strong sense of comfort and security. There are blue-light phones available throughout campus in case of emergencies, and security responds quickly and effectively to crises.

> **Questions?**
> For more inside information and survival tips, pick up College Prowler's full-length book on this school, written by an actual student! Check it out at www.collegeprowler.com.

Students Speak Out
ON OVERALL EXPERIENCE

Q "**AU is a small school, which some people like and some people don't**. Personally, I enjoy walking around campus, seeing familiar faces, and then seeing those same familiar faces at bars and clubs. AU really is a small community inside of DC. Walking from your dorm to class, it is very easy to see your friends and people you know. This is usually a positive, but the downside is that gossip moves fast, and everybody seems to be connected through friends or somebody they know, especially inside the Greek system."

Q "When I first came, I hated it and wanted to transfer. **It was difficult for me to adjust** to such a diverse population, and I had trouble finding people I could relate to. Also, the lack of sports really got to me. But after some time, I loosened up a little, met some new people, accepted the school for what it was, and had a blast."

Q "I wish I had studied more when I was there. **AU is kind of too easy**."

Q "I've had frustrations thanks to the bureaucracy that surrounds any such institution, but I'm happy I chose AU, and **I would recommend it to anyone who cares about diversity**, government, and high, second-tier academics with more than a few shining stars."

STUDENT AUTHOR: Though the school's population is relatively small and has fewer parties compared to state schools, many claim that it is worth it for the culture present in DC. Upon arrival at AU, the adjustment period can be tough. However, making friends is quite easy here for even the shyest of students because of the small, tight-knit AU community.

Amherst College

220 South Pleasant Street; Amherst, MA 01002-5000
(413) 542-2000; www.amherst.edu

THE BASICS:

Acceptance Rate: 18% **SAT Range:** 2000–2290*
Setting: Rural **Control:** Private
F-T Undergrads: 1,683 **Tuition:** $35,580

Most Popular Majors: Social Sciences, Foreign Languages and Literature, Psychology, English

*of 2400

Academics	A	Guys	B
Local Atmosphere	C	Girls	B
Safety & Security	B+	Athletics	B
Computers	A	Nightlife	B
Facilities	A	Greek Life	D-
Campus Dining	B	Drug Scene	B
Off-Campus Dining	B+	Campus Strictness	B+
Campus Housing	B	Parking	A-
Off-Campus Housing	C-	Transportation	B
Diversity	B+	Weather	C+

Students Speak Out
ON ACADEMICS

Q "I personally know dozens of professors here, and they will pretty much sit down with you at any time. They are **genuinely interested** in what you have to say and will really try to get at exactly what you're thinking of. You can also chat with some of them about everyday stuff, and even joke around with some of them."

Q "All the teachers are really helpful, and they **enjoy what they are teaching**. If you have trouble getting an assignment in, they are usually accommodating in giving you extra time."

Q "Professors are **really accessible** here. Some have even abandoned set office hours and will make themselves free for students who wish to come and see them almost at any time. It's great to be able to be lectured formally and then come talk about the class with the prof one-on-one."

Q "It feels kind of homey to go to school here. You really need to put work, and during the week people usually study in the evenings. In every class I've taken, it took the teacher about 30 seconds to **make me feel comfortable**."

STUDENT AUTHOR: Amherst allows for complete freedom of course selection. The academic atmosphere is much different from that of other schools, because the students have not been forced to take their class by a distribution requirement. Plus, there are no graduate students here to vie for the professors' attention. The open curriculum, however, does require students to have a higher level of self-discipline.

Students Speak Out
ON LOCAL ATMOSPHERE

Q "People in town are ridiculously nice. There is a surprising **variety of stores** and restaurants. That's pretty much it. Thank God the College has a lively social scene, otherwise I'd shoot myself."

Q "Even though UMass is a five-minute bus ride away, there is **very little interaction** between the two institutions. There are also three other colleges nearby, and we have more to do with them. There isn't much to visit here. We are away from it all."

Q "The atmosphere around here is really good. This is **an area for thinking people** who are friendly and want to cooperate. UMass is present, so it's not too small-townish. A lot of concerts and things like that come to the area, which is another big appeal."

Q "There's not a lot to do around here, but I like the town. **It's clean and beautiful**, and the people are friendly. Whenever I need to go to town to do something, I feel happy to do it."

STUDENT AUTHOR: There is not much in Amherst outside of the College. Amherst is the epitome of a college town. Main Street is right next the College, and there you'll find CVS, Starbucks, Fleet Bank, as well as various local shops. The locals are nice to a degree that stupefies most students from New York City, and you can't walk down the street without a complete stranger nodding and saying hello. Northampton is a 30-minute free bus ride away. It's a town bigger than Amherst and, as such, it is bubblier and livelier as well.

Students Speak Out
ON FACILITIES

Q "**The facilities are excellent** at Amherst, both athletic and computers. We have a very nice campus center, which makes me feel very cozy whenever I am there."

Q "For a small college, the facilities are very **impressive and modern**. The Campus Center is very small, though, and is not really a place where too many people are prepared to hang out. The athletic and computer facilities are top-notch and could cater to a lot more people than they currently do."

Q "I think the Campus Center is a little small, and it gets crowded around noontime, when everybody goes there to check their mail. The lecture and conference rooms are very nice. **The athletic facilities are great**, although the gym is a little far away from everything. The computer labs have modern computers, and they are quiet and a good place to do your work."

Q "The campus center is **really beautiful**. The furniture is lovely. There are sofas, love seats, and armchairs. I love the fireplace in the dining area of Schewmm's coffee shop."

STUDENT AUTHOR: At first glance, the sole coffeehouse, the lone theater, and the single gym may seem a bit slim to satisfy a whole college. Still, for the relatively small number of students at Amherst, the variety of things you can do and places you can do them in is overwhelming, and students regularly complain that they've missed out on some event or show, because they just didn't have time. The gym is state-of-the-art and has become a campus-wide hangout as well.

Famous Alumni

Henry Ward Beecher, Dan Brown, Rob Brown, John Cariani, Calvin Coolidge, Jonathon S. Keats, Charles E. Merrill, Raymond J. Teller

Students Speak Out
ON CAMPUS DINING

Q "**The food is nutritional**, and there is a pretty good variety, particularly among the salad bar and cereals (if that's a big deal). But the entrées are generally bland."

Q "There is Valentine, whose dinner dining hours are not convenient (**dinner is from 4:30 p.m. to 7:30 p.m.**). The Campus Center serves sandwiches and other things until 2 a.m. Usually, people order off campus at night. There are a lot of places that stay open until 3 a.m."

Q "Well, **the food in Val is pretty terrible** most of the time. I find myself ordering takeout and going to restaurants more often than I want to. What I do like about Val is that everyone meets up there, and it's fun to meet your friends everyday and eat together."

Q "There are some appetizing dishes, like the chicken nuggets and some of the soups. I was **pleasantly surprised** at the level of the food, but I wouldn't go as far as praising it."

Q "Except for Valentine, whose food I don't even want to talk about, **we have Schwemm's**. The sandwiches there are kind of expensive, but most people don't seem to mind."

STUDENT AUTHOR: Central dining has a huge impact on the campus social life, in that it brings everybody together on a daily basis. The huge social plus to central dining almost compensates for what many students believe are serious flaws in the current dining system. Dining hours should be adjusted. Nobody gets up at 7:30 a.m. to eat breakfast!

Student Body

African American:	10%	Male/Female:	50/50%
Asian American:	12%	Out-of-State:	84%
Hispanic:	9%	International:	7%
Native American:	<1%	Unknown:	18%
White:	44%		

Popular Faiths: Catholicism, Protestantism, Judaism

Gay Pride: The prevailing notion at Amherst is that a person's sexual orientation is their business. The campus is very accepting of homosexuality.

Economic Status: Most students come from wealthy families, and there is a considerable part of the student body that comes from a lower economic status, as well.

Students Speak Out
ON DORMS

Q "The upperclass dorms are huge and are surprisingly in **very good shape**. The College really takes care of the dorms. Most freshman dorms are significantly worse, but I'd say Pratt is definitely up to sophomore standards."

Q "Tyler and Plimpton are usually thought of as too far away, and Williston is sometimes thought of as having **very small rooms**. However, none of the dorms are bad. Even the Mudds are okay, they're very social and are good for freshmen who are trying to get to know each other and find friends."

Q "When you're a sophomore, **room draw can be quite cruel**. A good way out is applying to a theme house. Most theme housing is better than regular housing, at least for sophomores."

STUDENT AUTHOR: **Freshmen live amongst themselves, which is usually a cool thing, because it facilitates the sometimes-difficult process of making friends. Sophomores are usually the ones getting screwed, being at the bottom of room draw. Most dorms have that New England look: brownstones and white windows and all.**

Did You Know?
98% of undergrads live on campus.

Students Speak Out
ON GUYS & GIRLS

Q "**The guys are nothing special**. If you like the up-turned polo collar, though, you'll love it here. And if you can't find what you want on campus, there's UMass and Hampshire College nearby. The guys here complain about the girls, but they've got Smith and Mt. Holyoke (women's colleges) nearby."

Q "To dispel any beliefs guys may have on all women's colleges, let me just say that Smith and Holyoke girls are, by and large, **not hot**. Sorry. It's better not to get your hopes up regarding parties in these colleges."

Q "The guys at Amherst are attractive, generally. **The girls are about average**."

STUDENT AUTHOR: **Both great couples and sizzling one-night stands** have been known to flourish at Amherst, so don't worry about finding your college sweetheart, or the danger of eternal abstinence. You stand a decent chance at finding either one at Amherst. Guys have more options than girls do, since Amherst is in close proximity to two all-women colleges, whose students often make their presence felt at Amherst parties.

Traditions

Winter Traying
Slide down Memorial Hill on a dining hall tray on the first day of snow, maybe with your shirt waiting for you at the bottom.

Amherst–Williams
Go and cheer in the last football game of the season against archrivals Williams College.

Overall School Spirit
Current students, in their time here, normally become slowly, but surely, proud of their school, both in terms of athletics, academics, and otherwise.

Students Speak Out
ON ATHLETICS

Q "There are 1,600 students, and a little over half of them play a sport. We are Division III in varsity sports. The IMs have about **20 to 40 people per team**."

Q "At first it may seem strange that players in such a small, and presumably insignificant, school work so hard to win. But I guess this is how most **Amherst students take on challenges**. I like going to games when I have time, and I wish more people would go."

Q "The basketball team is a favorite among students. I've noticed that **a lot of alums** come and cheer in games."

Q "Varsity sports are quite a big thing here, since Amherst offers **athletic scholarships**."

STUDENT AUTHOR: **Amherst maintains a highly developed and competitive** athletic regimen. Most intercollegiate games don't see capacity crowds, but loyal groups of alumni and parents keep things lively. Nonetheless, in big games, either in the postseason, or against Williams College, seats can be hard to find. Above all, students love their football and men's basketball teams.

Students Speak Out
ON DRUG SCENE

Q "A lot of people use marijuana occasionally. **Alcohol is big here.** Also, a lot of 'nerds' drink. Harder drugs are more marginal, as you'd probably expect."

Q "If someone has something to do that evening, or they have to wake up early the next day, they **won't drink that night**. Academics and other responsibilities definitely come before partying for most people."

Q "I think that the most important fact about drinking here is that hardly anyone drinks just to get drunk, or if they do, it's very rare. This is why **drinking is not a major concern** on this campus, even though the state of Massachusetts apparently thinks it should be."

STUDENT AUTHOR: Amherst nights—and for some, the days, too—involve respectable amounts of alcohol. For many Amherst students, alcohol consumption is part of a weekly routine. This is, in part, due to generous seniors who frequently pick up the tab for the poor underclassmen.

12:1	Student-to-Faculty Ratio
96%	Freshman Retention Rate
88%	Four-Year Graduation Rate
52%	Financial Aid Applicants Receiving Aid

Students Speak Out
SAFETY & SECURITY

Q "There were some cases of **property damage** on campus, but about half of the crimes I've heard of were perpetrated by students from one of the other schools nearby. Usually, things don't get out of hand here. People don't get so drunk as to be violent, and campus police are always on alert and respond quickly to calls."

Q "**The campus is very safe**. You can walk around undisturbed at any time of the day or night."

Q "Amherst has got to be one of the safest schools ever. **The town is so quiet**, and the crime rate is low. On campus, there is a kind of honor code among students. A lot of people don't bother locking their doors and leave their packs unattended in class."

STUDENT AUTHOR: Amherst College has a certain homey atmosphere that drives away thoughts of crime. Students feel comfortable leaving their room doors unlocked. Even still, cases of theft are rare. Dorm front doors can only be opened with a personal code that only students and custodians possess.

Questions?
For more inside information and survival tips, pick up College Prowler's full-length book on this school, written by an actual student! Check it out at *www.collegeprowler.com*.

Students Speak Out
ON OVERALL EXPERIENCE

Q "I really love the **small, tolerant atmosphere** at Amherst. I am extremely happy here, and even though there are some shortcomings (like the housing and the food), they are not crucial to your existence here. It is very easy to settle in, and very easy to meet a huge portion of the people on campus—something you could never hope to do at a large university or college."

Q "I learned a lot, not only from classes, but from the people around me as well. You just have to be willing to engage in conversations. I know this is corny, but I really love this place. I led a very stimulating life here, and **I grew up a lot**."

Q "Although **I was somewhat disappointed** with the academics, the interesting people more than made up for it, and in the end, I am happy to have gone to Amherst."

Q "This place offers **a perfect environment to learn** and find out who I am. The open curriculum is incredible because I take only the classes that I think are interesting and not the classes some random person who doesn't even know me thought were important to take."

STUDENT AUTHOR: Students usually don't choose Amherst because of its academic reputation. Rather, students come here because of the promise of experiencing an eclectic array of stimulating peers, professors, classes, and activities. Some become disillusioned, not finding their niche within the abundance of opportunities and freedom. A place like Amherst, though, with so many accomplished and bright people threading its grounds, is bound to have more oddities than the average university.

Arizona State Univeristy

University Drive & Mill Avenue; Tempe, AZ 85267
(480) 965-9011; www.asu.edu

THE BASICS:

Acceptance Rate: 95%
Setting: Mid-size city
F-T Undergrads: 30,363

SAT Range: 960–1220*
Control: Public
Tuition: $17,697

Most Popular Majors: Business, Communication/ Journalism, Education, Engineering

*of 1600

Academics	B-	Guys	A
Local Atmosphere	A-	Girls	A+
Safety & Security	B .	Athletics	A-
Computers	C+	Nightlife	A+
Facilities	A	Greek Life	B-
Campus Dining	A-	Drug Scene	B-
Off-Campus Dining	A+	Campus Strictness	B
Campus Housing	C+	Parking	D
Off-Campus Housing	B+	Transportation	C-
Diversity	C+	Weather	A

Students Speak Out
ON ACADEMICS

Q "Most of **the professors are great**. I didn't expect to meet any of the top professors until I was a junior, but in three semesters I've had a former dean, a Regent's professor, and two department chairs, all of whom were personable and wanted to get to know their students."

Q "Classes at ASU may have as many as **200–400 students**. Fortunately, the professors hold office hours every week and there are usually a number of TAs available as well. As you move up in your major, you'll have an opportunity to take much smaller classes."

Q "It varies from class to class. The classes taught by **TAs are generally not very good**. This is also true with some professors, however every once in a while you will find a professor that can make any subject interesting and fun to learn, and consequently, those are the classes with the highest attendance. This is true no matter how hard the subject is."

Q "I think the classes and coursework are a lot easier at ASU, but there are still students who manage to fail their classes. I think **ASU is not as challenging** as it could be."

STUDENT AUTHOR: ASU is home to a wide spectrum of professors and teaching assistants (TAs). Many are nationally-recognized for their work, some have relocated from the Ivy League and other renowned institutions, and a few come across as less competent than the students they teach.

Students Speak Out
ON LOCAL ATMOSPHERE

Q "Tempe and Scottsdale **have loads to do**. Phoenix, on the other hand, disappointed me for supposedly being one of the largest cities in the U.S. It's large and spread out, but there's absolutely nothing to do there."

Q "Tempe has to be **the biggest party town** in the universe. Anywhere you go on any given day there is a party."

Q "There's always something to do and **plenty of nature nearby**. We have mountains and Papago Park (hiking, desert botanicals, and the zoo). There's even a lake near campus."

Q "ASU is in a great location. Tempe is a fairly populated area and there are tons of restaurants, bars, clubs, and places to shop. If you like going out, **Tempe is the place for you**. The campus is surrounded by bars and restaurants that range in price and style. Students often go into Scottsdale (five minutes away) for a change of scenery. Scottsdale has a wide mixture of high-end clubs as well as more low-key places, too. Tempe is literally five minutes away from the airport, very convenient."

STUDENT AUTHOR: Tempe is undoubtedly packed with plenty of fun activities for college students. Tempe is filled with infinite young and vibrant people who possess many different personalities, qualities, and interests. ASU is the only university in Tempe and the Phoenix metropolitan area.

5 Best Things	5 Worst Things
1 Atmosphere	1 Cowboy hats
2 Nightlife	2 Police and thieves
3 Beautiful girls	3 Community bathrooms
4 Fall and winter	4 Heat
5 Academics	5 Campus food (price)

Students Speak Out
ON FACILITIES

Q "ASU is expensive for out-of-state people, but the campus is beautiful, including all of its facilities. Almost **everything is well-kept and clean**."

Q "ASU's facilities are very up-to-date and top-of-the line. We have one of the biggest student recreation centers in the country. **Our union is huge** and includes a bowling alley, arcade, pool hall, post office, hair salon, music store, student bank, and credit union."

Q "Since the University likes to charge its students for services that are not requested, you might as well **go and work out at the SRC** because you're going to pay for a membership whether you like it or not."

Q "I'm pretty impressed with everything I have used on campus. There's **just about everything you could want**—a record store, Starbucks, all kinds of restaurants, multiple computer labs, and much more. My one complaint is that most of the restaurants on campus are too expensive."

STUDENT AUTHOR: **Most facilities on campus are excellent. The Student Recreation Complex (SRC) is considered among the country's elite. The Memorial Union is located in the center of Arizona State's campus, and is passed through by pretty much everyone at some point of the day. The MU basement is filled with places to grab a bite to eat, as well as many other games, shows, and activities. The computer complexes all provide computers with high-speed connections and have a spectacular software collection.**

Famous Alumni

Steve Allen, Barry Bonds, Reggie Jackson, Al Michales, Phil Mickelson, David Spade, Gary Tooker

Students Speak Out
ON CAMPUS DINING

Q "The Memorial Union has it all—Taco Bell, Burger King, Schlotzky's, Jamba Juice, Chick-fil-A, Pizza Hut, and even home-cooked style food. **There's food all over campus**."

Q "Campus food is in three words: **expensive, not cheap, and costly** (okay four words). That is my only gripe. However, there are some nice places to eat on and around campus where the food is good enough that you will look past the price."

Q "I hardly ever eat big meals on campus; I get **bored really quick with food**, and I feel like most of it is bad for your health."

Q "Food on-campus is pretty good. I feel like there is enough variety so that I don't really get sick of anything and **I eat on campus pretty much every day**. I love the food in the new section of the MU, but it's also nice to have the common places like Taco Bell and Burger King."

Q "I love that we have **fresh sushi** in the MU. I live on it."

STUDENT AUTHOR: **The on-campus dining has gotten some type of complaint from pretty much everyone. However, ASU has taken measures to increase the variety of food in the MU and the feedback has been wonderful. I think it's safe to say that everyone has a problem with the prices, definitely the biggest issue. While ASU scores points for having a good variety, and good-tasting food, it definitely loses points in all aspects of pricing. Overall, dining on campus is an accommodating and convenient experience.**

Student Body

African American:	4%	Male/Female:	49/51%
Asian American:	6%	Out-of-State:	25%
Hispanic:	13%	International:	3%
Native American:	2%	Unknown:	5%
White:	67%		

Popular Faiths: The most popular one is probably Christianity. There is also a pretty big Mormon population.

Gay Pride: The campus is very accepting of its gay population as well as its diversity in general. The gay community is neither overly outspoken nor particularly quiet.

Economic Status: ASU is economically diverse.

Students Speak Out
ON DORMS

Q "**Send in your housing application ASAP** to reserve the best dorms. The nicest residence halls are San Pablo, Sonora Center, and P.V. East and West. Avoid Manzanita, Best, Mariposa, and Ocotillo."

Q "Avoid Manzy. It is **strictly a freshman dorm**, and is not in very good condition. I've heard stories of people puking and urinating in the halls."

Q "The dorms are a pain because you have to show ID to get in. There's always **a person buzzing students in** from around 6 a.m. to 6 p.m. It's very secure."

Q "Live in the dorms your first year. **You'll meet lots of people** and have good times."

STUDENT AUTHOR: **With the immense number of freshmen who enroll every year, it's necessary to sign up and request housing early for the best results. There are many options for living situations the first year, depending on the type of hall you want to live in. There are many dorms to choose from, and one may fit your personality better.**

Did You Know?
17% of undergrads live on campus.

Students Speak Out
ON GUYS & GIRLS

Q "Tempe is an area of **beautiful people**. We've got the best of the best. It's a good idea to come here unattached."

Q "There are a lot of very hot guys here and a lot of attractive people in general. My friends who have visited from other schools always say that the **people here are really good looking and friendly** compared to those from their own schools."

Q "There are a lot of pretty people on campus; unfortunately, **a majority of them act fake** (speaking on personalities). However, like anywhere, there are always good, decent people; you just have to find them."

STUDENT AUTHOR: **There's something about the climate, the money, and possibly even the water surrounding Tempe that generates an exceptionally attractive gene pool. Aside from everyone on campus being characterized as eye candy, students have much to say about personalities as well. It's certainly easier to find a hottie than it is to find a real down-to-earth person at ASU.**

Traditions

"A" Mountain
Painting the large "A" on A-mountain is a tradition among ASU students. Fraternities and sororities have also been known to paint the A during rush week.

Overall School Spirit
ASU football at Sun Devil Stadium holds much tradition within itself. Students, faculty, and alumni dress in gold (and sometimes maroon), and sometimes even paint their faces with the ASU symbol. It's quite a sight seeing an entire stadium dressed in gold.

Students Speak Out
ON ATHLETICS

Q "ASU is a **PAC 10 powerhouse**. Football, girls' basketball, golf, wrestling, baseball, and track are all nationally ranked. Intramurals are huge."

Q "Varsity **sports are big**, but tough to get into. I've heard that intramurals are great."

Q "When I think of ASU sports, I think of **football and Sparky**. Sparky does pushups every time ASU scores."

Q "**ASU football is huge**, even when we're not doing well. Freshmen are probably more into it than upperclassman, or at least have more time to be into it."

STUDENT AUTHOR: **ASU students definitely agree that football is the primary sport that's followed and talked about here. The students who are into the other sports here usually either play a sport or know someone on a team. While intramural and club sports are not as popular as the varsity sports, there is still an impressive number of students who participate in them. ASU pride and support are highly visible.**

Students Speak Out
ON DRUG SCENE

Q "You can get them if you want or you can easily avoid them. Drugs at ASU are **not overwhelming** but are readily available."

Q "**Drinking and smoking pot** are the most popular drugs at ASU. I've met people that did other stuff like cocaine, or experimented with Ecstasy, but only a couple."

Q "If you want it, you can get it. ASU is a big campus in a big city, **an environment conducive to drug use**. It didn't take me long to know where I could get what I want."

STUDENT AUTHOR: As at many major universities, drugs are readily available and easily accessible. If you want them, you can get them. Marijuana is generally present at most off-campus parties and in the dorms. Harder drugs such as cocaine, mushrooms, ecstasy, and various painkillers are less visible but can be acquired with minimal effort. However, underage drinking and DUI arrests greatly overshadow illegal drug possession or consumption in Tempe.

23:1	Student-to-Faculty Ratio
78%	Freshman Retention Rate
28%	Four-Year Graduation Rate
76%	Financial Aid Applicants Receiving Aid

Students Speak Out
SAFETY & SECURITY

Q "I've been a student at ASU for four years and **I've never felt that I was in danger**. There is usually a police officer in site during the late night hours, and I have never seen any instances during the day."

Q "**Security at ASU is very good**. There's a police station on campus, and there are call-boxes all over."

Q "The biggest crimes at ASU are **bike theft** and the University's unorthodox method of charging way too much for tuition."

STUDENT AUTHOR: Instances of serious crime at ASU are few and far between. Most cases of violent crime are unrelated to the school or its police department. The city of Tempe in general is a pretty safe neighborhood. To avoid crime, be careful and make smart decisions.

Questions?
For more inside information and survival tips, pick up College Prowler's full-length book on this school, written by an actual student! Check it out at www.collegeprowler.com.

Students Speak Out
ON OVERALL EXPERIENCE

Q "ASU has **exceeded my expectations**. It's everything I've ever wanted in a school. Visit campus if you can. It'll be worth your while."

Q "I love ASU; I think it's an awesome school to go to, but **it all depends on what you make of it**. If you really want to get into Greek life or if you are looking for a small college town, then it's not for you here."

Q "I've had a good experience at ASU so far. **It can be competitive sometimes**, but on the whole I am happy I went here."

Q "I love it here at ASU in Tempe. I've been to a couple other schools, and this is **by far the best one overall**. I feel that you can get the full college experience at ASU, because college isn't only about just reading and studying; it's about socializing and learning about life. I've really had the chance to do that here."

STUDENT AUTHOR: Any student with a capacity for commitment and initiative, as well as a certain social aptitude, can tell you that Arizona State is a terrific environment in which to achieve the sort of growth, both personal and academic, that is expected of a college education. ASU is a large school with a diverse culture and a lot of great people. Students feel that they have met people that have all changed their lives in some way. While the Greek life here is nothing to brag about, parking sucks, and the campus police are kind of a pain in the butt, ASU students still have plenty to be thankful for.

Auburn University

South College Street; Auburn, AL 36849
(334) 844-4000; www.auburn.edu

THE BASICS:

Acceptance Rate: 69%
Setting: Rural
F-T Undergrads: 18,148

SAT Range: 1020–1230*
Control: Public
Tuition: $15,750

Most Popular Majors: Business/Marketing, Communication/Journalism, Education, Engineering

*of 1600

Academics	B-	Guys	A
Local Atmosphere	C+	Girls	A
Safety & Security	B	Athletics	A
Computers	C	Nightlife	C
Facilities	B+	Greek Life	A
Campus Dining	B+	Drug Scene	B+
Off-Campus Dining	B-	Campus Strictness	C+
Campus Housing	C-	Parking	B-
Off-Campus Housing	A	Transportation	B+
Diversity	D	Weather	B

Students Speak Out
ON ACADEMICS

Q "When it comes to teachers at Auburn, it all depends on who you get. Some are **easier than high school teachers**. Others are really hard, but there are only a few of those."

Q "Most of the teachers I've had have been very supportive and interested in their students' needs. **Get to know your professors**, and they will usually be even more willing to help you out. Most teachers here want to benefit their students, not fail them."

Q "All the math and science professors are going to **speak a different language**—that's almost a given. I am in the business department, and I like most of my professors. It also depends on the class. It doesn't matter who I have for accounting; I'm going to hate the class."

Q "The teachers at Auburn are **very approachable**. They're eager to help students understand all of the class material."

STUDENT AUTHOR: **Most students seem satisfied with their teachers at Auburn. However, as with any university, there are some teachers that don't meet the standard. The biggest problems that students encounter with their teachers are difficulty understanding foreign teachers, particularly teacher assistants (TAs), and getting stuck in lecture classes. As a freshman or sophomore, large classes are usually hard to avoid. However, students feel that personally confronting any teacher with a problem you might have will definitely be a benefit to you.**

Students Speak Out
ON LOCAL ATMOSPHERE

Q "Auburn is a small town, so it has that small-town atmosphere. Sometimes, the smallness will get on your nerves, but **Atlanta is only an hour and a half away**, so you get your city fix and come back."

Q "Auburn is a great little town. There's plenty to do to keep you occupied. The nightlife is pretty good, and, overall, it's just a classic 'college-town.' We are about an hour and a half drive from Atlanta, which kicks butt since there is so much to do there. One of the best bar scenes in the country is in **Atlanta at Buckhead**. I always end up going to Atlanta for concerts and Braves games."

Q "I'm not going to lie; **this town is down-home countrified**. It's fun, though. I've always loved going here. There is a junior college, called Southern Union, down the street. There's a state park, called Chewacla, that's pretty close. The best time to be here is during the spring when they have a lot of music festivals."

STUDENT AUTHOR: **Most students claim to feel right at home with Auburn's warm and friendly atmosphere. They enjoy the slow pace of the Southern University town, and at the same time, are able to engage in a variety of activities. While there are a few drawbacks, such as lack of entertainment during the breaks, larger cities are just a short drive away. For those of you who crave the fast life of a big city, Auburn may not satisfy your craving. In Auburn, there is something for everyone!**

5 Best Things	5 Worst Things
1 Gameday	1 No parking!
2 Rolling Toomer's Hill	2 On-campus housing
3 School spirit	3 Gameday traffic
4 Friendly atmosphere	4 Computer labs
5 Off-campus dining	5 The humidity!

Students Speak Out
ON FACILITIES

Q "They're about to start building a new student center. What's great is there's a place to work out in the student activities center. It can be kind of **crowded at certain times**, but it's pretty nice."

Q "The facilities are beautiful here. The buildings are amazing to look at. **The athletic facilities are awesome**, especially the baseball stadium, Plainsman Park, voted consistently as one of the top collegiate baseball stadiums in the nation. Everyone who visits the campus talks about how beautiful everything is here."

Q "The campus is really nice. It is clean and safe. It is an old Southern campus. It has big trees and lots of landscaping. A lot of the facilities are getting makeovers. **There is a new women's sport center**, as well. They built a new student center a few years back and they recently renovated a lot of the dorms."

Q "All of Auburn's athletic facilities are in mint condition. The same can't be said about all the buildings on campus, unfortunately, but they're **working to change** that. They also built a new student center, which should be nice. Foy Student Union was getting pretty run down. Other than that, everything on campus is great."

STUDENT AUTHOR: **Most students rave about the facilities on campus, especially the athletic facilities. Auburn University knows what it has to do to make the campus a pleasant place for students and faculty to attend. The campus is under constant revision. While that often means that a lot of construction is going on, students feel that it's worth it.**

Famous Alumni

Charles Barkley, Jimmy Buffet, Samuel Ginn, Bo Jackson, Don Logan, Carnell Williams

Students Speak Out
ON CAMPUS DINING

Q "**Food on campus is okay**. Since campus and town are pretty much right there with each other, I found myself eating many meals in downtown Auburn and spending too much in the process."

Q "Chick-fil-A is the best place for on-campus eating, but Auburn has this cool little thing called the 'Tiger Club.' You can basically eat and shop at any place in the Auburn area. It can work as either a debit card or a credit card. **Every student has one**, and you can choose how you use it so eating at Auburn is great!"

Q "Names of the food spots on campus are: Terrell, which is located on the Hill, Lupton Deli (**sandwiches and pizza**) located in the Quad, and Foy Student Union located in the middle of campus. There are also little places to get smoothies and coffee (Starbucks) in the library and Haley Center."

Q "They regularly update the cafeteria on the Hill. The food is good. There is also a food court in Foy Union. **They just redid that also**. It has sub shops, pizza, Southern cooking, a coffee shop, Chinese, wraps, smoothies, and junk food."

STUDENT AUTHOR: **Opinions vary when it comes to eating on campus. Many students enjoy the food that AU has to offer. Terrell Hall and the War Eagle Food Court are the two most popular places for students to eat. There are also several little snack and coffee stands throughout campus, if you need a meal on the run. While both Terrell Hall and War Eagle Food Court offer a variety of foods, some students still prefer to eat off campus.**

Student Body

African American:	9%	Male/Female:	51/49%
Asian American:	2%	Out-of-State:	31%
Hispanic:	1%	International:	<1%
Native American:	<1%	Unknown:	2%
White:	85%		

Popular Faiths: Southern Baptist and Methodist seem to be the dominant faiths on campus.

Gay Pride: Auburn has a few gay/lesbian clubs that will hold certain events, but Auburn's conservative atmosphere prevents them from having as large a presence as you might find at other schools.

Economic Status: Most students are lower- to upper-middle-class.

Students Speak Out
ON DORMS

Q "If you're going to live on campus, then sign up for it quickly! I got a place to live for my first two years, but both times, **I got my second choice**. I thought I signed up early enough! Guess not."

Q "Dorms are nice, but **the rules suck**. You can live in the Hill, Quad, Extension, or Village. The Quad dorms are in the middle of campus, a minute walk away from Haley Center. They are pretty nice and in the prettiest area of campus; they are also mainly coed by floor. I stayed there (Harper Hall) my freshman year, and it was great being able to sleep until 9:55 a.m. for a 10 a.m. class."

Q "**The Quad dorms are the nicest** dorms on campus. I would avoid getting a dorm anywhere but the Quad, the Hill, or Noble Hall."

STUDENT AUTHOR: While students mostly agree that living in the dorms isn't a luxury, they do say that spending at least your freshman year there is a good experience. Students with experience in the dorms claim that the Quad and the Hill are the best choices, while the CDV Extension and the Village are not as pleasant as the dorms to live in. The Quad and Hill are mostly coed but have a few all-girls dorms—particularly the Hill.

> **Did You Know?**
> 14% of undergrads live on campus.

Students Speak Out
ON GUYS & GIRLS

Q "At AU, there is someone for everyone, but what is most important is how nice and kind people are to each other. **Everyone here is awesome**, in one way or another."

Q "You'll find all sorts of guys here: city boys, ravers, rednecks, and lots of good ol' country boys. The girls are just Southern belles. **They are incredibly hot** (for the most part). If you aren't from around here, then it'll take a little while for you to get used to the accent."

Q "The guys are great. **Very cute**!"

Q "I have never seen so many **wonderful, attractive, genuinely nice girls** anywhere. It truly is amazing. Everybody that comes and visits notices that I have made some great girl friends."

STUDENT AUTHOR: Well, there's no question about it: students at Auburn look pretty good. And if socializing and drunken revelry is just as important to you as studying, then Auburn may be right for you. Guys and girls both generally tend to take good care of themselves by working out. On top of good looks, students at Auburn are also friendly and outgoing. If you're looking for a relationship or just a one-night stand, then you can make it happen if you try.

> **Traditions**
>
> **Hey Day**
> A day when students all over campus are given a nametag and everyone says hello to each other.
>
> **Rolling Toomer's Corner**
> After every football win during the season, AU students gather in the streets and toss toilet paper all over the large tree that stands on Toomer's Corner.
>
> **Overall School Spirit**
> Overwhelming! School spirit thrives at AU, especially during the football season. The town transforms into a booming metropolis during home games.

Students Speak Out
ON ATHLETICS

Q "Varsity sports are big, especially football. Everyone goes to football games and the six or seven weekends when Auburn is at home are the **biggest party weekends of the year**."

Q "Well, in football **we are top 25, on average**. A few seasons ago, we were the first unranked team to beat a #1 team (Florida) in NCAA history—it was awesome."

Q "Varsity sports are a major part of Auburn. The football games are unbelievable. It is so much fun. The student body is so supportive of all the sports. We have parades and pep rallies for games, and **the spirit is unbelievable**. Tailgating before games is also an experience. It's just a lot of fun and something that makes Auburn what it is. And it's not just football; it's every sport."

STUDENT AUTHOR: Auburn is football, as some people say down here. Students rave about the high energy and school spirit that is displayed on game days. You don't have to worry about getting bored, if you're a sports fanatic! Attend a varsity game or get involved in an intramural sport if that's your thing. Students promise that you'll have fun, no matter what you choose.

Students Speak Out
ON DRUG SCENE

Q "**Pretty much everyone smokes weed**. Well, everyone that I know and have met. It's not like a drug-dealing ghetto, though; it doesn't take over the town. But at least one person you meet knows someone who can get stuff for you, if that's your pleasure."

Q "Apparently, **Adderall and Ritalin** prescriptions are pretty easy to obtain, if you want. I know a lot of people who use that stuff to help them study."

Q "The drug scene is there, of course, but it does not rule the school. The whole time I was there, I think I saw cocaine only once. **The pot is not great**, but if you find good stuff, then they charge an arm and leg for it."

STUDENT AUTHOR: Like any other college, Auburn does have to deal with the presence of drugs. Fortunately, if you're not looking for that kind of recreation, then you probably won't come across it. Most students cite alcohol and marijuana among the most commonly used drugs at Auburn. If you choose to take that route, do so at your own risk.

18:1	Student-to-Faculty Ratio
86%	Freshman Retention Rate
34%	Four-Year Graduation Rate
57%	Financial Aid Applicants Receiving Aid

Students Speak Out
SAFETY & SECURITY

Q "Security is great on campus, especially at the dorms. **I never felt scared** or vulnerable at the dorms or when I was walking on campus."

Q "A few years back, there were three sexual attacks on campus, but after that security and safety became **a huge priority**. There have been very few since. There are security shuttles and escorts available anytime you need them."

Q "Auburn is a safe campus, but like any town, it has had **its fair share of rapes**. The basic thing to remember in any college atmosphere (and in general) is to have a good head on your shoulders and be wise to the situation you are in. Auburn has a personal escort service and police that patrol the campus."

STUDENT AUTHOR: Students agree that they feel very safe at Auburn, especially on campus. Like any other town, Auburn has its bouts of crime, but students advise that if you take the necessary precautions, your time at Auburn will be a safe and enjoyable one. Because of Auburn's friendly atmosphere, it may be easy to take safety for granted.

Questions?
For more inside information and survival tips, pick up College Prowler's full-length book on this school, written by an actual student! Check it out at *www.collegeprowler.com*.

Students Speak Out
ON OVERALL EXPERIENCE

Q "The only reason that I have ever wished that I went anywhere else is because my best friends go to other schools. If you do come to school here, then **get involved in something**. That's the only way you're gonna meet other people."

Q "I think it is the best school to go to! My overall experience has been amazing. When I graduate, **I am going to miss all my friends**, all the fun we had, and everything in between. I would never have wanted to go anywhere else!"

Q "My overall experience here has been great. No problems at all. The one thing you'll notice if you come here is how friendly everyone on campus is. That friendliness goes with you everywhere. You can be walking down the street, in some place far away from Auburn, see a fan or alumni, and exchange a hearty War Eagle (the typical Auburn greeting). The campus is big enough for **a large-university experience**, but small enough that you don't get overwhelmed."

Q "I have met so many great people, made so many life-long friends, and learned so much about life in general in just one year that **it blows my mind**. It has just been indescribable. And I think that if you talk to anyone else that goes here, then you will hear the same thing."

STUDENT AUTHOR: Overall, students are very happy to be in Auburn. They love the people around them and the experiences, too. College is what you make of it. If you sit at home and don't do anything, then you won't enjoy yourself no matter where you go. With all the options you have offered to you at Auburn, you have to try to not have a good time. And with a student body that is so happy to be here, it's also hard not to get swept up in the excitement.

Babson College

Babson Park; Wellesley, MA 02457
(781) 235-1200; www.babson.edu

THE BASICS:

Acceptance Rate: 37%
Setting: Suburban
F-T Undergrads: 1,799

SAT Range: 1130–1320*
Control: Private
Tuition: $36,096

Most Popular Majors: Business, Management, Marketing, and other related support services

*of 1600

Academics	B+	Guys	B-
Local Atmosphere	B-	Girls	C+
Safety & Security	A-	Athletics	B-
Computers	A-	Nightlife	B
Facilities	B+	Greek Life	B-
Campus Dining	B	Drug Scene	B+
Off-Campus Dining	B+	Campus Strictness	C
Campus Housing	B	Parking	B+
Off-Campus Housing	C-	Transportation	D+
Diversity	B+	Weather	C-

Students Speak Out
ON ACADEMICS

Q "The classes are interesting; the faculty is very knowledgeable as far as business classes are concerned. **Science teachers are terrible**, and interesting liberal arts classes are far and few in between."

Q "In general, classes that are revolved around solid concepts like economics, marketing, accounting, and more are very well taught and interesting. Things like organizational behavior (OB) and literature are quite dry and not inspiring. Faculty are very available to students and, in general, are **passionate about the subjects they teach**, which rubs off on the students."

Q "My faculty is very caring and interesting, and they make sure I have the best time possible here at Babson. Teachers here at Babson are like none I have seen. Even coming from a private Christian school, **the teachers at Babson are one up**. They are never afraid to offer their help, time, and support to those who need it and also to those who just need a confidant on campus."

STUDENT AUTHOR: The competitive business atmosphere at Babson is felt all the time and everywhere by students and teachers. Although the curriculum is extremely challenging the classes are interesting and very informative. The teachers take their work seriously and almost never miss class or meetings with students. They work almost as hard as the students on trying to teach them the basics of business in the business-oriented classes and even in some liberal arts classes.

Students Speak Out
ON LOCAL ATMOSPHERE

Q "**There is Boston**, which is everything you could ever want. Wellesley is a sweet town and a nice place to just get away from campus, but it is a little too expensive."

Q "**Wellesley is not a friendly place**. There is tons of traffic, and many local businesses there do not like dealing with college students. Needham is just as close, and it has many better places to eat."

Q "Wellesley is a rich and conservative town. It's a good place to walk around during the day and a great place not to be at during the night. There is no alcohol in Wellesley, and all shops close down early. **Wellesley College is nearby**, but I personally don't like going there. I have friends at Babson who go there all the time and love it."

Q "Wellesley is a very upscale suburb. Downtown consists of pretty nice restaurants, retail stores, and specialty shops. Wellesley College and Olin College are there, too, so there are **plenty of college students** to hang out with and make friends."

STUDENT AUTHOR: Wellesley is not exactly a 'college town,' but Boston is. The atmosphere revolves around pastry shops, some decent restaurants, very expensive retail clothes stores, and a few movie theaters. With such slim pickings of things to do, most students tend to stay on campus or travel into Boston, of course. Framingham and Natick are popular student destinations, where you'll often spot a group of Babsonians in the Natick Mall or in Lowes theater.

Students Speak Out
ON FACILITIES

Q "The facilities are very nice and well-kept. The computer center (Cutler Center) has **state-of-the-art computers** and is available most of the day for students to use."

Q "Most of the classrooms are nice; with state-of-the-art technology. Classrooms vary from lecture, to stadium-style seating, to a standard floored room. The athletic center is a great facility, but during rush hour, **there is a line to use some of the cardio machines**. The gym doesn't offer amenities like towels, shampoo, and other things."

Q "Webster is nice, usually available, although sometimes, there are scheduling conflicts where students don't have access to the pool for example. **The library and computer center are serviceable**, nothing special, although the access to Bloomberg on some of the computers is very nice. The campus center is beautiful, though having it closed on weekends, at least the food part, is not student friendly."

Q "I like the facilities on campus. Some are a bit **outdated, but they are all adequate**. There are nicer computers in the library this year; it shows that the school is spending money in that area."

STUDENT AUTHOR: **Reynolds Center is located in the middle of campus, with Trim Hall on one side and the Sorenson Center of Fine Arts on the other. It contains the Crossroads Cafe and the Campus Bookstore. You will find many students sipping on a cappuccino, reading a** *Wall Street Journal,* **or chatting with friends outside the Horn Library.**

Famous Alumni

William J. Allard, Craig Benson, Arthur Blank, Roger Enrico, Daniel Gerber, Jason Kosow

Students Speak Out
ON CAMPUS DINING

Q "I enjoy Reynolds most days, though the food there is **not necessarily healthy**. Trim has variety, which is nice, though the hot food often lacks any true flavor."

Q "As with most colleges, campus food gets old. But in comparison to other schools, Babson has quite good food. **Reynolds is good**, although we can only eat there a limited amount during the year with only a certain amount of money allocated to the OneCard, depending on the meal plan."

Q "I prefer Reynolds more than Trim, because it offers sushi and freshly-made wraps. It takes forever to get through the sandwich line at Trim, while at Reynolds **the wraps are pre-made** and take seconds to grab."

Q "The dining hall food gets very boring, very quick. **The lines are way too long**, and the halls are way too crowded. There are many great restaurants around Babson, in both Wellesley and Needham, many of which deliver. Ordering food is sometimes a better option than what is offered at Trim, and probably about as healthy."

STUDENT AUTHOR: **Even with all the incessant complaints about long lines, nutrition, and food variety, everyone admits that the food here is the best in comparison to other local colleges. A relevant issue that some students bring up is that all resident students are required to be on the meal plan. With the average meal plan costing over $1,800 per semester, it is reasonable for some to be upset.**

Student Body

African American:	4%	Male/Female:	60/40%
Asian American:	11%	Out-of-State:	65%
Hispanic:	8%	International:	18%
Native American:	<1%	Unknown:	15%
White:	44%		

Popular Faiths: There is a Christian Fellowship group on campus that holds meetings and goes to church on Sundays.

Gay Pride: The campus is generally accepting of its gay students and has an on-campus organization, The Gay-Lesbian-and-Everybody-Else Club (GLEE).

Economic Status: Babson College has a very diverse population, but it is apparent that students from wealthy backgrounds dominate Babson College.

**Students Speak Out
ON DORMS**

Q "I enjoyed Forest because of its **huge windows and high ceilings**, but I would have to say that I like South because of the convenient location."

Q "**The dorms are all wireless and heated**. The best dorms are McCullough, as they just were revamped a while back with new furniture, windows, and carpeting for students to throw up on. McCullough is made up of suites and is the center of our party scene. On weekends, people are seen pouring in this dorm in huge crowds."

Q "**Coleman and Van Winkle** are the nicest dorms on campus, but they are located at the top of 'Coleman Hill', which is twice as far from Trim and the campus center than most other dorms."

STUDENT AUTHOR: The majority of freshmen live in Forest Hall, which is good because of its closeness to Trim Hall. But many freshmen quickly find out that they are not only far away from other halls, but from virtually any place except Trim Hall and BABO. Since the first-year curriculum is ranked as one of the hardest in the country, many find themselves lured into the social scene found in dorms like McCullough, the Canfield Frats, and some suites in Pietz Hall.

 Did You Know?
83% of undergrads live on campus.

**Students Speak Out
ON GUYS & GIRLS**

Q "The guys seem to be very confident, and so do the girls. **This can be a good thing** and a bad all at once. For example, it's one thing to act confident in front of the class, but another to be that way because you want to show off. Kids at this school can be immature, sometimes."

Q "**Most guys are stuck up**, especially the jocks. Watch out for the soccer team guys, they only associate with each other and don't really care about anybody else."

Q "Guys and girls on campus are definitely **sub-par in the looks department** compared to state schools. But hey, they are probably going to work for us someday."

STUDENT AUTHOR: The average Babson student is well-groomed and quite intimidating to the outside observer and some students, too. But most people understand that this is purely to impress the professors who are in charge of giving out grades. If one gets below the surface of this facade, they would probably find shared interests and similarities in their personal lives.

Traditions

BDE Performance
The Babson Dance Ensemble is recognized for its amazingly choreographed dances and awesome lighting. Shows range from ballet to hip-hop.

Mr. and Mrs. Babson Competitions
Students compete on the basis of their looks, smarts, and talents. The competition is usually held in Knight Auditorium and is a favorite among the student body.

Overall School Spirit
A bit underrated. Despite the poor sports attendance, most students are proud to be at Babson. They are just trying to manage their time better.

**Students Speak Out
ON ATHLETICS**

Q "Sports are huge on campus; **they are almost like fraternities**. They foster good attitudes, competitiveness, and teamwork."

Q "**Our school is Division III**, so pretty much anyone can find some varsity sport to join. Intramural sports are also getting very popular, especially coed basketball and volleyball."

Q "**Sports are so small here**. I am a huge fan of sports, and I have no idea what goes on with sports. I feel that this is a huge determination of just how unimportant sport is at Babson. The only thing that is fairly important is men's basketball, which I do cheer for during the season."

Q "Varsity sports are **very popular at this school**. Intramurals are not as popular."

STUDENT AUTHOR: Varsity sports are very competitive, contrary to popular belief. In terms of popularity, it is true that few students attend games, but it's not true that few students play them. Considering the small-school atmosphere, neither the sports game attendance, nor athletic involvement can possibly be compared to other Division III giants.

Students Speak Out
ON DRUG SCENE

Q "Like any school college you can find people who abuse all types of drugs. **It is underground**, and you don't really see any of it, unless you seek it out."

Q "The most widely-used drug is probably marijuana. **I know some people who use it**. But if you want to get hold of coke, I'm sure that you can find a dealer here. Just be careful who you talk to, because of reputation issues. Prescription drugs are also common because they are used by kids to keep awake and for studying at night."

Q "A student can find a supplier for almost any drug, but **use beyond marijuana is rare**."

STUDENT AUTHOR: It's not too hard to find a dealer on campus, but not many students want people to know that they're actually seeking one out. Marijuana has been seen in rooms, and people have gotten caught smoking it in residence halls, but those incidents are few and far between.

14:1	Student-to-Faculty Ratio
97%	Freshman Retention Rate
87%	Four-Year Graduation Rate
54%	Financial Aid Applicants Receiving Aid

Students Speak Out
SAFETY & SECURITY

Q "I have never heard of a security issue worse than **a skunk spraying a drunken student** who had trespassed into his den."

Q "**The campus is too secure**, and the BABO (public safety team) doesn't always appreciate a good party. Truthfully, they thoroughly enjoy breaking up parties, and this has been getting stricter over the past four years."

Q "I always feel very safe on campus. Generally, the campus is pretty well lit during the night and even the lacrosse fields have bright lights on when it's dark. If I'm walking alone through the fields after a Knight Party, **I still feel safe** although I am far away from the residence halls."

STUDENT AUTHOR: The public safety team (BABO) is accepted by most students and is seen as a helpful agent in crime prevention, security, and argument mending. "BABO," the friendly nickname used for the public safety personnel, explains student's accepting attitude towards them. Babson is a safe town where crime is not an issue.

Questions?
For more inside information and survival tips, pick up College Prowler's full-length book on this school, written by an actual student! Check it out at *www.collegeprowler.com.*

Students Speak Out
ON OVERALL EXPERIENCE

Q "It was a little tough to get used to, but once I fit in, I didn't want to leave. The challenging academics along with **solid extracurricular activity** and strong social life make me not want to ever leave."

Q "Sometimes, I wish I had gone to a bigger school either in the city, out west, or down south. I've lived in the New England area my entire life, so **I am tired of the atmosphere**. The friends I met at Babson were the main reason I decided not to transfer."

Q "I love Babson. It is not a college for those who wish to do no work, not attend class, or just party. It is for people who want to do well in life. **Babson trains people for the rigorous business world**. The education here is priceless, especially because much of it is 'hands-on,' and I feel it's good practice for my future career."

Q "I like everything here, but I wish it was 8,000 students instead of 1,800. As a senior, I can honestly say that **I know most of the student body** except the freshmen, and I'm sure I'll meet tons of them this weekend if I stay on campus."

STUDENT AUTHOR: The best way to describe Babson is to say: at first you'll feel like a fish out of water, but as time goes on you somehow survive and become a lizard with tougher skin. No matter how hard you think your high school was, nothing can prepare you for the incredible and challenging academic life of a Babson freshman. Most students agree that the workload is by far larger than they initially expected. And although it takes some time to get used to the curriculum, students feel that the impeccable education is worth it.

Ball State University

2000 University Avenue; Muncie, IN 47306
(765) 289-1241; www.bsu.edu

THE BASICS:

Acceptance Rate: 72%
Setting: Small city
F-T Undergrads: 15,376

SAT Range: 1400–1710*
Control: Public
Tuition: $17,804

Most Popular Majors: Education, Business, Communication, Humanities, Health Professions

*of 2400

Academics	B	Guys	B
Local Atmosphere	C+	Girls	B
Safety & Security	C+	Athletics	C-
Computers	A	Nightlife	B
Facilities	B-	Greek Life	C-
Campus Dining	B	Drug Scene	C+
Off-Campus Dining	B	Campus Strictness	B-
Campus Housing	C+	Parking	C-
Off-Campus Housing	B+	Transportation	B+
Diversity	D-	Weather	D+

Students Speak Out
ON ACADEMICS

Q "It really depends on the type of class. I really enjoy the professors for my main focus of study. **Every teacher has his or her own quirks**, and you have to adapt to them in order to make the most of your college experience. It's rather easy to talk with the majority of the profs here, regardless of their field."

Q "The teachers were **a lot more personal than I thought they'd be**. I thought they'd be more strict and less approachable, but in class, I never felt like I had to hesitate about anything."

Q "**My professors like to work on a one-on-one basis**. Many will not hesitate to meet with you outside of class and help you with any problems you might have. But there are some that don't want to help; a few bad apples, but not many."

Q "I only had three or four classes with more than 100 students. **I had a few problems with English professors from other countries** who couldn't speak English very well, though."

STUDENT AUTHOR: **Over the years, Ball State University has earned a reputation as a party school. In many ways, this is true. Generally speaking, BSU students know how to have a good time. But the University has another reputation: one of academic excellence, especially in certain fields. Ball State is home to a renowned architecture school, as well as the nation's premiere journalism-graphics program. Overall, students say professors who teach core curriculum classes are approachable and understanding.**

Students Speak Out
ON LOCAL ATMOSPHERE

Q "**Muncie is a blue-collar town**, and there's an obvious divide between the students and Muncie residents. They aren't very welcoming, but they aren't hateful."

Q "I love Muncie. If you get off campus and away from the Village, go to Walnut and High Street. There's **all kinds of coffeeshops, art galleries, and just really interesting small shops**."

Q "It's **a pretty good atmosphere here**. It doesn't seem to get enough attention from the students. There's a lot of stuff that gets overlooked. It's not a big city, but you do have some things to do."

Q "Muncie has its ups and downs like virtually any town in America. Overall, it's a rather laid-back and friendly town. I guess Anderson and Indianapolis would be the closest places in terms of other colleges and universities. If you come here, **make sure to stay away from the bad ends of town**. A lot of undesirable things go down in the crooked parts, like in every shady piece of America."

STUDENT AUTHOR: **Ball State students have some mixed emotions when it comes to Muncie. Although much of the city is rundown, the victim of outsourcing and substantial urban decay, there are some things worth seeing. The city's downtown district is home to several art galleries featuring work by local and regional artists, a plethora of dining options, and a fairly decent bar scene. Students often overlook many of the city's festivals, which include Munciegras, Yart, and seasonal concerts.**

Students Speak Out
ON FACILITIES

Q "**Irving gym is wonderful**. You can reserve a racquetball court. The fitness area is good, too, but I don't like that it closes in the morning."

Q "Everything has been changing for the better here. **Every department that I know of has upgraded to better equipment**. The computer labs, for one, have been vastly improved in a matter of only six months. The graphics and animation labs have upgraded to G5 Macs, which are top-of-the-line."

Q "I don't know about the student center. **I think it would be nicer if it were more centralized**, but it's on the complete opposite side of campus from where everything is."

Q "**I haven't heard many complaints about the facilities on campu**s. Most people I know seem to enjoy them. In my personal experience, it can be a little crowded, but perfectly accessible, nonetheless."

Q "They vary from the dilapidated student center to the pristine music building. **There's really no consistent trend**."

STUDENT AUTHOR: The largest gym is Irving Gym, which features the latest in cardio and weight-lifting machines, as well as free weights, ab rollers, and other fitness devices. Most students prefer to hang out at the Art and Journalism Building's food court, which is known as the Atrium. A sort of de facto student center, the Atrium is well-lit, airy, and centrally located; a striking contrast to the Student Center's dismal, far-off, '80s-esque nightmare.

Famous Alumni

Jim Davis (creator of Garfield comics), Joyce DeWitt (actress), David Letterman (comedian, talk show host), John Schnatter (founder of Papa John's pizza)

Students Speak Out
ON CAMPUS DINING

Q "It's college food. **They don't really take care of vegetarians too well**, but there's lots of options for students with a normal diet."

Q "It's dorm food. **The repetition will get to you**, but places like Noyer have lots of choices. Most people tend to eat close to where they live, though. LaFollette also has some good things. A lot of friends of mine like Out of Bounds."

Q "Campus food is really good. **It's something you can stand to eat just about every day**. I really don't feel like I have to go off campus to eat somewhere."

Q "**They use a lot of preservatives**, and there's lots of junk food. They may have some organic items, but I haven't seen many."

Q "I personally haven't been much of an on-campus connoisseur lately. **I do occasionally eat at the Atrium with friends** since I practically live in the AJ building. From what I remember, I loved going to Woodworth for the stir-fry and paninis."

STUDENT AUTHOR: Although the myriad dining facilities on campus suggest a wide variety of eating options, this is generally not the case. Many of the foods served in The Food Mall are the same as those served at Court Side, which are the same as those served in Elliott Dining Hall. The deli-style sandwiches in the the Food Mall are popular, but the Food Mall is usually extremely busy at lunch time. All-you-can-eat buffets can be found at Elliott Dining Hall as well as in LaFollette and Noyer residence halls.

Student Body

African American:	7%	Male/Female:	48/52%
Asian American:	1%	Out-of-State:	7%
Hispanic:	2%	International:	<1%
Native American:	<1%	Unknown:	<1%
White:	90%		

Popular Faiths: The most prominent are Christianity, agnosticism, atheism.

Gay Pride: In general, BSU is a pretty gay-friendly place. Organizations such as Spectrum sponsor events and actively work to promote tolerance on campus.

Economic Status: It varies. Most students come from middle-class families.

Students Speak Out
ON DORMS

Q "**Stu-East was the most rundown**, but it had the best atmosphere. You should definitely try to get a dorm that has a food court, so you don't have to walk in the snow to get food in the winter."

Q "I liked the Z-shaped rooms in Johnson. It was hard to set the room up, but the atmosphere was good. **It was a real tight-knit group**. You meet a lot of interesting characters."

Q "**This all depends on the dorms**. Woodworth is pretty nice, but it's women-only. Dehority, LaFollette, and Stu-East tended to be the slums but the place to meet the coolest people. Noyer and Stu-West are the nicer dorms, but not much socializing went on, from what I know of."

STUDENT AUTHOR: **Most freshman students at BSU are required to live in the dorms, and as a freshman, the odds are pretty good you'll be living in LaFollette. Overall, Ball State students who moved off campus after their freshman year said they missed the social interaction they had experienced while living on campus but were willing to sacrifice it for the freedoms they had living in houses or apartments.**

 Did You Know?
37% of undergrads live on campus.

Students Speak Out
ON GUYS & GIRLS

Q "**Most guys here are stereotypical**. They wear baseball caps, khaki shorts, and flip-flops. The ones that aren't that way are stereotypical in other ways. Occasionally, you'll bump into someone worth meeting."

Q "**Some days, I look around and everyone's really attractive**. Other days, I'm like, 'God, there's a lot of ugly people here.'"

Q "Like at most colleges, **there are plenty of attractive members of either sex** at Ball State."

Q "Some of the girls are hot. **It's not like we live in Hollywood** or anything like that. I'm not one to make a judgment on that because I'm not that hot myself."

STUDENT AUTHOR: **For the most part, Ball State students feel that members of both sexes are pretty average. That is to say, they run the gamut from hideously ugly to strikingly attractive, with the majority falling somewhere in the middle. Almost all the students interviewed say they are satisfied with the overall appearance of the men and women at Ball State, and they feel it is about the same as most other schools.**

Traditions

Getting drunk at orientation

Getting drunk on your 21st birthday

Getting drunk

Overall School Spirit
For the most part, Ball State students are pretty apathetic when it comes to school pride. Attendance at sporting events is dismal, and the student government struggles to find and keep delegates, especially for the off-campus constituency.

Students Speak Out
ON ATHLETICS

Q "A lot of people don't pay attention to our athletic programs. **We're not very good at the mainstream sports**. If you're a football fan or a basketball fan, Ball State doesn't exactly have what you need, but there are worse schools."

Q "**Muncie is a hotbed for volleyball**. It's a big recruiting area, but it's not a big sport on campus. Basketball and football are big."

Q "Football is big, but we kind of suck. **I don't think sports are very big at Ball State**. They're there, but not enough to be in your face."

Q "We're not usually good, and **we don't have school spirit**. Varsity sports at Ball State are hard to talk about without a cynical tone."

STUDENT AUTHOR: **Sports attendance at Ball State University is dismal at best. Most students said they are often unaware a home football game is being played, and the team is almost never discussed in polite conversation, except maybe as the punchline to a joke. Despite all this, the University offers a strong intramural sports program with volleyball and rugby being among the most popular.**

Students Speak Out
ON DRUG SCENE

Q "I know a lot of people that are into marijuana. I hang out with these people, but I myself have never done it. **I haven't heard much on the subject lately**, so it seems like the people into any sort of drug on campus are keeping it hush-hush more so than four years ago."

Q "If you want it you can probably get it, but it's not like you can just walk up to someone on campus and ask them where to score. It's not Amsterdam. **You have to know the right people**."

Q "You can get just about any drug at Ball State. **Marijuana is probably the most popular**, but prescription drugs like painkillers are really close, as well."

STUDENT AUTHOR: **Despite efforts by the UPD, the Delaware County Drug Task Force, and other agencies, Ball State has a well-established drug scene. Many of the students interviewed agreed drugs are available to pretty much anyone who wants them. Marijuana is by far the most popular illegal drug on campus.**

17:1	Student-to-Faculty Ratio
77%	Freshman Retention Rate
27%	Four-Year Graduation Rate
75%	Financial Aid Applicants Receiving Aid

Students Speak Out
SAFETY & SECURITY

Q "I walk into my friends' halls without getting stopped, so **I'd say it's pretty weak**. I'll walk to my dorm at night by myself, but I won't walk anywhere else."

Q "I've noticed there aren't that many emergency call-boxes. I've only seen like four or five. Off campus, it's probably more dangerous, but that really depends on your circle of friends and what you like to do for fun. **It's still not that dangerous, though**."

Q "**It has improved immensely in the last four years**. There are call-boxes in the most likely and helpful of places. The pathways have been better lit than before, and if you're on campus later than the shuttles run, they have a cab-like service that will come pick you up if you call."

STUDENT AUTHOR: **Generally speaking, students say they feel safe around campus and agree the most important thing people need to do when it comes to safety at Ball State is to use common sense. If you know where you are, who you are with, and you aren't being an idiot, you should be fine.**

Questions?
For more inside information and survival tips, pick up College Prowler's full-length book on this school, written by an actual student! Check it out at *www.collegeprowler.com*.

Students Speak Out
ON OVERALL EXPERIENCE

Q "I feel that, had I attended IU, I might have better cultural and social opportunities, but generally, I feel that Ball State is a good school that has a lot to offer. Several of its academic programs are ranked among the top in the nation. Which major program you wish to pursue should factor heavily in your decision whether or not to come to BSU. I would definitely choose BSU over any smaller or private institution, and **it automatically wins out over Purdue for me** because of the female factor."

Q "So far I've really enjoyed college for the curricular and extracurricular activities alike. I've met some really awesome students and professors. **I don't wish I had picked someplace else**. Ball State is a good size and match for me."

Q "**I went to Ball State because my family could handle the cost**. I'm glad I ended up here. I've realized you won't get lost in the sea here. "

Q "As much as I hate Muncie at times, I wouldn't change my choice for the world. **I've met a lot of great people here** and have been given many a wonderful opportunity."

STUDENT AUTHOR: **Ask a Ball State student, and they'll tell you they're happy to be where they are. Sure, there's Parking Services to deal with, UPD crack-downs, and a ban on kegs, but these drawbacks pale when compared to the friends and memories students say they've acquired at BSU. Although recent policies threaten to end the party-school reputation, Ball State still has a strong social scene that continues to build friendships most students would be unwilling to give up. Whatever your field of study, it is important to focus and remember what you're here for.**

Bard College

1395 Lexington Ave; New York, NY 10128
(845) 758-6822; www.bard.edu

THE BASICS:

Acceptance Rate: 27% **SAT Range:** 1320–1430*
Setting: Rural **Control:** Private
F-T Undergrads: 1,801 **Tuition:** $37,574

Most Popular Majors: Visual/Performing Arts, English, Foreign Languages, Philosophy, Religious Studies

*of 1600

Academics	A	Guys	C
Local Atmosphere	B+	Girls	C
Safety & Security	A+	Athletics	C-
Computers	C+	Nightlife	B-
Facilities	B	Greek Life	N/A
Campus Dining	D+	Drug Scene	C-
Off-Campus Dining	B+	Campus Strictness	A
Campus Housing	C	Parking	B+
Off-Campus Housing	A-	Transportation	C
Diversity	C	Weather	D+

Students Speak Out
ON ACADEMICS

Q "I love my professors, especially the ones in the philosophy department—their classes rule. Most are easy to sit down with, and they're willing to talk about philosophy forever. I've had some **great conversations** at Bard."

Q "Bard professors are very available. My **advisors have had a strong effect** on my education. Overall, the classes are quite good, but of course some are better than others."

Q "I'm a math student, and Bard is not particularly known for its math department. For some reason, the department wants to keep its **bad teachers** and disregard or fire the good ones. I've been told that I was 'unteachable.' Overall, classes are pleasant when I'm not in contact with professors."

Q "In my experience, the professors at Bard are **knowledgeable and committed** to helping students learn. Classes are small and almost always run effectively. Most focus on discussion, rather than lecturing, so everyone participates. I can't picture just sitting in a lecture hall taking notes. That just wouldn't be Bard."

STUDENT AUTHOR: **Bard offers a diverse blend of structure and choice when it comes to academic exploration. Courses with an enrollment of no more than a dozen Bardians allow for the intimate discussion and one-on-one student-professor interaction, rather than an impersonal lecture hall setting. Many classes are writing-intensive, and others focus on performative acuity or artistic risk-taking.**

Students Speak Out
ON LOCAL ATMOSPHERE

Q "When I first came to Bard, we did a lot of **canoeing and rock-climbing**. That was great. I've also been camping with my friends since then, such as hiking in the Catskills. There are awesome sunsets here, too."

Q "I love Tivoli—it's an **artist town** to be sure, and there are lots of artists. I actually love all of Duchess County. People are nice and respectful. I think most people here just want to raise a family and live quietly."

Q "Red Hook offers all the **basic amenities**—health-food store, groceries, pharmacy, sandwich shop, bakery, burritos, ice cream places, and two movie theaters."

Q "It's boring—most of the time there's **nothing to do**. New York City is close, which is good. It's relaxing here, but definitely not exciting."

Q "The atmosphere around Bard is quite 'normal' and **conventional**. The town desperately needs a coffeeshop or a bookstore."

STUDENT AUTHOR: **The major complaint at Bard is that the surrounding area is rural and boring. Students who come from cities like New York or LA will find themselves in a world previously thought untenable. However, it's a beautiful area, full of history and scenic opportunity, and markedly unpopulated. When looking for something to do, students head to the nearby towns offering a small variety of coffeeshops, restaurants, clothing and craft stores, as well as bars.**

5 Best Things	5 Worst Things
1 Eclectic student body	1 Cliques
2 Small classes	2 Party scene
3 Beautiful campus	3 Bad dorms
4 Eminent professors	4 Parking
5 Freedom	5 Kline food

Students Speak Out
ON FACILITIES

Q "The Campus Center seems unwelcoming as it's big, gray, and concrete. Inside it's all right, but **too sterile**."

Q "The buildings at Bard are disorganized, but they all have potential. It's a **long walk** from one to another. I like the gym. The weight room is really nice, although it could be bigger."

Q "For some reason, I love the library. Most people think it's weird looking, but I truly enjoy its shape and form. It's an **eclectic mix** of the old Romanesque and the new Modern. Inside is like a cozy, well-lit lounge area. I go there to read, but I usually end up going to sleep. Why did they make the chairs so comfy?"

Q "The Richard P. Fisher Center for the Performing Arts is something—it's ostentatious, grandiloquent, and somehow **metallically turgid**. It's just one more alien shape on Bard's warped canvas of inconsistency."

Q "The Campus Center is solid. There's Internet, the post office, the bookstore, and a full-sized **movie theater**."

STUDENT AUTHOR: Bard's facilities are spread across the college's 600 wooded acres almost haphazardly, adding to the feeling that this school might actually be a state park rather than a place of learning. As the college has expanded over the past 150 years, new buildings have popped up to accommodate the student population. However, there's been no formal vision at work in uniting the hodgepodge of gothic and modern design, so the buildings tend to appear as a motley crew.

Famous Alumni

Chevy Chase, Blythe Danner, Larry Hagman, Todd Haynes, Christopher Guest, Anthony Hect, Daniel Pinkwater, Herb Ritts, Adam Yauch, Nick Zinner

Students Speak Out
ON CAMPUS DINING

Q "I think Kline is **worse than McDonald's**."

Q "I ate **pink chicken** the other day, and I haven't felt right since. Kline can make you sick, as it has done to me for years. But sometimes, there's just no other choice. I try to eat a lot of cereal and pizza. What else is there? Tofu? No thanks, Kline."

Q "Somebody has to do something about the food at Bard—it's embarrassing. Most people get **severe dyspepsia** after eating—eat off campus!"

Q "The best is when the vegans found out that the fries were being cooked in animal lard. Man, were they pissed. Once they changed the recipe, though, the fries **never tasted as good**. To be honest, I miss the animal lard."

Q "The food is okay. Kline has its edible and not-so-edible days; I'd like to see **more variety** there. I usually eat at the Campus Center more than not. I haven't tried Manor House Café yet, but I hear that it's excellent. The only problem is that I also hear how expensive it is. If there's one good thing about Kline, it's that it's all-you-can-eat."

STUDENT AUTHOR: With only two spots to choose from, most Bardians end up eating at Kline Commons, the school's central cafeteria facility, and the only truly affordable year-round eatery. Come to Kline two days in a row, and you're sure to see food from the day before, re-prepared and shabbily disguised to look like a new dish. Luckily, eateries like Manor House and Down the Road Café provide a well-needed respite from Kline.

Student Body

African American:	2%	Male/Female:	45/55%
Asian American:	3%	Out-of-State:	70%
Hispanic:	3%	International:	9%
Native American:	<1%	Unknown:	8%
White:	75%		

Popular Faiths: Most students are either unconcerned or quietly disapproving of religion. Religious clubs and services do exist, however.

Gay Pride: Bard is a highly-accepting community with a large and vocal gay population, and gay groups like the Queer Alliance are active on campus.

Economic Status: An inordinate amount of Bardians seem to come from wealthy, Northeastern families.

Students Speak Out
ON DORMS

Q "Manor is nice in an aesthetic way, although it's sort of **like that hotel in *The Shining***. Dorms like Tewksbury are notoriously bad—but it seems like that's just where they stick the freshmen."

Q "I love my suite in the Village. I live with my friends, and it's just like we have **our own apartment**. We have a bathroom, a kitchen, and a living room. It's nice."

Q "One year, I got the privilege of **living in a trailer**—literally, a trailer. It was because Bard over-booked and ran out of places to put freshmen. Some people had to suffer in an actual building with foundations and stairs and different floors, but I was lucky enough to score something that they use to transport horses."

STUDENT AUTHOR: **Many of the newer dorms (like the Village series) sport modern conveniences and eco-friendly devices, like auto-shut-off lights and geothermal heating. Older dorms, on the other hand, lack even basic amenities, like air-conditioning. Come fall, Bard continues to admit more students than it can accommodate, which inevitably leads to severe housing shortages.**

Did You Know?
77% of undergrads live on campus.

Students Speak Out
ON GUYS & GIRLS

Q "There are a **few extremely attractive girls**, but the discrepancy between these girls and the rest of the school is great enough to make you poke your eyes out."

Q "It's **slim pickings** when it comes to boys. As far as the female students go, there are many more hotties to choose from. If you're a good-looking guy, you'll do very well for yourself at Bard."

Q "Students look like **members of The Strokes**."

Q "Bard is one of the ugliest campuses ever. Girls here are the worst. I'd say find one and put a **paper bag** over her head, but that wouldn't work because most of them are fat anyway. The options are so limited that I usually go home to get laid. It's that bad."

STUDENT AUTHOR: **Students admit that Bard is not brimming with attractive people. While a lot of students take pride in dressing well and taking care of themselves, there's an equal number who throw personal hygiene to the breeze. Plus, a sizable percentage of Bardians are somewhat awkward and androgynous people who are uncomfortable when it comes to social (let alone sexual) interaction—approach them with caution.**

Traditions

Coming Out Week
A seven day series of events organized by Bard's Queer Alliance designed to encourage gay students to openly embrace their sexuality.

Bard vs. Columbia Rugby Match
Bard's most notorious rival on the rugby field—hated for their arrogance, feared for their hard tackling.

Overall School Spirit
The only spirit you'll find at Bard is a raging anti-spirit—it's hipper to knock an institution than to laud it. At Bard, it's the little guy who's important.

Students Speak Out
ON ATHLETICS

Q "I don't know much about the sports scene on campus, except for sometimes it seems rather non-existent. I went to a rugby game once, and **it was boring**."

Q "I think that the Bard sports program is getting much better and most of the teams' records are improving. The strongest teams for both sexes are the soccer and basketball teams. There is also squash, tennis, volleyball, and fencing, and each enjoys **mild recognition**."

Q "There isn't much of a sports scene here. Do I miss it? No—Bard is **not a sports-oriented college**. Most kids here don't even know how to throw a baseball. People are more interested in academics and arts. "

STUDENT AUTHOR: **When you take into account that the majority of students here couldn't catch a gently-lobbed softball, it's not surprising that the college suffers from a lacking sports scene. Most Bardians opt toward more academic and less physically-rigorous pursuits. Still, athletics do hold a tenuous place on campus, and a number of enthusiasts continue to participate in sports like soccer, basketball, and rugby.**

Students Speak Out
ON DRUG SCENE

Q "There are a lot of study **drugs such as Ritalin**. People take them a lot during finals, but some people do them for fun, which strikes me as stupid. I guess it's better than doing coke or heroine."

Q "There are some intense druggies at Bard, but it never gets out of hand. Once in a while you hear about someone having to leave school because of a drug habit. Normally, there is just **weed and beer**—pretty normal for a bunch of college kids."

Q "There is rare **usage of heroine**, but permanent usage of cocaine. Pharmaceuticals are more rare than usual. Of course, there is a ton of pot. Pot is everywhere you look. Also, a good amount of psychedelic usage—mushrooms and LSD."

STUDENT AUTHOR: **Cocaine can be rampant at parties and bars, and it's not uncommon for a group of friends to spend a day on acid or shrooms, wandering around Blithewood or the waterfall. Come finals, many Bardians also use Ritalin and Adderall to keep them awake and focused during cramming.**

9:1	Student-to-Faculty Ratio
88%	Freshman Retention Rate
67%	Four-Year Graduation Rate
90%	Financial Aid Applicants Receiving Aid

Students Speak Out
SAFETY & SECURITY

Q "Bard security is **cheerful and approachable**. They are strict enough when it concerns drugs and booze, but they generally let the students make their own decisions. Compared to my friends at other colleges, we're pretty lucky because security could be a lot more strict about breaking up parties."

Q "Security doesn't really need to do much. Bard is an **extremely safe** campus. Probably the most they do is give out parking tickets. I guess they have to keep busy."

Q "What could possibly happen here? We're basically in the middle-of-nowhere. The **crime rate is zero**. Everybody feels safe walking around at night, pretty much. I don't know anyone who's had a problem."

STUDENT AUTHOR: **What threats that do exist on campus are reprimanded accordingly by Bard's competent and dependable Safety and Security team. Most school years pass without major incident, and students generally walk the campus at night feeling safe and well-protected.**

Questions?
For more inside information and survival tips, pick up College Prowler's full-length book on this school, written by an actual student! Check it out at *www.collegeprowler.com.*

Students Speak Out
ON OVERALL EXPERIENCE

Q "People can get lost at Bard. Like, they get so much into a particular image, style, or major that they dissolve. **There's a strangeness** that doesn't wear off in some ways because so many people here are bringing so much strangeness to the table. It's easy to be lonely here."

Q "I think it's worth it because this is a small school with **interesting people**, smart professors, and a sense of community. People are unique and encouraged to express themselves in an open environment. Not many places have that."

Q "Bard has been a wonderful experience academically. My classes have been mostly inspiring and **totally entertaining**. There's a lot of work, and sometimes it feels like too much during exams."

Q "I came to Bard and didn't like it. As a freshman, I found it **weird and boring**. People were lame and dorky. This year, it seems better. Maybe I've somehow changed and become more of a dork, but I'm more into Bard now than I was. You can't complain about the classes, but sometimes the parties just suck. Bard is definitely a place that appeals to only certain people. I still don't know if I'm that person yet."

STUDENT AUTHOR: **Some students refer to the school as the Bard Bubble—an isolated, introverted space closed off from the rest of the world. Others recognize that thanks to the intimate classes, personal professors, and tightly-knit community in which people share similar interests and commitments, they could not picture themselves anywhere else. All-in-all, what Bard students esteem most about their "bubble" is that they've had the chance to develop a personal connection with the school.**

Barnard College

3009 Broadway; New York, NY 10027
(212) 854-5262; www.barnard.edu

THE BASICS:

Acceptance Rate: 29%
Setting: Urban
F-T Undergrads: 2,346

SAT Range: 1260–1440*
Control: Private
Tuition: $37,538

Most Popular Majors: Social Sciences, Psychology, Area and Ethnic Studies, Visual and Performing Arts

*of 1600

Academics	A	Guys	N/A
Local Atmosphere	A	Girls	B
Safety & Security	B-	Athletics	D
Computers	B-	Nightlife	A
Facilities	B-	Greek Life	D+
Campus Dining	C+	Drug Scene	A-
Off-Campus Dining	A+	Campus Strictness	A
Campus Housing	C	Parking	F
Off-Campus Housing	D-	Transportation	A+
Diversity	B	Weather	B-

Students Speak Out
ON ACADEMICS

Q "There is a **wide variety of teachers**; some are brilliant and teach very stimulating classes, and others are just boring."

Q "I would say the caliber is excellent and superior to most universities, based on my experience as a transfer. However, they are busy people and, as all professors seem to be, **concerned with publishing and their own research**. They demand that you be organized and efficient in dealing with them. Also, teachers at Barnard tend to nurture more, since they are accustomed to dealing with complicated women."

Q "The teachers are pretty accepting most of the time and **usually seem interested** in what they teach, although that doesn't necessarily mean they're good at teaching."

Q "While Barnard professors are often keeping themselves busy with teaching, grading papers, and responding to their students' needs and concerns, they still somehow manage to contribute their knowledge and insight to the academic world. They are **authors, researchers, translators, poets, scientists, and artists**."

STUDENT AUTHOR: The teachers at Barnard are really some of the College's best assets. For the most part, teachers at Barnard will accommodate students who need extra help. Barnard classes are open for cross-registration throughout Columbia University; you almost certainly will take a class at Columbia.

Students Speak Out
ON LOCAL ATMOSPHERE

Q "New York City is a very fast-paced environment. Since Barnard is located right next to Columbia, and NYU is only a subway ride away, there are **too many places to go and very few to avoid**. It makes doing work hard."

Q "Very few colleges can offer a small campus community **under the guise of a large university** in a big city. Essentially, that is what sums up the atmosphere at Barnard."

Q "There are many schools in the New York City area, it's very busy, and there are always places to visit or things to do. On the other hand, urban areas, especially **up near Harlem, can get dangerous** and people should use caution."

Q "A lot of **classes on campus take advantage of the fabulous cityscape** by arranging field trips to the Met, Central Park, or the theater. It can get kind of expensive, but if you know where to look, you can save a lot of money."

STUDENT AUTHOR: Morningside Heights is pretty much a neighborhood of just college students and professors that live nearby. There is an energy that comes from the city that a person might not find in many other places while still being able to enjoy the familiarity of a small neighborhood. Because there is nothing you can't find in the city, from Broadway to basketball to simple peace and quiet, Barnard is really located in a great city, and as New York asserts, it is "the greatest city in the world."

5 Best Things
1 Columbia affiliation
2 Street vendors
3 Subways
4 Manhattan skyline
5 Alumnae

5 Worst Things
1 No re-taking classes
2 Cold, cold winters
3 Frats behind dorms
4 Varsity sports
5 Parking

Students Speak Out
ON FACILITIES

Q "The athletic facilities could be better, as well as the student center, but basically, **we are connected to Columbia's facilities**, so it really doesn't matter."

Q **"Barnard's gym is very small and has weird hours**, but that has never been a problem since all BC students have access to Columbia's Dodge Fitness Center. Most people work out there. Our student center is quaint and by no means 'state-of-the-art,' but it does the job nicely."

Q "Our student center on campus is **pretty small, but it offers great food**, good coffee, mail service, music practice rooms, and a warm, comfortable environment."

Q "We have many things available to us. There's a small weight room available for us, as well as many computer labs. We have nice things but **nothing out of the ordinary**."

Q "The best part about our facilities is all the **people who run them!**"

STUDENT AUTHOR: **As a student on campus at Barnard, you'll be able to take advantage of all the facilities that the Barnard and Columbia University systems have to offer. Barnard's facilities are much more convenient to use. The one exception to this rule is the Dodge Fitness Center, which is Columbia's gym. Most of Barnard's facilities aren't great and most go unused, with the exception of McIntosh. Most students don't care too much, though, because, as part of Columbia University, they have access to everything on any campus. Whatever you are looking to use, it's out there.**

Famous Alumni

Zora Neale Hurston, Erica Jong, Jhumpa Lahiri, Margaret Mead, Cynthia Nixon, Anna Quindlen, Joan Rivers, Martha Stewart, Twyla Tharp

Students Speak Out
ON CAMPUS DINING

Q "The dining halls are not that great, but the food is edible most of the time. Luckily, there are many places to eat out close by. Lower-level **McIntosh, which uses points, is much better**."

Q "In my opinion, the food is excellent in comparison to what I've seen and heard about other campuses. And even if you don't like it, you're in the middle of NYC. There's **bound to be something to satisfy your hunger**."

Q "As a transfer and a girl who prefers to eat on my own time, I have never been required to buy a meal plan. **I use the fully-functional kitchens**."

Q "The food is good, and they have enough options, but **it can be a bit repetitious** if you're Kosher or have other dietary restrictions."

Q "Barnard's main dining areas offer a good variety of food, especially in comparison to Columbia's main dining area. The only inconvenience is that **Barnard and Columbia have different dining services**, so we can't use our points in the other campus dining areas."

STUDENT AUTHOR: **Don't be fooled by the school's Web site, which lists about six different places to eat. There are really only two. Although there aren't too many places to eat, there's quite a bit of choice at those few places. On any given day, you can find meat and vegan entrées. There's a Kosher section that is set off from the main serving area that serves breakfast, lunch, and dinner options. When judging dining hall food, think back to lunch in high school.**

Student Body

African American:	5%	Male/Female:	0/100%
Asian American:	17%	Out-of-State:	66%
Hispanic:	7%	International:	3%
Native American:	1%		
White:	67%		

Popular Faiths: There is a large Jewish population at Barnard that is very visible and tends to stick together. Christianity is also popular.

Gay Pride: Barnard is a very tolerant atmosphere for homosexuals.

Economic Status: Although there is a large economic range when it comes to Barnard students, the trend is overwhelming more affluent.

Students Speak Out
ON DORMS

Q "Dorms are **nice for the city**. Avoid Elliott and most Quad singles, and go for the 600s or 110th Street instead."

Q "Dorms are generally pretty nice. The Quad is good if you're looking for hall-style living. You're required to live there your first year, but there are **always really great options off campus**, but still within the realm of college housing."

Q "The dorms are pretty good compared to those of other colleges I've seen in NYC. Most girls get to **live in singles by their second year**, while in other colleges people don't get singles until their senior year."

STUDENT AUTHOR: **If you choose to live on campus at Barnard there are several housing styles to choose from, and after your first year on campus you may select housing based on what style appeals to you. One very important thing to keep in mind at Barnard is that some of the rooms and suites are very old, so there are a lot of exposed pipes and some rooms with very strange, small dimensions. Old also brings a lot of charm to some of the rooms that feature hardwood floors and fireplaces.**

> **Did You Know?**
> 90% of undergrads live on campus.

Students Speak Out
ON GUYS & GIRLS

Q "It's an **all-girls school**—what more can I say? And the guys at Columbia aren't that good-looking, to say the least."

Q "Columbia guys can be either arrogant or just **totally unaware of girls around them** because their nose is in a book. Columbia girls either don't care at all whether a girl is from Barnard or Columbia, or they absolutely hate Barnard girls for taking their guys."

Q "Most of the girls are average looking, but there are a few that **you can really tell have money**."

Q "A lot of people think Barnard is a school for lesbians, but **there really aren't very many** that go here."

STUDENT AUTHOR: **Looks rate very low on the priority list for girls at Barnard. When sleep is precious, and you're not trying to impress anyone, then what you wear to class doesn't matter. Other people, however, might show up in a dress and heels to class, usually because they have a fantastic interview downtown. Barnard is a college to be yourself; so even the ugliest of ducklings wouldn't feel left out.**

> **Traditions**
>
> **"I Love Barnard" Spirit Day**
> Once a year, Barnard holds a spirit day in which the school sells T-shirts, holds a barbecue out on the lawn, and gives away all sorts of Barnard goodies.
>
> **Greek Games**
> Each spring, Barnard brings together its students for friendly competition in games, such as tug of war.
>
> **Overall School Spirit**
> Barnard women really love their school. Each year this school spirit really comes out during the "I Love Barnard" spirit day.

Students Speak Out
ON ATHLETICS

Q "I **never hear about any of the sports**. I wouldn't know when a game was even going on."

Q "Sports take up a pretty large part of Columbia's activities. There are **lots of intramural games** like basketball at Barnard and Columbia."

Q "Either you're into sports here **because you know someone on the team**, or you're not."

Q "No one is very interested in sports because they take up so much time. Most people **can't afford to stay out every night** playing basketball."

STUDENT AUTHOR: **Playing sports and being active is great, so many people take advantage of the club and intramural sports, but very few can or want to afford the time commitment that varsity sports demand, especially for teams that aren't very good. At Barnard, you can find ways to get involved with athletics and be active, especially on a non-competitive level, but just don't expect to go cheer for the team at Homecoming.**

Students Speak Out
ON DRUG SCENE

Q "I don't think people at Barnard do drugs in the conventional sense. You **don't really ever hear of anyone looking for drugs** or worrying about being caught for using them."

Q "Most people at Barnard have probably tried drugs at one point, but **there are no real drug users here**."

Q "Girls at Barnard will probably say that there are no drugs on campus. There aren't drugs like heroin or anything, but there's **a lot of prescription sharing** and taking legal prescriptions illegally."

STUDENT AUTHOR: **It is possible to graduate from Barnard without ever seeing someone on drugs, taking drugs, or talking about taking drugs. New York City and the area right outside of Barnard are crawling with drugs—if you are into drugs, you'll be able to find them, but you probably won't want to because no one else will be doing them, and there's so much else going on.**

10:1	Student-to-Faculty Ratio
94%	Freshman Retention Rate
82%	Four-Year Graduation Rate
89%	Financial Aid Applicants Receiving Aid

Students Speak Out
SAFETY & SECURITY

Q "**Barnard really takes care of their girls**. We have 24-hour security booths on each corner all around campus and along the way towards the dorms. There are 24-hour desk attendants in every resident hall, as well as the security resources provided by Columbia."

Q "Security and safety are **very hard to achieve in New York City**, but I think they do the best that they can."

Q "Security is just fine. If you're walking home and it's dark, it makes you feel better to know that **a security guard is within yelling distance**."

STUDENT AUTHOR: **Most people know when they come to Barnard that the campus isn't located in the best part of town, but once school starts, very few feel concerned about their safety while on campus. Barnard's security is very visible and there are security guards at every entrance.**

Questions?
For more inside information and survival tips, pick up College Prowler's full-length book on this school, written by an actual student! Check it out at *www.collegeprowler.com*.

Students Speak Out
ON OVERALL EXPERIENCE

Q "Barnard is alright, although if I had it to do over, I would like **a college with a more 'college-y' atmosphere**. The girls at Barnard sometimes act like they're already grown professionals."

Q "Sometimes I wish I were elsewhere for the social aspect, but at other times, **I am so happy I decided to come to Barnard** that I can't imagine, nor would I want to be somewhere else."

Q "**I enjoy Barnard a lot**! I wouldn't want to be anywhere else."

Q "I've had a good experience in the city. It **offers a lot of things that other schools cannot**. Because it's in New York City, but not at the heart of the city, it becomes possible to create a sense of community, but still have outside attractions and lots to do."

STUDENT AUTHOR: **Barnard appears to work very diligently at making sure that it is both academically very rigorous, and that students have many opportunities to enrich their lives socially and financially. This is both a blessing and a curse because classwork takes up such a great deal of time. There is a nice, small college feel from small discussion classes and one-on-one advising while being able to take part in a large Ivy League university. Barnard is not the school for everyone, but the women that choose it are usually really glad they did. It provides a very unique college experience, much different than the pop-culture idea of college that includes rowdy football games and empty kegs lying on the lawns of frat houses.**

Baruch College

One Bernard Baruch Way; New York, NY 10010
(646) 312-1000; www.baruch.cuny.edu

THE BASICS:

Acceptance Rate: 26%
Setting: Urban
F-T Undergrads: 9,588

SAT Range: 1020–1230*
Control: Public
Tuition: $8,640

Most Popular Majors: Business/Marketing, Communications/Journalism, Psychology

*of 1600

Academics	B+	Guys	B
Local Atmosphere	A	Girls	B
Safety & Security	A-	Athletics	C+
Computers	B+	Nightlife	A
Facilities	B-	Greek Life	C+
Campus Dining	C	Drug Scene	A-
Off-Campus Dining	A+	Campus Strictness	B
Campus Housing	N/A	Parking	D-
Off-Campus Housing	B	Transportation	A+
Diversity	A+	Weather	B-

Students Speak Out
ON ACADEMICS

Q "**As many students hold part- or full-time jobs, I'd say the workload is fairly manageable**. In terms of quality of professors, I've mostly had good professors. There are a few that were highly intelligent people but not great educators or teachers. There were also a few who made me wonder how they ever received a Ph.D."

Q "The workload's not so bad, but the teachers aren't great. If you show genuine interest in the classes—asking intelligent questions or talking to them during office hours—**they'll be more willing to help you out if you need it**. However, it's not an excuse to slack off and hope for a good grade."

Q "Depending on your major, **the workload can be intense and the exams tough**. As a liberal arts major, I've had more writing-intensive courses than most Baruch students do."

Q "The cost of the school is incredible. **They are selective in who is accepted**, even though it's a public school. It makes Baruch more competitive and attracts better students."

STUDENT AUTHOR: **When it comes to critiquing the school's academics, there are as many opinions as students. With more than 900 teachers to choose from, class experiences vary from excellent to not so good. Most Baruch students major in a business-related discipline. Some say that the toughness of the workload and exams depend on the major, and the workload tends to increase at more advanced course levels.**

Students Speak Out
ON LOCAL ATMOSPHERE

Q "Since it is New York City, **the atmosphere is highly diversified**. There are limitless amounts of things to do provided you have money."

Q "The atmosphere in Manhattan is very fast-paced. During the morning and evening rush hours, people can be seen running on the sidewalks, trying to get wherever they are going in as little time as possible. Cars speed along streets as well, at times **creating hazards that pedestrians must navigate**. Having one's toes stepped on is not unusual, especially during the busiest times of the week."

Q "In the immediate area around Baruch, there is a music theater for concerts and a large amount of restaurants to visit. **Union Square is only eight blocks away**. NYU is further down but within walking distance."

Q "I love the area Baruch is in. **The Gramercy area is both beautiful and historic**. We are also well-situated near Fifth Avenue, 34th Street, and the youthful buzz of Union Square. We also share space with the NYU kids and SVU kids, who make life, shall we say, colorful."

STUDENT AUTHOR: **It's fast-paced. It's crowded. It's entertaining. Welcome to Manhattan, the heart of New York City. Some people love it; others wish they were somewhere else. But if you want to be in the epicenter of an urban life, study at Baruch. The neighborhood is filled with skyscrapers, cars, tourists, nightlife, and all the bells and whistles that come with living in The Big Apple.**

Students Speak Out
ON FACILITIES

Q "The facilities are great, especially when new students don't know about them yet, which keeps them less crowded. The gyms, the library, computer center, and theater are **all great and always functioning** with the best equipment."

Q "**I wish we could have a bigger cafeteria or student lounge** instead of having to fight for a seat during lunchtime. The library is huge with plenty of comfortable couches to sleep on!"

Q "The facilities on campus are above average, but due to overpopulation, they would be rated as poor. **Athletic facilities are always occupied, and it is impossible to use a machine** in the gym unless it is the weekend, late at night, or very early in the morning. The library is also overpopulated, and many students sleep there during periods when they do not have class. There is also a lack of cleanliness in such areas."

Q "The **cafeteria is always too crowded with not enough chairs or tables**. The seats available at the entrance are extremely uncomfortable."

Q "The library and VC (vertical campus) are some of **the best facilities CUNY has to offer**."

STUDENT AUTHOR: Aside from the complaints about overcrowding and broken escalators, students seem to be satisfied with the quality of campus facilities. Baruch College's wallet may not be as thick as some private colleges' pockets, but this affordable school still offers adequate facilities to its students. Overall, it has everything you need to succeed as a student.

Students Speak Out
ON CAMPUS DINING

Q "I don't like the food at Baruch. I think that the effort is not there to attract as many people as possible. I am not satisfied in the salads section at all—it's not tasty or mixed well. For this reason, **I buy lunch outside of Baruch**."

Q "Honestly, I don't like the food very much. One of the biggest reasons is that **lots of the food served is not very healthy**. In addition, they portions are too big per serving."

Q "I think **the food could be better**. I don't think that the food in the cafeteria is healthy enough, but it's okay."

Q "To tell you the truth, I usually don't eat in our cafeteria or on campus at all. **I was there once and had a sandwich**, and it was really tasty and fresh. Their coffee is good, too."

Q "**They are serving better tasting food** and have a moderate variety for all types of taste like the salad and soup bar, sandwiches, pizza, Chinese food, fruits, and the typical fried food."

STUDENT AUTHOR: When it comes to food at Baruch, students are quite divided. Some like it, while others aren't shy to slam the various aspects of campus dining. On the other hand, nearly every day—especially during the rush hours—plenty of students patronize both the cafeteria on the first floor of the Vertical Campus and the Starbucks. Once on campus, you may taste the food and fall in love. You can also become one of many students who take their hunger and money elsewhere in the vibrant Manhattan neighborhood.

Students Speak Out
ON DORMS

Q "It may be a surprise, but Baruch College **does not provide student housing**."

Q "When it comes to Baruch, **you just have to bear living off campus** as there is no other option."

Q "Baruch College is a **commuter school**."

STUDENT AUTHOR: For some Baruchians, the lack of dorms is the worst aspect of the school. Dorms help shape the overall college experience, often adding that special sense of communal living and belonging. If you still want to experience something close to a dorm-style living, check out the office of Educational Housing Services at 31 Lexington Avenue. It's right across the street from the Vertical Campus. The EHS offers affordable student housing. The residencies are located both in Manhattan and Brooklyn. They provide furniture and don't charge broker fees.

Did You Know?
0% of undergrads live on campus.

Students Speak Out
ON GUYS & GIRLS

Q "Students **don't fit the all-American image** here. Most of them speak more than one language and come from other countries. There is no specific look of a Baruch student."

Q "A typical guy is not very approachable and quiet. They seem very school-oriented and not really into looking for fun. The girls that I've met are really nice, but they are not into meeting new people. **They like to form cliques**."

Q "The **guys are okay**, and some girls are pretty."

Q "The guys on campus are generally not cute. If they are, they're probably gay. **The girls aren't too cute either**—most wear clothes that are too tight for them."

STUDENT AUTHOR: There is no specific look for a Baruch student. Clothes reflect lifestyles and cultures. In the same class, you can spot a flashy fashionista and a woman in a conservative Muslim hijab. No matter how diverse Baruch is, most students leave campus after studying is over. A lot of students are bookish and career-oriented, but there are also those who save some time for partying.

Traditions

Baruch Bash
An end-of-the-year party that celebrates graduating seniors and features an open bar, buffet, and DJ.

Club Fair and Spring Fling
Student clubs and organizations woo new members during the Club Fair in fall and Spring Fling.

Overall School Spirit
It may be rare to spot a Baruchian wearing a sweatshirt with the school logo, but you can find plenty of folks who are quite proud to attend one of the best public schools in New York.

Students Speak Out
ON ATHLETICS

Q "Baruch College is a Division III school, so our sports program isn't highly ranked. **There isn't an overwhelming amount of school spirit** among the general population of Baruch when it comes to attendance at games."

Q "Don't expect too much school spirit—you have to play for your teammates and yourself. If you are looking for to become a campus celebrity, transfer to Duke or Texas A&M."

Q "Sports aren't that big of a deal on campus. Our teams are good considering our division. **There aren't too many intramural sports**."

Q "In general, **sports at CUNY aren't that popular**. I think people don't give it a chance!"

STUDENT AUTHOR: For those who partake in the sports activities, the athletics department is a small, yet heartfelt community. In general, all the student athletes know and support each other. The Athletic Recreation Center, located underground in the Vertical Campus, offers a large swimming pool and a fitness center.

Students Speak Out
ON DRUG SCENE

Q "I know people who do drugs on campus, but I don't know where they do that. **Drinking is a bigger part of campus life** only because there is a bar around the corner."

Q "Students have been known to occasionally smoke marijuana outside the building. Since it is a business school, I'd imagine that **drug use is not as frequent due to frequent drug tests** from employers."

Q "I don't think the drug scene is a huge part on campus only because **we're a commuter school, so it's hard to really do drugs on campus.**"

STUDENT AUTHOR: If there's one thing you won't find at Baruch, it's an established drug scene. As an urban commuter school, it has managed to escape the active drug and drinking scene that's visible on so many campuses across the country. Baruch doesn't have dorms that would provide enough private space to do drugs. Some level of drug activity exists on campus, but it's most likely very small.

19:1	Student-to-Faculty Ratio
88%	Freshman Retention Rate
33%	Four-Year Graduation Rate
84%	Financial Aid Applicants Receiving Aid

Students Speak Out
SAFETY & SECURITY

Q "I have never really had a concern with Baruch's safety procedures since **security guards are always around campus**. In my opinion, crime at Baruch is very rare."

Q "Security on campus is poor and incompetent. The guards do not know how to handle an emergency situation well at all. There's not a lot of crime on campus per se, but **there is a lot of loitering and vandalism**."

Q "Baruch is actually **pretty safe, especially compared to the other CUNY schools**. The security guards are okay as long as you are courteous and don't give them an attitude."

STUDENT AUTHOR: Crime is low on campus. Safety officers patrol the campus in the evening, removing students who don't have permission to stay inside after hours. New York is a large city where anyone should practice a common sense caution.

> **Questions?**
> For more inside information and survival tips, pick up College Prowler's full-length book on this school, written by an actual student! Check it out at *www.collegeprowler.com*.

Students Speak Out
ON OVERALL EXPERIENCE

Q "Baruch is **a good school if you are set and focused on entering the business field**. They offer many opportunities and internships for such students. If you are a student in liberal arts or anything other than business, you will be most likely ignored."

Q "I can very honestly say that if I could do it all over again, **I would undoubtedly come back**. I was lucky enough to find my place at Baruch. I joined the clubs that most interested me, and I met a great group of friends within those clubs."

Q "It's a commuter school, so **you never really get the real college experience**. Most students have jobs, and a lot go to school at night. It's really hard to feel a part of the community, so the experience can be quite lonely, unless you are able to make friends quickly."

Q "I really enjoy going to Baruch College. I like how **the entire city is our campus** as opposed to all of my friends who are confined to a campus where there's little to do. I feel like I'm getting real life experience at this school since there are so many different people to interact with."

STUDENT AUTHOR: Baruch is a strong choice for a student who wants a quality education at a low price. Most Baruchians seem too busy studying, building resumes, and staying at home to hang out on campus. So unless you join a club or organization, it may be difficult to actively socialize. Demanding workloads can make studying hard, particularly if you plan to work. For many, it's a true business-oriented, urban environment that can make some folks feeling left out. It can be stressful, but overall, Baruch is capable of shaping you into a well-rounded, tough-skinned leader.

Bates College

23 Campus Avenue; Lewiston, ME 04240
(207) 786-6255; www.bates.edu

THE BASICS:

Acceptance Rate: 29% **SAT Range:** 1890–2150*
Setting: Suburban **Control:** Private
F-T Undergrads: 1,776 **Tuition:** $46,800**

Most Popular Majors: Social Sciences, English, Psychology, Biology, History

*of 2400 **includes room & board

Academics	A-	Guys	B
Local Atmosphere	C-	Girls	B+
Safety & Security	B+	Athletics	C+
Computers	B+	Nightlife	C
Facilities	B-	Greek Life	N/A
Campus Dining	A-	Drug Scene	C
Off-Campus Dining	C+	Campus Strictness	C+
Campus Housing	C+	Parking	C
Off-Campus Housing	C	Transportation	D+
Diversity	C-	Weather	C-

Students Speak Out
ON ACADEMICS

Q "Most importantly, I have almost always felt like they care about the students. For the most part, they have led interesting classes, although sometimes, I feel like **they rely too much on old teaching methods** that aren't very engaging for the students."

Q "The professors at Bates are **very intelligent and knowledgable**. Most seek active participation from their students and encourage classroom discussion. They are generally approachable and willing to talk or offer help outside the classroom."

Q "Overall, **the teachers have been pretty solid**. But honestly, some profs could not be any worse at their jobs. Classes are interesting, but I would have liked to see more diversity and not just standard courses one could find at any college."

Q "My professors at Bates have been friendly and down-to-earth. I feel like **they treat me more as an intellectual peer** that has something legitimate to contribute, rather than an inferior student."

STUDENT AUTHOR: **Most professors are experts in their fields, and they generally bring a high degree of enthusiasm to their classes. There are certainly some who, because they are tenured, don't care much about bringing new approaches to their courses, but most professors care very deeply about the subjects. Because so many classes are small and discussion-oriented, students are often deeply involved in their courses.**

Students Speak Out
ON LOCAL ATMOSPHERE

Q "It's pretty obvious to me that most people who live in Lewiston **don't like upper-middle-class students**, so I just try to be as friendly and polite as possible. There really isn't anything there except some restaurants and some strip malls."

Q "**Relations are tense** between Bates and Lewiston in the sense that they are almost nonexistent. I feel like most Batesies try to imagine that Lewiston isn't there. The students won't even give the town the benefit of the doubt. There is a reputation that there is nothing to do in Lewiston, and I think students stay on campus because of that."

Q "Bates actively tries to reach out to the community through service-learning and other initiatives, which will **hopefully improve our community relations**."

Q "Lewiston is **a New England mill town with a struggling economy**. The University of Maine in Auburn is a few miles away, although I have yet to notice any students from there in the area. I believe most of those students commute."

STUDENT AUTHOR: **Though the city of Lewiston is probably the biggest drawback about going to Bates, Lewiston probably isn't quite as bad as most students make it out to be. There are some nice trails only about 10 minutes from campus, and while there honestly isn't that much to do in Lewiston, Portland is less than an hour drive from campus. With few exceptions, though, Bates students prefer to stay in the "Bates bubble."**

5 Best Things	5 Worst Things
1 Strong academics	1 Parking
2 Improv comedy	2 Long winters
3 Computer network	3 Lewiston
4 The Quad	4 No cable TV
5 Snowball fights	5 Gen-ed requirements

Students Speak Out
ON FACILITIES

Q "Most facilities here are nice on the outside, but with the notable exceptions of the buildings less than 10 years old, **most are slightly dilapidated inside**."

Q "The gym is lacking in equipment. I think there is one treadmill and two bikes for a student body of 1,700. The student center is excellent for studying, but the student commons has **very little in the way of extra facilities** besides the dining hall and book store."

Q "I think the **facilities at Bates are very nice**. The athletic center, including the pool, the track, the ice rink, and the tennis courts, is great. I think the gym and cardio room could use improvements and updates, though."

Q "Some of the computer labs (Pettengill Hall and the library) have **new computers and a well-lit, comfortable atmosphere**. Some computer labs in other academic buildings are not as nice."

Q "We have a track and field complex, lacrosse field, and **a nice ice-skating area**. The rest of the athletic facilities, like the basketball gym, football field, indoor track, and field house are fairly standard."

STUDENT AUTHOR: The quality of facilities at Bates depends largely on the age of the building. Some of the classrooms have almost space-age technology, with remote controls for lights and window shades. Other classrooms are not so fortunate and look like they haven't been renovated since they were built decades ago. Facilities here are adequate, sometimes above average, but nothing more.

Famous Alumni

Frank Coffin, Robert Goodlatte, Bryant Gumbel, Benjamin Mays, Edmund Muskie, Louis Scolnik, James Tobin

Students Speak Out
ON CAMPUS DINING

Q "I like Commons food. I think that **it is pretty good**, in terms of college meals, and you can always find something to fill up on. How can you beat an all-you-can-eat buffet every single day?"

Q "The food is excellent here. However, it can be very hard to find a table in the one and only dining hall on campus. **They could definitely use a second dining hall**, but the food in the one they have is pretty good."

Q "The food on campus is great! **I love Commons**! There is only one dining hall on campus, which is nice, because it is a place where you can see everyone. There is also the Den, which is nice for late-night study breaks."

Q "Okay, there's only one dining hall; the food is fine, but let's face it, you're going to get **bored with the selection here**."

Q "Bates is a small school, so it only has one dining hall for the entire campus. The food here is great compared to other colleges I have eaten at, and they have quite a bit of variety with **plenty of vegetarian and vegan options**."

STUDENT AUTHOR: Dining services at Bates are generally excellent, with one outstanding flaw: there is only one meal plan. Students have unlimited meals, which can be a big advantage if you stop by Commons six times a day for coffee, but is also frustrating for students who only eat one or two meals in the dining hall a day. Though, on the whole, Bates Dining Services is outstanding, especially considering how small the school is.

Student Body

African American:	4%	Male/Female:	46/54%
Asian American:	6%	Out-of-State:	89%
Hispanic:	4%	International:	5%
Native American:	<1%	Unknown:	3%
White:	78%		

Popular Faiths: The ecumenical Christian Fellowship has a diverse membership, as does the Jewish Cultural Community.

Political Activity: The campus is overwhelmingly liberal, and many students are politically active. The school also has a small but vocal Republican element.

Economic Status: A majority of students are from wealthy families.

Students Speak Out
ON DORMS

Q "The nicest dorms are the suites in the Village, though you can forget about living there until you are at least a junior. I prefer the houses Bates owns because they are smaller and quieter, and you get to know the other people in the houses better. Adams is centrally-located, though it's just your average dorm. If you are a first-year, **try to get into Parker and avoid Page**."

Q "I think **the large dorms are mostly gross**, except for the Village. The Village is newer, and obviously has new furniture. However, public space gets trashed by parties."

Q "All dorms are very well kept, and most are very nice to live in. The majority of housing at Bates, though, is in **Victorian houses**, which are very popular."

STUDENT AUTHOR: **The best part about housing at Bates is the wide variety of options available to students. There are suites, quads, doubles, singles, halls, and houses, as well as theme houses. It can be difficult to get a single if you have a poor lottery number, but everyone will have a room, even if it's a forced triple in Page Hall.**

> **Did You Know?**
> 92% of undergrads live on campus.

Students Speak Out
ON GUYS & GIRLS

Q "**For us guys, it's really nice**. The females, for the most part, are hot, yet some can be stuck-up. Overall, we are an attractive campus."

Q "Anyone who is choosing colleges based on how attractive the people are would probably not choose Bates. **Students here do have fun with each other**, though."

Q "The guys and girls are **often hippies who don't shower**, so I'd have to say they're not that hot."

Q "There are **many different types of guys**. You've got your meathead, beer-chugging jock, you've got your greasy, smelly hippie, and you've got your nerdy, smart guys. And there's probably a few other types thrown in there, too."

STUDENT AUTHOR: **Bates has a preponderance of hippies, but there are also jocks, nerds, preppies, and so on. You'll find all ends of the spectrum at Bates. Batesies do tend to be attractive physically, but some people have complained about the general shallowness of the students on campus. Bates is a small campus, and before too long, students will be able to recognize just about everyone they pass by.**

> **Traditions**
>
> **The *Daily Jolt***
> The *Daily Jolt* is a student-run Web site that provides information and amusement to Batesies.
>
> **Newman Day**
> Each year, students try to drink a case of beer and then attend class. The college encourages students not to participate in this event.
>
> **Overall School Spirit**
> Many students are passionate, but few of them are passionate about Bates. People who play sports have lots of school spirit, but others remain fairly apathetic.

Students Speak Out
ON ATHLETICS

Q "**Sports are not huge on campus**, although if you want to participate, there is certainly an opportunity. I guess there is a whole scene for which sports is a big deal, but it is by no means pervasive. It's not like you are an outsider if you don't go to football games."

Q "I think **the majority of students here have participated** in either a varsity or IM sport. And if they haven't, they've probably been to a sporting event to cheer on their friends."

Q "**Bates isn't at the top of the pancake stack** when it comes to sports. We are more like the soggy one on the bottom. Although, I hear that our lacrosse team is good."

Q "Bates is definitely **more of an academic school**, but the sports are there if you want to play."

STUDENT AUTHOR: **IM sports are almost as big, if not bigger, than varsity sports at Bates. The football team has a less-than-stellar record, but the lacrosse team and basketball team enjoy more success. Generally, IM sports are the school's main attraction, though they can go unnoticed by people who aren't actually playing them.**

Students Speak Out
ON DRUG SCENE

Q "There is a **huge abuse of Adderall** here, and most people who party also regularly smoke pot. I know a handful of people who also do harder drugs like coke."

Q "It is there if you look for it. Pot and alcohol are pretty ubiquitous. You don't have to look all that hard for those. Harder stuff can be found if you're looking for it. It will not be shoved in your face, though. **It's not like they're selling heroin in the library**!"

Q "There is **quite a bit of pot on campus**, and I am sure every other drug imaginable, but the harder drugs are not visible. Most people party with alcohol or marijuana."

STUDENT AUTHOR: **Marijuana is definitely present, and you'd be hard-pressed to walk through the dorms without smelling pot. For students who don't want to get involved in the drug scene, there are a variety of chem-free housing options that really are chem-free; smoking and drinking are prohibited within 20 feet of these buildings.**

10:1	Student-to-Faculty Ratio
96%	Freshman Retention Rate
85%	Four-Year Graduation Rate
90%	Financial Aid Applicants Receiving Aid

Students Speak Out
SAFETY & SECURITY

Q "While security is **not as strict about alcohol** as other schools, they do their job, and I think students feel safe. In spite of the few past events at Bates, I think most students feel safe on campus."

Q "Security on campus is pretty good. There are **SafeRide shuttles at night** if you need them. However, I feel perfectly safe walking around campus alone at night."

Q "Unlike other schools, **students are happy to welcome security** into their rooms and parties, knowing almost all the officers by name. You get the 'we're in this together' feeling from security personnel, and so it builds a sense of community and responsibility when it comes to each other's safety."

STUDENT AUTHOR: **Since the rape and murder which occurred several years ago, security at Bates has become much more stringent. Proximity Cards now allow only students to enter residential buildings. Security officers are still very friendly, though.**

Questions?
For more inside information and survival tips, pick up College Prowler's full-length book on this school, written by an actual student! Check it out at *www.collegeprowler.com.*

Students Speak Out
ON OVERALL EXPERIENCE

Q "I do wish I was somewhere other than Bates. In high school, my big complaint in life was that I learned nothing from school and more from my peers. Now, I feel the reverse. Academically, I feel challenged by my classes and professors, now that I know how to pick good classes. However, **I do not feel challenged by my peers**. I think I would have done better in a more intellectually-driven school."

Q "I liked it here the first two years, although sometimes, **I wish I would have gone to a bigger school**. Now that I'm back for my senior year, I know I would have chosen a different place. There are just too many negatives in the surrounding environment."

Q "I'm glad I went to Bates because it's given me **the chance to make friends with the most amazing people**. I know I wouldn't have had as good a time anywhere else."

Q "I think Bates is a good school, and having a Bates degree will definitely help me for the rest of my life, but I still wish I hadn't gone here. It was mostly a matter of Bates being a good school, but not really the right school for me. I would have been much **happier in a larger school**, one in a real city, one whose student body isn't quite so homogenous."

STUDENT AUTHOR: **If you're looking for an intimate, close-knit campus, and an academically-challenging school, you'll probably enjoy Bates. If you want a big university with an exciting city nearby, you might be better off somewhere else. Even students who wish they were elsewhere will leave the school with a valuable degree and a unique learning experience.**

Baylor University

700 South University Parks Drive; Waco, TX 76798
(800) BAYLOR-U; www.baylor.edu

THE BASICS:

Acceptance Rate: 44%
Setting: Mid-sized city
F-T Undergrads: 11,641

SAT Range: 1110–1310*
Control: Private
Tuition: $23,664

Most Popular Majors: Business/Marketing, Communications, Health Professions, Biology

*of 1600

Academics	B-	Guys	A-
Local Atmosphere	D+	Girls	B+
Safety & Security	B+	Athletics	B+
Computers	B-	Nightlife	C
Facilities	A-	Greek Life	B+
Campus Dining	B-	Drug Scene	B+
Off-Campus Dining	C+	Campus Strictness	C
Campus Housing	B-	Parking	B
Off-Campus Housing	B+	Transportation	C
Diversity	C	Weather	B

Students Speak Out
ON ACADEMICS

Q "I had **good experiences** with most of my professors. Most were kind and willing to help, especially in the College of Arts and Sciences. It seemed like some of the business professors were a little stuffier."

Q "Unlike the stereotype, I have **not found much incorporation of Christianity** into the daily class agenda. This may or may not be a good thing."

Q "My teachers were very personable. Any time I had a question or needed help on something, they were **always available and willing to help**. I enjoyed their genuine interest in how I was doing in and outside of school."

Q "It's all **a matter of asking those around you** who have already taken those classes to find the good professors. For freshman-level courses, the material and assignments can be a little bit heavy, and if the class is in your major, the professor will most likely be difficult."

Q "Teachers in **upper level classes actually care** about students. While they may not always be available, they will find time to help."

STUDENT AUTHOR: When it comes to academics, the old cliché, "You get what you pay for," most encompasses Baylor's mentality. The biggest complaint from students working toward a Bachelor of Science is that they feel like there's too much emphasis placed on research, and for the most part, everyone feels that the teaching assistants are completely useless.

Students Speak Out
ON LOCAL ATMOSPHERE

Q "To be blunt, the atmosphere in Waco sucks. There is really **nothing to do** besides maybe go to the movies and get drunk, or get drunk and go to the movies."

Q "The atmosphere is friendly and pretty low key. For college students, there really isn't very much to do except **go to the movies**, go out to eat, or go to a small club (of which there aren't very many promising choices). I've heard that some people visiting Waco like to visit the Dr Pepper Museum and the Texas Ranger Hall of Fame, but people who live here don't usually go there."

Q "If you ever wanted to experience what the caste system of India might be like, this is the place for you. When you step out of the '**Baylor bubble**,' you can witness the plight of homeless Americans from the safety of your BMW or other equally expensive car."

Q "Waco the town is evil. It's the **armpit of Texas**."

STUDENT AUTHOR: The thing about Baylor, and especially Waco, is that if you don't get involved in something, you will die of boredom. There really isn't a whole lot that the town has to offer because, honestly, how many times are you going to visit the Dr Pepper museum? The biggest drawback is that, just like the motto says, everything is bigger in Texas, which also means more spread out. If you go without a car, you better start making friends fast, because otherwise, it's tough to get anywhere.

Students Speak Out
ON FACILITIES

Q "The facilities are nice, especially the SLC, where you can go to do things such as work out, play basketball, swim, or **climb the rock wall** . . . The computer labs are nice but usually a little crowded, and most of the computers are Dell with flat-screen monitors. The athletic complexes are also pretty nice. The baseball/softball complex is new. In general, the facilities are either new or well-maintained."

Q "Facilities are **top-notch**. The SLC is huge and beats out the majority of gyms you will ever encounter. It's totally state-of-the-art, with all new equipment and lots of it. Plus, it has a smoothie bar!"

Q "The school is **going into debt** to make itself look nice to the public and incoming students . . . so all facilities are in good shape."

Q "The facilities are really nice. The SLC is a really nice work out place, though you want to hit the weight room before 8 a.m.–9 a.m., or it becomes a **sweat sauna**."

Q "The SLC is awesome, especially if you actually use it. There are **plenty of activities** to keep a college student entertained."

STUDENT AUTHOR: **The list of amenities reads like a vacation on a cruise ship . . . Baylor definitely gets five stars because what the town lacks in atmosphere, the school makes up for in service. Short of having a butler bring up your dinner and keeping a personal assistant in-tow, Baylor really has gone above and beyond to offer students state-of-the-art facilities.**

Famous Alumni

Michael Brandt, Robert Fulghum, Derek Haas, Michael Johnson, Jason Jennings, Ann Richards, Mike Singletary, Kip Wells, Mark White

Students Speak Out
ON CAMPUS DINING

Q "The food on campus is good for about a month. Then, it gets old and the strange inventions the staff comes up with become **frightening** (e.g. some kind of apple dessert with stale frosted flakes on top)."

Q "The food is what it is—**mass-produced cafeteria-style goo**. Penland is good for food on the quick, Collins is good for lunch (try the Asian bowls), and Memorial for dinner—they have the best pizza."

Q "**I gained weight**, so it must not have been too bad."

Q There are several choices at Penland, which is the largest dining hall. Most freshmen eat there because it is so close to the freshman dorms. Memorial is more of an upperclassman dining hall, where a lot of Greeks sit at the same table each day. Collins tries to serve some of the **healthier choices on** campus, but most of the time there are only girls there."

STUDENT AUTHOR: **There has never been a Baylor student that starved to death . . . [T]he food on campus is so readily available, there really is no excuse not to eat. In fact, many of the students are often participants in binge eating, eating massive amounts of food just because it's there, not because they're hungry. All the gym junkies work out for a reason—over-indulgence . . . [U]nused meals at the end of the semester don't roll over, so a lot of the time you'll catch yourself eating meals just to use up your allotment.**

Student Body

African American:	8%	Male/Female:	42/58%
Asian American:	7%	Out-of-State:	17%
Hispanic:	10%	International:	2%
Native American:	1%	Unknown:	1%
White:	71%		

Popular Faiths: Baptist, Catholic

Gay Pride: It's incredibly low. Being a conservative, Republican, Baptist University, if you're looking for tolerance, go somewhere else. If you're really interested, read about Matt Bass. There is a group: Baylor Freedom. The University does not sanction any of their actions or even their existence.

Economic Status: Most students come from at least a middle-class background, usually upper-middle-class.

Students Speak Out
ON DORMS

Q "Collins and Dawson/Allen are as nice as it gets at Baylor. Ladies, avoid Memorial, and for men, Brooks. They are poor excuses for dormitories. Memorial is reputed to have rats/mice, and Brooks is called the **ghetto dorm**."

Q "They are all nice. Kokernot is small and cozy while Collins is **big, loud, and fun**. Take your pick."

Q "The dorms are fairly nice. They are well taken care of, and the staff is usually very helpful. The saying goes: **study with the Kokernot girls**, date a Collins girl, and marry a Russell girl."

STUDENT AUTHOR: **Most students move off campus as soon as possible.** Not because the on-campus housing is awful—it's mostly very convenient and respectable—but more because of Baylor's policy with visiting hours and alcohol. The dorms on campus (with some exceptions) aren't really that bad because the school does go out of their way to accommodate its students in terms of amenities and keep students on campus, but inhabitants refer to dorm life as white-collar prison.

Did You Know?
36% of undergrads live on campus.

Students Speak Out
ON GUYS & GIRLS

Q "Most people down here are pretty nice, hospitable types. Since it's a private school and expensive, **you get a lot of daddy's girl types**. There is an incredibly disproportionate ratio of girls to guys here."

Q "The guys and girls are both very good-looking, especially in the School of Business. **Eating disorders are known to be prevalent** on campus, though. Most of the students come from well-off families."

Q "I am disappointed that **students weren't more active in political issues** or taking active roles at their school. I think much reasoning for this is heavy work loads, but also because Baylor has strict rules and often punishes or shuns students that are different and break stereotypes."

STUDENT AUTHOR: **To a lot of people, Baylor and Waco are a complete anomaly.** The same girls that run in the social hookup circles on Friday night are taking you to church with them on Sunday. The guys practice the requisite Christian business principles, but blow through the Baylor babes that are in endless supply . . . just beware because Baylor has a penchant for smoke and mirrors. Don't get fooled, and be on the lookout for husband hunters.

Traditions

Bonfire
Students and faculty turn out for the Homecoming Bonfire no matter what the weather is like.

Diadeloso
A day off each spring, on a Thursday, for no other reason than to have fun.

Overall School Spirit
In terms of athletics, school spirit is very high, especially when competing against other teams in the state of Texas. Academically, students are also very supportive, but nothing compares to athletic events.

Students Speak Out
ON ATHLETICS

Q "Ha, we're Baylor and this is Texas. Since our football team is shamefully terrible, we are a failure to all Texans. Be prepared to be the butt of **many jokes** as a Baylor student. The IM sports seem to overcompensate for this shortcoming."

Q "The men's and women's **basketball, tennis, and baseball teams** are always the ones to watch, because more often than not they will actually win."

Q "This isn't a rah-rah school, and if I'm going to gauge the sport interest from one to ten (ten being a fanatic fan base), I'd say the campus interest level is **about a six**."

Q "Our **football team sucks**, but the other sports are pretty good and worth watching."

STUDENT AUTHOR: **Football is the reigning king of the South;** everyone knows someone who went on to play professional ball, completing the two degrees of separation that Baylor is famous for. Competing for a close second in popularity are basketball and baseball. When home games roll around, especially if Baylor is playing a rival school (pretty much anyone), the stands are packed.

Students Speak Out
ON DRUG SCENE

Q "From what I've seen, there isn't a lot that goes on. There are some who smoke pot, but it isn't really talked about. Other than that, the only things you hear about are **people taking Ritalin** or Adderall to stay awake and study."

Q "Boredom plus money equals a drug scene, for sure. It is **more of a tiny niche**, not really widespread. And like everything else here, it all depends on what you are into and what circles you run with."

Q "It's **what you make it**. You can find drugs anywhere if you are looking. A lot of that scene is hush since this is a private Christian school."

STUDENT AUTHOR: **The drug scene is as big as you make it. It isn't hard to find if all you do is ask around, and it's not tough to get whatever you want, because a lot of bored rich kids away from mom and dad want to experiment. Everyone knows someone, but generally speaking, illegal drugs aren't all that visible. Adderall is by far the most popular.**

15:1	Student-to-Faculty Ratio
86%	Freshman Retention Rate
48%	Four-Year Graduation Rate
82%	Financial Aid Applicants Receiving Aid

Students Speak Out
SAFETY & SECURITY

Q "The campus always feels safe, but with the **surrounding areas** being how they are, you can never be too sure. There have been a lot of cars broken into."

Q "**I always felt safe** on campus at all hours, though I know there have been problems with joggers around the Bear Trail at night."

Q "The campus is not that well lit, so it is sometimes **a little scary** at night if you are walking by yourself. The University advises students to always travel in groups of two or more at night. There are call boxes spread around the campus that you can use if you have an emergency or need help, and police like to patrol around the campus, but usually only to give out parking tickets and break up parties."

STUDENT AUTHOR: **This campus is, by far, one of the safest places to be. . . . Off campus is a slightly different story. Two blocks off campus, you'll find low-income housing, the industrial side of town, a strip club, a liquor store, and Dr. Daddy (a well-known local who frequents Baylor parties uninvited).**

Questions?
For more inside information and survival tips, pick up College Prowler's full-length book on this school, written by an actual student! Check it out at *www.collegeprowler.com*.

Students Speak Out
ON OVERALL EXPERIENCE

Q "I do not think that Baylor was worth the price, but I don't regret going there because **I made some wonderful friends**."

Q "I wouldn't trade it for anything. It is an interesting place to be; it can sometimes be frustrating with the **Baptist mindset** coating everything, but overall it's a good experience."

Q "I loved Baylor. I did not always agree with everything that Baylor did or stood for, but I do think that **it was the best place for me**."

Q "Overall, I really liked Baylor . . . For me, a middle-class, non-religious, non-sorority type female, I had a hard time relating to most of the other students on campus. I would have enjoyed **more diversity**. It would also be nice if alcohol wasn't outlawed so that students wouldn't have to go off campus or to extreme measures to drink. With that said, I am still glad I chose to go to Baylor, although I think I'd like to try somewhere else a little bigger and more open-minded for grad school."

STUDENT AUTHOR: **When polling immediate post-graduation opinions, it's pretty common to hear "Happiness is seeing Waco in the rearview mirror." However, most students are relatively satisfied with their time at Baylor after nostalgia has set in . . . For four years, at least, count on being frustrated with the social scene, overloaded with classes, poor, and running on no sleep and caffeine. The odd thing is, an unusual amount of graduates, despite their protests, never leave Waco. Everywhere you go, especially if it's in Texas, the Baylor degree is recognized, and the school itself is well known for networking.**

Beloit College

700 College Street; Beloit, WI 53511
(608) 363-2000; www.beloit.edu

Academics	B	Guys	C
Local Atmosphere	B	Girls	C-
Safety & Security	A-	Athletics	C
Computers	A-	Nightlife	D
Facilities	B-	Greek Life	B-
Campus Dining	B-	Drug Scene	B
Off-Campus Dining	C+	Campus Strictness	A+
Campus Housing	B+	Parking	B-
Off-Campus Housing	C+	Transportation	D
Diversity	D	Weather	C-

Students Speak Out
ON ACADEMICS

Q "**Most teachers are easily approachable** and willing to help or give extensions, even in situations when assignments weren't completed satisfactorily, solely due to an overabundance of work due in all courses at the same time."

Q "In my four years at Beloit College, **I never met a professor who was unwilling to help** his or her students or who flat-out refused to work with students when unusual circumstances arose."

Q "There has **only been one time that I was disappointed** and felt misled by a course description, and that sucked. Most profs at Beloit are pretty accessible and easy to get along with. You are bound to run into one or two that you hate with a passion, but one of your friends may love him."

Q "My teachers **purposely go out of their way** to give me opportunities that I don't even have to ask for. It's amazing the way that they watch out for you. I would consider many of them my friends. My classes are generally interesting, based completely on the professor."

STUDENT AUTHOR: One of Beloit's strongest points is the freedom it gives to its students to wander, experiment with, and mosey through different areas to find what they have a real passion for. And if the packaged deals aren't quite well-packaged enough, they have a "custom-made" option to please even the pickiest educational palate.

Students Speak Out
ON LOCAL ATMOSPHERE

Q "A serious drawback at the beginning of my college search—the lack of local activity—**meant very little once I visited the campus** and spoke with students and professors."

Q "The town seems to be a typical Wisconsin town: **fireworks, cheese, Wal-Mart trips, farms**, and bars. The problem is that there's a large portion of the community that is very poor, unfortunately, leading to high crime rates and unsafe parts of town."

Q "Fun stuff to do? Aside from Wal-Mart and Applebee's, there ain't a whole lot going on; at least, that's what you think until you discover **you can buy Blatz beer at seven dollars for a 24-case**, and that there's a restaurant called 'RESTAURANT' with concrete floors, and that the giant can of Hormel chili right off I-90 looks glorious in the moonlight."

Q "Generally, the people at student events plan so much for on-campus entertainment that is actually fun that **you wouldn't really need to leave**."

STUDENT AUTHOR: The thing you have to realize is that Beloit is boring, but Beloit College can always be entertaining if you're looking to be entertained. And if you're lucky, you might catch a flock of BSFFAs (Beloit Science-Fiction and Fantasy Assocation) in the middle of one of their midnight battles, or maybe you'll even be in one of their midnight battles, depending on your relationship with science fiction.

5 Best Things

1 Community
2 International programs
3 Flexibility in studies
4 Campus
5 Security reports

5 Worst Things

1 Isolation
2 Speed of gossip
3 Meal plan requirement
4 Power of BSFFA
5 Pretentious people

Students Speak Out
ON FACILITIES

Q "They range from fair to good—**not great, but good**. It depends on what year they were built. The workout room isn't so great; it doesn't have enough aerobics equipment and the weight machines are old. The Java Joint, which is kind of our student center is average. There aren't any facilities that wow me."

Q "Aside from a couple dormitories, the campus facilities are nice. The science center could use a makeover, but **the equipment and space is perfectly functional**."

Q "**The sports center roof leaks**, there aren't enough chairs in the art studio for all of the students, and most of the academic buildings don't have air conditioning. There are some very nice dorms (that even include sinks) along with some dorms that should be condemned."

Q "The school is **more than adequately equipped for student's computing needs** (though the classroom-used computer lab is entirely Apple)."

Q "There aren't enough computers on the residential side, but then again, **most students have laptops**. The athletic center is nice and the library is fantastic."

STUDENT AUTHOR: The campus is chock-full of computer labs, kitchens to cook in, and generally nice buildings. The library is pretty great, especially since half of its walls are windows, plus it has a good collection of books to mosey through. And there are some good movies down in AV that you can check out, too. For the most part, Beloit does a good job of providing students with what they need.

Famous People from Wisconsin

Willem DeFoe, Chris Farley, Harry Houdini, Liberace, Georgia O'Keefe, William H. Rehnquist, Spencer Tracy, Laura Ingalls Wilder, Frank Lloyd Wright

Students Speak Out
ON CAMPUS DINING

Q "Although there is a good-size population of vegans at Beloit, the menu does not cater to them very well, and I have been told by some that they live off of cereal, soy milk, and lettuce. I know one person who joined a fraternity **simply because it had a better meal plan**."

Q "Some students eat out; there is fast food close by, but that requires money. **There are also kitchens on campus**, and friends can get together and make dinner sometimes."

Q "The food in Commons is pretty good. **Some people like it, some don't**. There are always many options, though, so you will always find something that suits your fancy. If nothing looks good, you can always resort to the sandwich deli or to the cereal bar."

Q "DK's Deli and Grill is the alternative on campus which most people like. The Java Joint is the coffee shop, **which has good food**, drink, and a relaxed atmosphere."

Q "The cafeteria food is actually **not as bad as you'd expect**. We always have a huge selection of fresh salad stuff, and there is always a vegetarian and vegan dish offered."

STUDENT AUTHOR: Sometimes, the greatest part of the meal at Commons is the names they give their dishes. There's something they call "Enraged Pasta," and a couple times they made a cheese and hot dog soup that looked nauseating. The spaghetti is actually pretty impressive as far as mass production goes.

Student Body

African American:	3%	Male/Female:	39/61%
Asian American:	3%	Out-of-State:	80%
Hispanic:	2%	International:	5%
Native American:	1%	Unknown:	<1%
White:	86%		

Popular Faiths: There is a sizable Christian group, but the pagans are definitely a rival for them.

Gay Pride: Considering the liberalness of Beloit College, gay tolerance is pretty high.

Economic Status: The range starts at "scraping the bottom of the barrel" and climbs all the way to "I'm in the money."

Q "The dorms are nice, and many of the **rooms are big for dorm rooms**. Some of the nicest dorms are Aldrich, Maurer (all women), Chapin, and Brannon. None of the dorms are really too bad."

Q "There are dorms that are really nice, and there are some that are a little run down, but each has its benefits. In addition, **there are special-interest houses, Greek houses**, and townhouses to choose from for campus living."

Q "Turn in your housing application ASAP. If you can, get into Aldrich or Brannon (Brannon has sinks). Stay away from Peet **if you're not a drinker or a smoker**, and watch out for the dorms without AC."

STUDENT AUTHOR: **A person can get pretty spoiled living at Beloit. Campus housing is pretty comfortable—par for going to a private school. There aren't really any drawbacks to living on campus, unless you hate campus. Everybody's there, everything happens there, and you are right in the middle of it. A couple dorms need to be renovated, but for the most part, it's a giant lap of college-dorm luxury.**

Did You Know?
93% of undergrads live on campus.

Q "There really is every type of person at Beloit, so it's not hard to find a posse. We're very close and small so **hookups will not be kept secret** easily, but it's pretty much not an issue that causes people to get judged."

Q "Sorry, **no hot guys or girls** here."

Q "The **dating scene is twisted**, because after the first semester, any person you date has already dated a friend, teammate, roommate, or classmate of yours; it feels like incest. One should not come to Beloit to date."

Q "There are **lots of insecure people with major weight issues**. There are also lots of open gays, including faculty. It was hard as a straight guy with latent homophobia."

STUDENT AUTHOR: **The dating pool at Beloit is about the size of a very large puddle, and just about as dirty. Everybody who has dated someone at Beloit has, by association, dated a good portion of the campus. A good man is hard to find at Beloit, but certainly not impossible. People have made some catches in that dating puddle, and there are still catches swimming around.**

Traditions

Rocky Horror Picture Show
Every year around Halloween, a bunch of students get all Rocky Horrored up and go watch the movie at Wilson Theater.

Ultimate Frisbee Championship
A midnight rendezvous of the best Frisbee players we can find on campus.

Overall School Spirit
A lot of Beloit students have some fire in them, but that fire isn't necessarily burning for Beloit College.

Q "IM sports such as ultimate Frisbee seem to be more widely supported than any varsity sport. I was sad to find, upon going to my first soccer game, that the students have incredibly low school spirit. **The biggest game of the year is the ultimate Frisbee final game**, which is held at midnight under the football stadium lights—it's a lot of fun!"

Q "Varsity athletics are big on the Beloit campus in terms of percentage of the student body who participates; this is due to **the fact that there are not many students at Beloit**. IM sports are popular, too, in that some people get very serious and competitive about it."

Q "Varsity sports have a presence, but campus life certainly **does not revolve around them**."

Q "Both are pretty small, but **IM sports seem to be organized pretty well**. If you want to play, I can almost guarantee there will be a spot for you."

STUDENT AUTHOR: **I think students at Beloit would much rather wrestle with weird trivia than with their bodies. We're sort of a sit-down campus—watchers not doers.**

Students Speak Out
ON DRUG SCENE

Q "People do drugs here. It's a liberal arts school, and there are bound to be people here who do all kinds of drugs. **There's no pressure** to do it, and there's no one handing you a bong telling you to smoke up."

Q "Of those who do drugs, there are those who do any and every drug, and others who just stick to smoking marijuana. There are a lot of people who smoke marijuana, but overall, there **doesn't appear to be an out-of-control problem**."

Q "**Tobacco, alcohol, and marijuana** are probably the most used drugs on campus. A lot of people partake, a lot of people don't, and that seems to work out just fine for everybody."

STUDENT AUTHOR: Weed practically lives up to its nickname at Beloit, though. It sprouts up all over the place, and it is just about impossible to get rid of. But a simple "nah" will do to avoid the stuff entirely. Straight-edge people are a strong population at Beloit, and nobody gives them guff for it.

11:1	Student-to-Faculty Ratio
94%	Freshman Retention Rate
55%	Four-Year Graduation Rate
65%	Financial Aid Applicants Receiving Aid

Students Speak Out
SAFETY & SECURITY

Q "**I feel safe walking around campus** at night, but I wouldn't say the same about some nearby neighborhoods."

Q "Security is composed of probably around 10 officers (our school is only about 1,200 students) who patrol the campus at all times. **Most of them are 'pals' with certain students**, and we all have an understanding of what is acceptable and what isn't."

Q "**The campus itself is very safe**. The security officers (everybody loves them!) are always walking around campus. The areas around campus are not very safe, however, so don't walk around Beloit at night."

STUDENT AUTHOR: Students generally don't feel safe walking around the town at night. But the campus is pretty darn safe; the only real problems arise when people act stupidly or irresponsibly. There is definitely a good rapport between students and security officers.

Questions?

For more inside information and survival tips, pick up College Prowler's full-length book on this school, written by an actual student! Check it out at www.collegeprowler.com.

Students Speak Out
ON OVERALL EXPERIENCE

Q "**Sometimes, I wish I had gone to a bigger school** for a different social scene, but since I'm planning on going to grad school, I feel I'll get that large school experience at some point. But in terms of small, liberal arts colleges, I'm glad I chose Beloit. I do love it."

Q "Overall, I see Beloit as a place that offers a good education, but **little in regards to helping me grow socially as an adult**. If you know what you want to major in, and Beloit offers it, then you will get a great education. If you do not know what you want to major in, then Beloit is small enough that you can get into a variety of classes without a declared major, so you can explore."

Q "**I've had a lot of fun**, and every day is new and interesting. I have never had a night where there was nothing to do. I have never been buried under homework and not been able to keep up in my class."

Q "I just graduated. I'm glad I went to Beloit; it was a great experience. **Study abroad if you can**— it's worth it."

STUDENT AUTHOR: A four-year trudge through the thicket of Beloit education will put anyone in shape for a new challenge afterward. People either love Beloit, hate Beloit, or both, but it is pretty much guaranteed that whatever you feel for Beloit, it will be strong. Beloit can definitely provide students with an amazing experience if you use your resources right. Study abroad options are spectacular, and an overwhelming amount of students end up in a different country or a different part of the US at some point during their four years.

Bentley College

175 Forest Street; Waltham, MA 02452
(781) 891-2000; www.bentley.edu

THE BASICS:

Acceptance Rate: 38%   **SAT Range:** 1710–1960*
Setting: Suburban   **Control:** Private
F-T Undergrads: 4,016   **Tuition:** $33,030

Most Popular Majors: Business/Marketing, Computer
and Information Sciences

*of 2400

Academics	B	Guys	B+
Local Atmosphere	B+	Girls	A-
Safety & Security	A-	Athletics	B+
Computers	A-	Nightlife	B
Facilities	B+	Greek Life	C+
Campus Dining	C+	Drug Scene	A-
Off-Campus Dining	B+	Campus Strictness	B
Campus Housing	A-	Parking	B-
Off-Campus Housing	B	Transportation	A-
Diversity	C	Weather	C-

Students Speak Out
ON ACADEMICS

Q "Teachers are knowledgeable and always willing to help you whenever possible. Most classes are interesting and professors often **share their real-life experience**."

Q "The teachers are decent, but every teacher varies. I haven't had one that was terribly bad or extremely good. **My classes so far aren't really all that interesting**, but I think that's because I am a freshman and am taking filler courses instead of classes related to my major."

Q "All professors are more than willing to meet with you and **help you if you need it**. The classes are interesting. With tons of the elective choices, you can pick classes that are interesting to you."

Q "The core curriculum is great because it gives you some background in liberal arts and several aspects of business. Most of my teachers have been great and are very accessible, although, **I've had a couple of duds** that made me wonder why they were hired."

STUDENT AUTHOR: During your first two years, you will most likely be busy taking required classes and won't actually meet a professor in your major until junior year. However, this is not to be seen as a drawback because even professors outside your major are generally knowledgeable in their field and always available for consultation or extra help. One thing is certain; Bentley professors do not want to see anyone fail and are willing to go out of their way so that it doesn't happen.

Students Speak Out
ON LOCAL ATMOSPHERE

Q "Waltham is a pretty large city. It's close to Boston and has good amount of bars and nightlife during the week. **Brandeis is in Waltham too**, but we really do not interact too often. Boston's definitely a plus."

Q "There are a few other universities in the area. Many clubs and bars around tend to be 18 and over which is great. It makes it somewhat easy to switch it up on the weekends, so you aren't always on campus. **Waltham is an okay town**. However, having Cambridge and Boston only a few minutes away puts Bentley College at a great location."

Q "Waltham is a nice town. It is busy, but not too busy. For **those who crave craziness**, Boston is right next door, where the possibilities are endless. There are many other colleges and universities in the area, so if you need a change, just visit BC, Northeastern, or Harvard."

"Boston is great being that it is only a short **shuttle/car ride** away. There are so many young people in Boston!"

STUDENT AUTHOR: There is a strange, yet often unspoken love/hate relationship between Waltham and Bentley. Waltham loves to boost on its city Web sites how it has a rich academic tradition, yet does little to nothing to encourage college students to want to become part of their community. Unlike other colleges in suburban cities, local Waltham businesses do not offer a student discount on things like school supplies to Bentley students.

Students Speak Out
ON FACILITIES

Q "**Everything is nice**. The athletic center is older but they are keeping up with it, and rumor has it that there will be a new rec center in a few years with a new gym."

Q "Facilities here are really nice. The Student Center is **a new multi-million dollar building**. Computers are new and up-to-date. The gym has many prime machines to work out on, as well as a swimming pool that has open swim hours."

Q "**The Student Center is relatively new**. And all of the classrooms are run by computers, so with a touch, a computer screen turns the lights on or off and the window shades go down. The gym, swimming pool and playing fields are all top of the line."

Q "**Athletic facilities are nice**, but athletics overall are not really a main focus on the campus. Although very successful, the administration does not put a lot of emphasis on them. Computers are good and up to date. The Student Center is new and up-to-date."

Q "I think all of the buildings here are in good condition **compared to most schools**."

STUDENT AUTHOR: **The hub of student activity on campus can be found in the Student Center. Just over five years old, the Student Center quickly replaced the smaller, outdated former student center to become the mecca of anything related to student life. The administration has recognized how well the Student Center was received by students and the Charles A. Dana Center has been a success, as well—although many students complain about its inconvenient hours of operation.**

Famous Alumni

R. Marcelo Claure, Tim Harbert, Jay Leno, Robert F. Smith, Charles Taylor, Richard F. Zannino

Students Speak Out
ON CAMPUS DINING

Q "Seasons is the main dining hall on campus where an unlimited meal plan is offered. The food is good, but gets repetitive very quickly. **Lower Café is great** when you need a change."

Q "**Food on campus is nothing special**. It gets old very soon. Restaurants in the surrounding area, however, are worth a look at."

Q "The quality of the food in the cafeteria changes a lot. The pizza and grilled chicken are usually good, but there could be more options for vegetarians and a better salad bar. The Café, which is only open for lunch, has **good sushi and designer salads**."

Q "I don't mind the food on campus. All of the **fattening food is very good**, and some of the healthier stuff is good as well, and there's always a Panera down the street if you get sick of it."

Q "There is a lack of options; the only places you can go to eat are the main dining hall, which prepares **low-quality food** for the hefty price of the meal plan, and the Lower Café, which generally has the same offering as the main cafeteria (wraps, grill items, pizza)."

STUDENT AUTHOR: **For food on campus, the main option and place to go is Seasons dining room. Even though students love to complain about on-campus food, the truth is that the cafeteria is not really all that bad. Compared to other local college cuisine, Bentley has it pretty darn good. The company in charge of campus eateries is constantly changing meal plan options based on student feedback.**

Student Body

African American:	3%	Male/Female:	59/41%
Asian American:	8%	Out-of-State:	50%
Hispanic:	5%	International:	8%
Native American:	<1%	Unknown:	14%
White:	62%		

Popular Faiths: There are a variety of active Christian groups. A "Sacred Space" was created in the new student center for all religions to share.

Gay Pride: PRIDE, Bentley's gay, lesbian and transgendered club, is one of the best known, yet underappreciated, organizations on campus.

Economic Status: The majority of students here come from money. Designer clothes and the attitudes to go with it are far too common.

Students Speak Out
ON DORMS

Q "**Dorms here are good**. My friends who come to visit remark on how big my room is. Slade and Miller are the best freshmen dorms to get."

Q "**The dorms are good**; air-conditioning and heat that you control, clean carpets, and bathrooms are cleaned every day. No building is bad, some are louder then others, but you can pick where you want to be after your first year."

Q "The dorms here are pretty nice. They are all very well kept. Since they are building new ones all over the place things are looking better. Avoid any of the Trees. And try for Miller your freshman year. Other than that, **go for the new ones** such as Copley or Fenway, and then senior, go for the Falcone apartments."

STUDENT AUTHOR: **After the mandatory struggle of living in the freshman dorms, life will get much sweeter sophomore year as you make the choice between one of the three new suites on lower campus. Junior and senior year bring living to a new meaning as you begin your stay in an on-campus apartment. The major change happens after your tenure in the Trees, Miller, or Slade when you move into one of the Copleys or Fenway.**

> **Did You Know?**
> 82% of undergrads live on campus.

Students Speak Out
ON GUYS & GIRLS

Q "If you are a girl looking for a guy this is the perfect school for you. The ratio of girls to boys is **roughly 40:60**. And, yes, the guys are all really attractive."

Q "Bentley students tend to have a lot of money, nice cars, and nice clothing. I would say it's a good looking campus for guys and girls. If they aren't hot, **they have money** to do what it takes to be hot!"

Q "There are **a lot** of hot guys on campus."

Q "**The girls here are really pretty**, and most of them are close to perfect. The boys on the other hand, I know the good ones are around, I have yet to meet many of them."

STUDENT AUTHOR: **This is a campus filled with pretty people, and most of them know it, too. It's unfortunate, but the prettier girls do get stuck in the stereotype of being bitchy and high maintenance. The guys are generally laid-back in a social setting, but can also be ruthless in a business meeting. Some frat guys get a bad rap of being pigs and preying on freshman girls, and while those guys do exist, not all males give off the shady vibe.**

> **Traditions**
>
> **Black United Body Fashion Show**
> Each Spring, the BUB fashion show showcases the hottest styles from local stores. The music is kicking and the models are flawless at this unique event.
>
> **Breakfast by Moonlight**
> An event featuring faculty and administration serving students breakfast around midnight.
>
> **Overall School Spirit**
> Despite being home of the Division II National Field hockey Champions and having stars in the women's b-ball and football teams, Bentley students are not oozing blue and gold.

Students Speak Out
ON ATHLETICS

Q "**Varsity sports are big on campus**. Contests and prizes are offered to students who attended varsity games. Intramural sports seem to be big, but I don't really know much about them."

Q "There are some teams that stand out. There is a good crowd at most of the events. We have a super-fan program on campus that gets people to the events and gives out lots of free stuff. Intramurals are big, too. **Over 50 percent of the people here are involved**."

Q "The sports teams here are **all Division II** except hockey which is Division I. They are all really, really good especially the boy's football team and many of the women's teams."

STUDENT AUTHOR: **There is a harsh stereotype that exists at Bentley regarding student athletes: if a student is good in their sport it means they would have never gotten into Bentley for their grades. Varsity athletes are not exactly taken seriously by the rest of the population, but are given significant leeway. The football stadium isn't packed on the weekends with fans cheering wildly, but games are used as a way of "pre-gaming" for a party later on that night.**

Students Speak Out
ON DRUG SCENE

Q "**Some people smoke pot**, but I would say we are more an alcohol-drinking school rather then a drug-doing school."

Q "As far as I can see, there aren't too many drugs on campus. **People do them**, but they don't seem to be the biggest thing here. People would much rather drink at this school."

Q "There is an **abundance of marijuana** on campus, and you can pretty much call a number of individuals on any given night and pick up a nice bag. This is a big plus because there isn't usually much to do on week nights other than get high."

STUDENT AUTHOR: If the campus police log is any indication of which drug is the most prevalent, it would appear there are a lot of stupid pot smokers who don't put a towel beneath their doors. Alcohol use is widespread and not highly uncommon for students to start drinking Thursday night and go until Monday night. The peer pressure to indulge can be stronger in larger cliques such as sport teams and fraternities.

12:1	Student-to-Faculty Ratio
94%	Freshman Retention Rate
74%	Four-Year Graduation Rate
73%	Students Receiving Financial Aid

Students Speak Out
SAFETY & SECURITY

Q "Security seems **pretty tight** here on campus. I have never felt threatened or unsafe when walking on campus alone at night."

Q "I always feel very safe on campus because there is a **large campus police force**, and you always see them driving around. The campus police are also friendly."

Q "**This campus is very safe**, but it is not annoyingly strict by any means. The campus police let us have our fun with barely any problems, but they are right there in case of emergency and handle serious matters well."

Q "**Security is minimal**; anyone can come on campus, and there is no dorm check-in."

STUDENT AUTHOR: If there is one negative aspect about the security on campus, it is the fact that no matter where you are on campus, you can't avoid running into Campus Police (CP). Most students understand that the strong police presence isn't necessarily a bad thing and the joke is often, "Don't they have something better to do with their time?"

Questions?

For more inside information and survival tips, pick up College Prowler's full-length book on this school, written by an actual student! Check it out at *www.collegeprowler.com*.

Students Speak Out
ON OVERALL EXPERIENCE

Q "Bentley has a real good image. It is getting better and better. Socially, you meet a lot of great kids. **Nightlife tends to get repetitive**, but if you go into Boston and other school on occasions to switch it up its a good time. Overall, I like Bentley a lot."

Q "I think things need to be shaken up at Bentley. Overall, **the student body is pretty conformist** and conservative. There is strong Republican group. You won't find anyone with blue hair or a pierced chin at Bentley. There aren't many here with radical ideas, but you will find some promising entrepreneurs here and there."

Q "I love this school. It wasn't my first choice, but when I came here, I felt so comfortable and I loved the people. **I am very happy I came here** and wouldn't ever even think of transferring."

Q "**I am not particularly fond of Bentley College**. If you are looking for a large social scene with many diverse students don't come here. The student body consists of primarily middle-to-upper-class white kids, and there is very little to do in order to entertain yourself on campus."

STUDENT AUTHOR: The Bentley experience is hardly a normal college experience. From day one, you will be set off on a track to receive a unique business education. Hard work and effort are mandatory, but the rewards are endless. Students who are unhappy with their Bentley experience can actually attribute some of their issues to their own introverted-ness that keep them from exploring Waltham and Boston and the events, concerts, and meeting the school offers.

Binghamton University

West Drive; Binghamton, NY 13902
(607) 777-2000; www.binghamton.edu

THE BASICS:

Acceptance Rate: 39%
Setting: Small city
F-T Undergrads: 11,042

SAT Range: 1180–1340*
Control: Public
Tuition: $10,610

Most Popular Majors: Social Sciences, Business, Psychology, English, Biology, Health Professions

*of 1600

Academics	B-	Guys	B
Local Atmosphere	C+	Girls	B
Safety & Security	A-	Athletics	B-
Computers	B+	Nightlife	B-
Facilities	B+	Greek Life	C+
Campus Dining	B	Drug Scene	B
Off-Campus Dining	B-	Campus Strictness	B
Campus Housing	B	Parking	B-
Off-Campus Housing	A	Transportation	A-
Diversity	B	Weather	D

Students Speak Out
ON ACADEMICS

Q "**It's hit or miss**. We have some of the most qualified teachers in the world in their fields that teach really interesting, small, intensive classes. Then there are others who teach the same class every semester and throw darts at a board to figure out grades. It's the same with the departments, in general. Some are great and some are not."

Q "I had my share of good and bad teachers, but I must admit that **I always felt comfortable talking to them** when I had any questions."

Q "Professors are **just as jaded and dispirited as the students**. They seem to consider their teaching duties a distant second to their research. There are some good ones, don't get me wrong, but I have found that most of them don't respect the students."

Q "The professors have been very knowledgeable in their fields and willing to listen to student opinion. **They also have been really good about making time to meet with me** when I had questions about projects or classes or relating to my career. They really seem to care."

STUDENT AUTHOR: The prevalent student opinion on professors and academics seems to be that "it all depends." While some professors are knowledgeable and helpful, others would rather not be bothered with their teaching duties. Still, most agree that someone, be it a professor, graduate student, or teaching assistant, will be there should you seek their help. The key word here is "seek."

Students Speak Out
ON LOCAL ATMOSPHERE

Q "There is a lot of stuff to do, given you have a car, although I only started to realize it towards the end of my freshman year. **There are lots of natural attractions**, such as big waterfalls and the gorges in Ithaca. The only other universities are about 45 minutes away, such as Cornell, Ithaca, and Syracuse."

Q "There's always some kind of campus activity to get involved in, but town-wise, **most people can't find much to do** besides billiards, bars, clubs, movies, and bowling. There are community events, local points of interest, a playhouse, and the standard mall. But most people aren't interested in community-type events anyway."

Q "**Binghamton is kind of a hole, but the surrounding area can be pretty**. Don't go into certain parts of downtown by yourself, but you'll learn that soon enough. I haven't been to the zoo or carousels. They're supposed to be nice."

Q "The town of Vestal is very much a college town. **There is a mall, Wal-Mart, Wegmans, and little shopping centers**. There are a bunch of clubs and bars downtown, too."

STUDENT AUTHOR: If you are looking for a big city atmosphere, you are not going to find it at Binghamton. There is not much to say about a place when a trip to Wal-Mart can be considered a night on the town. People who enjoy outdoor activities will enjoy what Binghamton has to offer far more than those who need the bright lights and vibrant street life of a city.

5 Best Things	5 Worst Things
1 Price	1 Weather
2 Safety	2 Parking
3 Academics	3 Ugly campus
4 Off-campus housing	4 Campus dining
5 Nightlife	5 No football team

Students Speak Out
ON FACILITIES

Q "**They finished the Union** and are constantly constructing new facilities and improving the campus. It's really easy to get around 'the Brain,' as we call it, and you never have to walk more than 20 minutes to class, if that."

Q "The facilities are good; I can't complain about that. **The athletic and computer facilities are great if you use them**; they're super-convenient. The University Union is also improved since the mini mall is in there now. That is where we have all our publications and student organization offices. The newspapers, radio station, television station, post office, and bank are all there. There are also places to get munchies, play billiards, go bowling, and rent videos."

Q "There is a gym called Fitspace if you are into working out, but you have to pay something like $130 for the year to have access. The equipment is good, but it can get crowded during peak hours. **It's definitely not the ideal fitness center**. There are two main athletic facilities on campus—the West and East Gym—both have Olympic-sized pools and weight rooms."

STUDENT AUTHOR: Okay, so Binghamton is not going to win any campus beauty contests. The older buildings are unattractive red brick, the dorms were designed to look like prisons, the newer buildings are concrete and glass behemoths, construction blocks the scenery, and absolutely nothing matches. If you are majoring in 20th century ugly architecture, you should definitely come to Binghamton. Function over aesthetics—what do you expect from a school shaped like a brain?

Famous Alumni

Tony Kornheiser (Sportswriter, Talk Show Host), Paul Reiser (Actor, Comedian), William Baldwin (of the Baldwin Brothers)

Students Speak Out
ON CAMPUS DINING

Q "The food on campus is just that, campus food. **It's not horrible, but it's no five-star gourmet restaurant**. Some of the nice places to eat are Susquehanna and the Chenango Room—they are open to students, but these are where the teachers hang and eat their lunch."

Q "The food isn't home cooking, but it isn't awful, either. **I am still alive, so it can't be all that bad**. Don't get into the habit of munchies or the Nite Owl—they will all lead to the Freshman 15."

Q "The best dining hall so far is CIW, although the new Hinman Hall is pretty good, too. **Chenango Room is nice for a more expensive lunch**, and the Susquehanna Room is overrated. The Union is alright but really expensive."

Q "The food is disgusting and is rumored to contain laxatives to make sure we don't get food poisoning. **The only nice place is a hidden spot called the Chenango Room**, located in the Science I building, which few students know about."

Q "The food on campus is alright. **You can eat it and not pass away** (except for a few of the dishes, that is). It's really give and take."

STUDENT AUTHOR: Campus dining is not a major plus at Binghamton, but it is not a major minus, either. Dining hall food is just simply there. Most students prefer the convenience of Binghamton's á la carte system over a fixed number of meals per semester, especially since any money not used can carry over from semester to semester.

Student Body

African American:	5%	Male/Female:	55/45%
Asian American:	13%	Out-of-State:	7%
Hispanic:	7%	International:	8%
Native American:	<1%	Unknown:	23%
White:	44%		

Popular Faiths: Christian and Jewish groups are the largest.

Gay Pride: The gay community on campus is small and relatively quiet.

Economic Status: While there are plenty whose parents promised to buy them cars in exchange for the low tuition of a state school, there are just as many who are paying their own way through college.

Students Speak Out
ON DORMS

Q "Try to get into Mohawk. **It's the newest dorm, and it's actually rather nice**. If you want to live in a single room, I recommend Susquehanna over Hillside."

Q "**Each community has a personality**. Hinman is very scholastically oriented and can be cliquey, CIW is really friendly, but if you're not into drugs, it can be kind of a bad place for you, Dickinson people study a lot, and Newing is for the future frat boys and sorority girls of America."

Q "CIW and Newing are probably the best. CIW is very diverse and social. **Newing just does not care and lets you do your own thing**. Dickinson and Hinman are like two giant study lounges."

STUDENT AUTHOR: **The most important part of having a pleasant dorm experience at Binghamton is finding the community that best suits you. Student descriptions of the different communities may indeed be stereotypes, but they have been established for many years now and are probably the best guide for picking the community that matches your personality.**

> **Did You Know?**
> 56% of undergrads live on campus.

Students Speak Out
ON GUYS & GIRLS

Q "**I've found a lot of decent, nice guys**. It's hard to say who's hot and who's not because it depends on your taste, but let's just say there's something for everyone."

Q "No, seriously, Binghamton is **a good-looking campus that parties, but does its work**. We're the best of them all, man."

Q "**Some of the guys and girls can be jerks**, but the majority of the people on campus are friendly."

Q "People are very nice at Binghamton. At first I thought differently, but **through the years, my view has changed**. There are good-looking girls on campus so one doesn't have to worry."

STUDENT AUTHOR: **Students seem to agree that no matter what your scene, you should be able to find a fair share of attractive people. Binghamton students may lack supermodel-caliber looks, but they make up for it with personality, as many describe the people around campus as friendly. People at Binghamton are looking for everything, from long-term relationships to quick hookups, so no matter what you want, it can be found.**

Traditions

Purim Carnival
The annual Purim Carnival offers great games, rides, costume contests, and of course, delicious food.

Spring Fling
The annual celebration of the return of warm weather, even though it often continues to snow after the event has passed.

Overall School Spirit
There is more respect for the teams now that the school is Division I, but without a football team, the spirit will only grow so much.

Students Speak Out
ON ATHLETICS

Q "Even though we're up there in Division I now, unfortunately **not many non-athlete students show all that much support**. We have home games, but attendance is poor. You can get involved with intramurals and club sports no problem. They are just for fun, although some people tend to get a little competitive at times. The dance team, cheer team, and kick line are always looking for new people to try out."

Q "**Our basketball team is pretty good**, and there are games almost every week during the season. The baseball team is also very competitive, and attendance is rising with each passing year."

Q "Intramural sports are cool. **A lot of people play just for fun**. They are well organized, and there are multiple sports to partake in."

STUDENT AUTHOR: **As several teams have started finding success at the Division I level, the popularity of the programs have increased, while the new Events Center draws in even more fans. Furthermore, intramurals are very popular at Binghamton, and competitive and non-competitive leagues offer people of all skill levels the chance to participate.**

Students Speak Out
ON DRUG SCENE

Q "**It's there, but it isn't staring you in the face**. You may not know how to get drugs and your friend may not know how to get drugs, but you can rest assured that your friend's friend knows someone who can score some weed for your weekend enjoyment."

Q "**A lot of people smoke weed**; it's just the way it is. There is really no pressure to do it, but if you talk to people, you see just how prevalent it is."

Q "It is there, but it's not really a problem. **Weed is sort of popular, ecstasy is less popular**. I never knew anyone that did anything else, although I am sure it goes on somewhere."

STUDENT AUTHOR: **Students at Binghamton are not regularly exposed to any major drugs, and the most common ones are alcohol and marijuana. But no matter what drug you are into, you can probably find somebody to either buy from or sell to at Binghamton. As students say, it is not that drugs are a big deal on campus, but it is a big school, and there is a niche for just about any taste.**

20:1	Student-to-Faculty Ratio
90%	Freshman Retention Rate
70%	Four-Year Graduation Rate
69%	Financial Aid Applicants Receiving Aid

Students Speak Out
SAFETY & SECURITY

Q "**Security is great**. The University Police Department employs real police officers. We have a volunteer ambulance team called Harpur's Ferry, which is run by very qualified students that are certified by EMS."

Q ."I would have to say that **security and safety are very tight.** There are cops all over the place. I was toking in the woods like a mile away from any road, and I still got caught by the cops."

Q "The campus is relatively safe, and the University police are strict—they even carry guns. **They are fully-commissioned state police officers**, on par with the troopers who stop you on the highway. The thing is, though, that instead of focusing on real crime, they use their time giving kids criminal records for pot, booze, and fake IDs."

STUDENT AUTHOR: **With a closed campus, fully-trained police officers, on-site ambulance service, blue-light emergency phones, and Safe Ride vans making the rounds at night, most students would feel safe anywhere on campus, and at any time.**

> **Questions?**
> For more inside information and survival tips, pick up College Prowler's full-length book on this school, written by an actual student! Check it out at *www.collegeprowler.com*.

Students Speak Out
ON OVERALL EXPERIENCE

Q "Binghamton is a great school, but **honestly, the first two years are general education**, which means English, history, math, and science. If I had to do it all over again, I would just go to a community college for two years to save some money, and then transfer to a good school such as Binghamton."

Q "The friends I've made during the last few years have been amazing. There are truly a lot of good, hard-working people. Binghamton attracts a lot of students **who just can't pay for an Ivy League school**, but could probably attend one."

Q "I loved Binghamton, man. **They were the best years of my life**. It's a great school and you meet great, down-to-earth people. I highly recommend attending our University."

Q "I personally think Binghamton is a great school. **It is cheap and affordable, the neighborhood is safe, the people are extremely friendly**, the town is not totally dead, the students are motivated, and the professors are willing to teach. The education is a plus; at Binghamton, you will get more than what you paid for. There are many successful people who graduate from Binghamton, and of course, Binghamton is the number one SUNY."

STUDENT AUTHOR: **It is true that Binghamton is not a school for everyone. If you are looking for the atmosphere of a party school or the hands-on attention of a small private school, you will not find what you are looking for at Binghamton. However, if you are looking for a balanced experience that combines strong academic pursuits with a lively social atmosphere, Binghamton might be a great match for you.**

Birmingham-Southern College

900 Arkadelphia Road; Birmingham, AL 35254
(205) 226-4600; www.bsc.edu

THE BASICS:

Acceptance Rate: 66%
Setting: Urban
F-T Undergrads: 1,294

SAT Range: 1040–1290*
Control: Private
Tuition: $24,780

Most Popular Majors: Biology, Business, English, Psychology

*of 1600

Academics	B+	Guys	B+
Local Atmosphere	B-	Girls	A-
Safety & Security	B-	Athletics	B
Computers	B+	Nightlife	B+
Facilities	B+	Greek Life	A+
Campus Dining	C+	Drug Scene	B+
Off-Campus Dining	A-	Campus Strictness	B+
Campus Housing	C+	Parking	B+
Off-Campus Housing	C-	Transportation	C-
Diversity	D-	Weather	A-

Students Speak Out
ON ACADEMICS

Q "Some professors excel at discussion-based classes, some with lecture style, and some with collaborative learning. **You just have to figure out what kind of class you're signing up for**, and pick the professor accordingly. Once you learn who to avoid. it's smooth sailing."

Q "Most of my teachers are great, and I really enjoy the classes for my major and the faculty in the education department. **I've found that the entire faculty is very open to any questions** I might have, and they are always willing to lend any help they can give in any situation."

Q "The teachers are close to the students and they actually keep an eye on how you're doing. **Classes just depend on the teacher**, but usually, there's some unique trait that a teacher has that makes class fun."

Q "No matter where you go, you're going to find a class that you just don't like and a professor that isn't your favorite. But I've found that most of the teachers at Southern are **willing to listen to you**, help you when you're struggling, and even talk to you about other subjects."

STUDENT AUTHOR: **Southern specializes in small classes, and there is a pleasantly small ratio of temporary or adjunct teachers. Most classes are discussion-based and require a sizeable amount of group work. The academic standards tend to be fairly high, and while parties do happen, Southern isn't really what you would call a "party school."**

Students Speak Out
ON LOCAL ATMOSPHERE

Q "Birmingham is not the most exciting city in the world, and **there's not a lot to do if you're not into the bar scene**. Still, there are lots of great restaurants in town (Surin West and Dreamland BBQ, for example), and enough concerts to tide you over until you can move to a bigger place."

Q "Birmingham is an active Southern city. Read deeply into that Southern part. There are other schools in the city, the biggest, of course, being UAB. Don't walk around the campus after dark, because **the local neighborhood is a little frightening**. But in the other parts of the city there are great places like Five Points, Vulcan, and the Galleria."

Q "**There are several other schools in the area** like UAB and Samford. Birmingham is fairly large (at least, for Alabama), so there's plenty to do. I think Five Points in downtown is a fun place to visit, as long as you don't go alone. You can find good food, music, dancing, and other things like that. There's also Vulcan, the Birmingham Zoo, several parks, and malls like the Summit and the Galleria."

STUDENT AUTHOR: **Being in an enclosed campus makes it hard for students to interact directly with the local neighborhood. The malls are usually a good place to start, then the local restaurants, and finally the downtown clubs and bars. It's a comfort to be able to go out on the town and be able to return to a place that feels more like home than a big city. Southern has the best of both worlds.**

Students Speak Out
ON CAMPUS DINING

Q "The food is a very controversial subject at BSC. **You either love it or hate it**. I love it. They serve made-to-order breakfast from 10 p.m. to 12 a.m., which is a big hit. The omelets should be their own food group."

Q "**Breakfast is probably the best meal they serve**, which is probably why so many people go back late at night to get breakfast again. On pretty days, people like to take their food outside and eat at the tables around the fountain."

Q "The food on campus is paid for with our meal cards, which we are required to buy. **The food isn't all bad**, but we don't have a lot of options."

Q "The campus café is **not bad at all**, but the selection is such that you start desiring different types of food after the second month or so."

Q "The cafeteria isn't bad, although **there isn't a whole lot of selection**, and it gets boring pretty quickly. If you live on campus, you're forced to buy a meal plan, which is the biggest complaint for most people. The cafeteria and the Cellar are the only places to eat on campus."

STUDENT AUTHOR: The meal plan situation is simple at Southern: You have to buy one if you live on campus, and there are only two places to use it. Probably the biggest problem with this simplicity is that there is very little variety when it comes to food choices. The staff in the cafeteria is what makes all the blasé food bearable, however, with friendly, familiar faces and great service.

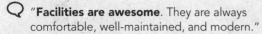

Students Speak Out
ON FACILITIES

Q "**Facilities are awesome**. They are always comfortable, well-maintained, and modern."

Q "I think the facilities on campus are very nice. **I use the gym almost every day**, and they have everything I need for my workouts. The student center has a theater and lounge with a big-screen TV; I think they have everything we need."

Q "Though the school has recently celebrated its 150th anniversary, **the facilities are still in top condition**. We recently finished building a brand new science building and renovating many of the other buildings on campus. Renovations are ongoing to continue to keep campus in top-notch shape."

Q "Everything is crazy new. That's one of the immediate things that struck me about the school. **All the facilities look new, save for the library**. My favorite building is Striplin. Even though I'm really not athletic or anything, I always feel at home in there."

Q "The exercise center is great, and all the computers are relatively new. **For a small school, it really has a lot to offer**."

STUDENT AUTHOR: Nearly all the facilities at Birmingham-Southern are new or newly renovated. Furthermore, the staff at BSC is very good about maintaining all of the facilities. There are always people outside working on the grounds, as well as a friendly maintenance crew that is quick to take care of problems. There is always something that is being improved so that students can have access to the best facilities possible.

Famous Alumni

Elton B. Stephens, Howell T. Heflin, Sena Jeter Naslund, Howell Raines, Richard Kirkland, Rebecca Gilman

Student Body

African American:	8%	Male/Female:	49/51%
Asian American:	3%	Out-of-State:	31%
Hispanic:	1%	International:	<1%
Native American:	<1%	Unknown:	4%
White:	85%		

Popular Faiths: Most religious activity on campus is from Christian denominations.

Gay Pride: The gay community is so small or so quiet that it seems to slip under the radar.

Economic Status: Given that BSC is one of the more pricey schools in the state, the majority of students come from middle- to upper-class families, and there are few from lower-class backgrounds.

Students Speak Out
ON DORMS

Q "The dorms aren't too bad. Upperclassmen get first pick of the dorms, so they tend to be arranged by year. **It also helps to have a good GPA** because they rank you based on that, too."

Q "**I think the freshman dorm experience is fundamental**, and sophomore year living with a suite of close friends is one of the best chances to build deeper relationships. Dorms may not always be the nicest housing options, but they are the most convenient, and it's college life, so get used to roughing it a little."

Q "**The dorms are nice enough**, in my opinion. Lots of people think they are too small or outdated, but I don't mind them."

STUDENT AUTHOR: **All students at Birmingham-Southern are required to live on campus until they are 21 or are of junior status, unless they are local and can live with family. This means that you end up getting to know the people that you go to school with very well. Some people like living in suites with their friends, while others prefer only one roommate or a single. Either way, there are different options for everyone to try.**

Did You Know?
76% of undergrads live on campus.

Students Speak Out
ON GUYS & GIRLS

Q "**The freshman girls seem to all have boyfriends back home**, and they often don't leave their dorm rooms until their sophomore year. It's like anywhere, I guess."

Q "The guys tend to have high opinions of themselves, and the girls tend to be nice once you get to know them. **We do have a lot of attractive people at BSC**."

Q "**Every person at BSC is ridiculously good-looking**. There are no exceptions."

Q "The girls are extremely attractive and tend to be pretty open to new friendships. **The small-college atmosphere tends to help** with meeting people."

STUDENT AUTHOR: At first glance, some people may be intimidated by the number of attractive people on campus. But don't let this facade fool you; not everyone is as perfect as they seem. Most students on campus are open to new relationships and are surprisingly non-stereotypical. Since there are more girls than guys, it seems that guys have a pretty good chance of getting to know at least one special person before they graduate.

Traditions

E-Fest
A miniature version of SoCo; it's a free concert and a great way to relax during the fall.

SoCo
SoCo is BSC's two-night concert series that is a spring celebration of youth and entertainment.

Overall School Spirit
It's not very common to see anyone walking around with a BSC tattoo, but the students at Southern are at least enthusiastic when the time calls for it.

Students Speak Out
ON ATHLETICS

Q "**Sports are pretty big here**. We're Division I, so we get to play all these real big schools in sports. The best part is that we actually beat them. It's amazing. We're like the little engine that could. Our men's basketball and baseball teams are both among the top teams in the Big South Conference."

Q "Basketball is fairly big. **I think sports aren't as big of a deal for us** as for most other schools, since we don't have a football team."

Q "**Men's basketball is by far our biggest sport**. People come from all over to watch basketball and baseball. IM sports are mostly played by Greek organizations; however, you can find some independent teams."

STUDENT AUTHOR: **While sports are not the most prominent thing on campus, there are a few die-hard groupies that you will see at almost every game. At basketball games, guys with their shirts off gather in the "Panther Pit" to hassle the other teams during free throws. And intramural sports are almost as big as varsity sports. BSC students tend to be active, whether or not it is on the varsity level.**

Students Speak Out
ON DRUG SCENE

Q "There are a decent amount of smokers, but the drug scene is **fairly low-key and centered on a few loners**. There isn't any pressure to try them because there aren't any addicts trying to push stuff on you."

Q "I personally don't know much about the drug scene on campus, except that it is there. Whether or not you're big into drugs, you need to be aware that **they will be present in almost every campus in the world**."

Q "**I don't really know much about the drug scene** because you never hear about it. I know that there are drugs on campus, but it's kept very quiet."

STUDENT AUTHOR: It would be dishonest to say that drug use doesn't happen on campus, but you almost never hear about it. Most students tend to stick to alcohol if they are looking for a perception-altering experience. Because of the low profile of drugs, there is little to no pressure to use drugs, so non-users don't have to feel intimidated.

12:1	Student-to-Faculty Ratio
85%	Freshman Retention Rate
60%	Four-Year Graduation Rate
83%	Financial Aid Applicants Receiving Aid

Students Speak Out
SAFETY & SECURITY

Q "**Campus Police are, by and large, excellent**. They wave you through the gate, patrol the grounds, and are quick to help if you need them. There are a couple of jerks, but the rest of the guys are as nice as can be."

Q "The campus is safer than anywhere else. **I feel comfortable going for a run at midnight**, or calling one of the security guards to unlock my room when I've lost my key."

Q "**The school itself is in a rough neighborhood**, but the campus is well lit, there's a gate, and security usually does a good job of monitoring who comes through it. I've always felt comfortable walking alone."

STUDENT AUTHOR: From the time you enter the gates until the time you leave, you can feel the presence of security on campus. With 18 full-time officers, security seems to be a high priority on campus, and most students feel safe in the somewhat questionable neighborhood.

> **Questions?**
> For more inside information and survival tips, pick up College Prowler's full-length book on this school, written by an actual student! Check it out at *www.collegeprowler.com*.

Students Speak Out
ON OVERALL EXPERIENCE

Q "I have loved being at Birmingham-Southern, and **I wouldn't trade my experiences with anyone at any other school**. Sometimes the classes are difficult, but the teachers will help if you ask. The people are extremely friendly, and everyone always has a smile on their faces."

Q "**My first year on campus was greater than I could have ever imagined**. I formed lifetime friendships, which made me happy, and I excelled in my academics, which really made my parents happy, so BSC has been a wonderful experience for my whole family."

Q "I've really enjoyed my experience at BSC so far. **It is definitely a challenging school, but I've enjoyed my experiences** both in and out of the classroom. I'd definitely recommend it to anyone who is looking for a small school where they can get a good education."

Q "I love Birmingham-Southern. I have had a great time here and have made so many new friends. **The school is such a warm and welcoming place** with so many opportunities for you to get involved on and off campus. It is a good place to make new contacts, also."

STUDENT AUTHOR: The whole school feels like one big family. While there are struggles, it seems as though everyone at BSC is looking to improve upon their mistakes and make it a place that everyone can enjoy. The administration is always changing curriculum to fit the needs of the students, and the students are always challenging the faculty in order to improve upon the status quo. Academics are a high priority at Southern, but it's still possible to have a life while you're here, as well.

Boston College

140 Commonwealth Avenue; Chesnut Hill, MA 02467
(617) 552-8000; www.bc.edu

THE BASICS:

Acceptance Rate: 27%
Setting: Suburban
F-T Undergrads: 9,080

SAT Range: 1250–1420
Control: Private
Tuition: $35,150

Most Popular Majors: Finance, Communications, English, Political Science, Economics, Biology

*of 1600

Academics	B+	Guys	B+
Local Atmosphere	A	Girls	A
Safety & Security	A+	Athletics	A
Computers	B+	Nightlife	A
Facilities	B+	Greek Life	N/A
Campus Dining	A	Drug Scene	B-
Off-Campus Dining	A	Campus Strictness	B-
Campus Housing	B	Parking	D-
Off-Campus Housing	B+	Transportation	B+
Diversity	C-	Weather	C-

Students Speak Out
ON ACADEMICS

Q "The **teachers are very knowledgeable** and most are very willing to give you any extra help you may need in their classes."

Q "The professors here are absolutely wonderful! Most of mine have reached out and really tried to **get to know me as a person**. Sometimes it is a good idea to attend their mandatory office hours so that they get to know you one-on-one, especially near grading time!"

Q "After finishing the core requirements, I was able to pursue my greater interests. Accordingly, I **found myself enjoying classes** more in the latter part of my college education."

Q "The teachers, for the most part, were fairly willing to accommodate students' needs. Most teachers take their jobs very seriously, and they're **dedicated to challenging the students** in their classes."

STUDENT AUTHOR: Most of the professors at BC are passionate and extremely intelligent individuals who inspire their students to follow the BC motto, "Ever to excel." Of course, there are a few bad apples that just can't seem to relate to their students, typically because of an age gap that can span decades. Luckily, misdirected professors are in the minority. To increase your chances of finding a good professor or interesting class, check out the professor evaluations where students have chimed in regarding the teacher's aptitude.

Students Speak Out
ON LOCAL ATMOSPHERE

Q "Boston is a college town, and anywhere you go you will see people your age. There are literally some **50 colleges within a 15-mile radius**. Though we are technically in Chestnut Hill, we are only a half-hour train ride from Boston."

Q "I think BC is ideal because it's not exactly in the heart of the city. This way you get the real **college campus experience**, since campus isn't in the middle of a busy city, but you're close enough to the city that you don't feel like you're in the middle of nowhere."

Q "We're close to BU, Northeastern, Harvard, Babson, Bentley and a bunch of other smaller schools. There are **plenty of attractions**, namely the Museum of Fine Arts, the aquarium, the Charles River, the Fleet Center, and Fenway."

Q "Not only is Boston **an incredible city** with plenty of fun things to do, but it's also the biggest college town in America."

STUDENT AUTHOR: Boston is a wonderful city with loads of American history. The area definitely has that youthful, alive feel that a lot of places do not. Boston College is located right on the outskirts of the Boston metropolis, which gives students a mix of low-key suburbia and thrilling city living. One of the worst mistakes you can make is to stay on Chestnut Hill and put off exploring the awesome city that surrounds you. Harvard, Northeastern, and Tufts are all fairly close to BC.

5 Best Things	5 Worst Things
1 Athletics	1 Diversity
2 Professors	2 Weather
3 Atmosphere	3 BCPD
4 Tradition	4 Administration
5 Senior Week	5 Moving days

Students Speak Out
ON FACILITIES

Q "Many of the dorms have secret little work-out rooms in the basements. **All have weight rooms** that never get crowded."

Q "The gym is a little lame, which is surprising for a Division I school, but it gets the job done. It has a nice **track and tennis courts** and lots of cardio equipment."

Q "Many of the dorms are updated and connected, which adds to a sense of community for the freshmen. These new conglomerations of buildings have really **nice study rooms** with vending machines, and some have laundry rooms in the basement."

Q "Some **facilities are state-of-the-art**, while others need some work. The computer center is nice, and fairly efficient. We have the worst student center I have seen."

Q "Hillside is the **fantastic new dining hall** in the base of the building. This building also has tons of teacher offices, a smaller bookstore, and the BCPD office."

STUDENT AUTHOR: **Throughout the last few years, the school has undergone a complete campus beautification program, and the results are awesome. The athletic center for the athletes is excellent, but only a small portion of campus is allowed to use it. McElroy, which currently acts as a student union, should never be called a student union. It has two chairs, a couch, and a few vending machines. This may change, as a new building is being planned.**

Famous Alumni

Doug Flutie, Matt Hasselbeck, Jack Kerouac, John Kerry, Leonard Nimoy, Chris O'Donnel

Students Speak Out
ON CAMPUS DINING

Q "The **food is actually really good**, although any campus food gets a little monotonous. Go visit your friends at other schools and you will appreciate BC food so much more."

Q "The **exorbitant price** aside, the food has never posed a problem for me. I really enjoyed the posh and cozy Hillside Café, complete with made-to-order sandwiches and Starbucks."

Q "There are basically **three major dining halls** and three smaller ones. McElroy is where freshmen primarily eat, or at Stuart on Newton Campus, and Lower is where upperclassmen eat, both of which have just about everything."

Q "The **meal card is such a huge convenience** at BC, because you never realize how expensive some of the food is that you're eating because it just gets deducted from your meal points."

Q "There is the Eagle's Nest, which serves wraps and salads but **can get insanely crowded**. The Rat is located in the Quad and is like McDonald's—serving fast and fried food."

STUDENT AUTHOR: **The food at Boston College is excellent, but it can feel monotonous after a while. Dietary concerns are very important to BC, and the school does its best to provide a variety of foods for students with special dietary needs. BC allows students to use their pre-paid meal cards at off-campus locations like Pizzeria Uno and Flatbreads. This is one of the greatest ideas the administration has conjured up for students.**

Student Body

African American:	6%	Male/Female:	49/51%
Asian American:	10%	Out-of-State:	72%
Hispanic:	8%	International:	2%
Native American:	<1%	Unknown:	0%
White:	73%		

Politcal Activity: Students are politically active on both the Republican and Democratic side.

Gay Pride: There are a couple organizations on campus, but only one, Allies of Boston College, is recognized by the school. its constitution states that it is there to provide support, but not advocacy.

Economic Status: Most students are middle- to upper-class.

Students Speak Out
ON DORMS

Q "You **don't get much of a choice as a freshman**, and you are basically put where you're put. There are two main areas where freshmen live: Upper campus and Newton campus."

Q "Newton just becomes its **own little community** and everyone knows everyone else. At least it feels like they do. From what I can tell, the Upper campus kids aren't as close or friendly, though they all think they're a lot cooler than we are."

Q "**Dorms are decent** at Boston College, and they are getting better. All dorms are coed, by floor freshman year and by room every year after that. Upperclassmen live in suite-style housing, some with kitchens."

STUDENT AUTHOR: **The living arrangements at Boston College are very comfortable, mostly modern, and very well kept. The main downside to BC's housing is the fact that the freshman dorms have communal bathrooms. If you're one of those people who absolutely cannot shower with others while wearing flip-flops, then you might want to pick another school with newer dorms that offer private bathrooms.**

> **Did You Know?**
> 82% of undergrads live on campus.

Students Speak Out
ON GUYS & GIRLS

Q "Students are **mostly preppy**, like at any private college. There aren't many alternative-looking people and everyone basically blends in. If you are looking for a lot of diversity, don't go to BC."

Q "We have a beautiful campus, and I'm not talking about the Gothicic buildings. BC **isn't really a dating school**, though."

Q "There are a lot of **beautiful, rich people**, but everyone is very nice."

Q "**Everyone looks the same** for the most part. Girls are very fit and are usually perfectionists. Guys are usually of average height and have little fashion sense."

STUDENT AUTHOR: **Overall, Boston College is a remarkably attractive campus, although very homogenous. Most students place a lot of emphasis on appearance. This is not the kind of place where you walk around in ripped jeans and flip-flops or come to class still in your pajamas. The overall image for both sexes is a fairly preppy. Most people on campus fit that description. There are people with other styles on campus, but they are few and far between.**

Traditions
Most traditions at Boston College center around sporting events. Students at BC go to games to cheer for their team. They tailgate before and party after. They also know every word of the fight song.

Overall School Spirit
Students at Boston College have a lot of pride and spirit in their school. Come to a football game, and you'll see what it means to have school spirit.

Students Speak Out
ON ATHLETICS

Q "Varsity **sports are a huge part of BC life** because we are a Division I school. Football games are a big deal, with tailgating all across campus. Hockey is also huge, as we have graced the Frozen Four with our presence often."

Q "If you get the chance, definitely **buy season tickets** to at least hockey and football games. You won't regret it!"

Q "Club sports and intramural sports have a pretty good following. It was **one of the most fun things I did** at BC."

Q "The sports at BC are enormous. The BC sports scene **could rival any other school**."

STUDENT AUTHOR: **Sports are huge at BC! If you're not into sports, BC might not be a great place for you. You certainly don't have to get into sports, but you might feel a little left out as everyone revs up for game day and you don't really care. There's always the other option of going to the games just to hang out with people, which can be fun and doesn't require actually knowing the rules or caring about sports.**

Students Speak Out
ON DRUG SCENE

Q "You can't miss pot, and I've seen coke a few times. You can probably **find most drugs if you look hard enough**."

Q "The **hardest thing I've seen on campus is weed**, though I'm sure that there are people doing harder things."

Q "Police are **overly strict concerning alcohol**. They treat it like manslaughter, but they brush all drug violations under the rug, which is mighty convenient for the growing number of coke-heads on campus."

STUDENT AUTHOR: Alcohol is where it's at for BC. Whether it's house parties, the bar or football games, people on campus love to drink. It can be difficult when you're under 21, because it seems like everyone is drinking but you. The BCPD is very strict about underage drinking. The illicit drug scene is not at all out in the open. It fluctuates in its popularity, but is usually very quiet and not center-stage. You can certainly avoid it if you're not interested.

13:1	Student-to-Faculty Ratio
96%	Freshman Retention Rate
88%	Four-Year Graduation Rate
87%	Financial Aid Applicants Receiving Aid

Students Speak Out
SAFETY & SECURITY

Q "I have **never felt unsafe** around Boston College. You just have to be smart and use common sense whenever you leave campus."

Q "Our campus is extremely safe. It is located in one of the wealthiest suburban areas around, and we're not directly in the city. We have our own **police force and escorts** who will travel with you if you ever think you might need them. I have never felt scared walking alone at night since there are always people around."

Q "It's all very well lit and there are **emergency lights with phones** that connect directly to the BCPD everywhere."

STUDENT AUTHOR: All in all, Boston College is a safe place for students to go to school and hang out. Incoming students are made aware of the potential dangers around them and are told about the best ways to avoid being victimized in any way. Also, police officers are always extremely friendly and helpful.

Questions?

For more inside information and survival tips, pick up College Prowler's full-length book on this school, written by an actual student! Check it out at *www.collegeprowler.com*.

Students Speak Out
ON OVERALL EXPERIENCE

Q "There are times when I wish I went somewhere more diverse, or to a smaller liberal arts school, but for the most part I've had a really great time and I've **met some wonderful people**."

Q "I had an incredible four years. I took some **wonderful classes**, made several amazing friends, worked hard, and had plenty of fun."

Q "As a recent BC grad, the only place that I wish I were now is back there. The **connections and relationships that you form** while at a school like BC define the greatness that the University embodies. It follows you in everything you do and in every town or city you find yourself in. There will always be a BC grad looking to help you out. It's a sensation that is unparalleled."

Q "I absolutely love it here. The teachers are great and the **classes are very interesting**. The city has offered so many opportunities. I'm glad I'm here and I don't want to be anywhere else."

STUDENT AUTHOR: Boston College is a wonderful institution with dynamic people that will challenge you. However, the first few years can be tough, as you may not be prepared for the enormity of the college experience. While parties and tailgates are enjoyable, they are not the only things college life is about. Yes, you want to have fun, but there are other reasons to came here. Remember that you are here to receive an exceptional college education, and Boston College will certainly deliver that. If you give the school a little time to grow on you, it certainly will and you'll be really glad you gave it a chance.

Boston University

1 Sherborn Street.; Boston, MA 02215
(617) 353-2000; www.bu.edu

THE BASICS:

Acceptance Rate: 59%
Setting: Urban
F-T Undergrads: 17,206

SAT Range: 1330–1530*
Control: Private
Tuition: $34,930

Most Popular Majors: Business, Communication, Psychology, Engineering, Health Professions

*of 1600

Academics	B+	Guys	C+
Local Atmosphere	A+	Girls	B+
Safety & Security	B+	Athletics	B-
Computers	B+	Nightlife	A-
Facilities	B+	Greek Life	C
Campus Dining	A+	Drug Scene	C+
Off-Campus Dining	A	Campus Strictness	B-
Campus Housing	D+	Parking	D-
Off-Campus Housing	B+	Transportation	B+
Diversity	B-	Weather	C-

Students Speak Out
ON ACADEMICS

Q "Freshman year, you'll have at least one class that is small—a writing class with 15–25 people in it. Other than that, most of the 100-level classes are large. The TFs (teaching fellows) are always glad to help out, but they don't teach the class, and **sometimes they don't speak English** very well."

Q "As a freshman, you will have **huge lectures**, and depending on your major, that might not change too much. The teachers are brilliant, but you might get lost in the crowd."

Q "The teachers are there if you need them. It's what you make of it. If you go to them for help **they are usually happy to talk to you**. If you don't make a point of going to their office hours and allowing them the opportunity to learn your name, they might know you only as a number."

Q "A lot of classes are lectures, so you don't have any one-on-one time with your professors. But if you **go to their office hours**, they usually love to meet with students and will help you out. Some professors aren't so much interested in teaching as in hearing themselves talk."

STUDENT AUTHOR: Everyone seems to agree that the best way to choose a class is by first learning about the professor's teaching style from other students. Don't get frustrated with your 100-level introductory classes; they are universally described as "a waste of time," "boring," and "impersonal." Get through your requirements, but keep in mind that the best classes are the upper-levels.

Students Speak Out
ON LOCAL ATMOSPHERE

Q "Boston is a college town. There are **a million schools and a million students**, making Boston a very young city. Stay away from overpopulated cliché traps like Landsdowne Street. Instead, explore the city and find places like Central Square, Jamaica Plain, and the South End."

Q "Boston is the place to be if you're a college student. There are so many things you can do and visit. There are shopping malls, nice restaurants, clubs, 'Broadway' shows, sporting events, museums . . . Plus, **the city is so rich with history**."

Q "There are so many other colleges around, and it makes for some crazy times and lots of opportunities to meet people. Boston is **definitely a college town**. There are so many things to see when you're there. The historic aspect of Boston is fascinating, and it is beautiful all year round."

Q "The vibe in Boston is chill if you are in the right area; otherwise, you may find that the people are **a bit on the conservative end**, which is restricting at times."

STUDENT AUTHOR: Recently, the administration has put a lot of money and effort into improving student facilities on campus. Depending on the particular colleges—which tend to receive different amounts of funding—some buildings are in better condition than others. Unfortunately, all of these changes also imply that a lot of construction is constantly taking place on campus.

5 Best Things	5 Worst Things
1 Selection of courses	**1** Conservative school
2 The professors	**2** Large size
3 Convenience Points	**3** Bureaucracy
4 Boston	**4** Grumpy security workers
5 Research opportunities	**5** Student apathy

Students Speak Out
ON FACILITIES

Q "Some buildings are **old and crappy**, but others are new and state-of-the-art."

Q "The **facilities are well kept**. The student union is mostly commercial, as exemplified by the food and the expensive booths selling gifts, jewelry, clothes, CDs, movies, and video games that litter the lobby; but then again, activities and organizations are not really BU's forte."

Q "For the most part, all the facilities at BU are **definitely high-quality**. They have just about everything. The computer center's all right, except that there are not enough computers down there. Anyway, the student union is pretty phat. There is some good food and a lot of seating. Some people spend their entire year doing work there, but it's still not the best student union."

Q "Everything on BU's campus is very nice. It's either new, or it's **old but architecturally beautiful** . . . [I]t is a city campus, so it's very concrete-looking; no big fields of green grass like other places."

Q "The **gym is decent** . . . There is a lot of fast food that you can burn off at the decent gym."

STUDENT AUTHOR: Recently, the administration has put a lot of money and effort into improving student facilities on campus. Depending on the particular colleges—which tend to receive different amounts of funding—some buildings are in better condition than others. Unfortunately, all of these changes also imply that a lot of construction is constantly taking place on campus.

Famous Alumni

Martin Luther King, Jr. is certainly the most-celebrated alum from BU. Noted celebrities Howard Stern, Jason Alexander, and Bill O'Reilly have also studied at BU.

Students Speak Out
ON CAMPUS DINING

Q "The food, for the most part, is pretty good. There are **a lot of dining halls** around campus, and each one is slightly different, which is good."

Q "West Campus renovated their dining hall; it has a restaurant atmosphere, and the food is awesome. Food at **Warren Towers is okay**, and the dining hall is very convenient since it's in the middle of the campus."

Q "On-campus food is actually pretty good. When they have **annual lobster nights**, the line is out the door."

Q "I'm sorry, but BU food is **stupendous** compared to some of the crap I've eaten at other universities. Almost every dorm has a dining hall, so it's pretty convenient."

Q "If you're a picky eater, there's always pasta, sandwiches or salad to eat. At the student union, they also have a food court where you can use your **dining points** . . . The food does get repetitive, but the good thing about being in Boston is that there are tons of places to eat."

STUDENT AUTHOR: While it is not uncommon to hear complaints about the food, all students will agree that BU is pretty hooked-up in that department. There is a huge variety and tons of places to use your meal plan around campus. The big suggestions for getting your money's worth are to check out the specialty nights and the smaller eateries on campus. Remember, the meals are not refundable . . . If you do the math, each meal costs about nine dollars, so eat up.

Student Body

African American:	3%	Male/Female:	41/59%
Asian American:	12%	Out-of-State:	77%
Hispanic:	6%	International:	9%
Native American:	<1%	Unknown:	19%
White:	52%		

Popular Faiths: Catholic, Protestant, Jewish, and students who claim no affiliation.

Gay Pride: BU has been in the spotlight for the surprisingly conservative views of the administration. However, there sometimes seems to be more gay men on campus than straight ones. The lesbian scene is slightly more concealed, but definitely prevalent.

Economic Status: BU students span a wide range, however, the majority is middle- to upper-class.

Students Speak Out
ON DORMS

Q "All the nice dormitories are located in West Campus, but you'd be pretty far from your school, **at least a 15-minute walk** . . . The Towers are not coed within floors. All of the girls on one floor, and all guys on another floor."

Q "It is impersonal, overcrowded, severely regulated, small, and **the communal spaces get trashed daily by the inhabitants**. Try to go for smaller buildings like the Towers, South Campus, and Bay State Road."

Q "Definitely avoid Warren Towers. It's where most freshmen get put, and **it's a hellhole**. But it is the best . . . because it's small, and you get to know everyone on your floor really well."

STUDENT AUTHOR: **Whatever you do, stay away from Warren Towers. It is the largest non-military dorm in the United States, and it is a freshman machine. It even resembles a factory in appearance . . . Other, smaller dorms are usually a safe bet, but they tend to be more secluded from campus life. If you can get a hold of a brownstone, don't give it up. They are by far the nicest living on and (in many cases) off campus.**

 Did You Know?
65% of undergrads live on campus.

Students Speak Out
ON GUYS & GIRLS

Q "There are lots of **hot guys and girlies**, but there are lots of snobs, too. Expect to get looked down upon if you're on financial aid, or if you're not a trust-fund baby."

Q "BU is approximately 60 percent girls and 40 percent guys, so it's kind of rough meeting a cute, heterosexual guy . . . There are so many other schools around, too, so **inter-school dating** is fairly common."

Q "**I am asexual**. I believe that sex is overrated."

Q "In general, the guys are more of the "pretty boy" variety . . . The ladies are very good looking, but also not much for intelligence or personality. There are some very good-looking people here, but **looks can be deceiving**."

STUDENT AUTHOR: **If you are a guy . . . you are way ahead. There are girls to go around, and around again. The student body is notoriously described by those both on and off campus as shallow and materialistic. This is obviously not universally accurate, but BU certainly serves up its fair share of these sorts of individuals. Just remember that finding people at such a huge university is easy; finding your niche, however, takes some time.**

Traditions

The Beanpot Hockey Event
It occurs in the fall between Boston University and Boston College each year, and it's always a party. Attended by the city at large.

Midnight Madness
This occurs in the hockey rink to celebrate the beginning of the season.

Overall School Spirit
Conservative BU truly lacks a strong base of students who care about University life. It is really hard to get a good turnout at both on- and off-campus events.

Students Speak Out
ON ATHLETICS

Q "All varsity sports are Division I, but hockey gets the largest turnout in terms of fans who actually attend the games. Basketball would be the second largest, and we also have soccer teams. Our **school spirit isn't on the level of UNC** or Duke, but if you enjoy watching sports, you can attend all games for free."

Q "BU is not known really for sports. **We don't have a football team**; our major sport is hockey."

Q "**Hockey is huge**, and the Beanpot is crazy. It all depends on whether or not you're into sports to begin with."

Q "Sports are **pretty much negligible** at BU, unless you are part of some genetic upper caste."

STUDENT AUTHOR: **Hockey is, by far, the most celebrated varsity sport at BU. There is a "Beanpot" game every year between BU and BC, which always escalates into a party. While BU is not a huge sport mecca, pretty much everything is offered, from Frisbee golf, to basketball, to snowboarding, to sailing. Except . . . there is no football team, so if that is your thing, your best bet is to look elsewhere.**

Students Speak Out
ON DRUG SCENE

Q "I don't do it, but **it's the usual**. Alcohol is big, of course. Weed is the biggest of the drugs, then I would say E, coke and K. Everything is here; it is a city. "

Q "The drugs scene on campus, itself, is not very big. There is always pot and a ridiculous amount of **smuggling of alcohol** . . . However, the harder drugs are not around campus as much as they are around certain circles."

Q "Honestly, I can say that I know more kids that use drugs recreationally than those that do not. Never, however, have I witnessed someone being forced to try something that they did not want to do themselves. If drugs are something that you wish to do, they are **not hard to come by**."

STUDENT AUTHOR: It is pretty readily agreed by most students that drugs are certainly a prevalent and available source of recreation on campus and off. No one, however, felt that this sort of activity was so rampant that it put a strain on campus life. The drug scene, while visible, is easily avoidable.

14:1	Student-to-Faculty Ratio
91%	Freshman Retention Rate
76%	Four-Year Graduation Rate
90%	Financial Aid Applicants Receiving Aid

Students Speak Out
SAFETY & SECURITY

Q "Security is a major issue at Boston University. It is very strict, which is **good and bad** . . . It's complicated and very stringent, but no matter what, you will be safe."

Q "There are **blue-light phones** on every corner at BU, which are phones you can use to call campus security. I've walked home from the library at 1 a.m. a couple of times, and felt completely safe."

Q "Boston University is **very strict** about who can and cannot enter dorms, and this is one of the biggest issues at BU that people get upset about. There are many dorms on campus, but unless it is a mealtime, you can only get into a dorm other than your own if you are signed in by someone who lives there. After midnight, you can't sign anyone in."

STUDENT AUTHOR: There is no question, students feel safe on campus. Most people even report feeling perfectly comfortable roaming the area alone at night. The overwhelming presence of campus security, however, does put a significant strain on student life in the dorms.

Questions?
For more inside information and survival tips, pick up College Prowler's full-length book on this school, written by an actual student! Check it out at *www.collegeprowler.com*.

Students Speak Out
ON OVERALL EXPERIENCE

Q "Overall, I'm glad I'm where I'm at . . . There are some days when everyone says they'd like to transfer because it gets to be too much or because it gets really cold . . . BU has some administration issues, but **overall, it's livable** . . . At the end of the day, it can be a hard place to meet people and make friends, but once you get a core group, you're golden . . . I'm going back, so that should tell you something."

Q "I was wait-listed and rejected from most places, but I did get into BU with a scholarship, so I decided Boston was the place for me. I am very happy at BU—now I know **everything happens for a reason**."

Q "BU is a good school and I'm glad that I go there. **I love Boston completely**. It's a fun city, it's clean and safe, and it's a total college town."

Q "I did enjoy my time here, and besides the **administration is a very convenient scapegoat** for all of your problems; just ask the student body. I definitely could not picture my college experience anywhere else. And if you really do not belong here, no one has any problem leaving. More than 50 percent of my friends dropped out or transferred freshman year."

STUDENT AUTHOR: While BU certainly has its downfalls, most of which are due to the sheer size of the University, there are plenty of opportunities to take full advantage of all that it has to offer. For the resourceful and motivated individual, a little effort will go a long way. If you are looking for a taste of city life, and think that you would be able to establish yourself at a big university in a high-paced atmosphere, it is definitely possible to find your niche here.

Bowdoin College

5000 College Station; Brunswick, ME 04011
(207) 725-3000; www.bowdoin.edu

THE BASICS:

Acceptance Rate: 19%
Setting: Suburban
F-T Undergrads: 1,710

SAT Range: 1300–1470*
Control: Private
Tuition: $36,370

Most Popular Majors: Political Science and Government, Economics, History, English, Biology

*of 1600

Academics	A+	Guys	A-
Local Atmosphere	B-	Girls	B-
Safety & Security	A+	Athletics	B+
Computers	B+	Nightlife	C
Facilities	B	Greek Life	N/A
Campus Dining	A+	Drug Scene	B+
Off-Campus Dining	B	Campus Strictness	C+
Campus Housing	A	Parking	B-
Off-Campus Housing	C	Transportation	C-
Diversity	C	Weather	C-

Students Speak Out
ON ACADEMICS

Q "The **professors spend ample time with students** in order to answer any questions posed. Classes are stimulating and provoke a great deal of thought. To help students do well, professors conduct night study sessions weekly."

Q "I liked most of my professors a lot. **The classes were challenging, but I learned a lot.** Therefore, I don't regret taking them."

Q "The **faculty is as diverse**, if not more so, than the student body. Professors come from all across the world to teach at Bowdoin and involve their students in research. As rich as the humanities are at Bowdoin, so are the sciences."

Q "Frankly, coming from a large public school where teachers reached out to you (namely, the top tier of the senior class), and students didn't have to take the initiative, Bowdoin seems **artificial**. Basically, if you are the least bit timid, it is unlikely that your professors would think very much of you."

STUDENT AUTHOR: Receiving help and support from your professors 24/7 at Bowdoin is the norm. They want to see you succeed and will do their best to offer what constructive criticism they can. Professors maintain office hours, but with a heads-up, they will make time to meet with you. The small student faculty ratio of 10 to 1 allows them to cap enrollment at 50 students per class. (Less than five percent of classes enroll more than 40 students.)

Students Speak Out
ON LOCAL ATMOSPHERE

Q "The town is a **typical college town**. There's not much to do, but there are a couple of interesting shops and nice restaurants around."

Q "Brunswick is apparently a major retirement spot, but you wouldn't necessarily know it if it wasn't for the retirement home near campus that advertises bingo on Thursday nights. The town has a **small, intimate feel** with diners, dry-cleaners right out of the 1950s, an independent theater offering student discounts, a gaming store, a DVD place, and a modern music store. It's a great blend."

Q "Brunswick is a very small town, which seems **separate from the college**. I've found that one can live on campus and still not have contact with Maine culture if that is what you want from your time at Bowdoin."

Q "The town is **small and quiet**, with many pretty residential neighborhoods nearby and a quaint little downtown area. There are no other universities or colleges nearby."

STUDENT AUTHOR: The quaint little town of Brunswick offers a New England feel with antique stores, boutiques, and restaurants dotting Maine Street. Brunswick's tranquil location creates a warm setting with tree-lined streets, open parks, bed and breakfasts, nice shopping stores, eateries, and much more. Town-gown relations could be better, but compared to many other schools, student-resident relations are excellent.

5 Best Things	5 Worst Things
1 The warm atmosphere	1 The long winter
2 The dining halls	2 The preppy campus
3 Nearby cities	3 Being towed
4 The Outing Club	4 Brunswick closes at 8 p.m.
5 Awesome housing	5 No public transportation

Students Speak Out
ON FACILITIES

Q "The architecture here is beautiful. From Hubbard Hall and the Art Museum to the Field House—each building carries a distinct ambience. They are **welcoming, soothing**, and pleasant inside and out. There are many updated computer labs and a number of places for students to mingle or study quietly."

Q "The facilities are amazing for a school of this size. I **couldn't ask for better**."

Q "**I love our facilities**! The athletic facilities are great. The dining halls are clean and pretty. The big dining hall is beautiful and spacious, and the small dining hall is a cozy place that begins to feel like your very own dining room after awhile. The student center is very cool with multiple levels, a café, a pub, space for dancing or concerts, and on the balcony, there are little tables for studying."

Q "For the most part, the facilities on our campus are **better than one would expect**."

Q "The student unions are **great**. Students seem to utilize them a lot; I sure do."

STUDENT AUTHOR: **On its 200-acre campus, Bowdoin pampers its student body with six athletic centers, two dining halls, a convenience store, a pub and grill, 25 computer labs/centers, a music library, science library, general purpose library, special collections department, government document collection, and much more. Students agree that the facilities available to them are more than adequate for a school of Bowdoin's size.**

Famous Alumni

Joshua Lawrence Chamberlain, Nathaniel Hawthorne, Oliver Otis Howard, Henry Wadsworth Longfellow, Donald B. MacMillan, Robert E. Peary, Franklin Pierce, John Brown Russwurm, Calvin Stowe

Students Speak Out
ON CAMPUS DINING

Q "After 20 weeks, the food becomes 'eh,' but compared to what my friends at bigger universities are served, it's still **top-notch**!"

Q "The food at Bowdoin is excellent. There are two dining halls, with different menus for each meal. There are lots of great **vegetarian and vegan** options. They also serve great theme and holiday dinners—it's very good!"

Q "**If it wasn't for the food** Bowdoin serves, I wouldn't have made it through the busy and stressful years that come along with this school."

Q "During winter recess, I went home and my mom made me a great dinner. I told her that it was almost as good as the food I ate at Bowdoin. The food they serve is **just that good** (my mom is a great cook)."

Q "Holy Crap! Dining Services is amazing! They're always serving something new, and the staff will often **greet you by name**. Students are split on which of the dining halls is the best; Moulton is smaller and homier, whereas Thorne is the type of upscale place where they have Trustee dinners."

STUDENT AUTHOR: **Yes, believe the hype. Bowdoin Dining is spectacular! All first-year students purchase the 19-meal plan, which basically translates into a lot of good food a lot of the time. This makes gaining the Freshman 15 much, much easier. Many students across campus joke that they spend more time in the dining halls then they do in classes.**

Student Body

African American:	6%	Male/Female:	48/52%
Asian American:	13%	Out-of-State:	88%
Hispanic:	7%	International:	3%
Native American:	1%	Unknown:	2%
White:	68%		

Popular Faiths: 33% claim no religious preference. Protestants make up 29%, Catholics 23%, followed by Jews at 8%, and Hindus, Muslims, and Buddhists all making up 1% of the population.

Gay Pride: There are numerous organizations that provide support.

Economic Status: Social houses tend to attract crowds with a higher socio-economic population.

Students Speak Out
ON DORMS

Q "**The dorms are pretty spacious** here. The coed floor dorms tend to be the louder ones."

Q "Housing at Bowdoin is great. Pretty much everything but Chamberlain doubles are sought after. On the plus side; **the Chamberlain doubles are the newest**, so at least they are nice even if they are insanely small."

Q "Make sure you really visit the dorm before you sign up for housing; check out all the options, and the distance from campus and facilities. **Dorms can be a very important part of college living** because it affects how you arrange your time."

STUDENT AUTHOR: First-years at Bowdoin get to live in rooms better than many upperclassmen get at competing schools. There are six dorms, commonly referred to as "The Bricks." Hyde Hall is the oldest un-renovated Brick on campus (almost 70 years without repair) and is the only Chemical/Substance-Free housing option. Coleman Hall is known as the more eclectic dorm. Moore Hall is the party dorm . . . [I]f you say you smoke, you'll probably get placed in Moore.

Did You Know?
92% of undergrads live on campus.

Students Speak Out
ON GUYS & GIRLS

Q "If girls draped in Abercrombie, Gap, American Eagle, Ralph Lauren, and other **name brands** are your type, then this is your school. With close to 50 percent of the student body coming from private schools, the campus is definitely not eclectic."

Q "From talking to friends, it seems that Bowdoin has a reputation for its **good-looking guys**, but that reputation doesn't seem to exist for the girls on this campus."

Q "To be fair, Colby does have an anti-Bowdoin hockey chant consisting only of the words 'Ugly chicks.' . . . [F]or a school of this size, there's plenty of hotness to go around. The entering **first-year classes get hotter**, honestly."

STUDENT AUTHOR: Bowdoin is a very athletic school . . . Many suggest how Bowdoin looks like a modeling agency brought to life not only because of the attractive students, but in how people can become too wrapped up in their image . . . The Bowdoin men might be some of the hottest at any college in Maine . . . The girls at Bowdoin get the shorter end of the stick when it comes to perception of attractiveness.

Urban Legends

The Ivy League invited Bowdoin to join their athletic conference.

Britney Spears considered Bowdoin as a school to attend if she took a break from show business.

Overall School Spirit
Students who attend Bowdoin believe in their school. It's not uncommon seeing students wearing Bowdoin hats, T-shirts, sweatshirts, sandals, gym pants, and rings. Spirit for athletic teams is strong when it comes to games against rivals.

Students Speak Out
ON ATHLETICS

Q "Varsity sports are cool if you're into the mafia-like cliques that they create. **IM sports are fun**."

Q "You can tell by how the student body carries themselves, what they wear, and how they talk, that **sports are big on campus**."

Q "Varsity sports are big here. For those not playing varsity, they can play either club or intramural sports. **IMs are popular** because there are three different levels from beginner to expert."

Q "I'd rather not comment. I might get hurt by what I have to say about them. **They live in the majority at Bowdoin**."

STUDENT AUTHOR: For a school of almost 1,700, varsity sports play an integral part in students' lives. More than 35 percent of the student body plays an intercollegiate sport. The school spirit for each team is amazing. Men's ice hockey, basketball, and lacrosse bring in big crowds. What the Harvard-Yale game is to the ECAC, the Middlebury-Bowdoin and Colby-Bowdoin games are to the NESCAC. Playing a varsity sport at Bowdoin is serious.

Students Speak Out
ON DRUG SCENE

Q "There's **a lot of pot**—I'm not aware of other heavy drug use."

Q "It exists, but you can do what you want with it. **The drug scene here is not as big as it is at other schools**. It's not like they're selling crack in the library!"

Q "It seems to be **mostly weed** at Bowdoin, but there is definitely some harder stuff going around underground."

STUDENT AUTHOR: **Once upon a time, Bowdoin had a slight reputation for chemical research in drugs, but today, our campus is more known just for having a fair share of alcoholic beverages and marijuana. Although some hard-core drugs may be used on campus, it's definitely kept private and hidden from the main stream of campus life. The pressure to participate is relatively tame. Students at Bowdoin respect the wishes of other students and will not put them in situations they are not comfortable in. The thing to remember is that participation is up to you.**

10:1	Student-to-Faculty Ratio
98%	Freshman Retention Rate
86%	Four-Year Graduation Rate
85%	Financial Aid Applicants Receiving Aid

Students Speak Out
SAFETY & SECURITY

Q "**Security is wonderful**—they really care about the safety of the students. They manage to be extremely vigilant without being omnipresent and are generally very friendly and polite. There are many blue-light emergency phones across the campus and near dorms. The Safe Ride Service is another great program."

Q "Personally, **I feel very safe** on and around campus. Campus security can often be seen making their rounds on campus."

Q "Although Brunswick is not a very threatening place, I feel like when an incident occurs, **Security keeps the campus informed** and takes the appropriate action to follow-up and investigate the situation."

STUDENT AUTHOR: **Campus Security and Bowdoin Student Government provide shuttle services, cab services, and escorts to promote a sense of security. There are some areas on the Quad that are darker than others, but with 15 certified officers on the security staff, not much slips by.**

> **Questions?**
> For more inside information and survival tips, pick up College Prowler's full-length book on this school, written by an actual student! Check it out at *www.collegeprowler.com.*

Students Speak Out
ON OVERALL EXPERIENCE

Q "I'd have to say, **overall, I have had a wonderful experience**. I've met lots of interesting and awesome people here. Advising from the faculty could be better, but then again, I should be more willing to take the initiative, too. I don't want to be anywhere else besides inside this 'Bowdoin bubble'—where the food is always good, Colby is forever despised, and everything is generally in good condition."

Q "With so much opportunity and so many great people, I always feel like I could have done more, but considering my maturity, **I feel I gained a lot from my education at Bowdoin**. Even though I may not have loved the school while experiencing it, I love it now and would recommend it to anyone. You become more of a unique person by attending this small institution."

Q "Going to school here is a mixed bag. I've met very nice kids, but **the typical day and lifestyle is so repetitive**. I have my days when I question my stay at Bowdoin, but on others, I couldn't be more psyched."

Q "I had a strong selection to choose from, but **I chose Bowdoin and remain glad I did**."

STUDENT AUTHOR: **When it comes down to it, most students are glad that they made the decision to attend . . . Many students choose Bowdoin as their first choice school because of the intimacy between the administrators, faculty, coaches, alumni, and students; the size, the resources available, the convenient suburban location with accessibility to bigger metropolitan areas, and overall reputation.**

Bradley University

1501 West Bradley Avenue; Peoria, IL 61625
(309) 676-7611; www.bradley.edu

THE BASICS:

Acceptance Rate: 64%
Setting: Urban
F-T Undergrads: 5,057

SAT Range: 1020–1280*
Control: Private
Tuition: $22,814

Most Popular Majors: Business, Engineering, Communication, Health Professions, Education

*of 1600

Academics	B+	Guys	B
Local Atmosphere	A-	Girls	B+
Safety & Security	B-	Athletics	A-
Computers	C+	Nightlife	B+
Facilities	C	Greek Life	A-
Campus Dining	C	Drug Scene	B-
Off-Campus Dining	A-	Campus Strictness	B-
Campus Housing	C+	Parking	D
Off-Campus Housing	B	Transportation	C+
Diversity	C-	Weather	D+

Students Speak Out
ON ACADEMICS

Q "The professors at Bradley are very diverse. They know what the right amount of work is to push a student to be at his or her best. **At times the workload gets tough**, but they are usually flexible to work around other classes."

Q "The workload is not unmanageable, but it's not a breeze. **I definitely have to put in my fair share of hours at the library**, but I still manage to write for the paper, sing in the choir, and have a position on my sorority's executive board."

Q "**Most Bradley professors are sharp**. They enjoy what they do and like helping kids become professionals. But there are some who you can tell probably ate lunch by themselves when they were kids in school."

Q "The teachers seem too lax sometimes. They are really helpful, but **sometimes they don't convey information clearly and efficiently**. Bradley is known for its nursing and engineering schools, although students complain the technology isn't up to date for them. The communications school is technologically advanced, but it needs more knowledgeable staff."

STUDENT AUTHOR: Bradley is known for quality academics, and the reputation isn't unwarranted. Most professors aren't lax and challenge students, but the workload isn't unmanageable. Everyone gets personal attention in mostly small classes. All things considered, Bradley lives up to its reputation of above-average academics, and employers value the education students receive.

Students Speak Out
ON LOCAL ATMOSPHERE

Q "I feel like Bradley is in a good location because **we are pretty close to many other schools**. Illinois Wesleyan and Illinois State are a 45-minute drive away. University of Illinois is an hour and a half down I-74, and Eastern Illinois is also nearby. St. Louis is a three-hour trip, and there are many schools there as well."

Q "I come from a suburb of Chicago, so I am used to more hustle and bustle, but **I am glad that Peoria is an actual city** and we're not stuck in the middle of nowhere. I feel like some areas of Peoria are kind of rundown, but other areas are well-kept and beautiful. Like any city, it has its good parts and bad parts."

Q "As a 'townie,' there's nowhere I'd rather be than Peoria. I grew up here, so I don't really know what it's like not to be here. **It's a mid-size city with plenty to do**, but without the lights and traffic of Chicago. You just have to know what parts to stay away from. There are two movie theaters, two malls, and plenty of chain restaurants and local establishments to entertain yourself with."

STUDENT AUTHOR: Peoria has the attractions of a big city, but as a mid-size Midwestern city, the traffic is reasonable, and there are still good old-fashioned outdoor activities to enjoy in some of Peoria's scenic areas. Many students appreciate Peoria's mix of small-town traditions and big-city attractions, but the lack of transportation to off-campus destinations is frustrating to those without cars.

5 Best Things
1 Personal attention
2 Quick walk to class
3 Sense of community
4 Low cost
5 Men's basketball

5 Worst Things
1 Parking
2 Registering for classes
3 Campus food
4 Student apathy
5 Lack of landscaping

Students Speak Out
ON FACILITIES

Q "Our facilities are okay. The library could be better, but it has what you need to do your work. Athletic facilities are good, too. The student center is pretty lame. **Compared to other campuses, ours is pretty boring** and could use a major overhaul."

Q "Facilities are kind of pathetic. **The cafeterias are too small and crowded all the time**, the student center is virtually nonexistent, and the library is one of the worst in the nation. It costs way too much money to go to Bradley for the facilities to be this terrible."

Q "**The facilities on campus are well-maintained**, with the exception of the recreation center. The library isn't great either. As for the cafeterias and dorms, they are really dated, but overall, there always seems to be something under construction, which is a good sign."

Q "The facilities are nice, and the campus is expanding, but **the school is outgrowing all of this stuff**, which is not a bad thing provided the administration continues to listen to students and address their concerns."

STUDENT AUTHOR: **There's good news and bad news. The bad news is that Bradley lacks in facilities—at least in the important ones. But the good news is that the administrators recognize this, and the campus is constantly changing. The to-do list is huge. In August 2006, Bradley announced its 15-year plan, which is supposed to transform the look of campus. However, even when the 15-year plan is finished, the campus will still need help.**

Famous Alumni
Jack Brickhouse, Neil Flynn, Hersey Hawkins, Tami Lane, Gen. John Shalikashvili, Charlie Steiner

Students Speak Out
ON CAMPUS DINING

Q "The dining halls aren't terrible, and Geisert was my favorite because **it was convenient to just run downstairs in my pajamas and grab lunch** on the weekends. But compared to other universities and what they have to offer, our food is much more bland and not so Grade A."

Q "In terms of food, tacos seem prevalent. Williams Hall cafeteria features them at least three times a week. Center Court is the best place to go on campus. It's fine American cuisine. **The dining halls are repetitive and usually chaotic**. They're also cheap, though, so I'll keep coming back."

Q "**Food on campus isn't great, but it's edible**. The nice thing is Bradley is a small campus, so it's very easy to walk across the street to other restaurants if you get bored or grossed out by Bradley food."

Q "The food on campus is edible, and **brunch is by far the best meal at the dining halls**. Geisert Hall's brunch is phenomenal and has almost any breakfast food imaginable. Plus the omelets are made fresh in front of you."

STUDENT AUTHOR: **Overall, it's not hard to find something to eat that fits with the meal plan. While there isn't gourmet food on campus, lines move relatively quickly in the dining halls. No one has to walk far for a meal because campus is so compact, but students get tired of eating the same meals over and over. Bradley doesn't compare to most schools in dining services, but those who've never been anywhere else might not notice.**

Student Body

African American:	6%	Male/Female:	45/55%
Asian American:	4%	Out-of-State:	13%
Hispanic:	3%	International:	1%
Native American:	<1%	Unknown:	2%
White:	84%		

Popular Faiths: Christianity and Judaism are the most prevalent religions on campus.

Gay Pride: Bradley is somewhat liberal, so students are accepting to the gay community, though it isn't prevalent.

Economic Status: Bradley is said to be populated by rich kids from Chicago suburbs, but the population is generally middle class.

Students Speak Out
ON DORMS

Q "The dorms are dorms. They aren't very spacious, but you can live in them, no problem. There aren't any to avoid or favor because **they all have pros and cons**. As long as you are willing to wander outside your room, you'll make a lot of good friends just by walking around your floor."

Q **"The dorms are fairly decent for a campus this size**. I lived in both Geisert and Harper, both my favorites. Harper is probably the biggest and most attractive dorm room, though I've heard lots of praise for Williams' dorm sizes."

Q "Dorms are a good time, and you won't even notice you're sharing a tiny space with another person. The best years of college are in the dorms because **the dorms are where you make all your best friends**."

STUDENT AUTHOR: Bradley dorms aren't unusually poor or impressive. They are typical college dorms— average in size, decently maintained, and relatively clean. Some people complain that living in Bradley's dorms is like living in a jail cell, and other people say they don't mind them at all. Either way, they're livable, and people get by because it's college.

> **Did You Know?**
> 63% of undergrads live on campus.

Students Speak Out
ON GUYS & GIRLS

Q "I've found that **most Bradley students are concerned about their grade**s and realize they're here for their education above all, but I wouldn't describe them as geeky. Like every campus, BU has a diverse group of people."

Q "Guys here are generally okay. **Some are nerdy, and others are jerks**. Most girls are alright. The typical student has a million people to say hi to, but they have a close-knit group of friends to make plans to chill with."

Q "When I came to Bradley freshman year, I was pretty excited because **there were hot guys everywhere**! But I've also met quite a few nerdy guys that only leave their rooms to talk about video games."

STUDENT AUTHOR: Bradley is like a big high school. Every stereotypical clique is represented. But no matter where a student falls into the mix, they're likely to find someone to suit them. Everyone is as least mildly intelligent, which makes for good conversation most of the time. Walking to class isn't like walking the catwalk with a bunch of models, but there are plenty of people from both sexes who are attractive, and plenty who aren't.

> **Traditions**
>
> **Block Party**
> At the start of the year, students attend a campus-wide block party with plenty of music and food.
>
> **Senior Bar Crawl**
> Every graduating class makes T-shirts and hits up the bars for a day-long bar crawl. Many students don't make it to the end.
>
> **Overall School Spirit**
> The Braves garner a lot of support. The men's basketball team gets praise during most of the games, but school spirit otherwise is low.

Students Speak Out
ON ATHLETICS

Q "**Basketball is Bradley's biggest claim to fame around here** due to the fact that we have no football team. But I find that other sports don't get as much glory."

Q "Varsity sports here are intense. People must be dedicated to keep that up. **Intramural sports are good, too**. People who are playing them are just as passionate as those on varsity."

Q "Basketball is huge here at Bradley. I would say it's the biggest sport, hands down. Students get so crazy at the games. **Soccer is the second biggest sport**, but support for soccer is way less than basketball. When the team made it to the Elite Eight this year, it wasn't as exciting as when the basketball team made it to the Sweet 16 a few years ago."

STUDENT AUTHOR: If Bradley were only known for one thing, it would be men's basketball. Thousands of people turn out for men's basketball games, both home and away. However, most other sports don't garner the same fan attention, whether they're having a good season or not. Intramurals are always popular, though. Just about every sport is offered, and they are prominent on campus.

Students Speak Out
ON DRUG SCENE

Q "**Weed is pretty prevalent on campus**, but you'll only find it if you're looking for it. I know people that do everything from 'shrooms to crack, but they're not going to give you any unless you really want it. It's easy to avoid, which is nice."

Q "There are people that do drugs around here, but **it doesn't seem like people pressure others to do it**. It's not really noticeable to me, although I do hear about it going on."

Q "Some people do drugs, but it's not hugely popular. **It seems like everybody is content with alcohol most of the time**, but if you want something different, you can probably get a hold of it. Marijuana is out there, and it's really easy to get if you're looking and asking for it."

STUDENT AUTHOR: **Aside from alcohol, marijuana is seen occasionally, but it's not a noticeable part of student life. Other hard drugs are available too, but they're even less visible than marijuana. People seem to stick to small gatherings or off-campus bars rather than all-out parties, which has made campus quieter.**

14:1	Student-to-Faculty Ratio
89%	Freshman Retention Rate
54%	Four-Year Graduation Rate
97%	Financial Aid Applicants Receiving Aid

Students Speak Out
SAFETY & SECURITY

Q "**I have never felt like my safety was compromised on campus**. I think there could maybe be more lights, but there is a new lighting system to be installed soon that will take care of that concern. I think there may be a lot of crime in certain parts of Peoria, but crime on campus isn't too bad."

Q "Security is okay. We have campus police, but I feel like **sometimes they're only out there to hand out drinking tickets** instead of making sure you don't get mugged or robbed."

Q "Crime is a hot topic, but **there actually isn't that much that you hear about**. Bradley and Peoria as a whole probably compare to anywhere else. Security is average."

STUDENT AUTHOR: **West Peoria isn't the best part of the city. Crime is common in surrounding areas, and police sirens are frequent. However, the University police watch over the campus and keep most crime away from the school. Overall, there's more talk about security issues than real threats.**

Questions?
For more inside information and survival tips, pick up College Prowler's full-length book on this school, written by an actual student! Check it out at *www.collegeprowler.com*.

Students Speak Out
ON OVERALL EXPERIENCE

Q "Bradley is a good place to be for someone who likes **the small-school atmosphere and personal attention**. There are some downs, such as the outdated buildings and horrible parking, but there are also plenty of ups. The professors are mostly intelligent people who have worked in their fields. They know how to challenge you, but they don't work you too hard. It's easy to make friends, and I know I've made some lifelong relationships. There is a lot of school pride, especially from alumni. It's a great place to be, and I don't want to graduate."

Q "**Bradley is a great college, and I've loved being here**. Yes, there could be better food and better parking, for example, but I've had a blast."

Q "Bradley is exactly what you pay for. For a private school, it's relatively inexpensive, so there are some shortfalls. But, **for the most part, you get a lot for your money**."

Q "Bradley wasn't perfect for my major, **but the small-school opportunities are irreplaceable**. Having professors who know your name and give you individual attention has been amazing."

STUDENT AUTHOR: **If students want a school where they'll get personal attention from professors, a short walk to class, and a solid, reputable education, Bradley is worth looking into. But it's not for everybody. Some people want to focus on the negatives, but those people don't get much out of their experience. Peoria doesn't offer the big-town buzz, and Bradley doesn't have all the draws of a large state school, but people who choose Bradley—love it or hate it—walk away in the end with a strong education and usually a couple of good stories to go with it.**

Brandeis University

415 South Street; Waltham, MA 02454
(781) 736-2000; www.brandeis.edu

THE BASICS:

Acceptance Rate: 38%
Setting: Suburban
F-T Undergrads: 3,242

SAT Range: 1270–1440*
Control: Private
Tuition: $34,566

Most Popular Majors: Economics, Biology, Political Science, Psychology, Sociology

*of 1600

Academics	A-	Guys	C
Local Atmosphere	B+	Girls	C+
Safety & Security	A-	Athletics	C
Computers	A-	Nightlife	B+
Facilities	B	Greek Life	C-
Campus Dining	A-	Drug Scene	B
Off-Campus Dining	B+	Campus Strictness	A-
Campus Housing	B-	Parking	B-
Off-Campus Housing	B	Transportation	A-
Diversity	C-	Weather	C-

Students Speak Out
ON ACADEMICS

Q "I've really liked my professors at Brandeis, with the exception of one I had in the economics department. They all have convenient office hours, and **they generally treat me as an equal, not as a subordinate**. Classes can be interesting depending on the department, the topic, the style of class, and the amount of students."

Q "The teachers are probably the best thing about Brandeis. They are very keen in their subjects, especially the history teachers. However, I am upset that **TAs teach some classes**, not professors."

Q "While the teachers here are **generally knowledgeable and interesting**, I think they're overrated. I definitely don't think most of them are that stimulating, and I question why students constantly laud their professors. I just don't feel as passionately about them as they do."

Q "I have had **very positive experiences** with practically every one of my professors. Some classes have been more interesting than others. University requirements aren't as much fun to take as classes in your major."

STUDENT AUTHOR: Brandeis offers students the opportunity to learn from well-known individuals, including . . . the likes of Robert Reich, Anita Hill, and Dennis Ross. Grad students, or TAs, do not actually teach any classes other than UWS (University Writing Seminar) and Introductory Calculus. [O]ne-on-one interaction with professors is not the exception, it's the rule.

Students Speak Out
ON LOCAL ATMOSPHERE

Q "**The town has not been very receptive to the college in the past**, but it is improving. The restaurants are getting better, and the bars seem to love us. Bentley College is in Waltham, too, but neither college seems to admit that the other exists."

Q "As a college town, **Waltham's not so happening**. Boston, on the other hand, is probably the greatest city for college students. It really opens up the social network."

Q "**Brandeis is kind of isolated** because it's self-contained, but Moody Street is a great place to have a nice meal, and if you have a car, anything is within five minutes."

Q "Waltham is **practically in Boston/Cambridge**, so the atmosphere is comparable. There is a ridiculous number of other universities in the area that are all easy to go to. Exploring Boston and the surrounding areas is a must for any student looking to fully experience New England."

STUDENT AUTHOR: While Waltham isn't exactly the most exhilirating place in the universe, it does include some bars, a supermarket, and other stores essential to college life. Less than a mile and a half from campus is Moody Street, which provides a bit of excitement for Brandeis students. If one is not satisfied enough by this selection, Boston and Cambridge, home of Harvard and MIT, are extremely close by. Both are reachable by either taking the Brandeis shuttle, the Commuter Rail, the T-line (Boston's subway system), or by car.

Students Speak Out
ON FACILITIES

"A lot of the architecture on campus is ugly, but then again, you're not buying the architecture. The athletic facilities are nice. The student center isn't bad, although it is an incredibly inefficient use of space. Classrooms are fine, though—nothing thrilling, but nothing terrible. **Dorms aren't great** but the facilities department has a great response time if you harass them enough."

"The **facilities are fairly nice**, especially the student center and residence hall [Village] which looks more like a hotel. The gym is always crowded, so don't count on getting to use a machine, especially around 3 p.m."

"The facilities for the sciences and the graduate schools are very nice. But it seems that Brandeis has ignored the rest of campus. **The Humanities Quad is in dire need of renovations**. For a school that doesn't seem to pay attention to sports, Brandeis has beautiful sports facilities. The student center is also great, minus the 'Emerald City' exterior, of course."

STUDENT AUTHOR: **Brandeis has a relatively small endowment, and sometimes the facilities reflect that. While many schools with more money are better able to update facilities and pay for the upkeep, Brandeis has a few problems. Administration is always involved in capital projects that try to get money to improve existing buildings or build new ones. Recently, however, they have made great strides. [U]ntil they make strides at updating all of their buildings, their facilities will not make an "A" grade.**

Famous Alumni

Mitch Alborn, David Crane, Thomas L. Friedman, Gary David Goldberg, Marshall Herskovitz, Marta Kauffman, Roderick MacKinnon, Debra Messing

Students Speak Out
ON CAMPUS DINING

"**The food on campus is better than expected**. We outsourced our food services to Aramark, and besides ripping us off daily on the prices, the quality is high. It's better than most schools I've been to. Obviously, it's not mom's cooking, and after three months, you'll want to go back to home-cooked food; but for a college campus it is good. Good spots include the Stein and the sandwich/salad bar in Usdan. The dining halls are in good shape, but the 'Jewish-ness' of Sherman can be intimidating and disrupting."

"Usdan Café is definitely better than the other dining halls. The food is actually quite good, and relatively varied, though one would probably still hear me complaining about the food, mainly because **it gets monotonous after a while**."

"**The food leaves something to be desired**. It's not absolutely terrible, but it's pretty bad sometimes."

STUDENT AUTHOR: **The food at Brandeis is edible, but it's nothing to rave about. Brandeis dining consists of only a handful of options. There's Sherman, broken down into Kosher and non-Kosher sides . . . both all-you-can-eat. The food here is only good if you keep Kosher, if you're really hungry, or if you have meals instead of points as a dining plan. Usdan is an à la Carte dining area . . . Upstairs from Usdan is the Boulevard . . . The food here is good, but the selection rarely, if ever, changes. Aramark, who runs the dining services, is very hesitant, it seems, to give the students what they pay for.**

Student Body

African American:	3%	Male/Female:	44/56%
Asian American:	7%	Out-of-State:	63%
Hispanic:	4%	International:	8%
Native American:	<1%	Unknown:	14%
White:	64%		

Popular Faiths: Brandeis is famous (although sometimes infamous) for being very, very Jewish.

Gay Pride: The Brandeis gay community is very strong. It is a very comfortable place for people who choose to come out. The gay community also throws some of the best parties at Brandeis.

Economic Status: All socio-economic backgrounds are represented at Brandeis.

Students Speak Out
ON DORMS

Q "The dorms are nice, except for East Quad which is loud, full of bugs, and extremely **ghetto**."

Q "Most dorms are in good shape, though they all look old, except for **the Village**. Some are really decrepit, such as Ridgewood. Since at any time except for freshman year, good options are living in a suite, a townhouse, or a hallway. Dorms to avoid include East with small rooms and hallways, and the Castle which is very anti-social. Nice dorms include Rosenthal, Ziv, Ridgewood, the Mods, and the Village."

Q "The **freshman dorms are the nicest**, while the sophomore dorms are the worst. Junior and senior housing isn't guaranteed, but if you are in need of housing, you will most likely receive it."

STUDENT AUTHOR: The quality and experience of on-campus housing at Brandeis really depends on whom you ask. Most people agree that East is the worst of the dorms, but many people who live there end up loving it because of the social opportunities. It's all about where your friends live. It is a testament to Brandeis's on-campus housing that so many students choose to stay on campus.

Did You Know?
80% of undergrads live on campus.

Students Speak Out
ON GUYS & GIRLS

Q "Two words: **Brandeis goggles**. Oh and there are three Gs to describe guys at Brandeis: 1) Girlfriend; 2) Gay; 3) God, not in this lifetime."

Q "Well, there are **a few winners** in both the guys and the girls categories, but Brandeis isn't exactly known for its hotness factor."

Q "The guys are quite similar to each other, and are **not very talkative**—although, you can find the occasional great guy! The girls are more vibrant and willing to go out and meet people. Brandeis, unfortunately, lacks general attractiveness of the opposite sex."

Q "Brandeis has a reputation for being an ugly campus. While there are cute guys here, they're not falling into your lap . . . **I like ugly guys**."

STUDENT AUTHOR: To really talk about Brandeis guys and girls, you need to know your standards. If you come to Brandeis with really high standards . . . you're in big trouble. There are some very attractive people on Brandeis's campus, but most of them are dating the other attractive people. That leaves a lot of average-looking people without a partner. Sometimes it seems that the gay community actually has more success.

Traditions

Bronstein Weekend
This is one of the best weekends of the year, and occurs in the spring. Bronstein usually features a couple of concerts and lots of camp-like activities.

Modfest
Modfest is a big block party that goes on in the senior housing area twice a year. The whole campus gets drunk and goes to this party to relieve stress.

Overall School Spirit
School spirit is underwhelming. Some say it stems from a lack of sporting prowess and a football team.

Students Speak Out
ON ATHLETICS

Q "Varsity sports are what you make them. Obviously, this is a **Division III** school, so we don't recruit like Division I schools. As a result, the talent level, facilities, funding, and venues are not like you'll find at a big D-I school (Big Ten, Pac Ten, ACC, Big East, and so on). The spirit is also not the same as you will find at a larger university. I think this is just because we don't have the resources, talent, money, or venue to bring in 100,000 fans to root for the football team we don't have."

Q "**Sports are not big**, although some have a small cult following like ultimate Frisbee and IM basketball."

Q "**We have sports** at Brandeis?"

STUDENT AUTHOR: The lack of a football team puts focus on the normally less popular sports. However, you will not find much in the way of athletic pride or support at Brandeis. While sports do exist, they are not much of a big deal, and are not a main attraction of the school. Recently, Brandeis has made great strides in recruiting more and more talented athletes to play for their teams.

Students Speak Out
ON DRUG SCENE

Q "Drugs are there if you want them. Weed is pretty prevalent, but **harder drugs aren't really that popular in my experience.**"

Q "There is **quite a bit of pot being smoked all over campus**. The school doesn't really do much to prevent it. Drinking is prevalent, but that's everywhere—I wouldn't say there's an extraordinary amount of alcohol consumption here. I would say there's a lot more pot being smoked than at the average school."

Q "**I do not find that drugs are a problem**. The drugs that exist don't interfere with the lives of students who choose to ignore them, which is quite easy."

STUDENT AUTHOR: Marijuana seems like it's everywhere on campus, especially over the weekends. You can certainly avoid it if that's not your scene, but if you want it, it is there . . . About half of the Brandeis population smokes weed at least once within their four years at Brandeis. The other half tends to take a very anti-drug stance.

8:1	Student-to-Faculty Ratio
94%	Freshman Retention Rate
84%	Four-Year Graduation Rate
82%	Financial Aid Applicants Receiving Aid

Students Speak Out
SAFETY & SECURITY

Q "While Brandeis seems to be in its own secure bubble away from the world, **security on campus isn't always trusted**. Dorms are easy to get into, and anyone can come and go."

Q "There are no big problems, and **in general, I feel safe**. I know many people who leave the door to their suite and room unlocked."

Q "Security is great. There are cops on duty 24/7, plus there's the blue-light system, which equals a **pretty safe environment**. I always feel comfortable walking around at night. The only bad thing was that someone attempted to break into my car in a Brandeis parking lot and caused $1,000 worth of damage, and nobody witnessed it. Other than that, security and safety at Brandeis is sufficiently high."

STUDENT AUTHOR: Although not located in the most affluent or nicest of towns, Brandeis, surprisingly, boasts a peaceful campus. While the rent-a-cop police officers seem incompetent at times, they actually do their jobs well . . . [T]heir main objectives are giving out parking tickets and breaking up parties.

Questions?
For more inside information and survival tips, pick up College Prowler's full-length book on this school, written by an actual student! Check it out at *www.collegeprowler.com*.

Students Speak Out
ON OVERALL EXPERIENCE

Q "I love Brandeis, but **if I could've done it again, I probably would've gone to another school**. The social and sports scenes are both lacking, and there is a lack of overall school unity. While the small size of Brandeis allows for students to have a more hands-on experience in their classes and with the activities they are involved in, you do not get to constantly meet new people, and there is also a limit in what a liberal arts university can provide in terms of course offerings."

Q "Overall, **this is the best place for me when you combine everything together**. I wish people were smarter. I think admissions standards should be raised. I expected that a top 35 school would be more challenging. It would definitely make me happier to have a more academic environment."

Q "**I really love it here**. I do, at times, wish I were at a more exciting school, but there is a feeling of family and closeness that you get."

Q "In some ways I wish I was at another school, and in some ways I don't. But in no way should you base your decision to enroll here on someone else's first year. Great people, teachers that truly care, and **a safe growing environment** would definitely be among the top elements I have loved so far at Brandeis."

STUDENT AUTHOR: They may complain a lot, but Brandeis students on the whole seem to be more than happy at Brandeis. More so than a lot of colleges, Brandeis is truly what you make of it. There are so many opportunities out there, but you need to be willing to put forth the effort to get the most out of them.

Brigham Young University

A209 ASB; Provo, UT 84602
(801) 422-4636; www.byu.edu

THE BASICS:

Acceptance Rate: 76%
Setting: Suburban
F-T Undergrads: 24,948

SAT Range: 1120–1340*
Control: Private
Tuition: $3,410

Most Popular Majors: Family and Consumer Sciences, English, Psychology, Accounting, Education

*of 1600

Academics	B+	Guys	A
Local Atmosphere	B-	Girls	A
Safety & Security	A+	Athletics	A
Computers	B-	Nightlife	C-
Facilities	B+	Greek Life	N/A
Campus Dining	B+	Drug Scene	A+
Off-Campus Dining	A-	Campus Strictness	D-
Campus Housing	B-	Parking	C-
Off-Campus Housing	B-	Transportation	B
Diversity	D-	Weather	B

Students Speak Out
ON ACADEMICS

Q "A nice thing about BYU is that it's a very **undergraduate-oriented** school. The professors are very willing to speak with the undergraduate students as well as the graduate students."

Q "I have never come across a bad teacher since I've been here. **They are all intelligent**, fun, flexible, and concerned with your progress in their class."

Q "I have had a lot of experience with teachers outside the classroom, and they have been quite helpful. Most of the professors really want to be there, and want to **see the students succeed**."

Q "The vast majority of my teachers have been **exceptional**. One or two here or there exhibited some flaws, like an excessive attachment to bland homework projects or slightly boring lectures, but I have found that, overall, my teachers are good friends. In particular, their lectures tend to reach beyond informational and educational, to exhibit an inspirational quality that develops a greater love and appreciation for the topic."

STUDENT AUTHOR: **BYU has top-caliber professors. There is no question that academics at BYU are important, and the administration strives to hire excellent teachers. One way to avoid the large classes as an incoming freshman is to go the "freshman academy" route. This is a program where you take all your generals in smaller classes with the same kids. You also live with these same kids, however, so it can be stifling.**

Students Speak Out
ON LOCAL ATMOSPHERE

Q "It's a very prim, proper, decent, and **boring town**. The neighboring city of Orem has a state college. So the off-campus housing available in the area tends to be populated by students from both our school and theirs."

Q "I really **enjoy Provo's atmosphere**. It truly gives me a warm feeling. Utah Valley State College is about 15 minutes away, and up in Salt Lake City is the University of Utah. There are tons of things to do—hiking, visiting the hot springs, or just hanging out."

Q "Provo is home to BYU and UVSC, both of which boast enrollments in excess of 30,000 students. With that many college-aged kids in one happy little valley, you would think there would exist something resembling nightlife. Not so. Provo unofficially **shuts down at 10:30 p.m.**, and if late-night studying is your speed, you would do well to develop a taste for Denny's or Village Inn, as these are the only two places to 'hang out' in Provo after the sun sets. However, in the daytime one will find mountains, canyons, lakes, and ski resorts all in close proximity, which makes Utah Valley an outdoor enthusiast's dream."

STUDENT AUTHOR: **While Provo is beautiful, nestled at the foot of the Rocky Mountains, it is by no means a big city. The majority of residents are college students, so activities like movies and restaurants tend to be fairly crowded. Provo's charm is in the nearby mountains and river; in the summer, bonfires up Provo canyon are a nightly occurrence.**

5 Best Things	5 Worst Things
1 Student involvement	1 Knee-length shorts
2 The Creamery	2 Parking
3 Football season	3 Lack of diversity
4 Studying abroad	4 Construction
5 Friendly student body	5 Honor Code

Students Speak Out
ON FACILITIES

Q "**Facilities are great**! Pretty much all of BYU's facilities are excellent, up-to-date, and useful; everything is really big. The library has seven floors, and it's really nice."

Q "Anyone can use the sports facilities. They are open to all students as long as they present their student IDs. You can play racquetball with your friends or go running. **The Wilk is nice**, too. People go there to study, talk, and hang out."

Q "BYU is **constantly renovating**, so we have some of the most up-to-date stuff that you can get. The student center was remodeled and is fantastic, complete with a bowling alley, arcade, and pool hall, all of which was actually already a part of the student center."

Q "Sports **facilities are awesome**. I use them a lot, and everything is free for students. The student center is also pretty good."

Q "Overall, the facilities on campus are really nice and clean, which is great. The athletic facilities for the athletes are much nicer than those for the average student, but the average student **facilities are adequate**."

STUDENT AUTHOR: **BYU is constantly striving to provide the most up-to-date facilities and classrooms, which means that there is always a big hole somewhere in the middle of campus. The majority of classrooms are wired with projectors and computers for the teachers, and more than a few professors resort to PowerPoint presentations during lectures. In the business building, some classrooms have Internet hookups for students, as well.**

Famous Alumni

Orrin Hatch, Steve Young, Aaron Eckhart, Jon Heder, Julie Stoffer

Students Speak Out
ON CAMPUS DINING

Q "Freshmen get a Dining Plus card, which is good because you can use it to eat on campus, in the dormitory cafeterias, or in the Cougareat. The food in the **Cougareat is wonderful**! It's great, and it's right in the middle of the Wilkinson Center, which is the main student center. The Creamery is also good, and you'll find that that's where a lot of freshmen go."

Q "Food is **very good** at BYU. Everyone loves the food, even though it's expensive. The Creamery shop is probably the most popular place to eat on campus."

Q "Don't expect to find any coffee or tea around. It's **against our religion** to drink the stuff."

Q "The dining halls on campus are almost entirely frequented by the freshman set, and although dining services gets credit for trying, **'cafeteria' and 'food' are two very mutually exclusive terms**."

Q "The food is decent. Pizza Hut and Burger King take Flex and are great to fall back on. Everything **closes too early**, however."

STUDENT AUTHOR: **The cafeteria food is not generally regarded as being amazing cuisine. But the glory of BYU meal options is that you don't have to live on cafeteria food alone! BYU offers a couple of different meal plan options; the most popular (and slightly more expensive) option is Dining Plus. This option gives students a daily allowance that they can spend anywhere, which is great if you don't want to trudge to the cafeteria for lunch.**

Student Body

African American:	<1%	Male/Female:	51/49%
Asian American:	3%	Out-of-State:	69%
Hispanic:	3%	International:	4%
Native American:	1%	Unknown:	0%
White:	89%		

Popular Faiths: The mian faith is Mormonism.

Political Activity: Most students are fairly conservative. While there are both College Democrats and College Republican groups on campus, political participation is not very high.

Economic Status: Most students are middle-class, upper-middle-class, or upper-class.

Students Speak Out
ON DORMS

Q "We have gobs of Mexican restaurants off campus, or maybe I'm just more aware of them because I'm from an area that lacks Mexican cuisine—but they're all over the place around here. There are tons of places to eat, because **people like to go out on dates here**."

Q "Good food is not hard to find in Provo. My favorite places are Café Rio—the best Mexican food in town, and Brick Oven Restaurant, which has **great pizza** and a salad bar."

Q "**American Pie Pizza** will forever be a hallowed establishment for the poor, starving students of Provo."

STUDENT AUTHOR: Provo has a plethora of great restaurants. Any type of chain restaurant can be found here, and there are also lots of good little local places. If you are coming from a place without great Mexican food, you are in luck, because there are plenty of authentic Mexican and South American restaurants. There are plenty of great little restaurants, so don't be afraid to tread off the beaten path and explore new cuisines!

> **Did You Know?**
> 6% of undergrads live on campus.

Students Speak Out
ON GUYS & GIRLS

Q "For the most part, there are guys and girls with **high standards**, focus, and direction in their lives. Just to get into BYU is tough enough, and typically only those students who maintain good grades get accepted."

Q "Lots of dorky guys, but lots of **cool guys**, as well. I met my husband here. There are mostly churchy guys, but it's cute when they are tough guys, but churchy, too!"

Q "Girls are **very cute**, although they wear too much makeup, and there's a lot of competition for the hot guys. Guys are usually nicer than they are cute, so if you meet a hot guy, odds are he's very nice and usually has a girlfriend."

STUDENT AUTHOR: BYU students are well known as being uncommonly friendly and inclusive. Although they may look intimidating at first with their seemingly uniform blond hair and Abercrombie & Fitch clothing, the majority is surprisingly nice, and, if you look hard enough, you may even notice that not quite all of the students are from Utah. Most people are outgoing, although the dorms can be a little cliquish.

> **Urban Legends**
>
> There are dinosaur bones buried under the football stadium. BYU stores them there because they didn't have anywhere else to put them.
>
> BYU is building a parking garage. This can also be varied by saying that the honor code is changing, tank tops will be allowed. It's never going to happen!
>
> **Overall School Spirit**
> Cougars are proud to be cougars! Many BYU students come from a long line of BYU graduates and have grown up watching BYU sports.

Students Speak Out
ON ATHLETICS

Q "It's so **fun to go to the games**, if you like football or socializing. Intramurals are fun, I hear; I never did them, but I know people who did and had a blast."

Q "Everyone comes to the games where we play our rival, University of Utah, and the games are **really fun**. IM sports are big, and we have some unusual ones—inner tube water polo and ultimate Frisbee are just some of them!"

Q "Sports are **very big**. Football games are huge, basketball is pretty big, and volleyball and soccer get pretty good turnouts."

Q "**Sports are huge** at BYU—all kinds of sports. IM is really well organized, and the varsity sports are competitive and fun to watch."

STUDENT AUTHOR: BYU football is a Utah County tradition. BYU takes a lot of pride in athletics, and student support is consistently consistent. The fall semester is punctuated with comments around campus supporting/bemoaning the football team. We do have sports aside from football, but they aren't really noticed unless they are doing well.

Students Speak Out
ON DRUG SCENE

Q "I haven't ever been around anyone that has done drugs on campus. They are hard to find anyway, because we sign our name saying we **won't do drugs**."

Q "The drug scene is almost nonexistent. I think I heard that someone was into LSD or something like that, but he was **expelled immediately**. You can always find stuff if you really want to, but most people don't care enough to."

Q "Fortunately, if there are problems, they're not major. Whereas at other campuses you sneak out to drink a beer or something, but at BYU it's like, '**Let's be rebels and go drink a Coke**.' Just kidding, it's not that bad!"

STUDENT AUTHOR: Due to the Honor Code, drugs are strictly prohibited and rarely seen or heard of. Students deeply appreciate the problems that are avoided by having a drug-free and dry campus and community. Due to the Mormon culture at BYU, it is unlikely that there would be drug or alcohol problems—even without the Honor Code.

20:1	Student-to-Faculty Ratio
93%	Freshman Retention Rate
27%	Four-Year Graduation Rate
39%	Financial Aid Applicants Receiving Aid

Students Speak Out
SAFETY & SECURITY

Q "BYU's campus is **pretty safe**, I guess. I know that if you ever have a problem walking home at night, there are blue boxes all over campus with a button you can push that calls someone to help walk you home. Honestly, though, I don't think that safety issues are a huge problem here."

Q "**I've never known of anyone or anything really bad happening** on campus, besides a stolen purse or something trivial."

Q "Provo has one of the **lowest crime rates** in the nation. BYU students participate in campus safety programs such as Safewalk, which makes sure that people don't have to walk home alone from campus at night."

STUDENT AUTHOR: Few campuses in America can boast the safety that BYU does. The Safewalk program is well designed and set up to make sure that students get home from campus safely late at night. Fellow students are friendly and look out for one another. It's the BYU way.

Questions?
For more inside information and survival tips, pick up College Prowler's full-length book on this school, written by an actual student! Check it out at *www.collegeprowler.com*.

Students Speak Out
ON OVERALL EXPERIENCE

Q "I had opportunities to attend other academically-prestigious schools, but I'm so **happy that I chose BYU**. However, I'm not sure I'd recommend it, unless you are comfortable with Mormons and our culture."

Q "I love BYU so much that I hate being home for the summer. I have had the opportunity to do a lot of things that I wouldn't have been able to do at other schools. BYU has even helped me to **spread my wings** to things I never thought I could do. I would never pick to be somewhere else, and I am glad that I chose to go to BYU."

Q "I have had a **really positive experience** here. I love the education, the students, and just the atmosphere, in general. I would never consider attending another university after being here."

Q "I've had friends transfer into here, and they say that it's **so much better** than where they were before. I wouldn't trade this experience for anything."

Q "I really do like it, and I wouldn't have gone anywhere else. The people and the atmosphere are great. **You will love it**."

STUDENT AUTHOR: A BYU experience is unlike anything else. The things that you will learn go far beyond what is taught in the classrooms, and the people that you will meet are exceptional. Researching the school, and being familiar with the rules and expectations of students, will make the transition smoother and help you get the most out of your BYU experience. If you decide that BYU is what you want, then jump in and enjoy it! You are in for a great and character-building experience.

Brown University

45 Prospect Street; Providence, RI 02912
(401) 863-1000; www.brown.edu

THE BASICS:

Acceptance Rate: 14%
Setting: Urban
F-T Undergrads: 5,790

SAT Range: 1330–1530*
Control: Private
Tuition: $36,928

Most Popular Majors: Social Sciences, Biology, Business, History, Visual and Performing Arts

*of 1600

Academics	A	Guys	B
Local Atmosphere	A-	Girls	B
Safety & Security	C+	Athletics	C+
Computers	B+	Nightlife	B+
Facilities	B	Greek Life	C+
Campus Dining	B-	Drug Scene	B-
Off-Campus Dining	A-	Campus Strictness	A-
Campus Housing	A-	Parking	C+
Off-Campus Housing	B+	Transportation	B+
Diversity	B+	Weather	C

Students Speak Out
ON ACADEMICS

Q "Because there is no core curriculum, you aren't typically forced into any bad courses. The skills and styles of teachers at Brown vary widely—as they probably do everywhere. But Brown does tell you to judge for yourself. The first several weeks of every semester is a '**shopping period**' during which you can try out as many classes as you can pack into your day."

Q "A lot of classes I have taken in my first two years have been taught by **graduate students**. You have to take initiative and go to office hours to get to know your professors."

Q "Almost every semester I have taken **at least one course that has had a profound impact** on my life."

Q "Brown has a **cross curriculum** with the Rhode Island School of Design; you can take up to four courses there for Brown credit."

STUDENT AUTHOR: At Brown, persistence and personal responsibility play a big role in defining the undergraduate career. Students are rewarded for learning to work within Brown's small and intimate academic departments. Many students come to Brown uncertain of their concentrations, and many switch their concentrations more than once in their undergraduate career. Brown's academic philosophy encourages exploration into new areas of study which can spark new interests or projects . . . Unlike other elite universities, Brown's primary focus is on undergraduate students.

Students Speak Out
ON LOCAL ATMOSPHERE

Q "Providence is **an ideal city for college**. The city is easily navigable, not overpowering, and still has plenty to do. Brown students have enough clout to influence city council elections. It's an easy commute to Boston, and weekend trips to NYC are cheap and easy. Less than an hour's drive gets you to at least three beaches in Rhode Island and Massachusetts."

Q "Personally, I can't imagine not going to school in a city. Brown is in the perfect location for a school. **It is on a hill, so it seems secluded**, but just walking down the hill puts you in the center of downtown Providence. Providence definitely has a city feel. There are always things to do and places to go. The Providence Place Mall, the largest mall in New England, is a 15-minute walk away."

Q "Providence is definitely a city that is on the up-and-up. There are art galleries and neat movie theaters—both **artsy, independent** foreign places as well as multiple theaters that show Hollywood movies."

STUDENT AUTHOR: Providence is a city, but it's not a big city. Sometimes the desire for the city to grow and incorporate new and exciting features is at odds with its efforts to maintain the small-town feel. If you want to go to a club one night, a museum the next day, a hip-hop show, and eat a few meals, you can cram it all into a weekend. And, of course, there is New York City and Boston, both easily accessible by bus and train.

5 Best Things	5 Worst Things
1 The New Curriculum	1 On-campus cable
2 The student body	2 The paltry endowment
3 Ruth Simmons	3 Long winters
4 Thayer Street	4 The meal plan
5 The College Greens	5 Providence parking laws

Students Speak Out
ON FACILITIES

Q "The athletic facilities aren't the greatest or the newest, but **they get the job done**. The computer labs are pretty good."

Q "**Nothing is crazy nice**. They are doing better jobs on newer classrooms, but most of the buildings from the '60s and '70s are pretty bad."

Q "The facilities are very nice. They're very state-of-the-art and **Ivy League-ish**. We don't have an official student center, but Faunce Hall acts as one, since it houses the Student Activities Office, the mail room, a mini-arcade, the Campus Market, and various other things."

Q "I participate in gymnastics and the facilities could use some attention. We're **donor funded**, so our facilities compared to other school's gymnastics facilities are not the best. But we can deal with it, we're fine."

Q "Brown **needs a better central place**, something like a student center or rec center."

STUDENT AUTHOR: Brown's facilities reflect student's needs; the average Brown student would tell you they spend much more time in the library than at the gym. Therefore, it makes sense that the libraries and computer centers are constantly renovated and updated, while other facilities may receive less attention. That being said, Brown is not completely lacking any facilities, but it is easy to see which interests are given priority. Compared to other Ivies, Brown's facilities are modest and reflect a degree of frugality . . . Most students have everything they need, though it may take them a little time to find it.

Famous Alumni

Todd Haynes, Charles Evans Hughes, John F. Kennedy, Jr., Laura Linney, Lisa Loeb, John D. Rockefeller, Jr., Duncan Sheik, Ted Turner

Students Speak Out
ON CAMPUS DINING

Q "The main dining-hall food is below average to **average cafeteria food**. Special snack bars are pretty good and give you good variety."

Q "**The meal plan rips you off**. The Ratty was disgusting. I was on the full meal plan. I'm definitely going off of it even though I'm living in a dorm without a real kitchen, which should tell you something. I think the V-Dub is a little better. Being off meal plan without a car might be a little difficult."

Q "I went to both cafeterias. I went to the Ratty more, but the **V-Dub is nicer**. The atmosphere at the V-Dub is nice; they play music, and it feels more like a restaurant. It's the same food no matter where you go."

Q "I was on full meal plan my freshman year. After that, **I switched to seven meals**. I was done [with the meal plan] by junior year."

Q "**I hated meal plan** when I was on it! The Ratty is the pits, but I hear it got better. The V-Dub is a better option. Josiah's and the Blue Room are better alternatives if you have points, and the Gate is a good place to get a piece of pizza."

STUDENT AUTHOR: From your first week on meal plan, you will undoubtedly enjoy meals with friends, meet lots of new people, and sing karaoke with your fellow Brunonians at the V-Dub. Good or bad, surviving meal plan freshman year is a defining experience and undoubtedly a right of passage . . . [Y]ou'll find the right balance of splurging for off-campus meals and eating creatively at the dining halls.

Student Body

African American:	7%	Male/Female:	48/52%
Asian American:	15%	Out-of-State:	95%
Hispanic:	8%	International:	7%
Native American:	1%	Unknown:	14%
White:	48%		

Popular Faiths: The majority claims no particular affiliation, but services are provided for all religions.

Gay Pride: The effort to promote queer politics and acceptance is spearheaded by the Queer Alliance. Twice a year, the organization hosts a huge dance that is among the most popular campus parties.

Economic Status: The average Brown student comes from the upper-middle class.

Students Speak Out
ON DORMS

Q "The dorms aren't bad, and many freshman rooms are **actually very nice**. As a freshman, everyone is assigned a roommate and a dorm, so you have no say in the matter. No matter what, housing is guaranteed all four years."

Q "Dorms are pretty decent. Some are much nicer than others, though. As a freshman, you'd want to be in **Keeney**—that's where most freshmen are, and it's located on the convenient side of campus."

Q "Don't worry if you get a so-called 'bad dorm' because **you end up bonding** with your dormmates over that anyway."

STUDENT AUTHOR: **Brown guarantees housing for four years if the student wants it. They also require students to live on campus for the first six semesters of their Brown career. Although many students complain about this policy, it makes life easier for rising sophomores and juniors, and relieves a lot of the stress between freshman and junior year. Despite complaints about the frustrating lottery system, Brown's housing system is better than most. A little finesse is all it takes.**

> **? Did You Know?**
> 80% of undergrads live on campus.

Students Speak Out
ON GUYS & GIRLS

Q "The **guys at Brown are a lot cooler** than the girls at Brown."

Q "We're certainly **hotter than Harvard** or Columbia. Dating depends on your clique. There's a lot of sex, but I don't know how many relationships there are."

Q "There are **two kinds of relationships** here: major serial monogamy and screwing a lot of people."

Q "I've met a lot of people that are socially **awkward**, but I think that's why we get along so well. It's funny when they all come together."

Q "Like everything at Brown, you have to be **persistent**."

STUDENT AUTHOR: **Students tend to agree that the admissions office did a fabulous job choosing enjoyable classmates, but they are a little more critical when it comes to sharing anything more than intellectual curiosity. The only real consensus is on the state of the dating scene: there isn't one . . . While this is a common complaint on Friday nights, the system is probably perpetuated because it suits the busy Brown lifestyle.**

Traditions

The Van Winkle Gate
Every student walks through the main gates of the University exactly twice in their undergraduate career. The first week of freshman year, the gates are swung inwards toward University Hall, inviting new University members to enter the Brown campus. Years later, upon graduating, the gates are opened out, ushering the grads back into the world.

Overall School Spirit
School spirit at Brown is strong, but it's not necessarily reflected by the turnout at athletic events or other school functions.

Students Speak Out
ON ATHLETICS

Q "**What's a varsity sport**? No, seriously, if you're looking for colleges where you can be a celebrity on campus because you are an athlete, then look elsewhere. My friends that are varsity athletes work very hard, and it is difficult for them to have social lives outside of their teams. Some of them end up dropping the team; others have a great experience so they stick with it and love their teammates and their sport."

Q "It can be **as intense as you want it** to be. There's a really great community of people who are athletically-minded but want something less intense than varsity but still highly competitive."

Q "A lot of **students just don't know** about Brown athletics at all. Only the biggest games are well attended."

STUDENT AUTHOR: **Brown is not an overly athletic school. Almost every student played some varsity sport in high school, but, for most students, academics and other extra-curricular activities come before athletics. However, there are a full range of varsity sports and less intense club and intramural sports.**

Students Speak Out
ON DRUG SCENE

Q "Most **Brown students are responsible** about drinking and drugs."

Q "If you want to find the scene, you can find it pretty quickly. If you don't want to, you can stay away from it. **People are pretty open** about their personal habits."

Q "Pot is the most used and accessible illicit drug at Brown. However, coke, acid, mushrooms, and ecstasy also seem to be around from time to time. **The scene is avoidable** if you so choose. I haven't really heard anything about heroin, which is a good thing."

STUDENT AUTHOR: **While you can guarantee some exposure to drugs, it is by no means a social prerequisite. There is enough to do at Brown and in Providence to stave off the boredom that makes the drug scene thrive at other less-entertaining schools. Many students drink and smoke cigarettes and pot casually. From there, the scenes are more obscure and are neither prominent nor hard to find.**

8:1	Student-to-Faculty Ratio
98%	Freshman Retention Rate
84%	Four-Year Graduation Rate
88%	Financial Aid Applicants Receiving Aid

Students Speak Out
SAFETY & SECURITY

Q "**My computer got stolen freshman year from my room**. I left my window cracked open, and someone crawled in . . . Still, I feel relatively safe on campus."

Q "I think that **there are certain areas off campus that you should avoid** when you are walking alone, but on campus, you don't have to worry about much."

Q "I never had a problem with security. They respond well when you lock yourself out of your room and don't hassle you too much when drinking is involved. However, you have to watch your back at night because **there have been a lot of muggings**, and security isn't everywhere. There has also been much dispute over arming Brown police with firearms."

STUDENT AUTHOR: **Brown students receive an alert by e-mail every time there is a major crime committed on campus or the University perceives a specific safety threat. Students should feel safe, but not be naïve about the threats that do exist in cities and on College Hill.**

> **Questions?**
> For more inside information and survival tips, pick up College Prowler's full-length book on this school, written by an actual student! Check it out at *www.collegeprowler.com.*

Students Speak Out
ON OVERALL EXPERIENCE

Q "Given the choice to do it over again, I would **definitely come to Brown**. Before I came to college, I never thought that the size of the school would be something really important to me. Now I know I would never want to go to a school that was any bigger."

Q "My biggest qualm about Brown is the fact that the University **doesn't have a large endowment**. I know a lot of programs are in danger of being cut."

Q "You really make Brown what you want it to be. There's not one social life that you have to lead. There's **not one academic life** or one extracurricular life either."

Q "Brown is an Ivy League school that places more **emphasis on the quality** of a liberal education than on the way they are perceived by other schools. Therefore, students at Brown are generally not competitive with each other; they do not feel the need to define their credibility by their GPA. Instead, Brown students are known for choosing to study what truly interests them, uninfluenced by economic or social pressures."

STUDENT AUTHOR: **Many students redefine and rediscover themselves in college, and Brown's biggest strength is that it promotes individual development and self-discovery over the course of the undergraduate career. Internally, you have a lot of chances to make mistakes, which the University calls "discoveries," in the course of your studies. It's easy to change your concentration in the fifth, or even sixth semester. Few people who choose Brown regret it. While it's not the school for everyone, almost anyone can find what they are looking for at Brown.**

Bryn Mawr College

101 North Merion Avenue; Bryn Mawr, PA 19010
(610) 526-5000; www.brynmawr.edu

THE BASICS:

Acceptance Rate: 49%
Setting: Suburban
F-T Undergrads: 1,266

SAT Range: 1820–2120*
Control: Private
Tuition: $35,700

Most Popular Majors: English, Political Science, Biology, Mathematics, Psychology

*of 2400

Academics	A	Guys	N/A
Local Atmosphere	B-	Girls	C+
Safety & Security	A	Athletics	C-
Computers	B+	Nightlife	B-
Facilities	B	Greek Life	N/A
Campus Dining	A	Drug Scene	A-
Off-Campus Dining	B	Campus Strictness	A
Campus Housing	A	Parking	C-
Off-Campus Housing	D	Transportation	C-
Diversity	B-	Weather	B-

Students Speak Out
ON ACADEMICS

Q "At a small school, **course selections can seem limited**. However, with options at Haverford, Swarthmore, and Penn, it's hard to complain."

Q "Professors are more like students. **They act as fellow learners** in the classrooms who can learn as much from you as a student as you learn from them as professors. They often invite students out for coffee or for dinner parties in their homes at the end of the semester, and they really make students feel important."

Q "Professors are, for the most part, **excellent, compassionate, engaging and brilliant** people. Teachers here treat you as intellectual equals and are willing to go out of their way to ensure that you succeed."

Q "I would say that the professors and classes I have been privileged to have at Bryn Mawr are **extremely intense**, but they have provided me with an invaluable, multi-faceted base of knowledge."

STUDENT AUTHOR: **Bryn Mawr is known for its strong academics. That said, your academic experience here really depends on your own interest in what you study, your own hard work, and more of your own hard work. Professors are typically characterized as helpful, encouraging, and enthusiastic, but you are pretty much also guaranteed to encounter several professors who are aloof or impatient. One unifying feature of the Bryn Mawr professor is his or her open door.**

Students Speak Out
ON LOCAL ATMOSPHERE

Q "Bryn Mawr is **a fairly boring suburb**. I spend most of my time on campus or at Haverford. I like Roaches, a local bar, and the Point, a local coffee shop and music venue."

Q "I love Bryn Mawr. Though **a mecca for Landrovers and Tiffany necklaces**, the mansions and crowded parking lots are part of the charm. There are a plethora of restaurants and coffee shops along with bookstores and bars."

Q "What I like is that there are a bunch of other colleges in the area, so it's pretty easy to meet and socialize with other students. **Haverford and Villanova are each five minutes away**, Swarthmore is about 20, and Penn is just a short train ride into the city. If I didn't have these schools nearby, as much as I love Bryn Mawr, I think I'd die."

Q "For a real escape, **Philadelphia is a great college town**. I highly recommend University City's used bookstores, West Philly's Ethiopian restaurants, pay-what-you-want day at the art museum, the Italian Market and Fairmount Park."

STUDENT AUTHOR: **Some students feel that the "little bit of everything" aspect of Bryn Mawr's location results in a whole lot of nothing. Philly is too far, Bryn Mawr and the mainline too suburban, and all the colleges in the area are too wrapped up in their own scenes, making them available, but not welcoming. When students overcome the shortcomings, they find that what the area does offer can make for some good diversion.**

5 Best Things	5 Worst Things
1 Timeless traditions	1 No guys
2 Honor Code	2 No diversity
3 Beautiful campus	3 Lack of parking
4 Inspiring professors	4 Guild closes at 2 a.m.
5 The administration	5 Lack of party scene

Students Speak Out
ON FACILITIES

Q "The facilities are gorgeous on campus, and hours are **pretty amazing** for the gym and all that. Also, as a dancer I enjoy being able to use the dance space without too much of a hassle."

Q "The student center isn't the most happening place at all times, but **nice to relax, study, or meet friends** if you want, and can also be a lot of fun when activities are planned."

Q "The Campus Center is **small but functional**."

Q "The gym is old and **needs to be modernized**. The buildings here are nothing compared to the wonderful facilities at the other seven sisters, but they're good enough!"

Q "The gym's great, though **it's inconveniently far from the center of campus**."

Q "**The Campus Center is used as the student center**, mail room, café and bookstore, and they are actually working on it to improve the living room area so that more students will use it to study."

Q "The dance studio is beautiful and **Thomas Great Hall is a wonderful place** to see a speaker or a concert."

STUDENT AUTHOR: Students are quick to gush about the school's architecture, but are quieter when asked about the actual facilities provided on campus. Sports teams, individual Mawrters, and some Haverford students frequent the fitness center to use its female friendly equipment, but all three groups demand more machines, especially for use at peak hours.

Famous Alumni

Julie Beckman, Edith Hamilton, Katherine Hepburn, Hanna Holborn Gray, Nettie Stevens

Students Speak Out
ON CAMPUS DINING

Q "I really like the food. Sure, it might be repetitive and limited, but **it's of good quality**. I was talking to Steve, one of the managers earlier this summer, and he said we might have kangaroo. Cool."

Q "The food is excellent. It's on a six week rotation. You do not eat the same foods that often. It is highly, **highly vegan and vegetarian friendly**. There isn't really anywhere else to eat but the dining halls."

Q "I thought **the food was really good** at the beginning of the year, but toward the end, I started to get tired of it."

Q "I love the dining hall food so much that I miss it when I go home. The options are always plentiful, and BMCDS does a wonderful job of mixing up the menus every once in a while with theme dinners. **Hours are good**."

Q "The sesame tofu soup and chicken fingers are **to die for**. I would choose Bryn Mawr just for the food."

STUDENT AUTHOR: Some Mawrters marvel over the quality and quantity of foods offered in the campus's three dining halls, while others argue that none of the choices offered by Dining Services are appetizing. Judging by the awards our cuisine has won, the food is not too shabby. Dining Services is giving students a few more options regarding how many meals you can pay for. Students are likely to continue to make the dining hall a popular place.

Student Body

African American:	5%	Male/Female:	2/98%
Asian American:	11%	Out-of-State:	80%
Hispanic:	3%	International:	8%
Native American:	<1%	Unknown:	0%
White:	73%		

Political Activity: Visibility of the Campus Democrats and Republicans varies year to year.

Gay Pride: Rainbow Alliance is an active club that attracts many freshmen. Drag Balls at Bryn Mawr and Haverford are popular.

Economic Status: The majority of students are middle- to upper-class.

Students Speak Out
ON DORMS

Q "The dorms are beautiful! If you have ever wanted to live in a palace, go to Bryn Mawr! There are **no cinderblock, cookie-cutter rooms** at BMC. Every room is unique and has its own history."

Q "I like the dorms. Sure there is the occasional bug, **sloppy bathroom**, or that two-week hesitation to turn on the heat, but it's the most social place going. I've loved my hall the last two years."

Q "Overall, **the dorms are clean**. Some of the rooms Bryn Mawr tries to pass off as freshman quads, though, should really not house more than three people max."

STUDENT AUTHOR: **For better or worse, everyone, from rambunctious freshmen to thesis-writing seniors, lives in one of Bryn Mawr's dorms. Occasionally, this creates abrasive situations, but far more often, this amalgamation leads to an atmosphere of beneficial social mingling and a strong, united community. Freshmen who do not specify a preference could wind up in any dorm, with none of the results being too disastrous.**

? Did You Know?
97% of undergrads live on campus.

Students Speak Out
ON GUYS & GIRLS

Q "The women at Bryn Mawr are **some of the most amazing people I will ever meet**. They are caring, funny, unique, independent, intelligent, confident and ambitious."

Q "I would not characterize Bryn Mawr as a 'lesbian school,' but there are quite a few girls who like girls on campus. But certainly, **the dating pool is much wider here**, if you like girls, than it would be at a coed institution."

Q "The **girls are hot**, until senior year when you get tired of them. And the drama."

Q "As is expected when you have over a thousand girls in one place, **there's a wide variety of personalities** and temperaments."

STUDENT AUTHOR: **Mawrters are not known for their beauty, but as long as puffy bags under the eyes and wrinkled clothes do not detract from attractiveness, there are a lot of very beautiful woman here. In fact, as a whole, Mawrters are a good-looking crowd. While no one spends very much time primping for class each day, those who completely neglect their personal hygiene stand out more than those who do not.**

Traditions

Athena
Students present gifts to the statue of Athena in return for good luck and wisdom.

Free Boxes
Each dorm has a box or space for students to deposit clothes or anything else that they want to get rid of.

Overall School Spirit
More apparent on a daily basis is "Department Spirit," demonstrated by department T-shirts and most students' excitement when talking about their major.

Students Speak Out
ON ATHLETICS

Q "Sports are **not very big here**. Many students play sports for the fun and exercise of it, but there are not many spectators and supporters at events."

Q "Due to the fact that **our athletic facilities are lacking in quality**, sports are not popular. Girls do not come to Bryn Mawr for the sports. We are in Division III. Academics take priority. We are always studying or feeling guilty for not studying."

Q "Girls don't put a lot of emphasis on sports, although I've been hearing that **the badminton team is amazing**."

Q "**Rugby games are always a good time** if you don't mind violence."

STUDENT AUTHOR: **The fact that sports are big here reflects a large student involvement, not massive crowds at games. Still, students who are involved in sports praise the coaches and play their sport with the same intensity that they devote to academics. Reasons for playing range from wanting to learn an exciting new sport to wanting to be part of a competitive team.**

Students Speak Out
ON DRUG SCENE

Q "There is **none that I perceive**. There is likely some recreational pot use, as there is at any university in the world. There is somewhat of a stronger drug culture at Swarthmore."

Q "I don't really know about a drug scene on campus. **Some students smoke pot**, and I have heard of some students' problems with harder drugs, but it's not really a part of the social scene for most Mawrters."

Q "The drug scene really centers on Radnor and is mostly pot. Around exam time, people seem to take **a lot of those ADD pills** to make themselves concentrate and do work—mostly seniors writing their thesis' I think."

STUDENT AUTHOR: **Any drug scene on campus is very low-key. There is hardly any visible drug use, though the scent of weed occasionally wafts through the dorms' halls. Radnor, formerly the only dorm that permitted smoking (but now smoke-free), and Brecon are considered the drug dorms.**

8:1	Student-to-Faculty Ratio
90%	Freshman Retention Rate
76%	Four-Year Graduation Rate
81%	Financial Aid Applicants Receiving Aid

Students Speak Out
SAFETY & SECURITY

Q "Safety services at Bryn Mawr are brilliant! You can do whatever you want, and **you're perfectly safe**."

Q "No campus could be safer! While firm and effective, Public Safety is very lenient of every Mawrter's idiosyncrasies. Public Safety is not the Big Brother on campus, **it is the Big Bro**—always looking out for Mawrters without intruding in our independence."

Q "Not only are we located where no danger is present, there is heightened security at all times, and campus safety is always developing better ways and **making more changes to keep us safe**."

STUDENT AUTHOR: **The disagreements about safety revolve more around Public Safety's role on campus than whether they generate safety on campus. With emergency phones aplenty, and lights keeping the most traveled night paths bright, the basic safety on this suburban campus is unarguable.**

Questions?

For more inside information and survival tips, pick up College Prowler's full-length book on this school, written by an actual student! Check it out at *www.collegeprowler.com.*

Students Speak Out
ON OVERALL EXPERIENCE

Q "I love it here. For a small liberal arts education, it is most assuredly one of the best and **the all girl situation is not all girls**. Guys from Haverford and Swat can take classes at BMC, and we can go to those schools."

Q "Bryn Mawr College offered me everything I wanted in one package: small-town life, big-city fun, efficient transportation, challenging professors and classes, travel opportunities, lots of learning and growing, skills for the future, **friendships that will last a lifetime**, and what might be the most stunning college setting with the most memorable traditions I've ever experienced."

Q "**Adjusting to Bryn Mawr was rough for me**. You have to actively seek a social life if you want one, and it is easy to isolate yourself here. However, the classes are amazing, the professors top quality, and the mix of students always keeps things interesting."

Q "BMC is **a hard place to be sometimes**. You will most likely be more than happy to be away from it when you graduate, but eventually, you'll appreciate it again."

STUDENT AUTHOR: **In the end, students are most proud of their academic work, but also fond of the school and experiences that they had here. Mawrters come to Bryn Mawr to benefit from the faculty and coursework the school is known for. Some women find the lack of boys on campus difficult to adjust to, or the general smallness of the campus undesirable, but in the end, most stay for the same reason they came: academics. When it's over, few look back on the decision with regret.**

Bucknell University

Moore Avenue; Lewisburg, PA 17837
(570) 577-2000; www.bucknell.edu

THE BASICS:

Acceptance Rate: 30% **SAT Range:** 1230–1400*
Setting: Rural **Control:** Private
F-T Undergrads: 3,492 **Tuition:** $37,934

Most Popular Majors: Social Sciences, Engineering, Business/Marking, Biology, English

*of 1600

Academics	B+	Guys	A-
Local Atmosphere	C+	Girls	B+
Safety & Security	A+	Athletics	B
Computers	B+	Nightlife	B
Facilities	A-	Greek Life	A+
Campus Dining	B	Drug Scene	B+
Off-Campus Dining	C+	Campus Strictness	C+
Campus Housing	B+	Parking	A-
Off-Campus Housing	B-	Transportation	C
Diversity	D-	Weather	C+

Students Speak Out
ON ACADEMICS

Q "In my opinion, the majority of professors at Bucknell **truly want to see their students succeed** and do well in their classes. I find most classes interesting, but I am uninterested in some of Bucknell's core requirement classes."

Q "It's great to have **published poets/fiction writers as your professors** and hear what they've written along with you in the class."

Q "The professors at Bucknell are some of the most accommodating people I've met. They are there to help their students improve upon their work and are **more concerned with their students' achievements** and positive progression through their course, rather than grading."

Q "I attended **a picnic for the physics department at a physics professor's house**. They just invited me along because I'm friends with some physics majors, and I spent the afternoon launching toy rockets and laughing with other students, physics professors, and their families."

STUDENT AUTHOR: **Bucknell's academic community truly is a community. If you're looking for a more intimate college atmosphere, Bucknell is a great school for you. Classes are small, so students have a voice and can express themselves during lectures and discussions. And while most schools are either described as workaholic schools or party schools; at Bucknell, there is a great balance that allows students to excel academically, graduate with a degree from a top university, and have a great time doing so.**

Students Speak Out
ON LOCAL ATMOSPHERE

Q "Bucknell organizes days where University students go downtown to help local businesses with planting and painting, which is a lot of volunteering and fun. Lewisburg is a nice little town and has **a lot of hidden treasures**, like Purity Candy and the Magpie."

Q "**The town is pretty weak for a college town**, but it could be worse. There are about three bars in town you can walk to and many restaurants a few blocks from campus. There are a few other universities within about twenty minutes, but there is very little mixing between the colleges."

Q "While it may seem like there's not a lot to do in Lewisburg, I'd disagree. A friend of mine wrote a year-long column for the campus newspaper entitled '**What to do in the Middle of Nowhere**.' She explored different museums, amusement parks, recreational centers, shopping, sports facilities, and more."

Q "The atmosphere is homey and comfortable, but not exactly exciting; there is far more entertainment on campus, and **the town is usually a place to run errands**."

STUDENT AUTHOR: **Students often say they wish they could pick up Bucknell's campus and community and transplant it closer to a city. It's an upscale town, and the main street, Market Street, is well-kept and safe. However, the economic differences between the academic community and the lower class is very obvious. Often, students see Amish and Mennonites shopping in the local Wal-Mart!**

Students Speak Out
ON FACILITIES

Q "The facilities on campus are **some of the nicest I have seen** on any college campus."

Q "The Langone Center, **our student center, is very nice**. It houses our bookstore, which offers plenty of Bucknell apparel, any items you need for class and even some toiletries and food. A lot of students will shop in our bookstore."

Q "Everything at Bucknell is modern, and a lot of money has been spent to keep the school **equipped with the latest technology**. The gym is unbelievable; many would consider it to look like a country club. A multi-million dollar athletic center opened in the last couple of years with an Olympic-sized pool, new basketball stadium, and gym. Most computers have flat screen monitors, and the computer technology is up-to-date."

Q "One of the best facilities on campus (that sometimes goes without mention) is the music building. It has **classrooms, practice rooms, and abundant storage space** for instruments."

Q "You could really go a whole year and **never once have to leave** the Bucknell campus."

STUDENT AUTHOR: **Most of Bucknell's facilities have recently undergone face-lifts. A fitness center, pool, and basketball stadium were finished within the last couple of years. The computers in the library and academic buildings are all very nice and new. However, there are a few buildings still in need of some help. It seems, though, that Bucknell is always undertaking some kind of renovation to improve the campus.**

Famous Alumni

Susan Sullivan Dunlap, D'Anna Fortunato, Edward Herrmann, Leslie Moonves, Philip Roth, Tim Williams

Students Speak Out
ON CAMPUS DINING

Q "The cafeteria is where I eat dinner; **they have different options** like Chinese food, stir fry, an ice cream bar, make your own pizza, and fajitas."

Q "**I can't complain about the food** on campus. The Bostwick dining hall (our cafeteria) is one of my favorite places to eat. It offers a wide variety of food for every meal, along with fantastic desserts and a constant choice of ice cream."

Q "The food on campus is good; **it's nothing special**, but definitely tolerable for college food."

Q "Compared to other campuses, the food at Bucknell is some of the best. The cafeteria has been renovated recently, and the **selection is rather impressive**."

Q "The 7th Street Café is great; it has really good coffee, live music on weekends, and muffins, cookies and biscotti. A lot of people go there to study, meet up with friends or study groups, or play chess. Some **professors hold their classes there** if the classes are small."

STUDENT AUTHOR: **The Bucknell Dining Services does an excellent job of providing students with a wide range of food. Bostwick has a pasta and pizza place, homestyle cooking, the Grill, Smart Market (salads, fruit, and vegetarian), the salad bar, Pacific Rim (stir-fry, egg rolls) the deli, and an egg bar. The egg bar is amazing. Many students will go for a long, extended meal with friends— perhaps just another way to put off their work! However, the food can get boring after awhile.**

Students Speak Out
ON DORMS

Q "The dorms are decent. Bucknell guarantees on-campus housing all four years, and because of that, there are many different dorms to choose from with many different qualities, but overall they are **all nice places to live**."

Q "McDonnell and Smith are two of the nicest dorms. I'd say that **Swartz, Vedder, and Larison are the worst**, yet they're always being redone, so by the time you read this, one of those might be the nicest."

Q "There is a distinction between **'uphill' and 'downhill' dorms**. If you are uphill, you are closer to the library and fraternity row. Downhill is closer to food and the 'downtown party' scene."

STUDENT AUTHOR: **Freshmen cannot choose what dorm they live in, but after freshman year there's a housing lottery. Still, Bucknell has very nice dorms for all class years. Probably the worst dorm, Swartz, is actually fairly nice according to many college students' standards. Many of the older, less popular dorms have been renovated recently, adding to their desirability.**

Did You Know?
87% of undergrads live on campus.

Students Speak Out
ON GUYS & GIRLS

Q "Bucknell has a freakishly vast population of beautiful people. A large portion of the student body looks like they just stepped **out of an Abercrombie & Fitch catalog**."

Q "I would describe Bucknell students as very preppy. Sometimes the school is referred to as the **'country club school of the east.'** Most people are from the New Jersey or New York area; a large population is from the West Coast."

Q "The **campus is so smiley**."

Q "Everyone on the campus is very intelligent, but somehow we manage to get **very attractive people** to come to our school. The guys are all preppy, and the girls are all skinny."

STUDENT AUTHOR: Most Bucknellians are very conscious about health and fashion and care about their physical appearance. Students report that it's strange to go back into the real world after a stint at Bucknell because it really becomes evident how unrealistic the standards of beauty are at Bucknell. On the downside, like many college campuses around the country, the issue of eating disorders is pretty common.

Traditions

First Night
The freshman class gets together to get the class flag, crest, and colors, and sing the alma mater.

Houseparty Weekend
An entire weekend of partying, occurring in the spring at the end of Greek Week.

Overall School Spirit
Because there is not a great deal of attendance at athletic events, school spirit is sometimes lacking—except for big events, such as Homecoming weekend and Midnight Madness.

Students Speak Out
ON ATHLETICS

Q "**We are a very athletic campus**. Pretty much everyone I know played at least one sport in high school, and many of us were captains of our teams in high school, although not all of them play a varsity sport now. Almost everyone I know has participated in one IM sport at one point, and club and IM sports are growing."

Q "Here's the perspective of someone who has never played a varsity sport at college: you hear them mentioned, but you can go your entire college career **without ever going to a single game**."

Q "A lot of people turn out for football and basketball games, but **Bucknell isn't really a sports-obsessed school**."

STUDENT AUTHOR: **There are many athletes on Bucknell's campus, as well as successful sports teams. However, since the school is small, there's not a significant amount of team spirit amongst fans. Still, individual students are very athletic, with most students participating in some kind of physical activity, whether it's a varsity sport, an IM sport, or just hitting up the gym.**

Students Speak Out
ON DRUG SCENE

Q "It exists, like on any college campus, but it's not like there are sketchy men waving you into back alleys. You'll read about the **occasional 'drug bust'** in the campus newspaper."

Q "Yeah, there are a lot of drugs around campus, but it is more of an **under-the-table kind of thing**. In certain circles, there is heavy drug use, but it's really not too bad."

Q "There isn't much of one, as far as I have seen. **We are a campus of boozers**, for the most part. A lot of people smoke pot, that's a fairly common thing to encounter, but I've never seen anything harder than that."

STUDENT AUTHOR: Just like most college campuses in the country, there's drug use at Bucknell, but it's certainly not very visible. Marijuana is fairly typical, but usually students will smoke it in privacy. There are some groups that are notorious for cocaine usage. Overall, though, if the typical Bucknellian wants to be under the influence, they're going to choose alcohol.

11:1	Student-to-Faculty Ratio
94%	Freshman Retention Rate
86%	Four-Year Graduation Rate
85%	Financial Aid Applicants Receiving Aid

Students Speak Out
SAFETY & SECURITY

Q "I've never been in a situation where I've felt unsafe at Bucknell. Anywhere you stand on campus, you can see a blue-light to call, and **Public Safety is patrolling 24/7**."

Q "While on campus and even in town, I feel extremely safe, since I know that Bucknell Public Safety and the Lewisburg Police both take their responsibilities very seriously. Plus, knowing that the town **does not have a high crime rate** at all and is not a very dangerous area is reassuring."

Q "Public Safety serves as Bucknell's 'police system.' They are on an enormous power trip. As for Bucknell, I feel **completely comfortable** walking around campus late at night."

STUDENT AUTHOR: Bucknell's campus is laid out in a manner that further isolates it, as the southern end of campus is lined with acres of cornfields, and the northern and eastern ends are surrounded by neighborhoods consisting of mostly upperclass students. Because the town is small, there isn't much crime.

> **Questions?**
> For more inside information and survival tips, pick up College Prowler's full-length book on this school, written by an actual student! Check it out at *www.collegeprowler.com*.

Students Speak Out
ON OVERALL EXPERIENCE

Q "I usually describe **my feelings about Bucknell as love/hate**. The thing I hate is the cliquey, exclusive institution of the Greek system and the unnecessary social divisions it creates at such a small school. I also hate the so-called 'Bucknell bubble,' wherein pretty much no one at the school knows or cares what's going on in the outside world, as well as the relative lack of diversity and cultural flavor that I was used to, growing up on the outskirts of a fairly large city. The things I love are the small classes, interested and interesting professors, beautiful campus, great parties, good concerts, and the genuine community feeling of the school—on any given walk across campus."

Q "I love the people I've met at Bucknell, and my academic experience has been **irreplaceable thus far**."

Q "I feel like the thought of transferring crosses each college student's mind at some point or another, but it was never a serious consideration for me. Bucknell has provided me with so many wonderful opportunities, and **I appreciate the possibilities offered here**."

STUDENT AUTHOR: Bucknell is a place where students can flourish both academically and socially in a small, supportive environment. Professors are deeply committed to the students and the students in turn seem to be genuinely interested in learning. The campus is breathtaking physically, though Bucknell may not be located in the hustle and bustle of a city, but Bucknell has is a very real sense of family—something that no city school could ever achieve.

Cal Poly

1 Grand Avenue; San Luis Obispo, CA 93407
(805) 756-1111; www.calpoly.edu

THE BASICS:

Acceptance Rate: 45%
Setting: Small city
F-T Undergrads: 17,843

SAT Range: 1080–1290*
Control: Public
Tuition: $15,213

Most Popular Majors: Engineering, Business, Agriculture, Architecture, Social Sciences, Art

*of 1600

Academics	B	Guys	B+
Local Atmosphere	B	Girls	A-
Safety & Security	C+	Athletics	C
Computers	B+	Nightlife	B+
Facilities	B+	Greek Life	C+
Campus Dining	C+	Drug Scene	B+
Off-Campus Dining	B-	Campus Strictness	C+
Campus Housing	C+	Parking	D
Off-Campus Housing	B	Transportation	B
Diversity	B-	Weather	A

Students Speak Out
ON ACADEMICS

Q "Most teachers at Poly put students first over research projects and other activities. Poly stresses the importance of quality teaching. **Classes are interesting** and engaging because of the teachers' dedication."

Q "Some teachers are okay, **some are not**. It's hard to tell sometimes, but a good guide is *www.polyratings.com*."

Q "Teachers **seem to be very educated** on the subjects. I have found some to be okay, while others I didn't get a memorable impression."

Q "As with any school, **there are a few bad apples**, but all of the rest are extremely dedicated and knowledgeable. Some of the professors here have become more than just my educators, they've become my friends."

STUDENT AUTHOR: **The quality of professors really depends on the department. The English department, for example, is known for its small class sizes and professors who will not only know your name but also be willing to help you with anything, even other classes! Overall, Poly professors tend to be down-to-earth, practical, and personable. Most are easy to approach and all have weekly office hours. This makes it convenient to discuss issues with your professor, even though you may have a full schedule and very little time. Throughout their four (or five or six) years here, students will generally form friendships with at least one of their favorite professors.**

Students Speak Out
ON LOCAL ATMOSPHERE

Q "San Luis is an amazing blend of college town and retirement community. People from all walks of life converge in San Luis. Being halfway between SF and LA, the convergence of techno-geek, and surfer dude, fast-paced, and laid-back is both fun and friendly. There isn't much pressure to conform to any one thing, so the **atmosphere is very tolerant and very comfortable**."

Q "I love the atmosphere. The **community is very peaceful**. You don't feel pressure to act or be a certain way. You can be yourself."

Q "SLO has a fun atmosphere, and of course, there is always stuff to stay away from anywhere you go. **Not too much to visit**, but enough to stay relatively not-bored."

Q "San Luis is a small town with some sophistication. The atmosphere is close and friendly. The **downtown is good to visit**, and there is nothing to really stay away from."

STUDENT AUTHOR: **Although SLO is a college town, it is also a tourist destination, so there are occasional tensions between college students, locals, and business people, but in general everyone gets along. The students, especially those used to large cities, are disappointed by the lack of pop culture activities available. Whether or not they are the athletic type, all students will end up trying some sort of physical activity, such as surfing or hiking.**

5 Best Things	5 Worst Things
1 Educational quality	1 Cost of books
2 The weather	2 Lack of any real diversity
3 The teachers	3 Campus police
4 Coastal location	4 No parking
5 Local atmosphere	5 Campus food

Students Speak Out
ON FACILITIES

Q "The health center is always pleasant and the doctors are great. I **have little to say that's bad** about the various facilities on campus."

Q "The facilities are great and **really convenient**."

Q "All of Cal Poly's facilities are **pretty clean** and loaded with resources."

Q "**Facilities are all good**, though the gym could be bigger. The UU is a really good place to do all sorts of activities."

Q "**Athletically, the school is amazing**. Basketball courts, volleyball courts, fully stocked weight rooms, racquetball, even Ping-Pong is available to all who want to participate. Classes are taught year-round on everything from yoga to fencing."

Q "Everything is **crowded**, but good."

Q "The gym on campus has great hours and **everything you need to stay in shape**. The athletic center is good."

STUDENT AUTHOR: The facilities open for use by all students (and therefore financed by everyone) are excellent. When it comes to individual departments, however, conditions vary. High-profile and profit departments like engineering and computer science, receive large donations, therefore are able to maintain their buildings. So, other departments seem to be living in the dark ages. The campus is covered with trees, green grass, and flowers. Since the weather is perfect, why be inside? Most buildings are at least efficient and serve their purposes well.

Famous Alumni

Robert "Hoot" Gibson, Mike Krukow, John Madden, George Ramos, Monty Roberts, Frederick W. "Rick" Sturkow, "Wierd Al" Yankovic

Students Speak Out
ON CAMPUS DINING

Q "The **food on campus seems good at first, but the novelty wears off quickly**. Some people began to wish for other options within a week. I managed to go nearly three months without wishing for my own cooking. I don't cook well. Most of the food wasn't exactly bad, just not really good. It gets monotonous after a while. Although it is more convenient than going to the supermarket, the campus dining experience is full of minor inconveniences."

Q "When living in the dorms, **campus dining is essentially all that is available**. On holidays, this may be restricted further, and you might not remember until it was too late. Of course, the best places to eat always have huge lines. If you do have to eat on campus, I recommend the Sandwich Factory. The food there mostly tastes good and isn't too overpriced."

Q "The **food is typical**. Not the best, but not the worst. Plus, you can always live on pizza."

STUDENT AUTHOR: Campus food is, well, campus food. Since everyone comes from different culinary backgrounds, it's impossible to please everyone. But, you become accustomed to it. There are many options to choose from. Freshmen are required to have a meal plan, but can choose from three. In each, there are a specified number of meals allotted each week. Campus dining also offers a meal plan for off-campus residents, but don't bother; it's more expensive to purchase the plan than to buy five meals with cash.

Student Body

African American:	1%	Male/Female:	57/43%
Asian American:	11%	Out-of-State:	3%
Hispanic:	11%	International:	1%
Native American:	1%	Unknown:	10%
White:	65%		

Popular Faiths: Christianity is the major religious force in the community.

Gay Pride: Cal Poly leaves a little to be desired in this area—there have been incidents where people have been harassed. However, it seems to be getting better.

Economic Status: Economically, Cal Poly is quite diverse.

Students Speak Out
ON DORMS

Q "I think it is good to experience dorm life. You meet a variety of different people in the dorms. It may lack some privacy, but is **definitely worth the friendships that you make** while living in the dorm."

Q "**Dorms are great**. After all, it is part of the whole college experience. I wouldn't want to live any other way. I have had so much fun and have met so many people."

Q "Something is always going on in the dorms. It's **hard to get a little peace and quiet**."

STUDENT AUTHOR: **Since dorm life is relatively crowded and not always pretty, it is tempting to upgrade to an off-campus apartment. However, living on campus is a must for social life. Those late-night chats in common areas about life and the universe will make your first year truly unique. Most of your friends will come from the hall you live in. Dorms at Poly are usually safe and clean, but also small and cramped. The bathrooms are adequate, but sometimes it feels like you've been placed in a minimum-security prison without privacy privileges. It's all part of the experience.**

> **Did You Know?**
> 22% of undergrads live on campus.

Students Speak Out
ON GUYS & GIRLS

Q "Poly's hottie ratio is one of the best on Earth. I swear every time I go somewhere fabled to have hot people, I just want to come home. The people are **amazingly friendly**. You can walk up to people and say hi and smile, and they'll say hi back."

Q "It doesn't matter if you are looking for a girl or guy, you'll find either to suit your taste. Everyone is really cool and **makes you feel comfortable**. This makes it easy to approach someone."

Q "Most people are **friendly**."

Q "The **guys are okay**. I think there is someone for everyone. I found mine, that's for sure."

STUDENT AUTHOR: **According to guys, most girls at Cal Poly are pretty good looking. If you're talking to girls, the guys are okay, mostly of all varieties. Good news for guys—most girls generally don't care as much about what guys look like, as long as they are showering and shaving. Weather here is usually warm, and a lot of skin is on display. The reality is that there is someone for everyone here. Someone will fit the type you are looking for.**

> **Traditions**
>
> **Egg Drop**
> Students compete to build the best "egg cushioner" from a selection of odd items.
>
> **Open House**
> On the specified weekend, clubs and colleges open up food and game booths.
>
> **Overall School Spirit**
> In all, Cal Poly students feel secure in the school's identity. Cal Poly has a healthy sense of school spirit.

Students Speak Out
ON ATHLETICS

Q "Cal Poly **sports are as big as you make them**. If you go and cheer with running thunder, you'll feel like sports are big on campus. A lot of people might tell you that Poly is missing some spirit and that our sports are a distant factor of the school, but I know so many people who play/cheer at/pay attention to sports on campus that it seems like a big part of my life anyway."

Q "I have to say that I don't think that sports is a big issue here at Cal Poly. I think **the focus is more on the classes**."

Q "Sports, in general, are **not a major priority** for Cal Poly students and administration alike."

Q "**IM sports** are quite popular."

STUDENT AUTHOR: **Poly is not exactly known for its athletics. It's not that Poly students don't care for athletics. In fact, they care most about playing them, rather than watching from the stands. Intramural sports are becoming increasingly popular. Let's face it, there are a lot of computer nerds here, and computer nerds as a group are generally not too excited about sports.**

Students Speak Out
ON DRUG SCENE

Q "I don't see a lot of drugs. Especially on campus, **alcohol is much more prevalent**, but I still don't think its use is rampant."

Q "Cal Poly has a 'no tolerance' policy in terms of drugs on campus. While **some people do get hold of and use drugs**, they're fewer than many other campuses I've been to. In general, marijuana is the most prevalent, but like most college towns, there is access to much harder stuff in the area."

Q "I really have no clue when it comes to illegal substances. I **haven't even seen any people with drugs**."

STUDENT AUTHOR: Like Greek life, the drug scene at Cal Poly only seems to be present if you want it. Students who have no affiliation with illegal substances are not at all likely to be approached or even exposed to drugs at all. People like to get drunk and have a good time, not drift into the twilight zone on something weird. Even then, peer pressure is minimal.

20:1	Student-to-Faculty Ratio
90%	Freshman Retention Rate
23%	Four-Year Graduation Rate
64%	Financial Aid Applicants Receiving Aid

Students Speak Out
SAFETY & SECURITY

Q "Campus seems really safe. Just don't be stupid, and don't walk alone at night if you're female. There are **police escorts available**."

Q "I tend to **feel pretty safe here**. With proper precautions, like anywhere in the world, I feel that San Luis and Cal Poly both are very safe places to live."

Q "It's **pretty safe** here. You just want to use common sense."

Q "Safety is fine. **Security staff is never seen**, except when people are skateboarding."

STUDENT AUTHOR: Security on campus is sufficient, but not exemplary. Most of the favorable comments about safety came from males. San Luis Obispo is certainly much safer than any large city, but be sure to use good judgment.

Questions?
For more inside information and survival tips, pick up College Prowler's full-length book on this school, written by an actual student! Check it out at *www.collegeprowler.com*.

Students Speak Out
ON OVERALL EXPERIENCE

Q "Poly has been a great choice for me. I plan to live in SLO after graduation if at all possible. The **teachers are good, the classes are fun** on occasion, and I have made some great friends. I keep convincing more of my friends to move to SLO and go to Poly."

Q "**Fun experience**. A lot of times, I wish I were at a more well-known school like UCLA."

Q "My **experience has been amazing** here, especially being a minority. I am happy at Cal Poly."

Q "Going to college here has been a great experience. San Luis Obispo is **a great town with a lot of outdoor activities**."

Q "Being at Cal Poly has been a good experience. I wish I had known that the **people were really friendly**."

Q "This school overall is good and **I like it here**. Be ready for something new when you come to college."

STUDENT AUTHOR: Any visitor would be hard-pressed to find alumni who are unhappy with their stay at Cal Poly. In fact, graduates tend to be very sentimental about their college days. The education is hands-on and prepares students well for professional life. So many people enjoy their stay at Cal Poly that they decide to settle down either in San Luis, or one of the adjoining cities. The overall student attitude is that the time at Cal Poly will definitely become some of the most memorable years of your life.

Cal Poly Pomona

3801 West Temple Avenue; Pomona, CA 91768-2557
(909) 869-7659; www.csupomona.edu

THE BASICS:

Acceptance Rate: 53%
Setting: Mid-sized city
F-T Undergrads: 15,925

SAT Range: 910–1150*
Control: Public
Tuition: $10,170

Most Popular Majors: Business, Engineering, Liberal Arts/General Studies, Architecture, Social Sciences

*of 1600

Academics	B-	Guys	B
Local Atmosphere	B-	Girls	B-
Safety & Security	B-	Athletics	C+
Computers	B+	Nightlife	A-
Facilities	B	Greek Life	C
Campus Dining	A-	Drug Scene	B
Off-Campus Dining	A-	Campus Strictness	A
Campus Housing	C+	Parking	D-
Off-Campus Housing	C+	Transportation	D+
Diversity	A+	Weather	A

Students Speak Out
ON ACADEMICS

Q "Psych teachers are awesome, except for a certain few, but the classes are really interesting. **The teachers are so down to help with projects** and give advice on what to study; also, many teachers are very approachable."

Q "I would have to say that **the professors at CPP, for the most part, are exceptional**. They truly care about the student, and are willing to really help you out if you need it. I especially like the professors and classes in my major."

Q "So far, I've mostly been doing just my gen eds, and a **lot of the teachers don't really seem to be into it**. I've had a few that really cared how well you did, though. I think it all depends on if you get lucky."

Q "I've had a lot of different kinds of teachers, but I've also been lucky enough to end up with awesome, caring teachers who'd go that extra mile to give you the help you really need. I've found quite a few of my classes very interesting. **I'm actually looking forward to quite a few of my upcoming core classes.**"

STUDENT AUTHOR: **The most important thing to be aware of is that Cal Poly Pomona is on 10-week quarters. Most general education classes range from 30 to 50 people, with the exception of those held in the lecture halls, which can hold a couple hundred (but this is rare). Also, don't be surprised if you are taking a communications class and it says you have an "activity" alongside with a class. CPP lives up to its motto of "learning by doing."**

Students Speak Out
ON LOCAL ATMOSPHERE

Q "**Pomona itself is a little quiet**, but you're minutes away from downtown Fullerton, and there's always Greek parties and restaurants in the area—ooh, and the 24-hour Wal-Mart! Woo-hoo for indoor football!"

Q "The atmosphere is very bland, with **very few things to do during the day**, but since it is in such a close area to many things, if you have a car, fun is just a few miles away. The beach, the mountains, the desert—everything is no more than an hour away."

Q "**Pomona is not really a college town**. It's a smaller town, but there are plenty of things within 15 minutes, and Hollywood isn't far—timing depends on traffic. There are a few junior colleges, like Mt. SAC and Citrus. Cal State San Bernardino and Cal State Fullerton are close by."

Q "Unfortunately, it is not a big college town. It is a commuter school; therefore, the majority of students **live at home or in apartments in nearby cities**."

STUDENT AUTHOR: **Pomona is a very rich city, full of various cultures, and it is close to everything that a college student would want, but Pomona in itself is not exactly the best city. It's far from a typical college town, and it's definitely not "the place to be" for college kids. When you are in Pomona, though, you are literally 45 minutes away from anywhere you could want to go: Huntington and Newport Beach, Mountain High ski lifts, Disneyland, Magic Mountain, Hollywood—everything!**

5 Best Things	5 Worst Things
1 Diversity	**1** Parking
2 Concerts put on by ASI	**2** Long lines for lunch
3 Hands-on classes	**3** Animal smells on campus
4 Free wireless Internet	**4** It's a commuter campus
5 Residential Suites	**5** No football team

Students Speak Out
ON FACILITIES

Q "The New Bronco Student Center is **probably the only updated facility**; other than that, a lot of the buildings are older."

Q "**Our Bronco Student Center is one of the best in the whole CSU System**. Several other universities visit the BSC to get ideas to improve their campus. This gives me a sense of pride about our campus that we are so fortunate to have such a reputable facility."

Q "The facilities on campus are usually kept up rather nicely. **The restrooms are always stocked with the proper necessities** and are generally very clean. The computer labs are nice and well-maintained. The student center on campus is very nice, considering it is basically brand new, but again, very nice with plenty of places to sit and relax."

Q "**The athletic centers are very convenient and have good hours**. They have nice areas for working out, as well as for cleaning up after a hard workout. The student center is one of the best places on campus. There are computers, meeting rooms, an arcade, food court, and a mini art gallery. It is a favorite place for many students."

STUDENT AUTHOR: The BSC is the most advanced out of all of the facilities on campus. As for the rest of the buildings on campus, they are average—nothing too exciting, just regular classrooms. Just about every building has at least one computer lab, and you can use it if it's open and no class is in session.

Famous Alumni

Robert Balzer (publisher of the *Inland Valley Daily Bulletin*), James Chick (of Chick's Sporting Goods), Carol Vaness (opera singer), Forest Whitaker (actor)

Students Speak Out
ON CAMPUS DINING

Q "If you are looking for a nice snack or a quick breakfast or lunch, **my favorite spot is the ENV Café**. The atmosphere is nice, the people are friendly, there's places to sit. They even serve toasted bagels and have doughnuts."

Q "U-Hour at Round Table is always a hotspot for Greeks. In the morning, a lot of people hang out at Carl's Jr. or up on the hill by the ENV Café. Sometimes there's a lunch truck that comes by in the morning, too. **Basically, if you need food, you're in good shape on campus**."

Q "Dining halls are very good for living on campus, especially since it's all-you-can-eat buffet style at the Los Olivos Commons. **The sandwich and salad bar is usually the safest bet**, and also the healthiest. Other food on campus is mostly fast food. The only place I'd recommend is Subway."

Q "The Commons are good at first, but **after a while, you really only have one favorite food**. Like, I would wait for a certain meal to be cooked that week. I usually just ate sandwiches. But that buffet style is what makes the freshmen fat, because you keep going back to get more!"

STUDENT AUTHOR: Eating on campus is the same as any other campus: you eventually get tired of the food because it's the same thing over and over again. However, the food in the Commons has gotten better over the years, thanks to Los Olivos. It's mostly buffet-style, with a variety of food to choose from. Once you find something you like, you'll probably stick to eating that.

Student Body

African American:	4%	Male/Female:	57/43%
Asian American:	28%	Out-of-State:	1%
Hispanic:	30%	International:	5%
Native American:	<1%	Unknown:	9%
White:	24%		

Popular Faiths: Many organizations on campus represent the Christian religion. Buddhism, Judaism, and Islam are represented as well.

Gay Pride: Since Cal Poly is such a diverse campus, the gay community receives a lot of support through organizations like the Pride Center and QSAFE.

Economic Status: Most students come from middle-class families.

144 | Cal Poly Pomona

Students Speak Out
ON DORMS

"The dorms are small, but it is what you make of it. **It's a great way to meet people**, and living on campus is very convenient. Encinitas and Montecito are nice ones."

"**The new dorms (the Residential Suites) are really nice.** The older ones are unrealistic in my eyes—way too small, and way too crowded."

"**Fitting three people in a living space made for two just sucks.** But if it's your first time in Southern California, or if you just want to meet new people, the dorms are the best place for it! I lived in the dorms for two years. It was bearable, but meeting new people made up for it, because I knew no one coming down here from 'Frisco."

STUDENT AUTHOR: The Residential Halls aren't exactly what you would call luxury living. Each room is anywhere from 165 to 184 square-feet, with two to three people crammed into each room—would you call this comfort? If you have an evil roomie, you're out of luck, because you have nowhere to escape to! But the upside of the dorms is that it's a great way to meet new friends and have the full college experience.

> **? Did You Know?**
> 9% of undergrads live on campus.

Students Speak Out
ON GUYS & GIRLS

"The girls are okay. **They all have different personalities.** There are a few hot girls, but it's not like you are at a modeling convention or anything. You gotta look for the good ones."

"My best friend and I have come to the conclusion that CPP guys are mediocre. In fact, even the girls are mediocre. Not that everyone is, but the vast majority is. **We call it 'the school of the mediocre.'**"

"Hot-looking men on campus are **just as rare as finding a good parking spot on Tuesday at 10 a.m.**"

"You're in a confined area with a large amount of people in your age group. **If you don't find hotties, you're not looking!**"

STUDENT AUTHOR: If you are looking for a campus full of blonde-haired, blue-eyed guys and girls, you aren't going to find them here! If you want to check out the good-looking crowd, you can look for them at the fraternity parties, but otherwise, you will probably have a few in your classes. It's been said that a lot of freshmen that come to CPP come single on purpose, so they can "start over" in the social department.

> **Traditions**
>
> **Bronco Fusion**
> An event to help new students get acquainted with the campus that provides food and entertainment.
>
> **Hot Dog Caper**
> Every October, thousands of hot dogs are given out to students to celebrate the new school year.
>
> **Overall School Spirit**
> The University and ASI try their best to promote school spirit by hosting events and handing out things like Bronco spirit bands, but it doesn't seem to make much of a difference.

Students Speak Out
ON ATHLETICS

"**I played IM volleyball and had a blast.** I met so many people through those games, and even from watching the other teams play. You'd see people you knew all over campus from one night of volleyball."

"**Varsity sports besides basketball seem almost nonexistent.** IM sports are pretty big if you have a big group of athletic friends who want to have a good time."

"We don't even have a football team, for crying out loud! **How do you expect to have a school with school spirit without a football team**? My theory is that if we had a football team, attendance at all other sporting events would increase, and Cal Poly's school spirit would rapidly increase!"

STUDENT AUTHOR: Since CPP doesn't have any school spirit to begin with, there really isn't any spirit shown at many sports games. The only sport that has somewhat of a crowd is basketball. The intramural (IM) sports are fun to get into if you aren't a pro but still want to play for the fun of it. It's definitely worth it to try and get on a team one quarter.

Students Speak Out
ON DRUG SCENE

Q "It is inevitable to have a drug scene on a college campus. Cal Poly's is not that severe. **It is mostly prevalent in small get-togethers** and parties. It is up to the student to partake in it or refuse."

Q "**Just like any other college, there are drugs on campus**—mostly weed. I've seen people getting high behind the dorms and off balconies in the Suites. It's nothing new. Students can make their own choices to do what they want. Do it if you want, don't do it if you don't want to do it."

Q "I hung out with a variety of people and never ran into hardcore drugs. I did meet a few people who smoked weed, but **it never happened on campus**. The risks are too high for a person that's pursuing their education to chance expulsion."

STUDENT AUTHOR: Besides weed, the most common drugs are the obvious: alcohol and caffeine. And it's been said that drugs like Ritalin and Xenadrine are used to stay awake during finals and midterms. This is a new trend that is unfortunately starting to catch on at campuses around the nation.

25:1	Student-to-Faculty Ratio
84%	Freshman Retention Rate
13%	Four-Year Graduation Rate
79%	Financial Aid Applicants Receiving Aid

Students Speak Out
SAFETY & SECURITY

Q "The security is not so bad. There are police that patrol the campus along with Parking Services. **There are also call-boxes around the parking lots you can use to call the campus police.**"

Q "At night when I get out of class, **I make sure to walk with someone to my car** or call for an escort from Parking Services. I don't feel safe walking by myself when it's dark out and there aren't many people around."

Q "**I still get scared at night because I don't see security**. All I do see are the blue-light emergency phones that you can run to, but you still have to wait for security. I do hope to see more security around. I wasn't this scared in the beginning until I heard about my friends getting robbed."

STUDENT AUTHOR: Safety-wise, University Police are pretty much on top of it. They have their own station on campus and are constantly patrolling the campus for any criminal activities. Escorts can also be called at night if you feel uncomfortable waiting for a shuttle or walking by yourself to your car.

Questions?
For more inside information and survival tips, pick up College Prowler's full-length book on this school, written by an actual student! Check it out at *www.collegeprowler.com.*

Students Speak Out
ON OVERALL EXPERIENCE

Q "I've had a lot of fun at school, and I've gone to visit friends at 'better' schools and really felt them to be overrated. Sure, it's not an Ivy League school, but **for what we have and what we pay, we've got the best school around**. I just wish we had more funding to be able to do more for the students and gain a better reputation."

Q "I like Cal Poly a lot. **Of all the Cal State schools, Cal Poly is the best**. The only thing that we lack is school spirit. If you are looking for one of those schools, I wouldn't pick Cal Poly. But other then that, Cal Poly is a good school."

Q "My overall experience has been terrible at Cal Poly. **The administrators are rude and very unhelpful**. The instructors I have had at Cal Poly have been pretty good, so I have no complaints about the instructors. My only complaint is about the administrators. When you have to deal with them, it is like dealing with the DMV."

Q "Overall, my experience at Cal Poly is one that I will always remember. **I enjoy Cal Poly's small tight-knit community**. The campus has a laid-back atmosphere that I've enjoyed these past few years."

STUDENT AUTHOR: CPP is a very kicked-back campus as far as students' ways of life go. We are in Southern California, and a lot of the students live up to the reputation of being mellow and relaxed (sometimes a little too much when it comes to going to class), but they still manage to crack down on the books when they need to. Many students come to Cal Poly Pomona not expecting to have a very good experience, but then it turns out to be everything they had hoped for in a college.

Cal State Northridge

18111 Nordhoff Street; Northridge, CA 91330
(818) 677-1200; www.csun.edu

THE BASICS:

Acceptance Rate: 69%
Setting: Suburban
F-T Undergrads: 23,166

SAT Range: 810–1050*
Control: Public
Tuition: $11,187

Most Popular Majors: Business/Marketing, Social Sciences, Liberal Arts, Humanities, Psychology, English

*of 1600

Academics	B-	Guys	B
Local Atmosphere	C+	Girls	B+
Safety & Security	B-	Athletics	C
Computers	B	Nightlife	B-
Facilities	B+	Greek Life	C+
Campus Dining	B+	Drug Scene	A-
Off-Campus Dining	B+	Campus Strictness	B
Campus Housing	B	Parking	D
Off-Campus Housing	B+	Transportation	D+
Diversity	A+	Weather	A-

Students Speak Out
ON ACADEMICS

Q "**Each teacher has their own style**. Basically, we have a little bit of everything. Professors that become your friend and others that become your worst nightmare. I think that it depends on the individual to keep the classes interesting. If you motivate yourself to learn something new every meeting, then that'll pay off."

Q "Teachers are cool, depending on who you get. **There are good professors, and there are bad professors**. Use www.ratemyprofessor.com to help you out. As for classes, if it sounds boring, it's probably going to be boring."

Q "The professors at CSUN are very nice. **They engage in conversations with students**, they will meet students during their office hours, they have compassion for their students, and they are willing to help them in every way possible."

Q "I have been at CSUN for three years, and so far, **all of my teachers have been really nice and understanding**. They have done their best at trying to make the class exciting and interesting, and most of them have succeeded."

STUDENT AUTHOR: **All professors, with a few exceptions, teach their classes, and they maintain a small student-to-teacher ratio. Although general education classes average about 45 people, upper-division classes shrink to about 20 to 30 people. Most of the professors take roll, but you won't hear students complaining, because the majority take school seriously. Many teachers call for group discussion, so be ready to participate.**

Students Speak Out
ON LOCAL ATMOSPHERE

Q "I live in Northridge, and CSUN is the only college around, except if you go into Los Angeles. **There isn't too much going on around CSUN**. You might want to go into the city for some action."

Q "The atmosphere is pretty laid-back. There is a lot to do in the area. There are many museums to visit in Los Angeles, and Universal Studios is close by. **There are also many clubs to go to in Hollywood**. I like Clockwork Orange on Friday nights at 7070 Hollywood Boulevard. The crowd is really nice and relaxed."

Q "**Northridge is not a college town**. I wish it was. CSUN is more of commuter school, so a lot of the students are just here for classes. CSUN is close to a lot of fun cities. It is 15 minutes from Westwood, and it's close to Hollywood, Santa Monica, and Malibu."

Q "The local atmosphere is **rather progressive and diverse**. The nearest universities, Pepperdine and UCLA, are about 25 miles away."

STUDENT AUTHOR: **For the most part, CSUN students agree that Northridge lacks the youth and edginess of a college town. However, in many ways, the town has shaped itself around the college and its students. For example, most of the bars in town offer a college night, and most restaurants offer a student discount. Since there are a limited number of college hangouts in Northridge, it's best to go to LA to party every once in awhile.**

5 Best Things	5 Worst Things
1 Wireless Internet	1 Parking
2 The events	2 Lack of school spirit
3 The weather	3 Printing costs
4 Diversity	4 Campus cliques
5 The library	5 Commuter campus

Students Speak Out
ON FACILITIES

Q "**The facilities on campus are nice**. They are in the process of finishing up the new student union. There is a new parking structure in the works, and everything just looks nice and clean."

Q "The library, computers, and the athletic facilities are nice. **Sometimes, it tends to get crowded in the Matador Gym**, because of the men's and women's basketball, and the playoffs for men's and women's volleyball teams."

Q "The facilities that I have used have all been nice. The only thing is **they are slightly crowded**, but they are always trying to get new things."

Q "**I really like the photo lab that just opened** because I am a photography student. I think CSUN needs to step up on providing materials for their art students."

Q "The facilities on campus, the ones I have visited, are nice. I like them because **they are very clean and organized**. And the staff is very helpful."

STUDENT AUTHOR: CSUN is only a 50-year-old campus. When put into perspective, CSUN is a very young school compared to most, and since the earthquake in 1994, almost everything has been rebuilt. The downside is that there tends to be a considerable amount of construction. CSUN's fitness center offers the typical gym activities including cardio machines, weight machines, free weights, and an aerobics room, but nothing super impressive. Although CSUN doesn't have a movie theater or bowling alley on campus, the surrounding area makes up for it with four theaters and two bowling alleys close by.

Famous Alumni

Richard Alacron, Stephen Bollenbach, Robert Englund, Barbara Fairchild, Larry Feldman, Bill Griffeth, Mark Lester, Linda Lingle, Jeri Taylor

Students Speak Out
ON CAMPUS DINING

Q "The food is great. **The Sierra Center is fab**! The pub is also really good, and so is Subway if you want to eat fresh."

Q "I like the variety of food choices on campus. **The variety of restaurants reflects the diverse student body** and the culturally diverse community of Los Angeles. You can eat Chinese, Japanese, or Mexican, plus the convenient mercantiles are so helpful. They stock everything you need, but don't have time to stop and buy at a market. They stock everything from beef jerky to Advil to disposable cameras. It's awesome."

Q "We have **a wide variety of food on campus**, a sports bar-type place just opened up so that could be a fun place to hang out. We also have a Jamba Juice, and a Burger King."

Q "The truck by the parking structure across from the education building is really good. **Try their chicken caesar salad**."

Q "**The food is grub, but not very healthy**. The few healthy selections don't taste very good."

STUDENT AUTHOR: With the addition of the Sierra Center, students can use their plan to eat a variety of food. The majority of eateries are on the south side of campus, so if you are taking classes in the education building, art building, or business building, your only options are vending machines or the Mercantile store that doesn't sell the healthiest of foods. Also, a disappointing factor in CSUN's meal plan offerings is that you can't use your meal plan anywhere off campus.

Student Body

African American:	8%	Male/Female:	43/57%
Asian American:	8%	Out-of-State:	2%
Hispanic:	28%	International:	6%
Native American:	<1%	Unknown:	19%
White:	31%		

Popular Faiths: Christianity, Islam, Buddhism, Catholicism, Judaism are the most prominent faiths.

Gay Pride: CSUN has a very relaxed vibe. This makes CSUN a very tolerant atmosphere where you will find all types of people comfortable with who they are.

Political Activity: Although many students at CSUN are apathetic, you can usually find a political group assembling on campus.

Students Speak Out
ON DORMS

Q "The dorms suck. **They charge during months that you do not live there**. They overcharge, they are dirty, unfriendly, people vomit in the elevators, and people are rude. RAs are pretty rude, and you can't get out of a lease."

Q "The dorms are **probably the nicest dorms in the University System**. They are pretty new. They were designed as two-bedroom apartments (which is much better than the closets most universities put you in). Most of the dorms have a full kitchen as well."

Q "I do not like all the dorms because **there are too many stupid kids**. Stay away from any rooms that face the parking lot because you will hear alarms all night long."

STUDENT AUTHOR: **One of the most exciting aspects about living on campus is the apartment-style housing of the dorms. All rooms have a large bathroom, two large bedrooms, kitchen, TV room, and dining area. Many students agree that the dorms lack that social buzz that carries throughout many other university dorms. However, this makes the dorms a more study-friendly environment.**

> **Did You Know?**
> 8% of undergrads live on campus.

Students Speak Out
ON GUYS & GIRLS

Q "**There are a lot more girls than guys on this campus**. And in my opinion, there aren't that many attractive people in this part of California."

Q "The guys are hot. **They are the emo/skater-type boys**. The girls are good-looking, too."

Q "What I love about CSUN is that **there are people from all over the world**, and from different ethnicities. It provides such a great variety of people to meet. There is a little bit of everyone, very good-looking, so-so, and others. The girls are cute, too."

Q "I think **too many girls dress like they are going to a club**; it's ridiculous. But most of the people I meet are fairly mild mannered, so it is easy to get along with people."

STUDENT AUTHOR: **Considering that Northridge is only a half hour from Hollywood, you can bet many CSUN students take their appearances to another level. Not all CSUN students pay attention to trends, though. There are as many types of people at CSUN as there are clothing stores on Melrose including surfers, skaters, scenesters, valley girls, bad asses, musicians, preps, jocks, and the girl/boy next door.**

Traditions

The Big Show
Five years strong, this free concert event is one of the most popular at CSUN.

Bull Pit
A group of student fans, who stand the entire game and cheer the CSUN athletes.

Overall School Spirit
CSUN students may love their school, but have mixed feelings when it comes to showing their school spirit. Although most students wear their CSUN sweaters, not many people actually attend games.

Students Speak Out
ON ATHLETICS

Q "Now that I got myself involved in AS and the Greek community on campus, **I realized that we have some good team**s like our men's basketball team, track and field, men's volleyball, and girls' water polo."

Q "**Intramural sports are a little more popular than varsity sports**, but mostly with the fraternities and sororities."

Q "When it comes to IM sports, **they are fun if you are in a fraternity or sorority** because there is always a rivalry going on."

Q "**We don't have a football team**, that pretty much sums it up; although, the basketball teams seem to be pretty good."

STUDENT AUTHOR: **Despite CSUN's success as a Division-I school, not many students attend the games. Certain teams are more popular than others. The men's basketball team has their faithful Bull Pit made up of students who attend every game and stand the entire time yelling obscenities at the other team, and turning their back when the opposing team enters the court. But most teams don't receive the same recognition.**

Students Speak Out
ON DRUG SCENE

Q "The campus is not big on drugs, but then again, it all depends on the people you hang out with. **You can always find drugs everywhere**, no matter if you are at CSUN or another school."

Q "**I don't think drugs are a big problem**. I think there is a lot of drinking in the dorms, but I think that is how college dorms are, and I know it can be a lot worse on other campuses."

Q "Not enough people do drugs here. It's depressing. I am from a small hippy town, where my entire high school class were a bunch of stoners. Now I am here, and everyone is about work, work, work. **Chill out and pass the J, Northridge**—or at least get drunk every night or something."

STUDENT AUTHOR: **If CSUN students are using drugs other than caffeine, alcohol, or tobacco, then they pretty much keep it to themselves. Although it's probably not impossible to search for people using drugs, drugs don't have a large, outspoken following that CSUN students are aware of.**

23:1	Student-to-Faculty Ratio
75%	Freshman Retention Rate
10%	Four-Year Graduation Rate
60%	Financial Aid Applicants Receiving Aid

Students Speak Out
SAFETY & SECURITY

Q "I feel okay at school. **I would like it more if those on-campus escorts would just leave me alone**. I guess I don't want them to ask me if I need to be walked to my car."

Q "I don't think the security is very high. **My car was broken into twice** while parked in the dormitory parking structure, and the police did nothing but take down my information. I think for such a huge parking lot they should at least install cameras."

Q "**I barely realized how great our security is at CSUN**. I stumbled upon this realization after I stupidly locked my keys in my car. Campus security came and got my keys out in less than 20 minutes. Plus, they also offer a service to jump-start your car if your battery dies."

STUDENT AUTHOR: **CSUN's security network has a strong presence on campus. CSUN also hires and trains students to become CSOs (community service officers). At night, the CSOs close down all but two entrances to the dorms, and request that students show their housing ID card to enter.**

Questions?
For more inside information and survival tips, pick up College Prowler's full-length book on this school, written by an actual student! Check it out at www.collegeprowler.com.

Students Speak Out
ON OVERALL EXPERIENCE

Q "**I come from a Big Ten university, and I wish I were still there**! The size of classes and the weather at CSUN is more desirable. It's hard for a transfer student who lives off campus to meet people because people aren't very friendly. But if you just want to go to school, then it's the place for you."

Q "I enjoyed my experience at CSUN. If you like a beautiful landscape and wearing flip-flops and tank tops in January, then CSUN is the place for you. **It's close to the beach, mountains, and downtown**. It's really a homey place."

Q "I like CSUN because it is close to my house, and **I feel I received a good education**."

Q "I guess it's been a growing experience. I've stopped messing around with my life and got serious. **At times, I wish I were somewhere else**, but I don't dwell on that. There isn't a perfect place out there, you just deal with your situation and make the best out of it. As for now, Northridge is a good fit. It can be as tough, as easy, as fun, as academically intense, and as costly as you want it to be."

STUDENT AUTHOR: **CSUN is a commuter school, meaning that most students live at home and commute to school, and because so many students are native to the area, they are not compelled to meet new people and participate in school activities. Years later, many of these commuter students say that the school lacks a social scene and they wish they had moved away from home to go to college. On the other hand, other CSUN students move from small, rural towns to go to a college in the city, and they absolutely love the campus.**

Caltech

1200 East California Boulevard.; Pasadena, CA 91125
(626) 395-6341; www.caltech.edu

THE BASICS:

Acceptance Rate: 17%
Setting: Suburban
F-T Undergrads: 913

SAT Range: 2150–2350*
Control: Private
Tuition: $31,437

Most Popular Majors: Engineering, Physical Science, Mathematics, Biology, Computer Science

*of 2400

Academics	A+	Guys	C
Local Atmosphere	B+	Girls	C-
Safety & Security	B	Athletics	D+
Computers	A+	Nightlife	C
Facilities	B	Greek Life	N/A
Campus Dining	B	Drug Scene	A
Off-Campus Dining	A-	Campus Strictness	A-
Campus Housing	B	Parking	B
Off-Campus Housing	C	Transportation	C
Diversity	B+	Weather	A

Students Speak Out
ON ACADEMICS

Q "The professors try to be nice, but because Caltech is heavily research-oriented, it's very obvious that most **professors consider teaching as a secondary job**. This shows in their lack of enthusiasm towards the class and lecturing skill. Having visited other colleges and sat in on classes, there are a markedly higher number of professors who can teach well in such a way as to help students understand. In the professors' defense, there are some that do actually try and have interesting and challenging courses."

Q "It's the grad student **TAs that are the real problem**. Most professors are happy to talk to the students, and generally helpful. I suggest you talk to them, ask them questions, and ask them to write you recommendations for stuff."

Q "The teachers at Tech are **undoubtedly brilliant**; they just don't teach very well."

Q "The teachers are decent. They're very smart, but they're not always the best at explaining the concepts that they teach (especially in the lower-level classes). Also, some of them can be **exceptionally mundane**, while others are phenomenal speakers."

STUDENT AUTHOR: Caltech has a rigorous academic program having much to do with the brilliant teaching faculty. Still, many professors are research scientists first and teachers second, creating a conflict of interest. In these cases, TAs can oftentimes be more useful than professors, especially in large classes.

Students Speak Out
ON LOCAL ATMOSPHERE

Q "The actual city of **Pasadena is pretty varied**. We have trendy spots (such as Old Town), run down parts (such as Northern Pasadena), and yuppie parts (like the homes around South Lake, near the Rose Bowl, and near the Huntington Gardens)."

Q "I like Pasadena a lot, but I wouldn't want to walk through it by myself at night. I would advise staying away from fast food places (like Carl's Jr.) on nights, since the **homeless and crazy locals** tend to accumulate there in the evening hours."

Q "**Trader Joe's is awesome**! Everyone should also visit the Orean Health Express and partake in yoga at Bikram's Yoga College of Pasadena. Furthermore, I strongly encourage patronizing the Equator Café in Old Pasadena."

Q "Old Pasadena is the main influence on the city. There's **Pasadena City College**, PCC, which is located about a block away from campus, but you'll want to avoid it at all costs. The people are more attractive than your average Techer, but they're too stupid to carry on any sort of conversation."

STUDENT AUTHOR: Caltech is in an affluent section of Pasadena, neighboring large estates and expensive houses. Attractions include the Rose Bowl and the Rose Parade, as well as tons of coffee shops. It is also a mere 30-minute drive from the California coastline. Malibu, Puma, and Ventura beaches are all easily accessible if you have a car or the money (and patience) for public transportation.

5 Best Things
1 Tight-knit campus
2 Honor Code
3 Research
4 Location
5 IM sports

5 Worst Things
1 Lots of work
2 Campus gossip
3 Social awkwardness
4 Scheduling
5 Professors

Students Speak Out
ON FACILITIES

Q "The facilities are well maintained in all aspects. **The gym is small**, and not the most fully-stocked location on campus, but it's clean, has good architecture, and serves its purpose. The houses are best described as unique."

Q "Kitchens are nice; their service is pretty quick. Some of the **lecture halls are a little old** and have uncomfortable seats; your lower half gets numb after a while. The undergraduate dorms are a bit old, but they are a lot of fun to live in."

Q "Lots of library space to study in the Fairchild Library. The extra space can be very useful. The SAC is good; **Coffeehouse, movie room**, and lots of club rooms."

Q "Caltech has a very nice gym—not grand, but nice. **Student centers are lacking**, though. There aren't very many of them. We students pretty much make our own student centers in the dorms."

Q "Facilities are alright, though they're **nothing to brag about**."

STUDENT AUTHOR: **Caltech's facilities offer two gyms with plenty of space and a complete set of weight lifting machines, three large swimming pools, and a track. Some houses (dorms) have hot tubs or trampolines, which are always fun and way cool. The Student Activities Center (SAC) has tons of stuff for students to do, and houses a general screening room for movies and TV, as well as pianos and practice rooms for musicians. In addition, there are numerous small libraries and three coffee shops on campus, one of which is student-run.**

Famous People from Pasadena
Octavia Butler, Julia Child, Sally Fields

Students Speak Out
ON CAMPUS DINING

Q "Food on campus is very good. It's usually all-you-can-eat, served by student waiters. That said, the board plan is **pretty expensive**. It's convenient for the first couple of years, but believe it or not, you mature a lot by having to eat out or cook with friends."

Q "Chandler is pretty good; unfortunately, there are no dinners. Avery is okay, but not much good vegetarian stuff—the **veggie burritos and quesadillas are horrible**. I really hated house food. The vegetarian bar is always nasty mushy green or brown stuff which just looks scary and inedible. And generally, there just isn't much choice."

Q "Food is overpriced, but there's **always something healthy to eat**. On-campus eating gets monotonous after a while. One thing is for sure, you will never go hungry."

Q "Many **entrees are unidentifiable**, especially the vegetarian stuff. The on-campus convenience store isn't open past 1 a.m., and it is incredibly overpriced. The student-run Coffeehouse food is pretty greasy, and it's also overpriced."

STUDENT AUTHOR: **Caltech is a small campus with four dining hall equivalents. There's the South Kitchen, the North Kitchen, Avery, and Chandler. Dinners are comprised of family-style sit-downs at a meal table in each dorm. Students work as the wait staff. The school also has two cafés, (Red Door and Café at Broad) and a convenience store. There is also a student-run [place], Coffeehouse.**

Student Body

African American:	<1%	Male/Female:	69/31%
Asian American:	38%	Out-of-State:	65%
Hispanic:	5%	International:	9%
Native American:	<1%	Unknown:	4%
White:	43%		

Popular Faiths: Caltech has a Jewish Community, a Muslim Students Association, and other religious groups, but the school is predominantly Christian.

Gay Pride: There are several gay organizations on campus, including PRISM, Lambda, the LA Gay and Lesbian Scientist group, and more.

Political Activity: The Caltech voter's association encourages and helps students to vote.

Students Speak Out
ON DORMS

Q "The South Houses are incredible. They are heavily customized, have murals everywhere, a large number of singles, sinks in each room, porches, balconies, well-equipped kitchens, and oh yeah, **they're also falling apart**. For example, the roof in Dabney's Alley leaks."

Q "In my opinion, they are great. They aren't the cleanest of structures, but they're a great social community. The south houses have some of the most **interesting architecture** I have ever seen. They are even considered historical buildings."

Q "Avery is good for people who want **peace and quiet** but still want to go to their house to socialize (or not). The building is new, there's good air conditioning in the rooms, and everything's very nice."

STUDENT AUTHOR: **Caltech housing is its own breed. All houses have their own traditions, murals, slang, and somewhat of a stereotypical personality attached to them, but people in all the houses intermingle in class and otherwise. The bad part is that some of them were built during the Hoover administration and are extremely outdated.**

Did You Know?
90% of undergrads live on campus.

Students Speak Out
ON GUYS & GIRLS

Q "Men are generally too interested in commitment and lose in the numbers game. Accordingly, women are fairly disinterested in commitment and spend time thinking about things like getting a PhD. In too many relationships, women realize they have control of the situation and take advantage of it, developing a boy-toy. **Neither sex is generally experienced** at relationships."

Q "The people here are really great. A lot are very nerdy, especially a lot of guys. The girls are generally less girly, as far as caring about their looks or salivating over boys. The **girls definitely do not tend to backstab** one another."

Q "**Most of the guys are antisocial trolls**. I didn't know we had girls at Tech."

STUDENT AUTHOR: **The gender disparity on campus is a focal point for much discontent—the school has about three times as many men as women. Guys complain about how women here are not primarily concerned with dressing to impress, but instead worry about graduate school and publishing papers. Some of the girls complain about men who don't seem to shower on a regular basis or guys who don't talk about anything but science.**

Traditions

Ditch Day
Underclassmen barricade seniors' rooms on senior skip day, and seniors attempt to distract them with elaborate puzzles and activities.

Rotation
This is the week-long meeting of freshmen and upperclassmen at the begging of the school year.

Overall School Spirit
Athletically speacking, students seem apathetic. However, students are enthusiastic about Caltech in research areas or if a professor wins a Nobel Prize.

Students Speak Out
ON ATHLETICS

Q "For IM sports, which we call **interhouse sports**, we usually have around two to three games a week in sports that change throughout the year. The popularity varies a lot among houses. A couple houses have been pretty diehard about it, and one or two will sometimes go planning to win but will have to forfeit for lack of players."

Q "We literally **lose at least 90 percent** of our intercollegiate games."

Q "We're NCAA Division III. In other words, sports really aren't a big deal. It's a big thing if any of our teams goes over .500, but if you're interested in playing varsity sports, for most teams, **anybody can join**. Since we're such a small school, the teams are looking for players whether you've even played the sport before or not."

STUDENT AUTHOR: **Though Caltech doesn't have a football team, there are many sports for men and women, intramural and intercollegiate. The difference here is that sports are rarely a high priority. This can be advantageous—those who are on the sports teams play for fun, and there is no pressure to win. The downside? There aren't any playoffs.**

Students Speak Out
ON DRUG SCENE

Q "Alcohol is present, and smoking **marijuana is available** to a much smaller extent. Other drugs are not very pervasive or seen much, although I doubt they're not hard to find if one was interested."

Q "People are **too busy with schoolwork** to do drugs."

Q "I would say that drugs are not too common on this campus. The only thing I've ever seen is weed, but even that is pretty uncommon. People here do **like to get hammered**, though!"

Q "Almost **nobody smokes** cigarettes."

STUDENT AUTHOR: Like every college campus, Caltech has some drug use. Drugs certainly are not an integral part of Caltech culture, though. Some students drink or smoke pot, but there is no peer pressure to try drugs. There are students who have never had a drink before, and many who abide by the law and do not drink until they are over 21.

3:1	Student-to-Faculty Ratio
96%	Freshman Retention Rate
82%	Four-Year Graduation Rate
86%	Financial Aid Applicants Receiving Aid

Students Speak Out
SAFETY & SECURITY

Q "On campus, things are pretty safe, but it's still best to take precautions because people have been **accosted near campus**."

Q "**Stealing can be a problem**. Don't leave stuff in the hallways, even though the houses are on combo (combination), it's not safe! People leave the doors open or give combos to random people a lot, and not all of the doors work."

Q "Security and safety on campus is very good. I haven't had anything stolen, and security people have always been very friendly and helpful. I once noticed a security officer following me and my friend back to our dorm at about 10 p.m. It's things like that that **make me feel safe** on campus."

STUDENT AUTHOR: Pasadena is one of the safest cities in California; the crime rate is extremely low compared to LA or San Diego. Caltech security guards are also friendly and very helpful. They roam the campus in golf-cart-like things and give people rides across campus if they need them.

Questions?
For more inside information and survival tips, pick up College Prowler's full-length book on this school, written by an actual student! Check it out at *www.collegeprowler.com*.

Students Speak Out
ON OVERALL EXPERIENCE

Q "**Caltech is hell** only because the work is ridiculously difficult, and it's made me hate a lot of subjects that I formerly loved. Don't ever think it'll be any different for you because everyone here was exactly like you in high school . . . valedictorian, perfect student who loved learning, never met a person smarter than them. Don't get me wrong, though. I'd rather be here than any other place in the world."

Q "**I'm pretty happy here**. The combination of a small school with nice weather and challenging academics is a good fit for me. Sometimes I wonder if I would be happier at a larger school with more activity choices, but in the end, I think the intimacy of a smaller school is a better match."

Q "This is one of the most depressing places you will ever go to. Sorry to say it so bluntly, but it is. When you meet upperclassmen, you will find almost everybody is bitter and depressed in some respect. **Bitterness and depression** will generally set in around the middle of sophomore year. This is all because of the workload and the ridiculous things professors have you do sometimes."

STUDENT AUTHOR: Although students here complain about the workload or lack of sleep (and girls), students are generally happy. They know what they are getting themselves into before they come—a top-notch education for the price of a few years of insanity. Many students know they could not find the camaraderie, traditions, research experience, opportunity to meet famous scientists, and hundreds of people who are interested in math and science anywhere else.

Carleton College

1 North College Street.; Northfield, MN 55057
(507) 646-4000; www.carleton.edu

THE BASICS:

Acceptance Rate: 27%
Setting: Rural
F-T Undergrads: 1,983

SAT Range: 1960–2240*
Control: Private
Tuition: $37,860

Most Popular Majors: Economics, Biology, English, History, Psychology

*of 2400

Academics	A	Guys	C-
Local Atmosphere	C	Girls	C-
Safety & Security	A-	Athletics	B
Computers	B+	Nightlife	B-
Facilities	B+	Greek Life	N/A
Campus Dining	C+	Drug Scene	B-
Off-Campus Dining	B+	Campus Strictness	A
Campus Housing	B	Parking	C-
Off-Campus Housing	B	Transportation	B-
Diversity	C+	Weather	C-

Students Speak Out
ON ACADEMICS

Q "The teachers are, for the most part, entirely **devoted to teaching** and their students. In many classes, they encourage students to take an active role in classes."

Q "Classes are interesting if you choose the right ones. I've had some phenomenal profs and **some who are terrible** by my standards, but my guess is that they're not terrible by more universal standards; they're okay."

Q "**While I struggled** during my freshman and sophomore years to find those small liberal arts professor-student relationships you expect coming into the school, in the last year or so things have really started to come together. Meaning, if you seek a closer relationship with a professor, it's definitely there."

Q "Most teachers are quirky; class is all right. There's **a lot of learning going down**."

STUDENT AUTHOR: The professors here get to know their students. They know their stuff, and they're passionate about their work. This can lead to impossible homework assignments and endless amounts of papers, but there's a reason for all of it. The professors never cease to challenge or lower their expectations for any of their students. Classes are rarely all lectures; they usually revolve around group discussion. Needless to say, you'll be challenged at Carleton, but you'll also have fun—even if you average more than one all-nighter a week.

Students Speak Out
ON LOCAL ATMOSPHERE

Q "Northfield isn't the most exciting of places, but it does have **its own bit of charm**. Carleton's desolate, rural Minnesota location actually works to the school's advantage in that the people choosing to come here are coming for the school itself. Northfield adds to Carleton's quirky atmosphere, and people embrace it as a result."

Q "Northfield is small and can get confining, but it's quaint. **Stay away from St. Olaf**—there's a semi-good-spirited, long-standing cross town/river rivalry, so people mainly talk a lot of smack."

Q "Northfield sucks. The 'historic downtown' is full of craft stuff, and things are overly neat and expensive. **There's no club scene**, college bar scene, or cheap alcohol. The town has an elitist attitude towards other small towns, so you don't get the All-American townies and shotgun holes in the speed limit signs."

Q "There's not much to say about Northfield; **not the best place ever** (unless you like small towns). St. Olaf is just across the river; however, there's little to no contact with them."

STUDENT AUTHOR: Northfield is a small town. You get a quaint feeling as you walk downtown and see family-owned businesses. Known as the town of "cows, colleges, contentment," Northfield is a classic slow-paced Midwestern town that has its fair share of little quirks and eccentricities. While students generally get along with the townies, there have been some disagreements between Carleton students and Northfield residents.

5 Best Things	5 Worst Things
1 Malt-O-Meal smell	1 The football team
2 Traditions	2 The cold weather
3 The library	3 Musser
4 The alcohol policy	4 The food
5 Burton	5 The Frisbee obsession

Students Speak Out
ON FACILITIES

Q "All of the facilities on campus are very nice. The **Rec Center is very modern** and can host a wide variety of activities. The computer labs have new computers and are also very nice."

Q "I think the facilities are mediocre. The Rec Center is great, and the computer facilities are good. **The student center is adequate** but not exciting, and people don't make much use of it."

Q "The grounds seem to be kept up well during the fall and spring. Aside from that, most of the facilities **don't leave much impression** either way. Except for the smoking lounge. That place is kept up well and will be around forever."

Q "They're **not bad**. There's no hot tub or outdoor pull-up bar, though."

Q "The Rec Center is the bomb. The student center could use some **more cool things in it**, but the snacky-poo (the Snack Bar) is always on point."

STUDENT AUTHOR: Far a small campus, Carleton has plenty of unique facilities to go around. The Rec Center is tremendous. You can play all the free pool and ping pong you want in the Great Space, and you can go swimming at the pool in West Gym. Carleton makes sure to keep all of its services up to date and modern. Computers in the public labs are recycled for faster models every couple of years. Science labs are never lacking, and all classrooms have access to overhead computer projectors and television sets. As far as facilities go, Carleton puts your $36,000 tuition to good use.

Famous Alumni

Paul 'Doc' Evans, Jack Carson, Michael Armacost, Peter Thorkelson, Barrie Osborne, Jane Hamilton

Students Speak Out
ON CAMPUS DINING

Q "Food on campus is somewhat lacking. Marriott provides more food than a person should eat. **It's not always good**, but lately things have improved. The Snack Bar offers a reprieve from the monotony of dining hall food."

Q "The dining hall food **leaves much to be desired**."

Q "Food is okay. The dining hall takes some getting used to, but once you learn how to eat there, East, at least, is pretty good. **The Snack Bar is terrible**. The junk food they serve there is exciting for about a term, and then it gets gross."

Q "I know many people like to complain about the food at Marriott, but I don't think it's all that bad. At least we have **a fair number of choices** for every meal."

Q "The dining halls are not great but provide the needed sustenance. No one comes here for the food, and almost **everyone complains about it**."

STUDENT AUTHOR: Carleton has two dining halls, Burton and East. East is a fairly new facility and serves more than 60 percent of the campus; Burton is older and caters mostly to Burton, Sevy, Davis, and Musser Hall residents. The food isn't terrible, but it won't knock your socks off, either. Any food that's not home cooking gets repetitive and stale after a while. The food that Marriott serves is definitely heavy and high in fat, but they do a good job of offering vegetarian options and a salad bar. The biggest problem with campus dining is its ridiculous prices.

Student Body

African American:	6%	Male/Female:	48/52%
Asian American:	9%	Out-of-State:	71%
Hispanic:	4%	International:	5%
Native American:	1%	Unknown:	0%
White:	75%		

Popular Faiths: Religious interest clubs include the Carleton Christian Fellowship, Jewish Students at Carleton, and the Reformed Druids of North America.

Gay Pride: Carleton is a very tolerant community in general, and this doesn't change regarding gays and lesbians.

Economic Status: The majority of students are wealthy.

Students Speak Out
ON DORMS

Q "Most of the dorms are very nice. I've seen lots of dorms at other colleges, and **one could easily do worse**. Goodhue is pretty far away from the rest of campus and is slightly isolated for that reason."

Q "All the dorms are a lot more spacious than any room I saw while visiting larger state universities. It's also nice to know that **if you want campus housing it's available to you**, no matter what year you are."

Q "The dorms are all right for the most part. Burton is the place to be, and **the newer townhouses are quite nice** to live in if one gets lucky enough."

STUDENT AUTHOR: **Carleton has an interesting set of dorms. This is the building block for social life at Carleton. Many students that shared a floor find themselves getting houses together as seniors. For freshmen, the dorms provide an opportunity to get involved with their community. The only complaint from upperclassmen is that freshmen stay up all night in the hallways playing UNO.**

> **Did You Know?**
> 82% of undergrads live on campus.

Students Speak Out
ON GUYS & GIRLS

Q "This is the **ugliest campus in America**. Bar none. Enough said. But we'll make money when we grow up, so that's a plus."

Q "The appropriate answer to this question would be no. There are **some who are very hot**, but personality is really the big thing with students at Carleton, not hotness. If you try too hard to look good, it's likely people will call you a tool or a slut."

Q "Girls are not hot. Repeat: **girls are not hot**."

Q "Third year and not a single Carleton girlfriend. It's best for the college that **I plead the fifth** on this one."

STUDENT AUTHOR: **The biggest stigma about Carleton is the non-attractive students. Carls are in the red end of the ugly alert. However, the longer you're at Carleton, the hotter the campus becomes. Whether these are the "Carleton goggles" or your parameters for attraction have simply readjusted, by the time you leave you'll have a new understanding of having a personality.**

> **Traditions**
>
> **Mai Fete**
> Every Wednesday night during Spring Term, there is a party thrown by the seniors on Mai Fete Island on Lyman Lakes.
>
> **Rotblatt**
> Carleton's famous all-day softball game/kegger, which is curiously named for '70s Chicago White Sox relief pitcher Marvin Rotblatt.
>
> **Overall School Spirit**
> Students are proud to say they go to Carleton, and no one is ever ashamed of wearing Carleton's maize and blue colors.

Students Speak Out
ON ATHLETICS

Q "I don't feel like there is too much emphasis on sports. **We are a Division III college**, so school is always first, but professors and coaches are also very understanding. It's a nice balance."

Q "Women's basketball. 'Nuff said. **Everyone plays Frisbee**. Other IMs are very popular."

Q "IM sports are pretty huge. **Varsity sports are pretty small**. The nice thing about that is if you want to stay active, you can almost certainly find an IM team you can play on. IMs are a lot of fun."

Q "The **talent in the IM basketball league** is like that in the NBA Development League."

STUDENT AUTHOR: **For a Division III academic school, varsity sports aren't a big draw. It's difficult for Carleton to field competitive teams because the academic standards are so high. There are a few varsity teams that capture the hearts of fans, the women's basketball team continually holds a top ten national ranking, and the women's swimming and cross country teams sent athletes to the U.S. Olympic team in Athens. On a down note, the football team loses more than it wins.**

Students Speak Out
ON DRUG SCENE

Q "Some people choose to smoke dope; those people also **choose to be losers**."

Q "I'd say it's strong to very strong. There's lots of pot, a little less mushrooms, and occasional spurts of cocaine. **People stay high** without much problem. In fact, you could conceivably smoke weed everyday and never buy any—there are just that many smokers."

Q "We are not a dry campus, enough said. There's also **a fair amount of marijuana**. Other drugs are harder to find."

STUDENT AUTHOR: **Drugs seem to linger in the background at Carleton. There's rarely anything harder than marijuana present at parties. That isn't to say that pot doesn't play a role in defining the campus infrastructure. There's not an overwhelming presence of drugs because it's very difficult to do and keep up your grades. Those that smoke weed excessively or get into harder drugs usually find themselves failing out by the end of the year.**

9:1	Student-to-Faculty Ratio
95%	Freshman Retention Rate
87%	Four-Year Graduation Rate
64%	Financial Aid Applicants Receiving Aid

Students Speak Out
SAFETY & SECURITY

Q "Carleton is **very safe**. I don't fear walking alone at night. Security is there, and they'll protect you if something goes wrong. Otherwise, they're in the shadows; they're not intrusive at all."

Q "Security is really cool. **They don't hassle people** about anything, they're only there for our protection, and they react quite quickly when called."

Q "Security is lax, but that's because it can be. **Campus is a safe place**, and the freedom that results is nice."

Q "I can't recall **ever feeling unsafe** here."

STUDENT AUTHOR: Not many students at Carleton feel that safety and security is an issue. Northfield is a small, family-oriented town and there's a very low crime rate. The campus is safe and well-lit. The biggest problem is bike theft, usually by people too lazy to walk from one class.

Questions?
For more inside information and survival tips, pick up College Prowler's full-length book on this school, written by an actual student! Check it out at www.collegeprowler.com.

Students Speak Out
ON OVERALL EXPERIENCE

Q "I love Carleton. I feel as though this is a place where one can study really hard during the day, and then relax and party with your friends that night. **Carleton is very challenging** and also very rewarding."

Q "I don't wish that I had gone anywhere else, though I take every chance I get to **visit other schools**. Most things that are lacking here are able to be resolved some way or another."

Q "Carleton is **exactly the right place** for everyone who comes here, only nobody is willing to admit it."

Q "Mostly, **I'm glad I'm here**. It's a small place, so it's not too hard to get claustrophobic or sick of the social scene. But the people are wonderful, the academics are great, if a bit limited in scope, and Minnesota's an interesting place to be, especially if you come from either one of the coasts."

STUDENT AUTHOR: **Given Carleton's high percent retention rate, it's pretty evident that Carls are satisfied with their school. Most people are surprised at how accepting other students at Carleton are and how easy it is to make friends, no matter who you are. As long as you're accepting and understanding, you'll get along just fine. The main reason why people usually end up choosing Carleton is its academics, but the main reason they stay is because of the people. Unlike at larger schools, you will not get lost at Carleton unless you make a conscious effort to do so. Sure, the academics are stressful, but the friendships and life experience you'll gain at Carleton is invaluable.**

Carnegie Mellon University

5000 Forbes Avenue; Pittsburgh, PA 15213
(412) 268-2000; www.cmu.edu

THE BASICS:

Acceptance Rate: 28%   **SAT Range:** 1310–1510
Setting: Urban   **Control:** Private
F-T Undergrads: 5,645   **Tuition:** $38,430

Most Popular Majors: Engineering, Visual and
Performing Arts, Business, Computer Science

*of 1600

Academics	A	Guys	C
Local Atmosphere	B+	Girls	C-
Safety & Security	B	Athletics	C+
Computers	A+	Nightlife	B
Facilities	B-	Greek Life	B
Campus Dining	C	Drug Scene	B+
Off-Campus Dining	A-	Campus Strictness	A-
Campus Housing	B	Parking	D-
Off-Campus Housing	A-	Transportation	B+
Diversity	A	Weather	C+

Students Speak Out
ON ACADEMICS

Q "The quality of education depends on your major, I guess. From the few classes I've taken in H&SS (Humanities and Social Sciences), I think the University's humanities department isn't that great—at least, the introductory courses aren't. If you're into a technological field, then the school is not bad. The computer science program is not bad at all. The teachers usually know what they're talking about, unlike most other places. Regardless, **it really depends on your major**."

Q "Professors tend to be **better as you get older**. Unfortunately, there are a lot of teaching assistants and lower-level professors who speak in strong accents and make things difficult."

Q "Teachers and academics are awesome! If you come here, you'd better be serious about learning, because you will get swept away if you aren't. Pretty much everything we do here is good. All of **our sciences kick butt**, and our drama and theater programs are really exceptional, too. We are cool like that; we have both nerds and artists. It makes things interesting."

STUDENT AUTHOR: It often feels like CMU is just a school with brilliant students struggling to get by in a never-ending onslaught of hard work . . . That said, CMU professors run the gamut from "I'm a pioneer in my field" to "I'm teaching this class so I can do research here." One thing that can be said about all the professors, though, is that they're very approachable.

Students Speak Out
ON LOCAL ATMOSPHERE

Q "One thing that sucks is that stuff tends to close really early around here. I don't get it at all, but it's true. Besides that, we have the Steelers, the Penguins, and the Pirates not even 10 minutes away by car. Museums, downtown, and Kennywood's roller coasters are all really close. **You can always find something** cool to do."

Q "I like Pittsburgh. It's a **nice medium-sized city**. I think it's beautiful because of the mountains and rivers, and I find enough to do here . . . We also have a big park adjoining our campus."

Q "There are **tons of museums** around campus, if you're into that kind of stuff. My favorite place to go on the weekends is the Waterfront. They've got shopping, great restaurants, and a huge movie theater."

Q "Yeah, **there are tons of other universities** present . . . but chances are, if you are at CMU, you won't have any desire to socialize with these people anyway. Most likely, you'd prefer a quiet evening of staying in your dorm room and gaming online with your friends. Go to a Pirates game because the stadium is sweet beyond words."

STUDENT AUTHOR: Allegheny County may be one of the most elderly counties in the nation, but that doesn't make Pittsburgh any less of a college town. During the school year, you can't go wrong walking down Forbes or Fifth Avenue—chances are you'll stumble upon some concert, restaurant, party, or bar. There are always activities going on.

Students Speak Out
ON FACILITIES

"The UC is a place to come hang out, but as of right now, there's **not too much to do** there besides relax and eat."

"Mostly everything on campus seems to be **newly-remodeled**. Since we have such a big computer department at our school, computer companies fight to give us computers. We have brand-new Macs and IBMs in all the labs. The gym is pretty nice, but if you are a hardcore athlete and you work out a lot, you may have to wait for a machine once in a while."

"I think the facilities are pretty nice. There is **always construction** being done on campus because they're always trying to improve what we have. The architecture is a little weird, but it's huge, new, and inviting. Computers are always state-of-the-art, and I swear that there are more of them than there are students."

"The computer places are good. I've never used the athletic stuff, although they seem decent for a fairly un-athletic school. Part of CMU's problem is that it doesn't have one main gathering area for students to meet and build a student community. Therefore, **school unity suffers** and the school becomes segregated into cliques which mingle on occasion."

STUDENT AUTHOR: **The University Center is the focal point of campus life at CMU. It contains numerous eateries, a gym, basketball court, and meeting rooms. It's also a great place to just sit and chill between classes. On the whole, the campus is aesthetically pleasing.**

Famous Alumni

Ted Danson, Holly Hunter, Vinod Khosla, Rob Marshall, Andy Warhol, John Wells, Ming-Na Wen

Students Speak Out
ON CAMPUS DINING

"The food sucks. The school has made a huge effort to diversify the selection of food, and in the process has made it **so confusing and crappy** that being on the meal plan is a hassle. You look forward to the times of day when you don't have to eat at the irritating establishments around campus. The meal plan is of poor value, overly complicated, and worst of all, it's very unsatisfying because the food is always too greasy, too bland, too overcooked, or too weird. . . . The best dining on campus is the selection of vans parked next to Posner Hall—there's Chinese, Thai, Greek, and Indian. It's all fresh and fairly tasty and at a very good value."

"If you come, **get as few meal plans as possible** with money to spend wherever . . . [M]ost people skip some meals and have a lot of their weekly plan leftover by Sunday. It doesn't carry over, so I bought a giant pack of orange juice the last day because I had so much left over that I needed to spend it."

"**Food is okay**. If you are a vegetarian, you may have some qualms, but check out Si Señor. I ate there every night my freshman year.

STUDENT AUTHOR: **All but the most optimistic students have problems with campus dining. The most disappointing thing about eating on campus is the small amount of food you receive for the high price you pay. The food isn't all bad. For freshman year, the meal plan is bearable, but after that, most students stay off campus when grabbing a bite to eat.**

Student Body

African American:	5%	Male/Female:	61/39%
Asian American:	24%	Out-of-State:	77%
Hispanic:	5%	International:	15%
Native American:	<1%	Unknown:	11%
White:	40%		

Popular Faiths: There are a lot of Christian groups. Most religious activity takes place off campus.

Gay Pride: The campus is very accepting of its gay students and has on-campus student groups such as SoHo, CMUout, ALLIES, and SafeZone. However, like most of CMU's student body, the sizable gay community is relatively quiet.

Economic Status: Most seem to have wealthy parents.

Students Speak Out
ON DORMS

Q "I lived in Donner Hall my freshman year and had an on-campus apartment sophomore year. I loved living in Donner. At first, I was wary of **community bathrooms**, but it was actually pretty cool, because Donner's where I met my best friends."

Q "Morewood and Mudge are nice because they are coed and near the fraternity quad. Donner looks **good on the inside**, but it's pretty ugly on the outside; it's coed as well. Stay away from the Hill dorms: Boss, McGill, Hamerschlag, and Scobell."

Q "In general, the **dorms are decent**. There aren't many singles, so get used to the idea that you're going to have a roommate."

STUDENT AUTHOR: **Most students are thankful for their experience in the dorms and feel that they wouldn't have adjusted well to life at CMU without it. As a freshman, you'll want to live in first-year housing, as it provides a social atmosphere among the most affable students. This means living in Morewood E-Tower, New House, Donner, or some of the all-freshman floors in Mudge.**

> **Did You Know?**
> 64% of undergrads live on campus.

Students Speak Out
ON GUYS & GIRLS

Q "It's not that hot both ways. There are lots of **'freaks and geeks'** . . . Attractive girls are in extremely short supply, but they have quite a choice due to the . . . male/female ratio."

Q "During my freshman year in the computer science department, there were more guys named David than there were girls, period. I wouldn't say that the majority of the girls are 'hot,' but there are **plenty of good lookers** if you know where to go. You are better off 'sightseeing' down the street at the University of Pittsburgh."

Q "A lot of **people tend to stick to their own** . . . [I]f you're decent-looking where you live now, then your attractiveness multiplies by 10 here."

STUDENT AUTHOR: **CMU students will unabashedly tell you that their campus is not an attractive one . . . The lopsided male/female ratio is hard for both sexes, but especially for the guys. All the physical praise for CMU's artistic students isn't unfounded; most of them are pretty fine. Many of the students studying less technical fields are actually pretty normal-looking.**

> **Traditions**
>
> **Bagpipes**
> CMU has a strange and storied tradition of bagpipe-playing.
>
> **Buggy**
> Buggies are small, cylindrical push carts that students race around the campus streets during Carnival, CMU's spring festival. They are piloted by a "pusher" and steered by the driver, a female student who is situated within the buggy. Students prepare all year.
>
> **Overall School Spirit**
> Students are usually contain more stress than school spirit. Individual majors/schools often see more unity.

Students Speak Out
ON ATHLETICS

Q "Varsity sports aren't very big; we're **Division III**. I think IM [intramural sports], on the other hand, is huge. I'd say about 75 percent of the campus plays some sort of IM sport."

Q "**What varsity sports**? If you love sitting in the bleachers with your friends and cheering on the football team, Carnegie Mellon is not for you."

Q "**IM is much bigger than varsity**. CMU is hardly a school for jocks, but it is good for people that just want to have some fun. There's some nice competition. There's even a golf course basically on campus."

Q "What? We play sports here? You mean the chess team or the **ping-pong club**, right?"

STUDENT AUTHOR: **Varsity sports may feature competitive play, but their popularity falls short when compared to the enormous success of intramural sports on campus. If you've always dreamed of coming to a college where you could cheer the football team to victory every weekend, you need to go down the street about half a mile to the University of Pittsburgh (or become a Steelers fan).**

Students Speak Out
ON DRUG SCENE

Q "I don't think that many kids at CMU use drugs, but the ones who do have **enough money** to hit the scene hard."

Q "It's there, but it's not rampant. The only drug use I personally encountered was people out in the dark smoking pot. **You can certainly avoid it** if you want to."

Q "**If you look hard enough**, you can find whatever your heart desires. I'd start with the frats. I'm not saying we're all a bunch of druggies, but it is college, and everyone experiments on those cold winter nights. I mean, what else are you going to do? It's too cold to step outside."

STUDENT AUTHOR: **CMU has less drug use than your average high school.** It's true that students sometimes freak out before a test and begin to fiend for caffeine. There are also rumors of Ritalin use, but like most drug use on campus, no one ever really admits to seeing it happen. Drugs are not a dominant force in CMU culture, even though it isn't that hard to obtain them.

11:1	Student-to-Faculty Ratio
95%	Freshman Retention Rate
70%	Four-Year Graduation Rate
85%	Financial Aid Applicants Receiving Aid

Students Speak Out
SAFETY & SECURITY

Q "I feel pretty safe on campus, even walking around late at night. There are blue call boxes around campus, just in case there is an emergency . . . This past year, I lived off campus and used the **CMU escort service** several times. It's a van that picks you up . . . and then drops you off at your residence."

Q "The crime rate has been very low; most crimes involve **stealing bikes** and unattended laptop computers or underage drinking on campus."

Q "The campus has had its share of assaults—sexual or otherwise—but they are few and far between. CMU is in a city with plenty of dark alleys to walk down, so you have to exercise caution and judgment, but if you act somewhat appropriate, **you should be safe**."

STUDENT AUTHOR: **Although there is crime on and around campus,** students are in agreement that they feel secure and not too concerned about their safety. Campus initiatives like Safe Walk and the escort van service have really helped students feel safer.

> **Questions?**
> For more inside information and survival tips, pick up College Prowler's full-length book on this school, written by an actual student! Check it out at *www.collegeprowler.com*.

Students Speak Out
ON OVERALL EXPERIENCE

Q "It's **a lot of work**, that's for sure. I would definitely say that we get a lot more work than most Ivy schools, from what I've heard. If you're at CMU, and you're majoring in something that we're not known for, then I would definitely go elsewhere."

Q "Job-wise, you can't do better than here. It's a very good school, and there are a lot of opportunities. I'm not kidding about that; it's a **great academic institution**, but you have to be serious about it. You will work harder than you've ever worked before."

Q "I wanted to transfer to NYU for sophomore year, but as the semester went by, I met a lot of people, and they really made my experience at CMU a good one. Another friend wanted to leave initially, but now she **absolutely loves it**. Honestly, I really enjoyed my freshman year."

Q "This school is **not for everybody**. CMU is a good institution that requires a lot of patience when dealing with the social scene and academic community. People here are weird. The campus is split into many subgroups of interests and studies."

STUDENT AUTHOR: **In appraising CMU, most students are appreciative** of the fantastic education they're receiving and the one-of-a-kind experience that the campus offers. Students who are unhappy with their experience are often frustrated with the sub-par social situation or the massive amount of work. No matter how fed up students get with the amount of work, the social scene, or the bad weather, students are often glad they came to CMU when they think about the unique experience the school has given them.

Case Western Reserve University

10900 Euclid Avenue; Cleveland, OH 44106
(216) 368-2000; www.cwru.edu

THE BASICS:

Acceptance Rate: 75%
Setting: Urban
F-T Undergrads: 3,996

SAT Range: 1200–1410
Control: Private
Tuition: $34,450

Most Popular Majors: Engineering, Biological/Life Sciences, Social Sciences, Business/Marketing

*of 1600

Academics	A-	Guys	C+
Local Atmosphere	B	Girls	C-
Safety & Security	B-	Athletics	C+
Computers	A+	Nightlife	B-
Facilities	B+	Greek Life	A
Campus Dining	C	Drug Scene	A-
Off-Campus Dining	A-	Campus Strictness	B
Campus Housing	B+	Parking	D+
Off-Campus Housing	B+	Transportation	B
Diversity	C+	Weather	C

Students Speak Out
ON ACADEMICS

Q "Most of the **faculty is focused on research**, though, and not teaching. Many of them cannot even speak English. There are a few gems, and they make it worth it."

Q "Engaged students always come out on top, and if anything, a **Case education is best at stripping students of their delusions**—you have to really want to do what you do at Case, or it'll be painfully obvious to everyone else but you that you're not cut out for what you've selected."

Q "I must say, the bulk of professors are really good and are really approachable. No matter what you major in, the **professors are all really approachable** and willing to talk after class and during appointed office times. This is a very academic school with very high standards and the school has some of the best professors you will find anywhere, bar none!"

Q "Almost all classes are taught by professors, so you get instructors who really know what they are talking about. I also think that so many of these people are big on research, and sometimes they care more about that than their students, but you **get some good ones and some bad ones**."

STUDENT AUTHOR: **Case is a unique research institution because unlike many other prestigious institutions, research is not limited to graduate students and Ph.D's. Many professors at Case embrace challenging innovations and new experiences—much like the students.**

Students Speak Out
ON LOCAL ATMOSPHERE

Q "John Carroll University is close. Stay away from East Euclid after dark; it's not such a nice area. Museums and botanical gardens are essentially right on campus, both are very nice to visit, and either free or very cheap to Case students. Visit **the Flats and the Warehouse District; they provide great times**."

Q "Cross the Cuyahoga River, and you wind up on the West Side which is that **college-friendly mix of cheap and hip amusement**. Clubs, bars, thrift shopping, ethnic food stores and restaurants, and salons—the West Side is definitely worth finagling a ride or catching the Rapid."

Q "**Cleveland is a pretty low-key town**. The city is more attractive to families than to young people. In addition to Case, John Carroll, Cleveland State and Baldwin Wallace are close."

Q "The area surrounding the campus varies **depending on the direction you go**. There are some run-down areas around campus, but these can be avoided."

STUDENT AUTHOR: **The local atmosphere on and around campus varies depending upon which direction you go and dramatically so. The campus itself and the outlying areas are jammed with cultural institutions. Northeast of campus is not a very safe place and southeast of campus are wealthier neighborhoods of Cleveland Heights, Little Italy and Coventry. If you travel 20 or so minutes West, you hit downtown Cleveland.**

5 Best Things	5 Worst Things
1 Campus events	1 Meal plan
2 Research opportunities	2 Parking
3 The Film Society	3 Frigid weather
4 Prep for the real world	4 Lack of political activism
5 Student diversity	5 Male-to-female ratio

Students Speak Out
ON FACILITIES

Q "The libraries and labs are all state-of-the-art, offer convenient times and are pleasant to work in. However, **don't let the labs replace having a computer**; having one is as much of a necessity as having a textbook."

Q "You can do almost anything you want to with access to the state interlibrary loan, OhioLINK (which **allows you to get almost any book that's ever been published**, from other schools in Ohio, within a week, and for free); with the online research databases, and the printing facilities."

Q "There are plenty of places on campus where **one can go to quietly study** and most are open 24 hours."

Q "**Thwing is a great place to socialize**, have coffee, and eat lunch. The bookstore is located there along with a Subway, a burger joint, a pizza place and Jazzman's Coffee as well as the student activity office."

Q "If you want something at Case, **there's a way to get it**—you just have to be resourceful and think the problem through."

STUDENT AUTHOR: Case students feel spoiled with the high-tech and readily available array of facilities and student resources. The libraries are the apple of the undergraduate student's eye. They go beyond the average undergraduate's comprehension as to the volumes of usefulness contained therein, the resourcefulness of which slowly and beautifully becomes apparent over the writing of many lab reports, papers, and defenses.

Famous People From Cleveland

Halle Berry, Drew Carey, Tracy Chapman, James A. Garfield, Arsenio Hall, Bobe Hope, Toni Morrison, John D. Rockefeller, the Wright Brothers

Students Speak Out
ON CAMPUS DINING

Q "The cafeteria food may seem good at first, but like any school, **it becomes redundant** after a couple weeks."

Q "**If you're vegetarian or vegan, plan on shopping frequently** if you want a variety of protein options, or post tons of comment cards in the dining halls. There are many on-campus vendors like Subway in addition to a good vegetarian spot called Schtick's located in the law school. Other than that, your best bet is to look off campus for nutritious food."

Q "The **cafeterias fry just about everything**, but they do have accommodations for lactose intolerance and vegetarians. They even make lunches for you to pick up in the morning if you have class all day."

Q "There are several coffeehouses located on campus and that is **where most people go to eat**."

Q "The **food in the campus dining halls is average**—there are good nights and there are awful nights."

STUDENT AUTHOR: I have hosted several prospective students and many have gone as far to say that the food here is "pretty good." Pretty good, by most students' standards, tends to mean that there is edible food that is appetizing if you're hungry or need something to keep you awake for a few more hours, but it still leaves you with a reason to eat out or make your own meal at least a few times each week.

Student Body

African American:	6%	Male/Female:	58/42%
Asian American:	16%	Out-of-State:	46%
Hispanic:	2%	International:	3%
Native American:	<1%	Unknown:	13%
White:	60%		

Popular Faiths: There are many Christian groups, and Judaism, Islam, and Hinduism are also visible.

Gay Pride: The campus is fairly accepting of the GBLTQ community; Spectrum, a student group, works to educate campus on sexuality issues.

Economic Status: Case's generous financial aid results in a relatively economically diverse student body.

Students Speak Out
ON DORMS

Q "If you take mostly engineering classes on the quad, **South side is a good choice** for your sophomore year. If you plan to major in the liberal arts or humanities, North side is a shorter walk to class."

Q "Housing isn't the best here. The dorms are somewhat small and **you are somewhat stuck on campus** till your senior year."

Q "Dorms are dorms. You will always have to deal with their smallness and living with a roommate. They're nice for the most part and **you really get to know other people** fairly well."

STUDENT AUTHOR: **Residence halls are on the whole are well-equipped, well-lit, warm enough and bug-free. Freshmen are required to live in doubles or quads which are well-furnished and have Internet and phone lines. Economically speaking, the price students pay for living in campus housing seems high compared with the price that a student would pay living off campus; location and residence life benefits (asked for or not) seem to buffer the sticker shock.**

Did You Know?
82% of undergrads live on campus.

Students Speak Out
ON GUYS & GIRLS

Q "**For girls, Case is heaven**. There are so many guys and so few (attractive) girls. If you are an attractive girl, you will have every guy hanging on you."

Q "There are some hot guys. Many are really nerdy, though, the kind that **don't leave their rooms often and are afraid of light**, girls, etc."

Q "It's not that hot both ways. There are lots of **'freaks and geeks,'** including me."

Q "The guys say there are no hot girls at Case. The girls say that yeah there are a lot of guys here, but **while the odds are good, the goods are odd**."

STUDENT AUTHOR: **A particular mentality proliferates among the male population with complaints for lack of dates and hot girls, though some report that the situation is improving as the gene pool continues to expand and new harvests of hotties penetrate the Case nerd barrier. For females, unless your tolerance for conventional nerdiness is nil, the options are endless.**

Traditions

The Hudson Relays
Held annually since 1910, the event commemorates the 1883 move of Western Reserve College from Hudson to University Circle.

The Sci-Fi Marathon
The Science Fiction Marathon comprises over 36 hours of back-to-back science fiction. It's popular with Cleveland as well as people from other countries.

April Fools Edition of *The Observer*
This is often an amusing way for students to be sarcastic and brutally honest.

Students Speak Out
ON ATHLETICS

Q "Athletics are not that big—if you have a little high school experience with a sport then you'll probably make the team. Our **strong points are track (the official sport of nerds)**, women's basketball, and swimming."

Q "Our varsity sports are pretty lame. **We are nerds, not athletes**."

Q "Varsity sports are a novelty. IM sports and clubs are pretty big, and any involvement is well worth it, **even if you never seem to be winning**."

Q "With Division III athletics, Case isn't too serious about sports, but there are still **plenty of students involved in varsity sports** and a good number cheering them on."

STUDENT AUTHOR: **Although Case is a Division III school, it would be safe to say that its student body too often acts like it, with a few exceptions when our teams start winning. Intramurals, on the other hand, tend to overflow with participants. Intramurals are open to anyone that wants to play anytime and often on short notice; sometimes it's just the right thing to kill the insomnia or motivate a power-study sunrise session.**

Students Speak Out
ON DRUG SCENE

Q "The drug scene is almost nonexistent. Most students are probably **more afraid of the actual drugs than getting caught** with them."

Q "Marijuana is the most common drug used on campus, and acid is used because **some people know how to make it**."

Q "Kids do drugs, yes, but mostly pot. I've known kids to deal prescription drugs like Adderall to help them study. Otherwise, everyone's totally cool. The University has the really great stance of: here are the facts, if you chose to do drugs and drink and you screw up, **you're an adult and can deal with the consequences**."

STUDENT AUTHOR: **Although there are pockets of students who dabble in illegal substances, marijuana is basically the extent of illicit substance use on campus. The academic rigor in combination with its predominant conservativism and general geekiness makes for an environment where there is little place for substances other than the occasional keg or 12-pack.**

9:1	Student-to-Faculty Ratio
91%	Freshman Retention Rate
59%	Four-Year Graduation Rate
89%	Financial Aid Applicants Receiving Aid

Students Speak Out
SAFETY & SECURITY

Q "Security is everywhere, and you can call them from phones on the quad and main walking paths all over the place. **I have never really been too worried**, even walking home at 2 a.m."

Q "Using common sense and taking advantage of campus security are two things that will help students avoid crime on campus. Students always **receive security updates** when crimes on campus occur."

Q "Security on campus is very good. **There are emergency call boxes everywhere**."

STUDENT AUTHOR: Case is an urban campus, so crime is a lingering concern, but not a constant threat. Common sense and listening to the advice of students with experience in navigating areas around campus are best bets to remain cautious but still be able to venture outside University Circle.

> **Questions?**
> For more inside information and survival tips, pick up College Prowler's full-length book on this school, written by an actual student! Check it out at *www.collegeprowler.com*.

Students Speak Out
ON OVERALL EXPERIENCE

Q "After completing seven semesters here, I have an extreme feeling of accomplishment and gratitude. **I've even impressed myself**."

Q "I enjoyed being at Case and as a recent alumnus, I already miss it. In retrospect, I might have gone to a school that had a more comprehensive focus on the humanities, but **a Case experience is what you make it**; the programs are so flexible."

Q "Students who wish to get the most out of a Case education have to be pro-active and not wait for good things to come their way. I am **taking advantage of every opportunity** that has come my way through Case and do not regret it."

Q "Case students are uniquely independent and succeed on many different levels and in many different ways. The academics are unquestionably good, but a general lack of spirit and **prevailing get-in-and-get-out attitude** makes it difficult for student leaders and students interested in areas other than their major to make any changes."

STUDENT AUTHOR: **Case is best-suited for self-motivated, goal-oriented students with a firm grasp on reality. Most students have professional aspirations and a solid idea where they want to be in 10 years. The largest amount of concern from students comes from issues such as social atmosphere and male-female ratio. The Case campus offers freedom, and the city of Cleveland affords opportunities. Case can be a school to fit the plans and aspirations of any ambitious and intelligent student in virtually any field.**

Catholic University of America

620 Michigan Avenue NE; Washington, DC 20064
(202) 319-5000; www.cua.edu

THE BASICS:

Acceptance Rate: 80%
Setting: Urban
F-T Undergrads: 3,058

SAT Range: 1550–1850*
Control: Private
Tuition: $30,520

Most Popular Majors: Architecture, Social Sciences, Visual/Performing Arts, Health Professions, Education

*of 2400

Academics	B	Guys	A-
Local Atmosphere	B	Girls	B+
Safety & Security	C	Athletics	C-
Computers	B	Nightlife	A
Facilities	C+	Greek Life	N/A
Campus Dining	B	Drug Scene	B+
Off-Campus Dining	A	Campus Strictness	C+
Campus Housing	B	Parking	C
Off-Campus Housing	B	Transportation	A
Diversity	C+	Weather	B-

Students Speak Out
ON ACADEMICS

Q "The teachers are mostly good, but the bad ones really stand out. Most of the teachers know what they're doing, but **there are a select few who ruin the reputation of the others** by being inconsiderate of students. The workload isn't bad, but there are times when it seems that all of the teachers planned on giving students a lot of work at one time."

Q "This semester my classes weren't as interesting as I had hoped. However, **my theology class was interesting**, even though I don't agree with Catholic principles."

Q "I believe that we have **a lot of very intelligent professors that came from really good schools** like Yale. My media professor studied at Yale, while another one came from Brown. I think that it's essential for smaller schools like CUA to hire teachers like this so that it makes our campus more formidable."

Q "**Workloads are often demanding but reasonable, especially senior year** since CUA is one of the few schools that still require senior comprehensives."

STUDENT AUTHOR: Generally speaking, teachers at CUA debunk the popular myth that professors care more about their research than they do their students. They tend to be warm, sociable, funny, and readily accessible to students. Class sizes tend to be small as well. Sure, many programs may not rank in the top ten, but they are still good programs with intelligent and determined professors.

Students Speak Out
ON LOCAL ATMOSPHERE

Q "CUA is nice because it is somewhat separated from the busy city life with its own well-defined campus on the northeast side. This does not, however, mean the CUA is out of touch with the city. **Metro access is incredibly convenient**, allowing students to get downtown for various events, museums, sites, games, and shows. The campus is also in close proximity to a number of other universities that lie within the district (like UMD, GW, and Georgetown to name a few)."

Q "**The city is great, but the neighborhood CUA is in is dangerous**. The best thing to do in the city is to discover new parts instead of just going to the monuments. Students should try their hardest to stay away from Anacostia, which is difficult because RFK Stadium is located there. The city is working on a new stadium, but that one isn't in the best neighborhood either."

Q "I do like the fact that the campus is not as structured as a normal city school. However, **I do wish that it were closer to other universities** and more centralized."

STUDENT AUTHOR: The Brookland neighborhood of D.C., where the University is located, barely makes the grade. There has been a history of crime in the area, with the unfortunate, yet perpetual feeling that things are never 100 percent safe. But Washington, D.C. itself is an incredible city for a college student. The Metro makes mobility so easy and affordable, and the monuments, museums, and historical elements galore make the city interesting and engaging.

5 Best Things	5 Worst Things
1 Plans for improvement	1 No anti-Catholic speaking
2 Caring professors	2 Lack of diversity
3 The Metro	3 High tuition/living costs
4 Proud Catholic identity	4 Small dorm rooms
5 Warm, friendly students	5 Ineffective student gov't

Students Speak Out
ON FACILITIES

Q "The main athletics center is somewhat distant from campus, and the main fitness center—while new and well-equipped—is quickly being outgrown. **There is no real student center**. The Pryzbyla center in the middle of campus is the closest thing to it, but this space has not necessarily been planned out well. It is easy to see that, with a growing student body, this space is also becoming very small."

Q "**The facilities here are average at best**. I mean, renovations have been made in the Pryz (the student center), but it doesn't feel like I'm going to a $40,000-a-year school."

Q "The library and athletic center are pretty nice, but there is **not much else to brag about here**."

Q "**Most of the buildings here are new or have been remodeled**, so they are a source of pride, so to speak."

STUDENT AUTHOR: **The problem lies not in what the University has, but rather what it does not have. For being a $40,000-a-year university, one would hope that it shows. But alas, the campus facilities are generally small and unimpressive. The campus itself is pretty, with green grass and attractive horticulture and plant life, but that is pretty much the extent of the positives. The DuFour Center, CUA's athletic facility, while a little distant from central campus, is big and helpful for student athletes, though most students don't trek across campus to use it. And while the library is pleasant, it is continuously ranked as one of the worst libraries in the country.**

Famous Alumni

Ed McMahon, Susan Sarandon, Jon Voight, Stephen Lynch, Brian Williams, Edward Gillespie, Terrence McAuliffe

Students Speak Out
ON CAMPUS DINING

Q "They're trying. **The dining halls are gradually responding to pressure** to improve quality and convenience. Unfortunately—as with many other facilities—the dining halls have already been outgrown by the growing student population."

Q "The food is good until you get used to it. **We joke that it dulls your senses**."

Q "**I really enjoy the new salad bar** because it provides a variety of vegetables as well as bread and other condiments. In general, the food is pretty good."

Q "For the most part, I've been impressed with our campus dining facilities. **We have the 'anytime' dining plan**, which means we can eat as many meals as we want throughout the day, anytime from open to close. The student restaurant is really a great socializing spot. It's nice being able to eat there with any friends at any time without having to worry about swiping away one of your meals just to hang out with some friends. Compared to other schools, we're really lucky."

STUDENT AUTHOR: **There is no simple way to describe the food at Catholic University. On one hand, students with a meal plan can eat as much and often as they want—so A+ in the quantity department. But the quality is another story. The main problem is that the "daily specials" are put out for a limited time, so many times students are stuck with pizza, burgers, fries, and strawberry ice cream. It may seem like a college student's paradise, but eventually it gets old.**

Student Body

African American:	5%	Male/Female:	46/54%
Asian American:	3%	Out-of-State:	94%
Hispanic:	6%	International:	2%
Native American:	<1%	Unknown:	14%
White:	69%		

Popular Faiths: Roman Catholicism is the dominant religion, for obvious reasons.

Gay Pride: It is tricky, given that the University is an official university of the Vatican. There are no clubs specific to gay pride or gay students, but there is a formidable gay presence on campus.

Economic Status: Most students are from affluent or well-off families but are generally modest about it.

Students Speak Out
ON DORMS

Q "**I suppose the rooms are fine**. They are a bit small and plain, but they are adequate. But there are some really bad dorms on campus. I was lucky to live in the nicer, newer hall, and I thank my lucky stars I never had to live on the south side."

Q "It's all on how you look at it. **Sure, the rooms are not as nice and big as Georgetown or GW**, but that really doesn't matter. You are more than capable of living it up in college, regardless of a mediocre room."

Q "How is living on-campus? **One word: fun**! But really, it all depends on where you lived. If you lived on the south side (Spellman, Conaty), you swear up and down how much fun you had, but those from the north side are indifferent. You decide."

STUDENT AUTHOR: **On one hand, there is nothing special about housing at CUA. Many of the rooms are small and uninviting, while the common areas look dated and out-of-whack. On the other, students will get used to their dorms and make them their own. And lucky for them, as they progress in their academic career at Catholic, the residence halls get a little better; that is, if one is lucky enough to find a room.**

? Did You Know?
68% of undergrads live on campus.

Students Speak Out
ON GUYS & GIRLS

Q "The mostly accurate assumption is that **students here are either Bible readers or bed hoppers**. I think there are more textbook 'pretty' girls while guys are more diverse and different."

Q "The one thing I like about Catholic is that the **guys and girls can be both fun and religious**. It's totally common to see the very same guys and girls who partied hard on a Saturday night attend Mass Sunday morning. They may be hungover, but they are at Mass nonetheless."

Q "The guys take on the three Gs: **gay, God, or girlfriend**."

Q "The girls, in general, are **sluttier than the guys**, but there are definitely promiscuous guys. You'll know them."

STUDENT AUTHOR: **Most girls, blonde or not, fill the bill of generally smart, dedicated, attractive young women. The only problem, really, is that they look like everybody else on campus. As for the guys, it's a little different. There are the beefy jocks, the dedicated nerds, the colorful music majors, the deeply religious theology majors, the party animals, the funny guys, etc., with not so many familiar resemblances with the ladies.**

Traditions

Luaupalooza
The McMahon parking lot is transformed into a luau, with food, carnival rides, music, and more.

Metro Madness
Campus Ministry organizes a massive scavenger hunt throughout Washington, D.C. at the start of each year.

Overall School Spirit
When it comes to school spirit in general, there is a healthy dose. But at the same time, there are a lot of students who openly (and regrettably) say that CUA was not their first choice school.

Students Speak Out
ON ATHLETICS

Q "I absolutely love it. It's a great way to meet people and friends. **You have your own little family in your team**."

Q "While CUA does not excel in sports as much as other schools, **there is a good variety of sports and facilities** for students to enjoy."

Q "The sports teams are okay—**not the best, since we're Division III**, but we pull off surprises."

Q "Students here really need to improve their school spirit. **Most games are played to an empty stadium or bleachers**. We may not be ESPN material, but we work hard and do pretty well, so there is no excuse for students here to not get up and go to a game once in a while to support their fellow students."

STUDENT AUTHOR: **Catholic University is all over the place in athletics. Most students have favorable opinions about the fitness center, and we have a modest (sometimes impressive) record. But students rarely show up to support the CUA Cardinals, even at home games, and only if the team is doing well. Most would agree that CUA needs a heavy dose of school spirit.**

Students Speak Out
ON DRUG SCENE

Q "Are drugs noticeable at Catholic? No, but **they are definitely here**."

Q "Yeah, there are drugs, but **not as many as the average university**. You could always find weed, but most students here aren't that interested. It's very underground."

Q "If you wants drugs, you can find them. **But more than likely, they won't find you**. However, most kids here won't admit that taking Adderall that their doctor didn't prescribe for them is taking drugs, but I guess it could be worse."

Q "**The worst I have seen here is cocaine**, but that was only recently, and it isn't very prevalent."

STUDENT AUTHOR: **Rather than saying there is a drug scene at CUA, it is more accurate to say that there are a few drug addicts and some dealers who bring the drugs. Maybe it is the Catholic identity, or the abundance of entertainment available, or the over-abundance of alcohol, but the average CUA student is just not interested in taking drugs.**

10:1	Student-to-Faculty Ratio
82%	Freshman Retention Rate
60%	Four-Year Graduation Rate
81%	Financial Aid Applicants Receiving Aid

Students Speak Out
SAFETY & SECURITY

Q "**The security is always present**. In years past, there has been a lot of crime but currently not so much. Still, they have a text messaging system if you sign up. They text everyone on the list if something big goes down."

Q "**There has been improvement, but they can do better**. It only takes one unresponsive cop to put my well-being in danger."

Q "Campus is situated in a rough part of town, but security measures have really been stepped-up over the past two years. **The administration takes student safety seriously**, and even though crime rates are lower than other schools in the district, they have implemented measures to increase the presence of campus police all over campus at all times of the day and night."

STUDENT AUTHOR: **The University's Department of Public Safety has things more or less under control, but there is room for improvement. It's true that in the past crime was more rampant, but campus has been safer since, with a stronger patrol car presence and more emergency phones.**

Questions?
For more inside information and survival tips, pick up College Prowler's full-length book on this school, written by an actual student! Check it out at *www.collegeprowler.com*.

Students Speak Out
ON OVERALL EXPERIENCE

Q "CUA is okay, but it's getting better. The last three years has really been a time of transition for Catholic, whether it be construction, renovations, new academic programs, etc. **It is truly an exciting time to be here**. It is hard for CUA, since it shares D.C. with other prestigious schools, but I think Catholic holds its own, and I look forward to its progress."

Q "**It was so important for me to come to a school where people share my values**, and I really found it here at Catholic. And at the same time, I have met others who do not share my values, and I have learned from them and vice versa. It has been a really great experience so far, mainly because the student body has been really nice and really reached out to everyone. Overall, I really couldn't have picked a better school."

Q "I've had a great time here, for many different reasons. **The people here are really easy-going and cool**, which makes it easy to find friends. This school isn't necessarily crawling with God warriors as everyone assumes, but those who are really strong in their faith are mostly understanding of others' lack of faith, which is always good."

STUDENT AUTHOR: **The Catholic University of America blends the best of both worlds: a small, conservative, Catholic community of devoted students and a liberal arts university located smack-dab in Washington, D.C. Its Catholic identity and pride does not hinder or isolate those with different faiths or no faith. Catholic University lives up to the liberal arts curriculum it boasts and does its best to accommodate those who adore and those who are apathetic to the Catholic aspect.**

Centenary College of Louisiana

2911 Centenary Boulevard; Shreveport, LA 71104
(318) 869-5011; www.centenary.edu

THE BASICS:

Acceptance Rate: 64%
Setting: Urban
F-T Undergrads: 839

SAT Range: 1010–1280*
Control: Private
Tuition: $20,940

Most Popular Majors: Business, Psychology, Mass Communication/Media Studies, Biology

*of 1600

Academics	B	Guys	C+
Local Atmosphere	C+	Girls	B-
Safety & Security	B	Athletics	C+
Computers	B	Nightlife	B-
Facilities	B-	Greek Life	A-
Campus Dining	C-	Drug Scene	B
Off-Campus Dining	A	Campus Strictness	C+
Campus Housing	B	Parking	A-
Off-Campus Housing	B-	Transportation	B-
Diversity	C-	Weather	B+

Students Speak Out
ON ACADEMICS

Q "The teachers are overworked—the entire history department consists of two professors, who have to teach all the history ever. So if you decide to go into certain majors, **you'll have very fried, exhausted—but still fun—teachers**. And they do try to keep things interesting."

Q "The teachers at Centenary are a unique blend of individuals, **from the super intellectual to the downright kooky**. We have a wonderful staff. Furthermore, it serves to reason with a staff like that, classes are almost always worthwhile and interesting."

Q "While there are a few teachers you should definitely stay away from (other students will alert you to these early on), **most teachers are great and are more than willing to help you out** with things if you take the time to develop a relationship with them."

Q "The teachers are helpful and **actually care whether or not you pass or fail**. The classes are, for the most part, interesting. Occasionally you'll get a dull one."

STUDENT AUTHOR: **Centenary is small—very small. Most of the classes have around 15 students. Classes tend to be more discussion-oriented than lecture, which makes them much more interesting. Almost all the classes are taught by professors, as well. Though the professors make themselves available, they are extremely busy. Some are impossible to track down unless you know their schedule and how to corner them.**

Students Speak Out
ON LOCAL ATMOSPHERE

Q "**Shreveport is the buckle of the Bible Belt**. The nearest under-21 club is in another town and the nearest universities . . . well, we don't talk to them. Stay away from the ghetto (duh). But there are good things you shouldn't miss, like the Red River Revel, the new River Walk, and when you hit 21, the casinos. They're anything but classy, but that's what makes them fun for a college student."

Q "Shreveport's hick-ish, but there's a lot of catering to the college crowd. **Under-21s can't even enter bars or clubs**, which sucks."

Q "Shreveport is halfway between big city and small town. **There's plenty to do (if you're over 21)**. Gambling addicts, beware."

Q "Shreveport is okay. **I am from a much bigger city, so it was hard to adjust to it**. They are building a lot of new stuff, especially down on Youree, so that makes it better! Downtown is really fun to just walk around, so be sure to check that out."

STUDENT AUTHOR: **Next to the quality of campus food, Centenary students complain about Shreveport the most. Although Centenary has been in Shreveport for nearly a hundred years, it rarely feels like a college town. Entertainment is aimed toward families and tourists looking to gamble. Though people in the community are really supportive of Centenary in terms of attending campus events, businesses generally don't go out of their way to attract the college crowd.**

Students Speak Out
ON FACILITIES

Q "**The gym is amazing**, considering that we are a small, privately-funded college."

Q "The facilities are **somewhat old, for the most part, but kept in good repair**. The computer labs in the dorms are not always in the best shape, but that is to be expected with the abuse they endure from drunk students."

Q "Centenary is always looking for ways to improve their facilities, and it shows. The residence halls are better than most I've seen, and there are no hall showers. It's only suites, which I think is great! The art building is small, and often there's not enough room for everyone to work and store their things. **The library is small as well, but you can order pretty much anything you need** through inter-library loan."

Q "**Athletic facilities on campus are rather nice**. The Fitness Center was just rebuilt a few years ago, so nothing is really old. There is a pool that is mostly for laps, workout equipment, a gym, and an indoor track."

Q "**Some areas of campus are nicer than others**. The Fitness Center is very well-kept, but the residence halls aren't."

STUDENT AUTHOR: Because the College only spans a city block, the facilities are limited to a small space. While the small size of the campus is good for the community and academics, the facilities suffer under the cramped conditions. What makes up for the small space is the fact that the campus is gorgeous. The people that keep up the grounds do an amazing job.

Famous Alumni

John Corrington (poet and author), Dr. Michael Mann (inventor of Lasik surgery), Robert Parish (basketball star), Hal Sutton (pro golfer)

Students Speak Out
ON CAMPUS DINING

Q "The food in the Caf at Centenary leaves a little to be desired. **Perhaps a few more vegetarian choices would help**. However, the food at Randle's, however unhealthy, is not bad."

Q "Cafeteria food is not bad. **The pizza is good, fries are good**, and sometimes the bagels are good. I, however, do not eat meat and do not really feel I can completely comment on all the food. Randle's isn't bad. I eat there every once in a while."

Q "Food is **a terrible, awful, greasy, bland, deep-fried, salt-soaked mess**."

Q "**In a word, the food on campus sucks**. It's all the same, and there's never anything new to look forward to. It does, however, make eating out that much better."

Q "The food has its moments, but mostly, it's pretty sketchy. The good thing is that **there's always pizza, salad, bagels, and cereal**, and it's really hard to mess up that food. Don't come expecting gourmet food at all. It's pretty mediocre, and you can't expect much out of cafeteria food anyway."

STUDENT AUTHOR: The general consensus is that the food sucks. There are a total of two places to choose from: the cafeteria and Randle's Place. It's generally a good idea to get more money toward Randle's because you'll rarely use all the Caf meals, and Randle's is open all day. Make sure to put some money aside to visit a restaurant once in while. It's the only way you'll survive.

Student Body

African American:	8%	Male/Female:	43/57%
Asian American:	3%	Out-of-State:	44%
Hispanic:	4%	International:	2%
Native American:	1%	Unknown:	0%
White:	82%		

Political Activity: The student population is divided in terms of politics. There's a pretty even division of liberal- and conservative-minded students.

Gay Pride: For such a small school, Centenary has a relatively large and vocal gay community.

Economic Status: A large majority of students are in the middle- to upper-middle-class bracket.

Students Speak Out
ON DORMS

Q "The dorms are okay, but **the RAs seem to think they're running a summer camp**. Prepare to have cutesy activities crammed down your throat every single week. James is top pick, since it's the only dorm with a kitchen."

Q "**The residence halls are pretty good**. There's an awesome sense of community among the smaller halls (Sexton, Hardin, James Annex). Ideally, the nicest place to live is Rotary, but it's only available to upperclassmen in good standing. It's also pretty lonely there."

Q "The dorms are great. **If you like to party and live in small rooms, stay in Cline**. If you're a guy, you don't have much of a choice until you become a junior."

STUDENT AUTHOR: There are five dorms at Centenary, and all of them have suite-style rooms, which means absolutely no hall bathrooms. Most students would advise living on campus because it's cheaper and easier. All your classes are no more than a five- to ten-minute walk away, and students are always around if you need help with homework.

> **Did You Know?**
> 70% of undergrads live on campus.

Students Speak Out
ON GUYS & GIRLS

Q "**The guys are few in number, and they know they're in demand**. Even the ugly ones get cocky with odds like that. The girls are all quietly pondering bisexuality."

Q "There are a lot of beautiful girls at Centenary. **With a two-to-one girl-to-guy ratio, you can't complain (being a guy)**. In addition to this, there is the fact that about 50 percent of those guys are gay, making your odds even better."

Q "**A lot of the guys are hot**. The girls are hot, too. The girl-to-guy ratio is way slanted to the girls side. They're everywhere."

Q "There's a fair amount of guys, even though the stats say more girls than guys. **But really, there's all of Shreveport to look at**."

STUDENT AUTHOR: Most of the girls on campus complain about the lack of male students. Centenary desperately needs more guys. Guys will sometimes complain about being one of two or three guys in a class. The girls tend to ignore them or grin apologetically when the conversation steers toward feminism in any class. It can be rough for male students, but they know the numbers work for them when it comes to dating.

> **Traditions**
>
> **Corrington Award**
> Annually, the College presents the John William Corrington Award to an established writer.
>
> **Freak Week**
> During the week of Halloween students paint pumpkins and decorate the campus with ghouls.
>
> **Overall School Spirit**
> Since Centenary has no football team, school spirit doesn't reach the frantic, frenzied mania of most universities. You'll rarely see students wearing face paint and large foam hands.

Students Speak Out
ON ATHLETICS

Q "**It's always fun to go watch both varsity and IM sports**. It's also fun to play IM sports. It's easy to get involved in those. They are trying to build up our program right now on our campus, so it should be fun!"

Q "I don't really follow athletics, **but ultimate Frisbee is really cool to watch and play**."

Q "I don't know much about varsity, but I play club lacrosse and really enjoy it. **The home games can be fairly big events**."

Q "**Varsity sports are kind of a big deal, but really only basketball**, and then just when they are winning. People attend the events, but basketball always draws the largest crowd. Intramural sports on campus are huge."

STUDENT AUTHOR: Though athletics are an important part of life at Centenary, they tend to take a back seat to academics and other student organizations. The absence of football makes Centenary much different than most other colleges. There is not much sports fanaticism, and school pride is not confined to athletic events.

Students Speak Out
ON DRUG SCENE

Q "There are drugs on campus. **You don't tend to see them, though, unless you are into that.** People that do that sort of thing work very hard to keep it concealed."

Q "**There are definitely drugs on campus.** It seems like it's mostly pot and stuff to help keep you awake. It seems more like a social activity than anything else."

Q "There's not really a 'drug scene' at Centenary. Drugs are mostly low-key and mild, like pot. If someone at Centenary does drugs, it's not likely that anyone knows about it. It is Louisiana, however, so **people do like their drive-thru daiquiris and liquor in general.**"

STUDENT AUTHOR: **You could get through all four years at Centenary without ever seeing any drug use. Drinking, though, is something you can't get away from. Even though the campus is dry, you'll hear your suitemates playing drinking games and see students sitting on dorm porches drinking alcohol from inconspicuous glasses.**

12:1	Student-to-Faculty Ratio
78%	Freshman Retention Rate
43%	Four-Year Graduation Rate
83%	Financial Aid Applicants Receiving Aid

Students Speak Out
SAFETY & SECURITY

Q "I'd say the safety on campus is pretty good. We have **a police force that always has officers on duty**, and students can call them at any time to get into buildings or request escorts."

Q "I feel pretty safe. **I've never had my car vandalized or anything stolen**, but I do know it happens. Still, I don't worry."

Q "**Centenary has had a problem with cars being broken into in past years** but has addressed it and has already started to stymie criminals. The school is very well-lit, and has well-spaced emergency boxes with warning sirens. Campus security patrols every night, and in my two years here, I have yet to see or hear about anyone having a real problem with people from the surrounding neighborhoods."

STUDENT AUTHOR: **Centenary is surrounded by an eccentric and moderately shady neighborhood. Although you're aware that the neighborhood is not the safest area of Shreveport, you rarely feel unsafe on campus. The worst problems have been car thefts, and those were dealt with quickly.**

> **Questions?**
> For more inside information and survival tips, pick up College Prowler's full-length book on this school, written by an actual student! Check it out at *www.collegeprowler.com*.

Students Speak Out
ON OVERALL EXPERIENCE

Q "**During my freshman year, I contemplated transferring many times.** Now, I don't know why I ever considered it, because I really am happy where I am. I wanted a small school where I wouldn't just be another random student, and that's what I got. I really enjoy Centenary, and I don't wish I was anywhere else."

Q "I have always loved Centenary. I suppose I could have gotten some good opportunities at other schools, but **I would never want to give up the relationships and the experiences** I've had at Centenary. I can't picture myself anywhere else."

Q "I would never trade my experience at Centenary for anything. There were some tough times, but **I loved almost all of it!**"

Q "At first I really disliked Centenary, but now that I'm involved with organizations on campus and have had time to find friends like me, **I adore it**. I'm glad I made the decision to come here. The great thing is that if there's anything you don't like about Centenary, and you're willing to put in the effort, there's a good chance that you can change it. If you're interested in going to a small school where your voice counts and you can get a great education, Centenary is a great choice!"

STUDENT AUTHOR: **Most of the students that enter Centenary are looking for a school where they won't be just a face in the crowd. There's a wonderful sense that anything you want to accomplish can be done. The most important thing about Centenary, though, is the quality of the academics. The teachers at Centenary work hard to make you learn. If you take full advantage of everything at Centenary, you will leave feeling confident and proud of the education you received.**

Centre College

600 West Walnut Street; Danville, KY 40422
(800) 423-6236; www.centre.edu

THE BASICS:

Acceptance Rate: 63%
Setting: Rural
F-T Undergrads: 1,196

SAT Range: 1700–2040*
Control: Private
Tuition: $30,700

Most Popular Majors: Social Sciences, Biology, English, History, Visual and Performing Arts

*of 2400

Academics	B+	Guys	B
Local Atmosphere	C-	Girls	B
Safety & Security	A-	Athletics	C+
Computers	B+	Nightlife	C
Facilities	A-	Greek Life	A+
Campus Dining	C	Drug Scene	B+
Off-Campus Dining	B-	Campus Strictness	B+
Campus Housing	B	Parking	A-
Off-Campus Housing	D+	Transportation	D+
Diversity	D-	Weather	B-

Students Speak Out
ON ACADEMICS

Q "Centre offers a particular advantage when it comes to teachers. Unlike a larger college or university, where students are commonly subjected to TAs and have less personal interaction with professors, Centre offers an environment where professors prioritize much differently. **Teaching comes first, and research second**."

Q "The teachers at Centre are wonderful because **they are always willing to help students, in and out of the classroom**. Centre classes are interesting because of the amount of class discussion and creative thinking involved."

Q "**The teachers are personable**, and many make class interesting. One of the best things about Centre is getting to know some of your professors on a more personal basis."

Q "The teachers are all wonderful. They all care about their students and how they are doing in class. **The classes are so diverse**, and every one of them provides a new learning experience. You are never really bored with a class."

STUDENT AUTHOR: The academic reputation Centre enjoys is what usually attracts potential students. Centre C also boasts an established practice of networking—around campus, it's known as the "Alumni Mafia." While Centre may not make any big party-school lists or have Ivy League credentials, its strength is in fostering an academic environment that produces well-balanced graduates with bright futures.

Students Speak Out
ON LOCAL ATMOSPHERE

Q "Danville is a very small, fairly conservative town. **It's a great place to go walking around**, as many of the buildings are quite historic and pretty, but there isn't much to do other than that. There's nothing I can really think of that you just have to see outside of campus."

Q "The atmosphere around town is pretty quiet. The town itself and the people are very nice, but **there is not a whole lot to do in Danville**, especially not at night. There is always something to do on campus but, if you are into the club and bar scene, then you'll have to go to Lexington."

Q "**The atmosphere in Danville is very quaint and friendly**. Danville is the stereotypical small American town. It is very beautiful with many old historic houses and buildings. Most activities that students participate in will most likely be on campus."

Q "Danville is a small town. However, recent policy changes have created growth and positive change. **The relationship between the campus and the town is good** and vital to the existence of both."

STUDENT AUTHOR: True to the town's Southern heritage, locals are friendly and helpful, which can be refreshing after a day in the big city. The downtown area is a nice walk during good weather and boasts a long-standing history with even older buildings. Overall, Danville is unpretentious, clean, and small; although even going to the mall involves a 45-minute drive.

5 Best Things	5 Worst Things
1 Photo of the week	1 The registrar's office
2 Nevin dorm	2 Interlibrary loans
3 Midnight movies	3 Diversity
4 Strong academics	4 Nevin dorm
5 Carnival	5 Classes in Grant

Students Speak Out
ON FACILITIES

Q "For a small college, they're fairly nice. The gym is amazing, but **the academic buildings could use some renovation**. I think that the technology's pretty on spot."

Q "We just got a freaking amazing new workout facility on campus, which is **huge and has any kind of machine you can imagine**. It's really posh, in my opinion, with all these TVs stuck in the walls, an indoor track on a high-up ledge, and a really good café that actually has some healthy food."

Q "The athletic facilities and library have just gone through a major update to be at the top of their game. The new facilities there are great, everywhere else on campus is **better than I've seen at other schools** (even the ragged-on dorm computer labs). The student center is well-equipped but doesn't get as much traffic as it can handle other than the Grille upstairs."

Q "**Centre has a really amazing campus all around**. I love the new athletic center. I would not consider myself a person who enjoys working out, but I can't wait to get back and exercise."

STUDENT AUTHOR: Perhaps one of the best facilities Centre has is the hot glass studio, run by world-renowned glass artist Steve Powell. The College Centre, the complex containing the athletic facilities, has recently been remodeled. The library is a great place to study, with private tables and work lamps to study under, but doesn't have the books and information on hand that are needed for higher-level research projects.

Famous Alumni

Joshua Fry Bell, John Cabell Breckinridge, John Marshall Harlan, Adlai Stevenson, T. Hunton Rogers, Alfred Nugent "Bo" McMillin, John Sherman Cooper

Students Speak Out
ON CAMPUS DINING

Q "We're catered by a private company, and frankly, **their food isn't the best**. They could do much better. Freddie's, Guadalajara, and Applebee's are good places to go to grab some food."

Q "It's campus food. **The cafeteria is actually better than about any other I've seen**, and The Grille is a great place for some late-night food, especially if you are craving something greasy and unhealthy."

Q "Cowan's food is okay. The salads and sandwich lines are pretty much guaranteed to be good, but the other lines are a toss-up. **The Grille has good food**, but only if you don't mind eating something fried."

Q "Food on campus has declined over the years, but **the administration has been shopping around to make it better**. There are basically three places to eat on campus: Cowan (the cafeteria), The Grille, and the Café. The Café is the place to go for fancy coffee drinks."

STUDENT AUTHOR: The campus dining has a tendency to be a little bit of a cattle call, especially with the monotony of the food choices. The food served in Cowan is basically good, but can get boring, and there are few healthy or vegetarian choices. Most students enjoy a steady diet of meat and potatoes, sometimes fried, baked, roasted, or broiled, but rarely varied. The kitchen facilities that some dorms have can also provide needed relief from campus food.

Student Body

African American:	4%	Male/Female:	46/54%
Asian American:	2%	Out-of-State:	38%
Hispanic:	2%	International:	2%
Native American:	<1%	Unknown:	0%
White:	90%		

Popular Faiths: There are a lot of Christian groups on campus; Wednesday night is the popular CCF meeting.

Gay Pride: Although relatively small, the gay community is established, although quiet, within Centre's campus.

Economic Status: Most Centre students are from middle- or upper-middle-class families.

Students Speak Out
ON DORMS

Q "**There's nothing special about the dorms**, they are typical college dorms. Freshman guys will have it the worst, but that's to be expected. The dorms aren't amazing, but they are livable."

Q "Dorms are your standard cinderblock prisons that all college students must experience at some point in their lives. Most have undergone renovations in the past few years, but the rooms are still too small to live in. Honestly, though, it's college—**what do you expect, the Ritz**?"

Q "The dorms aren't too bad. You can make them as homey as you would want them to be. It really all **depends on how much effort you want to put into decorating your room**."

STUDENT AUTHOR: **Campus housing is one of those experiences that everyone needs to have, and as they say, misery begets camaraderie. Suffering through early roommate wake-ups, fire drills, farm animal appearances on your hall, and breaking visitation rules are part of the college experience. Centre's small size is beneficial to the close friendships that are created, especially during group all-nighters or cram sessions.**

? Did You Know?
98% of undergrads live on campus.

Students Speak Out
ON GUYS & GIRLS

Q "Some of the guys are just snobby white guys, but **most of them are down-to-earth**. The girls are a mixture of cute chicks who are actually nice, and some of them are just shady."

Q "Everyone at Centre is very nice. Centre has **some very nice-looking people, both guys and girls**. However, looks, while important, are not the main focus on this campus."

Q "Some of the guys are hot, but **most of the girls aren't**. If you are a hot girl, then there's much less competition!"

Q "**Centre is like high school**. After your freshman year, everybody knows your business, which can be annoying if you're trying to date. However, I find most people are pretty attractive here."

STUDENT AUTHOR: **Everyone on campus will tell you that academics are why they chose to attend Centre, but don't let that convince you that Centre doesn't have its fair share of hotties. Almost everyone on campus knows each other, and learning who is who, even for newcomers to Centre, is easily and rapidly done. Dating at Centre is fairly easy, as are having midnight trysts, but finding your lifelong mate tends to be more common.**

Traditions

Carnival
A weekend-long theme party held each spring that features bands, events, and a cookout.

Kissing on the Seal
If two students kiss while standing on the school seal at midnight, they are destined to be married.

Overall School Spirit
Centre students are proud of their school, and the boys have been known to get rowdy at sporting events by painting themselves, making signs, and yelling snobby things at other teams.

Students Speak Out
ON ATHLETICS

Q "Varsity sports are somewhat big on campus. **Students especially like attending the football and soccer games** in the fall. IM sports are also pretty big. A lot of the sororities like to compete in IM Powder Puff football, and the fraternities seem particularly fond of IM basketball."

Q "**IMs are pretty popular** as far as participation, but I never went."

Q "At a D-III school, varsity sports are **just another extracurricular activity for most people**. People go to games if they want to support their friends, and it gives people a chance to keep playing their sport competitively, but also to concentrate on their school and other activities as well. Lots of people get involved in IM sports through their Greek organization, dorm hall, or other organization."

STUDENT AUTHOR: **Athletes will tell you that participating in a varsity sport at Centre was one of the best choices during their college careers, but non-athletes may barely notice they exist. Varsity athletics are taken seriously by the athletes who participate in them, while other students view the games as more of a social event.**

Students Speak Out
ON DRUG SCENE

Q "The drug scene is not very obvious, but if you run across it, it's hard to avoid noticing it thereafter. **There are quite a few potheads** and a small minority of snorters of various types."

Q "The drug scene on campus is **larger than anyone really expects**. Put 500 rich kids anywhere, and you will have people blowing loads of cash on different substances."

Q "There are **a lot of kids with too much money** that have nothing better to do than drink, smoke pot, snort pills, and ask around for cocaine, but it's really hard to get that on campus."

Q "I have no idea. **I've never seen drugs on campus**, and I don't think there are any."

STUDENT AUTHOR: If the College catches students with drugs, or paraphernalia, they are automatically expelled, period. That said, there are still students who risk it. Most students who do partake in drugs tend to be quiet about their actions, and most students just don't do illegal drugs.

11:1	Student-to-Faculty Ratio
83%	Freshman Retention Rate
81%	Four-Year Graduation Rate
86%	Financial Aid Applicants Receiving Aid

Students Speak Out
SAFETY & SECURITY

Q "**I rarely locked the door to my room** all three years that I have been at Centre. You're more likely to lose money due to parking tickets than from any theft."

Q "Campus feels very safe, for the most part. **Danville is a really safe town**, and I never really feel threatened around town or on campus."

Q "It's a small, relatively well-lit campus, and DPS can occasionally be seen **making rounds in their golf cart all night**. There are usually a few incidents each year with petty theft where students have left their doors unlocked (I hear they're working on the outside door situation), but overall, I think it's pretty safe, and I was never afraid to walk alone at night or anything."

STUDENT AUTHOR: DPS officers know almost all the students by nickname, even the freshmen, and this speaks to the security and community emphasis on Centre's grounds. Safety and security is taken very seriously at Centre, and the security the students feel reflects it.

Questions?
For more inside information and survival tips, pick up College Prowler's full-length book on this school, written by an actual student! Check it out at *www.collegeprowler.com.*

Students Speak Out
ON OVERALL EXPERIENCE

Q "I thought about transferring once. Then, I realized that once you make a place for yourself at Centre, you can get a whole lot more out of your education than cruising through a public institution. It was rough being so far from home, but **I really found out who I was** and how to get by on my own, and I had faculty and staff, as well as my friends, supporting me the whole way."

Q "I have no regrets about coming to Centre; the best experiences of my life came from this college, including meeting my best friends and the love of my life, traveling the world, and getting a thorough, **personal education that I don't think I would have gotten elsewhere**. I love it."

Q "It's been pretty cool. I've had some knocks, but I figure I would at any college. **I wouldn't want to be anywhere else**; it's a good fit for me. You just need to find your fit, and you'll have a blast."

Q "Centre has prepared me to go on to grad school and has helped me become a more adjusted adult. **Centre is the perfect choice for me from every aspect**—academics, social, class size, location, athletics."

STUDENT AUTHOR: Centre graduates emerge as well-rounded leaders, activists, and the prominent who's who of their generation. Centre is a place that takes away all the boring parts of high school but keeps all the spirit and fun. At Centre, each day is a healthy combination of work and play. Centre C is a few hours of class and homework blended with living with or next to your best friends, that hot crush, and your professors. Centre offers a remarkable experience for the whole person.

Claremont McKenna College

500 East Ninth Street; Claremont, CA 91711
(909) 621-8000; www.claremontmckenna.edu

THE BASICS:

Acceptance Rate: 22%
Setting: Suburban
F-T Undergrads: 1,209

SAT Range: 1910–2210*
Control: Private
Tuition: $36,825

Most Popular Majors: Social Sciences, Business, Psychology, History, Interdisciplinary Studies

*of 2400

Academics	A	Guys	B+
Local Atmosphere	C+	Girls	B+
Safety & Security	A-	Athletics	B
Computers	A+	Nightlife	B
Facilities	B+	Greek Life	N/A
Campus Dining	A	Drug Scene	A-
Off-Campus Dining	C-	Campus Strictness	A
Campus Housing	A	Parking	B+
Off-Campus Housing	D-	Transportation	D-
Diversity	B+	Weather	A

Students Speak Out
ON ACADEMICS

Q "To a science student, Claremont seems to be **full of government, international relations, and econ people**, so people who aren't one of those feel like they should take at least a few government or econ classes, because that's what the school seems to be known for."

Q "What's great about having more of a balance of views is that **it leads to some awesome debates in and out of class**, and you tend to learn more if you're not hearing the same point of view all of the time."

Q "**It's a friendly kind of competitiveness in terms of academics**. I have heard horror stories from Ivy League schools of students sabotaging other students' projects and such, something that would never in a million years happen here. Healthy competition that makes everyone better and smarter is how we operate."

Q "**The workload is perfect for me**; I feel like I worked so hard to get into CMC, and I'm paying so much money that if I wasn't getting everything out of my academic experience here, it'd be a waste."

STUDENT AUTHOR: **Professors at Claremont McKenna are friendly, hands-on teachers who care about the general well-being of their students. While there is a hefty workload, Claremont is not a grind school, and generally, the work ebbs and flows in regular cycles. It is not unusual to have two weeks of intense paper-writing and midterm-taking followed by a few weeks of reading.**

Students Speak Out
ON LOCAL ATMOSPHERE

Q "**Claremont (the town) is full of old, rich, white people**, but overall, it's a nice little bubble to live in protected from San Bernardino county to the east, and crappy LA everywhere else."

Q "The Claremont Village is small but has a very pleasant atmosphere. **There are a number of restaurants and a few good ice cream places**. The stores in the Village are catered more to an older, wealthier crowd, rather than college students. However, as you stray out of the city of Claremont and drive along Foothill, there are plenty of other options."

Q "The other four schools surrounding CMC's campus create **a lively environment filled with students and bustling with activities** that many other small liberal arts colleges lack. Instead of feeling like I go to a small, isolated school, Claremont McKenna feels more like a mid-sized university (but with all the benefits of a small school). Plus, our biggest sports rivals are only a block away! How convenient is that?"

STUDENT AUTHOR: **Going to college in Southern California means that it is a drive to get just about everywhere. The only sign of life within walking distance is the Village, a small town most often described as "sleepy." While not far off the mark, this description is slightly unfair. The Village is home to quite a few good, moderately pricey restaurants. Claremont McKenna sits on one of the main thoroughfares of the Inland Empire, however, so there are many college-student-friendly establishments within an easy drive.**

Students Speak Out
ON FACILITIES

Q "**In a word: utilitarian**. Everything works, it's user friendly, but if there was a pretty way to build it, we didn't do it."

Q "Everything's super nice—we're trying to build a new gym, but we keep running out of money. **The library is fantastic**, and we don't really have a student center, but it's okay for what it is."

Q "The facilities of CMC are fantastic, clean, and aesthetically pleasing. The Hub and Student Center lack personality, in comparison to places like the Motley at Scripps and the Grove House at Pitzer. **The library is quite dingy, and not a very comfortable place** to spend long periods of time."

Q "**The student center is pretty lacking**, but to be honest, with a small school, it's tough to really do too much. Plus, there are other student centers on the 5Cs that are usable, too. The library is awesome, though."

Q "We are not the prettiest college (**I say Scripps and Pomona are**). Our gym, however, is awesome."

STUDENT AUTHOR: **Claremont McKenna's campus is well groomed and maintained, almost to the point of obsessive compulsiveness. The grass is mowed religiously, the planters are replanted seemingly every month, and building interiors are spotless every morning. The oldest buildings on campus are only 60 years old. Mostly beige, utilitarian structures with red Spanish tile roofs, the buildings aren't spectacular, but they aren't eyesores either.**

Famous Alumni

Robert Nakasone (former CEO of Toys 'R' Us), Karen Rosenfelt (former president of Paramount Pictures), Robin Williams (actor, comedian—didn't graduate)

Students Speak Out
ON CAMPUS DINING

Q "One of the nicest things about the 5Cs is the ability to eat **at a different dining hall almost every night of the week**."

Q "Collins is great until you get used to it around sophomore year, but you can always change things up by going to the other campuses' dining halls and getting something new. The Hub's okay, **I like the Coop at Pomona a lot better**, and the Motley is good for coffee unless you mind all the hippie free trade stuff."

Q "**Food on campus is terrible**. I scoped out the local dining scene, and I prefer to eat off campus instead."

Q "I love the food. **Good variety, six main dining halls in total**, and lots of opportunities to make stuff yourself if you don't like it. There is also one restaurant on each campus, making basically four greasy spoons and one excellent coffeehouse (the Motley at Scripps). The three best dining halls are Collins (CMC), Frary (Pomona), and Scripps. The quality of the cafeteria food is pretty good, considering it's dining hall food."

STUDENT AUTHOR: **Claremont McKenna students are spoiled by the availability of five other dining halls within a five minute walk. Everyone quickly learns to catch the best of all the campus eateries, like Pitzer lunch, sushi night at Scripps, steak night at Harvey Mudd, and Little Italy day at Claremont. Dining halls are all-you-can-eat, but for mid-meal snacks there are cafés or coffeeshops on all of the campuses.**

Student Body

African American:	4%	Male/Female:	54/46%
Asian American:	12%	Out-of-State:	54%
Hispanic:	11%	International:	6%
Native American:	<1%	Unknown:	17%
White:	50%		

Popular Faiths: Christianity is the dominant religion, but there are many Jewish students, as well.

Gay Pride: Claremont's student body is relatively laid-back, but sexual orientation makes more CMC students uncomfortable than any other diversity issue.

Economic Status: Because CMC gives such generous financial aid, students come from all different walks of life.

Students Speak Out
ON DORMS

Q "Dorms are great, a lot bigger than most other schools' I've seen. Avoid Mid Quad because those dorms are ugly (except for Benson, that's nice). **North Quad is for parties, and South Quad is for studiers**. I'm in the Student Apartments, which are fantastic."

Q "**All of the dorms are very spacious**. There aren't really dorms to avoid on campus unless you are looking for a particular social scene."

Q "I've lived in Berger, Phillips, and Beckett. I liked them all—**there was nothing wrong with any of them**, but in the end, I preferred living in Beckett because girls can live on the first floor, which makes moving in and out much easier."

STUDENT AUTHOR: **Because a vast majority of students live on campus, dorm quality is a high priority at Claremont. North Quad hosts most of the on-campus parties and tends to be a loud place to live— South Quad is relatively quiet, and Mid Quad flip-flops in between. Dorm rooms are roomy, especially doubles, and adjustable furniture allows students to make space by lofting their beds to different heights.**

Did You Know?
98% of undergrads live on campus.

Students Speak Out
ON GUYS & GIRLS

Q "There are hot girls and guys, and there are not-so-hot girls and guys. The range is definitely out there. **A typical student would be a good-looking, bring-home-to-the-family type**, but nothing to swoon over for days."

Q "**People are laid-back, funny, and athletic**. Some of the girls are superficial, but a lot are really chill and so much fun to hang out with."

Q "To me coming to CMC was **like stepping into an Abercrombie and Fitch catalogue**. The style is stereotypically preppy, more upper-middle-class white than what I was used to. It was sort of culture shock for me. Now I'm more accustomed to it. I would say that there are just lots of average-looking people at CMC."

STUDENT AUTHOR: **CMCers like to get out and meet people, whether it's at a party, a concert, a movie, or any other social event. That means tons of chances to meet the one—or just someone, depending on who you're looking for. CMCers dabble in both the one-night stand and the long-term commitment. The five colleges in the Claremont consortium provide a deep pool of all different types of people with hugely varied interests, as well.**

Traditions

Monte Carlo
For Homecoming each year, ASCMC turns the dining hall into a giant casino. Outside there is a hardwood dance floor where couples can swing dance to big band music all night long.

Overall School Spirit
CMCers love CMC, but it isn't school spirit in the traditional sense. People don't turn out to every football game to root for the Stags (although we'll always come out to talk trash to Pomona), but the school spirit manifests itself mainly through the social life on campus.

Students Speak Out
ON ATHLETICS

Q "At CMC, **it's nice that varsity sports are so popular** that it doesn't put you at too much of a disadvantage academically. I opted out of participating in two sports until junior year, once I felt I had a handle on academics, but it is nice to play at a school where people are there because they want to be—there is nothing binding them to staying on the team if they want off."

Q "Varsity sports at CMC may not match up to D-I type events, but **being able to know all of the athletes on the court personally** makes the games a lot of fun."

Q "To be perfectly honest, **varsity sports aren't that great**. IM sports might actually be better because they're so fun to watch."

STUDENT AUTHOR: **There is a great sports rivalry built into the Five Colleges because the schools split into two Division-III teams: the Claremont-Mudd-Scripps Stags/Athena and the Pomona-Pitzer Sagehens. The stands are always packed for games between CMS and PP, and the atmosphere is electric. Other games are typically quieter, but because everyone knows athletes, there are always friends cheering on friends in the crowd.**

Students Speak Out
ON DRUG SCENE

Q "Like most college campuses, **pot is pretty readily available**, but harder drugs are fairly hard to come by. Not too many people smoke cigarettes. Drugs are there if you want them, but definitely not in your face if you don't."

Q "**I believe there are drugs there for those who seek them**, but if you do not want to take part, there is no pressure to do so."

Q "Drugs are as prevalent as you want them to be. There are kids who do them, and **if you go looking, you can find them**. However, everyone is really chill, and peer pressure is extremely low in relation to drugs and slightly higher in relation to drinking."

STUDENT AUTHOR: **There is beer at most major parties, and although at the biggest parties there is generally a pretty secure carding system, the same cannot be said for smaller dorm parties. Marijuana is by far the most prevalent controlled substance on the campus, but strict school policies keep users discreet.**

8:1	Student-to-Faculty Ratio
97%	Freshman Retention Rate
90%	Four-Year Graduation Rate
89%	Financial Aid Applicants Receiving Aid

Students Speak Out
SAFETY & SECURITY

Q "**Camp Sec is usually good at letting kids have their fun** and stepping in when things get out of hand. Some of them do have power trips, though."

Q "**I hear about stuff occasionally going on around the campus**, but I have never witnessed, experienced, or known anyone who has had anything happen to them. No school is 100 percent safe, because they are all publicly accessible, but CMC is definitely up there."

Q "**Most people leave their doors unlocked**, although since that is the case, stuff does get stolen from time to time. In general, it's very safe, though. We are kind of in the middle of suburbia, so the biggest threat is basically an angry soccer mom or something."

STUDENT AUTHOR: **In the dorms, most students live with their doors unlocked and open to make it easier for friends to come visit. There is the occasional theft, but even those are rare, while serious crimes are almost nonexistent. Dorms require ID cards to enter at all times.**

Questions?
For more inside information and survival tips, pick up College Prowler's full-length book on this school, written by an actual student! Check it out at *www.collegeprowler.com.*

Students Speak Out
ON OVERALL EXPERIENCE

Q "If I could do it all again, I would still pick CMC. It's a wonderful place with professors and staff who really care about the students, and overall, all they're trying to do is keep the kids happy and having fun. **The best thing about CMC is the quality of the education I'm getting**, the feeling that we're a community, not a school, and that everyone really cares about what happens to each individual student."

Q "**I am so glad I came here**. At a bigger school, I would be competing for opportunities that, at CMC, are here for the taking. It's incredibly easy to get involved, get jobs, and make friends. I feel so successful here, and I know that if I didn't, it would be easy to get help."

Q "I've loved CMC since I first visited, and **that love has only gotten stronger**. I would share a personal memory, but I can't think of anything legal at the moment."

Q "My experience has been incredible, and I would do it again in a second. **My favorite parts have been the people**, and my least favorite parts have been the finals—however, I'm pretty sure those are unavoidable."

STUDENT AUTHOR: **Claremont McKenna College fits in well with its easygoing Southern California surroundings. The quality of life is great, despite the academic challenges presented by classes. While CMCers don't leave learning and in-class discussions at the door, they aren't bookworms with one-track minds. Academics is mixed into daily life and woven into each individual's interests. The Five College Consortium makes available huge numbers of classes, far more than the typical 1,000-student school.**

Clark Atlanta University

223 James P. Brawley Drive SW; Atlanta, GA 30314
(404) 880-8000; www.cau.edu

THE BASICS:

Acceptance Rate: 53%
Setting: Urban
F-T Undergrads: 3,375

SAT Range: 830–970*
Control: Private
Tuition: $17,038

Most Popular Majors: Business, Communication, Security/Protective Services, Biology, Psychology

*of 1600

Academics	B-	Guys	B
Local Atmosphere	A-	Girls	A
Safety & Security	C	Athletics	D+
Computers	B-	Nightlife	B+
Facilities	C	Greek Life	B+
Campus Dining	B+	Drug Scene	C
Off-Campus Dining	A	Campus Strictness	C+
Campus Housing	C	Parking	C-
Off-Campus Housing	A-	Transportation	B-
Diversity	D-	Weather	B+

Students Speak Out
ON ACADEMICS

Q "Most professors here are very parental and strict, but that's only because **they truly want to see students succeed in life**. If you're the type of person who likes to goof-off or come to class only on test days, then be prepared for a few embarrassing moments, because some teachers will call you out in front of everybody."

Q "When I was taking my core curriculum classes, **there were definitely some professors that I attempted to avoid**, but I learned it's impossible to shake the hard ones every time. My best suggestion to prospective students is to immediately find a few upperclassmen and ask them who to register for and who to avoid at all costs."

Q "**It can be really difficult understanding some of these professors** because of their thick accents. The main reason why my pre-calculus class was so difficult was because of the teacher's heavy accent and his refusal to further explain what exactly he was saying. Usually, the hardest math classes are going to be taught by foreign teachers that you can't understand."

STUDENT AUTHOR: **Clark Atlanta University is a great institution for higher learning among HBCUs and other universities around the world. Small class sizes and constant student attention from caring professors are what continue to give this university the ability to produce excellent leaders in every aspect of society. Prospective students must come prepared for a few embarrassing moments if they are prone to slacking off in class.**

Students Speak Out
ON LOCAL ATMOSPHERE

Q "Ummm, **we are located in the hood**. Being in the urban community really gives you a sense of aspiring to become successful in college. I really want to become successful so that I can help this poor community, not do like some ignorant but prominent African Americans do and just leave it and never look back."

Q "For people who like shopping, **there are plenty of malls** that range from dirt cheap to stupid expensive. Personally, I think the Perimeter Mall is the best overall, because you can find good quality clothes on sale, and when you have a few extra dollars you can splurge on designer clothing from Bloomingdales."

Q "**I never got a chance to experience the FreakNik**, and I was highly disappointed about that because I heard that's when the city use to be real sick. Until they bring the FreakNik back, I'll never give Atlanta any props, Real Talk."

Q "There are a lot of things to do in this city. **Being in the big city can be a bit confusing at first**, especially if you're coming from a small town, but it's not hard to adjust."

STUDENT AUTHOR: **Although Atlanta is not the traditional college town in which a lot of activities are conducted on the actual campus itself, no one can deny the fact that there is always something to do in this restless city. One of the social benefits of choosing a school in Atlanta is that there will always be several parties after events that you have attended that are guaranteed to be crunk.**

5 Best Things	5 Worst Things
1 Atlanta	1 The administration
2 CAU pride	2 No support for athletics
3 Lifetime friendships	3 On-campus food
4 School of Business	4 Male-to-female ratio
5 Homecoming	5 Parking

Students Speak Out
ON FACILITIES

Q "Some of Clark Atlanta University's facilities need to be rebuilt, such as the business building, but it is supposed to be getting rebuilt in the near future. **Other facilities just need to look better, because some look a hot mess**."

Q "Clark is not making good enough efforts to improve some of the facilities that could use some renovations. **The gym is by far the worst building on campus**. The best buildings are the CAU Suites and the Carl and Mary Ware Academic Center."

Q "**I believe that the facilities here at Clark Atlanta are pretty good**, especially compared to some of the other HBCUs I have visited. For Clark to be a private school and an HBCU, I think it does a good job in maintaining the campus and the buildings."

Q "The equipment in places such as the student center can be outdated. At most schools, students enjoy hanging out in the student center because it's fun. **It's hard to create a fun environment in our student center** when all we have in our game room is an air hockey table."

STUDENT AUTHOR: **At first glance, the facilities at Clark Atlanta University may not appear to be the most outdated buildings in the South, but they could certainly stand some renovations. Many students feel that some of the freshman dorms are small and old-fashioned. There are a few other spots on campus that might need a few construction touch-ups here and there, but none are in horrid condition.**

Famous Alumni

Marva Collins, James Weldon Johnson, Emmanuel Lewis, Ma$e, Eva Pigford, Lt. Henry O'Flipper, Jackie Reid, Carl Ware, Louis Tompkins Wright

Students Speak Out
ON CAMPUS DINING

Q "Simply put, **campus dining is cafeteria food— nothing more, nothing less**. Eating on campus sucks because it's almost like you're in high school all over again. The food at Bumstead is not that bad because they usually switch it up a bit. Pork chops from Bumstead are crème de la crème."

Q "**The food is not so bad after you add necessary condiments** such as salt, pepper, and the infamous Texas Pete hot sauce! The key to a good meal is the seasonings."

Q "The Café serves some pretty decent food. Jazzman's is good for smoothies, but that's just about all they have to offer. The problem and difference with this school compared to others is that **we have no real fast food restaurants on campus**. The nearest Popeye's is like a mile or three away from campus, and people get tired of taking the beat-down shuttle bus."

Q "**The fruit man has the best fruit** in the whole city because it's cheap and tasty!"

STUDENT AUTHOR: **Clark Atlanta's main eatery, the Café, provides what seems to be a variety of food for the first few months, but then suddenly the meals become extremely repetitive. The best thing about the Café is that you can always choose to eat pizza, a burger, salad, or breakfast, if you're not into the special meal they have planned for the day. Bumstead also hosts a semi-annual party/ barbeque that gives Clark Atlanta students time to fellowship while they eat.**

Student Body

African American:	87%	Male/Female:	27/73%
Asian American:	<1%	Out-of-State:	77%
Hispanic:	<1%	International:	1%
Native American:	<1%	Unknown:	10%
White:	<1%		

Popular Faiths: Clark Atlanta is affiliated with the United Methodist Church, so most students are either Methodist or Baptist.

Gay Pride: Clark Atlanta University does not have any gay support groups on campus. Homosexuals are generally accepted on Clark Atlanta's campus.

Economic Status: There are some "rich kids," but many attend through scholarships and financial aid.

Students Speak Out
ON DORMS

Q "**I have heard of a lot of unhappy people complain about dorm life**, so I just chose to stay with my mom in our house. I might be missing out on the whole 'freshman experience' thing, but at least I'm living rent-free in a clean house."

Q "Campus housing sucks! Every few years Clark builds a nice new complex for students to rest their heads, **and every few years the knuckleheads trash the place**. It's better to just get a place of your own so you won't have to be bothered with these knuckleheads that seem to have no home training."

Q "I do not think that RAs should live in Heritage Commons. Heritage Commons is supposed to operate as an apartment complex, but **they still have people trying to watch over us**."

STUDENT AUTHOR: **Staying on campus can be an exciting experience for both first-year students and upperclassmen. Clark Atlanta's dormitories are not all fancy and state-of-the-art like some better-funded colleges, but they do provide a comfortable place to lie down. And the dorms' annual freshman step show is always highly anticipated.**

? Did You Know?
27% of undergrads live on campus.

Students Speak Out
ON GUYS & GIRLS

Q "Most of the guys and girls are mature and aware of issues of the opposite sex such as STDs and other gender issues. Although you have some girls who are golddiggers, **most have a focused attitude and know what they want out of life**, and they have the determination to achieve."

Q "Atlanta is the place to be for the grown and sexy crowd. **I don't think any other city compares to Atlanta's black social crowd**. The black women here are absolutely beautiful, and the fellows don't act like knuckleheads."

Q "Being at Clark is almost like being in high school all over again. The girls here bring so much drama, and **most of these boys aren't even worth a penny with a hole in it**!"

STUDENT AUTHOR: **Clark Atlanta University has a diverse student body that includes pretty girls, pretty boys, collegiate thugs, India Aries (the naturals), and almost every other kind of student you can imagine. But the most dominant social assembly is the future businessmen and women at Clark Atlanta University, because future businessmen and women at Clark Atlanta have a top priority, and that is to graduate with a job that pays well.**

Traditions
Clark Atlanta University freshman students are required to attend an introductory ceremony at the beginning of the fall semester.

Overall School Spirit
Clark Atlanta University lacks a lot of school spirit. There is not much school spirit shown by students until the Homecoming game or any game against Morehouse College.

CAU Urban Legends
Clark Atlanta University's cafeteria puts a form of laxative in the food to keep students regular.

Students Speak Out
ON ATHLETICS

Q "**Nobody really cares about the sports at this school**. If you're looking for a school with high school spirit and energy for the sports teams, you will not find it at Clark Atlanta, Morehouse, or Spelman."

Q "I didn't even know we had a basketball team until my sophomore year. **I don't really care too much about sports** because the teams are not that great, and I really don't understand them too much anyway."

Q "Coming from a multicultural high school where other sports besides football were also popular, it was **strange attending a school where nobody cares about the other sports**. As a member of the volleyball team, it disappoints me to see the empty seats at all of the volleyball games."

STUDENT AUTHOR: **Clark Atlanta University has a good athletics department; unfortunately, most students are either unaware or choose to not support their fellow Panthers. Although the total school spirit for the various sporting teams is low, many of the students that are actually involved love their teams and have high expectations of growth in the athletic department.**

Students Speak Out
ON DRUG SCENE

Q "**The weed man has a full-time job on campus**; weed is its own economy. A lot of these weed sellers pay their way through school by selling weed."

Q "**Drugs are really not a big issue on this campus**. Although I know of a few friends who smoke weed, the majority of friends with which I surround myself are very straightforward and law abiding. I have never heard of anyone smoking anything other than weed."

Q "The main illegal substance on our campus is weed, but it isn't anything to worry about, **unless it starts to get in the way of your schoolwork**. Smokey said weed is from the earth!"

STUDENT AUTHOR: **Drug use is not a huge problem here at Clark Atlanta. Students who choose not to smoke marijuana here are never pressured or put down for choosing to stay away from this drug. There are extremely rare cases of reports of study drugs or prescription drug usage, and even rarer are reports of cocaine or crack usage.**

18:1	Student-to-Faculty Ratio
69%	Freshman Retention Rate
19%	Four-Year Graduation Rate
95%	Financial Aid Applicants Receiving Aid

Students Speak Out
SAFETY & SECURITY

Q "**Clark Atlanta University, like most HBCUs, is in the hood**, and we do have some crime that happens every now and then."

Q "I feel secure to walk where I like because the surrounding area is really not that bad compared to Northern ghettoes. **I don't rely on the police or campus security to protect me** because they're fishy."

Q "Even though Clark Atlanta is located in the heart of the city, it's still a decent place to go to school. I have found that most of the people who live in the surrounding area are **very nice people who tend to their own business**. Bottom line: As long as you treat others with respect, they will (for the most part) treat you with respect."

STUDENT AUTHOR: **When students decide to attend Clark Atlanta, they quickly learn where to go, when to go, how to go, who to go with, and what to do when they arrive. Whether it is day or night, Clark Atlanta students are advised not to venture off-campus without the companionship of a friend.**

Questions?
For more inside information and survival tips, pick up College Prowler's full-length book on this school, written by an actual student! Check it out at *www.collegeprowler.com*.

Students Speak Out
ON OVERALL EXPERIENCE

Q "My overall experience at Clark Atlanta has been very exciting. **I've learned so much within my matriculation**. I've learned things about myself, my friends, and life, period. One of the best experiences at Clark Atlanta is meeting friends from so many different places all over the world."

Q "**I have absolutely no regrets in my college decision**. Both my father and mother attended Clark Atlanta when it was simply called Atlanta University, and they loved their experience too!"

Q "My experience at Clark Atlanta has been amazing so far. I'm proud to say that I have met people who I believe will be in my life from now until forever. **The best thing about Clark is the connections and friendships** that you get a chance to build with people from Clark, Morehouse, and Spelman. If I had the chance to do it all over again, I would definitely choose Clark Atlanta University."

Q "You learn so much from your peers, and it's an awesome feeling. **Most of your college friends will remain your friends throughout life**. If I could do this all over again, I probably would, because I think it has been one of the most memorable times of my life. I don't think I would have been the same person if I wouldn't have come to Clark Atlanta."

STUDENT AUTHOR: **The experience that Clark Atlanta University provides its students is one that is incomparable to any other institution of higher learning. Atlanta is arguably the greatest city for successful African Americans (past and present), and that in itself makes Clark Atlanta University one of the best Historically Black Universities to attend in the entire U.S.**

Clark University (MA)

950 Main Street; Worcester, MA 01610-1477
(508) 793-7711; www.clarku.edu

THE BASICS:

Acceptance Rate: 56%
Setting: Mid-size city
F-T Undergrads: 2,169

SAT Range: 1090–1310*
Control: Private
Tuition: $34,220

Most Popular Majors: Psychology, Political Science and Government, Business, Sociology

*of 1600

Academics	A-	Guys	C-
Local Atmosphere	C-	Girls	C+
Safety & Security	C	Athletics	D
Computers	B+	Nightlife	B-
Facilities	C	Greek Life	N/A
Campus Dining	C	Drug Scene	B
Off-Campus Dining	A-	Campus Strictness	B
Campus Housing	B	Parking	B-
Off-Campus Housing	B	Transportation	B
Diversity	C-	Weather	C-

Students Speak Out
ON ACADEMICS

Q "Professors, for the most part, are very helpful. I definitely **appreciated some of the passion the professors had** for what they were teaching. I do find most of my classes interesting, although there will always be that one required course that is a big yawn."

Q "Teachers can either be interesting, fun to talk to in and out of class, or like watching paint dry. Some classes in particular are interesting, but it **really depends on how interested you are in the subject** and how the professor presents the material."

Q "I had excellent teachers at Clark—they were engaging and **offered meaningful, hands-on learning opportunities**. I found almost all of my classes to be very interesting."

Q "**The teachers are amazing**. The majority of professors work hard to develop personal relationships with their students. Academically, most set the bar quite high, but they are always available to help you with questions."

STUDENT AUTHOR: In most cases, students are primarily attracted to Clark because of its noted academic programs. Although the general public may not think of Clark as a household name, other universities do. Special degree options like the fifth-year free accelerated master's program are also a huge draw to the campus. Yet, while students tend to love the classes within their major, they seem to bemoan the non-major classes required for their degree.

Students Speak Out
ON LOCAL ATMOSPHERE

Q "**When I first came to Worcester, I wasn't impressed**, but as I got to know the city, I really began to love it. Worcester has some of the best restaurants ever, and they're often cheap. The nightlife can be fun, too, if you ever motivate yourself to leave campus."

Q "It isn't the most secure area. **It's good to be cautious, just like any other area**. There are other universities very close, but Clarkies tend to only fraternize with WPI, for the most part. Don't walk around certain streets after dark, because some areas are more 'hostile' than others. Definitely try the ethnic restaurants around the area. They're great."

Q "The city of Worcester has nice areas; unfortunately, Clark is not in one of them. There is a feeling among the students that **the immediate surroundings of the University are not as safe as they could be**. Main South is definitely considered an area to stay away from, even though many students walk around at all times of night and never run into any problems. Other universities in Worcester are situated in better locations."

STUDENT AUTHOR: Worcester has its good spots and its bad spots. However, Clark happens to be in one of its worst spots. The average student can certainly have an enjoyable time without running into any trouble in Worcester so long as they use a little bit of common sense and pay attention to their surroundings.

5 Best Things	5 Worst Things
1 Clarkies	1 Construction noise
2 Spree Day	2 Worcester winters
3 Professors	3 On-campus food
4 Freshman dorms	4 Living in Main South
5 Diversity	5 Student apathy

Students Speak Out
ON FACILITIES

Q "Facilities are adequate and are **kept clean and operational**."

Q "**The gym is nice**—it has a good amount of machines, and there normally isn't a wait. The computer labs are also very nice. The student center is great because it's the one central place, and you're always guaranteed to run into many familiar faces."

Q "Much of the Clark campus is **made of old buildings much in need of repair**, but the newer facilities, such as the University Center and Maywood suites, are very nice and in great condition."

Q "**All the facilities are decent**, and they are making improvements to each slowly. The campus is set up pretty well so that everything is not too far of a walk, and you don't need to leave campus to find stuff to do."

Q "Clark has comfortable facilities. **Many of the buildings are old and loved**. The histories of the buildings give the campus its character. They give the University a sense of continuity."

STUDENT AUTHOR: **Clark is not constructed to be a fully self-sufficient island apart from the surroundings of Worcester. That is why the administration chose to have an open-campus policy and not implement some features that some other campuses have such as on-campus movie theaters, clubs, or bowling alleys since they are all so close and easy to get to. But, even without the need for such things, they still do their best to use each building to its fullest potential for the students.**

Famous Alumni

Steven DePaul, Mark Freedman, Matthew Goldman, John Heard, Jeffrey Lurie, Ron Shaich, Debra Jean Strimike

Students Speak Out
ON CAMPUS DINING

Q "Food on campus is okay. They try to have options for every type of eater, but if you're a vegetarian, **it can be hard unless you really love salad**."

Q "The food included with the meal plan isn't anything to brag about, but **Worcester has some of the best restaurants I've ever been to**. Shrewsbury Street is filled with amazing places to eat."

Q "**Campus food is never great unless it's parent's weekend**, and Clark isn't any different. The Bistro has some good food, though, and it is definitely preferable to the caf. It's more like a restaurant than a cafeteria, which is nice."

Q "The food on campus is fair. **It is typical cafeteria food**, but there are always a lot of options, so there is never a day when you can't find anything to eat."

Q "**The food is great in terms of convenience and quantity**, but its quality leaves much to be desired."

STUDENT AUTHOR: **The biggest gripe with the food always comes down to quality and selection. It was once rumored that the Clark University Dining Services was using meat that was of lower quality than dog food, and there are few vegetarian options. Of course, there are a few oases in the barren wasteland of Clark food. The Bistro makes some palatable entrees, albeit for a high price, and the greasy fast food mozzarella sticks at Moonlight can make your night much better.**

Student Body

African American:	2%	Male/Female:	39/61%
Asian American:	4%	Out-of-State:	60%
Hispanic:	2%	International:	8%
Native American:	<1%	Unknown:	18%
White:	66%		

Popular Faiths: Catholics, Muslims, Pagans, and all types of religions are represented at Clark.

Gay Pride: Clark is very tolerant of gay students and has student groups such as GLBTA that promote acceptance throughout the campus.

Economic Status: Clark provides excellent financial aid packages, so chances are that differences between economic strata are not likely to be noticed.

Students Speak Out
ON DORMS

Q "The dorms are better than most schools I've seen. Dodd has the biggest doubles next to Maywood, and Johnson has the biggest singles aside from the year-round houses. **Some of the houses could use fixing**. Maywood is the best all around."

Q "Most of the dorms are showing their age, but they are still functional. The dorms that are on **the far side of Downing Street can seem quiet and isolated from the rest of the campus** at times."

Q "Dorms are fairly nice compared to some of the ones that I've seen. **They're all comfy, if you make them comfy**. The best one is Maywood."

STUDENT AUTHOR: **The best things about Clark housing are that it is spacious and it is guaranteed all four years.** Clark may not have the newest buildings, but they are all well-maintained, and the size of the rooms more than makes up for their age. On top of that, all the housing options are within two minutes' walking distance from any classroom. Many consider the dorms to be the preferred way to live at Clark.

 Did You Know?
74% of undergrads live on campus.

Students Speak Out
ON GUYS & GIRLS

Q "There's a mix at Clark. **I didn't find too many that appealed to me until my junior year**, but that was probably just me."

Q "The nice thing about Clark guys is that, without football, you don't get the big macho jock types. **If you like the soccer player/swimmer build, you'll be happy at Clark**!"

Q "Appearance isn't typically what the students are known for, but **there is the same range of looks at Clark as there is at most places**."

Q "**A lot of Clarkies end up finding their future spouses at Clark**, but it all depends on what you're looking for. If you do it all for the nookie, and you're not satisfied with what's on campus, it's not far to visit the other colleges in the area."

STUDENT AUTHOR: If you wanted to shoot a video about hot college students going crazy, you would not choose Clark as your location. The people at Clark are neither all that hot, nor all that crazy. It may be true that Clark won't win first place in any beauty contests, but aesthetics and looks are not what Clark is about. If you can look past the blandness of the population, you could definitely find the right person to spend your time with.

Traditions

Midnight Breakfast
Each semester, before finals, the campus is invited to the caf to be served breakfast by the faculty.

Spree Day & Pre-Spree Day
Each year on Spree Day classes are cancelled and events are held. Students treat the day before Spree Day as an additional holiday, as well.

Overall School Spirit
Clarkies may not look all that spirited on the surface, but deep down, they know that it means something special to be a Clarkie.

Students Speak Out
ON ATHLETICS

Q "**Basketball is the big thing, because there is no football** at Clark. Since the school is so small, sports are fun to watch, and you know the people playing. Intramural sports are really big with pretty much everyone who gets involved."

Q "**Varsity sports are present, but not huge, on campus**. Going to sporting events is fun, though. Intramurals are pretty popular and a great way to play without committing time to practice."

Q "Clark is not a big sports school, but all those involved treat it like it is. **The intramural sports are fun**, less stressful and demanding, and you get to play on teams with all your friends."

Q "Varsity sports are fun, but **don't expect to win very much**. Intramurals are tons of fun."

STUDENT AUTHOR: At Clark, the sports seem to exist in another world. There is no huge football team to rally behind, and the basketball and baseball games are usually attended by people that are involved in some other sport at Clark. To many Clarkies, it seems that IMs are the real sports action on campus since those competitions are the ones you are most likely to talk about in the UC.

Students Speak Out
ON DRUG SCENE

Q "I wasn't a part of it, but I know that some girl fatally OD'd. **If you're going to do it, be safe about it**, and don't be stupid enough to get caught."

Q "If you want it, you can find it, but you might have to ask around. If you want to avoid it, it's **pretty easy to avoid everything except alcohol and weed**, and it's possible to avoid those, too. One of my best friends stayed straight for all four years, and he was one of the most involved and well-known kids on campus."

Q "I can't comment. **I'm still on parole.**"

STUDENT AUTHOR: Not only is drug use not a large problem among Clark students, most of the drugs seem hard to find. Marijuana is the main illegal drug, but the chances of being pressured by another Clarkie into trying it are slim to none. It is entirely possible for a Clarkie to get through their entire four years at the University without trying any substances.

10:1	Student-to-Faculty Ratio
88%	Freshman Retention Rate
69%	Four-Year Graduation Rate
54%	Financial Aid Applicants Receiving Aid

Students Speak Out
SAFETY & SECURITY

Q "Campus always felt very safe to me. I wouldn't walk far off campus at night, but **the paths around campus are always well-lit**, and there are call-boxes everywhere."

Q "Security and safety on campus are minimal. Efforts are being made to make dorms more secure and inaccessible, but **campus is currently pretty open to the public**. Despite this, I have not, personally, been involved in any incidents."

Q "The campus is **surprisingly secure, considering the neighborhood**. Most people make common sense decisions about their own safety when it comes to traveling around the area, and most don't encounter any problems."

STUDENT AUTHOR: Despite its poor location, Clark maintains an open campus. That means no fences, no security desks in dorms, and no parking garage attendant. Clark does have a swipe-card system, patrols, and cameras, and these small measures do seem to keep the campus population feeling safe.

> **Questions?**
> For more inside information and survival tips, pick up College Prowler's full-length book on this school, written by an actual student! Check it out at *www.collegeprowler.com*.

Students Speak Out
ON OVERALL EXPERIENCE

Q "**Clark fits like a glove**, and you'll know if it's for you relatively soon. I've loved meeting different people, hanging out until 6 a.m., water fights on Spree Day, checking out campus events and lectures, taking the walk of shame, trying out different campus groups, exploring the library, and oh yeah, the academics are good, too."

Q "At times, **it feels as though the school doesn't care very much about the individual students**, but more about the institution as a whole. The school is very strict about transferring credits from other schools. I personally am interested in learning some things that Clark doesn't offer, and I have been told that I can't get credit for any of the classes I want to take."

Q "I am glad I ended up at Clark. I was tempted to transfer at one point, but **I stuck it out and ended up falling in love with the school** and the people."

Q "I loved Clark. I am glad I went, and **I don't think I could've been happier anywhere else**. The kids are very friendly and open-minded; it's also easy to meet many different kinds of people."

STUDENT AUTHOR: The students say it best: Clark is a great place to spend four important—perhaps the most important—years of your life. Those that go to Clark report being glad they went. They say that they learned what they wanted to learn in their major, had a lot of fun, and grew up in the process. No campus is perfect, but despite Clark's flaws, students still manage to fall in love with it and pursue their degrees until the end. Clark's strengths lie in its academics, its community, and the city in which it resides.

Clemson University

106 Sikes Hall; Clemson, SC 29634
(864) 656-3311; www.clemson.edu

THE BASICS:

Acceptance Rate: 55%
Setting: Rural
F-T Undergrads: 13,135

SAT Range: 1650–1940*
Control: Public
Tuition: $19,480

Most Popular Majors: Business, Engineering, Education, Social Sciences, Health Professions

*of 2400

Academics	B-	Guys	A
Local Atmosphere	B-	Girls	A
Safety & Security	A-	Athletics	A
Computers	B	Nightlife	B
Facilities	A-	Greek Life	A
Campus Dining	B	Drug Scene	B+
Off-Campus Dining	B	Campus Strictness	B
Campus Housing	B-	Parking	D
Off-Campus Housing	A	Transportation	B+
Diversity	D-	Weather	B+

Students Speak Out
ON ACADEMICS

Q "The ratio is about 16:1 or 18:1. **Certain classes are huge**, but professors generally try to get to know you as more than just a face in the class."

Q "I've had really good experiences with my teachers. There are a couple professors that I go out with for lunch or for coffee. There are a lot of **professors whom I consider to be friends** of mine first and professors second."

Q "Professors are on average really good at Clemson. You can go to a Web site that my honor fraternity, Phi Sigma Pi, runs: *http://people.clemson.edu/~psp/ryp.htm* and within it, there is a tool called '**Rate Your Professor**' where you can look up how other students rate the teachers."

Q "About **80 percent of my professors are great**. Like every other school, there are some bad apples (jerks that don't care, old people who are a little out of their minds, etc.), but you can always find someone who cares and is willing to offer support."

STUDENT AUTHOR: **Although Clemson is no Ivy League school, it is still an outstanding public university devoted to educating and preparing its students for life after college. As the years go by and the standards for entrance get higher, Clemson is becoming more and more distinguished. The University's strong academic programs are only getting stronger, but with state budgets running in the red, the road ahead may be a little rocky.**

Students Speak Out
ON LOCAL ATMOSPHERE

Q "If you are looking for nightlife and clubs, this isn't the school for you. Don't get me wrong—it's a total party school if you want it to be. It's just that it's more of a **college bar and frat party scene** and not a night club thing."

Q "There are a lot of **places nearby where you can go hiking** and see waterfalls and camp. It's also good to make friends with someone who has a boat or Waverunner because it's fun to go out on Lake Hartwell. Also, Lake Keowee is about 15 minutes away, and it's beautiful! Supposedly Oprah has a lake house on it."

Q "Clemson University makes the town of Clemson. If it weren't for CU, Clemson would not be on the map! The **town survives because of the college kids**."

Q "Clemson is definitely a 'college town.' Without the school, there is not much to it. Downtown consists mainly of one street. Outside of Clemson there is **not much to do**; I can't name any outrageously cool museums, clubs, or restaurants to go to. The one thing that's great is gathering a group of friends and going camping."

STUDENT AUTHOR: **Some students say there isn't much to do in or around Clemson, while others say they can't get enough of the outdoor activities the region has to offer. Clemson has a golf course and an enormous man-made lake on the outskirts of campus. Greenville and Atlanta are great for the club/bar scene, and the Appalachian Mountains offer everything from camping to water skiing.**

5 Best Things	5 Worst Things
1 Athletics	1 Little diversity
2 School spirit	2 Dorms
3 Safety & Security	3 Strictness
4 Friendly town	4 No parking
5 Modern facilities	5 Far from nearby cities

Students Speak Out
ON FACILITIES

Q "Our **facilities are constantly upgraded** to ensure that they are top-notch."

Q "The student union is brand new. It has a **bowling alley, hair salon, and lots of other things**. It is awesome! The athletic building is called 'Fike.' There are weights, aerobic classes (all sorts), exercise equipment, and an Olympic-sized pool."

Q "The athletic facilities in general have undergone major updates, including **renovations to Death Valley**, which is still one of the largest college stadiums in the United States. Littlejohn, the basketball arena, just received major renovations."

Q "A lot of the **classes are in really old buildings that have been retrofitted** with necessary technology such as wireless Internet and digital projectors. Many of these buildings don't look especially good on the interior, but they serve their purpose."

Q "Lots of computer labs on campus, though they will be crowded. The varsity **athletic facilities have all undergone facelifts** and, wow, this place looks absolutely fantastic."

STUDENT AUTHOR: It seems like there is always yellow tape somewhere on campus—construction is never-ending. The Hendrix Student Center, Fike Recreation Center, Littlejohn Coliseum (basketball), Tiger Field (baseball), and Clemson Memorial Stadium were all recently renovated. Although some of campus is outdated, Clemson is perpetually engaged in improving its services to students.

Famous Alumni

David Beasley, W.B. Camp, Dale Davis, General Earl Morris, Phil Prince, Strom Thurmond

Students Speak Out
ON CAMPUS DINING

Q "There are usually about **five main dishes to choose from at each meal**, and there are 'standards' at every meal, too—cereal, pizza, pasta, sandwich wraps."

Q "There is cafeteria food; nothing more, nothing less. It's not bad, and they usually offer a good variety and have theme days to try and spice it up; there are several other places on campus, too, that are good. For instance, the student union has a food court with things like **Burger King and Chick-fil-A**."

Q "The first semester, you won't mind the food at all. I will warn you, however, that **second semester you probably will be tired of it**. There are also other choices aside from the meal plan. The food court in the Hendrix Center, Fernow Street Cafe, and the Canteen in the Student Union are great alternatives."

Q "The dining halls have a good variety, and nobody can screw up cereal, so you've always got a safety net. In short, it's not bad, but it's **not as good as cooking for yourself**."

STUDENT AUTHOR: When at college, what you're given is what you eat. Clemson is no exception. Students say the food is tolerable, and there are certain places that are better than others. Clemson House and Schilleter are agreed to be better dining halls than Harcombe. Other alternatives are the Hendrix Center's East Side Food Court and the Fernow Street Café. However, students do complain about early dining hall closing hours.

Student Body

African American:	7%	Male/Female:	55/45%
Asian American:	2%	Out-of-State:	33%
Hispanic:	1%	International:	<1%
Native American:	<1%	Unknown:	0%
White:	90%		

Popular Faiths: The most common religion at Clemson is Christianity.

Gay Pride: There is a gay-straight alliance club, but the student body's attitude tends to be less accepting of the homosexual population than it should be.

Political Activity: College Democrats and College Republicans do exist, but they are seldom the center of attention on campus.

Students Speak Out
ON DORMS

Q "I lived in Johnstone, the worst dorm on campus. Everybody knows it, and everybody makes fun of it. The walls are all metal, for starters. However, the experience is awesome. Right away, **you bond over the terrible building** and start friendships. You're in college; you don't need a room worthy of the Four Seasons."

Q "The apartments, for the most part, are nice; particularly Lightsey Bridge and new east campus apartments. New east campus is a little pricey, but **man, are those nice**."

Q "Shoeboxes are nice, but they are exactly what the name implies—**a shoebox**. Go for the high rises; they are really nice."

Q "The best dorms are **Holmes, McCabe, and Calhoun Courts** (on-campus apartments)."

STUDENT AUTHOR: **Dorms at Clemson range from outdated to top of the line. A lot of construction has taken place in recent years to improve student living conditions, and if you can't find a dorm that feels like home after your first year, there are many off-campus housing options to choose from.**

Did You Know?
47% of undergrads live on campus.

Students Speak Out
ON GUYS & GIRLS

Q "Clemson has the **hottest girls of any campus** I've ever seen, and I have probably been to over 20 large school campuses. They are even better than UF and UGA."

Q "The guys like to watch sports and drink beer. A lot of the girls are **looking for their MRS degree**. Most of them look pretty good."

Q "Get used to **doors being opened** for you."

Q "Since it's in the Southeast, it's a whole 'Southern hospitality' thing we've got going here. The majority of people from the South talk to the people they pass whether they know them or not—or if we don't talk, **we'll definitely smile**."

STUDENT AUTHOR: **Coincidentally, once the weather gets warm, class attendance for males seems to reach an unusual high, just as the number of females sunbathing on Bowman Field increases. Needless to say, Southern "gents" and "belles" at Clemson take pride in their appearances. Although some say there is a certain degree of superficiality, it certainly isn't enough to detract from their enthusiastic opinion of the guys and girls here.**

Traditions

Homecoming and Tigerama
On Homecoming game day, Tigerama is the largest student-run pep rally, and it includes the crowning of Miss Homecoming and student-performed skits.

Running Down the Hill
Clemson Tigers still run down the grassy field before each home game, even though it's no longer necessary after the building of the west stands.

Overall School Spirit
Clemson students' blood runs orange, especially for their football and basketball teams.

Students Speak Out
ON ATHLETICS

Q "Varsity sports are enormous. IM sports are enormous. If you like sports, there's no better place. In the fall, there are two things you can bet on and never lose: **church on Sunday morning and football on Saturday afternoon**. College football is an absolute institution here."

Q "**I hated football when I came**, but being here made me love it. "

Q "**We are Division I and on ESPN a lot**, so that's cool—Clemson has a tradition of being really strong in almost every sport that we offer on the varsity level."

Q Aside from football, there are tons of other sports to be a part of or support, from club level ice-hockey and crew, to ultimate Frisbee, soccer, baseball, and golf. **We've got it all**."

STUDENT AUTHOR: **Sports are a way of life at Clemson. It is perhaps one of the best schools for you to watch or play any sport imaginable, from Division I to intramural. Club and intramural sports give you the opportunity to try something you wouldn't believe a university would even sponsor—just don't tell your parents that you're skydiving.**

Students Speak Out
ON DRUG SCENE

Q "If anything, people smoke marijuana, but that's about it. Lots of people either don't do drugs or hide it very well—**drinking is a different story**, though!"

Q "**Nothing heavy** such as heroin or cocaine, but I've seen marijuana and some different pills. It's not that bad at all, especially for a major university."

Q "I don't use drugs, and **people who do don't bother me** in any way."

Q "The most popular drugs are **pot and ecstasy**, but I don't think there's a huge problem with them. However, there are quite a few smokers."

STUDENT AUTHOR: Students at Clemson speak positively of the drug scene. Besides the heavy alcohol consumption, drugs are only available if you're looking for them. Those people who do drugs don't tend to pressure those who don't. Heavy drug usage such as cocaine and heroin is rather scarce—a good sign.

16:1	Student-to-Faculty Ratio
89%	Freshman Retention Rate
40%	Four-Year Graduation Rate
71%	Financial Aid Applicants Receiving Aid

Students Speak Out
SAFETY & SECURITY

Q "CU has its own police department, and every year they have a '**Safe Walk**.' Members of the school and community are invited to attend and share ideas on ways to improve security."

Q "**Clemson acts as a municipality**, so it has its own police force, fire, and EMS."

Q "It's pretty good. There are campus cops, sign-ins with ID at all the dorms, and other stuff like that. It is still part of a city at night, but I'm a chick and **I haven't seen any big problems**."

Q "It's a small town atmosphere with a **very low crime rate**. Maybe once a year or so, you hear about someone getting attacked on campus, but it is definitely the exception, not the rule."

STUDENT AUTHOR: Security phones, police escorts, and lights all over campus help make Clemson a safe environment for students. Clemson also holds an annual Safe Walk involving students and community members who walk the campus and discuss ways to improve safety.

Questions?
For more inside information and survival tips, pick up College Prowler's full-length book on this school, written by an actual student! Check it out at www.collegeprowler.com.

Students Speak Out
ON OVERALL EXPERIENCE

Q "Clemson got inside me. You'll see bumper stickers around here that say '**my blood runneth orange**,' but nobody really understands that's the way it works until you get here."

Q "I'm from Orlando, so **it took me a while** to get used to the small-town, 'heavily Southern' atmosphere, but once I did, it really started to grow on me. It's an awesome school—a lot of fun."

Q "I didn't want to come to Clemson at first. My mind was set on UNC my entire life, but UNC doesn't accept many out-of-state students. So, when I was deferred until May, I had to make a choice, and I went with Clemson—**best decision I've made** regarding my education."

Q "I never had 'that' school where I wanted to go. I simply had an idealized vision of having a **classic college experience**. Clemson is pretty close."

Q "I am definitely glad I picked Clemson, and it's not just me—people love the school. Clemson (and SC) pride are definitely in the air. **People are friendly and happy** to be here . . . It's a little secluded, so it's kind of our own little world. I wouldn't have it any other way!"

STUDENT AUTHOR: Clemson offers an amazing college experience. Students return for the rest of their lives to see how the campus has changed and to support the Tigers. Although it is located in a small town, the school is big enough that there is never a dull moment, and the location only makes the student body closer to one another. As anyone who has been to Clemson knows, the Clemson spirit is contagious for almost anyone who attends.

Colby College

4000 Mayflower Hill; Waterville, ME 04901
(207) 872-3474; www.colby.edu

THE BASICS:

Acceptance Rate: 32%
Setting: Rural
F-T Undergrads: 1,867

SAT Range: 1910–2150*
Control: Private
Tuition: $41,770**

Most Popular Majors: Social Sciences, English, Race and Ethnic Studies, History, Biology

*of 2400   **includes room & board

Academics	A-	Guys	B
Local Atmosphere	C-	Girls	B+
Safety & Security	B+	Athletics	B
Computers	C	Nightlife	B-
Facilities	B	Greek Life	N/A
Campus Dining	A	Drug Scene	B+
Off-Campus Dining	B+	Campus Strictness	C+
Campus Housing	C+	Parking	B-
Off-Campus Housing	D	Transportation	D
Diversity	D+	Weather	C-

Students Speak Out
ON ACADEMICS

Q "Generally, courses are as interesting as you make them. **Students have so much liberty** to choose their own classes. It would be ridiculous to take a class that you didn't find interesting."

Q "The teachers are terrific and always willing to help outside of class. They encourage you to ask for help whenever needed. The classes I took as a freshman were mostly introductory courses, and from what I hear, are **not nearly as interesting** as the upper-level courses."

Q "The professors are generally really great; some of them are phenomenal. Some classes at Colby are irreplaceable. You have to take them because **they're that powerful**. Of course, there are a couple of standard classes with standard professors, too."

Q "Teachers are all different, of course, but all of them are **highly qualified**. Some teachers are super-organized, and others are scattered. I've never had one that I hated too much. Classes are interesting depending on how much you like the subject. I hate math, but when I took 'Math as a Liberal Art,' I still found myself interested in much of the subject matter."

STUDENT AUTHOR: Colby is a liberal arts school through and through. While we haven't eliminated core requirements entirely, we've whittled them down to seven "distribution requirements." Upperclassmen are always raving about their favorite teachers, so talking to them is a great way to get a handle on which teachers are Colby legend, and which can be skipped.

Students Speak Out
ON LOCAL ATMOSPHERE

Q "The Colby campus is generally viewed as **separate from the surrounding area**. Students have little interest in interacting with the local town, and those of the town feel the same about Colby."

Q "Not too many people spend that much time in Waterville. If you go off campus it's usually to Portland, Freeport, **Sugarloaf (the ski mountain)** or to other mountains to hike or climb. But Waterville provides everything we need; great pizza, pharmacies, hospitals, and a few awesome places to take the parents."

Q "The town we technically live in, and I say technically because campus is separated from the town, is a **somewhat depressed Maine town**, and our relationship with the people of Waterville is not at its best."

Q "Don't be afraid of the townies! Take a regular visit to **Mainely Brew or the Bob In**. They only think you're stuck up if you actually are, so feel free to hang out at some of the dives and make a few friends."

STUDENT AUTHOR: Waterville is typically viewed as a quaint and impoverished town. It's definitely a far cry from the Main St. college towns of many universities. While it provides Colby students with what they need, it is definitely not an attraction. Most students see a divide between the school and the town, although the Colby Volunteer Center, and groups like the South End Coalition are working hard to improve town-gown relations.

5 Best Things
1 Great professors
2 Friendly people
3 Activities
4 Getting Involved
5 Hot people

5 Worst Things
1 The weather
2 Nasty beer
3 The Jitney
4 Poor dance music
5 Rural surroundings

Students Speak Out
ON FACILITIES

Q "Colby is uber-pristine—they take great care of all the facilities and buildings, and are always trying to **offer the best to the students**. If anything falls below par, they re-do it."

Q "Some buildings are old and crappy but others are new and state-of-the-art. There's a wide variety. Overall, the buildings are **up-to-date on technology**, and they are going through a lot of renovations."

Q "The facilities on campus are state-of-the-art. I remember when I first visited Colby it looked like someone daily polished the lettering on every building. **The athletic center is very nice**; it gets crowded at high times (four or five in the afternoon) when everyone goes to work out, but if you go at the off times, you'll be fine. I love the town hall theme in Page Commons, where many speakers and dances are held."

Q "**All the facilities are top notch**. When it comes to physical buildings and their contents, I couldn't ask for more. One big problem is that the athletic center is as far away from the dorms as it can be. And as for the student center, it's only a student center in name. The only reason students go there at all is because it houses the post office and the ATM."

STUDENT AUTHOR: **Some students claim to have chosen to come to Colby because all the buildings matched. The buildings and landscaping are definitely top-quality, and the view from the Miller Library steps is nothing short of breathtaking. The athletic center is well liked and well used—sometimes, a little too well used.**

Famous Alumni

Billy Bush, Doris Kearns Goodwin, Elijah P. Lovejoy, Annie Prouix, Alan Taylor

Students Speak Out
ON CAMPUS DINING

Q "For college food, Colby does pretty well. I have always been pleased, and **surprisingly impressed** by the selection and quality."

Q "The food is amazing—I never get sick of it. Foss has, hands down, the best atmosphere, and really the most quality food (including the best salad bar). **Dana and Bob's are fairly tasty**, too, but not quite as exciting. The omelet and grilled cheese bars are amazingly one of a kind."

Q "All of the dining halls are good. Where you eat says a lot about you. I like that they all have good salad bars, and there is **always fresh fruit**. The desserts are dangerous, though. Beware: there are so many, and they all taste so good!"

Q "The food on campus is extraordinarily good. All three dining halls serve different, but high quality, food. Just be careful to know exactly what you're eating at Foss or you might get a nasty surprise. After a year, the food can get a little drab, but there's huge potential for mixing foods to keep things interesting. My favorite is cutting up the Sunday night chicken fingers into a salad, and pairing it with a mug full of root beer and a scoop of ice cream. **Creativity is the difference** between dorm food and cuisine."

STUDENT AUTHOR: **Dining is integral to Colby social life, and the individual characteristics of the three dining halls are part of what defines campus politics. Tables in the dining halls are big, as they are meant for large groups of friends, and they usually end up overcrowded anyway.**

Student Body

African American:	2%	Male/Female:	45/55%
Asian American:	8%	Out-of-State:	90%
Hispanic:	3%	International:	6%
Native American:	1%	Unknown:	5%
White:	75%		

Gay Pride: In general, the campus is very supportive of gay-rights issues, but tends to get uncomfortable if things get too loud.

Economic Status: Most students seem to come from very well-off backgrounds. Although the school is economically diverse, these differences aren't easy to see, which contributes to the perception of the school as entirely populated by rich, white, New Englanders.

Students Speak Out
ON DORMS

Q "**The dorms are adequate**. Some of the dorms have been newly renovated, and they are nicer than others. Johnson, Averill, and AMS are really nice; Treworgy and Grossman I would avoid."

Q "Since the remodeling and revamping of the dorms on campus, there really aren't any dorms that are truly awful. **Heights is ugly**, but has two room doubles, and is close to a dining hall. The Hillside dorms (or 'ugly white buildings') aren't so hot, but the rooms are big. Frat Row has smaller rooms, but isn't bad for location."

Q "The dorms are spacious and comfortable, but there are some that are tiny. Dorms on Frat Row don't have **the best bathrooms**. All are equipped with one or more common rooms, kitchens, televisions, and vending machines."

STUDENT AUTHOR: **Dorms are pretty hit-or-miss. There aren't really any phenomenal rooms, but nothing's too abysmal either. Dorms are renovated on a 20-year rotating schedule, so no building is more than 20 years old, and something is always being updated. Chem-free is a surprisingly popular living option, and carries no stigma whatsoever.**

> **Did You Know?**
> 94% of undergrads live on campus.

Students Speak Out
ON GUYS & GIRLS

Q "I feel that the Colby students are generally attractive. **The dating scene is interesting**. You are either dating (which means you are practically married) or you are just hooking up. It is very hard to find an in between."

Q "One can find pretty attractive women and pretty loud and annoying girls. Colby has an online dating service called '**Mulematch**'—use it at your discretion."

Q "Colby is **notorious** for its beautiful people."

Q "**Everyone is so friendly**; I was struck when I first came here that everyone smiled at you, even if you didn't know who they were. Although, all the Ralph Lauren, Tiffany's heart bracelets, and pastel matching seemed a little over-the-top."

STUDENT AUTHOR: **Most people choose to come to Colby because of the friendliness of the students. Colby folks smile at each other, make conversation easily, and are overwhelmingly optimistic. Alcohol is definitely a huge part of the social scene, though, and can get to be a bit much at times. Work-hard, play-hard is a term practically modeled off social life at Colby. Classes are rigorous and homework does pile up, but for most students, weekends are a time for debauchery.**

Traditions

The Miller Steps
The steps leading to Miller Library are a symbolic beginning and end to life at Colby.

Champaign Toast
On the last day of classes, seniors gather on the Miller Steps (surprise, surprise) to toast the school.

Overall School Spirit
While varsity sports might not be huge, Colby spirit is alive and well. Some are apathetic, but rivalries with Bates and Bowdoin, can incite even the least spirited students to bouts of chanting.

Students Speak Out
ON ATHLETICS

Q "Because Colby is so small, sometimes it feels as though almost everyone plays a sport, whether varsity or club. Colby is a very athletic and **outdoorsy school**—most students are active."

Q "There's a significant group that plays varsity sports, but an equally significant one that doesn't. The interaction between these groups is fairly good. If you play a varsity sport, there's a strong tendency to **get sucked in** and have few friends outside the team, though."

Q "Varsity sports are pretty big and intramural sports are really fun—**Go Mules!**"

Q "The Colby-Bates football game and the Colby-Bowdoin hockey game are famous. Around the time of the **Colby-Bates football game**, you see many students wearing 'Buck Fates' T-shirts."

STUDENT AUTHOR: **"Real" sports don't get too much attention here, certainly not as much as they do at major universities with big football teams. Lacrosse and soccer can be pretty popular, and hockey games are comparatively well attended. The Bates football rivalry and the Bowdoin hockey rivalry boost the attendance at those games, as well.**

Students Speak Out
ON DRUG SCENE

Q "When it comes time to turn papers in, kids stick a bunch of **Ritalin up their noses** and turn things in on extension."

Q "The illegal drug scene is overall weak and deep underground. Everyone knows someone who smokes pot, and someone else who smokes up all the time, but no one will try to pressure you to. **Alcohol is everywhere**. It's rare for there to be pressure to drink, but it does happen. Binge drinking is really common."

Q "The only drugs you can easily obtain are marijuana and **ADD medication**. Prescription meds are difficult to come by, and I have not yet seen cocaine. If this is what you are looking for, try a city university."

STUDENT AUTHOR: **There is no cocaine in the bathrooms for Colby students. We may be reliant on alcohol for fun, but drug use is rare and kept quiet. Marijuana is the biggest illicit vice; certain dorms never really lose that stoner smell. Hard drug use does exist, and those who are looking for drugs know exactly where to find them.**

10:1	Student-to-Faculty Ratio
93%	Freshman Retention Rate
84%	Four-Year Graduation Rate
89%	Financial Aid Applicants Receiving Aid

Students Speak Out
SAFETY & SECURITY

Q "Colby does an excellent job of making students feel secure. My only complaint about security is that they are often **too interested in breaking up parties** and fining students."

Q "I've never felt in danger at Colby. Security works incredibly hard to keep us safe, and is always in the process of improving their equipment and methods. There's a **student escort system**, so no one has to walk anywhere by themselves. All you have to do is call the security office and ask for the escort to walk you where you're going."

Q "**Security is very good** at Colby. They've recently improved it even more, and they're always around and available to help."

STUDENT AUTHOR: **Colby's isolated location is certainly a reason for this sense of safety. Also, Colby security is very visible and very well known. Most students can tell you the names and nicknames of at least one security officer, and it's not uncommon for students to stop and chat with whichever officer is prowling around outside dances.**

> **Questions?**
> For more inside information and survival tips, pick up College Prowler's full-length book on this school, written by an actual student! Check it out at www.collegeprowler.com.

Students Speak Out
ON OVERALL EXPERIENCE

Q "I absolutely adore being at Colby, even though it's an hour and a half to the nearest airport. The faculty is great, **the people are nice** and friendly, and the school does its best to take care of us and give us the best education that it can."

Q "I have never had any regrets about going to Colby. **The time has gone too fast**, and as I begin my senior year, I only wish I could do it all over again."

Q "I love it at Colby. It seems like everyone is just so happy to be there and loves this school as much as I do. Everyone is always looking for fun things to do and **more cool people to meet**. The people at this school are what make it so amazing. They are down-to-earth and love what they're doing."

Q "Colby academically far surpasses all of my expectations. Classes are great, teachers are amazing, and the workload, although heavy, is **manageable if you forgo sleep**, but socially, Colby seems to be drastically stunted. Life at Colby tends to revolve (like many other colleges) around alcohol."

STUDENT AUTHOR: **Colby students love Colby. While they can always find something to complain about—the weather, the town, the lack of diversity, and the homework—they tend to be happy here. Most cite the academics and the friendly atmosphere. Classes and professors are undeniably wonderful, and the student body tends to be happy, friendly, and optimistic. The school is not for everyone. However, being up on Mayflower Hill all the time can drive you crazy if you can't find a way to get into town every now and then.**

Colgate University

13 Oak Drive; Hamilton, NY 13346
(315) 228-1000; www.colgate.edu

THE BASICS:

Acceptance Rate: 26%
Setting: Rural
F-T Undergrads: 2,753

SAT Range: 1260–1430*
Control: Private
Tuition: $37,405

Most Popular Majors: English, Political Science, Economics, Sociology

*of 1600

Academics	A-	Guys	A-
Local Atmosphere	C+	Girls	A
Safety & Security	A+	Athletics	A-
Computers	B+	Nightlife	B
Facilities	A-	Greek Life	A-
Campus Dining	B+	Drug Scene	B+
Off-Campus Dining	B-	Campus Strictness	B+
Campus Housing	A-	Parking	B-
Off-Campus Housing	C	Transportation	B-
Diversity	C-	Weather	D+

Students Speak Out
ON ACADEMICS

Q "Classes in the afternoon interest me more than classes in the morning. As for classes being fun and interesting, Colgate offers a wide enough variety of such a **high quality** that class is always interesting."

Q "My Western Traditions class, which **everybody has to take** (and most people hate), was my absolute favorite class I've taken at Colgate, because the prof was enthusiastic and fun."

Q "For the most part, you can usually find out from other students which classes and **professors to avoid**. I only find my classes to be boring when they turn out to be much different than I expected."

Q "The quality of teaching at Colgate is excellent. Colgate pays a great deal of attention to student feedback regarding the **quality of the classroom** experience when extending professorships—there are no publishing jockeys with poor classroom presence here."

STUDENT AUTHOR: **Colgate professors make the learning experience interesting and worthwhile. Because Colgate has only a handful of graduate students, undergrads have many opportunities to gain lab and research experience. Be persistent—profs can, and usually will, sign you into a course with a demonstrated desire to get in it. In summary, Colgate's top-notch curriculum and accessible professors will challenge your mind, but course registration is a nightmare.**

Students Speak Out
ON LOCAL ATMOSPHERE

Q "It's such a small town, but such a community because of it. Colgate does a really nice job of organizing '**Town and Gown**' events, and letting students know about things going on in town."

Q "The town is really quaint and friendly, but it is sleepy, and there is **nothing to do beyond partying**. The school tries to say that they promote other things besides drinking, but good luck trying to find stuff to do if you don't drink."

Q "**Colgate is not a suitcase school**. In any given weekend, roughly 96 percent of the student body is present on campus at any given time."

Q "If you want a busy, sprawling metropolis, Colgate is not the school for you. It's quite small, and the closest **Wal-Mart is about 30 minutes away**. However, I think that because Hamilton is so centered around Colgate, it makes a student feel like they are connected to the community."

STUDENT AUTHOR: **Colgate is a small, college-oriented community that doubles in size when Colgate's students arrive in the fall. While Hamilton totes a limited array of shops and eateries, these businesses completely cater to the college kid. This is the kind of town where the pizza places deliver right to your dorm room door, where local restaurants offer special rates for student events, and where September kicks off with a "Streetfest" featuring student bands, sidewalk sales, and a game of twister sprawled across the pavement on a blocked-off Lebanon Street.**

5 Best Things	**5 Worst Things**
1 Resources	1 Course registration
2 Weekends	2 Hit-or-miss professors
3 Accessible staff	3 Cold winters
4 Beautiful campus	4 Tiny dorm rooms
5 Work hard, play hard	5 Housing lottery

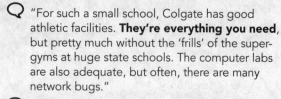

Students Speak Out
ON FACILITIES

Q "For such a small school, Colgate has good athletic facilities. **They're everything you need**, but pretty much without the 'frills' of the super-gyms at huge state schools. The computer labs are also adequate, but often, there are many network bugs."

Q "Our facilities are the best. They bought all new computers in the past few years, and **completely renovated both the Coop** (student center) and the fitness center."

Q "For a small Division I school, the athletic facilities are pretty nice. The fields could use some improvement, but the athletic center is in great condition, and the field house is **convenient and well kept**."

Q "The student center has been dubbed a 'ski lodge,' and athletic **facilities have been recently replaced**, too."

Q "I would describe Colgate as very decked out— **except for Gatehouse** (a freshman dorm). Everything is very nice and state-of-the-art."

STUDENT AUTHOR: Since receiving new furniture, floor tiles, bathrooms—new everything—the Coop is one of the most stylish and high-traffic places on campus. In addition to modern and aesthetically-pleasing facilities, Colgate's beautiful campus is one of its biggest selling points. The campus boasts attractive limestone buildings stretched across a hilly, tree-lined campus. Because it is a small school, all the facilities are within a 10-minute walk. On sunny days, kids blast music from their dorm rooms and lay out in the Quad.

Famous Alumni
Monica Crowley, Ray Hartung, Andy McDonald, Eugene Robinson, William P. Rodgers, Andy Rooney, Ed Werner and John Haney, Bob Woodruff

Students Speak Out
ON CAMPUS DINING

Q "As far as college food goes, **Colgate isn't really that bad**. Frank, the main dining hall, has many food options for a student to choose from. The Coop has good food, including stir-fry, loafer sandwiches, and wraps."

Q "Frank (main dining hall) has the best food on campus. You get **the biggest selection** for your money. I'm not a very picky eater, but I've never had a problem finding something satisfying to eat."

Q "The food is okay. **Better than most campuses**, I think. There's always cereal, salad, and sandwiches as backups, in case you don't like the main option."

Q "When giving campus tours, I usually tell prospective students and families that campus food is good enough that you can easily **gain your Freshman 15**, if you are not careful."

Q "My favorite thing about Frank is the workers! They're so **nice and very funny**."

STUDENT AUTHOR: The dining plan includes several eateries, with the infamous Frank Dining Hall being the biggest. Frank offers a large variety of food and plenty of vegetarian options. The food is satisfying for the first few months, but after a while, picky eaters will find the regular rotations predictable and monotonous. The Coop has higher quality food than general Frank fare, but since they serve the same thing every week, there is also little variety. Lazy weekend brunches are a staple to both freshman social life and the rumor mill.

Student Body

African American:	5%	Male/Female:	48/52%
Asian American:	7%	Out-of-State:	68%
Hispanic:	4%	International:	5%
Native American:	<1%	Unknown:	4%
White:	75%		

Popular Faiths: Christianity is the main religion on campus, but 20 percent of Colgate students are Jewish.

Gay Pride: Colgate is an open-minded community with a small LBGTQ population.

Economic Status: Colgate students carry designer handbags, flip the collars on their Polo shirts, and drive new models of SUVs.

Students Speak Out
ON DORMS

Q "In the first-year dorms, **go for a suite**, they offer a lot of space, and up your odds for getting a roommate that you really like."

Q "**Andrews suites are the nicest**—they have large bay windows and mantelpieces over old fireplaces that make the common rooms really feel like a homey living room. Gate House was temporary housing that they never tore down."

Q "One hall to avoid is the Gate House. It was built as temporary housing in the '80s, and well, 20 years later it's still here. You're guaranteed to see holes in the drywall and **unidentifiable substances** in the bathrooms after parties."

STUDENT AUTHOR: **For first-year students who all live in neighboring dorms on "the hill," the popular spots are Andrews and Stillman, the two residential halls that offer suite-style living. Two double bedrooms share a common room, so the extra space is a key attraction. Students agree that freshmen should avoid Gate House, the butt of every campus housing joke. The Townhouse Community is rather new, and hence the best housing available for upperclassmen.**

Did You Know?
94% of undergrads live on campus.

Students Speak Out
ON GUYS & GIRLS

Q "Many of the boys and girls at our school are fresh-faced and exercise regularly, and are thus quite **physically attractive**."

Q "There's practically **no dating scene** at Colgate, but the people are all good looking. Guys and girls alike seem to just be looking for weekend flings."

Q "My mom told me when I was applying to Colgate that it was the '**school of beautiful people**.'"

Q "Everyone on the campus looks the same. I can never remember whom I do and do not know. It's like a walking **J.Crew catalog**. People dress alike, act alike, and think alike, for the most part."

STUDENT AUTHOR: **Colgate is a beautiful campus, regarding both the grounds and the students who attend it. Most everyone is wealthy, well-dressed, and fit. Sometimes it can be a bit overwhelming, with guys sporting pink shorts and girls wearing their characteristic pearls to class. Couples do date, but relationships for the most part are casual. More often than not, the case is either sexile your roommate, or be sexiled yourself.**

Traditions

Thirteen
The University was supposedly founded by thirteen men—each with $13 and 13 prayers.

Salmagundi
The current name of Colgate's yearbook. The word means "miscellany" or "medley."

Overall School Spirit
Colgate students exude a lot of school spirit for such a small institution. Many come out for large athletic contests, such as football and hockey, and support their friends in less intense sports, like IM softball.

Students Speak Out
ON ATHLETICS

Q "Most of our teams end up seeing post-regular season action. Our hockey team has won the Patriot League championship, as well. **Hockey games are intense**, especially against Cornell, when basically the entire student body shows up to see the Raiders versus the Big Red."

Q "**Raider athletics are big**. We are one of the smallest Division I schools, and everyone goes out to support our teams. A few years ago, the football team made it to the D I-AA final game. Everyone was so psyched up."

Q "A large percentage of those not involved in varsity sports play IM. There are **so many sports** to choose from, and you can always start a team, if you have enough players."

STUDENT AUTHOR: **Athletic competition has long been an important aspect of Colgate tradition. All of its varsity teams are DI, and their many championship titles merit recognition. Fittingly, students support Raider athletics whenever the opportunity arises. But there isn't as spirited a following as large Southern universities or Big 10 schools have.**

Students Speak Out
ON DRUG SCENE

Q "The drug scene can be summed up by saying 'most have tried it; **few do it regularly**.' Marijuana has been smoked by a majority of Colgate students, but few are regular smokers."

Q "Nearly all Colgate students drink, and nearly all of them **drink to get drunk**. Alcohol is readily available and regularly abused."

Q "Marijuana is there if you want it. **Adderall or Ritalin** is also there if you want it. Cocaine and opium are there if you are willing to look for it. 'Shrooms are there if you want them. You will learn to get along with people drinking, smoking, or getting high in most situations."

STUDENT AUTHOR: **Like most other college campuses, drugs are part of the scene, but at Colgate, they are not a major problem. There are the regulars who smoke up weekly or more often, but the most common drug is alcohol, not narcotics. If people do smoke, they do it quietly, not blatantly; doors are closed, windows are opened, and fans are switched on out of respect for one another.**

10:1	Student-to-Faculty Ratio
94%	Freshman Retention Rate
84%	Four-Year Graduation Rate
88%	Financial Aid Applicants Receiving Aid

Students Speak Out
SAFETY & SECURITY

Q "I always feel safe on campus, even late at night. There is usually someone else walking around, and there are blue-light emergency stations everywhere. I think I've heard that **it was only used once**, and the culprit was someone who needed directions."

Q "I've never locked my dorm room. I always walk alone at night. **I've hitchhiked a few times** in the cold weather. Colgate is sort of like that movie, *Pleasantville*, where the fire department dedicates their time to saving cats in trees."

Q "Someone told me once that they were pulled over twice in the same night for having **a burnt-out taillight**. That's how little Campo has to do."

STUDENT AUTHOR: **At Colgate, there are rarely worrisome incidents, so most students do not hesitate to walk alone late at night or leave their dorm room unlocked. Patrolling Campus Safety officers are practically omnipresent at all hours of the day, as well.**

> **Questions?**
> For more inside information and survival tips, pick up College Prowler's full-length book on this school, written by an actual student! Check it out at *www.collegeprowler.com*.

Students Speak Out
ON OVERALL EXPERIENCE

Q "The opportunities and freedom one has to shape his or her college experience at Colgate makes it a **great undergraduate experience**. We have the academics of an Ivy League school, but a student body that can better balance their books with their beer."

Q "I love Colgate. **It's a perfect fit for me**. I just wish I didn't only have two years left! It's been an incredible experience—the people, the classes, the teachers, the activities, and the entertainment."

Q "The best part about Colgate is the size. Nearly all classes have **less than 40 students**, and in my first two years, all but two have been under 35 students, and a handful have been less than 15."

Q "There are kids who drive a Mercedes everywhere and fly to Europe when they get bored, but there are always financial aid kids who hang out in the library, because they don't have their own computer—**it's a hell of a place**. It's an amazing place once you have learned to love it, and you are able to meet people that will make your life that much fuller."

STUDENT AUTHOR: **Simply put, Colgate students love Colgate. Prospective students pick Colgate as much as Colgate picks them. It is the best combination of a small liberal arts college and a major university. It has the strong sense of community and warmth of a small college, but the impressive faculty and staff of a major university. Their pride and enthusiasm for the school are contagious, and this sucks anyone in who was not convinced from the beginning.**

College of Charleston

66 George Street; Charleston, SC 29424
(843) 953-5507; www.cofc.edu

THE BASICS:

Acceptance Rate: 65%
Setting: Mid-sized city
F-T Undergrads: 9,034

SAT Range: 1140–1300*
Control: Public
Tuition: $20,418

Most Popular Majors: Business, Social Sciences, Communications, Visual/Performing Arts, Education

*of 1600

Academics	B	Guys	B-
Local Atmosphere	B	Girls	A
Safety & Security	B	Athletics	B-
Computers	B-	Nightlife	B
Facilities	B	Greek Life	B
Campus Dining	C+	Drug Scene	B-
Off-Campus Dining	A+	Campus Strictness	B-
Campus Housing	B	Parking	C-
Off-Campus Housing	B	Transportation	B
Diversity	D	Weather	B+

Students Speak Out
ON ACADEMICS

Q "I don't think that the College of Charleston is negligent in their responsibility to hire professors who are capable in their field, but sometimes professors are **just unfair**—not giving enough warning before assignments, changing due dates, or testing on things that weren't discussed in class. Some professors just suck, but I guess that happens at every college."

Q "It's normal in college to skip a few classes, or even a lot of classes. But I've learned from my own personal experience, that teachers test on lecture material and **hardly ever open the book**. So skipping classes too much is pretty much the stupidest thing you could do at this school."

Q "This school is not easy, but I've learned that if you **get help from your advisor** and know what classes you're getting yourself into, you should never find yourself in a situation that's impossible to get out of."

Q "At first I was wondering about the quality of education here, but since I've declared my major, I've gotten **so many opportunities** and so much encouragement."

STUDENT AUTHOR: **Students will experience a range of emotions when it comes to their professors. This is true no matter where you go, but what makes the College of Charleston unique is the relationship between professors and students. With a student-to-teacher ratio of fourteen to one, you can always be certain that availability and attention will be provided in abundance.**

Students Speak Out
ON LOCAL ATMOSPHERE

Q "I love Charleston because we're in an urban setting, but it's not a big city that overwhelms you. The **beach is 20 minutes** in practically every direction, and so are the suburbs. There are so many places to go, but why would you want to go anywhere else? It's Charleston!"

Q "The **history here is so rich**. Sure, not a lot of celebrities are from here, or come here to visit, but I've seen a few. Everything is so old and authentic, and we get the privilege of living in it every day. Everywhere you go, there's an interesting story."

Q "I'm from Atlanta, and this city seems kind of small and quaint in comparison. But it's peaceful and quiet. You can still get crazy though, don't get me wrong. It's fun. It's **just not big**."

Q "It's hard with **all the tourists** sometimes. Charleston isn't that big to begin with, and when huge buses clog the streets, it's pretty annoying."

STUDENT AUTHOR: **Charleston is a city preserved by care and untainted by change and novelty. This isn't to say that Charleston is outdated or boring. Aside from being a beautiful and historic city, Charleston offers a variety of activities and events to choose from. Two other colleges, CSU and the Citadel are nearby, so even though Charleston is not a huge college town, there are enough college students to go around. Whether you're into sports or art; shopping or surfing, there is always something to do.**

5 Best Things	5 Worst Things
1 King Street	1 The smell
2 The Market	2 The sidewalks on campus
3 Beaches are close	3 HomeZone's food
4 The Waterfornt	4 Not enough boys
5 Marion Square	5 Bugs in some buildings

Students Speak Out
ON FACILITIES

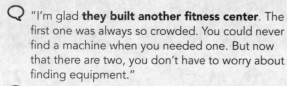

Q "I'm glad **they built another fitness center**. The first one was always so crowded. You could never find a machine when you needed one. But now that there are two, you don't have to worry about finding equipment."

Q "Recently they've built a new dorm, a new garage, remodeled the Stern Center, remodeled Barry Hall, and built another library. I love how they are always **trying to make things newer** and better for us."

Q "**They show movies** a couple times a month at the Sotille, and they're brand new, too. There are always packs of kids walking down George Street to go see whatever they're showing."

Q "**I love the arena**. The energy during a game is so high; you can't help but enjoy yourself, even if you're there only for social reasons."

Q "If you're not on an athletic team, the facilities here can be **frustrating**. The pool hours for general use are ridiculous, and unless you're on the team, you can hardly ever use it."

STUDENT AUTHOR: **Students feel that for the most part the amount of facilities provided by the College of Charleston is suitable, and the school is making further attempts to accommodate its students. The Stern Center, which is the best-equipped building for student needs, houses meeting rooms, a food court, a swimming pool, and a large ballroom for various events. However, sometimes it may seem that the College of Charleston has tried to cram too many things into a small amount of space.**

Famous People From Charleston

Andy Dick (comedian and actor), Dubose Heyward (author of *Porgy*), Padgett Powell (author of *Edisto* and *Aliens of Affection*)

Students Speak Out
ON CAMPUS DINING

Q "There's really **no reason to get a meal plan** after your freshman year. If you get Dining Dollars, you have a lot more options, and you can always eat at the cafeteria if you want to. But you shouldn't limit yourself to just a meal plan."

Q "I hate the HomeZone. If there wasn't a dorm above it, I would want someone to burn it down. There is no excuse for our parents paying the money they pay for the crap they call food in the HomeZone. It **makes me sick just looking at it** sometimes."

Q "I hate the cafeteria sometimes. When it's cold, it **seems so far away**. But you can really fill up there, and there's such a good variety of stuff. Salads there are awesome."

Q "I think the Champ Card is a rip-off. You're not getting a deal, or getting free meals. You're **paying for every scrap of food** you eat, just all at once instead of in increments. Don't be fooled. It's a good arrangement, but it's not like the College is getting shafted."

STUDENT AUTHOR: **There will always be mixed emotions when it comes to campus dining, but every student can pretty much agree that the dining hall leaves much to be desired. Most students agree that a combination of Dining Dollars, meals, and the Champ Card is the way to go. Whatever your needs are for dining at the College of Charleston, something can be arranged with the limited but sufficient options provided by campus dining.**

Student Body

African American:	6%	Male/Female:	36/64%
Asian American:	2%	Out-of-State:	37%
Hispanic:	2%	International:	2%
Native American:	<1%	Unknown:	5%
White:	83%		

Popular Faiths: Given that C of C is a Southern college, the most popular religion is Christianity.

Gay Pride: The Gay-Straight Alliance is the only student organization dedicated to gay students, and the gay community at the College of Charleston remains relatively low-key.

Economic Status: The majority seems to come from upper-middle or upper-class families.

Students Speak Out
ON DORMS

Q "I loved living in **College Lodge**. Yeah, it was kind of gross, but so much fun! Three of my neighbors either moved out or flunked out of classes because they partied too much. It's definitely not the place to live if you need peace and quiet."

Q "McAlister Hall and Kelly House don't even qualify as dorms. They're basically just **swanky** apartment buildings owned by the College. I was always expecting room service to knock on the door and bring us our breakfast."

Q "I'm so glad that most of the dorms on campus don't have **community showers**. I wouldn't mind one so much in a girls' dorm, but if I lived in McConnell and I had to use the same shower as 200 college guys, I would probably never shower."

STUDENT AUTHOR: **On-campus housing is a good way to meet new people, form friendships, and meet roommates for next year's housing plans. For this reason, many students choose to live on campus their first year, even though freshmen aren't required to do so.**

> **Did You Know?**
> 34% of undergrads live on campus.

Students Speak Out
ON GUYS & GIRLS

Q "This school must be like a playground if you're a guy. There are girls everywhere, and I hate to admit it, but for the most part, the girls at this school are cute. **Clones, but cute**."

Q "There are T-shirts on campus that say 'Charleston Girls, **Best in the World**,' and I have to agree. For every unattractive girl at this school, there must be 100 hot ones."

Q "Yeah, the guys are cute if you can tell them apart. After a while they all start to look the same—**shaggy hair** under a baseball cap, collared shirt, khaki shorts. All those guys tend to be from Virginia and North Carolina, though. Strange."

STUDENT AUTHOR: Usually what you'll find is that girls are sweet and conservative during the day and provocative at night, while guys will most likely roll out of bed after an afternoon nap and wear the same thing to a party that they've been wearing all day. There seems to be an abundance of preppy girls, and preppy guys who have gotten a little bit lazy, but no student ever complains about a dearth of attractive people. They're everywhere.

Traditions

The Booze Cruise
A popular event among students, the Booze Cruise is a boat party that occurs a couple times a month for students to basically get drunk and socialize while cruising around the battery.

Overall School Spirit
Athletics at the College of Charleston are no more popular than theater, music, or any other area of interest, and school spirit seems to be expended on all of these things. The pride that students have in each other and in the College of Charleston reaches to all areas and goes far beyond athletics.

Students Speak Out
ON ATHLETICS

Q "Sporting events aren't like a school obsession or anything, but they're very popular. A lot of people go simply for **the social factor**. But since it's free, there are always a lot of people at sporting events."

Q "Our gym, as well as our entire school, was used to film the basketball scenes in the movie *O*. Our gym is awesome. The energy in there during a game is **through the roof**, and even if basketball isn't really your thing, you can't help but get into it."

Q "One of the first things you'll find out about athletics here is that we have **no football team**. But basketball more than makes up for it."

Q "The **girls' teams** don't get enough recognition."

STUDENT AUTHOR: **While most of the teams on campus have their fair share of achievements, only with basketball do you get any real athletic excitement at the College of Charleston. Being very arts-driven, the overwhelming majority of the student population didn't come here because of a certain team or because of the College's athletic reputation.**

Students Speak Out
ON DRUG SCENE

Q "My neighbors in the dorm always had a bottle of **wine and a six-pack in their fridge**. Alcohol is a normal part of the College of Charleston experience. But you can stay away from it if you want."

Q "**Kids do basically what they want** here. I know there are lots of kids that probably try coke or something more dangerous, and some that are just plain users. But the people I've seen offering cocaine and ecstasy are not college students."

Q "I've heard people say that **cocaine** is becoming really popular at Charleston. But I haven't seen any evidence of that."

STUDENT AUTHOR: **Many students find that drugs are not a dominant force on this campus despite growing talk that cocaine is becoming a popular accessory to College of Charleston life. Drugs are passed around at parties and are used in the residence halls, but there is no pressure to use them. Alcohol is a different story. Many students think that getting a little wild with drinking is normal.**

13:1	Student-to-Faculty Ratio
82%	Freshman Retention Rate
42%	Four-Year Graduation Rate
70%	Financial Aid Applicants Receiving Aid

Students Speak Out
SAFETY & SECURITY

Q "Obviously, since the college is located downtown, **there are going to be crimes** and incidents that public safety can't always stop. But when I am on campus, I know that public safety officers are the ones around the street corner at night, not a mugger."

Q "It's not like we have fat, slow, lazy security guards 'protecting' us. They're real cops, and they have **real guns**, and as bad as that sounds, I feel safer around an officer with a gun than a security guard without one."

Q "The police on campus do a really good job, even though sometimes **they can be jerks**. But they're just doing their jobs, I guess. They make me feel safe, so they must be doing something right."

STUDENT AUTHOR: **Sometimes students feel that campus security is more like campus surveillance; police officers are on just about every corner, they even check your bags when you enter the residence halls after a certain hour of night. Overall, students feel that security officers are doing a good job (in spite of occasional bike thefts here and there).**

Questions?

For more inside information and survival tips, pick up College Prowler's full-length book on this school, written by an actual student! Check it out at *www.collegeprowler.com*.

Students Speak Out
ON OVERALL EXPERIENCE

Q "C of C doesn't have a reputation for much of anything. You're not getting the most exceptional education here, you're not participating in the craziest parties, or supporting the most successful teams. But I wouldn't want to go anywhere else. I feel like **this is my home** now."

Q "I met a lot of really unfriendly people when I first got here. I was thinking 'oh, southern hospitality will be nice,' and there wasn't any. This **isn't a typical Southern school**. It's about as metropolitan as you're going to get except for Atlanta."

Q "Sometimes I wish Charleston was bigger. It's so **laid-back and small-town**. But I can tell you one thing, Charleston is unique, and so is the school."

Q "It's **not a big place**, so if you're looking for career opportunities, you should use your time here to lead you to other cities and other places. But I know people who have gotten really good jobs and have stayed in Charleston, and they're happy."

STUDENT AUTHOR: **One cannot truly understand the appeal and rarity of attending the College of Charleston until they have been here awhile, and though students do transfer out for various reasons, those who do remain here for all of their college years look back on their memories with nothing but contentment and pride. Charleston does its best to encourage its students and residents to enjoy the time they spend here, and students here will never be lacking in opportunity for their career or further education goals.**

College of the Holy Cross

1 College Street; Worcester, MA 01610
(508) 793-2011; www.holycross.edu

THE BASICS:

Acceptance Rate: 34%
Setting: Mid-sized city
F-T Undergrads: 2,866

SAT Range: 1180–1350*
Control: Private
Tuition: $38,180

Most Popular Majors: Social Sciences, Psychology, English, History, Foreign Languages

*of 1600

Academics	B+	Guys	B
Local Atmosphere	C-	Girls	B+
Safety & Security	A-	Athletics	B
Computers	B	Nightlife	B+
Facilities	B	Greek Life	N/A
Campus Dining	B+	Drug Scene	B
Off-Campus Dining	B+	Campus Strictness	C+
Campus Housing	B-	Parking	C+
Off-Campus Housing	C+	Transportation	C-
Diversity	D-	Weather	C-

Students Speak Out
ON ACADEMICS

Q "The teachers at Holy Cross are great! They are always willing to provide students with extra help if it is needed. **They love students** to come and see them!"

Q "The teachers are **about as varied as the classes.** I've had some really good ones and some really bad ones. On the whole, I would say that there are more interesting classes than uninteresting ones."

Q "The teachers at Holy Cross are **caring and always available.** They really take pride in their jobs and are genuinely concerned for their students. The classes offered touch on a wide range of topics within each discipline."

Q "The professors at HC are **continuously the brightest part of my college education.** I count many of my teachers as good friends. Professors within my major (as well as professors outside of it) have always been both well prepared to teach their subjects and extremely accessible and personable outside of class."

STUDENT AUTHOR: The students almost unanimously praise their professors for their interest in course material and their efforts to make potentially boring classes interesting. Professors at Holy Cross are true educators. They all want to see their students develop into not just informed individuals, but critical-thinking men and women. Professors' passion for their subject matter carries through into the classroom, where students are inspired and enjoy their classes.

Students Speak Out
ON LOCAL ATMOSPHERE

Q "Worcester is a very industrial town and not very friendly looking. Although there are many other colleges, it is **definitely not a college town.**"

Q "The atmosphere in Worcester is kind of dull. Since freshmen and sophomores are not allowed to have cars, it is hard to go downtown without paying for a cab. However, many of the **upperclassmen love Worcester**. It is just a city that you need to explore for yourself. There are some great 24-hour diners."

Q "There are **lots of other colleges**, but Holy Cross kids tend to stay with other Holy Cross kids—that's just how it is."

Q "Worcester is **not exactly a thriving metropolis**. The city offers little for the college-aged kid to do. The atmosphere is like that of a plague-ridden medieval city: dark, depressing, and dull. There are a few clubs in town but nothing to write home about. They are only bearable because everyone who goes there is from HC."

STUDENT AUTHOR: Worcester is not the most college-friendly city. Unlike colleges in Boston, where the city is a real selling point for the school, Holy Cross is located in a city with a less stellar reputation. It is spread out and tough to navigate without a car, and the locals are not always the friendliest toward Holy Cross students. Although there are nine or ten other colleges in Worcester, few establishments cater to the entire college-age community, most likely due to Worcester's sprawling geography.

Students Speak Out
ON FACILITIES

Q "The buildings on campus are in great shape. Although **some of them are extremely old**, you would never be able to tell from the inside."

Q "The campus facilities are awesome and new. The athletic center (Hart) is great, especially the gym, although **it could use more elliptical machines**! The student center (Hogan) is also really nice, but they could focus the building more on the students."

Q "Since Holy Cross isn't a big school, we don't have anything that is overly state-of-the-art. The facilities definitely suit the needs of the average student. However, the campus center definitely tends to be more of an administrative center than a student center. It's a six floor building and only the first three are for students! The rest **seem all to be for administration**."

Q "The Hart Center provides an Olympic-sized swimming pool, ice-skating rink, basketball courts, racquetball courts, and an excellent weight training room. My own personal peeve is the **inaccessibility of basketball courts**. During certain sports seasons, it can be difficult for students to find available basketball courts. The school also has outdoor tennis courts and a good track for student use."

STUDENT AUTHOR: While most respondents agree that Holy Cross's facilities are pretty good, the availability of cardio machines at the gym is a common gripe. The Hart Center is well equipped—it has free weights and offers many aerobic classes. It has been said in the past that the Hogan Center has become more of an administrative center than a student center.

Famous Alumni
Joseph Califano, Chris Matthews, Clarence Thomas

Students Speak Out
ON CAMPUS DINING

Q "Kimball is pretty decent—**it's not like home cooking**, but then, what cafeteria food is? We have an awesome salad bar, and the food has a pretty good variety. We also have Crossroads (for upperclassmen) and Lower Kimball for a quick on-the-go!"

Q "**The food is not horrible**, but it's not great either. If you know what to eat and what to stay away from, then you can definitely get by without a problem. Kimball is one of the largest dining halls in the country, I think, so its sheer size makes meals interesting."

Q "Food gets a bad rep. It's tolerable and at times enjoyable. **Crossroads is the best place to go** if you're not a freshman. Upper Kimball has its good days and its bad days."

Q "Surprisingly, the food at Holy Cross really isn't that bad. **I'd even go so far as to call it good most of the time**. The main dining hall is called Kimball. It has ridiculously high ceilings, fine furniture, and even chandeliers. It is served buffet-style, and offers classic entrees, a grill selection, deli meat, pasta bar, and a healthy stir-fry line, not to mention cereal/breads, and a soup and salad bar."

STUDENT AUTHOR: Holy Cross is pretty average in terms of food. Most students seemed to agree that while the food isn't anything fantastic, it isn't toxic, either—although one student did say that the food was great! Dining options on campus are fairly limited, with only three dining halls (and only two for freshmen).

Students Speak Out
ON DORMS

Q "Dorms are nice and pretty big for freshmen. Once you hit junior year, **the situation gets dicey**. The school is making improvements, though—new apartments were recently built."

Q "All of the dorms are pretty much the same. They are decent-sized with two beds, two desks, and two closets. The apartments are awesome because **they have a kitchen and living room**. Wheeler should be avoided because the rooms are smaller and further away from other dorms."

Q "The dorms are pretty average. Different dorms offer different things. **Wheeler has small rooms** for freshmen but huge rooms for sophomores, plus it's a pretty good party dorm."

STUDENT AUTHOR: Almost everyone seems to agree that Holy Cross's housing is good for underclassmen, but decidedly lacking for upperclassmen. At the beginning of the 2005–2006 school year, a new apartment-style dorm opened, designed to keep upperclassmen on campus—and this option has proven very popular. The Hill Dorms house the majority of underclassmen and are more or less identical to one another.

> **Did You Know?**
> 89% of undergrads live on campus.

Students Speak Out
ON GUYS & GIRLS

Q "This is a hookup campus; no dating. As with any other institution, **some guys are hot and others not so much**. A lot of the girls try to look good at all times."

Q "On the whole, **HC is a clean-cut campus**. Everyone looks like they just stepped out of an Abercrombie or J.Crew catalog. Some people are attractive, and some not so much. But 99 percent are preppy."

Q "I don't think I've **ever seen a fat person**."

Q "The girls sometimes like to **dress up a bit too much**—when you're wearing designer fashion to a 9 a.m. class, it shows you care a little too much about what you look like!"

STUDENT AUTHOR: Given the general lack of diversity at Holy Cross, it's not surprising that most of the guys and girls are "cut from the same mold," as one student put it. The campus, as a whole, is extremely preppy, and most students seem to be from upper-middle-class backgrounds, so comparisons to catalog models are particularly apt. The majority of guys and girls are good looking in the clean-cut, preppy way and everyone, on the outset, seems friendly.

> **Traditions**
>
> **Spring Weekend**
> The first weekend in May is an excuse for campus to celebrate spring. The school sponsors a large carnival, among other events.
>
> **BC–HC Rivalry**
> The traditional rivalry with Boston College is still strong, despite the fact that the two schools haven't competed athletically since the 1980s.
>
> **Overall School Spirit**
> Purple Pride Day is dedicated to enlivening school spirit. Spirit is most evident at athletic events, particularly football and basketball games.

Students Speak Out
ON ATHLETICS

Q "**Football is huge despite** the fact that we stink. Basketball is also very popular, and we've been doing well for the past few years. Intramural sports are not big at all—in fact, I have never heard of any before."

Q "Holy Cross is not Notre Dame, but varsity sports are not ignored. The basketball teams—both women's and men's—are at the top of their class and **quite competitive**. The football team draws a crowd, but this is basically because of tradition's sake and the tailgating—the stands grow sparse after halftime. The soccer team is always solid, as is the women's tennis team."

Q "**Varsity sports are pretty big**—basketball is huge. Intramural sports could be better organized and better publicized."

STUDENT AUTHOR: There is no question that basketball is the most popular sport on campus. Holy Cross is in the Patriot League, the champion of which is guaranteed a place in the NCAA tournament. The school is now focusing on strengthening both its men's and women's programs. Football is also popular, but it's mostly about the tailgating.

Students Speak Out
ON DRUG SCENE

Q "Excluding weed, I haven't seen anything except **a little coke**. Definitely nothing hardcore."

Q "There are definitely those who use drugs, but they are in the great, great minority. I have never seen any at parties. **Holy Cross is definitely a drinking school**. Cocaine is present but never done openly, and you can count the number of people who have done it."

Q "I haven't encountered any drugs here. I know a **few people who smoke pot**, but it doesn't seem to dominate the culture like drinking does."

Q "Pot is **hard** to come by here."

STUDENT AUTHOR: With the exception of marijuana and a little cocaine, there is virtually no drug scene at Holy Cross. Pot, too, is not used as widely as it is at other colleges and is often difficult to find. Students prefer to drink, rather than smoke, their problems away. Ecstasy, heroin, and meth are practically unheard of on campus.

10:1	Student-to-Faculty Ratio
95%	Freshman Retention Rate
92%	Four-Year Graduation Rate
89%	Financial Aid Applicants Receiving Aid

Students Speak Out
SAFETY & SECURITY

Q "The campus is very safe—Public Safety's tactics ensure that. **But watch out**! They have been known to run down a student or two with their Public Safety vans—I was a victim!"

Q "As a female, **I have always felt safe**, even when walking back from the library at 1 a.m."

Q "Security on campus is pretty good. We have Public Safety minivans, an 'unmarked' Crown Victoria, and a few bike cops. **There are callboxes all around** campus, in case you need some assistance."

Q "**I always feel very safe walking anywhere** on campus. Campus security is always roaming around here and there!"

STUDENT AUTHOR: The lack of crime at Holy Cross is almost comical. An incident such as the theft of a wallet from an unlocked locker generates campus-wide safety alerts and a Herculean investigation from Public Safety. This also leaves officers time to spend time dealing with other quality of life issues.

Questions?

For more inside information and survival tips, pick up College Prowler's full-length book on this school, written by an actual student! Check it out at *www.collegeprowler.com*.

Students Speak Out
ON OVERALL EXPERIENCE

Q "I cannot see myself anywhere else. **I really loved the past three years** here and can't wait for this one."

Q "**I think I'm getting the best education** money can buy, but the social life here is really stifling and really boring, especially if you don't want to follow the crowd."

Q "**Holy Cross wasn't my first choice**, but I'm really happy I ended up here. I couldn't have asked for a better school. It's the perfect size, and I can tell the teachers really care about me as a person and my education. Now, I can't picture myself anyplace else."

Q "I love it—**anyone could find their niche at HC**. I wouldn't want to be anyplace else right now, but four years is definitely enough."

Q "Overall, **I'm happy with my HC experience**. The friends I have made are really great. I'm sure I could be happy somewhere else, too, but I'm really happy here!"

STUDENT AUTHOR: Students were mixed, though generally positive, in their feelings toward HC. The social scene seems to be the victim of most criticism. There is no question, however, that Holy Cross provides all its students with a first-rate education. Most students are friendly, outgoing, and fun, and making friends is not a problem. However, some students do complain about the school's homogeneity. Few students seem to want to do anything that is outside of the norm. In all, most students are very happy at Holy Cross, as is evidenced by the school's unusually high retention rate.

College of William & Mary

102 Richmond Road; Williamsburg, VA 23187
(757) 221-4000; www.wm.edu

THE BASICS:

Acceptance Rate: 34%   **SAT Range:** 1250–1450*
Setting: Rural   **Control:** Public
F-T Undergrads: 5,703   **Tuition:** $23,110

Most Popular Majors: Social Sciences, Business, Interdisciplinary Studies, English, History, Psychology

*of 1600

Academics	A	Guys	B-
Local Atmosphere	C+	Girls	B
Safety & Security	B+	Athletics	C
Computers	B	Nightlife	C
Facilities	B	Greek Life	A
Campus Dining	B-	Drug Scene	A
Off-Campus Dining	B+	Campus Strictness	B-
Campus Housing	B-	Parking	F
Off-Campus Housing	B-	Transportation	B-
Diversity	C-	Weather	B

Students Speak Out
ON ACADEMICS

Q "Professors are awesome. **They are there to teach, not to do research**, and they're incredible, intelligent, interesting people. I've had a few duds, that I'll admit, but the rest of them totally made up for it."

Q "All of my intro level classes have been very interesting. Every time I take one I always want to continue taking more classes in that subject. **The professors are so passionate** about their studies, and their interest seems to rub off on students."

Q "The professors rock! Okay, so you'll get the **occasional boring loser**, but mostly they're excited about what they are teaching and are good at it."

Q "It depends what department you're in. If you have a very popular major, you'll get to know your profs less-well than if you were in a tiny department. In general, the teachers are great. **TAs don't teach**, they only assist with grading and lab sections."

STUDENT AUTHOR: **On the whole, students are very happy with their classroom experience at William & Mary. Class sizes are small, which makes it easy for teachers and students to bond, be it over sandwiches at one of the delis or a conversation during office hours. The faculty is focused on instruction, not research, and no classes are taught by teaching assistants. Great teaching and a well-rounded liberal arts curriculum prepare students for any number of future endeavors.**

Students Speak Out
ON LOCAL ATMOSPHERE

Q "Williamsburg is probably **the weirdest college town in the world**. As the home of Colonial Williamsburg, a huge section of the town is a 'living museum' theme park—in other words, pretending to be in the 18th century. This means it's beautiful and there's lots of interesting stuff to see. We also have Busch Gardens Williamsburg, one of the best theme parks in the country."

Q "Williamsburg has a tendency to **completely die out around nine o'clock**. With no other universities closer than 45 minutes, you're really on your own to find a fun time. 2 a.m. Wawa hoagie runs are a must—one of the few things to do after hours."

Q "While some people claim there is not much to do, there is plenty if you take the time to look around. **Try taking a ghost tour** around Colonial Williamsburg, taking some friends for dessert at the Trellis, or having a picnic at W&M's Crim Dell outdoor amphitheater."

Q "The town is **half tourists and half retirees**. Go to Busch Gardens and Virginia Beach, but stay on campus for social outlets."

STUDENT AUTHOR: **Students label Williamsburg as quiet, touristy, and historic but wouldn't call it a town with a thriving college atmosphere. While it's a beautiful city, it can become overrun with tourists at times and can lack fun activities at other times. With enough creativity, however, students can make the best of the tepid atmosphere.**

5 Best Things

1. The professors
2. The architecture
3. A cappella groups
4. Late-night eating
5. Strong community

5 Worst Things

1. Lack of AC in dorms
2. Smelly woods path
3. Course registration
4. Rainy weather
5. Heavy workload

Students Speak Out
ON FACILITIES

Q "**The UC basement rocks**! It has pool tables, skee-ball, and a whole bunch of other stuff. It's very student friendly."

Q "The academic facilities range from beautiful and old **to ugly, modern, or nearly condemned**. The athletic facilities are nice, with a beautiful baseball park, a nice football stadium, and a large basketball arena, plus good tennis courts, soccer, and field hockey fields."

Q "The computer science building is pretty new and quite technologically advanced. The business building isn't bad, either. And the library was renovated. Most of the science buildings are outdated, but **they're gradually improving**, one by one."

Q "Since the Rec Center has been renovated, it's really nice. **They added a huge climbing wall**, a juice bar, another court, a massage room, and wireless Internet access."

Q "**The facilities are pretty nice**. One of the student centers has pool tables and video games."

STUDENT AUTHOR: For hours of entertainment, students flock to the University Center basement, where there are video games and pool, as well as a bar and a late-night eatery. Students sweat away their stress at the Rec Center, which features weight machines, weight rooms, an indoor pool, racquetball and basketball courts. The most common complaint is that the older academic buildings could use some improvement.

Famous Alumni

Glenn Close, Thomas Jefferson, John Marshall, James Monroe, John Tyler, Jon Stewart

Students Speak Out
ON CAMPUS DINING

Q "Food is alright. **Not that good, but passable**. The Marketplace has some pretty good food, but not as much variety as other places."

Q "The food on campus is okay. It was good at the beginning, but **it got old after awhile**. There are three main on-campus food spots: the Commons, the Marketplace, and the University Center."

Q "Although **'food' might be a bit of an exaggeration**, The Caf (the Commons), UC, and Marketplace are the main places to eat."

Q "Food on campus is fine. There are three dining halls, two all-you-can-eat, one à la carte establisment. **All freshmen are required to get the biggest meal plan** so they won't starve, and wherever students go, there's always something they can eat. The school has been making an effort in recent years to include more vegetarian and vegan options, as well."

Q "Food on campus is **one of the favorite things to gripe about**, but it's really decent. There's a huge selection, and you get a lot of choices. Even if you want to eat healthy, there are lots of options."

STUDENT AUTHOR: Some students think the campus food is above average, some find it below par. There are two all-you-can-eat cafeterias, offering rotating menus, and several à la carte eateries. Though greasy food won't help ward off the infamous Freshman 15, the hours of operation are pretty accommodating, and most students admit that the food really isn't all that bad.

Student Body

African American:	7%	Male/Female:	46/54%
Asian American:	7%	Out-of-State:	31%
Hispanic:	6%	International:	2%
Native American:	1%	Unknown:	13%
White:	64%		

Popular Faiths: There are many active Christian, Jewish, Muslim, and Unitarian organizations.

Gay Pride: There is a large gay community on campus, and they are mostly accepted by other students without conflict.

Economic Status: There is some diversity in this area, but most students seem to be middle class or upper-middle class.

Students Speak Out
ON DORMS

Q "Dorms are really decent. Ask to live in Yates freshman year; it's the 'party dorm' and very fun. As an upperclassman, Old Dominion Hall and the Randolph Complex are the nicest, in my opinion. **Make sure to try to get dorms with A/C**; not all of them have it."

Q "Your first year you'll be placed in a dorm, and from then on you'll know what's going on fine enough to make good decisions. Housing on campus, though, is **controlled by the lottery**. Each person gets a random number (seniors the best numbers, while sophomores get the worst) and places are given out in a first-come-first-serve fashion."

Q "For freshmen, **Dupont and Yates are the best dorms**."

STUDENT AUTHOR: Students say the quality of housing at William & Mary heavily depends on which dorm they end up in. Despite complaints, on-campus housing can't be all that bad—75 percent of W&M students reside on campus, and there's always a demand for more space.

> **Did You Know?**
> 75% of undergrads live on campus.

Students Speak Out
ON GUYS & GIRLS

Q "**Both sexes complain** of the lack of hot members of the opposite sex, but loads of people date, so it can't be that bad."

Q "Errrr . . . well, being a girl, let's just say I didn't come to William & Mary for the huge selection of hotties. There are some really cute, nice guys that I've met, though. Hey, **at least you know they're all smart**!"

Q "I must say the **girls here are particularly hot**."

Q "William & Mary's reputation for hot women may not be legendary, but **our status betrays us**. You only have to look to the person sitting next to you in Intro to Biology to see a face that'll make you fall in love."

STUDENT AUTHOR: Okay, so William & Mary isn't known for its exceptionally great-looking people. Superficiality aside, guys and girls at William & Mary are great people. They aren't the hottest students around, but there are more than a few very highly attractive people, and a whole lot of cuties. At least students at W&M can be assured that their entire selection gets an A+ in the brains department.

> **Traditions**
>
> **A Cappella**
> There are a zillion (or at least eleven) a cappella groups on campus. They perform for freshman dorms and at the William & Mary Sings competition.
>
> **Blowout**
> A campus-wide alcohol fest held on the last day of classes in both fall and spring semesters.
>
> **Overall School Spirit**
> You won't see hordes of W&M students painted up for football games, but most know all the lyrics to the alma mater and proudly sport W&M bumper stickers.

Students Speak Out
ON ATHLETICS

Q "Some varsity sports are 'big.' **Football at W&M is not as big as it is at other schools**. Many people participate in IM sports, though."

Q "**IM (intramural) sports are huge**, varsity sports are fun, but not too much winning in major sports."

Q "Varsity sports are big enough, but they're not a huge deal and neither are IM sports. But **most students do participate** in some sort of sport."

Q "To the average student, varsity sports don't exist. IM and club sports are much more widely used, and there are **dozens of options to choose from**."

STUDENT AUTHOR: The bottom line is that W&M is a school full of nerds; some are athletic, but a lot aren't. There is ample opportunity for those who want athletic action to get involved in something, though.

Students Speak Out
ON DRUG SCENE

Q "**Pot is easy enough to find** if you're interested, but if you're not the type, then you'd probably think that there wasn't any at all on campus. Anything else is extremely rare."

Q "I know there are some scenes into that, but **I really couldn't give you specifics**. It's not widespread, though."

Q "There is little or no drug scene on campus. The most popular drug, naturally, is pot, and you can seriously go all four years without even knowing anyone smokes up if it's not what your friends are into. But it's also not overly difficult to find people who do if that's what you are into—it's just **a very low key, non-blatant thing**. And drugs don't get much harder than that."

STUDENT AUTHOR: William & Mary's drug scene is only really evident to those who participate in it. Students say pot is available if they look for it, but if they don't, they probably wouldn't even notice. Alcohol use is pretty widespread, but use of harder drugs is almost non-existent.

11:1	Student-to-Faculty Ratio
95%	Freshman Retention Rate
84%	Four-Year Graduation Rate
59%	Financial Aid Applicants Receiving Aid

Students Speak Out
SAFETY & SECURITY

Q "I feel pretty safe on campus. **There is an after-hours escort service** that will walk you anywhere on campus. There are also emergency call boxes almost everywhere. The lighting at night is pretty good, too."

Q "**I feel pretty safe on campus**. It's not smart to walk around at night by yourself, but that's anywhere."

Q "Security is good on campus. It's a small campus, and most people, if anything, find the police officers annoying because they seem to be around all the time and interfere with people's social 'adventures.' **There are parts outside campus that aren't great**, but overall I feel safe walking around late at night."

STUDENT AUTHOR: The small-town atmosphere and tight-knit college community of W&M create a sense of safety that may not be present at larger universities. Serious crimes, such as assault and rape, are rare; most students don't fear this kind of incident, even late at night.

Questions?
For more inside information and survival tips, pick up College Prowler's full-length book on this school, written by an actual student! Check it out at *www.collegeprowler.com*.

Students Speak Out
ON OVERALL EXPERIENCE

Q "I really like William & Mary. **There are some problems**, namely the lack of nightlife, the lack of enthusiasm for varsity sports, and the parking problems. But the school is very good as far as nurturing education, and the professors are top-notch. I chose between William & Mary and UVA, and I'm still positive I made the right decision."

Q "I'm very happy with my school. The only thing I'd do differently is get involved in more activities. **There are so many organizations on campus to participate in**, you should definitely look around for what interests you and join in. I don't think I would have fit in anywhere else."

Q "**I'd do it all over again**, and love it. Go here."

Q "In terms of history, W&M is hard to beat. W&M has educated three U.S. presidents and has been around since the 17th century, which means it's filled with rich tradition, but is also very modern. There's something very cool about **sitting in the same classrooms Thomas Jefferson sat in** when he was a student here. I highly recommend W&M. I love it here, and I'm sure you would, too."

STUDENT AUTHOR: You hardly ever hear anyone expressing regret for choosing William & Mary. Alumni come back year after year and wish they could attend college there all over again. They love the sense of history, the size, the faculty, and their fellow students. Williamsburg may not be a bustling hub of activity, but the students form their own community that cannot be beat.

College of Wooster

1189 Beall Avenue; Wooster, OH 44691
(330) 287-3000; www.wooster.edu

THE BASICS:

Acceptance Rate: 80%
Setting: Suburban
F-T Undergrads: 1,794

SAT Range: 1650–1970*
Control: Private
Tuition: $31,870

Most Popular Majors: History, Psychology, Communication Studies, Political Science, Sociology

*of 2400

Academics	B+	Guys	B
Local Atmosphere	C	Girls	B
Safety & Security	B-	Athletics	B+
Computers	C+	Nightlife	B
Facilities	B	Greek Life	C
Campus Dining	B+	Drug Scene	B+
Off-Campus Dining	B+	Campus Strictness	C
Campus Housing	B+	Parking	C
Off-Campus Housing	D	Transportation	D
Diversity	D	Weather	C+

Students Speak Out
ON ACADEMICS

Q "The professors are **very keen on giving individual attention when needed**. Students do not need to be shy when contacting professors personally. Most classes are very engaging, with the occasional very boring and uninteresting one."

Q "**The professors here at Woo are a ton of fun**. All that I have had are interesting, absorbed in their subjects, and interested in me. I feel that they all know me, even though I may not speak individually with all of them. Classes are always interesting, especially the small ones!"

Q "My professors are really passionate and interested in what they're doing. **My classes are challenging and a lot of work**, but I'm also learning a lot, which will help me out in the real world."

Q "The teachers at the College of Wooster are **dynamic, enthusiastic, and care deeply** about each of their students' health and success."

STUDENT AUTHOR: **Students at Wooster regard academics in a serious way. From the classes to the professors, Wooster stands apart from the crowd because of its small class size, personal attention from professors, and individualized educational experience. Classes at Wooster average 21 students, and never top 50. The professors all have office hours, and they are very willing to find time to meet with you after class, or respond to your e-mails. Some will even host special dinners at their houses, which is always a treat.**

Students Speak Out
ON LOCAL ATMOSPHERE

Q "Wooster is cute! **There's not much to do in town except eat and watch movies**. It's fun to look out your dorm room window and watch an Amish buggy go clip-clopping by. I find it hugely ironic that there is a McDonald's right across the street from a huge Catholic church."

Q "**Wooster is a black hole**. There is nothing to do. If it weren't for the campus, this place would be totally dead. The only other place is OSU/ATI, but they dig in the dirt and feed cows."

Q "The community our college is in is a very close-knit one. There are a lot of churches in the area. There are also lots of Amish and Mennonites in the area, and it is interesting to see their way of life in comparison to my own. Ashland University and a branch of OSU are nearby. **Cleveland and Columbus are not too far away**."

Q "**The town have little festivals**, and I love the restaurants. There isn't much to do at night besides the movie theater, but I always find something on campus, so I'm never bored. I know friends who go to the bars in town, but most aren't for college students. They are kind of sketchy."

STUDENT AUTHOR: **Let's face it, the city of Wooster is a small, quaint, Midwestern town in the heartland of Amish country. Wooster is the county seat of Wayne County. There is also a great downtown with many quaint shops that students frequent during the day. Wooster is, needless to say, not a college town.**

5 Best Things	5 Worst Things
1 Small classes	1 No 24-hour food places
2 Great community	2 Crazy Ohio weather
3 Dorm rooms	3 Boy/girl ratio
4 The spring	4 Townies
5 Professors	5 Construction

Students Speak Out
ON FACILITIES

Q "Honestly, I feel that for the price of our tuition, **things should and could be better** on this tiny, rural campus. Some of the dorms are badly in need of an upgrade."

Q "The majority of the buildings are really nice, and efforts are continuously being made to improve and redo them. **They aren't ostentatious, but they're elegant**."

Q "Overall, facilities are okay. I admit that many things need to be renovated so they are more up-to-date, but **they get the job done**. Severance Hall and the science library are gorgeous, but Lowry could definitely use some more appeal since it is the student center. The PEC is also a little small, but they are going to be upgrading that soon, we hope."

Q "I am a huge fan of the science library, which was built over 100 years ago, but is **utterly gorgeous and very modern**, too. It's my favorite place to study."

STUDENT AUTHOR: Wooster is old and lovingly maintained. The grass is clipped, the flowers are bright, and the beautiful old stonework on the buildings glistens in the sun (on the good days). The majority of the academic buildings have been restored in the past 10 years, which makes for great working facilities. The student end of campus, though, is a different story. That isn't to say that they aren't great buildings. It's just getting to be a tight fit. Students are crammed into dorms and small houses, crammed into the student center and packed into the Physical Education Center.

Famous Alumni

Karl Compton, Stanley Gault, John Dean, Timothy Smucker, Stephen R. Donaldson, Vince Cellini, Duncan Jones, Alex Reed

Students Speak Out
ON CAMPUS DINING

Q "Kittredge has your mom's home-cooking feel to it, while **Lowry is more like the food court at the mall**. The food is pretty good; you just have to be careful how you eat or else you will gain a lot of weight."

Q "The dining halls are pretty nice, but it's the usual problem that **familiarity breeds contempt**, and by the end of the year everyone is sick of it all."

Q "The Food Services work really hard to make great meals for us. Even though the food can get repetitive, it's still **awesome compared to anywhere else**. What other college feeds you sushi, cous cous, and omelets every day; where else takes an entire dining hall outside for a barbeque with 1,000 students?"

Q "**Both dining halls serve excellent food**. I'm a vegetarian (who is slowly going vegan), and I have yet to get sick of the food here at Wooster. I'd recommend Lowry's international food line."

STUDENT AUTHOR: Overall, the College seems to have a very good system. The all-you-can-eat buffet style is one not seen often at colleges and universities anymore. The College keeps tweaking with the meal plan, and every year, Wooster takes baby steps in the right direction. The big improvement is the ability to swipe your meal card any three times a day you please, and the new grab-n-go lunches downstairs in Lowry Student Center. However, students still would like to be able to use their meal card in Mom's Truck Stop and the Shack down the road.

Student Body

African American:	5%	Male/Female:	47/53%
Asian American:	1%	Out-of-State:	45%
Hispanic:	1%	International:	7%
Native American:	<1%	Unknown:	0%
White:	86%		

Popular Faiths: Wooster was originally a Presbyterian college. There are many Christian groups, a Jewish group called Hillel, plus Muslims and Hindi present.

Gay Pride: For the most part, gays are accepted, although not entirely considering that Wooster is a conservative area.

Economic Status: The major economic group at the College seems to be middle class.

Students Speak Out
ON DORMS

Q "**The rooms are big, the bathrooms are clean, and there are very nice large public lounges**. Armington Hall has very small rooms, but is fairly new and redone. Holden Hall is popular as it is close to everything on campus. Douglass Hall is the oldest on campus and has very nice big rooms, as well as Kenarden Lodge, which houses upperclass students and was redone in the past 10 years or so."

Q "Don't stay in Bissman, Stevenson, or Wagner. The rest **all have their advantages and disadvantages**. And don't be afraid of program dorms or the small house programs; they're really neat."

Q "I like the dorms in general, but **the small houses are awesome**, too. Get your friends together and get a cool program house; you'll definitely appreciate it in the end."

STUDENT AUTHOR: **The dorms are well maintained, and exude an architectural grace that students say makes them feel like they are living in mansions. Most students are satisfied with the rooms they get every year, and the program dorms are thriving parts of the community.**

Did You Know?

99% of undergrads live on campus.

Students Speak Out
ON GUYS & GIRLS

Q "Students here tend to be **pretty diverse in their personal styles**, so it depends on what you're looking for. I'd say yes, depending on personal preference, there are hot girls and guys at Woo."

Q "I always thought the guys at Wooster were nice looking overall, and I believe that **generally everyone is rather friendly**. Of course, there are people that might be hard to approach and are not the most gorgeous. They say beauty is inner, and if you like a close knit community, you'll find someone who values that also."

Q "There are **some really smart girls here and some really ditzy girls**. And I never knew guys could be ditzy."

STUDENT AUTHOR: **While they'll admit that some people are nicer looking than others, this is not a campus that you step onto and immediately think everyone else has stepped off of the cover of Vogue. The general consensus is that most people on campus are nice-looking girl/guy next door types, with an average amount of pretty people and not-so-pretty people. Wooster students are also not very concerned with looks.**

Traditions

Bricks
Bricks have become a symbol for the College of Wooster with brick pathways intersecting the different parts of campus.

Kilts
The Scot band uniforms are one of the most recognized symbols for the College of Wooster.

Overall School Spirit
Whether it is cheering for the football team or helping out with the recycling crew, Wooster students jump in wholeheartedly.

Students Speak Out
ON ATHLETICS

Q "Sports range medium at Wooster. Varsity sports depend on how well the sport is doing in the season. **Wooster's men's basketball is by far the most popular**. IM is pretty popular, too, and can be great fun without the practice, with such sports as softball, floor hockey, and Frisbee."

Q "Varsity sports take over some of my friends lives. They get a lot of **support from peers, alumni, and faculty**, but sports aren't as big a priority as they would be at a DI school. IM sports get a lot or participants, though."

Q "**Football is a really well-attended sport**, but we are a Division III school, so some people have never been to a game. Many people do IM sports here. Those are really fun."

STUDENT AUTHOR: **Wooster's athletics are well respected by other colleges in the conference. Most sports teams are very competitive in the conference, if not nationally, and most teams get fairly decent support from the student body and the school in general. Even while academics are number one, sports don't lag here. Although IMs are popular here, this is still a DIII school.**

Students Speak Out
ON DRUG SCENE

Q "The kids that do drugs heavily **don't last a second at Wooster**."

Q "Sometimes, you get a whiff of pot, but **by no means are drugs a major player** at Wooster."

Q "I know a few people on campus who do. I don't know how they get it, but they always do. Be careful heading out to the Holden lot, **you're bound to get a contact buzz**."

Q "Drugs exist, just like anywhere else, but they aren't really big at all on this campus; if it is big, **it's mostly marijuana**. I have never seen any drugs on campus, but I know they're around."

STUDENT AUTHOR: **Drugs at Wooster are there, treading below the surface of student activity, but they are reasonably hard to find. Marijuana is probably the hardest drug out here. Probably the most commonly used drug on campus is alcohol, or sometimes Red Bull or another energy drink mixed with alcohol, which is never a good idea. Drugs may not be hard to find on campus, but they also aren't used by many, and the drug scene is miniscule.**

12:1	Student-to-Faculty Ratio
87%	Freshman Retention Rate
63%	Four-Year Graduation Rate
87%	Financial Aid Applicants Receiving Aid

Students Speak Out
SAFETY & SECURITY

Q "Safety and Security seem to always be around in the wrong places (parties) and **absent when needed** (vehicle break-ins). But the guys are always friendly and do help when needed."

Q "**I feel pretty safe at Wooster**. I am from a small town myself, so Wooster doesn't make me nervous. There are a lot of little blue safety phones. However, now that I think about it, I really haven't seen too many adult security officers around."

Q "The campus is fairly safe. Occasionally, we have the stupid drunks, and security can be very slow sometimes. Most of the time, though, there's **nothing to worry about**."

STUDENT AUTHOR: **Many students grow easily disgruntled with safety and security at Wooster. Security is normally seen as an enforcer of alcohol policies instead of a protector of the night. Certainly, serious security issues do come up, but compared to a big city, Wooster is the type of town where no one would steal a thing.**

> **Questions?**
> For more inside information and survival tips, pick up College Prowler's full-length book on this school, written by an actual student! Check it out at *www.collegeprowler.com*.

Students Speak Out
ON OVERALL EXPERIENCE

Q "The reason I came to Wooster was because of my first visit, **I felt comfortable**—like I belonged. Now, reflecting on my years spent here, I have been able to grow, get involved, and truly feel like I have made a difference on campus and in the community. Because of Wooster, I have priceless memories to always look back on."

Q "I love Wooster mostly because of the people. This has to be one of the greatest schools on earth when it comes to people. The professors are mostly fabulous, friendly, and helpful. And as for the students, I'll just say **I have more friends here than I've had in my life**!"

Q "Everyday of my life, I wish I was somewhere else. Wooster would be great if it was in a big city, but it is too isolated for my tastes. Plus, **I think it's way too expensive**."

Q "I love getting to know people so well and **creating a great rapport with my professors**. I know that I made the right decision by attending Wooster, and would never change it. Wooster has been a fabulous part of my life."

STUDENT AUTHOR: **Wooster students are very glad they chose to come to this college. They say that it's something about the atmosphere, something about the personal touches you see all over campus, and something about the friendships you make here that does it for them. They know that they are receiving a great education that will last them far into their future careers, forming friendships that may last longer than even their marriages, and gaining a wonderful background for becoming a richer person and living life to its fullest.**

Colorado College

14 East Cache La Poudre Street; Colorado Springs, CO 80903
(719) 389-6000; www.coloradocollege.edu

THE BASICS:

Acceptance Rate: 32%
Setting: Urban
F-T Undergrads: 2,034

SAT Range: 1230–1390*
Control: Private
Tuition: $33,972

Most Popular Majors: Social Sciences, Biology, Visual/Performing Arts, History, English

*of 1600

Academics	A-	Guys	B
Local Atmosphere	C	Girls	B
Safety & Security	B-	Athletics	B
Computers	B	Nightlife	B
Facilities	C+	Greek Life	B
Campus Dining	B-	Drug Scene	C+
Off-Campus Dining	A	Campus Strictness	A-
Campus Housing	B	Parking	C
Off-Campus Housing	B	Transportation	D
Diversity	D	Weather	C+

Students Speak Out
ON ACADEMICS

Q "The professors at CC, although highly educated, are **extremely approachable** and not intimidating. I feel that most teachers treat the students as equals, not as inferiors."

Q "Professors are usually **really animated**. Most of them know how to get students into what they are studying, rather than just reading and talking in class to get a good grade."

Q "Having taken many history and political science classes at CC, I find that the history department has its act together. I have yet to take a class that is poorly taught in history. However, I haven't had the same experience with political science. While we have many of the **top political minds** in the country, their egos many times interfere with their ability to teach, leaving the class hating political science as opposed to loving it."

Q "The professors make the class. If you have a boring professor teaching a very interesting subject, the class is still going to be boring. Although, here at CC, what is nice is that all the students do **teacher evaluations** at the end of each block. The school takes these evaluations very seriously."

STUDENT AUTHOR: **Professors at CC are quick to befriend students, invite them to engage in conversation, and debate both in and out of the classroom. Despite being friendly, professors demand much from their students. Many students spend six to eight hours per night on homework and may still go to class feeling unprepared.**

Students Speak Out
ON LOCAL ATMOSPHERE

Q "Colorado Springs **seems really big**, so everything is very spread out. There are other universities around here, but we don't interact with them very much, which makes it seem like it isn't a college town."

Q "The atmosphere of Colorado Springs is unique in that it's **so spread out** that there doesn't seem to be much of an epicenter. Downtown is small and lacks in cultural activity."

Q "Colorado Springs has a **great atmosphere**. There are many activities to keep you occupied during your down time, and the scenery will blow your mind. The town is nice as well, with many restaurants and stores."

Q "If you're interested in the outdoors and love the mountains, Colorado Springs is where you need to be. With the ski mountains only two hours away, winters are an exciting time. Colorado Springs is **an ideal location** for a college."

STUDENT AUTHOR: **Colorado Springs is a city of 500,000 that can often feel like one of the one-horse, one-saloon cow towns that dotted the West during the gold rush. The city's decentralized structure creates a far different, less metropolitan atmosphere than other cities of similar size. Downtown is comprised of eight or nine blocks, which, while offering several rows of tasty restaurants and coffeehouses, do little to spice up the dismal nightlife. There are, however, plenty of opportunities to explore the outdoors.**

5 Best Things	5 Worst Things
1 Caring professors	1 Lack of diversity
2 Free time galore	2 Nightlife
3 The Rocky Mountains	3 Residence halls
4 300 days of sunshine	4 Gossip
5 Intramural sports	5 Townies

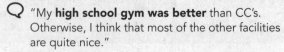

Students Speak Out
ON FACILITIES

Q "My **high school gym was better** than CC's. Otherwise, I think that most of the other facilities are quite nice."

Q "The facilities on campus are **very clean** and have very accessible hours. The dorms and theme houses have been improving every year as far as safety, cleanliness, and the overall state of the rooms goes."

Q "The facilities are really nice if you're a science major. All the newer buildings are science buildings. A lot of the humanities majors are in the **older buildings**, but they're are still perfectly fine for lectures."

Q "I think the **facilities are nice**, but they're nothing compared to the facilities at other universities, especially bigger ones."

STUDENT AUTHOR: The student experience of CC facilities depends largely on the life that the student leads and the activities that he or she is involved in. Classrooms are rarely packed, due mostly to the school's self-imposed class limit of 25 students. There's no doubt that the College needs to improve its athletic facilities if it ever wants to build a strong sports program. The facilities are by no means dilapidated, but a little modernization would attract more students and especially more athletes. Perhaps the greatest "facility" that CC offers isn't on the campus itself, but two miles to the west: the Rocky Mountains. If the gym is too small, students can go for a hike or mountain bike ride.

Famous Alumni

Lynne Vincent Cheney, Tara Nott Cunningham, Alison Dunlap, James Heckman, Ken Salazar

Students Speak Out
ON CAMPUS DINING

Q "The on-campus food is **terrible**. Rastall dining hall is notorious for tearing one's stomach to pieces. At no point have I ever enjoyed eating at the dining hall. However, I will say it's convenient not having to prepare your own food."

Q "The food on campus is edible, although **in no way gourmet**. Rastall can be a source for a good meal if you learn how to eat there. Benji's sandwiches and burritos are always a favorite."

Q "Food options on such a small campus are sometimes limited, but there are **good places** if you know where to go. Benjamin's Café and the Herb 'n Farm are both good places for sandwiches, as well as a change from the traditional dining hall experience."

Q "Rastall is the main dining hall. There you have everything from **vegetarian options** to the order-up grill. You can tell them anything you want to eat (within reason), and they make it."

STUDENT AUTHOR: Students joke about the principal cafeteria, Rastall, with such names as Rat-Stall and Nasty Rasty. These less-than-generous nicknames are exaggerated. While the "Stall" doesn't serve up gourmet fare, the food isn't so inedible as to warrant totally avoiding the place. The cafeteria chefs serve up a variety of choices every night. The problem is that "variety" becomes repetitive after the third month of eating it. Most agree that the key is to be creative with food selection and try new things on occasion.

Student Body

African American:	2%	Male/Female:	46/54%
Asian American:	5%	Out-of-State:	72%
Hispanic:	7%	International:	3%
Native American:	1%	Unknown:	4%
White:	78%		

Popular Faiths: Christian and Jewish groups have a dedicated, if sparse, following on campus.

Gay Pride: The Queer-Straight Alliance and EQUAL demonstrate the strong and important presence that the gay community has established on campus.

Economic Status: The stereotype is that CC students walk around in beat-up Birkenstocks and Goodwill clothes and drive up to Vail in their Land Rovers.

Students Speak Out
ON DORMS

Q "The dorms are nice. I recommend Loomis for your freshman year. It can **get a little wild**, but it's a lot of fun and close to everything. Slocum is really nice if you want a quieter atmosphere. I don't recommend Mathias unless you don't want any sleep and are just coming to school to party. It's a noisy one, but tons of fun."

Q "Avoid Loomis at all costs. After freshman year, avoid the bigger dorms. They're **kind of smelly** and crazy."

Q "It's nice to live in a substance-free or **quiet wing** because you can go party hardy elsewhere, but then be able to sleep and work in peace in your own room."

STUDENT AUTHOR: **Incoming freshmen are faced with few housing options, the largest of which are two first-year residence halls, Loomis and Slocum. The two buildings offer a very typical, "thrown into the mix" dorm experience. Most freshmen leave unscathed with a few stories to tell their friends back home. CC has made a concerted effort to keep students on campus as long as possible, thereby creating a closer-knit student body.**

Did You Know?
74% of undergrads live on campus.

Students Speak Out
ON GUYS & GIRLS

Q "I've always said that we're an 'outdoorsy' school, and the rugged, tough male seems to be a much more attractive type than the rugged female who **doesn't shower or shave**."

Q "The great thing about the students is that most of them are **athletic, smart, and motivated**. They're not all hot, but that's not always the most important thing."

Q "Everyone here is **hot**!"

Q "It's inspiring how many **brilliant people** there are here. And yes, even though the population of the school is small, there are many hot guys and plenty of beautiful girls, more than enough to go around, so don't worry."

STUDENT AUTHOR: **Girls and guys both are athletic and outdoorsy, and most students seem to have a glow about them that can only come from the Rocky Mountain air. CC girls save the lipstick and mascara for the parties, and tend to opt for an earthy, natural look. The guys will complain about this apparent lack of effort at times, usually while sporting ratty sweatpants and a torn T-shirt from the nearby thrift shop.**

Traditions

Harley Party
Each year, the Sigma Chi fraternity throws this bash for the entire campus. Students dress as Hell's Angels and other Harley-Davidson-riding gangs.

TWIG
On each block, a group of student comedians puts on an improvisational comedy show. The jokes seem to get raunchier every time.

Overall School Spirit
Despite a lack of consistently strong sports programs, CC enjoys a fun, vibrant sense of school spirit.

Students Speak Out
ON ATHLETICS

Q "Varsity sports are okay. With the exception of CC hockey, swimming, and women's soccer, most people actually **mock varsity athletes** because they aren't very good."

Q "Sports **seem to be popular**. All of the students are very active, so they like playing and watching. Varsity sports like hockey get a lot of attention."

Q "IM sports are **really good fun**—ice hockey, field hockey, volleyball. They're all great ways to get out and do something."

Q "The big varsity sport is hockey. If you don't come to CC already **loving hockey**, you will by the time you leave."

STUDENT AUTHOR: **Many students seem to dedicate their lives to becoming the best, while others participate only so they can eat and drink more without getting too fat. The point is that students usually play to have fun, not because they're getting paid, and the result is a fun atmosphere with a serious, competitive side for the truly passionate. Club and intramural sports also form a backbone of CC life. Over three-quarters of the students participate in one of these sports.**

Students Speak Out
ON DRUG SCENE

Q "There are **definitely drugs here** if you want them, but I wouldn't say that they dominate the 'social scene.' You can go your whole career here without even being tempted to try drugs."

Q "There are groups of **people that do lines** at every opportunity, but more often it's just people who have recreationally experimented with every drug in the book."

Q "I feel we have a **huge cocaine problem**, even more so than marijuana. As a person who believes greatly that drugs are wrong, I feel we have a problem, and more should be done to prevent drug use."

STUDENT AUTHOR: After alcohol, the drug of choice seems to be pot. Marijuana is a hugely popular drug, used frequently in residence halls in the early afternoon hours. Students can buy pot without any problems, and lax enforcement of drug policies makes it an even more attractive option. Harder drugs, such as cocaine, are no harder to come by, but are far less visible on the campus.

11:1	Student-to-Faculty Ratio
96%	Freshman Retention Rate
74%	Four-Year Graduation Rate
88%	Financial Aid Applicants Receiving Aid

Students Speak Out
SAFETY & SECURITY

Q "Security and safety on campus is **fairly good**. The lighting on campus isn't very good at times. Personally, I don't feel entirely comfortable walking across campus late at night by myself. Don't get me wrong, I don't fear for my life when walking across campus by myself, but there have been a small number of rape cases on campus."

Q "The security guards are great. They're very approachable. I feel **really comfortable** with the security of the housing on campus."

Q "Security on campus is adequate for a community our size. At times, dealing with them **can be frustrating**, but for the most part, they do what they can with the resources available to them."

STUDENT AUTHOR: Colorado Springs isn't necessarily a dangerous town, but there have been enough cases of serious crime to keep students on edge. Students commonly complain about the lack of light on campus and the slow call response time of CC security.

Questions?
For more inside information and survival tips, pick up College Prowler's full-length book on this school, written by an actual student! Check it out at *www.collegeprowler.com.*

Students Speak Out
ON OVERALL EXPERIENCE

Q "I give **my full endorsement** to this school. However, like any school, the atmosphere has to fit with the student. It's not for all people, but come and look. Within 10 minutes you'll know if this is where you want to be."

Q "CC is **a great place** to be. A very intensive learning process starts from day one with the small class sizes. The liberal arts degree seems very useful. There are tons of activities, and it's easy to get involved."

Q "My overall experience here at CC has been amazing. I've been stretched beyond my limits intellectually, and I've had **nothing but positive experiences**. I couldn't have received a better education at any other school."

Q "I love being at CC. I can't see myself anywhere else. The people are great, the Block Plan is great, and it's where I need to be. As a senior, I've **learned so much** here, and it's because of the atmosphere that CC provides. With the exception of a few things, I would recommend anyone who is interested to come to Colorado College and check it out."

STUDENT AUTHOR: With the caveat that a few students do transfer (usually due to the intense Block Plan), incoming students and those planning to apply should drop in for a visit, either over a morning and afternoon, or overnight. Aside from social and academic elements, CC makes amazing speakers and activities available. More than most other colleges, CC earns the respect of its current students and graduates for the training they receive in many areas, which will serve them throughout life.

Columbia University

3000 Broadway; New York, NY 10027
(212) 854-1754; www.columbia.edu

THE BASICS:

Acceptance Rate: 11%
Setting: Major city
F-T Undergrads: 6,367

SAT Range: 1330–1540
Control: Private
Tuition: $39,326

Most Popular Majors: Social Sciences, Engineering, History, Visual and Performing Arts

*of 1600

Academics	A	Guys	C+
Local Atmosphere	A	Girls	C+
Safety & Security	B-	Athletics	D
Computers	B	Nightlife	A
Facilities	B-	Greek Life	C-
Campus Dining	C+	Drug Scene	B-
Off-Campus Dining	A+	Campus Strictness	A-
Campus Housing	C+	Parking	F
Off-Campus Housing	D-	Transportation	A+
Diversity	B+	Weather	B-

Students Speak Out
ON ACADEMICS

Q "There is a **core curriculum** that will take up about two years of your studies. Although the classes are helpful, if you aren't so sure what you want to do with your life, the core could also hurt you because it prevents you from being able to try out a lot of different things with your credits. No matter what you think, don't take more than 19 credits in one semester. It is not worth it; trust me."

Q "Every professor I had was excellent. I found that they were **all approachable**. My psych professor got me a summer job."

Q "You have those who are so amazing that you can't believe you're in their class, and you'll have those that you won't be able to believe Columbia hired. That's college life, but there is a cool Web page that you can access through the Columbia Web site, called **CULPA, that allows you to read students opinions on teachers**. It helped me a lot second semester."

Q "Most of my experiences with teachers have been great. Columbia has **a lot of grad students** and TAs, but you would never know it. They are brilliant, young, and entertaining. Most of the time, all of my teachers have been accessible and approachable."

STUDENT AUTHOR: **The major problems that Columbia students cite are the huge egos of the senior faculty and the lack of individual attention. If a student is sincere and persistent, however, it is possible to find stimulating mentors.**

Students Speak Out
ON LOCAL ATMOSPHERE

Q "I do not like the atmosphere of Morningside Heights. It is **stuffy and overcrowded** with too many screaming children and stroller moms. Get out into the real New York, away from the Upper West Side or Morningside Heights. Alphabet City, St. Mark's Place, the NYU area, Greenwich Village, TriBeCa, and Soho, all make up a thriving, exciting, diverse atmosphere. You can see all of the movies, concerts, ballets, dance performances—anything you can imagine. It's a wonderful city, and there is nothing like New York."

Q "Dude, **it's New York**."

Q "I love living in New York because you can taste and **see all levels** of status. You can walk off of the campus after getting a bad grade on a test and see a man begging for food. You remember how lucky you are; it just keeps things in perspective."

Q "The campus is beautiful, and you will have so much **fun on and off campus**. You have the whole city to travel."

STUDENT AUTHOR: **New York City has something for everyone, and it does not take much for the staunchest suburbanite to find their niche somewhere in Manhattan. Sometimes, students feel like the city is going to eat them alive, but after making some friends and getting to know the environment, New York City becomes more inviting and less scary for those unfamiliar with über-urban life.**

5 Best Things	5 Worst Things
1 The Core Curriculum	1 Sluggish bureaucracy
2 New York City	2 Expensive costs
3 Diversity	3 Choice to study/explore
4 Professors and peers	4 Cramped housing
5 Culture and excitement	5 Getting used to things

Students Speak Out
ON FACILITIES

Q "The **facilities are good**, and they are making improvements constantly."

Q "The libraries are staffed by people who actually know what they are doing, and the stacks are **well maintained**. The media centers can be crowded, especially in the course reserve section. If you have to watch a video for a class, watch it early because there are usually only one or two copies on reserve."

Q "The facilities are **beautiful**. No other campus in NYC rivals it. And it is one of the only places in New York where grass is present. The gym is crowded but nice—truly the best place on campus to spot hotties."

Q "Lerner Hall, the student center on campus, is the only building that does not look like it belongs here. In a community of brick and ivy stands this **awkward glass structure** that houses cafés, computer rooms, theaters, and general meeting space. Once you get past the offbeat design of this place, you can enjoy the social atmosphere."

Q "Overall, I'd say the facilities on campus are **pretty decent**, although some of the classrooms are still kind of old."

STUDENT AUTHOR: **Students have been critical of the media centers located within the libraries, but with a little planning, you can get what you need. Lerner Hall has cafés, computer labs, a bank, a copy center, mailboxes, club meeting spaces, music rooms, and theaters to serve the student populace. Many students consider the gym as one of the best things about the campus.**

Famous Alumni

Maggie Gyllenhaal, Anna Paquin, Julia Stiles

Students Speak Out
ON CAMPUS DINING

Q "The dining hall is bad, I admit. The places where you can swipe your **Columbia Card** to use dining points are great. There's stir-fry, sushi, sandwiches, and Pizza Hut. You can get pretty much anything you want."

Q "During your first year at Columbia, they make you enroll in a meal plan that includes cafeteria food at John Jay. All I can say is that you should pick the meal plan with the least amount of meals but **more points**."

Q "**Save your money** to eat downtown on the weekends. Manhattan is rich with culinary delights for the Epicurean in all of us."

Q "Dining hall food is the same as anywhere. 212 is a great place for sandwiches, and Ferris Booth features **healthier dining options** like fresh fish with vegetable side dishes."

Q "**On campus, food is okay**, and there is a place to eat in the student center called Ferris Booth Commons, which is nice. Also, the grad schools have good places to get food, like Uris at the business school—I always eat there."

STUDENT AUTHOR: **Freshmen are required to have dining plans during their first year at Columbia, and there is only one dining hall on campus where they can eat breakfast and dinner (lunch is purchased with points at eateries mentioned previously). Sophomores and upperclassmen who go off meal plans often voice regrets about not being able to have food at their fingertips, but many rectify this problem by getting a Flex Account.**

Student Body

African American:	8%	Male/Female:	52/48%
Asian American:	18%	Out-of-State:	67%
Hispanic:	9%	International:	8%
Native American:	<1%	Unknown:	13%
White:	43%		

Popular Faiths: Judaism and Christianity are the most prominent faiths on campus.

Gay Pride: Columbia is a fairly liberal school in a very diverse city, so there aren't many problems with gay tolerance.

Economic Status: A lot of Columbia kids come from privileged backgrounds, but there's also a large number of students on financial aid from different countries and walks of life.

Students Speak Out
ON DORMS

Q "**Carman is a freshman favorite**. If you want the roommate experience or have a tough time meeting people, then it is totally the dorm for you because you are guaranteed to know three people—your suitemates. Whatever you do, don't go for a John Jay double; you could get a walkthrough and those are nice, but you could get an L shape and those are not so nice, so don't risk it. For a double, pick Carman. Furnald is also a really nice dorm, though it's less social than the others because it is half sophomores."

Q "Dorms are nice. **Columbia gives you singles** if you want them. I have actually lived in both of the freshman dorms. Carman is known to be more social; I liked it a lot. But having a single is really sweet, so I'd honestly go for John Jay if I had to do it over."

STUDENT AUTHOR: **Columbia housing is not created equally. All Columbia College and SEAS freshmen are required to live on campus, and the University saves decent living space for them. Once you have to undergo the housing lottery, you'd better hope that the housing gods are with you. Most students choose to stay on campus because there is no better deal in New York.**

> **Did You Know?**
> 94% of undergrads live on campus.

Students Speak Out
ON GUYS & GIRLS

Q "The dating scene here is strange. People don't really date. They just hang out as friends, and maybe a relationship develops, but that is rare. There is an abundance of **happily single people** at Columbia."

Q "**Hot isn't the word** I'd used to describe Columbians. We are better known for our 'good personalities.' You want hot? Head down to NYU."

Q "Socially, you get people who think they're the ultimate mix of being smart and cool. They leave **a lot to be desired** in both cases."

Q "Columbia is **nerdy** but hot."

STUDENT AUTHOR: **Many students say that they came to Columbia to study, not to focus on romance, and they are unfazed by the school's reputed lack of eye candy. That said, the students are usually ambitious and interesting, so sometimes mental attraction is more possible, and even sought after. There are all types here, from the high-maintenance princesses, to the shower-and-wear-jeans crowd.**

> **Traditions**
> At midnight, the night before finals begin, you can hear Columbia students lean out their windows and scream at the top of their lungs. To some, it's a stress reliever, to others, it's an unpleasant sleep disturbance.
>
> **Is It True?**
> According to a local saying, "Barnard to bed, Columbia to wed."
>
> **Overall School Spirit**
> Students are often very proud of going to such a well-respected university, but you won't hear anyone screaming "Go Fighting Lions" on game day. It's an intellectual spirit, not necessarily an athletic one.

Students Speak Out
ON ATHLETICS

Q "Many people are surprised to learn that Columbia even has football, basketball, baseball, and soccer teams. They are there for those who enjoy watching and competing in collegiate sports, but **not many people attend** these events. This is due in part to the fact that the fields and stadiums are nowhere near campus, and the activities are not widely publicized."

Q "**We have sports** at Columbia?"

Q "It's **embarrassing**, but they try so hard."

Q "There are many athletic opportunities at Columbia, but they are usually **not as popular** as they are at other schools."

STUDENT AUTHOR: **Some students are surprised to learn that Columbia has sports teams at all. Athletics are not a priority on campus, except for those who participate in them. Columbia is known for its academics, not its athletics, and many non-athletes (that is, most Columbians) rip on campus athletics any chance they can get. Those interested in athletics should check out the *Spectator* (Columbia's primary student newspaper) to learn more about our Lions.**

Students Speak Out
ON DRUG SCENE

Q "**Alcohol, nicotine, and caffeine** are the drugs of choice on campus, and they are in great abundance."

Q "Marijuana is the illegal drug of choice, and it is almost always available, as it's tough not to be exposed to a possible contact high at most parties. There's **very little peer pressure**, though. The potheads would rather keep their stash than waste it on someone who does not even want to try it. This drug is highly visible in the social scene, but it is the individual's choice on whether or not to partake in this vice."

Q "I really didn't see much of the drug scene since the crowd I hung with was **more into alcohol** than anything else, but I hear it's around."

STUDENT AUTHOR: **Caffeine is the drug of choice, but alcohol, nicotine, and marijuana are not far behind. For those who do not wish to imbibe or get stoned, you do not have to be exposed to those things if you choose your friends wisely; however, it is commonplace to see the squarest of students guzzling vodka and/or sharing a joint at a party.**

6:1	Student-to-Faculty Ratio
98%	Freshman Retention Rate
86%	Four-Year Graduation Rate
91%	Financial Aid Applicants Receiving Aid

Students Speak Out
SAFETY & SECURITY

Q "Columbia is **the safest place** in New York City."

Q "The campus itself is **like a citadel**."

Q "They close the main gates at 116th Street after a certain hour, and a security guard is posted 24/7. It's a pretty small campus, and while Morningside Heights was pretty sketchy 10 years ago, it's really cleaned up. I mean, I've definitely walked home at like four or five in the morning by myself; **no problem**!"

Q "Campus security and safety is great. When you walk through the gates, you walk into a totally different world. I have **never felt unsafe** on or around campus. It is very busy in addition to being well-patrolled."

STUDENT AUTHOR: **Most students feel safe at Columbia. It would be difficult not to, since Columbia security and the NYPD have such a high profile on campus. Even though the area surrounding the school has been gentrified, there are still some sketchy areas that should be avoided at night.**

> **Questions?**
> For more inside information and survival tips, pick up College Prowler's full-length book on this school, written by an actual student! Check it out at *www.collegeprowler.com.*

Students Speak Out
ON OVERALL EXPERIENCE

Q "I am **really happy with Columbia**. I love pretty much everything about it! I don't think that I could be happier anywhere else. The school is awesome, classes are hard but not impossible, and the core is a pain but a blessing in disguise—I have learned so much because of it, and sometimes, it can actually be fun."

Q "Columbia has been **like a dream** to me. There's no place I would rather be. It truly is the consummate urban campus, and I have really grown to love the city."

Q "It was the most amazing experience of my academic life, both as an undergrad and graduate student. As part of the **Ivy League**, this makes you special and separates you from the rest of the pack."

Q "The one thing that you should make sure about when coming to Columbia is whether you want a school where people will hold your hand or one where you're on your own. There is very little hand-holding at Columbia, and you are more or less **on your own**. Your support system is primarily the friends you make. However, if you are independent and want to take advantage of all of the opportunities that New York has to offer, Columbia is definitely the right place for you."

STUDENT AUTHOR: **Most students absolutely love Columbia. Columbia has the potential to give any student what they are looking for—be it prestige, socialization, culture, or a degree from one of the finest schools in the world. The city is not for the weak-hearted. Those who need hand-holding may not find that kind of support here, but then again, they might, if they look in the right place.**

Connecticut College

270 Mohegan Avenue; New London, CT 06320
(860) 447-1911; www.conncoll.edu

THE BASICS:

Acceptance Rate: 37%
Setting: Suburban
F-T Undergrads: 1,736

SAT Range: 1870–2130*
Control: Private
Tuition: $49,385**

Most Popular Majors: Economics, English, Psychology, Political Science, History

*of 2400   **includes room & board

Academics	A-	Guys	B-
Local Atmosphere	C-	Girls	B+
Safety & Security	A-	Athletics	B
Computers	C	Nightlife	C
Facilities	B	Greek Life	N/A
Campus Dining	A-	Drug Scene	B
Off-Campus Dining	B	Campus Strictness	B+
Campus Housing	B+	Parking	B
Off-Campus Housing	D	Transportation	D+
Diversity	C-	Weather	C-

Students Speak Out
ON ACADEMICS

Q "The professors at Conn are amazing. **Each has his or her individual story**. You'll take a class for a month, and then find out that your professor did something amazing, such as live in New Sudan for six months and write about the behavioral patterns of native tribes. Since most of the professors have accomplished such amazing things, they are able to make their classes more intriguing."

Q "Class discussion is almost always encouraged, with some of the larger introductory classes being the exception, sometimes to the point where **the originally planned topic is pushed aside** to follow the controversial/exciting/thought-provoking discussion/argument that has ensued."

Q "The more you put into a class, **the more you learn**. You not only learn from professors, but from your fellow students in class discussions."

Q "The teachers are personable and **have more interest in our success than we do**. They go to great lengths to make classes interesting."

STUDENT AUTHOR: Often referred to as a "Little Ivy," Connecticut College has strong and innovative academic programs. Rather than follow a predetermined list of classes, students are encouraged to actively plan out their education at Conn. Students usually get to know the professors in their majors very well, which makes it easy to seek out help after class, or fall into research and intern positions.

Students Speak Out
ON LOCAL ATMOSPHERE

Q "New London is **not a nice college town**. There isn't much to do, and it's not the safest place to be at night. The Coast Guard Academy and Mitchell College are both in New London."

Q "Conn College is a community within itself. I am on the sailing team, so I get to leave campus and travel all the time, but students who don't do sports **sometimes find they stay on campus** a lot. We do, however, have Mystic Seaport and many beaches, and Boston is only an hour and a half away."

Q "New London isn't very exciting, but Conn is the kind of school that has an active social life on campus. It is safe outside the school grounds, but **there is not much reason to leave campus** except to run errands or go out to dinner."

Q "New London is a great place for volunteer work, but students don't usually leave campus for anything else. There are a few really fun shops and cafés; **they just aren't very accessible**."

STUDENT AUTHOR: New London's claim to fame—its once booming whaling industry—won't make any students (aside from a few scrimshaw fans) rush to Conn. History buffs will appreciate the many historical homes, monuments, and museums nearby. The drawbacks to New London include safety issues at night and its isolation from campus. However, there is still some fun to be had in New London County.

5 Best Things

1 Professors
2 Self-scheduled finals
3 The arboretum
4 Meal plan
5 Shared governance

5 Worst Things

1 Social scene
2 Diversity
3 Off-campus housing
4 Rumor mill
5 Freshman registration

Students Speak Out
ON FACILITIES

Q "The library is nice, and the inter-college exchange system gives students access to even more resources. The athletic complex is too far away, and there isn't a good place for non-athletes to work out. The student center is nice—**nothing too special**, though."

Q "As a prospective theater major, it was really important to me to find a nice theater facility, and **Tansill Theater is beautiful**. When I visited Conn, I walked into Tansill and said, 'This could be my new home!'"

Q "The student center is basic. Because we're a small school, it isn't the greatest, but **it works for us**. The library is fine—they're always improving it."

Q "Conn sometimes is **a little bit behind technologically**. Its Internet connection has many problems, and people want to be able to use their ID cards in more places than just the snack shop and dining hall."

Q "The **classrooms are kind of run down**. Most of them have really old, uncomfortable desks."

STUDENT AUTHOR: The student center at Conn, diminutively known as Cro, is the heart of campus activity and the best place to look for students or professors between classes. Conn's students are blessed with a visually pleasing campus, which is beautiful in fall and winter. The granite and limestone buildings tie the school together aesthetically without making the architecture boring. Green space is plentiful, and it opens up the small campus. The College Green holds everything from soccer matches to Harvestfest booths.

Famous Alumni

Scott Lowell (actor, *Queer as Folk*)

Students Speak Out
ON CAMPUS DINING

Q "We have **innumerable options in the main dining hall**, but the smaller ones are the best for the atmosphere. We also have an all-vegetarian dining hall, Freeman, that does make-your-own stir-fry twice a week."

Q "The food is basically the same at each dining hall. I've heard food is a lot worse at other schools, but **our food really isn't that great**. The insides of the dining halls are nice though, and you do get lots of choices each meal."

Q "The food is really good. **Harris is the most popular dining hall**. In fact, I'm going to miss the food when I leave."

Q "All of the food on our campus is second to none. Most **people eat in dining halls 99 percent of the time**. There really are no other colleges in the country that have food as good as ours."

Q "The smaller **dinning halls on the south side of campus are best**, but have fewer choices."

STUDENT AUTHOR: Students are locked into a meal plan at Conn, so there's no reason not to take advantage of it. Harris Refectory serves all-you-can-eat buffet style breakfast, lunch, and dinner to most of the campus. Wherever you go, the Dining Services staff is incredibly friendly and accommodating. If you have any special requests—even if it's just to request your favorite cereal—you can drop them a "Napkin Note," and you'll have a response in about two weeks. You can't always get what you want, but it's nice to know input is heard.

Student Body

African American:	4%	Male/Female:	40/60%
Asian American:	4%	Out-of-State:	76%
Hispanic:	4%	International:	7%
Native American:	<1%	Unknown:	0%
White:	81%		

Popular Faiths: Most students are not outwardly religious, but there is a sizable population of Christians.

Gay Pride: The campus is very accepting of all sexual orientations and transgender and questioning students.

Economic Status: Most students predominately come from well-to-do backgrounds.

Students Speak Out
ON DORMS

Q "The dorms are great. Some of the bathrooms aren't that great. Really, **there are no bad rooms**, although most people say to stay away from the old Plex dorms. Even if you get one of those, you'll see that they have their charm, and a lot of people actually really like them."

Q "The dorms vary a lot. **All are mixed-class year and mixed-gender**."

Q "Lots of people want to live in certain dorms for so many different reasons, but what it comes down to is they all are pretty much the same. You will have the time of your life in any dorm so long as you are with your friends. **The people make the dorms great**!"

STUDENT AUTHOR: Dorms at Conn feel like little communities. Each has its own entirely student-run House Council, which manages day-to-day affairs and plans the dorm's social events. Dorms are located all over campus, and where you'll live depends a great deal on what area suits you best. All of the bathrooms are coed, which some initially find strange. In any case, students are quick to make themselves at home and develop dorm pride.

Did You Know?
99% of undergrads live on campus.

Students Speak Out
ON GUYS & GIRLS

Q "There are definitely more girls than guys on campus—it's about a 60-to-40 ratio. The guys are **either rich jerks or nice dorks**, but sometimes you can find good ones."

Q "The girls are either very hot or very not. There are plenty of cool guys around; it's all about **finding your little group of friends** that you fit in with."

Q "**The guys aren't hot**. There are more girls than boys, and all the good ones are therefore instantly taken."

Q "Conn College is, and has always been, high up in the rankings for the **most beautiful student body contest**."

STUDENT AUTHOR: More often than not, Conn students aren't looking for long-term relationships, but serious relationships can develop from random hookups. If you like to take it slow in relationships, however, Conn may not be the place for you. Conn's small size and plentiful single rooms could effectively make you roommates with your new boyfriend/girlfriend before you know it. Students at Conn, guys and girls, are friendly and outgoing people.

Traditions

Fishbowl
After consuming copious amounts of alcohol, body image is thrown out the window as seniors streak across the campus in various states of undress.

Meliora Weekend
The largest celebration on campus; includes Alumni Reunions, Parents Weekend, Homecoming and the Stonehurst Regatta.

Overall School Spirit
School spirit isn't rampant but occasionally bubbles to the surface.

Students Speak Out
ON ATHLETICS

Q "It seems like **everyone plays a sport**. We are an athletic bunch. The people who play truly love what they are doing, so that makes it so much better."

Q "Intramural sports are bigger than varsity. Lots of people play intramurals. Since it's Division III, **athletic events aren't that well attended**. The most successful sports are water sports."

Q "Sports in general are not too big on campus; **drinking games seem to draw bigger crowds**."

Q "There are some varsity sports that are big, such as lacrosse and soccer, but I think that the **intramural sports are just as important** if not more."

STUDENT AUTHOR: Connecticut College places an emphasis on developing "student-athletes." In other words, Conn is more interested in GPAs than field goal percentages and winning championships. The Camels typically don't get a lot of fan support at home, which is a shame, because all sporting events are free and easily accessible.

Students Speak Out
ON DRUG SCENE

Q "**Drinking is a significant part of our social life**, but that is not to say we don't all keep up with our schoolwork. There are not a ton of drugs coming into Conn, but it's not hard to find marijuana, coke, and maybe 'shrooms."

Q "Eh, there's a lot of pot, like every other campus. There's also booze, of course. Students hit up pills to keep themselves awake during crunch time, but **nothing more serious than that**."

Q "Drugs of all sorts are popular. Smoking is the most popular pastime. **There is no pressure**, however; people are chill and drugs are not an issue."

STUDENT AUTHOR: Without a doubt, Conn's poison of choice is alcohol. Pot is also available on campus and widely used, but students who get high are far more discrete. All in all, if alcohol is discounted, Conn has a minor drug scene, but it's really not that visible in the day-to-day goings on of the campus or its party scene. Then again, you don't exactly have to be Sherlock Holmes to uncover it.

11:1	Student-to-Faculty Ratio
90%	Freshman Retention Rate
83%	Four-Year Graduation Rate
79%	Financial Aid Applicants Receiving Aid

Students Speak Out
SAFETY & SECURITY

Q "**As a woman, I really don't feel threatened** walking around campus late at night. Never once was I scared that I would be in danger, and plus, because we're far away from downtown New London, the campus is isolated; no one ever comes up here."

Q "The **campus is incredibly safe**. I've never felt the least bit threatened or unsafe."

Q "Most people say that Campus Safety is really there **to protect us from ourselves**, and I would have to agree. I think most students are more scared about Campus Safety breaking up parties than they are of intruders."

STUDENT AUTHOR: If a student notifies Campus Safety of an alcohol or drug overdose, the patient will be immediately treated and rushed to the hospital—no questions asked. Campus safety is primarily concerned with students' well-being and will not severely discipline the patient or the reporter.

> **Questions?**
> For more inside information and survival tips, pick up College Prowler's full-length book on this school, written by an actual student! Check it out at www.collegeprowler.com.

Students Speak Out
ON OVERALL EXPERIENCE

Q "I love it. I would never want to be anywhere else. Once you find your group of friends, you are set. **It really is a great place to learn**. The weather keeps you on your toes. The teachers either make you laugh or push you really hard. The sports are fun and up-and-coming. The kegs keep you happy, the food keeps you full. Who wouldn't want that?"

Q "**I don't really fit in at Conn**, but I know so many kids that love it more than anything. I think I would have been happier at a bigger school."

Q "I never wished I had gone anywhere else, but I did **take advantage of studying abroad** for a semester and would recommend doing so to everyone, as Conn is a bubble on a hill, and it is very important for one to experience the outside world. Your time at Conn is what you make it out to be—if you don't do anything, you will be miserable."

Q "I'm very glad I'm here. If you look for it, the **academic environment** is there. I've met great people."

STUDENT AUTHOR: This is a great school for students who don't know what they want to major in. Conn's General Education requirements make it mandatory to take a variety of courses, and faculty are always available to advise students. The most common complaint among students who don't like Conn is its small size. Because of this, it's important to visit overnight or at least take a tour to try the campus on for size.

Cornell University

349 Pine Tree Road; Ithaca, NY 14850
(607) 255-2000; www.cornell.edu

THE BASICS:

Acceptance Rate: 21%
Setting: Rural
F-T Undergrads: 13,510

SAT Range: 1290–1500*
Control: Private
Tuition: $34,600

Most Popular Majors: Engineering, Agriculture, Business, Biology, Social Sciences

*of 1600

Academics	A-	Guys	B
Local Atmosphere	C+	Girls	C+
Safety & Security	B	Athletics	B-
Computers	A	Nightlife	C+
Facilities	A-	Greek Life	B+
Campus Dining	A+	Drug Scene	B+
Off-Campus Dining	B	Campus Strictness	B-
Campus Housing	A-	Parking	C+
Off-Campus Housing	B+	Transportation	B-
Diversity	B+	Weather	D

Students Speak Out
ON ACADEMICS

Q "It **depends on your major**, but in general, they are good. You get more attention in the smaller majors."

Q "It's Cornell. Need I say more? When you're lucky enough to have an actual professor instead of a TA, you really are receiving an education from the **best of the best**."

Q "Professors are generally very good, though they are rather boring. TAs are almost always useless and **don't speak English**. They teach writing seminars, sections, and labs."

Q "The teachers are excellent. The thing you must keep in mind about college teachers is that they are **not there to teach**. They are at Cornell to do research and they just teach on the side. I am speaking mostly of physics, math, and engineering professors."

STUDENT AUTHOR: All professors are highly qualified and are experts in their respective fields of study. TAs, on the other hand, may not be so proficient, and some, in certain cases, may not communicate as well with their students as professors could. With Cornell's intellectually dynamic faculty base, it's hard not to get one of the best educations around, second to none. However, Cornell is notorious for its intense workload. Most professors are unsympathetic, and while willing to accommodate personal needs, they make sure their students are kept very busy. On the average you should expect to work harder here than anywhere else.

Students Speak Out
ON LOCAL ATMOSPHERE

Q "The town is **full of hippies**—lots of vegetarian and eco-friendly people. Ithaca is fun, but sometimes it gets a little boring because you're far from any major city. There are always things going on around campus."

Q "I love Ithaca. It is so diverse and has **amazing waterfalls, and gorges**, and nice parks. Ithaca College is also fairly close."

Q "Ithaca is decent-sized with Ithaca College on the other side of town. **There's really not much to do in town**, but there is so much that is offered on campus."

Q "It's no secret that Ithaca is **remote and isolated**; it's thanks to Cornell University and Ithaca College that it has a place on the map. But surprisingly, the town is dynamic and vibrant, not only when school is in session, but during the summer as well. There are many things to do: visit Buttermilk Falls and Cascadilla Creek, swim in the gorges when it's warm (but steer clear of the cliffs), go on booze cruises at Cayuga Lake when it's warm, and ski at Greek Peak in the winter."

STUDENT AUTHOR: While Ithaca may be sheltered from aspects unique to urban life, the town is actually quite dynamic and teems with action. With two college campuses, there is always something going on, and the outdoor scenery is quite stunning. Those seeking a more fast-paced lifestyle characteristic of the city might be disappointed.

Students Speak Out
ON FACILITIES

"The facilities on campus are a mix between **Gothic architecture and modern buildings**. Most of the athletic facilities are modern and very impressive. The computer labs as well stay current with new programs and software."

"Cornell does a good job of keeping everything **up-to-date**. They are building new facilities constantly."

"The facilities on campus are always being **revamped and improved**. The computer labs have fully loaded PCs or Macs—though they tend to crash a lot. And many buildings are now equipped with wireless Internet capabilities. Classrooms on the arts quad are a bit cramped at times, especially in seminars, but rooms in the hotel school are a lot more comfortable and spacious. Uris and Olin libraries have their own coffee lounges—ideal for relaxing study and caffeine breaks. The gyms are equipped with state-of-the-art equipment, and Helen Newman multi-purpose center has its own Olympic-sized swimming pool, basketball courts, and weight room."

STUDENT AUTHOR: **Most students seem very satisfied with Cornell's facilities. Construction is continually in progress to improve older buildings and revamp outdated ones; unfortunately this construction is sometimes disruptive to classes. The architecture of many of these facilities lends itself to a traditional, gothic, Ivy League atmosphere. In general, students feel that Cornell's innovative facilities help foster its multitude of research, as well as academic and recreational opportunities.**

Famous Alumni:

Pearl S. Buck, Adolph & Joseph Coors, Dave Edgerton, Ruth Bader Ginsburg, Bill Maher, Toni Morrison, Bill Nye, Janet Reno, Christopher Reeve

Students Speak Out
ON CAMPUS DINING

"The food here is **supposedly the best** in the country; I think partly because we have such a good hotel school. For dining hall food, it's great. We make fun of it anyway, though. The best dining halls are on north where the freshmen are. I like RPU on north and Okenshield's on central campus."

"Some of the dining halls are all-you-can-eat, while others are á la carte. You have different varieties of food from Chinese to Italian to all-American. I have to give an A+ for food at Cornell. But **watch out**—a lot of people gain a substantial amount of weight their first year."

"The food, as you have probably heard, **is amazing**. I am seriously excited to go to dinner everyday."

"The **dining halls are excellent**. I find it difficult to get better food than what you find here on campus."

STUDENT AUTHOR: **Campus dining is first-rate and compensates for the hefty meal plan pricing. Hardly any students have qualms with it. Diversity of selection is impressive, and the all-you-can-eat facilities offer a variety of buffet assortments: deli, pasta bar, grill, stir-fry, chef's corner, Kosher corner, waffles, salad bar, smoothies, and freshly-baked desserts. Furthermore, special Cross Country Gourmet occasions take place at a variety of dining halls over the course of the semester, introducing students to marvelously exotic cuisines prepared by some of the world's leading chefs.**

Student Body

African American:	5%	Male/Female:	50/50%
Asian American:	16%	Out-of-State:	62%
Hispanic:	6%	International:	8%
Native American:	<1%	Unknown:	15%
White:	50%		

Popular Faiths: Christianity and Judaism are popular. While Buddhism, Islam, and Hinduism also exist, many students claim no religious affiliation.

Gay Pride: There is a lesbian, gay, bisexual, and transgender resource office that is very active on campus.

Economic Status: Students are from various socio-economic backgrounds.

Students Speak Out
ON DORMS

Q "There are **two types of dorms**: program houses and traditional halls. Program houses have a specific theme, like music or culture, for instance. If you are interested in a program house, then you apply to that house and hopefully get accepted. The traditional halls are regular. They're all quite nice, although some are better than others."

Q "Pray that you get Donlon! It's not the nicest in terms of quality, but it's **the most social**—you'll meet tons of people and make great friends. I loved living there this year. The new dorms, Court and Mews, are really nice, too. Dickson is okay, and Balch isn't because it's so quiet."

Q "As a freshman you'll be on north campus, which is nice. Sophomore year, try for **Cascadilla because it's in Collegetown**; there's a better upperclassmen scene there."

STUDENT AUTHOR: **Students tend to agree that campus housing for freshmen is much more convenient and enjoyable than on-campus housing for upperclassmen. Mews and Court Halls are the envy of every freshman, so consider yourself lucky if you end up there.**

> **Did You Know?**
> 42% of undergrads live on campus.

Students Speak Out
ON GUYS & GIRLS

Q "If this matters to you, **then you are shallow** enough to go to Cornell."

Q "Guys like to say that the **girls are busted** and that the guys are much better looking. I don't know if that's true. I think there are enough people here to assume a fairly normal distribution in terms of attractiveness."

Q "**You'll find someone** if you look extremely hard—harder than you've ever looked before, anywhere!"

Q "I think girls here are skinnier than anywhere else I've ever seen. They're always going to the gym or for a jog. I think we should start a campaign to **feed them**."

STUDENT AUTHOR: **Although the guys seem to be rated slightly higher than the girls, Cornell University is huge, so there are plenty of choices. There's really no reason to think that all the males and females are complete dorks either. There are also a lot of organizations to meet gay, lesbian, bisexual, questioning, or transgender students if that's what you are looking for.**

Traditions

Slope Day
On the last day of classes, students gather on Libe Slope to celebrate the end of the year. It used to be an unstructured event full of very drunk students, but now it is organized by the University. On Slope Day, there are food vendors, a carnival area, and bands.

Overall School Spirit
students don't necessarily have a tremendous amount of "ra-ra" spirit in support of its athletic teams. School spirit seems to be more contained to specific groups like colleges (the School of Hotel Administration), departments (applied economics and management), organizations and clubs, and fraternities and sororities.

Students Speak Out
ON ATHLETICS

Q "There are **a lot of IM sports**—soccer, softball, basketball, even inner tube water polo. Varsity sports aren't so big, except for hockey. We're not too good at anything else."

Q "**Hockey is unbelievable**. You will never see any school cheer for a team more than we do for Cornell hockey. You should definitely get season tickets. It's worth it."

Q "There is not much student support for the varsity athletic programs here aside from hockey. The student body gets so much work, and our sports teams are generally not very good. This combination contributes to **empty stands** and a lack of school spirit."

STUDENT AUTHOR: **Although Cornell isn't seriously focused on its athletic program like one of the Big 10 schools, we still come to dominate in several sports, including hockey, lacrosse, wrestling, and polo. In the future, it is without a doubt that Cornell will become increasingly more competitive and progressively more powerful in Division I athletics. Cornell is well-known for its men's hockey team, which constantly ranks in the national top 10.**

Students Speak Out
ON DRUG SCENE

Q "There's **not much** of a drug scene. I don't do drugs, and I've never really been confronted with them at school. Again, it depends on the crowd. There is a lot of drinking, though."

Q "In my experience, there is either not much of a drug scene on campus, or I **never saw it** firsthand."

Q "I personally do not think that the drug scene is that big here at Cornell. I never run into many problems, and I'm **never pressured** by any of my friends to do drugs."

Q "**The drug scene is underground** and not as bad as some issues at your normal university."

STUDENT AUTHOR: Although drugs are by no means prominent on campus, some say that if you want them, they're easy to find. Fortunately, there isn't a lot of pressure to get involved, and Cornell has much less of a problem than many other schools. Students tend to agree that they have never witnessed an obvious drug culture at school.

9:1	Student-to-Faculty Ratio
96%	Freshman Retention Rate
84%	Four-Year Graduation Rate
46%	Financial Aid Applicants Receiving Aid

Students Speak Out
SAFETY & SECURITY

Q "Personally, I have never had a problem, and it's **never been a major concern** of mine. There are blue-light phone systems, and I have only heard of a few people getting mugged. I've never been really worried; just try to walk with someone else if it's past dark. The campus is pretty well lit, and my car has always been safe as well."

Q "Safety is pretty good. It isn't a city or anything, so when you are on campus, you are pretty much safe. There are **random incidents**, but everyone feels safe on campus."

Q "I always feel **pretty secure** on campus. There are escorts and blue-light phones that are available if you're walking at night, so you feel better. I've never had to deal with any crimes, but there have been some racial issues in the past."

STUDENT AUTHOR: Most students agree that Cornell is a very safe campus since it's had few seriously consequential incidents in the past. Culprits aren't usually Cornellians, but Ithaca townies. With Cornell's diligent police force, safety hazards and security issues have been kept to a minimum.

> **Questions?**
> For more inside information and survival tips, pick up College Prowler's full-length book on this school, written by an actual student! Check it out at *www.collegeprowler.com.*

Students Speak Out
ON OVERALL EXPERIENCE

Q "I like it here; **I like it a lot**. The school is beautiful over the summer. You can take so many awesome classes—classes on wines, scuba diving, and sailing. I also like skiing, so that is a plus. The nightlife is lacking as far as I am concerned. However, I'm usually very busy with schoolwork, so it's kind of nice to not be so tempted. Bottom line, I like it here and would not want to be anywhere else."

Q "It's all right; I am happy I went here. Out of the Ivy League schools, Cornell is known for giving the most work. It's perhaps the most difficult. This school makes you **work your butt off** and it is no joke. It is a good school, but be prepared to work hard."

Q "Overall, I wish I had gone to a smaller, more personal school with smaller classes, fewer TAs, and a less competitive environment. Students here are **very cutthroat**, so get ready."

Q "I don't think that Cornell is for everyone. I think that it is a great school, but plenty of people **might be miserable** here. It's actually quite intense."

STUDENT AUTHOR: Students express both praise and criticism of their overall experience at Cornell University. Comments on the whole, however, seem to suggest that most students have had more positive experiences than negative ones. Many students are very grateful for the discipline and work ethic that they have developed here, which has become integral to their progress and success. One student clearly articulates, "The one thing I can say about Cornell is that nothing is handed to you." These words summarize the Cornell experience.

Creighton University

2500 California Plaza; Omaha, NE 68178
(800) 282-5835; www.creighton.edu

THE BASICS:

Acceptance Rate: 82%
Setting: Urban
F-T Undergrads: 3,830

SAT Range: 1550–1880*
Control: Private
Tuition: $27,282

Most Popular Majors: Health Professions, Business
Nursing, Communication, Psychology

*of 2400

Academics	B	Guys	C
Local Atmosphere	B-	Girls	B
Safety & Security	C-	Athletics	B
Computers	B	Nightlife	C+
Facilities	B	Greek Life	B+
Campus Dining	B	Drug Scene	A
Off-Campus Dining	A-	Campus Strictness	B+
Campus Housing	B-	Parking	A
Off-Campus Housing	B	Transportation	C
Diversity	D	Weather	C+

Students Speak Out
ON ACADEMICS

Q "My teachers have all been amazingly attentive. **They really pay attention to us**. I was tired and not really participating in class one day, and my professor came up to me at the end and asked if everything was okay, saying her door was open. They're always like that."

Q "Sometimes, I think the teachers are into talking more than communicating. **They like to lecture at you**. Then again, I'm in a bigger department (biology), so maybe it's different than others."

Q "Don't think you don't have to study just because it's not the hardest school in the country to get into. **It's hard here**. I spent all my time studying freshman year and came out okay. My roommate didn't, and she ended up losing her scholarship and having to drop out."

Q "**Since classes are small, it is easy to express your opinion without feeling uncomfortable**. Classes are fairly interesting, and even if you aren't particularly interested in a subject, sometimes just the arguments made in class can spark your interest."

STUDENT AUTHOR: Open-door policies, quick e-mail responses, and general concern for both academic progress and personal happiness have students singing their teachers' praises. Students also agree that most classes have heavy workloads. However, it can be surprising to discover that a relatively little-known school is so challenging. Here, you can't expect to spend as much time partying as your state school counterparts.

Students Speak Out
ON LOCAL ATMOSPHERE

Q "**Omaha is a really fun town**. The Old Market has a ton of great restaurants and shops. There are a couple of other schools in Omaha—St. Mary's and UNO, for example. Stay away from North Omaha, though. It's a little scary."

Q "This is one of the coolest places to live. I know it sounds pretty stupid to say, given that this is Omaha, but come on. **The people are friendly and the rent is cheap**—actually, everything is cheap. We have museums and concerts and everything like a normal big city, too."

Q "I didn't get out on the town all that much during my first couple years at Creighton because I did not have a car, but I like the atmosphere of the town because **it moves at a much slower pace than where I'm from in Florida**. The people are friendlier, as well, which is very refreshing."

Q "**It's very quiet during the night**. I'm from a suburb of Chicago, so I'm used to it being very noisy with cars and various things. All I hear outside are the interstate cars sometimes and noisy drunk people walking around late on the weekends."

STUDENT AUTHOR: Seriously, it's Omaha, it's Nebraska, it's the Midwest—it's 15 minutes to the nearest cornfield. But this is the most urban part of one of the least urban parts of the country. Many people retain that small-town simplicity and humbleness. If this irritates you, steer clear of the suburbs. Stay near campus where there's plenty to do.

Students Speak Out
ON FACILITIES

"The student center is a nice place to sit and listen to other students play the pianos or talk to people. **It's a great place to meet up with people**, because almost everyone knows where it is. And, since it is being remodeled, you will have more spots to sit around."

"As far as the facilities on campus go, **they are all pretty nice**. I think that some of the computers in a few of the residence halls could be upgraded, but most of them aren't too bad. The student center is still under renovation, and it will be even nicer than it was before."

"**The gym is oftentimes too full**, but that's the only problem. It has very nice equipment, and the staff keeps it well-maintained. Our facilities are nice compared to other universities that I've visited."

"The facilities aren't the greatest, but **the new stuff is good**, and the stuff they're building now should be really great. Opus Square, a junior apartment building, plus two garages are all new. The student center thing will be opening fall of 2008. How cool is that?"

STUDENT AUTHOR: **Overall, what Creighton has for facilities is adequate, and there is much more to come. Everything new at Creighton is, well, either just finished or still being built. Essentially, the past has been ho-hum for students, and the present is atrocious in some ways because of all the construction to maneuver around, but the future should be so wonderful that it's hard to hate Creighton for the effort.**

Famous Alumni

Kimera Bartee, Benoit Benjamin, Mike Boyle, Rodney Buford, Mike Fahey, Bob Gibson, Kevin McKenna, James Edward Murphy, John Dale Ryan, Lee Terry

Students Speak Out
ON CAMPUS DINING

"Dining halls are okay. **They have their basics covered**, and then they have some things that vary day to day, but nothing too special. The dining in the student center is alright, as well. It just has the typical things, but going there is convenient."

"I transferred here, and **this school's food is totally underappreciated**. I mean, I'm sure people get sick of it after awhile, but with all the choices of places to eat and all the different stuff they have within the cafeterias, it's tough to go wrong."

"Brandeis had a 'fresh food week,' which I liked a lot. It was pretty healthy, so if we end up having that type of food all the time, I would not mind the food at all. Actually, I guess **it's kind of nice that they offer us a lot of options**, at least, since not every school does that."

"**I think the food is not worth what we're paying for**, but it's better than some other places. Actually, since my mom and dad don't like to cook, I'd say it might be better than my own home."

STUDENT AUTHOR: **With two buffets, Blimpie's, Davis Diner, Irma's Bistro, and Java Jay Coffeehouse, all among the choices, what's not to love about Creighton campus dining? Apparently, a few things, according to students. Some say the food is too cold. Others feel their options are limited. Many just grow tired of repeating their dining hall routines day after day.**

Students Speak Out
ON DORMS

Q "**The dorms are not that bad**. Yes, they are small, but if you arrange things and organize it, the room can seem very big."

Q "I really enjoyed living in the new apartment-style dorm because I had my own room, a full kitchen, and a living room, and it was all brand new. I would highly recommend living on campus your freshman and sophomore year, at least, because **it is a good way to meet people**, and it's more convenient."

Q "The nicest dorms are obviously the newer ones, but **as freshmen, you will be in the older dorms**, and those all basically have the same size rooms."

STUDENT AUTHOR: **Time-saving is by far the greatest advantage of campus housing. That's why many choose to stay on campus, even after sophomore year. While it is true that certain freshman residence hall rooms contain fewer square-feet per person than the state of Nebraska requires for penitentiary inmates, most students are thrilled with their humble cells. Campus housing makes a great place to bond.**

Did You Know?
62% of undergrads live on campus.

Students Speak Out
ON GUYS & GIRLS

Q "Maybe it's just me, but it's awfully hard to get a date here. I think everyone is too stuck up—guys and girls. And **nobody's really that hot**. We all go to class looking like we just got out of bed."

Q "The problem with girls is, **if they're pretty, they're probably snooty**. I've heard it's like that with the guys, too; if we're hot, we're jerks. I don't know. Everyone here is good-looking, if you ask me."

Q "**It's both good and bad that this is a smaller school**. It's good because you might get a chance to get to know and fall in love with someone. It's bad because you're constantly bumping into your latest hookup. I mean, running into. You know what I mean."

STUDENT AUTHOR: **Everyone seems to whine and moan about the dating scene. The real problem, however, is that an abundance of attractive males and females are wandering around this campus, but they're so used to seeing one another all the time that they can't fathom approaching one another, because if rejected, he or she will probably be seated next to the other person in Spanish class next semester.**

Traditions

Candlelight Mass
Popular among Catholic students, but also attended by others, is the Sunday night Candlelight Mass.

JayWalk
A recent tradition, the JayWalk is a benefit for the Jesuit Middle School of Omaha.

Overall School Spirit
There are students who have wall-to-wall white and blue bluejays embroidered on their underwear, and then there are students who aren't sure what the school mascot is.

Students Speak Out
ON ATHLETICS

Q "Men's soccer and basketball seem to be our biggest sports. **We just built a new soccer stadium, which is awesome**! It's one of the best facilities in the country. The programs themselves have improved, and most are doing very well."

Q "**IM sports, especially flag football, basketball, and soccer, are huge on campus**. There are also many other IM sports, including ultimate Frisbee and volleyball. There is something for everyone!"

Q "I grew up in Omaha and have gone to the College World Series for a few years now. **I'd say it's the biggest athletic event in town**. And, of course, there are the Huskers games, too."

Q "I don't go to games. **I think there's school spirit, but I don't go**. I'm always busy."

STUDENT AUTHOR: **Creighton seems to have a fair mix—it knows better than to try to compete with fans for football in the Husker state, so it steers clear of football entirely and instead focuses on building a relatively successful men's basketball team. Creighton soccer and basketball, as well as the wide intramural offerings and large student participation in them, is redeeming.**

Students Speak Out
ON DRUG SCENE

Q "**Drugs won't be a problem, in general**. However, I had a friend whose first roommate used drugs. That was okay, until he started stealing from my friend to buy stuff."

Q "**Creighton is relatively drugless**, but the area of town immediately outside campus seems to be somewhat more drug-prone, so I guess if you needed to buy some, you could probably find it out there."

Q "You'll find **some pot-smokers amongst the frat crowd and a ton of major alcoholics**, but that's all I know about. Some of my friends are really into that stuff, but I try to stay away."

STUDENT AUTHOR: If you want to toke up, it's here. Just don't expect everyone else to join you. Even meth, the Midwestern drug of choice, doesn't seem to have soaked too deeply into the fibers of campus life. Without a doubt, some students may feel pushed into drinking, but many others say they have no problem finding fun without ever cracking open a cold one.

11:1	Student-to-Faculty Ratio
86%	Freshman Retention Rate
67%	Four-Year Graduation Rate
81%	Financial Aid Applicants Receiving Aid

Students Speak Out
SAFETY & SECURITY

Q "Campus is safe. **You just have to be smart and not walk around by yourself late at night**. Also, don't go north of the McDonald's on Cuming Street."

Q "**I think the campus is very safe**. I have walked across campus before around 8 p.m. for a night class, and even later to go to the convenience store by myself, and I wasn't afraid or anything. I have always felt safe."

Q "I think security and safety is very good on our campus. There are students all over the Mall during the day, and **pretty much everyone looks out for each other**. There are also Public Safety officers around campus looking out for the students."

STUDENT AUTHOR: The overwhelming advice given by Creighton students regarding security is: don't be stupid. The problem stems from the fact that Creighton quickly feels like a small town, and you think you know everyone, and so you start to think that there's no way anything bad could ever happen.

Questions?
For more inside information and survival tips, pick up College Prowler's full-length book on this school, written by an actual student! Check it out at *www.collegeprowler.com*.

Students Speak Out
ON OVERALL EXPERIENCE

Q "I can't help but wonder why anyone wouldn't want to go to Creighton. **It's such an awesome school**. The students are smart; they can be uptight sometimes, but they are generally really fun on the weekends to compliment their extreme studiousness. It's a great place to have a classroom debate, as well as to have a party."

Q "I was so scared of the Jesuits here. **I'm not Catholic**. They are the most generous, thoughtful, nonjudgmental, intelligent people I've met in my life, and that spirit is absorbed by students. This place makes you a better person."

Q "Creighton is the perfect place to be. All of my friends are here. It just fits. **Everyone is so nice, and the teachers are so dedicated**. You really can't put a price on the chance to live and learn with such amazing people."

Q "**I know there are people who don't like Creighton**, but I don't know very many of them. I think the best advice I can give is to try a lot of different activities and get to know as many people as you can; that way, if the first people you meet don't fit, you'll find others who do. There are so many opportunities here!"

STUDENT AUTHOR: Creighton students overwhelmingly seem to believe they are involved in a passionate love affair with their college. It's tough to blame them, though. You not only take classes, you really grow and develop with the school. The professors, and even administrators, will guide you and offer you support at all times, encouraging you to seek them out in office hours to help you reach your potential.

Dartmouth College

6061 McNutt Hall; Hanover, NH 03755
(603) 646-1110; www.dartmouth.edu

THE BASICS:

Acceptance Rate: 13%   **SAT Range:** 1330–1550*
Setting: Rural   **Control:** Private
F-T Undergrads: 4,109   **Tuition:** $36,690

Most Popular Majors: Social Sciences, Psychology, History, English, Engineering, Ethnic Studies

*of 1600

Academics	A+	Guys	B-
Local Atmosphere	C-	Girls	C+
Safety & Security	A+	Athletics	B
Computers	A	Nightlife	D
Facilities	B	Greek Life	A
Campus Dining	A+	Drug Scene	B+
Off-Campus Dining	C-	Campus Strictness	B
Campus Housing	A-	Parking	C-
Off-Campus Housing	B	Transportation	C
Diversity	B+	Weather	C

Students Speak Out
ON ACADEMICS

Q "**Academics at Dartmouth are unbeatable**. Since we aren't in the classroom very much compared to students at other schools, there is a lot of independent work, and it moves quickly. If you like to be challenged and move at a quick pace, you'll love Dartmouth."

Q "As for academics, they're amazing. The **professors are great**; you get to talk to them a lot more than you do at other colleges of similar merit."

Q "Honestly, there's **not enough discourse in classes**. I've lost my ability to speak in groups from being out-of-practice in class. Some professors are wonderful and have become mentors and friends, but on the whole I'm disappointed by the academics. Many college courses are a waste of time."

Q "While classes vary in difficulty, **it's not very hard to get a B plus**, which is the campus-wide median. Go to class, do your reading, and you should do just fine."

STUDENT AUTHOR: **Attending Dartmouth is a surefire way to avoid those troublesome TAs, as all classes are taught by professors. While there are some duds to be avoided, Professors are rarely sidetracked by research, which makes getting to know your instructors a breeze. Classes are challenging, professors are brilliant, and academic experiences are positive in the vast majority of cases. "Work hard, play hard" is an appropriate motto.**

Students Speak Out
ON LOCAL ATMOSPHERE

Q "Hanover is a very, very, small New England town. We are **literally in the middle of nowhere**. It's a very beautiful campus—anyone who has been to Dartmouth will tell you that."

Q "The town **life revolves around the college**. This is one of the coolest things about Dartmouth—being immersed in an environment that is totally devoted to education. There isn't so much to see in the town, but there's enough stuff to do on campus to make up for that."

Q "It's quaint; very small. **We have everything we need and nothing else**. It's boring at times, but it's also cute and I like it. It's very isolated, though."

Q "Dartmouth's atmosphere blends New England architecture and history with Southern hospitality and West Coast relaxation to create the perfect environment for a successful and happy college career. The **city of Hanover has a fruitful partnership with Dartmouth**."

STUDENT AUTHOR: **Most Dartmouth students are so busy that they rarely ponder what's beyond Wheelock Street. Those who do are usually thrilled by their placid surroundings. Hanover is consistently praised for its peaceful New England beauty. With nowhere to go and little to do, students form tight-knit bonds that foster a love for the "College on the Hill." While culture junkies should expect boredom, the rugged type will enjoy the region's unparalleled outdoor opportunities.**

5 Best Things	5 Worst Things
1 Tight-knit community	1 Dark winter days
2 Friendly professors	2 Isolation
3 The D-Plan	3 Hanover nightlife
4 Outdoor opportunities	4 Student apathy
5 The green campus	5 Crackdown on Greeks

Students Speak Out
ON FACILITIES

Q "On the whole, the **infrastructure is a bit old**, if well-maintained. Most of the dorms date from the 1920s and have not been changed much since. But what is lost in modernity is made up for in charm."

Q "Lots of people don't like Berry Library, but I don't mind it. There are **plenty of places to study**, and be sure to check out the Tower Room when you visit. It's on the third floor of Baker, and it provides the most ideal Ivy League setting anywhere on campus."

Q "**Novack Café is the most social place** to be on Sunday night or right before midterms. It's open till 2 a.m., and everyone goes there to procrastinate and hang out while they're ostensibly studying."

Q "The gym has been renovated, and the facilities here are top notch. The great thing is that **undergraduates have access to anything** the College owns. If you want to do some research with the MRI Dartmouth owns, you don't need to wait until you're a med school student."

STUDENT AUTHOR: Most structures are of a classy brick-and-stone structure and remain well-maintained on the inside despite their age. Newer buildings, such as the Rockefeller Center, generally fit in well with the other historical-looking decor. While Alumni Gym meets the needs of many, the cramped weight room, Kresge Fitness Center, has finally been rennovated. The enormous Baker and Berry libraries have plenty of study space, although many students despise the antiseptic look of Berry's interior.

Famous Alumni

Louis Gerstner, Paul Gigot, Robert Frost, Theodore ("Dr.") Seuss Geisel, Paavo Lipponen, Nelson Rockefeller, (Mister) Fred Rogers, Daniel Webster

Students Speak Out
ON CAMPUS DINING

Q "There's an abundance of greasy/fried food if that's your thing. Dining Services also does a good job of providing **healthy meals** (especially at the ever-trendy Collis). What we seem to lack is the more 'normal' food. The Kosher dining facility is great, though—there are never any lines, and the food is of outstanding quality."

Q "You're **forced to get a meal plan** by the college, so you just have a card to eat at the various dining halls, and they subtract it from you account. It's kind of a rip-off, unless you shop smart. There is also a Dartmouth convenience store where you may also spend your meal plan dollars, but the prices are pretty high there."

Q "Aside from the fact that the food is overpriced, Dartmouth dining services offer **more variety and higher quality** food than most colleges do."

Q "The food here is **actually really good**. I'm a fairly picky eater (and a vegetarian), and I have never had trouble eating on campus."

STUDENT AUTHOR: Dartmouth is that rare school where students speak fondly about their campus food. While all the selections in the cafeteria are certain to get old, sumptuous options like the nutritious Home Plate or the greasy Courtyard Café will almost make you forget about mama's secret-recipe lasagna. Variety and flexibility are the name of the game. With no set meal times, they can do so whenever they want. Moreover, students can spend they're declining balance account however they wish, meaning no meals are lost once you stop waking up for breakfast.

Student Body

African American:	7%	Male/Female:	50/50%
Asian American:	13%	Out-of-State:	97%
Hispanic:	6%	International:	7%
Native American:	4%	Unknown:	6%
White:	57%		

Popular Faiths: Catholics, Muslims, Jews, and Protestants of several denominations.

Gay Pride: Though it seems there is a more conservative outlook at Dartmouth, acceptance is generally growing toward gay and transsexual groups.

Economic Status: There is little old money at Dartmouth—few affluent students flaunt their wealth. Many students work their way through college.

Students Speak Out
ON DORMS

Q "While the sizes of rooms vary, the smallest rooms at Dartmouth are generally the size of the biggest rooms at larger schools. People in the Choates and the River will have slightly smaller rooms than usual, but most other dorms have **incredibly spacious rooms**. East Wheelock, in particular, has gigantic rooms with terrific views. Greek Houses also are an integral part in the housing situation, and many Greek-associated people choose to reside in their respective houses."

Q "They're pretty sweet. Some have big rooms. I had a fireplace last year, and **personal bathrooms are common**."

STUDENT AUTHOR: **Of Dartmouth's residential clusters, the Choates and the River are regarded as the worst digs. However, the freshmen who are stuck there often say that the bonding experience makes up for the cramped quarters. East Wheelock arguably has the nicest dorms, although its students are known for their 10 p.m. bedtimes. Dartmouth's community is made stronger by the fact that almost all students, even seniors, live on campus in dorms or Greek houses.**

> **? Did You Know?**
> 86% of undergrads live on campus.

Students Speak Out
ON GUYS & GIRLS

Q "Guys are much more attractive than average, and girls have really been on the rise since the inception of the **Dartmouth Beautification Project**, a little-known program that means to increase student happiness by only admitting the most attractive of qualified applicants."

Q "The guys here are not too bad. There are plenty of **attractive, driven men** for any girl to be pleased. Whether or not you'll actually form a meaningful relationship is a completely different question."

Q "The guys are pretty cool, laid-back, and love to party. The girls are pretty good, but usually way **below par in the looks**, which really sucks."

STUDENT AUTHOR: **Don't drop that high school sweetheart just yet, but Dartmouth students think they look all right. The disparity between guys and girls is very real, although recent female classes are quickly closing the gap, regardless of whether or not the Dartmouth Beautification Project actually exists. Hookups dominate in a nonexistent dating scene. Most students are able to locate a hottie or two, though sometimes with a pair of beer goggles.**

> **Traditions**
>
> **Homecoming**
> The big party in the fall. Freshmen are the focus of the weekend, as they are officially welcomed into the Dartmouth family.
>
> **Green Key**
> Arguably the biggest party weekend of the year. Barbeques and concerts abound, as students bask in the sun for three or four straight days.
>
> **Overall School Spirit**
> Dartmouth students are imbued with a fierce love of their unique and historic institution. The College's small size fosters a single Dartmouth community.

Students Speak Out
ON ATHLETICS

Q "The **varsity sports are not so big**. If you're looking for a school where athletics are an integral part of campus life, then Dartmouth isn't going to be your first choice."

Q "The **main draws are football and hockey**, although we have great success in several other areas, including nationally-ranked lacrosse and crew teams. Our football team draws huge crowds, especially for the Homecoming and Harvard games. While our teams, are not always terribly successful, a good time is had by all. With hockey, on the other hand, Dartmouth has seen a great deal of success."

Q "Some of our teams have been ranked in the top 10 nationally for several years. Club and **intramural sports are enormously popular**."

STUDENT AUTHOR: **Very few students watch Dartmouth sporting events religiously, but most hike, ski, or otherwise enjoy the great outdoors. This small school supports an amazing number of NCAA teams, meaning that almost a full half of Dartmouth students are varsity athletes. Winter hockey games are usually a favorite.**

Students Speak Out
ON DRUG SCENE

Q "It's there but doesn't influence the campus very much. Not many people use drugs, it's mostly **just drinkers—really big drinkers**."

Q "The **drug scene is pretty low-key**, but it does exist. Most people stick to alcohol, although I've seen tons of pot, and ecstasy is starting to become popular."

Q "Drugs exist, but **they aren't a big issue**."

Q "The two biggest drugs are pot and ecstasy. Quite a few people smoke up, but it's not a big deal. Personally, I don't smoke, and I have **never been pressured** into smoking at Dartmouth."

STUDENT AUTHOR: While the average student may run across quite a bit of pot, Dartmouth's drug scene has a very low profile. While ecstasy or the occasional mushrooms might show up at parties, students generally pass on everything but the grass. People in the know claim that the hard drugs are out there, and certain fraternities at Dartmouth have a reputation as substance abuse hot-spots.

8:1	Student-to-Faculty Ratio
98%	Freshman Retention Rate
89%	Four-Year Graduation Rate
84%	Financial Aid Applicants Receiving Aid

Students Speak Out
SAFETY & SECURITY

Q "Coming from a big city, it was quite a shock to be able to **stroll around campus at the wee hours of the morning with impunity**. Many people don't even lock the doors to their rooms."

Q "As for security and safety, don't worry. The biggest crime at Dartmouth is bike theft, and **perpetrators usually return your bike when they're done with it**."

Q "The College has installed security cards in all the residence halls. If it weren't for the Greek system, Safety and Security would likely have nothing to do at all. **They mostly handle drunk frat boys**."

STUDENT AUTHOR: With little outside crime, occasional theft is virtually the only security concern. Blue-light security phones are numerous in case you need a late-night escort or feel unsafe, and Safety and Security have a vigilant presence on campus. Students feel safe as they freely stroll campus at all hours.

> **Questions?**
> For more inside information and survival tips, pick up College Prowler's full-length book on this school, written by an actual student! Check it out at *www.collegeprowler.com*.

Students Speak Out
ON OVERALL EXPERIENCE

Q "Dartmouth was the time of my life. **Academics were spectacular**, and the social life was a blast. Greek life was definitely a large part of the social scene, but I was in a house and loved every minute of it; lots of extra-curricular activities."

Q "**Dartmouth students are often in love with their school**. My personal passion for Dartmouth has exceeded my own expectations, and I have found myself enormously happy at Dartmouth, despite initial misgivings. The people, resources, and general campus activity have made my Dartmouth experience so far entirely successful, and I am utterly content at Dartmouth."

Q "You can't walk out your door without being **invited to go somewhere**, play some sport, or eat."

Q "**After four years, I was ready to leave**, but I thoroughly enjoyed my time there. I can't imagine fitting in better, or having a grander time anywhere else."

STUDENT AUTHOR: With a gorgeous campus, delectable food, spacious dorms, and a vibrant party scene, why shouldn't students be happy? There are certainly a host of minor drawbacks to attending school in Hanover—isolation and no parking. However, unique positives like the study abroad program, top-notch academics, and numerous outdoor opportunities blow these negatives out of the water for most students. Dartmouth students have perhaps the strongest love for their school of any college kids in the country. Such passion is what motivates alums to trek to Hanover for big weekends and party like teenagers, long after their heyday has passed.

Davidson College

102 North Main Street; Davidson, NC 28035
(704) 894-2000; www.davidson.edu

THE BASICS:

Acceptance Rate: 26%
Setting: Suburban
F-T Undergrads: 1,668

SAT Range: 1900–2190*
Control: Private
Tuition: $34,776

Most Popular Majors: English, Economics, Political Science, Psychology, History

*of 2400

Academics	A	Guys	B+
Local Atmosphere	C+	Girls	B
Safety & Security	A+	Athletics	A-
Computers	A-	Nightlife	C
Facilities	A-	Greek Life	A-
Campus Dining	B	Drug Scene	A-
Off-Campus Dining	B-	Campus Strictness	B
Campus Housing	B+	Parking	A
Off-Campus Housing	A-	Transportation	B-
Diversity	D-	Weather	B+

Students Speak Out
ON ACADEMICS

Q "The teachers at Davidson make or break the classes. The student-teacher ratio is such that everyone has the potential to develop a personal relationship with their teachers. My most interesting teachers have taught my most interesting classes; **the material shines through** whatever lens the teacher wants to show it through."

Q "What they say about Davidson professors is right: they are **unbelievably brilliant**, and their classes are endlessly fascinating. I have enjoyed and learned many things from classes outside my English-major interests, like astronomy and other sciences."

Q "I've had **very few professors who I found intimidating** or hard to relate to (one). Also, I've had few problems getting into classes that I wanted to take. There's almost always room, or the prof is willing to work with you and raise the ceiling. Yeah, they have the power to do that."

Q "The teachers were one of the first things that impressed me about Davidson. They are always willing to offer students **every opportunity for help**. Teachers here often give out office and home phone numbers."

STUDENT AUTHOR: Davidson's excellent academic reputation is what attracts most students to the school in the first place. Students come here with the expectation that they will work hard and find it's virtually impossible to 'slide by' academically once they're in.

Students Speak Out
ON LOCAL ATMOSPHERE

Q "In terms of places to visit, there aren't really any exciting ones. **Charlotte is the closest city**, and it's about 25 minutes down Highway 77. I think the lack of 'stuff to visit' contributes positively to Davidson's academic environment. There are not as many distractions as people might have at other schools."

Q "The relationship among students and town's people is strong, with the exception of the occasional noisy off-campus party. **There are several places to visit** within Davidson's small town, including the Brickhouse (the only bar in town), Joel's, the Soda Shop, and Ben & Jerry's."

Q "Davidson is a quaint town, **surrounded mostly by countryside** (no other universities) and Highway 77 (with extensive suburbs). The people of Davidson are very friendly, and very supportive of sports, theater, and outdoor activities."

Q "There really isn't much to the town of Davidson except the Soda Shop, Ben & Jerry's, and CVS. **Christmas in Davidson is well worth experiencing** though, as are Concerts on the Green."

STUDENT AUTHOR: Franchises are barred from the town, so you won't find any Taco Bells marring the landscape. If you're looking for more than the town can provide, don't worry—just hop on I-77 and you're minutes away from any and all forms of entertainment that a big metropolis can offer.

5 Best Things	5 Worst Things
1 Self-scheduled exams	1 Heavy workload
2 Faculty	2 Grade deflation
3 Division I sports	3 Homogeneity
4 The Lake Campus	4 Dating scene
5 Close-knit community	5 Stressed students

Students Speak Out
ON FACILITIES

Q "Davidson is **not afraid to spend money**. The school is committed to making sure we have the best facilities, given the size of the student body and the limited donor pool. As a result, a lot of the facilities here are new, renovated, or simply well maintained."

Q "Davidson definitely **shows a long term dedication** to growth and improvement in its facilities. At the same time, Davidson cannot offer the same facilities that bigger schools can."

Q "The facilities are very nice. Davidson completed a student union a few years ago, which is fantastic. The **computer labs are state-of-the-art**, and there is also wireless Internet available for laptops."

Q "Baker Sports Complex is incredible for a small school. But the **crown jewel** is the student union. With the bookstore, post office, Union Café, weight room, climbing wall, offices for student organizations, wireless Internet access, state-of-the-art theater, and quiet corners to study, this has become the center of student life."

STUDENT AUTHOR: **Davidson's facilities aren't only well-equipped on the inside, but also appealing on the outside. All buildings on campus are constructed in a Georgian, neoclassical style, merging the old and the new in a stately theme of red brick and columns. And despite the relatively small student body, Davidson's campus spans some 450 acres, creating a true sense of space.**

Famous Alumni

John M. Belk, Patricia D. Cornwell, Dean Rusk, Tony Snow, Floyd J. Walters

Students Speak Out
ON CAMPUS DINING

Q "The cafeteria is good as far as cafeteria food goes, and there is **a lot of variety**. Not many schools can say that."

Q "A little under half of the guys and about 75 percent of the girls join Greek organizations and eating houses, which **have their own cooks**."

Q "There aren't as many choices as there are on larger campuses, but there's enough to **find something you're happy with**. I'm a big fan of the frozen yogurt machine in Commons. I'm also a fan of the huge cookies in the Union Café."

Q "The food is one of my few significant complaints about Davidson. When I ate at Commons last year, **I was frustrated by the lack of traditional dishes** that they replaced with a diverse ethnic food selection."

Q "In general, **most students agree that the food is pretty good**. Vail Commons dishes out breakfast, lunch, and dinner each day. Aside from the main entrees and sides, they offer a salad bar, pasta bar, sandwich bar, pizza bar, and quesadilla bar everyday."

STUDENT AUTHOR: **There simply is not too much to choose from in terms of on-campus dining at Davidson. Even despite the limited number of places to eat on campus, most students feel Commons and the Café do a good job of maintaining variety. Breakfast here is a favorite, with endless stacks of pancakes, bowls of fresh fruit, and even a place to make your own waffles.**

Student Body

African American:	6%	Male/Female:	49/51%
Asian American:	2%	Out-of-State:	81%
Hispanic:	4%	International:	3%
Native American:	<1%	Unknown:	0%
White:	85%		

Popular Faiths: By far, most students are Christian (predominantly Protestant, some Catholic).

Gay Pride: Davidson is not what you would call a gay-friendly campus.

Economic Status: The stereotype that most kids at Davidson are upper-middle class is generally true.

Students Speak Out
ON DORMS

Q "Most of the dorms are really nice, and Richardson is the only dorm people usually complain about. Fortunately, **it's only for freshmen**, so if you avoid it your first year you don't have to worry about it ever again. The senior apartments are really nice, with fully-equipped kitchens, living rooms, cable, and Internet access."

Q "I think the **dorms are pretty nice**, as far as college dorms go. Try to avoid Richardson. Belk is nice and very convenient. Cannon and Sentelle have pretty big rooms with huge windows, but they are mostly for upperclassmen."

Q "Dorms are in pretty good shape, but **they lack character and are overpriced**."

STUDENT AUTHOR: Given that over 90 percent of Davidson students live on campus all four years, dorm quality is a pretty important aspect of Davidson life to consider. Fortunately, the college has been working to renovate each summer. After three years of dorm life, seniors are welcomed into the college-operated senior apartments. While there is certainly a downside to dorms at Davidson, for many it's ultimately a matter of preference.

> **? Did You Know?**
> 95% of undergrads live on campus.

Students Speak Out
ON GUYS & GIRLS

Q "I've been here for four years, and there are no hotties in sight. **Maybe they're hiding** in their library carrels."

Q "I frequently comment to my friends when I come home for the holidays that the world seems to get a lot **more attractive as soon as I leave** Davidson's campus."

Q "An alarming number of **guys wear loafers**."

Q "Davidson is not the hottest college campus in the U.S., but in terms of **outstanding and interesting people**, it's full of them."

STUDENT AUTHOR: If intelligence is a big turn-off for you, don't come here. Students at Davidson come from a wide range of backgrounds, and are here because of their passion and enthusiasm for academics. Also, Davidson kids tend to do quite all right in the categories of attractiveness beyond physical appearance. They aren't afraid to say intelligence is sexy, but on weekends, they're looking to hook up with something other than a chemistry textbook.

Traditions

Court Selection Night
Freshmen girls are inducted into eating houses for the first time, by way of ceremony involving ketchup, shaving cream, and extremely cheap champagne.

Flickerball
It's most basically described as a mix of touch football and ultimate Frisbee.

Overall School Spirit
Wildcat spirit is pretty abundant at Davidson, and with a whole quarter of the student body playing Division I varsity sports.

Students Speak Out
ON ATHLETICS

Q "Davidson is one of the **smallest schools to participate in DI** athletics, so sports are pretty big. Despite that, admission to all athletic events is free for students."

Q "Lots of people **participate in intramural leagues**. Varsity sports are supported pretty enthusiastically."

Q "Sports are pretty big here, but not so big that you feel left out if you don't participate. **Flickerball is really fun** and is a great freshman hall-bonding activity."

Q "As one of the smallest Division I schools, the popularity of varsity sports **varies from sport to sport**."

STUDENT AUTHOR: If students aren't among the 25 percent playing a varsity sport, chances are they're participating in club or intramural teams, or out in the stands rooting everyone else on. If you're seeking a highly selective liberal arts college, and the highest level of athletic competition around, you'll be hard-pressed to find a better option than Davidson.

Students Speak Out
ON DRUG SCENE

Q "The chronic **potheads are fairly easy to weed out** (no pun intended). I have many friends who recreationally smoke marijuana and a few who have done more heavy-duty drugs in the past like ecstasy, LSD, or cocaine, but they keep their habits fairly quiet."

Q "On campus, **I never saw any drug use**, but I assume certain kids were probably smoking pot. I have not heard of the use of any harder drugs at all."

Q "The main drug one will find on campus is marijuana. **Alcohol is still the favorite**, however. Many people here don't even view alcohol as a drug."

STUDENT AUTHOR: **Generally speaking, Davidson is much more of an alcohol campus than a drug campus, and most narcotics use takes place pretty discretely. While drugs are available to those who want them, you definitely won't be bothered by any sort of drug culture on campus if you don't want to be.**

11:1	Student-to-Faculty Ratio
96%	Freshman Retention Rate
90%	Four-Year Graduation Rate
72%	Financial Aid Applicants Receiving Aid

Students Speak Out
SAFETY & SECURITY

Q "The campus is safe, although there have been some recent thefts. **Students leave their doors unlocked** because they feel too safe. Students here are gullible like that."

Q "Davidson's campus is extremely safe. I have **never felt threatened walking home** alone late at night. Nor have I felt particularly worried about leaving my book bag sitting on a step outside."

Q "**We have an Honor Code** that is taken very seriously by students and faculty, so most students leave their doors unlocked and feel free to just leave book bags and other things in public places, knowing that they'll be there when they come back. Most crime that does occur is instigated by people not associated with the college."

STUDENT AUTHOR: **At Davidson, the Honor Code is an unspoken agreement that students here will not lie, cheat, or steal during their four years on campus. Campus tour guides tell of a student who lost a 20 dollar bill, and later found it taped above the spot where he had dropped it.**

Questions?
For more inside information and survival tips, pick up College Prowler's full-length book on this school, written by an actual student! Check it out at *www.collegeprowler.com.*

Students Speak Out
ON OVERALL EXPERIENCE

Q "This school is tough as nails. If you aren't interested in **working your butt off** and learning a lot, then don't bother filling out the application."

Q "I think that most students, at one point or another, imagine themselves going to another school, and getting as far away from Davidson as possible. However, when all is said and done, I think each and every student at Davidson **walks away proud** of what they have accomplished."

Q "Davidson has certainly been a challenge. I have frequently **felt frustrated at the lack of a social scene**, and I have often found that many students lack open-mindedness. However, I also realize that the education my professors have given me is top-notch."

Q "The social scene at Davidson is small and can get frustrating, but **close friends are always there** to ease the pain. I would rather be surrounded by a few close friends that know me well than a campus of thousands of students who, if I'm lucky, I will see more than once."

STUDENT AUTHOR: **Fortunately, for the majority of Davidson students, the net result usually favors the positive. Students here do get frustrated about any number of issues, and certainly won't hesitate to vent over them—from the claustrophobic dating scene and small town setting, to the lack of majors and diversity. The rigorous academics are what give Davidson its tradition of excellence to begin with, and that all the hard work is, in the end, well worth the name on the diploma.**

Denison University

1 Main Street; Granville, OH 43023
(800) 336-4766; www.denison.edu

THE BASICS:

Acceptance Rate: 39%
Setting: Suburban
F-T Undergrads: 2,211

SAT Range: 1160–1360*
Control: Private
Tuition: $35,200

Most Popular Majors: Social Sciences, Communication, English, Biology, Psychology

*of 1600

Academics	B	Guys	B
Local Atmosphere	D+	Girls	B+
Safety & Security	B+	Athletics	C
Computers	B-	Nightlife	C
Facilities	B	Greek Life	A-
Campus Dining	C+	Drug Scene	B-
Off-Campus Dining	B-	Campus Strictness	C+
Campus Housing	B-	Parking	B-
Off-Campus Housing	D	Transportation	C-
Diversity	D	Weather	C+

Students Speak Out
ON ACADEMICS

Q "The professors are awesome. They really know their stuff, **and most of them are really cool** people. I like classes, though sometimes I feel like I'm bogged down with busy work."

Q "Teachers at Denison are **more on the liberal side**, which I like. Since it is a small school, teachers make an effort to know students individually. It is easy to get in touch with professors as well."

Q "I've had a few teachers that no one has liked, but I've worked with many people in the Spanish and religion departments and loved all of them. For the most part, **they make classes really interesting**. It also depends on your major and what you want to do. Some of the departments are weaker than others, and the teachers aren't as good as those in another department, hence, the classes can be boring and dull."

Q "My teachers are **very passionate about their work** and like to communicate with students in and out of the classroom. Some of my classes have been interesting, but several were dull."

STUDENT AUTHOR: Academics at Denison are challenging, which is generally the basis of Denison's appeal. The students are largely in agreement that the professors at Denison are excellent. Obviously, every department has one or two professors that students shy away from, but generally all professors are understanding and try to help students in any way possible.

Students Speak Out
ON LOCAL ATMOSPHERE

Q "Granville is a small, rich community of wealthy **old retirees, doctors, and lawyers**. There isn't too much to do for fun, but it is pretty and safe."

Q "**Granville is very small**, quiet, and rather far from any other universities. Ohio State is 45 minutes to one hour away. However, the town is old and beautiful. The people in the town are friendly. I have met really nice, older people from Granville at my church, St. Luke's. If one is religious, the religious communities here are friendly and very receptive to college students."

Q "Granville is the quintessential small town. Some students call it boring because there are no clubs and only two bars, but it's peaceful. I love that I feel safe walking around the town at three in the morning, and **I love that there are still things to do**. For example, I've had the greatest time walking down to Whit's at night with my friends, getting ice cream, and then just looking around."

Q "Ah, G'ville. It's **such a quaint, peaceful village**. While areas around the area have developed into cities (like Columbus and Newark), this town has managed to stay in a time warp."

STUDENT AUTHOR: Granville is not a typical college town. There are no clubs to frequent, and while there are coffee shops, a lot of things close early. Five o'clock is when most businesses shut down for the day. The atmosphere is, in a word, quiet. Denison University is not in an urban setting, so students looking for the excitement of big-city life won't find it here.

Students Speak Out
ON FACILITIES

Q "All of the facilities are nice. The athletic facilities are **nice and accommodating** for winter workouts. Students use the facilities frequently."

Q "**The athletic center is amazing**, and most of my classes have adequate facilities. However, the student union is kind of lame. It's getting better, but it's still kind of lame."

Q "Denison is, it seems, constantly trying to improve facilities on campus. The athletic center is awesome—**the machines are in perfect condition**. The student center could use some improvement, but for having as many things in it as it does, the center is decent. Sometimes the downstairs section is a little too dim, but that's not really a big problem."

Q "I like the facilities on campus. Some of them are kind of run down, but they're definitely still workable and usable and nice to be in. The student center basement was just renovated and is actually **somewhat well-lit** (although the rest of the building is still dark)."

Q "Facilities, huh? **Do you like bathrooms**? Now those are some nice facilities. There is toilet paper as far as the eye can see!"

STUDENT AUTHOR: Denison is an aesthetically-pleasing campus, with a lot of green on the quads and immense brick buildings. But the appearance of the buildings is not merely a façade—the facilities are in good condition. The effort to keep them in good condition, however, results in a lot of construction on campus. Most find it easy to forgive it in exchange for both the entertainment and the convenience they provide.

Famous Alumni

George Bodenheimer, Jim Cromwell, Chris Curtin, Michael Eisner, Jennifer Garner, Susan Whiting

Students Speak Out
ON CAMPUS DINING

Q "The food's usually decent, but there are definitely days when the **food is either good or bad**. There's enough at the dining halls to find something to eat, though."

Q "The food on campus is alright. College food is college food, and **I don't think it can get much better than what we currently have**. The dining halls, both Curtis and Huffman, are good, but I actually prefer Curtis. Slayter Hall offers a meal exchange program, which is pretty good."

Q "The dining halls are okay sometimes, but generally **they are just blah**. On-campus restaurants are limited to Taco Bell and Pizza Hut. There's not much else to say."

Q "Food on campus sucks. But I don't know of any campus where the students are required to eat the campus food that doesn't say the same thing. Basically all students who have to eat campus food hate it. We've got Pizza Hut and Taco Bell for late night, as well as **snack-food type places**. The dining halls are okay. The majority of the campus is required to eat cafeteria food, so everyone is in the dining halls, and it ends up being a very social place."

STUDENT AUTHOR: Campus dining is adequate, but there are problems with it. You won't starve at Denison, but if you come to campus expecting gourmet food, you will definitely be disappointed. The dining halls try to offer a variety of foods to satiate everyone's appetite—hence, the salad bar and the vegetarian line. Another good point to the dining halls is that it's such a social experience.

Students Speak Out
ON DORMS

Q "**Avoid Shorney and Smith**. Taylor is awesome. The Sunsets are pretty nice as well. In general, the dorms aren't that bad, although Residential Life sucks, and they don't have enough housing for everyone."

Q "The dorms are good. However, Shorney and Crawford are considered the party dorms, as well as the trashed dorms. For upperclassmen, the Sunset Apartments are desired living because they give students the ability to get off the meal plan and provide individual bathrooms. **The nice dorm for freshmen is East Hall**."

Q "In general, special interest housing dorms are in **better condition** than non-designated housing."

STUDENT AUTHOR: **Essentially, everyone is required to live on campus. However, requiring everyone to live on campus creates a real sense of community, which is especially important as a freshman. All first-years are now housed in all first-year housing, and if not, will usually be on an all-freshmen floor. This is nice because it immerses students in a social atmosphere immediately, and most students feel that dorm life helps them to adjust to Denison.**

Did You Know?
98% of undergrads live on campus.

Students Speak Out
ON GUYS & GIRLS

Q "**The guys are okay**, but they don't seem too receptive to the freshmen and are kind of intimidating. The girls seem pretty nice, but a lot of them are preppy."

Q "I've never dated anyone on campus, and I've been told that I made a very smart decision. The campus is so small that **you tend to run into your exes** (if you have any) all the time, which can make for a real pain depending on how harsh the breakup was. But everyone on campus is really cool, and I have a ton of hot friends."

Q "There are a lot of **pretty people**, but they are usually in the sororities and fraternities. Everyone is nice, nonetheless. You pretty much have to be beautiful yourself to date any of them."

STUDENT AUTHOR: **Students are pretty mixed in their opinion about guys and girls. Some find them fairly attractive, and others find them to be average. It's a common opinion that girls are more attractive than guys, but hot guys are not extinct—just hidden. Denison is a preppy school, and this is reflected in the way students present themselves. Especially in the warmer periods of the year, students are polished and well-dressed.**

Traditions

D-Day
D-Day is a concert Denison holds every year. Students can go for free and bring one or two guests for a reduced price.

Anchor Spalsh
Anchor Splash is a yearly swimming event put on by Delta Gamma sorority.

Overall School Spirit
Most people own sweaters or shirts with the Denison insignia. But overall, the spirit of Big Red isn't overwhelming.

Students Speak Out
ON ATHLETICS

Q "I think IM sports are almost bigger than varsity sports. You don't tend to hear too much about the varsity sports (depending on who you hang out with). Actually, **they might be an even mix**. I don't know."

Q "Varsity sports are not that popular unless its rugby or the swim team. **Soccer is the most popular IM sport**."

Q "**Varsity sports are not really a big deal**. Neither are IMs, but both get a fair amount of participation."

Q "You aren't going to get a **crowd of tailgaters** and diehard fans for football Saturday. In fact, you would be lucky if you get much more than the parents and alumni there."

STUDENT AUTHOR: **Athletics are fun, but they are not a big deal here. Denison is a DIII school, and admittance into sporting events is free to Denison's students. It's true that Denison has excellent rugby and swimming teams, but most have never watched the swim team compete. A few more students go to the rugby games, but while varsity sports are important to the athletes, playing them they are not a driving force on campus.**

Students Speak Out
ON DRUG SCENE

Q "There is much heavy drinking on campus and a good bit of marijuana use. **Cocaine, LSD, and ecstasy** are also popular among certain groups of people."

Q "**I absolutely don't do drugs**, and I have very few friends who do. It's not just because I like hanging out with people who don't do drugs, but that my friends aren't into the drug scene. Drugs and their users are really kind of hard to find."

Q "For the most part, drugs aren't a big deal at Denison. **There's a lot of pot smoked**, and drinking is almost a hobby. I mean, I have friends who know how to make more drinks than they can count. But as far as harder stuff, if it is here, I have no idea how to find it."

STUDENT AUTHOR: **You have to look to find any serious drug use. The administration has worked hard to eradicate Denison's reputation as a party school, and they have been successful. Alcohol can get out of hand, a lot of weed goes around, but drugs are nothing more than at any other campus.**

11:1	Student-to-Faculty Ratio
93%	Freshman Retention Rate
72%	Four-Year Graduation Rate
43%	Financial Aid Applicants Receiving Aid

Students Speak Out
SAFETY & SECURITY

Q "**The security is good** because it's a small, safe community. However, the security officers are kind of incompetent and useless."

Q "Compared to other campuses, Denison is very safe. Most students feel safe walking alone at night. However, **there have been several sexual assault cases** in the last couple of years; it is good to be careful. Security does its best to ensure student safety."

Q "Security has never been an issue for me. Perhaps that's because Granville is so small and quiet. I've never felt uncomfortable walking across campus. Besides, **a large part of safety is being aware** of your surroundings and no amount of security will do that for you. It's something you have to do for yourself."

STUDENT AUTHOR: Most students agree that Denison's campus is safe. Security is not terribly visible, but that does not mean that the campus is unruly. It's true that seeing an actual security guard is rare during the day, but at night they are more visible. In addition, there are blue-light boxes scattered around campus for students to use in case of an emergency.

> **Questions?**
> For more inside information and survival tips, pick up College Prowler's full-length book on this school, written by an actual student! Check it out at *www.collegeprowler.com*.

Students Speak Out
ON OVERALL EXPERIENCE

Q "I like it here. I recognize that there are some problems, but all in all, **I like the people** I have to deal with most of the time, and that makes all the difference in the world."

Q "Sometimes, I wish I were somewhere else. **Denison has screwed over a lot of students**. However, the financial aid has made me happy, and I've met a lot of nice people; even though they were hard to find. Overall, I'm pretty happy with where I am right now."

Q "Socially, **I had problems with Denison life**. I found it to be very conservative and elitist. It took me a year and a half to find decent friends. I wanted to transfer really bad. However, once I got into my major courses, I realized just how wonderful the education at Denison was, and I stayed."

Q "I wouldn't give Denison up for any other school in the country. The friends I have and the teachers I've gotten to meet have just made such a lasting impression upon me that I wouldn't leave them to study anywhere else. Especially Dr. Wise and Dr. Carlson. They just make learning **the most awesome experience in the world**."

STUDENT AUTHOR: **Most who come to Denison absolutely love it. While some find it a mediocre experience, very few say they hate it. The quality of education is exceptional, and that alone is enough to convince some that this is the place they belong. A lot of people fall in love with the intimate atmosphere that seems to pervade the University. Not only do you live among your peers, but most people are also friends with their professors, which results in a feeling of belonging.**

DePaul University

1 East Jackson; Chicago, IL 60604
(312) 362-8000; www.depaul.edu

THE BASICS:

Acceptance Rate: 64%   **SAT Range:** 1550–1880*
Setting: Urban   **Control:** Private
F-T Undergrads: 12,728   **Tuition:** $25,490

Most Popular Majors: Business/Marketing, Social Sciences, Communications/Journalism, Liberal Arts

*of 2400

Academics	B	Guys	C+
Local Atmosphere	A-	Girls	B
Safety & Security	B+	Athletics	B-
Computers	A	Nightlife	A-
Facilities	A	Greek Life	C-
Campus Dining	C+	Drug Scene	B-
Off-Campus Dining	A	Campus Strictness	B+
Campus Housing	B+	Parking	D-
Off-Campus Housing	A+	Transportation	A
Diversity	A-	Weather	D

Students Speak Out
ON ACADEMICS

Q "The professors at DePaul are generally very friendly and helpful. It's nice that **they almost always get to know your name** and what kind of student you are."

Q "The **amount of work students have is completely dependent on the major** they have. The science and business students seem to have a lot more work. As a political science major, I have to read a lot and write term papers."

Q "DePaul has a good mix of professors. I have some more difficult professors and some laid-back ones. I am a communications major, and I feel the professors in this field have a lot of experience. My journalism professor worked at the *Chicago Tribune* as an editor for quite some time, so I really feel that **I am getting a solid education**."

Q "I feel that the professors at DePaul are fair, knowledgeable, and helpful. **The workload is fairly large**. I am a commerce major, and I feel the commerce classes alone are especially hard. Finals week is especially grueling."

STUDENT AUTHOR: The academic experience for most students at DePaul is pretty different from those at a lot of other universities. DePaul has a nine different colleges, with the Liberal Arts and Sciences College as the largest. All of the colleges have their benefits and bragging rights. The academic experiences of each student are highly dependent on their college. Overall, classes are generally very small, and professors will almost always know each student's name by the end of the first week.

Students Speak Out
ON LOCAL ATMOSPHERE

Q "Living in Chicago is great! **It is probably the best part about going to DePaul**. The atmosphere varies depending on where you are. In the Lincoln Park/Lakeview area, where a lot of students live, there is always something going on. The majority of the people who live there are pretty young."

Q "The best parts of the city are the bars, restaurants, and museums. **Walking through Chicago is amazing**. The beach and Millennium Park are extremely fun and relaxing places, too."

Q "The atmosphere at DePaul is a very urban one. It is almost as though the students here go straight from high school into the real world. The campus is fairly spread out over city, between the Lincoln Park and Loop campuses. **The lifestyle can be very intense**, especially for those students who commute throughout the day."

Q "DePaul and Chicago are pretty interchangeable environments. **Even on campus, you know you in an urban setting**—a quality I think is pretty fantastic. I feel extremely blessed to be able to attend college in such an amazing environment."

STUDENT AUTHOR: The local atmosphere of DePaul is truly unparalleled to the atmosphere of any other university in the city. Lincoln Park is the neighborhood to reside in for college students and those in their 20s, and DePaul's campus is in the center of it all. For the most part, businesses cater to the wants and needs of college students in the area, and they are generally glad to have students around.

5 Best Things

1 Chicago
2 FEST
3 Lakefront
4 Open-mindedness
5 U-Pass

5 Worst Things

1 Weather
2 The EL Brown line
3 Cost of tuition
4 Parking
5 No football teamt

Students Speak Out
ON FACILITIES

Q "The **facilities on campus are extremely nice, organized, and clean**. The library, student center, dorms, and fitness center are all relatively modern and a pleasure to use."

Q "DePaul's campus is very modern. You can tell both students and faculty respect their environment by the way everything on campus is kept in good condition. The quality of DePaul's facilities is **proof that your tuition dollars are being relatively spent well**."

Q "I have no complaints about DePaul's campus facilities, except for the fact that I **wish there were more of them**—the campus is so small. I think we definitely have one of the nicest and most modern campuses in the city of Chicago, and probably one of the higher-quality campuses of most universities in general."

Q "**The Ray alone is pretty impressive**. The four-floor fitness center provides a workout environment that is more up-to-date and of better quality than a lot of the high-end fitness centers you'll see around Chicago."

Q "I love the library. There are lots of places to study, and **the whole building is beautiful**."

STUDENT AUTHOR: The facilities at DePaul are generally regarded as phenomenal. Despite the fact that the University is smack dab in the middle of a crowded, urban environment, DePaul's campus has managed to carve out a beautiful little haven for itself. Students have the privilege of stepping onto the quad and forgetting they are in the middle of one of the biggest cities in the United States.

Famous Alumni

Gillian Anderson, Anne Burke, Richard Daley, Benjamin Hooks, Timothy P. Knight, Raymond Manzarek, William W. Moreton, John C. Reilly

Students Speak Out
ON CAMPUS DINING

Q "**The food on campus is decent**, but I don't think we have nearly as many on-campus options as many of the bigger state schools."

Q "I prefer the downtown dining hall. Neither dining halls have a cafeteria feel—**they are much more modern and sophisticated** than the dining halls at other schools I have visited. The food is made for you when you order. It isn't pre-made, and so you often get what you pay for."

Q "**DePaul's campus has some pretty good food**, but you're in Chicago—a city that offers some of the greatest food in the world."

Q "While extremely pricey, the food on campus is pretty decent. The Lincoln Park Student Center offers food from just about any ethnic group you could want. There is never a problem finding vegetarian options—something that is important to a number of students at DePaul. There is definitely **a pretty good balance of healthy and unhealthy food choices**."

Q "It's easier to **eat more cheaply and healthily by cooking in your own apartment**, or finding some favorite restaurants around campus."

STUDENT AUTHOR: Students tend to have mixed feelings about the on-campus dining options at DePaul. There are a lot of choices for students, and the University at least tries to address a number of diverse ethnic and nutritional needs of students and faculty. Food on campus is definitely the easiest option for freshmen, who are required to purchase some form of a meal plan their first year at DePaul.

Student Body

African American:	8%	Male/Female:	45/55%
Asian American:	8%	Out-of-State:	16%
Hispanic:	12%	International:	2%
Native American:	<1%	Unknown:	13%
White:	57%		

Popular Faiths: DePaul is a Catholic university but is welcoming to all religions.

Gay Pride: Gay pride is fairly strong on campus. There are a number of student organizations, activist groups, and support groups, including LGBTQ.

Economic Status: The high tuition in combination with scholarship money makes for a rather split student population, as far as economic status goes.

Students Speak Out
ON DORMS

Q "The dorms at DePaul are decent. Even the worst one—Corcoran Hall—wields **a sense of pride from many of the people who live there**."

Q "The dorms are very nice. **Some of them have weird social scenes or no social scenes** at all. Clifton-Fullerton Hall is very nice but not as busy or as fun as a lot of the other dorms. Seton Hall is always the most social dorm and is generally partying about seven nights a week."

Q "The **dorms are a pretty important part of the college experience**. Almost all students move into off-campus apartments after freshman year anyway. A year in the dorms is pretty essential to meeting a large number of different people."

STUDENT AUTHOR: The dorms at DePaul are extremely nice and often well-received by prospective students and their parents. While pretty expensive, in most cases students get what they pay for. Many of the dorms are fairly new, and all are very well-maintained. The dorms are also all right on campus—no matter what dorm students live in, they're no more than 10 minutes away from anything on campus.

Did You Know?
18% of undergrads live on campus.

Students Speak Out
ON GUYS & GIRLS

Q "**There really isn't a typical student at DePaul**. I would say DePaul's population is pretty attractive and outgoing. DePaul students probably play a lot more than they work."

Q "The quality of girls versus the quality of guys on campus is pretty unbalanced. Most of **the males on campus seem pretty apathetic** to dating."

Q "The **guys who aren't completely oblivious to the female presence** are probably still writing songs for that girl they met in 10th grade."

Q "There are **a number of good looking people** on campus, but they are sometimes not the most outgoing. It takes a bit of effort to meet people, especially if you are looking to have a relationship beyond friends."

STUDENT AUTHOR: The dating scene at DePaul isn't the greatest. There are pretty much three extremes: those students who've dated the same person since high school, those who open their bedroom up to a different person every weekend, and those students who appear to be oblivious to the fact that intimate human relationships exist. On the plus, campus diversity and the prevalent nightlife scene make it very easy to meet a lot of new people.

Traditions

FEST
A concert in the quad, generally held in an academic lull between spring quarter and spring finals.

Vincentian Service Day
A university-wide day dedicated to community service, in which students and faculty participate.

Overall School Spirit
School spirit is seemingly non-existent, at least in the conventional sense. While students don't frequent sporting events, school spirit is more often directed toward volunteerism, social activism, and advocacy.

Students Speak Out
ON ATHLETICS

Q "**Varsity sports are pretty mediocre**, but intramural sports are a lot of fun. They are not always that popular but definitely worth trying."

Q "It's pretty hard to get to the basketball games when **the team doesn't play on campus**—and basketball is pretty much the only varsity sport anyone pays attention to."

Q "**I wish athletics were a bigger deal** on campus. I know DePaul's basketball team used to be a pretty big deal."

Q "I have played intramural football and softball. **I highly recommend intramural sports**—you meet lots of people and have really great time!"

STUDENT AUTHOR: The athletic scene at DePaul is one that tends to be a big draw for the young alumni crowd and less so for current DePaul students. Even though students do get free tickets to all DePaul sporting events with their student ID, the most popular sport—basketball—is not played on campus. Most of the local bars are great about playing DePaul games on television, so if students are dying to catch a game, this atmosphere is generally a lot of fun.

Students Speak Out
ON DRUG SCENE

💬 "A lot of students smoke weed, but that's really just college. It isn't something that affects the social scene or causes any sort of problems. **Alcohol is definitely the drug of choice**."

💬 "As far as drugs go, **you can basically find what you're looking for** on and around campus, but it is not hugely noticeable. Beyond alcohol and weed, you have to really be looking for a larger drug scene to find harder drugs."

💬 "I think for a lot of students, the drug scene is not noticeable at all. For a lot of others, **it's an extremely prevalent aspect of campus life**. It really depends on who you are and what you're looking for."

STUDENT AUTHOR: The drug scene at DePaul is contingent with what each individual student makes of it, and the choices students make in regards to drugs vary across all ends of the drug-use spectrum. Chicago provides students access to any drug they could imagine, but most students seem to stick alcohol and occasional recreational use.

16:1	Student-to-Faculty Ratio
85%	Freshman Retention Rate
44%	Four-Year Graduation Rate
76%	Financial Aid Applicants Receiving Aid

Students Speak Out
SAFETY & SECURITY

💬 "Security is pretty good on campus. Public Safety cars are always driving around campus at night. **I generally feel safe when walking around or nearby campus**. We have blue-light boxes all over for emergencies. After 6 p.m., Public Safety will escort you anywhere on campus."

💬 "There is not enough crime to seriously worry about, **only the occasional low-profile crime** that could occur in any area of a large city."

💬 "Due to the fact that DePaul's campus and Lincoln Park are relatively safe areas, **it's easy to forget that you are in a big city**. No matter how comfortable you get in your surroundings, you can't let your guard down too much. It's important to be aware of your surroundings, especially late at night."

STUDENT AUTHOR: For a campus in one of the biggest and most urban areas in the States, DePaul manages to stay very safe. There are a number of precautionary measures the University takes to ensure the safety of students and faculty, including Public Safety officers constantly patrolling campus.

> **Questions?**
> For more inside information and survival tips, pick up College Prowler's full-length book on this school, written by an actual student! Check it out at *www.collegeprowler.com*.

Students Speak Out
ON OVERALL EXPERIENCE

💬 "I think I would probably not come to DePaul again, but not because of anything the school is responsible for. For someone who loves city life, DePaul is probably the best school to experience this. **I find the hustle-bustle atmosphere and pollution a bit overwhelming** at times, but DePaul itself is really great!"

💬 "I have had a pretty good experience at DePaul. If anything, I wish it were more intellectually stimulating and that I was actually forced to work a bit harder for good grades. At the same time, I like the fact that **I am able to balance school, work, and activities pretty equally**."

💬 "My experience at DePaul has been really good. I've loved **getting involved with the many groups around campus** and embracing the Vincentian mission of service to the poor."

💬 "I really love DePaul. **I have found it to be the perfect fit for me**. I have made a lot of good friends and had a lot of good times. I've learned about the world, the city, and myself. I love being in Chicago."

STUDENT AUTHOR: DePaul students are not shy about their complete infatuation with the University—just as they are equally not shy about the few things dissatisfying about it. DePaul students seemingly either love or hate the school, with very few feelings in between. The DePaul experience is definitely unique to the University, so students have to know what they are signing on for when attending DePaul—be it the overt and sometimes overwhelming political scene, the liberal-minded majority, or the expensive and hectic nightlife. The DePaul experience equates to the Chicago experience.

DePauw University

313 South Locust Street; Greencastle, IN 46135
(765) 658-4800; www.depauw.edu

THE BASICS:

Acceptance Rate: 69%
Setting: Rural
F-T Undergrads: 2,362

SAT Range: 1680–1970
Control: Private
Tuition: $29,300

Most Popular Majors: Communication, English Composition, Economics, Biology, Psychology

*of 2400

Academics	B+	Guys	A-
Local Atmosphere	C-	Girls	A
Safety & Security	A	Athletics	C+
Computers	B-	Nightlife	C
Facilities	B	Greek Life	A+
Campus Dining	B+	Drug Scene	B-
Off-Campus Dining	B-	Campus Strictness	B
Campus Housing	B	Parking	A-
Off-Campus Housing	C-	Transportation	D-
Diversity	D-	Weather	D

Students Speak Out
ON ACADEMICS

Q "The teachers cover the spectrum in any and every area, whether it is experience, teaching styles, beliefs, or goals. I haven't yet had a teacher that didn't intrigue me in one way or another, nor have I ever had a teacher who didn't go **above and beyond the call of duty** in making themselves available to students."

Q "The atmosphere is very relaxed in the sense that it is very much a **two-way lesson** involving dialogue from both parties."

Q "One of the aspects I like most about DePauw is the **classroom setting**. The student/teacher ratio is great. Professors always want to talk to you after class and are usually around. I feel like many of my professors are my friends."

Q "Classes are so small here that it is easy to really get to know your professors. With some professors, I feel comfortable talking about my personal life and they do the same. Of course, **not all professors makes themselves that accessible**, but the majority of faculty is very open to getting to know their students. It is not strange to be invited to a professor's house for dinner or for a class meeting."

STUDENT AUTHOR: You can't make it through DePauw without having a professor who went to or taught at Harvard, Yale, or Princeton, or who has written a book that now sits on the shelf at Barnes & Noble. If not for Depauw, why else would extremely intelligent adults move to "middle-of-nowhere, Indiana" unless they truly loved to teach?

Students Speak Out
ON LOCAL ATMOSPHERE

Q "**There is definite tension** between the citizens of Greencastle and the students at DePauw. However, Greencastle seems to offer itself to the students the best it can through the Fine Print Bookstore and certain small restaurants."

Q "Greencastle is pretty uneventful, but it helps to **keep you focused on school**."

Q "It's a small town, but I really like the atmosphere around campus. There is a laid-back and friendly feeling. It's really easy to meet people and **feel like you belong**."

Q "It's a difficult adjustment to make if you aren't from the Midwest or if you're from a bigger city. I grew up in the Chicago suburbs, and I struggled with Greencastle's size at first. I've gotten used to it, but **it lacks diversity in everything**—the people, the restaurants, the stores, and the nightlife. There just isn't much to do in Greencastle."

Q "The town is quaint and old. Buildings and restaurants are **not very updated** or conducive to college students."

STUDENT AUTHOR: Greencastle does not consist of more than about 15 stoplights. Although many students consider one of DePauw's drawback to be the local atmosphere, the town allows full focus on college life. If you can handle life without traffic or nightclubs, you can find the simpler pleasures in Greencastle's great nature trails, covered bridges, elk farms, and mom-and-pop shops.

5 Best Things	5 Worst Things
1 Honors programs	1 Workload
2 Travel abroad	2 Gossip
3 Winter term	3 Eating disorders
4 Campus ambition	4 Competition
5 Monon weekend	5 No diversity

Students Speak Out
ON FACILITIES

Q "We have **one of the nicest** tennis and indoor track facilities in the nation."

Q "Overall, the facilities are beautiful at DePauw. However, our workout room in **the Lilly Center is awful**. The machines are old and poorly maintained. The room is small, always hot, and just not nice to look at. It gets crowded quickly, especially when the football team takes over the weight area, or between 4 and 7 p.m."

Q "**DePauw is blessed with funds**, and so students are blessed in return with great campus facilities."

Q "The **academic buildings are beautiful** and are efficient to serve student needs. Most of the classrooms at DePauw have technological systems (computer, screen, VCR, DVD) which is helpful for better learning. There are plenty of nice places to study on campus as well."

Q "The student center hosts a ton of activities and is very nice. Also, there are a lot of **very nice performance halls**."

STUDENT AUTHOR: **DePauw has a $412 million endowment and has put much of that money towards improving campus facilities and aesthetics. Campus is constantly changing and growing with a multitude of new buildings or improvements and additions to existing buildings. The Lilly Center could use updated equipment, a better air conditioning system, and more machines, but this neglect is definitely abnormal. The majority of facilities are top-of-the-line inside and out, adding to both the function and beauty of campus.**

Famous Alumni

Joseph Allen, Patricia Ireland, Barbara Kingsolver, Jack McWethy, William Rasmussen, Dan Quayle

Students Speak Out
ON CAMPUS DINING

Q "Depends on where you eat. It is usually good, but **it can be very expensive**."

Q "The food at DePauw is awesome. The **sorority food is first-class**, especially the cooks at Pi Beta Phi, and could honestly rival any first-class restaurant in New York City. For freshmen, Longden is a nice treat for the hungry, all-you-can-eat folk."

Q "The food on campus is exceptionally good. DePauw hires a special dining service, and the **meals are typically well-balanced and tasty**. Additionally, the Gate is a DePauw restaurant which students can use their meal plans to have a comfortable sit-down dining experience."

Q "Even if you don't like everything, there are a ton of other options (such as subs, peanut butter and jelly sandwiches, salads, cold cuts, cereal, and Pizza Hut pizza and breadsticks). **The meal-plan card offers more than enough** money to feed you for the whole semester. There is also a convenient store on campus where you can use your meal-plan card."

STUDENT AUTHOR: **DePauw offers two types of dining venues; Longden dining hall, which offers cafeteria-style eating with a different meal daily, and the Hub, which offers assorted fast-food options and is generally a hang out for first-year students. The Hub is valuable, not only for midday munchies, but the essential face time of the freshman meet and greet. Upperclass Greek students utilize a different meal plan that runs through their Greek houses.**

Student Body

African American:	6%	Male/Female:	44/56%
Asian American:	3%	Out-of-State:	54%
Hispanic:	3%	International:	3%
Native American:	<1%	Unknown:	3%
White:	82%		

Popular Faiths: Protestant and Catholic religions seem to be the most common on campus.

Gay Pride: Campus is relatively open to gay and lesbian students. LGBT offers Coming Out Week, in which campus-wide awareness activities take place.

Economic Status: Scholarship opportunities are abundant, allowing many students without the financial means to attend DePauw.

Students Speak Out
ON DORMS

Q "South Quad is **extremely nice compared to other schools** I visited. North Quad is older, but Rector Village, recently finished, is amazing."

Q "College Street **needs to be torn down**."

Q "My friends who visited from **other schools were so jealous** of my dorm."

Q "The dorms are extraordinarily nice! They are **air conditioned and cleaned daily**. Additionally, floors typically do not exceed 30 people, so you will share a comfortable living environment and make close friends. The nicest of the dorms include Longden, Bishop Roberts, and Humbert."

Q "I enjoy the **baby grand piano** along with the marble tile in the lobby of Longden!"

STUDENT AUTHOR: All first-year students are required to live in dorms on campus, which is helpful for adjusting to campus life and building a sense of belonging and community. South Quad is all freshman housing and where most of the first-year fun goes down. North Quadders are often forgotten on the freshman scene—they are sometimes distanced from their peers.

Did You Know?
99% of undergrads live on campus.

Students Speak Out
ON GUYS & GIRLS

Q "Girls and guys are both **rich, snotty kids** who have great book-smarts, but little to no common sense because Daddy will take care of them forever."

Q "Most people on this campus are very appearance-conscious. They dress very well, have trendy haircuts, work out, diet, and go tanning. There are a lot of extremely attractive people of both genders at DePauw, although sometimes it seems as if **everyone kind of looks the same**."

Q "The guys like to wear North Face fleeces, flip their collars up, and **act like fools**."

Q "You can always find someone in a class who is **nice to look at**!"

STUDENT AUTHOR: DePauw is home to some gorgeous people. Most everyone who goes here was "a somebody" in their high school, which provides for an extremely competitive scene. Due to the amount of attractive people and nature of a college campus, the random hookup is definitely not hard to find. Even if you're in class at noon on Friday, you will see people dressed to the nines!

Traditions

Monon Weekend
The Wabash and DePauw football rivalry is intense, and Tiger fans past, present, and future show up. The victor leaves with the an old Monon Railroad bell.

Lil' 5
A cycling race in which fraternities, sororities, non-Greeks, and even faculty race a track around campus.

Overall School Spirit
DePauw's school spirit is relatively high. Sporting event attendance is sparse, but loyal fans and tailgaters make it out. Basketball is also popular.

Students Speak Out
ON ATHLETICS

Q "Varsity sports are big on Monon weekend. Aside from then, you have to be on a team to realize that they exist. **IM sports are fairly big**."

Q "DePauw sports are not as well-followed as they are at bigger schools—or even at my high school. That's too bad. **We have good teams**!"

Q "Sports are still **not going to draw the numbers** that Division I schools will. On the other hand, at a small, intimate campus there is a better chance that students will not only know the names of players, but identify with them as friends and classmates. Therefore, there is more support among the student body."

Q "It honestly seems like **IM is hotter** than varsity."

STUDENT AUTHOR: DePauw's D-III status offers a great atmosphere for sports. It allows students to play sports and still be students, as well as be involved in other clubs or activities. The complaint of some student athletes, however, is that the fan base is not as strong as other schools. Intramural and club sports are also highly attended and very competitive.

Students Speak Out
ON DRUG SCENE

Q "I think pot is the most available drug, besides the obvious alcohol. If you're looking for it, it's easy to find, but I've seen **less of it than I have in high school**."

Q "A lot of **students use Adderall** to get all their work done."

Q "If you want drugs, you can get them. Marijuana is probably the most widely used drug—I see it a lot. People take Ritalin and Adderall for studying, or just for fun. And there is definitely an **emerging cocaine problem** on campus."

Q "The drug scene is quite small compared to other schools I've visited. While there are drugs on campus, most of the individuals who choose to use them are **private and discrete** about it."

STUDENT AUTHOR: **Marijuana is the easiest and most popular drug at DePauw. The prescription drugs Adderall or Ritalin come in at a close second. Harder drugs, such as cocaine, can be found on campus, but it is kept extremely quiet—so quiet most students aren't even aware that such things are going on.**

10:1	Student-to-Faculty Ratio
87%	Freshman Retention Rate
71%	Four-Year Graduation Rate
85%	Financial Aid Applicants Receiving Aid

Students Speak Out
SAFETY & SECURITY

Q "The **security is really reliable** on campus; there are emergency phones placed at what seems to be every 10 feet."

Q "I usually feel pretty safe, but the streets are dark here, and there are so many trees/bushes that it **kind of freaks me out when I am alone**."

Q "I always feel very safe here, even when I'm walking around campus alone at night. Many students leave their doors unlocked or do not shut their doors at all, even when they're away from their rooms. **Greencastle is a relatively crime-free city**. As long as you use common sense, there's no reason not to feel safe."

STUDENT AUTHOR: **DePauw safety goes out of its way to host events on self defense, safe drinking, and fire safety. They like to be a presence on campus that students feel safe contacting. Campus police can be reached by dialing 0 from any University phone, and safe walks or rides are always available.**

Questions?
For more inside information and survival tips, pick up College Prowler's full-length book on this school, written by an actual student! Check it out at *www.collegeprowler.com*.

Students Speak Out
ON OVERALL EXPERIENCE

Q "I am thankful that I can go out at DePauw, and not only meet new people with whom I'll come in contact again, but also see more than an occasional familiar face. I also enjoy getting to be a key part in my **small classes**. I could never speak out in a discussion group of 100, but I can easily give my input in a seminar of 14."

Q "**I applied to transfer** half-way through my freshman year, but changed my mind because of the friendly atmosphere amongst students and staff, the numerous opportunities to participate in civic education (volunteerism), and the liberal arts education environment."

Q "It is a very **nourishing environment**, both academically and socially. Students here study hard and party hard."

Q "I'm starting my senior year at DePauw, and I wouldn't want to be anywhere else. I get **frustrated with the small size and small town**, especially after spending a semester in New York, but I love this school. People are friendly, the campus is beautiful, my classes are exciting and fun, and I feel 100 percent comfortable here."

STUDENT AUTHOR: **A DePauw education has a multitude of benefits, including the allowance to try many different fields and explore areas outside your specific major. The different disciplines teach you how to think, learn, and question. Within the cornfields of north western Indiana, you will learn everything from formulas of physics to the values of friendship. The DePauw network extends across the country and maintains ties between classes, houses, and majors. With all of this, DePauw is definitely home to the quintessential college experience.**

Dickinson College

College Street; Carlisle, PA 17013
(717) 243-5121; www.dickinson.edu

THE BASICS:

Acceptance Rate: 42%
Setting: Rural
F-T Undergrads: 2,355

SAT Range: 1190–1370*
Control: Private
Tuition: $37,900

Most Popular Majors: Social Sciences, Foreign Languages, English, Biology, Business, History

*of 1600

Academics	B+	Guys	B-
Local Atmosphere	C	Girls	A-
Safety & Security	A	Athletics	B-
Computers	B	Nightlife	C+
Facilities	B+	Greek Life	B+
Campus Dining	B+	Drug Scene	B
Off-Campus Dining	B-	Campus Strictness	C-
Campus Housing	B-	Parking	D+
Off-Campus Housing	B	Transportation	C+
Diversity	D	Weather	C+

Students Speak Out
ON ACADEMICS

Q "The professors here are fabulous; **they are all super smart** and care a lot about their students. They'll do anything to help a student in need, from meeting after class to finding you a tutor."

Q "Some profs are interesting and some aren't. The same goes for classes. I like most of my classes for my major, but when it comes to graduation requirements, **some can be a bit tedious**."

Q "Professors are very reasonable. They are always available outside the classroom; many give their home and even cell phone numbers. They are very knowledgeable and approachable. **Classes at Dickinson are definitely engaging**; I've never had a class I wasn't interested in."

Q "For the most part, teachers are great. They are really understanding and are interested in what the students have to say about the course and course materials. It's great to see **teachers who enjoy what they teach**, and the professors at Dickinson are very passionate about their fields of interest."

STUDENT AUTHOR: **Without its reputation as an enriching learning environment, Dickinson would not have become the prominent institution it is today. The college demands excellence from each student, and the faculty and administration go to great lengths to see that this is achieved. From the freshman seminar to the senior workshop, students will receive the nurture, guidance, and support they need to accomplish whatever academic and career goal they set for themselves.**

Students Speak Out
ON LOCAL ATMOSPHERE

Q "The town is **generally quiet**. Dickinson is very isolated from the Carlisle as a whole, and interaction between townspeople and students is rare. The college and borough of Carlisle are working to strengthen this relationship, however."

Q "Carlisle is a small town in central PA. There are colleges within a short driving distance, but I never go. I would tell prospective students that Carlisle is **your typical suburban town**, nothing especially great about it and nothing especially bad."

Q "There are **many little shops downtown** that I love to visit. There are a lot of good breakfast cafés, as well."

Q "Carlisle is a small town but it has everything we need for the most part, short of a decent mall, but I am pretty sure they are building a new one of those, too. **Other universities are not in the immediate vicinity** but are only a short drive away."

STUDENT AUTHOR: **Dickinson was once ranked in the top 25 for "Worst Town-Gown Relations." It's true; the college and town of Carlisle have not always had the best of rapports. However, things are starting to look up. Yet, Carlisle still is not the ideal college town. While it has its share of bars and movie theaters, there is virtually nothing else to do downtown on weekend nights, which is the reason most students stay on campus for weekend activities.**

5 Best Things	5 Worst Things
1 Study abroad	1 Strictness
2 Guy/girl attractiveness	2 Overcrowding
3 Prof accessibility	3 Reliance on Greek life
4 The food	4 The online registration
5 The library	5 Room selection process

Students Speak Out
ON FACILITIES

Q "The fitness center is great, they even give you towels to use while you work out! Everything is new, and they are always adding new machines. **The Hub is nice**, too, although it would be nice if it were bigger."

Q "The facilities here are very nice and well-maintained, although **they are sometimes very crowded** due to the fact that it is hard to expand them on such a small campus."

Q "New computers were just put in all over campus. In the gym, **they just restored the hardwood floor**. I think these efforts show that Dickinson is really trying to put some effort forth to benefit the student body."

Q "Dickinson's facilities are beautiful and almost **everything is state-of-the-art**. This isn't a school that lets things go. Everything is always taken care of and clean."

Q "The **facilities are great**. Everything is modern. You don't have to worry about having old, ugly stuff here."

STUDENT AUTHOR: Dickinson has nice, relatively new facilities. The Kline Athletic Center is a favorite of most students, as it encourages a variety of sports activities, from squash to swimming to scaling a rock wall. The gym was outfitted with a new floor in the summer of 2003, and the fitness center is relatively new and nicely equipped. The library at Dickinson houses over 500,000 volumes and 6,000 periodicals. Students love the library, but like the fitness center, it is often crowded during peak hours.

Famous Alumni

James Buchanan, Spencer Baird, Alfred V. du Pont, Jennifer Haigh, Rosie O'Donnell, Roger Brooke Taney

Students Speak Out
ON CAMPUS DINING

Q "The food on campus is as good as it can be. **The dining hall has a wide selection** of meals, even for vegans. Don't worry about not wanting to eat on campus because there is always something good to be found."

Q "The lunches in the caf are the best. However, you'd better get there either really early or really late, because **lunchtime is the most crowded time** for meals at this school."

Q "Our food is good. There isn't always tons of variety among the hot meals, but whatever's there is usually really tasty. **The Quarry is excellent** for snacks and sandwiches coffee-shop style. The Snar lets you order what you want, a nice change from the Caf."

Q "There **aren't enough options** for food on campus. Also, when you eat in the caf, each sorority and fraternity has its own table. Be sure you don't sit at the wrong place."

Q "**I love the food** here. It's kind of annoying that there are only four places to eat, but for the most part, they are nice and well run."

STUDENT AUTHOR: There is one thing you can be sure of about the students at Dickinson—they love their food. The cafeteria is very popular, so much so that it is usually crowded during the peak eating hours. Newly remodeled, the HUB Cafeteria is adored by students and is relatively well run and organized. The problem most students find with dining on campus is the lack of options.

Student Body

African American:	4%	Male/Female:	45/55%
Asian American:	5%	Out-of-State:	75%
Hispanic:	5%	International:	6%
Native American:	<1%	Unknown:	2%
White:	78%		

Popular Faiths: Protestantism, Catholicism, and Judaism are the most prominent religions.

Gay Pride: Dickinson was recently ranked as one of the top 20 most "gay tolerant" schools in the country. Pandora, the gay-lesbian-bisexual-transsexual group is very active on campus and is generally accepted by the student body.

Economic Status: Most students come from middle- to upper-class backgrounds.

Students Speak Out
ON DORMS

Q "Our dorms are okay. I would definitely never want to live in the all-girls dorm, though. **For freshmen, Adams is pretty nice** because it has big rooms, and Drayer is cool because of the large social environment."

Q "The dorms are fine. **They are all pretty clean** and spacious. There really aren't any to avoid. Of course, not everyone always gets what they want at room draw, but you can be assured you'll get to live in the good dorms at least one of your four years, and usually more."

Q "The dorms for freshmen are alright, but in my opinion the upperclassman dorms are **lousy compared to other schools**."

STUDENT AUTHOR: **On-campus housing at Dickinson varies greatly. For freshmen, it currently leaves a lot to be desired, however, plans are in the works to renovate most of the freshman dorms, including the Lower Quads. For upperclassmen there are a lot of options, and those who receive good numbers in the room-draw lottery end up with really nice, new rooms. Off-campus housing is only available to seniors.**

> **Did You Know?**
> 92% of undergrads live on campus.

Students Speak Out
ON GUYS & GIRLS

Q "We're a real life Abercrombie & Fitch commercial. **Girls are very thin and very hot**, and there are tons to choose from. Guys just aren't as impressive when you compare them to all the gorgeous girls."

Q "A lot of **people are stuck-up**; I'm not going to lie. It's probably because most kids come from really wealthy families."

Q "We have tons, and by tons I mean **hundreds, of hot chicks**. You could date a different girl every day of the week and have still have a very slim chance of dating someone unattractive. I would highly recommend this school to guys, because hey, we're outnumbered and it's awesome!"

STUDENT AUTHOR: **Students normally have impeccable physical appearances and are intelligent in to boot. If you're looking for a campus with a lot of ditsy eye-candy, look elsewhere, because kids here are smart enough to know when they're being played. "Random," in the complete sense of the word, hooking up is pretty common. Overall, however, it is easy to say that Dickinson has an average amount of sexual promiscuity.**

> **Traditions**
>
> **Signing In**
> Each student walks up the stone steps into the lobby and officially "signs in" to the college.
>
> **The Seal of Dickinson College**
> The school motto, "Religion and learning, the bulwark of liberty," is found on the school seal, along with a liberty cap.
>
> **Overall School Spirit**
> Because the idea at Dickinson is that academics come before athletics, school spirit and student attendance at sporting events is less than stellar.

Students Speak Out
ON ATHLETICS

Q "Varsity sports aren't huge here, and **it isn't a big pastime** to go to sporting events for some reason. Intramurals are a lot more popular than varsity sports and rotate every season."

Q "Varsity **sports aren't popular** here at all, which sucks. I would really like to see more people come out to support the sports teams at sporting events."

Q "Varsity sports are reasonably big. **Intramural sports are a much bigger deal**, though, and pretty much every club and organization has their own team in something."

Q "Both varsity and intramurals are pretty big, but there are lots of **other ways to show school spirit**, too."

STUDENT AUTHOR: **Dickinson is a school where students can successfully participate in one or more varsity sports and not get caught behind in their workload. It isn't uncommon for athletes to participate in multiple varsity sports, something that many students love about Division III athletics.**

Students Speak Out
ON DRUG SCENE

Q "I don't think drugs are a problem here. I would say **weed is the most popular drug** among the smokers. I haven't ever actually seen the 'harder' drugs, but I've heard stories about them and who uses them."

Q "If you want drugs, **you can get them easily**. I think that's true anywhere you find large groups of students. Not many kids are actually part of the drug scene though, and there isn't really any pressure to be involved either."

Q "The **wealthy students love their cocaine** and designer drugs. Prescription drugs are also used fairly heavily by the drug crowd. Certain social groups are known for partaking of drugs a lot more than others."

STUDENT AUTHOR: **Drugs at Dickinson, like everywhere else, are available to those who are trying to find them. Marijuana, prescription painkillers, stimulants, and cocaine can be found. There are certain social groups with whom they are more prevalent than others.**

11:1	Student-to-Faculty Ratio
91%	Freshman Retention Rate
79%	Four-Year Graduation Rate
84%	Financial Aid Applicants Receiving Aid

Students Speak Out
SAFETY & SECURITY

Q "Morgan field could use more lighting at night, but in general **this campus is safe** 24 hours a day, 7 days a week. Safety is not a big concern here at all. Pretty much nobody worries about it."

Q "The Department of Public Safety is out and about at all hours of the night. **We have well-lit areas** covering the campus and emergency call-boxes in case a person feels threatened."

Q "This campus is about as safe as it gets. Anywhere you have large groups of people living together, **you'll have at least a few minor problems**, and Dickinson is no exception, but it's nothing that makes people scared to go where they want to go. Kids feel safe pretty much everywhere all the time."

STUDENT AUTHOR: **Dickinson employs such a tight-knit safety squad (Dickinson Public Safety or DPS) that security has never been much of a concern among students. There have been a few minor incidences, but they are few and far between. Students generally feel safe walking anywhere on campus.**

Questions?
For more inside information and survival tips, pick up College Prowler's full-length book on this school, written by an actual student! Check it out at *www.collegeprowler.com.*

Students Speak Out
ON OVERALL EXPERIENCE

Q "Overall, I really enjoy being here. You can find the right groups of friends very easily. The atmosphere is friendly, and the majority of kids are very social. **The academics are intense**, but very worthwhile. I think this is a great school."

Q "My freshman year, I wanted to transfer to be honest. But now I am a sophomore and I simply love it here. I think **it is such a great school**. It sometimes takes awhile to find your social niche, but once you find that, you are able to see all the other great things about this institution."

Q "I have loved my four years here so far, and I would never want to go anywhere else. **This school has its faults**, but on the whole, it's a great place, and I would recommend it to anybody."

Q "I like this school a lot. I think we have a great academic program, and I'll be proud of my degree when I graduate. At times, **I do wish I was at a larger school** that was closer to more nightlife and entertainment, but that's the trade-off you make for earning a private-school education over a state-school one."

STUDENT AUTHOR: **Kids come to school here because they are serious about their futures. Academics are always the top priority, and everything else comes second to classes and coursework. College is the success you make of it, and Dickinson is no exception to this rule. Thus, be prepared for Dickinson to push you to your limits academically. You can rest assured that after graduating from Dickinson, you'll have the skills and confidence to be successful in whatever walk of life you should choose.**

Drexel University

3141 Chestnut Street; Philadelphia, PA 19104
(215) 895-2000; www.drexel.edu

THE BASICS:

Acceptance Rate: 72%   **SAT Range:** 1070–1300*
Setting: Urban   **Control:** Private
F-T Undergrads: 10,393   **Tuition:** $28,500

Most Popular Majors: Business/Marketing,
Engineering, Nursing, Information/Computer Science

*of 1600

Academics	B-	Guys	C+
Local Atmosphere	A-	Girls	C
Safety & Security	C	Athletics	C+
Computers	B	Nightlife	A-
Facilities	C+	Greek Life	C
Campus Dining	C	Drug Scene	B
Off-Campus Dining	A-	Campus Strictness	B+
Campus Housing	C-	Parking	D-
Off-Campus Housing	A	Transportation	B+
Diversity	C+	Weather	B-

Students Speak Out
ON ACADEMICS

Q "The teachers in Information and Systems Technology are very helpful, and let me emphasize this, **very easy to understand**. Engineering is very much different. I find most classes interesting, but I think they should be more hands-on."

Q "I am a fashion design major, and the teachers in my program are very much involved in the industry. They are **true professionals**. One teacher that I have now actually comes straight from her job as an interior designer to teach an orthographic drawing class."

Q "Some of the education teachers are a **complete waste of time**. I enjoy the communication classes, however. There are a lot of good teachers on the whole at Drexel. During my first year, I had some tough courses, but I had some good teachers teaching those courses."

Q "Few teachers here are very interesting. Most teachers are intelligent, but are very poor teachers. Some engineering and physics teachers literally **can't speak English**."

STUDENT AUTHOR: Drexel is a very intense school with more of a technical focus than an academic one. True, the academic rigor of our classes does not match most top schools, but Drexel is expanding each academic program. Most Drexel students will tell you that it is difficult to actually learn all of the material within a 10-week term. While the intellectual challenge is not as demanding as other colleges, the pace is very fast and our students work very hard.

Students Speak Out
ON LOCAL ATMOSPHERE

Q "Drexel campus is **not as bad as people say**, but once you step off campus towards Spring Garden and 36th Street, it immediately becomes very ghetto and does not feel safe at all."

Q "Drexel is located **right next to Penn**, and the atmosphere changes as soon as you enter their campus. They have nicer stores and restaurants, and people dress differently."

Q "There are a few other universities in the area, so there is a **large college student population** here. There are many historical places to visit such as the Constitution Center, which houses the Liberty Bell, and Independence Hall where the U.S. Constitution was drafted."

Q "The atmosphere is **very upbeat**. Coming from a suburb, I was a little lost at first, but city life gets easier and easier each term. A few universities are present including Penn and Temple."

STUDENT AUTHOR: University City isn't very pretty, with the exception of Locust Walk on Penn's campus. There are tons of things to do in University City, like dine, shop, play sports, and more. Don't forget Center City is only minutes away within walking distance. There, you can witness many historical landmarks that have housed many significant events in American history. You can even see the original Constitution! In addition to all the culture, you can shop 'til you drop in the upscale shops that line Walnut and Chestnut Streets downtown. If you are a bit more frugal, check out the Gallery Mall, or South Street for great shopping districts.

Students Speak Out
ON FACILITIES

Q "Everything is kept very well, but **there isn't enough here**. There's one 60-yard turf field, one basketball court, and one gym."

Q "Don't use the commuter center. It's **infested with loud nerds**. It's hard to hear the TV when people, who are sitting right next to each other, are yelling about which superhero would beat the other!"

Q "The athletic center is pretty nice. I spend a lot of time there, and it's usually **clean and nicely kept**. The Student Center (Creese) is usually well kept. It's is a cool place to hang out between classes because the food places are there and it's nice and cool."

Q "The **facilities are okay**, if you're a guy. Drexel doesn't have enough women's bathrooms, and no feminine product dispensers, either."

Q "**Facilities are mediocre**. The honors lounge printer almost never works. The gyms are okay, but are nothing special."

STUDENT AUTHOR: The Athletic Center has extensive facilities—there is a nice pool, a weight room, and well-maintained basketball and squash courts. You can tell that some of the buildings desperately need some renovations and repairs. Nevertheless, the DAC is a great place to work out, take a dip, or engage in some friendly competition on the court. The Creese Center offers a lot, but delivers little. There really is nothing there but a few comfy chairs and some overpriced food. It's a good place to talk, but a bad place to study, as it's normally very busy and loud.

Famous Alumni

Paul Baran, Chuck Barris, Ruth Hale, Robert Hall, Malik Rose, Joseph Woodland

Students Speak Out
ON CAMPUS DINING

Q "Let's just say the cafeteria food will **make you feel sick in the morning**. It just does not settle well. Two words: Kelly Deli. You can always find something to eat in there, but it gets rather expensive after a while."

Q "The food is not too bad on campus. I just wish there were more healthier places for us to eat besides **cheesesteak stands**."

Q "There are two main pizza places next door to each other, and there are a few others in the area with pretty good food. **Taco Lou's** is the best drunk food ever. The new student center, the Ross Commons on Powelton Avenue, has good food but is a little expensive."

Q "**Corn on pizza**? Who came up with that? Inspect the pizza from the food hall. I didn't realize until I took a bite that they put corn on the pizza."

Q "The dining hall sucks, but what dining hall doesn't? The best place on campus is definitely **Pete's Little Lunch Box**. It's a lunch cart by Nesbitt. It's the best food and really cheap."

STUDENT AUTHOR: If you don't have a meal plan, watch out. You'll pay close to $10 for lunch on campus if you go anywhere but the lunch trucks. If you do have a meal plan, you can use it to buy some good food at the Creese Café or in Ross Commons. Many students do their best to balance cost and healthy eating because the only cheap food is very unhealthy and the only healthy food is very overpriced. Remember that you are in Philadelphia, home of the cheesesteak.

Student Body

African American:	9%	Male/Female:	58/42%
Asian American:	13%	Out-of-State:	40%
Hispanic:	3%	International:	8%
Native American:	<1%	Unknown:	5%
White:	62%		

Popular Faiths: Christianity (with a strong fundamentalist presence on campus)

Gay Pride: The campus is generally accepting of its gay students. The gay community is relatively quiet. There is only one student organization that is specifically gay oriented: the Straight & Gay Alliance.

Economic Status: Drexel has students from diverse economic backgrounds. The majority are lower-middle-class.

Students Speak Out
ON DORMS

Q "**Dorms are tiny**, the air conditioning breaks all the time, and fire alarms go off all the time. But if you meet the right people, none of that matters."

Q "Kelly Hall is **the best hall around**! The rooms are small, but it's a really social building, and everyone ends up knowing everyone."

Q "**Dorm life is cool**. You get to meet people, you live on campus, get access to the network, you don't pay utilities, and you don't have to worry about moving furniture. The worst dorm is Calhoun because the furniture is nailed in place."

STUDENT AUTHOR: **Freshmen must live on campus, which is good because it forces them to become involved in campus life and allows them to begin a social life at the University. Despite people's initial negative reactions to dorm life at Drexel, most students look back on their time living in the dorms fondly. With that being said, Calhoun is a pretty dismal dorm, but the rest are not that bad. Most students really don't mind the furniture that's bolted to the floor. The students in Kelly really have a sense of pride. You will invariably make friends, and your experiences living in any dorm will be positive.**

Did You Know?
35% of undergrads live on campus.

Students Speak Out
ON GUYS & GIRLS

Q "The girls here are okay. They aren't exactly hot, and they are somewhat stuck up. But UPenn girls are very hot, and they are way **more fun than Drexel girls**."

Q "In general, it's **a big mix of freaks**, geeks, hotties, uglies, smart, dumb, and any combination in between. The guy to girl ratio is in the girls' favor, though."

Q "**The girls are mediocre**. A few girls are really hot, but for the most part, they're nothing to fantasize about."

Q "It's **a real kick in the groin** to go from classes with all girls except for two guys (nursing), to about 50/50 (business), to all guys except for two girls (computer science)."

STUDENT AUTHOR: **There are simply more guys than girls here, and they are not much to look at. It's true; we can be a very "geeky" bunch, as most tech schools will admit. There are a lot of relatively unkempt guys walking around in big hooded sweatshirts and baggy cargo pants or jeans, but that just means we're harder workers! As for girls, every once in a while, you'll bump into a real hottie, but then you never see her again. The good-looking girls, however few, are spread out over curricula.**

Traditions

The Crystal Ball
CB is an annual charity ball that has a homecoming king and queen, who are selected based on the amount of money they raise for their respective charity or charities.

Spring Jam
This is an annual concert in the spring. There are several bands, but only one big headliner. Past headliners have been the Roots and Common.

Overall School Spirit
Students at Drexel have a lot of school spirit. We might not show it at sporting events, but it's there.

Students Speak Out
ON ATHLETICS

Q "Varsity sports **aren't huge**. Basketball is pretty big. The players get treated like gods here. Intramurals are a pretty big deal. There is always some kind of game going on, on Buckley Green."

Q "Varsity sports? **What varsity sports**? You mean basketball? I think basketball is the only popular one. I see other teams in uniform practicing all the time, but all you hear about is basketball. I was on the women's crew team, but I quit—it was too hard."

Q "There is **no football team**. B-ball is probably the biggest, then soccer. Sports are not that big."

Q "Varsity what? I am **a big fan of IMs**, but the administration and officials for it are horrible."

STUDENT AUTHOR: **Some people may not realize it, but yes, Drexel does have an athletic program—varsity sports are very limited at Drexel. We used to have a baseball team and a women's volleyball team, but they were cut for financial reasons. We've never had a football team. Basketball is the only one we hear about, but chances are, most students at Drexel couldn't tell you how the team finished last season.**

Students Speak Out
ON DRUG SCENE

Q "I wouldn't say the drug scene is any worse than any other campus. As a side comment, though, most suppliers **originate from UPenn**."

Q "The drug scene at Drexel is almost non-existent. I know that **Drexel is very strict** when it comes to drugs, so I have never been exposed to anyone doing drugs."

Q "From what I have noticed, there are not too many drugs on campus. Every now and then, I see people **smoking weed at parties**, but that's about all I see."

STUDENT AUTHOR: Drugs are not a pervasive problem on Drexel's campus. There is a lot of drinking, and marijuana use is common. It wouldn't be uncommon to hear boasts from our students about the quality of marijuana they are able to obtain at any given moment. Most people would probably be surprised to hear that harder drugs are much rarer here than at other schools, but it's true. Our drinking policies are very strict, though. There is a no-tolerance policy for alcohol on campus.

9:1	Student-to-Faculty Ratio
84%	Freshman Retention Rate
13%	Four-Year Graduation Rate
73%	Financial Aid Applicants Receiving Aid

Students Speak Out
SAFETY & SECURITY

Q "**Security is okay**—just be street smart. Avoid eye contact with strangers; don't handle or talk about money in public. Try not to walk alone at night. Basically it's like any other city."

Q "I have **never felt unsafe on campus**. There are almost always security guards within reach or vision, and emergency alarm posts are scattered throughout campus. Each post can be seen from the next."

Q "**Security is poor**. Someone was stabbed in the 'rape garden' a block away from my house. This was across from two different dorms. Security was stationed there afterwards for a while, and now it is back to normal, which is dangerous."

STUDENT AUTHOR: Yes, there have been some criminal incidents at Drexel. Drexel has taken steps to work at preventing serious crimes in the future. Students do generally feel safe with the strong presence of campus security. All throughout University City you will see Drexel security officers, Philadelphia police, UPenn Police, and emergency posts.

Questions?
For more inside information and survival tips, pick up College Prowler's full-length book on this school, written by an actual student! Check it out at *www.collegeprowler.com*.

Students Speak Out
ON OVERALL EXPERIENCE

Q "I'm glad **I came for the co-op experience**, and I love Philly. It's an awesome city, especially for the cheaper cost of living compared to other expensive places like Boston or New York."

Q "**I'm glad that I am here**. The 10-week terms are hard sometimes, with learning so much in such a short time. But I am challenged, I've met great people, and I really like Drexel."

Q "My experience at **Drexel has been fair**. I do wish I were at UPenn, but I really can't even afford to be at Drexel, so I know I could never afford UPenn. Maybe I'll go for grad school?"

Q "Drexel is okay. It sucks in the sense that the semesters are **only 10 weeks long**, so things get really hectic and crammed into the terms. Drexel is kind of a weird school to go to. There is a lot of crap to put up with, with regards to the administration, and you can easily see that Drexel is a public school that is very interested in making money any way possible."

STUDENT AUTHOR: A lot of students here complain about the "Drexel Shaft" screwing up their scheduling or billing, or how poor their teachers are. The truth is that you will find red tape headaches and poor teachers at just about every university. Even at the top universities, students complain that teachers of freshman-level classes are terrible. I've had first-rate teachers during my time here, even in some 100-level classes. Co-op scheduling can be spoiled by administrative error ("Drexel Shaft") easily, but if you stay on top of things, and be proactive, you will have very little trouble working things out for the long haul.

Duke University

2138 Campus Drive; Durham, NC 27708
(919) 684-8111; www.duke.edu

THE BASICS:

Acceptance Rate: 23%
Setting: Urban
F-T Undergrads: 6,197

SAT Range: 1350–1540*
Control: Private
Tuition: $34,335

Most Popular Majors: Economics, Psychology, History, Public Policy Analysis

*of 1600

Academics	A	Guys	B+
Local Atmosphere	C	Girls	B
Safety & Security	C	Athletics	A-
Computers	A-	Nightlife	C+
Facilities	A	Greek Life	A
Campus Dining	A-	Drug Scene	B-
Off-Campus Dining	C+	Campus Strictness	B+
Campus Housing	B-	Parking	D+
Off-Campus Housing	C-	Transportation	B-
Diversity	B+	Weather	B+

Students Speak Out
ON ACADEMICS

Q "Teachers at Duke are both great and personable. I worked for two professors and got really close to them throughout my college career. At the same time, though, **you have to take the initiative** because you could easily get overlooked. The classes are small, depending on your major (except for your intro classes), so you can easily form relationships with your professors."

Q "**Professors at Duke are all highly qualified**, and most are distinguished in their field. In my first year of classes, my professors included a renowned fiction writer, a Nobel prize laureate, a member of Jimmy Carter's presidential cabinet, and a former military commander."

Q "I had been warned that college professors were a little on the intimidating side, so I stayed clear of them in my first semester. After getting my grades, I realized I had to speak up if I wanted to do better. I was encouraged to come to office hours and lunches, or just to e-mail my professors. Even if you're struggling in a class, you can do better if you **show the professor you want to do well** by just talking with them."

STUDENT AUTHOR: All Duke professors are well educated and established in their field, and most students will tell you that the professors here do their best to relay their knowledge to the students in a way that is easily comprehensible, yet challenging at the same time.

Students Speak Out
ON LOCAL ATMOSPHERE

Q "There are two colleges near Durham. One is 15 minutes away in Chapel Hill (UNC), and the other is 20 minutes away in Raleigh (NC State). Durham has the Durham Bulls baseball team, the Carolina Hurricanes play nearby, and all of the college basketball teams in the area are stellar, so sports are huge. There's also a cool museum in Raleigh. There's **plenty to do in and around campus**."

Q "Durham is one big bore. However, Chapel Hill is nice because it's a town built around a large university. Duke makes its own social scene since Durham doesn't provide one. There are **at least six other colleges in the area**."

Q "Duke and Durham are almost two completely separate worlds. Durham is a rather small city, and it isn't a typical college town. Don't expect to find the same culture or entertainment options you'd see in New York or Boston. Wandering into the wrong sections of town will leave you in a **high-crime low-income area**."

STUDENT AUTHOR: As much as the students love Duke, there are some shortcomings that simply cannot be overlooked. The atmosphere, or lack thereof, is at the top of the list. While East Campus is not situated near the nicest part of Durham, there are a few nice, quiet, little residential areas around East Campus, as well as some adequate shopping centers and restaurants within driving distance. West Campus is much more isolated from Durham, so students won't really sense the Durham atmosphere.

5 Best Things

1 Caring professors
2 College hoops
3 Ethnic diversity
4 Unlimited meal plan
5 Pleasant weather

5 Worst Things

1 High school-style cliques
2 Communal showers
3 Long periods of rain
4 Catching the bus
5 No parking anywhere

Students Speak Out
ON FACILITIES

Q "The exterior of practically **every building at Duke is breathtaking; old and Gothic or Georgian**, new and innovative, exciting even. The inside sometimes doesn't evoke the same pleasant adjectives, particularly in the older buildings. The buildings on East Campus are nice, but the ones on West Campus are somewhat dark and cramped. All of the newer buildings I have seen are great, and the athletic buildings are made in the mode of shrines and palaces for kings."

Q "Duke facilities are excellent. They are convenient, up-to-date, clean, and provide a very enjoyable environment. **I'd rank Duke facilities among the best in the country**."

Q "The recreation center is excellent, the computer labs are above average, and the student center is okay—but it's mostly just a place to put the on-campus restaurants. The **school movie theater is a little lacking**, as far as quality is concerned."

Q "The facilities are **hardly ever lacking**. Our tuition money does not get wasted."

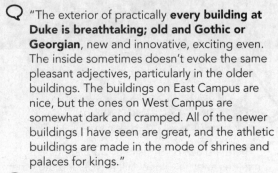

STUDENT AUTHOR: Duke is a beautiful campus, and the buildings are well kept. The original Gothic buildings on Main West quad and the Georgian buildings on Main East are simply stunning. The libraries make up for any lack of outer beauty with their extensive collections. This is not to say that all of the buildings on campus are spacious and immaculate—but it should be made clear that Duke, like so many of its students, is physically beautiful and well groomed.

Famous Alumni

John Feinstein, Annabeth Gish, Kelly Goldsmith, Kevin Gray, Christian Laettner, Richard M. Nixon, Robert Richardson, Jim Spanarkel, Judy Woodruff

Students Speak Out
ON CAMPUS DINING

Q "Though you will undoubtedly hear griping about the food from Aramark and jokes about Marketplace food, Duke food is considered some of the **best among the universities in this nation**. I don't know whether that's a testament to Duke, or to how bad food is at every university."

Q "As a freshman, **you'll eat breakfast and dinner in the Marketplace** over on East Campus. On West Campus, we have a pizza and burger joint called the Loop, a Mexican place, McDonald's, a really good cafeteria, a couple of delis, and a restaurant called the Oak Room. There are also many places off-campus that will make deliveries on food points."

Q "The food on campus is **way better for upperclassmen than for freshmen**! Freshmen are required to buy a dining plan that includes 12 meals a week in the Marketplace, the dining hall on East Campus, and while the food there isn't bad, it gets really monotonous. However, for the other meals, freshmen have the same options as everyone else. My favorites are the Loop, which serves gourmet pizzas and sandwiches, and Armadillo Grill, which serves Mexican food."

STUDENT AUTHOR: Although the food is really not nearly as bad as everyone will tell you, it really wears on you after a while. Duke's food service is known to be among the best in the nation, but students will complain anyway. If you can't find something you like on campus, you can use points to order from off campus.

Student Body

African American:	10%	Male/Female:	52/48%
Asian American:	17%	Out-of-State:	85%
Hispanic:	7%	International:	6%
Native American:	<1%	Unknown:	7%
White:	54%		

Popular Faiths: The most popular faiths are Protestantism, Catholicism, Judaism, Islam, and Hinduism.

Gay Pride: The gay scene is not very visible at Duke, but gays are not generally singled out or persecuted.

Economic Status: The Duke student body is astoundingly wealthy. Duke is remarkably image-conscious.

Students Speak Out
ON DORMS

Q "**Some things are nice about the dorms**, but some things definitely aren't. On East Campus, the laundry machines are really pathetic, although I hear they get better on West. However, we do have housekeeping staff that clean the bathrooms and halls every weekday."

Q "I find that the plan of **having all first-year students on East Campus is a good idea**, and it allows the new students to be together and share new experiences. I didn't hear about any particularly terrible dorms, except that Southgate is far from many facilities."

Q "You're **randomly assigned to a place for your freshman year**. After that, there is a housing lottery in which upperclassmen get the first shot at choosing rooms."

STUDENT AUTHOR: **Students agree that there are very few dorms on Duke's campus that really ought to be avoided. The tradeoff is usually pretty simple: classic beauty on one of the main quads, air-conditioning and brand-spanking newness in one of the newer dorms, or a level of autonomy. One thing's for sure—whichever dorm you choose, it will grow on you.**

Did You Know?
83% of undergrads live on campus.

Students Speak Out
ON GUYS & GIRLS

Q "The majority of people at Duke are **very attractive and very career-oriented**. There isn't much time or interest in starting serious relationships, so most don't make it past the weekend—which opens doors to getting to meet new people."

Q "Given the typical upper-middle class origins of most students, most are attractive. In all seriousness, **the guys here are more often attractive than the girls**. I kid you not."

Q "At Duke, you got your hot ones, you got your nice ones, and you got your 'others.' A nice plus, is that although all Duke girls do not rank a perfect 10, many have **great personalities and very interesting conversation skills**, and that ends up being more important, right?"

STUDENT AUTHOR: **A lot of the students have gotten a bit too caught up in their appearance to worry about personality and relationships. Students are much more likely to have a Friday night hookup than to build a lasting relationship. Although Duke students are generally attractive, image-conscious, and rich, they're also smart. Usually, school comes before relationships, but you've got to keep yourself looking good for those few exceptions.**

Traditions

Bonfires
After Duke beats UNC in a home game, Duke students run over to West Campus to light stuff on fire.

Blue Devil Mascot
The Blue Devil mascot appears to pump people up at all the basketball games.

Overall School Spirit
Duke spirit centers around the basketball season, and during the spring, people are so avidly into Duke it's amazing.

Students Speak Out
ON ATHLETICS

Q "Varsity sports are big here, of course, headlined by basketball. Students participate in bonfires on campus after big wins, and the basketball team is the rallying point for much school spirit. As freshmen, **many IM sports are organized by dorm**, contributing to a sense of unity, rather than anonymity."

Q "Duke has some of the top-ranked sports on campus. **Being a basketball fanatic is key**, and even if you're not now, you'll eventually start seeing blue after a while. It's hard not to catch the school's basketball fever."

Q "**Duke football is the worst**, but people still go to games for school spirit and social activities. Basketball games are, of course, the most popular."

STUDENT AUTHOR: **The current of basketball fanaticism pulses through everyone and everything at Duke. Ironically, the classic college sport, football, is just laughable at Duke. However, the other varsity and IM sports make a better-than-decent showing each year, and there's a good team for just about everyone out here. Mostly, though, there's basketball.**

Students Speak Out
ON DRUG SCENE

Q "**Alcohol is by far the most common** drug of choice, and I think a lot of people take their drinking way too far. A few people smoke. I don't take part in any of that, though, so I don't know exactly what's going on."

Q "Alcohol is most definitely the drug of choice. **There's a weed presence**, but I'd say it's a distant second."

Q "**Students can avoid it**, but if you're looking for drugs, you're basically presented with a buffet (if you know the right people). Marijuana is the most popular drug, and it can be found in most any social group."

STUDENT AUTHOR: **There are drugs on campus, but no one seems threatened by it. Alcohol is more prevalent and widely used than any illegal substance. There will always be the opportunity to use alcohol and drugs, especially if your group of friends uses them, but the pressure and prevalence of drug use shouldn't scare anyone away from Duke.**

8:1	Student-to-Faculty Ratio
97%	Freshman Retention Rate
90%	Four-Year Graduation Rate
90%	Financial Aid Applicants Receiving Aid

Students Speak Out
SAFETY & SECURITY

Q "Security is good on campus, but a girl can't walk around by herself at night because **the East Campus area isn't the best**. There are lots of emergency phones and police around, though, so I never feel unsafe, as long as I'm not alone."

Q "I've never really felt unsafe on campus. The University has its own campus police, and there are phones scattered across campus to call for help if you need it. You'll need a student ID in order to enter any of the dorms. Most other buildings require ID on nights and weekends. Unlike some schools, **officers don't regularly guard campus or building entrances**."

Q "Security and safety could definitely be improved on campus. Many **walkways and parking lots are poorly lit at night**."

STUDENT AUTHOR: **Duke tries hard to keep its students safe. However, the old real-estate maxim ("location, location, location") should serve to remind us that Duke has some inherent problems simply because of the instability of the surrounding area.**

Questions?
For more inside information and survival tips, pick up College Prowler's full-length book on this school, written by an actual student! Check it out at *www.collegeprowler.com*.

Students Speak Out
ON OVERALL EXPERIENCE

Q "I would never go anywhere else after having been at Duke this past year. Though I had my gripes about not getting into Harvard or MIT, I'm over that now. Duke offers a great educational opportunity, especially for undergraduates, and if you can **take advantage of the Freshman Focus program**, do so. It's a great program for your first semester."

Q "I came into this experience with very high expectations, and even so, I've been completely blown away. The Duke student philosophy is '**work hard, play hard**,' and we do. Duke offers students the chance to tailor their experience to whatever it is that they're looking for. Duke offers an environment where students are surrounded by success. The drive to succeed is key to Duke students' success."

Q "Duke is great; I find that the academic life is demanding, but awesome in nearly every way: the professors, the classes, the dedication of the students. I love having been able to meet people from **all over the world with diverse backgrounds**, and I'm most happy with my decision to attend Duke."

STUDENT AUTHOR: **Duke is one of the top academic schools in the country, but that's not its hook. You'll never see Harvard's basketball team in the Final Four or Yale students camping out for a week to get sports tickets. There's an emphasis on friends, social life, and fun here, and it's important to consider these aspects as well as academics when you're choosing a school. Remember— you're choosing the place you'll spend the next four years of your life, not just the name that shows up on your degree at the end.**

Duquesne University

600 Forbes Avenue; Pittsburgh, PA 15282
(412) 396-6000; www.duq.edu

THE BASICS:

Acceptance Rate: 74%
Setting: Urban
F-T Undergrads: 5,250

SAT Range: 1530–1810*
Control: Private
Tuition: $23,470

Most Popular Majors: Business, Education, Health Professions, Communication, Liberal Arts

*of 2400

Academics	B	Guys	B+
Local Atmosphere	B+	Girls	A
Safety & Security	B+	Athletics	C+
Computers	B-	Nightlife	B+
Facilities	B	Greek Life	B
Campus Dining	B	Drug Scene	A-
Off-Campus Dining	A-	Campus Strictness	C+
Campus Housing	C+	Parking	D-
Off-Campus Housing	B+	Transportation	B+
Diversity	D-	Weather	C+

Students Speak Out
ON ACADEMICS

Q "Professors are great! The classes are all pretty small, so they will know you on a first name basis. Also, **they will go out of their way to help you** with class work, and even finding internships and jobs. Most are very well connected with companies in Pittsburgh."

Q "If you want a really easy first semester or first year of college, **take all of your core classes—** but be warned! You'll be so bored sometimes, that you'll go out of your mind!"

Q "I would describe the professors as 'okay.' **There are some that are excellent**, some who are poor, but most seem to fall somewhere in the middle."

Q "Most of the teachers that I have are pretty great. They're always willing to meet outside of class with anyone who needs extra help. **Class sizes are pretty small**, but it also depends on your major. The major concentration and core classes usually run anywhere from 25–50 students."

STUDENT AUTHOR: **For the most part, students appear satisfied with their academic experience at Duquesne University. Professors make themselves available to the student body, and most will go out of their way to help their students. There are, of course, a few exceptions to this assessment, but they are generally few and far between. Duquesne's professors are extremely knowledgeable and expect students to put forth a strong effort into attendance and coursework.**

Students Speak Out
ON LOCAL ATMOSPHERE

Q "Pittsburgh is a great city! There is always something to do. Pitt and CMU are close and **one can easily find a party there**. You'll want to avoid the Hill district after dark. Make sure to visit Station Square, the Waterfront, and take a ride on one of the inclines. The skiing is great for those who enjoy it."

Q "There are loads of universities and colleges around Duquesne. **It's definitely a college town**. I was surprised by the large numbers of young, vibrant people to mingle with."

Q "What I like best about Duquesne is that even though we are so close to downtown Pittsburgh, it doesn't feel like you are in the city at all (when you are on campus). **The closed campus atmosphere makes me feel safe** and secure."

Q "Pittsburgh is a football town—make no mistake about it. The majority of students at Duquesne are from Pittsburgh, and **they love all Pittsburgh's sports teams**—particularly the Steelers and the Penguins."

STUDENT AUTHOR: **There is no shortage of atmosphere or things to do in Pittsburgh. Although many of the downtown attractions close early, the surrounding areas stay open late. From the University of Pittsburgh and CMU, to the clubs, bars, and eateries in the South Side, Station Square, or the Strip District, a Duquesne student should never be bored. Pittsburgh is overflowing with shopping areas, dining spots, and other attractions. Pittsburgh is a friendly city to everyone from all walks of life.**

Students Speak Out
ON FACILITIES

Q "Facilities are nice and are constantly improving. There are a few older buildings, but **most are newly remodeled** with up-to-date equipment and supplies."

Q "Everything is really good, and the computer **labs are always being updated**. Everyone has access to all the facilities—no strictly 'athletes only' spots."

Q "The school owns the A.J. Palumbo Center—they have concerts, sports, and **a great exercise facility**. It's always a good time when I am on campus. There are always concerts or something going on—especially when the weather is nice."

Q "We have a **really gorgeous campus**! We always brag about it to everyone at Pitt."

Q "**Union isn't that great**. I don't know about too many people hanging out there—the place is mostly for commuters to hang out between classes."

STUDENT AUTHOR: Overall, most students are proud of the Duquesne campus. The University goes to great lengths to maintain its pleasant landscaping and tidy walkways. It offers some of the only plush, green lawns for miles, and many students take advantage of them during the warmer months for sunbathing or studying. The majority of the buildings are well maintained and constantly updated throughout the year. The size of the gym seems to be a major gripe among students, though its new sign-up procedures have improved its efficiency.

Famous Alumni

Chip Ganassi, Norm Nixon, Art Rooney, Dan Rooney

Students Speak Out
ON CAMPUS DINING

Q "The food is not bad, surprisingly. **The best places to eat are Off Ramp and Options**. There is another cafeteria-type eating place called Towers, but sometimes their food isn't that great."

Q "We have a variety of food places on campus that you can choose from and use your meal plan for. **It's more a matter of acquired taste** for some of the food around campus."

Q "When my friends and I first started going to Duquesne, the food didn't really bother us, but after a while, **we started to crave a good home-cooked meal**."

Q "There are lots of eateries. **The dining halls have improved** since I started here. There's a wide variety of things to eat and selection is growing. I love the sushi stand in Options."

Q "**Food is all right**, but I would stay away from Towers dining area for the most part. The best place is Options, and then Off Ramp."

STUDENT AUTHOR: Duquesne offers a wide variety of eateries, and most students rate them between adequate and good. Towers cafeteria is the most convenient out of the dining halls but has the lowest quality food (aside from Saturday and Sunday morning brunches). Options, according to students, offers the best food and the most variety; one can even find sushi there. The Locust Street Subway and the Union's Duquesne Deli offer excellent food, but do not accept meal plans.

Student Body

African American:	3%	Male/Female:	42/58%
Asian American:	2%	Out-of-State:	19%
Hispanic:	1%	International:	2%
Native American:	<1%	Unknown:	12%
White:	80%		

Popular Faiths: Christianity, and more specifically, Catholicism, is most prevalent.

Gay Pride: Minimal. The first gay-straight alliance was formed in the winter of 2005, however, student support is not 100 percent.

Economic Status: An upper-middle-class background is most prevalent among Duquesne students.

Students Speak Out
ON DORMS

Q "I would recommend living in the dorms **just for the whole experience of it**, but come your junior or senior year, living off-campus is the thing to do."

Q "Towers (the big dorm) is where most people live. The **rooms are small, but livable**. The best dorm is called Vickroy, but only upperclassmen can live there. There's more room in that dorm than you'll know what to do with!"

Q "I've seen worse, and I've seen better. **Go with St. Ann's as a freshman**. Rules are easy to bypass in any of the dorms; just don't get caught."

STUDENT AUTHOR: Students give mixed feedback about the dorm situation. About half of the students either like living in or remain neutral towards the dorms. The other half dislike the facilities. The on-campus living experience declines for those who choose to remain on campus after their first year. Upperclassmen want to abandon the smaller dorm rooms for more spacious apartments near the campus. Towers is the least liked dormitory among all of the students.

> **Did You Know?**
> 56% of undergrads live on campus.

Students Speak Out
ON GUYS & GIRLS

Q "Hot, hot, hot! **Nicely dressed and very personable**! This is the very first thing I noticed about Duquesne!"

Q "Yes, the **guys are extremely hot**! There are also a lot of girls that are very pretty, too. I hear from other people that don't go to Duquesne that Duquesne girls are stuck up, but I don't think so."

Q "The guys are like everywhere else: some are stuck up, **some are nice**, and some are indifferent—same with the girls."

Q "As a guy, I love every second at this place. The girls outnumber us, and most of them are smoking. **I've never seen a hotter campus**! The hotties just seem to migrate here. I mean, wow!"

STUDENT AUTHOR: The popular opinion on the quality of Duquesne's guys and girls can be summed up in three words: they're high quality. When asked, most students will simply reply, "Duquesne is hot!" In reality, there is a wide mix of students. Duquesne boasts an abundance of attractive students with a good sense of fashion. One also notices a variety of personalities on campus as well, from the sexually promiscuous to the timid and cautious.

> **Duquesne Slang**
>
> **Student Rush**
> Refers to the special ticket deal the Pittsburgh Penguins offer to Duquesne students.
>
> **The Bluff**
> What students sometimes call the hill on which Duquesne sits.
>
> **Overall School Spirit**
> Duquesne students are very proud of their school. It is not uncommon to see half the student body sporting an article of Duquesne clothing. Athletic events could use a larger turnout, but fans are proud of their teams.

Students Speak Out
ON ATHLETICS

Q "Football wins their conference every year, but it is because **they are in an easier conference** than the rest of the teams. You can probably go weeks without ever talking about the varsity sports."

Q "Varsity **sports in one word: joke**. Not too many of the students follow the sports. I played soccer, and none of my friends ever cared."

Q "**We have Intramural sports**? I wasn't even aware."

Q "There isn't much school spirit for sports. Good football team, but **no one watches**. Actually, most of the sports teams do well, but no one goes to the games!"

STUDENT AUTHOR: Most students are quick to point out the odd athletic situation at Duquesne: the basketball team is "not that good," but the games are well attended, while the football team is "very good," yet without much of a following. The general consensus is that, except for the most hardcore of fans, few students concern themselves with sports at Duquesne.

Students Speak Out
ON DRUG SCENE

Q "People who smoke and drink don't force it on anyone else, so **there is no pressure to experiment** or anything. If you don't want to do something, no one's going to make you."

Q "Alright, **beer and alcohol are the easiest drugs** to get on campus. Pot—easy as well. Coke, heroin, LSD, ecstasy—they are not that prevalent."

Q "I hardly hear anything about drugs on campus. I assume they're easy to find if you know the right people, but it **doesn't seem to be that big a deal**. The only problem arising out of this is that when drug busts happen, the whole campus buzzes about them."

STUDENT AUTHOR: **Duquesne students stress the invisibility of the drug scene on campus. As with most other universities, there is some drug usage. The most important issue regarding drug use is the lack of peer pressure. Students generally turn a blind eye toward drug usage, which is not hard considering it is not readily visible.**

15:1	Student-to-Faculty Ratio
87%	Freshman Retention Rate
55%	Four-Year Graduation Rate
66%	Financial Aid Applicants Receiving Aid

Students Speak Out
SAFETY & SECURITY

Q "The **security on campus is great**! No one ever gets hurt on campus or anything."

Q "School is directly adjacent to a rotten part of town. However, **I feel safe there**, and there is an obvious police presence."

Q "Campus security is very good, but not suffocating. The Duquesne Police make their presence known and are very friendly. **They always offer assistance** to students. In the evening, students can call security if they want to be escorted in the dark."

Q "Duquesne is very safe and **very secure**. There is a 24-hour police presence. Very, very safe!"

STUDENT AUTHOR: **Although Duquesne lies right smack in the middle of downtown Pittsburgh and the Hill District, one never really feels in harm's way. The Duquesne Police take their job very seriously and respond quickly to any emergency. Residence halls are extremely safe.**

> **Questions?**
> For more inside information and survival tips, pick up College Prowler's full-length book on this school, written by an actual student! Check it out at *www.collegeprowler.com*.

Students Speak Out
ON OVERALL EXPERIENCE

Q "The education is worth it, **but there are little things** like parking, dorm rules, high tuition, and dining hall hours that make me sometimes wish I was somewhere else."

Q "My first year here, I wanted to transfer because I really missed my boyfriend. But I am glad that I stayed, because **I feel that it is a very good school**, and I have made some really good friends."

Q "I have been at Duquesne for five years and have loved it from the moment I stepped onto campus. **The location of the campus is great**. It's in the city, yet being up on a hill, you feel like you're on some suburban island."

Q "Duquesne is great for my major. **I wish that it was a little more open** to gay people and families, but I can't expect too much, because it is a Catholic school."

Q "Sometimes, **I wish I went to a bigger school** with a more diverse campus, but I'm surviving."

STUDENT AUTHOR: **Students gripe about issues like tuition and parking, but overall, most feel the education and experiences found at Duquesne are worth every penny. Presenting a wide range of majors and programs, the University offers something for prospective students from all walks of life. Duquesne continuously invests time, effort, and money into improving both the physical surroundings and educational content of the campus. Most think the campus beautiful, even in its urban setting. Students feel safe, welcome, and challenged here. The University emits the feel of a large institution, while still promoting the individuality of each student.**

Earlham College

801 National Road West; Richmond, IN 47374-4095
(765) 983-1200; www.earlham.edu

THE BASICS:

Acceptance Rate: 75%
Setting: Rural
F-T Undergrads: 1,168

SAT Range: 1670–2030*
Control: Private
Tuition: $33,274

Most Popular Majors: Biology, Art and Art Studies, Psychology, Interdisciplinary Studies, Sociology

*of 2400

Academics	B+	Guys	B-
Local Atmosphere	C	Girls	B
Safety & Security	A-	Athletics	C
Computers	A-	Nightlife	C
Facilities	B+	Greek Life	N/A
Campus Dining	C+	Drug Scene	B
Off-Campus Dining	D	Campus Strictness	C+
Campus Housing	B	Parking	A-
Off-Campus Housing	B	Transportation	C+
Diversity	C-	Weather	C+

Students Speak Out
ON ACADEMICS

Q "In my short time at Earlham, I have been able to look at Islam from the perspective of peace, look in depth at social deviance in our society, and discuss human nature and social change through the guise of religious philosophy. **I never wanted to skip class**, simply because I was afraid I would miss an incredible discussion or informative lecture."

Q "The teachers **really care about the education they provide for their students**. They are more than willing, for the most part, to take some time out of their busy schedules to sit down and talk. The classes that I have taken have definitely interested me."

Q "**I've never had a bad teacher at Earlham**, though I have heard of a couple. From the sound of it, students do actually have a say in whether a teacher stays for the long haul or not. That is a good thing! My classes have all been good. I've noticed that how long classes last tends to reflect the students more often than the teacher (if they are already a good teacher)."

STUDENT AUTHOR: At Earlham, all classes are taught by professors, and every department is chock full of great educators who are willing to work their hardest to give students the tools they need to succeed. Individual teaching styles aside, Earlham professors also almost invariably share the one quality that counts most: a passion for their subject matter. If you work hard, you'll reap the benefits of this inspiring academic community.

Students Speak Out
ON LOCAL ATMOSPHERE

Q "There's an imaginary rift between the Earlham community and the Richmond community, but if you just get off campus and interact with people, you will find that **people are really friendly and open and not as mean as you hear they are**. I hear the Whitewater Gorge in town is quite beautiful, although I've never been there myself."

Q "There are a lot of stereotypes about Richmond being a really conservative town. My experience as a youth soccer coach was fun, though, and I never had any problems. I also ran a psychological case study on a child in Richmond, and the people that I encountered were very friendly. However, **I have been called names and honked at by the townspeople**, and that made me feel unsafe."

Q "The town sucks, with some exceptions. It's a fairly conservative town, **in strong opposition to our hippy-dippy liberal college**. There's not much in town—on the surface, at least. You've got to dig deeper to get to the good stuff. There aren't any other schools around us."

STUDENT AUTHOR: Don't let the abundant conservative bumper stickers get you down. Despite the general contrast in political leanings between Earlham students and Richmond dwellers, if you walk down the sidewalk with a smile, you'll be greeted with the same. Those addicted to metropolitan culture, a happening music scene, or ethnic food should look elsewhere, or tighten their belts for the long haul.

5 Best Things	5 Worst Things
1 Professors live next door	1 Professors live next door
2 Farm Day	2 Richmond
3 Quaker ideology	3 Dorm drama
4 Shoes optional	4 Liberal infighting
5 Laptops on loan	5 Meal plan requirements

Students Speak Out
ON CAMPUS DINING

Q "The cafeteria food was okay when I first arrived on campus but **got increasingly bad throughout my second year**. Maybe I just got sick of the place. The Co-Op on campus makes awesome and healthy food. Especially if you like garlic, it's the place for you!"

Q "Food on campus is **a lot better than the majority of campuses around the nation**. Our one cafeteria gets old quick (by the end of your first year); however, we do have other options. The Coffee Shop houses a couple different possibilities, including Subway and Jazzman's Coffee."

Q "The Dining Hall is like any other corporate dining service. **It's good for the first couple weeks, and then it gets tired** after you see the same stuff rotated. But the manager is really responsive to suggestions. We have a Co-Op that has a good lunch plan, and we have a Coffee Shop with a Subway. Learn to cook your own food!"

STUDENT AUTHOR: **Earlham's dining hall, SAGA, may be all-you-can-eat, but good luck getting your money's worth. All in all, semi-greasy SAGA food will get you though your first year and give you time to decide for yourself how you want to eat for the next three years. Even if you don't cook, delicious treats are there if you know where to look for them. Don't miss out on a free gourmet meal on Farm Days (every Saturday at Miller Farm) or at Sabbat dinner in the JCC on Friday nights.**

Students Speak Out
ON FACILITIES

Q "The athletic facilities are absolutely wonderful. I spend much of my time there, and all of the employees are great people and wonderful to get to know. The student center is nice as well. **There are a few things that could be changed**, but honestly, nothing too serious."

Q "The athletic center has **everything you need to beat your body into a healthy bruise**. The student center was adequate but lacked a few things. I don't really know what, because I was satisfied, but my friends complained. If you need something, just ask for it enough, and you will get it."

Q "The Athletic and Wellness Center was remodeled recently and is open throughout the day to all students, staff, and members. Our student center has a coffeeshop in it, as well as the bookstore, post office, TV areas, pool and Ping-Pong tables, and places for bands to get together and practice. **Our campus is kept up very nicely**, and all of the academic buildings are in good shape, as well."

Q "The student center, Runyan, is **sorely lacking**."

STUDENT AUTHOR: **For the campus's small student population, Earlham has high standards for facility maintenance and construction, providing students with a great environment for learning, socializing, and recreating. With a few exceptions, anything you can't locate on campus you should be able to find in Richmond. It can be scary, however, to realize how long some students can go without leaving campus.**

Famous Alumni

Wendell Stanley, James Fowler, Thomas Gottschalk, Sybil Jordan Hampton, Frances Moore Lappe, Manning Marable, Michael C. Hall, Andrea Seabrook

Student Body

African American:	6%	Male/Female:	45/55%
Asian American:	2%	Out-of-State:	78%
Hispanic:	3%	International:	11%
Native American:	<1%	Unknown:	11%
White:	67%		

Popular Faiths: Quakerism plays a large role in campus ideals (equality, simplicity, so forth) and has a long tradition of promoting religious freedom.

Gay Pride: Earlham is a safe and welcoming place to people of all genders and sexual orientations.

Economic Status: Earlham outpaces many colleges by reaching out to lower-income students with substantial financial aid packages.

Students Speak Out
ON DORMS

Q "Don't avoid any dorms. **They are all completely livable**. Norwich Lodge is the best for an introvert, and Barrett is best for a partier. The others have their respective nooks and crazy floors, but it changes from year to year, depending on where the upperclassmen are."

Q "**I strongly advocate living in a College-owned house**, as this can a very rewarding experience (and costs the same or less than living in a dorm). Dorms are fine if you don't mind collective billing."

Q "Hoerner was designed by an architect of prisons (allegedly). Bundy is nice, except maybe the basement if you don't like low ceilings. **Barrett smells funny often**, but it serves its function. The new dorms are nice, if a little sterile."

STUDENT AUTHOR: **While some dorms may offer more spacious and attractive living spaces, and others host more eccentric bands of students, all campus housing is clean and livable. If you want to stay on campus all four years, Residence Life will be delighted, and you shouldn't have too much trouble accommodating your maturing demands.**

Did You Know?
87% of undergrads live on campus.

Students Speak Out
ON GUYS & GIRLS

Q "The guys and girls are all definitely unique. **There are some good-looking ones and some not-so-hot ones on both sides**. If you are looking for a huge pool of hot girls and guys, Earlham is probably not the place to go. You can still find a great catch, however."

Q "I think Earlham has some of the most beautiful people I've ever seen in my entire life. It's funny, though: when I first arrived, I didn't really feel this way, but after a few weeks I woke up and was like, '**Oh my Goddess, these people are really beautiful**.'"

Q "**Everyone is very 'Earlham,'** though the incoming classes seem to be preppier and more aware of appearance."

STUDENT AUTHOR: **Standards of beauty at Earlham are not necessarily so standard. Students often value an off-beat style and unique personality over bra-size. This isn't to say we Earlhamites are so high and mighty we are above noticing some nice abs or legs, but makeup and a bottle of bleach might not get you as far here as the University of Miami. One man's beauty queen may be another man's geek-of-the-week.**

Traditions

The International Festival
A week-long celebration, complete with eclectic cultural events, presentations, and foods.

Little Two
Every Tuesday night between 11 p.m. and midnight, students hold a bicycle relay race around the Heart.

Overall School Spirit
Earlham pride is only beginning to translate into excitement on the sidelines. Those who do come to games are small in number but enthusiastic enough for a crowd of hundreds.

Students Speak Out
ON ATHLETICS

Q "Although varsity sports are prevalent, **they are definitely not the focus of the campus** as in Division I schools. They are merely a nice addition if you are interested in playing or attending sporting events. There are also plenty of intramural sports offered, which are a great way to meet new people."

Q "**We have lots of IM sports that have many willing and enthusiastic members**. I am a varsity tennis player, and I absolutely love it. It is another way to get a close group of friends."

Q "Varsity sports are big to those who play them and their friends. **We don't do particularly well, but we have good spirit**. IM sports are big and lots of fun. Everyone gets out to play soccer or basketball."

STUDENT AUTHOR: **Varsity sports are a great way to get involved on campus, and most teams welcome walk-ons and first-timers. You don't have to sign your life away to play on a varsity sport, but our final records can be a bit dismal. That's not to say that our small pockets of fans aren't as die-hard as the crowds at some of big-name schools, there's just not quite so many of them.**

Students Speak Out
ON DRUG SCENE

Q "Honestly, I cannot really comment much, other than to say that it is prevalent. **It seems to be mostly restricted to marijuana and alcohol**, though I am sure there is more there I am not seeing."

Q "Although the drugs are still present, **they are not that noticeable**. The most common thing on campus is a hookah."

Q "There are some hard drugs that creep into the walls of the dorms, but people usually don't last long while on them. **Cocaine is a small problem, simply because it exists**. Most everyone has access to three or four on-campus dealers. But the weed isn't very good, and all else is sub-par, so drugs just end up wasting time and money."

STUDENT AUTHOR: **While drugs are present on campus, they're not going to be in your face. Most people aren't averse to responsible use of lighter recreational substances like alcohol and marijuana, but if you're not interested in taking part, you won't be pressured.**

12:1	Student-to-Faculty Ratio
85%	Freshman Retention Rate
64%	Four-Year Graduation Rate
93%	Financial Aid Applicants Receiving Aid

Students Speak Out
SAFETY & SECURITY

Q "Overall, there were **no points in my undergraduate experience when I felt unsafe**. The most threatening thing around this place is the skunk. He lives in the pines behind the Coffee Shop."

Q "Security is very good at Earlham. I have never felt unsafe on campus. **Security's primary purpose seems to be busting parties** where people are drinking, or coming to people's dorm rooms to write them up after they are caught drinking by their RA."

Q "Security patrols regularly. They are quite selective, in my opinion, as to who they chose to target at times for violating school policies. **Safety on campus is fine**, for the most part."

STUDENT AUTHOR: Earlham's Campus Safety and Security Office can be reached 24 hours, and they are an inconspicuous, though reassuring, presence on campus. There are no blue phones or escort services, but the campus's small size means that security is never far away.

Questions?
For more inside information and survival tips, pick up College Prowler's full-length book on this school, written by an actual student! Check it out at *www.collegeprowler.com.*

Students Speak Out
ON OVERALL EXPERIENCE

Q "Earlham is a great experience if you make it one. You have to be willing to give up what you are used to. **The size of it makes you work really hard to find things that you like** and people that you want to spend time with. There are days, weeks sometimes, that you'll be frustrated and want to go back to what you are used to. But the people are friendly, motivated, and excited about life. If you smile and go in with a good attitude, you'll have a great time. You'll start calling it the 'Earlham bubble.'"

Q "I loved Earlham. I loved it all. **It was the most significant experience of my life**, and it changed my parents, as well. I think if someone comes away from there without having changed, they were either beautiful to begin with, or too stupid to know when to fall in love."

Q "I wish I were at Evergreen for the alternative curriculum design and laid-back attitude, but I've had some good experiences at Earlham. Unfortunately, **Earlham needs to reconcile how you are to be trained for a changing world** when they discourage students from making that change at Earlham. Overall, it's left of center, but by no means radical."

STUDENT AUTHOR: People come to Earlham for the academics, the Quaker principles, and the community. And, for the most part, they fall in love with the off-beat professors and student body. Classes are compelling, and professors have a real love for their subjects and an investment in the students they teach. The opportunities are endless, and if Earlham's right for you, you're going to have an incredible four years. Surviving the weather and the dismal dining scene will all be worth it.

East Carolina University

East Fifth Street; Greenville, NC 27858-4353
(252) 328-6131; www.ecu.edu

THE BASICS:

Acceptance Rate: 84%
Setting: Small city
F-T Undergrads: 17,309

SAT Range: 1360–1630*
Control: Public
Tuition: $14,920

Most Popular Majors: Nursing, Elementary Education, Broadcast Journalism, Business

*of 2400

Academics	B-	Guys	B
Local Atmosphere	B+	Girls	B+
Safety & Security	B	Athletics	B-
Computers	B	Nightlife	B
Facilities	B+	Greek Life	C+
Campus Dining	B	Drug Scene	B+
Off-Campus Dining	B+	Campus Strictness	B-
Campus Housing	B-	Parking	C+
Off-Campus Housing	A-	Transportation	B+
Diversity	C	Weather	B+

Students Speak Out
ON ACADEMICS

Q "Personally, **I have only disliked a few of my professors for different reasons** (hard to understand, bad teaching style, etc.), but generally, I have enjoyed all my English professors. My classes are interesting because I choose which classes I am taking. Some of the general education classes are not very interesting, but if you like history and chemistry, then I suppose you would like those classes. It is all subjective."

Q "The Dowdy Student Store and the University Book Exchange (UBE) will give some money back for used books at the end of the semester, but the amount depends on how many marks there are in the book. So if students think they are going to need a few extra dollars at the end of the semester, they need to not write so much in the books. So, new students, **remember to keep the books clean**!"

Q "**Some people just aren't ready for college**. I just can't believe that there are so many students out there who don't understand that going to class and doing homework is something college students are supposed to do to make it worth the money to even be here."

STUDENT AUTHOR: The professors are what really makes ECU a great school. Professors are willing to help students who are willing to help themselves learn and develop professionally. ECU's professors are diverse, fascinating, and usually dedicated to student development.

Students Speak Out
ON LOCAL ATMOSPHERE

Q "**Greenville really needs to have more live music**. There's some here, but there really needs to be more. The older clubs that had it have closed, and the Folk Arts Society of Greenville occasionally has concerts, and there's that RA Fountain place, but that's a half-hour away."

Q "I'm from Greenville, and **I really miss the putt-putt place** that used to be out past Hastings Ford. The one at the Fun Park is okay, but the holes aren't that challenging. Let's have more putt-putt!"

Q "For people who love the outdoors, there's quite a lot to do in Greenville and in the surrounding areas for people who are willing to travel a bit. **There's kayaking and canoeing and camping and fishing**! Eastern North Carolina is beautiful."

Q "There are a lot of dance opportunities in Greenville. Of course there's the stuff at the clubs, but that's not really like real dancing, not like ballroom and salsa dancing. **There's even swing and contra dancing** down at that Willis Building, along with salsa and ballroom stuff."

STUDENT AUTHOR: Greenville's population is about 70,000, making it the largest town east of Raleigh. The Greenville area is also home to Pitt Community College, and most Greenvillians are connected to ECU, PCC, or the regional medical center. Some locals affectionately refer to Greenville as a "black hole" because many people who leave tend to eventually return, and many who come from other places tend to stay.

5 Best Things	5 Worst Things
1 Trees and green space	1 Strictness
2 Professors	2 Too much partying
3 Friendly students	3 Poor local job market
4 Diversity	4 Parking tickets
5 Affordable tuition	5 Conservative students

Students Speak Out
ON FACILITIES

Q "I heard recently that between 2001 and 2007, ECU spent about $300 million on construction. And we can definitely see it, too, because **there's always something blocking my way to class**, and I have to allow extra time to get there. As soon as one thing's done blocking pedestrian traffic, there's something else somewhere doing the same thing. I guess it'll all look better after it, though."

Q "**I love the Aqua Theater at the Rec Center**. It's something they have in the summers where a bunch of people hang out at the outdoor pool in the chairs, on air rafts in the pool, or just treading in the water, or any of the above, and watch a movie that they show on a giant screen out there. It's really cool, and a perfect date for a muggy night."

Q "I think all the athletic places we have on campus are awesome. **The football stadium is great, especially the upper deck**. Anybody who gets vertigo doesn't need to go up there, though, because it's so high up that it feels like it's moving. The new baseball stadium is really great too. I went to almost every game there last year when they were winning so much."

STUDENT AUTHOR: The Rec Center is very popular among students, as are bowling and billiards in the basement of Mendenhall. In addition, Wright Auditorium, Hendrix Theater, McGinnis Theater, and Fletcher Recital Hall provide venues for events, movies, plays, and concerts. ECU also has an abundance of athletics facilities, even though the teams are not the best.

Famous Alumni

Rick Atkinson, Ronnie Barnes, Sandra Bullock, Ron Clark, Elizabeth McDavid Jones, Al Maginnes, Vince McMahon, Emily Proctor, Bill Roberson, Kay Yow

Students Speak Out
ON CAMPUS DINING

Q "I used to get a small coffee drink at Java City every day when my friends and I would meet at the Wright Place, but then they posted the 'nutrition' facts, and **that scared me away from those drinks right then and there**. I haven't had one in probably a year, actually."

Q "Of course, **the campus Asian food isn't as good as what my family makes** or what I cook in my room, but they try, I guess."

Q "**My friends and I are boycotting the West End Dining Hall** because they tore up the old amphitheater that a lot of students loved. They ignored our protests, so now we're ignoring their desire for our money."

Q "Back when I lived on campus, I had a meal plan because I had to, but I can't afford it anymore. **It's too expensive** compared to what I can fix at my apartment, which is better than the junk stuff on campus anyway."

Q "The dining hall food is **surprisingly good**."

STUDENT AUTHOR: Despite gross amounts of money spent on expansion and catchy location names in recent years, the food on campus has not improved much. The food is decent for the first week of the semester, after breaks, or whenever parents are expected to be in town. The rest of the time, especially before breaks, the food is questionable. Those who are worried about the "Freshman 15" during their first year away from home-cooked food should plan to not be dazzled by the food options at ECU.

Student Body

African American:	16%	Male/Female:	41/59%
Asian American:	2%	Out-of-State:	10%
Hispanic:	2%	International:	1%
Native American:	1%	Unknown:	4%
White:	75%		

Popular Faiths: Christianity is the most common religion on campus.

Gay Pride: B-GLAD (Bisexuals, Gays, Lesbians, and Allies for Diversity) is a campus organization that strives to promote tolerance of diverse sexual orientations on campus and in the community.

Economic Status: ECU is accessible to students from a wide range of economic backgrounds.

Students Speak Out
ON DORMS

Q "As an upperclassman living off campus, **I miss the familiar feeling of knowing people** in the halls, doing things on campus, and not having to drive to the gym, library, or work."

Q "The mattresses in Umstead fit perfectly in the doorframes. It was really funny to watch drunk students try to find the doorknob through the mattress. **We only tried that once, and it was so funny** we figured we might get caught next time."

Q "I like the rooms. **Everything is bolted to the floor or to the wall**, but I like it, and my roommate has turned out to be really nice, too."

STUDENT AUTHOR: **Most dorms are tobacco free, but students can smoke outside. Dorm entry is by key, the loaning of which is punishable by "death." Actually, students caught loaning their keys, even to parents or a roommate, will be restricted from campus housing. There are RAs on every floor, some stricter than others. Both roommates pay for rooms, so they should collaborate on "house rules."**

Did You Know?
26% of undergrads live on campus.

Students Speak Out
ON GUYS & GIRLS

Q "**I love it when the guys grow up a bit and wear nice shirts**. Their jeans can be worn, but if the shirt's nice, even casually not tucked in and with the sleeves rolled up and the collar unbuttoned, then they look really good. Girls will notice, and may even compliment the guys if they look good."

Q "**I think the guys and girls at ECU are average**, but there are a few hotties here and there."

Q "Not everyone parties and has a lot of sex like some people think college students do. There are still students out there—around here, I mean—**who have some control and aren't just looking to get laid**."

STUDENT AUTHOR: **Guys and girls at ECU are often both intellectual and good-looking. Some ECU students are sexually promiscuous, but there is also a significant portion of students who are protection-conscious, and some who have decided not to be sexually active until later in their lives. No matter which category new students fit into, there will be others who share their ideas.**

Traditions

Halloween
Greenville's annual Halloween celebration is a huge and widely-known outdoor event.

Pirate Palooza
Students may get free stuff, like key chains and pens, and compete for free tuition and textbooks.

Overall School Spirit
No matter how bad the teams are and how much students complain about the sports teams, there are still fans (usually alumni) who will paint themselves purple and gold.

Students Speak Out
ON ATHLETICS

Q "Club sports really should not be overlooked at ECU. **We're tough, too, and we compete just like the big varsity teams**, except we don't have the same degree of funding—sometimes none—and we are usually better. We actually win. Try that, varsity teams!"

Q "**Freeboot Friday is awesome**! The Friday before every home football game, Freeboot Friday is held downtown in the public parking lot on the corner of Fifth and Evans streets. It's a really fun event, and seeing everyone interact there—students and members of the community—betters my opinion of Greenville."

Q "I love going to games with my friends from student organizations. **We don't care if the teams win or lose**. It's all about having fun with the people there."

STUDENT AUTHOR: **ECU baseball has been worth following in recent years, and football is steadily improving under the new coach. Despite chronic losses, however, fans still wear purple and gold, drive around with Jolly Roger flags waving from their vehicle windows, go tailgating, and attend games.**

Students Speak Out
ON DRUG SCENE

Q "**I am really not a fan of the zero-tolerance policy**. There should be at least one warning for us. That saved some of my friends before, and all they had to do was community service with Habitat for Humanity, but I'm not so sure I can get by with it now on campus without getting kicked out. My RA is really strict."

Q "Sure, I know where you can get some of that stuff. It's available, but I'm not going to tell you where or from whom. **There are some students who sell on campus, but more off campus**. Some are from Pitt Community College. Some are not from either."

Q "I'm a freshman and I love it at ECU. **Get ready to get drunk!**"

STUDENT AUTHOR: ECU has been labeled a "party school," partly because of the enthusiastic tailgating that occurs despite chronic football losses and because of the annual Halloween celebration; yet, a lot of students choose not to drink excessively or use illegal drugs.

20:1	Student-to-Faculty Ratio
77%	Freshman Retention Rate
25%	Four-Year Graduation Rate
73%	Financial Aid Applicants Receiving Aid

Students Speak Out
SAFETY & SECURITY

Q "**Don't use the ATM machines downtown at night**, because if you do, you'll probably get assaulted or robbed."

Q "All the new security guards freak me out. **They are always there** when I come in the door at my dorm. It seems like most of them are men, too, which can be kind of creepy."

Q "Most of those alerts we get are about stuff that happened in the middle of the night, usually around 2 a.m. or a little after. That seems to tell me that **that's a good time to get robbed and assaulted**. That also seems to tell me that people should not walk by themselves after leaving bars and parties. Students always need to walk in groups and watch out for their friends so they don't get date raped or something."

STUDENT AUTHOR: The ECU Police have a visible and friendly presence, yet they do not hesitate to arrest or cite people for various offenses, which should make students feel safe and secure. Fortunately, criminal offense rates are low here.

Questions?
For more inside information and survival tips, pick up College Prowler's full-length book on this school, written by an actual student! Check it out at *www.collegeprowler.com.*

Students Speak Out
ON OVERALL EXPERIENCE

Q "**The professors are great**, but a lot of the students I've interacted with don't have any intellectual interest in their field. I sometimes wish I had gone to a school where the students are more serious about academics. The professors are the only thing keeping me here."

Q "My dream when I was growing up was always to attend ECU. After two years at a community college about 45 minutes away, I transferred here, and I was really nervous at first, like being a freshman all over again. **ECU has lived up to all of my ideas from when I was younger**, and coming to ECU has helped get me set up for what I really want to do with my life."

Q "I didn't know that ECU didn't have the program I wanted when I came here, and now I'm making plans to transfer. **I guess I didn't do enough research, but now I know**, and all my classes will transfer, so it won't be so bad. I love the school, but it's not the place for me right now."

Q "**I regret not taking some of my classes as seriously as I could have** and not taking advantage of every opportunity to learn, instead of just doing assignments and turning them in for grades."

STUDENT AUTHOR: The quality and enthusiasm of the professors who care about their students is what attracts and retains students who could have gone to larger and more prestigious schools. Although the campus police are friendly, ECU is quite strict, perhaps in an effort to downplay the "party school" reputation. ECU has been through sports losses and administrative shake-ups in the past, but some of the political damage seems to be getting straightened out.

Elon University

2700 Campus Box; Elon, NC 27244
(336) 278-3566; www.elon.edu

THE BASICS:

Acceptance Rate: 41%
Setting: Rural
F-T Undergrads: 4,832

SAT Range: 1.130–1310*
Control: Private
Tuition: $24,076

Most Popular Majors: Business, Communications, Social Sciences, Parks and Recreation, Education

*of 1600

Academics	B	Guys	B+
Local Atmosphere	D	Girls	A-
Safety & Security	A	Athletics	B-
Computers	B	Nightlife	B+
Facilities	B+	Greek Life	A-
Campus Dining	B+	Drug Scene	A-
Off-Campus Dining	C+	Campus Strictness	B
Campus Housing	A	Parking	B-
Off-Campus Housing	A-	Transportation	D
Diversity	D	Weather	B+

Students Speak Out
ON ACADEMICS

Q "**The teachers at Elon are unique**. They are very interested in their students inside and outside of the classroom. I have had teachers ask me how other important things in my life are going, i.e. interviews or presentations in other classes. They are always willing to meet with you for help in their class. My professors bring a light to the classroom; I can tell they love their job and that directly affects how much I learn and how hard I work in their class."

Q "The teachers are great. They know a lot about the subjects in which they teach, and I am very impressed by the success they have had in their respective fields. **The classes that interest me are the subjects I love**. I have had a few other classes that aren't in my major, but the teacher made all the difference, allowing me to really understand the subject at hand."

Q "My professors are great and always available— **they're my favorite part of Elon**. I can get tutoring and personal help whenever I need it."

Q "**Every now and then you'll get a weird professor**, but they're cool. Class is usually interesting, but sometimes it's hard to stay interested (especially if it's an 8:00 class)."

STUDENT AUTHOR: The academics at Elon are very rigorous. Despite that, Elon is still a very small school. Classes are small enough that students can ask lots of questions, professors get to know names and faces, and there's never such a huge crowd that you have to fight to see your professor during office hours.

Students Speak Out
ON LOCAL ATMOSPHERE

Q "Elon is just the right distance from everything. Though there is **not much to do in Elon/ Burlington itself**, entertainment and activities are no more than an hour's drive."

Q "At Elon University, there are no other universities within a 15-mile radius. The town of Elon surrounds the campus, so that both coexist as one entity. It feels like a small town, almost **resembling Andy Griffth's town of Mayberry**, with many of the amenities of a larger college town."

Q "There are always going to be sketchy places, but I like the town. It's good because it's near **Greensboro, Raleigh, and Winston-Salem**, so you can go there for concerts and such."

Q "Well, the **town itself lacks in things to do**, but within Elon there is always something going on, so it's balanced out. We're in a good location as far as cities down the road from us. Chapel Hill, Durham and Raleigh have good stores, restaurants and concerts. Greensboro is okay."

STUDENT AUTHOR: The town of Elon is really small, around 5,000 to 10,000 inhabitants (including University students). The city of Burlington (which is about five minutes away) has a population of 44,917 inhabitants. Many students complain about Burlington being too boring. If you're looking for a city with buildings taller than three stories, buses, metros, and people always busy and going somewhere, Burlington is not the best area. The most fun thing to do is go to Wal-Mart—that says a lot.

5 Best Things

1 Study abroad programs
2 Beautiful campus
3 Accessible professors
4 Opportunities abound
5 State-of-the-art gym

5 Worst Things

1 Lack of diversity
2 Lack of laundry facilities
3 Dining hall hours
4 Lines in dining halls
5 No music practice rooms

Students Speak Out
ON FACILITIES

Q "Elon has done a wonderful job in 'keeping up with the times.' Some of the facilities are still very new because Elon has begun to grow, but they **try their hardest to meet the needs of the students** by constantly asking us to fill out evaluations or surveys."

Q "**The gym is really nice**, but sometimes crowded. The computers are great, and in enough places if you look hard enough, and the student center is nice but I wish they had more stuff to do there!"

Q "The facilities are all renovated, **extremely usable and accessible**. Some of the rooms don't have a digital projector or DVD drive, but that should be standard soon."

Q "The facilities are exceptionally nice on the campus. **Elon takes great pride in creating a welcoming warm environment** for the students in all different buildings. Each classroom has one wall painted a different color that helps brighten the room and make it more interesting than a white box. I have never seen trash around campus; it is immaculate."

STUDENT AUTHOR: **All the facilities are state-of-the-art. For those into sports and fitness, we have two gyms, an indoor pool, and three aerobic studios, as well as soccer, baseball, and football fields. Our Student Center is beautiful, with the marble floors. McCrary Theatre is the largest and is where most musicals are held. Then there's the Yeager Recital Hall, Whitley Auditorium, and Black Box Theatre. Finally, Acorn Coffee Shop and West End Station and Lighthouse bars are close enough to campus.**

Famous Alumni

Rich Blomquist, Dan Callaway, Jack McKeon, Allison Spant

Students Speak Out
ON CAMPUS DINING

Q "Compared to other friends' schools and meal plans, ours is really user friendly: **lots of options** from wraps, pastas, salad, sushi, coffee, pastries, to pizza or Chick-fil-A. The Acorn makes good sandwiches and baked goods. Freshens has good smoothies and ice cream."

Q "The food is amazing on campus. **We have two dining halls that are all you care to eat**, and then there is a sandwich shop and a fast food place, all which take meal plans."

Q "The food on campus is pretty good; there is variety and options for vegetarians. Harden is the best dining hall because it offers the most healthy options combined with junk food if you want it. There are also **several restaurants in the area that take Phoenix Cash**."

Q "The food is alright; **it gets a little boring**, but I guess it would anywhere. Some of the meal plan rules are dumb."

Q "I think the food **isn't that great**; however, I have been told it is much better than other schools. I find it hard to find meals that aren't just carbs, because I don't eat meat."

STUDENT AUTHOR: **Elon has had a lot of success with their meal plan program. There is a variety of foods, so each student is accommodated; from the student with stomach problems to the pickiest vegetarian. And if the menu doesn't please you, there is always the fast food in Octagon Café. Octagon has a pizza bar, Chick-fil-A, Grille Works (burgers, cheese steaks), and Ben and Jerry's ice cream!**

Student Body

African American:	6%	Male/Female:	41/59%
Asian American:	1%	Out-of-State:	72%
Hispanic:	2%	International:	2%
Native American:	<1%	Unknown:	6%
White:	83%		

Popular Faiths: Catholic, Baptist, Episcopalian, and Methodist are the most prominent religions.

Gay Pride: There is a high tolerance for homosexuals at Elon. The University not only has a policy of non-discrimination based on sexual orientation, but offers same-sex domestic partner benefits to staff members.

Economic Status: Elon is a private school, and the majority of the students are upper-middle class.

Students Speak Out
ON DORMS

Q "West, Virginia, Carolina, Smith, and Sloan are the **coolest on-campus dorms** and they have pretty decent room sizes. Hook, Barney, Brannock, and the others are a little rowdy and always have people in and out. Danieley is good, but it is pretty far off campus especially for freshmen. Jordan Center is ghetto."

Q "The dorms are nice; **they all have air-conditioning**. I have lived in Chandler for two years and it is wonderful to have a balcony to walk around on and sit outside on nice days."

Q "The dorms have **fairly large rooms**! They include Internet, cable, phone and other amenities. They're all nice, and I haven't had problems anywhere."

STUDENT AUTHOR: **Although no dorm could ever have all the space most students crave, the rooms at Elon are big enough to fit most, if not all, your needs. One concern for some is that none of the dorms have elevators; this can make moving in and out a more difficult task. These drawbacks are relatively minor compared to the beautiful housing facilities Elon provides for its students.**

? **Did You Know?**
58% of undergrads live on campus.

Students Speak Out
ON GUYS & GIRLS

Q "There are a lot more guys than girls on our campus. A lot of the girls are very nice, sincere people, but there are also those who are stuck up snobs. There are a lot of hot guys at Elon, but then again they are **usually rude, taken, or gay**. You wanted the truth, right? Since there is such a variety of people here though, it's not hard to find people with the same interests and form great friendships."

Q "The girls and guys here are very attractive. But **sometimes the girls may come off as easy or snobby**, with their bleach-blonde hair and layers of eye make-up. But that's not to say you can't find a very attractive person who is down-to-earth and sweet as can be."

STUDENT AUTHOR: **Like any other private university, you will have girls who come from wealthy families and can afford to dress in all Juicy Couture and wear make-up they bought at Sephora. Guys can be the same, with their Gap and Banana Republic clothes. However, none of this is a social requirement. Beneath the surface, students really appreciate a down-to-earth person who likes to put their best foot forward while maintaining an air of level-headedness.**

Traditions

College Coffee
Every Tuesday from 9:50 a.m.–10:20 a.m., students, staff, and faculty get to meet and talk over coffee and continental breakfast.

Chapel
Every Thursday morning in Whitley Auditorium, everyone is welcome to chapel on campus.

Overall School Spirit
We show a lot of school spirit at the games, but otherwise we're a pretty neutral campus. However, Greek pride is especially prevalent all over campus.

Students Speak Out
ON ATHLETICS

Q "Sports are pretty big, but sometimes there is **trouble getting students to support them**. Intramural sports, on the other hand, are huge. They are for fun and attract more of a crowd."

Q "Our football program should pick up since we're under a new coach now. **Basketball is amazing**. The games are really interactive—lots of spirit. IM sports are huge, easy to participate in."

Q "Intramural sports are pretty popular, and my friends who are involved in them get really excited for the competition. Varsity sports are horrible; **we are not an athletic school**."

Q "**Basketball is big**, and football really isn't, although I wish it was."

STUDENT AUTHOR: **Intramural sports are very big on campus—probably bigger than many varsity sports. Elon offers 17 varsity sports and 12 intramurals on campus. In 2003–2004, the school was brand new to a higher division—the Southern Conference. This advance has been very exciting for students and staff alike, and has helped our reputation grow. A good percentage of students play either varsity or intramurals at some point in their college careers.**

Students Speak Out
ON DRUG SCENE

Q "I have **never had any encounters with drugs** or have heard of any since I arrived at Elon two years ago."

Q "The **drug scene is pretty minimal**. While a fair number of students smoke pot every now and then, other drugs are much rarer in terms of the overall student population."

Q "There are always certain crowds that do drugs on campus, **nothing out of the normal**. It is not a huge issue."

STUDENT AUTHOR: This is college, so naturally there is going to be a certain population that chooses to use illegal drugs. However, this sort of thing isn't at all prevalent at Elon. Room checks are regularly conducted by RAs, so if anyone has drug paraphernalia they are immediately written up; there are different levels of punishments for different infractions, but the University won't go easy on those who break the law. If you're looking for a school where you will not feel pressured into drugs, Elon is definitely it.

14:1	Student-to-Faculty Ratio
90%	Freshman Retention Rate
65%	Four-Year Graduation Rate
73%	Financial Aid Applicants Receiving Aid

Students Speak Out
SAFETY & SECURITY

Q "Elon is a very safe campus and any severe security incidents are reported to all students via e-mail. **I have never felt unsafe** on the campus and if I ever did I know security would gladly come walk with me or check out the situation."

Q "The campus is amazingly safe—I sleep with my door open and don't think twice. **The people here are really honest**; we swipe our own cards for meals!"

Q "I always feel like Elon is a safe place, but we are **always encouraged to take safety precautions** regardless. Campus Security is a good department with good, smart people running it."

STUDENT AUTHOR: Elon is located in a smaller area, so it's naturally going to be more secure than some city schools. Elon has many programs that acquaint students with the security services offered on campus and what to do in a dangerous situation. With safe rides, blue lights, and escort services, students should feel pretty safe.

Questions?
For more inside information and survival tips, pick up College Prowler's full-length book on this school, written by an actual student! Check it out at *www.collegeprowler.com.*

Students Speak Out
ON OVERALL EXPERIENCE

Q "There is **so much opportunity here** as far as study abroad and internships. Besides, Elon's reputation is growing. I'm glad to be a part of that."

Q "I love it here. I'm becoming the person I'm meant to be and growing as an individual through the organizations and classes I take. My collective experience is amazing. From Greek to organizations to studying abroad, **I know I will leave Elon with a strong sense of self** and be equipped with what I need to live and function in our society."

Q "I love this school. The **people are a little on the shallow side sometimes**, but there are a lot of intelligent, warm people that make Elon one of the best universities I've ever seen."

Q "I love Elon. There always certain drawbacks to any school, but I can't imagine myself anywhere else. I have been given great opportunity for leadership on campus, and have really come **much closer to discovering my passions** through a small university environment."

STUDENT AUTHOR: The community is small and quiet, but students still can't imagine being anywhere else. Socially, there is a Greek scene and an abundance of nightlife that is in Greensboro, which is only 20 to 30 minutes away and well worth the trip. The academic curriculum can be rigorous at times, but the professors are willing to help in any way that they can. Elon's student body is great, even though they can be a little difficult to deal with at times. There are not a lot of complaints about the University other than its diversity issues and the size of the town.

Emerson College

120 Boylston Street; Boston, MA 02116
(617) 824-8500; www.emerson.edu

THE BASICS:

Acceptance Rate: 37%
Setting: Urban
F-T Undergrads: 3,346

SAT Range: 1710–1990*
Control: Private
Tuition: $28,352

Most Popular Majors: Cinematography, Creative Writing, Radio/Television, Marketing, Dramatic Arts

*of 2400

Academics	B+	Guys	B-
Local Atmosphere	A+	Girls	A-
Safety & Security	B	Athletics	D-
Computers	B	Nightlife	B+
Facilities	B	Greek Life	D
Campus Dining	B+	Drug Scene	B+
Off-Campus Dining	A	Campus Strictness	A-
Campus Housing	A-	Parking	D-
Off-Campus Housing	B+	Transportation	B+
Diversity	D+	Weather	C-

Students Speak Out
ON ACADEMICS

Q "I think for a lot of the teachers, **teaching is their passion**. Many professors encourage students to come by their office, if not to ask questions about the class, then just to chat."

Q "Most of the professors are at least competent and **securely educated** in their subject matter. I have also had my share of arrogant, pompous professors who I would recommend staying away from. As for the classes, a lot of times I was surprised at how interesting I found them to be, but I was disappointed at times!"

Q "Teachers are on **both ends of the spectrum**. They're either engaging, excellent, and teach fun, interesting courses; or they are boring, painful to listen to, and don't seem to have much knowledge in the subject."

Q "Professors are amazing, but **very liberal**. It can be hard to think of the other side of the argument, because one voice is normally so prevalent in class."

STUDENT AUTHOR: Emerson is perfect for students who have always wanted to be on stage, writing the next bestseller, editing a magazine, or studying communication disorders. Classes are generally small. Very few are lecture size, and you'll never be in class with 100 students, as can happen at larger universities. When it comes to majors, don't come to Emerson without one. Though the college does allow students to enter undeclared, Emerson is so specialized, that it doesn't make sense to come without a strong desire to pursue.

Students Speak Out
ON LOCAL ATMOSPHERE

Q "There's lots of stuff to do—if you're a tourist. There are lots of **galleries and museums**. There's always something going on in the city. You just have to worry about if you can afford it."

Q "Cambridge is a lot more relaxed than Boston will ever be. Mass Avenue is a plethora of fun, with all the music venues and mixes of people. Shops like Pearl Art and Harvest Co-Op draw an **artsy, young crowd** that keeps the area fresh."

Q "It's Boston. Everywhere you look, there are college students. Sometimes it's kind of annoying, but it's also cool, because there are **tons of people to meet** that are close to your age."

Q "Emerson is seated in the heart of Boston's downtown area, right at the edge of the Boston Common (**a kind of Central Park, Jr.**) which has become Emerson's unofficial campus and a haven for underclassmen."

STUDENT AUTHOR: Filled to the city limits with colleges, Boston offers everything imaginable for entertainment. Because of the high numbers of young people, Forbes.com's 2005 survey rated the city number five in its list of best singles cities. The survey also voted Boston number one for best culture. From theater to live music, from sports to art, there is plenty to keep you occupied. Some say Boston's best shopping is located on Newbury Street. Replete with restaurants and high-end retail stores, Newbury Street attracts many tourists and locals looking to spend some cash.

5 Best Things	5 Worst Things
1 Student organizations	1 Administrative offices
2 WERS-FM	2 Campus comedy troupes
3 Creative students	3 The weather
4 Internship opportunities	4 Parking
5 Castle & LA programs	5 Fitness center costs ($$$)

Students Speak Out
ON FACILITIES

Q "The facilities are new and pretty, but small. The gym sucks. The facilities are feeling the crunch of **bigger incoming classes**, but they still manage. I'm sure it will be updated with the uber-pricey tuition here."

Q "To join the gym, you have to pay, which is ridiculous, since the school is so expensive. But overall, **the facilities are really nice** and well-furnished (whether they have computers or camera equipment)."

Q "I really like our gym. **It's definitely tiny** compared to a lot of schools I've been to, but there also aren't as many people working out here. The cool thing about it is that the classes are free (though you do have to pay gym membership), and the staff are professionals who know what they're doing and talking about."

Q "The Student Union is beautiful, and it will be sad when Emerson sells the Back Bay buildings, because they really provide a warmer atmosphere than the **new sterile buildings** going up on Boylston and Tremont Streets."

STUDENT AUTHOR: Emerson doesn't have a "traditional campus." This means that the campus is more or less integrated into the city, and that there are few fun and convenient facilities for students. Yes, there is a student union, but because it is across campus from where the classes are located, it's more for business than socializing. There's also a 10,000-square-foot fitness center, which houses treadmills, a couple rowers, some bikes, and Stairmasters.

Famous Alumni

Kevin Bright, Vin DiBona, Dennis Leary, Jay Leno, Richard Levy, Harvey Miller, Henry Winkler

Students Speak Out
ON CAMPUS DINING

Q "The dining hall is **the best I've been to** of all the cafeterias I visited at other Boston schools. The selection's always good, and the food is good quality."

Q "Try not to eat on campus—seriously. I'm amazed that, despite being two blocks away from Chinatown, **students rarely go there** for really good food."

Q "The food's very good compared to other schools. You will definitely get sick of it after living there for a semester, but Aramark is pretty good at giving us a **wide selection**. If you're a vegetarian or vegan, they often give a lot of alternative choices."

Q "For those of you who just have to have that weekly dose of tacos, but are so absentminded that you often find yourself taco-less by the end of the week, have we got a solution for you! **Taco Tuesdays**!"

Q "**Get the block meal plan**. It definitely seems worth it, because your time in the dining hall fluctuates each week. It seems stupid to lose your meals at the end of each week."

STUDENT AUTHOR: Plenty of students gripe about the dining hall, but that's because Emerson students like to complain. The meal plans are generous, and few students complain about not getting enough food. The dining hall is all-you-can-eat, which means if you run out of meals, you can always stay in the dining hall all day and keep eating for the price of one meal.

Student Body

African American:	3%	Male/Female:	43/57%
Asian American:	4%	Out-of-State:	79%
Hispanic:	7%	International:	3%
Native American:	1%	Unknown:	13%
White:	69%		

Popular Faiths: Emerson students are known for fearing holy water and all things religious.

Gay Pride: The campus welcomes gay and lesbian students.

Economic Status: Let's just say that the phrase, "Do you know who her father/uncle/mom/brother is?" isn't uncommon. Emerson students are loaded.

Students Speak Out
ON DORMS

Q "It depends on what you like. The older dorms, like **6 Arlington and 100 Beacon**, have originality because they are older buildings. The Little Building is newer and cleaner, but all the rooms look the same."

Q "The Little Building **feels like an asylum** after a while. It's big enough to allow students not to leave it for entire weekends (dining hall, fitness center)—which can be damaging to students."

Q "The dorms that are located in old brownstones are homey and comfortable, but with the school relocating all the classes across campus (across the Common) it's much easier to live in the Little Building, since **everything's right there**."

STUDENT AUTHOR: **Freshmen aren't required to live on campus, and they aren't even guaranteed housing. Those who send in their housing deposit by May 1 will almost always be assigned a bed, though the school occasionally has to put up some freshmen in the DoubleTree Hotel. Most Emerson students are the kind who look forward to moving off campus sophomore year anyway, and you should.**

Did You Know?
49% of undergrads live on campus.

Students Speak Out
ON GUYS & GIRLS

Q "It seems like there are a lot of different types of people at Emerson, **as far as styles go**. There are mod kids, or hip-hop kids, or indie rock kids. Okay, they're mostly indie rock kids."

Q "The guys are gay for a large part, and the girls like to hang out with them and date guys from other schools and graduate students. The remaining **guys are lonely**, or they have girlfriends from back home."

Q "It seems like there are lots of kids who look like they were on the **style fringe** in high school."

Q "They all **start to mix together**. Some guys act like girls; some girls look like guys. There's a good variety in both genders."

STUDENT AUTHOR: **Emerson's population likes to look good; though, "good" is a subjective term. There are some really well-dressed kids, who look good by anyone's standards, and some interesting styles that are attractive in their own unique way. On the whole, Emerson isn't a campus of slobs who roll out of bed and trudge to class, but this is probably because most students normally don't live on campus.**

Traditions

The Evvys
The Evvys is an annual awards ceremony, held in the spring to honor students who submit creative works.

Overall School Spirit
Emerson students have a quiet way of showing school spirit. In fact, many don't show any at all. But just because sports events don't rally school spirit, that doesn't mean that Emerson students aren't proud of their education and the opportunities they have to get their hands dirty in their particular field.

Students Speak Out
ON ATHLETICS

Q "As far as I know, **sports aren't big at all** on campus. The last that I heard, the basketball team held practice in the gym of a local high school, but maybe things have changed."

Q "**Lacrosse and soccer** for guys are the only sports I've ever heard anything about."

Q "**Sports aren't big here**. There are some great athletes, but they have clearly chosen academics over sports by attending Emerson."

Q "**I've never been to a game**, and it's not in the foreseeable future."

STUDENT AUTHOR: **The average student doesn't play varsity sports at Emerson, and chances are his or her friends don't either. In fact, it's possible that the average student doesn't even know that Emerson has sports teams. Though team members and their roommates, friends, and parents may attend Emerson's varsity sports events, there is very little awareness—and even less support—on campus. Without owning any fields, it's nearly impossible for Emerson to provide club sports, since the play spaces are rented.**

Students Speak Out
ON DRUG SCENE

Q "The cool thing about Emerson is that there are enough people who are **straight edge**, or rarely ever drink, that you can find some people to hang out with who want to stay sober."

Q "The drug scene is definitely more prominent than the Greek scene, but **you have to go off campus** to do anything."

Q "The drug scene on campus is **pretty quiet**. Students don't smoke weed in any of the buildings (aside from dorms), as a friend of mine who goes to another school said happened there on a regular basis."

STUDENT AUTHOR: **Emerson is not a haven for drug dealers or addicts. This is not to say that there aren't the occasional pot smokers and alcoholics. But what school isn't that way? While living in the dorms, it is very easy to avoid drugs. On the other hand, if you're looking for weed, you'll most likely be able to find it. There aren't many drug busts on campus; usually, students who get caught are in the Common while burning one.**

14:1	Student-to-Faculty Ratio
90%	Freshman Retention Rate
69%	Four-Year Graduation Rate
82%	Financial Aid Applicants Receiving Aid

Students Speak Out
SAFETY & SECURITY

Q "The **building security guards** don't seem to do anything. You just need to not walk through the Boston Common at night."

Q "The security guards at 100 Beacon Street definitely **get plenty of sleep while on duty** overnight, but the doors are locked, so nobody who doesn't belong will get in."

Q "The dorms at Emerson are pretty well guarded, and no one will be getting in without a valid resident ID or guest sign-in. **I always felt safe** at the school, but the police officers who work downstairs in the Little Building have been known for being rude and hard to approach. That is definitely a department within residence life that needs a bit of revision."

STUDENT AUTHOR: **Despite the fact that Emerson is located in the heart of a city, the campus is quite safe. Dorms are secure with sign-in procedures in operation 24 hours a day. Students must swipe their IDs before accessing residence floors, and all guests must be signed in and out.**

Questions?
For more inside information and survival tips, pick up College Prowler's full-length book on this school, written by an actual student! Check it out at www.collegeprowler.com.

Students Speak Out
ON OVERALL EXPERIENCE

Q "**I really enjoyed Emerson**. I just graduated, and I feel like Emerson really prepared me for the real world. It was much more interesting and creatively stimulating than the state school I transferred here from."

Q "Emerson is a great academic experience. Financially, I could have made wiser decisions about college. **My funding sucks**. It often feels as if people are just trying too hard socially, and that is irritating, but I would imagine that the 'traditional' college social scene would have been more maddening."

Q "**The Castle Program** was the most amazing semester of my life, and I'm very grateful that Emerson gives their students that opportunity to explore the world, and to get to know each other in such an amazing setting."

Q "Emerson has so much to offer, but you have to be willing to take advantage of everything to get your money's worth. You must make strong relationships with faculty in your department. You must **take advantage of the opportunities** to get involved in the student organizations, or create your own."

STUDENT AUTHOR: **From the professors, to the production equipment, to the classes, many students feel they're being well-prepared for the real world, at Emerson. Students here have more internship opportunities, well-known industry professionals as profs, and quality classes than many larger schools. Emerson students are matchless in their excitement to learn, and though it's common to boo-hoo about the weather, the dismal parking, and early curfews, most Emerson students are proud to call Emerson their temporary home.**

Emory University

201 Dowman Drive; Atlanta, GA 30322
(404) 727-6069; www.emory.edu

THE BASICS:

Acceptance Rate: 16%
Setting: Suburban
F-T Undergrads: 6,806

SAT Range: 1960–2240*
Control: Private
Tuition: $35,800

Most Popular Majors: Social Sciences, Business, Psychology, Health Professions, Biology

*of 2400

Academics	A-	Guys	B-
Local Atmosphere	A-	Girls	C
Safety & Security	A-	Athletics	C-
Computers	B+	Nightlife	B+
Facilities	A	Greek Life	B+
Campus Dining	C	Drug Scene	C
Off-Campus Dining	A	Campus Strictness	B-
Campus Housing	B	Parking	F
Off-Campus Housing	A-	Transportation	B-
Diversity	B	Weather	B+

Students Speak Out
ON ACADEMICS

Q "The classes and **professors are great**! They are truly one of the only reasons to stay at Emory."

Q "Some teachers are amazing, and **some are amazingly bad**. The best advice is to ask around upperclassmen to find out which teachers are best for you. Any senior can give you a great list of good and bad apples."

Q "The General Education Requirements make it so your first two years here can get **mighty boring**, but once you get into your major, that all changes. Upper-level classes are great."

Q "At Emory, **your grades hinge on class attendance**. If the teacher knows your face and you participate, it's a lot easier to work with them if you are having problems. Don't expect any teacher to help you if you never show up, though."

Q "Some teachers are **too interested in their own research** and writing to help the students, especially in the undergraduate business school."

STUDENT AUTHOR: **Academics are certainly Emory's strong suit, and they're the reason most students apply here in the first place. Many teachers and departments at Emory are nationally recognized, and some are award-winning. Emory's small enrollment and extensive class offerings make for small class sizes, especially in the arts and humanities. This can be a real blessing for students in terms of how much knowledge they get out of their classes.**

Students Speak Out
ON LOCAL ATMOSPHERE

Q "Everyone down here is so nice, you really do **get a glimpse into Southern culture** and hospitality living in Atlanta. There are some places to avoid, like downtown and anyplace in southern Atlanta."

Q "**Atlanta is great**, but you don't really realize that until after freshman year when you can have a car on campus. There isn't much interaction with the other universities in town, even though there are about 14 others."

Q "Emory is **isolated from the rest of Atlanta**, but this is a good thing in some respects. The school is a short driving distance from everything in the city, but the key word is driving. The public transportation is not that great."

Q "Atlanta has a huge population of African Americans and some really great culture. **The music scene is cool**, even though the radio sucks, and there is always a concert to go to."

STUDENT AUTHOR: **Atlanta has tons of things to do for fun, but the poor quality of transportation and Emory's isolation sometimes restricts students' social life. The atmosphere in the immediately surrounding town provides its own interesting dynamics. Emory is situated in North East Atlanta, about a ten-minute drive from Buckhead (a restaurant, club and bar district) and a 15-minute drive from Midtown and Downtown (more restaurants, major league sports, etc.). Overall, it's hard to beat such a young and vibrant city to spend four years in.**

<table>
<tr><td>

5 Best Things
1 Atlanta
2 The professors
3 The campus
4 Spring Band Party
5 Dooley's Week and Ball

</td><td>

5 Worst Things
1 Cliques
2 New Yorkers
3 Administration
4 Division III varsity
5 No football team

</td></tr>
</table>

Students Speak Out
ON FACILITIES

Q "Emory has some top-notch facilities. The gym, the libraries, and nearly all of the buildings are impressive here. **Anyone would be impressed** by the buildings on campus, which is why the tour here is such an easy one to give."

Q "This school's campus is so nice and perfect that they filmed the movie Road Trip here a few years back. There are constantly people working on the maintenance and upkeep of the campus, which is nice, but **the construction can be overbearing** sometimes. Overall, it looks like you go to school on a golf course or something."

Q "Emory's facilities are very impressive, and when you look at them and use them, you can really **see where all of the money** goes here."

Q "The facilities, like the newest one, Cox Computer Lab, are very nice and almost too nice sometimes. They make you feel like you are **going to a country club** and not a college."

Q "Everything about **Emory exudes money**, especially the facilities."

STUDENT AUTHOR: **Emory's facilities as a whole are very attractive and well maintained. Nearly every building's exterior is made of marble, and most feature beautiful terra-cotta roofs and copper fixtures. Emory's athletic facilities are some of the nicest in the entire Southeast. The baseball and soccer field have been described as a "joy to play on" by members of other schools' teams. In one word, amazing.**

Famous Alumni
Newt Gingrich, Kenneth Cole, Emily Saliers and Amy Ray (Indigo Girls)

Students Speak Out
ON CAMPUS DINING

Q "At first everything seems great because it is all so new, **but that wears off** after first semester, and when you come back, it seems like everything gets a lot worse."

Q "The food isn't amazing, but it is good enough that most girls put on around fifteen pounds their freshman year. There are **a lot of greasy options available**, and when those are your only options, you have no choice."

Q "To put things simply, **the food could be better** here. The DUC is mediocre and Cox is, too, and the other options are way overpriced."

Q "The cafeteria has a lot to offer, and the food's pretty good for college, but after eating anything every day for a year, you get really sick of it. We have **Chick-fil-A and Burger King** at Cox Hall, but it gets old."

Q "Food here is better than some other schools I've been to, but it could definitely **use some more variety**. It gets old real fast."

STUDENT AUTHOR: **At first, freshmen are excited by the idea of a food court featuring a Burger King and Chick-fil-A, but the excitement soon wears off. Freshmen are required to purchase a meal plan through the school, which allows them to eat a certain number of meals at the DUC, and provides a certain amount for eating at Cox or Dooley's Den at the Depot. Overall, the food on campus is just okay, but certainly livable, and provides just enough variety to get through freshman year.**

Student Body

African American:	10%	Male/Female:	45/55%
Asian American:	20%	Out-of-State:	70%
Hispanic:	4%	International:	8%
Native American:	<1%	Unknown:	7%
White:	51%		

Popular Faiths: There are a lot of Jewish people at Emory, so there are also a lot of Jewish groups.

Gay Pride: This campus is very accepting of gay students and teachers alike. There are safe zones for gay students, and also clubs, as well as the Office of Gay/Lesbian/Bisexual/Transgender Life.

Economic Status: Emory is very expensive, and most students do not have any trouble paying their tuition.

Students Speak Out
ON DORMS

Q "The dorms are all relatively new, and **all have air conditioning units** that keep you cool during the hot spring and summer months."

Q "Freshman dorms are overall pretty good. I really don't know about upperclass dorms, although Clairmont Campus is **getting pretty nice** with the addition of a huge pool and activity area."

Q "The dorms are nice, although it would be wise to check ahead, because some are larger than others and **location is key**—Turman is far from campus and Dobbs has really small rooms. I lived in Harris, which is an exceptionally nice dorm— big room, newly remodeled."

STUDENT AUTHOR: **As a whole, the dorms on Emory's campus are nice, but there is nothing all that special about them. Each dorm has its differences from the next, and some are better than others in terms of location, etc. Each floor has both a Sophomore Advisor and a Resident Advisor, both there to help you out and get you in trouble at the same time. The dorms on campus are some of the few Emory facilities that don't feel like a country club.**

> **Did You Know?**
> 66% of undergrads live on campus.

Students Speak Out
ON GUYS & GIRLS

Q "The guys are short, and the girls are pretentious and annoying. **Some are good-looking**."

Q "Because of the money here, there are some gorgeous girls. But keep in mind there is also a **ton of mediocre girls**, too."

Q "**People are in pretty good shape** at Emory, so a lot of guys and girls have nice bodies. The problem is that most of them don't have nice faces to match."

Q "I would say that **Emory is an average school looks-wise**. People complain about the girls, but it's just like anywhere else in my opinion, although a lot of girls dress exactly the same here."

STUDENT AUTHOR: The Emory student body rates at a six out of ten overall. Not horrible, but certainly not great either. Fashion is very important to many students at Emory, and it is noticeable when a new dress trend hits the school. The amount of money girls and guys spend on clothes can get ridiculous, but also helps the campus to appear more attractive at face value. Fitness is also very important to Emory students.

> **Traditions**
>
> **Bid Night**
> New fraternity pledges run down the Row to their chosen fraternities in the evening, a precursor to a raucous party night.
>
> **Songfest**
> A dormitory singing competition for freshmen during Orientation Week.
>
> **Overall School Spirit**
> Emory is not a very spirited school. Having no sports teams to rally around hurts school spirit.

Students Speak Out
ON ATHLETICS

Q "**No one cares** about varsity sports, but men's and women's tennis and swimming, baseball, and softball have been very successful."

Q "What varsity sports? **IMs are huge** and very competitive and allow for a range of skill levels to have fun."

Q "There is **no football team**! That is the worst thing about Emory, by far, bar none."

Q "Some of the teams are very successful here, yet no one seems to care. **IM sports garner more interest** than varsity. For instance, people read a weekly ranking of IM teams with more excitement than any report of varsity sports."

STUDENT AUTHOR: **Varsity sports are all but nonexistent here, an aspect of Emory that many blame school-wide apathy on. There is no football team at Emory. Intramural sports make up for the overall lack of sporty school spirit here. Competition between fraternities is the most exciting, and occasionally an independent group will offer up a great team as well. The great athletic facilities make playing IM sports here a joy.**

Students Speak Out
ON DRUG SCENE

Q "There are **a lot of kids who smoke pot** at Emory. I would say that pot is by far the most prevalent drug, although I hear there is a big underground cocaine scene."

Q "Emory is a school of well-functioning **habitual drug users** of all kinds—it's surprising how successful some students are."

Q "Lots of people smoke marijuana, and **everyone drinks**. Other than that, everything else is kept a secret. I'm sure there are some people doing hard drugs, but they keep that to themselves. Pot smokers and drinkers are very open about it."

STUDENT AUTHOR: Alcohol is by far and away the poison of choice for Emory students, with marijuana and pills coming in tied for second. The amount of money students have here definitely facilitates the drug scene, and especially contributes to the amount of students doing cocaine. Of course, some students choose not to do drugs at all, but they are not bothered or harassed for abstaining.

7:1	Student-to-Faculty Ratio
95%	Freshman Retention Rate
82%	Four-Year Graduation Rate
86%	Financial Aid Applicants Receiving Aid

Students Speak Out
SAFETY & SECURITY

Q "Security and safety are **really never issues** on campus, unless you get too drunk and get yourself into trouble."

Q "Emory provides blue safety lights, you can call an escort, and there are patrolling Emory Police. **Campus is well lit** at night. Also, Emory offers health services for your physical and mental stability and security."

Q "The security and safety on campus is **stellar**."

Q "The **campus is very safe**, with the occasional locker break-ins at the gym and some laptop thefts; but other than that, you can always feel safe here."

STUDENT AUTHOR: In a city with a sometimes-disturbing crime rate, Emory could not be any safer. Situated in a suburban enclave more than 15 minutes from any high-crime area, Emory's few crimes are primarily committed by students themselves.

> **Questions?**
> For more inside information and survival tips, pick up College Prowler's full-length book on this school, written by an actual student! Check it out at *www.collegeprowler.com*.

Students Speak Out
ON OVERALL EXPERIENCE

Q "Like most people I know, I went through my time of wanting to leave, or **not feeling comfortable**, but everyone has a niche to fill at Emory, and once I found mine, I never looked back."

Q "My experience at Emory has been like being attacked by a grizzly bear. It starts off bad and **only gets worse**."

Q "Going to Emory was the **best decision of my life**. I have met some amazing people and learned from some of the leaders and great thinkers in their fields. I was able to study abroad in Africa and learn from the diversity of Atlanta. Overall, I would recommend Emory to anyone."

Q "Emory, if you plan on being serious, can really hook you up. There is a great Career Center and also an alumni resource center where you can easily find jobs, and good ones at that. If you have drive here, **you will succeed** and come straight out of school with a great job waiting for you."

STUDENT AUTHOR: Overall, the Emory experience is a good one, albeit very interesting. Emory can be trying at times with its restrictive and sometimes uncooperative administration, cliques, and strange lack of diversity. It can also be very rewarding, with great teachers, classes, and a fun, lively city to explore. Finding your niche is the most important thing to do to ensure a good four years, and trying to avoid the rampant Emory apathy is solid advice as well. Overall, the Emory students receive an amazing education on a beautiful campus in a fun city, and there's a lot to be said for that.

Fashion Institute of Technology

Seventh Avenue at 27th Street; New York, NY 10001
(212) 217-7999; www.fitnyc.edu

THE BASICS:

Acceptance Rate: 43%
Setting: Urban
F-T Undergrads: 6,769

SAT Range: N/A
Control: Public
Tuition: $11,140

Most Popular Majors: Fashion Merchandising and Design, Advertising, Commercial Art, Illustration

Academics	A-	Guys	D+
Local Atmosphere	A	Girls	A
Safety & Security	B+	Athletics	D-
Computers	C+	Nightlife	A+
Facilities	B	Greek Life	N/A
Campus Dining	C-	Drug Scene	B+
Off-Campus Dining	A+	Campus Strictness	D
Campus Housing	B-	Parking	F
Off-Campus Housing	D-	Transportation	A+
Diversity	A-	Weather	B-

Students Speak Out
ON ACADEMICS

Q "The teachers are very interesting and extremely qualified for the job, since many of them have worked or still work in the industry they are teaching about. **Students at FIT hear first-hand experience about the industry** that they are going into."

Q "I love my classes because **my teachers really challenge me as the industry would**. They want to see how you will perform, and not just on tests and papers. They give you real-life projects that make you really work and prove your potential."

Q "**For the most part, I love all my classes**, especially the ones that are related to my major. The teachers are really great, and they get to know you on a personal level so that if you have any problems, you can approach them and actually get a response."

Q "**Don't waste your time at FIT if you don't plan on going to class**. You have to do your best here because there is a lot to be learned. Get in good with professors, and take advantage of the night and online courses."

STUDENT AUTHOR: **SATs and ACTs are not required for admission to FIT. The college focuses on a hands-on education for its students. With career preparation in mind, FIT offers internship and mentoring programs in many of its majors. The courses taught here offer real-life assignments. The projects you will work on are not just out of a textbook; they are real situations; the outcomes come to life once the project is complete.**

Students Speak Out
ON LOCAL ATMOSPHERE

Q "New students **should take advantage of the cultural and tourist attractions** around the city, though in moderation. Most people who've been here for a bit stay as far away from the touristy places as possible, as the novelty wears off quickly. Students should try to stay in the city for the summer, though, since it's a great time to be in New York, if you can stand the heat."

Q "New York City is crazy, fun, energetic, wild, and **safe despite what you read in the newspapers** or hear on TV—it really is safe."

Q "Parsons is the FIT rival, but you don't interact on a daily basis with them. You could go down to NYU, but **the students there are either snotty or have a frat mentality**. Visit whatever floats your boat. It's all here."

Q "Since living in the city, I have been given the opportunity to dip into so many people's cultures. **New York is almost like a bigger and better Epcot Center**. And as far as the trite expression goes, it really is the city that doesn't sleep. There is always something to do at literally any time of the day."

STUDENT AUTHOR: **FIT is located in Chelsea, one of Manhattan's most fashionable and trendy neighborhoods. Perhaps the best thing about New York City is that it can be many things to many different people. You can be a loner or a partier, and you will still fit in. Whether you love it for the business or the hustle, the culture or the challenges, New York City has something to offer everyone.**

5 Best Things	5 Worst Things
1 Real-world experience	1 Too many girls
2 New York City	2 Not a typical campus
3 Student-made clothing	3 Dry campus
4 Experienced professors	4 Cafeteria food
5 Small class sizes	5 No school spirit

Students Speak Out
ON FACILITIES

Q "**The classrooms and buildings need some remodeling**, especially the bathrooms."

Q "Some of the facilities are nicer than others. The computer facilities are really great, while the gym is comparable to the standard high school gymnasium. **There isn't a problem with any of the facilities**; just some have updated features, while others lag behind."

Q "FIT got a new cafeteria and bookstore, and both are pretty nice. The computer labs are modern, as well. **The school overall may seem a bit rustic**, but you can't judge a book by its cover."

Q "**I can't say much for the facilities**. There's a basketball court, locker rooms, and a closet-like space they call a gym. The computer labs are sufficient, though they're nothing special."

Q "The bookstore and cafeteria are remodeled, and both areas are pleasant spaces. The computer lab gets hot, but it's clean, and **the student center is small but friendly** and a great place for a commuter student to catch an in-between-class nap."

STUDENT AUTHOR: **Unlike many colleges in Manhattan, FIT's campus is contained within only two city blocks. There are no grassy areas or parks on campus, but Central Park is only a subway ride away. The Museum at FIT houses one of the world's top collections of costumes and textiles. FIT has a variety of other special facilities including a toy design workshop, lighting laboratory, and fragrance studio—all unique to the campus.**

Famous Alumni
David Chu, Nicky Hilton, Carolina Herrera, Calvin Klein, Michael Kors, Marti Galovic Palmer, Daniel Vosovic

Students Speak Out
ON CAMPUS DINING

Q "The food on campus has **gotten a lot better since they have opened the cafeteria**. Plus, this is NYC—if you want Greek, Chinese, or Italian, you can walk three blocks and get it any time of the day."

Q "**The food at FIT is overpriced**. You can get a huge slice of pizza for $2 up the street on 7th Avenue, rather than buying pizza from the cafeteria."

Q "There is only one cafeteria, the Retail Food Court. The food there is average; **some of the dishes are hit or miss**, although they do work hard to keep it vegetarian-friendly. There are plenty of delis, pizza places, Chinese places, and fast food restaurants in a three-block radius."

Q "There is a cafeteria, which is not too bad. There are fresh grilled foods and sandwiches. **Just don't plan on eating there every day**, because it can get pricey—unless you are stuck with the meal plan."

STUDENT AUTHOR: **FIT is unlike a traditional college when it comes to campus dining. A majority of the people found in the cafeteria are students forced into the meal plan because they live in a dorm room that does not have a kitchen. The typical types of college food are available here—pizza, fried foods, junk food—and gaining that Freshman 15 can definitely happen if they don't watch what they eat. Students have so many cheap options all over New York City that the cafeteria is the last place they tend to go to for food.**

Student Body
African American:	7%	Male/Female:	15/85%
Asian American:	10%	Out-of-State:	27%
Hispanic:	10%	International:	8%
Native American:	<1%	Unknown:	17%
White:	48%		

Popular Faiths: Religious choices vary from Catholic to Muslim to Judaism to everything in between.

Gay Pride: There is a large population of gay students at FIT. If you are uncomfortable with this scene, realize that FIT is also located in Chelsea, which is a predominately gay community.

Economic Status: Many students rely on financial aid, and FIT is cheaper than many other fashion schools.

Students Speak Out
ON DORMS

Q "Alumni rooms are nice since **you get your own bathroom and kitchen facilities**. Coed suites are great, too, since you only have one other roommate, and you also have your own bathroom and kitchen facilities."

Q "I guess if I were forced to live on campus, I would live in Alumni Hall. **The dorm is coed, and students live in mini-suites** with private baths and kitchens."

Q "The dorms are more about convenience; living right across the street from school has many perks. **Students that don't dress up are the ones that live in the dorms**—they roll right out of bed."

STUDENT AUTHOR: Convenience and location are the major perks of living on campus. The dorms also offer residents a chance to live in one of the most expensive neighborhoods in Manhattan for a fairly reasonable price. Students that live in the dorms are more likely to take advantage of the social activities that happen on campus. They inevitably end up meeting more friends at FIT compared to someone who commutes.

> **Did You Know?**
> 17% of undergrads live on campus.

Students Speak Out
ON GUYS & GIRLS

Q "There are a good number of girls who are models. **I've found that most of the girls date older, professional guys** rather than FIT guys. As for the male population, I'd estimate the guys are split in half between gay and straight."

Q "**Guys are either gay or extremely metrosexual**—meaning they are straight but have a lot of gay qualities—and only a few are straight without a girlfriend. The girls are pretty, and most dress to impress."

Q "Everyone is so different and original here. **There are the fake, prissy people, of course**, since it's a fashion-based school, but overall, there is no problem fitting in and meeting friends for life."

STUDENT AUTHOR: You will notice that in certain classes, there are only two guys, and one is most likely gay, while the other is straight. This means that the one straight guy likely has over 25 potential girls to hook up with! In fact, men that work in Manhattan sit near campus to eat lunch, hoping to meet a girl. You will see groups of guys in business suits talking to any FIT girl that gives them a chance.

> **Traditions**
>
> **Graduation at Radio City Music Hall**
> FIT students do not graduate in the school gym, they graduate in Radio City Music Hall.
>
> **WOW Week (Week of Orientation)**
> This is an orientation held for incoming students in the beginning of the fall and spring semesters. The students learn about FIT through planned activities.
>
> **Overall School Spirit**
> You will see students here wearing clothes with the FIT logo on them, but not many will wear anything that has do with the sports here.

Students Speak Out
ON ATHLETICS

Q "Apparently, **our basketball team is very popular**. One of the reasons why I love FIT so much is that there isn't a big emphasis on sports. If you hated high school for that reason, you'll love FIT."

Q "**I played on the basketball team here** and met a lot of great people. Most students at FIT that I meet don't know about the sports, so I have become used to telling them about them."

Q "FIT is only really known for their basketball team, and **that's the only sport anyone cares about**, unless they are on a team for something else."

Q "**Sports are not big at all**; although, there is a girl's basketball team and a dance team."

STUDENT AUTHOR: A majority of students here have no clue about the sports offered at FIT. Athletics are not a priority here. Ask a student if they are going to the basketball game, and they will look at you dumbfounded, maybe even thinking you are talking about the Knicks. It also may not help that there are mostly women here, since men tend to be more fanatical about sports.

Students Speak Out
ON DRUG SCENE

Q "I personally have never seen anyone do drugs on campus. But FIT is in New York, and it should be expected that **people want to come here to experience new things**."

Q "FIT may be **a dry campus and strict against drug use**, but if students want to take drugs or drink, they are going to do it anyway."

Q "**I haven't seen a big drug presence at FIT**, compared to other schools where I hear of students taking pills to cram for finals. FIT is more of a drinking and partying school, and that happens off campus."

STUDENT AUTHOR: Since the school is strict about drug use, anyone that is involved with them keeps it quiet. Those who admit to usage tend to pick marijuana as the drug of choice. The only students that have real issues with the strict drug rules at FIT are the ones who live in the dorms. Dorm residents caught using drugs are subject to academic probation and can, in some cases, be kicked out of the dormitory.

11:1	Student-to-Faculty Ratio
84%	Freshman Retention Rate
63%	Four-Year Graduation Rate
66%	Financial Aid Applicants Receiving Aid

Students Speak Out
SAFETY & SECURITY

Q "**Security is tight on campus**. No one is allowed in the buildings without a current FIT ID. I personally have never felt unsafe at school, and just about all the colleges in Manhattan operate security in a similar manner."

Q "Security is strong. You don't have to worry about random people or strangers coming off the street and being able to hang out on campus or in your dormitory. FIT has it together so that students feel safe while they are on campus. **I haven't worried once while here**."

Q "Out of the many universities I have visited, **FIT is one of the strictest, security-wise**. We have to show our ID when entering any building on campus, where in other schools, they only require an ID shown in computer labs or the library."

STUDENT AUTHOR: Security is tight at FIT. Students, faculty, and staff must show their ID when entering any of the buildings on campus. It can be a pain, but it makes sense to take these precautions when attending a school located in New York City.

Questions?
For more inside information and survival tips, pick up College Prowler's full-length book on this school, written by an actual student! Check it out at *www.collegeprowler.com.*

Students Speak Out
ON OVERALL EXPERIENCE

Q "FIT is the perfect place for me. **My classes are great and very insightful**. I don't feel pressure to be part of a social scene, yet I have made many great friends through school. FIT doesn't have a big campus life, but we have New York as our campus. I have developed a strong sense of independence, all while enjoying myself just about every day."

Q "FIT students all want the best industry education they can get, and they know that FIT is the school for them. **FIT students have an academic industry pressure on them** that many other university professors don't put on their students. FIT students strive for similar goals—to be the best in their desired fields and to be a step ahead of all the rest."

Q "**If you are interested in fashion, this is the place to go**! FIT has great programs that consist of creative and technical techniques. There are always costume exhibits on display."

Q "I had a great experience at FIT. **You can get as involved as you want to be** and really be included in some different on-campus communities, or simply get lost in the crowd. If you're goal-motivated and job-oriented, this is the place for you."

STUDENT AUTHOR: A majority of students at FIT are in agreement that they are receiving a quality education at a fair price in the best city. Most of the teachers have extensive knowledge of their industries and offer their students real-world experiences. The students that do have a negative view of the college tend to be the ones who are uninvolved and unsure of their career goals.

Florida State University

540 West Jefferson Street; Tallahassee, FL 32306
(850) 644-2525; www.fsu.edu

THE BASICS:

Acceptance Rate: 47%
Setting: Mid-sized city
F-T Undergrads: 26,378

SAT Range: 1110–1290*
Control: Public
Tuition: $17,171

Most Popular Majors: Business, Social Sciences, Family and Consumer Sciences, Education

*of 1600

Academics	B-	Guys	A
Local Atmosphere	B	Girls	A+
Safety & Security	B+	Athletics	A
Computers	B	Nightlife	B
Facilities	A	Greek Life	B
Campus Dining	C+	Drug Scene	C+
Off-Campus Dining	B	Campus Strictness	B-
Campus Housing	C	Parking	D
Off-Campus Housing	A-	Transportation	B+
Diversity	C	Weather	A-

Students Speak Out
ON ACADEMICS

Q "Florida State offers some of the best instructors in the nation. In my experience, classes for majors are taught by **the most competent faculty**, and you will get your money's worth once you're on track."

Q "Many of the teachers are wonderful, and of course, **some of them suck**. The truly good teachers obviously love what they are teaching, and their enthusiasm spills over onto the students."

Q "Of course, you have to watch out for the instructors in the lower-level classes. Some are good, and some are bad. The best thing to do is **ask around** when you register."

Q "Despite the party-school reputation, FSU professors are **serious about academics**. If you want to be challenged, this is definitely the school to attend."

STUDENT AUTHOR: **Academics are important at Florida State University, especially among the tenured professors. Don't expect to coast through the higher-level undergraduate classes. It's college; you're here for the academics, so expect to work hard. The consensus among the Florida State University student body is that the faculty is both easy to get along with and dedicated to its profession. The school has recently received recognition for a broad range of scientific research projects, and they have just created a new College of Medicine.**

Students Speak Out
ON LOCAL ATMOSPHERE

Q "The town I am in is very much a college town. Besides FSU, there is also FAMU and TCC. There is **a lot of partying and bar hopping**, but it would be nice if there was more to do (especially in the downtown area) other than party."

Q "Tallahassee is a Southern town, and off-campus, the attitude can tend to **run towards the conservative**, but it hasn't marred anyone's ability to have fun here."

Q "The beach, especially Panama City, is an hour and a half away, and there are a lot of parks and other recreations. **Florida A&M and Tallahassee Community College** are in Tallahassee, which makes for a lot of fun because the groups support each other."

Q "It's a small town. There are two universities and one community college, and when the students are gone, **half the town is gone**. It's a great place for law and social science majors, because it's the state capital."

STUDENT AUTHOR: **This is a Southern town, so expect things to move at a slower pace. However, don't be fooled into thinking that nothing happens here. Tallahassee is home to two universities and a community college, so there is a large student population present, and not with just FSU students. This means there are twice as many bars, parties, and other activities to keep the average student entertained. Just keep in mind that appearances can be deceiving, and there is more to do in Tallahassee than meets the eye.**

5 Best Things	**5 Worst Things**
1 FSU Seminole football	1 Student parking
2 Warm weather	2 Humidity in August
3 Fsu Flying High Circus	3 Airfare to Tallahassee
4 The "student bodies"	4 Bad roads near campus
5 Lake Bradford	5 Musty buildings

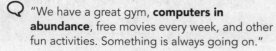

Students Speak Out
ON FACILITIES

Q "We have a great gym, **computers in abundance**, free movies every week, and other fun activities. Something is always going on."

Q "Everything is really nice. The only problem with FSU is that there is **a lot of construction** around campus all the time, as many of the buildings are being remodeled because they've been around for so long."

Q "Some of the buildings are really old looking. They look **kind of grimy**. The gym is nice, and we have a really nice stadium! Most of the facilities are decent."

Q "The Leach Athletic Center is **absolutely incredible**. The student center is nice, too. It includes a movie theater, lounge, coffee bar, study areas, and even the student counseling center."

Q "Several libraries offer resources and help for students, as well as **a comfortable place to get work done**."

STUDENT AUTHOR: **FSU has been actively remodeling and renovating older buildings on campus, as well as providing students with modern entertainment venues. The Student Life Building, which was recently completed, boasts a movie theater (showing a number of new releases each semester) and a Cyber Café. If exercise is more your style, then the Leach Recreation Center and Stults Aquatic Center are great places to break a sweat and check out the talent. At a school like FSU that offers an abundance of things to do, you have to try pretty hard to be bored.**

Famous Alumni

Alan Ball, Tara Christensen, Rita Coolidge, Lee Corso, Barabara Harris, Burt Reynolds, Richard Simmons

Students Speak Out
ON CAMPUS DINING

Q "The food court in the union is okay; **it's pricey** though. I don't really eat on campus if I can help it. I prefer some of the restaurants on the edge of campus. I get burned out on the same fast food menu every day."

Q "There are a couple of cafeterias on campus and a food court. It's enough, but the selection is not that great—**mostly fast food**. I also tried the meal plan my first semester here, but I didn't care for it. I'd rather make food for myself or scrounge off my roommates."

Q "If at all possible, **I suggest eating off campus**. It is more expensive, but your body will thank you."

Q "There are small snack and coffee stands littered through out campus where you can get lemonade or a quick junk-food fix before class. The **food is pretty good**; the Trading Post is a good convenience store."

Q "Some people will tell you that **they hate it**, but if you are the sort of person who adjusts easily to foods, you'll be fine."

STUDENT AUTHOR: **The food scene on campus has been steadily improving over the past several years, offering more choices and better quality than in the past. But still, it is cafeteria food and in no way can compare to the food your mom makes at home. You won't starve, but you won't be amazed, either. Most students will complain about on campus dining, but ironically, the restaurants and dining halls are usually busy.**

Student Body

African American:	11%	Male/Female:	45/55%
Asian American:	3%	Out-of-State:	11%
Hispanic:	12%	International:	1%
Native American:	1%	Unknown:	0%
White:	72%		

Popular Faiths: FSU is mostly Christian, but many other religions are also represented.

Gay Pride: While Florida State is in the south, both the FSU and the local community show a high degree of acceptance for alternative lifestyles.

Economic Status: The economic status of the student body varies, and FSU does a good job of bringing in students from all walks of life.

Students Speak Out
ON DORMS

Q "Dorms are pretty good, but it **depends on where you end up**. Some are renovated and some aren't. You just have to see for yourself to decide what you want."

Q "The more money you spend, the better the dorms. I stayed in Kellum my first year. That wasn't going to happen my sophomore year. The dorms here suck—**moldy, grimy, and nasty**."

Q "The quality totally depends—dorms like Dorman and Smith are nasty, while Salley and Murphree are nice. The other underclassman dorms **are pretty standard**."

STUDENT AUTHOR: **On-campus housing can be hit-or-miss. A small percentage of students love living on campus, where they have all the amenities of home and are close to their classes. Florida State is working hard to renovate the older dormitories and bring them all up-to-par with the newer facilities. As far as suggestions go, your best bet is to visit campus and see the dorms for yourself. If nothing else, dorm living is a great way to meet people and make friends.**

Did You Know?
19% of undergrads live on campus.

Students Speak Out
ON GUYS & GIRLS

Q "It's the Sunshine State, so you know there are some **fine women here**. There's just something about a nice tan that can drive a guy crazy! Girls I hang out with say the guys here are pretty hot, too, so I guess there's something for everyone."

Q "FSU is notorious for its beautiful people. Lots of 'blonde bombshells' from the beach, as well as **'Latin lovers'** from South Florida."

Q "There are beautiful men and women here. The guys are incredible, and there are so many different types to choose from. They are all gentlemen. The girls vary more so. They can be really sweet Southern belles, or they **can be snobby**, but they're the types of people you will find anywhere you go."

STUDENT AUTHOR: **Most students at FSU will admit that one of the more popular pastimes on campus is admiring the student body. The warm weather offers ample opportunity to bask in the sun. It also gives people a chance to show a little more skin. It can sometimes be distracting during the summer months, but you'd be hard-pressed to find someone that complains about it.**

Traditions

Planting of the Spear
Prior to kickoff, Chief Osceola, riding his horse, Renegade, gallops onto the field and plants a flaming spear at midfield to begin every home game.

Fountain Fling
Another demented tradition is skinny dipping in Westcott Fountain.

Overall School Spirit
School spirit is taken to the extreme at Florida State, especially during football season. Game days are completely nuts.

Students Speak Out
ON ATHLETICS

Q "Varsity football is the most popular, but FSU is a **very athletic campus** in all sports, including intramurals."

Q "Everything at FSU and Tallahassee revolves around the FSU football team. I never even cared for the sport until it sucked me in after the first year, and now **I try to attend every game**."

Q "Sports are crazy at FSU. We have some of the **best teams in the nation**. IM sports are easy to get into—there are tournaments between teams made up of people from dorms, frats, sororities, and just groups of friends getting together."

Q "Football and baseball are big. **Volleyball is pretty good**, as well."

STUDENT AUTHOR: **For varsity sports at FSU, football is arguably the biggest thing on campus. When fall rolls around, you can feel the excitement in the air. Tickets can be difficult to come by, especially for the big games, but everyone is usually able to attend the games they want. Florida State University prides itself on having one of the most competitive athletic programs in the country.**

Students Speak Out
ON DRUG SCENE

Q "Lots of drugs are available for those who want them. However, both the Tallahassee Police and **FSU Police are completely unforgiving** if you get busted."

Q "I'd say that more students abuse alcohol than drugs. **Heavy drinking** can be a problem, but I don't hear much about drug problems."

Q "There is a drug scene, though **it's kind of hush**. People don't walk around talking about it. If you use drugs, you won't have trouble finding them, but if you don't, you won't have to worry about being surrounded by the drug culture."

STUDENT AUTHOR: FSU has a very strict drug policy. While illegal drugs are present on campus, they aren't highly visible, and most students don't pay much attention to them. Alcohol and marijuana are the drugs of choice, although harder stuff, like ecstasy and amphetamines are available if you know where to look. Although some hard drugs are present, serious abuse is not a problem here.

21:1	Student-to-Faculty Ratio
89%	Freshman Retention Rate
48%	Four-Year Graduation Rate
55%	Financial Aid Applicants Receiving Aid

Students Speak Out
SAFETY & SECURITY

Q "Security and safety on campus is good during the day, but at night, I would advise you to always walk with someone else. **Never walk alone at night** on the FSU campus. It's just like any other big city."

Q "Not only does FSU have its own police department, but you also have the Tallahassee Police, **the Leon County Sheriffs**, and the Capital Police. It's a government town, so there's a lot of security."

Q "I've been here for four years and have yet to see any real trouble. There's usually petty crime and stuff, but **nothing serious ever happens** on campus."

STUDENT AUTHOR: Perhaps because Tallahasee is such a friendly town, people tend to take for granted that serious crimes rarely ever happen. Still, the University's Office of Safety and Security has done everything possible to ensure that the campus is extremely safe.

> **Questions?**
> For more inside information and survival tips, pick up College Prowler's full-length book on this school, written by an actual student! Check it out at *www.collegeprowler.com*.

Students Speak Out
ON OVERALL EXPERIENCE

Q "I think the school does an acceptable job—it is mostly dependant upon **how much you apply yourself** to your education."

Q "Overall, my time here at FSU has been like **one giant party**! If you value meeting people, great kegs, and a fun time, this is the place. It's a great college experience."

Q "I really like FSU, and it has been a **great experience for me**. Most people here seem to like it. It's a really beautiful campus with lots of activities."

Q "FSU is a quality school. They put a little too much emphasis on the football team, but other than that, I think **they have their priorities in line**. They are building a solid reputation as a research university, and as a science major, that means more opportunities for me to pursue. I highly recommend coming here."

STUDENT AUTHOR: You would be hard-pressed to find a graduate of Florida State University who doesn't have fond memories of the years they spent on campus. Current students will also agree that they are happy with their decision to attend school here. There is something for everyone, from athletics to academia, and you would have a hard time finding a more comfortable setting than Tallahassee. Although it bears the reputation of a party school, FSU also has a growing reputation for turning out some of the best and brightest graduates in the entire nation. Choosing which college to attend is not an easy decision, but if you're looking for the perfect combination of a good education and a good time, you can't do much better than Florida State University.

Fordham University

Rose Hill Campus; Bronx, NY 10458
(718) 817-1000; www.fordham.edu

THE BASICS:

Acceptance Rate: 47%
Setting: Urban
F-T Undergrads: 7,104

SAT Range: 1700–1990*
Control: Private
Tuition: $34,200

Most Popular Majors: Business, Social sciences, Communications, Visual/Performing Arts

*of 2400

Academics	B-	Guys	C+
Local Atmosphere	B+	Girls	B
Safety & Security	B-	Athletics	C
Computers	C	Nightlife	A
Facilities	C+	Greek Life	N/A
Campus Dining	D	Drug Scene	B-
Off-Campus Dining	A	Campus Strictness	D
Campus Housing	B	Parking	D+
Off-Campus Housing	B-	Transportation	A
Diversity	C	Weather	B-

Students Speak Out
ON ACADEMICS

Q "Try to **research your professors** before you register. There are some nightmare courses out there, but most teachers are awesome, really accessible out of the classroom, and stimulating inside the classroom."

Q "The theater professors are the best. They really form a community with the entire department and become your **friends and mentors**. As far as my core classes go, I can barely remember any of my professors' names."

Q "It's a shame. Professors here just **teach and go home**. I haven't really had any close relationships with any of mine."

Q "Make an effort to get to know your profs. They can seem really intimidating during class, but most are really friendly and open to helping students. Plus, most are working professionals in their area. They can land you **internships or even job connections** in the future!"

STUDENT AUTHOR: Many Fordham students find themselves surprised by the rigid nature of the core curriculum. Generally, students complete the core in their first two years of study while honing in on their chosen major. One of the most popular reasons for undergrads to come to Fordham is the school's size. The number of students in any given class rarely exceeds 25, making for a comfortable and open environment between classmates and professors. In terms of academics, both Rose Hill and Lincoln Center maintain impressive records.

Students Speak Out
ON LOCAL ATMOSPHERE

Q "Initially, I was really nervous about living in the Bronx, but now I love it. You'll feel completely safe inside the campus walls, and **outside isn't so bad** during the day."

Q "There's so much to do in the Bronx that I can go a month without **needing a Manhattan fix**. There are plenty of bars to hang out in."

Q "Outside the Fordham bricks, **the Bronx gets pretty real**. I think the neighborhood looks worse than it is, but at first, it's kind of shocking to see some of what you see."

Q "There are some advantages to living here. The **Bronx Zoo and Gardens** are a must-see, and the surrounding neighborhood has everything you need, but it's not quite New York City."

STUDENT AUTHOR: Although the Bronx may seem intimidating at first glance, most students come to embrace their neighborhood in one way or another. The campus itself is fairly self-contained, so those who ultimately feel uncomfortable outside Rose Hill's walls have little to worry about in the long run. Outside, however, is a bustling, lively area that offers a diverse mix of local businesses, popular bars, and national landmarks. Lincoln Center draws a good portion of its students based on its location. The campus stands right about where Midtown meets the Upper West Side. The Hudson River, Central Park, the Theatre District and Uptown Manhattan surround Fordham, giving students plenty of options when it comes to leaving the building.

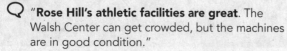

5 Best Things	5 Worst Things
1 Location	1 RH vs. LC campuses
2 Free theater	2 Student apathy
3 Free laundry	3 Lack of parking
4 Walsh Library	4 Poor food quality
5 Internships	5 Paying for RamVan

Students Speak Out
ON FACILITIES

Q "**Rose Hill's athletic facilities are great**. The Walsh Center can get crowded, but the machines are in good condition."

Q "If you go work out in the morning, then you'll **beat the crowd**. The worst time to go is at night after 7, especially when shows like *Sex and the City* or *The Sopranos* are on HBO. People come just to watch cable on the TVs."

Q "Athletics aren't bad, considering we don't have any sports here. It's nice to have **access to a free gym**, even if it just has a few treadmills and weight machines. You just hop in the elevator from the dorms to work out."

Q "Lincoln Center's gym isn't bad, since it's free, but **heavy-duty workout folks** seem to get really frustrated with it. I go more now that they put in TVs."

Q "The public bathrooms here are nasty. There's **never any toilet paper** and they always smell."

STUDENT AUTHOR: Lincoln Center and Rose Hill students offer very different takes on their respective school's facilities. Although some of the Bronx's buildings are over 100 years old, the campus remains in peak condition. It sometimes seems as if you can't turn around without a new renovation in the works. The entire Manhattan [LC] campus is contained in one 12-story building. Both are home to grassy areas that draw the sunbathing crowd (LC's Plaza is considerably smaller, though). Rose Hill's claim to fame is the Walsh Library, one of the most beautiful of any American campus.

Famous Alumni

Alan Alda, Patricia Clarkson, Bob Keeshan, Vince Lombardi, Dylan McDermott, Denzel Washington

Students Speak Out
ON CAMPUS DINING

Q "People really complain about the food, but we're in college. **We're not supposed to be eating gourmet**. You have something of a variety. I don't mind it."

Q "**The food here is gross**. I can handle the salad bar and anything prepackaged, but the cooking is greasy, slow, and bad. They use the same grills for everything, so vegetarians beware: that veggie burger is being cooked right where the cow left off."

Q "I **never eat on campus** if I can help it."

Q "Food at Lincoln Center is **awful and expensive**, but you really don't get much of a chance to eat it since the cafeteria is never open. There are no Sunday hours, and it's open Saturday until two, Friday until five, and during the week, it gets so crowded that you don't even have time to get something fresh."

Q "**Freshëns** is a welcome addition to the otherwise disgraceful cafeteria. It's expensive, but a smoothie beats the stuff they call food on the grill."

STUDENT AUTHOR: Rose Hill offers a modest variety of options, but students are still left unimpressed. The cafeteria (currently under renovation) at least allows for an all-you-can-eat style (though how much you actually want to eat is another matter). None of the eateries offer 24-hour dining. Lincoln Center fares even worse. Students have two dining options, both of which maintain absurd hours for normal, nocturnal college students.

Student Body

African American:	6%	Male/Female:	43/57%
Asian American:	6%	Out-of-State:	49%
Hispanic:	12%	International:	2%
Native American:	<1%	Unknown:	17%
White:	56%		

Popular Faiths: Catholicism and Judaism

Gay Pride: Despite what you might think about its Catholic affiliation, Fordham is extremely comfortable with homosexuality. Lincoln Center contains a high population of gay students, and both LC and Rose Hill have gay support clubs.

Economic Status: Fordham students are a mixed bag of economic backgrounds. There is a fairly high number of private school graduates, though.

Students Speak Out
ON DORMS

Q "**I guess they're roomy** compared to a lot of other colleges, but I wouldn't mind having more room. During my first year, I was crammed into a double with two other freshmen. That sucked."

Q "**Lincoln Center dorms are amazing**. My only complaint is that they're so self-sufficient that you don't really form a community with your neighbors. Since you don't share a bathroom, why go outside?"

Q "The dorms themselves are great, but Res Life is **the Gestapo of college**. They regulate the number of guests you can have, and of course, they try their best to keep you from having fun in every which way."

STUDENT AUTHOR: **Dorming at Rose Hill has its high and low points. Even the smaller, freshman buildings like Alumni North and South are of decent size, and the housing situations only improve with each Housing Lottery. Unlike Lincoln Center, Rose Hill's dorms create tight communities, something that's inevitable when sharing bathrooms is a necessity. Lincoln Center's apartments receive near unanimous praise, and at only 11 years old, the large suites deserve every word of it.**

Did You Know?
56% of undergrads live on campus.

Students Speak Out
ON GUYS & GIRLS

Q "As a female, the dating scene on campus sucks. We outnumber the guys, and most of them are gay anyway. Plus, our competition includes a **whole gang of dancers**. Go off campus to meet someone!"

Q "Someone's always throwing a party on Rose Hill, so there is an **opportunity to meet guys**. Too bad us girls have so much competition."

Q "Guys are **kind of jockish** here, and I'm not into that. The alternative ones seem to be taken, so I guess the dating scene is pretty bad."

Q "Just remember the cohabitation policy: you **can't check in members of the opposite sex** after 3:30 a.m."

STUDENT AUTHOR: **Lincoln Center females are easily frustrated by their overwhelming numbers on campus, and also the fact that a good number of the available males are gay. The lack of a social community doesn't help them either. Unfortunately, Rose Hill women tend to find mostly jock-and-beer men. The males at both campuses have it good. There is also a better variety of females, ranging from the "really, we do eat" dancers to the "really, we do date" liberal feminists.**

Traditions

Homecoming
This October Rose Hill event brings football and school spirit to its apex.

Spring Fling
Lincoln Center hosts this special spring day with a carnival on the Plaza.

Overall School Spirit
For a Division I school, Fordham's school spirit runs pretty low. Lincoln Center is proudest of its theatre and dance program, while Rose Hill students get so frustrated with their athletic teams' performances that it's difficult to maintain a high level of pride.

Students Speak Out
ON ATHLETICS

Q "I wish Lincoln Center had some kind of sports, even in intramurals. It would be a really fun way to form a community that **we're so lacking**. The most athletic we get here is playing Frisbee on the lawn."

Q "I like watching the games, but **I don't like buying tickets**. Especially since our teams aren't that good."

Q "I don't like that **so much money** goes into sports when nobody really cares about them, other than the people that play."

Q "Our football team has produced quite a few **professional players**."

STUDENT AUTHOR: **At Fordham College, sports are not necessarily a major part of student life. Any trace of athleticism is absent from Lincoln Center, while many Rose Hill students are merely bored by their school's poor athletic record. On the other hand, club sports are growing in popularity as they prove to be an enjoyable, low-stress alternative to the varsity world, as well as a distraction from the humdrum monotony of class work.**

Students Speak Out
ON DRUG SCENE

Q "On campus, drugs aren't really around, but off-campus, **there's definitely a scene**. This is New York, for Pete's sake. You won't find any needles on the street, but you can tell who is selling."

Q "There are **pot dealers on campus**, and everybody knows where they live—that's fine. They're not in anybody's way; they're just doing business for those that want it."

Q "Pot is kind of big here. Now that student smoking is banned from the dorms, I think residents are a little **more scared to smoke** inside, but it's still a college."

STUDENT AUTHOR: The two campuses offer different types of "drug scenes." Rose Hill houses numerous beer parties amid its buzzing social community, while Lincoln Center's festivities remain off-campus, usually at bars and clubs. Neither school has a significant drug problem, although students at both campuses admit that "if you seek, you shall find." Alcohol is, without a doubt, the University's biggest illegal substance.

12:1	Student-to-Faculty Ratio
90%	Freshman Retention Rate
76%	Four-Year Graduation Rate
80%	Financial Aid Applicants Receiving Aid

Students Speak Out
SAFETY & SECURITY

Q "**I've never felt in danger** at Fordham. I used the late-night escort van once, but I've never felt like I needed supervision walking at night."

Q "**Safety is good—too good**. You can't really sneak guests in after sign-out times, which can be annoying. There really isn't much nightlife on the [LC] campus itself, so once you go out, you just have to use common sense."

Q "Living in the residence hall is like living with a really **nosy mother**. The Res Life's favorite rule is the cohabitation policy, which prevents students from having guests of the opposite sex stay overnight. All you have to do is get someone else of the same sex to get a pass for you, but it's a hassle, though."

STUDENT AUTHOR: The long-debated, Catholic-founded cohabitation policy at Fordham is rigidly enforced, although students that sign in guests of the opposite gender without signing them out ultimately pay a mere $15 fine (hence giving way to Fordham's occasional nickname, "The Cheapest Hotel in New York").

Questions?
For more inside information and survival tips, pick up College Prowler's full-length book on this school, written by an actual student! Check it out at *www.collegeprowler.com*.

Students Speak Out
ON OVERALL EXPERIENCE

Q "The professors are awesome here, especially once you talk to them after class. **You can learn a lot** from the professionals alone. That's the best part of the Fordham experience."

Q "**This isn't your typical college**. We don't have frats or even a main social gathering point. The LC community is what you make of it, and there are times when I wish I was more involved here. I got a great education and am really happy and proud to go to grad school next year."

Q "Fordham isn't bad, but there's a lot I think can be improved. The administration doesn't always treat you like an adult. **Individuals can get shafted** if they don't know the right people. Classes are good, but some of the core requirements are just too much."

Q "I was disappointed with the level of academics here, but I found **a lot of resources outside** the school to be extremely helpful. I interned at a major network and made some big connections that way. So, if nothing else, Fordham opened a lot of doors for me."

STUDENT AUTHOR: Neither Rose Hill nor Lincoln Center offers the traditional college experience. The Jesuit tradition, the core curriculum, and the vital location of Fordham define the school's base foundation as a hands-on liberal institution. Once you split the University, you'll discover two different worlds: the green community-feel of Rose Hill and the urban buzz of Lincoln Center. At Fordham, the small class sizes create a tight-knit intellectual community. Classes are not about lecture notes, but about the students and how they interpret and mold their educations.

Franklin & Marshall College

415 Harrisburg Avenue; Lancaster, PA 17604
(717) 291-3911; www.fandm.edu

THE BASICS:

Acceptance Rate: 36%　　**SAT Range:** 1230–1390*
Setting: Small city　　　**Control:** Private
F-T Undergrads: 2,055　　**Tuition:** $38,580

Most Popular Majors: Business, Government, English, Biology

*of 1600

Academics	B+	Guys	B
Local Atmosphere	C-	Girls	B
Safety & Security	B	Athletics	C
Computers	B	Nightlife	C-
Facilities	A-	Greek Life	A-
Campus Dining	B	Drug Scene	B-
Off-Campus Dining	B	Campus Strictness	B-
Campus Housing	D+	Parking	C
Off-Campus Housing	A-	Transportation	D
Diversity	C-	Weather	C+

Students Speak Out
ON ACADEMICS

Q "My teachers have been inspiring. They have enriched my life. Classes have been interesting for the most part, especially when teachers **abandon the traditional lecture format** and engage us in dialogue, discussion, and use multimedia."

Q "As for the classes, I try to take what I'm interested in, so **I usually find them interesting** (naturally). Why suffer through honors calculus if your passion is the current lifestyles of aboriginal Australians, or vice versa?"

Q "The professors are generally rather passionate about their pursuits and definitely take the time to talk to students, get people engaged, and make plenty of time for office hours and appointments. I have had several profs who took an active interest in me beyond my grades, and **we have become good friends**."

Q "I have loved all of the government classes I took. The teachers were interesting, and also interested in what the students had to say. They **always encourage discussion, and also debate**, which is what really made the classes interesting."

STUDENT AUTHOR: Although all teaching styles may not appeal to all students, most students feel that the quality of education they're receiving at F&M is very high. Academics are top-notch here at F&M, with steep admission requirements and devoted faculty at the top of their fields.

Students Speak Out
ON LOCAL ATMOSPHERE

Q "**Lancaster is actually a really cool place** despite what a lot of people say. I have recently met some wonderful non-F&M people that I definitely don't want to lose touch with."

Q "In Lancaster, we explore art galleries every First Friday, see shows, shop, enjoy the outlets, tour the Amish farms, go bowling, and laser bowling. **I have never been left with nothing to do**!"

Q "I've been wandering into town on 'adventures' and **I have fallen in love with the city**. With five schools in the area counting us (Millersville, E-town, the Lancaster School of Art, Steven's Technical College, F&M), there are a lot of young people around."

Q "I don't really like Lancaster because I don't feel that the school and the community are close. I think that some of the Lancaster residents consider us rich, spoiled kids and **don't give us much of a chance**."

STUDENT AUTHOR: Lancaster is no New York City in terms of its theater, but the local downtown theater, Fulton Opera House, is nationally known to be of extremely high caliber. There's plenty for students to do around town, but local college-town relations have traditionally been strained. The James Street Improvement District is busily building relationships and helping students and "townies" get along better. But there are a few more fences to be mended.

5 Best Things

1 Cricket matches
2 Frisbee on the Quad
3 The professors
4 The wireless network
5 Coed halls

5 Worst Things

1 The football team
2 The mascot (Diplomat)
3 Attacking squirrels
4 Complaining students
5 Student apathy

Students Speak Out
ON FACILITIES

Q "The facilities are nice and updated; **I have no complaints**."

Q "The ASFC (Alumni Sports and Fitness Center) and computer workrooms are kept orderly and clean. **The student center is also a big hangout** for most students, and it's comfortable."

Q "**If you're into the arts, you're in luck**! We've built a gorgeous theater, the Roschel Center for the Performing Arts. This is on top of the Barshinger Hall and puts musicians, singers, dancers, and actors in seventh heaven. It's too bad, of course, that they didn't allot funds to staff the new building; the Department of Theater, Dance, and Film stretched its staff's resources to the limit to run the Center in its first year."

Q "These two performance centers have been built to **help strengthen the arts at a very science-focused school**. The chemistry, biology, and geology departments have typically been the most popular and most heavily-funded departments on campus, with excellent resources."

Q "Construction has been heavy on campus, and the administration is tirelessly **looking for new ways to improve the campus**."

STUDENT AUTHOR: **A number of new student buildings have popped up over the last decade, and students love the new spaces. Expect to see construction nearly constantly, but then again, that means that students will have new buildings pop up around them each year.**

Famous Alumni

James Lapine, Franklin Schaffner, Roy Scheider, Glen Tetley, Treat Williams

Students Speak Out
ON CAMPUS DINING

Q "The new changes on campus are great. The overall appearance of the dining facilities, specifically the dining hall are wonderful. They **bring a new life to a part of the campus** that was in dreadful need of repair."

Q "The food is, in all honesty, okay. The first week you're there, you think, this isn't so bad, and then **you stop attempting to be overly cheerful** about cafeteria food. You also learn to avoid the dining hall on weekends, as it is worse than normal."

Q "**There is a lot more variety** on campus than there once was. The dining hall serves more options and of better quality, particularly their produce."

Q "I am definitely glad I live off of campus and can **cook for myself now**."

Q "All I can say is that I definitely liked the food. Instead of gaining the Freshman 15, **I did the Freshman 25**. But, now that I'm starting to play sports again, I feel a little better about it all!"

STUDENT AUTHOR: **Although most agree that the food is better due to recent changes, with a larger variety and a better presentation, many seem to feel that the trade-offs in terms of space just haven't been worth it. However, the changes at the dining hall are heralded with more optimism. Hopefully, as the school gathers feedback on the changes, they will make a corresponding shift in practices.**

Student Body

African American:	4%	Male/Female:	51/49%
Asian American:	4%	Out-of-State:	61%
Hispanic:	4%	International:	8%
Native American:	<1%	Unknown:	8%
White:	72%		

Popular Faiths: Judaism, Catholicism, Protestantism, Islam, Unitarian Universalism, Orthodox Christianity, and Buddhism: we've got it all!

Gay Pride: The gay scene on campus is decent for a fairly conservative campus. The LGBTA (Lesbian, Gay, Bisexual, Transgender and their Allies) is active.

Economic Status: The students at F&M tend to be sheltered, suburban, and well-to-do.

Students Speak Out
ON DORMS

Q "Avoid all the dorms—they are all awful. Weis is probably the nicest of them all. The Bens are the worst, but they all are bad. They are small, ugly, and have bathrooms that are far away and halls that are too big. But **it's just a place to crash**; it's not that important."

Q "The dorms are like the food—not bad. But I feel that **it really depends on your hall** to make or break the dorm experience for you."

Q "The rooms are generally on the smaller side, and the furniture isn't so great, but it's not uncomfortable or poor. The kitchens suck in the sense that they only have a microwave and you can't actually cook in them. **The bathrooms are all communal**, which can be good or bad depending on whether it's coed or single gender."

STUDENT AUTHOR: **Many students stay on campus happily all four years at F&M. Many who choose to leave the dorms do so for special-interest houses or the West James Apartments. The special interest houses are a wonderful option for community living.**

> **Did You Know?**
> 99% of undergrads live on campus.

Students Speak Out
ON GUYS & GIRLS

Q "I think we're a smoking bunch honestly, and in all the shallowness I can muster, **there are no hideously deformed people** on campus. Something to keep in mind."

Q "**Dating on campus is very conservative**. It seems like all the guys are looking for someone to marry, which can be a lot of pressure on an independent, college-aged woman. There is a good deal of random hooking up, but any dating relationship seems to get very serious, very fast, and is generally overly traditional."

Q "The **preppy look is in** here, just flip through the pages of J.Crew and Gap and you'll see F&M students in it."

STUDENT AUTHOR: **Few students can complain that there are no hot prospects. The girls complain that the guys are self-involved twits, and the guys complain that the girls are self-absorbed airheads, but they continue to go after each other. Hot is relative—we'll never be at UCLA for the sun-bronzed hotties, but we're pretty content with our contents.**

> **Traditions**
>
> **Ben-in-the-Box**
> Late at night, young coeds urinate at his base as an initiation rite of sorts. Don't touch the statue!
>
> **Flapjack Fest**
> The day before finals, FSA serves breakfast all day while teasing scholars about their upcoming exams.
>
> **Overall School Spirit**
> Dips get rallied for basketball games, but few other sports. Of course, we'll wear F&M gear until the cows come home (never an idle threat in Amish country), and that's good enough for most of us.

Students Speak Out
ON ATHLETICS

Q "Varsity sports are kind of in-between. People go to the games, especially basketball, but **life does not revolve around them**. IM sports are also kind of in-between. People play them and people watch them, but they aren't all dominating or anything."

Q "I personally haven't attended varsity sporting events. However, a lot of students do go to basketball games. As for IM sports, **rugby is very popular**, and I, like many students, usually attend these games."

Q "Basketball is big **cause they win**."

Q "**We have varsity sports**?"

STUDENT AUTHOR: **And although several teams at F&M have winning seasons, the relatively low profile of varsity sports on campus limits the number of spectators. One-third of the guys play a varsity sport, and one-fourth of the women do. The number of intramural players is higher than that. Dips certainly aren't lumps of inactivity, even if they aren't the most spirited fans!**

Students Speak Out
ON DRUG SCENE

Q "**There's a lot of drinking**, weed (although it seems a lot more visible freshman year), and blow (cocaine)."

Q "**I was surprised** to see how big the problem was."

Q "Pot is more common than coke, and Ritalin or Adderall abuse is even more common than pot use (in my experience). But, all-in-all, the drug scene is one that's very avoidable. No one's going to force them down your throat. In fact, **you probably won't even see it** unless you go looking for it."

STUDENT AUTHOR: F&M runs an intense anti-drug campaign, but statistics on posters don't discourage the truly committed. By far, the most common drug on campus is GHB: the date-rape drug. Girls—watch your drinks. This is a problem at any campus—F&M's Red Zone program tries to make first-year women aware of their risk and make sure that they have the resources they need to find help, if necessary.

11:1	Student-to-Faculty Ratio
91%	Freshman Retention Rate
79%	Four-Year Graduation Rate
84%	Financial Aid Applicants Receiving Aid

Students Speak Out
SAFETY & SECURITY

Q "Safety and security . . . well, they try hard. Mostly they ride around on their bikes and let kids in their rooms if they've been locked out. However, to be fair, **I feel a lot safer if i'm walking home late** at night/early morning, and I see them posted around campus."

Q "**I have never felt unsafe** at F&M; I feel that the public safety people do a pretty good job."

Q "You always see security walking around campus, or even riding bikes down the nearby streets that some students live on. Plus, the campus security car is **constantly circling the roads around campus**. So overall, I feel pretty safe. I've never personally had a problem, and hope that it stays that way."

STUDENT AUTHOR: Over the past couple years, the Department of Public Safety has more than doubled. F&M is near a not so good neighborhood where muggings have been known to occur, although the rise of public safety officers has dramatically curtailed this risk.

> **Questions?**
> For more inside information and survival tips, pick up College Prowler's full-length book on this school, written by an actual student! Check it out at *www.collegeprowler.com*.

Students Speak Out
ON OVERALL EXPERIENCE

Q "So far, my experience has been amazing. Through my activities, I have found some of the most wonderful people ever, and I feel **I have grown a lot as a person**."

Q "I've loved my experience at F&M. I've made great friends, I've learned a lot from my professors in and outside the classroom, and had many great opportunities. **I wouldn't trade my college for the world**."

Q "I love it here! I wouldn't be a tour guide here in the middle of the summer **if I didn't love it**!"

Q "I enjoyed being in college and F&M itself was okay. I do wish that I was somewhere more liberal. I feel that the students and faculty here are **not as open-minded as the school portrays** them to be."

STUDENT AUTHOR: However much they may complain, Fummers love it here. Once they've found their niche, they're the happiest little bunch of workaholics you'll ever meet. The most usual F&M experience follows a pattern: as you come to know the school, you get to know people, and your initial high hopes are met with reality. After a brief stint of disillusionment and dissatisfaction (this bit is optional), you'll come to recognize the wonders of F&M and meet the people whom you will hopefully stay close with, and you'll close out your experience having grown both academically and socially. Not a bad job for your four years!

Furman University

3300 Poinsett Highway; Greenville, SC 29613
(864) 294-2000; www.furman.edu

THE BASICS:

Acceptance Rate: 57%   **SAT Range:** 1760–2050*
Setting: Small city   **Control:** Private
F-T Undergrads: 2,678   **Tuition:** $34,048

Most Popular Majors: Political Science, History,
BusinessAdministration, Biology, English

*of 2400

Academics	B	Guys	B
Local Atmosphere	B	Girls	B+
Safety & Security	A	Athletics	B-
Computers	B+	Nightlife	C
Facilities	B+	Greek Life	A
Campus Dining	B+	Drug Scene	A
Off-Campus Dining	B+	Campus Strictness	C
Campus Housing	B	Parking	B+
Off-Campus Housing	C+	Transportation	C-
Diversity	D-	Weather	B+

Students Speak Out
ON ACADEMICS

Q "Overall, I've found the professors to be extremely helpful and interested in their subjects. On the average, **they are passionate** about their material and work hard to inspire that same passion in their students."

Q "The teachers at Furman are generally helpful, attentive, and knowledgeable. The **small classes are great** because professors know their students' individual scholastic abilities and their personalities."

Q "I found that both the professors' knowledge of their field, and their **desire to help students** set Furman professors apart from others I have studied under."

Q "Almost all of them love to take **one-on-one time with their students** and encourage visits to their offices. I have been to one of my teacher's houses for dinner, and I know that is not a rare occurrence at Furman."

STUDENT AUTHOR: Furman prides itself on the high level of personal attention each student receives from professors. Many choose to work at Furman over larger, more research-oriented schools because of their strong commitment to teaching undergraduates. While professors are required to hold office hours everyday, most are available whenever students decide to drop by to discuss a project or just to chat. This consistent quality of educators makes for a broad base of strong academic departments in every field of study.

Students Speak Out
ON LOCAL ATMOSPHERE

Q "Greenville's downtown is my favorite thing about being a Furman student—Main Street has **hundreds of places to go**, from restaurants to stores, and there are always concerts and other activities on Friday nights."

Q "The town has a Southern feel, and **everyone is pretty friendly**. I see it as a mix of urban, suburban, and rural. Furman is close to downtown, local neighborhoods, and mountainous areas."

Q "There are **a few other universities here** but nothing that rivals Furman's prestige. We're the big cats here, and the University gets a lot of attention from the community and media."

Q "The atmosphere in Greenville is **'buckle of the Bible Belt' meets cosmopolitan downtown**. Although it seems somewhat schizophrenic, this duality is a nice balance that allows you to enjoy what both sides have to offer."

STUDENT AUTHOR: For a city of its size, Greenville has much to offer. There is an array of restaurants and interesting cultural activities. Although Greenville does not have a college-town atmosphere, students don't seem to mind. The friendly Southern tone makes it an inviting place to live. Although many students find it difficult to venture out of the Furman bubble during their freshman year, as soon as they immerse themselves in the downtown atmosphere, they will wish they had done it sooner.

5 Best Things	5 Worst Things
1 The lake	**1** Parking tickets
2 Professors	**2** Dating scene
3 The president	**3** Winter term
4 Freshman halls	**4** Rain
5 Academics	**5** Homogeneity

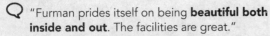

Students Speak Out
ON FACILITIES

Q "Furman prides itself on being **beautiful both inside and out**. The facilities are great."

Q "Everything on **campus is the best** you could ask for from a university. I'm very pleased with all of the services that the University provides."

Q "Furman has **great athletic facilities** for a school of its size. Even the club teams have good fields to practice and play on. The computers offered are relatively new and fast, and the student center is pretty modern."

Q "The best thing about campus facilities is that you **can walk or bike to almost all of them**. The Student Center is nice and has a decent variety of food and a small movie theater where the student activities board hosts free movies. The PAC is also nice and has a good selection of workout equipment and a pool."

Q "Overall, I think the facilities are nice. Nothing compares to the **natural beauty of the lake** and trees, but the buildings are well kept."

STUDENT AUTHOR: Furman's campus is known for its beauty. The lake, bell tower, rose garden, fountains, and traditional architecture create a picturesque and idyllic setting. The facilities offered are remarkable for a university this size. The Physical Activities Center, has a large gym with a climbing wall, indoor pool, and workout facility. The student center perpetuates Furman's reputation for having the atmosphere of a Southern country club. It houses the bookstore, post-office, copy-center, food-court, theater, and coffee shop.

Famous Alumni

Beth Daniel, Brad Faxon, Herman W. Lay, Keith Lockhart, Dottie Pepper, Dick Riley, Charles Townes

---

Students Speak Out
ON CAMPUS DINING

Q "I have **no complaints about the food**. There are many options, and there is always the trusty salad bar if the options are not suitable."

Q "The only problem is that after about eight or nine at night, there is **nowhere on campus to get a meal**, although the Wendy's drive through is only about five minutes off campus."

Q "The food is good, **it just gets repetitive** and boring after a while."

Q "There is only one dining hall at Furman. That's good because it's **a great place to socialize** and see everyone, but it's bad because it's often a bit crowded, especially during lunch time."

Q "Don't let others mislead you; Furman's food is **some of the best you will find** in a university setting. Every college student complains about the food at their school; however, students who complain at Furman should be ignored. Furman's food is some of the most innovative and healthy I have ever experienced."

STUDENT AUTHOR: Eating anywhere every day will get old, and the same is true with dining at Furman. There are really only two places to eat, the Dining Hall and the Pala Den food court, but each offers a wide variety of food. Dining Services truly tries to serve the students by giving them what they want. There are comment cards that students can fill out, and some things really do get changed. A problem is there are no places to get food on campus after 9 p.m., an early hour in the life of a student.

Student Body

African American:	6%	Male/Female:	43/57%
Asian American:	2%	Out-of-State:	71%
Hispanic:	1%	International:	2%
Native American:	<1%	Unknown:	0%
White:	90%		

Popular Faiths: Most religious groups on campus are some variation of Christianity.

Gay Pride: Furman's (openly) gay community is small. There are organizations, such as FLAG (Friends of Lesbians and Gays), whose presence on campus is remarkably visible.

Economic Status: True to its country-club atmosphere, most students are upper-middle-class.

Students Speak Out
ON DORMS

Q "Compared to other schools, the **dorms are large and nice**. There are two areas, South Housing and Lakeside Housing, and the rooms are bigger in South usually."

Q "Guys would probably prefer to live in South housing. It's closer to the gym and to the athletic fields—and so would girls who like those boys. Lakeside housing is good for those who'd like to **focus a little more on their studies**, especially freshman year."

Q "The dorms are nice, and it is especially nice that **suites are offered to freshmen**."

STUDENT AUTHOR: All freshmen and sophomores live in the dorms, and most students feel that this is a valuable part of connecting with other students. There are few complaints about Furman's dorms. While many cringe at the community bathrooms, others are glad to live in a place where the bathroom is professionally cleaned everyday, and they force freshmen to interact with their hallmates. The social atmosphere of dorm life seems to overshadow most shortcomings of the dorms themselves.

> **Did You Know?**
> 90% of undergrads live on campus.

Students Speak Out
ON GUYS & GIRLS

Q "There is definitely the prototype Furman girl and Furman guy. They're **preppy, and overall, pretty attractive**. Most are very nice."

Q "Furman has an **unusually attractive** student body. People work out all the time and generally dress rather well for classes."

Q "Some are hot, some are not. It just depends on what you think is hot. There's **not a lot of dating** on campus, just groups of people hanging out."

Q "The guys are preppy and portray themselves as **complete gentlemen**. And overall, I would say the people at Furman are incredibly nice."

STUDENT AUTHOR: Whether running around the lake or heading to the mall, Furman students work hard to keep up their appearances. But even without all the work, Furman has attractive people. Everyone seems to admire everyone else's polished conservative style. The girls seem to stay in shape so they can fit perfectly into their Banana Republic chinos, and the guys have a conservative frat look.

> **Traditions**
>
> **Beach Weekend**
> Students skip Friday classes one weekend every May and head to the beach.
>
> **President's Picnic**
> During Orientation Week, the entire freshman class is invited to a barbecue picnic on the lawn of the president's house.
>
> **Overall School Spirit**
> While Furman may not have as much school spirit as other schools, most are full of pride. With an acronym like FU, it's not difficult to have school spirit.

Students Speak Out
ON ATHLETICS

Q "Lots of people go out to the football and soccer games, but for some reason, no one is really a die-hard fan until they come back as alumni. You see them all get really **crazy and excited**."

Q "Intramural sports at Furman are great. There are several **levels of competition** and a lot of good players."

Q "Most of the **dorm halls create their own teams** and compete just as competitively as the fraternities and sororities."

Q "Varsity sports are not as big as at large public universities, but the **quality of our teams is incredible for the size** of the student body."

STUDENT AUTHOR: Football gets the most attention on campus and has the best turnout, but the soccer and golf teams are also very competitive. Intramural and club sports have a strong presence on campus with a high level of participation. Students actually seem to get more excited and competitive about their intramural team than varsity sports. Furman's teams are great for a small school. They just need more support.

Students Speak Out
ON DRUG SCENE

Q "There really is **not a big drug scene**. If anything, pot is used occasionally, but nothing more than that really."

Q "The drug scene on campus is remarkably small, although **one can easily find pot**, and sometimes cocaine, at off-campus parties or residences."

Q "There are drugs on campus, but they are much **less common than on other campuses**. They are easy to avoid because there is no pressure to try. In fact, if you want drugs you really have to look for them because they aren't around very often."

STUDENT AUTHOR: **As it turns out, the squeaky clean image that Furman students project is more than just an image. Drugs are a difficult thing to find on Furman's campus. Many students say they know of one or two people who use drugs, but a large majority have never even seen an illegal substance on Furman's property. Although there are drugs around, their users are hardly numerous enough to have an actual "drug scene."**

12:1	Student-to-Faculty Ratio
92%	Freshman Retention Rate
77%	Four-Year Graduation Rate
76%	Financial Aid Applicants Receiving Aid

Students Speak Out
SAFETY & SECURITY

Q "**I never feel at risk or in danger** on Furman's campus. I would trust that if I left my wallet somewhere accidentally that it would be returned to me safely."

Q "Furman's **Public Safety goes overboard** sometimes, writing underserved tickets and things of that nature. Many times, they seem to be overzealous, almost on a power trip."

Q "On the whole, **the campus is pretty secure**, and I don't have a lot of qualms about walking by myself at night. That doesn't mean incidents don't happen, but it's very rare. It's such a small campus that Public Safety can intervene quickly should something happen."

STUDENT AUTHOR: **About half of students never lock the doors to their rooms during the day or at night. Security may not be as tight as it is on other campuses, but that's because there isn't a need. Serious crimes rarely happen on campus. Public Safety maintains a visible presence on campus.**

Questions?

For more inside information and survival tips, pick up College Prowler's full-length book on this school, written by an actual student! Check it out at *www.collegeprowler.com*.

Students Speak Out
ON OVERALL EXPERIENCE

Q "**I absolutely love it**, and I'm totally happy. I never had second thoughts about being here, and I have never wished I was anywhere else. Really, it never crossed my mind. I love Furman."

Q "I was shocked at first by the 'Bible Belt' mentality that everyone seemed to have, but you learn to **find your own niche**. There are people who are not so conservative, and then you learn how to appreciate the ones who are. Learning how to overcome those differences had been a great life lesson."

Q "Furman is an **incredible place to explore** your calling and to find enjoyable people to join you on your journey."

Q "I knew that Furman was a place where I would get a **great education** and make excellent friends. I was right, and I couldn't be happier that I stuck it out. I have incredible friends and professors, and a major that I couldn't be more excited about. The trick is to throw yourself into the new experience and get involved quickly."

STUDENT AUTHOR: **Although it's not for everyone, the ones who decide to attend usually find it a great match. The academic programs at Furman are a huge draw. Students appreciate the quality of education they are getting and the personal attention they get from their professors. It's true the Furman bubble may seem out of touch with the real world at times. But despite a few complaints, no one seems to want to leave. Furman students love to talk about why they love their school.**

Geneva College

3200 College Avenue; Beaver Falls, PA 15010
(724) 846-5100; www.geneva.edu

THE BASICS:

Acceptance Rate: 68%
Setting: Suburban
F-T Undergrads: 1,639

SAT Range: 940–1210*
Control: Private
Tuition: $20,300

Most Popular Majors: Theology and Religion, Human Resources Management, Elementary Education

*of 1600

Academics	B	Guys	C+
Local Atmosphere	C-	Girls	B-
Safety & Security	B+	Athletics	C+
Computers	C	Nightlife	D
Facilities	C	Greek Life	N/A
Campus Dining	C+	Drug Scene	A
Off-Campus Dining	B	Campus Strictness	D
Campus Housing	B	Parking	B+
Off-Campus Housing	D+	Transportation	C-
Diversity	D-	Weather	C+

Students Speak Out
ON ACADEMICS

Q "**The majority of teachers are exceptionally student-friendly**. Oftentimes, students can find a better friend in one of their teachers as opposed to their classmates."

Q "It can be argued that one of the best qualities that Geneva offers is its professors. Not only are these individuals extremely knowledgeable and passionate concerning academia, but **they also employ deep personal connections** with their students."

Q "The teachers I have had for class had different expectations as far as following the syllabus, reading, and turning in assignments. **Each professor has their own teaching style**, and it is up to you to adapt to it. I found my classes interesting. With each class, whether economics, Bible, or biology, I saw how each subject was connected, especially in a Christian atmosphere."

Q "Geneva profs are fantastic, overall. I'm a senior English major, and **I've loved most of my classes**. Besides being fountains of knowledge, and besides really making me think, they give helpful advice and really care."

STUDENT AUTHOR: **Academics at a liberal arts school focus primarily on developing a worldview. Being that Geneva is a Christian institution, all the classes are focused on developing a Christian worldview. This is not to say that Geneva does not foster an environment conducive to all beliefs, but Christian values are definitely mainstream.**

Students Speak Out
ON LOCAL ATMOSPHERE

Q "The atmosphere surrounding Geneva is **a very diverse one, to say the least**. Unfortunately, it seems that the area in which Geneva is located is laden with great struggles."

Q "It seems that every attempt I make to engage the community reveals to me that **there is an invisible wall** between Geneva College and the Beaver Falls community. I am aware of some of the poverty problems that exist within the community, as well as some of the areas downtown that you don't want to visit at night."

Q "I honestly think **if the College wasn't here, the town would become deserted**. But there are plenty of other places to go, like Pittsburgh, Cranberry, and Monaca to escape the confines of Beaver Falls."

Q "Beaver Falls does not have the most pleasant atmosphere. It is an old town with nothing to do. **If you travel about 10 to 20 minutes, you can go to Chippewa, Beaver, or Monaca**, where there are malls, restaurants, and a movie theater. There are no other colleges in Beaver County besides community college."

STUDENT AUTHOR: **First, Geneva is not a party school, and the policies prohibit a party atmosphere even off campus. When you do have free time, there is almost nothing to do without a car. However, most students at Geneva have a car, so finding a ride to Monaca (for the mall and Starbucks), Cranberry (for wings), or the local Wal-Mart is not a problem.**

5 Best Things	5 Worst Things
1 Committed professors	1 Strict dorm policies
2 Parking	2 Limited facilities
3 Online registration	3 Small student body
4 The student body	4 Humanities core classes
5 Student activities	5 The town of Beaver Falls

Students Speak Out
ON FACILITIES

Q "They're **adequate, but nothing to write home about**. The facilities are functional, but there are not a whole lot of them to use. The Student Center is the only place to go to study besides McCartney, and there aren't many hang-outs."

Q "**Facilities aren't Geneva's forte**, but overall, they're certainly adequate. It seems like the bigger the school, the better the facilities tend to be, but also the less personal they are."

Q "What is here isn't bad, but **there is not enough to go around**. The cardio machines are always full, and the benches are always full. They need more equipment. Also, Old Main is beat. They have built some new buildings; other than that, it is adequate for a small liberal arts college."

Q "The facilities on campus, like the Student Center or field house, are **not the most attractive places, but you learn to look past it**."

Q "The facilities on campus are nice. **They are well-kept, and the hours are acceptable**. While there are limits to the different activities available (for example, there is no pool table in the Student Center), there are great places to study or shoot some hoops with friends."

STUDENT AUTHOR: **Geneva has made a conscious effort to improve the aesthetics of campus life. They recently renovated Clarke and Pierce Halls and the Student Center, and they installed new building markers to aid students and guests in more easily locating their campus destinations. Still, Geneva's facilities grade is low because of its biggest problem: the lack of them.**

Famous Alumni

Cal Hubbard – the only athlete ever to be inducted into the pro football, pro baseball, and the college football halls of fame

Students Speak Out
ON CAMPUS DINING

Q "The dining halls (Alex's and the Brig) certainly get old after a while, but **they do have pretty good variety**. Also, you can use meal points at a local pizza joint, which is good eatin'."

Q "I don't care for any of the food the school meal plan provides. **It is always fatty and gross**. There are some amazing desserts, though. It's like Willy Wonka's here—ice cream and cake flowing all around. And it shows—there are girls and guys bustin' out all over."

Q "The food is pretty good. There are two spots on campus to eat, and both can be visited and charged to the student meal plan by using an ID card. **The food is not gourmet, but it is possible to maintain a healthy diet**."

Q "I guess, for a college campus, the food in the dining hall is pretty decent. **There is a different meal for lunch and dinner every day**, and they always have lots of ice cream and desserts. The Brig is a cool place to eat and hang out. You can grab your food to go or eat it there."

STUDENT AUTHOR: **When you first get to school, the variety of food is overwhelming. Alexander's offers unlimited ice cream, its dessert bar is inviting, and the various wrap and pizza stations are a dream come true. However, after a couple of weeks, your dreams turn to nightmares, and you are stuck with the same choices day in and day out. The Brig is the only other option for on-campus dining. It is a nice change of pace, but the Brig's options are limited as well.**

Student Body

African American:	9%	Male/Female:	42/58%
Asian American:	1%	Out-of-State:	27%
Hispanic:	1%	International:	1%
Native American:	<1%	Unknown:	0%
White:	88%		

Popular Faiths: At Geneva, 86 percent of the student population is Protestant.

Gay Pride: There is no gay activism on campus. Although there may be an isolated homosexual here or there, rarely does anyone "come out" on campus.

Economic Status: The majority of students fall in the middle-class range.

Students Speak Out
ON DORMS

Q "I have never lived in the dorms. However, I think that they are pretty nice and **the sense of community-building that takes place** is very apparent."

Q "The apartments are the best places to live; however, **you need to have that freshman experience in the dorms**. I would suggest Memorial or McKee, and request a bottom floor so you don't have to haul everything upstairs. After that, room 103 Geneva Arms is the best for guys. It is the only big, four-man apartment for guys."

Q "**The dorms are decent**. There is not one that is really bad or one that is really good."

STUDENT AUTHOR: Campus housing has a list of policies that are taken seriously by the school. If you are caught breaking policy there will usually be some form of repercussion. These policies include violating open hours (dorm visiting hours for the opposite sex), drinking, smoking, or drug use. The strictness of the staff is unfortunate, but it is something that comes with attending a Reformed Presbyterian school.

Did You Know?
69% of undergrads live on campus.

Students Speak Out
ON GUYS & GIRLS

Q "**Guys play video games; girls go tanning**. I think video games and fake tanning are very hot."

Q "The guys are guys. **There are many hot guys, and not so hot**. Unfortunately, lots of times the hot ones are rather lacking in the personality and character arena, while the not-so-hot ones are more often the personable ones. I suppose that's just the way it goes."

Q "There are some hotties here, but there aren't a whole lot. The ones that are more attractive get picked up quickly. There are a good number of average girls. **Guys and girls alike are into keeping their virginity**, so there are a lot of stressful nights on campus."

STUDENT AUTHOR: At Geneva, the focus is mostly on inner beauty, which isn't all that bad. Frequently, you'll find a very attractive girl with a physically sub-par guy, but it's likely that they both have a deep, spiritual connection. The majority of students at Geneva are average, but there are handfuls of cute guys and girls, with a few knockouts. Overall, guys and girls at Geneva are looking for a soul mate, not a hookup.

Traditions

Midnight Breakfast
The night before finals, the faculty serves breakfast to the student body.

Midnight Madness
The basketball teams' season kickoff. Usually, there is a dunk contest and other fan activities.

Overall School Spirit
The Golden Tornadoes do not have a huge following. Of course, there are diehards here and there, but school spirit is kept at a low level. Students do have Geneva hoodies and T-shirts, but that is about it.

Students Speak Out
ON ATHLETICS

Q "Until coming to Geneva, I never even heard of the NAIA. **If you're looking for a big sports school, Geneva isn't the place for you**. The school does offer some decent intramural programs, and attending sporting events can be fun when there's nothing else to do, but the school spirit is really lacking."

Q "**The biggest varsity sports on campus are football and basketball**. Geneva offers a lot of intramural sports, as well, that people can get involved in."

Q "Personally, I think intramural sport are more popular than varsity sports. **Most of the students participate in intramural sports**, whereas most of the varsity games are not attended by the students."

STUDENT AUTHOR: Being that Geneva is not a NCAA Division-I powerhouse, students don't expect the athletic program to provide never-ending excitement. During football season, a good number of students attend the home games. Intramural basketball and indoor soccer are definitely the most popular.

Students Speak Out
ON DRUG SCENE

Q "Very rarely do you see or hear about drugs on campus. Since most of the students have strong religious beliefs, **drug use is looked down upon** and therefore isn't very prevalent."

Q "**There are people on campus who do drugs**, but I do not know how prevalent drug use is, so it must not be that prevalent."

Q "The drug scene is present, but **it is not visible**. Very few individuals partake in this activity."

Q "Geneva has **a no-tolerance policy for drugs and alcohol**. You are not allowed to do them on campus."

Q "Let's just say **even if you're high on life, it's not allowed!**"

STUDENT AUTHOR: **If you want to be exposed to drugs, as with anywhere, attending enough parties will subject you to casual drug use. However, at Geneva, there are few incidents of drug use on campus. Most students at Geneva avoid using drugs altogether—at least the illegal kind.**

14:1	Student-to-Faculty Ratio
76%	Freshman Retention Rate
45%	Four-Year Graduation Rate
85%	Financial Aid Applicants Receiving Aid

Students Speak Out
SAFETY & SECURITY

Q "Security is pretty much non-existent, although **there isn't much need for concern at Geneva**. Although there isn't a lot of security presence, I'd say most students feel safe."

Q "The security on campus consists of a group of older gentlemen equipped with flashlights and personal transmitters. Don't allow this fact to induce concern. **The fact is that this is all that security needs!** Geneva is located in an area in which very little security is required."

Q "**The campus is very quiet.** Occasionally, there is a security concern after dark, but the security staff is available, and there is an organization of college men who escort women to and from classes after dark, if they so desire."

STUDENT AUTHOR: **There are few places I've felt more safe at than Geneva's campus. Students often leave computers unattended, don't lock (or even close) room doors, and are generally pretty trusting of their student body. Geneva is an open community where everyone trusts each other.**

Questions?
For more inside information and survival tips, pick up College Prowler's full-length book on this school, written by an actual student! Check it out at *www.collegeprowler.com*.

Students Speak Out
ON OVERALL EXPERIENCE

Q "My Geneva experience has definitely been one to remember. I've made some great friends that I intend to keep for life. **I cannot imagine choosing a different school**. It was hard to adjust to college life, but Geneva did a pretty good job aiding in that transition."

Q "**Overall, I have had a positive experience with Geneva College**. This has mostly stemmed from the personal investment that many members of the faculty and staff have openly made so that my time in school would be a positive time of learning and growth. I do not wish that I was somewhere else."

Q "Sometimes I wish I were at a different school because **Geneva does not have a lot of things that other schools have**, but the people here are genuine, and it's nice to be in that kind of setting."

Q "My overall experience has been great at Geneva. **If you're looking for a place to be challenged in every area of your life** and have a great time while you're at it, Geneva's a good choice."

STUDENT AUTHOR: **Obviously there are the aspects of Geneva that few people like, such as the food, some aspects of the administration, the policies, and the parking, but overall, Geneva is a safe place to go for an opportunity to have the best four years of your life. If you get involved, continue traditions, start some of your own, join some clubs, and partake in the student activities—your experience will be a positive one. Geneva is an open community that flourishes on the good of man and whose members come together to support one another.**

George Washington University

2121 Eye Street NW; Washington, DC 20052
(202) 994-1000; www.gwu.edu

THE BASICS:

Acceptance Rate: 37%
Setting: Urban
F-T Undergrads: 9,654

SAT Range: 1800–2070*
Control: Private
Tuition: $40,392

Most Popular Majors: Social Sciences, Business/Marketing, Psychology, English, Health Professions

*of 2400

Academics	B+	Guys	B-
Local Atmosphere	A	Girls	B
Safety & Security	C+	Athletics	C
Computers	B-	Nightlife	A-
Facilities	A-	Greek Life	B-
Campus Dining	A-	Drug Scene	B
Off-Campus Dining	A-	Campus Strictness	B-
Campus Housing	A	Parking	D-
Off-Campus Housing	C	Transportation	A
Diversity	C+	Weather	B-

Students Speak Out
ON ACADEMICS

Q "I don't think academics at GW are much harder than high school. I do the bare minimum for most of my classes and still have a 3.9 grade point average. You learn that for some classes or professors you really need to do all of the reading and assignments, but for others you really **don't have to do anything**—not even show up for class."

Q "The required courses are pretty boring, but the classes I have to choose from are really interesting. The teachers are **hit or miss**. I tend to get a lot of professors with very thick accents, which makes learning harder."

Q "Teachers vary—as a freshman, you will be in a lot of large, impersonal classes, but as you move into upper-level courses, they get better. Professors are very knowledgeable in their subject matter. They are accessible to answer your questions during their office hours, and they are especially **good with e-mail**."

STUDENT AUTHOR: GW requires freshmen to take a significant number of General Curriculum Requirements (GCRs), so history majors may have to suffer through "Baby Bio," and pre-med students may be forced to plow through art history. Most undergrads agree that as they move into more specialized classes, professors are more engaged in the subject matter and more experienced in their fields. The University's location in the heart of Washington allows for top experts in every field to teach a course or two at GW.

Students Speak Out
ON LOCAL ATMOSPHERE

Q "There are **tons of things to do** in DC—take in a show at the Kennedy Center, party, go for monument walks, see museums, visit historical sites, listen to different political speakers. The atmosphere is very political, obviously."

Q "DC is **very eclectic**. There are people from all different backgrounds, ethnicities, religions, and socio-economic situations. There are lots of colleges and young professionals in the area."

Q "DC is amazing. There are lots of college kids and other young professionals in town. There is so much to do and **so many opportunities**, but you definitely have to make an effort in order to benefit from such opportunities. Some people think DC is really dangerous, just being in the city and with terrorism concerns, but if you are careful and smart, it's not a problem."

Q "DC is a **great place to go to school**. It's certainly a city, but in a very real sense, it has the qualities of an intimate town. It's the most unique gathering of people and ideas I've ever experienced. Some parts of the city are sketchier than others, so make sure you know where you're going when you get on the Metro."

STUDENT AUTHOR: With government officials working nearby, the school often seems to blend into the city, but GW's five-by-six block radius definitely feels like a traditional college campus. The University's close proximity to bars, clubs, museums, national monuments, sports arenas, and theaters exposes students to the entire experience that is DC.

Students Speak Out
ON FACILITIES

Q "Facilities are pretty nice. In fact, I would say they're **too nice**. This is a flaw—our University spends too much money on image and not enough on functionality."

Q "I absolutely love the campus facilities. The **student center is the best** I've seen on any other campus, the main computer centers are all of the newest quality, and the athletic facilities are accessible to everyone. But if you are on a sports team, traveling to the Mount Vernon campus for the main fields can be a hassle."

Q "One of the best things about GW is that it is **constantly building new facilities** for the students, and they are always beautiful. Several years ago, the University built a state-of-the-art gym with basketball courts, a track, squash courts, and workout rooms. It also recently built a new location for the School of Media and Public Affairs (SMPA) and finished a new International Affairs building. The student center is very modern and clean."

Q "Facilities are **top-of-the-line** at GW. I just wish they would put more money into academics and less into building new facilities."

STUDENT AUTHOR: GW students have always griped that the University spends too much money on facilities and goes overboard when renovating or building new structures—the infamous "Gold Pillar" in the Marvin Center is a perfect example of the University's extravagance—but no one complains when using brand new equipment in these multimillion-dollar structures.

Famous Alumni

Arnold "Red" Auerbach, Abby Joseph Cohen, Kent Conrad, Edward Liddy, Abe Pollin, General Colin Powell, John Snow, Mark Warner, Scott Wolf

Students Speak Out
ON CAMPUS DINING

Q "Food's okay. I am not a huge fast food fan, and we have a lot of that, but there's **a ton of options** because we are in DC."

Q "They really try to give students lots of food options at GW. Because there are tons of spots around GW's campus to grab a sandwich or a bagel, they are **constantly changing the menus**. The dining halls at GW are only located in the freshman dorms. Sometimes they have visiting chefs come in and cook dinners, but other than that, they aren't that good."

Q "As a freshman, **you can survive** eating campus food for the majority of the year. But for upperclassmen, Chipotle on F Street is a cheap yet tasty break, the shops at 2000 Penn have some good restaurants, and going to the special Tuesday meals on the Mount Vernon Campus are worth the trip. On special Tuesdays, lobster, steak, and assorted visiting chef meals can be served."

STUDENT AUTHOR: Although some universities work on a "meals per week" plan, GW's system is a little different and much more convenient. At the beginning of the semester, freshmen and others living on campus must purchase a meal plan, which works as a declining debit card. Extra points are carried over from the fall semester to the spring semester, but not from the spring to fall. Students like the convenience of GW's meal plan—no one tells them what to eat or when to eat it, and the variety of options is decent. One common complaint: a lack of healthy options.

Student Body

African American:	6%	Male/Female:	45/55%
Asian American:	10%	Out-of-State:	98%
Hispanic:	6%	International:	4%
Native American:	<1%	Unknown:	11%
White:	62%		

Popular Faiths: There is a relatively large Jewish population. Several Christian organizations as well as Muslim and Sikh groups also exist.

Gay Pride: The student body is very open and friendly toward the active and present gay community. Several groups exist on campus.

Economic Status: Several students complain about all the "rich kids" who like to show off their money.

Students Speak Out
ON DORMS

Q "Dorms are awesome. Stay in the ones that have your own bathroom in the room. Freshman year, almost everyone lives in Thurston, the party dorm. **HOVA is really nice** because it's an old Howard Johnson. Sophomore year, you can live in the Dakota, but it's impossible to get into. But if you can, they're awesome apartments. After that there's New Hall and E Street, but pretty much all other dorms are nasty, small, and dirty."

Q "All the dorms on campus are really nice in comparison to other schools. As a freshman, **you'll want to be in Thurston**. It's the most fun by far."

Q "With a few exceptions, the **dorms here are like palaces**."

STUDENT AUTHOR: GW's dorms are definitely some of the sweetest in the country—the majority of them are converted apartment buildings or hotels, or recently-built facilities. About half of the freshman class will live in Thurston Hall, GW's largest dorm. Because of its reputation as a "sexually active party dorm," most residents either love it or hate it, with the majority loving every minute.

> **Did You Know?**
> 64% of undergrads live on campus.

Students Speak Out
ON GUYS & GIRLS

Q "I love everyone at GW because they are so diverse. However, many of the **hot guys** at GW are actually gay. It's something to keep in mind."

Q "The biggest secret about GW is that a lot of the students are Jewish, so sometimes it's a little bit of a religious question when dating. The guys, overall, are pretty nice and definitely hot. The girls are pretty nice. I will admit that there are some really **stuck-up girls**, but there are some good people at GW."

Q "Lots of people on the campus are **very snotty and pretentious**. It's hard to get over people like that, but you will find them everywhere. But DC is a great place for meeting people, so you never know!"

STUDENT AUTHOR: The best word to use when describing guys and girls at GW is "average." You'll find very good-looking guys and girls and less attractive individuals, but most students fall in the middle of the spectrum. You have to pick your way through the self-absorbed guys and stuck-up girls, but many GW students are worthy of your friendship. More than looks, people's passion for the activities in which they are involved make them desirable.

> **Traditions**
>
> **Commencement on the Ellipse**
> Unless there are severe weather conditions, GW students graduate on the Ellipse in front of the White House every year.
>
> **Midnight Breakfast**
> Each fall and spring during finals, the University hosts a Midnight Breakfast at the Marvin Center. There are also games and activities to help students de-stress.
>
> **Overall School Spirit**
> Because GW athletics are not overwhelmingly popular, school spirit is definitely lacking.

Students Speak Out
ON ATHLETICS

Q "GW is Division I athletics, but we do not have a football team. For the most part, people attend basketball games, but usually not other sports. **Intramural sports** are relatively popular. GW also offers one-credit exercise and sports activities classes in everything from squash to horseback riding, golf to weight training."

Q "I'm not the most athletic person, but even I realize that GW is really **lacking on spirit**."

Q "GW's best varsity sport is women's gymnastics, but nobody here really cares about that. The biggest varsity sport at GW is basketball and the games can be fun, but most of the student body here is **pretty much apathetic** toward sports. Being an urban school with a lack of greenery and a football team might have something to do with it."

STUDENT AUTHOR: GW is not a sports enthusiast's dream come true. At GW, there are opportunities to play and watch sports, but if early morning tailgate parties before jam-packed football games is what you crave, then you'll be better off looking elsewhere.

Students Speak Out
ON DRUG SCENE

Q "I have heard there is a cocaine problem on campus, but I don't know much about it. There is **a lot of pot** and some ecstasy that I know of, but I'm not sure what else. If you are looking for it, it's there, and if you are trying to avoid it, you can—I have for the past four years."

Q "I think you will find what you are looking for. If you just want to drink, you will find those friends. If you want to smoke, you can find friends that do, too. Anything more? There are people into that. You can **avoid what you want** to, as well as find what you are looking for."

Q "Drugs are there if you want them, but they're not the center of social life, per se. A lot of kids smoke weed and **some particular groups do use coke**. Ecstasy is not very popular anymore, and harder stuff is around but not big."

STUDENT AUTHOR: **Alcohol is the most popular "drug." GW students love getting drunk; many are taken to the GW Hospital each week. Harder drugs are definitely not as visible as alcohol, pot, and study drugs.**

13:1	Student-to-Faculty Ratio
90%	Freshman Retention Rate
73%	Four-Year Graduation Rate
80%	Financial Aid Applicants Receiving Aid

Students Speak Out
SAFETY & SECURITY

Q "I can honestly say that **I feel safe** on campus. I often walk around at night alone. However, there have been incidents of robberies and violence at GW. We live right in a city, so it's something to think about. You definitely need to have street smarts."

Q "I feel very safe on campus. In all the freshman dorms, there are cameras everywhere. There are security guards at the desk to make sure that only GW students and their signed-in guests are entering the dorm. I would say that, all in all, the campus is pretty safe, with some isolated **instances of crime** . . . The campus provides minivan and shuttle transportation at night. The area where GW is located, Foggy Bottom, is one of the nicer and safer areas of DC."

STUDENT AUTHOR: **The University places great emphasis on security and safety. The security presence on campus is three-fold, with University Police, Metropolitan Police, and the Secret Service constantly monitoring the area. Overall, GW makes an effort, and the majority of students feel secure on campus.**

Questions?
For more inside information and survival tips, pick up College Prowler's full-length book on this school, written by an actual student! Check it out at *www.collegeprowler.com.*

Students Speak Out
ON OVERALL EXPERIENCE

Q "It was hard for me to adjust to GW at first. Actually, **it was really hard**. It can be a very image-conscious place, and the urban location did grate on me. I even applied to transfer but ended up deciding to stay. I would not want to be anywhere else now, though. It is a school with a lot of very intelligent, open-minded, and generally cool people, and there is a lot to do. You will just have to make an effort to seek out people who you like and avoid those who are shallow and petty. If you work at it, GW can be a fantastic place, but it can also seem like a trap if you let things pile up."

Q "The administration is horrible, and it is a complete joke to get anything done with financial aid, but the professors are wonderful, and there is **so much to do and see** in the city."

Q "I absolutely loved the past four years at GW. I just graduated and cannot think of a better place to have gone to school. Washington, DC was the most exciting and amazing city in which to attend college and live. The shopping, restaurants, bars, clubs, historical sites, and cultural things leave nothing to be desired. They are all top-notch and make going to GW that much better. Although there is a lot of red tape at GW, the overall experience you'll have here and **all the positives** of the school and the city far outweigh the negatives."

STUDENT AUTHOR: **GW students want the best and sometimes the University does not live up to their expectations. Although GW provides students with a large variety of on-campus activities, students can also enjoy the city. GW would not be the same, or as wonderful, if it were not located in DC.**

Georgetown University

3700 O Street NW; Washington, DC 20057
(202) 687-0100; www.georgetown.edu

THE BASICS:

Acceptance Rate: 21%
Setting: Urban
F-T Undergrads: 6,853

SAT Range: 1300–1490*
Control: Private
Tuition: $37,536

Most Popular Majors: Social Sciences, Business/Marketing, English, Foreign Languages and Literature

*of 1600

Academics	A-	Guys	B
Local Atmosphere	A+	Girls	A-
Safety & Security	B	Athletics	B
Computers	C-	Nightlife	A-
Facilities	B-	Greek Life	N/A
Campus Dining	C+	Drug Scene	A-
Off-Campus Dining	A-	Campus Strictness	B
Campus Housing	B+	Parking	D-
Off-Campus Housing	C	Transportation	B+
Diversity	B-	Weather	B-

Students Speak Out
ON ACADEMICS

Q "Most of them are great. **Grab as many Jesuit priest instructors as you can**—they're great teachers, very knowledgeable, and lots of fun."

Q "You should find that the **professors are brilliant**, available, and considerate. All but the last of those terms apply to professors in the SFS [School of Foreign Service]."

Q "You must work to get to know the professors. By visiting office hours and **participating in class**, professors understand that you're someone who is prepared and interested in learning."

Q "I still keep in touch by e-mail and go and visit my professors. They're **very accessible**, and they were a major plus to my Georgetown experience. I joke that I was 'coddled' (in a good way) through Georgetown because I was so taken care of."

STUDENT AUTHOR: An instructor can make or break a college class, and although there are always a few bad apples in every basket, the vast majority of Georgetown professors are respected and admired for their commitment to undergraduate education. Students speak with special fondness of their Jesuit professors, who are praised for showing a deep interest in students' lives beyond the classroom. The only common complaint is that the TAs and younger professors who are saddled with the task of teaching lower-level classes can be a little rough around the edges in terms of teaching style. Also, foreign TAs may have trouble with English.

Students Speak Out
ON LOCAL ATMOSPHERE

Q "Whatever interests you, DC is guaranteed to have. The best part about Georgetown is that it is close enough to the busy part of the city that activity is easy to find, yet Georgetown is its own **private community** that is very nice to retire to at the end of the day."

Q "DC and the suburb of Georgetown are awesome. There are **tons of landmarks to visit**. As far as memorials, go to the FDR memorial, it's amazing. There are also a lot of restaurants, shopping, performing arts (go to the Kennedy Center), and sports (rowing on the Potomac River)."

Q "There are a good many other universities in DC: George Washington, Catholic, Gallaudet (for hearing impaired), American, and a ton in northern Virginia. People would probably say stay away from southeast, since it's considered the dangerous part of the city. Definitely visit the museums, and pick up calendars of what's going on at them. It's fun to **get out in the city** and realize that there's life outside Georgetown. Lots of people have internships that get them out in the city. Georgetown is very pre-professional."

STUDENT AUTHOR: Georgetown students love their environment. During the day, Washington offers internships and employment opportunities. At night, DC is just as happy to cater to the needs of college students. Washington's main weakness is that you've got to pay to play, and like any major metropolis, everything costs more than it should.

Students Speak Out
ON FACILITIES

Q "Facilities are **dated**. Seriously, my roommate and I would always joke 'where does the 35 grand a year go?'"

Q "The gym is really nice—use it, since you're charged for it regardless. The student center is useful with its convenience store and coffee shop, however, there is definite room for expansion. The food court **could be better**."

Q "**Athletic facilities are okay**; we had a really large gym. It is huge, has weights, machines, basketball courts, racquetball, squash, and indoor tennis. There is a pool, aerobics room, massage room, and more. The student center is the Leavey Center, and it is nice. There is a large lounge, offices for all the student organizations and clubs, a small grocery store, a film developing place, the bookstore, and a food court. Most people, however, don't go to the student center to hang out."

Q "There are plenty of places on campus where students can go to do stuff. Sellinger lounge in the Leavey Center is nice and so is Hoya Court. . . . **Our gym is hot and gross and sweaty**, but I've grown to prefer it that way."

STUDENT AUTHOR: **It is difficult to get much of a consensus on the question of Georgetown's facilities. Athletic Hoyas decry the outdated state of the main campus gym, while participants in the Corp (the large, student-run business) praise their offices and retail spaces. Performing arts groups are perpetually in a state of near-revolt over the issue of rehearsal and performance space, while GUTV has its own studio.**

Students Speak Out
ON CAMPUS DINING

Q "It goes like this. The first semester, or at least the first month, you'll think the dining hall food is awesome—so much choice, so many options. Eventually, **you get sick of it**. Everyone does. If you choose to keep eating in the dining halls, you have to get creative with what you assemble. If you want to stay on campus, there's also a food court that has some okay stuff to eat, a grocery store, and the medical cafeteria (for the doctors)."

Q "Meal plans are done by any one of a number of plans, including 21, 14, 10, or 7 per week, a block of 90 or 45 per semester, or unlimited. You can also put Munch Money on your ID card, which allows you to use it **like a debit card** and buy food at one of the other food places on campus."

Q "We are **catered by the Marriott**, which means that we have lots of food all of the time, but it's all pretty similar to what we had last week. Are you vegan? Vegetarian? No worries, we have you covered."

STUDENT AUTHOR: **For the most part, Georgetown students maintain an enlightened air of resignation when it comes to campus food: they don't love it, but they have enough friends at other universities to know that what they're getting is at least as good as the East Coast average. The cafeteria and meal-planning staff is grudgingly credited with doing the best that they probably can, though students are often incredulous that, given the high price of Georgetown meal plans, the quality and variety of the food isn't higher.**

Student Body			
African American:	7%	Male/Female:	45/55%
Asian American:	9%	Out-of-State:	91%
Hispanic:	7%	International:	5%
Native American:	<1%	Unknown:	5%
White:	67%		

Popular Faiths: As a Jesuit school, most students at Georgetown are Catholic, though there is a sizeable Jewish population, as well.

Gay Pride: The campus is very accepting, and there are on-campus student groups. However, the sizable gay community is relatively quiet.

Economic Status: The vast majority come from wealthy families.

Students Speak Out
ON DORMS

Q "I think two of the three freshman dorms are better than anywhere else in the country. There are four you choose from in your freshman year: Darnell, New South, Harbin, or Village C. New South is **the biggest partying dorm**, though its rooms are probably the worst. It's the second largest dorm, but it's bland and kind of dirty. It has four floors, which are all coed, long floors, and hallways. About 15-20 people share a bathroom with three showers. Harbin is the most popular dorm. It got renovated recently, has nice rooms, and is very clean and sterile inside. It's organized into three clusters of eight rooms per floor. Each cluster is single-sex. Village C is the newest dorm. The rooms are the smallest, but each has its own private bathroom and shower; it's the quietest dorm. I lived there my freshman year, and I absolutely loved it. Darnell was renovated in 1996, and still has small rooms, but is in a good location and has the dining hall."

STUDENT AUTHOR: **Students have mostly good things to say about on-campus housing. Most speak lovingly of the freshman dorms which, if occasionally a bit "well worn," generally redeem themselves with various eccentricities.**

> **Did You Know?**
> 71% of undergrads live on campus.

Students Speak Out
ON GUYS & GIRLS

Q "Someone said that there are so many pretty girls here at Georgetown, but the boys are all trolls. I, personally, take offense at this, but yeah, there are **a lot of hot girls** on campus. Guys aren't that ugly either, I guess. Anyway, everyone has money, so everyone can do a lot to look good (or at least try)."

Q "**Students tend not to date a lot**, and instead, they go go out in groups and have more casual relationships and hookups until senior year."

Q "Guys are hot; girls are hot. There are lots of rich kids, so there's **a lot of expensive clothing**. You won't find a lot of hippies on campus; no goths, either."

STUDENT AUTHOR: **There is, in fact, a famed difference between the attractiveness of Georgetown students and those of other universities in the area. Word on the street has it that the girls have a reputation for being haughty and hard-to-get, but the word on the street has a funny way of forgetting that this might be because most of the guys have a reputation for thinking about sex, alcohol, sleep, and career opportunities—in that order.**

> **What's a Hoya?**
>
> Years ago, Georgetown's sports teams were known as Stonewalls. Back in those days, both Latin and Greek were required courses at Georgetown. And so it happened that one day, a Georgetown fan began shouting "Hoia Saxa," a combination of Greek and Latin equating roughly to "What Rocks." The slogan caught on. The spelling of Hoia was changed to aid pronunciation, and Georgetown's team nickname was later officially changed to the Hoyas. Ironically, asking "What's a Hoya?" is something like Abbott and Costello's "Who's on First?" routine; "Hoya" really does mean "what."

Students Speak Out
ON ATHLETICS

Q "**Basketball and lacrosse are huge**. They both have intramurals, but they're hard to get on. Crew is, by far, our biggest sport. You can compete or try out at all levels and ranges of commitment. Sports can provide a way for you to make lots of friends (if you can deal with the quasi-frat atmosphere). We have intramural [IM] teams for pretty much everything."

Q "From what I've heard, **about 55 percent of Georgetown students play IM sports**."

Q "Sports aren't huge, although, students tend to be 'athletic' and go to the gym a lot. I'd say basketball is the biggest sport, but unfortunately, the team plays in the MCI center downtown, so **games aren't on campus**."

STUDENT AUTHOR: **Hoyas are, as a rule, active people; working out at the on-campus gym has come to rival Catholicism as the most-practiced religion. Except for the basketball players, most varsity athletes are treated like humans rather than demi-gods. Basically, the athletic environment has a grass-roots flavor that is more populist and pick-up than professional.**

Students Speak Out
ON DRUG SCENE

Q "Georgetown is probably **more socially conservative than many college campuses**, so while a drug scene exists, it is definitely very underground. The major activity here is drinking."

Q "I knew a few people who smoked pot, but that was **relatively rare**."

Q "**Alcohol is the drug of choice**. There's some pot, and I knew of a couple of people using coke, but you can really stay away from it. I didn't feel affected by it, and I didn't make a major effort or anything. I think it's pretty minimal."

STUDENT AUTHOR: Most Hoyas characterize the Georgetown drug scene as low key and underground. Whatever you want can certainly be found, but drug use does not bother those students who do not want to be bothered by it. In the end, a prospective Hoya needs only to know that aside from alcohol use, the drug scene at Georgetown is, in a word, tame. Binge drinking, however, is as popular here as it is anywhere in the country.

11:1	Student-to-Faculty Ratio
96%	Freshman Retention Rate
90%	Four-Year Graduation Rate
84%	Financial Aid Applicants Receiving Aid

Students Speak Out
SAFETY & SECURITY

Q "We have a non-campus security force called the **Department of Public Safety**, and they're always around, which is good. The Metro Police (the force for DC) is always right off campus."

Q "Georgetown is in a city, so there are muggings reported from time to time in the area, but I really think these are rare. **I always felt safe**. I'd just recommend using common sense, as it is in a very urban area."

Q "Safety and security on campus are **very good**. I wouldn't leave your laptop lying around or your door unlocked all day when you're not home, but it's pretty safe otherwise. Off campus is a little more of a concern. But, if you follow common sense (no walking alone drunk at night), you'll be fine."

STUDENT AUTHOR: Off-campus muggings are becoming more common, as are burglaries of University-owned townhouses. As the Department of Public Safety is fond of reminding students, however, most of these incidents are wholly avoidable. For the fortunate majority, security is only a peripheral concern.

Questions?
For more inside information and survival tips, pick up College Prowler's full-length book on this school, written by an actual student! Check it out at *www.collegeprowler.com*.

Students Speak Out
ON OVERALL EXPERIENCE

Q "DC is awesome. There are so many opportunities for **fabulous internships**, which you must do while you are here. If you are into international or political stuff, my advice would be to come here, for sure."

Q "The Catholic thing is definitely something you need to think about in your decision. Do not let anyone tell you that you won't realize that the **Catholic presence** is there."

Q "**I used to wish I was someplace else**—I took a year off in the middle—but I had a great couple years when I came back. The weather and the conservatives were the biggest negatives to me."

Q "I absolutely loved my four years there. I found the courses to be great, the student population to be diverse, and the extracurricular and social scene to be well rounded. There are so many different clubs on campus, which more than makes up for the **lack of a Greek system**."

STUDENT AUTHOR: Georgetown is a great university doing its best to become the Stanford of the East . . . [but its] reputation has begun to outstrip its resources; in almost every category except academics, you're going to get better bang for your buck at a state school. At the end of the day, it's almost impossible to predict whether or not Georgetown is the right school for you. The best you can do is to think about your priorities and decide if they and the school intersect. Whatever you do, do not come to Georgetown simply because you didn't get into Princeton, or Berkeley, or wherever else. There are far too many kids on the Hilltop who are there because it's there, and not for actual reasons.

Georgia Institute of Technology

225 North Avenue NW; Atlanta, GA 30332
(404) 894-2000; www.gatech.edu

THE BASICS:

Acceptance Rate: 63%
Setting: Urban
F-T Undergrads: 12,565

SAT Range: 1240–1420*
Control: Public
Tuition: $23,770

Most Popular Majors: Engineering, Business/Marketing, Computer Science, Architecture, Biology

*of 1600

Academics	A-	Guys	B-
Local Atmosphere	A-	Girls	C-
Safety & Security	B-	Athletics	A
Computers	A+	Nightlife	B+
Facilities	B	Greek Life	B+
Campus Dining	C	Drug Scene	B-
Off-Campus Dining	A	Campus Strictness	B
Campus Housing	C	Parking	D
Off-Campus Housing	A-	Transportation	B-
Diversity	B	Weather	B+

Students Speak Out
ON ACADEMICS

Q "There are some teachers here **just to do their research**, but most of the ones I've had were pretty decent. Always ask upperclassmen about individual professors."

Q "Some teachers are great—you learn a lot, and you are **treated as a person**. However, there are some professors who are not so good and seem like they are just out to get you."

Q "There are teaching assistants for most classes and many free tutors on campus. **All Freshman Experience dorms have tutors** in the study lounges throughout the night, and the Office of Minority Education has many free and knowledgeable tutors."

Q "I've had good ones and bad ones, as to be expected. The good ones are really good, though. They're very understanding and incredibly good at teaching. Of course, **they expect a lot**, but Tech is a well-respected school."

STUDENT AUTHOR: **If you choose to attend Georgia Tech, you can expect that the professors in any given course of study will be among the most recognized and respected names in their fields. Doctorates from Princeton, MIT, Stanford, Caltech, and Georgia Tech roam the halls, instructing the next generation's leading scientists and engineers. Overall, you will be expected to learn things without supervision, and you will be held to very high standards.**

Students Speak Out
ON LOCAL ATMOSPHERE

Q "Atlanta is a huge town with lots to offer. Also in Atlanta are Georgia State University, which is right next-door, and Emory. About an hour away is the University of Georgia, **our big rival**, which is a big party school."

Q "Downtown is great. There's always **somewhere new to go** or something to try out."

Q "**Atlanta is pretty fun**. It has most anything you could want in a big city—restaurants, museums, symphony, theater, movies, bars, dance clubs, music, you name it. There are also a lot of things like running and biking clubs."

Q "Atlanta is a great city to be a part of. **Stay away from some of the shady places** at night, and definitely travel in a big group."

STUDENT AUTHOR: **Georgia Tech is in the heart of midtown Atlanta, which provides a very urban environment for students. Along with all of the amenities and luxuries that Atlanta's city life provides, there are also drawbacks, as is the case with any city. City life in general can sometimes be dangerous. Caution is a virtue; however, Atlanta is an exciting city with a vibrant local music scene, which has helped produce the likes of John Mayer and Collective Soul, four major league sports teams, and several attractions. Atlanta is the biggest and fastest-growing city in the Southeast, and students will always have access to a wealth of options for entertainment.**

5 Best Things	5 Worst Things
1 Academic reputation	1 Parking
2 Athletic facilities	2 Overwhelming size
3 Sunny weather	3 Profs too into research
4 Freshman dorms	4 Public transportation
5 Meal plan	5 Crime on campus

Students Speak Out
ON FACILITIES

Q "The facilities on campus are really nice. Everything is pretty new and **very technologically advanced**. Our facilities are much better than any other university I've ever visited."

Q "GT has done some things to **make the campus nicer**, but it's not one of those campuses that people describe as beautiful."

Q "Facilities are extraordinary! When the Olympics came, they built new, **incredibly nice dorms** and athletic facilities. I've visited many campuses, and Tech has the best dorms, classrooms, and student areas. All of the facilities are just phenomenal."

Q "Most of the classrooms are decent, at best. The Student Athletic Center (SAC) is pretty good (for **a free health club**). I will complain that they don't have enough weights for the demand."

Q "Some of the facilities are nice, and **some are not so nice**. The Student Center is who-knows-how-old."

STUDENT AUTHOR: The Student Center is the hub of student activity on campus. Located squarely in the middle of campus, it houses a computer cluster, a music listening room, a food court, a ballroom, and a theater. Many functions are held in the ballroom, and the theater regularly holds free screenings of popular movies, along with occasional concerts. The Student Center has also recently undergone renovations which integrate the facility more completely with the adjacent area.

Famous Alumni

Jimmy Carter, Mike Duke, Nomar Garciaparra, Bobby Jones, Arthur Murray, Sam Nunn, John Portman, Jason Varitek, John Young

Students Speak Out
ON CAMPUS DINING

Q "The Student Center food court is okay. **Avoid the dining halls** at all costs."

Q "Junior's, which is the oldest restaurant on campus, is pretty cool. It's a tradition to go there before football games or after staying up all night (they open at 6 a.m.). **The French toast special is awesome!** Also, the Student Center has a food court with gyros, smoothies, Chick-fil-A, and Taco Bell."

Q "The cafeteria food here just gets redundant, and **then it gets bad**. On the west side of campus, there's a West Side Market, so you can buy 'real' food."

Q "Food from the cafeterias **isn't anything to get excited over**. In fact, I wouldn't recommend getting a meal plan. There are many other places accessible on campus and near campus."

Q "There is a **wide selection of food** in the dining halls. If you go during peak lunch and dinner hours, there is fresh, hot food made every day that is really good."

STUDENT AUTHOR: While the dining halls are definitely no place to take a date, or anyone for that matter, to have a nice meal, they are adequate for everyday use. Georgia Tech is served by two dining halls, Brittain and Woodruff, which are located at opposite ends of the campus. The quality of the food has improved steadily over the last five years. Breakfast food is always your best bet at these dining halls, and students are free to make their own sandwiches and salads at the salad bar.

Student Body

African American:	7%	Male/Female:	70/30%
Asian American:	16%	Out-of-State:	29%
Hispanic:	5%	International:	5%
Native American:	<1%	Unknown:	1%
White:	67%		

Popular Faiths: Christianity and Islam are popular.

Gay Pride: Historically, Georgia Tech has not been particularly accepting of the GLBTQ community, but with on-campus organizations like Gay and Lesbian Alliance and Safe Space, the school has become much more accepting.

Economic Status: A majority of students are middle- to upper-class.

Students Speak Out
ON DORMS

Q "The **dorms are small**. The Freshman Experience is a good program, and I would definitely recommend it. You should upgrade to on-campus apartments after your first year."

Q "Housing is limited, and you're only guaranteed housing for the first two years. **They're all pretty nice** because the older ones have all been renovated, and all the apartments were built for the Olympics when they were in Atlanta, so they're pretty nice, too."

Q "Some dorms are decent, and others are in poor condition. **Avoid West Campus** freshman dorms."

STUDENT AUTHOR: **Dorms on campus are notoriously expensive, and accommodations leave something to be desired. Freshman dorms on East Campus are mostly small, two-person rooms about 12 feet by 14 feet in size. The West Campus dorms house mostly upperclassmen and athletes, and they are markedly nicer. If you are trying for the best possible facilities on campus, request housing in the Graduate Living Center (GLC) across 10th Street.**

Did You Know?
59% of undergrads live on campus.

Students Speak Out
ON GUYS & GIRLS

Q "The students are kind of dorky, as tech nerds would be expected to be. If you're looking for hot, **check out Georgia State**."

Q "What girls? The ratio at Tech is almost three to one, so there are lots of guys. **The guys are all really sweet**, though."

Q "Tech has always been thought of as a '**geek school**,' but it's not really."

Q "You can find very decent, very cute guys, but they are hard to come by. The good thing is that **they're smart** and that Buckhead and midtown are only 10 minutes away. "

STUDENT AUTHOR: **Typical Tech students are very hard-working and highly- motivated, regardless of their gender. Georgia Tech has a small contingent of stereotypical, laid-back, party-animal guys and girls. However, many guys tend to follow more of an academic persuasion and are not as interested in large social events. Guys at Georgia Tech outnumber girls by almost three to one.**

Traditions

Midnight Madness
During finals week, from 12 a.m. to 12:30 a.m. every night, students emerge from all over campus and scream.

Stealing the "T"
It is a common practice for the giant T that spells out Tech on the Tech Towers to be stolen each semester.

Overall School Spirit
School pride is rampant at Georgia Tech. The Swarm is the cheering section at sporting events of students wearing yellow T-shirts.

Students Speak Out
ON ATHLETICS

Q "You will learn **the joys of tailgating**, which is a huge deal in the South. There are lots of cool traditions mixed with lots of great parties."

Q "Varsity sports are pretty big. Football games are a ton of fun, and we recently renovated the football stadium and built a new baseball stadium. The sports scene at Tech is a lot of fun, and our alumni still come back for everything. **Intramurals are also pretty big**; everyone can play."

Q "Everyone loves the **Yellow Jackets**. It is a big part of our lives."

Q "Sports are huge. I mean, **we are an ACC school**. Whatever sport you want, we've got it."

STUDENT AUTHOR: **It is highly recommended that all students attend the home football games, and also the basketball and baseball games when possible. In addition to varsity sports, intramural sports are made available for all students and offer great social opportunities for fun and games. Sporting events are always great fun for students to attend, and they really complete the college experience.**

Students Speak Out
ON DRUG SCENE

Q "Hard drugs are **not that popular**, but drugs such as marijuana are readily accessible, though that does not mean that they pose a threat to those who wish not to partake."

Q "After three years at Tech, **I've never been asked for any drug**. I know some people that like to get high on the weekends, but they never pressure anyone else. It's totally an independent decision."

Q "There **aren't too many drugs apparent** on campus. If you don't want to see drugs, they won't be there."

STUDENT AUTHOR: Georgia Tech's academic rigor is most likely a deterrent for widespread drug use. The drug scene is not overly visible on campus, so many parents and students might be completely unaware of its existence. However, don't assume that the drug scene's lack of prominence means that it's not there at all; drugs are available on campus and are used heavily in some communities of students.

14:1	Student-to-Faculty Ratio
92%	Freshman Retention Rate
33%	Four-Year Graduation Rate
42%	Financial Aid Applicants Receiving Aid

Students Speak Out
SAFETY & SECURITY

Q "We have a police station right on campus, so **they can respond pretty quickly** to things. Tech is in midtown Atlanta, so you have to be alert and not do dumb things like walking alone at 2 a.m."

Q "On-campus **security isn't a problem**, but off campus, some parts of town are a little shady."

Q "Security and safety on campus is high, given its neighborhood. Although there have been some **robberies and car thefts**, campus is very safe, for the most part."

Q "It is **pretty safe**, for the most part. Just be cautious and use some common sense."

STUDENT AUTHOR: Georgia Tech has a good campus police force that patrols the campus extensively at night. Campus Police officers are just as competent as Atlanta City Police, and they have every intention of protecting the students.

> **Questions?**
> For more inside information and survival tips, pick up College Prowler's full-length book on this school, written by an actual student! Check it out at *www.collegeprowler.com*.

Students Speak Out
ON OVERALL EXPERIENCE

Q "I truly enjoy Georgia Tech, but I work really hard. You **get your money's worth**, but you really have to try your hardest."

Q "I love it at Tech. It's not a place where you can breeze through the classes, but if you work hard, **it's not hard to pass**. A Georgia Tech diploma is something that people respect."

Q "Tech is great school to get an education, but not the best place to **get the whole college experience**. Personally, Atlanta is all right, but I don't plan to stay here after graduation."

Q "I didn't like Tech at first, but when the semester was over, **I realized that it wasn't that bad**; it wasn't as hard as people had said. Just don't spend too much time goofing off."

Q "I wanted to go to Tech since I was in fourth grade. **I love it**, and there is nowhere else that I'd rather be."

STUDENT AUTHOR: It is true that many Tech students might sometimes wish that they had chosen another, less demanding school for college. Georgia Tech is very academically demanding, to an extreme that alienates many students and parents. Many see the school as a sort of "proving ground" for professional life. However, the size of the student body is not overly large, and it is easy for one to get involved socially and academically without straining your GPA. The rigorousness of academic life at Georgia Tech instills a rare motivation in the students there that will prepare them well for professional life. Most students feel that an education at Tech was worth all the work.

Gettysburg College

300 North Washington Street; Gettysburg, PA 17325
(717) 337-6000; www.gettysburg.edu

THE BASICS:

Acceptance Rate: 38%
Setting: Rural
F-T Undergrads: 2,451

SAT Range: 1220–1360*
Control: Private
Tuition: $37,850

Most Popular Majors: Business Administration and Management, Political Science and Government

*of 1600

Academics	B	Guys	B
Local Atmosphere	C	Girls	B
Safety & Security	B	Athletics	C+
Computers	B	Nightlife	B
Facilities	B	Greek Life	A
Campus Dining	B	Drug Scene	B+
Off-Campus Dining	B+	Campus Strictness	B
Campus Housing	B	Parking	A-
Off-Campus Housing	C-	Transportation	D
Diversity	D-	Weather	C+

Students Speak Out
ON ACADEMICS

Q "I find that **teachers at Gettysburg are willing to help and are always reachable**. I think most classes are interesting, but then again, I only take classes that interest me."

Q "The teachers are **really involved and very interesting**, and yes, the classes are, too."

Q "The vast majority of the teachers I've had have been very good, and their classes have been very interesting. **Most teachers here are in their given fields mainly to teach**, so there are very few who don't seem to like teaching. Some teachers don't seem to like intro classes, which tend to be very formulaic and streamlined."

Q "The professors that I have had here at Gettysburg have been **very qualified in their fields**. Speaking mostly for instructors in the Psychology Department, many of them are published and are currently working on research which I feel gives them more of a well-rounded grasp on their classes. This goes to show that professors here are not purely teaching from a book, they have first-hand knowledge about the courses."

STUDENT AUTHOR: The students, administrators, and faculty at Gettysburg College should be proud of the school's academics. It is not exactly the degree of difficulty that makes the academics so demanding, it is perhaps the level of student interest in every class that makes learning a satisfying and effective endeavor.

Students Speak Out
ON LOCAL ATMOSPHERE

Q "Gettysburg is a small town. Gettysburg is the only college around. The town is poor in areas and very ritzy in others. **There is not much to do in the town**, but I feel that I don't really have a need to leave the campus—it is pretty self-contained."

Q "**The campus and the town have two separate identities**. For the most part, I only venture into the town when I need something, not just to hang out. Since we live in Gettysburg, it's mostly tourist."

Q "There's a nice mix of townspeople and students surrounding the school. There are lots of bars too; though, some are labeled as either 'townie' or 'college' bars. However, there are many that do have a good mix. **Be sure to visit the battlefields** and Ernie's Texas Lunch."

Q "Gettysburg is a small town without any large institutions within a 20-mile radius. I think the town itself lends a special identity to the college community, particularly for historians. **Waitresses recognize you when you go to eat**, and there are unique little shops and nearly everything is within walking distance."

STUDENT AUTHOR: Gettysburg is a bit of a culture shock for anyone coming from a large town or big city. The town is a blend of small-town, rural America and a commercial tourist trap. Gettysburg offers the essentials to students, but if a little exploring is undertaken, a wide range of interesting (albeit out-of-the-way) destinations can be discovered.

<table>
<tr><td>

5 Best Things
1 Springfest
2 The students
3 Beautiful campus
4 The faculty
5 The food

</td><td>

5 Worst Things
1 Rural location
2 Lack of diversity
3 The food (after a year)
4 Class requirements
5 The Greek system

</td></tr>
</table>

Students Speak Out
ON FACILITIES

Q "I think things are generally pretty nice on campus. **The CUB and the Attic and stuff are usually fairly clean**, and they serve their functions well."

Q "**The athletic facilities, like the gym in Bream need some real updating**, but the rest, like the rugby pitch, the new soccer fields, and the football stadium are all pretty fair."

Q "All of the facilities on campus are top-grade. The furniture, computers, athletic facilities, classrooms, media, online databases, student union, and art facilities are **almost all new, renovated, or in good condition**. The grounds (landscaping, cleanliness) of the campus are incredibly well-kept and certainly high standard."

Q "**The CUB and Musselman library are nice**. The gyms really need some work, but they're building a new complex, so hopefully that will change."

Q "**For the most part, everything is well-maintained**. The computers are decent and so is the College Union Building."

STUDENT AUTHOR: **Your impression of the quality of Gettysburg facilities depends almost entirely on where you happen to be on campus. While some areas are recently renovated and are very clean and modern, other areas have yet to receive the same treatment and are quite unpleasant. The school has accepted so many students in the past few years that they have basically run out of conventional housing. Fortunately, the school has plans to renovate or improve most of the remaining areas on campus in the future.**

Famous Alumni

Bruce S. Gordon (head of the NAACP), George M. Leader (former PA governor), Jerry Spinelli (author of *Maniac Magee*)

Students Speak Out
ON CAMPUS DINING

Q "The food is alright, but **there isn't a lot of variety**. The Bullet Hole is good for quick meals, and Servo is better if you want more of a home-cooked kind of a meal."

Q "Food at Gettysburg is **great, when compared with other campuses**. Our dining halls aren't much, but they definitely provide a number of choices and variety for the size of the student body they serve. There are also awesome off-campus places to eat, like the Dobbin House and the Gettysburg Family Restaurant (probably my favorite)."

Q "I love Ike's, though **you can really only eat so much Mexican food** before your insides start to melt."

Q "**The food on campus is decent**. I do not have a meal plan this year due to living off campus, but it is pretty good."

Q "**I think the food sucks, but there is variety** and I heard it was much better than other schools. Ike's is good."

STUDENT AUTHOR: **For the first year of your career at Gettysburg, you will eat at Servo. Almost always. The consensus at G'burg agrees on two things: 1) The food here is better than at the majority of other colleges, and 2) Chances are, your taste buds will not be disappointed. At Gettysburg, food is not a problem. The quality, and to an extent the selection, tends to be quite good, with the occasional peak of delicious.**

Student Body

African American:	3%	Male/Female:	49/51%
Asian American:	1%	Out-of-State:	74%
Hispanic:	2%	International:	2%
Native American:	<1%	Unknown:	0%
White:	92%		

Popular Faiths: Students are mostly Lutheran and other Protestant religions.

Gay Pride: A strong and active campus chapter of ALLIES ensures that gay tolerance is quite high on campus.

Economic Status: Students generally come from upper-middle to upper-class backgrounds.

Students Speak Out
ON DORMS

Q "**The dorms on campus aren't too bad**. The nicest dorms are, by far, Quarry and Huber Hall. The theme house option is another option that makes Gettysburg different from other campuses. There is nothing better than getting to live in a house with some friends."

Q "Dorms are good here. **The college has bought numerous motels in the area** in which it houses students, but they are fine as well."

Q "Freshman dorms are alright when compared to other schools. Though, **only some of the dorms have air-conditioning** and some dorms are smaller than others. Huber Hall is the newly-renovated freshman dorm that is like a hotel and, by far, the best freshman dorm on campus."

STUDENT AUTHOR: Since Gettysburg is a residential college, living on campus is required for first-years, and strongly recommended for everyone else. The administration really had to make an effort to provide decent and varied housing for both first-year and upperclass students and, for the most part, they succeeded.

Did You Know?
94% of undergrads live on campus.

Students Speak Out
ON GUYS & GIRLS

Q "**The guys are short**. Well, not all the guys, but I am like a 5'6" girl, and I am considered tall. There are some pretty hot guys here, though."

Q "The girls and boys of Gettysburg are, **for the most part, an attractive, intelligent lot**. Girls tend to be either in a sorority or totally against them. Guys tend to be the same way. There are, of course, those who just don't care one way or the other."

Q "Everyone is **pretty good looking** here."

Q "I guess the guys aren't too bad. **Many can be huge asses**, but can also be nice when they want to (or when they get something out of it). I'd say no worse and no better than your typical campus."

STUDENT AUTHOR: The typical guy on campus wears fashionable, name-brand clothing, is friendly, vaguely attractive, and hangs out at the Greek houses on weekends. The typical girl is much the same. Since it is a liberal arts school, there are relatively few nerdy types on campus, generally restricted only to closet Star Wars fans and the odd live-action role player in the English department.

Traditions

Midnight Madness
Once or twice a month, Servo opens up its doors around midnight and offers a free buffet.

Springfest
Usually held during the last weekend of April, Gettysburg celebrates spring by holding a huge festival on Stine lake.

Overall School Spirit
Gettysburg sweatshirts and shorts are omnipresent, but that's just about the extent of displays of school spirit.

Students Speak Out
ON ATHLETICS

Q "We are Division III. **Football is the most well-attended event, which is not saying much**. There are also many intramural and club sports that a lot of people are involved with on campus. Probably everyone at one point or another has played on a club or intramural sport."

Q "**Varsity sports aren't big at all**. Never done intramurals, but I hear they're awesome."

Q "I don't remember the last time I went to any varsity sport game. Some of the sports draw a crowd once and a while, like basketball or football, but, **for the most part, I don't think anyone cares** if they aren't actually on the team."

Q "**Intramural sports are pretty big**, and there are many different ones offered."

STUDENT AUTHOR: If you crave the excitement and intensity of Division I-caliber athletics, do not come to Gettysburg. Sports are simply not a priority for most students at Gettysburg, and despite having perennially excellent men's lacrosse and women's field hockey teams, athletics generally fail to stir much excitement or support among the student body.

Students Speak Out
ON DRUG SCENE

Q "**S&S and borough police have been fairly attentive to drug trafficking** on campus, but of course, it will never be completely eliminated."

Q "Marijuana is probably the most popular drug on campus and **hard drugs are pretty low key**. I have noticed a significant decline in the amount of drugs on campus since they started renovating the Majestic Theater. I have heard that part of the renovation contract included keeping drugs to a minimum on campus. When 'dealers' get scared, they stop dealing."

Q "There are lots of good drugs at G'burg. **There's mostly pot, though, and it is fairly prevalent**."

STUDENT AUTHOR: **While alcohol permeates the school, present in dorms, fraternities, and off-campus housing, less socially acceptable drugs, such as marijuana and cocaine, are also accessible for those who want to find them. Abuse of prescription drugs such as Adderall has escalated sharply in recent years, as students want help cramming during midterms and finals.**

11:1	Student-to-Faculty Ratio
90%	Freshman Retention Rate
70%	Four-Year Graduation Rate
83%	Financial Aid Applicants Receiving Aid

Students Speak Out
SAFETY & SECURITY

Q "**Most of the officers are really friendly and helpful**. They really aren't trying to get the students in trouble as much as they are trying to keep the campus safe. Just don't piss them off and they will try not to piss you off."

Q "I think S&S does a pretty good job of keeping the campus safe and secure. **I have never had a terribly unfair encounter with them**. They also offer an escort service for anyone who wants it."

Q "Gettysburg's campus is a relatively safe one; there is some bad stuff that happens, but if you are smart and walk home safely in groups, you should be safe. **I occasionally walk around by myself at night, and I am still here**. S&S is always available to escort any one home if the person so desires."

STUDENT AUTHOR: **While Gettysburg is not totally devoid of crime, it is quite easy to avoid getting into situations where your life is in danger. As long as you take minor precautions, you are unlikely to fall prey to crime. S&S does do a good job of keeping students in line most of the time.**

Questions?
For more inside information and survival tips, pick up College Prowler's full-length book on this school, written by an actual student! Check it out at *www.collegeprowler.com*.

Students Speak Out
ON OVERALL EXPERIENCE

Q "Sometimes, I think I wish I was somewhere else, but generally I have come to love my friends and professors so much that **I don't think I could have made out any better elsewhere**. Gettysburg is so beautiful, it makes it hard to see yourself somewhere else."

Q "I am glad I am here. **I love this school, and I am glad this is the one I am at**. I have been here for two years and have had a great time."

Q "I think every experience is what you make of it, I'm happy I stayed because I've made some really good friendships. **The one thing I miss is city-life**. Sometimes, it gets very claustrophobic here on campus because it's so small."

Q "Overall, my experience at Gettysburg has been an excellent one. I am incredibly grateful that I was able to come here and have the privilege meeting a wide range of talented students and faculty. **A lot of the campus is geared towards the social scene**, but as admission has become increasingly competitive over the last four years, the student body is also becoming more focused on academia."

STUDENT AUTHOR: **Gettysburg will never be a UNC or Ohio State in terms of diversity, class offerings, or athletics. Then again, you'll never be in a class of 350 people, and you will never feel lost and or ostracized. The faculty is, for the most part, awesome. You have the chance to get to know your professors, as well as your classmates. The academics are challenging and rewarding. The more you put in, the more you get out. Its beautiful campus and challenging coursework are what make Gettysburg College, overall, a great place to spend the best years of your life.**

Gonzaga University

502 East Boone Avenue; Spokane, WA 99258
(800) 986-9585; www.gonzaga.edu

THE BASICS:

Acceptance Rate: 77%   **SAT Range:** 1090–1280*
Setting: Urban   **Control:** Private
F-T Undergrads: 4,344   **Tuition:** $28,162

Most Popular Majors: Business, Management, Marketing, Social Sciences, Engineering

*of 1600

Academics	B	Guys	B-
Local Atmosphere	B-	Girls	B
Safety & Security	C+	Athletics	B+
Computers	C+	Nightlife	B
Facilities	B	Greek Life	N/A
Campus Dining	C-	Drug Scene	B
Off-Campus Dining	A-	Campus Strictness	B-
Campus Housing	B-	Parking	A-
Off-Campus Housing	A-	Transportation	C-
Diversity	D	Weather	C+

Students Speak Out
ON ACADEMICS

Q "The teachers are all over the map. Some are tough, and some are easy. **Some give a damn, and some don't**. Some want to help you, and some have tenure and couldn't care less. However, it is a good school with professors who, at the very least, will know your name."

Q "The professors are generally pretty eccentric. **Sometimes cool and fun eccentric, sometimes snarky eccentric**. They tend to assign a lot of actual work, but in my experience, the grading is fair."

Q "**Classes are a mixed bag at Gonzaga**. In fact, pinning down a consistent style would have to be limited to fairly general things, like frequent small group discussions or regular postings on Blackboard. On the whole, classes can be as fascinating as they can be hopelessly boring."

Q "**I think that most of the professors are really laid-back**. Some are hard, but you'll be fine if you just do your work. But if you don't, don't make excuses. They'll tolerate honest laziness over obvious lying."

STUDENT AUTHOR: Gonzaga is a relaxed, moderately difficult, student-friendly university, which entails benefits and drawbacks. Gonzaga's focus is on teaching rather than research, so you won't be rubbing elbows with "leading lights." Students are taught mostly by professors, not TAs or adjuncts. This fosters a relaxed attitude. Students help their fellow students, and cut-throat competition is unheard of.

Students Speak Out
ON LOCAL ATMOSPHERE

Q "Spokane is **the least redneck city you can find in eastern Washington**, but that's not saying too much. If you find the beautiful spots and parks in the area, you've found the best it has to offer."

Q "The city of Spokane seems to be in the midst of **a mini-urban revival**. Nice restaurants and music venues are popping up in this once-depressed agricultural center. Downtown has nice shopping, a decent opera house, and some cool pubs."

Q "As a girl from Seattle, I can say that Spokane may lack a few amenities afforded to bigger, more well-known cities. Spokane is generally **more conservative, more working-class, more industrial**, and less cosmopolitan. However, the chill, down-to-earth feeling of Spokane is also reflected in Gonzaga."

Q "Having come from a big city, Spokane is a breath of fresh air. There is a small-town community feel, yet **a modern and sophisticated downtown is only a quick hop away**. There are many things to do and see, such as the local wineries, local bar scene, camping, hiking, skiing, and listening to live music."

STUDENT AUTHOR: If Spokane were a glass, one could spend days arguing whether it were half full or half empty. The half-full Spokane has a quiet upscale downtown nestled picturesquely on the banks of the Spokane River. The half-empty Spokane is notable for low-rent housing, ugly and abandoned buildings, and congestion. Gonzaga is positioned somewhat between the two.

5 Best Things	5 Worst Things
1 Basketball	**1** Bone-numbing wind
2 Fall colors	**2** COG food and prices
3 Community spirit	**3** Easy, boring classes
4 Walking along the river	**4** Student apathy
5 The student chapel	**5** The computer network

Students Speak Out
ON FACILITIES

"The facilities on campus are very nice. The athletic fitness center is state-of-the-art, as are many of the new buildings. The only facilities that are somewhat lacking are the older dorms. Although they may not be posh and modern, **they are quite livable and a great place to meet people**."

"On-campus facilities are very nice. **The library, arena, and fitness center are all new**, and there's plenty of green space to toss the Frisbee or play football."

"**We have a pretty loaded fitness center**. Our student center can be crowded, which can be good for social reasons, but bad if you're trying to get work done."

"**The fitness center is incredible**; they have a pool, a free weights area, a machine weights area, treadmills, elliptical machines, stationary bikes, stair climbers, and a lot of classes. It is kept clean, and it has a great atmosphere and an awesome staff."

"The fitness center is new, the library is big and beautiful, and **the student center is friendly and bustling**."

STUDENT AUTHOR: Over the past few years, Gonzaga's facilities have improved immensely. Functionality still rules the day at Gonzaga—it doesn't have luxuries such as an on-campus movie theater, concert venue, or full-blown coffeeshop. But once you get used to the idea that concerts are in Crosby, movies are shown in lecture rooms, and any number of spots can be a coffeeshop, it's not so bad.

Famous Alumni

Jason Bay, Tony Canadeo, Bing Crosby, Thomas Foley, Christine Gregoire, Carl Maxey, Carl Pohlad, John Stockton

Students Speak Out
ON CAMPUS DINING

"Sodexo gets a lot of criticism, only some of which is deserved, but **what would college be without whining about the dining hall**?"

"The food on campus is quoted as being **the best of any college or university in the state of Washington and Idaho**. Whether or not this is true, it's ridiculously overpriced."

"**Be wary of the COG**. I characterize the uncomfortable chain of events following a meal there as 'Mach 5,' in reference to the speed at which the food rushes through the lower intestine and beyond."

"Dining hall food, while it's a far cry from healthy, is **better than decent and a little under great**. A wide selection is offered at each meal, with the best menus being breakfast and lunch, in my opinion."

"**The COG is a place you should stay away from**, but Sodexo makes you buy a meal plan, so you're stuck with it. As for other campus options, Spike's and the Sub Connection are usually good when the lines aren't long."

STUDENT AUTHOR: Rare is the Gonzaga student who hasn't poked fun at the COG's suspect dishes, effects on digestion, or unhealthy properties. But most admit that it has a significant array of food that is edible. Weekend brunches are popular, as are theme nights. Bulldog Bucks (money put on your student ID, usable at all on-campus locations) is convenient. Nearly everyone likes the myriad coffee stands that dot the Gonzaga landscape.

Student Body

African American:	1%	Male/Female:	46/54%
Asian American:	6%	Out-of-State:	49%
Hispanic:	4%	International:	1%
Native American:	1%	Unknown:	0%
White:	87%		

Popular Faiths: More than half of the student body is Roman Catholic, and it shows.

Gay Pride: The gay and lesbian presence on campus is not a major one. There is HERO (a gay-straight alliance club), which sponsors awareness and activism events throughout the year.

Economic Status: Gonzaga students come from a wide variety of economic backgrounds.

Students Speak Out
ON DORMS

Q "I lived in DeSmet and Campion. **If you want peace and quiet, then go for Campion**. If you want a fraternity-like atmosphere and don't mind the loud noise or the puke in the bathrooms, then you'll want to go for DeSmet."

Q "The dorms all have their unique features—**none of them are bad, per se**. It all comes down to what type of environment you want to live in."

Q "My first year at Gonzaga, I lived in Catherine/Monica. If you are looking to meet a large number of classmates and you love to socialize (keep your door open), then C/M is for you. **The people I met in C/M are among my best friends**, even today—post-graduation."

STUDENT AUTHOR: Nearly everyone would agree that Gonzaga's policy requiring all freshmen and most sophomores to live in dorms is good. They are the center of social life. If upperclassmen look back with fond nostalgia, it's solely because of the friendships forged and times enjoyed, not the small rooms, grungy tiles and carpets, and communal showers.

Did You Know?
52% of undergrads live on campus.

Students Speak Out
ON GUYS & GIRLS

Q "**A quick trip to the Martin Centre will show you plenty of kids who look good** and spend a long time working to get that way."

Q "I don't know how Gonzaga compares to some So-Cal bimbo school, but I do know that there are **way more hot girls here than in the real world**."

Q "From my experience, **there is a lack of hot guys**."

Q "**Gonzaga is definitely a hooking-up school** as a result of the prevalence of partying and binge drinking. The typical Gonzaga student is probably upper-middle class, likes sports, takes an active role in politics, believes in God, takes studying seriously (to a point), and likes to party."

STUDENT AUTHOR: Because of the climate and the Catholically-tinged atmosphere at the school, Gonzaga is not a major meat market. Fashion plays a minimal role at Gonzaga; snobbishness and competition between or among the sexes is not particularly virulent. It's far too relaxed a school to be into social discrimination. Girls outnumber guys, and they seem to feel more pressure to find a relationship before they graduate.

Traditions
Around the World
Seniors go to six houses in six hours, each with a different alcohol theme, like Margaritaville or Ireland.

Boat Cruise
Gonzaga rents a cruise boat on nearby Lake Coeur d'Alene on two nights during the year.

Overall School Spirit
Many students wear Gonzaga apparel and are reasonably proud of their school. However, very few are given to boasting about Gonzaga or dissing other universities.

Students Speak Out
ON ATHLETICS

Q "**Varsity sports, specifically men's basketball, are the biggest events on campus** and provide a great source of pride and unity among the student body."

Q "**Basketball is huge**, which is compensation for no football. I know a lot of people who play IM or club sports, like basketball, soccer, and rugby."

Q "Men's basketball, and increasingly women's basketball, is **perhaps the defining element of campus life for most people**. I've also been surprised at how many students are involved in IM sports. Allegedly, 80 percent of the students are involved in IM sports in one form or other. No other activity comes close to that percentage of involvement."

STUDENT AUTHOR: Any student call tell you that basketball is the saving grace of Gonzaga athletics. The men's team is consistently very good, games are raucous and electrifying, and students get in for free. As for the intramurals, there's an A, B, and C league, so you can pick your level of involvement and competition. There isn't a huge variety of IM sports, but there's enough to keep everyone happy.

Students Speak Out
ON DRUG SCENE

Q "The number of students that do drugs harder than marijuana (like meth, ecstasy, or cocaine) is very low, and **even marijuana is mainly used recreationally**."

Q "More students smoke weed than you might think. **The boozing is wasteful and overdone like it is at most colleges**, and other drugs are definitely around, but fairly rare."

Q "**I think the average kid might smoke weed now and then**, and that's about it. But let's be honest here, GU has its drug scene just like any university. Once you know the people who do the harder drugs, a whole network of students is opened."

STUDENT AUTHOR: The majority of students party, but the contingent of students who are seriously dedicated to imbibing alcohol is much smaller. Since there are no truly wild parties, no fraternities, and not enough academic or social stress to justify excessive medication, most Zags seem to be content with caffeine and alcohol.

12:1	Student-to-Faculty Ratio
92%	Freshman Retention Rate
58%	Four-Year Graduation Rate
70%	Financial Aid Applicants Receiving Aid

Students Speak Out
SAFETY & SECURITY

Q "**The security staff on campus is wonderful**. The officers are easy to approach, generally have a great sense of humor, and are infinitely helpful. They deal with problems quickly and professionally."

Q "Girls shouldn't walk alone on the outskirts of campus after dark. **Bikes are at risk any hour of the day or night**. But other than that, there's not much to worry about."

Q "**Because it is a small campus, there is a sense of security**. Gonzaga is flanked by the river and three main streets (Sharp, Hamilton, and Division) that enclose the campus. There are no main roads that cut through, so it is very much in its own little world."

STUDENT AUTHOR: Surrounded by heavily student-populated neighborhoods, one rarely sees anyone on campus who isn't a part of the University. Campus Security patrols around the clock, and there are many blue-light emergency phones around. Bike theft is the preeminent crime.

Questions?
For more inside information and survival tips, pick up College Prowler's full-length book on this school, written by an actual student! Check it out at *www.collegeprowler.com*.

Students Speak Out
ON OVERALL EXPERIENCE

Q "I have loved my experience at Gonzaga, and I know that **I made the right choice to obtain my undergraduate degree**. There is no other place I would have preferred to spend the last four years."

Q "Overall, I've been very satisfied with the school, but I've known people who were very unsatisfied with the school. **I'd recommend visiting the school before deciding to come here**, to see if it's your style."

Q "There are many exceptional liberal arts colleges in America. What separates Gonzaga from the rest and makes it a truly unique experience is its location in the city of Spokane, **the Jesuit community**, and the incredible student community."

Q "The people at GU are special. My theory has been that, because GU draws from a lot of surrounding small towns, **we get students with that small-town kindness**. I think that the relationships here run deeper than they might at other schools."

STUDENT AUTHOR: Most students at Gonzaga are very happy to be here. Few would argue that Gonzaga isn't flawed. Common complaints include that it isn't strong enough academically, classes are too big, it's too Catholic or not Catholic enough, and Spokane is a lousy city for a college student. But most students admit their love for it anyway. Perhaps the primary reason for this is the tightness of the Gonzaga community and the relaxed and friendly atmosphere that comes with it. One can cope with shortcomings more easily when living in a comfortable and friendly environment.

Goucher College

1021 Dulaney Valley Road; Baltimore, MD 21204
(410) 337-6000; www.goucher.edu

THE BASICS:

Acceptance Rate: 66% **SAT Range:** 1590–1940*
Setting: Suburban **Control:** Private
F-T Undergrads: 1,472 **Tuition:** $32,168

Most Popular Majors: Psychology, Visual/Performing Arts, Social Sciences, Communications/Journalism

*of 2400

Academics	B	Guys	C
Local Atmosphere	B+	Girls	B-
Safety & Security	B+	Athletics	C-
Computers	B+	Nightlife	B+
Facilities	C+	Greek Life	N/A
Campus Dining	B	Drug Scene	B-
Off-Campus Dining	A-	Campus Strictness	B
Campus Housing	C+	Parking	C
Off-Campus Housing	D	Transportation	C-
Diversity	D	Weather	B-

Students Speak Out
ON ACADEMICS

Q "I had some professors and classes that blew my mind and others that just didn't inspire me. **I felt that I could have been challenged a lot more** in class discussion than I was. The papers and assignments were usually challenging, but the day-to-day class activity could have been more stimulating."

Q "A few professors **share too much info about their prescription drugs**. Students don't care if teachers are depressed."

Q "For the most part, professors are well-qualified, friendly, and helpful. **They care whether or not you do well**, and in the small classroom setting, that makes a big difference."

Q "Most professors are knowledgeable, enthusiastic, approachable, and involved in both their discipline and their students. **They are always willing to work with students** who are having difficulty in their courses. Because of Goucher's excellent professors, I have found most of my classes very interesting and enjoyable, especially within my majors."

STUDENT AUTHOR: **If you aren't used to receiving personal attention from teachers, Goucher professors may startle you at first. The professors are very accessible and participate in all aspects of the campus. They post office hours each week for students to stop by to ask questions about class, get feedback on assignments, or just to chat about life in general. Smaller classes also mean that there are no teaching assistants.**

Students Speak Out
ON LOCAL ATMOSPHERE

Q "**Towson is a bustling 'college town'** with a mall, a small concert venue, bookstores, movie theaters, and many restaurants. Be careful, however, not to be out alone once it gets dark, especially if you are a girl; it's not the safest area once you get past the mall."

Q "It's a very convenient town. **Everything you need is within a two-mile radius of Goucher**. On Friday nights, the bars can be low-key and fun. They're definitely not as exciting as those in Baltimore, but parking is free and it's easy to get home."

Q "Towson is fairly small, so **the number of things to do is limited**. This doesn't necessarily mean you can't have a good time. Towson University is just up the street, so if you're bored of Goucher by the weekend, you can always visit there."

Q "**Towson is fun, but only if you're over 21** and can get into bars and clubs. There's not much to do in Towson besides getting a bite to eat or seeing a movie. The mall is nice, but it gets boring after one too many visits, and it puts a hole in your bank account."

STUDENT AUTHOR: **Towson is a middle-class town with a population of about 50,000. Between Goucher and Towson University lies the "college atmosphere," where stores, restaurants, and bars line the streets. It's nice to know that everything you need is only a short walk away. When students venture into Baltimore City or Washington DC, it's usually out of boredom rather than necessity.**

Students Speak Out
ON FACILITIES

Q "If you're looking for big facilities and lots of them, you probably won't like what you see, but **they're still pretty good, overall**."

Q "Facilities on campus are **really nice and excellently maintained**. Some buildings are showing their age, but efforts are being made to remedy the situation."

Q "Facilities on campus are pretty nice and improving regularly. **The FMS crew does an excellent job maintaining the facilities** we have so that everything is clean and in working order 99 percent of the time."

Q "**I honestly love the facilities on campus**. I feel that the campus is beautiful, and there is so much for the students to do on campus."

Q "**Athletic facilities are lacking (to say the least)** and need to be completely renovated, especially the cardiovascular and weight training equipment."

Q "The social centers are **very attractive and convenient for students**, and they have always satisfied me. Pearlstone is a great place to chat and eat with friends."

STUDENT AUTHOR: The facilities on campus are well-maintained and aesthetically pleasing. The gorgeous landscape and architecture are a pride of Goucher. Each building added to campus is carefully designed to match the existing buildings: stone exteriors, beautiful angles, and tall windows. However, many buildings are too small for the growing student population.

Famous Alumni

Sara T. Hughes (first woman to serve in Texas State Court), Mildred Dunnock Urmy (actress), Jeanette R. Wolman (founder of the Women's Bar Association)

Students Speak Out
ON CAMPUS DINING

Q "The food is **excellent compared to other colleges**. There are so many options, many of which have choices of organic, vegetarian, or vegan. You are guaranteed to find something you like everyday."

Q "**Excuse me, I just threw up in my mouth a little**. The food was okay at first, but towards the end, I stuck to tuna sandwiches."

Q "I have no complaints about the food. **There's lots of variety for all types of eaters**. They make an effort toward organic and healthy options."

Q "The food is okay. **It's kind of greasy, but it's tolerable**. You should definitely save up money to go out to eat every now and then, because you'll need it."

Q "Stimson always has the same things to eat. The hot entrees usually have some strange sauce that no one likes. **Pearlstone is good for sandwiches and quick meals**, but if you go at the wrong time, you'll have to wait in line for a long time."

STUDENT AUTHOR: Students either love campus dining or hate it. Some say the food tastes like cardboard, while others say it's just like home cooking. The main problem with Bon Appétit, the company that provides food services for Goucher, is that they try to be too creative and often ruin a basic meal. Bon Appétit always takes student complaints seriously, though, and tries to accommodate students with special food requests.

Student Body

African American:	6%	Male/Female:	33/67%
Asian American:	3%	Out-of-State:	23%
Hispanic:	4%	International:	1%
Native American:	<1%	Unknown:	11%
White:	74%		

Popular Faiths: The student body seems equally split between Judaism and Christianity.

Gay Pride: The Goucher community is very open and accepting of students of all sexual preferences.

Economic Status: While students from all economic levels are represented in the student body, most hail from the upper-middle class.

Students Speak Out
ON DORMS

Q "**There is a huge disparity in dorm quality** and no reduction in price. If you're a freshman, chances are that you will be put in Stimson, which is mouse infested and deemed the 'ghetto.'"

Q "**Most dorms are spacious and clean**. Mary Fisher is the oldest, but it's also the best. It has character, huge rooms and a dining hall. There are also newer dorms with air conditioning that some consider 'the best,' but those dorms don't have as much personality."

Q "A lot of people give Winslow and Probst a bad reputation. **I actually think they're the most fun dorms around**, even though they're dirty and smell pretty bad. The rooms are big, so it's a small sacrifice."

STUDENT AUTHOR: **The quality of each dorm depends on what is important to you: comfort, convenience, character, or community. All of the dorms are livable, but Stimson and Froelicher are not well-maintained. Residents complain of mice, roaches, broken lights, clogged toilets, and awful stenches. If comfort is your priority, stick to the newer dorms.**

> **Did You Know?**
> 80% of undergrads live on campus.

Students Speak Out
ON GUYS & GIRLS

Q "Most people are very open-minded and friendly. **I don't know if I'd call them hot by societal standards**, but I have had no problem finding boys to date. There are certainly many girls to choose from because of the ratio."

Q "**We are pretty diverse, looks-wise**. You can go from an Abercrombie & Fitch kid to an artsy kid to anything in between."

Q "If a girl is looking for 'Mr. Right,' she'd better look elsewhere. Between the jocks, the computer science guys, and the homosexuals, the options are few. From the boys' side, however, the phrase **'the odds are good, but the goods are odd'** has been heard more than once."

STUDENT AUTHOR: **Jocks, hippies, airheads, preps, geeks, goths, and punks are all well represented at Goucher. As far as physical beauty goes, Goucher is lacking in both male and female hotties. Those that are attractive are either taken or extremely egotistical. However, the majority of students on campus are intelligent, humorous, and have great personalities. There is also a large LGBT scene.**

> **Traditions**
>
> **Goucherdales**
> An annual House Council fundraiser in which male Goucher students compete in stripping performances.
>
> **Winter Meltdown**
> An afternoon of stress relieving events held before finals week of the fall semester.
>
> **Overall School Spirit**
> Despite the close-knit community at Goucher, there is a serious lack of school spirit. Athletic events are not well attended by students outside the athletic social circle.

Students Speak Out
ON ATHLETICS

Q "Goucher has a good equestrian team and a decent ultimate Frisbee team. We also have lots of people interested in lacrosse, an increasingly better women's soccer team, and a good track team. **We're not exactly a top-rated school, but we do okay.**"

Q "Sports are not really big at Goucher. We have them, but **not a lot of students go to the games or events**. If you are looking to play as a student athlete, where your sport is more of a hobby, then this is the way to go."

Q "We have many varsity athletes, the teams are good and many are very competitive programs, but **there's not much support for them from the community as a whole**."

STUDENT AUTHOR: **The majority of Goucher students would rather read a psychology textbook than go to an athletic event on campus. The only thing students watch the sport teams do is try to fit 30 people at two small tables in the dining hall. While the student body is apathetic toward sports, the athletes that participate love it and have a guaranteed social circle.**

Students Speak Out
ON DRUG SCENE

Q "I like the drug scene. **It's not too strong, but it's strong enough** that I have been able to use pot as a great ice-breaking interconnective facet."

Q "**Almost everyone I have met smokes pot all the time**, but there are some people who don't. Some people seem to be getting into heavier drugs lately, but it's a very small minority."

Q "Drug use has gotten more prevalent recently, and I am kind of scared to see where it will go in the future. **There are a lot of pretty serious drugs, not just pot**. With that said, people are usually pretty low-key about it, and I never felt any pressure to partake if I didn't want to."

STUDENT AUTHOR: Many students rely on alcohol and pot for their weekend entertainment, so use is very prevalent at on-campus parties. While many students participate in this recreation, you don't have to smoke or drink to fit in; those who do partake are cool about not pressuring others to join in.

9:1	Student-to-Faculty Ratio
82%	Freshman Retention Rate
62%	Four-Year Graduation Rate
84%	Financial Aid Applicants Receiving Aid

Students Speak Out
SAFETY & SECURITY

Q "The security officers aren't constantly visible, but **you know they're there if you need them**. I thought it would be scary at night being surrounded by woods, but I never once felt intimidated."

Q "I never encountered a problem with security, but **I'm not so sure how safe the campus really is, when anyone can walk in at any time**. At least I feel safe."

Q "Sometimes, I feel like security is so focused on collecting revenue through parking tickets that they forget about the safety of the students. **There seems to be a sense of mutual disrespect between the students and security staff**. Most of the time, we don't like them, and they don't like us."

STUDENT AUTHOR: Campus is completely safe. Students feel confident walking across campus alone at night. Crime is sporadic, and offenders are usually Goucher students rather than off-campus perpetrators. Security provides escorts, and blue-light emergency phones are posted all over campus.

Questions?
For more inside information and survival tips, pick up College Prowler's full-length book on this school, written by an actual student! Check it out at *www.collegeprowler.com*.

Students Speak Out
ON OVERALL EXPERIENCE

Q "Overall, I have been very satisfied with my experience at Goucher. **I have especially enjoyed the community atmosphere**, as well as the nurturing staff. I've been blessed with many leadership and academic opportunities at Goucher that would not have been available to me had I attended another school. Though there have been times I have questioned my decision to attend Goucher, I am confident that there is no better place for me."

Q "No school is perfect, and that's true for Goucher, but **I still had a great experience**, and I am glad that I chose to go there."

Q "**I absolutely love Goucher**. At first, I was hesitant to come, but now that I'm here, I never want to leave. The people are awesome. Everyone seems to find their own little group, no matter what their interests are."

Q "I loved Goucher. I would not exchange my experience for anything. **It is extremely well respected, which helps after graduation**. My Goucher education prepared me for life post-college and made me into a more humane, compassionate, and open-minded person."

STUDENT AUTHOR: Goucher provides an atmosphere for students to grow and learn without being restricted or criticized. With an attentive and experienced faculty, freedom to design one's major, endless leadership opportunities, and a series of lectures, discussions, and performances, the Goucher experience is one of a kind. Despite complaints on parking, public transportation, the social scene, and campus facilities, the majority of Goucher students have great overall experiences.

Grinnell College

1103 Park Street; Grinnell, IA 50112
(641) 269-4000; www.grinnell.edu

THE BASICS:

Acceptance Rate: 43%
Setting: Rural
F-T Undergrads: 1,646

SAT Range: 1235–1450*
Control: Private
Tuition: $35,428

Most Popular Majors: Social Sciences, Foreign Language, Biology/Life Sciences, History

*of 1600

Academics	A-	Guys	C
Local Atmosphere	C	Girls	C
Safety & Security	A-	Athletics	C+
Computers	B+	Nightlife	B
Facilities	B	Greek Life	N/A
Campus Dining	D+	Drug Scene	C-
Off-Campus Dining	B-	Campus Strictness	A
Campus Housing	A-	Parking	B+
Off-Campus Housing	C+	Transportation	D-
Diversity	C+	Weather	C+

Students Speak Out
ON ACADEMICS

Q "Most of the professors I've had truly invested themselves in the students and the material. **They also had high expectations** for their students."

Q "There aren't a lot of options in the course catalog, which is one disadvantage of having a small school. Luckily, though, **the few classes that are available have excellent professors** who know what they're talking about, and they are more than happy to devote individual attention after class. It's also usually a good idea to stay away from temporary profs. Fortunately, they are few and far between."

Q "Your academic experience here depends entirely on the department you choose. They are all very willing to have one-on-one interactions with students; **they enjoy their subjects**, and they are genuinely interested in helping you in whatever way they can."

Q "The **professors at Grinnell are amazing**! They all seem so interested in what they are teaching. My classes have all been really fun and interesting."

STUDENT AUTHOR: **The pride and joy of Grinnell College is its academic reputation. Most classes are challenging but very rewarding; most professors challenge students to think critically and demand a lot. Anything assigned helps student understand what they're studying, rather than just passing on a deadline. The only course required is the Freshman Tutorial.**

Students Speak Out
ON LOCAL ATMOSPHERE

Q "The town is **really cute and charming**, but the townies resent the presence of the students."

Q "I'm a minority, and for me, **the atmosphere is fine most of the time**. However, on the weekends the townies (especially the teenagers) make comments both racial and sexual. I disregard it, though, because they are from Grinnell, Iowa. What do they know?"

Q "Grinnell is **a small one-college town**. Most people in town are very friendly and personable."

Q "**No other colleges are in town**, and there really isn't anything to stay away from because there isn't much to do here."

Q "The town resembles a 1950s farm-community— **pretty boring stuff**. Most students use downtown for random commerce, the bars, and for daily necessities. However, due to the residency requirement on campus, social isolation isn't a problem; the social scene is great and localized entirely within the campus."

STUDENT AUTHOR: **A 10-minute walk is all it takes to reach downtown. The setting is extremely rural. Many feel constricted by the small size. Every store can be found on either Broad or Main Street. Unless you plan on traveling on a regular basis, a car is unnecessary. While Grinnell isn't very big, there are always things to do. Those who are driven completely insane by living in the middle of nowhere usually leave after a year or two.**

Students Speak Out
ON CAMPUS DINING

Q "**The food in the dining hall is terrible**. It would be much better if dining services would spend as much time on the food as they do thinking of more diabolical ways to cheat students out of money!"

Q "The food is awful, but **the quad cafeteria looks exactly like Hogwarts** dining hall, so the ambiance makes up for it."

Q "The dining halls aren't as bad as everyone makes them out to be. **There isn't much variety**, but the food isn't terrible."

Q "Food on campus is bad—it's just plain bad! **They try really hard**, and the cooks are really nice. Basically, it's a bunch of Midwestern women trying to make something that the European chef likes. They are constantly trying to mass-produce meals that cannot be successfully expanded to feed that many people."

Q "If you have to be in the dining hall, **you could assemble something edible** from the options they do provide for you. Also, if you like salad, you might be okay."

STUDENT AUTHOR: **Most of the student body would agree that the current dining situation at Grinnell is quite dismal, but students make the most of it. The two college dining halls are Cowles on North Campus and Quad on South. In terms of the food they serve, the two are almost identical. Both eateries have a main line, which includes various main courses and hot side dishes. There are always dishes for vegans and vegetarians.**

Students Speak Out
ON FACILITIES

Q "Everything at Grinnell is top-notch. **I might complain about the computer labs** if anything, but there's almost always a computer open somewhere."

Q "The **campus is very well-funded**, and Grinnell is in the midst of building a new athletic facility and student center. I've always found the facilities adequate to serve about any purpose I could want."

Q "I think the facilities are nice. Still, the College is making an effort to improve them. I was pleased with the old dorms; still, **the College built new dorms**. I was pleased with the Forum (student center); now, the College built a new Campus Center. I was pleased with the PEC (athletic building); however, the college felt that building a new one was necessary. Grinnell seems very concerned with keeping up to date, for better or for worse."

Q "The **soccer fields are the best** I've ever seen."

Q "We have nice buildings here. **They fit very well with the atmosphere** on campus."

STUDENT AUTHOR: **Grinnell is going through a revamping of its facilities. Within the next few years (by 2007), many that are now near and dear to Grinnellians' hearts will disappear or be altered beyond recognition. The first step was the construction of East Campus. The process continued with the demolition of Darby gym. Although intentions were good, the move failed to appease the student body, and many students voiced their opinions by sporting "Save Darby" T-shirts.**

Famous Alumni

Kevin Cannon, Emily Bergl, Amy Johnson, Thomas Cech, John Garang, Robert Noyce, Gary Cooper

Student Body

African American:	5%	Male/Female:	47/53%
Asian American:	8%	Out-of-State:	90%
Hispanic:	6%	International:	11%
Native American:	<1%	Unknown:	7%
White:	62%		

Popular Faiths: The Christian community on campus tends to be the most visible.

Gay Pride: Grinnell is amazing when it comes to gay tolerance and is one of the most open colleges in the country.

Economic Status: There are a good number of upper-class and upper-middle-class students.

Students Speak Out
ON DORMS

Q "The dorms are extravagant, with the exception of Norris, a temporary building that's just a horrible sight. The floors are small, and the students living together have very tight-knit relationships. **Don't expect to get a room to yourself** before your third year, though."

Q "All the dorms are pretty nice; you really can't go wrong with any of them. There is the very occasional tiny shoebox room, but generally, **there is plenty of space**, and they are pretty comfortable."

Q "The dorms here are **very clean** and not at all crowded. I would personally suggest avoiding south campus if you do not like smoke. Also, east campus is new, so it is always a fine choice to live there."

STUDENT AUTHOR: Since incoming freshmen are not around to pick a room or dorm, the college selects their rooms for them. While some first years end up randomly scattered across campus, a good majority end up in Norris. There is nothing that can cement friendships faster than shoving 60 bewildered 18 year olds into the same building.

Did You Know?
87% of undergrads live on campus.

Students Speak Out
ON GUYS & GIRLS

Q "The **guys and girls are super intelligent** and cool. People here are very attractive, although not in a traditional way."

Q "Everyone gets so used to each other here that no one bothers to dress up, which gives Grinnellians **a reputation for being ugly**. Personally, I think that we're just comfortable with each other. For the most part, though, they are very accepting, wonderful people."

Q "The girls are **not super-model quality**, but many of them are attractive."

Q "While **there are some attractive individuals**, Grinnell is not the hottest school, though guys are generally considered more attractive than the girls on the whole."

STUDENT AUTHOR: Grinnell students are rarely hot. While there are a few tan, thin, blond girls, and a handful of buff guys with chiseled features and moussed hair, if you come to looking for them, you'll be disappointed. Grinnell students are intelligent, socially concerned, fun-loving, friendly individuals. While finding a makeout buddy on a Saturday night is usually not that difficult, finding a girlfriend or boyfriend might be.

Traditions

2 a.m. Bakery Run
On weeknights the Danish Maid Bakery finishes baking it's pastries at 2 o'clock in the morning. If you're up late studying it's traditional to take a quick run downtown to get something fresh out of the oven.

Overall School Spirit
School spirit at Grinnell isn't a very visible phenomenon. You won't find any cheerleading or pep squads here.

Students Speak Out
ON ATHLETICS

Q "Grinnell is **a Division III college**, but we still take sports seriously. The intramural sports are pretty big as well. Intramural soccer is growing by the year!"

Q "A fair number of people play varsity sports, but academics are top priority at Grinnell. Grinnell has **a no-cut policy**, though, so if you want to be on the team, you can be."

Q "Sports are **much bigger than one might expect**; college wouldn't be the same without a select few dumb jocks."

Q "Varsity sports? **We have varsity sports**? The people attending the games are the players and/or whoever the players cajoled into going to watch."

STUDENT AUTHOR: Aside from basketball, athletics aren't a big deal at Grinnell. Few students who aren't friends with someone on the team show up to games. Teams try to advertise sporting events as much as possible, but some would be hard-pressed to tell you where the outdoor track is. The fact that we don't have any kind of stadium doesn't help.

Students Speak Out
ON DRUG SCENE

Q "There are a lot of potheads at Grinnell, but there's no pressure to become one. **Alcohol is generally the preferred drug**, but it gets pretty old pretty fast."

Q "Grinnell is a very wet campus. Alcohol is almost always prevalent at parties. Weed is also present, and **sometimes harder drugs rear their ugly heads at parties** off campus."

Q "Hard drugs (i.e. crack, cocaine, ecstasy) are rare, but there are a lot of students on campus who smoke marijuana. However, **there is never any pressure for a student to experiment** with any drug. It's not like they're trying to sell students crack in the library."

STUDENT AUTHOR: The administration and a large majority of students believe that Grinnell has a drug problem. The college's alcohol policy is almost non-existent. While students are not permitted to have open containers on or around campus grounds, this is not enforced. Local police rarely get involved in school functions.

9:1	Student-to-Faculty Ratio
94%	Freshman Retention Rate
81%	Four-Year Graduation Rate
88%	Financial Aid Applicants Receiving Aid

Students Speak Out
SAFETY & SECURITY

Q "Dorms are on 24-hour lockdown, but for the most part, **security is pretty lax**, and students don't feel the need to lock their doors."

Q "First, **there's absolutely no crime here**. I've left my door unlocked 24/7 and have never had any problems; the last serious crime the campus experienced happened before I enrolled."

Q "**Security is great here**. I know most of the security guards, at least by sight, and say hi when I see them. They check up on people who have had too much to drink to make sure they're okay."

Q "We're in the middle of Iowa. **Security is as good as it gets**."

STUDENT AUTHOR: The security department at Grinnell is pretty inactive, but there's not much of a reason for them to exist. Violent crime on campus is unheard of, and Grinnell's Self Governance policy means that security guards are discouraged from poking around in students lives.

Questions?
For more inside information and survival tips, pick up College Prowler's full-length book on this school, written by an actual student! Check it out at *www.collegeprowler.com*.

Students Speak Out
ON OVERALL EXPERIENCE

Q "My experience has been great! You'd be hard-pressed to find a school where more freedom is granted than Grinnell. **The college really makes you feel alive!**"

Q "I applied early decision to Grinnell, and I've never regretted that decision. However, Grinnell is not for everyone. **Students here are given a lot of responsibility**, and if a prospective student cannot handle responsibility, well, they shouldn't apply. That also applies to students who are poor at handling stress, because you will get stressed out at some point if you come to Grinnell."

Q "Grinnell is **the only place I could see myself**. I love it here. To quote *Field of Dreams*: 'Is this Heaven?' 'No, it's Iowa.'"

Q "Grinnell has its perks and jerks, but I wouldn't change schools for the world. **I'm getting a great education**, and I'm constantly meeting people who teach me about the world. My peers are the men and women who really are going to make a difference someday."

STUDENT AUTHOR: A vast majority of Grinnell students love it. Students who choose to come here love the challenge they get from academia and their peers, and they love the amount of freedom that the administration gives them (mostly through Self Governance). Grinnell students are free to learn and grow into responsible, conscientious adults, and the students here are thankful that the school they've chosen has given them the opportunity to thrive. Overall, most of the students here are happy with the decisions they've made and the direction they're going in their lives.

Grove City College

100 Campus Drive; Grove City, PA 16127
(724) 458-2000; www.gcc.edu

THE BASICS:

Acceptance Rate: 55%
Setting: Rural
F-T Undergrads: 2,489

SAT Range: 1140–1390*
Control: Private
Tuition: $12,074

Most Popular Majors: Business/Marketing, Education, Biology, Engineering, English

*of 1600

Academics	B+	Guys	B-
Local Atmosphere	C	Girls	C+
Safety & Security	A+	Athletics	C
Computers	B	Nightlife	D+
Facilities	B-	Greek Life	C+
Campus Dining	C+	Drug Scene	A
Off-Campus Dining	C+	Campus Strictness	D-
Campus Housing	B	Parking	B+
Off-Campus Housing	N/A	Transportation	C-
Diversity	F	Weather	C

Students Speak Out
ON ACADEMICS

Q "I have loved almost every one of the professors I've had at Grove City. They all have been really willing to give you extra help, even giving you their home phone numbers and addresses— **some even invite you to their homes for dinner**. I even see a large majority of the professors at church on Sundays, and they usually will say hello to you by name."

Q "Classes are challenging, but to really make you know the information, not just to fail you. Though it may not seem so at the time, the classes really do **help you in shaping your worldview**."

Q "I've been to three other colleges and universities before coming to Grove City. I would be **hard-pressed to find a better learning experience** somewhere else."

Q "Many of the professors are wonderful and encourage their students to learn. However, many also do not try to help students explore viewpoints beyond their own or learn about other cultures. **Do not expect to learn much about non-European cultures** at Grove City."

STUDENT AUTHOR: **Engineering and biology majors are known for long hours at the library, and education majors seem forever occupied with lesson plans and projects. These hard workers blend in with their peers because the student body is known for its strong work ethic and wide range of interests. Profs at GCC carry more classes and focus less on personal research projects than their associates at other highly-ranked institutions.**

Students Speak Out
ON LOCAL ATMOSPHERE

Q "**Grove City is a dry town**, and I like that because there isn't a lot of drinking going on and trouble being caused in the town. There are no other universities in Grove City."

Q "Grove City has a population of around 2,000 Anglo-Americans who are **asleep by 10 p.m.**"

Q "The overall town is old. Not fun, not interesting, **nothing to do** for a normal college kid."

Q "There really isn't any atmosphere outside the campus. It is a dry town with nothing to do, unless you feel like going to eight different churches on a Sunday. The Wal-Mart isn't even open 24 hours. I'd say the big "hot spot" in Grove City would be the Sheetz. **The outlet mall is a few minutes down the road**, so if you have the money that is a good place to spend some time. Pittsburgh is about an hour away."

Q "It's pretty quiet, and it's easy to stay on campus for long periods of time (unless you go for long runs through the streets of Grove City). The atmosphere is pleasant and safe, although not exhilarating in itself. But there are **lots of green fields**, a must for me."

STUDENT AUTHOR: **Grove City, a safe, small town surrounded by the rural landscape of Western Pennsylvania, is well protected from any urban bustle. Grovers have access to attractions like the Grove City Prime Outlets and the Guthrie—a retro single-screen movie theater. Pittsburgh is about 40 mintues away; Slippery Rock University about 15 minutes.**

5 Best Things	5 Worst Things
1 Low tuition	1 No diversity
2 Worship sessions	2 21-meal plan only
3 The Gee's ice cream	3 FitWell
4 Ultimate Frisbee	4 The rumor mill
5 President's office hours	5 Expensive parking

Students Speak Out
ON CAMPUS DINING

Q "**It's sustenance**, but some days, you have to search really hard to find something edible."

Q "The dining hall service **does not always offer the healthiest selections** and is the lowest price level offered by Bon Appetit."

Q "The cafeteria food is not great, but **there are places on campus to get good food**. The Gee (student union) offers good finger foods, especially the chicken tender wrap, a favorite of GCC students. The Gee is where many students spend their evenings studying and hanging out with friends, so good snack foods are a must. The dining hall food is okay, and they are trying to make it more pleasing to students."

Q "I generally like it—**I don't have to cook it** and I don't have to pay for it (at least not directly). The food is basically a story of tight budgets—the food service does the best it can with a very limited budget, and they are creative."

STUDENT AUTHOR: While many students cast a suspicious eye on Hicks and MAP cafeteria entrées, the cereal options, salad bar, and dessert options make it rare for students to leave meals hungry. Weekday breakfasts at MAP cafeteria offer a wide selection of fresh fruits and a while-u-wait omelet bar. Specialty salads and carved meats or other chef specialties often bring students much closer to the home-style cooking they inevitably miss. The Geedunk (Gee) in the student union provides a break from cafeteria food, offering a bistro, grill, and a wood-fired pizza oven.

Students Speak Out
ON FACILITIES

Q "There is a new **student activities center that is open 24 hours**. That will be nice for anyone who needs a place to study when the library is closed."

Q "The architecture of the school is beautiful and adds to the beauty of the campus. The new academic building and the student union are technologically well equipped but still retain the character of the campus. **Some of the buildings are old** and could use some renovations, but everything is pretty nice overall."

Q "The athletic building is spacious. It has a great Intramural room, where anyone can come and play basketball or volleyball or indoor soccer—you name it, and it probably can be played in there. The **weight room is on the smaller side**."

Q "The computer lab, aside from the fact that many of the computer don't work all the time, is adequate, especially considering that **each student has his own laptop**. The new Student Center just opened, and is amazing with a full snack bar, bistro, pizza parlor, grand hall, meeting rooms, offices for student organizations, and a two-story bookstore."

STUDENT AUTHOR: GCC has more than 20 buildings spread on about 150 acres in a layout designed by Frederick L Olmstead (who also designed Central Park and the Washington DC Mall). And to keep campus up to speed, the recently built Student Activities Center has two-story windows, an open dining area, balconies, and a fireplace that should turn alumni who missed out green with envy.

Famous Alumni
Karin Hendrickson, Brian Leftow, J. Howard Pew, David and Joann Stauffer

Student Body

African American:	<1%	Male/Female:	51/49%
Asian American:	2%	Out-of-State:	53%
Hispanic:	1%	International:	1%
Native American:	<1%	Unknown:	1%
White:	95%		

Popular Faiths: The College is a broadly evangelical Christian institution. Students are active in service organizations, local churches, and campus religious organizations as a demonstration of their faith.

Gay Pride: Most students believe that homosexuality is immoral. The marginal gay presence is ignored.

Economic Status: Most of the student body comes from a middle-class background.

Students Speak Out
ON DORMS

Q "The newer dorms are the nicest, with bigger rooms, lounges, and better lighting. Memorial (freshman guys) is the best men's dormitory. Many of the frats live in Hopeman and parts of Hicks—**avoid their halls**."

Q "North, the freshman dorm, is great if you're in a double. Forced triples, three put in a room for two, sound awful but work out fine if you get along with your roomies. Most freshman girls are put in triples. It's cozy, but there is still a decent amount of floor space. **The best women's dorm is South** (West is similar, but older). It has suites—two dorm rooms sharing a bathroom. The other dorms, Harker and MEP are decent but have hall bathrooms. The disadvantage of these two is that the furniture is bolted down and the floor space is minimal. MEP has a good amount of storage space, however."

STUDENT AUTHOR: **Full-time students are required to live on campus unless they are married, have significant health concerns, or commute from their parents' home. This policy keeps several hundred students in close quarters and lends itself to a closer campus community. All dorms are single sex.**

> **Did You Know?**
> 93% of undergrads live on campus.

Students Speak Out
ON GUYS & GIRLS

Q "Good-looking guys; **fewer good-looking girls**. Great place to meet a Christian boy/girl and hold their hands for four years. If you are looking for those overnight flings, you have only a select few to pick from."

Q "I think the guys are great. They are **mostly nice guys that act like gentlemen**—they open doors for you and let you get in front of them in food lines. There is a wide spectrum of girls—from Britney Spears wannabes to homeschoolers. There aren't very many ugly people or extremely hot people, but most are attractive guy- and girl-next-door types."

Q "**You need 'Grover Goggles'** when looking for a potential date."

STUDENT AUTHOR: **The average Grover girl is pleasant and sharp minded. She wears minimal makeup, works out at least a little, avoids dressing flashy, and goes to church. Grover guys get higher marks for physical attractiveness than their female counterparts, but character is such an important factor for many Grove City College students that students may readjust shallow first impressions and crushes after the initial weeks of orientation.**

> **Traditions**
>
> **Rainbow Bridge**
> This stone bridge over Wolf Creek is a favorite campus spot for a romantic moment.
>
> **Creeking**
> Creeking involves carrying a fellow student across campus chanting "Wolf Creek" and then depositing him (or her) in the muddy water.
>
> **Overall School Spirit**
> School spirit isn't huge, except for the "Crimson Crazies," who cheer for their peers both on the field and the court with a touch of paint and a hearty yell.

Students Speak Out
ON ATHLETICS

Q "Varsity sports draw a medium-sized crowd, I would say. But if you would compare them to the sports of other schools, **the crowd is kind of pathetic**. School spirit is not very present, and people usually attend games for lack of anything else to do. Plus the varsity sports are not known to have a very good record, which doesn't help with the crowd situation. IM sports, however, are widely participated in."

Q "I believe **IM sports tend to get heavier crowds** than the varsity sports. With Christian students come more 'important' things such as studying and being good role models. Sports are for more of the rebellious types."

Q "I maintain that GCC has a football team **in order to keep us humble**."

STUDENT AUTHOR: **GCC's Wolverine Arena is never filled to its 1,600-person capacity. Student-athletes frequently feel under supported and dislike the interference of the College's academic rigor upon them. In addition to varsity sports, GCC also offers club and intramural sports, which tend to be more popular, and less of commitment.**

Students Speak Out
ON DRUG SCENE

Q "Drug use is not high. **I have seen and smelled people smoking marijuana** on campus, but rarely anything else, although I do know a few people who do 'hard' drugs quite frequently on campus."

Q "There is a **zero-tolerance policy** about drugs and drinking on campus. If you're caught, you will be suspended or expelled."

Q "No. I do not use drugs. **There are just the people who smoke cigarettes** and cigars, and the people who hide bottles of alcohol in their room."

Q "There are little to no drugs on campus—and if there are, **you never see it**."

STUDENT AUTHOR: **A few students hide alcohol in sock drawers or under beds, but the Grove City College Smoker's Club has created an interesting but entirely legal scene. Around 30 students have brought out their cigars and pipes for a Wednesday evening smoke fest.**

15:1	Student-to-Faculty Ratio
90%	Freshman Retention Rate
75%	Four-Year Graduation Rate
79%	Financial Aid Applicants Receiving Aid

Students Speak Out
SAFETY & SECURITY

Q "Grove City is not the type of town where a lot of bad things happen. I have never personally had to deal with campus security, but I have heard stories where **they were slow getting to a site**."

Q "Grove City College, being majority Christian, **adds a moral compass that further discourages sin**. Every once in a while, somebody gets out of hand and rolls right past the campus stop sign without making a complete stop. In those cases, campus security is sure to deal swiftly and justly to rectify the situation."

Q "There are several emergency phones stationed around campus, and if you don't feel safe walking back to your dorm alone, you can use these, and they will send a security guard to **escort you to your dorm**."

STUDENT AUTHOR: **Close your eyes and imagine a place where students leave laptop computers unattended in the library, don't lock their dorm rooms, and misplaced ID cards are returned before they are even discovered missing. Open your eyes—no, it's not Eden, just Grove City College.**

Questions?
For more inside information and survival tips, pick up College Prowler's full-length book on this school, written by an actual student! Check it out at *www.collegeprowler.com*.

Students Speak Out
ON OVERALL EXPERIENCE

Q "**I love Grove City College**. I believe in what it stands for—freedom from government control, and adherence to conservative lifestyles."

Q "After thinking long and hard I am glad I stayed at Grove City. It has provided a little net for me. It held me accountable so I didn't get in to too much trouble, but I was also able to grow up a bit while at college. The **academics are incredible** and I love the challenging scene."

Q "**Students here are very hardworking and driven**—you have to be to make it at GCC. But all in all, it is a very good college to be at. I wouldn't want to be anywhere else."

Q "The school has definite ups and downs. Its small size allows people to get involved in many organizations easily, and there are many friendly people at the school. It is a friendly environment, but I think at times too friendly. Many students come from sheltered backgrounds, and they're **never really challenged to grow beyond those backgrounds**. Also, the college's rules are rather stringent, and some of them, such as inter-visitation rules, seem to only hurt those who care about following them, as those who don't care break the rules constantly."

STUDENT AUTHOR: **Some students complain their way through four years of killer academics, narrow-mindedness, and local boredom, but by the time most of them actually finish they have enjoyed GCC, despite their gripes. Other students rave about the school from the start. They thrive on the academic challenges, accept Christian values, and change the local atmosphere with their passionate desire to serve God and others.**

Guilford College

5800 West Friendly Avenue; Greensboro, NC 27410
(336) 316-2000; www.guilford.edu

THE BASICS:

Acceptance Rate: 58%
Setting: Urban
F-T Undergrads: 2,268

SAT Range: 1590–1860*
Control: Private
Tuition: $26,100

Most Popular Majors: Business, Psychology, Forensic Science, Criminal Justice, Elementary Education

*of 2400

Academics	B	Guys	B-
Local Atmosphere	B-	Girls	B
Safety & Security	B+	Athletics	C
Computers	B	Nightlife	B
Facilities	B	Greek Life	N/A
Campus Dining	D	Drug Scene	C+
Off-Campus Dining	A-	Campus Strictness	C+
Campus Housing	B-	Parking	B-
Off-Campus Housing	B+	Transportation	C+
Diversity	B-	Weather	B+

Students Speak Out
ON ACADEMICS

Q "It's **a decent mix** of good and bad. It can be hard to avoid the ones you don't like because the school is small."

Q "Some teachers make their **liberal leanings** very obvious. Some classes are stimulating and interesting—you have to work to get the most out of it."

Q "Teachers on the whole are fantastic. They usually explain concepts very well and give students **personal attention**. The classes are interesting because they are frequently discussion based, and they provide real world examples and applications."

Q "Some teachers are too interested in teaching **their own philosophy**. It kind of makes me want to puke."

STUDENT AUTHOR: **Although many end up dissatisfied with one particular professor, they are often pleased with the rest of their classes. The majority of professors are very approachable and caring. You'll never have any 200-student intro classes at Guilford—and hardly any classes over 30, for that matter. Many classes are primarily discussion based. Some classes require that you participate or risk a lower grade. Everyone is on a first name basis, which, at the very least, gives the feeling and illusion of a friendly relationship with your teachers. At Guilford, there are no teaching assistants, and there is often a focus on peer group work and review.**

Students Speak Out
ON LOCAL ATMOSPHERE

Q "There are **many colleges in town**, but it's not a college town. Most social interaction revolves around campus."

Q "Greensboro is **pretty boring** in my experience. I don't really leave the campus much beyond walking distance."

Q "Greensboro's **kind of a strip mall**, but the Weatherspoon (Art Museum) and the Civil Rights Museum are nice places to visit."

Q "It's **somewhat Southern**: the accent, the hospitality. It's also stereotypical, but progressive, in part because of the consortium of colleges located in G'boro."

Q "It's a city of about 200,000 that just keeps sprawling and sprawling. It is very commercial with lots of chain restaurants and **big-box stores**. There are some really nice parks and public gardens, though."

STUDENT AUTHOR: **Some call Greensboro a college town, but others insist that it's anything but. It really depends on how much time you spend at the local college hangouts, such as the trendy and popular Tate Street. There is a great arts and culture scene, but you have to actually get off campus and venture into other parts of the city to find it. Many students are quite satisfied with the numerous activities on campus and stay absorbed in the "Guilford bubble."**

5 Best Things	5 Worst Things
1 Professors	**1** Meal plan food
2 The beautiful campus	**2** Construction
3 Small classes	**3** Campus Life's mothering
4 Friendly people	**4** Poor public transportation
5 All four seasons	**5** Party ban

Students Speak Out
ON FACILITIES

Q "There isn't much in the way of common space (the lounges are mostly for watching TV), but in general, the **facilities are decent**."

Q "**Campus isn't extravagant**, but I feel like I've got what I need. The only exception is laundry; the machines are usually in disrepair, and they cost way too much."

Q "We mostly **hang out in the woods**, meadows, or the dorms."

Q "The campus is beautiful. Computers are above par from what I've seen at other schools. The athletic center leaves **something to be desired**, despite recent renovations."

Q "Facilities are **always clean** and grounds are well kept."

Q "It's pretty **beautiful on the outside**, a little old on the inside, but still nice."

STUDENT AUTHOR: Some of the campus facilities are currently under major renovation and have been for the past several years. Guilford's reconstruction is moving slowly from one building to another, due to needed classroom and office space. Some of the buildings' interiors ring of 1970s décor, but have recently been updated, repainted, and redesigned. Most of the exteriors fit perfectly with the scenic campus, designed with red brick that complements the branching brick walkways. The theme of large white pillars invokes Georgian architecture throughout the campus. Overall, the aesthetics of campus are a main draw in many students' decisions to come to Guilford.

Famous Alumni

Mary Ann Akers, M.L. Carr, Howard Coble, Harrison Hickman, Keith Holliday, Warren Misofsky

Students Speak Out
ON CAMPUS DINING

Q "The food is **edible**, but not desirable."

Q "For God's sake, if you can get off the meal plan, do! The coffee Co-Op is the only thing worth your money, with **vegan pastries** and fair trade coffee."

Q "**The Caf is awful**, and it's only open during short and inconvenient windows."

Q "The dining hall is **unimpressive** and made worse by the fact that, one, the meal plan is mandatory for on-campus students and, two, you can't take food out of the Caf."

Q "Gross! The food here makes me **want to curl up in a ball and die**."

Q "There isn't a such thing as 'good' food on any campus, but Guilford does have **various foods** for everyone."

STUDENT AUTHOR: Many first-year students agree that if there were any way to get off of the meal plan, then they would do so in a heartbeat. However, others say that Guilford's fare is quite edible—at the very least tolerable—for cafeteria food, most notably because of the diverse selection. Both food and service have been getting progressively better throughout the years, despite outsourcing to Sodexho and a reduction in dining hall hours. There is always at least one hot vegan and one vegetarian option per meal, as well as available soy milk and a salad bar for lunch and dinner. It can be horrible, but any attempt to mass-produce food is usually futile.

Student Body

African American:	24%	Male/Female:	48/52%
Asian American:	1%	Out-of-State:	61%
Hispanic:	1%	International:	1%
Native American:	1%	Unknown:	1%
White:	71%		

Popular Faiths: Most students are Quaker or are of various Christian denominations.

Gay Pride: The Guilford community is open to all students, regardless of sexual preference. There is a presence on campus, but not an overwhelming one.

Economic Status: Most Guilford students come from middle-class backgrounds, although there are people from both economic extremes.

Students Speak Out
ON DORMS

Q "Avoid Bryan unless you like noise and drunken revelry. **Avoid Milner** if you're not a fan of living in closets."

Q "The **houses are nice**, but wait until your third or fourth year to live there. It is much more isolated, and there aren't as many chances to meet people."

Q "Binford is the unofficial freshman dorm, Milner has a variety of people, Bryan is the party dorm. Shore, an **all-female dorm** has some problems with mold. Mary Hobbs, another all-girl dorm, probably has the nicest rooms on campus. For guys, English is very good."

STUDENT AUTHOR: **Most of the dorms are in central campus, so Guilford students can roll out of bed and stumble to all the major academic buildings in a matter of minutes. Two of the biggest dorms—and the most common placement for unwary freshmen—are Milner and Binford. Some males say avoid Mary Hobbs, probably due to outgoing women and the large lesbian population that traditionally resides there. English is the solo, men-only dorm. It has alternately been a refuge for jocks, gays, and more studious men looking to get away from the coed atmosphere.**

> **Did You Know?**
> 80% of undergrads live on campus.

Students Speak Out
ON GUYS & GIRLS

Q "Not many people at Guilford shave—boys or girls—but there are **lots of hotties** of both genders."

Q "For the most part, I'd say the large majority of students on campus were nice. Most students didn't go through their four years at Guilford without **at least one relationship**."

Q "Most people are **open-minded** and nice to talk to. There are hotties around, too!"

Q "I have enjoyed Guilford. There are a lot of really **unique and wonderful people**. I've made some great friends."

STUDENT AUTHOR: **Dating and the social scene on Guilford's campus has a lot to do with the individualist nature of the students and the small, community-centered campus. There is a large lesbian population at GuilCo. There is much intermingling between the classes (freshmen, seniors), as well. Guys, in general, seem more compassionate and considerate than your average college male. Girls appear to be a bit more relaxed about relationships, as well. People are friendly. Expect smiles, glances, and hellos when you are new, and much of the same when you are not.**

> **Traditions**
>
> • Activism in all respects
> • Balls—the Gender Bender and Coming Out balls
> • Bonfires by the lake and secretly in the woods
> • Homecoming
> • Quaker tradition
> • Religious Emphasis Week in January
>
> **Overall School Spirit**
> Guilford students don't express their school spirit in terms of attending sporting events, but rather as critical and concerned members of the school's community.

Students Speak Out
ON ATHLETICS

Q "Some believe **Guilford is divided** between athletes and non-athletes more than between races. So sports have a presence on campus, but it is not as big as it is in state schools, by any means."

Q "Intramural sports, like rugby, are cool. Everything else is not. Jocks who come for scholarships are **always in opposition** to the rest of campus."

Q "The **athletes think sports are bigger** than they really are."

Q "Varsity is its own thing (big division between varsity sports and the rest of campus). Club teams are amazing though, and have great people (i.e., **ultimate Frisbee**)."

STUDENT AUTHOR: **Varsity sports are a sore point with the college and those who attend. Although varsity sports participants represent a significant part of the college population, few come to Guilford just to play sports.**

Students Speak Out
ON DRUG SCENE

Q "**We have a reputation** for being a pothead school, but there are plenty of people who don't enjoy smoking."

Q "The biggest drugs on campus are **tobacco and alcohol**."

Q "To give you an idea, you aren't going to walk down a dorm hall and see any drugs. The times when you see them are if you move within certain circles or start doing them yourself. It's **not an open thing** here."

Q "Some **people seem to care** about smoking weed more than they do their classes."

STUDENT AUTHOR: At Guilford, if you want to do drugs, you can do drugs. If you want to ignore their existence, you can do that, as well. Many students were not even aware that drug circles existed on campus. Others commented that they know students who use drugs on a regular basis, but do not feel pressured or threatened by the presence of drugs. The most visible drug is alcohol.

15:1	Student-to-Faculty Ratio
67%	Freshman Retention Rate
46%	Four-Year Graduation Rate
80%	Financial Aid Applicants Receiving Aid

Students Speak Out
SAFETY & SECURITY

Q "I feel great! Guilford is towards the Western edge of Greensboro; people on campus are free-spirited, and I have **never felt threatened** at Guilford."

Q "I haven't had to deal directly with security, but I generally feel comfortable leaving my **door unlocked** if I'm not leaving for a while."

Q "Security is wack. Safety is **not an issue**. Wherever I go, I feel safe constantly."

Q "Security once locked me into the library after doing their check to make sure the building was closed. I was studying on a couch in a public room when the lights went out. Plus, security staffing has changed three times during my stay at Guilford. Our security is **inadequate at best**."

STUDENT AUTHOR: Although most students feel very safe at Guilford, it is not necessarily because of the present security measures, but rather the side of town on which campus is located. A common complaint is that Security arrives quickly to break up parties, but takes longer when other, perhaps more serious, events occur.

Questions?

For more inside information and survival tips, pick up College Prowler's full-length book on this school, written by an actual student! Check it out at *www.collegeprowler.com*.

Students Speak Out
ON OVERALL EXPERIENCE

Q "I sometimes wish that the school administration would get its act together, since they seem very confused about the school's identity. However, there are really awesome teachers and classes here, and it's **not hard to get in**. We're lucky."

Q "**I used to love it**, but now I just want to be left alone by the administration."

Q "Yes, **I wish I was somewhere else**. Only basketball keeps me sane."

Q "I love the campus, the teachers, and the students. Guilford is **a really unique place**, and I can't imagine being happier at another college."

Q "I haven't found my groove academically, but there are **some cool people** to hang out with."

Q "I can't wait for grad school. I like the school, but I am **not really crazy about most of my fellow students**."

STUDENT AUTHOR: Guilford is a wonderful place to be if you are looking for a small liberal arts college experience. Guilford does not attract the types of people who go to standard, huge state schools with flourishing Greek scenes and near-professional football programs. Guilford students are good at voicing their opinions. Sometimes this is productive, while other concerns and suggestions are disregarded by the college altogether. Guilford's traditional ideals are geared toward community involvement and in major decisions that affect all that are connected to the college. Despite any gripes that students have with Guilford, most think that the other aspects weigh out enough that they stay and love it.

Gustavus Adolphus College

800 West College Avenue; St. Peter, MN 56082
(507) 933-8000; www.gustavus.edu

THE BASICS:

Acceptance Rate: 80%
Setting: Rural
F-T Undergrads: 2,571

SAT Range: 1160–1350*
Control: Private
Tuition: $30,320

Most Popular Majors: Corporate Communications, Business, Biology, Communications, Psychology

*of 1600

Academics	B	Guys	B+
Local Atmosphere	C-	Girls	A-
Safety & Security	B-	Athletics	B+
Computers	B	Nightlife	B
Facilities	A-	Greek Life	B-
Campus Dining	A-	Drug Scene	B
Off-Campus Dining	C	Campus Strictness	B-
Campus Housing	B	Parking	B
Off-Campus Housing	C	Transportation	C
Diversity	D-	Weather	D

Students Speak Out
ON ACADEMICS

Q "**I've had really positive experiences with the professors here**—they chose Gustavus, too, and part of why they come here is to work closely with students. It's great to grab a cup of coffee with a prof or drop by their office just to chat."

Q "I love the professors at Gustavus. **This is a staff that is truly passionate about their jobs**. They go out of their way to help you because they genuinely want you to succeed."

Q "Because I picked classes I wanted to take, **almost every class was very intriguing**. The teachers were, on the whole, excellent; they really taught well. They were not just extremely knowledgeable about their chosen fields, but passionate about instilling the love of learning in their students."

Q "Every teacher I have had the pleasure of meeting has **taken the time to get to know me and sincerely converse with me**. Most of them care about what you have to offer to the class, campus, and life in general."

STUDENT AUTHOR: Gustavus likes to tout that there is an average of only 17 students in a classroom, and professor attention is one of the school's biggest draws. Most professors genuinely care about the students, take time to learn more about them, and always have their doors open. Virtually no classes, with the exception of a few science labs, are taught by TAs, but small class sizes and individual attention means that professors notice when you are not there.

Students Speak Out
ON LOCAL ATMOSPHERE

Q "I would say that one of the drawbacks about Gustavus is its location. **It is located in a small town with virtually nothing to do** besides going to a movie or one of the many local bars. Because of its small-town nature, though, St. Peter is virtually as safe as a city can be."

Q "To be completely honest, **I find the town of St. Peter to be completely dull**. There are many people who might call it quaint, and while I think it's a nice town, I find it boring and feel a little bit suffocated by its tiny size."

Q "While St. Peter itself is a sleepy little town and lacks what most students require in a college town, **it does have a sufficient grocery store, pizza place, liquor store, and a few bars** within walking distance of the campus."

Q "**St. Peter is a small town, which is a blessing and a curse**. I love the fact that once a year, college students go into the town to help residents by doing home repairs. On the other hand, though, there seems to be some bad blood between local residents and college students."

STUDENT AUTHOR: You can't talk about Gustavus without talking about Mankato. Though the community of St. Peter has fewer than 10,000 residents, neighboring Mankato houses Minnesota State University, and Gustavus students can oftentimes find reprieve there and not be as noticeable in a community where college students don't stick out nearly as much.

5 Best Things
1. Close-knit community
2. Nobel Conference
3. Excellent academics
4. Brand-new facilities
5. Caf food

5 Worst Things
1. Gossip
2. Rural atmosphere
3. Housing options
4. Limited parking
5. Lack of underage options

Students Speak Out
ON FACILITIES

Q "Wonderful! **We paid a ton of money for state-of-the-art facilities**. You should love them and use them often, since they are free."

Q "**The Lund Center has vastly improved the cardiovascular and weight machine areas**. Other than improvements initiated by the Student Senate and required after the tornado in 1998, everything is 'okay'—nothing spectacular, nothing too bad. Our pool is beautiful, though!"

Q "**Because of the tornado some years ago, our campus has extremely nice facilities**, seeing as how we had to rebuild a lot after the storm. Our Campus Center is quite new, as is our athletic complex. We just recently remodeled our cardio and lifting centers, so students have much accessibility when it comes to finding a machine to work out on."

Q "I thought all the facilities were very nice. **It had everything I needed**, and lots of things I never took advantage of."

Q "They are quite nice, **improvements are often made**, and student input is heeded rather often, actually."

STUDENT AUTHOR: After suffering a massive F5 tornado in 1998, most of the campus was leveled and had to be rebuilt, preempting campus conversations as being either "pre-tornado" or "post-tornado." Though the tornado devastated the campus, it gave the College a reason to improve facilities that had been wearing down. As a result, many of the buildings are less than a decade old and are equipped with new amenities.

Famous Alumni
Allison Rosati Dennis (news anchor for NBC5 Chicago), Kurt Elling (jazz artist), Peter Krause (actor), Tim Latta (founder of Koku Dance Theatre)

Students Speak Out
ON CAMPUS DINING

Q "Only one real shot for food on campus: the 'Caf,' otherwise known as the Evelyn Young Dining Room. **The food is good, with a wide variety of options**. I've never seen a better cafeteria on any other college or university campus. It does get old, however, and a lot of people put on weight."

Q "**The cafeteria doesn't have enough overall variety** to keep the kids shoving in with the same enthusiasm they had moving from disgusting high school cafeterias to eating in the big world."

Q "I have heard prospective students say that if they pick a school based solely on the dining hall, they would without a doubt choose Gustavus. And it's not a lie. **I didn't realize how much I liked the Caf until I moved off campus** and had to cook my own meals."

Q "Most of the food is the same, which makes it repetitive after a while. One thing that is nice is that **you are only charged for what you buy**, instead of having so many meals a week. Some good things are the pizzeria, the bakery, and stromboli Wednesdays."

STUDENT AUTHOR: Though the Courtyard Café caters to the coffee and pastry crowd, the Market Place (otherwise known as the Caf) will have to satisfy the rest of your hunger pangs. The food itself is not bad for being a school cafeteria. Centrally located in the Campus Center, and open every day from 7 a.m. to 11 p.m., there is never any reason to miss a meal.

Student Body

African American:	1%	Male/Female:	43/57%
Asian American:	4%	Out-of-State:	19%
Hispanic:	2%	International:	1%
Native American:	<1%	Unknown:	0%
White:	92%		

Popular Faiths: Most are Lutheran, Catholic, or Protestant.

Gay Pride: Though a Coming Out Week is held each fall, Gustavus doesn't do much to show continuing support of the homosexual community during the rest of the year.

Economic Status: Students generally come from middle-class backgrounds.

Students Speak Out
ON DORMS

Q "I enjoyed living in Coed my freshman year because so many other freshmen are all in the same building. I also had a great section, and **we would do a lot of fun activities together** (funded by the school)."

Q "**All of them have their bad points**. Going into GAC, at first I loved Norelius (a.k.a. Coed) because it was always happening, and there were always people around to hang out with or study with."

Q "In my opinion, the best dorm is Coed (Norelius). It has the best setup, with **double rooms and a large common room for each section** to enjoy."

STUDENT AUTHOR: Though students are required to live on campus for at least the first two years, the majority of students retain residency on campus all four years, thanks to the school's push to keep students on campus and increase alternative campus housing outside of typical dorms. Students view the housing situation subjectively: some crave the quieter dorms (South Side), while others would go crazy without it being louder (North Side).

? **Did You Know?**
83% of undergrads live on campus.

Students Speak Out
ON GUYS & GIRLS

Q "**The dating pool is pretty diverse**. It helps living on both the North and South Sides if you want to meet the typical representatives of each group."

Q "The guys are fairly good-looking, but **it all depends**. The girls are fine, though, too."

Q "**I'll be honest: GAC has a good-looking campus**. There are far too few guys compared to girls, but both sexes can be stuck-up and not worth it sometimes."

Q "Some are hot, some aren't. Some are a-holes, some aren't. Some are skanky, some aren't. Some are soulmates, some aren't. **You'd find this anywhere**."

STUDENT AUTHOR: Gustavus has a good-looking campus. Men and women are attractive here, and prospective date-hunters can take comfort in the fact that the dating pool is wide open. Whether you are looking for a buff athlete, a latte-sipping hipster, a God-fearing Bible-thumper, the fraternity or sorority coed, a band dork, the boy or girl next door, the strikingly beautiful, or the tech guru, Gustavus offers them all.

Traditions

Christmas in Christ Chapel
In December, the school celebrates the season of Advent with five performances in Christ Chapel.

Nobel Conference
Nobel laureates come to campus to discuss different science-related topics each year.

Overall School Spirit
While tailgating may not occur before the big home game, and ESPN doesn't cover the big rivalry against St. Olaf, students and faculty are proud to be Gusties.

Students Speak Out
ON ATHLETICS

Q "I only ever played IM sports twice. It seems like a big program, but you don't hear much about it. Varsity sports seem to be successful, but again, it seems like **you don't hear about them unless the team does really well** (like wins nationals)."

Q "**Basketball and football are the most supported sports on campus**. People also love to go and watch IM basketball."

Q "**IM sports are bigger, I think**. Varsity sports are big for the athletes, but our school doesn't have a huge following of varsity sports that I noticed."

Q "If you put the time and effort in, they can be rewarding, and there are crowds that support your team of choice. **The IM sports are a huge hit**; I think this is because of the wide array of choices that can appeal to everyone."

STUDENT AUTHOR: The majority of varsity athletics at Gustavus have solid seasons and are free to students (with the exception of games that go beyond the regular season), so it's a cheap way to spend a weekend evening, or the perfect excuse to stop studying on a weekday.

Students Speak Out
ON DRUG SCENE

Q "**Marijuana is plentiful**, as I imagine it is at most schools, but I am not sure about anything harder. Binge drinking is by far the bigger problem."

Q "**I know very little about the drug scene on campus**. Most of what I have heard involves certain groups and the use of marijuana, but drug use is not rampant on campus and involves a very small percent of the population."

Q "Drugs seem to be used more and more on campus, but **our college recognizes this and not only has a no-tolerance policy**, but they are also in the process of developing a penal system for those who choose to use on campus."

STUDENT AUTHOR: **Recreational drugs exist at Gustavus, but in order to find them, you have to actively seek them out. Though some students are known to sell, it is not a prominent part of the culture of Gustavus, and it is a juicy piece of gossip when anyone is picked up for a drug offense other than alcohol. But the College has recently toughened alcohol policies to discourage underage drinking.**

12:1	Student-to-Faculty Ratio
89%	Freshman Retention Rate
79%	Four-Year Graduation Rate
64%	Financial Aid Applicants Receiving Aid

Students Speak Out
SAFETY & SECURITY

Q "I always feel safe at Gustavus, and **I enjoy taking walks around campus at night**. It's very peaceful. You can also arrange for an escort to walk you back, as well."

Q "I had great experiences with campus security. If you are respectful and understand that they have a job to do, you'll get along great. **Tick them off, and you will probably get what you deserve**."

Q "I don't think Safety and Security functions in a way which makes students feel particularly safe. I do think that **underage students are less likely to roam the campus while intoxicated** because of their presence, but at the same time, I don't think they are all that threatening. From my perspective, it seems like they are a bit of a joke."

STUDENT AUTHOR: **Safety and Security at Gustavus is made up of reasonable individuals looking out for the best interest of the students. Are they ticket happy at times? Certainly. But when it comes to student safety, there is no messing with them. They actually enforce the rules.**

Questions?

For more inside information and survival tips, pick up College Prowler's full-length book on this school, written by an actual student! Check it out at www.collegeprowler.com.

Students Speak Out
ON OVERALL EXPERIENCE

Q "Even though I have some negative things to say about the College, my overall experience has been wonderful. Yes, **there have been times where I wished I was elsewhere**, but I think that's common among college students, especially in high-stress moments. I'm so happy that I chose Gustavus, and I feel blessed to have had the experience I've had."

Q "I absolutely loved Gustavus, and if **I had to do it over again, I would have been a Gustie**. I made lifelong friendships with the faculty, professors, and with students. Even though all of my friends do not live in Minnesota, I know we will be friends for life!"

Q "**I loved every minute of it (well, most of it)**. I would never have gone to another school. Being a Gustie is such a special thing, and it makes you part of a larger family—yeah, I realize it's sappy, but it's actually true; Gustavus has a great alumni network."

Q "I think that when deciding to attend Gustavus, no one knows what they are getting into, but after a year, **the student really starts to latch onto the campus society**."

STUDENT AUTHOR: **Regardless of the times of frustration, stress, and anger, students always seem to firmly believe that Gustavus was the right choice for them. Students who enter Gustavus know many of the "downfalls" before they enroll: the small-town atmosphere, limited majors, and the social politics that will be involved by attending a college the size of many high schools. However, the benefits of the small school are experienced right away: small class sizes, personal attention, and the ability to quickly develop friendships.**

Hamilton College

198 College Hill Road; Clinton, NY 13323
(315) 859-4011; www.hamilton.edu

THE BASICS:

Acceptance Rate: 28%
Setting: Rural
F-T Undergrads: 1,835

SAT Range: 1300–1450*
Control: Private
Tuition: $38,220

Most Popular Majors: Social Sciences, Foreign Languages, Physical Sciences, Visual/Performing Arts

*of 1600

Academics	A-	Guys	B+
Local Atmosphere	C+	Girls	B+
Safety & Security	B+	Athletics	B
Computers	B	Nightlife	B-
Facilities	C+	Greek Life	B+
Campus Dining	B+	Drug Scene	D-
Off-Campus Dining	B-	Campus Strictness	B-
Campus Housing	B-	Parking	C-
Off-Campus Housing	D-	Transportation	C
Diversity	C	Weather	D+

Students Speak Out
ON ACADEMICS

Q "Most of the professors that I've had have been fantastic. **I have had many challenging, interesting courses**. I have found that the introductory courses are not usually very interesting but are designed to provide a good base of knowledge."

Q "Some of the professors seem like they make courses difficult **for the sake of being difficult**. It's almost anti-grade inflation here—an A is so much harder to get."

Q "Some professors are great, but you should **ask upperclassmen before registering** to avoid disappointment."

Q "Some of the professors really seem to care about making their classes interesting. Others, though, definitely take the '**this is an introductory class** and therefore it should be boring' approach."

STUDENT AUTHOR: One word: fantastic. It might sound overenthusiastic, but it's true. The professors might be the number one reason students love this school. Professors will go out of their way to help a student with schoolwork as long as they aren't afraid to ask. Classes are hard, and the greatest professors are often the most demanding of their students. They challenge their students to think independently in the classroom, and it is very rare for a professor to only lecture. Our faculty is also renowned across the country, especially the government and economics departments.

Students Speak Out
ON LOCAL ATMOSPHERE

Q "On-campus, it is nice. **Off-campus, it is a bit depressing**. Coming from a suburb of Boston, I feel like I am in the middle of nowhere."

Q "My favorite time in Clinton is during FallFest. The Hamilton community sets up a tent on the village green for all of Clinton to gather. FallFest features a battle of the bands, free food, raffles to raise money for the fire department, and pumpkin decorating for the children. **It really unites Hamilton with Clinton** and makes you feel at home."

Q "There's not much to visit in Clinton. We have a CVS Pharmacy, Bistro 7, the Alexander Hamilton Inn, pizza places, the Nice-n-Easy, and a grocery store. **It's no booming city**."

Q "There is very little in town. However, the scenery around Clinton is gorgeous. Although clubs and bars are not close to numerous, **there are tons of things to do**. There are cute small stores in town."

STUDENT AUTHOR: If you are looking for a bustling urban center; Hamilton College is not the school for you. The middle of central New York is predominantly farmland, and lacks the excitement of a big city. Some students begin their four years at Hamilton without fully understanding this fact. It has been a problem, especially for first-years who lack the mobility of a car to escape the Hill. In the winter, options for entertainment are limited to College-sponsored events.

Students Speak Out
ON FACILITIES

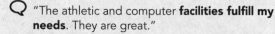

Q "The athletic and computer **facilities fulfill my needs**. They are great."

Q "Fitness and weight rooms are sub-par for serious athletes. **The computer centers are crowded**, and the amount of people selling stuff in Beinecke is ridiculous! It's not a mall."

Q "The Margaret Bundy Scott Field House is beautiful, with **an indoor track and a hardwood basketball court** that assembles on the gym floor. The Bristol pool is Olympic-sized, with a moveable divider that adjusts the length of the lanes."

Q "The facilities are nice, and those that are not are being refurnished. I think that **student life spaces will be greatly improved** over the next few years."

Q "I wish we had a student center where everyone would hang out. Beinecke is great and so is Bristol, but **neither is used like a typical student union**. Kids usually hang out in commons more than they ever would in one of those two places."

STUDENT AUTHOR: **Ade Fitness Center is small. In addition to the fitness center, Alumni Gymnasium includes Bristol Swimming Pool, Sage Rink, Scott Field House, two weight-lifting rooms, an additional basketball court, squash courts, tennis courts, and an indoor track. Hamilton College is planning a new student center in the old Emerson Literary Society building (ELS), but for the time being, our student center is Beinecke Village.**

Famous Alumni

Henry Allen, Paul Greengard, David Grubin, Thomas Meehan, Ezra Pound, Elihu Root, B.F. Skinner, Melinda Wagner, Steve Wulf

Students Speak Out
ON CAMPUS DINING

Q "Any dining hall is going to seem boring after eating there everyday, but as dining halls go, Hamilton is at the top of the list. **Options are limited**, however, for those with special food preferences or restrictions."

Q "The food is **not as bad as people make it out to be**. Going to the Howard Diner late at night is awesome!"

Q "I wish the dining halls wouldn't try so hard to make fancy things. If they just stuck to easy dishes, **the food would taste much better**. Crushed goldfish on mac-n-cheese is just wrong!"

Q "**Sushi in Commons** and stir-fry in McEwen make me a happy girl. The new ice cream freezer in Commons is incredible, too."

Q "**I wish we had better real meals**. I'm getting sick of pizza, hot dogs, burgers, pasta, and salad."

STUDENT AUTHOR: **The best thing Hamilton has to offer is the 21-meal plan. Students can come and go as they please. Between classes, you can grab a cup of coffee and still be able to come back an hour later for lunch. Despite glowing praise of the food, there are a few problems. A Howard Diner dinner costs $6.00, and with that money, you are limited to a sandwich, fries, and a drink. Equivalency dollars are based on the time of day, which means you don't get the same exchange value at breakfast and dinner. On the weekends, McEwen is closed.**

Student Body

African American:	4%	Male/Female:	48/52%
Asian American:	7%	Out-of-State:	66%
Hispanic:	5%	International:	5%
Native American:	1%	Unknown:	8%
White:	70%		

Popular Faiths: The majority religion at Hamilton is Christianity, although most students do not actively identify with any religion.

Gay Pride: The majority of the campus is very accepting of the gay community, even though it is a fairly silent presence.

Economic Status: Students generally come from an upper-middle-class background.

**Students Speak Out
ON DORMS**

Q "Generally, the rooms are spacious, beautiful, and provide a good living environment. The dorms are also a great way to meet people. Places like North are extremely social, and the **residents form tight bonds through the year**. Be careful when choosing substance-free housing for your freshman year; they are too quiet and mostly anti-social."

Q "Dorms **range from miserable to exquisite**. There's a huge range, and god help you if you draw Kirkland as a freshman."

Q "They **need improvement**, especially on the Kirkland side."

STUDENT AUTHOR: Upperclassmen have first pick of housing and are guaranteed to live in the nicest residence halls. The former fraternity houses have been renovated and are gorgeous. Most first-year housing is cramped and somewhat dumpy. Freshmen cannot live in a single, and their dorms are shared by students of all class years. Each dorm is a unique experience with an atmosphere like no other.

> **? Did You Know?**
> 98% of undergrads live on campus.

**Students Speak Out
ON GUYS & GIRLS**

Q "One word: **preppy**. Attractiveness, of course, depends on who you're looking at."

Q "The whole campus is **very attractive, fun, and friendly**. A typical student is fun, adventurous, and open."

Q "The **guys just want hookups**, and the girls are all looking for Prince Charming."

Q "Flip up your collar, puff out your chest, ignore your friends when you pass them on the street, develop a virgin-whore complex, complain bitterly about any and all work you're ever assigned, and **buy a North Face Jacket**. There, you're a student at Hamilton."

STUDENT AUTHOR: Predominantly a social student body, sometimes it is shocking to see the shy boy from history class out for a Thursday night party in Carnegie. The stereotypical Hamilton student is confident, well-dressed, and conventionally attractive. Perhaps unfortunately, this norm for Hamilton guys/girls is pervasive, and it can be frustrating rarely seeing other types of students who don't fit the mold.

> **Urban Legends**
> It's said that if you walk across the bronze map you won't graduate.
>
> It is said that the Admissions Building and Alumni House are haunted by the ghosts of the families that once lived there. Lights turn on and doors open that were left shut.
>
> **Overall School Spirit**
> The Dog Pound is made up of students that want to support Hamilton sports, primarily basketball and football. Nobody knows how to excite a crowd like the Dog Pound.

**Students Speak Out
ON ATHLETICS**

Q "Varsity sports are popular, and IM sports are also. **It is easy to get involved** with anything."

Q "Varsity sports are quite big here; however there are **not many jocks on campus**. If you want to spend your Sundays watching good college football, look elsewhere."

Q "**The typical student plays a sport** and drinks like a fish."

Q "Varsity **sports are fairly big here**. We have a good deal of athletes, but from the administration's point of view, football is, by far, the largest—and, incidentally, the largest embarrassment. IM sports are definitely big here."

STUDENT AUTHOR: The vast majority of students are involved in athletics of some form. As far as varsity sports are concerned, Hamilton students go all out. Intramural sports play a gigantic role in the social and athletic lives of most Hamilton students. Competition is high during these events, and during certain IM seasons, IM games are all you will hear about.

Students Speak Out
ON DRUG SCENE

Q "Alcohol is the center of the weekends. **Weed is prevalent**, and so is cocaine to a lesser extent."

Q "Always a bag of **weed to be had**."

Q "Hamilton is a hard drinking school. I don't know anything about the drug scene personally, except that **drug use seems widespread**. Not just weed—harder drugs, too."

Q "Scene? Try '**way of life**' for a Hamilton student."

STUDENT AUTHOR: The drug scene on campus is mostly weed and alcohol, with a handful of students using harder drugs. For the most part, drug use is limited to a recreational use and comparable to the scene at any other college or university across the country. Harder drug use is limited to a small portion of Hamilton students. Adderall and Ritalin are popular study drugs, and students are willing to pay the price. Cocaine and mushrooms are also used, but done in private and only within certain social circles.

10:1	Student-to-Faculty Ratio
96%	Freshman Retention Rate
86%	Four-Year Graduation Rate
86%	Financial Aid Applicants Receiving Aid

Students Speak Out
SAFETY & SECURITY

Q "I feel perfectly safe, although Campus Safety needs to **calm down on busting parties** and handing out parking tickets. Their one true passion is parking tickets."

Q "**I could not feel any safer** on campus. Nobody is going to do anything if you're just walking around."

Q "The campus is largely secure, though there have been occasional break-ins to cars, **largely attributed to people from off campus**. There is no problem walking alone at night, and I leave my dorm room unlocked."

Q "As a female, I have **no problem walking around alone** at night."

STUDENT AUTHOR: Hamilton College might be one of the safest places in the world. There is plenty of security for a small school in a very rural part of central New York. Blue emergency phones and alarms are clearly marked and decorate the campus grounds. Our Campus Safety staff is very visible.

> **Questions?**
> For more inside information and survival tips, pick up College Prowler's full-length book on this school, written by an actual student! Check it out at *www.collegeprowler.com*.

Students Speak Out
ON OVERALL EXPERIENCE

Q "When I first got here, I hated the place, but over the past year, **I have come to love it**. Hamilton is beautiful, the classes are challenging, and there are a lot of cool people here."

Q "Academically speaking, I couldn't ask for much more from Hamilton. Athletically, **I have had great opportunities** that I probably would not have had elsewhere. However, socially, this place can be very limiting."

Q "Everyone here bitches endlessly about the weather, the people, the social life, the dorms, and the food. I can't think of a single person who isn't grossly upset about something on campus, but **I don't think I can name you a person who's unhappy about attending here**, either."

Q "Hamilton is a great school. **As long as you embrace the experience**, academically and socially, there's no reason it can't be a positive experience for you."

STUDENT AUTHOR: As long as you don't ask a Hamilton student about how much they love their school in the dead of winter, you are likely to receive an overwhelmingly positive response. Complaining about our school can sometimes appear to be the new cool thing to do, and becomes increasingly more popular as the days grow darker, and both homework and snow seem to endlessly pile up. But if you listen to what students say, it's more than likely you will find a strong undertone of affection for life at Hamilton College. Current students are happily planning for the days when the entire nation will come to recognize what a great liberal arts experience Hamilton College is.

Hampshire College

893 West Street; Amherst, MA 01002
(413) 549-4600; www.hampshire.edu

THE BASICS:

Acceptance Rate: 53%   **SAT Range:** 1150–2060*
Setting: Rural   **Control:** Private
F-T Undergrads: 1,428   **Tuition:** $37,789

Most Popular Majors: Visual/Performing Arts, Social Sciences, English, Area and Ethnic Studies

*of 2400

Academics	B+	Guys	B-
Local Atmosphere	C	Girls	C+
Safety & Security	B+	Athletics	C-
Computers	C+	Nightlife	B
Facilities	C	Greek Life	N/A
Campus Dining	B-	Drug Scene	C-
Off-Campus Dining	B+	Campus Strictness	A-
Campus Housing	B+	Parking	A
Off-Campus Housing	C-	Transportation	B
Diversity	C-	Weather	C+

Students Speak Out
ON ACADEMICS

Q "For the most part, Hampshire professors are spectacular. Sure, there will be the occasional flaky hippie who is incapable of evaluating a single paper, but **most professors are willing to lavish a great deal of personal attention** on students."

Q "**Hampshire has the best and the worst teachers I've ever seen**. Often students disagree with the administration about what is valuable or important in our academic system. It's tough to predict if a class will be good or not, but Hampshire has a long shopping period, so you'll have time to check classes out before committing to them."

Q "I like my professors, but I do feel like griping about academics. First off, the Div-I system sucks, but too many people already say that. Most of the classes seem lecture/discussion based and focused on the humanities. **It would be really nice to have more science labs and equipment**. I was also surprised to find that Hampshire, which I thought was more of an artsy school, does not have a kiln for ceramics."

STUDENT AUTHOR: Academics at Hampshire can be frustrating and rewarding at once. All students design their own academic concentrations, receive written evaluations instead of grades, and write papers and create projects instead of taking quizzes and exams. This freedom has its pitfalls, however, and securing faculty support for independent endeavors can be really difficult.

Students Speak Out
ON LOCAL ATMOSPHERE

Q "Amherst is not a town, **it is the shopping district of UMass**, Amherst College, and Hampshire. Imagine the respective communities of those three schools, and you have a perfectly accurate representation of Amherst."

Q "The atmosphere is primarily chill, punctuated by **random and sustained periods of profound intellectual intensity**, that are often matched by emotional intensity brought on by stress and lack of sun."

Q "I love Amherst! **The town feels very alive, vibrant, and full of color**. There's no shortage of stuff to do, but it can be hard to find out what's going on sometimes. The Daily Jolt helps somewhat, but what could really help is if there were more noteworthy events on the campus itself, no offense."

Q "**There is a very nice atmosphere**, to the point where I would like to live there over the summer. I wish it were not such an early place, though. Everything goes dead by 2 a.m., and most places are closed in general by 10 p.m."

STUDENT AUTHOR: Nestled in the Pioneer Valley, Hampshire is surrounded by college towns: Amherst, Northampton, and South Hadley. The three towns are fairly consistently abuzz with lectures, indie music performances, art shows, and political protests. Those who are comforted more by the constant hum of traffic than the rustle of rural life might think twice before coming to the Valley, however.

Students Speak Out
ON FACILITIES

Q "Let's get this out in the open: **Hampshire is the ugliest college in the entire world.** Hideous, dilapidated '60s architecture haphazardly strewn around a filled-in swamp."

Q "**Sometimes not having a student center is annoying,** but the upper RCC and the library building make for a makeshift student center. It does suck when I want to use the gym but it's closed for events that would normally be held in a student center."

Q "In general, the facilities are not great, but **for 1,300 students, they suffice.** Sometimes I really wish we had a student center and another study lounge. But like I said, we make it work."

Q "Well, we're not Smith, but I think our facilities are pretty good. **Not top-of-the-line, but I haven't felt like it's a major problem.** It's just that most things are old or hand-me-downs from other colleges, but they work."

Q "Facilities on campus are okay compared to UMass. **Compared to Smith and Mount Holyoke, they are gross, outdated, and crappy.** The facilities grow on you, and it's easy to make do with what they have to offer."

STUDENT AUTHOR: **Hampshire College would not win any architecture pageants. The library is small and dingy, the theater spaces are limited, and the main basketball gym is scruffy. A big concern is that the College lacks a student center. The key culprit is the College's meager endowment. Luckily, Hampshire students have access to the other four colleges' facilities.**

Famous Alumni

Xander Berkeley, Chuck Collins, Daniel Horowitz, Toby Driver, John Falsey, Mike Ladd, Eugene Mirman, Liev Schreiber, Elliott Smith, Barry Sonnenfeld

Students Speak Out
ON CAMPUS DINING

Q "The dining hall food can get redundant, though **it's not the worst I've ever tasted.** I love the food in the Bridge Café, especially the tofu and cheese sandwiches."

Q "**The main dining hall, Saga, is okay.** Most people complain about it, but it's institutional food. You can't expect much."

Q "The food isn't that bad, but the monotony gets to people. However, **this is a very vegetarian- and vegan-friendly campus.**"

Q "For students living in the dorms, a full meal plan that is only usable at the College's one dining hall is mandatory. **This one dining hall is a wildly overpriced crime against humanity.**"

Q "Sometimes, I'll be so hungry and go to Saga and **just not want to eat anymore because nothing looks appealing.** There are no other options for food on campus other than the Bridge Café, which isn't really that substantial, and the school store, which is even less substantial."

STUDENT AUTHOR: **Even the most enthusiastic and grateful student can find dining options repetitive and uninspired. The main eatery, the Dining Commons (called Saga), prepares three hot meals a day during the week and a brunch and dinner on the weekends. Complaints about Saga are commonplace, but the place is not as bad as some students would suggest. Its ratings ought to hover around the "decent" mark.**

Student Body

African American:	3%	Male/Female:	42/58%
Asian American:	4%	Out-of-State:	82%
Hispanic:	6%	International:	4%
Native American:	<1%	Unknown:	8%
White:	74%		

Popular Faiths: Of the religious affiliations, Judaism is perhaps the most visible.

Gay Pride: Hampshire is, for many, a welcome respite from many less tolerant places. The atmosphere of the College and the surrounding area lends itself to open experimentation.

Economic Status: The general trend on campus is privilege, if uncomfortable privilege.

Students Speak Out
ON DORMS

Q "The main drawback of living in the dorms is the fact that living in them comes with a mandatory full meal plan that can only be utilized at the comically terrible Dining Commons. That aside, **Hampshire's dorm rooms are overwhelmingly singles**, which is a unique pleasure."

Q "**I would advise first-years to live in the dorms as opposed to mods**. Being a first-year in a mod isn't easy."

Q "Merrill C's pretty quiet. The rest of Merrill's good if you never want to sleep. Most of Dakin's been renovated (unlike Merrill), but **the halls are connected through the bathrooms**, so people are always walking through. Dakin has way more fire alarms than Merrill."

STUDENT AUTHOR: **Hampshire is a residential college, and housing is guaranteed to all students for all four years. Most of the rooms are singles, meaning no roommates, a rare luxury on college campuses. Also, all residential bathrooms are mixed-gender. Technically, students are supposed to register guests, but it's common for them to ignore this rule and have long-term squatters.**

Did You Know?
90% of undergrads live on campus.

Students Speak Out
ON GUYS & GIRLS

Q "**Hampshire booty is pretty awful on both sides**. I think the girls have it much worse, though, as none of the boys are 'the pick of the litter,' let's say. They lack both personality and looks, so there's not much left."

Q "Dating at Hampshire—wow, that's a challenge! **The guys are too shy or politically correct to make the first move**, so the girls take initiative and ask the other girls out!"

Q "The general rule of thumb is that **you don't date Hampshire guys; you train them** so that one day after college they can functionally date other people. Then again, I'm dating a Hampshire boy now, and it's working out well."

STUDENT AUTHOR: **Hampshire is small, and while that can mean comfort, when relationships sour, it can make folks downright claustrophobic. That being said, gender fault lines are not a problem, nor are there any enforced visiting hours, restrictions, or penalties for consensual sexual activity. For the most part, the social atmosphere enables and encourages experimentation.**

Traditions

Drag Ball
A spring dance party organized by campus GLBT groups where students dress in drag.

Keg Hunt
Every Easter, groups of students hide kegs in the woods on campus and others go out in search of them, cups in hand.

Overall School Spirit
Whatever mascot students decide to embrace, Hampshire school spirit is often coupled with a bit of wry humor about the school's many quirks.

Students Speak Out
ON ATHLETICS

Q "**I don't think that Hampshire really attracts the sporty kind of people** who care much about varsity sports. We do have very active Frisbee, soccer, and basketball teams. People just play for fun; it's not a big deal."

Q "**If you like nonstandard hippy athletics**, Hampshire athletics are quite good!"

Q "We have no varsity sports. **Our biggest team is the Red Scare, a very good ultimate Frisbee team**. Students can organize teams for whatever sports they want, like basketball, football, soccer, and rugby. Our big attraction is being one of only a handful of schools that offer kyudo (Japanese Zen archery) with Marion, one of the most amazing people I've ever met."

STUDENT AUTHOR: **After a few days on the Hampshire campus, it should be no surprise that athletics are not top priorities. Hampshire offers no sports scholarships and pointedly remains out of organizations like the NCAA. The school does attract active athletes and avid outdoorsy folks, but few, if any, are drawn to the school for athletic offerings.**

Students Speak Out
ON DRUG SCENE

Q "My neighbor snorted coke with her door open, **there was always acid in someone's mod freezer**, and someone is always selling pot, but if you don't use, you won't feel out of place. There are a lot of straight-edge people, too."

Q "**Trillions of tons of pot**, though the obnoxious faux-'80s hipsters enjoy a good line of cocaine."

Q "Marijuana and cocaine are pretty big at Hampshire. In distant third is heroin, and ecstasy use is almost nonexistent. **Drugs are readily available**, but the school has begun cracking down, forcing drug users to be a little more subtle about their need."

STUDENT AUTHOR: **Substance use is definitely prevalent around campus, with alcohol and marijuana being the substances of choice. It's also acceptable for students to remain dry, though it can make socializing a bit awkward. Some circles of friends seem to primarily bond around a shared joint. However, lately the school has been taking steps to discourage smoking.**

11:1	Student-to-Faculty Ratio
79%	Freshman Retention Rate
53%	Four-Year Graduation Rate
89%	Financial Aid Applicants Receiving Aid

Students Speak Out
SAFETY & SECURITY

Q "Since Hampshire is so isolated, **it's easy to take your safety for granted**. Assaults happen on campus, in dorms, and in mods; there are sketchy people everywhere."

Q "**This seems like a very safe little campus**. I've noticed the undercover cops and heard about kids with guns, neither of which makes me feel safe, but generally, it seems very safe. It's way safer than my high school, for sure."

Q "We have Public Safety officers that roam around campus all night. I've never felt unsafe walking around campus late at night. Then again, I'm a guy. The most serious crimes that take place on campus, at least from my own observation, involve **laptops and bikes getting stolen**."

STUDENT AUTHOR: **For the most part, Hampshire is a safe campus, and many students leave their dorm rooms unlocked. The nights can be dark, but aside from the occasional fear associated with the lighting problem, most people do not feel afraid on campus.**

> **Questions?**
> For more inside information and survival tips, pick up College Prowler's full-length book on this school, written by an actual student! Check it out at *www.collegeprowler.com.*

Students Speak Out
ON OVERALL EXPERIENCE

Q "The type of education kept me interested in staying in college, and the people kept it exciting. **I transferred here and was very happy with my choice**."

Q "**Adapting to Hampshire can take a while**. It's not the most regular place in the U.S.—that you can be sure of—but it is a great place for independent students to acquire a higher education."

Q "I think knowing what I know now about the school's lack of money, I might have considered going elsewhere. But I adore my teachers, and I love how flexible I can be with my studies. Hampshire is so unique in giving me the place to forge my own intellectual destiny. I can't see that happening anywhere else, but **this place is far from perfect** and has a lot of trouble addressing its weaker aspects."

Q "I am absolutely, wholeheartedly in love with Hampshire College, and **I can't imagine being anywhere else right now**. I can't even describe how cool and eye-opening this place can be if you let it. Maybe I say that because I am not jaded by the whole thing yet, but that's what I'm feeling right now."

STUDENT AUTHOR: **Hampshire students have no shortage of complaints about the place, but the harshest critics are also likely to be the most vocal advocates of the College. There are few, if any, places quite like Hampshire, and the love-hate relationship many have with the College is based on the passion with which they view alternative, experimental education. Criticize they may, but most students would be quick to defend their college if someone dismissed it.**

Hampton University

Tyler Street; Hampton, VA 23668
(757) 727-5000; www.hamptonu.edu

THE BASICS:

Acceptance Rate: 45%
Setting: Mid-sized city
F-T Undergrads: 4,886

SAT Range: 945–1220*
Control: Private
Tuition: $16,392

Most Popular Majors: Business, Journalism, Biology, Psychology, Nursing

*of 1600

Academics	B-	Guys	B
Local Atmosphere	C+	Girls	A+
Safety & Security	B+	Athletics	B-
Computers	B-	Nightlife	C-
Facilities	B	Greek Life	C-
Campus Dining	C-	Drug Scene	B-
Off-Campus Dining	A-	Campus Strictness	D
Campus Housing	D-	Parking	D
Off-Campus Housing	D+	Transportation	D
Diversity	D-	Weather	B

Students Speak Out
ON ACADEMICS

Q "There are **too many foreign teachers** at Hampton, and they are the ones teaching the hard stuff like math and science. It's hard to understand what they are saying with their accents."

Q "Most of the teachers I've had at Hampton have been helpful and understanding. I've had the occasional teacher who tries to act like they can't accept a valid excuse for a late assignment. I give my opinion on that teacher at evaluation time, **but overall, I like my professors**."

Q "I can honestly say that in three years, I haven't really had a professor that's given me a lot of problems. **They're always real cool** and pretty lenient when you need them to be."

Q "For real, one of the reasons I've stayed at Hampton is because most of my professors really do help me. **I like the fact that I'm not a number**—I'm a first and last name. When you see the professors on campus, they still remember your name, even after you've moved out of that class."

STUDENT AUTHOR: The smaller class sizes and the fine teachers are greatly appreciated by the students and alumni. Foreign professors with thick accents, however, are a major concern of the students. The most recognized department is the School of Journalism and Communications because it is globally funded and occupies the newest building on campus.

Students Speak Out
ON LOCAL ATMOSPHERE

Q "What fun is there here? **Everything closes so early** and you see the same people everywhere you go."

Q "I'm from California, so clearly, **I'm not used to this drab town**. It's like two clubs with the same locals there every other night."

Q "Hampton bores me to death. Like, I think I've seen everything in Hampton and in Norfolk for the most part. I only go to Norfolk when my big sister picks me up because I don't have a car. **I like going to Virginia Beach a lot** to get away from here."

Q "Hampton itself is a nice place as far as scenery, but as far as things to do on a scale of 1 to 1 to 10, I'd have to give it a 2. I like the locals because they are funny, but **the only real hang out place is Wal-Mart** because it's open 24 hours."

STUDENT AUTHOR: Hampton part of a larger area known as Hampton Roads, which consists of several cities that all run together: Hampton, Newport News, Norfolk, Portsmouth, Virginia Beach, Suffolk, and Chesapeake. The area consists of primarily suburban sprawl from Norfolk, which is home of the largest naval base in the world, placing Hampton in the middle of a major military area. Still, there is not a lot for a college student to do or be attracted to in the immediate area. Across a little bridge, we have Downtown Hampton, and there is a little shopping area for the locals.

Students Speak Out
ON CAMPUS DINING

Q "Food is food, but I've been to schools that have some great food. This definitely is not one of them. **The selection is small** and it seems like it's the same stuff all the time in the cafeteria."

Q "There is way too much chicken for me. **I used to love chicken before I came here**, but it seems like that is what I'm forced to eat each and every day if I eat on campus. I would eat more in the student center, but that costs money, and that gets old, too."

Q "I like the food in the student center, but **the cafeteria definitely is a no-no**. I've gone broke buying food, so I don't have to go in there. I just want to know how many different ways can you prepare a chicken each and every day?"

Q "**The food in the student center is bangin**,' but the cafeteria food is absolutely, positively, by far, the most terrible food that has ever touched my tongue. It can't even compare to other colleges and universities I have visited. Other schools have a plethora of eateries, and they can use their meal card—not here, and that is the worst."

Q "Our on-campus eating is the worst. It gets old real quick, and **the choices are nothing**."

STUDENT AUTHOR: **Gourmet Services is what the HU cooking staff is called, but frankly, there is nothing gourmet about the food at all. Many students feel that, the food in the cafeteria should be healthier and, perhaps, a little tastier. Also, most students agree that they should not be limited to eating the same thing everyday.**

Students Speak Out
ON FACILITIES

Q "**The student center is the main attraction** where everything is and mostly everyone chills."

Q "The student center is the spot. There's always someone in there to hang with either when classes are over or just between classes. **I like when they have the DJ** in there playing music like it's a party."

Q "Most of the facilities here are good. **They are clean and well kept**. I'm not really the athletic type, but I've seen the gym, and it's pretty nice. There are computers in every building to be used by students, so those labs provide enough access to the 'net for students. The student center could use some better eateries, but it's nice, too."

Q "I think there are enough computers and labs on this campus **but not enough access to them**. Sometimes, there's a class in the rooms, or they seem to close too early. That's one thing I don't like."

Q "Some of the facilities are excellent, and **some could use improvement**. The cafeteria, dorms, and the workout room in the gym all suck and need a makeover."

STUDENT AUTHOR: **Hampton's campus is one of the most attractive in the nation. However, some of the dormitories are not at all pleasing to the eye. HU takes much pride in both the appearance and structure of the classroom and administrative buildings, but focuses less on the residence halls. Although future renovations are inevitable, HU still has a long way to go.**

Students Speak Out
ON DORMS

Q "**Most people can't wait to move off campus**—if they have the funds and opportunity. The bathrooms are the worst part. White is one of the nicer dorms only because it's still pretty new and people haven't had the chance to destroy it yet."

Q "These dorms are fair. Of course, some are better than others. **Overall, I think they are okay**, for the most part. The only things I really hate about living on campus are all the rules. Visitation from the opposite sex is so limited, and they yank it away whenever they feel the need."

Q "**The residence halls have improved a lot** over the years. They aren't perfect, but the University looks as if it is at least making steps to make improvements."

STUDENT AUTHOR: The typical HU dorm is a roof over your head and a place to lay your head, but most residence halls here do not constitute the most luxurious style of living. Most students are thankful for their experience in the dorms and feel that they wouldn't have adjusted well to HU without it. The most fun and happiness in a dorm is normally acquired during a student's freshman year.

? Did You Know?
59% of undergrads live on campus.

Students Speak Out
ON GUYS & GIRLS

Q "The **girls outnumber the guys** here by a lot. The girls here go way too far to get all dressed up and put on all this makeup just to see the same guys each and every day of each and every year. It's not that serious."

Q "I'm quite content with the girls here. **I see a new girl every day**, and some seem to be more beautiful than the one before. I'm sure any guy would be pleased with the selection."

Q "The girls here are picturesque. **It's truly a portrait of perfection**."

Q "The guys and girls here **seem to interact well**. Most people, in general, are pretty social. Guys don't try to impress the girls like it seems the girls try to impress the guys."

STUDENT AUTHOR: HU girls have the reputation of being "high class, bourgeois" females. Some are actually considered "ditsy" and materialistic. Most, however are very smart, party hard, and even go to church on Sundays. The only downfall is that all these gorgeous ladies way outnumber the guys. Unlike the girls, the guys tend to wear designer, baggy jeans and a T-shirt, instead of looking traditional or clean cut.

Traditions

Step Show
Step is an event in which current freshmen step and former residents wildly cheer for their old dorm.

Miss HU Pageant
At Miss HU, the males have the joy of seeing the ladies dress to impress in evening gowns, swim wear, and business wear.

Overall School Spirit
Hampton has some sense about school spirit, though it isn't as predominant here as in other places, particularly since it lacks any outstanding sports teams.

Students Speak Out
ON ATHLETICS

Q "The football team always seems to do pretty well. I know I enjoy going to a lot of the football games **because the girls get all dressed up**, and you can tell they're not there to watch the game. It's really easy to get distracted from the game."

Q "The teams are consistently strong, and they usually display a lot of teamwork, and **they don't get as much recognition as they should**. The IM sports give people that usually don't have as much time to organized team sports a chance to be full-time students and also keep in touch with their love of sports."

Q "I couldn't say much about the games because I haven't been to the games since my sophomore year. **I don't know anything at all about the IM teams**."

Q "Go Pirates! I absolutely love going to Hampton games. I have to admit **I don't really support the Lady Pirates** games like I should."

STUDENT AUTHOR: Currently, the Pirates are a Division II team. However, die-hard HU fans who follow sports religiously hope to see them turn DI in the near future.

Students Speak Out
ON DRUG SCENE

Q "I don't know a lot of people who smoke weed, but I do know people who **smoke Black & Milds** [cigars]."

Q "There's a lot of weed smoking by students that attend the University, but as far as students doing it on campus, that's not too prevalent. What students do in their private quarters is their business, and the University can't control that, but **I think students respect the University** by not doing it on campus."

Q "I don't think these students **want to sniff anything or put anything in their veins**, but I definitely believe they will roll up any kind of herb with anything available and smoke it."

STUDENT AUTHOR: The main drug on campus is alcohol. Students drink regardless of age, time, place, or who may surround them; and often times carrying around "disguised" drinks. In conjunction with alcohol is marijuana. According to most students, marijuana has a highly visible existence on campus.

16:1	Student-to-Faculty Ratio
85%	Freshman Retention Rate
52%	Four-Year Graduation Rate
90%	Financial Aid Applicants Receiving Aid

Students Speak Out
SAFETY & SECURITY

Q "**I feel completely safe** when I'm on campus. It's well lit, and as a female, I don't worry about anyone trying to grab me as I'm walking back to my dorm in the late night hours from the library."

Q "I think Hampton is a pretty safe campus. **You always see the police patrolling** day and night making sure no one is up to no good. It makes me feel a little bit safer, as corny as that might sound."

Q "I don't feel threatened by anyone or anything on campus. The way the police are always around, it seems like **they could almost spot someone who isn't a student** anyway. I don't even hear of anything crime related for the most part on campus."

STUDENT AUTHOR: Students genuinely roam the campus at all hours of the day and night and feel comfortable and safe doing so. There are blue call-boxes around campus that allow you to call campus police for help, and there is 24-hour emergency assistance ready and waiting.

Questions?
For more inside information and survival tips, pick up College Prowler's full-length book on this school, written by an actual student! Check it out at *www.collegeprowler.com.*

Students Speak Out
ON OVERALL EXPERIENCE

Q "On one hand, Hampton University felt like being in high school again and, on the other hand, it was an experience that will take me into the real world. **I've never experienced more irritation or drama before I got to HU**. However, I've learned a lot about life at this University, and there are details of my life that I would not have been able to have had anywhere else."

Q "Though it has taken me five years to get out of this piece, **I don't hate HU, completely**. I've learned a lot of lessons like studying will pay off and how you react in college is how the real world will view you. I learned if you want to be somebody you have to want to get to where you want to be, which will not be easy."

Q "I learned a lot at HU. It was a great school, and I **learned a lot of the facts of life**."

Q "They were always telling me that HU is a very good school, and that my experience would be one to remember, and it was. **The academics I have received are superb**. I especially like the fact that the classes were small, so my teachers could focus on me."

STUDENT AUTHOR: The HU experience is definitely one-of-a-kind. At Hampton, you come in with the feeling that this is going to be the best experience of your life, when in actuality, it has become a lesson of choice and decisions, yet not regretted. The campus scenery will entice you, the academics will challenge you, the student body will enthrall you, and everything else will, without doubt, fall into place.

Hanover College

359 LaGrange Road; Hanover, IN 47243
(812) 866-7000; www.hanover.edu

THE BASICS:

Acceptance Rate: 67%
Setting: Rural
F-T Undergrads: 929

SAT Range: 1490-1830*
Control: Private
Tuition: $25,220

Most Popular Majors: Social Sciences, Psychology, Biology, Visual/Performing Arts, Communications

*of 2400

Academics	A-	Guys	B+
Local Atmosphere	B-	Girls	B+
Safety & Security	A	Athletics	A
Computers	B-	Nightlife	B-
Facilities	B+	Greek Life	A
Campus Dining	B	Drug Scene	A
Off-Campus Dining	B-	Campus Strictness	B
Campus Housing	B-	Parking	A-
Off-Campus Housing	D+	Transportation	C
Diversity	D	Weather	C

Students Speak Out
ON ACADEMICS

Q "My professors are very knowledgeable, and **the classes are engaging**. While some are not always fun, I still feel that I learn a lot."

Q "**Many of the required courses are boring** because the teachers are sometimes forced to teach subjects they don't enjoy or don't know much about. But when you get a professor teaching in their specialty, it can be a lot of fun."

Q "Some professors are very friendly and let you know what they expect out of you as a student. For the most part, **they are all willing to help you outside of class**, and they are willing to work with you on difficulties you're having with the subject matter."

Q "My teachers are all extremely interesting, creative, capable, and well-educated people. All of my classes are interesting, but **the work is really difficult**."

STUDENT AUTHOR: The teachers at Hanover are incredible—the majority, at least. Most have open minds and are willing to work with their students. There are no teacher's assistants, so the professors teach their own classes. The unusual student-teacher camaraderie at Hanover is unlikely to happen at a large school. And it's not just the College's small size that makes the teachers so willing to help their students—it starts with Hanover's president and the dean of students, who are both approachable and personable. This attitude then trickles down to the teachers and the students.

Students Speak Out
ON LOCAL ATMOSPHERE

Q "**There is nothing to do in Hanover, and it's by no means a college town**. But I guess that could be considered a good thing because I don't have anything to waste my money on."

Q "It's pretty boring around campus. There isn't a whole lot of nightlife, and the social atmosphere is very limited. **Downtown Hanover is very nice**, but the other parts are underdeveloped."

Q "The festivals are pretty cool. Every fall, there is the Madison Chautauqua Festival of Art, which has lots of arts and crafts booths. The famous regatta races are held here in the summers, and **there is a Spanish festival downtown that is really interesting**."

Q "Hanover is a **friendly town that reminds me of home**. The downside is that there isn't much to do off campus. But there is always a lot to do on campus, so you never have to leave to have a good time or to experience different things."

STUDENT AUTHOR: The area surrounding Hanover is a rural community nestled within the cornfields of Indiana. Glamorous? No, but the town just outside Hanover is Madison, which is where most Hanover students go to eat and shop. There are many fairs and festivals held in lower Madison, making it a tourist stop at different times throughout the year. Upper Madison is where you'll find clothing and retail stores and many restaurants. The bowling alley and movie theater are also in upper Madison, making it the place for students to go for fun off campus.

5 Best Things	5 Worst Things
1 Friends	1 In the middle of nowhere
2 Class sizes	2 Cold winters
3 Hinkle's restaurant	3 No city life
4 Greek life	4 Low GPAs
5 Frat theme parties	5 Campus Center food

Students Speak Out
ON CAMPUS DINING

Q "**The food on campus is blah**, but The Shoebox is the best place to go."

Q "The food here is alright. **The Underground and The Shoebox tend to be student favorites** and have more enticing foods."

Q "**The dining hall has its ups and downs**. There is always cereal and other things to eat when the main dish doesn't seem appetizing."

Q "The food is okay in the cafeteria, but The Underground is a little bit better. **The best food is at The Shoebox**, which is a restaurant on campus where you can use the declining balance from your meal plan."

Q "The food **options are very limited, especially if you don't live in a Greek house**. The Shoebox is too expensive. The Campus Center dining hall has too much access to unhealthy food. Food in the Greek houses is very nice because we can pick our own menus. Plus, there is always access to other food in a small kitchen, which is great!"

STUDENT AUTHOR: Since there are only three places to use your meal plan on campus, eating becomes a social event. This is especially true freshman year when everyone eats in the same places—at least before students who decide to go Greek are split up into Greek houses. While some may complain about the quality of food, the administration is constantly looking for ways to improve the food quality. There is also a student committee that discusses dining issues.

Students Speak Out
ON FACILITIES

Q "The newer buildings—Horner, Science Center, and the Campus Center—are very nice and well-kept. **The other facilities on campus could use a little maintenance**. The best living facilities are Greenwood Suites and File House. The Greek houses could all use some renovations."

Q "The facilities are wonderful, and they are only getting better. They are functional and well-designed to fit the needs of a college student. **Everything is accessible to the students**, and I appreciate that. A Hanover committee is currently putting together a strategic plan to renovate many buildings and modernize them."

Q "The facilities on campus are excellent. Horner Center is the **perfect place to work out no matter what type of exercise** you are looking to do. It offers aerobics classes, yoga, and karate. There is an indoor track, a weight room, and four basketball courts."

Q "**The athletic facilities are so-so**. The Horner Center gym is the best we have. Everywhere else on campus could use remodeling and updates."

STUDENT AUTHOR: The buildings on Hanover's campus are anything but bland. While a few of the structures on campus are older, the majority has recently been remodeled. The Horner Center, as many students commented, is up-to-date and user-friendly. The athletic center has features that many other schools of Hanover's size do not, such as racquetball courts, an indoor track, dance aerobics rooms, three basketball courts, and a weight-lifting room with high-tech equipment.

Famous Alumni

Thomas Andrews Hendricks, Woody Harrelson, Carol Warner Shields, John Shoemaker, Harvey W. Wiley

Student Body

African American:	1%	Male/Female:	46/54%
Asian American:	2%	Out-of-State:	34%
Hispanic:	1%	International:	4%
Native American:	1%	Unknown:	5%
White:	86%		

Political Activity: There are several political groups on campus, including the College Republicans and the College Democrats.

Gay Pride: In recent years, Love Out Loud, an advocacy group focused on LGBT issues, has gotten great support from Hanover students.

Economic Status: Students are mostly from upper-middle-class backgrounds.

Students Speak Out
ON DORMS

Q "The nicest dorm I've seen is Blythe because it is usually the quietest, air-conditioned, and spacious. **I don't think there are any dorms to really avoid**."

Q "Almost all of the dorms are nice because you can have guys and girls in them, so you don't have to worry about being able to have your boyfriend in your room. **You are treated like an adult in the dorms**."

Q "Living in a coed dorm—Katharine Parker—is so much fun! **I love hanging out with people whenever I want**. There are no visitation hours for guys or girls here."

STUDENT AUTHOR: **The dorms are the worst facilities on campus, but they are not unlivable by any means. In fact, they are actually quite enjoyable because they still operate under the blueprint of older dormitories, which have small rooms and large, common bathrooms. But a major plus to living in the dorms, especially during freshman year when students can get homesick, is having a large group of people close by, which can be very comforting.**

Did You Know?
95% of undergrads live on campus.

Students Speak Out
ON GUYS & GIRLS

Q "**There are a lot of good potential wives and husbands** at Hanover. People really get a chance to know one another in multiple social situations."

Q "I think Hanover is the place to come if you are looking for people to spend the rest of your life with. I don't necessarily just mean a boyfriend or girlfriend—lifetime friendships are also found here. I am biased, but **the hottest guys on campus are frat guys**."

Q "I've found that many of the students on campus are **very attractive young people**."

Q "**Everyone dresses pretty well here** and acts like adults. It is very Abercrombie or Gap."

STUDENT AUTHOR: **The guys and girls at Hanover are diverse, and there are people from all over the country. Most students come here not knowing anyone else, and it's very easy to make friends your first year while living in close quarters on campus. A large percentage of people marry a fellow Hanover student. The close campus community and no restrictions on visitation among guys and girls may explain this.**

Traditions

Bell Game
The annual football rivalry against the Franklin College Grizzlies. The winner keeps the victory bell.

Wiffleball Tournament
A hugely popular coed tournament hosted each spring by the Lambda Chi Alpha fraternity.

Overall School Spirit
School spirit is definitely alive at Hanover. At football games, it is common to see hundreds of students and alumni dressed in red and blue to support the team.

Students Speak Out
ON ATHLETICS

Q "Varsity sports are pretty big here. A lot of people come to Hanover because it is a Division III school, and they know **they will be able to keep playing their sport of choice**. IM sports aren't huge, but if you know how to get involved in them, they are really fun."

Q "**Most of the students here are athletes or played sports in high school**. Anyone is welcome to play intramural sports, and there are a variety of options."

Q "**Football and basketball are the biggest sports here**. IMs are fun for the rest of the campus."

Q "Sports are very big at Hanover. IM sports are very casual, but **they are a fun way to liven up spring term**."

STUDENT AUTHOR: **As a part of the general degree requirements at Hanover, students take physical activity courses during their four years here. Because Hanover is Division III, many students who would not get to play sports at a larger college have the opportunity to continue their athletic careers here. Many students and alumni support the teams, and tailgating before games is popular.**

Students Speak Out
ON DRUG SCENE

Q "**There's probably a number of users, but you never see them**. There are drugs from weed to ecstasy to alcohol, but I've never seen any hardcore drugs like cocaine."

Q "**The drug scene is limited here**, but there are people here who do drugs. Marijuana is the most common. I have also encountered hallucinogenic mushrooms and ecstasy, but these two are only available periodically. Drugs are available if you are looking for them, but I can't think of one time where a drug dealer randomly approached me."

Q "There **does not seem to be a big drug problem** at Hanover."

STUDENT AUTHOR: Students who do not use drugs far outnumber the small number who do. Every drug is available to those who want them, although it is typically more difficult to get drugs in such a remote town. Just like at every college, there are people who use drugs, but it is not a big part of the social scene here.

10:1	Student-to-Faculty Ratio
77%	Freshman Retention Rate
55%	Four-Year Graduation Rate
94%	Financial Aid Applicants Receiving Aid

Students Speak Out
SAFETY & SECURITY

Q "I have always found security to be helpful. Whether you need a ride to your dorm from the parking lot or you need help with an emergency, **security has always been quick to respond**."

Q "I feel really safe on campus, but it's not really because of security. **I feel like the students watch out for one another here** and know more about what is going on than security does."

Q "**One of the many things that sold me on this campus was the amazing safety and security**. There aren't 'normal' problems here that one might find at a much bigger university. I know I am safe here, and the odds that something will happen are slim to none."

STUDENT AUTHOR: The safety and security of Hanover's campus is excellent. Crimes are rarely committed here. Underage drinking is the most frequent offense that campus security will ticket students for, and even then, it is usually because the offender was acting out of control.

> **Questions?**
> For more inside information and survival tips, pick up College Prowler's full-length book on this school, written by an actual student! Check it out at *www.collegeprowler.com*.

Students Speak Out
ON OVERALL EXPERIENCE

Q "I can honestly say there is no better campus for me than Hanover College. It fits my personality the best. I cannot see myself anywhere else, and I'm very happy I'm here. There are so many opportunities in front of me, which is great. I love this campus, and **my experience has been nothing but great!**"

Q "**I love Hanover because the atmosphere is so friendly**. It's nice to walk around campus and to be able to say hello to your friends when you're on your way to class. The academics are very challenging, but you learn a lot of good time management skills and really improve on your academic skills. It's been a great experience. I've made lots of really good memories and even better friends."

Q "**At times I wish I were somewhere else** because of being 21 and not being able to do what I want. The College has good intentions, but I don't agree with some of the rules. For the most part, the administrative rules could force me to leave, but I wouldn't leave for any other reason."

Q "Hanover is a wonderful place, as long as you're prepared for a small school **where you pretty much know everyone**."

STUDENT AUTHOR: Hanover is only for you if you can accept the fact that it is a small school in a rural area and you will have to go out and look for things to do. A student at Hanover cannot party every night and think they will be successful here. If you want to go to graduate school, be aware that your grades at Hanover will be lower than if you went to a state school. But if you go to Hanover, you have a better chance of getting into grad school and being successful there.

Harvard University

University Hall; Cambridge, MA 02138
(617) 495-1000; www.harvard.edu

THE BASICS:

Acceptance Rate: 8%
Setting: Urban
F-T Undergrads: 6,641

SAT Range: 2080–2370*
Control: Private
Tuition: $32,557

Most Popular Majors: Economics, Political Science, Psychology, Social Sciences

*of 2400

Academics	A	Guys	B
Local Atmosphere	A+	Girls	B-
Safety & Security	B	Athletics	B-
Computers	A-	Nightlife	A-
Facilities	A-	Greek Life	D+
Campus Dining	B+	Drug Scene	B+
Off-Campus Dining	A	Campus Strictness	A-
Campus Housing	A+	Parking	C-
Off-Campus Housing	D-	Transportation	A
Diversity	A	Weather	C-

Students Speak Out
ON ACADEMICS

Q "You're lucky if you ever meet your professor in almost every class. **Graduate students** do the majority of the instruction. Some of them are good teachers, and some of them are not. Classes can be interesting, but those are often the hardest ones. A lot of requirements are painful experiences, such as statistics."

Q "The teachers are great in terms of teaching, but **they are also busy**—just like the students. They all hold office hours though, so you can find them."

Q "The **teachers are amazing**. Some of them are a bit pompous and hard to deal with, but they are all brilliant. With a little initiative, you can forge a strong relationship with a Nobel Laureate in chemistry, or whatever it is that you are interested in."

Q "The teachers are incredibly passionate, deep people. Sure, they often can be difficult to understand and obnoxiously tough, but if you **take the time to talk with them**, their passion is inspiring."

STUDENT AUTHOR: The school's unmatched resources and wide array of fields of study make it the ideal place to pursue nearly any academic interest. However, some students complain that professors are too far-removed from undergraduate life, and that in some cases, teaching assistants are left with too much responsibility. Most students are quick to indicate, however, that nearly everyone with any teaching duties is downright brilliant.

Students Speak Out
ON LOCAL ATMOSPHERE

Q "Boston is neat, and **it's all fairly accessible** by subway. There are a few bad areas, but it is a pretty safe city, overall. There are historic things, museums, sporting events—whatever you want—all about a 15-minute subway ride away from campus."

Q "Boston is amazing; **the city is so young**. There are at least four other colleges that have buses that go right to Harvard Yard, and there is never a dull night—never."

Q "Boston is the best college city in the world. BC, BU, Northeastern, and Tufts are all there, plus countless others. The only problem is that the city shuts down at 2 a.m. And Cambridge is too **high class**. Go downtown to Newbury Street, Quincy Market, the Aquarium, and places like that when you have a chance."

Q "**Harvard is in the best possible place** for a college to be . . . The only thing Harvard Square is missing is a cheaper bar scene."

STUDENT AUTHOR: In addition to the excitement and variety of activities of Cambridge and Boston, Harvard undergraduates have the opportunity to socialize with college-age students from the numerous universities surrounding the city. Most students find nothing wrong with the local atmosphere, but all of Boston's vivacity does come at a price. And most students will find it at the cash register because the city does tend to carry a slightly hefty cost of living.

Students Speak Out
ON FACILITIES

Q "I don't know what to compare them against, but I think they are nice. They combine state-of-the-art stuff inside, but the exteriors maintain Harvard's **elegant style**."

Q "They're second to none; **it's Harvard**."

Q "They're **really, really nice**. We're the richest school in the country or something like that, right?"

Q "Facilities are generally state-of-the-art. Harvard has the **nation's largest endowment**, and most of the time it shows. Nearly all classrooms are equipped with amazing technology, some of which seems like it's never used, but was added just so they could write about it in their admission guide. The athletic facilities were a bit pathetic, but Harvard renovated the MAC (Malkin Athletic Center), adding more space and equipment."

Q "Harvard has no real student center. The Loker Commons, an area that offers pool tables, computers, study areas, and some mediocre restaurants, is Harvard's most novel attempt at a student center. Undergraduates have placed a **great deal of pressure** on the University to build a student center."

STUDENT AUTHOR: **Harvard does lose points due to its lack of a true student center and the absence of any concrete plans to resolve the issue. Regardless of these complaints, Harvard receives high marks for providing top-notch facilities to aid undergraduates in pursuit of improving the life of the mind, as well as the body.**

Famous Alumni

Michael Crichton, Matt Damon, Ralph Waldo Emerson, Bill Gates, Al Gore, John F. Kennedy, Conan O'Brien, Natalie Portman, Henry David Thoreau

Students Speak Out
ON CAMPUS DINING

Q "I won't lie—freshman dining is awful. Annenberg is rightly called '**Annenbarf**.' But once you're assigned a house at the end of first year, the food is much better, with all kinds of variety for vegetarians and meat-lovers alike."

Q "First year food is **tolerable**. Upperclassmen Houses are a little better. You are stuck with the meal plan all four years, so you just have to accept it. The best dining hall is Adams House Dining Hall. However, they're a bit pretentious there and only let non-Adams residents eat there at certain hours."

Q "All freshman—and only freshman, except at breakfast—eat in Annenberg Hall; it's a huge, beautiful building that looks much more like a church than a dining hall. Granted, the building is **more impressive than the food**, but the food is not bad at all. Plus, once you become a sophomore and you're living in your upperclassmen House, the food is much better, because they are only cooking for about 200 people or so."

STUDENT AUTHOR: **Opinions on the quality of campus dining at Harvard run the gamut from total disgust to lavish praise. In general, students admire the beautiful architecture of Annenberg and most of the House dining facilities, but many don't believe that the ambience of the dining halls make up for the less-than-stellar cuisine served up by Harvard University Dining Services (HUDS). However, students can use their Crimson Cash at a select number of restaurants in Harvard Square.**

Student Body

African American:	8%	Male/Female:	50/50%
Asian American:	16%	Out-of-State:	86%
Hispanic:	7%	International:	10%
Native American:	1%	Unknown:	13%
White:	45%		

Popular Faiths: Harvard is a secular University in which no one religion dominates the University.

Gay Pride: Harvard is tolerant of homosexuality, and the Bisexual, Gay, Lesbian, Transgender and Supporters Allliance (BGLTSA) is constantly rallying to increase tolerance for homosexuality on campus.

Economic Status: Some students work their way through school; others never worry about finances.

Students Speak Out
ON DORMS

Q "It's **by far the nicest** housing out of anything that my high school friends have at other schools. You can't pick your dorm, but if you could, it would be a toss-up—each has its own strengths and weaknesses."

Q "Dorm rooms are amazingly nice and spacious, with **views of the river**, big suites with common rooms, and fireplaces."

Q "There are many different arrangements, but almost everyone I know likes their dorm and develops a good deal of **House pride**! All of the freshmen live in Harvard Yard (or close by, in the Union) for their first year. After that, you're able to choose a group of seven other people (collectively, called a blocking group) who you want to live with for the following years, and all of you are assigned to the same upperclass House—you don't get to choose. I think it's a pretty good system."

STUDENT AUTHOR: **From its rich history and beautiful architecture, to the close-knit House communities and central location, Harvard campus housing is matched by few, if any universities, in the country.**

> **Did You Know?**
> 98% of undergrads live on campus.

Students Speak Out
ON GUYS & GIRLS

Q "You've got your drop-dead-gorgeous, good-looking, okay, and **dog-ugly**."

Q "There are some '**beautiful people**,' though I'd say all of the Ivies have more than their share of people that could stand to get out of the library a little more."

Q "Taking into consideration that about 25 percent to 50 percent of the students don't leave their rooms, the student population you actually see out is **a fun, good-looking bunch**."

Q "There are some very hot Harvard girls, but there are also some really unattractive girls. Trust me, you'll find your own group, and regardless of appearances, the students are definitely **Harvard's biggest asset**."

STUDENT AUTHOR: **Don't let *Van Wilder* or *Girls Gone Wild* give you any crazy ideas about college and what girls and guys will look like at Harvard. The lack of looks at Harvard shouldn't get you down just yet, though, because Boston is home to a myriad of other universities to find potential partners. But for those who believe looks are not everything, then Harvard students' individuality should provide plenty of options.**

> **Traditions**
>
> **Old John Harvard**
> Every student must urinate on the John Harvard statue found in the Old Yard.
>
> **Studying Hard**
> Every student is supposed to hook up in the stacks of Widener Library.
>
> **Overall School Spirit**
> Harvard students are proud, almost snobbishly arrogant when it comes to their University's reputation, though athletics receive little support, if any. Students wear their colors proudly, especially on the weekend of the Harvard-Yale football game.

Students Speak Out
ON ATHLETICS

Q "We offer dozens of sports and play over a thousand IM games per year. Freshmen play in their own league, and upperclassmen Houses compete against each other. Harvard has more varsity teams than any other school, and many teams are comprised of students other D-1 schools would call '**amateurs**,' so if you want to play a varsity sport, Harvard is much more open. Attendance at athletic events is, however, unfortunately light."

Q "Varsity is **not too big** at all, except within the team. IM sports are big among the people who do them. It's all relative, but you don't hear much about either unless you're really into them."

Q "Above all else, Harvard is an academic institution, but taking that into consideration, our teams are **pretty good**."

STUDENT AUTHOR: **Originally founded as an athletic league, the Ivy League, including Harvard, has lost its reputation as an athletic powerhouse in major sports . . . [T]he only time Harvard fans even resemble true college sports fans is on the day of the Harvard-Yale football game.**

Students Speak Out
ON DRUG SCENE

Q "I never was involved with it, which means that in four years I never really came across it. I know it exists, but it's **not rampant**."

Q "I don't do them. It's there, no question, but it's **really understated**. You can get them if you want them, or you can easily avoid them if you're like me."

Q "Pot is pretty common and not that hard to get. There is a small scene (often associated with specific finals clubs) that does ecstasy. Also, if you really want, you could find coke. But drugs are by no means a dominant scene on campus. In fact, if you weren't interested, you wouldn't even know they existed. People are **very respectful** if you don't drink or do drugs."

STUDENT AUTHOR: **Drugs have a very small presence at Harvard. Marijuana is certainly the most prevalent, while harder drugs such as cocaine are often rumored to be the drug of choice for a small minority. All in all, Harvard receives high marks for its ability to keep drug use to a minimum and facilitate an academic and social life that is not inhibited by drugs.**

7:1	Student-to-Faculty Ratio
96%	Freshman Retention Rate
88%	Four-Year Graduation Rate
90%	Financial Aid Applicants Receiving Aid

Students Speak Out
SAFETY & SECURITY

Q "It's unsurpassed. The Harvard police are **expertly trained**. Many are ex-marines and SWAT members. They are extremely approachable and friendly. Also, the blue-light phone system is all over campus and very easy to use. Crime happens, but the HUPD prevents almost everything, and if they don't prevent it, they catch the criminals."

Q "**I always feel safe**, and I've never heard of anything bad happening. It's a city, so you have to use common sense, but I've never been uncomfortable, not even once."

Q "The campus is **pretty safe**. The Old Yard is enclosed and guarded by police."

STUDENT AUTHOR: **Students should always keep in mind they are in an urban setting and be alert, especially when walking alone at night. In the past, Cambridge crime waves have alarmed local citizens, but law enforcement still works to combat the trend with an increased presence. In general, Harvard students rightly feel safe, but prospective students should not be lulled into believing Cambridge and Boston are crime-free.**

> **Questions?**
> For more inside information and survival tips, pick up College Prowler's full-length book on this school, written by an actual student! Check it out at *www.collegeprowler.com.*

Students Speak Out
ON OVERALL EXPERIENCE

Q "I like Harvard. **It is a challenge**, but that is to be expected. The class sizes are often too large, but every now and then a professor will prove to be human and make himself accessible outside of class."

Q "Hmm . . . life is difficult. **It's a great place**; the opportunities are overwhelming, and so is the coursework. But it pays off."

Q "Overall, **my experience has been positive**. I love the people I've met at Harvard and can't imagine having gone anywhere else. My only gripe is that I have realized that I may have been academically better off going to a school that wasn't liberal arts-oriented, such as Wharton, which is more professionally oriented."

Q "**I love it**. The things I thought I would look for in a school (lots of school spirit, good professor to student ratio, prestige) ended up not mattering at all. What is important is the location and the people. Harvard has the best of both."

STUDENT AUTHOR: **Challenging, rigorous, and positive all describe students' overall experience at Harvard. The academic challenge initially seems daunting to many students, but the intellectual growth facilitated by this academic powerhouse leaves students pleasantly surprised. The social life of most Harvard students acts as a counterbalance to the intellectual challenge, and not surprisingly, students forge lifetime memories and friends throughout their four years at Harvard. Students leave the College satisfied, prepared, and as a stronger, more aware global citizen.**

Harvey Mudd College

301 Platt Boulevard; Claremont, CA 91711
(909) 621-8011; www.hmc.edu

Students Speak Out
ON ACADEMICS

Q "Some of the best classes I've taken here, amazingly, were humanities classes. The economics class I took at Mudd was absolutely fantastic. I'm really looking forward to the philosophy class I'm taking this fall. **The professors are just wonderful**."

Q "**A lot of the teachers are focused**, and they really care about whether or not you understand a concept. Questions are welcome during office hours, recitation sections, and even lectures. Since it's an undergraduate college, they're here to teach."

Q "Generally, I think the professors are **brilliant and very dedicated to their students**. I think all of my classes have been interesting, but many have been made more so by the professor's enthusiasm. Without the outstanding teachers, the courses would be rather bland."

Q "I've had one bad experience with a professor that just wasn't a good teacher, but for the most part, **the teachers are great at what they do** and really passionate about their teaching."

STUDENT AUTHOR: **Plain and simple—Mudd is about academics. Mudders are always looking for new challenges to push themselves academically. It's a rough time at Mudd if you've always been used to getting good grades, because high scores won't happen here automatically. Sometimes, the stress level can run high because academics are so competitive; however, Mudders are generally less combative than students at other schools.**

Students Speak Out
ON LOCAL ATMOSPHERE

Q "**Claremont is a really quiet town**, so don't expect any excitement coming from that direction. In fact, the local police can be real sticks in the mud, especially with noise complaints. It seems like the 5C community keeps itself apart from the rest of Claremont, to a large extent."

Q "One of the great things about Mudd is the fact that it is one of the Claremont Colleges. This group of five undergrad schools (plus a few graduate ones) gives a broader atmosphere to our small campus. It is nice, because you get both the intimacy of our school, along with **the variety of the other four colleges**."

Q "Of course, you visit the other four colleges. **Visit the village, visit Los Angeles**, but stay away from nothing."

Q "I like being in such a nice and safe town. I don't have to worry too much about off-campus people coming in to steal stuff, and **we're close enough to LA** that you can find good stuff to do."

STUDENT AUTHOR: **Although Claremont's small-town charm might be** appealing to many, it does get a bit monotonous at times. A lot of students get up-in-arms when the Claremont Police Department shuts down a party—Claremont residents did elect to live next to five colleges; what did they expect? Also, it is nice to be close enough to Los Angeles to experience a big city without actually living in a big city.

Students Speak Out
ON FACILITIES

Q "The LAC rents out **sports equipment and movies free of charge**, which is really convenient."

Q "They're institutional and very drab. Mudd leaves **no room for artistic expression**. They must assume that math and science people have no sense of aesthetics. The LAC is okay for a quick workout, though."

Q "I've seen prettier campuses, but there is **something kind of homey about Mudd**. The student center is more than enough for a school of 700. The computers are very good. The laboratories are very nice. The classrooms are nice, too."

Q "Mudd has **some good facilities**, like the Linde Activities Center, where everything is free (popcorn, pool, movies, sports stuff, foosball, and more)."

Q "The computers on campus work as well as could be expected for frequently-used public terminals. **Many departments have their own labs** with specialized software, which are of course maintained better than the general use labs."

STUDENT AUTHOR: **The best thing that can be said about HMC's facilities is that resources are shared with the other 5C colleges, especially Scripps and Pitzer. The biggest downside concerning Mudd's facilities is their aesthetic appeal, or lack thereof. HMC certainly doesn't have the prettiest campus around. The facilities are practical, first and foremost.**

Students Speak Out
ON CAMPUS DINING

Q "Food overall isn't too bad; it could be worse. **There are six dining halls** on the 5C, so there is also variety available. And they're all within walking distance. If the dining halls don't work for you, each college usually has a late-night, cafe-type place to grab a sandwich or pizza."

Q "Pitzer has good sandwiches, and CMC has good hamburgers for dinner. Down at Pomona, the breakfasts are varied. I think **Mudd's breakfasts are the best**, though."

Q "Um, it's good for cafeteria food, but **you get sick of it after awhile**."

Q "Dining hall food has always been and always will be universally mediocre. Luckily, at Mudd you have **the option of rotating** through all the dining halls on the 5C, so that you have forgotten what was particularly mediocre at any one before you get back to it."

Q "The food **varies from good to okay** to innovative to sometimes plain bad. But there are six dining options (six different dining halls), so that helps."

STUDENT AUTHOR: **There are a lot of ways to avoid the dining hall blues. Rotation is the key to avoid eating the same meal day in and day out. The food on campus is, in many ways, not so terrific. For lunch and dinner, though, the other 5C and off-campus spots are infinitely superior. One good thing about living in a five College Consortium is that you have many more options for dining.**

Students Speak Out
ON DORMS

Q "The dorms are great, but **choose the dorm based on the friends you have**. If you're living in Linde just because you want a kitchen, you'll hate it. Mostly, Mudders try not to step on each other's toes during room draw. There are some suites that are actually permanent, 'invitation only' kind of suites, and people respect that."

Q "It depends where you're living, but **I've always had plenty of space**, and the suite system is wonderful for keeping extra junk. I have way too many books, so they spill over into the suite, where anyone who wants to can borrow them."

Q "The outer dorms are all very nice, but there your selection of friends is limited—**halls and suites usually stick together** and only befriend each other."

STUDENT AUTHOR: **The outer dorms of Case and Atwood are quiet,** and well, bland. South dorm is substance-free and provides a very stable environment—if you want to study, go to South, home of the unicyclists. East is a world all in its own, where D & D tournaments and role-playing games reign supreme.

Did You Know?
99% of undergrads live on campus.

Students Speak Out
ON GUYS & GIRLS

Q "If you want hot girls, go to Scripps. If you want hot guys, go to CMC. If you want someone who is smart, **Mudd's the place to be**."

Q "It is impossible to make generalizations about the guys or the girls. Neither group is particularly attractive. However, once you're here for long enough, you start to **see people in a new light**."

Q "The girls here really aren't hot; **you'll have to cross the street** for that."

Q "The **guys are nerdy**, the girls are secretly nerdier. This does not necessarily guarantee or preclude hotness, but you might have something to talk about. I shouldn't have been, but I was shocked at how many more people here shared random interests with me than in high school."

STUDENT AUTHOR: **Mudd is definitely not a happening place for guy-girl interaction. Sexual promiscuity is rare on campus, since gossip runs wild at such a small school. There are exceptions, however, but for the most part, Mudders aren't all that good-looking. Most Mudders were nerds in high school, and not surprisingly, are nerds in college. It's not unusual for students to arrive at HMC having never had a boyfriend or girlfriend.**

Traditions

Bar Monkey
Steve Avery, Brad Greer, and Dustin Cooper built the Linux-based Bar Monkey, an automated bartender.

Puddle Jump
Every year a group runs through the 5C, jumping in all of the fountains and pools of each college.

Overall School Spirit
If you were to look in from the outside, Mudd seems apathetic. However, every student at Mudd knows that they are part of a wonderful community, and it does show at times.

Students Speak Out
ON ATHLETICS

Q "It is said that when you come to Mudd, you have three Ss (sleep, socialize, and study) and you get to pick two. Sports just add another option, and it's **hard to manage**."

Q "Athletics are **not very big** on Mudd's campus, but they are pretty big down at CMC and Pomona's campuses."

Q "Mudders aren't all that competitive (for the most part) and just want to have a good time. So intramurals are the biggest opportunity to have fun without worry. Some of the CMC teams get way too serious playing, but for Mudders it's all about having fun. The cheerleaders include everyone from the dorm who doesn't want to play. Some of the **cheers get pretty** rowdy, especially if they've had some drinks beforehand."

STUDENT AUTHOR: **Harvey Mudd gets the reputation of being too focused on academics; however, a lot of Mudders did play a sport in high school. Yes, there are people here who wouldn't exercise if they didn't have to, but there are also tons of exercise buffs who play sports, work out, and kick butt in the intramural games.**

Students Speak Out
ON DRUG SCENE

Q "**Some people get high**, and a lot of people drink on weekends, but there is virtually no peer pressure to do either."

Q "There are some people who do **drugs like pot or 'shrooms**, but they do them around friends that will take care of them. We usually don't have any trouble with crazy people who take drugs."

Q "It seems a lot worse than it is, but that's mainly because the handfuls of people that do drugs are generally **pretty vocal** about it. They're accessible if you want to experiment, but there's no pressure."

STUDENT AUTHOR: There isn't a lot of drug activity happening at Mudd, aside from the occasional pot smoking. If you go looking for them, they're easy to find, but you can go through Mudd not even noticing them. When doing drugs, the Honor Code still applies to all students. Students are expected to file a self-report if they do anything stupid. Campus Security will, leave students alone, unless they get too rowdy or cause trouble.

9:1	Student-to-Faculty Ratio
95%	Freshman Retention Rate
83%	Four-Year Graduation Rate
85%	Financial Aid Applicants Receiving Aid

Students Speak Out
SAFETY & SECURITY

Q "**Campus Security is good**. You always hear stories about how somebody tried to break into a lab or something in academics at four in the morning, but there are usually Mudders inside working. Really, it's our sleep deprivation that keeps us safe (wink, wink)."

Q "At the beginning of the school year, during orientation, **the sponsors pass out whistles** to every student. Each student then has a whistle on their key chain in case they need help. Everyone knows what to do if they hear a whistle. It's a small thing, but it really helps you to feel safe."

Q "I once left my wallet in the computer lab by accident, and I never worried that anything would happen before I could come back and get it. **Mudders take care of each other's things**."

STUDENT AUTHOR: The Honor Code system is one of the most powerful security devices on this campus. People live by the Honor Code here, so the only thing to be remotely worried about are occasional random incidents that happen off campus. There is a very trusting environment at Mudd.

> **Questions?**
> For more inside information and survival tips, pick up College Prowler's full-length book on this school, written by an actual student! Check it out at *www.collegeprowler.com*.

Students Speak Out
ON OVERALL EXPERIENCE

Q "As the saying goes, learning here is like drinking from a fire hose, but that's okay by me. I've **learned an amazing amount**, and of course, I've met some wonderful people. If you want to get a degree with four years of partying and slacking off, this is not the place for you, but if you have a strong desire to learn and are willing to put in the work, Mudd can be very rewarding."

Q "I love Mudd. It has hurt me, time and time again, but like a puppy, I keep crawling back to be kicked. There's a real **love-hate relationship** here, but I would never go to another school, ever—Mudd is the best."

Q "People here work hard, party hard, do laundry hard—I've never been around so many **passionate people**. Students do crazy spontaneous things, like prank friends for no reason, but that, well, the spaghetti is sitting right there, and I might as well use it. Mudders are great—absolutely insane, but great."

Q "Ask me Sunday night and I'll tell you that Mudd is horrible. Ask me on a Friday and I'll tell you that Mudd is heaven on earth. I guess the right answer is more like a Wednesday—**Mudd is hard as anything**, but loads of fun."

STUDENT AUTHOR: At Harvey Mudd, the workload is immense, the tests are sometimes impossible, and a two question homework assignment can take all night. The reason most of us came to Mudd has a lot to do with the academic integrity of the College and a lot more to do with the people themselves. The professors here are amazing; everybody knows the deans by name and can walk into their offices anytime. The students are all respectful and careful not to hurt each other.

Hastings College

710 North Turner Avenue; Hastings, NE 68901
(402) 463-2402; www.hastings.edu

THE BASICS:

Acceptance Rate: 79%
Setting: Rural
F-T Undergrads: 1,069

SAT Range: 890–1180*
Control: Private
Tuition: $20,912

Most Popular Majors: Business/Marketing, Psychology, Interdisciplinary Studies, Biology

*of 1600

Academics	A-	Guys	B+
Local Atmosphere	B-	Girls	B+
Safety & Security	B+	Athletics	A-
Computers	B+	Nightlife	C+
Facilities	B+	Greek Life	B
Campus Dining	C	Drug Scene	B
Off-Campus Dining	C+	Campus Strictness	C
Campus Housing	A-	Parking	B+
Off-Campus Housing	B+	Transportation	C
Diversity	D-	Weather	B-

Students Speak Out
ON ACADEMICS

Q "Since it's a liberal arts college, **you may discuss topics in class that you would never cover** at a large university. Professors engage in discussions with students and respect their opinions."

Q "One thing I really enjoy about Hastings is the small class size, which means you get more interaction in your classes, and your teachers really get to know you. The teachers are very easy to get along with and very approachable for questions and assistance. **They actually care whether or not you pass.**"

Q "While it is true that **the education department is exceptional** and there are a lot of education majors, that is not the only department that shines. The science and music departments are also very good. Hastings College is also known for its Lilly Endowment program."

Q "At a large university, you don't get the professors' personal attention, but, at HC, they give you their home addresses, home phones, and are **up for calls at night when you don't understand a problem**."

STUDENT AUTHOR: Classes are small, usually between 10–20 students, so professors get to know students individually and are readily available for extra help. Most classes will leave students with important pieces of knowledge related to their major. Students even get something out of many of the courses they have to take to fulfill their liberal arts requirements, many of which are fun and creative.

Students Speak Out
ON LOCAL ATMOSPHERE

Q "The atmosphere is cozy. There aren't a lot of businesses in Hastings, but it has some interesting cultural spots. There's an art gallery and The Listening Room, which is a small concert venue that **features local musicians and a few major artists**."

Q "Hastings' atmosphere is friendly and welcoming. **The community is always willing to help you.** They love having college kids around."

Q "The atmosphere is pretty quiet around here. Drive a mile east of campus, and you'll hit the corn and bean fields. **People like to golf, go to the waterslides, and go to the movies** for fun. We do have a very nice IMAX theatre and a local museum."

Q "Hastings was given the title of **Greenest City in the U.S.** a few years back, and it sure is! The city planners do a wonderful job of keeping Hastings beautiful. I love how the town has a great museum and offers some recreation such as Champions and YMCA."

STUDENT AUTHOR: Hastings is a friendly place with a welcoming community. Everything is easy to find and close enough to campus. There is bowling, movies, mini-golf, go-carts, and other outdoor activities when the weather permits. The shopping is lacking, aside from small downtown shops, and there isn't a large variety of nice restaurants. Hastings isn't the most exciting place in the world, but it definitely offers enough to keep college students happy.

5 Best Things	5 Worst Things
1 Accessible professors	1 Campus food
2 Friendly student body	2 Housing requirement
3 Student organizations	3 Guest policy
4 J-term	4 Lack of diversity
5 Small class sizes	5 "Suitcase" campus

Students Speak Out
ON FACILITIES

Q "The Gray Center **media building features a lot of great technology** that students learn to use for the campus radio station, television station, newspaper, yearbook, and Web site."

Q "The facilities are very nice. There are four gyms on campus and a huge weight room in the arena. The meeting rooms get the most use in the student union. The real hangout is the library. It is extremely cozy, has a **wide array of comfortable seating spaces, and free coffee**."

Q "The music building is really nice. There are around 20 practice rooms for student use with pianos in each that are very well maintained. There is a **nice auditorium with a small stage** for student and faculty recitals. The French Chapel is a beautiful building that gets used for many events including chapel services, visiting speakers, and talent shows."

Q "Our athletic **arena is just a few years old** and has a great weight room and athletic training area."

Q "The facilities are very clean and student friendly. The **recent changes to the student union** are great."

STUDENT AUTHOR: **The College certainly doesn't skimp when it comes to facilities. The library has enough resources for students and access to more through inter-library loan, there are computer labs in almost every building, and the athletic facilities are very nice. The student union was recently remodeled, adding a coffeeshop, more computers, and a cardio and strength training workout room. For the most part, students can't complain about the facilities.**

Famous Alumni

Clayton Anderson, Tom Osborne

Students Speak Out
ON CAMPUS DINING

Q "I like the convenience of eating in Sodexo—called the 'Ho'—but once I moved into an on-campus apartment, I mostly cooked for myself. I enjoyed the interaction eating with the other students, but **I wasn't fond of the food, except for breakfast**."

Q "It isn't mama's cooking, but **there is a wide selection of food**: breakfast foods, salad bar, pizza, deli sandwiches, burgers, fries, hot dishes, dessert, and more. For the most part the dining hall is very clean, and the kitchen staff is very friendly and helpful."

Q "The food on campus, contrary to the popular belief, is actually **very good and healthy**. There are almost Subway-quality sandwiches made to order at lunch and dinner. Sodexo provides nutritious meal options for students."

Q "**I go to Sodexo at least twice a day**. I personally like going to eat at the Sodexo because it does have a good variety of food. It's also in a good central location on campus."

Q "The dining hall is okay. **The meal plans aren't very flexible**, and the variety of food is usually on a fairly predictable schedule."

STUDENT AUTHOR: **Students don't have much choice when it comes to where to eat on campus—the "Ho" is it—but there are usually quite a few choices there. The food isn't the best, especially for the cost of meal plans, but it is slowly improving. For healthy eaters or vegetarians, the more appealing options are usually not the healthiest.**

Student Body

African American:	2%	Male/Female:	54/46%
Asian American:	1%	Out-of-State:	33%
Hispanic:	3%	International:	1%
Native American:	<1%	Unknown:	1%
White:	92%		

Popular Faiths: Most students are Christian.

Gay Pride: There are many students who are open and accepting of all genders and sexual orientations. There are also some students who are openly—but not violently—opposed.

Economic Status: Most students seem to come from about the same amount of money, usually somewhere in the middle class.

Students Speak Out
ON DORMS

Q "The dorms are nice. Bronc is for the athletic guys, and Babcock is for the athletic girls. Taylor is for girls who want rules to be followed. Weyer tends to be where music and art guys live because it's right next to the music building. And Altman, **the only coed housing, is where the most different types of people live**."

Q "Campus apartments are nice because they offer a lot more freedom and privacy than the dorms. The dorms are **very student-friendly with lots of space**. I would never say to avoid any dorm."

Q "I have lived in each of the all-female dorms and felt that Taylor was more my style because it seemed to be **more friendly and was a better environment to study in**."

STUDENT AUTHOR: **The dorms are conveniently near the academic buildings, and the campus apartments are a short walk or bike ride from class. The one con for many is that members of the opposite sex have to sign in if they're visiting someone in the dorms, and they can't be in each others' room past a certain hour at night. But, the social perks of on-campus housing at HC pretty much trump any negative.**

Did You Know?
73% of undergrads live on campus.

Students Speak Out
ON GUYS & GIRLS

Q "There are all types of students. There are those who are 'geeky, and those who are especially outgoing. A typical student at HC would be involved in at least two organizations and **probably belong to a sports team**."

Q "There seems to be two groups on campus that resemble high school: athletes and artists. The difference from high school, though, is that a good deal of **athletes and artists run in the same social groups**."

Q "Most of the **guys are well mannered**. They open doors, say hi, and are pretty respectful."

Q "The guys are mostly athletic, but there are some intellectuals, as well. **The girls are mostly very friendly and athletic**."

STUDENT AUTHOR: **There plenty of available guys and girls to date at Hastings College, many of which you would be proud to take home to meet your parents. Guys and girls don't often bounce around between love interests in a short amount of time, especially since everyone knows everyone, so it's hard to keep a secret. Many HC alumni and even some current students have walked down the aisle together right around the time they walked down the aisle in their caps and gowns.**

Traditions

Boar's Head
Semi-formal dinner served by the professors around Christmas time. A boar's head is displayed at the head table.

Mr. & Ms. Bronco
The winners of a campus-wide talent show hold the coveted titles of Mr. Bronco and Ms. Bronco.

Overall School Spirit
School spirit comes and goes at HC depending on the event, and, if it's a sport, depending on the quality of the team and who the opponent is.

Students Speak Out
ON ATHLETICS

Q "Sports play a pretty big role at Hastings College, especially depending on the opponent. A good amount of **students participate in athletics in some way or another**. Intramurals are tons of fun and always provide a chance to do something physical and be competitive."

Q "We have a wide variety of sports for everyone, from the **normal sports to Nintendo Wii tournaments**."

Q "Many people think this is a sports college. In many ways this is true because **a lot of students come here on scholarship to play sports**, but there are a lot of us that do not play sports, as well."

Q "The varsity **sports on campus are very popular**, especially volleyball."

STUDENT AUTHOR: **Hastings College is very big on sports. A high number of students participate in the wide selection of intramural sports offered. There is also a wide variety of varsity sports, as well as a good number of scholarships given out to students who participate in them. There is strong, continued support of all athletics here.**

Students Speak Out
ON DRUG SCENE

Q "I know a handful of people that do drugs, but it's not a big part of campus life. I think that because so many students do sports, **drugs are not a big problem** at Hastings College."

Q "**Hardcore drugs really aren't in the picture**. There is pot and alcohol, but what campus doesn't have them?"

Q "In a small town like Hastings, any drug incident that brings criminal charges definitely gets noticed, but I've only heard about one of those. For the most part, students are drug-free, partly because of all the athletes we have and partly because **there's just not a lot of interest**."

STUDENT AUTHOR: **Marijuana is the only drug really found on campus, and while drinking isn't really pushed on campus, there are a good number of students who enjoy their alcohol. But, the nice thing about Hastings is that there are groups of students to hang out with that don't choose to drink or do drugs, so you won't be left out if that's your choice.**

12:1	Student-to-Faculty Ratio
73%	Freshman Retention Rate
52%	Four-Year Graduation Rate
85%	Financial Aid Applicants Receiving Aid

Students Speak Out
SAFETY & SECURITY

Q "There is very little crime. I never had issues walking on campus. The actual campus is so small and **everyone knows everyone else**, so you feel very safe."

Q "**Public Safety walks through all the dorms at night** and monitors campus. In every dorm/apartment and building you can find Public Safety's phone number. We really don't have a big crime rate here on campus, just an occasional bad apple or two."

Q "There is practically no crime. Safety measures include coded fob key systems to access dorms and the apartments. There are emergency poles everywhere, though they don't really see any use. **I feel totally safe** almost 100 percent of the time."

STUDENT AUTHOR: **Most students find the College and town pretty safe. And, if they didn't, they could call Public Safety or find a buddy to escort them somewhere. Students do a good job of looking out for each other. At a school where everybody pretty much knows everybody else, there isn't much that can go unnoticed.**

Questions?
For more inside information and survival tips, pick up College Prowler's full-length book on this school, written by an actual student! Check it out at *www.collegeprowler.com*.

Students Speak Out
ON OVERALL EXPERIENCE

Q "I was a little nervous about coming to HC at first, but once I was here it became my second home. I cannot imagine being at any other college but HC. It is a friendly campus where **everyone says hi to you as you walk to class**. You just get a sense of belonging here."

Q "Overall, the school is a great institution that produces educated, productive individuals. If I could do it over, I would choose HC in a heartbeat. Having transferred from a larger university, **I find Hastings College a much better fit**."

Q "I wouldn't recommend getting too involved your first year. I was tempted with all the great organizations, and I put too much on my plate. You should take part in a few things to begin with because **there are so many amazing groups and organizations** on campus."

Q "I like the size of campus, the student population, small class sizes, and low student-to-teacher ratio. **I like the feasibility of being able to do a double major**."

STUDENT AUTHOR: **HC students are usually high achievers, and there are many things to take advantage of on campus. J-term, a one-month class session in January, features many week-long or longer class trips. The possibilities are endless—and not only in academics. Hastings College offers more than 70 student organizations. Students have to try hard to not find something to their liking. Not every student is happy here, but those who put in the time and effort find they can get what they want out of Hastings College.**

Haverford College

370 Lancaster Avenue; Haverford, PA 19041
(610) 896-1000; www.haverford.edu

THE BASICS:

Acceptance Rate: 27%
Setting: Suburban
F-T Undergrads: 1,169

SAT Range: 1960–2230*
Control: Private
Tuition: $37,175

Most Popular Majors: English, Biology, Psychology, Political Science, Economics

*of 2400

Academics	A-	Guys	C+
Local Atmosphere	B-	Girls	C+
Safety & Security	A	Athletics	B-
Computers	B	Nightlife	C
Facilities	B	Greek Life	N/A
Campus Dining	C+	Drug Scene	B+
Off-Campus Dining	B+	Campus Strictness	A
Campus Housing	A	Parking	B+
Off-Campus Housing	D	Transportation	C
Diversity	B	Weather	B-

Students Speak Out
ON ACADEMICS

Q "**The professors are incredibly helpful**. Almost all of the classes have discussion sections so that if you don't understand something, there is much less pressure to ask a question than if it were in front of a class of 100. The classes I'm taking really suit my interests, and they're very exciting."

Q "**The professors try really hard to be accommodating** and monitor how the class is going. As a frosh, you inadvertently end up in a lot of huge introductory classes, but your advisor tries to make sure you have an even balance of large intros and small discussion groups."

Q "**It is hit or miss with professors** at Haverford. While some professors are entertaining and bring the material to life, others are insipid and do an absolutely terrible job. That being said, it is hard to judge a professor by just one class—while a professor may be poor at teaching an introductory level class, they may be better at higher level courses. The classes at Haverford are generally interesting."

STUDENT AUTHOR: **A large percentage of professors live on or near campus, and it isn't uncommon to be invited to their homes for dinner. The Haverford faculty is an excellent group on the whole. We also benefit from very small class sizes—it's rare to find a class with more than 50 people, even at the introductory level. Higher level classes frequently run under 15. Haverford students can also take classes at Bryn Mawr, Swarthmore, and the University of Pennsylvania.**

Students Speak Out
ON LOCAL ATMOSPHERE

Q "The town around here is very pleasant, though some areas are very white and ritzy. Haverford has a great class-swapping and activity-sharing program with nearby Bryn Mawr College and to a lesser extent Swarthmore College. **Having Philadelphia nearby is awesome**; everyone should try to experience Philadelphia's night and cultural life."

Q "**Bryn Mawr comes to Haverford on the weekends**. There is the Main Line, with many shops and restaurants, and South Street in Philadelphia is obviously a great hangout."

Q "**The atmosphere is mostly quiet and relaxed**. Bryn Mawr and Swarthmore are constantly present since their students can take classes here, and we can take classes there. Bryn Mawr is a big part of the social scene. Buses run between Bryn Mawr and Haverford like every 15 minutes or so. Definitely visit Philly (museums, zoos, historical monuments), and if you are into shopping, King of Prussia is the place to be."

STUDENT AUTHOR: **Haverford is a very wealthy suburb of Philadelphia with plenty of supermarkets, convenience stores, movie theaters, and bars. Our unique relationship with Bryn Mawr, the all-girls school a mile or two west of Haverford, is central to the local atmosphere. Philadelphia is right in our backyard, only five or six miles east of the college. Some of Philly can be a little seedy, but if you avoid walking around West and North Philadelphia at night, you'll be fine.**

Students Speak Out
ON FACILITIES

Q "The facilities on campus are really nice; there is **a nice balance of old and new buildings** that makes you feel like we're somewhat modern, but with enough antiquity that it feels historic."

Q "The gym is perfect as far as I'm concerned, but I know many other students would like to see a nicer, more pleasant gym built. **We can use Bryn Mawr's pool**, but it would be sort of nice if we had a pool right on campus. The computer facilities are fine, and the student center is alright. It has a nice game room."

Q "**The computers are updated by Haverford about every three years** and work quite well. The campus center serves its purpose, but it could have been so much better if the school put a little more thought in it. The building tries to fit as much as possible into it, and it therefore seems cramped. And since it is isolated from campus (to some degree), students don't really congregate there at all, except for a few people at the student-run eatery."

Q "The facilities on campus are very good. **Given our size, the facilities are wonderful**."

STUDENT AUTHOR: **The general feeling among Haverford students is that the campus is improving, but is not spectacular. The few hangouts that exist now, though, are frequented and appreciated by students. Those who think the campus could do a little better in the way of facilities will only have a short while to wait until the college finishes up its current round of construction and renovation. In the meantime, Haverford provides a nice place for its students.**

Famous Alumni

Dave Barry, Chevy Chase, Mark Geragos, Frederic Jameson, Gerald Levin, Drew Lewis, Rob Simmons, John C. Whitehead, Juan Williams,

Students Speak Out
ON CAMPUS DINING

Q "There is only one dining hall on campus, called the Haverford Dining Center, and a small eatery located in the campus center, called the Coop. While most students bond on how terrible the Dining Center food is, it really isn't that bad. Unfortunately, **all students, including upperclassmen, must be on the meal plan**, unless you live in the college-owned Haverford College Apartments or live off-campus."

Q "There is **one main dining hall** which is good. Food variety is not amazing, but they are always open to suggestions and constantly improving. Skeeter's is good for late-night breadsticks, and Lunt Café is good for coffee and smoothies."

Q "**Food on campus is decent**. If you are on the meal plan, the Dining Center can get old. It has a six-week rotating menu, so it does offer some kind of variety that allows you to survive one way or the other. Nevertheless, sometimes, you need to eat something else. For those times, you can go to Skeeter's (pizza place), the Coop (hamburgers and sandwiches), or Lunt."

STUDENT AUTHOR: **Haverford's food is a big complaint among students. The College has only one main Dining Center (DC), and students who live in all dorms (except for the on-campus apartments and a couple of specialty houses) are forced into purchasing the full meal plan. Vegetarian and vegan options are offered at every meal. On the plus side, Haverford students are allowed to eat their meals at any of Bryn Mawr's three dining halls, which have significantly better food.**

Student Body

African American:	6%	Male/Female:	47/53%
Asian American:	13%	Out-of-State:	81%
Hispanic:	6%	International:	3%
Native American:	1%	Unknown:	0%
White:	71%		

Popular Faiths: Haverford is not a particularly religious campus.

Gay Pride: Most students feel Haverford is a comfortable place to be gay, though some have felt an unspoken intolerance.

Economic Status: A clear majority of the student body comes from upper- and upper-middle-class backgrounds.

Students Speak Out
ON DORMS

Q "The dorms are very nice, and Haverford gives nearly every student **the option of living in a single room all four years** if that is what appeals to him or her. This is a luxury that many colleges cannot offer. The apartments are a bit of a walk from the main campus, but even so, they are a comfortable and viable option for a student."

Q "For freshmen, Barclay is great—really big rooms (unless you get cramped into what was supposed to be a single with two people). Gummere has narrow halls, but they're all singles. The apartments are pretty far away, but they're really spacious. Overall, people are pretty happy with their living arrangements; **my room is bigger than my room at home!**"

STUDENT AUTHOR: **A majority of the dorms are singles, which suits most students very well. The rooms can be a little on the small side, though. The awfully complex (and arguably unfair) room draw ensures that the best dorms are kept to upperclassmen. Fortunately, there aren't any really bad dorms, though. With some of the comforts from home incorporated into on-campus living, you'll find that you will be content in most of the college's residence halls.**

> **Did You Know?**
> 99% of undergrads live on campus.

Students Speak Out
ON GUYS & GIRLS

Q "The people at the college are very nice and it is **easy to develop friendships with many people**. Everyone is relatively focused on their schoolwork during the week, and the social scene only really opens up on the weekend, but people are nice and helpful at all times."

Q "Ha! It's tough to define hot. Like at any other school, we have beautiful, pretty, normal, ugly, and hideous people. **It depends on your taste**. We are kind of a nerd school, so we have a lot of dorks. I mean that in a good way. Or maybe I don't."

Q "There are a **good number of attractive people here**, but honestly, we care more about more important things than looks."

STUDENT AUTHOR: **Much of Haverford's student body, both male and female, is on the socially-awkward side. Everyone is fairly intelligent, but some wear it on their sleeves more than others. Everyone tries to be extremely nice—even those who aren't the most dynamic. We do know, however, that in a school with only 1,100 people, a few attractive ones can really shift the balance. You definitely have an interesting choice of mates here at the College.**

> **Traditions**
>
> **Haverfest**
> The aforementioned orgy of food, music, and liquor that occurs during the first weekend before finals week.
>
> **La Fiesta**
> Very popular dance held by the Latino organization on campus (ALAS).
>
> **Overall School Spirit**
> Although Haverford students have minimal school spirit in the traditional "rah-rah" sense, most are very proud of the college.

Students Speak Out
ON ATHLETICS

Q "**A very sizable portion of the student body plays some sport**, either at the intramural or varsity level. Because we do not have a football team and we play in Division III, varsity sports may play a slightly smaller role than at other schools, but we are still competitive, and athletics are well attended on campus."

Q "**Intramurals are big on campus**, and so are varsity sports. Teams tend to sit together in the DC, but they aren't normally terribly exclusive. Intramural and club sports are very popular to get through fitness requirements, but most people who start a sport stay with it after they have met their requirements."

Q "**A lot of people participate** in a sport. The crowds at varsity basketball games can be large."

STUDENT AUTHOR: **Although athletes take their own sports seriously, athletics aren't a very big part of the overall Haverford experience. One nice thing about Haverford athletics is that participation is very high. A large number of students are involved in a club sport. We might not be terribly good, but we do like to play, and the college requires us to.**

Students Speak Out
ON DRUG SCENE

Q "**Alcohol is the drug of choice here**. Pot would be second, and, other than that, the drug scene is almost nonexistent."

Q "As for alcohol, you can do it and never get in trouble, even if you get sick and go to the hospital. **They're lenient on pot**, as well, but harder drugs, although they are used, definitely aren't popular."

Q "Drugs are here. Pot is a stone's throw away. But there is **absolutely no pressure to do drugs**. The people are very relaxed about that sort of thing. If anyone has a bad reaction to drugs, Safety and Security will take them to the hospital without getting the police involved."

STUDENT AUTHOR: The drug scene at Haverford is small and not very serious. There is certainly some recreational pot use, but it's actually less prevalent than at your average suburban high school. Overall, it's a pretty low-key college, and free from many of the pressures found at other schools.

8:1	Student-to-Faculty Ratio
96%	Freshman Retention Rate
86%	Four-Year Graduation Rate
90%	Financial Aid Applicants Receiving Aid

Students Speak Out
SAFETY & SECURITY

Q "Safety and Security is on campus, but **they stay behind the scenes** and do not disrupt daily life. However, in a time of need, they are at the scene necessary in a heartbeat and are helpful."

Q "The **Haverford College campus is very safe**, but that has to do with the area the school is in, not the Haverford Safety and Security Department, which is pretty incompetent. They don't have to do much and have no idea what's going on."

Q "**Safety and Security is there for the students**. They are very nice if you have lost something or need a new ID card. They take care of students, especially late at night if for some reason you don't feel safe walking home."

STUDENT AUTHOR: The campus is safe, though there are occasional petty thefts. It's important to remember that going into Philadelphia is another matter entirely. Provided you know where you are at all times, however, Philadelphia should present little more personal risk than campus does.

Questions?
For more inside information and survival tips, pick up College Prowler's full-length book on this school, written by an actual student! Check it out at *www.collegeprowler.com*.

Students Speak Out
ON OVERALL EXPERIENCE

Q "My experience here, so far, has been wonderful. **The College is challenging** and has pushed me to work hard. However, I have still had time to develop friendships and relationships, and this balance is typical of a Haverford student."

Q "There are a lot of things about this school that I like: the sense of community, the Honor Code, the fact that professors really care about you. There are people here that I am certain I will love for the rest of my life. When it comes down to it, **Haverford is academically hard and, perhaps, socially awkward**, but it has transformed me in so many ways that is impossible not to be attached to it. Sometimes, I wish I was somewhere else, but then I realize I don't have time to be thinking about that because I need to study."

Q "I love Haverford. **The students are amazing**, passionate, interesting people from diverse backgrounds, who come together to create a school community based on trust and respect, which is amazing to live in for four years. People say its unrealistic to live under the Honor Code for four years because it's not like the real world, but that's why were here, to try to change the real world to make it more like the 'Ford."

STUDENT AUTHOR: On the whole, students are satisfied with their experience at Haverford. Academically, the school has a spirit of reflective intellectualism that discourages students from becoming too detached from the real world. Social relations are guided by honor and civility. The student body generally has a sense of purpose and perspective, and knows how to relax while tackling a challenging school curriculum.

Hofstra University

340 Hempstead Turnpike; Hempstead, NY 11549
(516) 463-6600; www.hofstra.edu

THE BASICS:

Acceptance Rate: 53%   **SAT Range:** 1090–1270*
Setting: Suburban   **Control:** Private
F-T Undergrads: 7,570   **Tuition:** $27,600

Most Popular Majors: Business/Marketing, Communications/Journalism, Psychology, Education

*of 1600

Academics	B-	Guys	B
Local Atmosphere	A	Girls	B
Safety & Security	C	Athletics	C+
Computers	B+	Nightlife	A
Facilities	B	Greek Life	C
Campus Dining	B+	Drug Scene	D+
Off-Campus Dining	A-	Campus Strictness	B
Campus Housing	C	Parking	B
Off-Campus Housing	C-	Transportation	A
Diversity	B+	Weather	B-

Students Speak Out
ON ACADEMICS

Q "From my own personal experience, I have found that all professors in my major are **incredibly dedicated to their profession**, and especially their students, in teaching and support. However, I've also found that the majority of professors who've taught my core courses aren't nearly as passionate or supportive."

Q "Regardless of what I've thought of any professor here, there has **never been one that I felt afraid to approach**. It's like anything else in life; just have the confidence to approach anyone."

Q "I've noticed a **drastic change in the quality of the professors** as I've progressed here at Hofstra. A lot of the classes that you have to take in your freshman and sophomore years are going to have bad professors, either because they're new or they just don't care. But since I've gotten more into my major, the professors have been great and very understanding."

STUDENT AUTHOR: **While Hofstra's academic reputation has been climbing in recent years, our president is set on improving it even more. Under his supervision, we have seen several improvements to academic facilities, including new classrooms, new faculty offices, and even a completely new building with state-of-the-art everything. By overseeing the incoming of new programs and faculty, and by slowly enhancing the admittance standards, Hofstra is becoming more and more of a powerhouse among private universities in the Northeast. Be prepared to show that you have what it takes in a rapid-paced environment.**

Students Speak Out
ON LOCAL ATMOSPHERE

Q "If you have a car, there are plenty of things to do locally that don't even need to involve drunken nights at sleazy bars. **There are lots of things to do in Long Island during the day** and at night, but if you don't have a car, your options are limited pretty much to the mall and meat-market bars."

Q "I love when the spring comes and it gets nice enough to skip class, **go to the beach all day, and get to the city at night**. And then, get home in time to do it again the next day."

Q "It's a **perfect mix between a small city-type atmosphere and smaller communities**, not to mention we're so close to the beach and several state parks. It's very common on nice days to find your fellow students over at Eisenhower Park picnicking or to run into them down at the beach. This is a very hard place to get bored."

Q "The campus is so nice, and there are so many good things to do that are so close, yet there are areas around here where you just don't want to be at night. Especially when you're a freshman, it's very important to **learn where the safe areas are to go at night**."

STUDENT AUTHOR: **Nassau County may be one of the most densely populated areas in the country. The only drawback is that you really do need to have a car in order to have the freedom of exploring all there is to do. Without one, your only option is to take a bus or cab around, or of course you can get good at bribing others for rides.**

Students Speak Out
ON FACILITIES

Q "The facilities here are great; there's always a movie to catch, a sporting event to watch, a concert or play going on. We are constantly getting great performers here. And even when there's nothing going on, **there's always people hanging out in the courtyards**, throwing a Frisbee around, or a game of hoops to join."

Q "I spend a lot of time at the Recreational Center because of intramural basketball. It's really a great place once you start spending a lot of time there. I used to be intimidated to go in, because I wasn't really into working out, but then I realized that there's a lot more to do in there besides work out. There's a **nice-sized lounge area that has televisions and table games** that are perfect for anyone who's looking for something to do."

Q "**The Student Center is always nice**, mostly because you always know that you'll run into someone you know when passing through."

STUDENT AUTHOR: There is always something to do, and your own fun and enjoyment is largely what you make of it. The facilities are only here to help you along. Certainly, the school has put enough money into things to keep them modern. The gym is nice, but not dazzling; the arena looks cool on the outside, but more than average on the inside. The Student Center looks the same, although they have changed and added a lot to the dining there. The movie theater, unknown to many, and the courtyard set-up seems to please pretty much everyone, as it creates an area that is less open and prone to more social activity.

Students Speak Out
ON CAMPUS DINING

Q "Hofstra's dining is **better than most schools I've visited**, but not better than most restaurants. They have everything including Asian, Mexican, Mediterranean, grills, delis, an advanced salad station, and vegetarian. You can buy everything with your meal plan, so you don't notice how high the prices are sometimes, but the convenience usually makes up for the prices."

Q "The sushi place was a great addition to the Student Center, and they've added more options to all the grills, so you're not just stuck with getting burgers anymore. Also, all of **the new snack places that keep popping up are great**, especially for commuters just looking to grab a quick bite before class."

Q "I haven't paid for a meal plan for the past two years. This way, **I save money and eat better food**."

Q "The fact that Kate & Willie's is open until 2 a.m. is a huge lifesaver. **Everything that a drunk college student could possibly hope for** is just a minute away."

STUDENT AUTHOR: Our food on campus is honestly not bad at all, and the dining facilities are all very pleasant in atmosphere. The one problem seems to be falling into a cycle of eating the same things very often. They've also added a Mediterranean grill and announced that Dutch Treats will be open 24 hours. One last thing; the food at Sbarro's has gotten tremendously better.

Students Speak Out
ON DORMS

Q "**If you're lucky, you'll live in the Netherlands your freshman year**, but it's all left to the luck of the draw. It's great there, because you'll be with all other freshmen, plus the rooms are very nice. But if you get stuck in one of the High Rises, you may be bound to get a bad first impression of the school."

Q "Campus housing is probably the worst thing about Hofstra. **The rooms are extremely small and expensive**. The fire alarms love to go off at three o'clock in the morning, and the security they have now is just way overboard."

Q "Campus housing has its ups and downs. On the upside, **there are some really cool environments to live in**. On the downside, you have the Towers where everyone is pretty segregated and forced to socialize mainly with the students on the same floor."

STUDENT AUTHOR: **Many feel that it is an integral part of the overall college experience. For all of Hofstra's shortcomings when it comes to campus housing, one thing that it does extraordinarily well is accommodate its freshmen. Another problem they've always had and still do is the crowding of rooms. In one of the High Rise buildings, they tried to squeeze three freshman girls together.**

Did You Know?
47% of undergrads live on campus.

Students Speak Out
ON GUYS & GIRLS

Q "Overall, I would say that **there's a large variety of guys here at Hofstra**; you have the jocks who fool themselves into thinking that playing a sport at Hofstra is cool, the business guys who think they already own their own corporation, the film and television guys who think you're stupid if you don't like the same movies they do, and then the guys in the drama and fine arts area who are usually really nice, but not all that available."

Q "I think we have a great-looking campus. I mean, all of the flowers and trees, and girls. I mean, we live close to the beach, so **you get the type of girl that would go to the beach a lot**. And usually, those girls are really attractive."

STUDENT AUTHOR: **It's a miracle that guys and girls are able to live harmoniously together on the same campus. A majority of the guys describe the girls as superficial and difficult to communicate with. While according to the ladies, most guys can be summed up rather briefly: not worth it. Actually, pretty much everyone seems to be getting along just fine. Many students have good friends, but hardly anyone brings up long-term relationships.**

Traditions

Float Building and Bonfire
Organizations build floats the week leading up to Homecoming, and all the extra wood are scraps are used for a bonfire outside of the Student Center.

Freak Formal
Every Halloween, Entertainment Unlimited sponsors the largest party of the year.

Overall School Spirit
Though we have plenty of school spirit from cheerleaders, a dance team, two mascots, and a pep band, there remains a lack of spirt from students not involved in these organizations.

Students Speak Out
ON ATHLETICS

Q "Hofstra sports teams are only mid-major teams at best. It makes it hard to get into the games because they're **not playing against other schools that students would know**."

Q "**The Homecoming game is always great**. Not necessarily because of the actual game, but we always have a huge parade around town and everyone starts tailgating early in the morning."

Q "There's **always a lot of sporting activity going on around campus**; whether it's soccer, basketball, or Frisbee, you always see students out on the intramural fields doing something. We have a lot of leagues and sports that aren't actually sponsored by the University."

STUDENT AUTHOR: **The fairest assessment of Hofstra's athletic programs is that while they are certainly not eye-popping, they don't go completely unseen either. With the arrival of the Hofstra Arena and the Hofstra University Soccer Stadium, the school hopes to send a message that its athletic programs deserve more attention. Perhaps they do, but the football program still struggles to break into Division I-A, and the basketball program falters in a very weak conference.**

Students Speak Out
ON DRUG SCENE

Q "I've seen pretty much all kinds of drugs here, and I'm pretty new to this whole experience. There weren't a lot of drugs in my high school, so it's kind of **intimidating to find out that there are so many students here who do drugs**. It can put a lot of pressure on you as a freshman."

Q "Drugs are a huge part of the social scene here on campus. I've never met anyone here who hasn't at least tried something drug-related. It's even not that rare to walk by a group of students sitting in the courtyard smoking a joint right out in the open. **We have a lot of hippie students** here, so that probably helps contribute to the enormous drug culture."

STUDENT AUTHOR: **There is no hiding the fact that there are a lot of drugs on campus, not to mention the huge popularity of alcohol. However, while students paint a pretty dismal picture, drugs are not at all a huge problem on campus. True, things can get pretty dangerous when you're talking about some of the higher priced drugs like cocaine and ecstasy, but overall, their presence on campus is very much on the decline.**

14:1	Student-to-Faculty Ratio
80%	Freshman Retention Rate
39%	Four-Year Graduation Rate
80%	Financial Aid Applicants Receiving Aid

Students Speak Out
SAFETY & SECURITY

Q "The Public Safety officers are great people. They're very friendly, honest, and understanding. As far as I know, they do their jobs well, and they **don't get a rush out of busting people**."

Q "**The school has improved a lot** by adding security devices around campus such as call-boxes, so that if you are in trouble, hopefully you can get to one and call for help."

Q "Being on campus, I always feel very safe and at home. However, **there are several areas around that just aren't safe to be in at night**. It's like if you go east out of the school, you arrive at beautiful parks and shopping and restaurants, but head west, and it's straight into the ghetto."

STUDENT AUTHOR: **It's very true that there are some extremely rough neighborhoods around campus. There are now about 10 spots where they have installed call-boxes. Another new measure of safety is the escort service. These are student volunteers who will walk with you to and from any point on campus at any time of the day or night.**

Questions?
For more inside information and survival tips, pick up College Prowler's full-length book on this school, written by an actual student! Check it out at *www.collegeprowler.com.*

Students Speak Out
ON OVERALL EXPERIENCE

Q "**Hofstra has its ups and downs**, and it can be extreme on both sides. One of the most exciting times I've had here was during my freshman year. We would party in the Netherlands courtyard every night once the weather was nice. We'd have live music, football, Frisbee, and just an overall mecca of social activity. All of the good friends I've made here are the ones that I met my first year. After freshman year, it's all downhill; things get way more serious and complicated."

Q "I wouldn't change anything that's happened since I decided to come here. **There are lots of good people here**, both in the student body and the faculty and staff. I've been able to make a lot of good connections that should help me after graduation."

Q "One thing that certainly turns me off is the massive amounts of people all segregated into their little areas. This is **one of the most segregated areas in the whole country**, and sometimes it's a little disturbing. On the other hand, there are plenty of things that turn me on when I think about Long Island."

STUDENT AUTHOR: **While academics may not be the foremost thought on everyone's mind when thinking of Hofstra, they have no doubt increased in credibility over recent years. With the improvement and additions of more technically-advanced facilities, a strong commitment to providing limitless computing power, and a keen awareness of student's ever-growing needs, Hofstra is showing the world that it is willing to invest in the future and to correct what has been done wrong in the past.**

Hollins University

7916 Williamson Road; Roanoke, VA 24020
(800) 456-9595; www.hollins.edu

THE BASICS:

Acceptance Rate: 88%
Setting: Small city
F-T Undergrads: 755

SAT Range: 1510–1860*
Control: Private
Tuition: $26,955

Most Popular Majors: Visual/Performing Arts, English, Social Sciences, Psychology, Communications

*of 2400

Academics	B	Guys	N/A
Local Atmosphere	B-	Girls	B
Safety & Security	A+	Athletics	C
Computers	C+	Nightlife	C+
Facilities	B+	Greek Life	N/A
Campus Dining	B	Drug Scene	B+
Off-Campus Dining	B	Campus Strictness	B+
Campus Housing	A	Parking	B+
Off-Campus Housing	D	Transportation	C+
Diversity	C-	Weather	B

Students Speak Out
ON ACADEMICS

Q "All of my professors have been very engaged in both my academic and personal life. **They are relaxed and approachable**. I've found that classes at Hollins have definitely broadened my interests and sparked my imagination."

Q **"The teachers are very involved with each student as an individual**. They are concerned and sympathetic, while also brilliantly creative and assertive. My classes force me to stay focused and interested so much that they are daily discussion even outside of the classroom."

Q "Most of my classes are very interesting. I'm rarely bored in class. Most professors are fantastic, knowledgeable and interested in our educations. **I have only had a truly negative experience with one professor** out of the many I have been in class with."

Q **"I never feel as though I can't speak during class**. Whenever I have something to say, I say it. I never felt like this in high school. Would it be cheesy to say that I feel as though Hollins has liberated me in a way?"

STUDENT AUTHOR: For many Hollins students, the professors are the highlight of the academic experience. They encourage and inspire. Full-time professors usually focus more on teaching than on their own personal projects, and the English department is the only place you'll encounter a teaching assistant. Students report that not only will professors make time for students, but that they seem genuinely happy to do so.

Students Speak Out
ON LOCAL ATMOSPHERE

Q "Downtown Roanoke is terribly charming. There are a lot of **cute shops and independently-owned restaurants**. Blacksburg (VA Tech) is a 45-minute drive away. It has quite a social scene if you're willing to make the drive (and believe me, a lot of people do)."

Q **"Downtown Roanoke is my favorite area**. You'll see the occasional Roanoke College student wandering around, but for the most part, it's just us Hollins girls. There are many other universities within a reasonable driving radius, though."

Q **"Hollins University has a peaceful small-town atmosphere**, but at the same time, it is so close to downtown Roanoke and other colleges that there is always something to do."

Q "Roanoke isn't the best town compared to some real college towns. However, there's a great downtown district with shops, restaurants, bars, and the like. Also, **there are great outdoor activities in the area** like hiking, camping, and rafting."

STUDENT AUTHOR: Roanoke, Virginia is a small city that boasts lots of nearby natural beauty. There are some cultural events that take place, but nothing near what you would find in a larger city. Hollins sponsors a number of rafting, rock climbing, and hiking trips throughout the year. These are popular options for students who want to take advantage of the gorgeous surroundings.

5 Best Things	5 Worst Things
1 Thinking is encouraged	1 The network going down
2 Friendly professors	2 The printers
3 Tinker Day	3 Noisy heaters
4 Freya (secret society)	4 Lack of fun local bars
5 Library study nooks	5 Parking tickets

Students Speak Out
ON FACILITIES

Q "**The athletic complex is very nice**. There's a weight room and an exercise machine room, which I use often. There is also a great swimming pool. Not too many outside-community members use the pool, so you don't have to worry about it being crowded."

Q "The facilities at Hollins are always clean and well-equipped. **Sometimes I feel like I'm in a museum**. There is well-preserved antique furniture everywhere."

Q "The facilities are definitely sufficient for the size of the school. **Our pool is awesome, and there are tons of places to hang out**. If you want to find people at Hollins, you can. However, if you just want to be by yourself, Hollins has plenty of secluded areas where you can take a breather."

Q "The library is top-notch. There is a friendly staff, great e-resources, and comfy reading nooks. Also, there is a movie projector and a TV studio. I think that **the library is absolutely inspiring**. It just sparkles."

Q "I go to the gym early in the morning, because once 3:30 hits, there is a line for the treadmills. **There are only three**. There are plenty of other machines, but no one likes them all that much."

STUDENT AUTHOR: **The oldest buildings at Hollins are truly stunning. Students love learning in such a historic and beautiful setting. Everything stays clean and, with the occasional exception of the computers, in good working order. Among the more modern student favorites are the Wyndham Robertson Library and the Visual Arts Center.**

Famous Alumni

Margaret Wise Brown, Ann Compton, Annie Dillard, Elizabeth Valk Long, Elizabeth Saab, Lee Smith, Carol Semple Thompson

Students Speak Out
ON CAMPUS DINING

Q "If you like starchy food, you will love our food. Honestly, the dining staff tries very hard to give us decent food. They are friendly and will always work with you to try to meet your dietary needs (not always accomplished, **but they do try**)."

Q "Moody does a great job of preparing meals three times a day, but **the diversity of those meals is not impressive**. Be careful not to go to the grill station more than a few times each week, as the food there is always greasy and unhealthy! My friends and I always head off campus to eat for a break."

Q "**The food is not the best, but it is acceptable**. The dining hall is under the meal plan. I mainly go to see my friends. The Rat is rather expensive, so I only go there when I am desperate. It is nice to have a place besides the cafeteria, especially since it's open late."

Q "Food on campus is like a bipolar person— **great for four days and then horrible for two weeks**."

STUDENT AUTHOR: **Hollins is crawling with vegetarians and vegans, but you'd never guess it from checking out the daily menu. However, students report that new management promises a more receptive atmosphere for suggestions. If you are satisfied with bagels, grits, and eggs for breakfast and burgers for lunch, you'll be pleased with the status quo at Hollins. If that doesn't suit you, you'll find plenty of comrades to join in the movement to change the cuisine scene.**

Student Body

African American:	8%	Male/Female:	0/100%
Asian American:	1%	Out-of-State:	48%
Hispanic:	2%	International:	2%
Native American:	1%	Unknown:	1%
White:	85%		

Popular Faiths: There are student groups for Baptist and Catholic students that have a lot of participation.

Gay Pride: Hollins has a vibrant and vocal lesbian and bisexual population. The student group, Outloud, is among the most active on campus.

Economic Status: There are plenty of wealthy students, but there is a wide range of economic backgrounds represented.

Students Speak Out
ON DORMS

Q "**All of the dorms are really nice and very beautiful**. Tinker is the only dorm with air conditioning. West, Main, and East are the oldest and all sit around Front Quad. They all have high ceilings."

Q "The dorms hold a lot of character. Since Hollins is such an old campus, **most of the dorm ceilings are high**, and the windows are large and antique looking. Tinker feels a bit like a hospital, but it is the only one with air conditioning."

Q "The dorms for the first-year students are nice and new. The upperclass dorms aren't as new, but are old and are just stunning. **Living in old buildings or old houses is a lot of fun**."

STUDENT AUTHOR: **Hollins makes an effort to keep as many students on campus for all four years as it can, and most students agree that this is a good thing. Students find that their time on campus enhances their social life and creates a sense of community. Most RAs will always be available when you need them. Each hall develops their own standards in terms of quiet hours and visiting policies.**

Did You Know?
80% of undergrads live on campus.

Students Speak Out
ON GUYS & GIRLS

Q "**There are beautiful women at Hollins**. Everyone walks around with a smile on their face. If you're looking for a college where you can be dark and angst-filled, don't expect to find many people like you here."

Q "If you think Lily Pulitzer dresses and pearls are hot, you'll find someone. **If you think Harry Potter capes are hot, you'll find someone**."

Q "The students are friendly and hot enough to keep the lesbians **knee-deep in drama**."

Q "**Sorry, no guys here, and the girls just look like either guys or bookworms**. We are close to VMI, so you can always go there and find you a man in uniform."

STUDENT AUTHOR: **There aren't really any coherent profiles of Hollins women. They are preppy, bookish, artsy, nerdy, butch, and hippie. However, do expect to find more obviously wealthy and primped women than you would in the general population. Also, definitely expect to encounter more unshaven women. There is a good amount of support for individuality at Hollins, and so many students develop a lot self-confidence here.**

Traditions

Freya Walks
On nights of special events members of the secret society Freya walk across campus wearing black hoods and holding candles.

Tinker Day
Classes are cancelled for the day and students hike up Tinker Mountain dressed in crazy costumes.

Overall School Spirit
Ask an enthusiastic student how she feels, and she'll immediately tell you about the rich history of Hollins as one of the first women's colleges.

Students Speak Out
ON ATHLETICS

Q "**Riding is huge on campus**. There are a lot of people in the program, including some beginners. A lot of people go to the shows in support of the team. We are so proud of them!"

Q "There aren't a lot of athletes on campus, but **those who are in varsity sports are very dedicated**. I don't think they get enough credit sometimes. I have a lot of admiration for those students who can make all those practices and games and still keep their grades up."

Q "Sometimes I'll be walking around the loop, and I'll see a team out in the field. I can't tell if it's a game or a practice, because **no one goes to the games**."

STUDENT AUTHOR: **Hollins University embraces the country-club end of sports, with heavy emphasis on horseback riding and tennis. These are the teams that tend to attract the most attention, success, and funding. In recent years, other sports have not received the same kind of success, and turnout to games has been pretty low. For those students who are not athletes (and they are the majority), the sports scene does not play a very visible role.**

Students Speak Out
ON DRUG SCENE

Q "Drinking happens frequently, but rarely with incident. **There's pot, I hear, but not enough that I've seen a lot of it.** Compared to the high school I went to, it's nothing."

Q "**There aren't many hard drugs on campus.** Pot and stay-awake-type drugs for studying are about it. When all is said and done, I think that we are pretty tame when compared to most other colleges."

Q "Drugs are not a big part of Hollins. **I think we've got a good attitude here about it.** We recognize that substances are around, but no one goes crazy over cracking down on drug users, and students don't go overboard in their drug usage."

STUDENT AUTHOR: **While there are drugs on campus, they do not constitute a visible presence. The only truly visible substance is alcohol. Students feel as though there is not a high degree of availability of anything but alcohol and marijuana. Overall, it's up to the student.**

10:1	Student-to-Faculty Ratio
68%	Freshman Retention Rate
55%	Four-Year Graduation Rate
62%	Financial Aid Applicants Receiving Aid

Students Speak Out
SAFETY & SECURITY

Q "**Security officers are always visible on campus**, but sometimes it feels that they are more concerned with minor infractions (like ticketing students for rolling stops at stop signs) than they are of more important issues like drug and alcohol abuse."

Q "Hollins is such a safe campus, and **being so small means that help is never far away.** Campus security does their job, but I think I feel safer knowing that my friends are around."

Q "Campus security is friendly and accommodating. **They want to help as much as possible** while also allowing us to enjoy our time on campus. Other than the occasional NEFA party break-up, I rarely see Campus Safety telling anyone not to do something."

STUDENT AUTHOR: **Most students do not at all fear for their safety while they are on campus. The most talked about testament to this is the ease that students feel while walking alone at night. There is always one security car circling the campus, and most officers will wave to everyone they pass.**

Questions?
For more inside information and survival tips, pick up College Prowler's full-length book on this school, written by an actual student! Check it out at *www.collegeprowler.com*.

Students Speak Out
ON OVERALL EXPERIENCE

Q "It's funny: **Hollins attracts a lot of weirdos and a lot of clean-cut kids.** We end up with a unique balance in our social atmosphere. If you're up for a change, come to Hollins. Just don't expect the expected."

Q "If you are looking for the traditional big school with a party atmosphere, you won't find it at Hollins. **We have our own way of partying, and we have our own way of learning.** If you're not willing to give new ideas a chance, you'll have a hard time at Hollins."

Q "My experience here has been amazing. My fellow students are **incredibly smart, resourceful, and driven.** I'm likewise amazed by the alumnae. They are excited to help you. You've heard of 'the old boy's network.' Hollins alumnae are all about creating that for women!"

Q "**I love the small-school atmosphere.** There is a world of difference between a good education and a good personalized education. If you are the kind of person who does not like to participate in class or who does not like to collaborate with other students, Hollins will either change that or you'll transfer."

STUDENT AUTHOR: **Hollins students love their school. Many become very sentimental and enthusiastic in expressing this. Due in large part to its devoted alumnae recruiting system, Hollins remains poised to succeed in the future. Students also have a lot of say in what and how much they want to put into their educations. If flexibility and individuality are important to you, you'll appreciate the academic environment. If you crave academic structure, Hollins might not provide you with what you are looking for.**

Howard University

2400 Sixth Street NW; Washington, DC 20059
(202) 806-6100; www.howard.edu

THE BASICS:

Acceptance Rate: 54%
Setting: Urban
F-T Undergrads: 6,766

SAT Range: 1310–1960*
Control: Private
Tuition: $14,205

Most Popular Majors: Biology, Journalism, Radio/Television, Marketing, Psychology

*of 2400

Academics	B+	Guys	A-
Local Atmosphere	A	Girls	A+
Safety & Security	C	Athletics	C+
Computers	C+	Nightlife	A
Facilities	B-	Greek Life	C
Campus Dining	B	Drug Scene	A-
Off-Campus Dining	A-	Campus Strictness	C+
Campus Housing	B-	Parking	D
Off-Campus Housing	C	Transportation	A
Diversity	D-	Weather	B-

Students Speak Out
ON ACADEMICS

Q "Some of the professors are wonderful, some are evil. **A lot of them have really great personalities so their classes are interesting**, which makes it harder to deal with if you happen to end up with a professor with a not-so-great personality and a boring class."

Q "Most of the teachers are **nice, fair, and knowledgeable in their field**. All of my classes have been very interesting, from English to African American history."

Q "The professors create a nurturing environment, and they are very helpful. The classes are interesting because **the professors present the material with an innovative style**."

Q "**The professors are interesting, smart, knowledgeable, and thorough**. I've had very few boring classes, and it's been really great experiencing my professors being there not just as people teaching me stuff, but also as people who actually care about me and want me to do well and not just pass me through."

STUDENT AUTHOR: From day one at Howard University, students get a sense of the level of academic intensity that they can come to expect. While there's a heavy workload that goes along with most classes, most students still manage to balance a decent social life. This definitely becomes a little harder to accomplish the further you go into your major, but some students are still able to cope, regardless.

Students Speak Out
ON LOCAL ATMOSPHERE

Q "The University is in an urban scene that is **very stylish and liberal**, and it's a very exciting town to live in. There are many other universities present, lots of young people around, and there's always something fun to do."

Q "I love DC! **You can eat, watch a movie, and go shopping, all within the same block**. And even though it makes it so easy for you to overspend, it's all worth it when you think about the great experience you're having."

Q "Howard is a little too urban for my liking. It's a very exciting place to visit and hang out in, but **it's not all that wonderful for me to be living in such a noisy and crime-ridden atmosphere**. The museums are really nice, though, and you could spend a whole day in just one gallery without realizing it."

Q "There's always something going on in DC, and you can always get a chance to find whatever you feel like doing. **Some really nice places to go are U Street and Adams Morgan**, which have very nice restaurants and clubs."

STUDENT AUTHOR: Washington DC is a fast-paced city that literally has a scene for everyone. Howard University is located in the ritzy Shaw district, minutes away from downtown DC, and is flanked by seven other universities. For a large city, DC is relatively safe. However, the lower southeast side of DC should be avoided at all costs. DC gleams with life and personality. You will never long for things to do or places to go while here.

Students Speak Out
ON FACILITIES

Q "Athletic facilities are decent, but they can get crowded a lot. **Computer facilities are good, if insufficient in number**, and the student center is improving and adding new features every year. For example, the Punch Out wasn't as good or didn't have as much variety as it does now."

Q "Some of the facilities need to be upgraded, but **overall, they are nice and are maintained properly**. I have access to everything I need in order to do well in school, so that's the most important thing."

Q "**Most of the facilities on campus are nice**. I've never been to the gym, but I think it was just remodeled. The computer lab is nice, if a little crowded, and the food court is amazing."

Q "Not all the facilities on campus are up-to-date, but **most of them operate correctly**. You stand to suffer if you're in a department or club that doesn't have many members because your needs might be overlooked if you don't have someone to advocate for you to get the facilities you need."

STUDENT AUTHOR: **Generally, all the facilities on campus are well-maintained and much of campus receives high praise from students. However, there are some classrooms in some of the more sparsely populated departments that are in less-than-ideal condition. Whether this is due to an oversight by the administration or a matter of priorities, the fact still remains that there is a definite disparity between the condition of some departments over others at Howard.**

Famous Alumni

Zora Neale Hurston, Dr. Ossie Davis, Thurgood Marshall, Phylicia Rashad, Debbie Allen, Richard Parsons

---

Students Speak Out
ON CAMPUS DINING

Q "**The food in the Punch Out is very good but kind of pricey**. I usually just get something from the vendors or eat off campus."

Q "Food services are not the best right now. The food is good, but **everything is closed by midnight**. So, if you're hungry really late, it's on you to find yourself something to eat. Basically, dining on campus is not set up very well at Howard."

Q "The food on campus is decent, but **it can get repetitive and boring**. I always try to mix it up with eating off campus or going home on the weekends to get some of my mom's cooking."

Q "The food and dining choices are okay. If you eat at the dining halls long enough, you'll get bored with some of the selections, but you can always go and eat off campus or cook at a friend's apartment or house like I do. **You can have a fridge and microwave in your dorm**, so storing and reheating food cooked somewhere else shouldn't be a problem."

STUDENT AUTHOR: The Freshman 15 could very easily become the Freshman 30 if you get carried away by the amount of good, albeit unhealthy, food available at the campus dining halls. Some of the dining halls have themes depending on the day of the week as well (e.g., Soul Food Thursday, Barbeque Tuesday). Even though they are not as readily available as traditional eating options, vegetarian and vegan meals are available in Blackburn and Bethune Annex dining halls.

Student Body

African American:	89%	Male/Female:	33/67%
Asian American:	1%	Out-of-State:	93%
Hispanic:	1%	International:	9%
Native American:	<1%	Unknown:	0%
White:	<1%		

Popular Faiths: Christianity and Islam seem to be the two dominant religions on campus.

Gay Pride: Because the entire student body is so diverse, everyone is very tolerant of each other's sexual orientation, as well as their beliefs and cultures.

Economic Status: There are students from wealthy as well as humble backgrounds, but it's usually hard to tell because so many dress really well.

Students Speak Out
ON DORMS

Q "A lot of students try and move off campus because **dorm life can become a drag after about two years**. It's great those first two years when you have an active social life and you can interact with all the people on your floor, but after that, sometimes you just want to be alone and not have to deal with someone playing music at three in the morning."

Q "**Campus housing is decent freshman year**. You might get stuck with no air conditioning, but after that, dorms are reasonable."

Q "The housing is better than it used to be, but it needs improvements. There is sufficient housing for all freshmen, but **after that year, housing is no longer guaranteed** and it is given through a lottery system."

STUDENT AUTHOR: All of the freshmen-designated dorms are located less than five minutes away from the heart of campus. There's always been a lack of housing for non-honors upperclassmen, but freshmen and grad students are always well taken care of, even though the latter very often opt to live off campus.

> **Did You Know?**
> 55% of undergrads live on campus.

Students Speak Out
ON GUYS & GIRLS

Q "**Every day is a fashion show at Howard**. The guys and girls are very good-looking, but there is a disparity in the ratio of guys to girls, so that's kind of wack."

Q "**The girls outnumber the guys by far**, and sometimes this is a bad thing, but it kind of makes the student body more nurturing and affectionate, in my opinion."

Q "This is the first school I've been in that has such **a large number of attractive girls who are not conceited** or think they should be treated in a special way because they are beautiful. The guys are also very good-looking, and everybody dresses very uniquely."

STUDENT AUTHOR: With a male:female ratio of 30:70, there is often fierce competition between the girls to snag a good guy. Because there are so many hot girls, however, they all really have to go the extra mile in terms of trying to stand out. Most Howard girls are genuinely friendly and have great personalities. And since HU students come from all over the globe, they all have something unique to offer.

> **Traditions**
>
> **Bison Ball**
> A yearly event to honor the accomplishments of individual students and organizations on campus.
>
> **The Yard**
> The initials of various leaders and noted alumni are carved into trees and bricks in the Yard.
>
> **Overall School Spirit**
> Howard is all about showing school spirit. Take a walk on the Yard on any given day, and you will see the HU logo on shirts, key chains, sweatpants, backpacks, you name it.

Students Speak Out
ON ATHLETICS

Q "Sports are not big on campus at all. There's a sports page in the *Hilltop* (school paper) every day, but **nobody really pays much attention to sports until Homecoming**, and then the game is just another one of the many events."

Q "If Saturday morning tailgate keggers and March Madness mayhem are what you desire, **then Howard is probably not the school for you.**"

Q "I'm practically obsessed with sports, but I'm in the minority here. **Some people don't even know about all the teams we have**. Even the people on athletic scholarships are not that crazy about sports."

Q "Varsity sports aren't that big, but **IM sports are very popular.**"

STUDENT AUTHOR: Even though there is a very high level of school spirit and pride among students, Howard is not a very sports-oriented school. Most students, except for those who are on athletic scholarships, are not particularly preoccupied with school sports, at least not until the big Homecoming football game when students turn out in droves.

Students Speak Out
ON DRUG SCENE

Q "I've never known drugs or drinking to be a problem on campus. Most people are naturally high on life, so they don't need to be drinking or taking any drugs."

Q "I don't know about there being any drugs on campus. There are probably a few people who use drugs, but I've never met or gotten to know any and neither have any of my friends."

Q "Some crack dealers used to hang around the campus a few years back, and it was probably really easy to get drugs then, but now that the police have driven a lot of them away, it would be harder to have drugs on campus at all."

STUDENT AUTHOR: Drugs are virtually nonexistent at Howard, but realistically speaking, there are definitely a few individuals who take it upon themselves to use and sell drugs. Most students don't use drugs, however, and a new student would have to work kind of hard to find a regular hookup. There is no social pressure at Howard to do anything to fit in other than just to be yourself.

8:1	Student-to-Faculty Ratio
85%	Freshman Retention Rate
43%	Four-Year Graduation Rate
89%	Financial Aid Applicants Receiving Aid

Students Speak Out
SAFETY & SECURITY

Q "The neighborhood could be better, but there are campus police making rounds constantly on campus, and safety is usually left to the students to behave in a responsible manner."

Q "The closer you are to the main campus, the safer it is and the less likely it is for you to run into any shady characters that could harm you. There are lots of campus police around, especially by the dorms, and the city police patrol the area frequently, too."

Q "Safety is a serious issue at Howard, which is located in the heart of urban DC. Shuttle buses are available to transport students to and from the Metro station, dorms, and various campus locations. So, I think the University is doing their part to make sure students are safe."

STUDENT AUTHOR: Howard's campus, itself, is relatively safe. In the past, however, the surrounding Shaw district has been ranked by *USA Today* and several other national publications as one of the most dangerous areas in the country. However, there is a visible police presence on campus, especially after dark.

Questions?
For more inside information and survival tips, pick up College Prowler's full-length book on this school, written by an actual student! Check it out at *www.collegeprowler.com.*

Students Speak Out
ON OVERALL EXPERIENCE

Q "I've only been here a semester, and I already feel like I couldn't bear to leave. I love the diversity, the history and legacy of Howard, the Howard spirit, and practically everything that has the Howard stamp on it. Howard is such a cool place to be, and I'm so excited and happy to be here."

Q "I kind of have a love-hate relationship with Howard. As much as I love this school, its history, the people, and everything in between, there are just some things that are not right and should be straightened out, especially since we are the mecca."

Q "I love Howard. They could have chosen anyone else, but they chose my application. It is a good school with a good reputation, and I'm getting a very good education."

Q "There's nothing like being able to get a good education while forming lasting relationships with such warm and interesting people. It's like being part of a family, especially with some of the professors that I've had who became friends and surrogate parents in addition to being my professors."

STUDENT AUTHOR: Students are more than satisfied with the quality of education that they are receiving at Howard. Students seem to have no trouble meshing with their peers, as well as the faculty. In fact, the only qualm that students seem to have is experiencing the difficulties of dealing with HU administration. But even with all the little frustrations that come with dealing with the administration, there is a firm consensus among the students that there is no better place for them to be.

Hunter College

695 Park Avenue; New York, NY 10021
(212) 772-4490; www.hunter.cuny.edu

THE BASICS:

Acceptance Rate: 35% **SAT Range:** 970–1140*
Setting: Urban **Control:** Public
F-T Undergrads: 10,891 **Tuition:** $11,199

Most Popular Majors: Psychology, English, Economics, Film and Media Studies, Political Science

*of 1600

Academics	B-	Guys	C+
Local Atmosphere	A	Girls	B
Safety & Security	B	Athletics	D
Computers	B-	Nightlife	A+
Facilities	C	Greek Life	D
Campus Dining	C-	Drug Scene	B+
Off-Campus Dining	A+	Campus Strictness	B
Campus Housing	C+	Parking	F
Off-Campus Housing	D-	Transportation	A+
Diversity	A+	Weather	B-

Students Speak Out
ON ACADEMICS

Q "The teachers range from graduate students and adjuncts to researchers, professionals, and very experienced professors. **The introductory courses can be somewhat painful**, and higher-level courses tend to attract the better teachers, challenging courses, and best experiences. In general, the classes vary greatly and are difficult to predict."

Q "The teachers are a crapshoot, like any school. **Some are genuinely interested in their jobs, some are not.** Ask students about their experiences to find the better teachers. I find most of my classes interesting. Course descriptions are, unfortunately, often not enough to choose carefully by."

Q "I find **the classes taught by teaching assistants (TAs) or adjuncts more interesting** than the tenure professors. I think everything depends on what the student's interested in."

Q "Teachers are good overall. Some are not that professional, but **the majority are good**. Some classes are interesting, others are not. It depends on what you take."

STUDENT AUTHOR: Hunter is often referred to as a place where you get the most bang for your buck. The classes tend to have talented professors in the field, result in interesting discussions, and prepare students well for future study or work. The sciences, in particular, tend to be tough but worth the pain, and each department has its handful of exceptional professors.

Students Speak Out
ON LOCAL ATMOSPHERE

Q "New York City is really lively and exciting. There is a great mix of people, attractions, restaurants, and things to do. There are many universities. **I'd take advantage of the museums and theaters** in NYC. We get student discounts to museums, plays, and other cultural attractions."

Q "**Go around in packs, and you'll be fine**. There are tons of other universities. The only way to find out what to stay away from and what to visit is to get out and explore."

Q "In Brooklyn, there's not much. I live close to Flatbush, so it's rough, but I get by. **New York is filled with lots of places to go for walks**: Times Square, Fifth Avenue, Central Park, and the Coney Island boardwalk."

Q "**Since Hunter is a commuter school**, it depends very much on what borough you live in and what neighborhood you live in. In the Washington Heights area, there is another university around, but I wouldn't exactly say it's the most fun place to hang out. Most of the things to visit are the parks and museums, but I just happen to be a fan of those."

STUDENT AUTHOR: Hunter's campus is essentially New York City itself. With the subway a few steps outside of the buildings, you could be anywhere in minutes. Not that there's a lack of anything to do around town. The streets within walking distance of the campus are primarily lined with stores, though most of them, such as children's boutiques or antique stores, students may quickly pass over.

Students Speak Out
ON FACILITIES

Q "The facilities are okay, but **they are aimed at commuters and not residents on campus**. At the dorm, they are more standard college grade."

Q "**I found the exercise gym to be way too small for me**. Everything else is pretty typical for a city school."

Q "Honestly, I haven't visited many of the Hunter facilities. I know that **the counseling office is always packed and overcrowded**. But, if I've really needed help, I was guided to a place that could help me solve my problem. Somehow, things always work out, if not at the first place you look."

Q "The library is somewhat depressing, oddly deserted, and offers a lot of books (circa 1900). The gym has a lot of equipment. **The student center is surprisingly small** for a student body of 15,000, and there are few locations for socializing and relaxing. In general, the facilities are decent, standard for public universities, but improving each year, with new computers, a renovated student center, and motivation within the student government."

STUDENT AUTHOR: Except for the skywalks, there is nothing particularly interesting or attractive about Hunter's campus. Its library is not the belle of the ball, either, though students are able to use other CUNY libraries. Because the campus was founded in 1870 yet includes recent modifications and improvements, the campus has an interesting look to it, mixing the old with the new.

Famous Alumni

Bella Abzug, Ruby Dee, Gertrude Elion, Terrance Lindall, Rhea Perlman, Volanda Vega, Rosalyn Yalow; Didn't Graduate: Bobby Darin, Vin Diesel

Students Speak Out
ON CAMPUS DINING

Q "The cafeteria is **overpriced and rather unhealthy**. It's better to walk outside and get something from a nearby restaurant."

Q "The Hunter cafeteria leaves a little to be desired. They have prepared salads, sandwiches, a questionable daily 'blue plate special,' and an assortment of fried options. **I'd much rather go to one of the places within a few blocks** up or down Lexington."

Q "**Hunter's cafeteria is really bad**. But, you have no excuse, because most delis and restaurants on Lexington between 65th and 70th offer discounts to Hunter students."

Q "Well, I like to eat healthily, so there is hardly anything I can eat on campus. **There are no good spots—everything is so crowded**! Probably, outside is your best bet."

Q "**Food is not great and too expensive**, but it doesn't really matter. It's Manhattan, and you can go anywhere."

STUDENT AUTHOR: Students, on the whole, have mixed feelings about Hunter's cafeteria. There isn't much of a break on food (though, for $4.99 you can get their "blue plate" special that includes an entrée, two sides, side salad, fountain beverage, and dessert), but it's really convenient if you're too lazy to walk a few blocks. In July 2004, the city threatened to shut down the cafeteria because of health code violations. The school passed inspection, though, after cleaning up its act.

Student Body

African American:	12%	Male/Female:	32/68%
Asian American:	24%	Out-of-State:	5%
Hispanic:	21%	International:	10%
Native American:	<1%	Unknown:	0%
White:	35%		

Popular Faiths: In general, religion is not a very strong presence on campus.

Gay Pride: Sexual orientation is not a big deal at Hunter. It is a very open campus that has a visible gay presence.

Economic Status: Because Hunter is a very affordable school, it has students coming from broad economic backgrounds.

Students Speak Out
ON DORMS

Q "**They're good because they're singles**, but the construction of the forensics building is unbearable, hence, that side is cheaper (by less than 200 dollars). Avoid it if you can."

Q "I have no idea about the dorms. **Most people live off campus**—it's a commuter school."

Q "If you can get into the one and only dorm, you're lucky. The rooms are singles, and the building is nice. A word of advice to the newly applying: don't believe anything anyone tells you about dorm application rules or eligibility until you have had it confirmed by three or four other reliable sources. **You can also check out other college's dorms**. Some of them will allow in students from other colleges."

STUDENT AUTHOR: Located two miles from the main campus, which equates to a 30-minute subway ride or a 20-minute ride on the free shuttle, the Brookdale Campus houses about two percent of the people that attend Hunter. The dorm rooms are all singles, so there is no chance for the roommate-bonding experience, but that also means having the comfort of your own spacious room.

Did You Know?
2% of undergrads live on campus.

Students Speak Out
ON GUYS & GIRLS

Q "Don't we have an eight-to-two girl-to-guy ratio? **The hackey sackers outside intrigue me**, but that's because I like the silent, geeky, and/or brooding types."

Q "Okay, so 70 percent girls, 30 percent guys. **Of that, 30 percent to 50 percent are gay**. I have very little to say about the other half. Let's just say I look out of school for my eye candy. As for the girls, I guess they're hot."

Q "**The girls are numerous, well dressed, and often pretty**. For the last two years, I would have launched into a diatribe about the nonexistence of guys at Hunter. There still aren't men—I can go through a semester with a total of about 10 in all my classes."

STUDENT AUTHOR: All types of personalities go to Hunter; it truly is a diverse school. Hipster, grunge, preppy, nerdy—whatever you go for, you're likely to find. The campus leans towards having a lot of attractive students, either conventionally or unconventionally. Once students leave 68th Street, their lives are pretty much private; everyone is too wrapped up in their own lives to care too much about everyone else's.

Traditions

Overall School Spirit
If you got a nickel for every time you saw a Hunter sweatshirt, in a semester's time, you wouldn't have enough money to buy that sweatshirt. The most tangible way to measure school spirit is by sports attendance, and most students aren't even aware of the sports teams, let alone motivated to attend the games. Students have worked very hard just to be sitting in the classroom, and that tends to lead to pride in the school, but by the time senior year rolls around, most students are more than glad to graduate.

Students Speak Out
ON ATHLETICS

Q "Well, considering **I don't even know what the hell sports we have** or what the team mascot is, I don't think they're that big."

Q "**Varsity sports are big with the sports crowd**. Two- or three-sport athletes are not uncommon, and Hunter kicks ass. We usually win at least seven CUNY Athletic Conference championships a year. Hunter is the rival team to beat in most sports, particularly basketball and softball. Games are pretty interesting, particularly playoffs and championships."

Q "Sports are in no way as big as they are in other schools. **People play on teams, but it's not such a big deal**. We have no football team."

STUDENT AUTHOR: It is a rare occurrence that you hear anything about collegiate sports at Hunter College. You may catch wind of Hunter's annual Homecoming, though Hunter does not have a football team. The world of athletics exists in the lower levels of the school that extend below the subway line. Hunter does have facilities for those looking to get in shape, such as a gym, and the school offers intramural sports and recreation for the non-athletes with some time to spare.

Students Speak Out
ON DRUG SCENE

Q "I don't know much about the drug scene. **There were rumors about a huge coke trend** two years ago, but I don't know about the validity of the rumors."

Q "I don't know anything about the drug scene at Hunter. **If it's there, it stays out of the way of people who aren't involved**. If it's not—well, it's NYC, so I'm sure there's something."

Q "I don't do any, and **I would hope there wasn't a scene here**."

Q "Since it is such a commuter school, **no one really does drugs**."

STUDENT AUTHOR: Without a large percentage of students living on campus, whatever they do outside of the classroom is their own business. The only place where a "drug scene" could be analyzed would be downtown at the dorms. Drug use does occur in the dorms, despite prohibition. For those who want nothing to do with it, it can be out of sight, but not necessarily out of smell.

14:1	Student-to-Faculty Ratio
81%	Freshman Retention Rate
10%	Four-Year Graduation Rate
97%	Financial Aid Applicants Receiving Aid

Students Speak Out
SAFETY & SECURITY

Q "**I've never been asked for my ID** when entering any of the buildings, but it seems to work out somehow. I feel safe on campus, most of the time (not considering the times when you have to stay there late, like 11ish at night)."

Q "I see campus security officers around, but I don't know exactly what they do besides make their presence known. **I can say that I feel safe most of the time**, and perhaps it's a good sign that I don't see the security guards working too hard."

Q "**The CUNY police are everywhere**—walking around, on bikes, and in cars. Security in the dorms is tight, which is a good thing. Around the city, the NYPD are everywhere as well, so there's nothing to worry about."

STUDENT AUTHOR: Unlike most campuses or buildings in New York City, Hunter is open, so literally anybody can walk in. The only time you need your ID is to get into the library or computer lab. That doesn't mean the campus isn't safe. In fact, students feel very safe getting to and from class.

Questions?

For more inside information and survival tips, pick up College Prowler's full-length book on this school, written by an actual student! Check it out at *www.collegeprowler.com*.

Students Speak Out
ON OVERALL EXPERIENCE

Q "I really like the school. I must say, I was a bit hesitant to accept Hunter's non-traditional college setting, but **after two years, I began to love it**, and I have realized that your experience is what you make it."

Q "This is just where I want to be. Right now, I would say my college experience is good to great. And, **you can't beat the price**. You can get a bachelor's degree for under half the cost of a year at a private school."

Q "**I really enjoy being at Hunter**. It's in a great location. I've had many good experiences here, and I have met wonderful people."

Q "From the point of view of **being in the Honors College and living rent free** and not paying tuition, not even paying for all my books, I'd say it's not a bad deal."

Q "I like the school. It's been great to me. **I do wish I was somewhere else**, but it's not the school's fault. I came here first to get some classes I need for my major, and I ended up staying to finish up my degree."

STUDENT AUTHOR: As an overwhelming number of students commute to school, a lot of the student body fears they are missing out on the "traditional" college experience, if traditional means living on campus with parties every day of the week and buckets of school spirit. A lot of students went to Hunter specifically to avoid that environment, though; their life isn't focused on, nor does it depend on, the school. On the whole, it can be safe to say that the students who attend Hunter feel very fortunate to be here, and they work very hard to stay here.

Idaho State University

921 South Eighth Avenue; Pocatello, ID 83209
(202) 282-3620; www.isu.edu

THE BASICS:

Acceptance Rate: 80%
Setting: Small city
F-T Undergrads: 11,024

SAT Range: 910–1185*
Control: Public
Tuition: $11,566

Most Popular Majors: Health Professions, Mechanic and Repair Technologies, Engineering Technologies

*of 1600

Academics	B-	Guys	B-
Local Atmosphere	B	Girls	B+
Safety & Security	A	Athletics	B
Computers	B	Nightlife	B-
Facilities	A-	Greek Life	C+
Campus Dining	B	Drug Scene	A
Off-Campus Dining	B+	Campus Strictness	C
Campus Housing	C+	Parking	B-
Off-Campus Housing	A	Transportation	B+
Diversity	C-	Weather	B-

Students Speak Out
ON ACADEMICS

Q "For the most part, **the teachers at ISU are willing to help any student**. Most know what they are teaching. They all teach in different ways, so it's hard to compare, but I haven't had a teacher yet that I despise!"

Q "The teachers here are really knowledgeable. Some are frustrated because they **don't have enough funding**, so they can't do all that they could to give us a complete education. I do find my classes interesting but, of course, I like my major a lot."

Q "In general, **my teachers are wonderful**. They work really hard to ensure that the information they are teaching comes across in a manner that is easily understood, and they make themselves available to help students when needed."

Q "Most of my **teachers are thoroughly involved with their students**. That is the major advantage I see to attending a smaller university—the time the professors have to help students rather than research for their whole career. I personally find my classes very rewarding, but I am done with generals, so every class has some appeal to me."

STUDENT AUTHOR: **ISU is known as a health college, but not everybody wants to be a doctor or dental hygienist. All the major health programs receive money and improvement before any other program on campus. This is not to say that the other programs cannot operate adequately. They are still excellent programs with excellent faculty, but they are not reaching their full potential.**

Students Speak Out
ON LOCAL ATMOSPHERE

Q "**The atmosphere in Pocatello is pretty low key**. The town itself isn't really all that great, but the college makes up for it. The University always has something going on if you can't find anything in the town to do."

Q "I love the atmosphere of Pocatello. It is small enough to avoid the problems that larger metropolitan areas have, like traffic, pollution, and crime, and at the same time **it gives me all the things I need**."

Q "Pocatello is a very laid-back community. It is a liberal stronghold in an otherwise conservative state. The closest major university is Utah State, an hour and a half away. **Definitely stay away from the railroad tracks** unless you like carnies and other transients. Any mountain around Pocatello offers great chances to engage in many outdoor activities like hiking."

Q "The atmosphere is small but not too small. As far as stuff to stay away from, **there is always naughty stuff to stay away from**—stuff that challenges you as a person regardless of the size of the town."

STUDENT AUTHOR: **The Pocatello area does offer a wide variety of activities and fun for students including hiking, hunting, camping, snowmobiling, and boating all within a two-hour drive. The only problem is that there is not a lot to do without driving half an hour or more. In-town choices are limited to bowling, rollerskating, and going to the movies.**

Students Speak Out
ON FACILITIES

Q "The facilities on campus are great. **I love the rock climbing wall**. The gym could use a bit of an update."

Q "The facilities are fairly nice. **Students have access to decent sports equipment** and nice academic areas. We are very excited about the new Rendezvous Center that has many more student amenities. One thing I would like to have is a study area that can be accessed 24/7."

Q "The Holt Arena brings in a lot of great events from state wrestling to First Security Games to rodeos. **The facilities are really nice and well taken care of**. Most of the time it's free for students to get into these activities."

Q "I really enjoy our campus facilities. The new all-purpose building houses a dorm, a student union, classrooms, and a game center, among other things. Our gym, although not the newest, is well-maintained and **provides a large number of choices for activities**."

Q "The Stephens Performing Arts Center is an incredible addition to ISU. **Many more concerts, symphonies, and even plays** are starting to take advantage of this great facility—which is really nice for students, too!"

STUDENT AUTHOR: **With the various facilities the University provides, ISU has plenty of activities to offer to a wide range of students. Then again, the facilities are old. The only thing to say is that this is an old campus. A lot of the buildings have been continuously updated and remodeled time and again. The University definitely strives to keep up with the maintenance of these old buildings.**

Students Speak Out
ON CAMPUS DINING

Q "Campus dining is rather limited. **The dining halls do have plenty of options**, and you can always be consoled by the knowledge that they always have burgers and fries at the grill section."

Q "There are two dining locations on campus. Turner Hall, a typical all-you-can-eat cafeteria, is mainly for those who live in the residence halls but is open to the general public as well. The student union has a variety of food like soups, crepes, burgers, wraps, and even smoothies. It is always nice to go to the SUB on a cold day and get a hot chocolate before class, too! The staff is always very friendly, and I think that **the food in the SUB is great and very affordable**!"

Q "**The cafeteria food is alright**. I mean, it's cafeteria food, so it can't be that great! I actually had a smoothie from the SUB, and it was delectable. I strongly recommend peach!"

Q "Food on campus is rather limited, but **there are tasty places to eat at nearby**, right off campus, like Goody's."

STUDENT AUTHOR: **The ISU food service works to make meals as scrumptious, delicious, and nutritious as possible. Turner Hall is not very popular because mostly students living in residence halls eat there. The student union building is continually full of students taking advantage of on-campus dining opportunities. When students have the time, they are more likely to hit Goody's across the street. A hungry student is definitely more likely to be seen eating fast food than eating on campus.**

Students Speak Out
ON DORMS

Q "**I would recommend dorm living for all incoming students** for at least a semester. If nothing else, it will expose you to the vast differences that exist on campus. Turner Hall is the main, tower-style dorm. Any of the South Complex dorms will have a more intimate setting with fewer people around."

Q "They are pretty expensive because you have to buy the meal plan. **Students have to pay for a semester's worth of meals** all at once, so it seems like they are expensive."

Q "Dorms are dorms in my opinion: **always loud, experimental, and like living in a Motel 6** for months!"

STUDENT AUTHOR: The quality of ISU's campus housing varies. Some of the dorms are well-kept and maintained; others have more problems. Turner Hall is definitely the dorm to live in to get to know a lot of different people. The single-sex dorms are more intimate and not as crazy. The dorms are also more convenient for students with classes on upper campus, and they are close to Reed Gym, so that is always good motivation.

> **Did You Know?**
> 6% of undergrads live on campus.

Students Speak Out
ON GUYS & GIRLS

Q "There is a wide variety of girls on campus, but **you have to take the good with the bad.** But the good are very good."

Q "From a guy's perspective, **I would say there is a fair amount of good-looking guys on campus**. As for ladies—there are tons of girls on campus into just about any activity that you like, whether it's Ultimate Frisbee or choir or anything in between."

Q "From someone who has done a great deal of traveling, **I am not impressed with the selection pool**."

Q "Just like any other place, **there are some that spark your interest**, and then there are some that your mom wouldn't approve of!"

STUDENT AUTHOR: ISU is a big pond with many diverse fish. Since the students are extremely diverse with different backgrounds, standards, religions, ethnicity, and looks, anybody can find a mate at this school. It is a great way to find love, probably due to the laid-back community and the lack of things to do. Since there is not much to do anyway, guys and girls tend to get more creative, making things click on a different level.

> **Traditions**
>
> **March through the Arch**
> The Arch, originally part of Swanson Hall, which was built in 1903 and torn down in 1973, was dedicated to the memory of ISU alumni who attended classes in this first building. It is an annual tradition for freshmen to march through the Arch.
>
> **Overall School Spirit**
> Overall, the student body has Bengal pride. The school spirit can be seen by the amount of alumni support the school receives. ISU graduates are proud to call themselves Bengals, and it shines through in the spirit of students now.

Students Speak Out
ON ATHLETICS

Q "Varsity sports are big on campus. Many students attend all of the home football games, and both the football and basketball teams receive good fan support. They are almost always exciting to attend. **There are IM teams for almost every sport you can think of**. Flag football and basketball can get very competitive."

Q "**Idaho State is home to mediocre athletics with some exceptions**, including the women's soccer and volleyball teams. The intramural sports are participated in by a small group on campus."

Q "Varsity sports on any campus are big. You either like 'em or you don't. If you do, you support them and talk about them. **Typical class gossip isn't about the last football game** we played. IM sports are pretty big."

STUDENT AUTHOR: Athletic needs are a high priority at ISU. Between sports teams, the popular intramural program, sports clubs (competitive and non-competitive), and the athletic center, everybody can be involved. The one thing ISU athletics is missing is school pride. The new Bengal Battalion, a pep club of super fans, is hoping to improve Bengal pride.

Students Speak Out
ON DRUG SCENE

Q "I am not a part of the drug scene, but I know that it is there. If it is not something that you are into, then **there is no problem finding things to do and people to hang out** with who also share your feelings."

Q "I really don't know too much about the drug scene, but like any other place, **I'm sure drugs are accessible** if you know where to look."

Q "Alcohol is always a problem. **There are always these sorts of problems** no matter the density of the population and town."

Q "**The drug scene on campus is not noticeable** if you don't look for it. But, like any other university, drugs are accessible if you look for them."

STUDENT AUTHOR: The ISU drug scene is basically whatever you want it to be and whatever you make it. Drugs can definitely be found, but students have to look for them. This makes drugs not a major issue on the ISU campus. Students can find social scenes that have drugs and those that do not.

14:1	Student-to-Faculty Ratio
57%	Freshman Retention Rate
3%	Four-Year Graduation Rate
85%	Financial Aid Applicants Receiving Aid

Students Speak Out
SAFETY & SECURITY

Q "**Public Safety is always on duty**, so that provides some sense of security. I have always felt safe while on campus."

Q "**ISU is one of the safest campuses** in the nation. I think that is more due to the Pocatello community rather than any efforts by Public Safety. My experiences with them have been less that satisfying."

Q "Although I have only been here a semester, **I feel extremely safe** on campus."

Q "Safety and security are pretty good. I feel safe when I am on campus—not to mention Public Safety that patrols all day long! That is somewhat annoying because **you know they are just waiting to give you a ticket** or something."

STUDENT AUTHOR: Most students feel safe on campus due to the high patrol of Public Safety and the few minor crime reports and just because of the laid-back campus ISU has. Pocatello is generally a conservative town with a low crime rate. Most crime reports are related to parking issues or fender benders.

Questions?
For more inside information and survival tips, pick up College Prowler's full-length book on this school, written by an actual student! Check it out at *www.collegeprowler.com*.

Students Speak Out
ON OVERALL EXPERIENCE

Q "For the most part, ISU is awesome! The academic programs are awesome, and the social life is out there if you want one! **You definitely will make memories**."

Q "My overall experience at Idaho State University has been positive. Though it isn't an enormous university, I feel **it provides a great college atmosphere for its students**. The people of Pocatello are very nice and make it feel like home. I recommend ISU over any other university in the state of Idaho."

Q "I love ISU. It is inexpensive, but I get everything that comes with larger, more expensive schools. **The faculty is great, and the programs are wonderful**. I don't really wish I were anywhere else. Well, maybe the University of Hawaii, but hey, who doesn't?!"

Q "ISU is a good school to come to, especially for those living in-state. It offers a decent education, **lots of extracurricular activities, and a nice environment for a cheap price**. I just wish that more students would be more involved in student organizations and activities provided by the program board. With more participation, the school would do more fun things."

STUDENT AUTHOR: ISU is what someone might call one-of-a-kind. It has the city setting without actually being in a huge city. It is an institution with diverse programs, qualified professors, and a field of interest for any student. The student experience at ISU really comes down to what the student wants out of it. Pocatello can be viewed as an amazingly boring town, or it can be a fun, chill place enjoy life. That is definitely the word for Pocatello and ISU life in general—chill.

Illinois State University

700 West College Avenue; Normal, IL 61790
(309) 438-2111; www.ilstu.edu

THE BASICS:

Acceptance Rate: 64%
Setting: Small city
F-T Undergrads: 16,959

ACT Range: 22–26
Control: Public
Tuition: $14,310

Most Popular Majors: Education, Business/Marketing, Social Sciences, Health Professions, Communications

Academics	B	Guys	A
Local Atmosphere	B-	Girls	A
Safety & Security	A-	Athletics	B
Computers	B+	Nightlife	A-
Facilities	C+	Greek Life	B+
Campus Dining	B	Drug Scene	B-
Off-Campus Dining	B+	Campus Strictness	C-
Campus Housing	B-	Parking	C-
Off-Campus Housing	C+	Transportation	B+
Diversity	C-	Weather	C+

Students Speak Out
ON ACADEMICS

Q "When it comes to professors, it is hit or miss. Some are awesome while others hardly speak English. The professors are very knowledgeable, though, and **they are always willing to help out**."

Q "All but one of my classes are interesting. The history classes in general are very boring. **Students need to make sure that they like their major** because they will be spending a lot of time taking classes centered around it."

Q "I've had a lot of great classes here at ISU, but some classes I can never get into. A lot of the most interesting and **fun classes are really tough to get into** because everyone registers for them first."

Q "**The teachers are very personable**. They care about their students and the success of their students. The first two years are primarily general education classes, which seem to be less interesting than major classes during your junior and senior years."

STUDENT AUTHOR: **The relationships created and maintained by students and professors are one of ISU's greatest strengths. Most teachers will be available at any time for a student, some even willing to give out home phone numbers. Many professors work with students to make sure they are learning the material and understanding difficult concepts. On such a large campus this may not seem possible, but ISU strives to be different and to make an impact on its students' lives.**

Students Speak Out
ON LOCAL ATMOSPHERE

Q "The atmosphere on campus is a mixture of a big school and a small school. Bloomington-Normal is a college town, so **the whole town comes to athletic events**, and college students are employed everywhere."

Q "It is very calm here, but the weekends are hectic. **You will be almost certain to find something to do**, no matter what you like. Students here definitely love their weekends."

Q "The atmosphere is very diverse but welcoming. **People around here are always willing to help you out**, which comes in handy when you are a first-year student."

Q "**The town is very clean and college-friendly**. Since the town holds two separate universities, it is a real college town."

Q "The town is loud and busy with a lot of party-like activity. **You can always count on ISU to give you a good time**. Illinois Wesleyan is present as well. Students from both schools tend to hang out together once in a while."

STUDENT AUTHOR: **Bloomington-Normal is the typical college town and environment, and downtown Bloomington is one of ISU's greatest social scenes. The streets are full of restaurants and small boutiques to explore during the day, and at night people flock to check out the local bar scene. During the day in downtown Normal, students can ravage through thrift shops and local pizza joints.**

5 Best Things	5 Worst Things
1 Laying out on the Quad	1 School spirit
2 Bar scene	2 Residency requirements
3 The campus	3 Number of cornfields
4 Weekends	4 No 18-and-older bars
5 Watterson Towers	5 The girl/guy ratio

Students Speak Out
ON FACILITIES

Q "The facilities are clean for the most part, and the **computers are adequate in getting information**. There is a lot of work that goes into making ISU look presentable."

Q **"The current buildings are great, and even the older buildings are well-kept**. Considering how long ISU has been around, you would never know how old some of the buildings are."

Q "The computer labs, especially in the library, are really nice. The workout centers in Atkin-Colby and Hewett are nicely done, and **they are a great way to meet people**."

Q "The football field needs a little work, and the student center is nice. It kind of stinks coming onto campus and **seeing how dingy the football stadium looks**. The dorms are about average."

Q "The buildings are nice, and they accommodate the college population. **The rooms are never terribly crowded or anything**. ISU has done a good job with the facilities."

STUDENT AUTHOR: One of the drawbacks of ISU's facilities is the age of many buildings, though some are undergoing renovations. One of the newest areas that ISU is taking pride in is the renovated athletic weight room, the largest in the Missouri Valley Conference. The Bone Student Center is also a popular area where students can see concerts, enjoy food, study, or just hang out. Another nice touch that the University added is a tunnel that goes under College Avenue and Main Street and allows students to access all parts of campus without crossing the busy intersection.

Famous Alumni

Suzy Bogguss, Doug Collins, Sean Hayes, Felissa R. Lashley, PhD, John Malkovich, Donald McHenry, Laurie Metcalf, Dan Roan, Robert Wagner

Students Speak Out
ON CAMPUS DINING

Q "The dining hall food is really good. McAlister's and Pizza Hut are probably two of the best. It's nice that **ISU has brought some chain restaurants onto its campus**."

Q "The food on campus is great, and there is a variety of places to choose from. **Whatever you feel like eating, you can get it that day**. Having a lot to choose from is one of the best things about ISU's on-campus dining."

Q "The food in the dining halls is your basic fast food, which means it probably isn't that healthy, and **that could be why so many people gain weight in college**."

Q "There are pros and cons to all the various dining halls. Overall, **there is always something good to eat**. McAlister's is awesome; it is like a T.G.I. Friday's-style restaurant, and you can use your meal card."

Q **"The dining hall food isn't bad, but it gets old fast**. Watterson Food Court is the best."

STUDENT AUTHOR: Few will admit that they enjoy on-campus dining, but for ISU students, many do not complain about it either. ISU has made sure to offer a variety of food choices to its students. Students are able to taste food from different cultures while staying loyal to the true American cheeseburger. The portions that are given to students are also very reasonable, and many are satisfied after each meal. But while the variety of the food may be great, it is not always healthy.

Student Body

African American:	6%	Male/Female:	43/57%
Asian American:	2%	Out-of-State:	1%
Hispanic:	4%	International:	<1%
Native American:	<1%	Unknown:	4%
White:	84%		

Popular Faiths: Christianity and Catholicism are the most common religions on campus, but there are many student religious organizations on campus.

Gay Pride: ISU is very respectful of all sexual orientations, and many students at ISU accept everyone for who they are and do not discriminate.

Economic Status: Many ISU students hail from the suburbs of Chicago, so the economic status is generally middle class.

Students Speak Out
ON DORMS

Q "Try and **visit the dorms so you can get a feel for the set-up and atmosphere** you like. Watterson may have the biggest rooms, but it is not very social."

Q "None of the dorms are nice, but at ISU, **you are forced to live in them** your freshman and sophomore years. If you only had to live there for one year, then it would be okay, but two years is pushing it."

Q "The dorms are good. **Some rooms are kind of small, but that is what's to be expected**. Sharing a room with someone isn't that bad either. I haven't heard many stories of people getting horrible roommates or anything."

STUDENT AUTHOR: **While many may prefer an alternative to dorms, ISU tries to make the experience as painless as possible. Students may feel cramped in the small rooms, but each floor has a large lounge for studying purposes or even just for hanging out. A convenient aspect of the dorms is the numerous affordable washing machines and dryers in each building. Many students living off campus try to sneak back to do their laundry.**

> **Did You Know?**
> 35% of undergrads live on campus.

Students Speak Out
ON GUYS & GIRLS

Q "The guys are pretty hot, and the girls are pretty down-to-earth. **Like usual, though, the really hot guys and girls know they are hot**, so approaching them isn't that easy."

Q "There are a lot of hot guys, but **there aren't as many boys on campus as girls**, which is sad. It is a little disappointing to be a girl, but there are still a lot of hot guys to run after."

Q "**The guys here are cocky and have big egos**. The girls are pretty nice, but everyone pretty much has their cliques and keeps to themselves."

Q "There are very hot girls and guys! It's awesome going to school here because of that. **Everywhere you look, there is someone hot around**."

STUDENT AUTHOR: **At such a large university, there is bound to be a wealth of hot guys and girls. ISU is known for its hot student body, and many students are proud of that. In order to see these hotties at their prime, many go out frequently to make sure they do not miss a beat. Since many students party hard on the weekend, their sexual promiscuity comes along for the ride as well. ISU students are hot, and they are not afraid to admit it.**

> **Traditions**
>
> **Battle Bird**
> Before each home athletic game, each athlete will touch the Battle Bird.
>
> **May Day**
> The first weekend in May is considered May Day at ISU, and numerous fraternities come together and throw a huge party.
>
> **Overall School Spirit**
> School spirit may not be present during every athletic event, but students are proud to represent ISU wherever they go.

Students Speak Out
ON ATHLETICS

Q "ISU has a variety of sports. **The most popular sports here are men's basketball and football**. It is also really easy for students to get involved with IM sports, and everyone always has a great time."

Q "If you do not play sports, then you really don't get involved with them here at ISU. **I don't think our football stadium has been sold out in years**."

Q "Basketball is pretty popular, and there are many IM sports to get involved in. **You will hear a lot of people talking about the IM sports** once their season starts."

Q "Men's basketball here is huge! **Everyone goes to the Bradley game**. It is fun to see so many people excited over a game."

STUDENT AUTHOR: **Many athletes support each other at ISU, but it is difficult to get the student body to follow. With the lack of student support, it can be difficult for athletes to stay motivated and competitive. The popularity of IM sports continues to rise, and the only way for students to understand how much fun it is to sign up first thing when they get to school.**

Students Speak Out
ON DRUG SCENE

Q "It is here, but I am just too naïve to ever see it. I've never seen anything worse than pot. Drinking here is huge, though, and not just for the over-21 crowd. **Students here drink a lot**, but I don't think they are too serious about hardcore drugs."

Q "Drug usage is present here, but it is not overwhelming. It is probably average for college students. **If students here want to use drugs, then they can**, and they most likely won't get caught if they are smart about it."

Q "I'm sure half of all the students here do drugs. While some may just be smoking pot, I know a lot of people that are using cocaine. **It is not very hard to get it here at school**."

STUDENT AUTHOR: To find drugs at ISU, you do not need to look hard. The main drugs that are used at ISU are marijuana, prescription drugs, and cocaine. Many students also do not consider alcohol a drug because it is so widely talked about and used. Students tend to only use these drugs on the weekends or during partying-like situations.

19:1	Student-to-Faculty Ratio
83%	Freshman Retention Rate
39%	Four-Year Graduation Rate
70%	Financial Aid Applicants Receiving Aid

Students Speak Out
SAFETY & SECURITY

Q "Security is good, and **I have never felt unsafe on campus**. That is a big plus because safety should be a main concern for people when choosing a school."

Q "**There are 'blue-light specials' all around campus**. If you push the button on one of them, a police officer will be there in about one and a half minutes. This is a good relief for a lot of people who have to walk around at night."

Q "**I've never felt threatened or unsafe here**. In fact, cops are everywhere, so no one can get away with anything. This may also be a reason why so many ISU students will end up with some type of ticket before they graduate."

STUDENT AUTHOR: Safety is one of ISU's main concerns. Fortunately, ISU does not have much crime to respond to. Police can be seen driving around campus constantly, which is also a reason why the campus has such a low crime rate. NiteRide, a free bus service for students during late-night hours, is also provided.

> **Questions?**
> For more inside information and survival tips, pick up College Prowler's full-length book on this school, written by an actual student! Check it out at *www.collegeprowler.com*.

Students Speak Out
ON OVERALL EXPERIENCE

Q "I would never transfer from here because I love it too much. **Everything from the people and the parties to the classes** make this school so special. ISU is truly a unique university."

Q "**It is a fun state school that has a growing reputation around the state** and the country. I've met great friends here and have made awesome memories. There is no other place I'd rather be."

Q "I've enjoyed my time here so far, but **I have had a lot of bad experiences because of the police**. Sometimes I do wish I were somewhere else. Overall, it is an okay school, but there are a few things I would love to change about it."

Q "I love it here and absolutely could not see myself anywhere else. **ISU is giving me a great education** and a handful of unforgettable memories along with it."

Q "I couldn't imagine myself being anywhere else. I am so glad I decided to come here and not anywhere else. **Everyone here is so welcoming**, and it is so easy to make friends."

STUDENT AUTHOR: With so many colleges to choose from, many will say that they do not regret coming to ISU. The social scene is outstanding and guarantees students a great time on the weekends. Academically, ISU provides students with a well-rounded education and prepares them for the real world. Teachers dedicate themselves to their classes and make certain that their students understand the content. From the outside, ISU may seem like a very typical state university, but once you experience it, you come to understand that ISU is one of the most unique universities around.

Illinois Wesleyan University

1312 Park Street; Bloomington, IL 61702-2900
(309) 556-3034; www2.iwu.edu/home.shtml

THE BASICS:

Acceptance Rate: 52%
Setting: Small city
F-T Undergrads: 2,113

SAT Range: 1140–1400*
Control: Private
Tuition: $32,260

Most Popular Majors: Business/Commerce, Psychology, Biology, English, History

*of 1600

Academics	B+	Guys	B-
Local Atmosphere	B-	Girls	B
Safety & Security	B+	Athletics	B-
Computers	B+	Nightlife	B-
Facilities	B+	Greek Life	B+
Campus Dining	B	Drug Scene	B+
Off-Campus Dining	B+	Campus Strictness	B+
Campus Housing	B-	Parking	A
Off-Campus Housing	B+	Transportation	B-
Diversity	D-	Weather	C+

Students Speak Out
ON ACADEMICS

Q "The teachers here all have a passion for what they do, so **their enthusiasm makes going to class interesting**. Some classes only permit so much flexibility in teaching style, given the subject matter, like economics and math."

Q "**The teachers are well-educated, but not all of them can teach**. It's up to you to find classes that sound interesting. The selection is not bad because even lower-level classes offer diverse subject matter."

Q "The majority of the faculty is **well-qualified and professional**. It varies from class to class, but generally there is a nice balance between interesting subject matter and enthusiastic professors."

Q "One of the best parts about my experience at Wesleyan so far has been working with some of my teachers. For the most part, **they are very good about having flexible office hours**, keeping in contact via e-mail, and are willing to help out those students who are really seeking that help."

STUDENT AUTHOR: **The liberal arts approach is apparent in the wide range of general education studies required for graduation. Students here definitely work hard. Pressure to perform can translate into perfectionism and anxiety, but the professors' expectations are generally more accepting than students' personal standards. Most classes are small, which is conducive to intimate conversation and enthusiastic debate.**

Students Speak Out
ON LOCAL ATMOSPHERE

Q "Bloomington has **a diverse population and a growing arts community**. Downtown is sprinkled with shops and galleries. There are three other schools in town, Illinois State, Heartland Community College, and Lincoln College in Normal."

Q "I love Bloomington. You don't really realize how much you love it until you've been away for a summer. **The campus is absolutely beautiful in the fall**. ISU is down the road, which makes the college student population in the town quite a bit larger. One of my favorite spots is downtown Bloomington."

Q "Bloomington-Normal is like **the LA of the Midwest**. ISU is in town as well, and that is the place to go for the attractive ladies and cheap beer."

Q "**Bloomington is a small, small town**. Downtown is nice, so is Miller Park. Definitely avoid the west side of Bloomington because it is mostly low-income residential."

STUDENT AUTHOR: **There is always something to do in town, but oftentimes, it turns out to be the same thing: catch a movie, go downtown, or visit ISU. Downtown is really the only redeeming quality of Bloomington. Shopping, restaurants, local festivities, and just enough bars to foster debauchery make Bloomington more than just a quaint Midwestern town. Luckily, larger attractions are within an hour drive.**

5 Best Things	5 Worst Things
1 Small classes	1 The "Wesleyan bubble"
2 Knowledgeable profs	2 Small main quad
3 Outspoken students	3 Freshman dorms
4 Tight-knit community	4 Class registration
5 Men's basketball	5 Cafeteria food

Students Speak Out
ON FACILITIES

Q "**Most of the facilities are either very new or recently renovated**. The Ames Library, Hansen Student Center, and Shirk Gymnasium were all constructed within the past 15 years. There are ongoing projects and additions planned. In another 10 years, campus will look entirely different."

Q "**Two new multimillion-dollar facilities have gone up in the past few years**. I think they're planning another addition in the near future."

Q "The Ames Library is great. **It's new, and there is more than enough space to study**, hold meetings, or sleep. The other facilities are nice as well. The Hansen Student Center is a renovated basketball court with the original wood floors still intact."

Q "Shirk Center is really nice, but the climate control is off by like 15 degrees. **The gymnasium and pool are nice and clean** and always busy, which makes for a good environment to work out and socialize."

Q "**The facilities are really great**. They're easily accessible, have great hours, and are really clean."

STUDENT AUTHOR: **Most of campus was built within the last 15 years. Most of the buildings have wireless Internet access, and every building has a lounge area for studying. The facilities at IWU are equal parts luxurious and functional, without being overly elaborate. The construction is scheduled to continue, so within a few years, the campus may have entirely newly-built facilities.**

Famous Alumni

Edward B. Rust (State Farm CEO), Jack Sikma (NBA All Star), Dawn Upshaw (opera singer), Andy Dick (ridiculous-behaving person; didn't graduate)

Students Speak Out
ON CAMPUS DINING

Q "On-campus dining is pretty good for a small school. **There are a lot of options besides the usual cafeteria food**, and even that isn't half bad."

Q "**The food at Commons is not the best**. I wish it reminded me of home cooking, but it really doesn't. The Dugout is pretty good but repetitive. Tommy's is by far the way to go."

Q "Commons, the dining hall, serves decent food. **They boast a lot about how they're better than most other colleges**, but it's still college dorm food. There is a good place to buy sub sandwiches, though."

Q "**Commons isn't bad**, but Tommy's is definitely better, quality-wise."

Q "Sub Connection (which is like subway) and Grill 105 (burgers) are a nice alternative to Commons. They try really hard at the cafeteria, but **it's still cafeteria food**."

STUDENT AUTHOR: **You will get sick of the food on campus, but not nearly as quickly as you'd imagine. The cafeteria is accommodating, and the selection of food varies from day to day. There are enough buffet options available at every meal that you won't fall into the rut of eating the same thing every day. The alternatives to cafeteria dining are exceptional but are generally overpriced. The nice thing about the on-campus restaurants is the quality of food served. It may not be as affordable, but the quality is worth it.**

Student Body

African American:	4%	Male/Female:	43/57%
Asian American:	3%	Out-of-State:	14%
Hispanic:	3%	International:	2%
Native American:	<1%	Unknown:	0%
White:	88%		

Popular Faiths: The most prominent religion on campus is Christianity, though many students do not affiliate with any one faith exclusively.

Gay Pride: The gay and lesbian community is strongly supported, and nearly all professors take part in the Safety Zone program.

Economic Status: Most students come from the suburbs of Chicago and are upper-middle-class.

Students Speak Out
ON DORMS

Q "**If at all possible, live off campus**. Otherwise, avoid Magill and Pfeiffer. Do not live in Martin Hall for the life of you, it's about a 15-minute walk from campus."

Q "Munsell and Ferguson are standard for freshmen, but after that, housing is pretty accommodating. **The small halls are the place to be**; Blackstock is the unofficial art fraternity, and they host pretty cool gatherings."

Q "If you can live in a small hall, you should. The environment is much more relaxed, and you are more responsible for yourself. Most of the dorms are about the same, with the exception of Harriet House, which is very nice. **Tall ceilings, large suites . . . very nice.**"

STUDENT AUTHOR: If the dorms have a redeeming quality, it's the lounges, fireplaces, study areas, and recreation rooms. Every dorm has some sort of common area, all have comfortable chairs and a TV, and some even have a fireplace. These touches make even the most cramped dorm seem a little more like home. Student housing at Wesleyan is always an issue but never a problem.

> **Did You Know?**
> 75% of undergrads live on campus.

Students Speak Out
ON GUYS & GIRLS

Q "**Most students that attend IWU are bright, civil young men and women**. There are those that got in on sports scholarships and the like, but they constitute most of the good-looking ones."

Q "There are plenty of good-looking people on campus, lots of hot guys. **All different kinds of people, too**: frat guys, sorority girls, athletes, scientists, poets, musicians. Everyone is just finding out what they really like, so everyone is passionate about it, and that makes for a lot of fun."

Q "**There are as many good-looking girls as there are not-so-good-looking girls** on campus. But the lookers are really, really good-looking."

STUDENT AUTHOR: Guys that don't at least try to hit the weights make up for their lack of physical prowess with wit or charm. A lot of the guys don't need to work out because they've got a really great sense of humor. For as many girls that work out and live in sororities and are conventionally beautiful, there are as many girls that stay far away from frat parties and are unconventionally beautiful.

> **Traditions**
>
> **Passover Party**
> Every year, Passover is celebrated by students, both Jewish and Gentile. The celebration consists of a strange game of hide-and-seek accompanied by a night of partying. The only reason it's celebrated as Passover is because spring is on the way.
>
> **Overall School Spirit**
> School spirit is strong in name only. Lots of people, athletes and non-athletes, wear IWU athletic brand clothing. Lots of people participate in the Homecoming activities. But not as many students support the actual teams.

Students Speak Out
ON ATHLETICS

Q "The football and basketball games are well attended and always exciting. **Intramural sports aren't as popular as they used to be**, but there are a few groups that get together once a week or so."

Q "**Varsity sports are huge at Wesleyan**. There are a lot of athletes who attend. Intramural sports are pretty big also. There's just about anything you're looking for here."

Q "Football games are popular among students, but **the basketball games attract just as many local fans**, which makes for great atmosphere at the games. The excitement at the games can't be matched."

Q "No matter how horrible we did the year before, **football will remain the sole excitement of the fall season**."

STUDENT AUTHOR: Athletics aren't an essential part of campus life, but this isn't a Big 10 school. Many students are involved in the varsity sports, but even more take part in recreational and intramural games. This relaxed attitude toward sports emphasizes the role of academics and other student interests.

Students Speak Out
ON DRUG SCENE

Q "**There isn't so much of a drug scene on campus**, but there certainly is drug use. There are no X-induced raves or anyone doing rails off urinals at the '80s dance parties, but people will use drugs on their own time."

Q "People smoke and trip. Some roll, but not many. **People here don't get too tied up into that sort of thing** because they know it affects their performance on every level."

Q "**People smoke and drink**. Not much else goes on here. I'm sure there are harder drugs around, but maybe 1 student in 100 does anything besides drink."

STUDENT AUTHOR: There really is not much of a drug scene at IWU. It's safe to say that no one is trafficking drugs onto campus. Weed comes onto campus off the streets of Bloomington, usually via some food service employee or townie student. Harder drugs are virtually nonexistent. The drug of choice at IWU is alcohol, without exception.

12:1	Student-to-Faculty Ratio
90%	Freshman Retention Rate
77%	Four-Year Graduation Rate
92%	Financial Aid Applicants Receiving Aid

Students Speak Out
SAFETY & SECURITY

Q "Security has become more visible, and **campus has always felt pretty safe**. Watch yourself once you step off campus, though, some of the neighborhoods that are closer are a little sketchy."

Q "Because campus is so small, Security is able to make rounds nearly every 15 minutes. **There are plenty of blue-light phones all over the quad** in case of emergency. Besides, this part of town is pretty low-key."

Q "**I feel safe on campus**, and I've never known anyone to feel as though their safety was compromised on campus. Occasionally, we'll get strange people wandering around campus, but sometimes they end up being visiting speakers or professors."

STUDENT AUTHOR: Most students overestimate the crime rate in the area. There have been instances of theft and property damage, but these are never very extreme incidents. IWU is an altogether safe campus that poses a minimal risk to students and local residents as well.

> **Questions?**
> For more inside information and survival tips, pick up College Prowler's full-length book on this school, written by an actual student! Check it out at www.collegeprowler.com.

Students Speak Out
ON OVERALL EXPERIENCE

Q "At first, I was bummed I didn't get into University of Chicago or Washington University, but from what I've now learned about those institutions, **I'm thankful for the smaller community and atmosphere here**."

Q "Wesleyan is a good school, for the most part. Consider your intended major. **If you could get the degree at a state school, do that**. If you are a theater, art, music, nursing, or philosophy major, you should strongly consider IWU."

Q "**I'm pretty happy at Wesleyan**. I've seen a lot of other schools by visiting friends, and I am still glad I chose this place. I've felt academically challenged and greatly expanded my social and moral horizons."

Q "I have awesome friends here, and I love IWU. Everyone has their days, even weeks or months, where they just want to get out, but looking back, **I wouldn't rather be anywhere else**."

Q "**IWU is a great school**. I could go somewhere else, but I choose to go here. That can probably be said about everyone on campus."

STUDENT AUTHOR: For many students, IWU could be substituted with a more affordable institution. The business and economics school at IWU is respectable, but not worth the amount of tuition as compared to state schools. For business majors, there are more sensible options. IWU is a respectable school on par with other small schools in Illinois, but is not as academically intense as the University of Chicago or Washington University. Students who go to Illinois Wesleyan would like the powerhouse academics of U of Chicago or Wash U, but appreciate a smaller community and more relaxed approach.

Indiana University

107 South Indiana Avenue; Bloomington, Indiana 47405
(812) 855-4848; www.iub.edu

THE BASICS:

Acceptance Rate: 71%   **SAT Range:** 1040–1260*
Setting: Small city   **Control:** Public
F-T Undergrads: 30,079   **Tuition:** $23,906

Most Popular Majors: Business/Marketing, Education, Communication/Journalism, Education, Public Admin.

*of 1600

Academics	B+	Guys	A-
Local Atmosphere	B-	Girls	A-
Safety & Security	B+	Athletics	A
Computers	A-	Nightlife	B-
Facilities	A	Greek Life	B
Campus Dining	C	Drug Scene	B
Off-Campus Dining	B+	Campus Strictness	B
Campus Housing	B	Parking	D-
Off-Campus Housing	A-	Transportation	B
Diversity	C-	Weather	D+

Students Speak Out
ON ACADEMICS

Q "The professors all seem to know what they're talking about, because they teach and research in really specialized fields. The only downside is that IU is a **very big school**, so if you want to have a close relationship with professors, you have to go and talk to them during their office hours. The classes are often too big for them to get to know you. They love to have students come and talk to them, and they are very willing to help."

Q "They often have **graduate students** teaching lower-level courses, which I feel is a rip off for us paying for the classes, since they are not very experienced. I would ask people about this before registering for a given class, if possible."

Q "A lot of times it's **hit-and-miss** with your professors. Before you register for classes each semester, it's a good idea to talk to other people in your major about what professors are good and which ones you should avoid. It's much better to spend a couple hours researching teachers than to spend a whole semester hating your class."

STUDENT AUTHOR: **IU is widely recognized as an institution that can turn floundering freshmen into impressive, work-ready professionals in four short years. Regular access to professors outside of class can make or break some classes, and a student might have to go out of his or her way to dodge the anonymity that can accompany a huge student body.**

Students Speak Out
ON LOCAL ATMOSPHERE

Q "Bloomington is a **perfect college town**. It's not too big, not too small. IU is definitely the heart of Bloomington, though; IU is what gives it style."

Q "There are lots of different things to visit in Bloomington. The downtown area is really quaint, and it has good shopping. There are many ethnic restaurants, and you can find just about anything you need in Bloomington. **Indianapolis is only an hour away**, and it's not too long of a drive to just go up and back for dinner or a day trip."

Q "Bloomington is in a cool little town, but that's the thing—**it is little**, which means there is not much to do. If you like doing stuff outdoors, there are a lot of state parks around. Lake Monroe is really close, and it's the largest lake in Indiana."

Q "The atmosphere is **very laid-back**, but stay away from the townies at Peoples' Park. Visit Kirkwood. See an IU basketball game. Go to Hoosier National Forest or Lake Monroe sometime."

STUDENT AUTHOR: **One of the chief draws to Bloomington is the beauty of the surrounding environment. You're apt to find locals who chose Bloomington for the surrounding countryside and students from major cities who add to the mix, making the small town eclectic and refreshing. As in any small town, close-mindedness is not unheard of. Fortunately, this negative way of thinking is mostly drowned out by the liberal attitudes on campus.**

Students Speak Out
ON FACILITIES

Q "SRSC (workout center) is great but can be crowded at night. The Union has everything you need, **even a bowling alley**, a place to get you hair cut, a post office, and a travel agency, so if you don't have a car, you never have to go off campus if you don't want to."

Q "**The student center is a huge hotel** connected to a mall (some of which is underground) with bowling alleys, a movie theater, pool tables, a video arcade, the IU bookstore, and other shops."

Q "There's one word to describe the facilities: **beautiful**. A lot of the buildings on campus are old, and they look that way on the outside—that is why they are so pretty. They are getting renovated on the inside one by one to make them even better. We also have an awesome state-of-the art fitness center with multiple floors, where you can do just about anything: work out, go to class, or play practically any sport, including swimming."

Q "**Everything stays clean** on campus. The gyms are clean, the computer labs are clean, the Union is clean, and pretty much every other public area is clean. The custodians do a great job."

STUDENT AUTHOR: IU does a great job of finding ways to keep students entertained by and enamored with the college lifestyle. If you are unable or unwilling to go off-campus, you don't have to. Although it might be somewhat monotonous to live for four years within a few square miles, the nearby facilities are what make IU a convenient, fun, and pleasant place to be.

Famous Alumni

Joshua Bell, Kevin Kline, Jane Pauley, Trista Rehn, Will Shortz, Mark Spitz, Isiah Thomas, Wendell Willkie

Students Speak Out
ON CAMPUS DINING

Q "On-campus food is **crappy and overpriced**. This is one of the biggest issues I have had with IU. A $1.29 can of Ravioli from one of the C-Stores is $2.99. The food at the dining halls is generally greasy and crappy. The salad bars are overpriced and of poor quality."

Q "Campus food is really one of the top student gripes, along with parking. It's just one of those things that you have to get used to. It's not dog food, but it's **not home cookin'** either."

Q "The food on campus is okay. It gets old really quickly, but it also gets expensive to eat off campus if you live in the residence halls. Dorms Wright and Foster have **big food courts**, plus there are C-stores (like mini grocery stores where you can use your meal points) at McNutt, Willkie, Read, Wright, and Eigenmann, and there's even a McDonald's and a Starbucks where you can use your meal points in Read. Read and Collins also have all-you-can-eat buffets."

Q "The good thing about the dining halls is that they're **not all the same**. If you want a certain kind of food, you can definitely get it. Unfortunately, most of it is pretty awful, and you'll get sick of it pretty quickly."

STUDENT AUTHOR: Although there is a lot of variety available to IU students . . . the general consensus seems to be negative. IU requires freshmen to buy an expensive meal plan. Be sure to use every last point before the end of the year, because IU takes back whatever you have left over.

Student Body

African American:	5%	Male/Female:	50/50%
Asian American:	4%	Out-of-State:	34%
Hispanic:	2%	International:	5%
Native American:	<1%	Unknown:	1%
White:	82%		

Popular Faiths: Christianity is clearly predominant, and there are many Christian groups and clubs, but there are also representatives from all major religions on campus, with just as many groups and clubs.

Gay Pride: Most people on campus are very accepting of a relatively large GLBT population.

Economic Status: Most students come from an upper-middle-class background.

Students Speak Out
ON DORMS

Q "The Northwest neighborhood (McNutt, Foster, Briscoe) is known as the partying place. It's filled with **lots of freshmen who just get crazy** when they come to college. It's not a place to live if you are very serious about your studies."

Q "Read is where a lot of music students live because it's right across from the music school. They also have the most and best options for food. Ashton is all singles and stays pretty quiet. Teter and Wright can be a little bit crazier, but are still good. Eigenmann was recently remodled, so those **rooms are nice**. Willkie is the most expensive, but the rooms are great. If you can afford to live there, it's the best place to live on campus. You only have to share a bathroom with one person, and it's like a hotel room."

STUDENT AUTHOR: At IU, there's a wide range of dorm types, and your dorm experience is what you make of it. There aren't necessarily any "bad" dorms or "good" dorms, because each one has something different to offer. Living on campus will probably never compare to living off-campus, but it's a way to get a first taste of that freedom without too much responsibility attached. Besides, if you're a freshman, you don't really have a choice.

Did You Know?
36% of undergrads live on campus.

Students Speak Out
ON GUYS & GIRLS

Q "There are many very, **very attractive people** on campus. People are pretty friendly here also, so it's not hard to meet new people if you want to. We have everything from Midwest people to West Coast people and a ton of East Coast people."

Q "The student body at IU on the whole is approximately **two parts hot and one part not**."

Q "One of the great things about Indiana is its stock of **pretty girls** . . . The sooner you get comfortable with who you are and what you want to do, the sooner you're going to meet people who you'll actually like spending time with."

STUDENT AUTHOR: At IU, the guys come from all over the country, but there are a lot of Midwestern boys with Midwestern attitudes; the phrase "I grew up on a farm" is not exactly rare . . . And, because the Greek scene is definitely prominent, there are also a lot of guys who typify the frat boy stereotype. Girls at IU are of the same mold as the guys. Also like the boys, girls are generally very, very attractive.

Traditions

Basketball
We're the "Hoosier State." Enough said.

Little 500
IU is the proud home to what's known around the country as the "World's Greatest College Weekend," a non-stop party that centers around a bicycle race. Check out the movie *Breaking Away*.

Overall School Spirit
School spirit is one of the things IU thrives on. Particularly strong when basketball season rolls around, students are proud to be Hoosiers.

Students Speak Out
ON ATHLETICS

Q "When you say the word 'basketball,' one of the first things that should pop into your head is the **IU Hoosiers basketball** program. It is world-renowned, and the film Hoosiers showcases the famous work ethic of the team and the common love for basketball that most of Indiana's residents share. Football is not so hot, as the team is lousy year-in and year-out. Soccer isn't very popular, but the team is one of the most successful in college history. Intramural sports are fairly popular as well. IU offers basketball, baseball, flag football, and ultimate Frisbee among others."

Q "**Varsity sports are a blast to watch**! I don't do IM, but they seem to be pretty popular, too. Plenty of exercise equipment, two big gyms with weight rooms, pools, cardio rooms, tracks and multi-purpose rooms for students, and lots of good eye candy for men and women."

STUDENT AUTHOR: While men's basketball is the obvious draw, other varsity sports are not overlooked. If sitting on the sidelines isn't enough, athletically-inclined students are very much encouraged to participate in intramurals.

Students Speak Out
ON DRUG SCENE

Q "This campus sports some of the best weed I've ever seen in Indiana. There are also mushrooms, but no acid. Ecstasy used to be big, but I think that everyone finally found out just how bad it was for them, and it hasn't been around much. **Adderall is huge**, as it helps kids stay up all night and focus on whatever it is that they're studying. Other chemicals are much less common (crack, speed, coke, and heroin), but can be found in Indianapolis."

Q "**Alcohol is the most prominent** drug on campus, but there's some marijuana, too. Every once in a while, you'll see some harder drugs, but it's easy to avoid all drugs if you want to. Nobody's sticking them in your face."

STUDENT AUTHOR: **IU is a big school, where you can be as wild as you want to be. There are plenty of police around to make sure that nothing gets out of hand . . . Alcohol is, by far, the most prominent drug at IU, and that's the reason most students get in trouble.**

18:1	Student-to-Faculty Ratio
90%	Freshman Retention Rate
51%	Four-Year Graduation Rate
68%	Financial Aid Applicants Receiving Aid

Students Speak Out
SAFETY & SECURITY

Q "**I feel safe** on campus; however, there is not really an IUPD presence. This makes it seem like there is not much security."

Q "I feel very safe on campus. There are safety phones (phones with blue lights at the top) all over campus, and you can call the campus safety escort van to **pick you up for free** if it's late and you don't want to walk alone in the dark. The van goes off campus as well. IU also has its own PD."

Q "Security is **very good**. The campus police department regularly patrols campus, and there are plenty of emergency call boxes around. As far as I can tell, the campus is very well-lit at night. Rape and other violent crimes are very low for a campus of nearly 40,000 students."

STUDENT AUTHOR: **Students can access dorms only by key or ID card, . . . [and] police regularly patrol campus and are quick to respond to a cry for help. Safety concerns will mostly involve your fellow students, and at such a large school, it's up to you to take preventative measures.**

> **Questions?**
> For more inside information and survival tips, pick up College Prowler's full-length book on this school, written by an actual student! Check it out at *www.collegeprowler.com.*

Students Speak Out
ON OVERALL EXPERIENCE

Q "I love Indiana! There is nowhere else I would rather be. This is a great school, both academically and athletically, and there are also just **so many opportunities** available. It has all the advantages of a large university, but a lot of my classes were still very small, like 30 people or smaller, and the professors seem genuinely caring."

Q "**I couldn't ask for better**. I chose to stay here for the next two years over some other really good schools. I think your experience depends on how much you want to put into it, though. Getting involved in something definitely helps to make the school feel smaller, and you get to know a lot of people. It's a big school, which I personally like, but if you want personal attention, I would recommend going somewhere smaller. It can be intimidating at first, but it didn't take me long to start calling Bloomington home. It helps that the campus is beautiful."

Q "**Everything is well-organized**, and overall, it is just a really, really good school. The students can really annoy me sometimes, though. Most people here live for partying, but I'm not the type that likes to party a whole lot, so that's why it bothers me."

STUDENT AUTHOR: **Most of the complaints about IU involve its large size, and if you're looking for the kind of school where everybody knows everyone else's names, this isn't the right place for you. However, the faculty, staff, and general population of Indiana University all work together to make an otherwise intimidating atmosphere feel a bit more accepting. There are so many opportunities here that your experience is what you make of it.**

Iowa State University

2300 Lincoln Way; Ames, IA 50011
(515) 294-4111; www.iastate.edu

THE BASICS:

Acceptance Rate: 90%   **SAT Range:** 1050–1330*
Setting: Small city   **Control:** Public
F-T Undergrads: 20,004   **Tuition:** $16,919

Most Popular Majors: Business/Marketing, Engineering, Agriculture, Education

*of 1600

Academics	B-	Guys	B+
Local Atmosphere	B	Girls	B
Safety & Security	A-	Athletics	A
Computers	A-	Nightlife	B
Facilities	A	Greek Life	B
Campus Dining	B	Drug Scene	B+
Off-Campus Dining	B	Campus Strictness	B
Campus Housing	B-	Parking	C-
Off-Campus Housing	A-	Transportation	A
Diversity	D-	Weather	B-

Students Speak Out
ON ACADEMICS

Q "My teachers are all pretty great, although some **class sizes are beginning to get out of control**. As of right now, I am waiting to get into several of my classes for the fall semester."

Q "Most of my teachers have been quality. Of course, there are a few that I really don't know how they keep their jobs. For the most part, **I've been happy with the teachers**."

Q "The majority of Iowa State professors are very knowledgeable, but some **aren't as adept at teaching as they are at research** in their subjects. It is a big research university, and some of the professors are better researchers than they are teachers."

Q "Teachers depend on the college and individual class. In my experience, **most of the LAS teachers are nice and helpful**, especially if you aren't taking a huge lecture class. In the College of Engineering and the LAS math department, a lot of times, you'll get a teacher that doesn't speak English well and you'll spend the semester reading the book and hoping they don't put anything weird on the tests, for the most part."

STUDENT AUTHOR: While a few students do profess hatred of their teachers and subject material, most students tend to be content with the quality of education these teachers are providing. Cultural differences seem to be the biggest problem teachers and students have with each other, but these kinds of differences better prepare students for life in the real world.

Students Speak Out
ON LOCAL ATMOSPHERE

Q "Ames is about the best place in Iowa. **Iowa is a cultural wasteland**, but Chicago is eight hours away, and the Mall of America is about three."

Q "The city of Ames is really strict. They want to keep up their reputation of being a really nice, clean place to live, and sometimes, it's a pain in the butt for college kids. They make **a lot of really stupid laws**. They can really suck the fun out of college sometimes."

Q "It's a small town with a huge, world-class university in its midst. I loved it there, despite its shortcomings (meager nightlife). Des Moines has a variety of little community colleges, and there are Simpson College and Grinnell College not too far away. Boone is a tiny town right outside Ames; the Des Moines River runs through and **it's fun to go tubing**. Lake Okoboji is about two hours northwest of Ames, and it's one of the largest lake systems in the country."

Q "Ames is a very nice town. It is mostly middle- and upper-class because of the University. It is **the perfect size** in my opinion, not too big, but not so small that it doesn't have anything."

STUDENT AUTHOR: Students coming from densely-populated areas, such as Chicago, may find Ames to be a boring small town. Ames may also be seen as too strict by many students—the city council passed a ban on putting indoor furniture outside. But students generally make due with what Ames has to offer, and most of the students who attend ISU are generally satisfied with Ames.

5 Best Things	5 Worst Things
1 The people	1 Parking
2 Ethernet	2 Tuition hikes
3 VEISHEA events	3 Walking in the winter
4 The beautiful campus	4 Lame city ordinances
5 Sports	5 Budget cuts

Students Speak Out
ON FACILITIES

Q "Most of the facilities on campus are **very, very nice**—so nice, in fact, that sometimes I wonder if the niceness is at the expense of my out-of-state tuition."

Q "Our recreation facility is fabulous! One of the best in the country. **Computer labs are all over** and you can always use them. Our student center, the Memorial Union, is a great place to study, eat lunch, have meetings, and buy concert tickets. It has everything."

Q "**The athletic facility is great**. It's big and really nice. Sometimes, it's hard to get a basketball court at night, but otherwise it is pretty open. It's all pretty new, and they keep it updated. Computers are good, not the top of the line, but better than any other school I have been to."

Q "Computer labs are plentiful and stocked with decent technology. The library is very nice, with a lot of very comfortable chairs for a nap in between classes. The rec center is free for all students and has **most everything you could want out of an athletic center**."

Q "**Facilities are great** on campus. The athletic center is quite huge."

STUDENT AUTHOR: **Whether you prefer athletic events, bowling, live entertainment, eating out, working out, or hanging out, it can all be done at ISU without ever leaving campus! The students seem to be more than satisfied with the facilities that are available to them. Whatever your personal tastes, ISU has adequate facilities to meet your needs.**

Famous Alumni

John Atanasoff, Carrie Chapman Catt, George Washington Carver, Jamal Tinsley

---

Students Speak Out
ON CAMPUS DINING

Q "There are a ton of fast food spots. The Memorial Union has a lot of choices, and everything I have had is good. **The dorm food is alright**. I live in a fraternity, and the food there is really good."

Q "There are five or six dining centers in dorms, and they are like any normal cafeteria food. They get old after awhile, but everyone still eats there. There are other options, though. There is a student center on campus which has **a food court with a Subway**."

Q "In Campus Town, eat gyros and Cocost. **Stay away from dining services** if you can help it."

Q "What the food in Iowa State dining halls lack in quality, they make up for in quantity. The hot dishes range from pretty good to pretty awful, but you can get **as many servings as you want at each meal**."

Q "**The only bad food on campus is in the cafeterias**. Everywhere else is good. I especially enjoy the food at the Union and the Hawthorn Market & Café."

STUDENT AUTHOR: **While it is not gourmet quality, Iowa State offers pretty decent food choices. Whether or not you like cafeteria food, Iowa State has a place to eat when the need arises. Students need to find their niche in dining. If hot meals really don't appeal to you, make sure you eat when the deli sandwich line is available, and the salad bar is always available during dining hours. Variety keeps food from being totally unbearable for those who miss mom's cooking.**

Student Body

African American:	3%	Male/Female:	57/43%
Asian American:	3%	Out-of-State:	29%
Hispanic:	3%	International:	4%
Native American:	<1%	Unknown:	3%
White:	84%		

Popular Faiths: Christians, atheists, Buddhists, Mormons, and Muslims all share the campus.

Gay Pride: Although few hate crimes do occur on campus, there is a support center for homosexual students. LGBTSS offers support for homosexual, bisexual, and transgender issues for students.

Economic Status: Many students come from humble farming backgrounds; there are not many rich kids.

Students Speak Out
ON DORMS

Q "I enjoyed dorm life. I like apartment life better, though. **Maple, Willow, and Larch are good dorms**. I hear the new Friley dorms are nice. Frederiksen Court is now my preference. Stay away from Towers. They were built as temporary housing, and they're still standing."

Q "The dorms were okay, though **not all of them are air conditioned**. The Maple-Willow-Larch complex isn't bad. Friley Hall is okay, too, but stay away from the Towers. They're so far away from everything, and they sway in the wind. It's weird."

Q "I lived in Maple-Willow-Larch last year, and I thought the dorms were pretty good. **They weren't five-star hotels**, obviously, but they weren't falling apart by any means."

STUDENT AUTHOR: **Even if the dorms are less than lush, students tend to** make strong friendships and find places to party. Undeniably, dorm life is an important part of the freshman college experience. Maple, Willow, Larch, and Friley receive positive recommendations, and the Union Drive suites are a good choice, though more expensive.

Did You Know?
39% of undergrads live on campus.

Students Speak Out
ON GUYS & GIRLS

Q "The hot chicks **only come out when the weather is nice and warm**. But people in general are really nice."

Q "There are **significantly more guys on campus than girls**, which is really nice for the girls. You tend to see more and more girls in male-dominated fields, so the guys can still meet a lot of girls, even with the shortage."

Q "As far as guys go, there are **plenty of single hotties**! I suppose it depends on which parties you go to, but the girls are usually nice. I have met many nice hot men that are available!"

Q "Well, remember that ISU is primarily an agricultural school. We have a lot of farm boys. You know, **Wranglers, belt buckles, the works**."

STUDENT AUTHOR: **Iowa State's students tend to be casual in their dress and manners. With more than 20,000 undergraduate students, it is not difficult to find good-looking guys and girls. Some complain that many students blend together as they dress and act similarly, but there are always exceptions. If you're looking for romance or just looking for someone you can have fun with, you can find it at Iowa State University.**

Traditions

Homecoming
ISU alumni return to campus every year to celebrate with fireworks, lawn displays, tailgating, and more.

Lake LaVerne
If you walk around Lake LaVerne three times with your beloved, you will be destined to be together.

Overall School Spirit
School spirit is especially visible whenever one of the varsity sports teams plays the University of Iowa. Students have a great love for Iowa State and it's not uncommon to see students sporting ISU gear.

Students Speak Out
ON ATHLETICS

Q "Varsity sports are huge: our football team has gone to bowl games, and they'll probably do it again. The games are a great experience. Basketball is also great. Our women's team was ranked it the top 10, our men's team are on the upswing and have one of the top recruiting classes. **As for IM sports, they are huge**—there is everything from flag football and broomball, to foosball and bowling."

Q "**Football is huge**, but the basketball team sucks. Intramurals are huge. There are a ton of them, every sport possible. They are very easy to participate in and get information on if you choose."

Q "**Varsity sports get too much attention** and money. IM sports are great; there are so many different types of sports to try."

STUDENT AUTHOR: **The football team is especially a big part of Iowa State life, and students seem to enjoy attending and supporting the various sporting events. For those who just want to participate in sports for fun, intramural sports leave nothing to be desired. Students from all walks of life find something that tickles their fancy.**

Students Speak Out
ON DRUG SCENE

Q "Though **there is an occasional drug bust** in a student's dorm room, there is not much talk about drugs. Next to alcohol, marijuana is probably the most commonly used drug on campus, but there are not enough reports of it for it to be an issue."

Q "The drug scene is somewhat extensive, as would be expected in a small city with a large university, but if you don't go looking for it, it won't intrude on your life. You'll almost never run into pushers, and **you won't have to worry about being surrounded by drugs** if you don't want to be."

Q "**There are drugs to be found**, of course, but it's not like there are a lot of people that do anything openly."

STUDENT AUTHOR: The drug scene exists at Iowa State, but it is not very visible. If you are into drugs, you will find friends who can help to hook you up, but the rest don't need to worry about drug pushers or usage around them.

16:1	Student-to-Faculty Ratio
85%	Freshman Retention Rate
32%	Four-Year Graduation Rate
87%	Financial Aid Applicants Receiving Aid

Students Speak Out
SAFETY & SECURITY

Q "Safety on campus is great. There are emergency phones everywhere and the lighting is very good. **I feel safe at all times**."

Q "Although the Department of Public Safety here at Iowa State is **very disliked by students**, they do a very good job at keeping the campus safe for us. The parking division of DPS is what makes them hated so much. If you have a car to bring to campus, you will learn what I am talking about. You will get your share of parking tickets."

Q "I have never had a problem and haven't heard of many. If you need to go somewhere on campus late at night or walk from your car to your dorm, **they have an escort service**. Ames is a really nice place, and actually, I don't think there is much crime anywhere here."

STUDENT AUTHOR: The most prevalent crimes are liquor-law violations and petty theft. Other than that, Ames is a very safe community. ISU does a good job of patrolling campus and making sure that students feel safe at all times. Students have no qualms about venturing out on campus alone or at night.

Questions?
For more inside information and survival tips, pick up College Prowler's full-length book on this school, written by an actual student! Check it out at *www.collegeprowler.com.*

Students Speak Out
ON OVERALL EXPERIENCE

Q "Overall, I'd say my ISU experience so far has been **difficult but fun**. It was a huge change coming to college, and my first few months were kind of rough, as I was getting used to living in the dorms, college-size classes, new people, and all that. Toward the end of the year, I really started to find my niche and enjoy the new lifestyle."

Q "Frankly, if you aren't doing engineering, architecture, computer anything, or maybe physics or math, think about applying elsewhere. The people are nice, but tuition was just under $10,000 when I came here, now it's over $15,000 and **will climb again next year**."

Q "The experience was pretty good. If I didn't have a few factors that kept me there—friends, a good advisor, a few favorite places off campus—I might have looked into transferring schools, but **ISU was a good four years**."

Q "I have never wished that I was at another school. My experiences here were **life changing**, and I wouldn't change it. I always tell everyone that I wish I could go to college forever. I never want to leave."

STUDENT AUTHOR: For the most part, students enjoy their Iowa State experience. Iowa State is a large school with a beautiful campus and a reasonably diverse population. The first year can be difficult for many students, especially those who are not from the Midwest and are away from their families. Iowa State is large enough to be able to have great athletics and a huge social scene, but small enough that students get individualized attention in their classrooms and are easily able to make solid friendships.

Ithaca College

953 Danby Road; Ithaca, NY 14850
(607) 274-3011; www.ithaca.edu

THE BASICS:

Acceptance Rate: 66%   **SAT Range:** 1630–1920*
Setting: Rural   **Control:** Private
F-T Undergrads: 5,951   **Tuition:** $30,606

Most Popular Majors: Visual/Performing Arts,
Communications/Journalism, Business/Marketing

*of 2400

Academics	B	Guys	B+
Local Atmosphere	C+	Girls	B+
Safety & Security	A-	Athletics	C
Computers	C+	Nightlife	C+
Facilities	B+	Greek Life	D
Campus Dining	B+	Drug Scene	C-
Off-Campus Dining	B-	Campus Strictness	B
Campus Housing	B	Parking	C+
Off-Campus Housing	B+	Transportation	B-
Diversity	D	Weather	D

Students Speak Out
ON ACADEMICS

Q "I love my classes, especially those in my major—organizational communication, learning, and design. The professors are great; they lead interesting classes, and **they are really friendly and accessible**."

Q "**The professors really vary**. I've had some great ones and some that weren't so great. Overall, though, the professors I've had really seem to love what they do, which is a definite plus."

Q "Ninety percent of the classes I can say I learned something from, which is the true measure of success for me. Most of my history and journalism professors **I know outside of the classroom**."

Q "I have not come across one professor that I haven't liked. Professors at Ithaca look for methods of teaching that make classes fun and interesting. **They go far beyond what is required** of them and what a textbook would teach. I look forward to every class for one reason or another. One word that stands out when it comes to professors and courses at Ithaca College is 'creative.'"

STUDENT AUTHOR: With the atmosphere of a small liberal arts college, Ithaca offers a world of possibilities. First-year seminar classes help turn high school seniors into college freshmen, and internships help students get experience in the working world. Through it all, the faculty and staff at IC is ready to assist their students.

Students Speak Out
ON LOCAL ATMOSPHERE

Q "Ithaca is very friendly. I was pleasantly surprised after coming here from a big city. **There isn't really one dominant type of person** or clique, which is very nice and refreshing. I have yet to encounter someone from Cornell, but it's pretty to visit, and it's nice to know it's so close. Definitely hike around at least one gorge and get friendly with the 24-hour Wegmans."

Q "**Take advantage of hiking** before it gets really cold. If you like movies, there are great theaters in town, like Fall Creek Pictures, Cinemapolis, and Cornell Cinema. The downtown Commons is really cool, too, if you like that kind of thing."

Q "The atmosphere is very laid-back and laissez-faire. It's great to have a huge university on the other hill because it provides many more opportunities for cultural learning, socializing, and intense academic study. **Visit the gorges**, Buttermilk Falls, Treman Park, and the Commons."

Q "The college is also set on a hill with a beautiful view overlooking Cayuga Lake. Every time I look at it, **I get a sense of pride and pleasure** to be gaining a degree in such a fantastic location."

STUDENT AUTHOR: Ithaca is the home to both IC and Cornell University. With quaint coffeehouses, excellent theaters, large used bookstores, happening bars and dance clubs, boutiques, great restaurants, and mom-and-pop shops, there's always something to do or see in Ithaca.

5 Best Things	5 Worst Things
1 Friendly people	1 Winter
2 Extracurriculars	2 Located on a hill
3 Cortaca Jug	3 The price
4 Campus facilities	4 Hit-or-miss professors
5 The college town	5 No big visitors

Students Speak Out
ON FACILITIES

Q "**The gym is probably the gem of campus facilities**, but everything is well maintained and convenient. The library is especially useful for studying and reflection."

Q "**The non-alcoholic pub is one of the best student-gathering places** on campus. Students often meet there for coffee, sandwiches, or breakfast, and it is also a popular place for groups to meet to complete group projects."

Q "The Fitness Center is state-of-the-art: all new cardio machines, weight machines are always kept in good working order, classes are offered in yoga, tai-chi, pilates, and cardio-kickboxing. If the fitness center does not offer something and you want it, **you can request it**."

Q "Ithaca College has top-of-the-line facilities. **Our computer labs have recently been upgraded**, our gym is full of exercise machines, and our student center, well, it has a big screen TV. What more could you ask for?"

Q "At a first glance, t**he architecture of this campus is rather dull and outdated**. However, when you enter the buildings and classrooms, they're comfortable and technologically advanced."

STUDENT AUTHOR: **At first glance, many of the buildings on campus seem like a flashback to the disco era. IC doesn't have the prestigious, historical looking buildings that other universities have because of the overall newness of the campus, but most of the classrooms are state-of-the-art.**

Famous Alumni

David Boreanaz, William D'Elia, Arnald Gabriel, Barbara Gaines, Robert Iger, Gavin MacLeod, Jessica Savitch, Anthony Wise

Students Speak Out
ON CAMPUS DINING

Q "Dining halls are okay. **I don't eat in them**; I only take my food to go."

Q "The dining halls have gotten steadily worse each year that I've been here. Food is best at the Terrace Dining Hall and worst at Campus Center Dining Hall. **Thankfully, there are plenty of places to order from.**"

Q "The food on campus is not bad, compared to other food services. But after two years of eating it, **I was ready for a change**, and so I moved into an apartment to do my own cooking. The Terrace Dining Hall has the most selection."

Q "My favorite place to go alone or with a friend is the Pub. **It's a good atmosphere** to talk, do homework, or play a game of cards. Then you can walk over and get a cup of coffee, or whatever you want. They have the best hot chocolate ever, by the way!"

Q "At every meal, there are both old-fashioned American favorites, as well as a healthy array of foods. **It is always fresh**. Plus, the chefs and management do their best to appeal to everyone's tastes. They're always looking for feedback and new ideas to keep the meals different but delicious."

STUDENT AUTHOR: **All in all, campus food is pretty decent. Compared to other schools some students have visited, the food at IC is gourmet. Sometimes, what is served in the dining halls seems a bit repetitive, but students find that varying which dining halls they go to leaves them more satisfied.**

Student Body

African American:	3%	Male/Female:	46/54%
Asian American:	4%	Out-of-State:	55%
Hispanic:	4%	International:	2%
Native American:	<1%	Unknown:	12%
White:	74%		

Popular Faiths: Muller Chapel holds services for Catholic, Jewish, and Protestant faiths.

Gay Pride: Every April, the college celebrates "Gaypril," a month long event that strives to make the public more tolerant and increase awareness of homosexual students.

Political Activity: The city of Ithaca is known as one of the most liberal cities in the country.

Students Speak Out
ON DORMS

Q "**I like all the dorms**. The best, of course, are the Circle Apartments. They rock. I also like the Upper Quads. The Terraces are removed but nice."

Q "The dorms are small, but there are a lot of them. **Live in the Terraces if you want to have a pretty view and a long walk to class.** Live in the Circles if you want to believe you're not on campus and want a really long walk or a heck of a time finding a parking spot. The Upper Quads are really convenient, but they can get rowdy."

Q "I liked freshman housing for the experience because **it was very easy to meet people**. We had an open door policy, and it was comforting to know all the people in your building."

STUDENT AUTHOR: **IC is a residential college, which means that all students, except for seniors, are expected to live on campus. IC offers many housing options, and most are generally happy with where they live. The special housing dorms can be very beneficial for those who are interested. Those who spend some time in the dorms, though, often cite strong bonds and a community feel.**

> **Did You Know?**
> 70% of undergrads live on campus.

Students Speak Out
ON GUYS & GIRLS

Q "There are a lot of skinny girls here, if you think that's hot. I think it all just depends on preference, **but there isn't an over-abundance of trolls roaming around campus**, if that's what you what to know."

Q "Lot's of alternative people here, very few Abercrombie-esque models. **It's an okay mix, with lots of girls.**"

Q "**Everyone's pretty good-looking** here. I'd say a good 65 percent of the student body population can be considered hot."

Q "**Everyone is wonderful, period**. The personalities are what make this campus interesting and fun."

STUDENT AUTHOR: **Many feel that while some Cornell students have more brains, the students at Ithaca have the upper hand when it comes to looks. With a campus that's very open to sex and any sexual orientation, if someone wants to be promiscuous, he or she can find plenty of opportunities to do just that. If students want to try and find serious significant others, they can do that, as well.**

> **Traditions**
>
> **Convocation**
> Freshmen attend the convocation ceremony where the college president and other school officials address the class.
>
> **Cortaca Jug**
> Everyone on campus gathers at the football stadium to watch the Bombers take on their rivals, the Cortland Red Dragons.
>
> **Overall School Spirit**
> School spirit is not as prevalent here as it is at other schools.

Students Speak Out
ON ATHLETICS

Q "Sports aren't that big on campus, but there's always a game going on. If you're a sports fan, **there are plenty of opportunities** to catch a football or basketball game."

Q "**Varsity isn't a huge deal** since we're only D-III, but I've heard of a lot of students who really like intramural sports."

Q "With the exception of the Cortaca Jug, **nobody on campus really cares about college athletics**, except for the athletes themselves."

Q "Varsity sports are not too big of a deal on campus, but athletes enjoy their fair share of fans. **Intramural sports are very enjoyable**, from what I hear, and there are a broad range of sports for people to choose from."

STUDENT AUTHOR: **Despite the talent some of the teams at IC have, students fail to attend games or show school spirit. The college administration doesn't stress athletics, and the school's overall lackluster spirit shows it. The talent and athletic opportunities are there—students just have to take part in Bomber pride.**

Students Speak Out
ON DRUG SCENE

Q "**Pot is around a lot**. I haven't had much experience with people doing much else. I wouldn't say that harder drugs are used a lot on campus."

Q "Yes, there are a lot of drugs here. Pot is the most heavily used drug, then 'shrooms, then opium. **There are some harder drugs, but they're seldom used**. If you do not want to do drugs, and you want to stay away from all illegal activity, it is very easy to do so here."

Q "I don't know about any hard core drugs, but marijuana is fairly common, especially given the pot signs in the downtown Commons shops. They sell some **very pretty bongs, bowls, and hookahs**. You get the idea."

STUDENT AUTHOR: **Although some students use illegal substances, the scene isn't so prevalent to make other students uncomfortable if they want to be drug-free. The Health Center's drug counseling program is there to help students if they need it, and Public Safety officers work to control any substance problem that arises on campus.**

12:1	Student-to-Faculty Ratio
84%	Freshman Retention Rate
71%	Four-Year Graduation Rate
86%	Financial Aid Applicants Receiving Aid

Students Speak Out
SAFETY & SECURITY

Q "**I have always felt safe on campus**. Blue-light emergency phones dot the landscape, and the town and city of Ithaca are generally very safe areas."

Q "I haven't really had to use any of their services, but they seem pretty good. I'm not sure, but when my car battery needed a jump once, the **campus police were very helpful**."

Q "For the most part, I feel really safe on campus. I have **never worried about walking back to my room, even at 3 a.m.**; though I do keep my eyes open on the weekends when the drunks are out."

STUDENT AUTHOR: **IC has a very low crime rate, and Public Safety takes every precaution to keep it that way. Still, students need to use common sense. Valuables such as money, jewelry, or laptops should always be safeguarded.**

Questions?
For more inside information and survival tips, pick up College Prowler's full-length book on this school, written by an actual student! Check it out at *www.collegeprowler.com.*

Students Speak Out
ON OVERALL EXPERIENCE

Q "I love it here. **There are good opportunities to be found**, with a fairly good mix of decent people. You just have to go out and find it, but that's what college is all about."

Q "I love it here. **My overall experience has been great**. Yeah, there are things that have pissed me off with the administration and the weather and stuff, but not enough to make me want to be anywhere else."

Q "I've had a great experience here. I had considered transferring, **but I held on another semester**, and it turns out to have been a great move. College is what you make of it. I don't think it matters where you go, as long as you're learning, meeting people, and having a good time. I've succeeded in all three at IC."

Q "Even though I have enjoyed the journalism program, I'm still not sure what I want to do as a career. **It has not been a waste of time, though**. The lasting friendships I have made, the connections with professors, and the experiences of living in a small town have all contributed much to my education."

STUDENT AUTHOR: **The most common complaints are how much it costs to attend IC and the bitterly cold winter months that students have to endure. With many things in life, students' experiences with IC are simply what they make of them. If you sit in your dorm room for four years, you will be miserable. If you experience the life Ithaca has to offer outside of the four walls of your room, you most likely won't regret your decision to attend Ithaca College.**

IUPUI

425 North University Boulevard; Indianapolis, IN 46202-5143
(317) 274-5555; www.iupui.edu

THE BASICS:

Acceptance Rate: 70%
Setting: Urban
F-T Undergrads: 13,942

SAT Range: 890–1120*
Control: Public
Tuition: $19,919

Most Popular Majors: Business, Liberal Arts, Health Professions, Education, Communications/Journalism

*of 1600

Academics	B-	Guys	B-
Local Atmosphere	B+	Girls	B-
Safety & Security	B	Athletics	C
Computers	A	Nightlife	B+
Facilities	C+	Greek Life	D
Campus Dining	C+	Drug Scene	A-
Off-Campus Dining	B+	Campus Strictness	B-
Campus Housing	D+	Parking	D
Off-Campus Housing	A	Transportation	B-
Diversity	C	Weather	C+

Students Speak Out
ON ACADEMICS

Q "**The teachers are quite diverse**. In some classes there are part-time instructors who only have a master's, and in others there are well-regarded academics. You must do your research when deciding whose class to take."

Q "**Some classes are boring**. These are normally the required classes, such as history or writing, but if you plan your electives well, you will always be interested."

Q "Most of my classes are very interesting, and we generally cover a lot of important information. All my professors have **weird and funny personalities**—this makes them pretty unique."

Q "I find that the teachers at IUPUI are very knowledgeable, and although some are less interesting than others, **they are overall very enthusiastic about their topics** and the subjects they teach. I have found all my classes, for the most part, are interesting. This is influenced by the fact that I tend to choose only those classes which spark an interest."

STUDENT AUTHOR: **IUPUI includes two very well-known universities: Indiana University and Purdue University. The student-teacher ratio at IUPUI is as attractive as a private institution's. Students at IUPUI have much more access to professors than do their fellow students in Bloomington or Lafayette (where Indiana University and Purdue University are based). There are times when it will seem like you're getting a private education for the cost of a public one.**

Students Speak Out
ON LOCAL ATMOSPHERE

Q "The town seems to be **growing and yet dying at the same time**. People are moving out, but some are also trying to build a city for people to move back into. Stay away from 38th Street."

Q "IUPUI is central to the heart of downtown Indianapolis. The University sits just a few blocks away from the center of the downtown business district. **There are several other Universities and colleges in and around the city**, but none are as vital to downtown as IUPUI."

Q "The atmosphere in Indianapolis is very sports oriented, in my opinion. **I find that there are not enough cultural things going on**. I think the museums here in Indianapolis are definitely worth seeing! Also, the race track is, too."

Q "Attending a university in a downtown location makes all the difference! **There is a ton of stuff to do**, from the IMAX theater to the Irish Fest to free stuff (for IUPUI students), like at the Eiteljorg Museum. Close to downtown Indy are other colleges and universities, but each has their own specialty."

STUDENT AUTHOR: **Indianapolis is a great city with a lot of potential, but the way in which some people limit themselves can be disappointing. Many college students spend their entire week waiting for the moment when they can escape into a local pub or nightclub. Intellectual stimulation is everywhere in Indianapolis, though. There are a number of cultural districts in this city that just aren't taken advantage of by the young adults who live in it.**

Students Speak Out
ON FACILITIES

Q "As a student who has just recently cracked the 40s age barrier, I find that **all facilities that I use are quite adequate**."

Q "**Campus facilities are undergoing changes.** We have an okay athletic complex, which could be enlarged. Computer access is at a premium, but a student who wants to ensure access may want to consider purchasing a notebook with wireless capability."

Q "They seem nice. **There are brand-new computers and a 24-hour lab to use them in.** The only thing that I would watch out for is the athletic facilities. IUPUI doesn't exactly have a recreational sports facility worth bragging about. I mean, it's there, but it costs about $21 to use and it's not very up-to-date."

Q "The actual facility on campus for students to work out (**after paying the semester rec fee**) is not that nice. However, students get a discount membership to the National Institute for Fitness and Sports (NIFS), which is a nationally-known center and an excellent facility."

STUDENT AUTHOR: Students at IUPUI seem to desire improvement of the facilities around campus. Most of the computer facilities are satisfactory, and the new student center should really start to turn the campus around, but students typically respond negatively when asked about IUPUI facilities in general. The conditioning rooms, especially, are something that students would like to see renovated and improved upon. However, the IU Natatorium is a world-renowned facility.

Famous Alumni

Harry Day and Joseph Muhler (discoverers of fluoride for use in toothpaste), Dan Quayle (former U.S. vice president), David Wolf (astronaut)

Students Speak Out
ON CAMPUS DINING

Q "**The food is average.** There are two main food places on campus, as well as a restaurant and bar across the street at University Place Hotel. There are numerous vending machines and eating areas."

Q "I don't really like the food on campus. It's kind of cheap, but the quality is more important to me. In addition to that, **the dining halls are way too crowded.** You can never find a seat."

Q "Food on campus is **adequate at best**. Some of the best spots for eating are downtown, which will be a short walk or drive away from campus."

Q "The food on campus is expensive. **I suggest bringing your lunch**—it is cheaper and will be better for you. There are only about five spots on campus to buy food that is not from a vending machine, but there is a McDonald's in Riley Hospital for Children, which is on campus."

Q "I have never eaten on campus, so I don't know anything at all about that. **I just go straight home for food.**"

STUDENT AUTHOR: Most students vehemently agree that on-campus dining is "adequate at best." Some students bring sack lunches but most endure the low-quality cuisine that is served on campus. Also, if students are hungry after 3 p.m., it is pretty difficult to get a bite to eat on campus. But it should be noted that Chancellor's, the campus sports bar, is supposed to be one of the first steps in improving the IUPUI campus dining scene with its quality food and later hours.

Student Body

African American:	11%	Male/Female:	41/59%
Asian American:	2%	Out-of-State:	2%
Hispanic:	2%	International:	2%
Native American:	<1%	Unknown:	0%
White:	83%		

Popular Faiths: There are several religions on campus, but the one that is most active is Christianity.

Gay Pride: IUPUI has a significant gay community and supports it through organizations like the Advocate.

Economic Status: Many students at IUPUI are non-traditional adults that have had work experience and are looking to advance in their careers.

Students Speak Out
ON DORMS

Q "I have not lived in the dorms, but on visiting them, they are okay. **I would avoid the campus apartments**, as they are extremely expensive and you can get more for less by staying off campus."

Q "**Ball Hall is kind of beat up**, especially compared to IU-Bloomington's dorms. I used to go to Bloomington, and the residence halls are way better there."

Q "**There is brand-new housing on campus, but it is expensive**. The freshman dorm is in an old building on campus, and the new housing is apartments, with separate areas for international and honors students."

STUDENT AUTHOR: **Most students, even freshmen, live off campus. Compared to off-campus living, the dorms should be a second choice. Although the campus apartments are fairly nice, they cost much more to live in than off-campus apartments that are just as nice. Besides, the rules that come with living in the campus apartments—no candles, no incense, no pets—aren't worth the worry when students can just get a place a few blocks away.**

> **Did You Know?**
> 3% of undergrads live on campus.

Students Speak Out
ON GUYS & GIRLS

Q "Everyone seems to be relatively friendly. **A lot of the guys on campus are hot**, and they all have their own styles and trends. The same could be said of the girls."

Q "There are definitely a lot of hot guys around. They seem very arrogant, though. IUPUI being a commuter college, **people often seem to be very distant and reserved** toward one another."

Q "Most people are friendly. There are some young girls that come to school in high heels, and some girls come to school in pajamas. Most of the guys wear jeans and a T-shirt and are more laid back. It seems like **there are more pretty girls than hot guys**."

STUDENT AUTHOR: **Hookups and hotties are not very big concerns for most IUPUI students. Several of the students here are married and have family lives outside of their academics. The younger, single students do present themselves as such by hanging out at clubs or bars, but there is not a very prominent dating scene in general. There is also not very much competition for guys and girls, partly because the average student is 25 years old.**

> **Traditions**
>
> **Carnival in the Courtyard**
> This event kicks off the beginning of the year with musical acts and carnival rides.
>
> **Movie in the Courtyard**
> A huge screen is placed in the University College courtyard and a free movie for students is played.
>
> **Overall School Spirit**
> School spirit is not exactly high at IUPUI, but the students that have it are very loyal and excited. The students with the most school spirit are the happiest students.

Students Speak Out
ON ATHLETICS

Q "Campus sports are not that big, but **they are growing**. We don't have a football team, but we do have many NCAA Division I teams, like basketball, tennis, soccer, cross-country, and swimming."

Q "IUPUI has many sports teams but lacks a football team. IUPUI is located in Indianapolis, so **it's a given that basketball is a big sport**."

Q "**Varsity sports aren't that big**. I think that basketball is getting more and more popular, and the swimming team is well-known. There are many IM sports—basketball, softball, racquetball, tennis—you name it."

Q "**Men's basketball is the sport you hear most frequently about**. They keep getting better."

STUDENT AUTHOR: **In general, IUPUI students' attitudes toward sports are apathetic. Very few students attend sporting events at all, but the ones that do are pretty loyal fans. Students pay a $30 athletic fee, which is included in their tuition for the year. This gets them in to any event as long as they show their Jag Tag (IUPUI student ID). Unfortunately, very few students take advantage of this.**

Students Speak Out
ON DRUG SCENE

Q "I, personally, do not know much about the drug scene, but **I've heard talk about marijuana** from listening to the students that sit around at lunch."

Q "I have not heard anything about drugs on campus, but **I have heard a lot about smoking pot among young people**, so my guess is that the campus isn't an exception."

Q "IUPUI is supposed to be a drug-free, wet campus. Most students are not involved in illegal drugs while on campus, but **there is a bar, and students over 21 may drink** when outside of the classroom (unless you are taking a drink-tasting course)."

STUDENT AUTHOR: **Underage drinking is the one thing that might fit into this category, but most students that live on campus do not get very involved with drugs. There are surely some off-campus parties and gatherings where students can find drugs, but it would probably take a bit of effort on a student's part to get some marijuana or any other narcotics.**

17:1	Student-to-Faculty Ratio
68%	Freshman Retention Rate
7%	Four-Year Graduation Rate
79%	Financial Aid Applicants Receiving Aid

Students Speak Out
SAFETY & SECURITY

Q "Personally, I feel very safe on campus, and **I see a lot of security present at all times**. There are poles up around campus—if I ever feel in danger, I can just press a button and the police will come to me."

Q "**I think they have it pretty much organized**. Campus police are all over the place, and if there is ever a fight or anything, they always get it taken care of."

Q "Security is pretty average. Just like everywhere else you go, you should use caution. If you're walking on campus at night, **campus police offers a driving service**. You can call them up from any campus phone, and they will take you where you need to go on campus."

STUDENT AUTHOR: **The IUPUI campus is exceptionally safe, considering its urban location. Campus police remain very present during the day and night. Although there have been instances of car break-ins and muggings, there is action taken immediately by campus police for these matters.**

Questions?
For more inside information and survival tips, pick up College Prowler's full-length book on this school, written by an actual student! Check it out at *www.collegeprowler.com*.

Students Speak Out
ON OVERALL EXPERIENCE

Q "I love IUPUI! **I don't want to be anywhere else right now**! It is a very mature and serious learning environment and not the typical 'college-town school.' It is worth experiencing!"

Q "I am only a part-time student here at IUPUI, and I am slightly over 40. With that in mind, I would say that **my experience at IUPUI has been pleasant**, and I hope to graduate from here soon."

Q "I can't complain too much. There will be problems everywhere you go. **My concern is with parking and the athletic facilities**. I love my professors and they seem to care about my success. I have many home phone numbers of my professors—this is nice, and it has come in handy on many occasions. I feel challenged yet befriended by my teachers, and this makes for a quality education."

Q "**IUPUI has been a really good school**. For the money and for the convenience, I don't think I could have done better. I now have a degree from both Indiana University and Purdue University, and did not have to move from my home in Indianapolis, or commute long distances."

STUDENT AUTHOR: **IUPUI may not be a traditional campus with frat parties and hookups, but students really seem to appreciate its function and purpose, which is to promote professionalism, diversity, and urban learning. Athletic facilities are not yet to the standard that the students can accept, and parking is way below the needs of the students, but as long as you take the bad with the good, IUPUI will be, at least, a satisfactory and educational experience for you.**

James Madison University

800 South Main Street; Harrisonburg, VA 22807
(540) 568-6211; www.jmu.edu

THE BASICS:

Acceptance Rate: 65%   **SAT Range:** 1580–1870*
Setting: Rural   **Control:** Public
F-T Undergrads: 16,205   **Tuition:** $17,386

Most Popular Majors: Business/Marketing, Social
Sciences, Health Professions, Communications

*of 2400

Academics	B	Guys	B+
Local Atmosphere	B-	Girls	A
Safety & Security	A	Athletics	B-
Computers	B+	Nightlife	B
Facilities	A	Greek Life	B
Campus Dining	A-	Drug Scene	B-
Off-Campus Dining	C	Campus Strictness	B
Campus Housing	B+	Parking	D-
Off-Campus Housing	B+	Transportation	B-
Diversity	D	Weather	B

Students Speak Out
ON ACADEMICS

Q "Every teacher I've had here, no matter whether they were exciting or boring, good at teaching or just good at their subject, seemed to be **really interested in the students** and the students' well being."

Q **"I did not enjoy the general education classes** that I had to take as requirements. I found that they were boring, and the teachers were just as uninterested in them as the students were. However, now that I am in my major classes, I find that I am having more fun."

Q "For the most part, my teachers have been very good. They're **passionate about their subjects** and knowledgeable in their fields. I'd have to say that all of my classes have been interesting."

Q "I'm taking mostly general education classes this semester, and on the whole, these professors could be summarized, in a word, as 'liberal.' They are very opinionated and **vocal about current events** and historical interpretation, and they often add a liberal slant when teaching their course."

STUDENT AUTHOR: The majority of JMU professors really harbor genuine care for their pupils. Most professors are not only knowledgeable in their various subjects, but enthusiastic, as well. It's quite easy to make an appointment with a prof, and the rewards (improved grades, happy parents) are sweet. At JMU, it's not easy to slack off and squeak through with a decent grade.

Students Speak Out
ON LOCAL ATMOSPHERE

Q "Harrisonburg is **going through a huge transition right now** from a small town to a larger suburb, so it gives off this vibe that's a mixture of Southern country life and the more fast-paced suburban lifestyle."

Q "Harrisonburg is **unlike any other town**! It is a small college town with not much in it, considering that a third of it's population is college students. However, there are other universities that are very close to JMU: Bridgewater, EMU, and UVA."

Q "The atmosphere here is pretty chill, on campus and off. Harrisonburg **isn't really the most exciting town to live in**, but I wouldn't say there's anything to stay away from either. Eastern Mennonite University is across town; University of Virginia and Bridgewater Community College are pretty close, too."

Q "The town is full of welcoming people. Many of them have lived here most of their lives. There's always something to do, and **the mountains are close enough** to go on hikes."

STUDENT AUTHOR: Harrisonburg may lack huge shopping malls, dance clubs, and big city thrills, but the town's historic setting and several local attractions suffice nicely. The relative proximity of three other universities also creates opportunities for interaction and community. And, in the dire circumstance that you crave some sort of megalopolis, Washington DC, Richmond, and Roanoke are a mere two hours down the freeway.

5 Best Things	5 Worst Things
1 The Quad	1 Long winters
2 The Arboretum	2 Guy-to-girl ratio
3 Festival dining hall	3 Lack of nightlife
4 Movies at Grafton	4 Parking
5 Theme parties	5 Lack of diversity

Students Speak Out
ON FACILITIES

Q "I love the campus facilities. Some are a little old, but they're still relatively nice. **The new buildings and facilities are amazing**, especially UREC and ISAT."

Q "Computer accessibility and networking is excellent. Food is incredible and easily accessible. Also, UREC is **an amazing recreation facility** which rivals even the big business gyms."

Q "I really like the campus because it's really pretty, and it has character. The Quad is the best when it's hot outside because everyone comes out to be social. We also have a really great library, dining hall, gym, and all sorts of other cool places to go. **TDU is really good for commuters** and for anyone who needs a quick nap in between classes."

Q "Facilities here are so cool! I go to the gym and weight lift almost every day, but sometimes, it gets a little too crowded. All the other buildings are pretty nice, too. They're all old, so they kind of seem to fit with each other. And **the Quad is so wonderful**, if only just so we can see chicks sunbathing in bikinis in the spring. I love JMU."

STUDENT AUTHOR: **Elegant gray stone buildings with white trim dot the main part of campus that is intersected by a railroad and christened with a lake and a fountain. Although most of the campus consists of the original buildings in their aged beauty, the newer part of campus is splendid, as well, equipped with state of the art computer labs, air-conditioning, and expert interior and exterior design.**

Famous Alumni

Marcia Angell, David Gill, Robert "Phoef" Sutton, Phil Vassar, Charles Haley, Delvin Joyce, Curtis Keaton

Students Speak Out
ON CAMPUS DINING

Q "Personally, I like the food on campus. There are **a ton of different places to eat**, and as long as you don't let yourself go to the same place all the time, you won't get sick of what's around."

Q "The food on campus is amazing. You have a wide selection of food ranging from the typical pizza to sushi. There are tons of places to satisfy your appetite, and they are located at different places on campus. Some good places to eat are D-Hall (the main dining hall), Let's Go, Mrs. Green's, and Festival. **The main dining hall has anything you want**, depending on the day you go. They have everything from salad to cheeseburgers."

Q "As far as campus food goes, JMU's is pretty good. There is a wide variety of what to eat on campus, **from Sbarro to Mexican**, Italian, delis, and turkey dinners. D-Hall is always good because it's all-you-can-eat, as is Mrs. Greens, which is a salad bar."

Q "The food isn't bad for college food. I've heard some real horror stories about college dining, so **I consider myself fortunate**."

STUDENT AUTHOR: **A plethora of dining choices are available to students and faculty at JMU, regardless of the size of your appetite. Whether you feel like you could eat a rhino or merely a small salad, you'll be able to find whatever you desire. From do-it-yourself carry-out salad bars, to home-cooked turkey and mashed potatoes, it is inevitable that no stomach will leave unfilled.**

Student Body

African American:	4%	Male/Female:	40/60%
Asian American:	5%	Out-of-State:	29%
Hispanic:	2%	International:	5%
Native American:	<1%	Unknown:	2%
White:	82%		

Popular Faiths: JMU is mainly Christian, with a large Protestant and Catholic population.

Gay Pride: Madison students are accepting and supportive of the various sexual orientations present on campus. Clubs like Harmony promote awareness, tolerance, and equality for all sexual orientations.

Economic Status: The majority of students are from middle-class and upper-middle-class backgrounds.

Students Speak Out
ON DORMS

Q "The dorms are pretty nice, but some of the newer ones are all the way across campus, which is very inconvenient. They have nice accommodations, and most dorms are **strategically located within walking distance** to food and other resources."

Q "All of the dorms have their ups and downs. I have lived in the Village for two years, and it's nice because it is so central to everything on campus (the Quad and ISAT). However, it **doesn't have air-conditioning**. It definitely feels more like a community here. Logan and Gifford are the nicest dorms because they've been renovated."

Q "I lived in the Village my freshman year, and they were pretty nice. They didn't have AC, but they were **well furnished and fairly clean**."

STUDENT AUTHOR: An integral part of a typical college student's experience includes living in a residence hall. Students at JMU have plenty to choose from; 35 residence halls house nearly half of the undergraduate student body. The most popular dorms, hands down, are those with air-conditioning, Potamac and Chesapeake.

Did You Know?
36% of undergrads live on campus.

Students Speak Out
ON GUYS & GIRLS

Q "The guys are few and far between, but there are some cute ones when you find them! As for girls, most of them would **fit the sorority stereotype of skinny and blonde**. However, there are many different circles here, so if you look, there is something or someone for everyone."

Q "Guys here are pretty chill. They like to party, and they love JMU because **the ratio here is 60:40**. The girls here are mad hot, and there are so many of them. Most of them love to party too, so that's cool."

Q "There are **some really, really hot guys here**, but there are also some really hot girls. Unfortunately, there really is a shortage of males around here, which makes life interesting."

STUDENT AUTHOR: For the guys at JMU, it takes a glance or two to find some eye candy; for the girls, it may take some serious elbow grease, but they do exist. The imbalance of maleness on campus does account for a certain amount of cattiness and competition, both of which alcohol can augment. However, there are thousands (literally) of down-to-earth, friendly JMU girls out there, as well.

Traditions

Godwin Field Festival
A pep rally held on the Saturday of Homecoming Week with live entertainment, games, and food.

Homecoming Week
Homecoming is held during the last week of October and features talent shows, and of course, football.

Overall School Spirit
Madison is a friendly school where students are involved in their campus and community. Whether it is politically, musically, journalistically, athletically, or socially, they want to be associated with their school.

Students Speak Out
ON ATHLETICS

Q "Unfortunately, the sporting events that most people think to go to are not the ones that JMU excels at. **Our football team is terrible**, and our basketball team isn't that much better."

Q "Varsity sports are around, but I don't think any of them are exceptionally good or high ranked. However, there's **a lot of school spirit anyway**. Intramural sports are really popular, and they are a lot of fun. Since you can pick coed and the level, you can be as serious or as laid-back as you want with it."

Q "Well, the football team sucks, but they're still fun to watch. **Intramurals are huge** on campus, as well as clubs. There are tons of teams and sport clubs to get into."

STUDENT AUTHOR: JMU athletics isn't known worldwide for its talent and success. However, students agree that they can still have school spirit without a winning team. If you really need to root for a team that wins once in a while, follow water polo, archery, or one of the surprisingly talented but less mainstream teams at JMU. JMU has the ability to create a popular and successful intramural infrastructure.

Students Speak Out
ON DRUG SCENE

Q "I haven't really seen or heard of a lot of hardcore drugs on campus. There is **a relatively large amount of marijuana and drinking**."

Q "There are drugs here, and if you say you don't use them, you're lying. There's **not much hard stuff** that I know of, but it does happen. Mostly, pot and alcohol are the things to do at parties."

Q "A good number of people smoke weed, and there are all different types of people, too. If people are doing it at parties, they're almost always very secretive about it and do it in a bedroom because **it's still not universally accepted**. Heavier drugs aren't really talked about, and I haven't seen a lot of drug activity other than weed."

STUDENT AUTHOR: **The drug of choice at JMU is alcohol, and students have taken notice of the large amount of partying that goes on around the Harrisonburg vicinity. However, most people also admit to not feeling horribly pressured to be involved in the scene if it doesn't suit their fancy.**

16:1	Student-to-Faculty Ratio
91%	Freshman Retention Rate
64%	Four-Year Graduation Rate
36%	Financial Aid Applicants Receiving Aid

Students Speak Out
SAFETY & SECURITY

Q "I have never felt unsafe while on this campus, be it at two in the afternoon or two in the morning. There **always seem to be police around**, for example the Harrisonburg PD, JMU officers, or the Campus Cadets."

Q "**Campus itself is very safe**. Personally, I've never felt threatened or in danger, but I also try to avoid stupid situations. Don't be that girl who walks home alone at three in the morning; it's just not a good idea anywhere."

Q "Security is tight on campus. **I always see at least two police cars** during the day patrolling the campus, and even more during the weekend. The blue telephones around campus are there in case of any emergencies."

STUDENT AUTHOR: **Students pretty much agree when they say they feel snug as bugs in a rug walking around campus. Doors that access residence halls are locked 24/7, regular inspections occur to ensure complete and effective security exists, and heavy-traffic areas are well lit.**

> **Questions?**
> For more inside information and survival tips, pick up College Prowler's full-length book on this school, written by an actual student! Check it out at *www.collegeprowler.com*.

Students Speak Out
ON OVERALL EXPERIENCE

Q "**I love JMU**, and I've learned a lot since I've been at college. Sometimes, I've wondered if I'd be happier at a bigger school where sports were more important and the school was better known, but I can't imagine feeling more at ease than I do here. The campus is beautiful, the people are nice, the teachers are great, and I really can't complain."

Q "Being a transfer student, I couldn't be more pleased. **I wish there was more of a bar scene**, but other than that, everything around here runs really smoothly. The people are so friendly (staff and students), and you can feel welcome anywhere. Not to mention the beautiful campus buildings and landscape!"

Q "I can't see myself anywhere else but here at JMU. The atmosphere here is friendly and fun, but people are also here to get an education. I feel like it's a good mix, **not too big or too small**, but just right!"

Q "There is a lot to do around here, **if you are into being outdoors** or into traveling a little to go to DC or Charlottesville or somewhere. I am very glad I that chose this school. I have no regrets."

STUDENT AUTHOR: **Although students will lodge some minor complaints about the excessively flourishing festivities, the whimsical weather, the perpetual parking pitfalls, and the lack of notable nightlife, the overall consensus is that JMU is a lovely location in which to live. The amiable attitude around town and campus has created a truly welcoming environment at James Madison University and has helped Harrisonburg live up to its nickname, "the Friendly City."**

Johns Hopkins University

3400 North Charles Street; Baltimore, MD 21218
(410) 516-8000; www.jhu.edu

Students Speak Out
ON ACADEMICS

Q "Despite its reputation as being cut-throat, in most subjects, there's **a lot of teamwork**. Students who do best usually work together, especially in math and physics. Most of the teachers seem to care about how students do and are accessible."

Q "Because JHU is a research university, and many of the **professors are high profile**, you are less likely to receive personal attention. You are often really on your own."

Q "The **professors here absolutely are amazing**. I haven't encountered a single one I haven't liked as a professor or as a person."

Q "They are definitely hard and **expect a lot from their students**. Most of them genuinely care about the students and will challenge your mind! Most of my classes were big freshman year because I was taking all the preliminary pre-med classes. I didn't get as much of a chance to meet my teachers. However, by sophomore year, classes are all relatively small."

STUDENT AUTHOR: **Students disagree on the quality of teaching. In large lecture courses, professors don't really get to know students, while in upper-level courses, most make the effort, although some are more interested in their own research. There is a consensus that almost all teachers appreciate it when students attend office hours. Students are generally pleased with academics. If you ask what the deciding factor in choosing to attend Hopkins is, academics tops the list of reasons.**

Students Speak Out
ON LOCAL ATMOSPHERE

Q "Hopkins has an **excellent shuttle service**, which is a great way to get around the immediate area. As far as things to visit, DC is just a stone's throw away, and there are a number of options there. Baltimore itself has the things you'd expect from a city of its size (a zoo, sporting events, museums), and some unique stuff, too. See the aquarium at least once."

Q "There are **three other universities down the street from Hopkins**: Loyola, Towson University, and Goucher. I have a couple friends at Loyola, and it's not hard to get there. The atmosphere is very suburban right around the school, and more city-like towards Mount Vernon and the Harbor."

Q "The area right around Hopkins is geared towards the school with **coffee shops and cafés**. The Baltimore Museum of Art is next door, which is great to just walk around on a day off."

Q "The more people actually explore Baltimore, the more they seem to like it. The **city has charm**, but it's hidden."

STUDENT AUTHOR: **Baltimore takes time to love. It also might take a car and a friend who knows the way around. It does not have a city center where residents hang out. It is a city of neighborhoods, and each has a distinctive feel. From early spring through fall, each hosts festivals that celebrate the particular feel of their neighborhoods with food, vendors, and games. Keep in mind that it is within four hours of Washington DC, Ocean City, Richmond, Philadelphia, Pittsburgh, Newark, and NYC.**

5 Best Things	5 Worst Things
1 Research opportunities	1 Professor research
2 The green campus	2 Construction
3 Lectures	3 Athletics
4 Low cost of living	4 On-campus dining
5 Off-campus dining	5 Health center

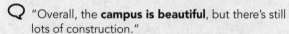

Students Speak Out
ON FACILITIES

Q "Overall, the **campus is beautiful**, but there's still lots of construction."

Q "The library is really nice, with **lots of space to study**, but it's underground, which is weird. It's open until 2 a.m. during the semester and 24/7 during finals period. It also has Café Q, which is a good place to get coffee and hang out."

Q "The **athletic center was renovated**, and an addition was put on. It has several basketball courts, squash courts, a weight room, a cardio room, a rock-climbing wall, a pool, and a room for classes like yoga, kickboxing, and aerobics. There are also additional basketball courts in the older portion of the AC that are used by the varsity teams. There are two tracks, an indoor 1/10 track, and an outdoor 1/4 track."

Q "The new student arts center, the Mattin Center, just opened up recently. There are quite a few things that go on there by different performing groups. It has soundproof music rooms, (some with pianos), and has **a Black box theater**, an Internet café, and darkrooms."

Q "The varsity facilities aren't very new or modern, but **they get the job done**."

STUDENT AUTHOR: **Hopkins is continuing to renovate many facilities on campus due to students' complaints. Students have responded well to the renovations that the administration has made. There are plenty of places for student groups to meet, and the campus is well maintained. The campus itself is beautiful. The quads are landscaped well and surrounded by flowers and trees.**

Famous Alumni

John Astin, John Barth, Michael Bloomberg, Wes Craven, Woodrow Wilson

Students Speak Out
ON CAMPUS DINING

Q "The food on campus leaves a little to be desired. All in all, **food is not a strong suit**."

Q "The **food isn't awful in the dining halls**, but it isn't spectacular, either. The best food on campus is probably in Megabytes or Levering, but you only get credit for half the money you pay for your meal plan, so it's really a rip-off."

Q "Overall, it's not too bad, but you have to mix it up. The **best part about dining is seeing everyone**! I spend almost an hour at every meal just talking with everyone."

Q "There are also lots of great places around campus where you can **use J-Cash to buy meals**. This means you get 50 dollars included in your meal plan each semester, and you can use that money at a nearby Middle Eastern place, a couple cafés, grocery stores, Ruby Tuesday, and Orient Express, a sushi place."

Q "Whenever upperclassmen go back to the dining halls, they always talk about how much better the food has gotten. Although the dining halls don't have the highest quality food, it's not bad, and you have **lots of choices about what to eat**. Also, breakfast is the best meal if you're awake."

STUDENT AUTHOR: **On-campus dining isn't great, but it's edible. What they lose in quality, they make up for in quantity. There are two all-you-can-eat dining halls located near the dorms, which always offer pizza, cereal, salads, burgers, soup, pasta, desserts, and a mix of meats and vegetables. Terrace Court has vegan and Kosher selections.**

Student Body

African American:	6%	Male/Female:	53/47%
Asian American:	25%	Out-of-State:	85%
Hispanic:	7%	International:	5%
Native American:	1%	Unknown:	10%
White:	46%		

Popular Faiths: It would be difficult to find a religion not represented at Hopkins, although many students do not practice any religion.

Gay Pride: There is a very active group on campus for homosexual, bisexual, and transgendered persons—the Diverse Gender and Sexuality Alliance.

Political Activity: There is a split of Republicans and Democrats. Students are more conservative.

Students Speak Out
ON DORMS

Q "Live in the AMRs freshmen year if you want an experience similar to that described in movies. It's really chill and **so easy to meet people**. You probably won't get a single, so try to find something in common with your roommate."

Q "The dorms are typical of any college. I lived in the AMRs freshman year, which are the most social, although not as nice. They are typical double rooms on a hallway, with bathrooms down the halls. **All dorms, except a few, are coed**. The downfall of the AMRs is that there is no air-conditioning; however, fans in the fall and spring are more than sufficient."

Q "The dorms are nice. My room as a freshman was huge. If you want **big rooms**, live in Buildings A or B. Their only downfalls are central heat."

STUDENT AUTHOR: **On-campus housing is required for freshmen and sophomores. The dorms are social and people form close friendships. Buildings A and B and Wolman and McCoy are great options. They are a mix of freshmen and sophomores, which gives them a more mature feel. The arrangement is suites with a common room on each floor.**

> **Did You Know?**
> 60% of undergrads live on campus.

Students Speak Out
ON GUYS & GIRLS

Q "It's a college. There are a several thousand people. Just about **any type you'd be looking for, you can find**. If you can't, there are four other colleges nearby to look at, too."

Q "They sometimes tend not to care about their appearances and may appear less attractive physically. They may also **need to work on their social skills**."

Q "Most students at JHU **don't put as much time into their appearance**."

Q "I must say that the aesthetically-pleasing pool of men is larger than the women's. The girls are ugly, and the guys are okay. A few are **hot here and there**, but not really amazing."

STUDENT AUTHOR: **People get accepted into Hopkins because of their intelligence, not because of their attractiveness. The population is diverse, so there's no traditional look here. Most of the students are pretty down-to-earth and studious. It isn't hard to meet people of the opposite sex since almost all dorms are coed. If you are upset by the selections at Johns Hopkins, you can travel to several other area colleges to meet more people.**

> **Traditions**
>
> **Outside Society**
> Students run naked through the main campus library to break the monotony and seriousness of studying.
>
> **Spring Fair**
> A concert, student plays, musical performances, craft vendors, and a beer garden for those of age.
>
> **Overall School Spirit**
> Students at Hopkins are not particularly spirited. The only sport that warrants excitement is lacrosse. crowds. Students get very spirited about their majors, often comparing themselves to other schools.

Students Speak Out
ON ATHLETICS

Q "Lacrosse is pretty much the sport at Hopkins. I'm from an area where football is big, so it was surprising to me that the crowds at lacrosse were so much bigger than those at football games. **Homecoming is actually in the spring because that's lacrosse season**."

Q "A lot of students don't really care about athletics. Many students don't exercise, and **IM sports are mostly frats** and dorms."

Q "Hopkins men's lacrosse is big, but that's the **only Division I sport** we have. Other than that, people sometimes watch the games, but they aren't a major deal."

Q "People on **varsity sports tend to stick together**. They are more high-profile than other people on campus."

STUDENT AUTHOR: **Athletics are not a major focus at Johns Hopkins. Even lacrosse, the most popular sport, doesn't bring out the whole student body. Tickets to events are free for students. Hopkins has one stadium, which is small by university standards. At Hopkins, school spirit is defined by academics and research as opposed to athletics.**

Students Speak Out
ON DRUG SCENE

Q "There is some drug use, but it is **relatively low-key**."

Q "As with any college, there are **definitely drugs and alcohol available** on campus. They are especially rampant at frat parties. It all depends on where you choose to go and who you choose to associate with. The most important thing, though, is that no one is pressuring you to do anything at Hopkins."

Q "I haven't encountered any hard drug use. Some students smoke pot. Alcohol use is prevalent. **Almost everyone drinks**. Moreover, people drink to get drunk."

STUDENT AUTHOR: **Alcohol is the top drug on campus, followed by pot. Students use caffeine pills to help them stay awake. They use them not to escape the world, but because they need to study. Drug use at Hopkins is a matter of choice. It is uncommon to hear about anyone allowing their use to interfere with their studies. When people choose to use drugs, it is usually on the weekends to relax.**

12:1	Student-to-Faculty Ratio
97%	Freshman Retention Rate
84%	Four-Year Graduation Rate
83%	Financial Aid Applicants Receiving Aid

Students Speak Out
SAFETY & SECURITY

Q "Although Hopkins is not in the best part of Baltimore, **campus security is superb**."

Q "Security is quite good. Most of the Hop Cops are **retired police officers**. They're very capable and pretty friendly."

Q "The campus itself is pretty safe, but as soon as you're **two blocks away, watch your back** or go with a friend."

Q "We have Hopkins Police patrolling the campus at all hours. There are **emergency phones throughout campus** that respond immediately when they are pressed. Four of the dorms are accessible with access cards and keys to the rooms, and security guards sit at the front desks of two of them."

STUDENT AUTHOR: **The presence of Hop Cops and other security guards 24 hours a day allows students to walk around campus safely. In addition, there are walking and driving escort services to take students where they want to go within a mile of campus. There is never an excuse for walking alone after dark.**

Questions?

For more inside information and survival tips, pick up College Prowler's full-length book on this school, written by an actual student! Check it out at *www.collegeprowler.com*.

Students Speak Out
ON OVERALL EXPERIENCE

Q "Hopkins provides **incredible opportunities** to undergraduates that aren't possible at other institutions, especially in research. Socially, it's what you make of it. There's a lot going on, but it's not force-fed to you the way it is at some other schools."

Q "I appreciated the challenge. I enjoyed the fact that I **actually had to work to succeed here**. This is a great place for some people, but it's not for everyone."

Q "I complain about it all the time, but it's really been the best, yet **most challenging, experience** I've ever had. Some keys to success at Hopkins: time management, love your major, love your friends, and have some fun."

Q "At Hopkins, we **study hard and play hard**! There is a ton of stuff to do in Baltimore. I think that it is a difficult school, but I am having a wonderful time, and I think that I am doing really well."

STUDENT AUTHOR: **Both students who love Hopkins and students who hate it recognize that it isn't the school for everyone. Many students wish that Hopkins offered grade inflation, as other top schools do. Even people who work hard end up with low grades. This encourages some students to put studying above any social activity. Some students wish that Hopkins encouraged students to get involved in all aspects of University life, but once you realize that it doesn't, you can make your own choices about how you want to spend your time. Even though students complain, most say that they've enjoyed being challenged by their experiences at Hopkins.**

Juniata College

1700 Moore Street; Huntingdon, PA 16652
(814) 641-3000; www.juniata.edu

THE BASICS:

Acceptance Rate: 67%   **SAT Range:** 1065–1260*
Setting: Rural   **Control:** Private
F-T Undergrads: 1,431   **Tuition:** $29,610

Most Popular Majors: Biology, Business/Marketing, Education, Social Sciences, Interdisciplinary Studies

*of 1600

Academics	B	Guys	B-
Local Atmosphere	B-	Girls	B-
Safety & Security	A	Athletics	B
Computers	B	Nightlife	C+
Facilities	B+	Greek Life	N/A
Campus Dining	C+	Drug Scene	A-
Off-Campus Dining	B	Campus Strictness	A-
Campus Housing	B	Parking	C+
Off-Campus Housing	A-	Transportation	D
Diversity	D-	Weather	C

Students Speak Out
ON ACADEMICS

Q "One of Juniata's top draws is the professors, in my opinion. **They are exceptional at their jobs and extremely student-oriented**. With that said, the classes range from boring to very interesting, much like most colleges. It mainly depends on personal preference."

Q "Most professors are nice and easy to get along with. There are always the hard classes that students don't like, but **most classes are at least interesting** on some level, and encourage you to think beyond what is taught in the classroom."

Q "Generally, the teachers are very helpful. **It is rarely a problem to meet after class** or in their office for extra help. Classes are small, so in-class discussion is useful, plus it helps keep the classes interesting."

Q "**The teachers are generally good, wholesome people**, very available for students to go and see them. The classes—well, I have found most of them to be very intellectually stimulating. As it would be anywhere else, it depends on the class subject matter and the particular professor's teaching ability."

STUDENT AUTHOR: **Most students agree that the professors play a huge role in furthering the spirit and feeling of community that Juniata prides itself on. In exchange for such high accessibility and support, professors have equally high expectations. While classes vary in size and difficulty, most tend to be small and challenging, and students respond by working hard.**

Students Speak Out
ON LOCAL ATMOSPHERE

Q "There are no other major colleges or universities in Huntingdon. **There are generally good relations between Huntingdon and Juniata**, despite rumors to the contrary. It's an undeniably small town, with limited things to do and see, but in my opinion, it's a town that feels like home."

Q "The town is very small. **There really isn't a lot of anything around Huntingdon**, but there are some nice restaurants, like Billi's Bric-a-Brac Café (a bagel sandwich shop)."

Q "**There isn't much to do in the city of Huntingdon besides go to the movies**. We are very close to Penn State and Altoona, which is a plus, because there is a tremendous amount to do in these two areas."

Q "The town is mostly blue collar. There is the DuBois College of Business down the street from Huntingdon. I stayed away from dark alleys and didn't go far when I was alone. **There are a few nice places to visit**: the park by the river, the Peace Chapel, Raystown Lake, the cliffs, and the playground behind Weis."

STUDENT AUTHOR: **Love it or hate it, the town has atmosphere. While Juniata wouldn't be Juniata without Huntingdon, that doesn't mean students don't get claustrophobic sometimes. The town is somewhat economically depressed and rather isolated, and it's small, small, small. However, students can usually get what they need from Giant or the various shops around town.**

Students Speak Out
ON FACILITIES

Q "Facilities are great. **The student center is kind of nonexistent**, but people hang out in Muddy Run Café anyway. The fitness center has plenty of equipment and all that."

Q "The facilities on campus are nice, and **everything is kept clean**. There is a lot to be offered to the students that they don't realize at first, but over time, they take advantage of what is offered."

Q "**The athletic centers are top-notch**. The computers are great, but it would be helpful if there were more of them. Ellis Hall, which is the closest thing to a student union, is pretty far from it, but the basics are there."

Q "The weight room is awesome. I loved going there. **Computers are in top condition**. The buildings are kept very clean!"

Q "As far as I'm concerned, **I feel that all of our equipment is really nice**. I was really shocked at how clean the gym facilities are, and though our pool isn't brand new, it's very well-maintained. The computers work 90 percent of the time unless some jerk clicks on one of those virus links and crashes the system."

STUDENT AUTHOR: As a general rule, when it comes to facilities, the ones that are good are very, very good, but the ones that are older could use a little work. While there is much to applaud about the facilities on campus, there are a few complaints as well: the lack of a true student center tops the list, and the art studios and Good Hall, while they get the job done, fall short of excellent.

Famous Alumni

Scott M. Beatty, Robert M. Biter MD, Sammy K. Buo, Carli K. Dale, Bruce Davis, Michael A. Trim, Alexander M. Jones, John D. Irvin, Charles R. Knox

Students Speak Out
ON CAMPUS DINING

Q "The dining hall is atrocious. **I cannot overstate how awful it is**. Every once in a while, you'll get something decent, but that is about it. Cherish the mediocre days."

Q "To be honest, **the food isn't all that great on campus**. Like other campuses, it has its good and bad days, and when it's a bad day, there is a place called Muddy Run where you can get hamburgers and hoagies made."

Q "**We have Baker and Muddy Run**. If the food in Baker sucks (our main cafeteria), you can always go to Muddy Run and get a burger and fries or a sub."

Q "**The food is not good in Baker**. No other way to say it. The food in Muddy Run isn't bad, but you have a limited amount, unlike Baker, so that's the trade off."

Q "I alternated between hating Baker (the dining hall) and liking it well enough. There are a bunch of options, but **it's still pretty bland cafeteria food**, usually. I ate there for most of my meals at Juniata, and it was okay."

STUDENT AUTHOR: Most students would probably agree that if the food in Baker were as pleasant as the people who serve it, they'd all be better off. However, most also recognize that a cafeteria is a cafeteria, and while it gets old pretty quickly, there's enough variety and sheer quantity to satisfy anyone's appetite. Muddy Run is considered the main escape route for anyone not up for what Baker has on the menu.

Student Body

African American:	2%	Male/Female:	47/53%
Asian American:	2%	Out-of-State:	28%
Hispanic:	1%	International:	3%
Native American:	<1%	Unknown:	0%
White:	92%		

Popular Faiths: Juniata is affiliated in name with the Church of the Brethren, and Christianity is easily the predominant religion.

Gay Pride: Juniata is a very tolerant and accepting campus, but the gay community is fairly quiet.

Economic Status: You can find students from many different economic backgrounds at Juniata, but the majority hail from middle-class suburbia.

Students Speak Out
ON DORMS

Q "**The dorms are livable**. For underclassman, TnT (Tussey and Terrace) is the best location, and for upperclassmen South or Cloister are top choices. Sherwood is the most dreaded dormitory as it's cramped and dirty."

Q "The dorms are pretty nice compared to other campuses I've seen. Avoid North and Sherwood at all costs. Girls, Lesher has the biggest rooms and biggest closets. **South is always fun**."

Q "South is the most spacious. **Sunderland and Sherwood are crowded** and more often the louder dorms. Tussey and Terrace are very quiet. East has a nice common room, surrounded by four two-person dorms. They are the farthest from campus, though."

STUDENT AUTHOR: **Non-commuting freshmen are required to live on campus, and this is a good thing, as it's the best way to get sucked into the Juniata bubble and meet the people who will become your family over the next few years. The rooms can be a bit cramped at times, but all dorms are only a short walk from all the key places on campus, except for East, which is a bit farther away.**

Did You Know?
83% of undergrads live on campus.

Students Speak Out
ON GUYS & GIRLS

Q "**Most Juniata students are intelligent, unique, and independent**. However, there are a lot of guys who are only here for the sports and partying (though who knows why they pick Juniata for that). Our community is more close-knit than any other I've been to."

Q "I would say you see the same personalities at Juniata that you've seen or would see at a high school of similar size. **There are a few good-looking folks and a lot of average folks**."

Q "**Most everyone is friendly and pretty cool**. There are plenty of hot people on our campus."

Q "Hot is a relative term; **there's definitely something for everyone**."

STUDENT AUTHOR: **Guys and girls alike tend to be intelligent, focused, fun, and easy-going. Socially, everyone's pretty casual. You'll have your share of pretty girls—and pretty boys, for that matter—but overall, everyone is laid-back when comes to anything from how you dress to who you hang out with on the weekends. Odds are, if you're comfortable with yourself, you'll find your niche and probably find what you're looking for.**

Traditions

Madrigal
A dinner/dance held every November. Half the school attends and students camp out to get the best tables.

Mountain Day
Classes are cancelled on a random day in the fall and students flock to the state park for picnics and games.

Overall School Spirit
Most students are proud of Juniata, whether it's because of its academics or just the friendships, independence, and good vibes they've found from nearly everyone there.

Students Speak Out
ON ATHLETICS

Q "**Juniata's biggest sport is volleyball** (both female and male). There aren't any scholarships given to athletes, so Juniata doesn't compete with high level universities. IM sports are participated in, but not hardcore."

Q "**Our volleyball teams go to the national championships every year**. All our other sports teams are pretty cool, too, even if they don't make the championships."

Q "Volleyball is our 'best' sport. **Football is dismal**. Rugby's pretty popular, especially during Storming of the Arch. I'm part of the equestrian team, which is a lot of fun, but a little expensive ($23–$26 per lesson)."

Q "It depends on the sport. Ultimate Frisbee is big. Volleyball is big. **Same with basketball**."

STUDENT AUTHOR: **Athletic teams at Juniata are supported with general goodwill—if not always attendance—from most of the students. Many teams have small but loyal followings. A good portion of Juniata students are athletic, whether they're on a varsity or IM team or just head to the gym to work out.**

Students Speak Out
ON DRUG SCENE

Q "It's by no means pervasive, but if you wanted to smoke some weed, you wouldn't struggle to find it, I don't think. It is just like everywhere else. I think **marijuana is about it, though**. I'd be surprised if there were any 'harder' drugs on campus."

Q "I'm not part of that scene so I don't know anything about drug dealing or using on campus. **I imagine it's probably a little less than the average college**."

Q "I'm sure there is one, **I just don't know where it is**. A few kids I know smoke pot, but there are no dirty needles around."

STUDENT AUTHOR: **Drugs at Juniata just aren't a problem, to the point that the school's newspaper attempted to investigate drug use on campus and came up with next to nothing. There's just not much of a drug scene to report on. If you're looking for drugs, yes, you can find them, but you'd have to look pretty hard to find anything harder than marijuana.**

13:1	Student-to-Faculty Ratio
84%	Freshman Retention Rate
67%	Four-Year Graduation Rate
88%	Financial Aid Applicants Receiving Aid

Students Speak Out
SAFETY & SECURITY

Q "Juniata takes security seriously, as there is always an officer patrolling either on a bike or in a marked SUV. **There are emergency buttons located in key places on campus**. It's a safe campus."

Q **"Safety and security is more than adequate**. Campus security is friendly and helpful; if you need them, they will be there."

Q "I always felt very safe on campus. **I was never afraid to walk anywhere at night**. There are emergency call-boxes around campus, but I've never used one, and I don't know anyone who's had to use them. I'm not naive enough to think that nothing ever happens, but I was never worried about safety."

STUDENT AUTHOR: **Safety and security aren't really a problem at Juniata. While students aren't naïve and common sense is always necessary when it comes to protecting valuables, the community on campus is really freakishly trusting. Most students have no qualms about walking anywhere on campus.**

Questions?
For more inside information and survival tips, pick up College Prowler's full-length book on this school, written by an actual student! Check it out at *www.collegeprowler.com.*

Students Speak Out
ON OVERALL EXPERIENCE

Q **"I am going to miss Juniata**. I think I will appreciate being out because the underclassmen seemed pretty immature after awhile, but I will miss my friends, the classes, the campus, and the cool activities/events."

Q "At first I didn't like it, but **once I found my place I loved it and am happy where I am**. At times, I wish I was someplace else, but I think at every college you get that. Overall, I am happy with where I am and I love Juniata, even though at times I hate it. I know that I will benefit a lot from what I have learned and to an extent have already."

Q "I love my choice of Juniata, and **I can't imagine having gone anywhere else**. Each person's experience will be different, but for me, it was absolutely the right choice."

Q "I don't know how I got here, but I'm here and it fits. **I wouldn't trade it unless I was accepted to Princeton**. Everyone is helpful and most people are very nice."

STUDENT AUTHOR: **Overall, most Juniata students really do love Juniata. If something's going to kill your experience, it's bound to be its smallness. But overall and overwhelmingly students and professors are warm, welcoming, and largely open-minded. Opportunities on campus and around the world are literally endless and growing. Students work hard, have fun, find their passions, and prepare for the world and the future. They also occasionally pull their hair out from claustrophobia. But in the end, they do appreciate Juniata, both while they're there and after they graduate.**

Kansas State University

1700 Anderson Avenue; Manhattan, KS 66506
(785) 532-6011; www.k-state.edu

THE BASICS:

Acceptance Rate: 84%
Setting: Suburban
F-T Undergrads: 16,186

ACT Range: 20–27
Control: Public
Tuition: $15,175

Most Popular Majors: Business/Marketing, Agriculture, Education, Engineering, Social Sciences

Academics	B-	Guys	A-
Local Atmosphere	C	Girls	A
Safety & Security	A-	Athletics	A
Computers	B+	Nightlife	B+
Facilities	A-	Greek Life	A
Campus Dining	B	Drug Scene	B+
Off-Campus Dining	B	Campus Strictness	B-
Campus Housing	C+	Parking	C-
Off-Campus Housing	A-	Transportation	C-
Diversity	C-	Weather	B-

Students Speak Out
ON ACADEMICS

Q "As a student of humanities, I have developed some great relationships with professors from various departments. Since K-State is more of a teaching institution than a research institution, **the professors put more energy into their students than their own work**."

Q "**Most of my teachers are very funny and willing to help** in any way possible. They take joy in teaching and want more than anything for students to understand the content."

Q "A majority of **my teachers have been full professors**, not graduate teaching assistants or instructors."

Q "As at any university, professors at K-State range from the energetic, fascinating ones who truly put their students first to the lethargic, somnolent ones who are biding their time until retirement. That said, my professors have been generally excellent, and **they took a genuine interest in helping their students learn**. My advice to pick your profs: Ask around and find out which ones are the best."

STUDENT AUTHOR: **Academics at Kansas State are a decidedly ominous grab bag. Depending on your major, the academic experience can prove either top-of-the-line or bottom-of-the-barrel. Though the years have dimmed its identity as a cow college considerably, K-State continues to preen its technical disciplines with far greater care than its liberal arts programs. There is no shortage of standout faculty, but class offerings can be slim.**

Students Speak Out
ON LOCAL ATMOSPHERE

Q "I absolutely love living in Manhattan. Everyone is so friendly. **If you even look like you are lost, people will stop and ask if you need help**. They reach out to you."

Q "Personally, I don't like Manhattan. I love K-State and the **'town within a town' atmosphere** that the University puts off, but this town is considerably boring unless you're a partier."

Q "Manhattan is smaller than most college towns I know, but **it still has a fun and comfortable atmosphere**. In spite of its size, it has a wide range of restaurants and good shopping."

Q "Manhattan has a small-town feel, and many of the activities center around the University. Despite not being in a big metropolitan area, the 'Little Apple' does have its share of things to do. There is unique shopping to be found on Poyntz Avenue, which is also home to an art museum, gallery, and public library and is near the local mall. **The Konza Prairie offers a spectacular view of Manhattan** and is equipped with nature trails for your walking or running pleasure."

STUDENT AUTHOR: **Manhattan itself is a flavorful blend of small-town sleepiness and college-community chutzpah. During the day, you'll encounter passersby here and there, but by 10 p.m., the streets are as vacant as the windows. Aggieville, on the other hand, doesn't really do bedtime. Essentially a continuous string of bars with the occasional coffeeshop or bookstore, it's practically off-campus housing for some students.**

5 Best Things	5 Worst Things
1 Physiology of Lactation	**1** Bacon cheeseburger pizza
2 Bosco Plaza water feature	**2** George Strait on repeat
3 Wrist-wrestling	**3** Purple
4 Horticultural therapy	**4** White
5 Grant Reichert's columns	**5** Together

Students Speak Out
ON FACILITIES

Q "The gym, pool, computer labs, and student union are nice, but **many of the classrooms are older and slipping into disrepair**."

Q "The facilities are well-maintained, and their **hours accommodate a wide range of student schedules**. Places like the rec center and Hale Library are open from early in the morning until late at night."

Q "Although I don't know enough about other campuses to make a comparison, the facilities at K-State seem nice. I really don't use many of the facilities on campus beyond the library and the rec center. **The library is spacious and modern with friendly staff**, and the rec center, if a bit crowded before spring break, contains a wide range of activities and ways to stay fit."

Q "**The recreation complex is probably one of the nicest facilities I have worked out in**. For the most part, you don't have to wait for machines, and there are many aerobic machines available to work out on."

Q "**I love the prairie Gothic architecture** of the campus."

STUDENT AUTHOR: Of all the buildings on campus, none boasts a higher quality quotient than the Charles E. Peters Recreation Complex. As slick and well-maintained as the students who frequent it, the rec center is a case study in University funds effectively spent. Its fellow facilities are functional, if less overtly impressive. The Union meets the baseline student center requirements—food court, bookstore, bowling alley, and movie theater all included.

Famous Alumni

Kirstie Alley, Thane Baker, Erin Brockovich, Herb Diamond, Marlin Fitzwater, Steve Grogan, Connie Ramos, Bernard Rogers, Jerry Wexler

Students Speak Out
ON CAMPUS DINING

Q "Having eaten at several campus dining halls in my day, I can honestly say K-State has the best residence hall dining food I've tasted. Much of K-State's dining hall **food comes straight from the K-State dairy** or other agricultural departments, so it's really fresh. The dieticians take great care to get to know students and serve them delicious, well-balanced meals."

Q "The food at K-State is expensive and mediocre. There is **a smattering of fast-food joints that form a grease gauntlet in the Union**. Call Hall ice cream is a treat, though."

Q "I've lived in the residence halls the three years that I've been here, and the food is pretty good. There are always a ton of choices at all three meals. My favorites are the Thanksgiving and Winter meals. **It's just as good as grandma's home cooking**."

Q "They **cater to students with specific dietary lifestyles**, such as vegetarians."

Q "The food in the dorms is a pick-and-choose kind of thing. **Some days it is really good, and other days there is no way I would touch it**."

STUDENT AUTHOR: For the first couple months, the quantity of doughnuts, ice cream, and Cinnamon Toast Crunch at your fingertips in the campus dining centers is dizzying. You could make a meal of desserts alone. Not that you'd need to—the fruit table and salad bar are just as extensive as the dessert menu. After the initial delirium, however, the selection turns monotonous.

Student Body

African American:	4%	Male/Female:	52/48%
Asian American:	1%	Out-of-State:	13%
Hispanic:	3%	International:	3%
Native American:	<1%	Unknown:	3%
White:	85%		

Popular Faiths: More than 80 percent of students on campus practice Christianity in one form or another.

Gay Pride: K-State's sizable queer community, the "Safe Zones" across campus, and a widespread attitude of acceptance make the University a hospitable place for the GLBT student.

Economic Status: Twenty-seven percent of students received a Pell grant in the 2004-05 academic year.

Students Speak Out
ON DORMS

Q "I love the dorms, as dorky as that sounds. **Each dorm is so different**, which makes it easier for students to find their fit."

Q "A lot of the dorms have been remodeled lately to include suites. I would avoid Marlatt (an all-guy hall that smells continually). **Coed halls tend to smell more than all-girl halls**. Putnam-Boyd-Van Zile are smaller and usually house more upperclassmen. The Derby complex (West, Ford, Haymaker, and Moore) is louder and more active. Goodnow and Marlatt are the only halls on the west side of campus."

Q "The dorms aren't bad at all; I enjoyed my time there. **The best dorms for the lowest price are double rooms in the Strong complex**: bigger rooms and closets, and they come with lofts."

STUDENT AUTHOR: **It's not where you end up that matters so much as the company you keep. Nevertheless, if peace and a pre-dawn bedtime are important to you, listing Putnam and Van Zile as your top preferences on the housing application is strongly advised. Goodnow is cleaner and kinder. Moore, Haymaker, West, and Boyd are hit or miss, subject to the floormate factor.**

> **Did You Know?**
> 34% of undergrads live on campus.

Students Speak Out
ON GUYS & GIRLS

Q "I would say that I have a lot of motivation to go to the rec center. **There are a lot of very fit guys here and quite a few hotties**. There is definitely eye candy here for the prowling girl/gay guy."

Q "I suppose the guys and girls at K-State are rather like the guys and girls everywhere, although **we do have a good selection of cowboys, if that's your type**."

Q "The girls are girls. **You have the down-to-earth ones all the way up to the sorority girls**."

Q "**There are lots of hot guys on campus**, although many of them are stereotypical frat boys. But almost all of them are really nice and open doors for girls and that sort of thing."

STUDENT AUTHOR: When speaking of the student body at K-State, the emphasis belongs on "body." K-State boasts a top-of-the-line recreation center, and it's obvious a lot of students have been putting it to good use. If the tan, taut, all-American specimen is what gets your motor running, you'll find no shortage of fuel in Manhattan. But if you look beyond the purely physical and into the personality department, the pickings become somewhat less appetizing.

> **Traditions**
>
> **Call Hall**
> Though not officially stipulated by the University, a trip to Call Hall for ice cream is practically a graduation requirement.
>
> **Midnight Madness**
> On the third Thursday of each month, students congregate in the Purple Masque Theater for a night of sketch comedy and exultant hullabaloo.
>
> **Overall School Spirit**
> Purple Pride reigns. Such is the dedication of K-State's student fan base: They're loud, and they're proud.

Students Speak Out
ON ATHLETICS

Q "**It's all about Wildcat football at K-State**. On Saturdays in the fall, the population of Manhattan doubles."

Q "Basketball is fun to go to, but **the team isn't amazing like KU**."

Q "I never was much into sports, but football, of course, is king. **K-State wouldn't have the reputation it does without it**. It can come off as fanatical sometimes, but I never felt excluded from the K-State community just because I wasn't into the football scene."

Q "**Sports are really, really huge**. I mean, this is a state college."

STUDENT AUTHOR: The influence exercised by the football program at K-State is truly epic in scope. This zeal by no means fizzles after graduation; alumni snap up season tickets and watch parties are organized by spirit clubs everywhere from Alaska to Florida. Though football often upstages other sports, it is by no means the only player on the scene. The equestrian team is ranked first in its league, and women's volleyball made quite a name for itself. Also, IM and club sport participation is huge.

Students Speak Out
ON DRUG SCENE

Q "**I've never seen any drugs on campus**, and it has never been an issue, although I would know where to go to find drugs."

Q "I like to pretend that this doesn't happen on campus, but I know it does. **I have overheard people talking about smoking weed** and doing other things, but I have never seen it first hand."

Q "I know that it must go on, but **I don't think drugs are absolutely huge on campus**. I think it's a lot more about the drinking."

STUDENT AUTHOR: Illegal drugs at K-State are a little like international students. You know they're out there, and with some effort you can track them down, but their presence is barely perceptible. Keep in mind, too, that "drugs," in central Kansas vernacular, translates as "marijuana." On those exceedingly rare occasions when reports of students busted for something harder turn up, it's a good bet they're from Kansas City area. And legal drugs? Alcohol is without a doubt the intoxicant of choice on campus.

20:1	Student-to-Faculty Ratio
78%	Freshman Retention Rate
25%	Four-Year Graduation Rate
74%	Financial Aid Applicants Receiving Aid

Students Speak Out
SAFETY & SECURITY

Q "**The biggest danger is being glared at by wallflower frat boys** whilst wooing their ladies on the dance floor."

Q "**As a woman, I feel safe on campus**, even at night. It's pretty well lit, and there are help buttons on certain lampposts around campus."

Q "**On a scale of one (worst) to ten (best), I would say our campus is about a seven**. There are emergency phones within view wherever you are, security guards patrol campus at night, and the sidewalks are generally well lit. I've heard of a couple of attacks that occurred at night on campus, but there's only so much our university can do, and then it's up to students to be smart and take their own precautions."

STUDENT AUTHOR: To call the grounds grandmother-friendly would be an understatement. Students walk across campus at all hours of the night with few to no fears for their personal safety. The emergency intercoms dotting the sidewalks serve a primarily decorative function.

> **Questions?**
> For more inside information and survival tips, pick up College Prowler's full-length book on this school, written by an actual student! Check it out at *www.collegeprowler.com*.

Students Speak Out
ON OVERALL EXPERIENCE

Q "I could not imagine myself anywhere else. I love K-State, the town, the people, and the lifelong friends that I've made here. I visited other schools before choosing KSU, but none of them felt right, and the people were not as friendly. **I've grown here, learned here, and made friends here**, and for now I consider it my home."

Q "I can say, without a doubt, that my experience at K-State was amazing and has changed me for the better. The faculty really took an interest in me and nurtured me, making me into the person I am today. **The classes I took opened my mind to new ways of thinking**, challenging my preconceived notions and encouraging me to embrace diversity."

Q "The atmosphere is great: **Everyone is so friendly, and it's got that small-town feel**. The classes, generally, are great, and there are lots of opportunities to get involved and pursue activities that interest you. I've met so many great people and had a great educational experience."

Q "I chose this school because they went out of their way to make sure I was comfortable. I didn't feel like just another kid they were shuffling around campus. **They took the time to get to know me**."

STUDENT AUTHOR: You can laud it as Middle America magic, or you can write it off as institutional brainwashing, but there's no denying that Kansas State has a way of winning the hearts of its students. Not everyone is thrilled to matriculate, but by the time graduation rolls around, all but a handful of curmudgeons are smitten with the school. The welcome, the warmth, and the willingness to help are all part of what makes K-State great.

Kent State University

800 East Summit Street; Kent, OH 44242
(330) 672-3000; www.kent.edu

THE BASICS:

Acceptance Rate: 80%
Setting: Suburban
F-T Undergrads: 15,425

SAT Range: 900–1130*
Control: Public
Tuition: $15,862

Most Popular Majors: Business/Marketing, Education, Health Professions, Communication/Journalism

*of 1600

Academics	B-	Guys	B
Local Atmosphere	C+	Girls	B+
Safety & Security	A-	Athletics	C+
Computers	B	Nightlife	B
Facilities	B-	Greek Life	C+
Campus Dining	B-	Drug Scene	B
Off-Campus Dining	B	Campus Strictness	C-
Campus Housing	C+	Parking	C-
Off-Campus Housing	A-	Transportation	C-
Diversity	D+	Weather	C

Students Speak Out
ON ACADEMICS

Q "A lot of students think they're going to study every night. Don't kid yourself. **You're only going to study a day or two before a test**, so you better get used to that when you come to Kent State. If you get to know your professors and participate in class, you're going to get a better grade."

Q "I don't think there are enough classes to take in my major. **I don't feel like I have a big enough choice of classes** to take."

Q "**Don't be afraid to drop a class**, even if it's because of something that seems stupid. Dropping because you can't handle the course load will really help your GPA, and you won't have trouble finding the time to take the class again later."

Q "**I asked my friends which professors to take**, so I always get the best teachers. Though, I didn't like my foreign teacher because he was hard to understand."

STUDENT AUTHOR: **The majority of freshman classes are taught in large lecture halls, with more in-depth classes being taught in smaller, more manageable class sizes. Students really won't dive into their major classes until sophomore and junior years, after they've finished their liberal arts requirements. Many of the lower-division classes aren't too difficult, and students don't have too many problems balancing their social lives with their academic lives.**

Students Speak Out
ON LOCAL ATMOSPHERE

Q "**Kent is a quaint college town**, but the people don't really like college students. A few of the crazy drunkards give everyone a bad name. Make sure you walk around the downtown area before you graduate. It's adorable. Also, the trails by the Cuyahoga River are really awesome."

Q "I don't know how to describe Kent without using the word 'sucks.' Other than a couple of random clubs and the bar scene, **there isn't much to do in Kent**. Kids looking to have a good time should venture out to Akron or Cleveland."

Q "It's nice and quiet here, and **there is not a lot of crime**. There are a lot of local businesses that are student-friendly and sometimes offer discounts."

Q "Kent is an old city. **I wish it was more modern**. I know it's a college town, but I wish it was cleaner."

STUDENT AUTHOR: **Kent is definitely a college town, as can be seen by the groups of drunken students stumbling down Main Street at all hours of the night. Other than the action on campus and a few local bars and restaurants, there isn't a whole lot to do. From the decades of wear by college students, the city is a little rundown. Most of the necessities are within walking distance, and a campus bus is available to cart hungry students off to the grocery store or Target. Sometimes, it's nice just to take a walk during the day and absorb the old city feel of Kent.**

5 Best Things	5 Worst Things
1 The Rec	1 The weather
2 Black squirrels	2 Parking
3 The abundance of clubs	3 The football team
4 Friendly people	4 May 4
5 Student publications	5 The bus system

Students Speak Out
ON FACILITIES

Q "**The buildings on campus are hit-or-miss.** Some are really nice and clean like Mouton Hall, and some are just nasty like those in the Small Group complex."

Q "My favorite place on campus is the Rec. I always love spending time there, and it's **nicer than gyms I've seen at other campuses**."

Q "Overall, the facilities are nice. I know the classroom buildings Satterfield and Bowman have problems with air-conditioning, but most of the buildings are good. Every year, they fix up a new building. **The University is well aware of all the problems** with the facilities."

Q "The classrooms are in pretty good shape. They are in just as good of shape as any high school. The auditoriums are usually in better condition than the smaller classrooms. There aren't any buildings that are in really bad shape. The **residence hall rooms are in good condition**, but the furniture is kind of tacky."

STUDENT AUTHOR: The new buildings on campus are pretty, and the older buildings are, well, not so pretty. But most likely, you won't be in the older buildings too much anyway. The University seems to be making an effort to keep its buildings up-to-date as much as it can afford by building many new residence halls. Anything you could possibly need is sold on campus. There is a bowling alley, arcade, and bar available to students, and if you're ever bored, the Rec Center is always a great place to go with friends to swim, run, lift weights, or play racquetball.

Famous Alumni

Bertice Berry, Drew Carey (dropped out), Carol Costello, Joshua Cribbs, Ben Curtis, Antonio Gates, Matt Guerrier, Arsenio Hall

Students Speak Out
ON CAMPUS DINING

Q "Food is always available on campus. It's pretty good, if you are into greasy carbs. But **there are healthy options available**. Einstein's Bagels is in the Hub, and there are salad bars at various dining halls. Eastway always has good food. Rosie's is open 24 hours, but the line is ridiculously long at mealtimes and late at night."

Q "I think, especially since the University turned its attitude towards nutrition, that **the food is not only better, but better for you**."

Q "Let's not kid ourselves—what they serve on campus is not food. It's **the University's attempt to package tasteless crap** and market it to a college audience."

Q "The food isn't that bad. Eastway's pasta is very good, and so is the pizza. **Watch how much you eat if you have a meal plan**. An entire meal can add up and become very expensive. The Hub is a nice place to go when you're sick of the same old cafeteria food."

STUDENT AUTHOR: Though it's pricey, the food on campus really isn't as bad as it could be. There are dozens of food stands and cafeterias strategically placed throughout campus, so a meal is never more than a five-minute walk away. Kent State residents are required to be on the meal plan until the end of their sophomore year. Many upperclassmen opt out of the meal plan option and just add FlashCash money to their FlashCard. This allows your FlashCard to be used like a debit card at all the on-campus places covered by the meal plan.

Student Body

African American:	8%	Male/Female:	41/59%
Asian American:	1%	Out-of-State:	10%
Hispanic:	1%	International:	1%
Native American:	<1%	Unknown:	4%
White:	83%		

Popular Faiths: Christian groups are the most prevalent; there is also a strong Muslim presence.

Gay Pride: The gay community isn't prominent on campus, but it's definitely there. Fusion, Kent State's LGBT magazine, rated Kent State as one of the five most gay-friendly universities in Ohio.

Economic Status: The majority of students are middle class, though there are exceptions.

Students Speak Out
ON DORMS

Q "I think **the current housing situation is troubling**. There seem to be a lot of dissatisfied residents on campus, but I think that speaks to the diversity of the campus rather than the condition of the dorms."

Q "The dorms are nice. Wherever you live, your classes are pretty much a 15-minute walk, maximum. **The only dorms that are really far away is Small Group**. The Eastway dorms are called '24-hour quiet' and 'substance-free,' but that doesn't mean no one's drinking there. They're just quiet parties. It's a very nice place to live."

STUDENT AUTHOR: Unless you live in the Kent area, you'll probably be living in the dorms your first two years of college. No matter how many horror stories you hear about the dorms, you will probably enjoy your stay, even if you add one or two of your own tales to the bunch. Most of the freshmen live in Small Group, which is unofficially called "Small World." This is because the freshmen dorms are clustered together on the far end of campus and even have their own cafeteria, so in a way, it's like its own small universe.

> **Did You Know?**
> 35% of undergrads live on campus.

Students Speak Out
ON GUYS & GIRLS

Q "**Kent State is a pretty good place to meet people**, but keep an open mind, and don't expect to meet people in a 'traditional' way. The best way to find someone at Kent State is to stop looking."

Q "I think there are **a lot more attractive girls** than there are guys."

Q "If you want to hook up, then you want to get into the fraternities and sororities, which is where a bunch of single people go to mingle. If you join sports or clubs, they always have opportunities to meet people of the opposite sex. It's also nice that **the dorms are coed, so you can meet people where you live**. Most of the guys are pretty nice here, unless they're in frats."

STUDENT AUTHOR: It doesn't matter if you're into Abercrombie or Wal-Mart. It is almost impossible not to find people on campus you're attracted to. You've got your geeks, your thugs, your jocks—all kinds of people to interact with. The general sentiment on campus leans toward hookups over relationships, but that's not everyone's scene. Most students at Kent State are generally outgoing, so if you're shy and standoffish, you may find yourself in a loveless rut.

> **Traditions**
>
> **Black Squirrel Festival**
> There is live music, great food, prizes, merchandise, and a fun atmosphere throughout the entire day.
>
> **Portfolio**
> Every year, the fashion merchandising and design majors put on a fashion show called Portfolio.
>
> **Overall School Spirit**
> Though most of the sports teams are nothing to write home about, There is definitely a pro-Kent State atmosphere on campus.

Students Speak Out
ON ATHLETICS

Q "**Varsity sports aren't very popular** on campus. Basketball is well attended, but everyone knows the football team blows."

Q "I've only ever been to softball and basketball. I don't care about the sports on campus. **Some people care a little bit**, but you never hear people saying, 'I can't wait to go to the game.'"

Q "The **intramural sports like broomball are bigger than other sports on campus**. Mostly freshmen attend the football games, because they might not have anything else to do."

STUDENT AUTHOR: It is only on occasion that one of Kent State's athletic teams will have a season that really gets students excited about KSU sports, though Kent State's basketball team went to the NCAA tournament in its 2005 season. For the most part, students are generally apathetic about the various teams on campus, and they only occasionally go to sporting events for social reasons. For most students, sports excitement comes out during intramural (IM) sports. This is also a great way to meet and form a lasting bond with people.

Students Speak Out
ON DRUG SCENE

Q "There is a lot of marijuana on campus. And you only hear about a few cocaine incidents. Only small minorities of my friends use drugs—most **people's drug of choice is alcohol**."

Q "**If you want drugs, you can find them**. If you don't, you won't see them or know about them."

Q "Alcohol is the biggest 'drug' available on campus. **There are a lot of hippies here who smoke weed**. Some of my friends talk about drugs, but they don't necessarily do them on campus. The dangerous drugs aren't that big here."

STUDENT AUTHOR: **If you want to, you can go through your entire Kent State career without seeing anything worse than a cigarette. The beauty of the drug scene is that it's underground and not something you see every day. Those who use drugs know better than to flaunt them. This doesn't mean that you won't be offered them at least once at a party, or in a group of new friends. If you say you're not interested, that will most likely be the end of it.**

17:1	Student-to-Faculty Ratio
73%	Freshman Retention Rate
19%	Four-Year Graduation Rate
85%	Financial Aid Applicants Receiving Aid

Students Speak Out
SAFETY & SECURITY

Q "**I feel really safe**, even coming from a small town. I thought living in a bigger city would be dangerous, but I never feel unsafe. Use common sense, and you won't run into problems."

Q "I've always felt relatively safe on Kent State's campus. **Most areas are well-lit**, and even at 2 a.m., people are outside talking or smoking. Security patrols the dorms every night, too."

Q "Security in the dorms is good. **It's not only the personnel who are looking out for students, it's also the students themselves**. I was trying to visit one of my friends, thinking someone would randomly let me in, but the residents told me I needed a key."

STUDENT AUTHOR: **There is a strong police and security presence at Kent State, but it makes students feel safe rather than paranoid. There are blue emergency phones everywhere, and there are few, if any, crimes committed against students on campus. Students should have no worries in this department.**

Questions?

For more inside information and survival tips, pick up College Prowler's full-length book on this school, written by an actual student! Check it out at *www.collegeprowler.com*.

Students Speak Out
ON OVERALL EXPERIENCE

Q "**Sometimes, I really wish I was somewhere else**. Most times I rationalize it all, and I realize that this school has the program that I want, and it's a pretty good program at that. I could be much worse off."

Q "I almost went somewhere else, but within one semester, I absolutely loved it here. I don't think I would be nearly as happy or nearly as involved if I went somewhere else. **I am really glad I made the last-minute decision to come here**."

Q "I actually came to Kent State planning on transferring after my first year, but after I got here, I decided I didn't want to leave. It's a great campus, and it's just far enough away that I can go home for the weekend if I want. **It's a nice area, near some major cities with lots of things to do**. I'm glad I didn't transfer."

Q "I love Kent State. **I'm so happy I go here**, and I have never wished to be at another school. It's so friendly, and there are great profs, administrators, and just people in general. Everyone's just so down-to-earth."

STUDENT AUTHOR: **At the end of the day, there are very few students who would trade their college experience at Kent State for anything else. Other universities are fun to visit on the weekends, but Kent State has an atmosphere that is welcoming to students and feels like a home away from home. If you ask an alumni of Kent State about his or her college years, most will think back on them fondly, and some will even say they were the best years of their life. Year by year, Kent State is gaining more and more prestige in the university world by improving its programs and facilities.**

Kenyon College

Ransom Hall; Gambier, OH 43022
(740) 427-5000; www.kenyon.edu

THE BASICS:

Acceptance Rate: 31%
Setting: Rural
F-T Undergrads: 1,636

SAT Range: 1870–2150*
Control: Private
Tuition: $39,080

Most Popular Majors: Social Sciences, English, Health Professions, Interdisciplinary Studies, Psychology

*of 2400

Academics	A-	Guys	B-
Local Atmosphere	C+	Girls	C+
Safety & Security	A	Athletics	C
Computers	B-	Nightlife	D+
Facilities	B-	Greek Life	B-
Campus Dining	B	Drug Scene	B-
Off-Campus Dining	C	Campus Strictness	B-
Campus Housing	B	Parking	B-
Off-Campus Housing	D-	Transportation	C+
Diversity	D	Weather	C+

Students Speak Out
ON ACADEMICS

Q "I've enjoyed the majority of the classes I've taken here. The professors are knowledgeable and interested in the subject. They want you to succeed, and are generous with their time and energy in helping you reach academic goals. For the most part, I've gotten the classes I want. **Registration is very easy** and non-competitive. Professors are often willing to sign for you to enter the class, even if it's filled."

Q "Overall, **the academics are fantastic**. Kenyon students often forget that, compared to 95 percent of colleges and universities, we have great teachers, challenging courses in a wide variety of subjects, and outstanding facilities. The faculty, though, differ from department to department."

Q "Kenyon has a lot to offer. Because it is a small school and the **student-to-faculty ratio is low**, I think that in a lot of cases, the faculty and administration are willing to bend over backwards for all of the students. It is a really hard school academically."

STUDENT AUTHOR: **The traditional selling point of Kenyon College has been its English and Humanities program. However, we are expanding from our English focus. The science quad and other changes have helped to rope in a wide range of majors. History and classics also attract many students, and the anthropology and sociology majors are also very popular. Kenyon prides itself on its small classes and close student-professor relationships.**

Students Speak Out
ON LOCAL ATMOSPHERE

Q "Gambier is very cute and very pretty; Mt. Vernon is very commercialized. Kenyon's location is a positive and a negative; the quaint stuff is fun for a while, but **in the end you do crave better food and more culture**."

Q "Once you get beyond the initial 'middle of nowhere' factor, **you really begin to love the village of Gambier**. Cars stop for you, everything is really clean, and you are able to interact with other students, faculty, and residents every day just walking through. Mt. Vernon, for what it is, a place to get all life's necessities, is fine."

Q "Gambier is **very picturesque and quiet**. Mt. Vernon is a good place to get away. Mt. Vernon has all the staples like McDonald's and a Wal Mart, movie theaters, and bowling alleys, plus a pretty, historical section of town. I think Kenyon's location is a positive. If you're from a big city, it takes a little adjusting."

Q "Kenyon's **location is definitely a plus because it is gorgeous**. It's the perfect location for any student who wants to concentrate on his or her studies."

STUDENT AUTHOR: **While Kenyon students are modern, everything around them is in a time warp. Downtown Gambier is a single block long, and features a market, deli, bookstore, coffee shop, post office, bar, and a barber. If all this becomes too much to bear, there is a fair amount to do in the surrounding towns and counties.**

5 Best Things	5 Worst Things
1 The people	1 Facilities
2 The campus	2 Surrounded by cornfields
3 The professors	3 Parking
4 Great education	4 Language classes
5 Isolation of the hill	5 Isolation of the hill

Students Speak Out
ON FACILITIES

Q "We **don't necessarily need a student union** because I think that the library, Pierce, Town, and Gund Commons in any season is a fine and a good meeting point. It also adds to the uniqueness of the campus."

Q "The academic facilities, particularly in the sciences, are excellent. We have some beautiful classrooms, more historic buildings than you can shake a stick at, and several good performance spaces. The art facilities could use some work, and **while there are a few exceptional residences, student housing is fairly primitive**. The lack of a student union is not a problem. Gambier's various gathering spaces serve the purpose more than adequately."

Q "The architecture is amazing, but **the insides of the buildings aren't all that great**. I am a little bit afraid of the athletic center. I am afraid that it might take away from the role that the town now plays as a sort of a student union, as a meeting place for the students. I think that is a real problem."

STUDENT AUTHOR: **Kenyon is very proud of the fact that we have no student union. The truth is, we don't need one. The village is built around students, and the campus is not big enough for us to lose track of each other without a central meeting place. Downtown Gambier serves as the center of student life Many students are excited about the recently completed $60 million Kenyon Athletic Center, which opened up much-needed space on campus for athletics and offers a gorgeous workout room.**

Famous Alumni

Rutherford B. Hayes, Laura Hillenbrand, Allison Janney, Robert Lowell, Wendy MacLeod, Paul Newman, William Rehnquist, James Wright

Students Speak Out
ON CAMPUS DINING

Q "The 21 meal plan courtesy of Avi Foodsystems is automatically a part of the Kenyon education. The general consensus of the student body is that **the quality of the food leaves much to be desired**. It is possible to sustain oneself on the food, but gaining the Freshman 15 from the dining hall food is not a concern."

Q "Surprisingly, **I really do love the food here**. I think most college students expect to go out to eat when they go to the dining hall or something. Kenyon doesn't have tons of options sometimes, but for the most part, it's all really good."

Q "**Campus dining could be worse and seems to be improving**. The dining service managers are extremely receptive to student input and try very hard to provide for everyone and supply us with a great deal of daily options. With a little creativity, one can put together decent, healthy meals in the dining halls."

Q "It's a typical college dining service. **Not great, but not disgusting**. As far as Avi, it was good for the first few weeks, but then it got old."

STUDENT AUTHOR: **If a Kenyon student stops eating in the cafeteria, they are either going to starve or go broke within days. It is not that our food is bad. As college food goes, it is actually pretty decent. But you will get to know all the campus food options very well, very soon. That is why the school recently started an initiative to make the dining experience resemble "real food" opposed to what students have experienced in the past.**

Student Body

African American:	4%	Male/Female:	47/53%
Asian American:	5%	Out-of-State:	80%
Hispanic:	3%	International:	4%
Native American:	<1%	Unknown:	2%
White:	82%		

Popular Faiths: The school was founded as Episcopalian, and Christians are still the biggest group on campus.

Gay Pride: Most students at Kenyon are fairly tolerant in terms of homosexuality. The school recently opened a unity house.

Economic Status: The typical Kenyon is the product of a suburban upbringing and a private school.

Students Speak Out
ON DORMS

Q "There is a range of on-campus housing. We have a few beautiful dorms, mostly doubles and triples, with a few singles, which are populated primarily by frat boys and party kids. The **freshman housing is grim**, but fosters a real sense of community."

Q "No matter how nice your dorm is, **it will feel like a dungeon by the end of the first month**."

Q "The **rooms in the freshman quad are huge**. These are some of the biggest I've been in anywhere, and I did a lot of college touring. The dorms are all really nice if you want to make them nice."

STUDENT AUTHOR: In the interest of maintaining a community, Kenyon maintains a strict residential campus. Most students live on campus all four years, and in these times, the dorms function as centers of non-academic student life. Kenyon housing can be evenly divided into two categories—dorms and apartments. Freshmen all live in dorms, and they live in the same area of campus. Some of the most desirable of the upperclass apartments are the Bexley Apartments (all singles).

> **Did You Know?**
> 98% of undergrads live on campus.

Students Speak Out
ON GUYS & GIRLS

Q "People **either get engaged or hook up**. There's nothing in between. There are a lot of attractive people, but most of them are engaged."

Q "Everyone is different, but I think that since **you will be living with the same people for four years**, some people are intimidated by the fact of hooking up and having relationships early in their Kenyon career."

Q "In terms of relationships on campus, I'd say the campus is pretty divided. There are those who want random hookups, but as time goes on, often you hear stories from the same individuals over and over, and realize it's more of a 'hookup circle.' The **people who want relationships are often harder to find**."

STUDENT AUTHOR: There are a great many cuties, but genuine hotties run few and far between. As a result, ordinary and slightly-above-average looking people find it extremely easy to find dates and hookups. It is not that we are overly promiscuous, but dating tends to happen within certain social circles. Everyone knows everybody else's business, and it hard to meet someone with a clean slate if you have any kind of history on campus.

> **Traditions**
>
> **Summer Sendoff**
> The school throws Summer Sendoff in early May as a sort of last hurrah before finals begin.
>
> **Vendors on Middle Path**
> When the weather is nice, merchants will set up stands on middle path for student shoppers.
>
> **Overall School Spirit**
> Kenyon students are insanely proud of their college, but they rarely have occasion to express this. There is a great understood sense of accomplishment in going to Kenyon.

Students Speak Out
ON ATHLETICS

Q "Kenyon is **definitely not a jock school**. The typical Kenyon student is very intellectual and very interested in classes; a lot of people talk about their classes outside of the classroom. Everyone seems to think pretty strongly about everything that goes on at Kenyon. They are very conscious of the community around them, and athletics are important, but there is definitely not that much of an emphasis put on them."

Q "We excel at geeky, patrician sports like swimming, and are laughably bad at jock sports like football. With that said, a huge number of people here are active and athletic without being jocks. **Intramural sports are popular** and a lot of fun."

Q "While there are some successful programs, the majority of **Kenyon teams are mediocre**."

STUDENT AUTHOR: On a campus comprised of many talented writers, artists, and scientists, sports simply do not occupy a significant spot on the Kenyon student's agenda. About 15 to 20 percent of the school tries to recapture their high school glory by playing in one of the IM leagues.

Students Speak Out
ON DRUG SCENE

Q "**Kenyon's drugs of choice are cheap beer and Camel Lights**. There's a fair amount of pot kicking around, some hallucinogens, a spot of E here and there. It's not really a big scene at all."

Q "There is **more cocaine than I thought there would be**. I never expected it, but people say it's easier to find cocaine than marijuana."

Q "It is evident that pot has its place at Kenyon. It is difficult to gauge the percentage of active smokers, however, it is strong enough that it necessitates acknowledgement. However, it is also **very possible to avoid it entirely without shutting oneself off from campus activities**."

STUDENT AUTHOR: Surprisingly, Kenyon's remote location and general affluence have not fostered any major hard drug scene. Drugs do not come looking for you, but if you want them, they are not hard to find. Many students are casual smokers, but becoming a serious stoner would impede on one's drinking life, and no one at Kenyon wants that to happen.

10:1	Student-to-Faculty Ratio
94%	Freshman Retention Rate
85%	Four-Year Graduation Rate
89%	Financial Aid Applicants Receiving Aid

Students Speak Out
SAFETY & SECURITY

Q "I started out as a freshman feeling as if security was always out to get me. Whether or not I was throwing a party in my room or going to a party, I always felt as if they were the enemy. As I have gone on and now am a senior, I appreciate their role; I realize they are not out to get us. They have done a lot for the school, and **at least 90 percent of the time, they care about the good of the students**."

Q "The **campus at large is very safe**, and although lighting is a concern, most girls, I believe, feel comfortable walking alone at night."

Q "Safety and security's role is to hassle students and to occasionally provide a helpful service. **They are a presence**."

STUDENT AUTHOR: Kenyon is about as non-threatening as a school can get. Dorms and academic buildings stay unlocked, and people leave their backpacks unattended for hours at the library. Security is there mostly as party monitors. They check to make sure underage students aren't drinking.

Questions?
For more inside information and survival tips, pick up College Prowler's full-length book on this school, written by an actual student! Check it out at *www.collegeprowler.com*.

Students Speak Out
ON OVERALL EXPERIENCE

Q "Kenyon has poisoned me forever. I desperately want to get on with my life and I never, ever want to leave. **This place is perfect and deeply dysfunctional**. It is not in any way shape or form like real life, and why should it be? It's college."

Q "If you had told me in the winter of my senior year of high school that I would be spending my college years in Gambier, Ohio, I would have questioned your sanity. In truth, **the three years have met the cliché as the best of my life**."

Q "**Kenyon's a place where all the smart but quirky kids from high school came**. We like to learn for learning's sake, but we also like to have fun. We play sports, we sing a cappella, we star-gaze, and we play ultimate Frisbee. There's definitely something to be said for 1,600 kids who want to spend four years in the middle of nowhere."

Q "The best part about the Kenyon experience is the feeling that you get from being there—a feeling that is not quantifiable, and requires a first-hand knowledge of the place to understand. It is not merely one aspect of community, but rather the sum of many things that contribute to this **feeling of comfort and warmth that Kenyon seems to exude**."

STUDENT AUTHOR: Kenyon casts a spell on everyone that passes through it—all the things that might initially make it sound unappealing are, in the end, what make the place so special. Everyone at Kenyon is there for the simple reason that they want to be. They have not come for the glamour of a big city, and they have not come because of an Ivy-league name to drop at parties. They have chosen Kenyon in spite of all its deficiencies.

La Roche College

9000 Babcock Boulevard; Pittsburgh, PA 15237
(412) 367-9300; www.laroche.edu

THE BASICS:

Acceptance Rate: 57%
Setting: Suburban
F-T Undergrads: 1,139

SAT Range: 800–1030*
Control: Private
Tuition: $20,938

Most Popular Majors: Business, Architecture, Visual/
Performing Arts, Education, Health Professions

*of 1600

Academics	B	Guys	B+
Local Atmosphere	B+	Girls	B
Safety & Security	B-	Athletics	D+
Computers	C	Nightlife	B
Facilities	B+	Greek Life	N/A
Campus Dining	D	Drug Scene	A-
Off-Campus Dining	B+	Campus Strictness	A
Campus Housing	A-	Parking	C
Off-Campus Housing	C	Transportation	C-
Diversity	B-	Weather	C+

Students Speak Out
ON ACADEMICS

Q "The teachers here tend to encourage their students to reach their goals. **They will go to any length to help their students** achieve anything they want."

Q "It's not hard to get into La Roche. They'll let anyone in so they get money. Really, **things only get difficult junior year**."

Q "For the most part, I feel like I'm being well prepared for prospective jobs. There is a variety of classes, which allows students to be more well-rounded. In addition, all the professors are really willing to help students out with internships and networking. **The fact that the school is small aids in helping students** prepare for the future."

Q "The professors are **the main reason to go to La Roche College**. They're excellent and well-diversified."

Q "Sometimes I feel like I'm not challenging myself with my major and my classes. I don't know if they're too easy or if I'm just **not making the most of my opportunities**."

STUDENT AUTHOR: The professors at La Roche are generally friendly and very helpful, and they provide an inviting atmosphere conducive to the learning process. Many are highly active in their specialties outside the classroom as well. At a small school like La Roche, there is a lot of potential for any student, regardless of ability and previous experience. The professors make sure that no student is left behind or forgotten.

Students Speak Out
ON LOCAL ATMOSPHERE

Q "If you are not from Pittsburgh, it's harder to bond and become friends with people here. However, they are nice and friendly and **always willing to show you the cool places** in the city."

Q "**Unless you have a car and are 21 or older, you're out of luck** in regard to things to do around here. There aren't any other universities present unless you go into downtown Pittsburgh."

Q "Everyone on campus is very friendly. You can ask anyone for directions or help, and they'll always help you. People **always hold doors open** for others, too."

Q "The atmosphere here is **really quiet and sometimes boring**. There are no other universities or colleges near La Roche, but I can honestly say I feel really safe here."

Q "**The atmosphere in this town is very relaxed**. There are a few other universities nearby like Duquesne, Point Park, and Pitt."

STUDENT AUTHOR: La Roche is located approximately 20 minutes from downtown Pittsburgh in a suburban area. Access to entertainment is much easier for students with cars. If you do not have a car, the off-campus entertainment options are hard to get to due to the lack of public transportation in this section of the Pittsburgh area. Once you get to the heart of Pittsburgh, there is a large number of bars, clubs, and coffeehouses, which provide excellent places to mix and mingle with other people from the area.

5 Best Things
1. Small campus
2. Semi-private bathrooms
3. The bookstore
4. Close to Pittsburgh
5. The Booze Cruise

5 Worst Things
1. Long wait for public safety
2. Lighting in parking lots
3. Poor public transportation
4. High tuition
5. Long wait for maintenance

Students Speak Out
ON FACILITIES

Q "**The library is the best facility on campus**. We have an inter-library loan system with other local colleges, so you can always find what you need."

Q "It's always **too hot or too cold** in the classrooms. The jocks are always in the gym, so you cant really use it. Classrooms are okay, until the heat or air goes out."

Q "The gym is really nice. If the weight room is ever too crowded, there's **a workout room in the basement of Bold** that students can use, too. It's nice because it's not overpopulated by the baseball team."

Q "Most of the facilities are pretty nice, but I hold the utilities such as air conditioning and heat in question. The transition in climate really **screws with comfort level**."

Q "Most of the facilities on campus aren't that nice. Many things don't work, and **when one thing gets fixed, something else breaks**."

STUDENT AUTHOR: Since La Roche is a relatively new institution, the facilities are all fairly modern. The residence halls are kept clean, even over the summers. The library is in good condition, but the lack of updated books makes it less appealing to students in search of information. The gymnasium is in excellent condition and has new locker rooms. The major complaint students have about the facilities is that they are not open during hours that accommodate some people's schedules. But aside from this, the students seem to be extremely satisfied with the facilities and buildings on this beautiful, suburban campus.

Famous Alumni

Dr. Yvonne Hennigan, Angela Longo, Dr. Marija Vrlijic

Students Speak Out
ON CAMPUS DINING

Q "The food is pretty horrible in the cafeteria, but that's kind of expected at a college dining hall. The Red Hawk Café isn't bad, but **there's only so much of that stuff you can eat in a week**."

Q "The cafeteria can be good or bad, depending on what they're serving for the day. **They make some dishes better than others**."

Q "**Wraps are the only edible items** to eat. The food in the cafeteria is crappy. It's never good for the entire day. If lunch is good, then dinner will be horrible."

Q "Food on the weekend is limited and gross. Thanksgiving is the best here, and **desserts are awesome**. The caf can be easy to avoid sometimes, but you need to eat somewhere in order to survive."

Q "The food in the caf is hit or miss. Some days it's really good, and **some days you're stuck with cereal for dinner**."

STUDENT AUTHOR: While many colleges offer a variety of dining halls and eateries, La Roche offers only two—Cantellops Dining Hall (aka the cafeteria) and Red Hawk Café. In general, the food is not well received. Many resident students go grocery shopping every week and eat the bulk of their meals in their dorm rooms. Most commuter students don't even bother paying for a meal plan and either just eat at home or pay to eat at off-campus restaurants. The consensus? LRC's food is not worth the more than $1,000 students pay per semester.

Student Body

African American:	5%	Male/Female:	33/67%
Asian American:	1%	Out-of-State:	13%
Hispanic:	1%	International:	11%
Native American:	1%	Unknown:	7%
White:	74%		

Popular Faiths: Protestant, Roman Catholic.

Gay Pride: There are no current organizations or clubs for homosexual students. They are present, but homosexual students here are not excessively active for gay rights.

Economic Status: Most of La Roche's students come from upper- to lower-middle-class homes. Twenty-five percent of undergrads receive Pell grants.

Students Speak Out
ON DORMS

Q "My only complaint about the dorms is that the walls are too thin. **You can hear everything that goes on in the room next door**—and I do mean everything."

Q "The dorms are easily the best thing about La Roche. Every room has a bathroom, so you'll **never have to worry about shower shoes** or that dirty kid down the hall from you."

Q "Most of the people leave their doors open, so **it's easy to make friends** with people in your hall. No matter what time of day or night it is, someone will always be up and walking around the dorms."

STUDENT AUTHOR: **A college dorm usually conjures up an image of a small, cramped cinder-block room. La Roche's dorm rooms break that mold. They are spacious, fully furnished, carpeted, and equipped with private bathrooms and plenty of closet space. There is a "no sex on campus" policy instituted due to the College's Roman Catholic affiliation, and students of the opposite sex are not allowed in one another's rooms after 2 a.m. But not many people get caught breaking this rule.**

> **Did You Know?**
> 36% of undergrads live on campus.

Students Speak Out
ON GUYS & GIRLS

Q "Guys—let's see: You have the jocks, who are all jerks; the designers, who are all gay; and the IT guys, who are all nerds. **That leaves about five dateable guys**, and guess what! They're taken."

Q "Never date a guy who plays an organized sport—and basically **that's all the guys** here."

Q "There are a few really pretty girls and a few really handsome guys. **Everyone else is just kind of plain.**"

Q "**The girls at La Roche seem to spend more time trying to out-do the other girls** than they do trying to get good grades or achieving something worthwhile."

STUDENT AUTHOR: **Physically, there are the exceptional few on both ends of the spectrum, but generally speaking, students here are just average people. What seems to truly separate the genders at La Roche is personality. In general, the girls seem to think they are better than everyone else. La Roche guys, on the other hand, seem to have a better concept of what it means to accept people for who they are on the inside.**

> **Traditions**
>
> **The Booze Cruise**
> Each fall semester, La Roche hosts a dance cruise on the Gateway Clipper Fleet that is affectionately called the Booze Cruise.
>
> **The Spring Fling**
> Much like the Booze Cruise, the Spring Fling is a dance held by La Roche at a local hotel each spring.
>
> **Overall School Spirit**
> The words "school spirit" hardly exist at La Roche, but students do like to wear La Roche T-shirts and hoodies from the bookstore to class.

Students Speak Out
ON ATHLETICS

Q "We need a football team at La Roche. I think it would make the school more well-known and **would attract more students**. On the other hand, though, the athletics that are here are pretty good."

Q "Games aren't usually that crowded, but they're fun. The teams are pretty good, and **admission is free**."

Q "Intramural sports aren't advertised—if we even have any here."

Q "Wait a second—**do we actually have sports teams at La Roche**? Wow, you learn something new every day!"

STUDENT AUTHOR: **Athletics at La Roche are not well followed by the majority of the student body. This could be because there isn't a football team at La Roche, which is frowned upon in a city where football is the most prevalent sport. Or perhaps it is because there is little or no advertisement of the sporting events on campus. However, students who do attend games usually have a good time. Admission is free, and the most of the teams are pretty good.**

Students Speak Out
ON DRUG SCENE

Q "**Marijuana is the only drug strongly present** on the La Roche campus. Alcohol is much more popular among the students."

Q "Very few students experiment with drugs. The majority of students are **smarter than that**. I think you'll have a few druggies at every college, though."

Q "Most students here are smart enough not to get caught up in the drug scene. If you do get caught with drugs, **the penalties are outrageous**."

STUDENT AUTHOR: La Roche has a very low-profile drug scene, and while some students say they smoke pot, it's rarely done on campus. And on the rare occasion they do smoke, it's usually in an obscure place at night without any lighting. Alcohol is much more prevalent at La Roche, and it's rare to hear of students here getting caught doing drugs. The majority of students here seem to lead drug-free lives, making the drug scene the least of college officials' worries.

12:1	Student-to-Faculty Ratio
66%	Freshman Retention Rate
43%	Four-Year Graduation Rate
99%	Financial Aid Applicants Receiving Aid

Students Speak Out
SAFETY & SECURITY

Q "La Roche is a very safe place, which is a good thing because **our security guards are slow to respond to calls**."

Q "I think students feel safe here. I do. Nothing bad ever really happens. Since everyone knows everyone else's business, **it's hard to get away with things**."

Q "The security guards do nothing but smoke outside the dorms and drive around looking for cars to put tickets on. If you call them for an actual problem, **it takes them 20 minutes to get there**."

Q "**No one has died**, and nothing has hit major news, so I think our campus is pretty safe."

STUDENT AUTHOR: La Roche prides itself on the fact that it was voted one of the safest four-year colleges in the United States by a CAP Index study. The crime scene at LRC seems to be almost nonexistent. The major problem with safety here lies in the officers' lack of enthusiasm when responding to students' calls.

Questions?
For more inside information and survival tips, pick up College Prowler's full-length book on this school, written by an actual student! Check it out at www.collegeprowler.com.

Students Speak Out
ON OVERALL EXPERIENCE

Q "You are able to be a **big fish in a small pond**. The teachers and faculty know you by name and will write you a letter of recommendation if you need one. This is a huge benefit that you don't have at some other colleges."

Q "I'm confident in the education and experience that has been offered to me here. As the chair of the Young Conservatives Club at La Roche, I feel that **I will be recognized for my efforts** both by the school and future prospects."

Q "I'm glad I picked La Roche. If I would have gone to school somewhere else, I wouldn't have met **all of my best friends** at La Roche."

Q "I love the small community atmosphere of this school. **Teachers are always there for you**, and you never get lost in a mass of nameless faces."

Q "I like that **my teachers know my name**. They know what sports I play, and they care about my grades. That's really nice."

Q "The only bad side to La Roche College is that **it is way too expensive**."

STUDENT AUTHOR: La Roche is a small campus, but it has plenty of resources. With a library full of books and a spacious student union area, there's something for everyone. The teachers and students here have a very personal connection, and everybody knows your name. To most students, this is what their ideal college is all about. However, La Roche is very expensive and doesn't offer many of the things that larger schools have—Greek life, an on-campus health clinic, 24-hour dining services, and campus bars and restaurants to name a few—which turns a lot of people away from this beautiful campus.

Lafayette College

118 Marlde Hall; Easton, PA 18042
(610) 330-5000; www.lafayette.edu

THE BASICS:

Acceptance Rate: 37%
SAT Range: 1200–1380*
Setting: Rural
Control: Private
F-T Undergrads: 2,346
Tuition: $33,811

Most Popular Majors: Economics, Political Science, Engineering, Psychology

*of 1600

Academics	B+	Guys	B+
Local Atmosphere	C-	Girls	B+
Safety & Security	B+	Athletics	B-
Computers	B	Nightlife	C
Facilities	B+	Greek Life	A-
Campus Dining	C	Drug Scene	B-
Off-Campus Dining	B	Campus Strictness	B-
Campus Housing	B+	Parking	D+
Off-Campus Housing	C-	Transportation	D
Diversity	D+	Weather	C+

Students Speak Out
ON ACADEMICS

Q "The professors that I've met are terrific one-on-one, but this has no bearing on their ability to lecture. If you're smart, **don't worry about 8 a.m. intro classes**—you'll get plenty of sleep."

Q "The professors are **my favorite part of Lafayette**. Most of them are easy to talk to and really make an effort to get to know you. I have learned so much from them outside of the classroom; it's amazing."

Q "A great aspect of Lafayette professors is that many of them **care about a student's life** outside of the classroom. I cannot even count the number of times professors have asked me how other classes are going, what is new with extracurricular activities, and everything else; professors care more about the students than their grades."

Q "I have had my share of great teachers and bad teachers. Fortunately, at Lafayette, you can have access to teacher evaluations before you pick your classes, and your peers are normally very good at pegging amazing professors and ones that are **not as stellar**."

STUDENT AUTHOR: One of Lafayette's greatest strengths is its eclectic range of subject matter. From Film and Literature, to Invertebrate Studies, to Principles of Studio Art, Lafayette's plethora of interesting classes definitely makes registration difficult. Another of the college's strengths lies in the excellent student-to-professor ratio. This is a main reason why professor/student relationships flourish here.

Students Speak Out
ON LOCAL ATMOSPHERE

Q "The 'city' of Easton hardly deserves the name. There isn't much that happens, especially if you don't have a car. No other universities and not even a movie theater! **Good Thai food**, though."

Q "Easton isn't terribly exciting, but **it isn't a dump or in the boonies**, either. Lafayette itself is actually in more of the residential part of Easton, and as for town-college relations, it seems that the town and the college sort of keep to themselves. There doesn't seem to be a terrible amount of interaction, save for the community outreach groups on campus."

Q "Easton is **cute at best**, and a harmless dump at worst. The Crayola Factory and Two River Landing Museum are fun, and State Theater is right around the corner and brings in some pretty high-profile acts. There are also a few coffee shops, and recently, some new restaurants have been added. The rest of the city is pretty dumpy, but I would not say that it is unsafe."

Q "The atmosphere is rather strained. There is a big difference between life on the hill and life off the hill. It would be good for students to see the rest of Easton, but many don't leave '**the bubble**.'"

STUDENT AUTHOR: Easton, an old steel town, is definitely nothing to write home about. Most of the time, one that lives on the Hill tends to stay on the Hill. That's the problem with Easton, it does not reach out to its most valuable visitors—Lafayette College students. Easton lacks a certain spark, and it is not cut out to be a college town.

Students Speak Out
ON CAMPUS DINING

Q "For someone trying to eat healthy, the food is pretty bad. Basically, healthy options consist of **salad and more salad**."

Q "The food isn't nearly as bad as I thought it would be. Gilbert's and downstairs Farinon are my personal favorites. **Get the grilled cheese**! The dining halls are never horrible, but some nights are better than others, depending on what they are serving."

Q "The food is okay. However, it is extremely expensive if you do not have a meal plan (just flex). **Gilbert's is a great spot** for meeting friends and getting late-night food."

Q "Food on campus is relatively good. I was pleasantly surprised. Though the food is decent, there aren't many options. **Marquis is the best option** for a dining hall. They always have a lot of variety, and the quality of the food seems better than it does anywhere else."

Q "On-campus food is uniformly mediocre and repetitive. **Get off the meal plan** (tip: say you're vegan, and you'll get off with no penalty)."

STUDENT AUTHOR: **Lafayette food—what is there to say? After four years of it, students were ready to return to more appetizing options. There are two main dining halls, Marquis and Farinon which are buffet-style, and the food is incredibly repetitive and not that appetizing. "Upstairs Farinon," as upperclassmen like to call it, is boring except for the "fro yo" (frozen yogurt), which is always a nice treat and a Lafayette staple.**

Students Speak Out
ON FACILITIES

Q "The gym is an **excellent state-of-the-art facility**, and Farinon is a comfortable atmosphere for studying, relaxing, and meeting with friends."

Q "There are a lot of buildings and facilities on campus that are new, and if the buildings themselves aren't new, they're being renovated from the inside out. **The student center is great**, the sports center is amazing, and most of the classrooms are equipped with the latest gadgets and gizmos."

Q "The facilities are probably the best aspect of this campus. **Most of the buildings are new**, and most of the ones that aren't are in the process of being redone. The athletic center is the nicest and most modern that I have seen at any other college campus. It has so much to offer, and it's free (except rock climbing)! There are more than enough computers available to students to use whenever they need to, which is a huge convenience if yours is 'out of order.'"

Q "The school **doesn't play around with their money**; they really put a lot of time, money, and energy into the construction and renovation of a lot of the buildings. Kirby gymnasium is my utmost favorite—take one look at the architecture, and you'll see why."

STUDENT AUTHOR: **The campus prides itself on being modern, and it does not disappoint. Almost every month in recent years, a building has been renovated, or a new site was being planned to break ground. As stated, Skillman Library was completely renovated. It is a striking beauty on campus—glass windows, new computers, and a Tiffany window donated by the Class of '04.**

Famous Alumni

Stephen Crane, Joseph F. Crater, Haldan K. Hartline, Philip S. Hench, Dominique Lapierre, Joel Silver

Student Body

African American:	5%	Male/Female:	52/48%
Asian American:	3%	Out-of-State:	70%
Hispanic:	5%	International:	6%
Native American:	<1%	Unknown:	0%
White:	82%		

Popular Faiths: Although the Jewish population is relatively small (12 percent), the Hillel Society is the most active and well-known religious group.

Gay Pride: With groups like QuEST (Questioning Established Sexual Taboos), there are outlets for gay and straight students, alike, to voice opinions.

Economic Status: LC students are generally all white, upper-middle class, and most are from NJ, NY, or PA.

Students Speak Out
ON DORMS

Q "Some of the dorms are really nice, and **some are kind of sketchy**. The dorms that are really nice are South, Keefe, and Easton Hall."

Q "For first-year students, the best dorms are South College and Ruef Hall. They are big, so you have the potential of meeting great friends that you will know throughout college. South has a reputation for being **loud but fun**, and it also has air-conditioning. Ruef is generally more quiet because of the shape of the dorm, and it has individual walk-in closets that gives you a space of your own while you adjust to life with a roommate. I keep wishing I still had mine!"

Q "Guys, not worried about living only with guys? Kirby Hall is the best dorm on campus with its marble floors, **gorgeous study with piano**, and suite living."

STUDENT AUTHOR: The residence halls at Lafayette are more than decent for a small college. One of the best things about Lafayette is their guarantee of on-campus housing for all four years, which is something not many other schools provide. After acceptance, first-year students are given the choice of where to live.

Did You Know?
96% of undergrads live on campus.

Students Speak Out
ON GUYS & GIRLS

Q "There are a lot of great people on this campus who don't go along with the **usual flock of sheep**. The girls who wear less than three designer accessories are generally very nice."

Q "When looking for schools, I was looking, however subconsciously, for places that felt familiar. That being said, the people at this school are a lot like people I went to high school with. On the whole, these are people that I get along with: people with a sense of humor, a brain, a sense of dedication and responsibility, and a burning desire to do lots of crazy things like **karaoke, bake-offs, and dance parties**."

Q "Guys can be summed up like this: Abercrombie, **Abercrombie, Abercrombie**. Girls can be summed up like this: Tiffany's, Tiffany's, Tiffany's."

STUDENT AUTHOR: Lafayette College can definitely be considered somewhat of a "meat market." Not only are the academic buildings and facilities aesthetically pleasing, but the students who grace their halls are equally beautiful. People should come to Lafayette expecting that they will be somewhat intimidated by the opposite sex at first (actually, even members of your own sex can be quite intimidating, to say the least).

Traditions

100 Nights/1000 Nights
These are two semi-formal dances sponsored by the college. Freshmen attend 1000 Nights on campus; seniors pay $40 to attend 100 Nights off campus at a banquet hall with open bar—great fun!

Dance Marathon
An all-night dance contest in which organizations and other Greek houses participate.

Overall School Spirit
It's lacking when it comes to athletics, but it's evident that students have pride for LC by all the clothing.

Students Speak Out
ON ATHLETICS

Q "**Sports are really big**. Sometimes, I feel like I might just be the only person on campus that isn't an athlete. I still take classes at the gym to make up for it, though."

Q "Sports are pretty big on campus. A lot of students participate in sports on all levels. Since we are such a small Division I school, that means a large percentage of students do participate in varsity sports. IM sports are a lot of fun, and they range from **basketball to bowling**."

Q "Varsity sports seem to be big here at times, especially football around **Lehigh-Lafayette weekend** and homecoming. As for IM sports, I really have no idea."

Q "IM sports are quite common; varsity sports, a bit less so. **Games aren't very well attended** because the playing fields are far away."

STUDENT AUTHOR: Sports at Lafayette are a mixed bag. We are in the Patriot League competing with Lehigh, Holy Cross, Bucknell, and others. Varsity sports are popular; basketball and football are the largest teams, but lack much student attendance for home games—another sign of student apathy.

Students Speak Out
ON DRUG SCENE

Q "As on most college campuses, a number of students **indulge in all types of drugs**. I dislike this aspect of campus life, but I have not let it affect my experience."

Q "**Leopards like to booze**, and we will ingest anything alcoholic. Enough people smoke marijuana that if you want your fix, you can simply walk down the hall in any dorm and inhale. Cocaine, on the other hand, is rare."

Q "The **drug scene is pretty popular at Lafayette** because of boredom. Easton offers very little to entertain college students, and Public Safety is pretty stringent about busting up parties, so disgruntled students turn to drugs and vandalism."

STUDENT AUTHOR: At Lafayette, weekends revolve around alcohol and partying. As said before, we work hard and play hard, and at the end of the week, our bottles of vodka and rum are put to good use. As for hard drugs, pot is definitely on campus, and if you want it, you will get it. Cocaine is here, but behind the scenes.

11:1	Student-to-Faculty Ratio
93%	Freshman Retention Rate
88%	Four-Year Graduation Rate
90%	Financial Aid Applicants Receiving Aid

Students Speak Out
SAFETY & SECURITY

Q "The campus is pretty safe compared to most. Public Safety is **constantly patrolling the campus** and local off-campus housing areas."

Q "Lafayette is safe! Security, I am sure, is responsible and **equipped to handle an emergency**, but my experience is that they are too preoccupied with busting kids for alcohol."

Q "To be honest, I don't think I have really ever felt scared or nervous walking around campus by myself, even at night. The campus isn't all that large, and there are dormitories nearby, as well as stores that could provide shelter for someone who is in need of help. In addition, student government has just provided **more lampposts for the students** to ensure a safer campus."

STUDENT AUTHOR: Public Safety, as an entity, is kind of a catch-22 on campus. Many students criticize the department for administering too many parking tickets, busting fraternity parties, and driving around campus in their "$36,000 SUVs." However, Public Safety is available 24 hours a day, seven days a week, and provides a free escort service.

> **Questions?**
> For more inside information and survival tips, pick up College Prowler's full-length book on this school, written by an actual student! Check it out at *www.collegeprowler.com.*

Students Speak Out
ON OVERALL EXPERIENCE

Q "I think if I went to a larger school, I might be having an even better time, but **Lafayette is excellent** for its academics, teaching staff, location . . . and campus."

Q "I would not have changed my decision for the world. Because the school is so small, you make so many friends, which could be a good or bad thing. The experience here has made me who I am today, and **I feel confident** with entering the 'real world' next year."

Q "**The academics are great here**, but the rest is lacking. It would be nice to be in a larger town."

Q "My overall experience so far has been a positive one. I think Lafayette has a lot to offer. There is so much to get involved in on campus, and the academics are really strong. Overall, the people are nice, and there is a lot of fun to be had. Though the school might feel too small at times, it does have a really nice **sense of community** that really makes you feel like you are a part of it. I think the size of the school helps a great deal in the transition from high school. The school really does cater to your needs, and it makes living away from home that much easier."

STUDENT AUTHOR: For the Leopards who take the time to meet people, and dive into their academics, Lafayette can be a very rewarding place. One of the best qualities of the college is its community atmosphere; in certain aspects, it is definitely like a family. Students support one another, and spend almost every waking moment together. Sure there are problems, and sure no one is happy 100 percent of the time, but Lafayette College definitely allows for growth of the individual.

Lawrence University

East College Avenue; Appleton, WI 54912
(920) 832-7000; www.lawrence.edu

THE BASICS:

Acceptance Rate: 59%
Setting: Small city
F-T Undergrads: 1,442

SAT Range: 1810–2130*
Control: Private
Tuition: $33,006

Most Popular Majors: Visual/Performing Arts, Social Sciences, Biology, Foreign Languages, English

*of 2400

Academics	A-	Guys	C
Local Atmosphere	C+	Girls	C
Safety & Security	A	Athletics	C+
Computers	B	Nightlife	C+
Facilities	B-	Greek Life	B-
Campus Dining	C+	Drug Scene	B+
Off-Campus Dining	A	Campus Strictness	A
Campus Housing	A	Parking	D+
Off-Campus Housing	D-	Transportation	C-
Diversity	B-	Weather	C

Students Speak Out
ON ACADEMICS

Q "I find most of my classes to be quite interesting. Lawrence is good about letting you take things when you want, so **you don't need to do all your gen-eds right away**, allowing for more fun classes that are tailored to your major."

Q "I have found, for the most part, that the teachers are pretty helpful, obviously some more than others. **Most of the professors I have had are extremely accessible** and willing to help their students. I have found a majority of my classes to be very interesting and intellectually stimulating."

Q "Lawrence is what you make of it, but the fact that the staff and faculty are so great really helps. I think that the professors are extremely knowledgeable, very well educated, approachable, willing to help, and accessible. I would say that **the students are very hard working and academically driven** as a whole."

Q "Teachers can go two ways: nice and friendly and will help you with anything or don't seem to notice that you are working hard. Either way, all of **the professors at Lawrence are very intelligent and experienced**."

STUDENT AUTHOR: **Students do not come to Lawrence thinking they can slack on their studies. Whether they are athletes, frat guys, or total burnouts, they study. With such small classes, professors will notice when students skip class, but more importantly, the size allows professors to know each of their students on a personal level.**

Students Speak Out
ON LOCAL ATMOSPHERE

Q "Residents of Appleton seem to have a lot of respect for the school. People in Wisconsin are generally very friendly. It's a safe, quiet place to go to school, which parents love, but **that can get boring for students**."

Q "The town itself isn't great. There are things to do, but **most of them are within driving distance**, not walking distance."

Q "Appleton is a really safe town, and the restaurants are great. There are many choices for dinners and dates. Appleton is generally supportive of Lawrence, but I often feel that Lawrence is more of a supporter of Appleton. At times, **Lawrence is also like a bubble inside of Appleton**. Not a whole lot goes on between them other than the bars."

Q "The town is one of the safest towns in the United States. **We hardly have to worry about robbery or other dangers**. We are located on College Avenue with cute coffee shops and many great bars. There could be more to do, but considering the size of Appleton, we're getting a good deal."

STUDENT AUTHOR: **Appleton may not be a cosmopolitan destination, but the area is unique and has its own endearing qualities that Lawrence students soon come to appreciate. Appleton is a blend of Midwest charm and suburban blasé. College Avenue offers a strip of unique shops, but if it gets too stifling for you, Madison is only a short drive away.**

5 Best Things	5 Worst Things
1 Professors	1 Appleton
2 Convocations	2 Size
3 Conservatory	3 Winters
4 Free concerts	4 Parking
5 Community	5 Public transportation

Students Speak Out
ON FACILITIES

Q "For the most part, the facilities are really nice, especially compared to a lot of other schools I have visited. It also seems that **the school is constantly trying to improve** and update the facilities to better serve the students."

Q "The facilities on campus are all kept up nicely. The union has a coffeehouse, dining area, and **large room for group meetings or special occasions**. The Center for Teaching and Learning is a wonderful resource on campus where students can go to get help on their schoolwork from their peers."

Q "The facilities are continually getting better. They aren't great, but at least the school is working on improving everything. **The library has improved drastically since my freshman year**."

Q "**Most facilities are very nice, well maintained, and clean**. The rec center is especially nice now that new equipment has been added."

Q "I find the facilities comfortable. **They're clean and resourceful**, and they're nice whether I'm studying, talking, eating, or just hanging out."

STUDENT AUTHOR: The average reaction to facilities on campus is that they are satisfactory. They serve their purposes and fit the school, but only for now. The school population increases every year, but the school doesn't seem to keep up. Lawrence is a very old school, so some of the buildings stand a little sub-par, but others are extraordinary. Much of the campus has been newly rebuilt, or is in the renovation process, so campus facilities are quickly improving.

Famous Alumni

Dale Duesing, Ashely Haase, Jeffrey Jones, Terry Moran, David Mulford, Alice Peacock, Campbell Scott

Students Speak Out
ON CAMPUS DINING

Q "The food on campus is fine. I've always found something to eat that I enjoy, but **more options would be nice**. By the end of the year, I was sick of eating Mexican food and pasta, which were common occurrences at Downer."

Q "The food on campus is **probably the only real complaint I have about Lawrence**, but even that isn't a huge problem. Although there isn't as much variety as I'd like to have, the food isn't terrible, and usually the campus grill can make a good substitute if the food at Downer is bad."

Q "Lucinda's seems to be more of the favorite cafeteria because it has more of a restaurant-style buffet where you don't have a tray and can actually **feel like you're enjoying a nice lunch with friends**."

Q "The food is mediocre but easy to get used to. **Our dining halls conveniently offer vegan and vegetarian meals**, as well as a salad bar."

Q "**Eating out starts to become regular** around here, especially toward the end of the term when you can't stand going to Downer anymore."

STUDENT AUTHOR: Meal plans are mandatory, so mealtime is an inescapable event for the entire campus. There are two dining halls on campus, only one of which is open for all three meals. There are always vegetarian and vegan options, butmost students complain about the odd choices. Food is not something students at Lawrence look forward to, but they gain favorite dishes (and weight) as their standards lower with time.

Student Body

African American:	2%	Male/Female:	46/54%
Asian American:	3%	Out-of-State:	61%
Hispanic:	2%	International:	8%
Native American:	<1%	Unknown:	10%
White:	75%		

Popular Faiths: There is a Christian group and a Jewish group, but neither is substantial on campus.

Gay Pride: The gay community on campus is pretty sizable, and the campus is extremely welcoming.

Economic Status: Lawrence students cover a large range of economic backgrounds, but they do not seem to lean toward the wealthy like at many other private schools.

Students Speak Out
ON DORMS

Q "The dorms at Lawrence are way bigger than dorms at other colleges. **Each has a unique history and unique characteristics** that fit a variety of personalities."

Q "Freshman dorms are definitely the way to go when you are starting out at school, as the **upperclassmen tend to be more secluded**. Trever is very open, and there are always people doing things. If you're more into studying, pick Kohler, but on a campus this size, it really doesn't matter where you live."

Q "I don't have a problem with any of the dorms. Hiett and Sage are definitely the best. All of them have positives and negatives, but **it's nice to have everyone on campus**."

STUDENT AUTHOR: **Mandatory on-campus housing for students can seem stifling, but it does preserve the home-away-from-home sentiment. If dorm life isn't for you, after freshman year there is an option of living in small theme houses. These houses have a much more personal atmosphere (and a full kitchen). Otherwise, the upperclassmen dorms also offer apartment-style living in a dorm setting.**

Did You Know?
89% of undergrads live on campus.

Students Speak Out
ON GUYS & GIRLS

Q "Most of the guys are very amiable—and big sweethearts. It's probably half hot, half not-so-hot. Most of the girls are very nice, too. Everyone is **eager to get to know one another** and very generous with their time and friendship."

Q "Let's be honest. Neither sex is putting its best foot forward at this school. But, if you do find someone who is physically attractive, there is no doubt **they also have a personality to back it up**, especially at this school. That's what makes both genders worthwhile at Lawrence—they have more to offer than their appearance."

Q "If you're asocial person, **hookups seem to happen more often** than finding actual lasting relationships."

STUDENT AUTHOR: **One would think that putting mature, well-educated college students together would spawn deep, long-lasting relationships, but not here. Most students would likely say they are too busy for a serious relationship. With life at such a fast pace, relationships tend to be short-lived and cursory. Be prepared to don the "Lawrence goggles"—suddenly intellect and talent will strangely overshadow a person's attractiveness.**

Traditions

The Nipple of Knowledge
Students climb up to the top of the original Lawrence building to sign their name in paint on what is designated as the Nipple of Knowledge.

Trivia Week
Founded in 1966, the "World's Largest Trivia Contest" is an annual trivia extravaganza that lasts 24 hours a day for three days.

Overall School Spirit
A winning sports team at Lawrence is rare, so school spirit tends to be uncommon as well.

Students Speak Out
ON ATHLETICS

Q "As a Division III school, **sports aren't that big**, but everyone usually goes to the games, which are fun. Hockey and basketball are probably the most popular spectator sports at Lawrence."

Q "Varsity sports aren't huge, but you do know all of the athletes at the school. It's cool to go to class and meet some pretty talented kids who can old their own academically, too. Intramural sports are pretty big. **Most of the people playing do it for exercise and fun**, so the competition is light, but it's a blast."

Q "There are **lots of classes or intramural sports** you can sign up for at the rec center, and many people take advantage of the chance to meet more people and do more activities."

STUDENT AUTHOR: **It's not a good sign for the athletic department when most students don't know what the school mascot is, but this is a Division III school, so sports aren't extremely serious anyway. Varsity, club, or intramural sports can be as serious as you want them to be. Most use them as a break from the rigor of academia but do not consider them a bigger priority.**

Students Speak Out
ON DRUG SCENE

Q "Students, for the most part, control themselves on campus. **Alcohol has a strong presence on campus**, like at any college, but if a student prefers not to drink, it is not looked down upon."

Q "There is little to no pressure to do drugs or drink alcohol. People respect others' choices, and if you don't feel comfortable in a situation, people usually respect that and **try to make sure that you are comfortable**, or you can leave without being questioned."

Q "Like most places, you get your groups of people that do drugs. **Lots of people smoke pot** at Lawrence. Some do a bit more than pot."

STUDENT AUTHOR: **Like on most campuses, alcohol consumption is everywhere at Lawrence. Drinking is kept to responsible levels, and problems from people drinking excessively are almost unheard of. In terms of other drugs, marijuana is widespread and available, but it's not a threatening force to non-smokers. Harder drugs are on campus, but most students remain oblivious to them.**

9:1	Student-to-Faculty Ratio
90%	Freshman Retention Rate
63%	Four-Year Graduation Rate
94%	Financial Aid Applicants Receiving Aid

Students Speak Out
SAFETY & SECURITY

Q "The security people will be there for you whenever you need them. As far as safety goes, **you will run into your fair share of drunken people**, but they're friendly."

Q "Since our campus is so small and intimate, everyone knows everyone, and **people will watch your back** if they see you getting into a confrontation. If you need a ride or feel unsafe, our security is always dependable."

Q "The security and safety on campus is great. There are never any huge security problems, so the **presence of security guards on campus** is always easy-going. They also maintain comfortable relationships with students on campus."

STUDENT AUTHOR: **Security is not a campus department that students fear. Students instead look forward to running into the guards, even on the weekends. Completely approachable, security guards maintain a comfortable atmosphere on campus and lively, friendly relationships with students.**

> **Questions?**
> For more inside information and survival tips, pick up College Prowler's full-length book on this school, written by an actual student! Check it out at *www.collegeprowler.com*.

Students Speak Out
ON OVERALL EXPERIENCE

Q "I really love Lawrence. The students are smart and talented. I think **everyone leaves feeling like they made great friends**, not to mention received a great education."

Q "At times I have wished that I went to a bigger school, but then I realize that the **small classes and individualized attention** teachers can give at a small school is extremely rewarding."

Q "I am really happy at school. I have found some great friends and had great experiences. There have been difficult times, and at times I wished I were somewhere bigger or somewhere easier, but really **I wouldn't change anything about my experience so far**."

Q "I absolutely love Lawrence. The students, staff, and faculty are amazing! I can't imagine going anywhere else. **I can't wait to go back in the fall!**"

Q "My time here has been awesome. As long as you **have a healthy relationship with your adviser** and listen to his advice, classes will be beneficial. If there isn't a specific class offered, you can do a tutorial or internship under a professor that has knowledge in that area of interest."

STUDENT AUTHOR: **it is easy for students to complain about the school they attend. Lawrence has a unique environment, and it has its oddities and drawbacks, but most students can't imagine being anywhere else. The opportunities in both the college and the conservatory are exceptional, and a student can achieve as much he or she aspires for. So the food is terrible, the town is dull, and your wild party fantasies may remain unfulfilled—it's all part of the school the students love to hate and hate to love.**

Lehigh University

27 Memorial Drive; Bethlehem, PA 18015
(610) 758-3708; www.lehigh.edu

THE BASICS:

Acceptance Rate: 28%
Setting: Small city
F-T Undergrads: 4,825

SAT Range: 1240–1390*
Control: Private
Tuition: $37,250

Most Popular Majors: Business/Marketing, Engineering, Social Sciences, Psychology, Biology

*of 1600

Academics	B+	Guys	B+
Local Atmosphere	C	Girls	B-
Safety & Security	C+	Athletics	B+
Computers	B+	Nightlife	C+
Facilities	B+	Greek Life	A
Campus Dining	B	Drug Scene	B
Off-Campus Dining	B+	Campus Strictness	C+
Campus Housing	B-	Parking	D
Off-Campus Housing	B	Transportation	C
Diversity	D	Weather	C+

Students Speak Out
ON ACADEMICS

Q "The teachers are mostly accommodating to your individual needs, but don't expect to learn everything in class; stress is put on home study time. **Class can occasionally be interesting**, unless it is an upper-level business class."

Q "The teachers' abilities and interest in their classes depends on the type of class, as well as their interest in it. I have found that being in the business school, very few of the teachers there provide interesting and **thought-provoking classes**. However, when the teacher is an outside professional and just teaches for fun, they provide a wonderful classroom environment."

Q "Most of the teachers are **pretty approachable** and easy to talk to—especially in smaller classes. I think most of my classes are pretty interesting, once you get past the distribution requirements."

Q "One constant I have found about the teachers at Lehigh is that they all care about their students doing well and are always willing to help. Most teachers have office hours and many go above and beyond by answering e-mails and even **talking to students on the phone**."

STUDENT AUTHOR: Students agree that, when it comes to Lehigh's academics, if the professor makes the class interesting, the student will become much more fascinated by the subject. Students in the business schools tend to complain more often about boring classes, while liberal arts students seem more likely to praise their professors. A professor's passion for the subject really makes all the difference.

Students Speak Out
ON LOCAL ATMOSPHERE

Q "I wouldn't walk around town—**it's very unsafe**. There's a nicer part of Bethlehem, but it's not within walking distance, which makes it very hard to get to."

Q "The town of Bethlehem is very **centered around Lehigh** and its students. The other residents are hardly involved in our daily lives, but the businesses and restaurants depend heavily on their Lehigh business. The fact that Gold Plus is now accepted virtually everywhere in town is wonderful."

Q "Bethlehem is **relatively boring** and fails to provide the students with extracurricular activities. On top of that, the people living in the town generally do not get along with the students. There are two other universities present in the town and they come and hang out at Lehigh, occasionally. Things to stay away from are some of the bars and the townies."

Q "The restaurants are good if you know where to go. **The town is worse than Jersey**, and there is little interaction with other colleges. There is stuff to visit within a relatively close distance like Dorney Park and the Crayola factory."

STUDENT AUTHOR: It's no secret that Bethlehem isn't exactly NYC, but changes over the last few years have improved the economy—most notably on the south side, near campus. The north side, historic Bethlehem, is five minutes from campus by car. A stroll down Main Street can make you feel like you're in a completely different era, with the old-fashioned sidewalks and storefronts.

5 Best Things	5 Worst Things
1 Greek life	1 Local cops
2 Playing Beirut	2 Parking tickets
3 Good friends	3 Bethlehem winters
4 Frat parties	4 Sporadic weather
5 Tailgates	5 Bethlehem

Students Speak Out
ON FACILITIES

Q "The facilities are very nice on campus, although the gym could use a refurbishing and some more equipment. **The gym is adequate** for a good workout, but it could be better."

Q "The facilities are nice and constantly being improved. The computers are all fast and contain almost all programs a student at Lehigh could need. The student center is also **very inviting for freshmen** and upperclassmen to meet each other."

Q "The facilities are awesome on campus, except for our gym. The computer labs and student centers are **easily accessible** and provide comfort and security. But the gym at our school totally sucks."

Q "The gym for non-athletes isn't that nice, but the **athletic facilities are beautiful**. All of the other student resource centers on campus are good."

Q "Well, if you are on the football or wrestling team, the athletic facilities are pretty good. Otherwise, be prepared to wait through long lines and **overcrowded facilities**."

STUDENT AUTHOR: There aren't many complaints about Lehigh's facilities, save for the gym. The gym is one of the most crowded facilities on campus, but the students feel it's in serious need of an upgrade. Most of the cardiovascular machines are old, and the stationary machines are outdated, not to mention there aren't nearly enough stations. Lehigh's other facilities are quite nice; the University Center is a beautiful building, and its dining hall is the largest and most popular.

Famous Alumni

Robert Durst, Terry Hart, Al Holbert, Lee Iacocca, Donny Most, Joe Perella, Tucker Quayle

Students Speak Out
ON CAMPUS DINING

Q "The dining halls aren't too bad on campus, but a lot of Lehigh off-campus eateries now take **Lehigh's GoldPlus**, which is a huge benefit to students. I'd recommend Pastaficio or Subversions on campus."

Q "I don't like the food in the dining halls at all. Although, once you join a sorority or fraternity, you **have your own kitchen** so you have a lot more variety in what you can make."

Q "Food on campus is good. The hotspots are **Pandini's and Subversions**. Also, GoldPlus is accepted at a lot of restaurants located right off campus, so many people eat at those places, too."

Q "The food is decent in the dining halls, and the school has opened up some new eating facilities on campus which are actually quite good, like the Cup, an **ice cream parlor**."

Q "Freshman year, I ate at the Cort Student Restaurant all the time and thought it was fantastic, until I had real food again and **realized how bad it actually was**. Sophomore year, I ate at Rathbone religiously because I was on the volleyball team. The salad bar is amazing."

STUDENT AUTHOR: Most students agree that both the University Center and Rathbone dining halls effectively get the job done, but as you move past freshman year, you will seldom eat at on-campus facilities. Those students who join fraternity and sororities will have a cook. There is also a food court above the UC dining hall which houses two atrocious eateries, one Chinese, and the other Mexican.

Student Body

African American:	3%	Male/Female:	59/41%
Asian American:	6%	Out-of-State:	75%
Hispanic:	5%	International:	3%
Native American:	<1%	Unknown:	9%
White:	74%		

Popular Faiths: Catholicism and Judaism. Many students attend church at Packer Chapel on Sundays, or synagogue on holy days.

Gay Pride: The campus is accepting of the gay community, but you wouldn't know it by looking at the students.

Economic Status: Lehigh students generally come from a lot of money. Lehigh may as well adopt Audi's A4 as the official school car.

Students Speak Out
ON DORMS

Q "**Dorms are all pretty similar**, but the most social dorm always seems to be M&M. Stay away from Lower Cents, it has a long walk to nightlife."

Q "Since they changed the dorm selection policy, there aren't really any 'cool' dorms, which is a lot better for the freshmen to meet each other. All the dorms I've been in are nice—**definitely not disgusting or old**."

Q "The dorms are okay. I would say that the dorms in the quad (**Drinker, Dravo and Richards**) are the best options. The rooms in M&M are really tiny, and Lower Cents isn't near anything else."

STUDENT AUTHOR: **It seems that freshmen have fond feelings for whichever dorm they wind up in. M&M has been the most popular freshman dorm. Despite its outdated furniture and small rooms, its close proximity to the Hill makes it the number one choice of many incoming students. Lower Cents has seen a dramatic increase in popularity over the last few years, due to its status as the newest dormitory, which also offers the only floor of coed housing and the easiest walk to classes. After freshman year, many sophomores will move into the fraternity and sorority houses.**

> **Did You Know?**
> 69% of undergrads live on campus.

Students Speak Out
ON GUYS & GIRLS

Q "I think the guys are hotter than the girls. I'm sure there are many hot girls who I've never met, but on the whole, I think there are a lot **more attractive men than women**."

Q "Every year, fraternity guys get really excited because the new freshmen come up to their houses, because after freshman year, many girls tend to gain weight. We're not a 'hot' school, but there's a fair share of **really attractive people**."

Q "Lehigh is a **very** good-looking campus."

Q "The guys are mostly East Coast preppy frat guys—**polo shirts, flip-flops, and beer cases**. They know how to party and are always happy to invite girls over to share their booze. On the whole, they're not bad."

STUDENT AUTHOR: **Let's get one thing straight: Lehigh is a very good-looking campus. The guys are mostly pretty boys and preppies. Guys are a little more reluctant to call the girls hot, but the hesitation is borne out of many girls' personalities. While there are a lot of chill, fun girls, the hotter ones tend to be very bitchy and either already have boyfriends or some kind of borderline personality disorder, or both. In short, some girls here can be childish.**

Traditions

Fraternity Rush
The time during which freshmen interested in going Greek must decide which house fits them best.

Lehigh-Lafayette Football Game
The oldest rivalry in college sports, the Lehigh-Lafayette football game is a true classic. This weekend sees more alumni return than any other weekend throughout the entire year.

Overall School Spirit
Lehigh's school spirit comes out at random occasions, but on the whole, you'd find most students to be fairly apathetic about school spirit, in general.

Students Speak Out
ON ATHLETICS

Q "**Varsity sports are big**, but I think it's great that the athletes are just like everyone else when they're in class and when people go out."

Q "Varsity sports are pretty big on campus given the small student body. **Football games tend to be huge** (tailgates), and basketball and wrestling get a good showing, also. IM sports are participated in by every fraternity and freshman halls, so you can imagine the intensity."

Q "Varsity football is almost half as big as the **tailgate parties** preceding it. Most people are too drunk by 12:00 in the afternoon to attend the games. The other sports do not get too many spectators, though."

STUDENT AUTHOR: **Lehigh's greatest athletic tradition is waking up at 8 a.m. on Saturday mornings and getting wasted before home football games. Kidding aside, morning cocktails and tailgates are some of the most popular events during the whole school year. Few attend the actual football game, which is unfortunate. Wrestling is the other insanely popular sport at Lehigh, although it's more revered by alumni and the town of Bethlehem.**

Students Speak Out
ON DRUG SCENE

Q "I wouldn't say there's a huge drug scene, but **every type of drug** you could possibly think of is at Lehigh. If that's not your thing, it's very easy to not be around drugs."

Q "I like drugs, especially marijuana and mushrooms. You can find anything you want on campus. I've actually **never run into heroin**, but I'm sure some kids did it."

Q "The scene is smaller than at most schools, I think. You have the standards: **marijuana and a bit of cocaine**. You probably see more prescription pain killers than anything else. Study drugs, like Adderall, are also around."

STUDENT AUTHOR: Many students will experiment with drugs at some point or another (if they haven't already). That being said, Lehigh's drug scene is really no more prevalent than at any other school. Pot is almost always available as long as you know the right people, although the police are far more attuned to the drug scene that many students realize. There has been a significant number of drug-related arrests over the past few years.

9:1	Student-to-Faculty Ratio
93%	Freshman Retention Rate
72%	Four-Year Graduation Rate
77%	Financial Aid Applicants Receiving Aid

Students Speak Out
SAFETY & SECURITY

Q "I've always heard of violence on campus, but in four years, I've never seen anything besides the normal **fraternity-against-fraternity fight**."

Q "On campus, the security and safety is above average. **I feel safe walking anywhere** on campus by myself, day or at night. There are always cops, and it is a very safe place."

Q "There is a lot of security on campus. There are bike cops, brownies, and cop cars. There is also the **T.R.A.C.S. van service** which takes kids on and off the Hill. I would not walk alone at night, but I wouldn't do that anywhere. Also, I do feel safer on campus then directly off campus. Some parts of this town are shady. However, compared to New York, or some parts of Jersey, it's cool."

STUDENT AUTHOR: Lehigh students feel incredibly safe on campus, and in certain cases, the police can seem almost too overbearing. Off campus is where the problem lies. The areas immediately surrounding campus aren't terrible, but a few blocks either east or west of campus can be considered somewhat dangerous, especially at night.

Questions?
For more inside information and survival tips, pick up College Prowler's full-length book on this school, written by an actual student! Check it out at www.collegeprowler.com.

Students Speak Out
ON OVERALL EXPERIENCE

Q "It's the best school ever. **Join the Greek system** and you're guaranteed to make the most of college. I wouldn't want to be anywhere else."

Q "People always talk about how great it used to be, but I had a crazy four years that I wouldn't trade for anything. My only complaint would be the size of the student body. If I change anything, I'd bring some more people there because after awhile **everyone knows your business**, and you need to find girls in the weirdest places."

Q "I wish I went to school in Los Angeles or someplace **a bit more exciting** than Bethlehem, PA."

Q "There's something about this school that you **just can't put into words**. Walking to class in the winter with the town of Bethlehem opening up underneath you, trudging up a steep hill at four in the morning with a Natty Ice in your hand, or just watching TV with your best friends in the frat house—I wouldn't change anything. Also, the academics are just as solid as many other good schools."

STUDENT AUTHOR: There's nothing quite like being an undergrad at Lehigh University. There's a reason why many people call college "the best four years of your life," and that statement applies to Lehigh perfectly. It may not be in the greatest town in the world—the winters can be harsh, and the student body is incredibly homogenous, but Lehigh students love their school. The professors are mostly knowledgeable and friendly, and academics play a huge role in any college student's experience, but the friendships forged and the outstanding social life are what make Lehigh students fall head over heels.

Lewis & Clark College

0615 SW Palatine Road, Portland, OR 97219
(503) 768-7188; www.lclark.edu

THE BASICS:

Acceptance Rate: 56%
Setting: Urban
F-T Undergrads: 1,952

SAT Range: 1790–2060*
Control: Private
Tuition: $33,490

Most Popular Majors: Social Sciences, Psychology, Biological/Biomedical Sciences, Foreign Language

*of 2400

Academics	B	Guys	C
Local Atmosphere	B+	Girls	C+
Safety & Security	A-	Athletics	D+
Computers	B	Nightlife	B+
Facilities	B-	Greek Life	N/A
Campus Dining	B-	Drug Scene	B
Off-Campus Dining	A-	Campus Strictness	A-
Campus Housing	B	Parking	C
Off-Campus Housing	B-	Transportation	A
Diversity	D+	Weather	B-

Students Speak Out
ON ACADEMICS

Q "The teachers, for the most part, are phenomenal. The same is true with the classes. A good majority of them are **very interesting**."

Q "Some of the teachers assign too much work. It actually makes you learn a lot if you can keep up. But if you fall behind, catching up seems impossible, and you stop learning. Sometimes, **you have to drop a class** if one of your teachers assigns an insane amount of work."

Q "The professors at LC are dedicated to their fields, committed to **high-quality teaching**, and successful in providing thought-provoking, insightful classes. I find most of my classes very interesting."

Q "My teachers have so much knowledge crammed into their brains that I'm surprised their heads don't explode. This can be a good and bad trait. **Classes are interesting**, but sometimes the professor will go on a tangent and will have to be pulled back to the day's theme."

STUDENT AUTHOR: **Don't be fooled by LC's stereotype as a stoner school. The academics here are demanding. Teachers seem to be enthused about their subjects and are more than willing to help students outside of class. The teachers here require you to think outside of the box. The core course that freshmen must take, Inventing America, is a weak point. Teachers from different areas of study teach this course. Depending on the teacher, it can be a great introduction to college or a boring waste of time.**

Students Speak Out
ON LOCAL ATMOSPHERE

Q "Portland is a phenomenal city. The atmosphere is **totally welcoming to college students**. The city is eclectic, anyone would fit in here. Visit the zoo—it rocks!"

Q "Portland is a fabulous town. Lewis & Clark is isolated enough to have a gorgeous, forested campus, but close enough to the city to be only minutes away from a vibrant nightlife, great restaurants, fun attractions, a good music scene, and then some. In addition, it's a perfect location from which to **explore the Northwest**."

Q "If you come to Portland, the Japanese Garden is a must-see. It's gorgeous! Plus, all the different neighborhoods are just waiting to be explored. **The Pearl District is artsy**, Hawthorne has a more bohemian feel, and sophisticated Nob Hill is a great place to window shop."

Q "Lewis & Clark's immediate vicinity is a big disappointment. Burlingame, or 'Boringame,' has a few shops and a supermarket, but **if you want a cool atmosphere** or are looking for a place to eat when you're up late studying, you'll need to venture out farther."

STUDENT AUTHOR: **While Portland is a phenomenal city, LC's immediate vicinity is a sleepy suburban area, and you need wheels to get anywhere. Portland's neighborhoods range from bohemian and grungy Hawthorne, to the artsy and upscale Pearl District. There are great coffee shops, excellent bakeries, and prime second-hand shops. There are also forests and beaches nearby.**

5 Best Things
1 Great professors
2 Beautiful campus
3 Study abroad
4 Library hours
5 Pioneer Express

5 Worst Things
1 Summer-camp feel
2 The grapevine
3 Guy-to-girl ratio
4 Weather
5 Campus food

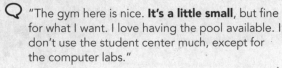

Students Speak Out
ON FACILITIES

Q "The gym here is nice. **It's a little small**, but fine for what I want. I love having the pool available. I don't use the student center much, except for the computer labs."

Q "Generally, the facilities are nice. **The student center is confusing and dim**, but it's in the process of being rebuilt. The library has huge windows, which makes it very pretty, but also really cold at night."

Q "**Athletic facilities are so-so**, but then again they aren't a priority on campus. The student center is functional but bland. It is the outdoors that makes the campus beautiful."

Q "The facilities here are **pretty nice** and always improving. The student center leaves something to be desired, but there are plans to spruce it up. The same goes for the athletic facilities."

Q "The facilities at LC are all **fairly average** compared to the surrounding universities, but many LC students don't utilize them as much as they should."

STUDENT AUTHOR: **The facilities on campus are functional and well kept. The newer buildings are well designed and environmentally friendly, while the older ones are a bit dilapidated. The student center is criticized for its non-central locations, but it serves its purpose. Templeton Student Center is home to the two dining halls, the mailroom, a computer lab, the Student Health Center and the student club offices. Pamplin Sports Center is a fine facility for the size of this campus, and the track is great, but usually empty.**

Famous Alumni

Earl Blumenauer, Serena Cruz, Monica Lewinsky, Markie Post, Kim Stafford, William Stafford

Students Speak Out
ON CAMPUS DINING

Q "Well, **the dining hall has good food**, but they serve the same thing everyday! After a while, you don't care what you eat or where you go, so long as you don't have to eat hard pizza."

Q "Food here is good, but it's **getting progressively worse**. There's great variety, including plentiful vegan and vegetarian options. The Trail Room is great for meals, and Maggie's is great, too. They're catered by the same company, though, so the food is similar."

Q "The food at LC, overall, is okay. In the Bon (the dining hall) there's always a vegetarian-vegan option, which is usually your best bet for quality food. **LC gets Noah's Bagels**, which is so awesome! The baked goods are decent, but stay away from the beans."

Q "I was impressed by Bon food overall, especially on special occasions like finals brunch. **They go all out**, and you can get anything from crepes to sushi. I think LC students who complain about the Bon are spoiled."

STUDENT AUTHOR: **If you have a meal plan, you pretty much have to eat in the Bon (Fields Dining Room) for most meals because you can only use flex points in the Trail Room, Maggie's, and Dovecote. This can be restricting because the Bon is only open during certain hours, and sometimes it's tough to juggle the hours with your classes. On the bright side, it is all-you-can-eat. However, that can be problematic when it comes to the Freshman 15. Bon Appetit, overall, does a fine job at LC!**

Student Body

African American:	1%	Male/Female:	39/61%
Asian American:	5%	Out-of-State:	78%
Hispanic:	4%	International:	4%
Native American:	1%	Unknown:	0%
White:	85%		

Popular Faiths: There are some Christians, but you have to look hard to find religious students.

Gay Pride: The campus is very accepting of its gay students and the on-campus group, Unisex, is very active and visible on campus.

Economic Status: There seems to be an abundance of snobby rich kids milling around, despite LC's many generous financial aid programs.

Students Speak Out
ON DORMS

Q "**Odell is top-of-the-line**, but you don't want to live in the projects (Platt) if you can help it."

Q "The dorms vary, but are mostly pretty good. Akin has big rooms and walk-in closets, but there's **a ghost in the lower bathroom**. Forest used to be office buildings, and it definitely shows. If you hate bunk-beds, Stewart, Odell, or Akin are your best bets."

Q "Copeland is definitely more of a party dorm. **Stewart and Odell are quiet**, but have really nice rooms. Personally, I like Forest and Platt-Howard for a mix of fun and privacy."

Q "**I love it at Platt-Howard**. VAPA rules (Visual and Performing Arts floor). Avoid Copeland at all costs; it's confusing."

STUDENT AUTHOR: While the not-so-originally named Apartments are the nicest on-campus housing, the other dorms each have their own charm. Akin, Odell, and Stewart all have large rooms with moveable furniture, but the biggest perk is their central location. Copeland is huge and mazelike, but the social scene and community atmosphere is great.

Did You Know?
70% of undergrads live on campus.

Students Speak Out
ON GUYS & GIRLS

Q "I just realized that all the guys I've hooked up with play Dungeons & Dragons. I don't know if that reflects poorly on me or on **the sad guy population** at LC."

Q "There aren't too many muscle-bound jock types walking around, so if that's your cup of tea, then this wouldn't be the school for you. In regards to girls, most of them are really **down to earth**, which is great. They are beautiful because most of them are very comfortable with who they are."

Q "Most of the people here are super-fit and outdoorsy, and yes, there is the 'non-bathing' contingent. You have everything from scary, vaguely nervous-looking RPGers to **tan gorgeous Hawaiian girls**."

STUDENT AUTHOR: While LC has more than its share of nerdy types, most students are fairly attractive. The earthy, natural look is in, which is both good—most girls don't wear layers of makeup and overprocess their hair—and bad—some people don't smell very fresh. Maybe the main problem is the shortage of athletic students. They tend to be preppy, but there are very few and they get snatched up within weeks of the school year starting.

Traditions

Lu'au
Held annually, this colorful festival of costume, food, and dance celebrates native Polynesian culture.

Naked Mile
In April, daring students run a mile around campus to celebrate being comfortable with their bodies.

Overall School Spirit
Most students here seem proud to go to LC. School sweatshirts are commonly worn on campus, and activities like Casino Night and the Lu'au are well-attended by students.

Students Speak Out
ON ATHLETICS

Q "If you're looking for a school that gets all wild and crazy and **tailgates every weekend**, you might want to look elsewhere."

Q "Varsity sports aren't huge here, especially among students who don't participate, but they do have a following. **Crew is pretty popular**. IM sports seem even bigger, but I wish there was a better IM girls soccer opportunity."

Q "Sports here are not a main focus of the students. However, there are **plenty of casual club sports**, which are fun, but not very competitive."

Q "Sports are not pervasive, but they are there if you want them. **Most students play pick-up games** rather than varsity sports because academics are important."

STUDENT AUTHOR: Athletics are not a focus at LC. Rowing, or crew, is the most popular sport. This alone sums up the overall significance of athletics here. While Lewis & Clark's Division III sports are important to students who play them, none of the sports have much of a following. IMs are played sparingly, even by those who choose to participate in them.

Students Speak Out
ON DRUG SCENE

Q "**Drugs are around**. If you're into drugs, you'll find them. If you're not, then they're not that hard to avoid."

Q "I'm happy to say that there are **no hardcore drugs here on campus**. I'm not into drugs, so I may be a little biased, but that's one of the reasons I chose Lewis & Clark. It's not a big party school. Pretty much the only thing you'll find here is pot. It seems to be the drug of choice."

Q "If you are someone who is really sensitive to smoke, you won't have to worry because it is required that smokers stay **at least 25 feet** from any building on campus."

STUDENT AUTHOR: It is a well-known fact throughout the West Coast that marijuana is very popular at LC. However, there are many students who don't smoke pot and there isn't a problem with peer pressure. It's not like students are offered drugs in the library or anything like that. The school seems to be doing their best to recruit new students with cleaner backgrounds when it comes to drug use.

12:1	Student-to-Faculty Ratio
88%	Freshman Retention Rate
59%	Four-Year Graduation Rate
81%	Financial Aid Applicants Receiving Aid

Students Speak Out
SAFETY & SECURITY

Q "For the most part I feel safe, but campus safety leaves a lot to be desired. **Don't walk alone at night** and you should be fine."

Q "Lewis & Clark serves as a kind of **protective bubble**. I have never felt safer on any of the campuses I've visited. Everyone here, including girls, feels comfortable walking back from the library at three in the morning by themselves. This is definitely something that can't be said for all colleges."

Q "I've taken the safety issue for granted here until I recently visited a big university in Washington where you need keys to get into the bathrooms because **they have had incidents** of strange men walking in while girls are taking showers and assaulting them."

STUDENT AUTHOR: There is very little crime around campus, so students feel safe enough to walk around alone during all hours of the night. The lack of crime could be attributed to the mostly female population (there just isn't enough testosterone to cause problems) or the fact that LC is in a laid-back suburban area.

> **Questions?**
> For more inside information and survival tips, pick up College Prowler's full-length book on this school, written by an actual student! Check it out at *www.collegeprowler.com*.

Students Speak Out
ON OVERALL EXPERIENCE

Q "I transferred to LC and have been very happy with the move. Both the academic atmosphere and the social environment are interesting and exciting. **The classes are very challenging** but provide excellent training for further education or the workplace. Overall, I feel extremely lucky to be an LC student."

Q "Academically, Lewis & Clark has been much more stimulating than I had expected— challenging, despite the laid-back atmosphere. Most students seem **genuinely passionate about learning**, while others seem content to do the bare minimum while their parents drop huge amounts of money on tuition."

Q "The social scene is fairly suffocating here. Living off campus is an entirely different scene, but on campus, if you get drunk and hook up with someone, **you're bound to bump into them** everyday in the dining hall."

Q "I missed the community feel of Lewis & Clark. I liked being able to walk around campus and recognize people. It made me feel more grounded. Also, at Lewis & Clark, **I never felt like just another face** in the crowd. I never felt lost or invisible. I had been so afraid before entering college that I would just become another number, but that is definitely not the case at Lewis & Clark."

STUDENT AUTHOR: Lewis & Clark has a lot to offer, but it depends on the student's motivation and ability to work hard. Some students just sail by with average grades, living it up and smoking up a lot, without really challenging themselves. However, there are many students who are very active and make the most of the opportunities that are available.

Louisiana State University

156 Thomas Boyd Hall; Baton Rouge, LA 70803
(225) 578-3202; www.lsu.edu

THE BASICS:

Acceptance Rate: 73%
Setting: Urban
F-T Undergrads: 21,811

SAT Range: 1530–1890*
Control: Public
Tuition: $11,281

Most Popular Majors: Business/Marketing, Education, Biology, Liberal Arts, Social Sciences

*of 2400

Academics	B-	Guys	A-
Local Atmosphere	B+	Girls	A
Safety & Security	B-	Athletics	A+
Computers	A-	Nightlife	A+
Facilities	B	Greek Life	A-
Campus Dining	B	Drug Scene	C+
Off-Campus Dining	A-	Campus Strictness	B
Campus Housing	C+	Parking	D-
Off-Campus Housing	B-	Transportation	C-
Diversity	C-	Weather	B

Students Speak Out
ON ACADEMICS

Q "The **teachers are like the bars** in Baton Rouge—a few good ones, a whole lot of bad ones."

Q "I've had maybe one or two teachers that I really like. Most of them are **either foreign or extremely prejudice** and just don't know how to teach whatsoever. The classes for my major tend to be much more interesting than the general education classes I have to take; those are awful."

Q "If you want a small school, LSU is not for you. The lecture classes are a pure representation of it. It is very hard to be in **a class with 300–375 students**. As hard as the University tries, it becomes apparent in these lecture classes that you are truly just a number in a massive university."

Q "If you take the opportunity to seek their assistance, nine times out of ten [professors] are delighted to help. I've had the occasional language barrier issue with a foreign language teacher, but usually, **as long as they see you putting forth effort** to understand and do your best, they're lenient about basic cultural and linguistic differences."

STUDENT AUTHOR: **LSU has always been a school whose reputation for raucous partying and great athletics precede its academic standing. And in a school with over 30,000 students in all different fields of study, it's hard to feel like your personal education matters that much to anyone.**

Students Speak Out
ON LOCAL ATMOSPHERE

Q "Baton Rouge is **one of the best places to go to college**. Everyone is really laid-back, and there is always something fun to do. The night life is great, there are great bars and live music playing just about every weekend."

Q "This is a college town. We have shirts that say '**Baton Rouge: A Drinking Town with A Football Problem**,' and they ain't kidding. The entire town revolves around LSU and football games in the fall. Southern University is across town, but they don't really count."

Q "I'd watch out when leaving campus, because **directly off campus is ghetto**—only for about 10 or so minutes, afterwards, you're clear."

Q "It's pretty laid-back down here. **This place isn't exactly Harvard**, so there are always people sunbathing at the nearest swimming pool or drainage ditch hammering away at case of beer at noon time."

STUDENT AUTHOR: **From hints of French snuck into conversation, cooking and architecture, Baton Rouge is different from other places above the Mason-Dixon line. The city adores LSU, and almost everyone here is a Tiger fan. Everyone is relaxed and friendly, from downtown capitol workers to those in the immediate areas outside of campus. The entire town has the vibe of a laid-back college atmosphere. Football games and LSU news are just as crucial to the adults living in the area as to the LSU students themselves.**

<table>
<tr><td>

5 Best Things

1 Football season
2 Party atmosphere
3 Attractive coeds
4 Walking the lakes
5 The size

</td><td>

5 Worst Things

1 The size
2 Parking on campus
3 Pollen in the spring
4 Scheduling classes
5 Waiting for CATS bus

</td></tr>
</table>

Students Speak Out
ON FACILITIES

Q "**Anything having to do with the athletes is new and nice**; the rest is falling apart and real old. Some of the classrooms are underground and have pipes going through the halls that are low enough to hit your head on."

Q "The facilities are very good, **some buildings are older and not as nice**, but overall, they are good. But I still wouldn't go and lick the bathroom floor."

Q "All of the facilities are very nice especially the Rec Center. There are plenty of machines, **even a swimming pool**. There are racquetball courts and weights. The computer labs are also very nice."

Q "**Computers are good**—brand new pretty much. I don't find anything wrong with the Union, other than a lack of quiet areas for studying. Bathrooms are usually pretty nasty."

Q "The Union is pretty nice, **aside from the retro décor**. The food selection is fairly decent, and there are lots of rooms for meetings and open areas for studying or socializing."

STUDENT AUTHOR: Students said it, athletic facilities are top-of-the-line. From Tiger Stadium to the Rec, students can't argue with the high-quality equipment and constant maintenance these areas receive. But there is plenty outside of athletic facilities at LSU. LSU architecture with its Italian Renaissance style gives the campus a gorgeous overall appearance, and the many nationally-recognized buildings make LSU a work of art.

Famous Alumni

Elizabeth Ashley, Billy Cannon, Bill Conti, Pete "Pistol" Maravich, Shaquille O'Neal, Rex Reed, Stephen Stills, Y.A. Title, Joanne Woodward

---

Students Speak Out
ON CAMPUS DINING

Q "If you can, eat at the Pentagon dining unit, that's **where the athletes eat** and their food is always better. Highland cafeteria is okay, too."

Q "Dining halls are pretty decent, you can almost have anything you want there, its pretty diverse. **The Union has the best food**, but the most fattening foods so if you don't want to gain the Freshman 15, stay away from there."

Q "There are too many **good restaurants near campus** for people to continue eating on campus."

Q "When I was a freshman, I tried not to eat in the dining halls because there didn't seem to be much healthy food to pick from. **There's always something fried**, and there's an ice cream machine."

Q "**Food is decent on campus**. I wouldn't make a daily living off of campus food, but if you're hungry and don't have anything to eat it serves its purpose."

STUDENT AUTHOR: Several students would rather talk the brisk five or ten minute walk of campus to restaurants in the North Gate area, as opposed to eating from campus dining options. However LSU dining is not something to run screaming from. Most students can find something to fill their hungry bellies for a reasonable price. Both the Pentagon and Highland dining halls offer a wide variety of meal options for those looking to use their dining meals. Though it may be cafeteria food, it's a little more advanced than your high school's offerings.

Student Body

African American:	9%	Male/Female:	49/51%
Asian American:	3%	Out-of-State:	14%
Hispanic:	3%	International:	2%
Native American:	<1%	Unknown:	2%
White:	81%		

Popular Faiths: There are a slew of Christian groups, and several churches are located on campus.

Gay Pride: The campus gay community takes an active part in ensuring that other LSU students learn to be more accepting of the gay community.

Economic Status: LSU has students from every economic background.

Students Speak Out
ON DORMS

Q "**The dorms are pretty fun**, towards the end of the second semester, the only thing you want to do is get out so be prepared. The dorms are what you make of them. Any dorm can be made into something worth living in, they never look nice when you first move in. Live with someone you know though, 'cause people you don't know can go schizoid on you."

Q "None of 'em are too nice. I stayed in Kirby Smith, a 12-story, all-male dorm aptly dubbed the 'sausage tower.' **Guys, you have to check in girls**, and they have to be out by midnight. If you're staying in this dorm, be prepared to sneak the ladies up to your room through the 'ho door,' the side door in Kirby."

Q "I lived on campus, and **I loved it**. Sure, you don't have a lot of space, but you're so close to all on campus events and right there for class."

STUDENT AUTHOR: **Students at LSU will blatantly tell you the dorms are gross, but in the same breath, students will tell you it was the best time of their life. On-campus housing is a great way to make friends, survive your classes, and save some money.**

Did You Know?
23% of undergrads live on campus.

Students Speak Out
ON GUYS & GIRLS

Q "The guys and gals at LSU are top notch! We have all kinds here, and **you're bound to find your group of people** and people to have a great time with. And of course, they're hot!"

Q "There are lots of pretty people here, as there will be at any big Southern school. But **it's not stuffy or a daily fashion show** like at some schools. Most people save their hotness for the nightlife, and it shows when they roll out of bed hung over to come to class in T-shirts and shorts."

Q "There are **lots of hot guys**, but unfortunately, just as many really pretty girls."

STUDENT AUTHOR: **The male/female ratio is fairly even, and though students may go through dry spells, rarely will you meet a student who hasn't had at least a few dates in their college career. But serious courtship can be a whole other matter. It's hard to deny that it can be more difficult to find someone who is not Republican and into the conservative lifestyle.**

Traditions

Chancellor's Pancake Breakfast
Just swipe any working LSU ID for a huge plate of pancakes and a chance to meet the man in charge of your education.

Homecoming
From the all day scavenger hunt to the crowning of the queen and king, to the nearly 20 foot decorations, Homecoming is the pinnacle of LSU traditions.

Overall School Spirit
The football slogan "I Bleed Purple and Gold" is not an understatement.

Students Speak Out
ON ATHLETICS

Q "Football is a way of life. **The University revolves around football!** during football season. Basketball (men's) and baseball are probably the next biggest sports that are attended by students."

Q "Football games are the highlight of my college career. Every other sport is free to students. **Intramurals are also pretty big** and a lot of fun."

Q "**LSU's sports program is huge**. Our baseball program has been a national contender for over a decade, the football program is currently one of the best in the nation, and basketball is always a threat."

Q "Even if you're not a big sports fan, **you will be a big Tiger fan** because it's a weekend-long party seven times a year."

STUDENT AUTHOR: **Beyond football, many men's and women's varsity sports are known for staying near the top of the rankings each year. Club sports offer a great chance for those with athletic prowess a chance to get in on the action, but don't expect a strong following.**

Students Speak Out
ON DRUG SCENE

Q "There is a drug scene, but it is **overshadowed by the drinking and going-out scene**. Not much is said about drugs. I think because alcohol is so easily accessible for most students, drugs are not as big a part of the college culture here as at other places."

Q "Not many people I know do drugs. Campus is not swamped in drugs. There are people that do drugs, but there are also **just as many people who do not** do drugs. I also have never heard of hardcore drugs on campus, mostly weed."

Q "**I don't know too much about it**, I don't see many people at all who look like 'druggies.' However, I'm sure they are out there to be found if that's your thing."

STUDENT AUTHOR: LSU football games usually go by the standard of "win or lose, we booze." Binge drinking is a competitive sport. Overall, LSU's drug scene does not overshadow the school. Plenty of students don't do drugs, and if they do, most of them don't talk about it.

20:1	Student-to-Faculty Ratio
85%	Freshman Retention Rate
26%	Four-Year Graduation Rate
69%	Financial Aid Applicants Receiving Aid

Students Speak Out
SAFETY & SECURITY

Q "I've always felt very safe on campus. There are a number of highly visible emergency call-boxes around campus, and **free transit that will pick you up** and bring you anywhere on campus after 5 p.m. In addition, there are always patrolling campus police and plain-clothes cops."

Q "Since the tragic incidents that happened, our **security is better than ever**. Drastic measures have been taken to make sure students feel safer on campus."

Q "I've never had a problem with security on campus but it is **very dark at night** because of the trees on campus. It makes me a little nervous to be walking around on campus at night, which is probably why they tell us not to do it."

STUDENT AUTHOR: Safety has become a serious issue at LSU. LSU police, including some undercover officers, constantly patrol campus. Dorm security has been tightened, with all of the dorms requiring some sort of card-swipe access.

> **Questions?**
> For more inside information and survival tips, pick up College Prowler's full-length book on this school, written by an actual student! Check it out at *www.collegeprowler.com*.

Students Speak Out
ON OVERALL EXPERIENCE

Q "LSU has an awesome atmosphere and a thriving social scene. **Plenty of fun** is to be had if one attends sporting events and participates in the campus and local social scene. There is no place like LSU."

Q "I never wanted to come to LSU. But the moment I stepped on campus, I fell in love. There is something about this place that you can't describe that gets in your skin and makes you enjoy everything about this school. It has something for everyone. There are **more than 350 organizations** to get involved in, so you're bound to find something you like."

Q "I love LSU and could not see myself anywhere else. **There is a unique camaraderie** and pride shared by LSU students, faculty, and alumnae."

Q "I don't feel like the vastness of LSU is a bad thing. At LSU, **they don't hold your hand** and spoon feed you, and I feel that it really gives students fresh from high school a chance to sink or swim on their own. In my opinion, that's what college is for."

STUDENT AUTHOR: It's the experiences of community, whether it be through football games, nightlife, through more academic organizations, or through living on campus. Students appreciate at the fact they are at something far bigger than themselves. The size of the University presents students with opportunities to do so much, from getting involved academically to finding a boyfriend or girlfriend. There is an overwhelming sense of pride and allegiance to the University that unites all LSU students. The phrase "I bleed purple and gold" holds more true than anyone could imagine.

Loyola College in Maryland

4501 North Charles Street; Baltimore, MD 21210
(800) 221-9107; www.loyola.edu

THE BASICS:

Acceptance Rate: 69%
Setting: Urban
F-T Undergrads: 3,671

SAT Range: 1650–1930*
Control: Private
Tuition: $35,140

Most Popular Majors: Business/Marketing, Communications, Social Sciences, Foreign Languages

*of 2400

Academics	B	Guys	A-
Local Atmosphere	B+	Girls	A+
Safety & Security	B-	Athletics	C+
Computers	B+	Nightlife	B
Facilities	A-	Greek Life	N/A
Campus Dining	B+	Drug Scene	B-
Off-Campus Dining	A	Campus Strictness	B-
Campus Housing	A+	Parking	D
Off-Campus Housing	B+	Transportation	B+
Diversity	D-	Weather	B-

Students Speak Out
ON ACADEMICS

Q "The teachers you can get at Loyola range in quality just like any other university. One of the better things about LC is you will usually get a teacher who is actually personable, friendly, and always eager to give any extra help needed. **Class size is always small**, as well—between 15–30 kids on average—something very unique over other schools where they have lectures with more than 60 kids."

Q "Some classes are long lectures, but **most are entertaining** and interesting. I can honestly say I have enjoyed almost all my classes and teachers—they try very hard to get to know the students."

Q "The Jesuits are generally some of the best professors on campus. I had microeconomics with a well-known, well-liked Jesuit, and even though I was not particularly skilled in economics, I took macro and environmental economics, as well. **I learned more than economics** in that class from the professor and that is why I chose to come to a Jesuit school."

Q "In my opinion, **we have a whole variety** of teachers here on campus. Some are dumb as door nails and can't teach, some are really smart but still can't teach, and some are smart and can teach very well."

STUDENT AUTHOR: The classes are interesting, but of course, there are boring, difficult, and no-fun classes everywhere. Fortunately, Loyola participates in the site, *ratemyprofessor.com*.

Students Speak Out
ON LOCAL ATMOSPHERE

Q "Baltimore is a big city, just like Philadelphia, DC, and New York City. There are **plenty of great things to do around the city** besides the bars, if you have both the imagination and the means of doing so. Getting around without a car can be annoying and expensive, though."

Q "**Baltimore definitely has a lot of great spots** including the Harbor for showing visitors and your family, Fell's Point, Federal Hill, and Canton for great restaurants and bars, and of course, Loyola's own York Road, which all Loyola students will get to know very well in the first week of school!"

Q "**You have to be smart** about areas in Baltimore. Feel safe on campus but don't let your guard down."

Q "The atmosphere here is a really odd mix. We have multi-million dollar homes on one side of us, then the not-so-nice area on the other. Notre Dame College, Towson, John Hopkins, BCC, and a few other schools surround us. Stay away from parts of York Road, but **visit everything at least once**."

STUDENT AUTHOR: When asked, one usually compares Baltimore to New Orleans, because they are set up in such a way that the "nice" and "bad" areas are practically intertwined. One of the best places to spend a few hours is walking around downtown in the Inner Harbor and at Harbor Place Mall.

Students Speak Out
ON FACILITIES

Q "The facilities on campus are really nice. Most of the buildings and facilities you deal with **all feel brand new**. The gym and student center are both really nice."

Q "They are nice and **accommodating**."

Q "Excellent. The athletic center is great and very well kept. The library is good. The student center is nice. **Everything is top-notch** and well maintained."

Q "We have a very nice athletic center. Loyola has great facilities; **they are always working on improvements** and technology. Everything is beautiful."

Q "In all of the schools I've looked at, Loyola's Fitness and Aquatic Center is, by far, the nicest workout center I have seen. It includes an indoor track, two basketball courts, an indoor soccer court, rock climbing, squash, racquetball, and a full weight and cardio room. There is a sauna and hot tub. **It has everything**, and everyone is there. It's quite the hangout."

STUDENT AUTHOR: **The Fitness and Aquatic Center, is gorgeous—no exaggerations included. One downfall is that sometimes our gym turns into a bit of a fashion show. Some students feel the need to wear only the most fashionable workout clothes with a matching sweat towel. Obviously, the gym can sometimes seem more of a social hangout than a fitness center. Not to worry though; a good number of students realize the purpose of the place and actually go there to get in a good workout.**

Famous Alumni

Tom Clancy, Jim McKay, Barbara Mikulski

Students Speak Out
ON CAMPUS DINING

Q "**The food is good at first**, but it becomes tiresome. The service and prices in the dining halls are terrible."

Q "As far as the quality of the food, **I feel they could be more diverse** to different cultures. Where's the soul food, West Indian, and Middle Eastern? An alternative way is cooking your own food in your dorm room. There is access to a kitchen either in your dorm room or floor kitchens in freshman dorms."

Q "The food is really good. Everything gets boring after a couple years, but **I wouldn't complain about it**."

Q "The food is good, but **it's way overpriced**. You get sick of the same old thing, too."

Q "Food can get boring, and you get sick of the choices after a few months. But by then, it's almost the end of the semester, so you stick it out. I'm a transfer student and **it's definitely far better than my old school's food**."

STUDENT AUTHOR: **The food on Loyola's campus is catered by a company called Sodexo. You wouldn't call any eating area at Loyola a dining hall because they are just not that big, messy, crowded, or cheap. The meal plan is debit-based, which is all well and good, until you notice all of your parents' money being swiped away and you still have three weeks of school left. That's when you realize that all those flavored bottled waters and Bagel Bites have left you with a balance of zero dollars and zero cents.**

Student Body

African American:	4%	Male/Female:	41/59%
Asian American:	3%	Out-of-State:	81%
Hispanic:	4%	International:	<1%
Native American:	<1%	Unknown:	3%
White:	85%		

Popular Faiths: The majority of students are Catholic, as the school's affiliation is Roman Catholic.

Gay Pride: At such a religious school, gay pride is limited. While there are no overt anti-gay sentiments, most gay or lesbian students keep their orientation a private matter.

Economic Status: Not every student is rich, but the majority are upper-middle to upper-class.

Students Speak Out
ON DORMS

Q "The dorms are great. **They are beautiful and fully equipped** with all the necessary amenities. They are rated very well in comparison to other college dorms."

Q "The dorms are great; they are large, mostly apartments. They are very nice but sometimes **the rules suck**."

Q "**You can't go wrong with the dorms** at Loyola. All the housing is great here. Even though on-campus apartments sound great as a freshman, I strongly suggest living in the doubles if you can. It's good because you are living in an all-freshman environment and are able to make great friends with those around you."

STUDENT AUTHOR: You can call them dorms if you want to, but they are the nicest student apartments you'll ever see. We have been praised for our dorms like palaces. All of the dorms have wall-to-wall carpeting, controllable air conditioning and heat, and Internet access for students who bring their own computers. Here's what's guaranteed: it will be nicer and more operational than your parents' first apartment. Sorry mom and dad.

Did You Know?
79% of undergrads live on campus.

Students Speak Out
ON GUYS & GIRLS

Q "I find the guys to be okay. There are hot guys here, **you just have to look**. The girls are hot, too."

Q "The **girls at Loyola are gorgeous**. One will walk by and before you can comprehend how pretty she is, another one will draw your attention. Almost all of the campus is from Long Island or New Jersey, so take that as you will."

Q "There are **pretty boys and easy girls**. Everyone's hot when you are drunk."

Q "The majority are preppy, rich people, and almost entirely white upper-class. Everyone is relatively good looking, but that should not matter. **There are no morals here**. The girls are easy and the guys promiscuous."

STUDENT AUTHOR: Almost 80 percent of the kids that go to Loyola are from New York and New Jersey, so if you don't like the Yankees (in every sense of the word) steer clear. Many students at Loyola have a secure financial dependence on their parents. The campus is severely preppy. The kids here do not wear sweats, baggy clothes, spandex, or too much makeup or jewelry, and they don't have piercings or tattoos.

Major Alumni Events

Milestone Reunion
Loyola annually honors its five-year milestone alumni with a weekend full of celebration, which includes campus tours to see changes made in the years passed, the Wild West Family Hoedown, a reunion reception and dinner, and lectures.

Overall School Spirit
Sometimes, campus seems to lack all school spirit because Loyola doesn't have much to celebrate in the way of sports. Students still feel a pride for their school and support it in other ways, like joining clubs and attending special events around campus.

Students Speak Out
ON ATHLETICS

Q "Lacrosse and soccer are pretty big. Basketball is re-developing itself. There are **no varsity football or baseball teams**. But club and intramural sports involve a lot of people."

Q "**Sports are not very big**. School spirit is lacking."

Q "**No one really cares**. People seem to spend the same amount of time thinking about club sports."

Q "IM sports are pretty big, though. Almost **everyone I know is on some team**. It's a good way to do something active, yet not get so involved."

STUDENT AUTHOR: Without a football team, Loyola seems to be lacking in the school spirit department. The basketball team isn't known for their playing abilities, so few spectators attend the games. Many students join in athletics through intramural teams. There are teams for sports from inner tube water polo, to squash and flag football.

Students Speak Out
ON DRUG SCENE

Q "It's not that bad, **but it is present**. The only real drug I've seen used with any kind of regularity is marijuana."

Q "I personally don't do drugs, but drugs are used and available on campus. **There really is no pressure** to partake in them if you don't want to. Drinking is definitely bigger than drug use."

Q "The drug scene is relatively prominent, but it's done more secretly. All grades are involved. Pot, coke, and **pills are the most popular**."

STUDENT AUTHOR: **The majority of students that dip into the mystical realm of drugs are turning to Adderall, Ritalin, and weed for writing those 12-page papers the night before they're due. Alcohol, however, is a bit different. Most people say Loyola is a big drinking school. On the rare occasion that students have ventured out to other schools, they have collected liquid proof of our abilities to drink other schools under the table. We will beat you at A$$hole, beer pong, flip cup, and moose, just to name a few.**

12:1	Student-to-Faculty Ratio
91%	Freshman Retention Rate
81%	Four-Year Graduation Rate
82%	Financial Aid Applicants Receiving Aid

Students Speak Out
SAFETY & SECURITY

Q "Security is good on campus. **I have never felt unsafe**. Security and lighting always makes me comfortable."

Q "The campus security isn't the best that it should be in preventing crimes such as theft and alcohol abuse, but they do try their best to make sure the students are safe from outsiders. **Most crimes are because of the carelessness of students**, such as binge drinking and leaving their dorm rooms unlocked."

Q "I wouldn't say I feel completely safe, but it is **reasonably safe for a school in the city**."

STUDENT AUTHOR: **Loyola students feel pretty safe on campus, but most agree that off-campus areas are where the trouble might lie. One wrong turn can lead you to some dangerous areas of the cities. Stay in large groups and make sure you know what area you're heading to.**

Questions?

For more inside information and survival tips, pick up College Prowler's full-length book on this school, written by an actual student! Check it out at *www.collegeprowler.com*.

Students Speak Out
ON OVERALL EXPERIENCE

Q "Loyola is a good school with great facilities, dorms, girls, and generally lots of good professors. I have loved Loyola. **It has ups and downs** just like any other school."

Q "I love it here; I'm so glad that I attended Loyola. I've had **some of the best experiences of my life**, and I have formed great friendships."

Q "**I had trouble adjusting**, but I am very happy here now. It's a great educational opportunity."

Q "So far, so good. I've made a few good friends, had good times, but I wish I was somewhere with a more diverse and larger student body. **Everyone here is basically the same**, and everything is based around drinking. I wish there was more to do that had nothing to do with alcohol."

STUDENT AUTHOR: **For freshmen everywhere, the first few weeks, maybe even semesters, of college life can be a daunting experience. Sharing a room with a total stranger, making a whole new circle of friends, and learning how to cope with professors and lecture classes can be enough to make anyone rethink the decision to go away to school. Fortunately for students at Loyola, these anxieties are quickly replaced by school pride and affection for the intelligent professors, gorgeous dormitories, and exciting nightlife. While Loyola has a great list of pros, there are some cons to life on campus. There is little diversity among the student body. For some, that's a major downfall.**

Loyola Marymount University

1 LMU Drive; Los Angeles, CA 90045
(310) 338-2700; www.lmu.edu

THE BASICS:

Acceptance Rate: 52%
Setting: Suburban
F-T Undergrads: 5,766

SAT Range: 1070–1280*
Control: Private
Tuition: $33,266

Most Popular Majors: Business, Visual/Performing Arts, Communications, Social Sciences, English

*of 1600

Academics	B	Guys	A
Local Atmosphere	A-	Girls	A+
Safety & Security	B	Athletics	C+
Computers	B-	Nightlife	A+
Facilities	A-	Greek Life	C
Campus Dining	B-	Drug Scene	B+
Off-Campus Dining	A	Campus Strictness	B-
Campus Housing	B	Parking	C
Off-Campus Housing	B-	Transportation	B-
Diversity	B+	Weather	A

Students Speak Out
ON ACADEMICS

Q "In general, all the teachers are extremely accessible and **really nice**. Many are aware of the stresses we students face and are willing to work with us when it comes to deadlines. Others are less lenient, but certainly don't have expectations that are too high or impossible. Some classes were more interesting than others."

Q "Before coming to LMU, I received a DVD in the mail containing interviews with the professors, and I was a bit concerned at how young they all seemed. **I have been pleasantly surprised**, however. Most of the professors at LMU have a PhD or are currently working towards one. My specific professors are mostly good, and it seems as though they average out; I have one who is a Yale-educated, highly intellectual woman and another who is about as sharp as the broad side of a cello. About half of the classes I've taken I find genuinely interesting, while the other half I find purposeless."

Q "I had a history professor who never gave above an A-, but that's the only time I ever felt like a professor was out to get her students. Most professors want their students to succeed and are **willing to give you a break** if you need extra time."

STUDENT AUTHOR: LMU's strength is in the strong relationship between students and professors. On the negative side, the attendance policy is usually very strict. Although the strict policy can seem intimidating, most classes at LMU are worth attending.

Students Speak Out
ON LOCAL ATMOSPHERE

Q "This is LA! LMU is near UCLA and USC. You're next to Venice Beach! You're near Hollywood. There's **nowhere better to be**. This is the place to visit. Besides all that, LMU is beautiful. You are on a bluff overlooking a beautiful view. The classes are small. The dorms are big and spacious. Grass and trees are everywhere. We're also very close to LAX! We even have a wonderful religious community and beautiful church. And for all those religious people—our school is in the shape of a cross. In my opinion, there is no better place to be!"

Q "The town is **not a college town**. It's a residential area on one side and the back of an airport on the other that has a mix of minivans and wandering travelers. LMU seems sort of out of place in Westchester, but it's LA. It's not as though you really have to stay within the 10 blocks that surround campus."

Q "LMU is a in **a good location**, not too deep in the city or completely away from it. It is also minutes from LAX, which does not pose that much of a problem."

STUDENT AUTHOR: The University prides itself on being simultaneously part of LA, yet separate from it. LMU is close to the culture and nightlife that makes LA so unique, but the University lacks the crime and concrete of the city. The University has a Los Angeles address, but the campus sits in Westchester, a quiet suburb in the western half of Los Angeles.

Students Speak Out
ON FACILITIES

Q "The facilities are absolutely awesome and modern. The gym has many modern machines (more than just your basic treadmills), including jacks for headphones, which let you watch the TVs! A gym with four TVs is totally awesome. The student centers, such as the Lion's Den, are great places to hang out, relax, read, get coffee, and talk to people. I definitely have **no complaints** about the facilities."

Q "They put a ton of money into the buildings here, except for West Hall. I always feel like the **walls will collapse** in an earthquake."

Q "The **facilities are beautiful**. You'll know where your tuition goes when you step into the gym, the computer labs, or sit by the trickling fountain in the fully stocked library. You always see people doing maintenance on campus, gardening and painting and repairing to keep it gorgeous."

Q "There is a center for first-year students, which has helped me a lot with any questions I had and made college bearable and doable. Most of the **computers are up-to-date**, with some few exceptions (like the engineering computer lab)."

STUDENT AUTHOR: **Facilities at LMU fall into two categories: new and old. All classrooms are large and comfortable; they feature a projection system, computer, Internet, and cable. Overall, the entire campus is extremely clean. The University employs a huge staff to maintain the plants and clean the classrooms. The maintenance staff even cleans the sidewalks and dusts the escalators. The campus eyesore is West Hall.**

Famous Alumni

Linda Cardelini, Kim Costello, Steve Franks, Brian Helgeland, Steve McEveety, David Mirkin, Darin Morgan, Glen Morgan, Van Partible, James Wong

Students Speak Out
ON CAMPUS DINING

Q "It's **not gourmet**, but it's so much better than most schools. We have the snack shop and the cafeterias. We have two stands and another snack type shop in University Hall. Also special events such as the Valentine's Day dinner and the Etiquette Dinner have really good food. We also have a Jamba Juice. Yes, there are good restaurants all around that you can choose from. One is Little Italy's, which is really close and accepts Flexi. You can also buy a Domino's pizza delivery with Lion dollars, but you can't put the tip on your Lion dollars."

Q "Well, if you're a newcomer, the Lair will seem like option heaven, but after awhile the food **tastes the same**, and you never know what to decide between pasta, Mexican, a burger, or a sandwich. The Roski dining hall in University Hall is better, obviously, because all the teachers' offices are close by. Go to the Boar's Head for the best sandwiches ever! You have a nice view of the waterfall and the waterworks in the dining hall there."

Q "I am a **vegetarian**, and there are almost no vegetarian options."

STUDENT AUTHOR: **Walk into the dining hall on your first day of school, and the Lair is overwhelming. Is it possible to try everything the Lair offers in one school year? Unfortunately, the answer is yes. For students determined to eat healthy, food selection can be a frustrating process. With or without a meal plan, you will pay significant amounts of money to eat on campus.**

Student Body

African American:	8%	Male/Female:	41/59%
Asian American:	13%	Out-of-State:	25%
Hispanic:	20%	International:	2%
Native American:	<1%	Unknown:	0%
White:	56%		

Popular Faiths: Most students are Roman Catholic and hail from parochial schools.

Gay Pride: While there is no active anti-gay sentiment on campus, this is a Catholic institution, and therefore there are certainly a number of people on campus who are not entirely accepting.

Economic Status: There is a wide gulf between the "haves" and "have nots" on campus.

Students Speak Out
ON DORMS

Q "Avoid Whelan, Rosecrans, and the quad near them if you don't like rowdiness. Rains, McCarthy, and **the Leaveys are nice** because they're new. East Quad dorms are decent."

Q "If you are a freshman or sophomore, your housing options are great. After that, well, **good luck**, because LMU doesn't care where you live as long as they get their money."

Q "The dorm I lived in was coed in that guys lived on the first floor, and girls lived on the second and third floors which required **keycard access**. It was really fun, and I also felt safe knowing that you needed to swipe your keycard three times, entering a secret code on the third time, in order to get into my room."

STUDENT AUTHOR: **Dorms are well-equipped with a reasonable amount of closet and drawer space. Students who are unhappy with sharing a bathroom with an entire floor can opt for one of the many suites on campus. Non-smoking and quiet dorms are available. Overall, the dorms offer students a variety of room types and buildings. The trick is getting a spot after your sophomore year.**

> **Did You Know?**
> 49% of undergrads live on campus.

Students Speak Out
ON GUYS & GIRLS

Q "There are a lot **more girls on campus** than guys, and for some reason the hot guys are in hibernation until second semester. Then, they are worth the wait: hot and relatively intelligent. It's a nice thing. What isn't nice is that the girls are just as hot, and the competition is tight."

Q "Students are nice, and **this is LA**, so of course everybody is nice to look at."

Q "One thing I can say is that this school is **definitely a "beach" school**—girls go out to the dorm courtyards in bikinis, and guys go out shirtless in order to get tans–and "beach" fashion, meaning flip-flops, tans, bleached hair, and a large flower on your ear, is very popular here."

STUDENT AUTHOR: **LMU students reflect LA's obsession with appearance. Everyone here looks good and dresses well. The general attitude of students is that the student body is hot. While that may seem intimidating to some, students are mostly friendly and outgoing. The ratio of guys to girls on campus means that when finding members of the opposite sex, the guys have a greater advantage. Even though LMU is a Catholic school, students are not strangers to sex.**

> **Traditions**
>
> **Charter Ball**
> In past years, LMU hosted a annual prom-like event to celebrate the merger of Loyola University and Marymount College in 1973. Cancelled after 2004.
>
> **Sunset Concert**
> The annual concert that brings bands to play at LMU.
>
> **Overall School Spirit**
> LMU athletics are not overwhelmingly popular, so school spirit is lacking when it comes to sports. However, school spirit becomes apparent whenever the volleyball team defeats Pepperdine (a major rival).

Students Speak Out
ON ATHLETICS

Q "Neither varsity or IM sports seemed to be too important, even though they were publicized and held. **More support seems to be needed**!"

Q "I don't think sports are that huge. I wish they were, though, because that would bring more boys. **We don't have a football team**, which is a big downer. The school wanted to be small, so they got rid of the football field. Our biggest sport is basketball, and I don't think we're that good. Our rival is Pepperdine. I say we forget the small school crap and build us a football and track field before it's too late!"

Q "**Volleyball is pretty big** here, but I haven't been to any games."

Q The most popular sport at LMU is basketball, and even then, it is **not a big deal**."

STUDENT AUTHOR: **Athletics are huge among the athletes, but the ordinary student body is generally apathetic to the school's sports teams. Although the school does offer IM sports, the challenge is to get students to participate and stick with them. LMU is not a major sports school.**

Students Speak Out
ON DRUG SCENE

Q "**LMU is not a dry campus**, but it's not overtaken by drugs. As far as drugs go, it's all about potheads. If anyone is caught with a drug, it is usually marijuana. A ton of people smoke, but cigarettes are not considered an illegal drug. There are very few cases of those heavy drugs used, but it is usually those potheads."

Q "Oh, **everyone drinks**, it seems."

Q "No matter how hard the University tries to control it, alcohol is a big problem here. Drinking a few beers occasionally is one thing, but so **many people take it too far** and end up in the hospital. Then, they get kicked out of school."

STUDENT AUTHOR: Most students drink, and some students drink heavily. It was no surprise to many students when the annual Charter Ball was canceled after numerous alcohol-related emergencies. Drugs are not a significant problem when compared to alcohol. However, it is very unlikely that you will find a student who openly admits to trying other illegal drugs because of the severe penalties from the University.

13:1	Student-to-Faculty Ratio
87%	Freshman Retention Rate
63%	Four-Year Graduation Rate
71%	Financial Aid Applicants Receiving Aid

Students Speak Out
SAFETY & SECURITY

Q "We have our own security that we call Public Safety. **They don't do much** except hand out parking tickets. When a real problem emerges, they call the LAPD."

Q "Well, it's not **Fort Knox**, but I've felt pretty safe."

Q "**It's a safe campus**, especially for LA. I almost went to USC, and that place is right in the middle of a ghetto."

Q "I once saw a homeless woman gathering up and **eating the stray french fries** on the countertops at the Lair. It made me question the security a bit, but it wasn't like an everyday occurrence. The campus has always felt very friendly, clean, safe, and secure, except that day."

STUDENT AUTHOR: The flaw in LMU security is in the gated entrances. Anyone can enter the campus on foot, and usually, guards at the security booth do not stop cars that do not have a University parking permit. But overall, students do not worry about physical safety because serious or violent crime is almost non-existent.

> **Questions?**
> For more inside information and survival tips, pick up College Prowler's full-length book on this school, written by an actual student! Check it out at *www.collegeprowler.com*.

Students Speak Out
ON OVERALL EXPERIENCE

Q "So far, I really enjoy the size of LMU. I like that I see at least one person I know every time I walk out of my dorm room. Everyone is really friendly and the environment is beautiful, clean, and comfortable. You feel like **you are taken care of** here. The teachers are caring, and despite a few bad seeds, LMU is a great place."

Q "Personally, **I am pretty content** at LMU. Almost all of my experiences from professors to students to the student center have only been good. Students seemed to be laid-back, relaxed, mellow, and friendly, which really helps when coming on to campus every day because you do not feel so alienated. LMU is in such a wonderful area, and the atmosphere is pretty lively. My only complaint is the efficiency of the administration, especially in financial aid. They are very disorganized, which is not good; that can really turn off prospective students."

Q "This is a tight-knit school. You can't just hide in a crowd because there aren't any. While you get to know everyone, sometimes there is a huge **pressure to fit in**—have the right clothes, right car. Sometimes it's intimidating, but I'm happy with the atmosphere."

STUDENT AUTHOR: Students here are quick to point out that LMU differs from its neighbors USC and UCLA. Overall, LMU is quiet and intimate. Students cite a small student body and close ties with professors as the main advantages to an LMU education. Another plus is the lavish facilities, especially the Burns Rec Center. Students repeatedly report problems with a disorganized administration, especially financial aid.

Loyola University Chicago

1052 West Loyola Avenue; Chicago, IL
(773) 274-3000; www.luc.edu

THE BASICS:

Acceptance Rate: 73%   **SAT Range:** 1050–1270*
Setting: Urban   **Control:** Private
F-T Undergrads: 9,167   **Tuition:** $28,700

Most Popular Majors: Business, Social Sciences, Psychology, Biology, Health Professions

*of 1600

Academics	B-	Guys	B-
Local Atmosphere	A-	Girls	B
Safety & Security	C	Athletics	C+
Computers	C+	Nightlife	A-
Facilities	B-	Greek Life	D+
Campus Dining	C	Drug Scene	C+
Off-Campus Dining	A	Campus Strictness	C
Campus Housing	B+	Parking	D-
Off-Campus Housing	B+	Transportation	A
Diversity	B	Weather	D

Students Speak Out
ON ACADEMICS

Q "A lot of universities have faculty that focus a great deal more on their own research, but Loyola's professors possess, above all other career motivations, **an immense desire to teach**—not only on their area of specialization, but also other valuable life lessons and skills."

Q "In general, the professors at Loyola were very good. I found most of them **easily accessible** and motivated to perform well."

Q "The trick for me is not to be intimidated or overly skeptical about the fact that you may have a Jesuit priest as your professor, because **Jesuit priests are smart as all get out**. And some have been kicked out of the Catholic Church before, indicating they're rebels, willing to smite tradition in favor of social justice."

Q "I knew students who baby-sat for their professors' kids, who had beers with their professors after class, who knew their profs' office hours by heart, and called them by their first names. **If it got any more intimate, we'd all be going to class naked**."

STUDENT AUTHOR: **Although there is certainly disagreement on the topic, most students agree that the best thing about studying at Loyola is the care professors put into teaching their classes. Unfortunately, because of constant budget cuts, it is sometimes impossible for professors to provide their students with the materials necessary for learning, but graduates from all of Loyola's departments leave with a strong sense of social justice.**

Students Speak Out
ON LOCAL ATMOSPHERE

Q "**Chicago is a fantastic city** with plenty of other schools in town. There is plenty to do and see in Chicago: museums, sporting events, parks, architecture. Just stay away from Cabrini Green."

Q "Chicago is **the city for 21 and older**, so you'll be spending your time drinking in your dorm/apartment anxiously waiting for your 21st birthday. It's a lot of waiting. We don't like to talk about the other universities present in Chicago—they are inherently evil."

Q "Loyola is in Chicago, not Boulder, and not Madison. There's crime. There are bums. There are **cars on fire in the alleys**. If you want a college town, complete with lax liquor laws, *Animal House* antics, and townspeople who wear your school's colors and shout, "Go Wildcats!" or whatever, go somewhere else."

Q "There is **something for everyone** in Chicago. There are other colleges and universities around, but they don't interact to that great of an extent."

STUDENT AUTHOR: **It is next to impossible to become bored in Chicago unless you try really, really hard. Chicago is the heart and soul of the Midwest. The Second City pulses with the combined energy of an entire region. The first thing a student must know is that Chicago is likely much larger than anywhere he or she has ever lived before. As intimidating as this idea can be, Chicago manages to remain friendly and inviting to those unused to its hustle and bustle.**

Students Speak Out
ON FACILITIES

Q "The athletic facilities are for the most part run down and old. The computer labs are **cramped and hot**. And there really is no student center."

Q "Facilities **range from great to sub-par**. The gym is too small, and at peak hours it is too crowded. If you want to use it, make sure to have an alternate plan for staying up late or going very, very early. If you're smart, you'll learn to start using the gym at the downtown campus, which sees much less traffic."

Q "There is no 'student union,' only a lobby with some uncomfortable chairs and some tables. The computer labs have decent computers (Gateways or Dells with Pentium IIIs) and the libraries are **well stocked with books**."

Q "The student center, simply put, isn't. It's a big area with some tables, but there's nothing really that interesting going on there. When big events happen, **such as a band playing**, it's a great gathering place."

Q "**They've been renovating**, so in a few years everything should be up to par."

STUDENT AUTHOR: **Loyola is not a big, rich, state-run university. Therefore, you probably will not find many of the standard college amenities, such as fraternity houses, student unions, and an adequate athletic playing field. Aesthetically speaking, though, Loyola's buildings on both campuses, with a few notable exceptions, are architecturally magnificent. Many students cite the ivy-covered red brick walls of Dumbach and Cudahy Halls as main factors in their decision to come to Loyola.**

Famous Alumni

Susan Candiotti, William Daley, Richard A. Devine, Richard L. Flanagan, Neil F. Hartigan, Bob Newhart, Don Novello

Students Speak Out
ON CAMPUS DINING

Q "The food on campus is doable, though **not exactly cheap**. Dining at one of the residence halls costs roughly the same as it would cost to eat at a fast food restaurant. Even so, it's probably a good idea to go with a minimal dining plan and add money onto it later if need be, as your balance is not rolled over at the end of the semester."

Q "The food is adequate; it's **nothing to write home about**, though."

Q "**Don't expect to avoid the Freshman 15**, even if you only hit the salad bar. None of the fare offered can be considered health food. Avoid Lake Shore Dining at all costs, except for brunch on Saturdays and Sundays. Wolf and Kettle at Water Tower is a good snack stop."

Q "The food is **best accompanied by cheese dip**. Pour it on everything and anything. Simpson Dining Hall is by far the best option on campus for food. You can get your fair share of grease, meat, veggie, and pizza here. They also have gummy bears, which automatically boosts them into an entirely different level."

STUDENT AUTHOR: **It could be worse. That seems to be the attitude most students have about Loyola's on-campus dining options. This doesn't sound like the greatest endorsement, but Loyola does try to mix it up a little bit. Vegetarian and vegan options are always available, and the University goes out of its way to bring in various ethnic foods.**

Student Body

African American:	5%	Male/Female:	35/65%
Asian American:	12%	Out-of-State:	34%
Hispanic:	9%	International:	1%
Native American:	<1%	Unknown:	11%
White:	61%		

Popular Faiths: It is mostly Catholic, being a Jesuit university, but Loyola is inclusive of all faiths.

Gay Pride: Loyola is quite accepting of its gay population and it was one of the first private US institutions to sponsor gay student organizations.

Economic Status: Many backgrounds are represented, but most are upper-middle-class and middle-class.

Students Speak Out
ON DORMS

Q "The dorm rooms are **extremely nice**, which was one of the major draws to Loyola. Simpson Living Learning Center has the newest rooms. The biggest rooms on campus can be located here, as well as the smallest dorm rooms. If you want mice for company, then Mertz is the place to go. If you're lucky enough to get a corner room, you'll have an awesome view of Lake Michigan."

Q "Simpson has **coed floors and private bathrooms** for every three rooms, but it is usually the preferred dorm, and hard to get into. Mertz, though the victim of frequent fire alarms, is truly 19 floors of fun. Each floor by year's end has its own identity, for people bond quickly due to the ordeal of living there. The motto of Mertz is 'Mertz 'till it hurts!'—but I loved it."

STUDENT AUTHOR: **Loyola requires freshmen to live on campus. This may not sound like a blast, but sharing a communal bathroom and living under the tyrannical boot of an RA can be the perfect bonding experience for those who have not lived away from home before. The people you live with freshman year will probably be some of your best friends four years later.**

> **? Did You Know?**
> 39% of undergrads live on campus.

Students Speak Out
ON GUYS & GIRLS

Q "There are **lots of hotties on campus**; check out Hamilton's on a Thursday night and you'll see what I mean."

Q "The girls, frankly, stink. There are no knock-outs, but most of them act like they are. A lot of the girls have crabby, selfish personalities and drink way too much, way too often. **Most of them are teases**. I'm one of them."

Q "There are **two girls for every guy**, and some of them are even pretty cute."

Q "There are some pretty fine looking people at Loyola. The Lakeshore campus is cool because you meet **many different kinds of people** with different interests. And most of them are decent looking, too."

STUDENT AUTHOR: **GQ is definitely not knocking down the doors to get to Loyola's guys, and you won't see the girls on the cover of *Cosmopolitan*. Still, the campus overall is a fairly attractive one. The trick is to get people out of their cold weather clothes. Then they're hot. The best part about students is that they all come from different backgrounds, making it very likely you'll find someone to curl up with on a cold night.**

> **Traditions**
>
> **President's Ball**
> The closest Loyola comes to a Homecoming celebration, featuring dancing and awards.
>
> **The Sixth Man**
> A group of fanatical Rambler fans dressed in maroon and gold shirts attend every men's basketball game.
>
> **Overall School Spirit**
> School spirit is almost nonexistent at Loyola. Perhaps the most telling sign of the students' love for their school is their willingness to protest about it and fight the administration tooth and nail.

Students Speak Out
ON ATHLETICS

Q "This school is spirit-deficient. **The teams are ho-hum**, and nobody even tries to get the student body rallied around them. Club intramural teams are fun to get involved with, though the draw there isn't even that huge."

Q There's no football team; in its place is club rugby, the players of which **do more drinking than playing**."

Q "**Intramural sports are relatively big**, especially softball and volleyball, and especially with the coed leagues. Typically, the same students that participate in intramurals as freshmen still participate as seniors, and not many newbies join in later on in their academic careers."

Q "Intramurals are never that big, but **always fun**."

STUDENT AUTHOR: **In stark contrast to its varsity squads, Loyola's intramural and club teams thrive. Fueled by a sizeable population of former high school athletes, intramurals are always popular. There is nothing (well, almost nothing) that can ease fragile nerves around finals time like a good game of flag football or indoor soccer.**

Students Speak Out
ON DRUG SCENE

Q "**The main drugs are alcohol and nicotine**. Lots of students smoke cigarettes, and many drink socially. There is a good deal of pot on campus, but other drugs are not that prevalent. Be warned, though, Chicago is a big city. If you want it, you can get it."

Q "You can get pretty much anything you would want on campus if you know where to look and who to ask. However, **students' drug use is not prevalent**, nor is it obvious to notice which kids use. Sometimes stoners, in actuality, are just lazy kids."

Q "Everyone knows someone. I wouldn't say it's anything of a problem or an epidemic, but it's **definitely there**."

STUDENT AUTHOR: **Not many students at Loyola resort to hardcore drug use, but there are certainly those that do. No one at Loyola will shove a joint in your face and demand that you smoke it. If you choose to do drugs, it will be of your own volition. Just remember, drugs are bad, okay?**

14:1	Student-to-Faculty Ratio
84%	Freshman Retention Rate
57%	Four-Year Graduation Rate
88%	Financial Aid Applicants Receiving Aid

Students Speak Out
SAFETY & SECURITY

Q "The campus is well lit and small enough to have buildings (and people) nearby at all times. There's **a sense of seclusion** from the bad neighborhood around campus."

Q "**The campus police are ineffectual**; all they're useful for is getting you written up, and for taking you to the hospital when you're sick. The heaviest artillery I've seen them carry is a Maglight, so if you're getting mugged, don't count on much help."

Q "The area around Loyola is somewhat troublesome, but Loyola doesn't seem to have much more crime than any other university. Being in the city, I think Loyola students pay more attention to security and **tend to keep their guards up**."

STUDENT AUTHOR: **The most troubling fact about Loyola is that it's located in an area of Chicago that can be dangerous. While the neighborhood is well patrolled by both campus and city police, students would be well advised to keep their eyes peeled for danger when in Rogers Park.**

Questions?
For more inside information and survival tips, pick up College Prowler's full-length book on this school, written by an actual student! Check it out at *www.collegeprowler.com*.

Students Speak Out
ON OVERALL EXPERIENCE

Q "I really enjoy Loyola. The school is **just the right size**, and having the city around is really great. Sometimes I do wish that I had gone somewhere with college football or a bigger party scene, but no matter where you go, there will always be something you are missing. Given everything that I gained by going to Loyola, I would never do it differently."

Q "The actual campus is awesome, the people are great, **the administration is Big Brother** to the extreme, and I wish I blew $50,000 playing one game of blackjack instead of going to Loyola."

Q "Nothing beats the faculty, student body, and location, but **the administration needs to get its act together**. If they don't, there are plenty of other universities in Chicago to go to."

Q "Loyola still has **a lot of issues to sort out**, including the administration's seeming witch hunt for anything at all that could be wrong with student life, as well as some budget problems, but with ever-increasing class sizes, the financial problems should be a thing of the past."

STUDENT AUTHOR: **Loyola's students are quick to point out the school's faults. There is little sugar-coating in their appraisal of the school as a financial mess that is so rife with incompetence that it is hard to accomplish even the simplest administrative tasks without putting up a fight. That said, most Loyolans love their school. They see its faults as nothing more than additional challenges they must face on their way to graduation. Loyola is starting to come slowly out of its period of financial distress as incoming class sizes grow in size. Outside of the classroom, the University is actually growing and improving by the day.**

Luther College

700 College Drive; Decorah, IA 52101
(800) 458-8437; www.luther.edu

THE BASICS:

Acceptance Rate: 80%
Setting: Rural
F-T Undergrads: 2,385

SAT Range: 1500–1950*
Control: Private
Tuition: $32,140

Most Popular Majors: Visual/Performing Arts, Business/Marketing, Social Sciences

*of 2400

Academics	B	Guys	C+
Local Atmosphere	C-	Girls	B-
Safety & Security	A	Athletics	B-
Computers	B	Nightlife	C+
Facilities	B	Greek Life	C-
Campus Dining	B-	Drug Scene	A-
Off-Campus Dining	B	Campus Strictness	B+
Campus Housing	B-	Parking	C
Off-Campus Housing	D+	Transportation	C-
Diversity	D	Weather	C

Students Speak Out
ON ACADEMICS

Q "The professors are all very knowledgeable, and they do seem to care about the students. **The workload varies from class to class**. I've had classes with almost zero actual work and others that have homework every single night."

Q "In general, the professors are friendly and capable and do want to see their students succeed, which is something particularly necessary to classes that are taken to fulfill general-education requirements. I also find that they do enjoy talking to their students, and they **treat their students as responsible adults**."

Q "A lot of teachers understand that students want to just get through a class sometimes, and I don't think that's a bad thing. **They try to make your experience within the class the best it can be**, but they know it's not going to be your life's work."

Q "When people see grades from Luther, they'll know that the student worked hard if they got an A, at least based on what I've heard about grade inflation. **Professors will make you work for a grade**, even in 'easy classes,' even to the point of looking for a reason not to give you an A."

STUDENT AUTHOR: **Luther is not Yale or Harvard, but you'd never know it by the way the College is respected. The workload can be heavy at times, but many students find relief by building their schedule around a mix of general-education requirements and upper-level classes for their major, and professors are often eager to work with students on schoolwork or a mutual collaboration.**

Students Speak Out
ON LOCAL ATMOSPHERE

Q "Decorah is anything but exciting, but for people originally from small towns, it's perfect. There's not much to do—there's the **typical movie theater, bowling alley, and smattering of bars**, but if you want to truly experience some nightlife, you'll have to travel at least an hour away, if not more. However, the town itself is by all means charming and friendly, warm and welcoming, just as you might expect from a small, rural town."

Q "I love the outdoor life here—the biking/hiking trails make for more exciting and unique dates than a typical dinner and a movie. And if it's warm enough, **tubing down the Upper Iowa River with your buddies never gets old**, especially with a cooler of beer."

Q "The College wants us to disassociate ourselves from the community and vice versa, it seems to me. That's fine. **There's plenty of fun to be had on campus** without running into town."

Q "**It's a beautiful area**, especially if you like wildlife. You can't come to small-town Iowa and expect the big city."

STUDENT AUTHOR: **For the student who appreciates a small town, the transition will be easy. But for those who are used to big-city lights and sounds, the sounds and smells of cow pastures cannot compete. Decorah is great for the student who wants to be within a reasonable distance of big cities but still wants the quiet peace of a small town.**

Students Speak Out
ON FACILITIES

Q "The athletic facilities are really nice, but they're always busy during peak hours. **Our Union is brand new and pretty darn good-looking.** We've also got very nice classrooms, and our library is designed for art and study."

Q "Our new Union is great looking, and along with the Center for the Arts, it sets a nice bar for where our campus is headed. I know **I like the buildings here a lot more** than at other private colleges—we're old-school, but not in an ancient way."

Q "I think our facilities are good for the size of our school. We've got a lot of lecture halls, the gym is nice, and **many buildings will be remodeled in the coming years** or have recently been done."

Q "I think we've got good facilities for those people who want a bit of everything. **I really enjoy the new art building for studying**, and I love the Regents Center, especially the racquetball courts."

Q "The new Union is an awesome building that serves a lot of campus needs. Our concert halls in the CFL and the music building are great as well, and **the gym is a great place to work out, especially in the morning**."

STUDENT AUTHOR: When it comes to facilities at Luther, it's "out with the old and in with the new." The state-of-the-art Dahl Centennial Union serves nearly all of the eating and entertainment needs of students. In general, Luther knows that progress needs to be made in a few buildings, and steps are being taken to ensure that every building on campus is viewed as a pinnacle of design and function.

Famous Alumni

Cheryl Browne, Clarence Norman Brunsdale, Marty Haugen, Adolph Herseth, Mark Johnson-Williams, Weston Noble, Jim Nussle, Jacob Aal Ottesen Preus

Students Speak Out
ON CAMPUS DINING

Q "I know many students don't like it, but **I think the Caf is actually really good**; it's far better than any state school I've ever been to, and much better than many colleges of our size as well."

Q "When I got to Luther, I really liked our Caf, Marty's, and Oneota. But after eating the same meals on a routine basis for nearly four years, **I've grown tired of it**. The key is variety, whether it's in switching up where you eat or going off campus on occasion."

Q "I think our Caf is amazing for a school our size. **We've got a great variety of food for almost any appetite**, including a lot of things you can cook yourself like the pasta line, the sub line, or the stir-fry."

Q "The food at Luther is college food, plain and simple. Supposedly, it's better than other places, and I can believe that. I've never seen anything in the Caf that's made me want to go throw up. But it's not going to be the end-all, be-all dining experience you might think it is. **After a while, everything tastes the same**."

STUDENT AUTHOR: The food itself at Luther, from any of the dining establishments, is top choice, as long as you mix it up. Eating in the Caf every day will be as boring as eating in Marty's every day, but if that's your cup of tea (or your tall double macchiato caramel latte with espresso), so be it. Like anything else, variety is the spice of life, no crappy puns intended.

Students Speak Out
ON DORMS

Q "**Sophomores and juniors really get the shaft from Luther**. Seeing the freshman dorms makes you think that dorm living won't be so bad, but that's because those got remodeled and are actually fit to live in."

Q "Luther does a great job of **spinning the housing situation to make it seem great** when you're on a tour by showing you Farwell and Brandt (which are, admittedly, really nice buildings) but skipping Towers, which is where almost every student will live at some point."

Q "Freshman year = very nice. Middle years = hell, unless you can get into Farwell or get an Olson suite. Senior year = **Baker and Farwell; these are the pinnacle**, but College Apartments aren't bad."

STUDENT AUTHOR: **Campus housing is a bookend kind of deal: freshman and senior year, most of the living arrangements are very solid, but in the middle years, things get a little musty. Since almost all of Luther's students will live on campus all four years, it is important to consider where you'll wind up and what you want to get out of it.**

Did You Know?
88% of undergrads live on campus.

Students Speak Out
ON GUYS & GIRLS

Q "The **typical guy is nice with a good sense of humor**. Girls can be really hot, and some aren't. For the most part, they are attractive in one way or another."

Q "Neither the guys or the girls will blow you away, but **there is someone for everyone** at Luther."

Q "The typical student dresses to fit their personal style but dresses nicely and, for the most part, **looks nice and polished when they go to classes**, even during finals."

Q "The girls here are very down-to-earth and don't wear a lot of makeup. **The girls are cute, but I wouldn't say any of the Luther girls are hot**! This goes with the guys as well."

STUDENT AUTHOR: **Luther College seems to be an average collection of college students. All fashions, lifestyles, and partner aspirations are welcome here. More importantly, they act how young people are supposed to act, and deeper connections are made. Most students on campus, when asked about their partner, will talk about how much they connect rather than how hot the person is. That's a standard that anyone can live with.**

Traditions

Christmas at Luther
This four-day, six-performance event is a cornerstone of the music program, particularly for the choirs.

Flamingo Ball
A dance that happens over Homecoming, often with a live band and a theme.

Overall School Spirit
School spirit at Luther is more about pride for the campus than athletics. You'd be hard-pressed to find a student without a single piece of Luther clothing. Most students support athletics at big games.

Students Speak Out
ON ATHLETICS

Q "Don't come here if you're looking for a huge strength in sports. Luther definitely believes in the term student-athlete, so they're **not that big on student sports**. The coaches believe in the teams, but getting the school and student body to do the same is a difficult task."

Q "Varsity sports are very competitive and definitely fun. **Sports teams are very united on campus** and are very good friends. Intramural sports are actually very competitive also since many athletes do both a varsity sport and an intramural sport. "

Q "In recent years, our teams have been really great. The women's basketball team recently made it to the Sweet 16, and whether we're good or bad, **the football games are always a good time**."

STUDENT AUTHOR: **Sports at Luther are like your appendix: You can go your whole life and never know they're there. Both varsity and intramural sports are available, but they don't play at all into the landscape of what defines a student. If you're looking into playing varsity sports but still want to be a student first, Luther could be the place for you.**

Students Speak Out
ON DRUG SCENE

Q "House parties are fun, and it seems like a lot of theme parties (golf pros and tennis hos, '80s rock star, beach party, lumberjack party) take place on the weekends. **Just don't go to the same party over and over**, and you won't get bored."

Q "Learn how to play beer pong before you come here, and **you'll make a lot of friends**—it seems to be the most popular game on campus. You'd do well to learn how to play flip cup, too."

Q "The parties are predictable, and not always in a good way. Drink at home, walk with everyone to the bar, drink in one of two clubs, dance, go home, order pizza, and pass out. But **if you like structured fun, look no further**."

STUDENT AUTHOR: **Being that Luther is a small town in the Midwest made up of primarily Lutheran students, you shouldn't expect to find much nightlife. Drinking in the dorms is fun for a while, but after a few semesters of it, students go batty. Off-campus parties are a lot of fun, but they're rarely open-invitation. You'll need a car to find other options.**

12:1	Student-to-Faculty Ratio
85%	Freshman Retention Rate
61%	Four-Year Graduation Rate
85%	Financial Aid Applicants Receiving Aid

Students Speak Out
SAFETY & SECURITY

Q "**I am amazed that students leave their bags out in the open on campus**. While at lunch, a ton of students just leave their stuff outside, no matter how much they have in their bags—laptops, iPods, you name it. Being from a big city, I still haven't made that transition."

Q "**I feel safe leaving my bookbag out** in the library and leaving to get dinner, knowing it'll be there when I get back. I don't lock my doors, and I can walk across campus anytime I want."

Q "The atmosphere on campus is very safe and community-like. I have no hesitation walking past any person on campus or doing anything at night. The town itself is small and convenient, and **I feel comfortable doing all the things I normally do**."

STUDENT AUTHOR: **Luther College could not be any safer if it came straight out of a '50s sitcom. The campus, city, and surrounding areas are all places where students feel comfortable at all times. Students can be assured that they will be living, working, and playing in a safe location.**

Questions?
For more inside information and survival tips, pick up College Prowler's full-length book on this school, written by an actual student! Check it out at *www.collegeprowler.com*.

Students Speak Out
ON OVERALL EXPERIENCE

Q "My Luther experience has been fine. I'm happy with where I've wound up. I looked at other schools and almost transferred at one point, but I know **I'm not going anywhere now because of the friendships I've made** and the memories we've created."

Q "I can't imagine myself anywhere else. **Luther has helped me realize who I wanted to become** and who I really was. Without one or the other, I don't think I'd be as happy as I am now."

Q "Luther is a wonderful school, but it's not for everyone. **You have to be able to deal with a few inconveniences** (no nightlife, small classes, lack of weekend fun), but if you surround yourself with the right people, you can have the time of your life. I know I have, even though it took me a while to realize it."

Q "My life changed when I went to Luther. It was the only place I applied, and **it's given me everything I wanted from a college experience**. There have been highs and lows, but I can't imagine that being any different somewhere else."

STUDENT AUTHOR: **The Luther bubble creates an experience that cannot be duplicated, and many students hold that near to their hearts. Many students love Luther for the simple fact that the bubble allows students to experience all kinds of fun. Academics aside, many students come to Luther to play sports, make a difference in student government, or contribute to the campus's vibrant performing arts society. College is not about ivory towers, old brick buildings, and a false sense of importance—it's about finding and creating yourself. For many students, there's no better place to complete that project than Luther.**

Macalester College

1600 Grand Avenue; St. Paul, MN 55116
(651) 696-6000; www.macalester.edu

Students Speak Out
ON ACADEMICS

Q "I have had wonderful experiences with most of my professors. Mac profs are, for the most part, inspiring and interesting. Most of my classes have been **extremely engaging** and have exposed me to information that has had a profound effect on me."

Q "Overall, the **teachers and classes are excellent**. Obviously, there are a few rotten eggs in the bunch, but overall both are great. I have been to a few other colleges, and in comparison, I find that Mac is the most academically challenging and academically diverse."

Q "For a while, I taste-tested various departments, but ultimately came home to English. The English department at Macalester boasts **fiercely intelligent**, witty, and interesting professors. I don't know a lot about departments outside of my major, however."

Q "Some teachers at this college are **truly incredible** and others really shouldn't be teaching at Macalester. However, I've been very impressed with the majority of my professors, and my classes have been very interesting."

STUDENT AUTHOR: At a small school like Macalester, students inevitably grow to know their professors as people rather than as distant specks at the head of the lecture hall. Likewise, most Macalester professors grow to know their students on a personal basis—even a lecture-course professor is likely to recognize his or her student outside of the classroom.

Students Speak Out
ON LOCAL ATMOSPHERE

Q "The Twin Cities are **really fun**, although most of the students I know (including myself) are too lazy to get off campus much. Lots of yummy food, cool ethnic neighborhoods, theater (some cheap and some not-so-cheap), clubs, and bars. The bus system kind of sucks, but for most of us without a car, it works well enough."

Q "**Saint Paul rocks**! What more can I say? Macalester is in the Mac-Groveland area of the city, and it is a beautiful residential neighborhood. I would suggest going to Carmello's, an awesome Italian place."

Q "Although it sits in a residential area of quiet Saint Paul, Macalester is not as isolated as it seems. With main bus lines running along Snelling and Grand, the big city atmosphere is **easily accessible** with nearby destinations such as the Mall and downtown Minneapolis."

STUDENT AUTHOR: As a first-year student, chances are that your dorm windows will either face the attractive Macalester campus or the historical and beautiful Summit Avenue, part of a four-mile stretch of some of the best-preserved Victorian mansions in the country. Either way, leaving the Macalester campus to explore what the Twin Cities have to offer can be tough, especially when numerous bars, restaurants, shops, and supermarkets are all within walking distance of the campus. For this reason, many students will attest to the fact that it's easy to get stuck in the "Macalester bubble."

5 Best Things	5 Worst Things
1 International diversity	1 Freezing walks to class
2 Small classes	2 Scorching walks to class
3 Friendly people	3 Outdated facilities
4 Quick walks to class	4 Housing requirement
5 Funny professors	5 Required meal plan

Students Speak Out
ON FACILITIES

Q "The **Field House is okay**, although I'm sometimes too intimidated by the hardcore jocks to work out there much. The open pool hours are definitely a plus, and a great way to blow off steam."

Q "The athletic facilities are **adequate at best**, but they are fortunately not very crowded. The student center is one of the best I have come across. Computer-related issues are not a point of pride for Macalester, however."

Q "The rule for Mac is that **things are small**. This applies for everything. Yeah, it would be nice to not have to fight over gym space, but I guess that just isn't possible on a campus that's squeezed into two blocks."

Q "I think the facilities are all right. That the school built a 20 million-dollar student union and initially left out a game room seems shortsighted. Overall, there are opportunities around, and for a small school, the resources seem **satisfactory**."

Q "The facilities are nice. They don't blow you away in a gaudy, overwhelming way, but they are not totally lacking. The athletic department could use a little more work, but it is **still sufficient**."

STUDENT AUTHOR: **Considering the fact that Macalester has invested $80 million into campus facilities since 1994, it comes as no surprise that students tend to praise the new facilities and criticize the old ones. The new facilities are not only attractive and functional, but also state-of-the-art in design. The indoor athletic facilities, while fully functional, are somewhat outdated and cramped.**

Famous Alumni

Kofi Annan, Siah Armajani, Gary Hines, Carl Lumbly, Walter Mondale, Tim O'Brien, Shaw Lawrence Otto, Flip Schulke

Students Speak Out
ON CAMPUS DINING

Q "**The food is amazing**. There is always a wide variety in the cafeteria, even for vegetarians and vegans. The student dining hall is out of this world. However, just by being cafeteria food, it stops being enticing after eating it day after day for two years."

Q "The food on campus is **good for a while**, but it becomes pretty ordinary after a long stay. The attempt of our food service is to spice up the food to make it unique, but that doesn't always work in a mass-produced food system like a cafeteria."

Q "On-campus food is **very good**, but it has one huge drawback. Everything closes down on campus before I get the munchies. This means you can't just go to the cafeteria and get some Cheetos whenever you want."

Q "Regrettably, the only dining option on campus is Café Mac. Although the food is some of the **best cafeteria food on college campuses nationwide**, one can easily tire of the options when forced to eat there for the first two years at Mac. After all, it is required, along with mandatory on-campus living."

STUDENT AUTHOR: **Mac students share a certain unspoken guilt when it comes to complaining about the food options on campus. Yes, cafeteria food does get old after eating it day-in and day-out for a minimum of two years. In comparison to most other college cafeterias, however, Café Mac has a much greater and healthier array of choices.**

Student Body

African American:	3%	Male/Female:	43/57%
Asian American:	6%	Out-of-State:	76%
Hispanic:	3%	International:	14%
Native American:	1%	Unknown:	0%
White:	73%		

Popular Faiths: Macalester hosts several religious groups, but no single dominant religion.

Gay Pride: The gay community is widely accepted on campus, and discrimination of any kind is unquestionably taboo.

Economic Status: Macalester draws students from a variety of states and countries, so everybody comes from a relatively different economic background.

Students Speak Out
ON DORMS

Q "First-year dorms are not the nicest, but they often have the best floor chemistry. **Dupre is a great dorm** for first years, for example, but the sophomore single rooms are some of the least desirable. Wallace is the party dorm."

Q "The dorms **get progressively nicer** as you move further along in college, with the freshman dorms being the small doubles and singles. George Draper Dayton Hall is the dorm to be in as an older student because you live in a suite with your own bathroom."

Q "I'd say that **Turck is cool** for first-years. It's got a homey, community atmosphere to it."

STUDENT AUTHOR: **The key to getting the nicest dorms on campus? Aging. There's no getting around living in a standard dorm your first year at Macalester. The good news is that all of the freshman dorms are relatively similar, so there's no need to worry about where you're going to end up in terms of comfort or convenience. After freshman year, however, students start to think about options. The quality of your dorm as an upperclassman really depends on luck of the draw.**

Did You Know?
68% of undergrads live on campus.

Students Speak Out
ON GUYS & GIRLS

Q "There are more girls than guys on campus, but the guys who are here come in **a wide variety**. The diversity of the girl and guy population in terms of looks, interests, and background is quite diverse. There is really no one typical Macalester guy or girl."

Q "Actually, the ratio of girls who are hot and want to date to guys that are hot and want to date is approximately **15:1**."

Q "Guys are really, **really hot**. I mean, just look at me. I don't know, I'd say that girls are just as hot here as on any other campus. What you do see is less makeup and designer clothing."

STUDENT AUTHOR: **There's someone for everyone at Macalester. For the most part, Macalester students don't tend to spend too much time worrying about their looks, but by no means is the populace exceptionally unattractive. Students don't really go for one particular look, style, or fashion here. Guys and girls run the gamut in overall appearance, so don't expect to find any specific "look" in bulk at Macalester.**

Traditions

Bagpipes
If you live on campus, you're bound to startle from sleep one early morning to the sound of bagpipes.

Spring Fest
Held in April at Shaw Field, Spring Fest includes a beer garden, a moonwalk, and live music.

Overall School Spirit
For a small college that's so low-key about sports, there's a surprisingly large amount of students wearing Mac shirts, sweatshirts, and sweatpants on campus.

Students Speak Out
ON ATHLETICS

Q "Varsity soccer is huge, but if you're interested in football, **stay clear of Mac**. IM sports are what you make of them. They tend to get really competitive and enjoyable if you take them seriously."

Q "Some varsity sports are more successful than others. **Men's and women's soccer** and men's basketball have the biggest followings and rosters. The cross-country, tennis, volleyball, baseball and softball teams offer good experience for members. Football and women's basketball are both having trouble getting members and fans to watch their games. Intramural sports, especially indoor and outdoor soccer, are quite popular."

STUDENT AUTHOR: **Both varsity and intramural sports are there if you want them, but sports are so minor on campus that self-designated "not sports people" can spend the rest of their Macalester careers without ever learning what "IM" stands for. If you're looking for an opportunity to play on a dedicated team or cheer on at a game without having to pay a ticket price, however, Macalester is the right place for you.**

Students Speak Out
ON DRUG SCENE

Q "Macalester is notorious for being a **pot-smoking school**, but that is only partially true. My group of friends has both regular pot-smokers and people who have never tried and never want to try any drugs. Hard drugs, like cocaine, are rare and are used only by a tiny minority."

Q "Let's just say our school cheer is: '**Drink Blood, Smoke Crack**, Worship Satan, Go Mac!' Now exchange the crack with weed and you're set."

Q "My first-year roommate was heavy into drugs, but he is a rarity. Mostly, students limit themselves to **smoking pot**, if anything."

STUDENT AUTHOR: Students seem to attribute a certain "stoner school" reputation to Macalester College, and yes, some students certainly live up to the expectations that such a status entails, but they are by no means in the majority. A large number of students choose to refrain from using any drugs whatsoever, and have no difficulty fitting in at Macalester or having fun at the parties.

11:1	Student-to-Faculty Ratio
92%	Freshman Retention Rate
74%	Four-Year Graduation Rate
92%	Financial Aid Applicants Receiving Aid

Students Speak Out
SAFETY & SECURITY

Q "I am actually very surprised by how **honest and good-natured** the students who go to Mac are. I've never heard about people who steal or vandalize."

Q "I may be a bit naive, but I walk around at night and leave things unlocked and nothing's ever happened. I feel **pretty safe**."

Q "Security guards stroll around campus, but who knows how effective they are? They're pretty **protective of the foliage**, though. Last fall I got busted for climbing a tree with a friend. The guard said it was outlined in the student handbook as being against school policy. He lied."

STUDENT AUTHOR: 19th-century Victorian mansions, family homes, and small shops surround the dorms and buildings. The pleasant atmosphere of the Mac-Groveland area, not to mention the honest student body, certainly allows Mac students to feel secure and at ease both on campus and off.

> **Questions?**
> For more inside information and survival tips, pick up College Prowler's full-length book on this school, written by an actual student! Check it out at www.collegeprowler.com.

Students Speak Out
ON OVERALL EXPERIENCE

Q "I can't imagine myself somewhere else. **I've had a blast**. There are a few things that are annoying about Macalester (network outages, no public transportation, no domestic diversity, limited dating opportunities), but in the larger scheme of things, they are but mere trifles."

Q "Mac is about **finding your own niche**; it's not like a university where you can go to some frat kegger and meet a lot of people. Here, you kind of have to make an effort. But it is worth it in the end. If you are really going to college to get an education and have some fun while you are at it, then this is the place to be. If you want to party your butt off, go somewhere else."

Q "I love this place. **At times, it feels a little claustrophobic** due to the small size, but overall, I love it. The people tend to be smart but not too pretentious, and they're always willing to engage in a good conversation. Classes tend to be challenging enough to keep one's interest, but they're usually not too stressful (my peers might disagree with that last part)."

STUDENT AUTHOR: You'll be hard pressed to find a student at Macalester who doesn't want to be there. The intimacy of the small Macalester campus gives students a sense of community and support, yet the liberal spirit of the college gives students the space and independence they need to make their own decisions and experiences. If you're looking to join a fraternity and party after all of the major football games, however, most Mac students will agree that you're probably better off somewhere else. Macalester is a very small campus, so whether you like it or not, you're never going to get lost in the crowd here.

Manhattan College

Manhattan College Parkway; Riverdale, NY 10471
(718) 862-8000; www.manhattan.edu

THE BASICS:

Acceptance Rate: 51%
Setting: Urban
F-T Undergrads: 3,072

SAT Range: 1510–1795*
Control: Private
Tuition: $24,140

Most Popular Majors: Business, Engineering, Education, Communications, Social Sciences

*of 2400

Academics	B	Guys	B+
Local Atmosphere	A	Girls	B+
Safety & Security	B+	Athletics	B
Computers	B-	Nightlife	A+
Facilities	B-	Greek Life	D
Campus Dining	C+	Drug Scene	B-
Off-Campus Dining	B+	Campus Strictness	C-
Campus Housing	B	Parking	C
Off-Campus Housing	B-	Transportation	A+
Diversity	C	Weather	B-

Students Speak Out
ON ACADEMICS

Q "**Many of the teachers are very passionate about their material**. Some of the readings are very heavy."

Q "My experience with the teachers has been that they are, for the most part, genuinely concerned with the education of their students. **The workload depends on the major and commitment of the student**."

Q "The teachers are concerned for the students for the most part. The workload is fair—some weeks are worse than others. **The school is primarily known for its engineering department**."

Q "I feel the teachers are fair. Workloads vary from major to major. The business majors tend to have less work, while **history and English majors tend to spend many hours in the library**."

STUDENT AUTHOR: Manhattan College is a very good academic school that not a lot of people know about. The strongest school at Manhattan College is the School of Engineering. This school was founded in 1892—tied with the School of Arts as the oldest in the College. Yet, this school is one of the most successful engineering programs in the country. It is also the College's most well-known program. Manhattan is known for having a good education and preparing students for the "real world." The school's reputation may actually not give the school enough credit, as the academics may be better than that reputation suggests. Teachers at Manhattan are always friendly and eager to help the students.

Students Speak Out
ON LOCAL ATMOSPHERE

Q "Well, we are a small school located in Riverdale, New York, which is a very nice area in the Bronx. It is very close to anything you could want and **just a quick train ride to anywhere you want to go**. The best place to go is into the city to just walk around and learn about new and different things."

Q "The city is that of New York City. There is a plethora of things to do, such as sightseeing or hanging out in the various parks. **It is important to avoid some areas**, especially the parks at night. The universities in New York populate each borough of the city."

Q "The atmosphere in Riverdale is very nice. **Everything that you could want is here**. I like the fact that we have a lot of different bars and places to party. If you can't find something to do, you can always hop on the train and go into the city."

Q "**The city is close by and is a resource most students take advantage of**. There is also a good amount of energy at the nearby bars."

STUDENT AUTHOR: Manhattan College is located in the city of all cities—New York. There is a vast number of opportunities to succeed here. The internship possibilities are great for any student looking for one. This is the perfect city for any college student because you meet a lot of people and have lot of opportunities to go to major sporting events, shopping, the theater, restaurants, and clubs. New York has its own saying: "New York, New York, so nice they say it twice."

5 Best Things	5 Worst Things
1 New York City	1 Not enough parties
2 Small campus	2 Suitcase school
3 Great people	3 Athletic facilities
4 Caring professors	4 NYC winter weather
5 Great school tradition	5 No football team

Students Speak Out
ON FACILITIES

Q "**The library is very nice**, but the athletic facilities are a little bare."

Q "The facilities are well-kept for the most part. The gym, however, is too small, and **the hours are inconsiderate of non-athletes**."

Q "**There are only eight treadmills to satisfy the entire student body**, and the weight room closes to non-athletes from 4 p.m. to 6 p.m. every day. The unfortunate part of that is the fact that everyone uses the gym at those times."

Q "Well, being a member of the basketball team and an exercise science major, I can work with just about anything—weights are weights. **We do have a new fitness center that is open** to all students. The weight room is old, but it always being used even though it could be better."

Q "The **facilities are very nice**."

STUDENT AUTHOR: Manhattan College's library is very nice, very clean, and a comfortable place to hang out and study. There are three computer labs that cater to everyone on campus. The athletic facilities need some extra help. The fitness center gets really crowded, and although the machines are up-to-date, a lot are often broken. Overall, the facilities at Manhattan College are good enough to get you the results you need, whether it is to study and get an A or to work out and look your best for the beach. We also have a brand-new five-level parking garage that is a great and useful addition to the campus.

Famous Alumni

Sam Belnavis, Luis Castro, Jesse Darcy, Nick Derba, Luis Flores, Rudy Giuliani, Raymond W. Kelly, Mike Parisi, James Patterson, Matt Rizzotti, Jim Ryan

Students Speak Out
ON CAMPUS DINING

Q "They do take into consideration **the need to improve food services**."

Q "Food on campus is provided by Sodexo, and **I guess you get use to it**. At times, it is very good, but at other times, it's bad."

Q "**You are really flipping a coin on your chances of getting a good meal**. Sometimes, I am surprised and pleased; a lot of times, I just eat it to suit my needs despite the horrible taste."

Q "The food on campus isn't that good. **The dining halls serve basically the same foods all the time**, but the good thing is the places off campus. We have Burger King, McDonald's, diners, and lots of delis where you can eat good food."

Q "**There is always a good variety** of any type of food from vegetarian to Chinese. We have three dining halls that are open to all students."

STUDENT AUTHOR: The Manhattan College dining halls are unpredictable to say the least. At times, students can be very pleased with the food and love it. The very next day, the students could be upset with the food and hate it. Students may complain about the dining inconsistency with good food, but there is something for everybody—you will never see a student not eating. We may not be like other colleges and have some big time restaurants or fast food places, but the dining halls are decent. If you don't want anything from there, you could always walk right down to Broadway and eat at many of the off-campus spots.

Student Body

African American:	2%	Male/Female:	51/49%
Asian American:	3%	Out-of-State:	31%
Hispanic:	9%	International:	<1%
Native American:	<1%	Unknown:	17%
White:	68%		

Popular Faiths: Catholicism is the most common religion, but there are plenty of other religions at the school as well.

Gay Pride: Manhattan College has an extracurricular club called Standing Together, the lesbian, gay, and bisexual student support group on campus.

Economic Status: The economic status of nearly all the students is that of the middle class.

Students Speak Out
ON DORMS

Q "**The dorms on campus are pretty decent**. Horan Hall is the biggest dorm and the famous one because most of the cool people live in Horan Hall. The men's basketball, lacrosse, and baseball teams, as well as the women's sports teams, for example, live in Horan. The nicest dorm is the newest dorm, of course."

Q "**Every dorm has its own unique characteristics** that make it different for better or worse. It really depends on what you want."

Q "The dorms are nice at Manhattan College. **Chrysostom is a dorm to stay away from**. They are very small and have no air conditioning."

STUDENT AUTHOR: The on-campus housing at Manhattan College is very comfortable. Students really have no complaints about any of the dormitories because they all have advantages. Chrysostom is well liked because it is small and all freshmen, which makes the transition to college life very easy. The dorm has no AC, which is a problem when school starts and it's very hot. In Fall 2008, a new on-campus dorm will be opening, which should be nice since it is the twin of Horan Hall.

> **Did You Know?**
> 68% of undergrads live on campus.

Students Speak Out
ON GUYS & GIRLS

Q "**Everyone at the school is pretty good**. You have the diversity of everyone, so it is a good environment."

Q "A majority of the student body is from Long Island. I think I can say 'nuff said' with that comment. **Many students do fall into that stereotype that I have heard about Islanders** for so long."

Q "In my experiences, **everyone is outgoing**."

Q "Everyone is nice. Think about it—no one really knows anyone to start off with, so they're not going to be mean when they first meet. **They're going to be nice or have no friends**, so it's really what you put out."

STUDENT AUTHOR: Being that Manhattan College is a small campus, you pretty much will get to know 50 percent of the campus if you hang out on campus and go out. The majority of girls on campus are pretty, and there are a few hot girls. The majority of guys on campus are into working out and looking their best, which a lot of girls may like. The school has a good ratio of guys to girls. Everyone at Manhattan College is very outgoing and very nice.

> **Traditions**
>
> **Founder's Week**
> This is a week-long celebration about when Manhattan College was founded.
>
> **Senior Week**
> After the school year and finals are completed, the seniors have a week to celebrate before graduation.
>
> **Overall School Spirit**
> The men's and women's basketball teams can say that they have the greatest fans in the world—they are always supportive and come out to cheer on the teams and show school pride.

Students Speak Out
ON ATHLETICS

Q "The varsity sports at Manhattan College are good. I like the fact that **there are so many athletes on campus**. I think that if your team is successful, you will get a lot of support from the student body. Intramural basketball is very popular at our school, and it is very competitive."

Q "**Our basketball team is the highlight** of our school as many people attend the games."

Q "**Manhattan is Division I** in all the sports, so they are good. I really don't know about the intramurals, though."

Q "The only varsity sport that we have that anybody cares about is basketball. **Sadly, there is no football team**."

STUDENT AUTHOR: Athletics are a driving force for the school. The success of the many Manhattan College sports teams is what helps bring money and exposure to the school. The school gained significant exposure from the success of the men's basketball team, which is the highlight of the school. The baseball team has experienced a renaissance as of recent years and recently had three players drafted to the major leagues.

Students Speak Out
ON DRUG SCENE

Q "It's not noticeable on campus, but **this is New York City—if you want it, go find it**."

Q "A lot of students smoke cigarettes and also drink, but that's really all I know. **If someone does drugs, they're not going to do it in the open** and shout it out."

Q "**A lot of people smoke marijuana**. It is not a noticeable part of campus life unless you want drugs. If you want them, it is easy to get them."

STUDENT AUTHOR: **Sadly, there is a drug scene at Manhattan College.** Unlike a lot of colleges, this is not a major problem. The most common drug is marijuana. The majority of students do not even get involved with drugs, but that is not saying they haven't tried them. Most of the campus drinks and smokes cigarettes. Other than that, you really have to look carefully to find any sort of drug problems or make friends with the wrong people. This isn't a college that gets involved in that sort of stuff, and there are a lot of responsible students that attend Manhattan.

13:1	Student-to-Faculty Ratio
88%	Freshman Retention Rate
58%	Four-Year Graduation Rate
84%	Financial Aid Applicants Receiving Aid

Students Speak Out
SAFETY & SECURITY

Q "Security is very important on campus. I think **Manhattan College is one of the safest schools in NYC**. There aren't many crimes on campus beside students being drunk on Thursdays. The campus offers e-mails, text message alerts, security guards, and a police station only a few blocks away."

Q "**Students must always be careful because we are in the city**. But, there is generally a low level of crime, and most students feel safe."

Q "The campus is fairly compact, so there is not that much ground to cover. In my time at this school, **I have only heard of a few cases of incidents happening**, including alcohol poisoning and muggings."

STUDENT AUTHOR: The security department does a magnificent job of protecting the students of Manhattan College and ensuring that the campus is safe at all times. The campus is not very big, so they do not have a lot of ground to cover. The College is not the safest in America, but it is pretty close to the top.

> **Questions?**
> For more inside information and survival tips, pick up College Prowler's full-length book on this school, written by an actual student! Check it out at *www.collegeprowler.com*.

Students Speak Out
ON OVERALL EXPERIENCE

Q "I love MC. I love how it's small. I love how all the teachers know your name and generally care about you. It's a wonderful experience, and I would come here again. My favorite part is the freedom we get. My least favorite part will be saying goodbye to this wonderful place. **MC is my home away from home**."

Q "I had a great experience. **You meet good people here**. It's kind of sad that there are not as many on-campus parties, but oh well."

Q "This school for the most part is wonderful, and **I would definitely come here again**."

Q "**I have had an incredible time at MC**, from the teachers to the academics to the people I've met and experiences I've had. I would definitely do it again."

STUDENT AUTHOR: **Manhattan College is a small college located in the greatest city in the world.** The best part of this college is the people. You have the opportunity to know half of the College, which is something you can't always do at other colleges or universities. There is a great student-to-faculty ratio, so the teachers will likely know you by your first name. The professors care about the students and make sure they graduate and are prepared to succeed in the real world. There are some things that are missing from this college, like a football team, but it still has a lot of energy and life. The school gives you everything you could want from a small and comfortable atmosphere to the thrills of a Division I school. At Manhattan College, you will get the experience of a lifetime and will not regret coming here.

Manhattanville College

2900 Purchase Street; Purchase, NY 10577
(914) 694-2200; www.manhattanville.edu

THE BASICS:

Acceptance Rate: 52%
Setting: Suburban
F-T Undergrads: 1,842

SAT Range: 1490–1830*
Control: Private
Tuition: $31,620

Most Popular Majors: Business, Visual/Performing Arts, Social Sciences, Psychology, English

*of 2400

Academics	B	Guys	B
Local Atmosphere	B+	Girls	B+
Safety & Security	A	Athletics	B-
Computers	A-	Nightlife	A-
Facilities	A-	Greek Life	N/A
Campus Dining	B	Drug Scene	B
Off-Campus Dining	B+	Campus Strictness	B
Campus Housing	B	Parking	B+
Off-Campus Housing	D-	Transportation	A
Diversity	A-	Weather	B-

Students Speak Out
ON ACADEMICS

Q "The teachers vary from very good with a lot of enthusiasm to dry and boring and cannot teach that well. The work depends on the teacher, but **the workload in general is not that bad**. It is a sufficient amount of work that can become overwhelming at times."

Q "Workload is average, but students in the arts programs—music, theater, and visual—require longer classes, and **art students have long hours in the studio**."

Q "I'm getting a great education here, and **I don't feel bad that my parents are spending so much** money to send me here."

Q "I transferred to Manhattanville because I wasn't doing well at my other school. This is the place for me. **My grades have improves significantly**, and I am happy with my progress."

STUDENT AUTHOR: The average class size is between 13 and 17, meaning professors will know their students' names. The small class size is one of the benefits of going to a private college like Manhattanville. All professors have office hours, but many go above and beyond that. Professors at Manhattanville genuinely care about how well their students do and recommend that their students meet with them whenever necessary. With that being said, it is no surprise many professors will work with students around other schedules if time is an issue. Manhattanville has an exceptional School of Education, and the theater program also stands above the rest.

Students Speak Out
ON LOCAL ATMOSPHERE

Q "**Purchase is so boring**. Luckily, White Plains and NYC are close by. If they weren't, I would probably go crazy!"

Q "Purchase is a rich area with no attractions in it. **When I'm off campus I go to New York City**. I can find things to do there for days."

Q "White Plains, the town next to the college, is **very accessible both by a public bus and the college's shuttle**. The best things to do include going to the cinema, Mamaroneck Avenue, bars, and restaurants."

Q "SUNY Purchase is down the road. The Manhattanville campus is very small but **close to White Plains**, which has two malls, The Galleria and The Westchester, several bars, restaurants, and a movie theater."

STUDENT AUTHOR: Aside from being able to enviously gaze at the big houses that line Purchase Street, Purchase, N.Y., is a little town with no attractions. There is nothing to do here, but luckily, it borders White Plains and is a short train ride from the Big Apple. White Plains is a city that is continuously growing as big shots like Donald Trump break ground and build up. Wal-Mart, Target, and Stop and Shop are places where college students on a budget can shop for necessities like snacks and Red Bulls to pull all-nighters. New York City is also another place many students spend their time on the weekends. It is just a short 40-minute train ride and is filled with so many attractions that serve as day-long entertainment.

5 Best Things
1. Hanging out in the Quad
2. The Castle
3. View of NYC
4. Living in Spellman
5. Affordable trips to NYC

5 Worst Things
1. Red trays in FLIK
2. Portfolio system
3. Lack of school spirit
4. No football team
5. Male-to-female ratio

Students Speak Out
ON FACILITIES

Q "The library is open 24 hours, which is amazing. Also included in tuition is a fee for supplies, so **printing at the library is unlimited and free**."

Q "The facilities on campus are nice. They are actually building a new student center, which should be open at the end of this year with a new gym, theater, radio station, and more. However, the one building that stands out the most is the Castle because of the **amazing architecture and design, inside and out**."

Q "**The gym in the new building is wonderful**. The whole building in general is high-tech and very modern. I like it a lot."

Q "My favorite place to go is the Castle. I find something new in it every day, and **how many people can say that their school has a castle**? It's awesome."

Q "I spend a lot of my extra time in the Game Zone. I have friends who work there, so **we play pool and stuff**."

STUDENT AUTHOR: **Even though Manhattanville has such a small campus and population, there is always something to do. The Game Zone is rarely empty, and good tunes are always flowing out of the jukebox. Students enjoy the Game Zone's relaxed and carefree atmosphere. The students who like to get on top of their studies enjoy the library. The librarians and student workers are friendly and more than helpful. The library's atmosphere is calm and is a reasonable escape from the average quick-paced day.**

Famous Alumni
Rose Kennedy, Eunice Kennedy Shriver, Ethel Kennedy, Carmen Marc Valvo

Students Speak Out
ON CAMPUS DINING

Q "FLIK does the food across campus. **The Pub is the hot spot for easy food on the run** like fries, burgers, and chicken fingers; the library café is good for coffee; and the Brownson café by the commuter lounge has Starbucks coffee and quick snacks."

Q "**I don't eat meat, and I never have a problem finding food in FLIK**. That was something that I was scared about when I came to college."

Q "The food is good at first but gets very old. The Pub is overpriced but tasty. **There's not much variety, but it is a really small school**."

Q "The food on campus is edible but not that enjoyable because **after a few weeks it becomes the same thing** over and over again."

Q "I like that **FLIK is all-you-can-eat**. I can eat 10 different things at each meal if I wanted to."

STUDENT AUTHOR: **The food at Manhattanville is provided by FLIK, which stands for Food and Love in the Kitchen. Students often wonder what they consider "love" to be. As with any school food, there are good days as well as bad. The best thing about FLIK is that it is all-you-can-eat, so if you don't like something you got to eat, you can easily get something else. The cafeteria also has a Cook to Serve station, which is home to Sushi Wednesdays, Dosa Delhi on Thursdays, and other special meals cooked at lunch and dinner. Vegetarians never fear: The salad bar is here and it also serves for students who want to eat on the lighter side.**

Student Body

African American:	7%	Male/Female:	33/67%
Asian American:	2%	Out-of-State:	37%
Hispanic:	15%	International:	8%
Native American:	1%	Unknown:	14%
White:	53%		

Popular Faiths: Christianity, Judaism, and Islam.

Gay Pride: The gay population at Manhattanville is evident and shows through the efforts of the Gay Straight Alliance (GSA).

Economic Status: The students here represent all facets of the economic scale. No matter what a student's economic status is, though, no one is singled out or discriminated against, and other students are not aware of others' situations unless they disclose that information.

Students Speak Out
ON DORMS

Q "The dorm rooms—with the exception of Spellman—are very small. The nicest dorm is Spellman because **the rooms are very big and spacious** and people tend to be very friendly there."

Q **"The freshmen don't know how lucky they are** living in Spellman, but I guess they will realize when they have to pack up and move out!"

Q "Spellman was amazing. I miss it so much! **If I could live there all four years, I would**."

STUDENT AUTHOR: **With rooms that have an ample amount of storage and enough space to actually sit on the floor, freshmen have the luxury of living in Spellman Hall for their first year. The rooms here provide enough space for more than just a student and roommate to hang out. Founders Hall, on the other hand, is quite the opposite. While some students live in triples and quads, the doubles are more confining. Originally designed to be occupied by one student, doubles in Founders have been renamed "dingles."**

> **Did You Know?**
> 85% of undergrads live on campus.

Students Speak Out
ON GUYS & GIRLS

Q "As a girl at Mville, it really sucks because **there are so many girls**, but the boys who do go here are pretty good looking. Most of them are nice, too, which is a plus."

Q "There are a lot of fairly attractive guys on campus. The athletes, in particular, are nice, although **many are typical jocks who just want to hook up**. There is a much higher percentage of girls, which makes it a problem to find a guy but provides a more female-directed curriculum."

Q "No matter where you go, **you will never get away from cliques**. It's just something that never goes away."

Q "Manhattanville has a wide range of guys and girls, from the **geeky to the jocks and everything in between**. It makes the campus very diverse and enjoyable to be in."

STUDENT AUTHOR: **Since there are way more girls than guys, on this campus it's a downer to be a single, straight girl who really wants to find her future husband! The guys are lucky and have the pick of the litter, for lack of a better term. They have hundreds of pretty girls to choose from. Not all of the guys on campus fall into the stereotype that men are just after sex. Some of them actually have morals and know how to treat women, but of course there are jerks sprinkled here and there.**

> **Traditions**
>
> **Fall Fest**
> This takes place in September, and there is a lot of fun food and activities, student performers, and if everyone is lucky, bright, warm weather.
>
> **Quad Jam**
> This takes place in April and entails a lot of fun, food, and a headline performer. In the past, 112 and the Gin Blossoms have performed.
>
> **Overall School Spirit**
> Manhattanville is a small school, and many students are not as enthusiastic as students at other schools.

Students Speak Out
ON ATHLETICS

Q "**Hockey is the big thing** because our team is really good. Many of the other sports get ignored but are available. There are a lot of intramural tournaments organized by faculty that can be lots of fun, including dodgeball."

Q "There are a great deal of sports on campus. We are Division III, and since **our school does not have a football team**, the next biggest thing for us is our hockey team."

Q "Basketball games are the unifying athletic events because **other sports teams, like the baseball team, come and cheer the team on**."

Q "**The female teams don't get enough praise**, but the funny thing is that most of them are better than their male counterpart teams!"

STUDENT AUTHOR: **On and off the field, all of the men's and women's teams work their butts off, but the school spirit at Manhattanville is disappointing to an extent. The attendance at the games is moderate but usually inconsistent. The pride isn't where it should be, but when students go to athletic events at Mville, they get decked out in their gear to support their teams.**

Students Speak Out
ON DRUG SCENE

Q "A handful of people do drugs on campus, but I believe that every campus has drugs. And it is noticeable because **if you listen to people talk, you hear them talking about getting high** and whatnot."

Q "**All I ever hear about is people smoking weed and drinking**. I don't think drugs are as noticeable as the drinking because people are more cautious about talking about doing drugs."

Q "Two words: The Hill. Lots of people smoke a lot, and it's not hard to find them. **Harder drugs are much less popular**, though."

STUDENT AUTHOR: The drug scene at Manhattanville is not showcased, but it still exists. On campus, pot is the most used drug. It is the cheapest and easiest to find, but that does not mean students don't do any other drugs. Ecstasy, cocaine, mushrooms, and acid are also used by students. Drinking is easier to hide, but smoking anything inside a residential building can get students into a lot of trouble. It is harder to mask the distinct smell of weed, and students who partake in this activity indoors are just asking for trouble.

12:1	Student-to-Faculty Ratio
76%	Freshman Retention Rate
56%	Four-Year Graduation Rate
89%	Financial Aid Applicants Receiving Aid

Students Speak Out
SAFETY & SECURITY

Q "There have been a few fights on campus, like at Castle parties, but the security guards were so quick to break them up. **I hope they get paid a lot of money because they do their jobs well**!"

Q "Campus Safety is always on top of everything. They make me feel comfortable when I am on campus, and **I know that if anything became dangerous, they would be ready** to take care of the situation."

Q "Security is very vigilant. **Crime is pretty much nonexistent on the Manhattanville campus**. I feel very safe on our campus, and I am confident with the job that our Campus Safety staff does."

STUDENT AUTHOR: Parents who send their students to Manhattanville have little to worry about when it comes to safety. Campus Safety here makes sure that everyone is safe. For example, when entering campus, if a car does not have a Manhattanville parking decal, the driver is required to announce his or her purpose and who he or she is going to see on campus. There are blue-light stations located in different spots on campus. The stations have a button, which students can push when they find themselves or others in an emergency situation.

Questions?
For more inside information and survival tips, pick up College Prowler's full-length book on this school, written by an actual student! Check it out at *www.collegeprowler.com*.

Students Speak Out
ON OVERALL EXPERIENCE

Q "I love it. **The people and atmosphere are amazing, and we have a castle**. You don't really need anything else. The teachers really care, and classes are small, which is wonderful. While the small size does limit options, it creates a very familial atmosphere that is very welcoming."

Q "I have had nothing but good times at Mville, but **it was hard to see some of my friends transfer after freshman year**. It's too bad that they didn't find their perfect school right away like I did."

Q "I didn't like Manhattanville at first. I refused to enjoy myself and make friends, but then I realized **college is what you make of it, and I changed my outlook**."

Q "Mville has its **good and bad aspects, but there are more good than bad**, thankfully. I enjoy the people and teachers here, but I wish the tuition were less."

STUDENT AUTHOR: Many students either love or hate Manhattanville. Some see that after a few semesters they are not happy or doing well, so they usually transfer. But the students who stay end up loving the atmosphere, the people, and, of course, the Castle. Some who stick it out at Mville take a while to get used to the college atmosphere, but it helps to get involved so you meet new people and grow your circle of friends. In general, most students say that their experiences have been great.

Marlboro College

2582 South Road; Marlboro, VT 05344
(802) 257-4333; www.marlboro.edu

THE BASICS:

Acceptance Rate: 58%   **SAT Range:** 1100–1340*
Setting: Rural   **Control:** Public
F-T Undergrads: 337   **Tuition:** $32,180

Most Popular Majors: Social Sciences, Foreign
Languages, Interdisciplinary Studies, Biology

*of 1600

Academics	B	Guys	B-
Local Atmosphere	B-	Girls	B
Safety & Security	B+	Athletics	F
Computers	B-	Nightlife	B
Facilities	B-	Greek Life	N/A
Campus Dining	C+	Drug Scene	C-
Off-Campus Dining	B+	Campus Strictness	A+
Campus Housing	B	Parking	B-
Off-Campus Housing	B+	Transportation	B-
Diversity	D-	Weather	D

Students Speak Out
ON ACADEMICS

Q "Marlboro is what you make of it. **Don't come to Marlboro if you need to have your hand held.** Don't come to Marlboro if you want to be spoon-fed anything—from a social life to an academic program. Nothing is going to be given to you here except opportunities."

Q "Professors at Marlboro are consistently excellent. **I've never studied with one that didn't challenge me in some way.** I admit, I don't need much help getting excited about my academics, but my professors always help me find some new way to look at things that I hadn't considered. Also, I'm happy to be in a school where I can relate to my professors outside of class."

Q "I have **never been as intellectually challenged** as I am at Marlboro."

Q "**Classes are small** and revolve around discussions rather than teacher-dominated lectures."

STUDENT AUTHOR: If there is one thing Marlboro College is known for, it's a passion for learning. Students are encouraged to study broadly but also to keep their own interests and passions in mind. By the end of your years, you will have incorporated all of your classes into one comprehensive project. "The Plan" is one of the most sought after assets Marlboro has to offer. Can you imagine applying to graduate school having already research and prepared your own thesis?

Students Speak Out
ON LOCAL ATMOSPHERE

Q "**Marlboro is very serene**. The closest gas station is 10 miles away. We're pretty tucked away from everything, but we still have everything we need (the outside world) in neat, hip, happening Brattleboro, which is only 20 minutes away."

Q "Marlboro the town has relatively few residents, but it's a beautiful little New England town, with locals more than willing to get to know you. Brattleboro, of 12,000 residents, is a 20-minute drive away. **It has a very New England, crunchy-granola ambience**. There's not much of a bad area to stay away from as far as I know. There is a plethora of tiny shops, a few nice coffeehouses, two movie theaters, a museum, that sort of thing."

Q "The closest donwtown-ish area is Brattleboro. Brattleboro is, in many ways, a typical college town. Coffeeshops and boutiques full of 'hip,' crunchy-granola merchandise abound. There's also the hospice, for those who enjoy cheap and interesting clothes. **We're fairly close to New Hampshire**, known for its lack of any sales tax."

STUDENT AUTHOR: Marlboro is considered to be an isolated, cloistered, and somewhat cabin fever-inducing college. Students who live on campus tend to get a little itchy for outside interaction just about all the time. Luckily, the town of Brattleboro is just down the mountain. In this eclectic hippy village you can find all sorts of fun things. There is an enormous collection of bookstores, a handful of cafés, and lots of great restaurants.

5 Best Things	5 Worst Things
1 Dedicated community	1 Friday night dinners
2 Professors	2 Price of tuition
3 Conversations	3 Hike to the library
4 Weekend brunch	4 Deciding your Plan
5 Open-mindedness	5 Choosing your classes

Students Speak Out
ON FACILITIES

Q "Our 'athletic center' is pretty pathetic, but our **campus is centrally located in a gorgeous network of hiking trails**. The student center is serviceable, although you can expect to be too busy with homework and studying to see much of it."

Q "The facilities at Marlboro are nice, in a rustic kind of way. A beautiful new performing arts center is being built, and **the inside of the library is great** (the outside is a total eye-sore) and run by a superhero of the media world. The Campus Center is very homey, though illegally smoky, and if your lungs are already dead to the world, it is very uncomfortable. The athletic facilities are minimal. Very minimal."

Q "Most facilities are good, especially since we're a small campus. They have their own kind of charm. **Some are really top-notch and state-of-the-art, and others are not**. It goes back and forth. They grow on you. They are most certainly secondary to what you're learning."

Q "This is what we have: the Campus Center, with **a small coffeeshop, a small bookstore**, a Ping-Pong table, a pool table, and foosball."

STUDENT AUTHOR: **Marlboro College: land of the reconverted dairy farm. That's right! Our academic building, dining hall, administrative offices, health center, admissions building, and even one of our dorms used to be part of a working dairy farm. Here at Marlboro, we've got what we need to learn and be happy, but high-tech expensive facilities are not in our near future, nor do most students want them to be.**

Famous Alumni

Sophie Cabot Black (Native New England poet), Robert MacArthur (Noted American ecologist), Jock Sturges (Controversial American photographer)

Students Speak Out
ON CAMPUS DINING

Q "**The hub of Marlboro culinary life is the Dining Hall**. The Dining Hall is a place of social gathering for students, whether they eat there every day or simply grab a free drink or piece of fruit on the way to class."

Q "I have no complaints about the food, but I feel I may be in the minority. **There is always a vegan option at every meal**. It's not great, but its mediocrity encourages the students not to overeat. I think one of the main reasons students move off campus is to get off the meal plan."

Q "The Dining Hall is pretty decent for college food. Lunches are almost always nice, though dinners can be iffy. Don't expect more than one or two options at dinners. It's not a food-court style dining hall like many campuses; it's one line, high school cafeteria-style. But **it's all-you-can-eat, and you can take food out, too**."

Q "The Dining Hall is where most of the students and some faculty eat. **Students sit down with their teachers** and make conversation as easily as they do with their peers. Because it is one of the easiest places to find a friend or teacher, many students come to the Dining Hall, although they definitely don't come for the food."

STUDENT AUTHOR: **Marlboro has one dining hall, and one café. Most meals at Marlboro have a bit of home cookin' to them. Each dish is prepared with love and often will taste like it's right out of the oven. You can imagine meals at Marlboro as dinnertime for a family of 300. Everyone eats together.**

Student Body

African American:	1%	Male/Female:	48/52%
Asian American:	4%	Out-of-State:	89%
Hispanic:	4%	International:	1%
Native American:	<1%	Unknown:	0%
White:	90%		

Popular Faiths: Though religion is a very popular subject at Marlboro, religions are not readily practiced at Marlboro.

Gay Pride: Marlboro is very receptive to the GLBTQ community. Our most active group on campus is Marlboro Pride.

Economic Status: There are some rich kids, some not-so-rich kids, and lots of people in between.

Students Speak Out
ON DORMS

Q "I think **the dorms tend to be the most rundown buildings on campus** (probably because Marlboro's major donors never have to see them). There are some pretty nice ones, though. In my opinion, Out of the Way is by far the best, but it's also a bit of a hike from the center of campus."

Q "**Dorms are small—the biggest one is only 30 residents, and it's split in half**. I'd say dorms are pretty much a toss-up; there's no one that's better than any other. Our triple-wide trailer, Marlboro Gardens, gets a lot of snide remarks, but it has the biggest hot-water heater of any dorm on campus, and it's the only dorm with air conditioning."

STUDENT AUTHOR: **Most of the housing on Marlboro's hillside campus is rustic and homey. Generally, students are very satisfied with their housing arrangements. Most dorms become a place students can call home. Each dorm is small in population, which results in a family-like atmosphere to come home to. The dorm rooms here are cozy and comfortable, but if luxury living is what you're looking for, then living on campus is not your best option.**

> **Did You Know?**
> 80% of undergrads live on campus.

Students Speak Out
ON GUYS & GIRLS

Q "I think **Marlboro has some of the truest beauty in the world**. We have traditional 'hotties,' but you really can't define the true beauty that Marlboro has. I didn't see it at first, but after a couple of weeks, I was head over heels for, yeah, everyone."

Q "**We don't have your conventional hotness**. As with anything else associated with Marlboro, we're talking kooky. It's also often buried under heavy, very practical winter clothing. The dating scene at Marlboro presents a unique set of challenges."

Q "The people here are typical small liberal arts college students: **earnest, liberal, a bit scruffy-looking**."

STUDENT AUTHOR: **Many of the guys at Marlboro are "Vermont, granola, crunchy, bearded-teddy-bear" hot. Many of the girls are "hippyville, vegan, I-don't-shave-a-lot" hot. Anybody you are in A relationship with, you're gonna have to be willing to see a whole lot of them—and I mean, like, just turn the corner, and there they are again. But there's a diverse crowd for such a small school. Furthermore, with 300 students, the selection here is rather limited.**

> **Traditions**
>
> **Cabaret**
> Cabaret is held twice a year as a "roast to the student body" given by soon-to-be graduates.
>
> **Five Fires**
> A party given by upperclassmen at the beginning of every semester with five bonfires and live music.
>
> **Overall School Spirit**
> Marlboro's spirit could be thought of as its support for the community government. Because we are a self-governing community, our town meetings and constitution are extremely important to us.

Students Speak Out
ON ATHLETICS

Q "Ha ha! Seriously, though, **if competitive athletics are your thing, Marlboro may not be the place for you**. We have a soccer team composed of students and professors that has won about two games in the last 10 years. We do have an active fencing community, though."

Q "Oh man, they're big! **Varsity sports are nonexistent**. Theater is our spectator sport, the biggest sport we have. There are some seasonal sports, like four-square and broomball."

Q "If that's what you're looking for, go to a different school. **The word 'sports' is not in our vocabulary**."

STUDENT AUTHOR: **Apart from watching the "big game" as a joke at a local bar, sports are as laughable to Marlboro students as Botox injections. We're just not interested. But, when it comes to competition and athleticism, Marlboro certainly has its share. Marlboro is more inwardly focused when it comes to physical competition. If you seek varsity football, Marlboro is not your place. But if it's fun, friendly sportage you're looking for, Marlboro has sure got it.**

Students Speak Out
ON DRUG SCENE

Q "It exists, and because Marlboro has such a lax policy, **you have people doing drugs of all kinds**. If you have a problem, you can definitely get help."

Q "**Lots of pot, lots of alcohol, some LSD, some mushrooms**, a little bit of cocaine, a little bit of every prescription drug that can possibly be abused (particularly Ritalin). There's delightfully little pressure to do anything, which is nice. If you're not a big drinker, no one is going to try and force you into anything."

Q "There is a lot of pot smoking but not much else, and there's **not a lot of pressure to join in** if you don't want to."

STUDENT AUTHOR: **Though widely used, drugs and alcohol are almost never pushed upon individuals. If there is a party where drinking and smoking is going on, people will offer you what they have, but will not criticize your decision to say no. Drugs are not necessarily a problem at Marlboro, though they are widely used.**

8:1	Student-to-Faculty Ratio
75%	Freshman Retention Rate
45%	Four-Year Graduation Rate
93%	Financial Aid Applicants Receiving Aid

Students Speak Out
SAFETY & SECURITY

Q "We have a couple of security guards, they're nice guys. In a place where nobody locks the doors to their dorm rooms, and very few even have the keys that go to them, I think **safety is created by the trust in the community**."

Q "**I've never felt safer**. We have one security guard, and his main job is to keep cops off campus."

Q "Things are very safe in our community. We have a nighttime campus safety patrolman, but because of our community atmosphere, we don't have problems with safety on campus. **If someone steals something from you, there's a good chance you'll get it back**."

STUDENT AUTHOR: **This may sound odd, but Marlboro has no campus police. In fact, we have a policy to keep police off of our campus until a necessary situation arises. That way, we are solely responsible for what goes on up here. Though generally calm and safe when it comes to security, thefts do occur.**

> **Questions?**
> For more inside information and survival tips, pick up College Prowler's full-length book on this school, written by an actual student! Check it out at *www.collegeprowler.com*.

Students Speak Out
ON OVERALL EXPERIENCE

Q "I have a very love-hate relationship with Marlboro. I think I'm incredibly lucky to be able to work so closely with such amazing teachers, and I feel the praise Marlboro has been getting for its academic program is absolutely justified, but on a social level, I've often been very unsatisfied. The Marlboro student body is so small and insular that **gossip spreads like wildfire**, cliques develop far too easily, and the dating pool is just too small, even at the best of times. Still, there are some wonderful students going to Marlboro, and I feel truly honored to have met some of them."

Q "A college is supposed to be a place of intellect and social development, but it is only when the college makes the student want to be a better and more complete person that the college has truly succeeded in its mission. I'm sure I could find a more well-rounded college, with more teachers and a greater variety of classes, but **I don't think I would be able to find myself as well as I have at Marlboro College**."

Q "**I love Marlboro**. There are always things you can complain about no matter where you are, but I feel like I am getting a great education from happy and enthusiastic professors."

STUDENT AUTHOR: **Consistently growing in its respectable reputation, this school will forever strive to keep the learning process focused on and around the students. Walter Hendricks wanted to make education a conversation, and that's what Marlboro College continues to do. Not everything is possible at Marlboro, but once a student graduates, they have the power to imagine anything and act upon their dreams.**

Marquette University

1217 West Wisconsin Avenue; Milwaukee, WI 53201
(414) 222-6544; www.marquette.edu

THE BASICS:

Acceptance Rate: 67%
Setting: Urban
F-T Undergrads: 7,511

SAT Range: 1090–1290*
Control: Private
Tuition: $27,720

Most Popular Majors: Business, Communication, Social Sciences, Engineering, Health Professions

*of 1600

Academics	B	Guys	B+
Local Atmosphere	B	Girls	B-
Safety & Security	B-	Athletics	A-
Computers	B-	Nightlife	A-
Facilities	A	Greek Life	C
Campus Dining	C-	Drug Scene	B+
Off-Campus Dining	A	Campus Strictness	B+
Campus Housing	C+	Parking	C
Off-Campus Housing	B	Transportation	A
Diversity	D-	Weather	C

Students Speak Out
ON ACADEMICS

Q "I have found that most of my teachers have been **friendly, interesting people**. Occasionally, you come across one you may not see eye-to-eye with, but most of them have been very accommodating of opposing viewpoints and treat students fairly and like adults."

Q "The professors here are very cool, for the most part. If you are going to take a foreign language, test out of the introductory classes by taking a pre-test. It's only an hour of your time and you'll get **free credit** without having to take the intro class; plus, it saves you some dough."

Q "One thing that I don't like about Marquette is that they employ a lot of **teaching assistants** who are from foreign countries. It's really hard to understand those teachers sometimes."

Q "The classes at Marquette vary widely in their intensity. Freshman classes are not nearly as demanding and are similar to classes at other colleges, but here at MU, the professors tend to be more **engaging**, knowledgeable, and passionate about their respective fields."

STUDENT AUTHOR: **Marquette employs a number of teaching assistants as extra help for the professors of most lab sections. Depending on what TA you have, your class experience can be a lot different. If you stumble upon a TA whose teaching style is difficult for you to understand, check in with the professor, and he or she will help sort everything out. Also, you can browse the Web site, www.dogears.net for student feedback.**

Students Speak Out
ON LOCAL ATMOSPHERE

Q "**Milwaukee is a great city**. Marquette is located right downtown and is close to all of the downtown attractions, whether it be a Bucks game, a Brewers game, the art museum, or a lovely stroll on the lakefront. The closest university is UW Milwaukee, and occasionally you might find yourself down there."

Q "Some things to stay away from would be areas past the Rave (28th–55th Street) and some of the areas further south across the interstate, at least when you're alone at night. I would highly recommend checking out Water Street, with its bars and restaurants, Brady Street, with its shops and eating galleries, and the festival grounds, where Milwaukee has multiple festivities year-round. **The lakefront is also gorgeous** in fall, with many miles of trails along the shore to walk or run."

Q "Milwaukee is a rather tough, **blue-collar town**—at least, where Marquette is situated it is. The town is also very diverse, with many ethnic districts . . . Still, there is plenty to do in Milwaukee, and the various ethnicities bring with them their own arts, festivals, music, and food."

STUDENT AUTHOR: **Downtown Milwaukee is only a few blocks away, and with so many great things to do, it is hard to be bored. One part of campus borders a slightly sketchy area that some students get concerned about. The ethnic diversity of the area can be overwhelming to some, but the different groups add something special to the Milwaukee mix.**

5 Best Things
1 Academics
2 Off-campus restaurants
3 Friendly atmosphere
4 Entertainment
5 Pick-of-the-litter faculty

5 Worst Things
1 Meal plans/dining
2 High-priced tuition
3 TAs
4 Unpredictable weather
5 No diversity

Students Speak Out
ON FACILITIES

Q "There's a wide variety of buildings on campus; some are new, and some are old. The old ones are really beautiful on the outside, covered in ivy and such, and they are still **new and up-to-date** on the inside."

Q "The Rec Plex is perhaps the nicest in terms of athletics, because it was **once a YMCA**; the weight rooms are very nice there. Valley Fields is also nice, but due to Milwaukee's long periods of cold and drizzle, there needs to be an enclosed area for club sports to practice."

Q "There's a very nice rec center, and lots of people make use of it. It's very nice and well-kept on the inside. The union is a pretty popular study spot. **No one really has any complaints** about facilities here."

Q "The facilities here are great! MU has a wonderful rec center with tennis courts, workout areas, and an Olympic-size pool. It's all very nice. MU also recently built a huge new **computer center**, renovated the science buildings, revamped the dorms, and added several new residence halls."

STUDENT AUTHOR: **From the digital state-of-the-art John P. Raynor Library to the Al McGuire Center athletic facility, there are a lot of interests taken into consideration on this campus. There are almost always a few minor renovations happening to the numerous other facilities. With facilities like the Chapel of the Holy Family, Rec Plex, Helfaer Tennis Stadium and Recreational Center, Haggerty Museum of Art, Helfaer Theater, St. Joan of Arc Chapel, or the Golden Eagles Spirit Shop, the campus is in top shape to begin with.**

Famous Alumni
Chris Farley, The Incomparable Hildegarde, General Douglas MacArthur, Joseph McCarthy, Lech Walesa

Students Speak Out
ON CAMPUS DINING

Q "Food on campus is **the worst thing about MU**. After eating at O'Donnell Hall (OD) my freshman year, I thought the food couldn't be possibly get any worse than OD, but I was wrong—Schroeder Hall sucks. I can't remember how many times we have had baked potatoes for dinner (at least two times per week)."

Q "Dorm food is dorm food, and one cafeteria isn't really that much different from the next; they're limited selection and **questionable dishes** can make mealtime interesting, to put it nicely. Luckily, there are some non-cafeteria options: Marquette Place in the Union has a few more choices (and generally better-tasting food), as does the Annex."

Q "There have been numerous surveys conducted to try and improve conditions, and they all seem to prove unhelpful, as nothing has changed. O'Donnell has, by far, the best breakfast on campus. Mashuda Hall is known to have a wider variety, but Schroeder and Straz (East) Halls have, reportedly, the best food. The general consensus, however, is that the food is **putrid, greasy, bland**, and many kids prefer to stock up on food in their own rooms. Meal plans are also greatly overpriced, and the dining hall hours are absurd."

STUDENT AUTHOR: **Nearly all Marquette students will agree that campus food could definitely use some fixing. While each residence hall has its own dining facility, each offers a similar buffet selection, usually with the same menu.**

Student Body
African American:	5%	Male/Female:	46/54%
Asian American:	5%	Out-of-State:	53%
Hispanic:	5%	International:	2%
Native American:	<1%	Unknown:	1%
White:	83%		

Popular Faiths: Most students boast they are either Catholic and Protestant.

Gay Pride: In general, the Marquette campus is quite accepting of gay students. There are several gay tolerance groups on campus though, the relatively small gay community is more or less quiet.

Economic Status: Given that Marquette is not the cheapest of places, a fair number of students apply for financial aid. On the whole, MU seems to have a predominant number of wealthy attendants.

Students Speak Out
ON DORMS

Q "Avoid Mashuda; it is the furthest away from classes. **East Hall is the nicest dorm**, and McCormick is the most popular freshman dorm (it's called 'the beer can' because of its shape). McCormick is coed and pretty cool."

Q "East Hall is by far the nicest dorm to live in. That's where I stayed last year, but the only way that you can get in as a freshman is to be in the honors program. Otherwise, your choices will most likely be **Cobeen or McCormick**. Cobeen is all-girls dorm, but the rooms are nice. At McCormick, the rooms are tiny, almost like a dungeon, but if you don't mind the small rooms and want to be in a place where there is non-stop action, that's the place to be. You'll meet a ton of people very quickly there. Orientation Week will help with that, too."

STUDENT AUTHOR: **Dorm preference at Marquette is a toss-up. The school provides places from down-and-dirty to clean-and-classy, so there are dorms to suit any student's needs or interests. Options include coed, single-sex, private bathrooms, and specialty housing floors for nursing, engineering, and honors students.**

Did You Know?
51% of undergrads live on campus.

Students Speak Out
ON GUYS & GIRLS

Q "I wouldn't say that there are lots of drop-dead hotties, but there are definitely **plenty of cuties**. I'd say that the guys are about the same. I haven't really heard many girls complain about the guys on campus. A lot of students at Marquette are from the Midwest, mostly Wisconsin or the Chicago area. I grew up outside of Chicago, and I know that the people there can be pretty good-looking in general. So I'd say that if you come here, you won't be disappointed."

Q "That stereotype about people from the Midwest looking **more homely** has a bit of truth to it. The problem is that people tend to be less active in the long winter, so they get fatter (not to mention that people are always wearing two layers of clothing)."

STUDENT AUTHOR: **Marquette males and females agree—the initial reaction seems that Marquette's male population is composed of mainly handsome hunks, whereas the female population consists of, for the most part, plain Janes. Above all, the students seem to recognize the fact that good-looking males and females are both here; it is just a matter of finding the right fit. On the whole, Marquette is definitely not a dog pound.**

Traditions

Hunger Clean Up
MU's largest one-day community service project. Over 2,300 students, staff, and faculty come together to make a difference in the Milwaukee community.

Senior (Citizens) Prom
This spring event provides an opportunity to spend time socializing, and even dancing, with seniors from the surrounding neighborhood.

Winter Flurry
Winter Flurry is a culmination of events put together during the first week of classes after winter break.

Students Speak Out
ON ATHLETICS

Q "Basketball is the only **Division I** sport that everyone attends. The games are really fun to go to. Everyone there goes insane, and you have a bunch of "different" people that dress up like they just came out of a circus. As for the other sports, they just reap the athletic benefits of the basketball team. Other than that, no one really pays any attention to the other teams. Intramural teams are pretty fun; the competition is good there . . . IM basketball, I hear, is pretty intense, but it's rewarding. I would definitely suggest trying an IM sport."

Q "Basketball is our biggest sport on campus, but overall, **sports don't receive a lot of attention** from the student body."

Q "Intramural sports are great and **a lot of fun**."

STUDENT AUTHOR: **MU athletics can be summed up in one word: basketball! The popularity of varsity basketball surpasses the popularity of all other varsity, club, and intramural sports combined. For this reason, other sports are overlooked and do not receive as much funding or attention.**

Students Speak Out
ON DRUG SCENE

Q "The drug scene is there, though it's not crazy. I mean, it's **not a predominant part** of campus."

Q "I party a lot, and at the parties I've held or been to, **all I've really noticed is weed** every once in a while. It doesn't seem to be a big problem at all."

Q "**Alcohol is big**, but other drugs aren't."

Q "The drug scene is **not bad at all**. Occasionally, you'll find some kids with drugs, but for the most part, it's the bums you need to worry about."

STUDENT AUTHOR: While there is a certain degree of drugs on campus, rarely do you ever notice drug usage. Overall, the act is kept mostly secret, and those who so choose to participate, which is a minor population, do not enforce peer pressure or create a highly visible threat. As for the existence of other drug types—alcohol is, of course, a biggie, with a small side order of marijuana coming in second. On the whole, the environment is safe and relatively drug free.

15:1	Student-to-Faculty Ratio
89%	Freshman Retention Rate
57%	Four-Year Graduation Rate
82%	Financial Aid Applicants Receiving Aid

Students Speak Out
SAFETY & SECURITY

Q "One of the great things about Marquette is the public safety department. Marquette is located close to a bad part of town, but **I do feel pretty safe** when I am on campus. Bad things are going to happen, but the public safety officers and student members of public safety patrol often."

Q "Since MU is downtown, safety and security are of **high importance**. MU public safety does a very good job protecting the students and faculty."

Q "I haven't had any major problems in Marquette's immediate community. Public Safety seems to be effective in controlling security on campus, and major crimes on campus are generally few and far between. Overall, **I feel safe** on campus. As long as you use common sense, you'll be fine."

STUDENT AUTHOR: The primary objectives of student safety programs include placing safety escorts and transports throughout campus, observing and reporting suspicious or unusual activity, and providing an active presence in the off-campus area. They know there is a potential safety problem, and they want to help keep students safe.

> **Questions?**
> For more inside information and survival tips, pick up College Prowler's full-length book on this school, written by an actual student! Check it out at *www.collegeprowler.com*.

Students Speak Out
ON OVERALL EXPERIENCE

Q "The city experience has been well worth it, but overall, **I wish I had gone elsewhere**. Marquette is not worth the money or the stress that comes from dealing with all the problems the University tries to deny it has. Oh, and the weather is mostly terrible, along with the smell of dead fish, yeast, or tanning chemicals."

Q "In general, I feel that **Marquette duped me** into coming here with false advertising, and I think that the school commends itself much more than I or anyone else would."

Q "I really like Marquette so far, and I do not wish I was at a different school. I like that I have to take religion classes, and I like that Marquette is large enough to be in Division 1 but small enough that **the atmosphere is personal**."

Q "**I love Marquette**—I wouldn't ever want to be anywhere else; leaving for summer vacation has been next to impossible both times I've done it! For those who want a more 'college-town' atmosphere, Marquette isn't for you; it also isn't for those who don't like an urban setting. But if you can put up with crazy weather, a basketball-crazed student body, and the ups and downs of city life, then MU is the place for you."

STUDENT AUTHOR: In the college selection process, Marquette, more often than not, is one of the top picks amid college prospects, due to a number of factors. Sure, students are fast to recognize the drawbacks, but most acknowledge the beneficial qualities Marquette can provide, such as the strong academic foundation, top-quality professors, and entertainment opportunity in a major city location.

McGill University

845 Sherbrooke Street West; Montreal, QC, Canada, H3A 2T5
(514) 398-4455; www.mcgill.ca

THE BASICS:

Acceptance Rate: 46%
Setting: Urban
F-T Undergrads: 20,181

SAT Range: 1870–2020*
Control: Public
Tuition: $15,420

Most Popular Majors: Social Sciences, Biology, Business/Marketing, Engineering, Health Professions

*of 2400

Academics	A-	Guys	B-
Local Atmosphere	A+	Girls	A-
Safety & Security	B	Athletics	C-
Computers	C-	Nightlife	A
Facilities	C+	Greek Life	C-
Campus Dining	B	Drug Scene	B
Off-Campus Dining	A	Campus Strictness	A+
Campus Housing	B	Parking	D
Off-Campus Housing	A	Transportation	A-
Diversity	B	Weather	C-

Students Speak Out
ON ACADEMICS

Q "**Most of my classes are interesting, with the occasional dud**. Since I am a first year, most of them are very generalized with a high population density, and there is little or no interaction with the teacher on my part, except for the occasional in-class question with an impersonal response. I am sure this will get better, though, with more specialized classes."

Q "It really depends on the class and the semester. Some classes were a dread to go to, and some professors put me to sleep. However, there were also many professors that I loved and whose lectures I enjoyed. Overall, I'd say that **there were more interesting professors than disappointing ones**."

Q "For the most part, my teachers have been very good. They are very knowledgeable in their area of interest, and **they present information in a way that is easy to understand**. That being said, I have had some teachers that could have improved their presentation style."

STUDENT AUTHOR: McGill is one of the, if not only, top universities in Canada. However, about equal with the smarties are the mediocre, and a handful of morons to boot. The mixed student body does have one major upside: a very doable grade curve. If you do your work and have some natural intelligence, your grades will be fine without having to tear your hair out. Whether it's the great faculty, the omnipresence of the grad students, or the mixed student body, McGill offers a really good education that is unique to itself.

Students Speak Out
ON LOCAL ATMOSPHERE

Q "**Montréal is very chill and eclectic**. Lots of festivals and cultural events going on, especially in the spring and summer."

Q "Montréal has **an extremely lively atmosphere; there is never a loss for stuff to do**. This can be frustrating or dangerous when exam time comes around. If you lock yourself in your room or chain yourself to a library table, the distractions can be avoided, though. Plenty of nightlife in diverse clubs and bars, and plenty of culture in the many museums and historical attractions, if you are into that."

Q "Montréal's a vibrant, multicultural city. It's very accepting of different people and is a big melting pot of leftie-liberals. Republicans beware. Other big schools in Montréal include Concordia University, University of Montréal, University of Québec at Montréal, and University of Sherbrooke, as well as some large CEGEP schools. **Montréal's quite the party city**, as you really have to take advantage of the gorgeous weather before winter hits."

STUDENT AUTHOR: Montréal is one of the most cosmopolitan cities in North America. The nightlife, the shopping, the restaurants, and the culture make this one of the most exciting cities for a student to live in. To top it off, it has one of the lowest costs of living for a city of its size. Along with McGill, Montréal is the home of many other universities and colleges. When it comes down to it, Montréal makes McGill.

5 Best Things	5 Worst Things
1 Montréal	1 Bureaucracy
2 The campus	2 The weather
3 Low tuition	3 The hills
4 The profs	4 8:30 a.m. classes
5 Diversity	5 Huge lectures

Students Speak Out
ON FACILITIES

Q "Most of the buildings are old and pretty, the Faculty of Arts has a really nice building placed just in the center of the campus. The gym is fairly good, although **the fitness center is not very big**."

Q "The **facilities on campus are definitely adequate**; during the school year, McGill offers both a free-weight room and a nicer one, which costs 20 dollars per semester. Also free (if you don't count student fees) in the McGill gym is tennis courts, squash courts, an Olympic-size swimming pool, a running track, basketball courts, and the list goes on."

Q "I have no qualms with the facilities on campus. **I have never had to go far to get something I need**, and there is nothing that is rundown or needs improvement. The athletic center is state-of-the-art, the libraries are nice, and the bookstore has everything you need."

Q "Computers and student study center are not that bad, but **the McGill gym complex is so ghetto**! A lot of the equipment is a little bit outdated, and the pool is very small!"

STUDENT AUTHOR: **McGill has a very large campus, student body-wise, but a relatively small campus facility-wise. Almost all of the buildings circle around a good-sized quad, which makes going from class to class much easier and helps the large school feel much smaller. This setup, however, limits the amount of buildings and venues the campus can fit. Like most universities that are located in the heart of large cities, the city picks up the slack for whatever is lacking in the school.**

Famous Alumni

Burt Bacharach, Leonard Cohen, Marie-Claire Kirkland, Cameron Mathison, William Shatner, Vaira Vike-Freiberga

Students Speak Out
ON CAMPUS DINING

Q "The food depends basically on where it is purchased. The Bronfman Bistro and the Arts Café are my favorite places. Although the food is usually good around campus, **it tends to be overpriced**."

Q "**The food on campus is pretty much on par with most university food**. Big food industry corporations have taken over most, but not quite all, of the food on campus, meaning it's not much different than going to a café or a fast food joint. The cafeterias stands out as having exceptional food, especially the cafeteria in New Residence, and all can be used by people with the meal plan, however, they do cost a pretty penny."

Q "I think that compared to other universities, McGill has far fewer places to eat. Indeed, there are snack bars in just about every building, and there are several cafeterias, but if I am going to spend my money, I would much rather go one step off campus and get something at one of my favorite restaurants. **McGill is at the heart of downtown Montréal**, so there are tons of great, interesting places just steps away."

STUDENT AUTHOR: **Dining in residences requires a meal plan that is included with the rent of your dorm. Main campus dining consists of a bunch of eateries in a food court in the Shatner Building and some scattered throughout other buildings. It's about as good as one might expect at a mall food court, sometimes worse. Overall, campus dining is highly mediocre, especially considering the accessibility of the restaurants around the area.**

Student Body			
Native Language		**Geographic Diversity**	
English:	53%	Quebec:	57%
French:	18%	Other Provinces:	24%
Other:	29%	International:	19%

Popular Faiths: Christianity is the dominant religion at McGill, but the most visible religious groups are probably Islamic and Jewish.

Gay Pride: Queer McGill is an organization very active in promoting its hotline and services for the GLBTQ population of McGill. McGill is a fairly liberal school with liberal administration, and Montréal is a very liberal city.

Economic Status: International students tend to be much wealthier than Canadian or Québec students.

Students Speak Out
ON DORMS

Q "**Upper Rez didn't seem at all great because of the huge hill to climb** and the small jail cell rooms. New Rez was very fancy, but I couldn't imagine living in a hotel for a year, plus it is really expensive, for not all that great of an experience, I would imagine."

Q "Dorms in McGill are not your typical dormitories. We do not have stringent rules, such as visitation hours. **You are given responsibilities as tenants with official rents**; the school isn't here to baby you."

Q "MORE housing is not for everyone, but some love it. New Residence has a reputation for being very 'rich,' and **Upper Rez is a cool place to hang out**, a little dirty at times, but nonetheless, cool."

STUDENT AUTHOR: No one lives on campus after first year. Many students at McGill are actually from the Montréal area, and they use McGill as a commuter school. For the 11 percent of students who do live on campus, there are many, many housing options to choose from. New Rez is the Rez people either love or hate, so it would be wise to check it out before listing it as a first choice.

Did You Know?
12% of undergrads live on campus.

Students Speak Out
ON GUYS & GIRLS

Q "McGill has **a pretty bad guy-to-girl ratio, for girls that is**, it's at least 1:2. As for the attractiveness level of each sex in general, to each their own, but most of the girls are pretty hot."

Q "Like everywhere else, there are good-looking people. The best about Montréal is that you not only have the guys from this university, but guys (and girls) from other universities like Concordia. There's definitely **plenty of attractive people to go around**!"

Q "Not really, a lot of metro men (not my favorites, but some people like them), but **lately, random hot guys have been appearing**."

STUDENT AUTHOR: McGill, and Montréal in general, has some of the most beautiful women in North America. Maybe it's the French influence, but it seems that there are an unusual amount of thin, well-dressed women. Guys at McGill are another story. The ratio is not in favor of women at all, and the men are much less attractive. Sure, there are plenty of good-looking guys, but it's not unusual to find an attractive girl with a mediocre-looking guy.

Traditions

Frosh
At the end of August, McGill welcomes its newest class to a week of debauchery in Montréal.

Open Air Pub
At the beginning of the fall semester, and the end of the winter semester, McGill has OAP with live music, Molson beer, and food on the lawn.

Overall School Spirit
McGill students are proud to go to McGill. There is an intense academic rivalry between McGill and University of Toronto.

Students Speak Out
ON ATHLETICS

Q "**Not so big, unless you are on the team**, which I am not, so I couldn't tell you. I might have been on the field hockey team, that is until I learned that it does not get funded at all by the University. The University definitely has its priorities in varsity sports. I am pretty sure football is big, which surprises me, sort of, or just disappoints me."

Q "**People at McGill are definitely active**; it's just that their activity is not really a focus point for campus culture."

Q "**Varsity is a joke**. Nobody really watches IM, but a lot of people play."

STUDENT AUTHOR: Looking at the list of varsity sports, McGill athletics look pretty impressive. However, do not let them fool you. It's not so much that our teams are terrible, it's more that considering its size, there is not a lot of participation. If you are dedicated to your sport, and you would like to play varsity, you have a decent chance of making the team. The nice thing about athletics at McGill is that you don't need to be on a team to do something physical.

Students Speak Out
ON DRUG SCENE

Q "It is **very laid-back when it comes to marijuana**, users of which I would say are abundant here."

Q "Hard drugs, like speed, ecstasy, and cocaine, are much less obvious among McGill students. There are **definitely those who experiment**, and some who use, but it is just not a major part of student culture in the way that alcohol and marijuana use is."

Q "There are drugs, mainly pot, I've never heard of any stories of people trying harder stuff. **Nothing to worry about**."

STUDENT AUTHOR: Considering the nightlife, it is definitely no surprise that McGill is a bit of a party school. Most people drink, and most people get drunk at least once a week, with a good portion getting drunk multiple times a week. That said, McGill is also a demanding school, so as much as there is partying, there is also studying. As far as illegal substances are concerned, marijuana is the most prevalent.

16:1	Student-to-Faculty Ratio
92%	Freshman Retention Rate
65%	Four-Year Graduation Rate
56%	Financial Aid Applicants Receiving Aid

Students Speak Out
SAFETY & SECURITY

Q "I always feel safe on campus, and even in most places off campus. There are security vehicles all over the place, the blue-light phones, and plenty of student-run organizations geared toward making you feel safe. There are a few streets in Montréal to stay away from when alone, but, otherwise, **it is a really safe city, just don't take it for granted**."

Q "In my experience, safety is good on campus. They have **lighted pathways at night** and Walksafe to get you where you need to go."

Q "As far as I know, things are pretty safe, but, **occasionally, I do hear of people getting mugged** and beat up, so don't let your guards down going home late at night."

STUDENT AUTHOR: Given its large student body, McGill is surprisingly safe. There is a lighted pathway through campus to make night travel as safe as possible. As for the area surrounding McGill, it is also fairly safe for a city, but that safety is dependent on the street smarts of the students.

> **Questions?**
> For more inside information and survival tips, pick up College Prowler's full-length book on this school, written by an actual student! Check it out at *www.collegeprowler.com*.

Students Speak Out
ON OVERALL EXPERIENCE

Q "I am **only disappointed in the limited interaction with professors**. I am glad that McGill leaves students pretty much to fend for themselves and be mature about it. Sometimes, though, this can be daunting."

Q "**I love Montréal, I love McGill** (even though, according to my report card, it may not love me), and I couldn't have asked for a better school."

Q "I love being here because of the cultural scene in the city and because, **in general, McGill gives you a solid education**. I was a bit disappointed in the music program because there are not a whole lot of playing opportunities for performance students. The school seems less goal-driven and less intensive than American music conservatories."

Q "I found my first year here extremely challenging, lonely, and stressful. However, I think these feelings are experienced by all students at some point, no matter where they go. McGill is a great university, and **if you decide it's the place for you, you can be confident in your choice**."

STUDENT AUTHOR: Looking at the school as a whole, most students would say that they are pretty content to call McGill their university. It's so easy to get overwhelmed with decisions about majors, where to live, when to study, and when to party, that succeeding here can seem unlikely at best. However, despite the red tape and faceless crowds, McGill is an amazing opportunity for those who want to make it one. It really is a school that you can mold to fit your needs. McGill makes kids grow up fast; for some it's terrifying, but for others, it's the ideal.

Miami University

501 East High Street; Oxford, OH 45056
(513) 529-1660; www.muohio.edu

THE BASICS:

Acceptance Rate: 80%   **SAT Range:** 1110–1300*
Setting: Rural   **Control:** Private
F-T Undergrads: 14,508 **Tuition:** $25,771

Most Popular Majors: Business, Social Sciences, Education, Biology, Communications

*of 1600

Academics	B	Guys	A-
Local Atmosphere	C+	Girls	A
Safety & Security	B+	Athletics	B
Computers	B+	Nightlife	B+
Facilities	B+	Greek Life	A-
Campus Dining	B+	Drug Scene	B+
Off-Campus Dining	B-	Campus Strictness	B
Campus Housing	B	Parking	D-
Off-Campus Housing	B+	Transportation	B
Diversity	D-	Weather	C+

Students Speak Out
ON ACADEMICS

Q "Most of the **professors are kind and considerate**, especially if you have a problem. Some professors go out of the way to make things interesting, and some just seem to recite the textbook."

Q "The classes that I find the most interesting are the ones where **I end up working the hardest**. These are also classes where my grades are below my personal average. They like to push students, and they make each class challenging."

Q "Several of my computer science classes were very interesting. I've had the entire spectrum of professors. I've had the **inspiring and insightful** teachers, and also the horrible and unfair teachers. For the most part, they have been pretty good. The best way to find good professors and classes is to ask upperclassmen."

Q "I think that there's probably a difference in professors from department to department, and **there will always be bad professors**. However, I think that the professors here are really good. I am a literature major, and most of the professors I have had from the English department have been excellent."

STUDENT AUTHOR: **At Miami of Ohio, the professors are capable of both captivating their students with oratorical wizardry, and sedating them with drabble read monotonously from a teacher's manual. Good and bad experiences also depend upon subject matter and whether or not you are interested in a particular subject at all.**

Students Speak Out
ON LOCAL ATMOSPHERE

Q "**The town is quaint, to say the least**. There's one Wal-Mart, one Kroger's, and 12 bars. That's about it. However, Cincinnati is less than an hour away. Overall, I think Oxford was a good place to be in college."

Q "Oxford is quite an isolated town. It's small and quaint, yet it has a lot of history. Unfortunately, there are no other universities anywhere near Miami. **This only adds to the isolation**. Local news seems like the only news that's talked about. Few students seem to really pay attention to national issues."

Q "Oxford is a small town. The population is around 8,000, but including students, it moves up to 21,000. Townies are never seen uptown. Oxford is secluded in **its own little bubble**, but it has everything you need."

Q "With Cincinnati close by, there is always something to do. In Oxford, **there are a lot of great restaurants**, a movie theater, a couple of dance clubs, and quite a few bars for when you are over 21."

STUDENT AUTHOR: **Although students often describe Oxford as a "typical college town," readers should not be misled and signify Oxford with say, Chapel Hill, NC or Columbus, OH. While there are a few local activities to keep students entertained, people who are used to having big-city amenities may have problems adjusting to the cobblestone streets, small, private-owned businesses, and historic buildings of Oxford.**

5 Best Things	5 Worst Things
1 Lifelong friends	1 Parking tickets
2 Exceptional professors	2 Isolation
3 Beautiful campus	3 High tuition
4 Broomball	4 Registration
5 Uptown Oxford	5 Anorexics

Students Speak Out
ON FACILITIES

Q "The buildings at Miami are **examples of beautiful architecture**. Coupled with the campus, the atmosphere will make you want to stay. The facilities, in general, are excellent."

Q "On West Campus, **there's an art museum, which is free and very nice**, but few students go there. They had a rock n' roll exhibit on every band you can think of from the '60s and '70s."

Q "Our student center isn't really the greatest. It has food and some entertainment, but nothing like a movie theater or anything—**they do show weekly movies** for various programs. They're usually good movies, too. We also have a drive-in movie night every fall on Cook Field where they set up a giant screen, and everyone brings blankets out to the field to watch a movie."

Q "The workout facility at Miami is called the Rec—it's great. **It has huge pools**, a hot tub, a rock-climbing wall, an indoor running track, a weight room, and tons of cardio machines. Also, they have lots of fitness classes, like kick boxing and cardio hip hop. It does get crowded at certain times of the day, so sometimes, you have to wait if there's a certain type of machine you want."

STUDENT AUTHOR: **All students agree that the Recreational Center is the crown jewel of Miami's campus, offering a wonderful location for students to work out. However, if the Rec Center is Miami's sparkling diamond, the Phillip R. Shriver Student Center most definitely represents its lump of coal. Almost all students agree that what serves as the "student center" is mainly an administrative building with a food court thrown in—perhaps to justify the term.**

Famous Alumni

Paul Brown, Benjamin Harrison, Nick Lachey, Ben Roethlisberger, Wally Szczerbiack, Ron Zook

Students Speak Out
ON CAMPUS DINING

Q "The food is okay. There's no fast food on campus. **There isn't much variety**, and after a year or so, you will really start to notice this. However, the food is health conscious, and there are decent vegetarian options."

Q "The food on campus is seriously really good. Compared to other colleges, the dorm food is great. **There are delis** in a lot of the dining halls with soft pretzels and fresh sandwiches, too. And the best dining hall here, by far, is Bell Tower. So if you do visit, be sure to eat there."

Q "We have amazing food on this campus: made-to-order smoothies, fresh-baked goods, stir-fry, sushi, pasta bars, pizza, grill stuff, Mexican—**basically anything you could want**. The best places are Bell Tower on academic quad, and Erickson Dining Hall on east quad."

Q "**The food can be disgusting** at some of the regular dining halls, like Martin. However, it is absolutely wonderful at the more upscale places like Bell Tower, with many different types of food to choose from."

Q "**The food is very good**. Bell Tower seems to be a campus favorite followed by Shriver and Erickson."

STUDENT AUTHOR: **College food is notorious for being vile and disgusting. However, at Miami, students actually enjoy a variety of tasty options either at à la carte locations, buffet-style cafeterias, and sprawling marketplaces. While the menu can become repetitious, it is agreed among students that Miami has fairly good food compared to most other colleges.**

Student Body

African American:	4%	Male/Female:	46/54%
Asian American:	3%	Out-of-State:	30%
Hispanic:	2%	International:	2%
Native American:	1%	Unknown:	4%
White:	85%		

Gay Pride: The Gay Lesbian Bisexual Transgender Queer Straight Alliance is a group on campus that promotes gay tolerance and attempts to make Miami's gay community visible.

Economic Status: Miami has a reputation for being home to upper- and middle-class students who all drive nice cars. While this is true to some extent, there are students from various walks of life.

Students Speak Out
ON DORMS

Q "Dorms are dorms, but I liked the ones on Western Campus the best. **Peabody Hall is a beautiful building**. They all look pretty much the same otherwise: red brick, Georgian-style architecture."

Q "All of the dorms are gorgeous on the outside. I think the nicest setups are in Flower and Hahne Halls, where **four people live in two bedrooms** and share a bathroom. You can also control your own heat and A/C by individual room in those dorms. The dorms on East Quad and Western Campus are the farthest from the action."

Q "**I lived in Dorsey and loved it**. Peabody's on Western, so you'd only be over there if you were in the Western College Program, which is for architecture majors and students who create their own majors."

STUDENT AUTHOR: **Students agree that the atmosphere of the dorms freshman year cannot be beat, although the rooms could stand to be a few feet larger. Many students have a good experience in the dorms; by junior year, however, moving off campus seems to be the most desirable option.**

> **? Did You Know?**
> 46% of undergrads live on campus.

Students Speak Out
ON GUYS & GIRLS

Q "Almost everyone knows Miami is synonymous with 'J.Crew U,' but I don't really agree. We have **a lot of good-looking guys and girls**, and there are some ugly ones, too. Sometimes, the guys are too 'pretty,' and sometimes, the girls are way too obsessed with their looks. If you're not into that, then you just have to seek out the ones who are more laid-back."

Q "The guys are often kind of cocky, but some are very nice. The girls are very, very pretty—and what you might call high maintenance. There are usually **many types of people overall**, so everyone can find a group they mesh with well within their dorm."

Q "**This is Miami**. You can see some of the most attractive students, boy or girl, at this school."

STUDENT AUTHOR: **Most students will agree: beautiful people abound at Miami. However, it is also true that everyone has some kind of niche at the school. Miami students feel it is important to stay in shape, which explains the multitude of joggers that can be found at any given time. The constant crowds at the Rec—not to mention around the salad bars— is also a testament to the overall health consciousness of the student body at Miami.**

> **Traditions**
>
> **Upham Arch**
> If you really want to marry your sweetheart, kiss him or her beneath the Upham Arch at the stroke of midnight.
>
> **Victory Bell**
> The bell travels between Miami and the University of Cincinnati depending on which football team wins the rivalry each year.
>
> **Overall School Spirit**
> Students at Miami tend to have spirit if their teams are winning—I think "bandwagon" is the proper word.

Students Speak Out
ON ATHLETICS

Q "Varsity sports are not great, since we aren't very good at many things. **Hockey is the biggest**, and football is up there. Baseball is growing because we just got a tight new stadium."

Q "Sports aren't quite as big of a deal as other schools of the same size or bigger, but they still have **a loyal following**."

Q "Varsity sports are somewhat supported. We usually have good teams, but **lack school spirit**. Our largest fan base is hockey. I've yet to see a basketball game. IM sports are huge!"

Q "Football is not as popular as one might expect. However, hockey is a favorite on campus. Many students play IM sports, **especially broomball**."

STUDENT AUTHOR: **Students support athletics at Miami, but most agree that school spirit could improve when it comes to football and basketball attendance. Hockey is the most popular varsity sport at Miami, always drawing large, often inebriated crowds to Goggin Ice Arena. Many students participate in intramural sports, especially broomball. Broomball participation has been known to peak at 2,000 participants per tournament season!**

Students Speak Out
ON DRUG SCENE

Q "As far as drugs go, **there is a lot of weed**, but not much else. So, based on the people you know, different things are available to you, but it's up to you what you choose to do or not do."

Q "Honestly, **all I do is drink**. I never got into the drug scene, and I don't know many people who ever did it. Of course, no college campus is 100 percent clean. It all depends on whom you hang out with and what you like to do. I'm sure if you wanted to get into it, you could."

Q "**Drugs are kind of big** on campus, especially on east quad and Western. Students here do drugs, but I'm not sure about how strict the police are about it."

STUDENT AUTHOR: Drugs are present at Miami, even if they aren't always visible. Students agree that marijuana tends to be the most prevalent drug on campus. Some feel Western Campus and East Quad are areas where drugs are most likely to be found. However, Oxford and Miami police, with the help of RAs and officials, prosecute drug offenders quite harshly.

16:1	Student-to-Faculty Ratio
89%	Freshman Retention Rate
67%	Four-Year Graduation Rate
68%	Financial Aid Applicants Receiving Aid

Students Speak Out
SAFETY & SECURITY

Q "I have always felt very safe in Oxford. **If you're smart, you'll be fine**. Miami has its own small police force just for the University. Plus, there are the Oxford police. It's a safe town in my view."

Q "They have a van that will pick you up anywhere on campus and take you anywhere at night, free of charge. We also have **emergency phones** around, but I've never felt scared on campus. It's well lit, and you'll rarely walk anywhere alone."

Q "Compared to other universities, Miami has a good safety level. A few sexual assaults have occurred. **Theft, however, is not much of a problem**. Nobody I know has had anything stolen, which surprises the heck out of my friends at other colleges."

STUDENT AUTHOR: With emergency call-boxes, the CAPP van, and police force, there are many precautionary measures for Miami students to take advantage of. The use of student ID cards to enter the residence halls has cut down on theft, assault, and a number of other unwanted intrusions, especially at night.

> **Questions?**
> For more inside information and survival tips, pick up College Prowler's full-length book on this school, written by an actual student! Check it out at *www.collegeprowler.com*.

Students Speak Out
ON OVERALL EXPERIENCE

Q "Miami is **amazing for its academic reputation**. But just like every college, some people love it, and some people hate it. I happen to be the sixth person in my family to attend Miami. So we obviously like it enough to keep coming back."

Q "I wouldn't send my worst enemy to Miami. It's a great school academically. Socially, it is a cookie cutter factory. The weather is drab and bland—some sun, but **mostly gray skies**. Oxford is a cow town in the middle of nowhere. There is nothing to do on the weekends. I knew a girl from Beverly Hills who came here and struggled. It's a big cultural difference for big-city people."

Q "There have definitely been times when I've thought about transferring. But this is a really good school. It's got a **small-school atmosphere with big-school advantages**, like a modern rec center, good libraries, competitive sports teams, and interesting classes."

Q "This is a nice college town—it's geared totally toward college students. Classes, unless you're, like, a finance or business major, usually aren't . that bad. It's never too much work that you can't handle it—if you put forth some effort, that is. There is always something to do here, and there are mostly good, **fun people everywhere**."

STUDENT AUTHOR: There's an old saying, "You can make a big school small, but you can't make a small school big." Most will agree that the former part of this statement is representative of Miami. Miami is not a huge school, but it is large enough to feel like a big university without being overwhelming. Nobody enjoys school 100 percent of the time, but the students at Miami have a plethora of options, both social and academic, at their doorsteps.

Michigan State University

West Circle Drive; East Lansing, MI 48824
(517) 355-1855; www.msu.edu

THE BASICS:

Acceptance Rate: 74% **SAT Range:** 1000–1270*
Setting: Suburban **Control:** Public
F-T Undergrads: 33,088 **Tuition:** $22,260

Most Popular Majors: Business/Marketing, Biology, Communications, Social Sciences, Engineering

*of 1600

Academics	B-	Guys	A-
Local Atmosphere	B-	Girls	A-
Safety & Security	B+	Athletics	A
Computers	B	Nightlife	A-
Facilities	B+	Greek Life	B
Campus Dining	B	Drug Scene	B+
Off-Campus Dining	B+	Campus Strictness	B
Campus Housing	B	Parking	C+
Off-Campus Housing	A-	Transportation	B+
Diversity	C	Weather	C-

Students Speak Out
ON ACADEMICS

Q "Before starting college, I had always imagined that classes and professors were going to be really difficult and strict, but it's pretty **laid-back**."

Q "While taking University-required classes, I found that there could be **up to 450 people** in one room."

Q "The **math department stinks** for undergraduates: most classes are taught by teaching assistants who don't speak English well. Some professors teach those classes, though, so when you sign up you need to make sure that there's a professor's name next to the class; otherwise, a TA is probably teaching it and that might make the class difficult for you."

Q "All of my teachers had **office hours** that made them easily accessible for me. They're required to have three office hours a week, I believe, and were willing to set up appointments to provide additional help if necessary. I think they're pretty good."

STUDENT AUTHOR: **Most students find the professors at MSU helpful and approachable. However, many students find that it can be difficult to vie for a professor's attention in some of the University's crowded required classes. Also, try to do as much research on professors and courses as possible before you enroll in classes. The advantage of attending such a large school is that there are plenty of other students who can offer advice about the class or let you know what level of coursework you are in for.**

Students Speak Out
ON LOCAL ATMOSPHERE

Q "It's a very **relaxed and friendly** atmosphere. It's very scenic and naturally beautiful. No other universities are present, but there is a community college not far from here. There's not too much to stay away from, but the city of Lansing can be pretty shady in some spots. Most of the stuff to do is in East Lansing around or on campus, such as sporting events, concerts at the Breslin, plays and performances at the Wharton, the Kresge Art Museum, and the Children's Garden, among other places."

Q "The atmosphere here is **perfect for the typical college student**. I see people walking down the street with 12-packs frequently."

Q "The main street near MSU is called **Grand River** Avenue. It's a nice strip filled with bookstores, restaurants, music stores, and clothing stores. It's a nice place to hang out."

Q "East Lansing is all about MSU. **It's great here**; there's green and white all over the place and everyone in East Lansing loves the students. The town is pretty much MSU."

STUDENT AUTHOR: **East Lansing has a wonderful atmosphere— surrounded by trees and Red Cedar River, a walk through campus during the fall colors is breathtaking, as is a stroll downtown to the shopping strip and restaurants. The backdrop of the Lansing Capitol is visible from certain parts of campus, making the landscape feel intimate but still spread out.**

Students Speak Out
ON FACILITIES

Q "I think the facilities on campus, for the most part, are **very nice**, considering how many people use them."

Q "They are **clean and updated**. I like using the athletic equipment at the IM. They have a good variety of machines and weights. The International Center and the Student Union are quite nice. They offer plenty of services and activities that I enjoy."

Q "**MSU does a good job** of maintaining the facilities. Most buildings are renovated or are planning on being renovated to keep the campus looking great."

Q "The music building is **old and crappy**, but it's like home, so we get along. Facilities here that I have been to are very nice and new, especially on the south side of campus."

Q "The facilities are **pretty nice**. Everything is clean and well taken care of."

STUDENT AUTHOR: Most students agree that MSU's facilities are adequate enough to suit their needs. The University makes consistent efforts to update computer labs, fitness rooms, and campus buildings, and it maintains the grounds nicely. MSU recently unveiled a plan called "2020 Vision: A Community Concept for the Michigan State University Campus." The goal of this plan is to create an updated campus environment that facilitates the mission of the University, preserves MSU's heritage, and responds to the needs of campus users. Most students agreed that it is a step in the right direction.

Famous Alumni

James Caan, John Engler, Clare Fischer, Richard Ford, Kay Koplovitz, Bill Mechanic, R. Drayton McClane Jr., Frank Price, Robert Urich, John Walters

Students Speak Out
ON CAMPUS DINING

Q "Not terrible, but it tends to get **a little greasy** sometimes. Landon Hall had some pretty good fresh and non-greasy food."

Q "I mostly eat in Shaw Hall, and I think the food and selections are pretty good. I'm not really a picky eater, though. **You can always get a salad** and sandwich if the other choices look bad."

Q "The food served at the cafeterias in the dorms was better than I had expected. I have heard that the best dorm for food is **Brody Complex**. The problem with the food is that it's pretty much the same thing all the time. You have to get creative towards the end because the food gets old. There are also many food courts located on campus, one in the International Center, and the other in the Union."

Q "The dorm food gets a little old after a while, but what food doesn't. You'll have your favorite meals, though; **taco night** was always a big thing."

STUDENT AUTHOR: Campus dining is convenient, but the quality of food lacks consistency. Sometimes it's good, sometimes it's bad, and other times, well, it's really bad. Don't get discouraged, though, because the next day, the cafeteria crew will bounce back with something you can stomach. Dorm food might not be top-notch, but the University really does try hard. Other than Sundays, there's a lot of variety. On special dinner days, the cooks step it up a bit and the food takes a small leap toward divinity.

Student Body

African American:	8%	Male/Female:	47/53%
Asian American:	5%	Out-of-State:	8%
Hispanic:	3%	International:	5%
Native American:	<1%	Unknown:	1%
White:	77%		

Popular Faiths: Christianity is the dominant religion, but there are outlets for other forms of worship.

Gay Pride: Most students are very accepting of people, regardless of their sexual preference. Twice a year, a gay pride week is held.

Economic Status: Although social and economic standing can vary, most students who attend MSU belong to middle-class families.

Students Speak Out
ON DORMS

Q "The **dorms are decent**, but nothing special. Shaw has really nice dorms and facilities. West Circle has good food and is very pretty. Brody has big rooms and is going through some excellent changes, too. I would avoid Hubbard, Akers, and the South Complex. I don't like their setups or their locations."

Q "Dorms aren't as bad as some people say. It's **very convenient**—you're right on campus, you don't have to cook, and you meet a lot of people."

Q "The views of different residence halls vary by preference of location on campus, community bathroom, or suite preference. Shaw Hall at central campus was recently remodeled and has been the **latest craze** for on-campus housing."

STUDENT AUTHOR: **If you're a freshman at MSU, you have to live in the dorms—it's not a punishment, it's an experience you won't forget. Most students favor the old mansion feeling of dorms in West Circle on North Campus. However, most freshmen are placed in Brody Complex, the dorms most poorly thought of by most students.**

Did You Know?
43% of undergrads live on campus.

Students Speak Out
ON GUYS & GIRLS

Q "Hmm, not too sure; I don't judge based on looks. But most people here are **super nice**, if you're hot."

Q "MSU's size provides a great ratio of guys to girls, and there are people of every kind. The greatest part about the students is that almost everyone is really friendly and fun. You have both your beautiful and ugly people in both sexes, but MSU is **known for its attractive men and women**. I never had any complaints."

Q "We've got about 30,000 students and most of them **range in appearance** from good- to great-looking. Getting caught up with girls is what got me on academic probation my first semester!"

STUDENT AUTHOR: **How you approach the MSU dating scene depends on whether you are just looking to meet new people or if you are ready for a committed relationship. This is the time to figure out what you like, what you don't, what kinds of people you are attracted to, and whom you cannot stand being with. No matter what your sex or sexual preference, you will likely find a connection with at least one other person.**

Traditions

Painting the Rock
Anybody may paint it after sundown as long as they "control" it. After sunrise, you are not allowed to paint it until the next sundown.

Tennis Court Tailgates
The place to be at 10 a.m. Saturday mornings before home football games.

Overall School Spirit
MSU is bursting with school pride. There's a good chance that if you scream "Go Green" from anywhere on campus, you will be answered with "Go White."

Students Speak Out
ON ATHLETICS

Q "Varsity sports here are huge. We're in the Big Ten conference, which is one of the best and biggest conferences, so **it's quite competitive**. As for the IM sports, they're quite good, too. They're a lot of fun to participate in."

Q "Varsity **sports are huge** on this campus. If you don't like sports, you'll be a minority here."

Q "Varsity sports are huge at MSU. We are one of the top colleges in all sports. Our biggest sports are basketball, football, and hockey. I highly recommend getting football tickets, and if you like basketball, get those tickets, too. Football is amazing; every home game, thousands of people **tailgate and party**. It's an amazing experience, and few schools can compete with the atmosphere that we create for our sports."

STUDENT AUTHOR: **Athletics are an extremely influential part of Michigan State University, but that's to be expected from a Big Ten school with a national following and several national championship titles. Whether it is basketball, hockey, or football games, students gather their friends, don their green and white apparel, and root for the MSU Spartans.**

Students Speak Out
ON DRUG SCENE

Q "There is a drug scene, but I don't have the connections to say whether it's big or small or good or bad. At many of the larger social gatherings, **there's marijuana**, but that's about it."

Q "**It's there**, but not overabundantly or intrusively."

Q "It's not too bad. **You have to go looking** for that sort of stuff. Of course it's here like everywhere else, but it isn't widespread."

STUDENT AUTHOR: Students didn't have much to say about the drug scene, which speaks to its general absence around East Lansing. On the whole, the students at MSU agree that drugs are rarely seen on campus, much less heard of. The most commonly-reported drugs were, by far, alcohol and marijuana. It's pretty rare to attend a party with someone selling or using drugs. There are a few students who admit to smoking pot in their dorm rooms, but these only represent a small percentage of students at MSU.

17:1	Student-to-Faculty Ratio
91%	Freshman Retention Rate
44%	Four-Year Graduation Rate
71%	Financial Aid Applicants Receiving Aid

Students Speak Out
SAFETY & SECURITY

Q "After certain hours you must have an ID to get back into the dorms, and if you have a guest, you must check them in and they too must present ID. Cops respond pretty quickly to any calls. There's **barely any crime**; just make sure that you lock your doors in the dorms and are sensible about whom you trust. There is a good atmosphere here."

Q "I've **always felt safe** on campus; walking back to my dorm late at night can be slightly unnerving, but passing by the green lights have always given me a sign of assurance that safety is nearby. The campus police are there to do their job, and they work hard to make sure we feel safe and protected, which shows."

STUDENT AUTHOR: Michigan State University often gets a bad reputation as a "party college" because of its previous national exposure (involving student riots). Since those unfortunate events, MSU has taken extreme precautions to tighten up its security measures on campus in general.

> **Questions?**
> For more inside information and survival tips, pick up College Prowler's full-length book on this school, written by an actual student! Check it out at *www.collegeprowler.com*.

Students Speak Out
ON OVERALL EXPERIENCE

Q "On a scale of 1–10 with 1 being the worst and ten being the best, **I give MSU a nine**. I wouldn't go anywhere else."

Q "MSU has been great! There are a lot of nice people to meet and plenty of parties on the weekends. MSU also has several great academic programs such as Education, Business, Law, Communications, and Agriculture. I definitely **don't regret my decision** to come here."

Q "**I love MSU**, and I could not picture myself at any other school."

Q "My college experience at MSU was the best time of my life. I've wished many times that I could **go back and do it all over** again. I would never have chosen a different school because MSU offers the most out of any college in Michigan. The people are great, friendly, and fun. You can party all the time and still get a great education in almost any degree you can imagine."

Q "A college experience at MSU is four years you'll never forget. It's a beautiful campus during every season and the **students are extremely friendly** and helpful. You'll never run out things to do. I couldn't even imagine having gone somewhere else."

STUDENT AUTHOR: Most students are very satisfied with their decision to attend Michigan State University. New students sometimes complain that the size of MSU can be overwhelming and that it's pretty easy to get lost while walking to classes. However, it only takes a few weeks and the campus starts to look familiar and feel more like home.

Middle Tennessee State University

1301 East Main Street; Murfreesboro, TN 37132
(615) 898-2300; www.mtsu.edu

THE BASICS:

Acceptance Rate: 65%
Setting: Suburban
F-T Undergrads: 18,159

SAT Range: 900–1160*
Control: Public
Tuition: $15,618

Most Popular Majors: Business, Visual/Performing Arts, Communications, Interdisciplinary Studies

*of 1600

Academics	B-	Guys	B
Local Atmosphere	B	Girls	B+
Safety & Security	C	Athletics	C
Computers	B-	Nightlife	C-
Facilities	A-	Greek Life	C
Campus Dining	C	Drug Scene	B-
Off-Campus Dining	B+	Campus Strictness	A-
Campus Housing	C	Parking	C-
Off-Campus Housing	A	Transportation	D+
Diversity	B-	Weather	B

Students Speak Out
ON ACADEMICS

Q "**Most professors are stretched way too thin**. You can't get as much individualized attention because of the large number of students on campus. I haven't had that many professors, but I loved two or three. The others were just there to present the material whether you learned it or not."

Q "The professors here respect the students' opinions, and **they understand that we have other classes**."

Q "**The classes you take later in your college career are more interesting** because it's what you want to study. I like my teachers."

Q "There are **some classes that are a huge waste of time**. Then there are some I really enjoy because they're rewarding and worthwhile, which is generally because of the professor."

STUDENT AUTHOR: MTSU has a diverse mix of students majoring in arts and sciences and everything in between. As a liberal arts school, the University offers a multitude of subjects to improve the overall knowledge of students. This environment is conducive to well-rounded intellectual and social development. The professors are varied in their commitment and interests, but there are more who care than who do not. Some programs seem to suffer more than others. The biology and photography programs don't always seem to have the equipment they need, while the aerospace and recording programs seem to have plenty.

Students Speak Out
ON LOCAL ATMOSPHERE

Q "Murfreesboro is a party town. Most people are so bored that **they have nothing to do with their lives but drink**. Nashville is 40 minutes away and has a lot of universities, but there's nothing here."

Q "**There's a lot of drinking and partying here** because the college takes up a large portion of the town. But overall, it's pretty laid-back. I haven't participated in anything I'd recommend staying away from, but I haven't really participated in much."

Q "During the week, the atmosphere in this town is much like at any large university. **On the weekends, however, the campus is very vacant** due to students' proximity to home."

Q "**Murfreesboro is a hang-out kinda place**. There are lots of coffeehouses, and you can go to the movie theater."

STUDENT AUTHOR: The local atmosphere is quaint with a mix of country and progressive youth. Murfreesboro is trying to maintain its historical architecture and environment while managing to be the fastest-growing city in the state. There are parks everywhere, and many students take advantage of the mild weather by heading to one of them. If you're looking for a bigger city atmosphere, Nashville is only a 30-mile ride down the interstate. Music is the staple of entertainment around here, and Murfreesboro and Nashville have a significant number of venues for local and regional artists.

<table>
<tr><td>

5 Best Things
1 Beautiful environment
2 Lots of opportunities
3 Availability of help
4 Starbucks
5 Homemade muffins

</td><td>

5 Worst Things
1 Parking and driving
2 Tuition increases
3 Sexual assault
4 Mandatory exit exam
5 Overloaded programs

</td></tr>
</table>

Students Speak Out
ON FACILITIES

Q "Most of the facilities on campus are fairly modern. The rec center is very nice. **The only places that are substandard are the science labs.**"

Q "I never use the athletic center, so I have no clue what it's like. The KUC is kind of cool—there's a movie theater. It's handy that the KUC has the **mailboxes, store, food, post office, and movie theater all in one spot.**"

Q "**The rec center is awesome**, but sometime it gets crowded between 7 p.m. and 9 p.m., which makes it hard to go there."

Q "The café in the Mass Comm Building is only open for an hour or two a day. It needs to be open more. **The KUC looks better since they remodeled it.**"

Q "**I love the rec center, and I actually enjoy going over there**. It's probably the only reason I'm not 250 pounds. MTSU is a big, flat campus so when my allergies aren't acting up, I can run outside because it's not hilly like the campus at the University of Tennessee."

STUDENT AUTHOR: Some of the facilities available to students include the recreation center, intramural fields, a music library, various dining facilities, and a post office. The recreation center, which has an indoor pool with a slide, an outdoor pool, a rock-climbing wall, a weight room, aerobics, and fitness testing, is very popular. The four-story library is a proud point for the campus. Currently, new campus buildings are cropping up, while others, such as a science building and student union, will be breaking ground soon.

Famous Alumni

Bill Boner, James M. Buchanan, Tyrone Calico, George S. Clinton, Albert Gore Sr., Ph.D., Kelly Holcomb, Amy Lee, Terry Weeks, Chris Young

Students Speak Out
ON CAMPUS DINING

Q "The food is a **grade better than high school food, but at least there is a lot of variety**. There are good fast food places, but they are overpriced."

Q "From a vegetarian point of view, go to the grocery store. The KUC is okay—Quiznos is good, but it's expensive. **There's not a lot of variety of full meals for a vegetarian**. Cybercafé has a Subway, which is cool, but I'm real mad that they got rid of Taco Bell."

Q "Everything you find here is a higher price than what you're going to find off campus. Until gas starts going to $6 a gallon, **you're better off driving the 20 yards off campus to get food.**"

Q "Campus food is okay. **The café in the Mass Comm Building needs to be open more.** The KUC looks better since they remodeled it."

Q "I don't eat on campus that much, but it's not bad. **It's a little expensive.**"

STUDENT AUTHOR: MTSU offers a wide variety of dining options, but they're not exactly cheap—you can expect to spend about $7 for a square meal. Some of the restaurants on campus include Burger King, Chick-fil-A, Pizza Hut, Quiznos, Starbucks, and Subway, but the prices tend to be higher than they are at their off-campus counterparts. A major downfall is the lack of a 24-hour dining facility. But remember, freshmen who live on campus are required to purchase a meal plan, so you may eat a majority of your meals on campus, whether you like it or not.

Student Body

African American:	15%	Male/Female:	48/52%
Asian American:	3%	Out-of-State:	5%
Hispanic:	2%	International:	1%
Native American:	<1%	Unknown:	1%
White:	78%		

Popular Faiths: Catholic, Protestant.

Gay Pride: There is 100 percent tolerance here. The gay community is not isolated and is seen throughout the campus community.

Economic Status: Most students are middle-class and from the Tennessee area. Lower-income students have additional financial-aid options that give them resources needed for their education.

Students Speak Out
ON DORMS

Q "The dorms are not good. **Corlew and Cummings have nice atmospheres**—they're coed, house freshmen only, and you're near the center of campus—but those are the only two I know anything about."

Q "**I like having more freedom than the dorms allow**. I don't need some establishment telling me what hours I can have visitors."

Q "I lived in a dorm my first year, and it can be pretty rough living. **It was pretty crowded, and there was no privacy**, but it was alright. I wouldn't recommend Corlew, but that's the only one I know."

STUDENT AUTHOR: **With 22 residence halls, one would expect the MTSU campus to be crawling all the time. But the truth is most students only stay in the dorms during the week and go home on the weekends. This is convenient for the students who do stay on campus, as it gives them some alone time away from their roommates. MTSU is also different because, unlike at most other schools, the University does not require freshmen to live on campus.**

Did You Know?
12% of undergrads live on campus.

Students Speak Out
ON GUYS & GIRLS

Q "**Most of the guy are preppy, except for the mass communication majors**, who are grungier and wear mostly jeans and T-shirts. Most of the girls are invisible in cold weather but dress very provocatively when the sun is out and it's above 70 degrees."

Q "I don't pay much attention to the guys, but the girls are beautiful. You have to get to know folks a little, but I've found that once you do, **everyone is very friendly**."

Q "**The guys are all hippies around here**. The girls are pretty cool, I guess."

Q "People are the same way everywhere, and **you find your niche eventually**. MTSU has an extremely large population, so there's a lot to weed through."

STUDENT AUTHOR: **You will find good and bad in both sexes, but for the most part, people here are kind and social. Since most students are from the Tennessee area, it can sometimes be difficult to break into an established clique—a lot of students come to MTSU knowing who they will live, eat, and socialize with—but some come here not knowing a soul. When it comes to dating, clubs and bars are good places to meet the excitable type. If you are not looking for a relationship, you can find a fly-by friend at any local pub.**

Overall School Spirit

Tailgating is an extremely important activity. On Saturdays, the campus fills with trucks, campers, and people with grills. School spirit is increasing as the population grows and the athletics department advertises the games better.

Students Speak Out
ON ATHLETICS

Q "Varsity sports are not that big here because there is **hardly anyone on campus on the weekends**."

Q "Varsity sports could be a lot bigger—**I don't think that we get the fan support**. IMs are pretty big, and a lot of people participate."

Q "It seems that IM sports gets more excitement around here than varsity sports. **All the Greek kids just love IM sports**, and they seem to have dominated them pretty well. But there are a lot of students who participate—it's not just a Greek thing."

Q "Fewer people show up for basketball because there is less community involvement, but **people get more excited about basketball than football**."

STUDENT AUTHOR: **MTSU offers a variety of sports in which students can participate or watch. On any given evening in the spring, 40 students could be playing touch football on one end of campus, while the other end reverberates with cheers from a baseball game. Many students simply gather on a regular basis to participate. Increased advertising has improved attendance and gotten students and faculty excited about the football team. But overall, the athletics here could be greater when compared with other schools of its size.**

Students Speak Out
ON DRUG SCENE

Q "**It's easy to be around drugs, and it's easy to avoid it**. It's possible to get anything you want, but that's if you're in a specific circle. It's up to an individual to surround themselves with it or not."

Q "I have friends who do drugs around here. Apparently **they're easy enough to get**, so they can do them fairly easily, which is probably not a good thing."

Q "Drugs are available on and off campus. From what I've heard, **you can get anything you want on campus**."

STUDENT AUTHOR: **Everything is available, but it is not in your face. Nothing is flaunted, and no one seems to be pressured—drugs aren't just going to present themselves to you. The most widely used drug at MTSU is marijuana. There are a couple of shops in town that sell glass pipes and other paraphernalia for "tobacco use only." Alcohol is much more of a problem at MTSU. Students can show up to any number of keg parties and drink themselves stupid—and do they ever. Alcohol is not hard to get, but MTSU is a dry campus, and security will enforce that rule when they find alcohol.**

22:1	Student-to-Faculty Ratio
71%	Freshman Retention Rate
14%	Four-Year Graduation Rate
61%	Financial Aid Applicants Receiving Aid

Students Speak Out
SAFETY & SECURITY

Q "Security is very visually present. However, there are some **concerns about campus safety, especially for women**."

Q "I've never had a run-in with security. You can go through the parking lot sometimes when it's late and feel a little concerned, but **I don't particularly feel threatened**."

Q "I was attacked my freshman year, and after that I had the patrol officers escort me at night. But you have to initiate that phone call. **I recommend staying in groups**."

STUDENT AUTHOR: **Security on campus is effective but not overwhelming. The University and the campus safety department offer self-defense classes where students can learn to be aware of their environment, how to prevent an attack, and what to do if they are attacked. The city of Murfreesboro is safe, especially around campus.**

> **Questions?**
> For more inside information and survival tips, pick up College Prowler's full-length book on this school, written by an actual student! Check it out at *www.collegeprowler.com*.

Students Speak Out
ON OVERALL EXPERIENCE

Q "I don't find the school very challenging. The departmental organization is horrific. No one has any idea what anyone else is doing, and you'll spend most of your time running from one place to another with re-done paperwork because someone lost it, didn't send it through the proper channels, or gave you the wrong paperwork in the first place. **There is a great lack of communication among the administration**, which it makes it extremely difficult to get anything done."

Q "MTSU is close enough to home, yet far enough away. **It's a big school, but it's not too small and not too large**. It fits my personality just right."

Q "I'm glad I chose MTSU, and I can't think of anywhere else I'd like to be. **I like the people and the laid-back atmosphere**."

Q "I'm not a big fan of Murfreesboro, but I really do like MTSU. **I like the people I've met here, and it's been a good experience**. I think I'm where I need to be. There are good students and faculty members here—you just have to know where to look for them."

STUDENT AUTHOR: **Not everyone is keen on the town of Murfreesboro, but almost everyone loves MTSU—it's a safe and rewarding environment. Anyone who chooses to become active in outdoor pursuits will not be let down. Between the inspiring Tennessee landscape and the technical and logistical assistance of MTSU, an outdoor enthusiast can enjoy wonderful experiences here. Remember: If you ever need help while you're here, all you have to do is ask. The faculty and staff at MTSU want nothing more than to see you succeed.**

Middlebury College

College Street; Middlebury, VT 05753
(802) 443-5000; www.middlebury.edu

THE BASICS:

Acceptance Rate: 17%
Setting: Rural
F-T Undergrads: 2,430

SAT Range: 1910–2200*
Control: Private
Tuition: $49,210**
**includes room & board

Most Popular Majors: Social Sciences, English, Visual/Performing Arts, Ethnic Studies

*of 2400

Academics	A	Guys	A-
Local Atmosphere	C+	Girls	A-
Safety & Security	A	Athletics	B+
Computers	B+	Nightlife	D+
Facilities	A	Greek Life	N/A
Campus Dining	A	Drug Scene	B
Off-Campus Dining	B-	Campus Strictness	B+
Campus Housing	A	Parking	B-
Off-Campus Housing	D+	Transportation	C+
Diversity	C+	Weather	C-

Students Speak Out
ON ACADEMICS

Q "The teachers are really laid-back and all have interesting projects and research of their own. **They make class fun** by talking about their research, using real-life examples, and bringing in interesting, and often famous, speakers."

Q "**Middlebury is widely recognized** for having some of the most engaging professors and class discussions. Most Middlebury professors present even the most mundane class material in a way that promotes active, involved, and thought-provoking discussions."

Q "I have to say, I've never taken a course at Middlebury that has bored me. As at any institution, we have our good professors and our not-so-good professors, but for the most part, every prof is passionate about what he or she teaches and **committed to teaching undergrads**. This is the greatest gift of a Middlebury education."

Q "Overall, **I've been very impressed** by my professors at Middlebury. Having such brilliant professors is definitely one of the college's biggest assets. Most classes are interesting, although students can be unengaged at times."

STUDENT AUTHOR: The primary reason that most students come to Middlebury is for the academics. Even in the biggest classes, your professors are approachable—and you'll want to approach them. You will be disappointed, however, if you thought you might have a rich and ripe social life, especially on the weekdays.

Students Speak Out
ON LOCAL ATMOSPHERE

Q "The town of Middlebury is **small but enjoyable**. What it lacks in entertainment and culture, it makes up for in coziness and charm."

Q "The town of Middlebury is tiny and **pretty much revolves around campus life**. Walking through town is pleasant and scenic; there are also lots of cute little shops to browse through."

Q "It's a **classic New England village**—charming, cold, and sleepy. There's pretty steady tourist traffic year-round, which keeps the downtown alive with restaurants and shops."

Q "Middlebury maintains positive relations with the town, and **the two exist symbiotically**, as the college employs a very large percentage of the town's population. A large proportion of hockey game spectators are residents of the town, and between plays at a recent NESCAC men's championship game, the commentators even congratulated the high school girls' hockey team for their record. Being Vermont, the Ben and Jerry's beside Otter Creek is a popular destination for visitors, so don't forget that, either."

STUDENT AUTHOR: If you're a country bumpkin, a lover of the magnificent outdoors, or are simply anxious to be liberated from the noise and pollution of the city, Middlebury is for you. The atmosphere caters well to those more inclined toward outdoor activities—particularly winter sports, hiking, and swimming.

Students Speak Out
ON FACILITIES

Q "The facilities are beautiful—**Middlebury has a lot of money**, and it shows."

Q "**I don't think many colleges could rival the facilities** Middlebury provides its students. The athletic facilities are amazing, both for sports teams and for working out on your own. The student center is a convenient meeting place, with great food available at the Grille as an alternative to the dining halls."

Q "The computers are all fairly new and work well. They are scattered around campus so you can usually find one. The student center is nice and has everything that you might really need, as well—a store, restaurant, study room, social hall, mailroom, and other stuff, as well. **The buildings are really confusing** until you get familiar with them, but you will adapt to them quickly."

Q "**Middlebury's facilities are unbelievably, even excessively, beautiful**. I especially appreciate the Grille and the student center, which is a nice, alternative place for studying and meeting friends."

Q "**Construction is always active** on campus, providing students and alums with a visible indication of how their tuition dollars are being spent."

STUDENT AUTHOR: Older buildings and furniture have been left standing around Middlebury's campus to preserve the charming, antique feel; they've been restored and modernized throughout the years, however, to compliment the new facilities that continue to be added.

Students Speak Out
ON CAMPUS DINING

Q "**Middlebury has won various awards** for the quality of its food, and three dining halls provide three uniquely enjoyable dining experiences."

Q "I am quite content with the food on campus. Middlebury **supports local farmers** and offers organic vegetables in its salad bars. Its dining staff isn't afraid to try creative dishes, and, usually that's not a problem."

Q "Ross dining rules! The food is above average in all Middlebury dining halls, but **Ross always has great selections**. Visitors are consistently in awe of the quality of food that we get there."

Q "Outstanding food—in fact Middlebury won the prestigious Ivy Award for food. Sorry if I sound like a public relations agent, but the food is incredible. **One will not go hungry**."

Q "Everyone complains about the college food, but once you spend a weekend at another college, **you'll know just how great the Midd food is**. Proctor offers the opportunity to create. The microwaves, panini grill, and fantastic salad bar enable you to eat something different every night."

STUDENT AUTHOR: The fact that you're required to be on the meal plan freshman year may feel confining, but remember that you're going to be busy. Besides that, the food is phenomenal for a college and truly unlimited. How many other college students can choose between fried calamari, fresh stir-fry, grilled chicken, and three varieties of pizza for lunch?

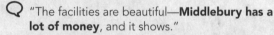

Students Speak Out
ON DORMS

Q "The freshman dorms aren't great, but the options are great for upperclassmen. I like to avoid the new dorms and **stick with the older ones** that are right in the heart of campus."

Q "The dorms are a really mixed bunch because some of the newer ones, like Ross, are absolutely lovely, while others, like Coffrin, are less pleasant. Overall, **the rooms are comfortable**."

Q "**There is something for everyone**. There isn't one specific dorm to avoid because in any given dorm some rooms are smaller than others. The location tends to make a 'good' or 'bad' dorm."

STUDENT AUTHOR: **Freshman rooms and some sophomore rooms are just big enough for you and your stuff. Junior and senior rooms, however, will not only fit you and your stuff, but allow your guests a bit of room to breathe at an impromptu party, as well. If you're lucky, you may even get to live in a house or a suite your senior year. Room draw will typically allow you to choose a better room every year, depending on your random draw number and whether or not you stay in your commons.**

Did You Know?
97% of undergrads live on campus.

Students Speak Out
ON GUYS & GIRLS

Q "Midd kids are infamous not only for wearing J.Crew, but also for **looking like J.Crew models**. At Middlebury, it certainly doesn't seem like blond hair or blue eyes is a recessive trait."

Q "Everyone is either **preppy or crunchy**. Most are preppy New Englanders, but a few are more of the outdoorsy, environmental-types."

Q "Middlebury has an **attractive student body**. We have lots of young, spry blonds."

Q "The place is 80 percent right out of an Abercrombie catalog. Most people are really gorgeous in both sexes. **People-watching at meals is a big pastime** here."

STUDENT AUTHOR: **If one opinion sounds off more loudly than any other, it's that we think we're pretty hot. This could mean that we're arrogant, but we like to call it honesty. As for personality, students tend to have lots of it, or at least make an effort to seem like they do. To better fit the Middlebury mold, see if you can't work for a foreign embassy, or at least learn to surf in Australia before you arrive.**

Traditions

Polar Bearing
As soon as Lake Dunmore thaws, students take to the icy waters for midnight Thursday dips—naked.

Waking the President
Students march down to the President's door at 5 a.m. on graduation day to ask him whether or not the procession will take place outside that year.

Overall School Spirit
Middlebury College is just small enough to foster a substantial amount of school spirit.

Students Speak Out
ON ATHLETICS

Q "Sports are important at Middlebury, but students who don't play sports aren't shunned or beaten. I think **there's a pretty healthy balance** among the student body."

Q "**Middlebury is a very athletic campus**, and a number of the varsity programs are very strong and successful. Some IM sports, particularly broomball during J-term, are famously cultish."

Q "Ultimate Frisbee is the other really popular option here, and the **team members form a tight group** who like to have a good time."

Q "Hockey is the best! **Tons of people turn out** at free men's hockey games during the winter, complete with face paint, cheers, and a love for heckling the opposing team's goalie. However, hockey is the only popular sport, and almost no one goes to football and basketball games."

STUDENT AUTHOR: **Whether you want to play with some of the most driven, hard-working, and talented athletes in the country, or you simply want to take part in an IM here or there, when it comes to athletics, it would suffice to say that Middlebury's got it all.**

Students Speak Out
ON DRUG SCENE

Q "Like on any college campus, **people do a lot of pot**. Other than that, I haven't really encountered much of a drug scene, and it has certainly never been a problem."

Q "**A lot of drinking and smoking goes on** here due to the stress. People smoke marijuana, and there are some other hard drugs that appear once in a while. No-Doz and caffeine are popular, but there are plenty of people who do not use drugs."

Q "Like anywhere, the drugs are here if you're looking for them, but **they're not in your face** if you're not. Pot smoking is fairly common, and a few kids use other drugs, but for almost everyone, alcohol is the drug of choice."

STUDENT AUTHOR: Your exposure to drugs simply depends on who you hang out with and what you expose yourself to. At a school so focused on academics and achievement, rest assured there are many Middlebury students who don't spend their time or money on drugs.

9:1	Student-to-Faculty Ratio
95%	Freshman Retention Rate
86%	Four-Year Graduation Rate
87%	Financial Aid Applicants Receiving Aid

Students Speak Out
SAFETY & SECURITY

Q "I feel like **this is an extremely safe campus**, and I have never had any problems with crime here. The officers are almost too much of a presence at times."

Q "**We feel kind of bad for security officers** here on campus. They have nothing better to do than ride around in minivans and break up relatively docile parties at two in the morning—a pretty cushy job if you ask me."

Q "My biggest fear walking around campus is that **I'll slip on the ice that covers the campus** grounds for a good five months out of the year. I've never been worried about my safety, otherwise."

STUDENT AUTHOR: Overall, Middlebury is an entirely safe locale, from the town to the College. Even if you black out in the middle of the main quad on a Saturday night—which isn't to say you should—you'll most likely be left to sleep peacefully until morning (assuming you don't freeze to death first).

> **Questions?**
> For more inside information and survival tips, pick up College Prowler's full-length book on this school, written by an actual student! Check it out at *www.collegeprowler.com.*

Students Speak Out
ON OVERALL EXPERIENCE

Q "Sometimes I wish I'd gone somewhere where **I would have had more free time**, but when I think about the opportunities that are open to me because I went to Middlebury and excelled in such a rigorous academic environment, I'm happy that I stuck it out! Middlebury is a great place brimming with talented and fun people, and a generally friendly and helpful staff. I would come here again if I had to choose."

Q "**I have had an unbelievable time** at Middlebury. I'm glad I chose a small liberal arts college over a university. I've really benefited from the tight community and academic rigor. Looking back, I made the right choice."

Q "I like Middlebury. It's a **funny, little, isolated culture**, and it's not much like real life. On the other hand, it's a fun place and I'm glad to be here."

Q "I sometimes wish I did not have to devote as much time to academic work as I do. I know there are **many schools that are less intense** than Middlebury. This being said, Middlebury has been a wonderful place for me, and I never wished I had chosen someplace else for college."

STUDENT AUTHOR: Middlebury provides an incredibly varied experience—an opportunity to stick your paintbrush in all shades of colors, so to speak. Students often wish they toiled less at the books and more at the booze, but the pristine facilities tend to distract us from scholastic misery. The on-campus social scene is lively and shot through with school spirit. The athletics put us at the top of our division, and the area is quaint ("quaint," unfortunately, being the opposite of any adjective suggestive of "nightlife").

Millsaps College

1701 North State Street; Jackson, MS 39210-0001
(601) 974-1000; www.millsaps.edu

THE BASICS:

Acceptance Rate: 77%
Setting: Mid-sized city
F-T Undergrads: 1,043

SAT Range: 1090–1320*
Control: Private
Tuition: $23,352

Most Popular Majors: Psychology, Business, Biology, English, Sociology

*of 1600

Academics	B	Guys	B+
Local Atmosphere	C	Girls	B
Safety & Security	C	Athletics	C
Computers	B-	Nightlife	C+
Facilities	C+	Greek Life	A+
Campus Dining	C+	Drug Scene	B+
Off-Campus Dining	B	Campus Strictness	B
Campus Housing	C	Parking	A+
Off-Campus Housing	D+	Transportation	C
Diversity	C	Weather	A-

Students Speak Out
ON ACADEMICS

Q "Except for a few situations, **I love every teacher that I've had here**. They never seem aloof or too self-important. For better or worse, they never push their own research on you. They really have gotten me to see the earthiness of the material, and I see my education for what it is: the blueprint for the rest of my life."

Q "They call it **reading and writing intensive**, and as you might imagine, that isn't an admissions gimmick for your parents. You should expect three or four big essays a class, several essay tests a semester, and more rarely, daily writings. If you take them seriously, though, you'll have to become really involved in the subject matter, and you are more engaged during the period."

Q "There's a lot of talk about the difficulty of classes, but most of the students seem to be in the humanities, so you know how heartfelt they are. **By sophomore year, most students are coasting** anyway. From what I hear from some of my friends at big prestigious state schools, we have a pretty good deal."

STUDENT AUTHOR: **Students that make it through the core curriculum, in which foci vary from history to lab science to modern culture, discover their callings and come to understand which paths they should pursue. In every department, you will find well-versed professionals on almost every level who are willing to advise. Many courses, especially in the humanities, center around discussion.**

Students Speak Out
ON LOCAL ATMOSPHERE

Q "The city has really got a lot going for it, even though it is dead after seven on weekdays. It should have blossomed a long time ago into a niche city, with the blues scene, the history, and all of those famous writers, but it remains **a good college town with job opportunities** in the capital and downtown businesses."

Q "The grass is not greener on the other side. One side of campus borders the ghetto, the roads are absolute trash, and **the nightlife needs to be rejuvenated**. But I can't say too many negative things—I bought a place here and plan to stay in the city after I graduate."

Q "Half the people find what they enjoy and do it; the other half sits around pining for something or other. Most people get so deep into one aspect of campus life that they don't care. **Either you really 'love' Jackson, or you wish it was a very different city**."

STUDENT AUTHOR: **Jackson is often cited as a "burgeoning" city. Some think that various proposed changes that could potentially stimulate the capital are much belated. Also, there has been a recent downturn in the off-campus dining scene, since several favorite restaurants were closed. However, the city does offer tremendously diverse cuisine, from Greek to Japanese. Many Millsaps students become increasingly insulated over their four years, causing the campus to be informally dubbed "the Millsaps Bubble."**

5 Best Things	5 Worst Things
1 The personal touch	1 Administration
2 Strong academics	2 The dorms
3 Well-maintained facilities	3 Gossip
4 Beauty of campus	4 Lack of diversity
5 Safe environment	5 Gloomy seasonal weather

Students Speak Out
ON FACILITIES

Q "**Millsaps campus is like that Batman villain, Two-Face**, because you have the Bowl during spring, and you have the south side and the AC during winter. I suggest just staying away from both the upperclassman side and the Academic Complex. That way you can enjoy your time here rather than loathing it."

Q "The aesthetic on campus is not going to win over most prospective students, which is why **they've been talking about tearing down so many of them** in the past few years. The buildings are well-maintained, but that would be like restoring a disaster."

Q "**I sincerely have no idea what all the complaints are about**. The AC is my favorite building."

Q "Typical of Millsaps campus, I heard all of this negative stuff about the AC and the south side of campus, and how the admissions department for a long time hid the latter from prospective students. When I discovered I had already seen both and had not gotten a bad impression from either, it did leave the impression that the **students here have super-intense criticisms of everything**."

STUDENT AUTHOR: **In the past few years, schools across the States have been in a furious race to provide the best facilities. Providing high-quality academic programs is always top priority, however, and schools with more limited funding, such as Millsaps, may appear to be losing the race in this regard. Everyone agrees, though, that the worst facility is the Ford Academic Complex.**

Famous Alumni

Michael Beck, David Herbert Donald, Ellen Gilchrist, Lewis Nordan, Claude Passeau

Students Speak Out
ON CAMPUS DINING

Q "I had the same experience as every one else. **As a freshman, I was surprised by how good it was**. As a sophomore, I ate more fast food than I ate on campus. By my junior and senior years, everyone asked me whether I had transferred because they never saw me in the Caf' or Kava House. By the 7,000th chicken breast or ham and cheese sandwich, I needed a serious change."

Q "**The Caf' closes at 7 p.m.**, and I don't know anyone except Millsaps students that begins dinner at 6:30 p.m. They begin closing at about that time, so you have to get there well in advance. Breakfast is a lost cause, unless you're an insomniac and are willing to be there an hour before class."

Q "In the Caf' you get a relatively nice selection. **Soups, salads, hot sandwiches, and some ethnic foods are popular**. The Kava House has some choices where you can get a quick bite. Other than that, you'll make good use of High Street, which has a nice line-up of fast food joints that are open late."

STUDENT AUTHOR: **Anyone that has diverse tastes sighs when they watch students line up for the Grille, whose menu includes such "variety" as hamburgers, cheeseburgers, and bacon cheeseburgers. Despite the boring menu, there has been no attempt to court more diverse food options. The Kava House is a more social area with a large television and a stage used for open-mic nights and small events.**

Student Body

African American:	11%	Male/Female:	49/51%
Asian American:	4%	Out-of-State:	50%
Hispanic:	2%	International:	1%
Native American:	<1%	Unknown:	<1%
White:	83%		

Popular Faiths: There are a lot of Christian groups.

Gay Pride: In 2004, Rusty Walker managed to pull off a double coup within the small but vocal gay and lesbian community on campus: he founded a campus chapter of Family and Friends Pride Coalition and managed a campus stay for the AIDS quilt.

Economic Status: There is some diversity here, but it does lean toward the wealthy.

Students Speak Out
ON DORMS

Q "**Forget hospitality if you're looking for it from the Residence Life group**. Other than the freshman RAs, which everybody thinks highly of, the RAs are garbage. They only command respect in that rude, uptight way. The people running Residence Life in the administration are really out of touch. They're rude and have no problem with putting students out, because it's more convenient for them."

Q "**Be prepared to deal with red tape**. My roommate dropped out of my housing selection, and I spent weeks dealing with the bureaucratic ramifications."

Q "There's a high premium on some dormitories, like New South, but **all of them are pretty good quality**."

STUDENT AUTHOR: Although freshman housing is very good, by the time most students have preference in their junior and senior year, they have moved off campus or onto Greek Row. The housing selection program has been changed recently, giving preference to high GPAs, which has gotten some negative criticism.

Did You Know?
81% of undergrads live on campus.

Students Speak Out
ON GUYS & GIRLS

Q "If you like sharp young professionals, you're in heaven. They are a dime a dozen. You must acknowledge the '**Southern belle and gentleman**' thing here. If you're a big fan of *Gone With the Wind*, you'll be welcome here."

Q "**Millsaps is incredibly superficial**. Fifty percent of the time, people are just trying to blow off some steam. They're looking for a hookup with someone with little long-term appeal. Neither the guys nor the girls are going to pay you any attention unless you can send off those signals: 'I'm hot, I'm fun, and I'm easy.'"

Q "**A good route to go is just joining a fraternity or sorority**. That way you can meet caboodles of people, find those that have your same interests, and get married before you're 22."

STUDENT AUTHOR: Again, Millsaps gives one the impression of high school more often than not. But that does fade away. The Greek scene is very inclusive, and that can be a nice meeting spot for singles on campus. Guys, by most estimations, are big-brother types, and if you're looking for a young professional type who is a bit weak-willed and from an upper-middle-class background, you have hit the jackpot. As far as 'the goods' are concerned, it's assumed that Millsaps College has a very good-looking campus. Two qualities that have a high value on campus are taste and style.

Overall School Spirit

The Millsaps campus doesn't not have an overwhelming amount of school spirit, but people will turn out for rival sports games and brag about their experiences at the school. Many students have a tremendous amount of pride for their Greek house and major. This develops into some friendly ribbing over the utility of an English degree or the excitement of accounting.

Students Speak Out
ON ATHLETICS

Q "**Students are lackadaisical in their support of teams**. As a result, a ton of players don't take the games very seriously. It works out well because it is just a game, and people that just want to go out and have a cultivated and well-rounded life can do it without having sports consume them."

Q "The teams are good quality at the level that they play within. **They're not allowed to give out scholarships**, so athletes really come here for an education."

Q "**People are involved in intramurals**. I get e-mails all the time with some trash-talking. It's like streetball with an element of the WWF mixed in. It's the biggest nerds out trying to validate themselves on the playing field and acting silly in the process. Students strut around like peacocks after victories."

STUDENT AUTHOR: Millsaps is a member of the SCAC (which also features rivals Sewanee and Rhodes). As a Division-III school, it is not allowed to give scholarships based on athletic ability. Intramurals are alive and well, however. The playing facilities are well-maintained and well-used. All students are given pretty much free reign to use the same exercise units that the athletes use.

Students Speak Out
ON DRUG SCENE

Q "**Most of the students experiment**, but no one really involved on campus gets into anything hardcore. Rarely, a freshman gets into it before their second semester, and then they leave for their own reasons."

Q "Millsaps is a very low-key campus. **Alcohol is the substance of preference**, and beer specifically. Then, maybe some pot, and that's it."

Q "**Most students use some substances**, whether it be alcohol or some marijuana, to blow off some steam. I can only imagine about five students on campus that don't."

STUDENT AUTHOR: The drug scene is probably the most predictable aspect of Mississippi. The state, the community, and the campus is conservative. Most students have been using alcohol since their early high school careers, and it's easily available on campus at frat parties or from upperclassmen. Marijuana is, predictably, considered a marginal drug; a majority of students have used it but frown on it somewhat.

11:1	Student-to-Faculty Ratio
82%	Freshman Retention Rate
63%	Four-Year Graduation Rate
81%	Financial Aid Applicants Receiving Aid

Students Speak Out
SAFETY & SECURITY

Q "At first, with all the buzz on campus about the violent crimes and the sirens (which are the local fire department, actually), you think you're in a real nasty spot. Inevitably, you realize that as long as you make sure that when you walk across campus you've got a friend, **you're in one of the safest places you could be**."

Q "Security is phantom-like. Safety isn't. People really are **far more conscious of protecting themselves**, rather than circumventing the authority types."

Q "It's gated. Each dorm is electronically locked. Security is easy to contact. The situation is really nice at Millsaps. **All you have to do is use good judgment** and muggers will find a much easier target on this campus."

STUDENT AUTHOR: Although a few high-profile attacks on students by people unassociated with the College were reported in past years, many students feel as though safety has become one of the most important benefits of Millsaps life. Security is often viewed as a friendly foil to students.

> **Questions?**
> For more inside information and survival tips, pick up College Prowler's full-length book on this school, written by an actual student! Check it out at *www.collegeprowler.com*.

Students Speak Out
ON OVERALL EXPERIENCE

Q "There are **more drawbacks than advantages to coming to Millsaps**. The price is ridiculous and is only going up. The professors are very firmly liberal and not always open to discussion. I got as much out of high school, which was absolutely free. I'm just not sure 10 years of debt is worth it."

Q "Millsaps has helped me come closer to achieving the things that I have always aspired to doing. **The student-to-teacher ratio is one of the best**, because it really enables an actual relationship. I have professors that are mentors, valuable guides, and genuine friends."

Q "**The campus is beautiful, the people are fantastic**, and I met the love of my life here. I don't know that anyone imagined me coming here, but now I couldn't imagine going anywhere else."

Q "**Millsaps is the place for an exceptionally ambitious student**. It's not mad competitive like an Ivy League school. It also isn't Suntan U. You can do anything you want: join a frat, do volunteer work, become active politically, join a club, or start an organization. But the students do blow off steam, and plenty of it."

STUDENT AUTHOR: Despite all their qualms with the academics, the facilities, and the social aspects of Millsaps, many students look on their years here as a great personal investment. Millsaps College prides itself on being a transformative experience, and many students come back more thoughtful, more liberal, and more mature. A freshman standing at the door of his college years at Millsaps College will be beginning an individual and unique process.

MIT

77 Massachusetts Avenue; Cambridge, MA 02139
(617) 253-1000; www.mit.edu

THE BASICS:

Acceptance Rate: 12%   **SAT Range:** 2040–2310*
Setting: Urban   **Control:** Private
F-T Undergrads: 4,119   **Tuition:** $36,140

Most Popular Majors: Engineering, Computer
Science, Biology, Physical Science, Mathematics

*of 2400

Academics	A+	Guys	C
Local Atmosphere	A+	Girls	C-
Safety & Security	B	Athletics	C+
Computers	A+	Nightlife	A-
Facilities	B+	Greek Life	A
Campus Dining	C+	Drug Scene	B+
Off-Campus Dining	A	Campus Strictness	B-
Campus Housing	B-	Parking	C-
Off-Campus Housing	D-	Transportation	A
Diversity	A	Weather	C-

Students Speak Out
ON ACADEMICS

Q "Teachers are the best in their fields, often having discovered, developed, or decoded the subject they are teaching. This makes them incredibly knowledgeable, although, not always the best teachers. Classes and assignments are not very interactive, but they are **intensely difficult**."

Q "Teachers are a mix of really energetic professors who are **truly excited to be teaching** us, and those who are old, crusty, and very out of touch with students today."

Q "Most professors really do care about feedback from their students, and they definitely do make **active efforts to improve** the content of their classes and their various methods of teaching."

Q "Sometimes, you have **foreign TAs** that may be a bit hard to understand, but the professors, for the most part, are really good."

Q "It is hard—don't take that lightly. At MIT, you'll **work your tail off for a C** and be proud of it. People do get As, but I'm just not one of them."

STUDENT AUTHOR: The academics at MIT are top-notch. Classes are designed so you learn as much as possible. Exams at MIT are designed to test your knowledge and understanding of the formulas, how to derive them, and how to apply them in all sorts of ways. Classes teach you how to think. Classes are rigorous, but academic opportunities outside the classroom are endless. This is what sets MIT apart as one of the best academic institutions in the country.

Students Speak Out
ON LOCAL ATMOSPHERE

Q "Since the Boston/Cambridge area is filled with colleges (Harvard, Boston University, Boston College, Wellesley, and Tufts). It is a definitely a **city with a college atmosphere**."

Q "MIT is a blend of work and play. It is in the heart of Cambridge/Boston, where a ton of other colleges are present. Throughout the week, MIT **students rarely experience the world outside** our campus due to the workload."

Q "There is so much to do. The shopping is great, and there is **no sales tax**. There is a lot of history, yet at the same time, there are so many colleges nearby that the city doesn't seem old and outdated."

Q "You can visit downtown Boston, which has museums, the **Symphony Hall** (where MIT students get a discount), shopping outlets, and food places."

STUDENT AUTHOR: Sandwiched between Harvard and Boston University, MIT is in the hub of the ultimate college city. With so many high-quality schools in the area, Boston is a city that is driven by young, hip, and ambitious students. Because of the thousands of college students wandering the streets, many Boston businesses cater to this population. Concerts, clubs, restaurants, and malls are everywhere. Going to college in Boston is an experience unlike any other. Unfortunately, some students at MIT get so wrapped up in their schoolwork that the only problem with living in Boston is finding the time to enjoy it.

Students Speak Out
ON FACILITIES

Q "Facilities are a mix of **beautiful new buildings** and older ones in need of renovation and repair. The Student Center is a good hang-out and meeting spot."

Q "The **Student Center** has nice couches, a convenience store, four dining places with a variety of foods, a campus store, a bank, and many rooms where activities are held throughout the year."

Q "The facilities on campus are really nice. The **athletic center is awesome**. You can go swimming, or use the machines on the second floor."

Q "Facilities are actually pretty good, and they're **constantly being upgraded**."

STUDENT AUTHOR: The highlight of MIT facilities is the gorgeous new athletic facility, the Zesiger Center. The Z-Center features two pools, six squash courts, an indoor track, and multi-activity courts for basketball, volleyball, and other IMs. Students have access to this state-of-the-art facility free of charge. Moreover, students also have access to personal trainers and certain other services at a premium. The other main student facility is the Stratton Student Center. The first floor was refurnished with comfortable couches, tables, and additional seating. Because dorms and living groups are so spread out, students often choose to meet in the Student Center to eat, work, and socialize. Overall, most facilities on campus offer students their own preferred places to hang out, study, and make themselves comfortable.

Famous Alumni

Edwin "Buzz" Aldrin, John T. Dorrance, George L. Eastman, Cecil H. Green, William R. Hewlett SM, Robert Metcalfe, Benjamin Netanyahu

Students Speak Out
ON CAMPUS DINING

Q "The dining halls aren't too good. There are food trucks that are pretty good (mobile kitchens in trucks). Lots of people that I know cook for themselves since many **dorms have kitchens**, and there is a supermarket nearby."

Q "Food on campus is average and kind of expensive. Most students have a declining balance on their ID card that they use to purchase food. **LaVerde's is good** for pretty much whatever you need."

Q "It's **horrible**. But the dorms all have kitchens, and the off-campus and delivery food is decent—some of it is even pretty cheap."

Q "MIT dining is rather odd, I think. There's **no one big dining hall**; there are bunches of smaller eating places."

Q "It's **pretty poor**, or so goes the popular sentiment."

STUDENT AUTHOR: One of the best things about MIT dining is that there are no required "meals" that you have to buy. Instead, you decide how much money to credit to your student ID. Then you can spend the money however you like on campus. You can also use your card at the market in the student center, LaVerde's. Although prices tend to be expensive, students should always be able to find something to eat. Most freshmen don't catch on to one of the best lunch deals, the food trucks. There are two food trucks at 77 Mass. Ave., and a large group of them next to the bio building.

Students Speak Out
ON DORMS

Q "Each dorm holds a personality of its own, so it's to each student's individual taste. While **some dorms are older** and perhaps more run-down, they may be more convenient."

Q "East Campus is famous for its eclectic mix of residents, who often choose to paint and decorate their rooms in **funky fashion**."

Q It depends what kind of person you are. McCormick is all women, very clean, **quiet, and kind of boring**. Baker is very social, pretty new, kind of loud, and party-ish."

STUDENT AUTHOR: **MIT is unique in that you get two chances to choose** where you live. The summer before your freshman year, you make a choice of dorms. But you also get another chance to choose which dorm you want to live in when you get on campus. There is a period at the end of orientation where dorms will have their "rush." Be careful when you make your choices over the summer. Your decision and dorm assignment could be permanent, for a while at least. After dorm rush, if you think you want to switch dorms, you can put yourself on a waiting list.

> **Did You Know?**
> 90% of undergrads live on campus.

Students Speak Out
ON GUYS & GIRLS

Q "MIT men—**the odds are good**, but the goods are odd.' There's also a saying about Boston women: 'Wellesley to wed, Simmons to bed, MIT to talk to.'"

Q "There're all kinds here—hot, not, geek, preppy, whatever. They're **all intelligent**, though."

Q "It's way too varied. Remember **beauty truly lies within**. I've met the most 'beautiful' people at MIT and I wouldn't have if I was simply concerned with hotness."

Q "The **guys are great**. It doesn't seem like there are many hotties, though. And those who are hotties are so arrogant that they aren't hot anymore."

STUDENT AUTHOR: **In terms of pure physical attractiveness, MIT isn't at** the top of any list. For the most part, many students opt to try to meet people from other schools. Lots of guys will date girls from Boston University or Wellesley College. In fact, a lot of MIT girls have a tendency to be bitter towards the Wellesley girls who show up at parties. One of the biggest barriers to having a relationship at MIT is finding the time to have one.

> **Traditions**
>
> **Steer Roast**
> This is a weekend-long event held at Senior House, including bands, mud wrestling, body painting and, of course, the roasting of a steer.
>
> **Bad Taste**
> Bad taste is an annual concert held by the Chorallaries, an MIT singing group.
>
> **Overall School Spirit**
> Most students have a love/hate relationship with MIT, and "spirit" is focused more within housing communities.

Students Speak Out
ON ATHLETICS

Q "People who play varsity think it's a big deal, but it tends to be **overlooked by the general population**. Many people do IMs though, because you don't have to be good, and they're fun."

Q "iM sports are pretty big. Most people who play do it because they to do want something that's not academic and they're **not hardcore athletes**."

Q "IM sports are really big. We have a fairly content athletic community, but MIT is just not that big on sports. We're **Division III**. "

Q Some of our sports teams aren't so great since we're **pretty big nerds**."

STUDENT AUTHOR: **Although MIT is obviously not one of the most** athletically competitive schools in the nation, many students here are, in fact, very interested in sports. IM sports are actually one of the favorite pastimes of MIT students. There are over 1000 IM teams with a 75 percent undergraduate participation rate. Most teams are organized through living groups, and IMs exist for everything from football to foosball.

Students Speak Out
ON DRUG SCENE

Q "**Alcohol** is definitely the most prevalent drug on campus, if you choose to classify it as one. Aside from that, pot would come in second."

Q "There are people who will strongly **discourage the harder drugs**, but the soft ones are quite common."

Q "There are actually several users scattered through a couple of dorms. Just ask when you get here; it's one of those **open secrets**."

STUDENT AUTHOR: Some people do use drugs at MIT. A surprising number of students use marijuana occasionally or have at least tried it. It is the most widely used drug, and users have an easy enough time getting their hands on it. After all, MIT is right in Boston, and as with any other urban area, drugs are there for those who want them. For those who have no desire to do drugs, you will never be forced to. And avoiding the drug scene is not hard. Even under peer pressure, you should not feel uncomfortable simply saying "no." People respect each other's choices here.

6:1	Student-to-Faculty Ratio
98%	Freshman Retention Rate
83%	Four-Year Graduation Rate
89%	Financial Aid Applicants Receiving Aid

Students Speak Out
SAFETY & SECURITY

Q "Campus security is great, though it is rarely needed. On this campus, **nothing happens**. There has never been a time when I feared for my life or was even too scared to walk to my dorm at 4 a.m. (yes, I was up doing work that late)."

Q "MIT is in a city and has **some problems with theft**, but keeping the door to your room locked usually fixes that. In general, the campus and the area around it is fine."

Q "MIT's campus is very safe. Despite being surrounded by heavy urban areas, MIT tends to have a **fairly isolated feeling**. There are places to avoid at certain times of day, but they're trivial."

STUDENT AUTHOR: As with any other city, Boston does have its share of safety issues and concerns. Since MIT is fairly self-contained, however, safety isn't a problem on campus. The most common crime on campus is theft, usually of bikes or laptops. If you own a bike, be sure to lock it up.

Questions?
For more inside information and survival tips, pick up College Prowler's full-length book on this school, written by an actual student! Check it out at *www.collegeprowler.com*.

Students Speak Out
ON OVERALL EXPERIENCE

Q "It's been an **incredible experience**: challenging academics, wonderful people, and actually some fun occasionally."

Q "I'm leaving here **pretty burnt-out** and somewhat unsure of my abilities in the real world. MIT arms you with a lot of educational tools and the ability to learn, but it takes about four years to regain your confidence and self-esteem."

Q "Despite all the work and stress, my two years at this crazy institute of learning have been **tremendously rewarding** and satisfying."

Q "It's really tough—you'll hate it, but you'll love it. **IHTFP is the local motto**—it has a double meaning of 'I have truly found paradise,' and 'I hate this #$%-ing place,' and we mean every word of it."

Q "Its hard, but worth it. I sometimes **wish it were easier**, but then, it wouldn't be MIT, would it?"

STUDENT AUTHOR: MIT students have a love/hate relationship with their school. They love the people and the atmosphere, and hate the boatloads of work. Overall, every student, at some point, will think that they made the wrong decision. But it's the fact that these people made the decision to attend MIT that sets them apart from the rest. Whether they knew what the school was like or not, students here were willing to take the chance. As a result, the people at MIT are the most creative, helpful, brilliant, and unique in the world. MIT is one of the most challenging schools in the country, but it is also one of the most rewarding.

Montana State University

201 Strand Union Building; Bozeman, MT 59717
(407) 994-0211; www.montana.edu

THE BASICS:

Acceptance Rate: 67% **SAT Range:** 1000–1250*
Setting: Rural **Control:** Public
F-T Undergrads: 8,996 **Tuition:** $16,997

Most Popular Majors: Business/Marketing, Engineering, Visual/Performing Arts, Education

*of 1600

Academics	B-	Guys	A
Local Atmosphere	B+	Girls	B+
Safety & Security	B	Athletics	B-
Computers	B	Nightlife	B-
Facilities	B	Greek Life	C-
Campus Dining	C	Drug Scene	B
Off-Campus Dining	A	Campus Strictness	B+
Campus Housing	B	Parking	D+
Off-Campus Housing	A	Transportation	D-
Diversity	D-	Weather	B-

Students Speak Out
ON ACADEMICS

Q "The most interesting thing I've come to appreciate about my teachers at MSU is that they **come from a wide variety of backgrounds and countries**. I have one professor from Morocco, one from Wooster, Massachusetts, and another from Brighton, England."

Q "My experiences with my professors have been positive, overall. I have come in contact with many **faculty members that are involved in cutting-edge research**, yet still are very much concerned with their students' learning. I have found most classes to be very interesting."

Q "MSU is like most other four-year colleges; it can be **as difficult or easy as you want** to make it."

Q "**The Honors College is a great program**, one that students should take advantage of. Other than that, you mainly get the standard lectures."

STUDENT AUTHOR: While MSU is gaining a reputation as a research school, many professors still choose to put their students before personal glory. Beyond the classroom, most teachers are generally accessible and are willing to meet with students in a local coffeeshop or in their office to discuss class material or grading policies. For students who thrive in smaller, more intense settings, the Honors College may be an appropriate option. The best professors throughout the school come together to teach honors seminars. Many incoming students find their classes require little of their time, but once they reach the 200-levels, the workload increases significantly.

Students Speak Out
ON LOCAL ATMOSPHERE

Q "Bozeman is a small town and feels like it, but it is growing fast. **The small-town feel pervades**, as does its reputation as one of the last true ski towns. It is a wonderful place to live. People are nice, and I think that, even as a small town, there is still plenty to do."

Q "Bozeman is **a very relaxed outdoors-oriented town. There are no other universities**. There are lots of places to visit nearby, to name a few: Yellowstone National Park, ski areas (Big Sky, Moonlight, and Bridger), and mountains (my favorites are the Beartooths, but there are also many others)."

Q "The town is wonderful—**very laid-back and friendly**. Bozeman is a very young, energetic town with lots of activities geared toward college-age people."

Q "Bozeman is totally **a ski town minus a ton of hippies**, and there are world-class ski resorts less than an hour away."

STUDENT AUTHOR: Bozeman is the type of town that tries to hang on to old traditions while bringing in new ones. Skiing is one thing nearly everyone living in the town or attending the University has in common. For those who either cannot afford or do not care for skiing, downtown Bozeman has a surprisingly large amount to offer for a town of approximately 35,000 friendly residents. You'll quickly discover the essence of Bozeman: outdoor country living with a splash of art and culture.

5 Best Things	5 Worst Things
1 Mountain setting	**1** Public transportation
2 Laid-back attitude	**2** Food service
3 The duck pond	**3** Apathetic attitude
4 People-watching	**4** Everyone is white
5 The Brewed Awakening	**5** Lack of cultural activities

Students Speak Out
ON FACILITIES

Q "The school is continually trying to update the facilities, but right now, they're **less than stellar** and definitely could use some work."

Q "The **training facilities for non-athletes could definitely be improved**. If you are an MSU athlete, the facilities are better, but if you're just a regular student looking to work out, then you're pretty much screwed."

Q "As far as campus beauty, this isn't Harvard or anything. What we do have are **a lot of choices for places to work out, places to study**, and places to chill with friends."

Q "The athletic facilities are more than adequate on campus. Tennis courts, an indoor track, intramural gyms, a climbing gym, racquetball courts, weight rooms, a cardio room, a swimming pool—it's more than most fit people actually use. The SUB is great because it offers everything you need in one building: **a bookstore, coffee, food, a copy shop, and recreation**."

STUDENT AUTHOR: **The library has study rooms students can reserve for quizzing one another, or for what often happens: laughing, talking, and not doing much studying. Mediocre is the most accurate way to describe MSU's buildings and design. The Planning Board is currently working to develop a campus plan to make everything more aesthetically pleasing, but so far, the only piece of evidence they have for their plan is the empty field on campus cleared to build a new chemistry research building. Noisy construction equipment and chopped down trees are not exactly the most beautiful thing to see while walking to class.**

Famous Alumni

Maurice Ralph Hilleman, Jan Stenerud, Kevin Donavan, Lance Deal, Craig Kilborn, Valerie Hemingway

Students Speak Out
ON CAMPUS DINING

Q "The food on campus is alright (**nothing to brag about, but definitely not bad**). However, there are many restaurants surrounding campus that are very good, and they are only a short hop, skip, and a jump away."

Q "Food on campus is actually a little scarce outside of the dining halls, but what you can find is decent. **Almost all restaurants on campus are in the SUB**. I would recommend trying Avogadro's Number. The dining halls have a good variety, but like all food services, leaves something to be desired."

Q "Food service is no home-cooked meal, but it's pretty good considering how many students they have to cook for. **It can get a little old, since they just repeat their meal cycle** over and over."

Q "The dorm food is not the best quality, but **I've always been able to find something to eat**. You might have to lower your standards a bit, but you can make up for the lack of quality with quantity."

STUDENT AUTHOR: **Your two choices when eating at University Food Service are to either eat things that taste good but carry loads of fat and sugar (Freshman 15, anyone?), or eat as healthy as possible but hardly be able to choke down the food. A first-year student's best bet is to choose the five-day meal plan rather than the week-long meal plan. This way, they save money on room and board and can go out for delicious meals around town on the weekends.**

Student Body

African American:	<1%	Male/Female:	54/46%
Asian American:	1%	Out-of-State:	31%
Hispanic:	1%	International:	3%
Native American:	3%	Unknown:	3%
White:	88%		

Popular Faiths: Christianity is the main religion at MSU, along with a few Jewish and Muslim students.

Gay Pride: For being in a conservative state, MSU is surprisingly open to homosexuals. There is a Queer/Straight Alliance group that is supported on campus.

Economic Status: As with many public universities, MSU has a wide range of economic statuses.

Students Speak Out
ON DORMS

Q "Dorms on campus are just like any other university's dorms: small, crowded, and the place to be. There are **nine different dorms to choose from for freshmen**, and each is tailored to certain preferences, so you can't go wrong."

Q "The dorms can be a less-than-fun place to live. **It's required for freshmen**, however, so good luck with that, and try to have a little fun."

Q "The dorms are **a little sketchy on the high-rise side of campus**. Lowrise is much more spacious and a little more low-key."

STUDENT AUTHOR: **By requiring freshmen to live on campus, MSU does everything it can to ensure its students will be well taken care of and meet plenty of people. For students who want to party, the highrises on the west side of campus are their best choice. These include Roskie and the two Hedges, North and South. The lowrises, including dorms such as Mullan, Langford, Hapner, Hannon, and the Quads are typically quieter than the other side of campus. The Quads are a favorite of the lowrises, and their residents do not normally venture out of the Quad courtyard to find a friend.**

> **Did You Know?**
> 25% of undergrads live on campus.

Students Speak Out
ON GUYS & GIRLS

Q "I try and explain this to my sister back home in Michigan: **the guys out here are very hot**. They're all interested in outdoor activities, so they're all in shape and gorgeous. You can easily spot freshman girls, because they're all dressed prim and proper, and then it snows and they freeze."

Q "So **MSU isn't on *Playboy*'s top 10 list** of attractive universities, but when you take a lady back to ma and pa, they won't say 'Her?'"

Q "There are plenty of outdoorsy guys here, and the **campus is just generally attractive** all around."

Q "There are **not enough girls** on this campus. The ratio is horrible."

STUDENT AUTHOR: **With a motto like "Mountains and Minds," a school is bound to attract a lot of outdoorsy students. This means guys and girls will have healthy, fit physiques and be very laid-back. The level of attractiveness is high at MSU for those who don't mind a bit of unkemptness in exchange for a great body and lots of energy.**

Traditions

Hike to the "M"
Freshmen and a few other students gather together with their residence floors at the beginning of the fall semester and go on a big group hike up to the MSU "M" on the Bridgers.

Tailgating
MSU Bobcat football fans love to do a little pre-gaming before the home games.

Overall School Spirit
While the Bobcats may not always be a winning team, students, faculty, and fans seem to forget that whenever the University of Montana Grizzlies are in town.

Students Speak Out
ON ATHLETICS

Q "**Intramural sports are all-inclusive and ever-present** on campus. It is a great way to stay in shape and stay involved, no matter what sport preferences you have."

Q "**Football and volleyball are fairly popular** as far as varsity sports go. There is also a lot of student participation in intramural sports."

Q "Football games are fun to tailgate for, and lots of people go to volleyball games. But they're not that big; they're more like big high school games rather than university athletics, in my point of view. **Intramurals are huge, and everyone is eventually on a team**."

STUDENT AUTHOR: **The MSU student body is a very athletic group overall. They love to hike, run, bike, climb, and ski. When it comes to varsity sports, however, the student support is usually lacking, unless the University of Montana Grizzlies are in town for a game—then all hell breaks loose, and everyone is given a sudden injection of adrenaline-packed school spirit. MSU is unique in some respects, as it has a nordic ski team, something offered at few schools across the nation.**

Students Speak Out
ON DRUG SCENE

Q "Lots of people drink, and some people smoke pot. But lots of people are totally clean, and there are **not too many hard drugs**."

Q "Everyone knows there are drugs around campus, but unless you choose to hang out with those people, **you won't be bothered by it**."

Q "Bozeman has the **school full of alcoholics**, Missoula has the school full of hippie potheads. Take your pick."

Q "The usual marijuana is common here, but there are also **a few hardcore drugs floating around**, such as 'shrooms, ecstasy, and meth, which is actually fairly common in Montana."

STUDENT AUTHOR: **Alcohol is a much more serious problem than drug abuse, and rumor has it that over half the drivers in Montana after dark have been drinking. Drugs are not a prominent part of campus life at MSU, and those who do choose to indulge in their illegal curiosities usually choose to do so off campus at a party or a friend's house.**

16:1	Student-to-Faculty Ratio
72%	Freshman Retention Rate
19%	Four-Year Graduation Rate
78%	Financial Aid Applicants Receiving Aid

Students Speak Out
SAFETY & SECURITY

Q "We have cops that do a pretty good job upholding order on campus. I have heard a few bad stories of things happening to people on campus, but I think **violence is kept to a minimum**. I feel just as safe walking around campus at night as I would anywhere else."

Q "For the most part, they do a really good job. I've seen statistics that show that **crime is down for the area**, and the stricter atmosphere of the dorms prevents anything really bad from happening on campus."

Q "The campus police are very good (perhaps too good, some people may argue). Also, if you are living in the dorms, **the people in charge do a very good job** of keeping everything under control and safe."

STUDENT AUTHOR: **Most students seem to feel safe and have few qualms about staying late at the library, then walking home bleary-eyed. The campus has no blue-light centers where students can pick up a phone and get campus police, but the cops patrol the campus in the cars throughout the night.**

> **Questions?**
> For more inside information and survival tips, pick up College Prowler's full-length book on this school, written by an actual student! Check it out at *www.collegeprowler.com*.

Students Speak Out
ON OVERALL EXPERIENCE

Q "Being at Montana State has been a great experience, hands down **one of the best choices of my life**. In Bozeman, there's no such thing as a stranger, just a friend you haven't made yet. There is always something to do, either scholastically or socially."

Q "**MSU's surroundings are phenomenal**, and I wouldn't give them up for anything. The mountains are huge, the rivers are amazing, the landscape is inspirational."

Q "When I first started looking at colleges, MSU was at the bottom of my list. Somehow, I ended up here, and I am so glad I did—it is my favorite place to be. The school and Bozeman have their ups and downs, but **I would never consider trading my time here for anything**."

Q "MSU has **everything that makes me happy**, along with a strong education system. It pretty much rocks."

STUDENT AUTHOR: **Many students at MSU, mainly those from out-of-state, are surprised that they ended up here. What they find even more surprising is that they never want to leave. Academics find a great research university and exceptional learning environment. Skiers look out their windows to see countless backcountry and ski hill opportunities. Overall, MSU is a place where the happiness is infectious, as is the relaxed state of mind. Everyone is accepted, and people from different backgrounds love to mix. Attracting people who love life and are happy in their current situations, MSU and Bozeman have a pleasant atmosphere. Most often, the people who are not happy here are those who dislike fun, nature, and getting an education.**

Mount Holyoke College

50 College Street; South Hadley, MA 01075
(413) 538-2000; www.mtholyoke.edu

THE BASICS:

Acceptance Rate: 53%
Setting: Rural
F-T Undergrads: 2,173

SAT Range: 1835–2120*
Control: Private
Tuition: $37,460

Most Popular Majors: Social Sciences, Biological/Life Sciences, English, Visual/Performing Arts, Psychology

*of 2400

Academics	B+	Guys	N/A
Local Atmosphere	C+	Girls	B
Safety & Security	A-	Athletics	C
Computers	B	Nightlife	C
Facilities	B	Greek Life	N/A
Campus Dining	A-	Drug Scene	A-
Off-Campus Dining	B	Campus Strictness	B
Campus Housing	A	Parking	D+
Off-Campus Housing	C+	Transportation	B+
Diversity	A-	Weather	C+

Students Speak Out
ON ACADEMICS

Q "Of course, I loved the classes for my majors, but a lot of the classes I took as distribution requirements were a lot of fun. **I'm glad that we had the distribution requirements**, because they really introduced me to areas that otherwise I might not have made time for, and they ended up being fun classes."

Q "Like any college, MHC has its boring and frustrating professors. But I've found it also has more than its share of truly inspiring ones. All the faculty members I've worked with are very concerned about the student's experience and **willing to go far out of their way** to make sure you're getting what you need—you only need to ask."

Q "Of course, the qualities of teachers varied. I had some great ones, as well as some that weren't so great—but overall, my teachers were wonderful. **They really listened** to the students, and they're all really accessible."

Q "The **teachers are amazing**. They're willing to take time out of their schedules and lives to sit and talk with their students over lunch at Blanchard and the dining halls."

STUDENT AUTHOR: Because this is a relatively small school, you're much more likely to get to know one or several professors on a more personal level than just as "that guy who stands up there and lectures." Some of these relationships continue beyond graduation, as the professor becomes a mentor to the student.

Students Speak Out
ON LOCAL ATMOSPHERE

Q "In the immediate town, there is nothing to do, **unless you like to go to Subway for pleasure**. However, if you have a car, there is a lot of stuff to do on Rt. 33 down the road. Of course, there is always Amherst and Northampton. But, if you are looking for something to do around Mount Holyoke, expect to spend money to do it."

Q "South Hadley itself is small. There is a **movie theater, coffee shops, a pizza place**, a Chinese food place, and some knick-knack stores right across the street, and there's a grocery store a short drive away (as well as a few restaurants)."

Q "MHC is part of the Five College Consortium—that means that **we can take classes, join clubs, and go to events at four other colleges**. I met my boyfriend by joining a club at UMass."

Q "There are some **often-overlooked fun places to visit** right on campus, including the botanical gardens, the art museum, and the forest trails near the Equestrian Center."

STUDENT AUTHOR: Some students go off campus almost every weekend to Boston or New York, but this is definitely not necessary, and in fact, most students will stick around and create their own fun. You might even find yourself falling in love with the somewhat rural charm of this part of the state. Of course, it's not Boston, but it is a place rich with history. This is also a great area for hiking and other naturalistic, outdoor pursuits.

5 Best Things	5 Worst Things
1 Beautiful campus	1 Academic burnout
2 Inspiring professors	2 Distance to grocery store
3 Rigorous academics	3 Length of winters
4 Sense of community	4 Swarms of geese
5 Students' attitudes	5 Forced meal plan

Students Speak Out
ON FACILITIES

Q "The facilities are great, and everything is maintained and kept in good condition. **The gym is just big enough** for any use a student might need to make of it, and it's usually not too crowded."

Q "Blanchard is definitely **the center of student activity**. It includes student organization offices, the campus store, mailboxes, a café, a full-service dining option, and a stage for student activities. There's something going on almost every weekend night, including a cappella concerts, drama skits, and so on."

Q "**Everything on campus is kept clean**, and given that many of the dorms are really old, that's pretty good!"

Q "The **facilities are excellent**, and I highly suggest wandering around every building just to see what each one offers and get the lay of the land, so to speak."

Q "I always appreciated the **computer labs being well stocked** whenever I had to print anything out."

STUDENT AUTHOR: **For a small school, there's a decent amount that you can find to do here on any given day. Mount Holyoke is bursting with cultural and educational opportunities. In general, the campus is very aesthetically pleasing. It was planned to be that way; the layout having been originally designed by Frederick Law Olmsted, who also designed Central Park in New York City. Even the newer buildings were designed so that they would blend in as unobtrusively as possible.**

Famous Alumni

Virginia Hamilton Adair, Dr. Virginia Apgar, Elaine Chao, Emily Dickinson, Priscilla Painton, Suzan-Lori Parks, Nancy Vickers, Wendy Wasserstein

Students Speak Out
ON CAMPUS DINING

Q "The food on campus can be weird sometimes. **They offer vegetarian alternatives** to mostly everything. (I recall one time seeing vegan veggie balls on the menu . . . ew.)"

Q "Compared to many college campuses, I think **we have pretty good food**. The worst option tends to be Blanchard Café, which is mostly fried food, but the other dining halls usually offer something nutritious."

Q "I never minded the food, but then again, **I'm not picky**."

Q "It's a fact of life: wherever there are dining halls, there will be complaints about the food. The food at MHC is actually very good, though. **Everything is usually very fresh**, and there is a wide variety of food options. So it might not be what your mother makes at home. Deal with it."

Q "I enjoyed Wilder dairy days and loved Prospect Sunday brunches. I don't remember one Sunday where I didn't go there to enjoy their omelettes and waffles. **Good stuff**. I also liked Blanchard a little more than I care to admit, though I am aware that it is bad for me."

STUDENT AUTHOR: **Because the board plan is required for all students who live on campus, food is extremely important. In general, the food is edible, and there are always vegetarian and vegan options. Some things, such as meatballs, just were not meant to be vegetarian. Despite these problems, the food at Mount Holyoke is rated better than the food at other schools.**

Student Body

African American:	5%	Male/Female:	0/100%
Asian American:	11%	Out-of-State:	74%
Hispanic:	5%	International:	17%
Native American:	1%	Unknown:	12%
White:	49%		

Popular Faiths: Catholicism boasts the highest representation, but campus has a multi-faith flavor.

Gay Pride: There are numerous "out and proud" lesbians on campus, though by no means is the college comprised solely of lesbians.

Economic Status: Economic class is generally not talked about. There is a whole range of students here.

Students Speak Out
ON DORMS

Q "Many of the dorms are absolutely beautiful and offer a comfortable living environment. Personally, I tend to **like the older dorms more** than the newer ones."

Q "I love the old dorms at MHC. **They've got grand sitting rooms**, old steam radiators, and funny little rooms that come in surprising shapes and sizes."

Q "The modern dorms are nice, with large rooms, and modern facilities. The old dorms are charming, and some of them have been renovated inside, although **the room sizes vary** greatly."

STUDENT AUTHOR: **This is a very residential campus, with 93 percent of students living on campus. This is undoubtedly one of the contributing factors to the strong sense of community you will find at MHC. All classes live in each dorm, providing many opportunities for inter-class friendships. There is friendly competition between dorms, especially during Disorientation, a tradition that occurs every fall and serves to unite first-years and seniors.**

Did You Know?
94% of undergrads live on campus.

Students Speak Out
ON GUYS & GIRLS

Q "No guys. There are girls that look like guys, but no guys. It's lesbian heaven, but a complete hell if you're a woman who **craves massive amounts of male testosterone**."

Q "There are no guys—it's **quite a diverse group** of women."

Q "The atmosphere is one of acceptance, whatever your orientation—the straight, the lesbian, the bisexual, and the undecided, should all feel at home here. There is **no pressure to be anything you don't want to be**. And yes, the girls are hot."

Q "The women of MHC are, for the most part: very **liberal, good students, not big on parties**, independent, and high achievers."

STUDENT AUTHOR: **Because the student body is composed of all women, and because of the open and somewhat experimental atmosphere on campus, there is perhaps more than average lesbian activity. But if guys are what you're looking for, you can find them at other places in the Pioneer Valley, most readily at the other three colleges in the area that have them.**

Traditions

Big/Little Sisters
Juniors are paired with one or more first-years who become their "little sisters."

Laurel Parade
This tradition brings together alumnae from reuniting classes with the graduating class, who become the newest alumnae.

Overall School Spirit
MHC is unique in so many ways, and those who aren't turned off by it come to love the school with a passion. Loyalty runs strong.

Students Speak Out
ON ATHLETICS

Q "Sports, in my experience, aren't that popular on campus. A lot of women play sports, but I do not know about the turnout. I know **I've never been to a game**."

Q "Although **my roomie was on the volleyball team**, and I knew a couple of water polo players, I never went to any of the games, and neither did any of my friends."

Q "Sports, overall, while they all have their followings, are **not especially big** on campus, but they are important. So if you're into watching or participating in sports, there's a lot for you, and if you're not, you won't feel left out."

Q "**A lot of women play** both varsity and intramural sports, and some of the teams are really into it (crew and rugby come to mind), but while playing a sport is a central part of the athlete's life, it's not necessarily a big part of campus life."

STUDENT AUTHOR: **Let's just say this isn't a sports-oriented campus. It's not that you can't find sports if you're looking for them, but the latest basketball statistics probably won't be a hot topic of conversation.**

Students Speak Out
ON DRUG SCENE

Q "MHC is **pretty tame in terms of drugs**. There is no substance-free housing, for the simple reason that it isn't usually a problem. Serious abuse of alcohol is rare (especially compared to other campuses), and I personally haven't encountered any illegal drugs on campus."

Q "Several of my roommates had pot in our rooms, and there were several times when I got stoned. However, it generally seems to happen off campus, and **drug use is typically frowned upon**."

Q "There is some drug use, but not very much. Neither drugs nor alcohol are central to campus life, although there are **some groups that are very into both**."

STUDENT AUTHOR: **You can completely avoid the drug scene at Mount Holyoke if you want to, as it's not that pervasive; although, if you remain at the school for any length of time, you'll probably encounter at least one person who regularly gets drunk or high.**

10:1	Student-to-Faculty Ratio
92%	Freshman Retention Rate
79%	Four-Year Graduation Rate
90%	Financial Aid Applicants Receiving Aid

Students Speak Out
SAFETY & SECURITY

Q "**I feel absolutely safe** walking around campus alone at night, although I know that's not something to make a habit of. Security is really good on the main part of campus (not so good on the outskirts), and I find that the guards make an effort to get to know the students."

Q "Public Safety, to me personally, is a little too much for the campus. They are **a bit too nosey**, but I guess some people find that as a comfort."

Q "Security is excellent—emergency 'blue-light' stations abound, Public Safety is constantly on patrol, and let's face it: an all-girls campus in a tiny rural Massachusetts town is **an extremely uneventful place** in terms of crime."

STUDENT AUTHOR: **Any crime on campus tends to be petty, involving loss of or damage to belongings, but no threat to anyone's physical well being. Still, Public Safety is a very visible presence on campus. Mount Holyoke maintains a very trusting atmosphere.**

Questions?
For more inside information and survival tips, pick up College Prowler's full-length book on this school, written by an actual student! Check it out at *www.collegeprowler.com*.

Students Speak Out
ON OVERALL EXPERIENCE

Q "My education was amazing, and the friends I made were all wonderful. It was **a home away from home**. This was the nurturing environment I wanted, and the opportunities I had going to MHC have shaped, and will always shape, my life."

Q "Mount Holyoke pushes me, and is **more academically rigorous** than my previous school, so even with all of the papers and projects, studying and stressing, I can't be thankful enough for being here."

Q "We have a **very strong alumnae association**, which tells of the commitment that many students feel for this school."

Q "Also, one of the great things about MHC is that it teaches you that you can do anything you put your mind to—that **gender is not a hindrance**. I have come into the 'real' world expecting people to be of that mindset, and the professions that I am looking at are careers that have been traditionally male-dominated."

STUDENT AUTHOR: **It seems that students come to Mount Holyoke for the academics and stay for the community. Women who come here either quickly discover that they hate it and transfer out, or fall in love with the school and become unable to imagine going anywhere else. You will undoubtedly be exposed to new influences during your time here, and you won't be afraid to call some of those new influences your friends—especially the ones who scared you at first. The atmosphere of care is catching—new students quickly catch it from older students, and so the tradition lives on.**

Muhlenberg College

2400 West Chew Street; Allentown, PA 18104
(484) 664-3100; www.muhlenberg.edu

THE BASICS:

Acceptance Rate: 44%
Setting: Medium-sized city
F-T Undergrads: 2,297

SAT Range: 1680–1980*
Control: Private
Tuition: $32,850

Most Popular Majors: Social Sciences, Biology, Business/Marketing, Dramatic/Theater Art

*of 2400

Academics	B+	Guys	A-
Local Atmosphere	C+	Girls	A
Safety & Security	A	Athletics	C
Computers	B-	Nightlife	C+
Facilities	A-	Greek Life	B+
Campus Dining	B+	Drug Scene	B
Off-Campus Dining	C+	Campus Strictness	B
Campus Housing	B+	Parking	C
Off-Campus Housing	C+	Transportation	C+
Diversity	D-	Weather	C+

Students Speak Out
ON ACADEMICS

Q "The teachers at Muhlenberg are awesome for the most part. They are very helpful, and **they love to get to know their students** and challenge you in ways that are interesting."

Q "For the most part, I have found the professors to generally be nice people, but not necessarily good teachers. Most professors do seem very willing to meet students outside of the classroom for extra help, though. I can honestly say that I have learned at least **one interesting thing from every class** I have taken at Muhlenberg."

Q "The classes here can be difficult, but you don't come to a college like Muhlenberg to sit back and relax. You want to have fun, but you also want to learn. I feel like **Muhlenberg has a great balance** of both of those things."

Q "At some schools, you can go through an entire semester without a professor even knowing your name. At Muhlenberg, **your professors will remember things about you** years after you take their class."

STUDENT AUTHOR: **Although there will obviously be a few professors who students don't like, the thing that stands out the most about Muhlenberg professors is how extremely accessible and personable they are. Along with this excellent personal support, Muhlenberg offers students a variety of academic opportunities. While Muhlenberg is known for its excellent pre-med program, it is also well known for theater and dance.**

Students Speak Out
ON LOCAL ATMOSPHERE

Q "A lot of people complain that there is nothing to do in Allentown, but I only agree to an extent. There is a nearby mall and a good amount of **restaurants, movie theaters, and coffee shops**; however, for the student looking for active nightlife, Allentown is not the best place to go. Lehigh and Lafayette are relatively nearby, and many students take advantage of the greater social opportunities."

Q "**This part of Allentown is very affluent**; it has a very suburban feel to it. Cedar Crest College is right down the street, but they might as well be on the other side of the country because we really don't do anything with them cooperatively. Try not to get lost and end up downtown by yourself; it can be scary!"

Q "While you may not expect it, Allentown has some **great cultural sites**. Try to take a look at them because they can be a great alternative to the usual weekend happenings. Also, go to the parks!"

Q "Allentown is really cool if you **explore everything you can**. People make fun of Allentown and say it's boring, but it has most of the same things that other towns have."

STUDENT AUTHOR: **In addition to having a lot of rewarding places to volunteer (such as an after school program called Casa Guadalupe), downtown also offers several social and cultural spots such as the Allentown Art Museum and the 19th Street Theater. There are also five other colleges that are nearby.**

Students Speak Out
ON FACILITIES

Q "The **facilities on campus are widely used**, which helps bring the campus together. I enjoy going to the gym and lounging in the Red Door."

Q "One of the reasons that I was finally sold on coming here was how beautiful the campus is. On a nice day, I just look around and think how pretty everything is. Everything is always clean, and they are constantly repainting. **It's a very picturesque campus**."

Q "I think the facilities are very nice. **They are maintained very well**, and the exteriors are appealing. They're always renovating to make buildings more up-to-date, functional, and better looking."

Q "My parents often joke that every time they visit Muhlenberg we're **having something painted or renovated**. Muhlenberg really does a lot to keep our facilities looking great."

Q "Most of the facilities are very nice. The student union has a cozy fireplace and **student 'hangout' spot**."

STUDENT AUTHOR: Muhlenberg has a nice mixture of both traditional and modern buildings that makes your walk down Academic Row interesting. Although the campus is small, there is plenty of open space for students to enjoy the outdoors. The walkways and fields are always clean and well kept, and the landscaping is attractive. Muhlenberg does everything it can to keep the older buildings well maintained. The facilities are always very clean, and they are constantly being repainted and refurbished to keep everything looking good.

Famous Alumni

Richard Ben-Viniste, Frederick Busch, David Fricke, Robert David Steele

Students Speak Out
ON CAMPUS DINING

Q "I really like GQ (General's Quarters) because it feels more like a café and less like a cafeteria. I do **start to feel like I eat the same food everyday**, but the Action Station has something different every day of the week. I know a lot of people like Garden Room because it has a really large variety of food, and Java Joe's has awesome coffee and really good cookies."

Q "The food is delicious, but we tend to get our favorites over and over, so it can become repetitive. I prefer the Garden Room because of **the variety, speed, and cost**. If you purchase five cents over a swipe in GQ, you must pay by cash or swipe again."

Q "Nothing compares to a home-cooked meal, but **bagel bombs at GQ** are the best breakfast food and late-night snack!"

Q "The **food is good for college food**, but you get sick of eating the same things over and over and over again."

Q "Although the food isn't bad, it can definitely get redundant because **GQ almost always has the same options**, and Garden Room has a weekly schedule that is repeated throughout the semester."

STUDENT AUTHOR: For many people, it could be easy to gain the Freshman 15 at Muhlenberg because the food is generally decent. "Pasta Day" in GQ is probably the most popular day for food on campus. One note of caution though: it seems that by the end of the week, the chefs take a break, and the pickings get very slim.

Students Speak Out
ON DORMS

Q "I think Muhlenberg's dorms are very nice. I can't complain about any of my experiences so far. Prosser is the 'party dorm' for freshmen. It houses the most freshmen, and is often referred to as the 'ghetto dorm.' **Walz is the newest** of the freshman dorms, and it is air conditioned."

Q "The dorms are actually quite nice. They aren't very big, so they give **the feeling of a close community**."

Q "I think **you can manage to be happy in any dorm** Muhlenberg has to offer. There are positive and negative things about each when you get right down to it. Even though it's a small campus, it makes things feel so much cozier when you can just wander to your friend's room at all hours."

STUDENT AUTHOR: **Housing freshman year is supposedly based on how soon you turn in your deposit with your housing preferences. For this reason, a large portion of Walz is made up of students who applied Early Decision. Some are newer and bigger than others, but there are very few rooms in any of the dorms on campus that are unbearable.**

? Did You Know?
91% of undergrads live on campus.

Students Speak Out
ON GUYS & GIRLS

Q "**You don't really find the 'tough guy' jocks** here, and the girls are sweet and hot! Students are admitted to Muhlenberg because they have a fun personality."

Q "Many **people get dressed up and made up for class**. It is not unheard of for girls to wear heels and straighten their hair regularly."

Q "I've definitely had friends from other schools comment that **Muhlenberg is a hot college**. I guess there are worse things we could be called."

Q "Sometimes, it seems like it's really hard to find people to date here because the school is so small. **You start to feel like you know everyone** you'd want to date."

STUDENT AUTHOR: **While you never know what will happen, Muhlenberg can be a good place to look for a random hookup, relationship, or even a future husband or wife. Since the school is so small and friendly, it can be easier to get to know people. The size can sometimes become as issue when considering the gossip circle, however.**

Traditions

Candlelight Carols
A tradition since 1958, they're held in Egner Memorial Chapel the weekend before finals during the fall semester.

Red Doors
As a sign of welcome, all of the doors on Muhlenberg's campus are painted bright red.

Overall School Spirit
The majority of students at Muhlenberg have a strong sense of school pride and are usually eager to tell others about how much they like it at Muhlenberg.

Students Speak Out
ON ATHLETICS

Q "**Varsity sports are really not very big** since we are Division III. People come here to be future doctors; they're not usually here to play sports. The biggest varsity sports are probably football, soccer, women's basketball, and rugby. A great deal of the campus participates in iM sports."

Q "**If you know people on the teams, you'll go to a game** to cheer them on. If you don't know people playing, Muhlenberg isn't really a school where you go out to a game because it's a popular thing to do on the weekends."

Q "If you're looking for somewhere that **you can play sports and have fun**, you can do that here. If you're looking for a school that puts a huge emphasis on sports, this probably isn't the right place for you to go."

Q "**Muhlenberg was appealing to me** though because I knew I could play competitively, but I wasn't at a school where sports were so important that I wouldn't have fun with it, too."

STUDENT AUTHOR: **Muhlenberg offers a wide variety of intramurals and club sports, and Frisbee golf is a popular pastime for students.**

Students Speak Out
ON DRUG SCENE

Q "Drugs are available if you're interested, but if you're not, **you wouldn't even know they were here**."

Q "I don't do drugs, and I have never felt the pressure to do them here. I do know of students who are involved in that 'scene,' but **it is done quietly**. I do not believe that it affects the overall college atmosphere at all."

Q "In three years, **I've never once been offered drugs** or felt like it was a pressure. Like most schools, I'm sure it's available if you're into that. It's just not something that you need to deal with if it's not for you."

STUDENT AUTHOR: In many respects, Muhlenberg probably has fewer students using drugs than a typical high school. The only drug that you see on a somewhat regular basis is alcohol. One thing that most students tend to agree on when it comes to drugs on campus is that there really isn't a pressure to try them.

12:1	Student-to-Faculty Ratio
93%	Freshman Retention Rate
76%	Four-Year Graduation Rate
77%	Financial Aid Applicants Receiving Aid

Students Speak Out
SAFETY & SECURITY

Q "I have walked home at all hours of the night, and **I have never felt unsafe** on campus. The campus is compact and very well lit. Campus safety is always patrolling on foot and by car."

Q "**I feel completely comfortable** walking around campus by myself at night. It's a very safe campus."

Q "I feel like **I see campus police everywhere I go**. Sometimes, I even see them when I'm off Muhlenberg campus just driving around! At times, I think that's a little weird, but it's also nice to know that they're available if I ever did feel nervous about my surroundings."

STUDENT AUTHOR: Just in case you do get worried, you can usually spot one of the Campus Safety vehicles or an officer on foot at most times of the day and night. You can even call Campus Safety and get someone to escort you to your room if you are really nervous.

Questions?
For more inside information and survival tips, pick up College Prowler's full-length book on this school, written by an actual student! Check it out at *www.collegeprowler.com*.

Students Speak Out
ON OVERALL EXPERIENCE

Q "**I can't picture myself going to any other school**. Sometimes I wish Muhlenberg was a little bigger, but that would be my only real complaint."

Q "The people I've met have been amazing, and I was **able to make friends really fast**. The campus is so small that you never feel like just one of the crowd. I really believe that everyone has a chance to shine here. Even though Muhlenberg may not be the biggest party school, I have had some of the most fun in my life just doing random things with friends."

Q "**The fact that we are so small can be annoying at times**. Sometimes, I wish I had chosen a larger university; yet, I know that I'd miss the personal attention I get here."

Q "Walking down Academic Row, people shout out your name as you look around and see a beautiful campus with students studying on the grass, playing games, or eating. **It feels like something from a movie**, but then you realize that you picked an awesome college because Muhlenberg is real!"

STUDENT AUTHOR: While no college experience can be completely flawless, most students claim that they can't see themselves being happier anywhere else. The work can be challenging at times, but you know that you will step into your future feeling as prepared as possible. You will be encouraged to think independently, and become actively engaged in whatever you are studying. It's also a huge source of comfort to know that there are always people behind you every step of the way.

New College of Florida

5800 Bay Shore Road; Sarasota, FL 34243
(941) 487-5000; www.ncf.edu

THE BASICS:

Acceptance Rate: 58%
Setting: Urban
F-T Undergrads: 785

SAT Range: 1820–2090*
Control: Public
Tuition: $23,766

Most Popular Majors: Psychology, Environmental Studies, Economics, History

*of 2400

Academics	A	Guys	C
Local Atmosphere	B-	Girls	C+
Safety & Security	A-	Athletics	F
Computers	B-	Nightlife	B
Facilities	C+	Greek Life	N/A
Campus Dining	C+	Drug Scene	C+
Off-Campus Dining	B-	Campus Strictness	A
Campus Housing	B+	Parking	A-
Off-Campus Housing	C+	Transportation	C-
Diversity	C	Weather	A

Students Speak Out
ON ACADEMICS

Q "**The whole point, mission, and meaning of New College is that there is no set curriculum** for majors, and students are expected to navigate their education according to their own interests and perceived needs. What that means is that the coursework is as difficult as you make it."

Q "**You will develop a close relationship with your professors and advisers**. This is one of the best aspects of academic life at New College."

Q "Academics are limited. We don't have a large course catalog, but that's the trade-off you get at a small college. **You're going to have a hard time finding what you want**."

Q "New College has mixed classes with students from different academic backgrounds at different levels of involvement. **It brings a lot of perspectives into the classroom**. I often feel like the professors teach to the top of the class, which makes it really hard for first-years in those classes. But I liked the challenge, and I liked being able to learn from other students."

STUDENT AUTHOR: New College professors are amazingly accessible and qualified. While there are no grades at New College, tests are still scored numerically, and a lot of feedback is given to assess strengths and weaknesses. The month of January is devoted to students completing Independent Study Projects. These range from internships to seminars, and they tend to be open-ended. At New College of Florida, academics reign.

Students Speak Out
ON LOCAL ATMOSPHERE

Q "Sarasota is pretty if you are into palm trees, lizards, and hazardous drivers over the age of 80. It's nice enough for a medium-sized Florida town. There are some pretty good beaches, but **you will run out of things to do if you are into parties or music**. For that, you'll have to drive to Tampa, which is an hour away."

Q "**Sarasota is definitely not the exciting city environment I was looking for**. This is a typical Florida town—full of retirees and tourists."

Q "The local atmosphere is very polar and not always friendly to New College. We are looked at strangely. I don't feel like we integrate well with the town. **There is a sharp socioeconomic divide in Sarasota**."

Q "It's nice to have an escape from New College. Siesta Key and Lido beach are great places to visit. **New College is a bubble**, and you have to push yourself to get off campus sometimes."

STUDENT AUTHOR: While Sarasota has more to offer than most students will admit, Novo Collegians tend not to take advantage of these resources. Located on the west coast of Florida, there are beautiful beaches with silky, white sand within a 10-minute drive. The weather is always beautiful, so it is possible to go to the beach all year long. Downtown Sarasota is a 10-minute drive away and offers nothing exciting. It has several art galleries and ritzy shops, but it caters to the rich, old folk of Sarasota.

5 Best Things	5 Worst Things
1 Palm Court parties	1 Townies at Walls
2 The free table	2 Being capped out of class
3 Towne meetings	3 Poor food in dining halls
4 Student e-mail forum	4 Town-gown relations
5 Four Winds Café	5 No weekday nightlife

Students Speak Out
ON FACILITIES

Q "I know the Hamilton Center a little too well as far as what's lacking, such as fully functional roof. There's archival material in the Hamilton Center, but it's by no means a dilapidated building. It will get better. **The classrooms are well outfitted**."

Q **"We take classes in a mansion with a view of the Sarasota bay**! The school is really good about getting new equipment if it is considered helpful for the academic experience."

Q "The classrooms in College Hall and the marine lab are beautiful. There is a lot of natural light almost everywhere. **Our facilities are a mix of behind the times and brand new**. The older facilities are not problematic, but they are definitely not ideal."

Q "The facilities are not very up-to-date compared to bigger colleges, but **we have a very good science building with all the equipment needed** for the typical undergraduate."

Q **"The facilities certainly seem to be sufficient** as I've never needed any more than what they offer."

STUDENT AUTHOR: While its image, rigor, and philosophy don't always reflect it, New College of Florida is a public school. This means that the bulk of its funding comes from the taxpayers. This provides students with an affordable education, but it affects some of the aesthetic aspects of the school. Most agree, however, that the trade-off is worth it. Others still yearn for the red bricks and ivy of peer institutions. The west side of campus is situated on the picturesque Sarasota Bay, where students enjoy watching the sunset.

Famous Alumni

David Allen, Lincoln Diaz-Balart, Rick Doblin, Jennifer Granick, William Thurston

Students Speak Out
ON CAMPUS DINING

Q "I don't like it at all. **I think that the food we are provided with is subpar**. For the most part, it does not taste good or look very appetizing. While I appreciate the choices given to vegans and vegetarians, it is irrelevant because the food quality is so poor."

Q "It caters to a large amount of vegans and vegetarians **who know better than to eat there**."

Q **"I actually like eating there.** There is enough variety, so it doesn't get too repetitive. I am vegetarian, and I appreciate all of the accommodations they make to have vegetarian food available."

Q "I don't feel like it is as bad as everyone says it is. **It's certainly not as good as the price would lead you to believe**."

Q **"I have never felt sick from eating here**. The Four Winds has really good food, but it is really expensive."

STUDENT AUTHOR: This is by far the most controversial issue on campus. Frankly, dining services at New College do not cater to the sophisticated and picky palates of students. There is one main dining hall on the east side. On the west side, the popular student-run Four Winds Café provides an alternative. Students and professors congregate there for discussion, tutorials, and relaxation. The Four Winds provides a necessary alternative to the Sodexo doldrums. When New College expands to a size that would offer another dining hall, hopefully the attitude will improve.

Student Body

African American:	2%	Male/Female:	38/62%
Asian American:	3%	Out-of-State:	23%
Hispanic:	10%	International:	<1%
Native American:	1%	Unknown:	6%
White:	78%		

Popular Faiths: Judaism and Christianity.

Gay Pride: New College is extremely gay friendly. The organization PRIDE is active, and "Queer Ball" has become a tradition on campus.

Economic Status: Mostly middle-class.

Students Speak Out
ON DORMS

Q "I've visited other colleges, and **honestly, these are like luxury suites**. Plenty of other schools pay double what we do for a fourth of the space."

Q "**The only problem with the dorms is the social aspect**. Because we have rooms that are spacious and have everything we need, we don't feel claustrophobic, so you don't feel forced out into common areas. You can compensate, though, by inviting friends to your room."

Q "**The rooms are big enough, and each has its own bathroom**. The only problem that can arise from having a triple is disliking your roommates."

STUDENT AUTHOR: The main dormitories were designed by renowned architect I.M. Pei. Replete with balconies, proximity to main buildings, unlocked doors, communal areas, and equipped lounges, there is little to complain about New College housing, though, of course, some may disagree. Most first-years begin at the social and communal Pei complex, which is made up of three courts. The courts border a central area known as Palm Court, which is the heart of social activity at New College.

Did You Know?
80% of undergrads live on campus.

Students Speak Out
ON GUYS & GIRLS

Q "In terms of aesthetics, we are lacking. It's more distinctive. **People don't embrace what is traditionally sold as attractive**."

Q "People don't really care about how they look. **If you're looking for pretty people, this is not the campus**."

Q "**If you are a heterosexual male or homosexual female, New College is great**. If you are a homosexual male or heterosexual female, then New College sucks."

Q "A lot of straight women complain about a lack of attractive heterosexual males. **The quality is high, but the quantity is low**. Our standards for what we think is attractive are different than what is typical."

STUDENT AUTHOR: Gay friendly, liberal, and eccentric—the guys and girls at New College don't reflect the mainstream. The decision to attend New College is not typically one that is completely rooted in social factors. People come for the academics. New College is a place where close relationships can form quickly and intensely. The environment is conducive for relationships because of the coed dorms and the fact that it is so easy to get to know everybody.

Traditions
Ben and Jerry's Devotional Society, Gatsby Party, Headphone Dance Party, Naked Potluck, Thesis Burning, Towne Meetings

Overall School Spirit
There is often a love/hate relationship with the school. The lack of large, organized extracurricular events makes it hard for people to show school spirit. However, most of the students who stick around are proud to be Novo Collegians, and they flaunt New College apparel. We have a lot of personal investment in the ideals and vision of the school.

Students Speak Out
ON ATHLETICS

Q "**Athletics would disrupt the academic focus**. Athletic programs are nice for larger places, but I'm glad we don't have that. The fitness center is fine."

Q "**Our stereotype of being 'dodgeball targets' is absolutely ridiculous**—it is possible to be smart and athletic at the same time."

Q "I wouldn't say that we lack athletics. **I would say we don't have a priority on athletics**. I'm satisfied with the facilities, and there are enough students to field teams when someone starts one."

Q "We're already academically competitive enough without grades. We're fighting against each other to be the best. **We benefit from not having organized sports**."

STUDENT AUTHOR: The beauty about athletics at New College is that, unlike most schools that don't have bustling sports teams and schools spirit, our student body just doesn't care. There are no intramurals and only two intercollegiate teams. The ultimate Frisbee team is open to all. The girls' soccer team also doesn't have a strict tryout procedure. New College doesn't attract the athletically inclined, so it doesn't become an issue.

Students Speak Out
ON DRUG SCENE

Q "The drug scene is prominent, but **peer pressure here is unheard of.**"

Q "The drug scene is very open and visible, but I think the visibility is not representative of the quantity of use. **People are open about their drug use because they are not ashamed** and do not see it as a bad thing. They are not hiding."

Q "The drug scene is good—I don't have complaints. **We usually get the crème de la crème of the drug world**."

STUDENT AUTHOR: Are there drug users here? Yes. But, are they irresponsible? No. To the extent that it is possible to do so, those who use drugs do so in a responsible manner. Peer pressure is virtually nonexistent. There is a vast amount of students who don't use drugs at all and are respected for their choices. Marijuana, alcohol, and cigarettes are used publicly. Students tend to be moderate with their usage, making sure their habits don't interfere with their studies.

10:1	Student-to-Faculty Ratio
82%	Freshman Retention Rate
45%	Four-Year Graduation Rate
68%	Financial Aid Applicants Receiving Aid

Students Speak Out
SAFETY & SECURITY

Q "I feel safe on campus dealing with New College students, but I have had experiences on campus with people who were not students that were unpleasant. **The New College Police Department was able to help me** with those unpleasant situations."

Q "**It's a safe place because everyone knows everyone, and outsiders are easily identified**. Computers in Ham have been stolen a couple of times. You can definitely go jogging at night, and you'll be fine. That's not true at most places."

Q "A friend of mine's costume fell off at the anything-but-clothes party, and **she walked back to her dorm across campus completely naked.** She was fine. No one cared."

STUDENT AUTHOR: By pure statistics alone, one can easily notice that New College is one of the safest campuses in the country. Few college campuses are home to unlocked doors, unattended laptops, and females walking alone in the middle of the night without fear.

> **Questions?**
> For more inside information and survival tips, pick up College Prowler's full-length book on this school, written by an actual student! Check it out at *www.collegeprowler.com*.

Students Speak Out
ON OVERALL EXPERIENCE

Q "We're a school that defied the norm of traditional education and built a new edifice of a liberal arts eduction. We've questioned typical university grading systems and discovered that evaluations are quite comparable and even better in some respects. I'm proud to have come here, and **the experience is something I'll cherish for the rest of my life**."

Q "I think the small social atmosphere is conducive to people who weren't popular in high school. **It is a warm and tight-knit community**. Overall, I really enjoy this school. It is inexpensive because of the great scholarship opportunities it provides. I'm happy to be here."

Q "If you've already chosen a career, New College is not a great idea. **If you are undecided, I would very much recommend coming here**."

Q "New College as an overall experience has been blossoming and has given me a lot of perspective. I am more accepting of certain qualities. **For the first time, I feel like I fit in somewhere**, and I don't feel like I'm being judged. I feel comfortable in my own skin."

STUDENT AUTHOR: New College is a special place. You cannot think of it as just another small liberal arts school in the South. There is not a single aspect of New College that can be considered traditional. From the progressive academics to the alternative social culture, it is a unique setting. This intensity does not bode well for everyone. Not everyone can hack it; many fail out, and many transfer. Most Novo Collegians believe in the intrinsic value of education, and they believe that their school is providing them with far more intellectually than most Ivy League schools can offer.

New York University

70 Washington Square; New York, NY 10012
(212) 998-1212; www.nyu.edu

THE BASICS:

Acceptance Rate: 37%   **SAT Range:** 1860–2140*
Setting: Urban   **Control:** Private
F-T Undergrads: 19,914 **Tuition:** $37,372

Most Popular Majors: Visual/Performing Arts, Social Sciences, Communications/Journalism, Liberal Arts

*of 2400

Academics	B+	Guys	B-
Local Atmosphere	A+	Girls	A-
Safety & Security	B-	Athletics	D
Computers	C	Nightlife	A+
Facilities	C-	Greek Life	D+
Campus Dining	B	Drug Scene	C-
Off-Campus Dining	A+	Campus Strictness	B
Campus Housing	B+	Parking	F
Off-Campus Housing	D-	Transportation	A+
Diversity	B+	Weather	B-

Students Speak Out
ON ACADEMICS

Q "The professors I had really help their students and are **always willing to meet outside of class** or have e-mail conversations with them. The only bad experience I had was with a TA."

Q "Most teachers at school are approachable and easy to work with. As for classes, they are **interesting as can be**, especially when dealing with core requirements."

Q "Honestly, the teachers and professors vary. I have had some good ones, but I think **the not-so-good may outnumber the good**. But the TAs are generally good. They definitely help and are available whenever you need them to be."

Q "The quality of teachers can vary. They are all very **qualified and are masters in the subject**, but some are more helpful and caring to the students than others. When you arrive, you should ask around for which teachers are favorites."

STUDENT AUTHOR: NYU students are divided when it comes to teachers. While some students feel the professors are at the top of their field, others feel they are lacking. Most teachers are willing to accommodate individual needs, but you must pursue them yourself through e-mail or direct confrontation; and some teachers are more approachable than others. Every now and then, a teacher comes along that will turn you on to a subject and perhaps even lead you down the road to a major if you are undecided.

Students Speak Out
ON LOCAL ATMOSPHERE

Q "**Nothing beats NYC**; everybody needs to be a part of that excitement at least once in their life."

Q "We are right by New School and Cooper Union. Pace is downtown, and Hunter and Columbia are uptown, so there are a bunch of other colleges, but they **don't really interact** all that much."

Q "The **campus probably isn't what you expect**; it's not a regular campus, it's a city campus. It surrounds Washington Square Park, and the classrooms are in buildings all over the area. The freshman dorms are all around that area, too, in the Village. The apartment-style dorms are all over NY, mostly in the downtown area."

Q "Although the city has gotten a lot nicer and safer, it's still **possible for bad things to happen**. There are tons of things to visit in NYC—Ground Zero being the most popular now. Broadway shows, Times Square, museums, and Central Park are all popular."

STUDENT AUTHOR: Any NYU student will tell you that if you want a traditional college campus, then NYU is not the school for you. The city atmosphere is fast-paced and hectic, and if you get too caught up in it, your grades could be affected. This is not to say that it is impossible to go to school here; you just need to find a balance between all the excitement of the city and your studies. Students love New York because it provides endless entertainment—plays, concerts, bars, clubs, restaurants—and there is never a reason to be bored. The atmosphere at NYU is exciting.

5 Best Things	5 Worst Things
1 Location	1 High tuition
2 Internships	2 Housing lottery
3 Nightlife	3 School spirit
4 Diversity	4 Housing
5 Subways	5 Cost of living

Students Speak Out
ON FACILITIES

Q "The facilities are always new and improving. NYU has a buttload of money, so they have a lot of **resources at your disposal**."

Q "The only big downside to going to school in NY is the space issue. Due to the **lack of space** in Manhattan, the facilities suffer. They're small, but they do the job. NYU does rent out Chelsea Piers (a sports facility uptown), though, for some of the teams. Basically, classrooms are small and weird looking, but you deal."

Q "The **computer facilities are nice and convenient**, offering both Macs and PCs. The gym is nice enough, and the student center has offices too small for the clubs and organizations they were meant to house. It doesn't look like a student center."

Q "The facilities are all very nice, very well maintained, and for the most part, equipped with the **most modern technologies**."

Q "NYU's music studio and the music department are pushing the poverty line. The thing I find most aggravating with NYU is the bureaucracy. **Money is poured in some areas and not others**."

STUDENT AUTHOR: The main downside to the facilities at NYU is not that they are in poor shape, but that they are not big enough for the volume of students who attend the University. Students complain most about the computer labs, and they learn to deal with the large numbers of people who crowd the gyms and classrooms. Expect to wait in lines for most of the facilities.

Famous Alumni

John Cusack, Neil Diamond, Nathaniel Goldstein, Ang Lee, Spike Lee, Charles Moskowitz, Ashley Olsen, Martin Scorsese

Students Speak Out
ON CAMPUS DINING

Q "It depends on where you eat on campus. There are **cafeterias in some of the dorms**. The older dorms have pretty mediocre food, but the new ones are pretty good. There are plenty of places to eat off campus."

Q "Food on campus is actually pretty good. Many campus **food spots besides dining halls** accept meal plans or Declining Dollars, which are very convenient."

Q "Food from the cafeteria is not gross, but they **serve the same food everyday**, and it can get pretty nasty."

Q "Around campus, **most places are pricey**, as in you'll find a hard time getting lunch for less than five dollars. If you are living in a dorm, chances are you that will get a meal plan. Personally, I like dining hall food."

Q "Dining halls are **fun during the first few months**. They tend to get disgusting after that."

STUDENT AUTHOR: NYU might boast a wide selection of campus dining, but it's still dining hall food, no matter how you slice it. One student favorite is the Weinstein Food Court. The monotony of choosing from the same meals bothers students after a few weeks, and freshmen have it the worst because they are required to be on a meal plan. Luckily, you can choose to live in one of the many apartment-style dorms sophomore year where you can prepare your own food. Students have many eateries right near campus that have great food, and some of them even accept Campus Cash, so they can use their NYU accounts to pay.

Student Body

African American:	4%	Male/Female:	38/62%
Asian American:	18%	Out-of-State:	64%
Hispanic:	7%	International:	5%
Native American:	<1%	Unknown:	17%
White:	49%		

Popular Faiths: In a city like New York, you can find any religion you can imagine.

Gay Pride: NYU is very supportive of its lesbian, gay, bisexual, and transgender student population. The NYU Office of LGBT Student Affairs offers many resources for interested students.

Economic Status: With a tuition as high as NYU's, there is a large number of kids from wealthy families.

Students Speak Out
ON DORMS

Q "The dorms are good. It depends on what style dorm you get. The traditional style is basically a room and a bathroom. NYU dorms have a **bathroom in every room**. Apartment-style is a room, bathroom, a common room, and a kitchen."

Q "Upperclassmen dorms are amazing, but some are far away. The **freshman dorms definitely have the best locations**, but they aren't that nice. Compared to the dorms at other universities, however, NYU does provide nice dorms."

Q "Because of **space issues**, the dorms are pretty small. They're all different sizes and are in lots of different locations."

STUDENT AUTHOR: An NYU tour guide once said, "Enjoy the NYU dorms while you live in them. They are probably the nicest apartments you will be able to afford in New York City for a looong time." There are no communal bathrooms whatsoever; of course, you do have to clean your own. The dorms are in some of the most coveted locations in the whole city, but they are very expensive.

Did You Know?
53% of undergrads live on campus.

Students Speak Out
ON GUYS & GIRLS

Q "There are some hot guys, but it's **hard to meet people outside of your dorm** or your classes since there is no campus."

Q "Think of our school: **actors and actresses are definitely hot**, but there are also nerdy students, like pretty much all of the Stern Business School."

Q "There are also some ugly people on campus and some **nice people on campus**; it's up to you to find your significant other."

Q "There are **lots of gay guys**, but there are definitely some hotties. The girls, I don't know. They're rich, I guess."

STUDENT AUTHOR: There is definitely a lot of eye-candy at NYU. In a city where models roam the streets freely, giving men license to openly gape at their leggy glory, the NYU chicks put up a pretty good fight. There are a lot of exotic-looking girls, and the guys are not too shabby either. Many prefer to date outside NYU, picking from the general NYC dating pool rather than trying to find a compatible classmate.

Traditions

Bobcat Day
Street festival celebrating NYU spirit and tradition, featuring live music, games, and NYC snacks.

Annual Strawberry Festival
An afternoon of strawberries, carnival attractions, food, and bands.

Overall School Spirit
Although sports are not a big school spirit factor, students are definitely proud of the NYU name. Students in each school at NYU have their own particular brand of pride.

Students Speak Out
ON ATHLETICS

Q "NYU is not the school for you if you're looking for a 'ra-ra' sports school. We are a Division III school, with our only D-I sport being fencing. **School spirit is not big** at NYU, and although we do have decent men's and women's basketball teams, there is little to no support for them."

Q "Varsity **sports are not a big deal**, and the college competitiveness is nonexistent."

Q "Sports don't play a big role in school life. We **don't have a football team** or a stadium for games. We have a gym with a basketball court and a pool where most of the games are played."

Q "**IM sports are kind of small**, I think; I've never seen or participated in one. There are tons of options if you want to take advantage of them."

STUDENT AUTHOR: If you come to NYU, don't count on the sports teams being a major part of your college life. The players are dedicated and love what they do; they just aren't appreciated as much as they would be at a state school.

Students Speak Out
ON DRUG SCENE

Q "**Drugs are a big part of NYC**, no matter whether you're in college or not. They are hot items, but I haven't had any problems with it. Drugs are easy to get, but they're also pretty easy to stay away from."

Q "There are drug dealers right in front of the dorms in Washington Square Park, but **the NYPD does their best to crack down** on that. As far as drug safety is concerned, though, it's not like you're gonna trip and fall right into a bong! Just don't let peer pressure get to you."

Q "**Weed is huge** at NYU with a large majority of students. But like anything else, you don't have to be a part of it."

STUDENT AUTHOR: Smoking weed is a popular pastime at NYU, and there is certainly no shortage of it on campus. As for other drugs, they're around, but one usually has to make a conscious effort to get them. Sure, Washington Square Park has its share of dealers, but these can easily be avoided by not walking through at night and staying uninvolved.

12:1	Student-to-Faculty Ratio
92%	Freshman Retention Rate
78%	Four-Year Graduation Rate
85%	Financial Aid Applicants Receiving Aid

Students Speak Out
SAFETY & SECURITY

Q "**Security is annoying**, but for the most part, nothing ever happens on campus. There is no real campus, so many times things that happen are out of their jurisdiction."

Q "Security and safety are great, as long as you have common sense. There are **24-hour guards** at all the dorms."

Q "Security is great, but there is a little too much in the dorms. You can only have three guests at a time without special permission, and they have to be signed in and show photo ID. Security will also **pick you up anywhere in the city** if you call and tell them you are stranded."

STUDENT AUTHOR: In a place like New York City, tight security is a must. NYU is much safer than you might think, but you should always be careful. Remember, you are in a big city where anything could happen, so take precaution. Be aware of your surroundings, and never walk alone at night.

> **Questions?**
> For more inside information and survival tips, pick up College Prowler's full-length book on this school, written by an actual student! Check it out at *www.collegeprowler.com.*

Students Speak Out
ON OVERALL EXPERIENCE

Q "Basically, I think NYU is the place to be. There is just so much out there. Anything you could want is waiting **right there at your fingertips**."

Q "It's a different experience for different people, depending on your major. I'm an actress, and it is perfect for me. **If you are artsy, go to NYU**. If not, then think it over, but it really is a great place to be."

Q "The major difference between NYU and any other school is that it's in the city, so there's not really a campus, which means **there's not really any campus life**."

Q "Another perk about being at NYU is the **opportunity that hits you in the face**. I work at MTV right now. I interned there for two semesters and then got offered a job as a production assistant for the news and docs department. I know that I wouldn't have had this opportunity if I wasn't here. So there are a lot of opportunities here at NYU."

STUDENT AUTHOR: NYU requires a certain taste and is not for everyone. Students say that the best part about attending NYU is living in New York City. The only complaints are that there is not much of a campus or student bond, and the school is run too much like a business. Whatever you're thinking when you apply to this school, just remember that if you attend, you should be prepared for a mix of demanding academics and wild experiences in the city. Finding a balance between the two is key at this big-city school.

North Carolina State University

2205 Hillsborough Street; Raleigh, NC 17695
(919) 515-2011; www.ncsu.edu

Academics	B	Guys	B
Local Atmosphere	B+	Girls	B
Safety & Security	B	Athletics	A-
Computers	A	Nightlife	B+
Facilities	B-	Greek Life	C
Campus Dining	B+	Drug Scene	B+
Off-Campus Dining	B	Campus Strictness	B-
Campus Housing	B-	Parking	C
Off-Campus Housing	B+	Transportation	A-
Diversity	C	Weather	B+

Students Speak Out
ON ACADEMICS

Q "I have had a very wide variety of teachers; some have been incredible, some have been terrible. The same with classes—**some have been interesting, and some have not**. It's the luck of the draw, in my opinion. There is going to be a bad egg in every bunch at every school."

Q "**My freshman year, my classes were so basic**, but this year, I find my classes more interesting because they relate to my major. The teachers are very in-depth and interesting with their lectures, too."

Q "Like most, I've had good and bad teachers. **I have had more good than bad**, though. As long as a student is putting forth effort, I think teachers, in general, are willing to help a kid out."

Q "All the teachers I have had at NCSU make it very easy to learn from them, and they are **very approachable with office hours**. Even if you have a conflict with their hours, they will help you some other way. I find my classes very interesting, and my teachers make it worth getting up to go to class."

STUDENT AUTHOR: Academics are held to a high standard at NC State, due to the top-ranked colleges within the University in combination with the dedicated professors. While NCSU has very strong academics in most fields, some are still developing. NC State holds its own with diverse areas of study and accessible professors, all of which provide an enriched learning environment.

Students Speak Out
ON LOCAL ATMOSPHERE

Q "Raleigh is a nice college town. There is a downtown area with **good nightlife and restaurants all within biking distance**. There also many good, convenient shopping centers around."

Q "Raleigh is a great town with lots of things to do in it. However, **at night, it sometimes sucks for people under 21**. Most of the bars and clubs allow only people 21 and over. Most of the time, there are parties to take care of that, though."

Q "In Raleigh, there is a more urban atmosphere around the campus. There is a good bar scene, many good restaurants, and NC State athletics—not to mention **Chapel Hill is only half an hour down the road**."

Q "The atmosphere in Raleigh is very urban, and if you find the right places, such as Glenwood Avenue, you can have a good time. Since Raleigh is the capital, if you are interested in historical landmarks and things like that, **you can visit the capital building and other things in downtown**."

STUDENT AUTHOR: **It's important for a student to find a college atmosphere fitting his or her needs. Raleigh is very upbeat, and after being voted one of the coolest places to live, more and more single young people are moving here and taking advantage of the dating scene. NCSU is surrounded by college students. It is never a question of what is going on—it's always hardest deciding what to do.**

Students Speak Out
ON FACILITIES

Q "Facilities are really nice around campus. **They are kept nice and decently cleaned**. I am impressed with how nicely we keep the buildings when we have so many students using them."

Q "**The gym is old and generally crowded**. The computers are up-to-date, for the most part. It's been a while since I've been in the student center, but the last time I went it was in good condition."

Q "On campus, **the computers are very up-to-date, the athletic facilities are tops** in the ACC, and our student center is a bit older but still nice. NC State is in the process of building new facilities on campus, as part of the seven-year-long One Billion Dollar Campaign to renovate the school."

Q "Facilities around campus are great. There is a lot to do. Our library—well, you will get used to being there. **The book stacks are a great place to study** and get away from distraction."

STUDENT AUTHOR: There is a variety of facilities for students to use, whether for academics or athletics. Students who are into athletics can go to Carmichael Gym and pick from a number of activities. For those interested in academic facilities, there is the Tutorial Center and the Career Center, as well as computer labs and internship offices. There are many computer facilities available to students, some open 24 hours, and all are well-maintained. Also, Students can get a jump start on finding a job through internship coordinators and the Career Center.

Famous Alumni

John Edwards, John Tesh, Bill Cowher, Pablo Mastroeni, Terry Holt, Philip Rivers

Students Speak Out
ON CAMPUS DINING

Q "There are many choices in on-campus dining. Taco Bell is a big hit, as is Chick-fil-A. The dining halls are nice, too. **They usually have a pretty big menu to fit anyone's needs**. The places to eat are convenient, too. You don't have to walk a long ways to get to a place to eat."

Q "I didn't mind eating on campus the first year. I **didn't get a meal plan my second year** and stuck to buying groceries and grabbing the occasional bite to eat on campus."

Q "**Personally, I think on-campus food is gross**. I don't eat fast food often, so the only place I ever visited was the C-Store or the smoothie shop. I think opting out of buying a meal plan and then just buying groceries is the way to go. Subway on Hillsborough Street is one of my main destinations. On a high note, at least it is possible to eat healthy on campus."

Q "Places around campus are good to eat at. I guess you get kind of tired of eating at dining halls and in the Atrium, but when you need something to eat between classes, you can't complain. **Dining hall food is not all that bad, it just gets old sometimes**."

STUDENT AUTHOR: Dining hall foods are not the best, but students here have heard of worse things. The dining hall isn't bad the first year, or maybe even two, but afterwards, you will learn it is a little cheaper to invest in groceries you want and make your own food, or have the occasional bite to eat on campus or out at some of the student-favorite restaurants.

Student Body

African American:	9%	Male/Female:	56/44%
Asian American:	5%	Out-of-State:	7%
Hispanic:	3%	International:	1%
Native American:	1%	Unknown:	2%
White:	79%		

Popular Faiths: Christianity seems to be, by far, the most common religion.

Gay Pride: NCSU has a very diverse set of students and is accepting of the gay community.

Economic Status: NCSU tends to have a lot of "middle of the road" kids attending. There are the wealthy, and there are some from lower socioeconomic classes.

Students Speak Out
ON DORMS

Q "**The dorms on campus are older**, but University Towers and anything like Owen or Tucker in Central Campus are good. Avoid those like Wood or Bagwell, because they are too far from all the action."

Q "The dorms, for the most part, are all pretty good. Almost all of them are air-conditioned, and **you meet a lot of people in the dorms**."

Q "It's a tough decision whether or not you should live with your best friend when coming to college. Think wisely about that—**you don't want to ruin a friendship by fighting over tight space**."

Q "It was **nice having someone clean up after you** in the bathroom and keep the lounge vacuumed."

STUDENT AUTHOR: NC State's dorms are about average; though this depends on students' standards. The housing Web site (*www.ncsu.edu/housing*) is helpful and easy to navigate. Each dorm is in good shape, for the most part; it is just important to look up the location in relation to your classes, the air conditioning and smoking status, and the alcohol policy to best fit your preferences.

> **? Did You Know?**
> 34% of undergrads live on campus.

Students Speak Out
ON GUYS & GIRLS

Q "For the most part, the girls on campus are pretty good. If you go out, **you are bound to run into someone you think is attractive**, and who knows where it will go from there."

Q "We have a very mixed campus here. I see a lot of hicks in the agriculture department. **If Southern boys are your type, you will definitely find some here**. I do see a lot of preppy boys, though, too, mostly in fraternities. It's all about your taste in guys."

Q "The girls are pretty hot on campus—they're prettier than us boys, I'm sure. I think a guy has a pretty good chance of finding a girl they can get into. I'm just glad **the boy-girl ratio is finally evening out a little**."

STUDENT AUTHOR: With more than 25,000 students, there is bound to be someone with the ideal personality for you. The girls, as a whole, seem to outshine the guys in looks, playing in a league above them, but with Raleigh being a top city for singles, the dating scene is hot for anyone. NC State, unlike UNC-Chapel Hill, is known for having more guys than ladies. Boys, don't be afraid to venture out and test the waters at Meredith and Peace College.

> **Traditions**
>
> **Homecoming**
> Each year there is a homecoming football game with a parade down Hillsborough Street.
>
> **Hillsborough Hike**
> Graduating seniors start drinking at Player's Retreat and try to hike their way up Hillsborough Street, going from bar to bar.
>
> **Overall School Spirit**
> School spirit is strong at NCSU. Remember, we do not like the Tarheels!

Students Speak Out
ON ATHLETICS

Q "Varsity sports, especially the revenue-generating sports like football and basketball, are very big on campus. Student tickets to these games are always in high demand. **Intramural sports are also pretty big on campus**. There are tons of leagues for different sports, and it's very easy to get involved in these activities."

Q "Athletics are big here at our school. I encourage everyone to support it and **get tickets to go to the football games and basketball games**. Going to events like these is what college is all about. Enjoy good and free tickets while you can."

Q "**Intramural sports are big**, especially with fraternities and sororities and different club organizations."

STUDENT AUTHOR: Athletics at NCSU are great. Even though the teams hit bumpy roads, there is still strong backing at football and basketball games. College is not just about varsity sports, though. NC State makes it very reasonable to partake in club sports or even intramurals. The University does a great job of organizing intramural functions and supporting the students' activities.

Students Speak Out
ON DRUG SCENE

Q "As with everywhere else, drugs are available. However, **one can avoid them** if they decide to."

Q "There are going to be drugs everywhere, in my opinion. I think **it depends on the type of crowd you hang out with** as to whether or not you're going to know about them. I haven't really heard of any drug problems around NCSU. That doesn't mean we don't necessarily have them, though; just don't go out looking for trouble, and you'll probably be okay."

Q "I've heard of a few incidents of students being caught with drugs, and all I really know is they were punished severely for it. I think one kid was expelled from school. **NC State takes illegal activity seriously**."

STUDENT AUTHOR: **Drugs do not seem prevalent at NCSU. Alcohol consumption is more of an issue than drugs. There is no heavy pressure to partake in drug use. It is easy to steer clear of drugs on and off campus. To get involved, it almost seems as if you would have to do research.**

16:1	Student-to-Faculty Ratio
89%	Freshman Retention Rate
37%	Four-Year Graduation Rate
69%	Financial Aid Applicants Receiving Aid

Students Speak Out
SAFETY & SECURITY

Q "There are **security stations all over campus where you can run up and call security**. This makes getting help very quick and convenient and should make every student feel safe. If you don't feel comfortable walking alone, you don't have to with NC State's escort service."

Q "**I do not see a very large security presence on campus** from our police officers. In fact, I get e-mails about crime alerts and people being robbed. There are safe walks, and rides you can get if you call the police if you are somewhere and it's late and you don't want to walk."

Q "I suppose **I feel safe everywhere around campus**. It is a little scary to walk around at night, but that is how I feel walking anywhere at night."

STUDENT AUTHOR: **NC State considers safety a top priority. The campus grounds are dotted with blue-light emergency phones, and Campus Police offers an escort service for students. Overall, students feel that Campus Police have the right priorities, but there is room for improvement in a few areas.**

> **Questions?**
> For more inside information and survival tips, pick up College Prowler's full-length book on this school, written by an actual student! Check it out at *www.collegeprowler.com*.

Students Speak Out
ON OVERALL EXPERIENCE

Q "My experience has been great overall. I've met numerous new people that have made me enjoy every moment at NC State. I have no regrets coming to NC State. **There is something here for everyone**."

Q "I have met so many people it is crazy. It has come to the point now, as I'm about to graduate this year, that I walk around and recognize more and more people from my classes. I think **attending a large university is a great experience for everyone**."

Q "I think **Raleigh is a great place to live if you're young and single**. I have enjoyed my NC State experience, and I'm happy I came here. The professors are so willing to help a student out. Thanks to the University, I have had the opportunity to co-op with engineering firms and will hopefully find a secure job after graduation."

Q "I have loved NC State so far. **I'm halfway through college and have no regrets**. In fact, I've enjoyed it here so much I'm considering attending NC State for graduate school. I don't think anyone would regret coming here, but if you like big schools, this is the place for you."

STUDENT AUTHOR: **Overall, the students' experience with NCSU is one that provides them with a rich learning environment. Students learn to balance play and work. NC State wants its students to succeed not only in academics, but in life, too. Here you learn important lifelong skills that are essential to your survival in the real world. Classes can be rigorous and stressful, but students find a way to overcome hardships and get through. You will come out of college ready to work in some of the most diverse settings.**

Northeastern University

360 Huntington Avenue; Boston, MA 02115
(617) 373-2000; www.neu.edu

THE BASICS:

Acceptance Rate: 39%   **SAT Range:** 1750–2010*
Setting: Urban   **Control:** Private
F-T Undergrads: 15,339   **Tuition:** $33,721

Most Popular Majors: Business/Marketing, Engineering, Health Professions, Security Services

*of 2400

Academics	B	Guys	B+
Local Atmosphere	A+	Girls	B+
Safety & Security	C	Athletics	B-
Computers	B+	Nightlife	A-
Facilities	A-	Greek Life	C-
Campus Dining	A	Drug Scene	A-
Off-Campus Dining	A	Campus Strictness	B-
Campus Housing	B+	Parking	D
Off-Campus Housing	B+	Transportation	B+
Diversity	C	Weather	C-

Students Speak Out
ON ACADEMICS

Q "Most of the teachers are **very approachable** and quite understanding. They usually try to make the classes somewhat interesting, although with some of the core business requirements, this is a fruitless labor."

Q "Northeastern specializes in the 'techie' fields, so these majors are more difficult; I hear the engineering majors **never sleep**."

Q "If you take an astronomy class, there are field trips to the Museum of Science to use their telescope. If you take a geology class, you may visit **Harvard's collection of fossils** and dinosaur skeletons. Campus is practically on top of the Museum of Fine Arts. Northeastern recently hosted the Boston Poetry Festival. You get the point."

Q "All of the classes in my major have been interesting, however, the general classes that I need for my core requirement (algebra, English, and history) are not only boring, but **a waste of time and money**."

STUDENT AUTHOR: The professors here can seem inconsistent. Some professors are merely assistants or adjuncts, and students can feel like they are not getting their money's worth out of the class. However, some professors are experts in their fields, such as former presidential candidate Michael Dukakis and criminologist Jack Levin. Our professors have won scholarly honors, written books, and appeared on television. Overall, the faculty help make the academic experience.

Students Speak Out
ON LOCAL ATMOSPHERE

Q "There is certainly no shortage of **things to do**. Even if you're screaming for a break from the city, Boston Common is a park large enough for anyone to find his or her own patch of grass."

Q "Boston is well-known for its culture and education. The NU campus is located along the **Avenue of the Arts**, which is another way of saying 'the section of Huntington Avenue where the Museum of Fine Arts is located.'"

Q "Boston is, without a doubt, **the ideal city** to go to college in. There are over 100 colleges and universities in the area, and the student-to-resident ratio is 5:1. The Christian Science Center is a beautiful area, located just a few blocks from campus. Also, the Prudential Center and Copley are just steps away from the freshman dorms."

Q "Northeastern has the benefit of being an urban university, and thus the local atmosphere is not limited to the campus pub and a greasy pizza pit. We're **a stone's throw away from Fenway Park**: the Green Monster, proud home of the Boston Red Sox."

STUDENT AUTHOR: Two words can accurately sum up the city of Boston: college town! Yes, Beantown is the ultimate place to be if you're a college student. No matter what you enjoy seeing, doing, or eating, the city of Boston and its suburbs, such as Brookline and Cambridge, have so much to offer, it's impossible to think of going to college anywhere else.

Students Speak Out
ON FACILITIES

Q "I think that the facilities are **very nice** and state-of-the-art. This campus is filled with many great places for students to chill. I never find myself without something to do."

Q "Just check out the pictures of our amazing campus. Everything is **new and sparkling**. The main gym has three floors with basketball courts, machines, weights, and an elevated running track. The gym across the street has an indoor soccer field and a pool. The student center is beautiful as well."

Q "The facilities on campus are pretty **technologically advanced**, and there are a lot of beautiful buildings. There is a fairly new gym on Columbus Avenue—the Badger and Rosen Squashbusters—which has squash courts and workout areas."

Q Our facilities that serve everyone are great, although some of the more specialized facilities (practice rooms, labs) are **not up to par**."

STUDENT AUTHOR: NU's facilities get better every year. The University has recently added brand new classrooms and dorms, and even the dining hall has been revamped with eight plasma TV screens. The Cabot center is available for students to swim, and for teams to meet for practice. Everything is so close by, it's only a matter of where to meet and what to do first! Northeastern also has something very unique—tunnels. Whether it's cold, snowy, raining, or you just plain feel like walking through them, most University buildings are attached by underground tunnels.

Famous Alumni

Darald Libby, Richard J. Egan, Robert J. Davis, Linda Connors, Kevin Antunes, Damien Fahey

Students Speak Out
ON CAMPUS DINING

Q "Our dining halls have by far **the best food** I have ever had at any college. They've got beautiful dining halls, plasma TVs, and more. There's everything from make-your-own-waffles to make-your-own-stir-fry."

Q "The food is **pretty decent** here. There are a lot of different places to go. There are always new restaurant chains springing up on campus, too."

Q "The food here is really good. Sign up for the **Kosher option**, even if you aren't Jewish, because the food is a million times better, and you can still eat the other food for the same price! There's no reason not to!"

Q "Like most other colleges, Northeastern's dining facilities **just aren't very good**. Somehow, no matter how much atmosphere you give a cafeteria (plants, flowers, fancy lighting, and booth seating), it's still a cafeteria. The most appealing dinner options on certain nights consist of cold cereal and bagels."

STUDENT AUTHOR: The food on campus is pretty good. There are healthy choices for the health-conscious, and with two dining halls, students can mix up their meals so they don't get bored. As a freshman, you are required to have a meal plan if you're living in the residence halls. You'll be spending a lot of time in the D-hall, as it's commonly known. Since you won't have a kitchen your freshman year, you'll be spending a lot of time in the D-hall, as it's commonly known. Some people complain about the food, but they'd be hard pressed to find a college campus with much better options.

Student Body

African American:	6%	Male/Female:	49/51%
Asian American:	8%	Out-of-State:	65%
Hispanic:	5%	International:	5%
Native American:	<1%	Unknown:	15%
White:	61%		

Popular Faiths: There are a few Christian groups, and Hillel for Jewish students on campus is also popular.

Gay Pride: Northeastern has NuBiLaga, the group for bisexual, lesbian, and gay students. They host Gay Pride Month events, which is well-received.

Economic Status: Some students are really poor, and others are astonishingly rich; chances are, you'll find someone in every economic group.

Students Speak Out
ON DORMS

Q "I enjoyed my time in the dorms, although I only stayed in them for my freshman year. All of them have their positive and negative aspects, but no matter where you end up your first year, keep in mind that it's the worst it's going to get. Upperclassman housing is **top-of-the-line**."

Q The dorms are **very nice**. I have been lucky! Freshman year is okay, but it sucks if you live in an economy triple! After freshman year, it gets much better."

Q "Dorms are **typical dorms** when you're a freshman, but if you can live in West Village after that, it's definitely worth it."

STUDENT AUTHOR: The University uses a lottery system weighted by seniority. Students are guaranteed housing for three years, but if you get your housing form and deposit in on time, you should have no problem getting housing for the last two years as well. After freshman year, you can decide whom you want to room with by entering the lottery with your friends. A few weeks after that, you will be assigned the same lottery number as those you want to room with.

Did You Know?
49% of undergrads live on campus.

Students Speak Out
ON GUYS & GIRLS

Q "All different types of people from all parts of the world—you're pretty much guaranteed to find someone that you'll enjoy hanging out with. There are a lot of **good-looking people** around."

Q "I think we have the most attractive campus around. I see the students at BU as being the 'nerdy-antisocial' crowd, and Northeastern's students being the '**popular-but-smart**' ones."

Q "Some of the guys are **gorgeous**, and some of the girls are very pretty, too."

Q "I guess the girls and guys here are okay. Like every other college, it just depends on where you are and how hard you're looking. Then again, Boston is a college town, so you'll pretty much **find anything out here**!"

STUDENT AUTHOR: NU is full of attractive people, and most of them are just waiting to hook up. The problem is the communication; students seem to need some sort of dating guide, because both girls and guys don't know how to treat each other properly. NU is a sexually-open campus; the school has events on sex (Sex Week) and students are always talking about who hooked up, who sleeps around, and who's still a virgin.

Urban Legend
The Husky, Northeastern's mascot, was adopted in 1927 when the first Husky, Sapsut, a canine with sled dog royalty, was brought to campus from Alaska. He received an honorary degree from the University president and was named forever more King Husky. For decades, it has become customary for students to come here and rub the Husky's nose for good luck.

Overall School Spirit
Students wear black and red, the school's colors, on Northeastern Day in May.

Students Speak Out
ON ATHLETICS

Q "Varsity sports are pretty big, but it's often difficult to get to the places where these events go on. **Intramural sports are pretty big**— broomball, played in the ice hockey rink, is a fun one."

Q "The only varsity sports games I've ever attended are the hockey games when **we play our rivals**, Harvard, BU, and BC. Other than that, I don't pay much attention to our teams' stats."

Q "With the exception of the Huskies football team, I never hear about any of the athletic stuff here. I know we have it, but it's so **not a big part** of college for me."

Q "I'm on the field hockey team, and **we work our butts off** every day. It would be nice to get some more freakin' recognition for what we do."

STUDENT AUTHOR: Though students don't always demonstrate a lot of school spirit over NU sports, the University does have its athletic draws. The Huskies consistently field a competitive hockey team, and students regularly turn out when Harvard, Boston University, or Boston College is in town. Regardless, most students readily admit that athletics aren't huge at NU.

Students Speak Out
ON DRUG SCENE

Q "I have a friend who had to drop out of NU during his sophomore year because of drug and **drinking problems** that, pretty much, began here. However, there are plenty of other alternatives for students at NU."

Q "Northeastern has a **very strict drug policy**, making it a rarity to hear about or see a lot of drug usage on campus. Other than marijuana, which is popular no matter where you go, there isn't a huge problem with the consumption of illegal substances."

Q "Drugs are **here if you want them**. However, if you feel uncomfortable being around them, then you don't have to be."

STUDENT AUTHOR: **Massachusetts enforces harsh penalties for marijuana possession, though this doesn't seem to deter those students who intend to look for it. Other, harder drugs, are probably around, but they aren't out in the open, and students certainly don't feel pressured to be involved if they don't want to.**

16:1	Student-to-Faculty Ratio
91%	Freshman Retention Rate
54%	Four-Year Graduation Rate
57%	Financial Aid Applicants Receiving Aid

Students Speak Out
SAFETY & SECURITY

Q "There is great security here. We have police patrolling **24 hours a day** and lots of guards outside of campus buildings. We can also get a hold of security at any time."

Q "Northeastern University has a **very visual security force** on campus. Police cars bearing the Northeastern seal are thick on campus, day and night. The officers are members of the Office of Public Safety, and there is also an additional hired contractor to keep the peace outside of the residence halls. You cannot enter any campus residence—dorm or on-campus apartment—without an NU student ID (and you must sign in guests that don't live there, even if they go to Northeastern)."

STUDENT AUTHOR: **Any city is going to be dangerous in some areas and intimidating at night, especially if you are not familiar with your surroundings. Boston is no exception. The NUPD, however, makes a huge effort to ensure our safety; NU is a well-lit campus, equipped with emergency call boxes.**

Questions?
For more inside information and survival tips, pick up College Prowler's full-length book on this school, written by an actual student! Check it out at *www.collegeprowler.com*.

Students Speak Out
ON OVERALL EXPERIENCE

Q "I love it here. I think **it's a great town** to go to college in, and maybe even to live in afterward. I would certainly look into staying here."

Q "I have had a **very good experience** at NU. I am from Virginia, so I wasn't quite sure that to expect, but you meet a lot of people. It's a big school, so everyone has a place."

Q "If you are an independent person and do not rely solely upon others for your happiness, you'll **have a good time**. Make the most of Boston— the experience is what you make of it."

Q "Overall, I am **very happy** with my choice to attend Northeastern. I can't think of a better place to attend college than here."

Q "**I love it here**. I wouldn't trade it for anything short of a professional baseball contract."

STUDENT AUTHOR: **Student complaints about Northeastern are generally the same complaints students have anywhere else: the advisors don't care enough, people slack off in their jobs, et cetera. Like any school, Northeastern has its setbacks, but these are easy to overlook, given the many advantages the University has to offer. The city of Boston offers an unparalleled experience for students. The Northeastern faculty is among the best you'll find anywhere, and student life on campus is fun and vibrant. Students may take issue with trivial matters here and there—parking's hard to find, the University can be too strict—but it's unlikely you'll find anyone who feels that Boston is boring, or that the University doesn't prepare students for post-college life. When it comes down to it, most students are happy to be here.**

Northern Arizona University

South San Francisco Street; Flagstaff, AZ 86011-4084
(928) 523-9011; www.nau.edu

THE BASICS:

Acceptance Rate: 75%   **SAT Range:** 990–1190*
Setting: Small city   **Control:** Public
F-T Undergrads: 12,844   **Tuition:** $14,428

Most Popular Majors: Education, Business, Liberal Arts, Social Sciences, Visual Arts, Health Professions

*of 1600

Academics	B-	Guys	B-
Local Atmosphere	A	Girls	B+
Safety & Security	B	Athletics	B-
Computers	B+	Nightlife	C+
Facilities	A-	Greek Life	B-
Campus Dining	C	Drug Scene	C+
Off-Campus Dining	A-	Campus Strictness	B
Campus Housing	B-	Parking	C-
Off-Campus Housing	C	Transportation	A-
Diversity	C	Weather	A

Students Speak Out
ON ACADEMICS

Q "I found the most valuable connections with the teachers in my major and minor departments. I have only come into contact with one difficult professor in over four years of NAU experience. The **classes were interesting**, but I was often disappointed to find that a class I wanted to take purely as an elective had prerequisites."

Q "My teachers in the College of Education are amazing. They all have been **nothing but helpful and encouraging** throughout my college experience. My classes are really easy. School is easy and enjoyable for me, so in turn, my classes have never been too hard."

Q "Many teachers are amazing. They are fun and relatable. However, **sometimes you get stuck with an awful, cruel professor**."

Q "I like most of the professors. I find most of my classes interesting—**definitely not a waste of my time**."

STUDENT AUTHOR: Most people don't generally view NAU as a highly-regarded academic institution; however, the school's small class sizes really give students the opportunity to ask questions and develop personal relationships with their professors. The instructors themselves are passionate about their fields. The salaries at NAU are not very high, so it's more likely that your teachers really enjoy what they do and aren't just here because it allows them to buy a Beamer. The education you receive is rewarding, it just takes time to get deeper into the upper-level courses.

Students Speak Out
ON LOCAL ATMOSPHERE

Q "**The town of Flagstaff is small and relaxing**. I like it because people are laid-back and nice. Plus, I am a fan of the outdoors and hiking. There are lots of students, which is cool, but I like the summers when it's quieter."

Q "I think that the atmosphere here in Flagstaff is very college-town-like. During the school year, there are lots of students and a lot for students to do. In the summer, the town dies. It seems as though a majority of the population leaves, only to return when school begins again. There are no other universities here, but there is a community college. In the winter, **Flagstaff can be a ski town if we get snow**, and in the summer, the temperatures are very moderate in comparison to the rest of the state, so it is the place to be."

Q "It's a hippie town. Lots of Birkenstocks, tie-dye, granola, and hand-rolled smokes. **For the most part, everyone is nice**. People tend to smile back at you or say hello."

Q "The environment is awesome. It's a college town, and it's a nice place to visit. Plus, the **weather is usually great**!"

STUDENT AUTHOR: The world famous Grand Canyon is in the neighborhood, and Phoenix, the state's capital and one of the largest cities in the country, is a short drive down the freeway. Flagstaff has been able to really balance the additions of modern day while still retaining the old-school look and feel of its Route 66 past. Plus, there's a ton of hippies.

Students Speak Out
ON FACILITIES

Q "The campus is undergoing major construction. **More buildings are popping up around campus**, and pre-existing ones are being upgraded. Unfortunately, our tuition is being affected by these major changes."

Q "All of the facilities are very nice. We have a great library and recreation center. NAU is also **doing well in keeping up with evolving technology**."

Q "**This campus has an identity crisis**. North campus is all original, all beautiful brick buildings and tall trees. South campus is all construction and pavement. Central campus is a mix. Generally speaking, everything is in good working order. It looks nice (with the exception of current construction). Everything serves its purpose. I can't think of anywhere on campus that is a hindrance."

Q "The facilities on campus are pretty nice, for the most part. I find that **NAU prides itself on being up-to-date** with their athletics, computer software/connections, as well as student union amenities."

STUDENT AUTHOR: **NAU is in the midst of a transition period. The campus is absolutely beautiful with its historic roots; however, the University is getting a bit of a facelift to keep up with the changing times. Even in the campus's older buildings, the University has done a good job of keeping them usable, clean, and technologically sound. NAU is doing a great job of giving students nice stuff to work with—just mind the mess until they're complete.**

Famous Alumni

J.S. Cardone, Diana Gabaldon, R. Carlos Nakai, Rick Renzi, Mark Thatcher, Steve Altman, Thomas P. Smith, Clarence Moore

Students Speak Out
ON CAMPUS DINING

Q "Unfortunately, **the food on campus is hit-or-miss**. Some days, it is delicious and the people are nice, and then there are the other days where the food looks like roadkill and the people are rude. Java is a pretty good place to go, and south dining, too."

Q "Pass! Halfway through freshman year, I couldn't stand any of the food on campus. **A lot of it is just crappy cafeteria food**. Gristly chicken, stale bread, brown lettuce, and the like."

Q "Despite popular belief, **the food on campus is surprisingly not bad at all**. There is a well-packed, fresh salad bar, as well as a personal choice everyday for vegan and vegetarian students, a deli that outdoes Subway with its fresh ingredients and bread selections for sandwich lovers, a Chick-fil-A and Pizza Hut for students that can't seem to get enough fast food, and an all-you-can-eat buffet for every jock on campus."

Q "By the end of freshman year, I was burnt out on campus food. **I wanted to actually use the dorm's kitchen**."

STUDENT AUTHOR: **Eating on campus is not necessarily bad, it's just very disappointing. The food itself is very much hit-or-miss. Some days, you will be pleasantly surprised; other days, your taste buds will strike and form a picket line right there on the table. When it comes to dining on campus, the service is bad, you have very few options, and you might as well just eat from the vending machines.**

Student Body

African American:	3%	Male/Female:	40/60%
Asian American:	2%	Out-of-State:	21%
Hispanic:	12%	International:	2%
Native American:	6%	Unknown:	4%
White:	71%		

Popular Faiths: Christianity seems to dominate the religious social scene and spiritual organizations.

Gay Pride: Gays and lesbians are openly accepted in this peace-loving, tree-hugging, hold-hands-and-sing-Kumbayah kind of town. Rainbows are everywhere, and NAU is a very warm and receptive community.

Economic Status: NAU is, by and large, enrolled with upper-middle-class students.

Students Speak Out
ON DORMS

Q "They are small, yes. There are communal bathrooms, loud neighbors at two or three in the morning, and the occasional squabble with your roommate is a given. However, **I haven't hated living in the dorms**, and I find that NAU prides itself on providing reliable, safe, clean, and nice dorms for all students who choose to live on campus. As far as dorms to avoid, McConnell (a freshman dorm located on south campus) is definitely not popular among many students at NAU."

Q "McConnell: party, trash, and **just plain old scary things happen there**."

Q "**For peace and quiet, Cowden**, the three-year-degree and honors dorm, is a great place to live."

STUDENT AUTHOR: **Campus housing at NAU is very good, especially after looking at the cost of living off campus. The halls on campus are all very nice and are all within distance of either the Doob or the Union. All in all, living on campus is a great experience—even the community bathrooms aren't that bad!**

? **Did You Know?**
40% of undergrads live on campus.

Students Speak Out
ON GUYS & GIRLS

Q "The girl-to-guy ratio sucks! **There are a lot more girls than there are guys**, so guys can take their pick. Girls might want to consider becoming lesbians. The guys are okay. Lots of hippie/skater/pothead types."

Q "Guys are either obsessed with working out, coffee junkies (hippies), **total outdoorsy types, or video gamers**. People think our girls are overweight, but they're not."

Q "**The girl-to-guy ratio is amazing if you're a fella**. I mean, you've got to like your chances. The girls here are all different types. You have every kind of stereotype, and then some. There are quite a few attractive ladies. Most are generally pretty friendly and easygoing."

STUDENT AUTHOR: **Dating is common on the mountain campus, but if you're looking to just hook up, there is plenty of action for that, too. Everyone is very laid-back and friendly. The University considers everyone an adult, so make sure to put on your big kid pants. When it comes to guys and girls at NAU, you'll find that the people are very friendly, receptive, and there's a group for just about everyone to fit into.**

Traditions

Bed Races
Businesses in town each sponsor a "bed," a metal frame on wheels that rolls down the street. The teams line up down the street and must try to complete the downhill circuit.

Greek Week
Greek Week is a weeklong celebration of Greeks and the brotherhood and sisterhood.

Overall School Spirit
For the most part, students are very proud of their school and seem to be content going here.

Students Speak Out
ON ATHLETICS

Q "Sports are popular, but **intramural sports are more fun**. Many people get involved, and it's a good way to meet new friends."

Q "IM sports are more popular than varsity sports. Everyone wants to participate and have a good time. **We suck at varsity sports!**"

Q "The **school spirit could be better**, but we try. IM sports are pretty big. There are a lot of different teams to play on, and they are always full."

Q "They are not big at all. **They are rather embarrassing**."

STUDENT AUTHOR: **NAU isn't known for its athletic prowess. The Lumberjack sports teams haven't been all that successful over the years. Intramurals are very popular on the mountain campus. The sheer number of different sports gives an opportunity for everyone to compete. If you're not into sports, it's no big deal. Sports at NAU can be enjoyable, and there are some great facilities, but most would rather sarcastically mutter "go team" while standing in line to grab a smoothie at Java.com.**

Students Speak Out
ON DRUG SCENE

Q "**NAU does have a drug scene**. There's always going to be marijuana and various other common drugs. Especially in a town like Flagstaff, there isn't much else to do, so many students turn to drugs as a sort of recreation or hobby. Drugs are going to be anywhere, but at NAU, it's not really a problem. Sure, they are there, but if you're not into them, no one bugs you. It's a very laid-back community, so it's an easy scene to avoid."

Q "**Nothing too bad**. There's lots of weed, but that's all."

Q "This school is the **marijuana school**. It seems like every week they bust someone for possession."

STUDENT AUTHOR: **Flagstaff is known as a hippie town, and the marijuana scene follows suit with the stereotype. Though alcohol abuse is quite common on campus in especially alarming numbers, nothing else is really a problem. There is the large following of marijuana users, but it's never a negative issue.**

17:1	Student-to-Faculty Ratio
71%	Freshman Retention Rate
27%	Four-Year Graduation Rate
72%	Financial Aid Applicants Receiving Aid

Students Speak Out
SAFETY & SECURITY

Q "I have found the campus to be safe. There are **emergency phones all around campus**. Some of the parking lots are a little dark, and some of the pathways don't have enough lighting; however, overall, I think that our crime rate is pretty low."

Q "Things could be a lot worse around here. If security spent less time trying to bust potheads and more time patrolling the streets at night, there would be less rapes and cars broken into. But **our crime level has gone down**, so that says something."

Q "There's an actual NAU Police Department, not just security. **Safety aids are available** to walk girls (or guys) across campus at night. I seem to hear about a lot of crime going on at McConnell Hall, though."

STUDENT AUTHOR: **No matter how you look at it, NAU is a safe place to be. Every once in a while, there is a sexual assault, usually on south campus, and students will feel a little spooked. The consensus of most people seems to be that if you practice common sense, then there is nothing to worry about.**

> **Questions?**
> For more inside information and survival tips, pick up College Prowler's full-length book on this school, written by an actual student! Check it out at *www.collegeprowler.com.*

Students Speak Out
ON OVERALL EXPERIENCE

Q "**I love NAU**. It's a small university and perhaps not as prestigious as other schools, but it's still great. The opportunities you will have here will far exceed anything you could imagine."

Q "I absolutely love it here. I could not imagine myself anywhere else, but I'm really liberal—almost a hippie. **If you live your life like *Laguna Beach*, you'll hate it here**. Go to ASU. If you're an activist, a hippie, a snowboarder, or any type of non-mainstream subculture, I think you'd love it here."

Q "I love NAU and don't want to go anywhere else. **I love my department and my teachers**. I love the smaller atmosphere and close-knit community. I am very happy with my choice to go here."

Q "I couldn't be happier at any other college. NAU has provided me with such opportunity to excel. The location is perfect, and teachers are more friends than professors. **NAU has shown me how to be a better person** and how to get involved. I love it here."

STUDENT AUTHOR: **When asked to reflect back on their time at NAU, the overwhelming majority of students give it the thumbs-up. Most will tell you that they love Flagstaff and would recommend NAU to anyone. The small class sizes and beautiful location make it a perfect spot to learn and develop within the confines of higher education. It's not the place for everyone, but most say the combination of a solid education and friendly social environment make NAU a great spot to chop down trees, grow a beard, and wear flannel just like a real lumberjack.**

Northern Illinois University

1425 West Lincoln Highway; DeKalb, IL 60115
(815) 753-1000; www.niu.edu

THE BASICS:

Acceptance Rate: 61%   **SAT Range:** 955–1155*
Setting: Small city   **Control:** Public
F-T Undergrads: 16,609   **Tuition:** $15,244

Most Popular Majors: Elementary Education, Accounting, Management, Marketing, Psychology

*of 1600

Academics	B-	Guys	B-
Local Atmosphere	C+	Girls	A-
Safety & Security	B-	Athletics	B+
Computers	B	Nightlife	C-
Facilities	B	Greek Life	B-
Campus Dining	B+	Drug Scene	B-
Off-Campus Dining	B-	Campus Strictness	B+
Campus Housing	C	Parking	D
Off-Campus Housing	B	Transportation	A-
Diversity	B-	Weather	C-

Students Speak Out
ON ACADEMICS

Q "A lot of the professors I had were surprisingly inspired and motivated. They didn't just have knowledge on the subject, **they got students interested and involved**. Some were just 'average,' in that they taught the subject and didn't seem interested in much else."

Q "The teachers are tough and seem to think that they need to be mean, rude, harsh, and basically just brutal **so they can show us what it is like in the 'real world.'**"

Q "The classes are interesting, and I get a lot out of most of them. However, **there are some that are a waste of time and poorly taught**, like those with a TA just reading off of PowerPoint slides."

Q "The teachers that I have are quite interesting in their own ways. **Some try to make class interesting by telling some funny stories** in order to break up the monotony of lecturing every day. I usually find my classes to be interesting because I am taking classes for my major, which is what interests me. But on some days, I find every class boring—even my favorite classes."

STUDENT AUTHOR: **NIU may not feature the same constellation of academic stars as a school like Harvard, but hey, our tuition costs about three SUVs less per year than an Ivy League school. There are many teachers who care about their jobs and their students with the same passion as professors at other schools with better academic reputations and more well-off students.**

Students Speak Out
ON LOCAL ATMOSPHERE

Q "DeKalb has an overall friendly small-town atmosphere. **I can't think of anything to really stay away from**. Places to visit are Corn Fest, the Paperback Grotto, and of course, all the bars that DeKalb has to offer."

Q "I think there are times when DeKalb has an amazing atmosphere, and then there are times when it is just a bore. **There seems to be a lack of options for students in the town**. However, I believe that people should definitely check out 'downtown' DeKalb because it has a number of dive restaurants and dive bars."

Q "DeKalb is in the middle of nowhere. Being surrounded by all the corn is sometimes very depressing. The level of culture here is basically nil. **I get to Chicago as much as possible**."

Q "DeKalb has a pretty sleepy atmosphere most of the time. **There are some really great park trails for biking and walking in town**, as well as a pool, but outside of NIU's Recreation Center, there's a surprising shortage of gyms or even sporting goods stores."

STUDENT AUTHOR: **The DeKalb community is very proud of its association with the University, and locals are a constant presence in the lives of students, usually for the better. Area businesses go out of their way to be welcoming and friendly, but there isn't much in terms of cultural destinations. Thankfully, Chicago is only a relatively short drive away.**

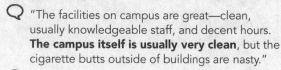

5 Best Things	5 Worst Things
1 The people	1 Finding parking
2 Independence	2 Winter weather
3 Tailgating	3 Academic reputation
4 The football team	4 Registering for classes
5 Thursday nights	5 Suitcase students

Students Speak Out
ON FACILITIES

Q "The facilities on campus are great—clean, usually knowledgeable staff, and decent hours. **The campus itself is usually very clean**, but the cigarette butts outside of buildings are nasty."

Q "The rec center is very well maintained and was just renovated with a snack bar. Everything's kept very clean, even the locker room, and **there are a ton of weight machines, treadmills, and ellipticals**. It's probably one of the best parts of campus."

Q "It can get very crowded. I like the rec and student centers, but mostly in the summer. **I try to avoid the congested areas on campus during the day**; otherwise, I want to scream at places such as downstairs in DuSable and Subway at HSC."

Q "**I would say all the facilities are very nice**. The rec center is great and offers so many different classes and activities. The convo center is amazing. The look of the campus is pretty good. Sometimes there is trash lying around, though."

Q "It has very nice places and semi-trashy places. The biggest problem is the construction. **They do it at inconvenient times**, like during move-in week.

STUDENT AUTHOR: University officials have been stepping up efforts to beautify campus—and it has paid off big-time. The necessity of buildings like the Convocation Center may be in question, but there is no denying how beautiful and advanced they are. Founders Memorial Library sees just as much student use as the Recreation Center, and for good reason—its staff is friendly, and its resources are seemingly unending. The Holmes Student Center is also a good place to chill between classes.

Famous Alumni

Joan Allen, Dan Castellaneta, Steve Harris, Dennis Hastert, Paul Sereno

Students Speak Out
ON CAMPUS DINING

Q "Dorm food is convenient but way unhealthy. I like using Huskie Bucks, but that means fast food. **Trying to go on a diet on this campus is impossible**."

Q "**The food is above average**. Grant North has its good and bad days, but there is always something to eat."

Q "It's dorm food, after all, so you have to lower your expectations. **It's comparable to what you would find in a good high school cafeteria**. Don't make a habit of eating a ton everyday because you will gain a ton of weight and burn through your meal plan."

Q "The food on campus is hit or miss. The two best places to go at any time are Stevenson's food court and the Dog Pound Deli in Douglas. Think of it as **Subway that you can buy with your Dining Dollars**. Avoid Lincoln late-night at all costs."

Q "The majority of the food is fried, and **the rest of the stuff, for the most part, will be disgusting**. If I were a student coming in and living in the dining halls, I'd be prepared to get acid reflux at some point while living in the dorms."

STUDENT AUTHOR: As long as you don't arrive with high expectations, the quality and variety of on-campus dining can be a pleasant surprise. Each dining hall offers a different menu, be it all-you-can-eat or à la carte, and the number of options is impressive. In fact, students might experience too much of a good thing, as freshmen pack on the pounds due to the availability of fried foods.

Student Body

African American:	13%	Male/Female:	46/54%
Asian American:	6%	Out-of-State:	9%
Hispanic:	7%	International:	<1%
Native American:	<1%	Unknown:	<1%
White:	74%		

Popular Faiths: There are several Christian groups on campus, but there doesn't seem to be a dominant denomination or faith.

Gay Pride: Most students and administrators are very accepting of gay students and go out of their way to make them feel comfortable.

Economic Status: NIU students are decidedly middle class.

Students Speak Out
ON DORMS

Q "**Not counting the students who lived there, the dorms were pretty lame**. School officials can get pretty rabid about calling them residence halls and not dorms, since the latter word apparently has a negative connotation."

Q "I lived in the suites in Lincoln, and they are very nice—not as expensive as Stevenson, but still really nice. **Stevenson's dorms, though, are definitely the nicest**. Some even have their own bathroom in them. I wasn't in Grant much, but it's the 'ghetto dorm.'"

Q "The dorms are average. Grant, on the whole, is the worst, and the best is Stevenson. Douglas and Lincoln are right in the middle but provide **the best amount of space out there**."

STUDENT AUTHOR: **Because they view them as more than living spaces, NIU prefers to call its dorms "residential halls." It's a nice thought, but dorm rooms don't compare all that favorably to jail cells—they are small and cramped, and you are stuck with your roommates whether you like them or not. NIU requires all freshmen to live on campus, but you could call it a necessary evil for the full NIU experience.**

? **Did You Know?**
33% of undergrads live on campus.

Students Speak Out
ON GUYS & GIRLS

Q "The guys and girls of NIU deserve each other. **The guys are not nearly as hot as they think** and are always on the make. The girls are teases and dress like it."

Q "Yes, the girls are hot. But **most of them are definitely not worth touching** with a ten-foot pole. There do seem to be a lot of 'sluts.' It is always funny to watch them freezing in their small skirts in January."

Q "The guys you will run into are the annoying ones that just want to get in your pants (if you're a girl). **All the nicer ones are hard to find**."

Q "There's a girl for every guy. **Although some are hot, some lack intellectual capabilities**."

STUDENT AUTHOR: **By and large, the men of NIU are an aggressive and horny bunch. The girls, who slightly outnumber the men, are fairly attractive. More importantly, they are approachable and rather easy to engage in conversation. Don't come to NIU looking for Amazonian beauties or studs that belong on Desperate Housewives. You will find neither in DeKalb. Still, there are enough decent guys and girls to make it worth your while.**

Traditions

Recyclable Boat Race
A Homecoming Week tradition featuring student organizations racing flimsy boats made out of recycled materials in the East Lagoon.

Gay Jam
It wouldn't be Lesbian Gay Bisexual Transgender Awareness month without this truly wild annual event, an extravagant drag show.

Overall School Spirit
Many students don't acquire a fondness or sense of pride for their educational experience until it's over.

Students Speak Out
ON ATHLETICS

Q "**They could do a much better job of promoting intramurals**. Unless you make the effort, you are not going to hear about what's going on."

Q "Varsity football is pretty huge, **especially pre-game tailgating**, which seems to draw the entire campus and then some."

Q "The football team has been improving in the past few years, and games are a blast. **The volleyball team is solid though under-appreciated**, but I wouldn't expect to see the basketball team playing in the NCAA tourney any time soon. Intramural sports are pretty big, and there are a lot of different sports offered at any given time."

Q "**Football is the sport on campus**. As for intramurals, I never saw much more than one or two flyers for them."

STUDENT AUTHOR: **Athletics at NIU begin and end with the football team, and luckily, there have been a lot of happy endings lately. The football team recently played and won its first bowl game in more than 20 years. Devotion to sports on campus is sub-par, and intramurals are generally a non-factor in student life.**

Students Speak Out
ON DRUG SCENE

Q "Maybe I have my head in the clouds, but there isn't much of a drug scene at Northern. Sure, students smoke grass and drink a lot, but beyond that **there isn't a lot of hard drug use**."

Q "Alcohol is by far the biggest thing. Everybody drinks, and **those who don't are pressured to do so to a ridiculous degree**."

Q "**I smoke some stuff and don't consider it that big of a deal**. As long as you do stuff in moderation, you'll be fine. Also, know where you are getting stuff from or don't use it. There are some very shady characters out there who will sell you crap."

STUDENT AUTHOR: **Alcohol is the No. 1 drug of choice on campus, and it's widely available to everyone, including minors. "Soft" drugs like marijuana are also quite prevalent and not hard to find if you know the right kind of people. Students make little attempt to hide these habits and often flaunt them. Thankfully, harder drugs like heroin and cocaine are not in wide use.**

17:1	Student-to-Faculty Ratio
78%	Freshman Retention Rate
48%	Four-Year Graduation Rate
72%	Financial Aid Applicants Receiving Aid

Students Speak Out
SAFETY & SECURITY

Q "**I was really proud how the police handled the Valentine's Day incident**. I felt like I had all the info I needed very quickly and knew exactly what to do. I think they could be more aggressive in making classrooms more secure, but I'm satisfied that they are serious about protecting students."

Q "**I don't think I'll ever feel completely safe** after what happened with the classroom shooting. The police can be as vigilant as they want, but if someone wants to do that again, nothing can really stop them."

Q "I would say it is pretty safe. They have the Husky Patrol, who will walk you to and from places at night. **The biggest issues would be probably just keeping your stuff safe** from drunk kids at night."

STUDENT AUTHOR: **If you believe lightning can't strike twice, then NIU is among the safest college campuses in America. The February 2008 killing spree by a former student came without warning, but the police response was rapid and disciplined, and the University is constantly updating its security policies as a result of this incident.**

> **Questions?**
> For more inside information and survival tips, pick up College Prowler's full-length book on this school, written by an actual student! Check it out at *www.collegeprowler.com*.

Students Speak Out
ON OVERALL EXPERIENCE

Q "Overall, I have had a positive experience at Northern. I feel it is **an excellent academic institution that offers many great opportunities** to succeed."

Q "I could sit and gripe about 800 things about this place, but you know what? **I've had a pretty positive experience here** despite all the crap. I feel prepared for what's next, and I had fun along the way."

Q "I have such a love-hate relationship with this place. There are days when I am so happy to be here, and then **there are days when I regret ever stepping foot here**."

Q "I came from the University of Michigan, and I was pretty pleased that unlike that school, NIU didn't have 80 percent of my classes taught by grad students from countries yet undiscovered by the modern world. There are definitely fewer options when it comes to extracurricular activities or social life, but **if you put effort into it you can really get a lot out of the school**."

STUDENT AUTHOR: **NIU isn't for everybody. It's a school in the middle of nowhere with a large student population and a less-than-stellar academic reputation. The toughest part is getting through the first year. Dorm life can be hell, and you can't take classes in your major until late in your second year. But in the end, the positives far outweigh the negatives. The people are down-to-earth, and there is always a bar or party or concert to go to, no matter the day of the week. Oddly enough, NIU can grow on you. It isn't a perfect institution by any means, but most students come to appreciate their time at Northern Illinois University in the quiet farm town of DeKalb.**

Northwestern University

633 Clark Street; Evanston, IL 60208
(847) 491-3741; www.northwestern.edu

THE BASICS:

Acceptance Rate: 27%　　**SAT Range:** 2010–2270*
Setting: Suburban　　**Control:** Private
F-T Undergrads: 8,111　　**Tuition:** $36,756

Most Popular Majors: Social Sciences, Journalism,
Engineering, Visual and Performing Arts, Psychology

*of 2400

Academics	A	Guys	C
Local Atmosphere	C+	Girls	B
Safety & Security	C+	Athletics	B
Computers	B-	Nightlife	C+
Facilities	B	Greek Life	A-
Campus Dining	B-	Drug Scene	B
Off-Campus Dining	A-	Campus Strictness	B+
Campus Housing	B	Parking	D-
Off-Campus Housing	C+	Transportation	A-
Diversity	B-	Weather	D

Students Speak Out
ON ACADEMICS

Q "I have **some amazing professors** and some that are awful. Northwestern has a really good system where you can read online what other students thought of classes and professors before making your decisions."

Q "It all depends on the department they are from. Personally, I have been very happy with the political science and **Euro history professors**."

Q "Graduate students don't teach classes here, but they do work as teaching assistants. It is important to get a good professor for your freshman seminar because he or she becomes **your freshman advisor**. There are some really renowned teachers here, but it's usually hard to get into their classes as a freshman."

Q "Read the course and teacher evaluations before you register for a class with a certain professor, and ask people (sophomores in your dorm are good resources) what they thought of the professor. Also, don't shy away from a professor just because **they seem intimidating**—often, they are the most brilliant ones."

STUDENT AUTHOR: **Professors at NU are hit or miss. You may have a class on Monday and Wednesday with a professor as dry as week-old bread, but on Tuesday and Thursday, you may be sharing the classroom with a Tony Award-winning diva. Despite this variation, one thing's for sure: you'll never suffer through class with an unprepared graduate student, so you always have access to instructors who, in many cases, are experts in their fields.**

Students Speak Out
ON LOCAL ATMOSPHERE

Q "Evanston is not much of a college town. There are a lot of retirees, and things close early. But there's always Chicago, and **Evanston really isn't that bad**. We have a theater, lots of shopping, restaurants, and we're right on the lake."

Q "Evanston's atmosphere is very nice. Generally, the school, as a whole, **does not have a good relationship with Evanston** on political matters, but it's a great place to shop, eat, and just hang out. There are no other universities in Evanston, but there are several schools in Chicago."

Q "**South campus is nice** because it's right near downtown Evanston. I don't see a lot of Evanston-Northwestern connections being made, except for necessary things like shopping, but I can't say that's really bothered me a lot."

Q "Evanston is a city in transition from a little North Shore town to imitation Lincoln Park. But the influx of new, **trendy businesses and restaurants**, along with the movie theaters, has definitely brought more nightlife to the place."

STUDENT AUTHOR: **Northwestern and Evanston have a notoriously bad relationship—including a several-million-dollar lawsuit leveled against the University by the city. Though these tensions often run high, students are satisfied with the small town's offerings, particularly its restaurants. And for those looking to escape the sometimes small, snobbish feel of the north suburb, Chicago is a short train ride away—$1.75 grants you access to one of the great cultural centers of the world.**

5 Best Things	5 Worst Things
1 Proximity to Chicago	1 The winter
2 Dillo Day	2 Dorky guys
3 The Lakefill	3 Expensive city to live in
4 Bright professors	4 Dining hall food
5 Well-rounded students	5 Sub-par athletics

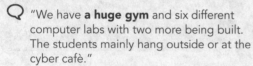

Students Speak Out
ON FACILITIES

Q "We have **a huge gym** and six different computer labs with two more being built. The students mainly hang outside or at the cyber café."

Q "Facilities here are fantastic, although it depends on what you're interested in and what school you're in. The Technological Institute, which houses all engineering and most science classes, is **the third largest building in the world** under five stories (behind the Kremlin and the Pentagon, I think)."

Q "The student center is okay, but definitely not one of the best features here. It has an eating area, a study area, and a game room, but that's it. The athletic center has been remodeled and is a definite plus. **The library is huge** and has everything you would ever need."

Q "Computer labs are nice, and most of the classrooms are state-of-the-art and air conditioned. A few buildings are **still living in the '60s**, but the school is constantly remodeling and updating the facilities."

Q "**I like the pool at SPAC** a lot, and I think the athletic facilities are generally in good shape. Norris is bland but useful."

STUDENT AUTHOR: **In recent years, NU has experienced a building boom—unfortunately, most of these buildings are for offices or specialty departments, not for undergraduates. The campus is a hodgepodge of different architecture, ranging from the classic University Hall, to the hulking behemoth of University Library to the clean, futuristic McCormick Tribune Center.**

Famous Alumni

Warren Beatty, Rod Blagojevich, Dick Gephardt, Charlton Heston, Julia Louis-Dreyfuss, David Schwimmer

Students Speak Out
ON CAMPUS DINING

Q "The food on campus is generally good. The dining halls are all pretty much the same and offer **a wide variety of foods** at each meal. Elder and Allison halls are probably the best, in terms of environment."

Q "Food really isn't bad. It just gets a little tedious. At first, I was really excited about all the possibilities in the dining halls, but they get old after a while. However, we also have Norris University Center, which provides more palatable choices, and you can use part of your meal plan for that. **Overall, it isn't bad.**"

Q "Dorm food stinks, and food at the Norris Student Center isn't much better. Yet, Evanston is known as **the dining capital of the North Shore**, so there are tons of restaurants off campus that are awesome."

Q "The Allison Dining Hall on South Campus is my favorite. There is a good variety of food. I was on the normal meal plan first quarter. Now, I'm on flex, which **gives me a bunch of Bonus Bucks** to eat at Norris University Center. Norris has better food, and if you don't use your entire Bonus Bucks, then you can get drinks and food at the end of the quarter."

STUDENT AUTHOR: **Each dining hall has unique characteristics, but all share a common thread. The food, though prepared by friendly chefs, gets tedious after a quarter— spaghetti and pizza day after day. Most students eventually convert to a meal plan that allows them to eat at Norris or the numerous coffee joints, which add a little more variety to the sometimes monotonous fare.**

Student Body

African American:	6%	Male/Female:	47/53%
Asian American:	17%	Out-of-State:	75%
Hispanic:	7%	International:	5%
Native American:	<1%	Unknown:	6%
White:	59%		

Popular Faiths: Christianity and Catholicism, as well as Judaism, are the main faiths on campus.

Gay Pride: One student group, Rainbow Alliance, addresses gay issues.

Economic Status: Most students' backgrounds are relatively high-end, considering this is a pricey, private institution.

Students Speak Out
ON DORMS

Q "Some dorms are known for being very social, very loud, geeky, **theater-major dominated**, or just all-around fun. You'll have no problem fitting in wherever you go, though."

Q "**We have all sorts of dorms**—suites, singles, doubles, triples, quads—with varying social scenes and room sizes. The northern dorms tend to be a little more party-oriented, being near the frats. The southern dorms are a little quieter, but not boring. Some dorms (the engineering residential college) are really tame and quiet."

Q "If you're a math or science type, you'll want to live on the north part of campus. If you're more liberal and artsy, live on the south. Allison is probably the best dorm to live in as a freshman, but **NMQ and SMQ** and Willard aren't bad."

STUDENT AUTHOR: **Generally, North Campus attracts engineering kids and students in the hard sciences, and South Campus is populated more by theater and journalism majors—originally anchored in proximity to certain academic departments. While some will say North attracts more partiers, wild dorm life can be found in every corner of campus—if you look hard enough.**

Did You Know?
65% of undergrads live on campus.

Students Speak Out
ON GUYS & GIRLS

Q "There tends to be a lot more good-looking girls than there are guys, but overall, **it's a good mix**. There's always Chicago, too, if you are looking for love."

Q "The guys are pretty nice. There are definitely **some hot boys on this campus**, but a lot are gay. The girls are nice. With both sexes, there are definitely all sorts of people here—from ditzes to geeks to really artistic people, it really varies."

Q "I tend to find that most people at Northwestern are either **very attractive or very unattractive**."

Q "We developed the phrase '**Northwestern cute**' for the guys. There are some good-looking guys, but the shortage makes your standards lower."

STUDENT AUTHOR: Dating still mystifies much of the Northwestern population. Almost all agree that the girls are more attractive than the men, on the whole. Students either seem to be in committed relationships, or having one fling after another with the acceptable members of the opposite sex who reside somewhere on campus. Ambition for academics often puts a damper on sizzling passion, which can be frustrating when looking for a date to the formal.

Traditions

Painting the Rock
NU students, typically Greek, take turns painting the huge rock on South Campus. Tradition holds that if a student wishes to paint something on the Rock, he/she must guard and paint it from sundown to sunup; many student groups start guarding even earlier, to ensure that they'll be first.

Overall School Spirit
At the kick-off of NU football games, students used to throw marshmallows. While Gary Barnett was football coach, he banned marshmallows because they supposedly detracted from the serious level of football that he wanted for the school.

Students Speak Out
ON ATHLETICS

Q "Football is big here. Students, although not usually Evanston residents, generally go to the games, even if we are not having a good year. **The games are awesome**, so much fun. Basketball is reasonably big."

Q "Our football team has performed well as of late. **Our basketball team blows**, though. I have no hope for them. A lot of our women's sports are ranked year after year. IM sports are huge."

Q "I guess there's a medium amount of support for varsity sports. None of the spectator sports are very good, so I'm sure that makes a difference. **IM sports normally seem pretty popular**."

Q "**Club sports seem pretty cool**—all the benefits of exercise without necessarily the commitment for varsity."

STUDENT AUTHOR: Although NU's football squad is up-and-coming, and even cracked the top 25 for a while in 2005, they still have a long way to go before they garner respect the likes of Michigan or Ohio State—two Big Ten rivals. Most students go to games for the camaraderie, and nothing more.

Students Speak Out
ON DRUG SCENE

Q "They're here. I mean, **pot is pretty much everywhere**, but there aren't too many people who do the hard stuff. There definitely are people who do, but it's not as pronounced as at a lot of other colleges."

Q "The drug scene is not very easy to break into at first, but **drugs are definitely around campus**. Most people just smoke weed, but coke and X (ecstasy) are around every once in a while, too."

Q "**Dude, where's my pot brownie**? You can usually do drugs without getting caught. Not many people do much more than pot. I've ran into people who do 'shrooms or trip occasionally, but many bookish students would be shocked."

STUDENT AUTHOR: NU students? Risking academics or an internship just to smoke a joint? As with any college campus, if you want marijuana, you'll find it, but most likely, you'll discover stockpiles of Smirnoff and Bacardi—perfectly legal, thank you very much. A lot of people partake solely in social situations, a nip of vodka at a mixer, or a toke off a communal joint at an off-campus house party.

7:1	Student-to-Faculty Ratio
96%	Freshman Retention Rate
86%	Four-Year Graduation Rate
87%	Financial Aid Applicants Receiving Aid

Students Speak Out
SAFETY & SECURITY

Q "I think people generally feel safe on campus. Certainly, **there are events that cause alarm**, but generally, people feel safe. However, going to school near a big city is evidently going to cause problems."

Q "Security has honestly been an issue as of late, but we have very little crime. I know that sounds odd, but all of a sudden we had a few assaults, so they are **beefing up security more**. That being said, I often leave my door unlocked and do not feel uncomfortable doing so."

Q "**Northwestern has its own police force**; they have all the authority and privileges that any town police force has, except their main task is to enforce the laws here at NU."

STUDENT AUTHOR: Most people feel safe on campus, but several incidents have been a cause for major concern. Racial epithets and threats to minority students destabilize the community, and attacks on female students leave some wary, to say the least. But for the most part, students report feeling very safe, and applaud campus security in all aspects.

> **Questions?**
> For more inside information and survival tips, pick up College Prowler's full-length book on this school, written by an actual student! Check it out at *www.collegeprowler.com*.

Students Speak Out
ON OVERALL EXPERIENCE

Q "I complain a lot, but in all honesty, **things here are great**. The people are interesting, professors intriguing, and there's never a dull moment. If Evanston sucks, Chicago is a stone's throw away. It's top-of-the-line, and people don't take enough pride in NU's strengths."

Q "I have enjoyed Northwestern. I don't like all the people, and I think it is unfortunate the partying has decreased and has moved into more expensive bars. But in general, **you will meet great people**, learn a lot, and have a lot of fun."

Q "I love Northwestern, and I admit I will miss it when I graduate next month. I am a typical party boy, and I was scared that NU would be a bunch of dorks, but it's really not. **I prefer the liberal, open-minded, intelligent atmosphere** at NU."

Q "I like it here. If anything, I'd change the social scene to include more non-Greek parties and less of a focus on the three bars in this town. The dating thing is frustrating, but not unbearable, and sometimes, you get lucky and find someone awesome. I really like Northwestern. **It's got natural beauty going for it**, too."

STUDENT AUTHOR: We bitch, we moan, but there's a reason Northwestern is one of the best overall undergrad experiences in America. Academics are stellar, but at the same time, students allow themselves to be students—once that 12-page paper is done, of course. At NU, you will be surprised at how much you learn—and how much of that learning is done outside of the classroom. NU students don't labor under any illusions that the school is perfect, but despite its shortcomings, most students admit that they wouldn't have had it any other way.

Oberlin College

173 West Lorain Street; Oberlin, OH 44074
(440) 775-8411; www.oberlin.edu

THE BASICS:

Acceptance Rate: 33%
Setting: Rural
F-T Undergrads: 2,793

SAT Range: 1900–2180*
Control: Private
Tuition: $38,012

Most Popular Majors: Music Performance, English, Biology, Political Science, History

*of 2400

Academics	A	Guys	C
Local Atmosphere	D+	Girls	C+
Safety & Security	A-	Athletics	C-
Computers	B+	Nightlife	C-
Facilities	B+	Greek Life	N/A
Campus Dining	C+	Drug Scene	C+
Off-Campus Dining	B	Campus Strictness	B
Campus Housing	B-	Parking	C
Off-Campus Housing	B-	Transportation	C
Diversity	C+	Weather	C

Students Speak Out
ON ACADEMICS

Q "Most professors are **really enthusiastic about what they teach**. They are available outside of class, and many students build a close relationship with their professors."

Q "The teachers are **extremely casual**, but expect a lot out of their students. Though many classes take an informal tone, the course work is often quite a load."

Q "It's easy to **see their commitment** not only to their area of interest, but also to students, and to teaching. 'Interesting' seems less apt an adjective than 'challenging,' 'engaging,' or 'extremely difficult.'"

Q "There are **lots of flavors and personalities**. I've enjoyed most of my classes, and nothing beats an excellent and inspiring teacher. They make you feel like studying more and more."

STUDENT AUTHOR: There are so many choices of interesting classes to take at Oberlin that students sometimes feel frustrated there isn't enough time for everything. It isn't uncommon for students to take a maximum number of credit hours, not because they have to, but because they don't want to miss out on a really great class. Oberlin students are almost masochistic about having busy schedules, and consequently, a serious work ethic prevails on campus. Without a doubt, one of the best things about classes at Oberlin is their size—the small-class environment leads to stimulating discussions and a more intimate rapport between students and professors.

Students Speak Out
ON LOCAL ATMOSPHERE

Q "It's actually a **pretty nice small town**, and it's really worthwhile to seek activities that involve town residents."

Q "Oberlin is a **pretty typical college town** with the usual mix of restaurants, bookstores, and bars. The downtown is small, and right next to campus, so it's very easy to get coffee or go shopping. There also is an old movie theater with a big old-fashioned marquee that plays late-run movies for a few dollars."

Q "Tiny town, and it's the only university around for at least an hour. There **isn't specific stuff to visit**, since it's so small, you end up going everywhere anyway."

Q "I think the college is the biggest influence on the town itself. You don't really run into people from other schools (though both the Cleveland universities and Wooster are only about an hour away), and so the **Oberlin-bubble feeling** is pretty pervasive, especially if you don't try and interact with the town itself."

STUDENT AUTHOR: While Oberlin is a typical small college town, its unique history and cultural assets lend it a distinctive air. Some of the best things about the town are its cozy, peaceful atmosphere, its numerous green areas, its quaint, old movie theater, and its thriving cultural scene. Students often joke that Oberlin is situated in between two cornfields. They often spend more time on campus than they do in the surrounding area. But Cleveland is only 40 minutes away.

Students Speak Out
ON FACILITIES

Q "The facilities that matter for getting a good education are awesome. The **libraries are huge and nicely designed**, and the labs and studio spaces are great."

Q "The **student union is too small** to hold the big events comfortably, which makes it charming."

Q "Phillips Gym, the main athletic facility, is fairly nice. There is **extensive weight and cardiovascular equipment**, as well as more esoteric stuff, like a climbing wall, a fencing room with armory, and many squash and racquetball courts. A small, but fairly nice indoor-track and tennis-court area is also a part of the gym."

Q "Athletic: for a Division III school of our size, we have sweet facilities. Computers: no complaints; CIT seems to have **hardware and software up to date**. Student center: we get great concerts."

Q "Oberlin has one of the best libraries and **best art collections in the country**."

STUDENT AUTHOR: At Oberlin, the facilities necessary for a good education are first rate. Oberlin's library collection of books and periodicals, scores, government publications, sound and video recordings, and software contains over two million items. The Environmental Studies Building is a cutting-edge experiment in a green building. Students gather in Wilder Hall, the student union building—a cozy space with couches, TVs, and a snack bar. It is also home to the WOBC radio station, which houses an extensive collection of music, and is the pride and joy of many students involved in radio.

Famous Alumni

Jim Burrows, Tracy Chevalier, Stanley Cohen, Jerry Greenfield, Herbert Morse, Liz Phair, Jane Pratt, Julie Taymor, Caroline Kovac, Laura Wendall

Students Speak Out
ON CAMPUS DINING

Q "Dining halls are sufficient, although most students dine less as they move up the class. Maybe a good idea to point out is the co-ops where students have **more freedom to choose what and how to eat**."

Q "The main dining hall, Stevenson, has multiple **vegetarian and vegan options**, and often uses locally grown produce, and makes an effort to supply fairly nutritional options, in addition to an 'everything fried' line."

Q "One of Oberlin's main selling points is the Oberlin Student Cooperative Association (OSCA), an entirely **student-run alternative** to campus dining services."

Q "**Dining halls suck**, no matter where you go. That's all I have to say."

Q "The food on campus is average, institutional food. There are about **five to six entreé options** in each of the two main dining halls."

STUDENT AUTHOR: All three dining halls, Dascomb, Stevenson, and Lord Saunders, include salad bars, fresh fruit, vegetarian, and fried-food options, as well as cereals and all the ingredients necessary for making sandwiches. Oberlin offers an excellent alternative for students who prefer to cook their own food, work communally, and eat healthier. The co-ops are entirely managed by students and they are cheaper. The downside: you must be prepared to eat at exactly the same time every day, or you run the risk of missing out on all the food. Students must cook and clean every week.

Student Body

African American:	6%	Male/Female:	45/55%
Asian American:	8%	Out-of-State:	91%
Hispanic:	5%	International:	6%
Native American:	1%	Unknown:	<1%
White:	74%		

Popular Faiths: There are Christian and Jewish groups, a Muslim Students Association, a Pagan Awareness group, and a vocal agnostic contingent.

Gay Pride: Campus is extremely accepting. Events include the Drag Ball and Transgender Awareness Week. There are also Queer Studies courses.

Economic Status: The majority of students are from predominantly middle- to upper-class families.

Students Speak Out
ON DORMS

Q "Dorms are okay. East Hall is quiet and boring. Talcott is beautiful. Burton, Noah, and North are good for meeting people freshman year. The co-ops are also a housing option—they're not that clean, but **they're cheaper, and you have more freedom**."

Q "Dorms are pretty small. Choose big dorms like South or East if you prefer quiet nights. Definitely **choose Barrows for freshman year**—one of the only all-freshman dorm on campus. There could be too much drama going for you there, but there's always lots of fun and beer."

Q "The **program houses tend to be nicer** than the regular dorms—Asia house, Baldwin, and J-house. If you're the co-op type, the housing co-ops have really nice rooms, and are less strict."

STUDENT AUTHOR: Many students (who could otherwise not get into a single their freshman or sophomore year) find that they have a better chance of securing a single room in a program house rather than in a regular dormitory. Program houses are popular amongst students who prefer smaller-sized dormitories and a tight-knit community.

> **Did You Know?**
> 75% of undergrads live on campus.

Students Speak Out
ON GUYS & GIRLS

Q "Both **guys and gals are hot, in their own way**. If you prefer an off-beat, hippie, relaxed, or artsy style that is not on reality TV, Oberlin will be like heaven to you."

Q "Oberlin attracts **an interesting crew**. There's some conventional hotness, but this is a dating community, which generally goes more for the 'beauty on the inside' than shapely tanned legs or big muscles."

Q "I think Oberlin kids are hot, and people are cool and good to be around. **Lots of queer stuff**, lots of straight stuff, lots of flexible stuff."

Q "I think people are hot here; people are special and **confident about themselves**, in any case."

STUDENT AUTHOR: Oberlin's reputation for unattractive students is not a fair assessment. Many Obies are physically appealing, albeit in a slightly offbeat kind of way. The main styles at Oberlin fall into: crunchy hippie, indie-rock hipster, metrosexual, gender-ambiguous, hopelessly geeky, the occasional preppy kid, and there are still enough jocks on campus. The main lesson in style is anything goes, as long as you give it a shot.

> **Traditions**
>
> **Drag Ball**
> A celebrity drag king/queen MC is hired for a catwalk competition to judge student costume designs.
>
> **The Rock**
> Designs and messages have been painted onto the six-foot-tall stone in Tappan Square since 1962.
>
> **Overall School Spirit**
> If apparel is any measure of school spirit, a significant number routinely don the letters. Many students harbor a deep pride for Oberlin and are quick to defend it in comparison with other colleges.

Students Speak Out
ON ATHLETICS

Q "Nobody really cares about varsity sports on campus except for the people who are recruited to play them and their significant others. Actually, that's not entirely true, but **guest lectures have bigger attendance** than football games."

Q "**Club sports are huge**. Varsity, no."

Q "Oberlin's new director from Stanford is transforming Oberlin from a 'jock-hater school' to an '**Ohio jock-school wannabe.**'"

Q "**Sports are becoming larger** on campus, or at least having a more-visible presence. Games are still under attended, even though the teams are generally performing better."

STUDENT AUTHOR: Because Oberlin is a liberal arts college, the focus is placed on education over athletics. Oberlin is not a place where athletes come to groom their talents in preparation for professional success. Athletics on campus are not of interest to anyone except to those who actively participate in them. Oberlin jocks tend to stick to themselves. Athletes have access to excellent facilities, and can choose from a wide range of competitive teams.

Students Speak Out
ON DRUG SCENE

Q "I certainly have heard plenty about it, but I never experimented myself, and I **never felt the slightest pressure** to. Whether you do it or not it really is up to you."

Q "Tons of kids smoke weed or drink alcohol, it just happens. But on the whole, kids seem to **take classes seriously** enough."

Q "Yes, you'll see coke; you'll **definitely see pot; drinking happens**. Occasionally, someone on acid will run into you, literally. It's not like you necessarily have to seek drugs to get them, but at the same time, you're not confronted with them all the time." ·

STUDENT AUTHOR: **A majority of Obies are motivated and determined students, so drugs and alcohol are not a huge part of the social scene. Oberlin has its share of stoners, but there is very little pressure to indulge in anything besides free-spiritedness. All sorts of drugs are available to those who want them, though pot and alcohol are by far the most prevalent.**

10:1	Student-to-Faculty Ratio
94%	Freshman Retention Rate
64%	Four-Year Graduation Rate
72%	Financial Aid Applicants Receiving Aid

Students Speak Out
SAFETY & SECURITY

Q "I generally feel pretty safe. For people who are used to big cities, Oberlin's a breath of fresh air. The campus security squad is usually pretty **reasonable and helpful**."

Q "Safety and security people can be **notoriously difficult to deal with**, but for the most part, the campus is pretty safe. The streets are relatively safe at night, and except for laptops stolen from libraries and the like, things are secure as long as you're careful."

Q "Safety and security is pretty cool. **They don't like busting people or breaking up parties**, they'd rather come in and help fix things, but they will do their jobs!"

STUDENT AUTHOR: Because Oberlin is a small town, people take for granted that serious crimes rarely ever happen. Emergency phones are attached to blue-light posts all around campus, and the Shuttle System allows students who feel either unsafe to walk or too inebriated to drive from running into trouble.

Questions?
For more inside information and survival tips, pick up College Prowler's full-length book on this school, written by an actual student! Check it out at *www.collegeprowler.com*.

Students Speak Out
ON OVERALL EXPERIENCE

Q "I really think **Oberlin is one of the best places** to get a good college education. Considering everything the school offers, there's no other place I'd rather be."

Q "It's not a place to go and laze around and not leave the house—**people tend to be active and passionate** about politics, art, food, sex, and everything else. I never wished I'd gone somewhere else, and Oberlin's the kind of place that makes you want to change things if you don't like them, not just sit around."

Q "I love the people. Oberlin is definitely a **stimulating place in terms of academics**. I've met many interesting people that I wouldn't have ever known otherwise."

Q "I got more than I ever could have bargained for at Oberlin. I wanted to enrich my mind, not only **academically, but also socially and spiritually**. Being at Oberlin will teach you things about yourself that you could have never even imagined."

STUDENT AUTHOR: **Most students are more than appreciative of the unique academic and cultural opportunities Oberlin offers. Students who are frustrated with their experience often complain about the small, insular environment, long, cold winters, and the heavy workload. For those who thrive from Oberlin's stimulating academics and interesting student body, they are willing to accept the challenges inherent to attending a small, liberal arts institution. The opportunities you will receive at Oberlin are countless, but it is up to you to find your place within the mosaic of different beliefs, interests, and passions, and to take advantage of all the available resources.**

Occidental College

1600 Campus Road; Los Angeles, CA 90041
(323) 259-2500; www.oxy.edu

THE BASICS:

Acceptance Rate: 44%
Setting: Urban
F-T Undergrads: 1,825

SAT Range: 1775–2080*
Control: Private
Tuition: $36,160

Most Popular Majors: International Relations, Economics, English Language/Literature, History

*of 2400

Academics	B+	Guys	B
Local Atmosphere	A-	Girls	B+
Safety & Security	B+	Athletics	B-
Computers	B-	Nightlife	A+
Facilities	C	Greek Life	D+
Campus Dining	B-	Drug Scene	B
Off-Campus Dining	A	Campus Strictness	B
Campus Housing	A-	Parking	A-
Off-Campus Housing	B-	Transportation	C-
Diversity	A	Weather	A

Students Speak Out
ON ACADEMICS

Q "If you pick the right programs, you can have an excellent experience at Oxy. If you don't pick the big ones, though, **you can have a very difficult time**."

Q "People look at an Oxy diploma very highly. Were I to take the same program from another school, I wouldn't have had nearly **as easy a time getting a job** after graduating."

Q "Take theater; it's an awesome major and it will make you a better person. Our theater program has a lot of help and **connections from people in the industry**, and the professors are some of the best in the country."

Q "While I hate to admit it, **the Core program did teach me how to write** and very quickly brought me up to a college level when it came to essays and papers. I know a lot of people in other colleges that didn't get anywhere near the same kind of help as freshmen."

STUDENT AUTHOR: **Occidental truly has some incredible degree programs, and it can be an excellent place to study for certain programs such as theater, diplomacy and world affairs, and English. The emphasis on creating a diverse liberal arts education allows students to earn a degree in a certain field while being able to pull in classes from as many different areas as possible. In the Core Program, all freshmen take one class the first semester and two classes the second semester of their freshman year that are devoted to emphasizing writing skills.**

Students Speak Out
ON LOCAL ATMOSPHERE

Q "What more could you want? It sucks if you don't have a car, but **that never stopped me**. I've had nothing but fun in this city."

Q "It's great to be right in the middle of everything in LA. As long as you're willing to go out and try something new, **you'll never have a boring night**. All the clubs are awesome, there's always a new movie to see, and even if you want to chill, you can find some cool place to go."

Q "**You can't do anything without a car**. People say you can take the bus places or get rides from friends, but that's nowhere near as easy as it sounds. The buses take forever to get any more than four or five miles away from campus, and it can easily take two hours to go from Oxy to some place like Sunset and Vine."

Q "**I hate Eagle Rock**, but once you get outside of it, you have a lot of awesome stuff to do. I go to the beaches, especially Venice, if I want to go have fun."

STUDENT AUTHOR: **While Eagle Rock is lacking for things to do, especially at night, the rest of Los Angeles more than makes up for it. Being in one of the largest metropolitan areas in the country has its advantages in terms of entertainment and cultural opportunities, and there's never a lack of things to do. With the many museums and concert halls, the level of culture in LA is remarkable.**

5 Best Things	5 Worst Things
1 The diversity	**1** Being secluded
2 Being in LA	**2** Needing a car
3 Weather	**3** Internet connection
4 Small size	**4** LA public transportation
5 Specialized programs	**5** Lame Greek life

Students Speak Out
ON FACILITIES

Q "I mostly just hang out in my dorm. There's not too much to do except for a few parties here and there. I would much prefer to **go off campus**."

Q "**I hate dances**, and that's all there is to do on campus. I go out a lot, as you can imagine."

Q "The **plays are always awesome**, and the movie series (put on every Wednesday) is a nice chance to chill out during the week. Other than that, the dances are kind of fun, but they do get old after a while, and there are only a few other events that go on here and there that aren't that great either."

Q "I buy a lot of food from the store in case I ever get hungry after about 11 p.m. on weekdays. There's just **nothing open on campus**, and I don't have a car to go get anything that late."

Q "If we had just some place that was **open during the weekends** for normal hours, I think we'd be fine, but the hours from Friday to Sunday are so weird that I still haven't figured them out after three years."

STUDENT AUTHOR: There is, unfortunately, not a lot to do on the Occidental campus, and the variety of events are often lacking. A lot of students complain about the dances, simply because most money for events goes to them, and very little else is put on that has much value. The weekends are particularly lacking, as the campus seems to shut down for Friday and Saturday nights. The academic facilities such as the library are top-notch, though, and most students have nothing but good things to say about them.

Famous Alumni

Ben Affleck, Olin Browne, Steve Coll, Todd Garner, Terry Gilliam, Jack Kemp, Barack Obama, Rider Strong, Owen Wilson

---

Students Speak Out
ON CAMPUS DINING

Q "Campus Dining cheats out a lot on the food if you ask me. I think **we could get a lot more** for what we pay."

Q "I love it, especially the vegan options. There's **always something available for a vegan** like me to eat, which is a nice change from most places where I have to just eat a salad all the time. They even make a really good vegan pizza, too."

Q "The quality of the food is good enough, but the selection sucks. After about three weeks, they start using a lot of the same menu options. They're good and all, but **if I have to eat chicken strips ever again, I'll go crazy**."

Q "My only complaint is the **eating hours for the weekends**. The food is good, but the hours are so screwy. I can never get there in time for breakfast on Saturdays, unless I wake up really early."

Q "Even though **I love the pasta** and a lot of the other stuff Campus Dining has, after eating it for a whole semester, it gets really hard to take."

STUDENT AUTHOR: A lot of students have taken up the smallest meal plan, and then supplemented that with buying groceries off campus and making their own food on weekends. Since a meal plan is required with on-campus living, this appears to be the most popular solution to the lackluster meal selection. Because of the easily accessible grocery stores and nearby places to eat, eating was very low on most students' lists of problems they had with the school.

Student Body

African American:	6%	Male/Female:	44/56%
Asian American:	13%	Out-of-State:	61%
Hispanic:	15%	International:	2%
Native American:	1%	Unknown:	5%
White:	58%		

Popular Faiths: The most popular faiths on campus are Christianity and Judaism.

Gay Pride: There are many clubs and activities on campus that show an active and openly gay community that is a cornerstone to the rest of the school.

Economic Status: Since Oxy is a private institution, most students are upper-class or upper-middle-class.

Students Speak Out
ON DORMS

Q "Lower Campus is the place to be. All the dorms are better, and you're really close to everything important on campus. **Nobody goes to Upper Campus** unless there's a party or they have to."

Q "I suggest living in nowhere but Braun. The dorm is definitely not the nicest, but it always has **the tightest community every year**, and we have always had the best time hanging out. I've lived there for two years and I wouldn't want to live anywhere else."

Q "I wish I didn't have to buy a meal plan with my room. **I like living on campus** and being so close to everything; it's unbeatable. But I don't like having to buy a meal plan to do that. It doesn't matter, though; I'll live on campus anyway."

STUDENT AUTHOR: **Living on campus at Occidental is definitely well worth it. The buildings are well maintained, if not completely aesthetically pleasing, and people in every hall have a strong sense of community. Each dorm has its own personality, and even the "ugly" dorms such as Braun have people living there who wouldn't want to live anywhere else.**

> **Did You Know?**
> 76% of undergrads live on campus.

Students Speak Out
ON GUYS & GIRLS

Q "The saying '**So-Cal girls are foxy, the rest go to Oxy**' is very true. There are some hot women, but not many. I wish I could find more people who were cool with just hooking up, too."

Q "There are a lot of hot girls—a lot. I transferred from a tech school, and the **situation has definitely improved**."

Q "**I'm pretty impressed** by the men and women here. They're all what I thought Californians were all like."

Q "Online dating is the way to go. The school is way too small, so it feels **a lot like high school** when you try and hook up with somebody or start dating. It's the one part of this school that really bugs me."

STUDENT AUTHOR: **While there is no over-abundance of beautiful people, there is no lack of them either. Most people at school seem satisfied with the hookup and relationship options, although several did say that they did not like the high school mentalities that a lot of people at Oxy have. While most people at the school are sexually promiscuous, it is very rarely talked about openly and still carries a small stigma.**

> **Traditions**
>
> **Getting Thrown in the Fountain**
> Oxy has a long-standing tradition of throwing someone into the fountain for their birthday.
>
> **Sex on the Beach Party**
> For over 20 years, the Residence Life staff of Stewart Cleland Hall puts on one of the best parties ever.
>
> **Overall School Spirit**
> Most people at Oxy don't have a very strong sense of school spirit. Very little is done to foster it, and it mostly comes about when a sports team has a winning season.

Students Speak Out
ON ATHLETICS

Q "When I get done with classes in the morning, it's so nice to go to the gym and work out for a while. **The whole place is nice**, and I can do everything I need to. It's also really close to everything else on campus, too. I would be really out of shape if I had to go very far to get to the weight room."

Q "Isn't the basketball team pretty good? I know we have a lot of stuff with athletics, but **I never really hear about it**."

Q "There are **a lot of options** for sports and stuff—they even have karate for people like me. Anybody who wants to play a sport can do what they want. My friend even does archery and gets a lot of help with it, too."

Q "**I love the club sports**, especially with the funding they get. The school is really supportive of us, and it helps when you're trying to find things to do."

STUDENT AUTHOR: **There is a good variety of men's and women's varsity sports, giving many options for those wanting to play, and each team is very well funded both from the school and from their own fundraising.**

Students Speak Out
ON DRUG SCENE

Q "A lot of people do it, but **it's never out in the open**. You just know someone down the hall is smoking weed right now, but you can't ever see it."

Q "We're not free of drugs, but **it's definitely not a problem**, either. College students are going to do stupid stuff like that, and you can stop quite a bit of it, but you can't stop it all."

Q "I don't see anything go on. I hang with a lot of different crowds, and I don't see very many people doing drugs at all. If people are going to do anything, **they're going to drink**."

STUDENT AUTHOR: **There are no drug dealers in the dorms or large epidemics of drug use, but drug use does go on. Most students that do use drugs smoke pot, although there are a rising number of students that have been reported to be using cocaine and ecstasy as well. Drug use is hidden, and when it does come out, it is dealt with quickly and strictly.**

10:1	Student-to-Faculty Ratio
92%	Freshman Retention Rate
76%	Four-Year Graduation Rate
76%	Financial Aid Applicants Receiving Aid

Students Speak Out
SAFETY & SECURITY

Q "I feel very safe on campus. **I have had no worries at all**. Campus Safety is always around, and even when something does go wrong, they always show up to help right away."

Q "I never worry about safety, but **I still don't walk alone** at night just to be safe."

Q "I've never had a problem with the health center, but **I do hear a lot of people complain** about it all the time. They are incredibly limited in what they can do, but when I've been sick with the flu and stuff, they've hooked me up pretty well."

Q "I only go to the health center if I absolutely have to. They can't do very much, and **they don't seem very responsive to what I have to say** at all."

STUDENT AUTHOR: **Because of the small size of the school, Campus Safety is able to field fewer officers, which allows for a greater personal relationship and a greater feeling of community on campus, which in turn leads most students to feel even safer amongst one another.**

Questions?
For more inside information and survival tips, pick up College Prowler's full-length book on this school, written by an actual student! Check it out at *www.collegeprowler.com.*

Students Speak Out
ON OVERALL EXPERIENCE

Q "I don't ever want to leave! I've had the best time at this school, and I wouldn't trade it for anything. The classes are awesome, the people are even cooler, and **I've been able to see so many different things** here. I know my life is definitely better for it."

Q "I didn't really know what I was getting into here. **It's a good school, but it's not for me**. I don't like the liberal arts way of learning, and I think people should be careful about that if they choose Oxy. I want to have a more intensive science program, but that means I have to go to another school."

Q "I would recommend Oxy to **someone who wanted diversity** in the way they learned, lived, and played. It's got a great way of teaching, and the people here make it truly spectacular."

Q "**Liberal arts schools are a different way to go to college**, but if you want to get the kind of diversity in your studies and social life that a liberal arts education implies, Occidental is definitely the place to go."

STUDENT AUTHOR: **Oxy is a highly diverse school in terms of those who attend, as well as the multitude of academic and extracurricular options available to all students. It also has a very tight community, both between the students amongst themselves, as well as students and the administration. There is a plethora of things to do on and off campus as well, and for those looking for a change or looking for a variety in culture or entertainment, there is nothing lacking in Los Angeles. Take a look at the school, and see if the programs it currently excels in may be right for you. If they are, definitely take a chance and visit campus.**

Ohio State University

154 West 12th Avenue; Columbus, OH 43210
(614) 292-OHIO; www.osu.edu

THE BASICS:

Acceptance Rate: 59%
Setting: Urban
F-T Undergrads: 35,716

SAT Range: 1130–1330*
Control: Public
Tuition: $21,918

Most Popular Majors: Business, Social Sciences, Consumer Sciences, Engineering, Biology

*of 1600

Academics	B	Guys	A-
Local Atmosphere	A	Girls	A
Safety & Security	B-	Athletics	A+
Computers	B	Nightlife	B+
Facilities	A	Greek Life	C
Campus Dining	C-	Drug Scene	B
Off-Campus Dining	C	Campus Strictness	B
Campus Housing	C	Parking	C-
Off-Campus Housing	A-	Transportation	B+
Diversity	C	Weather	C+

Students Speak Out
ON ACADEMICS

Q "The teachers here are **just as diverse as the student population**; they each bring something different to the picture. Classes are interesting once you get into your major. The general education courses (GECs) here stink."

Q "Most of my teachers give **good lectures and fair exams**, and they are always available and involved with their students. I've had a few, however, that are more interested in their research than teaching."

Q "Teachers are **pretty personable** here. You can e-mail them about something and get a reply within a few minutes."

Q "Occasionally, you will have **a foreign TA** or professor, but they are usually pretty easy to understand. All of my teachers have been eager to help, and most of them are very clever, inspiring characters."

STUDENT AUTHOR: Though feelings about the methods in which some courses are taught may differ a bit, one of the greatest advantages is the ease with which one can contact professors and TAs. OSU has a somewhat lax classroom environment compared to other schools, but don't be fooled: attending classes is vital. Many courses weigh attendance and participation in your final grade, and beyond that, subject matter moves quickly, and skipping even one class can put you in a deep hole. Don't make the mistake of thinking that a teacher will rigidly stick to the syllabus, either. Agendas change, and so do deadlines.

Students Speak Out
ON LOCAL ATMOSPHERE

Q "Columbus is the **perfect little big city**."

Q "Columbus is **a great town**; there's always something to do, or so I hear. I actually haven't had much of a reason to venture off campus, since virtually everything I need is right here."

Q "Just about **every major concert tour** comes to Cleveland or Cincinnati. The Columbus Zoo is awesome! It's best to go when the weather is nice."

Q "There are five concert venues, three major shopping malls, and a lot of cool museums such as the COSI Science Center and the Riffe Art Gallery downtown. There is an area of town called the Short North that has a lot of really funky art galleries, too. For a small, Midwestern city, it's pretty **cultured and sophisticated**."

Q "OSU is a very **chilled-out environment** with massive amounts of things to do every single day of the week."

STUDENT AUTHOR: You cannot discuss the local atmosphere without discussing Buckeye sports. During football Saturdays, everyone watches the game. The Buckeye vibe permeates all of the surrounding area, and students see Columbus as a friendly town. Don't be fooled by the Midwest stigma of blandness or ignorance—most of the townies are glad to see you, and they will greet you with a smile. The city is also very close—albeit, by vehicle—to cities such as Cleveland and Cincinnati, which provide even more activities.

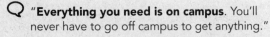

5 Best Things	5 Worst Things
1 Concerts	1 Parking
2 The band	2 Campus dining
3 Michigan Week	3 Greek scene
4 Brutus Buckeye	4 Unpredictable weather
5 Mirror Lake	5 Hemp Fest

Students Speak Out
ON FACILITIES

Q "**Everything you need is on campus**. You'll never have to go off campus to get anything."

Q "There are **tons of libraries**, several fitness centers, and four commons for the dorms; then there is the Ohio Union, which is nice, and has 10 different fast food places."

Q "OSU facilities are awesome—especially our athletic centers! Also, there are plenty of computer labs. As one of the biggest universities in the country, it definitely has **all of the resources you need**."

Q "Nothing to complain about with regard to the facilities here in OSU—there is always construction going on to **improve the outlook of the campus**."

Q "The athletic center is awesome. The computer labs are good, too. The Ohio and Drake Unions are the student centers—the **Ohio Union even has a bar!**"

STUDENT AUTHOR: OSU provides its students with facilities to meet both mental and physical needs. Food courts can be found throughout campus, though the Ohio Union is the favored rest area between classes. In addition to the Main Library, there are a lot of smaller specialized libraries and reading rooms for almost every type of interest. If you just like to work out regularly, you're in luck—numerous fitness centers around campus are available to students. Larkins has been renovated, and at over 45,000 square feet, it is one of the finest recreation centers in America. You don't actually have to leave campus for anything.

Famous Alumni

John Glenn, John Havlicek, Bobby Knight, Richard Lewis, John M. Matthias, Jack Nicklaus, Jessie Owens, R.L. Stine, James Thurber, Dwight Yoakam

Students Speak Out
ON CAMPUS DINING

Q "There are **tons of little places all over** that you can eat at, and some even let you use your Buck-ID (you can put money on it)."

Q "United Dairy Farmers (UDF) is a cross between 7-11 and Baskin Robbins, and **it is open 24 hours**. If you visit UDF at any given time, day or night, you're going to find students hanging around or making a quick stop."

Q "**I personally like Mirror Lake**. They don't have much of a variety, but I like their subs."

Q "I'll be honest, **the food is bad**; in fact, many people lose the Freshman 15 rather than gain it. Mirror Lake Café is the best bet for using your meal plan here. Oxley's is another decent place to go. Normal dining commons are awful, though, and the Buckeye Express gets old after a few weeks."

Q "There is also the Ohio Union, which has a **food court**."

STUDENT AUTHOR: OSU dining needs help, and fast. If you've seen what some universities offer, you'll be really disappointed by Ohio's cafeteria food. Opinions vary regarding the food in the commons, but most are negative. Many feel they are being ripped off with how much money they spend for their food. Mirror Lake is the most sought-after place to use your meal plan. Buckeye Express is also a student favorite, but fast food wears on you after a few months. The one redeeming part of OSU's dining halls is that the staff is nice. Too bad this doesn't translate into better food.

Student Body

African American:	7%	Male/Female:	53/47%
Asian American:	5%	Out-of-State:	11%
Hispanic:	3%	International:	3%
Native American:	<1%	Unknown:	10%
White:	80%		

Popular Faiths: Catholic, Protestant, Lutheran, Jewish, and Muslim beliefs are more visible.

Gay Pride: Columbus is an extremely open community with a large amount of gay and lesbian individuals. OSU has a number of gay/lesbian groups, such as Fusion and GLBT Student Services.

Economic Status: Most students range from lower-middle-class to upper-class.

Students Speak Out
ON DORMS

Q "We have three areas of dorms, with three **different reputations**."

Q "You definitely need to live in the dorms your freshman year. The dorms are really friendly; **everyone normally leaves their doors open**, and it's a great way for you to meet new friends. South Campus most definitely is the place."

Q "The **dorms are okay**. The rooms are kind of small, and floor bathrooms can get really sloppy. The North Campus dorms and the two Towers are better, for the most part, and have air-conditioning."

STUDENT AUTHOR: There are three main housing quarters on campus: North, South, and the Towers. North Campus is considered the place for quiet living and for those who don't seek out a huge social life. South Campus dorms are a bit louder. They house the majority of the incoming freshman class. Towers are nearly ignored because of their distance from the main campus. Most students agree that all the dorms could use some work—don't expect to be wowed. Choose an area based on what type of environment you want.

Did You Know?
24% of undergrads live on campus.

Students Speak Out
ON GUYS & GIRLS

Q "There are **lots of people to look at**. I personally think there are lots of very good-looking people on campus."

Q "Girls vary, in terms of personality, though—some are **very sweet, and some are stuck up**."

Q "There are definitely some hot guys here. People here are **a little preppy**, but pretty much every group you can imagine is represented here. There are people of all kinds."

Q "People at OSU are generally pretty cool. It's one of the biggest universities in the world, so there are **many different types of people**; you're bound to meet people you like, even though they may be completely different from you."

STUDENT AUTHOR: Guys and girls alike feel that there is enough variety to find any type of relationship you're searching for. The feeling around campus is pretty upbeat, and there are many places to go searching for a specific type of girl or guy. Just look around you: classrooms and residence halls are a great place to meet people. It's also a good idea to go around town and hit the different scenes, because there is a lot of variety out there.

Traditions

Ramp
The marching band proceeds down a long ramp to take the field and bursts out the OSU Fight Song.

Script Ohio
The band spells out "Ohio" on the field. As the sousaphone player dots the "i," the crowd goes wild.

Overall School Spirit
Everywhere you go, you can find students decorated in scarlet and gray. Outside of Ohio, it's kind of cool to hate OSU. This seems to make students even more proud of being Buckeyes.

Students Speak Out
ON ATHLETICS

Q "We are **a Big Ten school**! Sports are huge, and we love the Buckeyes! Let me tell you, football games are the greatest—they're so much fun!"

Q "One of the **largest intramural programs** in the country gives any sports lover the opportunity to compete in a wide variety of sports at many different skill levels."

Q "We have one of the biggest stadiums in college football, and on **game days the atmosphere is awesome**!"

Q "We have **a lot of good athletic teams**, men's and women's, that don't receive the attention football receives, because half of the school population is still gloating about being the 2002 national champions of college football."

STUDENT AUTHOR: Football, football, football! You'll be hard-pressed to find a more competitive football school than OSU. Columbus is filled with block parties and huge crowds getting ready for each game, and competition is always high. An abundance of intramural sports keeps the physically active students busy, as well. OSU intramurals offer nearly every type of sport you can think of.

Students Speak Out
ON DRUG SCENE

Q "**There is drug use**, of course; I mean, this is a huge university. However, there aren't junkies running around. The most common drug is pot."

Q "Drugs aren't a big problem. **Alcohol use and abuse** is honestly much more of a concern."

Q "**Every campus has drugs**. I don't feel as though it is a big problem here."

Q "**Marijuana is plentiful**. It makes an appearance at most parties. If you're looking to avoid drugs, though, don't worry; no one will force you."

STUDENT AUTHOR: Alcohol is, by far, the most prevalent drug on the OSU campus. The rest of the drug scene isn't terribly huge, and it is kept in check by factors such as price, since students claim that drugs around OSU are more expensive than most places. The legalization debate pops up frequently on campus, and "Hemp Fest" takes place each spring on the South Oval. While this marijuana subculture isn't officially supported in any way, it is pretty evident; however, it is also quite easy to avoid, and there isn't any social pressure.

13:1	Student-to-Faculty Ratio
92%	Freshman Retention Rate
40%	Four-Year Graduation Rate
79%	Financial Aid Applicants Receiving Aid

Students Speak Out
SAFETY & SECURITY

Q "OSU is really safe. We have **an escort service** that you can call 24/7. You are also never out of sight of a blue-light call-box that you can use to access the police, fire department, or an ambulance."

Q "You kind of **know what areas of campus to avoid** after dark, and those places are mostly off campus. It's generally very comfortable and secure."

Q "I find campus to be extremely safe; I have never had any problems with theft or vandalism at the dorms. **Off campus is a little more hairy**, but for a city as large as this, it's relatively safe. I have never once been scared to walk by myself anywhere on campus at all."

STUDENT AUTHOR: As with many areas, the off-campus spots are those most prone to problems, and generally speaking, students report few problems on campus throughout the year. A great benefit to being an OSU student is the courtesy shuttle that take students back to the residence halls.

> **Questions?**
> For more inside information and survival tips, pick up College Prowler's full-length book on this school, written by an actual student! Check it out at *www.collegeprowler.com.*

Students Speak Out
ON OVERALL EXPERIENCE

Q "Ohio State encompasses all aspects of the college experience. It's a place where you'll make your best friends, you'll meet people from all walks of life, and even learn a thing or two. It definitely offers a **unique and totally liberating college experience** to all who bear the scarlet and gray."

Q "I love OSU. The entire athletic program has really made it **memorable for me** so far."

Q "It's a really big school, so if you like a lot of personal attention and hand holding, this probably isn't the place for you. But if you want a **big school with lots of choices** and options, this may be a good place for you."

Q "I've met some wonderful people, and there are so **many options class-wise**. There's always something going on for you to get involved in. Ohio people are very friendly."

STUDENT AUTHOR: There is a reason the Buckeye Nation is considered to be so devoted; an overwhelming love for OSU is evident in student responses, and in the loyalty of alumni to their alma mater. Some feel that the academics are top-notch and have found exactly the programs they wanted; others lean toward the athletic success of the Buckeye teams. After only a quarter of classes, you won't be able to cross the Oval without seeing someone you know. Ohio State is truly the smallest large university you will find. The people are known for their friendly attitudes, and alumni are scattered across the nation. If you choose to go to OSU, you're choosing a school with a name that's well known, both in the workplace and in the college community.

Ohio University

20 East Union Street; Athens, OH 45701
(740) 593-1000; www.ohio.edu

THE BASICS:

Acceptance Rate: 82%
Setting: Rural
F-T Undergrads: 16,072

SAT Range: 970–1200*
Control: Public
Tuition: $17,871

Most Popular Majors: Communication, Childhood Education, Business, Social Sciences, Liberal Arts

*of 1600

Academics	B	Guys	A
Local Atmosphere	B-	Girls	A
Safety & Security	A-	Athletics	B
Computers	A	Nightlife	A
Facilities	A-	Greek Life	B
Campus Dining	B	Drug Scene	B+
Off-Campus Dining	B	Campus Strictness	B
Campus Housing	A-	Parking	F
Off-Campus Housing	B	Transportation	C+
Diversity	D-	Weather	C+

Students Speak Out
ON ACADEMICS

Q "The teachers in my major have been especially great. **They all have real-world experience** as well as teaching experience, so they have a lot more to offer than what is in a textbook."

Q "The teachers at Ohio University are like any other teachers at [any other] university. You will have teachers that are challenging and enthusiastic about teaching and then there will be teachers who act like they do not want to even be there. However, **more than 90 percent fall in the first category**."

Q "The teachers at OU are friendly and seem interested in what the students are involved in. Many teachers relate the topics they are discussing in class to something we, as students in a small southeastern Ohio town, **can understand within our daily lives**."

Q "Since the teachers are so interested and care so much about the students, **the classes stay interesting**. There are also a very wide variety of classes you can take to suit your individual interests."

STUDENT AUTHOR: At OU, each student will have at least one experience with an awesome professor and one with a professor that just plain sucks. With any professor, students need to take the initiative to form a relationship. Introductory classes can be large, but once you get into the higher levels, the classes shrink. Also, don't be afraid to ask advisors or other students, what classes they recommend and which ones to avoid.

Students Speak Out
ON LOCAL ATMOSPHERE

Q "**Athens is a college town**. The University population makes up a large majority of the town's population, and when classes aren't in session, it feels like a ghost town! But it's wonderful!"

Q "**Everything is within walking distance**, even if you live off campus. You could have a class at one end of campus and still make it to your next class on the complete other end of campus on time."

Q "The atmosphere at Ohio University is very different than any other college campus I visited while still in high school. The community of Athens cares about the school since the University is a huge part of their economy. With **the nearest city being over an hour away** there is a sense of community and pride in the school and city that is hard to find anywhere else."

Q "The atmosphere in Athens is great! Everyone is so friendly and **most people (who are not students) tolerate a lot of things** that people in small towns do not usually have to deal with."

STUDENT AUTHOR: Practically any student you ask will say that the atmosphere is one of the greatest parts of going to OU. Athens is the epitome of a college town: tree-filled greens, colonial architecture, brick streets, all of which makes for a very quaint and comfortable learning atmosphere. However, at times, it can seem like Athens is closed off from the rest of the world.

Students Speak Out
ON FACILITIES

Q "Our athletic fields are pretty nice. **We're not huge sports fans around here**, but the facilities still seem pretty nice."

Q "We don't have a student center (yet!), but **we're supposed to be getting one soon**."

Q "The facilities on campus are very nice. **They are constantly updating and renovating buildings** to accommodate students' wants and needs. They are in the process of building a new student center that will be completed soon."

Q "The facilities on campus are wonderful. The **Ping Center is a state-of-the-art gym and has everything that you can imagine**: from the climbing wall, to the top-of-the-line exercise equipment, to the track and the basketball courts. It has everything you could ask for."

Q "Baker Center is okay. It was in a convenient place, and **I really only went there though when I had an occasional meeting** or had to mail something. I'm jealous that I'm not going to be there when the new student center is done!"

STUDENT AUTHOR: Students love the Charles J. Ping Center, and it is by far one of the most popular places to be on campus. The new student center should be awesome. The current Baker University Center, though convenient for mailing packages and stuff, is less than exciting and mainly serves as a place for organizations to meet. Overall, the campus is beautiful. Many of the buildings are new or renovated, and the facilities are not only convenient and modern, but also aesthetically pleasing.

Famous Alumni

Nancy Cartwright, Joe Eszterhas, Arsenio Hall, Matt Lauer, Paul Newman, Piper Perabo, Mike Schmidt, Betty Thomas, George Voinovich

Students Speak Out
ON CAMPUS DINING

Q "The food in the dining halls is really not that bad. **There's a huge variety**, so everyone can find something to eat. They really try to accommodate peoples dietary needs."

Q "There have been times when **I wouldn't touch some of the things that were being served**, but for the most part, the food is pretty good."

Q "There are late-night dinners that are served, but none of the dining halls are open 24 hours. However, **there is now more variety that exists with new grab n' go services** that are equipped with full deli's, sushi, wraps, and just about anything else. "

Q "**I do know that there is a problem with the variety for many vegetarians**. One complaint that I always hear is that they are constantly eating bagels and living off the full salad bar. Ohio University was trying to appease many vegetarians when I left the campus."

Q "The dining halls didn't seem like they had the best food in the world when I ate there my freshman and sophomore years. It was just a great place to socialize! Although, when I moved out of the dorms, everyone I knew missed the dining hall food. **I really missed the mashed potatoes**!"

STUDENT AUTHOR: Overall, the dining halls provide good deals for students—they're convenient, the food is good, and changes are being made to accommodate vegetarians and those who want a healthier menu.

Student Body

African American:	5%	Male/Female:	47/53%
Asian American:	1%	Out-of-State:	8%
Hispanic:	2%	International:	2%
Native American:	<1%	Unknown:	0%
White:	91%		

Popular Faiths: Though the majority students are Christian, there are many clubs, organizations, and places of worship for a variety of faiths.

Gay Pride: Ohio University has a somewhat visible gay, lesbian, and transgender community.

Economic Status: You'll meet students who receive a steady allowance from their rich daddies, as well as students from slums and tenement buildings.

Students Speak Out
ON DORMS

Q "All of the dorms are fairly nice and offer pretty much the same things. All rooms come equipped with a computer and a Micro-fridge. **Some dorms have better locations** and some have elevators, so base your decision on that, rather than the name."

Q **"The dorms depend on what part of campus you really live on**. Of course you will hear that West Green has the most parties, the Front Four on South Green are the most fun, and the dorms on East Green are nicest and closer to everything."

Q "My sophomore year was probably my favorite year at OU. **My dorm was coed and it was so much fun**! I met some great people that year. We all did a lot of crazy things together."

STUDENT AUTHOR: **Suffice it to say, the dorms are a great experience for pretty much everyone and make the first couple of years at college, which can be the most difficult, easier. Thankfully, the residence halls are nice at OU—they are clean, convenient, safe, and comfortable. Another great thing about living in dorms is the amenities.**

> **Did You Know?**
> 44% of undergrads live on campus.

Students Speak Out
ON GUYS & GIRLS

Q "I think that the people at Ohio University are very good looking. I have had friends come visit from other colleges **who comment on the fact that most of our students are attractive**."

Q "The guys are hot and the girls are cute, but that's definitely no indication of relationship potential. I have tons of friends who met guys/girls at OU that they totally fell in love with and **will most likely end up marrying**."

Q "The guys are hot at our school and the girls are pretty. **Both are friendly** and tend to be pretty relaxed and low-key."

Q "I would say I had **just as many guy friends as girl friends** at OU."

STUDENT AUTHOR: **There are very attractive people at this school, and to make it even better, people are generally really friendly, outgoing, and relationship-worthy. While a fair share of jerks are thrown into the mix, students agree that both sexes are cool and even game for a serious relationship. Just keep in mind that whatever kind of relationship you may be after, it is, like in any other place, a two-way street.**

> **Traditions**
>
> **Family Weekends**
> Moms, dads, and siblings all have their own weekends to come visit OU, which make for some of the best times on campus.
>
> **Shuffles**
> Students usually partake in this ritual their senior year. Wearing T-shirts bearing their shuffle's name, they try to make it to every bar on campus.
>
> **Overall School Spirit**
> It is pretty hard to find someone who doesn't love going to OU.

Students Speak Out
ON ATHLETICS

Q "Sports are not that big at Ohio University. I have only been to a few varsity games, and those were only on the big weekends, **like Homecoming or when we played Miami of Ohio**."

Q "Intramural sports are huge at OU. **Broomball and flag football** seem to be two of the most popular."

Q "Basketball and baseball are probably the two biggest sports on campus. **Basketball games are probably the most fun to watch** because OU typically has a good team."

Q "Our football team isn't the best, but the games are still fun to attend (**so you can see the Marching 110 perform at half time**)."

STUDENT AUTHOR: **If you are looking for a school with obsessed football fans who never miss a game and tailgate into the wee hours of the morning, look elsewhere. On the other hand, intramural sports are really popular, so if you don't have the time (or talent) to play varsity, join one of the many intramural teams at OU.**

Students Speak Out
ON DRUG SCENE

Q "**The drug scene on campus is there if you know where to look**. There is not a heavy drug population, but mostly marijuana."

Q "Athens and Ohio University is fairly drug free, and **it is extremely rare to go into a party and see any drug usage** of any kind."

Q "To be completely honest, I do not know much about the drug scene at Ohio University, **but I am sure it is there; it's just not talked about**."

STUDENT AUTHOR: Most students know little about the drug scene because, obviously, they don't do drugs (or are just playing innocent). Either way, that's basically how it is on campus; you are unaware of the drug scene if you aren't a part of it. There's no pressure put on students to do anything they don't want to do. And sometimes it seems downright hard to find the things you do want to do. Alcohol is the drug of choice among OU's majority, and while hard drugs are no doubt on campus; they're not floating around. But as with any campus, it's there if you look hard enough.

19:1	Student-to-Faculty Ratio
78%	Freshman Retention Rate
47%	Four-Year Graduation Rate
69%	Financial Aid Applicants Receiving Aid

Students Speak Out
SAFETY & SECURITY

Q "Generally, I would say this is a really safe campus. I'm not saying nothing bad ever happens here, but **it's not something you're constantly worrying about**."

Q "Security and safety on campus are excellent. In all my years at Ohio University, neither my friends nor I have had any major crimes committed against us. **There are sporadic instances of criminal activity**, but these are common and quickly taken care of by either the Campus Police or Athens Police."

Q "Fortunately OU is a safe campus, and the police departments of Athens and Ohio University make sure to **stay in eyesight at all hours** of the day and into the late evening to continue the feeling of safety."

STUDENT AUTHOR: Though there are occurrences of crime like any other place, everyone agrees that OU is generally a safe campus for men and women. In addition to city police, OU has its own police department, so patrolling officers are a pretty common sight.

Questions?
For more inside information and survival tips, pick up College Prowler's full-length book on this school, written by an actual student! Check it out at *www.collegeprowler.com.*

Students Speak Out
ON OVERALL EXPERIENCE

Q "**I actually went somewhere else and transferred to Ohio University** and do not regret a second of it. It is a great place to be and I recommend it to anyone interested in having a good time."

Q "Many of my friends from other campuses loved to visit, go to the block parties, enjoy the good food and the many activities that always seem to be going on. **I can't believe people actually go to school at other places besides OU**."

Q "I love OU, and I think any student or alumni would agree with me. **It's a very close-knit and open community** where everyone is able to find their niche and circle of friends."

Q "OU is what I always envisioned my college experience would be like. Athens is a total college town. **Everything is so close together and convenient**. I made so many great friends that I'm sure will be my closest friends in life. Oh, and I got a good education, too!"

STUDENT AUTHOR: Whether it's the unique atmosphere, great classes, people they've met, or a combination of several factors, Bobcats are passionate about their school and feel confident about the choice they made. Once they graduate, it's inevitable they will return more than once to recapture the feeling of strolling along Court Street and hanging out with great friends over a beer or game of pool. What's most important about college is you make the most of wherever you choose to go. Thankfully, OU gives each individual many opportunities and amenities to enjoy this special phase of their lives.

Ohio Wesleyan University

63 South Sandusky Street; Delaware, OH 43015
(740) 368-2000; www.owu.edu

Academics	B	Guys	B+
Local Atmosphere	C	Girls	B+
Safety & Security	B	Athletics	B-
Computers	B-	Nightlife	B-
Facilities	B	Greek Life	A
Campus Dining	B+	Drug Scene	B
Off-Campus Dining	B+	Campus Strictness	C+
Campus Housing	B	Parking	C+
Off-Campus Housing	D	Transportation	D
Diversity	D+	Weather	C+

Students Speak Out
ON ACADEMICS

Q "I have had very positive experiences with all of my professors. They are **engaging, interesting, and interested in their students**. I am most amazed by their willingness to go out of their way to help students. A lot of professors are involved on campus and strive to make great programs for the community."

Q "OWU is on the small side, and **classes remain small in number**, which allows students to really form a bond with their professors if they choose to do so. Once the bond is formed, many professors will go out of their way to help the student now or even post graduation."

Q "The classes are interesting but challenging. **Be prepared for heavy reading**. Most classes are very open, and debate and discussion is encouraged, which leads to a richer intellectual experience. Working hard and making the most of your class, though, is definitely required."

Q "**Most of the classes that I have taken have been interesting**, even the ones I wouldn't have expected."

STUDENT AUTHOR: Academics at Ohio Wesleyan are nothing less than top-notch, and it is no secret among its students. As opposed to many larger universities, the professors come to OWU to teach, and they love doing so. Classes are small and allow personal interaction with every faculty member. There is no such thing as a teaching assistant here. Be warned—slacking off at OWU comes at a high price.

Students Speak Out
ON LOCAL ATMOSPHERE

Q "**The atmosphere in Delaware, Ohio leaves a lot to be desired**, as far as I'm concerned. I don't think that the little town of Delaware was ever intended to have a world-class liberal arts college in its midst."

Q "Being in Delaware is a great experience because the focus is on the University, but **students can escape to Columbus and the neighboring towns** whenever they want something different. Every year, the town hosts the Delaware County fair, which is in walking distance from the campus."

Q "The town atmosphere is pretty dull. Barring the two pubs we have on the main street of the town, there isn't really any nightlife in town. The good side to this is that there are ample parties and social events on campus to keep one occupied. Another big plus point is that Columbus is just 40 minutes away, so if you have a car, you can definitely enjoy the nightlife in a big city. **Ohio State University is in Columbus**, so there are definitely a lot of college students you can come across while in Columbus."

STUDENT AUTHOR: Students will probably never describe the town of Delaware as dynamic or exciting, but the fact does remain that it is a small, safe community that most students feel very comfortable walking around in, even at 3 a.m. The town is making strides to become more dynamic by adding new cafés and restaurants that will entice students to get more active in the community.

Students Speak Out
ON FACILITIES

Q "The student center, called Ham-Wil, is comprised of the **bookstore, food court, a lot of offices, and rooms for events**. It is a wonderful building where people meet for breakfast, lunch, and dinner. It has a couple of lounging areas, where friends can catch up or grab a coffee from the bakery on their way to class."

Q "**The academic buildings on campus are beautiful**. That was one reason Ohio Wesleyan grabbed my attention. I wanted a school with old stone buildings and history behind each wall. There are a few newer buildings, and those are extremely nice as well. The science center, for instance, is a nice place to hang out in between classes if you don't feel like walking back to you dorm room."

Q "The facilities are really nice. **The campus center is relatively new, so it's really nice** and is in the center of campus, so the location is perfect. The athletic building is well-equipped and has all the basic needs. The academic buildings are older but aren't intolerable to learn in."

STUDENT AUTHOR: **Ohio Wesleyan has very good facilities for a campus of its size. The campus offers a beautiful blend between architecturally-stunning, century-old buildings and state-of-the art facilities. There are some places in need of renovations, and those are on the University's priority list for a makeover. Overall, the buildings give the campus an old-fashioned feel that a great University should give its visitors, but most are still in very good condition.**

Famous Alumni

Charles Fairbanks, Branch Rickey, Robert Gillespie, Richard North Patterson, Wendy Malick, Fred Barron, David Wetherell, Susan Headden

Students Speak Out
ON CAMPUS DINING

Q "**The food situation on campus is improving**, with the recent introduction of a sushi bar in Ham-Wil and an ice cream area in the Bishop Café. The best part of campus dining is the coffee. Students have access to coffee carts in almost every academic building on campus."

Q "It seems that **pretty much any type of food you could want is available somewhere**. I also know students who have requested specialty foods to be ordered for their needs and had no problem doing so. Sandellas in Bishop Café is a great lunchtime spot with booths and TVs."

Q "For the most part, the food on campus is decent. It could be worse, and it could be better. **They each offer something a little different** so that the food does not become redundant and boring, but that is inevitable by the end of the year, anyway."

Q "The **food on campus is surprisingly good**. OWU is unique in the fact that it offers so many options. Smith Dining Hall is the main dining hall, serving lunch and dinner every day with an added weekend brunch."

STUDENT AUTHOR: **Food at Ohio Wesleyan is hit or miss, but one cannot argue that for a small school, a good number of dining options do exist. The University is always trying to improve their selection, and even added a sushi bar within the past few years that has become very popular with students. No matter what you are craving, there should be a place that can suit your needs.**

Student Body

African American:	5%	Male/Female:	47/53%
Asian American:	2%	Out-of-State:	41%
Hispanic:	1%	International:	8%
Native American:	<1%	Unknown:	0%
White:	84%		

Popular Faiths: Ohio Wesleyan is still affiliated with the United Methodist Church, although the average OWU student probably does not even know this.

Gay Pride: On campus, gays and bisexuals are mostly accepted, however that is definitely not to say that discrimination is nonexistent.

Economic Status: Most students are middle-class to upper-middle-class.

Students Speak Out
ON DORMS

Q "**All but two of the dorms are configured in a suite-style**, where two to four people share one bathroom, depending on whether you're in a quad or a double. Singles are available but highly coveted with most of them going to students with senior status."

Q "Another on-campus option is the SLUs (small living units). OWU has 10 of these themed houses on campus including the Creative Arts House, the Modern Foreign Language House (or MFL), the International House (I-House), and the Tree House (environmental studies). Each house member puts on one house program per semester, such as a seminar or hosting a speaker or artist. **The SLUs add a lot to the campus** and are a great way to live on campus with people of similar interests and still live in a house environment."

STUDENT AUTHOR: **Every student probably fits into one residence area or another. It all depends on the type of environment you want to live in. The majority of students will live in the residence halls for their entire tenure at OWU, so it is important to find out what place you can be happy to call home.**

Did You Know?
83% of undergrads live on campus.

Students Speak Out
ON GUYS & GIRLS

Q "To sum it all up in a nut shell: we have some very diverse personalities—some guys and gals are very nice and cool, some are self-centered and asses. **There are good-looking guys and gals**. I'd say for the most part, it's 50/50 each way."

Q "I would recommend **joining some clubs or organizations on campus**, and you would have a better likelihood of meeting your kind of people. On the 'hotness' front, guys are definitely hot! Gym and fitness is a big deal on campus, so a lot of guys and girls have awesome physiques!"

Q "Ohio Wesleyan is like any campus—there are **definitely good-looking students**. It's definitely possible to meet some great people!"

STUDENT AUTHOR: **Everyone seems to fit in with some group on campus. The constant blend of students often results in casual hookups at parties, which is the predominant way the social scene works. Long-term relationships do occur as well, but they are less common between the students. The best way to meet people is just by hanging out in the different residence halls, in classes, and in the Hamilton-Williams Campus Center.**

Overall School Spirit

The amount of school spirit runs the entire spectrum from those that could care less up to the students that love the fact that they can call themselves OWU Battling Bishops. School spirit at OWU, for the average student, develops very slowly but can become incredibly strong. The only drawback is that many times, this spirit doesn't become fully developed until their last semester, causing them to wish they would have had more time to immerse themselves in everything the institution offers. Overall, everybody from the school needs to work together in order to foster and strengthen school spirit in students as soon as they enter their freshman year.

Students Speak Out
ON ATHLETICS

Q "Varsity sports cannot be compared to a D-I atmosphere, as **OWU is only a D-III college**. Overall, our sports teams do exceptionally well. For most varsity sports, not many college students attend them, which can be seen when you look into the stands and mostly see parents sitting there."

Q "**Intramural sports are all over campus**. If it's not an interfraternity league, you'll find kids doing all sorts of stuff. In short, if you're into something, you'll probably find it here. Okay, so we don't have an intramural Sherpa team. Sue us."

Q "**Almost all the kids are involved** in a sport, whether it be varsity, club, or intramural."

STUDENT AUTHOR: **A very large portion of the student body chooses to take advantage of opportunities to get involved with intramurals or club sports. If you are looking for a school that will offer you a fantastic time in the stands cheering on your team, OWU may not fit the bill, but if you are looking for an opportunity to competitively play a sport in your free time, OWU might be worth taking a look at.**

Students Speak Out
ON DRUG SCENE

Q "Drugs are prevalent on campus—they seem to be pretty easy to obtain, because there are people doing it pretty often. However, **Public Safety is pretty vigilant about drugs**—their possession and abuse. There are pretty strict penalties if you're caught."

Q "I know this will come as a huge shock to all you college applicants out there, but it is possible to get drugs just about anywhere. Ohio Wesleyan University is no exception to this rule, but **it is relatively low-key here** and has rarely gone beyond marijuana, to the best of my knowledge."

STUDENT AUTHOR: **Drugs are not highly visible but are easily available** throughout the campus. The OWU drug scene would mostly be characterized by nothing more than hippies passing a marijuana joint around a circle. Students learn within their first two weeks at OWU where the drugs are prevalent and where they are not, and it is up to them to decide where and with whom they will be hanging out.

13:1	Student-to-Faculty Ratio
80%	Freshman Retention Rate
54%	Four-Year Graduation Rate
88%	Financial Aid Applicants Receiving Aid

Students Speak Out
SAFETY & SECURITY

Q "What I can say personally is that **it is really up to you to be in good company and in good hands**, especially during party nights. There have been isolated incidents regarding security of girls on campus, but to the best of my knowledge, they have been kept under control."

Q "The Public Safety officers at Ohio Wesleyan are **the nicest officers I have ever met**. They really care about the safety of the students. You can ask for assistance back to your dorm at any hour of the night, sober or drunk."

Q "**Ohio Wesleyan is a safe campus**. As with any campus, common sense is always the best weapon, but walking around at night is safe. Public Safety commonly patrols through University buildings and grounds."

STUDENT AUTHOR: **The University takes strides to make sure that** the campus community feels very secure by having keycard-only access to dorms and emergency phones placed around campus that alert the campus police. In addition, they offer free escorts at night across campus.

Questions?
For more inside information and survival tips, pick up College Prowler's full-length book on this school, written by an actual student! Check it out at *www.collegeprowler.com.*

Students Speak Out
ON OVERALL EXPERIENCE

Q "I'm glad to be at Ohio Wesleyan. **So far, it has been an enriching experience**. The campus encourages students to create and lead groups, and so far, that has been the best part of my experience."

Q "The campus is friendly, students get along, and we aren't overly competitive with each other. Everyone just sort of does what makes him or her happy. **It seems like there is a niche for every type**. The school encourages students to get involved, and the more you do, the more you get out of your time here. While it is a small school, I feel it is a place that offers students great opportunities on campus and beyond with internships, study abroad, and research programs. It is a great place for students who are eager to learn and take part in a community."

Q "After three years at Ohio Wesleyan, I am confident that I made the right decision. **The campus is great, as is the proximity to Columbus**. Most importantly, the students are amazing, and there are many worthwhile activities to get involved in. I wouldn't trade my experience."

STUDENT AUTHOR: **An Ohio Wesleyan student truly appreciates the opportunities that are given to them at this small liberal arts school. There is something special about OWU that the rankings seem to overlook. The students appreciate an Ohio Wesleyan education because it focuses on every aspect of character and knowledge and not just what is taught in the classroom. OWU students do not just learn about facts and equations; they learn how to think, and that is what sets them apart.**

Old Dominion University

5115 Hampton Boulevard; Norfolk, VA 23529
(757) 683-3000; www.odu.edu

THE BASICS:

Acceptance Rate: 72%
Setting: Urban
F-T Undergrads: 12,810

SAT Range: 1440–1730*
Control: Public
Tuition: $18,390

Most Popular Majors: Business, Health Professions, English, Engineering, Interdisciplinary Studies

*of 2400

Academics	B-	Guys	B
Local Atmosphere	B-	Girls	B+
Safety & Security	C-	Athletics	B-
Computers	C+	Nightlife	B
Facilities	B-	Greek Life	C
Campus Dining	C-	Drug Scene	B-
Off-Campus Dining	B+	Campus Strictness	B-
Campus Housing	C	Parking	C-
Off-Campus Housing	C-	Transportation	B-
Diversity	B+	Weather	B

Students Speak Out
ON ACADEMICS

Q "The professors that I've had have been generally easy to speak to, but you have to be really careful who you get or you're not going to do well in the class at all. **Your success or whatever really depends on the professor** you get."

Q "If you have a smaller class, the professors are pretty easy to talk to. But **the larger the class, the harder it is to get into contact with your instructor**."

Q "**I don't really feel a need to compete with anyone** in my courses. It's a very chill atmosphere, which I'm not used to because I went to a high school that was very competitive. I am much more laid-back here, and it's much easier for me to coast through my classes."

Q "I've had two **teachers where I was smarter than them in the subject** they were teaching."

STUDENT AUTHOR: Without the pressures of making the best grade in a course, student-teacher relationships are far more relaxed than they might be. Each of the colleges at ODU is equipped with a stunning gamut of professors who are well-read in their fields. Although ODU is mostly renowned for the degrees and majors it offers in the science and business fields, it too has a burgeoning College of Fine Arts and Education, providing for a dynamic dualism between the colleges on the campus. Without the hassles of competition, classes just flow more easily at ODU.

Students Speak Out
ON LOCAL ATMOSPHERE

Q "It has its share of nightlife and plenty of places to shop and eat. **Hampton University and Thomas Nelson Community College** are the two educational facilities present. As far as stuff to stay away from, I'd say, like any other city, you want to avoid the drug regions. Places to visit include: Jason's Deli, Hampton Coliseum, AMC 24, and Cinema Café."

Q "In Ghent, there are a bunch of restaurants, some coffeeshops, and a nice atmosphere of an old district. The Chrysler has an amazing collection, and keeps on growing and changing. The downtown area has some interesting places, as well, like Scottie Quix, which is a restaurant/club with some excellent music and great atmosphere. There is **Relative Theory Records that has just about any type of music you can wish for**, and the mall if you're up for shopping."

Q "I would definitely suggest visiting Waterside, the zoo, and Doumar's, which is a curbside burger joint. Oceanview is fabulous, and check out Ghent. It is very beautiful and aged. **Anyone that doesn't like Norfolk is just whack**."

STUDENT AUTHOR: There is definitely always something happening in either downtown Norfolk or Old Dominion's campus. Whether you're looking at going to a party or a clambake or a mixer, you kind of have to know at least one person who has a good sense of what is going down on campus or around campus, otherwise your weekends will be comprised of nothing but aimless wandering up and down 42nd trying to find something to do.

5 Best Things	5 Worst Things
1 Amiable professors	1 Construction
2 Clean campus	2 Parking
3 Proximity to beach	3 High crime rate
4 Wi-fi access	4 Off-campus housing
5 Academic programs	5 On-campus dining

Students Speak Out
ON FACILITIES

Q "The facilities are kind of old, but adequate. **We have a relatively new fitness center** in the University Village with a lot of cardio equipment. The weight side is very cramped, though. The computers are just a few years old, and OCCS is always doing stuff to speed them up."

Q "**Everything is pretty much clean here**. We have two workout centers, one pool, and two gyms, and they're all great. Everything is regulated, even locker rooms, so people tend to keep it clean because they know they will be back. It kinda sucks that you have to take a class to get access to all of the stuff—but it's only 15 minutes long."

Q "Personally, **I think the facilities here are great**. The athletic department gives access to facilities like the pool and even sauna, and the students and faculty are really helpful."

Q "**The H&PE Gym is going to be reconstructed**. That's good, because the gym looked really old."

STUDENT AUTHOR: Each and every semester and with every passing year, ODU continues to augment its campus by adding facilities. The facilities themselves, such as the gymnasiums and the computer labs, are terribly clean—which is very rare. The eateries, dining halls, computers, stores, and et ceteras inside of the Webb Center are often spotless. However, the campus is often covered in scaffolding, or masked by hideous cranes and/or disgustingly gross trucks carrying building materials to and from destination sites. Luckily, these things are temporary and are a means to an end.

Famous Alumni
Bootie Barker, Kenny Gattison, Nancy Lieberman, Oliver Purnell, Tom DiCillo

Students Speak Out
ON CAMPUS DINING

Q "When I lived in the dorm, I thought it was absolutely ick. I thought they put Ex-Lax in the food. There was some comfort in having all your meals prepared for you. Even if it was bland food that required Tabasco sauce, it was ready-made, and you didn't have to worry about buying it or making it. **It is cafeteria food, after all**. There were some things that they sold that were great."

Q "**The food here is junk**. ODU is ranked the sixth unhealthiest campus, I believe. Students here are fat. We have Taco Bell and Chick-fil-A. That's about it."

Q "I think I ate a lot healthier when I lived in the dorms, even though **the food was seriously disgusting**."

Q "The food on campus isn't fabulous, but **the Webb Center is pretty good**. We have a restaurant at night called the House of Blue. The food in the dining hall is edible. But who would trust it?"

Q "The first time I got there, I was like, '**Wow, cake every day**!' Then I was like, 'Gross.'"

STUDENT AUTHOR: Cafeteria food is stereotypically bad. In fact, cafeterias in general are often gross and just not fun to eat in. ODU has taken steps to remedy this stereotypical problem with café spots like House of Blue. But still, ODU students are sticking to their guns—on-campus food here is probably not the best thing for you. For the money you pay, the food could most definitely be better.

Student Body
African American:	23%	Male/Female:	42/58%
Asian American:	6%	Out-of-State:	8%
Hispanic:	3%	International:	2%
Native American:	1%	Unknown:	0%
White:	65%		

Popular Faiths: Religion isn't even visible on campus, although there are on-campus groups.

Gay Pride: Organizations such as ODU OUT are really active on campus, probably even more so than a lot of organizations—but they don't steal the scene.

Economic Status: ODU's students run the gamut, but a lot of students receive financial aid, and most are at ease because of parental aid.

Students Speak Out
ON DORMS

Q "The dorms are really clean, especially the newer ones like Powhatan. The University Village is new, but I don't think I'd want to live over there. A man once got shot and was killed there. Not a good environment—it's really close to a bad part of Norfolk. If you're looking for a dorm to stay, **freshmen should probably choose Rogers East**."

Q "**The dorms are tiny**. If you're used to sleeping in a huge bed, forget about it—you can only fit a twin in those small rooms. I used to live in Rogers Main, and we had two people in a dorm and four people shared a bathroom. And the bathrooms were kind of gross."

STUDENT AUTHOR: **A big problem with campus housing is more so based on security than the dormitories themselves; those are fine. They come furnished. But the locations of the dorms and apartments are not all that close to ODU's campus. The dorms themselves are safe, so long as students are actually inside them—but when walking alone at night from a class, do it in groups, or not at all.**

Did You Know?
25% of undergrads live on campus.

Students Speak Out
ON GUYS & GIRLS

Q "**The girls at ODU seem really approachable** most of the time. You could go and sit down and have a conversation with a girl you've never met before, and she'd be real cool about it. The whole campus is relaxed like that."

Q "We here at Old Dominion University are an attractive bunch, but divided **still in our cliques of style and social archetypes**. It's a broader version of high school at the very core."

Q "It's so funny here—everyone looks really good. And if they don't, they still dress really well and keep themselves well groomed. . . . If you come here looking for someone to hook up with or to date, the school is so diverse that **there is bound to be someone here for you**."

STUDENT AUTHOR: **The good thing about the guys and girls at ODU is that most of them are—on the average—extremely good-looking. The male-to-female ratio is pretty balanced here, so the chances for hookups are high, and flings as well. Clubs and other situations can be perfect for the proverbial one-night stand. But whether you're looking for a fling or a relationship, you'll most likely be happy with your options.**

Tradition

Climbing the Lion
It's tradition for seniors to climb the lion outside of Webb and get their picture taken with them on it before they graduate. The danger involved is that any senior that is caught will get expelled from the school.

Overall School Spirit
Old Dominion might seem apathetic during the school year, what with school work and jobs piling up on each other, students barely have enough time for themselves. But when Homecoming comes around, students are eager to paint their faces and join in the parades and the fun.

Students Speak Out
ON ATHLETICS

Q "**Basketball dominates** this campus. No question about it."

Q "When I think of ODU athletics, **I automatically think about the Lady Monarchs**. In fact, I didn't even know we had a baseball team until someone asked me if I wanted to go to one of their games or something. Is that bad?"

Q "I always hear about ODU's women's basketball team, so I rarely think about any of the other teams. From what I know, **we don't have really cool sports or intramurals**. That would be so much better than basketball."

Q "I'm glad **they opened up the University Village Gym**. It's really nice, even though it is kind of small."

STUDENT AUTHOR: **Whether you're looking to join a team or just hit up your nearest gym to quickly shed some pounds, ODU has the facilities and the opportunities. Sports don't really take center stage when compared to academics, but with all of the dangers of the Freshman 15, it's advised that students get to the gym often as possible.**

Students Speak Out
ON DRUG SCENE

Q "**There are drugs at parties around ODU but not at ODU itself**. I mean—it's a university, so you can't expect for there not to be drug use. I know when I go to parties, I usually always see people drinking and smoking marijuana— although the harder drugs I've never seen people using. But ODU is kind of in a bad area already, so if there were harder drugs—and I'm sure there are—I wouldn't be surprised."

Q "I don't know much about the drug scene. I think it all depends on who you hang out with. It's mostly an underground thing, and **it isn't really a visible 'threat,' or whatever**."

STUDENT AUTHOR: Very rarely can you find a student who will admit to taking or using drugs other than alcohol. However, that isn't to say that drug use doesn't happen on ODU's campus. Alcohol is the most obvious activity, but marijuana is most definitely the drug of choice on campus. But, virtually all of the students here are good at keeping their night life separate from their academic one, and there is no pressure for non-users to start.

18:1	Student-to-Faculty Ratio
80%	Freshman Retention Rate
22%	Four-Year Graduation Rate
79%	Financial Aid Applicants Receiving Aid

Students Speak Out
SAFETY & SECURITY

Q "**I believe a lot of people think it's worse than it actually is**. I've heard people say that 42nd is so dangerous, or it's so ghetto. But really, I've walked up and down 42nd Street in the middle of the night plastered and sober, and nothing has happened so far. I don't feel unsafe here. When you go down to 38th, that's when it's kinda creepy. All these people are walking around, and it's just really ghetto."

Q "There are many cops around here, but they don't have much interaction with the students. There are a lot of them **watching and making sure we're safe**."

Q "**I don't think Norfolk is all that dangerous**. It does look really scary at night, though."

STUDENT AUTHOR: It needs to be said that Norfolk just isn't very safe. Old Dominion police have made several efforts to improve the situation on campus, but the crisis really stems from the University's surrounding environment.

Questions?

For more inside information and survival tips, pick up College Prowler's full-length book on this school, written by an actual student! Check it out at *www.collegeprowler.com*.

Students Speak Out
ON OVERALL EXPERIENCE

Q "**A lot of times ODU gets a bad rap because it's still a growing school**. It's young. It has a lot of evolving to do, and so some people turn a nose up at it. I love this school, though, and I am glad to attend. It's fun growing as a person along with the school and looking back and saying, 'Oh, I remember when . . .'"

Q "The classes I've taken here have been so wonderful. **Professors are insightful and willing to take time out of their schedule to help you** if you have any questions. And it most definitely has the feel of a busy, bustling campus. There is so much going on, especially during the literary festival and the first few weeks of each semester. It's an engrossing experience."

Q "Overall, my experience is good here. I plan to graduate here. I think that there could be more events that ODU could sponsor. The **school could have a lot more interaction with the students**—that would better my experience here."

Q "Other than the fact that **I have to drive for 20 minutes just to get to a random store**, I like ODU."

STUDENT AUTHOR: Students gripe about workload and professors just like at any other university, but Old Dominion provides its students with so many opportunities to explore the world with study abroad programs, internship opportunities, and hands-on job experience that it is almost impossible for a student to fail in anything that they do—be it academic, athletic, or social. Old Dominion can simply be an institution for education, but most of the student body does not treat it as that.

Penn State University

210 Old Main; State College, PA 16802
(814) 865-4700; www.psu.edu

THE BASICS:

Acceptance Rate: 51%
Setting: Rural
F-T Undergrads: 36,749

SAT Range: 1100–1300*
Control: Public
Tuition: $24,248

Most Popular Majors: Business, Engineering, Communication, Social Sciences, Education, Psychology

*of 1600

Academics	B+	Guys	B
Local Atmosphere	B	Girls	B+
Safety & Security	B+	Athletics	A
Computers	B	Nightlife	B+
Facilities	B+	Greek Life	A
Campus Dining	B	Drug Scene	B
Off-Campus Dining	B+	Campus Strictness	B-
Campus Housing	C	Parking	D
Off-Campus Housing	A-	Transportation	B+
Diversity	C-	Weather	C

Students Speak Out
ON ACADEMICS

Q "You'll have **helpful, interesting professors**, and you'll also have know-it-all, uninvolved professors. The majority of classes are large, so it's hard to get to a one-on-one basis with the professors."

Q "The teachers at Penn State are, for the most part, really cool. Everyone here likes the sociology classes because those classes have the coolest teachers. There's work involved with all classes, but look for classes that **allow discussions and debates**."

Q "I think the teachers are good here. They know what they are talking about, but you do run into the **huge lecture classes**. Some TAs barely speak English, but I hear that happens elsewhere, too."

Q "The teachers are like prizes in Cracker Jack boxes: some are cool and worth trying for, while **others simply suck**. Some are here to do research and that's all they care about, so their classes put you to sleep faster than NyQuil."

STUDENT AUTHOR: From the foreign grad student who barely speaks English to the wise old department head who practically invented your major, all kinds of instructors can be found at Penn State. The majority of the professors are middle-aged and quite accomplished in their fields. Many of the teachers are there because they want to be, but there is, of course, a minority of professors who are more interested in their own research than instructing students.

Students Speak Out
ON LOCAL ATMOSPHERE

Q "State College is a relaxing, friendly college town that can make anyone feel at home. There isn't much to visit, though, since we really are in the **middle of nowhere**."

Q "The town is great. Everyone is there for Penn State. There is a lot of pride in being a Nittany Lion. There are tons of stores selling just PSU stuff. On the down side, University Park is in the middle of nowhere. Pittsburgh and Philly are both about three hours away; **New York City is about five**."

Q "It's entirely a college town, dominated by the University. The atmosphere is laid-back and that of a society run by 20-somethings and 20-somethings alone. It's kind of like *Lord of the Flies*, but with booze. **Don't leave town alone**, especially if you are going to interact with locals. Otherwise, it's worth a visit to Bellefonte, the drive-in theater, and Penn's Cave."

Q "If you're keen on drinking, there are more than enough bars to suit your fancy. There's also a little bit of shopping to do, although most of it is **Penn State apparel**, unfortunately."

STUDENT AUTHOR: State College has been fairly judged as a party town. The town's population and activity level rises and falls with the academic calendar. During the day, State College is a decent shopping ground for any 15–25 year old. The surrounding area is almost always undergoing development, with new shopping plazas, restaurants, and movie theaters being added every year.

5 Best Things	5 Worst Things
1 Work hard, play hard	1 Rural isolation
2 School spirit	2 Alcohol-centered culture
3 Joe Paterno	3 No parking
4 Beautiful landscape	4 No diversity
5 THON	5 Lack of dance clubs

Students Speak Out
ON FACILITIES

Q "All of the facilities here are really nice, and they are **relatively new**. There are plenty of places for sports, and there's just always somewhere to go."

Q "The facilities on campus are **above average**. Most of the facilities are handicap-friendly, and there are computer centers in almost every corner of the campus."

Q "The facilities are really good here. There are different gyms on campus for basketball, volleyball, and weightlifting—all that the YMCA has to offer—and then some. The student union (the HUB) was newly renovated a few years ago and is very modern. There are fast food joints, places to study, convention rooms, an art gallery, and a **record-breaking fish tank**."

Q "The facilities at Penn State vary in quality. Some of the computer labs are really nice, and the same goes for the athletic facilities and the HUB. The White building is shiny and new, and the old gym at **Rec Hall is not quite as new** and pretty, but it is still functional. The same goes for the computer labs."

Q "The HUB is a **teenage wasteland** come to life."

STUDENT AUTHOR: The student center, known as the HUB, is one of the nicest buildings on campus. An epicenter for all kinds of student activities, the HUB houses various fast-food spots, a Starbucks, an art gallery, study lounges, game rooms, and an auditorium with free movies. Penn State has every type of facility available to students: Olympic-sized swimming pools, full gyms, ice rinks, tennis courts, and more.

Famous Alumni

Charlie Dent, Jonathan Frakes, Roosevelt Grier, Franco Harris, Larry Johnson

Students Speak Out
ON CAMPUS DINING

Q "The dining hall food at Penn State is good when compared to **cafeteria food** at most other large universities."

Q "The food is excellent in the HUB if one is willing to pay the price. The 10 percent discount that the HUB offers is not enough for most students. Food in the commons is generally **nothing more than filling**."

Q "I don't like the food, and there is always some form of chicken for dinner. In East Halls, there is a sandwich shop that is good. **The Big O is good** if you have it sparingly, but it is expensive."

Q "On campus, the best quality and variety is in the West Halls dining commons. To grab a snack and do a little studying, Otto's Cafe in the Kern building is efficient and recently remodeled. The HUB has **tons of perks**—its central location makes it a good meeting spot. Even so, the HUB is best during non-peak hours."

Q "There is **quite a variety** of food on campus, and most of the restaurants are in the HUB building."

STUDENT AUTHOR: Some meals are universally enjoyed, while others will leave you gagging. The A-La Board meal plan is required for all undergrads living in dorms. No two halls serve the same menu. Depending on the size of the hall, options such as salad and pasta bars, stir-fry stations, and mini-bakeries may also be available. Each commons building also has a smaller alternative to the dining hall with different hours. There is also the HUB to fall back on, which is similar to a food court at a mall.

Student Body

African American:	4%	Male/Female:	55/45%
Asian American:	6%	Out-of-State:	25%
Hispanic:	4%	International:	3%
Native American:	<1%	Unknown:	0%
White:	83%		

Popular Faiths: There are about 46 active religious organizations on campus, the majority of which is affiliated with Christianity.

Gay Pride: The gay community actively participates and often spearheads debates and events promoting acceptance, understanding, and safe sex.

Economic Status: Thanks to generous and expansive financial aid programs, PSU represents a broad spectrum of economic backgrounds.

Students Speak Out
ON DORMS

Q "The dorms are horrible. They're dirty and small. However, the nicest dorms are in West Halls and the dorms in **the Honors College**."

Q "East is a great place for freshmen to live and meet other freshmen. West is the nicest dorm, but it is too quiet and uneventful for me. South is in a great location (right on College Avenue) and has decent-size rooms. Pollock has a great location and **fairly large rooms**."

Q "The freshmen dorms (East Halls) resemble little prison cells. You meet a lot of people and make friends. West has the best rooms, but **the kids there aren't as friendly**. You look forward to off-campus housing after the mandatory freshman year in the dorms."

STUDENT AUTHOR: **The dorms at Penn State vary widely in size and quality. In the campus housing booklet that advertises each dorm area, East Halls comes across as the best dorm. This is where nearly all incoming freshmen end up, but student opinion will tell you that it's, by far, the worst dorm. They are the farthest from central campus and downtown, and the rooms are the smallest.**

? Did You Know?
37% of undergrads live on campus.

Students Speak Out
ON GUYS & GIRLS

Q "The guys seem to be far more immature than the girls. Most guys don't like serious dating, so if you're looking for a relationship, good luck! And obviously, **the girls are cute**!"

Q "There are a lot of good-looking girls here, and it's always nice to see how the girls go out to filthy house parties in their skimpiest attire. It's **kind of funny** also."

Q "There is definitely a variety, and parties here can look like *People* magazine."

Q "There are a lot of good-looking women on campus: **blondes and brunettes**, as well as girls from all races and countries."

STUDENT AUTHOR: **On a Thursday, Friday, or Saturday night at PSU, the majority of girls get pretty dressed up, guys make themselves presentable, and people look to meet each other. True to the party school stigma, students seem to lean towards hookups rather than serious connections. It's also tradition that the student body gets hotter in the spring when clothes come off and the lawns are crowded with sunbathers galore.**

Traditions

The Mifflin Streak
Every year, the students of Mifflin Hall streak across campus. No one quite knows why, but it is a long-standing tradition.

THON
A 48-hour dance marathon intended to raise money for charity. One year, Penn State students raised $3,547,716 for the Four-Diamonds Fund.

Overall School Spirit
School spirit at Penn State is stronger than most schools you can name. Nittany Lion Pride is taken very seriously, as is respect for coach Joe Paterno and the famed Lion Shrine.

Students Speak Out
ON ATHLETICS

Q "Varsity sports are very big on our campus because **Penn State is Division I**, which means that in order to participate in PSU sports, you have to have a scholarship or be an absolutely amazing athlete."

Q "Varsity sports are great. The school spirit, when a sports team is doing well, is **tremendous**."

Q "Football games will send a chill down your spine when you attend your first game. And everyone I know who is **involved in IM sports** meets a great group of people and has a great time."

Q "Penn State football and JoePa reign supreme. At PSU, **tailgating is a contact sport**. We have championship volleyball, soccer, and hockey."

STUDENT AUTHOR: **Football is a big part of Penn State life. Other varsity sports pale in comparison to the aura of intensity that surrounds every home football game. Tailgating is a full-time, three-day occupation. If, for some insane reason, you'd prefer a sport other than football, Penn State does offer just about every IM sport from whiffleball to kayaking.**

Students Speak Out
ON DRUG SCENE

Q "Drugs are present, but in no way are they dominating. Drug pushers try to stay in hiding, as **Penn State is very anti-drug**."

Q "There is a lot of pot around; nothing too hard, though. There is **some 'E' and coke around**, but it's not open."

Q "**It's not a big problem**. If you look for it, it's there. But I dare say that the drug scene is more prominent in my hometown than away at school, though."

STUDENT AUTHOR: **Illicit drugs are available and relatively easy to get, but by no means have they taken over State College. The most prevalent drugs around campus are pot and ecstasy, though others exist in the area as well. The former may be a nuisance if you happen to live in a dorm room that overlooks an entrance used for smoking, and the latter is usually confined to bars and other off-campus areas. Alcohol is a problem for both the campus and the surrounding area, especially during football weekends.**

17:1	Student-to-Faculty Ratio
92%	Freshman Retention Rate
60%	Four-Year Graduation Rate
74%	Financial Aid Applicants Receiving Aid

Students Speak Out
SAFETY & SECURITY

Q "I have never had any safety problems on campus. There were a few incidents of people **breaking into dorms**, but I never knew any of the victims."

Q "Security is good here—almost too good. There's a ton of employees in the campus police force that like to show you how important they are. **They hold shifts 24/7** to make sure we can all sleep at night."

Q "**Security and safety are great here**. They don't seem to skimp on it. If you need an escort home, they'll provide one for you. If they can't, they'll call a cab to pick you up (and they'll pay for it, too). Campus police walk the campus checking up on the security of all the buildings."

STUDENT AUTHOR: **Security is a constant concern on the Penn State campus. Dorms are now on 24-hour lockdown. While dorm lockdown does make it harder for any random person to wander in, students do use their cards to bring in outside friends, and often let strangers in by politely holding the door, assuming they live there.**

Questions?
For more inside information and survival tips, pick up College Prowler's full-length book on this school, written by an actual student! Check it out at *www.collegeprowler.com*.

Students Speak Out
ON OVERALL EXPERIENCE

Q "I love Penn State. I wish to be nowhere else. The atmosphere is relaxed, and it is a nationally-recognized **Big 10 school**. There are lots of ways to get involved in different organizations, and the school spirit is tremendous."

Q "Penn State has something for everyone. **Try to get a car** if you can because it gets boring, but that can happen anywhere. I mean after living somewhere for a while, you do everything and then start looking for new options."

Q "Basically, there are two things that govern PSU: **drinking and football**. There are always parties going on, tons of frats and sororities, and when you do turn 21 or obtain a fake ID, there are plenty of bars."

Q "I have had **a splendid time** at school because of the people I've met and the subjects I've studied. I could've gone somewhere else, but I don't regret coming here. After a while, you do start to grow attached to this place and the people. I'm actually surprised there isn't a wall around campus."

STUDENT AUTHOR: **Despite common reservations about the location and climate, most Penn State students are fiercely loyal to their alma mater. Penn State boasts one of the largest alumni populations in the United States; graduates are proud of their degrees, and employers recognize the University's name immediately. Aside from academics, PSU is also known for its social scene, especially in relation to sports and parties. Nittany Lion football is a national draw and a point of pride for both the University and the town of State College.**

Pepperdine University

24255 Pacific Coast Highway; Malibu, CA 90263
(310) 506-4000; www.pepperdine.edu

THE BASICS:

Acceptance Rate: 35%
Setting: Suburban
F-T Undergrads: 2,934

SAT Range: 1690–2020*
Control: Private
Tuition: $36,650

Most Popular Majors: Business, Communications, Social Sciences, Psychology, Visual/Performing Arts

*of 2400

Academics	B	Guys	A
Local Atmosphere	B	Girls	A+
Safety & Security	A	Athletics	C+
Computers	B	Nightlife	B-
Facilities	B+	Greek Life	B+
Campus Dining	A-	Drug Scene	B+
Off-Campus Dining	B-	Campus Strictness	D
Campus Housing	A+	Parking	B-
Off-Campus Housing	C	Transportation	D
Diversity	A-	Weather	A+

Students Speak Out
ON ACADEMICS

Q "I found most teachers to be easily accessible and more than willing to help you with the class and its related material—except for the general education classes with hundreds of people in them. Teachers in these classes **seemed annoyed** with student questions, and they'd shun their TAs."

Q "Ironically, my most straightforward and non-religious class was religion. Expect **lots of ex-pastors** for professors."

Q "The **teachers are friendly** and are always willing to help. They will invite you over to their houses for dinner, and they'll give you their home numbers, if you ever have any questions at all. They can do this because of the small class sizes. Also, they all live on or close to campus."

Q "The teachers at Pepperdine are okay. I have taken classes at a community college during the summer, and the teachers there were a lot better, as far as being **open-minded and sensitive** to the needs of their students. But then again, I haven't had every teacher on campus, so this cannot be entirely accurate."

STUDENT AUTHOR: Pepperdine people seem genuinely satisfied with their instructors and their courses. Class sizes matter more than an incoming student might expect, and Pepperdine offers some of the smallest, most intimate classes in California. Also, the excellent international programs are an opportunity not to be missed.

Students Speak Out
ON LOCAL ATMOSPHERE

Q "Malibu is a very **nice, sophisticated town**. It's right next to the beach, which is really cool. The campus is almost like a resort. You don't really think of it as a school when you first get there."

Q "I found Malibu nightlife to be **excruciatingly boring**. It includes two bars in town and house parties. There are no cool frat parties due to the lack of frat houses. The one thing Malibu does not lack is beaches; there are many beautiful ones that I would highly recommend."

Q "Pepperdine is a **pretty isolated** place, tucked back next to the coast. If you want to have contact with other universities, your only real bet is to go to the sporting events, or meet through Greek organizations. No one would ever call Malibu a happening place, because other than going to the beach, there is nothing to do."

Q "It is a **gorgeous campus**; you will not find one that is any nicer than Pepperdine. It's right on the ocean, with most of the classrooms affording spectacular views."

STUDENT AUTHOR: To some, Malibu is an irritating 20-minute drive from anything interesting to see or do; while to others, it's a mere 20-minute drive from fabulous Santa Monica, or a thrilling half-hour jaunt away from LA. Some scoff at the trappings of wealth and celebrity that Malibu so quaintly celebrates, while others head down the hill to the Coffee Bean to sit and watch for movie stars. Everyone can agree, though, that Malibu is a truly unique place to go to college.

5 Best Things	5 Worst Things
1 The view	**1** Strict RAs
2 International programs	**2** Lack of diversity
3 Small classes	**3** Monotonous nightlife
4 Attractive people	**4** Long commutes
5 Fabulous location	**5** The "Peppervine"

Students Speak Out
ON FACILITIES

Q "The facilities are mostly **nicely kept**. The gym is great, as is the pool and hot tub. The student center suffers from the abuse of students, but it remains in decent shape."

Q "The facilities are very nice and pretty much new, for the most part. The gym is **kind of small**, but it is free. There is a pool and hot tub, too. The library is kind of small, but then there is also the law library on top of the hill."

Q "The campus has **nice, new facilities**. It's a small school, so you don't always have all the amenities of a big school, but it's quaint and the natural scenery is incredible. Pepperdine is on a hill that overlooks the gorgeous Pacific Ocean. You can't beat the view here."

Q "The weight room is sadly small. The buildings are nice, but after **four years of stucco**, you tend to crave some sort of architectural variation. The student centers (HAWC and Sandbar) are very comfortable, and usually filled with people to spend time with. The Sandbar looks like a spot from Chuck E. Cheese's, but it's all a matter of taste, right?"

STUDENT AUTHOR: **Pepperdine's beautiful campus is maintained in such a way that everything is white, immaculate, and uniform at all times. And what the architecture lacks in diversity and history, it makes up for with singleness of purpose and a becalming sterilized unity. One area in which Pepperdine could still improve itself is its single undergraduate library; the shelves seem filled with fragile, dusty tomes.**

Famous Alumni

Dain Blanton, Dough Christia, Bob Ctvrtlik, James K. Hahn, Montell Jordan, Bill Weir, Randy Wolf

Students Speak Out
ON CAMPUS DINING

Q "The Caf makes the **best veggie burgers** and fries I have ever tasted. I never really ventured off campus, because I always had a bunch of points left over."

Q "Make friends with underclassmen, because you never know when you'll find yourself with no points, and craving an **ice-blended mocha** with soymilk and a shot of raspberry."

Q "The food is **pretty good**. The dining system is à la carte, unlike most schools. You use a point system for what you take, so you can't go up again and again for more food. At least it kind of keeps you from pigging out."

Q "The food is great, compared to other schools. Go anywhere else, and you'll complain. Go to Pepperdine, and you'll be like, '**wow**.'"

Q "Campus food is awesome; they actually **served shark one night** for dinner. People complain about it, but I guess they haven't experienced bad dorm food."

STUDENT AUTHOR: **It's certainly safe to say that Pepperdine can number itself among the better-tasting American universities. The basic meal plan is more than sufficient, even for those who just can't resist getting double heaping portions of the ever-reliable London Broil, or succulent pork tenderloin sliced right before their eyes by the Waves Café personnel. Don't worry, there are also plenty of vegetarian offerings.**

Student Body

African American:	7%	Male/Female:	45/55%
Asian American:	10%	Out-of-State:	50%
Hispanic:	10%	International:	7%
Native American:	1%	Unknown:	5%
White:	59%		

Political Activity: Pepperdine falls somewhere between quietly conservative and blissfully apolitical.

Gay Pride: You can find liberal thought and social acceptance at Pepperdine, but don't expect them to run rampant.

Economic Status: The stereotypical Pepperdine student drives a BMW or a Porsche and never wears the same pair of designer jeans or high heels twice.

Students Speak Out
ON DORMS

Q "The dorms, I must admit, are **incredibly snazzy**. I've never seen dorms at another college to match them, and they played a big role in my decision to come to Pepperdine."

Q "In comparison to other schools, the dorms are like **palaces**—but they are still dorms. You want a dorm close to the center of campus. The Greek dorms, as they are called, are quite a walk."

Q "There are no coed dorms until you get into the Towers, which are where graduate students and upperclassmen get to live. No boys are allowed in your room after midnight, or in your dorm after one in the morning. Some people there are really **strict with the rules**—I'm talking students—so they might narc on you and get you kicked out."

STUDENT AUTHOR: **You know the campus housing is pretty impressive when such an affluent student body tends to use terms like "palace" and "castle" to describe it. Indeed, freshman dorms well reflect the University's eagerness to ensconce its students in comfort and splendor. The dorms' restrictive policies can grate on students who aren't used to random room checks.**

Did You Know?
67% of undergrads live on campus.

Students Speak Out
ON GUYS & GIRLS

Q "The **dating scene is awful**. There aren't nearly enough guys for girls, and the guys aren't always dating material. They're better as friends."

Q "Guys are cookie-cutter, Abercrombie-wearing surfers. Once in a while, you get your attractive, pensive, introspective bloke who loves literature. He is usually already dating someone. The girls have blonde hair, tanned skin, and carry around Louis Vuitton handbags. There is a small population of hippie-type alternative men and women. But, if you were an outsider looking in, you'd think the campus was made of all **model-type men and women** (a sort of Stepford University)."

STUDENT AUTHOR: **To sum up the general opinion on campus: a) the girls are hot, b) so are the guys, but c) a lot of them are gay, and d) no one dates. Students tend to conform, in terms of style and personality, and walking around Pepperdine is a little like watching a movie or attending a fashion show. Tight clothing and high heels do predominate, and accessories bearing the names of venerable fashion avatars are a mainstay.**

Traditions

Midnight Madness
Students pack the Firestone Field House to watch the men's and women's basketball teams take the court for their first practice at 12 midnight.

AWOL
The week-long senior sendoff—"A Week of Leaving."

Overall School Spirit
A few students dislike Pepperdine explicitly, and most students are happy to be Waves, but aren't particularly effusive about it.

Students Speak Out
ON ATHLETICS

Q "The sports get a lot of attention because we are good at a lot of things, **especially basketball**, tennis, and baseball. There is definitely a lot of school spirit and IM sport participation."

Q "Unfortunately, Pepperdine doesn't have much school spirit when it comes to sports. **IMs are fairly big**. I don't know about fan support, but lots of students are involved in IMs. Everyone goes to the basketball games. Those are fun, especially the big games."

Q "**Sports are huge**, but more like admired from afar, like a local team would be for a small town. We all go to the games, but no one really knows the players. They're a tight-knit group. Intramurals are where it's at, especially the rugby team. Very fun, very ferocious."

STUDENT AUTHOR: **Students can't seem to agree on the athletics scene at Pepperdine. They do agree, though, that men's basketball is by far the most popular sport, essentially occupying the vacuum left by the absence of a football team. Even so, the stands do not necessarily fill up for every game.**

Students Speak Out
ON DRUG SCENE

Q "It's a Christian school. **Not many do drugs**."

Q "There are a lot of underground pot smokers. **Some cocaine**, apparently, though I never saw it myself."

Q "There is definitely a good percentage of students on campus that **smoke weed**, and I'm sure there is other drug use. But, it's nothing out of control. Alcohol use, like on any campus, is definitely present. Not to say everyone drinks, but I bet over half the student population does."

STUDENT AUTHOR: Reading the disparity of student perceptions of the Pepperdine drug scene tells a lot about drug use on campus. Some have never noticed much of a drug scene at all, while others insist that expensive drugs are "very big" on campus. A logical inference is that whatever serious drugs students snort, swallow, or inhale are being used either off campus, or in an extremely covert manner. If they weren't, it would not be long before a sharp RA or Public Safety officer would catch the offending students.

14:1	Student-to-Faculty Ratio
88%	Freshman Retention Rate
74%	Four-Year Graduation Rate
67%	Financial Aid Applicants Receiving Aid

Students Speak Out
SAFETY & SECURITY

Q "I've always felt **extremely safe** at Pepperdine. It's a totally self-enclosed campus, and the only two entrances are monitored 24 hours a day by guards. Students joke that it's not hard to sneak on campus, and that's pretty much true, but I've never heard of any incidents that would make me feel uncomfortable."

Q "Public Safety is often **overbearing**, but I suppose as a result of that, I never feel endangered really."

Q "I've never had any concerns about my safety or security. As long as you use **common sense** and don't leave your laptop in the middle of campus, I don't think you have anything to worry about."

STUDENT AUTHOR: Whatever concerns Pepperdine students may have about their chosen school, safety obviously is not one of them. Every so often, one will hear of a theft or two, but hardly anyone ever expresses much anxiety over the security of their belongings.

> **Questions?**
> For more inside information and survival tips, pick up College Prowler's full-length book on this school, written by an actual student! Check it out at *www.collegeprowler.com*.

Students Speak Out
ON OVERALL EXPERIENCE

Q "Pepperdine is the **best university** in existence, and I'll tell that to anyone who asks. The opportunities given to students here are just awesome, most significantly in the area of international programs. I've been lucky enough to participate in three of them, and they completely changed my life and made my college experience."

Q "My experience has been great. **I love it**, and I don't wish I were anywhere else. If you're worried about being homesick, don't be. I got over it in a hurry. I went a long way and knew nobody, and I had a blast. I can't recommend it strongly enough."

Q "I'm **having a great time** at Pepperdine. I only wish I was elsewhere when I miss big Southern football. It's a once-in-a-lifetime experience, though. Also, I should note that Pep has amazing overseas programs that about half the students take advantage of. I'm going to London next spring to study."

STUDENT AUTHOR: Most Pepperdine students are happy with the college they picked, their minor critiques of particulars giving way to an overall appreciation of the experience and benefits Pepperdine has granted them that no other school could. While some find the small campus and even smaller student population comforting, others find that Pepperdine's quaintness inhibits their growth and restricts their social life. There's nothing small, though, about the 125-foot cross that stands at the forefront of the Malibu campus, whose job it is to proclaim loudly and clearly that Pepperdine's mission is not merely academic.

Pitzer College

1050 North Mills Avenue; Claremont, CA 91711
(909) 621-8000; www.pitzer.edu

THE BASICS:

Acceptance Rate: 22%
Setting: Suburban
F-T Undergrads: 976

SAT Range: 1160–1370*
Control: Private
Tuition: $34,500

Most Popular Majors: Social Sciences, Psychology, Visual/Performing Arts, Communications, English

of 1600

Academics	B+	Guys	B-
Local Atmosphere	C+	Girls	B
Safety & Security	A-	Athletics	C
Computers	A-	Nightlife	B
Facilities	B+	Greek Life	N/A
Campus Dining	A-	Drug Scene	B
Off-Campus Dining	C-	Campus Strictness	A
Campus Housing	B	Parking	B
Off-Campus Housing	D-	Transportation	D-
Diversity	B+	Weather	A

Students Speak Out
ON ACADEMICS

Q "Many of the teachers respect the students as equal peers, and almost **every class is somewhat unconventional**."

Q "The professors are so laid back, but incredibly smart, too. They are all unique and have so much experience that **they push students to new intellectual heights**. It's not unusual to have a class in the outdoor classroom or for your professor to sit out on the mounds and have lunch with you and your classmates."

Q "Most of the **classes were interesting**, but every now and then, you run into a subject that is just going to be boring—there is no avoiding it."

Q "The faculty makes Pitzer. They are wonderful people and brilliant scholars. They are also very conscious of what makes a class boring, and I think they do their very best not to be boring. There are, of course, **a few jerks in the faculty**, and they don't get along very well with one another (which is sometimes hilariously entertaining)."

STUDENT AUTHOR: Almost everyone agrees that the professors at Pitzer are the fundamental basis of the school. Every student at Pitzer has been influenced by a professor at some point in their college career. Profs here really go the extra mile and take care of their students. One of the greatest things about Pitzer is that a student can take a course at Pitzer or at any other of the Claremont Colleges. This allows for a small-school atmosphere with large-school resources.

Students Speak Out
ON LOCAL ATMOSPHERE

Q "Claremont is the most beautiful town in this area. It's stuck between two giant toilets (Pomona and San Bernardino). It has a cool, calming aspect in the middle of city life. The Village has **plenty of lovely shopping** and park benches upon which to read."

Q "Take advantage of the **proximity to Los Angeles**. Go see some art exhibits and take in a few concerts. The nearby 99-cent store is also a college student must—it's fabulous."

Q "Claremont is **boring, snotty, Republican, yuppie, and suburban**. There are a few good restaurants, and a few good shops (Rhino Records/Video Paradiso being standouts). Good luck finding a movie theater within walking distance, and give up your preconceptions about 'college towns' because the city of Claremont hates the colleges."

Q "The five-college Claremont community is **like nothing else in the world**. The small-college atmosphere combined with the spectrum of classes to choose from is unique and amazing."

STUDENT AUTHOR: There is always something to do in Southern California. Many students find the town of Claremont to be to quiet and dull, especially at night when most establishments are closed by 9 or 10 p.m. If you have a car, or a friend with a car, there are many options available. The Los Angeles area has activities going on to suit every taste from theater and shows to nightclubs and parties.

5 Best Things	5 Worst Things
1 Professors	1 The dorms
2 Small class size	2 Pitzer gym
3 Student involvement	3 Traffic
4 5C resources	4 False 5C stereotypes
5 Everyone is nice	5 Overzealous protestors

Students Speak Out
ON FACILITIES

Q "The facilities are very nice for such a small campus. We are lucky to be able to **take advantage of other student centers** and joint athletic teams on other campuses."

Q "The Gold Student Center rocks, although many of our **other buildings are very old**."

Q "The facilities of the five colleges as a whole are **very nice**, though at Pitzer they are a bit lacking. There is a current plan in action to improve the campus greatly."

Q "We have many facilities available due to the fact that we are a five-college consortium. **Our gym has a rock-climbing wall** and is located in the student center. The student literary journal and senate officers are upstairs in the student center as well."

Q "**Facilities are decent**, though most of the other colleges in the 5Cs have nicer ones."

Q "The fitness room is **getting better and better** each year."

STUDENT AUTHOR: Pitzer's heritage is reflected in campus aesthetics. The buildings and walkways are representative of the 1960s architectural design. At present, Pitzer is undertaking to redo campus; so many features of the campus (dorms, classrooms, office spaces, and campus layout) will be changed in the near future. One of the biggest highlights of the campus is the grounds. The gardens surrounding campus and the Grove House are beautiful. Also, if you play college sports, there is the well equipped Rains gym for your use.

Famous Alumni

David Bloom, Max Brooks, Mablean Ephriam, Mary Beth Garber, Jane Memel, John Landgraf

Students Speak Out
ON CAMPUS DINING

Q "At the Claremont Colleges, you can eat in any dining hall—enjoy it! **The food is not too bad**, although a little greasy. The food service management is very responsive to student suggestions."

Q "The dining hall is mediocre. As a third year student, I have gotten a bit tired of the same food, day in and day out. **The salad bar is excellent** the first 200 times. The best thing about Pitzer dining hall is that they try to provide for vegetarians, vegans, and carnivores as much as possible."

Q "The dining hall is **sometimes amazing** and sometimes drab."

Q "The dining hall is **good for only one thing— lunch**. Other than that, I think you are better off going to one of the other dining facilities."

Q "The Grove House has the best food within a 50-mile radius. It is **organic, fresh, home cooked**, and delicious!"

STUDENT AUTHOR: Pitzer students have six all-you-can-eat dining halls to choose from. Quantity is not an issue. Some students find that they get bored with on-campus dining. Flex Dollars, used at non-cafeteria eateries, helps to diversify the menu, yet for some it's still inadequate. For these students, it is best to opt out of the meal plan. Many students turn to off-campus dining to pacify the adventurous eater within. With LA's fantastic culinary, this isn't hard. Most students like to complain, but when asked sincerely, they admit the food is good.

Student Body

African American:	6%	Male/Female:	41/59%
Asian American:	9%	Out-of-State:	45%
Hispanic:	15%	International:	3%
Native American:	<1%	Unknown:	25%
White:	41%		

Popular Faiths: There are both large Christian and Jewish populations on campus.

Gay Pride: The Queer Resource Center and the Queeralicious Club promote gay-straight alliance and a sense of unity amongst the 5C gay community.

Economic Status: A majority of the student body is from moderate to wealthy backgrounds.

Students Speak Out
ON DORMS

Q "I hated living on campus because, even in the quiet hall, it was **often too loud to sleep**, there was no privacy, and it was hot. However living on campus means you can meet people and adjust to college life."

Q "The dorms are fairly nice, though **a bit on the small size**, compared to the average college dorm. The sooner you can get into Mead Hall, the better, as the living arrangements are nicer, and there are more lounges."

Q "The dorms are not amazing, but they are a good place to live. I have chosen to live on campus for all four of my years because I have been happy with them. One of the best features is that **we do not have common bathrooms**."

STUDENT AUTHOR: **Despite general complaints about housing facilities, most are satisfied with on-campus living. They like the convenience and constant excitement found in hall life. There is always something going on, and someone to study with. Themed halls are a campus favorite. Most recently a science hall has opened.**

Did You Know?
65% of undergrads live on campus.

Students Speak Out
ON GUYS & GIRLS

Q "There are more girls on campus then guys. I think that there are a lot of cute girls, **not too many guys** to pick from. That's why you take classes on the other Five Cs."

Q "The guys are cool; the girls are cool. Everyone's nice. **No one's really hot**; their awesome personalities make up for it."

Q "Most people at Pitzer tend to go the **hippie, au naturale look**, but it's about what you would expect at a private undergraduate institution."

Q "I hear Pitzer is known for its hot girls, but I think they are confusing us with Scripps. I think there are **a lot of very good-looking guys**. Everyone is really nice and supportive."

STUDENT AUTHOR: **There is a significantly greater female population on the Pitzer college campus. Girls sometimes complain about this, but with all five campuses, there is still a significant pool of single guys seeking out a date. For guys, Pitzer offers a few advantages; not only is there a disproportionate number of female students, there is an all girls school (Scripps) about 20 paces from campus. The dating scene is above average.**

Pitzer Slang

5Cs
Referring to the five undergraduate schools that make up the Claremont Colleges.

Sagehen
The Pitzer-Pomona mascot. A small extinct bird, resembling a small chicken.

Overall School Spirit
People grumble and complain about Pitzer a lot. However when it comes down to it, people are proud of the school and what they can learn. Sports do not overwhelm the campus with spirit.

Students Speak Out
ON ATHLETICS

Q "Sports are **not very popular**; I have not been to any game or tournament in all the years I have been here."

Q "You can play a varsity sport, and people might even come to watch, but I wouldn't count on it. Sports are **more of a hobby thing**. IM sports work the same way, it's fun but it is not your life."

Q "Varsity sports are not very big. More **people participate in IM** I think."

Q "There are some outstanding athletes at Pitzer College. Though varsity sports **don't have as large a fan base** as some schools they are defiantly respected."

STUDENT AUTHOR: **Pitzer's sports philosophy mimics the ideals on most subject matter. If you want it, it is available, and you can make it as much a part of your life as you want. Varsity sports get some recognition, however it is not a school-wide, drop-everything-and-run-and-cheer reaction that might be seen at a jock school. Intramural sports are enjoyed by many students, and there are numerous to choose from, but again there is no overwhelming sentiment towards the sport.**

Students Speak Out
ON DRUG SCENE

Q "Pitzer has pretty much a 'don't ask, don't tell' policy. If you are smart and quiet about it, you can do what you want, however, **I have never felt pressure** to use anything I don't want to here."

Q "There is **harder stuff around** I am sure, but all you ever hear about is pot."

Q "It is easy to fall into the alcohol/drug scene, especially if you find someone to do it with you. I do not think this is unique to Pitzer, though. I think **it is distinctive of college in general**. It is really easy to stay away if you want."

Q "If you are looking for it, **it's around**; if you aren't, you can avoid it."

STUDENT AUTHOR: **Many students at Pitzer drink, many smoke pot, many do neither. Of course, if you are considering going to college, you are smart enough to realize this will be the same at any school. Some schools have a reputation for their parties and excessive drinking; Pitzer is not one.**

12:1	Student-to-Faculty Ratio
92%	Freshman Retention Rate
64%	Four-Year Graduation Rate
52%	Financial Aid Applicants Receiving Aid

Students Speak Out
SAFETY & SECURITY

Q "While the security on campus is not all that great, **I still feel safe** in this area."

Q "I don't walk off the Pitzer campus by myself at night. I am consistently paranoid that my car will be broken into. **I don't lock my room** because I live with people I know I can trust, but I do lock my computer to my desk just in case."

Q "The **campus is pretty secure**, but it all depends on how safe you make it for yourself. It is important to remember that the Claremont Colleges are still part of the larger world. I mentor first-year students, and I tell them to lock their doors when they leave their hall."

Q "**Except for CMC**, a nearby sister college, the five colleges are very safe."

STUDENT AUTHOR: **Pitzer College is as safe a place as any. Sure, there's some crime, but in general you and all your belongings have no need for concern. Most students agree campus security does a good job, and keeps off-campus hoodlums and vandals away.**

Questions?
For more inside information and survival tips, pick up College Prowler's full-length book on this school, written by an actual student! Check it out at *www.collegeprowler.com*.

Students Speak Out
ON OVERALL EXPERIENCE

Q "Overall, I love Pitzer! This is my school! There are **too many great memories**, experiences, friends and teachers for Pitzer not to be my school."

Q "I was very surprised when I arrived at Pitzer to find how much time and energy was spent on nonsense. From poster plastering to student protests, it seems as if **someone is always dissatisfied**, and the mass e-mails are annoying."

Q "If I were doing it all over again, I would pick Pitzer, hands down. **My experience has been exciting**, enriching, challenging, and fun!"

Q "I love Pitzer! Though it was far from my first choice, now that I am here, I cannot imagine myself anywhere else. **I have grown in incredible ways** here and been able to participate in things I would have never dreamed of doing. I wouldn't want to be anywhere else, and I know that when graduation day comes I will be leaving college not only with an education, but with a deeper understanding of what my social responsibilities are, and how I can contribute in helpful ways."

Q "I think I've found **the best school for me**."

STUDENT AUTHOR: **There might be profit in "I love Pitzer" paraphernalia. Pitzer students almost unanimously "love Pitzer." Responses from students without that statement were hard to find. Like any institution, Pitzer also has problems. Students have complained about cost and unnecessary political activism. On the other hand, students have enjoyed: the five campus set up, the science department (JSD), the political activism, the social responsibility, the study abroad opportunities, and the friendships.**

Pomona College

550 North College Avenue; Claremont, CA 91711
(909) 621-8000; www.pomona.edu

Students Speak Out
ON ACADEMICS

Q "I haven't had one bad professor; **they're all so enthusiastic** about the material it's hard not to be interested."

Q "The teachers generally care about your well-being. Some are amazing, and **some are clinically insane**. Classes are usually unfocused enough that you can make them as interesting as you want to."

Q "The **teachers were smart** but apathetic about pushing students academically."

Q "The teachers, for the most part, are fabulous. They definitely **want to help their students** and are readily available outside of the classroom. I developed several close connections with my professors and am very grateful for their intelligence, enthusiasm, and patience."

Q "Most of the faculty are leaders in their fields. They are **extremely successful in their own research**, but more importantly, have a genuine love of undergraduate teaching."

STUDENT AUTHOR: Classes at Pomona aren't just small, they're intimate. If you are afraid of intimacy, be warned; you will be expected to participate at Pomona. You won't be listening to tape-recorded lectures in a hall full of 500 disinterested students. Classes are largely discussion based, and if you don't keep up you won't just be threatened with grade penalization, your peers might think less of you, as well! As for Professors, they are accessible and interesting.

Students Speak Out
ON LOCAL ATMOSPHERE

Q "The **campus is beautiful**, but the surrounding area leaves much to be desired. A car is very helpful."

Q "The town sucks! Most of it isn't geared to college students, despite the fact that we have a significant presence in the town. **There's nothing to do** at all. You need a car to seek any kind of off-campus entertainment."

Q "The atmosphere is sunny and sleepy in Claremont. It's an upper-class retirement community. **Thank goodness we have the other Claremont Colleges** with which to socialize."

Q "I don't spend much time in Claremont; it's **mostly just expensive antique stores** and mediocre restaurants. The close proximity of the other four colleges makes Pomona feel like a much larger school, which is good sometimes. You can always go eat at another school's dining hall for a change of pace. Also, having the other colleges adds to the social life."

STUDENT AUTHOR: Claremont is far more of a retirement community than it is a college town; you will exhaust its entertainment potential in about a day. There isn't anything to do except walk around and buy overpriced doo-dads. Los Angeles is a cultural Mecca, and you'll have a difficult time running out of things to do there. The other colleges provide a nice break from Pomona, but aren't, when you get right down to it, really different enough from Pomona to constitute an off-campus experience.

5 Best Things	5 Worst Things
1 Nurturing environment	1 Claremont
2 Climbing the flag pole	2 Chino winds
3 Free condoms	3 The network going down
4 Sneaking into Frary	4 Grade inflation
5 Imprormptu concerts	5 8:20 a.m. classes

Students Speak Out
ON FACILITIES

Q "All of the facilities are really nice and are **very impressive** for such a small school. Most of the stuff in the Rains Center is almost brand new, like the weight machines and stuff. The pool is really nice, too."

Q "I don't know what their dumb excuse is for **closing the weight room as early as they do**, but it's bullcrap."

Q "Our **facilities are wonderful**, of course—only the best."

Q "**The gym really sucks**. I used the Tulane gym all summer, and it has so many windows, new machines, wide treadmills, and other nice things. Not at Pomona. The Campus Center is charmless and creepy. "

Q "Facilities on campus are **beautiful and incredible**. Everything is nice and never crowded."

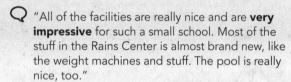

STUDENT AUTHOR: **Pomona students have mixed opinions on their college facilities. This could either be because the facilities are highly controversial, or it could be because, as liberal arts students, they are trained to always explore opposing viewpoints. The Campus Center, Rains Center, and library are all large and impressive, especially considering the size of the college, but many find them unappealing, unpragmatically designed, and even garish. Others, of course, rave about them, but it is a fact that the facilities generally seem designed more to impress than to, well, facilitate the activities that they were designed to facilitate.**

Famous Alumni

John Cage, Kris Kristofferson, James Turrell, Tom Waits

Students Speak Out
ON CAMPUS DINING

Q "The food is good. The quality is about standard, but there is a lot of selection. The school **pays special attention to special-needs eaters** like vegetarians and vegans and gives them a lot of special options, as well. To add more variety to the routine, we can eat at any of the dining halls on any of the five campuses."

Q "Food on campus is okay. **Scripps has better food**."

Q "The **dining halls rock**, but spoiled, bratty students love to gripe about the food. In Frary, you're dining in about as much style as you'll ever see on a college campus."

Q "By the time you're a junior, you know that the **food on campus sucks**. The best available food is actually at Claremont McKenna."

Q "Food on campus is delicious and **nicer than the food at many restaurants**."

Q "The food at Pomona is **not terrible**, but it's nothing to rave about."

STUDENT AUTHOR: **The quality of campus food service is a common target for complaint and ridicule among students, but Pomona actually does a pretty good job. No, it's not gourmet, nor probably even commensurate with your dear mother's cooking, but Pomona's dining halls offer a large variety of dining options. Students particularly laud the design-your-own meals, which range from pizza to stir-fry and have become more and more of a fixture in recent years.**

Student Body

African American:	8%	Male/Female:	50/50%
Asian American:	14%	Out-of-State:	67%
Hispanic:	11%	International:	4%
Native American:	<1%	Unknown:	15%
White:	46%		

Popular Faiths: Most Pomona students are either Protestant, Catholic, or Jewish.

Gay Pride: Generally Pomona is a very accepting environment; there is a QRC (Queer Resource Center), a Queer and Questioning club, and there are many queer-sponsored activities on campus.

Economic Status: New-moneyed, western snobs cleverly but imperfectly disguised hippies.

Students Speak Out
ON DORMS

Q "Dorms are classy, **renovated frequently**, and well maintained."

Q "The dorms are very nice. The rooms tend to be pretty big, and **the furniture is pretty nice**, too. Some dorms are really nice, but even the worst ones aren't completely bad by any means. Upperclassmen housing is practically palatial, some rooms have fireplaces and other amenities."

Q "The dorms at Pomona are great. There's a lot of variety, and **guaranteed four-year housing** takes a lot of stress out of college life. There are 12 dorms on campus, and one is renovated every summer, so no dorm is more than 12 years old in terms of paint, furniture, and fixtures."

STUDENT AUTHOR: Pomona's dorms are an eclectic bunch, and opinions regarding how nice they are vary widely. Something particularly nice about Pomona is that it is relatively easy to get a single if you want one. Dorms here are constantly being renovated, and as such, they tend to be relatively clean and well-appointed. Ninety-seven percent of students live on campus all four years.

> **Did You Know?**
> 98% of undergrads live on campus.

Students Speak Out
ON GUYS & GIRLS

Q "Everyone here is **kind of nerdy**, or used to be nerdy and now wants to pretend that they never were. That means we get a lot of variety in types of people and personalities."

Q "There are plenty of beautiful people, but in general, **students dress very casually** and don't wear a lot of makeup."

Q "Lots of hot girls, **lack of hot guys**. Most of the hot guys are gay!"

Q "My boyfriend's really hot, but the rest of the student body is mainly middling. If you have a fetish for **pale, weedy intellectuals**, you're in luck. My boyfriend's pale and intellectual, but he's not weedy."

STUDENT AUTHOR: It is a generally accepted fact that Pomona students just don't care that much about how they look. This is not to say that people here are ugly, because they're not. They just care more about drinking and hanging out than making devastating impressions on their chosen sexual targets. This makes a lot of sense when you think about the fact that everyone knows everyone else.

> **Urban Legends**
>
> **Pomona Trek**
> The Oldenborg dorm is the model for the ships ("cubes") of the Borg on the television show *Star Trek*.
>
> **Mufti**
> A secret society at Pomona whose sole function is to plant subversive fliers.
>
> **Overall School Spirit**
> Pomona students are happy, and they generally like their college, but they tend not to be all that fanatical about it.

Students Speak Out
ON ATHLETICS

Q "Many people play varsity sports, but **I wouldn't say that they're big**. At Pomona, you don't really get any prestige for being an athlete."

Q "Sports are **not that important here**. We are Division III. Most of the teams have good years and bad years. People go to games not so much because we're good, but because they know everyone on the team. IM sports are popular."

Q "**No one gives a damn** about sports here."

Q "Sports are **somewhat of a joke**. Pomona thankfully doesn't take itself seriously enough to recruit any nefarious testosterone-laden dunces."

STUDENT AUTHOR: As a small Division III school, Pomona doesn't put that much emphasis on athletics. The varsity athletes do get very involved in their sports and are often somewhat cliquish, but general student support and interest is relatively low. Athletes tend to attend the games of other athletes. Some intramural sports, such as ultimate Frisbee, and inner tube water polo generate a fair amount of excitement, as well. Football is really the only sport that gets any recruiting power.

Students Speak Out
ON DRUG SCENE

Q "I've never encountered anything harder than weed or 'shrooms. **People do it**, but it's not socially mandatory."

Q "There are quite a few people who smoke pot, but there are very few 'potheads.' Hard drugs are very rare. **Alcohol is common**, but people are generally responsible about it and only drink on weekends."

Q "The drug use I have witnessed has been primarily limited to tobacco, alcohol, and marijuana. **Some students also use mushrooms** and acid, and I have heard about but never witnessed the use of cocaine."

STUDENT AUTHOR: **Well, the fact is just about any drug one desires is available on campus, but they're not a highly visible part of campus life. Tons of people drink, and many smoke pot. Drugs aren't a necessity for a social life at Pomona; as often as not they're an escape from a sometimes overwhelmingly-present social scene. They can certainly be avoided if you want.**

8:1	Student-to-Faculty Ratio
97%	Freshman Retention Rate
90%	Four-Year Graduation Rate
80%	Financial Aid Applicants Receiving Aid

Students Speak Out
SAFETY & SECURITY

Q "Security is very good. Security guys zip around on golf carts all the time. There are lighted security stations with phones all over campus. **RAs are always on call** and are easy to get a hold of. I feel very safe walking across campus in the middle of the night."

Q "It's fine. **I never felt unsafe**, and I would frequently walk around at night alone."

Q "Seriously, it is like being back in the womb or something. You may get your bike stolen, but I **never ran into any dangerous people**. Most crimes on Pomona's campus are acts of petty vandalism committed by Pomona students who are generally given a slap on the wrist."

STUDENT AUTHOR: **Pomona security officers are generally laid-back, eager to help, and loathe to make your, and thus their, lives more difficult. They are far more likely to warn you than cite you for most minor infractions. Pomona is a safe campus: there are hardly ever any incidents.**

> **Questions?**
> For more inside information and survival tips, pick up College Prowler's full-length book on this school, written by an actual student! Check it out at *www.collegeprowler.com*.

Students Speak Out
ON OVERALL EXPERIENCE

Q "**I never wanted to be anywhere else**."

Q "I think **Pomona was pretty good**, but I sometimes wish I went to a school that more lay-people had heard of. It's so insulting to have paid all that money and still have people think you went to a two year community college. Alas."

Q "It's good. I probably would like to be in a city, but **I would put Pomona in the middle of a city**, not be at an inferior college that is already in a city."

Q "**I seriously considered transferring** or dropping out so many times I have lost count. I was too apathetic to actually do so, however. I honestly cannot fathom how this school has earned such a favorable reputation."

Q "I have loved every minute of my time here. **I love the small campus** and being able to see so many friends and people I know just by walking to class. The campus is gorgeous and a perfect size; small enough so you can walk everywhere easily, but large enough so that you don't feel closed in. All of the best classes I have ever taken have been during my time here."

STUDENT AUTHOR: **Just about any Pomona student will tell you that they truly enjoyed their college experience. The classes are good, and the professors are great, and that certainly plays its part, and it's an open, friendly campus, which is nice. Barring that, it must be that people here just really like the people they go to college with. Are Pomona students better people than other selective liberal arts college students? Probably not. However, Pomona puts a great deal of stress on allowing people space to find their own way.**

Princeton University

1 Washington Road; Princeton, NJ 08544
(609) 258-3000; www.princeton.edu

THE BASICS:

Acceptance Rate: 13% **SAT Range:** 2080–2360*
Setting: Suburban **Control:** Private
F-T Undergrads: 4,845 **Tuition:** $34,290

Most Popular Majors: Social Sciences, Engineering, History, Biological/Life Sciences, Public Administration

*of 2400

Academics	A+	Guys	B
Local Atmosphere	C+	Girls	B
Safety & Security	A	Athletics	B
Computers	A-	Nightlife	C
Facilities	B+	Greek Life	N/A
Campus Dining	A-	Drug Scene	B
Off-Campus Dining	B	Campus Strictness	B+
Campus Housing	B-	Parking	B
Off-Campus Housing	D-	Transportation	C+
Diversity	A+	Weather	B-

Students Speak Out
ON ACADEMICS

Q "Princeton's name pretty much speaks for itself here. The academic programs and professors are, by far, the best in the country. **All of the departments have world-renowned experts**, and you will definitely come out with an amazing education."

Q "Princeton faculty is **adept at adapting courses to academic and technological trends** and responding to student feedback. The result is a course offering of lectures and seminars that captivate and challenge."

Q "Outstanding! **Princeton is all about the undergrad program**. The classes are great, and the professors actually teach them. You can really get to know your professors if you make the extra step to try to meet them and do things like going to their office hours. That is the best part!"

Q "I loved my professors. **They are world-famous, yet they'd take me to dinner** to discuss educating inner-city youth, Melville's short stories, or why New York was on one of the largest fault lines."

STUDENT AUTHOR: The level of Princeton's academics makes it one of the best schools in the nation for undergraduate education, if not the best. Princeton professors place an emphasis on personal accessibility, and no graduate students are allowed to lead lecture courses. What results is an institution focused upon the education of undergraduates, not the research of professors.

Students Speak Out
ON LOCAL ATMOSPHERE

Q "It's a nice town. **It's quiet, and it has good shopping** if you prefer pricier stores and trendy fashions. The town people do not seem to be a problem. It's rather safe, as well."

Q "The town and University are fairly separate entities, but the town is small enough that most errands can be done conveniently on foot. The towpath that runs by Lake Carnegie is beautiful. There are **some great (but pricey) restaurants**."

Q "Rutgers University and the College of New Jersey are the closest other schools, but we really don't have anything to do with them. The town, itself, is **very quaint and community-oriented**. There are lots of little stores and restaurants, and the campus is one of the most beautiful places I've been to. The architecture and greenery is really breathtaking, especially in the spring and fall."

Q "New Jersey is the heart of everything, in the sense that you are **an hour and a half from the beach**, two hours from Atlantic City, three hours from DC, and 30 minutes from Trenton."

STUDENT AUTHOR: Princeton is a small town with a rich history, but many students complain that Princeton is trapped in time because of its older buildings and small town atmosphere. Despite its rich history, the University leaves much to be desired by way of a varied social life, so students are forced to look elsewhere to other places, such as New York and Atlantic City, for a little excitement.

Students Speak Out
ON FACILITIES

Q "They're great. **Princeton just got a new track** a few years ago, and the student center was remodeled and looks great! Everything is excellent. There's a new gym fitness room, new computers, and nice housing. The old buildings are all fixed up, and there are a lot of new buildings. They are all kept clean and safe, and there is a lot of history to them."

Q "Most facilities are excellent; there are lots of new buildings, centers, and libraries. **The new student center is excellent** and gives a reasonable alternative to dining halls."

Q "There was a new engineering building finished recently, the Friend Center, and its classrooms all have **projection TVs with the latest audio/video equipment** as well as some really nice chairs. The older classrooms are pretty standard."

Q "They just redid the gym, so it's really nice now. There's also another gym for athletes. Right now, they're in the process of **a 20-year dorm renovation**, where they take one dorm each year and completely redo it. I think Princeton is the richest school in the country, so they definitely have the money to provide the finest facilities."

STUDENT AUTHOR: Common student facilities, such as the gym and student center, are state-of-the-art. Princeton has made a lot of recent strides to catch up with other major universities in terms of campus facilities, though Frist Campus Center and Stephens Fitness Center both face overcrowding problems, which will only get worse as the University expands its student body.

Famous Alumni

Bill Bradley, Dean Cain, David Duchovny, Steve Forbes, James Madison, Ralph Nader, Donald Rumsfeld, Brooke Shields, James Stewart

Students Speak Out
ON CAMPUS DINING

Q "**For the first two years, students live and eat in Residential Colleges**. The food at the colleges varies greatly, with Rockefeller being one of the worst and Forbes being the best. Students have some flexibility because any underclassman on the meal plan can eat at any of the dining halls."

Q "The food here is great. The dining halls have a huge selection, and the Frist Campus Center is awesome. Meal times are **a really good time to hang out with friends**."

Q "Food is generally very average. It's your basic dining hall buffet food; we got sick of it pretty quickly. At the end of sophomore year, you join an eating club. There are 10 eating clubs on Prospect Street ('The Street'); they are where you will eat your meals and hang out. It's similar to a frat, I guess. **The food at eating clubs is generally much better than the dining halls**. The club I was in, Charter, probably had the best food on the street. We had pub nights two times a week, with international food on Wednesdays. All in all, the food was very good, although lunches could be mediocre. People who don't join eating clubs are independent and have to cook for themselves."

STUDENT AUTHOR: The strength of Princeton's dining hall facilities is that they have many options. Eating in the dining halls does get boring after two years, though, so the vast majority of students opt to go independent, join a co-op, or join an eating club. Though, the food quality at the co-ops and the eating clubs is varied.

Student Body

African American:	9%	Male/Female:	53/47%
Asian American:	14%	Out-of-State:	84%
Hispanic:	8%	International:	9%
Native American:	<1%	Unknown:	7%
White:	52%		

Popular Faiths: There are many groups like Agape, Athletes in Action, and the Center for Jewish Life.

Gay Pride: The community is accepting of gay students, as seen by the popularity of Pride Alliance events, though there remains a very small unaccepting minority.

Economic Status: Princeton now awards financial aid, allowing for more diverse economic backgrounds.

Students Speak Out
ON DORMS

Q "They are all rather nice and have lots of Gothic-type architecture. Appearance-wise, some of the newer buildings are not as impressive as others, but **all have similar living conditions**. I enjoy it very much. The social scene is a little monotonous, and some of the fellow students are a little pretentious, but on the whole, it's a great place to have a college experience."

Q "**Freshman year, there isn't a choice**, but you should be okay. Sophomore year, you live in the same general area but can pick your room. By junior year, you know where the best place to live will be—it varies with construction."

Q "The dorms are all really nice. **All the dorms are close to the academic buildings**, but Forbes dorm is pretty far if you want to get to the E-Quad."

STUDENT AUTHOR: **Princeton's housing options could be a lot better. With few affordable options within walking distance to campus, the University has little incentive to improve the conditions in the dorms; however, the University has started to renovate one large dorm or two small dorms a year.**

> **Did You Know?**
> 98% of undergrads live on campus.

Students Speak Out
ON GUYS & GIRLS

Q "There's probably a pretty big spectrum, but **hot guys are definitely available**. I'm quite satisfied with the guys on campus. As for the girls, well, I think we're really good-looking, as well."

Q "The guys are cool but a little pretentious, and **the girls are very pretentious**. The majority is ugly as sin—only a few good-looking ones exist, half of which have boyfriends. The idea of 'importing girls' is widely used."

Q "You have a nice selection of good-looking guys and girls if you go to the right places. Generally, if you go to the eating clubs on a Thursday or Saturday night, you'll find the best-looking people on campus. However, **don't expect to find too many in a 300-level math class**."

STUDENT AUTHOR: Socializing freshman year is awkward at best. Freshman girls are pursued by the more experienced upperclassmen while freshman boys wait for their turns to come, and after a freshman year of casual dating or hooking up, Princeton women plunge to the bottom of the dating totem pole by senior year when they see their male classmates attempt to chase the younger women on campus.

> **Traditions**
>
> **Baccalaureate Address**
> A "sermon" from a noteworthy speaker marking the start of Commencement for graduating seniors.
>
> **P-rade**
> Formally, the Alumni Parade, the P-rade occurs the Saturday of class reunions.
>
> **Overall School Spirit**
> Princeton students and alumni can never be accused of not having school spirit. They rally behind their respective residence halls, their rivalry with Harvard and Yale, and they always return for reunions.

Students Speak Out
ON ATHLETICS

Q "Varsity sports are very big. Sports on campus are huge; it seems that **nearly half or more of the student body participates** in some athletics—varsity or IM [intramurals]."

Q "We have a ton of varsity athletes; it blows me away. IM sports are fairly big, as well. **Not too many students attend football games**, but a heck of a lot attend men's basketball games. Our basketball team is always first or second in the Ivy League. Our lacrosse team has won the national championship in recent years."

Q "**IM sports are huge and so much fun**! We have everything from broomball (the best sport ever—hockey using brooms instead of pucks) to inner tube water polo. They were a huge part of my Princeton experience. Not only did I have an awesome time and get great exercise, but I also met a lot of my close friends through them."

STUDENT AUTHOR: **For a small Ivy League school, Princeton exhibits an athletic prowess that's almost surprising. The Ivy League provides a fantastic rivalry and gives Princeton students another venue for bragging about their abilities on and off the field.**

Students Speak Out
ON DRUG SCENE

Q "It's not bad. Of course **they are in circulation**, but it's nothing infringing."

Q "The drug scene isn't that bad. **Marijuana is the dominant drug**. I think very few people do the hardcore drugs."

Q "I'd say there's not really a drug scene. I mean, I would think that there would be some, like at any place you go, but I have never heard of any bad things in Princeton. **I think I heard of something only once** and it had to do with pot. All the drug scenes are in the big cities like Philly, New York, Trenton, and so on."

STUDENT AUTHOR: Other than alcohol, marijuana is the most prevalent drug on campus. Increasingly, a small minority of Princeton students have started to use drugs other than alcohol and marijuana, and because of the academic pressures, some students opt to use prescription drugs, such as Ritalin, to stay awake to do work, but it is by no means a widespread problem.

5:1	Student-to-Faculty Ratio
98%	Freshman Retention Rate
89%	Four-Year Graduation Rate
91%	Financial Aid Applicants Receiving Aid

Students Speak Out
SAFETY & SECURITY

Q "Princeton is very safe. There are people called proctors who make sure everything's going okay. **The building doors all lock automatically** and can only be opened by Princeton students with their ID cards."

Q "If anything, Public Safety has **too much of a presence on campus**. As long as you use common sense and stay out of certain parts of town by yourself after dark, there is nothing to worry about."

Q "We used to have rows of bushes by the tennis courts, but **these were cut down because people could hide in there** and attack people walking by."

STUDENT AUTHOR: As a town, Princeton is extremely safe. Some may even lament that the constant presence of Public Safety officers makes it difficult to have too much fun on campus, but the University has made personal safety a top priority.

Questions?

For more inside information and survival tips, pick up College Prowler's full-length book on this school, written by an actual student! Check it out at www.collegeprowler.com.

Students Speak Out
ON OVERALL EXPERIENCE

Q "I love it here. **It's a little conservative, but the opportunities are fabulous**. I love Princeton and have had incredible experiences. It's not the perfect place for me, but I don't think any college is perfect for anyone. Princeton is the kind of place that should be totally amazing but somehow is not. There is a weird vibe, but it also completely depends on who you know, where you end up, and what kind of person you are because most people love it."

Q "It has been, **by far, the best time of my life**, both socially and intellectually. I really wish I could stay here forever."

Q "My overall experience has been very positive. Initially, like many others, I wasn't that thrilled with the school because it is very much a closed campus, and there's not tremendous choice in terms of the social scene. But freshman year, I made some really close friends with people in my hallway, and from there, I started to like it more and more. **You get used to the uniqueness of the school**. I got involved in sports and had a great time. The four years have gone so fast, and I'm actually a little sad that it's time to move on."

STUDENT AUTHOR: Princeton is not just a school, it is an experience. Students who take full advantage of what Princeton has to offer have the opportunity to work with some of the most talented professors and scholars in the world on an idyllic campus. The historic buildings and eating clubs give Princeton its own sort of feel that may not mesh well with all students but certainly provide Princeton undergrads with a plethora of traditions and opportunities that are characteristically Princeton.

Providence College

549 River Avenue; Providence, RI 02918
(401) 865-2000; www.providence.edu

THE BASICS:

Acceptance Rate: 41%   **SAT Range:** 1610–1920*
Setting: Urban   **Control:** Private
F-T Undergrads: 3,951   **Tuition:** $28,920

Most Popular Majors: Business/Marketing, Social Sciences, Education, English, History

*of 2400

Academics	B	Guys	B+
Local Atmosphere	B+	Girls	A-
Safety & Security	B-	Athletics	B+
Computers	B-	Nightlife	A-
Facilities	B	Greek Life	N/A
Campus Dining	C+	Drug Scene	B+
Off-Campus Dining	A-	Campus Strictness	B-
Campus Housing	B+	Parking	C-
Off-Campus Housing	B+	Transportation	B+
Diversity	D	Weather	C

Students Speak Out
ON ACADEMICS

Q "Most professors at PC make a sincere effort to get to know their students personally. The **small class sizes make this possible** and create an excellent atmosphere for open class discussions. You can tell the professors love their jobs."

Q "I have found that all of **my professors have been very passionate** about their subject and also make themselves very accessible to the students. PC's academic setting can be a very advantageous environment to the undeclared student, as it is very encouraging of students to test the waters to discover subject matter that interests them before committing to a major."

Q "I feel the teachers can be anywhere from fairly liberal to extremely conservative. I guess you can't expect too much from a Catholic school. **Some teachers are cold, boring and confusing**, while others can be extremely interesting and fun."

Q "Students **take an active role** in their education rather than a professor lecturing the entire class."

STUDENT AUTHOR: **Professors at PC all possess a genuine concern for their students, often going above and beyond the average to make themselves accessible. Like all colleges, professors and their classes cover the entire spectrum from liberal and eccentric, to conservative and traditional. A central experience for the PC student is the Development of Western Civilization course (Civ). Although Civ may be a challenge, it is one every PCer is proud to have completed.**

Students Speak Out
ON LOCAL ATMOSPHERE

Q "The atmosphere of Smith Hill sharply contrasts with that of the one inside the 'PC bubble.' Surrounding the $30,000-a-year college is a neighborhood abundant with poverty and several **low-income housing projects**."

Q "Providence is **a wonderful city** with so much to do: shopping, eating, and theater. The one thing to stay away from is some of the scary streets that directly surround campus. It's not the safest ever."

Q "Being a New England city, Providence is **rich in history** and culture, so there are many attractions for its residents, but in any city, there are plenty of places that are dangerous and should be avoided, and Providence has its share."

Q "Personally, **I really enjoy Providence**. It's compact enough so that I can easily ride my bike to most places I need to go, but big enough to offer me opportunities for entertainment and growth outside of PC."

STUDENT AUTHOR: **While the area directly surrounding campus is one that anyone with presence of mind avoids, PC is minutes away from downtown Providence. Providence College has all the benefits of a small, close-knit school in an urban setting. For those who do not enjoy the drinking scene, there are countless options to keep you busy around town. Because of the poor area in the vicinity of the school, walking places is not the best idea, but biking, cabs, and free RIPTA buses are always an option.**

5 Best Things	5 Worst Things
1 Being in a city	1 Diversity
2 Restaurants	2 Parking
3 Bars and ticket parties	3 Civ
4 Movies on Slavin Lawn	4 Parietals
5 The library	5 No grass on the Quad

Students Speak Out
ON FACILITIES

Q "The student center and the computer labs are nice, not spectacular like you see at big state universities, but **appropriate for our small close-knit student body**."

Q "The facilities are **nice, open areas**. Especially with the recent addition of McPhails on our campus, it invites and accommodates more on-campus activity among students."

Q "They're alright; when I first visited the school, I really **didn't think anything special** of its appearance. For one, we're not big on grass. But again, the people and the spirit make that almost unnoticeable."

Q "**The student center is very nice**. We recently had a new campus bar and hangout built; it's a good place to go play pool, ping pong, or watch a baseball game on the big screen television."

Q "Some athletic facilities, such as Peterson, are **only accessible to non-athletes**, so that the facility is not occupied by varsity athletes."

STUDENT AUTHOR: Every year seems to be a year of renewal for Providence College. Returning students to the PC campus eagerly anticipate new structures and edifices upon return each September. With so many construction projects nearing completion the Providence campus will have an entirely new look for returning students and fantastic new facilities for the incoming class to utilize. Providence administration deserves a round of applause for addressing the needs of the student body.

Famous Alumni

Doris Burke, Robert C. Gallo, Mike Leonard, Elizabeth Flynn Lott, Arthur F. Ryan, Lindsay Waters, Lenny Wilkens

Students Speak Out
ON CAMPUS DINING

Q "Raymond Hall is our main dining facility on campus. **You can get almost anything** you want to eat, and it's open most of the day. The favorite meal of the week tends to be weekend brunch."

Q "It's all run by Sodexho, who serves 90 percent of the schools in the U.S., so it's going to be about **the same wherever you go**."

Q "The food is getting better every year I return to campus. The dining company has a wide variety of foods to choose from and **has started to become more health conscious** about what meals they are giving PC students."

Q "The food on campus is pretty good, not as good as home cooking, but **good for college food**. They have a huge variety and personally being a vegetarian, offered a lot of choices for me."

Q "The food is the one thing **I'm not looking forward to going back to**. It's fine if you don't have to be diet conscious, but Ray will add more onto the Freshman 15 than the local bars will."

STUDENT AUTHOR: There are two sources of food on campus: Raymond Cafeteria and Alumni Food Court in the Slavin Center. Ray Café is the best place to eat when they keep it simple and stick to the basics. Slavin is the place to be if you can tolerate noise and interruptions when you are studying. Slay, as it is affectionately termed, carries something for everyone. The drawback is that Slavin requires money that is put on your all-purpose Providence College ID card at the start of every semester.

Student Body

African American:	2%	Male/Female:	44/56%
Asian American:	2%	Out-of-State:	87%
Hispanic:	2%	International:	1%
Native American:	<1%	Unknown:	10%
White:	83%		

Popular Faiths: Catholicism. Pastoral Services and the Chaplain's Office direct numerous programs on and off-campus for multiple faiths.

Gay Pride: PC is very accepting of its gay community and even has clubs such as SHEPARD to increase awareness, tolerance, and acceptance of gays.

Economic Status: Students are typically from middle or upper-class economic backgrounds.

Students Speak Out
ON DORMS

Q "The dorms are a decent size; compared to other colleges I've seen, **they are about average**. If you are a freshman male and like to party and be loud, you want to live in Guzman Hall; its opposite would be Fennell Hall."

Q "**The dorms aren't beautiful** or anything incredible but they are fun. Living on the quad was the time of my life. Freshman year, I recommend the normal frosh dorms just because you meet all the other freshmen."

Q "For incoming freshmen I definitely would **suggest being in an all-freshman dorm**. For girls, McVinney or Raymond; boys Guzman or probably Guzman, unless you're more quiet and don't mind the walk from lower campus."

STUDENT AUTHOR: Ranging from old and in need of repairs, to newer suites, campus housing covers the entire gamut of possibilities. Everyone recommends freshmen choosing an all-freshman dorm to create solidarity with their class. Housing is assigned by Residence Life freshman year based on preference to buildings and room size.

Did You Know?
78% of undergrads live on campus.

Students Speak Out
ON GUYS & GIRLS

Q "I like to think we're **a pretty attractive campus**, at least that's what I've found in the past! You could classify the campus as pretty preppy, but everyone has his or her own twist of style."

Q "The guys and girls at this school are all the same dressed in Abercrombie and accessorized with a **silver spoon in their mouths**. Though the guys and girls are for the most part, attractive, they get kind of repetitive."

Q "The guys can be anywhere from really cool, smart, and **interesting to dumb**, mean, rude, and immature—the same goes for girls."

Q "On this matter, I would have to compare PC to a **typical high school**. There are different cliques like jocks, nerds, and those in the middle."

STUDENT AUTHOR: While PC may look like a page out of a J. Crew ad, one has to wonder if this conformity goes along with the lack of diversity at PC. Don't worry if you're not fashion conscious, you'll fit in just fine anyway because in the case of our campus beauty is accompanied by brains. Overall, everyone agrees that PC is a good-looking school, even if the look is slightly repetitive.

Traditions

The Clam Jam
It's a great way to start off the year, kick off the weekend, and spend a fun night on campus.

Midnight Madness
The night is spent in the Mullaney gym awaiting the strike of twelve when the basketball teams can officially begin practice sessions.

Overall School Spirit
Providence students are full of pep and vigor particularly when it comes to their school. Everyone owns a closet full of PC apparel.

Students Speak Out
ON ATHLETICS

Q "PC is a Division I school so **varsity sports are very popular**. Basketball, hockey and lacrosse are everyone's favorites, but all games have pretty good turn outs."

Q "PC men's basketball is **the team of Rhode Island**, so even non-students and alumni get really hyped up for the basketball season. Go Friars!"

Q "PC is a Division I school so varsity sports are a big attraction. Intramurals are **probably just as big**, though. The intramural department promotes a fun and easy going competitive sports program that includes everything from basketball to Frisbee and dodgeball."

Q "It's usually a big deal to win your IM championship game; the prize T-shirts are **sought after by many**."

STUDENT AUTHOR: Being a Division I school in the Big East, men's basketball is by far the biggest sport at PC. Because most students won't compete on a Division I team, intramurals are huge, yet anyone of any degree of athleticism can play and have tons of fun.

Students Speak Out
ON DRUG SCENE

Q "Truthfully, I don't believe there is a lot of drug use on campus. I'm a very social person and have **never come across any drugs** besides marijuana."

Q "I feel like the drug scene here is pretty mild. **Alcohol is much more prevalent** on campus than any drug. I suppose pot would be the biggest drug used on campus, but it's never been as widespread as alcohol by any means."

Q "From what I know, I do not think the drug scene is too bad at PC compared to other colleges across the country. However, there is heavy drinking all over campus, and it is pretty much **accepted as the norm**."

STUDENT AUTHOR: **By far the most widely used drug at PC is alcohol. The real drug scene is much more inconspicuous. While marijuana is the drug of choice, there are whispers about ecstasy, mushrooms and a small coke scene. The low-key use of drugs makes PC a comfortable atmosphere for the students who don't use.**

12:1	Student-to-Faculty Ratio
92%	Freshman Retention Rate
85%	Four-Year Graduation Rate
85%	Financial Aid Applicants Receiving Aid

Students Speak Out
SAFETY & SECURITY

Q "PC tries to provide students with the best security possible. The three **all-female dorms have night guards** that stay at the entrances. Three security stations at the River Avenue, Huxley Avenue, and Eaton Street entrances monitor incoming guests."

Q "The security on campus, to be honest, is **worthless**. Men in their 90s aren't my idea of adequate security."

Q "Providence College is a very safe campus. However, once you get off campus, it can be unsafe at times. There are **muggings and assaults on the nearby streets**."

STUDENT AUTHOR: **Overall, PC has put into place numerous security measures to ensure both student and parental peace of mind. The use of common sense and awareness of one's surroundings is the best preventative measure.**

Questions?
For more inside information and survival tips, pick up College Prowler's full-length book on this school, written by an actual student! Check it out at *www.collegeprowler.com*.

Students Speak Out
ON OVERALL EXPERIENCE

Q "School is pretty good. The **academic schedule at PC is very challenging** with teachers who really push their students to the limit, which is important for intellectual growth. Also, I have made long-lasting relationships with people on campus, so I really couldn't see myself anywhere else."

Q "I love the strong faith that many of my peers have. **I have grown spiritually** a lot since I have been here."

Q "We go to class but we know how to have fun. A teacher once told me, '**Never let class get in the way of an education**.' PC is a hands-on learning experience in all areas, and I would recommend it to anyone who can balance a social life and school."

Q "I've really enjoyed my time at PC. There is a good party scene and a lot of young people who want to have fun. However, it is also a good environment to get a solid, all-around education. There are also a lot of opportunities to **get involved in the Providence College community**. It all depends on how much you are willing to put into your experience."

STUDENT AUTHOR: **The brilliance of the education at PC is that it extends itself outside of the classroom. Your experience of PC can be anything that you want to make it. If you want to focus on academics you can. If you just want your college years to be the wild and crazy ones you've heard they can be, PC has that, too. The overwhelming majority of students look on their time spent at PC as a phenomenal learning experience.**

Purdue University

475 Stadium Mall Drive; West Lafayette, IN 47906
(765) 494-4600; www.purdue.edu

THE BASICS:

Acceptance Rate: 80%
Setting: Rural
F-T Undergrads: 29,051

SAT Range: 1060–1310*
Control: Public
Tuition: $19,824

Most Popular Majors: Liberal Arts, Engineering, Business, Agriculture, Education

*of 1600

Academics	B+	Guys	A
Local Atmosphere	C+	Girls	B+
Safety & Security	A	Athletics	A
Computers	A-	Nightlife	B+
Facilities	A	Greek Life	B+
Campus Dining	B	Drug Scene	B
Off-Campus Dining	B	Campus Strictness	C
Campus Housing	B	Parking	C
Off-Campus Housing	A+	Transportation	B+
Diversity	C	Weather	C

Students Speak Out
ON ACADEMICS

Q "During my freshman year, I had a lecture class with **over 600 students**, and during my junior year, I was in a class with only six other people. But, even in the big lecture classes, there are always teaching assistants and other students around who can help you. Professors often give their home phone numbers and e-mail addresses out, and they are pretty good about helping you out, or setting up appointments to meet with you."

Q "I graduated from the School of Liberal Arts with a degree in advertising, and I loved all of my professors. The academic atmosphere is **intense** and overwhelmingly full of information at times, but it's also fun."

Q "The professors that have **a passion for teaching** are wonderful! Those who educate for the sole purpose of maintaining their research potentials, not so much. I'm not all that impressed with many of the math teachers, but they get the job done."

STUDENT AUTHOR: Purdue's Ivy League-sounding title belies its public standing, but aptly describes its challenging curriculum—according to first-year engineering students. Purdue's engineering, management, and agricultural schools attract students from around the nation—and the world—because of their high academic reputation. The biggest complaint of Purdue students is the plethora of foreign TAs whose accents are almost incomprehensible.

Students Speak Out
ON LOCAL ATMOSPHERE

Q "West Lafayette is **basically just Purdue**, so the population is mostly us college kids. You don't really have to worry about offending older people with music or college stuff, because you rarely see people above the age of 23."

Q "West Lafayette is **pretty boring**. There's nothing too exciting to do, really. On the weekends, you can always find a party to go to somewhere. There are movie theaters, and our student union has a bowling alley (there are also others off campus). And when you are with friends, you can usually find something to do."

Q "West Lafayette is **not a place to visit**. Sporting events are the only reason for someone under the age of 21 to come visit, unless they know someone who lives there."

Q "Visit the Horticultural Park and the Main Street Ice Cream Parlor. By campus, there are **plenty of coffeeshops** as well as a new ice skating rink! There are hundreds of student clubs to provide you with entertainment of your choice and keep you out of trouble—and if you don't find one that suits you, make your own! I did."

STUDENT AUTHOR: Being in the middle of a cornfield doesn't seem like the most exciting of locales, but Purdue students take it all in stride. While West Lafayette revolves around Purdue University and very little else, the Lafayette area is filled with restaurants, parks, historical attractions, and other diversions that are very similar to other moderately-sized cities in the nation.

5 Best Things	**5 Worst Things**
1 Fountain runs	1 Boring surroundings
2 Big 10 athletics	2 Midwestern weather
3 Beautiful campus	3 Dead Week
4 Grand Prix	4 Saturday finals
5 Lunch tray sledding	5 Meredith Hall

Students Speak Out
ON FACILITIES

Q "All of the facilities are basically new. The computer labs are upgraded approximately every two years, and a new pool was built recently and is the **best in the Big 10**, just like our student center."

Q "The student center (the Union) is **pretty nice**. Students hang out upstairs, where they have a big screen TV and lots of couches and chairs that many people sleep on. Downstairs, there are restaurants and an arcade."

Q "The facilities are **getting better all the time**. They've done a lot of improvements to the recreational center, and they've done some renovations on the libraries and other classroom buildings. It's constantly improving all the time."

Q "Everything is kept **as clean as possible**. The football stadium was recently renovated, and it looks awesome now. The libraries are in need of a serious redecoration, but they still function fairly nicely."

Q "The Co-Rec is really nice now. **Excellent weight room**, plus the place has stuff for everyone else, too."

STUDENT AUTHOR: **Purdue's multi-billion dollar campaign has resulted in numerous renovations around the campus, including the recreational sports center, the residence hall dining rooms, the computer labs, and the libraries. The campus itself is compact, charming, and clean. Although it is large enough to accommodate over 30,000 students, the layout is such that a student can walk from one end to the other within 15 to 20 minutes.**

Famous Alumni

George Ade, John T. McCutcheon, Orville Redenbacher, Neil Armstrong, Eugene A. Cernan, Booth Tarkington, David Ross

Students Speak Out
ON CAMPUS DINING

Q "Food on campus is fine. Everyone will complain about the dorm food as a freshman, but trust me, it's **very good** compared to most other places. Once you are an upperclassman, you will try and snag underclassman IDs so that you can eat in the dorms."

Q "On-campus food basically comes from the dorms and the student union. Everything is pretty good, and there's a **nice variety**—it doesn't get old. The food is also designed to cater to a wide variety of diets, such as vegetarian and religion-specific diets."

Q "Meredith has **great food**. So does Cary! I've never been to Earhart dining hall, but I hear it's phenomenal. Villa Pizza in the Union is a dependable choice—it always has good food!"

Q "The food is terrible. Hands down, I have to say that Indiana (after being used to the great food in Chicago) is probably **the capital of crappy food**—next to England. On the other hand, if you like corn and other 'down-on-the-farm' food, you will love it!"

STUDENT AUTHOR: **Depending with whom you speak, dorm food at Purdue can be either excellent or inedible. On the whole, students seem to agree that what the residence halls serve is actually very good, especially at Meredith Hall or Cary Quad. The Union food, though overpriced, is good and easily accessible. If all else fails, there are numerous mini-marts to purchase microwave dinners, or there are grills for hamburgers, french fries, and other mainstay food staples.**

Student Body

African American:	3%	Male/Female:	59/41%
Asian American:	5%	Out-of-State:	26%
Hispanic:	2%	International:	7%
Native American:	1%	Unknown:	0%
White:	82%		

Popular Faiths: Christianity, Judaism, and Islam are the most popular religions on campus.

Gay Pride: The LesBiGay network sponsors events on campus, such as "Gaypril," in attempts to strengthen alternative lifestyle acceptance at Purdue.

Political Activity: Most students at Purdue are conservative Republican.

Students Speak Out
ON DORMS

Q "There is Windsor, which looks like a castle, and Hillenbrand, where most of the upperclassmen live. That one **looks like a hotel** and is very nice. And there is Meredith Hall. It looks the crappiest, and at first it was my least favorite, but that was the one that I ended up living in. Let me tell you, I absolutely loved that dorm."

Q "Ladies, **avoid Meredith** Hall. It's like living in a walk-in closet."

Q "I lived in Windsor the last three years. **I really liked Windsor**, because of the closeness to campus. It was convenient, and it's really close to everything (including the recreational center). Hillenbrand is a nice upperclassmen dorm, because it has its own bathrooms and air-conditioning."

STUDENT AUTHOR: **Freshmen attending Purdue are not required to live in the residence halls, but it is an unwritten rule that they do so. It's advisable to try and get out of living at Meredith Hall or Cary Quad. Hillenbrand is undoubtedly the most spacious of the residence halls, but students are only eligible to live there after their first year.**

 Did You Know?
40% of undergrads live on campus.

Students Speak Out
ON GUYS & GIRLS

Q "I think there is something like a six to four guy-to-girl ratio on campus, so that's good for the girls. The girls here are **usually good-looking**. But for some reason, when spring rolls around, they tend to take off some extra clothing—and they look even better!"

Q "Are the guys hot? The girls that go to school at Indiana University say they **prefer Purdue boys** to their own, so that is how I would answer that question. Everyone is generally really nice here; you will run into some snobs, but that happens everywhere. I get along well with almost anyone, so I'd like to think that we are a rather personable university."

STUDENT AUTHOR: No matter what you're attracted to, you'll be able to find it at Purdue. The girls come out the definite winners; with about one-and-a-half men to each woman, the odds are in your favor, ladies. Gentlemen, Purdue is not without its share of female beauties. The former Miss Indiana and her first runner-up were both Purdue students, and a jaunt past any sorority house will show you that pretty women are everywhere.

Traditions

Grand Prix
Campus-wide fraternity and sorority party the weekend before finals.

The Old Oaken Bucket
The winner of the Indiana/Purdue football game retains this trophy, along with bragging rights.

Overall School Spirit
Purdue students bleed black and gold. Boilermakers are proud of their top-notch athletic teams and are fiercely loyal to the University.

Students Speak Out
ON ATHLETICS

Q "Football is the biggest sport here. Everyone goes to the games, and **they are a blast** to attend! Tickets for the other sports are also available, but they aren't as popular. You can participate in intramural sports by going through the residence halls or the Greek system. There are a lot of athletic facilities on campus, especially the Co-Rec, which has weight rooms, gymnasiums, outdoor fields, tennis courts, and a new aquatics center."

Q "Football weekends in fall are **unbelievable**, and if you don't like football, you should still go to at least one game for the atmosphere. Football weekends are also big party weekends."

Q "At Purdue, for a true Boilermaker, **football is life**. Sports are huge here. Intramurals are very popular, especially with the Greeks and in the residence halls."

STUDENT AUTHOR: As a Big 10 university, Purdue students take great pride in their athletic teams. During football season, there is no other place to be other than tailgating before the games and cheering in the stands during the games.

Students Speak Out
ON DRUG SCENE

Q "The drug scene on this campus is **very limited**. Marijuana can be found anywhere in the country; you just have to know where to find it. If you don't want to see any drugs, you won't. No one will offer anything to you at a party or anything. Most drugs can't even be found at parties where there is alcohol."

Q "You can get anything you want, if that's what you're into, but the drug scene is mostly **underground** here. There's not a lot of drug use on campus, maybe some marijuana, but not even that drug is big."

Q "I am sure it exists, but just like the Greek scene, I have never had problems avoiding it. The drug scene is **not prevalent**."

STUDENT AUTHOR: The drug lifestyle is pretty much hidden away underground; you can't see it, but you know it's there. Students agree that if you wanted to find such substances, you would have no problem doing so, but you won't have pushers coming up to you on the Memorial Mall.

15:1	Student-to-Faculty Ratio
86%	Freshman Retention Rate
31%	Four-Year Graduation Rate
69%	Financial Aid Applicants Receiving Aid

Students Speak Out
SAFETY & SECURITY

Q "I've never had a problem, and I don't really know anyone who has. **I'm not scared** about walking alone on campus at night, but I am usually with friends, because I don't like going anywhere alone."

Q "Security is **very noticeable**, especially at night. Purdue has their own police department, and they do a good job keeping things under control."

Q "Security and **safety is good**. I've never felt uncomfortable, but I wouldn't recommend walking around by yourself in your jammies at four in the morning—unless you're on the way to a very early breakfast club."

STUDENT AUTHOR: Students at Purdue feel overwhelmingly safe and secure on campus, thanks to its 200-plus yellow call-boxes, its patrolling police, and its free evening escort service. Residence halls are about as well protected as Fort Knox, requiring IDs and several keyed doors to reach living areas.

Questions?
For more inside information and survival tips, pick up College Prowler's full-length book on this school, written by an actual student! Check it out at *www.collegeprowler.com*.

Students Speak Out
ON OVERALL EXPERIENCE

Q "**Purdue is a great place** to meet people. Sure, there may not be that much to do when you're under 21, but you can always find something on your own. I'm glad I chose to go to Purdue."

Q "I couldn't imagine myself anywhere else. I know it sounds cheesy, but I've had the **best three years** of my life here, and I am really going to miss this place when I graduate. I've met so many people, and I've had so many great opportunities. I wouldn't trade my experiences here for anything."

Q "**I love it here** at Purdue. It's a big university, but you aren't just a number here. The teachers actually take the time to get to know you. There is a very active social scene, but people are pretty smart here and still get their work done."

Q "I got my Bachelor of Science degree after four years at Purdue, and now **I have an awesome job**. Recruiters working for companies from all over the country come to Purdue to look for people to hire. "

STUDENT AUTHOR: Students could not have been more glowing in their praise about their time at Purdue University. Boilermakers unanimously appreciate all the opportunities that are afforded to students at a Big 10 university. From the thriving social scene, to the academics, to the prestige of a Purdue diploma, to the lifelong friends, Purdue students are grateful for their time in the heartland of the Midwest. The sheer size of Purdue may intimidate those students who feel that they will never be more than a number at Purdue, but as students have pointed out, there's a niche here for everyone.

Radford University

801 East Main Street; Radford, VA 24142
(540) 831-5000; www.radford.edu

THE BASICS:

Acceptance Rate: 74%
Setting: Rural
F-T Undergrads: 7,779

SAT Range: 920–1100*
Control: Public
Tuition: $13,201

Most Popular Majors: Business, Interdisciplinary Studies, Communications, Health Professions, Arts

*of 1600

Academics	B-	Guys	B
Local Atmosphere	B-	Girls	B+
Safety & Security	A	Athletics	C
Computers	B+	Nightlife	C+
Facilities	B	Greek Life	A
Campus Dining	B-	Drug Scene	B-
Off-Campus Dining	A-	Campus Strictness	C-
Campus Housing	B	Parking	D+
Off-Campus Housing	A	Transportation	D
Diversity	D	Weather	B

Students Speak Out
ON ACADEMICS

Q "**It's a hit or miss when it comes to the teachers**. You have your awesome teachers that actually help you learn, and then you have the plain idiots."

Q "The workload is average. I'm assuming that it is just as hard as any other university. **The teachers are usually very willing to help**. In such a small atmosphere, it is easy for them to know you personally and not just as a number."

Q "Depending on your major and assigned credits, **the workload is fairly easy**. As long as you space your days out, you should be fine."

Q "**The teachers at Radford University all have a lot of personality**, at least all the teachers that I have had. Most have an attendance policy because they want you to be able to enjoy and get the full experience of the class."

STUDENT AUTHOR: Radford has really been pushing for strong academic programs. Throughout the state of Virginia, Radford is becoming known for its nursing, psychology, and education programs. It is a small school, which allows for small class sizes—usually 20 to 40 students—and personal relationships with the professors. Small class sizes allow for more personal attention, more in-class discussion, and more in-depth coverage of material. Professors make themselves accessible to students with office hours, out-of-class appointments, and by staying after a class to answer questions. Radford has been improving its reputation as a party school and becoming known as a school with serious academic integrity.

Students Speak Out
ON LOCAL ATMOSPHERE

Q "Radford is a very small town in the Blue Ridge Mountains, so there is not too much to do besides staying around this area. **It is definitely a big drinking school** because of the lack of other things to do."

Q "The atmosphere is good if you like rural environments. **There are a lot of outdoor activities to do around here**. However, in the winter when the temperature is in the teens, there is absolutely nothing to do in this town other than party inside."

Q "The best thing to do is go tubing down the river near our campus in the spring and summer. **I usually go to Blacksburg and Roanoke**. There are actually things to do like go shopping, to the movies, or hang out with friends."

Q "**If you like small towns, this is certainly the place to be**. It is slowly building up into an actual city but has a long road ahead of it."

STUDENT AUTHOR: Located in southwest Virginia in the heart of the Blue Ridge Mountains, Radford affords an incredible view of the New River and the mountains surrounding it. Radford's closest shopping mall is 20 minutes away. The closest club is in Roanoke. With the majority of entertainment being located outside of city limits, many students spend their weekends away. The school has been nicknamed a "suitcase school" by students, as many prefer to visit Virginia Tech or to return home on the weekends.

5 Best Things	5 Worst Things
1 Professors	1 Lack of recycling
2 Nightlife	2 Public transportation
3 Variety of places to eat	3 Strictness of campus
4 Friendliness of students	4 Dining hall food
5 Campus activities	5 Rural location

Students Speak Out
ON FACILITIES

Q "All of our facilities are in good condition. There are two weight rooms, multiple sports arenas, and more-than-adequate student centers with bowling and pool. **They library is more extensive than you could ever need**, so don't worry."

Q "The facilities on campus are exceptional. **They are very useful and always full of students**. We could use some more machines at the gym on campus because they get a lot of use."

Q "**The student center is state-of-the-art** and has many things for students to do. The school also has free activities there throughout the week."

Q "**All of the facilities are top notch**. Everything from the bowling alley at the student center to the weight room in Peters is definitely on point."

Q "The Bonnie Student Center houses a movie theater, bowling alley, ping pong tables, and pool tables. **I think it's quite snazzy**."

STUDENT AUTHOR: **The University is constantly working to improve the facilities for the students. From movies to bowling, ping pong, and pool, the Bonnie Hurlburt Student Center provides many forms of entertainment. The McConnell Library contains five floors of books, journals, and other forms of media in order to meet the academic needs of students. The athletic centers are clean but often crowded. All the buildings are aesthetically pleasing and well maintained. While many of the facilities are older, the school works hard to make improvements and is constantly in the process of building new facilities or upgrading the quality of the existing facilities.**

Famous Alumni

Dr. Donald Newton Dedmon, Chris Skinner

Students Speak Out
ON CAMPUS DINING

Q "**I think the food on campus is just fine**. It is often 'uncool' to like school food, but I will admit that I do. There are two cafeterias on campus and multiple fast food places."

Q "It is not hard to find healthy food on campus; however, **they still have a wide variety of junk food** for those of us who just can't get away."

Q "**The dining halls have improved since my freshman year on campus**. The first year that I attended Radford, we did not have many of the places that are available now. We now have chain restaurants like Chik-fil-A and Wendy's."

Q "I can say that **our dining facilities are starting to really impress me**."

Q "The main dining hall, Dalton, has some room for improvement. **The food there is not the best**."

STUDENT AUTHOR: **Radford does not offer a wide variety of options where food is concerned. Most of the available food options lean toward fast food. Chik-fil-A, Wendy's, and Sbarro are the greasiest spots to eat on campus, although they all do offer small salad items. The dining halls are a different story. Dalton offers a variety of options every night, including soups, sandwiches, a salad bar, a pasta and pizza bar, a healthy menu option, and daily specials. However, the quality of food offered at Dalton is widely disputed among students. Many prefer Muse dining hall, although Muse lacks the convenience. The time constraints on the available options at Radford severely limit choices and offer reasons to complain.**

Student Body

African American:	6%	Male/Female:	43/57%
Asian American:	2%	Out-of-State:	7%
Hispanic:	3%	International:	1%
Native American:	<1%	Unknown:	2%
White:	86%		

Popular Faiths: The student body is mostly Christian.

Gay Pride: Spectrum is the gay, lesbian, bisexual, transgender, identity questioning, and straight ally activist club on campus that works to dispel myths and minimize prejudice.

Economic Status: Most students at Radford fall into the category of middle and upper class.

Students Speak Out
ON DORMS

Q "I lived in the dorms my first two years. I feel that if you really want to get a feel for the place, **you have to live in the dorms for at least your first year**."

Q "Dorms are small, but good for first-year students. **They are a really good way to meet new people your first year**. Avoid Muse—it draws too much attention to trouble-making freshmen."

Q "**Radford's dorms are doable**. My first year here, I lived in an upgraded dorm with air conditioning that was located close to all the classrooms and food locations."

STUDENT AUTHOR: **The dorms are on the older side, but they're well maintained. Seven out of the 15 dormitories have been upgraded within the last decade and—for a small fee—allow students to control their own heating and air conditioning on a room-by-room basis. The dorms are all set up suite-style with two rooms sharing a bathroom. While dorm living is vital to creating bonds with fellow students, especially during the first year of college, it does have its drawbacks. Dorms are not sound proof, and students often complain about a noisy neighbor or floor.**

> **Did You Know?**
> 37% of undergrads live on campus.

Students Speak Out
ON GUYS & GIRLS

Q "**Radford's typical student is attractive and outgoing**. I would say most clubs and organizations have a typical student for that club."

Q "I think that everyone is pretty in their own way. For the most part, people here are outgoing and attractive. **I wouldn't say we have many geeky people at all**."

Q "**The guys and girls at Radford are relaxed and fun people**. They are easy to get to know, and from what I've seen, most are outgoing."

Q "The guys are cool. The girls are, for the most part, attractive, but **they do have a reputation for being easy**. They also tend to put on weight after a few years of constant alcohol intake."

STUDENT AUTHOR: **Most of the students here are very good-looking.** Looking good is especially necessary with such a large number of available girls—everyone is trying to beat the competition. The guys at Radford are severely outnumbered, and that makes finding decent relationship material a lot harder. Because of the plethora of girls available, men have a very easy time finding a partner, whether for a relationship or a casual hookup.

> **Traditions**
>
> **Quadfest**
> Quadfest is a long-standing student-based tradition. It is usually the third weekend in April and involves an inordinate amount of people getting as drunk as possible. The school no longer sponsors it and has even tried to ban it, but students have kept the tradition alive and thousands still flock to Radford for a variety of drinking activities.
>
> **Overall School Spirit**
> School spirit has been given a lift recently with a new campaign called "Dread the Red," encouraging students to wear red at all Radford sporting events.

Students Speak Out
ON ATHLETICS

Q "**Varsity sports are kind of a bummer**. We don't have a football team, and our basketball team is dismal, but club sports are great."

Q "The varsity sports are pretty good. **The women's teams are better than the men's teams** based on past and present records and statistics. Of course, the men get praised more."

Q "**There is a wide variety of intramural sports available for everyone**. They are definitely well done and fun."

Q "During the winter, I joined the snowboarding club. **Those were some of the best times of my life**, but being in the club was so expensive."

STUDENT AUTHOR: **Athletics at Radford are not well respected by the student body. In fact, the only official sport that seems to be given any notice is basketball. The University has started several initiatives to get student attendance at basketball games to rise. School spirit has been almost nonexistent for several years but is on the rise with the new "Dread the Red" campaign. Intramurals are a much more prominent part of student life.**

Students Speak Out
ON DRUG SCENE

Q "I do not see a lot of drug use going on among students. There are the typical pot smokers but not a lot of hard-core coke addicts or anything like that. **Drinking is the main obsession among students**."

Q "**The drug scene is typical of a college campus**. You can find anything you want, but you have to know the right people."

Q "You would never guess, but drugs are everywhere. It's not noticeable from an outside perspective (other than the drinking of course), but **some people here get into some heavy stuff**."

STUDENT AUTHOR: **Every college is going to have a drug scene—there is no avoiding that. Unfortunately, Radford is no exception to the rule. Drugs can be found if one looks for them, but they are not prevalent on campus. Certain students do partake in illegal substance abuse, prescription drug abuse, and the obvious alcohol abuse. Radford maintains a three strike policy. An alcohol violation counts as one strike, and a drug violation as two. After the third strike, students are asked to leave.**

18:1	Student-to-Faculty Ratio
78%	Freshman Retention Rate
42%	Four-Year Graduation Rate
63%	Financial Aid Applicants Receiving Aid

Students Speak Out
SAFETY & SECURITY

Q "Since I've been at Radford, the security has gotten tighter and more serious around campus. **The events at Virginia Tech have made Radford more aware of the dangers at a university**. Our school has taken appropriate precautions for the students."

Q "The school has its own campus police. **They tend to circle around campus like vultures** when the evening sets in."

Q "The campus is really safe. There are blue-lights located around campus. If you don't feel safe, you can use them and get a safety escort back. **I have yet to hear of any serious crimes on campus**."

STUDENT AUTHOR: **Radford has always boasted a serious security program on campus. With the events at Virginia Tech, a school within 15 miles of Radford, the University has implemented many new security policies. There is no single place on campus where students feel unsafe walking, even at 2 a.m.**

Questions?

For more inside information and survival tips, pick up College Prowler's full-length book on this school, written by an actual student! Check it out at *www.collegeprowler.com*.

Students Speak Out
ON OVERALL EXPERIENCE

Q "**I love it here**. If I could start over as a freshman, I would do it again in a heartbeat."

Q "I love Radford! At this point, I can't see myself going anywhere else. Whenever I visit my friends at other schools, **I can't help but think that I have it better at Radford**."

Q "My overall experience has been amazing. I've made wonderful friends that I wouldn't trade for the world. **I couldn't imagine going anywhere else**."

Q "I like RU for the most part. **I've gone up and down with my feelings toward this school**. I am not a big fan of being in such a small town, and if I could do it over, I might go to a city school."

STUDENT AUTHOR: **Radford offers a unique experience in a small-town environment. The small size of the University allows for much more personal connections with both the faculty and other students. Radford social life is also a large bonus of such a small school. With a school so small, the majority of students know each other fairly well. They party together, go to classes together, and spend quality time together during campus activities and Greek Life. Our nightlife is a legend among colleges of Virginia, and the parties are incredible. The town is small but located within miles of several hot spots for action. Virginia Tech is 15 minutes away, Roanoke is less than an hour, and if the city is not what one is looking for, there are several mountainous hiking trails and camping areas. What it boils down to is that Radford is a "what you make of it" experience. If students put in the effort to go to class and engage in campus activities, their time at Radford will be incredible.**

Reed College

3203 Southeast Woodstock Boulevard; Portland, OR 97202
(503) 771-1112; www.reed.edu

THE BASICS:

Acceptance Rate: 32%
Setting: Urban
F-T Undergrads: 1,402

SAT Range: 1940–2210*
Control: Private
Tuition: $37,960

Most Popular Majors: Social Sciences, English, Biology, Psychology, Physical Sciences

*of 2400

Academics	A	Guys	C+
Local Atmosphere	A-	Girls	B-
Safety & Security	A-	Athletics	D+
Computers	A-	Nightlife	B
Facilities	B+	Greek Life	N/A
Campus Dining	C+	Drug Scene	C
Off-Campus Dining	A-	Campus Strictness	A
Campus Housing	A-	Parking	A-
Off-Campus Housing	A	Transportation	A
Diversity	C-	Weather	B-

Students Speak Out
ON ACADEMICS

Q "The classes are fantastic, particularly the conferences. The professors are **all very knowledgeable** and excited about their subjects, and more than willing to help their students."

Q "The teachers are very cool and very thought-provoking. None of them act as if they hold the right answers and that you are wrong, but rather they **approach everything like a discussion** that they could learn something from."

Q "I have found my teachers to be very dedicated to conveying the knowledge that they have to the students in an interesting and challenging way, and **always open to conversation** outside of the classroom."

Q "The professors at Reed tend to be some of the best around. They're **consistently fascinating and intelligent people** who teach fascinating and intelligent courses, though quite difficult. Though they're hard while you're taking them, I haven't regretted a single course I've taken."

STUDENT AUTHOR: As any good college-informer will say, Reed does not have any student teaching assistants; a professor leads every lecture, conference discussion, and seminar. Reed revolves around the concept of the conference system in which a minimal number of students and a professor critically discuss the subject of the class. No professor is an ivory tower; every person who educates at Reed College works to further the comprehension of any student in need.

Students Speak Out
ON LOCAL ATMOSPHERE

Q "Portland is a great city. It's small enough to not feel overwhelming, but big enough that you can find big-city amenities, like arts, little shops, and cool people. Plus, **public transportation here is great**."

Q "Portland's really fun. There's **a relaxed, casual atmosphere to the city** with a lot of independent coffee shops, restaurants, and bookstores. Just walk around and you'll find interesting things. Go to Powell's."

Q "Portland is **an awesome, friendly city**. Powell's is the largest independent bookstore in the world, and it's without a doubt my favorite part of the city. Portland's got everything! There are other schools, most notably the University of Portland and Lewis & Clark College. It also has Portland State University, the large state university just across the river. In general, I can't praise Portland enough; it has everything it needs to be self-sufficient. Portland has a small, but active theater scene, several wonderful scenic day trips, and some of the friendliest metropolitan people I've ever met."

STUDENT AUTHOR: Portland is an anomaly for modern-day cosmopolitan cities; it possesses both a big-city and a small-city feel. The city has the look, resources, amenities, and feel of a much larger metropolis. However, the close-knit nature of the city's community allows Portland a friendly atmosphere usually only afforded to smaller villages and towns.

Students Speak Out
ON FACILITIES

Q "The pool hall is awesome, and there is free pool for many hours of the day. I haven't used the athletic stuff, but it would be easy to do. **Everything is maintained well**, and use is not arbitrarily and excessively restricted."

Q "Facilities at Reed are clean, warm, and inviting. **The Student Union is pleasantly ratty**, the student darkroom is accessible and rad, and the fact that a band practice room exists is way cool. The pool hall is my second home, and you've got the print shop."

Q "The facilities are all very nice. Everything is kept clean—even the men's bathrooms. There are facilities for almost anything you could want. **Reed has a comic book library**, some fairly recent movies to check out from the library or rent from the bookstore, many well-maintained computers, and even a nuclear reactor if you need something carbon dated."

Q "Everything is nice here. **Some people complain**, but that's because they're spoiled and have never been to an actual college campus where stuff is falling apart and nobody cares."

STUDENT AUTHOR: **Although Reed may be small, the school's facilities allow for a wide range of activities. From sports or computing to studying or drinking coffee, Reed offers its students numerous state-of-the-art facilities to accommodate any desire or educational need. Students generally find Reed's campus to be one of the most well-maintained of any of the schools that they have visited.**

Famous Alumni

X James Beard, Susan Blosser, Arelene Blum, Suzan Delbene, Steven Jobs, Michael Levine, Peter Norton, Doros Platika, James Russell, Howard Vollum

Students Speak Out
ON CAMPUS DINING

Q "Food isn't bad, but then again, it isn't good. You can live off the food in the student center, but the selection **starts to get old after a few months**."

Q "Food sucks at Commons. The food is **overpriced and often inedible**. There are some nearby restaurants that are good, but that's even more money out of your pocket. I personally shop at Trader Joe's."

Q "The dining hall **isn't bad for the first year**. After that, the selection is repetitive."

Q "The food in Commons gets tedious, but Expo is usually good, and they do a good job of trying to offer variety. There's **a lot of catering to vegans, vegetarians**, and the occasional, barbaric meat-eater."

Q "Food here is fairly good. There are always several different options at Commons, the dining center, including vegetarian and vegan options. I can always find something I like. Also, there are **great kitchen facilities in some of the dorms** for when you get tired of Commons food."

STUDENT AUTHOR: **Unlike most institutions of higher education, Reed offers only one centralized dining hall for students choosing to dine on campus. However, while most students agree that on-campus college food usually lacks in comparison to what you could cook for yourself in an apartment, Reed students seem to appreciate what their campus dining experience has to offer. However fun it may be to dine on campus, though, it becomes rather tedious if done repeatedly.**

Student Body

African American:	1%	Male/Female:	45/55%
Asian American:	4%	Out-of-State:	86%
Hispanic:	5%	International:	3%
Native American:	1%	Unknown:	1%
White:	85%		

Popular Faiths: Several atheists, pagans, and Unitarians, as well as Christian and Jewish students.

Gay Pride: The many gay, lesbian, transgender, and bisexual students are given a stronger voice through the QA (Queer Alliance) organization.

Economic Status: Many students come from middle-class backgrounds, though there is a wide range.

Students Speak Out
ON DORMS

Q "There are pretty dorms, like Bragdon and Anna Mann, and there are dorms that look like they were erected in about three months and should really have been replaced a couple of decades ago, like Woodbridge and Chittick. Still, there's running hot water, heating, electricity, and Ethernet in all dorms, and **you can't really ask for much more than that**."

Q "The dorms are all pretty nice. There is definitely **some deviation in size** and ambient noise depending upon which dorm you are in. The only way to really know where you want to be is by checking out the dorms for yourself."

Q "Anna Mann used to be the president's house but has been converted into a dorm. **Many rooms have fireplaces**."

STUDENT AUTHOR: **Your enjoyment of living on campus at Reed depends on your willingness to sacrifice space and privacy for the ability to meet a ton of nice people in a close environment. Although campus rooms generally lack in size, the dorms themselves usually contain almost every amenity that a student could want.**

> **Did You Know?**
> 57% of undergrads live on campus.

Students Speak Out
ON GUYS & GIRLS

Q "To write about the condition that, according to the girls, afflicts the majority of the male population at Reed (namely that **their idea of courtship is ogling a person in class**), would take more space than I am permitted. I like girls, but there are not enough of them."

Q "Reed is not the place to go if you're looking to get booty or whatever. There are plenty of attractive people, but of those attractive people, I'd say about half are in seriously-committed relationships, and **the other half are socially retarded** in some way or another."

Q "Guys are generally attractive, white, and skinny. Same goes for girls. There are **a number of attractive catches** in both sexes."

STUDENT AUTHOR: Although not an overly-promiscuous campus, Reedies generally enjoy slightly more sexual liberation than the average society does. You can describe us according to our looks if you want, but doing so would do us a disservice, as such trivial concerns do not dominate our campus. To echo a few of the student quotes, you should not come to Reed if you're looking for a place where you can ogle the student body.

> **Traditions**
>
> **The Doyle Owl**
> A 400-pound stone owl statue that is passed around between students and which often appears at events.
>
> **Renn Fayre**
> A campus-wide festival held annually to celebrate the completion of the academic year.
>
> **Overall School Spirit**
> Although a few die-hards exist, most students remain apathetic to the sporting events of Reed. Academically, however, Reedies show a great deal of school spirit.

Students Speak Out
ON ATHLETICS

Q "**You're kidding, right**? If not, take your pick between women's rugby and Frisbee. The former is obviously limited somewhat by your gender."

Q "The concept of sports at Reed is **completely different from any other school**. Sports are played here, but with a joyful enthusiasm for the exertion and love of the game, not to keep scholarships or get somewhere in a career!"

Q "**Rugby, soccer, and Frisbee** are the only teams that really compete. Everyone else plays for fun."

Q "Here's a Reed joke that's an old favorite of mine: Why did the Reedie cross the road? To get his PE credit. Basically, there are sports here, but **they never come before academics**."

STUDENT AUTHOR: **Despite the dearth of athletic activities on campus and the complete absence of varsity sports, Reedies do enjoy sports (weather permitting). Reedies enjoy playing mainly for club teams. Otherwise, students generally prefer studying and partying to sporting; the usually inclement weather often prohibits all but the most extreme activities.**

Students Speak Out
ON DRUG SCENE

Q "Most students have used, or currently use, marijuana, and it's not that big a deal. Cocaine is prevalent, but decidedly less popular than it was in the '80s. Mushrooms are extremely popular, as is LSD. As for other psychoactive substances, most Reedies are **against the use of most synthetic drugs**, so there are not very many, though I'm sure you can buy anything you've ever heard or read about if you fall in with the right people."

Q "Drugs at Reed are plentiful, but **there is no pressure to drink** or do any kind of drugs."

Q "If you want drugs, they are **easily accessible**, and I guess that if you don't, it can seem like they are everywhere."

STUDENT AUTHOR: Most Reed students believe that, while Reed does possess a prevalent drug scene, that scene doesn't pressure students to become part of it. Although drugs do float rather freely around campus, those that choose to do those drugs respect other students while using them.

10:1	Student-to-Faculty Ratio
89%	Freshman Retention Rate
49%	Four-Year Graduation Rate
92%	Financial Aid Applicants Receiving Aid

Students Speak Out
SAFETY & SECURITY

Q "The campus safety officers are never far away when you need them. Even if you've just locked yourself out of your room or are uncomfortable walking back to the dorm at two in the morning, they're **always there to help out**."

Q "I don't find there to be a problem with it. Every now and again, a break-in of some kind occurs, but **I've never felt unsafe**, even alone at night."

Q "**The Honor Principle is taken very seriously**; it applies to life everywhere, not just at Reed or on campus. Here, if you lose a wallet, it will be returned to you within hours. You can leave your stuff in the library without fear of it being stolen. The CSOs [campus security officers] just try to keep people safe."

STUDENT AUTHOR: Reed students agree that, despite the occasional theft, Reed's CSOs do an outstanding job of protecting the community. Rarely do students feel in danger while on campus, and, if they do, Community Safety willingly provides an escort service at any hour of the night.

Questions?
For more inside information and survival tips, pick up College Prowler's full-length book on this school, written by an actual student! Check it out at *www.collegeprowler.com*.

Students Speak Out
ON OVERALL EXPERIENCE

Q "I wanted to transfer during freshman year, but I am so glad I stayed. **The workload pushes me to my limit**, mostly because my professors really seem to care about what I say and what I write. They seem to give everything they've got for each class, and I want to do the same. The friends I've made here are people I trust and respect—brilliant, thoughtful, and caring. They're just so fascinating! The people I've met here and the work I have done have changed my life; that's why I'm glad I stayed."

Q "Although this place is not without its flaws, and there is an **alienating cultish mentality** to being a 'Reedie,' I am happy here. I do not know of a place where I would rather be."

Q "Reed is very intelligent, a bit pretentious, somewhat insular, and **thoroughly insane**. I'm quite glad I came."

Q "Reed is a great place. There are so many incredible people here, so many incredible **resources, so much intensity**. You are on your own completely, which is hard at first, and may be a freedom abused by first-year students (hence the high attrition rate)."

STUDENT AUTHOR: Empirically, Reed's commitment to making critical thinkers and writers out of its students separates it from other academic institutions, and most students believe in Reed. Although feeling disenchanted with their institution of higher education at times, most Reedies accept their school's shortcomings for what they are, and accept that they can not see themselves anywhere else. Reed is not just a college, it is an academic, personal, and social experience, and Reedies respect and cherish Reed.

Rensselaer Polytechnic Institute

110 Eighth Street; Troy, NY 12180
(518) 276-6000; www.rpi.edu

THE BASICS:

Acceptance Rate: 44%
Setting: Mid-sized City
F-T Undergrads: 5,357

SAT Range: 1830–2100*
Control: Private
Tuition: $36,950

Most Popular Majors: Engineering, Computer Sciences, Business, Communication, Architecture

*of 2400

Academics	B+	Guys	C+
Local Atmosphere	D	Girls	C
Safety & Security	B	Athletics	B-
Computers	A+	Nightlife	C+
Facilities	B+	Greek Life	B+
Campus Dining	B+	Drug Scene	A-
Off-Campus Dining	C+	Campus Strictness	B
Campus Housing	B	Parking	C-
Off-Campus Housing	A-	Transportation	B-
Diversity	C+	Weather	D

Students Speak Out
ON ACADEMICS

Q "Many professors are **all about research**—but then, there are many teachers that really care about the students, are really smart, and have really interesting, amazing backgrounds and experiences."

Q "As a whole, I would say the teachers are what I expected. Overall, freshmen end up with a lot of classes which are **rather large lectures** (50–100 people, usually more like 50), so teachers can help but seem kind of distant."

Q "I think the professors are great. They really seem interested in the students, and if you go to their office hours, **they are always willing to help**. There are a few professors that don't seem to teach the material too well, and you might have to focus more on the book."

Q "**RPI is a tough school**. Lots of the classes you take even your first semester are among the hardest for other schools. Everybody knows this, including the professors, so the work goes along with that."

STUDENT AUTHOR: Your best bet is to talk to an upperclassman who has taken classes with professors before, and find out who is good and who to avoid. Pick a major that you're going to enjoy, but also pick one that you've got a good feeling about—again, talk to other students in the programs, because your major will make a huge difference. RPI is a demanding school, and students here are expected to do a lot of work, both inside and outside the classroom.

Students Speak Out
ON LOCAL ATMOSPHERE

Q "There is **Russell Sage College down the hill**. Troy is a small town, and it can be very boring, especially if you don't have a car. You need to go out of town for entertainment, mostly."

Q "**Downtown is a kind of sketchy place** at night. I'd say the atmosphere on campus is a deal better than in the city."

Q "Albany is a medium-sized city, and Troy is nicknamed the Troylet: not much to do there. **NYC, Boston, and Montreal are all three-hour drives away**."

Q "A city such as this leads to **an isolated campus**, where there is not a heck of a lot to do during the long winter months except concentrate on your studies. And when you are paying top dollar for a school such as RPI, that's probably not a bad thing anyway."

STUDENT AUTHOR: In general, students find Troy to be a boring and dangerous place where it is hard to have fun. Albany, Saratoga, and Grafton Lake are all good get-away spots if you have a car. As far as entertainment options, there are a few decent golf courses in the area at reasonable prices, not to mention plenty of hills to go hiking, and creeks if you feel like cliff jumping on a hot afternoon. RPI will tell you that you should never go downtown—it can be scary at night, as long as you don't wander off by yourself. Distractions are welcome to break the monotony of studying; whenever you have a chance to do something different, you should.

5 Best Things	5 Worst Things
1 Computer network	1 Male/female ratio
2 Frat parties	2 Weather
3 Big Red Freakout	3 Administration
4 GM Week	4 Commons food
5 Senior Week	5 Lack of activities

Students Speak Out
ON FACILITIES

Q "The facilities are **good and getting better**. RPI has been spending quite a bit of money on improving its facilities."

Q "We have a new fitness center, which is really good: **three floors and aerobics classes** are offered and stuff like that. It's a good resource."

Q "Computer labs are nice, not as abundant as some places because **all students are required to have laptops**, but they're around. The Student Union is pretty cool; it's a good place to go to do work, get food, or meet people. It has four bowling lanes, pool tables, and a small arcade. It also has a piano."

Q "Most of the facilities are 1800s looking on the outside and **modern on the inside**, combining the best of the old and the new."

Q "RPI has a **good student union**, although the bookstore is a little lacking."

STUDENT AUTHOR: The students of RPI are satisfied with the facilities on campus. The Union renovation and the Mueller Center give the students good places to study and relax, as well as work out and burn off some of the stress that can build up from classes. The computer labs and their availability have also scored big with the student body, despite the fact that everyone has a laptop anyway. The dorms are steadily improving with each year. The athletic facilities are top-notch and provide great equipment to help students stay in shape. RPI combines an older-style campus with the most modern technology, making it a perfect marriage of grace and practicality.

Famous Alumni

Kevin Constantine, Allen DuMont, George W.G. Ferris, J. Erik Jonsson, Joe Juneau, George Low, Adam Oates, Sheldon Roberts, Ray Tomlinson

Students Speak Out
ON CAMPUS DINING

Q "Compared to other colleges, the food is very good, but like **all mass-produced food, it can get old**."

Q "There are essentially three places to go for food: The Commons is the largest dining hall, and pretty much all your meals are there. Sage Dining Hall is the alternative main dining hall; the food at Sage is better overall, but the selection is a lot more limited. The Union has places where you can **buy food with cash or credits** on your meal account, and it's pretty good food but isn't unlimited dining."

Q "Every **freshman has a meal plan** that can be used at the big freshman dining hall (called the Commons), as well as Russell Sage dining hall on campus. You can usually find something."

Q "I would rank the food on campus as **average**."

Q "For a quick lunch, the Union and Rathskellar are excellent. In a lot of the buildings, you can find **bagel and coffee stations** which is nice if you are in a hurry."

STUDENT AUTHOR: The variety in the dining halls and the Union is good, but the food is passable and no better. Special-need diets, such as vegetarians and vegans, can find it difficult to find an appropriate meal. The smaller food carts scattered throughout campus provide students a quick bite between classes if they can't make it to a dining hall when they are in a rush. The dining halls themselves offer many different all-you-can-eat options, and though the food is rather expensive, it is at least filling.

Student Body

African American:	4%	Male/Female:	75/25%
Asian American:	12%	Out-of-State:	49%
Hispanic:	5%	International:	4%
Native American:	<1%	Unknown:	0%
White:	75%		

Popular Faiths: The major religions are Christianity (Catholic and Protestant), Judaisim, and Islam.

Gay Pride: There is a relatively small population of homosexuals, and the community is not biased.

Economic Status: There are students from all different economic backgrounds, although there are quite a few that come from very well-off families. Some argue there is too much "old money" at RPI.

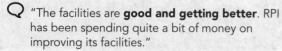

Students Speak Out
ON DORMS

Q "The quality of the dorms is rather varied. I'd say the **dorms at RPI are slightly less nice** than the dorms I saw at other colleges."

Q "Dorms are dorms: they all suck, except for Barton. **Barton is like a hotel**. All of the other dorms are pretty much the same as each other. BARH is mixed upperclassmen and underclassmen; it's a little farther from campus and off of Freshman Hill."

Q "Avoid North Hall or E-dorms; **good dorms are Nugent, Davison, BARH**, and maybe Warren. Single apartments are Colonie, those are good, too."

STUDENT AUTHOR: **The housing on campus is comparable to that at most colleges. Dorms provide excellent opportunities to meet new people and offer social outlets for the residents. Renovations to Freshman Hill and Cary Hall going coed means there is no longer a clear-cut "Worst Dorm On Campus" award winner, so freshmen don't have to worry about getting stuck in a complete dungeon. The dorms are expensive, which is why many move off campus after freshman year.**

? Did You Know?
56% of undergrads live on campus.

Students Speak Out
ON GUYS & GIRLS

Q "There are lots of guys, some cool, some computer dorks, but girls have all the power at RPI. Most of the girls aren't that great looking, but **the ones who are can do whatever**."

Q "**Some guys are hot**, while others are dorky."

Q "There is a very disturbing mix of kids here. Many very **sheltered, technical, computer people**; along with the little art groups of people who seem to stand out a lot."

Q "You'll find people with all sorts of eccentricities and idiosyncrasies. Believe me when I say there are **all types of people on the campus**. Whether you are the large football player type or the silent, quiet type, you're bound to find them somewhere."

STUDENT AUTHOR: **The men at RPI outnumber the women by better than three to one, and that makes it hard on both sides. For women, most of the guys seem to be dorks or jocks, and of the good guys left most seem to be taken. For guys, the numbers aren't favorable, even factoring in the women from Russell Sage. What girls are available seem to become stuck up, because they're in such a minority that they can afford to be very choosy.**

Traditions

The Big Red Freakout
A campus-wide hockey frenzy when students wear RPI clothing and go to the sold out hockey game.

Senior Week
A week at the end of the spring semester. Seniors take part in the Senior Banquet and Booze Cruise.

Overall School Spirit
School spirit is marginal at best. RPI clothing is commonplace. Grand Marshal Week is the biggest school spirit event on campus, which are student government elections, as well as other activities.

Students Speak Out
ON ATHLETICS

Q "RPI has **Division I men's ice hockey**; the other sports are Division III. There are IM sports that people participate in, and students can even start their own."

Q "A lot of people play sports, but the **social scene doesn't revolve around sports** at all. IM sports are pretty popular, more popular than varsity, and a lot of sports are available."

Q "Many people get involved. If you're not a hockey fan now, **you may get sucked in**."

Q "If you are on a sports team, there are usually a lot of social activities associated with it. Most of the **sports teams hang out a lot outside of practice and have parties**."

STUDENT AUTHOR: **While RPI is a Division III school, the student athletes take athletics very seriously. Hockey and football are the only two that draw a crowd, but the others are still highly competitive within their conference. Many students find they don't have the time to dedicate to the rigor of varsity sports, though, which is why intramural sports and clubs are so popular. They provide an opportunity for students to remain active.**

Students Speak Out
ON DRUG SCENE

Q "Public Safety and RDs are **really strict about drugs and alcohol**. RAs are okay about alcohol sometimes, but will still write you up for it."

Q "Well, as long as you are quiet, you are pretty much safe. There are drugs around RPI, yet not that much in the open, and drinking does occur—but for the most part, **it's at a party**."

Q "The illegal-drug scene here is mainly pot. People use a variety of others, of course, but the one most often seen, heard about, or smelled is pot. **Ritalin and Adderall are also popular for students cramming before tests**."

STUDENT AUTHOR: **RPI is not much different from most campuses. Most students prefer alcohol, with marijuana coming in a distant second. Overall, the campus has very few problems; even the number of reported incidents is low, considering the size of the campus. There is no pressure to do anything if you don't want to, and those groups that choose to use drugs mainly stick to themselves. You could go four years and never see a thing.**

14:1	Student-to-Faculty Ratio
95%	Freshman Retention Rate
57%	Four-Year Graduation Rate
64%	Financial Aid Applicants Receiving Aid

Students Speak Out
SAFETY & SECURITY

Q "Campus safety is **more concerned with giving people parking tickets** then they are with the blue-light at the emergency booth."

Q "Campus is very safe. I don't feel threatened while on campus, and if it's late, you can always ask campus police to **give you an escort to your dorm**."

Q "RPI's Public Safety officers function **essentially like police**, and they're really nice about helping and everything. There are public-access telephones all over campus."

Q "The town of **Troy isn't quite as nice** or that safe in certain areas. That's not to say that Troy is a bad place; there are some nice parts of Troy."

STUDENT AUTHOR: **If you leave things lying around for too long, such as a laptop or books, they may not be there when you come back. This is probably the biggest risk, but at least it's avoidable. Remember to lock your doors every time you leave—no matter how secure the dorms seem, you can't be too careful.**

Questions?
For more inside information and survival tips, pick up College Prowler's full-length book on this school, written by an actual student! Check it out at *www.collegeprowler.com*.

Students Speak Out
ON OVERALL EXPERIENCE

Q "Although the **social scene isn't the greatest** and there are a lot of cliques, I've found my niche among friends, and the education I'm getting is going to give me the opportunity to be a pioneer in my field."

Q "This school is **much more challenging** than most, and my fraternity life keeps me sane, but I definitely wish they ran things a little differently here so that we at least get the impression that the administration cares about its students."

Q "It's a good school, and it gives me a good education. People are nice, and **you just have to be outgoing** and you will meet a lot of people and have fun."

Q "If you have trouble with a class, you can find about five people **willing to take time and help you with the class** and your work."

Q "The **classes are good, but they are tough**; don't expect any breaks with the grading. Socially RPI is all right—probably better for girls than guys."

STUDENT AUTHOR: **RPI provides many advantages to its students; the most important of those are the prospects post-graduation. This is perhaps the most compelling reason to come to RPI Most find their way into the workforce with decent entry-level jobs. The social life isn't what you can find at other schools, but there are still fun things to do if you're willing to look for them; students who get into the social scene tend to remain friends with the people they meet, even after graduation. This is not a party school—work comes first. Partying is fine, but not at the expense of schoolwork. Manage your time well.**

Rhode Island School of Design

2 College Street; Providence, RI 02903
(401) 454-6100; www.risd.edu

Academics	A-	Guys	C+
Local Atmosphere	A-	Girls	B+
Safety & Security	B	Athletics	D
Computers	B+	Nightlife	B+
Facilities	B-	Greek Life	N/A
Campus Dining	B-	Drug Scene	B-
Off-Campus Dining	A-	Campus Strictness	B+
Campus Housing	C-	Parking	D
Off-Campus Housing	B+	Transportation	B+
Diversity	B+	Weather	C

Students Speak Out
ON ACADEMICS

Q "They are amazing, intriguing, and great. I learn so much from them. Everyone is **helpful and open to independent study**. I find my classes very interesting and challenging."

Q "For the most part, it really impresses me that there are **teachers who are willing to sacrifice their personal time to help their students**. I have professors who come in to give me extra help during Sunday mornings; I also had another teacher who came in late during the night and stayed with me until midnight to help me with my work. On that note, I feel like RISD teachers are some of the most dedicated and caring teachers I have ever met in my life."

Q "Most of the teachers I have had here **have a lot of expectations of their students**. They are dedicated and driven and will go out of their way to help students, giving them just as much back as the students put in. My classes are very interesting."

Q "Some studio classes are interesting, but most **liberal arts classes are jokes**."

STUDENT AUTHOR: The faculty is the driving force behind RISD's strenuous and exciting classes. It is safe to say that while there may be the odd professor that does not meet what the high-standard students expect from their faculty, professors at RISD are professional, knowledgeable, and dedicated to their students and their field. Regardless of major, studio classes are almost always challenging and enriching.

Students Speak Out
ON LOCAL ATMOSPHERE

Q "**Providence is a weird, big college/colonial town**. Stay away from the downtown transit area. Visit Wickenden St., Thayer St., Brown University, and Downtown. Visit the old buildings and the Capitol Building."

Q "The East Side and College Hill are rather student friendly. It's **not a large city**, it's pretty small actually, but it still has the same kinds of benefits that a larger city has. I wouldn't venture out into the south end of Providence alone at night."

Q "The atmosphere is okay, I guess. **I don't really think there is one distinct atmosphere** for the entire city. There are bad areas; ones to stay away from, but nothing close enough for a RISD student to really wander into."

Q "Honestly, I don't think there's much to do in Providence in terms of entertainment, since I grew up in a big city. **You really need to get out there to discover things you want to do**."

STUDENT AUTHOR: Providence, Rhode Island is absolutely New England. It is the largest city in New England outside Boston, and behaves accordingly. While culturally, Boston is a big leap from Providence, there are things about the city that make it wonderful. The main activity in Providence is built on the colleges of RISD, Brown, and Johnson & Wales, and so the town caters much of its business and attitude toward college students. The surrounding college neighborhoods are fairly quiet and pleasantly residential.

5 Best Things	5 Worst Things
1 The art community	1 Lack of financial aid
2 The professors	2 Timid social scene
3 The studio facilities	3 Restricted resources
4 Connection with Brown	4 Never sleeping
5 Student shows	5 Activity participation

Students Speak Out
ON FACILITIES

Q "We'll probably always want more in our studios. But I think **compared to other schools, we have amazing resources**. My department has equipment that only exists at a couple schools in the country."

Q "It **depends on your major**—my studios are unbelievable. They put a million resources at your fingertips. And the atmosphere is great for working. I haven't really heard people that upset about communal studios; it's more a fight for personal studio space. Some majors get more than others, and not until a certain year, if at all."

Q "I've been really impressed with my department. My class doubled the size of the previous class, and **they've found a way to accommodate us at every turn**. It's been tight in some cases, the CAD lab is the worst, but we've managed."

Q "**Some departments are a lot nicer and newer than others as far as facilities**. The computers are all pretty new and fast, the gym is mediocre, but we can use the very nice Brown gym instead."

STUDENT AUTHOR: When it comes to studio space, (which is the facility that students care about most), it's on a department by department basis. On the whole, people's needs are met one way or another. The equipment that RISD students are privileged to have access to during their college experience is impressive. When it comes to athletic facilities, Brown makes up for what RISD lacks. RISD's greatest resource is the Museum.

Famous Alumni

Chris van Allsburg, David Byrne, Dale Chihuly, Liz Collins, Martin Mull, Seth MacFarlane, Nicole Miller, Gus van Sant

Students Speak Out
ON CAMPUS DINING

Q "The food is actually really, really good. **Compared to other schools, it's excellent**. I've had friends come over excited to eat at the Met with me. Carr Haus (campus coffee house) is excellent. The dining halls don't have much atmosphere, but the food is good."

Q "The food at Carr Haus is the best, but that's where the longest line is, usually. With the Met, **you really have to be on the meal plan to afford the prices**. The Pit is good grilled stuff, but it gets real old real fast, and it's sometimes too greasy. I haven't eaten much at the Break because it's way out of the way. And Watermark Café is great, but really, really expensive for school food."

Q "The **food is good in comparison** to the other schools I've visited."

Q "For campus food, it's quite good. You get sick of it by the second half of your freshman year, but it's still pretty good. There are **always vegetarian and vegan options** and lots of 'do-it-yourself' salad/sandwich stuff. Carr Haus has good baked goods but vile coffee. The new RISD Watermark Café is great quality, but pricey."

STUDENT AUTHOR: Students will always, always complain about school food. Anyone eating the same things every day for every meal is bound to get sick of them. However, if you ask freshmen in the first month of school, they'll tell you how great the food is. It's diverse, there are always vegetarian options and vegan options, it's tasty, and it's healthy.

Student Body

African American:	1%	Male/Female:	33/67%
Asian American:	14%	Out-of-State:	83%
Hispanic:	4%	International:	16%
Native American:	<1%	Unknown:	25%
White:	39%		

Popular Faiths: The most popular faiths on campus are Christianity, Catholicism, and Judaism.

Gay Pride: The students at RISD are extremely proud of gay classmates, and the Lesbian, Gay, Bisexual Alliance is active on campus and sponsors a Freshman Outreach Program.

Economic Status: Most students come from a middle- to upper-class background.

Students Speak Out
ON DORMS

Q "**Being in the dorms is important because you meet so many people**. I lived in school housing for three years and made a lot of friends and stayed connected to what was going on because of that. Dexter House and Colonial Apartments are great."

Q "Dorms are dorms. **If you want to live in the lap of luxury, move off campus**. It's hard enough to get housing as it is. They are average. Not so new, but they function fine. They were all pretty equal for the first year."

Q "The **freshman dorms are really fun** and the rooms are a fine size. There's enough space. If you're a party kid, go for Homer 5, for upperclassmen, avoid Farnum."

STUDENT AUTHOR: It's true; you can't avoid dorm life if you come to RISD as a freshman. However, there are some definite pluses to living in the quad. You are right by food and studios, and there are always people around and awake to hang out with. If you're not so lucky as to get a suite, the communal bathroom is only for a year. Once you're out of the freshman dorms, life gets better.

> **? Did You Know?**
> 70% of undergrads live on campus.

Students Speak Out
ON GUYS & GIRLS

Q "Guys? **RISD is predominantly female**, completely so in some majors. I'm sure there are some hot guys out there. There are definitely lots of very attractive, stylish girls."

Q "**This is a ridiculous question**. Anyone who bases their decision to attend on this deserves to end up somewhere where everyone has prominent birth defects that are difficult to politely stop staring at."

Q "**Guys are few and far between**, but the girls are hot."

Q "**If girls need to find guys, I would recommend going to Brown**. I have a lot of guy friends on campus, but I see them more as good friends and not people to date."

STUDENT AUTHOR: It may sound like a lot of places, but it certainly doesn't sound like college: tons of young, beautiful women, surrounded by a small showing of fairly attractive, mostly gay men. That's art school. Both the gay and straight dating scenes are vibrant and energetic, and there are plenty of clubs, bars, and coffeehouses for both depending on what kind of experience is desired. The most important thing to remember at RISD is that it's personality that gets you the farthest.

> **Traditions**
>
> **Class Ring**
> In 1994, Tamara Mottl designed the RISD ring which students now wear proudly.
>
> **Studying in Rome**
> New juniors and seniors from the European Honors Program venture off to Rome to study art and architecture.
>
> **Overall School Spirit**
> People are here because they want to be, and they love the school, but they're sarcastic and cynical, and that's also part of the spirit.

Students Speak Out
ON ATHLETICS

Q "**Sports at RISD aren't big at all**. I don't even know if they're fun, but they're definitely funny."

Q "Sports are not big at all. It's gotten better from the past. The biggest thing is probably ice hockey, the Nads, and maybe the Balls. **Students are so busy getting their studio work done**, I don't think they have time to do extracurricular stuff."

Q "**Sports are nonexistent**. Some of them are fun clubs. They're more like fun and loose get-togethers."

Q "**Athletics aren't very big**, unless you count getting drunk to cheer on a giant, foam, rubber penis a sport."

STUDENT AUTHOR: While serious athletics is pretty much out of the question at RISD, students definitely have fun with what they've got. Imagine, during parents' weekend, half the campus drunk and yelling obscenities at a team of completely bewildered ice-hockey players while a giant penis in a cape leads cheers from the sidelines. Once in a while, there will be a scandal during which Scrotie has been kidnapped by an unnamed group.

Students Speak Out
ON DRUG SCENE

Q "**It's not a big thing here**. There is drinking, but not as much as most other colleges. There are drugs too, but once again, not as much as many other places. I think most RISD people are too dedicated to their work to want to waste lots of time getting really messed up. Caffeine abuse, that's rampant, but everything else is limited."

Q "The drug scene is there, if you do a little searching you can find most things. **It's not a problem**, though. Most people here are too serious about what they do to be involved with it."

Q "**Some kids do tons of drugs**, but it's not usually the kids you would expect. It's not in your face, but it's available."

STUDENT AUTHOR: The drug scene at RISD is something that exists behind closed doors. It's definitely around, but most people don't get mixed up in anything worse than pot. There is a manageable amount of drinking around, but for most people it's not for more than one night a week, if every week.

8:1	Student-to-Faculty Ratio
96%	Freshman Retention Rate
78%	Four-Year Graduation Rate
56%	Financial Aid Applicants Receiving Aid

Students Speak Out
SAFETY & SECURITY

Q "On campus, it's pretty good. The shuttle system has improved greatly, meaning you never have to be walking home alone at night. **For a city of its size, Providence is not a very dangerous place**, and the RISD area is the poshest section of Providence. You shouldn't be out alone at 2 a.m. or leave expensive electronics around, but I feel safe enough."

Q "I think campus feels pretty safe, most of the time, but I get a little skittish walking around at three in the morning. I wouldn't walk around on parts other than Thayer St. and Wickenden St. by myself after dark. **Definitely travel in groups after dark when off campus**."

Q "**It's safe**. Providence is a city; muggings are a reality, but happen infrequently."

STUDENT AUTHOR: Even though Providence is a city, most students feel safe while they're on campus and the close surrounding areas. The blue emergency phones, Public Safety Officers' patrol, strict building access, and Saferide system keep the feeling of on-campus safety high.

Questions?
For more inside information and survival tips, pick up College Prowler's full-length book on this school, written by an actual student! Check it out at www.collegeprowler.com.

Students Speak Out
ON OVERALL EXPERIENCE

Q "**I love RISD, and i can't imagine being in another school**. Everyone is so nice and friendly. You can talk to random people out of your major and feel perfectly comfortable talking to them. I was amazed at how much talent people have and how much you can learn from each other. It's very inspiring to be around a group of talented people, you get new ideas from your peers. I have also branched out a lot, and have many friends from other departments."

Q "I think I'm meant to be here. Despite a couple of minor drawbacks, this school has helped me hone my technical knowledge and fine-art capabilities. **A number of teachers have been life-alteringly inspirational**. It is an intense place, and I don't recommend attending unless you bring that same level of intensity to the table."

Q "Art school is the biggest joke and the best thing ever. **Don't take it too seriously**."

Q "It's been a good one. **There have been downsides**, things I didn't enjoy, but nothing I think I could have necessarily avoided by going anywhere else (all the dorms I've seen are equally crappy)."

STUDENT AUTHOR: The workload may be extremely demanding, but RISD students are not coming to receive the typical college experience. Students who come to RISD are coming to gain access to an amazing amount of resources and equipment. Once students let go of any ideas of what college is supposed to be, they will realize that what RISD offers is not only a completely unique and exhilarating experience, but a degree that holds a lot of weight in the professional world.

Rhodes College

2000 North Parkway; Memphis, TN 38112
(901) 843-3000; www.rhodes.edu

THE BASICS:

Acceptance Rate: 50%
Setting: Urban
F-T Undergrads: 1,651

SAT Range: 1160–1350*
Control: Private
Tuition: $32,136

Most Popular Majors: Social Sciences, Biology, Business, English Literature, Psychology

*of 1600

Academics	B+	Guys	B-
Local Atmosphere	B+	Girls	B
Safety & Security	B-	Athletics	C-
Computers	B	Nightlife	A-
Facilities	B	Greek Life	A
Campus Dining	C	Drug Scene	B-
Off-Campus Dining	A	Campus Strictness	B
Campus Housing	B	Parking	B+
Off-Campus Housing	B+	Transportation	C-
Diversity	D-	Weather	B

Students Speak Out
ON ACADEMICS

Q "Most of the professors at Rhodes truly care about your learning progress. I would say that the **professors at Rhodes are mentors** rather than simply teachers."

Q "The thing I like the most is that **Rhodes forces you to learn**. If you have even a half-open mind, you're going to be exposed to all sorts of things you probably have never heard of before."

Q "Classes are **largely discussion-oriented**, and on the whole, very interesting. Professors encourage you to think, not just imbibe what they say and regurgitate it."

Q "**I don't like the amount of work**. Yes, Rhodes is challenging, but it's not so much the quality of the work due, it's the quantity. Teachers really pile it on."

Q "Some are boring and deliver a lecture every day, but some teachers have **great indirect instruction techniques**."

STUDENT AUTHOR: **The workload at Rhodes is definitely challenging. It often feels like just as you've finished one paper another is due, and that right when you get through with one exam, you have to start studying for another. What really makes Rhodes's academics so phenomenal are the professors. If you make a good grade, you earn it. They put a lot of effort into their work, and they expect to get just as much back from you. Professors push you to push yourself, but they will also joke around with you.**

Students Speak Out
ON LOCAL ATMOSPHERE

Q "Memphis is **a nice, small community**. All Rhodes students must take at least one trip to Graceland during their four years here—it is a rite of passage of sorts."

Q "There is a **dichotomy here of the haves and have-nots,** but in Memphis, these two groups live within a block of each other rather than having buffer zones of middle-class housing. The other universities are more diverse in terms of the student body, but they lack the academic rigor of Rhodes."

Q "It's easy to judge Memphis too harshly, but if you spend the time to get to know it, it's pretty cool. Subculture is hard to find, but it does exist. So does **good local music of all types** if you know where to look. Go to the Caravan, the New Daisy, and the Riot if you like rock. Go to Beale as often as possible. Even if you can't drink, you can just sit around and listen to music."

Q "Memphis is **a city of rapid transitions**—one moment you're in a nice, safe area and the next, you've entered the ghetto."

STUDENT AUTHOR: **Memphis isn't the paradigmatic college town, but that's part of its charm. From the blues and bars on Beale to the quirky antique and vintage shops in the Cooper-Young District, Memphis has just about anything for anyone. The music scene is terrific, and you're almost guaranteed an impromptu concert somewhere. Crime is high; use the buddy system whenever you go out.**

5 Best Things	5 Worst Things
1 Honor Code	1 Meal plans
2 Academics	2 Tuition
3 Architecture	3 Athletics
4 Atmosphere	4 Bathrooms
5 Greek system	5 Rumor mill

Students Speak Out
ON FACILITIES

Q "The facilities on campus are top-notch and very versatile. No matter what your interests are, there is probably **some place that can accommodate** them."

Q "The gym is great, but it's **too small for the quantity of people** that work out at Rhodes. The machines are great, but usually one is broken. The classrooms are all pretty good."

Q "The buildings, architecture, and just the general **beauty of the campus** are in my top five things I love about Rhodes. The stone and ivy are just perfect."

Q "The facilities on campus are wonderful. You never feel like a place is unclean (even the bathrooms). The buildings are beautiful inside and out, and they make a **nice atmosphere for study**."

Q "Buildings, recreational facilities, and the campus as a whole are **all top-notch**."

STUDENT AUTHOR: The aesthetic aspect of the campus is arguably unequaled by any other college in the nation. The buildings' gothic architecture, stained glass, and abundant ivy give Rhodes an Oxford feel. At night, when the bell chimes and the windows glow blue, green, and red, it seems otherworldly. Many students who visit the campus simply fall in love with its beauty, and decide to seal the deal on their enrollment. But Rhodes isn't just a pretty face, it's the whole package. The College offers state-of-the-art, convenient facilities wrapped up in stunning exteriors, while continuing to expand and upgrade each year.

Famous Alumni

John Bryan, Lt. General Claudia J. Kennedy, George Hearn

Students Speak Out
ON CAMPUS DINING

Q "As much as we complain about them, the dining options are pretty good—there are **always healthy and not-so-healthy options** available."

Q "There is a great selection, and with the improved menu options recently, things have only gotten better. There is **something for every taste**, and a lot of healthy options that taste really good, too."

Q "The campus food is pretty good, considering. **Hours are restrictive**, but food is generally good, except on weekends. Rat food on the weekends should be avoided at all costs."

Q "The food here is horrible. You are **forced to pay for the meal plan if you live on campus**, and because of possible class schedules, one is apt to miss two meals a day due to the times they are served at."

Q "Java City makes decent coffee, their sandwiches and dessert items are good, but it can be a wee bit **pricey for a meager college budget**."

STUDENT AUTHOR: If you live on campus, you have to be on a meal plan. The only two places to eat using your plan are the Rat and the Lair. Because of the rather inflexible hours and sparse options, it's nearly impossible to make the most of your meal plan, and you usually end up wasting a lot of money each week. Surely everyone can find something that they consider appetizing, but because of the prices and time limits, they might not always be able to get it.

Student Body

African American:	4%	Male/Female:	42/58%
Asian American:	3%	Out-of-State:	72%
Hispanic:	1%	International:	1%
Native American:	<1%	Unknown:	1%
White:	90%		

Popular Faiths: Rhodes is predominantly Christian, but a lot of religious activity takes place.

Gay Pride: The campus is accepting of its gay students, but in general, the gay community is relatively quiet. FOSTER is an on-campus student organization that encourages acceptance.

Economic Status: Students come from a variety of backgrounds, but the majority seems to be wealthy.

Students Speak Out
ON DORMS

Q "The residence halls are okay. The rooms are a lot **bigger than most of the other colleges** I applied to, but the furnishings could be updated."

Q "Freshman year, I thought my room was fine. Not too big, but good enough. Then I visited a friend at a state university and realized my room was a palace compared to his room. And **it only gets better as you get older**. You couldn't ask for better housing."

Q "Most of the residence halls are **comfy and cozy**. The rooms can take a little getting used to depending on what you are used to when at home, but overall, the size is adequate."

STUDENT AUTHOR: **The biggest drawback of campus housing is the housing selection process. The lottery system is fair, and usually works out well in the end, but the whole ordeal is really just a big convoluted hassle. Most Rhodes students are moderately happy with their on-campus housing. All Rhodes students must live on campus for at least two full academic years, so having big rooms and clean amenities is a plus.**

Did You Know?
75% of undergrads live on campus.

Students Speak Out
ON GUYS & GIRLS

Q "Of course everyone is very smart, and there are many good-looking people, but when you go to such an academically-based school, you have to learn to **look at the inner beauty** of a person."

Q "The guys here are very intelligent and nice. It is very hard to expect a dating-type situation, however. The people at Rhodes are often either in a **serious relationship or they are just randomly hooking up** with people. Although there are a lot of cute, sweet guys, they are not often looking for a relationship."

Q "I'm really not quite sure where Rhodes finds all these attractive people. There are tons of well-dressed, smart, **cute guys and girls**. Kids are really friendly here, especially to new people."

STUDENT AUTHOR: No one would go so far as to say that every guy and girl on campus is swoon worthy, but in general, the student body is well over moderately attractive. You'll also see some artsy, intellectual types, a few who want nothing better than to be transported back to the '60s, and a number who are clean-cut. Nearly everyone is outspoken and intelligent, which are attractive qualities, and people are sincere.

Traditions

The Honor Code
All students pledge to uphold the code, which means refraining from dishonest acts, treating everyone with respect, and preserving the Rhodes community.

Rites of Spring
Nationally-known bands are booked for a three-day concert fest that is free to all students.

Overall School Spirit
Even though students don't rally on the bleachers, many adorn themselves, their cars, and their rooms with the Rhodes logo.

Students Speak Out
ON ATHLETICS

Q "Varsity sports are **for those who love the game and want to be competitive**. I love sports, but I think at the varsity level, they take too much away from other college things like studying and having fun. IM sports are great fun."

Q "Sports **games are fun here**, but if you are looking for a big school spirit college, Rhodes is not the place to find that."

Q "The sports programs are somewhat underappreciated in my opinion, but then again, **most people don't come to Rhodes for the sports**, they come for the academics."

Q "I think that the **athletes are a pretty tight-knit group**, and the athletic programs are definitely worth participating in."

STUDENT AUTHOR: Rhodes's status as a Division III school plays a large role in the general apathy of the student body towards sports. It seems that varsity sports are only important to those athletes who are involved in them. However, the number of students who participate in intramural and club sports is quite shocking considering the school's academics-only reputation.

Students Speak Out
ON DRUG SCENE

Q "Some students smoke out, but I don't think it is that prevalent and certainly not blatant. There is **not a lot of pressure to do drugs** here."

Q "I hear that cocaine is a problem, but I have never actually seen it. Drugs are definitely used here, but it is **not really out in the open**, and easy to avoid if that is not your scene."

Q "**Drinking is very evident** at every party. Though you may hear about someone going to smoke marijuana, it is rarely done in front of you. Other drugs are around, but no one talks about it."

STUDENT AUTHOR: **Rhodes is not completely drug-free, but drugs are definitely not a dominant force on campus. Alcohol is unquestionably the drug of choice (though it may be tied with caffeine), and even a number of students abstain from indulging in it. There's no pressure to partake in drugs if they don't want to, and the majority don't want to. Everyone seems to have heard of someone who does drugs, but few actually admit to it. If you're looking for drugs then you're able to find them.**

11:1	Student-to-Faculty Ratio
85%	Freshman Retention Rate
77%	Four-Year Graduation Rate
87%	Financial Aid Applicants Receiving Aid

Students Speak Out
SAFETY & SECURITY

Q "I **always feel safe**, even beyond the point of being reasonable sometimes."

Q "Safety on campus is good, and I've never felt unsafe. Since we're on an honor code, lots of kids **leave their doors unlocked**, leave their backpacks at the entrance of the Rat, and walk around at night with little apprehension."

Q "Our security is much better than any other Memphis school. Everywhere you look, there is a security camera, and you cannot get onto campus unless you go through security first. The beautiful but intimidating fence around campus **deters unwanted visitors**, and no one can enter the dorms without an ID card."

STUDENT AUTHOR: **Since the Honor Code plays a huge role in protecting students from dishonest acts, Campus Safety's main job is to protect students from people outside of it. It's easy for students to forget just how much crime is outside of the gates and how much is stopped everyday from getting in.**

> **Questions?**
> For more inside information and survival tips, pick up College Prowler's full-length book on this school, written by an actual student! Check it out at *www.collegeprowler.com*.

Students Speak Out
ON OVERALL EXPERIENCE

Q "I love it here. Though there isn't a lot of diversity, and there are definitely some things I would like to change, I feel like I am getting a **good education in a fun and comfortable environment**."

Q "The people are laid-back, smart, friendly, and civil to each other—everyone co-exists here in relative peace, even if we're not all best friends. It's **impossible to be anonymous here**, someone knows you and cares about you, especially your professors."

Q "I think everyone goes through a phase at Rhodes where they want to transfer. But for some reason, **most people stay** and end up having, for the most part, the time of their lives. I am so glad I came here."

Q "Rhodes is okay. The **social scene is pretty bland, but the academics seem good**. I think that I would be happier at a more liberal school; for all their claims of being liberal and committed to diversity, it hardly seems evident."

STUDENT AUTHOR: **When assessing their college experience, most students feel that Rhodes is the right place for them, and that they'd rather not be anywhere else. Students are constantly challenged to reach their potential, explore their interests, and take advantage of their talent. In the beginning, it's sometimes difficult for students to take all of this in. At some point, every student is going to dislike something about the college—the massive amount of work, the social scene, the food, even the weather. But overall, most students are very satisfied with their decision to attend Rhodes.**

Rice University

6100 Main; Houston, TX 77005
(713) 348-0000; www.rice.edu

THE BASICS:

Acceptance Rate: 22%   **SAT Range:** 1330–1540*
Setting: Urban   **Control:** Private
F-T Undergrads: 3,025   **Tuition:** $20,160

Most Popular Majors: Economics, English, Biology, Engineering, Social Sciences

*of 1600

Academics	A	Guys	B-
Local Atmosphere	B+	Girls	B-.
Safety & Security	B+	Athletics	B-
Computers	B+	Nightlife	A
Facilities	B+	Greek Life	N/A
Campus Dining	B	Drug Scene	B+
Off-Campus Dining	A+	Campus Strictness	A-
Campus Housing	A-	Parking	B
Off-Campus Housing	A-	Transportation	D
Diversity	A	Weather	B

Students Speak Out
ON ACADEMICS

Q "The professors at Rice are amazing. Almost every professor is incredibly receptive to questions and concerns. They are **tough but willing to help you do well** in any way possible. Most classes are interesting, and there are so many choices that you can always find something to take."

Q "In smaller classes, you can get to know your professors better than in the bigger ones. If you take the time to ask them questions, visit their office hours, and **show genuine interest**, your profs will open up to you."

Q "Teachers are so nice and enthusiastic about their subjects. They are also **very open-minded**; they are willing to listen to your thoughts both in and out of class."

Q "I found my classes at Rice University to be very interesting. They tend to be **quite challenging** but highly engaging, as well. Class sizes are much smaller than those at comparable universities, which provides a great deal of personal attention and guarantees that you'll always be able to speak to your profs."

STUDENT AUTHOR: **Rice students admit that most departments have both strong and weak professors. In order to earn a Rice degree, you must complete a certain number of classes in different areas of study. This allows students to explore areas outside of their chosen major. When you do have a choice about your courses or professors, there are many resources to help you avoid unwise decisions.**

Students Speak Out
ON LOCAL ATMOSPHERE

Q "**Houston is a huge city**, but I find it a little boring. Fortunately, because Rice has such a strong and tight-knit campus life, you don't really have to go out to have fun."

Q "Theoretically, you could go a whole year without leaving campus and still enjoy yourself. There are **other universities** in Houston, but since Rice is so isolated, you don't meet many people from them, unless you make an effort to do so."

Q "The atmosphere, I would say, is pretty decent. It's a **very fun place to live**. There's plenty to do—from clubbing, to partying, to museums, to visiting the zoo and the tons of restaurants—not to mention that it becomes an adventure when you try to get around Houston."

Q "Houston's **a city that grows on you**. Rice can be an island in the middle of the city—there's enough to do on campus that you never have to leave. But if you get out and look for stuff to do, there's plenty to be found."

STUDENT AUTHOR: **Houston does have something to offer for everyone. Overall, it is a fairly happening place for a young person to live. Go off the beaten path of typical Rice hangouts, and discover your own. If nothing else, you can keep things interesting by dining at a different restaurant every time you go out, and you probably won't run out of options before you graduate! Outside of the Rice bubble, there is a world of diverse cultural and social opportunities to explore.**

<table>
<tr><td>

5 Best Things
1 Faculty
2 Alcohol policy
3 Willy Week
4 Orientation Week
5 Extracurriculars

</td><td>

5 Worst Things
1 Pollution
2 Parking
3 Small campus
4 Tuition
5 Social life

</td></tr>
</table>

Students Speak Out
ON FACILITIES

Q "The facilities are awesome. The campus is quite beautiful, and many of the buildings are richly furnished, adorned, and **equipped for the 21st century student**."

Q "The gym is somewhat small, but since Rice has a small student body, it's never too incredibly crowded, and the equipment is in good shape. The college computer labs are of varying quality, but the **labs in the academic buildings are pretty nice**, though you can't get into those late at night."

Q "In the student center, there are also many different **lounges and conference rooms** available for Rice community use, as well as the campus bookstore."

Q "The facilities are first rate, among the best in the country. However, the athletic facilities are only average. The University's **main emphasis is on academics**, and you'll notice it."

Q "The gym is swank, outfitted with personal TV screens for every cardio machine and a huge weight room. It **gets very crowded**."

STUDENT AUTHOR: Students feel lukewarm about Rice facilities. Over the last couple years, there has always been one construction project or another going on to improve facilities. The movie theater is small and cozy, and shows an excellent variety of exotic movies (usually foreign or independent films). Students can enjoy the new and old food options at the student center, and afterward attempt to burn off these options at the Rice gym. The Rice Media center offers a photo lab.

Famous Alumni

Ron Bozman, Bill Broyles, Charles Duncan, Lynn Elsenhans, William Hobby, Howard Hughes, Mary Johnston, Larry McMurtry, Robert Wilson

Students Speak Out
ON CAMPUS DINING

Q "There is **a great selection**, and the lines are short. There has been a huge improvement from when I entered."

Q "Food on campus is not half bad. The residential college system allows for there to be a number of small cafeterias that make the dining situation better. At my residential college, **we have family-style dinners every night** where we sit down, and freshmen wait on upperclassmen. It's a really fun tradition."

Q "The Rice meal plan charges **rather steep prices** as a result of the improvements. The salad bar is pretty great, and the desserts are good."

Q "Food on campus is kind of blah; there are not a lot of options. The residential colleges are all getting these new serveries now that offer a lot more options, and the **food is better because it is fresher**—they don't have to ship it from one central location anymore."

Q "The **food is edible**. All things considered, it's pretty good. However, quality varies across campus."

STUDENT AUTHOR: Compared to larger universities, the number of on-campus dining options at Rice is very limited. The cost of the meal plan has steadily increased with the improvements, but students can choose from vegetarian options, a salad and fruit bar, sandwiches, pizza, grill food, soup, desert, baked goods, cereal, made-to-order omelets (only on weekends), or main dishes. The serveries will also occasionally offer a themed food night.

Student Body

African American:	7%	Male/Female:	51/49%
Asian American:	15%	Out-of-State:	47%
Hispanic:	11%	International:	2%
Native American:	1%	Unknown:	0%
White:	64%		

Popular Faiths: The most outspoken and visible religious organizations are Christian and Jewish.

Gay Pride: There is support provided through organizations such as ALLY, Pride, the Rice Counseling Center, and Minority Affairs. The city of Houston also has a sizeable and very visible gay community.

Economic Status: Rice is a "best-buy" university, and people from all socio-economic backgrounds attend.

Students Speak Out
ON DORMS

Q "The dorms are great. You don't have a choice, so you can't avoid any one over another. They all **have their pros and cons**, but generally they are very nice places to live."

Q "The residential college system creates buildings that are **more than just a dorm**. They house my friends, my 'Rice family,' my sports team, my theatre productions, my servery, my laundry facility, my computer lab, my pool table, my hammock, and my livelihood."

Q "I like all the colleges. Martel is the newest. All are supposed to be equal, but they aren't really because they were all built at different times, and they **all have different amenities**."

STUDENT AUTHOR: **As an incoming student you will be randomly assigned to a college, and most students stay at this college until graduation. You will be associated with the college even while living off campus. Transferring between colleges is an option, but no more than a handful of students take this route. Each residential college becomes something like a family unit, and each has a special personality, spirit, and unique traditions.**

Did You Know?
80% of undergrads live on campus.

Students Speak Out
ON GUYS & GIRLS

Q "I don't think it's really possible to characterize the entire male or female population of the school, but there is definitely **someone out there looking for what you are looking for**, whether that is a serious, deep relationship or a hookup."

Q "First, you must understand that the guys and girls at Rice are all very intelligent people at the minimum. Now, standard stereotypes would customarily dictate that all such people compensate for this gift with decreased social skills and **general unattractiveness**. There are plenty of jokes based on this concept told by those inside and outside of Rice."

Q "The saying around here goes: '**Brains before beauty** at Rice University.'"

STUDENT AUTHOR: **The truth is that the dating situation and experience at Rice varies for everyone. You may not find as many traditionally attractive hotties at Rice as you would at large state schools, but then again, we have fewer people. We tend not to attract many stereotypical "frat boys or sorority girls," although there are a few, and the number may be increasing. You can, of course, find whatever "type" you might be looking for.**

Traditions

O-Week
The week before school starts in the fall, intended to welcome and acclimate Rice freshmen and transfers.

Screw Your Roommate
Set up roommates on a blind date and brainstorm creative ways for them to meet.

Overall School Spirit
There is almost a fierce pride and camaraderie amongst Rice students. We identify with each other, and we are proud of our school. And we will cheer and wear the gear.

Students Speak Out
ON ATHLETICS

Q "Despite the fact that Rice is a Division I school, varsity athletics are not followed as much as at other Division I schools. However, IM sports are huge, especially when **Residential colleges are pitted against each other**. Most students participate in IM sports as players or fans."

Q "They are as big or small as you want them to be. Rice is **all about individuality**."

Q "Varsity sports on campus are taken fairly seriously, but are **not the epitome of college** life. Rice football is followed by most students, as is Rice baseball, but other sports are usually followed sparsely."

Q "It is **fun when you know certain players** from your college, or if you go with a student group to support."

STUDENT AUTHOR: **As the smallest Division I school in the country, we play against bigger schools, which unfortunately has not resulted in a fabulous record. Despite being Division I, students do not demonstrate much school spirit or support. A variety of club and intramural sports are available, and a high percentage of students participate.**

Students Speak Out
ON DRUG SCENE

Q "For a college campus, I think the drug scene at Rice is **very calm**."

Q "I never ran into drugs. It's not something there's a lot of or any peer pressure about—I knew some people who did a lot of drugs, some with whom I was very close, and I **never felt interested or bothered by it**. In terms of the alcohol scene, there's a lot of it, and it's easy to find."

Q "Pot is available and around, but I don't think that the majority of the student population uses it. **Alcohol is readily available** since it's a wet campus. There are plenty of 21 year olds around, and pretty much everyone drinks. It's a major part of the social scene."

STUDENT AUTHOR: Most students feel that drugs are a non-issue at Rice. People that want them can seek them out, but for the most part you will rarely encounter anything other than alcohol unless you go looking for it. At parties, alcohol plays a very key role and it's highly visible, but drugs are not. All in all, the drug scene here is practically invisible.

5:1	Student-to-Faculty Ratio
92%	Freshman Retention Rate
76%	Four-Year Graduation Rate
69%	Financial Aid Applicants Receiving Aid

Students Speak Out
SAFETY & SECURITY

Q "Considering that Houston is such a big city, I feel very safe on the Rice campus. The campus **police are amazing**, and their constant presence around campus makes me feel really secure."

Q "Crime is **virtually non-existent** here. The campus police are excellent, and they do a very good job of keeping things secure without making things difficult for the students."

Q "The security officers are helpful, but I would advise you not to go out at night alone, and always be around friends because it is in the downtown area. Since it's an open university, **people can get in and out easily**. So yes, the security is good, but nothing is perfect."

STUDENT AUTHOR: Although situated in the heart of a huge city, the Rice campus feels like it's sealed by an invisible, protective force field. The RUPD is not out to bust college kids and drain their bank accounts; they are here to protect the student body and make a productive learning environment.

Questions?
For more inside information and survival tips, pick up College Prowler's full-length book on this school, written by an actual student! Check it out at *www.collegeprowler.com*.

Students Speak Out
ON OVERALL EXPERIENCE

Q "I love Rice! It's a small campus, so you don't feel lost all the time. You get to know the people you see every day. The **college system is great**, and the classes are all good."

Q "There's plenty of stuff to do and a diverse population here, so you'll **find your right group of friends and something to get involved in**. If you were the quiet type in high school, you'll be fine here. If you like to party a lot, you'll be fine."

Q "Don't get in a rut your freshman year—try getting involved with a bunch of different groups of people, eating routines, and weekend hangouts. Then, **figure out what feels comfortable** and fun to you."

Q "It's got a wonderful atmosphere, a gorgeous campus, excellent academics, and a constantly fascinating student body. I wouldn't want to be anywhere else. I don't know if Rice is the best place for everyone, but if you're serious about learning, not dependent on social cliques, and just a little bit quirky, it **might be the perfect place for you**."

STUDENT AUTHOR: While students complain about some of the negative aspects of Houston (pollution, transportation, traffic, panhandlers), they also admit that there are many positive aspects to Rice's location. Rice's small campus and student body are nice because they create a personal environment and allow students to meet more people and not just feel like faces in the crowd. However, students also claim that it begins to feel confining at times. The traditions, high academic standards, and amazing people that make up the Rice community create an extraordinary and irreplaceable environment.

Rochester Institute of Technology

1 Lomb Memorial Drive; Rochester, NY 14623
(585) 475-2411; www.rit.edu

THE BASICS:

Acceptance Rate: 65%
Setting: Urban
F-T Undergrads: 12,555

SAT Range: 1090–1300*
Control: Private
Tuition: $27,624

Most Popular Majors: Computer Science, Business, Engineering, Applied Arts, Video/Photographic Arts

*of 1600

Academics	B+	Guys	B-
Local Atmosphere	C+	Girls	C+
Safety & Security	B	Athletics	B-
Computers	A	Nightlife	D+
Facilities	B	Greek Life	C+
Campus Dining	C+	Drug Scene	B
Off-Campus Dining	B+	Campus Strictness	C
Campus Housing	B-	Parking	D+
Off-Campus Housing	A-	Transportation	B
Diversity	C+	Weather	D

Students Speak Out
ON ACADEMICS

Q "The teachers at RIT **have always been there** to help. I have never had a class where I couldn't find the professor during office hours and talk over any problems that I might have had."

Q "The professors in the biology department are very friendly and helpful. They are always there if you need to talk to someone, whether it is about class work or **pesky personal problems**. I have a lot of respect for all of them, and I have made some lasting friendships and connections with many of the professors."

Q "I have had some very bad experiences at RIT. I have been put on academic probation and been nearly expelled because of my grades. This school is **really hard to get through**. Some of my professors were very understanding about things and others simply saw me as a number."

Q "**This is a hard school**, because the classes are tough and the professors can't afford to slow down for anyone. I have had a hard time keeping up with classes, and have barely kept a 2.5 GPA, which is awful because I was one of the top students in my high school class."

STUDENT AUTHOR: **RIT is consistently ranked among the elite colleges for technical degrees. The programs generally bring out the "intensive" in intensive learning and many departments are currently offering ground-breaking new majors. All of RIT's programs have the advantage of offering a hands-on approach to learning by way of the co-op system. Overall, the professors are intelligent and helpful.**

Students Speak Out
ON LOCAL ATMOSPHERE

Q "If you are content to go and wander around a park or Mt. Hope Cemetery, then it's a pretty cool place. However, if you're looking for wild-night clubs and bars, then this might not be the right place for you. **It depends on what you want to do** I guess."

Q "I hear a lot of people complain about Rochester and how there is never anything to do here, but I think these people **just aren't looking hard enough**. I can always find stuff to do if I want to."

Q "Rochester is a great place to live, but I wouldn't want to visit. **There is nothing to do on a whim**. There are no tourist attractions and no amusement parks. I, for one, wouldn't want to take a date to the George Eastman House."

Q "With Fisher, Nazareth, U of R, Genesseo, and Brockport all nearby, students here have opportunities to **meet other college students** that don't go to RIT. Plus, there is a good chance that you'll meet some Rochester natives that might have a better idea of what to do for fun."

STUDENT AUTHOR: **Rochester is NY State's third largest urban area. Within the city lie a number of interesting and stimulating experiences, that is if you don't mind all the brick (brick roads, brick buildings, and brick street signs). Home to leviathans Kodak and Xerox, Rochester has become a city full of opportunity, especially for people pursuing business and technical careers. There are eight colleges in the area, including U of Rochester, St. John Fisher, and SUNY Geneseo.**

Students Speak Out
ON FACILITIES

Q "The turf field is **the finest addition** I've seen to this campus since I've been here. The lacrosse team finally has a decent place to practice and play. There should be open recreation hours posted, though. It'd be a great place to get a game of ultimate Frisbee going, but no one knows when it is open for student use."

Q "I don't understand why the administration altered Sentinel. **That used to be a great quad** with a vast field of green grass to go hang out on. Now it is a paved area with a big metal thing stuck in it—I just don't understand."

Q "**The nature trails here are pretty good.** They're not the best I've seen, but they provide a pleasant getaway where students can walk around and not be surrounded by bricks the whole time."

Q "**Wallace Library could use some work.** Most of the students on campus don't actually take books out of the library since they can get to the information on the Web site. The problem here is that students who want to use the actual books have a hard time finding them, if the library has them at all."

STUDENT AUTHOR: **It is hard to not be impressed with the facilities at R!T. The Gordon Field House recently opened, and has since provided students with a spacious workout area as well as two new pools. It is the site for athletic events, seminars, and concerts throughout the year. Also, many classrooms are being transformed into "smart rooms" allowing professors to simply use their laptops to teach class.**

Famous Alumni

Bernie Boston, Daniel Carp, Tom Curley, Robert Fabbio, N. Katherine Hayles, Bruce James

Students Speak Out
ON CAMPUS DINING

Q "**Dining on campus is awful**—the food is gross and overpriced. I'm really glad they don't require students in the apartments to have a meal plan. I can go to Wegman's Groceries and get real food and cook it myself—it's cheaper and it tastes better."

Q "Gracie's food is the same thing everyday. It isn't bad food, but most of it is fried and the Global Vegetarian doesn't do a very good job with their meals—**the food is always mushy.**"

Q "I love the fact that the **Subway delivers to campus.** You can order subs and have them brought to your dorm. Then, you can pay the delivery guy with flex. It's really convenient, plus Subway makes great cookies."

Q "Most people joke about Gracie's, and how bad the food is, but I don't think it's that bad. Most of their food is deep fried, but it is **no worse than going to Ponderosa.** One of the best parts is that Gracie's is all-you-can-eat, so if you're really hungry, you don't have to pick what you want, you can have it all."

STUDENT AUTHOR: **Most students vehemently complain about Gracie's during their freshman year. Many students rarely opt to eat at Gracie's more than a few times after their first year. Gracie's is the main dining hall for freshman, and a specified number of meals are allotted in their dining plans. Even students who remain loyal patrons at Gracie's will tell you that the food isn't bad, just monotonous. The food at Gracie's is served in a buffet-style, but students find the same foods on the tables.**

Student Body

African American:	5%	Male/Female:	71/29%
Asian American:	7%	Out-of-State:	45%
Hispanic:	3%	International:	4%
Native American:	<1%	Unknown:	0%
White:	80%		

Popular Faiths: Christianity, Islam, and Judaism are all well represented on campus.

Gay Pride: RIT and the town of Rochester in general, are very accepting of the gay and bisexual population.

Economic Status: Students tend to be from middle to upper-class backgrounds. There is, however, a generous sprinkling of lower-class students.

Students Speak Out
ON DORMS

Q "The townhouses are nice if you keep them that way, but the **parties can get a little overwhelming**, especially if you aren't a party animal. I wish that I had opted to live in Perkins instead. Parties there are smaller, more intimate, and not as loud."

Q "The biggest problem I have is **the whole dry campus thing**. I am 22 years old! I just want to come back to my room after a hard day of work and have a beer. I don't see why I should be punished for that."

Q "Living in the apartments is a great experience. **Utilities are included**, and free access to the Internet is available. Here, students have on-campus luxuries without having to live in the dorms. I would definitely recommend living in the apartments if you can get a spot."

STUDENT AUTHOR: **Many students choose to live on campus all four years at RIT. A good majority of these students feel that living on campus is convenient, mainly because of the proximity to classes and school facilities and because they don't have to worry about paying rent every month. Also, utilities including Ethernet, local phone bill, and cable are included in rent.**

? Did You Know?
60% of undergrads live on campus.

Students Speak Out
ON GUYS & GIRLS

Q "You know what they say about guys at tech schools. **The odds are good, but the goods are odd**."

Q "It's hard to describe the girls at RIT because you see so few of them. I'd have to say **they are usually pretty cute**, and most of them are cool to talk to, but you have to be careful because most of them have boyfriends already."

Q "**There are girls on this campus**?"

Q "**I never really had to look for guys at RIT**. You just go to a party and there are a bunch of them there. It's nice, though, because I have never had to buy my own drinks."

STUDENT AUTHOR: **RIT is a technical school geared towards technical students. Therefore, the students here weren't exactly social gods in high school. This is not to say that everyone here wears glasses held together by tape and paperclips, or that we all wear pocket protectors. Chances are, if you are looking at RIT then you are a bit of a geek yourself. Overall, when discussing the social scene at RIT, there is no getting passed the high ratio of guys over girls.**

Traditions

Advertising on the Walls
The buildings that line the quarter mile make perfect bulletin boards and students from many organizations take full advantage of them.

Bagpipes
RIT has a history of busting out the bagpipes at any formal occasion.

Overall School Spirit
RIT students are constantly under scrutiny by the administration for many reasons, one of which is the lack of school spirit.

Students Speak Out
ON ATHLETICS

Q "**The hockey season isn't long enough**! We need hockey to be year round so we could have a good sports program the whole year."

Q "**The lacrosse team is really good**, but no one watches their games. Rugby is the same way."

Q "Soccer doesn't get enough attention here. We have some awesome teams, but the **administration is so apathetic** that no one really cares."

Q "We have a great hockey program, what more do you want? **Our hockey team is really talented**, and the games are fast-paced and exciting."

STUDENT AUTHOR: **If it weren't for athletics, RIT would rank miserably in the school spirit department. The hockey team has long had a cult-like following here, and many RIT students leave here with fond memories of either watching or participating in one of the best hockey programs in the nation. The Tigers are consistently ranked as one of the top teams in their division and often win the section title. All athletics on campus are highly competitive and well coached, either by professionals or fellow students.**

Students Speak Out
ON DRUG SCENE

Q "I've never seen anyone using anything other than alcohol on campus. I'm sure that people use drugs, but **I've never been approached** about it, so I don't really care."

Q "There are a group of students who go out and smoke pot on the nature trails. Other than that, though, I haven't really known of anyone doing any drugs. I don't bother them and they don't bother me—**it's pretty isolated really**."

Q "I've been at a few parties where **people were pretty stoned**, but it was always a couple of guys sitting in the corner. I've never really seen a large number of students getting stoned together or anything."

STUDENT AUTHOR: **If the rigors of a technical education are getting to you, and you feel that there is no other way to relieve the stress, then you will always be able to find the "stress reliever" of your choice. Normally, there are not a high number of referrals or arrests due to student drug use, and the most prevalent drug on campus is marijuana (many think it should be legalized anyway).**

13:1	Student-to-Faculty Ratio
84%	Freshman Retention Rate
33%	Four-Year Graduation Rate
91%	Financial Aid Applicants Receiving Aid

Students Speak Out
SAFETY & SECURITY

Q "The worst problem I've had on campus is having my TV stolen from my dorm room. It was before the school introduced **the 24-hour lockdown policy** for the dorms, and my roommate had left the room unlocked, so it was just stupidity."

Q "Because I'm a girl, I was worried that I would have problems **walking alone after dark**, but the campus- safety escort service is great. I don't have to worry about putting myself in situations where I don't feel comfortable."

Q "I've never really had to deal with campus safety, so I guess that is an indicator of how safe the campus is. **Parking services, on the other hand, are ridiculous**. I get tickets for parking even where I am allowed to park!"

STUDENT AUTHOR: **Overall, the RIT campus is incredibly safe, considering the number of students. Mostly what campus safety deals with are drug and alcohol-related problems, or occasional cases of automobile damage. Theft is not a notable problem on campus.**

Questions?
For more inside information and survival tips, pick up College Prowler's full-length book on this school, written by an actual student! Check it out at *www.collegeprowler.com*.

Students Speak Out
ON OVERALL EXPERIENCE

Q "So far so good. I still have three years left before I am done here, but I am confident I will stick it out until graduation. This school may have its problems, but **the positives far outweigh the negatives here**."

Q "I transferred in so I guess I stand a better chance of making it to graduation since I didn't have to spend five years straight here. I can definitely see why people leave. It is a pretty dead campus most of the time and **some of the professors can be jerks**. Overall though, I'm glad I came here."

Q "I love RIT! I have had so much fun here that I really don't want to leave. **I am transferring** to a different school for a year, though, because I need to see if I can make it outside of my native Rochester. I'll be back in a year to finish out my degree, though. I want my degree to say Rochester Institute of Technology on it."

Q "RIT has given me a lot of great opportunities. I have become more of a leader and made a lot of new friends. **This place has challenged me** in ways I never expected. I knew that the academics would be challenging, but I didn't realize how hard living away from home would really be."

STUDENT AUTHOR: **RIT does its best to provide students with a wealth of information, great facilities, top-notch academics, and a pretty good athletic program. Living in Rochester for four years teaches students a lot about who they are and what they want out of life (with the lack of student-oriented activities, you'll have a lot of time to think). Many choose to drop out or transfer schools due to the strenuous quarter system.**

Rollins College

1000 Holt Avenue; Winter Park, FL 32789
(407) 646-2000; www.rollins.edu

THE BASICS:

Acceptance Rate: 58%
Setting: Suburban
F-T Undergrads: 1,725

SAT Range: 1110–1280*
Control: Private
Tuition: $34,520

Most Popular Majors: Social Sciences, Business, Visual/Performing Arts, English, Psychology

*of 1600

Academics	B	Guys	B+
Local Atmosphere	A-	Girls	A
Safety & Security	B-	Athletics	B-
Computers	B	Nightlife	A-
Facilities	A-	Greek Life	A
Campus Dining	B	Drug Scene	C-
Off-Campus Dining	B+	Campus Strictness	B
Campus Housing	B-	Parking	C+
Off-Campus Housing	C+	Transportation	C+
Diversity	C	Weather	A

Students Speak Out
ON ACADEMICS

Q "I have yet to find a teacher at Rollins I dislike. The teachers are **always so excited** to be teaching their specific subject that they make you excited, too. There's never a dull moment."

Q "I find the teachers very nice and helpful. They are willing to make learning a fun experience, and I do find many of my classes interesting. **I loved my creating writing class** and many of my psychology courses."

Q "Professors are **extremely encouraging** at Rollins. One thing you get at a school of this size is teacher interaction. When I go to class my teacher knows my name—that's not something you get at larger schools."

Q "The teachers are great. They are liberal, while most of the students appear to be more conservative, so it's a nice change. The classes are all interesting, I find, and the teachers seem **passionate about their work**, as well as very easy to get in touch with."

STUDENT AUTHOR: This small liberal arts school deserves its reputation for academic excellence due to the quality of its faculty. The school's small size facilitates close interaction between students and faculty. At Rollins, no student is just a number. Teachers generally know not only your name, but you major, plans after college, and academic strengths. They are always available to help or simply to talk. The majority of professors at Rollins are here because they have a genuine desire to impart knowledge in their field.

Students Speak Out
ON LOCAL ATMOSPHERE

Q "I'm from the Orlando area originally, so nothing is new to me, but I love this town. There is **always something to do**. There are other universities present, such as UCF and Stetson. Of course since you're in Orlando, you should visit the theme parks and take advantage of the beaches."

Q "Rollins is **next to Orlando**, the home of Mickey Mouse and other tourist traps. Downtown Orlando's scene has its highlights, but the 2 a.m. alcohol curfew is quite a buzz kill. UCF is right down the road, well a few miles down the road, and if someone tells you they go to Full Sail turn and run as fast as you can!"

Q "**UCF is nearby**, which is nice, because there are other college students downtown in the area. There is Orlando five minutes away to go downtown and Disney is close if family and friends come into town."

STUDENT AUTHOR: Winter Park itself is a small, relatively quiet town abutting the bustling city of Orlando. This provides the best of both worlds, as Rollins students can relax in the small-town atmosphere surrounding the college and also visit the multitude of attractions Orlando has to offer with just a 15-minute drive on I-75. Within walking distance of campus are a variety of upscale clothing stores and elegant restaurants. Though the quaint town of Winter Park is beautiful and ritzy, you really need a car to experience more of the area.

5 Best Things	5 Worst Things
1 Fox Day	1 Parking
2 The weather	2 Small student body
3 Downtown Orlando	3 Lack of diversity
4 Park Avenue	4 Materialism
5 Frat parties	5 No football team

Students Speak Out
ON FACILITIES

Q "The student center always has something going on where you can meet a ton of people. The clubs are always holding some program or another. It depends what you're interested in, but **you will always find something** that you enjoy."

Q "The facilities are **fabulous**! They are one of the best parts of the school. The student center is brand new and overlooks a lake. The sports center is new and gorgeous. The grounds are beautiful. You can always find a nice spot on campus to sit around."

Q "The athletic center is a great place, and it offers **free group exercise** classes that are really fun."

Q "I think the facilities on campus are very nice. The people who work here are friendly, and they always make sure that the students are in good hands. The athletic center is fairly new, and the computers in the library are only a couple years old. **Everything's clean** and very well kept."

STUDENT AUTHOR: It isn't uncommon to hear people visiting Rollins for the first time remark something like "This looks more like a country club than a college!" Rollins's campus is a picture of paradise, combining traditional Florida flair with a Northeastern feel that is difficult to pinpoint. The Cornell Campus Center offers breathtaking views, almost making the common cafeteria food served there feel like more upscale dining. Many students are initially drawn to Rollins for its beautiful campus, and it is hard to surpass the sheer splendor of this petite tropical paradise. Rollins takes great care to build and maintain its facilities, and it's rare to find a college so clean and new.

Famous Alumni

Donald Cram, Buddy Ebsen, Dana Ivy, Fred Rogers

Students Speak Out
ON CAMPUS DINING

Q "The food at Beans is **some of the best** college cafeteria food anywhere. The vegetarian place is great, and the pizza slices are huge!"

Q "The **food can be iffy**. In the cafeteria, I usually found myself eating just a salad or sandwich. But the Grille has some good options; however, they get tiresome after a while because it's all greasy."

Q "The food on campus is very good (considering I came from boarding school). Although the meals are **a bit repetitive** and the price range a little steep, the quality is still very good. Beans, the Grille, and Dianne's seem to be the hot spots."

Q "Food is **surprisingly good** for a college. Dianne's café is the best, and it is covered by the meal plan. The panini caprese with vegetable chips and a frozen strawberry lemonade is the best."

Q "Dianne's Café has **great sandwiches** and coffee. The C-Store has everything you could possibly need, as far as food goes. The cafeteria is mediocre."

STUDENT AUTHOR: Campus dining is generally not criticized heavily, and many students find the food at Rollins far superior to that at other colleges. Food on campus can be extremely overpriced, and it is easy for students to pay little attention to the cost of meals only to find themselves without meal plan money left by the end of the semester. The inflated prices cause more cash conscious students to forego the meal plan and turn to the variety of off-campus food sources.

Student Body

African American:	5%	Male/Female:	40/60%
Asian American:	4%	Out-of-State:	51%
Hispanic:	8%	International:	3%
Native American:	1%	Unknown:	0%
White:	79%		

Popular Faiths: The church on campus offers services for multiple Christian denominations.

Gay Pride: The campus is tolerant and accepting of gay members. The Gay, Lesbian, Bisexual, Transgender Alliance (GLBTA) is recognized and supported.

Economic Status: Rollins seems to consist of students from wealthy economic backgrounds.

Students Speak Out
ON DORMS

Q "I'd say the best dorm if you want quiet is Holt. It's **always clean** and the people are so friendly. If you want constant parties, check out Ward."

Q "**Yikes**. The dorms are not the brighter side of Rollins. Ward is probably one of the nicer ones. I lived in McKean my freshman year. It wasn't that great. So now I'm living in the Sutton Apartments, which are definitely an upgrade from the dorms, but they're for mainly upperclassmen."

Q "For the money, the **dorms could be better**, and they could turn on the heat when it gets cold in Ward, but they are decent enough (it could be worse), and the cleaning people work really hard."

STUDENT AUTHOR: **Rollins now requires all students with fewer than 60 semester hours to live on campus, which essentially forces most freshmen and sophomores to live in the dorms. For a college with immaculate facilities, the dorms are a source of disappointment. Many freshman dorms have tiny rooms and always seem dirty, despite the genuine efforts of cleaning staff.**

Did You Know?
66% of undergrads live on campus.

Students Speak Out
ON GUYS & GIRLS

Q "The guys are, for the most part, **stuck-up jerks**, and the girls for the most part are, well, stuck-up jerks. Look for transfer students and the exceptions to these descriptions."

Q "The 'stereotypical' Rollins guy is as follows: **cocky, good looking, rich**, Republican, non-monogamous, lacking in intelligence, and often drunk. The girls are the same. Throw in some cocaine and you have the stereotypical Rollins relationship."

Q "The girls are really attractive. The guys are, too, but it seems like a lot of the guys are **arrogant**. It's quite annoying."

STUDENT AUTHOR: **The student body at Rollins is an unusually attractive one. Girls are typically thin, dressed in designer clothing, and immaculately well kept. Guys are preppy, rich, and many are very good-looking. Girls are also known to be snobby, and guys generally cocky. Entering Rollins, you quickly realize that this campus has extreme materialistic tendencies and an abnormal amount of students with excessive wealth.**

Traditions

Peace Jam
Each year, the community comes together with a Nobel Prize recipient and meets for leadership-building activities and an address by the honoree.

Fox Day
Once a year, in the spring, the current president puts a fox statue on Mills Lawn to cancel classes for the day.

Overall School Spirit
Many students are proud to go to Rollins, yet they fail to get actively involved. The lack of attendance at varsity and intramural games reveals this.

Students Speak Out
ON ATHLETICS

Q "A sport's popularity depends on the crowd. The spirit on campus is miniscule if anything. However, our sports teams win many competitions and are of good quality. IM sports are **fairly popular** on campus, but there is always room for more people."

Q "**Varsity sports are big**. Soccer, baseball, golf, and basketball are the big four that always do well. IM is so-so. Since Rollins is so small, most of the good athletes are already on teams and don't do much IM stuff."

Q "Sports are definitely supported but not very big on campus. We don't even have a football team, but our soccer boys and girls are **pretty good**."

Q "Sports are **pretty big**—soccer especially. There's also volleyball, crew, basketball and a ton I know I'm missing."

STUDENT AUTHOR: **Rollins has some amazing athletes, and many of our varsity teams consistently rank well in their divisions. However, much of the student body is unaware of this. The most popular sports, mainly soccer, basketball, and baseball, receive some degree of attention.**

Students Speak Out
ON DRUG SCENE

Q "Drugs are prevalent at Rollins. It is often said it's 'snowing in Florida' from **Rollins' cocaine problem**. Painkillers such as Valium are popular, as is Adderall. I'd estimate that at least 50 percent of the students do some sort of drug (including pot)."

Q "I have heard many rumors, but never actually seen anything going on. Many people smoke cigarettes (probably **more than 50 percent** of the population), weed is talked about, and the rumors are that a surprising number of students do cocaine, but like I said I've never seen it."

Q "There are **many drugs** on campus. No one ever notices that there are, though."

STUDENT AUTHOR: **Drugs are certainly a presence on campus, and they are easily obtained. Marijuana runs a close second in popularity to alcohol. Pot users range from the typical frat guy to even the best of students that secretly light up in their rooms. During finals, and for some all year round, students in need of Adderall abound.**

11:1	Student-to-Faculty Ratio
85%	Freshman Retention Rate
51%	Four-Year Graduation Rate
41%	Financial Aid Applicants Receiving Aid

Students Speak Out
SAFETY & SECURITY

Q "The campus feels **pretty safe**. I almost always see Campus Safety riding around on their little golf carts. At the same time, I wish that there were more of the blue safety lights around campus."

Q I have not had much experience with Campus Safety, but there are **call boxes all around** campus, and I know that they are available at night to give you an escort if you so desire."

Q "I've **never really needed assistance** from Campus Safety, but I haven't really heard good things about them. Basically, just better security is needed, but I feel safe for the most part. It's a very well-lit campus."

STUDENT AUTHOR: Most students feel safe on campus, due largely to the extremely small size of the campus and infrequent crime. Campus Safety seems to always be a presence, riding around both day and night on their golf carts. Call boxes are located all around campus.

Questions?
For more inside information and survival tips, pick up College Prowler's full-length book on this school, written by an actual student! Check it out at *www.collegeprowler.com*.

Students Speak Out
ON OVERALL EXPERIENCE

Q "Overall, I do **like Rollins a lot**. I do not wish I was somewhere else. This was my number one school of choice, and for the most part, I have been happy with my education here so far."

Q "My overall school experience so far has been **pretty good**. I've made friends and learned to laugh at the stupid people. My classes and the valuable resources that professors offer us is the reason that I won't leave Rollins."

Q "Besides the profound capitalist nature of Rollins, it is **pretty decent**. If there was another school that is in the South with a small campus, small classes, wonderful professors, and my major, but has normal people, I would be there in a flash."

Q "This is my third school, and I'm not a big fan of the student body. Though UCF is down the road and Orlando is home to many **do-nothing-neo-Bohemians** working at Starbucks or some other corporate venue to pay for their art supplies or tattoos to hang with. This is not to say that I do not love the academics at Rollins. I have yet to have a bad professor and the bio and chem departments are top-notch. Also the professors will bend over backwards for you."

STUDENT AUTHOR: **Starting college can be a major change, and entering Rollins feels a little like entering another world. Maybe it has something to do with the paradise-like setting or the constant notion of being at an expensive country club. Whatever the cause may be, Rollins is different from most other colleges. Academically, Rollins doesn't disappoint and frequently exceeds the expectations of entering freshmen. In regards to social life, the small size of Rollins is not always considered a plus.**

Rutgers New Brunswick

65 Davidson Road; Piscataway, NJ 08854
(732) 932-1766; www.rutgers.edu

THE BASICS:

Acceptance Rate: 56%
Setting: Small city
F-T Undergrads: 24,416

SAT Range: 1110–1310*
Control: Public
Tuition: $15,599

Most Popular Majors: Social Sciences, Psychology, Biological/Life Sciences, Business, Engineering

*of 1600

Academics	B	Guys	B
Local Atmosphere	B+	Girls	B
Safety & Security	C-	Athletics	B+
Computers	B+	Nightlife	A-
Facilities	A-	Greek Life	B
Campus Dining	B	Drug Scene	B+
Off-Campus Dining	B+	Campus Strictness	B
Campus Housing	B	Parking	C
Off-Campus Housing	C+	Transportation	B+
Diversity	A-	Weather	B-

Students Speak Out
ON ACADEMICS

Q "I've had teachers that didn't speak English very well, teachers who were dry and boring, but also **teachers like those you see in the movies** and would imagine college to be like. Some teachers have done things like sing in a lecture hall and throw paper airplanes out of the window."

Q "Professors at Rutgers, compared to other schools, seem **a bit more distant from the students**. Rutgers is a more 'do-it-yourself' or 'seek-out-help-on-your-own' kind of college. No professor here is going to hunt you down for a paper or specially come to you to help you."

Q "There are **strong academics and strong competition**, which a lot of Rutgers' students don't realize when they come here. In-state students think Rutgers is going to be an easy ride since it's a state university with cheap tuition. They assume that it's going to be like high school or community college, which it definitely isn't!"

Q "Rutgers professors are best described as **unique, quirky, and always very interesting**. You never know who you will get—a liberal, conservative, homosexual, or Marxist."

STUDENT AUTHOR: Some prospective students are scared at first about coming to a university that seems so tremendous. It is large; that's for certain. There are five campuses, and they all have a different atmosphere, as well as college focuses, so it is extremely important to visit RU and take a university tour, and figure out what college or campus "fits" you.

Students Speak Out
ON LOCAL ATMOSPHERE

Q "**Rutgers isn't on an isolated campus**. You're put in the middle of a city, so you learn to 'buddy up' when you walk, and the police presence is very obvious. New Brunswick is in the center of New Jersey, less than an hour train ride to either New York City or Philly. The shore is also less than an hour away, too, so the local atmosphere is awesome."

Q "I love going to school in one of the most prominent theater districts in the state. There's so many great theaters, restaurants, cafés, nearby clubs. There is really **no reason to have to go home**."

Q "The city of New Brunswick is great. There is an active nightlife, and **something for almost anyone in the area**, with little need for a car. No other universities are really nearby. People should not go really far into downtown because it can be dangerous."

Q "New Brunswick is **definitely a college town**. There is plenty of off-campus housing which is, in reality, is as close walking distance as on-campus housing."

STUDENT AUTHOR: Rutgers is like its own self-sufficient world. It has five campuses, on-campus dining, various student organizations that provide entertainment—there's really never a reason to leave campus. One of the best and most unique aspects of Rutgers is how versatile the atmosphere is. Depending on the campus, you can have a country college experience, as well as a city one.

5 Best Things	5 Worst Things
1 Diversity	1 The administration
2 Division I sports	2 Rutgers Buses
3 Busch Dining Hall	3 WebCT
4 Clothing box sales	4 Recitations
5 The Kissing Bridge	5 Teaching assistants (TAs)

Students Speak Out
ON FACILITIES

Q "The student centers are nice and **make you feel welcome to college**. They always have fliers and stuff saying what's going on at Rutgers, like mall trips, concerts, and trips to Manhattan."

Q "There are a handful of gyms with all different styles, hours, equipment, and location. I live in the Easton Ave. apartments, and **there's a gym that is connected to the dorm**, which is amazing. The student centers have campus shops, restaurants, convenience stores, computer labs, and lots of tables for studying, eating, or hanging out."

Q "**It varies from campus to campus**, yet if you take pieces of each campus's facilities, they're amazing—for instance, the athletic center and dining hall on Busch, or the student center at College Ave."

Q "**The facilities on campus are amazing**! None of my friends' colleges have the amenities that Rutgers has. Student centers offer everything from Wendy's to Dunkin' Donuts to cute cafés. As for the athletic centers, they are absolutely state of the art."

STUDENT AUTHOR: **The Sonny Werblin Gym on the Busch campus is known as the best gym and is absolutely spotless, featuring Olympic-sized swimming pools, exercise bikes placed near cable TVs and more. Student centers are a main part of RU life, and they become a meeting spot or simply a place to hang out when you want to leave your dorm. At each student center, there is a food court similar to those seen in malls.**

Famous Alumni

Mario Batali, Deron Cherry, Calista Flockhart, James Gandolfini, Edward Jordan, Clifton Lacy, Robert Pinsky, Paul Robeson, David Stern

Students Speak Out
ON CAMPUS DINING

Q "Dining hall food is never good at any college, but **Busch dining hall is somewhat decent**. The other dining halls, though, are another story."

Q "The dining halls offer **a variety of meal options**, and the take out is helpful if one has a late class. There are many pizza places in the adjacent area of College Ave., although they don't offer very healthy choices. But, if you are on Busch or Livingston, the dining hall is really your only choice unless you have a car."

Q "What can you really expect of college food—it's nourishment. **There are many dining halls to choose from**, the Busch dining hall being my favorite."

Q "**Too many people complain about the food**, but I think it's not so bad; just stay away from the dining hall on weekends. I don't like the breakfast, but for lunch, they have a deli line, which is good."

Q "**The food is a natural laxative**. Buy a case of Pepto Bismol or Maalox."

STUDENT AUTHOR: **Rutgers's dining halls are not like eating at home, and it is easy to fall into the trap of eating burgers and fries every day. Dining services host numerous "RU Eating Right" sessions in the dining halls to warn freshmen about the dangers of eating unhealthy. However, most students are satisfied with the dining halls because they all feature something that they would eat, even if it's Cookie Crisp cereal or a crunchy peanut butter sandwich on white bread for dinner.**

Student Body

African American:	9%	Male/Female:	48/52%
Asian American:	22%	Out-of-State:	8%
Hispanic:	8%	International:	2%
Native American:	<1%	Unknown:	0%
White:	59%		

Popular Faiths: There is a diverse array of religions on campus, mostly due to the large student body.

Gay Pride: Rutgers University is very accepting of the gay, lesbian, transgender, and bisexual community. The gay community is outspoken on campus, like most of Rutgers' social and political groups.

Economic Status: RU's prestige and low tuition costs lead to a wide range of economic backgrounds.

Students Speak Out
ON DORMS

Q "Now that I live off campus on College Avenue, I feel like I'm actually at college—unlike when I lived in the Busch dorms. Busch is not a fun place to live. The dorms are alright, but **nobody is social**."

Q "**Dorms could be better**; freshman dorms especially. Bathrooms need renovation, and the buildings need air-conditioning. The river dorms are nicer. Easton Avenue Apartments are the nicest."

Q "The dorms are very pleasurable and accommodating. Room sizes may vary, but I think that **dorm life is a must** at least for the freshman year. It will make you get to know a lot of people and help you to be much more sociable."

STUDENT AUTHOR: **Freshman dorms are always the most fun— doors are always open, people hang out in the lounges every night, and everyone is friends. As you become upperclassmen, students are more reserved and focus on studying; primarily to fix their freshmen GPAs made from bad study habits in their freshman year halls.**

? Did You Know?
47% of undergrads live on campus.

Students Speak Out
ON GUYS & GIRLS

Q "**If you're out-of-state, you will be cool** at Rutgers. It makes things interesting because everyone is from Jersey."

Q "**It's what you make it**. Since it's a state school, a lot of people kept boyfriends and girlfriends from home."

Q "**There's a lot of diversity**, which is the best part of it."

Q "You can date easier here, because **everyone is from New Jersey**, so when you go home, you can still see the person you're with."

Q "There's **all different types of people**, different ethnicities, social backgrounds; it keeps things interesting."

STUDENT AUTHOR: **If you come to Rutgers with a "type," chances are you will be able to find 300 guys or girls to satisfy it. It is definitely not hard to meet people at Rutgers. Douglass alone is a campus of only girls. Although love isn't always lingering in the air, it seems as though Rutgers students are happy. Plus, the parties are always free and hosted by the fraternity, which provides a good opportunity for meeting someone.**

Traditions

Cap and Skull
A secret prestigious honorary society established in 1900. Members are initiated in a secret ceremony.

Homecoming
A major day at Rutgers where students, faculty, and alumni celebrate with pep rallies and float-making.

Overall School Spirit
Most feel school pride for their particular college. Cook and Douglass show pride during their "Ag Field Day," Rutgers celebrates "RutgersFest," and Livingston puts on "SpringFest."

Students Speak Out
ON ATHLETICS

Q "Varsity sports may not be as big as they are at other universities, but Rutgers has a lot of school spirit. **We may not have the best football team**, but a lot of our other teams make it really far like lacrosse and soccer. Intramural sports are big on the Cook Campus; we definitely have the best intramural sports program."

Q "They're pretty big deal, but there's a lot more going on too, so **it doesn't overpower other clubs and organizations**."

Q "**I guess football is pretty big**, and I really love women's soccer, but that's about all I know about Rutgers sports."

Q "Varsity sports suck; they want to be a big deal, but **they just don't have the chutzpah**."

STUDENT AUTHOR: **Sure, our teams may not win all the time, but Rutgers students have a lot of pride in athletics. Intramural sports are big deal on campus, and often become extremely competitive. Many students thrived in high school sports, but didn't make the cut for Division I making RU intramurals a tremendous part of student life.**

Students Speak Out
ON DRUG SCENE

Q "There is a drug scene on campus, but it's not prevalent. **It can be easily avoided**, but it is up to each individual to use drugs. This is not to say that a problem does not exist, but I don't feel that it's something major."

Q "Drugs are great, and **they're plentiful on campus** if you know the right people. I highly recommend introducing yourself to as many people in your dorms because they'll be invaluable resources for pharmaceutical needs."

Q "It's not as much of an issue as you would think it would be, since there are so many people at Rutgers. I mean, there are the potheads, and kids that do other drugs, too, but **they don't make up any large majority** at Rutgers."

STUDENT AUTHOR: **People can do what they want to do, and it isn't crazily talked about. Students really don't seem to get caught smoking weed or taking other drugs, although it is a common problem to get caught drinking in the dorms.**

14:1	Student-to-Faculty Ratio
89%	Freshman Retention Rate
46%	Four-Year Graduation Rate
78%	Financial Aid Applicants Receiving Aid

Students Speak Out
SAFETY & SECURITY

Q "Security is non-existent, **the police have sublet out their responsibilities to CSOs** (community service officers), which are little more than students with flashlights and no authority. The only police presence you'll feel is a hassling of students for noise and garbage violations."

Q "We always get e-mails about the stuff that goes on like rapes, thefts, attacks; **obviously, something is wrong at Rutgers**."

Q "Although safety is an ongoing concern, the main streets of campus, such as College Avenue, are **reasonably safe on any given night**, although the Drunk Bus and police officers driving around make things seem safer, but I still don't feel safe walking back to my house off campus at night."

STUDENT AUTHOR: **Many students openly admit they don't feel safe off campus and are extremely upset about the RUPD. RU Safety is a controversial subject, and e-mails reporting theft and other crimes fill students' inboxes while police ticket jaywalkers.**

Questions?
For more inside information and survival tips, pick up College Prowler's full-length book on this school, written by an actual student! Check it out at *www.collegeprowler.com*.

Students Speak Out
ON OVERALL EXPERIENCE

Q "I have had an amazing experience at this school. There is something for everyone here, although I would not suggest this school to people looking for small class sizes. This school offers **education at a bargain price if you live in state**. I could not imagine myself at any other school."

Q "I'm glad I'm here. The education has challenged me, for the most part. **There are a lot of things to get involved in** no matter where your interests lie. Also, because Rutgers is so big, you are bound to find people who share your interests. I could have gone to Brandeis, but I'm glad I chose Rutgers."

Q "I may be one of 36,000 students at Rutgers New Brunswick, but at the same time **I get a small college feel out of the place**."

Q "I love this school. **I never wish I was anywhere else**, and if I could do it all again, I'd just wish I had more advice at the start about which classes to take freshman year. But all experience is good, since it helps you learn. Too many people come here with a negative attitude and just want to transfer because they ended up here because of 'not getting in' somewhere else."

STUDENT AUTHOR: **The courses are tough at Rutgers. TAs mainly don't speak English, and you can never find a parking spot. However, despite these things, after the first week of your freshman year, you realize Rutgers is different then other schools. Diversity is definitely something that makes Rutgers stand out. Students will learn to live with all different people, despite different backgrounds, and smile and laugh the nights away in the dorms.**

Sacramento State

6000 J Street; Sacramento, CA 95819
(916) 278-6011; www.csus.edu

THE BASICS:

Acceptance Rate: 67%
Setting: Urban
F-T Undergrads: 18,472

SAT Range: 820–1060*
Control: Public
Tuition: $13,218

Most Popular Majors: Business, Social Sciences, Communication, Protective Services, Health Professions

*of 1600

Academics	B-	Guys	B-
Local Atmosphere	B	Girls	B
Safety & Security	C+	Athletics	C-
Computers	B-	Nightlife	B-
Facilities	C+	Greek Life	C-
Campus Dining	B+	Drug Scene	C+
Off-Campus Dining	A-	Campus Strictness	A-
Campus Housing	D+	Parking	D-
Off-Campus Housing	B+	Transportation	B+
Diversity	A	Weather	B+

Students Speak Out
ON ACADEMICS

Q "Truthfully, it depends mostly on the individual's enthusiasm. But on the whole, Sac State has very **'student-oriented' and 'teaching-oriented' professors** who care for the learning process, not research."

Q "The teachers and classes are interesting, I think. I think **they're outgoing and produce an intelligent environment** for their students. They provide what we need and help students to their best ability."

Q "Most of the teachers I have had are **very competent in the courses they are teaching** and very knowledgeable in general. They are often willing to meet with you personally. The classes are usually only as interesting as the professors. The majority of my classes have been interesting and engaging."

Q "**In smaller classes, teachers take time to work with you**. In my larger class, it's hard to ask the teacher for help because she's always busy. The larger classes have too many people. I don't know my geology teacher at all."

STUDENT AUTHOR: Most Sac State students have high opinions of their professors but still feel like something's missing in their classes. This is more common in lower-division general-education classes where students aren't always worked too hard. Frequently, professors go easy on them when they could be making them turn in harder assignments. If you're smart, there's nothing Sac State can throw at you that you can't handle.

Students Speak Out
ON LOCAL ATMOSPHERE

Q "As a commuting student, I really don't get off campus too much, but **Sacramento does have the usual bar and club scene**, and the American River bike trail is a stone's throw from campus. The Lake Natomas Aquatics Center is right up Highway 50 for water sports, too."

Q "Sacramento has an interesting atmosphere. **The city population is very large and diverse**. However, an almost rural feeling exists. UC Davis and a few community colleges exist nearby. There are plenty of historical places and artifacts scattered throughout the city."

Q "**Rather unfriendly, in my opinion**. In Sacramento, it is so crowded that people seem eager to communicate but unwilling to put in the effort. A couple of community colleges and UC Davis are around. I just moved here, and I'm not familiar with it yet."

Q "**The atmosphere is fun but, at times, very quiet and calm**. I don't really know the area too well, but alcohol is a big thing people are trying to stay away from."

STUDENT AUTHOR: Sac State is right in the middle of a lot of shopping and dining venues, so if you like to spend money in a consumer paradise, you're in luck. If, however, you like to enjoy great landmarks and unique local attractions, you're going to have to work harder to find them. There are museums, concert halls, and sports arenas, but they're not as impressive as the ones in larger and more famous cities.

Students Speak Out
ON FACILITIES

Q "**I thought the gym was really kept up well**. It's clean. I've only seen it set up for gymnastics, though."

Q "The equipment's good. Everything's in the right racks. In the free-weight room, the 50s are with the 50s and the 30s are with the 30s. At the school I went to in LA, if you weren't an athlete, you had to pay for the athletic facilities, but **here, they're free**."

Q "**Some facilities are better than others**. Carpet would be a nice thing to add to some rooms since it cushions the feet more, even though I know it would be harder to keep clean. The bathrooms should be equipped with air-freshener devices, though."

Q "The facilities are acceptable. I recently transferred from the University of Oregon, though, and the campus was much nicer. **At CSUS, buildings don't try to be beautiful**, and athletic facilities are not very good."

Q "**Some of the facilities could use some updating**, but they still serve their purpose."

STUDENT AUTHOR: There are things to do on campus, but there could be more. Arcade rats and pool junkies love the Union, which is always crowded with people doing all sorts of things. The Union is the focal point of student life, with the River Front Center coming in a close second. River Front Center is basically all eateries, so it's naturally a hotbed of activity. However, the Union has more than just food, and pretty much all of the recreational options are located there.

Famous Alumni

Wayne Thiebaud, John Weborg, Janice Rogers Brown, Giselle Fernandez, Dale Carlsen, Rene Syler

Students Speak Out
ON CAMPUS DINING

Q "**The food on campus is good**. We have a good variety, such as Gordito Burrito, TOGO's, and others. The dining halls are good and have a good variety."

Q "Food on campus comes in a large variety, including places like Round Table Pizza, Mother India, and Kung Fu Fat's. **The dining hall foods resemble most cafeteria-style foods**; however, the hours of operation are limited."

Q "I feel that the food on campus is good. **You really can go anywhere and get good food**. It depends on what you like, though."

Q "I like the food in Dining Commons. Last semester, I was on Meal Plan A, but I'm on Meal Plan B now because I can get more food with it. **They have a lot of selections on the menu**."

Q "The food on campus is great. I love Java City Café, Leatherby's, Kung Fu Fat's, and Burger King. However, **why does everything have to close so early**? There are students here until about 8 p.m."

STUDENT AUTHOR: There's a lot of food on campus, and if you like commercialized fast food, you'll be happy. Burger King, TOGO's, Gordito Burrito, and others provide a familiar dining experience that's no more or less healthy than most other places in the world of American dining. Just be prepared for the lines, which are longest in the afternoon. You'll frequently find yourself eating at your second or third choice because the line for the first one was just too long.

Student Body

African American:	7%	Male/Female:	43/57%
Asian American:	19%	Out-of-State:	1%
Hispanic:	15%	International:	1%
Native American:	<1%	Unknown:	17%
White:	40%		

Popular Faiths: Most students at Sac State are Christian, but they don't dominate in any way.

Gay Pride: Overall social acceptance for openly gay people is moderate to favorable, but the organized collective gay voice isn't that prominent.

Economic Status: Sac State has students from all over the economic spectrum, but most are middle class and lower-middle class.

Students Speak Out
ON DORMS

Q "I don't mind the dorms, but I don't feel very independent with RAs and stuff. It's a great way to meet people, but you can't get away from them, either, in those small, loud rooms. **I was happy to live in the dorms**, and I'm happy to be out."

Q "**The dorms are convenient and close to campus**, which avoids the commute madness. However, they are old and in need of repairs. The rooms are small, but the students in the dorms make it a fun atmosphere, and they offer many ways to make friends."

Q "I think that the dorms are **a great opportunity to meet people on campus**. I wasn't too fond of sharing a room, but I stayed in a triple."

STUDENT AUTHOR: For a school with so many undergrads, it's surprising that there are only five three-story dorms to accommodate them. But then again, Sac State was designed to be a commuter school, so not as much attention is paid to dorm quality. The major saving grace for students is the social atmosphere. Making new friends is worth the experience, or almost worth it, at least.

Did You Know?
5% of undergrads live on campus.

Students Speak Out
ON GUYS & GIRLS

Q "**There are lots of good-looking girls here**. A nice number. I'm not complaining. And there's more enrollment now, so there are more girls."

Q "Unfortunately, the guys are attractive, but **they all dress the same**—khaki shorts and cotton striped shirts with flip-flops. Boring. The girls are pretty, but again, they all look the same."

Q "When the sun is shining and girls are comfortable, they look great. **For guys, the frat-boy look is common**."

Q "I've heard there are some better people at other colleges, but **there are some hotties here, I just haven't seen any of them**. Just kidding! There really are some cuties."

STUDENT AUTHOR: Taking all the different responses into account, Sac State is an okay-looking campus. There are some people who dress sharp, but few of them look like supermodels or personal trainers. Then again, not everyone is into that look. Also, male students usually think more highly of their female counterparts' looks than vice versa, so if you're a guy who likes girls, you'll at least have a lot to look at.

Traditions

The *Calaveras Station*
The campus literary magazine that's published by the English department.

Chickens and Squirrels
For years, Sac State was well-known as a place where chickens and squirrels ran freely around campus. But some time ago, the chickens mysteriously vanished.

Overall School Spirit
Sac State could definitely use some help in the school spirit department, but every once in a while, the spirit bug comes around.

Students Speak Out
ON ATHLETICS

Q "**Sac State is not a sports school**. Most people just come here for class and then leave. A lot of people have jobs or kids, so they have things to do instead of just go to college games. If more people stayed on campus and lived here, then sports would be bigger."

Q "People get riled up at that Davis game. Sports are never down. **I don't think games are difficult to get into**. A lot of people go to games and then leave."

Q "I'd say we're not really a big sports school. **Lots of students don't pay attention to them**. I know I don't."

Q "Sports don't seem as important here. **IM seems much more visible than varsity**, though."

STUDENT AUTHOR: The few students who are sports enthusiasts are so vocal about their passion that they'll almost convince you that the whole school is just like them. But just the opposite is true—Sac State students aren't really into campus sports. Most games have lots of empty seats, and a lot of students don't pay attention to the teams.

Students Speak Out
ON DRUG SCENE

Q "**I think it just deals with who your friends are**. I haven't seen many drugs on campus. However, students seemed too open about other things."

Q "There's a lot of meth. You can tell because of pockmarks on people's faces. The way people behave too, and the excuses they give. **They're doing some meth**. It is cheap, and a lot of people buy it."

Q "**Not as bad as at my former school**. The occasional pothead is often seen, but the dealers tend to run things off campus. Even the new policies on cigarette smoking have lessened the sightings of users."

STUDENT AUTHOR: Hardcore drugs are less popular with students, but they exist as well. A lot of people talk about meth, and a few about cocaine. Dealers operate away from campus, for the most part, but users and dealers both come to school. And, of course, there is caffeine, which is very easy to come by on campus because of the unlimited supply of Java Cities.

22:1	Student-to-Faculty Ratio
78%	Freshman Retention Rate
12%	Four-Year Graduation Rate
82%	Financial Aid Applicants Receiving Aid

Students Speak Out
SAFETY & SECURITY

Q "Although there is a visible presence of security and law enforcement, **many students are concerned with their personal safety**. Items like cars, bikes, and belongings are often reported as vandalized or stolen. On a danger scale of one to ten, I'd say we're a seven."

Q "**Security is good at some things, like writing tickets and crap like that**. However, we have some of the worst car theft statistics in California. Security would rather bust you than protect you."

Q "I feel safe, and I think people are honest. I left my laptop in class, and a dude picked it up and put it on the counter. I think I can trust people in class. **I'll leave class and my things won't be missing when I come back**."

STUDENT AUTHOR: Most students feel safe and secure on campus, and they're not too concerned about being victims. However, sometimes thefts occur. But the frequency of car thefts and break-ins isn't enough to make everyone afraid of parking at the school.

> **Questions?**
> For more inside information and survival tips, pick up College Prowler's full-length book on this school, written by an actual student! Check it out at www.collegeprowler.com.

Students Speak Out
ON OVERALL EXPERIENCE

Q "**It's been a good experience, besides parking**. The schedules of my classes are very good. Availability of resources and tuition is decent. Anything you need for your classes is on campus. The school provides a good opportunity for education at a minimal cost. Unfortunately, they're taking more students than they have parking for. They need to have a designated area for full-time seniors because they've been here the longest, and it's their last year here."

Q "The school's pretty good. **I could be doing worse things—smoking crack, joining a gang**. It could be a more on-campus school with more spirit, but it's a commuter school."

Q "I don't stay on campus enough. **I come here for class and leave**. I don't feel Sac State has an inviting atmosphere."

Q "It's cool here. It's better than it was last semester. The people make it better. I joined an organization here, and social connections made it better. I haven't been to a lot of other schools, but I know **this one could be more of a community school**. It could have more togetherness and unity—more school identity."

STUDENT AUTHOR: Most students appreciate Sac State because it's pleasant, but they often wish it had more school spirit. A majority of people who attend Sac State just want a degree so they can get out. They know not to expect the typical college experience that makes for legendary times and awesome memories. Too many of them commute. Although most Sac State students don't think their education is lacking, when they voice concerns, it's obvious that they feel something's missing.

Saint Joseph's University

5600 City Avenue; Philadelphia, PA 19131
(610) 660-1000; www.sju.edu

THE BASICS:

Acceptance Rate: 86%
Setting: Urban
F-T Undergrads: 4,528

SAT Range: 1580–1850*
Control: Private
Tuition: $32,710

Most Popular Majors: Business, Social Sciences, Education, Psychology, English

*of 2400

Academics	B+	Guys	B
Local Atmosphere	A-	Girls	B+
Safety & Security	B+	Athletics	B+
Computers	B-	Nightlife	A-
Facilities	B	Greek Life	C+
Campus Dining	C	Drug Scene	B
Off-Campus Dining	A-	Campus Strictness	B-
Campus Housing	C+	Parking	B
Off-Campus Housing	B-	Transportation	B+
Diversity	C	Weather	B-

Students Speak Out
ON ACADEMICS

Q "Some of my friends try to pick classes and teachers by word of mouth if they find out teachers are easy. It's a smaller school, so you can do that, but it's good that it's smaller, too, so that **you can form more personal relationships with your teachers**."

Q "I like that a lot of the general requirement classes are taught by adjunct teachers. At first I thought this was weird, but **the adjuncts tend to be younger and energetic** and care about the students' learning."

Q "I'd say about **75 percent of my teachers knew everyone's names by the end of the semester**. Some don't bother to learn, and it's hard in the few really big classes. I still talk to or say 'hi' to a few of the teachers I only had one class with freshman year."

Q "**I'd like a little more diversity in the course offerings**, but overall I'd say they've been good. One thing that's weird is, if you take night classes, there are a lot of older students who can be overly competitive with the typical college-aged students also in the class."

STUDENT AUTHOR: St. Joe's academic reputation has been on the rise as of late and with good cause. New school President Rev. Timothy Lannon, S.J., has encouraged serious growth in the school's physical property and in the students' education. The broad spectrum of majors offered and its fine reputation are mainly what attract students to the University.

Students Speak Out
ON LOCAL ATMOSPHERE

Q "Philly is a good time, but **it's taken me almost three full years to figure out my way around** the city. Around St. Joe's you can check out some of the stuff on the main line, like bars on Lancaster Avenue and shops on Montgomery."

Q "I love St. Joe's because you can jump on the train and go west and you're at Villanova, or head east and you can go to Penn, Drexel, or even Temple. **There's plenty to do** around St. Joe's, too, like Main Street, Manayunk."

Q "Philly is filled with all sorts of restaurants. If you're into food, **it's got fancy stuff and local and exotic fare**. Everyone has their own favorite place to grab a cheesesteak, but by far Pat's is the best. I think the art museums are free like one day a month, so that's cool if you're into that."

Q "Philadelphia is a complex city. You have different sections of the city like the Northeast, South, University City, and West Philly. There's a lot to do around St. Joe's, but **definitely make sure to check out the whole city**."

STUDENT AUTHOR: **Philadelphia has a distinct character in its city and people. Some will complain that it's not as big as New York, but that is often beneficial to younger college students. The city is definitely large enough to explore over and over again and not get bored, yet it's not so impossibly large that one can never actually see all of it. At St. Joe's, students get access to a major city but are also able to avoid the hassle of living directly in a city atmosphere.**

Students Speak Out
ON FACILITIES

Q "The movie theater is new, so that's cool. But too many of the **campus facilities are closed too early for students studying late** at night. The only good part of late-night studying is that you can have 24-hour visitation to any dorm if you have a friend sign you in."

Q "A lot of the campus buildings are really old, and I like how the newer buildings are styled to look like that old brick style. But then on the inside, like in Mandeville, **it's all state-of-the-art, with TV screens on walls and things like that**."

Q "The fieldhouse is pretty nice and very historic. Duke's men's basketball coach was once quoted as saying he thinks it's the **toughest place to play besides Duke's Cameron Indoor Arena** because of how loud and crazy it gets."

Q "I would say our facilities are mediocre, but **they have been updating everything** since my freshman year, so that is a good sign, I guess."

Q "The new gyms they installed are mostly just treadmills, a machine or two, and free weights. That's better than nothing, I guess, but they **really don't benefit the upperclassmen since they're all in freshman dorms**."

STUDENT AUTHOR: **The campus has expanded but is still relatively compact. Overall, St. Joe's has a lot to offer. The school continues to make visible efforts to modernize campus. In just the past few years, the University has built a movie theater, updated the computer lab twice, built two dormitories, renovated the radio station's booth, and broke ground on an expansion to the field house.**

Famous Alumni

Dr. Andrew von Eschenbach, Joseph McKenna, Vince Papale, Mary Lou Quinlan, Dr. Jack Ramsay, Sr. Mary Scullion, Jack Whitaker

Students Speak Out
ON CAMPUS DINING

Q "For freshmen, the food's okay, but **speaking as a junior, I rarely would touch the stuff** other than grabbing a sandwich at lunch."

Q "Freshman year, I came home at Thanksgiving, and my parents thought I was on drugs. They were expecting the Freshman 15, but I came home **20 pounds lighter thanks to the cafeteria food**. Honestly, it's improved since I was a freshman, but it's not as good as some other schools I have visited."

Q "The food has really improved, but **it's got a long way to go** from friends' colleges that I've visited."

Q "My biggest complaint about St. Joe's and food is that **you can't eat anywhere on campus past 11 p.m.**, and that kind of stinks for girls who don't want to go traipsing around Philly looking for late-night study food."

Q **"I live and die by the spicy chicken wraps** during lunch. They are my manna from heaven."

STUDENT AUTHOR: **Students often complain about the quality of the food at dinner but rate the lunch options significantly higher. Mass-produced cafeteria-style food is tough to pass off as home-cooked, and this could explain the higher rating for simple sandwiches and fast food options during lunch. Older students tend to reluctantly agree that the food quality has improved since they've been here, but it has a long way to go. Many students keep a declining balance after freshman year and forgo the meal plan option.**

Student Body

African American:	3%	Male/Female:	48/52%
Asian American:	3%	Out-of-State:	60%
Hispanic:	3%	International:	1%
Native American:	<1%	Unknown:	4%
White:	86%		

Popular Faiths: Catholic; there is a chapel on campus where some students have made Sunday night Mass a popular destination.

Gay Pride: The campus is very tolerant of gays and lesbians. Programs such as SafeZone and Unity Week are strong examples of this.

Economic Status: St. Joe's has students from a variety of economic backgrounds.

Students Speak Out
ON DORMS

Q "There are drawbacks to all of them: In Overbrook, you're far away from the rest of the freshmen; in McShain, you don't have a suite; LaFarge makes me claustrophobic; and Sourin has no AC and is the nastiest dorm. **It all depends on how you get along with your freshman suite or hallmates** if you're going to like it or not."

Q "Pretty much everywhere on campus you get stuck as a freshman has community showers unless you get stuck in a random house with sophomores, in which case they'll probably be annoyed by you anyway, so **you'd be better off with other freshmen**."

Q "If you're **looking to party and hook up**, the two best places to live are Ashwood and Lancaster Court."

STUDENT AUTHOR: St. Joe's requires freshmen and sophomores to live on campus. There is still work to be done, but St. Joe's has begun updating its housing, as is evidenced by the new buildings and improvements in older dorms such as Sourin that the University plans to continue. One of the keys to living on campus is making friends with your RA.

? Did You Know?
61% of undergrads live on campus.

Students Speak Out
ON GUYS & GIRLS

Q "We have a lot of hot girls here, and **everyone is obsessed with going to the gym**. At least, that's what their AIM away messages say, but I don't always buy it."

Q "**This school is night and day**. This girl in my English class looked like she got hit with a bomb in class, but I saw her out that night, and she didn't look like that anymore, that was for sure."

Q "It's a really small school, so **you have to be careful who you date or hook up with**."

Q "We have **some good-looking guys and girls**. But for the most part, the girls think they're more attractive than they really are. Being that it is a small school, many of the guys are idiots and buy into how hot many of the girls think they are."

STUDENT AUTHOR: Many students disagree on the attractiveness or personalities of the opposite gender, but for the most part, St. Joe's is your average-looking college. It definitely has its share of cover girls and attractive guys. Two complaints seem to plague a bulk of the population, however. The guys need to be a little bit neater, and girls need to stop thinking so highly of themselves—but isn't that how it is at most colleges?

Traditions

The Hawk
The student chosen to be the Hawk receives free tuition and board, but he or she can never stop flapping the mascot's wings while in costume.

Hawk Mates
The name for two St. Joe's alumni that get married.

Overall School Spirit
Saint Joseph's is steeped in tradition, and its students bleed crimson and gray, as do alumni. This fierce pride is evident in the school's motto: "The Hawk will never die."

Students Speak Out
ON ATHLETICS

Q "St. Joe's varsity sports are **really taking off**."

Q "**Basketball hasn't been as crazy since Jameer Nelson graduated**, but the games are still just as fun and almost as crazy."

Q "**What St. Joe's needs is a football team**, even if it isn't very good; the whole atmosphere in the fall in college is so different here than at other schools with football teams. There's no homecoming game for alumni, and a lot of the pep rally stuff is held over for basketball season."

Q "IMs are fun but not as big as they are at some of the schools I've visited. **Kids take it seriously**, but there isn't a lot of organization or refereeing. It's a good chance to get exercise and play sports, though."

STUDENT AUTHOR: Varsity sports are dominated by the men's basketball team, and Coach Phil Martelli is slowly becoming a Philadelphia icon. Women's basketball also has a larger spotlight on it than other sports. Men's and women's crew have recently become more popular, and students have started making the trek to where the races are held.

Students Speak Out
ON DRUG SCENE

Q "Everyone seems to have tried pot at some point, but **mainly kids just drink** and, if they're into it, do Adderall. I think a drug company would make a fortune on St. Joe's if it were allowed to sell Adderall to the students."

Q "Every once in a while, my friends who smoke pot say mushrooms or LCD are going around, but I think **the most widely used drug is Adderall** because some people take it to party and some people take it to help them study."

Q "Basically, by sophomore year, **kids have experimented here and there**. There are those kids who smoke weed multiple times a day and those who have tried it and moved on."

STUDENT AUTHOR: **The most prevalent drug on campus is Adderall because students take it for both studying and pleasure. Marijuana is around and can be easily found if you look for it, but students would say there is rarely peer pressure. Like at most colleges, there are stories about some crazy kid who freaked out on LSD, but there are never any eyewitness accounts.**

15:1	Student-to-Faculty Ratio
88%	Freshman Retention Rate
68%	Four-Year Graduation Rate
85%	Financial Aid Applicants Receiving Aid

Students Speak Out
SAFETY & SECURITY

Q "I feel pretty safe, but **watch out for stupid kids stealing your stuff.** My roommate had her laptop taken out of her room while she was in the shower, and I got my jacket stolen off a caf table while I was refilling my soda."

Q "Campus is safe, but I would say **be careful driving at night** if you're not familiar with the area. It's nice around school, but a couple wrong turns and you're in pretty bad neighborhoods."

Q "The school is pretty safe, and **most of the crime is silly stuff**. My friends and I sit around Friday afternoons in the caf and read the incidents of crime in the school paper and see what drunk frosh pushed over what garbage bin this week."

STUDENT AUTHOR: **Don't leave your iPod, laptop, wallet, or anything else of value in plain view in a public place when you're not going to be attending to them. That being said, students agree they feel very safe when on campus. Security guards and police cover the grounds 24 hours a day.**

Questions?
For more inside information and survival tips, pick up College Prowler's full-length book on this school, written by an actual student! Check it out at *www.collegeprowler.com*.

Students Speak Out
ON OVERALL EXPERIENCE

Q "St. Joe's is a good school because it mixes a lot of things together. There's kids who party their way through and have bad grades, and then there are geniuses and hard workers who have great grades and go to the same school. **It's an interesting cross-section**."

Q "My sister went here, and I visited her a couple times, and she said she loved it. **I've been here two years, and it's okay**. I guess it's up to the person."

Q "**St. Joe's is great if you're looking into the business world**. My friends in that school all had job offers months before graduation. One of my friends actually got a job with a young investment banking firm that hired exclusively St. Joe's kids this year. Also, the school gets tons of money for the food marketing department."

Q "Philly's not like New York, so don't expect to be having Manhattan part two in your backyard. However, Philly, much like St. Joe's, is quirky and **really grows on you after you've been here awhile**."

STUDENT AUTHOR: **Everyone at St. Joe's takes the school with a small sense of humor. There are some who love it and a small percentage who pretend they hate it, but most people agree this quirky school in an even quirkier city is endearing. The biggest complaint is the cost of attending; however, this is often offset by the large number of scholarships given out. A lot of students have the "grass is greener" syndrome when reflecting on their time here. However, ask a St. Joe's student if they would rather be down the road at UPenn or Villanova, and you might get a fat lip.**

San Diego State University

5500 Campanile Drive; San Diego, CA 92182
(619) 594-5200; www.sdsu.edu

THE BASICS:

Acceptance Rate: 47%
Setting: Urban
F-T Undergrads: 21,630

SAT Range: 970–1180*
Control: Public
Tuition: $12,690

Most Popular Majors: Business, Social Sciences, Liberal Arts, Security, Psychology

*of 1600

Academics	B-	Guys	A
Local Atmosphere	A	Girls	A+
Safety & Security	B	Athletics	B-
Computers	B	Nightlife	A-
Facilities	B+	Greek Life	B
Campus Dining	B-	Drug Scene	B-
Off-Campus Dining	A-	Campus Strictness	B-
Campus Housing	C-	Parking	D
Off-Campus Housing	B+	Transportation	C+
Diversity	A-	Weather	A+

Students Speak Out
ON ACADEMICS

Q "Teachers do a good job with inspiring students to study. The **lectures I've had in classes weren't always exciting**, but the subjects and the assignments were."

Q "I like most of my professors. The majority of them are pretty cool, but there are anal ones as well. I especially like my classes this semester, because **I am finally taking classes which have something to do with my major**, as opposed to the classes that I had to take before for graduation requirements."

Q "Most of my teachers are very good with their material and very passionate about their teaching. **Other teachers are not quite as enthusiastic** about their teaching subjects, and it makes the classes seem boring. These classes put me to sleep."

Q "Teachers are knowledgeable and understanding. **They genuinely care for their students**. My classes are appealing simply because I like my major. You have to enjoy what you want to do with your life to find your classes attractive. The teachers sometimes make classes interesting as well."

STUDENT AUTHOR: The school could use improvement with the quality of teaching in its introduction and lower-division courses. Many are taught by graduate students rather than professors. Overall though, most of the professors know what they're doing, love what their doing, and genuinely care about their students.

Students Speak Out
ON LOCAL ATMOSPHERE

Q "The atmosphere in San Diego isn't one of a typical 'college-town,' but in the surrounding college area **there is a feeling of student life creeping around** here and there. There's not really anything to stay away from. It's all pretty safe and hunky dorey."

Q "The atmosphere is wonderful in San Diego. **You've got the beach, clubs, restaurants, casinos**, and anything else you can think of. There are two other major universities present, UCSD and USD. Definite places to visit would include Balboa Park, which is occupied with museums and beautiful scenery, and Coronado, which is home to one of the most beautiful hotels in the nation, the Hotel Del Coronado."

Q "San Diego is definitely a chill city. With so many options, there is always something to do here. **Just make sure to stay away from the border** if you aren't going with someone who is familiar with it. I've heard numerous horror stories from friends about the corruption of the police in Tijuana."

Q "The atmosphere in San Diego is very relaxed. **Individuals of all sorts can find comfort and entertainment here**."

STUDENT AUTHOR: With plenty of young people, a lot of affordable housing, and a fun atmosphere, the area surrounding San Diego State's campus can be very desirable for a college student.

Students Speak Out
ON FACILITIES

Q "**I think San Diego State has a really nice campus**, as compared to the other schools I have been to."

Q "Facilities on campus are very nice. I go to the gym all the time and **it's one of the best gyms in San Diego**. I've been to other college gyms and they don't hold a candle to the ARC."

Q "The ARC is very nice, but Aztec Center could use a minor facelift. The campus itself is beautiful and it has very nice athletic facilities. Overall, the campus is very pleasant, but **it is located in rather bad area**."

Q "I have never been to the athletic center. It looks very nice from the outside, but I hear that it is always very crowded and that there are long lines for the machines. The computers facilities are nice, and we have a huge library. **The student centers are okay; I have seen better** at other campuses."

Q "The facilities on campus are very good. The gym is especially nice and **the equipment is frequently maintained**, so it is always comfortable to workout in there. The staff in the ARC is pretty cool, and they are always helpful. The bowling alley needs some improvement, it seems to be quite outdated."

STUDENT AUTHOR: San Diego State's campus is, for the most part, in good condition. Several of the school's facilities are state-of-the-art. If some of the older buildings were more frequently maintained, there would be nothing to complain about in regards to the facilities on campus.

Famous Alumni

Michael Cage, Jamal Duff, Marshall Faulk, Tony Gwynn, Art Linkletter, General Merill A. Mcpeak, Maureen O'Connor, Gregory Peck, Marion Ross

Students Speak Out
ON CAMPUS DINING

Q "I do not eat on campus aside from going to the market to get coffee and water. **The food on campus is mainly fast food**, but there are few healthy alternatives within walking distance such as 4.0 Deli."

Q "The food is good. **The campus offers a variety of general food places** like Panda Express, burrito restaurants, some pizza places, and a deli. I guess you could say it has all the bases covered, at least the junk food ones."

Q "There are plenty of fast food joints on campus, as well as healthy dining alternatives. There is something for everyone. I have heard that the dinning hall food is pretty good, **although I've never eaten there myself**."

Q "The food on campus is decent. I like Sub Connection and Panda Express the most. The dining hall is **quite crowded during lunch hour**, and eating there can be quite a hassle."

Q "The Dining Room is pretty good and they have a different menu every night. **Everyone loves breakfast night** because it has got the best food. While not the best, the foods here is no worse than at any other school."

STUDENT AUTHOR: San Diego State offers a plethora of fast food options and not much else. The Dining Hall facility is rather nice, and the food it offers is above average, granted that it is produced in masses. The selection of fast food is decent, but there is not much else besides it. You'll quickly grow tired of it.

Students Speak Out
ON DORMS

Q "**I have never lived in the dorms**, but when I visited friends I noticed they were small, kind of old, and not too nice."

Q "Everyone needs to **experience the ups and downs of living in the dorms**. Cuicacalli is a much easier experience because of its luxuries that the other dorms don't offer, such as single rooms and a kitchen."

Q "Oh the dorms. The dorms are seriously a good place to start. You meet most of your friends and acquaintances there and it's just an experience no one should miss out on. **The dorms are bearable like a Motel 6**, but nothing extravagant. Still, the dorms are the best!"

STUDENT AUTHOR: Compared to other schools, San Diego State is far behind in the quality of its standard dormitories. Even though the quality of these traditional residence halls lags behind, it is still the place you want to be if you're looking to meet lots of new people your first year at school. Living in the dorms is quite an experience, and I think that everyone should do it for a year regardless of the quality of the facilities.

> **Did You Know?**
> 15% of undergrads live on campus.

Students Speak Out
ON GUYS & GIRLS

Q "Yes, it's true what they say. **San Diego has a lot of good-looking people**! Everywhere you turn, there's a pretty face."

Q "The **guys are mainly So-Cal surfer dudes**, and the girls are ridiculously good looking. The girls are gorgeous and definite eye candy."

Q "The pleasant scenery definitely includes the ladies. **The gorgeous weather adds to the attractiveness of the coeds**."

Q "Of course there are hot guys and girls; it's a college in Southern California. Some are idiots and some are nice. **Hopefully there are a few people on campus who are here to learn** instead of worrying about hot guys and girls."

STUDENT AUTHOR: To be blunt, San Diego State is home to lots of gorgeous people. Girls at SDSU are known to be some of the prettiest in the state, and you would be hard-pressed to disagree. Guys are known to be almost as equally attractive, but they care a lot less about their looks than the women. With some of the most beautiful college students around, you couldn't ask for much more out of San Diego State.

Traditions

Homecoming
Homecoming week involves numerous events for both current SDSU students as well as alumni.

Welcome Week
Welcome Week encompasses a variety of programs that welcome students to San Diego State University and campus life.

Overall School Spirit
School spirit is generally a lightly felt presence. The majority of the campus is divided into cliques, and they have spirit only for themselves.

Students Speak Out
ON ATHLETICS

Q "Sports are semi-big on campus, at least to those who care enough to watch. And unfortunately, **that is not too many people**."

Q "Varsity and intramural sports are big on campus. Football, baseball, and basketball are the big varsity sports on campus. Almost every common sport is played as an intramural at SDSU, and **anyone can join up or create a team for themselves**."

Q "I am a junior and I have never attended a sporting event. **There does not seem to be a great deal of support** for our teams around campus."

Q "**There are sports at my school**? I had no idea. Guess they don't have a large influence on campus."

STUDENT AUTHOR: Sports at San Diego State have the potential to be huge, but they're not, because of both the quality of the teams and the apathy of the student population. Home games can be exciting, especially when we are squaring off against big teams such as UCLA—even if the Aztecs don't win.

Students Speak Out
ON DRUG SCENE

Q "The drug scene is there, but if you keep yourself away from it, **you won't get caught up in it**."

Q "I don't know a lot of people who do drugs other than smoke weed. **There are a lot of people who smoke weed here**. I am positive that more goes on here, but I don't involve myself with it."

Q "Yeah, there are a lot of drugs in San Diego, but nothing more than you would see at any other college. Marijuana and cocaine are the two big ones here; **marijuana more so than cocaine**."

STUDENT AUTHOR: Hardcore drug use, the kind Hunter S. Thompson would be proud of, is for the most part absent. If you truly wanted to get into some heavy stuff, I've been told that you could find it. On the contrary, if you want to surround yourself in a clean and drug-free environment, you could just as easily do that. Living off campus you will see a lot more marijuana use than on campus. Be prepared to see a lot of booze and some weed, but not much else.

20:1	Student-to-Faculty Ratio
81%	Freshman Retention Rate
10%	Four-Year Graduation Rate
70%	Financial Aid Applicants Receiving Aid

Students Speak Out
SAFETY & SECURITY

Q "I hear about an incident maybe once or twice a year. **We have escorts for late at night**, which makes the campus a whole lot safer."

Q "The cops make breaking up parties their life because they have nothing better to do. **Every big house party will eventually get broken up** by the San Diego Police Department."

Q "I have never felt like I was in any danger while on campus. The blue-light poles make me feel safe. They make me feel like if I ever was in trouble, **I would be able to get immediate help** from an officer."

Q "From what I've heard, **car theft could be considered a problem**. Several cars have been reported as stolen the past year."

STUDENT AUTHOR: With abundant blue-light emergency stations located throughout campus and a 24-hour escort service, students feel they are being protected by campus security. Most incidents tend to take place in fraternity houses and house parties, where there is little security and regulation.

> **Questions?**
> For more inside information and survival tips, pick up College Prowler's full-length book on this school, written by an actual student! Check it out at *www.collegeprowler.com*.

Students Speak Out
ON OVERALL EXPERIENCE

Q "I have had a great experience at this school. I always hear about SDSU's bad reputation and about how it's just a party school, but **college is what you make of it**. I am here to learn and get a degree. I have learned a lot, and I have had some wonderful professors and mentors. I have gotten involved with a few activist groups on campus and met friends who share my drive. Other than that, my social life exists outside of campus, and that's what I want."

Q "**I was very skeptical about SDSU** when I first came here, but now I could not have been happier with my decision."

Q "**I love my school** and everything I've experienced in San Diego. I wouldn't trade my time spent here for anything else."

Q "San Diego has a lot to offer and there is so much to do here. **It's not dominated by the colleges**, so you can go out and experience plenty of other things. I love it! I am so glad I moved to San Diego for school!"

STUDENT AUTHOR: San Diego State is essentially defined by its social culture, and if students relate to it, they love the school, and if they don't, they can loathe their time here. With the beauty of the campus, the quality of the teaching, and the fun social environment, it is difficult to dislike much about the school, but some do. Those who tend to dislike San Diego State have reservations about the social scene, which is heavily conducive to partying and Greek life. SDSU is a very well-rounded school that has a lot to offer, but if you are searching for a strictly academic experience, you should look elsewhere.

Santa Clara University

500 El Camino Real; Santa Clara, CA 95053
(408) 554-4000; www.scu.edu

THE BASICS:

Acceptance Rate: 57%
Setting: Mid-sized City
F-T Undergrads: 4,316

SAT Range: 1110–1300*
Control: Private
Tuition: $28,899

Most Popular Majors: Business, Social Sciences, Engineering, Communications, Psychology

*of 1600

Academics	B	Guys	B
Local Atmosphere	C+	Girls	B+
Safety & Security	A	Athletics	C+
Computers	B-	Nightlife	C-
Facilities	A-	Greek Life	C-
Campus Dining	B+	Drug Scene	B-
Off-Campus Dining	B+	Campus Strictness	C-
Campus Housing	B	Parking	D+
Off-Campus Housing	B	Transportation	B
Diversity	A-	Weather	A

Students Speak Out
ON ACADEMICS

Q "Classes are not easy, but if you are having trouble, go to the teacher's office hours and stuff. They will **help you out a lot**, and showing them you're serious about it always helps."

Q "I don't like the quarter system. I don't know why they can't make the schedule closer to the way other schools are. It also kind of sucks to have to take **three sets of finals every year**."

Q "People say the **work load at Santa Clara is just as hard as at Harvard** or other Ivy League schools, and that it's just getting in that's harder. I don't know if that's true, but SC is definitely a tough school."

Q "The teachers at Santa Clara take a special interest in making sure that **students are engaged with the subject matter**. Most will take the time to sit down personally with a student and address any confusions or concerns the student might have, or even just discuss a particular concept in more depth."

STUDENT AUTHOR: If you think recruiting offices over-emphasize the importance of class size and student/teacher ratio, I can tell you right now they don't. It really does make a difference when you know your professors, and more importantly, they know you. Classes are more intimate and productive. The quality of a Santa Clara education is very high. Each course is taught by an SCU professor, not a teaching assistant, so every class is led by someone knowledgeable and experienced.

Students Speak Out
ON LOCAL ATMOSPHERE

Q "The campus is **somewhat isolated**, but there are lots of cool places to go to not far away, like San Francisco, Santa Cruz, and parts of San Jose."

Q "Santa Clara is not the most exciting city. I spend the majority of my time within **a mile radius of the University**, where there are a lot of student houses and apartments."

Q "Santa Clara is definitely not a college town or activity center, but there are **many interesting things to do and see** within driving distance. There are tons of bars, restaurants, and music in San Fran. If you like the outdoors, there's camping in Big Sur, skiing/snowboarding in Tahoe, and the beach in Santa Cruz."

Q "The campus and right around it are cool, but then there is a **big dead zone**. If you're leaving the immediate area, you have to pretty much go all the way out of San Jose to do anything cool."

STUDENT AUTHOR: Aside from the student housing next to campus, the nearby neighborhoods are not geared toward young people. Many feel that nightlife suffers because of the lack of bars and clubs near campus. It also does not help that El Camino Real, the "main" street in the area, is considered one of the ugliest streets in the country. There are many interesting places nearby like San Francisco, Santa Cruz, Berkeley, and Monterrey to appeal to both the urban and outdoorsy types. The students seem to appreciate the options that the location affords them.

Students Speak Out
ON FACILITIES

Q "Our **stadiums are all really good**. All we need is some good sports teams to go with them, and we'd be set."

Q "The school really goes all out to make sure all the **facilities are top-notch**. That goes for the landscaping, too. The dorms are pretty plain, though. I mean, they're not bad or anything, but since they spend so much time and money improving the gym and library and stuff, you'd think the dorms would be really nice, too."

Q "Malley is our gym and it is incredibly nice. The equipment is all state-of-the-art, there are three **basketball courts, a lap swimming pool, and a workout area**; a well-kept secret is the saunas in the bathrooms."

Q "The Bronco is really nice, but it's not like a real college bar. They card really hard, so it never gets really wild. You **go there to hang out**."

Q "The **grounds are very well kept**. Almost too well kept."

STUDENT AUTHOR: SCU spends huge amounts of money each year to maintain the grounds and facilities, and it shows. The campus is always clean and beautiful, and it seems like the facilities are constantly being upgraded. A new addition to the Orradre Library has doubled its size. The computer labs have plenty of machines. The sports fields and stadiums are high quality as well. The dorms seem to be a little behind the rest of the facilities, but the University has begun improving a few of them as well. SCU spares no expense when it comes to facilities.

Famous Alumni

Andy Ackerman, Edmund G. "Jerry" Brown, Jr., Brandi Chastain, Shemar Moore, Steve Nash, Leon Panetta

Students Speak Out
ON CAMPUS DINING

Q "Bronco food is a **late-night guilty pleasure**. It's all terrible for you, but it's nice to take a break from studying."

Q "The food on campus is overall of a high quality, but it is becoming more and more expensive each year. There is a main dining hall where most freshmen and sophomores eat because they have dining plans. However, for those that live off campus, there are many **more price conscious options**. There is also a market that sells many nonperishable items and frozen goods."

Q "It's **good for cafeteria food**. But that doesn't mean it's good."

Q "Bon Appetite provides a quality product that tends to go unappreciated until students move off campus, and realize they don't have easy access to it anymore. However, there are a wide variety of restaurants that **students can use their Flex money** at."

Q "The quality is good, but it's **way overpriced**, and there's nothing you can do about it."

STUDENT AUTHOR: All students living on campus receive a dining plan as part of their housing costs. Every quarter, the student receives dining points that can be used to buy food in the cafeteria, the Bronco, the Cellar Market, and a few other places. Quality-wise, the food is much better than most college cafeterias. There are several stations (a burger grill, an Italian station, a vegetarian station) that each have a permanent menu and lunch and dinner specials every day.

Student Body

African American:	3%	Male/Female:	43/57%
Asian American:	19%	Out-of-State:	32%
Hispanic:	13%	International:	4%
Native American:	1%	Unknown:	0%
White:	60%		

Popular Faiths: A majority of the student body is Christian, with Roman Catholic being the most common denomination.

Gay Pride: The gay community at Santa Clara is relatively small and accepted by almost all.

Economic Status: While by no means made up entirely of "rich kids," much of the student body seems to come from fairly wealthy backgrounds.

Students Speak Out
ON DORMS

Q "Not one of the dorms is terrible. There are several newer ones that tend to be in high demand—Sobrato and Casa. But **it's more about the people you're living with** than where you're living."

Q "The rooms are like any other dorm rooms. It's nice that they **all have Ethernet connections**."

Q "I liked living in the dorms, but I was ready to move off campus after the first year. Campus Safety and the **RAs are just too strict**. Sometimes it felt like they were trying to baby-sit me. Then other times I felt like they were trying to get me arrested."

STUDENT AUTHOR: **The dorm rooms at SCU are just that—dorm rooms. They are not particularly large or small, and they come with minimal furnishings. The biggest complaint students have about the dorms is the strictness. While this varies to some degree depending on the RA, they are all fairly strict. Campus Safety will check into any noise or activity they think is suspicious, and sometimes search the rooms of students. This is more of an annoyance than anything.**

Did You Know?
48% of undergrads live on campus.

Students Speak Out
ON GUYS & GIRLS

Q "There seems to be a **high-school mentality** among both sexes, but this is particularly noticeable in the fraternity-oriented groups. Guys seem to know how to dress nice, but not how to take care of themselves."

Q "Girls are on the attractive side, but there is **too much emphasis placed on looking good**. I wouldn't be surprised to find out many girls spend more time on their outfits and makeup than they do on their studies."

Q "Most of the guys are cool. From my experience, the **hot girls are often snobby**, stupid, and rich, but there are exceptions."

Q "The social scene here **isn't conducive to meeting people and hooking up**."

STUDENT AUTHOR: **Pledging with a fraternity or sorority ensures that you will have plenty of opportunities to interact with drunk members of the opposite sex, but since they will mostly be other Greeks, it can have a limiting effect on your selection. Combined with the small size of the school and the RLC system that groups students together in both classes and the dorms, one's options can seem narrower than they really are.**

Traditions

Dads and Grads
The morning of graduation, students and their fathers go to the Hut bar to "prepare" for the ceremony.

Midnight Breakfast
This significant social event is held in the Benson Center for new students every fall so they can get to know each other.

Overall School Spirit
Even though sports aren't huge at SCU, almost half the student body is part of the Ruff Riders booster club.

Students Speak Out
ON ATHLETICS

Q "Athletics seems to attract minimal attention compared to other universities. Though our teams are good, and the athletes extremely devoted, there always seems to be a **considerable lack of supporters** present, even at home games."

Q "Our teams are really good for our size, and it's really cheap if you **join the Ruff Riders**."

Q "**Soccer is the SCU big thing**, and then of course men's basketball when we play Gonzaga only. Intramurals are cool; a lot of people get involved."

Q "Varsity sports are not very big. There's no football team, and thus **no real school spirit**."

STUDENT AUTHOR: **Varsity sports are not a huge part of Santa Clara life. The most notable example is the lack of a varsity football team. This means no tailgating, no Homecoming, no Bowl games, and less school spirit. And although it is a Division I school, SCU's small size makes it hard for the school to be competitive in many major sports. Recreational sports are very popular on campus. It seems like everyone is on one intramural team or another.**

Students Speak Out
ON DRUG SCENE

Q "**Marijuana is a definite staple** among the students, as is alcohol. Other drug use is not widely publicized."

Q "**Drugs aren't big here**; it's not a party school. A lot of people smoke weed, but that's about it."

Q "Drugs are not all over the place or anything, but it's like everywhere—**you can find them if you look**. Well, you might have a problem if you wanted crack or something. But how many college students smoke crack anyway? And Santa Clara's a really good, hard school, so that kind of thing is even more uncommon."

STUDENT AUTHOR: **The drug scene at SCU is miniscule compared to most colleges. There is some hallucinogenic use, but it's pretty covert. Prescription painkillers are common in a few circles. There is use of study aides like Adderall and Ritalin, especially during finals. The only drug that is prevalent around campus is marijuana. If you searched every off-campus student apartment or house, you would probably find weed or paraphernalia in a most.**

12:1	Student-to-Faculty Ratio
92%	Freshman Retention Rate
76%	Four-Year Graduation Rate
71%	Financial Aid Applicants Receiving Aid

Students Speak Out
SAFETY & SECURITY

Q "The **only thing you have to fear** on campus is Campus Safety."

Q "It's never really occurred to me that campus might be dangerous. **Campus Safety is so strict**, and the police station is so close, that it's hard to imagine anything really crazy happening."

Q "You'll be **fine as long as you're not an idiot**. If you leave your bike or laptop laying around, it might get stolen, but that's kind of your own fault."

Q "You **couldn't get hurt on campus if you tried**. If you got a paper cut, Campus Safety would show up and carry you to the hospital, and there'd be a write-up about it in the *Santa Clara* (student paper)."

STUDENT AUTHOR: **The SCPD is very well funded and well staffed. If there was an emergency, a swift response is pretty much guaranteed. There are emergency phones all over campus, and Campus Safety is always patrolling the grounds. Some students even think that the campus is a bit too safe.**

> **Questions?**
> For more inside information and survival tips, pick up College Prowler's full-length book on this school, written by an actual student! Check it out at *www.collegeprowler.com*.

Students Speak Out
ON OVERALL EXPERIENCE

Q "Santa Clara is an awesome school if you make the most of it. This **requires some effort on your part to get involved** in the many different things there are to do here. But nobody's going to make you do it, so you'll have to be motivated coming in."

Q "The **teachers give you a lot of attention** and are good about hooking you up with jobs or grad school applications after graduation."

Q "The desolation of the surrounding area forces the students into a **tight-knit community**. I like that community."

Q "The **small size has benefits and drawbacks**. It's a pretty tight community, but sometimes it is too much like high school."

Q "Campus is beautiful, the surrounding area blows, **small classes**, bunch of loser frat guys, bunch of hot girls, no football, basketball's getting good, and facilities are good."

STUDENT AUTHOR: **Santa Clara is not like most schools. It is a small, Jesuit University, and its strengths and weaknesses stem from that. It depends what you want from college. If you want a high-quality education, you should definitely come; if you want *Girls Gone Wild* to do a special at your frat house, probably not. If you like surfing, skiing, hiking, climbing, or the outdoors in general, you will like the area; if you want to go clubbing four nights a week, you probably won't. The academics and facilities are top-notch, and the school spares no expense on the facilities. The size of the school makes it difficult to be competitive in Division I sports. The social scene is limited compared to larger schools, but it is also less exclusive and stressful.**

Sarah Lawrence College

1 Mead Way; Bronxville, NY 10708
(914) 337-0700; www.slc.edu

THE BASICS:

Acceptance Rate: 44%
Setting: Suburban
F-T Undergrads: 1,198

SAT Range: 1160–1350*
Control: Private
Tuition: $34,042

Most Popular Majors: Liberal Arts and Sciences

*of 1600

Academics	B+	Guys	C+
Local Atmosphere	C·	Girls	B
Safety & Security	C+	Athletics	D+
Computers	B	Nightlife	C+
Facilities	C+	Greek Life	N/A
Campus Dining	C	Drug Scene	D+
Off-Campus Dining	B-	Campus Strictness	B
Campus Housing	A-	Parking	C-
Off-Campus Housing	C-	Transportation	B-
Diversity	D+	Weather	B-

Students Speak Out
ON ACADEMICS

Q "There is no rigid distinction between student and teacher, but there is, rather, a sense that someone **well-versed in his or her field** is welcoming you into it."

Q "My history and theater classes remind me why I went to SLC—dorky as it sounds. They **inspire my interest** and various curiosities inside and outside of the classroom."

Q "Projects really depend on your own ambitions. Fortunately, most **students here are very motivated**. I'm always impressed with all the hard work that goes on here."

Q "Though it depends on the classes, for the most part, my teachers are **phenomenally smart** people who sincerely love what they do. Some of them are quirky and awkward, some are confident, suave, and glamorous, and a surprisingly large number of them have keen senses of humor."

STUDENT AUTHOR: **What's vital to understanding SLC academics is its emphasis on the individual. Classes consist of round-table discussions in which speaking your mind is mandatory. Professors push you to your intellectual limit, then push you more. Skipping readings or homework assignments can be disastrous. While the grading system is flexible, professors write detailed evaluations of your performance, and they'll come down hard if you've been slacking.**

Students Speak Out
ON LOCAL ATMOSPHERE

Q "Bronxville doesn't have much to offer in terms of entertainment. It's a wealthy town with quaint little stores, but that's about it. If you want entertainment, **take advantage of New York City**."

Q "SLC has a **contentious relationship** with Bronxville; the townspeople benefit from having the college there, but they seem to resent its presence. There are definitely businesses that are less than friendly to students."

Q "Bronxville is not exactly what could be described as a bustling college town. And although **Manhattanville College is close by**, there doesn't seem to be much, if any, student mingling going on."

Q "It can be inconvenient to get to Yonkers. To get there, you have to walk over major roads that are poorly lit and in no way pedestrian-friendly. I **don't feel comfortable walking there at night**. I like Bronxville more. It's easier to get to because the school runs shuttles there, and the walk is always on a sidewalk."

STUDENT AUTHOR: **You may find yourself trapped between two unfriendly opposites. Walk in one direction, you'll hit Bronxville, a ritzy town with showcase windows and high-priced boutiques. Walk two miles in the other direction and you'll be in Yonkers, a working-class suburb. Campus clears out on weekends as students flee to NYC for entertainment, as well as hospitality.**

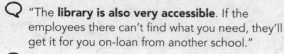

Students Speak Out
ON FACILITIES

Q "The **library is also very accessible**. If the employees there can't find what you need, they'll get it for you on-loan from another school."

Q "The facilities are amazing because there are new buildings popping up everywhere, and the old buildings are constantly being upgraded. But the **rustic charm of the old buildings** is still intact."

Q "**Classrooms are always sufficient**, and many have flat-screen televisions and DVD players. The tables are all round tables to facilitate discussions, and you'd be surprised how well this works."

Q "The **movie theaters on campus** are good. Heimbold is beautiful and polished, like the 'real thing,' while the PAC theater is perfect for rowdy, bring-your-dinner-with-you kind of events."

Q "The gym is a really excellent resource on this campus. It's very new and clean and **has almost anything you would want** in order to work out."

STUDENT AUTHOR: SLC is changing in a big way. Widespread renovations are planned. The absence of a student center has been a gaping hole in student life for several decades. Now, renovations intended to improve public student spaces in Bates are underway. One problem that has arisen in recent years is the major lack of handicapped-accessible pathways, doors, and dormitories. This is being addressed. Campbell Sports Center houses a full gym, as well as a basketball court, swimming pool, yoga and fencing studio, rowing tanks, and squash courts.

Students Speak Out
ON CAMPUS DINING

Q "The Pub is where you can go **pretty much any time of the day** and get candy, snacks, and greasy food like pizza and hamburgers."

Q "People like to complain, but I really don't have a problem with the food on this campus, except for it being **outrageously overpriced**. The Health Food Bar is my favorite place to eat."

Q "Brunch is always superb at either Bates or the Pub. But to keep it healthy and cheap, you're **better off cooking your own meals** (if your dorm has a kitchen)."

Q "As college dining goes, I think **we've got it pretty good**. I usually stick to the Health Food Bar because I end up eating too much at Bates."

Q "Compared to other universities, I think our food is great, but since we pretty much have the same options every day, it gets old pretty fast. I enjoy Bates because you get **all-you-can-eat meals** there. Things at the Pub and the Health Food Bar get pricey, and you get very little food for your allotted amount."

STUDENT AUTHOR: The flagship of SLC eating is Bates Dining Hall, an all-you-can-eat venue that serves lunch, dinner, and brunch. The Pub's greasy, repetitive fast food options are only worth it if you're on the go. The Health Food Bar is a favorite among students for its more nutritious cuisine and cozy ambience. There's a reason why students flock to dormitories with kitchens—on-campus meals, although culturally diverse, are questionable in terms of nutrition and taste.

Students Speak Out
ON DORMS

Q "It's pretty **easy to get a single** after freshman year, and it's also feasible to get a kitchen if you'd like. The dorms here are generally a lot less cookie-cutter and institutional than other colleges."

Q "**Group housing is by far the most popular** housing on campus. Usually, groups petition for an apartment with a full kitchen, a living room, and two floors. Everyone wants these, hence, they are hard to get."

Q "It seems like the **New Dorms are the lousiest** on campus, unless you like non-stop noise, cigarette smoke creeping under your door, and filthy hallway bathrooms."

STUDENT AUTHOR: It seems that at Sarah Lawrence, single rooms are in hot demand, and roommates are perceived as burdens. When the housing lottery rolls around, students often join forces and petition for one of the on-campus houses, which offer singles, a kitchen, shared bathrooms, and a common room. In general, dorm furniture is adequate, bathrooms are manageable, and the college is quick to respond to problems and repairs.

Did You Know?
86% of undergrads live on campus.

Students Speak Out
ON GUYS & GIRLS

Q "The **guys are sparse; there are too many girls**! Many of the guys abuse this fact and many of the girls are so desperate that they allow it."

Q "Both the guys and girls are extremely smart, well-spoken, interesting, and artsy. **You won't find any 'dumb jocks' or 'dumb blondes'** here."

Q "The **guys are gay and hot**. The girls are lesbians and hot."

Q "Being a **single, straight girl is, well, frustrating**. The girls here range from the hippiest of hippie-chicks, to wanna-be runway models and fashionistas."

Q "For me, **there are some wonderful, amazing, talented, attractive men** here."

STUDENT AUTHOR: There are three times more girls than guys, and yes, it is noticeable. Straight SLC guys, on the other hand, are notoriously promiscuous. On such a small campus, this can lead to a lot of fighting, backstabbing and jealous love triangles, so watch out. However, the significant gay, lesbian, and transgender population on campus means that exploratory relationships are encouraged and an open-mind is required.

Traditions

Bacchanalia
Students flock to the North Lawn for a day of dancing, live music, games, free food, and free beer.

Cabaret
Anything goes on stage, as long as your performance is good, funny, sexy, or comically bad.

Overall School Spirit
There's a feeling that everybody at SLC has something intellectual to offer. School spirit is evident in the massive turn-outs for student art shows and performances.

Students Speak Out
ON ATHLETICS

Q "Sports are a joke here. The **only 'cool' sport is ultimate Frisbee**, and that's just a club activity that involves a bunch of shirtless guys chasing a Frisbee back and forth across the North Lawn."

Q "I guess that Sarah Lawrence just **lacks a sports-competitive spirit**."

Q "The men's basketball team usually gets a larger crowd. If you do play sports, **we have an amazing sports center** with a fitness center, lap pool, rowing tanks, a track, and a huge gym."

Q "We **don't have big varsity sports**, and intramural sports are a small group of about 40 people who play all the sports."

STUDENT AUTHOR: The general consensus is that Sarah Lawrence students are brainy, weak creatures, and any attempts at physical contests are promises of pathetic failure. But that isn't entirely true. Many sports are offered at the varsity level. Turnout for games is low, which may frustrate athletes who work hard to represent the school, and don't receive respect or encouragement. The athletic crowd on campus may be small, but their morale is high and the facilities are top-notch.

Students Speak Out
ON DRUG SCENE

Q "The drug scene here is huge. Everyone smokes pot and is **always looking for a new drug** to try. Luckily, everyone is pretty open minded, too, if you don't do drugs."

Q "There's also **no pressure**—kids totally respect if you're straight edge or just not in the mood."

Q "Private college plus rich, artsy kids plus independent studies (a.k.a. too much free time) equals—you guessed it—**a thriving drug scene**."

STUDENT AUTHOR: The dismal social scene, the anti-social demeanor of many students, and the insular campus atmosphere are popular scapegoats for SLC's drug predicament. And despite the college's numerous movements to educate students on safe partying habits, more and more kids get hospitalized for substance abuse every year. Fortunately, students who aren't into the drug scene aren't typically pressured or harassed by those who are.

6:1	Student-to-Faculty Ratio
92%	Freshman Retention Rate
66%	Four-Year Graduation Rate
88%	Financial Aid Applicants Receiving Aid

Students Speak Out
SAFETY & SECURITY

Q "If you're worried about campus safety, don't be. There is a **student shuttle at night**, so you don't have to walk home in the dark. There are also security cars patrolling the campus all day long."

Q "When it comes to things like thefts and violence, I think **security does a great job** trying to keep those to a minimum. On the other hand, however, I've seen people getting stoned (and sometimes drinking) right in front of security, and they ignore it."

Q "Security works hard to make the campus safe. However, I think the **campus is very poorly lit**. There are areas that I feel very uneasy in at night. I also think that security needs to enforce a speed limit on Kimball because cars do not slow down for pedestrians crossing the street."

STUDENT AUTHOR: Security guards are a familiar, reliable presence, and the numerous emergency towers make it easy to contact them if you're in trouble. Students agree that the campus feels safe, but its urban surroundings can get creepy at night.

> **Questions?**
> For more inside information and survival tips, pick up College Prowler's full-length book on this school, written by an actual student! Check it out at *www.collegeprowler.com*.

Students Speak Out
ON OVERALL EXPERIENCE

Q "I love the academic structure and mentality of this school. There is much more **freedom to choose what it is that you want to study** here than any place else I know of. This is also the kind of environment where you take out what you put in, so you can pretty much work as much or as little as you want, depending on the kind of results you want for yourself."

Q "I **find the people pretentious**, Bronxville boring, Yonkers frightening, the social scene claustrophobic, the classes often intolerable, and the dating options nil."

Q "SLC is not perfect, but nothing is. You will pay a ton of money, and for that, you get **classes that will blow your mind**."

Q "I love SLC more than anything. **Ridiculously expensive? Yes**. But it is my ideal school. It has helped me become a person I'm proud to be; it has given me confidence. I've made tons of great friends and experienced many new things."

STUDENT AUTHOR: Careers, money, and business are seen as secondary in comparison to the joy of learning. The one-of-a-kind curriculum gives you the freedom to choose what you want to learn and how you want to learn it. Being a student here equals spending four years immersed in a community of intellectual young people and world-renowned professors. What students report as the biggest setback is the anemic social scene. Traditionally, SLC students are introspective, private, and socially-awkward people. Still, the retention rate is high; students seem determined to endure the College's weaknesses for the sake of its unique strengths.

Scripps College

1030 Columbia Avenue; Claremont, CA 91711
(909) 621-8149; www.scrippscollege.edu

THE BASICS:

Acceptance Rate: 43%
Setting: Suburban
F-T Undergrads: 947

SAT Range: 1910–2170*
Control: Private
Tuition: $37,736

Most Popular Majors: Social Sciences, Visual/Performing Arts, Area Studies, Psychology

*of 2400

Academics	A	Guys	N/A
Local Atmosphere	C+	Girls	A-
Safety & Security	A-	Athletics	C-
Computers	A-	Nightlife	B-
Facilities	B+	Greek Life	N/A
Campus Dining	A	Drug Scene	B
Off-Campus Dining	C-	Campus Strictness	B+
Campus Housing	A+	Parking	C-
Off-Campus Housing	D-	Transportation	D-
Diversity	C	Weather	A

Students Speak Out
ON ACADEMICS

Q "Teachers do more than encourage discussion, **they demand it**. Classes are always interesting and educational, both in the material they examine and the way in which we discuss and apply it."

Q "Academics are **the most important thing** to everyone here."

Q "The teachers at Scripps are phenomenal. Scripps encourages students to **find connections between wildly different disciplines**; interdisciplinary professors, interested in several different fields besides their specialization, help in this process."

Q "My classes are definitely interesting. I enjoy the discussion and hearing from other students, and for the most part, the **subject matter is pertinent** and engaging."

STUDENT AUTHOR: Scripps's academics are focused wholly on the process of learning and the pursuit of knowledge. Students do not find learning to be a chore and constantly challenge each other. When asked what drew them to Scripps, nearly all students will state that academics was the primary factor. The small size of the school permits its professors to focus their attention on the education of a tight group of undergraduates. Tradition and the classics do indeed have a strong presence in Scripps learning and teaching style. However, students will find that most professors are open to the ideas of their students.

Students Speak Out
ON LOCAL ATMOSPHERE

Q "Claremont is a tiny town and mostly residential. It has a quiet, laid-back atmosphere that is relaxing, especially when you know that **the bustle of LA is only a short trip** down the freeway."

Q "**Claremont as a town is pretty dull**. It's quaint, and a trip to the Village is nice because it feels like small-town USA. The Claremont Colleges feel pretty secluded in their own environment."

Q "The Claremont near the colleges is **a sleepy residential town** that snuggles close to the San Gabriel Mountains. The Village is a quaint, over-priced section of Claremont about a mile away from Scripps."

Q "**Your parents will love Claremont—** guaranteed. The campuses are directly surrounded by an upper-middle-class neighborhood that exudes a sense of security and safety you won't find at larger urban campuses."

STUDENT AUTHOR: The local atmosphere is very peaceful and conducive to learning. Most students will say that there is really nothing for young people to do in Claremont, and this is pretty much true. Everything shuts down soon after night falls, and while the local Village area is charming, it is geared more towards families and the elderly, the main inhabitants of the city. The lack of social venues result in most Scripps students leaving campus on the weekends, and it is known that most who can, do.

5 Best Things	5 Worst Things
1 No men	**1** Its small size
2 Tradition-bound	**2** Cost
3 Humanities focus	**3** Off-campus nightlife
4 Individual growth	**4** Rigid rules
5 Challenging classes	**5** Gossip

Students Speak Out
ON FACILITIES

Q "**There isn't really a student center**, but there is the Hampton Room, which is very nice. The school holds dinners and lectures there."

Q "Scripps is **on the Historic Register** for our beautiful buildings, and the grounds are immaculate."

Q "We **share a lot of facilities**, so I never feel like we are lacking anything."

Q "Facilities are known to be beautiful and almost antique. Scripps has **this sort of culture ingrained into the physical appearance** of the college, which gives the environment of the college a romantic element."

Q "The athletic facilities are shared with Claremont McKenna and Harvey Mudd, and they are **very well equipped and have long hours**. There are eight tennis courts, two pools (one more for serious swimming and one for hanging out and tanning and playing inner tube water polo), a bunch of gyms, a weight room, and a track."

STUDENT AUTHOR: **While the Scripps campus, with its vast fields of grass, quaint gardens, and courtyards, gives off an aura of history and past generations, there are plenty of modern facilities that are widely used by students as well. Facility improvement and expansion has been occurring at Scripps at a rapid rate. The only complaint that students have is that individual dorms are not equipped with individual miniature facilities and televisions are not always working up to par so everyone has to gather at a central school facility. Also, there are very few pay phones and no ATM vestibules.**

Famous People from Claremont

Ben Harper, Mark McGwire, Snoop Doogy Dogg, Robin Williams

Students Speak Out
ON CAMPUS DINING

Q "The dining hall is good. There's usually something good to eat, **even if you are vegan or keeping Kosher**. It does get a little repetitive near the end of the year, but compared to anywhere else, it's heaven."

Q "Malott is generally considered to have **the best dining-hall food of the five colleges**. The food is better than the average dining hall, with high points like fresh-baked pizza, bread from a local bakery, and sushi Fridays. Even the greatest dining hall can become boring, however."

Q "**I get bored** of eating on campus every day, but the food is generally very good."

Q "Let me put it this way—while most of my friends at other colleges and universities yearned for home-cooking, I began to dread my mother's cuisine as summer neared. This is not for my mom's lack of culinary prowess, but rather a **direct result of the quality of on-campus dining** at Scripps."

Q "The food on campus is great. Scripps is known for its good dining hall food. Sometimes they get **a little creative with leftovers**, but they really have a great selection."

STUDENT AUTHOR: **In 2003, Malott had become so crowded during meal times that Scripps students decided to have "Scripps Only" hours so that Scripps students could eat at their own dining hall without fighting a crowd. Students do get tired of Malott day in and day out, but compared to most colleges, the food at Scripps is gourmet.**

Student Body

African American:	4%	Male/Female:	0/100%
Asian American:	13%	Out-of-State:	59%
Hispanic:	7%	International:	2%
Native American:	<1%	Unknown:	24%
White:	50%		

Popular Faiths: The most popular religious student groups are Christian.

Gay Pride: There is large proportional gay population at Scripps, and there's safe space for queer and questioning students to freely discuss issues.

Economic Status: A very large proportion of Scripps's students are from upper-middle to top income level.

Students Speak Out
ON DORMS

Q "The 'old dorms' built in the 1930s are some of **the most beautiful places** I've ever been to, and even the newer dorms, built around the 1970s, are palatial compared to any other college's dorms."

Q "The architecture of them and the campus in general is beautiful. The older dorms are really nice **because of their architecture** and the feel they have to them. I appreciate how Scripps takes care of their dorms because there is such a focus on it being a residential college."

Q "Overall, the dorms are **clean and well maintained**. The common areas, which include the living room and the browsing room for every residential hall, are useful for studying and for taking naps."

STUDENT AUTHOR: Most dorms have more space than any other college-living space, and comfort is a top priority. All dorm buildings are unique, with not any one like another. There are dorms that are preferred less than others, but there are no dorms deemed unlivable or hated by students. Comfort is a top priority.

> **Did You Know?**
> 96% of undergrads live on campus.

Students Speak Out
ON GUYS & GIRLS

Q "Males are there if you want them to be, but they are not a persistent presence, **which is very nice**."

Q "Scripps claims to be a women's college, but because of the Consortium, **it isn't actually like a women's college**. Most Scripps classes have guys in them, and Scripps women can take classes on the other coed campuses."

Q "There are a lot of beautiful and intelligent people here. Guys live on other campuses around us, because it's a women's college, but I've never had a hard time finding them. And **there's a fairly sizable queer community**, so there's lots for the gay community to choose from as well."

STUDENT AUTHOR: Many students lose interest in Scripps once they find out that it is all female, but this is something that the student body holds great pride in. Unique and intelligent, Scripps females are all beautiful; each in their own way. The women of Scripps can be intimidating and sometimes exclusive, which has led many to describe Scrippsies as overly proud and arrogant. While the college is indeed only female, males are far from scarce.

> **Traditions**
>
> **Afternoon Tea**
> Once a week, Scripps holds afternoon tea, at which time students gather for a snack and some punch or tea.
>
> **Matriculation**
> The ceremony symbolizes and celebrates the right of passage and journey that the students go through.
>
> **Overall School Spirit**
> Students show their school spirit through the way that they influence the outside world and through the changes that they can make in their lives.

Students Speak Out
ON ATHLETICS

Q "However, although we may hear the roar of a football game at CMC, most Scripps students **don't keep track of sports** unless they or their friends are involved. In general, your interest determines your level of involvement."

Q "If you want to attend a college that doesn't revolve around its basketball or football programs, **Scripps might be a good fit** for you."

Q "A lot of people **play for fun** here and it is not their goal in life to become a professional."

Q "**It's not popular** among the Scripps students. The retention rate of Scripps athletes is really low."

STUDENT AUTHOR: Unlike at large universities, there is not a huge emphasis on games and rallies. There are a good number of Scripps students on teams, but sports are for the most part not their main priority. The team spirit and support from the general student body is not always that great in that sports events are not widely attended, but the small following is very loyal.

Students Speak Out
ON DRUG SCENE

Q "Scripps has **a mild drug scene**. Many students choose to smoke marijuana at parties or with friends, but anything more dangerous is hidden from the public eye. Doubtless, if you wish to find it, you will be able to, if not on Scripps then at another campus."

Q "Alcohol is definitely **the drug of choice**, and marijuana is fairly prevalent as well. The usage of harder drugs is far less out in the open."

Q "Scripps students **aren't known for being hardcore partiers** to begin with, so women who choose not to participate in the scene do not feel tremendously pressured or uncomfortable with their decision."

STUDENT AUTHOR: There is a sizable substance-using community on Scripps as well as on the other colleges, but abstinence is respected and most social scenes and social groups have a mixture of extreme, occasional, and non users. Most students do not feel peer pressure to conform or fit in through drugs.

10:1	Student-to-Faculty Ratio
90%	Freshman Retention Rate
79%	Four-Year Graduation Rate
78%	Financial Aid Applicants Receiving Aid

Students Speak Out
SAFETY & SECURITY

Q "Scripps is an extremely safe place. Claremont is not a highly urban area, so the colleges and the surrounding area have **a quiet, community feeling**."

Q "The **Claremont Colleges go out of their way** to provide a safe, comfortable atmosphere and a security force that students are comfortable going to for help."

Q "Aside from the eerie quiet at nighttime, the air of safety makes walking back to your dorm at 3 a.m. a breeze. Regardless of the lack of criminal activity, emergency phones that directly connect to Campus Sec are scattered around campus and **students are equipped with whistle keychains**."

STUDENT AUTHOR: Security is taken very seriously at all five campuses. Most crimes that occur in Claremont are relatively small and occur off-campus or on the outskirts of campus at night, when security is more plentiful and patrols are on duty all around campus.

Questions?

For more inside information and survival tips, pick up College Prowler's full-length book on this school, written by an actual student! Check it out at *www.collegeprowler.com*.

Students Speak Out
ON OVERALL EXPERIENCE

Q "I love Scripps more than I can say. It is the best place in the world to grow and develop your mind and your identity. My dad says he sent a girl off to college and **got an adult woman back**. I think that's true. I feel lucky every day to be in such a beautiful place among women who are so amazing."

Q "I hated my first semester here. **It's a tough place to be**, but once you realize that everyone is in the same boat and help each other, it's terrific. You just have to give yourself some time to adjust and settle in before making any judgments."

Q "I have had a great experience being here at Scripps. **Getting involved was the key** to adapting quickly and taking advantage of the opportunities that abound here."

Q "I like the women's college part because the faculty and staff are dedicated to building us up and encouraging us to challenge ourselves in every part of life. That said, **it's not all touchy-feely**; there is a good sense of competition. It's all what you make of it."

STUDENT AUTHOR: The emphasis on learning, the openness to exploration, and the acceptance of what is different and exceptional are all things that I love about the school and things that contribute to a positive overall growth and development, as well as self realization. The atmosphere here has a sense of healthy competition that encourages students to feed off each other and mature together. Stress is a constant here, but over time it becomes a motivational factor that does not allow you to give up on yourself.

Seattle University

901 12th Avenue; Seattle, WA 98122
(206) 296-6000; www.seattleu.edu

THE BASICS:

Acceptance Rate: 64%
Setting: Urban
F-T Undergrads: 3,951

SAT Range: 1560–1890*
Control: Private
Tuition: $28,260

Most Popular Majors: Business, Health Professions, Engineering, Psychology, Social Sciences

*of 2400

Academics	B	Guys	B-
Local Atmosphere	A-	Girls	A-
Safety & Security	B	Athletics	C+
Computers	B-	Nightlife	A-
Facilities	B	Greek Life	N/A
Campus Dining	B	Drug Scene	B
Off-Campus Dining	A	Campus Strictness	C+
Campus Housing	B+	Parking	C
Off-Campus Housing	B+	Transportation	A-
Diversity	A-	Weather	C-

Students Speak Out
ON ACADEMICS

Q "The teachers on campus are fantastic. I feel very lucky to have such **educated, sincere, and devoted people** to learn from daily."

Q "The teachers are usually really great. They tend to be passionate about their subjects and are ready to help you out whenever you need it. My classes so far have been really interesting. Be careful, and **ask around to see who's a good professor**; it really makes a difference."

Q "Teachers at SU are, simply put, amazing. They are excited about their subjects, interested in their students, and **they focus on teaching and campus involvement** rather than research."

Q "For the most part, the teachers are willing to go out of their way to offer help and meet with students outside of class when they have questions or are struggling with the class. Most of them are challenging, and they **push their students to think critically**. I found very few of my Core classes interesting, but all of the classes that I have taken for my major, minor—and those I took just for fun—have been extremely interesting, and I have gotten a lot out of them."

STUDENT AUTHOR: **The Jesuits have an exceptional academic reputation. Not all professors are Jesuits, but their mission permeates the campus. This does not mean that every class has Catholic overtones, but it does mean that all professors are passionately committed to what they teach. The focus is to educate the whole person, not just provide the student with information.**

Students Speak Out
ON LOCAL ATMOSPHERE

Q "Seattle is comfortable most of the year; not too hot, not too cold. **UW is 5–10 minutes away**, for you frat-going types. Some neat places to visit are Pike Place Market, the Space Needle, the Experience Music Project/Science Fiction Museum, and the giant stone troll under the Fremont Bridge."

Q "The atmosphere in Seattle is **very easy-going and diverse**. Walking around, you see business people, homeless people, college students, and many different ethnic groups. There are other universities, but none of them are right next to the SU campus."

Q "Seattle is wonderful, and SU is in walking distance from almost anything in the downtown area. Capitol Hill is great, with lots to do and see. Broadway Ave., which runs on the west side of school, can get a little sketchy at night, so walk in small groups after 10 p.m. The atmosphere is great, the downtown location takes its toll on the vivacity of the on-campus party scene, but there's **an abundance of great places to go and things to do in Seattle** in general and around SU especially."

STUDENT AUTHOR: **One of the unique aspects of SU is its location. It has both a college feel and the flavor of an urban setting. With a mixture of landmarks, distinctive buildings, museums, theaters, and parks, Seattle has everything. In any given place, there are street performers or businessmen. This combination creates the cozy hustle a city ought to have.**

Students Speak Out
ON FACILITIES

Q "The facilities are so-so. **The gym is a little seedy**, and the Student Center has a tendency to feel like a high-school cafeteria. Other than those two weak points, the campus itself is a fairly welcoming place."

Q "The new Student Center is **very beautiful and well furnished** with everything to keep students from going too insane during hectic college life. There are also some nice areas around campus to play any number of sports, from soccer to Frisbee to bocci ball. The indoor astro-gym allows protected play in times of bad weather or for night games, and the basketball courts are right next door."

Q "The buildings for liberal arts studies, such as English, are **terrible and feel like high school**."

Q "With the Student Center, Law School, and Chapel, the campus looks nice, but the gym looks like a hideous warehouse, and **the library still looks like 1960** with avocado/orange dominating the interior. Luckily, they are going to be redone soon."

Q "**The library needs to be renovated badly**, and the Connolly Center does, as well. The Student Center is okay, but it could offer more services."

STUDENT AUTHOR: The Student Center houses two dining places, a few collegiums, a game room, and a TV lounge where students can rent game systems. The Connolly Center houses two gyms, two pools, racquetball courts, an astro-gym, and a weight-room. Watch out for rushes—it can be hard to get a machine.

Famous Alumni

Mohamed Ali Alabbar, General Patrick Brady, William Foley, Jerry Grundhofer, Leo J. Hindrey Jr., Carolyn S. Kelly, Kirk R. Nelson, Chen-Jen K. Tan, Jim Whittaker

Students Speak Out
ON CAMPUS DINING

Q "Overall, the food is pretty good—better than I was expecting for cafeteria food. My biggest complaint is the lack of variety. With **only two dining halls on campus**, I often felt as though I was eating the same two meals every day."

Q "Compared to other nearby universities (UW), **the food on campus is fantastic**. You'll probably be hankering for something new and different by the end of the year, but that could be said of almost any college food."

Q "Food on campus is decent for the most part. **It gets a bit old by the end of the year**, but I have definitely had worse. The only words of wisdom I can muster here are to caution you to avoid C-Street on Sunday nights, because they pull out the leftovers from Saturday and Friday."

Q "Food on campus is actually quite good, especially compared to other colleges. There are off days, though. However, salads can always, always, be made well. It's also great that the company that does our catering **does their best to buy organic local products**."

STUDENT AUTHOR: SU's dining services don't have many horror stories. Students are more apt to complain about prices and availability rather than the quality of the food. Campus dining is expensive, too, and this turns many commuter students off to buying anything more than the occasional sandwich. All students who live on campus are required to have meal plans, which can be quite a drain on financial resources; though points do roll over.

Student Body

African American:	5%	Male/Female:	39/61%
Asian American:	22%	Out-of-State:	39%
Hispanic:	7%	International:	9%
Native American:	1%	Unknown:	0%
White:	56%		

Popular Faiths: About half the student body is Catholic, though other faiths are represented, as well.

Gay Pride: With campus next door to a large gay population, Capitol Hill, there is not a mere tolerance of homosexuality, but an accepting and even welcoming atmosphere.

Economic Status: The range of available scholarships makes SU economically diverse for a private school.

Students Speak Out
ON DORMS

Q "For the most part, the residence halls are good places to live, especially because they are located on campus. I would not say there is any one hall to avoid; like individuals, each hall has its own personality and must match with one's personal taste. I have had good experiences living on campus, and **I would highly recommend it**."

Q "It doesn't quiet down very often in any of the dorms, but there are plenty of other places to study. **Cohabitation is against the rules**, but people are expected to be responsible for themselves. The all-girls floors are weird. There is way too much estrogen!"

Q "**If you don't like to have sex** or throw up after drinking, don't live in dorms."

STUDENT AUTHOR: SU requires freshmen and sophomores to reside on campus. Students agree that it is essential to achieving the full college experience. While there are all-freshman floors, the dorms are mostly a mixture of all undergrads; only the Archbishop Murphy Apartments have the junior- and senior-only restriction.

 Did You Know?
36% of undergrads live on campus.

Students Speak Out
ON GUYS & GIRLS

Q "The women outnumber the men by a long shot, and **the gay community in Seattle is prominent**. Therefore, it is a little different from other schools. Boys do still exist—you just have to keep your eyes peeled."

Q "With a **girl to guy ratio of 60 to 40,** girls totally outnumber guys. Out of that, a good percentage of the guys are gay. What does a girl have to do around here to find someone decent?"

Q "**Half of the guys are gay**. The ones that aren't are metrosexuals, or they all dress the same."

Q "Guys—**there are so few of them** that they always look scared during their first year. Then they're overwhelmed with 'options.' Haha!"

STUDENT AUTHOR: The campus's location results in a noticeable population of gay students. This somewhat limits the options of straight girls. However, regardless of sexual preference, the girls and guys on campus are definitely good-looking. From the relaxed granola styles, to the young professionals, to the spunky fashion risk-takers, there are dynamic categories within the basic understanding of attractive.

Traditions

Battle of the Bands
SU student bands compete, and local DJs choose the winners who become the opening act for Quadstock.

Quadstock
A huge concert held in the Quad each spring featuring big-name national acts.

Overall School Spirit
School Spirit is definitely an aspect SU needs to work on. The athletic programs have a small, faithful following, but the majority of the time, the crowds are made up of as many parents as there are students.

Students Speak Out
ON ATHLETICS

Q "I would say that IM sports are more popular than the varsity sports. We just are **not much of a sports school**, and so I think that it is more fun for people to play IM sports than to watch other sports. Basketball and soccer can usually draw crowds to cheer them on, and it is fun to go watch varsity sports."

Q "Varsity sports are not very big; **soccer is probably the biggest sport**. IM sports are present, but they're also not very big."

Q "**IM sports seem to be bigger than varsity sports**—there isn't really any college sports scene to speak of. The varsity soccer teams are pretty darned good, though."

Q "The IM scene is robust and pretty friendly, not to mention **the best flesh market going at SU**."

STUDENT AUTHOR: Sports are not a highly visible part of SU campus life. Nevertheless, there are impressive varsity and intramural sports thriving, though many students are unaware of their successes. Intramurals are popular, and they are a great arena to try something new or keep up on a sport you played before coming to college.

Students Speak Out
ON DRUG SCENE

Q "**Most students will either drink or smoke weed**, which causes little or no problem on campus. Many students will go off campus to do these things so as to not even worry about involving the school. On a few occasions, I have heard of other students doing drugs harder than alcohol and weed."

Q "SU probably has the normal amount of drugs for a college campus; there **seems to always be someone getting in trouble** for smoking pot, and you hear about 'shrooms and various other minor drugs fairly regularly."

Q "There are drugs on campus, but not a prevalent problem. It's **very secretive and low-key**."

STUDENT AUTHOR: Students agree the drug presence on campus is average for what you would expect to find on a college campus. There is marginal evidence of marijuana and other illegal drugs around campus, but there is little pressure for non-users to convert.

13:1	Student-to-Faculty Ratio
86%	Freshman Retention Rate
46%	Four-Year Graduation Rate
80%	Financial Aid Applicants Receiving Aid

Students Speak Out
SAFETY & SECURITY

Q "With **card-access-only dorms and elevators**, it makes it hard for non-students to get in. I'm comfortable walking on campus, especially when I know the security guards personally."

Q "There seems to be plenty of security around campus to deal with the normal amount of crime seen in any area. **Rarely do you hear of any violent crimes**; however, petty vandalism and theft are unfortunately a natural occurrence."

Q "Of course, there are the usual problems—car theft/break-ins, assault, and tons of incidents where students are still convinced that they are the first ones to discover underage drinking. However, the incidents here could happen anywhere. **The officers are all great**, and they get along with students well."

STUDENT AUTHOR: Because SU is in a sprawling urban setting, it would be impossible to walk around after dark, but this is not the case. Crime is present in the surrounding neighborhoods, just as it is to a degree on campus, but with appropriate precautions, there is little reason to be worried.

> **Questions?**
> For more inside information and survival tips, pick up College Prowler's full-length book on this school, written by an actual student! Check it out at *www.collegeprowler.com*.

Students Speak Out
ON OVERALL EXPERIENCE

Q "I love it here. I have found different opportunities to really grow, both mentally and physically. I have found programs that challenge me and open up the world to me, and for that, **I will always adore SU**. I can't think of anywhere else that I would be."

Q "I'm very happy I chose SU. **I like the small class sizes**, the small campus, the availability of the professors, and the tight-knit community. I like being able to see people I know every day walking around campus instead of running into someone maybe once a week."

Q "I love the school. **The administration leaves a little something to be desired**, but there are so many amazing people on and around campus that it's difficult not to have a great time here."

Q "Seattle University is the best place ever. I am very, very happy with my choice to come here. Seattle is **a wonderful city to be a college student in**, and the actual University has a very unique and wonderful balance between being small enough to accommodate the needs of students and big enough to accommodate their interests."

STUDENT AUTHOR: Looking at Seattle University as a whole, most students would not exchange their experience for anywhere else. The University provides an outstanding academics program, a unique location and atmosphere, and boasts a highly acclaimed personal connection to students. The regimented nature of the campus and the close attention of the staff and administration might frustrate some, but most find it a help as opposed to a hindrance.

Seton Hall University

400 South Orange Avenue; South Orange, NJ 07079
(973) 761-9000; www.shu.edu

THE BASICS:

Acceptance Rate: 77%
Setting: Suburban
F-T Undergrads: 4,889

SAT Range: 980–1190*
Control: Private
Tuition: $29,630

Most Popular Majors: Business, Health Professions, Communication, Social Science, Education

*of 1600

Academics	B	Guys	A-
Local Atmosphere	B-	Girls	A-
Safety & Security	B	Athletics	B+
Computers	A-	Nightlife	B+
Facilities	B-	Greek Life	B-
Campus Dining	C+	Drug Scene	C
Off-Campus Dining	A-	Campus Strictness	C+
Campus Housing	B	Parking	C+
Off-Campus Housing	B-	Transportation	B+
Diversity	B-	Weather	B-

Students Speak Out
ON ACADEMICS

Q "It is a relatively small school, so **professors will actually know who you are** and are willing to talk to you. Professors and students alike seem to care, and a majority are nice people."

Q "All the professors are different. **They vary from easy to hard.** The best way to find out which professors to take is to ask people. Overall, the ones I had were very helpful."

Q "It mostly depends on the department. It's **pretty awful in my department (computer science),** but I've heard lots of good things about the psychology, communications, nursing, and business departments."

Q "I have found all of the teachers to be excellent. They genuinely care about their students. **They really consider students' feedback** and try to build on their suggestions."

Q "Teachers are okay, but **it's not the toughest education in the world.** I transferred from Montclair State University, and I don't see any difference in the teachers."

STUDENT AUTHOR: Probably the biggest issue facing Seton Hall academics at the moment is general education requirements. In order to graduate, students must fulfill these requirements, which, coupled with a student's major requirements (most of which involve writing a senior thesis) can be very difficult for a student to complete in four years. Aside from the gen ed requirements, students have few complaints about classes and professors at Seton Hall.

Students Speak Out
ON LOCAL ATMOSPHERE

Q "This is a small school in the middle of the greater New York City area. For internships, and job opportunities after school, **you won't find a better location,** depending of course on your chosen career."

Q "South Orange is **a town full of ancient relics.** And when I say that, I am not talking about the buildings, but rather all the old people who hate anyone that goes to Seton Hall."

Q "There are so many things to visit, and places to go, with **New York City a short train ride away.** There are other universities around, so you can easily go to a party on another campus."

Q "The local atmosphere is strange because we are **so close to slums,** but the town is really nice. I think in a few years Newark is going to creep into the South Orange area, and it will be all slummy."

Q "South Orange could be the worst college town in the world. There is **literally nothing to do.**"

STUDENT AUTHOR: South Orange is a very rich, suburban town that does not usually embrace the school or the students. Due to the fact that local citizens tend to vote and attend town meetings, their say is taken more seriously than the thousands of students. The town cracks down hard on parties, and much harder on parking, as most of the streets surrounding the campus now have a three-hour parking limit. That is not even enough time to take two day courses back-to-back.

5 Best Things	5 Worst Things
1 The parties	1 Arrogant teachers
2 The guys and girls	2 Parking
3 Organizations	3 Monotonous food
4 Laptops with Wi-Fi	4 High tuition
5 Basketball games	5 The neighborhood

Students Speak Out
ON FACILITIES

Q "**Computer facilities are good**. There are a lot of labs on campus, although we could use a few more printers."

Q "The student center is where you'll find the cafeteria, Pirate's Cove, the Theater-in-the-Round (which is **a small theater designed after the Coliseum**), the Main Lounge (home to Thursday night parties among other things), the Greek room, and offices for many organizations and clubs."

Q "**The field house is huge** and actually very good. It houses an indoor track, as well as a number of basketball courts. We also have racquetball courts, and a very nice swimming pool, both of which can be used by the entire student body."

Q "The computer labs are **stocked full of new computers**, most with flat screens and zip drives, and the usual computer accessories."

Q "The student center is okay, and runs a lot of activities, but **not too many people normally go to them**."

Q "On Thursday nights, **the student center turns into a hip-hop club**; everybody always goes to that."

STUDENT AUTHOR: The Recreation Center, while it does have a workout room open to all students, does not have free weights. It does have treadmills, bikes, and other workout machines, but no bars. The University Student Center is the heart of the school where you'll find the cafeteria, a coffee lounge, the theater, and a game room.

Famous Alumni

George Abbot, Craig Biggio, Joseph Clark, Bob Dubill, Michael Kanfer, Bill Raferty, Avie Tevanian, Mo Vaughn, Dick Vitale, Max Weinberg

Students Speak Out
ON CAMPUS DINING

Q "Besides the cafeteria, there is another place to eat on campus known as the Pirate's Cove. It serves food that is a little better, but, of course, **the menu is somewhat limited**."

Q "If you are a commuter, don't buy a meal plan, **you can put money on a debit system** where you can swipe your ID in the bookstore or the cafeteria, and you get back what you don't spend."

Q "**I really like the food at the Cove**, but it takes the ladies behind the counter so long to get to you, and if you don't give them exact change, they huff and puff."

Q "**They just changed the caf to buffet-style** a few years ago. Since then, the food has gone straight downhill."

Q "The cafeteria has Nathan's, a pizzeria, a sandwich shop, an ice cream shop, and the there is also a buffet. **When you buy a meal card you prepay for meals at the buffet**, and if you do not use them you still have to pay for it."

STUDENT AUTHOR: I have one piece of advice on picking out a mandatory meal plan if you are going to live on campus: choose the smallest one possible. You prepay to eat three meals a day from the buffet, so if you sleep in, you will have paid for breakfast and missed it. You may be lucky that you missed it, as it was probably not that good, but you can save money, and your stomach, by simply ordering delivery from off campus.

Student Body

African American:	11%	Male/Female:	46/54%
Asian American:	6%	Out-of-State:	17%
Hispanic:	11%	International:	1%
Native American:	<1%	Unknown:	19%
White:	51%		

Popular Faiths: Seton Hall is a Catholic school which recognizes every holy day with a mass service.

Gay Pride: The campus is not very accepting of its gay students. There has been some uncertainty with the Catholic beliefs on gay rights, but the student body does not actively discriminate homosexuals.

Economic Status: There is a predominant amount of upper- and upper-middle-class students.

Students Speak Out
ON DORMS

Q "Boland is huge and half of it has community bathrooms (which you don't have to clean) while **the other half has suite bathrooms**, which are shared with the room next to you."

Q "Aquinas is nice because **it's all freshmen**, and it has air conditioning. Your only other choice is Boland, which has most of the freshmen, but smaller rooms and no air-conditioning."

Q "There are **seven dorms total**. Two are for freshmen—Boland and Aquinas—three are for upperclassman—Xavier, Cabrini and Serra, which are coed—Neumann is all female, and Ora Manor is also for upperclassman and is two miles off campus."

Q "Housing on campus is run by HRL, and **they keep you on your toes**."

STUDENT AUTHOR: If you are a freshman, and live on campus, drop down on your knees and beg for Boland. Boland Hall houses over 1,000 freshmen, and half of them are of the opposite sex. This will be the first time that most of the students will be living on their own, which will form special bonds within the confines of the dormitory.

> **? Did You Know?**
> 44% of undergrads live on campus.

Students Speak Out
ON GUYS & GIRLS

Q "There are **definitely some really cute guys** on campus, but you have to watch out for some of them because some of them are really shady. And just like anywhere you go, some of the girls are nice, and some of them aren't. It's just really important to surround yourself with a positive crowd."

Q "Word to the wise, **pour your own drink at a fraternity party**, and never ever let it down. I know a girl who put her drink down for one minute, and someone slipped a roofie (date rape drug) in it."

Q "I was surprised at how many good-looking girls there are on this campus. Tons! And now that I think about it, I guess the **same goes for guys**."

STUDENT AUTHOR: The guys are undeniably pretty boys who care more about their own looks than the girls do, and the girls are really fake and materialistic. In general, the guys and girls are extremely hot, but their beauty is, unfortunately, only skin deep. If you want to have a good time and be with the beautiful people, you have come to the right place. Understand that you may not find your soulmate within the gates of Seton Hall.

> **Traditions**
>
> **Greek Week**
> A week of festivities held in the spring where the fraternities and sororities compete for dominance.
>
> **Parties on the Green**
> When spring first arrives students throw enormous parties on the campus green with hidden kegs.
>
> **Overall School Spirit**
> I don't know if it is school spirit or just the hatred of rival Rutgers that makes the students go insane during games. Students make T-shirts, posters, and colorful cheers for the big event.

Students Speak Out
ON ATHLETICS

Q "**Intramural sports are good**. I've played football, basketball, hockey, soccer, and volleyball and had lots of fun. Football, which is not an official school sport, is played during the day. The others are all night sports."

Q "Seton Hall has **a good baseball program**. A bunch of pro players have gone through here!"

Q "The baseball team **won the Big East championship several years ago**, and the soccer team was in the elite eight of the NCAA Tournament, as well."

Q "Games for most basketball and baseball teams are played off campus. Tickets are about $6, and the school provides **free bussing** to the games."

Q "**Intramurals are more competitive** than the real sports here."

STUDENT AUTHOR: The real excitement for sports on campus is the intramurals. The intramural office offers over eight different intramural sports throughout the year. In the fall, Seton Hall could care less that they don't have a football program, because intramural flag football captures the campus.

Students Speak Out
ON DRUG SCENE

Q "If you smoke weed, you will have plenty of friends. There is **always somebody who has some**. You'll never have a problem getting a hold of some. As far as I know, that's about the only drug that's big on campus."

Q "There are definitely ways to get drugs on campus, if you want to. The **main drug of choice is marijuana**. There really haven't been any issues with other kinds of drugs."

Q "Ask one person and he or she will say that drugs are a big problem, ask another and the response will be that we have no such scene. It all depends on **what environment you put yourself in**."

STUDENT AUTHOR: No Seton Hall handbook will be able to provide the information that I am about to give you; there are ridiculous amounts of drugs on campus. Sometimes, it is easier to find a dime bag of marijuana than it is to find a six pack on campus. However, there is little peer pressure about doing drugs at Seton Hall.

13:1	Student-to-Faculty Ratio
80%	Freshman Retention Rate
40%	Four-Year Graduation Rate
66%	Financial Aid Applicants Receiving Aid

Students Speak Out
SAFETY & SECURITY

Q "Seton Hall is **really wired for security**. It's what they call a 'gated community,' meaning that gates, which can only be opened by an ID, surround the campus."

Q "There have been **a minimal number of violent crime on campus**, and when they are, it's usually by students. I have never personally been mugged or anything, but it can happen. I feel perfectly safe on campus."

Q "To even enter the campus, you must go through guarded gates. I always see police on bikes around the campus, and there are emergency phones almost everywhere you look. I did my undergraduate work at Rutgers University, and **I didn't feel as safe at Rutgers** as I feel at Seton Hall."

STUDENT AUTHOR: Seton Hall's proximity to Newark has precipitated a solid security system. In the past 10 years, they have enclosed the University by a large fence. The only way to get in or out of campus by foot is to swipe your student ID card through a magnetic lock system.

Questions?
For more inside information and survival tips, pick up College Prowler's full-length book on this school, written by an actual student! Check it out at *www.collegeprowler.com*.

Students Speak Out
ON OVERALL EXPERIENCE

Q "Academically, if you put in the effort, you'll get the education you're looking for. **Socially, it's a friendly place**."

Q "One thing that I recommend is that **you should live on campus your first year**. I made that mistake and commuted. I really missed out on a lot, and don't really have much of a social life at school. So, even though the dorms may not be satisfying, you may get lucky and get one of the nice ones. Besides, it's only for one year, and then you get the bigger dorms."

Q "I've gone back and forth on this one, but I enjoy the School of Diplomacy very much. **I know that SHU is right for me**. The professors are helpful, and the school is generally close-knit."

Q "**The school is a perfect size**. You don't get lost in it, yet you can always see someone that you don't know."

Q "It's been okay. I've had issues with guidance counselors making me waste money on classes I didn't need. **Be informed about what kind of classes you are signing up for**, and have a direction in mind as to what you want to major in. You'll be better off."

STUDENT AUTHOR: Part of your education is being around people from different walks of life, and no place is better for that than Seton Hall, one of the most diverse campuses in the country. The social scene at Seton Hall is very trendy and fast paced. Seton Hall's education is good depending upon your major. Business, nursing, computer science, and diplomacy are what make Seton Hall a Tier II school. The people you meet here, and the friendships that you form, make this school a community.

Simmons College

300 The Fenway; Boston, MA 02115
(617) 521-2000; www.simmons.edu

THE BASICS:

Acceptance Rate: 55%   **SAT Range:** 1530–1810*
Setting: Urban   **Control:** Private
F-T Undergrads: 1,891   **Tuition:** $29,900

Most Popular Majors: Health Professions, Social
Sciences, Communication, Psychology

*of 2400

Academics	B	Guys	N/A
Local Atmosphere	A	Girls	B+
Safety & Security	A-	Athletics	C
Computers	B	Nightlife	A-
Facilities	B	Greek Life	N/A
Campus Dining	B	Drug Scene	A-
Off-Campus Dining	A	Campus Strictness	B+
Campus Housing	B-	Parking	D-
Off-Campus Housing	B+	Transportation	B+
Diversity	C	Weather	C-

Students Speak Out
ON ACADEMICS

Q "Despite the single-gender atmosphere, **students bring a rich diversity of experience and opinion to all discussions**, both in and out of the classroom. While I've learned a great deal from my professors, I feel that I have learned more and been perhaps even challenged more by my classmates. I have not had a single class at Simmons where I did not learn an important lesson."

Q "The teachers at Simmons College are amazing and really interact with the students. The majority of the classes **engage the students in and outside the classroom**. You're not a number at Simmons College. The teachers remember who you are and know you by name."

Q "There are many classes at Simmons, and each professor makes them interesting and enjoyable. **It's a joy to go to class to debate about a topic in the news** that is related to the class or a theory you may have learned."

STUDENT AUTHOR: Because of its small size, teacher attention is one of Simmons's strengths. First-year students are paired with faculty for scheduling and the planning of their time at school. Many students select additional advisors later in their college career based on their majors. Networking is emphasized at Simmons, and faculty members are easily reached as a resource for connecting many students to future employers. Teachers are well qualified in their fields, and students do not learn from teaching assistants.

Students Speak Out
ON LOCAL ATMOSPHERE

Q "**Boston is the best town to go to school in**. It is surrounded by all different colleges and universities, in a really hip, fun setting with plenty to do. It does get expensive, but there are cheap ways of having a fabulous time without overdrawing your bank account."

Q "Boston is a great place to be as a college student! **There are about five other colleges located right on the same block** as Simmons, which makes for a lot of students, both male and female, everywhere. Definitely visit the Boston museums and the public gardens. Boston is beautiful in the spring, summer, and fall, but the winters here get pretty messy, so bring boots and an umbrella!"

Q "**Boston is great or terrible, depending on what you make of it**. There are places to go when you are sick of staying in one place, which is great. There are parks and squares for people-watchers, and there are clubs and everything else for people who want action. Boston is great for all interests."

STUDENT AUTHOR: Simmons is located in the heart of Boston, which opens up a vast sea of opportunities for its students. In the quintessential college town, the streets of Boston produce a feeling of intellectual stimulation. With nearly 50 colleges, the atmosphere is hip and youthfully urban. In between classes, you may find yourself roaming an urban city walking through the many niche communities Boston has to offer.

5 Best Things	5 Worst Things
1 Living in Boston	1 Parking
2 Small class size	2 Freezing winters
3 Caring professors	3 Limited dining options
4 All-women environment	4 Required meal plan
5 Intelligent students	5 Geese

Students Speak Out
ON CAMPUS DINING

Q "**There is only one dining hall, known as Bartol Hall**. It is okay, and has a lot of variety, but students get sick of it quickly. There is a little convenience store on campus, too, which has things to order, like fries and hamburgers—not too healthy! On the main campus, there is Java City (a coffeeshop) and also the Fens, another dining area, which is good."

Q "The food is up-in-the-air, just like all other college and university dining halls. It has its good days and its bad days. Usually, **students will get tired of eating cafeteria food** after a few weeks."

Q "Bartol Dining Hall has its ups and downs, but if you can be creative with your food, I would say **it's actually pretty good**."

Q "The food is **usually not too bad**, but it's sometimes terrible, just like it would be at any other school."

Q "The food stinks, but **there are cheap eats around campus**."

STUDENT AUTHOR: There are five locations for students to eat on campus. **Bartol Hall, the main dining location, is located on the Residence Campus. Students living on campus are required to carry a meal plan with at least seven meals a week. Located in lower Smith Hall, Quadside Café hosts live bands, pool, arcade games, and movie nights. The food matches this lax environment, with a snack bar within a convenience store.**

Students Speak Out
ON FACILITIES

Q "The athletic center is great! If you enjoy working out, it's an excellent place to do so. There is a free-weight room, as well as a room full of weight machines, a cardio area with treadmills, bicycles, elliptical machines, and a suspended track over the gym. Also, there is **an Olympic-size pool, basketball court, and racquetball courts**, as well as a dance studio."

Q "Most of the facilities on campus have been renovated within the last 10 years, so they are all fairly nice. **The freshman dorms have not been renovated**, but come on—they are freshman, so they can't be too picky."

Q "Since Quadside Café has been redone, it seems that it is **a great place for students to get together and study** or just hang out."

Q "The facilities are nice. **The gym is used by a lot of other people besides students**, so sometimes that's weird, but not too much. Computers are good, the fast Internet rocks. The student center is cute, there's really no other word for it. There are pods (areas with a couch and two chairs and a table) and a coffeeshop upstairs, and the Fens (where the best food is) is downstairs."

STUDENT AUTHOR: Simmons is growing, and improvements are rapidly being made to campus facilities. Future plans continue to please alumnae and students. A rebuilding program has modernized the classic Main Campus Building, with a new College center, conference center, computer kiosks, and the updating of classrooms.

Famous Alumnae

Marie Celestin, Denise Di Novi, Ann Fudge, Nnenna Freelon, Gwen Ifill, Lisa Mullins, Carolyn Noyes, Suzanne Yalof-Schwartz

Student Body

African American:	6%	Male/Female:	0/100%
Asian American:	8%	Out-of-State:	39%
Hispanic:	4%	International:	2%
Native American:	<1%	Unknown:	5%
White:	75%		

Popular Faiths: Judaism, Catholicism, and Bahai are the most common faiths.

Gay Pride: The alliance makes efforts to make students comfortable with their sexuality. Recent discussion has expanded to transgender students.

Economic Status: The cost of tuition and room and board dictates that the average student tends to be middle-class or upper-middle-class.

Students Speak Out
ON DORMS

Q "I've seen other campuses, and I think our dorms are very nice. The **freshman dorms are the dorms to avoid**, but they are all being remodeled and updated."

Q "**The dorms are pretty average**. They re-did Smith Hall to include singles and private bathrooms in each suite. Most of the other halls are generic small rooms, but the closet space is pretty good."

Q "Of course, the freshman dorms might not be the greatest, but **the newer dorms are awesome**! They look quite contemporary and have air conditioning and elevators."

STUDENT AUTHOR: **With the expansion of Simmons, Residence Life has quickly renovated many of the dorms on campus. Within the last five years, six of the nine dorms have been renovated, with plans for the rest within the next five years. Rooms are assigned through a housing lottery, and seniors are given priority. Much to the disappointment of students looking for on-campus housing, the increase in the number of undergraduates has eliminated the four-year housing guarantee once offered.**

> **Did You Know?**
> 55% of undergrads live on campus.

Students Speak Out
ON GUYS & GIRLS

Q "**What men**?! The men of Boston are fun, but there are none on campus."

Q "Well, it's an all-girl school, except for the graduate programs. Mainly, the only guys you see on campus are employees or boyfriends. But **there are many good-looking guys around Simmons at Wentworth and Northeastern**! There is a good-size lesbian population on campus, too, so if you're into girls, then there are plenty of people for you to socialize with!"

Q "Guys? What guys? It's great being in Boston and at an all-girl's school. I feel that you get the great education from this women's college but **can meet anyone and everyone from the surrounding colleges**."

STUDENT AUTHOR: **Simmons women are extremely independent and focused. The all-women environment creates a bond among students, who are all experiencing the college life together. Students looking for guys will have to focus their attention elsewhere. Many students find guys at other colleges in the area. Though it is an all-women's college, Simmons is not a nunnery. Boston offers opportunities to meet all kinds of people.**

> **Traditions**
>
> **Simmons Cup**
> This annual field day event pits each residence dorm against the other in a day of outdoor events.
>
> **Tea**
> There is a lot of tea brewing on campus. Resident students meet each month or once a week to socialize and eat.
>
> **Overall School Spirit**
> Apathy is a feeling on campus many students are guilty of, but it is those same students who are involved in many activities.

Students Speak Out
ON ATHLETICS

Q "What sports? Our sports teams are fun to go watch, but **we are definitely a D-III school**."

Q "Some sports are big on campus, mainly basketball, soccer, and field hockey. I know that there are **some great intramural teams** through the Colleges of the Fenway organization, and there are a good number of students who participate."

Q "Sports are **definitely secondary to academics** at Simmons."

Q "Simmons is a D-III school, and **sports are a big part of some of the students' lives**. Many of the teams have won the conference in their division, so the sports teams are pretty good."

STUDENT AUTHOR: **The idea that student athletes are students first is stressed. Unfortunately, while the teams have been successful in their divisions, there is still little attendance at games. In order to maintain student health, the College offers the Lifelong Exercise and Activities Program (LEAP). LEAP offers classes for students without the stress of competition, while still encouraging an active lifestyle.**

Students Speak Out
ON DRUG SCENE

Q "I have not encountered much of a drug scene at Simmons. For the most part, the students here are very oriented toward school and their grades. **Alcohol is definitely the number-one drug of choice**. I think after that would have to be pot."

Q **"I don't feel that it is to a point where it is a problem**. You know that it is around, but you aren't bothered by it. Girls drink and smoke, and if it gets to the point where you know about it, someone needs to be notified, like an RA or an RD."

Q "I think it's similar to any other campus. People drink and smoke, but it is **not overwhelming**."

STUDENT AUTHOR: **Drugs are not a serious problem at Simmons. You need to dig pretty hard to find any activity on campus. The smell of marijuana occasionally appears on the Residence Campus, but this does not happen with enough frequency to cause concern. Campus programming is focused toward alcohol abuse rather than drug abuse. There is no pressure for non-users to use drugs.**

13:1	Student-to-Faculty Ratio
85%	Freshman Retention Rate
66%	Four-Year Graduation Rate
97%	Financial Aid Applicants Receiving Aid

Students Speak Out
SAFETY & SECURITY

Q "You would never even know that you are in the middle of a big city. We have **a large iron fence around the Residence Campus that is locked at night**. You need to be with a Simmons student who has her ID to enter the campus. We have security guards who do routine checks of the campus, and an escort service that provides someone to walk you from the Main Campus Building to the residence halls at night."

Q **"I have never felt unsafe on campus**, even if I'm walking alone from one dorm to another. I like the concept of having the dorms with gates around them, and the gates being locked after 11 p.m., except for one, which you have to walk past Public Safety and use your student ID to get through."

STUDENT AUTHOR: **The flexibility of Simmons's policies is generally appreciated by students who feel like an adult, not like they are still under their parents' watchful eyes. Within the iron gates of the Residence Campus, students generally feel a strong sense of security.**

> **Questions?**
> For more inside information and survival tips, pick up College Prowler's full-length book on this school, written by an actual student! Check it out at *www.collegeprowler.com*.

Students Speak Out
ON OVERALL EXPERIENCE

Q "This will be my senior year at Simmons, and I have had my ups and downs with the school overall, but my experience has been positive. I would suggest this school to anyone who likes a quiet campus. **It's not that we just sit in their rooms and study, but we know the right time to do so**."

Q "I have loved Simmons since I first got on campus. **There are certainly some times where I wish it was coed**, because, as we all know, being around all girls all the time can get a little tough. But I have no doubt that I am receiving an excellent education at a great location."

Q "I love Simmons! It took some getting used to, but what doesn't? I think it was the best decision I could have made. **I love who I have become at Simmons**."

Q "I love it. This is the sixth college that I have attended (over ten years), and I have to say I think I made a good choice for myself. If I was younger, the all-girls thing might bother me. **I have never lived in the dorms, and I think it's a good idea** because you're more likely to meet people."

STUDENT AUTHOR: **It is the mix of extracurriculars, academics, environment, and nurturing that leads Simmons women to enjoy their experience. Being in Boston provides professional opportunities for its students when it comes to picking internships and finding jobs after graduation. The urban environment fills a social gap that the absence of a Greek life or men on campus could create. But Simmons students don't just come to school to party, but rather to become women.**

Skidmore College

815 North Broadway; Saratoga Springs, NY 12866
(518) 580-5000; www.skidmore.edu

THE BASICS:

Acceptance Rate: 37% **SAT Range:** 1750–2040*
Setting: Suburban **Control:** Private
F-T Undergrads: 2,612 **Tuition:** $38,114

Most Popular Majors: Social Sciences, Visual/Performing Arts, Business, English, Foreign Languages

*of 2400

Academics	B	Guys	B-
Local Atmosphere	C-	Girls	B+
Safety & Security	B+	Athletics	B-
Computers	B	Nightlife	C+
Facilities	B	Greek Life	N/A
Campus Dining	C+	Drug Scene	C+
Off-Campus Dining	B-	Campus Strictness	B-
Campus Housing	A	Parking	C-
Off-Campus Housing	D+	Transportation	C+
Diversity	D	Weather	D

Students Speak Out
ON ACADEMICS

Q "If you pick them right, the **professors can be amazing** and the classes fascinating. If you make a mistake, the wrong professor will make your life hell."

Q "The professors are the schools best and most enduring assets. **They are an incredibly passionate**, bright, and well-informed group who thrives on their students' positive achievements. It is the norm for students to have close relationships with their professors that carry on even after they leave."

Q "**It depends**, but overall, the teachers are all very good. Entry-level professors who are just visiting campus for a year or two are not the greatest. The best are those who have been around campus the most, love the college, and respect the students."

Q "Teachers are, generally, an energetic and eager bunch. Some of the older faculty are **a bit too into their own work**, but most teachers are very accessible, especially in the government department."

STUDENT AUTHOR: One of the huge advantages of class size at Skidmore is that they are anything but huge. Classes average about 20 to 30 students and offer a tight-knit environment with a closer student-professor relationship than your typical state university. The professors are about as outspoken and quirky as the students. If you want to stay on their good side, show up on time and hand in your work.

Students Speak Out
ON LOCAL ATMOSPHERE

Q "Skidmore students often get stuck in their own little bubble, but if they venture out, Saratoga has a lot to offer. **There are a lot of cultural and community activities** that are fun to attend."

Q "Saratoga Springs, New York, is **home to only one college**—Skidmore. The next nearest university or college can be found in the greater Albany area, which is a half-hour drive south of Saratoga Springs."

Q "Saratoga is a really fun town! I would not call it a "college town" because it doesn't depend on us for survival (more on the wealthy people from the track), so it **doesn't really cater to college students** all the time, but there is still plenty to do."

Q "I think Saratoga is the ideal college town. It's quaint and unique, but **far from boring**. The nightlife, restaurants, and shopping attract people from all over."

STUDENT AUTHOR: Saratoga is an ideal college town—a cozy area with many attractions. It is quite the tourist spot in the summer months when the race track is open (July-September). There are tons of trinket and clothing shops, restaurants, and coffee nooks. Union College and Rensslaer Polytechnical Institute (RPI) are the two colleges most likely to cross paths with Skidmore students. It has been said that Skidmore students don't really notice the other inhabitants of the town, but they do exist. There are local folks and high school students, and there is even a Naval base.

Students Speak Out
ON FACILITIES

Q "We're not a really big school so we don't have all the amenities some places have, but the **facilities are generally fine**."

Q "Overall, I think the facilities are excellent. The gym is well kept up and open almost all day. The student center is a good place to stop by in between classes since **there are always people hanging out there**. There is also music and entertainment sometimes in the evening. It makes a nice, convenient environment to meet with people. The cyber café is open until 1 a.m., which is also great because nothing else on campus is open that late."

Q "The sports center has just been redone and **it is amazing**. For the most part, everything is up to date and relatively new."

Q "The facilities are all very new; we have a beautiful library, beautiful on campus museum, beautiful art building, and a poor music building that **needs more classrooms and maintenance**."

Q "The facilities are getting better every year. **Skidmore is trying to keep up** with the competition of other schools."

STUDENT AUTHOR: Skidmore is a small school, and it has proportionately nice facilities that are generally stocked with up-to-date equipment. Activities tend to center around eating and movie watching. The number one complaint about academic facilities is the inconvenient hours. Palamoutain Hall houses a number of computers and comfortable work spaces; however, the building closes at 11 p.m.

Famous Alumni

Hessa Hamad Al Thani, Eddie Cahill, Nancy Evans, John Hall, Grace Mirabella, Ariana Richards, Sybil Shearer

Students Speak Out
ON CAMPUS DINING

Q "The food is crappy. The D-Hall is the bane of a lot of students' existences. The Spa, which sells hamburgers, grilled cheese, quesadillas, and so forth, is pretty good, and the Burgess Café is just **what you'd expect** (except the lady who works there most of the time is super nice, which is a plus)."

Q "The food on campus is only mediocre. It can be **difficult to find vegetarian options** in the dining hall, and the food is usually really greasy."

Q "Students frequently complain about the food, although the most common complaint regards not the quality of the food but **the lack of options**."

Q "Eating at the same place, with **the same choices day after day can get boring**, no matter how good the food is. Overall, the quality of food in the dining halls is good."

Q "The **food is alright**. The dining hall can be repetitious, but the Spa is always good."

STUDENT AUTHOR: At Skidmore, campus food has a bad a reputation. It's served in two dining halls, Aikens and Murray, which are located on opposite sides of the same building. The same food is available on each side. If you get tired of the dining hall or are hungry after it has closed, you can go to the Spa. This is a grill/café located in the student center. It is often preferred over the dining hall because it is less crowded, Esperanto's pizza and Doughboys (student favorites) are available, and there is a cappuccino maker.

Student Body

African American:	4%	Male/Female:	40/60%
Asian American:	7%	Out-of-State:	68%
Hispanic:	5%	International:	3%
Native American:	<1%	Unknown:	15%
White:	66%		

Popular Faiths: Religious clubs include Newman Club (Catholic), Christian Fellowship, and the Jewish Student Union.

Gay Pride: The campus is very accepting of the gay community. Student groups include Student Pride Alliance (SPA) and a sexuality-awareness house.

Economic Status: Skidmore students are stereotyped as "rich kids."

Students Speak Out
ON DORMS

Q "For the most part, the **dorms are really nice**, much nicer than some of the other colleges I visited."

Q "Our rooms are huge, and almost all the upperclassmen (including sophomores) get singles. South Quad, excluding Wieking Hall, is **worse than North Quad**, but all the dorms are nicer than those of most places."

Q "All of the dorms are basically identical, and there is very dry air in Tower (Jonsson). There are large rooms, and **it is easy to get a single** after freshman year."

STUDENT AUTHOR: **Campus housing is divided into two Quads: North and South. Every dorm, with the exception of Weiking Hall, has a laundry room, lounge with cable TV, and is arranged in suites. Though it changes slightly from year to year, South Quad has a reputation for parties and jocks (because of its proximity to the sports center) while North Quad has a reputation for being nicer, although quieter. Every room on campus has a window seat.**

Did You Know?
85% of undergrads live on campus.

Students Speak Out
ON GUYS & GIRLS

Q "There are a lot of attractive people here. I would say that there are **more cute girls than cute guys**. Styles range from Abercrombie ad to dirty hippy to uber-stylish."

Q "All Skidmore girls and guys act in a certain way. There are a lot of very wealthy students on campus, so **there is a certain snob factor**, but it isn't so bad as to make me feel uncomfortable."

Q "I can't say much on the girls' behalf, but I think most men are either **gay, taken, or not worth it**."

Q "Well, for one thing, the split campus is about 40 percent guys, 60 percent girls—so **girls be warned**."

STUDENT AUTHOR: **There is no doubt that Skidmore has a reputation—girls, girls, girls. Most of the male population undoubtedly recognizes that the ratio leans in their favor. Dating exists, but according to students, it seems to be minimal. Hookups are more common, and girls often complain that guys have more power in the dating scene than women. The downside of a smaller school is the rampant gossip.**

Traditions

Bagpipes
The graduation procession and recession each year are led by a bagpipe band,

Under the Big Top
Skidmore's dance and musical groups perform in this show for Parent's Weekend and Graduation.

Overall School Spirit
Skidmore students seem to be more involved in individual interests and issues, rather than in the school community as a whole. Also, Skidmore doesn't have a football team.

Students Speak Out
ON ATHLETICS

Q "Sports don't really play a large part at Skidmore expect to serve as some sort of **quasi-social club** or fraternity/sorority scene. Sports seem to be the only chance to meet people."

Q "We are not a big sports school at all. We are **Division I in Equestrian sports**, and that's about our sports program's only claim to fame."

Q "I think that **intramural sports are more popular** than varsity sports. I hear a lot about IM soccer and softball."

Q "People **aren't really into attending sports games**. Spectators can only be found at a capella jams."

STUDENT AUTHOR: **For the most part, Skidmore students feel apathetic about athletics. Teams make their presence visible through flyers, the school newspaper, *Skidnews*, and e-mail announcements about games. Skidmore athletes have a great deal of energy and spirit, but athletic spirit has yet to infect the non-athletic portion of the student body. Many students that enjoy athletics seem to prefer intramurals and club sports.**

Students Speak Out
ON DRUG SCENE

Q "There's a lot of pot smoking and a mild amount of cocaine use, but for the most part, I think **Skidmore students limit themselves** to alcohol and marijuana."

Q "It's **a big scene** at Skidmore. Almost everyone I know drinks or smokes weed."

Q "If you don't use drugs, don't worry. Though many people do, **there is not really peer pressure** to do things that you are uncomfortable with."

STUDENT AUTHOR: The bottom line is that drugs are available in the on and off campus scenes. Alcohol and pot are considered the most prominent, although cocaine takes a close second. Alcohol is not as big a problem at Skidmore as it might be at a school with Greek life. Alcohol is not Skidmore's most prevalent drug. The school is actually infamous for marijuana. The positive side to Skidmore's drug scene is the idea that they are available if you are into it, but there are plenty of kids that are not, so pressure is not a factor.

9:1	Student-to-Faculty Ratio
94%	Freshman Retention Rate
78%	Four-Year Graduation Rate
87%	Financial Aid Applicants Receiving Aid

Students Speak Out
SAFETY & SECURITY

Q "It's so safe that I never really thought twice about safety or security. You can always call Campus Security to have an escort. A plus is that **it's a closed campus** so you don't leave your living area to get to class or the library."

Q "I can't count the number of times **I walked home from downtown** without worrying. I have even passed out drunk in someone's front lawn and nothing happened."

Q "I imagine it's safe, but it is **no thanks to the Campus Security officers**. The biggest thing to be worried about for guys is theft. For girls, it's drunk guys."

Q "It's a very safe campus and town. **Locking doors feels like an option**."

STUDENT AUTHOR: The College's Campus Security guards are available 24 hours a day. They are on-call and can be contacted for reasons ranging from locking yourself out of your room to helping your roommate regain consciousness. The area of Saratoga Springs has proven to be low in crime.

> **Questions?**
> For more inside information and survival tips, pick up College Prowler's full-length book on this school, written by an actual student! Check it out at *www.collegeprowler.com*.

Students Speak Out
ON OVERALL EXPERIENCE

Q "I love Skidmore. There might be some policies and priorities I would change, but I do not prefer to be anywhere else, and **I value the education** I am getting, both inside and outside of the classroom."

Q "I think one of Skidmore's biggest problems is a **lack of diversity** in economic/class/backgrounds. It is enough to make me wish I had chosen a different school."

Q "There was never a time I regretted going to Skidmore. The town is wonderful, the professors are great and the friends I made are irreplaceable. I would say it felt small at times, but this can be a nice feeling to feel like you are **truly a part of a tight-knit community** of students and faculty."

Q "Skidmore has a lot of really great programs and other things going for it, but **I do wish I were somewhere else**, as do many people I know. I know that I am getting a really good liberal education from this school, but I 'm often very frustrated with the student body, which is often apathetic and concerned more with partying."

STUDENT AUTHOR: We aren't going to lie to you—Skidmore has its down points. It is cold for most of the school year, the total student body is small enough to breed gossip, and there isn't always a lot of excitement for students under 21. Campus apathy is not uncommon around sophomore year when "the slump" kicks in for a while. However, most upper-class students can attest to the fact that Skidmore grows on you. Its strongest points are the closeness you will find in friends, classmates, and very importantly, professors.

Slippery Rock University

1 Morrow Way; Slippery Rock, PA 16057
(800) SRU-9111; www.sru.edu

THE BASICS:

Acceptance Rate: 59%
Setting: Rural
F-T Undergrads: 7,149

SAT Range: 1370–1670*
Control: Public
Tuition: $8,038

Most Popular Majors: Education, Business, Parks/Recreation Studies, Health Sciences, Communications

*of 2400

Academics	B-	Guys	B
Local Atmosphere	C-	Girls	B+
Safety & Security	A-	Athletics	C
Computers	B	Nightlife	C+
Facilities	B-	Greek Life	B-
Campus Dining	C+	Drug Scene	B-
Off-Campus Dining	B-	Campus Strictness	C
Campus Housing	B	Parking	C-
Off-Campus Housing	B-	Transportation	B-
Diversity	D-	Weather	C

Students Speak Out
ON ACADEMICS

Q "**Most professors here are down-to-earth and understanding**. The workload can be pretty heavy, but as long as you pace yourself, you'll be fine."

Q "All I know is, **after a few years at SRU, I gained a new appreciation for higher learning**. Yet, I still feel close to my roots. I was an ignorant kid when I came here. And now, at least, I'm a semi-ignorant adult."

Q "The professors here are, for the most part, phenomenal. You really start to get to know them and **get a feel for your major when you get past the liberal arts requirements** and get to focus more on your major classes."

Q "All of my **homework seems to be busy work**. It can be really frustrating."

Q "What's great is that we have **professors here from all over the world**, but it's sometimes a struggle to understand them during lectures."

STUDENT AUTHOR: At SRU, it is not uncommon to have lunch with your professors or to have a friendly chat about politics and literature during their office hours. Students are not just a number here. Most professors know students by name and greet them accordingly, while trudging through the snowy quad. Class sizes are kept small and taught by real professors, never by TAs. Also, across the board, veteran SRU students advise to know your professor before you walk into his or her classroom.

Students Speak Out
ON LOCAL ATMOSPHERE

Q "Often SRU is described as 'rural,' 'boring,' and 'small,' but with **so many students in one small, close-knit place**, there is always something to do (even if that something is a midnight field trip to Sheetz)."

Q "Slippery Rock is your **typical hick town** in Western PA. I've never seen so many 'Get 'er Done' bumper stickers in my life."

Q "Slippery Rock is a cool place to spend your college years. With the campus facilities at your disposal, **there should be more than enough options to keep you busy**. However, if you find yourself living there well after you graduate, then you need to get your priorities together—there are just too many hicks and closed-minded people."

Q "The town here is pretty calm. **You have to drive to Butler or Grove City** to go to a movie theater or do any real shopping."

STUDENT AUTHOR: Slippery Rock is a rural town that thrives off of the University's presence. If students want to catch a movie or do some serious shopping, they must drive to the adjacent towns of Grove City and Butler. However, campus itself offers many programs during the week, including art exhibits, plays, and movies. When night falls, the parties get started, and the bars become animated with SRU's finest. Though many complain that the town is small, quiet, and boring, others argue that with so many students in one place, there is always something going on.

5 Best Things
1 The people
2 Off-campus parties
3 Low tuition
4 No TAs
5 The ARC

5 Worst Things
1 Low school spirit
2 Miserable weather
3 Local police
4 Parking tickets
5 Dry campus

Students Speak Out
ON FACILITIES

Q "**The Union is a great place to hang out**, watch TV, read, study, play pool, or nap between classes. It's really comfy, and there's usually something going on there. It's an ideal place for commuters to relax."

Q "When I graduate and have to pay $80 a month for a gym membership, that's when **I'll truly miss the ARC**. The place is just immaculate! I just wish they would turn the heat down a little bit in the weight room in the warmer months."

Q "**The library is so old** and all of the books are ancient. With all of the construction going on, I think they should redo the library."

Q "**Most of the classrooms are old**, and the hallways of Eisenberg and Spotts are tight. The doors, of course, open outward, which doesn't help that problem."

Q "**Spotts and Eisenberg classrooms are pretty plain**, but who really cares. We don't go to class to get a show or anything. Class is class."

STUDENT AUTHOR: **Bulldozers and wrecking balls are a common sight these days at the Rock. The University is undergoing a multi-million dollar facelift— knocking down many of the 1970-something residence halls and replacing them with new-and-improved residential suites. Campus is currently a hodgepodge of new and old. One of the most popular places to hang out on campus is the campus recreation center, the ARC. Overall, the University continues to rebuild and expand to make way for the growing on-campus population and to keep up with, and hopefully surpass, the competition of surrounding universities.**

Famous Alumni

Greg Hopkins, Robert J. Stevens, C. Vivian Stringer, Kenneth L. Wilcox

Students Speak Out
ON CAMPUS DINING

Q "After freshman year, I'd recommend getting one of the intermediate meal plans, like 14 White or 10 Green. This allows a student to balance eating off campus with eating in the dining halls throughout the week. **If you do this right, campus food will not seem that bad at all**."

Q "**If you love your stomach, don't eat too often at the dining halls**. Weisenfluh, or 'the Fluh,' has a better selection and longer hours than Boozel, but the food is equally bad. I survived three semesters on cereal and cheese pizza."

Q "I don't understand how you can gain the Freshman 15 if you constantly puke and poop out the food you just ate at the Fluh. Their new slogan should be, '**Weisenfluh is not just a place to eat, it's an epidemic**.'"

Q "The Fluh is okay sometimes, but mostly crappy. **Rocky's is the best, but the prices are too high**. Flex doesn't grow on trees. The wraps are, by far, the best choice of food."

Q "Weisenfluh isn't as bad as people say. It's all-you-can-eat, and **there's a lot to choose from**."

STUDENT AUTHOR: **Let's face it, campus dining at any university is not first-class gourmet, nor is it expected to be. Slippery Rock is no different. Slippery Rock offers the typical cafeteria à la carte buffet at Weisenfluh and Boozel dining halls, and fast food options at Rocky's Grille. The number one place to eat on campus is Cyberfresh, a section of Rocky's Grille, which serves highly-recommended wraps and fresh soups.**

Student Body

African American:	5%	Male/Female:	44/56%
Asian American:	1%	Out-of-State:	5%
Hispanic:	1%	International:	1%
Native American:	<1%	Unknown:	0%
White:	92%		

Gay Pride: Homosexuality can be a sensitive issue on any campus. Through Lesbians, Gays, Bisexuals, Transgender, and Allies (LGBTA), students who are a part of the gay community, or support those in the gay community, can come together to support each other, educate others, and build connections with the University community.

Economic Status: Slippery Rock is made up of mostly students with middle-class backgrounds.

Students Speak Out
ON DORMS

Q "When I moved into Patterson Hall my freshman year, I thought I was moving into a bomb shelter. However, I lived the typical dorm experience and learned that it wasn't all that bad. **Dorming is a great experience**. You get to live in a cool little community and meet some great people."

Q "I live off campus now and must confess that I somewhat miss dorm life. **The dorms are always full of interesting characters**, and you can always find something to do and someone to hang out with."

Q "The dorm rooms aren't that bad after you spruce up the walls with posters and pictures. Otherwise, **you realize that you're living in a cement cell**."

STUDENT AUTHOR: **Slippery Rock is replacing the old, cement cell blocks that were the traditional dorms that SRU students knew and loathed. The new suite-style residences are welcomed, but the price of on-campus living is skyrocketing due to this major upgrade in quality. About half of the on-campus housing is brand new; the rest of the housing transformation should be completed by fall 2008.**

? Did You Know?
39% of undergrads live on campus.

Students Speak Out
ON GUYS & GIRLS

Q "The campus seems like **a larger version of high school** in that every possible clique is represented. It's just natural that some people, due to majors, clubs, or whatever other factors, flock together."

Q "The girls on campus always seem like they're dressed up and ready for the club, while the **guys seem to be stereotypical frat boys**."

Q "**There are a lot of hotties at SRU**. There is a girl for every guy, and every type of girl is here. You have your brains, your athletes, your party girls, shy girls, small girls, fat girls, tall girls, short girls, all girls. You are bound to find one you like."

STUDENT AUTHOR: Slippery Rock guys and girls are, for the most part, a diverse bunch of crazy kids. Casual relationships and "hookups" are not a rare occurrence, upholding the party school stigma in a very sexually-charged atmosphere. However, there are some students with morals and monogamy. Overall, campus is a mixed bag of attractiveness and morals. There is always someone for everyone, even if it's just for one night.

Traditions

Midnight Madness
Every October, students flock to the the ARC to celebrate the beginning of the basketball season.

Homecoming
A king and queen are crowned at halftime of the football game, and a ceremony is held in their honor.

Overall School Spirit
Although Slippery Rock clothing and paraphernalia abound on campus and around town, the average SRU student is pretty apathetic when it comes to supporting his/her alma mater.

Students Speak Out
ON ATHLETICS

Q "I always hear about how great our football team was a billion years ago and how there was a cult-like following. It's anything but these days. I think **a lot of school spirit, in regards to sports, has faded away**, especially since the University recently cut certain teams."

Q "There are **lots of intramural sports teams** at SRU. I wish there was as much pride in varsity sports as there is in intramural sports."

Q "I didn't really expect much out of the sports program when I first came here. I'm from Western PA, and I knew that SRU didn't compare to Pitt or Penn State, as far as athletics. I now know that, if anything else, **SRU is an athletically-oriented campus**, and if you want to get involved here and play a sport, you certainly can."

STUDENT AUTHOR: **The glory days seem to be over for SRU varsity athletics. Intramural sports teams are, believe it or not, far more popular and, in many cases, taken more seriously than varsity sports. IMs carry a cult-like following, as students create their own teams and come out to the ARC to have fun, more than anything.**

Students Speak Out
ON DRUG SCENE

Q "Other than **pot and alcohol**, I don't think there is much drug use."

Q "I know about a lot of drug use on and off campus. It's **more than you would imagine** in such a small town."

Q "If you're here to do drugs and party, then you'll be able to do so—but why even bother attending? **Save yourself the money** because, in the end, you're just going to drop out and be a nobody."

STUDENT AUTHOR: **Move over Cheech and Chong, hello SRU. Marijuana is, by far, the most prevalent drug on campus. There is also rumor of harder drugs, such as cocaine, floating around and taking hold of a small minority of the student body. However, it is safe to say that the majority of Slippery Rock students have chosen a drug-free lifestyle and other avenues of entertainment. The majority of students who do decide to participate in the drug scene usually find out the hard way that drugs and academics don't mix.**

21:1	Student-to-Faculty Ratio
78%	Freshman Retention Rate
24%	Four-Year Graduation Rate
71%	Financial Aid Applicants Receiving Aid

Students Speak Out
SAFETY & SECURITY

Q "There is a section of campus called 'East Lake' and it's basically **a big parking lot that's not very well lit** and there is a small, creepy pond right next to it. I affectionately call it 'rape lake,' although I've never heard of anyone being attacked there."

Q "**You have to get into the dorms by ID card** and get onto floors by key. It's pretty well-locked down and safe. I guess it's a great thing, but it's irritating when you have your hands full and have to juggle doors."

Q "My car has been broken into several times. **Be smart about what you leave in your car**, and always lock your door. It's the same idea anywhere."

STUDENT AUTHOR: **Every residence hall is on lockdown with ID access, locked doors sealing every stairway, video surveillance, and on-site University staff. One may say that all of these measures are excessive, but it keeps the crime rate here extremely low.**

Questions?
For more inside information and survival tips, pick up College Prowler's full-length book on this school, written by an actual student! Check it out at *www.collegeprowler.com*.

Students Speak Out
ON OVERALL EXPERIENCE

Q "My favorite SRU memory is waking up to find a cow and other various livestock outside of my window at Patterson. It ended up being some kind of farm show to promote whole foods or something. I just remember laughing and thinking that this was somehow **typical of what it is like here: ridiculous**."

Q "People don't consider SRU a prestigious school because it has been **plagued by the label of 'party school**,' but I'm not even graduated and already have some pretty good job offers."

Q "I think that a lot of people who transfer do so only because **they didn't make much of an effort to meet people** and get involved."

Q "I love SRU, and **I would definitely choose it again if I could**. The size of the campus is just right and the people that I've met here have made it a memorable experience."

STUDENT AUTHOR: **At SRU, you are not treated as a number, but, in many cases, as a family member. Most students here agree that the people are what make this place. You will not only make lifelong friendships and connections with fellow students, but with professors and local townspeople as well. Slippery Rock has been trying to overcome the party school stigma that has overshadowed its sophisticated academic programs. Known for many programs including education, physical therapy, and parks and recreational management, Slippery Rock offers high quality at a low price. It's highly recommended that you get involved and make the most of your time here. At Slippery Rock, we play hard, we work hard, and most agree that they would do it all over again in a heartbeat.**

Smith College

7 College Lane; Northampton, MA 01063
(413) 585-2700; www.smith.edu

THE BASICS:

Acceptance Rate: 48%   **SAT Range:** 1760–2090
Setting: Rural   **Control:** Private
F-T Undergrads: 2,588   **Tuition:** $33,940

Most Popular Majors: Social Sciences, Foreign Languages, Visual/Performing Arts, Psychology

*of 2400

Academics	A	Guys	N/A
Local Atmosphere	C	Girls	B
Safety & Security	B+	Athletics	C
Computers	B+	Nightlife	C+
Facilities	A-	Greek Life	N/A
Campus Dining	B+	Drug Scene	C
Off-Campus Dining	B+	Campus Strictness	C
Campus Housing	A	Parking	D
Off-Campus Housing	D+	Transportation	B
Diversity	B	Weather	C+

Students Speak Out
ON ACADEMICS

Q "One of the best parts of Smith is **the low faculty-to-student ratio**; it's something that a lot of us just take for granted."

Q "My American government class is really cool, because we're talking about the presidential nomination. In a lot of my government classes, the **professors make the information relevant to current politics**."

Q "Academics are intense. **You really have to figure out time-management and prioritize**. Sometimes, that means not having a social life and coming home at 3 a.m. every night for two weeks. Professors sometimes think we're geniuses and give us way more than we can actually handle. In the end, though, it's worth it because it makes you know your stuff really well."

Q "The professors have very unique approaches to the material, and they are usually very engaging. The classes are small for a college, so **there is rarely a boring lecture**."

STUDENT AUTHOR: The school's academic reputation is the reason many get interested in Smith in the first place. There is no such thing as an "easy" class at Smith. Smith has a tradition of hiring distinguished, intelligent professors. Students at Smith work extremely hard since academics are of Ivy League caliber and all-nighters are common, but the all-female environment makes it feel less competitive.

Students Speak Out
ON LOCAL ATMOSPHERE

Q "Northampton is indescribable. You'll have to see it for yourself. I'd say it's a funky town, but also has **the feel of a safe, close-knit town**. There are plenty of places to visit in town, and of course, there's the five-college system, which provides more to do if one doesn't want to be in Northampton. Another thing I love about Northampton is that it's a small town, but has three sushi places."

Q "**The town is too ritzy**. It doesn't know the meaning of poverty, and it's very narrow-minded when it comes to socioeconomic politics. Everything closes at 10 p.m., too."

Q "NoHo is really laid-back. There are street performers that engage passersby. They are really cool. You're able to make eye contact and have conversations with people. **There's pleasant human interaction** that so often gets cut out of communities."

Q "It's cutesy, but coming from a big city, it was hard to adjust. But it's not the small stereotype; Northampton has a thriving cultural and political community. **Plus, it has a lot of lesbians!**"

STUDENT AUTHOR: Northampton is off-beat and has a bustling cultural atmosphere. It is "bourgeoisie bohemian:" predominantly liberal, white, and an upper-middle-class suburb. Northampton's big-city aspirations are obvious by its nickname NoHo, a take off of the areas in Manhattan, SoHo and NoHo. Despite these aspirations, the word most often used to describe the town is "quaint."

Students Speak Out
ON FACILITIES

Q "The facilities are great. Some of the buildings look a little old, but **Smith has done a pretty good job of rebuilding things** that need to be fixed. We have a new gym and a new Campus Center which look great on campus."

Q "I think the facilities are amazing. **The Campus Center is beautiful and functional**. It's the center of campus, and every time I'm there I see someone I know, which is the point. It's clean and modern; I think it's really comfortable and visually fun. I think it works wonderfully. It has the bookstore, café, post office, and offices."

Q "The gym is sweet. It's very pretty, it has glass walls, and you can look out over the campus or over the pool. **In a lot of the labs, the computers are new**, and they usually have staff to help you out. The Campus Center is amazing! It's really sunny and cheerful, and a lot of people hang out there, including faculty, professors, and local high school students. It's a great place to run into people."

Q "I really like Campus Center, because **you run into people that you wouldn't normally** run into because of the way the housing and dining systems are set up."

STUDENT AUTHOR: In case you didn't notice, the Campus Center is really the only public space to hang out on campus. Since opening in the fall of 2003, the it has become the hub of the Smith community. With the constant up-keep of existing facilities and the development of new projects, Smith ensures that its students learn and live with the best amenities possible.

Famous Alumni

Barbara Bush, Julia Child, Madeleine L'Engle, Ann M. Martin, Sylvia Plath, Nancy Reagan, Gloria Steinem

Students Speak Out
ON CAMPUS DINING

Q "The food is good. I love my kitchen. I really like knowing my kitchen staff. I feel that there really is a lot of choice here, considering that it's still a small school. The cooks are very accommodating, too. For instance, this morning they served scrambled eggs for breakfast. I was dying for some fried eggs, and **one of my cooks made me fried eggs**. That really made my morning!"

Q "The food is good for college, but **there's not always a lot of variety**."

Q "The food is palatable, but it's a lot better than other schools where everything is fried. I've been to a lot of other schools, and **we have a unique dining set-up** that makes our community really special."

Q "When I first came, **I thought it was like being at an expensive, catered party everyday**. After a while, it doesn't seem as exciting anymore. What is great is the kitchen staff. They work really hard to make sure that we're happy with the food. I can't have pierogies without applesauce, and they are always happy to get it for me. They are really concerned about helping us out."

STUDENT AUTHOR: To try to accommodate the desire for more options while dealing with a budget crisis, Smith submitted a proposal for a more consolidated dining system. As a result, several dining rooms have been closed altogether, while some are only open for dinner during the week. However, students are unlimited in the number of meals they wish to attend.

Student Body

African American:	7%	Male/Female:	0/100%
Asian American:	13%	Out-of-State:	77%
Hispanic:	7%	International:	7%
Native American:	<1%	Unknown:	23%
White:	43%		

Popular Faiths: The most popular religion is Christianity, and there are several Christian groups.

Gay Pride: The gay community is one of the most vocal and present groups on campus. Some students, however, complain that Smith is too focused on the gay community.

Economic Status: There are a few very wealthy and a few very underprivileged, but mostly middle-class.

Students Speak Out
ON DORMS

Q "I'm partial to Lower Elm, but **different parts of campus are better for different things**. If you're an athlete or a science major, you might choose Green Street because it's near everything. If you like to party, go to the Quad. I do not recommend the Quad if you want quiet all the time. Lower Elm and Upper Elm are very similar, and they have a nice balance between partying and studying."

Q "I love the housing, **especially the bathroom situation**. They're really clean. I love having a single. A lot of people have singles their sophomore year."

Q "It's unique. Each area of campus has its character, history, and flavor. **Some are big houses, and others are smaller and intimate**."

STUDENT AUTHOR: **The houses at Smith are more like sorority houses than dormitories. They are self-governing and can be quite insular. Though the houses are not as different as people make them seem, it is important to find one that fits your personality. It cultivates a great sense of community, but it can be hard to make friends outside of your house.**

Did You Know?
90% of undergrads live on campus.

Students Speak Out
ON GUYS & GIRLS

Q "I suppose **it's great, as long as you aren't straight**, but many people do go to the other four colleges for activities and classes. Many people also have long-distance relationships."

Q "It's sometimes difficult to find guys who want to stick around for more than the night. However, **according to guys at nearby schools, Smithies are in high demand**."

Q "The dating scene is **a little messy**."

Q "It appears to be very homosexual. Although, that doesn't mean that everyone identifies as a lesbian. There seems to be **a lot of free love happening, as in no commitments**. Some people are committed, but they seem to live on Green Street."

STUDENT AUTHOR: **A lot of questions about dating focus on the trouble that girls have meeting guys. For the gay student, being at a school with so many women offers dating opportunities that most coed schools do not, but that does not mean that every gay student is happy with the dating scene. The best bet for meeting guys is usually to take classes off campus, or get involved in activities that interact with other campuses.**

Traditions

Convocation
The evening before classes begin, the Smith community gathers to listen to an opening address and a performance by the Glee Club.

Mountain Day
On a beautiful day in the fall, the president announces a surprise holiday, and all classes are cancelled.

Overall School Spirit
While there is not much of a fan-base for any of the sports teams, Smith students tend to develop a deep sense of community with their fellow classmates.

Students Speak Out
ON ATHLETICS

Q "In my opinion, **sports are one of Smith's last priorities**. There's so much else going on, people just don't notice sports. The people that play sports are really intense about their experience. Spectators really aren't a major presence, however."

Q "**A fair amount of students participate**, but few students consider themselves more than fair-weather fans."

Q "Varsity sports are supported, but not huge. **The team with the most support is the rugby team**, which is a club sport, but it is treated as a varsity sport because of all of the student support."

Q "Club sports are thought of as **merely social scenes that encourage drinking**, as opposed to varsity sports, which are taken seriously."

STUDENT AUTHOR: **For athletes, sports are a major time commitment. Many club sports (particularly rugby) are known for the social life that comes along with joining the team. Usually, people are at games to cheer on their school and their friends, not because sports are a major part of Smith.**

Students Speak Out
ON DRUG SCENE

Q "**Marijuana is prevalent, as is alcohol** (particularly in the Quad). There is some cocaine use, but it's pretty much underground. There is also some prescription drug usage."

Q "From my experience, there are a lot of drugs on campus. If drugs are your thing, you can find most things. **Mostly it's weed and coke**. A lot of people have money to spend on drugs."

Q "There is **a huge underground cocaine scene**, which is surprising, but this is only if you get in the loop. There is definitely more pot smoking than drinking. Smith is a very herb-friendly school."

STUDENT AUTHOR: **Though drug-use is fairly significant on campus, it's mostly underground. People do drugs with other people that do drugs, and non-users feel very little pressure to indulge in drugs because of how insular the various drug-using groups are. Those that want to stay away from it don't have a problem doing so.**

9:1	Student-to-Faculty Ratio
90%	Freshman Retention Rate
78%	Four-Year Graduation Rate
88%	Financial Aid Applicants Receiving Aid

Students Speak Out
SAFETY & SECURITY

Q "It is very safe. You can't say that it's 100 percent, but **I have never felt threatened**, even when I was walking alone in the dark. It is one of the safest campuses I have been to. But Public Safety sucks."

Q "Many of my friends in other schools (especially large universities) have to sign in their friends in order for them to get into the building. **There are no security cards here**."

Q "I feel really safe on campus, but **I'm not a fan of Public Safety**. I feel that they don't really know what they're doing, and they don't do that much to begin with. I've also seen them harass students occasionally and not take their problems seriously."

STUDENT AUTHOR: **Students agree that they feel secure and are not concerned about their safety, but though there are few security issues on campus, students still complain about Public Safety's lack of efficiency. While there are officers patrolling 24 hours, they are rarely seen.**

Questions?
For more inside information and survival tips, pick up College Prowler's full-length book on this school, written by an actual student! Check it out at *www.collegeprowler.com*.

Students Speak Out
ON OVERALL EXPERIENCE

Q "The amazing financial aid and JYA are what brought and kept me here. But Smith is notorious for refusing to talk about its negative aspects. And there are negative aspects, like the lesbian atmosphere. It's amazing and it brings a lot to the school's diversity; but **no one talks about sexual harassment**. I've been grabbed at parties, and girls have tried to make-out with me, and that's not okay. If that was some guy, it wouldn't have been okay, and it's not okay for girls to do it."

Q "I love that it's an all-female environment. Everything caters to you; you're in an environment that depends not on how you look, but on your ideas, beliefs, and opinions. **I'm straight, and I'm really glad that I'm here**."

Q "If you get bored easily, Smith may not be the school for you, unless you are looking for **a highly academic, anti-*Animal House*** college experience."

Q "I love being here. It's been **positive and challenging in the best way possible**. I keep learning more about myself. I've met so many people who think differently, and I really value that. I miss it when I'm not here. It's a great place to be."

STUDENT AUTHOR: **One thing is for sure: Smith is not for everyone. Talk to any student, and you'll probably find that they have a ambivalent relationship with the school. Some people cannot handle the single-sex environment, while others find it to be their favorite part of Smith. It's not a huge party school, and it's not a stereotypical college experience; but, for most Smith students, that's exactly the way they like it.**

Southern Methodist University

6425 Boaz Lane; Dallas, TX 75205
(214) 768-2000; www.smu.edu

THE BASICS:

Acceptance Rate: 64%
Setting: Urban
F-T Undergrads: 5,882

SAT Range: 1110–1300*
Control: Private
Tuition: $26,880

Most Popular Majors: Business, Social Sciences, Communications, Psychology, Visual/Performing Arts

*of 1600

Academics	B+	Guys	A-
Local Atmosphere	A-	Girls	A
Safety & Security	B-	Athletics	C+
Computers	C+	Nightlife	A-
Facilities	C	Greek Life	A
Campus Dining	B-	Drug Scene	C-
Off-Campus Dining	A	Campus Strictness	B
Campus Housing	B	Parking	D
Off-Campus Housing	B+	Transportation	C-
Diversity	D+	Weather	B-

Students Speak Out
ON ACADEMICS

Q "I find most of the professors here to be **very sharp and on task in the classroom**. Besides being very intelligent, most professors are also easy to confront with concerns, or to just have a friendly chat with. I believe a class only to be as interesting as the professor who teaches it. All my classes in the political science and Italian department are challenging, yet all the classes have an environment that is conducive to learning but also fun to be in."

Q "The teachers are great. Although way too many of them **do not speak English well enough** for an hour and a half of pure lecture. Overall, the classes are very interesting, especially when you get all of the boring prerequisites out of the way."

Q "SMU has a great reputation, but I really don't think the classes are that much harder than Texas Tech, even though we are supposed to be so much better. I think we just have better PR. **SMU is not the 'Harvard of the South**,' or whatever the saying is."

Q "Quite honestly, **I've only found two professors that are interesting**."

STUDENT AUTHOR: SMU can make no guarantees, just like any other institution, but at least they offer a number of intelligent professors that are interesting. The courses are noteworthy and challenging enough to force you to find the library. Most students say that the academics become harder every year—so be prepared to lose sleep.

Students Speak Out
ON LOCAL ATMOSPHERE

Q "The atmosphere is **better for natives** than for international students."

Q "Dallas has a lot of things to do, especially if you seek them out. There are **various arts venues and decent shows and exhibits**. There are several other universities in the general Dallas-Ft. Worth area, though I have yet to come into direct contact with any students from other schools."

Q "**Dallas is a great college city**. There are tons of restaurants and bars, and there is plenty to do on the weekends. If you are into the party scene, you can't go wrong with Greenville Avenue. It is so close to campus, and Deep Ellum is right downtown."

Q "The atmosphere in Dallas is vast. It is a fast-paced, big city, but it still keeps the pride and character of Texas. There are universities around, but I haven't had much interaction with them. As with any big city, **stay away from the sketchy parts of town and the strip-clubs**. Visit all the landmarks of Dallas: the museums, art galleries, historic monuments—anything you can get into your sight, go see it."

STUDENT AUTHOR: In Dallas, not only do you have the best of what's around, but if you're low on cash, you can still find something amusing to do on any given day. There is always something to do, and everything is at your fingertips—if you have a car. I am still finding little treasures in the most remote parts of the city.

Students Speak Out
ON FACILITIES

Q "The athletic department facilities stink. But **they are renovating . . . like always** . . . not to mention raising tuition for it . . . like always."

Q "The newer facilities found in the engineering buildings are up-to-date and enjoyable. Computers outside of the engineering facilities are not that great, but you also do not need ~ that much. Some of the places seem **a bit crowded and stuffy**."

Q "The facilities on campus are adequate. **They are not very elaborate**, but they get the job done."

Q "The dorms vary. There are the yucky ones, nice ones, quiet ones, loud ones, fun ones, and cozy ones. **The computers vary by location**, but the best ones are in the libraries. The student center is nice . . . much like any other."

Q "Well, **if you're a business student**, then you have the best facilities money can buy, and there are more great facilities on the way. If you are any other major, just be happy that you don't have to study outside because your buildings aren't ever getting repaired."

STUDENT AUTHOR: Every year, SMU makes new plans to improve each and every school building as well as things like roads and parking garages. The plans are available online and so is their expected completion date. The more you walk around this campus, the more you will see how nice the facilities look. Don't be dismayed if you see sidewalks and buildings being ripped apart—construction never ends here.

Famous Alumni

Kathy Bates, Powers Boothe, Laura Bush, James Cronin, Paige Davis, Lauren Graham, Steve Lundquist, Patricia Richardson, Aaron Spelling

Students Speak Out
ON CAMPUS DINING

Q "Dining halls get old fast. They **should be 24-hours**. The best place to eat on campus is Chick-fil-A."

Q "The dining halls are good at first, but **they get old really quickly**. Really quickly. The breakfast at Umph [Umphrey Lee Center] is the best. Besides that, Subway and Chick-fil-A are okay, depending on your mood."

Q "Dining halls are dining halls. **Other food around campus is decent**. La Madeleine, Roly Poly, Stromboli Cafe, and Jimmy John's are all within walking distance."

Q "In the student center, the food is great. There is a Subway, a Chick-fil-A, and another sandwich place. The cafeterias are okay. I mean, **what can you really expect from a cafeteria anyway**?"

Q "The food is all right. **It's nothing special**. The hours are not that great, especially for college students. The dining halls are nice and are always clean. One of them has a baby grand piano. Really, I wish there was something 24-hours where you could hang out and get a meal. There's food to walk to off campus that accepts the student card, which is a bonus."

STUDENT AUTHOR: Almost every student will admit that the dining on campus is great . . . until their breaking point surfaces and they wish they were still eating mom's homemade pot roast. However, having someone else clean your dishes and cook several different types of food is the upside of having a meal plan.

Student Body

African American:	5%	Male/Female:	45/55%
Asian American:	6%	Out-of-State:	31%
Hispanic:	9%	International:	4%
Native American:	1%	Unknown:	0%
White:	75%		

Popular Faiths: SMU is a Methodist school, but there are also many Catholics and Protestants.

Gay Pride: The gay community is widely accepted in the Meadows School of the Arts. Acceptance has yet to be fully incorporated by the rest of the campus.

Economic Status: Most SMU students come from upper- and upper-middle-class economic backgrounds.

Students Speak Out
ON DORMS

Q "Perkins is great. It is an older dorm, but those dorms have a fun and homey feel. Boaz is crazy, but **good for people who stay up** until 4 a.m. every day."

Q "Every dorm has its own experience. Some say that you should stay away from Boaz (the party dorm), but I had a great experience. **You meet many people and make friends**. But after a while, you want some peace and quiet, and you move to better dorms like Cockrell-McIntosh."

Q "The dorms are a lot of fun. **A lot of the dorms have been completely renovated** with new walls, ceilings, carpet, and 90 channels of cable."

STUDENT AUTHOR: It is required by the school that all first-year students live in the dorms. Even though some students choose to complain about their living situations, many will agree that the experience was worthwhile and essential to their introduction to SMU. The only downside to living on campus is that some of the residence halls have not been renovated in a while.

Did You Know?
40% of undergrads live on campus.

Students Speak Out
ON GUYS & GIRLS

Q "The girls at SMU are top notch. They wear short, tiny little skirts, and their wardrobe probably costs more than my car. Most of the guys are worried about the sun burning their necks and light getting through their aviators at the night club. **Most of the frat boys look like they just got off a sailboat**."

Q "A lot of girls and guys are **stuck up rich kids**. They've never had a real job and live off their parents for the rest of their college career. The girls are great to look at, but in reality, most of them are fake or have some fake part that daddy paid for."

Q "It's more like **a museum with pretty pieces that you can't touch**."

Q "Labels, proof of wealth, and social status **plague our school**."

STUDENT AUTHOR: SMU has some of the most stunning and beautiful girls from all over the nation. Most of the guys walk around campus with their jaws dragging, and some of them are even lucky enough to date a couple of SMU's fine and polished ladies. Sadly, the men at SMU are not up to par with the women. It is not out of the ordinary for a girl to date the same attractive guy that her friend has also gone out with.

Traditions

Mane Event
A giant annual festival held in front of Dallas Hall which includes live music, food, games, and more.

Brown Bag
Every semester, the dance department showcases student-choreographed pieces in the Bob Hope lobby.

Overall School Spirit
Students may not be able to sing the "Pony Battle Cry," but they can tell you about SMU's several top programs in the nation. Students are proud to say that they attend SMU.

Students Speak Out
ON ATHLETICS

Q "We have a great soccer team and swimming team, but **no one cares about sports**. Football is awful. They spend more and more money to get better, but all they do is help the players drive nicer cars. We have the potential to be excited about sports but lack the motivation from the players and the crowds. Intramural sports are fun. They are huge among frats and sororities."

Q "**Sports aren't as big a deal as the parties** before and after the games. We may not have won a game last year, but our tailgating skills are unmatched."

Q "We love to tailgate for football, and we'll go to a bit of the game. Soccer gets a lot of fans and so does basketball. **IM sports are fun, and a lot of people participate**, especially Greek groups."

STUDENT AUTHOR: Where there's a will, there's a way . . . well, maybe to tailgate incessantly. SMU is home to some of the top teams in the nation, yet the majority of students would rather check out the weekend bar specials than actually go to a sporting event. Maybe if $1 beer specials were offered to students at all sporting events, the attendance would not be so depressing.

Students Speak Out
ON DRUG SCENE

Q "Of course they're here. If you want something, you can get it. **Drugs are prevalent here**, especially pot and coke."

Q "There are drugs on every campus, and this one is no different. But you usually don't see it out at parties. I think **people's drug use here is usually pretty private**."

Q "Adderall seems to be the new study drug, and I think people from every group or type can be prone to using it. **Party drugs like cocaine seem to be popular** among some of the more upper-class Greek people on campus. And who can forget GHB? It's popular among the frat boys for sex assistance."

STUDENT AUTHOR: **SMU is similar to every typical college; it has drug users and alcoholics. You can get access to any kind of drug you wish. The most prevalent drugs are marijuana and Adderall. On the surface, this campus is drug-free—minus the few stoners and fans of bar specials found on every campus.**

12:1	Student-to-Faculty Ratio
87%	Freshman Retention Rate
56%	Four-Year Graduation Rate
82%	Financial Aid Applicants Receiving Aid

Students Speak Out
SAFETY & SECURITY

Q "I have heard of some instances of car jacking and minor theft, but besides that, the campus, from my perspective, has been **a very safe place to be, even at night**."

Q "You always see the cops on campus. They are only a phone call or blue box away. But, you should still use common sense. **Don't walk in dark or sketchy areas**. Robberies and other incidents do happen."

Q "I think security is pretty good; I always see SMU police driving around campus. However, there are **a lot of places on campus that are not that well lit**, which can be a little scary when walking back from a night class or back to your dorm/apartment."

STUDENT AUTHOR: Even though University Park and SMU Police work together to patrol the city, SMU PD pays more attention to parking violations than a screaming girl whose hair is in flames. On the other hand, nothing too out of the ordinary ever occurs here on campus, so what else is there for them to do?

> **Questions?**
> For more inside information and survival tips, pick up College Prowler's full-length book on this school, written by an actual student! Check it out at *www.collegeprowler.com*.

Students Speak Out
ON OVERALL EXPERIENCE

Q "SMU is great for some, but not for others. If you are from out-of-state, you won't like it because **Texans love Texas, and outsiders may not**. But this is from my experience. I would rather be on the East Coast."

Q "**I wish I was in a more crowded area** like New York, where people are more open and don't mind diversity."

Q "**I think Dallas and the school offer so much**, no matter what you are into. Dallas has great concerts, good bars, and a friendly community. The campus is beautiful (when there is no construction), safe, and most importantly, a great place to learn."

Q "Even though I hate the frats, and our football team sucks, I have made so many friends here. **The faculty in Dedman have helped me do so much** that I can't imagine being anywhere else. Besides that, the fact that so many guys at our school act like total tools just increases my chance with some of the hottest and richest women in the United States."

STUDENT AUTHOR: **While some SMU students will gladly tell you that this school was their first choice, there are plenty of others that will admit that they're not sure how they got here. An exuberant school spirit in terms of athletics might be missing, but SMU pride in the sense of academic excellence and social atmosphere is highly evident. Students get irritated with parking and other little issues, but in the long run, most of them are satisfied with their level of education and their experience.**

Southwestern University

1001 East University Avenue; Georgetown, TX 78626-0770
(512) 863-6511; www.southwestern.edu

THE BASICS:

Acceptance Rate: 66%
Setting: Suburban
F-T Undergrads: 1,252

SAT Range: 1150–1360*
Control: Private
Tuition: $21,900

Most Popular Majors: Social Sciences, Business, Visual/Performing Arts, Communication, Biology

*of 1600

Academics	B	Guys	B-
Local Atmosphere	C+	Girls	B+
Safety & Security	A+	Athletics	C-
Computers	B	Nightlife	B
Facilities	B	Greek Life	A
Campus Dining	B-	Drug Scene	B+
Off-Campus Dining	B	Campus Strictness	C+
Campus Housing	B	Parking	B
Off-Campus Housing	B-	Transportation	D
Diversity	C-	Weather	A-

Students Speak Out
ON ACADEMICS

Q "I enjoy my teachers and classes. **I love the small class size**, and for the most part, the professors care about who you are as a person, and they want to help you out."

Q **"Classes at Southwestern are easier than I expected**. I remember during FYS (first-year seminar) a bunch of people were freaking out over writing a five-page paper, double-spaced. I was writing 10-page papers in high school!"

Q "The professors here are very interesting and love to teach. They also love interacting with students, and go to great lengths to meet and help students out. The majority of classes are very interesting, but **there are always those few that are totally boring** and a waste of time. I think that no matter where you go, you can't escape those dull classes."

Q "Most of the professors are amazing, really care about student learning, and are **always available to work with students outside of class**. A few are downright crazy, but that's what makes it interesting!"

STUDENT AUTHOR: **Southwestern derives much of its academic strength from personal attention, small class size, and accessible/accomplished professors. Southwestern's academics are, overall, quite strong, and the coursework is appropriately challenging for the students. The school is not well known, and therefore, the school does not attract the most sought-after students. But SU's programs and prestige are growing every year.**

Students Speak Out
ON LOCAL ATMOSPHERE

Q "There are no other universities in Georgetown, and sometimes it **seems like the community resents us college kids** for breaking into their peaceful little town."

Q **"The proximity to Austin is the only redeeming factor of SU's location**. Of course, there is a wealth of stuff to do there, but the 30-minute drive can get tiring when you end up making it every weekend. Georgetown itself is small and conservative, and everything closes before 11 p.m. (except Wal-Mart)."

Q **"The surrounding town is very small but cute**. I really enjoy the historic town square that is in walking distance from the school because it has cute little antique shops, and it makes me feel all warm inside. There is also a lake nearby called the Blue Hole; I haven't been there yet, but I hear it is a fun place to be. Other than that, there really isn't a whole lot to do in Georgetown. Most people drive the 30 minutes to Austin."

STUDENT AUTHOR: **SU students can be divided into two categories: the ones who revel in Georgetown's small town-ness, and those that dislike it and flee to Austin at every chance they get. It's definitely not an exciting place to live when you're a roving 20-something-year-old. Georgetown isn't a very college-friendly place—it is mostly a retirement community filled with bed and breakfasts and antique shops. However, lots of students enjoy the cozy, sleepy atmosphere—especially the students who grew up in similar places.**

5 Best Things	5 Worst Things
1 Accessible faculty	1 Georgetown
2 Fine arts department	2 Lack of diversity
3 Proximity to Austin	3 Boy/girl ratio
4 Strong academics	4 Quiet campus
5 No TAs	5 No football team

Students Speak Out
ON CAMPUS DINING

Q "**The on-campus food is tolerable for a while**. It does get old after a year or so, but it's not terrible. A lot of people decide to eat in the Cove or buy their own food, especially if they get an apartment."

Q "The food on campus is not very good; **there is a lack of selection most days** with the food in the Commons. But, there are quite a few fast food restaurants and grills near campus that are easy to get to."

Q "Sodexo food is **pretty darn good for college food**. I eat more there than I do at home. The Cove is always there if you miss the Commons meal, and it's not bad, either."

Q "The food is pretty good. There is a decent amount of stuff for vegetarians, but **certainly not enough for vegans**. But overall, there are lots of choices."

Q "I'm not a fan of the Commons. The Cove is pretty good, but **it doesn't open for dinner until 7 p.m.**, and by that time, I'm usually starving."

STUDENT AUTHOR: **Southwestern only offers two on-campus dining choices: the Commons (a traditional cafeteria) and the Cove (more like a snack bar/coffeehouse). Everything in the Cove is pretty tasty, but it's about as healthy as fast food. The food in the Commons is on the high end of the scale when it comes to college dorm food, but it is bland enough that one trip to Chipotle will make you realize what you're missing.**

Students Speak Out
ON FACILITIES

Q "The couches in the student center are nice places to do homework or just hang out. The Cove in **the student center is also a fun place to eat, hang out**, play pool, and do homework."

Q "The gym could be much better. There are only a few machines (both weight and cardio), which are often broken. As far as academic and computer facilities, **everything is very modern and very beautiful**. In fact, our Physical Plant workers are kind of poked fun at for keeping everything too immaculate. The same is true of the Commons. Every weeknight, at about 11 p.m., you will see the housekeeping staff doing a very thorough cleansing of the dining area."

Q "The facilities are very nice. **My dorm room is the envy of all my other college friends**, due to its sheer size and general cleanliness. The buildings are lovely, and the lawns are always in perfect order—perhaps this is why so few students dare tread on the grass?"

Q "All the **facilities are almost too nice**. I feel like I'm intruding into some fancy-pants school, when really, it's just my Southwestern."

STUDENT AUTHOR: **The student center is the sun around which all of Southwestern galaxy revolves. It contains the mail center, the Commons, the Cove, the bookstore, the ballrooms, and a spacious lounge. Southwestern's facilities, from gym to student center, are all very well kept. Southwestern is very well prepared to provide students with all the facilities they need, and the Physical Plant staff is always working hard at keeping up the appearance of the school.**

Famous Alumni

J. Frank Dobie, Jerry Hardin, Red McCombs, John F. Murrell, Mike Timlin, John G. Tower

Student Body

African American:	4%	Male/Female:	41/59%
Asian American:	4%	Out-of-State:	9%
Hispanic:	13%	International:	1%
Native American:	1%	Unknown:	0%
White:	77%		

Popular Faiths: There is a very active Christian community on campus; all other religious groups are quiet and/or ignored.

Gay Pride: Many high-profile students feel pressure to remain in the closet for fear of being labeled as "the gay one."

Economic Status: Most students come from upper-middle-class families.

Students Speak Out
ON DORMS

Q "The dorms here range from decent to really nice. **Luckily, there aren't really any total crapholes**. The quirk about the dorms at Southwestern is that the level of community and fun is inversely proportional to the quality of the dorm. For instance, Brown-Cody is the nicest dorm on campus, but most of the girls can't even name everyone on their hall. Ruter is the worst dorm on campus, but the boys there are the closest of any dorm and often make 'Ruter Alumni' shirts."

Q "**All the dorms are nice**—especially the girls dorms! Some of the dorms are pretty old (Moody-Shearn and Mabee) but are kept in good condition."

STUDENT AUTHOR: **All of the dorms at Southwestern have their own unique atmosphere. All of the dorms provide everything students need to live comfortably (except for Lord Centers, which you furnish yourself), and they tend to be bigger than your average dorm room. Where students are happiest tends to depend upon their personalities and interaction in the different residence halls.**

Did You Know?
83% of undergrads live on campus.

Students Speak Out
ON GUYS & GIRLS

Q "**There aren't many people here**. Get used to incestuous dating, where you've dated your best friend's ex-girlfriend, who's dated your brother, who's dated your current girlfriend's best friend, who's dated . . ."

Q "**The male-to-female ratio is definitely not beneficial to girls**. The guys are almost nonexistent. And if you date one person, you pretty much blow your chances of dating his or her friends, and almost everyone is friends in some way."

Q "The only real problem I have with Southwestern is that **it is difficult finding a female who is interested in just dating**, not like, getting married."

STUDENT AUTHOR: **The dating scene is one of the most interesting aspects of Southwestern. If you're not careful, everyone on campus will know about your sexual activities due to "Mouthwestern." In general, the campus is filled with two types of people: the type that is looking to get married within the next five years, and those that just want to make out with as many people as possible. When it comes to guys at SU, "the goods are good, but the odds sure aren't."**

Traditions

Late-Night Breakfast
The Commons opens its doors for one hour only, from 10 p.m. to 11 p.m. on the Monday of finals week.

Candlelight Service
Candlelight is the annual Advent service held in the Chapel the week before winter finals.

Overall School Spirit
Pretty much all of the students at SU are happy with the school, and partake in on-campus activities.

Students Speak Out
ON ATHLETICS

Q "**Intramurals are a pretty big deal**. There are always fun IM sports and outdoor excursion events throughout the year. And I don't think the school would function without ultimate Frisbee."

Q "Our sports teams are pretty good, but **we're Division-III athletics**, so that mean we're non-scholarship."

Q "**Sports aren't really that big of a deal here**. Intramurals are fun for some. I'm not really a sports person, but I hear that people who are have a lot of fun with intramurals. And even some of the varsity teams aren't that hard to get on to, like swimming."

STUDENT AUTHOR: **It isn't that no one plays sports on campus, it's just that the campus community isn't very involved in cheering them on. No one comes to Southwestern expecting it to be a powerhouse basketball school. And really, as long as Frisbees precariously whiz by students on the mall, most SU students will feel like they're getting their fill of sports. While sports may not play a pivotal role on campus, most students do enjoy a friendly IM game every now and then.**

Students Speak Out
ON DRUG SCENE

Q "There are people who do and people who don't do drugs, but **it doesn't really affect the overall social scene**, unless you prefer to hang out only with the people who do drugs."

Q "I know there is pot relatively often, and **alcohol is plentiful**, especially if you're Greek."

Q "The drug scene is here, like any other campus, but **it is hardly a problem**."

Q "I have some friends who smoke pot occasionally, but it's not some kind of epidemic or anything. I **recently heard of some guy getting in trouble for having cocaine** in his room, which really surprised me because that's the only hardcore drug I've ever heard of here on campus."

STUDENT AUTHOR: **The typical SU student has never tried a hard drug,** rarely indulges in pot, and drinks on the weekends. If you want to avoid even that meager amount of drug use, it can be done pretty easily. At Southwestern, drugs are not very visible on campus, nor do they interfere with campus life.

10:1	Student-to-Faculty Ratio
86%	Freshman Retention Rate
64%	Four-Year Graduation Rate
80%	Financial Aid Applicants Receiving Aid

Students Speak Out
SAFETY & SECURITY

Q "**Campus security and safety is generally very good**. Sometimes, bikes are lost or stolen, but that happens anywhere. But, like anyplace, you probably shouldn't go walking around at night alone, just to be safe."

Q "**Security concerns—are you kidding me**? I never lock my door, and if you lose your wallet, people return it to you over campus-wide mail. I even run around the campus at midnight sometimes."

Q "Southwestern is **extremely secure and safe**. It is a small university, so everyone watches out for one another. Even complete strangers will take care of you if need be. You could drop 50 dollars on the sidewalk, and nine out of ten times, you would get it back."

STUDENT AUTHOR: **There is a general sense of trust within the student body. The campus is essentially very safe. The sidewalks are all well lit, the school itself is in a good neighborhood, and anyone who wanders onto the campus that doesn't belong there is quickly apprehended.**

> **Questions?**
> For more inside information and survival tips, pick up College Prowler's full-length book on this school, written by an actual student! Check it out at *www.collegeprowler.com.*

Students Speak Out
ON OVERALL EXPERIENCE

Q "Overall, I love it here, and **I can't picture myself anywhere else**. I like the individualized attention I get from the professors and my academic advisor. They really help make me feel comfortable with the academic life. And the overall social scene is almost perfect for me, though there could be a few more guys."

Q "I love Southwestern; I don't think I could have picked out a better school to fit my personality. I am from a small town, so **I enjoy the small-town vibe that Southwestern and Georgetown give off**. The people here are very enjoyable to be around, and they're always willing to help you out if you have any problems adjusting to college life. I have found some of my best friends here, while also getting an incredible education!"

Q "I really love Southwestern University. If you are looking for **a challenging academic and intellectual environment**, this is the place for you. Everyone discusses everything, and you really get a chance to learn about new things and have new experiences."

STUDENT AUTHOR: **Essentially, Southwestern provides top-notch and unique educational opportunities for its students. Some students take advantage of study abroad and internship opportunities, others do not. Some students take advantage of the thriving social and Greek scene, others do not. Because Southwestern tends to be isolated, it takes effort on your part to go out and find things to do. To get the most out of your time at Southwestern, you have to be prepared to make the school work for you. If you invest lots of energy and work in Southwestern, it's bound to return the favor tenfold.**

Spelman College

350 Spelman Lane; Atlanta, GA 30314-4399
(404) 682-3643; www.spelman.edu

THE BASICS:

Acceptance Rate: 35%
Setting: Urban
F-T Undergrads: 2,151

SAT Range: 960–1120*
Control: Private
Tuition: $20,181

Most Popular Majors: Social Sciences, Psychology, Biological Sciences, English Language/Literature

*of 1600

Academics	B	Guys	N/A
Local Atmosphere	A-	Girls	B+
Safety & Security	A-	Athletics	D
Computers	B	Nightlife	B+
Facilities	B-	Greek Life	B
Campus Dining	C	Drug Scene	A-
Off-Campus Dining	A	Campus Strictness	D
Campus Housing	B	Parking	D-
Off-Campus Housing	A-	Transportation	B-
Diversity	D-	Weather	B+

Students Speak Out
ON ACADEMICS

Q "The professors in both the department of biology and department of philosophy were amazing. Not only had they all been published, **they all knew innovative ways to convey the information**, had the right questions to ask to spark further interest, and made themselves available to students outside of class."

Q "Overall, the teachers are great! They're enthusiastic about teaching, dedicated to academic advancement, and committed to their subject matter. Teachers are **very concerned about developing the 'whole woman.'**"

Q "I find the classes in my major to be interesting. Some of the other core classes that are outside the rest of my life don't really apply. My teachers seem to be passionate, so **they try to make it interesting**, and that counterbalances and keeps me motivated."

Q "I would say that 90 percent of my teachers were **brilliant, warm, and caring**, and they were genuinely concerned about me as an individual."

STUDENT AUTHOR: **Spelman is academically sound, and not only because of its well-known and published professors or the recognition it receives in the press. All students are challenged to take on both group and individual projects meant to expand their knowledge, as well as enhance their approach to problem solving. Spelman has always had a strong reputation as a liberal arts college. In recent years, the college has widened that reputation to include the sciences.**

Students Speak Out
ON LOCAL ATMOSPHERE

Q "For sports, there are major arenas, leagues, and constant activities. For arts, there are **museums, festivals, theaters, galleries, and classes**. For food, there are plenty of restaurants that will satisfy any taste bud. Shopping malls, delectable restaurants, and clubs are located throughout the area. If you need a break from the city life, the suburbs offer great getaways, with spas, retreat centers, and hotels."

Q "**Atlanta has a very vibrant party atmosphere** that will quickly encompass your life. Luckily, by sophomore year, you will realize that every party is basically the same, with the same people doing the same things, and you don't have to go to the club every time its doors open."

Q "Atlanta is **a black mecca in terms of education and opportunity**. It's also home to many historic sites, including the archives at the Auburn Avenue Library, the history center, and the national registry near the capital that holds documentation of births and deaths back through the days of slavery."

STUDENT AUTHOR: **Atlanta, lovingly known as HotLanta, is one of the fastest growing cities in the South. Attending Spelman College provides an opportunity to experience the small community setting nestled within the gates, as well a chance to venture out and explore all that Atlanta has to offer. You'll find the people in Atlanta to be friendly and inviting. Nothing beats Southern hospitality, and there is enough to go around in this town.**

5 Best Things	5 Worst Things
1 Homecoming	**1** Parking sucks!
2 Unique traditions	**2** Controlled male visitation
3 Market Friday	**3** Convocation
4 The Grill	**4** Read Hall gym
5 Freshman Week	**5** Crowded computer labs

Students Speak Out
ON FACILITIES

Q "In recent years, **campus buildings have been upgraded** to remain competitive with larger universities; however, the beauty lies in the fact that the new construction blends beautifully with the historic structures, like Giles & Packard."

Q "Depending on the building you're in, the facilities are older, yet functional. The student center is evolving. It's not as large as other campuses', and it could have more things for students to do besides watching TV. The gym is really dated and small. For a women's college that promotes healthy living, **I'm surprised that there isn't a larger gym**. We go over to Morehouse to use their student center and gym. It's huge!"

Q "**The student center (Lower Manley) is the place to be** to find out what events are going on, to connect with friends, to meet up with visitors from other campuses, to play pool, and to get some good food. The indoor part of the center is on the floor under the cafeteria, and then there is an outside area where Market Friday is held. This is when local vendors come to offer their services and products."

STUDENT AUTHOR: On the campus of a college that was founded over 100 years ago, you should expect some older, smaller buildings, but the facilities on Spelman's campus are mixed when it comes to design and modern amenities. Students complain most about the gym. Spelman is a work in progress, and students can expect that there will be more renovations to come to make the campus competitive with other schools.

Famous Alumnae

LaTanya Richardson Jackson, Shaun Robinson, Rolanda Watts, Keisha Knight-Pulliam, Danica Tisdale, Sherri A. McGee, Iris Little Thomas

Students Speak Out
ON CAMPUS DINING

Q "**The cafeteria sucks**. We have good days. Wednesday is fried chicken day, and it is crowded so get there early. In addition to the cafeteria menu, a woman makes fresh pasta to order and another prepares vegetarian. You can specify what you want in the order; for example, 'no onions.' The pasta line and vegetarian line won't let you down."

Q "I haven't eaten in the caf since my freshman year. **It doesn't look very good**. The Grill is good, it's just kind of overpriced."

Q "**Food on campus is really not that great**. There is one dining hall and one grill/fast food place. The food could really use improvement."

Q "As far as the main dining hall, I never really ate there much, except for freshman year because I was forced to live on campus. **The dining hall is okay, but the Grill is better**. They serve hamburgers. More people eat there than in the actual cafeteria. They have wings, smoothies, and those types of things."

STUDENT AUTHOR: The Spelman meal plan is included in your tuition, and your ID card gives you access and is preloaded with $25 for the the Grill. After that, you have to stock up the card on your own. It seems like the highlights of the week for most students are fried fish Friday, fried chicken Wednesday, and the Spelman Sunday brunch. Other than that, students don't have much to say about eating on campus. It is safe to say that perhaps this is not one of the strong points of the College.

Student Body

African American:	92%	Male/Female:	1/99%
Asian American:	<1%	Out-of-State:	77%
Hispanic:	<1%	International:	2%
Native American:	<1%	Unknown:	1%
White:	<1%		

Popular Faiths: Christianity is popular, as well as Islam.

Gay Pride: The lesbian community on Spelman's campus is supported, and the organization Afrakete provides support and a "safe space" for gay, bisexual, and transgender students.

Economic Status: Spelman has students from all socioeconomic backgrounds.

Students Speak Out
ON DORMS

Q "The **dorm rooms are mostly small**, and most have no air conditioning. LLCI and LLCII have air, but the rooms are still small."

Q "The **memories are more important** than the dorm you choose."

Q "Of course you have your 'no air' issue, but we all come to Spelman expecting that. The dorm rooms are extremely small everywhere, so it is hard to feel at home when you feel like you are in a closet. **They do their best to make you feel like you are in a family environment**. I suggest LLCI and LLCII because they are air-conditioned. In the older dorms, like Morehouse James, the rooms are bigger. You have to decide what to sacrifice, space or air."

STUDENT AUTHOR: **For first-year students at Spelman, living on campus is mandatory. The best dorm for you will depend on your personality. Front doors are locked in each dorm late at night and visitation, specifically male guests, is only allowed during certain hours. Overall, living conditions on campus are decent. The dorms are very conducive to studying and provide a safe and quiet environment.**

Did You Know?
43% of undergrads live on campus.

Students Speak Out
ON GUYS & GIRLS

Q "Being in the AUC was a unique experience because **I got to meet a ton of different guys** from different backgrounds with differing goals. The dating scene can be intense because of the close proximity of the schools and occurrences of conflicts over relationships. But the guys are great as friends and for networking. In general, the student bodies in the local schools are intelligent, fun, and easy to get along with. Students got together for fun and for studying."

Q "The guys are pretty attractive at other schools. At Spelman, **a lot of our male interaction is with Morehouse men**, and while there are a lot of cute guys, due to the small size of our schools, you tend to see the same eligible guys all the time."

STUDENT AUTHOR: **The dating scene on Spelman and in the surrounding Atlanta University Center is always full of surprises. The consensus seems to be that guys and girls are nice, but anyone can be up to no good. Spelman, as well as the other schools in the AUC, advocate safe sex and provide students with information and contraception. There seems to be no short supply of attractive, eligible, and ambitious bachelors.**

Traditions

Ivy Oration
This is a speech given by the senior class valedictorian during Class Day, two days before graduation.

Spelman Hymn
The hymn is sung at the conclusion of many significant events on campus.

Overall School Spirit
School spirit is high, primarily during special events like Homecoming, Founders Week, Freshman Week, or graduation. You will always see students wearing Spelman paraphernalia.

Students Speak Out
ON ATHLETICS

Q "**Varsity sports are not such a big deal**. We attend all of Morehouse's football and basketball games for entertainment and to see people."

Q "**IM sports are nonexistent**. Varsity sports don't get much support at all. The good athletes don't come, nor those who really have a love for sports. That area needs improvement. The facilities aren't what they should be."

Q "There isn't a great emphasis on sports, which is kind of sad because some people come looking for sports activities. Spelman is working hard to put more spotlight on the sports scene. In the past, **this just hasn't been a big thing at Spelman**."

STUDENT AUTHOR: **Athletics is second to academics at Spelman, which some might argue is a good thing. However, there are many students who believe more emphasis and support should be given to sports programs. It seems as if there are some ad hoc IM and club sports that go on through smaller groups, but for the most part, even with the recent promotion to Division III, the school has a long way to go in the athletic department.**

Students Speak Out
ON DRUG SCENE

Q "Drugs are easy to obtain and easy to avoid, it all **depends on where you go and whom you decide to hang out with**."

Q "**Spelman is pretty strict with any violation**, so the use of drugs would be too much of a gamble. You can't even smoke cigarettes out in the open at school. Now, off campus, there is probably more drug use because there is more privacy, but I honestly didn't see too much of that."

Q "**Drugs are everywhere in the world**, but not too much was available at Spelman, outside of weed, and that wasn't often."

STUDENT AUTHOR: **The drug scene outside of some who smoke marijuana or drink liquor and beer is seemingly nonexistent. Most of the drinking amongst Spelman students takes place during key events, such as Greek Week, Senior Week, Homecoming, and graduation weekend. Spelman seems to be a relatively drug-free campus with only certain students who participate in the heavy drug and alcohol scene.**

12:1	Student-to-Faculty Ratio
89%	Freshman Retention Rate
65%	Four-Year Graduation Rate
87%	Financial Aid Applicants Receiving Aid

Students Speak Out
SAFETY & SECURITY

Q "I felt very secure on campus, and I even feel like our Public Safety on campus tries to help us off campus. What I mean by that is they will be posted by the MARTA or down the street. They also have **self-defense classes to make sure we are prepared**."

Q "It is handled well. The gate is protected. I feel secure on campus. There were times I had to stay overnight to finish an art piece, and **I always felt safe**."

Q "Spelman is guarded by the Spelman College Public Safety office. **Security is tight**, and Spelman is gated. Men can visit dorms and dorm rooms, but must be off campus by midnight. Spelman dorms lock after midnight, but Spelman women can come and go as they like."

STUDENT AUTHOR: **Spelman takes on-campus security very seriously. Spelman has set visitation hours in the dorms specifically for males. This decreases the likelihood of non-Spelman students wandering the grounds after hours. You won't find too many campuses safer than Spelman College.**

> **Questions?**
> For more inside information and survival tips, pick up College Prowler's full-length book on this school, written by an actual student! Check it out at *www.collegeprowler.com*.

Students Speak Out
ON OVERALL EXPERIENCE

Q "Overall, the Spelman experience, which included academics as well as extracurricular activities, **helped prepare me to face the challenges of the real world**. Oftentimes, it had me juggling far more projects than the average person could manage."

Q "Attending Spelman was **one of the best decisions that I ever made**."

Q "I love Spelman. It has been a wonderful experience. I was nervous coming to an all-girls school because of females and drama. It is the first place **I have had the opportunity to form real friendships**. It's been great."

Q "I wouldn't go anywhere else. **It is very diverse, even though it was all women**. I got to do a lot more than what I would have done up North. You have three other schools that you can take classes in."

STUDENT AUTHOR: **Spelman students generally embrace both the good and the bad elements of their college experience and emerge with a positive overall view. The sisterhood, challenges, and nurturing environment are aspects of their time at Spelman that they cherish the most. Spelman is seen as a journey into womanhood for many young ladies. It is also an opportunity for many students to meet other women of color like themselves, for the first time in their lives. Spelman brings together a plethora of women who might not otherwise have met or ever discovered the common bonds they share. Academically, Spelman ranks high and has been recognized in the media for producing successful women who go on to be recognized in all fields of study, industry, and business.**

St. John's University

8000 Utopia Parkway; Jamaica, NY 11439
(718) 990-2000; www.stjohns.edu

THE BASICS:

Acceptance Rate: 56%   **SAT Range:** 960–1180
Setting: Urban   **Control:** Private
F-T Undergrads: 11,763   **Tuition:** $28,100

Most Popular Majors: Communication, Finance,
Computer Sciences, Criminal Justice, Psychology

*of 1600

Academics	B-	Guys	C
Local Atmosphere	B+	Girls	C+
Safety & Security	C+	Athletics	B
Computers	D+	Nightlife	A-
Facilities	C	Greek Life	C
Campus Dining	C	Drug Scene	C+
Off-Campus Dining	B	Campus Strictness	B
Campus Housing	D	Parking	C
Off-Campus Housing	C-	Transportation	A
Diversity	A	Weather	B-

Students Speak Out
ON ACADEMICS

Q "Not only are the teachers knowledgeable, but they **make the classes interesting**, and they want to help all of their students as much as possible. Many of the teachers go out of their way to help the students learn so they can pass and be prepared for their intended majors."

Q "There is absolutely **no flexibility in choosing your courses**. I can understand as a freshman they start off the students by choosing their required classes, but I notice as an upperclassman, even, when you are choosing your own classes, you still have to go by their required curriculum."

Q "My professors seem to make things very hard for us by **giving us lots of work**. However, they never seem to teach me what I really need to know. Most of what I learn just seems like unnecessary knowledge and wasted time."

Q "There are **some really good teachers**; the curriculum is not challenging at all, though. Most of the classes you can easily pass by just showing up and handing in your assignments; they don't even need to be on time."

STUDENT AUTHOR: St. John's mission through its academic program is to implant a rewarding education to individuals wishing to succeed in all aspects life. Many areas of study, which include more than 100 majors, are designed to prepare students for the future, while focusing on a highly dynamic, increasingly global society. The good thing about St. John's is the abundance of coursework assistance.

Students Speak Out
ON LOCAL ATMOSPHERE

Q "It's a good area with a **residential setting and an urban feel**. For the majority of the time, it is quiet, but when you come off campus, just a few miles down, especially in Jamaica, it is more noisy."

Q "It is a nice area, not too big and busy, but **near transportation** and all the necessities."

Q "At St. John's, we are lucky that we are **so close to Manhattan**. There is just so much for students to do and see. It provides a very unique experience, especially for those students that are not from the city. The diversity alone gives ways to learn new things, such as food and culture."

Q "It is a more homey environment than my old school, which was in Manhattan. I felt lost and [like I was] just another student, but here at St. John's, the **community is really tight knit**, where people are out to help you around here."

STUDENT AUTHOR: St. John's is located in the Jamaica Estates, which is a development designed as a residential park. It is a nice mixture of an abundance of homes, but at the same time, there are many stores that help to cater to the student's needs. Even though the campus isn't in Manhattan, it's hard to escape the hustle and bustle of city life. Crowded buses and noisy neighbors (particularly high school kids) are to be expected. On the plus side, there are so many things to do that students will rarely have to think for long to come up with something to do on a weekend. It's mostly a matter of outlook and motivation.

5 Best Things	5 Worst Things
1 Different backgrounds	1 Tuition
2 Close to Manhattan	2 Lack of campus housing
3 Student organizations	3 Computer labs
4 Public transportation	4 Parking
5 Hofstra	5 High school kids

Students Speak Out
ON FACILITIES

Q "I don't really use the facilities because most of the **athletes overcrowd them**."

Q "The **facilities are decent**, especially in the University Center; everyone has a good time, you have a variety of choices for entertainment, which include the gym or just chilling out and watching the big-screen TV."

Q "Campus is pretty nice; they are adding many new buildings and trying to **accommodate the students better**. Also, the best thing is that mostly everything is within walking distance which makes it easier for the students."

Q "Overall, I would say that the campus facilities are very nice, although there are some areas, such as the UC, that **could use renovations**."

Q "The **campus is just the right size**. All of the facilities are within walking distance, especially the dining hall and classes. This is definitely a big plus, because after classes when I just want unwind, I don't have to walk off to Guam for some enjoyment. There are also a lot of selections that I can do just to chill out without having to come off campus."

STUDENT AUTHOR: The University Center features several activities to keep students occupied and entertained. The UC gym, while crowded, is still relatively up-to-date. And updates are on the way. Some grumble that the athletic facilities are monopolized by athletes at certain hours. Other students say that a social order develops and precludes students not within the loop from partaking in the bounty of facilities at St. John's.

Famous Alumni

Hugh L. Carey, Nickolas Davatzes, Regina Dolan, Thomas J. Donohue, Susan Kropf, Patrick Purcell, Linda S. Sanford, Ian Schrager, Ron Silver

Students Speak Out
ON CAMPUS DINING

Q "I don't think the on-campus food is that good; it's **all fast food, no healthy food**. They give the best food to the Law School."

Q "The food is good; there are **four different cafeterias** and you never have to pay for anything because of the meal plan, it's great. I eat there all the time, and there is a wide selection of delicious food to choose from."

Q "It's **not as bad as everyone says**; the food is not excellent, but it is not bad at all. A lot of schools serve worse food."

Q "After a while, it is very easy to become bored with the food selections on campus, especially when you end up eating basically the same thing every day. Also, the **prices are on the high side**. I would not mind paying if the food was better, but the food selection never changes."

Q "Avoid Marillac! The **Law School Café is the best example of real food**. Marillac and the Law School Café are about the same price, but the quality of the Law School is way better."

STUDENT AUTHOR: The quality of food is supposed to be an important aspect of campus life, but it seems as though the menu selections are limited, and prices are on the steep side. Resident students have to get a meal plan and might as well make the best of it. Students should add money to their card and try not to pay with cash because that will eliminate the tax, saving money in the end. Try to mix up your meals and eat at a variety of on-campus selections.

Student Body

African American:	17%	Male/Female:	42/58%
Asian American:	15%	Out-of-State:	10%
Hispanic:	15%	International:	3%
Native American:	<1%	Unknown:	0%
White:	49%		

Popular Faiths: Fifty-three percent of students are Catholic, and 11 percent claim they are unsure.

Gay Pride: Not many gays or lesbians are open on campus. Also, there are not any clubs or organizations dedicated to them.

Economic Status: St. John's accepts all walks of life, from low-income to upper-class students. Everybody is mixed together here.

Students Speak Out
ON DORMS

Q "I lived on campus for four years and loved it. The **suites are extremely nice**. Sometimes sharing the bathroom with a lot of people was a pain, and there were a lot of rules to follow, but it was totally worth it."

Q "The dorm **situation is absolutely terrible**. First the school lures a whole lot of students here by promising housing for four years, then they recently started instituting a lottery thing where the only people guaranteed to live on campus are freshmen."

Q "It's horrible; I feel sorry for those that stay on campus. It is **not worth the money at all**, and they are basically robbing the students for the amount they have to pay each year."

STUDENT AUTHOR: St. John's should invest more money building new dormitories. Upperclassmen have to participate in lotteries to see who will get housing. Many are on waiting lists, but in the end, are left without housing because priority goes to freshmen and out-of-state students. The dorms are set up nice and have recreation areas. The best thing is that every room has one or two bathrooms.

> **Did You Know?**
> 17% of undergrads live on campus.

Students Speak Out
ON GUYS & GIRLS

Q "The girls and guys act like they are in high school; **they are so cliquish**. The point of college is to branch out and meet new people and learn new things."

Q "I am not going to say all the guys are bad; there are some very respectful men on campus. The **girls think it is a fashion show** and sit there just to criticize others."

Q "The **guys are crazy** on campus."

Q "Most **students here are very immature**; they don't do work, and they act like they do not want to be here. This is a distraction to those that want to be here and are paying their money to come."

STUDENT AUTHOR: The biggest complaint from both guys and girls on members of the opposite sex is that they act like they are still in high school. The guys feel they can have all the girls on campus, and the girls take school as a fashion show. Also, gossip seems to run rampant. Finding a serious relationship at St. John's can, at times, be hard, but it's not impossible. Finding a weekend hookup is significantly easier.

> **Traditions**
>
> **Red Storm Volunteers**
> Athletes volunteer service to school kids. When not playing hard on the field or court, many of them assist as tutors in elementary classrooms throughout the tri-state.
>
> **Overall School Spirit**
> School spirit is really big towards the basketball and soccer team, but it's not that big on Greek life and other events. When there is any event, even if it is a just an organization holding a picnic, there is always a crowd supporting and serving as spectators. There could be more student engagement, though.

Students Speak Out
ON ATHLETICS

Q "St. John's is **definitely a sports school**. Our basketball team has always been popular, and we have one of the best soccer teams in the nation. Also, there is always a packed stadium."

Q "I really don't keep up on the sports because it is **not as exciting as everyone makes it**."

Q "They **shouldn't have done away with the men's football** and track & field teams. I can't understand that."

Q "It's great at the games because they always **give out free stuff** like T-shirts and they always hold a raffle."

STUDENT AUTHOR: There are a wide variety of interest club sports and intramurals for those that enjoy the recreation but don't want the competition and travel. The University works hard to provide all students with opportunities to exercise and partake in recreational activities. On the national level, the Red Storm is a well-respected program. Athletics are a big thing on campus, but it is not fair that many of the sport teams are overshadowed by the popularity of the basketball and soccer team.

Students Speak Out
ON DRUG SCENE

Q "I don't understand why legal age undergraduate students can't drink, but Law School students can. That does not make any sense. They call us **a dry campus**, so that means no one should be allowed to drink on campus."

Q "Everyone knows about it, **they just turn their heads**. If you are in the dorms, you especially know the deal."

Q "**Drugs happen all the time**, and basically at every school."

STUDENT AUTHOR: Despite the fact that drugs are not a visible threat, they are definitely still done on campus. Most smoke or drink in their rooms, or at campus parties. Many drink or smoke because they feel that it is the way to have a good time or because of the stress affiliated with school. These activities are hardly done in the open, and even though many people know what is happening, it is kept on the hush. When students are sharing a room, if one roommate is caught in possession of alcohol, all the roommates are expelled.

18:1	Student-to-Faculty Ratio
79%	Freshman Retention Rate
40%	Four-Year Graduation Rate
96%	Financial Aid Applicants Receiving Aid

Students Speak Out
SAFETY & SECURITY

Q "Public Safety **officers are always around**. You can walk around freely on campus without being scared. They are always on the lookout and are very helpful in assisting at any time."

Q "The campus hired a **police force full of idiots** on power trips."

Q "Our school **doesn't have a major crime rate**, and I think it would be unfair for the school to become more strict on safety, which will discourage the students from doing a lot."

Q "I rarely ever see Public Safety, except standing by the front gates, and there is usually a group of them. They **should spread out to keep watch** of the whole campus."

STUDENT AUTHOR: St. John's Department of Public Safety maintains frequent contact with the local police. What disturbs many students is that security is not in full view, patrolling the campus, and accessible in an event that something may occur. St. John's needs to make security one of its top priorities.

> **Questions?**
> For more inside information and survival tips, pick up College Prowler's full-length book on this school, written by an actual student! Check it out at www.collegeprowler.com.

Students Speak Out
ON OVERALL EXPERIENCE

Q "I really enjoy it; it is a really good school with a good name. St. John's is **a good place to make connections** to the New York business world, so use that to your advantage. Also, take part in internships and activities; it will make so much of a difference in your college experience."

Q "I like St. John's; I just **wish the costs weren't so high** and the students weren't so childish. I don't regret going to St John's, but I wish they would get their priorities together."

Q "It's **an excellent school**; it's just too expensive, but if you can afford it, it's definitely worth it. The name alone will take you far in the workforce."

Q "I don't feel the school is all that its cracked up to be; it is **unnecessarily expensive**, and they try to get money out of people in every way. I went to this school because I got caught up by the name, but I must say, I am highly disappointed."

STUDENT AUTHOR: Some argue that with the high tuition cost, students should receive better student services and facilities. They need more dorm rooms, better computers, and better safety and security. These things are not luxuries, but rather necessities to keep the students and the institution running smoothly. Going here is a good experience, and the name itself seems to impress many people, which is a good trademark to use in the workforce. The majority of teachers care about their students and know what they are teaching. But, the costs are going up each year and the financial aid is basically staying the same, making it hard for students to attend because of the lack of funding. There's plenty to enjoy and benefit from, but don't get caught up in hype.

St. Louis University

221 North Grand Boulevard; St Louis, MO 63103
(800) 758-3678; www.slu.edu

THE BASICS:

Acceptance Rate: 80%
Setting: Urban
F-T Undergrads: 6,521

SAT Range: 1080–1320*
Control: Private
Tuition: $30,628

Most Popular Majors: Finance, Marketing, Nursing, Psychology, Communications

*of 1600

Academics	B-	Guys	B+
Local Atmosphere	B+	Girls	A-
Safety & Security	C+	Athletics	C+
Computers	B-	Nightlife	B+
Facilities	B+	Greek Life	B-
Campus Dining	B-	Drug Scene	B+
Off-Campus Dining	B+	Campus Strictness	B
Campus Housing	B-	Parking	D
Off-Campus Housing	B+	Transportation	B+
Diversity	D+	Weather	B_

Students Speak Out
ON ACADEMICS

Q "It is a Catholic, Jesuit school, but the influences are only there as much as you want them to be. So, if you want the whole religion thing, it's there. If you don't want it, it's not like it's shoved down your throat. Everyone has to take **at least one theology class**, but they are usually pretty interesting."

Q "SLU is an **outstanding school** with solid professors and a top-notch communication program (which I highly recommend). Find out the opinions of students about the professors; this way you will know who to avoid. As with any school, one sour grape can spoil the whole batch of wine."

Q "Teachers are **absolutely wonderful**! They are so helpful in whatever you need. They'll even give you their home phone numbers and e-mail addresses, so you can reach them anytime."

Q "This is a private school, so the teachers are among the **cream of the crop**. They are professionals who also work in the fields they teach, so you actually feel like they are prepping you for the real world."

STUDENT AUTHOR: SLU has very few classes that are larger than 100 students or are taught by teacher's assistants. Because of this, teachers are highly accessible outside of class, and the class atmosphere itself is more conducive to discussion rather than lecture. Teacher involvement, though, is entirely on the shoulders of the students and their willingness to interact with the professors.

Students Speak Out
ON LOCAL ATMOSPHERE

Q "I love St. Louis! It's **the best town** out there. They have everything—a great park right by SLU and a couple other colleges and universities really close by. Don't go north on Grand Boulevard past the Fox. The Arch, the zoo, Forest Park, the Fox Theatre, and the Muny are all great places to visit."

Q "SLU is a beautiful campus with lots of green space, flowers, and the whole landscaping deal. It's right in the middle of the city. You can take the Metro to downtown; it's only three miles to the Arch. The Central West End area of town, about a mile west of campus, is great, with a bunch of **coffee shops, artsy stores**, and vintage clothing and record stores."

Q "It's a city with a population of approximately 350,000 people or so. Washington University is a few miles away, and University of Missouri (in St. Louis) is about 10 miles away. **You should visit the Landing** and the Anheuser-Busch Brewery. I hear the zoo is cool here, too. You shouldn't visit the 'projects'—unless you really want to."

STUDENT AUTHOR: As far as the Midwest goes, St. Louis is a fantastic city for students. There are bohemian areas such as the Loop, bar districts like Laclede's Landing and Soulard, fine restaurants and coffee houses in the Central West End, and excellent Italian dining on the Hill. Musicals and jazz acts frequent the Midtown theatres and clubs; and for the less cultured, there is a Six Flags amusement park located about 30 minutes outside the city.

Students Speak Out
ON FACILITIES

Q "For athletic purposes, we have a recreation center with a 40-meter pool, a track (7.5 times around is a mile), and six full-court basketball courts. The **equipment is great**, with a lot of weight machines, free weights, bikes, and much more."

Q "Facilities are **really excellent**! The volleyball and basketball practice gym is nice, but old. Everything is pretty kept-up and very nice. There aren't too many crappy places on campus."

Q "The recreation center is huge; computer labs are new, and the athletic facilities are **top-notch**. Our basketball games are played downtown in the gigantic city arena where the Blues play. Shuttles run to give students a way to get there."

Q "The facilities on campus are nice and improving. There is an entirely renovated student center with a radio station, a newspaper office, cafeterias, **restaurants, a theater**, ballrooms, and offices."

Q "Our **facilities are amazing**. Simon Recreation Center is the athletic center; it's just like a YMCA. It has an Olympic-sized pool, a hot tub, locker rooms, indoor track, racquetball courts, basketball courts, a weight training area, dance and aerobic rooms to practice in, an outdoor pool with sand, and a volleyball court."

STUDENT AUTHOR: **You shouldn't come to SLU because of the facilities—while they're more than adequate for the student body, they're nothing to dazzle the eye. The present buildings and construction projects seem to fit the pocketbook of the current administration.**

Famous Alumni

Enrique Bolaños, Larry Hughes, Eugene Kranz, Brian McBride, David Merrick

Students Speak Out
ON CAMPUS DINING

Q "**Not great**, but not terrible. There is, of course, cafeteria food, along with a food court with Subway, a pizza place, an ice cream place, and a grill where you can get burgers and things like that."

Q "The cafeteria food is **pretty bad**, but the food court food is very good. The meal plan includes both. The student center has a lot of good places to eat, and Fusz Food Court is popular."

Q "The campus dining service came under a new name, Chartwells, and seems to be a **great improvement**. Good places to get food include the Busch Student Center and the Ameren Café in the business school. A quick place to get food is the Fusz Food Court."

Q "Food is not one of SLU's strengths. The dining halls are **mediocre**, and the variety of food isn't much better. "

STUDENT AUTHOR: **The food at SLU is not very good, even by cafeteria standards. Most students prefer to use their "flex points"—dollars included in most meal plans that go toward campus food courts and restaurants—rather than play "Name That Meat Product" in the dining halls. Students can also use Billiken Bucks, which is currency used throughout the school and kept on the student ID. Overall, food on campus is nothing to write home about; it may even be something to consider when you're deciding whether to live on campus after freshman year. The lack of options makes dining a weak point at SLU.**

Students Speak Out
ON DORMS

Q "If you don't mind being a block off campus, **Reinert Hall is nice**; it has the biggest rooms. It's really great! Each room has its own bathroom, and there is a cafeteria."

Q "**Stay in Griesedieck**, if you can, because it is in a central location. Fusz is good, too. I would avoid Reinert, Marguerite, or DeMattias. For upperclassmen, the Village is the best. You also have Grand Forest and Marchetti Towers; they are pretty nice."

Q "The dorm rooms are pretty nice, but **the rules suck**. As a Catholic school, they can make whatever rules they want."

STUDENT AUTHOR: **Each residence hall has its own little charm. In many cases, the housing at SLU wasn't built by the University originally—dorms include a former hotel and retirement home, among others—the rooms themselves are in good condition and have some entertainment options available for students. Even though first-year living arrangements are somewhat limited, hang in there, because as you become an upperclassman, you'll have more of a choice.**

Did You Know?
52% of undergrads live on campus.

Students Speak Out
ON GUYS & GIRLS

Q "Girls at SLU are **really cute**. There are a couple of really hot ones, but the girls tend to be just cute. As for the guys, we are a pretty attractive group. Overall, the SLU guys are great."

Q "Well, a lot of the guys are hot, and the **girls are very pretty**. If you go down the road to a party at Washington University, the guys love SLU girls (they say we are way cuter than any of their girls)."

Q "I really haven't dated anyone on campus yet. The **guys are really cute**, and I have been looking for the cutest one on campus. Every time I think I found one, I discover another guy who's even hotter!"

STUDENT AUTHOR: **The girls and guys around campus are attractive, but probably nothing that would stun an outsider. What SLU lacks in super hotties, however, it makes up for with a generally laid-back attitude. Usually, there is a girl for every guy, no matter what the physical attributes of either party. Comparatively speaking, however, the attractiveness level at SLU has other St. Louis schools beat by a long shot.**

Traditions

10 p.m. Mass
The priests realize that no student would wake up early on Sunday to go to mass, so they created the 10 p.m. mass for students to attend.

Ted Drewes Frozen Custard
Ted Drewes has been a city landmark since its inception in the 1950s.

Overall School Spirit
Students' attendance at soccer games is a national standard, which really isn't saying much, but their attendance at other events is sub-par.

Students Speak Out
ON ATHLETICS

Q "I'm not sure about intramurals, but **basketball is pretty big**, and the soccer team is great! Basketball games are lots of fun, and they are always packed."

Q "Soccer games are a big deal in the fall. A lot of people go to them, and they are **awesome to watch**. Basketball is also fairly big, but other than that, it depends on whom you ask."

Q "Varsity sports are pretty big at Saint Louis University, but men's basketball and soccer definitely dominate. There are lots of different intramural sports that one can get involved in. Intramural sports are big on campus, and it is very **easy to get involved**. You can sign up by yourself, or with a group of friends, to be in everything from water volleyball to flag football."

STUDENT AUTHOR: **In all honesty, SLU is an apathetic sports college. Students care more about the Blues, Cards, and Rams than their own SLU teams. Then again, those professional teams actually win. Yes, the soccer team is well supported, but soccer games are more of a social event than a sporting event for students.**

Students Speak Out
ON DRUG SCENE

Q "I'm not into the drug scene, but I don't think there is a big scene with drugs. I suppose drugs are present everywhere, but **I haven't seen any** here."

Q "At SLU, drugs are **not prevalent**. I know a couple people who smoke pot, but that's about it. I don't know too many who do other stuff like hard-core drugs. It's a personal choice. I don't see drugs, and it's rare that I smell pot."

Q "SLU's biggest drug problem is alcohol. **Drinking is huge** on campus. Some people smoke weed, but other than that, I don't think there is much of a drug problem on campus. Ecstasy would probably be the second most-used drug."

STUDENT AUTHOR: In SLU's urban setting, it's not all that difficult to find drugs. Be that as it may, however, the drug scene on campus is not major by any standard. The few who do choose to take drugs hardly ever venture past marijuana, or occasionally, mushrooms. Peer pressure to take drugs, however, is minimal to nonexistent.

12:1	Student-to-Faculty Ratio
87%	Freshman Retention Rate
55%	Four-Year Graduation Rate
77%	Financial Aid Applicants Receiving Aid

Students Speak Out
SAFETY & SECURITY

Q "The area is not the best, but the campus itself is **very well patrolled**. The surrounding areas are not great, but they are starting to get better—nothing changes overnight. I lived in a dorm about a block off campus. I felt that I could walk around at 3 a.m., and no one would bother me. Overall, I would say that Public Safety does a nice job in keeping the campus safe."

Q "Campus **security is great**! I have never felt unsafe at SLU during my three years, so far. The Department of Public Safety officers are all over. Being that we are located in the middle of the city, off campus is not exactly unsafe, but I wouldn't go walking around off campus (especially north of campus) alone."

STUDENT AUTHOR: Inside campus, students feel safe to roam around at all hours of the night—though it might still be a good idea to travel in groups. Problems only start when students wander off campus into the surrounding areas, which don't have the same cloak of safety that the campus does.

Questions?
For more inside information and survival tips, pick up College Prowler's full-length book on this school, written by an actual student! Check it out at *www.collegeprowler.com*.

Students Speak Out
ON OVERALL EXPERIENCE

Q "You need to **live on campus or join a club**, and it doesn't necessarily have to be a frat or sorority. This was the biggest mistake I made because I only got to know a few people all four years I went there. I think if I had become more involved, I would have had a fuller education. Also, when you come, you need to forget the tour of the campus, or at least put it off as the last thing you do."

Q "I like it here. It's an **excellent school**, and it's well worth the cost. You get so much out of Saint Louis University. The academics, the activities, and the people all contribute to a great experience."

Q "My overall experience has been **wonderful**. This school has definitely worked out for me. I enjoy the program of study I am in, and I have met many amazing friends."

Q "I know people who hate the school, and I know people who love it. **I would not go anywhere else**. I'm one of those who love it! I think it is an awesome school, and it is beautiful. It also is a good education. So, I hope no matter where you go, you feel the same way."

STUDENT AUTHOR: SLU gets largely positive reviews from students, and few have complaints about the academics or the campus itself. It's certainly safe to say that no one attends for the cheap tuition, so the size of the student body speaks for itself. Above all else, however, it's important to understand that you get out what you put in at SLU. Of course, this can be said for any college, but given the large commuter population at St. Louis, it's especially applicable here.

St. Olaf College

1520 St. Olaf Avenue; Northfield, MN 55057
(507) 786-2222; www.stolaf.edu

THE BASICS:

Acceptance Rate: 59%
Setting: Rural
F-T Undergrads: 3,016

SAT Range: 1760–2090*
Control: Private
Tuition: $35,500

Most Popular Majors: Biological/Life Sciences, Social Sciences, Visual/Performing Arts, English

*of 2400

Academics	A	Guys	B+
Local Atmosphere	B	Girls	A+
Safety & Security	A-	Athletics	C
Computers	B+	Nightlife	C
Facilities	A	Greek Life	N/A
Campus Dining	A	Drug Scene	B+
Off-Campus Dining	A-	Campus Strictness	C+
Campus Housing	B+	Parking	C
Off-Campus Housing	C	Transportation	B-
Diversity	D-	Weather	C-

Students Speak Out
ON ACADEMICS

Q "The professors at St. Olaf are unique in that they, from the first day, make a conscious effort to get to know the students on an individual and personal basis. **The profs are also very accessible**."

Q "The teachers are generally brilliant and very accessible to students seeking out academic or personal support. **My classes have been insightful and challenging** to the appropriate degree."

Q "**Professors at Olaf are freakishly accessible**. For the most part, they all seem to be passionate not only about their subject and students but about the school and the St. Olaf community."

Q "At Olaf, **you are a name instead of a number**. Your questions are answered by your professor instead of a teacher's assistant."

STUDENT AUTHOR: **The professors are the most notable element of St. Olaf's academics. They are all, for the most part, extremely accessible, personable, and caring. They exhibit a genuine passion for their respective subjects and for teaching undergraduate students. St. Olaf is proud to be a school, not a research facility. The fact that Olaf is an undergraduate-only institution ensures that no professors are forced into introductory courses when they would rather be working with graduate students. It also means that all courses will be taught by professors and not TAs or graduate students. One thing you can count on is that, over four years, every student will have taken plenty of truly challenging classes.**

Students Speak Out
ON LOCAL ATMOSPHERE

Q "Northfield is very gentle, safe, and comfortable. **Parts of it have a small-town charm** that would probably be dissatisfying for an individual hoping for a lot of partying or city action."

Q "I admit that we Oles don't get off campus enough, but Northfield has a great downtown. **They've managed to keep the chains out for the most part**, so there are lots of interesting local restaurants and shops."

Q "Northfield is a small town with a small-town feel. With Carleton College just a few minutes a way, **many of the local coffee houses and restaurants are shared between the two colleges**."

Q "**Northfield is an academic town that smells like Malt-O-Meal** or the Cannon River, depending on the day."

STUDENT AUTHOR: **Northfield, Minn., is an unusual town. It's about a 35-minute drive away from Minneapolis, so all the amenities of cosmopolitan urbanity are accessible but never an unwelcomed distraction. Do not get the impression, however, that Northfield is some sparse little cow town. The warmly welcomed presence of two nationally ranked private liberal arts schools sets this rural Minnesota city far apart from its kin. After all, it is not every small town that boasts a yoga studio, Zen center, and arts guild. Northfield can be briefly summed up as quaint, but in a hip way.**

Students Speak Out
ON FACILITIES

Q "The campus is beautiful. **All the facilities are very nice**, like the new athletic center and student center."

Q "**Oh gosh, we are spoiled**. Our athletic center, Tostrud, and our student center, Buntrock, are beautifully designed buildings that we all enjoy."

Q "Buntrock Commons was just built a few years ago. **It's a top-notch facility**. My main complaint is that there aren't as many practice rooms in the music building as there ought to be."

Q "Skoglund and Tostrud, the athletic centers, are incredibly nice with great gyms, several weight rooms, a pool, a great rock wall, an indoor track, and tennis courts. The student center is nice, too, and **there's a small student-run radio station in it**."

Q "The athletic, computer, and student centers are **the nicest I've seen anywhere in Minnesota**."

STUDENT AUTHOR: None of the buildings on campus are ridiculously old. St. Olaf has a tendency to demolish or totally revamp its more ancient facilities—except for Old Main, which was the first building erected on campus. St. Olaf's two most recent building projects, Tostrud Athletic Center and Buntrock Commons, are truly the gems of the campus. Buntrock is the epicenter of student activity. The building is truly beautiful inside and out, but it can get a little bit crowded between afternoon classes when everyone heads to lunch. Incoming first-years can look forward to the completion of Olaf's next big building project, a new science center.

Famous Alumni

Nancy J. Anderson, Dr. Jennifer Thompson Braaten, Gary M. Christensen, Arlen Erdahl, Ambassador Robert A. Flaten, Gretchen Morgenson, Barry Morrow

Students Speak Out
ON CAMPUS DINING

Q "It's not home cooking or fine dining, but **it's better than typical cafeteria food**."

Q "**Food on campus is actually really good**! Stav Hall provides a wide range of options, and the school-run Cage makes some awesome chicken tenders. The Lion's Pause is student-operated, and they make really good, really cheap pizzas."

Q "**The Caf food is of high quality**, but it can get monotonous after a while."

Q "We just have one cafeteria, Stav Hall. **It's ranked as one of the best college food services in the nation**. The other college I applied to when I was a prospective student had terrible food—definitely not the case with St. Olaf."

Q "On-campus dining tastes very good, and it offers a tremendous variety for people with various meal limitations. **The dining hall itself is beautiful with vaulted wooden ceilings**. There are also always flowers on the tables."

STUDENT AUTHOR: With more than 90 percent of students living on campus all four years, St. Olaf is a very residential campus. School policy dictates that living on campus means having a meal plan. To those unfamiliar with the school, that probably sounds awful, but the St. Olaf cafeteria was actually ranked ninth in the nation for college food, so it isn't nearly as bad as you may think. There is only one cafeteria on campus, and it can get pretty crowded. But what the Caf lacks in elbow room, it more than makes up for in quality.

Students Speak Out
ON DORMS

Q "The dorms in general are larger than those of public campuses. St. Olaf is also unique in that **students are encouraged to stay on campus all four years**, creating a close community within the campus."

Q "All the dorms are relatively nice, and **each has its own personality**, so choosing the best dorm depends on your individual taste."

Q "**The dorms are always immaculately clean**. Most people enjoy whatever dorm they are in."

STUDENT AUTHOR: **Because the school is almost exclusively residential, dorm life is central to the St. Olaf experience. Through all four years, students will maintain loyalty to their first-year dorm. Although all the dorms offer all the typical amenities and are well maintained and cleaned, your options for on-campus housing are terribly limited. If you really want something different from dorms but still on-campus, you can opt to live in an honor or foreign-language house. Honor houses offer an almost frat/sorority house-like atmosphere, but you have to develop an ongoing service project in order to live in one.**

> **Did You Know?**
> 96% of undergrads live on campus.

Students Speak Out
ON GUYS & GIRLS

Q "**Students at Olaf are gorgeous**, and they're pretty intense when it comes to relationships—you're either single or deeply committed."

Q "The guys are okay, and they have their pick of the girls. **As a girl, it is frustrating to look for a guy**—they are either gay, unattractive, or already have a girlfriend."

Q "It is a very attractive campus, but **the dating scene is pretty lame**."

Q "The girls are hot! Never again in your life will you be surrounded by so many attractive and intelligent females. **As a guy, you will be in heaven**."

STUDENT AUTHOR: **St. Olaf certainly has its fair share of attractive and eligible young guys and girls. Heterosexual gentlemen take note: There are more women than men. However, despite what some uninformed students may say, the ratio is definitely not two girls for every guy. Sorry kids, but it is common knowledge that Oles don't know how to casually date one another. Why this is so remains a mystery.**

> **Traditions**
>
> **Midnight Breakfast**
> Each semester before finals, Stav Hall fires up the stoves at 11:30 p.m. and offers eggs, bacon, hash browns, and other breakfast fares to late-night crammers.
>
> **President's Ball**
> This annual dance provides students the opportunity to get all gussied up and dance the night away.
>
> **Overall School Spirit**
> Just as everyone's a little bit Irish on St. Patrick's Day, so is everyone a little bit Norwegian when they attend St. Olaf.

Students Speak Out
ON ATHLETICS

Q "**Sports on campus serve to strengthen camaraderie and athleticism** more than to actually promote school spirit. If you want to go somewhere with record student turnouts, check out a music group's event."

Q "**IM sports are huge** at St. Olaf."

Q "Sports on campus are not really anything big varsity-wise. Aside from the standards, **kickball and dodgeball are fun intramurals**."

Q "I definitely noticed a **lack of concern for varsity sports at St. Olaf**."

STUDENT AUTHOR: **The average Ole is more likely to attend a choir concert than a football game. Some people love this fact, and some people hate it, but like it or not, it's the truth. Varsity and intercollegiate sports are not paid much attention by the student body. Even though the games are all played off campus, hockey seems to be the sport that students are most likely to get excited about. Intramural sports, however, are huge—around 60 percent of students participate.**

Students Speak Out
ON DRUG SCENE

Q "There is a small drug scene on campus. **Marijuana is semi-prevalent** with other harder drugs less so."

Q "**There are drugs on campus for anyone who is interested**, but some of the harder drugs that have made it to other campuses are not yet at St. Olaf."

Q "**It's pretty hush-hush, but access to drugs is fairly easy**. Apparently, Northfield is one of the easiest places to get drugs. Ask around."

STUDENT AUTHOR: **Most Olaf students are not into drugs, and this is even truer if we're talking about drugs more serious than marijuana. However, if you are into drugs, you'll be able to find friends on campus who feel the same, and you'll be able to find drugs, too. The drug scene is not an obvious presence. Some students don't even know it exists, but it does, and finding out how to be a part of it is not difficult. Overall, however, the drug scene is not a major part of life at St. Olaf unless you choose to become a committed affiliate.**

13:1	Student-to-Faculty Ratio
92%	Freshman Retention Rate
83%	Four-Year Graduation Rate
76%	Financial Aid Applicants Receiving Aid

Students Speak Out
SAFETY & SECURITY

Q "**The close-knit St. Olaf community breeds an extremely safe campus**. We don't even have locks on our P.O. boxes!"

Q "**I've always felt safe**. There are lights and walking paths everywhere, and public safety is only a phone call away for a safe ride to a nearby dorm."

Q "Public safety officers drive around regularly in their Jeeps, although they never seem to be doing anything except issuing parking tickets. **St. Olaf is an extremely trusting campus**—students tend to leave their personal belongings in open, public areas with the confidence that they will be safe."

STUDENT AUTHOR: **St. Olaf is an extraordinarily safe place. Students usually feel comfortable leaving their doors unlocked. When you head to the cafeteria, you're likely to see piles of student backpacks, and even computer bags, left unguarded without any worry. Of course, there are occasional incidents.**

Questions?
For more inside information and survival tips, pick up College Prowler's full-length book on this school, written by an actual student! Check it out at *www.collegeprowler.com*.

Students Speak Out
ON OVERALL EXPERIENCE

Q "**Olaf has been a delightful experience that has allowed for me to grow as a person**. It really fosters your ability to be a leader and to find out what you can excel at. As much as I love the quaintness of St. Olaf, I do miss the hubbub of the city."

Q "Sometimes I do wish I were somewhere else, but the whole college choice thing is mostly a wash anyway. **It doesn't really matter where you go, just what you bring with you**."

Q "If you are looking at liberal arts schools, definitely consider St. Olaf. **I really look forward to my next three years at St. Olaf**."

Q "St. Olaf is an incredible place with hundreds of resources at each student's fingertips. There is much opportunity to grow for students who pursue it, and the campus is beautiful. The faculty and abroad experiences I've had at St. Olaf have taught me to think in a critical new way, which **allows me to see and understand the complexities of life** and the world in a way I could have never learned to anywhere else."

STUDENT AUTHOR: **It's not uncommon at St. Olaf to run into second-, third-, or even fourth-generation Oles. This fact, coupled with the school's outstanding 94 percent retention rate, shows that there is something that keeps drawing students, alumni, and their children back to the Hill. Despite the long winters, the course work, and the stress of life in general, campus is an extraordinary place to be—and it shows. The school makes a point of nurturing the entire individual. You are seen as a person who needs a social and spiritual life in addition to a scholarly one. Olaf truly is a healthy place to be.**

Stanford University

450 Serra Mall; Stanford, CA 94305
(650) 723-2300; www.stanford.edu

THE BASICS:

Acceptance Rate: 9%
Setting: Suburban
F-T Undergrads: 6,504

SAT Range: 2000–2300*
Control: Private
Tuition: $36,030

Most Popular Majors: Social Sciences, Interdisciplinary Studies, Engineering, Biological/Life Sciences

*of 2400

Academics	A+	Guys	B
Local Atmosphere	B-	Girls	C+
Safety & Security	A	Athletics	A
Computers	A	Nightlife	B
Facilities	B+	Greek Life	B-
Campus Dining	B+	Drug Scene	B+
Off-Campus Dining	A	Campus Strictness	A-
Campus Housing	B-	Parking	B
Off-Campus Housing	D-	Transportation	B
Diversity	A+	Weather	A

Students Speak Out
ON ACADEMICS

Q "**The professors here are excellent**. The personal attention you receive from your professors—all of whom are among the best in their field—is unbelievable."

Q "In my experience, professors really want students to come to their office. **They like talking to the undergraduates**. Most dorms have 'faculty nights,' where everyone can invite professors to come have a nicer-than-usual dinner."

Q "The information that my professors presented was fascinating. The professors here at Stanford are **some of the best in the world**, and not only are they the top minds in their fields, they also know how to teach in a way that is comprehensible to a beginner."

Q "To be honest, I didn't really feel like I had a good relationship with a professor until senior year. When you start out as a freshman, you have to take a lot of large lecture classes with sections and TAs. Those classes tend to feel a lot more competitive, and it's **easier to get lost in the crowd** if you're not the most vocal student."

STUDENT AUTHOR: **Most Stanford students are quite pleased with their academic experiences. Professors are highly accessible, and truly make an effort to get to know undergraduates. Some students may feel that their introductory classes are too large, or poorly designed, but the overwhelming sentiment is that the education you get here truly is first-rate.**

Students Speak Out
ON LOCAL ATMOSPHERE

Q "There are some great restaurants off campus, but most of them are **quite pricey**. There are a few bars, but I haven't found a single good dance spot. I go to 'Frisco' to party."

Q "Palo Alto is a **small, upscale town**. Mountain View, to the south, is more of a 'normal' town area, and Atherton, to the north, is one of the most exclusive, blue-blood places in the nation. There's not much to see off campus until you get to San Jose and Silicon Valley, which are about 20 minutes to the south, or 'the city,' which is about 40 minutes to the north. Be forewarned that rush hour travel is terrible here, but that affects very few students because the majority lives on campus."

Q "**Palo Alto is definitely not a college town**! There is a dire shortage of 24-hour places, although more stores are gradually extending their hours. There is a plethora of good restaurants on University Avenue, but they are by no means cheap. Shopping at Stanford Shopping Center is pricey, too. In other words, Palo Alto is an affluent town, and the shops cater to residents, not to college students. You'll have to go to Berkeley to get a college-town feel."

STUDENT AUTHOR: **Students are happy with the food offerings and the safety of Palo Alto but don't think of it as a college town. Campus is large and isolated, so you either need access to a car or the patience to endure public transportation in order to explore.**

5 Best Things	5 Worst Things
1 The weather	**1** Stringent administration
2 Beautiful campus	**2** Palo Alto
3 San Francisco	**3** Egomaniacs
4 Excellent professors	**4** Cost of living/tuition
5 Great parties	**5** All-nighters

Students Speak Out
ON FACILITIES

Q "The facilities here are awesome. The gyms are nice, and so are the computer labs. It's a private school, so there is **nice stuff pretty much everywhere**."

Q "As far as athletic facilities are concerned, we have a couple of small gyms. I hear that the Arrillaga Gym is pretty good, but I've never been there, and most of the time, its use is **restricted to our athletes**. The student center flat-out sucks, especially compared to Berkeley or UCLA."

Q "The only thing that we don't have on campus is **a real student union** where everybody can hang out."

Q "Every summer they build something new. Most people say this is one of the **nation's prettiest campuses**."

Q "The facilities on campus are generally newer and very well maintained. All that tuition money has to go somewhere, doesn't it? The 'student union' is **something of a disappointment**. The available food there isn't the greatest, and amenities like an arcade or a bowling alley are completely absent."

STUDENT AUTHOR: **Students are pleased with computer clusters, labs, and libraries—all provide a good venue for studying and getting work done. However, students are unified in their distaste for the current student union, Tresidder. Most think there are some reasonable options for working out on campus. Some, however, think that these facilities are overly crowded, or don't have convenient hours.**

Famous Alumni

Steve Ballmer, Sergey Brin, Lawrence Page, Sandra Day O'Connor, John Elway, Herbert Hoover, Ted Koppel, Sally Ride, Sigourney Weaver, Tiger Woods

Students Speak Out
ON CAMPUS DINING

Q "There's good food at the dorms. **The smaller houses have better food** and fully stocked public kitchens. Restaurants in Palo Alto are fairly good, but some are expensive."

Q "The food on campus isn't very good. However, when you come to campus for freshman orientation, **they give you a listing of all the off-campus eating places**, and almost all of them are good."

Q "**The dining halls here are above-average**, but their fare gets repetitive after a while. There are a lot of good little places on campus, but no chain restaurants."

Q "I'm not a picky eater, so I think that all the food is okay. I definitely like some places more than others, but since **most of the dining halls have been revamped** within the last few years, they're all pretty good."

Q "Dorm food is pretty good, but it depends on where you live. Some dorms have better food than others, but **none of the food is so bad that it will kill you**. There is a Mexican restaurant and a coffeehouse on campus that are alternatives to the dorm food. I don't complain about the food, although I do try to go off campus for a meal once a week, just for a change from dorm food."

STUDENT AUTHOR: **Anyone can get tired of the dining hall after several months of it, but there are ways to keep it interesting. Try some different sandwiches at lunch, or go out with some friends instead.**

Student Body

African American:	10%	Male/Female:	51/49%
Asian American:	23%	Out-of-State:	58%
Hispanic:	12%	International:	7%
Native American:	3%	Unknown:	7%
White:	38%		

Popular Faiths: Most are Christians (Protestants and Catholics), and Judaism is also popular.

Gay Pride: There are many gay students on campus and their presence is very visible. There are gay parties and an unofficial gay co-op.

Economic Status: There are some students from lower-class backgrounds, but most are fairly wealthy.

Students Speak Out
ON DORMS

Q "The dorms here are **generally nicer than the dorms at most other universities**. You can't avoid living in any particular dorm because you'll be a freshman, and freshmen are randomly placed into dormitories."

Q "As a freshman, **I would recommend that you opt for an all-freshman dorm** because you get to know the most people that way, and it will also be more fun. I probably wouldn't do SLE (Structured Liberal Education) because you'll have a lot more work than the other freshmen."

Q "All the dorms are okay, but **avoid four-class dorms if you want a really social atmosphere** as a freshman. Conversely, if you are planning on getting some serious studying done freshman year, avoid all-freshman dorms, especially Branner."

STUDENT AUTHOR: **Stanford definitely has one of the most diverse housing systems of any university, and there's a large disparity between the qualities of different options. Some students live in crowded one-room triples and have mediocre food, while others live in singles and have a house chef.**

Did You Know?
89% of undergrads live on campus.

Students Speak Out
ON GUYS & GIRLS

Q "The consensus seems to be that Stanford guys are pretty good-looking, and **Stanford girls are not**."

Q "I have a lot of attractive guy friends, and a lot of people have also made this observation. A lot of the girls complain that **the guys don't take the initiative**. It's kind of hard to date here, but plenty of people do."

Q "Most people are attractive, though **it is a very academically-oriented school**."

Q "Don't come here for the girls. Stay here long enough and your standards will take a nosedive, also known as getting '**Stanford glasses**.'"

STUDENT AUTHOR: **The level of attractiveness at Stanford is definitely up for debate. A lot of students, particularly the male ones, will express the controversial opinion that at Stanford the guys are hot, and the girls are not. Most of the students were nerds in high school, and the ineptness in the social scene has, not surprisingly, carried over into higher education.**

Traditions

Full Moon on the Quad
At the first full moon, freshman females and senior males come out onto the Quad and kiss at midnight.

Big Game
The week of the annual football game between Stanford and Berkeley marked by rallies and pranks.

Overall School Spirit
Your average Stanford student is a walking advertisement for the University. Expect a bit of cynicism around midterms and finals, but otherwise students are overwhelmingly excited about the University.

Students Speak Out
ON ATHLETICS

Q "Varsity and IM sports are both pretty big here, but **varsity sports are particularly big**. My family and friends are local, so I'm off campus too much to participate in sports very much, but Stanford offers classes for volleyball, and many other sports (though no basketball class, to my dismay), so even if you can't play in an IM sport, you can still find athletic activities in which to take part."

Q "Varsity sports are pretty big here because we do so well in them, **especially in women's sports**. Intramural sports are also pretty big, and they are there if you want to participate in them. We have a fair amount of Olympic athletes here, and all that, which is pretty cool."

Q "We have the **best athletic program in the nation**, but most people only recognize us for our academics."

STUDENT AUTHOR: **Stanford really does have one of the nation's best overall athletic programs. Having so many athletes at Stanford adds a strange dimension to what is generally considered a academic institution. If you don't play a sport, there is no better institution at which to be a fan.**

Students Speak Out
ON DRUG SCENE

Q "I can assure you that the **presence of drugs is very limited** due to the stringent academic requirements of this school. You'd have to cross the Bay and go to Berkeley to find that sort of 'scene.'"

Q "I never notice much of a drug scene. I know **there are certain dorms that have a reputation**, or at least one dorm in particular does. But even so, I don't think it's that big."

Q "From what I can tell, hard drug use is quite rare. **Marijuana, however, is extremely common**. Within the dorms, you're not really at risk of arrest. Drinking is even more common."

STUDENT AUTHOR: **Drugs don't appear to be a major part of life at Stanford. The most popular substance used (or abused) is alcohol, and the only drug that students mention with frequency is marijuana. At a school where academics outweigh nearly every other scene, you're not likely to find many students willing to compromise their studies for a quick fix of any kind.**

6:1	Student-to-Faculty Ratio
98%	Freshman Retention Rate
79%	Four-Year Graduation Rate
85%	Financial Aid Applicants Receiving Aid

Students Speak Out
SAFETY & SECURITY

Q "Security is really good. **They have blue phones, which are conveniently located** for you to use if you ever feel unsafe. Just don't leave your bike unlocked, because it will get stolen."

Q "It's extremely safe. There are a few thefts in the dorms every year, but Stanford is **basically a self-contained community**, so it's not a big issue."

Q "I have felt so safe at Stanford. Granted, I don't walk around all the time at night in dark areas by myself, because I'll either bike or be with other people. **I've never had anything stolen**, and I never had anything bad happen to me or to a friend. Some people will leave all their books and their laptop at the library for hours while they go eat, and no one takes their stuff."

STUDENT AUTHOR: **Students are overwhelmingly satisfied with the level of campus safety. Given the huge size and isolated nature of campus, it is rare that outsiders venture here at night. The police forces do a good job of patrolling. Students feel at ease when walking or biking around late at night.**

> **Questions?**
> For more inside information and survival tips, pick up College Prowler's full-length book on this school, written by an actual student! Check it out at *www.collegeprowler.com*.

Students Speak Out
ON OVERALL EXPERIENCE

Q "I honestly can't imagine being anywhere else, but I think everyone says that about his or her school. I genuinely love Stanford, though, because it is an awe-inspiring institution, while managing to be **quirky and personal**. I wouldn't trade my experiences here for anything."

Q "**There is a misconception about Stanford** that I would like to correct. Everything you have heard about Stanford being a laid-back school is false."

Q "This is definitely the best place that I could be. It is **academically rigorous, sometimes to the point of being painful**, but there are also a lot of opportunities to have fun."

Q "Stanford gives you great opportunities. The downside to attending Stanford is that **it can feel competitive at times**, and you might feel intimidated by that. The big thing to keep in mind is that many people are so smart and study so hard that they tend to be a little weird. But I have some great friends that are very down-to-earth. I am kind of bummed about the dating scene right now because I had a few girlfriends in high school, and now that's not the case. But I am here mainly to learn, so I am happy."

STUDENT AUTHOR: **The combination of challenging academics, undergrad-oriented faculty, diverse students, beautiful weather, and a fairly social campus environment all combine to make Stanford a great four years of college. Perhaps the biggest challenge students face here is dealing with the other students, who range from hippies to hyper-competitive pre-meds. However, if you immerse yourself in it long enough, it will eventually start to feel reasonably normal.**

Stetson University

421 North Woodland Boulevard; DeLand, FL 32723
(386) 822-7100; www.stetson.edu

THE BASICS:

Acceptance Rate: 64%
Setting: Suburban
F-T Undergrads: 2,273

SAT Range: 980–1190*
Control: Private
Tuition: $27,100

Most Popular Majors: Business, Social Sciences, Visual/Performing Arts, Biology, Education

*of 1600

Academics	B	Guys	B+
Local Atmosphere	B-	Girls	B+
Safety & Security	A-	Athletics	B-
Computers	A	Nightlife	B-
Facilities	B	Greek Life	A-
Campus Dining	C-	Drug Scene	B
Off-Campus Dining	B-	Campus Strictness	C+
Campus Housing	B-	Parking	C-
Off-Campus Housing	B	Transportation	B-
Diversity	B	Weather	A

Students Speak Out
ON ACADEMICS

Q "They try to make well-rounded students, but I think that they try too hard. **There are a lot of general education requirements** that preclude me from focusing on my major and interests."

Q "The school is really easy academically, and **I feel the professors are really lacking**. I think for the money we pay, it shouldn't be an extension of high school academically and socially."

Q "**I think academics at Stetson are good, especially in the business school**, for their real-world application and experience. I appreciate the fact that they have special programs and degrees like the family business degree and the Roland-George program."

Q "You will fail at some point at this school. **All the work is set up to fail you eventually**. This makes me really think that the academics are not properly taught at certain levels."

STUDENT AUTHOR: The academics for most majors are comprehensive and taught by passionate professors. There is always a catch though. Most will find that the academics can be overwhelming, as the required amount of credits per semester is an average of 15 credit hours. The positive notes of Stetson's academics are the professors and small class sizes. The ability to receive help is easy in almost any subject and readily available at designated office hours. Overall, Stetson has impressive core professors but could use some needed improvements in a few departments.

Students Speak Out
ON LOCAL ATMOSPHERE

Q "I like downtown DeLand and all the shops. I have my favorites, but **serious shopping and clubbing is best done elsewhere**. There are malls all around for people to go to, and they are relatively close."

Q "From what I've done so far, I like the local atmosphere very much. **The little cafés and town activities that happen are really neat**."

Q "The local atmosphere has a little bit of everything. The malls nearby are especially nice since there are two good-sized ones within a 15-minute drive. **Everyone should be able to find what they want** for their shopping needs."

Q "About the local atmosphere, I have to say that **it's nice with a lot of cool small shops but not very much to do**. However, there are some local bars that students go to."

STUDENT AUTHOR: The first thing that everyone should understand is that DeLand has a limited amount of stuff to do because it is such a small town. Luckily, there are plenty of things to do elsewhere. But if anyone is planning on doing anything in town, here are some tips. At night, college student should look toward the main college hangouts. The best suggestion is to go to Orlando or Daytona for serious clubbing. There are more things to do locally during the day, when there is a variety of restaurants and little stores open. When students have a chance, they should take a drive with a friend and have fun exploring.

5 Best Things	5 Worst Things
1 Small classes	**1** Limited dining options
2 Approachable profs	**2** Dorms
3 Small-town atmosphere	**3** Attendance policies
4 Location	**4** Professors notice absences
5 Beautiful campus	**5** Limited club funding

Students Speak Out
ON FACILITIES

Q "I feel that there are great facilities on campus, but **I think there is a need for a place for bands to perform**."

Q "If Stetson would give the students a few more recreational things, such as a student bar or movie theater, **it would make this campus a whole lot better**."

Q "Facilities at Stetson University are new and old, all at the same time. There are things being done to renovate the old structures, while at the same time new structures are being created. **It shows that Stetson has foresight and cares for the students**."

Q "**The facilities are well-kept and very clean**. The Hollis Center is a great facility with a student lounge area, exercise room, game room, and pool."

Q "The places here at Stetson are pretty nice with the exception of the fact that the dormitories are too moldy, Elizabeth Hall is too hot, and **there is nowhere besides a few lounging areas for students to go to**."

STUDENT AUTHOR: **There is a wide variety of things happening on campus, created either by individual organizations or the school itself. Concerts are held with performances ranging from well-known bands to local artists to those in the music school. On the downside, there aren't any student bars. In all, the facilities seem to meet the needs of the students, and the University does its best to make sure there is more than enough to do on campus.**

Famous Alumni

Ted Cassidy, Max Cleland, Craig Crawford, Roy Geiger, Richard J. McKay, Charles E. Merrill, James Merritt, Jessica Rafalowski

---

Students Speak Out
ON CAMPUS DINING

Q "The food selection is limited and can get old. Plus, **if anyone is a vegetarian or vegan, it can be hard to find something to eat**."

Q "I think the food they serve is unhealthy, and you have to buy all the healthy stuff. **I feel like they are trying to rip me off**. A meal cost around $9 according to the meal plan, but if I want yogurt, I have to pay extra. Rarely do I get my $9 worth of food."

Q "**There needs to be more variety, or at least for the most part, better food served**. Like, who eats shrimp pizza? I don't want to have that stuff! Yet they keep serving it over and over."

Q "**I think they should serve more organic food and less preservative-laden food**. Sometimes people get really sick from the food they serve."

Q "Although there is a salad bar and a few choice selections for a vegetarian, **eating virtually the same thing every day gets old**, and anyone would agree with that."

STUDENT AUTHOR: **To say the least, people here do not like the fact that there is a horrible selection of on-campus dining. In the defense of Stetson, it's a small campus, and they feel that three serving facilities is adequate. Of course, as students, we know otherwise: There must be selection. What I hope for are some needed improvements on selection and the dumping of bad menu items. After a while, most students decide to not get a meal plan and use cash as they go.**

Student Body

African American:	5%	Male/Female:	41/59%
Asian American:	2%	Out-of-State:	19%
Hispanic:	9%	International:	3%
Native American:	<1%	Unknown:	6%
White:	75%		

Popular Faiths: The main religion on campus is Christianity.

Gay Pride: The gay community has been quiet but is starting to move to a more active level due to past incidents on campus.

Economic Status: Mainly students from wealthy families attend Stetson University due to the high tuition cost.

Students Speak Out
ON DORMS

Q "The rooms in the freshman dorms are small, and **it is almost impossible to live in them without at least one of the beds lofted**. The other dorms are more spacious."

Q "Thankfully, **they are building new buildings that will hopefully be better** than the ones already on campus."

Q "**I think the dormitories are way too expensive for what you get**. They need to lower the prices and not penalize the students who wish to move off campus."

STUDENT AUTHOR: **The on-campus housing leaves something to be desired. There are problems with mold, mildew, and the age of some of the buildings. Some students seriously mistreat the buildings and seem to have no regard for responsibility. There are plans to build better dorms, and there are always things being done to improve the ones already here. The thing to remember is that the rooms are small, but with careful furniture management and roommate cooperation, it can be a decent place to live.**

> **Did You Know?**
> 72% of undergrads live on campus.

Students Speak Out
ON GUYS & GIRLS

Q "**Some of the guys can be really obnoxious because they get drunk a lot**. But, there are a few guys out there that are good-looking and aren't drunk 24/7."

Q "Generally, Stetson is friendly, and people tend to keep to themselves. But since this is a small campus, students are forced to interact with each other. **It's a well-rounded community**."

Q "**There aren't enough** openly gay, lesbian, and bisexual people on campus."

Q "**I think there is someone for everyone**. It's just sometimes hard to find someone to fit your personality or your wants through and through."

STUDENT AUTHOR: **Both guys and girls are sexual promiscuous, which is not surprising to anyone who knows what college is like. For the most part, the student body is not looking at having anything casual. Remember that Stetson is a small campus, so just like in high school, rumors run rampant, and perceptions will be made based on the way you dress and act. The best advice for the girls and guys on campus is to be realistic about expectations.**

> **Traditions**
>
> If you're a freshman and you have a birthday during the school year, it is tradition to get thrown into the fountain. But beware, there is a $50 fine if you're caught by a strict Public Safety officer.
>
> **Overall School Spirit**
>
> The school spirit at Stetson is mediocre. It's not too strong, but it's not absent. Students are constantly wearing Stetson gear, and there is a decent turnout for the games. There is more school spirit if you're involved in Greek life.

Students Speak Out
ON ATHLETICS

Q "Even though we don't have a bunch of sports on campus, the ones that we do have are relatively good. **They are definitely a force to be reckoned with**, and they know how to hold their own."

Q "For the few sports that we have here, they're good. **I wish our school had a football team**."

Q "**There isn't enough school spirit on campus**, which takes away from the experience."

Q "I feel that the **funding for the athletic teams is not dispersed fairly**."

STUDENT AUTHOR: **Stetson really cares about its athletics, especially basketball. During the season, students can check out games and become involved. But, not all sports share the same support. For the most part, only certain sports get attention. Other sports teams, such as crew, tennis, and soccer, receive less funding and support. In terms of athletic facilities, the fields and courts are well maintained. The facilities also keep hours that mesh well with students' schedules, which allows them to workout outside of the team practices.**

Students Speak Out
ON DRUG SCENE

Q "I'd say that drinking is more of a prevalent scene on campus compared to the drug scene. The drugs are there and sometimes go hand-in-hand with drinking."

Q "It's college—drugs and alcohol are supposed to be here. This is the place where students learn from stupid mistakes and grow from them."

Q "I haven't noticed drugs to be a problem on campus. I know there are a lot of people who drink, but I haven't noticed there being a lot of drug problems."

STUDENT AUTHOR: The campus itself is fairly good on keeping drugs to a minimum. There is not too much of anything hard like cocaine or heroin. However, that isn't to say that it is not on campus. Most of the drugs on campus are pretty much just marijuana. Underage drinking is very prevalent at Stetson. The administration does deal with that alcohol problem accordingly when students are caught drinking.

11:1	Student-to-Faculty Ratio
81%	Freshman Retention Rate
55%	Four-Year Graduation Rate
93%	Financial Aid Applicants Receiving Aid

Students Speak Out
SAFETY & SECURITY

Q "The campus is relatively safe and protects itself well. It also doesn't have strict rules, except for the weird ones about how we can only have beer and wine and not just whatever we want."

Q "Public Safety seems to be doing its job fine, but I hate the stupid parking tickets we receive, especially since we have such a dire need for parking itself. Another ticket that was amazing to get was for speeding."

Q "Health Services needs to have a doctor on the weekends and have one for longer than they do now. People don't just get sick on the weekdays and during office hours."

STUDENT AUTHOR: Safety responds to any calls from students on campus. They have placed blue-light call boxes all over campus in case of an emergency. The campus and the town are relatively safe anyway. Stetson is so safe that even John Walsh of *America's Most Wanted* let his kid go here.

Questions?
For more inside information and survival tips, pick up College Prowler's full-length book on this school, written by an actual student! Check it out at *www.collegeprowler.com*.

Students Speak Out
ON OVERALL EXPERIENCE

Q "I've had a very good overall experience based on the knowledge of my professors and how they teach their material. I'm also pretty satisfied with the facilities that they offer us and the activities that they have on campus."

Q "I enjoy the University, although I think that there are too many prerequisites. The University is small and the classes are small, so you can become very close to your professors. The downfall to that is that the classes can be very tough, and you can fail some of them easily."

Q "The experience that I've had at Stetson has been very eclectic. The attitude has been along the lines of work hard and party hard."

Q "My overall experience is that it's very challenging to go here. It is easy to become overwhelmed. Even though certain classes are more important than others, any bad grade will really take a toll on your GPA."

STUDENT AUTHOR: The overall experience of Stetson University can be described as intimate. The campus itself isn't big, so of course that has its pros and cons. The pros are that students get to know one another well, and finding and walking to classes is easy. Of course, if it's a really rainy or hot day, then it can be a hassle. However, with a small campus, students are able to get to know their professors well, which is great. On the downside, if you miss a class, the professor will notice. Another contributing factor of the overall experience is the small class size. Small class sizes are nice for those who like it, but they correlate with a higher tuition rate.

Stony Brook University

100 Nicholls Road; Stony Brook, NY 11794
(631) 632-6000; www.stonybrook.edu

THE BASICS:

Acceptance Rate: 43%
Setting: Suburban
F-T Undergrads: 12,620

SAT Range: 1650–1920*
Control: Public
Tuition: $12,870

Most Popular Majors: Business, Psychology, Computer Science, Economics, Health Professions

*of 2400

Academics	B-	Guys	B
Local Atmosphere	C+	Girls	B-
Safety & Security	B	Athletics	C
Computers	B+	Nightlife	B-
Facilities	B	Greek Life	D+
Campus Dining	C-	Drug Scene	B-
Off-Campus Dining	B	Campus Strictness	B
Campus Housing	C-	Parking	D+
Off-Campus Housing	C+	Transportation	B-
Diversity	A+	Weather	B-

Students Speak Out
ON ACADEMICS

Q "For most of the classes, I feel I walk away having learned something new that may help me later on. **Many teachers are willing to work with me** and explain things further if I need it."

Q "I have mixed feelings about the classes offered here. **Good teachers make a class more interesting**, and if you really want to do what you're studying, it doesn't matter who the professor is."

Q "**No one in the math department speaks English**. Almost every professor and TA I've had for math was from Eastern Europe and talked like Arnold Schwarzenegger, except they were not nearly as hilarious."

Q "Most teachers are willing to teach you things on their own time if you are willing to **take time to ask for their help**."

STUDENT AUTHOR: Many professors actually work "in the field," and so they are cognizant of most new advances in their profession. This is important because it adds to the amount of enthusiasm for learning in the classroom. A majority of the faculty use current media applications to assist in teaching, like PowerPoint and Flash, which always keeps education new and intriguing. Classroom discussions generate good, and sometimes, intense exchanges of ideas. Professors are almost always accessible at their office hours. Most are flexible and will schedule around your needs if the allotted time isn't convenient. On the whole, they are willing to work with you.

Students Speak Out
ON LOCAL ATMOSPHERE

Q "Stony Brook is a **quaint little town**, with a carriage house and a grist mill. Other than that, there's a diner and a mall. There's not enough stuff to separate it into categories."

Q "Stony Brook is not a college town, but the Bench is nearby. **Port Jefferson is a great place to go visit**, and it's good for night life."

Q "**Stony Brook is too quiet**. There are not that many places to go out, but on the other hand, this makes me concentrate on my education."

Q "The atmosphere isn't that bad. Some places are pretty cool, e.g. the Velvet Lounge on 25A. They have **live bands performing and it's a relaxed environment**. Stay away from the Rumba Sky (which has a new name every semester)."

Q "Stony Brook Village is **secluded, dead, and in retirement**. Stay away from the woods! The Sports Complex is a must see!"

STUDENT AUTHOR: Aesthetically, the beaches and surrounding villages are quaint and really quite beautiful. Shady streets and antique storefronts, juxtaposed against the Victorian homes create the *Our Town* setting, with a relaxing cool breeze that rolls in off the shore. The campus is fairly removed, so a car is desirable. However, public busing is available, and a Long Island Rail Road (LIRR) station is located on the northern tip of the campus. Malls, bars, supermarkets, and other amenities are within 10 minutes of the campus by car, but can be a far walk.

5 Best Things
1. Computers
2. Real life experiences
3. Close to the city
4. The scandalous women
5. Friendly people

5 Worst Things
1. High-priced food
2. Class sizes
3. Parking/ticketing
4. Attitude of some staff
5. Bad advisors

Students Speak Out
ON FACILITIES

Q **"The Health Sciences side of the campus gets all the money**. Their library is a palace, quiet, with working lighting fixtures. We pour money into the athletic facilities, while the arts facilities get next to nothing. The computer centers are really good, all over, and always open."

Q "Many computers are available with good hours. **The 24-hour commuter lounge is great**! Buses from South P are also good."

Q **"Stony Brook needs a much bigger gym**. The computer centers are nice. The Student Center isn't used as much as one would expect."

Q "The facilities on campus are okay. **Some stuff in the weight room needs to go**, like the equipment, because it's old and rusty."

Q **"The SINC sites are fully high tech** (at least the popular ones). There are gyms, an indoor swimming pool, outdoor game areas, and a stadium. I think it's much better than most of the colleges nearby."

STUDENT AUTHOR: Stony Brook University is a relatively young university, at only 49 years old. Work is always being done to make the campus better able to handle the growing numbers of students. The Student Activity Center, or "the SAC" for short, features a state-of-the art exercise facility, art gallery, and student lounge. The athletic facilities are immense, with courts for every kind of sport. There are at least a dozen computing sites on campus, some open as late as 4 a.m. The Student Union is also a large hub of the campus, with a deli, cafeteria, and an outside café.

Famous Alumni

Craig Allen, Christine Goerke, John Hennessey, Scott Higham, Russell Lewis, Jef Raskin, John Reiner

Students Speak Out
ON CAMPUS DINING

Q "Campus dining is mediocre at best. There are **no vegetarian or healthy foods in the Roth Dining Quad**. The SAC is okay. Campus Dining is trying, but a lot of the food is expensive."

Q **"I get sick from it once a day**. Roth Dining Quad is bad. Generally, campus food is very greasy. The Wang Center, Kelly Quad, the SAC, and the Bleachers Club are alright."

Q "I actually like the campus food (although it's pricey). End of the Bridge has some good food. And **when in doubt, there's always Burger King**."

Q "The food here sucks. The **good spots are at the End of the Bridge, Jasmine's**, and sometimes at the Student Activities Center."

Q **"The food is mostly unhealthy**! Be prepared for Taco Bell, Burger King, and Chinese/Indian. The healthy options are very limited to salads and sushi, that's about it!"

STUDENT AUTHOR: Inside the dorms, one can find fast food restaurants, like Burger King and Taco Bell, along with Kosher dining, vegetarian restaurants, Asian, and Mexican. The largest dining hall is in the Student Activities Center, and can accommodate any appetite, from fresh pizza made in a brick oven, to sushi, and Philly cheesesteaks. The Wang Center features the Jasmine Food Court, with authentic chefs making sushi and other Asian dishes. The End of the Bridge restaurant is perhaps the most elegant dining on campus.

Student Body

African American:	10%	Male/Female:	51/49%
Asian American:	23%	Out-of-State:	3%
Hispanic:	8%	International:	5%
Native American:	<1%	Unknown:	0%
White:	54%		

Popular Faiths: There are about 15 active religious groups on campus, including Muslim, Protestant, and Catholic campus ministries and foundations.

Gay Pride: The LGBTA, the Queer Alliance, and the AFFIRM Network are the main organizations on campus devoted to students with alternative lifestyles.

Economic Status: Seventy-three percent of students applied for financial aid, and 59 percent were found to have needed it.

Students Speak Out
ON DORMS

Q "There is a **vast difference between dorms**, such as the H and Mendelsohn Quads compared to Kelly and Roosevelt Quads. Greeley is the worst, also Stimpson."

Q "The dorms are usually noisy, and no one seems to enforce the rules. **Most people are quiet, but some are out of control**!"

Q "It depends on which dorm you are assigned. Avoid Roosevelt Quad! **Irving, O'Neill, and Roth are too dark**. Benedict College, James College, and the apartments are nice."

STUDENT AUTHOR: **Living on campus offers lots of amenities that one can't get just by living at home. Fitness centers, computer labs, cafés, and dining halls can give students the recreation and relaxation they need, while affording more time to study and take part of campus life. On the other hand, campus housing is expensive, especially to live in the apartments. The consensus overwhelmingly positions Roosevelt Quad as the worst dorm. However, it is a corridor-style dorm, which tends to be enjoyed most by the social butterflies who leave their doors open for anyone to pop in.**

Did You Know?
59% of undergrads live on campus.

Students Speak Out
ON GUYS & GIRLS

Q "**The guys at SBU are not ready for commitment**. They are immature. The freshman girls are easily manipulated into doing things with upperclass men."

Q "The guys are very diverse. The girls are unfriendly. **Everyone leaves to go home all the time**."

Q "The girls are okay, but **most of them are crazy**. I have acquired a lot of stalkers on campus."

Q "The girls are not really that hot. Other universities seem to have more attractive girls. **The guys are so-so**. Some are good looking."

STUDENT AUTHOR: **The ratio of males to females at Stony Brook is pretty evenly balanced, so competition for the opposite sex isn't arduous. The more challenging task is to find someone that is open to meeting others. Many of the students at Stony Brook can be stand-offish, with the typical princesses and jocks that wander the social scene. Most of the student body is more concerned with day-to-day life, and doesn't focus on the way they look.**

Traditions

G-Fest
G-Fest is an annual carnival held in G-Quad, featuring popular bands—always a great success.

Homecoming & Wolfstock
To "kick off" Homecoming, the players and cheerleaders are out to meet everyone. After the game, Wolfstock continues with bbq's and live music.

Overall School Spirit
The unique thing about Stony Brook is that everyone is very excited about how much they feel USB sucks. Apathy is something everyone here can get behind.

Students Speak Out
ON ATHLETICS

Q "Varsity sports are not too big. **This isn't a sport-focused school**. Most people will not be able to name or point out sport players unless they are wearing the school uniforms."

Q "Stony Brook University sports teams suck. **I'm surprised they're Division IA**. They do try their best, though."

Q "Varsity sports are not that big on campus. **Intramural sports are much more known** than the varsity sports."

Q "Sports in general are a big deal on campus. SBU is **very spirited with athletics**—whether it is varsity or intramural."

STUDENT AUTHOR: **Stony Brook University's Kenneth P. LaValle Stadium has created a lot of new excitement for our Division IA teams. The Seawolves play some the best schools, but they also lose most of the time. If our teams had a better reputation for winning, there would be a very large following. Intramural sports are really where all the action is. IMs have an enormous popularity and a very large following in all the different varieties offered.**

Students Speak Out
ON DRUG SCENE

Q "Being a resident assistant, I can testify that there are **quite a bit of drugs, mostly weed**, if that's what you're looking for. However, you shouldn't be focusing on that."

Q "People are **more likely to drink than to do drugs**, but as is the case everywhere, drugs are around."

Q "**It's beyond flagrant**, and the campus is infested with potheads. You know, one of the nicknames for this school is Stoner Brook."

STUDENT AUTHOR: It is generally alcohol and marijuana that students use, but there are cases of harder drugs. That's not to say that there is any kind of pressure to indulge. Students do what they like, and it can be easily avoided. However, it is a pretty common sight to witness drunken stupidity at all hours of the night. Don't let the noise get out of hand, or you will find the University Police banging at your door, and the consequences can be harsh. Community service is no fun when there are finals to study for.

14:1	Student-to-Faculty Ratio
86%	Freshman Retention Rate
37%	Four-Year Graduation Rate
68%	Financial Aid Applicants Receiving Aid

Students Speak Out
SAFETY & SECURITY

Q "Although I haven't encountered a dangerous situation, there are **many areas that are dark, hidden, and isolated**, which can make me feel uneasy at times."

Q "Very tight. **Everything is well organized** from RHDs to RAs, security, and police officers. Everyone follows protocol."

Q "**For the most part, it's safe**; they have a security desk at the gate, which is intimidating, but they let anyone in and sometimes no one's there. They have RSP desks, but they can't prevent people from coming in propped doors."

Q "The main campus is safe, but **the residence halls need a little more security**, because any stranger can get into the halls very easily."

STUDENT AUTHOR: At midnight, the gates on South Drive are locked, and access by car is limited to the main entrance. Drivers must stop at the guard booth and show a valid Stony Brook ID. University Police are always seen driving around at any time of day. Programs like the RSP and University Police Personal Safety Ride Program also help students to safety.

> **Questions?**
> For more inside information and survival tips, pick up College Prowler's full-length book on this school, written by an actual student! Check it out at *www.collegeprowler.com.*

Students Speak Out
ON OVERALL EXPERIENCE

Q "Overall, I think Stony Brook University is **great for people who are serious with their career**, otherwise people can find better places to hang around or party. This is not a party school."

Q "My experience here was okay. However, I do wish I was somewhere else sometimes. The activities have been really slacking in quantity and quality. As for your social life, it doesn't matter where you go; it'll be what you make of it. **Lots of great down-to-earth people** are here from every background."

Q "Well, **I think SBU needs to brush up on certain things**: taking care of residence halls properly (my floor), especially things like showers and toilets. We have had little or no hot water for almost an entire semester now."

Q "**People complain about Stony Brook, but I enjoy it** a lot. I've made good friends. I'm very involved in clubs, and enjoy college to the fullest. Don't stress the tests, finals, Orgo—whatever. Buddhism teaches the moment."

STUDENT AUTHOR: Students are friendly and engaging, there are always different activities for students to get involved in, as well as numerous clubs and organizations. However, like any school, there are some negatives. Since more than half of the student population consists of commuters, there is a real barrier to student contact. This is a large contributing factor to the low student morale Stony Brook has attained. In recognition of this, the University has been making a large push to try and combat this issue by providing things like street fairs, and Midnight Madness, an all night long party in the gym with giveaway prizes.

Susquehanna University

514 University Avenue; Selinsgrove, PA 17870
(570) 372-4260; www.susqu.edu

THE BASICS:

Acceptance Rate: 86%　　**SAT Range:** 1050–1220*
Setting: Rural　　　　　　**Control:** Private
F-T Undergrads: 1,903　　**Tuition:** $30,980

Most Popular Majors: Business, Creative Writing, Biology, Elementary Education, Psychology

*of 1600

Academics	B+	Guys	A-
Local Atmosphere	C+	Girls	A-
Safety & Security	A	Athletics	C+
Computers	B+	Nightlife	C
Facilities	A	Greek Life	B-
Campus Dining	B	Drug Scene	B+
Off-Campus Dining	B-	Campus Strictness	C
Campus Housing	B	Parking	A-
Off-Campus Housing	C+	Transportation	C-
Diversity	D-	Weather	C+

Students Speak Out
ON ACADEMICS

Q "The teachers are extremely helpful. Since the classes are small in size, **one gets to interact with the teacher on a one-to-one basis**. I feel that teachers really care about the students and are always there when you need them."

Q "Every class that I have taken has been extremely interesting. **I actually look forward to going to class every day**. Professors at SU always have new and exciting ways of keeping students involved and intrigued."

Q "The teachers are very helpful. Depending on what major you are in, **your teachers will be different**. Some will be fun, others will be crazy, and some will just be plain old boring. I found my classes to be interesting. There are always going to be those one or two classes that are just boring, but for the most part, I enjoyed going to my classes."

Q "Many times, teachers will go out of their way to accommodate every student's needs. However, **not every class is interesting**. I find that classes that interest me are more appealing, but not every class is like that."

STUDENT AUTHOR: **Susquehanna academics are challenging and not to be taken lightly. That said, the classes are not so hard that nobody stands a chance of succeeding. In any course encountered, the amount of effort that a student puts into a course is the biggest determinant of how well he or she will do. All classes are taught by professors; teachers' assistants are there to aid professors, not teach for them.**

Students Speak Out
ON LOCAL ATMOSPHERE

Q "Selinsgrove is a tiny town. **It would be the most boring town in the universe if SU didn't exist**. The locals are a little strange, so I prefer to stay on campus as much as possible. This is great because there is always something fun to do at SU. Bucknell and Bloomsburg aren't far, so it is easy to make an overnight/weekend trip to one of the two. Most of the people I know would rather visit me at SU, though."

Q "Being in a small town, away from any big cities, **the atmosphere is really quiet**. There is not much happening."

Q "I don't know if there's anything that someone might want to stay away from or that they necessarily want to visit, either. You end up visiting everywhere before you graduate, but it's a small town, and for people who are from a town bigger than 5,000, **I think it can be a hard adjustment**."

Q **"The atmosphere in Selinsgrove isn't lively**. The only activity in the town occurs when school is in session. Without the Susquehanna students, the town is pretty dead. However, I find that, within the vicinity, there are things to do."

STUDENT AUTHOR: **While the area may be far from hip, it is important to note that everything is within a 15-minute drive from campus. There is a Wal-Mart, the Susquehanna Valley Mall, a movie theater, and tons of places to eat. It is also possible to run down to the river or along country roads without worrying about safety. There is also a lot of open space, and the town is not overdeveloped.**

Students Speak Out
ON FACILITIES

"Compared to other schools, **all of the facilities at Susquehanna are state-of-the-art**. The gym is top-of-the-line, and the student center was already nice but underwent renovations. It's amazing that SU looks so beautiful and old on the outside but is so up-to-date on the inside."

"The athletic center is extremely nice. The pool is a little bit old, but the rest of the facility is great. The field house is pretty big, and **the football field is top-of-the-line**. The computer labs vary. The campus center lab is decent, while the Apfelbaum labs are extremely nice. The academic building labs (Steele and Bogar) are pretty old-looking."

"All the facilities are very nice, and **the entire campus in general is very beautiful**."

"The facilities are very nice. **The gym has newer equipment and a nice track**. The computers are newer, and they are continually updating them."

"The facilities on campus are very nice. The cafeteria and **a portion of the student center recently underwent renovation**. The computers are all fairly new with flat-screen monitors, but the printers aren't always working well."

STUDENT AUTHOR: While we don't have a movie theater per se, Charlie's Coffeehouse has a big-screen TV to show movies that are no longer out in the theaters but have yet to come out on DVD. There isn't a bowling alley on campus, but there is one not far away; the same applies for bars. Charlie's is always a good place to hang out and just sit on one of their comfy sofas and drink coffee.

Students Speak Out
ON CAMPUS DINING

"The food is okay. **It's not the best, but it's better than other places** I have heard of, and there are definitely a lot more choices to eat than at other schools. The dining hall is good, but it's crowded at lunchtime."

"At first I did not think that the food at SU was very good. Anything compared to my mom's home cooking is, at best, mediocre. When I tasted food at other schools, though, SU food seems amazing. **For cafeteria food, SU's is definitely the best I've tasted**."

"My favorite place to eat at SU is the dining hall. There are a bunch of different stations, which offer a lot of different kinds of meals, and **if all else fails, there is always the salad bar**."

"The dining halls, on average, are pretty good. It can get kind of boring because **the food doesn't vary as much as would be nice**, but for the most part, people are pleased and fed."

"I am a vegetarian, and I was worried that there wouldn't be anything for me to eat. I made some suggestions and complaints, and the menu was quickly changed. **The food staff is very open-minded and truly cares** about the needs of students."

STUDENT AUTHOR: Students eat most of their meals in the cafeteria, where there are lots of options. There is a station that serves home-style foods such as meatloaf, mashed potatoes, and boiled vegetables. There is also a grill line that serves burgers, fries, and the like. There are lots of hits and misses in the cafeteria. The worst-case scenario is when all of the "misses" occur on the same night.

Students Speak Out
ON DORMS

Q "If I had to avoid any dorm, I would probably avoid Hass because, **while it's quiet and still has a good location, the rooms are really small**—especially if you aren't used to sharing a room. Most students try for Smith, and I definitely agree with that."

Q "**All of the dorms are mediocre**. But as an upperclassman, the suites and townhouses seem like great places to stay."

Q "The only dorm I would say to stay away from is West because there is no air conditioning. If you like to make any noise whatsoever, stay away from Scholar's and Seibert because **they are serious when they say 24-hour quiet hours**."

STUDENT AUTHOR: **Dorm rooms at SU are larger than most, with plenty of closet space. However, some dorm rooms are better than others. Hassinger Hall, a freshman dorm, has rooms that are far smaller than any other dorm on campus, and West Hall does not have air conditioning. In recent years, the trend of putting freshmen in forced triples has increased, but this setup is doable after a little experimenting with bed and desk placements.**

Did You Know?
80% of undergrads live on campus.

Students Speak Out
ON GUYS & GIRLS

Q "One would assume that at a rather small school there wouldn't be many good-looking people—this is a false assumption. There are many hot guys and girls. One might also assume that these hot people would be snotty and mean, but this is also false. **It is quite possibly the most pleasant place I've even been**."

Q "**There are some hot people on campus**. It's not like in the movies, but there are a lot of good-looking people."

Q "**The guys can be arrogant, but some are nice**. The girls can also be the same way, but you have a mix of everyone."

Q "I find that you have the **same kind of guys and girls you did in high school**."

STUDENT AUTHOR: **Overall, the campus has a very friendly atmosphere created by the comfort level of the students. The students are attractive for the most part; it is certainly not hard to find a significant other (or drunken hookup) who has similar tastes as you and is also aesthetically pleasing. In the dating game, guys have a slight advantage because the campus is roughly 45 percent male and 55 percent female.**

Traditions

Fall Frenzy and Spring Weekend
Although these weekends are infamous on campus because of their "out-of-control drinking" (this is a myth), they are a lot of fun because of the activities. There are usually obstacle courses and different carnival-type attractions, as well as live concerts.

Overall School Spirit
The school spirit isn't really overwhelming. If you want to go for a school that has crazy, passionate fans, this is not the place. "Fairweather fans" is an ideal term to describe the spirit at SU.

Students Speak Out
ON ATHLETICS

Q "I think that it is fun to go to games and watch, but SU is **not as competitive and serious as other schools** in better divisions. I know that the athletes do put a lot of time and effort into their sports. It is definitely time-consuming."

Q "**Varsity sports are big**. IM sports are not that big, but we still have them."

Q "I started an intramural team fall semester my freshman year. It was quite possibly the best decision I ever made. I met a lot of awesome people and had a ton of fun! A lot of people play, and everyone has a great time. **The intramural program is one of the most fun things at SU.**"

Q "The school has cracked down on wild cheering at basketball games, so **the games are about as dull as a middle school basketball game**."

STUDENT AUTHOR: **The team on campus that receives the most attention is undoubtedly the football team, even though other teams have far better records. The turnout to many matches, meets, and games is pretty low when compared to the size of the student body. The intramural leagues and sports that have the title "club" instead of "team" are popular.**

Students Speak Out
ON DRUG SCENE

Q "Some people do drugs, but **it is not really out in the open**. If that is your thing, it is available for you. If it is not your thing, you most likely won't be confronted with it. Nobody asks anybody to buy drugs or anything. People who do drugs basically keep it quiet."

Q "I do not personally do drugs, but **there are many on campus**, and they're not that hard to obtain."

Q "I don't do a lot of drugs, but I smoke weed sometimes. **It's not hard to find someone with it**—I have no idea where they get it from, though. I just always use other people's and never try and get my own."

STUDENT AUTHOR: **Every weekend, rumors circulate of scores of students being caught drinking, but rumors about those caught with drugs are far more rare. While there is drug usage on campus, it is not forced on students, and it seems that, while students readily use alcohol, many do not partake in other illegal substances.**

14:1	Student-to-Faculty Ratio
84%	Freshman Retention Rate
80%	Four-Year Graduation Rate
64%	Financial Aid Applicants Receiving Aid

Students Speak Out
SAFETY & SECURITY

Q "Because Selinsgrove is a relatively safe town on its own, the police force is not extremely large. **Public Safety on campus is very responsive to any problems**, and it handles everything appropriately. They're also really down-to-earth people as well; it's nice to see that they really do care about the students' well-being."

Q "It's rare to find a time when you are the only one wandering around the campus, even at one o'clock in the morning. And when living in the dorms, **there's always an RA on duty throughout the day**, so if an accident happens, there's always someone to find."

Q "We have public safety officers who **drive around most of the night looking out for things**. They aren't breathing down your back constantly."

STUDENT AUTHOR: **Public safety and health services at SU are great. All of the public safety officers are approachable and not intimidating or commanding. The campus itself feels very safe; students frequently walk by themselves late at night on their way from one building to another.**

Questions?
For more inside information and survival tips, pick up College Prowler's full-length book on this school, written by an actual student! Check it out at *www.collegeprowler.com.*

Students Speak Out
ON OVERALL EXPERIENCE

Q "I love my school. It is the best choice I could have made. **It has the right number of people**, and you can know everyone or know only a few people. I couldn't ask for better friends than what I have made here."

Q "Overall, I love SU. At first, I used to wish that I had gone to a bigger school because I was so scared of meeting people, but once I started, I was happy that I had stayed. SU has a lot to offer, and the classes are, for the most part, really fun and interesting. **I wouldn't trade my experience at SU for anything**."

Q "The professors go out of their way to help you, and **everyone is friendly, holding doors open and saying 'hi.'** It's not unusual to walk around campus and say, 'Hi, how are you?' if you see someone you just know by their face."

Q "I love Susquehanna. I was disappointed when they wouldn't let the fraternities have on-campus parties anymore, but otherwise I couldn't be happier. It is a gorgeous campus, and the people are really nice. The professors are friendly, and **it is really easy to get involved and play a large part** in an organization."

STUDENT AUTHOR: **Susquehanna is an amazing place to go to school. While some people see it as their worst nightmare, for those who want a small liberal arts school, there aren't many better places to go than SU. However, there are a lot of catch-22s. Campus security is really strict, but at the same time, the campus is incredibly safe. Professors live close so there are rarely snow days, yet they care deeply about their students and open up their homes to them. If you want a smaller school, then Susquehanna really is the place to be.**

Swarthmore College

500 College Avenue; Swarthmore, PA 19081
(610) 328-8000; www.swarthmore.edu

THE BASICS:

Acceptance Rate: 16%
Setting: Rural
F-T Undergrads: 1,478

SAT Range: 2010–2280*
Control: Private
Tuition: $36,154

Most Popular Majors: Social Sciences, Biology, Philosophy, Psychology, Visual/Performing Arts

*of 2400

Academics	A	Guys	C
Local Atmosphere	B-	Girls	C
Safety & Security	A-	Athletics	C-
Computers	B	Nightlife	B-
Facilities	B	Greek Life	D
Campus Dining	B-	Drug Scene	B+
Off-Campus Dining	B-	Campus Strictness	A-
Campus Housing	B-	Parking	D
Off-Campus Housing	B	Transportation	B
Diversity	A-	Weather	B-

Students Speak Out
ON ACADEMICS

Q "All the professors here have unique personalities, but the common threads are amazing intellects and a genuine concern for their students. They're also obsessed and **very knowledgeable** about their subjects, but can hold a discussion on anything you can imagine."

Q "They expect a lot out of you, but are **accessible and willing** to answer any questions. Also, though they're all very intelligent, they won't talk down to their students."

Q "The best thing has been finding professors that have been able to challenge and guide me. Without those kinds of profs, I don't think I would have pushed myself to try things that are outside of my comfort zone (i.e. taking honors seminars), and I wouldn't have taken certain risks. So in that sense, I **really have found mentors** at Swat."

Q "At Swat, I've never had a teacher who was absolutely awful. On the other hand, our professors are **definitely demanding**—they expect their students to put in the effort to really understand course material."

STUDENT AUTHOR: As the brochures say, "it's not about competing to learn what has already been learned, it's about creating new knowledge." Yeah, whatever. Creating new knowledge can be especially painful in Swarthmore's classroom experience. At a larger school, it might be possible to hide behind your notebook in a lecture hall. But Swatties must be prepared to learn in a different ways and see the world through new eyes.

Students Speak Out
ON LOCAL ATMOSPHERE

Q "The atmosphere in Swarthmore is very relaxed, since a lot of old people live here. It's a family-oriented town and the stores close kind of early, so the majority of your shopping won't be done in the town of Swarthmore. You can escape to nearby **Springfield or Philly** for restaurants and shopping, though."

Q "Swarthmore feels like a small town, even though we're actually really close to suburbia. We're less than a mile from a major road where you can find basically **every chain store** you can think of, and Swarthmore should definitely be considered a suburb of Philadelphia."

Q "The atmosphere is very small-town, **suburban, and liberal**. No other universities are around, and it's not really much of a college town (no bars or good coffeeshops). The Ville people try to keep a distance from the college students, therefore preserving their quiet way of life."

Q "Prospective students beware: the Ville is a business district that isn't really geared for college students. Unless you go to bed at 7 p.m., you'll become frustrated because everything (restaurants, gyms, bars) **closes early**."

STUDENT AUTHOR: Philly is 20 minutes away from Swarthmore, and provides an excellent getaway from the "Swarthmore bubble," but Swarthmore itself is a quaint little town consisting mainly of college professors and retirees. It provides little for college students aside from a co-op food store, a pizza place, some restaurants, and a few shops.

5 Best Things	5 Worst Things
1 Intimate classes	1 The Ville
2 Professors	2 No Wawa
3 Diversity	3 The bubble
4 Arboretum	4 Snobs
5 Traditions	5 Weather

Students Speak Out
ON FACILITIES

Q "Public computers are okay. They're also put in a big **new commons area** in the center of Parrish, which is really nice."

Q "The **gym here is ghetto**. Otherwise, the facilities are excellent for a small school. They may not look as modern or high-tech as you'll find at a state school, but I'm sure that's intentional."

Q "In general, the academic **buildings are gorgeous**—almost all of the classroom space is either new or renovated within the last 10 years."

Q "There is a **great fitness center** and tennis center. The athletic centers have been recently renovated, so they are all really nice. Computers are updated with current operating systems, and they are all Dells and Macs."

Q "Our school hates its athletes . . . and that gym sucks! On top of that, it's **always crowded**. The field has nice turf, though."

STUDENT AUTHOR: **Campus is home to the Scott Arboretum, whose employees are constantly working on the upkeep of the carefully manicured landscaping around campus. Sometimes students feel like they're walking through a five-star resort in the English countryside instead of a liberal arts college in suburban Philadelphia. On the other hand, students' number one complaint is that they only having one major dining hall on campus. At busy times, Sharples, can be overwhelmed with students, many of whom are tired of eating the same food in the same place everyday.**

Famous Alumni

Christian Anfinsen, Diane Di Prima, Michael Dukakis, Jonathan Franzen, Samuel L. Hayes III, Beth Littleford, James A. Michener, Alice Paul, Howard Temin

Students Speak Out
ON CAMPUS DINING

Q "Despite the variety, almost everything at Sharples **tastes the same**, and most of the people I know wind up eating the same thing every week. No one starves, but the food selection does flirt with monotony."

Q "The food here **ranges from good to tolerable**, but I've grown to hate it simply because we're forced to stay on the meal plan for each of our four years, if we live on campus. It's certainly not worth the high price we have to pay for it."

Q "As a vegetarian, I know I'm pretty lucky to be at Swarthmore. There's a good variety of **vegetarian/vegan options**. And although the dining hall can be a bit repetitive, Donny's grill station is always an option, and you can always make your own waffles!"

Q "Essie Mae's is very good. You can use your meals there and **customize your food** if you are feeling inventive. Weeknights, you can go to Paces, a student run café, that has very good food, but you have to pay out of your own pocket. Qub is a chill spot where you get tea for the most part, but it's a good place to hang out."

STUDENT AUTHOR: **There is only one real dining hall on campus— Sharples. Either learn to like it, which usually isn't hard the first year or two, or bring large amounts of cash to either spend at Pace's or off-campus restaurants. You can use the meal plan in Essie Mae's snack bar also, but sandwiches and curly fries can get old really quick. For the hungry Swattie, Sharples is the most frequent choice.**

Student Body

African American:	9%	Male/Female:	48/52%
Asian American:	17%	Out-of-State:	87%
Hispanic:	11%	International:	7%
Native American:	<1%	Unknown:	11%
White:	44%		

Popular Faiths: Swarthmore has fairly active Christian, Muslim, and Jewish student groups.

Gay Pride: Swarthmore is notorious for being one of the most queer-friendly schools in the country. The active Swarthmore Queer Union (SQU) sponsors two queer pride weeks during the school year.

Economic Status: Swatties usually come from wealthier backgrounds than average college kids.

Students Speak Out
ON DORMS

Q "**Mertz, Wharton, and Parish** are the nicest dorms, in my opinion. The worst dorm is probably Willets. The halls smell really bad! There are some good parties that go on there, though."

Q "The dorms here are **mostly quiet** on every day except Friday. Depending on a student's personality, that can be a good thing or bad thing."

Q "Willets is known as 'the **party dorm**' on campus. Filled with mostly freshmen and sophomores, there is always someone awake there at all hours of the day and night. There's always a mini-party going on in one of the rooms or in the hall lounges."

STUDENT AUTHOR: **Majority of Swarthmore students live on campus all four years, and for good reason. In general, the dorms are pleasant to look at, and even the least attractive dorms are lovely when compared to the dorms (prison cells) at larger universities. A good number of Swarthmore's dorms are converted, older buildings, once used for boarding school housing or private homes, and the buildings are beautiful.**

? Did You Know?
95% of undergrads live on campus.

Students Speak Out
ON GUYS & GIRLS

Q "Students develop '**Swat goggles**.' Like beer goggles, 'Swat goggles' make average looking people seem attractive once you have been here a while."

Q "Swarthmore girls rarely wear a lot of makeup and are very **low maintenance**. Boys often wear their hair a little bit long. People on the whole are very open-minded about sex. Although long-term relationships are definitely the norm, it is easy to find a hookup if you want one."

Q "Swatties are generally considered some of the **least attractive people** of any college. That may not be that far off, although there definitely are some cute girls here. Still, most people aren't all that interested in how they look."

STUDENT AUTHOR: **If you are looking for a school where curvaceous blondes and rugged, chiseled Abercrombie models outnumber textbooks, you should turn the page right now. It's not that Swatties are downright ugly, but their general apathy towards outward appearance sometimes makes them seem that way. However, there's always Philly to escape to—hitting the club and bar scene can serve as a quick remedy.**

Traditions

Crum Regatta
Student racers construct boats for this annual anything-that-floats race on the Crum Creek.

The Graduate
On the night before fall classes begin, tradition insists that there be a showing of the movie *The Graduate*.

Swarthmore Urban Legend
The plot for the movie *Dead Man on Campus* originated at Swarthmore. A student whose roommate died received all As for the rest of the year because of a "dead-man's clause" in college policy.

Students Speak Out
ON ATHLETICS

Q "Varsity sports aren't big at all. I'm a pretty big fan of pro sports, but I've never been to a varsity sporting event here. Also, I don't think it is unusual that a lot of **people here couldn't care less about sports**. IM sports are a little more popular, I think, but they're not huge."

Q "**IMs were great** this year; some of the teams could have beaten some of the varsity teams. I'm seriously not kidding."

Q "If you want big time sports, **go to Penn State** or Villanova, Certainly don't come here!"

Q "IM sports are pretty big, actually, and there's a wide range of competitiveness as far as that goes. Some people **take IMs very seriously**, while some just goof around and shoot the basketball over the hoop, so to speak."

STUDENT AUTHOR: **Sports almost always take a backseat to academics. Despite the percent of the population involved in athletics of some type, funding and support from the administration and the student body remains low. The lack of team spirit is not just the student body's fault, either. The teams tend to lose frequently and, well, pretty badly.**

Students Speak Out
ON DRUG SCENE

Q "There is **moderate drinking** and moderate pot smoking at Swarthmore. However, the drug problems I've seen here pale in comparison to the problems at larger state schools."

Q "Sometimes I **wish there were more** drug use on campus. I'm an occasional pot smoker, and when I decide to smoke, I feel like an outcast. I guess this intolerance for illegal substances is a good trait for a school to possess, though."

Q "You can get a hold of any kind of drug you desire, but who has time to do them? Oh, I know, **the dropouts!**"

STUDENT AUTHOR: The drug scene on campus is present, but is not at all intimidating. Like any "we-put-the-liberal-in-liberal-arts" college, marijuana use is pretty widespread, and the administration generally turns a blind eye to any petty use that may rear its head. Alcohol, however, the other widespread drug on campus, is very easy to come by, particularly on weekends when campus parties are often flowing with it.

8:1	Student-to-Faculty Ratio
96%	Freshman Retention Rate
88%	Four-Year Graduation Rate
97%	Financial Aid Applicants Receiving Aid

Students Speak Out
SAFETY & SECURITY

Q "It's safe, but Public Safety is annoying sometimes, especially when **they don't answer the phone.**"

Q "If you do feel unsafe, there is always Public Safety, and they usually can **give you an escort** to any building on campus. There have been a couple of instances where they forgot to pick me up, though. So I guess, like anyplace, it's never perfectly safe."

Q "The campus is **generally safe**. Public Safety handles security. They are kind of loose sometimes, but they handle business when it comes down to it. You really don't see too many sketchy characters around here either."

STUDENT AUTHOR: Swarthmore is a relatively safe campus; there is a low occurrence of crime, and Public Safety is generally there when needed. As far as crime prevention, however, students complain that the sidewalks are poorly lit, and that there could be a few more emergency phones around campus.

> **Questions?**
> For more inside information and survival tips, pick up College Prowler's full-length book on this school, written by an actual student! Check it out at *www.collegeprowler.com*.

Students Speak Out
ON OVERALL EXPERIENCE

Q "My favorite thing about Swat is definitely the students. Everyone I have met has **an interesting story**. The seemingly typical, quiet boy in your biology class may be writing a novel, or the friendly girl from down the hall could lead the Sierra Club student coalition. You'll just never know, unless you get involved. I have stayed up until 3 a.m. with friends doing everything from taking tequila shots, to discussing the problems with globalization, to mud wrestling in the softball field."

Q "I'm really happy to be at Swarthmore. If you want to meet incredible, intelligent, motivated people and you're okay with **sacrificing sleep**, social life, sports, or schoolwork (I manage all of them, somehow), come to Swat. I know it's one of the best decisions I've ever made."

Q "You can get **a better education** here than at an Ivy League school. Getting a degree here is an arduous task, but in the end it's worth it."

Q "Let's get this straight, Swarthmore is **not for everybody**. You have to be willing to work hard or else you'll be miserable during your tenure here. You also have to be pretty idealistic to be comfortable here. Finally, the vast majority of students here were nerds in high school, so if you don't feel comfortable around us, you won't be happy here."

STUDENT AUTHOR: Many students that do happen to find their niche at Swarthmore here are generally happy that they came. So, what type of student is Swarthmore suited for? Well, in the broadest sense, someone who is open-minded, ultra-liberal, and possesses a true passion for intellectual stimulation tends to thrive.

Syracuse University

900 South Crouse Avenue; Syracuse, NY 13244
(315) 443-1870; www.syr.edu

THE BASICS:

Acceptance Rate: 51%   **SAT Range:** 1110–1330*
Setting: Mid-sized City   **Control:** Private
F-T Undergrads: 12,981   **Tuition:** $32,180

Most Popular Majors: Business, Communications, Social Sciences, Visual/Performing Arts

*of 1600

Academics	B	Guys	A-
Local Atmosphere	B	Girls	A
Safety & Security	C+	Athletics	A
Computers	B	Nightlife	B-
Facilities	B+	Greek Life	A-
Campus Dining	C+	Drug Scene	C
Off-Campus Dining	B	Campus Strictness	B-
Campus Housing	B	Parking	C-
Off-Campus Housing	A-	Transportation	A-
Diversity	C	Weather	D+

Students Speak Out
ON ACADEMICS

Q "The teachers are willing to work with you, but you have to make the initial effort and seek them out first. **They are fair in their teaching** and easy to get in contact with if you need some additional help with the class. You have your good teachers and your bad teachers. It really just depends on who you get."

Q "My teachers are great; I don't know about all the teachers at this school. Professors come from all over the place. **Some have even written their own books** and use them in class."

Q **"The quality of professors varies wildly.** Sometimes, you'll get an excellent professor, and sometimes you'll get a horrible professor. Pray that you don't get a foreign grad student f or a teacher because they can't even speak English well."

Q "Overall, I would say that the teaching here is good. Most teachers are very helpful if you approach them. But there are a few of them, sadly, who **lack a personal touch** and will not make any extra effort to reach out to you."

STUDENT AUTHOR: SU has over 200 majors in nine undergraduate colleges; a few of SU's schools are world-renowned. The faculty at SU is generally compliant with students' needs. If you make use of the availability of your professors, go to class, do your homework, and study for the big tests, you should have no problem getting excellent grades.

Students Speak Out
ON LOCAL ATMOSPHERE

Q "The city of Syracuse survives because of SU. **Syracuse doesn't have much of a downtown atmosphere**, but the bar scene and Greek life make up for this loss."

Q "The only place to stay away from is the ghetto. If the people who live there see you walking around there, they won't bother you, but you need to act confident. **Don't be scared**."

Q "The atmosphere in Syracuse is pretty nice, I think. Nearby, you have Onondaga Community College and Le Moyne. Sometimes, you'll run into students from those other schools in bars and stuff. **Niagara Falls isn't far away**, either."

Q "You do have quite a lot to do in Syracuse. We have the Carousel Mall to brag about, **one of the most complete and largest malls** in New York state. If you are a gaming freak, Shoppingtown Mall is the place for you. There are also the outdoor arts and antique shows, annual festivals and fairs, Sunday-night bowling, ice-skating, the Syracuse Zoo, the Jamesville Lake, and so many other exciting places to go to."

STUDENT AUTHOR: Since Syracuse is a large university, most students find contentment in staying on campus because there is usually something going on. For those students that wish to venture off the campus, there are still options for them in the city of Syracuse. You can bowl, barhop, or catch a movie at Carousel Mall. Your best option to get out of the routine for a weekend is to head to Montreal, only a four-hour trip.

Students Speak Out
ON FACILITIES

Q "The gym sucks. It's too crowded, and there are not enough machines. **They use very outdated equipment**."

Q "I can't complain about the facilities on campus. The Schine Student Center has a good dining center, a bookstore, and a large auditorium for various events. **All the computers on campus are updated** with the latest operating systems (Windows XP)."

Q "The facilities are really nice. The computers are good, **the student center has pretty much everything** you could need, and the gym has a pool and huge weight room. In addition, you can take physical education classes for credit in any sport from golf, to kickboxing, to horseback riding."

Q "There is a state-of-the-art gymnasium on campus that anyone can use, and there are also some great recreational facilities. The student center is good, too—nothing amazing, but **it gets the job done**."

Q "All of the facilities at Syracuse are state-of-the-art. I'm at the gym everyday, and it definitely gets **two thumbs up from me**! Seriously, though, it rocks."

STUDENT AUTHOR: **If you were to go on a tour of SU, the tour guides would deliberately highlight certain facilities on campus and avoid others. The buildings on the campus, especially the older ones, can be breathtaking in their architecture. The Crouse building looks like a castle, and the Hall of Languages is a beautiful piece of history.**

Famous Alumni

Marv Albert, Dick Clark, Bob Costas, Taye Diggs, Ted Koppel, William Safire, Vanessa Williams

Students Speak Out
ON CAMPUS DINING

Q "**Dining halls are okay**. Sometimes, you have to pick and choose what to eat. But the food courts and the faculty dining center are both awesome."

Q "**The food here is decent**, and you also get the Supercard, which can be used at the various dining centers located around campus."

Q "If you enjoy onion rings, french fries, and chewy hamburgers, then you've come to the right place. Usually, I go for the food from the vegetarian section, not because I'm a vegetarian, but because the **food there seems better prepared** than the rest."

Q "The Kimmel Dining Center, however, is very good because **it consists of many large fast food franchises** (Taco Bell, KFC, Burger King, Sbarro, and Dunkin' Donuts)."

Q "I personally didn't care too much for the dining hall food. The simple things like cereal, bread, bagels, and stuff like that are all good because you can't go wrong with any of that. **You'll always find something you like**, though."

STUDENT AUTHOR: **There are two types of food at SU: dining hall food and Supercard dining facilities food. The dining halls are the places on campus where you may use your meal plan; it's also where you will need the skills of Emeril Lagasse to concoct something even remotely tasty. The Supercard areas more than make up for the gross grub in the dining halls. These places are designated for use with cash or your prepaid Supercard.**

Student Body

African American:	7%	Male/Female:	44/56%
Asian American:	8%	Out-of-State:	59%
Hispanic:	6%	International:	4%
Native American:	<1%	Unknown:	10%
White:	64%		

Popular Faiths: There is a large variety, although SU probably has more Jewish students than most colleges.

Gay Pride: The city of Syracuse has a fairly active gay community.

Economic Status: Most are either in the middle- or upper-middle-class category.

Students Speak Out
ON DORMS

Q "**As a freshman, you have no choice** about where you live, so you'll figure it out after your first year. All of the dorms are pretty nice, though."

Q "When I was a freshman, the Mount seemed like the most fun. It might have been a hike to get there, but **there was always something going on**."

Q "Overall, the dorms are awesome. **Location is the problem**. Brewster/Boland is really far away from everything, and Flint and Day (on the Mount) require walking up and down over a hundred steps to get to campus."

STUDENT AUTHOR: **All dorms have their perks, and most dorms have their downfalls. The students in Day and Flint Halls live on Mount Olympus, literally and figuratively, but you must field over 100 stairs to get to the top. Brewster and Boland dorms are the farthest away from campus. Although you have no say whether you end up in an open or split double room, cross your fingers for the split. This way, if you and your roommate clash in any way, you have some separation between you.**

Did You Know?
75% of undergrads live on campus.

Students Speak Out
ON GUYS & GIRLS

Q "It's impossible to describe all the guys and girls. **So many different people go here**. They're all unique. Some are hot . . . some not so much."

Q "SU has many good-looking women. It's interesting because most of the women at SU are very attractive, and it is rare to find a woman that is below the standards of most men, **although they do exist**."

Q "Some Syracuse guys are hot, but this campus is very diverse, so **you can find just about whatever** type of guy you're looking for. I honestly don't look at the guys that much, but there are some true studs around."

STUDENT AUTHOR: It's easy to meet people at Syracuse, mainly due to its slightly-larger-than-average student population. On the personality scale, however, SU is home to a host of different character traits. Students seem to think that a significant number of egotistical, rich students (both males and females) attend this university. Still, that number is balanced easily by the broad range of other personalities on campus.

Traditions

44
The number 44 has come to encompass all that is successful with both sports and the University in general.

Otto the Orange
In 1997, it was made official that the team was the Orange, and Otto the Orange would remain the University's mascot.

Overall School Spirit
Syracuse is an Orange town through and through; on the SU campus, the sentiment is not as pronounced.

Students Speak Out
ON ATHLETICS

Q "**Sports at Syracuse are huge**, as one might expect of a Division I school. They tend to bring a lot of money to the school. You'll definitely enjoy watching them, and they are a huge part of campus life."

Q "In football and basketball, we have **some of the best teams in the NCAA**, and a lot of people come to school because of that. Intramural sports are great here, and I've taken part in both an indoor soccer league and a broomball league."

Q "Have you ever seen a Syracuse football game or basketball game on TV? Being in **the Carrier Dome is crazy**!"

Q "This is a huge sports school, **especially for football and basketball**. We have a really big intramural program, as well."

STUDENT AUTHOR: One main reason students love varsity sports is the Carrier Dome—the setting for all football, men's basketball, and men's lacrosse home games. The Dome is great for football, especially when it's snowing outside, as well as basketball. The best part about the Dome is its location—right in the middle of the SU campus.

Students Speak Out
ON DRUG SCENE

Q "The drug scene is serious. The biggest drugs on campus are **marijuana, alcohol, and cocaine**. The scope of the drug scene is one that seems to be far-reaching and widespread."

Q "Getting drugs on campus is **as easy as ordering a pizza**."

Q "Drugs are definitely present. Of course, there's weed on campus, but there's also ecstasy, coke, acid, and 'shrooms. All that stuff is present anywhere you go, though, and **you really don't notice it unless you are involved** with it. The drug scene is no bigger than it is on any other college campus that I've visited."

STUDENT AUTHOR: The drug scene at Syracuse University is more than likely no different than at most schools across the United States. The drug scene at Syracuse University is more than likely no different than at most schools across the United States. The Options program in the Health Center is excellent for students who feel they have a problem.

15:1	Student-to-Faculty Ratio
91%	Freshman Retention Rate
71%	Four-Year Graduation Rate
83%	Financial Aid Applicants Receiving Aid

Students Speak Out
SAFETY & SECURITY

Q "Security and safety is good, but the school **security guards are on a serious power trip**. They think they are the FBI or something."

Q "As long as you take the proper precautions to protect yourself and your stuff, you'll be fine. **Public Safety is very prevalent on campus**. Often, I leave my studio class at 3 or 4 in the morning and have never felt any danger when walking back to my dorm."

Q "Overall, security is pretty good. **They could do more**, but for the most part, the campus is pretty safe."

STUDENT AUTHOR: The area around the Syracuse campus is not the safest place to be at night. Despite the fact that Syracuse is surrounded by a fairly rural area of central New York, it still is a city and has a city-like crime rate. Just be careful, but don't get overly stressed.

> **Questions?**
> For more inside information and survival tips, pick up College Prowler's full-length book on this school, written by an actual student! Check it out at *www.collegeprowler.com.*

Students Speak Out
ON OVERALL EXPERIENCE

Q "Let's just say that I've had friends from home come to visit and they've decided **it's blown away their colleges**. I've even had one of them transfer to Syracuse last year because he had such a good time visiting."

Q "For my major, Syracuse has one of the best schools in the nation. If it wasn't for that, I wouldn't come here to be **tortured by the winters** that last from October to May or the roving bands of sorority girls."

Q "I love SU. **Be sure to pick your major early** because if you switch from, let's say, the Arts and Sciences into the VPA program, you could get caught having to stay an extra year due to different program setups. I love it there, and I wish I were back there now."

Q "**I can't say enough good things** about this place. I've loved every second of it. Syracuse is just so much fun, and you're getting a great education at the same time."

STUDENT AUTHOR: SU has a laundry list of good qualities about it, and very few flaws. The main thing to remember is that SU and its students refuse to be pigeonholed. There are so many varying interests at Syracuse University, as well as a broad array of extracurricular activities. The on-campus and off-campus housing is excellent, the computer facilities are top-notch, and the nightlife can be a major draw. Also, students generally have a lot of genuinely interesting events going on around campus. Whatever the reason, students who come to SU tend to stay here.

Temple University

1801 North Broad Street; Philadelphia, PA 19122
(215) 204-7000; www.temple.edu

THE BASICS:

Acceptance Rate: 63%
Setting: Urban
F-T Undergrads: 22,306

SAT Range: 980–1180*
Control: Public
Tuition: $17,236

Most Popular Majors: Business, Visual/Performing Arts, Education, Journalism, Psychology

*of 1600

Academics	B-	Guys	B-
Local Atmosphere	A-	Girls	B
Safety & Security	B	Athletics	B
Computers	C+	Nightlife	A-
Facilities	B+	Greek Life	C-
Campus Dining	C	Drug Scene	C+
Off-Campus Dining	A-	Campus Strictness	B
Campus Housing	C+	Parking	C
Off-Campus Housing	B	Transportation	B+
Diversity	A	Weather	B-

Students Speak Out
ON ACADEMICS

Q "Don't suffer alone; join one of those clubs that are part of your major, so you can meet people who have taken classes that you need to take. You can also **save money on books**."

Q "Hardly anyone graduates in four years, it takes like four and a half to five, and it's because of these **core classes** you have to take."

Q "I understand we have to **take some of those basic classes** before we can really start taking classes in our major. There's some that we haven't got a choice one, but then we do have the option of picking something that we have an interest."

Q "I heard that they were trying to make Temple an **Ivy League**, which is good for students like me who got in with a low SAT score."

Q "I got a **pretty good mental workout** in my time there. Some departments need to take more heed when students complain about poor teachers."

STUDENT AUTHOR: The foundation of education at Temple is based on core classes along with core requirements for majors. Temple has a goal for each student to be well rounded. There are mixed feelings about the teachers. Many feel the staff is not enthused about their subject, but overall, they feel that the teachers aren't that bad. Get to know your professors, and ask them for assistance if you need it.

Students Speak Out
ON LOCAL ATMOSPHERE

Q "I thought Philly was a **big city** like New York, but it really doesn't compare."

Q "Philly is the worst; there are dirty streets, too many bums, and the **city shuts down at midnight**."

Q "Philly has **a lot of attractions** and things to do. They always seem to have a festival or concert happening."

Q "**Philly isn't bad**, it has a lot of history and lots of places to go if you take the time to see it all."

Q "I think it's an okay city for some people. **It is very historic** and definitely has its good parts and bad parts."

Q "Philly has great food, and a **great college atmosphere** with all the other colleges close, but I'm not big on Philly."

STUDENT AUTHOR: Center City is the heart of Philadelphia and is packed full of historic places, such as museums and shopping areas, making it a great place to hang around or take the family. There is a mural of former Temple professor Sonia Sanchez that has become a part of Philly's culture. Another cool place to check out is South Street, which is what Philly has to offer as far as a social scene. Great bars and good food lie on this strip, which is very accessible. South Street is similar to the Village in New York, so things are very expensive, but definitely worth at least one visit.

5 Best Things	5 Worst Things
1 Diversity	1 Staff attitudes
2 Bar on campus	2 Not enough computers
3 Spring Fling	3 Financial aid office
4 Aeropostle box sales	4 Teachers
5 City campus	5 Malls are far away

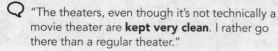

Students Speak Out
ON FACILITIES

Q "The theaters, even though it's not technically a movie theater are **kept very clean**. I rather go there than a regular theater."

Q "The gym has a lot of **different exercise equipment**, and I like the classes that they offer such as yoga and Tae Bo."

Q "The **pavilion was cool**; it is a nice facility. You could play ball and not worry about someone off the street coming to rob, shoot, bully, stab, or harass you."

Q "The new SAC and Tuttleman and all that is pretty good, too. Tuttleman's lab is pretty nice in my opinion. Overall, it seems like the facilities are **in fairly good shape**."

Q "The turf on 15th and Norris is bad, its just **Astroturf** with concrete under it."

STUDENT AUTHOR: **There are numerous facilities available, including basketball courts, weight rooms, and swimming pools where students can enjoy numerous recreational activities. There are also racquetball/handball courts spread throughout the campus. These gyms also offer classes such as yoga, Pilates, and aerobics. Best of all, they are never crowded. Sometimes, the gym offers free snacks or contests. A favorite among students is the "Take a Break Tuesdays," where a student can get a caricature done and free pretzels. Unfortunately, there is a $5 charge for visitors to these facilities. Thankfully, however, some dorms on campus have a game room or a fitness center, for which there is no charge.**

Famous Alumni

Bill Cosby (honorary degree), Mark Jackson, Eddie Jones, Dan Klecko, Aaron McKie, Bob Sagat

Students Speak Out
ON CAMPUS DINING

Q "I **always eat at the lunch trucks**; it's faster, and the prices are cheaper, and also the people that serve the food are nicer. The cashiers and food preparers at Temple always have an attitude."

Q "The little dining areas in the dorms **should stay open later**. Often, I get hungry when I'm studying, and I don't want to walk all the way to 7-Eleven for something to eat."

Q "They have lots of different delis that all serve the same thing; it seems kind of **wasteful**."

Q "No one liked the caf [cafeteria] because the **food got old**, but at the same time, if you go to the SAC to eat, all they served you was processed fast food."

Q "I usually had no problem with the SAC, and the caf is fine if you know what to avoid and how to **mix it up**."

STUDENT AUTHOR: **Though there are a lot of places to eat on campus— about half don't accept a meal plan. They either accept cash or Diamond Dollars, accessible with your ID card. Fair warning: don't get a big meal plan; it's a waste. The smallest meal plan available is a block five, which is five meals per week, and only to be used at the SAC or the cafeteria. The largest plan is the Super Value Carte Blanche plan for unlimited feasting. The cafeteria specializes in different cultural foods, as well as the usual pizza, sandwich, pasta, and salad entrees. The Student Center carries fast food restaurants and snacks.**

Student Body

African American:	17%	Male/Female:	49/51%
Asian American:	10%	Out-of-State:	22%
Hispanic:	3%	International:	3%
Native American:	<1%	Unknown:	9%
White:	58%		

Popular Faiths: There are a few Christian clubs and groups that hold events. The Muslim Association is probably the largest religious club on campus.

Gay Pride: The campus is tolerable to those who are gay. There also are clubs and events geared towards this minority.

Economic Status: The students at Temple come from different financial backgrounds.

Students Speak Out
ON DORMS

Q "The housing situation was a little strange. The school takes in too many freshmen and it creates a **logjam in housing**."

Q "I love on-campus housing. It allows you to **meet a lot of people**, and the facilities are nice."

Q "It's fun junior and sophomore year, but as you get older, the **rules can seem confining**."

Q "The freshman dorms are like living in a **mansion with 400 bedrooms**. It was the best."

STUDENT AUTHOR: **The freshman dorms at Temple allow people to meet each other with communal showers and weekly activities. The Kardon building is an apartment-style dorm that sits back, away from campus. 1300 offers single, double, and quadruple suites and apartments. They have a fitness room, game room, computer lab, mini-food store, and TV and study lounges. This dorm is located near classrooms and the Student Center. Temple Towers offers the same features. Park Mall is conveniently located near a hair salon, 7-Eleven, and classroom halls. Park Mall is clean with good amenities, but there is no apartment-style housing available.**

> **? Did You Know?**
> 20% of undergrads live on campus.

Students Speak Out
ON GUYS & GIRLS

Q "**No sense of variation** with the looks."

Q "No one had a sense of **individuality**; everyone wanted to do what the next person was doing."

Q "I think its **better to be a guy** at Temple. They seem to get more attention from the girls than the girls get from the guys."

Q "People are **free with sex** when they live on campus; a lot of people go out of character when they go away to school."

Q "There are people I know in **serious relationships**, there are people I know who are in serious relationships and who cheat, there are those people just looking for a good time here."

STUDENT AUTHOR: **Students at Temple find that, thanks to the large population of people from all over, it's easy to find someone that sparks interest, at least for a few days. As far as anything serious—come on, it's college! Live a little. Temple has a lot of potential for relationships, both short term and long. Temple has a handful of students who are models and actors. They are attractive and educated.**

> **Traditions**
>
> **Bill Cosby**
> All graduates look forward to seeing funnyman Bill Cosby speak at their graduation. He's never a disappointment.
>
> **Block Parties**
> Twice a year, campus turn into a giant outdoor party. The parties consist of food, music, games, and tons of fun.
>
> **Overall School Spirit**
> From the decorated dorm rooms of Temple paraphernalia to the painted bodies at games, Temple students are proud to be owls.

Students Speak Out
ON ATHLETICS

Q "Temple doesn't do a good job recruiting; they don't look for players that are **eligible grade-wise**."

Q "Certain teams, like the football team, get **lots of privileges** but can't win a game."

Q "**Football sucks**! The basketball team was great, but is now okay. Our rowing teams are outstanding, but nobody knows."

Q "I'd say we have **school pride** when it comes to our sports because we always want to be good and have one up on UPenn, LaSalle, and St. Joe's and so forth."

STUDENT AUTHOR: **The football team sucks, and the basketball team isn't much better, and because of this, you can be sure that tuition is going to increase. Nevertheless, Temple has phenomenal gymnastics, fencing, tennis, and swim teams. All of the sports are Division I teams. There is a bigger hype around the intramural teams. There are numerous intramural and club teams that students can get involved in. Temple also offers funding and promotional opportunities to help clubs become established and grow.**

Students Speak Out
ON DRUG SCENE

Q "Drugs aren't out there at Temple, but I'm pretty sure **behind closed doors**, there are students doing stuff."

Q "I know of a couple of people shooting up and snorting coke—crazy stuff, not to mention the plethora of **drunk and high people**."

Q "I think that if there was a problem with any kind of drug, it would be **alcohol**."

Q "They stress how much **underage drinking** is so much on the campus, yet they build a bar right in the heart of campus."

STUDENT AUTHOR: Alcohol is tolerated if you are of age, and only a certain amount can be brought into the dorms. Students find ways to get around the red tape, but there are RAs that take their job seriously. Besides alcohol, students report marijuana as the most commonly abused substance on campus. As far as other types of drugs, there are a lot of rumors of doing hard drugs, but usually it's from students that "have a friend that knew this guy."

17:1	Student-to-Faculty Ratio
85%	Freshman Retention Rate
30%	Four-Year Graduation Rate
71%	Financial Aid Applicants Receiving Aid

Students Speak Out
SAFETY & SECURITY

Q "I always see the Temple **police on their bikes** or eating a donut at 7-Eleven."

Q "They were good; **campus is lit very brightly**, and the new security phones are darn near everywhere you could possibly need one. Police respond very quickly (you'd know if you ever called them)."

Q "I probably sound naïve, but I don't think a lot of crime happens on campus. You hear about people getting their cars broken in to and people getting things stolen from their rooms, but I don't know, I would think that was a **minor issue** for Temple."

STUDENT AUTHOR: Temple University is maintained with Temple police, city police, and security guards. Temple has a vast lighting system. To make up for the bad location, the administration makes sure it has a top-notch security system. Thanks to the administration's importance on security, crime rates have been low.

Questions?
For more inside information and survival tips, pick up College Prowler's full-length book on this school, written by an actual student! Check it out at *www.collegeprowler.com.*

Students Speak Out
ON OVERALL EXPERIENCE

Q "It really wasn't much about education, it was more about experience. Since the school was located in a city, I think I **learned more outside the classroom** than I did in it."

Q "The college experience, more so the Temple experience, was great for me, personally. It **taught me a lot about myself**."

Q "Temple is a pretty cool school. **They didn't seem to expect much**, academically; it was kind of, like, you making the best of everything Temple had to give their students."

Q "I like it, and I have **a lot of fun**. I just wish the weekends weren't so dead."

Q "I love Temple. I love it because there is **always something going on**, there's always something to get involved in, and I have never had any type of problem that made me think differently."

STUDENT AUTHOR: Some people don't feel as though they are prepared for the real world once they leave campus, but others say it's been an incredible learning experience. Those students that love their experience at Temple all have their own reasons. Some love the atmosphere and found it to be a lot of fun. Others found it to be a great place to grow-up and discover themselves. Lots of students take away more from living in a big city than they do from the University. But one thing that most students agree upon is that the people at Temple University are what really make it a worthwhile experience.

Tennessee State University

3500 John A. Merritt Boulevard; Nashville, TN 37209-1561
(615) 963-5000; www.tnstate.edu

THE BASICS:

Acceptance Rate: 66%
Setting: Urban
F-T Undergrads: 5,754

SAT Range: 1185–1435*
Control: Public
Tuition: $15,162

Most Popular Majors: Business. Education, Biological Science, Engineering, Mathematics and Statistics

*of 2400

Academics	B-	Guys	B
Local Atmosphere	B+	Girls	A-
Safety & Security	C	Athletics	B
Computers	C	Nightlife	B+
Facilities	B	Greek Life	B
Campus Dining	C	Drug Scene	B+
Off-Campus Dining	B-	Campus Strictness	B-
Campus Housing	C+	Parking	D
Off-Campus Housing	B-	Transportation	B
Diversity	C-	Weather	B

Students Speak Out
ON ACADEMICS

Q "The classes in my major and the ones that I want to actually be in are interesting. The teachers that I have are animated; thus, I learn more. But there are **a lot of dry, by-the-book teachers here**, and that doesn't always work for everyone."

Q "I find that my classes don't focus on the aspects of the subject matter that most students find interesting. I think that **teachers are usually more concerned with humor** than trying to find ways to engage in the subjects that are actually exciting and fun."

Q "**My teachers have been the backbone of my career**; I really don't know where I would be without them. They are very supportive, and they will do everything they can to make the class enjoyable."

Q "The classes are well-taught, and **most teachers seem very dedicated** to their work."

STUDENT AUTHOR: Most of the TSU student body and faculty take academics very seriously. The University prides itself on having a large graduating class every year, and most of the classes are very interesting due to the teachers who teach them. TSU offers a wide variety of professors who either make or break the class. Most teachers are confident in their subjects and work diligently to create a fun, safe learning environment. Professors are required to keep office hours, so students who need to speak with them can come by with no appointments.

Students Speak Out
ON LOCAL ATMOSPHERE

Q "There are lots of other colleges and universities here: Vandy, Fisk, Belmont, Lipscomb, and other little community colleges and stuff. **There is always something to do in Nashville**. I love music, and this is a music town. And since I'm old enough to partake in it, the bar scene is great here, too! There is a cult church here, though, and some seedy clubs; stay away from those."

Q "**Nashville is very quiet**. There are plenty of 'tourist attractions,' but as a student, you can only visit those things a few times before it becomes boring. The crime rate is on the rise, so I spend a lot less time in the slums."

Q "Nashville is **not much of a college town**. There aren't places that cater to students, unless they are directly next to the campus. There's a lot to do socially, however."

Q "I think Nashville is a great town. It has pockets of many of the things desirable about student and urban life. **I find the city to be much more interesting than the campus**."

STUDENT AUTHOR: In Nashville, there is always something to do for fun; the key is to know where to look. Campus is five minutes away from West End and Charlotte avenues, which will carry you to the hottest clubs, restaurants, and shopping areas. The campus itself is very friendly; however, the surrounding area can be somewhat unsafe at times. Overall, the people in Nashville are great to socialize with, and despite the South's reputation, we are certainly not all hicks.

5 Best Things
1 The students
2 The teachers
3 Football games
4 Parties
5 Beautiful atmosphere

5 Worst Things
1 Parking
2 Registration process
3 Admissions department
4 Fickle weather
5 The dorms

Students Speak Out
ON FACILITIES

Q "The school is currently undergoing improvements, but **most of the facilities are outdated**."

Q "The facilities are very nice. Although they appear old on the outside, **the inside is very well managed and kept**. The computer areas are busy but well-maintained and updated. The student center is very welcoming and has almost everything you need to live on campus, including restaurants, a café, the bookstore, an ATM, and all of the offices, like student affairs."

Q "**The Wellness Center is new and a great place to work out**. Trainers will work with you and guide you. Equipment is well labeled. Other facilities, such as the student center, are clean and well-kept. TSU tends to take pride in the maintenance and cleanliness of campus."

Q "The facilities are great. Most notable is the student center because it has **everything a new student needs** from the bookstore to financial aid."

STUDENT AUTHOR: **The administration at TSU has spent millions of dollars making sure the facilities are nice and hospitable to students. The best facility is definitely the Floyd-Payne Campus Center. It houses all the really important offices such as records, financial aid, the bookstore, post office, as well as a huge lounge area. There are, however, older buildings that need to be remodeled badly. The newer buildings are kept up really well, and the administration is trying to remodel parts of the campus that are not in great condition.**

Famous Alumni
Jimmy Blanton, Moses Gunn, Jesse Russell, Ed "Too Tall" Jones, Oprah Winfrey

Students Speak Out
ON CAMPUS DINING

Q "The campus **food is good in certain periods of the semester**. Whenever there is someone of influence (alumni, congressmen, guest speakers) around, the cafeteria food tastes better."

Q "Overall, **the food is not very good**, but it's a college campus, so you can't really expect home cooking or anything."

Q "The food needs work. **The meals in the cafeteria are bland**, to say the least. The best place to eat is the coffeeshop."

Q "This campus is a little too far on the greasy, junk-food end of things. **It is not accommodating to vegetarians**."

Q "With so many fast food restaurants around, **I have never even considered eating in the cafeteria**. Rumor has it that it is not really good anyway. I'd rather eat food I know I'm going to like."

STUDENT AUTHOR: **The food on campus is mediocre at best. There are meal plans available to students who live on campus, but it is a generic menu every day. TSU students love their junk food, so the cafeteria is the least popular place on campus for students to eat. Freshmen are required to have a meal plan, and usually that's about all it takes for them to realize there is better food available. Students' options are limited because this is a Southern school, and therefore, greasy food is in! Soul food and junk food are the most popular diets, but the cafeteria really tries to serve well-balanced meals, as they should.**

Student Body

African American:	84%	Male/Female:	35/65%
Asian American:	1%	Out-of-State:	23%
Hispanic:	<1%	International:	1%
Native American:	<1%	Unknown:	0%
White:	13%		

Popular Faiths: The campus is mostly Christian, especially Southern Baptist and Methodist.

Gay Pride: The gay population is accepted around campus. Everyone pretty much just minds their own business, and people are really respectful to one another.

Economic Status: TSU represents a wide range of economic diversity.

Students Speak Out
ON DORMS

Q "The dorms are okay. **They're not great, but they're not completely horrible either**, at least the ones I've lived in. (Some people might not agree.) Rudolph is a nice place from the outside, but the rooms are small as hell."

Q "**The freshmen dorms are death traps**. It's much better to be a female than a male student when it comes to housing options. Men have only two dorms: the freshman dorm and the dorm for everybody else."

Q "The dorms are okay if you are used to it, but I had a pretty big room at home, so **the space limit is hard to get used to**, because the rooms are so small."

STUDENT AUTHOR: **On-campus housing at TSU is not the best aspect of the school; however, the students who live on campus seem to be pretty happy with their living arrangements. The rooms are really small, but they are not terribly out-of-date, and they are kept pretty clean. Most students seem to be satisfied with the dorms, aside from the rooms being so small. If you want to experience TSU mostly for academics, consider living off campus, because you will have much more privacy.**

Did You Know?
73% of undergrads live on campus.

Students Speak Out
ON GUYS & GIRLS

Q "**The girls are hot**, as long as you like African American girls. Other groups, including Caucasian, are underrepresented at the school."

Q "Some of the guys are cool, more are like associates. The **girls are okay, some are good-looking**, you know. I could go on all day with that."

Q "The women are lovely beyond compare. The ratios are so skewed with relation to male and female that **it's a virtual buffet for guys**."

Q "There are some hotties, but **you do have the tragic cases that should be avoided**. This campus had a big STD outbreak the year before I was here."

STUDENT AUTHOR: **The guys and girls at TSU are really attractive. TSU has a great variety of cliques, and a little bit for each individual to choose from. There is a lot of competition for guys because the ratio of girls to guys is almost 2:1! This is actually an inside joke on the campus, because guys love the fact that they are surrounded by girls. The campus is pretty accepting of everyone who is a part of the social scene.**

Traditions

Alma Mater
Each student must learn the alma mater in their freshman orientation classes. It is a necessity to know in order to survive football games and graduations. Some teachers will even test you on it to make sure you know it by heart.

Overall School Spirit
The TSU school spirit is extremely high. Before every football game, the student center is full of royal blue and white decorations everywhere. Throughout the week, students flaunt their TSU Tiger sportswear across campus to show their support.

Students Speak Out
ON ATHLETICS

Q "Some sports are bigger than others. Football and b-ball are big. **The IM sports draw a good crowd**, too."

Q "Football is king. **Basketball is gaining popularity**, as the team is creating a buzz in the city."

Q "**The varsity sports are not supported too well**, though many students enjoy competing in the IM sports, especially basketball."

STUDENT AUTHOR: **Student participation is pretty high in football and basketball for the guys and volleyball and basketball for the girls. Football games are by far the most popular, and basketball is a close second in participation and attendance. The IM sports are played for bragging rights, and everyone who participates in them gets pumped up about them. Students will not have a difficult time fitting in regardless of whether they like sports or not, though. There are many students who do not play or attend any of the sports; however, a student cannot help but keep up-to-date, because students talk about the previous games frequently.**

Students Speak Out
ON DRUG SCENE

Q "Just like any school, **you don't see it unless you are looking for it**."

Q "There is a lot of marijuana usage, but other than that, **it's pretty clean**."

Q "There is a lot of weed smoking around here, but you really don't notice it unless you go searching for it. **It's kept pretty low-key**."

STUDENT AUTHOR: Students are aware of marijuana usage around campus, but most don't even acknowledge it as a problem. Caffeine is by far the leading drug on campus, though, and you will usually see students walking around with a coke of some kind or a coffee from Starbucks. Students at TSU will not openly admit using any drugs, and you will not notice it much. There is not peer pressure to take any drugs. Cigarette smokers are still a minority at TSU, and marijuana users tend to be secretly spread throughout the campus. For an incoming student, the drug scene is not really something to worry about.

12:1	Student-to-Faculty Ratio
74%	Freshman Retention Rate
46%	Four-Year Graduation Rate
87%	Financial Aid Applicants Receiving Aid

Students Speak Out
SAFETY & SECURITY

Q "For people, it is safe; for their things, no. There aren't many snatchings, but **people will break into your car** very quickly."

Q "TSU **has increased security** procedures and installed video cameras within the last few years."

Q "I **mostly feel unsafe because of the security guards**. They have a tendency to abuse their power on campus."

Q "It **needs much improvement**. It seems like only a matter of time before something serious happens because of a lack of proactive policing."

Q "Security is average. I mean, I've heard things about cops busting people for different things and stuff, and I've also heard that **people's cars are getting broken into**, too."

STUDENT AUTHOR: Safety on the TSU campus is certainly not its greatest attribute; however, it is slowly but surely getting better each year. Off campus, it is entirely different. The surrounding area is in poverty, so it is best to not travel alone, especially after dark.

Questions?
For more inside information and survival tips, pick up College Prowler's full-length book on this school, written by an actual student! Check it out at www.collegeprowler.com.

Students Speak Out
ON OVERALL EXPERIENCE

Q "I am happy to be going to TSU. **I feel I am getting a great education**. I have had no major issues dealing with school that would make me think anything else. I am proud to be attending TSU, and I would recommend it to everyone."

Q "I'm not really satisfied with the school. They don't have the major that I'm looking for. The administration is upsetting, and they never have anything together. Yes, **I do wish I was somewhere else**, and I'm transferring after my sophomore year."

Q "It's great. **I enjoy the atmosphere of the campus being downtown**. It would seem to be congested, but it's like a whole separate world from the rest of downtown."

Q "I really like it. I believe that the environment is very easy to learn in, and **the diversity of students allows all to be comfortable**. I did feel a little skeptical about going to a mostly African-American school, but I did not notice it after the first week."

STUDENT AUTHOR: Students at TSU seem to be happy with their experiences thus far. There are a few improvements that could be made such as parking, registration, and some building renovations, but most of TSU's drawbacks are related to the same problems the city itself has. The University's motto is "Students Matter Most," and they truly try to aid students in any way they can. TSU students are satisfied with the school as a whole, and in order to get the best ideas of what to do and not to do, talk to the students. TSU students are friendly, energetic, and always able to help someone in need.

Texas A&M University

Houston Street, College Station, TX 77843
(979) 845-3211; www.tamu.edu

THE BASICS:

Acceptance Rate: 76%
Setting: Small City
F-T Undergrads: 34,495

SAT Range: 1070–1300*
Control: Public
Tuition: $22,474

Most Popular Majors: Business, Engineering, Agriculture, Social Sciences, Biological/Life Sciences

*of 1600

Academics	B-	Guys	A+
Local Atmosphere	C+	Girls	A
Safety & Security	B	Athletics	A
Computers	A	Nightlife	B
Facilities	A	Greek Life	B
Campus Dining	B+	Drug Scene	A-
Off-Campus Dining	A	Campus Strictness	B
Campus Housing	B-	Parking	C--
Off-Campus Housing	B+	Transportation	C+
Diversity	D+	Weather	B

Students Speak Out
ON ACADEMICS

Q "I think **our school is very academic-minded**, and most professors that I have run into are very helpful if you show you care about your work and education."

Q "All my professors have been very helpful and nice. They are **extremely challenging**, but they also care a lot for their students and try to help you out as much as they can."

Q "I really liked most of the teachers I have had. **Some of them are just there to do research** and don't really care about us, but a lot of them are really nice. If you are a science major, you are more likely to get the ones that don't care or have bad English, but I had a teacher last semester that let me borrow her textbook before every test because I lost mine. She had my cell phone number and I had her home phone number!"

Q "I dropped a class because the teacher was from China, and **if I closed my eyes I couldn't understand her**. I have trouble concentrating as it is!"

STUDENT AUTHOR: **Most of the teachers at A&M are extremely qualified in their field and very knowledgeable in their subject matter. There are a large number of international graduate students that may teach introductory courses. Academically, a lot is up to the student. Students need to make the effort to get to know the professors. The teachers actually view their students as fellow human beings, and not just some pesky pupils.**

Students Speak Out
ON LOCAL ATMOSPHERE

Q "I love artsy stuff and was very disappointed coming here. There are **very few cultural things to do**, with hardly any museums or exhibits in sight. The closest things to art are some tiny exhibits in the MSC that change every few months. Go to Austin or Houston if you want that kind of stuff."

Q "The atmosphere is really good. Coming from Dallas, a huge city, I think we're in a pretty small town. There is not really a downtown because the College is the main thing, but Bryan has a cute little downtown right next to C.S. **Austin is an hour and half away, and Houston is the same**. Galveston and the beach are two hours from us. We did a bunch of little weekend road trips around Texas."

Q "**You can walk up to total strangers** and start conversations with them. That's what sold me on going to A&M."

Q "**I hate College Station**. I made a T-shirt that says 'College Station Sucks' that has been wildly popular. I'm thinking of selling it. I could make a million."

STUDENT AUTHOR: **College Station is a small town in rural Texas. The town definitely revolves around A&M. The entire city works around the University's calendar, especially the athletic events. If students do get bored—and they will—they can always take a road trip to Austin or Houston. Overall, there is a thick conservative and Christian atmosphere in and around College Station.**

5 Best Things	5 Worst Things
1 Traditions	1 Parking
2 Unity	2 Athletes are spoiled
3 Respect for history	3 Lack of diversity
4 Football	4 Standing for whole game
5 School spirit	5 School is huge

Students Speak Out
ON FACILITIES

Q "The **Rec is a multi-million dollar facility**, housing an extremely nice weight room and workout facility, a rock-climbing wall, basketball courts, indoor volleyball courts, indoor soccer facilities, racquetball courts, aerobics rooms, an indoor running track, an indoor Olympic-sized pool, an outdoor pool, outdoor basketball courts, and sand volleyball courts."

Q "Everything is awesome. **It's all new or recently upgraded**. You always see something being done on campus."

Q "**The Browsing Library is my little study secret**. It is always quiet, and you can get headphones to listen to any CD they have there while you study. It's on the second floor of the MSC."

Q "The **track is on the third floor** and has really good terrain. It's great to run on, because it's always too hot outside."

STUDENT AUTHOR: Most students are very happy with the facilities at A&M. The libraries are nice, and the Memorial Student Center is the Grand Central Station of campus. It has everything you could possibly want, from practical things, like a post office, to the entertainment of a game room and bowling alley. The Rec Center is state-of-the-art. There is a rock-climbing wall inside, as well as a nicely stocked weight room, racquetball courts, inside and outside pools, and a hot tub. If a facility is not new already, it's probably under construction. A&M gives a lot of attention to making students satisfied with their facilities.

Famous Alumni

Chet Edwards, Aaron Glenn, Davey Johnson, Robert Earl Keen, Chuck Knoblauch, Kandace Krueger, C.E. "Pat" Olsen, Rip Torn, Gene Wolfe

Students Speak Out
ON CAMPUS DINING

Q "**Sbisa is like a wonderful food dream**. You walk in and it's like an acre-wide buffet serving everything you can think of. I run them out of money since it's all-you-can-eat. You can always get your money's worth from your meal plan."

Q "The food isn't horrible, but after a while, you get kind of tired of it. **We do have Chick-fil-A and Whataburger on campus**, which make up for the cafeteria food at times."

Q "No matter which dorm you choose, you do not have far to go to find a good meal! **Both Northside and Southside dorms offer students a cafeteria** including meal plans that are accepted at any on campus dining hall, cafeteria, or snack stand."

Q "For a late night of studying, **Rumours is the hot spot**!"

Q "I am not too picky about food, but I can tell the difference between good and bad, and I think we have **pretty good food**. I am an athlete, and we have our own dining hall, but I have eaten at other dining halls and the food was good there."

STUDENT AUTHOR: There are several all-you-can-eat cafeterias, giving A&M students the option of taste-testing as little, or as much, as they desire. There's also pizza, burgers, and everything you can think of that's both tasty and fattening. For those of you looking to fend off the Freshman 15, there are salad bars and delis where you can build your own healthy sandwiches. The best kept secret on campus is Cain Dining Hall in the athletic dorm.

Student Body

African American:	3%	Male/Female:	50/50%
Asian American:	5%	Out-of-State:	4%
Hispanic:	13%	International:	2%
Native American:	<1%	Unknown:	<1%
White:	76%		

Popular Faiths: Christianity is by far the most popular religion on campus. There are over 70 religious organizations on campus, as well.

Gay Pride: There are a couple groups for gay and lesbian Aggies, but they are definitely in the minority and are not highly visible on campus.

Economic Status: Most students are middle-class, but there are students from every economic level.

Students Speak Out
ON DORMS

Q "**The Commons are nice**. Made up of Mosher, Kruger, Dunn, and Aston Halls, they're mostly for freshmen. I found I really enjoyed my experience in Mosher. The Commons is the main place on Southside. The modular dorms are really nice, too. They are pretty big and offer private bathrooms."

Q "The dorms were **built decades ago and are older than dirt**. The fluorescent lights disgust me, so we took them out and just used lamps. Depending on your roommate, you can usually dress up your room and make it feel homier. You can bring a TV, microwave, and fridge, but there's not much room for them."

STUDENT AUTHOR: **A&M is divided into two parts, Northside and Southside. Every person on each side will tell you their side is the best. The dorms on Northside are generally cheaper, and the Northside dwellers, in general, are a close-knit, anti-frat, anti-Corps group. Southside is home to the Corps Dorms and the Commons, which houses a lot of sorority girls. You'll just have to take a guess about which side you think you'd like best, because they really are very different.**

? Did You Know?
25% of undergrads live on campus.

Students Speak Out
ON GUYS & GIRLS

Q "Both the girls and the guys are great. **It's a super-friendly campus**, and we do have some major hotties here and there."

Q "Wow, the guys are amazing! They're adorable, with good manners and **sweet Southern charm**. Bonus points if he looks good in Wranglers."

Q "**I think they all look kind of the same**, which is good if you like that style. Most everyone's clean cut, and there are very few punk or skater-types."

Q "The Corps guys are hot! People are nice enough, but **it is hard to make friends** and keep them, just because there are so many people that it's hard to stay in touch."

STUDENT AUTHOR: **Most of the guys and girls seem to be clean cut and conservative dressers, but you can find anything out of the thousands of students here. Due to the conservative atmosphere and influence of the Corps, you will find that welcoming Southern hospitality all around town and on campus. Also, most of the guys are very chivalrous. It is very common for strangers to give up their seat on the bus to a lady and to hold doors open, even if the girl is 20 feet away.**

Traditions

Every Time the Aggies Score, You score
At a football game, if the team scores a point, you kiss your date.

Midnight Yell
At midnight before every home football game, Aggies gather at Kyle Field for yell practice.

Overall School Spirit
There are lots of loyal fans who keep all the traditions. Aggies love their sports, and students come decked out in maroon and white, some standing or shouting during the entire game—quite a sight to see.

Students Speak Out
ON ATHLETICS

Q "**We're part of the Big 12**, so when it comes to varsity sports, like football, it's definitely a big part of what our school is all about. I have yet to find a school with as much spirit as Texas A&M."

Q "Varsity sports are really big here, especially football. There are tons of intramural sports here, too, and lots of people are involved in them. **Texas A&M is very proud of its unity** within the student body. At football games, we have fight songs that the entire crowd knows. If you are from Texas, you have probably heard tales of the intensity of the Aggie football games! They are a blast, and I haven't missed one yet."

Q "Aggie football is the biggest thing ever. It's like a **big party going on at the stadium**. There are so many traditions that it's unbelievable. Baseball is a really big thing too, but sports are just big in general here."

STUDENT AUTHOR: **Football is, by far, the biggest and most overshadowing sport at A&M. Most students enjoy football games and the traditions that go along with them. Kyle Field is always filled to capacity with screaming fans.**

Students Speak Out
ON DRUG SCENE

Q "I know for a fact that there are people on campus who smoke up, but there are very few. The **drug scene here is almost nonexistent**. It's better that way, in my opinion."

Q "I'm sure there is a drug scene here. If you want it, I'm sure you can find it. If you're not into it, it's hard to see it. I think, for the most part, **A&M parties are known for having large quantities of alcohol**."

Q "I don't know much about it, except that there's **some pot smoking** and a little coke here and there, but nothing's too big as far as I know."

STUDENT AUTHOR: Alcohol is probably the only substance that all students have a wide exposure to, although other drugs are likely still available on campus. Of all the illegal drugs on campus, marijuana is the most popular, but even that isn't very common. College Station is a small town with little influence from the drug culture. It's mostly a clean town, which gives you a better chance to stay in school and pass your classes.

20:1	Student-to-Faculty Ratio
91%	Freshman Retention Rate
40%	Four-Year Graduation Rate
68%	Financial Aid Applicants Receiving Aid

Students Speak Out
SAFETY & SECURITY

Q "The on-campus security is great. If you are out late, you can always call one of the Corps guys to escort you home. **There are lots of lights, and people are always out**. I personally do not like to walk around alone at night, but it's never a problem at A&M."

Q "I lost my wallet once and got it back from Lost and Found with all the money still in it. A&M really is a cool place, and **people look out for each other**."

Q "There are people walking around constantly, even late at night, and there are always security guys around—not to mention all the lights. These are the benefits of being at a big school—the campus never goes to sleep. The worst thing that happened to me was when **my bike got stolen**!"

STUDENT AUTHOR: Living inside the Aggie bubble leads many people into believing they're always safe. In the not-so-distant past, there have been reported cases of assault and even rape, on campus. This is not to mention the crimes on campus that are not detected, mentioned, or reported.

> **Questions?**
> For more inside information and survival tips, pick up College Prowler's full-length book on this school, written by an actual student! Check it out at *www.collegeprowler.com*.

Students Speak Out
ON OVERALL EXPERIENCE

Q "I love A&M for its **small-school feel on a big campus**. The tremendous school spirit makes you feel like you are a part of a huge family. I wish, in a way, that I would have gone out-of-state for a more challenging experience, in the realm of diversity at least."

Q "My dad and grandpa both went here, and the strength of the traditions really attracted me to A&M. **The school is really consistent and stable**, and I like that."

Q "It's like someone said, '**Looking in from the outside, you can't understand it**. Looking out from the inside, you can't explain it.' It holds true for me. I can't explain to you how much spirit there is, or how much I love A&M. I don't want to leave. I loved it, and A&M will always be my second home."

Q "I think the traditions are stupid, and too many people have their entire identity wrapped up in the school. It's a neat place, but **it shouldn't be your whole life**."

STUDENT AUTHOR: Most students either love or hate A&M, and those who hate it usually transfer out their first year. A&M offers an incredible educational and lifetime experience that most students thoroughly enjoy. If you have a problem with life at A&M, it's most likely because you haven't found a niche and you still feel lost in the crowd. It can be difficult to find people with common interests that you really click with, but if you get involved in student organizations and your classes, you'll figure it out. A&M isn't just about going somewhere for four years to learn—it's like becoming part of a society that will continue to shape and mold your life.

Texas Christian University

2800 South University Drive; Fort Worth, TX 76129
(817) 257-7000; www.tcu.edu

THE BASICS:

Acceptance Rate: 49%
Setting: Urban
F-T Undergrads: 7,050

SAT Range: 1060–1260*
Control: Private
Tuition: $26,900

Most Popular Majors: Business, Communications, Health Professions, Education

*of 2400

Academics	B	Guys	B+
Local Atmosphere	B+	Girls	A-
Safety & Security	B	Athletics	B
Computers	B	Nightlife	B+
Facilities	B+	Greek Life	A
Campus Dining	C+	Drug Scene	B+
Off-Campus Dining	B+	Campus Strictness	B
Campus Housing	B-	Parking	C
Off-Campus Housing	B-	Transportation	B+
Diversity	C	Weather	B-

Students Speak Out
ON ACADEMICS

Q "The teachers that I have encountered at TCU have **all been very supportive and very reasonable**. I haven't come across any 'I am mightier than thou, bow down in awe before my massive PhD' type of professors that you hear about or see on TV."

Q "The teachers at TCU are pretty decent, but it **seems like a lot of them leave for other opportunities**. The foreign language teachers seem especially great."

Q "**All the classes are small enough**, and you can easily talk with your professors. The professors are very personable, and it isn't scary talking to them at all. This is definitely a positive thing about TCU, and something that drew me to it."

Q "Teachers really vary depending on the subject. You're going to have some that are really tough, and others that aren't so bad. I found my professors to be very friendly and helpful. They were very adamant about letting us know they **were there if we needed assistance**."

STUDENT AUTHOR: **With accessible and mostly understandable teachers, there is an emphasis on the learning process. Small classes create an intimate setting between professors and students, which makes the whole learning process more personal. Most TCU professors take an active interest in their students' performances and are willing to help them succeed. Less personable professors are generally the exception; though, most students will encounter them at some point.**

Students Speak Out
ON LOCAL ATMOSPHERE

Q "When you're on campus, **you feel like you're not part of the city**. However, the downtown area, museum district, and historical district are only about 10 to 15 minutes away. There are places to eat, see, and fun things to do."

Q "This is how it works: Fort Worth has the good bars and Dallas has the great clubs. TCU is in a city that's big, but not too big, and you have tons of other cities to choose from. Dallas is only 30 minutes away. Don't expect to see cowboy types around here; the **majority of people are conservative**."

Q "There is so much to see and do within Fort Worth and the entire area. There's the Botanical Gardens, Water Gardens, **stockyards, museums, pro sports teams, a ton of concerts**."

Q "Fort Worth is awesome. It has everything you might need. If not, **Dallas is a mere 30 minutes away**. Southern Methodist University (SMU) is in Dallas, and University of North Texas (UNT) is in Denton—both are only about 30 minutes away. The University of Texas at Arlington (UTA) is 20 minutes away, too."

STUDENT AUTHOR: **Though it is a small town, Fort Worth has restaurants, bars, clubs, and movie theaters close to campus. The small-town atmosphere blends well with the University, making it a good environment for students to work and play. For students who want a change of scenery, nearby cities such as Dallas and Arlington provide more entertainment and activities.**

5 Best Things	5 Worst Things
1 Clean campus	1 No parking
2 Modern technology	2 High tuition
3 Nice landscaping	3 Lack of diversity
4 Good facilities	4 Everything is expensive
5 Close to Dallas	5 Living in the TCU bubble

Students Speak Out
ON FACILITIES

Q "We have a nice recreation center. It has **everything from a rock-climbing wall to saunas**. Each aerobic machine has a 15-inch LCD screen attached to it, so you can watch whatever you want while working out. We have a new baseball stadium, our basketball facility is pretty nice, and our football stadium is huge! The student center is one of the next projects to be considered for renovation on campus. Many of the residence halls have been recently redone. We also have two fairly new academic buildings on campus. Even the oldest buildings have been upgraded and have plans for renovations."

Q "The student center is alright. It's sometimes really crowded, especially around noon. The recreation center is really nice. The **computers in the library are really nice**, too—they just upgraded the Macs. The only facilities that I have a problem with are the food places. For breakfast and lunch, it's okay, but at dinner, there's only one place to eat, and that is kind of annoying."

Q "**Everything is something to show off**. Everything is so well-kept. TCU is constantly renovating and updating!"

STUDENT AUTHOR: **The Rickel Recreation Center features many of the newest machines and a variety of weights, as well as a climbing wall, saunas, and racquetball courts. The Brown-Lupton Student Center is also well equipped for many student affairs, but in reality, it may fail to provide enough variety in the restaurant department. Overall, campus is very well kept, and anything that hasn't been renovated lately is sure to get its chance soon.**

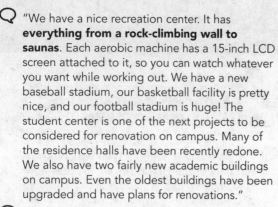

Famous Alumni

Aaron Chimbel, Gordon England, Reggie Hunt, Davey O'Brien, Rod Roddy, Rob Schieffer, Bo Schobel, Matt Schobel, LaDainian Tomlinson

Students Speak Out
ON CAMPUS DINING

Q "We have several places on campus to eat. The Main is the biggest place to eat. It's cafeteria-style food with pasta, burgers, chicken fingers, and there's usually something different everyday. There's a big salad bar, which is pretty good, too. Eden's is my favorite place for lunch. There's **Mongolian style stir-fry that is amazing**! They are only open for lunch, though, which is a pain. I usually eat a big lunch there, and then just have a little dinner at Frog Bytes, the convenience store. Deco Deli is a sandwich place connected to Eden's, and it has great sandwiches, too."

Q "The food on campus is occasionally tasty, but **mostly just expensive**. It needs to have more variety."

Q "Food on campus **isn't as bad as I thought it would be**. The best places to eat are Eden's Greens, a salad shop, and a Chinese food place. Deco Deli is a sandwich shop, and it also has hot Campbell's soup. All of these places are very good."

STUDENT AUTHOR: **There aren't many options for on-campus dining at TCU, though some are appetizing. The cafeteria-style Main Grain, Eden's Greens, and the sandwich-lover's Deco Deli and Sub Connection offer a bit of variety for a short time. Some groceries and other food are available in Frog Bytes, the cyber café, which is usually open late. The food tends to be overpriced, and it is easy to lose interest in the selection within a semester. Despite the limited hours, many students are satisfied with the dining options.**

Student Body

African American:	5%	Male/Female:	40/60%
Asian American:	2%	Out-of-State:	20%
Hispanic:	8%	International:	4%
Native American:	<1%	Unknown:	5%
White:	76%		

Popular Faiths: Christianity is obviously very prominent, but other religions are met with tolerance.

Gay Pride: There is a TCU chapter of eQ Alliance, which meets regularly throughout the year and sponsors some events.

Economic Status: The student body is made up of people from either upper-class or upper-middle class, along with a good deal of scholarship students.

Students Speak Out
ON DORMS

Q "The **freshman and the all-male dorms are the worst dorms on campus**. They're really bare—there are community showers and bathrooms, and they're just not very private. My freshman year, I stayed in Colby Hall, which is okay if you're just going to live there for one year, but the nicer dorms are Foster and Waits. The ideal living situation are the on-campus apartments, the Upton Brown/Pete Wright community."

Q "Dorms are great. **Most of them have been newly renovated**. I would stay away from Colby, the all-girls dorm, because it's older than all the rest. I lived in Brachman my first year, in Worth Hills, and it was awesome. I like living down there because you always know what is going on with the fraternities. Worth Hills is where most of the fraternity and sorority houses are located."

STUDENT AUTHOR: Housing at TCU revolves around money—each dorm comes with its own price tag. Most of the nicer on-campus housing is reserved for upperclass students, although none of the facilities are entirely exclusive. All freshmen are required to live on campus, which can be a great way to get involved with the school and meet new people.

Did You Know?
46% of undergrads live on campus.

Students Speak Out
ON GUYS & GIRLS

Q "TCU girls were **ranked among the hottest girls in the nation**, and the guys are pretty good looking, too! TCU has been trying to balance the girl-to-guy ratio. My favorite part is that the guys will open the doors for you! What Southern hospitality!"

Q "As a general rule, **TCU has a lot more attractive people than most universities** around. I visited a lot of other schools—hanging out with friends—and can confirm this. With that, however, also comes a good number of people that know they are the attractive people."

Q "The **girls here all seem to be blonde** and clones of each other."

STUDENT AUTHOR: Most girls at TCU are the sorority type, but if you come looking for something different, you're sure to find it. TCU guys are not known for being quite as attractive, though most are quite appealing to the eye and by manners. Most students at TCU take part in Greek life, which makes it harder to find someone outside of that. Finding someone new and interesting is by no means impossible, and most of the people are at least somewhat attractive.

Traditions

Purple and White
The purple signifies royalty, and white, the other school color, represents a good, clean game.

Ol' South
At the Ol' South Pancake House, the menu is cheap, and the 24-hour restaurant has been a popular attraction of TCU students for decades.

Overall School Spirit
From the stickers on their cars to the sold-out football games, students clearly take pride in the school. It is not uncommon to see a sea of purple at sporting events.

Students Speak Out
ON ATHLETICS

Q "**All TCU sporting events are free with your student ID**. It's fun to dress in purple and head to the games to cheer on the Frogs! Intramural sports are also pretty competitive. There are several teams that compete each year, and it's fun to watch them!"

Q "Unfortunately, most school sports aren't too popular, except when the teams are winning. The Intramural sports are a big deal. **The guys get really competitive**. Lots of people go and watch the games during weeknights in the winter."

Q "TCU's sports programs are the **largest-funded organization** (including all the schools) on campus. They take money away from the music program and theater school, but the games are fun."

STUDENT AUTHOR: Football is the most popular sport on campus; basketball's a distant second, and most others trail by a significant margin. Intramural sports, with options ranging from inner tube water polo to sand volleyball, provide a variety of interesting and new athletic experiences for students who have a bit of time and money to spare.

Students Speak Out
ON DRUG SCENE

Q "I never came into contact with drugs. At TCU, people have a tendency to put on a front because of the whole Christian thing. Honestly, TCU is a regular school with regular people. **Drugs do exist, but they are certainly not dominant**."

Q "There **are a lot of people who have tried pot**. There are also a number who regularly use ecstasy. I hear there are several girls in each sorority, and no doubt elsewhere, who use cocaine. I would say the drug of choice on this campus, however, is alcohol. There are also a lot of people who are very sober."

Q "You don't notice until you start to go to parties, but **people don't pressure you**."

STUDENT AUTHOR: **A survey conducted by the Office of Alcohol and Drug Education found that marijuana use is common among TCU students, but still under the national average. Campus Police uphold strict guidelines for students who violate TCU's alcohol and drug policy, ensuring student safety and stability.**

14:1	Student-to-Faculty Ratio
86%	Freshman Retention Rate
55%	Four-Year Graduation Rate
79%	Financial Aid Applicants Receiving Aid

Students Speak Out
SAFETY & SECURITY

Q "I've never had a problem, and I don't hear about them really. There are emergency phones, and it's relatively well lit. **The campus police are always driving around** giving people parking tickets, so at least they're keeping the cars safe."

Q "I feel fairly safe. The police seem to keep tabs on thefts and other incidents, and **Froggie Five-0 helps keep us ladies safe** at night."

Q "I felt safe living on campus until two girls were raped in a nearby apartment building. However, I live in an **apartment building that has 24-hour security and gates**, so I feel a lot safer. TCU certainly doesn't have abnormal safety issues, though."

STUDENT AUTHOR: **The combined efforts of the campus police and Froggie Five-0 make TCU students feel safe on campus. The patrol service, which includes foot, bike, and automobile patrol officers, ensures the 24-hour protection of students and University property. TCU also offers free self-defense classes.**

Questions?
For more inside information and survival tips, pick up College Prowler's full-length book on this school, written by an actual student! Check it out at *www.collegeprowler.com.*

Students Speak Out
ON OVERALL EXPERIENCE

Q "**Nobody here is unfriendly or truly snobby**— just very separate, in a noble sort of way. You make your education on your own here, but I still wish I were someplace that had a little bit more diversity."

Q "I've loved my experience at TCU. Fort Worth has about half of a million people living in it, but it is very suburban and quiet. **I think the best thing about TCU is the faculty**. They really love to teach, and they will work with you if you have problems. It's an aesthetically pleasing campus, complete with domesticated squirrels and Oak trees."

Q "I love both TCU and Fort Worth. If I find a job there, I plan to live in Fort Worth when I graduate. **I have no desire to be anywhere else** at all. Although it is a Christian school, nothing is forced upon anyone. You are required to take one religion class, which is either Bible or World Religions, and those are both just awesome classes."

STUDENT AUTHOR: **Most students at TCU are pleased with their education and the opportunities presented to them. While diversity continues to be an issue on campus, strong academics, good facilities, and countless organizations play a larger role in student life. TCU isn't a stuffy church school. It's a place where students are encouraged to spread their wings, try new things, and branch out. A few organizations—Greek ones in particular—tend to discriminate between social groups, but the overall student body is quite friendly. Academically, students are eager to learn, and a small student/faculty ratio allows students to interact closely with each of their professors.**

Texas Tech University

2500 Broadway; Lubbock, TX 79409
(806) 742-2011; www.ttu.edu

THE BASICS:

Acceptance Rate: 72%
Setting: Mid-sized city
F-T Undergrads: 21,226

SAT Range: 1470–1780*
Control: Public
Tuition: $12,740

Most Popular Majors: Business/Marketing, Consumer Sciences, Engineering, Communications, Agriculture

*of 2400

Academics	B	Guys	A
Local Atmosphere	C+	Girls	A+
Safety & Security	A-	Athletics	A
Computers	A	Nightlife	A-
Facilities	A	Greek Life	A
Campus Dining	B+	Drug Scene	B
Off-Campus Dining	B	Campus Strictness	B-
Campus Housing	B	Parking	C
Off-Campus Housing	A+	Transportation	C+
Diversity	C+	Weather	B

Students Speak Out
ON ACADEMICS

Q "I think sometimes Tech gets the reputation as being a party school, but what school isn't? **Tech is becoming more and more well-rounded**, and I believe students in Texas are beginning to take our school more seriously."

Q "I am an early childhood major, and **so far I have loved every single one of my teachers**. My classes are smaller in my major, and the workload is always appropriate for the class. As I take more advanced education classes, the work becomes more intense in order to prepare me for student teaching."

Q "It seems like the best teachers I had were in my last four semesters of school. All the good teachers were **people who had real careers prior to teaching**."

Q "The teachers at Tech are hit-or-miss. You can easily get a teacher who is **fun, cool, and willing to help**, but other classes are more challenging. The teachers there are hardcore and eat, live, and breathe their subjects."

STUDENT AUTHOR: **What's important to figure out from the start is how that teacher is going to conduct class and how to mold yourself to it. These teachers are teaching 200 students at one time sometimes, and it is impossible for them to change to fit each student. As you get deeper into any major, the teachers get better. Your freshman year will be packed with classes that focus more on attendance and memorization than retaining concepts.**

Students Speak Out
ON LOCAL ATMOSPHERE

Q "Lubbock is a great place to go to school. It is the perfect size—small enough to get that college-town feel, but **large enough to have all the comforts of a big city**. It has a major mall, great restaurants, and a fantastic and diverse nightlife."

Q "**Lubbock is the most laid-back town that you will ever come across**. There are some smaller universities and community colleges, but Texas Tech is the catalyst that keeps the town thriving."

Q "The atmosphere in this town is a little boring. You have to really try to find things to do, and **Lubbock natives take life in the 'slow lane.'**"

Q "Lubbock seems to have a stereotype of being flat, boring, and dusty. **It is a wonderful town filled with friendly people**, and it can be exactly what you make of it. I wouldn't have changed a thing about our dusty little college town."

STUDENT AUTHOR: **It's not until you graduate and bump into other Lubbock alums that you realize the bond this small town builds between people. Once you have lived in Lubbock, you just get it. It may not have the best shopping, the prettiest landscape, or the greatest service at the one trillion fast food and chain restaurants, but that's what everyone loves about it! Lubbock is small, but not too small; slow, but not too slow; and fun, but not too fun. Either you love it or you hate it, and that's the bottom line.**

Students Speak Out
ON FACILITIES

Q "**The library is great**. It's very big, with lots of quiet places to work."

Q "The facilities on campus are amazing and are improving every semester. Although the construction does get a bit tiring, all of Lubbock is being redone, so this is nothing new to me. **These inconveniences have proven to be well worth it, though**, in that our new health facility and student union are incredible. We have an amazing fitness center, and although old, the libraries are all really quite nice."

Q "The student union center functions as it should—as a **hub for all students**. Chances are you will pass by it at least a few times a day and eat at their surprisingly varied and tasty food court."

Q "**The rec center is absolutely beautiful**, boasting ping-pong tables, a rock-climbing wall, 12 racquetball courts, seven basketball courts, multiple random workout rooms, and enough workout equipment to keep your body tight."

Q "The facilities around campus are amazing! The Student Union Building (or SUB) is my favorite place on campus. It is beautiful, and **it has everything in it that you could possibly need**."

STUDENT AUTHOR: Since 2000, Tech has spent about $6 million on construction around campus, and more than $1 billion in future construction is planned. Walking into the United Spirit Arena is like walking into a professional basketball venue. The other newcomer is the Student Union. Tech also does its best to help you keep off those extra college pounds by giving all students free access to the Robert H. Ewalt Recreation Center.

Students Speak Out
ON CAMPUS DINING

Q "The Student Union is **your best bet for the most varied and delicious fare**. The Market is also a nice alternative."

Q "The food on campus is actually pretty good. I don't think I have ever eaten anything I haven't enjoyed. **My favorite place is by far the Market in Stangel/Murdough**. The SUB (Student Union Building) also has great food, as well as the Sam's Place in Murray Hall. Most of the dining halls on campus are food-court style, and they have anything you can imagine eating."

Q "The food in the dining halls is fairly good-tasting, but **they don't provide many healthy choices**."

Q "**Sam's Place in the dorms was amazing**. Freshman year, it was fun to see your friends during lunch in the market."

Q "I think the Market is a good place to start out. It has a variety of food. The other dorms, such as Hulen, are nice because **they have an all-you-can-eat counter** that is a lot cheaper than the Market, and dessert is provided."

STUDENT AUTHOR: Due to the dining arrangements in the dorms, the Freshman 15 is no myth at Texas Tech. In the bottom of several of the dorms, a small convenience store called Sam's Place is open until late-night cravings are satisfied. The Market, located on the first floor of the Stangel/Murdough complex, is an on-campus eatery that is a hotspot for freshmen to hang out between classes. The Student Union has a wide variety of food to choose from, but for the dieter or even the casual healthy eater, campus dining is not the place for you.

Students Speak Out
ON DORMS

Q "The dorms are sick. But **if I have to say one of them is nice, it'd be Stangel**—then Chitwood because of the dining hall."

Q "The dorms are good for dorms. **I loved living on campus because I met so many people**! Most of the freshman dorms have the exact same floor plans, but the popular dorms are Stangel/Murdough and Chitwood/Weymouth."

Q "I lived in Gates/Wall, **the dorm that has the reputation of 'The Gates of Hell.'** I have found that, wherever you end up, you will find some incredible people. This was the case for me and will likely be for anyone who attends. You will find your place wherever you are; Tech is just that kind of place."

STUDENT AUTHOR: **Every incoming freshman must live in one of the dorms. Some of the dorms have movable furniture, but the most popular dorms (Chitwood/Weymouth, Stangel/Murdough, and Horn/Knapp) have the furniture built in. There are six dorm complexes that have guys living in one building and girls living in another connected by a common foyer.**

 Did You Know?
26% of undergrads live on campus.

Students Speak Out
ON GUYS & GIRLS

Q "**Tech girls are so beautiful**. There is something about Tech that just attracts smart, sexy girls who are going to be successful. The guys are, in my experience, not of the same caliber. Most of them are very set in experiencing all the pleasures of college, and their bodies show it. However, as long as you don't mind a little mush around the middle, you'll find great southern hospitality from them."

Q "Guys are sexy. **Girls are sexier**."

Q "There is no typical student **except good-looking and laid-back**."

Q "**I think Tech has the best-looking students ever**! I have always heard that Tech has good-looking students, but after visiting other colleges and attending Tech, I can say it is definitely true!"

STUDENT AUTHOR: **On a Tech visit, it is almost impossible to walk around town or campus without bumping into an attractive and friendly girl. The problem is that many Tech girls tend to be overly friendly with the opposite sex, branding Tech's female population as somewhat less than classy. Girls at Texas Tech are given a lot of credit for their looks, but the guys are the real gems. Unlike the female population of Tech that is relatively uniform in appearance, the male population mixes it up.**

Traditions

Carol of Lights
This tradition, which has been in existence since 1959, takes place each year during the month of December. A lighting ceremony brings out thousands of students and people from the Lubbock community.

RaiderGate
This is a huge tailgate for which a band is hired to play, and it is held in a parking lot on campus.

Overall School Spirit
Although the alumni and student fans may not agree on the proper way to express school spirit (some use vulgar lyrics in the school songs), there is definitely an abundance of it.

Students Speak Out
ON ATHLETICS

Q "Sports are a big deal for pretty much everyone. You can hear your dorm shake and rattle with the noise from everyone on game day during football season, and you will see **lines of people walking throughout campus in red and black** when there is a basketball game."

Q "Sports are a huge deal at Tech. **We live in Texas—of course they are a big deal**."

Q "Football and basketball are great at Tech. **IM sports are more competitive than they probably should be**, but that makes it fun."

Q "**Basketball is always highly supported**. The rest of the sports tend to be only so-so."

STUDENT AUTHOR: **Football season is huge. Spirit is shown in the windows of buildings around town, and on game days the town is desolate because everybody is on the Tech campus tailgating. When it comes to basketball games, "Bobby Knight" is all that need be said. Although his son Pat Knight is sitting on the bench these days, Bobby Knight made the Tech basketball program one to watch.**

Students Speak Out
ON DRUG SCENE

Q "I would say there is a good group of potheads at Tech and probably a crew that blows cocaine, but **in my four years, I never saw coke**. It's one of those things that, if it is your scene, you can find it, but if you don't want to hear about it, then you won't even know it's going on. More people booze than do drugs, for sure."

Q "There are not a lot of drugs, but **of the drugs there are, it's mainly pot**."

Q "**Drugs are everywhere**. They are in college as much as they are in high schools. No one college is different from any other when it comes to the drug scene."

STUDENT AUTHOR: **Tech has no problem living up to its reputation as a party school. Marijuana makes its appearance at parties, but if you don't want to see it, you won't. It would be naïve to think that no one on the Tech campus is dabbling in hard drugs like cocaine, but the percentage is small. Tech has its fair share of heavy drinkers and potheads, but when it comes to heavier drugs, Tech students in general just say no.**

19:1	Student-to-Faculty Ratio
80%	Freshman Retention Rate
30%	Four-Year Graduation Rate
63%	Financial Aid Applicants Receiving Aid

Students Speak Out
SAFETY & SECURITY

Q "Texas Tech is one of the largest campuses around, and I never felt unsafe. **They have emergency phones everywhere on campus**, and you can always count on those campus cops to check on you when you need them and when you don't need them, too."

Q "**Campus has a natural feeling of security and safety**. It may not be anything specific that the University does to achieve this, but I usually feel safe on campus."

Q "There is **not really a place you can go on campus without seeing a patrol car nearby**, which I really love."

STUDENT AUTHOR: **Texas Tech is a contiguous and extremely self-contained campus. When you are on it, it seems like you have stepped out of Lubbock and into a new town or neighborhood. And like most neighborhoods, Texas Tech has campus police officers who patrol all day and night.**

> **Questions?**
> For more inside information and survival tips, pick up College Prowler's full-length book on this school, written by an actual student! Check it out at *www.collegeprowler.com*.

Students Speak Out
ON OVERALL EXPERIENCE

Q "My favorite thing about Texas Tech would have to be the sporting events. In football, we are always fighting for a Big 12 championship, and the atmosphere is great. Before games, RaiderGate is where the students tailgate and listen to the music—**we're the only school in the Big 12 that allows tailgating on campus** grounds. My least favorite part about Tech would have to be the wind storms."

Q "My overall experience at Texas Tech was a great one! I wouldn't take back one minute of it. The city has grown so much, and **the people here are great**. It really is a college town where the students run everything about it."

Q "I love Texas Tech! I would come here again, and **I would encourage everyone I know to come here as well**. My favorite parts were the people that I have met and the memories I have made. It is easy to get very involved on campus and make an obvious difference."

Q "Overall, I enjoyed my college experience. **It definitely was different from how I thought it would be.** I thought it would have been a more intellectual experience, but I have realized that the college system is quite bureaucratic."

STUDENT AUTHOR: **It's stereotyped as a party school in the middle of nowhere, where going to class takes a backseat to having a beer. Although Thursday nights are big in Lubbock, students who attend Tech get not only a great education but a chance to explore who they are and what they are good at in a laid-back environment. Texas Tech has it all, or all you need anyway. This is a place where friends are easy to find and grades are easy to get, as long as you put in the effort.**

Towson University

8000 York Road; Towson, MD 21252
(410) 704-2000; www.towson.edu

THE BASICS:

Acceptance Rate: 60%   **SAT Range:** 990–1160*
Setting: Suburban   **Control:** Public
F-T Undergrads: 14,180   **Tuition:** $15,120

Most Popular Majors: Business, Education, Social Sciences, Health Professions, Communications

*of 1600

Academics	B-	Guys	C+
Local Atmosphere	B+	Girls	B+
Safety & Security	B	Athletics	B-
Computers	B	Nightlife	A
Facilities	B	Greek Life	C
Campus Dining	B	Drug Scene	B
Off-Campus Dining	A	Campus Strictness	C+
Campus Housing	B+	Parking	C-
Off-Campus Housing	A-	Transportation	B+
Diversity	C-	Weather	B-

Students Speak Out
ON ACADEMICS

Q "My **professors were all amazing**. It is hard to believe that Towson is a public school sometimes because my classes are so small that I really get to know my professors."

Q "Towson has some great professors that **truly care about their students**. It seemed that most of my professors at Towson recognized and awarded the students who actually put in the effort."

Q "The teachers at Towson make themselves very accessible and available to the students at all times for meetings or questions. Most **teachers are friendly** and quite knowledgeable in their area of teaching."

Q "Professors are generally very **engaging** and open for dropping by whenever you need them."

Q "Professors are good, but the classes have often put me to sleep. The **classes are small** if that's what you're into."

STUDENT AUTHOR: Towson has some outstanding professors, but every now and then, people encounter some less intriguing ones. They are usually accommodating and accessible to students outside of class during scheduled office hours or even beyond those hours via e-mail. Unlike other universities, it is rare for a class to be taught by a graduate student or teaching assistant. There are many good, hands-on learning opportunities that provide interaction with the professors.

Students Speak Out
ON LOCAL ATMOSPHERE

Q "The **town is very accessible** and offers many places to shop and to eat. Towson is a good distance from the Inner Harbor and downtown Baltimore."

Q "I love the Towson area; there are bars to go to have fun, and the people there are mostly friendly. There are **many other colleges around the Towson area.**"

Q "Everyone, including faculty and students, at Towson seems to be **pretty friendly**. However, most people stay within their 'circle' (Greeks, sports, SGA, and so on)."

Q "The atmosphere is great. It's nice to be right near a city but not actually in one. There are plenty of things to do and places to go in Baltimore. The aquarium is really nice, and so is Little Italy. **The Inner Harbor is beautiful** as well, with lots of good places to eat and shop."

Q "Towson is pretty **metropolitan**. You have the population and atmosphere of a city."

STUDENT AUTHOR: The area of Towson has it all. It is the ideal college town with everything to offer, aside from school spirit. It is obvious that there is a lack thereof. Students love the fact that Towson has a selection of many bars, restaurants, a great mall, movie theaters, and a bookstore, all within walking distance of the University. The local community is, for the most part, friendly toward the students, but the interaction among students and locals is not that frequent.

5 Best Things	5 Worst Things
1 Power Plant Live!	1 Parking on campus
2 The Patuxent	2 Wait at the Health Center
3 Inner Harbor	3 The Glen
4 Towson Hot Bagel	4 Dorm kitchens
5 Tiger Fest	5 Lack of school spirit

Students Speak Out
ON FACILITIES

Q "Facilities on campus are mostly very nice. The older portion of campus includes half academic buildings and some housing, with **elaborate architecture** and aesthetic landscaping. The other portion of campus is newer and not as attractive, but offers a student union with lots of food choices, lounge areas, and a large University store."

Q "The facilities are nice; **the gym is the best** out of them all. Our gym really is outstanding and beautiful."

Q "I think that the campus is **getting a little old**. The classrooms mostly need the most renovation."

Q "Towson has some pretty and **clean buildings** and some ugly ones. My biggest complaint about the facilities is the Health Center."

Q "All of the facilities on campus are up to scale, as well as being clean. The **classrooms are the perfect size**."

STUDENT AUTHOR: **Students express their appreciation for most of Towson's spacious dorms and the beautiful gym. There are many advantages to the facilities Towson offers, in terms of being spacious and having classrooms in proximity to the dorms. Furthermore, Towson has invested a lot of money in order to improve the facilities on campus. So far, students approve of the renovations that have taken place, but agree that more can still be done in terms of updating some of the older buildings. The facilities at Towson are standard, suitable, and are currently undergoing improvements.**

Famous Alumni

Charles "Roc" Dutton, John Glover, Shonda Brewer Shilling

Students Speak Out
ON CAMPUS DINING

Q "There is **a lot of food selection** on campus. The Union offers the best spot, the Patuxent, with gourmet selections for lunch Monday through Friday."

Q "Newell is probably the second best. It is a basic cafeteria that has a large selection of anything you could possibly imagine, including a good salad bar, waffles, and **stir-fry anything**!"

Q "The **Patux is the most popular place** to eat on campus. Therefore, it is quite difficult to find a seat. Nevertheless, the wait is certainly worth the outstanding food."

Q "The food is edible, but there are **not a lot of healthy choices**."

Q "Food on campus is actually **the best I've seen** in comparison to other colleges. The dining halls are nice. Newell Dining Hall is about two or three years old, and the other (the Glenn) was renovated."

STUDENT AUTHOR: **Campus dining can be good or bad depending on what dining hall you choose to go to. The Susquehanna Food Court in the University Union is a decent eatery, where a student can find Chick-fil-A, pizza, and a deli. Students express their love for the Patuxent because it provides an alternative to the typical mess-hall food. As a whole, students find the food okay at Towson. It is safe to say, though, that the food on campus lacks appreciation because of the outstanding off-campus dining selection.**

Student Body

African American:	11%	Male/Female:	39/61%
Asian American:	4%	Out-of-State:	17%
Hispanic:	2%	International:	3%
Native American:	<1%	Unknown:	9%
White:	70%		

Political Activity: The Student Government Association (SGA) serves as a liaison between the administration and the student body to promote the best academic and social environment possible.

Gay Pride: The student body and administration are tolerant of a diversity of sexual preferences.

Minority Clubs: There are many cultural clubs that increase awareness of their culture by coming together on campus.

Students Speak Out
ON DORMS

Q "Try to **get housing in the Towers**! Avoid housing on the old side of campus. (They have no air-conditioning.)"

Q "The dorms are okay, but **most are kind of old**. Stay away from the Residence Hall."

Q "If you want a very quiet dorm and hope to never get woken up while you are sleeping, go for Newell Hall. They have the nicest bathrooms, too, and some nice rooms as well, with **quads for three to fifteen people**."

STUDENT AUTHOR: **The dorms in Towson are good. In fact, about a third of the undergraduate students at Towson live on campus. However, each has its pros and cons. The dorms at Towson are all unique in their own ways. Some are clearly better than others, depending on what you are looking for in on-campus living, what would make your life more convenient, and what would make you the happiest. The dorms really are about what you would like from your college experience. Students agree that housing in Towson is, for the most part, superior to other colleges that they have seen.**

Did You Know?
22% of undergrads live on campus.

Students Speak Out
ON GUYS & GIRLS

Q "The **girls at Towson are beautiful**. On the other hand, the guys on campus are not very attractive. However, they think they are God's gift to humankind, basically because the beautiful girls lower their standards and date these boys."

Q "So, so, so many girls. There are definitely a lot more girls than guys here, but for the guys that are here, they are **pretty good looking**."

Q "As a girl, you kind of **lower your standards**—it is pretty sad."

Q "This is the school where you will find **unattractive men** with gorgeous girls. So, have fun, guys, and good luck, ladies."

STUDENT AUTHOR: **Towson has many more girls than guys. With this ratio, guys are granted many more options, and the girls tend to settle with what they can get. Even though the ratio of guys to girls is beginning to level off a bit more, it still has a great affect on the opportunity pool. Since there are so few good-looking guys, the ones who are tend to become overly conceited. However, as always, there are some exceptions.**

Traditions

Tiger Fest
It is the annual spring festival that is open to the campus community. The greatest thing about Tiger Fest is that it gathers all of the students together with games, novelties, a beer garden, food vendors, and concerts. It is held on Burdick field on the first Saturday of May.

Overall School Spirit
It is clear that Towson lacks school spirit. Towson is most spirited around Homecoming, but many students still end up partying in the parking lot and missing the game.

Students Speak Out
ON ATHLETICS

Q "**IM sports are big**, and I would highly recommend joining a team if you are decent at anything. You meet so many people and go on some pretty cool trips."

Q "It seems as though sports are big, but **school spirit is a joke**."

Q "**Football and lacrosse are pretty big**; I guess baseball and basketball are, too, and we have a really good dance team."

Q "Varsity sports are popular because people make a huge deal out of **tailgating** before and after the games."

STUDENT AUTHOR: **It is always enjoyable to be on a sports team at Towson, whether it is a varsity sports team, club, or intramural. Being involved with a team is a good way to meet people. There is great camaraderie among the students on all sports teams. Many students especially love being on the intramural teams because the teams are less competitive. Since there is a lack of school spirit, many excellent teams are not recognized enough, either.**

Students Speak Out
ON DRUG SCENE

Q "Many of the students do have a **tight budget** since this is a public school, so I do not think that the drug scene is that bad."

Q "**Booze dominates** much more than drugs."

Q "It's pretty underground. Lots of **people smoke weed**, like everywhere, and you hear of harder drugs, like coke, but it really isn't seen. I would say that people that do drugs are a minority."

Q "Pot is the most popular, but other than that, **harder drugs are found much less often**."

STUDENT AUTHOR: As with a majority of college campuses, alcohol dominates the social scene. Illegal drugs can be found, but it is marijuana that is the most popular. Some people are engaged in the scene more than others. It comes down to who you choose to associate yourself with, since some are more engaged in it than others. Essentially, the drug scene at TU is easy to steer clear of but not difficult to access. Harder drugs are present in Towson, but they are only used by a small number of students.

18:1	Student-to-Faculty Ratio
82%	Freshman Retention Rate
38%	Four-Year Graduation Rate
68%	Financial Aid Applicants Receiving Aid

Students Speak Out
SAFETY & SECURITY

Q "TU is well secured. All on-campus and the majority of off-campus housing requires an ID card or key to get into the buildings. Campus police are seen all over campus, and **escorts are available**."

Q "I have heard of assaults on campus, but they have **beefed up security**, and it seems that security is getting the job done."

Q "I **feel safe on campu**s because neither I, nor anyone I know, has ever had a problem."

Q "I think that the security on campus is good. There have been a couple rapes on campus, but the school is not silent about this, which I think is **very admirable** compared to other schools."

STUDENT AUTHOR: Crime is not a primary concern for TU students, but the TU police department still chooses to keep students well informed. Another great safety feature is that there are 24-hour emergency telephones and lit sidewalks all over campus.

Questions?
For more inside information and survival tips, pick up College Prowler's full-length book on this school, written by an actual student! Check it out at *www.collegeprowler.com*.

Students Speak Out
ON OVERALL EXPERIENCE

Q "This is a school that I feel takes getting involved in to enjoy. The more you put into it, the more you will come out with. Towson has great class sizes, and you will **never just feel like a number** in this school. If you love going to bars, meeting people, the Baltimore area, the Ravens, and the Orioles, you will love Towson."

Q "I love TU. The academics have a good reputation, **Greek life is amazing**, and campus has a lot to offer. The nightlife is so much fun and so convenient."

Q "I think it is the **perfect size** and perfect atmosphere. Its academic reputation keeps getting better and better."

Q "I have encountered some of the nicest people, the most caring professors, and in a **great working atmosphere**. I would never, ever, want to go anywhere else."

STUDENT AUTHOR: Towson is the type of school that, if you find the right people, you will have a wonderful experience. For those who have trouble making friends, it is highly recommended to get involved on campus. There are many organizations and sports teams that thrive in Towson and are strongly recommended in order to assist students in finding a solid group of friends. Towson is a school that becomes what you make of it. It is clear that the students who are engaged in their work or are interested in an organization gain a greater sense of appreciation for Towson. Some students express how rewarding their experiences at Towson have been while acknowledging the fact that Towson is not for everyone.

Trinity College

300 Summit Street; Hartford, CT 06106
(860) 297-2000; www.trincoll.edu

THE BASICS:

Acceptance Rate: 40%
Setting: Mid-sized City
F-T Undergrads: 2,092

SAT Range: 1820–2120*
Control: Private
Tuition: $33,630

Most Popular Majors: Political Science, Economics, History, English, Psychology

*of 2400

Academics	A-	Guys	A-
Local Atmosphere	C-	Girls	A-
Safety & Security	C-	Athletics	C+
Computers	B-	Nightlife	A-
Facilities	B	Greek Life	B
Campus Dining	C+	Drug Scene	B-
Off-Campus Dining	B+	Campus Strictness	A-
Campus Housing	B-	Parking	C+
Off-Campus Housing	D	Transportation	C-
Diversity	C	Weather	C+

Students Speak Out
ON ACADEMICS

Q "The teachers can be **a bit egotistical**, but they are always there to listen to what you have to say. The most interesting classes are the challenging ones taught by professors who are really into what they teach."

Q "I have had teachers who have **cared more about my personal happiness** than about how I do in their class."

Q "The teachers are really **good about giving help**. Most of them care, and they're flexible if you're a good student. I've been blown away by so many of my professors, and most of the classes still have me thinking."

Q "The professors at Trinity are great. They are able to answer all your questions no matter what the subject. If they don't know the answer to your question, **they'll help you** figure it out, either by referring you to other sources or approaching the problem themselves."

STUDENT AUTHOR: Not surprisingly, there are good professors and bad professors at Trinity. Because the school and class sizes are so small, students feel they receive a lot of individual attention—something you just won't get at larger universities. Trinity students almost always find their classes interesting. Because students feel that the majority of Trinity professors respect them and are genuinely concerned with their academic well-being, students respect their professors in return and want to listen to what they have to say.

Students Speak Out
ON LOCAL ATMOSPHERE

Q "A lot of students get intimidated by the **Hartford ghetto**, which is right by Trinity, but there are a lot of opportunities to make a difference in Hartford."

Q "Hartford is often seen as the 'downside' of going to Trinity. However, by the time a student has reached his or her junior year, it becomes obvious that the city adds much to the experience of college. Students are able to **secure internships at the Capitol** or perform in local bars and clubs. The problems facing Hartford have created an opening for Trinity and its students to take a part in the reinvention of the city."

Q "Hartford is a city, plain and simple. It offers all the **good and bad points** other urban areas have to offer their students. It is a city with bad neighborhoods and high crime rates as well as amazing restaurants and captivating theater productions."

Q "Visit **New York and Boston** every chance you get."

STUDENT AUTHOR: The local atmosphere of Trinity and the surrounding area is not what you would call ideal. While Hartford is a surprisingly cultural town, it is not very student-friendly. There is not much to see in downtown Hartford, which always catches out-of-towners off-guard, given that it's the capital of Connecticut. There is very little interaction between students and locals.

5 Best Things	5 Worst Things
1 The Quad in spring	1 Budget cuts
2 The professors	2 The location
3 The small campus	3 No parking
4 Thursday nights	4 Horrendous campus food
5 The '80s party	5 The awful weather

Students Speak Out
ON FACILITIES

Q "Most facilities have been renovated or are in the process of being renovated. Trinity has been **trying to update all facilities**."

Q "There's really **no good student center**, and it would be nice if the dorms had kitchens, but there's plenty here to be impressed by."

Q "Trinity has a history of grateful alumni, and their gratitude is shown through the **excellent facilities**. The Ferris athletic center is small but well equipped, and popular among the student body. The computer labs are quiet, clean, and a great aid to restless students trying to get work done."

Q "The athletic facilities are comprehensive, and the squash courts are **the best in the country**. If you don't know what squash is when you come to Trinity, you will very soon after."

Q "The athletic center is very nice, although **you should expect to wait a while** for a free treadmill."

STUDENT AUTHOR: **Trinity is making a step in the right direction, in regards to campus facilities. For one, the library is fantastic. There are plenty of places to study with a variety of sweeping, panoramic views of campus. Overall, Trinity's facilities are indicative of just how small this school really is. Don't expect any big-university-type efficiency here. Buildings are definitely designed for aesthetics as well as for a particular use. Living at Trinity, you don't feel as though you are one person living in a huge complex; rather, you feel like one big family living in a really big house.**

Famous Alumni

Edward Albee, Timothy Horne, Thomas Chappell, Elizabeth Alden, Joseph Kluger, Joanna Scott, Liesl Odenweller, Mary McCormack

Students Speak Out
ON CAMPUS DINING

Q "While Trinity kids tend to complain about 'Mather food,' it is widely understood that the food is **pretty good in comparison to most places**."

Q "Mather, the main dining hall, tends toward the **heavier, fried variety**. However, it does have a fabulous pasta bar where you can get vegetables sautéed and then the pasta added, pick your sauce, and end up with a fairly healthy, really tasty meal. Mather also has a vegetarian section."

Q "All in all, **the food's pretty tasty**. Students are required to be on a meal program if they're living on campus, so they might as well enjoy it."

Q "Food is usually **somewhere between awful and decent**. It varies. The main dining hall isn't good, but I love the Bistro. And the meal plans are really pretty flexible."

Q "The food on campus is **barely digestible**, and the Cave serves all their food fried, but people think that the Bistro is nice."

STUDENT AUTHOR: **First off, don't expect gourmet food at Trinity, but do expect enough to get by. The three dining centers—Mather, the Cave, and the Bistro—are all operated by Chartwell's, which means that they aren't in competition with one another (hence the mediocre food). Mather, the main cafeteria, has a wide variety, with vegetarian selections, a grill, and specials each night. The food is cooked for the masses, though, and thus can be rather bland. The Bistro is by far the best choice for a nice meal. You can get wraps and fresh-blended smoothies.**

Student Body

African American:	5%	Male/Female:	50/50%
Asian American:	6%	Out-of-State:	80%
Hispanic:	5%	International:	2%
Native American:	<1%	Unknown:	0%
White:	82%		

Poltical Activity: Democrats and liberal Republicans seem to be about evenly matched on Trinity's campus.

Gay Pride: EROS is a Trinity club open to any student interested in GLTB rights issues.

Economic Status: Most students at Trinity seem to be from upper- or upper-middle-class families.

Students Speak Out
ON DORMS

Q "Most dorms are very comfortable. All rooms are equipped with an **Internet connection, cable, and phone lines**. Freshman dorms tend to be the ones to avoid, such as Little and North. All upperclassman dorms are good places to live."

Q "One of the advantages of Trinity is that you are **guaranteed housing** all four years, so you never have to worry—no matter how bad your housing lottery number is."

Q "For the most part, the dorms are **clean, functional, and in good condition**. However, the dorms at Trinity are nothing to brag about."

STUDENT AUTHOR: **No matter where you live, you'll do fine with housing at Trinity. Every dorm room comes well-equipped with furniture, a telephone jack, and Internet and cable TV connections. While two of the freshman dorms, Little and Frobb, come across as rather small and unkempt, most other dorms are considered "good" or "bad" based primarily on location. Because there is plenty of housing, you will almost always be able to find a nice place to lay your head at night.**

> **? Did You Know?**
> 95% of undergrads live on campus.

Students Speak Out
ON GUYS & GIRLS

Q "The **guys are jerks**, and the girls are hot, and every stuck-up, tanned, skinny inch of them tells you that they know it, too."

Q "Trinity is known as **a 'beautiful people' campus**. The typical Trinity look for girls is brightly flowered Lily Pulitzer dresses, pearl earrings, designer jeans, Polo shirts with the collar flipped up, and CK Bradley accessories. The typical Trinity male wears jeans or khakis, and purple or pink polo shirts with the collar also flipped up."

Q "Bottom line for now—it is pretty hard to go to a Friday night party or to take a walk down the Long Walk without **bumping into someone** whom you find attractive."

STUDENT AUTHOR: **Trin students care about their looks. Bright colors are everywhere, and most every guy and girl on campus owns a pink polo shirt. The guys and girls are, to use an overused but appropriate word, pretty nice. You will be able to find a social group where you feel that you belong. Hookups are, in general, more common than relationships. Trinity has a reputation as a party school, and it is not undeserved.**

> **Urban Legends**
>
> **Plaque on the Long Walk**
> There is a plaque on the Long Walk that commemorates a visit FDR made to Trinity in the 1930s. The legend is that, if you walk on it, you will not graduate.
>
> **Overall School Spirit**
> Although the student body is somewhat apathetic regarding their alma mater, as a whole, there is a lot of support and respect for the Trinity sports teams— illustrated by the pride students show in their mascot, the infamous Bantam.

Students Speak Out
ON ATHLETICS

Q "Tons of people play varsity sports. Squash, football, and basketball get spectators. Nothing else really gets a lot. We are **five-time national champions in squash**. Intramural sports have a small but loyal membership of enthusiastic people."

Q "Varsity sports at Trinity are **pretty much ignored** by those not actually playing them."

Q "Homecoming at Trinity tends to **revolve mostly around the tailgating**, rather than the big game at hand."

Q "Sports come **in and out of fashion** at Trinity. When our athletic teams are doing well, the stands are packed, but when the scores are not as high, most students find something else to occupy their free time."

STUDENT AUTHOR: **Given that Trinity is Division III, it can't exactly be called a big-time athletic school. If you are into squash, however, then it is worth a trip to the school just to see the courts. Although our sports teams may not get much recognition, they are still a big part of the school. If you are a freshman, sports are a great way to network.**

Students Speak Out
ON DRUG SCENE

Q "Rumors and stories indicate that **marijuana is easily available** to any student with the money to purchase it, and that cocaine is always able to be found on campus."

Q "There is **way more drinking** than drug use."

Q "Although most students find their partying limited to alcohol, there are pockets of students who **rely heavily on drugs** for their weekend festivities. Although the most abused drug appears to be marijuana, Trinity students will sometimes dabble with cocaine, heroin, and Special K. Several years ago Trinity lost two students, both to drug overdoses. Since then, students have begun to wise up and party with a little more caution."

STUDENT AUTHOR: You won't find prevalent hard-core drug use at Trinity. Marijuana is around, but the heavier drugs, like cocaine and ecstasy, are harder to come by. However, alcohol abuse can seem pretty outstanding at times. Some students will blow off steam by downing a few brewskis.

10:1	Student-to-Faculty Ratio
91%	Freshman Retention Rate
77%	Four-Year Graduation Rate
86%	Financial Aid Applicants Receiving Aid

Students Speak Out
SAFETY & SECURITY

Q "Security has **long been an issue** at Trinity—we are located in a city, and with that comes city problems. We're an open campus, but with common sense, anyone can avoid trouble."

Q "Safety is a **controversial topic** right now."

Q "I usually feel safe on campus. I have never personally had any problems, although each year **several muggings occur on campus**. For those who don't feel comfortable walking, Trinity runs several shuttles around the campus and the Hartford area."

Q "Being safe calls for **using common sense** and sticking to groups."

STUDENT AUTHOR: Students tend to express varying opinions about the safety of Trinity's campus. In general, however, students agree on the basic facts: we are in the center of a large urban area; there is crime. Don't walk alone at night. Trinity definitely tries to control the crime on campus.

Questions?
For more inside information and survival tips, pick up College Prowler's full-length book on this school, written by an actual student! Check it out at *www.collegeprowler.com*.

Students Speak Out
ON OVERALL EXPERIENCE

Q "Trinity is a small school, and as such, it **can get on one's nerves**. However, Trinity became my home within the first semester I was there."

Q "My first year at Trinity was a big adjustment. Coming from a public high school and being submerged in a crowd of boarding school graduates, **I was overwhelmed** with the preppy clothes, the drugs, and the elitist attitudes. I definitely had thoughts of transferring. But during my second year, I found a group of students I automatically clicked with."

Q "Trinity is a great school where you can **excel academically** as well as maintain a decent social life. Without question, this is the place for me."

Q "Trinity is a good place to **hide from reality** for four years, but I wouldn't mind being abroad, or in California."

STUDENT AUTHOR: Everyone seems to experience a similarly hard freshman year; Trinity is not perfect. Once you accept that, you can begin settling down, grow comfortable, and view this little oasis in the middle of Hartford as a home for the next four years. Quite a few Trinity students can't wait for the beginning of September just to get back to school. Another experience everyone else seems to have in common at Trinity is a fierce loyalty to their alma mater—the love for the Bantum is only one example. Whether you decide to spend the next four years of your life at Trinity or choose another college, learn to accept the college or university that you selected. If half of the students who felt frustrated initially chose to leave Trinity, they never would have discovered what a great place it really is.

Trinity University

One Trinity Place; San Antonio, TX 78212
(210) 999-7207; www.trinity.edu

THE BASICS:

Acceptance Rate: 52%
Setting: Urban
F-T Undergrads: 2,447

SAT Range: 1210–1380*
Control: Private
Tuition: $26,664

Most Popular Majors: Business, Social Sciences, Foreign Languages, Liberal Arts, Communications

*of 1600

Academics	B	Guys	B+
Local Atmosphere	B+	Girls	A-
Safety & Security	A-	Athletics	C+
Computers	B	Nightlife	B+
Facilities	B	Greek Life	B+
Campus Dining	A-	Drug Scene	B+
Off-Campus Dining	A-	Campus Strictness	B+
Campus Housing	A	Parking	B+
Off-Campus Housing	B	Transportation	C
Diversity	C-	Weather	B-

Students Speak Out
ON ACADEMICS

Q "Trinity has great professors. **They get to know you personally** and take great interest in your learning experience. Also, classes are small enough to foster lots of interesting discussions, especially when students are willing to speak out and participate."

Q "Academically, Trinity is the '**Ivy League of the South**' that it is reported to be. However, if you want to find the less than redeeming classes, ask around, and you'll find easy As."

Q "Trinity is **definitely a teaching institution**, rather than a research institution. At Trinity, the primary goal of the professors is to educate and aid the students. The majority of them are more than willing to spend time with students after class."

Q The quality of the class itself depends almost entirely on the department. **Trinity excels in history, chemistry, and technical theater**, and is mediocre at best in psychology and religion. Trinity also has a lot of pre-med students, although a vast majority of them will eventually change their major to business."

STUDENT AUTHOR: Here at Trinity, it seems as if every faculty member **works hard to help each student fully live up to his or her potential. Any student who asks will be able to receive personal attention from a teacher. The homework can seem overwhelming. Yet with some hard work and help from classmates, there should never be more work than you can handle.**

Students Speak Out
ON LOCAL ATMOSPHERE

Q "San Antonio is an excellent city. There is a lot for tourists to do, like visit the River Walk, or go to one of the parks. **Ask professors and locals for recommendations** of fun things to do, and you'll get plenty of answers. Austin is only 45 minutes away, if you don't mind the drive."

Q "The cultural background and diversity of San Antonio makes for **a very interesting, laid-back city**. Other universities are present, but San Antonio doesn't have the feel of a college town. Downtown is mostly tourist attractions, but there are some good clubs, theaters, and museums."

Q "Compared to what I'm used to in Philadelphia, the city is extremely clean in the downtown areas, and they always seem to be throwing a party or festival. **The diversity of culture is wonderful**, too, and instead of riots, they just have fun when Fiesta and other celebrations are occurring."

Q "This is **kind of a hick town in a big city**. There are clubs and things, and of course, there are malls and the River Walk, but not as many natives go there because it's so touristy. For the most part, the energy off campus is very subdued."

STUDENT AUTHOR: In San Antonio, the culture is rich and inviting, and **when it is embraced, will give you more and more reasons to fall in love with the city. More of the fun activities take place in the daytime, but fun nightlife can be found if you look in the right places. You'll be able to party in any fashion that you so desire.**

5 Best Things	5 Worst Things
1 Dorm life	1 Parking
2 Professors	2 Computer lab hours
3 Ethernet	3 Lack of diversity
4 Coates Dining Hall	4 Cardiac Hill
5 The coffeehouse	5 Attendance at games

Students Speak Out
ON FACILITIES

Q "They are very nice. Different than what you would expect for a college, not so imposing, but modern and nice. **They make the environment pleasant**, and the school is in a beautiful part of town."

Q "The **athletic facilities are excellent**, complete with headphone jacks and televisions in the aerobic fitness room. The computer labs have new computers with flat-screen monitors, and the Tiger's Den has a very nice pool table and videogame equipment. In general, the campus facilities are very nice—the only exceptions being the recreational rooms in the North/South dorms."

Q "The athletic center on campus is very nice, which is to be expected considering all the scholarships that Trinity gives for sports. The computer centers are pretty good, too, but they do get crowded and loud at times. **Printing is expensive and sometimes slow**, and the computers are not open all night long (neither is the library). You should definitely bring your own computer—this is a necessity."

Q "All of Trinity's facilities **freaking rock**! The Bell Center is my life."

STUDENT AUTHOR: **A friend of a Trinity student commented that "every time I walk onto that campus, they're building something new." This is not an exaggeration. Trinity is constantly building new facilities and trying to fix the old ones to keep up with new technology and create a comfortable campus so that parents feel justified paying the high tuition.**

Famous Alumni

John Cornyn, Douglas Hawthorne, Chuck McKinley, Bob West

Students Speak Out
ON CAMPUS DINING

Q "The food is **really good compared to most other colleges**, however, it is also more expensive, and the dining halls have pretty terrible hours."

Q "Food on campus is good, for college on-campus dining. The quality and diversity of food options are both very impressive. Dining options like **vegetarian, vegan, or 'low-carb' are possible**, but much more limited in variety. Options also include the Java City coffee bar in the main library, which serves a variety of coffees, cookies, and light sandwiches."

Q "It's really fine, despite the students' complaining. Try the University of Texas's food and **you'll be grateful**."

Q "**Our food is recognizable**, and very often edible. It's not low-cal, it's not low-fat. You can eat healthily on campus if you make the effort, but it costs a bit more on the meal plan, as you buy a lot of fruit and veggies."

STUDENT AUTHOR: **Since buying a meal plan is part of living on campus, and most students are forced to do so for three years, it is difficult to escape the campus food. It is also expensive because of the catering company that the school uses (Aramark), but the food is of good quality, and there is more than enough to go around. The problem that most students face is that, after four years of dining in the same cafeteria, they have practically memorized the menus, and none of the options seem very appealing anymore.**

Student Body

African American:	4%	Male/Female:	46/54%
Asian American:	6%	Out-of-State:	30%
Hispanic:	11%	International:	5%
Native American:	1%	Unknown:	13%
White:	60%		

Popular Faiths: The campus is predominately Christian with several different Christian groups.

Gay Pride: The student body also appears to be generally accepting of homosexuality. There are certain groups that might morally oppose it, but they do not raise protest, and there is an LGBSA.

Economic Status: Many are able to attend because of student loans, but a vast number come from wealthy families.

Students Speak Out
ON DORMS

Q "The dorms at Trinity are rated some of the best in the nation for a reason. They're actually really nice. They're spacious, **many have limited heat/air control**, and they all have data and TV access. We're on a suite system, so there are no communal bathrooms."

Q "**All the dorms are a suite-style** (two rooms connected by a bathroom) and most have balconies. The best dorms, in my opinion, are Miller and Calvert in the freshman quad, or South and Prassel for the upperclassmen."

Q "**You have no choice your freshman year** on what dorm you want. But even the 'ghetto' dorms are better than most colleges. Pray for Witt or Winn."

STUDENT AUTHOR: **Trinity students are required to live on campus for the first three years of their education, but you won't hear much complaining. The dorms are so nice and so well kept that most students live those three years in comfort. Both the freshman and upperclassman dorms are structured so that students can get to know each other just by walking down the halls.**

Did You Know?
73% of undergrads live on campus.

Students Speak Out
ON GUYS & GIRLS

Q "The guys are generally good-looking, but not necessarily dateable. **A lot of them just want to party**, and the rest seem to be in really long-term relationships."

Q "Hot? Yes. Attractive? **Maybe, if you like men who can crush beer cans with their foreheads**. There are some nice guys, but overall, the girls are hotter than the guys. But maybe that's because the guys don't wear halter-tops all the time."

Q "People always tell me that I'm good looking, but at this school, even I felt ugly. **God, are they ever hot**."

Q "The guys like to party, but **really can be quite nerdy**, as they love their video games."

STUDENT AUTHOR: **Trinity students are a pretty attractive group, yet, aside from random hookups, there is a prevalent feeling on campus that nobody at Trinity dates. It is as though by going on one date, a girl and guy have committed themselves to a lifelong relationship! Because San Antonio is hot and muggy most of the year, students are fairly desensitized to seeing people wearing short shorts and small shirts.**

Traditions

Night In Old San Antonio (NIOSA)
A yearly city-wide celebration. The streets are blocked off and flooded with music, food, and alcohol.

Tigerfest
A week of events leading up to Homecoming, including an armadillo hunt, a dance, and a parade.

Overall School Spirit
Trinity students love their school, and know that they are getting a great education; however, they don't often feel the need to attend sporting events, even when the team is doing really well.

Students Speak Out
ON ATHLETICS

Q "Varsity sports are a big deal on campus when they are winning a lot. Soccer is very popular and so is basketball. IM sports are huge on campus. The beginning of the year is host to **Hallympics, where dorms compete in various sports** such as flag football and Wiffleball. Intramural sports are held throughout the year in all sorts of events from soccer to racquetball to ultimate Frisbee."

Q "People like IM sports because you don't have to be great to play, and **the competition really is friendly and fun**."

Q "They're good, but **completely unappreciated**. No one really cares unless you are actually the one playing."

STUDENT AUTHOR: **While students normally fail to support the varsity sports in droves, the football games draw in moderate crowds. However, the intramural sports are far more popular, especially the Hallympics that are held every year. Dorms form their own teams and compete against each other for T-shirts and bragging rights. There is a sense of fun and competitiveness, and points are awarded to the most sportsmanlike teams.**

Students Speak Out
ON DRUG SCENE

Q "The drug scene on campus is not as bad as you would think. If anyone does drugs **they usually just smoke pot**. And who doesn't do that in college?"

Q "Mostly, it's people smoking marijuana. Sometimes, people get hooked on something heavier, but for the most part, drugs are for social use. People smoke pot on the balconies, and **they're rarely reported**."

Q "On campus, drugs don't seem to be a big issue. Sure, some people do them, but unless you do drugs yourself, you really aren't aware of them being much of a big deal. Instead, more students border on being alcoholics, as **binge drinking tends to be the replacement for drugs**."

STUDENT AUTHOR: **Alcoholism is a bigger threat to the Trinity campus than drug abuse, but if you want to find drugs, you won't have to look too hard. Pot is not the only drug available on campus—cocaine, speed, and various other drugs will sometimes be used, but students are never pressured to try them.**

10:1	Student-to-Faculty Ratio
90%	Freshman Retention Rate
67%	Four-Year Graduation Rate
76%	Financial Aid Applicants Receiving Aid

Students Speak Out
SAFETY & SECURITY

Q "I never worried about anything on campus. The good thing about Trinity is that everyone is so rich that they already have everything they want and don't steal. **Nobody goes on to campus unless they have a reason**, too, so strangers aren't a common sight."

Q "Trinity is located, almost literally, in the center of San Antonio. Nonetheless, it always feels like a safe and insulated campus. This is partially due to **a very intentional absence of city streets** running through campus."

Q "There are always officers patrolling campus and emergency phones are set up all around. There was **never a time when I did not feel safe** walking alone."

STUDENT AUTHOR: Part of the reason that the Trinity campus is referred to as "the Bubble" is because of the safety that comes along with living there. Overall, DCS is great at creating an atmosphere where students can, and often do, take their personal safety for granted.

> **Questions?**
> For more inside information and survival tips, pick up College Prowler's full-length book on this school, written by an actual student! Check it out at *www.collegeprowler.com*.

Students Speak Out
ON OVERALL EXPERIENCE

Q "Trinity was not my first choice of schools. That said, **I can't imagine having gone anywhere else**. I have met some amazing people, taken some stellar classes, had super professors, and had an amazing time in general. It hasn't all been easy, and there have been some pretty trying times, but that could, and does, happen anywhere."

Q "I love Trinity. I couldn't be happier here or anywhere else. Like the perfect pair of pants—**it doesn't fit everybody**, but if it does, it's University bliss."

Q "The University was **very accommodating to student needs**, and listened to the students' opinions, which was refreshing. The campus at times feels like its own world or bubble, but at least it is safe and in a great location. All in all, I loved my experience at Trinity and would highly recommend it to any potential students."

Q "It is nice to get to know classmates in these smaller classes, but if you are looking for an adventure, then do not come to this school. All in all, it is great, but the place **can definitely be plain vanilla**. And that can wear you down. Do not come to this school if you are easily bored."

STUDENT AUTHOR: **Most students that come to Trinity find a niche, and have a wonderful four years at the University. The experience can be as exciting or as mundane as you make it, but no matter what you do outside the classroom, the academic standards never fall, so you will find that there is a lot of work to do, but the education that makes it all worthwhile. Grads wind up happy that they worked hard and gave up sleep for such an educational experience.**

Truman State University

100 East Normal Street; Kirksville, MO 63501
(660) 785-4000; www.truman.edu

THE BASICS:

Acceptance Rate: 79%
Setting: Rural
F-T Undergrads: 5,842

SAT Range: 1110–1390*
Control: Public
Tuition: $11,543

Most Popular Majors: Business, English, Psychology, Biology, Recreation/Fitness Studies

Academics	B	Guys	B-
Local Atmosphere	C+	Girls	C
Safety & Security	A+	Athletics	C
Computers	B	Nightlife	C-
Facilities	B+	Greek Life	A-
Campus Dining	C	Drug Scene	B+
Off-Campus Dining	C+	Campus Strictness	B
Campus Housing	B+	Parking	B-
Off-Campus Housing	A-	Transportation	C
Diversity	C-	Weather	C+

Students Speak Out
ON ACADEMICS

Q "It has been my experience that the teachers at Truman are good overall. **They are very knowledgeable and helpful**, and they don't avoid answering questions if they don't know the answer—they will find out. This is only my third semester, but I've enjoyed my classes and the professors that I have had."

Q "**For the most part, the teachers are very personal**. They are focused on the students' success and care about the individuals. In my experience, they have always been reasonable in extreme circumstances and are typically available for help."

Q "Truman's professors are a diverse, knowledgeable group. In my experience, their dedication to presenting information and ensuring that students understand it is second to none. Plus, **most are friendly, approachable people who are flexible** and willing to work with you to help you succeed."

Q "I like most of my teachers. They all have office hours and are **completely willing to talk with students outside of office hours** as well. They are generally friendly."

STUDENT AUTHOR: Academics are not just a background against which to enjoy the weekends, and it shows. If a student here makes the effort to attend class and get involved, he or she can graduate with not only a slew of heartfelt recommendations, but also a few close professor friends. All in all, the courses are Truman's strongest asset.

Students Speak Out
ON LOCAL ATMOSPHERE

Q "The atmosphere is very similar to any Midwestern small town. **The locals, for the most part, are strongly rooted in rural culture**. The presence of the college does bring some life into the town, though."

Q "The atmosphere is very homey if you look in the right places. A lot of the business owners are very supportive of the school and the students. **It's the only time I've been treated well at a post office or a license bureau** if that tells you anything. There's little to do unless you want to go to Columbia, although the campus provides entertainment."

Q "Kirksville is not exactly what one would call a bustling metropolis, but **this small town can be quite peaceful and offers a safe environment** with everything one could possibly need."

Q "Kirksville is kind of small. **The University sponsors a lot of activities to keep us busy**, but for the most part, it can be a bit of a drive to find something to do that is not alcohol-related."

STUDENT AUTHOR: If you are looking for museums or big-city sports teams, you're not going to find them in Kirksville, so it is a testament to the University that so many students choose Truman. Nearly any kind of entertainment or nightlife you'll find is on campus. The city of Kirksville is sleepy, which makes it a great escape from the hustle of campus life. Spend a Saturday wandering through the shops on the square.

Students Speak Out
ON FACILITIES

Q "I really love the recreation center. It has an **awesome weight room, an elevated track, a huge gymnasium**, tons of treadmills/bikes/elliptical trainers, an indoor soccer room, and aerobics rooms. All of the equipment is well kept and easy to use."

Q "If you walk on campus, you will always see construction because **Truman is continually updating its facilities**. Nothing ever gets overly old; everything is pretty new."

Q "The rec center is very nice because it has all sorts of options. **The library is very welcoming, but it doesn't always have everything you need**. The computers have recently been updated to mostly flat screens, which are really easy to navigate, but sometimes the network itself is temperamental."

Q "**The athletic facilities are not up to par.** I guess athletics are not top priority here, and that can clearly been seen by the facilities that the basketball team uses."

Q "The facilities at Truman are **very impressive for the size of the university**."

STUDENT AUTHOR: **The pretty campus is routinely one of the deciding factors for prospective students, according to Truman's admissions office. The campus may be small, but picturesque brick buildings and majestic, shady trees give the University a grander, almost Ivy-League feel. Like most universities, Truman's facilities could always stand to be better, but for the price, everything is relatively effective and in good condition.**

Famous Alumni

Lenvil Elliott, Jenna Fischer, Harry Gallatin, Alphonso Jackson, Glen Jacobs, Mike Morris, Al Nipper, Ken Norton, John J. Pershing, Gregg Williams

Students Speak Out
ON CAMPUS DINING

Q "Cafeteria food is cafeteria food. There's a pretty **decent amount of variety, at least if you don't have any special dietary concerns**."

Q "I think **the food is pretty good for how cheap it is**. That said, it did seem to go downhill as the semester wore on. Definitely go to a dining hall during family day so your parents can see exactly what you have to eat. They will give you money for food."

Q "**The food on campus is nowhere near as bad as the horror stories one may hear**. The residential dining halls usually have a variety of choices every day. The Student Union Building also has a large cafeteria that offers alternatives, such as Godfather's Pizza, Blimpie Subs, and a full grill."

Q "Should you have an affinity for eating absolute filth, Truman is for you. **The food is terrible.** You can spend all your money for a halfway decent—not healthy, just decent-tasting—meal at the SUB, but you use up your money quickly, and you will pack on the pounds."

Q "Unfortunately, there is just **not much of a chance of finding good food on campus**."

STUDENT AUTHOR: **Meals at Truman are something you learn to deal with. The food isn't always the healthiest, but there are always vegan options. The lack of 24-hour dining facilities is inconvenient, but students stock up on late-night munchies for studying. Plus, with the off-campus dining nearly as limited in selection as on-campus establishments, students mostly resign themselves to becoming a little less choosy.**

Student Body

African American:	4%	Male/Female:	43/57%
Asian American:	2%	Out-of-State:	25%
Hispanic:	2%	International:	5%
Native American:	1%	Unknown:	3%
White:	83%		

Popular Faiths: Catholic, Protestant.

Gay Pride: The campus is very accepting of gay, bisexual, and transgendered students. Nearly all tolerance activities, including an incredibly popular semiannual dance and drag show, go through an umbrella organization called PRISM.

Economic Status: All levels, but most students here are from rural or suburban middle-class families.

Students Speak Out
ON DORMS

Q "**All of the dorms are pretty much equal**. The choice really only depends on whether you would prefer a community bathroom, which you do not have to clean and maintain, or a suite-style bathroom, which you share with four people and have to maintain."

Q "Centennial is one of the nicer coed dorms in terms of quality and location. Missouri Hall is **great for freshman art, music, and theater majors** as it is 30 feet away from the fine arts building, Ophelia Parrish. If you can, avoid dorms with no cafeteria because in the winter you have to walk out in the cold when you want to eat. That means no shorts and flip-flops."

Q "I would avoid any dorm that has community bathrooms, but that's just me. **I'm not a fan of having to wear sandals into the shower**."

STUDENT AUTHOR: **Truman has recently been overhauling many of the residence halls, so if you end up with a dorm room, it won't be so bad. Having to share a toilet with 20 other people might be unsettling, but the dorm atmosphere is great. All freshmen are required to live on campus, so it's something to moan and groan about together.**

> **Did You Know?**
> 47% of undergrads live on campus.

Students Speak Out
ON GUYS & GIRLS

Q "**Truman folk are about as plain as they come**. There are a few interesting personalities floating out and about, but most people tend to subscribe to the same generic form of personality as the rest."

Q "People are generally nice. I like a lot of the people around here. Many, however, are pretty big dorks, but that's okay. **They're usually semi-attractive dorks** anyway."

Q "**Half of the guys are gay, but gay guys are hot**, I suppose."

Q "**Most of the student population is pretty friendly and open**, and it's not hard to meet someone with similar interests. Beauty is always in the eye of the beholder."

STUDENT AUTHOR: **Everyone tends to adopt a love-the-one-you're-with perspective. The guys may not be buff, and most of the girls aren't models, but there are some remarkably attractive people walking around if you're looking for the kind with black-framed glasses and an iPod in tow. People have been known to go to Mizzou, an hour-and-a-half drive, for the purpose of a good hookup. There may be many fish in the sea, but Kirksville, unfortunately, is as landlocked as they come.**

Traditions

The Gum Tree
Lore has it that the gum tree originated in the 1920s, when it was against the rules to chew gum in class.

Statue of Joseph Baldwin
During graduation, valedictorians ceremoniously lay a wreath at the base of the statue of Joseph Baldwin, the founder of the University.

Overall School Spirit
There's a lot of support for the school. Both the Truman and Kirksville communities participated in the search for a new name for the University in the 1990s.

Students Speak Out
ON ATHLETICS

Q "**If you're into a school for its sports, you should probably look somewhere else**. The women's teams at Truman are fantastic, and the men get lucky every once in a while. However, interest in any sport at TSU is poor at best and pathetic most realistically."

Q "IMs are awesome, and **almost everyone I know participates in them**. Varsity sports definitely have their followings, but they're not huge."

Q "Our men's teams suck. Seriously, **the football team is a huge joke among Truman students**. It's pretty funny just to go to games to see them get trampled. The girls' teams are pretty decent. They win a lot more often."

Q "IM sports seem **bigger than varsity sports**."

STUDENT AUTHOR: **If you prefer to spend weekends decked out in your school colors, cheering on the University football team to a landslide victory, Truman just isn't the place. Intramural sports garner the most spectators, and during soccer matches between frats, cheers can be heard from across campus.**

Students Speak Out
ON DRUG SCENE

Q "Personally, I don't even notice a drug problem on campus. Thus, I think it's safe to say that if you work at avoiding it, **no one's going to bother you.**"

Q "**I know people who do drugs**, but I wouldn't consider any of them 'druggies.'"

Q "There's so much alcohol here that I'd consider that the most dangerous drug. It's kind of ironic that Truman is a dry campus. And although a lot of kids smoke pot recreationally, **there do not seem to be too many smokers.**"

STUDENT AUTHOR: **Kirksville has a powerful reputation for meth, as does the entire state of Missouri, which has the highest rate of meth lab activity in the United States. Yet, despite the culture that rages outside of the University, the campus is pretty much drug-free. There are a couple of fraternities inextricably linked with marijuana and some mildly harder drugs, but you won't find any visible drug use unless you go looking.**

16:1	Student-to-Faculty Ratio
88%	Freshman Retention Rate
46%	Four-Year Graduation Rate
97%	Financial Aid Applicants Receiving Aid

Students Speak Out
SAFETY & SECURITY

Q "**Since it's such a small town, I always feel safe.** I have no problems walking around campus by myself late at night. There are help phones all around campus, and there are usually lots of other people walking around."

Q "I've never had a problem. The campus is well-lit, and **there are almost always a lot of people around, even late at night**. And there is an escort service if you want it."

Q "Personally, I've never felt unsafe while on campus or even in the town. The campus is well-lit at night, and if someone is ever worried about anything, they can press an emergency blue-light located on poles around campus, and help will come immediately. **The department of public safety is monitoring the campus 24 hours a day.**"

STUDENT AUTHOR: **Kirksville has its share of advantages, and a safe campus atmosphere is definitely one of them. In this case, fewer people seems to equal fewer crimes. Even for girls, walking through campus late at night never brings a sense of fear or distrust. The dorms are locked after 10:30 p.m., and Truman recently equipped the night monitors with ID-swiping machines to make the process a little more official. Theft seems to be uncommon as well.**

Questions?
For more inside information and survival tips, pick up College Prowler's full-length book on this school, written by an actual student! Check it out at www.collegeprowler.com.

Students Speak Out
ON OVERALL EXPERIENCE

Q "I love this school. I feel that I fit in from the start. **Sometimes I wish that the location of the school were different, but I love Truman**."

Q "Sometimes I think about the places I didn't go, but **overall I am very happy and satisfied with my decision to come to Truman**. I also think that very few people are dissatisfied with Truman when they leave here."

Q "I've had a great overall experience at Truman. I've met a lot of amazing people who have become great friends. Even most of my classes have been pleasant experiences. **The small school atmosphere is perfect** because I love being able to walk to class and see four or five people I know along the way."

Q "I like the school itself, and I love the classes for the most part. However, **I do not like the town**. It's a downer sometimes, and it can be hard to get excited to come back after vacation or a break."

STUDENT AUTHOR: **For in-state kids, Truman is a fabulous deal, especially because the school gives out so many scholarships. But however majestic the buildings are, how impressive and wonderful the professors are, or how many scholarships are awarded, it's the other students who make or break the college experience. Truman students are a pretty motivated, involved, and accepting bunch of people. Plus there is always something to do on campus: plays, concerts, lectures, and demonstrations for every interest under the sun.**

Tufts University

419 Boston Avenue; Medford, MA 02215
(617) 628-5000; www.tufts.edu

THE BASICS:

Acceptance Rate: 28%
Setting: Suburban
F-T Undergrads: 4,976

SAT Range: 2010–2230*
Control: Private
Tuition: $38,840

Most Popular Majors: International Relations, Economics, Psychology, Political Science, English

*of 2400

Academics	A	Guys	C
Local Atmosphere	A-	Girls	C+
Safety & Security	B+	Athletics	C-
Computers	B	Nightlife	A-
Facilities	B	Greek Life	C
Campus Dining	A-	Drug Scene	B+
Off-Campus Dining	A	Campus Strictness	B+
Campus Housing	B-	Parking	B-
Off-Campus Housing	B-	Transportation	B+
Diversity	B+	Weather	C-

Students Speak Out
ON ACADEMICS

Q "The teachers are one of the best aspects of Tufts because they are so **open and accessible and willing to help**. Upper-level courses are designed to bring students' diversity and range of experiences into the classroom to make the material more tangible and meaningful."

Q "Classes **totally depend on the teachers**. Some of the teachers are really great and make class interesting, while others make class boring and hard to follow. Overall, I would say most teachers are pretty good."

Q "A good portion of the teachers at Tufts have worked in their respective fields for long periods of time, and since Tufts is **just underneath Ivy League status**, they are professionals."

Q "Most **teachers have high expectations** of the kids, but are also very fair. I have no complaints about the teachers at Tufts, although I've heard some of the TAs are annoying. You run into TAs mostly when you have a lab for a class."

STUDENT AUTHOR: **Tufts has an excellent faculty, and academics that are some of the news makers in modern studies. Classes are what students make of them, and for the most part, so are relationships with faculty. Office hours are an excellent time to get to know a professor outside of the classroom setting and find out about research projects and possible internships. Professors are really just grown up students, and if you take the opportunity to get to know them outside of class, you will really enhance your college experience.**

Students Speak Out
ON LOCAL ATMOSPHERE

Q "Tufts is like its own little world, but as soon as you hop on the T, the **whole city of Boston appears on your doorstep**. There are endless restaurants, bars, clubs, shops, historical sites, and museums to visit. It's a college town."

Q "Boston is the biggest college town in the country. There are **over 500,000 students** in the city, so there are always things to do and people to meet."

Q "The **Tufts campus spans two towns**, Medford and Somerville. Medford, which is more towards the uphill side of campus, is quieter, but right along the edge of campus is Boston Avenue."

Q "Medford itself is a small town and doesn't have much other than Tufts and its downtown area, Medford Square. Boston's a huge town with a ton of colleges that you can visit, and a city with lots of places to go. Boston's about 15 minutes away through the subway, and it's readily accessible. **Harvard and MIT are within 10 minutes** reach, and there's a lot to do in Harvard Square. There aren't many places to stay away from—you're in college, so you might as well experiment with everything."

STUDENT AUTHOR: **Tufts has the advantage of being just a 15-minute T-ride from the center of a city where there is plenty of nightlife, concerts, and entertainment for the Tufts student body and the other 55 Boston-area schools. Once you've explored the area, you'll find there really is something for every taste in this varied, college-friendly region.**

5 Best Things	5 Worst Things
1 Spring Fling	1 Walking uphill to class
2 Research opportunit	2 Parking tickets
3 Free movies	3 Freshman bathrooms
4 Sunday brunch	4 Liberals vs. Conservatives
5 Guest speakers	5 Small endowment

Students Speak Out
ON FACILITIES

Q "The computer labs have **up-to-date, fast computers**. The Campus Center is a chill place for people to hang out and get some food."

Q "The Campus Center is pretty cool. It's a good place for people to meet up, and there are a **bunch of little study nooks**, and a couple big-screen TVs (with cable) located upstairs. The library is nice with its cozy armchairs."

Q "I love the Campus Center and our athletic facilities. We have a new track, and we **get new weight equipment every year**. Timing for the gym is important because crowds come in during the afternoon."

Q "The gym is **a lot nicer than at most other colleges**, and has become very popular. It's probably your best chance to see someone socially, but all the academic facilities are good."

Q "Some of the facilities are a little on the older, 1970s side, but there are **rarely complaints**."

STUDENT AUTHOR: **Tufts takes a lot of pride in its campus buildings and facilities, and they are always well kept and maintained. Generally, students complain that the buildings are a little too small. There are minor problems with overcrowding, but with such a small student body, this is only noticeable during busy times. There has been a flurry of construction over the last 10 years, with more new buildings and renovations every year. There is something new on campus every fall, and Tufts is steadily trying to keep up with the growing needs of the student body. They wish they could compete with the facilities at larger schools.**

Famous Alumni

Hank Azaria, Rob Burnett, Tracy Chapman, Pierre Omidyar, Bill Richardson

Students Speak Out
ON CAMPUS DINING

Q "Food on campus is **good, for mass-produced cafeteria food**. People complain about the tedium of it, and many sophomores order in on Points instead of going to the dining halls."

Q "The food here is so good! Tufts food is ranked **second best in the country, I think**. It's a little tough to ward off the Freshman 15, but it's worth it!"

Q "They **try to meet every student's needs**, and they do a good job at it. The required purchase of an unlimited meal plan for freshmen is a bummer because not that many people will actually use up any more than half of the 400 meals given a semester!"

Q "It **can get repetitive**. You just have to get a little more creative!"

Q "Once you get to be an upperclassman, you usually eat at the Campus Center, which I love as much as the cafeterias. There's plenty of selection, and **a huge salad bar**."

STUDENT AUTHOR: **The majority of students will tell you that the food on campus is great. Students who have been to other university cafeterias agree that they are lucky. There are always fresh vegetables and fruits in the dining halls, Campus Center eateries are generally packed, and Sunday brunch is one of the largest social events on campus. The unlimited meal plan is required for the first year, which some students resent. It is true that you probably won't get to eat all the food you pay for before the end of the semester.**

Student Body

African American:	6%	Male/Female:	49/51%
Asian American:	12%	Out-of-State:	72%
Hispanic:	6%	International:	6%
Native American:	<1%	Unknown:	12%
White:	57%		

Popular Faiths: There are a number of active religious communities on campus, including Christian, Jewish, Islamic, and Eastern religious groups.

Gay Pride: Except for a few isolated incidents every once in a while, the campus is very tolerant, and most students are very supportive of the gay community.

Economic Status: There is a huge population of very wealthy kids, many of them international students.

Students Speak Out
ON DORMS

Q "Dorms are, on the whole, pretty decent. Big dorms like South are **fun and modern**, but can also be isolating freshman year if you don't land on a good hall. People in Bush and Metcalf seem to have good bonding experiences. Stratton is good if you want big rooms and no noise. But it is so quiet sometimes, the place feels empty."

Q "I've seen better dorms, but I've also seen dorms much worse than ours on other campuses. It's a **conflict between uphill and downhill** at Tufts: uphill has Miller and Houston, and the best downhill dorm is Bush. Tilton is the all-freshmen dorm, which is great for making friends."

Q "You're **assigned a room freshman year**, so you don't have any choice."

STUDENT AUTHOR: Tufts dorm rooms aren't the size of hotel lobbies, but they aren't the size of hotel closets, either. Some dorms are slightly better than others, but most rooms are medium-sized, and living in any one of them is a similar experience. The fact remains, however, that no matter what dorm you're assigned during your first year, the differences are going to be small.

Did You Know?
66% of undergrads live on campus.

Students Speak Out
ON GUYS & GIRLS

Q "Lots of people just hook up with other people, and then you have your **die-hard couples** who are joined at the hip and rarely go anywhere unaccompanied by their other half, but I think there are plenty of people who don't do either, be it because they are dating someone at another school, or just not really dating anyone."

Q "The **girls at Tufts are definitely better looking than the guys**. Although it's true that people don't really fix themselves up at Tufts as much as at schools, say, in the South."

Q "The guys at Tufts aren't the best part, but you **can find your match**, and the other benefits outweigh this seemingly negative aspect."

STUDENT AUTHOR: You can generalize Tufts guys and girls, and still be fairly accurate. They aren't the best looking—usually a bit on the dorky side—and probably weren't super-popular in high school, but still really enjoy partying and socializing. Never fear—Boston has thousands upon thousands of college students passing through every year, so there is always hope and plenty of opportunities to meet new people.

Traditions

First Night
The first night of Freshman Orientation, the entire class and alumni gather in the Gantcher Center for dinner and the story of Jumbo.

Painting the Cannon
Every night, students paint advertising on the Cannon. Painting may only be done in the dark.

Overall School Spirit
Tufts school spirit extends further than sports. It is hard to avoid, since the Tufts Spirit Coalition is always cooking up something.

Students Speak Out
ON ATHLETICS

Q "Varsity sports, depending on which, are big on campus. I think the biggest ones are track, soccer, softball, crew, and sailing. Those teams have **recently won championships** at a national level, and are really popular."

Q "Tufts is not big on its sports. People definitely play and **enjoy going to games**, but it is not a campus spirit builder."

Q "Tufts is **only a D-III school**, and nobody really watches the sports. There are people who go to games, but they're not really Tufts' students. There are a lot of older people coming to watch the games."

Q "The **teams are competitive**, but school spirit is low. It's one of Tufts biggest flaws."

STUDENT AUTHOR: The University certainly doesn't own any kind of athletic bragging rights over any other schools, which is why those who believe sports are the essence of college have probably never heard of Tufts. Tufts has a long-standing tradition of athletics, but most students find that school spirit is not focused around sports at all.

Students Speak Out
ON DRUG SCENE

Q "There are certain circles where drugs are commonplace, but overall, the **only widespread substance use appears to be alcohol**."

Q "A lot of people **don't do drugs at Tufts**, so the scene is really limited to a few groups who pretty much all know each other."

Q "Drugs are **available if you want them**, like on any campus, but they're by no means prevalent. The same with drinking—you can if you want, but nobody will think any less of you if you don't."

STUDENT AUTHOR: One thing's for sure, there isn't any social pressure to do drugs at Tufts. As a matter of fact, a student here could very well go their entire college career without seeing anything more than alcohol and cigarettes. Generally, where there is smoking and drinking, marijuana isn't far away. There are also a few rich fraternity boys here and there that are known for their coke habits. The average Tufts student will probably drink on weekends and smoke from time to time, but as for the drug scene, there is virtually nothing to worry about.

8:1	Student-to-Faculty Ratio
95%	Freshman Retention Rate
87%	Four-Year Graduation Rate
85%	Financial Aid Applicants Receiving Aid

Students Speak Out
SAFETY & SECURITY

Q "Tufts is a very safe place, with a large sense of **community and courtesy**. Most security violations come from local residents."

Q "The campus police **offer a self defense class** for girls, and have made many efforts to remind students that they aren't always as safe in the 'real world' as they are on campus. It's easy to take our safety for granted."

Q "**Dorms are always locked**, but entrance is easy. That may seem a bit unsafe, but it's never been a problem. In fact, you'll find that it's much nicer to have easy access to dorms, and not have restrictions on who can stay over like at other schools. I feel totally safe at Tufts, and in Boston, for that matter."

STUDENT AUTHOR: Tufts has gone to incredible lengths to make students feel safe. With safety services like TEMS (an emergency medical service), police escorts, and a strong police presence, Tufts students feel safe walking around their well-monitored, well-lit campus, even at night.

Questions?
For more inside information and survival tips, pick up College Prowler's full-length book on this school, written by an actual student! Check it out at *www.collegeprowler.com*.

Students Speak Out
ON OVERALL EXPERIENCE

Q "The **school is growing**, and it's nice to be a part of that. I wish we had better race relations, more school spirit, and a bigger endowment. But I feel like I'm getting a real-world education."

Q "**Extracurriculars are huge** at Tufts—there's something for everyone, from the Tufts Dance Collective to a society that discusses Simpsons episodes. Honestly, I haven't met any freshmen who didn't love their first year, and couldn't wait to go back."

Q "It doesn't have a lot going for it that would make you jump up and down in joy, but if you **get involved**, there's no reason you shouldn't have a good time."

Q "I used to wish I were somewhere else, but not any more. I have been through many great things at Tufts and have had met many wonderful people. I even got to go to Cuba! College is definitely what you make of it, no matter where you go. Just be open-minded about things, and make sure that you look for the good things as opposed to the bad. When I did that, I saw that I was at **a great school with a great reputation**, and that it has a lot to offer me."

STUDENT AUTHOR: The Tufts experience goes beyond the classroom, and provides students access to the ideal academic and social surroundings. The combination of school opportunities and local culture give Tufts its own distinctive flavor that allows students to grow in ways they never could have imagined. Most of the negative experiences that Tufts students gripe about are also good growth experiences. Students who graduate from Tufts enter the real world focused, confident, and prepared to face even the toughest challenges.

Tulane University

6823 St. Charles Avenue; New Orleans, LA 70118
(504) 865-5000; www.tulane.edu

THE BASICS:

Acceptance Rate: 27%
Setting: Urban
F-T Undergrads: 5,173

SAT Range: 1890–2140*
Control: Private
Tuition: $38,664

Most Popular Majors: Finance, Psychology, English, History, Marketing, Biology

*of 2400

Academics	A-	Guys	B
Local Atmosphere	A-	Girls	B+
Safety & Security	C	Athletics	B-
Computers	B	Nightlife	A+
Facilities	B+	Greek Life	A
Campus Dining	B-	Drug Scene	C+
Off-Campus Dining	A+	Campus Strictness	A
Campus Housing	C+	Parking	C+
Off-Campus Housing	A-	Transportation	B-
Diversity	B	Weather	B

Students Speak Out
ON ACADEMICS

Q "The workload is absolutely reasonable, but that depends on what you are studying. You will see a large chunk of the student population going out on weeknights fairly often, though, especially first semester, so **I can't imagine the workload is that hard across the board**."

Q "The workload is pretty tough. Prepare not to sleep during midterms or finals weeks. **We have a lot of great programs here**, especially Latin American studies, business, architecture, and now political science."

Q "Most of the professors I've had were knowledgeable and good at transferring information to their students. They're fascinating people, too—I'm only a freshman, but **I've had a sitar-playing hippie for English** and a Chilean native for Spanish."

Q "The workload depends on your major **Architecture students never sleep**, but business majors can virtually party 24/7."

STUDENT AUTHOR: Since Hurricane Katrina, the school has implemented a renewal plan to improve its academics. The addition of a public service graduation requirement helps incorporate the classroom with the rebuilding of New Orleans, and the Tulane Interdisciplinary Experience Seminars (TIDES) for freshmen are designed to help students integrate into college life. Tulane's efforts have paid off—with each progressive year, the freshman class continues to raise the academic bar.

Students Speak Out
ON LOCAL ATMOSPHERE

Q "New Orleans is a very unique city with a culture all its own. It's possible to walk or take the street car basically anywhere of interest in the city. Obviously, the French Quarter is infamous, but **there's more to do there than just party**."

Q "There is a lot of live music around New Orleans—**almost any day of the week there is some kind of free show** somewhere. There are a few museums and art galleries that are nice, and, of course, everybody who comes to visit has to go to the French Quarter and Bourbon Street if they've never been."

Q "New Orleans is so fun to explore and get lost in. Audubon Park is literally right across the street, and it's great to people watch and run or bike. New Orleans is a checkerboard city, though, so make sure that you don't get caught in a wrong area. You can literally **walk one block from million-dollar houses to a bad neighborhood**."

Q "It's slow, it's friendly, and there's good food, good music, and good parties. The **locals are eccentric and interesting**, not to mention incredibly generous and helpful."

STUDENT AUTHOR: New Orleans is an old city with lots of beautiful architecture and interesting history. Regardless of your interests, you'll never be able to say there is nothing to do in New Orleans. There is always some sort of festival, parade, game, gallery opening, book reading, or musical group performance going on.

5 Best Things	5 Worst Things
1 City of New Orleans	1 Rain and humidity
2 Weather	2 Safety issues
3 Unique culture	3 High tuition
4 Nightlife	4 Parking
5 Local music scene	5 Public transportation

Students Speak Out
ON FACILITIES

Q "The Reily Center (the gym) is amazing—it has two pools and a ton of workout equipment. The LBC (the student center) is **new since Katrina and is an 'all green' building**. All the facilities are nice, and the school works hard at keeping them up."

Q "The LBC building is very nice as it was just finished a few years ago. As far as classrooms go, the Business School has the best. Otherwise, I'd have to say most of the facilities on campus **range from okay to good to poor quality**."

Q "The **library isn't one of those really gorgeous old-fashioned buildings** some schools have, but it's a good place to study. It has some amazingly comfortable couches that people like to read on."

Q "The athletic center is huge, and offers lots of classes and nice equipment. It's a lot **bigger and nicer than any other gym** I've been to."

Q "**Everything's pretty modern**, and the academic buildings are beautiful. They've been doing quite a bit of renovation since I've been here."

STUDENT AUTHOR: **The student center is one of Tulane's newest and nicest buildings on campus. The LBC is not only a great facility in terms of its environmentally friendly structure, it also has great functionality and is every Tulane student's one-stop shop. In terms of athletic facilities, Reily is an excellent gym with fairly new cardio equipment and a large weight room. Most buildings on campus, especially in the academic quad, are beautiful and go well with the green spaces.**

Famous Alumni

Geoffrey Beene, Neil Bush, Newt Gingrich (MA, PhD), Lauren Hutton, Bruce Paltrow, Jerry Springer

Students Speak Out
ON CAMPUS DINING

Q "Campus food is pretty decent, especially the local stuff they serve. They pull out all the stops for Parents' Weekend and when prospective students come, but even the rest of the year is **nothing to complain about**."

Q "Freshmen mostly eat at Bruff, where **the food is decent by most people's standards**. And some people actually really love Bruff. Other places on campus, like the student center and Le Gourmet, are better. They're pretty expensive, but you get meal plan dollars called Greenbucks for those places."

Q "It seems somewhat obnoxious that freshmen have to purchase an unlimited meal plan, but it is also really **nice to be able to eat whenever you want** and as many times a day as you want."

Q "Bruff leaves a lot to be desired, and other eateries on campus are **ridiculously overpriced**."

Q "The dining hall is usually pretty good, but it doesn't offer much variety. **Switch things up by going to the LBC food court** and you'll be fine."

STUDENT AUTHOR: **All freshmen are required to have an unlimited meal plan at Bruff, and the sentiments toward this requirement depend on who you talk to. While some complain that the food gets old, the staple foods are always available, and Bruff is constantly trying to improve the quality and selection of its food. The other eateries on campus are set up so that meal dollars—or Greenbucks—buy essentially the same things as real cash.**

Student Body

African American:	9%	Male/Female:	46/54%
Asian American:	5%	Out-of-State:	77%
Hispanic:	4%	International:	2%
Native American:	2%	Unknown:	6%
White:	71%		

Popular Faiths: It seems most students are Jewish, Catholic, or Protestant.

Gay Pride: New Orleans and Tulane are fairly liberal climates, so all sexual preferences are welcomed.

Economic Status: You cannot pay full tuition here if you're not rich. But, a lot of students are here on scholarship, so there is also a population of middle- and lower-class students.

Students Speak Out
ON DORMS

Q "The nicest dorm is Wall—seriously, **it's like a Hilton**—but you have to write an essay to get in. All other dorms are more or less the same in niceness. It gets better for upperclassmen."

Q "The freshman dorms are pretty typical: smallish with communal bathrooms. They're **better than some dorms I've seen** at other schools, though. I have decent closet space."

Q "Monroe and Sharp are the most popular and also the most populated. They are the biggest, so **most of the freshman class lives in these two dorms**. They are the party dorms, so they are fun."

STUDENT AUTHOR: **Monroe and Sharp house a majority of the freshman class. Most agree that they are old, ugly, and pretty gross, but there's a big social factor about living in these dorms. In terms of the other freshman dorms, JL is the all-girls dorm, Butler is the honors dorm, Paterson is the wellness dorm but is known as the hippie dorm, and Wall is the newest dorm on campus and is completely suite-style. Students are required to live on campus their freshman and sophomore years, and most choose to live off campus after that.**

> **? Did You Know?**
> 48% of undergrads live on campus.

Students Speak Out
ON GUYS & GIRLS

Q "The guys are largely athletic, really good looking, decently intelligent, and, sadly, think quite highly of themselves. The girls are generally pretty, and **a lot of them are either artsy or obviously sorority girls**."

Q "There are a lot of **really attractive people here**. The majority of people are fun and outgoing."

Q "Students are pretty varied but not overly so. **Most love to drink and party**, although a fair amount are very serious about school."

Q "A lot of people are from the Northeast, so expect **a lot of really skinny people**—we don't look like typical Louisianians here. But, we also have lots of Southern guys and girls—it's really pretty diverse."

STUDENT AUTHOR: **Tulane has a wide variety of guys and girls on campus. The girls tend to dress up more than at your average college campus, and most guys tend to look average and have the average college wardrobe. There a lot of cool and interesting people to meet, and a lot like to have a good time along with studying. There are more hookups than committed relationships, but you'll still find a lot of people with significant others that live elsewhere.**

Traditions

Senior Salute
Formal reception at the dean's residence to recognize all graduating seniors before commencement.

Nicknames
Tulane is called the "Green Wave," "Greenbacks," and "Greenies" because of the football jerseys' color.

Overall School Spirit
While there isn't huge enthusiasm for the sports teams on campus, Tulane students know how to show their pride in just about every other respect. They wear Tulane gear and are very supportive of their clubs and organizations.

Students Speak Out
ON ATHLETICS

Q "Our football team isn't so great, but **they play at the Superdome and games are fun**. Our baseball team is actually pretty good and competitive. All varsity games are free to students, too. Club sports are pretty popular, fun, and easy to join. I highly recommend them."

Q "**Intramural and club sports are huge**. Anyone can form an intramural team as long as they get enough people together."

Q "The athletic reputation is okay. Sports are popular, but **this isn't LSU**."

Q "**Sports are not so good here**. Basketball, baseball, and volleyball are fair, but if you live and breathe sports, this isn't going to be the best place for you."

STUDENT AUTHOR: **A number of things might come to mind when one thinks of Tulane, but its athletic department is not one of them. The baseball, basketball, and volleyball teams are good, but they're still not widely supported by the student body. But, a lot of students are involved in club sports. Intramurals are also fun to participate in, but these tend to be much less organized.**

Students Speak Out
ON DRUG SCENE

Q "The drug scene is big enough for our small campus and is definitely noticeable. However, **campus police are starting to really crack down on drugs**, so it's less of a problem now."

Q "There are a lot of drugs at Tulane—almost enough to match the drinking scene, I'd say. **People smoke often**, despite the awful risks you face if you get caught on this campus."

Q "I personally have never seen anyone do drugs. That being said, it is prevalent among Tulane students from what I hear. Cocaine, Adderall, and pot seem to be the main drugs of choice although **alcohol consumption is definitely more popular than anything**."

STUDENT AUTHOR: **Other than marijuana and cocaine, there are not that many drugs that are heavily used on campus. However, alcohol is considered a drug, and a lot of students abuse it. Also, given a city like New Orleans, there's going to be a certain amount of substances—legal and otherwise—no matter where you go.**

9:1	Student-to-Faculty Ratio
87%	Freshman Retention Rate
66%	Four-Year Graduation Rate
80%	Financial Aid Applicants Receiving Aid

Students Speak Out
SAFETY & SECURITY

Q "We live in the **most dangerous city in the U.S.**, and we knew that coming in. That said, Tulane does a lot to protect its students and inform of danger. We have a Safe Ride program, blue lights, officers all over campus, e-mails and signs about crimes, and regular e-mails with safety reminders."

Q "New Orleans is not a safe city, hands down. Campus is pretty safe, but **it is not okay to walk off campus alone** at night."

Q "**I've never felt unsafe on campus**. It's easy to be safe off campus, you just have to be smart about it. I think this helps students grow up during college."

STUDENT AUTHOR: **It's common knowledge that New Orleans has a high crime rate, but this does not mean that Tulane students are in constant danger. In fact, most say they feel very safe on campus. The most frequent crime on campus is theft, but even that is minimal. The real concern is when students travel off campus, especially at night and while intoxicated. Common sense is the best defense.**

Questions?
For more inside information and survival tips, pick up College Prowler's full-length book on this school, written by an actual student! Check it out at *www.collegeprowler.com*.

Students Speak Out
ON OVERALL EXPERIENCE

Q "I love Tulane and can't imagine going anywhere else. The workload can be really hard at times, and the people are really smart and dedicated to what they do, but the social and cultural scenes are amazing, as well. **Living in New Orleans is a unique experience** that makes Tulane one of a kind."

Q "The academics are good, but you don't have to be closed up in you room studying all the time to get good grades. **It's really easy to have a great social life** in conjunction with your academic experience."

Q "I love the school, and this is definitely one of my favorite cities ever! If I could do it over again, I would definitely come here again. In fact, I could definitely **see myself living here, even after graduation**."

Q "I wish I had gotten more involved right away, but it's easy to start late. There is a lot of partying but don't fall behind on your schoolwork. New Orleans is an amazing city and so unique. I highly recommend Tulane to students not from the South because **it's not too Deep South, but it's a whole new experience**."

STUDENT AUTHOR: **Living in such a culturally rich environment creates a unique learning opportunity that many kids who go to different schools will never get a chance to experience. It takes a very intelligent and well-balanced person to attend Tulane because the nightlife and 24/7 party scene can tempt students to blow off classes and just have a good time. There is no other school like Tulane, and there is no other city like New Orleans.**

UC Berkeley

110 Sproul Hall; Berkeley, CA 94720
(510) 642-4636; www.berkeley.edu

THE BASICS:

Acceptance Rate: 23%
Setting: Mid-sized City
F-T Undergrads: 23,863

SAT Range: 1820–2190*
Control: Public
Tuition: $29,540

Most Popular Majors: Social Sciences, Biological/Life Sciences, Engineering, Law, Business

*of 2400

Academics	A-	Guys	B-
Local Atmosphere	A-	Girls	C+
Safety & Security	C+	Athletics	B+
Computers	A-	Nightlife	B-
Facilities	B+	Greek Life	B
Campus Dining	B-	Drug Scene	C+
Off-Campus Dining	A	Campus Strictness	B
Campus Housing	B	Parking	D
Off-Campus Housing	C	Transportation	A
Diversity	A	Weather	A

Students Speak Out
ON ACADEMICS

Q "The staff at Berkeley is second to none and includes **numerous Nobel Prize winners**. In most of my classes, I've been impressed with my professors' abilities, but I have heard tales of bad professors."

Q "Generally, professors in your first and second years will be less personal and harsher graders, only because **the classes are large**, and they want to 'weed people out.' Once you start your core major classes in junior year, that's when the awesome teaching begins."

Q "A lot of professors are world-renowned scientists and researchers. There has never, in the history of man, been **a better collection of minds** in one place at one time, seriously."

Q "Go to class! I think if there is one thing I wish someone had drilled into my head when I came here, it would be that. The teachers are amazing, but you really don't get to see that unless you **go to class as much as possible**."

STUDENT AUTHOR: The majority of students at Cal agree upon one remarkable aspect of Berkeley that surpasses all else: its enriching academics. Berkeley is consistently ranked as the number one public university in the United States for several reasons, but perhaps the most dominant one is its challenging academic atmosphere. After talking to students from a wide variety of departments ranging from dance to electrical engineering, every student had at least a few positive things to say about their studies.

Students Speak Out
ON LOCAL ATMOSPHERE

Q "If you like the outdoors, Berkeley is definitely one of the best places to go to school. It's so close to **the ocean, the mountains, woodlands**—the weather from spring to early fall is sublime."

Q "San Francisco is where my friends and I go to hang out and party because, unless you're in a frat or sorority, **the town is pretty much dead**. Sure, there are places to shop and eat and socialize, but they get old fast, and you get sick of seeing your classmates and GSIs everywhere you go. The culture in SF is a lot more genuine, a lot more true to real life."

Q "Berkeley is an interesting place in itself. Students pretty much dominate the area, but **people love to visit** and walk up and down Telegraph—a street bordering campus that has smoke shops, Bohemian people selling trinkets, book stores, coffee and sandwich shops, and thrift stores."

Q "I came from a suburb in Southern California, so **Berkeley was shocking** to me when I first got here. I wasn't used to stepping over bums on my way to class and being surrounded by people all my age."

STUDENT AUTHOR: It may seem surprising to hear people refer to Berkeley as a "college town." At a school so large, you might not expect people to feel like they're regulars every place they go. The city of San Francisco is a nice escape from the college-town doldrums.

5 Best Things	5 Worst Things
1 Student body	1 Homeless people
2 Inspiring faculty	2 Academic pressure
3 Large facilities	3 Too many choices
4 Proximity to San Fran	4 Drug culture
5 Natural amenities	5 Rainy weather

Students Speak Out
ON CAMPUS DINING

Q "Crossroads is the **best thing to happen to campus food** since I don't know when. I was in the dorms before the dining commons was built, and the food was barely edible."

Q "If you're a freshman, I say a meal plan with lots of **Flex Points is probably the best way to go**. You have the freedom to eat at the dining halls when you feel like it, and other places on and off campus when you don't, without feeling pressured to get your money's worth."

Q "The dorm food at Berkeley is horrible. If I lied and told you the food was edible, I'd feel intense guilt. It's not. **Get the smallest meal plan you can**, because most people just end up eating cereal, wilted salads, and frozen yogurt."

Q "**Food on Campus is okay** at the Golden Bear Café, where you can use your meal swipes from the dining commons. There's also the Free Speech Movement Café, which is a great place to study and hang out with friends."

Q "The incoming freshmen have no idea **how big of an improvement** Berkeley's new dining options are over the old ones."

STUDENT AUTHOR: **While many students seem happy about the recent addition of Crossroads and the recent re-addition of the Bear's Lair to on-campus and residential dining options, many of the students deemed the remaining options as "barely edible." The flexibility of the meal plans is a real savior for Berkeley students. The huge, 800-person capacity commons is clean, modern, and gives students more of a buffet-style setting, rather than a cafeteria atmosphere.**

Students Speak Out
ON FACILITIES

Q "One of the reasons I chose Berkeley was because of its facilities. When I visited the campus, **I was impressed** by the huge, old-school libraries and stadiums, the nice gym, and the modern labs and buildings."

Q "Berkeley's **facilities are good enough**, unless you're looking for only the best. I think unless you came from an extremely wealthy high school, Berkeley's facilities will be a big improvement."

Q "The RSF is a pretty hopping place. **It's pretty big** compared to the athletic centers I've seen at other colleges, and access to the RSF also means access to the pools around campus and another gym up at Strawberry Canyon."

Q "The only big complaint I have about Berkeley's facilities is the **lack of career services** close to campus. There's a career library near the Tang Center, but the career center is down several blocks on Bancroft from campus, making it kind of an inconvenience to go."

Q "I've watched **a lot of performances** at Zellerbach because a lot of really interesting and famous acts come through here."

STUDENT AUTHOR: **From its athletic fields and basketball courts, to its enormous, resource-filled libraries and research laboratories, Berkeley's awesome facilities are some of the most raved-about features of the school. The extensiveness of Berkeley's facilities is undeniable, and their aesthetic appeal is almost unanimously agreed upon. Berkeley combines a modern-historic feel with the most up-to-date technology and resources.**

Famous Alumni

Jonathan Galbraith, Walter Haas, Julie Morgan, Gregory Peck, Nicklaus Wirth, Steve Wozniak

Student Body

African American:	3%	Male/Female:	46/54%
Asian American:	42%	Out-of-State:	10%
Hispanic:	12%	International:	3%
Native American:	1%	Unknown:	8%
White:	31%		

Popular Faiths: Christian, Muslim, spiritual but not religious.

Gay Pride: LGBT Center and clubs are very active and visible on campus.

Economic Status: Varied; mostly middle and middle-upper class.

Students Speak Out
ON DORMS

Q "Dorms aren't bad at all. Usually it works out kind of **give-and-take**; if you have a tiny triple, your roommates or floormates will be cool. If your room is roomy and nice, your roommates will be duds."

Q "Dorms are pretty nice. I'd say try for Foothill if you're willing to pay a bit more for comfort. **Dorms are a great way to meet people** and enjoy social life, especially as a freshman. I'd definitely recommend that you stay in a dorm for at least one year."

Q "The **co-op scene is cool** for a while; it's kind of neat living communally and feeling like you're really working for your room and board, but then when the place gets all trashed at parties, and people stop doing a good job on their chores, it's not so fun anymore."

STUDENT AUTHOR: **Students at Cal seem generally pleased with their on-campus housing options. Most students were placed in rooms of their preference, and few had seriously harsh remarks about their roommates or resident advisors.**

> **? Did You Know?**
> 35% of undergrads live on campus.

Students Speak Out
ON GUYS & GIRLS

Q "If you're only looking for blonde bimbos, male or female, **go to UCLA, UCSB, or USC**. Berkeley isn't for you."

Q "There's always talk of the lack of hot girls and guys at Berkeley, but I've definitely come across a lot of not only good-looking, but actually **interesting, nice people** here, especially in class and through Greek life."

Q "There are tons of beautiful men at Berkeley, but unfortunately, they're either **gay or taken**."

Q "There are around **20,000 undergrads at Berkeley**; I'm sure you can find a guy or girl that's good-looking enough for you."

STUDENT AUTHOR: Berkeley has never really prided itself on its "hot" guys and girls, maybe for good reason. Though some conventionally and exotically attractive men and women can be spotted on campus everyday, most Berkeley students choose to focus on their activities, schoolwork, and friends, rather than their appearances or clothing. The guys and girls at Berkeley appear to have their heads on their shoulders.

Traditions

SUPERB Spring Concert Series
These are noon concerts held on Lower Sproul every Friday that usually feature small or indie/alternative bands.

Cal vs. Stanford Football Game
The axe is the prize for the victor of this monumental annual game.

Overall School Spirit
The antagonism between Cal and Stanford has gone on for a century and continues to be one of the strongest signs of our school spirit to this day.

Students Speak Out
ON ATHLETICS

Q "Berkeley has **lots of school spirit** . . . and lots of spirit means that varsity sports are very big on campus. Our football team isn't the best, but you still have a great time at the game, win or lose. Our pride for Cal is incredible. Our basketball team is awesome! The games are lots of fun. IM sports are also big, and they're easy to join."

Q "Even though Berkeley is supposed to be a bunch of bookworms, there are still some **first-rate athletes** that go to this school, and people know it."

Q "**Sports aren't big** on campus. People like to have fun and occasionally go to games, but, overall, a lot of people don't pay attention."

Q "Any sport available anywhere in the U.S. is one we most likely have and are also **pretty good at**."

STUDENT AUTHOR: Berkeley's reputation as an academic school doesn't hinder its competitive athletic performance in several sports, most notably basketball, rugby, gymnastics, and football. Cal's heavy recruitment of athletes helps booster both sports scores and student body diversity.

Students Speak Out
ON DRUG SCENE

Q "It's out there—I've seen it. There's **a lot of weed** and a lot of coke. Students also now use Adderall to study here. Be prepared for weed world. There are way too many people who smoke weed."

Q "I personally have never seen students abusing drugs. I've heard of some people who smoke pot, but it's **definitely not the Berkeley of the '60s.**"

Q "I'd say there are **more drug users at Cal** than at most universities. That's probably because some of the people who come to Berkeley associate the school and the city with its hippie past and want to come here and relive it or something."

STUDENT AUTHOR: Students agree that drug use is far from nonexistent at Berkeley, and it's even seen as part of popular campus culture by many. Most people name pot and psychedelics as the most frequently-used drugs, while harder drugs are less-frequently used. Berkeley is a liberal place, and its liberalness often comes with a blind eye towards most drug use.

15:1	Student-to-Faculty Ratio
97%	Freshman Retention Rate
61%	Four-Year Graduation Rate
78%	Financial Aid Applicants Receiving Aid

Students Speak Out
SAFETY & SECURITY

Q "I find security to be pretty good on campus. Personally, I find Berkeley to be a relatively safe place. **There is crime**, but I don't see it that often."

Q "The campus has many different types of services to make you feel **as safe as possible.**"

Q "Inside campus, it's quite safe, and my female friends do not feel threatened. Campus paths are well lit, and we have a good night-walking program and lots of security. Around campus, the city of **Berkeley is a bit ghetto**, and although I personally have never felt threatened before, I've heard stories of people getting harassed."

STUDENT AUTHOR: Students concur that UC Berkeley has gone to great lengths to make its students feel safe. Though it may seem like a college town at times, Berkeley is nevertheless an urban area, and students should act with caution and conscientiousness.

Questions?

For more inside information and survival tips, pick up College Prowler's full-length book on this school, written by an actual student! Check it out at *www.collegeprowler.com.*

Students Speak Out
ON OVERALL EXPERIENCE

Q "I've **never been happier in my life** than where I am now, here in Berkeley. Both the campus and town are amazingly diverse and offer opportunities for just about everything."

Q "Although **it has been really tough for me**, I wouldn't want to be in another school. Berkeley is one of the toughest and most competitive schools in the country, and those two qualities allow Berkeley to prepare its graduates better than any other school."

Q "Maybe I've had a bad experience, but undergrads at a research university with 32,000 students are **not cared for at all** as individuals by faculty."

Q "Overall, my time here has been awesome. I've had such a fun and rewarding experience. I came to Berkeley without ever visiting, and I have never regretted my decision. I definitely do not wish that I went somewhere else. **I love Berkeley**, and I can guarantee that you won't find any other place like it."

STUDENT AUTHOR: Overall, students have very positive things to say about their experiences at Cal, stating that there is no other place they could have met the extraordinary people, professors, opportunities, and challenges. However, the majority of Berkeley students go through, at times, the exhausting process of acclimating and growing to love their large university, asserting that they've gained more academic strength, tenacity, and open-mindedness than they could have at any other institution.

UC Davis

One Shields Avenue; Davis, CA 95616
(530) 752-1011; www.ucdavis.edu

Students Speak Out
ON ACADEMICS

Q "Most of my classes have had **200-plus students**, so I have never really gotten to know many teachers."

Q "If anyone wants to become a vet, Davis is the place to be. Besides **being the top vet school** in the country, the animal science teachers are excellent."

Q "**All classes are really hard**, and I think the teachers vary, depending on the class. Some of my classes I found to be quite boring because the teacher was not that great. The course material was not that bad, but the teacher would just lecture the whole time. However, I did have some really good teachers, which would make the class very interesting and worthwhile."

Q "I'm sure that most of the teachers are really smart and educated in their fields, but **sometimes the thick accents make it hard** to understand them. The material is hard enough to understand without the added difficulty of deciphering every word they say. However, I have always found that they're willing to work individually with me after class, and that has been really helpful."

STUDENT AUTHOR: **With more than 110 undergraduate fields of study, Davis has the greatest academic diversity of all the UC campuses. This gives students the chance to take classes that interest them, and the majority seem to appreciate the opportunities. Despite the challenges, most seem satisfied with their courses.**

Students Speak Out
ON LOCAL ATMOSPHERE

Q "The atmosphere is awesome. People are open-minded and laid-back. You don't **get snooty intellectuals** the way you would at say, Stanford. Yuck."

Q "It's a definite college town; **everything seems to be catered to the students**. The food and movies are reasonably priced, and being able to get to Sac and San Fran so easily makes it so there's a lot to do."

Q "Davis is unique. We are way more liberal than the surrounding areas. Sacramento is to the east, and we make fun of their campus a lot. Woodland is a farming area so not much is there besides Wal-Mart and Target, **which is good for cheap college students**."

Q "**Don't come to Davis if you're lazy**. First off, you'll flunk out of school, and second, your social life will suffer. Here, parties don't come to you; you go to them. If you get up and get out, Davis has a lot to offer, but if you expect an invitation from the clubs, chances are you'll spend a lot of time sitting around by yourself complaining that there's nothing to do in this town."

STUDENT AUTHOR: **Students enjoy the convenience of a college town and the comfortable atmosphere of a community. Davis is also just a car ride away from Sacramento, San Francisco, Tahoe, and Cache Creek. It's close enough to the beach to throw together a full-day adventure or even a weekend camping trip.**

Students Speak Out
ON FACILITIES

Q "Shields Library is **the best library ever**! It's quiet when it needs to be, but you can also take friends there to study with."

Q "UC Davis's recreation hall is one of my favorite places to go, as well as the Quad. These places are usually crowded because **people are always up for staying in shape** and basically unwinding under the sun."

Q "The Memorial Union (MU) has the bookstore, a study lounge, and a **student-run coffeehouse that has a ton of tables** in and around it for eating, studying, and napping."

Q "We have an awesome recreation center, a great health center, great computer labs—**UCD takes good care of us**."

Q "We have a large array of student facilities on campus. We have this really huge recreation hall that's **open almost all the time** with tons of athletic equipment, a pool, and even a rock-climbing wall. They hold some classes there as well."

STUDENT AUTHOR: Overall, students seem very impressed with the facilities on campus. Besides being pleased with the quality of the facilities, students are also grateful for the accessibility. The options are there and plentiful, and students are nothing but satisfied. While UC Davis students enjoy many top-notch facilities, one establishment is particularly renowned. With 3.24 million library volumes, the Shields Library is one of the largest libraries nationwide. It is a priceless resource for students to utilize for both academic reasons and leisurely reading.

Famous Alumni

Gus Lee, Ken O'Brien, Mark and Delia Owens, China Boy Martin Yan

Students Speak Out
ON CAMPUS DINING

Q "I would **recommend exploring off-campus food**. I have three words for the dining halls: horrible crap meals. No, they aren't really that bad; however, they get old fast."

Q "The food on campus **depends on whether or not you are a picky eater**. Personally, I am a very healthy eater, and sometimes I do not like everything that is offered at the dining commons. But, there is always something I could eat. The salad bar at the dining commons is great, and there are quesadilla makers and a grill that I like. Frozen yogurt is always there, too."

Q "The food on campus is **not bad at all**. If you are going to be a freshman, you will be living in the dorms, and the DCs (dining commons) are pretty good."

Q "There's **every kind of food you can think of**. Across campus from that there's the Silo, which has Taco Bell, Carl's Jr., Subway, a crepe place (crepes are huge in Davis), and some other fast food places."

Q "Dorm food is nutritious, but I found myself eating chicken sandwiches, fries, and side salad for dinner all too often. Memorial Union has a student-run food court, which is also an option. Here you can find **pizza, burritos, soups, salads**, or entire meals."

STUDENT AUTHOR: The dining commons have plenty of vegetarian and vegan selections, and some theme nights (Luau night, Caribbean night) that students seem to enjoy. Whatever the dining commons lack in its entrees, it makes up with its desserts.

Student Body

African American:	3%	Male/Female:	45/55%
Asian American:	41%	Out-of-State:	2%
Hispanic:	11%	International:	2%
Native American:	<1%	Unknown:	7%
White:	36%		

Popular Faiths: There are several Christian groups and Asian American religious groups, but most religious activities are held off campus.

Gay Pride: The campus is very accepting of its gay students and even hosts "Gay Pride Day" in June.

Economic Status: UCD has students from very diverse economic backgrounds.

Students Speak Out
ON DORMS

Q "The dorms are great and **a good place to meet roommates** for the rest of your academic career. The best dorms on campus are the Cuarto area."

Q "Cuarto rocks! It allows privacy, but at the same time **you can meet people just as easily in traditional dorms**. They're also more spacious and give you a better feel of life after dorms."

Q "Cuarto, especially Castillian, is the best! Your own bathroom and living room make it more like home while still creating the dorm atmosphere. Steer clear of Tercero **unless you really like the smell of cows**."

STUDENT AUTHOR: **Davis dorms are set up differently to accommodate students' different living styles, and picking a favorite just depends on what's important to you. No matter what though, students agree that the dorms provide a once-in-a-lifetime experience that no student should miss. Students point out that Tercero has a better dining common. Cuarto is suite-style—more like apartments. If you're aiming to make a ton of really close friends, but not too many acquaintances, a big suite in Cuarto would suit you well. Segundo is designed in a typical dorm style.**

> **Did You Know?**
> 25% of undergrads live on campus.

Students Speak Out
ON GUYS & GIRLS

Q "The girls on campus are attractive, and as a guy, there is a slightly higher number of girls than guys—**less competition is good**."

Q "I really like the guys here . . . they're obviously smart, but **they're not stuck up**. More often than not, they play some sort of sport, so they're in good shape, but that's kind of superficial. All the guys I've talked to have been really nice, friendly, and going somewhere in life."

Q "All I have to say is girls plus bikes plus miniskirts equals **one great combination**."

Q "Guys have it great here; the odds are in their favor. The girls aren't superficial, and they are great to talk to; **I can't say enough about the women's personalities**."

STUDENT AUTHOR: **The majority of Davis students respond with appreciative comments based on personalities. Though many are quick to point out the merits of bike riding and free gym access, they also clarify that the personalities and attitudes of the students far outshine the physical appearances. Students are open minded and friendly, and with a large student body, you're bound to find someone that interests you.**

> **Traditions**
>
> **Picnic Day**
> The college version of the high school open house, Picnic Day takes place in early April and showcases the work of many departments. Picnic Day is a popular day for students, alumni, and prospective students to come get a feel for UCD.
>
> **Overall School Spirit**
> Besides packing the stadium for football games, hanging out on Picnic Day, and plastering the UC Davis logo over much of their clothing, Davis students show school pride in the support they show for each other.

Students Speak Out
ON ATHLETICS

Q "UC Davis has been a powerhouse in Division II sports over the last decade. Now as DI, the **sports programs are big** and very good."

Q "Sports are pretty big here, especially football— **it's our pride and joy**! Sporting events are always going on, and they are a lot of fun. IM sports are also pretty good, and there are plenty to choose from."

Q "Varsity sports are pretty big . . . but **just the main ones** like football and basketball. Baseball is good to watch, too."

Q "There are IM sports of all kinds, and **you will probably find what you like**. Most are coed."

STUDENT AUTHOR: **Football games draw big crowds, and the Aggie Pack (possibly the largest student-run organization in America) encourages masses by handing out free shirts, water bottles, and UCD gear. IM sports are pretty big here, too, and anyone can participate. There are the traditional sports like soccer, basketball, and volleyball, but Davis also has some less conventional teams: inner tube water polo, Hapkido, and ballroom dancing.**

Students Speak Out
ON DRUG SCENE

Q "Seriously, **we're a bunch of nerds**; we're too smart to be messing with that stuff."

Q "I don't know too much about the drug scene on campus and off campus; it's probably going on. I know that getting caught with drugs on campus is not a fun thing to do, and I think **they will prosecute you harshly**."

Q "I don't think there really is much of a drug scene. I mean, if you really wanted to get some, I'm sure you could search and find it. There are people from Humboldt and Chico going to school here, and those two areas are 'pot city,' but **you won't have to worry** about crazed drug dealers shaking someone down on your way to class or something."

STUDENT AUTHOR: With zero-tolerance policies for drugs and alcohol on campus, students find it easy to avoid exposure to the underground network of alcohol and illegal substances. Considering the enormity of the student body, Davis's drug problem can practically be considered nonexistent.

19:1	Student-to-Faculty Ratio
91%	Freshman Retention Rate
43%	Four-Year Graduation Rate
82%	Financial Aid Applicants Receiving Aid

Students Speak Out
SAFETY & SECURITY

Q "The campus is definitely a place where you can feel secure while still not feeling oppressed by overbearing security. Thanks to student-run programs such as the Student Escort Service and Tipsy Taxi, **there is always help when you need it**."

Q "I think that **Davis is the safest UC school** compared to UCLA or UC Berkeley. The town is basically a college town, so I think that that is why it is so safe. Let me put it this way—the number-one crime in Davis is bike theft."

Q "Of course no campus is 100 percent safe, but I'm proud to say that **you won't have to worry about violence** or other crimes in general."

STUDENT AUTHOR: UC Davis funds a free escort service that starts running every night at 6 p.m. There are self-defense classes on campus and plenty of campus safety phones. Despite the fact that UC Davis seems safe enough, there is still a huge effort striving to increase security on campus.

Questions?

For more inside information and survival tips, pick up College Prowler's full-length book on this school, written by an actual student! Check it out at *www.collegeprowler.com*.

Students Speak Out
ON OVERALL EXPERIENCE

Q "I am really glad I came to Davis. I met a bunch of wonderful people, I love the town, and the campus is beautiful. The atmosphere is very nice, especially when the weather warms up. **Everyone seems to be happy and relaxed**."

Q "I really like it here. I have no regrets about Davis. It's the **best environment for my major and my liberal attitude**, and I feel like there are opportunities to explore any avenue of academics, social life, and activities in general."

Q "**I love being able to ride my bike** for five minutes and find myself in the middle of some farm road in the middle of nowhere. I love being able to drive my car 10 minutes and end up at a varied social scene in Sacramento. I love being so close to the Sierra Nevada to ski and hike."

Q "Everyday I am surrounded by brilliant, talented people, people so diverse, but with commonalities, too. I love everything about Davis: the trees, the community, even the cows. I love the fact that I came in planning to major in biochemistry, changed to psychology, then to English, **and still may end up going to med school**."

STUDENT AUTHOR: With such a friendly campus and such competitive academics, many enjoy the dynamics between the bustling, active University and the laid-back college town. Not only are you likely to leave Davis with a priceless diploma and a starting salary that makes up for all those weekends spent in Shields, but you'll also leave with friends, memories, and the experience of a lifetime.

UC Irvine

Berkeley Place, Irvine, CA 92697
(949) 824-5011; www.uci.edu

THE BASICS:

Acceptance Rate: 49%
Setting: Urban
F-T Undergrads: 21,488

SAT Range: 1610–1930*
Control: Public
Tuition: $27,734

Most Popular Majors: Social Sciences, Psychology, Biology, Engineering, Interdisciplinary Studies

*of 2400

Academics	B	Guys	C+
Local Atmosphere	B-	Girls	B-
Safety & Security	A	Athletics	C-
Computers	B+	Nightlife	B-
Facilities	A-	Greek Life	B-
Campus Dining	B	Drug Scene	A-
Off-Campus Dining	B-	Campus Strictness	C
Campus Housing	B+	Parking	D-
Off-Campus Housing	B-	Transportation	D+
Diversity	A-	Weather	A

Students Speak Out
ON ACADEMICS

Q "Teachers are good. If you **go to office hours and get to know a professor**, they may even give your grade a boost at the end of the semester. Most students don't put in the extra effort, but the benefits are huge if you do."

Q "Teachers here seem all right, but they seem more distant and somewhat more difficult to contact. You **lose the personal relationship that was apparent in high school**. The level of interest for each class depends on the professor and whether or not you are personally interested by the subject that is being taught in the actual class."

Q "There are some good teachers, and some bad ones. My suggestion is to get to know your professors. **Once they know you care, they'll do anything to help you out**."

Q "I found **a lot of the teachers at UCI to be knowledgeable, but somewhat apathetic**. Most of my friends had good relationships with teachers they really liked."

STUDENT AUTHOR: What plagues many major universities, UCI included, is the lack of one-on-one, personal attention from some professors that most students are used to receiving from their high school teachers. It's up to the students to step up their effort and visit their professors during their office hours if they want any kind of direct interaction. It's fortunate for UCI students that even the busiest of professors will set aside time for students outside of class.

Students Speak Out
ON LOCAL ATMOSPHERE

Q "The atmosphere in Irvine is pretty boring; it **lacks a variety of student-oriented things** and places to go. There are no other universities around here worth visiting."

Q "To be honest, **most of the students do not like the city of Irvine** (as Irvine is mostly retired people, they don't seem to care for college students much), but the areas around are fun. Huntington Beach is all students and always fun. Also, San Diego and LA are both about 45 minutes away, Disneyland is about 20, and there are about five huge malls for shopping."

Q "The atmosphere here is okay. It's not very lively here. There's **plenty to do in Newport Beach and all the surrounding areas**. If you come here, four years is plenty of time to do it all."

Q "The University is located in a suburban setting, making for **a mostly quiet and laid-back atmosphere**."

STUDENT AUTHOR: For many students to say that Irvine "isn't a party town" would correlate with another frequently heard understatement in Irvine: "There are some old people here." Having a car dramatically reduces the social despair that most students will endure due to the hour driving distance between UCI and surrounding attractions. It's strongly advised that you bring your car to UCI, or else you may be stuck with only visitations to the University Town Center movie cinema across the street.

5 Best Things	5 Worst Things
1 Famous alumni	1 Parking
2 Beautiful weather	2 Student fees
3 Student center	3 Lack of things to do
4 Three libraries	4 High cost of living
5 Study abroad program	5 Huge lecture classes

Students Speak Out
ON CAMPUS DINING

Q "The food on campus is alright. It's better than other campuses I've eaten at, but after a while, eating the same stuff over and over again gets nasty. **Usually for freshmen, if you are living on campus, you have to buy a meal plan**. There are three places around campus where you can use your meal plan; Brandywine is usually the best, but it depends on where you live. If you live in Mesa Court, you usually eat at the place called the Commons because it's nearby. If you live at Middle Earth, the places nearby are Pippen's and Brandywine. Also, In-N-Out is a short walking distance away, and Del Taco and Taco Bell are a short drive away. But that's money out of your pocket."

Q "The food on campus is pretty decent. They have spaced out food places on our campus, so no matter where you go, **there's always someplace to eat**."

Q "All college students worry about food! Well for one thing, the **dorm food is above average, in my opinion**. Plus, right across the street there are at least 10 more dining spots."

STUDENT AUTHOR: **Yes, after months of the same food from the same menu, dining options can get really old, really fast. However, many transfer students at UCI agree that the food on other campuses is not quite as good as the food they serve here. You can always take on a low meal plan and walk yourself across to the University Town Center (UTC) and get some decent food. In-N-Out, Del Taco, and Taco Bell are all student favorites.**

Students Speak Out
ON FACILITIES

Q "The ARC (Anteater Recreation Center) is a huge two-story building with an Olympic-sized pool, tennis courts, indoor soccer, racquetball, basketball, free weights, yoga classes, and karate classes. **Everything at the ARC is offered for free**. The student center is nice, but not extraordinary."

Q "Facilities are awesome, because we are not an old campus; **most everything is fairly new**. Our recreation center is state-of-the-art and amazing. There are exercise classes that you can take as well, and every kind of workout equipment you can think of."

Q "We have **a nice and fairly big student center** that is located right next to the bookstore, pub, food court, and student quad. It's all kind of in a circular clump."

Q "The **dorms are kind of shabby and worn out, but they are definitely livable**. Other than that, the facilities on campus are very good; the Anteater Recreational Center (ARC) is especially nice."

STUDENT AUTHOR: **All of the facilities on and around campus definitely add to the overall physical attraction of UC Irvine, and most of these facilities are fairly new. Car-less students and commuters waiting between classes will not be left standing around. The ARC is a must see and do for the more physically conscious and active types. If you want to better fit the stereotypical image of a Southern California college student, it might be a good idea to make frequent trips to the ARC.**

Famous Alumni

Amy Bender, Davud Benioff, Michael Chabon, Roy Fielding, Allison Liddi-Brown, Jon Lovitz, Whitney Otto, Kelly Perrine, Alice Sebold

Student Body

African American:	2%	Male/Female:	50/50%
Asian American:	49%	Out-of-State:	3%
Hispanic:	12%	International:	3%
Native American:	<1%	Unknown:	0%
White:	34%		

Popular Faiths: Christian groups are by far the most numerous on campus.

Gay Pride: UCI has a Lesbian Gay Transgender Bisexual Resource Center, as well as the group organizations Irvine Queers and OUTspoken.

Economic Status: It's safe to say the majority of UCI students lean towards economically strong family backgrounds.

Students Speak Out
ON DORMS

Q "All of the dorms are very new. However, **only 30 percent of the students live on campus**. We're pretty much a commuter school."

Q "**Dorm life is the best experience**. It's so easy to make friends and stuff like that. I suggest living in Mesa Court if you are a social type. In general, that is where the more social people live. Middle Earth is the other dorm facility. It's quieter there, but it is closer to campus."

Q "The Middle Earth dorms remind me of cheap run-down motels because of the way they look and the way they are set up. However, the environment itself is very fun. **You get to meet new people, make new friends**, and just overall enjoy a good social environment."

STUDENT AUTHOR: **Mesa Court seems to be the favorite, even though it's a little bit away from the center of campus. Middle Earth, a runner-up, is right on campus. The students who occupy the dorms also do their best to form tight-knit social relationships with one another. Considering some of the housing costs around UCI, undergraduate housing becomes a steal, comparatively.**

? Did You Know?
33% of undergrads live on campus.

Students Speak Out
ON GUYS & GIRLS

Q "I don't know what your tastes are, but **people here generally spend a lot of time grooming and looking good**. There are a lot of attractive people at this school. The student body is predominantly Asian American, so if you're down with that, you're in good shape."

Q "The **girls are a lot better looking than the guys**. You'll learn what the term 'He's Irvine Cute' means real soon. In other words, the guys aren't the hottest, but they are nice, and for the most part, smart!"

Q "All the guys are pretty cool. There are lots of Asians here. Both guys and girls. There's also a fair amount of white people. The white guys are all mostly surfer and skater guys, not that I'm looking, but they look alright. The **girls are pretty hot**, too."

STUDENT AUTHOR: **Students generally agree on the fact that the girls at UCI are hotter, on average, than the guys. Many guys here are labeled "Irvine Cute," meaning that they are considered good looking because they go to UCI, but if they went to another school in the So Cal area, then they would be considered middle of the pack or maybe even lower. For the gals, this generally means that they're probably going to actually have to look for love that's beyond skin deep—which isn't all that difficult.**

Traditions

Wayzgoose Festival
A medieval themed carnival of jousting, fun, food, among friendly faculty, student, and club organizations.

Mardi Gras
This is one the campus's highlighted galas of gorging and trouncing along the paths of Ring Road.

Overall School Spirit
Without any major sports team to lead the way, it takes a few years for students to really start feeling any school spirit.

Students Speak Out
ON ATHLETICS

Q "I would say the **two biggest sports on campus are men's basketball and baseball**. The men's basketball team receives the greatest attention; as for intramural sports, the school's recreation facility (ARC) holds numerous tournaments and leagues every quarter."

Q "Varsity sports really only include baseball and basketball (**sports is actually our weakest area**). We only really have these two sports (we have soccer, track/field, and water sports as well, but not as well advertised). As far as IM sports go, we have a good sized crew team and swim team. Then there is volleyball, rugby, soccer, and many others."

Q "**I don't follow campus sports at all**. I'm not the only one."

STUDENT AUTHOR: **Despite IM sports being on the rise at other universities nationwide, at home, some UCI students could care less. The others either participate in IM or don't know they exist; it's very possible to be athletically ignorant on this campus. With an anteater for a mascot, UCI's student body almost takes a masochistic pleasure in its general apathy and ignorance of student sports.**

Students Speak Out
ON DRUG SCENE

Q "Drugs aren't that big on campus. No one is going to shove things in your face, but if you want them, **they can easily be found**. This is college, after all."

Q "The **drug scene here is shockingly low** for a college campus. Even at big parties in the drama department, I've only seen an occasional pot smoker and never anything harder."

Q "UCI **doesn't really have that much of a drug problem**. Underage and binge drinking are the larger problems here."

STUDENT AUTHOR: **Drugs are among the least of UCI's problems on campus. Beyond a few dabbling pot smokers here and there, everyone lives in a blissful bubble. The campus police, the local citizens, and the majority of the student body just wouldn't put up with heavy drug trafficking and usage on or around campus. The fact that many UCI students are so involved in their academics also plays a part in the relatively scarce drug scene here.**

19:1	Student-to-Faculty Ratio
94%	Freshman Retention Rate
41%	Four-Year Graduation Rate
76%	Financial Aid Applicants Receiving Aid

Students Speak Out
SAFETY & SECURITY

Q "Well, at one point, Irvine was rated the second safest city in the country (yes, the country) so there is hardly any crime here. If it's late at night, you can always call a campus number, which sends **an escort to take you to the parking garage or wherever you need to go**."

Q "**I feel completely safe** walking around campus at any time of the day. There are always police cars patrolling the area and on campus. I feel no threat in any way."

Q "The **campus is actually unbelievably safe**. The entire town is really safe. On campus, we have a system of emergency lights where you can push a button to activate the system and a person's voice will answer asking what kind of assistance you need."

STUDENT AUTHOR: **As far as the safety issue on campus, you won't be hard-pressed to find a blue-light post or a husky security guard in a golf cart nearby. There's still going to be an isolated occurrence of minor theft here and there, but that's common at any campus. The town of Irvine mostly consists of retired citizens and white-collar workers.**

Questions?

For more inside information and survival tips, pick up College Prowler's full-length book on this school, written by an actual student! Check it out at *www.collegeprowler.com.*

Students Speak Out
ON OVERALL EXPERIENCE

Q "Irvine is boring. **It's not a college city**. I'm a second-year here, and I'm transferring to UCLA. You're not missing out on anything here. I wouldn't come."

Q "I think it really depends what you're looking for in terms of academics and atmosphere because schools are really different. UCI is the biggest planned community in the nation, so it is extremely safe. You have the beaches 10 minutes away. I especially think if you want to come to the West Coast that you should come to Irvine. Also, **UCI has the largest minority population of any school**. The Greek system is also big at UCI."

Q "I like the campus a lot. It's very peaceful. The only thing I don't like is that there really isn't much to do around there. **You have to have a car to get around**."

Q "I'm happy with UCI. Even though I'm more of a city person, the suburbs aren't that bad. If you want to go somewhere fun, it's good to have a car or at least make friends with someone who has a car. **If you do have the chance, attend an overnight orientation** where you have the opportunity to stay in the dorms. I did, and it was one of the best experiences I've ever had."

STUDENT AUTHOR: **Many students here will admit that UCI wasn't their first choice, or even their second. While UCI still doesn't live up to the prestige of UCLA or UC Berkeley, it's increasingly gaining respect. With enough imagination, you should never be bored. The minimum course load is light, and this leaves plenty of time to socialize, hang out in the beautifully maintained park at the center of the campus, or do whatever else suits you best.**

UC Riverside

900 University Avenue; Riverside, CA 92521
(951) 827-1012; www.ucr.edu

THE BASICS:

Acceptance Rate: 78%
Setting: Urban
F-T Undergrads: 15,708

SAT Range: 1340–1650*
Control: Public
Tuition: $20,022

Most Popular Majors: Business, Social Sciences, Biology, Psychology, Liberal Arts

*of 2400

Academics	B	Guys	B-
Local Atmosphere	C+	Girls	B
Safety & Security	B-	Athletics	C+
Computers	B-	Nightlife	C+
Facilities	A-	Greek Life	B-
Campus Dining	B-	Drug Scene	B+
Off-Campus Dining	B+	Campus Strictness	C
Campus Housing	B	Parking	C
Off-Campus Housing	B	Transportation	B+
Diversity	A+	Weather	A

Students Speak Out
ON ACADEMICS

Q "Most of the teachers are great and have very **specialized knowledge**. The classes are interesting, but I don't think that has anything to do with the University, just the classes you happen to be enrolled in."

Q "Teachers are sometimes great and sometimes not. I think the best teachers are usually those in the **College of Humanities** because they don't tend to have high egos. Some classes are interesting, while others are boring. My philosophy classes have always been interesting, as were most social science courses."

Q "The teachers are okay at UC Riverside. Most lectures are done by professors, and discussions or **labs are taught by TAs**. Many professors are idiots, and some have trouble speaking English."

Q "**The classes are really easy**. You can get a passing grade with practically no work. If you're a decent student now, you'll probably get straight As. If you're lazy, it's good because you don't have to do a lot of work for classes. I've had some where I didn't even have to show up, except for the midterm and final."

STUDENT AUTHOR: Student opinions vary when it comes to academics at UCR. Some students claim that instructors are approachable, while others find interaction with the TAs easier and more worthwhile. Although some classes are relatively large, most of these courses have mandatory discussion sections along with them. This allows students to get to know the TAs in a much smaller setting.

Students Speak Out
ON LOCAL ATMOSPHERE

Q "Southern California is the best place to live. The weather is great all the time, and there are a lot of parties and **social stuff to do**. If you don't mind driving, it's a really wonderful place."

Q "You will notice that on University Street there are a lot of homeless people. It's sad, but just another part of life. We are **not far from some major theme parks**, about an hour from Los Angeles, Disneyland, and Universal Studios. At school, they even sell many tickets at discounted rates."

Q "The atmosphere in Riverside is good, except during the evenings in the downtown area where it's really not safe. Stay away from walking alone in downtown. Be sure to visit the Mission Inn and **the Botanical Gardens**. There are no close universities present, unless you consider Riverside Comm College or Cal State San Bernardino."

Q "Riverside is **right in between LA and San Diego**, so an hour and a half in any direction will take you to some really cool places."

STUDENT AUTHOR: While there is not much in Riverside, the students find their way into the surrounding areas in Southern California. The campus itself and immediate area create a nice college atmosphere. But, venture out into the city of Riverside, and you won't find a whole lot. The Orange Blossom Festival, Market Nights, and Mission Inn are a few of the highlights. It is strongly suggested that you travel in groups, especially at night, though.

5 Best Things	5 Worst Things
1 Small campus	1 Homeless people
2 Fast growing	2 Lack of local nightlife
3 Science program	3 Construction
4 Creative writing	4 Cafeteria food
5 Diversity	5 Pollution

Students Speak Out
ON FACILITIES

Q "We have an **awesome recreation center**, which has lots of exercise machines, a track, badminton courts, and a climbing wall. They also have field trips and classes you can take."

Q "There is a plethora of computers located in libraries and dorm facilities. The University Commons is cool, and it is being rennovated. The **campus keeps getting nicer and nicer**!"

Q "I lift weights pretty often, and I am pleased with the gym. They have a **really nice fitness center** for the students."

Q "**The facilities are okay**, and it's getting better. They recently finished six or so buildings and are slated to build a few more."

Q "The Recreation Center is very nice and well equipped. The computer labs are nice. The campus grounds are normally well kept. Overall though, there is **nothing terribly special** about most of them."

STUDENT AUTHOR: The campus is constantly improving upon buildings and places for students, but the Student Recreation Center definitely hogs the spotlight. Students love the up-to-date Rec Center with its huge weight room and frequently-updated and modern equipment, such as treadmills, elliptical machines, stationary bicycles, and stair-steppers. The Student Commons facility is currently under major renovations, and is scheduled to be completed in 2008. Once it is completed, the new 142,000 square foot commons building will include venues for food and entertainment and areas for students to lounge, study.

Famous Alumni

Mark Andrus, Ruben Barrales, Neil Campbell, Sally Fox, Ken Goddard, Gary McCord, Tina Nova

Students Speak Out
ON CAMPUS DINING

Q "Campus food is great! I love it! There's a place called the Campus Grille that makes an excellent Philly cheesesteak sandwich. There's also a Commons dining area on campus that has different selections of food ranging from **pasta to sushi to subs**."

Q "Food on campus is decent, although many would disagree. The campus commons has good food. **I recommend the Campus Deli** for sandwiches and Baja Sol for Mexican food. The Courtyard Café, not in the Commons, is pretty good, too. The dining halls serve good food, depending on the day."

Q "The food at commons is diverse, and Mama Mia's is good. The dining hall is alright, but the **food is greasy**."

Q "**Dorm food is so-so**. It tastes good at first, then it gets old fast! I think this is typical of all schools, though. I like our meal plan, where you use a 'meal' and then it's all-you-can-eat."

Q "Most of my friends and I enjoy eating on campus. There is **a wide variety of good food** and some discounts for students."

STUDENT AUTHOR: Overall, students seem to think the food options on campus are decent. Generally, food in the commons, and located on campus, tends to be better than that served in the residence hall cafeterias. The major complaint about the cafeteria food is that it is greasy, and it sometimes seems that the workers are not trained very well.

Student Body

African American:	7%	Male/Female:	47/53%
Asian American:	42%	Out-of-State:	1%
Hispanic:	24%	International:	2%
Native American:	<1%	Unknown:	0%
White:	25%		

Popular Faiths: Catholicism is the dominant religion on campus.

Gay Pride: People, for the most part are pretty tolerant around campus. Although, be advised that there have been a few hate crimes in recent years.

Economic Status: UCR has students from diverse economic backgrounds. Many students find themselves working their way through school.

Students Speak Out
ON DORMS

Q "The dorms are nice. I have lived in all three, and they are all nice. **Pentland Hills is the nicest**, especially if you want privacy and a good study atmosphere."

Q "The residence halls are nice. Pentland Hills is the most expensive, **A-I is the cheapest**, and Lothian is in between. The forms they use to pair up so-called compatible roommates are a waste of time, as the system seems to just ignore them. The air-conditioning is occasionally shut down on the weekends to save money. Room temperatures can rise to about 80 degrees."

Q "**The oldest dorm is Aberdeen-Inverness (A-I)—you don't want to live there**. I am in East Lothian, which is a lot of fun. One of the newer ones is called Pentland Hills, and it is very expensive, but nice and clean."

STUDENT AUTHOR: **A-I and Lothian dorms are the most social dorms. Pentland Hills are the newest and provide the most privacy. The cost, however, is higher to enjoy the luxuries that PH has to offer. Living in the dorms is highly encouraged for freshmen because it is an excellent way to meet people and get to know them on a personal level.**

Did You Know?
28% of undergrads live on campus.

Students Speak Out
ON GUYS & GIRLS

Q "**You have to go Greek** to find good-looking people. There are plenty of studs and hot chicks in the Greek community."

Q "**The guys here are usually sociable**, although some have a large ego and machismo issues. The girls are sociable as well, although the diversity in the types of girls is much greater. Some are very sweet and caring, while others seem like it's their time of the month every day."

Q "We're all **horrid-looking** three-foot trolls."

Q "UCR doesn't have the best looking people, but you have to remember that UCR is still **close to the beach and LA**."

STUDENT AUTHOR: **Students at UC Riverside are generally good-looking. Most people are nice, friendly, and down-to-earth. Students agree that the Recreation Center and the baseball fields seem like ideal places to scope out good-looking people. The beach is another place. Some students believe that the only attractive students are in the Greek community, or among the well-dressed law majors. Athletes are also in tip-top shape.**

Traditions

Bagpipes
Since UCR is home of the Highlanders, it is not uncommon to hear the odd noise of the pipes making their way through the entire campus.

Writer's Week
UCR holds an annual writer's week. During this week, a variety of writers, poets, and authors are invited to share their thoughts with the Riverside community.

Overall School Spirit
Over the years, UCR school spirit has become increasingly stronger.

Students Speak Out
ON ATHLETICS

Q "We have no football team, and the basketball team sucks. Even though the teams aren't that good right now, **we still like to celebrate** when there are games."

Q "We just moved into Division I a few years ago. School spirit needs to spread on campus. IM sports, however, are very big. It seems like more and more students are getting into the IM scene every quarter. In basketball alone, **hundreds are involved**, including myself."

Q "The biggest sport right now is basketball because **they are Division I**. We don't have a football team, and the college lacks school spirit. I guess the women's teams are pretty good, but they are not followed as much as the men's."

STUDENT AUTHOR: **Although support for athletics is on the rise, it will take more time before athletics at UCR gain full school support. Support is actually stronger for some intramural teams than for the varsity teams. However, more students are showing stronger support for the UCR basketball team. Sports are not as big at Riverside compared to a school like UCLA, especially since UCR has no football team.**

Students Speak Out
ON DRUG SCENE

Q "Drugs are **not a major problem** on campus, unless you consider cigarettes as drugs. Marijuana, however, does make its way into the residence halls occasionally."

Q "Drugs don't seem to be a big problem, but **alcohol is always a battle** for administration."

Q "**There are weed dealers**, and I heard it's not hard to get 'e' and shrooms. I don't hear too much about anything else, though."

Q "It's always there if you really want it, but I wouldn't say that it's pervasive. People aren't selling/using drugs **out in the open** or anything."

STUDENT AUTHOR: There are drugs on campus, but many students do not usually take notice. The campus police crack down hard on drug users and distributors, so most people take their drug business elsewhere. It seems that the majority of people do not do drugs, but where there is a will there is a way to find them. Occasionally, however, you'll run into some potheads or some pill poppers at parties around campus.

18:1	Student-to-Faculty Ratio
84%	Freshman Retention Rate
38%	Four-Year Graduation Rate
83%	Financial Aid Applicants Receiving Aid

Students Speak Out
SAFETY & SECURITY

Q "Campus Security is, from what I can tell, very active on campus. I personally don't know of anyone being involved in a violent crime, but I do know several people, including myself, **who've been robbed**."

Q "Security around campus is very safe from what I have experienced. I live across from the school, and sometimes I end up walking by myself at night. There are **escorts that can walk you home**, and sometimes they have shuttles that will take you near your place."

Q "Campus security is good, but downtown Riverside is a very bad neighborhood. It's very dangerous, **almost like LA**. The area immediately around the school is okay, but if you go about five miles in any direction, it's really bad."

STUDENT AUTHOR: Overall, students feel safe on campus. However, the sense of security lessens as students venture off campus and into the areas of downtown Riverside. The farther away from campus students go, the less safe they tend to feel. Students suggest traveling in groups, especially at night, both on and off campus.

Questions?
For more inside information and survival tips, pick up College Prowler's full-length book on this school, written by an actual student! Check it out at www.collegeprowler.com.

Students Speak Out
ON OVERALL EXPERIENCE

Q "My overall experience here has been positive. Of course, once in a while **I do wish I were somewhere else**. Then again, I think UCR has a better-looking campus then UC Berkeley and a safer one than say, UCLA or USC."

Q "I love this school. I just wish it was in a different city. If you are looking for a school that parties all the time and has dorms with good social atmospheres, don't come here. **This is basically a commuter school**. Most people that go here live nearby, so they go home on the weekends. It's a 'suitcase college' in that respect."

Q "I'm a very shy person, and I thought I wouldn't make any friends, but I did. The best thing you can do is **live in the dorms** for your freshman year. It's part of the true college experience."

Q "**This school is not like UCLA** or any of those colleges that you see in the movies. It's very quiet and pretty small. At first, I thought because it was a UC college, it would be similar, but it's really not."

STUDENT AUTHOR: UCR grows on its students. Those who are not excited and attached to the school from the beginning usually find that they cannot help but love it once they get there. The majority of students enjoy their time at UCR. While a number of students come into to UCR with the idea of transferring after their first two years, many often change their minds because they are pleasantly surprised with what a smaller campus atmosphere and community has to offer. In some ways, one could say that the positive aspects of UCR have been part of a well-kept secret that is making its way out into the open.

UC San Diego

9500 Gilman Drive; La Jolla, CA 92093
(858) 534-2230; www.ucsd.edu

THE BASICS:

Acceptance Rate: 42%
Setting: Suburban
F-T Undergrads: 22,205

SAT Range: 1700–2040*
Control: Public
Tuition: $28,083

Most Popular Majors: Social Sciences, Biological/Life Sciences, Engineering, Psychology

*of 2400

Academics	B+	Guys	B-
Local Atmosphere	A	Girls	B
Safety & Security	A-	Athletics	D+
Computers	B	Nightlife	B+
Facilities	B+	Greek Life	C
Campus Dining	B	Drug Scene	B
Off-Campus Dining	A-	Campus Strictness	C+
Campus Housing	C+	Parking	D-
Off-Campus Housing	C+	Transportation	C+
Diversity	A	Weather	A+

Students Speak Out
ON ACADEMICS

Q "Classes get much more interesting in your major, but there are some **random classes that everyone loves**, like some of the theater and music classes."

Q "Most of the teachers I've had at UCSD have been **genuinely interested** in their students. There are some professors that are only interested in their own research and teach because they have to. You can usually tell right away if they are a good professor by how organized and excited they are."

Q "It can kind of be the **luck of the draw** when it comes to professors, but we have a book that comes out each year where students rate professors, so you can have some idea of what you're getting into."

Q "Most of the teachers are good, although some are there just for research. Teaching is not their main concern. But depending on your major, there are **plenty of good teachers**—just ask around."

STUDENT AUTHOR: At UCSD, everywhere you look, there are intelligent people doing amazing things. UCSD has some of the top programs in the nation for sciences, social sciences, theater, and dance. The faculty is made up of world-class professors who rank at the top of their fields. Academics at UCSD are taken very seriously by the majority of students, and on any Friday night, you can find just as many students in the library studying as you can out partying.

Students Speak Out
ON LOCAL ATMOSPHERE

Q "La Jolla is **not a college town**. The beach is close, so that's nice, but most of the fun stuff to do is kind of far. San Diego is great—there are tons of different things to do."

Q "Our school is basically in the most **anti-college town** ever!"

Q "The atmosphere is really laid-back—it's going to be a **culture shock** for you if you're from a busy city. San Diego State, which is one of the biggest party campuses in the U.S., is only a few minutes away."

Q "La Jolla is **not very college-friendly**, since it's catered more towards rich, older retirees. If you are looking for a more 'college-like' atmosphere or a party school, go to San Diego State."

Q "The University is like its own town because La Jolla is full of rich old people. It kind of sucks, but **Pacific Beach and University City are both full of college kids**. Definitely check them out."

STUDENT AUTHOR: La Jolla is a ritzy, stuffy community filled with rich, retired old people. However, this does not stop UCSD students from enjoying the beautiful place where they live. With the beach just walking distance away from campus and sunny skies and water sports everywhere, it is hard not to enjoy living in San Diego. There are many exciting things to do away from the beach, as well. UCSD students are generally happy with the activities and environment San Diego has to offer.

Students Speak Out
ON FACILITIES

"Facilities on campus are **pretty good**. The athletic ones are sub-par in my opinion, but the University Center and Recreation Center are really nice."

"The facilities are pretty nice. If you like going to the gym, RIMAC is awesome. I've never worked out before, but RIMAC is **really motivating** for me. I've put on 15 pounds of muscle thanks to that place. I think, overall, we have good facilities."

"I think that the facilities are pretty good; **modern, clean, and available**. Although some things are so spread out it takes a long time to walk from place to place."

"Price Center has almost **everything you could ever need**: a book store, movie theater, travel agency, post office, meeting rooms, game room, computer lab, fast food, coffee shop, and lots of places to hang out. What you can't find there, you can find at the Old Student Center like the co-ops and the radio station."

The Old Student Center **could be improved** to be more student-friendly."

STUDENT AUTHOR: **The facilities on campus are excellent. You can find anything you need on campus. There are lots of new buildings, including a huge gym, RIMAC, and the Price Center. The Giesel Library, named after Dr. Seuss, a former resident of La Jolla, is well known, and has even been used in a few movies because of its interesting architecture. UCSD students are happy with the facilities on campus and enjoy using them.**

Famous Alumni

Benicio Del Toro, John Dobak, Nathan East, Raymond Feist, Zachary Fisk, Michael Greif, Mike Judge, Guy "Bud" Tribble, Dylan Voeller

Students Speak Out
ON CAMPUS DINING

"The dining hall food is **boring and bland**, but I've heard from friends that it is considerably better than some of the other UCs."

"I always had left over meal points at the end of the quarter, but you can use them at Earl's Place, a coffee shop, to **buy fun stuff** like lava lamps and butterfly chairs. At least that way they don't go to waste."

"Food on campus is mostly your **general dorm food fare**, but I've found that it's actually not that bad. Out of all of them I think Muir's Sierra Summit is the best. Anyway, you can't really go wrong with the salad bars at any of the halls."

"After trying dorm food from other universities, I thought the **variety at UCSD was great**—especially if you are vegetarian or vegan."

"The food was **much better** than I had expected. Summit has the best food, by far."

STUDENT AUTHOR: **Cafeteria food is one of those things that every incoming freshman dreads. However, UCSD students report that it is not that bad. It may be tasteless and unexciting, but it's not horrible. There are many different cafeterias on campus, each with different kinds of food so that students are sure to find some place they enjoy. Even if students absolutely hate dorm food, they are able to survive on it for the year. For a healthier option, the Food Co-op has vegetarian and health foods which are usually good and very cheap. It might take some work, but there is good and healthy dining on campus.**

Student Body

African American:	2%	Male/Female:	52/48%
Asian American:	45%	Out-of-State:	3%
Hispanic:	12%	International:	4%
Native American:	<1%	Unknown:	10%
White:	27%		

Popular Faiths: Christian groups, both Protestant and Catholic, are visible on campus.

Gay Pride: The Lesbian Gay Bisexual Transgender Resource Office connects students, faculty, and staff together to promote diversity and acceptance.

Economic Status: The majority of UCSD students are middle-class.

Students Speak Out
ON DORMS

Q "From what I've heard, dorms at UCSD are pretty **good compared to other campuses**, but they vary from college to college. I think the obvious choice for the best dorm is Roosevelt. Otherwise, they are pretty similar."

Q "Each college has its own dorms. I was in Sixth College, and I **really liked it** because they were smaller and more personable. There were also lots of grass and trees."

Q "Dorms are okay—**kind of small**, but livable. I got into the on-campus apartments. It depends what college you're in."

STUDENT AUTHOR: **There is no agreement at UCSD on which is the best or worst dorm; most people say they like the dorm they are in the best. Dorm assignments are completely arbitrary and only based on what college you are in. Most students find that the people they met and lived with influenced their dorm experience more than which dorm they lived in. Overall, as long as you are flexible and try get along with your roommate, the dorm you live in is not that important.**

> **? Did You Know?**
> 33% of undergrads live on campus.

Students Speak Out
ON GUYS & GIRLS

Q "**Everyone's nerdy**. If you find a hot guy, send him my way. There are a few beautiful people scattered around campus, but you have to look for them."

Q "When you're a freshman, you think you've gone to a school full of **beautiful people**, but as the years go by, they all start to disappear. Anyway, just because they are hot doesn't mean they are quality."

Q "San Diego has some of the **most beautiful people**—both men and women."

Q "As a guy that went to a high school with a lot of hot girls, coming to UCSD was actually a **disappointment**."

STUDENT AUTHOR: **Students were generally disappointed with the physical attributes of the opposite sex. They had dreams of coming to college and living in the midst of a campus filled with beautiful people, but these dreams come to a nightmarish end once the new students step foot on campus. With the beach minutes away and an emphasis on fitness, UCSD students are known to be surprisingly unattractive or lacking in social skills.**

> **Traditions**
> Going to class drunk during Sun God, Winterfest, and Fallfest, decorating the Sun God statue, celebrating Dr. Seuss's birthday with free cake, and attending the Unolympics during Welcome Week.
>
> **Overall School Spirit**
> The event with the most school spirit is the Sun God Festival. This is popular for all students, not just those living on campus. Campus is always filled on the Sun God Festival with students having a good time and participating in events all over campus. The day concludes with a concert at RIMAC field.

Students Speak Out
ON ATHLETICS

Q "The **impact of sports on campus is miniscule** at best. There are a lot of varsity sports, but they don't have a lot of funding or much of a fan base. Intramural (IM) sports are lots of fun, especially inner tube water polo, which is coed. Most people that play IMs live on campus."

Q "It's pretty sad when the **opposing schools** have more people in attendance at our home games than we do."

Q "I only went to a few sporting events, and they weren't a big deal. There's **no football team**, and that's the team everyone at college usually watches."

Q "The sports scene here is **nonexistent**."

STUDENT AUTHOR: **Athletics have become a joke at UCSD. Although UCSD moved from Division III to Division II, sports have very little support around campus. There is no football team, and although some of the teams have done very well in competition and have gone on to the national level, no one pays attention. Those who play on a team seem to enjoy it, but everyone else is oblivious to the sports on campus.**

Students Speak Out
ON DRUG SCENE

Q "Come on, **UCSD is pretty nerdy**. I know drugs probably circulate around campus, and I've encountered it here or there, but its pretty nonexistent."

Q "There is **not much of a drug scene** here. People I've come across look and sound like they've just discovered drugs—and that's usually just marijuana. Pacific Beach looks like a cloud of smoke some days."

Q "Let's say if you want to be a part of it, you can be, and if you don't, it will leave you alone. Drugs don't seem to be too big here, and **the drinking is mediocre, especially for college**. It's not something to worry about."

STUDENT AUTHOR: **There is very little drug use at UCSD besides marijuana. UCSD students are very conscious about studying, and oftentimes believe that drug use is detrimental to their success at school. Therefore, there are practically no hard drugs found at UCSD. Marijuana use is an entirely different story.**

19:1	Student-to-Faculty Ratio
94%	Freshman Retention Rate
56%	Four-Year Graduation Rate
82%	Financial Aid Applicants Receiving Aid

Students Speak Out
SAFETY & SECURITY

Q "I don't think that safety and security has ever been an issue for me on campus. One of the reasons my parents let me go away to school here is because it is **such a safe campus**."

Q "I've heard that **sexual assaults happen** and are not reported well, but I guess that happens on every college campus. Except for the occasional theft, I don't think there is much crime around campus."

Q "It's a **very safe campus**. I have never heard of any real incidents. There are stations with alarms everywhere on campus, should anything happen. You can also get a campus police officer to walk you back to the dorms or to your car if you're at the library studying late night."

STUDENT AUTHOR: **UCSD students are notorious for never thinking about safety and security; La Jolla is one of the quietest and safest cities in San Diego County. The UCSD police station has done such a good job at keeping campus safe that many students forget to think about their safety at all.**

Questions?
For more inside information and survival tips, pick up College Prowler's full-length book on this school, written by an actual student! Check it out at *www.collegeprowler.com*.

Students Speak Out
ON OVERALL EXPERIENCE

Q "**I love it here**. The school's a little antisocial at first, but once you meet some people it can be really fun. It's a beautiful campus surrounded by a really cool city with tons of things to do. It's a very good school."

Q "The academics and level of education here is one of the best in California and in the country, but I **hated the lack of social life**. I met a lot of friends, but never really felt like I belonged."

Q "I'm **pretty ambivalent** about it. My experience has been awesome just because of the people I've met and just living in San Diego for four years in itself creates a different mentality. I don't regret having gone to UCSD, but I know my college experience would have been fuller if I had gone somewhere else, like State. UCSD is definitely its own university unlike any other, in both good and bad ways."

Q "I have **really enjoyed** going to UCSD. I enjoyed the challenge of my classes and the friends that I've made. I love the San Diego area. I'm really glad that I lived on campus my first two years because it made it much easier to make friends and get adjusted to school."

STUDENT AUTHOR: **When students contemplate their overall experience at UCSD, they usually base their decisions around the friends they have made and the good memories they have. Although academics at UCSD are world-class, they are not always the most important factor in the overall experience. Social life at UCSD is known to be a little boring; many students wished they had a more active social life, but most still managed to find friends with whom they created lasting memories.**

UC Santa Barbara

552 University Road; Santa Barbara, CA 93106
(805) 893-8000; www.ucsb.edu

THE BASICS:

Acceptance Rate: 54%
Setting: Small City
F-T Undergrads: 17,960

SAT Range: 1600–1960*
Control: Public
Tuition: $29,181

Most Popular Majors: Social Sciences, Business, Interdisciplinary Studies, Biology, Psychology

*of 2400

Academics	B+	Guys	A
Local Atmosphere	B+	Girls	A+
Safety & Security	A-	Athletics	B-
Computers	B	Nightlife	A
Facilities	B+	Greek Life	B-
Campus Dining	B-	Drug Scene	C+
Off-Campus Dining	A-	Campus Strictness	C+
Campus Housing	B+	Parking	D+
Off-Campus Housing	C-	Transportation	B-
Diversity	A-	Weather	A+

Students Speak Out
ON ACADEMICS

Q "The classes offered are one of the reasons I chose to come here. Geological Catastrophes, **Death and Dying**, Vampirism, and Human Sexuality are as good as general education requirements get."

Q "Every teacher is different. If you want to have a relationship with your teacher, you pretty much need to seek them out, but **they are very helpful** in office hours. You also have TAs that are pretty accessible."

Q "I've done research with three different professors in my three years here, so there are plenty of chances to work with faculty, if that interests you. The school is also large enough so that, if you want, **you can remain just a name**, as well."

Q "UCSB is the secret spot for **really amazing professors**, and their credentials prove it. I think the professors have figured out that Santa Barbara is a great place to live, and they can get paid while they are here."

STUDENT AUTHOR: **Although each department might have its monotone, sleep-inducing professor, most of the instructors are experts in their fields, excited about what they teach, and very accessible. UCSB is unique in that it has very few graduate students, so teachers are focused on their undergraduates. The UCSB academic program has made a concerted effort to shed the "party-school" image and prove that the professors and students take academics very seriously.**

Students Speak Out
ON LOCAL ATMOSPHERE

Q "Isla Vista is probably **one of the best college towns** in the country."

Q "It's definitely a **laid-back atmosphere**—we live on the beach. Isla Vista (IV) is a condensed square mile of college kids squished together."

Q "Santa Barbara residents are, for the most part, **very affluent**, which can actually be an advantage when you are a student who needs a good-paying job and some career connections!"

Q "We live in one of the most beautiful places in the world. The mountains and oceans are both right here, and there is a lot less development than other cities in Southern California. There's **so much stuff to do** locally, and a lot of activism to get involved with."

Q "Serious students **avoid Isla Vista**, while the less academically-inclined seem to spend an inordinate amount of time there."

STUDENT AUTHOR: **With such a great atmosphere, productivity can be very low. Some students know that they will only stay focused if they live outside of Isla Vista. The two beaches by Isla Vista are Devereux and Sands. If it's at all sunny, you can bet that both will be crowded with tanners and surfers. Isla Vista also has casual and inexpensive restaurants, and most do not close before 2 a.m. Where else can you choose from 10 to 30 parties on the weekend, hang out on the beach, and stand in line at four in the morning for burritos and pizza?**

Students Speak Out
ON FACILITIES

Q "Everything is **fairly clean**. There's not too much to complain about."

Q "The Rec Center on campus is free, so that's always good. There are lots of classes and sports that take place there. You can get credit for classes like **scuba diving and sailing** through the Rec Center."

Q "There are **great athletic facilities** that are pretty up-to-date. The UCen is also great and usually busy."

Q "The UCen and Rec Cen stand out, however, the library could really use some improvements aesthetically—**orange floors and dark brown wood siding** were 'out' a long time ago. Another comment is that none of the buildings match."

Q "The University Center and the Recreation Center are **beautiful**."

STUDENT AUTHOR: **Although the library looks like it's from the Nixon era, other facilities are modern and more pleasing to the eye. UCSB has the Recreation Center (Rec Cen) that is free to all students, and the University Center (UCen), which is the student center that houses fast food restaurants, cafés with salad, pasta, pizza, and sandwiches, a coffee shop, the bookstore, and a computer lab. It's a favorite place to waste an hour while waiting for a class. Students like the new, clean facilities, and use them daily—the only major complaints are the crowded Rec Center and the not-so-attractive library.**

Students Speak Out
ON CAMPUS DINING

Q "I have a meal plan on campus. I eat at the dinning commons and think the food is awesome. **People sometimes complain about it**, but trust me, it's better than the cooking of anybody I know. They also have fast food places on campus."

Q "The food is good. In the dorms, you will get **tired of the food** no matter what. It just gets old."

Q "The **campus dining halls are scary**. Avoid them especially at the end of the week, when the week's leftovers are combined to make new treats."

Q "I lived in the on-campus dorms my first year. When doing so, you can go to any one of the different cafeterias. The food is decent for a cafeteria. At least **they always have a salad bar**; that's hard to ruin."

Q "I didn't even buy a meal plan. Any mass-produced food is bound to not be good. If you don't want to **gain the Freshman 15**, then the dorm food isn't going to help."

STUDENT AUTHOR: **Students say that the dorm food doesn't make them gag, but that it does become boring fairly quickly. Most enjoy eating in the on-campus restaurants instead, where the variety ranges from fast food to more café-like food and deli standards. The dorm cafeterias do have one advantage—they offer vegan and vegetarian options. All of the dorm cafeterias have a salad bar, a grill, frozen yogurt, and a hot-food line.**

Students Speak Out
ON DORMS

Q "Dorms are great. There are off-campus dorms in Isla Vista, as well as the on-campus dorms; both are great. It doesn't really matter which, but I think it would be **better to be on campus**."

Q "On-campus dorms are okay. The **rooms are kind of small**. Most rooms are doubles, but due to overpopulation, some are triples. On campus, you might have to only share a room with one other person, but you will have a common bathroom with toilets and showers that you share with about 50 people."

Q "I lived on campus, and I would definitely advise it! **It's really convenient** for your first year and a good way to meet a lot of people."

STUDENT AUTHOR: No matter which dorm you get, it's hard not to have fun when you are suddenly living with 50 other 18-year-old freshmen who just moved out of their parents' house. The only dorm I would steer clear of as a freshman is San Rafael—it has more upperclassmen. Usually, these students have already made all of their friends and are no longer going through the same transitions that freshmen are.

> **Did You Know?**
> 31% of undergrads live on campus.

Students Speak Out
ON GUYS & GIRLS

Q "Girls and guys are both **very attractive** on a general basis. You just have to find the ones that are cool."

Q "Guys are freaking hot here. It's like going to school with **Ken and Barbie** sometimes, but beware—some of them aren't too nice, but they are nice to look at, for sure."

Q "I don't know about guys, but the women, my god, they are beautiful. But after a while, your **standards start to increase** because you've adjusted, so it kind of backfires. At home, girls that used to be hot just don't do it for me anymore."

Q "There are **beautiful people everywhere**—it's Santa Barbara."

STUDENT AUTHOR: It's hard to beat a surfer boy biking to the beach with his wetsuit down to his waist and a surfboard under his arm, or a couple of bikini-clad girls playing volleyball on the sand. Students agree that the hottie level is high here, but they disagree on the inside beauty. Dating occurs, but just not as often as meeting up with your crush at a party or downtown at the bars.

> **Traditions**
>
> **The Loop**
> Drinking a beer at every establishment in Isla Vista before you graduate.
>
> **Overall School Spirit**
> UCSB school spirit is pathetic compared to some other big, Division I universities. Most blame the fact that we don't have a football team. But, Gaucho Locos, the student club that attends sporting events in bright yellow shirts, are fun, rowdy and very spirited. You can join for $5, get a T-shirt, and make lots of high-spirited friends!

Students Speak Out
ON ATHLETICS

Q "**Basketball and volleyball** are the biggest sports here. The IM program here is huge. You can play just about any IM sport that you want."

Q "Sports are not a big deal at our school. We're Division I, and no one seems to care. It just **doesn't get much hype**. Intramural sports are cool, though."

Q "There isn't as much school spirit as there is at UCLA sporting events. **Varsity sports aren't huge** events that everyone goes to, but they are fun events when you do go."

Q "Our **sports teams are good**, but you don't hear a lot about them."

STUDENT AUTHOR: Some of the varsity sports teams at UCSB are actually very good, frequently winning their divisions and making it to national tournaments, yet it seems like half of the school is oblivious. Basketball and volleyball games can usually draw large and loud crowds, but without a football team, UCSB lacks the media spotlight and big campus athletes that other campuses draw.

Students Speak Out
ON DRUG SCENE

Q "The drug scene **goes both ways**. If you want to get into it, great; if not, then you won't even know that it's there."

Q "I don't even think of pot as a drug anymore. Every job I have had here, **my co-workers and employees smoke**. Half of my friends' parents smoke. Seriously, I forget that it isn't legal."

Q "The most relevant drugs are pretty much just **alcohol and some marijuana**. The Greek system tends to have some harder stuff."

Q "**Everyone's tried something** at least once."

STUDENT AUTHOR: **Drinking and smoking pot are a big part of the culture here; however, many students choose not to partake and get through four years without feeling any pressure. A documentary was filmed at UCSB asking people on campus how long it would take them to "hook up a gram" and the average answer was 10 minutes. Obviously, drugs are definitely available. It really is up to you whether you participate.**

17:1	Student-to-Faculty Ratio
91%	Freshman Retention Rate
61%	Four-Year Graduation Rate
73%	Financial Aid Applicants Receiving Aid

Students Speak Out
SAFETY & SECURITY

Q "Campus **safety is good**. We have campus security officers who patrol, and whom you can call for an escort if you need it."

Q "There have been issues recently with safety, especially my senior year, but I think that's common with any college. I wouldn't worry about anything except maybe **bike theft**."

Q "Safety and security on campus seems to be really good. I don't know of anybody who has had anything happen to them while they were here, except a few who had their **cars messed up by drunk students** late at night."

STUDENT AUTHOR: **Students say that the biggest safety issues at UCSB involve bike theft and vehicle vandalism, and that they are pleased with the visibility of on-campus security. Campus police and student CSOs (Campus Security Officers) patrol the campus every night and are always available.**

Questions?
For more inside information and survival tips, pick up College Prowler's full-length book on this school, written by an actual student! Check it out at *www.collegeprowler.com*.

Students Speak Out
ON OVERALL EXPERIENCE

Q "I love this school. It definitely **has its positives and negatives**, like anywhere, but I can honestly say that I am very happy to be here."

Q "UCSB has some of the worst undergraduates around. But there are those that try hard and subsequently do well. Unfortunately, this is a 'party school,' and **it lives up to its reputation**. If you're serious about your classes, you can get a great education here and work with some fantastic professors."

Q "I absolutely love UCSB. Who couldn't love a school with oceanfront property to take your morning jog on? There's **a niche here for everyone**."

Q "Overall, my campus experience at UCSB has been awesome. **I love it here**. Coming to UCSB is the best thing that's ever happened in my life. It's very fun, and I'm happy with my choice."

STUDENT AUTHOR: **UCSB students can't say enough good things about this place—most never want to leave. Whether it's the academics, the weather, the social scene, or the laid-back atmosphere, practically all students fall in love with something here. Tourists pay money to get to hang out here for a vacation, and we get to live here, full-time! Give yourself a chance to get to know the school and the town. It can take a year to find your type of friends or your major or your favorite club, but if you are actively searching, you will be able to find what you are looking for at UCSB. Overall, UCSB is the true college experience that many high-school students have been anxiously awaiting.**

UC Santa Cruz

1156 High Street; Santa Cruz, CA 95064
(831) 459-0111; www.ucsc.edu

THE BASICS:

Acceptance Rate: 82%
Setting: Small City
F-T Undergrads: 13,909

SAT Range: 1020–1250*
Control: Public
Tuition: $19,584

Most Popular Majors: Social Sciences, Biology, Visual/
Performing Arts, Psychology, Business

*of 1600

Academics	B	Guys	C
Local Atmosphere	B+	Girls	B-
Safety & Security	B	Athletics	C+
Computers	B	Nightlife	B-
Facilities	B+	Greek Life	C-
Campus Dining	B	Drug Scene	C+
Off-Campus Dining	B+	Campus Strictness	C+
Campus Housing	B-	Parking	D
Off-Campus Housing	C+	Transportation	A-
Diversity	A	Weather	A

Students Speak Out
ON ACADEMICS

Q "At UCSC, I have always had attentive teachers. I feel like **they want you to succeed**, and TAs and profs alike all have office hours to make sure you don't fail."

Q "How good the professors are really varies from class to class. I am a psychology major, and there are some **incredibly good professors** in the area of psychology. Some seem a little crazy, but they are clearly brilliant, and they keep class stimulating."

Q "The teachers here are **generally pretty good**. It depends on your area of study, because sometimes teachers can be pretty one-sided, but I believe it can be like that at any school. This school is very liberal, and that can be annoying to some students."

Q "Most of the teachers are cool, but it really depends on your major. From what I have heard, we have amazing psychology teachers and a great film program. The **classes are fairly small**—they range from 20 students to 300."

STUDENT AUTHOR: The overall view of most students about academics at UCSC is that it varies from program to program, and person to person. There are great teachers, great classes, and great majors; you just have to get off your butt and find them. The main goal is finding out who's who before registration. Make sure to take advantage of the knowledge resting in the overblown heads of UCSC upperclassmen.

Students Speak Out
ON LOCAL ATMOSPHERE

Q "The **political and social activism** is strong. Environmental ethics and the hippie culture are huge here. Surf culture, anarchists, and the straightedge, hardcore scene are big in town. You have to go to Saturn Café and Tree Nine. You also must try dumpster diving. It's insane!"

Q "The atmosphere in Santa Cruz is one that could only be described as 'mellow.' The people are mellow, the **town is mellow**, and the parties are mellow (for the most part). The only other university present is Cabrillo College, located in Capitola, which is about 15 minutes from downtown Santa Cruz."

Q "Santa Cruz sometimes **feels like a bubble**. Coming from San Diego, it seems much smaller, but it does have a familiar beach atmosphere."

Q "The atmosphere is pretty **laid-back** here. There are actually a lot fun things to do at night, but you just have to keep your eye out for them, like midnight movies and bowling."

STUDENT AUTHOR: The local atmosphere is definitely an incentive to choose Santa Cruz over other UC schools. In Santa Cruz, the Pacific Ocean meets looming redwoods to provide one of the most beautiful campuses in the country. It is paradise for people who love the rustic outdoors. UCSC students participate in surfing, mountain biking, hiking, and many other recreational pursuits on a regular basis. Besides the beauty and the outdoors, most people seem to like the mellow, laid-back Santa Cruz vibe.

5 Best Things	5 Worst Things
1 Ocean views	1 Merrill Hill
2 Coed dorms	2 Distance from town
3 First rain streaking	3 Dirty hippies
4 Diverse professors	4 Lack of school spirit
5 Happy hippies	5 High cost of living

Students Speak Out
ON FACILITIES

Q "The East Field Gym is awesome. It is always crowded, but when you can find a spot, you can run on a treadmill where there is a **gorgeous view of the ocean** and downtown."

Q "UCSC has **the most beautiful fields** I have ever seen. There is no stadium because there is no football team, which is fine by me. There is a great workout gym, and a dance room. There are fast computers as well. I think that UCSC's facilities are fine."

Q "The athletic center could be bigger, but for its size, it is definitely **well equipped**. There is a beautiful dance studio over at the Rec Center, as well as two more at Theater Arts. They are all very nice and well taken care of. Some of the computers in the libraries are outdated, but in the computer labs the computers are good."

Q "The facilities here are so nice. The gym is one of the best I have ever been to and has a **gorgeous view of the ocean**. The computer labs are pretty nice, but I am not a fan of Mac computers."

STUDENT AUTHOR: In short, the facilities at UCSC are more than sufficient to meet student needs. Generally, students are pretty impressed with the athletic center, particularly the location with its amazing ocean view. Students seem to view the Rec Center as small but good in regards to what it has to offer. There is a state-of-the-art Olympic-sized swimming pool that is free and available to all students. The fields on campus are beautiful and well kept, and the dance studios and martial arts rooms are all modern, too.

Famous Alumni

Brannon Braga, Anne Flett-Giordano, Laurie Garrett, Camryn Mannheim, Katherina Roberts, Maya Rudolph, Kathy Sullivan, Don Wallace

Students Speak Out
ON CAMPUS DINING

Q "Dining halls have variety for about the first three weeks of school, then it's all downhill from there. I don't think I have ever eaten there and not **left with a stomachache**!"

Q "Dining halls at UCSC are nice, if you aren't too picky. I go to Porter for good vegetarian meals, and College 8 if I feel like buying authentic baked goods. **I really like the dining halls**, to be honest. This goes against the views of most everyone I know."

Q "From what I hear, the food on campus is much **better than many other schools**. I would say it's pretty good, and they give you many options to choose from. The Hungry Slug is my personal favorite, but if you are looking for a down home meal, I would say Porter is the best."

Q "The Hungry Slug Café at Porter has the **best cheeseburgers in Santa Cruz**, hands down. Also, the Stevenson Coffee House is the best place to eat on campus. Stevenson has really tasty salads, reasonable prices, and most excellent baked goods."

STUDENT AUTHOR: Most UCSC students can handle the dining halls and actually find the food edible, though by the end of the year, most students get sick of it (some literally). All of the colleges on campus have a café or eatery of some sort. These range from taquerias, to coffee shops, to pizza joints. It's easier than you think to empty your account once you start to grow tired of dining hall food. Oh yeah, don't forget the Tums.

Student Body

African American:	3%	Male/Female:	46/54%
Asian American:	21%	Out-of-State:	3%
Hispanic:	16%	International:	1%
Native American:	1%	Unknown:	8%
White:	51%		

Popular Faiths: The Jewish community at UCSC is prominent and is always advertising events.

Gay Pride: Santa Cruz is known as a very gay-friendly place. It is common to see openly gay couples, since the gay and lesbian community really thrives here.

Political Activity: Political groups and activities are plentiful at UCSC. Every month, there seem to be rallies and speakers in the central area of campus.

Students Speak Out
ON DORMS

Q "The dorms here are okay. Some are better then others for sure. In terms of environment, Porter and Kresge were the right places for me, but I really feel that the colleges **cater to different people** and their interests. It's a good idea to visit campus or stay with a friend at the dorms to get a feel for the ambience of the place you're staying before you commit."

Q "**I enjoyed the dorms**. The facilities are well maintained, clean, and of good quality. I enjoyed my stay at Cowell since it is close to the sports facilities, the library, and the bookstore."

Q "**Oakes is great**! The double rooms are huge, but you really get screwed if you have a triple."

STUDENT AUTHOR: It's very hard to say which dorms are good or bad because all of the dorms are so different. Each college comes along with a stereotype. While these generalizations could contain a grain of truth, they don't hold true for everyone in a particular dorm. While Cowell may be known as the jock or Southern California dorm, and Porter for its eccentric hippie residents, a new student can still find their niche wherever they stay.

> **Did You Know?**
> 47% of undergrads live on campus.

Students Speak Out
ON GUYS & GIRLS

Q "Girls are hotter then the guys at UCSC for sure. Sometimes the boys get here and **stop cutting their hair and showering**. Overall, I would say there is someone for everyone."

Q "Some SC guys are **lazy stoners**, and some are cocky. I've found enough people to date for five years, but the well is starting to run dry. Guys are generally mellow and friendly, though."

Q "I would say there are quite a bit of good looking men, but **not a lot of them are single**. Chances are that, if they are single, they don't have the personality to match the looks. Granted, there are exceptions, but this is my overall experience with the men. There are a lot of really good looking women with great personalities, too."

STUDENT AUTHOR: There seems to be a wide variety of different looks and styles here, but most agree that students are attractive in both the looks and personality departments. There will be hippies, punks, surfers, and your basic, average-looking people; you'll find it rather easy to find hot people here. Oh, and you're far more likely to see someone walking to class in Garfield pajamas than to see someone in a short skirt and heels.

Traditions

First Rain
The first time it downpours at UCSC, which is usually sometime in October, all of the students at Porter college get naked and streak around campus.

Halloween
The main street downtown is blocked off and flooded with all of Santa Cruz's most eccentric people.

Overall School Spirit
While people may not have much spirit for the sports teams at UCSC, many students are still proud to be Banana Slugs.

Students Speak Out
ON ATHLETICS

Q "We have **no football team**, which I don't have a problem with. The good varsity teams are men's soccer, men's and women's ultimate Frisbee, tennis, and swimming."

Q "I don't really hear much about varsity sports at UCSC. I think our basketball team kind of sucks, but water polo and tennis are good though. The **IM sports are awesome**. There are huge leagues for most sports, and they are pretty organized."

Q "Varsity sports are **not that big**. There is a larger selection of club sports. The overall athletic scene is pretty diverse, though."

Q "There are a **few varsity sports** on campus, but they are not big. There a few club teams that draw an athletic crowd."

STUDENT AUTHOR: There are only a few varsity sports on campus; the fighting Banana Slugs are not widely known for their school spirit or their school pride. Club sports and intramural sports are, however, very popular on campus. There are many sports clubs, which are between varsity sports and IM in terms of commitment and competition levels.

Students Speak Out
ON DRUG SCENE

Q "**Every drug imaginable** can be found somewhere in Santa Cruz. Without doubt, weed and mushrooms dominate the drug scene, but coke is around. Opium, LSD, and other stuff is fairly easy to get as well. There was even some heroin going around Kresge for a while last year, and Porter is a regular chemical smorgasbord."

Q "**Weed is ubiquitous** on campus and in town. Acid and 'shrooms are pretty popular as well. Ecstasy is next in line. Harder drugs are present on campus, but not that popular."

Q "There is a drug scene here. If you want to partake, you can, but if not **there's no pressure**. It's not like students are selling crack in the library."

STUDENT AUTHOR: **Students will say that many drugs exist and are available on campus, but other students will emphatically say that drugs are not all that prevalent and they can easily choose not get involved with them on any level. If you want, you can request to live on a sober floor in the dorms.**

19:1	Student-to-Faculty Ratio
90%	Freshman Retention Rate
46%	Four-Year Graduation Rate
73%	Financial Aid Applicants Receiving Aid

Students Speak Out
SAFETY & SECURITY

Q "At night, both campus **entrances are patrolled**, and a student ID card is required for entrance."

Q "Although the campus mostly consists of **dark forest at night**, I always feel safe walking around by myself. After all, what is the likelihood that someone is hiding in the bushes of some random path? There are two very useless security kiosks at the entrances of campus that operate at night. They basically serve to check if each person coming onto campus at night is a student, or a friend of a student."

Q "I lived on campus for my first year, and we all felt safe and secure to a point that we would even leave our doors unlocked at times. Cops are **everywhere during the day**, but I don't recall too many at night."

STUDENT AUTHOR: UCSC's location amidst many trees can make walking on the trails at night sort of scary, and it seems that students are sometimes afraid of the dark. While there are a number of theft-related incidents on campus every year, there are very few incidents of violent crime at UCSC.

Questions?
For more inside information and survival tips, pick up College Prowler's full-length book on this school, written by an actual student! Check it out at *www.collegeprowler.com.*

Students Speak Out
ON OVERALL EXPERIENCE

Q "**I don't like it here** at UCSC. I just don't like the people here. They are too laid-back and annoying. I wouldn't recommend going to school here, but maybe I just don't like it because I experience racism."

Q "I wouldn't want to spend my college years anywhere else. Studying amongst trees and walking past deer everyday is an **awesome** experience. I just hope I never see any mountain lions!"

Q "**I love it** in Santa Cruz. There are so many things to do, and so many strange and interesting people. It's beautiful, and the weather suits me. I belong in Santa Cruz."

Q "Coming to Santa Cruz was definitely the **best decision I ever made**. Whether you go to Harvard or Chico State, colleges are as good or bad as you make them. No one is going to force you to learn. So, that being the case, you might as well be somewhere beautiful and fun, both of which categorize UCSC."

STUDENT AUTHOR: **Most students seem pretty happy at UCSC, although many of them indicate that it took some time to adjust to the school and its surroundings—the town of Santa Cruz is small, but the University is pretty big. Many students say that it is a school that takes some getting used to but, once you find your niche, it is a cool place to be both socially and politically active, and also to receive a good education. The most problematic things students mentioned about UCSC were the lack of diversity, the overall resentment of Greek life, the student body's apathy for athletics and, in some cases, academics.**

UCLA

405 Hilgard Avenue; Los Angeles, CA 90095
(310) 825-4321; www.ucla.edu

THE BASICS:

Acceptance Rate: 23%
Setting: Urban
F-T Undergrads: 25,614

SAT Range: 1750–2110*
Control: Public
Tuition: $27,575

Most Popular Majors: Social Sciences, Biological/Life Sciences, Psychology, History, English

*of 2400

Academics	A-	Guys	A-
Local Atmosphere	A+	Girls	A
Safety & Security	B+	Athletics	A-
Computers	B+	Nightlife	A-
Facilities	A-	Greek Life	B
Campus Dining	A-	Drug Scene	C
Off-Campus Dining	A	Campus Strictness	C+
Campus Housing	C	Parking	F
Off-Campus Housing	B-	Transportation	C-
Diversity	A+	Weather	A

Students Speak Out
ON ACADEMICS

Q "Language classes are particularly good. Admittedly, some professors are more concerned with their research than with teaching an undergrad class. But for big lectures, the University tends to hire **excellent lecturers**."

Q "I had mostly science teachers. I had several teachers that were enthusiastic about their subject of expertise making the class both interesting and informative. Of course, some were boring and others incoherent; I swear one was **127 years old**."

Q "The teachers here come in a wide variety. Some are boring; **some are fun**. Some are easy; some are hard. I haven't had many problems with my professors, but that's just me."

Q "They cover the whole range from very good to very bad. I've probably had more mediocre/poor professors than good professors. Many are **preoccupied with their own research** and put minimal effort into teaching, and some are simply old and disorganized and unable to convey the material."

STUDENT AUTHOR: **The teachers at UCLA are qualified, as many of them earned their graduate degrees at some of the most prestigious American colleges, including the Ivy Leagues. Many of the professors are so involved that they've devoted their lives to their subjects, and not to teaching. However, many professors cannot communicate their innovative ideas clearly enough in one quarter of a class.**

Students Speak Out
ON LOCAL ATMOSPHERE

Q "LA's atmosphere is **awesome**. There are lots of other schools around the area, including USC. Boooooo!"

Q "Los Angeles is **a tourist's dream**; there are museums, amusement parks, water parks, movies, theater, musicals, beaches, and movie stars right outside your door."

Q "Westwood is a **good college town**. There are lots of little shops, restaurants, coffee shops, and theaters. As for Los Angeles in general, there is everything from the beaches, to Hollywood, all the clubs on Sunset, Disneyland, and Magic Mountain."

Q "There are **five big universities by UCLA**. They are, by distance: Mt. St. Mary's in Brentwood, Loyola Marymount by LAX, CSUN in Northridge, USC near Downtown/South Central, and Pepperdine in Malibu. I'd stay away from South Central; it's a much better place than before the riots, but I wouldn't go there alone, especially at night. The same goes for Hollywood; if you go there during the day, that's fine; at night, go with friends. Other than that, the area is pretty cool."

STUDENT AUTHOR: **Despite its reputation of being the capitol of face lifts and breast implants, Los Angeles actually has a casual style and many unique neighborhoods. There are many patches of culture and fun scattered throughout the city. To get around Los Angeles and see everything that the city has to offer, a car is necessary.**

5 Best Things	5 Worst Things
1 Movie premieres	1 Traffic
2 Close to the beaches	2 Smog
3 60-degree winters	3 School politics
4 Actors on campus	4 Expensive apartments
5 The quarter system	5 Necessity of a car

Students Speak Out
ON FACILITIES

Q "The administration makes a concerted effort to keep the facilities **in good condition**. The campus is always amazingly clean. Computer labs always have the latest software and hardware. The fitness center could use an expansion and an update in equipment, though."

Q "The facilities are **decent**. The gym is a little bit small for the size of the student body, though. It expands in size and quality every year."

Q "We have the Wooden Center, a **state-of-the-art** workout facility, complete with racquetball courts, a rock-climbing wall, and basketball courts. UCLA has the privilege of being the only campus to offer the real Tae-Bo taught by Billy Blanks's instructors. It's seriously a good workout!"

Q "**I like the gyms**. I know that they tend to get crowded, but the best part about the free time between classes is hitting the gym. The gym is so close and accessible that there is no way that people can't like it. I go in to lift weights or check out a basketball and just shoot some hoops. It's a great way to meet people. I love it!"

Q "Everything is **pretty cool**, but there is a lot of construction. The two buildings that aren't being worked on are up-to-date and nice, though."

STUDENT AUTHOR: The Wooden Center, the athletic gymnasium, is a true powerhouse with a weight room, three basketball courts, two volleyball courts, numerous racquetball courts, a rock climbing wall, a cardiovascular area, and private rooms that offer lessons in everything from martial arts to hip hop dance and dance aerobics.

Famous Alumni

Kareem Abdul-Jabbar, Troy Aikman, Nancy Cartwright, Jimmy Connors, Francis Ford Coppola, James Dean, Jim Morrison, Darren Star

Students Speak Out
ON CAMPUS DINING

Q "There are **many different eating areas** on campus. They have burgers, pizza, tacos, and Chinese food, to name a few."

Q "The food is great here. In the dorms, they pride themselves on the number of food options available, and the dining halls are nationally ranked as **some of the best food** at any university. On campus, there are a whole bunch of coffee shops, a Taco Bell Express, Panda Express, Rubio's, and Sbarro, just to name a few. And if you don't like any of those restaurants, you have Westwood right next door with many restaurants and cafés."

Q "The **dining halls are excellent**. They always change up the menu. On campus, there are three regular dining places plus there is a Taco Bell, Baja Fresh, Panda Express, and Sbarro."

Q "I'd say the **food is pretty good** compared to other college campuses. In my opinion, Rieber dining hall is the best dining hall, and Covel Commons is the worst."

STUDENT AUTHOR: Dorm dining on campus is truly hit or miss, but if you plan right you can hit big. Starting with the dorms, the best strategy is to plan ahead. Keep eating at the same place, and the pizza and hamburgers will start to taste too familiar. You'll soon find your feast in the cereal section. Realistically, the food is nutritious and delicious if you survey the scene ahead of time. Be sure to check out the late-night places to eat for a tasty midnight snack that will pack on the pounds.

Student Body

African American:	4%	Male/Female:	45/55%
Asian American:	38%	Out-of-State:	6%
Hispanic:	15%	International:	4%
Native American:	<1%	Unknown:	5%
White:	34%		

Gay Pride: There is campus resource center and major designed towards lesbian, gay, bisexual, and transgender education and awareness.

Economic Status: The economic diversity here spans the spectrum. There are rich and poor students of every ethnicity, but certain groups tend to attract a rich and snobbish stereotype. Don't let stereotypes speak for the group.

Students Speak Out
ON DORMS

Q "There are four high-rise dorms and three suite/apartment-style complexes. All of them have their own dining hall, a small computer lab, and some even have a fitness room and/or a recreation room with pool tables. I lived in Hedrick for two years and think that it had the best dining hall, Sproul is kind of blah, and **Dykstra is the most social**."

Q "The dorms are pretty good. Avoid Sproul Hall—its suites are the best, but are **way too expensive**. The Plaza's suites are not worth the money either."

Q "Dorms are **a problem**. UCLA is jamming three people into doubles, and it is nearly unbearable."

STUDENT AUTHOR: When living on campus, students basically have two lifestyle choices: 1) live like honeybees packed into a hive, all the while making many friends and living a very social lifestyle, or 2) enjoy peace, quiet, and spacious privacy (not to mention paying a little extra). UCLA works each year to expand the tight quarters of on-campus housing. Until then, underclassmen should just get used to the tenament-style living.

Did You Know?
36% of undergrads live on campus.

Students Speak Out
ON GUYS & GIRLS

Q "The girls at UCLA are **really incredible**. There are pretty girls all over the place—no joke."

Q "There are more girls at UCLA than guys—maybe that's because girls are smarter! In my opinion, the **girls are hotter than the guys**, and they're in really good shape, too."

Q "The guys and girls here are, for the most part, **stereotypically LA**. They are overly concerned with style, appearance, and whatnot."

Q "There are some pretty good looking guys and girls at UCLA. There is no shortage of eye candy! Although the guys may be hot, they are pretty arrogant. The girls are really pretty but kind of **catty and snobby**. UCLA is really influenced by Hollywood."

STUDENT AUTHOR: Despite having a reputation for cookie-cutter men and women, UCLA is a very diverse campus when it comes to its guys and gals. Students at UCLA are beautiful and intelligent, this goes for all the departments. If you are looking, which many UCLA students are, you are sure to find whatever type of physical attraction that suits your taste. The eclectic backgrounds of the students provide a variety of distinct looks.

Traditions

Book Reading Marathon
This little jewel is an English lover's delight, as the Undergraduate English Association sponsors a reading of a book in 15-minute increments.

Farmer's Market
Each Thursday, there is a large gathering of farmers that sell their produce (wholesale) on campus.

Overall School Spirit
Most freshmen are thrilled to make it into UCLA, and they carry their excitement and expectations of the school with them throughout their first year.

Students Speak Out
ON ATHLETICS

Q "**Basketball and football** are the only two college sports that get any serious attention at UCLA. Intramural (IM) sports don't seem to be that huge, but they are around."

Q "The **sports program is thriving**, although many students never pay attention to them. I've heard that IM sports are also popular."

Q "Football and basketball are huge. The teams are usually pretty solid. The **fans go all out**, and it's a lot of fun to go to the games."

Q "**Sports are very big**; especially football and basketball, as we always field a good team."

STUDENT AUTHOR: You can feel the anticipation in the air when fall rolls around, as the football team usually steam rolls the early season competition and sets up hope for another long-awaited national title run. Attending the games indulges the student in the frenzied action, and the ticket availability fluctuates with the success of the team. If the basketball team is winning, you'd better hope that you bought season tickets; the student section tickets will be more impossible to get your hands on than a nearby parking spot.

Students Speak Out
ON DRUG SCENE

Q "I know a guy who knows a guy. Seems like that is the way it is on this campus—**everyone knows**, but nobody does it."

Q "The drug scene is **not so obvious**, but I think everyone smokes pot. I think it's another story if you're in the school of Arts and Architecture though. I hear the students and professors enjoy doing a ton of drugs."

Q "**Weed is popular** and readily available. Some kids do harder stuff, and some kids would never touch a joint. There's a large variety."

STUDENT AUTHOR: Just because drugs are not always out in the open at UCLA does not mean that they do not exist. Many daring potsmokers won't hesitate to light up and smoke on any area of campus. The only day that there is noticeable drug usage on campus is on April 20 (the infamous 4/20) when hundreds of students openly light up on campus in a festive manner. Drugs are readily available, but that doesn't mean that each and every student is using them.

16:1	Student-to-Faculty Ratio
97%	Freshman Retention Rate
65%	Four-Year Graduation Rate
89%	Financial Aid Applicants Receiving Aid

Students Speak Out
SAFETY & SECURITY

Q "The campus is **pretty safe**. The UCPD does a good job of patrolling, and we have a program of student cops on bikes for more presence and visibility. There's also an escort service available for those late study nights."

Q "It's okay; there are campus security officers who think they're tough stuff. However, **there was a rapist** a few years ago, and people were afraid to leave their rooms for a few weeks."

Q "There is a **free campus escort service** all night, every night, and they will walk you from wherever you are back to your residence. There are security phones all over campus that connect you to the campus police, too."

STUDENT AUTHOR: The UCLA campus is one of the most secure in the UC system. UCLA employs its own police force, with officers that patrol the campus day and night. In the daytime, UCLA is extremely safe. Some people fall prey to petty theft, but for the most part, crime is not an issue.

Questions?

For more inside information and survival tips, pick up College Prowler's full-length book on this school, written by an actual student! Check it out at www.collegeprowler.com.

Students Speak Out
ON OVERALL EXPERIENCE

Q "**I love it here**. I like the people, the atmosphere, and being so close to the ocean. I like that there is so much to do. I was really unsure about the move to LA, but now I'm thinking of staying here."

Q "Well, I've just graduated. I'd say it was okay. UCLA is just **so darn big**, and it's hard to be involved, or really feel like you're actually a part of a school that has over 35,000 people."

Q "UCLA was a great school for me. I had a lot of fun. There are a lot of opportunities available, so take advantage of them. I was afraid it would be too large and impersonal for me, but I found that the opposite was true. **You get a great education** for the price of a state school."

Q "I definitely do not regret my choice when it comes to college. I have had **nothing but good experiences** here and would not trade it for the world. And I know that this sounds like a 'sell,' but honestly, I really think that if you're looking for nice people, a surrounding area full of experiences and fun, and a good academic experience, then come to UCLA."

STUDENT AUTHOR: There is a reason that UCLA is not a party school; the classes are too difficult to slack off for any prolonged stretch of time. Academically, students need to be prepared to focus on their classes beginning the first day of school. Socially, students are pressed to find a niche amongst a throng of 35,000 students. Through all of its challenges, UCLA is the ideal school to come to if you want to grow into a stronger person (physically, mentally, intellectually, socially) as students are sure to learn more than just what's inside the textbooks.

Union College

807 Union Street; Schenectady, NY 12308
(518) 388-6000; www.union.edu

THE BASICS:

Acceptance Rate: 43%
Setting: Small City
F-T Undergrads: 2,149

SAT Range: 1720–2010*
Control: Private
Tuition: $48,522**

Most Popular Majors: Political Science, Psychology, Economics, Biology, History

*of 2400 **includes room & board

Academics	B	Guys	A-
Local Atmosphere	C-	Girls	B+
Safety & Security	B	Athletics	B+
Computers	B-	Nightlife	B
Facilities	B	Greek Life	A-
Campus Dining	B	Drug Scene	B-
Off-Campus Dining	B	Campus Strictness	B
Campus Housing	B+	Parking	D
Off-Campus Housing	C+	Transportation	B
Diversity	D+	Weather	D

Students Speak Out
ON ACADEMICS

Q "The faculty are amazing. Because **the classes are small** you really get the chance to connect with your teachers. It's not uncommon for a professor to invite a group of students over to their house for coffee or dinner."

Q "The majority of **the professors are great**. There are always a few who aren't; but in general, they are interested in benefiting the students here."

Q "The teachers at Union College **are mostly very personable, intelligent people**. I have found that the majority of my classes have been interesting. The more you devote to a class, the more interesting it usually is."

Q "The majority of the professors really care about how you are doing in their class. While the intro classes can be large, the professors almost always know your name and make an effort to make sure that you are doing well in their class. The classes are interesting because the professors make sure that the subject matter they are teaching is done in an **effective and intriguing** way."

STUDENT AUTHOR: The academics here are challenging, which is something Union is very fond of. Since its founding in 1795, Union's academics have been some of the strongest in the country. It's evident from the students' opinions that academics are the priority of the college and of the professors. Each department feels like a tight-knit family. There isn't that much time for many electives.

Students Speak Out
ON LOCAL ATMOSPHERE

Q "The stockade is beautiful, and Jay Street adds some artistic flair to an otherwise industrial city. But if you don't enjoy Schenectady, **beautiful Saratoga is close by**, and hiking trails are plentiful."

Q "There isn't really anything to do in Schenectady. It's not the greatest neighborhood, but it's also not the worst. You want to be careful at night, but it's not necessary to be neurotic. **There are a few other schools** within a few miles of Union, as well as museums, concert venues, and sporting events."

Q "**The town isn't the greatest**, and if you don't have a car, you're pretty much confined to staying on campus. But the college tries hard to accommodate students, so there's really no reason why you have to leave campus at all."

Q "Schenectady is an old, struggling, upstate New York city, so it is not necessarily the most aesthetically pleasing place. However, they are starting to make some **nice improvements** and there are some nice areas such as Jay Street that carries a lot of local restaurants and business."

STUDENT AUTHOR: Based on the student's quotes about Schenectady, it is certainly fair to say that the city is a work in progress. Many students don't venture out into Schenectady until their sophomore year, but those that do find "hole in the wall" cafés with a lot of local flavor. While Schenectady has many things to offer students, the town itself is definitely not geared towards Union students.

Students Speak Out
ON FACILITIES

Q "The gym needs a renovation job. I refuse to go there because it's stinky and gross, and there is zero ventilation. **The Campus Center is reasonably nice**, there's a good game room and plenty of lounge space."

Q "Some of the buildings are 'iffy' about handicap accessibility, but overall **most facilities are nice**."

Q "Since many of the buildings on campus are older, **many aren't as nice** as schools that have done recent renovations. However, with all of the money that the school has begun to put into renovations, there should be major improvements coming."

Q "For the most part the facilities are very nice—the student center has a lot to offer (food, lounge, study rooms). **They are making a lot of changes with dorms** (the new ones are really beautiful), and eventually, they plan to renovate the athletic facilities, which now are a bit outdated, but will be really nice in a year or so."

Q "The **facilities are good**; it's nothing special, but more than enough."

STUDENT AUTHOR: **Though the facilities aren't state-of-the-art, Union is working on improving its facilities through renovations and technological advances. Many of the facilities on campus are very nice, and a lot of the buildings at Union have been either gone through or are in the process of going through renovation and upgrading. This is true, but the changes seem to be happening at a very slow pace. The gym, for example, is quite small when a large number of students use it.**

Famous Alumni

Chester A. Arthur, Baruch, Blumberg, Daniel Butterfield, Gordon Gould, Tom Riis, Phil Alden Robinson, Nikki Stone, George Westinghouse

Students Speak Out
ON CAMPUS DINING

Q "Thankfully, the food here hasn't been a disappointment. **There are enough choices** (salad bar, sandwich bar, and grille) that there's always something tasty to find. The only real problem is that the menus repeat themselves much too often."

Q "**Food on campus is good**, and it can be great when you don't eat too much of it. Eating the same thing day after day gets boring in any setting, and it's hard to avoid that eating on campus."

Q "The food on campus is decent. **The freshman dining hall is lacking**, though Upperclass Dining is good, and they respond well to requests. The Skellar is fabulous for a good sub and fried food—a nice late-night weekend spot."

Q "Overall, the food at Union is impressively edible. **There are plenty of options**; although by senior year, they seem redundant and old."

Q "The food at Upperclass is very good, with a **sandwich bar and salad bar everyday**, and various hot meals, which aren't as good, depending on the day."

STUDENT AUTHOR: **The biggest problem with Union dining seems to be that the students quickly get bored with the repetitious menu offered at the Upperclass and residential dining halls. Both upper and lower offer all-you-can-eat, buffet-style service though, and the salad bars are always well stocked and maintained. Freshmen are required to purchase the largest amount of meals per week.**

Student Body

African American:	3%	Male/Female:	54/46%
Asian American:	5%	Out-of-State:	55%
Hispanic:	4%	International:	2%
Native American:	<1%	Unknown:	0%
White:	86%		

Popular Faiths: People are pretty quiet about religion on campus.

Gay Pride: There aren't many openly-gay students, and most who are seem to come out senior year.

Economic Status: Even though a majority receives financial aid, one wouldn't be able to tell on campus. While not everyone is rich, there is a status quo of wearing your best at all times.

Students Speak Out
ON DORMS

Q "Most of the residence halls could use a sprucing up, but **generally they're not too bad**. The apartment houses on Seward and Huron Streets are very nice, and the newly renovated (former) Ramada Inn will make for very good living."

Q "The dorms are okay. The college has been putting a lot into fixing up the housing situation. I lucked out as a freshman and ended up in a suite in Fox, but **South is now the place to be**."

Q "The dorms are pretty comfortable. Union is implementing a new housing system, with **seven new dorms** on campus."

STUDENT AUTHOR: It seems pretty obvious that while your freshman year you'll be living in a smaller dorm room, your remaining years at Union will lead to living in some great dormitories. Over recent years, Union has put a lot of effort into revamping their housing system. And with Union's rapidly increasing student body, the college is increasing its number of housing options available to students. The college purchased a former Ramada Inn, now known cleverly as the Inn.

> **Did You Know?**
> 88% of undergrads live on campus.

Students Speak Out
ON GUYS & GIRLS

Q "Our campus is **a bunch of supermodels**. Everyone looks like a J.Crew model, and I'm pretty sure some are."

Q "The guys range all over the scale. You have jocks, frat brothers, engineers, and some guys are all three rolled into one. **This is not a big school for relationships**; people just tend to get together when they feel like it."

Q "The guys are preppy for the most part, while the girls tend to be **cliquey and sorority-esque**."

Q "A hot campus? I guess, but don't expect a dating scene. There is **a serious amount of conformity**; you can tell who's from Union and who's just passing through."

STUDENT AUTHOR: The girls here are very good looking in general. They are polished and well dressed on the whole, but they can also be very prim as well, although there are exceptions to that statement. The guys at Union are a mixed bag. You'll get a polo wearing jock, a few pop-punk rockers and many laid-back, "wear what doesn't smell bad" dressers. The guy/girl ratios are pretty equal at Union, too.

> **Traditions**
>
> **The Naked Nott Run**
> The Naked Nott run is something every student is supposed to do at least once before graduating from Union. Literally, you strip down and run circles around the historic, 16-sided building in the middle of the campus.
>
> **Overall School Spirit**
> When it comes to athletics on campus, especially hockey games, the student body gets involved. Students love to go to the game and cheer our ladies and gents on.

Students Speak Out
ON ATHLETICS

Q "Overall, I don't think there is too much enthusiasm for varsity sports, except maybe **hockey and possibly football**, for those who aren't on the teams."

Q "Varsity sports are great here whether you play them or not. **IM sports are a great alternative** for students who played sports in high school, but who don't want the commitment of a varsity college sport."

Q "This school is obsessed with the varsity hockey. **The games are fun**."

Q "I know **IM softball is big in the spring**, but I don't know much more. The rugby clubs are very popular."

STUDENT AUTHOR: For such a small school, the athletics here are really good. This is definitely an athletic student body. The Division I hockey teams (men and women) are always competitive, and everyone gets psyched for their games. The women's soccer team is stellar, as is the men's football team. Soccer, softball, broomball, and basketball are the most popular intramural activities.

Students Speak Out
ON DRUG SCENE

Q "There are **way more drugs** than a lot of people realize, especially in the frats, specifically cocaine."

Q "There is mostly pot on campus, but also some **people do coke** and take painkillers. It's easy to stay away from and also easy to find."

Q "Alcohol is the dominant drug. Cocaine is growing, but you see it rarely. Pretty much **everyone just wants to get drunk**."

Q "There is **a lot of pot** floating around campus. I believe cocaine, too."

STUDENT AUTHOR: The drugs are attainable if you want them, but they are totally avoidable if you don't. Keep your nose clean (no pun intended) and your eyes open, because as with anywhere else, having and/or doing drugs can get you into serious trouble here. Drugs at Union aren't necessarily a "scene" per se, but there is a market for them in some circles. Students here like to play hard, but they are also required to work extremely hard.

11:1	Student-to-Faculty Ratio
91%	Freshman Retention Rate
81%	Four-Year Graduation Rate
86%	Financial Aid Applicants Receiving Aid

Students Speak Out
SAFETY & SECURITY

Q "Campus safety is a good network for assuring security on campus. **They respond quickly** to the most serious of problems."

Q "I believe that the security is lacking on campus. The campus pathways are not well lit enough considering **we are an open campus**. There have been instances of sexual assault on the perimeters of campus, causing students to feel unsafe walking home at night."

Q "I have always found security to be reliable on campus. There are **a series of blue-light posts around campus**. If you feel threatened or there is an emergency, all you have to do is push a button and security is there in moments."

STUDENT AUTHOR: Students feel quite safe on campus, although, walking alone at night can be a little harrowing. The important thing when it comes to safety at Union, or any college for that matter, is common sense. When you're out walking at night, try to walk in groups.

> **Questions?**
> For more inside information and survival tips, pick up College Prowler's full-length book on this school, written by an actual student! Check it out at *www.collegeprowler.com*.

Students Speak Out
ON OVERALL EXPERIENCE

Q "I enjoy the interaction that I am able to have with my professors and my advisor, but I wish that the students cared a little bit more. There are certainly some who do care, but it is a **frustratingly apathetic campus**."

Q "I have had **a wonderful time** here, I think because I have taken advantage of the many opportunities that the school has to offer."

Q "Sometimes, yes, I am glad that I came here. Sometimes, I'm not. As with any other school or other organization, **there are both good and bad times to be had**. For the most part, looking back at the four years I've spent here, I must admit that I am glad I came."

Q "I have had a real positive experience at Union. I have **met some of the best people I know**, and I know they will be life-long friends. I was fortunate from the beginning to meet great people, and I never have questioned if this was the place for me. For the most part, the people I know have had similar experiences and have enjoyed their time here."

STUDENT AUTHOR: Sure, Schenectady isn't what you would call an "ideal college town," but that doesn't seem to affect the students' overall experience here at Union. Sure, the food gets old after awhile, but that seems to happen at every school. And students party hard at Union, too. First-year students seem to be split into two groups: those who hate it at Union and those that love it. Socially, it takes a bit to adjust to Union if you're not the outgoing type and not willing to jump on the academic bandwagon. But eventually, people really do find their niche at Union and seem generally happy.

University at Albany

1400 Washington Avenue; Albany, NY 12222
(518) 442-3300; www.albany.edu

THE BASICS:

Acceptance Rate: 52% **SAT Range:** 1060–1220*
Setting: Small City **Control:** Public
F-T Undergrads: 11,959 **Tuition:** $10,610

Most Popular Majors: Social Sciences, Business, Psychology, English, Communications

*of 1600

Academics	B-	Guys	B
Local Atmosphere	B	Girls	B
Safety & Security	B	Athletics	C-
Computers	B	Nightlife	A-
Facilities	C+	Greek Life	C
Campus Dining	B	Drug Scene	C-
Off-Campus Dining	B+	Campus Strictness	B
Campus Housing	B-	Parking	D
Off-Campus Housing	B	Transportation	A-
Diversity	C+	Weather	D

Students Speak Out
ON ACADEMICS

Q "In general, the classes are **long and boring**. However, towards the upper-level ones, the numbers start to thin out, and the teachers teaching them tend to be more personable. It also differs from major to major."

Q "I found that most of my professors were really nice and always made time outside of class to help students out who were having trouble. Most of them were very **into what they were teaching**, which helped me get more into what I was learning."

Q "The quality of the teaching staff varies amongst the departments. The economics department, in my opinion, has the worst teachers. I have found that my business, and many of my sociology professors, are **extremely interesting** and very intelligent."

Q "A considerable amount of your professors may be **graduate students**. They usually make classes easier for the students. But, if you really expect something from the class, find a professor who teaches it. The professors are always available to speak in their office hours."

STUDENT AUTHOR: The biggest issue currently facing Albany academics is likely gen ed requirements. These, coupled with a student's major requirements (which often include a Senior Thesis), can be very difficult to complete. Aside from the gen ed requirements, students have few complaints. The system may have a few flaws, but the professors and courses are above average, to say the least.

Students Speak Out
ON LOCAL ATMOSPHERE

Q "The town, I think, is **pretty awesome**. It's very diverse. Albany, the town itself, is pretty much a college town. I would stay away from Arbor Hill and anything past Clinton Avenue after dark. But there is a lot to see, such as the museums and Empire State Plaza. Plus, the music scene is pretty awesome, so there are a lot of shows going on throughout the year."

Q "**Albany is a bit odd**, but mostly pleasant. The other universities are around, but not too present in Albany social life. Stuff to stay away from would be Arbor Hill and the areas around there. Stuff to visit would be Lark Street, especially the bars down there."

Q "Albany is generally a **nice, cozy place** that offers big city opportunities with small town personality. There are lots of good restaurants, museums, and stores. Downtown Albany is something to be explored and experienced. Stay away from the shady areas and the 'college' bars, located on Western and Quail Streets."

Q "There are a **few other colleges in the area**. Nothing as big as SUNY Albany, though. Definitely visit Washington Park on a nice day."

STUDENT AUTHOR: Albany is a great city to spend four years getting an education in, but many students would not suggest settling down in the area after graduation. If you want to get a real feel for Albany, check out the downtown area (Lark Street and the Empire State Plaza).

5 Best Things
1 Fountain Day
2 Bars everywhere
3 Crossgates Mall
4 Big Purple Growl
5 Concerts at the RACC

5 Worst Things
1 The student ghetto
2 Parking
3 Dining halls
4 Winter
5 Common showers

Students Speak Out
ON FACILITIES

Q "Everything on campus is **pretty nice**. Not as nice as private schools, but recently a lot has been refurbished. University of Albany is on the up and up."

Q "They could use some help; they're a little dirty and **in need of a face lift**, like the campus in general."

Q "**The RACC sucks**. The equipment is outdated and minimal, and the hours of operation are limited. The gyms, such as the basketball courts, and also the swimming pool, are pretty nice. On Empire Commons, the campus apartments, they have a really nice facility with new equipment, but you have to be a resident there to use them."

Q "All of the facilities on campus are decent. The Science Library is actually **very beautiful** inside, and it's pretty big, too, so you can almost always find a quiet place to study."

Q "From the stuff I've used, it's all **pretty well kept** and functional."

STUDENT AUTHOR: **The facilities at the University at Albany are exactly what one would expect when a great deal of the place hasn't been updated since the 1970s. Most of the fitness centers are hot, dirty, and outdated, with the exception of the center in Empire Commons. The University does not offer much other than a pool, fitness center, and gym. In general, the campus is not a visually pleasing one; with cement accounting for the vast majority of the buildings' makeup. Most students view the buildings as gray, prison-like structures that blend in with the Albany sky.**

Famous Alumni

Steve Berkowitz, Catherine Bertini, Randy S. Cohen, John Devoto, Anthony Vinciquerra, Richard Wesley

Students Speak Out
ON CAMPUS DINING

Q "Frankly, the campus food is wretched. The only useful purpose it serves is character-building and cement mix. The Campus Center food is much better, albeit **much more expensive**."

Q "Well to be completely honest, **food sucks** in most of the dining halls. Get used to it, that's part of the experience. Out of all the dining halls, I found Colonial Quad to have the best food."

Q "Chartwell's is the school's food service provider, and they provide **the worst food**. The dining halls are horrible and have horrible selections. The Campus Center is not too bad, but how much Sbarro's and Burger King can one really eat in a week? The only thing I really enjoy is the Cee Cee's Deli, where you can get bagels, but they aren't open for very long each day."

Q "Dutch Quad's dining hall **isn't half bad**. If you get stuck in the downtown dorms, avoid that dining hall if at all possible."

STUDENT AUTHOR: **The food in the dining halls on campus leaves much to be desired. The food is fattening, and at times, very tasteless. On the other hand, they cater to vegetarians and to students who maintain a Kosher diet. During finals week, the dining halls re-open at midnight to serve free snacks to students who'd like a study break. Each quad (housing complex) has its own dining hall for the convenience of the students. The food court contains some familiar places, like Burger King, Sbarro's, Au Bon Pain (serves a variety of soups), and Freshëns (frozen yogurt and ice cream).**

Student Body

African American:	8%	Male/Female:	49/51%
Asian American:	6%	Out-of-State:	5%
Hispanic:	7%	International:	2%
Native American:	<1%	Unknown:	0%
White:	77%		

Popular Faiths: Christianity and Judaism are the most popular religions; religious activities take place off campus, except for the occasional holiday.

Gay Pride: The campus is very accepting of gay students. There are many gay organizations on campus that hold rallies and awareness events.

Economic Status: Though economically diverse, most students come from middle-class families.

Students Speak Out
ON DORMS

Q "The dorms are nothing to brag about—in general, they're **small, dusty, and poorly lit**. However, some of them are newly renovated, and are thus slightly better than the others. Empire Commons is a welcome, albeit expensive, on-campus housing alternative."

Q "The dorms **aren't so great**, but the University has been doing renovations, and they have improved considerably. The apartments on campus are pretty sweet, though, so try to get into them if you can."

Q "You are just going have to face it, **dorms stink**. If you are lucky, you'll get a bathroom in your suite. Every suite has three bedrooms and fills six people. If you don't want to be stuck with the hall bathroom, try to live in one of the towers. They have good furniture and more space."

STUDENT AUTHOR: The dorms on campus are not what you see on TV shows; they are small, dark, and dirty—unless you live in a newly-renovated dorm. Surprisingly, the Presidential Scholar dorms are two of the loudest. So, if you like a good night sleep on weekdays, bring earplugs.

Did You Know?
58% of undergrads live on campus.

Students Speak Out
ON GUYS & GIRLS

Q "The girls are **mostly from Long Island**, so if you like that, you're in luck. If you don't, you're out of luck, unless you look elsewhere."

Q "They are all just a little slice of **New York**."

Q "The **girls are pretty**. Sometimes you come across a decent-looking guy."

Q "The majority of the students on campus are from Long Island (no, that is not the city). A good portion of the student body are from the city (New York), and the rest from upstate. Some girls **dress like they're going to a club**. Some people look like they came right out of Woodstock. Overall, there are many guys and girls that are attractive. You will be able to find someone."

STUDENT AUTHOR: The University at Albany has something to offer everyone when it comes to finding the right guy or girl. There are plenty of students looking for a serious relationship, and there are even more who are looking to just hook up. On a typical Friday night, most guys are hunting to find the right girl to take home for the night. The phrase "one night stand" rolls out of the mouths of so many Albany students.

Traditions

Fountain Day
The first day the fountain is turned back on in early spring essentially becomes a campus-wide class-skipping, beer-drinking, all-day event.

Parkfest
An all-day music festival at the local fairgrounds. Students receive discounts and free shuttlling.

Overall School Spirit
Albany students take more pride in being—and maintaining the air of—a party school than they do in supporting athletic teams or school-sponsored events.

Students Speak Out
ON ATHLETICS

Q "Varsity sports are **fairly quiet**. There are events (i.e. Homecoming and 'the Big Purple Growl') periodically, but the majority of students don't pay any attention to them. I don't have much of a basis to judge IM sports, but from what I know they are fairly popular, and great for those who like sports but don't have time/talent for the varsity squad."

Q "Sports never really caught my attention. We **have good teams**, but nobody gets into the school spirit when it comes to sports on campus."

Q "Sports are **not terribly big** on campus. I, for one, have never attended any sort of sporting function. IM sports are pretty large, especially the SCAM team (ultimate Frisbee)."

STUDENT AUTHOR: Intramural sports are, by far, the most popular amongst Albany athletics. Hundreds of sport-loving students participate, and have an amazing time doing so. Playing intramural sports helps students stay in shape (and lose that Freshman 15), as well as meeting new friends, which can be difficult to do otherwise at such a large school.

Students Speak Out
ON DRUG SCENE

Q "**Everyone smokes cigarettes** and drinks. There are other drugs present as well, but they're not as much in-your-face as drinking and smoking cigs."

Q "**Lots of pot**, lots of alcohol, and a dappling of heavier stuff, depending on what the person can afford."

Q "Nothing out of the ordinary. A good amount of weed gets smoked, and **everyone is drunk**, but that's college."

Q "**Marijuana is the most common drug** on campus, and students are always getting caught using it. I've heard of other drugs on the campus, but can't say how often they are used."

STUDENT AUTHOR: **Drugs, like at every college, play a big role in many students' social scenes. If you want to get your hands on some type of drug, that option can be exercised, but is definitely not recommended. On the other hand, if you want to stay away from drugs and that entire scene, it is definitely possible.**

19:1	Student-to-Faculty Ratio
84%	Freshman Retention Rate
52%	Four-Year Graduation Rate
71%	Financial Aid Applicants Receiving Aid

Students Speak Out
SAFETY & SECURITY

Q "University Police Department—they keep me safe and make me smile. It's a big school, so some problems are to be expected, but **everything remains relatively quiet**."

Q "I have never run across a problem or ever felt unsafe while walking the campus at night. The University Police make themselves **very present** at all times on campus."

Q "Security on campus is **very good**, and there are blue-light emergency phones everywhere. There are programs like 'Don't Walk Alone' available, so that you never have to walk alone on campus at night."

Q "**Security is good**, but don't expect much help from Albany PD if you are off campus."

STUDENT AUTHOR: **Although there is crime on and around the campus, students still say they feel safe. Services like "Don't Walk Alone" and the blue-light phones are just two of the many things the University has done to ensure safety; the University Police maintain a very visible presence, day and night.**

> **Questions?**
> For more inside information and survival tips, pick up College Prowler's full-length book on this school, written by an actual student! Check it out at *www.collegeprowler.com.*

Students Speak Out
ON OVERALL EXPERIENCE

Q "The first two years of school I didn't really give it a chance, but the next two years I started joining things and had a great time. I learned so much about myself in college, and it was a great experience to live away from home for the first time. However, I do feel I **could have been more enlightened** educationally."

Q "It's so hard to generalize—from a social perspective, the school is **great if you're a hedonist**, as there are lots of cool people and lots of things to do. On the other hand, if you're looking to discuss philosophy or literature or modern physics, it's almost impossible to find anyone interested outside of the typically inaccessible professors. My main gripe with this university is the almost utter lack of intellectual curiosity its students exhibit. If I dwell on this enough, I begin to regret not going to the more prestigious schools I'd been accepted to, where I might have related better intellectually to more of the students."

Q "**Albany is awesome**. I have made the best friends up here and have had the best time. I'm loving everything about the school."

STUDENT AUTHOR: **Students at the University at Albany generally tend to enjoy the overall experience the school offers. They are pleased with not only the excellent education they receive, but also with their social experiences. From internships and community service to study abroad programs and hundreds of different clubs and organizations, the school offers something for everyone. Despite the bad weather, frustrating parking situation, and crazy party scene, most students are genuinely content with their college choice.**

University at Buffalo

3435 Main Street; Buffalo, NY 14214
(716) 645-2000; www.buffalo.edu

THE BASICS:

Acceptance Rate: 52%
Setting: Urban
F-T Undergrads: 16,509

SAT Range: 1050–1250*
Control: Public
Tuition: $11,740

Most Popular Majors: Business, Social Sciences, Engineering, Communications, Psychology

*of 1600

Academics	B	Guys	B+
Local Atmosphere	B+	Girls	B
Safety & Security	C	Athletics	C+
Computers	A	Nightlife	A
Facilities	A-	Greek Life	C-
Campus Dining	C	Drug Scene	B
Off-Campus Dining	A-	Campus Strictness	B
Campus Housing	B-	Parking	C
Off-Campus Housing	A-	Transportation	A-
Diversity	B-	Weather	D-

Students Speak Out
ON ACADEMICS

Q "The academics, like most things at any college, are what you make of them. **Gen ed requirements are a pain**—especially freshman year—but there's not much you can do except get them out of the way ASAP, and even then, they're not that bad."

Q "Freshmen are herded into the lecture halls like cattle to the meat grinder. The powers that be **shove up to 400 kids in a class**, mostly taught by TAs, while at the same time, glorifying the University for its renowned faculty. After freshman year, though, the classes thin out; now that I'm a senior, most of my classes are 20 kids, and they're taught by the professors the recruitment brochures had touted so highly."

Q "The fine arts programs are **worth every penny**, as are the humanities-related departments. I know many people who have gone to UB for an English degree, and they all say they've gotten a great education."

Q "The student body is usually pretty good at letting you know who the bad teachers are, so **make friends with a few upperclassmen** in your major!"

STUDENT AUTHOR: There's a small bunch of highly intellectual students who frequent office hours, take graduate classes, get involved in research, and sprint for fellowships. At first, these kids are often frustrated by the lack of intellectual energy at UB, but most seek it out in small classes, academic clubs, or professors' homes.

Students Speak Out
ON LOCAL ATMOSPHERE

Q "Amherst itself **doesn't really have a college town atmosphere**. South Campus and downtown Buffalo are pretty cool. There's usually something to do, but a car (or a friend with a car) is nice to have. The campus really grows on you."

Q "The area is terrific if you're into art and music. There are great scenes for hardcore and jam band aficionados. Also, while not as many popular acts stop here as in Toronto and New York, Buffalo is **one of the mainstay stops for most traveling bands**."

Q "There's **something for everyone in Buffalo**. Once in downtown, there's a gallery, theater, or movie house every few blocks. Buffalo boasts one of the most thriving art scenes in the state, from contemporary art to photography to sculpture and back again. The problem, it seems, is getting students to venture from the comfort of their dorms in Amherst into the city."

Q "There's a lot of fun stuff to do, including Sabres hockey and indie-rock shows. **The Bills play 30 minutes from campus** in Orchard Park."

STUDENT AUTHOR: The University at Buffalo exists in two parts of the city of Buffalo: Amherst and the Heights. Most students are immediately bored by the serenity of Amherst, but the Heights is a vibrant area chock full of shops, entertainment, and nightlife. Overall, Buffalo has a dynamic arts community, excellent museums, a fine orchestra, and the beloved Bills and Sabres, whose games most students go to see at least once.

5 Best Things
1 Strong academics
2 Laid-back people
3 The city of Buffalo
4 Last call at 4 a.m.
5 Lost cost of living

5 Worst Things
1 Parking
2 The football team
3 Dining halls
4 Large class sizes
5 Blizzards

Students Speak Out
ON FACILITIES

"The facilities on campus are all up-to-date and well maintained. All the buildings on North Campus are **connected through tunnels and bridges**, which is very useful on the winter walks to class. I have no problem with any of the complexes."

"Facilities on North Campus are **pretty modern**, and they offer you the luxury of walking inside through the academic buildings without having to go outside for the 10 months of the year when it's freezing."

"In general, the facilities on campus are fine. Alumni Arena is a perfect place to work out, play some basketball, or swim in an Olympic-size swimming pool. Aside from Alumni, the rest of the campus isn't exactly eye-candy. The academic buildings and dorms serve their respective purposes, but **nobody really went for broke when designing them**."

"The Student Union **leaves much to be desired**. It's a big open atrium that's never quite clean with bad food and poor acoustics. Fortunately, there are nicer places to visit and eat on campus."

STUDENT AUTHOR: Most students who come to UB hate the way North Campus looks at first; it's built like a '70s vision of a "college of the future." In time, though, nearly everyone gets used to the campus, and many grow to like it. South Campus has a more traditional feel. Its ivy-covered facilities are weathered and worn by the years, but its scenic quads and sloping lawns are beautiful.

Famous Alumni

Ellen Shulman Baker, Wolf Blitzer, Millard S. Drexler, Brad Grey, Howard Kurtz, Ronald A. Silver, Tom Toles, Harvey Weinstein

Students Speak Out
ON CAMPUS DINING

"It's not the best you'll find, but I think **it's edible in most places**. Bert's is one of the best. Pistachio's is pretty good, Putnam's serves its purpose, and the food in the Commons is pretty decent."

"**Two tips**: never eat anything called a 'Monster Burger,' and always get up in time for brunch on Saturday and Sunday mornings. Those brunches will be the best meals of your college career."

"**The campus food sucks**. The dining halls are always full of the same stuff you don't want because the quality is bad. The dining halls are very nice-looking, though, good lighting and good seats. Ellicott dining halls are the best."

"I really like the dining on campus. All sorts of foods are at your convenience and at a fairly reasonable price. The dining halls in Legoland (Ellicott) are **all-you-can-eat in a comfortable setting**."

"The food in the dorms is **very inconsistent**. Sometimes the food is great, and sometimes the best thing to eat is cereal."

STUDENT AUTHOR: Some students genuinely enjoy the campus food. But unless they're willing to eat the same three or four things every week, most students tire of it. North Campus's isolation means students are stuck with the campus-food monopoly one to three times a day. And with a couple of exceptions, the dining options in UB's food network are bland and overpriced.

Student Body

African American:	7%	Male/Female:	54/46%
Asian American:	9%	Out-of-State:	2%
Hispanic:	4%	International:	6%
Native American:	<1%	Unknown:	1%
White:	73%		

Popular Faiths: There are many Christians (Irish Catholics, especially), as well as Hindu and Muslims.

Gay Pride: UB has an open and vibrant queer culture, and more quiet gay students often find the privacy offered by UB's large campus to be liberating.

Economic Status: Most students are solidly middle-class and there is little classism present on campus.

Students Speak Out
ON DORMS

Q "The dorms are all right. I live in Governors, and I really love it here. **I highly recommend staying a night in the dorms** if you're deciding whether or not to come here—it's the only way you really get a feel for the place."

Q "Dorms—**not so hot**. Go to a private school if you want nice ones. Tiny rooms, ugly little floors, cinder block walls; but the décor doesn't really matter because you'll treasure the experience anyway."

Q "Ellicott, which everyone says looks like a stack of Legos, is kind of like **Governors's messier little brother**. He was the one who never cleaned his room and didn't really care if he showered that day. It's loud, it's fun, and my GPA is glad I didn't live there."

STUDENT AUTHOR: Only about one-third of undergraduates live on campus, so rooming at "Smellicott," "Governerds," or South Campus is an experience within an experience at UB. Most students love their experience in the dorms without having any special affection for the dorms themselves.

> **Did You Know?**
> 38% of undergrads live on campus.

Students Speak Out
ON GUYS & GIRLS

Q "The frat guys and sorority girls are **full of themselves**."

Q "Be sure to check out all the hot chicks in the first few weeks of school, while it's still warm, before they all migrate south for the winter. But be sure to **avoid Long Island girls**. They tend to be a bit pretentious."

Q "The girls in Buffalo are **like the wings**: the mild ones are hot, the medium ones are very hot, and the hot ones are very, very hot."

Q "Guys at this school are **either immature or quiet**. The immature guys are the one at the bars all up on every chick they see and throwing out their lines at you like those lines actually have ever worked on someone in the past."

STUDENT AUTHOR: In terms of looks, UB is a numbers game—there are thousands of hot guys and girls, but also, thousands of busted ones. UB's guy and girl scene is made up of different subcultures, as well. Many of those from upstate don't like Long Island girls, who are known for being rich, rude, and promiscuous. Conversely, those from downstate often find upstate students to be plain and dull.

> **Traditions**
>
> **Fall Fest and Spring Fest**
> A huge free concert held each fall and spring at Baird Point (weather permitting) featuring big-name acts.
>
> **Oozfest**
> An infamous campus-wide mud volleyball tournament held each spring.
>
> **Overall School Spirit**
> There is not much solidarity among students at UB. Most students are happy in their corner of the University, but can muster only lukewarm spirit for the larger institution.

Students Speak Out
ON ATHLETICS

Q "Though the school tries to promote it, **football doesn't get a lot of attention**, generally due to the fact that they lose a lot. When the basketball team gets on a roll, Alumni Arena is a great place to catch a game. Lots of students take part in a wide variety of intramurals and club sports."

Q "**UB just moved up to Division I**, and they have yet to become competitive or grow a fan base. It doesn't look like things are about to improve, either."

Q "Varsity sports would be big if the teams could put together some wins. The student body is **hungry for a good team**."

Q "**I'd rather go to Syracuse** and watch a real team play."

STUDENT AUTHOR: Despite huge levels of promotion, varsity sports (especially football) have failed to inspire much of a following on campus. Over 20,000 students usually come out for the home opener, but interest trails off as the losses mount. UB fields top-notch club teams, though, and many also join intramural sports leagues, which are generally taken very seriously at UB.

Students Speak Out
ON DRUG SCENE

Q "While it is definitely possible to get harder drugs like cocaine and ecstasy (mostly through sororities and seedy fraternities) around campus, softer drugs like marijuana and 'shrooms dominate the student population. Though there are periodic dry spells, **UB's proximity to Canada makes it easy to find pot** at fair prices with little hassle."

Q "If you are not interested in drugs, **they're easy to stay away from**. If you are interested in drugs, they're easy to find."

Q "The drug scene is **mostly hippies on pot and yuppies on coke**. Go, frats, go!"

STUDENT AUTHOR: It's easy to ignore the drug scene if you don't want to get involved, and the majority of students don't try anything more serious than pot, but nobody has any illusions that more serious abuses don't happen behind closed doors. Partly due to traffic in potent Canadian pot, the city of Buffalo is an infamous transfer point in the international drug trade.

15:1	Student-to-Faculty Ratio
88%	Freshman Retention Rate
34%	Four-Year Graduation Rate
69%	Financial Aid Applicants Receiving Aid

Students Speak Out
SAFETY & SECURITY

Q "North Campus is fairly safe, but South Campus is more urban and has a greater amount of crime. It's not uncommon to hear about **an occasional car break-in** or vandalism in University Heights."

Q "There is a **moderate amount of crime** in the University Heights area, though I have never heard of any major, serious crimes being committed on the dorms or on North Campus."

Q "South Campus lies at the edge of Buffalo's Eastside, **an area known for its crime and drug problems**. I live in University Heights, an area near South Campus. Last year, all the cars in my driveway were broken into; all the valuables from each car were stolen. The lesson I learned is that crime happens everywhere."

STUDENT AUTHOR: North Campus is nestled in Amherst, which is considered one of the safest towns in the U.S. However, South Campus is more dangerous. During the day, students can be confident in their safety, but at night, no one should walk anywhere alone.

Questions?

For more inside information and survival tips, pick up College Prowler's full-length book on this school, written by an actual student! Check it out at *www.collegeprowler.com*.

Students Speak Out
ON OVERALL EXPERIENCE

Q "I could not have had a more fulfilling college career. I switched my major twice, and you can do that here with so many programs to choose from. I have fallen in love with the area, the people, and the culture of Buffalo. It's vibrant and alive, and I have loved every minute of going to school here. **This place is full of idiosyncrasies**, but those are what make it great. You will not regret the choice to come to UB."

Q "I love UB—**good people and good parties**. You can't beat the price if you live in-state because the education you get for most of the majors is excellent. Most of the professors have won awards and written their own books."

Q "I have enjoyed UB to the fullest extent. I'm **happy to be here**, and I wouldn't trade it for anywhere else."

Q "I really enjoy being at this University. It is a great place, and **I love the city of Buffalo**. There is so much history, and it has so much potential (even if the city is in trouble now). UB is a major player in western New York life, and it has the potential to make even more of a difference for the city of Buffalo than it already has."

STUDENT AUTHOR: From the overwhelmingly diverse campus culture to the odd architecture, UB takes some getting used to. But nearly all students say they've gotten a lot out of their four (or five, or six) years here, and many simply love the place. If you're not intimidated by the diversity and the sprawling campus and if you get involved, you'll have an eclectic and inspirational experience. Students say UB is no utopia, but it's a lot of fun. And when it's over, nearly everyone remembers it fondly.

University of Alabama

739 University Boulevard; Tuscaloosa, AL 35487
(205) 348-6010; www.ua.edu

THE BASICS:

Acceptance Rate: 64%
Setting: Small City
F-T Undergrads: 19,361

SAT Range: 1000–1230*
Control: Public
Tuition: $16,518

Most Popular Majors: Business, Communications, Health Professions, Family Sciences, Engineering

*of 1600

Academics	B-	Guys	A-
Local Atmosphere	B	Girls	A
Safety & Security	B+	Athletics	A
Computers	B	Nightlife	A-
Facilities	A-	Greek Life	A
Campus Dining	B+	Drug Scene	B-
Off-Campus Dining	B	Campus Strictness	B-
Campus Housing	B-	Parking	C
Off-Campus Housing	A	Transportation	C
Diversity	C+	Weather	A

Students Speak Out
ON ACADEMICS

Q "Grad students are the best teachers. They're **more understanding**, and they know what it's like to be loaded down with work."

Q "Some teachers care a lot about their students' needs, while others don't care at all. The classes for your major are usually pretty interesting, while the **core classes are usually boring**."

Q "Most teachers I've encountered are **excellent**. There are, however, a few teachers I wish I had never encountered. The classes seem interesting based on the skill and likability of the teacher."

Q "Most of the **teachers are helpful** and generally care about their students. However, some are stuck on the PhD and they don't care whether you pass or fail or what problems or concerns you have about the class. My classes are interesting for the most part, but sometimes I feel like I'm on a merry-go-round, having the same information thrown at me over and over."

STUDENT AUTHOR: At the University of Alabama, the quality of the teachers and classes are, overall, exceptional. However, like at all universities, there are a few bad seeds. It's good to do a little research before picking a class. Just ask around—students love talking about teachers that made their learning experiences either better or worse. If you find yourself in a class bored or confused, contact your teacher through e-mail, during office hours, or by phone. If students talk to their teachers about problems, they can usually be fixed.

Students Speak Out
ON LOCAL ATMOSPHERE

Q "The atmosphere of **this town is incredible**! There are smaller colleges in the area, but it only makes Tuscaloosa more interesting. I would say you have to visit the Strip. It totally sums up the amazing atmosphere."

Q "There are two junior colleges within 15 minutes of UA. We have two malls in town, and there is also **a lot of historic stuff** that you can visit. Three of the buildings on campus were here during the Civil War and are still in use."

Q "The atmosphere in Tuscaloosa is a perfect example of the **common college town** stereotype. There's all-night partying, long nights at the bars on the Strip, and of course Alabama football games in the fall. Although partying and having fun with your friends is part of Tuscaloosa's nightlife for students, so is spending long hours in the University's libraries."

Q "The atmosphere provides a sense of community because of the population and size. There are many places for underage students to get in trouble, but also **many beautiful places** to go."

STUDENT AUTHOR: The University of Alabama is a typical Southern college town with a lot of attention devoted to football. To live in this town, you must be able to accept that Bama football takes over in the fall. When football season is over, there are still tons of things to do; on the Strip, you can always find good food and unique shopping. With all that's offered in Tuscaloosa, many students say there's never a dull moment.

Students Speak Out
ON FACILITIES

Q "Most of the buildings on campus are old and very **historic-looking**. That's not to say that they aren't good, but they aren't new. They are all designed in a Greek or Victorian architectural style. They are very beautiful and the Quad is very scenic. The athletic facilities are great."

Q "Most of the facilities are **clean and spacious**. It's evident that the University devotes a lot of time and money to making the environment here comfortable."

Q "The **Rec Center is great**, especially the new pool and waterslide. The Ferguson Center is nice as well. The facilities are maintained well."

Q "Many facilities are very nice. A few of the buildings seem ignored, but **there's always construction** going on to correct things."

Q "The athletic center is busy, but generally very well maintained. Computers are updated and clean. Student centers can range from grubby, to feeling as if you should be wearing a formal dress. The **aesthetics are gorgeous** and can really contribute to a feeling of academia."

STUDENT AUTHOR: UA students don't only enjoy using the facilities on campus, they also take pride in them. The Ferguson Center, or the student center, is one of the most visited facilities on campus. It offers students a post office, a supply store, numerous places to eat, and even pool tables; you can always find students there reading, studying, or hanging out around Starbucks. Overall, students enjoy the facilities and think the University strives to keep them clean and comfortable.

Famous Alumni
Shaun Alexander, Mel Allen, Hugo Black, Paul "Bear" Bryant, Winston Groom, Joe Namath, Latrell Sprewell, Bart Starr, E. O. Wilson

Students Speak Out
ON CAMPUS DINING

Q "The food **isn't too bad**. I recommend a meal plan for your first year, or at least your first semester, because it's a good way to meet people."

Q "The food on campus is **actually pretty good**! You have to try the Fresh Food Company at the Ferg; it's awesome!"

Q "Dining halls are **sufficient**, but off-campus eating is a great time because someone you know is always out and about."

Q "**Food on campus is good**, but the prices are high. Burke cooks the 'down-home' food, while the Fresh Food Company has a healthier selection."

Q "I personally **love the food** on campus. I don't know what I'd do without my meal plan at Burke. You always get a healthy all-you-can-eat meal there. The fellowships and friends that you make there are the best part."

STUDENT AUTHOR: Students enjoy the wide variety of food that UA's campus offers. The Ferg's Fresh Food Company seems to be the students' favorite. If you live on campus, meal plans are the way to go. However, they are not mandatory. If students need to grab a bite on the go, the Ferg offers many fast-food restaurants including Chick-fil-A and Burger King. If you're in a real rush, grab a snack from one of the many vending machines on campus by using your Action Card. If it is late, students can enjoy Paty's 24-Hour Diner. Also, many of the dorms have all-you-can-eat buffets for a set price.

Student Body

African American:	11%	Male/Female:	47/53%
Asian American:	1%	Out-of-State:	20%
Hispanic:	2%	International:	1%
Native American:	1%	Unknown:	0%
White:	84%		

Popular Faiths: UA boasts about 20 varied religious organizations (though predominantly Christian).

Gay Pride: The Queer-Straight Alliance organization is widely known around campus. However, the gay community is rather small and mostly quiet.

Economic Status: UA students hail from all economic backgrounds, though the Greeks are typically viewed as the "rich kids."

Students Speak Out
ON DORMS

Q "The dorms **aren't bad at all**. I lived in Rose Towers, which is an apartment-style coed dorm. We had three people sharing a two bedroom, one bathroom, fully-furnished apartment."

Q "It's college! Everyone has to experience dorm life! Tutwiler is the popular girls' dorm, which is fun because most of your friends will be living in there, just on different floors. That's the nice part—you don't have to drive to see them. You can just take the stairs or elevator. **Small rooms** and community bathrooms—it's up to you to make the most out of it."

Q "The only dorm I lived in was Tutwiler—it was an experience that I felt like I need to have as a freshman, but I **wouldn't want to do it again**."

STUDENT AUTHOR: **Tutwiler, the largest female dorm on campus, gets both good and bad reviews from students. If you are the type that needs your own space, then a place like Rose Towers may be best for you. Checking out all the dorms before deciding which one to live in is the best way to find where you belong; there are many to pick from and the options are growing.**

> **? Did You Know?**
> 29% of undergrads live on campus.

Students Speak Out
ON GUYS & GIRLS

Q "Just like everybody else, but I will say girls here are **beautiful Southern girls** and everybody dresses up to go out, so we always look nice. Guys are shaggy-haired, laid-back guys, and most of them always look really nice as well."

Q "There are plenty of guys and girls on this campus. Like anywhere else you might go, there will be some hot people and some not-so-hot people, some nice people and some not-so-nice people. But around here, there do seem to be **more nice people** than usual."

Q "If you are looking for **hot guys** with lots of ambition, check out the business school. Sorority girls have a reputation for being snotty, but I've found that's not always the case."

STUDENT AUTHOR: **There are more girls than guys here, and the guys say they're in heaven, but the girls aren't complaining, either. You won't find everyone to be a supermodel, but don't fret if that's what you're into. There's plenty of eye-candy to go around. With so many hot students roaming about, it is easy to hook up. The guys at the business school enjoy a reputation for hotness, and the girls are just gorgeous in general.**

> **Traditions**
>
> **Chalking the Quad**
> Organizations and students competing in Homecoming elections write promotional messages in colorful chalk.
>
> **The Iron Bowl**
> Auburn vs. UA is the biggest football game of the season; don't expect to get cheap tickets.
>
> **Overall School Spirit**
> Football is like a holiday here, and the students look forward to it all year. Sitting in the student section during one game will make you an instant Bama fan.

Students Speak Out
ON ATHLETICS

Q "Football, football, and football. In the fall, Tide fans are full of spirit and tradition. Mark your calendar—every Saturday will be booked for Alabama football. **Roll Tide!**"

Q "Varsity sports, and especially football, are the major focus of the entire University. Sports provide a social environment more than anything. Everyone goes to football games whether they like football or not because it's 'the thing to do.' I'm a huge Bama fan, and to me, there's nothing better than **85,000 people going nuts** at a Bama football game."

Q "Sports are a **great way to get involved** and meet people. Football games are the highlight of the year."

STUDENT AUTHOR: **Football is almost a religion in Alabama. It's a tradition that takes over the school and even the town. Students count down the days until the fall in anticipation of the start of the football frenzy, and people from all over pack into the Bryant-Denny Stadium for every home game to show their Crimson Pride. Game days are a tradition on this campus that will never get dull.**

Students Speak Out
ON DRUG SCENE

Q "There are going to be drugs everywhere you go, but the drug scene here **isn't bad at all**. Of course, you'll hear things every now and then, but this is mostly a drinking school."

Q "I don't know anything about the drug scene here. **I know it's out there**, and I've heard people talking about marijuana and once even cocaine, but I've never seen it. I tend to stay away from people who are a part of it and places where it would probably be found."

Q "People are always **looking for Adderall** during exam time, and it is easy to get. During exam time, it is everywhere."

STUDENT AUTHOR: There is a rumor that cocaine is big at UA; however, most students say they have never seen it. The most common drug among UA students is Adderall, which students use to stay up late cramming for exams. Marijuana is also popular for some, but police are usually looking out for it. One thing for sure is that this town is a drinking town.

19:1	Student-to-Faculty Ratio
87%	Freshman Retention Rate
38%	Four-Year Graduation Rate
73%	Financial Aid Applicants Receiving Aid

Students Speak Out
SAFETY & SECURITY

Q "You **just have to be smart**. Lock your car doors and bike. Don't leave your book bag or purse idle. It's just like anywhere else."

Q "I would say that safety and security are above average. Crime is not bad, and the police are always pretty much on top of things. The **dorms are patrolled well**, and most all-girls dorms even have parking lot escorts. Also, the most commonly frequented areas are well lit and have emergency phones installed nearby."

Q "I **haven't had much of a problem** with the security on campus. Now, I have heard stories of a few bad things happening over the past couple of years, but any university will have isolated occurrences."

STUDENT AUTHOR: At UA, there's no reason to walk alone at night since the school offers a free escort service, the Bama Escort Service, which provides students with free rides between campus locations. There are also plenty of emergency phones located all around campus if students have any problems.

Questions?
For more inside information and survival tips, pick up College Prowler's full-length book on this school, written by an actual student! Check it out at *www.collegeprowler.com*.

Students Speak Out
ON OVERALL EXPERIENCE

Q "I love everything about the University of Alabama—its traditions, its sports, and its activities. It feels like home. The minute you set foot on the Quad, or whenever you hear the fight song being played after one of the best college football teams in history scores a touchdown, you get chills. Game day is **one of the best experiences** of your life."

Q "I couldn't be any happier. I went to a small private school freshman year, and by October, I was ready to split. I wanted the **big football games**, Greek life, nightlife on the Strip, and the diversity of the many students."

Q "My overall experience at Alabama has been the best experience of my life. I have met so many great people and made friendships of a lifetime. The **education is great**, and the campus is absolutely beautiful. I would never choose to go to another school."

Q "I just graduated, and I am quite thankful that I chose UA. The school's traditions drew me in, and even now I take pride in having been a part of them. There is no doubt in my mind that I received a top education and an **excellent college experience** overall."

STUDENT AUTHOR: University of Alabama students constantly brag about their school's traditions and spirit, and their pride is shown throughout the town. Some say it's the incredible education that drew them here, and others say it's Bama football that brought them to this Southern school. But no matter what reason these students choose to come to UA, most believe it was the best choice they could have made.

University of Arizona

1042 East South Campus Drive; Tuscon, AZ 210066
(520) 621-3237; www.arizona.edu

THE BASICS:

Acceptance Rate: 81%
Setting: Urban
F-T Undergrads: 25,964

SAT Range: 980–1220*
Control: Public
Tuition: $18,408

Most Popular Majors: Business, Social Sciences, Biological/Life Sciences, Communications, Psychology

*of 1600

Academics	B	Guys	A+
Local Atmosphere	B	Girls	A+
Safety & Security	B-	Athletics	A
Computers	A-	Nightlife	B+
Facilities	A	Greek Life	B+
Campus Dining	A	Drug Scene	B-
Off-Campus Dining	A-	Campus Strictness	B
Campus Housing	B-	Parking	D+
Off-Campus Housing	A+	Transportation	B-
Diversity	B	Weather	A-

Students Speak Out
ON ACADEMICS

Q "A lot of teachers are very accommodating and understanding, but it all depends on the class and its size. I'd say, as a whole, **I had a lot of good teachers** and only disliked one each semester. Just do your work, go to office hours, and they like you."

Q "Classes are interesting depending on how good the professors are, how engaging the students are, and **how drunk I am at the time**."

Q "At the University of Arizona, they offer a place online where you can go and **find out the ratings on a particular teacher**. They have students grade the teachers based on respect and all that jazz. It was pretty helpful to me."

Q "In my experience so far, I have found the teachers to be very good, except for the occasional math teacher that **doesn't speak very good English**. They provide ample office hours, and there is a lot of free tutoring for all classes on campus."

STUDENT AUTHOR: So let's get this straight: the instructors are good, and non-English speaking TAs are bad (or just misunderstood). Sometimes, professors even give out their home phone numbers. What a great idea! Again, because it is a public university, general education classes tend to be large, and the instructor may appear to be unapproachable. You'll get both good and bad professors, but the same could be said of TAs, employers, and other University personnel. You just have to deal with it.

Students Speak Out
ON LOCAL ATMOSPHERE

Q "**There isn't really anything spectacular** about Tucson. The University is all it really has going for it. So, unless you're a student, or you just like to be hammered all the time, it's not really worth the visit."

Q "I would say, overall, people are friendly. I've never had anyone jump me or anything like that, and I'm not fearful for my life. **There are no other universities in town**, but there's one close enough to keep the rivalry spirit up. I like to go to the coffeeshop on campus. It's a good place to study and meet people."

Q "To be perfectly honest, if it weren't for UA, there wouldn't be much else to do in Tucson. At the same time, that just goes to show that **Tucson is a college town** because most of the nightlife revolves around the students."

Q "Some of the people are pretty nice, but many of them can be very **rude, unfriendly, and flat-out idiotic**. Plus, they can't drive for crap!"

STUDENT AUTHOR: Tucson is a chill town. It's the second-largest city in Arizona, but it's still vastly different from Phoenix in terms of vibe and size. Phoenix, Arizona's capital, has enough going on to keep its constituents cheering, clubbing, or eating out—that is, until they finally get sick of the California-like traffic jams. Phoenix is to New York (fast, crowded, and important) as Tucson is to the California coastline (relaxed, spread out, and still important but in a different kind of way).

Students Speak Out
ON FACILITIES

Q "Facilities here are always clean and are useful to the majority of students, but **they can get crowded**. Three especially crowded places: library computer lab, the student union, and the student recreation center."

Q "There's a student union that was recently built. There is also an underground building called the **Integrated Learning Center** that recently opened and is just amazing. It has a new computer lab and many new and awesome classrooms and furniture."

Q "We have a new student union with a food court downstairs as well as a Mexican restaurant, a coffee bar, and a **cafeteria-style restaurant** upstairs. It also has a mini mart, a hair salon, and a travel agency."

Q "For the most part, we have state-of-the-art facilities. **The Rec Center is beautiful**, and we just got a new student union that's really nice. Our bookstore has two levels. It's a beautiful campus."

Q "I think all the facilities here are **among the best in the nation**, and the campus is growing."

STUDENT AUTHOR: The underground center consists of glass study rooms, tons of computers, a multimedia zone, and fancy classrooms, all of which suggest that the UA is running out of surface area. The older buildings on campus, while nostalgic and historic, are kind of a nuisance. The bathrooms' pipes creak, the seats are small, and the acoustics create eerie echoes. But most of the UA really is well kept, and you can tell that a lot of money goes into the upkeep of new facilities.

Famous Alumni

Gilbert Arenas, Joan Ganz Cooney, Robert A. Eckert, Greg Kinnear, Craig T. Nelson, Geraldo Rivera

Students Speak Out
ON CAMPUS DINING

Q "Food is a problem on campus because it's pretty darn good. **I put on the Freshman 15 in my junior year**. The Cactus Grill cafeteria has a nice selection for breakfast, lunch, and dinner. It serves smoothies, bagels, fruit, and salad."

Q "Food on campus is great. There's starting to be a lot more options, making for more variety. However, don't get too attached to these places or you will be poor. My favorites are On Deck Deli, **Panda Express, Pei Wei, and Chipotle**."

Q "The food on campus is good. **You can put money on your student ID** card and use that at all food places on campus. It's great for not having to have cash on you."

Q "It's as good as it gets. The University of Arizona has very good student union food. If you don't want that, they have Domino's, McDonald's, Panda Express, Chick-fil-A, and Bruegger's Bagels where you can **purchase food with your Cat Card**."

Q "**The food is pretty good**. A new student union was built. It has a McDonald's, Domino's, Panda Express, and On Deck Deli."

STUDENT AUTHOR: UA has everything you need to gain the dreaded Freshman 15. On the flipside, however, UA also has a nice recreation center where you can work it all off. Our Student Union Memorial has more places to eat than the food courts in most shopping malls. Be careful, though, because it's easy to deplete your funds as you sample the various culinary offerings that abound.

Students Speak Out
ON DORMS

Q "I hear that living in a dorm is a lot **cheaper than living off campus**. However, I don't know if it's worth it to risk shacking up with a potentially psychotic roommate."

Q "**Coronado is pretty much all freshmen**, and it's pretty social—it's loud. I didn't have a hard time studying, but others have. I liked living in it because it was all first-year students. The other dorm that's popular is Colonia De La Paz. La Paz is really nice! It's new and pretty spacious, and it's in a great location. However, it's not all freshmen, and the bathrooms are community-style."

Q "**I recommend Kaibab/Huachuca** or Monzanita/Mohave. They're not the prettiest, but the rooms are the biggest, and this may be important when you have to share a room."

STUDENT AUTHOR: **Make sure you take a virtual tour before you decide on which dorm will suit you best. Take into consideration more than just price, since placement on campus, date of completion, and layout are important, too. All of the dorms that I've been in are small. I think Maricopa Hall might escape that tag, but dorm life is still dorm life.**

> **Did You Know?**
> 20% of undergrads live on campus.

Students Speak Out
ON GUYS & GIRLS

Q "There are a lot of California people here. There are also a lot from Chicago, New York, New Jersey, and of course, Arizona. I think the girls are hot. There are lots of blondes with blue eyes and tan skin—**all that *Baywatch* stuff**. Guys are the same. They have spiky hair, work out a lot, and drive nice cars."

Q "To be completely honest, **there are a lot more pretty girls** than there are nice-looking guys on campus. But I've found that most of those pretty girls are only at the University to be in a sorority."

Q "Guys here are so hot. Especially if you like ones in T-shirts and jeans or board shorts, sandals, and sunglasses. Guys at Arizona are **pretty much your all-American boys**."

STUDENT AUTHOR: We, at the UA, are not "everyday people." We are beautiful and hot. Well, most of us are anyway. The non-hot people would probably be hot anywhere else, but next to the cream-of-the-crop, super-hot UA students, they only come off as average looking. That's how hot we are. Hopefully, such claims won't make prospective students accumulate any eating disorders. You really should come as you are. If you're not hot, we just won't talk to you.

Traditions

The Bell
The bell housed on the USS Arizona was one of two bells rescued from the ship after Pearl Harbor and now rests in the clock tower of the Student Union.

"A" Mountain
At the beginning of each school year, freshmen repaint the "A" on "A" Mountain. For more than 100 years the "A" remains a Tucson/Wildcat landmark.

Overall School Spirit
School spirit here is pretty high, and is actually made sexy by the ever-popular girls' short shorts with the letters U and A printed on each butt cheek.

Students Speak Out
ON ATHLETICS

Q "If the sport is basketball or football, then it's huge. **The other varsity sports aren't as big**, but they still get attention. A few people play intramurals, but I don't hear much about them."

Q "Sports are a very big deal. Men's basketball and women's softball is doing really well, too. There's **a huge rivalry with Arizona State**."

Q "I played **IM softball and flag football**, and both of them were a blast."

Q "**The basketball team dominates** Arizona as far as sports are concerned because they are really, really good."

STUDENT AUTHOR: **UA is a huge sports school. Intramural sports are organized through the student recreation center and are wildly popular. The sunny weather in Tucson allows for a wide variety of these intramurals. The University community is especially passionate when it comes to basketball. We love Coach Lute Olson, and we will kick your butt if you say anything bad about him. We cheer wildly at games, we refuse to study during the Final Four, and we rioted when we made it to the national championships.**

Students Speak Out
ON DRUG SCENE

Q "I know a few dealers who've told me how easy it is to **sell drugs to students**. But there are too many dealers and users to be caught, so drug activity on campus is pretty rampant."

Q "If you are looking for them, they aren't hard to find, but if you don't want them, there's no pressure. **They don't have an overwhelming presence** on campus."

Q "There are plenty of people who take drugs, and you usually read about **someone being busted for marijuana**. If you want some, you can find some; if you want to stay away from it, that's not too hard, either."

STUDENT AUTHOR: Say no to drugs. Well, at least say no to the really hard ones. Marijuana seems to make a lot of friends on this campus. Are you going to be one of these friends? You don't have to experiment in college. And many "sober" AU students aren't deprived or setback in any way. Use your head and make decisions you're comfortable with. Otherwise, you'll end up feeling ripped off.

19:1	Student-to-Faculty Ratio
79%	Freshman Retention Rate
32%	Four-Year Graduation Rate
70%	Financial Aid Applicants Receiving Aid

Students Speak Out
SAFETY & SECURITY

Q "There are security phones all over campus, and **several buildings are open for 24 hours**. The University also has its own police force."

Q "I don't really have any complaints about the security on campus. I had two bikes stolen while I was here, but it was off campus and I had really crappy locks, so I blame myself. If you do plan to take a bike, **make sure you get a U-Lock** and not a lame cable lock like I had."

Q "I've never had a safety problem on campus, but I do hear of **occasional theft and violence**. Also, there's been a recent outbreak of sexual assaults on women, but I've never personally had a real problem."

STUDENT AUTHOR: The biggest complaint UA students have, according to the police Web site, is bike theft. Personal safety is a little better. The UA has placed emergency blue-light phones sporadically throughout the square mile of campus. Even if a crime victim is unable to talk into the phone, an officer will respond to the location if the button is pressed.

> **Questions?**
> For more inside information and survival tips, pick up College Prowler's full-length book on this school, written by an actual student! Check it out at *www.collegeprowler.com.*

Students Speak Out
ON OVERALL EXPERIENCE

Q "Sometimes I wish I was somewhere else, but it's usually during finals week. **Overall, everything's great**. I've had a really good experience here, and I have little to no complaints."

Q "Learning in college is great and **very beneficial in the long run**, but I never stop wishing I were somewhere else. Just knowing that I won't be here forever keeps me from driving a needle through my temple."

Q "**I made friends and memories that will last me a lifetime**. I really didn't think much of the quality of my education when I was there, but I've noticed that Arizona actually made me pretty smart now that I'm out in the real world and attending graduate school."

Q "I'm so happy at Arizona! I couldn't see myself anywhere else, and I think that's how it is for most people! I don't know many people who had a bad experience here! **It's amazing!**"

STUDENT AUTHOR: I'm going to go ahead and tip my hat to the UA. It's a great school in a chill city that has nice weather and beautiful, beautiful people. I've had long talks with friends in parking lots. I read John Updike for the first time here, rediscovered Faulkner in the Modern Languages Building, and pulled an all-nighter in the library. I stumbled through calculus with a teacher who hardly spoke English. How can I talk trash about my alma mater? Yeah, the UA has its problems, but how many students do you know that demand perfection. If you want a decent education and an interesting experience, you'll get them both at the UA.

University of Central Florida

4000 Central Florida Boulevard; Orlando, FL 32816
(407) 823-2000; www.ucf.edu

THE BASICS:

Acceptance Rate: 50%
Setting: Urban
F-T Undergrads: 31,050

SAT Range: 1070–1260*
Control: Public
Tuition: $17,821

Most Popular Majors: Business, Education, Health Sciences, Psychology, Liberal Arts

*of 1600

Academics	B-	Guys	B+
Local Atmosphere	A	Girls	A
Safety & Security	A-	Athletics	B-
Computers	B	Nightlife	A
Facilities	A	Greek Life	B+
Campus Dining	A	Drug Scene	C+
Off-Campus Dining	A-	Campus Strictness	C
Campus Housing	C	Parking	C-
Off-Campus Housing	A	Transportation	B+
Diversity	B	Weather	A

Students Speak Out
ON ACADEMICS

Q "Most general education courses tend to be **large and boring**, but once you're in your core track the subject material is much more interesting."

Q "I think the **teachers are ridiculous**. Out of my four years of experience at UCF, I have encountered about three good professors."

Q "A lot of teachers here **really care about educating their students** and really helping them get the most out of their classes. Then there are a few bad apples that take attendance and lecture word-for-word out of the book."

Q "Most of the teachers are accommodating and **flexible with their schedules**. My teachers have gone out of their way to make sure the students are really learning the material."

Q "For a lot of my teachers, **English is a second language**."

STUDENT AUTHOR: Many UCF professors are passionate and genuinely interested in their students learning. Like anywhere else, you have your bad seeds thrown into the mix. Most teachers will assist you anyway that they can, and they're there to work with you and your needs. I would advise asking around to see what professors are well-liked and which classes are most interesting. Students are a fountain of knowledge when it comes to recommending professors and courses. Be sure to listen when they give you their two cents.

Students Speak Out
ON LOCAL ATMOSPHERE

Q "There are **plenty of downtown areas** catering to all different interests, such as dance clubs, bars, unique shops, bookstores, and scenic parks."

Q "Rollins College is the only other university in the area. I'm pretty sure **it's a private school**, too."

Q "The atmosphere is **young, active, and trendy**. Orlando has a fun relaxing atmosphere as well. It's as fast or as slow-paced as you would like it to be."

Q "**Stay away from Orange Blossom Trail** (OBT, a road that runs through downtown) and you'll be fine."

Q "UCF is about **an hour from Disney World** and 30 minutes from Universal Studios. There are also several sports teams in the area worth seeing."

STUDENT AUTHOR: It's no understatement to say that you'll never be bored in Orlando as long as you take advantage of what the city has to offer. There's something for everyone, whether you favor a fast and upbeat tempo or a slow, relaxing day enjoying the outdoors. For the upbeat person, a day at the theme parks is only minutes away. For the laid-back person, there are numerous parks and recreational facilities around Orlando that you can enjoy, whether you fancy a canoe ride down a lazy river or a bicycle ride through one of the local parks.

5 Best Things	5 Worst Things
1 Athletic center	1 No parking
2 Spirit Week	2 Apathetic students
3 Wackadoo's	3 Lack of spirit
4 Wireless Internet	4 No football field
5 Campus shuttles	5 Rain storms

Students Speak Out
ON FACILITIES

Q "The facilities on campus are **nice and reliable**. Most of the facilities on campus are relatively new as well."

Q "Facilities are extremely nice and well-kept. So much money has been spent on **state-of-the-art technology** and equipment in every building—and it shows."

Q "**The gym is top-notch**. However, you should workout in the morning or you'll be waiting in line for everything. There's a lot of eye candy to help motivate your workout."

Q "Lets just say **we're getting our money's worth** when it comes to the facilities at UCF. Everything we need is only walking distance away—it's amazing!"

Q "The gym is beautiful, as is the student center; the computers are okay, but they seem a little slow. **There's an abundance of labs**. The lab in the Student Government building is very accommodating."

STUDENT AUTHOR: **The UCF gym has received great reviews from students and critics alike! It's definitely worth checking out. Not only can you workout there, but you can partake in Wellness Center programs, such as biofeedback and massages. Group exercise classes are energetic, fast-paced, and offer a rewarding workout with a chance to meet tons of people. Aside from the gym, the facilities at UCF are new and usually clean. The school hasn't been around long enough to have deteriorated or aged just yet. When that time comes, maintenance and administration will probably keep everything up-to-par.**

Famous Alumni

Lee Constantine, Daunte Culpepper, Robert Damron, Erika Dunlap, Cheryl Hines, Asante Samuel, Al Weiss

Students Speak Out
ON CAMPUS DINING

Q "The meal plan has such a variety; I never get tired of the assortment. I love how the chef makes your **food to order**."

Q "**Wackadoo's is the place to go** and is the social spot on campus. It serves great food, cold beers, and tasty snacks."

Q "The dining hall is great because it's all you can eat, and you can't beat that. The choice of food **accommodates everybody**."

Q "I worked for two months with dining services, so first-hand, the food is pretty good. Don't walk back to the meal-plan kitchen—it might change your mind (**bad smell**)."

Q "There's so much to pick from, as far as food on campus. My **favorite spot is Wackadoo's**. Most other spots on campus are certainly edible as well, though."

STUDENT AUTHOR: **You'll never go hungry while living on or visiting the UCF campus; there's enough variety for everyone. Conveniently, you can find tons of fast food all over the campus. There really is every type of food, ranging from hot dogs to Mexican. By majority vote, Wackadoo's is the top choice of places to eat on the UCF campus. It aims to please students, featuring things such as the "Fat Ass Burger," for the hungry student. Many meet up and work on group projects while taking advantage of the food establishments on campus. Although it doesn't seem to be a place to eat every meal, it provides students with easy eating and variety.**

Student Body

African American:	9%	Male/Female:	46/54%
Asian American:	6%	Out-of-State:	7%
Hispanic:	14%	International:	1%
Native American:	<1%	Unknown:	1%
White:	69%		

Popular Faiths: Christianity, Judaism, and Catholicism are the most popular religions at UCF.

Gay Pride: GLBT (Gay, Lesbian, and Bisexual Student Union) is a club at UCF consisting of students who share an interest in GLBT issues and concerns.

Economic Status: UCF is a state school. Therefore, its students receive a large amount of financial aid. Students vary from underprivileged to upper-class.

Students Speak Out
ON DORMS

Q "Why would you live on campus when there are so many **affordable off-campus apartments** right around the corner?"

Q "I met lots of people when I lived in Hercules. It was a **great social experience**."

Q "Academic Village is pretty nice, but the others are dumps. They're all way overpriced, and you can find much better places for $100; it's sometimes **$200 cheaper off campus**. Avoid Pegasus Landing at all costs. It's dirty and there have been numerous robberies and car thefts."

STUDENT AUTHOR: **There are many options available for all types of students, whether you're an incoming freshman or an upperclassman. UCF's housing service has dorms that will satisfy any incoming student. These include the magnificent Nike and Hercules complexes. The kicker here is that there are also many dorms, including Pegasus Landing and Apollo, that are revolting to just about everyone and aren't entirely safe. If you're planning to live on campus, Academic Village is the way to go. These dorms are new, and they're set up as apartment-style housing.**

 Did You Know?
21% of undergrads live on campus.

Students Speak Out
ON GUYS & GIRLS

Q "Everywhere you look on campus, there are **young, beautiful people**. Hugh Hefner should just set up a booth on campus!"

Q "**Boys are boys anywhere you go**, and UCF is no exception. You got hot ones and not-so-hot ones. Look out for the not-so-hot guys posing as hot ones."

Q "At UCF, male **pickings are slim**. There are lots of skinny, pretty girls, though."

Q "There are hot girls and guys everywhere. **Everyone is nice and friendly**, and it's really easy to make friends. Just be careful—a lot of the guys are players—or at least try to be."

STUDENT AUTHOR: **Overall, there are more girls than guys, so the guys have a better selection. Not to worry, though, because UCF's social scene makes it easy to meet people no matter what. The student body enjoys their mating and dating, and it's an important part of many students' lives. The campus seems to be fairly promiscuous as well. Not too many students are into relationships at UCF, most just want to explore, and conquer, all their options.**

Traditions

U-C-F
Over the years, many acronyms slandering UCF administration have sprung up including: Under Construction Forever.

Overall School Spirit
Every fall semester, UCF has a designated week called Spirit Week. The highlight of Spirit Week is "Spirit Splash." On this one occasion, students are permitted to jump into the Reflection Pond. Special preparation goes into this event, and thousands of students join in the fun and jump in the fountain while a band plays in the background.

Students Speak Out
ON ATHLETICS

Q "The tailgating during varsity football games probably gets more attention than the game itself. Our basketball team made the **NCAA tournament** in 2005!"

Q "I really enjoy **IM sports** at UCF. This program has also allowed me to continue being a referee official while getting paid a minimal amount."

Q "Our sports teams are getting better each year. As for intramurals, it's run by up-tight officials who look for ways to **take all the fun out of IM** as much as they can."

Q "IM is huge! **Varsity sports?** Do we have those?"

STUDENT AUTHOR: **While most couldn't tell you a thing about the athletes at UCF, they definitely could talk your ear off about their tailgating experiences. Students highly anticipate the football season and the tailgating parties that precede the games. The partying outside the stadium often prevents students from actually attending the football game itself due to their high levels of intoxication. This is a problem that UCF officials and UCF administration are trying to correct.**

Students Speak Out
ON DRUG SCENE

Q "There are **no drugs on campus**. Many students smoke marijuana and drink alcohol outside of campus events."

Q "My friends and I are drug free. We still go to parties and no one treats us differently just because we don't do drugs. There is **no peer pressure at all**, in that regard."

Q "Be careful, **drugs are everywhere**! Sometimes it seems like the whole town of Orlando is on cocaine. Other colleges in the area are no exception, either."

STUDENT AUTHOR: UCF students study hard and play hard. However, the drug scene on campus doesn't compare to the one around campus and in Orlando. Marijuana is used by many students. Study drugs and pills, such as Adderall, are also popular among students. The school offers counseling and educational programs about both drugs and alcohol. The Counseling Center can also give advice and support if you're having a problem with drugs.

30:1	Student-to-Faculty Ratio
84%	Freshman Retention Rate
31%	Four-Year Graduation Rate
83%	Financial Aid Applicants Receiving Aid

Students Speak Out
SAFETY & SECURITY

Q "There seems to be enough police around campus, so **I've never really felt unsafe**. Actually, I feel more apprehensive walking around in my own hometown at night."

Q "**Security is okay**; I never have had any concerns. This is certainly not the case at many colleges in America, so I feel lucky."

Q "Security on campus seems to be **very strict and clean-cut**. With the exception of a few loose cannons, officers take care of situations in a professional manner. They're there to help the students, not to get them in trouble."

Q "Drive very slow on campus or the cops will get you. I know a friend who got pulled over for **doing 27 in a 25** miles-per-hour zone!"

STUDENT AUTHOR: UCF has its own police station located on campus, and many officers can be found patrolling the campus. Always drive with caution and obey the speed limits; there's often an officer with a radar gun waiting in the wings. I guess if this is the worst thing that UCF students have to worry about, then it can't be all that bad. Right?

Questions?
For more inside information and survival tips, pick up College Prowler's full-length book on this school, written by an actual student! Check it out at *www.collegeprowler.com*.

Students Speak Out
ON OVERALL EXPERIENCE

Q "I love UCF! I have made some amazing, wonderful, **life-long friends** and have had a blast while getting a great education."

Q "I like the school a lot. I wish I was at a smaller school. There are **too many students**, and UCF needs to cut down on freshman admissions— please. Classes are just to large because of this."

Q "I have had **an overall good experience** so far. I kind of wish I went to a school with more of a college town atmosphere. Sometimes Orlando is just too 'touristy' for my liking."

Q "I'm so happy that I chose UCF for my college career! I would never change it even if I had the opportunity to. **I chose UCF over the University of Hawaii at Manoa**, and am extraordinarily happy that I picked Orlando."

Q "Overall, UCF is a good school that's **improving every year**. Things are definitely going to change here."

STUDENT AUTHOR: UCF is growing by leaps and bounds. The students love to hang out, and they all know how to have a good time. There's so much to do and there's something for everyone. Do you really need any more reasons to go to college in Florida? Orlando is an exciting city with tons of attractions and activities available to all. In many ways, going to school at UCF resembles a four-year vacation (Disney on Sunday, classes on Monday). Downtown Orlando on a Friday night can, at times, seem like Mardi Gras, and City Walk on a Saturday night isn't to be missed. Floridians are welcoming and friendly, and most students make friends that will last a lifetime.

University of Chicago

5801 South Ellis Avenue; Chicago, IL 60637
(773) 702-1234; www.uchicago.edu

THE BASICS:

Acceptance Rate: 38%
Setting: Urban
F-T Undergrads: 4,851

SAT Range: 1330–1530*.
Control: Private
Tuition: $36,891

Most Popular Majors: Social Sciences, Biology, English, History, Physical Sciences

*of 1600

Academics	A+	Guys	C+
Local Atmosphere	A-	Girls	C
Safety & Security	B-	Athletics	C+
Computers	A	Nightlife	B
Facilities	B+	Greek Life	B
Campus Dining	B+	Drug Scene	B+
Off-Campus Dining	A	Campus Strictness	A+
Campus Housing	B	Parking	D-
Off-Campus Housing	B+	Transportation	A
Diversity	A	Weather	D

Students Speak Out
ON ACADEMICS

Q "**I am satisfied with my education** here. With the exception of one, all of my teachers have been professors, and many of them are also doing research."

Q "My math teacher was a sixth-year grad student who recently accepted a prestigious fellowship for next year (after he gets his PhD). He often went off on **interesting tangents**, sometimes talking about things totally unrelated to math (his experience with skydiving or the Cricket World Championship). He also taught us how to solve Rubik's cubes."

Q "Academics are **tough but manageable**. It depends on classes and teachers. For the most part, the professors are willing to work with you and are usually readily available."

Q "**They're pretty good**. Make sure you shop around, ask around, and don't settle for less. Like any school, they just aren't going to give you the best. You have to put a lot of effort into it yourself."

STUDENT AUTHOR: The University of Chicago is one of the premier academic institutions in the world. Don't be surprised to see your professors quoted in the newspaper, cited in your textbooks (if they haven't authored them outright), or on the shelf at Borders or Barnes & Noble. At the same time, professors are required to teach undergraduates and often take outstanding students under their wing. If you are willing to work hard, it will be a rewarding experience.

Students Speak Out
ON LOCAL ATMOSPHERE

Q "Chicago is a huge city. There are plenty of things to do; **it all depends on what you like**. I shop a lot on the weekends and watch movies or go out to eat with friends."

Q "Hyde Park has a very contradictory atmosphere. **Rich, privileged teenagers** and sheltered academics reside next to a very historically-entrenched neighborhood and just a few miles away lays one of the most crime-ridden areas in the city. There are restaurants and fabulous bookstores here, but not much else. It becomes imperative to get out of the neighborhood from time to time, so as to keep your sanity."

Q "Chicago rocks; you do have to know where to go, though. It's very easy to lock yourself in your room and hate the fact that you don't go out of Hyde Park. **Chinatown is a great place to eat**; the North Side and Wrigleyville are awesome places to hang out; Wicker Park is also cool."

Q "It all depends. You will find that there is more to the city than meets the eye. Lake Michigan shore is near, and the parks are nice. Downtown is close as well. **Never walk alone at night**."

STUDENT AUTHOR: The University capitalizes on its location by heavily subsidizing student trips to cultural events throughout the city, like the Lyric Opera, the Field Museum, and the occasional Cubs game. There are the usual tourist attractions (Michigan Avenue, the Museums, Navy Pier, and more), but once you get past them, you realize that Chicago is a city of serious depth.

5 Best Things	5 Worst Things
1 The Core	1 The Core
2 O-Week	2 The weather
3 The House system	3 The Reg
4 Scav Hunt	4 The swim test
5 *Kuviasungnerk*	5 Cell phone reception

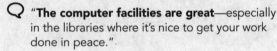

Students Speak Out
ON FACILITIES

Q "**The computer facilities are great**—especially in the libraries where it's nice to get your work done in peace."

Q "**Our student center is nice**—it has this study lounge that's like a big living room, and there's always a fire going in the winter. I study there all the time."

Q "The student center, Reynold's Club, is nice. You'll always **end up running into someone you know in there**. The athletic facilities at the Henry Crown field house aren't so good, but they are planning to open a brand new athletic center next year that is supposed to be state-of-the-art. Students don't have to pay to get into any of those."

Q "The facilities are okay. They just built a few new dorms, and a new dining hall was constructed a few years ago. **The campus buildings are beautiful, though**, with gothic architecture everywhere."

STUDENT AUTHOR: The University has, over the past several years, undergone a campus-wide effort to either refurbish or replace outdated facilities. In 1999, the Max Palevsky Residential Commons opened, consisting of three new 250-person dormitories clustered around a new dining hall. Half of the freshmen are assigned to one of the postmodern cubes. The Ratner Athletic Center opened in 2003, which also saw the opening of a new botanical garden on the midway right next to the ice skating rink, and a new building for the Graduate School of Business was completed in the summer of 2004.

Famous Alumni
John Ashcroft, Ed Asner, Milton Friedman, Phillup Glass, Edwin Hubble, Carl Sagan, John Paul Stephens, Paul Wolfowitz

Students Speak Out
ON CAMPUS DINING

Q "**All of the dining halls are decent**, but they lack variety and enough healthy food. The coffee shops that have area restaurants' takeout food help provide variety."

Q "The food on campus is good—for a massive catering service. **Bartlett is the best dining hall**. Uncle Joe's Coffee Shop (located in the Reynolds club) is also a good place to eat and get drinks. There's also Hutch, but it's fast food stuff."

Q "The food here is college food—**nothing worth noting**, and occasionally something that should be actively forgotten. With the opening of Bartlett, I thought there was a decent eating location, but the food quickly became indistinguishable from one day to the next. Don't come here for the culinary experience."

Q "Your first year, you eat on campus. **The best place to eat is BJ and Pierce tower**. The chefs there have interesting fire cooking displays once in a while. The food is okay by my standards."

STUDENT AUTHOR: Snide comments about dorm food aside, Chicago dining is surprisingly solid. The ingredients are fresh (including fresh-baked bread every day) and there is variety for every palate, including Asian Cuisine (Chinese, Thai, and Japanese) at Pierce. At all locations, though, vegan and vegetarian options as well as low-fat and low-carb healthy options are available and the bagel and cereal bar is always an option as well. Bartlett Dining Commons seems to be rated the best among students. The dining hall has a glass skylight running the length of a vaulted ceiling.

Student Body

African American:	5%	Male/Female:	50/50%
Asian American:	13%	Out-of-State:	68%
Hispanic:	8%	International:	8%
Native American:	<1%	Unknown:	19%
White:	47%		

Popular Faiths: Chicago is home to the second-largest number of Seminaries in the world (just after Rome). So, there will be a place of worship for you.

Gay Pride: The "LGBT" community at Chicago is relatively quiet. Annual events like "Drag Ball" and AIDS Awareness Week garner attention on campus.

Economic Status: The need-blind admissions policy means that students from all backgrounds attend.

Students Speak Out
ON DORMS

Q "**All of the dorms have pros and cons**. My least favorite was the Shoreland because you have to take a bus into campus or walk for 20 minutes—something you don't want to do in the winter."

Q "**The dorms vary widely**. However, because of the Residential College system (students are organized in houses within dorms), I think the general system works better than most dorm systems. If you want a close-knit, insular (and quirky) house, you can have that. If you want privacy, you can have that, too."

Q "The nice dorms include Shoreland, Max Palevsky, Pierce, and **Stony Island (for upperclassmen only)**. All others are not very good or fun places to live."

STUDENT AUTHOR: All freshmen are required to live on campus, but once you get settled in, you'll realize that the requirement is not simply to make you feel a part of your class, but it's also a direct integration into the University community. The centerpiece of the living arrangements is the "House System." It works by dividing up dorms into geographic areas like floors or wings, with no less than 35 and maxing out at around 120 students.

> **Did You Know?**
> 60% of undergrads live on campus.

Students Speak Out
ON GUYS & GIRLS

Q "They have these T-shirts: 'University of Chicago, where **the squirrels are more aggressive** than the guys,' and 'University of Chicago, where the squirrels are cuter than the girls.' That pretty much sums it all up."

Q "There are **more attractive girls** here than guys. Most attractive guys have significant others, usually from back home. Otherwise, they are going out with the attractive girls. The dating scene can be kind of depressing."

Q "You will have to work to find nice and cute girls. People are different and look for different things. If you like **sitting around and watching the hotness parade**, go to a state school, or Northwestern—but whatever."

STUDENT AUTHOR: There are usually four or five notable parties every weekend (fraternity and apartment), but aside from the fraternity parties (which are well publicized using the technologically-advanced techniques of spray-painting crude slogans on bed sheets and hanging them out the window), apartment parties are often invite-only, or spread through word of mouth. You simply need to know people who can tell you when and where the debauchery is scheduled to take place.

> **Traditions**
>
> **O-Week**
> O-Week tells how to pick classes, and how to plan your course of study.
>
> **Top of the World Reception**
> Every year, the College rents out the 98th floor of the Hancock Observatory, one of the tallest buildings in the world, for a reception for the incoming class.
>
> **Overall School Spirit**
> Students sport T-shirts claiming that Chicago is "Where Fun Comes To Die" in a perverse twist on the modern conception of "school spirit."

Students Speak Out
ON ATHLETICS

Q "Varsity sports as social events are non-existent, and **school spirit is very low** in terms of athletics. However, many students do play varsity sports. And many of the varsity athletes are smart, too!"

Q "**The IM scene is big**. There's everything from basketball to softball, broomball to euchre. There's not much pressure, and they're fun."

Q "**Varsity sports are popular**, but they're not a big part of total campus life. No one attends the events, but the athletes all love it."

Q "**Sports are not a big deal**. People enjoy playing club and IM sports for fun, though."

STUDENT AUTHOR: Despite having been a founding member of the Big 10 over 100 years ago, Chicago leased its spot in Division I long time ago (to Michigan State in 1946). Athletics take a back seat to academics; although that does not mean that the students here are not athletic. Athletics are a key component of the Chicago Education. A full year's worth of athletic participation—be it ballroom dancing, or intramural basketball—and a swim test, are required for graduation.

Students Speak Out
ON DRUG SCENE

Q "It's a city, and drugs are accessible. But there aren't that many habitual users here. **You hear about it from some rich kids**, but overall, it seems like it's a small thing."

Q "The drug scene isn't very important on campus; **people do drink or smoke up**, just like any other campus, but it isn't like it's a major factor in becoming cool—it's actually far from it."

Q "Well, there always **the local Walgreens Drugstore**, which students like going to, and then there's also the guy getting high in his dorm room and the clouds of smoke filling up the hall."

STUDENT AUTHOR: If you want to get technical about it, the most frequently abused drug on campus is caffeine. And if that doesn't clue you in, then perhaps you'll understand after reading a recent copy of *the Maroon* detailing the prevalence of Adderall, a prescription drug abused by students on campus for the purpose of—get this—studying more! Alcohol and marijuana are used more than Adderall, but Adderall serves more of a practical purpose, students will say.

6:1	Student-to-Faculty Ratio
98%	Freshman Retention Rate
84%	Four-Year Graduation Rate
73%	Financial Aid Applicants Receiving Aid

Students Speak Out
SAFETY & SECURITY

Q "From what I know, the most frequent crime around here is bike theft. **Students here get scared easily**, I'd say, but it's generally okay."

Q "Safety on campus depends on what you mean by 'on campus.' **On the quads, I have never felt in any danger whatsoever**, regardless of the time or conditions. In the larger neighborhood, I would urge anybody to use caution."

Q "After dark, if you plan to go more than a few blocks away from the quads, don't do so alone. This isn't to imply that the University is unsafe, because I personally believe that **the police do the best job possible**. It's simply that any urban environment requires alertness and caution."

STUDENT AUTHOR: For a child raised by overprotective parents, the University of Chicago, on the surface, can seem like a dangerous place. Located on the South Side, the reputation of the area far exceeds the reality of the security situation. However, the University has gone to great lengths to address these issues and more.

> **Questions?**
> For more inside information and survival tips, pick up College Prowler's full-length book on this school, written by an actual student! Check it out at *www.collegeprowler.com*.

Students Speak Out
ON OVERALL EXPERIENCE

Q "**I like it here but am not staying**. The kids here are so into studying. You will obviously get every different kind of person, but I need someplace where it's a wee bit more balanced!"

Q "I'm very glad I'm here; what I wanted most out of college was intense intellectual activity, and at the University of Chicago, I got exactly that. This is **not the place for either partying** or pre-professionalism. It's the place where every idea you have will be questioned, analyzed, and ripped apart to shreds."

Q "While the thought of transferring has crossed my mind more than once, I have enjoyed my experience and can say that **I am happy here**."

Q "I've really enjoyed my first year at U of C. There's always something interesting going on around campus, from panels and lectures, to concerts, art shows, plays, and usually some sort of free food. No one ever has any legitimate excuse for being bored; if nothing on campus interests you, **explore the city**. Being in Chicago is one of the greatest benefits of this school."

STUDENT AUTHOR: Everything at Chicago centers around providing students an ideal education. Not only the Core Curriculum with its balanced approach to the disciplines and rigorous opposition to mediocrity, but also the House System, the campus design, and the graduate-undergraduate dynamics all contribute to Chicago's continuing pursuit of the perfect academic experience. Is it hard? Yes. You will spend nights in the Regenstein Library wishing you were at some nameless, beach-side state school drinking martinis poolside.

University of Cincinnati

2600 Clifton Avenue; Cincinnati, OH 45221
(513) 556-0000; www.uc.edu

THE BASICS:

Acceptance Rate: 61%
Setting: Urban
F-T Undergrads: 17,334

SAT Range: 1510–1850*
Control: Public
Tuition: $22,419

Most Popular Majors: Business, Health Professions, Engineering, Visual/Performing Arts, English

*of 2400

Academics	B	Guys	B
Local Atmosphere	B	Girls	B
Safety & Security	C+	Athletics	A-
Computers	B	Nightlife	B-
Facilities	A	Greek Life	C+
Campus Dining	C	Drug Scene	B
Off-Campus Dining	A	Campus Strictness	B
Campus Housing	B-	Parking	D
Off-Campus Housing	B	Transportation	B+
Diversity	B-	Weather	C+

Students Speak Out
ON ACADEMICS

Q "I'd say **the most important thing UC is known for is the co-op program**. As a student who is worried about the transition between the academic and the professional world, it's the best thing that's ever happened to me. I've learned more than I thought was possible by spending every other quarter working in the field as opposed to the classroom. It's the most valuable part of my education at UC."

Q "I was somewhat **discouraged by the size of some of my lectures during my freshman year**, which sometimes had 200-plus students. Because of the size, I was hesitant to ask questions."

Q "English was not the first language for some of my TAs. At times, I became aggravated because **it was difficult to understand what they were saying**."

Q "**University-wide, several of our colleges are very well rated nationally**. Programs within the School of Design, Art, Architecture, and Planning and within the College Conservatory of Music are top-ranked, and the co-op program out of several of the colleges is well-known."

STUDENT AUTHOR: The faculty and staff truly care about students succeeding, and that's exactly why UC is home to some of the best programs in the world. Workload varies based on a student's major. Students in the College of Design, Architecture, Art, and Planning are notorious for being swamped with classwork, but for other students, it depends on the class and professor.

Students Speak Out
ON LOCAL ATMOSPHERE

Q "UC is located in the heart of an urban city and is close to downtown. I think this is a great advantage because students have access to a lot of different events or activities that are sponsored by the city. **Cincinnati has great museums and historical sites to visit**."

Q "Cincinnati is a mixed bag. **I feel like there is space for nearly everyone here**. Cincinnati is a place I've definitely grown to love over the years I've been here."

Q "This is a strange city—urban and rural at the same time. It's got its share of great things to do, but it's also got a lot of downtime. **Downtown is dead after dark**, but it's a different story when the sports teams are doing well."

Q "The city atmosphere is not too bad. Cincinnati is a nice-enough city. **It's not too big or too small**, and there can be quite a few things to do. During the winter at the zoo, there is the Festival of Lights, and anytime during the year it is not too bad going to Newport on the Levy for a movie or to hit the bars."

STUDENT AUTHOR: Going to college in Cincinnati is a great opportunity. Whether you have a passion for art, sports, music, or nightlife, there is something for everyone. The city is big enough to satisfy the student looking for a hip, urban environment, but it's not too big for someone coming from a small town. Plus, there is always something going on in Cincinnati, no matter what time of year, so students will never be bored.

5 Best Things	5 Worst Things
1 Diversity	**1** Parking
2 Accessible professors	**2** Off-campus crime
3 Internship opportunities	**3** Not a 24-hour campus
4 Co-op programs	**4** Weather
5 Facilities	**5** Lack of food options

Students Speak Out
ON FACILITIES

Q "The athletic facilities are very nice. UC is one of the only colleges I know of that **allows intramural sports to use the varsity playing fields**."

Q "The facilities at UC are amazing. **They have mostly just been revamped**, so they look great. The new rec center is phenomenal, and I use it every chance I get. The student center in TUC is also very nice—there are plenty of places to sit and study or socialize."

Q "I think most of campus is pretty nice, but it is a **bizarre mishmosh of architectural styles**."

Q "I study in Langsam library every day. **It's a nice and quiet atmosphere** to get reading and homework done. They also have a brand new computer lab that is open 24 hours, which is great for people who don't own computers or have Internet access in their homes."

Q "I think **we have state-of-the-art facilities**. I love the campus. It's the surrounding area I'm not too fond of."

STUDENT AUTHOR: The campus was ugly, but since big changes have been made in some of the most popular facilities, students have had nothing but positive things to say. The Campus Recreation Center, which opened in 2006, is a state-of-the-art fitness center. The Tangeman University Center has undergone changes, making progress on choices in the food court and hangout areas throughout the building. TUC is a great place to meet friends, grab a bite to eat, and kill time between classes.

Famous Alumni

Cris Collinsworth, Sandy Koufax, John Lutz, George Rieveschl, Oscar Robinson, Joseph Strauss, William Howard Taft, Kevin Youkilis

Students Speak Out
ON CAMPUS DINING

Q "**The food is questionable, but freshmen seem to love it**. The dining halls have won awards, but it tastes like dining hall food to me."

Q "**I wish the food was a little healthier**. It is kind of annoying to always eat Wendy's or Gold Star, and it's not a close walk to buy healthy food. Sometimes it's nice to eat junk food, just not every day. I've only been to the dining halls a few times, but I love their food, and they're spacious."

Q "UC does a good job of providing a variety of restaurants on campus. Most of them are located in TUC, and there is a Subway and Starbucks right outside TUC on MainStreet, which is nice. **During lunch time, lines can be long**, but they usually move pretty quickly."

Q "There are two dining halls on campus, and their food is not too bad, but **if you don't have a meal plan, it can be quite expensive**."

Q "**The food on campus is terrible**. The dining halls have decent food and a good selection, but everything else on campus is really crappy. It's all just fast food."

STUDENT AUTHOR: When it comes to on-campus dining, there aren't a lot of options. For the most part, if you visit the student center, expect to chow down on your typical fast food menu items: burgers, fries, pizza, and chili. It's not ideal to go to Tangemen if you're looking for a quick, healthy meal. The dining halls are decent but expensive if you don't have a meal plan. The food isn't amazing—it's basically dining hall food.

Student Body

African American:	11%	Male/Female:	49/51%
Asian American:	3%	Out-of-State:	10%
Hispanic:	2%	International:	1%
Native American:	<1%	Unknown:	6%
White:	77%		

Popular Faiths: Christian and Catholic religions are the most common, but students of other religions have a presence as well.

Gay Pride: UC is a diverse campus, so 99.9 percent of the time, LGBT students will not feel left out or discriminated against.

Economic Status: Though a majority of students come from middle-class families, there are students from higher- and lower-income families.

Students Speak Out
ON DORMS

Q "Some dorms are better than others, but there are a few you should try to get into if you can. **Calhoun and Daniels halls seem to be pretty fun places to live**. Turner and Schneider are also brand new and seem to be fairly nice places."

Q "If you're looking for a place that's nice and quiet for studying, then I would suggest Turner Hall because the **rooms give you a little more space and privacy**. If you're the type who wants to meet a lot of new people, then Daniels Hall is a good choice."

Q "Pick a dorm that seems like something you may be interested in because **everyone likes something different as far as dorms go**."

STUDENT AUTHOR: UC is primarily a commuter college, so most students don't live in a dorm throughout their years here. Living on campus isn't a bad option, especially if you are looking to meet new people and be close to everything UC has to offer. Some of the nicer dorms tend to be reserved for upperclassmen, so you need to be prepared to live in older buildings until you reach upperclassman status.

Did You Know?
20% of undergrads live on campus.

Students Speak Out
ON GUYS & GIRLS

Q "There are only a handful of guys on campus I deem worthwhile, but it's a huge campus. I have no opinion on the girls—really, **there's just a lot of furry boots and tans**."

Q "**There's a pretty decent mix** of models, skater boys, pot heads, rockers, jocks, nerds, and frat boys. The girls are all different, too. They're either chill, high maintenance, trashy, or average."

Q "The guys range from athletic to ghetto to nerdy to workout-aholics. The girls all wear the same clothes but **are generally friendly**."

Q "The campus is really a social hodgepodge. **Anyone can meet someone who has something in common with him or her**. The girls are mostly attractive, and they're pretty down-to-earth, too."

STUDENT AUTHOR: UC students have their own styles and personalities, so no two students are the same. Guys and girls are open about their culture and beliefs and who they are, and other students are generally accepting of differing lifestyles and ideas. Most students are in relationships or are looking to find someone special. Overall, the guys at UC are good-looking and take care of themselves. Most girls you meet on campus aren't "cliquey" and will befriend people who are not like them.

Traditions

Spring Concert
This event is free for students and the community and has included country artists, rock acts, and hip-hop artists. In 2007, the concert featured The Roots.

Welcome Week
This annual event is designed to help new (and returning) students become familiar with UC life.

Overall School Spirit
School spirit is hit-or-miss. If athletic teams are doing well, there tends to be more school spirit than when things aren't going so well.

Students Speak Out
ON ATHLETICS

Q "**Varsity sports are improving every year** thanks to the school's membership in the Big East Conference. The football team is finally worthy of discussion, and the basketball team's rebuilding appears to be well ahead of schedule."

Q "The basketball team does well almost every year, and **students are true Bearcat fans**. There are intramural sports like basketball, football, or baseball that students can participate in."

Q "The football team just had a great year, the basketball teams are fun to watch, and the **Shoemaker Center can get loud at times and be a good time**. The men's soccer team is pretty competitive. Intramural sports are fun and inexpensive."

Q "**Intramural sports are big** for fraternities and sororities, for sure."

STUDENT AUTHOR: Since UC joined the Big East Conference in 2005, the Bearcats have taken on bigger rivals and had some big games. The success of the football and men's basketball programs has put athletics at the forefront of student life at UC. Students are getting into the spirit of being a Bearcat.

Students Speak Out
ON DRUG SCENE

Q "Plenty of people smoke plenty of weed, but I wouldn't say it's noticeable, and **I certainly wouldn't say it's a problem**."

Q "If you go to a house party, someone will have pot there. Every party I've been to had joints or a bong or something. **It's not my thing though, so I just avoid it**."

Q "I'm not really familiar with the drug scene, but I'm sure there are people who do it. I hear people talk about getting stoned a lot. Especially after a holiday weekend or a big party night, it's all people talk about. But, as a majority, UC **students are more into drinking than drugs**."

STUDENT AUTHOR: **A lot of off-campus parties will have pot around, but smokers won't pressure you to do it. You'll very rarely hear about mushrooms, crystal meth, heroin, cocaine, or other "hard" drugs, so it seems the drug scene is very minimal in the area. If anything, the drugs that do exist are off campus because the dorms tend to be more strict and are harder to sneak things into.**

15:1	Student-to-Faculty Ratio
83%	Freshman Retention Rate
19%	Four-Year Graduation Rate
77%	Financial Aid Applicants Receiving Aid

Students Speak Out
SAFETY & SECURITY

Q "Although Clifton as a whole has a lot of problems with crime, the one place where that seems to be most under control is on campus. There are certain streets where walking at night is just not safe, but **I've always felt safe walking through campus at night**."

Q "During the day, safety doesn't seem to be an issue. **If a crime happens on or around campus, the University police will notify you via e-mail** to make you aware of the incident. The campus police are seen driving around campus a lot."

Q "They try to make it seem like we're safe but you are only as safe as you make yourself. Don't walk around alone at night. There is a lot of crime. **They do have a great shuttle system so we don't have to walk around the neighborhood**."

STUDENT AUTHOR: **Among UC students, safety still remains a big concern. In response, UC's police department has taken steps to make campus a safer environment for students and staff, particularly at night. They've added lighting, blue-light phones, and upped police presence on campus. Programs like Nightwalk provide students with escorts and rides home to keep them out of danger at night.**

Questions?
For more inside information and survival tips, pick up College Prowler's full-length book on this school, written by an actual student! Check it out at *www.collegeprowler.com*.

Students Speak Out
ON OVERALL EXPERIENCE

Q "I would say try to live on campus your freshman year and, if possible, don't commute any year. **The only people I know who didn't like UC were the ones who weren't involved** and didn't ever do anything with their peers on campus other than go to class. It is a better school than some people in Cincinnati believe, and lots of people in high school who said they wanted to get away from Cincinnati transfer here after their freshman year and love it."

Q "My four years at UC so far have been amazing. I've met great people and learned a lot about myself. I would definitely choose this place again because DAAP is a great school, and **I'm proud to be getting my education here**."

Q "I would choose to come to UC again. There are good and bad things here, but **the good things definitely outweigh the bad**."

Q "UC has not been too bad. I would come here again if I needed to. **It has gotten better each year I have been here**, with the rec center opening up and free Metro rides."

STUDENT AUTHOR: **The University of Cincinnati is ideal for anyone who is looking to come out of college with a solid education and experiences of a lifetime. At UC, there is something for everyone, no matter what background you come from and no matter what your goals are. The faculty and staff are helpful and passionate about helping students learn, so whatever program you choose, you'll get a good education. Plus, the University is always expanding the curriculum, so students have more options of what they can study.**

University of Colorado

552 CUB; Boulder, CO 80309
(303) 492-1411; www.colorado.edu

THE BASICS:

Acceptance Rate: 78%
Setting: Small city
F-T Undergrads: 24,414

SAT Range: 1070–1280*
Control: Public
Tuition: $25,400

Most Popular Majors: Business, Social Sciences, Biology, Psychology, Communications/Journalism

*of 1600

Academics	B-	Guys	A
Local Atmosphere	A-	Girls	A
Safety & Security	B-	Athletics	A-
Computers	B	Nightlife	B+
Facilities	B	Greek Life	B
Campus Dining	C+	Drug Scene	C
Off-Campus Dining	A-	Campus Strictness	B
Campus Housing	B+	Parking	C-
Off-Campus Housing	B	Transportation	A
Diversity	D+	Weather	C+

Students Speak Out
ON ACADEMICS

Q "As a freshman, I highly recommend making an appointment to **meet with a counselor to develop what they term a 'four-year plan.'** Although your original set of courses may change significantly, it will still keep you somewhat on track in regards to finishing core courses and other required credits."

Q "The teachers at CU are **pretty good in most cases, but it depends on your major**. I'm majoring in electrical engineering, and I have had some awful foreign professors in the past."

Q "As a journalism major, I would advise incoming students with equal interests to thoroughly evaluate their choice because the entire process is a true test of skill and patience. First-year students are initially classified as 'pre-journalism' because there are a number of required courses that one must complete to accumulate a competitive GPA. I applied three times before I was accepted! Once I gained access to register for the classes, I was still set back because I **found myself at the bottom of a long waitlist**."

STUDENT AUTHOR: **Some students rave over attentive professors, while others remain disappointed with teaching assistants. With well over 3,000 courses in 150 areas of study, CU offers countless opportunities that attract a multitude of interests. Once registered, incoming freshmen often find large class sizes intimidating, but many students later learn that upper-level classes within their major provide considerably smaller classes.**

Students Speak Out
ON LOCAL ATMOSPHERE

Q "The University has a **famous film festival, and occasionally puts on an opera**, or an excellent play. In the spring, there is the Conference on World Affairs, which is interesting and attracts some celebrities."

Q "Everyone is really chill here. I'm from New York (very close to the city), and **it is a huge shock to see how laid-back these people are**! You have to go on hikes; the views are amazing!"

Q "Boulder is **open, calm, and scenic**. But watch out for the low-income housing kids—they think they're gangsters. Pearl Street Mall, Flatirons, and the Hill are all entertaining places to visit."

Q "**Complete college town** if I've ever seen one! College students everywhere! Parties everywhere! You will love it!"

STUDENT AUTHOR: **There are few methods to understanding Boulder, but ask any student and they will provide you with countless ways to describe it. It is a place where people come to ski, but learn that invigoration can be sought beyond moguls and slopes. People breathe a little better and still enjoy a booming business environment, Starbucks is shunned, Shakespeare is a tradition, and finding parking is still a problem. A college town where local residents resent students for driving expensive SUVs, rioting, throwing parties, and renting a piece of their well-kept secret. Overall, Boulder is a town where students consider themselves lucky to spend four years.**

5 Best Things	5 Worst Things
1 The campus	1 Boulder police
2 Boulder	2 High cost of living
3 Ski season	3 Core requirements
4 Quality of life	4 Lack of diversity
5 Variety of courses	5 Rich kids

Students Speak Out
ON FACILITIES

Q "The student center has a CU Boulder store that is way **overpriced but relatively convenient**. It's modern, and it's home to many students doing late-night or last-minute cramming."

Q "The **athletic facilities are decent**. There's a climbing wall, ice-skating rink, racquetball court, and several pools. You can go to these places for free with your school ID. They also offer many classes for very reasonable rates, such as kickboxing and hip-hop dance."

Q "CU has a **very good center** with a hockey rink, gym, free-weights room, machine room, rock-climbing wall, two swimming pools, a bunch of racquetball courts, and volleyball courts."

Q "I guess the facilities are nice. The Recreation Center has **everything you could want** to work out, from pools, machines, weight room, and more. The UMC has a lot of tables, and some decent restaurants."

STUDENT AUTHOR: **Prospective students visiting the University of Colorado are often lured by the University's grandeur. The main campus alone maintains over 700 acres of towering trees and captivating landscape. Aside from the naturally inspiring campus grounds, the facilities at CU are especially inviting. To put it best, Colorado's campus is everything that one would expect from a major university. Most students will proudly admit that a simple walk around the campus was all it took for them to choose CU, knowing that they would spend adequate time walking on its grounds and within its walls.**

Famous Alumni

Chauncey Billups, Chris Fowler, Hale Irwin, Billy Kidd, Trey Parker, Robert Redford, Rick Reilly, Kordell Stewart, Matt Stone, Byron "Whizzer" White

Students Speak Out
ON CAMPUS DINING

Q "The food on campus is **pretty bad in general, but you can't expect much** from dorm food. Beef stroganoff, swiss steak, and all that great stuff is served on a daily basis. A good spot to eat for on-campus dining would probably be the Alley@Farrand, which has a buffet-style menu."

Q "You'll find good food anywhere you go. Cafeteria food always **leaves a great deal to be desired**, but we all have to go through it as undergrads, so it's nothing out of the ordinary."

Q "Dorm food is **not exactly great, but it's not too bad**. There are a lot of choices, and there's always cereal, fruit, salad, and sandwiches, if the meal on the menu isn't good."

Q "Food on campus is not so exciting. It's decent but definitely lacking. The Hill nearby has **everything you could want, from burritos to sushi**."

STUDENT AUTHOR: **While college dorm food, in general, is hardly appealing, you will most likely end your first semester feeling as if you couldn't get enough of it. CU provides its students with four different all-you-can-eat dining centers conveniently located in some of the most popular student dorms. In the past, CU's dining halls were generally loathed by all, but renovations have impressed even the pickiest eaters. Students often venture to University Memorial Center (UMC) where they can grab a bite to eat at the Alfred Packer food court—everything from burgers and fries to a Mexican cantina.**

Student Body

African American:	2%	Male/Female:	53/47%
Asian American:	6%	Out-of-State:	40%
Hispanic:	6%	International:	2%
Native American:	<1%	Unknown:	5%
White:	78%		

Popular Faiths: Colorado boasts on-campus associations ranging from the Zen Society to the Hillel Jewish Student Resource Center.

Gay Pride: The Chancellor's Standing Committee on Gay, Lesbian, Bisexual, and Transgender Issues has accomplished numerous projects since its inception.

Economic Status: The student body is generally upper-middle-class.

Students Speak Out
ON DORMS

Q "**Dorms are okay**. I loved Hallett Hall (everyone does), but students claim that the Kittredge dorms have a nicer interior. Sewell sounds like fun if you plan on going Greek, but avoid Will Ville at all costs."

Q "**Kittredge dorms are good overall** (on the edge of campus). Farrand is for arts and science students, Sewall for Greek kids, and the Quad is for engineers. I have heard that Cheyenne Arapahoe is known for its drugs, so be warned."

Q "The dorms are a great one-year experience. I would say, **try not to end up at Will Ville**. The best and most conveniently located dorms are Libby, Farrand, and Cheyenne Arapahoe."

STUDENT AUTHOR: **While some students complain about the requirement to live on campus the first year, they soon find that dorm life is fundamental to establishing a social life of any kind. The dorms are a place where relationships are formed and the beginning of the next four years of your life unfolds. Williams Village, a bus ride from campus, can be avoided by submitting residence hall request forms as soon as possible.**

Did You Know?
25% of undergrads live on campus.

Students Speak Out
ON GUYS & GIRLS

Q "There are **lots of gorgeous women** on campus, and lots of hot guys. It's a big, old meat market."

Q "There are a lot of **good-looking girls and guys on campus**, but sometimes I think a lot of people here are a little stuck up and snobby. But on the other hand, there are a lot of really cool people to meet in Boulder. I've met some of my best friends here."

Q "It's very liberal at CU, so get yourself ready for that. I was in for a change, being from conservative Texas. I will say that there are tons of hot guys and girls, but **everyone is really friendly here**, and it doesn't matter what 'class' you are in."

STUDENT AUTHOR: **With a multitude of beautiful people, many students find it hard to remain attached. The majority of the guys are scruffy snowboarders and skaters who barely shave, yet manage to still look great. Girls who prefer their men clean and conservative also have a variety of Abercrombie & Fitch-wearing fraternity boys to choose from. The girls, for their part, are mostly out-of-state bombshells from California, Illinois, and Texas.**

Traditions

Ralphie
In 1966, a six-month-old calf was chosen to represent the University; it was originally named Ralph, but upon realizing her actual gender, the name was amended.

The Sink
Students sign their names on the walls of the Sink before graduation, typically in the early morning.

Overall School Spirit
Throughout football season, school spirit is at its highest. Prior to the commencement of every season, students wait hours to purchase season tickets.

Students Speak Out
ON ATHLETICS

Q "**Football is really big**, and games are fun to go to. We have some other really good teams. The ski team and the cross-country team usually win nationals. Girl soccer games are enjoyable, and I've found that joining the cycling and triathlon teams are a great way to meet people."

Q "CU **football is a religion** here. For most students, women's basketball is pretty big, too. Men's basketball is fun to watch, but it certainly does not have a big following."

Q "When it comes to varsity sports on campus, it depends on who you ask. **Football is huge** for players and fans, as well as basketball. Everything else is low key unless you make the effort to play or be involved as a spectator. Intramural sports are all over. "

STUDENT AUTHOR: **Some students come to CU passionately anticipating the football season. Others are left with no choice, and eventually succumb. Even if you don't share the initial desire to paint yourself in yellow and cheer on the Buffaloes, there is a high probability that you will be swooped into the school spirit which flourishes at CU.**

Students Speak Out
ON DRUG SCENE

Q "There are lots of drugs to be had, so if you want it, it won't be very hard to find a connection. I'm not a user of any sort, but I know plenty that are, and they all agree that it is fairly easy to get what you want. It's also **pretty easy to avoid**, too. People are pretty laid-back about it."

Q "If you want it, you can get it. CU is **more of a drinking school**, but there are drugs around. Typically, you'll meet people who smoke pot and use rave drugs, but LSD is also popular. Not many people do coke or other hard drugs."

Q "**Of course there are drugs**, and they are easy to get, but if you're not into that and want to stay away from it, you can."

STUDENT AUTHOR: Though marijuana is the preferred drug of choice, mushrooms, acid, and ecstasy are used occasionally by the younger students who are still celebrating their newly acquired freedom. As students turn 21, there is a shift from hallucinogens to stimulants. Still, this is merely a "scene," comprising only a portion of students.

18:1	Student-to-Faculty Ratio
83%	Freshman Retention Rate
32%	Four-Year Graduation Rate
49%	Financial Aid Applicants Receiving Aid

Students Speak Out
SAFETY & SECURITY

Q "Safety is pretty standard on campus, neither exaggerated nor emphasized. But I've never felt threatened at all. **Boulder is a fairly safe place to be**."

Q "I have **never sensed any sort of danger**, though sometimes walking out at night can feel scary on campus, but I always felt safe in the dorms. If the dorms were any safer, I believe they would be too restricted."

Q "If it's late at night, there are **people you can call to walk you home**. There is also a car service that is free. They will drive you somewhere if you don't want to walk."

STUDENT AUTHOR: Though Boulder is a small, relatively safe town, CU remains a large campus that attracts a high volume of people. Attempted rapes have been the University's most pertinent safety issues, but great measures have been taken to protect students from being unsuspecting victims.

> **Questions?**
> For more inside information and survival tips, pick up College Prowler's full-length book on this school, written by an actual student! Check it out at *www.collegeprowler.com*.

Students Speak Out
ON OVERALL EXPERIENCE

Q "I just graduated from CU, and I loved my experience here! I wouldn't trade my college experience in Boulder for any other school, even Harvard. Where else in the United States can college students **receive a great education, party like animals, and ski** up to four times a week? This is the only place."

Q "It's the most amazing place I've ever seen in my life. **The lifestyle out here is so healthy and adventurous**; everyone seems so happy and content. The town is awesome, with so many cool restaurants, bars, and cafés. The school is gorgeous, and so are all of the facilities. I can't say enough about it. I'm so happy I came here. CU Boulder is amazing, and there are many opportunities here."

Q "The overall school experience at CU is very good. I enjoy outdoor activities, and **Boulder has tons to do**—from rock climbing to skiing. I also like the big campus because it gives me the opportunity to get involved in programs and activities that fit my interests."

STUDENT AUTHOR: There is not just one simple thing that separates CU from the countless number of universities that a student has to choose from; it could have something to do with the mountains. Being greeted every morning by Colorado's towering terrain never fails to put an inflated ego into place. Looking down from the highest peak in Vail is more than a subtle reminder of the benefits of dedication. Even fresh Aspen air is capable of lifting the lowest spirits. The knowledge you can gain at CU is immeasurable, but not everything in life can be based on an academic curriculum.

University of Connecticut

2131 Hillside Road; Storrs, CT 06269
(860) 486-2000; www.uconn.edu

THE BASICS:

Acceptance Rate: 49%   **SAT Range:** 1090–1290*
Setting: Rural   **Control:** Public
F-T Undergrads: 15,615   **Tuition:** $21,912

Most Popular Majors: Business, Social Sciences, Health Professions, Liberal Arts, Psychology

*of 1600

Academics	B	Guys	B
Local Atmosphere	D+	Girls	B
Safety & Security	B+	Athletics	A-
Computers	B	Nightlife	B-
Facilities	A-	Greek Life	B-
Campus Dining	B	Drug Scene	B
Off-Campus Dining	C	Campus Strictness	B-
Campus Housing	C+	Parking	D-
Off-Campus Housing	B	Transportation	B
Diversity	C	Weather	C+

Students Speak Out
ON ACADEMICS

Q "Most teachers and TAs (teaching assistants) are **enthusiastic individuals** that do their best to make learning enjoyable. However, every once in a while, you'll get one that is clearly just running through the syllabus in an attempt to get back to whatever research they were doing."

Q "Freshman classes are huge. **My lecture classes ranged from 150 to 350 students**. None of my classes, except English, were smaller than that. All of the TAs are from foreign countries. These TAs teach discussion classes for each of the lectures (it's a once-a-week, small class with kids from your lecture, meant to clear up anything you didn't understand in the big lecture), but not many speak English well. It's hard to learn from them or ask them questions."

Q "I get the feeling that my professors don't care that much about their students, but **care more about their research or experiments**. For the most part, my classes are interesting, except Psychology 132—that was painful."

STUDENT AUTHOR: There are simply too many students at UConn for a student to expect routine, one-on-one attention as an underclassman. The professors have office hours, and most are very accommodating, but they will never approach you. When you delve further into your major, classes will become progressively smaller. While fulfilling the general education requirements, however, you can expect classes no smaller than 100 students— you'll be expected to take the initiative.

Students Speak Out
ON LOCAL ATMOSPHERE

Q "There's not much else close by. UConn essentially is the town of Storrs. About a half-hour away is a **mall and movie theaters**. Hartford isn't too far if you need more to do."

Q "The town is a little quiet and a little slow, **there's nothing in particular to visit**. Eastern is about 15 minutes away. Try not to go to Willimantic."

Q "UConn is about one **hour and 20 minutes from Boston, which is always fun** to visit."

Q "Regrettably, Storrs is a **pretty, quaint town, which is okay if you're a farmer**, retired, or looking to raise a family—but not that great if you get tired of on-campus activities. Eastern Connecticut State University is nearby—about 20 minutes by car—so if there is a dull weekend on campus, you can always try your luck over there. If you have a car, that is."

Q "**Storrs is in the middle of nowhere**. There are no other universities and there is nothing to do— unless you count cow tipping. However, the University of Connecticut recognizes this and provides numerous activities for their students on campus."

STUDENT AUTHOR: The local atmosphere is rural and quaint, and those words should be setting off alarms. There's a reason every time someone mentions local atmosphere the words "New York and Boston are close" are in their carefully-worded response. UConn is Storrs, and the surrounding area is very beautiful, but also very empty.

5 Best Things
1 Basketball
2 Spring weekend
3 Football
4 Tons of people
5 Academic support

5 Worst Things
1 Parking
2 Math professors
3 Construction
4 Wind tunnel effect
5 Weather

Students Speak Out
ON FACILITIES

Q "The **athletic facilities aren't bad**, but crowding can often be a big problem in the weight rooms."

Q "The **student center has been rebuilt**, and now has a movie theater. The field house is nice, but it gets crowded."

Q "The athletic facilities are excellent. The field house has free weight rooms, plenty of exercise machines, a pool, basketball and volleyball courts, and an indoor track. There are also outdoor fields for the teams and IM sports. There are some good computer rooms. The student union is all right, but it's been completely redone (along with plenty of other buildings) with a **movie theater and all kinds of cool new stuff**. There's always construction, but the campus is looking really nice."

Q "The **library is open until 2 a.m.**, but there is a place called Bookworms in the library which is open 24 hours. The field house and gym are open from 6 a.m. until midnight, and they are often full. The student center is fine; I do not use it too much, but it's got some things students might like in there."

STUDENT AUTHOR: **Since UConn is a public university, it receives funding from the state and has poured over two billion dollars into the school to improve the campus and its infrastructure. The changes have launched UConn ahead of a lot of other higher education institutions, and they are very visible. However, Some of the academic buildings are in desperate need of refurbishment.**

Famous Alumni
George M. Carew, Fred Contrata, Alfred Covello, Ron Paolillo, Raymond J. Fonseca, Joette Katz, Tom Keegan, Richard Mastracchio, Meg Ryan

Students Speak Out
ON CAMPUS DINING

Q "The best cafeteria is South, as they have a grill chef, pizza, Chinese, pasta, and lots of other stuff everyday. North has a good cafeteria, too. All the **cafeterias are buffet-style eating**, so there are always plenty of choices."

Q "As an incoming freshman, you would probably be **required to buy the largest plan**, which is on-campus dining. It isn't great, but it doesn't suck."

Q "The South and Northwest dining halls both have very **high-quality food, as far as dorm food is concerned**. The lines can be long if you go on the quarter-hours.

Q "The food on campus is pretty good. I like the dining halls, plus **there are other spots around campus with delis** and things like that. There is also a McDonald's-like place in the student union."

STUDENT AUTHOR: **Food on campus is really good at all but a few dining halls. South and Towers are usually rated the best, with Northwest close behind. North and Buckley are usually held as the worst. Though you can eat at any dining hall with your card, a majority of students will find themselves using all their meals at one dining hall. Because so many students live in such a concentrated area and have wildly diverse eating preferences, the dining halls are forced to constantly prepare an equally wide variety of dishes.**

Student Body

African American:	5%	Male/Female:	49/51%
Asian American:	7%	Out-of-State:	24%
Hispanic:	4%	International:	1%
Native American:	<1%	Unknown:	8%
White:	74%		

Popular Faiths: Almost every religious club dedicated to a particular religion listed on the school's Web site is Christian, and that says it all.

Gay Pride: The Rainbow Center is working to promote gay tolerance, but the campus is definitely not as open-minded about gay rights as they would like.

Economic Status: Figures would probably show the bulk of the students coming from traditional, New England, middle-income families.

Students Speak Out
ON DORMS

Q "The new freshman dorms are **pretty nice, although they're substance-free**. They redid them, and I got to live in them the first year they were open. As far as niceness and cleanliness, they are the best."

Q "You definitely don't want Towers. They slapped a pretty **new face on the buildings, but the inside is still nasty**. It's dark and small, and it smells. I swear, every floor has this weird smell. Hilltop, McMahon, and South are really nice, but as a freshman, you can pretty much count on having no chance of getting into any of those. I didn't even have a chance this year."

Q "North has a good location, but the **dorm rooms are pretty run-down**. If you're a freshman, I'd definitely try getting into Northwest, or South if you're an upperclassman."

STUDENT AUTHOR: **Northwest and Towers are the best communities for** freshmen. Some students complain that Northwest is similar to high school, but you can't beat it for making friends. Towers are a bit far, but it also has a beautiful new dining hall, and buses that run to most parts of campus.

 Did You Know?
68% of undergrads live on campus.

Students Speak Out
ON GUYS & GIRLS

Q "The **people here are conceited**. Everybody thinks they are better than everybody else. There are decent amounts of hot girls, but most have bad personalities, or play games. Personally, I think all the guys here are nerds; they both look and act that way."

Q "Well, I can say **there are plenty of cute girls**. For guys, look at it like this . . . there are about 6,000 of them; they're bound to be a whole bunch you'd like."

Q "It's half-and-half. You'll see a lot of cute guys and girls, but then there are also **some busted-up people**."

Q "**Some guys are attractive**, some aren't. The cute ones are always mean or weird, darn it!"

STUDENT AUTHOR: There is a joke at UConn that the hot girls hibernate for the winter, but it's actually just the cruel contrast between their summer short-shorts and the parkas of early winter. The biggest problem is meeting people you're potentially compatible with. The best way to do it is to get involved in activities that interest you. With so many people on campus, it's guaranteed there will be someone you'll like—UConn is a very attractive campus.

Traditions

Ooze-ball
Volleyball played in mud during the senior week festivities.

One Ton Sun
Insert 2,000 lbs. of free ice cream into the middle of a college campus; college kids love free food.

Overall School Spirit
School spirit is very prominent on campus, and sports are one of the largest attractions, but that scene isn't for everyone. There are students who live and breathe Husky sports; there are those who couldn't care less.

Students Speak Out
ON ATHLETICS

Q "**Basketball pretty much runs the school**—the games are really fun to go to. The other sports, such as soccer, football, and baseball, have a following, but they're definitely not as popular as basketball. Intramurals are definitely fun, and there are a bunch of different leagues. So, depending on how competitive you want it to be there's pretty much a league that caters to everyone, which is cool. If you're just going to have fun, you don't have to play against people whose lives revolve around that sport."

Q "I could care less about sports, but **who doesn't love the women Huskies**?"

Q "I think that UConn is **one of the best athletic schools** in the country. We have almost all sports."

STUDENT AUTHOR: Husky-mania is unavoidable on campus at UConn, and during the peaks of the football and basketball seasons, the events garner a ton of attention. Much of campus pride comes from domination on the playing fields, making athletics one of UConn's greatest offerings. IM sports are also big, and offer something for every skill level.

Students Speak Out
ON DRUG SCENE

Q "**Beer flows like water**. The pot scene isn't that far underground."

Q "The drug scene isn't that prevalent. There have been some pretty decent busts, but you definitely won't walk down the hall and be swamped with drugs. **Pot is definitely common** among UConn students."

Q "Ecstasy and pot are both present, depending on where you live. Dealers come and go all the time because of the cops. **Watch out for narcs**. I wouldn't say there is too much drug use on campus, though."

STUDENT AUTHOR: Although alcohol is present in all of the dorms, and marijuana can be found with connections, the drug scene is not prominent. Marijuana is the most prevalent drug used on campus by far, and relatively easy to acquire, but you won't see it if you aren't looking for it. Willimantic hosts some off-campus students, and is known for drug problems. The drug scene can best be described as "isolated."

17:1	Student-to-Faculty Ratio
93%	Freshman Retention Rate
54%	Four-Year Graduation Rate
71%	Financial Aid Applicants Receiving Aid

Students Speak Out
SAFETY & SECURITY

Q "Security is pretty good. Whenever there's something wrong, like a door won't lock properly, it's always fixed quickly. The on-campus police **response time is good**."

Q "UConn has its own squad of state troopers, and its own fire and EMT station. **There are always tons of police around**, and there's an emergency call system all over campus. You can see the callboxes anywhere on campus and just push a button for help. The campus is very well-lit in most places. Buses run almost all the time to get you where you need to go, and you can call Safe Rides if they aren't running—they'll pick you up and take you anywhere on campus 24/7."

Q "I feel **very secure** on campus."

STUDENT AUTHOR: The UConn police force is large and very active, constantly patrolling for parking violators and drunk drivers. There is no large amount of any other crimes besides alcohol-related ones. The campus is in a small town, and the majority of students report feeling safe in general.

Questions?
For more inside information and survival tips, pick up College Prowler's full-length book on this school, written by an actual student! Check it out at *www.collegeprowler.com.*

Students Speak Out
ON OVERALL EXPERIENCE

Q "UConn wasn't my first choice last year, but I honestly am glad I went here. I wouldn't go anywhere else. It's kind of in the middle of nowhere, but at the same time, it's between any city you'd ever want to go to. It's really pretty out in the woods and mountains. It has lots of academic and extracurricular stuff to do, and at the same time, it has a really great party scene. You pretty much **have your pick of doing just about anything**."

Q "I love the school. It is very, **very challenging, and has very good majors** to choose from. I just wish I could move it down south somewhere, near the beach."

Q "I like it a lot, but it gets a **little dull with barely any cultural outlets** nearby. If you can deal with not much in the winter besides indoor sports, drinking in the dorms, and snowball fights, you'll be fine."

Q "I am very happy here. I have **never regretted coming here**. It really is a nice mix of academics, athletics, and social aspects. I feel like I'm getting a good education. I am pretty involved around campus, and I'm enjoying myself."

STUDENT AUTHOR: There is literally something for everyone at UConn. With over 15,000 undergraduates, you will not have your opportunities handed to you—it's a very large school, so a student must seek out their particular niche. Joining one of the 250-plus clubs on campus is the best way to get involved. It seems if you don't go out and get what you want, you'll sit idly in your dorm room. If you choose this approach, you may be one of the unhappy Huskies who get lost in the deep blue sea that is the University of Connecticut.

University of Delaware

210 South College Avenue; Newark, DE 19716
(302) 831-2000; www.udel.edu

THE BASICS:

Acceptance Rate: 61%
Setting: Suburban
F-T Undergrads: 14,649

SAT Range: 1680–1950*
Control: Public
Tuition: $20,260

Most Popular Majors: Business, Social Sciences, Education, Health Professions, Engineering

*of 2400

Academics	B	Guys	B
Local Atmosphere	C+	Girls	B+
Safety & Security	C+	Athletics	B+
Computers	B+	Nightlife	B-
Facilities	A	Greek Life	B
Campus Dining	C+	Drug Scene	C+
Off-Campus Dining	B	Campus Strictness	B-
Campus Housing	C	Parking	D+
Off-Campus Housing	A-	Transportation	B+
Diversity	D+	Weather	B-

Students Speak Out
ON ACADEMICS

Q "Some classes are huge, and you don't even get to know the teachers, but the smaller classes are great. The teachers are similar to high school. They know your name, and try to help you on a more personal basis. **It depends on the size of your class** and effort as a student to get to know your teachers."

Q "There are **many professors who will go out to the bars on the weekends**, young and old, and drink with their students. The professors who do this are mainly in the humanities."

Q "I think the teachers here are awesome. I became so close to many of them that we actually began to care about what was going on in each other's life. Many of the teachers will **spend lots of time with students outside of the class**. When I graduated, I missed my professors as much as my friends."

Q "The teachers here are **hit or miss**. If you know upperclassmen, it is a good idea to ask them who they like. A lot of professors are here because they are excellent scholars, but they are completely unable to teach a class without putting you to sleep."

STUDENT AUTHOR: Most students agree that their classes and professors fulfill their academic needs, especially in the more advanced courses. There is a tendency for introductory classes to be taught in large lecture halls, or to be taken over by TAs when there is a staffing shortage, and this is the major downfall of classes at UD.

Students Speak Out
ON LOCAL ATMOSPHERE

Q "In Delaware, you're in a great location. Newark is a typical college town, and you are 30 minutes from Philadelphia, an hour from Baltimore and DC, two hours from New York City, and about 30 minutes from Wilmington. **There is always something to do**, on or off campus. The Residential Life staff organizes a lot of student trips also. I went to NYC for a day and saw the *Phantom of the Opera* for $33."

Q "Most incoming students see Newark as a quaint little town that is **within driving distance of many major cities**. They find it cute in its simplicity, but this often gets boring very quickly."

Q "There is not too much to visit around here. **Philly is very close by**, and so is Baltimore. Once I turned 21, I would go up to Philly to see bands and go to the bars, but not around here."

Q "There are **no other colleges around** that are big like ours. The state of Delaware basically revolves around our school. Philly and King of Prussia Mall are good places to visit."

STUDENT AUTHOR: **The city of Newark basically consists of one street aptly named Main Street. Over the years, Main Street has become more commercial with the appearance of a Starbucks and numerous tanning salons. Some students appreciate this small-town feel and enjoy the scenic campus while others will drive to Philly every weekend. Most students will spend some time exploring the surrounding cities by the time they graduate.**

5 Best Things	5 Worst Things
1 Internet access	1 Parking
2 Academics	2 Dining hall food
3 Fitness centers	3 Lack of diversity
4 Theater groups	4 Excessive partying
5 Professors	5 Lack of air-conditioning

Students Speak Out
ON FACILITIES

Q "All the facilities are **always accessible whenever needed**. The athletic stadium area is kind of far though, so most people take the bus down to the field house."

Q "All in all, the facilities are good. There are two student centers, an indoor stadium, and an outdoor stadium. **They usually have a few concerts and comedians per year** at the indoor one—I got to see Bill Cosby and quite a few bands/musicians there."

Q "**The library has a nice copy center**, as well as a pretty good snack-bar-type place. Trabant has a good study area that not many students seem to know about. Perkins has one that even fewer kids use. Once you learn the nooks and crannies, then you'll be very happy with the facilities."

Q "The student centers are clean and kept up to date. The athletic facilities seem to get a large portion of our tuition funding; they are kept in very nice condition. **The computer centers are kept up to date** with the latest software and computers."

Q "All the facilities on campus are beautiful, clean, and **technologically advanced**."

STUDENT AUTHOR: **A main priority here at UD is to keep the campus as aesthetically pleasing and well equipped as possible. The University (quite amusingly) fights a losing battle to keep the grass growing in areas that are major student hangouts. Besides these few areas, the landscaping and architecture is stunning and many students have said they chose Delaware simply because "it was so pretty."**

Famous Alumni
Joseph Biden, Rich Gannon, Kevin Mench

Students Speak Out
ON CAMPUS DINING

Q "Dining-hall food is okay. Sometimes **it can seem repetitive**, but it's edible. Some days are better than others. Also, there are plenty of other eateries around campus to choose from in case you're not feeling the whole dining-hall food thing."

Q "I happen to be a very picky eater, but I still managed to survive four years of dining-hall food. It's not great, but **it isn't too terrible**. Unfortunately, if you live on campus, you have to purchase a meal plan, which gives you a certain number of all-you-can-eat meals per week, which can only be used at the dining hall. It also includes a certain number of points per semester, which can be used at the dining hall, and at a few other locations."

Q "College food is college food. Its not going to kill you, but it's not mom's home cooking. If I were you, I would **choose a meal plan with more points** and less dining-hall meals."

Q "The food on campus sucks; **you will get fat if you eat it**."

STUDENT AUTHOR: **There are some people who are tremendously fond of the dining hall and sing its praises, but most students find themselves looking for other options pretty quickly. After some time, students figure out which ones prepare which meals the best, and move between them to satisfy cravings. The food courts are a good place to use your points and students often find themselves choosing fewer meals in favor of points.**

Student Body

African American:	5%	Male/Female:	42/58%
Asian American:	5%	Out-of-State:	58%
Hispanic:	6%	International:	1%
Native American:	<1%	Unknown:	3%
White:	80%		

Popular Faiths: The most popular religion is Christianity, though other faiths are represented.

Gay Pride: There is tolerance of the gay community on campus although it is rare to hear from them. There is a campus club, called Haven, dedicated to preserving the rights of every sexual orientation.

Economic Status: Students are mostly upper-middle-class, and this seems to be a growing majority.

Students Speak Out
ON DORMS

Q "I lived in the Towers for my freshman year and **it was very anti-social**. I wish I had lived in a dorm. The one that you would want would be Rodney or Russell because it's right on the beach, an open area where everyone hangs out."

Q "The **dorms are okay**. Some have air-conditioning, but they tend to be the smaller ones that are far from campus. Rodney rocks if you need to use that health insurance that you purchased."

Q "The dorms are very small and crowded. Most people prefer South Campus because it is right in the middle of everything and prettier. The U of D has a problem with accepting more freshmen than they can house, so **tripling has become common in recent years**."

STUDENT AUTHOR: **Freshman housing tends to be cramped and overcrowded with three to a room becoming more common every year. While the rooms may provide little privacy, this can lead to the bonding that many freshmen long for from their first year. All students should try to live in a freshman dorm their first year.**

 Did You Know?
46% of undergrads live on campus.

Students Speak Out
ON GUYS & GIRLS

Q "My friends said that they heard that this **school has some of the hottest guys**. There are definitely a lot of hot guys on campus. You see more hot guys on campus each day than you would at most places."

Q "I can't complain, to tell you the truth. A lot of the people at UD are Abercrombie boys and girls. That means that they're **clean cut, well dressed, and attractive**. On a scale of one to ten, I would rate UD an eight on hotties."

Q "Guys and girls are **both extremely hot**!"

Q "The guys are overwhelmingly womanizers. There is this **huge frat boy mentality**, and most guys are just looking for a good time. You have to be really careful in finding a guy you can trust."

STUDENT AUTHOR: The main feature of this campus is its fascination for being completely put-together at all times. Even an ordinary looking person can put on makeup or flattering clothes and contribute to the campus level of attractiveness. Another contributor to the hotness-factor is the popularity of working out. There are so many fitness opportunities on campus that there is never an excuse not to go.

Traditions

Homecoming
Homecoming is a big deal at the UD and is generally celebrated with an all day drinking binge.

Greek Week
A festival involving all of the fraternities and sororities and featuring football, talent shows, and games.

Overall School Spirit
School spirit on this campus is about medium. The popular sports teams have a student following to support them, and most students have paraphernalia such as sweatshirts and stickers for their cars.

Students Speak Out
ON ATHLETICS

Q "If you like football and basketball, they are pretty big. **The teams are good and fun to go and watch**. I am not sure about IM sports. My friend was on a club team and she had fun, and they got to travel to other schools and play against them."

Q "Sports are big on campus, but not that big. **There's not that much school spirit** in those areas. The games do get packed, though. So maybe that's just my opinion."

Q "**Sports are not really big on campus**. Most people don't attend games unless they know members of the team. Football is, of course, the exception, and to a lesser extent basketball."

Q "Varsity football is huge. We're Division I football, as well as basketball. Our field hockey team is also well respected. **IM sports aren't that big of a thing**."

STUDENT AUTHOR: **Athletics are popular to those who care about them. The main spectator sports that draw crowds are football and basketball. Of course, every student wants UD teams to win, but few students follow the games or know the teams.**

Students Speak Out
ON DRUG SCENE

Q "My freshman year, some people on my floor really got into pot, and that's a pretty common thing. **Other drugs are out there**, too, like ecstasy, and mushrooms. They are not as commonly used, however."

Q "The drug scene at Delaware is **not out of hand at all**. A lot of people smoke weed, and it's pretty easy to get, but I haven't really seen any big drugs being used. I think I've seen E, 'shrooms, and coke one time. This school is definitely not full of crack heads and heroin addicts."

Q "The drug scene is probably no worse than on other campuses. There's mostly weed, some ecstasy, and a little cocaine, but **I wouldn't say there is a drug problem**."

STUDENT AUTHOR: **Most students will at least end up trying marijuana by the time they leave UD, if they haven't already. It is just around all the time. If you have no desire to be around marijuana, it isn't exceptionally hard to avoid it. You just hang out with those who are similarly-minded.**

12:1	Student-to-Faculty Ratio
91%	Freshman Retention Rate
64%	Four-Year Graduation Rate
62%	Financial Aid Applicants Receiving Aid

Students Speak Out
SAFETY & SECURITY

Q "In the four years that I've been there, the campus has **generally been quite safe**. The surrounding areas were not spectacular, but not too bad. In other words, a few muggings would happen here and there, but usually nothing serious."

Q "The campus has been having some trouble with robbery and smaller crimes of that nature. The city of Newark is **kind of a rough area**, but normally, it is totally hidden by the school."

Q "If you are a girl, it is **best to avoid fraternity houses or be very careful** if you choose to go. Many have been kicked off campus recently because of rape and hazing charges."

STUDENT AUTHOR: **On a day-to-day basis, most students don't really worry** about security. While it is always wise to keep an eye on your belongings, crime isn't a major focus. The number of muggings, attacks, and rapes has been quite high, with the result that students have been a little more aware of their actions.

Questions?
For more inside information and survival tips, pick up College Prowler's full-length book on this school, written by an actual student! Check it out at *www.collegeprowler.com*.

Students Speak Out
ON OVERALL EXPERIENCE

Q "Overall, my **experience at the University of Delaware has been a great one**. I have made a lot of friendships in my three years. I consider myself fortunate when I say that I never regretted coming to U of D."

Q "I hated it at first because I have gotten kicked out so many times. You are really treated like a number here. But now that I've been here two years, I sort of like it. **There isn't a lot of stuff to do in Delaware** if you're underage."

Q "I absolutely hated this school the first two years until I started to meet some people who weren't so typical. Now, I am okay with the school, but I know I would have preferred to go somewhere else. **I'm taking it for what it is**, and searching out those hidden departments, professors, and people that I believe are what college is supposed to be like."

Q "It's fun, but it gets boring very quickly. It is true that there isn't much else to do here. I would have **preferred a more intellectual atmosphere** that prized learning along with one's social life. Here, people forget that their main purpose is to learn; many truly believe that school is second to having a good time."

STUDENT AUTHOR: **While many students have a slow start here at Delaware, they all report that once they decided to give it a chance, they found their experience rewarding, not only academically but socially. This University tends to provide a nice balance between a social life and an academic one. There is always plenty of time to hang out and get your work done, so no matter what you are interested in, you have a chance to get it all done.**

University of Denver

2199 South University Boulevard; Denver, CO 80208
(303) 871-2000; www.du.edu

THE BASICS:

Acceptance Rate: 65%
Setting: Urban
F-T Undergrads: 4,772

SAT Range: 1070–1280*
Control: Private
Tuition: $33,710

Most Popular Majors: Business, Communications, Social Sciences, Biology, Visual and Performing Arts

*of 1600

Academics	B	Guys	B+
Local Atmosphere	B	Girls	B
Safety & Security	A-	Athletics	B-
Computers	B+	Nightlife	B-
Facilities	A-	Greek Life	A-
Campus Dining	C+	Drug Scene	B-
Off-Campus Dining	A-	Campus Strictness	A-
Campus Housing	C+	Parking	D+
Off-Campus Housing	A-	Transportation	B+
Diversity	C-	Weather	C+

Students Speak Out
ON ACADEMICS

Q "Most of my teachers have been really nice. I think the **best part of classes is the small size**. Usually classes only have about 20 or 30 students, unless it's a required core class."

Q "The professors are generally very engaging and **open to student comments**. Most of the classes include plenty of opportunities for students to voice their own opinions. The small class sizes make for great discussion."

Q "Usually, you can ask around and **find out from other students which teachers to avoid** and which are fun. People are pretty honest, and it helps going into a class if you have an idea of what to expect."

Q "Personally, I have found some of the professors' **teaching styles to be pretty dry**. Some of them talk very monotonously and just give lectures the entire quarter, every single class."

STUDENT AUTHOR: Some teachers are engaging, energetic, and personable, while others seem bland, uninformed, and not particularly driven for teaching. A handful of classes, especially some of the core requirements, can seem like a waste of time. The quarter system at DU ensures that even if students don't enjoy a particular class or professor, they only have to put up with it for 10 weeks. However, unlike semesters, the quarter system is a bit less forgiving on students who don't always make it to class. If you miss even one measly class, you run the risk of falling considerably far behind.

Students Speak Out
ON LOCAL ATMOSPHERE

Q "Denver is **a pretty fun city**, although I wouldn't really call it a 'college town.' There's a lot of variety here—outdoor sports, cultural outings, movies, and some great restaurants."

Q "DU is in Denver, but it is also its **own community within the big city**. All of the commodities of a big city are at hand, but the campus and student body are so small that a person never feels lost."

Q "Downtown Denver is the only really fun place in the city, and even that can get pretty old weekend after weekend. Plus, **some of the bars downtown are super expensive**."

Q "There are other universities around, but not very close to DU, so you don't really interact with students there on a daily basis. I definitely **recommend going to a sporting event** such as a Denver Broncos, Colorado Avalanche, Colorado Rockies, or Denver Nuggets game."

STUDENT AUTHOR: Perhaps the best part of living in this city is the best of both worlds—big-city living and a rural landscape. Connoisseurs of fine art, sports nuts, and entertainment fans alike can find something to do in the metro area, but if things get too hectic, peace and quiet is no more than 45 minutes away in the beautiful, majestic Rocky Mountains. You don't even need to get in a car to find something fun to do because the area surrounding DU's campus is constantly growing with new facilities, attractions, restaurants, and bars that appeal to DU's restless students.

5 Best Things	**5 Worst Things**
1 The city of Denver	1 Lack of diversity
2 10-week quarters	2 Parking
3 May Daze	3 Dorm food
4 Greek bar parties	4 Timing of breaks
5 Rocky Mountains	5 Snobby rich kids

Students Speak Out
ON FACILITIES

Q "The **facilities are awesome**! I love the pool—it's beautiful."

Q "The **Coors Fitness Center is beautiful**! I love working out there. It has two floors full of great cardio equipment, free weights, and weight machines."

Q "The athletic facilities at DU are great. There aren't a lot of places to eat on campus, but that's my only complaint. I hardly ever go to movie theaters anymore, because they **play recent movies for free** in Sturm."

Q "I'm a digital studies major, so I spend my life in the computer labs at school, and they're really nice. The machines are high tech, and they're **loaded with the latest software**."

Q "**I wish we had a better student center** at DU. I guess the closest thing is Driscoll, but I wouldn't really call that a student center."

STUDENT AUTHOR: Sidelines Pub is publicized as the "cool" place to hang out on campus, but most would rather go to an off-campus bar. Sidelines is the only sit-down restaurant on campus. All the other food spots are quick, on-the-go cafés. Also, a few buildings were left behind in the architectural makeover of the past few years. But a collection of beautiful architecture has replaced the campus's 1960s buildings. The music, law, and business schools attract and impress. The Coors Fitness Center, basketball courts, and giant swimming pool are available for a good workout or just a good time. Outside the Ritchie Center are beautiful tennis courts and soccer and lacrosse fields.

Famous Alumni

David Adkins (Sinbad), Peter Coors, Gale Norton, Condoleezza Rice, Andrew Rosenthal, Mark Rycroft

Students Speak Out
ON CAMPUS DINING

Q "Most places you go on campus have **vegetarian options**. It might not be the highest quality food, but I wouldn't say it's the worst."

Q "The dorm food actually isn't too bad, but a lot of students eat off-campus or **buy food to keep in their rooms and snack on**. The Commons is pretty popular because it's right in the middle of campus and right by Sturm Hall, where a lot of kids have class."

Q "When you first walk into the cafeteria, you're **blown away by all the food you see**, but a few weeks into the quarter, you're wondering why a meal plan with gross food is required."

Q "The best part about on-campus food is there's **coffee everywhere**!"

Q "I like eating at Sidelines because you can watch sports and play pool. The food's decent and pretty cheap. Plus, it's the **only place on campus that serves alcohol**."

STUDENT AUTHOR: Sodexo, the campus food and beverage supplier, tries to be creative and provide students with variation, but inevitably, some meals in the dorms are served repeatedly. The expense of eating off campus is eased by applying flex points at some off-campus vendors. Several cafés are located strategically throughout campus, boosting tired students with quick caffeine shots when needed. The cafés also have wired connections and plenty of outlets for computers, making them perfect study spots. Many healthy options are also available.

Student Body

African American:	3%	Male/Female:	45/55%
Asian American:	5%	Out-of-State:	56%
Hispanic:	7%	International:	4%
Native American:	1%	Unknown:	4%
White:	75%		

Popular Faiths: On campus are a number of religious groups, and Christians, Jews, and Muslims.

Gay Pride: You don't hear much about the gay and lesbian community on DU's campus, but student organizations, such as PRIDE, sponsor ongoing events and activities.

Economic Status: Most DU students come from affluent families, but many are on scholarships.

Students Speak Out
ON DORMS

Q "I lived in Towers last year, and I really liked it. It felt more like I was **living in an apartment** than a dorm room. There's access to a kitchen so you can cook for yourself, and it's just really laid-back. Everyone hangs out in the common living area and watches TV."

Q "I like being in Halls because **there's always something going on**, but I think it has the reputation of being the least-desired dorm on campus. It's a little rundown, but it's fun. Try to live on a coed floor. It definitely keeps things interesting."

Q "Freshmen have the choice of Centennial Halls or Johnson-McFarlane. They **both are pretty clean** and offer plenty of different living arrangements."

STUDENT AUTHOR: **Although freshmen are forced to live in either Halls or J-Mac, the experience is what you make it. Halls is known to be a bit wilder and louder, and J-Mac offers a delicate balance of partying and studying. Towers is a good if you want more of an apartment feel, but being on the north outskirt of campus, some complain they feel disconnected from the rest of the school.**

Did You Know?
41% of undergrads live on campus.

Students Speak Out
ON GUYS & GIRLS

Q "There are some really good-looking guys and girls on this campus! But you kind of have to **search them out**."

Q "The **guys are out to impress** each and every girl on campus. The girls are out to show off what daddy bought them before they came to school. It's kind of pathetic, and people care entirely too much about what others think of them."

Q "I wish people were **more real**."

Q "It's hard to really have time to think about having a relationship with school and other stuff always getting in the way. But if you're looking for **random hookups at bars or clubs** or whatever, yeah, there's a lot of that scene."

STUDENT AUTHOR: **It seems most of the good-looking crowd parties, studies, hangs out, eats, and basically has to be with each other at all times. DU's hotties tend to look similar to one another, with little sense of individuality or independence. Some of the best-looking guys on campus act much too superior for their own good, and some of the best-looking girls can be seasoned ice queens. The best place to meet hotties is in downtown bars and clubs.**

Traditions

Drag Queen Fashion Show
Beefcakes dress to impress in short skirts, pantyhose, spike heels, and bras, all while prancing around dancing and singing. Proceeds go to local charities.

May Daze
A week-long carnival in the spring on Driscoll lawn with games, activities, music, giveaways, and food.

Overall School Spirit
Most students only take great pride in DU when a sports team wins a big game. Many students don DU gear, such as hooded sweatshirts and T-shirts.

Students Speak Out
ON ATHLETICS

Q "Sometimes **school spirit is truly lacking**. Stands are hardly ever full unless it's a big game, and people don't seem to have much interest in the teams that aren't winning."

Q "**Hockey is, by far, the major sport** on campus. Lacrosse is also a student favorite to watch, and soccer is becoming more popular every year."

Q "IM sports are so fun if you get into them. You have to make the effort, but I say go for it. It's a **great way to meet new people** who have the same interests as you."

Q "Being **a Division I school** is pretty cool, but no one on campus seems to care."

STUDENT AUTHOR: **Many students remain unhappy with the lack of a DU football team, and some attend CU or CSU games to compensate. In recent years, there has been an increased effort to publicize DU's varsity sports in order to rally more student support at games. Varsity men's ice hockey takes center stage at DU. Games usually are well attended, but it's unfortunate that other athletic teams often don't receive the same degree of support and appreciation.**

Students Speak Out
ON DRUG SCENE

Q "I haven't seen too much of the drug scene around here, except for **weed and alcohol**. Some parties can get pretty crazy."

Q "I haven't heard about drugs on DU's campus. I don't even know if a lot of students smoke weed. **Drinking is really big**, just like on any other campus. I don't think most students here consider alcohol a drug, though."

Q "I haven't seen too many drugs around here. Then again, I haven't really looked. I'm sure if you were into that, you could find what you wanted, but **most students stay away from it**."

STUDENT AUTHOR: **Other than alcohol and marijuana, you don't hear much about drugs on the DU campus. Drinking is a popular activity, but there are other things to do if it is not your scene. At times, the campus buzzes with rumors of cocaine, but for the most part, hard drugs aren't a factor. Most students don't want to even think about the consequences of getting caught with hard drugs, much less live out those consequences.**

10:1	Student-to-Faculty Ratio
87%	Freshman Retention Rate
60%	Four-Year Graduation Rate
71%	Financial Aid Applicants Receiving Aid

Students Speak Out
SAFETY & SECURITY

Q "Our **campus is really well lit**, so that makes you feel safe."

Q "The campus has a lot of campus safety officers. There are **call boxes stationed all around** campus, and there is a SafeRide program that allows students to wait for a van to pick them up and take them home."

Q "All I know about the department of safety and security is that they **patrol the campus all day**."

Q "Really, the campus is so small that **getting into trouble is truly an effort**. Even at really rowdy parties I've been to, nothing horrible takes place. Maybe a couple of vandalisms, but no felonies or assaults or anything. Usually the cops break up parties before anything like that can happen."

STUDENT AUTHOR: **Although it's tempting to equate a big city with high crime rates, DU and its surrounding areas are exceptionally safe. Denver has one of the safest downtown areas in the country. Both DU's department and the Denver Police Department are quick to respond to campus concerns.**

> **Questions?**
> For more inside information and survival tips, pick up College Prowler's full-length book on this school, written by an actual student! Check it out at www.collegeprowler.com.

Students Speak Out
ON OVERALL EXPERIENCE

Q "**Denver is a great city to live in**. There's so much to do, and the people here are so nice. DU could definitely improve on some things, but I feel I've gotten a good education. I just wish it weren't so expensive, and I wish I had met more diverse people while I was here. The campus is kind of bland and boring."

Q "I **wish there was more diversity** represented on campus. Another thing is many of the students have a lot of money, and sometimes that can come across as snobbishness."

Q "I could do without the quarter system and the snobby Greek life people. But **my classes have been great**, and I've met some really interesting people by getting involved in student organizations. And I love living in Denver!"

Q "I love this school. At first, the people can seem really snotty and exclusive, but **once you find your niche, you really start to feel at home**. I think everyone's experience is very unique and different because the school has so much to offer. It all depends what you are interested in and what you decide to get involved with."

STUDENT AUTHOR: **Students generally enjoy their time at DU and are content staying for four years. Classes are interesting, professors are friendly, and the campus is in the middle of a growing, energetic city. DU offers a nice balance of academia and partying. If you're looking to dedicate your college years solely to developing your career and learning as much as you can, DU probably isn't the place for you. If you want to learn, but also want to have some fun in the process, DU might be the perfect fit.**

University of Florida

201 Criser Hall; Gainesville; FL 32611
(352) 392-3261; www.ufl.edu

THE BASICS:

Acceptance Rate: 42% **SAT Range:** 1140–1360*
Setting: Small city **Control:** Public
F-T Undergrads: 32,470 **Tuition:** $20,623

Most Popular Majors: Social Sciences, Business, Engineering, Communications, Agriculture

*of 1600

Academics	B	Guys	A
Local Atmosphere	B+	Girls	A
Safety & Security	A	Athletics	A+
Computers	B	Nightlife	B+
Facilities	A+	Greek Life	B+
Campus Dining	C	Drug Scene	B
Off-Campus Dining	B+	Campus Strictness	B
Campus Housing	C	Parking	D-
Off-Campus Housing	A-	Transportation	B
Diversity	B+	Weather	A-

Students Speak Out
ON ACADEMICS

Q "Almost all of my professors were very interesting and willing to **help outside of class**. Although some of my general education classes weren't my favorites, I loved the classes in my major."

Q "Most of the teachers are really accessible and check their e-mail all day long, which is very convenient. It's always good when you go out of your way to meet with them or talk to them, because then you're **more than just a face** in a chair in a lecture hall."

Q "I feel that I have had the opportunity to take a wide variety of classes here. I have done **multimedia projects** for visual anthropology, taken pictures for an ecology course in Mexico, learned about black holes in astronomy, and read fascinating short stories in Caribbean literature."

Q "Most freshman-level classes are so big that you might not get to know your instructors personally. The teachers are good though. In smaller classes, you'll get a chance to know them more personally. But they **always have office hours** when you can see them or their TAs."

STUDENT AUTHOR: With about 1,700 professors here, it can be difficult to characterize them as a single group. For the most part, though, they are extremely interested in their subjects and in sharing with whoever will listen, which can sometimes mean that you get your ear talked off. Usually, it just means that they're really easy to approach and totally interested in helping you get everything you can out of their classes.

Students Speak Out
ON LOCAL ATMOSPHERE

Q "Every type of student can find something to do in this town. Whether you're into the club scene, alternative music, or sporting events, **your needs will be met**."

Q "Some find Gainesville too small, while others think it's just right. **Gainesville is not Orlando** or Tampa, though both are within two to three hours' drive. Gainesville has a decent-sized mall and an active downtown for going out. There are also lots of restaurants and bars dispersed throughout the city."

Q "Well, the city is pretty much the college—and vice-versa. It's kinda strange because you have very little connection with people out of your age range. **FSU, UNF, and UCF are about two hours away** each in their respective direction, so it's a good spot."

Q "One of the best things about UF is that Gainesville is really a quintessential college town. Almost everything **revolves around the school**."

STUDENT AUTHOR: Gainesville could be an absolute prototype for the college town. UF is the only university here, and although there is also a huge, high-quality community college (Santa Fe C.C.) in our fair village, this place is pretty much centered on being the Land of the Gator. Of course, this town resembles neither New York City nor the backwoods of Alaska, so if you're looking for the extremes in population, setting, or events that go with those kinds of places, Gainesville may not be the ideal location for you.

5 Best Things	5 Worst Things
1 Options!	**1** Parking
2 Gainesville	**2** Traffic
3 Cool professors	**3** Gas prices
4 Changing majors	**4** Fire drills
5 Game days	**5** Class sizes

Students Speak Out
ON FACILITIES

Q "The Reitz Union is very nice, and constantly being improved on. It has clean, smoke-free **bowling alleys, pool tables**, and other games for a quarter each."

Q "We have excellent facilities. We have a number of gyms to work out at. You can also **run around the football stadium** or walk (or run) up and down the football bleachers. This makes for a good workout."

Q "UF's facilities are excellent. From the Reitz Union, where you can go to eat, play pool, bowl, study, or catch a flick, to **Lake Wauburg, with its free boats**, barbecue grills, and more, you'll find something to fill up your spare time."

Q "The HUB is where the old bookstore used to be, although now they built a massive new one by the Reitz Union. **The HUB is nice** for some Taco Bell or KFC, or to get some Gator gear."

Q "There's a huge new workout room and three new indoor basketball courts at the Student Rec Center, in addition to **a room full of treadmills**."

STUDENT AUTHOR: **With all the things going on at the Reitz, it's an ideal place to hang out if you don't know what you want to do—a strawberry smoothie from Freshens on the ground floor will never fail to make you feel better. And Lake Wauburg is definitely an untapped resource for an awful lot of UF people; it's a little slimy, and I would recommend washing your ears out when you get home, but hey, it's a lake—what are you going to do? Wauburg, like so many other attractions at UF, is totally free of charge.**

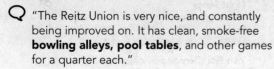

Famous Alumni

Chris DiMarco, Faye Dunaway, David Eckstein, Robert Love, Andy North, Forrest Sawyer, Bob Vila

Students Speak Out
ON CAMPUS DINING

Q "Every dorm resident has to at least try Gator Corner. Even if the food's not great, **there's a lot of it**. And I suppose if you're really ambitious, you can always pay for breakfast and hang around 'til dinner."

Q "The dining halls aren't bad. The cool thing about them is you can get a good, balanced, hot dinner every night of the week, and make a few friends with the staff (they will recognize you after a while) while you're at it. **It does get old** after awhile for most people, though."

Q "I have only eaten at Broward Dining, and it is excellent. In high school, I refused to eat at the cafeteria, but **Broward Dining is excellent** for breakfast. They have the best fruits and waffles I've had in a long time."

Q "I don't think the food on campus is anything to complain about. Gator Dining has a ton of selection, and it's **big enough** that you don't have trouble finding a seat. Broward Dining is a lot smaller, but it still offers quite a lot, and it's more convenient to a lot of classes."

STUDENT AUTHOR: **There are two kinds of on-campus food: the kind that uses up a meal block (Gator Corner/Broward Dining) and the kind that uses up declining balance (everything else). The meal-block variety is pretty cheap, very filling, and easy to get to, and it'll keep you eating your veggies. However, after a couple of semesters, you'll probably get tired of it, and it's not really anything to write home about to start with.**

Student Body

African American:	10%	Male/Female:	46/54%
Asian American:	8%	Out-of-State:	5%
Hispanic:	14%	International:	1%
Native American:	<1%	Unknown:	2%
White:	65%		

Popular Faiths: UF is home to one of the world's largest Jewish student populations (although it does not constitute the majority of students).

Gay Pride: Reasonably high—there are some fairly active lesbian, gay, bisexual, and transgender groups on campus.

Economic Status: Largely middle-class, although there is a fair-sized group of the extremely well-off and a slightly smaller group of those who aren't.

Students Speak Out
ON DORMS

Q "Lakeside was built in 2000 and is really nice, but it's on the **outskirts of campus**. You have to take a bus to the middle of campus. It has four small rooms, two bathrooms, a living room, and a large kitchen."

Q "There's no more fulfilling experience in your first year of college than spending your nights at Murphree Hall, where the lack of air conditioning invites the town's most social and outlandish **cockroaches**."

Q "Dorms are a lot of fun. You meet so many people and have a great time. You can check online; **some don't have A/C**. Avoid those. Some are suites, like apartments, and others are normal dorms, depending on preference."

STUDENT AUTHOR: **Dorms at UF all involve, to some extent, nasty linoleum or industrial-strength carpeting, cinderblock walls, possibly irritating neighbors, a lack of automatic dishwashers, and a bathroom to be shared with at least one (but as many as 50) other kids. On the other hand, you are offered all kinds of practice with choosing carpet remnants, getting along with your fellow (woman, and achieving high levels of immodesty.**

> **? Did You Know?**
> 22% of undergrads live on campus.

Students Speak Out
ON GUYS & GIRLS

Q "At UF, you have **so many different types of people**—it's not even funny. You're sure to find someone to get along with. In my opinion, there are lots of really hot guys. There are also good-looking girls, too."

Q "The people on campus are pretty nice. However, at the same time, **there are ditzes who tend to make you feel better** about yourself."

Q "Even Emeril will tell you there's **no better dish than a female Gator**."

Q "I think **the guys are preppy** and often interested in athletics and parties. Some of them are hot. The girls are pretty and often into the latest trends and fashions."

STUDENT AUTHOR: **Many people at UF—for some reason, mostly girls—tend to wear rather small clothes. Anyway, when they're not sun-worshipping, a good number of students here are busy praying to A&F or Hollister. As it turns out, guys in torn-up cargo shorts and button-down shirts are pretty easy on the eyes, as apparently are girls in low-cut rugby shirts and short tan skirts, and if Abercrombie is not your gig, there are more than enough people here who would agree with you.**

> **Traditions**
>
> **Fight Songs**
> During home football games, chants such as "The Hey Song," "We are the Boys," and "Orange & Blue Cheer" can be heard from miles around.
>
> **Two Bits (George Edmondson Jr.)**
> Ask any Gator about the 85+-year-old insurance salesman, and they'll tell you about UF's biggest fan!
>
> **Overall School Spirit**
> Everybody around here seems obsessed with UF—have you ever heard of an entire county closing schools so the students can march in a university homecoming parade? Alachua County does!

Students Speak Out
ON ATHLETICS

Q "As you may know, Gator football is huge. We have awesome football and basketball teams. **You should see this place** on game day."

Q "Sports are huge on campus. We have **Top 10 teams in baseball, football, and basketball** almost every year."

Q "IM sports obviously aren't as big as varsity sports. However, **they're still pretty big**. My friends that play the IM sports really like it."

Q "There are huge intramural sports on campus. They range from **extreme Frisbee**, to rugby, to football, to softball."

STUDENT AUTHOR: **As cool as badminton intramurals are, I have to tell you that it and its fellow IM/club sports are a little overshadowed by UF varsity sports. Golf, soccer, tennis, and others have recently produced national champions, and men's basketball has a very attached following, but it's Gator football that takes over the land in the fall. Even if you come here knowing nothing about the game, I can just about guarantee that you will be very familiar with football by the time you leave.**

Students Speak Out
ON DRUG SCENE

Q "From what I know, weed is the drug of choice for anyone who does drugs, but **it's normally select groups**, so it can be available if you want it. If you aren't into that, it's not something you have to deal with."

Q "There are people who do drugs on campus. You can choose to be involved or not. I myself don't do drugs, and no one seems to have a problem with that. **No one ever tries to pressure me** into doing them."

Q "There are drugs around, I won't lie, and you hear about it, but **it's not a huge problem** or anything. It's about the same as every other university in this country. It's not hard to stay away from it if you want."

STUDENT AUTHOR: **Most hard drugs, it seems, are not particularly popular on campus. Pot has something of a following (for better or for worse, this town is famous for its "Gainesville Gold"), and ecstasy, Rohypnol ("roofies"), and a few others have shown themselves in some places.**

22:1	Student-to-Faculty Ratio
95%	Freshman Retention Rate
54%	Four-Year Graduation Rate
78%	Financial Aid Applicants Receiving Aid

Students Speak Out
SAFETY & SECURITY

Q "I feel very safe here. The University has its own police force that **responds to calls**. In the residence halls there are also nighttime security assistants who patrol the area."

Q "I would say that security and safety are comparable to most colleges. But people do run into danger here. **A little common sense** will keep you safe and out of jail in Gainesville."

Q "I felt pretty good about the safety on campus when I first arrived, and it has only improved since then. The University Police are always available and, more often than not, eager to assist. **They patrol campus very thoroughly**, and they will help you get from point to point at night—the SNAP service, for example."

STUDENT AUTHOR: **UF's state- and nationally-accredited police department is not just some lame rent-a-cop force. They keep an eye on the campus 24 hours a day, 365 days a year—in patrol cars, on motorcycles and bicycles, and by foot. In an emergency, they can be just about anywhere on campus in what seems like an instant.**

Questions?
For more inside information and survival tips, pick up College Prowler's full-length book on this school, written by an actual student! Check it out at *www.collegeprowler.com*.

Students Speak Out
ON OVERALL EXPERIENCE

Q "I love UF. I think everything about it is great. **The faculty is nice and helpful**, students are friendly, and the school overall is awesome. I wouldn't go anywhere else. You should give UF a chance; it really is an amazing school."

Q "I like the whole spirit of the school and how everyone supports the Gators. I think UF is pretty diverse and has every kind of group that any school would have. Let me warn you about one thing—**UF is run like a government bureaucracy**. That's one big complaint I have."

Q "I'm from New Jersey, and I decided to come here not knowing anyone. It was the best decision I ever made. **I love Florida**! I have met amazing people and been able to go to every big city and beach in Florida."

Q "If I had it to do all over again, I would pick UF with no hesitation. I have now lived in Gainesville longer than any other place in my life, and the University has affected me in so many positive ways. **There's a bumper sticker** that reads 'UF: Worth Leaving Home For', and it's so true."

STUDENT AUTHOR: **Well, UF is not your typical state school, and Gainesville is certainly not your typical small town. Because this place is so big, we have all the libraries, dorms, athletics, courses, clubs, and services you could want at a good price, but if you put out just a little effort, you'll find that we also have more compassionate, down-to-earth professors, locals, and students that any small, private school could ever dream of having. In your final days, when you look back at your life, you may be hard-pressed to find any brighter memories than your time and experiences at UF.**

University of Georgia

212 Terrell Hall; Athens, GA 30602
(706) 542-8776; www.uga.edu

THE BASICS:

Acceptance Rate: 55%   **SAT Range:** 1690–1950*
Setting: Mid-sized city   **Control:** Public
F-T Undergrads: 23,418   **Tuition:** $19,156

Most Popular Majors: Business, Social Sciences, Education, Biology, Psychology

*of 2400

Academics	B	Guys	A-
Local Atmosphere	A-	Girls	A+
Safety & Security	B-	Athletics	A
Computers	B	Nightlife	A-
Facilities	A-	Greek Life	A-
Campus Dining	B	Drug Scene	C+
Off-Campus Dining	B+	Campus Strictness	B+
Campus Housing	B-	Parking	C+
Off-Campus Housing	A+	Transportation	C
Diversity	D-	Weather	B+

Students Speak Out
ON ACADEMICS

Q "Most of the professors I have had are very eccentric and more lively than my high school teachers. I find my professors to **hold a broad knowledge of their material** and present it with enthusiasm and a blend of personal background."

Q "**I found that there was a general apathy regarding many classes**, which I thought I left behind in high school. Since I am motivated mostly to perform well academically, I hated this aspect of UGA."

Q "I have had some wonderful teachers, and even though you will have some large classes your freshman year, your teachers will have office hours, and will be **very willing to provide help**."

Q "If a student takes the time to get to know their teacher, the teacher makes the effort to get to know the student. I have had teachers that have genuinely taken the time to help out when needed. Several of my teachers have made the content of their courses apply to my life and interests. There are lecture classes, as well as **small, intimate classes available** for students."

STUDENT AUTHOR: Oftentimes, UGA attracts both students who want to learn and students who want to party. UGA has a dubious reputation for being a "party school," but make no mistake about it, you will not be able to slack on your studies and leave here four years later with a diploma. Professors always encourage students to stop by their offices for help or for study reviews.

Students Speak Out
ON LOCAL ATMOSPHERE

Q "Downtown Athens is the place to be! There are theaters, restaurants, clubs, bars, and street performers, all of which are very cheap. You can't beat it. **Athens is a great town to be young and energetic**, because there is so much to do there. The weekend before I left Athens to come back home for the summer, I went to a carnival, saw a movie at a drive-in, went barhopping, kayaking, to a concert, and played basketball."

Q "Athens is what I had always imagined a college town would be like. **The school's campus is gorgeous**, and UGA is located in a large town that revolves around the University. There are tons of thing to do, and you are only an hour and a half away from Atlanta, which is a great city."

Q "Athens has a **great, small, Southern-town feel**! The town itself is beautiful. It's very historic and has lots of character. Visit the Arch when you come down here—it's the University's trademark."

Q "If I had to guess, I would say local Athenians probably get **tired of seeing college kids all the time**."

STUDENT AUTHOR: Athens, the "Classic City," is the quintessential college town. Downtown offers amazing nightlife, with numerous clubs, bars, cafés, restaurants, and shops on every corner. Music is a cornerstone of downtown Athens, with plenty of opportunities for students to see local and nationally-famous bands. Downtown is located within walking distance from the dorms, so nobody has to drive.

5 Best Things	5 Worst Things
1 The people	1 Constant construction
2 Football season	2 Humidity
3 Downtown	3 Lack of diversity
4 The weather	4 Parking
5 Music scene	5 Annual tuition increases

Students Speak Out
ON FACILITIES

Q "The athletic facilities are impressive and probably the most impressive aspect of campus. We have an **$83 million student fitness center** that houses an indoor track, indoor olympic-size pool complete with diving, numerous dance and aerobic studios, eight basketball courts, a gymnastics area, two volleyball courts, and two separate weight-training facilities."

Q "Our student center has a movie theater that run**s new movies, classic movies, and sneak previews of upcoming movies** (I saw *Road Trip* two months before it came out in theaters), as well as the Bulldog Café, study rooms, art galleries, the bookstore, and is the hub for advertisements and offices that can help get you involved in the thousands of activities that take place at UGA."

Q "The SLC is probably the nicest building I've ever been in on campus. There are **marble steps, leather chairs, and a really nice library**. I was actually pretty impressed by it all."

STUDENT AUTHOR: **The Student Learning Center (SLC) is a major asset to the campus. SLC boasts 26 new, state-of-the-art classrooms, 96 private-group study rooms, wireless Internet access, and the coffee shop. The libraries are extremely large, with many areas to study. The Tate Center houses a movie theater, game room, and several other venues. Ramsey is very popular with students. There are pools, basketball courts, aerobic rooms, a rock-climbing wall, racquetball courts, badminton courts, gymnastics facilities, volleyball courts, and state-of-the-art workout equipment. You can even sign up for a personal trainer.**

Famous Alumni

Anne Barge, Chris Carter, Neill Slaughter, Dominique Wilkins

Students Speak Out
ON CAMPUS DINING

Q "Personally, I find the food a bit bland, and sometimes they mix leftovers with other leftovers and call it a new dish. I don't feel like the meal plan saves much money on food or is a very healthy option. **The highlight of the meal plan is Sunday brunch.**"

Q "The food on campus is amazing. There is something for everyone, including extravagant foods such as tofu pizza, Philly cheesesteak sandwiches, salad bars, omelet stations, and ice-cream tables with every topping imaginable. Whether you are in the mood to eat healthy or not, there is always something for you. Another nice feature is that **the nutritional information of all the foods is available for you** so you can know exactly what you're eating. The dining halls also have specialty days, on which the dining hall is specially decorated with themes like 'Beach Party,' 'Under the Big Top,' 'Tastes From Around the World,' and 'Silver Platter Night.'"

STUDENT AUTHOR: **The Village Summit has been a big hit with students since its inception in 2004. It has two levels and offers items students can pay cash for on the bottom floor, like a restaurant, with another dining hall on the top floor. Most freshmen will be assigned to live in a high-rise dorm and will therefore be eating at Bolton a lot. Bolton has a great salad bar, and if grilled cheese and tomato soup is your thing, the dining experience will be comparable to heaven. Oglethorpe gets packed on Sunday's. The brunch is so good that local Athens residents choose to come after church.**

Student Body

African American:	6%	Male/Female:	42/58%
Asian American:	7%	Out-of-State:	11%
Hispanic:	2%	International:	1%
Native American:	<1%	Unknown:	1%
White:	83%		

Popular Faiths: There are a lot of very active Christian groups at UGA. Baptist groups probably have the largest numbers, though.

Gay Pride: The campus is not terribly tolerant toward gays and lesbians. There have been several protests at the Tate Center surrounding this issue.

Economic Status: There seems to be a predominant amount coming from wealthy families.

Students Speak Out
ON DORMS

Q "The dorms are a great community for students. There is a variety of sizes of dorms to meet your comfort. While you are sharing a room, **it is an experience like no other**. I recommend that all freshmen take advantage of the living situation by getting involved on campus and meeting new people."

Q "I'll just give the basic gist of the dorms. Russell has 10 floors and is coed by hall, and **there is always someone to party with**. It's a great place, in my opinion. Creswell has nine floors, and is coed by floor. It's a little bit rundown, but still fun. Brumby has nine floors and is an all-girls dorm. I enjoy hanging out with guys a lot, so I wouldn't want to live there, but some of my friends did, and they loved it. Mell Hall, Lipscomb Hall, Hill Hall, Church Hall and other places are smaller, usually comprised more of upperclassmen, and are a little more boring."

STUDENT AUTHOR: **Each hall has its own parties and socials every so often, and there is definitely a sense of community within every hall. And, get this—the bathrooms are usually very clean. All the dorms now have air conditioning.**

Did You Know?
27% of undergrads live on campus.

Students Speak Out
ON GUYS & GIRLS

Q "Most of the guys are good old Southern boys. **They drink too much, they're too loud**, and sometimes they're way too horny, but that's why we love them. Girls around Georgia are very friendly, for the most part. Southern people, overall, are pretty nice."

Q "The girls here are amazing. I'll be honest with you—one of the main reasons I came to school here is because the girls here are hotter than anything I've ever seen, and I'm coming from Atlanta. **You will not find hotter girls anywhere** else, trust me."

Q **"Everyone here seems to wear the same thing**—golf shirts and rainbows (flip-flops) for guys, sorority shirts and short black skirts for girls, and that's it."

STUDENT AUTHOR: **Most students at UGA are very good looking and friendly. There are a lot of tan, toned bodies walking around campus and downtown. Students have been classified as easygoing and down-to-earth, making it at least fairly easy to talk to people. Working out and sunbathing are very popular pastimes, so I guess it's only natural that the general population looks great.**

Traditions

Bulldogs
The term "Georgia Bulldogs" came from an article stating, "The Georgia Bulldog would sound good because there is a certain dignity about a bulldog, as well as a ferocity."

The Chapel Bell
Georgia fans ring the chapel bell after a Georgia football victory. The tradition began in the 1890s.

Overall School Spirit
Alumni support, both financially and being present at University events, is overwhelming. Football games unite thousands of students and fans that might have nothing in common but a love for the school.

Students Speak Out
ON ATHLETICS

Q "This is UGA! It's Bulldog country! You better get out of town on football weekends if you don't like football. It's a way of life, and the games are so much fun. **I didn't like football until I started going to school at UGA.**"

Q "Football rules at UGA, followed by basketball and baseball. Swimming and gymnastics are pretty big, mostly because our teams are excellent and win the national competitions frequently. You'd better get ready to learn how to tailgate for football games, though. Football game days are really fun. **Everybody dresses in red and black!**"

Q "I have grown to hate football season because you can't go anywhere or do anything on game weekends, and **everyone is drunk and obnoxious.**"

STUDENT AUTHOR: **Football is God for many at UGA. Alumni often show up in their RVs and trailers on Thursdays for a Saturday game. The other varsity sports programs have smaller followings. Basketball games are a lot of fun and usually draw a decent crowd. Intramural sports are also really popular.**

Students Speak Out
ON DRUG SCENE

Q "There is a lot of pot on campus, although I don't know how much relative to other campuses. That's the only drug I really hear about. There are rumors of wealthy kids doing cocaine. I guess that if you look hard enough, you can find all kinds of drugs, but **it's pretty easy to keep your nose clean**."

Q "Drugs are present at UGA. **Obviously, alcohol is quite prevalent**. I haven't seen much else, though, aside from marijuana. Stuff is available, but if you choose to 'say no,' people will not look down on you."

Q "I've heard that one of our dorms actually is rumored to be one of the 'top 10' pot-smoking dorms in the nation. Athens has been called a '**drinking town with a football problem**' to poke fun at the crazed UGA football fanatics."

STUDENT AUTHOR: Alcohol is probably the most abused substance on campus. There are lots of students, especially guys, who drink all the time. Smoking pot is pretty popular, but if someone is smoking in a dorm, he or she is usually caught pretty quickly.

18:1	Student-to-Faculty Ratio
93%	Freshman Retention Rate
48%	Four-Year Graduation Rate
58%	Financial Aid Applicants Receiving Aid

Students Speak Out
SAFETY & SECURITY

Q "I've never felt in any kind of danger on campus. There are some dorms located across the street from housing projects, but I lived there and I never once had a problem with anything. Sometimes **cars parked along that street get broken into during the day**, though."

Q "Security on campus has been **quite a problem for the past few years**. There have been several rapes, and a number of attacks on students. However, most of these attacks could have been avoided. Having some street smarts would prevent a lot of those incidents."

Q "**Most areas are sufficiently lit**, and campus police frequently circulate the campus."

STUDENT AUTHOR: Walking home from downtown can potentially be dangerous—some people have been mugged and even raped doing so. Students should always travel in groups. The downtown cops are mainly there to bust underage drinkers, and they are usually out in droves, so trying to run from them doesn't always work.

> **Questions?**
> For more inside information and survival tips, pick up College Prowler's full-length book on this school, written by an actual student! Check it out at *www.collegeprowler.com*.

Students Speak Out
ON OVERALL EXPERIENCE

Q "**My overall experience has been amazing**. I love it here, and I am so glad I came. I have had so much fun these past few years, while also getting a great education. In town there is always something going on, and there are always a ton of people around. It just makes for a great college experience."

Q "**The trick to succeeding at a big university is to find your niche**. I suggest getting involved. Whether it's in a Greek society or in any of our hundreds of student organizations, you can meet people with similar beliefs and interests while also being exposed to tons others!"

Q "UGA is great and I love it. Sometimes I wish that I had chosen a smaller school, but overall, I am happy that I am here. After my first year, I realized that this was a really big school and found myself feeling more and more like a number rather than an actual student. I had a great time and love this school, but **I think that you should consider the size** in making your decision."

STUDENT AUTHOR: UGA and Athens have so much to offer in so many different categories, that there really is something for everyone. The positive energy of 30,000 people who are happy to be here is captivating, and something you will instantly want to be a part of. Students are encouraged to explore their talents and make the most of their four years here, and most students are able to achieve their ultimate "college experience." It's exciting to be in Athens because there is always something going on, whether it is entertainment, a demonstration, job fairs, or just a chance to hang out with people you just met.

University of Illinois

601 East John Street; Champaign; IL, 61820
(217) 333-1000; www.uiuc.edu

THE BASICS:

Acceptance Rate: 71%
Setting: Small city
F-T Undergrads: 30,205

SAT Range: 1170–1410*
Control: Public
Tuition: $25,890

Most Popular Majors: Business, Engineering, Social Sciences, Biology, English, Psychology

*of 1600

Academics	B+	Guys	B+
Local Atmosphere	B-	Girls	A-
Safety & Security	B+	Athletics	A
Computers	B	Nightlife	A-
Facilities	A-	Greek Life	A
Campus Dining	D	Drug Scene	B-
Off-Campus Dining	B	Campus Strictness	B
Campus Housing	B-	Parking	D
Off-Campus Housing	A-	Transportation	A-
Diversity	B-	Weather	D

Students Speak Out
ON ACADEMICS

Q "**The faculty is pretty good**. I am in the math department, so there is a social intimidation factor—only in the math department, though. I don't know why they are like that."

Q "I have liked almost all of my classes. The teachers have always been available at office hours, and they are generally accessible. I have **no complaints**."

Q "**It's different than high school**—you have to do 70 percent of the teaching to yourself by reading a lot. You can always get help, whether you go to office hours or get a tutor."

Q "Many professors are approachable, research opportunities are available, and once beyond the first year or so, a student will have the opportunity to **directly interact with the professor in a classroom** setting."

STUDENT AUTHOR: **The University's business and agricultural programs are world-renowned and very popular. However, the liberal arts and sciences departments are not as prestigious. Students often complain that arts majors are passed over in favor of other majors. Many professors are dedicated to teaching and reaching out to their students. Most make themselves available, and a few have even been known to give out their home phone number. Still, it can be hard to get acclimated to a school of 30,000, which is why the University implemented discussion groups to accompany big lectures.**

Students Speak Out
ON LOCAL ATMOSPHERE

Q "The atmosphere is **just campus life, really**. The recreational areas are the places where everyone is. There isn't much interaction with other colleges in the area."

Q "The atmosphere is nice—that of a small, Midwestern city. **The people are nice**, and the town is cozy. It is large enough to have plenty to do without being too big and overwhelming. There is a community college in town and a few other colleges within an hour's drive away."

Q "For a state school, the University of Illinois is in an awkward spot. A little **more than two hours from Chicago** and three from St. Louis, the atmosphere of Urbana-Champaign is completely dictated by the events of the University."

Q "The historical Virginia Theater is located in Champaign, where **U of I alum Roger Ebert holds his annual Overlooked Film Festival**. The theater also plays classic or popular films that are well attended by the academic, student, and local communities."

STUDENT AUTHOR: **Urbana-Champaign is mostly farmland, except for the University, which is located in the middle of prairieland, bounded by farms and fields. The campus rises out of the middle of the twin cities, and even with its popular main road, Green Street, the city is not at all an urban center. U of I has truly kept the small-town feel as much as possible. It is not a fast-paced city attempting to build the tallest skyscrapers, but rather a small town seeking to keep its rural roots.**

5 Best Things	5 Worst Things
1 Meeting people	1 Feeling like a number
2 Gumby's Pizza	2 The dining halls
3 Close to home	3 No parking!
4 Huge facilities	4 Lack of diversity
5 Interesting classes	5 Core classes

Students Speak Out
ON FACILITIES

Q "**The Union is pretty nice**, and there are several places to stop and do homework or chill for a while. You can also grab some food when you don't want to go home to your dorm."

Q "The student union provides **a bowling alley and billiard room**, as well as an eatery with multicultural meal choices. There are several rooms for studying, coffee shops for fuel, Internet stations for checking e-mail on the UIUC server, ATM machines for convenient money withdrawal, and even the Courtyard Café where, at night, performances are given."

Q "The gyms at the University are well-equipped with a large quantity and wide variety of aerobic machines and weight lifting equipment, but even with two separate facilities (IMPE and Wimpe), it can be **hard to get a machine**. There is a sign-up process that reserves machines for students, and it is best to get to the facility early to get what you want."

Q "There are instrument practice rooms in every dorm, as well as **furnished lounges** and ping pong, pool, and foosball tables."

STUDENT AUTHOR: **U of I's campus has many places to keep students busy. At the Illini Union, students lounge between classes and eat in the food court, with a variety of food from Chinese, to McDonald's, to Blimpie. The student bank and computer lab are here, too, which is convenient for students who want to get work done between classes. The gyms also attract many students; they're up to par for DI Big Ten athletes, but even the athletically inclined like to chill there.**

Famous Alumni

Roger Ebert, Bill Geist, Hugh Hefner, Bob Miner, Andy Richter, Shel Silverstein, Carl Van Doren

Students Speak Out
ON CAMPUS DINING

Q "If you think U of I cooking is like mama's cooking, **you are sadly mistaken**. On the bright side, you will not starve with so many fast food places on campus."

Q "Lunch and breakfast in the dining halls are good. Dinner is bad. As for outside the dorms, there is **a good selection of food** on campus."

Q "Sometimes you just wish they would feed you regular food whenever they **try to get fancy with something like 'nut-crusted loin.'** Well, thank God for delivery pizza."

Q "The cafeteria food is **not as bad as it may sometimes seem**. I complained while I was living in the dorms of course, but now that I am off campus, I know that it was a blessing."

Q "Students do go wild over specialty restaurants that are held in different dorms like Wok on the Wild Side (Asian cuisine), Soul Ingredient (soul food), and the favorite: Fat Don's, where they serve steaks (and let me tell you, **those steaks they serve are big, juicy, and tender**)."

STUDENT AUTHOR: **The dining halls leave much to be desired. Most students agree that instead of working hard to make creative new foods and variety, the University should just stick to learning how to make Rice Krispie treats properly. Cafeteria food is always going to be cafeteria food, which means either boring repetition or outlandish creations that make you skip right to the cereal bar. Luckily, the University's dining is not limited to basic dorm fare.**

Student Body

African American:	7%	Male/Female:	53/47%
Asian American:	13%	Out-of-State:	7%
Hispanic:	7%	International:	6%
Native American:	<1%	Unknown:	2%
White:	66%		

Popular Faiths: There are many Christian groups on campus. Groups like Illini 4 Christ and Intervarsity are located right next to the Quad.

Gay Pride: Groups like PFLAG and LGBT encourage tolerance, and there are SafeZones on campus.

Economic Status: U of I is predominantly a middle-class environment. People generally come from small or medium-sized cities throughout Illinois.

Students Speak Out
ON DORMS

Q "Live in the Six-Pack [Peabody Avenue] if you want to live in the dorms. People are actually social there, not geeky. **You will meet more people in the Six-Pack** and have more fun."

Q "Illini Street Residence (ISR) is the best dorm, but not many freshmen are placed at ISR. The Six-Pack, a set of six dorms in Champaign, is where many freshmen end up staying. **The dorms there are nothing special**, a little smaller than the other dorms, but definitely livable."

Q "**The dorms vary**. They can be very different experiences. PAR has an open and closed lounge—there are no triples. The Six-Pack dorms have triples, though. And the tunnels are nice."

STUDENT AUTHOR: Housing at college can often be a nightmare. Luckily, the University offers many options for its students. FAR/PAR are the only dorms that are close to the student parking lot. Lincoln Avenue and Busey-Evans Residence Halls are the two women-only dorms, and students say they are also the cleanest and most aesthetically pleasing. The Six-Pack is a collection of six dorms beside one another. They are allegedly the wildest of the dorms.

Did You Know?
50% of undergrads live on campus.

Students Speak Out
ON GUYS & GIRLS

Q "To be honest, you really have to go past the exterior to get to know some of the individuals on campus better. **You will be surprised** by what you encounter."

Q "Girls here are too obsessed with getting a guy. **It is so 1950s.** They all get dolled up for class and run around in tube tops. No wonder McKinley is always running out of free condoms."

Q "Girls here are out of control. It is the sorority thing. **Sexy women, yeah.**"

Q "Most of the hot girls on campus can be found in the sorority houses, which is good because they travel in packs. **The hook-up culture is very prevalent** on our campus due to the insane amounts of alcohol we consume."

STUDENT AUTHOR: In a lot of ways, U of I can feel like high school instead of college. This is especially true of the bar scene. Not many people go out at night in T-shirts and sneakers. Most people get dressed up, especially on the weekends. Typical wear for a guy includes a button-down, long-sleeve shirt with vintage jeans and some kind of necklace, while girls wear mini-skirts, black pants, dark jeans, and some kind of low or tight top.

Traditions

Lincoln's Bust
Students with tests in Lincoln Theater often rub the nose on Lincoln's bust for luck.

Outdoor Movie
A couple times a year, U of I hosts movies outside on the Quad. People gather on the grass with blankets and food and just hang out.

Overall School Spirit
Everyone is very loyal during the first few weeks of the school year. Then the winter wind starts blowing in and none of us can figure out why we came to school here in the first place.

Students Speak Out
ON ATHLETICS

Q "University of Illinois is a **Division I Big Ten contender in every sport**. If nothing else, the weekend is always filled with sporting events to watch—football and basketball particularly, but it extends to every sport."

Q "**Varsity sports are pretty big**, but fans tend to be fair-weather fans. Intramural sports are pretty big, as well."

Q "If you are a sports fan, **invest in those season tickets early**. If you like the Illini and like going to every single basketball game (like some people I know), there is this club called Orange Crush where you and the team can benefit from student participation."

STUDENT AUTHOR: Athletics at U of I are big, and people take sports very seriously. Whether they are spectators or participants in the game, nearly everyone on campus is interested in the outcome of the varsity sports teams. As far as basketball and football are concerned, you'll find more students buzzing over and attending those games than you will any other sport on campus. But this is a Division I school, so that's expected.

Students Speak Out
ON DRUG SCENE

Q "The drug scene is pretty typical at the University of Illinois. There is **a zero-tolerance policy** in the dorms. If one has the desire to get drugs or alcohol illegally, it is possible."

Q "One word describes the general drug scene on campus: pot. There is lots and lots of marijuana. Your neighbor probably smokes. It's not just potheads, either. People smoke-up to write papers, do engineering homework, to study, to go out, to play Frisbee. **Everybody is smoking**, and everybody is selling."

Q "Well, **I have been offered pot and acid**. I have heard rumors of coke, and I know some people take cold and pain medicine to get more of a buzz when drinking. But most people just stick to beer. Hell, it's cheaper."

STUDENT AUTHOR: **The drug scene at U of I is limited to acid and pot for casual users, and even then, usage of these drugs is generally not very popular or extreme. These drugs are available, though, as most students say they either know of someone who has gotten drugs or someone who supplies drugs.**

17:1	Student-to-Faculty Ratio
93%	Freshman Retention Rate
63%	Four-Year Graduation Rate
71%	Financial Aid Applicants Receiving Aid

Students Speak Out
SAFETY & SECURITY

Q "Safety **services are really good here**. There are late bus services and SafeRides. There are options if you choose to utilize them."

Q "If one follows the advice from the safety classes the University requires every new student to take, such as never walking at night alone or always making sure one knows where a drink came from, **most problems can be avoided**."

Q "Orientation really prepares students to deal with campus safety. **Every female is issued a rape whistle**. We have a workshop called C.A.R.E., which is mandatory by the end of your first semester, and it is very informative in dealing with issues of date rape but approaches it in an open-minded forum."

STUDENT AUTHOR: **There are blue emergency phones all over campus, and even if they are used as unofficial ashtrays, they are there should you need them. Officers are on campus, whether they are patrolling the bars at night or monitoring speed limits in the daytime. SafeRides are also a valuable resource.**

> **Questions?**
> For more inside information and survival tips, pick up College Prowler's full-length book on this school, written by an actual student! Check it out at *www.collegeprowler.com*.

Students Speak Out
ON OVERALL EXPERIENCE

Q "**There are pluses and minuses**. What it offers is a quality education, a strong opportunity for activism, and a social scene that revolves around every individual's personal interests."

Q "When my mother exclaimed 'you made it—your first year,' I was so caught up in finals that I was so eager to leave. But ever since I returned home, I have thought about school every day. The **good times, the rough times, and how they were all worth it**."

Q "At times, I wish I was someplace warmer, but this is a great school. It's been **a truly unique experience for me**. I am proud to be at a place that has such a rich tradition."

Q "The University is big, and to some it is overwhelming, but I love seeing everyone on the Quad and knowing we all have stresses and tests but we make it through. A big part of it is finding a group or student organization to be involved in. Then, as you get to know people, **the campus gets smaller and smaller**, and you feel like you know a ton of people."

STUDENT AUTHOR: **Though students have had varied experiences here, many say that they are glad to be students at U of I. They are proud of the history, proud of academic accomplishments, proud of the social opportunities, and when finished, they are proud to be alumni. For so many students to view their time here as a positive experience after all the pros and cons have been taken into consideration, is a fantastic testament to the University's strength. The most encouraging fact was that so many people mentioned that they were leaving as better people ready to navigate through life's twists and turns.**

University of Iowa

107 Calvin Hall; Iowa City, IA 52242
(319) 335-3500; www.uiowa.edu

THE BASICS:

Acceptance Rate: 83%   **SAT Range:** 1070–1320*
Setting: Small city   **Control:** Public
F-T Undergrads: 18,669   **Tuition:** $19,662

Most Popular Majors: Business, Communications, Social Sciences, Psychology, Visual & Performing Arts

*of 1600

Academics	B	Guys	B+
Local Atmosphere	B-	Girls	A-
Safety & Security	B	Athletics	A
Computers	B	Nightlife	B+
Facilities	B	Greek Life	C
Campus Dining	C	Drug Scene	C+
Off-Campus Dining	B+	Campus Strictness	B-
Campus Housing	B	Parking	D
Off-Campus Housing	A-	Transportation	B+
Diversity	D-	Weather	C+

Students Speak Out
ON ACADEMICS

Q "Like in high school, some teachers are great, and some teachers suck; though I found that as I got **further into my major studies, my classes got smaller**, and my teachers got better."

Q "**The history department is outstanding**; I can't comment too much about other departments. Avoid the music department, though."

Q "**The general education courses suck**, but a lot of times, it's not really the professor or the course content that makes the class unbearable; it's more the students because you can tell that a majority of them have an absolute distaste for the courses, thus diminishing the quality of the learning environment. I feel as if my gen ed courses are a huge waste of time, and I'm glad I got most of them done in high school. The major classes are a lot better, and in terms of quality, my political science major is a lot better than my journalism major; although the journalism professors at UI are absolutely world-class."

Q "I have been very lucky; as a history major and an art major, my classes are very interesting. The **teachers are very energetic**, making you further interested."

STUDENT AUTHOR: Probably the biggest issue facing Iowa academics is general-education requirements. Students who are taking courses to fulfill gen ed requirements compete for places with students who are taking the courses for their majors, which creates crowding. Aside from this, students have few complaints about classes and professors at Iowa.

Students Speak Out
ON LOCAL ATMOSPHERE

Q "The bar scene at Iowa is pretty hip. Bars dominate Iowa City. The downtown areas at both places are pretty similar, but **Iowa City does have more of a bar atmosphere**—that can be better or worse for you, based on your tastes."

Q "I would say **Iowa City is two different towns**: in the summer, when there are no students, it is quiet, and when the students are here, it's a wild bar town."

Q "Iowa City provides **the right mix of academics and outside life**. I love walking through the Ped Mall on weekend nights to see all the people—most of whom are drunk. The west side of campus also is very lively, especially on game days. Vendors are lined up on Melrose, and it's almost as fun to walk up and down the street as it is to watch the game."

Q "**There are 20 to 25 bars in a four-block radius**, so you can imagine the scenes during the nights and weekends. Otherwise, it's a cool, casual atmosphere, and the only fights/brawls come from the drunks."

STUDENT AUTHOR: Iowa City is the world's biggest small town—at least, that is what the locals like to call it. Because of the essentially rural region, students from large metropolitan areas may find themselves bored with Iowa City life after a few months; however, UI and the city are growing—over the last decade, both have drastically changed and become much more accommodating to the college crowd.

Students Speak Out
ON FACILITIES

Q "**I did not have any problems** during my first year getting from building to building in the allotted time."

Q "Some majors/schools are definitely more equipped with better facilities and technology than others. I, being a liberal arts student, get stuck with the run-down rooms with windows that break easily. The engineering and business buildings are gorgeous. Overall, **the facilities are decent but not world-class**."

Q "**Athletic facilities are great**—they're big and really, really nice. It's hard to get a basketball court on some nights, but other than that, everything is pretty open. It's all pretty new, and they keep it updated. Computers are good—not the top of the line, but better than any other school I have been to. The student center is really nice. Be sure not to step on the Zodiac when you walk in, though—if you do, they say you'll fail your next test!"

Q "Everything is always made for your convenience, which is nice on such a big campus. Our student center is really cool, and they do a lot to get kids involved. During finals week, **they had masseuses come in and give free massages**, which was very fun."

STUDENT AUTHOR: Many of the UI's buildings add to the flavor of the community. Each building on campus has something unique about its design relating back to the state, like the Boyd Law Building, which looks like a corn silo and walkways that look like giant ears of corn.

Famous Alumni

George Abbot, James Van Allen, Paul Conrad, George Gallup, Charles Guggenheim, Avie Tevanian, Gene Wilder, Tennessee Williams

Students Speak Out
ON CAMPUS DINING

Q "I've found that the food on campus is good. Dorm food is dorm food, although it is much better now than it was when I was a freshman, and that wasn't even bad. Now they have much more variety, and overall, it is much better. They **keep improving that every year**."

Q "Since they revamped the dining halls, the school is presenting different themes of food selection, such as Italian, Mexican, Chinese, etc., giving you **the restaurant-style-food feel, but all in one big cafeteria**."

Q "**The dining halls are your typical cafeteria-type food**. You will get a few more choices and selections than you would at, say, a high school cafeteria."

Q "Cafeteria food at Hillcrest isn't bad at all, and Burge's cafeteria was renovated, so **it's pretty updated, and there's lots of variety**. Food at IMU is pretty good, too—everyone that lives in the dorms is given $100 per semester to spend there, and choices include sandwiches, Pizza Hut, salad, and stuff like that."

STUDENT AUTHOR: Dining at the University of Iowa is nothing for incoming students to get too excited about. Unlike other major universities, there are very few halls for students to use their meal plan around UI. However, in the past few years, the University has redone Burge Dining Hall and added many satellite cafés all over campus. You can take some consolation in the fact that most only have to eat in the dining halls for a year.

Students Speak Out
ON DORMS

Q "There's a **huge difference between the east and west side dorms**. They're both okay, but the east side may be a bit closer to your classes."

Q "I think they are, overall, very nice. **I was lucky to get a room with a bathroom**, which is always a plus. The residence halls have a study lounge on every floor, which makes it easy to study. They also have some sort of lounge that contains such things as pool tables and TVs. The staff is also a plus; they are friendly and can help you with any troubles."

Q "The residential halls are fun for the most part. **They make it easier for you to meet people** and make strong friendships. The food at Burge is terrible compared to the food at Hillcrest, but I love living in the dorms."

STUDENT AUTHOR: **Each dorm offers students a certain style of dorm life—some are extra quiet, and some are quite noisy. The general feeling is that the east side of campus is a little bit wilder. On the west side, residence halls seem to have a more laid-back, quieter feel. That isn't to say those students don't enjoy partying, though.**

? Did You Know?
30% of undergrads live on campus.

Students Speak Out
ON GUYS & GIRLS

Q "Well, there are the frat guys, the slacker guys, the smart guys, the engineers—**all the cliques you can think of**. In general, the guys are hot."

Q "I don't know what it is, but at least 90 percent of the people here are good-looking. I feel as though it's a different class of people here. We're **all very well-educated and clean**."

Q "**There are a ton of awesome girls** who are really nice and extremely friendly, but there are also a ton of girls that think they are better than everybody else."

Q "Iowa seems to be a very good-looking campus; however, **it's also laid-back**. You don't have to get all dressed up for class, but some people will."

STUDENT AUTHOR: The University of Iowa has many attractive members of both sexes. Guys around campus come off as a little defensive—it seems like everyone is trying to be better than any other guy they know. The girls around campus can be shy, but once you start talking to them, they open up. It seems like a strong majority of the campus is looking for a special person, either for a night or for a long-term relationship.

Traditions

One-Eyed Jake's on Your 21st Birthday
A staple for UI students, One-Eyed Jake's offers 21 pitchers of beer for $21 on your 21st birthday.

Weeks of Welcome
A city-wide celebration with barbeques and fireworks held during the first few weeks of classes.

Overall School Spirit
School spirit is very dominant on Iowa's campus. Students can often be seen wearing clothes with the Iowa logo, and, of course, sports and activities are very popular and have a high level of participation.

Students Speak Out
ON ATHLETICS

Q "Hawkeye sports rock! **This whole town is nuts when there's a game**, especially football. It's like Mardi Gras—I love it. We have so much spirit. If you don't like sports now, you will by the time you're a senior. It's a blast."

Q "**There are plenty of opportunities for IM sports**. Varsity football and basketball are obviously huge, as is wrestling. Girl's basketball is fairly high-profile, too, but the rest of the sports get little media coverage."

Q "Basketball **tickets for men's basketball are impossible to get** unless you order online ahead of time. IM sports are fun, though. I played soccer once, and it was really fun, although my team was really bad."

STUDENT AUTHOR: **All sports have a following around the UI campus, though none as big as football. The wrestling program is known as one of the best in the nation. Intramurals are also quite extensive at UI. There are dozens of sports offered of nearly every type, so there's something available for everyone. Anyone of any skill level can get involved in intramurals, and many use them to fill the void left by high school athletics.**

Students Speak Out
ON DRUG SCENE

Q "There are a lot of drugs in Iowa City, but I am sure it is **proportionate to any other college** town. If you want drugs, they aren't hard to find, but if you don't do that stuff, then it won't come looking for you, either."

Q "I haven't ever been caught for drugs or drinking, and I have had both pot and alcohol in my dorm room. Really, **the only way to get busted in a dorm is if you leave it out for your RA to see** or if you are way too loud and they come to check on you."

Q "Some drugs are all over campus. Sometimes I wonder how the University can be so blind to it. When they do catch people using drugs, they **often go too harsh on the punishments**."

STUDENT AUTHOR: **Most students do prefer a drink on the weekends, but** only some students drink enough to be noticeably drunk. If you are caught with an illegal substance, the University will give out the harshest punishments possible—even to first time offenders.

15:1	Student-to-Faculty Ratio
83%	Freshman Retention Rate
40%	Four-Year Graduation Rate
70%	Financial Aid Applicants Receiving Aid

Students Speak Out
SAFETY & SECURITY

Q "The campus is **well lit, and there are several emergency stations**. Campus police are available, as well. I think the campus is quite safe, but it's certainly not perfect."

Q "**Iowa City is pretty safe**. The majority of the problems happen when kids think they are totally free or they have too much to drink. Even if you have too much to drink, as long as you're not being a jerk, you won't get busted."

Q "Iowa is a safe campus. As always, proper precautions should be taken, and you shouldn't walk alone at night, but there are campus police, blue-light call-boxes, and other safety features. Since I have been at Iowa, **I cannot recall many, if any, attacks**."

STUDENT AUTHOR: **UI does do a great job in making students feel safe**—on weekend nights the UI police are always a visible presence. The University also has set up a number of emergency phones around campus so students can call if they ever have a problem.

> **Questions?**
> For more inside information and survival tips, pick up College Prowler's full-length book on this school, written by an actual student! Check it out at *www.collegeprowler.com.*

Students Speak Out
ON OVERALL EXPERIENCE

Q "I wouldn't change schools if I had to. I love Iowa and everything about it. The campus is absolutely beautiful, and they offer such a wide variety of services and things that are easy to take advantage of. **I wouldn't want to be anywhere else**."

Q "I'm happy here. It's a nice, casual college town, but with almost limitless opportunities for whatever you might want to do. **The emphasis on partying and drinking is a little too much**, though. I don't have a problem with other people drinking and socializing, but I think the amount of partying on campus is a little excessive, and drunks, while funny, are a nuisance, especially if they lie half-naked in the middle of the street while cars are driving by at 2 a.m. in February."

Q "I picked like nine schools I wanted to go to, and after visiting Iowa and seeing the campus, I was so in love! **It looks like a campus/college town right out of a movie**! I wasn't sure about going here at first, and I was hesitant about the sorority thing, but I cannot be any happier that I chose to come here. I love it so much! I have never met anyone who doesn't like it. Even when my friends come to visit, they all love our school. Its amazing academically, on top of having a great social scene. You would be crazy not to go!"

STUDENT AUTHOR: **Iowa isn't an Ivy League school, but it does provide a strong education with a focus on career choices; nor is Iowa a party school, but its students know how to relax and have fun while keeping up with their workload. With a combination of solid academics and a college town that caters to the social scene, UI students find themselves in a well-balanced environment.**

University of Kansas

1502 Iowa Street; Lawrence, KS 66045
(785) 864-2700; www.ku.edu

THE BASICS:

Acceptance Rate: 92%
Setting: Small city
F-T Undergrads: 19,131

ACT Range: 22–27
Control: Public
Tuition: $16,272

Most Popular Majors: Business, Social Sciences, Psychology, Biology, Journalism

Academics	B	Guys	B+
Local Atmosphere	B+	Girls	B+
Safety & Security	A-	Athletics	A-
Computers	B-	Nightlife	A-
Facilities	B+	Greek Life	B+
Campus Dining	C+	Drug Scene	B+
Off-Campus Dining	A-	Campus Strictness	C+
Campus Housing	B-	Parking	D-
Off-Campus Housing	B+	Transportation	A-
Diversity	D+	Weather	B-

Students Speak Out
ON ACADEMICS

Q "KU has some very good teachers. **Our business school is one of the top in the nation**, and it's very competitive. Our med school, of course, is at the top, and our education school is ranked nationally, too."

Q "The teachers are all incredibly helpful. All of them have at least four hours of office time each week, as well as e-mails, and most have Web sites for the class, as well. The first year, most classes are **taught by graduate teaching assistants and they are great**, very easy to talk to, and get a hold of for help."

Q "It depends—at any large-scale school, you are going to be dealing with a huge variance in the staff. I have had great professors and not so great ones. **You basically live and learn**, talk to older people and try to avoid the few 'bad' professors. But as a deciding factor, no matter where you end up, there will be teachers that bite!"

Q "I have found that TAs and GTAs can be more **willing to help and relate to students better** than some professors."

STUDENT AUTHOR: Overall, the teachers work to give students the best opportunity to learn. For students struggling in the classroom, the best thing to do is communicate with your teacher. They will help you out if you are struggling to understand something in class, and many are just normal people, too.

Students Speak Out
ON LOCAL ATMOSPHERE

Q "There is a lot to see and do in Lawrence, plus KC is only 45 minutes away, so there is a ton to do within driving distance. If you don't like to be bored, **there is always something to do**."

Q "There is **nothing to stay away from** [in Lawrence], and definitely go to Massachusetts Street. You'll probably be there a lot—shopping, dining, hitting up bars, etc."

Q "It's a college town with **a really fun downtown area where a lot of the bars are** located, making walking around easy. The only other college in town is Haskell, a small [American] Indian school. Clinton Lake is big and a lot of fun to go wakeboard on or camp around. It's just five minutes from campus."

Q "Lawrence is so much fun. It is totally diverse. **You get a great mix of people**. It's a pretty liberal area, also. Everyone I know has only good things to say about Lawrence. It's a fun place to be for college."

STUDENT AUTHOR: While Lawrence is a fairly small city, students like all of the great features of this college town. It has all the basics a student will need for fours years and beyond. You can find old-fashioned barbershops on just about every block, along with the popular stores, such as Abercrombie & Fitch and Gap. The atmosphere is a combination of a town entrenched in tradition and the youthful college students who keep it alive.

5 Best Things
1 Tradition
2 Men's basketball
3 Campus life
4 Local atmosphere
5 House parties

5 Worst Things
1 Parking
2 Weather
3 Common showers
4 Dorm food
5 Walking to campus

Students Speak Out
ON FACILITIES

Q "**The Unions are great places**. The Main Union is always undergoing renovations, but it is still a great place to hang out and have fun."

Q "Computers are everywhere. You could live in the Union. **It's got everything**: a bank, post office, restaurants, and an art gallery. There is even a little deal where you can look to see if anyone is driving to your hometown any time soon, so you can catch a ride. The only problem is that it's so far from where most classes are."

Q "Allen Fieldhouse is where the basketball team plays, and **it's such an exciting experience** going to a KU game. Jayhawk fans are some of the loudest in the nation, and it's amazing being there when they play big rivals like Missouri and North Carolina."

Q "The library, several classroom buildings, and some of the dorms are antiquated, but the campus architecture and facilities all blend the **old classical-style characteristic of Washington** with a modern academic look."

Q "The student center is a collection of food vendors, including Auntie Annie's Pretzels. No games (there is a television and lots of seating), but there's a big city out there; there's really no point in having a big student center, so we don't have one. **It's not really missed**."

STUDENT AUTHOR: The traditional buildings on campus are visually appealing and functional for all students. The Kansas Union is a popular area for students, along with Wescoe Beach and Wescoe Terrace.

Famous Alumni

Scott Bakula, Wilt Chamberlain, Bob Dole, William Inge, Don Johnson, Clyde Tombaugh

Students Speak Out
ON CAMPUS DINING

Q "Typical dorm food. The biggest cafeteria is Mrs. E's. It's up by most of the dorms, and is buffet-style food. There's always pasta, pizza, hamburgers, etc. **It does get old**, though."

Q "The food is **normal cafeteria food**. What more can I say? There is the dining center for those who live in the dorms, located right next-door, and both unions have food in them. The Kansas Union, the main one, has a really nice place to eat. There is a Burger King, Pizza Hut, and other small restaurants in it. It isn't that bad."

Q "Dorm food is **only as good as it sounds, but so convenient**. I miss it, actually. There's no cooking, no cleaning, and you'll be eating with all your friends. It's a fun time, if you're not too picky."

Q "Food in the coed dorms is actually not all the bad. There are **tons of options** and a pretty big variety each day. I've heard the food in the all girls dorm isn't as good, but you can always take the bus over and eat from the other cafeteria."

Q "The **food isn't the greatest**, but it's better than I expected. Eat at Mrs. E's."

STUDENT AUTHOR: The food on campus is good because of the variety offered in different locations. You can stop and get something to eat in pretty much any part of campus. Most agree that the Union is the best place to find food on campus. It has pretty much everything you can think of, and definitely all the essentials for a good meal. The student's favorite dining hall is undoubtedly Mrs. E's.

Student Body

African American:	4%	Male/Female:	50/50%
Asian American:	4%	Out-of-State:	23%
Hispanic:	4%	International:	4%
Native American:	<1%	Unknown:	3%
White:	81%		

Popular Faiths: The University is mainly dominated by Christian groups.

Gay Pride: KU is accepting of the gay population. However, there does not seem to be a large gay population here.

Economic Status: Most students range from middle- to upper-class.

Students Speak Out
ON DORMS

Q "**They all are decent**. The all-girls dorms tend to have a lot of sorority sisters. Templin and Lewis are the best. Oliver is nice, too. The scholarships halls are very nice, if you can stand communal living. Hashinger is the 'artsy' hall."

Q "The dorms are okay. I would **stay away from the all-girls dorms**. They have the nickname 'Girls State Prison,' but the others are okay."

Q "It really depends on what dorm you get and how social you are. I definitely recommend going to dorms like Oliver and Ellsworth, where it is an open atmosphere and **a community in and of itself**."

STUDENT AUTHOR: **Students usually weigh their dorms depending on the people they are surrounded by during their first year. Each dorm seems to have its own character or reputation. The dorms are a great chance to meet new friends and establish close relationships. Another perk is that KU gives students the chance to apply for all types of living arrangements, including the option to live off campus.**

Did You Know?
23% of undergrads live on campus.

Students Speak Out
ON GUYS & GIRLS

Q "There are a lot of different types of people. There are a lot of hotties on both ends, mostly Greek. There are some really hot alternative looking guys, though, too. Girls are all different, from very preppy to very freaky. There's anything you could want. Also, **it's a very liberal campus, so anything goes**."

Q "Like anywhere, there are lots of great guys, but there's also **a lot of losers**; it's the same with girls."

Q "All shapes, sizes, and styles. **There is someone for everyone**."

Q "The guys are pretty good-looking, and there are **lots of ways to get involved** so that you can meet both guys and girls."

STUDENT AUTHOR: At a big university in the Midwest, it is not uncommon to find a large majority of good-looking people. KU students like to hit both the bars and the gym, and either place is a great spot to find girls and guys. You can meet people by going to class, joining a student organization, or just hanging out around campus. The best chance, though, is to go out on the town and experience KU nightlife.

Traditions

Rock Chalk Chant
The chant is sung at every athletic event, and it's especially loud during KU basketball games.

The University Seal
A very important part of the University, the seal comes from a Biblical story in the third chapter of Exodus.

Overall School Spirit
KU students have an extreme amount of school spirit. Students love to wear the crimson and blue colors that have been a part of the KU athletic teams since 1896.

Students Speak Out
ON ATHLETICS

Q "Our football coach seems to know what he is doing, so hopefully our football team will do better in the years to come. We have a lot of other sports at KU, as well, like rowing, lacrosse, basketball, and baseball. **There's pretty much any sport you can think of**."

Q "KU basketball is huge, full of tradition, and by far the most intense sport season, for obvious reasons. **Intramural sports are fun, too**. I played coed softball this year and had a lot of fun."

Q "There is nothing like a KU basketball game. I can't even describe it. They are so much fun, and **the school spirit is unbelievable**."

Q "KU pretty much has **year-round intramural activities going on**. Anything you could possibly imagine, from rock-climbing to softball, we have it."

STUDENT AUTHOR: **With its rich tradition and frequent success, fans love everything about KU's basketball program and follow its every move. KU is in the Big 12 Conference, which is one of the premier sports conferences in America. Intramurals are a big part of the University, as well.**

Students Speak Out
ON DRUG SCENE

Q "Drugs are a part of every campus, but there are a lot of them in Lawrence. This doesn't mean that all the students do them, but in actuality, **Lawrence used to be a hippie town**."

Q "Just like anywhere, if you want it, you can get it. But it's not like the drug scene overruns campus or the social scene or anything. At least the people I know who do a lot of drugs **pretty much keep it to themselves**."

Q "There is **no drug scene on campus**. It is policed very well. Off campus, there are people who are into it, but it is no big deal. You probably won't see it if you don't want to see it."

STUDENT AUTHOR: **Marijuana is the dominant illegal drug used by students, but alcohol is much more popular. Most students choose to drink, and most parties revolve around alcohol. Non-alcoholic events are offered throughout the campus for students who do not choose to participate in the drinking scene.**

19:1	Student-to-Faculty Ratio
79%	Freshman Retention Rate
26%	Four-Year Graduation Rate
51%	Financial Aid Applicants Receiving Aid

Students Speak Out
SAFETY & SECURITY

Q "Security on campus is really good. We have officers that go around the campus often, and you don't have to worry about safety because **you can almost always rely on them**!"

Q "Safety and security are major issues at KU, and there **has not been one time that I have not felt secure and safe**. However, you must always remember to walk in groups. Never go out by yourself. That's just a given for whatever place you decide to go."

Q "**Security is top-notch at KU**. The campus is well lit, and Lawrence, overall, does not have a lot of crime."

STUDENT AUTHOR: Students feel that KU does provide all the necessary components to keep campus safe. The blue-light system makes students feel safe. The campus police are always patrolling, and the Lawrence police always seem to have the town under control.

Questions?
For more inside information and survival tips, pick up College Prowler's full-length book on this school, written by an actual student! Check it out at *www.collegeprowler.com*.

Students Speak Out
ON OVERALL EXPERIENCE

Q "I had the opportunity to go to many other schools, some with much better academic reputations and others that offered more money, but KU was definitely the best choice for me. The coursework can be tough, but there is plenty of help and tons of time for fun. And there is a lot of fun to be had in Lawrence. I **recommend KU over any other school in the Midwest**."

Q "I love KU. I've had a lot of friends from NY visit me and I've visited them at their schools, and not only do they fall in love with KU whenever they come here, but when I go to their schools, **I know I made the right choice**."

Q "KU is so awesome. The atmosphere is great, and it seems like **any type of person could find their niche** here. There are all the hippie pothead kids, the jocks, and the Greek system is pretty big. Everyone is really laid-back and cool, and the campus is so gorgeous. It's hilly, not like you'd think of Kansas at all, but really pretty."

Q "Oh, I really love it here at KU. The people are friendly, teachers are nice and fair, and the town is great overall. **You'll never get bored** here in Lawrence, and there are lots of activities and clubs to join at KU. I guarantee that you'll have a blast if you go to this school."

STUDENT AUTHOR: **KU students have the opportunity to get a quality education at a fairly cheap price, which is something that not a lot of schools can boast. The community around Lawrence offers all of the important features of a great college town. There is entertainment, nightlife, and fine dining seemingly around every corner. You'll have no problem finding everything you'll need for four years of good living.**

University of Kentucky

500 South Limestone; Lexington, KY 40506
(859) 257-9000; www.uky.edu

THE BASICS:

Acceptance Rate: 77%
Setting: Urban
F-T Undergrads: 16,779

SAT Range: 1010–1250*
Control: Public
Tuition: $15,018

Most Popular Majors: Business, Communications, Social Sciences, Education, Engineering

*of 1600

Academics	B-	Guys	A-
Local Atmosphere	B	Girls	A-
Safety & Security	C+	Athletics	A-
Computers	B	Nightlife	B
Facilities	B	Greek Life	A-
Campus Dining	B	Drug Scene	B-
Off-Campus Dining	A-	Campus Strictness	C+
Campus Housing	C	Parking	D
Off-Campus Housing	B	Transportation	C+
Diversity	D-	Weather	B-

Students Speak Out
ON ACADEMICS

Q "Some **teachers in upper-level classes are like mentors** and help you grow tremendously. My core classes I find interesting, but some of the extra stuff you have to take can be rather boring—especially electives."

Q "I **hated every professor I had during my first two years of college**, but I began to form better relationships with my professors during my last two years of college. I have found the majority of my classes to be interesting. Most of my first year classes weren't as beneficial as they could have been. The professors didn't care if you were there or not, because they get paid regardless."

Q "Most of the teachers are good at what they do, but one big problem is their availability. **They are not really personable**, so as a student, you are expected to find out info yourself and get things done that way. Sometimes they are not much help."

Q "Many of the **teachers in the intro classes are teacher's assistants** or graduate students who work under a professor. Generally, for the large intro classes, there isn't one-on-one contact."

STUDENT AUTHOR: As most large state schools go, students can feel a bit overwhelmed by the class sizes during their first semesters at Kentucky. However, getting to know your professors can be a wise decision to set yourself apart in large introductory classes. It can also be helpful to team up with other students in large classes and form study groups to help everyone keep up with the course load.

Students Speak Out
ON LOCAL ATMOSPHERE

Q "Lexington is **surrounded by distilleries** that are close enough to visit. The thoroughbred farms are fun to tour, and Keeneland racetrack is always a favorite."

Q "There is really some **Southern hospitality** at UK."

Q "The atmosphere is kind of **old-fashioned and not very progressive**. Lexington was once a pretty small town, so it still kind of holds those conservative ideals and ways of thinking. However, because there are so many people in Lex because of UK, there are a lot of liberal views, as well. There are some universities close by, such as Transylvania and Georgetown, but I wouldn't say that they really have much of an impact on UK."

Q "The atmosphere is fun. **Everyone in Lexington loves the school** and has a college sticker on their car. There are college kids everywhere! For things to visit, just go downtown; it's pretty cool. There are shops and places to eat, plus a cool waterfall."

STUDENT AUTHOR: Lexington is a town rich in the history of horse racing and the Old South. It's a fairly traditional city with down-home values and the mentality of a much smaller town, but is so close to Cincinnati and Louisville that there is also a city experience to UK. The various other colleges in the area give students tons of people their age to mingle with, as well.

Students Speak Out
ON FACILITIES

Q "The **facilities are state-of-the-art**. The library is really big."

Q "UK's **Student Center has improved** since we got a Starbucks. They've tried to clean it up and modernize it. They are trying to give it a new look. It seems to be pretty popular because there are always people there to meet for coffee between classes. It's quite small, and there isn't really enough room for people to sit and stay in there for any length of time."

Q "The Johnson Center is great to work out in. It's new and has easy-to-use machines if you go at certain times. The Student Center is a little outdated but nice if you have a dining card and can eat on campus because it's **close to the buildings**."

Q "There are **free workout facilities and a pool**; there's an outdoor center where you can rent camping equipment; the computers are updated regularly. As far as the Student Center is concerned, no one hangs out there except to wait for their next class or to eat lunch. There's a game room, but there's never anyone in there."

STUDENT AUTHOR: **The largest monetary commitment the University makes besides education is athletics (a close second). With the opening of the Johnson Center, students have a state-of-the-art workout facility to climb, run, swim, play, and take classes. The Student Center, however, is extremely outdated. Unattractive architecturally, it seems to be an afterthought to some of the more attractive and historical buildings on campus.**

Famous Alumni

Stonewall Jackson, Ashley Judd, William Lipscomb, Thomas Hunt Morgan

Students Speak Out
ON CAMPUS DINING

Q "**Food is fine, but not great**. Avoid the fast food places in the Student Center—grease, grease, grease. I liked the Commons, but many don't. K-Lair has good, greasy hangover food."

Q "**Campus food sucks** and costs more. Pazzos, Jimmy John's, Kashmir, and Qdoba are all around campus, so you'll never go hungry."

Q "Commons is on south campus and **has about everything you could ask for**, even hand dipped ice cream! The best place, by far, on campus is OVID's."

Q "My favorite is the Commons, which is a little food court right in the square of all the freshman dorms. The dorms are centralized by the Commons Food Court, which also has a small grocery market. My favorite there is Block & Barrel for sandwiches or Stir Fry station—you pick the meat and veggies, and they stir fry with your favorite sauces. Also, there is a café in the library—OVID's—which is really good, as well. They change their variety weekly, and it's all really good. **I really love all the food on campus**."

STUDENT AUTHOR: **Beware of the Freshman 15! Kentucky offers a variety of food that has the ability to more than double your size if you aren't careful. Still, most students seem to feel that it is overpriced because of the convenience, and nobody seems satisfied with the campus dining plan for the Wildcat Card. Good eats are available, however—if you live on central campus, definitely plan on trying the legendary K-Lair Grill.**

Student Body

African American:	6%	Male/Female:	49/51%
Asian American:	2%	Out-of-State:	19%
Hispanic:	1%	International:	<1%
Native American:	<1%	Unknown:	3%
White:	87%		

Popular Faiths: Christianity (Protestant and Catholic) is by far the most represented religion on campus.

Gay Pride: The Lavender Society and Lambda Lambda Lambda offer activities and support for gay students.

Economic Status: The University of Kentucky tends to attract students from middle-class backgrounds whose parents help pay for their educations.

Students Speak Out
ON DORMS

Q "The **north campus dorms are old**, but not so bad. The Kirwan and Blanding dorms are okay, too, but the towers have bars on the windows and feel like prisons. Haggin Hall is like a nightmare."

Q "I lived in the Wesley Foundation for Methodist students. Other denominations live there, but they want Christian people there. The one thing that I did like is that we **had our own kitchen**, so we could cook and not eat out all the time."

Q "Freshmen live in south campus dorms. They're **small and compact, but accessible to the Johnson Center** and the football stadium. Lots of the South Campus dorms became 24-hour visitation recently."

STUDENT AUTHOR: **Most students live in the dorms for at least one year and hate it the entire time because the rooms are old and small. Ask them a few years later, and they will tell you they had the time of their lives. Each section of campus dorms has its own stigma. South campus dorms are noisy and close to the fraternity houses; North is the more serious side where the honor students live.**

? Did You Know?
27% of undergrads live on campus.

Students Speak Out
ON GUYS & GIRLS

Q "Most of the guys are great, and the girls are, too. The **best part is Southern charm**; everyone is so friendly. No one here has ever met a stranger."

Q "**Guys are laid-back, girls are blonde**. Girls tend to make more effort in the way of appearances, normally, but many are very high maintenance. Guys are usually former athletes. Sorority girls think the campus is theirs, but guys get sick of them after the first year."

Q "We have super preppy geeks, a few punk rockers, and **a lot of country boys** around."

Q "The guys are fabulous. Have you met a boy from Kentucky?! **You're in for a treat**! The downside is that most girls are pretty hot, too— just a little friendly competition, right?"

STUDENT AUTHOR: UK has quite a reputation— attractive people are never in short supply. You'll find everyone at UK, from farm kids to upper-crust country club types with family money. There are plenty of opportunities to meet people at parties and in class, so a social life is not hard to come by at Kentucky. Just make sure that you are studying as much astronomy as you are heavenly bodies; Kentucky has some stunning eye candy for a walk to class.

Traditions

Mascot
The Wildcat mascot serves as a friendly ambassador for the University.

Blue and White
Originally, UK's colors were blue and yellow, but the University adopted white in 1892.

UK Urban Legends
It is lucky to sit in President Patterson's lap (the statue's, of course!) during finals week, unless the police are around. In that case, it could be very unlucky. Bonus points for having your picture taken.

Students Speak Out
ON ATHLETICS

Q "This is Wildcat Country. There **isn't anything much bigger than Kentucky basketball**. The football team also gets a lot of attention, but we have every sport you can think of for men and women. There's a huge intramural circuit, for sure."

Q "**Basketball and football dominate** the sport scene. But club sports like hockey can have a cult following. And intramurals are great to play."

Q "Varsity sports at UK are huge, especially basketball. UK basketball is life. Our football team . . . well . . . we like to root for the underdog. A lot of people **get season tickets and enjoy the tailgating before games**. It often becomes a bigger event than the actual game."

STUDENT AUTHOR: **Kentucky basketball is infectious and will bring you to your feet, giving you some great memories of your college years—even if you don't like the sport all that much. The football team doesn't exactly have a winning record, but the fans don't seem to care. Greek sports and intramurals are a great way to get involved and make some friends while staying in shape, as well.**

Students Speak Out
ON DRUG SCENE

Q "The **majority drink** on the weekends."

Q "I really don't know; I haven't run into too much other than a lot of people who **take pills to help them study** and stay awake, but I haven't ever been persuaded."

Q "**Marijuana grows on the side of the road** in Kentucky, so you can guess what it's like. Not everybody's into it."

Q "As far as drugs are concerned, marijuana is a cash crop in Kentucky, and you won't have trouble finding anything else you could want. But **if you're not into drugs, you'll never have to see them**."

STUDENT AUTHOR: **Just as in high school, there will be people at Kentucky who are interested in drugs and not in school. They will, however, probably be in college for the better part of a decade. Drugs are available depending on the sort of people you socialize with. For the most part, there are so many activities that don't involve drugs, you may never notice them.**

17:1	Student-to-Faculty Ratio
78%	Freshman Retention Rate
30%	Four-Year Graduation Rate
72%	Financial Aid Applicants Receiving Aid

Students Speak Out
SAFETY & SECURITY

Q "Last year, there were a bunch of incidents right on the outskirts of campus, but UK **police did a good job** of going door to door handing out fliers of wanted persons. Basically, just like any other place, don't walk alone at night—there are SafeCats to escort you anywhere on campus at night."

Q "**Carry pepper spray** or a tire iron."

Q "They seem to be trying to improve it, but I keep hearing about different things late at night— **attacks near the library** that have been going on for a while now. They don't seem to be able to control that."

Q "UK has its **own police force, cruisers, and bikes**. There are also panic posts all over campus."

STUDENT AUTHOR: **The Kentucky campus has had crime reports, especially crimes against women. However, drastic measures have been instilled; cellular phones are available for checkout at the library to make sure students have some way of being heard. What a great safety measure!**

> **Questions?**
> For more inside information and survival tips, pick up College Prowler's full-length book on this school, written by an actual student! Check it out at *www.collegeprowler.com*.

Students Speak Out
ON OVERALL EXPERIENCE

Q "Well, I spent my six years of college existence at UK. I have to say that my overall experience has been wonderful. I've made friends I'll have for the rest of my life. As far as Lexington is concerned, **I'm not staying, but I wouldn't change the time I've spent here**."

Q "I like to move around, so I am getting tired of Lexington, but I never wanted to go anywhere else. The population in Lexington has risen since I was a freshman, and traffic has become a problem, but it is livable. I am ready to move onto something new, but UK is **definitely a fun, fun school with a great reputation** for academics—being a wildcat has its perks. I love it here. It is a big campus, but it seems small."

Q "We have a beautiful campus, and really cool and friendly people. There's also a **sense of tradition that you love to be a part of**. There's nothing like walking across campus and seeing just a sea of blue and white and everyone wearing Kentucky baseball caps and T-shirts. They even started doing these 'roasts' where they block off the street and play music and have food and you can drink; it's really cool."

STUDENT AUTHOR: **Some students can feel overwhelmed by all the organizations and people when they first come to campus. It takes about a year to settle in and find your niche on campus. Once they do, they find that UK offers a well-rounded education and opportunity for networking and making friends, while staying in a mid-sized city with traditional values. With the exception of the parking problem, lack of diversity, and an annoying Greek population, Kentucky can provide a student with a great college experience.**

University of Louisville

2301 South Third Street; Louisville, KY 40292
(502) 852-5555; www.louisville.edu

THE BASICS:

Acceptance Rate: 70% **SAT Range:** 1010–1260*
Setting: Urban **Control:** Public
F-T Undergrads: 11,776 **Tuition:** $19,272

Most Popular Majors: Business, Social Sciences, Engineering, Psychology, Health Professions

*of 1600

Academics	B-	Guys	B-
Local Atmosphere	B+	Girls	B
Safety & Security	B-	Athletics	A-
Computers	C+	Nightlife	B+
Facilities	C+	Greek Life	A-
Campus Dining	C	Drug Scene	B
Off-Campus Dining	B	Campus Strictness	A-
Campus Housing	C-	Parking	C-
Off-Campus Housing	A-	Transportation	B+
Diversity	C+	Weather	B-

Students Speak Out
ON ACADEMICS

Q "The classes I've had so far haven't been that hard. **Most of the general education classes are easy**, and most of the teachers are ready and willing to help if you have any problems. A lot of classes also have graduate students for assistants that you can go to if you need help."

Q "One of the things I like about U of L is that **you can take some of your classes online**. It makes it convenient for people who can't always make it to class."

Q "The classes are alright. **They remind me a lot of high school, actually**. I don't really think they're that hard. You just have to do your work and not skip your classes all the time."

Q "The online classes aren't all they're cracked up to be. I've taken a couple of them, and sometimes they're more trouble than what they're worth. **It was hard for me to communicate with my teachers** and other students over the Internet. I also think the cost of Internet classes is too high."

STUDENT AUTHOR: While many people come to the University of Louisville to have fun and meet new people, the main reason they all come is for an education, and U of L doesn't disappoint. Several of the University's programs, including business and medicine, are some of the better programs available. The professors are some of the most helpful people you can find. The general education that is required of every student provides a sound foundation for each student's future.

Students Speak Out
ON LOCAL ATMOSPHERE

Q "I haven't been in the area long, but I've heard that you shouldn't wander around the neighborhoods around campus, especially at night. **It's supposed to be a heavy crime area** or something."

Q "**I like that U of L is in a large city, but I also like that it's close to other large cities**. Indianapolis and Cincinnati are only a couple of hours away, so if there's a concert in either one of those places, it's not a long drive."

Q "Louisville's a good city, but **traffic is horrible, especially during rush hour**. If you drive to class every day, leave early because you will need the extra time. There's not much to look at on your drive because it's mostly skyscrapers, interstate, and concrete."

Q "One reason I picked U of L was because I love the city. I've lived here all my life, and I can still find something new almost every time I go outside. **I love that it's urban but still has lots of green parks that you can walk around in**."

STUDENT AUTHOR: Being a large city, Louisville definitely has a lot to offer. From restaurants to shopping malls to parks and museums, it seems there is something for everyone. Like many cities, there are parts of Louisville that are rundown and subject to crime. The best thing to do is stay out of these areas. Besides those spots, the atmosphere in the city is vibrant and cheerful. Even though it is urban, most of the people of Louisville are as friendly as anyone you could ever meet.

5 Best Things	5 Worst Things
1 Location	1 Parking
2 Extracurriculars	2 Food
3 Diversity	3 Liberalism
4 Students' attitudes	4 Dorms
5 Professors	5 Noisy trains

Students Speak Out
ON FACILITIES

Q "I think the facilities on campus are OK. For the amount of students we have, it's no wonder that **some of the building look worn out**. There's just no way you can keep everything in tip-top shape. But everything is usable, and it doesn't look that bad."

Q "You would think the facilities would be nicer for what they charge for tuition. **Tuition goes up every year, and yet the facilities stay the same**. I don't know how long it's been since they worked on the SAC, but some places could use a mini overhaul."

Q "The libraries are pretty nice, especially Ekstrom since they added the new wing. **It's nice now that they have the new café in there**, so you can grab a cup of coffee to enjoy while you study. The SAC is alright, but it could use some work. Some parts of it look rundown."

Q "Intramurals are pretty popular on campus, and **the facilities for athletics are decent**. If you're into something besides sports, good luck because there isn't much else besides the libraries."

Q "Facilities are average here. **There's nothing outstanding, but it's not bad either**."

STUDENT AUTHOR: **With as many students as Louisville has, it needs a large number of facilities. There are several libraries with multiple computer labs scattered around, a large student center equipped with athletic facilities and restaurants, and a nice concert hall. However, some of the buildings are in need of work. On the other hand, some of the facilities are really nice.**

Famous Alumni

Larry Birkhead, Christopher Dodd, Bob Edwards, Shin-je Ghim, Stefan LeFors, Mitch McConnell, Robert Nardelli, Louie Nunn, Johnny Unitas

Students Speak Out
ON CAMPUS DINING

Q "There really isn't a lot of good food on campus. **It is mostly chain stores that sell unhealthy food**, and all of the places, especially the ones that do have a few healthy selections, are open fairly limited hours."

Q "It would be **nearly impossible to be a vegetarian and live on campus**, and it would be particularly difficult for vegetarians who plan their diets so that they are getting proper nutrients (or anyone else wishing to have a proper diet)."

Q "Imagine eating fast food every day for a school year. That's pretty much the option that U of L has to offer. **It's not good for you, and it doesn't even really taste that good**. You'll have to cook your own food if you want to eat anything good."

Q "We have burgers, chicken, and pizza. Those are the primary food groups at U of L. There are some veggies and fruit available, but they only have apples, bananas, oranges, and salads mostly. **There aren't a lot of vegetable options**."

Q "**You have to wait forever in line** to get it. They need to add some more food places so students don't have to wait as long."

STUDENT AUTHOR: **If you love fast food, you'll love the food available. With restaurants like Wendy's, Papa John's, and Chick-fil-A on campus, it's often the easiest for students to simply resort to these popular restaurants for their meals. One problem with the restaurants on campus is created by the large stampede of people during the lunch hours.**

Student Body

African American:	12%	Male/Female:	49/51%
Asian American:	3%	Out-of-State:	13%
Hispanic:	2%	International:	1%
Native American:	<1%	Unknown:	2%
White:	79%		

Popular Faiths: Catholicism is very prominent on campus, and Southern Baptist is probably the second most common. There is also a large Jewish presence.

Gay Pride: For the most part, gay rights seem to be respected on campus, but there are still several people on campus who aren't as willing to accept gays or lesbians.

Economic Status: It ranges from lower to upper class, but the majority are probably middle class.

Students Speak Out
ON DORMS

Q "**The majority of the dorms are old**, and it shows. Threlkeld doesn't even have an elevator. It sucks to have to walk up four flights of stairs to get to your room 10 times a day."

Q "If you're going to live on campus, **live in Bettie Johnson or Kurz**. They're newer and a heck of a lot nicer than the nasty older dorms. You can park next to the newer halls, too."

Q "I like living on campus because **I'm close to everything that is happening**. If I want to grab a bite to eat in the SAC, I'm just a few steps away. If there's a party near campus, chances are I can walk there. It makes everything more convenient."

STUDENT AUTHOR: **Living on campus is a lot like Valentine's Day—you either love it or you hate it. Those who love it do so because it's convenient, they can be close to their friends, they can walk to class, and they have free cable and high-speed Internet. Those who hate it complain about the nasty bathrooms, the small rooms, the people they get stuck rooming with, and the planes from the airport that fly overhead at night. The truth is, living on campus is what you make it.**

> **Did You Know?**
> 19% of undergrads live on campus.

Students Speak Out
ON GUYS & GIRLS

Q "If you're even remotely attractive, **you should have no problem finding a date** on or near campus. I mean, there are thousands of people around here, so surely you can find somebody."

Q "Hmmm, let's see. How I can put this nicely? A lot of the guys on campus are, well, let's just say they're not the nicest people in the world. To put it bluntly, a lot of the guys are jerks. Of course, **you can always find a nice guy, but you've got to look hard**. Sometimes it seems like guys just have one thing on their minds."

Q "There are hot people, ugly people, and then **there's a lot of average people** mixed in."

Q "There are **some pretty hot girls on campus**, especially if you hit the party scene. But then again, a lot of the party girls are also easy."

STUDENT AUTHOR: **If you can't find someone you like at U of L, then shame on you. There are almost endless possibilities on campus. Out of 20,000 people, there are at least hundreds, if not thousands, of people who could be considered "hot." If you're looking for a meaningful relationship on campus, you might have some trouble at U of L simply because there is a lot of hooking up and casual dating going on around here.**

> **Traditions**
>
> **Annual Foam Party**
> Often the wildest party on campus, the dance floor in the Red Barn is covered with tons of foam.
>
> **Symphony Orchestra Halloween Spooktacular**
> Every Halloween, the University Symphony Orchestra performs a collection of Halloween favorites, such as "The Sorcerer's Apprentice" and "Ghostbusters."
>
> **Overall School Spirit**
> You'll see hundreds of people wearing U of L attire every day. If you're not wearing red and black on game day, you're in the minority.

Students Speak Out
ON ATHLETICS

Q "Athletics is a big part of life at U of L. In the fall, it's football, and in the winter, it's basketball. **We're pretty proud of our teams**."

Q "I'm a soccer fan, and I know U of L has a soccer team, but I just don't hear that much about it. I think **they need to put more emphasis on the teams that are overlooked**."

Q "The intramural program at U of L is awesome. **They have something for everyone**. It's a great way to meet new people."

Q "It seems like **U of L revolves around athletics**. On game day, you'll see almost everyone walking around in red and black. I think it's great and really unifies us as a school."

STUDENT AUTHOR: **The athletics program is one of the major reasons that a lot of students choose to come to U of L. From basketball to football to field hockey to rowing, there is a seemingly endless list of athletic teams here. If you're not really into participating in sports but you like to watch, we've got that covered, too. Of course, if you want to get tickets to a men's basketball or football game, you better get them early because they will sell out.**

Students Speak Out
ON DRUG SCENE

Q "I'm sure people do all kinds of drugs on campus, but you never hear about it unless someone gets caught, and that doesn't happen very often. **The drug scene is hidden pretty well here**."

Q "Drugs are mostly done at parties. **I don't think that U of L has a drug problem**. I've never seen anybody busted for drugs on campus. There's not really pressure to do drugs here."

Q "Drugs are popular on any campus. **A lot of people use marijuana** or have at some point. It's just part of growing up."

STUDENT AUTHOR: You're not going to see anyone walking around campus passing out cocaine or smoking pot. When it comes to the U of L drug scene, there just isn't much to talk about. That's not to say that people around here don't do drugs—you just never hear about it. Drugs are used mostly at parties and in people's apartments, and if you don't want to use them, you won't feel any pressure to do so.

19:1	Student-to-Faculty Ratio
78%	Freshman Retention Rate
19%	Four-Year Graduation Rate
83%	Financial Aid Applicants Receiving Aid

Students Speak Out
SAFETY & SECURITY

Q "For a big city like Louisville, there's not as much crime as you would think, especially on campus. If something does happen, it's usually minor. I don't really worry about crime. **I sleep well at night**."

Q "I don't think I've ever seen a major crime on campus. **The only thing I've ever seen is a parking violation**. The only crime I hear about on campus, for the most part, is theft, and it's usually not actually on campus."

Q "I know they just implemented a crime and emergency alert system that students can get on their cell phones, and we get alerts through e-mail. **I see the University police around pretty much every day**. It seems like a pretty safe place to me."

STUDENT AUTHOR: For such a large campus, the University of Louisville surprisingly doesn't have that big of a problem regarding safety and security. Even though there isn't a lot of crime on campus, there are precautions that the University takes to keep everybody safe. There are several emergency lights with buttons that students can push if they need help during an emergency. You can also see University police patrolling the premises daily.

> **Questions?**
> For more inside information and survival tips, pick up College Prowler's full-length book on this school, written by an actual student! Check it out at *www.collegeprowler.com*.

Students Speak Out
ON OVERALL EXPERIENCE

Q "The school is good for a great education, but other than that, it just needs tons of work. Some **new younger people on the faculty might help** make some good decisions to help U of L strive to be the best."

Q "I know some people who have hated U of L and transferred, but I'm not one of them. I love it here, and I always will. **Everything just seemed to fall into place for me here**. My teachers helped me find the right major for me, and I've met some great people here."

Q "Sometimes I wonder if I should have gone to another school, but **in the end, I think I made the right decision**. They give good scholarships here, so it's not too expensive. The classes are informative, and the teachers are helpful. The food's not great, but it's edible. You can meet all sorts of different people here. It's a good school."

Q "U of L's a good school, especially if you're going into medicine or law. **It's got good business and engineering programs**, as well. Some of the programs aren't so great. I wouldn't get an English degree here, but nothing's perfect."

STUDENT AUTHOR: The University of Louisville isn't perfect. It has its flaws, but to those who love it, the flaws only add to the experience. Not everyone is going to like such a large university, but even with a huge student body, most people find a tight group of friends that they stick with throughout their time at U of L. The University has a lot to offer, you just have to jump in and grab it.

University of Maine

168 College Avenue; Orono, ME 04469-5713
(207) 581-1110; www.umaine.edu

THE BASICS:

Acceptance Rate: 77%.
Setting: Rural
F-T Undergrads: 7,892

SAT Range: 1430–1750*
Control: Public
Tuition: $18,414

Most Popular Majors: Business, Education, Engineering, Health Professions, Social Sciences,

*of 2400

Academics	B-	Guys	B
Local Atmosphere	B+	Girls	B
Safety & Security	A	Athletics	A-
Computers	C+	Nightlife	B-
Facilities	B+	Greek Life	B
Campus Dining	C	Drug Scene	B
Off-Campus Dining	B+	Campus Strictness	B-
Campus Housing	C	Parking	B-
Off-Campus Housing	B	Transportation	B
Diversity	D-	Weather	C-

Students Speak Out
ON ACADEMICS

Q "For the most part, classes are interesting, and the **professors are very knowledgeable about the subjects** they are teaching. There are obviously exceptions to this statement, but I find that classes are definitely worth attending and are interesting, as well."

Q "The teachers here at UMaine are **all quite different in many ways**. I have found that a good portion of my teachers require appointments for their office hours and can be difficult to find at times. Other teachers that I have can be really laid-back and allow us to stop by their office or stop them after class in order to ask questions and be reflective. Each teacher is different, and I am happy with a few of the professors I have had here at UMaine."

Q "The teachers are **mostly close-minded left-wing hippies.** My classes were pretty interesting, although most teachers frowned upon open discussion of varying opinions, which I didn't like."

STUDENT AUTHOR: **Attending class regularly and participating in class discussions is the most advantageous way to learn and to interact with your instructors. Most professors are very approachable and will meet with you either during their office hours or when you unexpectedly drop in. Getting to know your professors, and taking multiple courses with those who have the most significant impact on your education, is not only important, but will help you to achieve greater success in your academic endeavors.**

Students Speak Out
ON LOCAL ATMOSPHERE

Q "Orono is a college town. **If it weren't for the University, it wouldn't really be much** of a town at all. Neighboring Bangor is the 'big city' of the area. There are some historic sites to see there, as well as cultural experiences like the theater and art museum. There are bars and dance clubs in both Orono and Bangor—the favorite spots vary from year to year."

Q "The atmosphere of Orono is hip—**very liberal, very small town, very organic**. I love the local shops and the community center in town where there is live music, dancing, yoga, and other fun things that happen. I like living off campus because I get to know some local folks and feel like a part of the community. Definitely to visit: Farmer's Market, Ampersand coffeeshop (great pumpkin cookies), and Pat's Pizza of course!"

Q "Orono is a great little college town. There are **great local bars and restaurants within walking distance** to the campus and surrounding most off-campus apartments. There really isn't anything to stay away from in Orono, and the atmosphere is relaxed, fun, and outdoorsy."

STUDENT AUTHOR: **The small-town atmosphere in Orono provides students with the opportunity to blend in with the residents. It is not uncommon to find yourself on a first-name basis with local business owners and clerks. Orono is located at the convergence of the Stillwater and Penobscot rivers, which provide optimum conditions for canoeing and kayaking.**

5 Best Things	**5 Worst Things**
1 Extracurriculars	**1** Lack of diversity
2 Career resources	**2** Inadequate parking
3 Flexible scheduling	**3** Bursar's Office
4 Small campus	**4** Parking tickets
5 Low crime	**5** Ongoing construction

Students Speak Out
ON FACILITIES

Q "Most of the facilities are nice and are constantly being renovated and updated. The new fitness center **provides a lot more amenities** to students that the old center did."

Q "A majority of the facilities on campus are adequate. The University has an old and new feel to it depending on where you're at. I would say the **nicest areas are the Alfond, the Union**, and the upcoming recreational center."

Q "The Union is great. The **library staff is quick to respond to requests** for materials located at other schools or on UMaine campuses."

Q "The facilities are **always growing and improving**. The athletic fields and Alfond Arena are wonderful considering we are a Division I school for football and hockey. There are two gyms on campus, as well as tons of bike trails and fields to play soccer and club sports. There is a river very close to campus for canoeing and such."

STUDENT AUTHOR: **A majority of the facilities on campus are not only aesthetically appealing, but they are continuously being modernized and updated when necessary. Memorial Union is one of the busiest buildings on campus. The classrooms have the proper equipment required for instruction and are kept up-to-date with modern technology. Raymond H. Fogler Library is the state's largest research library. The noisy first floor of the library also houses the Oakes Room Café, where students frequently retreat for much needed caffeine boosts.**

Famous Alumni

Doug Hall (Founder of Eureka!), Don Holder (Tony Award winner), Paul Kariya (Pro hockey player), Stephen King (Best-selling author)

Students Speak Out
ON CAMPUS DINING

Q "This is always a source of contention among universities—it's like every other cafeteria food system, either you like it or you don't, and you already know how you feel about it. **The Union is nice to break up the routine of the commons**, but beware, because you will get tired of eating there if you go too often."

Q "**The commons are a hit-or-miss kind of thing**. There are good days, and there are bad days. You either know the menu so you can judge the good meals from the bad ahead of time, get used to the salad/wrap bar, or prepare to fork out some money for some good food."

Q "**Commons food is not that good**, but if you eat it, you should definitely work out."

Q "The food on campus was okay. It had variety most of the time and filled your stomach, but that's about it. **The student meal plans are a big rip-off and disappointment**. I am not pleased about spending money on something I have to as a first-year. To sum it up, the food is overpriced and not worth the money."

STUDENT AUTHOR: **If you didn't like any of the food in your high school cafeteria, then chances are that you won't enjoy the commons food at UMaine. There is a variety of available foods for all meals in the commons. You may also choose to eat at one of the more popular restaurants in Memorial Union. Just remember: your parents didn't mass produce a meal for hundreds of students, three meals a day, every day, so don't expect it to be like home-cooking.**

Student Body

African American:	1%	Male/Female:	49/51%
Asian American:	1%	Out-of-State:	16%
Hispanic:	1%	International:	2%
Native American:	1%	Unknown:	0%
White:	94%		

Popular Faiths: Catholic and non-denominational are most common.

Gay Pride: The University of Maine has a significant gay community. Many members of the gay community are active in campus organizations.

Economic Status: Students coming from out-of-state frequently seem to come from households with higher incomes.

Students Speak Out
ON DORMS

Q "Some of the dorms are quite beat up and are typical dorms with damage and funny smells. I lived in Kennebec, and it was always a mess. This is the same with Cumberland, Gannett, Androscoggin, Aroostook, York, Hancock, and Stodder. Although some are worse than others, these **dorms are the epitome of a college lifestyle, at least for the first two years** or so until students decide to move off campus."

Q "I think they lack up-to-date furniture and architecture. They are right from the '80s and make **things seem like you are in an old hospital at times**."

STUDENT AUTHOR: **First-year housing is mixed between all of the "dormitory-style" residence halls. These rooms consist primarily of doubles. The halls have all of the amenities that students need, including communal kitchens in the basement, as well as ample study lounges and areas to socialize. The University is very good about making the necessary changes and renovations to the housing, even though most of them lack modern aesthetic design features.**

Did You Know?
42% of undergrads live on campus.

Students Speak Out
ON GUYS & GIRLS

Q "Well, everyone jokes that everyone disappears in the winter months, but it seems so true. During the first weeks and the last, hot people are everywhere, and I sometimes wonder where they come from. It's all up to what you are looking for, but **most kids at this age just want to get laid and have no commitment**."

Q "**Beauty is all in the eye of the beholder**. UMaine does have a lot of amazing students, though; just take the time to get to know them."

Q "**Depending on what you like, you'll find it**. There are plenty of attractive people, plenty of average people, and plenty of 'leave me alone I just woke up and dressed in the dark' people. There are lots of hot guys and girls."

STUDENT AUTHOR: **Most students coming to UMaine are in search of a good-looking guy or girl to spend some quality time with, but fewer will actually attain it. Hooking up or settling down in a relationship is up to those who are participating in it. Most students will say that there are more unattractive people than not, and the appearance of students actually may coordinate with their area of study.**

Traditions

Bumstock
Annual springtime concert held for students at the concert park on Hilltop.

Class Gift
The graduating class supports UMaine by collecting donations to purchase a gift for the University.

Overall School Spirit
There is very high school spirit, especially when it comes to popular varsity sporting events, such as men's hockey.

Students Speak Out
ON ATHLETICS

Q "Intramurals are huge; **hockey is king here** for varsity. Better get in line early for your free student tickets."

Q "Varsity sports are huge, hockey being the most popular. But **UMaine has great football, basketball, and baseball games**, too. Don't forget women's sports; it is very exciting and competitive."

Q "**Men's hockey and women's basketball are huge**. You cannot come to UMaine and not go to hockey. You would be short-changing yourself massively. Intramural sports are big amongst the fraternities."

Q "The **varsity sports are so selective** that anyone who doesn't make the teams will end up doing IM sports."

STUDENT AUTHOR: **Hockey is definitely the most popular varsity sport at UMaine. Intramural sports are also very popular among students. Individuals can get friends together to participate in IM sports, or residence halls can coordinate teams. The athletic facilities and fields are great for individual and IM sports.**

Students Speak Out
ON DRUG SCENE

Q "I've heard some people say that drugs are easier to find on campus than your classes are, but I have never had a problem with them. I know that if I wanted to buy drugs, I could find people to sell them to me, but **it's not in your face all the time**."

Q "There are **a lot of drugs on campus**. More than any other college in the U.S., though? I doubt it."

Q "I didn't see too much of it, but it's there. I can't really say anymore about it, except that **you hear more about it these days** than when I first started here."

STUDENT AUTHOR: **Most of the drugs pushed around on UMaine's campus outside of marijuana are prescription medications. There are not many other widely-known abused substances around campus, although students are aware that the use of highly-addictive substances does exist. The campus has many programs available to provide education and information about drugs and their prevalence on college campuses.**

16:1	Student-to-Faculty Ratio
79%	Freshman Retention Rate
32%	Four-Year Graduation Rate
80%	Financial Aid Applicants Receiving Aid

Students Speak Out
SAFETY & SECURITY

Q "People at UMaine watch out for their own. We truly are a community, and most of the time, things are very respectful in regard to security and safety. Students get to know their Public Safety officials because they will see them at random times in random places. Some students even get the opportunity to work on the force. **You couldn't ask for a more safe and secure place**."

Q "The campus is extremely safe. They just finished installing more lights all over campus, so walking at night is not a problem. The UMaine police are great! Their goal is to be part of your community, not to bust everyone. **Don't be stupid, and you will find that the campus is very safe**."

STUDENT AUTHOR: **The campus has a very low crime rate and nearly nonexistent violent crime. Since walking alone is not recommended at night in even the safest environments, the campus has volunteers who will walk with students at night through the Campus Walking Companions program.**

Questions?

For more inside information and survival tips, pick up College Prowler's full-length book on this school, written by an actual student! Check it out at *www.collegeprowler.com*.

Students Speak Out
ON OVERALL EXPERIENCE

Q "Now that I have graduated, I can look back and say that **UMaine was the best time of my life**. I fell in love there. I had some firsts there. I met the greatest people I will ever know there. I got into some trouble, I got good grades, I loved my experiences there, and I can only hope that others will find UMaine as incredible as I did."

Q "Maine is the only place I would want to be. I am never bored. I love my hockey team, classes are great, and **if you get bored, it's your own fault**, because there is never a lack of things to do! Come on up, and we'll show you how to have fun Black Bear style!"

Q "My overall experience is great. Being an in-state student, **I couldn't have asked for better experiences**. The people are friendly, the scenery is scenic, and the campus life is prosperous."

Q "I loved UMaine. Great atmosphere, great opportunities for clubs, organizations, sports, and fitness. **So many choices of classes** and a scenic area—I'm glad to call UMaine my alma mater."

STUDENT AUTHOR: **The students who offered responses regarding their overall experience at UMaine have overwhelmingly praised the University for its effect on the students who attend it. Many of the students make Maine their home, even after graduation. The University has an abundance of assets of immeasurable value to offer to its students. There are activities and clubs for nearly every student interest. Nearly all students have enjoyed their experiences at UMaine and are proud to call it their alma mater, and even more whole-heartedly, their home.**

University of Maryland

1201 Turner Hall, Baltimore Avenue; College Park, MD 20742
(301) 405-1000; www.maryland.edu

THE BASICS:

Acceptance Rate: 47%
Setting: Suburban
F-T Undergrads: 23,788

SAT Range: 1170–1380*
Control: Public
Tuition: $23,076

Most Popular Majors: Social Sciences, Business, Biology, Engineering, Communications, Education

*of 1600

Academics	B+	Guys	A-
Local Atmosphere	B+	Girls	A
Safety & Security	B	Athletics	A-
Computers	B	Nightlife	B-
Facilities	A-	Greek Life	B+
Campus Dining	B-	Drug Scene	B
Off-Campus Dining	B	Campus Strictness	B+
Campus Housing	C+	Parking	C
Off-Campus Housing	B	Transportation	A
Diversity	A-	Weather	B-

Students Speak Out
ON ACADEMICS

Q "I always found the **younger faculty to be a lot more engaging and interesting** in the classroom. Sometimes, even the best were only adjunct, contractual faculty. Being a history major, it was tough getting stuck with some old white guy droning on for an hour about what he thought was historically important. It was when you had the chance to really interact with the younger faculty that you felt like you learned something."

Q "The teachers, for the most part, were **welcoming, warm, and full of interesting insight on their subjects**. From Death Education to Human Sexuality, you can't ask for a better selection of classes!"

Q "The Philip Merrill College of Journalism is amazing. The professors there are excellent because they are high-level journalists working for different, big-time newspapers across the country (like the *Washington Post* and *Baltimore Sun*). It's **one of the top schools** in the country."

Q "**Some classes are so big you can get lost** or take a nap, and no one will notice you."

STUDENT AUTHOR: **Academics at Maryland are delightful when students have a sincere interest in the subject matter. There tends to be a good amount of interaction between teachers and students throughout each school at Maryland, and because of this, students' satisfaction levels are pretty high; who would know that courses about human sexuality and death would be so popular?**

Students Speak Out
ON LOCAL ATMOSPHERE

Q "The town of College Park is not the most bustling college town. It lacks quality restaurants and a huge number of bars and shopping areas. However, the campus makes the most out of it, and there are **always things going on**."

Q "College Park is a college town that isn't really a college town. I don't think I realized this until I visited other schools that were truly college towns. The 'downtown' area is a **far cry from being student-friendly**, and there's little selection in shops and things to do, especially if you're under 21."

Q "There are over **a dozen universities within an hour and a half** from College Park. I recommend going to both the bar areas in DC and Baltimore. Each has a completely different scene and atmosphere. If you have never been to the museums and attractions of DC and Baltimore, I definitely recommend seeing them."

Q "College Park is very self-sufficient. You can get anything you need right there, and the **Metro is very accessible if you want to go to DC**."

STUDENT AUTHOR: **College Park would be a great town if only DC and Baltimore weren't so close by, and so easily accessible from campus with or without a car. These two great cities make College Park seem like a fair town. The business district seems to be flooded with places to eat, and while there are malls just minutes away, College Park can actually be the perfect size for getting your hands on basic necessities and returning to campus quickly.**

5 Best Things	5 Worst Things
1 Location	1 Parking hassles
2 Beautiful campus	2 Housing scarcity
3 Athletics	3 Little nightlife
4 Living/Learning dorms	4 Construction
5 Late-night dining	5 College Park is small

Students Speak Out
ON FACILITIES

Q "The athletic facility **rivals any in the country** and will stay modern for many years. For that reason, it's always crowded."

Q "The **libraries are amazing**. I know you're wondering who would say that, but I haven't been able to find a library as big or with as much information as that. You can get dazed and confused figuring out where to get the item you just spent an hour looking up on the computer."

Q "It's amazing. **Everything is amazing**. The gym, the pool, and the PAC are so nice."

Q "The athletic **facilities are fantastic**. Computers are great. The student union is fine; however, there's so much around town that the student union gets by without having to offer too much."

Q "The **CRC is awesome**. Huge! Clean."

Q "The new student center is really beautiful, but nothing compares to the **divine, unparalleled Comcast Center**. No college b-ball stadium can compare!"

STUDENT AUTHOR: **One of the most significant reasons for attending Maryland is its beautiful campus and awe-inspiring facilities. There's no avoiding the bountiful cherry blossoms and flower arrangements on the grounds, including an occasional rosebush. The CRC facility is so large that it sometimes feels like an airport. The pools are heated and have speakers mounted deep below. Thankfully, the CRC offers healthy, fun, and challenging experiences for students at all levels of fitness.**

Famous Alumni

Connie Chung, Larry David, Len Elmore, Norman "Boomer" Esiason, Jim Henson, Kathleen Turner, Scott Van Pelt, Dianne Wiest

Students Speak Out
ON CAMPUS DINING

Q "The food on campus is not terrible, but it gets **repetitive eating at the dining hall each night**. South Campus dining hall has the most variety, and the places at the Union do, too. I never eat at Adele's in the Union."

Q "It's fine—the **food is good** on campus. I liked the Co-Op in the Union. It's so good. I don't recommend any of the other places to eat."

Q "Dining hall food was pretty good. At the Ellicott dining hall, they had **late-night meals of good, greasy food to help you study** and gain the Freshman 20. At the end of the semester, you'll end up buying cakes, cookies, and meals for other people because you didn't budget right and have a lot of money left over."

Q "**There are different food plans**, depending on how much people wanted to eat in the dining hall and at other on-campus eating facilities, which was a nice option. There's also a sit-down restaurant, Adele's, which is good when you need to use up your points on the meal plan."

STUDENT AUTHOR: **One of the best things about UMCP is the availability, quality, and variety of food on campus. In addition to the overabundance of options and the staff's willingness to help students, both dining halls continue to offer their extremely popular "late-night" dining hours; students may purchase fast food snacks, sandwiches, ice cream, and plenty of beverages. Eating healthy on the campus is easy—the challenge is not having dessert at every meal.**

Student Body

African American:	13%	Male/Female:	52/48%
Asian American:	14%	Out-of-State:	23%
Hispanic:	6%	International:	2%
Native American:	<1%	Unknown:	8%
White:	57%		

Popular Faiths: Judaism and Christianity are quite popular on campus.

Gay Pride: Campus is very open to those students with a diverse interest in non-traditional sexual/gender preferences.

Economic Status: Students from all walks of life attend UMCP, and that's what makes it special, right?

Students Speak Out
ON DORMS

Q "Sure, a lot of schools brag that they have suite-style housing with private bathrooms, but there's nothing like living on a floor with a bunch of people your age and **sharing a bathroom**. Yeah, it can be gross sometimes, but it does help raise your 'scum tolerance.'"

Q "On floors with community bathrooms, you will find a stronger sense of community in which people know one another better and interact more. If you don't know anyone besides your roommate, **brushing your teeth can be a great place to meet people**!"

Q "Your dorm is only as good as your housekeeper. Due to the demand for housing, it's crowded. If you like living **on top of your roommates**, you're all set."

STUDENT AUTHOR: Living on campus at Maryland is so highly regarded that there can be a waiting list for students to move onto campus each year. Be prepared for healthy, safe, but possibly cramped living quarters. A quaint number of single rooms do exist for students with the highest on-campus living priority level.

> **Did You Know?**
> 48% of undergrads live on campus.

Students Speak Out
ON GUYS & GIRLS

Q "Well, frat guys and sorority girls are basically cookie cutter. If it's trendy, that's what they look like. Overall, it's a fairly **attractive campus—if you like a Long Island accent**."

Q "It's a mix. Guys: there's a strong showing from the NY tri-state area: NJ, Long Island, CT. You have your **princesses, whose mommies bought them BMWs**. You also have your mix of attractive-looking people and a mix of average-looking people."

Q "**Hot**, in a Long Island kind of way."

Q "It's a really good-looking crowd here. In fact, I find the girls here **the best looking** out of lots of places, and also the coolest and most down-to-earth."

STUDENT AUTHOR: The campus's emphasis on athletics and its state-of-the-art CRC facility motivates many students to keep in shape, especially during College Park's colder months. It's generally accepted here that there are more hot girls than guys, but not by an astronomical margin. Come the spring, when the CRC's outdoor pool opens on North Campus, you'll find already fit guys and girls getting sun, flirting, and showing off their bodies.

> **Traditions**
>
> **Getting Lucky**
> For a hint of good luck, students visit a bronze replica of Maryland's mascot, Testudo, which sits at the entrance to McKeldin Library.
>
> **The All-Niter**
> One night in September, the student body holds the campus's longest party of the year.
>
> **Overall School Spirit**
> Maryland's students are outrageously dedicated to the power and performance of the sports teams.

Students Speak Out
ON ATHLETICS

Q "Varsity sports are big, since Maryland is a Division I school. **Football and basketball are the most popular sports**, depending on how good our teams are doing. It's a lot of fun to go to the games with friends."

Q "Going to an ACC/Division I school made my college experience even better. My memories of football, basketball, lacrosse, and soccer games are some of the most fun I have of being in college. I can't imagine going somewhere without **so much school spirit**."

Q "It's huge—that's what's fun. I think IMs are pretty big, too. I played flag football. If you want to, you can get involved. There's **plenty of club sports**."

STUDENT AUTHOR: As it's a Division I school, varsity sports at Maryland are very popular. Student athletes at Maryland are so talented that even those who are not very passionate about sports will attend games to support them and to witness some awesome displays of competition. For those students not too keen on statistics, let's just say that when students say that the men's squad is the best, they are actually telling the truth.

Students Speak Out
ON DRUG SCENE

Q "**Pot is hot**—everything else is not!"

Q "Very **large, underground drug scene** on campus. It's very easy to get a variety of different drugs on campus."

Q "There's a **good amount of drug use**, but no more than other campuses. Kids are still pulling high GPAs."

Q "I can't comment on the drug scene because I've never done drugs. I'm sure that **many do drugs**."

Q "There was rarely anything more than **some pot** on campus."

STUDENT AUTHOR: Similar to other aspects of college life at Maryland, there is a perception of a big drug scene, but there is a relatively small amount of traditional drugs being abused on the campus. Surprisingly, despite some students making drug use one of their top priorities while at UMCP, they do excel in their courses, all while honoring the "Code of Academic Integrity."

18:1	Student-to-Faculty Ratio
93%	Freshman Retention Rate
58%	Four-Year Graduation Rate
68%	Financial Aid Applicants Receiving Aid

Students Speak Out
SAFETY & SECURITY

Q "**Safety is good**, but people will still do dumb things, like walk around at 3 a.m. without anyone else near the darkest and shadiest parts. So as long as you're acting safely, there are no worries."

Q "Security is **ever-present**, and the University does a good job with it."

Q "Personally, I **never had a problem**. There was always petty theft from dorm rooms. And every once in awhile someone breaks into cars. But the majority of serious crimes that are reported are from off campus."

Q "The **blue-light system** makes you feel like help is always just a flashing blue light away!"

STUDENT AUTHOR: It's the location of campus that causes potential concern, since no matter how many video cameras, emergency phones, or neighborhood watches there are at Maryland, trespassers, vagrants, and criminals will make their way beyond the gates after hours.

Questions?
For more inside information and survival tips, pick up College Prowler's full-length book on this school, written by an actual student! Check it out at *www.collegeprowler.com.*

Students Speak Out
ON OVERALL EXPERIENCE

Q "The professors were thoughtful and thorough, and I particularly enjoyed my professors who were professionals from DC, coming to UMD to teach a class or two after work. However, it was the **winning sports teams and social life that completed the experience**. Everyone I met wanted to enjoy their lives while in school, and we matured and lived life to the fullest in those three bars in College Park, in our dorms, and in our sorority house."

Q "Going to Maryland was **one of the best decisions I ever made** in my life. It wasn't always perfect, and I definitely did a lot of growing, but I couldn't imagine going anywhere else. The education I received and the opportunities I was given from my involvements are unparalleled."

Q "I **loved my time at UMD**, and I wouldn't change a thing."

Q "Amazing. I think it's the best college in the country, and I wouldn't recommend any other school, but of course I'm biased. **There's nothing bad about the school**. After attending, I wouldn't have gone anywhere else."

STUDENT AUTHOR: Most students who join the campus community stay a while, and some don't want to leave, even after being there for four or even five years. From their first year on campus, to their final days leading up to graduation, students' academic, personal, physical, professional, and social lives come together to prepare them for the real world. Once entering such a world, many alumni look back and agree that, even if they could, they wouldn't change a thing about their overall experience at UMCP.

University of Massachusetts

181 President's Drive; Amherst, MA 01003
(413) 545-0111; www.umass.edu

THE BASICS:

Acceptance Rate: 66%
Setting: Rural
F-T Undergrads: 18,646

SAT Range: 1030–1240*
Control: Public
Tuition: $20,499

Most Popular Majors: Business, Social Sciences, Communications, Psychology, Bological/Life Sciences

*of 1600

Academics	B	Guys	B+
Local Atmosphere	C	Girls	B+
Safety & Security	B	Athletics	B
Computers	C+	Nightlife	B
Facilities	B-	Greek Life	B
Campus Dining	C+	Drug Scene	B-
Off-Campus Dining	B+	Campus Strictness	B+
Campus Housing	B-	Parking	F
Off-Campus Housing	C-	Transportation	B
Diversity	C-	Weather	C+

Students Speak Out
ON ACADEMICS

Q "The teachers at my school are unbelievable! They're **willing to help you no matter what**, and they always strive to make their classes enjoyable. The general education professors I've had have been decent for the most part, and many of the University's faculty have won awards for their teaching and research."

Q "The **most respected majors at UMass** are engineering, computer science, psychology, communication, and anything in the school of management."

Q "My experience has been that **professors tend to be condescending**. I don't know if that is especially the case at UMass, but I have had a lot of teachers whose egos get in the way of their teaching."

Q "Professors at UMass are a mixed bag. **You could get a total idiot or a complete genius**. I personally have lucked out with teachers, but others haven't been so lucky. The teachers within your major are bound to be good, but don't expect too much out of general education courses."

STUDENT AUTHOR: Despite the overwhelmingly large general education requirements that each student must satisfy at UMass, the breadth and scope of classes involved allows students who have not yet picked a major become exposed to fields that they might not have previously considered. Due to UMass's size, students are sure to experience varying degrees of quality among the faculty.

Students Speak Out
ON LOCAL ATMOSPHERE

Q "Although very rural, Amherst is **in a convenient location to get to other areas**. Boston, New York City, Hartford, and New Haven are all within just a few hours from Amherst."

Q "Amherst is a **small town with two colleges**—UMass and Amherst College. Northampton is about five or six miles down the road. It's a trendy town with a lot of shops, restaurants, and music halls. The Northampton district is lively, while Amherst is more laid-back."

Q "In every way, Amherst is a college town. All the businesses are dependent on the colleges around them, but it's a very nice atmosphere. Down near Smith College is Northampton, and the bus goes right there. It's a **great town with a lot of history, culture**, and some very nice restaurants. Everyone loves the movie theater, where the shows are only five dollars."

Q "I was born and raised here and will probably never leave. This whole area is the most beautiful spot in the fall with the leaves and everything else; it makes you feel like you are in a movie. **The town is cute** and has so much history."

STUDENT AUTHOR: The richness and volume of culture in Amherst and Northampton is synonymous with the idea of college. During the winter, Amherst gets crowded and takes on the likeness of a metropolis, especially with Holyoke, Amherst, Hampshire, Smith colleges, all in the area. However, during breaks, Amherst is so dead that it could pass for a rural farming community.

5 Best Things	5 Worst Things
1 Parties	1 Budget cuts
2 Great professors	2 Parking
3 Low tuition	3 Technology department
4 Variety of majors	4 Expensive books
5 The library	5 Dwindling school spirit

Students Speak Out
ON FACILITIES

Q "The athletic facilities are **very close to the Southwest residential area**, and because sports are so huge here, the facilities are very well kept."

Q "The athletics department and **the computer labs definitely get hooked** up with cool stuff. The student union isn't bad, but it could use some work."

Q "There are some old-fashioned, typical New England-style buildings, and there are some **hideous, modern, concrete buildings**."

Q "We have a **nice stadium and two good gyms**. There are also fitness centers in various residence halls on campus."

Q "The gym has really crowded weight-lifting rooms, but **it's good for basketball** and aerobic exercise."

Q "I've had classrooms where I'd rather sit on the floor than in the chairs, and I've had classrooms where it was **hard to stay awake because the chairs are so darn comfortable**. They put an addition on Isenberg and I've never seen such beautiful, technologically-advanced classrooms."

STUDENT AUTHOR: **UMass facilities are well maintained and offer most of what students want. Some could use a facelift, as they appear to have been designed by an architect who lived in communist Russia. With some exceptions, the buildings on campus are not very architecturally pleasing, but they certainly possess a lot of history and character.**

Famous Alumni

Herbert Bix, Jack Canfield, Natalie Cole, Jeff Corwin, Bill Cosby, Julius Erving, Robert Meers, Bill Pullman, Briana Scurry, Jeff Taylor, Paul Theroux, Jack Welch

Students Speak Out
ON CAMPUS DINING

Q "There are **vegetarian meals, vegan meals**, and always subs and pizza in the dining commons. For delivery, there is awesome food!"

Q "Being a rather 'picky' eater, the quality of the dining commons and food was extremely important to me. After touring more than 20 colleges (between touring for myself and visiting my older siblings at their colleges), I can honestly say that UMass Amherst **allows for the best dining experience of them all**."

Q "There's a program called 'Off-Campus Meal Plan' (OCMP). You can **pay extra to put food from off-campus restaurants on a special card** they issue. It's kind of expensive, but it's definitely worth it."

Q "It's **mandatory to eat there** for your first two years, which is a huge pain in the butt. We have a few good places on campus, though. The Hatch, Bluewall, and Greenough Sub Shop are the most common favorites. They serve things ranging from soups and salads to pizzas and subs. Your campus meal plan swipes you into these places. The Hatch is the best place to eat on campus, though few freshmen know this valuable fact."

STUDENT AUTHOR: **UMass dining offers many options in terms of food served. If, at the end of the semester, you haven't fully redeemed all the meals you purchased, you don't get back the remaining balance. Therefore, buying the most basic and inexpensive meal plan is highly advisable. I promise you won't starve at UMass—if anything, you will gain weight.**

Student Body

African American:	5%	Male/Female:	50/50%
Asian American:	8%	Out-of-State:	19%
Hispanic:	4%	International:	1%
Native American:	<1%	Unknown:	9%
White:	73%		

Popular Faiths: If there is a "popular" religion on campus, it is probably Christianity.

Gay Pride: Homosexuals are prevalent on campus. There is an educational resource center, a yearly rally, and a special interest floor for the benefit and support of homosexual students.

Economic Status: UMass students illustrate an accurate depiction of middle-class America.

Students Speak Out
ON DORMS

Q "Southwest is a huge, concrete mess—the general rule of thumb is that **you go to there to party, but not to live**. I've lived in Central all three years, and I loved it. It's located near just about everything, and the dorms are nice and made of brick."

Q "Northeast has the biggest and cleanest dorms, but the **social life really sucks**. It's far away from everything, so if you like a fun social life and a clean dorm, or you want to be close to everything, live in Southwest in a low-rise."

Q "Sylvan sucks, Northeast is quiet, and Orchard Hill is nice and quiet. Central has a bit of a drug culture, but they're very open-minded and laid-back. **Southwest is big party area** with tall towers, and the people there are pretty shallow."

STUDENT AUTHOR: UMass is good about placing students in the buildings they requested; each is very different. Central and Orchard Hill have the best dorms. Southwest has "Z-rooms," which are worth checking out. Northeast is nice because they have a sand volleyball court outside. Sylvan and Orchard Hill have long walks to class.

Did You Know?
60% of undergrads live on campus.

Students Speak Out
ON GUYS & GIRLS

Q "UMass women are very **easy on the eyes**, and they are a dime a dozen. Most of them have their heads on straight, but some you'd swear do not belong in college."

Q "I think, because this school is so big, a lot of people try especially hard to stick out by wearing ridiculous clothes or hardly any at all. This place is **crawling with attractive people**; what am I doing inside?"

Q "Personally, I **never had any trouble finding attractive guys** on campus. There are jocks, hippies, and gangster-types. Depending on what area of campus you live in, you'll probably be exposed to different types of people. In general, UMass has a pretty attractive population."

STUDENT AUTHOR: On the whole, people are the same with a few exceptions; every stereotypical guy and girl can be found here in great numbers, but one can observe some beautiful scenery. On a scale from one to ten of sexual promiscuity, one being a convent, and ten being a brothel, UMass ranks about a seven or eight. Random hookups happen here, so "Closing Window Shades 101" is a valuable course.

Traditions

Streaking
Fall and spring streaking happens each semester before finals. As a way to blow off steam, hundreds of UMass students will run butt-naked through the Northeast Quad at night as a break from studying.

Overall School Spirit
The school spirit at UMass is not what it used to be, partially because the athletic department has been downsized over the last couple years. However, certain sporting events are still a big draw at UMass, like Midnight Madness and the Homecoming football game.

Students Speak Out
ON ATHLETICS

Q "The football team sucks, and not many people go to see the games. If they do, it's to see the marching band—no joke. The marching band is incredible! I'm not too sure about intramural sports, because a lot of them were recently **eliminated because of the budget cuts**."

Q "**Basketball is huge**. Other sports like lacrosse, soccer, softball, and baseball are very competitive but don't get too much attention. Hockey is okay. As far as intramural sports go, they are huge! There are tons of different sports to play for both semesters."

Q "Everyone loves football, and Midnight Madness, the first night the basketball team starts practice for the season, is a big deal. **Our teams really aren't that good**, even with our enthusiasm."

STUDENT AUTHOR: Varsity sports on campus are not very big, especially when compared to universities of similar size, like UConn. A lot of the less popular sports are now done away with, and you'll never have a problem finding a seat at a game. On the plus side, all tickets for sporting events are free for students. Conversely, intramural sports are big and a great distraction from homework.

Students Speak Out
ON DRUG SCENE

Q "There's lots of pot, but that's about it. You'll run into **ecstasy here and there**, but it's not like we have coke heads or heroine addicts running around."

Q "People **love their herb** out here—marijuana, if you're not down with the lingo. I haven't seen too many hard drugs, but they are there if you really want them."

Q "Once in a while, you will see people doing coke or **pills like OxyContin and Vicadin at a party**, but it is all very avoidable. Although, if you don't want to be around drugs, I suggest not living in Southwest or Central."

STUDENT AUTHOR: **Drugs can be found at UMass, but in no way are they unavoidable. Once in a great while, you may smell the odor of marijuana in a dormitory hallway, but almost never will you come across someone doing a harder drug—drug users at UMass are either few or very clandestine about their behavior. Still, drugs are the number-one cause of arrests on campus.**

17:1	Student-to-Faculty Ratio
84%	Freshman Retention Rate
49%	Four-Year Graduation Rate
70%	Financial Aid Applicants Receiving Aid

Students Speak Out
SAFETY & SECURITY

Q "The security on campus is very good, as far as I'm concerned. A couple of years ago, there were **several cases of rape, but since then, security has been tighter** than ever!"

Q "Every dorm building has security 'check-ins' on the weekends—you have to have a dorm sticker on your student card or be signed in by someone who lives in the building to get in. On campus there are **emergency phone boxes, and UMass police patrol the campus**. Overall, I feel safe."

Q "My freshman year, I heard about these people who were all dressed up and came to a Northeast building, telling people to leave for an hour so they could fumigate. Then, when the students got back, **all of their valuable stuff was gone**. What a great idea for a robbery!"

STUDENT AUTHOR: **Certain areas of UMass experience more crime than others. These areas include Southwest, parking lots, and the many off-campus apartment complexes. Thankfully, the police department keeps things from getting out-of-hand, and most students seem to feel safe.**

Questions?
For more inside information and survival tips, pick up College Prowler's full-length book on this school, written by an actual student! Check it out at *www.collegeprowler.com*.

Students Speak Out
ON OVERALL EXPERIENCE

Q "It's a great place with lots of opportunities. Despite some of the recent budget cuts, I am really happy here. I know that **the University will get back on its feet and fix things up**— hopefully by reinstating escort services, supporting some of the smaller sports teams, and providing child care."

Q "UMass really feels like home to me. **It's like living in a city with so many people** here, and I think it's more like real life because of the number of students."

Q "I love UMass. The people are great, and the classes and social life are a lot of fun. Sometimes, it's tough to get into classes because of the huge number of people, which gets annoying, but you deal with it. I'm a psychology major, and I love it. The department is great! Our business program is amazing, too. I wouldn't want to be anywhere else. I'm a city girl, and it was tough to adapt to 'cow country.' Once you do, though, you really **learn to appreciate the scenic area** and the great people here."

Q "In the beginning, I didn't like it because I wasn't very outgoing, and you have to be at any big school. **It's easy to slip through the cracks** if you're not. My advice is to join clubs and other activities right away."

STUDENT AUTHOR: **Despite the bad parking, unpredictable weather, and crumby campus dining, it's still hard to find someone who genuinely hates UMass. The size of UMass provides you with more resources and options, so do what I did, and have fun. Judging from the comments other students have made, coming to UMass has truly enriched their lives, academically and socially.**

University of Miami

1360 Stanford Drive; Coral Gables, FL 33146
(305) 284-2211; www.miami.edu

THE BASICS:

Acceptance Rate: 38% **SAT Range:** 1740–2020*
Setting: Urban **Control:** Private
F-T Undergrads: 9,677 **Tuition:** $34,206

Most Popular Majors: Business, Visual and
Performing Arts, Health Professions, Biology

*of 2400

Academics	B+	Guys	B
Local Atmosphere	A	Girls	A
Safety & Security	B+	Athletics	A
Computers	B	Nightlife	A+
Facilities	B+	Greek Life	B
Campus Dining	C+	Drug Scene	C+
Off-Campus Dining	A+	Campus Strictness	B
Campus Housing	B	Parking	C+
Off-Campus Housing	B+	Transportation	B
Diversity	A	Weather	A

Students Speak Out
ON ACADEMICS

Q "My teachers are all very friendly and willing to help out their students. They try their best to **make each class interesting**, and they stay up-to-date on current trends in society, allowing them to relate to each student."

Q "My teachers have **made each class challenging while also making them fun** by adding jokes into their lectures and having a surprise from time to time. I would say that I have had a positive experience with all of my teachers."

Q "I find that all the **teachers are accessible**, and that is a positive thing. They are also more than willing to help with any questions."

Q "The teachers **range from very passionate to extremely boring**, but this is the case with every school. In general, most classes are interesting. It really depends on the teacher and subject."

STUDENT AUTHOR: UM has done a great job in climbing its way into the top tier of American colleges. Although Miami is still a great party town, most of UM's students are here with academics in mind, as well as nightlife and beaches. As a school becomes more prestigious, it builds a strong faculty, and that's exactly what UM has done. Students seem to like their professors, even if they complain regularly about homework and exams. Although complaints about the amount of work and grading are common, it's rare to hear anyone claim that a professor does not know the subject he or she is teaching.

Students Speak Out
ON LOCAL ATMOSPHERE

Q "The city of Miami always has something going on, though for those under 21, things can become a bit limiting at some times. **There are other schools around**, but not within 20 miles or so. There are many movie theaters, bars, clubs, and general places to hang out. However, there are also a lot of areas to be avoided."

Q "Miami is a **very fast-paced city**. There is always something to do. I would recommend going to Coconut Grove many times, South Beach once, and always avoid Grand Avenue. Coconut Grove is always a fun place to shop, eat, and catch a movie. South Beach is fun to people watch."

Q "The town is **perfect for a college campus**. It has its great spots, good spots, and the ones you need to avoid, as well. Other universities are present and are a noticeable factor in the community. The city atmosphere provides a good cultural, as well as career-oriented atmosphere."

Q "The atmosphere of the city is one of the main draws of the University. It truly is a city that never sleeps. You **can always find a place to go** and eat or party."

STUDENT AUTHOR: It's hard not to be impressed by the aura of Miami. Whether it's the authentic Cuban culture in Little Havana or the neon frenzy of South Beach, Miami has plenty to do and see. Sports fans are impressed by the mixture of professional and collegiate athletics, while entertainment-savvy students love music and art scenes. Few cities can match Miami's 24-hour atmosphere.

5 Best Things	5 Worst Things
1 Sports teams	**1** Traffic
2 Nightlife	**2** Parking
3 Weather	**3** Dining halls
4 Restaurants	**4** Hurricanes
5 24-hour culture	**5** Shared bathrooms

Students Speak Out
ON FACILITIES

Q "The Wellness Center is amazing and has a **zillion aerobics classes**. I've tried some at other schools, but they're much better here and offered at more times."

Q "The buildings are uglier than sin, but the landscape makes up for them. Inside, most of the major buildings are very nicely decorated and kept-up, and you forget what the outside looks like. The new **buildings are nicely designed**."

Q "The facilities, which span all interests, are all top-notch. The Wellness Center has top-of-the-line sporting amenities for any activity one may seek to pursue. The bookstore, University Center, and dining halls are all **clean and technologically sound**."

Q "The **library has a wide variety of sources** for students to access. The Whitten University Center is a nice place for students to just sit around and relax. The Storm Surge Café is a place where students can hang out, play billiards, and eat. The UC also has a lap pool for students to work on their tan."

Q "The facilities on campus are ridiculously nice. **Most are either new or newly renovated**."

STUDENT AUTHOR: The highlight of UM's facilities is, by far, the **Wellness Center—a huge gym located next to the dorms where most freshmen live. The building stays open until midnight on weeknights, allowing for late-night games of basketball, squash, or racquetball, which can provide a great study break. The multi-level gym has pretty much anything a student could want.**

Famous Alumni

Rick Berry, Gloria Estefan, Roy Firestone, Jerry Herman, Bruce Hornsby, Patricia Ireland, Dwayne Johnson, Suzy Kolber, Al Rosen, Sylvester Stallone

Students Speak Out
ON CAMPUS DINING

Q "The University does have a 'center' that has many **fast food-type establishments**, offering a change from the everyday monotony of dining hall food."

Q "At the food court, there is a Taco Bell, a sandwich place, Chinese food, sushi bar, juice place, **mini-Starbucks**, and an ethnic food place."

Q "I like the dining halls because **there are a lot of choices**, and you can either eat healthfully or not; whatever you like."

Q "The dining halls are, contrary to popular belief, actually **not that bad**. The food quality is usually decent."

Q "Fast food restaurants on campus are hot spots, with names like **Taco Bell, Sbarro, and Subway**."

STUDENT AUTHOR: **UM has two dining halls, both with pretty standard college buffet food. The variety sounds good— pizza, pastas, made-to-order sandwiches, hamburgers, hot dogs, fries, salads, and ice cream. Freshmen usually start with the comfortable 14 meal plan, which allows for 14 meals at the dining hall per week. UM has an excellent selection of fast food restaurants on campus. There's a food court with Taco Bell, Panda Express, Jamba Juice, and Starbucks, and there's even an overpriced takeout sushi bar if you feel like blowing all your dining dollars on the first day. Other places include a Sbarro, a Subway, a crepe stand, and the Rathskeller—a sports bar and popular meeting place.**

Student Body

African American:	9%	Male/Female:	46/54%
Asian American:	5%	Out-of-State:	74%
Hispanic:	23%	International:	6%
Native American:	<1%	Unknown:	9%
White:	48%		

Popular Faiths: Religion isn't a major issue, although there are plenty of clubs for more spiritual students.

Gay Pride: Miami citizens are very accepting of the gay community, and UM mirrors that tolerance with organizations like spectrUM.

Economic Status: Given the high cost of attending UM and the fancy clothing seen around campus, many students seem to come from wealthy homes.

Students Speak Out
ON DORMS

Q "I strongly **recommend living on campus**. It has been a lot of fun living with several people of different backgrounds, and I have enjoyed getting to know all of them. Some people complain about communal bathrooms, but they are cleaned twice a day."

Q "The dorms are a great environment. There are freshman dorms (Stanford and Hecht), which are a really fun time. They are **coed by floor, and the rooms are doubles**. There really is not a set of dorms to stay away from, as they are pretty much all the same set-up."

Q "I like living on campus and all of the benefits that come with it, which include waking up and **going to class without worrying about parking** and meeting more people."

STUDENT AUTHOR: **If you're lucky and you have a good RA, your floor will turn into a family. Video game tournaments and hallway sports are common, and chances are, at least a few people on your floor will be friends that you keep in touch with for the rest of college. A lot of upperclassmen try to get into the apartments, which are tough to reserve.**

 Did You Know?
45% of undergrads live on campus.

Students Speak Out
ON GUYS & GIRLS

Q "The girls are amazing. **They are all beautiful**, but the question is if it's on the inside or just outer beauty. The friends I have made have generally not been supermodels, but quality girls, and I leave the models for just looking."

Q "**Every type of person is represented** here. We have nerds, jerks, punks, rockers, and everything else."

Q "**Watch out** for personality."

Q "**People here are interesting**. A lot of Eastern attitude comes out, in my opinion. As a midwesterner, I am used to a little more hospitality. However, I do believe that this is no different from any other campus."

STUDENT AUTHOR: **Overall, the guys and girls look great, and some are great all around. But the amount of really intelligent, nice, caring people who are also hot seems to be low. If you're looking for a quick hookup, it's not hard. Most don't make it a habit, though. Perhaps the biggest problem is that guys and girls hide their real identities in favor of tight clothes and good tans, since that is the look most students are going for.**

Traditions

Hurricanes Help the Hometown
Students dedicate a Saturday morning and afternoon to volunteering at dozens of locations through Miami.

Sportsfest
This is a yearly competition where residential colleges battle one another in various sporting events.

Overall School Spirit
"It's great to be a Miami Hurricane!" Most students feel this way, with plenty of school-related things to be proud of. The sports teams, notably football and baseball, are always among the top in the nation.

Students Speak Out
ON ATHLETICS

Q "Miami is **one of the leading sports programs in the U.S.** There is nothing like Hurricane football and the history that comes with it. I am a huge sports fan, and one of the main draws was coming to watch the sports here."

Q "**IM sports are very prevalent**, particularly for fraternities. Arena football, flag football, and basketball are some of the more popular ones."

Q "It seems like varsity football is the only thing that matters here. **Basketball and baseball are just fillers until the football season**, even though we have an excellent baseball team."

Q "This is the University of Miami. **Do you really have to ask** about varsity sports?"

STUDENT AUTHOR: **UM has one of the most dominant college football programs in the country, and they show no signs of dropping out of the nation's top tier. A true sign of a student's devotion is how early they wake up for a game. Students line up outside the Orange Bowl gates as early as 8 a.m. to ensure good seats. By the mid-morning, the lines wind out into the parking lot, and the massive student section is generally buzzing.**

Students Speak Out
ON DRUG SCENE

Q "There is **a lot of weed** being smoked, but anything more serious than that isn't very apparent."

Q "I can honestly say that I have never run into anyone attempting to buy, sell, or use drugs. I'm **sure that they're out there**, but I suppose they hide themselves very well."

Q "**Alcohol is very prevalent**, and it definitely lives up to the stereotype of being everywhere on a college campus."

STUDENT AUTHOR: **Miami, like any big city, has its fair share of bad neighborhoods and drug addicts. But it's easy to stay away from them, especially around upscale Coral Gables. The only drug being really abused on campus is alcohol, and that's true of almost all colleges. There are groups of students that are into marijuana, cocaine, ecstasy, or various other drugs, but dealing is not really a problem on campus, and most RAs are pretty strict. Given UM's fairly difficult classes, most hardcore drug users aren't going to be around for long.**

12:1	Student-to-Faculty Ratio
90%	Freshman Retention Rate
63%	Four-Year Graduation Rate
86%	Students Who Applied for and Received Financial Aid

Students Speak Out
SAFETY & SECURITY

Q "The campus is very secure. There are several places on campus that have emergency phones in case an emergency ever arises. Also, police are always walking or driving around campus. After 10 p.m., **students entering a residential college must present their ID**."

Q "I feel perfectly safe walking around on campus any time of the day or night alone. Still, we sometimes **get reports in e-mails about some crime going on** around campus that we should watch out for."

Q "**Check-in booths at all entrances** ensure safety after 10 p.m. Moreover, you must swipe your ID at three locations before you may enter your dorm after 10 p.m., so there is a real sense of safety, especially in the nighttime hours."

STUDENT AUTHOR: **Even though Miami can be a dangerous city at times, UM is located in Coral Gables, which is a nice neighborhood. Public Safety should be commended for its honesty about what's happening around campus. Their truthfulness in matters makes students feel more comfortable.**

> **Questions?**
> For more inside information and survival tips, pick up College Prowler's full-length book on this school, written by an actual student! Check it out at *www.collegeprowler.com*.

Students Speak Out
ON OVERALL EXPERIENCE

Q "When you find the right situation, everything works out great. I strongly suggest people come and **enjoy everything this city has to offer** and the amazing experience that is Miami."

Q "My overall experience has been so positive, words can't describe it. The friends I've made, the learning I've done, and the culture I've become accustomed to have **made me much closer to the person I strive to be**."

Q "I love it here. There is **no place on earth I'd rather be** getting my education."

Q "Overall, UM is okay. **I am not really happy with how much I pay** to go to this place. Sometimes I wish I was somewhere else when I consider the money that I pay, but otherwise, it's a great school."

STUDENT AUTHOR: **Despite daily griping about tuition costs, parking, thunderstorms, and hard classes, most students really seem to enjoy UM. Excellent attributes, like the nightlife, weather, and culture seem to cancel out some of the bad things about being in Miami. For some students, these bad things include the unapproachable "hot" girls and guys on campus, while others find life in the dorms to be a challenge. The complaints about college are basically what you'd expect to hear anywhere. It appears that the bad things at UM really aren't that bad, but the good things are very good. Miami is one of the coolest cities in the world for a college student, and that goes deeper than just the superficial bar and club scene. Despite the initial challenges of coming to college, there are few cities in the world that are as fun as Miami.**

University of Michigan

503 Thompson Street; Ann Arbor, MI 48109
(734) 764-1817; www.umich.edu

THE BASICS:

Acceptance Rate: 50%
Setting: Mid-sized city
F-T Undergrads: 25,179

SAT Range: 1220–1420*
Control: Public
Tuition: $34,042

Most Popular Majors: Social Sciences, Engineering, Psychology, Biology, Business, English, Visual Arts

*of 1600

Academics	A-	Guys	B
Local Atmosphere	B+	Girls	A-
Safety & Security	B+	Athletics	A
Computers	A	Nightlife	B+
Facilities	A-	Greek Life	B+
Campus Dining	C	Drug Scene	C+
Off-Campus Dining	B+	Campus Strictness	B+
Campus Housing	C+	Parking	D+
Off-Campus Housing	B-	Transportation	B
Diversity	B	Weather	C-

Students Speak Out
ON ACADEMICS

Q "Nearly every program at Michigan is in the top 10 in its field. That's one cool thing about Michigan—its **academic reputation is incredible**, to say the least."

Q "The UROP (Undergraduate Research Opportunity Program) is amazing. It gives undergraduates the **opportunity to do ground-breaking research** with renowned professors and present their research."

Q "I was able to learn from professors who had genuine interest in teaching and who could make even the dullest subject matter seem exciting. I also learned that getting to know the professors outside of class was **well worth the effort**."

Q "**Be ready to work hard**. This school has no remedial classes, and because they know that students are smart, professors expect you to do a lot of work."

STUDENT AUTHOR: At a school as reputable as the University of Michigan, you are bound to find amazing professors who really care about teaching. They may have even written the book for the class you're taking. Although you'd expect some of the best experiences to be found in small classes such as seminars (of which there are plenty), some large lectures have surprisingly engaging professors. Students pack the lectures halls and fill the hallways outside simply to catch a lecture. Even with some less-than-stellar GSIs (Michigan-speak for TAs), everyone agrees that UM's academics are first-rate.

Students Speak Out
ON LOCAL ATMOSPHERE

Q "Ann Arbor is a really fun town. **The people are really friendly**, and there's always something to do whether you want to see a movie, hear a concert, go out to dinner, catch a play, or hit the museums. Ann Arbor really has anything."

Q "It's the **perfect college town**."

Q "Ann Arbor is a city in its own right, but **life is dominated by UM**. There are other universities nearby, but there is so much to do in Ann Arbor that there's no real need to go elsewhere."

Q "Well, Ann Arbor is a college town, make no mistake about it. **Take advantage of the shows** that come to Hill Auditorium. A lot of people visit Michigan State because it is supposedly a bigger party school than UM, and that's about 45 minutes away. You are four hours away from Chicago and Toronto, three hours from Cincinnati, and 45 minutes from Detroit."

STUDENT AUTHOR: The University and the city intertwine like threads into a rope. It's hard to determine where the University ends and where the city begins—they are virtually one. It is safe, charming, picturesque, and friendly. For a city the size of Ann Arbor, it is amazingly cosmopolitan. There is always something to do, and students don't have to leave town for a good time. The town has done well to steer clear of the rampant commercialism that has made towns across the country mirror images of one another. There are still used record shops, local coffee shops, and businesses as old as the University itself.

5 Best Things	5 Worst Things
1 Football	1 Dorm food
2 Ann Arbor	2 Parking
3 Academics	3 Tuition
4 Student organizations	4 Older dorms
5 Research opportunities	5 So much snow

Students Speak Out
ON FACILITIES

Q "Michigan has an amazing mix of buildings, both old and new. With all of the construction and renovation on campus, our **facilities get better every day**. The technology and resources available on campus are second to none."

Q "The campus facilities are top-notch, in my book. There is **always a library open** for you to study in if you need to get away from your room."

Q "The facilities here are **better than at many other midwestern universities**. There are two main athletic complexes for students to use, so that's not a problem. The student center (we call it the Union) is large, and it's also a pretty famous building. The Union has a bunch of food places, a bookstore, pool hall, libraries, coffee shop, and much more."

Q "A lot of the **classroom buildings are very historic with ivy, wood**, and the whole nine yards. Other buildings are state-of-the-art, brand spankin' new. Overall, UM provides its students with a very distinct learning environment."

Q "The research facilities on North Campus are **absolutely incredible**."

STUDENT AUTHOR: Although it has its fair share of older, historic buildings, they are all completely updated and well cared for. Constant renovations on campus can be a bit irritating to students at UM, but they must realize that not everything can get done in the summer months. From the stately law quad to the NASA-sponsored research facilities on North Campus, the University of Michigan's facilities are very tough to beat.

Famous Alumni

Selma Blair, Dan Dierdorf, Jim Harbaugh, James Earl Jones, Lawrence Kasdan, Lucy Lui, Gilda Radner, Carole Simpson, Chris Van Allsburg, Chris Webber

Students Speak Out
ON CAMPUS DINING

Q "The campus food is okay. Dorm food is pretty **consistent across campus**."

Q "Dorm food is dorm food, and it's no different here. East Quad is notorious for a lot of vegetarian dishes. There are Kosher meals somewhere on campus. West Quad and South Quad have great dining, and **most dorms have some sort of after-hours café**. West Quad is also attached to the Union, where you can buy things like Wendy's, First Wok, and pizza by using money on your M-Card."

Q "Although **few students have meal plans after freshman year**, many have Entrée Plus, so they can eat 'for free' in the Union, or other places around campus."

Q "The food at the dining halls might not be the best around, but they **offer much more than food**. They are a place to meet people, take a break from the studying, and just hang out with friends."

Q "There are **plenty of good places to eat** on campus; it's just that most of them are not in the dorms."

STUDENT AUTHOR: Everyone admits it's not the best food, but it seems to get fewer complaints than some schools. As compared to other schools, Michigan offers the typical: hot and cold entrees, a salad bar, and desserts. Weekend brunches are known by many students as the best cooked meals of the week, and don't be surprised to see tired and hungover classmates wearing pajamas and slippers.

Student Body

African American:	6%	Male/Female:	50/50%
Asian American:	12%	Out-of-State:	32%
Hispanic:	5%	International:	5%
Native American:	<1%	Unknown:	6%
White:	65%		

Popular Faiths: Judaism and Christianity are the most popular religions on campus.

Gay Pride: The University of Michigan, for the most part, is very accepting of the gay community.

Economic Status: Although Michigan students come from diverse economic backgrounds, there seems to be a preponderance of students coming from very wealthy families.

Students Speak Out
ON DORMS

Q "Those interested in the Greek system will want to stay on the Hill, although it's inconvenient and loud. **West Quad and South Quad are probably the nicest dorms**, and they certainly have the best location. East Quad is known for having a lot of independent-minded residents."

Q "**Living on the Hill is the best** place to be. It's mostly freshmen, and you're surrounded by lots of dorms."

Q "Dorms at UM are okay, but some suck. You **don't have a choice**, though. You go where they put you."

STUDENT AUTHOR: **Dorm life on the campus isn't really about being good or bad, comfortable or uncomfortable, fun or lame—it's just there. You can't pick your dorm, but you can request a specific area. Most people choose to live in them only for their freshman year. Most recommend choosing Central Campus or the Hill, and most choose North Campus last. Either way, students live with what they get. The dorms of U of M are nothing spectacular, but it doesn't seem to matter since the residents are what make all the fun.**

Did You Know?
63% of undergrads live on campus.

Students Speak Out
ON GUYS & GIRLS

Q "Whether you're looking for **Mr. Right or Mr. Right Now**, you'll find him at UM."

Q "There is **no lack of eye candy here**—whether you are male or female. The campus, overall, is pretty darn attractive."

Q "The guys are really hot, but there are a lot of gay men here. **Ann Arbor is a very liberal place**, and it's very diverse."

Q "If you want hot sorority chicks and sexy frat guys, then you've got plenty to choose from at UM. But, on the other end of the spectrum, there is a **large population of hippie types** who could care less about how they appear to others."

STUDENT AUTHOR: **Expect to find good-looking people if you come to the University of Michigan. The majority of the students here take time to look good, and many are on the forefront of the fashion world. A handful of students openly admit to not being able to pay attention in class because of the plethora of hotties that surrounds them. At a school as large as UM, you're bound to find a mixed bag when it comes to looks.**

Traditions

The Naked Mile
A Michigan tradition that is often emulated on campuses around the country.

Wade in the Water
Upon graduation, students walk through the fountain toward Michigan's Graduate Department.

Overall School Spirit
Spirit pervades every inch of the Michigan campus. Few schools have more spirit, especially when it comes to big sports. You'll soon know the words to the fight song by heart.

Students Speak Out
ON ATHLETICS

Q "Varsity sports are really big on campus. Michigan has a **great reputation for athletic excellence**! Plus, we have the Big House. If you've never seen a Michigan football game, then you won't know what I'm talking about. Michigan stadium is crazy; it's the largest stadium in the United States and holds over 110,000 crazy and screaming fans."

Q "At a school this big, **it's hard to be on the varsity team** unless you're a high school All-American, so club sports are often played at high levels of competition."

Q "IM sports are big here, and it's cool because many **IM teams are coed**. A lot of people do it just for fun, so competition isn't always a big issue."

STUDENT AUTHOR: **To put it simple, this is a sports fan's paradise. From football to broomball, Michigan's teams are stellar. It's worth coming here just to experience the Big House. The sports teams aren't simply teams, they are a way of life. It's fun to be the school everyone loves to hate. You'll find yourself wearing maize and blue in no time.**

Students Speak Out
ON DRUG SCENE

Q "Ann Arbor is **notorious for its lenient marijuana laws**. Each year, Hash Bash brings the sketchiest people stuck in the '70s to campus."

Q "There are so many different kinds of people here. You'll meet people who have never even seen marijuana, and people who've snorted enough cocaine to kill a small horse! It's just like anywhere else: **if you look for it, you can find it**, whatever 'it' happens to be."

Q "Drugs at UM and Ann Arbor are available but certainly **not overwhelming**."

STUDENT AUTHOR: Being that most students can comment on the subject, even if they choose not to be involved, only supports the fact that drugs are openly available at U of M. While drinking seems to be the popular form of entertainment on campus, some prefer other methods of enjoyment. Either way, you've got to love the fact that thousands of students and vagabonds alike fill the streets of Ann Arbor every spring for a daze-filled day called "Hash Bash."

15:1	Student-to-Faculty Ratio
96%	Freshman Retention Rate
70%	Four-Year Graduation Rate
82%	Financial Aid Applicants Receiving Aid

Students Speak Out
SAFETY & SECURITY

Q "**Residence halls have secured entrances**. To get in, you have to swipe your M-Card, so people who don't belong there can't get in."

Q "There are **blue phones all around** campus that signal the police and flash a blue light."

Q "I have **never really felt unsafe** at UM. It's a big school, but the main campus is pretty compressed. At night, it's not the best idea to walk alone, but that is the case at most any campus."

Q "Living off campus is a little different. The University **provides free transportation** to many areas. However, a lot of times it is easier and faster to walk."

STUDENT AUTHOR: The University has its own police force, and when teamed with the AAPD, look no further for assistance. Since Ann Arbor is a small city, most feel relatively safe. There are few worries of major crime, and despite a few robberies and peeping Toms, students feel secure.

> **Questions?**
> For more inside information and survival tips, pick up College Prowler's full-length book on this school, written by an actual student! Check it out at *www.collegeprowler.com.*

Students Speak Out
ON OVERALL EXPERIENCE

Q "There were times when the academic pressure was so much that I wished I was somewhere else, but I am glad I stuck it out. The engineering school is really good, but really tough, too. The **campus is absolutely beautiful**, and I had a great time."

Q "**You will be just a number here**. That was hard for me to adjust to. Ann Arbor is very expensive, especially for out-of-state tuition. It's a nice town and a great atmosphere."

Q "My **education is first class**, and my friends are excellent. There is nothing more I could have desired from college."

Q "The people here are great, campus life is wonderful, and **you can get involved with almost anything** that you want. Now I see the world through maize-and-blue-colored glasses."

STUDENT AUTHOR: Although many students gripe about the weather, the cost of living, and the calculus GSIs with incoherent accents, one thing holds true: the Michigan experience is one to be envied by all. Few schools have a greater academic reputation, better sports, and more opportunities for extracurricular involvement There are 900 student organizations to choose. As a Michigan graduate, your degree will be one of the most highly respected in the nation. Graduate schools respect the Michigan name. Nearly every academic area is in the top 10, the sports teams warrant immediate respect, and the social life is right with the times. By joining the ranks of the largest alumni population in the world, you'll be a member of a proud family for life.

University of Minnesota

100 Church Street SE; Minneapolis, MN 55455
(612) 625-5000; www.umn.edu/tc

THE BASICS:

Acceptance Rate: 57%
Setting: Urban
F-T Undergrads: 27,091

SAT Range: 1650–2040*
Control: Public
Tuition: $20,252

Most Popular Majors: Social Sciences, Engineering, Business, English, Psychology

*of 2400

Academics	B	Guys	B+
Local Atmosphere	A-	Girls	B
Safety & Security	B+	Athletics	A-
Computers	B	Nightlife	A
Facilities	B+	Greek Life	B
Campus Dining	C	Drug Scene	B
Off-Campus Dining	A	Campus Strictness	B+
Campus Housing	B	Parking	D
Off-Campus Housing	B-	Transportation	B+
Diversity	C	Weather	C-

Students Speak Out
ON ACADEMICS

Q "With most of your very large lectures, **they also break you down into 'discussions**.' This is a group of about 20 to 25 students from your class that meets once or twice a week to go over what is taught in lecture. Here, you have a teaching assistant (you have a real professor in lecture) that runs the discussion. You get to know some students in your class better, and it is easier to ask questions and form study groups this way."

Q "My only complaint is that some professors and teaching assistants, especially those teaching math and science courses, are sometimes foreign and a little difficult to understand. I have really only had this problem with the teaching assistants (TAs), but I have friends who have had this happen to them with their professors. This is a problem at any university of this size. However, our **professors are very accessible outside of class**—you just need to make the effort to go talk to them."

Q "The **class sizes are a little large at first**, until you begin taking classes specific to your major. Having large classes at first makes your major classes feel smaller."

STUDENT AUTHOR: **It can be frustrating trying to ask a question in a lecture hall with 100 to 400 other students trying to do the same thing, but the smaller discussion classes, which usually accompany large lectures, are a great place to bounce ideas off your classmates and a TA.**

Students Speak Out
ON LOCAL ATMOSPHERE

Q "The University is **close to downtown**, so you can easily forget that you are a student. At the same time, there is enough happening on campus that it's easy to take part in campus life, too."

Q "The **river runs through campus**, and it's beautiful. You can sit at the riverbank and look at the skyline of the city. Nicollet Mall is great. There are lots of places to visit and lots of art galleries."

Q "There are **many colleges around the Twin Cities metro area**. There are a lot of cool lakes and parks around, and of course there's the Mall of America."

Q "There are so many things to do and places to visit. Uptown—located in south Minneapolis—is the place for the truly hip and trendy. There are many specialty shops and unique restaurants, nice coffee shops, and a really cool atmosphere. Because it's located near the chain of lakes, there are **tons of walking and biking paths** and places to just relax."

STUDENT AUTHOR: **From a college atmosphere to a classy lifestyle, whatever your mood, you can find it in the Twin Cities. The urban life, the suburban life, and even rural elements of this Midwest state can be found on the boundaries of Minneapolis and St. Paul. There are many theaters, live music venues, art institutions, and a world-class orchestra with great student specials.**

Students Speak Out
ON FACILITIES

Q "The facilities are pretty good, and they're getting better. Since I have been here, the University began renovating many of our facilities (computer labs, medical buildings, student union). **I have no complaints**."

Q "The facilities on campus are **generally kept up fairly well and are pretty nice**. Everyone always complains about all the construction that goes on around campus—but, it's a sign that the University is continuing to grow, which is definitely a good thing."

Q "The **Recreation Center is very nice**. You usually do not have to wait for a machine, unless you go right at 5 p.m. There is also a gym on the St. Paul Campus that is very nice. The student union recently had major renovations, so now it is state-of-the-art. The main library on the East Bank reopened after undergoing major renovations, and it is also very nice."

Q "Our facilities rock—they're really great. We have everything we could need. The Rec Center is awesome, and the **St. Paul Student Center is very nice**."

STUDENT AUTHOR: Now that Coffman Union has been renovated, there are a lot of students and non-students alike venturing in to check out what has been changed. St. Paul Student Center is new. Everyone seems to be taken with the sheer amount of activities available there. The libraries offer a great place to study. The Rec Center is a student favorite with a wide variety of activities.

Famous Alumni

Loni Anderson, Norman E. Bourlaug, Bob Dylan, Kimberly Elise, Henry Fonda, Eugene McCarthy, Kevin McHale, Walter Mondale

Students Speak Out
ON CAMPUS DINING

Q "The food is decent, and they do a pretty good job of offering different things at each meal. One thing I like about the food in the dorms is that they offer a service where **you can make a bag lunch in the morning to bring with you**, in case you are not around for lunch. That way, your meals are not wasted."

Q "**Dining hall food is convenient, and that's it**. If you're looking for a great meal, look elsewhere. For what you spend per meal with University Dining Services, you can better spend your money at a restaurant eating food that doesn't leave you feeling sick. Although, Bailey is by far the best residence hall dining hall."

Q "The **food in the residence halls is okay**. Truthfully, at first you might like it. Although, after weeks of eating it over and over, it starts to feel like you are always eating the same thing. Each dining hall is different, though. Some are better than others, and you are allowed to go to any of them. There are also campus restaurants that are run by University Dining Services. These have better quality food than the residence halls, but they are a bit more expensive. You are allowed to use what is called FlexDine at these places—it is dining dollars that are held on your student ID."

STUDENT AUTHOR: The intention of stating that the dorm food at the University of Minnesota, Twin Cities is only average is to be truthful—this school's food is not one of its highlights. The food in the dorms is average at best; at worst, it's indigestible.

Student Body

African American:	4%	Male/Female:	47/53%
Asian American:	9%	Out-of-State:	27%
Hispanic:	2%	International:	2%
Native American:	1%	Unknown:	0%
White:	82%		

Popular Faiths: The University of Minnesota is religiously diverse and religion-tolerant.

Gay Pride: Minneapolis has one of the largest gay communities in the United States. The city holds a Gay Pride Parade and Festival every year.

Economic Status: Most students rely on some form of financial aid: whether it's a loan, a grant, scholarships, or work study.

Students Speak Out
ON DORMS

Q "The dorms were a fun experience for me. This is the quickest way to meet the most people. Choose your dorm based on the location of your classes. **If you want to meet a lot of people, pick the freshman dorms** (Territorial and Frontier). Here, no one knows anyone at first, so they all want to meet people."

Q "Well, dorms are okay. I only stayed in one during my freshman year. The food in the dorms is not wonderful, and they are always full. But, **the University is accommodating and listens to what students request** as far as housing."

Q "**Frontier is the best freshman dorm**. Comstock is nice, and Middlebrook is alright, if you are into the artsy, theaterish kind of life."

STUDENT AUTHOR: **Living on campus as a freshman is an especially excellent idea. Many friends are made in dorms, and the transition from living at home with parents, to moving out on your own, is made easier with having a sort of "support group" found in the dorms. Each dorm has a computer lab, video games, pool, kitchenettes on each floor, and study and relaxation areas.**

Did You Know?
23% of undergrads live on campus.

Students Speak Out
ON GUYS & GIRLS

Q "Well, it all depends what kind of guys you like. If you like white boys—**Abercrombie and Fitch-looking guys**—then you will be in heaven. As for hot men of color, they are few and far between—but they are out there."

Q "Guys and girls? Well, truthfully, campus is so huge that **there is always going to be someone to fit your taste**."

Q "Like anywhere, the guys and girls are nice, and some are cute. Don't worry, I think **there are plenty to pick from**."

Q "**There are good-looking people everywhere**; you just have to find them, like anywhere else."

Q "There is a mix—**lots of hot guys and girls**."

STUDENT AUTHOR: **Walking around campus, there is always someone you think is the hottest person you have ever seen. Just as there is always someone you find that has the worst sense of style you have ever seen. There are plenty of cuties, plenty of unattractive people, and a plethora of the in-between. Most of the students are really very nice and just looking for someone new to associate with.**

Traditions

Viennese Ball
The student union, Wilson Commons, is transformed for a night into an elegant ballroom where students dress in formal wear and waltz the night away, accompanied by the University Chamber Orchestra.

School Colors
English instructor Augusta Norwood Smith, "a woman of excellent taste," according to University president William Folwell, chose the school's colors: maroon and gold. First used between 1876 and 1880, the colors weren't officially approved by regents until 1940.

Students Speak Out
ON ATHLETICS

Q "Varsity sports are great. **It's a Big 10 school**, so no matter what you like sports-wise, you can get tickets (hockey sells out fast, though). A lot of students get varsity season tickets to lots of sports. There are lots of IM choices, too."

Q "We're a Big 10 school. **Sports are big, but you don't have to hang with the athletes** to fit in. I suggest buying season football tickets. They are reasonably priced, and it's a good time. IMs are big, too; lots of athletic and non-athletic people do those. They have lots of sports to choose from."

Q "Sports are big. I do not go to many games, but there is mad support for athletics. **The Rec Center here is great**, and there are always intramural sports going on."

STUDENT AUTHOR: **Golden Gopher sports have a huge following, of not only current students and alumni, but also by those who have never attended a single class at the University of Minnesota, Twin Cities. As a Big 10 university, there is a lot of media coverage of our teams. Even our non-rated teams and intramural sports are very popular, and students are mostly supportive of the sports programs.**

Students Speak Out
ON DRUG SCENE

Q "Like anywhere, **there are people who do drugs and people who don't**. I know both kinds of people. There is no pressure to do drugs, if you don't want to; but, if you do, you can probably find it pretty easily. If this is something you are into, my only advice would be not to do it in or near the dorms. They will kick you out on the spot."

Q "I don't know about major drugs, but you can find **weed all over the place**."

Q "**Drugs are not a problem on campus**. There are kids that do them and plenty that don't. You will have no trouble finding friends that do not do drugs."

STUDENT AUTHOR: **You will probably be around people using drugs somewhere, like a party, and they may offer you some. But, if you choose to say no, that decision will be respected, and nobody will think less of you. The drug scene can be really laid-back and no big deal, and if you do not want to partake, that will be just fine.**

15:1	Student-to-Faculty Ratio
88%	Freshman Retention Rate
29%	Four-Year Graduation Rate
73%	Financial Aid Applicants Receiving Aid

Students Speak Out
SAFETY & SECURITY

Q "Security on campus seems pretty good, although there are occasional problems. It's best to **just use common sense when it comes to issues of safety**. Try not to walk around campus alone after dark, and try to stay in areas that are well lit. Generally: mind your own business, and don't look lost."

Q "Campus is in a decent area of town. It's not too unsafe at all. Depending on where you live, though, it might be a slightly different story. **All of the residence halls are in okay spots**. It's just that some off-campus apartments are not in ideal neighborhoods. There is nothing here like the bad spots in some big cities, so don't worry. The campus does have security guards that walk around at night."

STUDENT AUTHOR: **For a campus of this size, safety and security efforts and successes are rather remarkable. There are emergency telephones throughout campus for students to use. The students at the University of Minnesota, overall, feel safe on campus, because they know that there is always security on and around campus.**

> **Questions?**
> For more inside information and survival tips, pick up College Prowler's full-length book on this school, written by an actual student! Check it out at *www.collegeprowler.com*.

Students Speak Out
ON OVERALL EXPERIENCE

Q "I am very happy with my experience here. Because I go to **such a great school in such a good city**, I have had so many opportunities that I would not have had at the other universities I was looking at. I have met great people in my classes and from my fraternity, and I have been able to get a great internship in downtown Minneapolis. My advice to you would be to get involved right away. It is the best way to make the most out of it."

Q "Going here was the best choice ever. I took it very seriously and visited a ton of schools, but I am so happy at Minneapolis. It's not only a great school in terms of reputation, but campus life is also a blast. It's great. If you want a bigger school, **there are huge benefits to being here at a Big 10 school**. And, if you want a big city, it's the best. If you want something smaller, it's probably not the right place for you."

STUDENT AUTHOR: **The University of Minnesota, Twin Cities provides admirable academic opportunities, an environment that facilitates those opportunities, and a surrounding in which students are able to construct their own unique opportunities and experiences. Being centered in a large metro area adds to this experience by exposing students to a wide range of people, ideas, and opportunities. In the midst of these two beautiful cities, in the classroom and out, you will build strong personal morals, refine your ideals, and structure your beliefs. When you leave the University of Minnesota, Twin Cities, you will better understand not only the world around you, but you will also know who you are.**

University of Mississippi

617 All American Drive; University, MS 38677
(662) 915-7792; www.olemiss.edu

THE BASICS:

Acceptance Rate: 84%
SAT Range: 920–1170*
Setting: Rural
Control: Public
F-T Undergrads: 11,628
Tuition: $11,436

Most Popular Majors: Marketing, Elementary Education, Family and Consumer Sciences, Psychology

*of 1600

Academics	B-	Guys	B+
Local Atmosphere	B+	Girls	A
Safety & Security	A-	Athletics	A-
Computers	B-	Nightlife	B
Facilities	B	Greek Life	A
Campus Dining	B-	Drug Scene	B
Off-Campus Dining	B+	Campus Strictness	C+
Campus Housing	C	Parking	D+
Off-Campus Housing	A-	Transportation	D-
Diversity	D+	Weather	B-

Students Speak Out
ON ACADEMICS

Q "My teachers were extremely personable. I felt as though **I could go to them at any time and talk about anything**. When it came time for me to apply to graduate schools, they went to unbelievable extremes to help me gather information, as well as write recommendations. My teachers seemed enthusiastic about the subjects they taught—and very educated!"

Q "For the most part, the teachers don't care about the students. **They are underpaid, and they're more interested in their research**. They will tell you that their job does not revolve around the students."

Q "I've had some good and some bad teachers. Mostly, I have had wonderful teachers that went out of their way to help me. Some classes I found to be very interesting, but a few of **the 'core' classes were really of no interest to me**. I only took them because I had to."

Q "The teachers really take an interest in their students. They care about more than just lecturing; **they want their students to succeed in class and in life**."

STUDENT AUTHOR: **Once you make it past those 100-level classes, it's smooth sailing. Teachers get more fun, and the subject matter becomes something that students enjoy, as it's more tailored to their interests. As you progress into the upper-level classes, you will meet students who are in the same field as you. This allows students to discuss subject matter outside of the classroom for a clearer understanding of the material.**

Students Speak Out
ON LOCAL ATMOSPHERE

Q "The **atmosphere at Ole Miss is definitely a warm one**. Everyone is friendly. The town and the University represent the idea of Southern hospitality. No other major universities are present, and the town is small, but the nightlife is great. There are many bars to go to, and you'll more than likely see many people you know when you go out."

Q "The atmosphere at Oxford is unique. During the infamous football months, the tiny, unique town of Oxford is so full of energy and school spirit that you can literally feel it in the air. Everyone of all ages and races gets extremely involved. The Grove holds an energy that you cannot find anywhere else in the world. The **pride that comes with Ole Miss Football** is representative of the love the students and alumni have for the school."

Q The Mississippi stereotype does not apply to Oxford. If you're interested in **music, art, sports, history**, and just bumming around, Oxford is the place."

STUDENT AUTHOR: **Oxford is like no other place on earth. It doesn't have that "Mississippi redneck" feel that one might expect. Oxford is a very artsy, intelligent town with a huge music and literary scene. You'll be able to experience all the literature, films, and music you can in the four or five years that you are lucky enough to reside in this little haven of a city. You will find as many options for entertainment as many big cities offer.**

Students Speak Out
ON FACILITIES

Q "The facilities on campus are kept very nice. Equipment is usually kept in good working order and is of **the latest technology**."

Q "The athletic center is busy, but generally very well maintained. Computers are updated and clean. Student centers can range from grubby to feeling as if you should be wearing a formal dress. The **aesthetics are gorgeous**, and they can really contribute to a feeling of academia."

Q "Ole Miss has excellent facilities. They have a **state-of-the-art workout center** available to all students. Ole Miss alumni continuously pour money into the school, so buildings are constantly being renovated. The Student Union could use some improvement. Having a decent place to eat between classes is hard to find, unless you are part of the Greek system."

Q "The school has updated many of the old buildings on campus. If a building is falling apart, it's either being worked on will be very soon. Get used to **construction tape and temporary walls**."

Q "The athletic facilities on campus are very nice, and **they keep getting better**."

STUDENT AUTHOR: **Even though some of the outsides of the buildings aren't the most appealing sights at the moment, the insides of these buildings have been continuously renovated over the years. These facilities are just waiting for their exterior faces to match the attractive surroundings within. The most popular facility is the Turner Center, which many students feel is a great athletic facility.**

Famous Alumni

John Grisham, Trent Lott, Eli Manning, Duce McAllister, Leonard McCoy, Shepard Smith, Larry Speakes, Stark Young

Students Speak Out
ON CAMPUS DINING

Q "The food on campus leaves a lot to be desired. The Union has a Chick-fil-A and excellent sushi, but most of the other dining areas on campus aren't very good. Most **students eat at fraternity or sorority houses on a regular basis**."

Q "The food has improved on campus, but it still doesn't compare to that of the surrounding restaurants or a home-cooked meal. The sushi bar in the Union isn't half bad (sounds scary but isn't). Johnson Commons is where you can get the most out of your buck. The **Union tends to be way overpriced** for certain items."

Q "The **food on campus isn't great**, but it's doable. I'd recommend eating at home."

Q "The **Union offers a wide selection of food**. Many students enjoy the addition of fresh sushi. There's a deli, a Chick-fil-A, and an area that serves hot plates of breakfast, lunch, and dinner."

Q "The food is **average**."

STUDENT AUTHOR: **It's a good thing that the meal plan is only required during your freshman year, because it's a waste for most people. Everyone says that the food is okay in the Union and in Johnson Commons, but you rarely meet a person who chooses to eat there instead of their fraternity or sorority house or an off-campus restaurant. It's probably safe to draw the conclusion that the food there isn't that great. Some of the chain restaurants on campus, like Chick-fil-A seem to be at least a reliable alternative.**

Student Body

African American:	13%	Male/Female:	47/53%
Asian American:	1%	Out-of-State:	33%
Hispanic:	<1%	International:	1%
Native American:	<1%	Unknown:	3%
White:	82%		

Popular Faiths: Christianity is the predominant religion at the University.

Gay Pride: Even though Mississippi is a very conservative state, Ole Miss tends to be pretty tolerant of homosexuality.

Economic Status: Ole Miss ranges in economic status from very poor to very wealthy. Most of the campus is probably middle- to upper-class.

Students Speak Out
ON DORMS

Q "The dorms are fun. **Everyone lives there their freshman year**. By sophomore year, only girls tend to still be on campus."

Q "Dorms are dorms. In the past few years, there have been renovations of bathroom facilities, common areas, and room furnishings. The University **has done away with all freshman dorms, which is sad**, because it did provide an excellent way for freshmen to bond. However, this does mean that there are more dorm options for everyone."

Q "Unless you love sharing showers, hearing doors slam throughout the night, and not having the opposite sex over, **move off campus**."

STUDENT AUTHOR: It's required at Ole Miss that all freshmen live on campus, unless they are from Oxford. Yes, I am sure that some of you were looking forward to getting out of the house and making your own rules; but living in the dorms isn't all bad. For those of you who are from out of state and don't know anybody at Ole Miss, living in the dorms is a great experience that will allow you to meet lots of new people.

? Did You Know?
28% of undergrads live on campus.

Students Speak Out
ON GUYS & GIRLS

Q "**Girls are pretty**; the boys are lacking."

Q "The **majority of guys are the classic 'good ol' boys' who love huntin' and drinkin'**. But then there are others who are really different. The girls, in general, have blond hair and wear lots of makeup. They live for their sorority sisters. But there are others who are really different and break the mold. There are a lot of pretty girls at Ole Miss. And every now and then, you'll see a beautiful boy."

Q "There **isn't a mold for guys or girls** on campus. You can find a little of everything, but during football weekends, everyone seems to turn into clones."

STUDENT AUTHOR: Chivalry is not dead in the South. Most of the time, girls can expect to be treated with courtesy and respect. The general consensus is that the girls are much more attractive than the guys here, though. If you are female and thinking about coming to Ole Miss, know that the guys will treat you well and take care of you. But, it seems like you're supposed to work out and keep a very trim, athletic frame—no matter how your guy is letting his body waste away.

Traditions

Groving
Ole Miss has a very unique way of tailgating called Groving that's been passed down through the generations. People get to the outskirts of the Grove at 5 a.m. when security lets them in to set up their tent. There are some families that have been setting up their tents in the same spot for 20 years.

Overall School Spirit
Ole Miss has a lot of school spirit! There isn't just an amazing amount of school spirit among the students, but the alumni as well.

Students Speak Out
ON ATHLETICS

Q "**Football time and the Grove are the best parts of Ole Miss**. It's a tradition, and no one will understand it until they are actually a student. If you're not born a rebel, you soon will be one."

Q "Sports are part of life at Ole Miss, and the school takes its sports teams very seriously. Whether it's soccer, basketball, football, or baseball, you'll always find a large crowd of students enjoying the game. **IMs are also a big part of life on campus**, and it gives people the opportunity to participate in friendly games for fun."

Q "Varsity **sports run the school**."

STUDENT AUTHOR: Ole Miss is all about football and its traditions. There's a canopy of trees covering a grassy area near the stadium, called the Grove, where families, fraternities, sororities, and fans set up tents. If you're worrying that you won't have a tent, don't. I didn't, but I joined organizations that did, and I had friends with family tents. People in the South, especially Mississippi, are hospitable and want to have all the friends they can.

Students Speak Out
ON DRUG SCENE

Q "There's certainly a drug scene on campus. Primarily, **drug use tends to lean toward alcohol and marijuana**, though the harder stuff is present, also. Many more people deal and use than meets the eye, but the use is there, if you know where to look."

Q "Though **I have seen people doing drugs and under the influence**, I think it's less prevalent on the Ole Miss campus than at other major universities."

Q "I **never see much drug use**. But I hear it's common in some of the fraternity houses."

STUDENT AUTHOR: Outwardly, Ole Miss appears to have no drugs, but inwardly, there are groups that do partake in drug use, whether prescription or illegal. No one really hangs out without alcohol present. Sure, there are some groups who are adamantly opposed to drinking, but those groups at Ole Miss are few and far between. So, if the drinking scene isn't for you, you may want to go in armed with similarly minded friends.

19:1	Student-to-Faculty Ratio
80%	Freshman Retention Rate
34%	Four-Year Graduation Rate
70%	Financial Aid Applicants Receiving Aid

Students Speak Out
SAFETY & SECURITY

Q "I feel **extremely safe on and off campus**. Oxford is a small community, so you always feel safe. The campus police make themselves very visible and are willing to come pick you up at any point on campus. Since Ole Miss has a large majority of students living on campus, I feel as though I am always surrounded by other students."

Q "Ole Miss basically has a safe campus. I always felt safe running at night, walking around alone on campus at night, or hanging out in a dorm. But Cobra Security, who is in charge of security on campus, is **not exactly highly visible, especially during a sporting event**. I always just hoped nothing ever happened during those times. This is a serious issue in regard to safety."

STUDENT AUTHOR: Even though Oxford is very safe, the University still takes extra precautions to ensure the students' well being. The best idea is to go out with a group. There's safety in numbers, especially for women, but being in a small town like Oxford is very comforting.

Questions?

For more inside information and survival tips, pick up College Prowler's full-length book on this school, written by an actual student! Check it out at *www.collegeprowler.com*.

Students Speak Out
ON OVERALL EXPERIENCE

Q "Never do I wish I had gone anywhere else! I love the Ole Miss experience, and I consider myself extremely fortunate for having the opportunity to meet the professors I did, to live in a unique location such as Oxford, and to have to the chance to be a part of such **an elite student body who takes pride in their school**."

Q "I loved Oxford so much that I stayed! You'll find that most students take their time when it comes to graduating, because **Oxford has so much to offer**."

Q "I love Ole Miss. No matter where I go, I seem to run into someone who has an Ole Miss connection. **Ole Miss creates a big family** network, and people are always excited to talk about the school."

Q "Although the academic demands are not equivalent to Harvard, I got a great education from Ole Miss by forcing myself to take harder classes with more demanding teachers. **You will get out what you put in**."

STUDENT AUTHOR: Overall, students don't want to leave Ole Miss or Oxford, even after they graduate. The University provides almost everything one could want in a college experience. There are great sporting events that are heavily attended by the student body. There's a hopping nightlife. There are many religions and church denominations available. There's a supportive faculty and a beautiful campus. Many students credit Ole Miss with making them who they are today and say that they have fond memories that will last a lifetime about a place that will be with them forever.

University of Missouri

104 Jesse Hall, Conley Avenue; Columbia, MO 65201
(573) 882-2121; www.mizzou.edu

THE BASICS:

Acceptance Rate: 86%
Setting: Small city
F-T Undergrads: 20,295

SAT Range: 1070–1300*
Control: Public
Tuition: $18,459

Most Popular Majors: Business, Communications, Engineering, Social Sciences, Education

*of 1600

Academics	B-	Guys	A-
Local Atmosphere	B+	Girls	A-
Safety & Security	A-	Athletics	A-
Computers	C+	Nightlife	B+
Facilities	B+	Greek Life	A-
Campus Dining	B	Drug Scene	B
Off-Campus Dining	B+	Campus Strictness	B
Campus Housing	C	Parking	D
Off-Campus Housing	A	Transportation	C+
Diversity	D	Weather	C+

Students Speak Out
ON ACADEMICS

Q "I have had many good teachers, even in large lecture classes. The **TAs (teaching assistants) can be kinda crappy sometimes**, but my overall experience with professors has been very positive."

Q "I have not encountered any professors who are unqualified. Some professors are difficult to understand, **some are just plain mean, and others are enthusiastic** and make you glad that you came to class."

Q "I had **some fabulous teachers**—and some I wanted to beat with my overpriced textbook."

Q "I was in a pretty specialized curriculum my final two years at MU; but overall, I found that the faculty and **professors were exceptionally knowledgeable, understanding, and eager** to help students learn. I can't think of a single one that I had problems with. I was in a medical field, and the resources and knowledge available were unbelievable."

STUDENT AUTHOR: **Mizzou's enormity is both a blessing and a curse for those who roam its hallowed grounds. Many students feel that some of the classes that are required (introductory economics, science, and math classes) are incredibly boring, time consuming, and due to overcrowding, not particularly fruitful. But in smaller, more intimate classes, you'll find the teachers very well qualified, fun to listen to, and more than willing to help if you have problems.**

Students Speak Out
ON LOCAL ATMOSPHERE

Q "I am impressed with how warm and welcoming everyone at the campus is. It is something entirely different from other colleges I've visited. Also, **the campus is the most gorgeous I've seen**."

Q "Columbia is a great town, with a wonderful old downtown area, and a refined uptown. **The town vibrates with the energy** and youth that only a large university can bring. There are other colleges in the area, Columbia College and Stephens College. It's always good to avoid being on a first-name basis with the alcohol patrol and other law enforcement agencies."

Q "St. Louis and Kansas City are about two hours from Columbia, so visiting them for shopping is a plus. There is also the Lake of the Ozarks, which is 45 minutes away. During the spring and fall, a lot of students **travel there for the beaches and boating**."

Q "**Downtown Columbia is a lot of fun**. There are so many different shops, restaurants, clubs, and bars. It's really a great place to just walk around, at any time."

STUDENT AUTHOR: **Scores of students like to go downtown to eat at the restaurants, watch some live shows, or just to admire the serene parkland sprinkled in between the strip malls, the bars, and the highway. Like any college town, Columbia becomes slightly edgy when night falls. Still, there is enough in Columbia to keep people satisfied and happy throughout their college tenure.**

Students Speak Out
ON FACILITIES

Q "**We have everything you could want** on the campus, from tanning salons to a bowling alley."

Q "MU has some of the **nicest facilities I have ever seen**, on par or above with the most prestigious campuses in the nation."

Q "**The Rec Center is tight**. I'm up there at least four or five times a week. We also have a Student Success Center where they give tutoring, writing labs, and computer training."

Q "The Student Center and the Rec Center are top-of-the-line. Facilities are **adequate, but getting better with expansions**."

Q "Facilities on campus are good. The Rec Center was great for me (I'm a workout freak). Computer labs are plentiful and accessible. Student **commons areas and unions are comfortable** and have convenient hours."

STUDENT AUTHOR: **Missourians love their exercise, and Mizzou delivers in spades. With its artificial turf and one-third mile track, Stankowski Field is a popular place for students to scamper to when the weather is sunny. Students also tend to agree that Brady Commons is a great hangout—with a decent food court, the campus bookstore, an arcade, and even a bowling alley. It is also an ideal place to do some studying for a group project, or to just chill out and relax. The classrooms inside the buildings are a little on the plain side, and some of the desks are small. For the most part, the campus facilities are well designed and functional; campus is attractive and unique to say the least.**

Students Speak Out
ON CAMPUS DINING

Q "The best places on campus are Eva J's in Johnston Hall and Romano's. Both offer a wide variety of great food. **Don't miss breakfast at Eva J's**—it's the best! If you want pizza, go to Rollins."

Q "Campus food is okay. At first it was great, but **once you get used to it, it gets old**. The four main diners are Eva J's, Rollins, Mark Twain, and Dobbs; not much difference between them. Other places have a point system, where you can come in and get snacks to take home and stuff."

Q "The food is what you'd expect from college dining halls: some is quite tasty; some is all right; and **some is better left to the imagination**. The best and probably most popular dining hall is Rollins."

Q "**Dorm food is dorm food**, but there are plenty of options to put on your student charge account."

Q "Campus food that is from the dorms is livable. I lived on campus for about two years and survived. It was nice to not have to prepare all of my meals, and **I was generally able to find healthy and tasty food**."

STUDENT AUTHOR: **Students agree that they have a bunch of fast-food restaurants on campus to choose from, including a McDonald's, numerous Subways, and Chick-fil-A. However, for all the quality fast food joints, there are some truly sub-par eateries concocted by the Mizzou bureaucrats.**

Students Speak Out
ON DORMS

Q "I'd rate the dorms on the upper half of the spectrum. I've seen many, but there are better. I would **recommend the all-girl dorms** because they are the nicest."

Q "**Dorms are mandatory for freshmen**, except for men joining fraternities. They are about average compared to others—I've seen much nicer ones while visiting friends at other universities."

Q "Better social dorms include Hatch, Hudson, Gillett. Johnston is a quieter dorm. The dorms certainly provide **a good opportunity to meet people**."

STUDENT AUTHOR: The dorm system is acceptable for entering the school, but many students tend to flee off campus after their freshman year. It is highly advisable to go into a dorm for your first year, just to let the overall feel of Mizzou sink in. Some residence halls have themed floors that reflect a particular major. Getting into these can be tricky, especially for the more popular halls. You are likely to meet plenty of new people, regardless of what dorm you're in freshman year.

Did You Know?
39% of undergrads live on campus.

Students Speak Out
ON GUYS & GIRLS

Q "Guys and girls **come in all shapes, sizes**, colors, temperaments, humors, styles, and religions."

Q "There are some really, really, really hot guys; **they're cute Midwestern boys**! I love the people here—I've made some of my best friends ever."

Q "The girls here are beautiful, but usually Greek. There is **no short supply of hot people** on campus."

Q "You know, **there's 25,000 people, so you basically have your pick**. Freshmen and sophomores are not serious at all; then you meet juniors and seniors and they are extremely serious, so it's kind of funny."

STUDENT AUTHOR: Students tend to think the enormity of Mizzou comes in handy when searching for the perfect companion or just a random hookup. Some can actually match their beauty with some intelligence. There are a ton of girls and guys at Mizzou to sort through when searching for either a longterm relationship or a fleeting hookup. It all depends on your taste.

Traditions

Walking Through the Columns
Walk through the Columns when entering the school freshman year. When you graduate, you will walk through the Columns again—backwards. This is supposed to represent your entrance into the world.

Speaker's Circle
Speak passionately on something you care about at Speaker's Circle at the entrance of Brady Commons.

Overall School Spirit
Generation upon generation grows up loving the Tigers.

Students Speak Out
ON ATHLETICS

Q "Everyone goes to all the football games and basketball games. Basketball is huge, so usually, the **games are standing-room only**. IM sports are only fun and intense if you are Greek."

Q "The good thing about Mizzou is that no matter how much the team sucks, people are still going to show up because of **one thing: tailgating**. I felt like football and basketball games generated campus-wide interest, and I know I definitely had a blast attending them. As for the other sports, I'm not sure."

Q "It's very easy to **get an all-sports pass**, which gets you to every varsity sport from gymnastics, to track, to baseball. I would have to say we have a lot of school spirit."

Q "IM sports are great. **There are plenty of them**. I played them all the time."

STUDENT AUTHOR: Nothing beats the experience of watching a Mizzou basketball game. There are a ton of them, and some games (like Kansas-Missouri) are the sporting events of the year. Beyond spectator sports, there are a lot of different sports you can play for IM.

Students Speak Out
ON DRUG SCENE

Q "You can probably find whatever you want, but **there's no pressure to do anything**. I think there's a bigger emphasis on drinking."

Q "It's not bad. A good number of people smoke weed, I would say. It's really under control though—the **people who use drugs are in their own groups**; and it really doesn't affect people outside of those groups."

Q "Drugs are bad, so stay away from them! It might be a little too easy to get drugs on this campus, but **I know the campus police are on top of things over here**."

STUDENT AUTHOR: **Students tend to drink more than experiment with drugs—but it's very possible to nab some pot, mushrooms, or acid if you search hard enough. Pot, especially, is very available. There are relatively few drug arrests, and hard drugs like crystal meth and heroin are far, far away. But to be perfectly honest, drugging is not a widespread pastime at Mizzou.**

18:1	Student-to-Faculty Ratio
85%	Freshman Retention Rate
38%	Four-Year Graduation Rate
70%	Financial Aid Applicants Receiving Aid

Students Speak Out
SAFETY & SECURITY

Q "Honestly, I feel comfortable walking outside at night because **you always see cops** around, and everything is well lit."

Q "I've never felt unsafe on campus. There is **nothing to worry about** over here, no matter what time of the night it is. Campus police are also present everywhere, although I don't think it's to keep us safe from anything. It's more to make sure we aren't misbehaving."

Q "I've always felt safe on campus. I never had any qualms about walking by myself at night. The blue-light security phones are everywhere. But **it's always smart to exercise caution**, no matter where you are."

STUDENT AUTHOR: **STRIPES, a free service run by hard-working student volunteers, gives tipsy students a van ride back to their dorms, and it's said that it's the best service the Missouri Student Association (MSA) ever created.**

Questions?
For more inside information and survival tips, pick up College Prowler's full-length book on this school, written by an actual student! Check it out at *www.collegeprowler.com*.

Students Speak Out
ON OVERALL EXPERIENCE

Q "After a year, I'm confident that I've made the right choice. Everything I love about college—the adventure of being away from home, the 'rah-rah' college spirit—**would not be the same anywhere else**."

Q "I would never wish to go anywhere else. **I love this school so much**, and so does everyone I know who goes here. This is definitely the school I want to graduate from, without a question. I've never been so happy before!"

Q "I love going to Mizzou. I never want to go home because of this. I learn a lot and party hard. **Every day, there is something new**. I've had some awesome experiences."

Q "My overall experience has been awesome. I have lots of fun, get to **meet great people, and get a great education**. There have been times when I've wished I'd gone to another university—but that has only to do with my major (occupational therapy) and the curriculum they have at Mizzou. But seriously, looking at it, I wouldn't change a thing!"

STUDENT AUTHOR: **Mizzou is not the best college in the country. But beyond its simple exterior, the University of Missouri is truly a complex, sociable, and at times, incredibly fun place to be. Diversity is certainly lacking, some of the dorm food is sub-par, and parking is difficult. But all of those drawbacks are compensated for by the thrill of screaming "screw KU" at the top of your lungs at the biggest basketball game of the year or participating in a meaningful club or organization that make Mizzou worth going to.**

University of Montana

32 Campus Drive; Missoula, MT 59812
(406) 243-0211; www.umt.edu

THE BASICS:

Acceptance Rate: 95%
Setting: Rural
F-T Undergrads: 9,940

SAT Range: 1390–1780*
Control: Public
Tuition: $15,576

Most Popular Majors: Business, Social Sciences, Environmental Science, Communications, Psychology

*of 2400

Academics	B	Guys	B
Local Atmosphere	C+	Girls	B
Safety & Security	B+	Athletics	A-
Computers	B-	Nightlife	B+
Facilities	A-	Greek Life	C+
Campus Dining	A	Drug Scene	C+
Off-Campus Dining	A-	Campus Strictness	B
Campus Housing	B+	Parking	C-
Off-Campus Housing	A-	Transportation	A-
Diversity	D	Weather	C+

Students Speak Out
ON ACADEMICS

Q "The teachers in the English literature/creative writing program are some of the best in the country. Missoula has been **rated in the top 10 American creative writing programs** for the past few years, but a lot of professors tend to be a bit more interested in their own work than the work of the students. Such is academia."

Q "The first year tends to be easier. After that, **get ready to study, study, study**. Teachers will make you work."

Q "**The 100-level and some 200-level classes are huge**. Sometimes they have 200 people. But as you get to upper-division classes, they are smaller, like 30 people, which is important because the workload increases dramatically."

Q "Get to know your teachers. Most will work in your favor if you know them and show you care. If anything comes up, most teachers are willing to work something out so your grade isn't ruined. Teachers are easy to talk to and very liberal. **This place is full of outstanding and genius professors**."

STUDENT AUTHOR: They flew in the best of the best to teach here. Students are drawn to the University of Montana because they will walk out of here with an outstanding education. The diversity of classes offered and the people teaching them make for an interesting curriculum that you might not see at another university. Professors are encouraged to teach what they know and are given leeway to come up with new class ideas and subjects.

Students Speak Out
ON LOCAL ATMOSPHERE

Q "I'm from California, so it was quite a shock to see how dressed down everyone is. At first I thought people were sloppy, but now I realize they are just dressing comfortably. **People here like to do stuff outside**, so they wear clothes for the outdoors."

Q "This town seemed a little boring at first. Yes, in the winter it can be boring, but if you're into skiing or snowboarding, then this is the place for you. **It's so easy to get to the ski areas**."

Q "I like walking across the bridge in the fall and seeing the kayakers at Brennan's Wave. It's cool that this town has **so many places to do things that don't cost a lot of money**."

Q "I think **the music scene is great**. There are a lot of shows for people 18 and older. I like that I don't have to be 21 to see live music since most shows are in bars downtown."

STUDENT AUTHOR: While Missoula is considered a small town in comparison to the rest of the nation, it certainly has big-city culture. From art walks every first Friday of the month to weekly readings by students, locals, and professors, as well as a bustling music scene, Missoula is not lacking in things to do. Missoula is definitely a town for outdoor enthusiasts. For students who are not the outdoorsy type, you can catch a movie, enjoy the relaxed life, or party if that's your thing. Just know that Missoula is not a hustle-and-bustle, "designer jeans and stilettos" atmosphere.

Students Speak Out
ON CAMPUS DINING

Q "I don't even leave campus, and I don't have to. There is so much food here, and **it's all really good**."

Q "There are signs all over the food court about the farmers that grow your food. **It's nice to know that the University is helping out local people**."

Q "I'm a vegetarian, and this school is very **accommodating to people with different food preferences**. I haven't had a problem finding something that is meat-free."

Q "UM is a very health-conscious place. I eat pretty healthy on campus. There is a lot of homemade food, and **it doesn't feel like cafeteria food**. If the food is included in room and board, then it's not that expensive, but as soon as I moved off campus, I realized that food is expensive here—expensive but good. I would say it's worth every penny."

Q "Be careful about what you are eating because **some food at the Food Zoo is very fatty**. If you watch what you eat, there are plenty of choices. Get the all-campus meal plan."

STUDENT AUTHOR: **All in all, food on campus is yummy, and there is a good variety. There are plenty of ways to gain the Freshman 15 if you are not careful. The campus is loaded with junk food, but there is also a wide variety of health food, too. There is food on campus to accommodate all. The University is like a town in itself with restaurants, grocery stores, and coffeehouses. So just because Mom isn't around to feed your tummy anymore, you don't have to worry about going hungry on this campus.**

Students Speak Out
ON FACILITIES

Q "All the buildings on campus are great, and they're clean too! The Rec Center is a real good gym. **It has a great environment for a college**. The University Center is great, and the library is fantastic."

Q "There is a lot of renovation going on now that makes walking across campus more difficult. But I guess renovation is good because **the University is updating all the buildings** and expanding others. I mean, this campus has been around for more than 100 years."

Q "**The athletic facilities are top notch**. The library is huge, and it has books on reserve, so you don't have to buy books—you can just use theirs. But you can't leave the library with them."

Q "All the University cares about is expanding the stadium. **It needs to get new desks in the old buildings** instead of adding more seating to the already gigantic stadium. The old desks are wooden, hard, and uncomfortable. The new classrooms have comfortable seats, though."

Q "I hardly even have to leave the campus because **everything I need is here**."

STUDENT AUTHOR: **The University wants to compete with some of the larger schools in the nation, so to do this many facilities are being expanded or rebuilt altogether. The School of Journalism just completed a state-of-the-art building that gives it room to grow for many years. There's a lot of work being done on some of the science buildings that will continue for the next few years. Students really seem to like places like the University Center and the Rec Center. Overall, campus has some great places to meet with friends, study, and recreate.**

Famous Alumni

Eric Braeden, Carroll O'Connor, J.K. Simmons

Student Body

African American:	<1%	Male/Female:	46/54%
Asian American:	1%	Out-of-State:	27%
Hispanic:	2%	International:	2%
Native American:	4%	Unknown:	8%
White:	83%		

Popular Faiths: Catholic, Christian, Jewish, and Protestant are most popular, but being spiritual and not religious definitely dominates here.

Gay Pride: The campus community is accepting of the gay lifestyle, and classes about gay and lesbian literature, facts, and myths are offered.

Economic Status: The people living here range from poor college students to healthy, wealthy, and wise.

Students Speak Out
ON DORMS

Q "Sometimes **the showers can be a little busy**. Luckily, my classes are a bit later than everyone else's, so I never have a problem getting bathroom time."

Q "I live in Turner Hall. Some people don't like that it's all girls in here, but **I like that the rooms are bigger and have sinks in them**, and that the building is older. It has a bit more class than the other dorms."

Q "I hate living in the dorms. **Everyone is so noisy, and it's hard to study**. I can't wait to get out."

STUDENT AUTHOR: Living in the dorms can be like living in your parents' garage. You might not live in the house anymore, but you are still under a watchful eye. Resident Assistants fill in for the parents and are watching your every move. So make friends with the RA, and life will be more pleasant. Living in the dorms is one of those experiences that every student should have. It will be fun, and it will be stressful, but at least you will be able to say you did it and made it out alive. Most students come out of the dorms with great friends and good times that will last forever.

Did You Know?
24% of undergrads live on campus.

Students Speak Out
ON GUYS & GIRLS

Q "The typical student on this campus is a non-showering, **dreadlock-wearing, khaki-and-green-wearing hippie**."

Q "**Students range from athletes to hippie-types**. Some are very attractive, others not so much. The typical students here come from all walks of life."

Q "I wouldn't say there is a typical student. We have everything from granola, tree-hugging hippies to dreadlocks to a gal in a business suit to hair-gelled-to-a-shoe-shine guys. **Someone could fit in anywhere**."

Q "**There are two types of guys: jocks or hunters**. There are two types of girls: wannabe Hollywood girls or straight-up Montana girls wearing flannels and Doc Marten boots."

STUDENT AUTHOR: It has been established that Missoula is a hippie town. But if you think this is a bad thing, think again. Hippies don't shower often, so if you are one of those people who gets up at 5 a.m. to dress to impress, you can leave that routine in the dust. Of course, there are the trendy students who do get up at 5 a.m. to get ready, but that tends to fade as the year goes on. With the variety on campus, everyone can find someone they are attracted to whether it's stinky or clean people.

Traditions

Cat-Griz Football Game
UM has a rival about two hours away in Bozeman, Montana. Their mascot is the Bobcat, and every year one of the schools hosts the Cat-Griz football game. The energy is crazy. Besides homecoming, it's the biggest crowd drawer of the year.

Overall School Spirit
"Go Griz" is a phrase everyone has uttered at least once. Even if people claim to dislike the football team, they still support the Griz, and everyone on campus seems to own at least one Grizzly sweatshirt.

Students Speak Out
ON ATHLETICS

Q "**There is so much school spirit here**. People paint their whole bodies maroon and silver. There is not a day that goes by that I don't see at least 50 people wearing Griz sweatshirts. There is even this one guy who wears a shirt that looks like it was attacked by a grizzly. UM is all about football spirit."

Q "Trying to get tickets for one of the football games is **more competitive than the game itself**."

Q "Football is a way of life for most students. Ultimate Frisbee is very popular. **Just being active is popular, no matter what sport you are doing**."

Q "I think that without the football team this campus would have nothing. Everything here is football. **The football players think they are immortal or something**."

STUDENT AUTHOR: The University of Montana and town of Missoula eat, sleep, and live "The Griz." And when you hear the words "The Griz," that applies to one sport: football. Tickets for the games sell like tickets to the most popular rock concert. And for a campus that loves recreation and being active, intramural sports are just as important as varsity ones.

Students Speak Out
ON DRUG SCENE

Q "Missoula is a hippie town. **It smells like marijuana all the time**."

Q "I know it's there because people talk about it, but I think **it's easy to stay away from, too**. If you are somewhere and they are doing drugs, it's easy to just leave. Nobody has ever pressured me."

Q "**I have seen every single drug possible here**. Drugs are everywhere. Everyone drinks and does drugs. Missoula is a party town."

STUDENT AUTHOR: **Most people keep their drug and alcohol for weekend extracurricular activities off campus. But this is a college town, and wherever there is a big college presence, there is partying. Scoring weed or getting alcohol is about as easy as putting on a shoe. It's everywhere, and everyone knows someone who has some. Although drugs and drinking are popular, nobody will tie you down to a chair to blow a hit in your face or pour beer down your throat. People respect others' wishes. Be careful not to get caught, though, Missoula and campus police are always keeping their eyes and nostrils open for offenders**

19:1	Student-to-Faculty Ratio
72%	Freshman Retention Rate
20%	Four-Year Graduation Rate
69%	Financial Aid Applicants Receiving Aid

Students Speak Out
SAFETY & SECURITY

Q "**Lock up your bike**. Bikes are like Benzes around here. There are so many bikes that people steal them and repaint them, and you will never get your bike back."

Q "The campus is pretty secure. **I haven't noticed a lot of crime** compared to other larger cities I have lived in. There are emergency phones all over the campus, and it is well lit. There are also security patrols."

Q "It seems like **every time I look up, there is a campus police officer**. They are pretty strict about alcohol and drugs on campus."

STUDENT AUTHOR: **Be sure to keep an eye on belongings in areas like the University Center, Mansfield Library, and the Rec Center. It is easy for thieves to walk away with unattended items. There have even been many reported cases of stolen textbooks, as they can be sold back to the bookstore during buyback. So be safe and aware, and you should be alright.**

Questions?
For more inside information and survival tips, pick up College Prowler's full-length book on this school, written by an actual student! Check it out at *www.collegeprowler.com*.

Students Speak Out
ON OVERALL EXPERIENCE

Q "UM has an amazing variety of people. Art and music are my two loves and Missoula's too. The art culture here has helped expand my mind and creativity to a place I didn't even know existed. If you choose to come to Missoula, be open and experience it fully—**it definitely has a lot to offer students**."

Q "I have been challenged by my teachers to point I thought I was going to break. As an English major, I have written hundreds of papers. And it's all paying off because **I just got a job offer from a prestigious magazine**."

Q "I had no idea that a small Montana town would know how to party like it does. I mean, **the school is great, but the social life is even better**. I have so much fun here. My schedule consists of five nights a week of partying. I take off Sunday and Monday to do homework. And can you believe that I am passing with a busy schedule like this?"

Q "UM takes a while to grow on you. **I have gone through moments of loving it and hating it**, but in the end, I always love it."

STUDENT AUTHOR: **Students at UM are quick to complain on a day-to-day basis, but if someone from out of town asks about the school, they will be quick to defend the good. It's a relaxing environment to receive an education. Students enjoy riding their bikes or walking to campus. They like the fresh air, beautiful mountains, lakes, rivers, and wildlife. The simple life is not just a TV show with Paris Hilton, it's a way of life at the University of Montana. People are proud to call it their college and usually miss it when they are gone.**

University of Nebraska

14th and R Streets; Lincoln, NE 68588
(402) 472-7211; www.unl.edu

THE BASICS:

Acceptance Rate: 63%
SAT Range: 1040–1340*
Setting: Urban
Control: Public
F-T Undergrads: 17,283
Tuition: $16,013

Most Popular Majors: Business, Education, Engineering, Communications, Social Sciences

*of 1600

Academics	B	Guys	B-
Local Atmosphere	B	Girls	B-
Safety & Security	A	Athletics	A-
Computers	B	Nightlife	B+
Facilities	A-	Greek Life	B
Campus Dining	B-	Drug Scene	B-
Off-Campus Dining	B+	Campus Strictness	C
Campus Housing	B	Parking	B-
Off-Campus Housing	B+	Transportation	B
Diversity	D-	Weather	C+

Students Speak Out
ON ACADEMICS

Q "The professors are hit and miss—**some great ones and others are not so great**. The classes within your major are usually the most interesting. General requirements can be dull depending on the subject."

Q "The teachers are hard to group together. Some I liked and some I didn't like. **I don't think anyone has ever been unfair, though**."

Q "The teachers are usually interesting and helpful—**especially for those with disabilities**. I could do without all of the PowerPoint presentations. They should try to make classes more interactive."

Q "The teachers here are really, really good. I went to a very good high school, so my college professors had a lot to measure up to, and I have not been disappointed yet. **I have always had a professor for an instructor and not a TA**, which makes a big difference. I was in a big lecture class last semester—probably about 150 kids—and the teacher knew about everyone's names, which is really impressive."

STUDENT AUTHOR: According to students, the average UNL professor is just that—average. Some are brilliant and some are wretched, and the rest fit somewhere in-between. If you want to meet a professor who is more than just your average, everyday Joe, then you'll need to take it upon yourself to actually meet them by attending office hours And, yes, there is much more to college than what's in the $120 textbooks.

Students Speak Out
ON LOCAL ATMOSPHERE

Q "The town is a basic college town and **football is a huge part of it**. There is a lot of culture available if you seek it. Stuff to visit: the museums, the Ross, the stadium, coffee shops."

Q "**Lincoln is like a big small town**. The people are friendly and welcoming. Being a college town, Lincoln is thriving with young people and social activities. Visit SouthPointe and the Haymarket."

Q "It's **very much a college town**. Many people of the same age group and background live in Lincoln. I feel very at home in any place around the college or outside and love the downtown scene. There are very cool people on campus and downtown, but the rest of the town is total suburbia man."

Q "The town has about 230,000 people. There are three other universities and one community college. There are two malls (neither of which are very good). **There is not a lot of stuff to visit**. Omaha is 52 miles away, though, and provides some entertainment."

STUDENT AUTHOR: It's obvious that Lincoln is a college town. There are four colleges in the area, which means there are tens of thousands of college students to run into. Omaha offers a nice change of pace for when students get tired of the usual Lincoln hangouts. While the city doesn't have a Broadway or any historical landmarks, it does have its share of nature and enough local landmarks to make it feel like home.

Students Speak Out
ON FACILITIES

Q "Our Union and Rec Center are **two of the best in the country**. You can go to the Rec Center for free and get a nice workout—a truly wonderful facility."

Q "The Rec Center is fantastic—the weight room is incredible. The Student Union is okay, kind of crowded and noisy during the day. **The baseball and football stadiums are amazing**, which makes the sports really fun to watch."

Q "The athletics are solid, the computers aren't bad (depending on which lab you go to), and the **Student Union isn't much** (mainly just offices, the food court, and the bookstore). The Health Center (a.k.a. Death Center) is not very good. I suggest doing your own diagnosis if you're sick."

Q "Most facilities are good. **There is room for some improvement**, though. They have made some changes since I've been here, and now it's better."

Q "**I freaking love the Union and Rec Center**. They should make classes more available at the Rec, though."

STUDENT AUTHOR: Nebraskans love their Huskers, and they treat both students and student athletes to some breathtaking facilities. Students also gush about the Rec Center, which in the minds of many, leaves nothing to be desired. The Student Union is a popular hangout for many students who enjoy its many amenities and great lighting. Whatever you're looking to do, UNL provides state-of-the-art facilities to accommodate the student body.

Famous Alumni

Warren Buffett, Johnny Carson, Willa Cather, Aaron Douglas, Ted Hustead, John J. Pershing

Students Speak Out
ON CAMPUS DINING

Q "**Dining halls are mediocre at best**. Food in the Student Union is average—Subway is by far the best restaurant on campus. There are restaurants near campus, however."

Q "Dining Hall food **gets old by the end of the year**. There are tons of places to eat downtown, though."

Q "The dorms actually served good food. The key was variety and **they serve about six or seven different options at every meal**. In the Student Union, they have the main fast-food restaurants."

Q "The on-campus dorm food is not so great, but I don't think it is that great anywhere. I am a vegetarian, and **the vegetarian meals were definitely bad**."

Q "**Dorm food is good**. There are always a huge variety of things to choose from so it is hard to not find something you like. There are also snack bars in all of the dorms that open at night if you need a study break or are just hungry. They serve everything from hamburgers and mozzarella sticks to sub sandwiches and ice-cream sundaes. Also, in the Student Union, there is a Sbarros Pizza, an Imperial Palace, a Subway, and a BK."

STUDENT AUTHOR: To put it simply, on-campus dining at UNL is not gourmet, but it is low maintenance. If you offered an off-campus student a free meal at a dining hall, he'd jump at the chance because, although it's not spectacular, at least he wouldn't have to shop for it, cook it, or clean up afterwards.

Student Body

African American:	2%	Male/Female:	54/46%
Asian American:	3%	Out-of-State:	18%
Hispanic:	3%	International:	3%
Native American:	1%	Unknown:	5%
White:	83%		

Popular Faiths: Lutherans and Catholics dominate the spiritual scene.

Gay Pride: The administration officially tolerates and supports homosexuality, but the student body has its fair share of homophobes.

Economic Status: The majority of UNL students drive a '97 Honda, wear Gap clothing, and pay $15 for a haircut.

Students Speak Out
ON DORMS

Q "The dorms are very fun. **I would recommend living in them your first year**. If you want to meet guys I would recommend living in Abel because there will be guys living on the same floor with you."

Q "**Dorms are the best**. I would suggest that if you do not rush, that you live in Selleck. That is where I live and I love it. It is the best dorm because it is the center of campus. Dorms to avoid: Abel/Sandoz is the party-dorm—most dropouts come out of there. And Harper Schramm Smith complex—it is pretty far from campus."

Q "The dorms were an experience, I guess. I lived in **Abel, which is historically the party hall**. Unless you're into academics hardcore, avoid Neihardt and Kauffman."

STUDENT AUTHOR: **When it comes to picking favorites, UNL students care more about the convenience and reputation of a dorm than the quality of its rooms. Some students are willing to sacrifice shut-eye for partying (Abel), while others are willing to walk three extra blocks to class so they can actually study in their rooms (at Harper-Schramm-Smith).**

? Did You Know?
41% of undergrads live on campus.

Students Speak Out
ON GUYS & GIRLS

Q "**The guys are average**. It seems to be like everywhere else I've been. There are definitely some hotties, and then there are those gross, nasty losers whom you'd like to get away from ASAP!"

Q "Guys and girls are **a little more casual and dressed down**, but that doesn't take away from their faces. They are both good looking."

Q "You have **really good and really bad**."

Q "Because the Greek system is somewhat big, **guys and girls tend to be competitive**, so people tend to dress well when they go out."

Q "There are **beautiful people of all types**—not just jocks. Seek, and you will find."

STUDENT AUTHOR: **Either UNL students have really low standards, or the guys and girls really are as good-looking as the students claim. Students commonly mention members of the Greek system as the Adonises and Aphrodites of UNL, but there's also a feeling among students that there are plenty of great and interesting mortals out there to spend eternity with.**

Traditions

Homecoming
One of the campus's largest traditions—a week-long schedule of festivities, floats, and football.

The Cornhusker
Former UNL team nicknames include the Bugeaters, the Tree Planters, and the Rattlesnake Boys.

Overall School Spirit
There's one thing that unites the gym rats, the band geeks, the engineers, the English majors, the frat brothers, and the dormies—a Husker football Saturday. The school spirit is highly contagious.

Students Speak Out
ON ATHLETICS

Q "Well, football is Nebraska. People bleed Husker Red here—it's pathetic frankly. **They even sell our parking spaces here for the home games** and make the students park elsewhere. Basketball isn't really supported here, but the women's volleyball team is. They just built a new baseball/softball stadium as well."

Q "[Nebraskans] **focus on their college team since they don't have any professional teams**. Other sports are big, too, as well as IM."

Q "**Husker sports are huge**. Football is the main attraction, although women's volleyball and gymnastics, and men's baseball are usually solid. IM sports have a lot to offer."

Q "Very good. **IM sports are really big on campus** especially with Greeks."

STUDENT AUTHOR: **Students are well aware that, to the rest of the world, Nebraska is synonymous with Husker football. Athletics are a typical UNL student's pride and joy. Even if they're not on a sports scholarship, many UNL students are active in intramural sports and rec center activities.**

Students Speak Out
ON DRUG SCENE

Q "**There are not too many drugs**, but I have friends who do them (mostly weed). Most people who I know that do drugs have been caught or got into minor trouble because of them."

Q "Well, **if you're looking to score anything besides weed, good luck**. Like I said before, don't do it in the dorms or the campus police will make rounds on the floors of the dorms and they will bust you."

Q "I am from Colorado, so I am used to a really large drug scene, and maybe it is just me but **I did not notice it as much as I do at home**. Maybe because all my friends at home do drugs, and not a lot at UNL. It is there, just like the drinking. I think alcohol is easier to find but just depends on what parties you hit."

STUDENT AUTHOR: For students with an itch to stretch the limits of their minds (and the law) it seems that weed is the drug of choice. Students say that the UNL campus is pretty tame when it comes to drugs, but there are ways to find what you seek.

20:1	Student-to-Faculty Ratio
84%	Freshman Retention Rate
25%	Four-Year Graduation Rate
59%	Financial Aid Applicants Receiving Aid

Students Speak Out
SAFETY & SECURITY

Q "**I've always felt very safe**. I've never heard of anyone I know being assaulted or robbed. There are lots of lights all over the place—very safe."

Q "Security and safety are pretty solid. They have emergency phones all over the campus as well as campus escorts to walk people home. **I can't remember any reports of a major crime** on campus since I've been here."

Q "All-in-all, I think it is very safe. In my three years, I have not heard of any incidents. The only thing is that campus is in a bad part of town. However, Lincoln is not that big, so I don't know what your definition of 'bad' is. **All of the trouble tends to stay in the neighborhoods** and not on campus."

STUDENT AUTHOR: UNL students feel overwhelmingly safe on campus. By day, students don't lock their dorm rooms and by night, students traipse through all corners of campus in the dark. Even seniors at UNL say they've never heard of any negative incidents that deserve any undue attention.

> **Questions?**
> For more inside information and survival tips, pick up College Prowler's full-length book on this school, written by an actual student! Check it out at www.collegeprowler.com.

Students Speak Out
ON OVERALL EXPERIENCE

Q "**My overall experience was a 7.5**. Classes were fine, but the youthful atmosphere could have been improved. Join clubs right away and just get involved in everything. Yes, I do wish I were somewhere else. However, don't let me discourage you. UNL is a good place to go to school."

Q "For a while, I wished I was somewhere else. **I had a little trouble adjusting**, but I really, really love it now. I wouldn't want to be anywhere else. I would recommend Nebraska to anybody. It is so much fun!"

Q "**It's no Berkeley or Madison**, but we can still have fun."

Q "I've had a good time. I'm ready to graduate, but that happens to everyone toward the end. I'll probably hang around Lincoln for a while, but who knows. **I don't really have too many complaints**. Overall, I've been happy here."

Q "The overall experience that I had at Nebraska was very good. **I met a lot of nice people and made a lot of friends**, which is really what made the experience for me."

STUDENT AUTHOR: All in all, it is quite common for prospective students to put UNL on the back burner and place the more glamorous private schools first on their agendas. But although it has its blemishes, most students just can't say enough about the University of Nebraska. They love the atmosphere, they love the activities, and most of all they love the people that they have met here. The students here believe that UNL can provide a great experience if you come to school with the right attitude and work ethic.

University of New Hampshire

105 Main Street; Durham, NH 03824
(603) 862-1234; www.unh.edu

THE BASICS:

Acceptance Rate: 59%
Setting: Rural
F-T Undergrads: 11,467

SAT Range: 1010–1230*
Control: Public
Tuition: $21,770

Most Popular Majors: Social Sciences, Business, Health Professions, Biology, English

*of 1600

Academics	B-	Guys	B-
Local Atmosphere	B	Girls	B
Safety & Security	A-	Athletics	B+
Computers	B-	Nightlife	C
Facilities	B+	Greek Life	C+
Campus Dining	B+	Drug Scene	C-
Off-Campus Dining	B-	Campus Strictness	B
Campus Housing	B-	Parking	C
Off-Campus Housing	B-	Transportation	B+
Diversity	D-	Weather	C-

Students Speak Out
ON ACADEMICS

Q "It depends on your classes and what you like in a teacher. At the end of the semester we fill out evaluations, which you can access in the library to **find out about teachers before you enroll** in their classes."

Q "Most of the teachers try and make themselves available to students, by making office hours. If you can't make it to their office hours, they're usually **good about making an appointment to see you**. Yes, all of the classes I have taken (with the exception of Economics and Propaganda) have been extremely interesting."

Q "Teachers are usually pretty friendly and some **seem more involved with their research** at UNH than their classes. Most of my classes are interesting."

Q "It depends on what you take, but **I've only had one teacher who really stunk**. Most professors are helpful and try to understand their students' needs, but they can also be frustrating."

STUDENT AUTHOR: Lecture classes tend to range in the hundreds, and every student has a set of general education requirements to reach before graduation. The Center for Academic Research (CFAR) is more than willing to give advice on what courses and professors to take, and can even show you student feedback that will give you a better idea of what direction you want to take. Also, professors always have teaching assistants on hand who are more than willing to help.

Students Speak Out
ON LOCAL ATMOSPHERE

Q "Newington and Portsmouth are 10 minutes away, with nice restaurants and theaters. If you're in the mood for some sun, **the ocean is only 20 minutes from campus**."

Q "**The town is small but quaint**, with a great college atmosphere."

Q "I love Durham! UNH is a big school in a quaint town. **Downtown Durham runs right through the campus**, so you see students sitting outside coffee shops or just hanging out at the restaurants all the time. New Hampshire is really beautiful, and there are a lot of things to do in the area."

Q "When it's nice out, the school sometimes has big barbeques where you can eat all you want for free. I thought that was cool when I first got here. It's a great campus. **Everything is within walking distance**, and the historic buildings make it so pretty."

STUDENT AUTHOR: Durham is probably one of the smallest towns in New Hampshire, and when you stick more than 12,000 students in the middle of it, you get an interesting mix of relaxed locals and wild college students. Durham, like any other small town, has a high school and elementary school, a post office, numerous gas stations, a few casual bars where the locals and students often mingle, and a small shopping plaza for all the necessities. The nightlife solely belongs to the students.

5 Best Things
1 Men's hockey
2 Outdoor barbecues
3 Close to beaches
4 Broomball
5 Student newspaper

5 Worst Things
1 Bell tower ringing
2 Lack of holidays
3 Mud season
4 Traffic on Main Street
5 Meal plans

Students Speak Out
ON FACILITIES

Q "UNH has a wonderful **gym that offers aerobics, workout facilities, an indoor tack**, racquetball, saunas, and basketball. The student center is pretty big and is a nice place to go for dinner, too."

Q "All of our facilities are very nice. **The student center doesn't have a ton in it**, but it's got the typical pool tables and living rooms that students need."

Q "The facilities on campus are top-of-the-line. The new dining hall has really good food and a nice atmosphere. There is the MUB, which is basically the student union, which is nice and has many things to do in it. The on-campus gym is really nice. **They're always adding new equipment** to it. The gym is air conditioned, too, which is a plus. We also have an indoor ice rink for ice skating and activities during the winter."

Q "The student center has really good food. Sometimes I sit and do my work there because **you see everyone you know**."

Q "The library was brand new my freshman year and is a **great place to study or take a nap**."

STUDENT AUTHOR: The UNH campus offers a lot to its students. They have recently renovated the athletic centers, library, and numerous dorms. Mostly due to the strength of the UNH hockey team, a prime ice-skating rink, open to all students, is located on campus. The rink can get a bit crowded, especially on the weekends. Overall, the students at UNH seem generally happy with the facilities provided for them.

Famous Alumni
John Irving, Richard M. Linnehan, Mike O'Malley, Louis Crosby Wyman

Students Speak Out
ON CAMPUS DINING

Q "The campus food itself is really good, but Holloway Commons (the main dining hall) **can be a bit frustrating** at times."

Q "Compared to most schools (so I've heard), our dining halls are pretty good. We **have unlimited meal plans** and a wide variety of foods at the dining hall."

Q "The **dining halls are alright**, but they get old quickly."

Q "On campus there isn't really too much besides some pizza places and buffet-style dining halls. **My favorite place to eat is the MUB** (Memorial Union Building), where they have a food court with pizza, sandwiches, Taco Bell, and other foods like that."

Q "We all complain about the food at UNH, but the **school has won many awards** for the food. It's actually very good. People complain because, like any other school, it can get old."

STUDENT AUTHOR: UNH Dining Services tries very hard to please as many students as they can, and they have won numerous awards for their efforts. While the food can get old on campus, Dining Services also has a "Cat's Cache" program that allows students to put money on their student ID card, which can, in turn, be used at certain shops downtown to purchase not only food but many other items. This adds a little variety and excitement to the UNH students' dining options. Overall, the campus food services genuinely go out of the way to please the students in any way they can.

Student Body

African American:	1%	Male/Female:	44/56%
Asian American:	2%	Out-of-State:	43%
Hispanic:	2%	International:	1%
Native American:	<1%	Unknown:	9%
White:	84%		

Popular Faiths: UNH has a very active Christian Fellowship and Jewish organization.

Gay Pride: UNH is very accepting of the gay culture, and they are very prominent on campus, holding many events tailored specifically to the gay community as well as gay awareness.

Economic Status: The economic status tends to lean more toward the upper-class.

Students Speak Out
ON DORMS

Q "The dorm you choose depends on what you want out of school. If you want to be able to **walk out your door and onto frat row**, you should stay in the biggest dorm, Stoke. Williamson and Christiansen are far away from the parties but close to the school. The Gables is in the middle of nowhere, but there are no RAs either, so you can have parties and stuff without anyone watching you."

Q "The dorms are all right; they're nothing spectacular, but **a great place to meet people**."

Q "Overall, the dorms are a good size and there aren't too many problems. Freshman dorms are kind of far from classes, but they are nice because **all the residents are freshmen**. You'll have some of the best times of your life here."

STUDENT AUTHOR: **Whether you're a double major in biology and mathematics who wants nothing more then a quiet living space to study and be in close proximity to the science and math buildings, or a party animal jock whose sole purpose in life is to be the center of attention, there is probably a dorm for you.**

> **Did You Know?**
> 55% of undergrads live on campus.

Students Speak Out
ON GUYS & GIRLS

Q "There are **a lot of hot mountain men**, but a lot of the guys/girls look the same."

Q "Like any place on this planet, there are beautiful people and people who are **beauty-challenged**."

Q "There are **large variations in the people** at UNH. We have a lot of hippies, but also a lot of the preppy, Abercrombie type, and the 'pretty-boy' type. For the most part, the campus is very much 'all American.'"

Q "In general, UNH is a very nice-looking campus. The guys are hot, but there are a lot of jerks. There are also a lot of awesome guys too, so it **all depends on who you involve yourself with**. I think that most girls at UNH are very friendly and chill."

STUDENT AUTHOR: **All students agree that no matter what your taste in guys or girls is, everyone is generally friendly and accepting of whatever type of beauty you may possess. As far as meeting people goes, it's all in the effort. Considering the size of UNH, finding companionship of the opposite sex won't be easy, but with the right attitude, at least you'll have fun trying.**

> **Traditions**
>
> **Boulderfest**
> Boulderfest is the UNH version of Woodstock. This event happens every year as an end of the year celebration.
>
> **Dead Fish on the Ice**
> The most popular men's hockey tradition is throwing a dead fish onto the ice after the first goal of every home game.
>
> **Overall School Spirit**
> UNH school spirit is strong in areas such as sports. Even, outside of sports, UNH pride is fairly strong.

Students Speak Out
ON ATHLETICS

Q "Hockey is the biggest sport we have and the games are always a lot of fun to go to. **Lots of people play intramural sports** and have a really good time with it."

Q "Intramural sports are big on campus. A lot of times people will play on an intramural team with their floor or residence hall. As far as varsity sports, UNH students take a lot of pride in the hockey team. **Games always sell out**."

Q "Both intramural sports and varsity athletics are huge. Many students at UNH **participate in athletics at some level**."

Q "I would say, besides men's hockey, the second most popular sport is ultimate Frisbee. There are **always people playing it somewhere** on campus."

STUDENT AUTHOR: **UNH is competitive in football, soccer, track and field, volleyball, basketball, and alpine skiing, and also boasts one of the best intramural programs in New England. Hockey draws the most students to its games, but ultimately, no matter which sport you choose to play you will always have students cheering you on.**

Students Speak Out
ON DRUG SCENE

Q "**We have a lot of potheads**. There are people who do the other stuff, but that's not as common as weed. Most people draw the line at alcohol and marijuana."

Q "The drug scene all depends on **the people you surround yourself with** at UNH."

Q "Drugs are a big issue with the police, as is underage drinking and transportation of alcohol. If you **drink somewhere private**, you'll probably be fine. Just carry alcohol in a backpack."

STUDENT AUTHOR: Although drug use is basically out in the open, it's rarely a hassle to the students. Some students aren't exposed to any drug use at all. The general consensus is that drugs are basically there if you want them to be. At UNH, the harder drugs are much less prevalent, and very few cases have been cited. Overall, UNH is a fairly harmless school when it comes to drugs, but ultimately the choice is up to the students.

18:1	Student-to-Faculty Ratio
87%	Freshman Retention Rate
58%	Four-Year Graduation Rate
78%	Financial Aid Applicants Receiving Aid

Students Speak Out
SAFETY & SECURITY

Q "The security system is pretty good. There are **safety lights and emergency call boxes** at regular intervals and Campus Security patrols the campus."

Q "Security is good. There are 24-hour lockdowns in residence halls, **two full-sized police forces** at all times, two minute response time at emergency call boxes, student security officers, bike cops, and more."

Q "At first I was hesitant, just because I was brought up being cautious of everything, but it is very safe. The majority of the town population is the students, so **everyone watches out for everyone else**, though you still need to be careful."

STUDENT AUTHOR: Since UNH is a small campus, it is much easier to keep safe. However, no place (not even Durham) is ultimately safe. The campus police have a great relationship with the students and greatly care about their safety.

Questions?
For more inside information and survival tips, pick up College Prowler's full-length book on this school, written by an actual student! Check it out at *www.collegeprowler.com*.

Students Speak Out
ON OVERALL EXPERIENCE

Q "I was accepted to all the schools I applied to, but I chose UNH because it was the one I could afford. To be honest, it wasn't my first choice. Let me tell you, though, that **I had a great time** while I was there. The school is wonderful and I had a good time."

Q "If I had to sum up UNH in a few words, I think it would be **party school**."

Q "I had a lot of trouble adjusting to college life my freshman year, as a lot of students do. But after being here for two years, I have come to love UNH as my home. All of the experiences that I've had here have **helped me to grow as a person**, and I'm sure that UNH will provide me with many more."

Q "UNH has many abroad programs and it was the greatest part of my UNH experience. This year was awesome. **I really got involved**, loved my classes, and had an awesome time with my friends. I write a column for the school newspaper, I'm in a theatre troupe, I was in a play this past semester, and I am always doing things on campus."

STUDENT AUTHOR: Most students did not choose UNH as their first choice. However, many of these same students will tell you that they learned to appreciate UNH and its well-rounded course curriculum, spectacular seasons, local "college town" atmosphere, and myriad of activities for students of all ages. It's safe to say that UNH is a school that caters to the needs of many different personalities. The campus also encourages students to explore all that they have to offer through many different organizations.

University of North Carolina

250 East Franklin Street; Chapel Hill, NC
(919) 962-2211; www.unc.edu

THE BASICS:

Acceptance Rate: 35%
Setting: Suburban
F-T Undergrads: 16,722

SAT Range: 1800–2090*
Control: Public
Tuition: $19,353

Most Popular Majors: Social Sciences, Communications, Psychology, Biology, Business

*of 2400

Academics	B+	Guys	A-
Local Atmosphere	B+	Girls	A
Safety & Security	A-	Athletics	A
Computers	A	Nightlife	B+
Facilities	A	Greek Life	B
Campus Dining	C+	Drug Scene	B+
Off-Campus Dining	B+	Campus Strictness	B
Campus Housing	B	Parking	D
Off-Campus Housing	B	Transportation	B+
Diversity	C	Weather	B+

Students Speak Out
ON ACADEMICS

Q "I have only run into a couple of bad professors. The good thing about college is that you can drop the class and get out. A **lot of the lower-level classes are taught by TAs**. Beware of the math department. A lot of those TAs don't speak very good English."

Q "Most teachers are very friendly, accommodating, and approachable. All the teachers that I have approached have been more than **willing to spend time with me outside of class** to help me learn."

Q "Many professors seemed to be uninterested in teaching, as they were **preoccupied with professional standards** (retaining tenure, being published, research, and personal interviews). This is the primary reason that the classes were less than interesting."

Q "Some teachers are great; some are horrible. Just **ask the upperclassmen which professors to take and which ones to stay away from**. This will make your academic life at UNC so much easier."

STUDENT AUTHOR: The faculty, like the student body, is diverse—UNC has over 100 African American faculty members. All professors are required to have office hours and many will arrange to meet with students by appointment if their office hours conflict with the student's schedule. Talk to upperclassmen to get the inside scoop on which teachers are interesting and fit your personal needs, and more importantly, which ones to avoid.

Students Speak Out
ON LOCAL ATMOSPHERE

Q "Chapel Hill is in a good spot: it's **two hours from the beach and two from the mountains**. There are several other known universities in the area, such as Duke, NC State, and Wake Forest. The area is absolutely gorgeous. I transferred from the University of Hawaii to UNC, and I think that the campus is every bit as beautiful as UH."

Q "The town of **Chapel Hill is definitely a college town**. UNC definitely makes the town what it is, and local residents respect that. But the location is pretty convenient. It is really close to Durham and Raleigh—cities with good restaurants and great malls. I think everyone in the area should go to Southpoint—it's great!"

Q "**Chapel Hill's campus is beautiful**. I definitely didn't want to be in a big city when I went to college, but I still wanted to have a nightlife. I wanted to be able to go hiking and have a lot of nature around me, but still be able to go out at night and have a few options. UNC is perfect for me."

Q "Chapel Hill is a **typical small town**. There's not very much to do around here unless a group or organization throws a party."

STUDENT AUTHOR: Chapel Hill is the epitome of a college town and has everything a college student could ask for. UNC is not the only school in the area: Duke, NC State, and North Carolina Central University are all close by. In a state that has a ton of universities and colleges, there's always somewhere to go and something to do.

Students Speak Out
ON FACILITIES

Q "The **facilities on campus are beautiful**. The Student Recreation Center (the gym) is well equipped with a wide variety of machines that function properly on a regular basis. The computers in the newly-renovated library are really nice and work pretty well. The new addition to the Student Union has plenty of room for studying."

Q "Most of the athletic facilities here are fabulous. Many are fairly new, in great condition, high-tech, and pleasant to go to. Many **computer labs and the student union have been renovated**. We have many famous alumni that contribute significant amounts of money so that today's students can live a better college life."

Q "The facilities on campus are pretty impressive. The Dean Dome, where all the basketball games are held, is **nothing short of immaculate**. The libraries, especially the newly renovated Undergraduate Library, provide comfortable, spacious, and quiet places to study."

Q "The facilities here are excellent. The Student Recreation Center is always full of people, and the **computer labs are wonderful and easily accessible**."

STUDENT AUTHOR: The UNC Student Union offers several conference rooms, study rooms, lounges, and a large computer lab open for students and faculty. The Student Recreation Center (SRC) has the latest exercise equipment and offers classes taught by certified aerobics instructors.

Students Speak Out
ON CAMPUS DINING

Q "The food on campus is pretty **good compared to other universities** I've been to. The dining halls provide a good combination of old favorites (pasta, pizza, salad, burgers, fries) and new choices (sushi, Mexican, Chinese, Greek, Thai)."

Q "The **food on campus at UNC is pretty good**. It certainly tastes better than some of the other dining hall food at other schools I have come in contact with. The good spots on campus are Top of Lenior, Lenoir Mainstreet, and Tar Heel Café."

Q "The food on campus is okay. **Don't be fooled by the food within the first week** of class, because it isn't always that tasty."

Q "You've got Lenoir as an option. Downstairs has fast food places and upstairs is the cafeteria. The **atmosphere in Lenoir is great**—it's a historic building, but inside is really modern. The food and overall variety is good. Your meal plan allows you to buy a certain number of meals per week at the dining halls and then get flex dollars for the fast food joints if you choose."

STUDENT AUTHOR: Just about every student agrees that all UNC dining options are a step above high school. Carolina's dining halls have sushi, grill, pasta, deli, pizza, a vegetarian corner, and soul food. Students are given the option of constructing their own meal plan. Just be prepared for long lines during lunch at Lenoir and in the morning at the coffee shops. With all the options available for UNC students, the Freshman 15 can very easily turn into the Freshman 30 if you're not careful.

Students Speak Out
ON DORMS

Q "**Live on South Campus your first year**. The dorms are new and you meet a ton of people! South Campus is usually where first-years end up anyways."

Q "The **dorms at UNC are decent compared to dorms at other schools**. While the North Campus dorms are bigger, closer to class, and all air conditioned; the South Campus dorms provide residents with private bathrooms, and balconies that allow students to meet people."

Q "The freshman dorms are Morrison, Ehringhaus, Craige, and Hinton James. **You will meet many interesting people** if you live in one of these four dorms. They are decent in size, and the community of the dorms is incredible."

STUDENT AUTHOR: **Overall, students at UNC seem happy with their living arrangements. However, a good majority of upperclassmen recommend that incoming freshmen stay on South Campus for the dynamic social life alone. Most of the dorms have a recreation area and parking. Whatever living arrangement you desire, there's a dorm that will suit your needs.**

Did You Know?
46% of undergrads live on campus.

Students Speak Out
ON GUYS & GIRLS

Q "UNC is a great place to meet that special someone. We have preps, **quite a few nerds, a lot of preppy white guys** who try to act like they're from the ghetto, a few that are truly ghetto, and a few surfers, skaters, and hippies. It's a great place, and most of us love it."

Q "The guys on campus are pretty hot. Also, most guys here are **extremely focused, motivated, and pretty friendly**, too. But they are limited. The females on campus are nice, come from a good background, are looking to prosper, and are focused."

Q "We have **more girls than guys**, so a lot of girls complain that finding a good guy is tough."

STUDENT AUTHOR: At UNC there is no shortage of places to meet members of the opposite sex. Parties, campus activities, clubs, sports, and Lenoir are all good places to meet people. Everyone is aware of the disproportionate ratio at UNC. Girls use it to explain why they're single, and guys use it to brag to their buddies. Most students are smart and outgoing. Everyone at Carolina is unique in his or her own way. That's what makes Carolina guys and girls the cream of the crop.

Traditions

Halloween on Franklin Street
Every year, thousands of people come to Franklin Street to celebrate Halloween.

Tar Heel Town
Before every football game, "Tar Heel Town" is created on the Quad.

Overall School Spirit
Every student is proud to be a Tar Heel. Because sports have such an impact on the Carolina culture, it's hard not to have any school spirit.

Students Speak Out
ON ATHLETICS

Q "Varsity sports are pretty big, but **many sports programs are overlooked**. Everyone focuses mainly on basketball and football."

Q "Varsity sports are a huge part of college life at UNC. We have a great academic and athletic reputation. People will line up to get basketball tickets pretty early in the morning, or even the night before the ticket distribution. **IM sports are pretty big** as the majority of people on campus are interested in athletics, though not on a varsity level."

Q "All sports at UNC are fantastic! **Tickets are free**, and there's always a sport to watch."

STUDENT AUTHOR: **If you are an athlete, a sports fan, or both, UNC is your paradise. All varsity sports are competitive, and walking on to any at UNC is a long shot because of the crop of talent that is shipped into UNC every year. It is not uncommon to have a class with one of your favorite school athletes. However, if you don't make the team, or if you're simply not interested in the varsity level, you can join a club or intramural sport.**

Students Speak Out
ON DRUG SCENE

Q "**It depends on who you're hanging out with**, but cocaine and ecstasy are big in the Greek and athletic scenes."

Q "**People do smoke weed on campus**, but it's not something everybody does. This type of illegal activity is usually isolated to that person's dorm room."

Q "There are drugs here, but they're very avoidable. There's really **nothing to worry about**."

Q "I don't think it is really a problem on our campus. **Binge drinking is the only real drug-related problem** you will encounter."

STUDENT AUTHOR: Security does a good job of warning students of the dangers of taking drugs and getting carried away with alcohol consumption. Drug prevalence at UNC is relatively small. Of course, if you are looking to do drugs, you will probably be able to find some rather easily. You will by no means be considered uncool for not doing drugs.

14:1	Student-to-Faculty Ratio
96%	Freshman Retention Rate
71%	Four-Year Graduation Rate
50%	Financial Aid Applicants Receiving Aid

Students Speak Out
SAFETY & SECURITY

Q "Security and safety at UNC are decent. We have **late-night escorts who pick you up anywhere on campus** if you want someone to walk home with. But then again, we've had some problems with assaults on campus. They were nothing major, but they still happened."

Q "The **security is very good here**. All the paths and greenways are lit up and have emergency boxes everywhere. The main library has a shuttle service at night to take you back to your dorm instead of walking alone."

Q "Security and safety is **definitely an area that UNC seems to take seriously**. Because of the amount of women enrolled, as well as for the concern of all students' well being, UNC has incorporated security posts every couple yards."

STUDENT AUTHOR: The safety and security of students is a top priority for UNC officials. The Department of Public Safety heads a first-rate division of police, security, and emergency services that ensures that students live in a safe and secure environment.

Questions?
For more inside information and survival tips, pick up College Prowler's full-length book on this school, written by an actual student! Check it out at *www.collegeprowler.com*.

Students Speak Out
ON OVERALL EXPERIENCE

Q "**I couldn't have picked a better, more well-rounded school** to go to. Academically, it's really challenging. Socially, there's always something to do. Diversity is something that's really embraced. And we're the Tar Heels—sports are great!"

Q "**I love it here at Carolina**. Even though it was not my first choice, it has become my home away from home. No other institution could give me the experiences and opportunities I gained here. Carolina is very close to other diverse institutions as well, which makes the college experience five times more appealing."

Q "Overall, I am glad I attend UNC at Chapel Hill because it's a well-known school throughout the nation. However, I do at times wish I were somewhere else because **the social life for blacks is not that great**. Academics can also be threatening when you walk into a class and you're the only black person or minority. Your success at Carolina will depend on your goals and how focused you are. My only advice is to not get caught up in the party scene your first year."

STUDENT AUTHOR: Students who attend Carolina are often happy with their choice—even if it wasn't their first. UNC is surrounded by a great college town, is one of the most prestigious public schools in the nation, and is one of the most diverse schools in the nation. It doesn't take long to adjust to Carolina. It's mainly common sense—hang out with old friends, make new friends, party, take a weekend trip or two (but don't forget to bring along your books). Students who attend UNC realize that they are receiving a great college education and an even better college experience.

University of North Carolina–Greensboro

1000 Spring Garden Street; Greensboro, NC 27412
(336) 334-5000; www.uncg.edu

THE BASICS:

Acceptance Rate: 72%   **SAT Range:** 1380–1680*
Setting: Urban   **Control:** Public
F-T Undergrads: 11,919   **Tuition:** $14,351

Most Popular Majors: Business, Education, Visual/
Performing Arts, Health Professions, English

*of 2400

Academics	B	Guys	B-
Local Atmosphere	A	Girls	B+
Safety & Security	B-	Athletics	C+
Computers	B+	Nightlife	A
Facilities	A	Greek Life	B-
Campus Dining	B-	Drug Scene	B
Off-Campus Dining	A-	Campus Strictness	B-
Campus Housing	B	Parking	D-
Off-Campus Housing	A-	Transportation	A-
Diversity	B	Weather	B+

Students Speak Out
ON ACADEMICS

Q "**The workload depends on the class and the professor's preferences**. It all has to do with the type of class. Academically, the University is known for its theater, education, nursing, music, business, and hospitality and tourism programs, so you can expect to have a heavier workload if your major involves any of these."

Q "Teachers, from what I've experienced and heard, **tend to be awesome when the classes are in your major**. I've had bad run-ins with the Latin department, but I love the theater department teachers. But I've heard from Latin majors that they love the Latin teachers, so it probably has to do with how well you get to know them personally."

Q "The teachers at UNCG are, for the most part, very willing to help you, but **the grad students who are teaching are the best teachers to have**. They have taught me the most by far and have been the most responsive and easiest to relate to."

Q "It would probably be best to find an older student or **ask at orientation which professors to take and who not to take**."

STUDENT AUTHOR: Just like at any other university, a few classes and professors at UNCG are "duds." Luckily, if you have to encounter them, it will most likely be in your general education classes. Thankfully, duds are not the norm at UNCG. The more involved you get with your major or program of study, the more you will appreciate the knowledge and talent of your professors.

Students Speak Out
ON LOCAL ATMOSPHERE

Q "The town is young and diverse with a large African American population from what I've noticed. There are many universities in the town and **lots of younger people**."

Q "I wish things would stay open a lot later. Late at night, **the only thing to do other than going to a bar is to go hang out at Wal-Mart**."

Q "Greensboro is one of the best places to live. **There is always something to do, and there are many places to shop and eat**. The downtown area keeps college students occupied most of the time. I would say it's what makes Greensboro so great."

Q "**The town is on the rise but slowly**. Tate Street offers a colorful, although fading, reminder of the diversity in the college area and differs from the other sides of the campus with social areas, small boutiques, bars, and the best coffee shop in Greensboro. The Guilford Battleground Memorial Park and Country Park are great for all kinds of activities."

STUDENT AUTHOR: Greensboro is a fabulous city. When people say there's always something to do, they mean it. Of course, most of the fun stuff requires that you have money, which can be a bit of a problem for the average financially challenged college student. But since Greensboro is a college town, several local businesses offer discounts if you present your student ID. It is also pretty easy to figure out fun things to do on a budget.

Students Speak Out
ON FACILITIES

Q "I love the facilities on campus. The EUC is a wonderful place to **hang out with friends and grab a bite to eat or a cup of coffee**. The campus bookstore is there, and it's also a great place to hold meetings for your campus organization."

Q "The rec center is really neat. It has an indoor pool, an indoor rock wall for climbing, an indoor track, and outdoor amenities, along with a ton of other **really cool resources for your enjoyment**."

Q "The libraries—all three: Jackson Library, the Music Library, and the TLC—are **wonderful places to use**. You can study in peace and quiet by yourself, meet friends to study in groups, or use the computers. And of course, they are great for research. There is material on almost every topic you can think of."

Q "The gym on campus is awesome. It is always crowded, but **it has everything you need**, including classes. The EUC is always crowded as well, but if you don't go around breakfast, lunch, or dinner time, you can find a seat. The computer labs in the library are always full, but the library is a great place to study."

Q "One great thing about the EUC is that **there are so many hidden bathrooms** inside that you are guaranteed to find one that you can use in private, if that's important to you."

STUDENT AUTHOR: If you notice anything while visiting UNCG, it will be the gorgeous campus. Many of the buildings have either been built or remodeled within the past few years, so everything is really top-notch. But more important than the pretty exteriors is how useful the insides are, and UNCG's facilities are definite crowd pleasers.

Famous Alumni

Richard M. Coffey, Claudia Emerson, Emmylou Harris, Beth Leavel, Alejandro Moreno, Cleveland Sellers Jr.

Students Speak Out
ON CAMPUS DINING

Q "There is variety of food in the Caf, but unfortunately it isn't good. I've never liked any of the Caf food except breakfast. My freshman year, **I lost 50 pounds because I didn't want to eat it**."

Q "Although some stuff is really gross, everyone usually finds food they can live with in the Caf. Generally, I find that the breakfast food, burgers and fries, and pizza are safe bets. If even these are suspect, **you can always have cereal**."

Q **"In the EUC, the food is great—there's a lot of variety**. The Caf is a bit nasty, but most freshman meal plans include unlimited visits there, so it works if you have no other option."

Q **"The Caf is very enjoyable for about the first year, and then grows extremely old after that**. There are other places to eat, like Chick-fil-A, but they can use up your declining balance really fast."

Q "The food could be better, but so could any school food. For the most part, there are many options. The Caf is okay most of the time, but **for special occasions there is Spencer's**, and the EUC offers many other choices."

STUDENT AUTHOR: The Caf is definitely not a favorite among students, but it isn't for lack of trying. There's a lot of variety, but the quality of taste is about equal to what you could find in your high school's cafeteria. Plus, the bulk of the food available isn't exactly healthy. The good news is that every meal plan comes with a "declining balance" that you can spend freely at the campus food court, coffee shops, convenience stores, and restaurants.

Student Body

African American:	21%	Male/Female:	33/67%
Asian American:	4%	Out-of-State:	7%
Hispanic:	3%	International:	1%
Native American:	<1%	Unknown:	6%
White:	65%		

Popular Faiths: Various forms of Christianity are probably the most prominent, but you will meet someone from every faith at UNCG.

Gay Pride: UNCG is known as UNC-Gay for a reason. A large number of students are openly gay in their everyday lives.

Economic Status: Most students receive some sort of financial aid, and the majority come from households with an average income.

Students Speak Out
ON DORMS

Q "A lot of people refer to the high rises as the 'ghetto; of campus because **they're the most rundown dorms with the smallest rooms**, and no one really wants to live there."

Q "I don't know how UNCG can get away with not having air conditioning in the dorms on the Quad. I lived in one, and **it was the most miserable year of my life**. I tried to stay out of the dorm as much as possible when it was hot."

Q "I was lucky enough to only have to stay in a dorm for one year, but the dorm that I did stay in—Ragsdale-Mendenhall—was **the nicest one, in my opinion, especially for the freshmen**. Mendenhall had just had the bathrooms redone, and the rooms were bigger than the ones in the other dorms."

STUDENT AUTHOR: **UNCG has a full spectrum of dorms, from ones you'd love to live in to ones you hope you never get stuck with. As is customary at most universities, freshmen have to tough it out in the rougher dorms before they can move up to the nicer places. At UNCG, freshmen will most likely find themselves in the high rises or the Quad.**

> **Did You Know?**
> 31% of undergrads live on campus.

Students Speak Out
ON GUYS & GIRLS

Q "There are hardly any guys on campus, so it's hard to describe one. **UNCG has a large population of homosexual men**. The campus is mostly women, so keep that in mind when choosing it. Most students are nice and outgoing."

Q "There are some pretty attractive ladies on this campus. **As a guy, I feel like the odds are in my favor here** because there are so many more girls than dudes."

Q "I dated around until **I found the person of my dreams**. I know that's probably not a common story here at UNCG, but I'm proof it can happen!"

Q "There are some people who don't even try to look decent, but for the most part, **the students seem pretty dateable**."

STUDENT AUTHOR: **Some things never change. UNCG used to be a teaching academy for women, and the population hasn't strayed too far from what it once was. If a major deciding factor in your choice of college is the number and quality of guys on campus, you might want to look elsewhere. Now on the other hand, if you're looking for a campus swimming with all kinds of attractive women, UNCG might be your kind of place. More than likely, you'll probably approach dating like the rest of us here: You'll take your chances.**

Traditions

Convocation
All new students are given a daisy and a Spartan pin after the Convocation ceremony each year.

Halloween
Every Halloween, the Mary Fousters turn their entire dorm into a haunted house. '

Overall School Spirit
Almost every student owns a UNCG sweatshirt, and many cars parked on campus sport UNCG bumper stickers, but that is about as far as the general school spirit goes.

Students Speak Out
ON ATHLETICS

Q "UNCG is definitely **not as famous for sports as some of the other North Carolina universities**, but the teams we have are decent."

Q "A lot of people are turned off by the fact that **we don't have a varsity football team**. I think all we have is a club sport version of football, which gets no attention at all. Soccer is the sport we're known for, but I wouldn't say that it's a big deal."

Q "The club sports on campus, such as football, rugby, soccer leagues, and basketball leagues, are **very big for students**."

Q "Some of our teams do respectably, but overall the school spirit and **attention UNCG sports brings to the school is minimal**."

STUDENT AUTHOR: **Many students say the reason athletics aren't more prevalent on campus is because UNCG has no football team. It's true. In a country where the most important game of the year is the Super Bowl, a university that is known for its soccer team isn't really going to stand a chance of making the headlines. That said, UNCG still provides a very athlete-friendly environment, and there are lots of club sports.**

Students Speak Out
ON DRUG SCENE

Q "There's always pot at every party I go to. I personally don't smoke, and it's not uncomfortable to me because no one ever tries to shove it down my throat. I try not to be around it, though, because if cops ever show up, I'm definitely not going down for something I didn't do."

Q "The drug scene is such where **if you want to look away from it, it's very possible to do so**. But if you are interested in it, there is an existing community for you to enter."

Q The drug scene isn't a noticeable part of campus life. **Most folks are straight-laced partaking just in booze and marijuana** but never noticeably because of the Gestapo-like presence of the UNCG Police, who operate under a zero-tolerance policy."

STUDENT AUTHOR: Let's be honest: marijuana and college go hand in hand. Most people don't smoke enough to fail out or get kicked out, but casual usage at parties or after big exams definitely happens. The general consensus among students is that it isn't really that big of a deal, and many can take it or leave it.

16:1	Student-to-Faculty Ratio
76%	Freshman Retention Rate
28%	Four-Year Graduation Rate
98%	Financial Aid Applicants Receiving Aid

Students Speak Out
SAFETY & SECURITY

Q "The security at UNCG is **pretty tight**."

Q "I'm a little disappointed that security on our campus is about the **same as it was before the Virginia Tech tragedy**. I feel like UNCG should step up in that respect to make students feel as safe as possible."

Q "**I definitely feel safe on campus**. It's when I walk down to Tate Street at night that I start to feel nervous about being by myself. It seems like there are always homeless people there asking students for money, cigarettes, or other things. I guess it's just something that happens in bigger cities like Greensboro."

STUDENT AUTHOR: UNCG has its own police station right in the middle of campus, and many students find comfort in this, while some feel that it is too intrusive in a Big Brother kind of way. Chances are, though, you won't need their services in your time at UNCG because the other safety features you will experience on campus are actually pretty useful.

Questions?
For more inside information and survival tips, pick up College Prowler's full-length book on this school, written by an actual student! Check it out at *www.collegeprowler.com*.

Students Speak Out
ON OVERALL EXPERIENCE

Q "I am so glad I made the decision to come to UNCG. When I first got here, I didn't know the area, and I especially didn't know any of the people. That's all changed now. I learned my way around Greensboro, and I've developed a fondness for this city. **I found people who became like a second family to me**. I wouldn't give up this experience for anything."

Q "There are definitely pitfalls when it comes to attending UNCG, but **I think every person's experience is unique**. I don't get along with the roommate I was paired with, I hate a couple of my classes, and the parking situation is stupid, but would I rather have gone to another school? No. I think I would have negative experiences at any college I could have chosen. But for the most part, I am comfortable here."

Q "Don't ever turn down anything, even if it causes you to miss studying. Everything is an experience that prepares you for something. Live life to the fullest and **enjoy everything Greensboro has to offer**."

Q "Without a doubt, **I'd do the whole UNCG experience again**. I respect the professors in my major so much. They reaffirm my desire to be in the field I'm in."

STUDENT AUTHOR: While there are always a few students who are critical of the University, most students are very happy with their experiences at UNCG. You will make friends that will feel like family, and you will keep in touch with them for years to come. You will learn to love Greensboro and all that it offers, and your mind will be broadened here.

University of Notre Dame

1600 Edison Road, Notre Dame, IN 46556
(574) 631-5000; www.nd.edu

THE BASICS:

Acceptance Rate: 24%
Setting: Mid-sized city
F-T Undergrads: 8,371

SAT Range: 1930–2230*
Control: Private
Tuition: $36,850

Most Popular Majors: Business/Commerce, Social Sciences, Engineering, Psychology, Pre-Medicine

*of 2400

Academics	A-	Guys	B+
Local Atmosphere	D-	Girls	C+
Safety & Security	A-	Athletics	A
Computers	B	Nightlife	B-
Facilities	A-	Greek Life	N/A
Campus Dining	A+	Drug Scene	A-
Off-Campus Dining	C+	Campus Strictness	C-
Campus Housing	B	Parking	C+
Off-Campus Housing	C+	Transportation	C
Diversity	C-	Weather	D-

Students Speak Out
ON ACADEMICS

Q "I really like all the teachers I've had. They are **very personable, and you can talk to them**. They're also very accessible, which is great if you have last-minute questions or problems. For the most part, the professors love what they're doing, and they make classes interesting."

Q "I love my teachers. Not only do they really know what they are doing, but if I have any problems, they are **always available during office hours** to answer any questions. Many of my teachers have invited classes over to their houses for holidays and for dinner during the semester."

Q "One of the great things about Notre Dame is that your classes are actually taught by professors. Classes are **interesting if you enjoy the subject matter**. If you register for classes addressing subjects you truly want to learn more about, then you'll find what you are looking for."

Q "Most of the teachers are great and are very **willing to give one-on-one assistance**. There is, of course, the occasional jerk who thinks he doesn't have time, but that's rare."

STUDENT AUTHOR: **Although some students occasionally encounter that one, bloodthirsty, Attila-the-Hun professor who slashes at them with a red pen, this is relatively rare. Most students have found their professors to be enthusiastic, accessible, and approachable. Even though they have all had some boring classes, the majority agrees that the classes required for their majors are more enjoyable and easy to praise.**

Students Speak Out
ON LOCAL ATMOSPHERE

Q "**South Bend is not a college town**. It is fairly dirty and not nice, but it won't really affect your day-to-day life. You might have a problem with theft if you move off campus. There are two other universities nearby, but interaction with them is very limited."

Q "The town isn't very big and often does not have the same 'college town' atmosphere that a state school might have, but **you can see the school spirit in the entire community**."

Q "South Bend is not a university town—Notre Dame is in a bubble. **South Bend is a very poor, industrial town** with a lot of problems. The University is physically separated from the city."

Q "South Bend, Indiana is **not a great place**. The school is the best, but its location kind of sucks. Although some may complain, it doesn't bother me. There's plenty to see on campus, and Chicago is only an hour and a half away."

Q "**South Bend is separated from ND**. I don't really feel like I live in a town, I just feel like I live at Notre Dame."

STUDENT AUTHOR: **At Notre Dame, a trip off campus is not a fun-filled vacation in Beverly Hills. The consensus is that South Bend is a dirty and somewhat dangerous small industrial city. While this may make it difficult for many students to feel comfortable venturing off campus, leaving the Notre Dame "bubble" to run errands is feasible, as long as you know what areas to avoid.**

Students Speak Out
ON FACILITIES

Q "Social space is kind of lacking, but other than that, everything is state-of-the-art. They're **always building something new**."

Q "Everything is pretty good. There are three fitness facilities, and they're all modern and easy to use. The student center has a lot of cool stuff, too. Basically, if you didn't want to leave campus, you wouldn't need to, because **everything's here— even a salon**."

Q "**The cafeterias are both nice, as are the athletic facilities**. Classrooms are comfortable, although at times rather chilly! The student center (LaFortune) has recently undergone many renovations to add several amenities to the building (Sbarro, Starbucks, and Subway) and has several other ideas brewing. Obviously, nothing is perfect, and there are always improvements to make, but overall, nothing is lacking."

Q "Notre Dame did not spare any expense while building any of its wonderful facilities. **They all meet the technologically advanced needs** of professors and students today, and almost all of the University's buildings, old and new, are architecturally beautiful to look at."

STUDENT AUTHOR: **Notre Dame offers a number of high-quality student facilities which are as nice to look at as they are to frequent. Student praise for the athletic facilities, restaurants, and the Hesburg Library helps to offset the complaints about the minimal space at the student center. Overall, the variety, number, and condition of Notre Dame's facilities earn excellent marks.**

Famous Alumni

Phil Donahue, Paul Hornung, Joe Montana, Regis Philbin, Condoleeza Rice, Nicholas Sparks

Students Speak Out
ON CAMPUS DINING

Q "I think the dining hall food is **a lot better than other schools**. I got lucky; my dorm is right by South Dining Hall, which is a lot better than North, in my opinion."

Q "Basically, the dining halls are pretty good, **offering wide varieties of food** from Italian, Chinese, and Mexican, to grilled food, a salad bar, desserts, and breads."

Q "**South dining hall is much better than North**. It would be wise to learn the habits of the dining hall so you can plan to eat during times when the food is the freshest. You do have the option of getting a 'Grab-N-Go' sack lunch if you don't have time to eat breakfast, lunch, or dinner."

Q "The dining halls offer a wide variety of foods. In each dining hall, there is a Mexican section, a cook-out section, a vegetarian section, a deli, a stir-fry section, a home-cooking section and a panini section. There's also a salad bar with fresh bread and soups! This may sound a little crazy, but **some parents want to eat in the dining hall when they visit** instead of going out to a restaurant."

STUDENT AUTHOR: **Notre Dame students are very fond of their dining halls. Combined with the generous meal plans, which range from 14 to 21 meals per week, meal points can be used at campus restaurants, in vending machines, and for "Grab-N-Go" sack meals. The variety of food at the dining halls gives Notre Dame a grade that most cafeteria lunch-ladies can only dream about.**

Students Speak Out
ON DORMS

Q "**The dorms are all nice**. If you get an older dorm, they have lots of tradition and a somewhat better atmosphere. If you get a newer dorm, they have air conditioning and the rooms are all a uniform size."

Q "The dorms are alright. How much you'll enjoy them **basically depends on who your rector is**. My rector sucked, so I really didn't like my dorm too much, but the majority of students truly love dorm life. That's why 85 percent of students live on campus all four years."

Q "You can't pick your dorm. Some are nice and some suck; it's the luck of the draw. Each one has positives and negatives—**you just have to deal with what you get**."

STUDENT AUTHOR: **Freshmen are not allowed to pick either their dorm or their roommates, but the majority feel that the University does a fairly good job in making the final decision. Of the 27 dorms, there's really no clear student preference. While the older dorms seem to be favored by some because of their traditions, the luxury and comfort of the newer dorms are preferred by others.**

> **Did You Know?**
> 80% of undergrads live on campus.

Students Speak Out
ON GUYS & GIRLS

Q "Although **the stereotype here is that the guys are hot and the girls are ugly**, the actuality of it is that most everyone is attractive."

Q "The hotness of the guys at Notre Dame is almost mythical. Students joke around that some girls attend Notre Dame because they know that the guys are smart and hot. High school girls even **take campus tours just so that they can look at all the hot guys**, and sometimes they even bring their cameras so that they can take pictures of them. No joke!"

Q It seems that **either people hook up or are in serious relationships**, but you find very few people in between. Whoever figures out how to change this could make a lot of money."

STUDENT AUTHOR: **The stereotypical Notre Dame guy is both intelligent and hot, while girls apparently run the gamut from uptight to simply unattractive. However, it's likely you'll find plenty of exceptions to both of these standards. While the Notre Dame social scene is quite skewed, it hasn't been pronounced dead on arrival—you will see the occasional serious couple walking arm-in-arm, and hookups are not uncommon.**

Traditions

The Fighting Irish
Tales of the origin of this nickname differ, but most agree that it perfectly sums up the spirit of the school.

SYR Hall Dances
SYR (Screw Your Roommate) dances held by the halls involve setting up one's roommate with a blind date.

Urban Legends – The Gipper
George Gipp, a Notre Dame football player in the 1920s, died of pneumonia, which, legend has it, he contracted by sleeping outside his hall in the rain rather than be caught breaking curfew.

Students Speak Out
ON ATHLETICS

Q "Notre Dame is a pretty big athletic school. Varsity athletics are big on campus. There's **nothing like a Notre Dame football weekend**, even if you aren't a football fan. Besides the varsity sports, there are also several club sports and countless intramurals. The intramurals become a great way to socialize and can be very competitive."

Q "Come on, this is Notre Dame! **Football practically has its own religious denomination** on campus. If you're a varsity athlete, you are worshipped and loved by everyone. The reason for this is because, overall, Notre Dame students are extremely athletic and know what it takes to be a varsity athlete."

Q "You won't find another university in America with better intramurals. **Sports obviously dominate the social scene** at Notre Dame."

STUDENT AUTHOR: **Make no mistake about it, sports are a huge part of life at Notre Dame. If it wasn't a Catholic university, it would be religiously affiliated with sports. The spirit, determination, student participation, and the expansive program vaults Notre Dame's athletics into a champion's spot.**

Students Speak Out
ON DRUG SCENE

Q "**The drug scene doesn't really exist** unless you look for it, and even then, it's barely there."

Q "While there is an **occasional isolated flare-up of drug use** on campus, there is absolutely no tolerance of this by the administration. Being caught means expulsion."

Q "My experience is that there is **more of it going on than the school cares to admit**. No one talks about it, but it is definitely around. You can avoid it easily or get into it easily, whichever you want."

Q "There's very little drug use to speak of. If you want drugs, I guess it's not too hard to find them, but **alcohol is, by far, the drug of choice**."

STUDENT AUTHOR: **Although alcohol can be found in excess, the University's strict zero-tolerance drug policy seems to be frightening enough to check the few students who are even interested in drug use. Whatever does happen is always in isolated circles. Of course, there are things around—this is the case at any campus.**

12:1	Student-to-Faculty Ratio
97%	Freshman Retention Rate
90%	Four-Year Graduation Rate
67%	Financial Aid Applicants Receiving Aid

Students Speak Out
SAFETY & SECURITY

Q "Safety is barely an issue. The campus is very safe, and the surrounding South Bend area is safe, as long as you know where you're going and **don't get mixed up in the wrong neighborhoods**."

Q "There is **generally a low crime level**. I can honestly say that I think I only locked the door to my room when I was leaving campus overnight and my roommate was not going to be there."

Q "The campus is pretty safe. **I leave my door unlocked all the time**, and I never feel threatened walking around at night. They have a program called SafeWalk—if you're out there somewhere and don't want to walk by yourself, just call and they come and walk with you. It's free."

STUDENT AUTHOR: Aside from the occasional bike theft, the majority of students agree: there is virtually no crime under the Golden Dome. South Bend, however, is a stark contrast to campus, and students recommend avoiding many areas of the small industrial city.

> **Questions?**
> For more inside information and survival tips, pick up College Prowler's full-length book on this school, written by an actual student! Check it out at *www.collegeprowler.com*.

Students Speak Out
ON OVERALL EXPERIENCE

Q "I definitely love Notre Dame—it was always my dream to come here. I knew it would be some work. I have gotten involved in student government, made some great friends, and we have had more than our share of fun. But don't expect Notre Dame to be like some state school with parties and beautiful girls everywhere. If you know how to have fun, then you can at ND, but here, **school should be your first priority**. If not, then this isn't the place for you."

Q "**Despite the weather, I love it**! Everyone you meet at Notre Dame will leave a lasting impression on you for the rest of your life. The only way I'd go anywhere else would be if you moved Notre Dame to a warmer location."

Q "In choosing Notre Dame, I am absolutely positive I made the right decision. I love it here. The classes are challenging, the teachers are outstanding, and the people are **some of the most wonderful people you'll ever meet**."

Q "Notre Dame is a hard place to live—you're **there to study and not have much fun**, besides drinking. Weigh carefully what you want from your college experience."

STUDENT AUTHOR: **Notre Dame is not an easy school, and it's important to remember that academics are huge. Above all else, you need to be willing to study and focus, or you're not going to make it through the University's workload. Students here are universally dedicated to their studies, and campus life reflects it. Students may find themselves frustrated by the value system or the lack of outside activities. Though often, the atmosphere alone is enough to sway your feelings one way or the other.**

University of Oklahoma

660 Parrington Oval; Norman, OK 73019
(405) 325-3011; www.ou.edu

THE BASICS:

Acceptance Rate: 89%
Setting: Mid-sized town
F-T Undergrads: 17,057

SAT Range: 1050–1300*
Control: Public
Tuition: $9,900

Most Popular Majors: Business, Social Sciences, Communications, Engineering, Biology

*of 1600

Academics	B	Guys	A
Local Atmosphere	B+	Girls	A-
Safety & Security	A	Athletics	A
Computers	B	Nightlife	B
Facilities	A	Greek Life	A
Campus Dining	A-	Drug Scene	B
Off-Campus Dining	B+	Campus Strictness	B
Campus Housing	B	Parking	D
Off-Campus Housing	A-	Transportation	B
Diversity	C-	Weather	B-

Students Speak Out
ON ACADEMICS

Q "The majority of the teachers that I've had have been **pretty good**. There have only been a few that I wanted to jump in a dark alley."

Q "OU has wonderful teachers who make class worth going to and really try to make the material interesting. Then, there **are those few who try to make things difficult for students**."

Q "**Some classes have 15 to 35 students**, and some basics, like Psychology that everyone has to take are like 200. I have talked personally with many of my teachers, and they are always open to meeting."

Q "**I haven't been happy with OU**. I feel like the staff is more interested in their careers than their students. The classes are big, and even though OU boasts of an impressive staff, the most you ever see until upper division are teaching assistants. I've been able to maintain a high GPA but due to an absence of personal relationships with faculty, it has been hard to build up recommendations for grad school."

STUDENT AUTHOR: Most students at the University of Oklahoma agree that the professors are a great addition to a strong academic program. Many are truly concerned with their students' success and possess a passion for their subject matter that can be felt through their daily lectures. Some common complaints were that the professors are not readily available to respond to their students' needs and that some majors were better and more accessible than others.

Students Speak Out
ON LOCAL ATMOSPHERE

Q "Norman is a **typical college town**. It's the only university there, but there are some small ones in Oklahoma City—about 20 miles away."

Q "The atmosphere is local and lively in Norman. **Thursday night is a night everyone goes out** with their friends. The weekends are sometimes more quiet when lots of students go home. The community is very involved with the campus."

Q "OU is the only college in Norman. Norman is a college town. You **can't go anywhere without seeing people who go to OU**, and they can usually be identified by their Greek T-shirts. This makes for a pretty fun town (lots of bars)."

Q "It's very good here—everyone loves OU. The **whole state loves OU**. OSU is in Stillwater, about two hours away. It's a big rivalry. And there are some smaller schools in OK City, as well. Many people visit the Memorial, and in OK City, there is also a theme park I haven't been to called Frontier City."

STUDENT AUTHOR: Norman is very college-oriented. It's smaller than Dallas, but bigger than Miami. (Miami Oklahoma, that is) As one student commented, the town really does feel a lot smaller than it is. People from larger towns often have preconceived notions that Norman is strictly a farm town. Upon arrival, one will discover that this is simply not true. The community itself is a mixture of small-town good ol' boys and girls from various parts of the state, along with many uptown snobs who grew up in the suburbs of Dallas.

Students Speak Out
ON FACILITIES

"The facilities are very convenient here at OU. We recently built a brand new face to the Memorial Football Stadium. The student center and the Union are both very nice. The Union **looks like an Ethan Allen store**. It's very clean and very big—it's a great environment."

"There's a workout center, the Huffman, or 'the huff and puff,' but it was just remodeled. There are b-ball courts, an indoor track, racquetball courts, **a huge cardio room, and separate weight rooms**. The student center or union is nice. It has all those restaurants, offices, meeting areas, and a post office. Also, there's a big screen TV and sitting area, pool tables, and a big theater they hold events in."

"**Campus is absolutely beautiful**. I had already sent in my acceptance to another college when I got to visit. The campus changed my mind. It is really green with tons of trees. The facilities are really good."

"**Everything is top-notch**. The student union is an awesome site in itself, as are the library and all of the buildings. The computers are as current as any I have seen at a college. They're about to double the size of the fitness center, too."

STUDENT AUTHOR: Sometimes, the facilities are kept so clean and so nice that the amount of tuition that goes to place old cherry wood paneling throughout the student union bathrooms seems a little excessive. However, after the initial shock, and if you try not to think about what it costs to keep the stadium lights on in order to do construction, OU is a more than comfortable place to inhabit.

Famous Alumni

Stephen Alexander, Mookie Blaylock, James Garner, Ed Harris, Michael F. Price, J.C. Watts, Roy Williams

Students Speak Out
ON CAMPUS DINING

"**The food's great**. The cafeteria is good for cafeteria food. There are good restaurants everywhere, especially on campus corner."

"There's a little place to eat in the bottom of Couch Center called Couch Express, and I'm going to miss the dorms because of it. I'm being serious here. They have the **best grilled cheese sandwiches and creamy potato soup**. They have little pizzas, little pasta salads, and pretzels. It's kind of like a fancy concession stand."

"The Food Court has a YoYo's (soup and sandwich), a Chick-fil-A, a Sbarro (pizza), a Taco Mayo, and a Wendy's. Crossroads is like a little restaurant where kids go and hang out, study, sleep, and eat. **It's open 24/7**. My friends and I, if we're starving at four in the morning, go and eat at Crossroads and get the cheese sticks or hamburger and fries—it's so good."

"The food in the cafeteria is surprisingly good. By the dorms, there is a building that houses a Taco Mayo, **a sandwich place, a pizza place**, and also a convenience store with snacks, groceries, and more."

STUDENT AUTHOR: OU definitely gives new meaning to the Freshman 15 because there is no lack whatsoever of fine cuisine on this campus. If you took the saying "You are what you eat" literally, then on any given day you could walk into a class at OU and see a chicken fried steak conversing with an Indian curry taco. Food at the University is as diverse as its student population.

Student Body

African American:	6%	Male/Female:	49/51%
Asian American:	6%	Out-of-State:	25%
Hispanic:	4%	International:	3%
Native American:	7%	Unknown:	0%
White:	74%		

Popular Faiths: Most students at OU practice some form of Christianity.

Gay Pride: The homosexual population at OU is not quite as large as it is in other state schools. Despite being in the Bible Belt, many OU students are generally accepting of people's sexual preferences.

Economic Status: Students from every economic status and race are represented.

Students Speak Out
ON DORMS

Q "Most of the dorms are suites, which means you share a bathroom with your roommate and two others. The three **best dorms are Walker, Couch, and Adams.**"

Q "The dorms are not about comfortable living as much as they are meeting new people and having the time of your life. I loved living in the dorms, but **would I live there again? No.** But would I trade that year and the experiences I had while living there? Absolutely not."

Q "The dorms are old, but I definitely think they are livable. I lived in Couch and it was just fine. Walker and Adams are cool, but Cate is pretty ghetto. **Get your contract in as fast as you can** so you'll have a better chance of not living there. You can always suggest a room change."

STUDENT AUTHOR: **Overall, the dorms at OU hardly resemble the Ritz-Carlton, but they are comfortable and decent places to live. Most dorms give you the options of a shared bathroom and bunked or regular beds. They are definitely livable for a year, and some of the best times of your college lives will take place within their hallowed walls.**

Did You Know?
29% of undergrads live on campus.

Students Speak Out
ON GUYS & GIRLS

Q "There are many attractive people here, both guys and girls. Some come with a little more attitude than others, but honestly speaking, it's probably **a more attractive school than most**."

Q "**They breed them best in the Midwest**, so people are generally pretty attractive at OU. I personally believe that Texas and Oklahoma have the hottest people per capita in the United States. I've lived in several different places, and I can say the hottest people are in the South and the Midwest."

Q "The guys are cute, but I'm from New York, and so **my taste in guys is different**. There are some hicks, but it's not too bad. The girls are cute, but there are a lot of Texas girls and a lot of small towners. Both are really nice."

STUDENT AUTHOR: **The guys and girls on campus are good looking, and most of them know it. The sororities and fraternities tend to produce carbon copies of one another, but if that's your style, then you will be in dating heaven, and if you break up with someone, then you are sure to find someone who reminds you of "the one that got away." People here are attractive and strangely tan no matter what the season—fake and bake.**

Traditions

BOOMER! SOONER!
Whether it is in a bar or in a bank, if someone yells "BOOMER," everyone in the immediate vicinity yells back "SOONER."

The Wire
The campus radio station is the Wire, which is programmed through OU's Gaylord College of Journalism and Mass Communication.

Overall School Spirit
Sooners, and their fellow statesmen, have more school spirit than other state school students.

Students Speak Out
ON ATHLETICS

Q "OU football is life. **Our basketball team went far in the NCAA tourney**, so basketball is big, too. Our softball team is always in the hunt for another national title, and our gymnastics team recently won the national title, as well."

Q "Football is huge! The games are always packed and are **lots of fun to attend**. Basketball is also very big at OU. IM sports are pretty popular, as there are many to participate in."

Q "I absolutely love football and basketball season. We have so much Sooner pride here. It's been a real experience to have so much pride in your school. **IM sports were pretty big this year**. We have basketball, softball, water polo, soccer, volleyball, and a lot of others I can't think of."

STUDENT AUTHOR: **At the University of Oklahoma, football isn't just a sport, it is a religion. Starting in August, the students and OU fans file like zombies to their temple (Gaylord Memorial Stadium) and worship the football team that they love so much. Not only is OU's football team one of the main reasons that people get up in the morning, they are also quite profitable to the town merchants and business establishments.**

Students Speak Out
ON DRUG SCENE

Q "If you're into drugs, you can get anything you like. I wouldn't say that drugs run rampant on campus, **just basic stuff like pot**."

Q "I know that some of the male crowd smokes weed. **It's not a big deal really**. There are places to go smoke and places to get away from it. You'll fit in anywhere in this place if you do drugs or not. Now I'm not sure about the hardcore stuff, but it would probably be easy to find out."

Q "It varies according to the people you hang out with. You **hear more about drugs in Greek life**."

Q "**Many people smoke pot**. There are certain groups that do other things, but only a few of my friends are into that."

STUDENT AUTHOR: **Drugs are not always visible on and around campus. However, if you ask around, students will tell you that they are easy to find. The common drugs of choice are marijuana and of course alcohol—yes, alcohol is a drug. Also, the state of Oklahoma was once known for having the most meth labs in the country.**

19:1	Student-to-Faculty Ratio
83%	Freshman Retention Rate
26%	Four-Year Graduation Rate
90%	Financial Aid Applicants Receiving Aid

Students Speak Out
SAFETY & SECURITY

Q "Campus is **pretty well lit at night**, and I know I can always call Safewalk to get someone to walk home with me."

Q "I've never felt unsafe walking across campus by myself, even at night. **There are usually people out walking around**, and the campus also has emergency phones that connect you directly to the OUPD."

Q "To my knowledge, security is good. We have a program called Safewalk, which allows a student to call up someone to escort them after dark if they feel unsafe walking alone. There are several emergency phones located across campus, and everywhere is well lit. **I have never heard of someone being attacked**."

STUDENT AUTHOR: **Students agree that safety on campus is not a huge issue. Although most college kids do have a feeling of invincibility anyway, the numbers actually back up the overall feeling of assurance. It is very unlikely to get attacked walking through campus at night.**

Questions?
For more inside information and survival tips, pick up College Prowler's full-length book on this school, written by an actual student! Check it out at *www.collegeprowler.com*.

Students Speak Out
ON OVERALL EXPERIENCE

Q "I've had an amazing overall experience on this campus. There are **so many opportunities** and activities to be a part of, as well as fun places to hang out with your friends."

Q "It seriously is amazing. First, I'll say we have one of the best presidents of a university at our school. **Everyone loves President Boren**. He cut down on the admissions because he didn't want to get over 30,000 students. He is big on a sense of community. He wants his students to hang out and get to know each other and has so many people to help you along your college career."

Q "The sports are so much fun. The Greek system will help you meet tons more people, too. But if you don't like that sort of thing, it's not a big deal. I love it here, and I feel like I'm at home. **You should truly think about coming here**. There are so many life-changing experiences and awesome people you will encounter. I promise you'll love it."

Q "I love it and I am so proud to be graduating from OU. My best memories have been here. My friends tell me about their other schools and they don't compare. **It's absolutely beautiful** and my whole family loved it."

STUDENT AUTHOR: **The majority of students were very satisfied with their time spent at OU. They feel that the small town of Norman offers a true college experience, along with the ability to give back to the community. Most feel that people in Norman are genuinely friendly and, for the most part, down to earth. The academics at OU are strong, and, generally speaking, the professors are understanding and qualified.**

University of Oregon

1585 East 13th Avenue; Eugene, OR 97403
(541) 346-1000; www.uoregon.edu

THE BASICS:

Acceptance Rate: 87%
Setting: Mid-sized city
F-T Undergrads: 15,077

SAT Range: 990–1220*
Control: Public
Tuition: $17,250

Most Popular Majors: Business/Commerce, Psychology, Sociology, Education

*of 1600

Academics	B-	Guys	B-
Local Atmosphere	B+	Girls	B
Safety & Security	B-	Athletics	A
Computers	A-	Nightlife	B-
Facilities	A+	Greek Life	C
Campus Dining	B	Drug Scene	C+
Off-Campus Dining	A	Campus Strictness	B
Campus Housing	B-	Parking	C-
Off-Campus Housing	B+	Transportation	A
Diversity	C-	Weather	B-

Students Speak Out
ON ACADEMICS

Q "The **teachers at Oregon are unique**. Each one has his or her opinion, and that is what makes classes interesting. They are really approachable, too. If you have trouble with anything, they will help you."

Q "Most of the teachers here are interesting and really knowledgeable. My classes are intriguing, but they're also **challenging on many levels**."

Q "Teachers have office hours where you can connect with them on a more personal level as opposed to being just another face in the class. **Graduate Teaching Fellows (GTFs) are like teacher aides**; they are graduate students who often teach the discussion sections. They are more down-to-earth because they know what you are going through and are generally easier to talk to."

Q "Most of the teachers are either more interested in writing books and doing research than teaching classes, or are disorganized and boring. I've had **very few teachers that I actually respected** after a 10-week period, and even fewer who have been able to keep me interested during that period."

STUDENT AUTHOR: Some students complain that the faculty seems to focused on research, and in certain cases this may be true. Professors at the UO, however, always make themselves readily available several times a week, both during office hours and outside of class. It's not Harvard or Yale, but the UO provides a wealth of opportunities.

Students Speak Out
ON LOCAL ATMOSPHERE

Q "I love this town, even if it is a little dull at times! You have to the visit the amazing outdoor stuff here: **camping, rivers, mountains, and skiing**. There is a great outdoor program on campus that will take you on cheap trips year-round if you like."

Q "The whole city of Eugene is behind the University. It's **the only large school in the area**, and the closest school to us is Oregon State University. Everyone you see around the city will be wearing a UO shirt or hat."

Q "The atmosphere is very liberal and political. I think all of the former flower children of the '60s moved from San Francisco to Eugene. However, this creates a diversity of opinions, although **conservative views are not usually welcomed** or accepted.

Q "Eugene is very well-known for being a very liberal and 'earthy' town. Some people call it '**Hippieville, USA**.' Most people say that Eugene is kind of boring, but if you have money, you can have fun."

STUDENT AUTHOR: The beauty of Eugene is that it's suited to fit any interests, from big-town business to small-town suburbia; it also happens to be an outdoor enthusiast's dream. Eugene has a very laid-back, relaxed atmosphere which offers the feel of a big city without the hassle of traffic on an eight-lane freeway. From time to time you will run into the occasional "hippie," but that's the beauty of Eugene—you never know what you will see next.

Students Speak Out
ON FACILITIES

Q "UO probably has **some of the most advanced facilities on the West Coast**. The founder of Nike went here, so he gives millions and millions of dollars to the UO. Our recreation center is amazing!"

Q "We are very fortunate enough to have very nice facilities. **All are very new, and if not new, they are extremely well-kept**. The University, like many others, is heavily geared towards our athletic teams. With that being said, we have some of the best athletic facilities, if not the best, in the country."

Q "Our school has been getting **a lot of donations from alumni recently**. They finished building the Law School and also finished Lillis Hall and Gilbert Hall. Also, the Museum of Natural and Cultural History has reopened, as well as the Living-Learning Center, a state-of-the-art facility with large residence hall rooms and two classrooms, a performance hall, Café, lobby, and meeting rooms."

Q "**Facilities are in excellent shape**! I have never seen a rundown building anywhere on campus, and I've never even seen a chair which had torn or stained fabric."

STUDENT AUTHOR: The University of Oregon offers some of the most extravagant, up-to-date facilities in the nation. The administration is always making the University more appealing, and recently, the University has revamped nearly every building to improve it in some way. You'll be hard pressed to find students who could ask for more.

Famous Alumni

Edwin Artzt, Ann Bancroft, Ann Curry, Rudolf Deutekom, Thomas Hardy, Ken Kesey, Phil Knight, Ahmad Rashad, Dan Wieden

---

Students Speak Out
ON CAMPUS DINING

Q "Campus food gets better every year! Students are **encouraged to submit recipes** of their favorite dishes, and the cooks try to make it."

Q "The dorm food is actually pretty good, and there is **a pizza place and a hamburger joint** where you can use your dorm allotment if you are sick of the traditional stuff."

Q "**The food on campus is alright**. There are a few places that are good, like Hammy's Deli."

Q "**Some dining halls are open until 2 a.m.**, and the Common Grounds, which serves coffee, bread bowls with soup, smoothies, waffles, grilled cheese, and all other sorts of foods, is the main place to go. My favorites place is the Grab 'N Go, which is a mini-mart type place."

Q "Campus provides an array of food choices. The only hard part is choosing what suits you best. Freshmen as of lately have had their food options increase dramatically. You **should not have a problem finding what you want**."

STUDENT AUTHOR: The University offers a selection to suit any appetite, from two dining centers providing all-you-can-eat buffets to the popular Grab 'N Go Marketplace and its fast-food options. Students see the food itself as standard dorm fare, but the variety of options makes it more palatable. One interesting feature of Oregon's meal plan is that students are encouraged to submit recipes to the Dining Services director and may even have their food incorporated into the dining hall offerings.

Student Body

African American:	2%	Male/Female:	47/53%
Asian American:	6%	Out-of-State:	22%
Hispanic:	3%	International:	4%
Native American:	1%	Unknown:	0%
White:	84%		

Popular Faiths: Christianity is the most popular religion on campus, but no single religion dominates.

Gay Pride: The majority of students are very open about their sexuality in Eugene, and it is well tolerated by both the school and town.

Economic Status: Both the town and the school are home to people from all walks of life, and both are essentially middle-class.

Students Speak Out
ON DORMS

Q "Everyone in the dorms is in the same boat as you, so it's not like you have to feel bad for being in such a cramped space. In the dorms, you have to **share showers and bathrooms**. You don't get your own."

Q "Well, the majority of freshmen live in the dorms for their first year, and I highly recommend it. Living off campus during freshman year is pretty unnecessary and dorms are **the best way to meet people**."

Q "As a freshman, **you can't really pick your dorm, just your hall**. I am in the Outdoor Pursuits hall where the people tend to be a bit wilder. Health and Fitness and Academic Pursuits halls are much quieter."

STUDENT AUTHOR: The University of Oregon has seven different dormitories, which cater to a range of needs, from the large rooms and private bathrooms of Barnhart Hall to the Bean complex, which is affectionately referred to as the "ghetto" dorm. You should definitely spend your first year in the dorms, because this is one of the best places to meet people and make friends.

Did You Know?
21% of undergrads live on campus.

Students Speak Out
ON GUYS & GIRLS

Q "Both guys and girls dress very casual, mostly **not too concerned about their appearance**. Overall, everyone's pretty laid-back."

Q "The guys here are nice, but I am used to diverse people and ethnicities, and **that is not represented as much here**. I wouldn't say the majority of them are what I would consider 'hot,' but there are a few worth taking."

Q "There's **no stereotype for the girls**. There are all different kinds and sizes, and they're pretty hot."

Q "All I have to say is, **thank God for spring** and the warmer weather! I would say we have a pretty good-looking campus for both sexes. You won't be disappointed."

STUDENT AUTHOR: While the University of Oregon certainly isn't Miami Beach, it's not Fargo either; you'll find a happy medium in terms of the eligible student body. Students all agree that spring term is the best time in Eugene, when you can see what's been hiding under all the clothes after a cold winter. Men generally aren't disappointed with the quality of women, whereas ladies offer mixed views of who's hot and who's not.

Traditions

Pit Crew
Sports-crazy students that attend every basketball game while making more noise that a 747 at takeoff.

Street Fair
A street festival held twice a year (once per semester). on 13th Street with plenty of food and arts and crafts.

Overall School Spirit
Almost everyone in Eugene owns some type of sports memorabilia, and everyone is supportive of the school in general. The whole community backs the University and its students with great support.

Students Speak Out
ON ATHLETICS

Q "**Football is huge**! If you come here, you have to experience both football and basketball first hand. The noise level at the Pit (basketball court) is crazy! IM sports are usually big, depending on what sport you play, and they can get pretty serious."

Q "**Sports are very big here**. Don't come here unless you are prepared to cheer on our teams."

Q "This is **an extremely athletic campus**. There are club sports, which are more intense than IM and less intense than varsity (with the exception of Frisbee and rowing)."

Q "Oregon has **the loudest stadium in the nation** because of the fans. They say it's one of the hardest basketball courts to play in because of them. The track and field team is good, and as for intramurals, they are greatly supported."

STUDENT AUTHOR: If you're interested in sporting events or think that weekends spent cheering on your favorite team are the way to go, you'll feel right at home with UO's athletic climate. Oregon is a fierce competitor in the Pac-10, and all of Eugene gets behind the University in support of our athletics.

Students Speak Out
ON DRUG SCENE

Q "There are a lot of drugs on campus, particularly marijuana. **We are very well known** for that. Mushrooms and all other soft drugs are common on campus."

Q "Well, according to most, pot is not a drug. There is **one frat that trades LSD for beer**, but other than that, those that do it are pretty quiet about it."

Q "Eugene is known for its marijuana. I still haven't figured out how, but it seems to be legally grown here and there is a pot farm somewhere off the freeway. **4/20 is a true holiday**, and I find it to be quite interesting. Due to a good number of hippies, it helps you understand why this lifestyle may thrive so much."

STUDENT AUTHOR: It's a well-known fact among many Eugenians that weed spreads like wildfire. UO's drug scene is very lifestyle-based, though which means that it's easy to avoid. If you choose not to hang out with people who do drugs, you may not even encounter them during your time on campus.

20:1	Student-to-Faculty Ratio
84%	Freshman Retention Rate
38%	Four-Year Graduation Rate
67%	Financial Aid Applicants Receiving Aid

Students Speak Out
SAFETY & SECURITY

Q "**Safety and security is present** and usually can be seen around fairly often. I'm never worried about my safety, but nighttime can be a different story."

Q "There have been some attacks on women, and a few isolated incidents, but what I can say is that the University is **placing a lot of emphasis on safety** and is constantly trying to make changes for the safety of the students."

Q "We always have a few attacks on campus every year, but usually it's someone walking alone late at night, which is never a good idea. There are **blue light stations all over campus** where you can call the Department of Public Safety (DPS) to come pick you up if you think you're being followed or in danger."

STUDENT AUTHOR: The University has had a few riots in the past, but fortunately no one was seriously injured. The University makes a good effort to provide the safest possible atmosphere on campus and prevent any further problems. With its bad track record, however, the UO has some work to do.

> **Questions?**
> For more inside information and survival tips, pick up College Prowler's full-length book on this school, written by an actual student! Check it out at *www.collegeprowler.com*.

Students Speak Out
ON OVERALL EXPERIENCE

Q "I love it here. **It's a laid-back lifestyle**, and I think it's pretty healthy. People like to have house parties and do the outdoors thing. Housing is cheap, easy, and nice. The campus is small with lots of trees and brick buildings, and has an excellent feel to it. You always run into someone you know. If you don't mind the rain, I think this is a great place."

Q "I love the UO. It's great! I'd just recommend to everyone who comes here to be very open and accepting. There are so many types of people around Eugene that **if you're prejudiced against anything, you will hate it**, but come with an open mind, and you will love it."

Q "It is fun here, and the people are great, especially if you like a small-town atmosphere. It **may not suit you if you like big cities.**"

Q "UO is a very liberal school, and Eugene is a very liberal town. Some people have had **a bit of culture shock** coming here, but the people are very friendly and accommodating. If I were to go somewhere else, it would only be because I wanted to see what else is outside of Oregon. Otherwise, I really do like it here."

STUDENT AUTHOR: The University of Oregon is a big school in a small town; Eugene is more liberal than many college towns, however, and offers a lot of atmosphere for its size. UO has something for every mind set, along with a wealth of opportunities to prepare you for the world outside college. At the UO, you'll find a school that is strong in both athletics and academics, as well as a school surrounded by the perfect area for outdoor activities. It can provide the quintessential college experience with few drawbacks.

University of Pennsylvania

3451 Walnut Street; Philadelphia, PA 19104
(215) 898-5000; www.upenn.edu

Students Speak Out
ON ACADEMICS

Q "Penn stands out among most universities in that it has great teachers available. In effort to generalize, I'd say that not all the teachers are great at teaching (are professors supposed to be good at teaching?!), but it's clear that **most are pretty brilliant in their field**. My classes are always interesting because I take classes dealing with subject matter that I'm interested in."

Q "The professors range from **uniquely dynamic to mind-numbingly intellectual** individuals. Each has his own view of the importance of his field and the contributions that he and his students can provide to society."

Q "There are both big lecture courses—which I never had a problem in—and courses with a small number of students, so **don't let people tell you that you'll get lost** in the system."

Q "**I have enjoyed both the breadth and depth** of the classes made available to me. The requirements are flexible enough to permit a wide range of study."

STUDENT AUTHOR: Penn students tend to be genuinely impressed with the knowledge and commitment of their professors but concede that, now and then, an uninterested or uninteresting teacher can slip into one's schedule. The enormous amount of classes offered at Penn (the course book is the size of a phone book) practically guarantees ample opportunities to find ideal classes and professors for each student.

Students Speak Out
ON LOCAL ATMOSPHERE

Q "It's definitely a city atmosphere, and **everything you need is within walking distance**. There isn't much to do uptown, but downtown there are a lot of clubs, stores, theaters, and museums."

Q "It's a city atmosphere, but at the same time, one could be in the middle of campus, standing on a green, and not know he or she was in a city. There are **a few universities present**—Drexel being the closest, with Temple, La Salle, St. Joseph's, and Villanova relatively close by."

Q "Stay away from people on the street who ask for money, potholes, construction areas, and scary parts of town. Visit most of the city east of campus, **sporting events, and definitely eat cheesesteaks**."

Q "Believe it or not, the city of Philly has a lot to offer. You can **head down to King of Prussia** or Liberty Place for some nice shopping, or you can go down to South Street or Penn's Landing to check out some very interesting people and shops."

STUDENT AUTHOR: Unique, vibrant, and artsy, the city of Philadelphia has absolutely everything a student could want. Music, food, sports, and more universities than Boston, as well as sections of the city which retain their friendly neighborhood feel, set Philly apart as a diverse and exciting place to go to school. Center City is a short walk away, and the historical richness of Old City is a cab ride from the heart of Penn's campus.

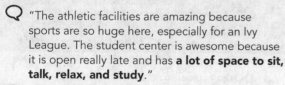

Students Speak Out
ON FACILITIES

Q "The athletic facilities are amazing because sports are so huge here, especially for an Ivy League. The student center is awesome because it is open really late and has **a lot of space to sit, talk, relax, and study**."

Q "Penn has undergone a number of remodeling projects during the past few years, improving both the interior and exterior of a number of buildings on campus, making the University both **an attractive and exciting place to learn**."

Q "The libraries have a lot of books; almost any book that you could ever need for a research project. There are a few libraries on campus: Van Pelt, Lippincott, the fine arts library, the law library, the biomedical library. It just goes on and on. **All the libraries are nice places to study** with comfortable couches."

Q "**Facilities on campus are beautiful**. Some of the buildings are old, others are new. There is constant renovation to make Penn a better place to be."

Q "There is a state-of-the-art fitness center and a brand-new Wharton building. Computers are available all over the place, but obviously, they can get crowded. The student center is beautiful—**perhaps the most collegiate thing on campus**."

STUDENT AUTHOR: **Penn facilities make it convenient for students to exercise, plan a vacation, grab a bite to eat, or simply round up a study group. There definitely is a range of quality, but the best-maintained buildings can be absolutely breathtaking.**

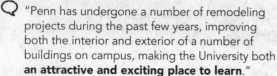

Famous Alumni

Sadie Alexander, Candice Bergen, William Brennan, Harold E. Ford, Jr., Doug Glanville, Rabbi Israel Goldstein, William Henry Harrison

Students Speak Out
ON CAMPUS DINING

Q "I am **really not a fan of on-campus dining**. I would definitely not recommend getting a meal plan. The food is really expensive, and for the price that you are paying, it should be really good. Plus, you have to mold your schedule around the dining hall hours."

Q "The food is crap. I'll be honest. But **most dining hall food in any school is horrible**. Restaurants are everywhere; take your pick."

Q "Dining is expensive, and I believe meal plans are required on campus. The food is not so great, but depending on what dining hall you choose to use, there may be a little better selection. Most students do not remain on the meal plan if they have a kitchen; otherwise **it's a lot of ordering out**."

Q "The dining plan sucks—I'm a vegetarian. The **good food places are the food trucks** on campus, especially along Spruce Street. They are cheap, safe, and tasty."

Q "I can remember so many times in my freshman year getting lip from the ladies that served me and **finding hair in my food**. Penn Dining is just a horrible experience."

STUDENT AUTHOR: **At Penn, students on a meal plan have three ways to pay for food. They can use a specific number of allotted meals per week or semester at the Dining Halls, Dining Dollars which can be continuously replenished at most retail locations around campus, and PennCash, which works somewhat like a debit card.**

Student Body

African American:	7%	Male/Female:	48/52%
Asian American:	17%	Out-of-State:	81%
Hispanic:	6%	International:	10%
Native American:	<1%	Unknown:	12%
White:	47%		

Popular Faiths: Judaism is a very popular religion among Penn students. Christianity is also common.

Gay Pride: Although the majority of students are very accepting of the gay community, students do not tend to be extremely aware or involved.

Economic Status: Most undergraduate students enjoyed a relatively privileged upbringing.

Students Speak Out
ON DORMS

Q "**Don't ever stay in North or Gregory**! North is the crappiest dorm in the world, and Gregory can't be any more isolated. Hill and the Quad are awesome fun places; High-Rise East rocks, as well."

Q "The Quad (Spruce, Ware, and Fischer Hassenfeld Houses) is the best place to live for freshmen. It's absolutely beautiful, the rooms are decently-sized, **it's in the middle of campus**, and they recently installed air-conditioning."

Q "The **high-rises are home to various floor events** that try to emphasize a certain program that students should follow. For example there is 'Latin America,' 'Arts House,' 'International Program,' and 'Ancient Studies,' among others. You have to apply to get into these."

STUDENT AUTHOR: **The Quad is the most popular for freshmen not because of the likelihood of making friends, but rather, because of its central location, air conditioning, and relatively nice rooms. Kings Court and Hill, however, are self-sufficient. Both have dining halls and activity rooms that the Quad lacks.**

Did You Know?
64% of undergrads live on campus.

Students Speak Out
ON GUYS & GIRLS

Q "A large percentage of students tend to hail from the Northeast and tend to be upper-middle-class. The **guys are better looking** than the girls."

Q "Unlike at many smaller, liberal arts school campuses, **hot is not defined by how good you can look without even trying** or who's the sexiest bohemian. At Penn, 'hot' for the girls usually means who can wear the most expensive ensemble while still sporting a relatively casual appearance. As for the guys, it's buff abs, preppy clothes, and hair gel all the way."

Q "**It's a big school, so you have a pretty good chance** you're going to meet 'your type.'"

Q "There are attractive people, but I'll be honest, **it's not UCLA**."

STUDENT AUTHOR: As picky as you may be about who you choose to "spend time with" at Penn, you pretty much automatically know the person hitting on you at that party is intelligent and has some good qualities, otherwise he would not be here. As far as promiscuity, people are definitely not prude, but if you come to school a virgin, you will not be alone.

Traditions

Spring Fling
Spring Fling is an incredible three days of vendors, bands, performances, and all out partying.

Penn Relays
The biggest track meet in the world, this yearly event draws visitors from all over to Penn's campus.

Overall School Spirit
School spirit is incredibly strong at Penn, especially at sporting events. Students can constantly be seen wearing Penn paraphernalia and bringing high school friends by to partake in the Penn experience.

Students Speak Out
ON ATHLETICS

Q "Varsity men's basketball and football seem to **garner the most support from students**. A longstanding rivalry with Princeton makes these sporting events hard to miss."

Q "Varsity sports are huge considering we're an Ivy League school. Penn definitely **has the most school spirit out of all the Ivies**. Football and basketball are big, but so are soccer, girl's volleyball, and lacrosse. IM sports aren't as big, but they're still nice to become involved with."

Q "People at Penn tend to be **very athletic and well-rounded**, so it's not very hard to find a new sport to pick up and some worthy competition."

Q "There's definitely school pride, especially against our rival, Princeton. In playoff games against them, **students all over campus wear their 'Puck Frinceton' shirts**."

STUDENT AUTHOR: **Penn has had many Ivy League Champion teams including men's soccer, women's volleyball, football, and men's basketball. Club sports are taken seriously by those involved, while intramural athletes tend to have a more laid-back practicing and training schedule.**

Students Speak Out
ON DRUG SCENE

Q "You can do drugs if you want, or you can stay away from them. There's **not too much peer pressure for it**, although there is definitely a large drug scene, especially in the fraternity and sorority system."

Q "Lots of people smoke weed. There are a few rich kids who insist on doing coke. Other than that, **it's your normal college thing**—mostly weed, some 'shrooms, whatever. It's not a big deal."

Q "The problems with drinking and drugs are baseline; **people are smart about not getting caught**, especially with drugs. There are occasional alcohol-related incidents but nothing major, in my memory."

STUDENT AUTHOR: **Not surprisingly, alcohol and marijuana are common and easily obtained at Penn. However, students feel that the drug scene is easy to avoid if you simply do not make an effort to become involved in it. It is easy to set your own standard of drug use while you are here.**

6:1	Student-to-Faculty Ratio
98%	Freshman Retention Rate
87%	Four-Year Graduation Rate
44%	Financial Aid Applicants Receiving Aid

Students Speak Out
SAFETY & SECURITY

Q "Penn is very safe; there are guards at every dorm and **plenty of Penn police everywhere**. There are, however, quite a few homeless people that always wander around and ask you for money."

Q "I never really feel unsafe on campus, but I know some people have. **Security is decent** compared to most schools."

Q "As a female, although campus itself is said to be safe, I'd be careful. There have been a few incidents within the past few years, and although security is getting tighter, you are in West Philadelphia. **Try not to walk alone at night**. There's a walking escort or van that you can call; do not be afraid to use it."

STUDENT AUTHOR: **Penn has proven that it is committed to improving the streets of West Philadelphia and making the area safer for students and local residents alike. Students appreciate the strong efforts made by the administration to improve security, increase the police force, and implement new technology.**

> **Questions?**
> For more inside information and survival tips, pick up College Prowler's full-length book on this school, written by an actual student! Check it out at *www.collegeprowler.com.*

Students Speak Out
ON OVERALL EXPERIENCE

Q "It's definitely a great experience. I love the city and the school. I would never want to be anywhere else. It has **the stellar academics of an Ivy**, a great city with tons to do, and wonderful people."

Q "**Penn has truly become a home-away-from-home**, and I'm hopeful that I can continue the Penn experience, if I get accepted to the law school. Its location is unmatched, its facilities are beautiful, and it remains home to a brilliant faculty (including a number of Nobel Prize winners)."

Q "Penn's great. **I wasn't sure about it coming in**, but it's definitely turned out to be the right place for me."

Q "My choice when I was applying came down to Penn and Yale, and **I could not be happier** that I made the decision I did. The people at Penn are very down-to-earth, and my friends at most of the other Ivies have become sort of pretentious since they have started school."

STUDENT AUTHOR: **Penn is not the school for everyone, but the student body consists of interesting, intelligent, and well-rounded people, which creates a stimulating and fun environment for most. Students seem to be extremely content and do not regret their decision to come to Penn, even though the school definitely has a pre-professional feel. Most students base the reasons for their happiness around the people, the academics, the urban environment, and the endless opportunities. You can feel confident that an education from Penn will prepare you for what lies beyond your undergraduate years.**

University of Pittsburgh

4200 Fifth Avenue; Pittsburgh, PA 15213
(412) 624-4141; www.pitt.edu

THE BASICS:

Acceptance Rate: 54%
Setting: Urban
F-T Undergrads: 15,662

SAT Range: 1150–1340*
Control: Public
Tuition: $21,616

Most Popular Majors: Business, Social Sciences, Engineering, English, Health Sciences

*of 1600

Academics	B+	Guys	B
Local Atmosphere	B+	Girls	B
Safety & Security	B-	Athletics	A-
Computers	B	Nightlife	B+
Facilities	A-	Greek Life	B-
Campus Dining	B-	Drug Scene	B
Off-Campus Dining	A-	Campus Strictness	B
Campus Housing	C+	Parking	D+
Off-Campus Housing	B+	Transportation	B+
Diversity	C-	Weather	C+

Students Speak Out
ON ACADEMICS

Q "I've had good teachers who actually care; I've also had bad ones who couldn't care less, barely spoke English, and were really inexperienced. On the whole, I think the teachers are pretty average. In bigger classes, the professors are usually pretty good, and the **teaching assistants are really helpful**."

Q "Generally, I think the professors do a good job of trying to **keep the classes interesting** and engaging. Some of them are a little bit out there, but I've never had trouble with a professor being unhelpful or disagreeable when you try your best."

Q "A lot of my teachers have taught directly from the book. Many times **I've felt like I could just skip going to class and just read the book**, and still be able to keep up with what was going on. As great as that sounds sometimes, I really think that it reflects poorly upon some of the professors at this school."

Q "There are **many very good professors**, and then many of them are primarily concerned with their research projects."

STUDENT AUTHOR: From a strong medical program based on UMPC's massive resources, to a well-known business program, to a distinguished philosophy department, Pitt has plenty of options for any sort of education you're looking for. With some programs that are stronger than others but some that are smaller and more personal, Pitt can meet the needs of nearly any student.

Students Speak Out
ON LOCAL ATMOSPHERE

Q "The campus is decent because it's spread out in Oakland, which is actually a part of the city of Pittsburgh. **There's stuff to do in the Oakland area, such as shop, eat**, and go out bar hopping. There are also a few clubs in the area."

Q "Pittsburgh is a big city, but it's not huge and scary. Most **bands come through here because we've got a bunch of venues** such as the Mellon Arena, Post Gazette Pavillion, Chevy Amphitheatre, and smaller clubs. There are plenty of places to go, depending on your interests; we have museums, galleries, and an awesome zoo."

Q "There is so much to do in this city, and all you have to do is travel a few miles to get out of the city. If you need trees and bike trails and grass, **Schenley Park is almost directly across the street**."

Q "Oakland is a wonderful place to study, with five colleges in the immediate area. There are also **ample opportunities to broaden your horizons** outside of the classroom, from the Carnegie museums across the street, to the concert venues on Forbes, to the symphony downtown."

STUDENT AUTHOR: Students love the busy, city life of Pittsburgh without the stress of being overwhelmed by an area too large to explore. There are so many things to do, with colleges to interact with, and restaurants, top sports teams, museums, and cultural districts to visit that students have few complaints about the well-rounded city atmosphere.

Students Speak Out
ON FACILITIES

Q "The **classrooms are nice and pretty new**. There are gyms all around campus, but they aren't that great, except for the one at the Peterson Events Center. The student union has a big pool table room and assembly rooms where they run new movies for a few dollars several nights a week. It's nice, but you really don't spend too much time in there unless you like to play pool a lot, I guess."

Q "The Peterson Events Center is a huge building that **looks like some sort of arena in Boston or DC**. The basketball team plays there, and May graduation also take place there. There are also eating and shopping places, another weight room, and all kinds of student facilities inside. I love it, even though it's a bit of a hike up the hill!"

Q "The **campus is filled with grass and trees**, so if you are not used to the city, it's not overwhelming. As far as the inside of the buildings goes, some classrooms are great, while others have uncomfortable chairs. The Cathedral is slowly getting air conditioned, which can be pretty painful for summer classes."

STUDENT AUTHOR: **If you're looking for first-rate athletic facilities, you won't be disappointed by what Pitt has to offer. The Petersen Events Center is a state-of-the-art basketball and recreation arena, and the main residence halls also have smaller gyms attached; though the equipment is older. Campus also offers Hillman Library, the University's four floor collection. Students can also access smaller subject-oriented libraries.**

Famous Alumni

Michael Chabon, Mike Ditka, Tony Dorsett, Dan Marino, Andrew W. Mellon, John Murtha, Leo Robin, Rick Santorum, Dick Thornburgh

Students Speak Out
ON CAMPUS DINING

Q "The Pitt dining plan is one of the main reasons I'll be moving off campus after this semester. Although every café presents a different image, there's really **very little variety in the food**. Many of the eateries are essentially fast food; not only is this unhealthy, but it gets old really quickly. The University claims to provide vegetarian and vegan meals, but these tend to be low-quality and hard to find."

Q "If you're diet conscious, C-Side, now the **Marketplace, is the best place to eat because you have more options**. It's also the best for any meal plan because it's buffet style. Eddie's, under Tower A, is probably the second best in terms of variety, but the most popular place to eat is Schenley in the Union."

Q "We have a lot of food choices, including Pizza Hut, a sub place, hamburgers, tacos, salad bars, and hot meals. There are buffet-style dining halls where you can **eat as much as you want**, as well as à la carte places where you can get single dishes, or stock up on cereal, milk, fruit, and chips for your dorm."

STUDENT AUTHOR: **There are a number of eateries on Pitt's campus— Eddie's and the Schenley Café are the busiest. Both are food-court style, and have a number of different features. The all-you-can-eat cafeterias boast more variety than any other eateries. Many students are satisfied with the quality of Pitt's dining services. However, meal plans can get costly—if you don't use up your meal blocks each week, you lose them.**

Student Body

African American:	8%	Male/Female:	49/51%
Asian American:	5%	Out-of-State:	17%
Hispanic:	1%	International:	1%
Native American:	<1%	Unknown:	4%
White:	81%		

Popular Faiths: Much of the campus is Christian or Catholic, but there is a sizable Jewish population.

Gay Pride: Most Pitt students are accepting of any lifestyle. There are a number of homosexual campus groups, as well as a few gay bars in the area.

Economic Status: There are students from every possible economic background you could imagine.

Students Speak Out
ON DORMS

Q "For freshmen, I would suggest the Towers. I know they **look, smell, and feel awful, but it really is the best way to meet people**. I lived in Holland Hall my freshman year. I wasn't crammed into a pie-shaped room, but I also didn't get the chance to meet as many people."

Q "My first year in Lothrop Hall sucks. It's old, there is **no air-conditioning, and right on top is a helicopter pad**. Every night, the hospital helicopter takes off and lands a ton of times; it doesn't exactly help you sleep."

Q "The Schenley quad is my favorite because all of the buildings are old and **have a lot of personality**."

STUDENT AUTHOR: When you first get to Pitt, you'll find most of your class living in Towers A or B, which are all freshmen. Many upperclassmen see the Towers as "the most fun you'll never want to have again." Forbes and Sutherland are regarded as the best dorms on campus, but they are the farthest from everything. If you live in either of these, you'll either learn to love walking up hills or spend a lot of time waiting for shuttles.

> **Did You Know?**
> 44% of undergrads live on campus.

Students Speak Out
ON GUYS & GIRLS

Q "I know that people from Carnegie Mellon come here in the spring to just look at the Pitt girls. They're **wonderful eye-candy**."

Q "Some people suck, and some don't. This place **isn't as cultured as San Fran or New York**; it's more like a college town filled with all types of people from bums to rich kids, drunks to sobers, and the thin to the obese."

Q "I always had a great time with the guys on campus. I made a lot of **great guy friends and dated a few sweethearts**."

Q "There are enough attractive people of both genders to go around. The variety's not too bad—there are jocks, punks, skaters, and many more. I've had **my share of male distractions**."

STUDENT AUTHOR: Pittsburgh is known for being one of the friendlier American cities, and there are enough students at Pitt to make for a smorgasbord of potential relationships—whatever type of relationship you're looking for. The student body varies widely; though, girls are almost universally considered better looking on the whole. Pitt guys have much less to complain about than the CMU students up the street.

Traditions

Hating Penn State
Anti-PSU shirts are sold on the streets in Oakland. Anyone who compares the Pitt Panther to a Nittany Lion is asking for trouble.

The Oakland Zoo
The official student section during basketball games; this is the place to be if you're a rabid fan.

Overall School Spirit
Pitt gear is abundant around campus, faces are painted blue and gold, cheers are shouted at major sporting events, and many games sell out.

Students Speak Out
ON ATHLETICS

Q "Pitt is **definitely a football and basketball school, for sure**. It's easy to get season tickets for football, but for basketball, good luck. IM football, rugby, and other sports are starting to attract a sizeable following, as well."

Q "**Tailgating at football games** is a highlight of the fall."

Q "I don't pay much attention to them, except when they're doing well. I think that's how most people are. Everyone goes to football games, though. I know a **bunch of people in IM sports**, and they all love it."

Q "If varsity sports aren't your thing, all you have to do is walk by the Cathedral anytime from late August into mid-November and you'll find 30–40 guys and girls **playing rugby or ultimate Frisbee**."

STUDENT AUTHOR: Athletics are off the hook at Pitt. The football team is often ranked in the top 25 and goes to a bowl game virtually every year. The men's basketball team has been nationally ranked over the past few seasons and looks to have a bright future ahead of them. There are also numerous IM and club sports, as well as constant pick-up games.

Students Speak Out
ON DRUG SCENE

Q "There is a decent-sized drug scene on campus. I wouldn't go so far as to say that it's becoming a huge problem, and **it doesn't seem like it's more prevalent here** compared to any other university or college. However, I know if I ever wanted to get drugs, I would know who to get it from."

Q "I really can't say because I don't ever buy, and I rarely do anything. I just stick to **drinking and occasionally weed**, but I never buy or know where to. I know a ton of people who do, though, so I'm guessing there is a pretty big drug scene."

Q "There is **not a big-time drug scene** on our campus. Most people are into drinking, though."

STUDENT AUTHOR: If you're in a position to see the drug scene at all, most of what you'll encounter will be alcohol and marijuana. Ecstasy, acid, and other "hard" drugs may appear, but use of these is even more subdued than marijuana. All drug use around campus is discreet; many students have never even encountered the drug scene at all.

17:1	Student-to-Faculty Ratio
90%	Freshman Retention Rate
55%	Four-Year Graduation Rate
50%	Financial Aid Applicants Receiving Aid

Students Speak Out
SAFETY & SECURITY

Q "It's pretty good. There are campus cops, **sign-ins with ID at all the dorms**, and other stuff like that. It is still part of a city at night, but I'm a chick, and I haven't seen any big problems."

Q "There is less hustle-and-bustle at smaller schools, and many more hiding places. Walking home from a party is a scary thing at those schools. On the contrary, Pitt's campus is well lit, and **there are always people on the streets**— all the drunk partiers find their way home by the light of the Cathedral of Learning. I feel much safer on an urban campus than a rural one."

Q "Pitt has its own police force—not just campus security officers, but **actual police officers**. They are everywhere, and there are posts with free phones and emergency buttons on campus."

STUDENT AUTHOR: The South Oakland area isn't known as the best location, but the police presence tends to deter any serious crime. The campus is always well lit—the University invested nearly a million dollars into lighting—and because of the urban location, there are always people around.

> **Questions?**
> For more inside information and survival tips, pick up College Prowler's full-length book on this school, written by an actual student! Check it out at *www.collegeprowler.com*.

Students Speak Out
ON OVERALL EXPERIENCE

Q "I have a great sense of pride in my school—I love the University of Pittsburgh, and I always will. I think it is an excellent school with a wide range of fields of study and an immense number of job opportunities in every line of work. No matter what major you choose, you can always **walk away with a well-rounded education and great experiences**. From partying with friends, to cramming for finals, I wouldn't trade my time at Pitt for the world. Hail to Pitt!"

Q "I love it. I would not go anywhere else. If you want a **diverse campus with lots to do** in the surrounding area, pick Pitt."

Q "I like Pitt. The education is good, and there's fun to be had. It's **not too pricey**, either."

Q "Pitt was a great choice. There is enough to do in this city to keep me occupied, and not too much going on so that I stay out of trouble. The teachers have been helpful and have motivated me to do **better than I have ever done in school before**. If Pitt adds a few more academic programs, it will be the perfect school."

STUDENT AUTHOR: Though some students dislike bad weather and city atmosphere, others love Pitt's high-caliber academics, many student organizations, and prime opportunities such as study abroad, cultural activities, and talented sports teams. If you're willing to be active on campus, there's so much to get from Pitt. The University's location can also be an advantage—Pittsburgh is a positive environment for students, thanks to the many colleges and universities in the area. The social scene is always jumping, locals are friendly, and there's always something to do if you explore a little.

University of Puget Sound

1500 North Warner Street; Tacoma, WA 98416
(253) 879-3100; www.ups.edu

THE BASICS:

Acceptance Rate: 65%
Setting: Mid-sized city
F-T Undergrads: 2,537

SAT Range: 1700–2000*
Control: Private
Tuition: $33,975

Most Popular Majors: Business Admin, Psychology, English, Economics, Biology

*of 2400

Academics	B+	Guys	C
Local Atmosphere	B-	Girls	C+
Safety & Security	A-	Athletics	C+
Computers	B+	Nightlife	C-
Facilities	B	Greek Life	B
Campus Dining	A-	Drug Scene	B+
Off-Campus Dining	C+	Campus Strictness	B+
Campus Housing	A-	Parking	A-
Off-Campus Housing	C+	Transportation	A-
Diversity	D	Weather	C-

Students Speak Out
ON ACADEMICS

Q "The profs are really good. Most of mine are **experts in their subjects** and have written the text books we use, which is really impressive."

Q "There are myriad opportunities available to fit anyone's interests. From the sciences to the arts, any one could feel at home with any major here. Even if **none of the available majors suit you, you can design your own** with the advice of any of our helpful professors."

Q "Sometimes I wish I went to a bigger school so that I would have more options for classes, but **UPS does have a good selection** for its size."

Q "Professors here are very demanding of students. They will push you to learn and think in ways you never have before, all in the spirit to help students. **Professors assign a lot of papers**, regardless of major, but they respond with an equal effort to read and critique your work."

STUDENT AUTHOR: In terms of academics, you will be running with a very fast pack at UPS. The professors hold their students to high expectations. UPS provides plenty of opportunities to do that through an array of interesting and engaging classes and independent research. Writing is stressed across all disciplines at UPS, and students can expect to do a lot of it. All classes, including labs, are taught by professors. Freshman students are assigned a professor from one of their classes to serve as an advisor for their first year.

Students Speak Out
ON LOCAL ATMOSPHERE

Q "It's pretty cold and rainy here, but when the sky is clear, you can see **Mt. Rainier practically right outside your window**, and it so beautiful, especially during a sunset when the sky is pink and purple. There aren't many universities close by, and there are some areas to stay away from, but none are that close to campus."

Q "Northern Tacoma (the Northend) is really a beautiful place. We're only a few blocks away from the Proctor and Old Town districts and also the Sound. Point Defiance Park is a few miles away and is **a beautiful spot to hang out**, enjoy the Sound, or go to the incredible zoo and aquarium."

Q "With a short drive, you can get to the mountains or the ocean and **there is no shortage of places to explore**. I love being in this place that is so close to the outdoors."

Q "When you tell someone at a restaurant or a store that you go to UPS, they tend to **greet you with open arms**. The school has a great reputation here, which you would not find at larger schools."

STUDENT AUTHOR: While many students complain of the campus bubble (a metaphorical bubble that separates the campus from the community), there are many chances to escape campus life and to explore Tacoma and other nearby locations. For the outdoor enthusiasts, Puget Sound offers several beaches within minutes of campus, and Mt. Rainier is about an hour and a half away.

5 Best Things	5 Worst Things
1 Small class size	1 Heavy workload
2 Beautiful campus	2 Rain
3 Campus food	3 Not much nightlife
4 Spacious dorms	4 Diversity
5 Location in Northwest	5 Guy/girl ratio (for girls)

Students Speak Out
ON FACILITIES

Q "We've got a pretty nice gym on campus, including a **student-run climbing wall** that I use all the time, and a pool that any one can use during open swim."

Q "The **architecture on this campus is amazing**, but even more amazing is the landscaping, always kept beautiful and freshly planted with flowers or whatever is in season here. We've got green grass year round because of all the rain, but be careful not to walk on it or you'll get muddy feet."

Q "The gym, computer labs, and student center are **usually full—a good sign** that the student population likes to use them and feels at home with the facilities."

Q "We have one of the **largest tennis pavilions in the Pacific Northwest** and our fitness center is really nice, too. There are many lounges on campus where students can go to drink coffee, relax, and visit with friends."

Q "The athletic facilities are a little shabby in my opinion. But **compared to other schools the dorms are really nice**. I've had friends come and visit and they are really jealous of the size and quality of the dorms here. The student center is also pretty nice."

STUDENT AUTHOR: With **red brick buildings covered in ivy, connected by arches and walkways through fir trees and green grass, Puget Sound is a beautiful place to spend four or more years. Students have a lot of respect for the well kept campus, and they enjoy the recent renovations to several buildings and hope for more in the future.**

Famous Alumni

Harry Brown, Dale Chihuly, Adam West

Students Speak Out
ON CAMPUS DINING

Q "The **food is excellent and diverse**, so everyone with different tastes can find something that they can enjoy. We have a vegetarian station, a Mexican station, a Chinese station, fresh sandwiches, a salad bar, and much more."

Q "Honestly, **we have it pretty good** when we eat on campus. The food is varied and cheap, and dining services does its best to make things taste good. We have good vegetarian and vegan options and plenty of meat available, too."

Q "Not only do we have pretty good food in the main cafeteria, if we get sick of that we can go downstairs and get a pizza made by fellow students, or get **really good, cheap coffee** and pastries at the café."

Q "Personally, I think the food serviced at the SUB (Student Union Building) is **better than most campus dining services**."

Q "Hooray for UPS food! I know, it seems like a strange thing to say—especially since I'm a senior, so I've put up with several years of the dining halls here. But UPS truly has good food—there are **lots of options, and it's cheap** (especially with a meal plan), quick, and easy."

STUDENT AUTHOR: The meal plan at UPS consists of a "point" system **where each student's ID card works like a debit card. Every food item is assigned a price in points, and points are deducted for whatever you choose to get. This allows students to eat whenever they want without the constraints of a lunch or dinner hour in a meals-per-week system.**

Student Body

African American:	2%	Male/Female:	42/58%
Asian American:	8%	Out-of-State:	70%
Hispanic:	3%	International:	<1%
Native American:	1%	Unknown:	0%
White:	85%		

Popular Faiths: While multiple groups are present on campus, the majority belong to the Christian faith.

Gay Pride: Tolerance for homosexuality is high at UPS. However, the number of openly gay students is relatively small.

Economic Status: UPS draws from a diverse economic background but most students come from double-income, upper-middle class families.

Students Speak Out
ON DORMS

Q "I am so thankful I go to UPS whenever I go to visit my friends at other schools. Compared to most schools, **the dorms here are amazing**—they are large, well kept, and very beautiful on the inside and out."

Q "Lucky upperclassmen get to live in on-campus houses, either by establishing a theme or getting a place in a lottery. These houses are **just like having your own house** off campus, except for no heating or water bills."

Q "The dorm rooms are **very large compared to other universities** and come with two desks, two beds, two closets and a bookshelf. I have not had to wait for a shower or a sink in the bathroom yet and the facilities are very clean."

STUDENT AUTHOR: **Freshmen live in one of nine well-kept residence halls, which are arranged in two quadrangles on the north and south sides of campus. Each building has recreational areas, vending machines, kitchen facilities, coin-operated laundry machines, a television lounge, a piano lounge, and study areas. If you are not a big fan of communal bathrooms, you can opt for suite-style living after freshman year.**

Did You Know?
59% of undergrads live on campus.

Students Speak Out
ON GUYS & GIRLS

Q "People on campus **tend to divide into groups**. Guys divide into nerds, regular people, and 'uber' jocks who spend large portions of time lifting. Girls divide up similarly, but not into the same groups. Girls either become very image-conscious, frumpy and nerdy, or somewhere in between (majority)."

Q "The **high girl-to-guy ratio is rather unfortunate if you're a college girl** looking for some love, but it provides a great selection for the guys."

Q "Social opportunities like Greek functions or other on-campus events like concerts are a good place to **meet members of the opposite sex**."

Q "People here are **great to have a good time with**."

STUDENT AUTHOR: **When students cite the reasons they chose to attend UPS, the dating scene would probably not come up at all. Given that the winters are chilly, most people are kept tucked under their jackets and hats between classes, making it hard to distinguish between potential date options. It does, however, make for nice surprises and spring flings when the flowers begin to bloom in May.**

Traditions

The Rail
The Rail is an organized set of parties every year during Halloween weekend.

The Luau
A dance and dinner hosted by the Hui O Hawaii club where more than 2,000 University and community members come together to share a traditional Hawaiian meal.

Overall School Spirit
While students here may not be bustling with athletic cheers and clothing, people are very proud of UPS.

Students Speak Out
ON ATHLETICS

Q "In terms of numbers of students involved, **IM sports are much more popular**. Four seasons of IMs a year and thirteen different sports provide an athletic output for nearly a quarter of the school."

Q "The nice thing about Division III athletics at Puget Sound is that you can participate very competitively, but **they do not take over your whole life**. Academics come first for most students here."

Q "Participation in both the varsity and IM sports is very good. It seems that **many people on campus get involved** in either one [type] or sometimes both."

Q "The **basketball games are intense**. A lot of students go to them to support our team."

STUDENT AUTHOR: **Puget Sound encourages participation in athletics as a means of achieving a more well-rounded education and balanced lifestyle. A number of school policies reinforce the value of academics—the school offers no athletic scholarships. But Puget Sound is proud of its accomplished athletes.**

Students Speak Out
ON DRUG SCENE

Q "I think it's pretty much **the same as on any other college campus**. [It's] not too bad. [If] you don't want to find it or hear about it, you don't. If you do, you do."

Q "I haven't really been exposed that much to drugs on campus. I know they're out there if you like [them], but **it's not a high pressure kind of thing**."

Q "Like any college campus, there are drugs available for anyone who looks for them. The difference is, here, **the drugs don't come to you**."

STUDENT AUTHOR: **Drug use is just not very common at UPS. Most students choose to drink at some point during their stay at UPS while very few get involved with drugs other than alcohol. Some students say that attaining drugs is surprisingly easy, and that pot is the most popular. There is a general sentiment that the drug scene at UPS is about the same as it is everywhere.**

12:1	Student-to-Faculty Ratio
85%	Freshman Retention Rate
66%	Four-Year Graduation Rate
88%	Financial Aid Applicants Receiving Aid

Students Speak Out
SAFETY & SECURITY

Q "Our **dorms and campus buildings are very secure**. Many people don't even lock the doors to their rooms, just because they know no one would steal from them."

Q "The **security people are always driving around** the parking lots or cruising through campus. You can always find one to help you if you need it."

Q "Security on campus is relatively safe. **I have never experienced anything bad**; however, that doesn't mean that nothing bad happens on campus. The school is very good about alerting the campus to incidents."

STUDENT AUTHOR: **The fact that security services are available 24 hours a day makes students feel very safe and comfortable on campus. Within the student body there is also a considerable level of trust as many students find that they can leave their dorm rooms unlocked.**

Questions?
For more inside information and survival tips, pick up College Prowler's full-length book on this school, written by an actual student! Check it out at *www.collegeprowler.com.*

Students Speak Out
ON OVERALL EXPERIENCE

Q "I have **met people from all over the world** and, even though this University is small, I still feel like there is a lot of room for me to open up, try new experiences, and meet new people."

Q "My experience here has been very good. I had such a wonderful time in orientation, being taken out into the woods and doing community service, and I got to be very good friends with some of the people in my groups. **Everyone on campus has been so welcoming** and many efforts have been made to help me feel at home here."

Q "I transferred here after one year at a larger university where my professors didn't even know my name. The **intimate atmosphere here provides a much better learning atmosphere**, with professors and students always willing to help or just talk about life."

Q "UPS is a great school. I had an initial concern about attending a smaller school—but trust me, **you really don't recognize everybody**. The actual discussion in class is much more valuable than some huge lecture class."

STUDENT AUTHOR: **Several students found their niche here early on during the well-crafted orientation program, "Prelude Passages and Perspectives," which gives freshmen a taste of the Northwest and the college lifestyle through academic sessions and community service. While every student will complain from time-to-time about the high workload, the rain, or a host of other issues, people here are proud to be a part of the Puget Sound Community.**

University of Rhode Island

8 Ranger Road; Kingston, RI 02881
(401) 874-1000; www.uri.edu

THE BASICS:

Acceptance Rate: 77%
Setting: Rural
F-T Undergrads: 11,210

SAT Range: 980–1160*
Control: Public
Tuition: $23,552

Most Popular Majors: Business, Journalism, Health Professions, Education, Engineering

*of 1600

Academics	B	Guys	B
Local Atmosphere	B	Girls	B+
Safety & Security	A-	Athletics	B+
Computers	B-	Nightlife	B+
Facilities	A-	Greek Life	C
Campus Dining	C	Drug Scene	B
Off-Campus Dining	B+	Campus Strictness	B
Campus Housing	B-	Parking	D
Off-Campus Housing	A-	Transportation	C+
Diversity	D	Weather	C

Students Speak Out
ON ACADEMICS

Q "**Just about every major has its own curriculum here**. Probably the best way to keep on schedule is to know your major going into college."

Q "Most of my classes are lectures, and there is a mix of about 20 people in each of my concentration classes. **The workload is decent and manageable.**"

Q "The most frustrating thing about academics is trying to get into the classes that you need. By the time that I am able to finally register for classes, they are already filled up. I sometimes have **trouble getting into classes that I need for my major**, and that really puts me behind. You can try to get an override into the classes, but not all teachers allow it. You don't want to count on getting an override, because if you can't get in, then you really have nothing to fall back on."

Q "I usually register for about five or six classes, (15 to 18 credits) and wind up dropping at least one. I think its **better to sign up for as many classes as possible** and then see which ones you like best and drop the others."

STUDENT AUTHOR: Since URI is a pretty big school (around 11,000 undergraduate students), students can find themselves in lectures with more than 500 students. However, no matter how big you class is, all teachers encourage students to contact them by going to their office hours, and some even give out their home phone numbers.

Students Speak Out
ON LOCAL ATMOSPHERE

Q "Rhode Island is so small! When you leave URI, **you can pretty much go anywhere locally**. I don't live on campus, and I love being in Narragansett. It's all college kids."

Q "**Narragansett is a college town**, definitely. My whole neighborhood is practically URI kids. It's fun, because there is always something to do. I'm always running into kids at Stop & Shop or Cumby's."

Q "I live off campus in Narragansett. Half of the people that I run into that live there year-round are pretty friendly, but **the other half hate college kids because of all the parties**. They like to call the cops on you even if you only have a couple people over, because they think it will turn into a party."

Q "All the **local shopping is pretty much all together in the same area**. If you just keep driving down the same street, you will surely run into something that you are looking for."

STUDENT AUTHOR: College students have taken over the local community and made it their own. With most students living off campus and in local towns, the atmosphere is going to be similar to what you would find on campus. Narragansett is your average town, but URI makes it stand out. Since Narragansett is a beach town, there are several boating and fishing opportunities available. This offers students something a little different than what you would find in a city atmosphere.

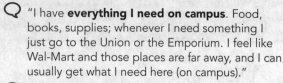

5 Best Things	**5 Worst Things**
1 Close to the beach	1 Parking
2 Parties	2 Class registration
3 The people	3 Overcrowded shuttles
4 Off-campus housing	4 Rainy days and snow
5 Ryan Center concerts	5 Campus is on a hill

Students Speak Out
ON FACILITIES

Q "I have **everything I need on campus**. Food, books, supplies; whenever I need something I just go to the Union or the Emporium. I feel like Wal-Mart and those places are far away, and I can usually get what I need here (on campus)."

Q "I love the Union. I'm always there in between my classes. You have the bookstore, a bank, the Ram's Den, Ronzio's, pool tables, and an arcade. It's a pretty chill spot. Grab some food, play some games, **you can even get your hair cut or buy some flowers**. Also, I love when people come and set up booths (mini malls)!"

Q "I like when **the Ryan Center has concerts**. It's a great building, and it's new. It's much better than Keaney where all the events used to be."

Q "The Union has everything a student might need, including the bookstore and a convenience store. I also **go to the information center a lot just to buy a newspaper or stamp**, stuff like that. Everything you need can be found on campus (except for alcoholic beverages)."

Q "**There are a lot of new dorms** and the whole Freshman Village."

STUDENT AUTHOR: There are little complaints about the lack of activities while on campus. The campus has a lot of attractions, like the Ryan Center, which holds a lot of sporting events and concerts. Also, the gym is a great retreat for students who have some extra time and want to workout. With all the facilities on campus, students have just about everything they need all within walking distance.

Famous Alumni

Christine Amanpour, Robert D. Ballard, Tom Ryan, Ross Kauffman

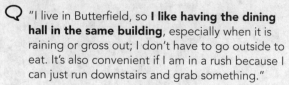

Students Speak Out
ON CAMPUS DINING

Q "I live in Butterfield, so **I like having the dining hall in the same building**, especially when it is raining or gross out; I don't have to go outside to eat. It's also convenient if I am in a rush because I can just run downstairs and grab something."

Q "**I wish some of the meals were healthier**; the hot meals, for example. They usually serve chicken nuggets or something fried. And it seems like all the hot vegetables are soaked in butter or oil."

Q "I like that **during the holidays they have special dinners** for Thanksgiving, Christmas, and Valentine's Day, too. They decorate and have special meals, like steak and all these gourmet side dishes. They make it all fancy. It's fun and good."

Q "I think the choices in dining are important. I usually get sick of eating the same thing, so I need options. I think **URI has a lot of dining options, so I'm pretty satisfied**. The food may not be the greatest, but what do you expect from college cafeterias?"

STUDENT AUTHOR: Variety is key in the dining halls. The more food you have to offer, the better the chances students will leave satisfied. Students need to feel like they can get the food they want and have it go down smoothly and stay down. Having multiple dining halls allows students to find their favorites and not be stuck with one option. Most agree that it could be a lot worse, and you learn to adjust to the food preparation and taste.

Student Body

African American:	5%	Male/Female:	44/56%
Asian American:	3%	Out-of-State:	50%
Hispanic:	5%	International:	<1%
Native American:	<1%	Unknown:	15%
White:	73%		

Popular Faiths: Christianity is the most popular, though other faiths are also represented.

Gay Pride: Several organizations and programs have been established to promote awareness and tolerance of gay students, including the GLBTA, Diversity Week, and the Rainbow Diversity house.

Economic Status: URI students are predominately middle-class, as is the surrounding area.

Students Speak Out
ON DORMS

Q "The dorms are very different from each other. They are **either brand new or really old**. There are good and bad parts for each one. In the older dorms, you can get away with a lot more because the RAs don't care as much, but the new ones are nicer."

Q "Even though the older dorms like mine, Burnside, aren't as nice, they are a lot of fun. The rooms are more private and **you basically have your own bathroom**. Kids don't get in much trouble, because they aren't as strict. Plus the balcony rooms are pretty cool."

Q "Sophomore year, I was in a triple with two other friends. It got a little tight at times, but we managed. Plus, **we got a good discount on housing for tripling up**. I thought it was worth it."

STUDENT AUTHOR: **Dorms are typically for freshmen and sophomores, although there is no requirement for living on campus. Housing and Residential Life also makes it easy for students to switch rooms if they aren't satisfied with the living conditions or roommate situation. No matter which dorm you live in, you'll have a good time.**

Did You Know?
45% of undergrads live on campus.

Students Speak Out
ON GUYS & GIRLS

Q "I had a boyfriend going into college, and I broke up with him within the first week I got here. **There are so many hot guys**, I wanted to be single."

Q "**I remember doing the 'walk of shame'** a couple of times my freshman year."

Q "I think **alcohol plays a huge part** in hooking up. Guys and girls get drunk and horny, so they hookup."

Q "It's hard to have a relationship here, because there's so much temptation. Part of me wishes that I was in a relationship because it would be more satisfying and fulfilling. But then again, it would be hard to trust someone because **there is such a temptation to cheat**."

STUDENT AUTHOR: **URI is the place to hook up, in every sense of the word. Students can potentially meet the guy or girl of their dreams just about anywhere on campus, as well as off campus. There are no limits to where you can meet attractive people of the opposite sex. Casual sex is not an uncommon thing at URI, but if you're looking for love, you might not be successful.**

Traditions

12th Night
A festival held on the twelfth day of classes to welcome returning students with games and events.

Midnight Madness
Celebration of the beginning of the basketball season with dance performances and live entertainment.

Overall School Spirit
Rhode Island has a lot of pride, and school spirit is something that encourages students. One of the first things that new students learn when they come to URI is the fight song.

Students Speak Out
ON ATHLETICS

Q "I was on the crew team my freshman year. It was good because I meet a lot of cool people and it was a good way to make friends. I definitely think that **joining a team is worth it**. A lot of the friends you make are on your team and those are the people you hang out with. It's nice to always have a group of friends there for you."

Q "Games are never sold out, and **you don't have to pay for tickets**. Basketball is big at our school, and I usually go to the games."

Q "**I love going to basketball games**. They are so exciting, and a lot of people go. I'm not that big of a sports fan, but the energy at the games makes it fun."

STUDENT AUTHOR: **Basketball is probably the most popular sport at URI. The team plays in the Ryan Center, and students can get tickets at any time. Athletics are an important aspect of college life to a lot of URI students Whether they are players or spectators, sports are popular at URI. Even though games may not be selling out in the box office, students do show their support. Rhode Island has a lot of pride, and this little state has a lot of big dreams.**

Students Speak Out
ON DRUG SCENE

Q "**URI had a rep of being a party school**. When I decided to come here everyone was like, 'You're going to URHigh!' Then when I got here, I didn't really run into that many drugs. Obviously, people drink, and I come across an occasional pot-smoker, but other than that, nothing."

Q "I think there is a good amount of drugs on campus, especially pot. I know **some kids who do coke** as well. I don't think there is any pressure with drugs, though. They aren't that important."

Q "The kids across the hall from me **would smoke pot every day**. They would do it in their rooms, on the balcony, or take a ride in their car. They never got caught."

STUDENT AUTHOR: You may be oblivious to the drug scene at URI, but it is there. Most students don't promote the fact that they do drugs or know people who do. It is not something that they brag about, but it is something that is being done. Although drugs are used at URI, they are not in popular demand.

17:1	Student-to-Faculty Ratio
80%	Freshman Retention Rate
40%	Four-Year Graduation Rate
63%	Financial Aid Applicants Receiving Aid

Students Speak Out
SAFETY & SECURITY

Q "I see cop cars parked outside of buildings and dorms sometimes, but I mostly see cops in the parking lots ticketing people. I think **police are mostly worried about illegal parking**, especially during the day."

Q "In order to get into the dorms, you need your ID. If someone doesn't have theirs, for whatever reason, I usually just let them in. **Kids are constantly going in and out of dorms** visiting friends and whatever. I'm not going to stop them if they don't have their ID."

Q "**I never locked my door** in my freshman year. My roommate lost her key for a little while so it was just easier to keep it unlocked. Nobody ever came in or stole anything."

STUDENT AUTHOR: URI is not in the middle of a city or surrounded by other main attractions, it is just a college campus. This limits the amount of outsiders that may straggle into URI. This setting allows students to feel safe and free to walk around campus without having to worry about any outside elements.

> **Questions?**
> For more inside information and survival tips, pick up College Prowler's full-length book on this school, written by an actual student! Check it out at *www.collegeprowler.com.*

Students Speak Out
ON OVERALL EXPERIENCE

Q "I like URI. I'm from Rhode Island, and half my high school goes here. I've stayed friends with a lot of them, so I feel like I never got to really go off on my own. I still hang out with a lot of my high school friends because they either go here or somewhere close by. **I kind of regret not going somewhere else** and getting the chance to meet all new people."

Q "There are some things that I don't like about URI. I can't graduate in four years because **I can never get into the classes that I need** to take. It's frustrating being behind and knowing that there is nothing you can do about it."

Q "I wish I went to a school with more to offer. I need a city near me, and I just don't find much excitement in farmland. I guess **I just don't like the location**."

Q "College isn't all about school; it's also about having fun and doing new things. It is your first time away from home and it's exciting. I'm having a great time here, and **I'm going to be sad when I have to graduate** and get a real job."

STUDENT AUTHOR: The biggest part of college is learning to adjust and knowing what is out there. URI is a friendly environment, and most students feel happy to be here. Academics are the biggest challenge, and getting into the right classes is often an obstacle. There are a lot of organizations and events that engage students throughout the year. Overall, students have a positive experience at URI. There's definitely something for everyone to enjoy.

University of Richmond

28 Westhampton Way; Richmond, VA 23173
(804) 289-8000; www.richmond.edu

THE BASICS:

Acceptance Rate: 40%
Setting: Urban
F-T Undergrads: 2,766

SAT Range: 1200–1380*
Control: Private
Tuition: $38,850

Most Popular Majors: Business, Social Sciences, English, Foreign Languages, Biology

*of 1600

Academics	B+	Guys	A-
Local Atmosphere	B-	Girls	A-
Safety & Security	A	Athletics	B
Computers	C+	Nightlife	B+
Facilities	B	Greek Life	A
Campus Dining	B-	Drug Scene	A-
Off-Campus Dining	B	Campus Strictness	B-
Campus Housing	B-	Parking	C-
Off-Campus Housing	B	Transportation	C-
Diversity	D	Weather	B

Students Speak Out
ON ACADEMICS

Q "Some of the introductory courses, like Psych 101, are taught by more than one professor in hopes of exposing the students to all the aspects of that concentration. This is a good idea, but doesn't turn out so well in practice because **each teacher has his own style**, and it can get confusing."

Q "I've found about all of my teachers to be understanding, interesting, and knowledgeable. The classes that aren't requirements are fun and interesting. **General education requirements can be boring** and CORE is terrible."

Q "The teachers with tenure don't really seem to care anymore. I like it when I have a young teacher because he tries to make the class interesting and still seems excited about the subject. Fortunately, there seem to be **a lot of energetic young professors here**, even if you do have to deal with the occasional old, boring one."

Q "I would honestly say that I felt like I was getting my money's worth from my teachers, and I walked away from school with **not only 'book' knowledge but 'life' knowledge, as well**, thanks to my intelligent, caring teachers."

STUDENT AUTHOR: Professors are very approachable because class sizes are small and intimate. If you choose your courses wisely, you will take courses that will prepare you for life after college without being overwhelmed.

Students Speak Out
ON LOCAL ATMOSPHERE

Q "Campus is in the suburbs of the city and feels that way. There is not a presence of other universities until you move downtown by VCU. There are definitely areas of the city to stay away from, but there is no reason to be in those places anyway, and there is a pretty good bar scene downtown to visit. **Virginia Beach also is not too far away**."

Q "Richmond is **a little too Southern for me**. I am from Boston, and I would be permanently pissed off if I lived down here all the time. Things move way too slowly."

Q "For all intents and purposes, the University of Richmond **could be located on the moon**. Hardly any of the students venture outside of the 'UR bubble,' which is the invisible barrier that seems to keep everyone on campus all the time."

Q "One thing that the students do take advantage of off campus is 'the River.' During the first two months of school, students (and just about everyone else in Richmond) go down to the James River to **enjoy the sun and the warm water**."

STUDENT AUTHOR: The city is situated on the banks of the James River, and on warm, sunny days, most of the town can be found swimming, canoeing or kayaking there. The only potential drawback to UR's location is that it is a bit too far from the city of Richmond. Also, depending on what region of the country you are from, Richmond's slow pace may be too much to bear at times.

Students Speak Out
ON FACILITIES

Q "The racquetball courts are great. You **can rent equipment from the gym**, and there is usually an open court. It's great exercise and lots of fun."

Q "**The student center is lacking a lot**, and I don't think that it is all that great. It has a bookstore, which usually has long lines, and a game room (with only a few pool tables and Ping Pong tables), and the headquarters of some of the student organizations (on the third floor and hard to find), but that is it. They could do more to make it a nice place to hang out."

Q "The gym is great, plus **it offers aerobics classes and hosts programs** to show you how to work out. As long as you don't visit during peak hours, you will be able to find a free treadmill or exercise bike."

Q "The athletic facilities are nice, but the weight-lifting gym is a little small. The computers are fabulous, and the student center is average but in a nice spot because **it looks over the majestic lake on campus**."

Q "The Robins Center is a **really nice basketball stadium, with recreational ball courts** and racquetball available to all students."

STUDENT AUTHOR: **UR has more than adequate facilities that are convenient and readily available to students. The fact that UR has an on-campus bar (the Cellar) is one of the biggest highlights of the school. With the exception of a few possible additions, the facilities at UR are extensive enough that you will never run out of things to do.**

Famous Alumni

Shawn Barber, Sean Casey, Maj. General Warren Edwards, Virgil H. Goode, Johnny Newman, Grant "Ed" Shaud

Students Speak Out
ON CAMPUS DINING

Q "The dining hall food is **what you would expect from a college food service**, nothing special, but not bad with a lot of variety and choices for each meal."

Q "**The vegetarian selection is miserable**, but it is nice that the school tries. The Pier offers salads, but they are usually gross, and the Cellar doesn't have much to offer except greasy food."

Q "The selection is wide enough that I haven't got tired of it yet, and since it is buffet-style, **you can eat until you explode** if you want to."

Q "The Pier has incredibly long lines all the time. They really need to come out with a new system for taking orders and giving out the food. You can **be in line for a half hour**, and the food is definitely not worth it."

Q "Food Services wants to make the students happy and it shows. The problem with the food on campus is that there **are only two main places to eat**."

STUDENT AUTHOR: **There really isn't much selection at all as far as on-campus dining is concerned. Undergrads usually eat all their meals at the main dining hall, E. Bruce Heilman Dining Center (D-Hall). The food isn't half bad here, especially at breakfast. There are also theme nights where exotic food is served. One of the strengths of the University is that it offers many different and flexible meal plan options. Although freshmen are required to buy the full plan, less extensive plans are favored by the upperclassmen.**

Student Body

African American:	6%	Male/Female:	51/49%
Asian American:	4%	Out-of-State:	83%
Hispanic:	3%	International:	7%
Native American:	<1%	Unknown:	7%
White:	73%		

Popular Faiths: Catholicism and Christianity are popular. There is also a sizeable Jewish population.

Gay Pride: Although there aren't any obvious examples of intolerance toward gay students, there isn't an outpouring of support, either.

Economic Status: Notoriously the "University of Rich Kids," most UR students come from wealthy or above-average economic backgrounds.

Students Speak Out
ON DORMS

Q "In general, the dorms are nice because they **provide a lot of variety for students** to arrange their room in the most comfortable way possible."

Q "**Living in the apartments is great**. It might be a long walk to classes, but it is worth it to have your own kitchen and bathroom. Try to live near the IM fields if you can because they seem to be the center of the action."

Q "Dorms are pretty standard, and **the quality doesn't vary too much** between them."

STUDENT AUTHOR: Freshmen are required to live on campus, which is good because it requires them to interact with other students and helps them develop relationships. After freshman year, it is possible to move off campus, but few students move off campus since on-campus housing is so convenient. Perhaps the biggest disadvantage to on-campus housing is that the dorms are segregated by gender. Fortunately, there aren't any regulations regarding visiting or spending the night in a member of the opposite sex's room.

Did You Know?
92% of undergrads live on campus.

Students Speak Out
ON GUYS & GIRLS

Q "The girls are hot, but also spoiled and stuck up. Most of **the guys are cool, except for the real rich ones** who think they are better than everyone."

Q "Everyone here is great. The **guys and the girls are fun and like to party** on the weekends, but during the week, it is all business and schoolwork."

Q "There is **no shortage of beautiful people** on campus. I mean this in terms of physical beauty, as well as inner."

Q "You'll learn quickly **not to judge a book by its cover**."

STUDENT AUTHOR: One of the best and worst parts about UR is that it is full of beautiful people. Don't worry—there are also lots of average ones. The bad part is that students are very concerned with appearance—maybe too much so. It is also very easy to get a reputation because the school is small enough that word will get around if a person hooks up a lot with different people.

Traditions

Beach Week
Following spring finals, most students visit the Outer Banks for a week of relaxing and unwinding.

Pig Roast
On the weekend before spring finals, the fraternities host the biggest party on campus.

Overall School Spirit
Students are proud of UR and proud to call themselves Spiders. The student body is solid in its support of most athletic teams, and because it is quite homogeneous, everyone gets along well.

Students Speak Out
ON ATHLETICS

Q "Basketball and baseball are huge because they are good. **Disband the football team** because it sucks, and give the other programs the money."

Q "**Varsity sports are not that huge** on campus. The football team is a joke, no one goes to the games, and I would say the basketball team is the most legitimate 'big/popular' sport that everyone goes to see."

Q "**I've been to almost every baseball game** because our team is so good and the fans get real excited. There is usually a tailgate in X-lot during games and people will cook burgers and bring beer. I also play most intramurals for my frat and they are always fun."

Q "Richmond has a bunch of talented teams, and it has **produced many professional players**. For its size, it has a very strong athletic program."

STUDENT AUTHOR: For students not gifted enough to play a varsity sport, club sports are a fun way to meet people, exercise, and compete against other schools. Intramural sports are bigger than club sports, and in some cases, bigger than varsity sports.

Students Speak Out
ON DRUG SCENE

Q "The only real big drug is Ritalin or Adderall. **Everyone uses these to study** or if they need energy. Weed isn't big, but I know a few people who smoke regularly."

Q "There are **a small number of stoners**, but mostly people avoid drugs."

Q "Overall, it is a small percentage of students who are seriously involved. **Campus police has begun cracking down** on the selling of drugs on campus, as well as the students' partaking of them."

STUDENT AUTHOR: UR doesn't have that big of a drug scene. This is probably because of the strictness of the University and that you will most likely get caught if you buy, sell, or use drugs on campus. Non-users won't feel pressured to use drugs because the scene is so underground. There really isn't any reason to use drugs because if you get caught, you will most likely be kicked out of school.

9:1	Student-to-Faculty Ratio
91%	Freshman Retention Rate
81%	Four-Year Graduation Rate
76%	Financial Aid Applicants Receiving Aid

Students Speak Out
SAFETY & SECURITY

Q "I've had beer stolen from my refrigerator, but that is the extent of the criminal activity at UR. **It is as safe as a school gets**."

Q "**You never need to worry** about your personal safety here, and the only incidents that you have to deal with are petty vandalism and some theft."

Q "I have never locked my door in three and a half years at this school. This campus is safe. **Theft is occasionally a problem**, but not unreasonably so."

Q "UR is **extremely safe**. There is nothing to worry about except for drunk students breaking stuff."

STUDENT AUTHOR: One of the biggest deterrents to crime is that the campus police maintain a very visible and active presence 24 hours per day. Students never have to fear for their own personal safety. The campus itself is very well lit, and there are cops everywhere.

Questions?
For more inside information and survival tips, pick up College Prowler's full-length book on this school, written by an actual student! Check it out at *www.collegeprowler.com.*

Students Speak Out
ON OVERALL EXPERIENCE

Q "I've had a great experience at UR, and am very happy that I chose to go here. Other than sometimes **wishing we had better sports teams or larger parties** like at a bigger school, I've never wished I was somewhere else."

Q "The academic and physical aspects of the school are fantastic. I wish that the human element were a little better. The **students act like they are still in high school** and can be huge snobs."

Q "The school is small enough that you will at least recognize most of the people you pass throughout the day. It's not so small that you can't escape or everyone knows your business. And **it's not too big that you would ever feel lost or overwhelmed**."

Q "The **friendliness took me by surprise** my first semester—everyone says hello and is willing to help you out. Overall, I feel proud having graduated from such an esteemed institution, and I feel honored to have worked with, and been challenged by, high-caliber professors."

STUDENT AUTHOR: Students really seem to enjoy UR and its retention rate seems to reflect that. The best part about UR is the intimate atmosphere that it has, being a somewhat small, private university. By the time senior year comes around, everyone in your class likes the school and knows one another. Students realize how lucky they are to be here and try to make the most of their opportunity by taking advantage of the great education, strong alumni network, and career preparation activities that the school provides.

University of Rochester

500 Wilson Boulevard.; Rochester, NY 14627
(585) 275-2121; www.rochester.edu

THE BASICS:

Acceptance Rate: 42%   **SAT Range:** 1910–2210*
Setting: Urban   **Control:** Private
F-T Undergrads: 4,839   **Tuition:** $37,250

Most Popular Majors: Social Sciences, Psychology, Biology, Musical Performance, Engineering

*of 2400

Academics	A	Guys	B
Local Atmosphere	C+	Girls	B-
Safety & Security	B+	Athletics	C+
Computers	B	Nightlife	C+
Facilities	A-	Greek Life	A-
Campus Dining	C-	Drug Scene	B
Off-Campus Dining	B+	Campus Strictness	B+
Campus Housing	B	Parking	C-
Off-Campus Housing	A-	Transportation	B
Diversity	C	Weather	D

Students Speak Out
ON ACADEMICS

Q "The staff is one of the high points of the University. No matter the department, they are **dedicated and really smart**. They have some impressive credentials and awards."

Q "The **classes are pretty small**, so there is a lot of interaction. Also, almost all of the professors schedule regular office hours so the students can come in to get extra help or discuss something about class."

Q "I feel that the professors are passionate about their subject matter and are **always willing to help their students** in any way possible. Classes are interesting and often convey a whole new perspective on the world, not just facts."

Q "Occasionally I find professors who are more **interested in their research** than their teaching, but generally they are genuinely interested in their students and their learning. My classes have a lot of reading and work."

STUDENT AUTHOR: Each professor has office hours, and many are willing to meet outside those hours. The workload is challenging, and students cannot coast through with ease, but the quality of teaching makes the work well worth it. There are professors who are enjoyable to listen to for hours based on their amazing wealth of knowledge. If you want to be in the class, you can be in the class. It's left up to you if you think you can handle it. The curriculum at UR is very open, and even as a freshman you'll have only one required class, so students are free to enjoy any class offered.

Students Speak Out
ON LOCAL ATMOSPHERE

Q "The city of Rochester is okay. Nothing really fun is super-close, which makes it **tough as a freshman since you can't have a car**. But other than that, there are malls, a park, and all of that."

Q "The city of Rochester seems fairly conducive to **fun for college students**. There is also RIT, St. John Fisher College, and Nazareth in the city. SUNY Brockport and SUNY Geneseo are very close by."

Q "Rochester is **pretty cool for a small city**. The other universities are all out in the 'burbs, so we don't really hang out with them. Definitely check out the East End and Park Avenue areas—that's where a lot of clubs, restaurants, and shops are."

Q "Rochester is a city, definitely not a college town, and **UR is pretty isolated** from the rest of the community because of it."

STUDENT AUTHOR: Considering the enormous amount of college students in the area, there isn't a specific area where you will find a concentration of college students. East Avenue and the Gibbs Street area have coffeeshops and theaters, and down Alexander Street are some nicer restaurants and bars. A lot of the suburbs outside the campus are quiet residential areas. Down in the St. Paul area are some clubs as well. If you go a few hours in any direction, you can find some fun. Niagara Falls is only an hour and half away, and Toronto is close. Being in upstate New York with lots of colleges around has its advantages.

5 Best Things	5 Worst Things
1 The academics	1 Campus food
2 Proximity of everything	2 Lack of parking
3 Professor accessibility	3 Meal plans
4 Rochester's fall	4 Bookstore prices
5 Career Center	5 Gray skies

Students Speak Out
ON FACILITIES

Q "The **aesthetics are gorgeous** and can really contribute to a feeling of academia."

Q "The **classrooms are clean and comfortable**, the dining areas are clean, and the library is in a class of its own. The dorms can get dirty, and sometimes the bathrooms don't work perfectly, but otherwise, everything on campus is in pretty good shape."

Q "The **athletic building was just redone** a few years ago, and it is really nice. The pool is in good shape and the gym has a lot of equipment that is in excellent condition. A lot of student life, like club meetings, takes place in Wilson Commons, but there really isn't a student union like there is on other campuses."

Q "I like the computer labs. A lot of them have some of **the latest technologies**, and you can even sign out some things (like video cameras and editing machines)."

Q "There is **no center of student life**, which is kind of annoying."

STUDENT AUTHOR: There aren't many negatives about most of the facilities at UR. The library is billed as one of the nicest buildings on campus, almost nice enough to make studying a pleasant experience. The student union is oddly constructed in the contemporary style of glass and weird angles, and thus not at all practical. It does not really do the job of uniting the students as much as one would see at other schools. As the one weakness in a collection of otherwise first-rate facilities though, UR averages out pretty well.

Famous Alumni

George Abbott, Myles Brand, Robert Forster, Michael Kanfer, Galway Kinnell, Deborah Jo Rupp, Avie Tevanian, Joseph C. Wilson

Students Speak Out
ON CAMPUS DINING

Q "It is **ridiculously expensive**. Dining services will rip you off, but unless you're a junior or senior, you're kind of stuck."

Q "The Meliora is a really good spot. It's a fancy dining hall that's **only open for lunch** during the week. Their food is definitely restaurant-quality. As for the regular dining halls, I prefer Douglass because I think they have the best variety."

Q "There are **all-you-can-eat dining halls** as well as places to buy food a la carte."

Q "The Pit has a grill, pizza, subs, wraps, and a few other selections. There is also **a coffeeshop in Wilson Commons**. Douglass has a grill, pizza, deli, rotisserie chicken, quesadillas, burritos, and a few other things. After eating on campus for a while, most people seem to get tired of the food."

Q "Stick with The Meliora and the Club Express—they're **faster and tastier than anyplace** else."

STUDENT AUTHOR: The lack of variety and low quality of food are the top two complaints by students. Meliora, the sit-down style dining area, is the best of the worst, but has limited hours—if you have class during the lunch hours, you're pretty much out of luck. The Pit is convenient, but it's the lowest rung on the ladder for food quality. UR Dining still has far to travel in terms of decent food (and acceptable prices) on campus and satisfied students. Many are angry that tuition must be so high, only to be given less-than-mediocre choices for food at high prices.

Student Body

African American:	4%	Male/Female:	48/52%
Asian American:	11%	Out-of-State:	37%
Hispanic:	4%	International:	4%
Native American:	<1%	Unknown:	15%
White:	77%		

Popular Faiths: Students mostly follow Catholic, Jewish, Hindu, Muslim, and Protestant faiths.

Gay Pride: There have been a few incidents with hate and discrimination, but the gay community is fairly visible. An organization called the Pride Network is active on campus.

Economic Status: Most students come from middle-class backgrounds.

Students Speak Out
ON DORMS

Q "We have freshman housing, so you can't really avoid any dorms. Once you get on campus, you will learn what meets your personal needs. We have **suite living, apartment-style living**, rooms with sinks, and many singles. There are tons of options."

Q "Burton and Crosby are the dream halls, and Hill Court is also pretty good. All of the dorms are decent enough. **Most freshmen live in Sue B.**, which has a lot of storage and nice rooms but is kind of small and crowded."

Q "Depending on how you want to live, different areas **offer different amenities**."

STUDENT AUTHOR: **Rooms can be arranged in a multitude of ways, so there's bound to be a way all roommates can be comfortable in their living space, with lofting beds and furniture-arranging. Rooms are guaranteed freshman and sophomore year, so there are no worries about whether housing will be available or not. Everyone agrees the quad dorms are the most desirable; there are some palace-like singles with in-room sinks right in the middle of it all on campus.**

Did You Know?
85% of undergrads live on campus.

Students Speak Out
ON GUYS & GIRLS

Q "We have an **overall good-looking campus**, but there's a big group of awkward girls and guys, a large section of generally attractive people, and a handful of hot guys and girls."

Q "Just about the entire student body is very **friendly and pretty easy to get along with**."

Q "Guys on campus are mid-range hot; there is not a whole lot of out-of-the-ballpark gorgeousness, but there are **lots of nice, sensitive guys** who are good to be friends with."

Q "There are some hot guys. There are attractive girls, too. I'd say, overall, it's a pretty attractive campus. But even more than that, **the people are just plain cool**."

STUDENT AUTHOR: **There is a geeky constituency, seeing that it is a science-intensive school, but there are a fair share of attractive guys. Intellectually, there is a good chance of finding a guy who is not lacking in the brains department. The girls tend to be attractive, and very put together. They are described in the middle scale of attractiveness. Everyone finds everyone else is friendly, so if nothing else, we all play well with others.**

Traditions

Boar's Head Dinner
Held since 1934, students gather for a traditional medieval times dinner served by the student choir.

Meliora Weekend
Alumni reunions, Parents Weekend, Homecoming, and the Stonehurst Regatta all in one weekend.

Overall School Spirit
Students will gladly wear UR gear around campus, but when it comes to attending games and cheering on their classmates, attendance is minimal. But UR students genuinely love where they go to school.

Students Speak Out
ON ATHLETICS

Q "Rochester is a Division III school, and sports are **not a big deal at all here**. Men's basketball is the most popular among the students, and there's usually a pretty good crowd at their games. Football is probably second-most popular, but most people who go to their games are from the community rather than students."

Q "Varsity sports are actually presenting excellent teams that are competitive and successful in the leagues. Unfortunately **school spirit is low** reflecting in firstly attendance and also general opinion."

Q "**IM sports are active**, but treated very much like pick-up games that happen to be scheduled. It's laid-back and fun."

STUDENT AUTHOR: **The general feeling on sports is there is not much reason to support UR varsity athletics. There is a large amount of students that participate in sports themselves, there's just not that many people watching. UR also does not give athletic scholarships, so no superstars show up. Intramurals are a way for students to stay active even if it's not participating in a varsity sport.**

Students Speak Out
ON DRUG SCENE

Q "**Some people smoke pot**, but other than that, there's not much. Alcohol is fairly easy to obtain, but there isn't really any pressure to drink if you don't want to. The drug scene is not very big on campus, though I'm sure if someone was interested, they could find what they want."

Q "There are definitely many students who do drugs, but it is **not a forefront activity** of the campus."

Q "There **aren't a lot of hard drugs**, and those who do smoke up are pretty discreet about it. It would be quite possible to ignore it entirely."

STUDENT AUTHOR: Security does enforce the policies, and if students are caught, it is dealt with accordingly. Each person recognizes that the other is old enough to make their own decisions about their choice of lifestyle, and as a result, people hang out with those similar to them, and it's no big deal. Marijuana is the drug of choice for UR students, similar to most colleges. There is harder drug use, but this is even less prevalent.

9:1	Student-to-Faculty Ratio
96%	Freshman Retention Rate
66%	Four-Year Graduation Rate
91%	Financial Aid Applicants Receiving Aid

Students Speak Out
SAFETY & SECURITY

Q "Security and safety on campus is **a major priority for the school**."

Q "There are **blue phones all over** the place that connect directly to security if you are in trouble. If one of the phones is off the hook, Security goes directly there. They are pretty nice and helpful."

Q "All the residence halls have card readers, so no one without a University of Rochester ID card can get in. There have been a couple of isolated incidents, minor thefts, over the course of these four years, the kind of thing you'd expect to find anywhere, but we have Security that patrols around and also students who work as security aides at night. I **never feel uncomfortable walking across campus alone** at any time day."

STUDENT AUTHOR: The crime rate on campus remains low, and students feel safe walking around campus at any time of day. Security is occasionally strict. Students feel comfortable walking around at any hour of the night, and there are multiple ways to contact security in the event of an emergency.

Questions?
For more inside information and survival tips, pick up College Prowler's full-length book on this school, written by an actual student! Check it out at *www.collegeprowler.com*.

Students Speak Out
ON OVERALL EXPERIENCE

Q "The people are great. The reason I chose here was because I loved the atmosphere so much. The campus is also beautiful, and I wouldn't want to be anywhere else. I **feel very academically challenged here**, even though they give a ton of work. It makes me feel rewarded."

Q "The weather is lousy, but I would have a hard time finding a better school for academics both in terms of quality and **freedom to study what I want**. Learning here is really easy and really fun. The amount of student activities and groups are also incredible."

Q "As a school it's a great place, unfortunately the school tends to **totally ignore the needs of students outside the classroom**."

Q "I am very happy here. I **like how the campus is set up and the fact that it is not a huge school**. The atmosphere is very nice, and the student body is very friendly. I guess the social life could be a little better, but it is not tough to find something to do."

STUDENT AUTHOR: The strong suits of academics and atmosphere make UR a perfect fit for many. Even if it takes a while to adjust and find your niche, once you do, you will easily fall in love with the school. Beyond the food and small inconveniences, UR comes out ahead for student approval. The student body as a whole is intelligent and ambitious, and the faculty are talented and welcoming. Rochester itself also provides an interesting melting pot, and if you look, you will never run out of places to go or things to do. The weather can get you down and the classes may seem unending and tough, but if you take a step back, you'll realize you're glad to go to UR and it has become home.

University of San Diego

5998 Alcala Park; San Diego, CA 92110
(619) 260-4600; www.sandiego.edu

THE BASICS:

Acceptance Rate: 52%   **SAT Range:** 1650–1930*
Setting: Urban   **Control:** Private
F-T Undergrads: 4,909   **Tuition:** $35,870

Most Popular Majors: Business, Social Sciences,
Communications, Psychology, Biology

*of 2400

Academics	B	Guys	A-
Local Atmosphere	A-	Girls	A+
Safety & Security	A-	Athletics	B-
Computers	B-	Nightlife	A-
Facilities	A-	Greek Life	C+
Campus Dining	B+	Drug Scene	C+
Off-Campus Dining	A-	Campus Strictness	C
Campus Housing	B+	Parking	B-
Off-Campus Housing	B+	Transportation	C+
Diversity	B-	Weather	A+

Students Speak Out
ON ACADEMICS

Q "The teachers are concerned with the students as individuals and **want each student to succeed**. The majority of the classes are interesting."

Q "I have found that some teachers play favorites, however, the majority of my classes have been decent. **Some majors are easier than others**."

Q "GEs (general education classes) are always going to be a drag. **I really struggled with some of them** just because they have nothing to do with my majors. The teachers are all really helpful, though. You have to listen to them and really do everything they ask in order to get an A."

Q "To be honest, only come here if you have a scholarship. It has been my experience that the **faculty is not top-rate**, and the school is not worth spending the money on."

Q "Sometimes USD teachers give **a pretty heavy workload, which can be grueling**, but that can also be avoided if you research and choose the right professors."

STUDENT AUTHOR: **Everything about academics at USD looks good, but we all know that sometimes looks can be deceiving. On the positive side, students recognize that USD professors are at the top of their fields and take a genuine interest in meeting students' needs. Class sizes are incredibly small. Some students feel passed over for the needs more interactive classmates.**

Students Speak Out
ON LOCAL ATMOSPHERE

Q "It's **laid-back and sunny**. San Diegans are your typical Southern Californians; they like to do their thing and then hang out and have fun."

Q "There are two other major universities in the San Diego area, but there are even more in the surrounding cities. University of California at San Diego, San Diego State University, Cal State San Marcos, and Mesa College, are the big draws, but other smaller community colleges populate the area. **San Diego is a great town**. It's a half-hour trolley ride to Mexico (Tijuana) that has both day and night activities."

Q "If students visit Mexico, it's important to go in a coed group, especially at night; and **the larger the size, the safer**."

Q "It seems like **you can always find something to do or something to visit** in San Diego. If you haven't done all the touristy things, you have to in order to experience the full culture of San Diego. It's good to make friends with some natives because they can let you know about all the cool things to do that might not be widely advertised, but are definitely worth your while."

STUDENT AUTHOR: **A young city filled with students from all over and a friendly, laid-back native population, San Diego is a student paradise characterized by near limitless variety. Wild San Diego State parties rage throughout the nights, and enormous beach barbecues and friendly athletic events populate the days. Finally, there is the beach.**

5 Best Things

1. The beach
2. Dorm life
3. The guys and girls
4. The weather
5. Close-knit classmates

5 Worst Things

1. Mandatory attendance
2. Parking
3. San Diego traffic
4. Cost of tuition
5. Dating in Camino

Students Speak Out
ON FACILITIES

"The **facilities are very nice**, especially the new science and tech building."

"All the facilities are very nice; **they are maintained very well**. We pay an insane amount of money to care for the grass and flowers every year. The gym is nice, they just built it five or six years ago. It is really big and there are lots of machines and weights."

"It's the most beautiful campus you'll ever set foot on. It has **beautifully-landscaped gardens** and peaceful Spanish-style facades."

"The facilities are good now and getting better. The gym is new. They also just built the Peace and Justice Center where they hold a lot of cool events. Lots of big-time politicians can be seen around campus from time to time. They are also built a new science building that has all the latest technology. **The computer labs are nothing special and neither is the student center**, but I don't have any complaints about them."

"All of the facilities on campus **have new equipment and are really nice**."

STUDENT AUTHOR: In a city known for its beautiful environment, USD stands out above the crowd. USD feels more like an elite country club or retreat than a college campus. Students often fall in love with their surroundings on day one. The one legitimate complaint about USD may be its size. It is a small campus, and popular buildings can be overcrowded, especially the gym. Few people would mind if USD were just a little bigger.

Famous Alumni

Bill Bavasi, Theo Epstein, Andrew Firestone, Taylor McKegney, Eric Musselman, Petie Ynachulova

Students Speak Out
ON CAMPUS DINING

"It's **very good, actually**. The staff at the University Center dining room is wonderful, and they have great food."

"The food is very good, no complaints here. Besides the cafeteria, there's the Torero Grille and the deli and bakery. **The dining hall is very nice** and meal cards work at all those places as well."

"Oh man, the food is bad. I mean if you are in the mood for a snack then I would say it's alright, but **if you are looking for a meal, keep looking**."

"Dining services is **very receptive to student suggestions on new food** and set-ups. They also continue to work so that the dining facilities are nice in appearance and have all the things us students want from them."

"I think the food at USD compared to the other college campuses I have visited is phenomenal! **The Main Dining Hall has great variety**— Mexican day in the caf is great. La Paloma has healthy, hearty sandwiches, salads."

STUDENT AUTHOR: Students find the food on the USD campus surprisingly good. There are six different places to eat in the University Center, and you are likely to see a large portion of your 5,000 or so schoolmates pass through there during lunch, munching on a sandwich or burger. La Paloma is perhaps the favorite spot. Meal plans may be used at the caf, La Paloma, Torero Grill, and the Deli. This flexibility leads many students to vary their meals during the week.

Student Body

African American:	2%	Male/Female:	42/58%
Asian American:	10%	Out-of-State:	40%
Hispanic:	14%	International:	3%
Native American:	1%	Unknown:	6%
White:	63%		

Popular Faiths: This is a Catholic school, and there are some very large Christian organizations.

Gay Pride: There are a significant number of gay students at USD, and the student body as a whole is very laid-back and tolerant.

Economic Status: Most students at USD are from wealthy backgrounds.

Students Speak Out
ON DORMS

Q "The dorms are okay. Camino/Founders, Maher, Vistas, and the Valley are all older dorms, but they are pretty nice. Manchester Village is awesome, and **there is an opportunity to have your own room**."

Q "The **dorms are pretty nice** if you get the Valley. I have always had on-campus apartments, which have been really big and nice."

Q "**The communal bathroom is nice** to have because it gives you the opportunity to talk to people on your floor and catch up with people. Some rooms are singles (quite small) and the rest are doubles but can be converted into triples without excessive crowding."

STUDENT AUTHOR: **Campus housing at USD is pretty good. Students know they have a good thing going, but they definitely have their favorites, and for the most part, it's Maher. Camino/Founders, the infamous "Virgin Vault," at least provides for an interesting conversation piece if not a dating challenge. Missions A and B in the Valley are very nice dorms; they are just a little farther away from classes.**

Did You Know?
49% of undergrads live on campus.

Students Speak Out
ON GUYS & GIRLS

Q "I've never seen more beautiful people than I have at USD. **Not only do we have quantity**, but quality as well. Hugh Hefner should just set up a booth on campus."

Q "There are definitely a lot of attractive people at our school. **There are lots of pretty girls**; unfortunately there are more attractive girls than guys."

Q "I feel like I keep repeating myself. If you want to see girls wearing a lack of clothing San Diego is the place to be. **USD equals white, upper-class beauties**."

Q "The **guys are cool**, and the girls are beautiful."

STUDENT AUTHOR: **USD students are definitely the closest thing you will find to an Aaron Spelling television campus in real life. And they know it. Not very many students have a complaint about how their classmates' looks. The guys are all very fit, active, and extremely well groomed for college kids. Students find the girls are generally blonde and beautiful and have impossible figures. Some students also find that there are too many girls.**

Traditions

Father Serra Foot Massage for Luck
Rub the toes of the statue in front of Serra Hall, and all will become clear.

Harbor Cruises
You will probably experience a harbor cruise on the big bay of San Diego.

Overall School Spirit
"Torero Pride" is often a sardonic cry from students, who are usually the first to mock their small size and major conference ineptitude. USD students will, however, defend their school to any outsider.

Students Speak Out
ON ATHLETICS

Q "Some sports are big like football and basketball. **IM sports are very big**; there are lots of people who are involved in them."

Q "USD is trying to increase student excitement about varsity sports by giving away free stuff, and you know that college students can't pass up free stuff, so **more people are going to the games**."

Q "**Basketball gets pretty intense** come tourney time. There are lots of IM sports."

Q "The only athletics to worry about are **keg-stands and surfing**."

Q "This is **not a big sports school** at all."

STUDENT AUTHOR: **Torero mania clearly has not taken hold of the students on the USD campus. The size of the school, and the fact that it is not considered a big time "athletic" program, definitely hurt its ability to draw fans in an era where everyone expects national championships. Students who follow their teams know that while they will most assuredly lose when Kansas comes to town to play basketball, but it's never really a walk in the park for the big boys.**

Students Speak Out
ON DRUG SCENE

Q "**There is some drug use** such as marijuana, and I've heard of people doing cocaine, too."

Q "I can't really comment too much; **most students drink on the weekends**, and some smoke marijuana, but other than that, I don't really have any idea."

Q "Everyone smokes weed. **Other drugs are not as common** at all, though."

Q "I personally don't do drugs, and never have, but there is some of that on campus. **There are a lot of rich kids**, so what do you expect?"

STUDENT AUTHOR: Here's the obvious thing about drugs at USD: students don't like to talk about them very much. Most students do not feel adversely affected by the presence of drugs and aren't bothered by the occasional use they may witness. Very few USD students feel that it is difficult to avoid drugs if they so desire. Students seem to think that what drug use exists is not a problem or danger to their daily lives.

15:1	Student-to-Faculty Ratio
85%	Freshman Retention Rate
64%	Four-Year Graduation Rate
84%	Financial Aid Applicants Receiving Aid

Students Speak Out
SAFETY & SECURITY

Q "It's pretty safe; there are break-ins of cars on campus, but it's probably just drunk college kids. **No big crime really happens** on campus—it's pretty safe."

Q "**Public Safety is a student's enemy**. They do whatever they can to send students to detox."

Q "**Security is extremely tight**. Public Safety does regular rounds to make sure everything is safe, and they have lighted telephone distress stations all over campus. There are also two extensions for the office of public safety, one for emergencies, and one to report disturbances, like noise or a car alarm."

Q "There are a lot of security officers always on call, and **you feel safe on campus**."

STUDENT AUTHOR: Students feel USD's small, familiar community plays a large part in keeping the campus safe. Campus crime has been limited to primarily burglaries and petty theft. Keen-eyed security members guard the two main entrances, and students are aware of a gated community feel.

Questions?
For more inside information and survival tips, pick up College Prowler's full-length book on this school, written by an actual student! Check it out at *www.collegeprowler.com.*

Students Speak Out
ON OVERALL EXPERIENCE

Q "I love USD! **I'm so happy** that I decided to come here."

Q "I had a hard time my freshman year at USD because **there isn't a college community around campus** and it is hard to meet people. Once I joined a sorority and moved off campus, I became much happier."

Q "**I love USD**. You have to find your niche and then you will be set. It's a great school to grow and learn and have fun altogether."

Q "Sometimes **I wish I went to a bigger school** where everyone doesn't know each other."

Q "It was good. I graduated in May, and by the end I was sorry to leave. I wanted to transfer my freshman year. **I hated it**, and I think a lot of people share that same sentiment. Luckily for me, I found a wonderful friend that I survived the four years with. I had fun with my job and my club activities, and once I found my niche I finally felt comfortable and got more out of it than others might."

STUDENT AUTHOR: It's hard to imagine a comparable experience to USD. By the end of four years, everyone has done so much growing and changing, and it's hard to tell how much of it depends on the University, your friends, yourself, and just blind luck. Whatever it is, the majority of USD students love their lives at USD. Sure they complain a little, but when asked about overall satisfaction, students have nothing but superlatives for their school. Beach life can become addictive, and for some, it is impossible to leave under any circumstances. Few people look back on their days at USD with regret.

University of San Francisco

2130 Fulton Street; San Francisco, CA 94117
(415) 422-5555; www.usfca.edu

Academics	B-	Guys	B-
Local Atmosphere	A	Girls	B+
Safety & Security	B	Athletics	C+
Computers	B	Nightlife	A-
Facilities	B	Greek Life	D+
Campus Dining	B	Drug Scene	C+
Off-Campus Dining	A+	Campus Strictness	B-
Campus Housing	B-	Parking	D-
Off-Campus Housing	B-	Transportation	A-
Diversity	A	Weather	A-

Students Speak Out
ON ACADEMICS

Q "Those teachers in my major have been **consistently wonderful**; I have found a few boring lecturers in required classes (namely European history and natural science)."

Q "Overall, the **teachers are quite good**. The young ones seem genuinely eager to mold their students into great people and the old ones seem comfortable in their well-worn-but-can't-miss routine."

Q "More often than not, the teachers are weird. If not weird, **they're definitely not normal**."

Q "Most of the teachers I have had have been very encouraging to my own personal well being and improvement as a writer; they have flexible office hours and are always more than happy to talk. Most of the teachers are **excellent mentors, as well as friends**."

Q "The teachers are competent, fair, and understanding. There are lots with accents, too, so **they can be hard to understand** sometimes."

STUDENT AUTHOR: At a school like USF, academics often take a back seat to the city and often times, the religious preference of the school. But the professors are one of the most important and inspirational parts of USF. Because the school is relatively small, it is extremely easy to get to know your professors on a personal level. The best thing to do at USF is to take advantage of office hours and get to know the professors.

Students Speak Out
ON LOCAL ATMOSPHERE

Q "I love this city. There are a million things to do and **a million little subcultures** to get into. You can do all the touristy stuff your heart desires, and most of it is honestly worth doing. The city is the best part of being at USF."

Q "City life is **busy but incredibly fun**. Visit downtown, the parks, and the museum, but stay away from bad areas like Hunter's Point, Tenderloin, and Mission Street at night."

Q "There are other universities around, but we don't have a rivalry or anything. There are three art schools, which make for a lot of pretentiously dressed people in bars. **I've met Berkeley people through internships**, but not really otherwise."

Q "The city of San Francisco is very tolerant and liberal. There are **people of all walks of life** here; college students (USF and others), adults, kids, everything."

STUDENT AUTHOR: San Francisco, large and bustling as it may be, provides an excellent backdrop for the university. Whenever school becomes too stressful, students can always escape to their favorite off-campus site. Also, the abundance of history, beauty, and culture makes classroom activities more tangible and relevant; often classes take field trips to the city's museums or historical sites, as well as perform community service and work with the homeless. If you're looking for a fun, exciting, cultural, and hands-on experience, San Francisco is definitely the place to be.

5 Best Things
1. San Francisco
2. Size of the school
3. Aesthetics of campus
4. Diversity
5. Quality of teaching

5 Worst Things
1. Cost of tuition
2. Parking
3. Lack of school spirit
4. Lack of parties on campus
5. Four-unit system

Students Speak Out
ON FACILITIES

Q "**Everything here is very up-to-date**. Computers, though I know nothing about them, are always speedy and easy to use, and the Koret Center facility is very nice. It has every kind of work out equipment anyone would ever need. The University Center is fun, too. It has a lounge, cafeteria, Jamba Juice, and a café. I spend a lot of time there."

Q "A variety of adequate facilities are available, most notably **an excellent gym**."

Q "Koret is a beautiful, gigantic health center, something to rave about in a big city like San Francisco. The computer labs and computers **could be nicer or more high-tech**, along with Parina Lounge, the campus common room."

Q "**Everything is pretty nice**, though sometimes, things are a little dingy in high-traffic areas. For the most part, there's nothing to worry about."

Q "The facilities are good, for the most part. Some of the buildings are getting pretty old and a few of the elevators get stuck at times. However, it seems that **a lot of renovating is being done**, so hopefully that all will be taken care of soon."

STUDENT AUTHOR: As far as buildings go, the majority of the campus is fairly old. Only the library, Koret Recreation Center, and Saint Ignatius Church appear new and refurbished; however, that is not to say the older buildings aren't aesthetically pleasing as well. The problem with the older buildings shows most on the inside. Students tend to complain that the dorms have an unpleasant odor and that the facilities are generally run-down or outdated.

Famous People from San Francisco:

Benjamin Bratt, Joe DiMaggio, Clint Eastwood, Robert Frost, Jerry Garcia, Danny Glover, Merv Griffin, Josh Hartnett, Jack London, Robin Williams

Students Speak Out
ON CAMPUS DINING

Q "The cafeteria food is **not too bad, but it's quite pricey**. Crossroads and Jamba Juice are quite affordable, but, other than that, I would pack my lunch."

Q "Campus food is good; however, a couple months with **the same menu can get tiring**. One can only take so many bagels, burritos, pre-made sandwiches, and pizza."

Q "The food is good, but **ridiculously expensive**. It doesn't make any sense."

Q "One of my friends told me that USF has the **best cafeteria among schools in the Bay Area**. World Fare offers different kinds of food, ranging from Chinese, western, vegetarian, and fast food. They have fruits, juices, cereals, pastries, ice cream, and yogurt. The only drawback is that the food can be too expensive."

Q "Food on campus is **horrible, apart from Jamba Juice**."

STUDENT AUTHOR: Campus dining at USF is a completely different experience than it was a few years ago. The company Bon Appétit handles every single food-related franchise on campus. Dining on campus offers many options, and only organic items are used; however, the prices reflect the quality. (Some say it's worth it, though.) Most students complain about the food on campus, but that dissatisfaction comes from repetition; because USF is a relatively small school, there are only a handful of places to eat. Fortunately, San Francisco has a million excellent restaurants, so you can always take a break from campus dining.

Student Body

African American:	5%	Male/Female:	36/64%
Asian American:	26%	Out-of-State:	24%
Hispanic:	13%	International:	7%
Native American:	<1%	Unknown:	1%
White:	48%		

Popular Faiths: All religions are represented throughout campus.

Gay Pride: Like San Francisco, USF is safe and accepting of its gay population. Students are encouraged to be open about their sexuality.

Economic Status: There seems to be a good amount of wealthy students.

Students Speak Out
ON DORMS

Q "Dorms are **a good thing to experience**. You get to meet all the students your age, and most likely that's where you will meet many of the friends that will stick with you after graduation. Make sure to bring shower slippers and a small fridge, if you can find one. Renting them isn't too expensive, though."

Q "The sophomore dorms smell, but it's good to live in the residence halls for the great experience. Lone Mountain is **great, clean, and fairly big**."

Q "Dorms are cool, but get old after the second year. While they are **good for social networking**, it's difficult to deal with no privacy and minimal personal space constantly."

STUDENT AUTHOR: **Living on campus is one of the most important experiences any college student can have. Most students make life-long friends from their roommates and hallmates; they share in the experience of all-nighters and group study sessions together. As any student can tell you, living on campus is also incredibly convenient.**

Did You Know?
48% of undergrads live on campus.

Students Speak Out
ON GUYS & GIRLS

Q "The guys are okay; they're not really that hot, though, and there are not too many of them. The ones that are hot are the athletes, but **they can be conceited**. The girls are fine, but there are too many of them."

Q "The girls are, by and large, smart, beautiful, exotic, and **way out of my league**."

Q "**Everyone is pretty trendy**, whether it's trendy-normal or trendy-in-their-own-style."

Q "There are a lot of attractive guys, but a lot of them are gay. It is San Francisco, after all! Also, the last time I heard, the ratio of women to men was 70:30—so **good luck ladies**!"

STUDENT AUTHOR: **For the most part, USF is an attractive campus with attractive people. Lots of the students dress to impress. Students at USF often complain about the ratio of girls to guys and the lack of available hotties to choose from, which stems from the fact that USF is a small school. Fortunately, as most will agree, the number of undergraduates has nothing on the number of attractive and intriguing people on campus.**

Urban Legends

Lone Mountain Ghost
Lone Mountain is said to be haunted by the ghost of a nun who killed herself.

USF Cemetery
USF is built on top of a cemetery and allegedly not all of the bodies were moved.

Overall School Spirit
While almost every student at USF owns some article of clothing bearing the USF logo, school spirit is practically nonexistent.

Students Speak Out
ON ATHLETICS

Q "Intramurals are pretty popular at USF. If there is a sport you enjoy, definitely **try to participate in the IMs**. Soccer, basketball, baseball, and volleyball are also popular."

Q "It's **not really a sports school**, though they are competitive, and you can see some good games, as well as some big-name schools. They're pretty fun, particularly when people come out to the games."

Q "Varsity sports aren't huge, but we support the Dons. **Intramural sports are easy to get in** and a lot of fun."

Q "There's an undeniable apathy about sports at USF. **School spirit is practically nonexistent**. Many people do intramurals, though."

STUDENT AUTHOR: **School spirit and sports at USF are a catch-22. Because there is little school spirit, students heavily involved in the sports scene at USF are few and far between. Because there are few Dons sports fans at USF, there isn't much school spirit. The best thing for any newcomer to do is to check out at least one game at USF, and then decide if the whole Dons scene is your thing.**

Students Speak Out
ON DRUG SCENE

Q "I have never had an experience with drugs on campus, and **I have never been offered drugs**. I do think, though, a lot of that has to do with the people I surround myself with."

Q "There is **plenty of weed** and a good amount of other fashion drugs, which can be easily obtained in a liberal, 'hippie' city like SF."

Q "It depends on who you hang out with, just like anywhere else. There are crowds that are heavily into everything, one drug, or just heavily into drinking. There are **even people strictly sober**. Pick the one that fits you best."

Q "I'm guessing the drug scene is **just like at any other university**."

STUDENT AUTHOR: **While the consequences are tough, anyone who has ever lived in the dorms will tell you that weed is a popular drug at USF and smelling it in the halls is not uncommon. The good news is that the drug scene is not terribly predominant, and few students ever feel pressured into taking drugs.**

14:1	Student-to-Faculty Ratio
85%	Freshman Retention Rate
46%	Four-Year Graduation Rate
66%	Financial Aid Applicants Receiving Aid

Students Speak Out
SAFETY & SECURITY

Q "I have never felt unsafe on campus. It's open, and usually, there are a lot of people around, but there are also emergency poles. You push a button, and **15 seconds later, security is there**. Public Safety is great and dependable."

Q "Public Safety kind of slacks off at times, but for the most part, I'd say **the campus is pretty safe**."

Q "Fairly good. **We get the occasional vagrant**, but they're pretty harmless. Nevertheless, it's easy (and bad) to forget that we are in a city, and there's always a measure of insecurity that comes with that."

Q "The **campus is very secure** with 24-hour public safety."

STUDENT AUTHOR: **USF Public Safety has an important influence on campus life. While some incidents are unavoidable and inevitable, Public Safety does its very best to give the campus and its students a safe, secure environment. Officers patrol the campus 24 hours a day.**

> **Questions?**
> For more inside information and survival tips, pick up College Prowler's full-length book on this school, written by an actual student! Check it out at *www.collegeprowler.com*.

Students Speak Out
ON OVERALL EXPERIENCE

Q "I like USF, and I'm not planning on transferring. However, **it is definitely a financial burden**, especially because they raise the tuition almost every other year."

Q "I love this city. The school has been pretty great. Some of my professors are really wonderful and have helped me a lot. **I'm planning on staying in San Francisco**, and I'm glad I had time in college to get to know the city a little. I feel like I'm at home here now (after four years) and that I've gained some skills."

Q "**I could not have made a better choice** for a university. My four years here are almost up, and I can definitely say it's been a fun ride. Oh yeah, and the education is great, too!"

Q "Overall, I would say that it has been a very good time at USF, with a good diversity of experiences. Going to **college in a big city is something I would recommend**, particularly if you want to do things apart from the school at times. The education is good, just try to find something you like to do and learn about. Personally, I am glad I am here, because I think that at a bigger school, I may have been lost in the crowd a bit."

STUDENT AUTHOR: **USF gives its students the opportunity to enjoy both the intimacy of a small college experience and life in the big city. When the campus feels too consuming or school work becomes too demanding, San Francisco provides an amazing release. Students here take advantage of the different cultures, views, restaurants, museums, and nightlife of the surrounding city. In the end, USF students find nothing better than this stunning combination of an amazing university and the city of San Francisco.**

University of South Carolina

1500 Pendleton Street; Columbia, SC 29208
(803) 777-7000; www.sc.edu

THE BASICS:

Acceptance Rate: 59%
Setting: Mid-sized city
F-T Undergrads: 18,289

SAT Range: 1080–1280*
Control: Public
Tuition: $21,232

Most Popular Majors: Business, Social Sciences, Communications, Biology, Psychology

*of 1600

Academics	B	Guys	B
Local Atmosphere	B+	Girls	A
Safety & Security	B	Athletics	B+
Computers	B+	Nightlife	A-
Facilities	A-	Greek Life	B+
Campus Dining	A-	Drug Scene	B
Off-Campus Dining	A-	Campus Strictness	B-
Campus Housing	B-	Parking	B
Off-Campus Housing	B+	Transportation	A-
Diversity	C	Weather	B+

Students Speak Out
ON ACADEMICS

Q "All of the teachers that I had thus far have been tremendous. They are willing to meet with you and give you as much help as you need. They will **meet with you during their office hours** or set up another time."

Q "Some teachers are fantastic, and a few are terrible. Many are extremely intelligent and **knowledgeable but just not very interesting**. The key is to do your research before signing up for classes."

Q "USC is a big school, though, so **there isn't always a lot of personal help** unless your classes have a graduate student TA."

Q "I've liked most of my teachers. I was interested in most of the honors classes that I took, but I didn't really like the non-honors classes. Also, **discussion-based classes are 10 times better** than lecture classes."

STUDENT AUTHOR: It seems impossible for students to categorize the teachers at here as good or bad. The difficulty is that the students have a range of preferences when it comes to teaching methods. While some think that the best teachers are the ones that give them an easy A, others prefer a challenge. There are all kinds of teachers with varying teaching methods and levels of personal involvement with the students. Academic advisers are helpful when trying to find out information about particular teachers, but sometimes students are forced to rely on word of mouth.

Students Speak Out
ON LOCAL ATMOSPHERE

Q "This is the South. **The biggest adjustment is a cultural one**. The people are incredibly warm and friendly (almost suspiciously so to an outsider), and you have to deal with the eccentricities and the sometimes backwards thinking."

Q "I love Columbia! It's a great place, and we are only **two hours from the mountains and two hours from the beach**! Charleston is a great place to go."

Q "It is a busy campus. There are relaxing locations on campus such as the Horseshoe, but other than that, it is a **'go, go, go' atmosphere**."

Q "Since South Carolina is one of the original slave states, there are different cities you can visit that still have **historical houses and things for you to look at**. In Columbia, there's a pretty cool museum. And downtown Columbia has historic houses."

STUDENT AUTHOR: Located in the heart of Columbia, many students are delighted by the mix of Southern charm on campus and the fast pace of the urban setting. The campus grounds are scattered with gorgeous greenery and secluded gardens. USC also harbors a vast array of historical treasures. Being in the South and smack in the middle of the "Bible belt," there is a lot of conservative thinking. This appeals to some and frustrates others. Many are also involved in the political scene. Students make their voices heard.

5 Best Things	5 Worst Things
1 Football games	1 Parking
2 Cocky the mascot	2 Tuition increases
3 Int'l Business School	3 Close-minded people
4 Honors College	4 Hot summers
5 Fitness Center	5 Incompetent advisors

Students Speak Out
ON FACILITIES

Q "The Russell House is the student union, and there's quite a lot to do there—a lot goes on there. Often, they show **free movies at the Russell House Theater** before they even come out, and there's always free fun stuff to do."

Q "I think that the new gym is the largest workout gym in the whole state; it also **has an Olympic-sized pool**! The student center has restaurants, and lots of people are always there."

Q "Campus facilities at USC are amazing. The **recreational center is a phenomenon**. It's up-to-date equipment and technology make it easy for any student to come and go at their own convenience. Academic tutoring is another one of USC's perks."

Q "The new gym is really nice and has something for everyone to enjoy. The **library has so many resources for students** to use."

Q We also built a coliseum for our basketball teams that brings **great events and concerts** to the University."

STUDENT AUTHOR: **Students seem to be very satisfied overall. The Strom Thurmond Wellness and Fitness Center houses five basketball courts, an indoor and outdoor pool, an indoor track, a climbing wall, and strength training equipment. Students really enjoy taking advantage of the long hours and brand new equipment in this multi-million-dollar facility. The Russell House University Union is where students get food, check their mail, get tickets for sporting events, watch movies, and attend group events.**

Famous Alumni

Andrew Card Jr., Alex English, Leeza Gibbons, Charles Frazier, Jim Hoagland, Hootie and the Blowfish, Robert C. McNair, Dan Reeves

Students Speak Out
ON CAMPUS DINING

Q "**I love the food**! There are like 20 different places to eat on campus. You hardly ever get tired of it. And they have this thing where you can eat at a bunch of off-campus restaurants as well."

Q "There is great food! We have main restaurant chains, and we also have many cafeterias with numerous buffet lines with things like pasta, stir-fry, salads, hamburgers, chicken, subs, and **anything you want**—it's available."

Q "The food is all right. It's better than some cafeteria food. **The GMP has decent food**, though toward the end of the year, it gets really old."

Q "Food on campus ranges from average to good. **It's not fantastic**, but it's not bad either. The main student union in the middle of campus contains everything."

Q "The food is decent. A few **dorms have cafeterias in them**."

STUDENT AUTHOR: **Chicken Finger Wednesday! Yes, USC students do get excited about their chicken fingers. But, if for some reason chicken fingers don't tantalize your taste buds, there are plenty of other options. The Russell House University Union has the biggest variety of food options. It houses an Italian cuisine restaurant, a sub place, a juice bar, several fast food restaurants, and the Grand Market Place. Students generally seem to rate the food on campus anywhere from average to good.**

Student Body

African American:	12%	Male/Female:	45/55%
Asian American:	3%	Out-of-State:	24%
Hispanic:	2%	International:	1%
Native American:	<1%	Unknown:	9%
White:	72%		

Popular Faiths: Christianity is by far the most prominent religion on campus. There are a lot of religious clubs and organizations, most of which are Christian-oriented.

Gay Pride: Anti-gay sentiments are not expressed visibly at USC, but this may be in part because the gay population remains relatively quiet.

Economic Status: The majority of USC students are middle- to upper-class.

Students Speak Out
ON DORMS

Q "The nicest freshman dorms for girls are Patterson and Bates. The only negative thing about Bates is that it is very **far from campus**."

Q "When you become an upperclassman, I'd recommend East Quad, South Quad, or anything on the Horseshoe—it's **probably the prettiest place on campus**."

Q "You get what you pay for. **You could pay for an elegant room** in the South or East Quad and live like a queen, or you could opt to live in one of the Towers buildings and gag whenever someone uses the restroom in the large communal bathroom."

STUDENT AUTHOR: **There are advantages and disadvantages to living on campus. Most students find that living on campus freshman year allows them the opportunity to interact with students more and get involved in activities without having to worry about commuting. Visitation policies in some dorms can be a hindrance since they restrict members of the opposite sex. There are mandatory hall meetings, rules about quiet hours, and the occasional RA from hell.**

Did You Know?
40% of undergrads live on campus.

Students Speak Out
ON GUYS & GIRLS

Q "Guys are really Southern and **have a great deal of Southern pride**, especially the fraternity guys. They all wear rainbow flip flops, croakies, short khaki shorts, and shaggy haircuts."

Q "The girls from up north are usually pretty nice, but they can also be kind of rude. **Girls from the South are nice and sweet**."

Q "As far as the girls go, there's a lot of eye candy. If you're into girls, there's a whole lot of them. There seems to be a big **stigma here against homosexuals**, though."

Q "**Dating material?** I'm not so sure about that one."

STUDENT AUTHOR: **It's true that down here in South Carolina the weather is sweltering, but the guys and girls are even hotter! According to students, the guys tend to be more chivalrous and charming than the average, and the girls are beautiful, even if many of them may fall into the typical southern belle category. This is not to say that all girls and guys are good-looking. It just depends on what you find attractive.**

Traditions

Tiger Burn
The week before the big Clemson/USC football game, the cheerleaders, pep band, and students come out to get pumped up about the big game.

First Carolina Night
The night after moving in, freshmen are transported by shuttle bus to a secret location where a special program awaits them.

Overall School Spirit
Students at USC are teeming with school spirit, especially during football season. USC T-shirts, shorts, bumper stickers, and caps are seen all around the city.

Students Speak Out
ON ATHLETICS

Q "USC is in the SEC, which is the biggest sports conference in the nation. **Gamecock football is absolutely huge** at USC."

Q "You haven't experienced football until you've gone to a SEC football game in the south. It is the **most ridiculous fun**, even if you aren't a big football fan."

Q "**Football dominates** the varsity sports, but the basketball teams are also very good. IM sports on campus are also pretty good."

Q "There are 80,000 plus people in our stadiums during the games and **over 100,000 people that tailgate**."

STUDENT AUTHOR: **Football is pretty much the focus of the sports calendar for USC students. Students really make a big deal out of tailgating and attending the games, even if they just do it for the social aspect rather than actually watching the game. On the other hand, intramural sports experience minimal fan turn out, but are still a fun way for students to get together and have fun. Anyone can join an intramural team, and there are several to choose from.**

Students Speak Out
ON DRUG SCENE

Q "The only illegal drug you see on campus is weed. A lot of people smoke weed; it's not hard to find. There are a lot of other drugs used, but **people usually keep it on the DL**."

Q "There are a lot of drugs on campus—**a lot of X** (ecstasy) and pot."

Q "Every college campus has its drug scene. You **don't have to look very far** to find someone that uses or knows someone that uses drugs."

Q "If you want something, it can be found, but **it is not the predominant thing** on campus."

STUDENT AUTHOR: **Marijuana is the most common drug of choice, but ecstasy and cocaine are available, as well. The prominence of the drug scene depends on the crowd a student chooses to associate with. When students do choose to get high, they usually do it in privacy with their circle of friends or at parties. You will not see anyone pressuring anyone else into doing drugs.aking money by selling it. But if a student wants the drugs, they are there for the taking.**

16:1	Student-to-Faculty Ratio
87%	Freshman Retention Rate
40%	Four-Year Graduation Rate
73%	Financial Aid Applicants Receiving Aid

Students Speak Out
SAFETY & SECURITY

Q "We have campus police, and you see them riding around on their bikes or in the cars, but unfortunately, **there is crime everywhere**. I think that the security does all they possibly can."

Q "I've never had any problems, but there are some incidents that occur every once in a while. Mostly **everything is pretty well lit**."

Q "There are tons of **emergency boxes spread across campus** that allow anyone to access help from police at any given time."

Q "Security is fine, just don't be stupid and think you're invincible just because you're in college and on your own—stay in groups after dark. **Use your intuition and common sense**."

STUDENT AUTHOR: **Being in the middle of a city, there are dangerous people. However, the University provides a number of services to ensure safety. In addition to the city police force, the USC Police Department (USCPD) patrol campus 24 hours a day.**

Questions?
For more inside information and survival tips, pick up College Prowler's full-length book on this school, written by an actual student! Check it out at *www.collegeprowler.com*.

Students Speak Out
ON OVERALL EXPERIENCE

Q "I've really enjoyed my transition to South Carolina. There is **a lot of school spirit** and plenty of nice people on campus to help you with problems or whatever the case may be. It's a really nice place to be."

Q "The **campus is beautiful**, with oaks, ponds, palmettos, and gardens. It is truly a special place. USC has over 20,000 students, but you cannot go two feet without seeing someone you know."

Q "I think that this is a great school. It's a place where **I feel truly at home**. The people here are extremely friendly and welcoming, which is nice."

Q "I have had a **really good experience here**, but it seems to me that the most important element that dictates your happiness at college is the friends you make."

Q "To be honest, I like USC. In-state tuition is a **good deal for a school of its size and caliber**. I've really enjoyed the past few years here, and I wouldn't take them back. I've enjoyed being educated here."

STUDENT AUTHOR: **If there is one word to describe the experiences you will have at USC, it would have to be unforgettable. Being away from home for the first time is one of the things that makes it so exciting, and even a bit scary at times. As at any college, the quality of the experience depends on what you put into it. There are thousands of new people to meet, there are activities going on, and there are things to learn both in and out of class. But those who don't take advantage of these opportunities will not get a lot out of their experience here.**

University of South Dakota

414 East Clark Street; Vermillion, SD 57069
(877) 269-6837 www.usd.edu

THE BASICS:

Acceptance Rate: 80%
Setting: Rural
F-T Undergrads: 4,456

SAT Range: 910–1130*
Control: Public
Tuition: $11,506

Most Popular Majors: Business, Education, Health Professions, Psychology, Social Sciences

*of 1600

Academics	B	Guys	B
Local Atmosphere	B-	Girls	B-
Safety & Security	A-	Athletics	B+
Computers	B+	Nightlife	B+
Facilities	B-	Greek Life	B+
Campus Dining	B-	Drug Scene	B-
Off-Campus Dining	B	Campus Strictness	B
Campus Housing	C-	Parking	D
Off-Campus Housing	A-	Transportation	C
Diversity	D-	Weather	B-

Students Speak Out
ON ACADEMICS

Q "I like the teachers. **Everyone is professional and very knowledgeable** in his or her field. Some classes are boring, but some are fun and interesting. The political science professors are really energetic and interested in the field, which makes classes a lot more fun and interactive."

Q "Psychology classes are my favorite. **Everyone wants to take 'Psychology of Sex'** before they graduate because it's an interesting class. What they don't realize is that the professor teaching the course is interesting, as well. I've learned a lot more in my major at USD than I did in Nebraska before I transferred."

Q "My favorite part is the emphasis put on critical thinking, which can be **a lot more trying than memorizing some terms** and definitions. It has definitely taught me a lot more. Professors here are big on interaction inside the classrooms, and it greatly benefits the students. They are also really open and honest to students and always willing to help out."

STUDENT AUTHOR: USD is home to an interesting range of faculty, professors, and classes. While most teachers are full-time professors, not all of them have teaching degrees. Freshmen can expect a number of their classes to be rather large and in lecture halls; however, most students never enter the lecture halls after their first year of class. Once into your major, classes will become smaller, usually between 12 and 22 students.

Students Speak Out
ON LOCAL ATMOSPHERE

Q "Other than watering holes and the occasional sporting event, **Vermillion doesn't offer much for entertainment**. Most of my friends and I head to Sioux Falls for entertainment. The cities are much larger and provide many more opportunities."

Q "There is a fantastic atmosphere in Vermillion. **It is very rare that a weekend will come along where there is nothing to do**. The people are very friendly and eager to get to know you. From the music and theater scene to just hanging out, I love staying in town on the weekends."

Q "**When it is nice, the river is a great place to be**. A lot of the students spend afternoons and weekends along the river playing football, swimming, or grilling out. Of course, many of us drink along the banks, too, but you don't need to drink there to have a blast."

Q "Vermillion is a town of college students. It's nice because **most businesses and services cater to students**."

STUDENT AUTHOR: Vermillion has never been considered a large community, which is what makes it so unique. The University is larger than the town and makes up almost half the Vermillion population. Many students would agree that USD's population tends to control the city, especially on the weekends, which typically start on Thursday nights.

Students Speak Out
ON FACILITIES

Q "**Old Main is lovely**, especially at night. It's also nice because it has 'smart' classrooms that can offer Internet access, so teachers can interact better during class hours."

Q "It's the **oldest campus in the state**, what do you expect most of the buildings to look like? Things are outdated, but the atmosphere really seems to make you forget about how old the building you're standing in really is."

Q "**The facilities are either new or ancient**. It's your luck where you have class or choose to hang out. Old Main is nice, and the basement of Noteboom Hall is creepy. My freshman English class was there, and it seemed like a dungeon."

Q "The facilities are nice. **There's not a whole lot to do in the student center**, but it's not too bad. I don't think the Dome's workout area is that great, and the ones in the dorms are pretty sad."

Q "**The DakotaDome is much improved** with recent renovations. I especially like the pictures hanging from the ceiling, and the new locker rooms were well-needed."

STUDENT AUTHOR: USD doesn't have the best campus facilities in the nation. But for a smaller campus in a smaller town, the school offers up-to-date buildings with more remodeling currently taking place. USD may not have any bowling alleys, movie theaters, and convenient stores, but these can all be located within walking distance from campus. The CSC does offer some entertainment, including pool tables and a big-screen TV.

Famous Alumni

Tom Brokaw, Peter Dexter, Doug Einsel, Dorothy Cooper Foote, Tim Johnson, Robert Miller, Greg Nelson, Al Neuharth, Alton Ochsner

Students Speak Out
ON CAMPUS DINING

Q "**Charlie's is probably the best**, because it's quick and they have sandwiches. Plus, they have daily specials that are a little cheaper than the average Charlie's meal, and they have pizza and sometimes calzones ready to go."

Q "On-campus food is **deplorable and overpriced**. I hated eating it when I lived in the dorms."

Q "Are you ready to get fat? No, seriously, **just like high school, the food is high in fat content**. Students have really been complaining about it lately, but they haven't gotten anywhere. I ate most of my lunches in my dorm room with my roommate."

Q "The food is definitely a big step up from high school. **The Commons and Lacotah both have good food**, but my favorite is Charlie's for a quick lunch."

Q "**Get as much Flex Money on your meal plan as possible**, because you will use it most of the time. Plus, if you have extra Flex at the end of the semester, you can always stock up on your favorites at the Beede Bump and the Speed Bump."

STUDENT AUTHOR: Honestly, it is probably better than lunch at your local high school, but no one would attempt to put USD dining and Applebee's in the same category. In fact, many students complain about the taste, variety, and price of campus food. Unless you're an athlete or big eater, you will probably want the most Flex Money possible compared to Commons meals on your food plan.

Student Body

African American:	1%	Male/Female:	37/63%
Asian American:	1%	Out-of-State:	30%
Hispanic:	1%	International:	<1%
Native American:	2%	Unknown:	6%
White:	85%		

Popular Faiths: Most students come from Christian-based families, and a large number of the population remains religiously active on campus.

Gay Pride: USD is known in the area for being one of the most accepting schools around when it comes to different sexual preferences.

Economic Status: The majority of students come from middle- to upper-middle-class families.

Students Speak Out
ON DORMS

Q "**The dorms are small**, like most dorms are at any South Dakota university, but they are redoing some of them, and Richardson now is really nice. I would recommend living in the North Complex because it holds the most students."

Q "**Julian has big rooms, but they smell weird**. Don't live in Burgess; all estrogen is never a good thing. Go to the North Complex."

Q "The dorms are dorms, but you can make them nice. **The North Complex is nice** because it has air conditioning. Julian Hall has really big rooms."

STUDENT AUTHOR: **Don't bring a trailer full of stuff on moving day** because you'll only fit a small portion of it into your dorm room. Yes, USD dorms are small and old, but they're a great experience. And while it's true that not much else besides the bed, desk, fridge, and maybe a small couch will fit, you'll find the free cable, Internet, and utilities a big advantage. Most students move off campus after their sophomore year, but some stay on campus, and the University has no rules regarding how long you can live on campus.

> **Did You Know?**
> 31% of undergrads live on campus.

Students Speak Out
ON GUYS & GIRLS

Q "I think **a lot of guys are immature, especially a lot of frat boys**. I guess I wouldn't ever imagine dating a USD guy, and most of my past boyfriends have gone to universities in Iowa or Minnesota. There's nothing wrong with the guys here, they're just more concerned about the social scene than girls."

Q "I can't say I've noticed an overabundance of hot guys. **Some of them are pretty good-looking, but those guys are usually also in the frats**. Most guys at USD seem pretty friendly, though, and quite sincere."

Q "There are almost two girls for every guy; you can't go wrong with that. The **girls are also very good-looking**."

STUDENT AUTHOR: Hookups happen often, both on and off campus; however, not all students are concerned about looks, and you'll find a decent amount of both guys and girls who feel much more comfortable in a T-shirt and jeans than a miniskirt or button-down shirt. There are a variety of students at USD, and you're bound to find the crowd that interests you. We judge people more by who they are than by what they wear.

> **Traditions**
>
> **Dakota Days**
> By far the biggest event on campus, Dakota Days is USD's homecoming. It takes place each fall.
>
> **Kegs & Eggs**
> Part of Dakota Days, Kegs & Eggs takes place downtown the Saturday of the homecoming football game when anyone willing to participate heads to the bars at 8 a.m. for food and liquor.
>
> **Overall School Spirit**
> School spirit at USD, for the most part, is considered to be high.

Students Speak Out
ON ATHLETICS

Q "Varsity **sports get a pretty good following** on campus, especially football and basketball."

Q "**You can participate in pretty much any sport here through IM**, and they are competitive, but not too competitive, which makes them a lot of fun and a nice break from homework on a weekday evening."

Q "All sports are big. There is information up everywhere, and they are an important part of campus life. **I think club sports are becoming more important than varsity ones**, and I've attended a lot of the soccer and rugby games in the past year."

STUDENT AUTHOR: From the Coyote's football team to USD's rugby players, USD athletics are well known for their talent, support, and popularity. Varsity sports play at the NCAA Division II level, traveling primarily around Nebraska and Minnesota. Participation in varsity sports is mostly scouted, but all the sports welcome walk-ons. USD's club sports and IM sports are definitely growing, and most USD students can find a suitable sport to interest them.

Students Speak Out
ON DRUG SCENE

Q "**Drugs flow like water here**. I don't think the drug scene is extra-prominent, though, nor is it hidden. If you want drugs, you'll be able to find them. If you don't want to be around them, you don't have to be."

Q "A lot of the **professors talk about weed**, so I guess its been here for a while, but I haven't really seen any on campus yet. I know people do it, but it's just like alcohol, if you don't want to be around it, you won't be."

Q "There's a lot of pot, but **not very many harder drugs**."

STUDENT AUTHOR: Drugs, especially marijuana, are common in the Midwest. USD is no exception. Substance use and abuse happens on and off campus, and marijuana, opium, and mushrooms are probably the most prominent drug scenes. Besides mind-altering drugs, the use of tobacco, caffeine, and Stackers has become popular with a lot of students on campus. Smoking is popular in South Dakota, and the habit is very visible on campus.

15:1	Student-to-Faculty Ratio
72%	Freshman Retention Rate
22%	Four-Year Graduation Rate
72%	Financial Aid Applicants Receiving Aid

Students Speak Out
SAFETY & SECURITY

Q "For the most part, I feel safe on campus; there are always people out and about during the day, and **it's a small campus, so you don't have to walk far**. Even at night, I'm not worried about walking across campus alone."

Q "I feel safe on campus. It is a small enough school that I can't see too much going wrong. Plus, **Public Safety has enough staff on duty both during the day and night hours**. I get more worried once I'm off campus than I do when I'm on campus."

Q "I have **never had a problem feeling safe** on campus. That may be because the only times I have taken long walks at night is when I am drunk, and at that point, we don't tend to worry so much."

STUDENT AUTHOR: Students at USD feel safe on campus. On campus, students will find blue-lights in the parking lot behind the North Complex dorms and in the DakotaDome lot. Safety concerns have also made key/ID access mandatory to enter the dorms.

> **Questions?**
> For more inside information and survival tips, pick up College Prowler's full-length book on this school, written by an actual student! Check it out at *www.collegeprowler.com*.

Students Speak Out
ON OVERALL EXPERIENCE

Q "I've had a great experience at USD so far. There's nowhere else I would want to be right now for school. I didn't necessarily think I'd feel this way when I arrived, but **everything about USD has been comforting**. It's not too large, and you never feel lost, nor is it so small that everyone knows who you are."

Q "I decided to come here because I couldn't find another university with this many opportunities, whether it be **close interaction with my professors** or the great research and extracurricular programs. I never thought that I would see more of the world by going to an in-state school than I ever could have at an East Coast school. I love it here."

Q "**I came here kicking and screaming, and now I will graduate crying**, knowing that I'm going to miss it so much."

Q "I've been here for two years, and **I have loved every minute of it**. From my activities with a number of organizations to the off-campus social events and fantastic professors, USD has really become my second home."

STUDENT AUTHOR: The Midwest ranks many of the University's departments as some of the top ones in the area, and most of the students say they wouldn't wish to be anywhere else. If you're looking for the friendliness of a small community, the competition of a top school, and the educational opportunities of a private institution, USD has the ability to offer all three. You'll have every chance possible to do some hands-on researching, be part of some amazing organizations, receive some down-home attention, and make friends to last a lifetime.

University of South Florida

4202 East Fowler Avenue; Tampa, FL 33620
(813) 974-2011; www.usf.edu

THE BASICS:

Acceptance Rate: 50%
Setting: Urban
F-T Undergrads: 24,600

SAT Range: 1010–1210*
Control: Public
Tuition: $16,081

Most Popular Majors: Business, Social Sciences, Education, Psychology, English, Biology

*of 1600

Academics	B-	Guys	A-
Local Atmosphere	A-	Girls	A
Safety & Security	B+	Athletics	B
Computers	B	Nightlife	A
Facilities	B+	Greek Life	B+
Campus Dining	B-	Drug Scene	B-
Off-Campus Dining	A	Campus Strictness	B
Campus Housing	C-	Parking	C-
Off-Campus Housing	B+	Transportation	C+
Diversity	B+	Weather	A-

Students Speak Out
ON ACADEMICS

Q "Most of my **professors have been excellent**, but I have had some very lousy graduate student professors who should not be teaching."

Q "The teachers are great teachers. **They really know the material**, and during their office hours, they do what they can to help the students understand. The classes are, for the most part, very interesting; otherwise I would not be taking them."

Q "For the most part, the teachers here are quite good. On occasion, you get a teacher who is there to just make your life difficult, but everyone will leave USF with one teacher in mind who **left a great impression**."

Q "From what I have experienced, teachers in the science department are **not all bad, but the majority of them stink**."

Q "Some teachers are nice, but some of them are uncaring. **I enjoy most of my classes**, so far."

STUDENT AUTHOR: Professors at USF are knowledgeable about subject matter, willing to work with students, and intent on helping students pass. However, some end up with a graduate student who can barely speak English. Because of recent budget cuts, classes are sometimes crowded. USF is aiming to expand to get more funding and offer more classes. Although USF offers a variety of majors, clubs, and resources for its students, the hectic environment can sometimes make classes more difficult and confusing than normal.

Students Speak Out
ON LOCAL ATMOSPHERE

Q "Our town is **not a typical college town**. Over the past few years, it has gotten a little bit better with places displaying the signs, 'This is Bulls country!' Definitely visit Ybor at least once. Everyone should walk around Channelside and International Plaza."

Q "Tampa is a very interesting place, with **so many things to do**. You can go to the movies, go clubbing, go out to different dinner places, go bowling, and do all that good stuff."

Q "The atmosphere in Tampa is very inviting. There is not much to stay away from, except for the strip clubs. Busch Gardens and Adventure Island are the two main attractions in this city. There is also **Clearwater Beach that is about one hour south of Tampa**."

Q "Tampa is a **borderline hick town**. There is Ybor City where a lot of people ages 16–35 go clubbing."

STUDENT AUTHOR: The city is growing quickly, and there are more things for college-aged students to do every year. The area surrounding the school is dotted with bars and restaurants, and there are two amusement parks a short ride away. Those interested in veering a little farther can visit Ybor City or Channelside, which are excellent for shopping, dining, and movies. What remains a problem is that most of Tampa's exciting destinations are only accessible with a car, as the city buses are infrequent and often stop running early.

Students Speak Out
ON FACILITIES

Q "Facilities on campus are quite nice. **Everything you need** is conveniently located around campus."

Q "**I like the different facilities** on campus, especially the gym. Also, the computers that are available for us to use and print with no cost are sweet! I know I have saved a lot of money on ink and paper this year."

Q "The student center could be nice in the future because more renovations are in the works. The **recreation center is very nice** (and big) but usually gets crowded during peak hours."

Q "The Marshall Center, being the main student activities building, **could be improved greatly**. To have a nicer Marshall Center would definitely make coming on campus more fun, but obviously there is controversy on how to pay."

Q "Most of the facilities are pretty decent. They are **not as great of some other campuses** around the state, but they do what they can for the students."

STUDENT AUTHOR: As more students come to USF, the facilities will continue to grow. There is still plenty of space around campus to build, so the number of facilities will increase with time. Thousands of dollars are spent on the facilities at USF each year. The variety of activities on campus is superb, and most students can easily find something that suits their own personal interests. USF also plays home to the Sun Dome, a large arena that hosts concerts, conventions, lectures, and some sports competitions.

Famous Alumni

Chucky Atkins, Sandra Bailey, Leo Gallagher, Nicole Johnson, Tony LaRussa, Rick D. Olivera, Richard Oppel

Students Speak Out
ON CAMPUS DINING

Q "The **food is not very good** compared to other schools. But it has gotten better in the past years. There are several fast food places, and most are good but expensive."

Q "If you have flex bucks or something from your meal plan, then you might not mind paying for it, but for the poor college student, I would **recommend bringing your own lunch** here because sometimes the lines tend to be long and it costs a fortune. The eating areas are not all that great in the Marshall Center."

Q "The main dining hall is the Fresh Food Company, which has been remodeled and **serves better food**. There is also the Tampa Room located inside the Marshall Center, which has better food."

Q "Most students are on a limited budget and **don't want to spend $5 for a bagel**, but unfortunately, that's what it has come to. It is best to leave campus to get food. To prove my point, they have built a Starbucks inside the library."

STUDENT AUTHOR: The foods offered at USF are mostly sandwiches from Montague's Deli, Subway, and Chik-fil-A. SUSHI and Bène Pizza and Pasta add something different to the mix, but most places have high prices for a small amount of food. Students who can't really afford to spend all of their money on food still end up eating on campus, because it beats the hassle of leaving. USF is trying to keep students content with daily meals, but expensive food is gradually ticking them off.

Student Body

African American:	13%	Male/Female:	41/59%
Asian American:	6%	Out-of-State:	3%
Hispanic:	13%	International:	1%
Native American:	<1%	Unknown:	2%
White:	65%		

Popular Faiths: There are several clubs for Christians, but Judaism and Islam are also popular with students.

Gay Pride: USF is welcoming to all students, regardless of sexual orientation. The PRIDE Alliance often holds special events to promote awareness about homosexuality.

Economic Status: Wealthier students are few and far between at USF.

Students Speak Out
ON DORMS

Q "Since Gamma is new now and renamed Castor, it must be nice to live in, with new bathrooms and other facilities. I also lived in Holly, the apartment-style dorms, and they are really nice, too. **I don't think there are really any to avoid**."

Q "I loved staying at Magnolia! **Nothing beats lounging poolside** with a good book."

Q "Most of the dorms aren't that great, but they're **working toward building newer, nicer ones**."

STUDENT AUTHOR: Students can expect two things once the renovation project begins to wind down. First, complaints about the dorms' drudgery and miniscule size will gradually fade away. And second, on-campus life will become more enjoyable due to the fact that students will want to live in apartment-suite-style dorms. Although many USF students will vehemently argue that the current social activity on campus is lacking, small parties and get-togethers do go on, and there is a sense of camaraderie amongst each dorm and its members. It would not be the least bit inaccurate to say that USF's housing can go nowhere but up.

Did You Know?
13% of undergrads live on campus.

Students Speak Out
ON GUYS & GIRLS

Q "There are definitely **more girls on campus than guys, unfortunately**. Choosing from the guys that are here can be a little difficult because most of them have girlfriends."

Q "There are **so many beautiful girls here**, it is unreal! Every day, I fall in love with two or three new ones!"

Q "There are **plenty of hot women** wearing next to nothing in the Florida sun."

Q "The **guys, for the most part, are hot**—well, some of them, anyway. Some of these guys are a little bold for me, asking me if I have a boyfriend and then I say yes, they still say 'would you like to go out to dinner with me?'"

STUDENT AUTHOR: It's not difficult to find attractive people around campus. Girls can spot incredible eye candy in the weight room as the football players pump iron. Guys can catch USF's loveliest ladies basking in the summer sun in tank tops. Even the University's pickiest students find someone to crush on by the end of the semester. Whether it is a serious relationship or a not-so-serious hookup, USF has something for everyone.

Traditions

Bull Market
A marketplace where people share ideas, cultures, and sell homemade goods every Wednesday.

Movies on the Lawn
Students gather to watch movies every Wednesday night on the wall of the SEC.

Overall School Spirit
The school's athletic department has grown in recent years, pushing a rise in school spirit at the University. Because the Bulls are Tampa's only college football team, city residents are strong supporters.

Students Speak Out
ON ATHLETICS

Q "Varsity sports are very big on campus, especially basketball and football. They're not as big as other school's sports, but **it's getting better each year**. IM sports are very big, and there's a big turnout for most games. Greeks participate in most sports, as well."

Q "When you live on campus, it's easier and more **fun to become involved** with intramural sports because you have to get a team together."

Q "I swear, at times it seems like **IMs are bigger** than the varsity sports!"

Q "IM sports are a lot bigger than varsity sports. Our **football team has started to get bigger**, and our basketball team is still doing well."

STUDENT AUTHOR: Although varsity sports have become more popular with students in recent years, game turnouts are not nearly as large as they should be. However, fan support seems to be rising, along with the teams' winning percentages. Not all varsity sports are recognized as they should be, but these sporting events are increasing in popularity and will probably continue to do so as long as USF continues to recruit talented athletes.

Students Speak Out
ON DRUG SCENE

Q "It's always best to do all your business off campus. If a student is caught with drugs or alcohol twice, they can **possibly be expelled from all Florida universities**."

Q "USF is actually **pretty tame in terms of drugs** compared to other schools."

Q "You have to know someone who is going to hook you up with drugs because, apparently, they are not as easy to get as you might think they are. **I don't think it is an extremely bad problem**."

STUDENT AUTHOR: Although alcohol is consumed just about every place on campus where the residents are old enough to drink, drugs and alcohol are much more prevalent off campus than on campus. Marijuana is sometimes found in the dorms, but most students weigh the use of marijuana against the consequences and decide that it is safest to take their recreational drug use off campus. Those who are not interested in using drugs will have no problem staying away from them.

19:1	Student-to-Faculty Ratio
81%	Freshman Retention Rate
22%	Four-Year Graduation Rate
80%	Financial Aid Applicants Receiving Aid

Students Speak Out
SAFETY & SECURITY

Q "We have SAFE Team, which is helpful for girls at night, and the **cops are usually strolling around campus**."

Q "I think that this **campus is pretty safe**."

Q "As the campus has been growing, they have been **putting in more of the emergency call boxes**, which are good for students."

Q "There are those beacon things that someone can push in case of an emergency scattered all around campus. There are always police lurking around, and now there is an officer riding around on a motorcycle. **Theft is quite common** in the dorms because students often leave their rooms open or unlocked."

STUDENT AUTHOR: Students generally feel safe on campus. For those who are afraid to walk alone late at night, the SAFE Team will transport students anywhere on campus. SAFE Team's presence deters criminals from committing crimes because of the elevated possibility that their acts will be observed.

Questions?
For more inside information and survival tips, pick up College Prowler's full-length book on this school, written by an actual student! Check it out at *www.collegeprowler.com*.

Students Speak Out
ON OVERALL EXPERIENCE

Q "It's a different experience than a college that is in the middle of nowhere and in a 'college town.' So, **it really depends on what you want** to experience. It took me awhile to get adjusted, but now I love it."

Q "I love this place, but I **wish it was a little more of a college town**, where the town revolves around the campus."

Q "With every school **there is always a good and bad**, so you just have to make the best of the situation. That is what I have done, and it is just wonderful."

Q "When I first came here, I wanted to leave because I was going through the homesickness thing, but **now I love it**, and I know I wouldn't want to leave."

STUDENT AUTHOR: Students can look forward to meeting many people from diverse backgrounds, and the teachers here are strong role models for students. While classes are sometimes stressful and unbearable, the lessons taught outside of school are invaluable. With the various top-notch facilities on campus, nighttime activities, dining out, or just laying around in the sun, USF has much more to offer than rock-solid academics. Of course, college is what you make of it. Students who spend their time in their dorm rooms miss out on opportunities to make friends and grow as individuals. Those who get involved in student activities enjoy their college experience much more. That's why it is important to take advantage of the opportunities that USF presents. Overall, most students enjoy their time here, even if this was not their first choice.

University of Southern California

801 Exposition Boulevard; Los Angeles, CA 90089
(213) 740-2311; www.usc.edu

THE BASICS:

Acceptance Rate: 25%
Setting: Urban
F-T Undergrads: 15,684

SAT Range: 1310–1490*
Control: Private
Tuition: $37,114

Most Popular Majors: Business, Social Sciences, Visual and Performing Arts, Communications

*of 1600

Academics	A-	Guys	A-
Local Atmosphere	A-	Girls	A
Safety & Security	C+	Athletics	A+
Computers	A-	Nightlife	A+
Facilities	A-	Greek Life	A
Campus Dining	B	Drug Scene	B-
Off-Campus Dining	A	Campus Strictness	B+
Campus Housing	B	Parking	C+
Off-Campus Housing	B-	Transportation	C-
Diversity	A	Weather	A

Students Speak Out
ON ACADEMICS

Q "Teachers here are awesome. **You really get that personal attention** that you're not supposed to get at big schools. All are extremely approachable. To this day, I keep in touch with two of my favorite professors. Classes are taught by professors, not by teaching assistants (TAs). My only complaint was with one professor who had a bad accent; it was hard to understand his lectures."

Q "I'm indifferent on the teacher subject. I've liked almost all of mine, but **none have changed my life**."

Q "I have found many of my professors to be quite **approachable and easy-going**. Some of them are quite brilliant. I did have one teacher that I did not particularly care for, yet I still learned a lot in that course."

Q "I was flying home for winter vacation this year, and **I saw my religion teacher being interviewed on CNN**."

STUDENT AUTHOR: **All in all, students are happy with the academics at USC. Resourceful students are ecstatic about courses, and passive students have good and bad things to say. The most widely-discussed issue that students have is that teaching assistants tend not to be entirely fluent with the English language. Another issue is the grading curve at the Marshall School of Business. Students have a hard time dealing with the fact that a predetermined amount of As, Bs, Cs, Ds, and Fs are distributed at the end of a semester.**

Students Speak Out
ON LOCAL ATMOSPHERE

Q "**UCLA is only 14 miles away**, and LMU is only 10 miles away. There are tons of places outside of campus where you can go out and have fun—the beach, Westwood, Hollywood, Santa Monica, Old Town Pasadena, Dodger Stadium, and the Staples Center."

Q "Movie premieres are held in Hollywood, Westwood, and Santa Monica a lot. We're only a block away from the Shrine Theater where they hold the Grammys and Emmys. **USC is the most-filmed campus in America**, so you'll see movie stars on campus from time to time. Sunset clubs, Universal City Walk, Disneyland, and Disney's California Adventure are only 10 to 40 minutes away."

Q "Los Angeles is the greatest town on earth. I've been to **more concerts here** in the last six months than I'd been to in all my life!"

Q "You can do everything in LA. **From the mountains to the beaches**, I wouldn't go to any other school. I can go to the beach in San Diego for the day and be in Chinatown the next day."

STUDENT AUTHOR: **Once students develop a navigational sense of the area, they gain access to a world of mountains and oceans, city and country, shopping centers and art museums, movie stars, and job opportunities matched both in quality and quantity. People are friendly at any time of day, other than rush hour. The weather is beautiful. The food is amazing. Anything is possible in LA.**

Students Speak Out
ON FACILITIES

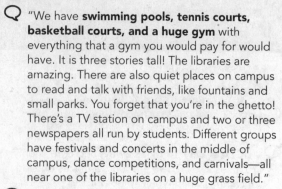

Q "We have **swimming pools, tennis courts, basketball courts, and a huge gym** with everything that a gym you would pay for would have. It is three stories tall! The libraries are amazing. There are also quiet places on campus to read and talk with friends, like fountains and small parks. You forget that you're in the ghetto! There's a TV station on campus and two or three newspapers all run by students. Different groups have festivals and concerts in the middle of campus, dance competitions, and carnivals—all near one of the libraries on a huge grass field."

Q "Given the amount we pay in tuition each year, you **better believe things are nice**!"

Q "The campus is beautiful. I sometimes forget that I'm in LA and think that I'm somewhere on the East Coast! The **brick buildings and the landscaping are amazing**. The facilities on campus are great, except for the student gym—it's very small and always crowded."

Q "The gym and computer facilities are great, but **there isn't a real student center**."

Q "All the facilities are great. Granted the buildings are old, but they are kept in top-notch condition. I love walking through campus because it really **does look like an Ivy League school**."

STUDENT AUTHOR: **New students usually don't think to leave campus until their second semester, since USC provides them with everything they need to manage their lives as college students. Varsity athletes have separate facilities for training and dining in Heritage Hall. Everything else on campus is pristine and newly renovated.**

Famous Alumni
Neil Armstrong, John Carpenter, Will Ferrell, George Lucas, John Wayne, Robert Zemeckis, Laura Ziskin

Students Speak Out
ON CAMPUS DINING

Q "The food is pretty good. Everyone seems to like Café 84 and Upstairs Commons. **We have a Wolfgang Puck, Colombo, Betty Crocker**, and La Salsa."

Q "There are two cafeterias. One is EVK and the other is IRC at Parkside. **Parkside is absolutely wonderful. EVK is not so great**. I personally did not eat there except for Sunday brunch, which was pretty good. The other places to eat are Commons, downstairs Commons, and Café 84. In those three areas, there are tons of things to choose from."

Q "**The food is not super-great at USC**. It's probably USC's only drawback. Upstairs Commons is a little bit more of what would be considered a restaurant because it serves dishes that are about $7–$10 in cost. Other than that, most of the food at USC is not that great."

Q "Upstairs at Commons is good. It's one place where **you can order a bottle of wine with your meal** and charge it to your meal plan."

STUDENT AUTHOR: **Upstairs Café, Parkside Residential, Wolfgang Puck's Express Café, La Salsa, and Wasabi Sushi all receive rave reviews. On the other side, the food at EVK is never very healthy or tasty, though servings are enormous. Meal plans that allow for freedom of discretion are considered to be the best. The great lunch secret on campus is at the Galen Center. Most people think it's specifically for athletes, but anyone can eat there during lunchtime.**

Student Body

African American:	6%	Male/Female:	50/50%
Asian American:	22%	Out-of-State:	51%
Hispanic:	13%	International:	9%
Native American:	1%	Unknown:	2%
White:	47%		

Popular Faiths: Christianity and Judaism are hugely popular on campus.

Gay Pride: Tolerance is high on campus. The Gay, Lesbian, Bi, Transgender Assembly is highly influential to school administration. Gay students who are harassed have strong support at the GLBTA.

Economic Status: Although a huge number of students are wealthy, there is even a greater number of students on financial aid.

Students Speak Out
ON DORMS

Q "**New/North are great dorms**; they're very social. I recommend dorms over apartment or suite-style units. If you can't get dorm-style, suite is the next best. Don't live in the off-campus apartment; you'll feel segregated. Marks and Pardee Tower also has good dorms, although they're not as much fun as New/North. Honors dorms are not nicer than regular dorms."

Q "I lived in Pardee and loved it. However, Pardee is coed by floors. You might want something that has coed floors, because those are so much more fun. Some good ones are Birnkrant, New/North, and Parkside. **I would not recommend Webb and Fluor**."

Q "Dorms are the best, and they are the **most fun I ever had**."

STUDENT AUTHOR: **All freshmen are required to live on campus. Of all the places to live, the adjacent New and North Residence Halls are the most sought after by incoming students and remain the most popular throughout the year. New and North are not the most modern dorms on campus, and their EVK dining hall is not the best place to eat.**

Did You Know?
41% of undergrads live on campus.

Students Speak Out
ON GUYS & GIRLS

Q "I think the guys are pretty cute, but some of them are cocky. I really like all the girls I have become friends with. I think you can always find and surround yourself with people who are like you. There is **definitely a lot of materialism** on campus, with guys and girls. Kate Spade, Louis Vuitton, Gucci, Prada . . . Not everyone is like this, though!"

Q "There is a **mixture of guys and girls alike**. You have your big jocks, your studious students, your 'how the hell did you get in here' kids, your 'why aren't you at Harvard' kids, your snobs, your sweeties, the good-looking, and the not-so-good-looking . . . Get my point?"

Q "It's Southern California . . . **doesn't get better**."

STUDENT AUTHOR: **People tend to be healthy and happy in Southern California. These simple traits work wonders for a person's attractiveness. Girls are downright beautiful, well dressed, and well spoken. Guys tend to be tall and in strong physical condition. Guys and girls get along at USC, but they seem to have come here to have fun, not to fall in love. There is a superficial element that keeps people from letting their emotional defenses down.**

Traditions

USC Marching Band
USC marching band is the only college marching band to be featured on a platinum-selling album and be nominated for a Grammy award.

Overall School Spirit
USC's transition from just a party school with amazing sports teams to a school with excellent academics, amazing sports teams, a more controlled drug scene, and a diverse student body has given students a new sort of Trojan pride. Students will always be loyal sports fans, but the school spirit has officially extended into the realms of academics, as well.

Students Speak Out
ON ATHLETICS

Q "**Football games are the best ever**; everyone goes. It's what makes you a Trojan—going to games, chatting with friends, and cheering for your team. It's the Trojan family."

Q "Sports are really big on campus. We have **excellent baseball, basketball, and football** programs. For fall, the school goes nuts over football, and everyone tailgates and parties before the game. Then we all walk towards the stadium following the band. It's really fun."

Q "Varsity football, basketball, and women's volleyball are all huge at USC. **IM sports are also really big**. University housing has teams, and the Greeks do their own IM tournaments."

STUDENT AUTHOR: **There is a resounding sense of pride among USC sports fans. Trojans are faithful to their sports teams, both as athletes and fans. Varsity athletes get royal treatment from the University in exchange for a commitment as demanding as a full course load. Although men's soccer was wiped out some time ago, USC's varsity sport teams are a threat to the best teams in almost every sport.**

Students Speak Out
ON DRUG SCENE

Q "**I don't think the drug scene is out of control**. I'm sure if you look for it, you'll find it. I haven't really noticed drugs while being here, and I went out and partied."

Q "There's a handful of rich kids in the Greek scene that have money to burn, so **you get the occasional coke or ecstasy users** at some parties. If you choose to stay away from it, you don't get any peer pressure and probably won't notice it. I'd recommend not getting involved."

Q "**Drugs are more 'undercover' here**. USC is a moderate school, not extremely right-wing or liberal. You get the occasional bud smoker here and there. If you plan on doing it, I'm sure you'll find a handful that will do it with you."

STUDENT AUTHOR: **The drug scene is considerably tame for a wealthy school in the middle of a city that is famous for partying. For the most part, there is a lot of drinking, less marijuana smoking (but still a significant amount), and a small amount of cocaine and ecstasy abuse.**

10:1	Student-to-Faculty Ratio
95%	Freshman Retention Rate
61%	Four-Year Graduation Rate
43%	Financial Aid Applicants Receiving Aid

Students Speak Out
SAFETY & SECURITY

Q "There is an escort service that you can use if you need someone to walk with you back to the dorms from a late class or from anywhere on campus. We also have this thing called Campus Cruiser that can **give you a ride after 5 p.m. to anywhere within two miles of campus**. I do suggest traveling with at least one other person at night."

Q "There are tons of blue-light posts set up around campus for you to use in case of an emergency. The average response time for a DPS officer (not a rent-a-cop) is supposed to be less than 20 seconds. **Unfortunately, the area surrounding the campus isn't all that great**, but no one that I know personally has been robbed or attacked in any way."

STUDENT AUTHOR: **Although most students would agree that campus is safe, there is no denying that bad things happen. The DPS and the LAPD have committed more officers to problem areas, and even though problems still exist, assailants tend to strike in the remote areas that most students avoid.**

Questions?

For more inside information and survival tips, pick up College Prowler's full-length book on this school, written by an actual student! Check it out at *www.collegeprowler.com.*

Students Speak Out
ON OVERALL EXPERIENCE

Q "If you're looking for a **school with old traditions, top-rate athletics**, the most effective job network, challenging academics, a beautiful and safe campus, and a metropolitan atmosphere with nonstop entertainment, USC is the place."

Q "I love USC! I have never been happier. The first few weeks were a little hard, but everyone that is a freshman feels the same way. **It's helpful to get involved** with study groups in order to meet people in the beginning. Go out when there is a big party on the Row to meet people. Smile to people and say 'hi.'"

Q "I really love the campus. It's really pretty, and I feel comfortable here. If you don't mind being around a lot of people, and if you usually get along with others, then LA should be good for you. The Trojan Family really is like a family. **People get hooked up everywhere with jobs**."

Q "I have no regrets about where I chose to go to school. **Southern California is the coolest place** to spend your college years. USC caters to the wants of most of its students. If you're into sports, it has great teams. If you like to party, plenty of people do that, too. If you don't like to party, you can also find those kinds of kids. If you like to get involved, it's easy to do so."

STUDENT AUTHOR: **Students from Southern California usually love USC from the beginning and strengthen their bonds with the school as time passes. Those who travel from long distances tend to adapt more slowly, dealing at first with the culture shock that inevitably comes with a first impression of LA. Universally, those who can survive the transition into the USC way of life for the first semester fall in love with the school.**

University of Tennessee

2712 Neyland Drive; Knoxville, TN 37996
(865) 974-1000; www.utk.edu

THE BASICS:

Acceptance Rate: 65%
Setting: Mid-sized city
F-T Undergrads: 20,328

SAT Range: 1070–1270*
Control: Public
Tuition: $18,086

Most Popular Majors: Psychology, Accounting, Biology, English, Journalism

*of 1600

Academics	B-	Guys	A
Local Atmosphere	B	Girls	A
Safety & Security	B-	Athletics	A+
Computers	B	Nightlife	A-
Facilities	B+	Greek Life	A-
Campus Dining	B	Drug Scene	B-
Off-Campus Dining	A	Campus Strictness	C+
Campus Housing	B-	Parking	D+
Off-Campus Housing	B+	Transportation	A-
Diversity	D+	Weather	B-

Students Speak Out
ON ACADEMICS

Q "While most of the distribution **classes seem to be large and impersonal**, the upper-level courses are the total opposite. As the classes get more in-depth in each field, both the classes and the teachers get more interesting and more individualized toward each student."

Q "While many teachers seem like jerks while sitting in class, **many are very friendly on an individual basis**, as long as you are not the student that constantly shows up late, sleeps in class, or never comes."

Q "**I've liked every single teacher I have had**. I went to a very competitive high school, so I feel like the teachers here almost baby us. They always end up curving grades, delaying due dates, and making other compromises with students. There are still a few sticklers, though, so watch out. All teachers are nice and willing to help you out after class hours anytime."

Q "If you ever mess up, there is one important thing to remember—most professors are like motorcycle cops. **They have heard every excuse in the book**, and they are usually on to any lame excuse you might make."

STUDENT AUTHOR: **After the first day of classes, you may feel that UT is a large school with cold and hard professors. As time passes, however, you will learn that they are human and want you to learn the material and develop as a student. Most professors want you to visit them during office hours, so don't be afraid to ask for extra help!**

Students Speak Out
ON LOCAL ATMOSPHERE

Q "Knoxville is a **city highly influenced by college football**. If you're not a football fan or you despise the color orange, you will be very unhappy being in Knoxville, during football season or not. Except for houses, orange is a highly-accepted color for most everything here."

Q "Knoxville is a great city. The campus is a major part of the city, but they have a historic downtown and two decent malls. You can always find something to do, and you are **only 30 minutes from the Smoky Mountains**."

Q "Knoxville **may seem like a big town trapped in a small-town mentality**. The people here cling to small-town values and traditions."

Q "Knoxville is **big enough that you can find whatever type of activity** or people you want. If you want to party till 5 a.m., you can—UT was rated the number one party school in the nation several years ago. If you'd rather study or get involved with student government or religious groups, you can do that here, too."

STUDENT AUTHOR: **Knoxville truly serves as a happy medium between a large city and a small town. It is an easy transition for students coming from either extreme. The people of Knoxville are rather relaxed (except on game day), and there are plenty of places to go to enjoy leisurely activities. You may find that Knoxville is the ideal size for a college student. Atlanta and Nashville are not too far away, and you can be in the mountains in even less time.**

Students Speak Out
ON FACILITIES

Q "They really **try to separate the athletes from regular students** at UT. The athletes have one of just about everything to themselves, and what they have is all cutting-edge and modern. Many of the long-overdue renovations to student facilities are now taking place, and they are now worth a visit."

Q "**We have some of the best facilities in the Southeast**, and we are getting more. Our athletes have the best fitness and study centers around. The computers are all kept up-to-date and are really fast, and the student center is a great place to meet people and catch a bite to eat, or to see a dollar movie."

Q "The **UC has a basement where you can bowl, play pool, air hockey, or ping pong**. You can even take bowling as a class! I never even learned how to check out a book from our huge Hodge Library until May!"

Q "While many of the buildings are new, others are **exactly the same as when your mother or father attended UT**. All that has been changed in some buildings are the light bulbs, while the desks, flooring, windows, and bathrooms are from the stone age."

STUDENT AUTHOR: **The crème de la crème of facilities is still reserved for athletes. The University does spend a few of the leftover dollars on facilities for students, and most of the students are satisfied with their quality. A university of this size suffers a lot of wear and tear. Anything new does not stay new for long, and no matter how hard they try to maintain facilities, some get worn quickly.**

Famous Alumni

Jeff Ashby, Howard Baker, James Buchanan, Tamika Catchings, John Cullum, Peyton Manning

Students Speak Out
ON CAMPUS DINING

Q "The food isn't bad. **We have about six dining halls across campus** with regular food like steaks, ham, and stuff like that. There's also a Burger King, Quiznos, and Edy's Ice Cream, so there is no need to complain about the food. There are even mini-grocery stores in some of the dorms."

Q "As a freshman, you will love eating the fast food in Presidential. It is quick and tastes pretty good, but I promise **you will miss home cooking** after a few weeks. Be forewarned, eating this stuff every day can pack on the pounds!"

Q "My best advice for subscribing to a meal plan is **keep track of your bonus bucks**! Many freshmen get in the habit of mindlessly scanning their card everyday. Since you will probably use them, even if you don't visit snack shops, they go pretty quickly. Since cigarettes can be purchased with bonus bucks, some freshmen take up smoking and spend them rapidly."

Q "I eat my meals in Gibbs Hall with all the athletes and non-athlete residents who live in Gibbs. A lot of the football players live in Gibbs, and since Tennessee cares so much about football, this **cafeteria has the best food by far**."

STUDENT AUTHOR: **Since you will be stuck with the UT Dining Services meal plan, why not make the most of it? The key is to read the meal plan rules. Keep track of your bonus bucks and eat during allotted dining hours. One thing is for certain, you will gain a whole new appreciation for your mother's cooking that you had taken for granted so many years.**

Students Speak Out
ON DORMS

Q "**The dorms provide a good experience**. If you like to be more social, try South Carrick or Humes. Morrell is too far away. Hess and Melrose are the closest to classes. It seems like anyone who randomly gets put in any dorm always raves about how it's the best, but I would avoid the ones across the street, like Clement, because they're too far."

Q "The dorms are **generally run-down and need a lot of remodeling**. The most popular dorms are around the Presidential Court area (Humes, North and South Carrick, and Reese). The dorms to run away from are Clement and Hess. If you like the tight-knit community opportunity, Hess and Morrill are your best bets."

Q "For a freshman, **Humes, South Carrick, and Morrill are all great**. Avoid Clement if you aren't into the old-building feel, and know that Humes has the best staff."

STUDENT AUTHOR: The dorms have somewhat improved over the last several years. Since there is no perfect dorm, and none that can really be a huge pain, try to make the most of whatever situation you have and make new friends.

? Did You Know?
33% of undergrads live on campus.

Students Speak Out
ON GUYS & GIRLS

Q "If you are a guy that prefers the blond-haired, **blue-eyed, classy, and posh Southern belles**, UT could be considered their capital."

Q "The guys are generally in between a slow-paced or a fast-paced kind of individual. The slow-paced, non-goal-driven guys generally do very little, including their school work. The fast-paced, goal-driven guys generally have a great grasp on what happens on campus, school, and social life. The girls are also the same way, although there are **more fast-paced, goal-driven girls than there are guys**."

Q "The only thing that really determines their dateability is their attitudes. **Many of them know they've got 'it'** and act like it."

STUDENT AUTHOR: Great looks, a fancy car, and impeccable clothing do not always guarantee success with the opposite sex at UT. The common denominator among those truly successful with the opposite sex is a positive attitude and confidence. Whether you seek a friend, a date, a hookup, or a relationship, there are unlimited choices. You will enjoy meeting the friendly, laid-back students of UT.

Traditions

Colors
UT's school colors, orange and white, were chosen by Charles Moore. He apparently chose the colors after the daisies he saw growing on the Hill. But it is possible that Moore was color blind, since no daisies of such colors are known to exist.

Mascot
The Volunteers get their name from one of Tennessee's nickname, "the Volunteer State," deriving from the overwhelming number of Tennessee citizens volunteering for military service in past wars.

Overall School Spirit
As far as UT football is concerned, no explanation should be needed.

Students Speak Out
ON ATHLETICS

Q "Everybody in Tennessee is a dedicated Tennessee football fan. I don't think there's a school around that can muster up a better crowd than our **107,000 screaming fans**."

Q "The intensity you will experience at a classic Tennessee football game is incredible. **It is almost like a European soccer match**, except without all the violence."

Q "**Football is high and mighty**, with basketball as the next best, and we get in to all the home games for free! IM sports are huge if you are Greek, but it's easy to get involved—even if you're not, just round up your dorm floor or friends who want to start a team."

STUDENT AUTHOR: Even if you are not a huge sports fan, you will enjoy the excitement and tradition that goes along with a football game. It is only fair to warn you that if you dislike sports, you may want to vacate Knoxville in the event of a football game. IM sports are popular to both play in and watch. There are great chances to play sports, whether it is something you participated in during high school or you want to make friends.

Students Speak Out
ON DRUG SCENE

Q "At UT, like any college campus, there is some drug use. People will not try to shove it in your face and will not put a lot of pressure on you to do it. People who do drugs are somewhat discreet about it—they slip away, do their thing, and come back. **If it isn't something you want to do, you aren't the only one**, and they won't force the issue."

Q "**When I came to UT, I was naïve about drugs** and drug use. Now that I have been here several years, I have learned more about it and seen how the whole drug culture operates. There will be a noticeable difference in those who start using drugs in college and an academic downturn is just one of many changes."

STUDENT AUTHOR: Marijuana is the No. 1 cash crop in the state of Tennessee and is easily the cheapest and most readily available drug. You will probably not have many encounters with drugs other than marijuana. With drugs in general, it is easy to maintain your stance, and people will handle your decisions as an adult the majority of the time.

15:1	Student-to-Faculty Ratio
84%	Freshman Retention Rate
27%	Four-Year Graduation Rate
92%	Financial Aid Applicants Receiving Aid

Students Speak Out
SAFETY & SECURITY

Q "It seems that **there are always cops cruising the streets**, no matter the time of day. You almost can't walk across campus without seeing a police car."

Q "UT has a **late-night van service**. My experience has been that it responds very quickly, usually in two to three minutes. There is a lot of room on the buses to accommodate your friends, as well."

Q "There are security phones all over campus, so if you get in trouble, you can find one of the blue-light phones and automatically call the UTPD. Most pathways are well lit, and you must be escorted by a dorm resident in order to get in the dorm's door. All dorm residents have keys to the dorm they live in and the **access doors remained locked at all times**."

STUDENT AUTHOR: Most students' opinions on safety and security boil down to one thing—using your common sense. The UTPD take their jobs very seriously and are always looking out for students' safety. For a school of UT's size, they are very successful, and the majority of students don't walk around with spray-mace key rings tightly in hand.

> **Questions?**
> For more inside information and survival tips, pick up College Prowler's full-length book on this school, written by an actual student! Check it out at *www.collegeprowler.com.*

Students Speak Out
ON OVERALL EXPERIENCE

Q "My experience in school has been a **mixture of positives and negatives**. The positives have been my social life, experience in the classroom, and overall outcome in life. The negatives have been how the administration treats me as a number rather than a person."

Q "**I absolutely love UT**, and I grew up less than 15 minutes away from it. If that's not convincing, I don't know what is!"

Q "I thought it would be real different, too different from what I am used to at home in Long Island, New York, but I actually found it to be very nice. **I love the mountains and the beautiful Tennessee scenery**. In the South, there are definitely the accents, and everything is a little more slow paced."

Q "My experience at UT has been wonderful. I think that every person can make UT what they want to make it. Getting involved seems to be the thing that separates the people who love UT and those who do not. Even if you do not want to go Greek, I would **suggest getting involved in some kind of club**."

STUDENT AUTHOR: UT draws students from all over, and it is little wonder why. UT has a personality all its own. The level of pride and tradition here is among the strongest in the country, and the amount of support Knoxville has for UT is amazing, especially with sports. You will love the laid-back Southern style UT has to offer, and you will enjoy spending time with the people you meet here. As long as you remember that education is the main reason for coming to UT and prioritize accordingly, you will be very happy during your college days.

University of Texas at Austin

1 University Station; Austin, TX 78712
(512) 471-3434; www.utexas.edu

THE BASICS:

Acceptance Rate: 44%
Setting: Urban
F-T Undergrads: 34,604

SAT Range: 1650–2020*
Control: Public
Tuition: $27,760

Most Popular Majors: Journalism, Social Sciences, Business, Engineering, Biology

*of 2400

Academics	B+	Guys	A
Local Atmosphere	A+	Girls	A+
Safety & Security	B	Athletics	A+
Computers	B-	Nightlife	A
Facilities	A	Greek Life	B+
Campus Dining	B	Drug Scene	C+
Off-Campus Dining	A	Campus Strictness	B-
Campus Housing	B-	Parking	D
Off-Campus Housing	B	Transportation	B+
Diversity	A	Weather	A

Students Speak Out
ON ACADEMICS

Q "**The teachers are very intelligent** and very scholarly. Sometimes the intensity of their own research causes them to be more apathetic about the progress of their students."

Q "For the most part, the teachers are awesome. **Teachers keep my interest, even in the 8 a.m. classes.** Dr. Brandl in the business school is a great lecturer, so much so that he got a standing ovation the last day of class. Most of my classes are interesting, but there are some that make me feel like I'm back in high school again. The good ones open my eyes to new perspectives about the world around me."

Q "**Some teachers are cool; others I'd like to punch in the face**. It's basically the same anywhere you go. Oh, and don't take any classes before 11 a.m."

Q "Professors are varied. For many of the lower division courses, (freshman, sophomore), more than one professor teaches the course, and invariably, one will be better than the others. **Ask someone who has already taken the course which professor they like**."

STUDENT AUTHOR: **The University of Texas is one of the top public universities in the country and is consistently ranked in the top 50 public universities in the country. The professors at UT run the gamut— some are great and genuinely care about their students, and some have written the textbooks that are used in their classes and aren't as interested in students' input.**

Students Speak Out
ON LOCAL ATMOSPHERE

Q "**It's always charged here in Austin**. There's always something to do, and if you're not careful, you could be sucked into spreading yourself too thin. The thing about Austin is that it is so great that you can enjoy both ends of the spectrum. You can go to a crazy concert in Zilker Park, or the quiet, cozy surroundings of Spiderhouse Coffeehouse."

Q "Austin is an amazing and liberal city. I grew up in Denver, Colorado, a very liberal environment in itself, but never before did I imagine a place where any type of person can fit in. Although the city itself is growing rapidly, **I still feel it maintains its small-town feel**."

Q "Austin is pretty friendly. West Austin has nicer neighborhoods. Don't go to East Austin, it's dangerous. South Austin is sometimes referred to as Bubba-Land by older Austinites. While it's openly liberal, there are conservative people if you know where to look. **It is a very political city, as there is always some issue**."

STUDENT AUTHOR: **You really couldn't ask for a much better college town than Austin, Texas, the Live Music Capital of the World. There is so much to do in Austin and definitely something for everyone—bars, museums, parks, lakes, running trails, kayaking, shopping, coffee houses, outdoor music venues, smoky blues clubs, naked swimming at Hippie Hollow. We even have our own little beach in central Texas—Volente Waterpark Beach. Austin is a city with a small-town feel, and that is what most people love about it.**

Students Speak Out
ON FACILITIES

Q "The facilities are satisfactory, but the better ones are usually in the business or computer science buildings. The plus to this is that you can use them even if your major is not one of those, but most people don't know that. Athletics are really impressive here. We have a **wonderful swim center and many great gyms**."

Q "The facilities on campus are very nice. The gym facilities are clean and contain the latest equipment. The computer labs carry the most recent technology. **Lots of people speak badly about the Health Center**, but my one experience was great and quick."

Q "All buildings (athletic center, computer labs, and student center) are nice and relatively new. There are older classrooms and buildings on campus; but **nothing is ever dirty or smells funny**. It's all nice."

Q "The facilities are extremely nice on campus. With so many students, **there is more money for these buildings**, and the University is one of the nicest I have ever seen."

STUDENT AUTHOR: **UT's gym and Rec Center contain machines, weights, a pool, volleyball courts, racquetball courts, an indoor track, and a climbing wall. The Texas Union is a great place to study, relax, grab a bite to eat, watch TV, or make copies. There is an Undergraduate Writing Center located on campus in the UGL where you can get help editing your papers and work on your writing skills free of charge. There are also career centers within every college.**

Famous Alumni

Laura Bush, Earl Campbell, Roger Clemens, John B. Connally, Walter Cronkite, Michael Dell, Farrah Fawcett, Janis Joplin, Dan Rather, Kevin Reynolds, Owen Wilson, Renee Zellweger

Students Speak Out
ON CAMPUS DINING

Q "The Union is definitely the way to go. There are many different options. Tortilla Flats and Chick-fil-A are favorites. I have tried Bene Pizza, and while it looks like it is really good, I didn't particularly like it. Texadelphia in the Union Underground or just on the Drag is also always a great choice—you can't really go wrong there. There is a Wendy's in the Union and Burger King in the business school. However, **a lot of them are only open a few hours every day**, so if you like to eat at odd hours, watch out."

Q "**Kinsolving is the best**, the Union is solid, but costs more than dining halls (Bevo Bucks rule!). Philly cheese or chicken strips are where it's at in Jester."

Q "My personal favorite is O's Café because it is not expensive, and it is fairly good. **Jester dorm food has mixed reviews**, and if you are into salad bars, I don't recommend going there."

Q "The food on campus is great and usually cheap. Good spots are Taco Bell and the egg roll cart on 21st Street by the South Mall. **It's heaven in Styrofoam**!"

STUDENT AUTHOR: **Overall, not many people love dorm food, especially on-campus dorm food. Some of the private dorms, such as SRD and Castilian, have pretty good food, but for the most part, Bevo Bucks are the best way to go because they can be used at so many places. The Union is a good bet with many different choices, and Wendy's is open late. Jest'A Pizza is a good option. Even as a vegetarian, there are always plenty of options.**

Student Body

African American:	5%	Male/Female:	48/52%
Asian American:	17%	Out-of-State:	4%
Hispanic:	18%	International:	4%
Native American:	<1%	Unknown:	0%
White:	55%		

Popular Faiths: Christianity is pretty popular on campus. There are several churches on campus.

Gay Pride: Austin is definitely the liberal bubble of Texas, so the gay acceptance is probably higher here than anywhere else in Texas.

Economic Status: There are wealthy and middle-class students, and students with very little money.

**Students Speak Out
ON DORMS**

Q "Always leave your door open at the beginning of freshman year so that you can meet everyone on your floor. Believe me, people will come in if your door is open. Talk to everyone you can, and don't just wait for people to talk to you. **Freshman year is the time to meet people**, and the dorm is the optimal place to do that, so meet everyone that you can. Try to be friends with lots of people on your floor, and have big floor parties because those are always fun. We would always take over the TV room on our floor and play drinking games together, and it was great."

Q "Jester sucks. Prather is quiet as hell, but you can get away with anything there. Moore-Hill is similar. **Live in either Towers or Castilian** because you'll have the most fun, and you will meet more people there. Get an apartment on West campus after freshman year."

STUDENT AUTHOR: **San Jacinto is the clear favorite of the on-campus dorms. Jester is where a majority of people live, it's really not as bad as it seems. Kinsolving and Littlefield are not bad choices. If you can afford to live in a private dorm, Castilian is coed, and a place where you will meet tons of people.**

Did You Know?
20% of undergrads live on campus.

**Students Speak Out
ON GUYS & GIRLS**

Q "I can't remember the last time I was walking around UT and didn't see a hot guy. They are everywhere. With about 25,000 men running around, you are bound to find a cute one! Many days, **I am overwhelmed with the hotness** around me in my classes, but that usually means I'll go, so that helps me out."

Q "**The guys are laid-back**, and the only reason I go to campus anymore is to see all the hot girls walk around in tank tops. I love warm Texas weather."

Q "They are incredible! There is **every kind of girl you could ever want to meet here**. We have one of the best-looking student bodies of any university I've ever visited."

STUDENT AUTHOR: *Playboy* has repeatedly named the girls at UT some of the hottest in the nation (supposedly), and the guys aren't too bad either. There is every type of guy and girl on this campus. Styles range from skater to sorority girl, hippie to prep, activist to stoner, model to "anything but," frat boy to thug, prissy girl to outdoorsy, and of course, there's a fair share of nerds and jocks. However, it is somewhat difficult to find someone who wants the same things that you want.

Traditions

Hook 'em Horns hand signal
Introduced at a Friday night pep rally before the Texas Christian University football game in 1955.

Mascot Bevo, a Longhorn steer
Stephen Pickney (1911) spearheaded a movement to provide a live mascot for the University of Texas, collecting $1 each from 124 alumni.

Smokey the Cannon
It creates the thunderous roar heard after each Longhorn touchdown, field goal, and extra point. Four blank 10-gauge shotgun shells are fired.

**Students Speak Out
ON ATHLETICS**

Q "If you come to Texas and you don't know about Texas football, then you came to the wrong school and should just turn around and go back to that cave you crawled out of. **Texas football madness never ends in Austin**. When the season ends, we start talking about next season. Football season is the most fun time of year, as you can feel the energy in the air on campus. Alums come in on buses, by car, by plane, and by limo. They have box seats, season tickets, and lifetime passes."

Q "**Can you say football? I don't know many other universities that have F-16 flybys at their football games**. Basketball would definitely come in second in terms of fun for fans. We're good at lots of sports, but who wants to watch golf or swimming?"

STUDENT AUTHOR: **Buy a sports package; it gives you the opportunity to draw for tickets for all of the major varsity sports games. Football at Texas is huge, especially since we won the National Championship in 2006. Basketball fans are almost as rowdy, and although our baseball team doesn't gather as many fans, the boys do have their loyal following.**

Students Speak Out
ON DRUG SCENE

Q "**It totally depends on who you are around**. You will probably know people who sell and use drugs from your dorm or apartment building, and you may or may not be friends with them depending on your preferences. But, even if you are around drugs, people at UT are not into peer pressure—this isn't high school. You could go through your entire college career without ever seeing anyone using drugs, depending on who you hang out with and where you spend your time."

Q "**Drug problems here are mostly with alcohol**, and the interesting thing here is that people don't know that drinking every weekend can turn into alcoholism."

STUDENT AUTHOR: **Most students at UT drink, no matter what their age, and getting a hold of alcohol if you are underage is fairly simple. Most students at UT consider weed not to be an illegal drug, but put it in the same category with alcohol. Whether you are a pot smoker or not, you will not feel pressure to do so at UT.**

18:1	Student-to-Faculty Ratio
91%	Freshman Retention Rate
47%	Four-Year Graduation Rate
73%	Financial Aid Applicants Receiving Aid

Students Speak Out
SAFETY & SECURITY

Q "Austin is known for its safety. I cannot really answer what security is like on campus since there is no need for it really. However, there are call-boxes placed sporadically throughout the campus, and **SURE Walk is available for people walking across campus** and the surrounding areas at night."

Q "Security on campus is **very impressive with phone booths lit up** all over campus. Police constantly patrol here, and I feel surprisingly safe for having grown up in a small town and moving to the city."

Q "I'm a girl, and I used to walk across campus to Gregory Gym at night. Campus was well lit, and there were always people there at night. I've felt safe, but **I always carry mace just in case**."

STUDENT AUTHOR: **Programs, such as SURE Walk and UTPD Escort Service contribute to better feelings of security to students; walk with others rather than alone. Campus police are usually seen on campus, and there are blue-light phones that will notify police of your location on campus.**

> **Questions?**
> For more inside information and survival tips, pick up College Prowler's full-length book on this school, written by an actual student! Check it out at *www.collegeprowler.com*.

Students Speak Out
ON OVERALL EXPERIENCE

Q "Both of my parents went to school here, so **I have been a Longhorn fan my whole life**. Once I got to school here, it was obvious why my parents loved it here so much. I have had more fun here than I ever expected to have in college, and I never want to leave."

Q "I love UT; it is the perfect place for me. I was going to go to the northeast to a small liberal arts college in Maine (Bates College), but I thank the Lord everyday that I am blessed to still live in Texas. **I can't imagine myself happy anywhere else**."

Q "I have wanted to be here since I can remember and never considered anywhere else. The faculty is good, but **the staff and advising departments leave much to be desired**, as they are often unorganized. The advisors seem to often be uninformed or not interested in going the least bit out of their way."

STUDENT AUTHOR: **Students get a great education while having an awesome college town with everything at their disposals. Don't try to graduate early. Enjoy your time at UT—go cheer on the Longhorns at all the home games for all sports: football, basketball, baseball, intramurals. See the amenities that the Forty Acres has to offer—the Harry Ransom Center, go to our libraries and see our more than eight million volumes. Go to Gregory Gym and the Rec Center—you have a free gym membership for four years or more—use it. All you have to do is find your niche, and everything else should fall into place. UT is not nearly as big as it sounds.**

University of Utah

201 South Presidents Circle; Salt Lake City, Utah 84112
(801) 581-7200; www.utah.edu

THE BASICS:

Acceptance Rate: 86%
Setting: Mid-sized city
F-T Undergrads: 15,242

SAT Range: 1440–1860*
Control: Public
Tuition: $13,371

Most Popular Majors: Social Sciences, Business, Communications, Engineering, Health Professions

*of 2400

Academics	B-	Guys	B+
Local Atmosphere	B	Girls	B
Safety & Security	A-	Athletics	B+
Computers	B-	Nightlife	C+
Facilities	B	Greek Life	C-
Campus Dining	B-	Drug Scene	A-
Off-Campus Dining	B+	Campus Strictness	C
Campus Housing	A-	Parking	B-
Off-Campus Housing	A	Transportation	B+
Diversity	D-	Weather	B

Students Speak Out
ON ACADEMICS

Q "The professors are knowledgeable and seem **genuinely interested in how a student performs** in class. The majority of my classes are interesting, although there are a few exceptions; usually, the general studies classes not pertaining to my major."

Q "The teachers are academics. They have never worked a real job and look down on anyone who does. Class is **only interesting when the students get involved** in the discussion."

Q "The professors at the U, well, it really is **the luck of the draw**. I have had some whose teachings I think about all the time. At the same time, I have had some that I would be embarrassed as a university to say they work for me."

Q "I thought I would be bored with the classes outside of my major, but I was **happy to find interesting courses** for several of the general education requirements."

STUDENT AUTHOR: If you're looking for the best academic institution in the world, the U isn't it—strictly "by the numbers." The trouble with "the numbers," though, is academic quality among teachers is generally gauged by research and publishing success, not teaching ability. The U has plenty of great teachers, and simply because of its sheer size, there's a wide variety to choose from. Because it's large, there are plenty of opportunities to take advantage of if you find them.

Students Speak Out
ON LOCAL ATMOSPHERE

Q "The University of Utah is a commuter college. Salt Lake is **a great town to be in**—it's safe, clean, and overall, has some really cool people."

Q "Salt Lake is a very calm city. The U of U is the major university influence, followed by Salt Lake Community College. Close to campus, there are many places to visit and hang out, especially in the downtown area, which is five minutes away. Anyone attending the U has to **take advantage of the close mountains** and everything they offer to recreators."

Q "The city's not as bad as many people believe. **There is a nightlife if you find your scene.** Stay away from Provo and BYU unless you are Mormon."

Q "The great thing about where I live is the **proximity to outdoor activities** like hiking, skiing, bicycling, and water sports. However, having spent a little time in a big city like Washington DC, I am a little disappointed in the availability of other cultural activities."

STUDENT AUTHOR: Salt Lake is a city of contrasts. Its population is split pretty much down the middle between people who belong to the Church of Jesus Christ of Latter-day Saints and people who don't. Salt Lake is a mid-sized city, so it lacks the small-town charm of a straight-up college town, or the big-city flair of a university in a major metropolitan area. However, if you are an outdoorsman/outdoorswoman, you will utterly relish your time at the U.

Students Speak Out
ON FACILITIES

Q "The facilities are nice, the athletic facilities are pretty good, but **the hours could be better** for students; the Union is great, and it offers tons of events to keep you entertained."

Q "**Athletic facilities are somewhat archaic**. They're in the process of building a new facility for students to work out in. The computers are nice and fast, and the student center is well organized and well staffed."

Q "The **facilities are very nice**, except for the Mines building."

Q "Athletic centers are great! Go Utes! Computers are **updated frequently with the latest technology**, and the student center is welcoming. You can either sleep and study or go crazy elsewhere."

Q "Most of the facilities are new and handsome looking. The Field House is a notable exception. It is an old facility **kept in tolerable condition**, but is often overcrowded."

STUDENT AUTHOR: One advantage to the U's large size is the number of facilities available. In addition to the gyms and other recreational facilities, there are plenty of student-oriented events. The gyms aren't the best in the world, but they're not terrible. The stadium and dorms were revamped for the Olympics and are, accordingly, world class. The U has a firm commitment to keeping its campus green, with stretches of lawn that beautify but aren't too annoyingly large. The U's vast expanse of green space includes a nine-hole golf course.

Famous Alumni

Rocky Anderson, Alan Ashton, Nolan Bushnell, Stephen Covey, E.J. "Jake" Garn, Gordon B. Hinckley, J. Willard Marriott, Keith Van Horn

Students Speak Out
ON CAMPUS DINING

Q "**Food is getting better**; four years ago when I started it was awful, but lots of complaining has really turned it around. Try the fresh food made in the Union—it's so awesome."

Q "The food on campus is of mediocre quality and a little expensive. But I think that is **fair for a college campus**. Recently, Chartwells, the food service provider on campus, has worked to add more vegetarian and vegan dishes."

Q "I **try not to eat on campus**; I can get ripped off anywhere in the city."

Q "What food? **All I have ever seen is slop**. The dining hall is dirty and dingy and needs to be remodeled."

Q "The food is done by Chartwells, and I have to say that it is pretty good. There are tons of options for every taste. The Heritage Center (residence halls dining area) is only a few years old and is fantastic. **The Union has tons of food options**, and it's a great place to socialize and grab a bite to eat."

STUDENT AUTHOR: The cafeterias on campus are located in the residence halls. If you live there, you must have a meal plan, but anyone can buy one if they want. The cafeteria food is okay, with quite a bit of repetition that gets old fast. There are two other options instead of the cafeterias, and they are the food court/restaurant-style eateries. There are also snack bars in the Annex and University Services Building. The cafeteria at the Union Building is mediocre, but there's a Chick-fil-A there, as well as options for vegetarians.

Student Body

African American:	1%	Male/Female:	55/45%
Asian American:	5%	Out-of-State:	8%
Hispanic:	4%	International:	2%
Native American:	<1%	Unknown:	0%
White:	88%		

Popular Faiths: A large plurality of students on campus belong to the Church of Jesus Christ of Latter-day Saints.

Gay Pride: Since 2001, the U has had a Lesbian, Gay, Bisexual, and Transgender Resource Center.

Economic Status: The U of U student population comes from a wide variety of economic backgrounds.

Students Speak Out
ON DORMS

Q "The dorms are all super nice. They are new and were **used in the 2002 Winter Games** as athletes' housing."

Q "Dorms are excellent; the houses on Officer's Circle (where I stayed) are incredible. The Residence Hall Association makes sure that there are **plenty of events and activities** to keep everyone interested and involved."

Q "I have heard they are unbelievably modern and clean, and **the Internet connection is very fast**. The friends I have living there are very happy where they are and have really enjoyed the experience of getting to know a new roommate through the matching program."

STUDENT AUTHOR: These buildings are absolutely fabulous. They have state-of-the-art security capabilities, they have fine cafeterias, and the apartments are large and comfortable. It can be a bit of a walk from the dorms to the campus, depending on where your classes are, but it's all downhill, and there's a nice, attractive pedestrian bridge over the only busy street separating main campus and the residence halls.

Did You Know?
7% of undergrads live on campus.

Students Speak Out
ON GUYS & GIRLS

Q "Lots of **hot girls here**, but unless you are of the faith, keep your hands off the merchandise."

Q "Most of the guys and girls are married at a very young age. **It's difficult to meet someone** of the opposite sex if you are over 25."

Q "The U of U has a very beautiful student body. It's **very white-bread** and maybe a little too sweet for some people's taste."

Q "The student body is about as homogenous as you'd expect. Lots of pert girls and clean cut boys with **Teutonic good looks**. It's a big school; there's plenty of fresh meat circling around."

Q "There are **a lot of cute boys** on campus, but a lot of them are married."

STUDENT AUTHOR: The subject of dating is perhaps the greatest example of the University of Utah being a land of contrast. Most Mormons aren't interested in dating someone outside of their church because they're looking to marry within their own faith. Now, having said all that, the campus is populated with some very good-looking people. But look for wedding rings before you waste any time.

Traditions

BYU-Utah Game
Nothing gets the crowds out more than a showdown between the Utah Utes and the BYU Cougars.

Classic Greek Festival
Every fall, the theater department stages a dawn showing of a classic Greek play (typically "Oedipus the King").

Overall School Spirit
Because it's a commuter campus, the U doesn't have a great deal of school pride, but for those involved with on-campus organizations, the pride swells.

Students Speak Out
ON ATHLETICS

Q "Football and basketball are huge; they are usually in the national rankings, and we've got an incredible ladies gymnastics team, though they definitely deserve more patronage. I'm **astounded by the variety of IM sports**—it seems like for anything you're interested in, there's group or a club waiting for you to join."

Q "Varsity sports are hardly an obsession, but **they're all well attended**. Men's basketball is the big draw."

Q "Lots of people get involved in IM sports at the U. I am doing an indoor soccer one. From what I have heard, **the organization is good**, and lots of people show up to play."

Q "This year, **football seems to be really big**."

STUDENT AUTHOR: Students are generally disinterested in athletics, which makes it that much easier for those who are to get good seats at sporting events. The only events that really get people's blood pumping are games against Brigham Young University, the U's rival. Alums, staff, and faculty love these grudge matches, so tickets go fast.

Students Speak Out
ON DRUG SCENE

Q "I know anyone who's in the market for marijuana **won't have to look too hard** or long, but there's no real drug 'problem' at the U."

Q "Don't know of one; it's **a fairly clean campus** from what I've seen."

Q "I have never seen drugs on campus, and I have only heard of a few busts over the years. **We have a dry campus**, which the drinkers gripe about, but the non-drinkers love. I think the latter group is happy to not have to put up with drunken college men and women on campus."

STUDENT AUTHOR: **Drugs are not a problem at the U, or at least, not a very large problem. Yes, if you're looking for drugs, you'll be able to find them, as with anywhere else in the United States, but the U population, particularly the Mormons, shy away from substance abuse. The administration has a zero-tolerance stance against alcohol, too, which annoys some, but they don't throw you in jail for drinking on campus if you don't annoy anyone or break anything.**

15:1	Student-to-Faculty Ratio
79%	Freshman Retention Rate
17%	Four-Year Graduation Rate
69%	Financial Aid Applicants Receiving Aid

Students Speak Out
SAFETY & SECURITY

Q "The campus is **very safe and non-threatening**. I feel safe walking around alone at 2 a.m. after the library closes."

Q "As a woman, I always felt very safe on campus. There is good lighting and close parking lots accessible for evening classes. **Many call-boxes are located throughout campus** for security."

Q "I once made the mistake of leaving my car window down for three days in the school parking lot while I was out of town. Luckily, and to the admiration of the local culture, **nothing was harmed**."

Q "**I feel very secure** on campus. I seldom hear of occurrences that would make me feel otherwise."

STUDENT AUTHOR: **The U is a big campus with lots of trees for prowlers to hide behind late at night, but if you aren't walking around late, you'll be fine. The dorms security systems were built with Olympic athletes in mind, so they're top notch. Security is a question of common sense.**

> **Questions?**
> For more inside information and survival tips, pick up College Prowler's full-length book on this school, written by an actual student! Check it out at *www.collegeprowler.com*.

Students Speak Out
ON OVERALL EXPERIENCE

Q "I love going to school here; the opportunities to participate in activities that change your life are abounding, and **my life is 10 times better than it ever was** before going to school here."

Q "**I hated the U of U** my first year, but now I can't imagine going anywhere else."

Q "It seems like there is a prevailing feeling of animosity on campus—**it's not nearly as friendly as I wish it were**. In this respect, I wouldn't hesitate to go elsewhere. Classes are a bit crowded, and many of the professors are just there to pick up a paycheck it seems."

Q "I love the University of Utah! I went to another school for a little while, and it doesn't even compare. Also, getting involved in student government, clubs, or the Greek system is one of the best things you can do! **It's so much fun**, you'll make tons of new friends, and you will definitely love the U!"

Q "The overall experience has been great; I have met a lot of people and have found **Utah is a great place to live**!"

STUDENT AUTHOR: **The trick to having a rich experience at the U is to get involved. If you live off campus and only come to school to "go to school" then your good, old college days will be very bland indeed. There is no campus community; there simply isn't. But there are dozens and dozens of sub-communities on campus to find and become a part of. People who enjoy the U are those who take ownership of their education and college experience. Those who complain about it are generally those who just sit back, waiting for someone else to make college great for them.**

University of Vermont

South Prospect Street; Burlington VT 05405
(802) 656-3131; www.uvm.edu

THE BASICS:

Acceptance Rate: 65%
Setting: Rural
F-T Undergrads: 9,723

SAT Range: 1080–1270*
Control: Public
Tuition: $26,306

Most Popular Majors: Social Sciences, Business, Psychology, Education, Health Sciences

*of 1600

Academics	B	Guys	B-
Local Atmosphere	A-	Girls	B
Safety & Security	A-	Athletics	B-
Computers	B+	Nightlife	B
Facilities	B+	Greek Life	C
Campus Dining	B+	Drug Scene	C+
Off-Campus Dining	A-	Campus Strictness	B
Campus Housing	C	Parking	D+
Off-Campus Housing	B	Transportation	B+
Diversity	D-	Weather	C-

Students Speak Out
ON ACADEMICS

Q "**You are not a number**, and that is important. If you want help, it is there. If you want to be left alone, that is also an option. It is really about what you want."

Q "I think that at UVM, the quality of your teachers depends on the effort that you make to get to know them. If you want to see them and get to know them, **they are there to help**, but they won't put that much effort into getting to know you unless you make the first move."

Q "I've encountered **a lot of professors with a great commitment to teaching**. Few have expressed their own work and research as more important and urgent than our education, at least in front of the classroom."

Q "Most **professors were easy to get in to see** and to get extra help from."

Q "For the most part, I've found professors enjoy teaching and are **interested and knowledgeable in their field**."

STUDENT AUTHOR: **Both professors and students approach their jobs with enthusiasm and dedication. As a result, UVM students experience satisfying relationships with professors, enhancing their academic experience. A laid-back attitude takes precedence over high-strung, fast-paced living. Professors here definitely possess personality, reflecting a variety of backgrounds resulting in many refreshing, unprecedented approaches to teaching.**

Students Speak Out
ON LOCAL ATMOSPHERE

Q "The atmosphere is great. It's Vermont! Burlington has a few other universities in the area; their presence is mostly a positive thing. The **commercial downtown area is beautiful**, but the surrounding area—Vermont's natural setting—can be a nice place to visit, too."

Q "Since Vermont is such a small state, and Burlington is the 'major city,' you can sometimes find **opportunities here that you couldn't find in larger cities**—it's a great place to get involved with the community."

Q "The atmosphere here in Burlington and Vermont, overall, is the reason I came to UVM. The tolerance, the crunchiness, the happiness, and the unabashed liberal and free spirit provide the necessary background for a college student—an **atmosphere in which everything and anything is accepted and supported**."

Q "The **atmosphere in Burlington is a laid-back, pretty outdoorsy feel**. There are other universities present."

STUDENT AUTHOR: **Burlington is a small but bustling city with five colleges in its vicinity. With majestic rolling fields, golden stalks sweeping in the wind, and the Green Mountains hailing in the background, Vermont is a visionary canvas. This is an obvious advantage for those who enjoy outdoor activities. Vermont boasts arguably the best region on the East Coast for this. The winter months give rise to the East Coast's best skiing at Killington and Stowe— the only eastern rivals to the Rocky Mountains.**

Students Speak Out
ON FACILITIES

Q "All the facilities are great. The gym is cool because **you can look out the window at the mountains while you bike or jog**. The computers are all pretty new, and the student center is also nice."

Q "The facilities are nice, especially the gym and weight room. The **student center is rather impersonal and complex-like**. It feels more like a maze than a place to go hang out. Computers, again, are available and usually not crowded, but most people have their own."

Q "Most **classrooms are nice, and the dining areas are clean**. People hang out all over the place. The lobby of your complex will have Ping-Pong tables and pool tables and stuff, but most people hang out in their rooms or halls and just chill in there."

Q "The athletic center is really nice and has pretty much anything you could want, from a climbing wall to a swimming pool. The buildings are all really nice, and there is an **ample amount of places for students to gather** and do whatever they want to do."

STUDENT AUTHOR: The athletic facilities are simply beautiful. This is due to the commitment of the school to provide its students with updated equipment. Best of all, the whole facility overlooks unobstructed views of the Green Mountains. The Billings Student Center houses numerous places to study, the University radio station, and club spaces. UVM provides students with a number of facility options ranging from the solitude of secret study places to the flurry of high-octane hockey games.

Famous Alumni

Grace Coolidge, John Dewey, Mike Gordon and Jeff Holdsworth of the band Phish, John LeClair, Libby Smith, Jody Williams

Students Speak Out
ON CAMPUS DINING

Q "Besides the dining halls, UVM also has food-court-type places where your food is made-to-order. These places include the Round Room, which offers a wide variety of sandwiches made on your choice of bread, and Cook Commons, located on the main campus, which offers a rotating selection of Chinese food, fast food, a homemade food place, and wraps, which are **really popular and really good**."

Q "If you are vegetarian like me, I have found that UVM is probably **more accommodating than most schools**."

Q "The food on campus is great. The system that UVM employs allows for a **wide variety of choices for any kind of eater**. We have two major dining halls in which you can use your dining points at the door, and then eat all you want from the typical offerings of pizza, french fries, hamburgers, garden burgers, a salad bar, bagels, breads, lunch meats, soup, pasta, grilled cheese, cereal, and a meal that changes for most of the day. In the morning, they offer waffles, bacon, sausage, potato tots or hash browns, omelets, and other breakfast foods."

STUDENT AUTHOR: The University of Vermont dining services receives high marks from students. The University actually has fairly good dining hall food compared with other schools. Taking the food for what it is—bulk-purchased, vitamin enriched, mass-produced cuisine—it is actually pretty tolerable. Everyone will have his or her fair share of complaints, but overall, they do a fair job.

Student Body

African American:	1%	Male/Female:	45/55%
Asian American:	2%	Out-of-State:	65%
Hispanic:	2%	International:	<1%
Native American:	<1%	Unknown:	2%
White:	92%		

Popular Faiths: All religions are present on campus, but Christianity seems to be the preferred religion of most.

Gay Pride: UVM is a tolerant place where people of all sexual orientations are accepted.

Economic Status: UVM consists of students, for the most part, who come from middle- to upper-class families.

Students Speak Out
ON DORMS

Q "Live in Harris-Millis your first year. I lived there my first year, and I thought it was great. Athletic Campus is the place to be during your freshman year, and Redstone Campus is the place to be for your sophomore year. People who live on Redstone already know everyone else there, so **it's easier to meet people when you live on Athletic Campus**."

Q "The **dorms aren't great**. They are all fairly modern, but they're all fairly small, as well."

Q "UVM offers **fewer dorm options than some other colleges**. Freshman and sophomore year, everyone is required to live on campus in dorm rooms with extremely limited access to suites and virtually no campus apartments exist."

STUDENT AUTHOR: **Most dorms at UVM do have adequate places to study for those who get stuck with a roommate who never studies. UVM does not offer many alternatives to the basic dorm room, but students feel that the required two years of on-campus housing allows students to develop important ties to UVM, both socially and individually.**

> **Did You Know?**
> 54% of undergrads live on campus.

Students Speak Out
ON GUYS & GIRLS

Q "Most people don't dress up for class, and a lot (including myself) wake up about 20 minutes before class to throw on a sweater or sweatshirt and jeans, and then just go to class. Nobody cares if you want to dress differently. I find it to be **a really comfortable atmosphere**."

Q "Neither guys nor girls can really be pigeon-holed at UVM. Dreadlocks and crew cuts are equally as likely to be pot heads, active members of clubs and organizations, and friends with one another. We do have a pretty physically-active student population, providing for **a fairly fit and attractive crowd**."

STUDENT AUTHOR: UVM is infamous for the "hippie" population, but all other types of people are here, too. There are attractive people from all spectrums. It is unanimous—both the guys and the girls are attractive. But if anything is missing, it is the mental or emotional connection between people in relationships. Hooking up and having fun seems to be the trend. There are certainly people in serious relationships, but many want nothing more than a casual relationship.

> **Overall School Spirit**
> Students at UVM love their Catamounts! Students can be seen sporting their UVM attire on any given day around campus. Both the men's and women's hockey teams are followed religiously by students and local residents alike. The UVM men's team, in particular, has been very successful over the years. They have won four conference titles in the last decade alone. The men's basketball team has also experienced recent success—particularly in the 2004 NCAA tournament when they defeated perennial the powerhouse Syracuse in the second round.

Students Speak Out
ON ATHLETICS

Q "UVM has **no football team**, but our hockey team is a big deal, and so is our basketball team. One of the things that kind of sucks about UVM is school spirit. We do lack a bit in that department, but it's hard when the school doesn't really promote varsity sports that much."

Q "**Hockey is big** at UVM. I recommend attending as many hockey games as possible, even if you don't like hockey. The social scene is great."

Q "Sports aren't that big. However, they are fun, and it's definitely worthwhile to participate in them. I was a member of varsity swimming for two months but found it **too difficult to manage my time with all of my classes**."

STUDENT AUTHOR: While UVM does not draw the best athletes from across the country, its reputation as a competitive Division I school is increasing. Moreover, the surroundings of Vermont entice many to take up independent sports such as climbing, hiking, or cross-country skiing. There is likely a sport for anyone who cares to participate in one.

Students Speak Out
ON DRUG SCENE

Q "If you want to avoid drugs and drinking, and can't stand people who choose to use them, you should **live in a substance-free dorm** or on a substance-free floor."

Q "There is **pot just about everywhere**. If you want to find some, it's pretty readily available, except when there is a lull in the market, probably the result of a drug bust or something. Substances come around in waves, so there are rarely other given drugs around, except maybe cocaine."

Q "There is a lot of weed on campus; UVM is well known for it. But if you're not into that kind of thing, don't worry about it. **Not everyone does it**. There are plenty of people at UVM that are not pot heads, trust me."

STUDENT AUTHOR: As with any college campus, there are drugs and alcohol, and there are students who use either, both, or none. Marijuana is the most prevalent illegal substance, along with alcohol. Pot is very common not only here, but in the surrounding Burlington community.

16:1	Student-to-Faculty Ratio
86%	Freshman Retention Rate
56%	Four-Year Graduation Rate
82%	Financial Aid Applicants Receiving Aid

Students Speak Out
SAFETY & SECURITY

Q "As far as I know, **security and safety at UVM are top-notch**. The campus police are actually a division of the state police, so they're good policemen, but if you do things like smoke weed in your room, they have a reputation for busting people, so watch out."

Q "For the most part, **UVM's campus, as well as Burlington itself, feels safe** and manageable. Incidents are generally well publicized and security is dependable, although, perhaps, campus police should be less discipline-oriented and more approachable with safety concerns."

Q "**Safety at UVM is great**. Like any campus, UVM's campus has call-boxes, campus police, and lighted walkways."

STUDENT AUTHOR: Students love the secure feeling they get having award-winning police services on campus. Be forewarned—they are not simply rent-a-cops. They hold the same jurisdiction as state police. Overall, UVM feels like a safe place. There continues to be little crime in the area.

Questions?

For more inside information and survival tips, pick up College Prowler's full-length book on this school, written by an actual student! Check it out at *www.collegeprowler.com.*

Students Speak Out
ON OVERALL EXPERIENCE

Q "I love it, and I fit right in with my school. You really have to be **very liberal, very open to new things, very open to homosexuality**, and very willing to be screwed over by the system, although everything will turn out fine in the end."

Q "I do wish that I was not at UVM. **I wish that I would have stayed in New York**, preferably in the city. I'm from New York, a little outside the city, and I just miss the city life."

Q "College was a huge decision for me. I wanted the best total college package, and I can't believe **how lucky I am to have found it here at UVM**. My father and I visited over 20 schools nationwide, and I chose UVM over all of them. You can walk downtown in Burlington wearing sweatpants or a prom dress, and no one will think twice about it."

Q "Overall, I think that **UVM is a blast**. There are lots of people, lots of things to do, the mountains are so pretty, and the lake is so beautiful. It's a pretty campus, the people are nice, and the academics are good."

STUDENT AUTHOR: Students are in agreement that the University of Vermont is a remarkable place to go to school. The refreshing environment and lovely surroundings meld well with the progressive, laid-back city of Burlington. The University of Vermont houses provocative and diverse thoughts, mixed with a dedicated student body and the additional flair of Burlington. The verdict is out: UVM is a beautiful school with a rigorous academic curriculum, mixed in a place that people come to enjoy, and surely, continue to love.

University of Virginia

1740 University Avenue; Charlottesville, Virginia 22903-2619
(434) 924-0311; www.virginia.edu

THE BASICS:

Acceptance Rate: 39%   SAT Range: 1230–1430*
Setting: Rural   Control: Public
F-T Undergrads: 13,378   Tuition: $24,100

Most Popular Majors: Economics, Business, Psychology, English, International Affairs

*of 1600

Academics	A-	Guys	A
Local Atmosphere	B	Girls	A
Safety & Security	B+	Athletics	A
Computers	B-	Nightlife	C+
Facilities	B	Greek Life	A
Campus Dining	C	Drug Scene	B
Off-Campus Dining	B+	Campus Strictness	A
Campus Housing	C+	Parking	D
Off-Campus Housing	A-	Transportation	B+
Diversity	C+	Weather	B

Students Speak Out
ON ACADEMICS

Q "There's more excellent teachers than bad teachers. Usually, **you will get a professor**, but in some classes, you end up with a graduate assistant (GA) or teaching assistant (TA)."

Q "I found that the **greatest challenge was the way the courses were structured**, and more specifically, the class size of most of the courses. For courses within my majors, it was not until my fourth and final year that I had a class where the professor was close enough to me that I did not need my glasses to make out his/her face."

Q "Some of the unknown teachers teach some of the best classes I have ever had. **I don't think I missed a thing** by not taking classes with some of the well-known professors."

Q "When you are still young, **most classes will be large lectures**, and as you declare a major, they get smaller. All professors have office hours, and if you go to them, you will get to know your teachers even more. I have yet to be disappointed by any of my teachers."

STUDENT AUTHOR: **Most students agree that the professors at UVA are outstanding. For the most part, students find that classes and professors in the College of Arts and Sciences (particularly the English, drama, and history departments) are more liberal and interesting. Some of the more technical courses and schools (biology or engineering) can be a necessary burden, even for students specializing in those fields.**

Students Speak Out
ON LOCAL ATMOSPHERE

Q "**There's a lot to visit in C-ville**. The places I would recommend are the Downtown Mall, Humpback Rock, Beaver Creek, Crabtree Falls, Monticello, and the Rotunda."

Q "Charlottesville has a small-town feel, which at times is **wonderful and relaxing, and at other times is stifling and insulating**. Overall, I always thought of Charlottesville as made up of college kids (mostly affluent and from other cities), the professors and their families, the ex-hippies who landed here because of the liberal-friendly feel, and all the other people affectionately referred to by the college kids as 'townies.' Definitely find time to visit the Downtown Mall. There is a free trolley from the Corner and Grounds."

Q "The town is really nice in areas that are generally populated with University students, such as the Corner, Barracks Road, and Downtown Mall. However, there are **some sections of town that you definitely want to stay away from**."

STUDENT AUTHOR: **Charlottesville has a unique, artistic, natural feel to it. It is surrounded by the beautiful hills and mountains of the Blue Ridge, which alone have much to offer—from hiking and picnicking, to a simple stroll along Skyline Drive. Although it can seem stifling at times, the area has more than enough for you to discover over your four years of college. If you're willing to be creative and explore new places, there's a lot to be found. There are plenty of lakes and ponds just outside of town where students like to cool off in.**

5 Best Things	**5 Worst Things**
1 Beautiful surroundings	1 Greek scene
2 Amazing professors	2 Advising system
3 Vibrant people	3 Parking
4 Fun social scene	4 Lack of diversity
5 Athletic facilities	5 Naïve students

Students Speak Out
ON FACILITIES

Q "**The AFC is great**—though I wish the pool was open more. I constantly wanted to swim when the pool wasn't open. In terms of fitness equipment, UVA is great."

Q "While all these facilities are nice, the **administration shows its bias toward athletics** at UVA, as students watch privileges like free and unlimited printing in the computer labs go down the tubes in the course of the same year in which ground is broken for the new basketball arena."

Q "The facilities depend on which school you are in. The engineering school's facilities (such as the library and computer labs) are **old, dirty, uncomfortable, and falling apart**. Most of the classrooms are in the basement with no windows, and students must sit in cramped seating. They recently constructed a new library, though."

Q "When it comes to facilities, Virginia has the best around. The gyms are great and have the most modern and safe equipment. There are **more computer labs than I can count**, and the libraries are renowned. All athletic events are free to students and so much fun."

STUDENT AUTHOR: **Students agree that the athletic facilities (especially the Aquatic and Fitness Center) are superb. However, despite the excellent gyms and new athletic-and fitness-oriented projects, UVA sometimes neglects other parts of the campus. Some students will complain about the condition of labs and classrooms within the various colleges; though, complaints about the lack of a proper student center have finally ceased with the renovation of the new Newcomb Hall.**

Famous Alumni

Ronde and Tiki Barber, Katie Couric, Tina Fey, Thomas Jones, Edgar Allan Poe, Woodrow Wilson

Students Speak Out
ON CAMPUS DINING

Q "Some of the food they serve is really sub-par, but the dining halls **all have some sort of ethnic/alternative meal station**, which is usually pretty good."

Q "I love the dining hall! I had a **meal plan for all four years**. Some days are definitely better than others, but I could always find something to eat—though, maybe not always the healthiest. Chick-fil-A was so clutch."

Q "UVA dining leaves a lot to be desired. Compared to other schools, UVA **doesn't really have a wide assortment of choices**. UVA needs more fast food on grounds."

Q "Food is great—well, **it depends on what you like**. If you are not a fan of the dining halls (O-Hill, Newcomb, Runk) you can hit up the Treehouse (Pizza Hut and the Grill) or the Pavilion (Chick-fil-A, Cranberry Farms, Smoothie King, Bene Pizza, and the Bagel shop)."

Q "On grounds, where all freshmen eat, it is definitely not bad at all; there are a lot of **options for even the most picky eaters**. The best dining halls are O-Hill and Newcomb."

STUDENT AUTHOR: **Most students find the on-grounds dining to be pretty standard. The salad, wrap, cereal, and ethnic/alternative food stations are normally pretty reliable. The biggest complaint seems to be that the food is always the same. It is sometimes difficult for vegetarians and vegans to find something that suits their needs.**

Student Body

African American:	9%	Male/Female:	47/53%
Asian American:	11%	Out-of-State:	28%
Hispanic:	2%	International:	5%
Native American:	<1%	Unknown:	0%
White:	73%		

Popular Faiths: There are a few prominent Christian groups within the University that regularly hold meetings.

Gay Pride: UVA is becoming increasingly more accepting of its gay and lesbian population. There are various active organizations at the University promoting gay awareness—the GLC, for example.

Economic Status: UVA students come off as pretty wealthy—with their cars, clothes, and drinking habits, it would seem they would have to be.

Students Speak Out
ON DORMS

Q "I lived in new dorms, but I wish I'd lived in the old dorms. The **old dorms are a lot closer to classes**. New dorms have some pros, though: suites and more diversity (old dorms are almost all white). Do not live in Hereford!"

Q "**Do not live in Hereford**, ever. Old dorms are the place to live, meet people, and have fun, but the dorms are crap. But at least that way you have something to complain about together!"

Q "I think it's good to live on grounds your first two years and then live in an apartment off grounds. It's a **good taste of the real world**—dealing with landlords and bills and all."

STUDENT AUTHOR: **Most students agree that the old dorms (McCormick Road Resident Area) are the place to be your first year. Despite the small double rooms, they are far more social, and the location is much more convenient for classes and other activities. In terms of quality, the dorm facilities at UVA are pretty standard. Because there are definitely those undesirable dorms, and because the housing office is not very courteous (especially to students who must move back on grounds after being off grounds).**

Did You Know?
46% of undergrads live on campus.

Students Speak Out
ON GUYS & GIRLS

Q "That first day of spring when all **the girls jump into skimpy summer clothing** for the first time and start sunbathing on the Lawn and the Quad is a great day. There are a bunch of attractive people at UVA."

Q "Everyone here is pretty attractive, guys and girls. There are **virtually no fat people**. Everyone runs and works out at the gyms. The gyms are really great, by the way!"

Q "**Everyone is laid-back and willing** to help you out or become friends with you. Guys and girls are both really nice. I find the Southern culture to be really genteel, on the whole. The boys are really cute, in a frat-guy sort of way."

STUDENT AUTHOR: **UVA students have a very refined look. Most really care about appearances, so you will certainly see a lot of dressing up for class, as well as a lot of working out at the gym. Some find this to be a cute and distinctive feature of UVA, while others find it really obnoxious and superficial. Most students agree the girls are way hotter than the guys. Personality-wise, however, there is some definite snobbiness within the girl population, and this detracts from their better looks.**

Traditions

The Good Ole' Song"
Many crazy Cavalier fans sing this after every UVA touchdown at football games.

The Bridge
Many students and their organizations get together and paint the bridge late at night.

Overall School Spirit
UVA has great school spirit, especially at football and basketball games, where among other things you can find bodies spray-painted in orange and blue, girls dressed in pearls, and guys wearing orange bow ties.

Students Speak Out
ON ATHLETICS

Q "**Basketball is big here**—some of the crazier fans (like me) have been known to camp out for weeks in the snow and rain just to get the closest seats to the floor. It's ACC basketball, need I say more?"

Q "I **don't think IM sports are that big** at all—I never really heard about them."

Q "**Sports are huge**! UVA has a couple dozen varsity teams that are extremely competitive. You don't become a UVA student until you go to a UVA football and basketball game!"

Q "You can try to walk onto a team at Virginia, but **you better be good**."

STUDENT AUTHOR: **Athletics at UVA have always been huge, and most everyone recognizes this coming into the school. Basketball and football in particular are very big sports here, no matter the quality of the team from season to season. Going to home football games is definitely a tradition at UVA; students get all dressed up, go to tailgates beforehand, and sing the "Good 'Ole Song" after every touchdown.**

Students Speak Out
ON DRUG SCENE

Q "There's a lot of alcohol use and abuse, but other drugs aren't as popular. I think **30 percent of students smoke**. In my substance abuse class, I think we learned that marijuana was the number one illicit drug used here."

Q "If you don't know about the drug scene, you'll never see it at all. There are certain sororities and fraternities known for certain drugs, particularly **coke and weed**."

Q "You can pretty much get whatever you want in town, but I don't know much about drugs, other than pot. I've heard that **the ecstasy here is sketchy, but it's big** at Virginia. Alcohol is the main drug that kids use here."

STUDENT AUTHOR: **The most-used drug among students is alcohol by far. Generally, if you don't know about drugs or aren't interested in knowing about them, you'll never see the scene around Charlottesville. Some students feel as though marijuana and cocaine are a problem, but for the most part no one sees heavy drug use during their tenures) here.**

15:1	Student-to-Faculty Ratio
97%	Freshman Retention Rate
83%	Four-Year Graduation Rate
24%	Financial Aid Applicants Receiving Aid

Students Speak Out
SAFETY & SECURITY

Q "I've always felt really safe here. I think most other students do, too. A lot of **being safe is just using common sense**."

Q "The security is great at Virginia. **We have our own Virginia police**. If you need a ride home from somewhere on the campus at night, you can dial UVA security and they will give you a ride home. I've personally never heard of any security problems at the campus."

Q "I've never really felt unsafe, but not a year goes by that there isn't talk of **someone getting hurt**."

Q "Coming from a guy, I've never had any problems walking alone at night, but the recent **assault and battery incidents** have caused me to worry about my female friends."

STUDENT AUTHOR: **Most students at UVA feel pretty safe. The UVA police are quite a noticeable presence on grounds—in addition to the school's 90 police officers, there is a staff of about 130 security workers. Standard campus security services are offered at UVA (blue-light phones, escort services), but the best tools are common sense and simply being aware.**

> **Questions?**
> For more inside information and survival tips, pick up College Prowler's full-length book on this school, written by an actual student! Check it out at *www.collegeprowler.com*.

Students Speak Out
ON OVERALL EXPERIENCE

Q "The school was really great, believe it or not. There's **a great party scene**. Some find it too preppy, but you can find just about any sort of crowd. I never once regretted going to UVA over Duke."

Q "Because I did not fit in well with the dominant social scene at UVA (**Greek-influenced, pretentious . . . shall I go on?**), I often thought I would be better suited elsewhere. But if you're in-state, it's a great deal for the money, and that is why I stayed."

Q "I miss college already. I just graduated and am already envious of my kid brother coming here in the fall. **I miss the UVA lifestyle**."

Q "There are great traditions. UVA has some really neat ones; you really end up feeling that you are part of the original scheme that Jefferson thought up. **The campus is beautiful**, and the memories made here are unique, but this sometimes gives us a reputation for being a snobby school."

STUDENT AUTHOR: **The University of Virginia has some of the most devoted alumni in the country. Of course, there are those who wished they had gone elsewhere, and those who were turned off by things such as the lack of diversity, the prominence of Greek life, student naïvety, or the pretentiousness that is, in fact, present on grounds. Those who really like UVA appreciate its traditions, the friendly and outgoing atmosphere, the beautiful setting, and the outstanding academic environment. Students definitely have their share of rough, sad, aggravating moments at UVA. But, for most, the hardships endured pay off big in the end.**

University of Washington

1410 NE Campus Parkway; Seattle, WA 98195
(206) 543-2100; www.washington.edu

THE BASICS:

Acceptance Rate: 65%   **SAT Range:** 1610–1950*
Setting: Urban   **Control:** Public
F-T Undergrads: 24,209 **Tuition:** $23,219

Most Popular Majors: Social Sciences, Business, Engineering, Psychology, Visual & Performing Arts.

*of 2400

Academics	B	Guys	B+
Local Atmosphere	A-	Girls	B+
Safety & Security	C	Athletics	A
Computers	A-	Nightlife	A-
Facilities	A-	Greek Life	B+
Campus Dining	B+	Drug Scene	B
Off-Campus Dining	A	Campus Strictness	B+
Campus Housing	C-	Parking	D
Off-Campus Housing	B+	Transportation	A-
Diversity	B+	Weather	C-

Students Speak Out
ON ACADEMICS

Q "I've found UW to have a wide variety of teachers. They vary in methods and approach; overall, however, the **quality of the teaching staff, I feel, is extremely competent**. Mostly after approaching them, I've found the staff to be friendly and open, and I would stress the importance of getting to know your teachers."

Q "I think the level of interest in a class is almost directly related to who the teacher or professor is. I've taken classes where the **course content could have been far more interesting** and engaging had the instructor been able to make it so and been able to keep my attention. Especially in long lectures, make sure you get into a class you are willing to sit through."

Q "I find classes very interesting—some more than others. I enjoy the challenge professors at UW present. **It is not like high school** where I would not see the benefit to attending class."

Q "The teachers were all pretty good. They're all very willing to help the students grasp the concepts being taught, and **they want to see the students succeed**."

STUDENT AUTHOR: Thanks to the size of the University, students have an expansive selection of courses and professors each quarter, and an equally impressive breadth and depth of ripe resources. And because so many students call UW home, professors don't usually cater to stragglers—most often, a student sinking in an intro-level class won't get help unless he or she asks.

Students Speak Out
ON LOCAL ATMOSPHERE

Q "Seattle is an amazing town to live in, and if it weren't for the weather, I would stay here forever. There are tons of sight-seeing, touristy areas to visit, gorgeous views, and great outdoor activities. SPU, the art institute, and the community colleges are the schools nearby, but it's just a quick drive to Western. And of course, **for the underagers, Canada is great** and close by, as well."

Q "When I was at a journalism conference in Las Vegas a few months ago, someone complained that their campus had no scene. The girl I was with chimed in that **at UW, 'the whole campus is a scene!'**"

Q "I personally don't really like the area around the UW that much. The Ave. is getting better, but **it seems really trashy to me**; U-village is really close, and it has a much nicer atmosphere."

Q "Even though there are other universities around, **it's mostly UW students**, and it's a great environment to be in."

STUDENT AUTHOR: Seattle culture is as inspired as the natural atmosphere surrounding it. A city of many neighborhoods, Seattle offers everything from the colorful Ave. to lush Capitol Hill, to cozy Queen Anne, to ritzy University Village, to bustling downtown Seattle, to zany Broadway. The vibrant-yet-chill Seattle scene threads the diverse group of neighborhoods together, and virtually everyone finds a niche.

5 Best Things	5 Worst Things
1 Springtime on Quad	1 Large class sizes
2 Mt. Ranier	2 Parking
3 The Husky Den	3 Rain
4 The IMA	4 Foreign professors
5 Husky football	5 Communal bathrooms

Students Speak Out
ON FACILITIES

Q "**I love the campus facilities**, but I think sometimes the priorities as to which buildings need renovations are messed up."

Q "I absolutely, positively **love the fitness facilities at the UW**. A recent remodel to the IMA has given students every reason in the world to get fit. It is free, and the facilities are first-rate. Also, the Washington Yacht Club is well-suited for providing students with cheap fun on the water. Otherwise, I'd say the UW is good at supporting students. The facilities are generally above average."

Q "**Everything is accessible**. Right down by the parking lot there is a huge athletic department called the IMA where you can go work out and play basketball or tennis. There is a pool and other facilities you can use, too. On campus, there is a big building called the Husky Den, and that is kind of like the student center; it's a place you can go for information."

Q "I love the whole campus; there are some old buildings, but it gives the school character. The new IMA is great, and the dorms aren't bad (of course, that depends on where you end up). **The Husky Den is a great place**, as well."

STUDENT AUTHOR: UW's facilities definitely meet the standards of most students. The Husky Den and the IMA are the heart of UW's facilities, and as a whole, the campus is visually stunning. The classic brick buildings and quaint brick walkways on the Quad evoke the Ivy-League feel—a look that peaks during spring when the cherry blossoms bloom.

Famous Alumni

Beverly Cleary, Patrick Duffy, David Horsey, Kenneth "Kenny G" Gorelick, David Guterson

Students Speak Out
ON CAMPUS DINING

Q "The Husky Den has the best on-campus dining. Subway is my personal favorite. But the best part about the Husky Den is the social scene at lunch hour. Once you meet some people on campus, if you go into the Husky Den around lunchtime, **there will be someone there you know**."

Q "It's really nice that UW has quite a few eating areas; however, **I think that they should be open more** and have longer hours than they do. Also, unless you eat off campus some, you won't get a very diverse food intake. McMahon and By George do not change their menus that often."

Q "The Husky Den has a ton of options and is moderately priced. Everything is very tasty, as well. The dining halls are **good, but a little overpriced**. The best place to eat if you're on a budget would probably be By George."

Q "As far as meals go, there are plenty of options on campus. What I have found, though, is that **eating on campus is not economically sound**. By grocery shopping and eating on the University Avenue (the Ave.), I have saved an average of $300 a month over eating on a meal plan."

STUDENT AUTHOR: As far as college campus menus go, UW has a pretty big selection and provides many different types of cuisine. Some students seem satisfied with the selection and the quality of eats, while others get bored of the limited options. Students agree that price inflation is a fairly large problem, but even so, students still eat at the Husky Den regularly.

Student Body

African American:	3%	Male/Female:	49/51%
Asian American:	25%	Out-of-State:	23%
Hispanic:	3%	International:	3%
Native American:	1%	Unknown:	0%
White:	65%		

Popular Faiths: Because UW is so big, there is a fairly wide range of religions represented.

Gay Pride: Seattle is a socially liberal area with a large gay scene concentrated around Broadway. UW has a high gay tolerance and a significant LGBT population.

Economic Status: Since it is a state school, there are some in-state low- and middle-income students, as well as students from high-income families.

Students Speak Out
ON DORMS

Q "The dorms were okay. **Some were crowded and too penitentiary-like**. The best is McMahon. I would stay away from Hansee, Haggett, and Terry-Lander."

Q "The dorms are actually a good place to live. It is a great community, and **I would strongly recommend it to first-year students** as a way to make friends. The best dorm is McCarty, then McMahon. The worst dorm is Mercer."

Q "Dorms are cramped, but it is a good experience. **You don't want to live there more than a year**, though; it's too strict."

STUDENT AUTHOR: **Residence halls run the gamut from buzzing social vortexes to socially-muzzled black holes. Because of over-enrollment, UW often squeezes three people into a room originally built as a cozy double. Proximity to campus also poses a huge variable. Lander, Terry, and Mercer, which have been referred to as "the boonie dorms," require a bit of a hike to central campus but only a short walk to the Ave., while McCarty, Hagget, and McMahon are nestled right in the Quad's backyard.**

Did You Know?
17% of undergrads live on campus.

Students Speak Out
ON GUYS & GIRLS

Q "The campus, overall, has an attractive student body, but for a public school, **there are more stuck-up and superficial people** than I would have expected."

Q "There are a lot of pretty girls on campus; I don't really look that way too much, but they are there. Guys are amazing; I've met a couple guys that the only way to describe them is beautiful—like, wow, **they're not hot, but they are beautiful**. So the guys are a good thing."

Q "Well, guys I can't judge too well. The girls are not too cute here. The thing is, **with the gloomy weather, nobody ever tries to dress up**, but as soon as the sun comes out, people start looking better."

STUDENT AUTHOR: **UW's size is the defining factor here. If you're looking for hot guys and girls, they are definitely to be found on campus, and many believe they are concentrated in the Greek population. If you're attracted to athletes, hippies, stoners, skaters, ravers, whatever, UW pretty much has it all. You won't confuse campus for Hollywood or Malibu, but there are definitely plenty of attractive people of both sexes.**

Traditions

Boat Races
Many students come out to the Montlake Cut on Lake Washington for the first crew races of the season.

Drumheller Fountain
Students like to take late-night swims in the Drumheller Fountain—but only after it's been cleaned.

Overall School Spirit
There is definitely no shortage of school pride at UW, but there is also a fair amount of resentment toward the UW, for whatever reasons. As with everything, there's a large range in the student body.

Students Speak Out
ON ATHLETICS

Q "Varsity sports are big on campus, especially football. I am a big fan of the **numerous clubs and IM sports options**. There's something for everyone. I think if you go to UW without being physically active, you'd be wasting an incredible resource."

Q "Both varsity and intramural sports are big in every way possible. Football makes the UW a lot of money. **In general, everyone loves the Huskies**. UW sweatshirts are big, and the games are packed. Basketball is pretty popular, too."

Q "With the IMA, **more people seem interested in IM sports**, and it's not difficult to join or start your own team. The IMA is also cool because of the classes it offers in everything from hip hop to karate."

Q "IM sports are a lot of fun, and they have **crazy ones such as innertube basketball**."

STUDENT AUTHOR: **Athletics are undeniably a huge part of the Husky experience. UW sports are a typical event for friends to partake in together. Many students get a big group together and go out to cheer for the Huskies, whatever the season or sport.**

Students Speak Out
ON DRUG SCENE

Q "I don't see many people doing drugs on this campus; however, I hear all the time about people on my floor going and getting high and such. I know there are a lot of people who smoke on campus; however, that is **typical for a big city and a university**."

Q "Drugs are there and available, but **it's not like campus is a drug flea market**."

Q "I don't see much focus on keeping the campus drug free and all that, but **it seems to be that people know the consequences** and make their decisions to use or what not privately, and then act on them."

STUDENT AUTHOR: **While many students drink alcohol, there are some that don't, and recreational drugs can be avoided or found fairly easily. Marijuana is definitely the most common drug, and some people do ecstasy or shrooms. Some students have encountered more hard-core drugs like crack, cocaine, or heroin, but those are much more rare—shooting up is definitely not a typical house-party activity.**

11:1	Student-to-Faculty Ratio
92%	Freshman Retention Rate
42%	Four-Year Graduation Rate
67%	Financial Aid Applicants Receiving Aid

Students Speak Out
SAFETY & SECURITY

Q "Campus feels really safe, but I live by what is called 'the Ave.,' which **has done a great job of cleaning itself up**, though there is still more work to do. A lot of bums hang around. I don't like it when they ask me for money. I'm like, 'Hey, I'm poor, too.'"

Q "I hardly ever see any security or police around campus at night, which makes me wonder if our campus is really that safe. **I hear all the time about people getting mugged** or things being stolen from their dorm rooms."

Q "I personally have always felt very safe on campus. **There are emergency booths all over the place** with big blue emergency buttons you can push."

STUDENT AUTHOR: **Certainly campus efforts cannot make students immune to violence and victimization, but there are fair precautions taken against dangers, and for the most part, students have many resources to protect themselves from danger.**

Questions?
For more inside information and survival tips, pick up College Prowler's full-length book on this school, written by an actual student! Check it out at *www.collegeprowler.com*.

Students Speak Out
ON OVERALL EXPERIENCE

Q "Overall, I am satisfied with the job the University of Washington has done with my education. I think that **it is a good school with its students' best interests in mind**. I feel that it is highly bureaucratic, which isn't good for students who are easily lost in the shuffle. But for me, it was a great experience."

Q "Overall, I like going to UW, but it's such a huge school. Sometimes, **I wish I was someplace a bit smaller** with a better sense of community and school spirit."

Q "I love the school, I love my friends, and I know that I'm getting the best education. **I have no regrets.**"

Q "The University of Washington was my last choice. I applied to six schools: University of San Diego, Loyola Marymount, Gonzaga, University of Portland, and Seattle University. With that said, I cannot imagine myself anywhere else right now—it is the best experience I'm having. I live in a sorority, and that helps make the student population smaller for me. You will enjoy any college, but **it is hard to find a Husky who doesn't love their school**. It is a difficult decision, but I know that I made the right one. Good luck."

STUDENT AUTHOR: **Perhaps for a less socially-motivated person, UW isn't the ideal school. In a bigger environment, maybe it helps to be a little more outgoing—you sort of have to put yourself out there in order to get anything back. In all, though, if a student is determined to make his or her time at UW a positive social experience, it's definitely within the realm of possibilities to do so.**

University of Wisconsin

500 Lincoln Drive; Madison, WI 53706
(608) 263-2400; www.wisc.edu

THE BASICS:

Acceptance Rate: 56%
Setting: Urban
F-T Undergrads: 27,680

SAT Range: 1170–1380*
Control: Public
Tuition: $21,780

Most Popular Majors: Social Sciences, Biology, Engineering, Business, Communications

*of 1600

Academics	B+	Guys	A-
Local Atmosphere	B+	Girls	A
Safety & Security	A-	Athletics	A
Computers	B+	Nightlife	A
Facilities	A-	Greek Life	B
Campus Dining	C	Drug Scene	C
Off-Campus Dining	A-	Campus Strictness	A-
Campus Housing	B-	Parking	D
Off-Campus Housing	A-	Transportation	B+
Diversity	D+	Weather	C

Students Speak Out
ON ACADEMICS

Q "Teachers are all great here, but you will have **many classes taught by teaching assistants—** which is common at any large university, really."

Q "The professors are all right, but it is a really hard school to begin with, so don't expect them or the TAs to help you much. **Madison gives you a lot of work**, so expect to study at least a few hours a day."

Q "It's hard to describe the teachers of this school since there are so many of them. Over the course of an education here, you're bound to find ones that you love, some that you hate, and many that you won't think either way about. On the whole, though, **they are excellent professors** who make the material interesting for their students, no matter the subject."

Q "There are so many teachers that you will find both great and horrible ones. Being at a **very liberal campus**, expect their viewpoints to be expressed, but not overbearingly so. The professors really do a good job at staying neutral."

STUDENT AUTHOR: Colleges attract students by promising high-quality academics and professional programs, and this is no different for the University of Wisconsin-Madison. With a school like the UW, however, its reputation for academic excellence almost precedes itself. The University of Wisconsin-Madison is ranked among the top 50 academic institutes in the nation, and many of its departments lead the country in education.

Students Speak Out
ON LOCAL ATMOSPHERE

Q "Also in Madison is Madison Area Technical College and Edgewood College, which are smaller. **The atmosphere is young**, like a typical college town in a movie. It is fun, with lots of outside activities and things to see, like the museum, the yearly film festival, and all kinds of plays."

Q "The community is awesome here because it is totally a college town. But since it's the capitol of Wisconsin, there are a lot of important things and people here too. **The campus is right between two big lakes**, which makes it very nice in the summer when you can go to the Union and get a beer."

Q "The atmosphere in Madison is **pretty much anything goes**. People do what they want and don't worry what others think of them."

Q "Madison is a very cool city. It is small enough that it isn't overwhelming, but there is still tons of stuff to do all the time. **There is a good live music scene**."

STUDENT AUTHOR: Madison itself is a comfortably-sized city located in the heart of the Midwest. Most students feel its locality creates a friendly and safe environment. The UW campus sits right next to the city's trendiest street, complete with shops, restaurants, and bars. Apart from the gorgeous aesthetics, students find the areas near campus to be very accessible.

Students Speak Out
ON CAMPUS DINING

Q "Food on campus is great. The food in the dorms isn't bad, and there are **tons of awesome restaurants within 10 minutes** of walking. Most restaurants stay open late, so there is plenty of food available late at night."

Q "Both student unions (Memorial Union and Union South) **offer great meal plans** for students living off campus."

Q "The food on campus isn't that great. I lived in the private dorms, and I heard that it is better in the public dorms because **you have more choices**."

Q "The dining hall serves just that—dining hall food. It's not great, **occasionally horrible, but mediocre overall**. The interesting thing about the dining hall is that they have cards with nutrition facts in front of whatever food you pick. That is so you truly know how many grams of fat you are taking in with your over-processed food."

Q "It pretty much goes without saying that most people **aren't going to like their dining hall's food**. Despite that, from what I've seen, they have decent things to eat."

STUDENT AUTHOR: **Try as they might, students cannot mask the inevitable, and universal, disappointment in campus dining. Students will admit that dorm cafeterias are convenient for location, price, and student socialization. While the dorm food options may be minimal, UW does offer a fair amount of dinning locations.**

---

5 Best Things	5 Worst Things
1 Number of people	1 Walking up Bascom Hill
2 Expansive academics	2 Distance to buildings
3 Educational resources	3 Lack of diversity
4 Atmosphere	4 Bar crowds
5 Student organizations	5 Lack of parking

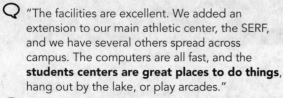

Students Speak Out
ON FACILITIES

Q "The facilities are excellent. We added an extension to our main athletic center, the SERF, and we have several others spread across campus. The computers are all fast, and the **students centers are great places to do things**, hang out by the lake, or play arcades."

Q "I enjoyed Memorial Union very much. There is **nothing like sitting next to the lake** on the Union Terrace, drinking a beer, and listening to a free concert."

Q "The main union, Memorial Union, has the Rathskellar (a bar), a cafeteria, an arcade room, a pool, a terrace, **a student travel center, a movie theater, and many other things**. There is another union near the engineering campus, and it is smaller than Memorial Union. It has places to eat, club meeting rooms, swim, arcade games, and bowling. There is also a motel there."

Q "I find that the **facilities on campus are more than acceptable**, with conveniently located gyms, and the main student union located very close to the center of campus."

Q "This place is **decked out**."

STUDENT AUTHOR: **While the unions and gyms are very popular, UW obviously has more to offer than just that—for example, the library system is extensive and spreads all over campus. One negative aspect of some facilities, however, is the location. Since the school is several miles in size, some academic buildings or libraries may not be within walking distance, which can be inconvenient for students during bad weather.**

Famous Alumni

Jerry Bock, Jane Brody, Joan Cusack, Jim Lovell, George Poage, Harry Steenbock

---

Student Body

African American:	3%	Male/Female:	47/53%
Asian American:	6%	Out-of-State:	32%
Hispanic:	3%	International:	4%
Native American:	<1%	Unknown:	3%
White:	80%		

Popular Faiths: The student population is filled with those who are Lutheran, Catholic, Jewish, non-denominational, and anything else you can imagine.

Gay Pride: There is a high acceptance for those who are lesbian, gay, bi-sexual, and transgender.

Economic Status: Students' financial backgrounds are as varied as the students themselves, but a majority comes from middle- to upper-class families.

Students Speak Out
ON DORMS

Q "The dorms are small, crowded, loud. Although one would never choose to live in them again, as most students move out after freshman year, **it is an experience** few would be willing to pass up."

Q "The dorms are all nice. **Avoid the Towers** unless you are planning on joining a frat, or unless you are from the East Coast. The Langdon is nice, clean, and has decent food."

Q "Every dorm will be fun, because you will make friends. However, **I wouldn't live in an all-girls dorm**. Dorm living is part of the experience of being a freshman in college."

STUDENT AUTHOR: **UW students have a complete range of options when it comes to on-campus living. When choosing a dorm, location sometimes becomes the largest factor. UW is very accommodating in terms of student housing. There are thirteen public (University) dorms, and about five private dorms. The public dorms are primarily for freshmen and sophomores looking to meet people. While some of your better days may not be spent in the dorms, the majority of students do defend this housing option.**

> **Did You Know?**
> 24% of undergrads live on campus.

Students Speak Out
ON GUYS & GIRLS

Q "There is **a large selection to chose from** at Wisconsin. The girls are very pretty and the guys are really hot. I have never had a problem on the guy front for sure! Plenty of eye candy here."

Q "It's hard to walk to class here without **checking out at least a dozen people** in this town. Most of the people you'll meet are Thursday through Saturday partiers, and Sunday through Wednesday studiers. It's all about trying to juggle work and play at this school. You have to do both."

Q "**They are hot**! I mean come on now—there's 40,000 students, so you have a whole range to choose from!"

STUDENT AUTHOR: **Students agree that the student body is very eye pleasing, literally. While there is a little more commentary about the girls, they do not discount the attractiveness of the male population. Looks aside, students do find most people to be accepting and friendly in nature. This "Midwestern mentality" makes it easy for new students or visors to feel comfortable at UW.**

> **Traditions**
>
> **Mifflin Street Block Party**
> Since 1960, residents on this street open their homes and liquor cabinets to anyone wanting to party.
>
> **Sledding on Bascom Hill**
> Bascom Hill is perfect for sledding down, and students will use everything from notebooks to cardboard boxes to travel its slope.
>
> **Overall School Spirit**
> School spirit is at a continuous high at UW. Football games bring out the most amount of school spirit. Students attend these events decked out in red and white.

Students Speak Out
ON ATHLETICS

Q "There is a lot of school spirit. Lots of people go to the **football, volleyball, basketball, and hockey games**. I know a few people that joined intramural teams."

Q "It's a **Big Ten school**, so we're very into our sports, especially football."

Q "Varsity sports are huge. Football, basketball, and hockey are all big. The fans are so fun and **the games are great**. Even if you don't like the sport, it's fun to go to the games."

Q "Both varsity and **IM sports are huge** on campus. Plan early for either."

STUDENT AUTHOR: **Nobody denies the intense role athletics play at UW. Overall, UW does not lack in providing athletic opportunities. For those needing serious and heavy competition, varsity sports are the place to be in. Students wanting something more low-key should check out intramurals. Lastly, if you're looking for something a little different, check out the club sports. Students can pick-up aikido, figure skating, or wakeboarding.**

Students Speak Out
ON DRUG SCENE

Q "**Drugs are pretty easy to obtain** at Madison, especially pot. You can smell people smoking it during most house parties and often at night."

Q "Drugs do exist at Madison, but **you don't have to partake in them**. Mainly, people just smoke weed, but I do have friends who do worse. Like any city and any campus, you always have the hardcore drugs, but they are definitely avoidable. Be careful at frat parties with drugs like roofies."

Q "I know of **prescription drug abuse**, cokeheads, and marijuana use, but none of it is forced on anyone. Or at least I haven't experienced that."

STUDENT AUTHOR: **Students do not deny the presence and habitual use of drugs at UW. The choice to use drugs is really just that—a choice. Students don't feel pressured to do drugs, and say the amount of drugs being used generally depends on the crowd with which you associate. If the campus or Madison police catch you with illegal substances, there will be consequences.**

13:1	Student-to-Faculty Ratio
93%	Freshman Retention Rate
47%	Four-Year Graduation Rate
69%	Financial Aid Applicants Receiving Aid

Students Speak Out
SAFETY & SECURITY

Q "I personally **have not had any issues** with security, and Madison itself really hasn't either. Campus and dorm security itself is very efficient as well."

Q "I have never felt threatened here at all. There are programs where you can have people escort you back to your dorm if you feel unsafe, but you probably won't even need them—**this campus is pretty safe**."

Q "I walked into this college with people telling me Madison is the one of the safest cities in the US. I realized later that this doesn't mean its 100 percent safe. If you have a bike, own a bike lock. **Lock your door** before you go out."

STUDENT AUTHOR: **Location plays a large role in how students perceive safety at UW. Certain areas are a little less safe than others are, and students try to steer away from these. In general, students feel safe walking around campus, State Street, and near the dorms.**

> **Questions?**
> For more inside information and survival tips, pick up College Prowler's full-length book on this school, written by an actual student! Check it out at *www.collegeprowler.com*.

Students Speak Out
ON OVERALL EXPERIENCE

Q "I love Madison and wouldn't want to be anywhere else. It was definitely one of the best decisions I made to go to Madison. **I have no regrets**."

Q "Overall, I couldn't be happier here. I know of no one here who has transferred, and I never hear people complain. Classes here are incredibly hard, but once you find the balance between partying and studying **you will never want to leave this school**."

Q "I love it, but I've always wanted a large school. I occasionally **wish that it was more racially diverse**, but that argument can be made for most schools across the country."

Q "I had a rough time the first couple of semesters, but overall, **I know I couldn't be this happy anywhere else**. I love the amount of people that I meet daily, the weather when it is summer, and the view of the Isthmus at Sunset from Lake Mendota. With State Street as my front lawn, how could I not be glad to be here?"

STUDENT AUTHOR: **Students put a lot of time and energy into their undergraduate education. Luckily for those at UW, many feel it has been a positive experience. The college atmosphere, expansive campus, and intense academics are only some of the reasons students enjoy UW so much. Students feel they are able to form relationships with other students, as well as their professors. Furthermore, UW leaves them prepared for their future. Wherever you deiced to spend your undergraduate years, definitely consider the University of Wisconsin as a practical and fulfilling option.**

University of Wisconsin–Stout

712 South Broadway Street; Menomonie, WI 54751
(715) 232-1122; www.uwstout.edu

THE BASICS:

Acceptance Rate: 81%
Setting: Rural
F-T Undergrads: 6,830

ACT Range: 18–23*
Control: Public
Tuition: $13,408

Most Popular Majors: Business/Marketing, Education, Visual and Performing Arts, Engineering

*of 36

Academics	B	Guys	B
Local Atmosphere	B-	Girls	B
Safety & Security	B+	Athletics	B-
Computers	A	Nightlife	B
Facilities	B	Greek Life	C-
Campus Dining	B+	Drug Scene	B-
Off-Campus Dining	B+	Campus Strictness	B-
Campus Housing	B	Parking	A-
Off-Campus Housing	A-	Transportation	C
Diversity	D-	Weather	C

Students Speak Out
ON ACADEMICS

Q "Most of the teachers really seemed to enjoy their jobs, but **some are stuck in their groove** and use outdated books and materials that have no new ideas."

Q "Some classes have a lot of daily work, others have generous portions of reading, and others have semester-long projects. Stout has **tons of online courses if you are a self-learner** and do not have time to attend classes. It is also a very hands-on school being a polytechnic university."

Q "UW-Stout is definitely known for specific majors such as **art/design, construction management, hospitality and tourism, and packaging**—there are not too many schools that offer that."

Q "The teachers at UW-Stout are great. They are well qualified and underpaid, so you know that **they are passionate about what they do**. The ratio of teachers to students is exceptional, along with the flexibility of office hours. Of course, you'll have teachers that just annoy you, but, hey, that's life."

STUDENT AUTHOR: **Most students at Stout say they are getting a good education but the workload is fairly easy. However, this depends on your major. Art and design students may be in labs until 4 a.m. waiting for paint to dry, while hospitality and tourism students take a wine and spirits class, and then go celebrate what they learned. Although the general academic rigor at Stout may not be intense, the professors are there to help if your grades do drop.**

Students Speak Out
ON LOCAL ATMOSPHERE

Q "I have always felt comfortable and welcome in Menomonie. **The town itself is adorable**, in my opinion. There is so much authenticity, and the community is great at embracing the college and students. Personally, I enjoy spending my time in a couple of my favorite local cafés."

Q "Menomonie is like a starter town for young adults—**it has everything you need, but there is still a young spirit**. A lot of people know everyone, it's easy to get around, the scenery is very pretty, and, contrary to what people may say, there are things to do besides go to the town bars or house parties."

Q "There are so many fun outdoor activities to do. **There are lots of trails and parks and rivers** that you can hang out by. The bars are fun, as well as all the little shops and restaurants along the two main streets in downtown."

Q "Menomonie is a town with a lot of historical sites. It has a small-town feel, but **Eau Claire and Minneapolis/St. Paul are close** enough to get anything that you want."

STUDENT AUTHOR: **Menomonie is a unique town with plenty of character. It has movie theaters, bowling, mini-golf, awesome parks great for barbecuing, multiple disk golf courses, and even a water park. City slickers will sometimes complain about Menomonie not having enough shopping, glamour, and city culture, in general, but Eau Claire is only 30 minutes away, and the Twin Cities are not much farther.**

Students Speak Out
ON FACILITIES

Q "The Fieldhouse provides a lot of things to do, including Stout Adventures, where **you can climb the indoor climbing wall**, and use the fitness center, racquetball courts, and swimming pool. At the student center, there are three different places to find food. At the library, there is a little food cart where you can pick up snacks if you get hungry while studying or working on a group project."

Q "The buildings are well-kept and clean. Some are even part of Menomonie history and have been around for many, many years. They are **better than other campuses I have been on**."

Q "The library is a **great place to go to, and it's pretty big**. I use the gym about three times a week, and I enjoy the equipment it has available."

Q "**The athletic facilities are awesome**—they're the best part of the school. The library is very nice, but people are really loud there."

Q "The student center is **large and has several places to eat** and the essential comfortable couches. The athletic complex is available to all students, and the rates for the weight room are cheap compared to other gyms in the area."

STUDENT AUTHOR: UW-Stout is no architectural gem, but the facilities are more than adequate. The student center offers plenty of eating spots, free meeting rooms for student organizations to use, and even a bowling alley! The fitness center offers a weight and cardio facility, two rock-climbing walls, an indoor swimming pool, and plenty of indoor and outdoor space for informal recreation. However, the size of the student body has outgrown both facilities, and they need to be expanded.

Famous Alumni

Vera Bushfield, Nancy Zieman, David Zien

Students Speak Out
ON CAMPUS DINING

Q "There are tons of places to eat on campus. There's the Heritage Café, a great sit-down place; the Terrace, which is a food court; and The Pawn, which **even delivers to dorm rooms**! The Commons was better than high school and gives you the freedom of tons of options for every meal. And, best of all, it is mostly all-you-can-eat for cheap."

Q "The food on campus is decent. Of the two dining halls, **I prefer Tainter because it always seems cleaner**. If you are willing to spend a bit more money, you can find some decent food at the Heritage Café in the student center."

Q "The food on campus is **really bad, especially if you are a vegetarian**. In about two semesters, I have only eaten on campus about 15 times."

Q "**Dining plans are very convenient** at Stout. You can use your dining dollars at a variety of places on campus. They even have 'Expressway Carts' in the academic buildings where you can buy snacks in between classes."

Q "There is **such a variety of things**, you should always find something to eat."

STUDENT AUTHOR: The two main cafeterias on campus offer the best value because students are charged for the meal, not per item. The á la cart options offer a wider variety, but the prices are more expensive. Stout doesn't offer dining plans with a certain number of meals a week. Instead, students add a certain dollar amount to their accounts, and at each meal, money is deducted off that account. So, you don't pay for the meals you don't eat!

Students Speak Out
ON DORMS

Q "The dorms are a little dated, but that's okay. Red Cedar Hall is by far the best because it is **set up more like an apartment building rather than a dormitory**."

Q "The dorms are a great environment to be in, especially your first year. I have such amazing memories of meeting so many people in the dorms my freshman year that I would not trade for anything. I would say **most of the dorms are exactly the same**, but there are one or two that have newer furniture."

Q "The dorms are typical. At Stout, **you never have to worry about being on the 16th floor** like at other schools."

STUDENT AUTHOR: The residence halls are clean and close to classes and campus services. Many extras are included at no extra charge, including lofts, a micro-fridge, and cable TV. The one negative is that all freshmen live on South Campus and have little interaction with upperclassmen. This segregation limits role modeling, which can be an essential step to becoming a more mature college student.

Did You Know?
40% of undergrads live on campus.

Students Speak Out
ON GUYS & GIRLS

Q "Lots of girls come to Stout for the apparel and retail majors, so many are fashionable, and some people say you can always tell who the fashion majors are. Most of the guys on campus are athletes, so **if you want to meet a hot guy, go to Rec Center** any time of day."

Q "Art students try to style their hair and clothes in a 'different' way. **Construction management students all wear Carhartts** and beer/camo baseball caps. Business majors mostly wear jeans and T-shirts."

Q "**A typical student at Stout is just that**—a typical college kid."

Q "The girls tend to dress up when going out but have no problem wearing sweats to class, though **they can seem catty**. The guys are pretty outgoing and somewhat attractive."

STUDENT AUTHOR: In general, the students at UW-Stout are good looking. The ratio of guys to girls is fairly equal, so everyone has a fair chance of meeting plenty of good friends, that special someone, or maybe even just someone to spend the night with. Most students don't get super dressed up for a day of classes, but on a Thursday night, you will see plenty of short skirts and cologne-scented guys dressed to impress.

Traditions

Hands-On Learning
As a polytechnic institute, UW-Stout has an academic tradition of "hands on" learning, which bridges theory and practice. The school has a long tradition of using applied learning, which was encouraged by founder Sen. James Huff Stout.

Overall School Spirit
Most students are proud of attending UW-Stout. Some link school spirit to athletics, but at Stout there doesn't seem to be much correlation. Students regularly wear Stout apparel and on-campus events are heavily attended.

Students Speak Out
ON ATHLETICS

Q "Varsity sports are great to be involved in or to simply watch. It is nice being a D-III school where **sports don't dictate the overall atmosphere of the campus**. There is not a ridiculous amount of pressure put on our athletes, but we are still competitive, and the coaches push us to our full potential."

Q "**There are year-round intramurals, club sports to join**, a rock wall to climb, and great fitness facilities. In fact, I don't think there is anything that we don't have!"

Q "The most popular varsity sports on campus are **football, basketball, baseball, and softball**."

Q "Intramurals are a **great way to meet people and stay in shape**, and there are many options."

STUDENT AUTHOR: Intramurals and other recreational activates are far more popular than varsity athletics. The stadium doesn't even fill up for the Homecoming football game. But intramurals are huge! You don't have to be any good to play, but the competition can get fierce during the playoffs. If you're good enough, you will win the coveted intramural championship T-shirt.

Students Speak Out
ON DRUG SCENE

Q "There are always parties—it's college. But it's a suitcase campus, so a lot of people go home on weekends if they don't live off campus, which **limits the drug scene**."

Q "There are quite a few smokers and drinkers. It seems as if **90 percent of campus has or does smoke pot**."

Q "While it would be unheard of to have a college without drug use, the **drug scene at Stout is relatively inconspicuous**. If a person is in search of drugs, he could probably find them with little effort; otherwise, the drug scene is pretty low-key."

STUDENT AUTHOR: At off-campus parties, small groups of students may go off and smoke marijuana or you may even smell it in the residence halls once in a while. However, hard drugs like meth and cocaine are not widely used by Stout students. Overall, drugs are not a noticeable part of campus life and students are definitely not pressured to use them.

19:1	Student-to-Faculty Ratio
72%	Freshman Retention Rate
16%	Four-Year Graduation Rate
68%	Financial Aid Applicants Receiving Aid

Students Speak Out
SAFETY & SECURITY

Q "Dorms lock up at 11 p.m. and stay locked until 7 a.m., and **the only way to get in is with a valid Stout ID card**."

Q "Stout is a small campus that is tightly compacted and well lit. I work at a bar on Main Street and walk home alone afterward and **have never felt threatened or followed**. We have tons of campus police patrolling."

Q "There are security workers roaming campus every night, as well as **video cameras in the dorms, and an RA on duty** in every dorm. The walkways are well lit and checked on a regular basis to make sure they stay safe for anyone walking home late at night. There is very little crime on campus, and although select incidents do occur, that can be expected on any campus or in any town."

STUDENT AUTHOR: Most students feel very safe on the Stout campus and in the Menomonie community. The UW-Stout Police Department and Menomonie Police are very visible—so visible, in fact, that you can't go from one end of town to the other without seeing a police officer.

Questions?
For more inside information and survival tips, pick up College Prowler's full-length book on this school, written by an actual student! Check it out at *www.collegeprowler.com*.

Students Speak Out
ON OVERALL EXPERIENCE

Q Attending UW-Stout is **not just an education, it's an experience**. It's the textbook rental program, the parking tickets you receive, the laptop program, the awesome Stout Adventures trip that you go on your junior year, the rugby club you join, the test you fail, the homecoming memories, the Thursday nights you don't remember, the friends you make, and the Grandwiches at the Heritage Café that make up the experience."

Q "More than anything, UW-Stout provides opportunity and community. Once you set your roots at Stout, **you'll never want to leave**. The perfect-sized student body allows students to build a community of friends that last a lifetime."

Q "When a Stout student walks across the stage during commencement, he or she is filled with feelings of excitement about their future and **sadness for a journey coming to an end**."

Q "Students have the opportunity to **meet one-on-one with their professors**, start and lead their own campus organization, take their education abroad, manage a restaurant on campus, apply theories, and make decisions for the entire campus by participating in student government."

STUDENT AUTHOR: The University of Wisconsin-Stout focuses on degree programs that lead to careers focused on the needs of society. Stout uses hands-on learning, which is why Stout has an unbeatable employment rate and is what makes the University unique. But, overall, there are many mixed opinions about the school. Prospective students are usually impressed, but there are still some who say "Stout, Stout, the easy way out."

UNLV

4505 Maryland Parkway; Las Vegas, NV 89154
(702) 895-3011; www.unlv.edu

THE BASICS:

Acceptance Rate: 68%
Setting: Urban
F-T Undergrads: 15,677

SAT Range: 910–1140*
Control: Public
Tuition: $15,100

Most Popular Majors: Business, Education, Journalism, Psychology, Visual & Performing Arts

*of 1600

Academics	B-	Guys	B
Local Atmosphere	A-	Girls	A
Safety & Security	B	Athletics	B
Computers	A-	Nightlife	A+
Facilities	B	Greek Life	C-
Campus Dining	C+	Drug Scene	B+
Off-Campus Dining	A-	Campus Strictness	B+
Campus Housing	D	Parking	C
Off-Campus Housing	B	Transportation	B-
Diversity	A-	Weather	B+

Students Speak Out
ON ACADEMICS

Q "I'd like to say it depends on the subject, but I've had classes that I would normally love that were just ruined by bad teachers, and then bad classes that were made fun by good teachers. Overall, **I've been pretty happy with the teachers** and classes. I just try to forget the bad eggs."

Q "Most of the teachers I've had are really great; they're usually helpful, informative, and flexible. Not all of my classes are very interesting. I really found that the **English courses here are limited**."

Q "They're all different and **bring their personalities into class**, at least in the computer science department. They're interesting really only if you're interested in the subject material."

Q "Some teachers are good, some are bad. Our math teachers suck, science is okay, English teachers are good (usually). **Word of mouth can save your GPA**. Classes are interesting, in general. In warmer weather, a lot of teachers let us have class outside."

STUDENT AUTHOR: As always, college is what you make of it. You can scrape by with a C learning virtually nothing, or you can try your best for the highest grades you can get, which is rewarding. Most instructors are, for the most part, friendly, approachable, and willing to help students with any problems. UNLV has many teachers who are, or have been, professionals in the field they are teaching, which is helpful because they can teach from experience, not just from a textbook.

Students Speak Out
ON LOCAL ATMOSPHERE

Q "**The atmosphere here sucks if you are under 21**. There are a few clubs for 19-and-up, but nothing much to do. A person can only go to the movies or get coffee so many times. There are a few other schools, but UNLV is the biggest. Stay away from the Strip! There is bad traffic and annoying tourists. It loses its appeal very fast."

Q "The area around UNLV is kind of ghetto, but the school is working on it. There are highrises within a block of campus that are age restricted to 35 or older (dumb). **It's not a very University-oriented community**. There are community colleges nearby and, of course, the Strip."

Q "I don't like the town I live in and can't wait to leave. There's **no sense of culture or community here**. There's only one university here. Don't gamble; the clubs are cool, and there's an art district."

Q "**This town is very exciting and tempting**. I'm a homebody, but I know those who are very into the nightlife. As long as you can stay focused at what you are trying to accomplish, you will have a great academic and social life."

STUDENT AUTHOR: The downside of living in Las Vegas is that it is a tourist town, and when people are on vacation, many tend to leave their manners at home. Jaywalking is expected, and many tourists are self-centered and rude. However, with the city's occupants changing constantly, there are also many fun and interesting people to meet and new things to learn.

Students Speak Out
ON FACILITIES

Q "The library is definitely something to boast about. It's pretty new and five stories tall. It has **beautiful architecture and a ton of computers**. As far as athletic areas go, I've only used the pool. It's kept clean at all times, and there's always a lifeguard on duty during lap swim times."

Q "**The Moyer Student Union is nice**. But it is now under construction, so I feel it is smaller than it used to be. It is still nice, though. Also, the library is great here."

Q "The facilities are okay, but **there is room for improvement or some modernization**. The area most in need of improvement is the restrooms, by far. They're crowded, dark, and very run-down. But other than that, the rest of the facilities are okay. The library is really nice."

Q "The facilities are always nice on campus. Everything is **almost always well-maintained**."

Q "**The Moyer Student Union is my life**. I love it there. It really is the hub of campus. It has all the info about what's happening on campus."

STUDENT AUTHOR: Despite some concerns of higher tuition fees, the school has gone ahead with upping the costs slightly to make way for new facilities, such as the revamped student union and new recreation hall. UNLV's master plan has a list of future renovation projects and additions, which includes five much-anticipated parking garages. UNLV's main campus is landlocked. It makes the administration more efficient in its planning, but it also means there cannot be any drastic increases in campus size.

Famous Alumni

Randall Cunningham, Larry Johnson, Jimmy Kimmel, Suge Knight, Kenny Mayne, Elizabeth Muto, Ronnie Vannucci, Anthony E. Zuicker

Students Speak Out
ON CAMPUS DINING

Q "The food on campus is alright—just alright. **We need more variety and more places to dine overall**. Cyber Wraps is a good place to eat. It's better than burgers or pizza. Jamba Juice has the best smoothies. They're healthy, and they fill you up."

Q "Food on campus is generally pretty good. The MSU and Sidewalk Café are the best, in my opinion. **The Dining Commons has its ups and downs**."

Q "The Dining Commons is okay at first; they charge too much, and **it gets boring and disgusting really fast**. It's not somewhere I ate after the first weeks. The union and fast food restaurants across the street are popular."

Q "The Dining Commons are decent, but the **selection quickly grows old**. Request 14 meals per week at most. The MSU has good burritos."

Q "The Dining Commons is the best, with a great buffet and a very good selection of meals for all needs: breakfast, lunch, and dinner. It is very reasonable in price, **a true campus secret to those who never go there**."

STUDENT AUTHOR: Campus dining has its perks, but it can get old. The Dining Commons has surprisingly good food. The Moyer Student Union choices are lacking, though good things have been said about some of the food. The presently small and frequently crowded indoor dining area will also receive a makeover; extensive seating will be scattered throughout the new MSU.

Student Body

African American:	8%	Male/Female:	44/56%
Asian American:	14%	Out-of-State:	25%
Hispanic:	11%	International:	4%
Native American:	1%	Unknown:	1%
White:	61%		

Popular Faiths: Christianity, in general, or more specifically, Catholicism, is the most common religion among UNLV students.

Gay Pride: As in any place, there are those tolerant of homosexuals and those who aren't.

Economic Status: All kinds go to UNLV, especially now that all Nevadan high school students are eligible to shoot for the Millennium Scholarship.

Students Speak Out
ON DORMS

Q "I've only been in the campus dorms once, and they seemed kind of like an ant hill. I'm claustrophobic, so going up in an elevator and getting off in this tiny cramped hallway only to smash myself further into a tiny, little room no bigger than my living room shared by two people was a little hard to digest. **If anything needs to be revamped, it's the dorms at UNLV**."

Q "The freshman dorms are **small, dismal, and poorly ventilated**. The Upper Class Complex is more tolerable. It seems that the nicer ones are achieved later in your involvement with UNLV."

Q "They seemed like the **typical jail-cell dorms** to me."

STUDENT AUTHOR: **Living in the dorms can be a great way to enhance the often-sought-out college experience. Because UNLV students are, for the most part, not very involved with campus life, the dorms are almost the only place to find some semblance of unity and student activity. The problem with dorm life is that UNLV dorms aren't very nice. All of the dorms are tiny, and many students joke that they look like jail cells.**

Did You Know?
7% of undergrads live on campus.

Students Speak Out
ON GUYS & GIRLS

Q "The **girls are amazing and also very mean**. Watch out."

Q "**Guys are egotistical, and girls are fake**. In early fall, girls show up to class in bikinis. It's a good university to meet a mate and forgo a degree."

Q "There is a **wide variety of boys on campus**, most of them are decent to hot, but there are some questionable ones. Many of them are usually very nice and approachable."

Q "The guys are mostly from California and could care less about muscles; it's more about keeping the surfer style. **The ladies are beautiful**; I have seen more at USC, but that is a bigger school."

STUDENT AUTHOR: **Whether it's the alluring nightlife or something in the air, the women at UNLV are definitely above par. There are attractive men on campus, but it's somewhat of a mystery as to where they hide. However, the Strip is close to UNLV, and many hot men hang out there. If you're new to the area, it could be a bit more difficult to really get to know people. However, the students get friendlier as faces become familiar.**

Traditions

The Fremont Cannon
A trophy won by the winner of the UNLV vs. UNR (University of Nevada, Reno) annual football game.

UnityFest
UnityFest is a week of events celebrating diversity. Entertainers, programs, and cultural experiences help to increase cultural awareness of students, faculty, and staff.

The Rebel Experience
This is UNLV's official tailgate party, which premiered in 1997 with 30,000 fans.

Students Speak Out
ON ATHLETICS

Q "The games are a big deal to go to because it **encourages school pride and unity**. It is also a great social function to get together with friends while supporting the school. Intramural sports are really important to Greeks; they promote friendly competition."

Q "**Nobody goes** to the games."

Q "The **varsity sports that seem to be big are basketball and football**. Besides those, I don't really hear much of other sports. Intramural sports are semi-known but not very popular."

Q "There is a **wide variety of intramural sports**, and they are very easy to sign up for."

STUDENT AUTHOR: **In every class, you will probably meet an athlete of varsity or intramural level, and there are more than enough willing to start new club or IM sports. So, if you were an athlete in high school, there is opportunity to keep that up here at UNLV. Over the last few years, UNLV has hired many elite coaches, and as soon as students start attending the UNLV games, sports will be improved tremendously around campus.**

Students Speak Out
ON DRUG SCENE

Q "There is **virtually no drug activity on campus**. I'm sure it's there, but it is almost never seen. Many people on campus smoke, though, but that's about it."

Q "There is **not too much drug stuff going on** from what I know."

Q "What drug scene? **Everyone seems pretty clean and boring** so far. More potheads would be nice. They sometimes say funny things in class."

STUDENT AUTHOR: The drug scene on campus is very small, almost inconspicuous. Stories of drug use are not popular, and drugs are practically never seen. When drugs hit the social scene, if at all, it's usually during a party, or it's kept behind closed doors with friends. Drinking is much more popular with students. Periodically, beer bottles can be found in the parking lot near the dorms, and with more than 500 bars in Las Vegas, drinking is a much easier and more socially acceptable habit to support.

20:1	Student-to-Faculty Ratio
75%	Freshman Retention Rate
14%	Four-Year Graduation Rate
71%	Financial Aid Applicants Receiving Aid

Students Speak Out
SAFETY & SECURITY

Q "**Campus police are awesome**. They are easy to become friends with. Their response time is amazing. They are understanding, usually. I've had night classes that ran until 10:30 p.m., and I was never afraid on campus."

Q "I rarely see the security guards on campus, but **I've never felt it is dangerous**."

Q "UNLV police do not have an overpowering presence on campus, but they are always around. With their central location just across Tropicana, **they are only a phone call away if they don't happen to be on campus**. If any ruckus is started on campus, they are usually there to check it out, even if the situation hasn't yet escalated to something dangerous."

STUDENT AUTHOR: For the most part, the UNLV campus is surprisingly safe. The neighborhoods around UNLV are not the best, but few major crimes occur on the campus, though there have been some. UNLV police officers and security patrol the campus, even at night.

> **Questions?**
> For more inside information and survival tips, pick up College Prowler's full-length book on this school, written by an actual student! Check it out at *www.collegeprowler.com*.

Students Speak Out
ON OVERALL EXPERIENCE

Q "**I really wish it wasn't a commuter school and there was more campus life to it**. Everyone complains about this, second to parking, but they are the same people who aren't doing anything about it. It is incredibly easy to get involved with groups. They stress that a ton at orientation, but you need to actually do it! It will make your college experience so much better. And if a large majority of people did it, we would be able to fill the stands at the basketball and football games and be like a real school with a home-field advantage. Sadly, I don't see that happening in the near future."

Q "**I like our school, our teams, and the friends that I have made here**, but I do plan on leaving after I graduate. This town isn't for me, especially when it comes to my career. Overall, I'd recommend it, though."

Q "UNLV is **better than the locals say** it is."

Q "**UNLV isn't how I imagined college**. Most people come to attend classes and then leave. It doesn't seem like there is much involvement nor any interaction. I would love to be somewhere where there was more college life."

STUDENT AUTHOR: Though there might be a bad egg here or there, UNLV is filled with caring, helpful faculty and staff members who actually believe that they are there for the students. And with Las Vegas overflowing with residents and expensive housing, business is booming. Because Las Vegas is such a transient city (about 2,000 people move away every month, while about 7,000 move in), jobs, internships, and other career advancement opportunities are almost always available.

Ursinus College

601 Main Street; Collegeville, PA 19426
(610) 409-3000; www.ursinus.edu

THE BASICS:

Acceptance Rate: 55%
Setting: Suburban
F-T Undergrads: 1,656

SAT Range: 1700–2010*
Control: Private
Tuition: $38,500

Most Popular Majors: Social Sciences, Biology, Psychology, English, Communications, English

*of 2400

Academics	A	Guys	B+
Local Atmosphere	C	Girls	B+
Safety & Security	B+	Athletics	B+
Computers	A	Nightlife	B-
Facilities	B+	Greek Life	A-
Campus Dining	C+	Drug Scene	A-
Off-Campus Dining	B-	Campus Strictness	B+
Campus Housing	B	Parking	B
Off-Campus Housing	D-	Transportation	B-
Diversity	C	Weather	B-

Students Speak Out
ON ACADEMICS

Q "The teachers are one of my favorite things about Ursinus. They are all very friendly and always open to helping you. **I love the fact that all of my teachers know my name**, and they get to know the students on personal levels. The workload is harder than high school, but it is manageable. College is supposed to be a lot of work, and it is, but it's not impossible."

Q "The faculty and staff at Ursinus College are, for the most part, extremely friendly and helpful. This is largely due to the **intimate atmosphere and small student-to-faculty ratio**, both of which help contribute to a sense of being part of a community."

Q "**I find the teachers to be very open and willing to help**. Their doors are always open. I find most of my classes to be interesting; others are boring but essential to building a solid knowledge base."

Q "The teachers are so much more than teachers— **they are mentors**. I respect and look up to them. They always invite students into their offices for extra help or just to chat, and they even invite you to their homes for meals."

STUDENT AUTHOR: **Academics are the College's strong point. The faculty is genuinely concerned with the students, and the teachers are extremely dedicated to their particular fields of study. Ursinus is one of the top undergraduate schools for research, and it has remarkable science professors. But don't worry—other departments are not neglected.**

Students Speak Out
ON LOCAL ATMOSPHERE

Q "It's a small town, right near King of Prussia and Philadelphia, making for **easy access into the city and other larger venues**."

Q "Collegeville is a quiet city, and there's not too much around. There are a lot of restaurants and little shops. The best things to do are to go to Wawa, the Soft Pretzel Company, or Rita's, or just walk around town with friends. **There really isn't anything to stay away from** because everything is very safe in Collegeville."

Q "**It is a friendly little town**. The King of Prussia Mall is close. Plus, there's a flea market down the street and a few diners nearby. There's stuff to do."

Q "**Collegeville is not a very exciting town to hang out in**, but it does have all of the necessities for any college student within walking distance. Wawa is conveniently located, and Target is only a short drive away. There are also a couple of different restaurants nearby for a night off campus, and the King of Prussia Mall is about a 20-minute drive."

STUDENT AUTHOR: **There is not a whole lot to do in Collegeville. It is a typical residential area that holds the bare necessities in terms of things to do: movie theaters, shopping centers, and restaurants. But on the positive side, students looking for a relaxing suburban setting and safe neighborhoods will find them here. Plus, Philadelphia is a fairly short trip away, and much, much more can be found to do there.**

5 Best Things
1 Free laptops
2 Wireless Internet
3 Jazzman's
4 Awesome professors
5 Campus scenery

5 Worst Things
1 Campus food
2 Bias toward sciences
3 Collegeville is boring
4 Some dorms aren't great
5 Students holed up in dorms

Students Speak Out
ON FACILITIES

Q "**Our performing arts center is breathtaking**. However, we don't even have a real student center. I guess everyone tends to hang out at the gym or in the cafeteria."

Q "The athletic facilities are amazing. Our fitness area and indoor track are the nicest I've ever seen—**even nicer than the Division I schools I've visited**."

Q "Most of the facilities on campus are nice, seeing as **most of the buildings have been built fairly recently or have been renovated**. The athletics facility was renovated in 2002 and has extremely nice equipment. A new state-of-the art performing arts center has just been built. Both of the science buildings are in great condition and have great labs. However, there are some buildings that are outdated and need renovations."

Q "**The facilities are very nice, especially when compared to other schools that I have visited**. The athletic facilities are new and extensive. There is an indoor field house for almost any sport you can imagine. The student center is nice, but it could use a game room."

Q "The library has a lot of study rooms so that you can **work in groups very easily**."

STUDENT AUTHOR: **The facilities are extremely nice. The campus has a good mix of old and new buildings making it a classic and traditional campus as well as a forward-looking, modern school. In general, there are true bright spots on the campus, but there are also a couple of not-so-great facilities that need to be renovated.**

Famous Alumni

Gerald Edelman, Hermann Eilts, Russell Conwell Johnson, Sam Keen, Joseph Melrose, J.D. Salinger

Students Speak Out
ON CAMPUS DINING

Q "The food is college food. It leaves something to be desired, but **no one is starving from a lack of decent things to eat**. I prefer Zack's to Wismer—I think of it as quality over quantity."

Q "**The worst part is that Zack's is not open on weekends**, so everyone has to go to Wismer during the shortened mealtime hours, which is not a highlight of the weekend, to say the least."

Q "Wismer is just 'eh.' I love it when I go back to school, but **I hate it by the end of the semester**. I wish we had pierogies every day."

Q "**The food on campus isn't bad for college food**. Wismer has a variety of foods at different stations, such as hometown, pizza, hot off the grill, and several others. There is a huge salad bar that is always open, and cereal, bagels, breads, and ice cream are always available."

Q "The food on campus is pretty good for a cafeteria. In Wismer, there are lots of choices. Zack's has fewer choices and is more expensive for what you get, but **it is okay if you are a small eater**."

STUDENT AUTHOR: **With only two places to eat on campus, there are not a whole lot of options. The food here gets really old really fast. To be fair, dining services tries to change things up a bit by offering something different each day, but in the end, it becomes one giant rotating schedule. Wismer, the main dining hall, is very much ostracized—it always has been and likely always will be. The food may not be the best, but you can eat as much of it as you want and stay for a while. Zack's, on the other hand, provides fresher food.**

Student Body

African American:	6%	Male/Female:	45/55%
Asian American:	4%	Out-of-State:	42%
Hispanic:	3%	International:	1%
Native American:	<1%	Unknown:	13%
White:	73%		

Popular Faiths: Christianity and Judaism.

Gay Pride: Thanks to the Gay Straight Alliance, gay tolerance and acceptance is usually the norm, although there have been a few recent incidents of graffiti containing hate messages.

Economic Status: Ursinus students are very diverse in this regard. Economic status has very little, if any, relevance on campus.

Students Speak Out
ON DORMS

Q "Any college kid will complain about the dorms. However, **compared to other schools, I'd say we have great ones**. The fact that more than 90 percent of students live on campus says that the dorms must be fine."

Q "The dorms are really great. The closets are a good size, and **the bathrooms are always extremely clean**. For freshmen, there are two dorms, and 44 freshmen also live in the new dorm."

Q "The freshmen are housed separately from all other students, which is helpful in getting to know people at the beginning of the year. Reimert, which is the loudest of the dorms, **is the place where all of the parties happen**, so it tends to be the least well-kept. I would not like to live there, but some people love the fact that it is the center of a lot of the social activities on campus."

STUDENT AUTHOR: **All incoming freshmen are clustered in one of three buildings—BPS, BWC, or on the first floor of New Hall. This ensures that all freshmen get to know people from their class and live with students who know as little about the school as they do. Since the campus is so small, all five dorm buildings are close to the center of things.**

Did You Know?
95% of undergrads live on campus.

Students Speak Out
ON GUYS & GIRLS

Q "**Everyone is extremely friendly, which is one of the things that attracted me to this school**. At other places, I always encountered individuals with a 'better than you' attitude, which really turned me off. Are the students hot? Oh baby, the girls are dead sexy!"

Q "**The guys are alright**—it depends on which ones, though. The girls are nice, too. Some are just drunk idiots, but that's everywhere, I guess."

Q "**There are a lot of good-looking people on campus**, and the best part is that most of them are usually smart and friendly, which is a bonus."

Q "I love the guys on campus. **A lot of them are smart, athletic, and pretty hot**."

STUDENT AUTHOR: **The social scene on campus is fairly flat during the week, but come Friday and Saturday night, watch out. Most of the campus is hitting the party scene with one of two objectives: get drunk and have fun or hook up and have fun. The campus is also fairly balanced in terms of appearance. Fashion is not too big of a factor, but it helps if you dress decently. And being relatively fit certainly increases everyone's chances.**

Traditions

Sledding on Trays
When it snows, students will steal trays from the Wismer cafeteria to use as sleds.

Sliding before Graduation
Between Pfahler, Thomas, Reimert, and BWC, there is a pair of fountains that have a downward slope, which students slide down before graduating.

Overall School Spirit
Ursinus students have a weird sense of school spirit. Most seem to genuinely love the school but sometimes have a strange way of showing it.

Students Speak Out
ON ATHLETICS

Q "Men's basketball is probably the biggest sport on campus. **Sports are becoming better attended and supported**. Intramurals are pretty big and lots of fun to be involved with. People don't usually come to watch them, but lots of people play."

Q "Ursinus is cool in that **it has a good number of intramural sports** for idiots like me who have no athletic genes in their bodies."

Q "Sports are a very big part of the campus, and since it is such a small school, **there are a lot of students actively involved in sports**."

Q "Football is pretty big, as is basketball, but otherwise, sporting events don't attract the numbers that they might at other schools. As far as intramural sports, **I know that rugby is a big deal here**."

STUDENT AUTHOR: **Athletics usually take a backseat to academics, but Ursinus students certainly play hard. There is a lot of participation in sports. Intramural sports are very popular. Perhaps it is because there is less pressure to succeed and more incentive to have fun, but whatever the case, students are more willing to play intramurals than varsity.**

Students Speak Out
ON DRUG SCENE

Q "There are bound to be people who do drugs on any campus. However, **you never hear about drugs on this campus**. Our school is not known for it."

Q "The drug scene here is pretty much nonexistent. I would say that it is not a noticeable part of campus life because **the students are normally smarter than that**. It's not a problem at Ursinus."

Q "I'm not involved with drugs, so maybe I'm just oblivious to it. However, **marijuana isn't terribly uncommon**, but harder drugs would be very, very minimal."

STUDENT AUTHOR: **Drug use is definitely not prevalent on campus. Hardly anyone seems to be heavily involved in drugs, and the substance of choice seems to be alcohol. If tobacco and caffeine are considered drugs, then there is a bit of that. Marijuana is probably the most accessible drug on campus, but students need to know the right people to get some. And most people who smoke pot do it at places where they are not likely to get caught.**

12:1	Student-to-Faculty Ratio
88%	Freshman Retention Rate
72%	Four-Year Graduation Rate
81%	Financial Aid Applicants Receiving Aid

Students Speak Out
SAFETY & SECURITY

Q "There is very little crime, if any. The campus safety office is located right in the middle of the campus, and it's always open. **They offer an escort service at any time** if you are afraid to walk alone on campus, which is really nice, especially for female students."

Q "I feel very safe on campus. **I don't feel that security is very strict**, but currently there is no reason for it to be so. If there were any type of threat, I am sure that security would be more strictly enforced."

Q "**I have never felt as though I were in danger at Ursinus**. Since the campus is so small and secluded, the College is able to keep the students under control without having to worry about violence from the surrounding town."

STUDENT AUTHOR: **Most students genuinely feel safe at Ursinus. There have been a few incidents of theft on campus, but the statistics have been declining every year. And to be realistic, most of these cases usually occur when students leave their doors unlocked, allowing easy entry into any room. On the whole, students are generally satisfied with their safety.**

> **Questions?**
> For more inside information and survival tips, pick up College Prowler's full-length book on this school, written by an actual student! Check it out at *www.collegeprowler.com*.

Students Speak Out
ON OVERALL EXPERIENCE

Q "I think that Ursinus is life-changing. As cheesy as that may sound, **Ursinus people build relationships unlike anywhere else I've heard**. In addition to making friends with people who truly care about you and understand you for you, we are all challenged to think about our own moral codes and beliefs, making us not only better students but better people."

Q "**My favorite parts are the students and the teachers**. I have the best friends I could ask for at Ursinus. I never thought I would have loved college as much as I do!"

Q "I love it, and I wouldn't change a thing. **No place is going to be perfect**. The problems I've faced here are a sample of what I'm going to face in the 'real world.'"

Q "I love Ursinus, and I can't imagine being at a better school. But, **as much as I love it, it's not for everyone**. If someone is looking for a big school with a lot of students, Ursinus isn't the school for you. If I could do it all over again, I would choose Ursinus, hands down."

STUDENT AUTHOR: **Students love this school, despite its drawbacks. It is not big or in a nice cultural area, the town offers little to do, and the food on campus definitely could use improvement. But Ursinus' strength lies in its excellent academic program, and the students and professors are a tight-knit group. Philadelphia is close but still far enough away for Ursinus to be removed from a large-city setting. In general, this is a small school in a small town. Most students will graduate having met almost everyone who goes here, while also receiving an excellent education.**

Valparaiso University

1700 Chapel Drive; Valparaiso, IN 46383
(219) 464-5000; www.valpo.edu

Students Speak Out
ON ACADEMICS

Q "It's easy to tell when a professor loves what they're doing. Many of them seem to have been here too long. They are in a rut and **teach more out of habit than passion**."

Q "I would contend that the professors at Valpo are the biggest draw to the University. I could never have imagined as a freshman at VU that in the next four years I would be **challenged intellectually, spiritually, and personally** by what I consider to be the best faculty anywhere in the nation. Sure, there are a few profs who you'd like to strangle, but for the most part, they will become lifelong influences on you, and more than that, become your friends. The classes are typically very stimulating (of course with some exceptions), and they all are taught by professors, not graduate students."

Q "The teachers are great, **very knowledgeable, and personable**. Most of the classes are interesting, and many professors try and bring in the real-world situations to the discussions."

STUDENT AUTHOR: One aspect of Valpo's academics that most students do not even take note of is the absence of TAs. Most VU students do not comment on this because having a TA just doesn't happen. VU is what many call a teaching school, and while the professors are strongly encouraged to do research and publish in journals, their primary focus and objective is to teach students. While some professors may not be the most personable, on the whole, they are accessible and ready to help you learn.

Students Speak Out
ON LOCAL ATMOSPHERE

Q "Valpo is small, but it does offer some interesting **only-in-a-small-Midwestern-town type activities**: Popcorn Festival and the Wizard of Oz Fest (in Chesterton, just north of Valpo). Valpo also takes full advantage of the Lake Michigan Dunes just a short 20 minutes up the highway."

Q "Valparaiso, Indiana is boring. Since the University is located just over an hour from Chicago, most students travel into the city to find activities. It's **nice to be so close to Chicago**, but it's almost essential to go there to find something to do."

Q "Valparaiso is **small compared to most college towns**, and the University is at the heart of the city. I normally go to the neighboring town (Merrillville) where there is a mall and a movie theater."

Q "A distinct division exists between Valpo the college town and Valpo the community. VU is the only university in town, but relations between the **college students and the locals are not always jolly**."

STUDENT AUTHOR: The small downtown section of Valparaiso is only about three blocks square, but contains enough specialty shops to keep you busy for a whole Saturday. Downtown Valparaiso is also the home to some of the "best town secret." If you can't find something to do in Valpo, you always have the option of going to Chicago. It has everything you could possibly think of with sports teams, concerts, theaters, museums, and shopping.

5 Best Things
1 Basketball games
2 Free movies on campus
3 On-campus concerts
4 Library
5 Academic programs

5 Worst Things
1 Lots of snow
2 Community bathrooms
3 Tiny cardio room
4 Dining hall food
5 Lots of rain

Students Speak Out
ON FACILITIES

Q The athletic building and pool are not the greatest. **They are getting pretty old**, and you feel a little like you're in a dungeon. The new library and computers there are amazing! The Union is getting pretty old, but still serves its purpose well."

Q "**The football field is embarrassingly small** and unattractive. The computer facilities, other than those in the new library, are rather pieced together and dingy. The student center is adequate, but it is in the 10-year plan to be rebuilt. The student center offers two dining hall options, two study lounges, and multiple meeting rooms, in addition to a large assembly hall."

Q "Valpo **built a new library with very nice computer labs**. As far as athletics, Valpo needs a bigger cardio and weight room for the students. My high school had better workout facilities than Valpo."

STUDENT AUTHOR: **A few of the buildings need remodeling or upgrading, while some have already received face lifts. While the facilities, in general, around campus are in good shape, some areas just need to be remodeled or expanded to accommodate the growing on-campus student population. The library, which is connected directly to the Union, is a great addition to campus. It brings a new state-of-the-art facility to a campus that is trying to move forward and expand. The places that students do agree need work are the workout facilities. The ARC, while nice in size, is usually overrun with athletic teams and their practices.**

Famous Alumni

Bryce Drew, Michael Essany, Paul Grammatico, Jackie Lyden, Lloyd McClendon, Douglas Rich, Al Seib, Kathi Seifert

Students Speak Out
ON CAMPUS DINING

Q "The food is typical cafeteria food—palatable mostly because it's **saturated in grease and salt**. The options are interesting; the staff tries to offer different ethnic cuisines, and a variety of fast food-quality options are always on hand."

Q "Food here is one of the biggest downfalls. It is very expensive, and it is not all-you-can-eat. Much of your food, like deli sandwiches and salads, are weighed, and **prices can get steep**."

Q "The café in the library has great drinks; most of the cafeterias serve the same food, but Lankenau and the Round Table offer sandwiches all day. The food is not the greatest, most of the time, but what can you expect from mass-produced food? They do have **several dishes and soups that are really good**."

Q "Food has been better in the past. The plus is there are **many choices for different diets**, and there are always sandwiches available at the Round Table."

STUDENT AUTHOR: **Campus food is better than most high school cafeteria food. The main gripe of most students is the á la carte meal plan, which charges you for each item of food instead of by the "meal." This pay-per-item system causes problems when making salads or sandwiches, since students are charged per ounce. Often the saving grace is the availability of fast-food-type burgers, chicken fingers, and other grill items. Favorite occasions for many students are theme nights. There is Mexican night, Picnic night, Hawaiian night, Disco night, and '50s night.**

Student Body

African American:	4%	Male/Female:	47/53%
Asian American:	2%	Out-of-State:	67%
Hispanic:	3%	International:	1%
Native American:	<1%	Unknown:	0%
White:	90%		

Popular Faiths: Christianity (largely Lutheran and Catholic) and a small Muslim population are the most prevalent religions.

Gay Pride: Valpo has Alliance, a GLBT group, but the overall attitude on campus is not extremely tolerant of these lifestyles.

Economic Status: Students come from mostly middle- to upper-middle-class families.

Students Speak Out
ON DORMS

Q "Scheele, Lankenau, Alumni, and Brandt are all old and not air conditioned. They are small and somewhat shabby, despite numerous attempts by the University to dress them up with new carpet. Guild and Memorial are both very nice and clean. Wehrenberg is also nice, but anti-social. Avoid Brandt—it's just dirty. Avoid Berg or GM if you enjoy interacting with your neighbors. Scheele is all sorority sisters. **Lank and Alumni are the freshman dorms—choose Lank**."

Q "All of the dorms are pretty similar. The freshman and sorority dorm have the same rooms, which include a sink and vanity. **Berg, Guild, and Memorial Halls have bigger rooms**, and are closer to the cafeteria."

STUDENT AUTHOR: **Without being a commuter student or a senior, it is pretty impossible to live off campus more than your last year. Everyone manages to find a dorm that they like. Some students loved the noise and constant movement of the freshman dorms. Other students move into 'Berg (Wehrenberg), Guild, or Memorial—all of which have been remodeled in the past 10 years.**

> **Did You Know?**
> 65% of undergrads live on campus.

Students Speak Out
ON GUYS & GIRLS

Q "I wouldn't say Valpo has the hottest-looking people, but there are **definitely some good-looking guys**."

Q "The **guys are the Midwestern farm-boy type**. They are, on the whole, not attractive. There might be five attractive young men on the whole campus. The general personality type is rather 'nice,' but without much substance. The girls are equally unattractive on the whole, and rather unpleasant towards each other."

Q "The girls are pretty cute. Most of them are the **girl-next-door type with Abercrombie clothes**. Although, there are definitely some on this campus that are not hot."

STUDENT AUTHOR: **"Average" is the most commonly used word when asking anyone at Valpo about the physical attributes of the opposite sex. There are few good-looking ones wandering around, but there is no promising that they aren't taken. There are the typical jocks, nerds, and artists hanging around campus, so if you are hoping to find someone of a particular brand, then it is easy to determine where you should be looking.**

> **Traditions**
>
> **Midnight Madness**
> Held the midnight of the day when practices officially start, thousands of fans and students gather to watch the first practice of men's and women's b-ball teams.
>
> **Late-Night Bingo**
> About once a month, the Union holds late-night bingo from 11 p.m.–2 a.m. Proceeds go to charity.
>
> **Overall School Spirit**
> The most blatant show of school spirit is the student cheering section at the basketball games. Students dress in VU apparel, temporary tattoos, even wigs.

Students Speak Out
ON ATHLETICS

Q "**Varsity basketball is huge**. Everyone goes. Unfortunately, other than basketball, most people don't go to other sporting events other than to cheer for their friends."

Q "Basketball is huge. Football is poorly supported. Women's volleyball is good. Softball is poorly supported, but improving. IMs are huge. **Greek life, and freshmen especially, keep the brackets full**."

Q "Our biggest varsity sport is men's basketball; that's what Valpo gets the most attention for, at least. Intramural sports are very big on campus, and we have **almost every sport you may want to play**."

STUDENT AUTHOR: **A large contingent of the student body makes regular treks over to the ARC to watch Valpo men's basketball. In the past year or two, the women's basketball team has been drawing a bigger and bigger crowd on a regular basis. The most passion seeps off the basketball court into intramurals. Intramurals are available to anyone who wants to play, and they are a great way for a large number of students to stay in shape and take a much needed break from studying.**

Students Speak Out
ON DRUG SCENE

Q "You can find **a lot of drugs off campus**. I don't know anyone on campus who does drugs."

Q "The drug scene on campus doesn't seem all that prominent. I know that there are kids that smoke weed, and I had heard some talk about ecstasy around my sophomore year. I'm sure that if you went off campus, either to a party or elsewhere in town, you could track down some drugs, but for the most part, **I don't know anyone who does drugs** or has done drugs."

Q "Quite simply, it happens. I know that it goes on, but **it's nothing that is right in your face** or an everyday thing. In fact, I don't know that I have ever seen someone doing drugs, and none of my friends do."

STUDENT AUTHOR: **Finding drugs on campus is a difficult task. The portion of the campus population that participates in drug use is minimal. Just about every student knows more people in his/her high school class who did drugs than people around campus who do drugs.**

13:1	Student-to-Faculty Ratio
85%	Freshman Retention Rate
58%	Four-Year Graduation Rate
85%	Financial Aid Applicants Receiving Aid

Students Speak Out
SAFETY & SECURITY

Q "Valpo feels very safe. A student can walk alone at night with minimal fear. The police do not necessarily contribute to this feeling of safety, however, as they have a cold relationship with the student body. The **familiarity amongst the students is what offers the sense of security** on campus."

Q "Police are always patrolling, and the student **van service is available at night** to take students around campus for free."

Q "VUPD isn't real visible, but it doesn't really matter because there isn't much of anything to be scared of. **Dorm security is another issue**. It's not that security in the dorms is bad, but it doesn't take much to slip past the DAs in the dorms you don't live in."

STUDENT AUTHOR: **It may be uncomfortable to walk alone from the main library back to the dorm, but it is definitely safe. Very few incidents have occurred on or around campus in the past few years. VUPD is not a very visible part of campus. You see them more often ticketing cars than actually patrolling campus, but patrolling is not really required of them.**

> **Questions?**
> For more inside information and survival tips, pick up College Prowler's full-length book on this school, written by an actual student! Check it out at *www.collegeprowler.com*.

Students Speak Out
ON OVERALL EXPERIENCE

Q "I wouldn't want to be anywhere else. The campus atmosphere is wonderful, and the staff and faculty **make you feel like you belong**."

Q "I enjoy the friends I've made and the excellent study abroad programs, but **I would rather have been in a real city** with more challenging peers. Everyone here is pretty similar and content with it. There's sort of a general acceptance of the mundane, and people don't strive too hard to really achieve great things."

Q "I really like my VU education, and I am very proud to be part of this institution. However, I have the distinct privilege of wanting to be here and not having any alternative plans. I don't need a job, I don't need a social life, and I don't need a man. So college is really what I make of it. **VU is not a 'worldly' experience**. It is in Indiana, for God's sake."

Q "I was able to get **involved in a whole bunch of activities** and do what I wanted without feeling pressured to be extremely active in every group I belonged to. I am incredibly glad that I picked Valpo."

STUDENT AUTHOR: **When trying to determine the best part about their VU experience, most students recount the great friends and the encouraging atmosphere the professors work hard to create. A great advantage to the students at Valpo is the willingness of professors to speak with you, even if you aren't in their class or even their department. Students consistently comment that they have left Valpo with lasting friendships and a deep appreciation for learning. Valpo is a one-of-a-kind place that just seems to draw you in.**

Vanderbilt University

2301 West End Avenue; Nashville, TN 37235
(615) 322-7311; www.vanderbilt.edu

THE BASICS:

Acceptance Rate: 33%
Setting: Urban
F-T Undergrads: 6,463

SAT Range: 1300–1480*
Control: Private
Tuition: $34,414

Most Popular Majors: Social Sciences, Engineering, Foreign Languages, Psychology, English, History

*of 1600

Academics	A	Guys	B+
Local Atmosphere	B+	Girls	A+
Safety & Security	B+	Athletics	B
Computers	B	Nightlife	A-
Facilities	A	Greek Life	A+
Campus Dining	B-	Drug Scene	B+
Off-Campus Dining	B+	Campus Strictness	A-
Campus Housing	B+	Parking	D
Off-Campus Housing	C-	Transportation	D+
Diversity	C	Weather	B

Students Speak Out
ON ACADEMICS

Q "I think that one of Vanderbilt's greatest strengths is the amount of student-faculty interaction. I have found my professors to be both approachable and genuinely interested in helping the students. Almost all of my classes have **centered on class discussion and participation**, and this provides a good opportunity to get to know other students, as well as the professors."

Q "In all my years at Vanderbilt, **I have never taken a single class from a TA**. Then again, I'm going to graduate without taking any math courses."

Q "The best advice I've gotten on teachers is that if you find a teacher you like, take another class with them no matter what it is. Just take it, because **it's the teacher that makes the difference**. Now I just have classes with the ones I like and relate to, and it makes class so much easier."

STUDENT AUTHOR: It goes without saying that an institution like Vanderbilt **will boast a tremendous faculty. As a research university, the offerings are unlimited, and between all the departments and post-graduate schools, there is ample opportunity for a student to fully explore any discipline he or she so chooses. Combine this with a reasonably small student body and a fabulous student-to-teacher ratio, and you have a learning environment in which undergrads are treated like upper-division students from the moment they step on Vandy's campus their freshman year.**

Students Speak Out
ON LOCAL ATMOSPHERE

Q "**Nashville is the sort of city that needs to be given a chance**. Many people from larger cities, notably New Yorkers (Yankees, in the Southern vernacular), are predisposed to disliking Nashville, and as a result, they miss out on what it has to offer. Truth be told, it is a smaller city, but that doesn't mean it is devoid of cultural events or good nightlife. It is just on a smaller scale than San Francisco or New York."

Q "Before students graduate from Vandy, they must **visit Memphis to see Graceland** and make the spring break drive to New Orleans to take in Mardi Gras."

Q "I don't really like Nashville. I'm from a small city, and I wanted to move to a big, fast city. Nashville got much of its big city notoriety from Opryland and the country music scene. **It can be described as a big small town**. Yes, there are lots of clubs, but I'm sure you won't be spending your weekends there. After awhile, the club scene gets boring."

Q "Vanderbilt is in Nashville, but **it's like its own little community**. We call it the Vander bubble. There are other universities around, but you rarely meet anyone from them. It's a great town."

STUDENT AUTHOR: Nashville is an insider's town—if you know the ins **and outs of the city, then there's something to do every day and night. This is a lot of fun because knowing about the cool restaurants or the special nights at various clubs makes you feel like you're privy to exciting information.**

5 Best Things	**5 Worst Things**
1 Strong academics	**1** Dominant Greek life
2 Urban environment	**2** Lack of diversity
3 Beautiful campus	**3** Southern food
4 Southern hospitality	**4** Undegrad requirements
5 Faculty	**5** The mascot

Students Speak Out
ON FACILITIES

Q "The facilities on campus are beautiful. Because of the school's enormous endowment, they are able to **continually build new buildings and renovate old ones**. It is very rare that you will find yourself in an architecturally unappealing or dated building."

Q "The Rec Center is amazing, and it provides great workout machines. It's often crowded, though. Go at off-peak hours. There are also good classes for yoga and aerobics. There is a **movie theater on campus** that shows movies—not brand new movies, but before-they-go-to-rental movies. There is an art gallery in the student center and art studios where they offer classes for a fee. The student center is where the dining hall is. It's a very central and busy part of campus. That's also the location of the bookstore and the mail room."

Q "All of our facilities are **nice, clean, and modern**."

Q "Facilities are awesome and state-of-the-art. The **campus is gorgeous**."

STUDENT AUTHOR: **Vanderbilt takes great pride in both its aesthetics and functionality. With the endowment and tuition prices as high as they are, the school has little trouble continually improving its facilities and does an excellent job in discerning what is the most effective solution. There is something very special about stepping out of the garden environment of the campus into a perfectly maintained building and being able to access a high-speed, wireless network on your laptop.**

Famous Alumni

Lamar Alexander, Roseanne Cash, Al Gore Jr., Tipper Gore, Amy Grant, Matthew Hart, Michael Kantor, Grantland Rice, Molly Sims, John Snyder

Students Speak Out
ON CAMPUS DINING

Q "It's good if you **realize it's going to be cafeteria food** and lower your expectations accordingly. The only complaint I ever had was that the meals were repetitive. Regardless, students are always going to complain about the meal plan. For breakfast and lunch, the cafeteria has a lot of very good options with any type of food you desire."

Q "Food is great if you aren't eating dinner on the Rand dinner plan. The **student center has several great eateries**; Stonehenge serves incredible sandwiches and soup bowls, but only during lunch. The Pub (officially called Overcup Oak) has good pub food, like grilled sandwiches, salads, hamburgers, soup bowls, chicken strips, nachos, and free popcorn. They serve beer, too, which is why it's called the Pub, and they have a tremendous happy hour special."

Q "Food has been top rated, and when Dining Services prepares a special event, it's usually excellent. The day-to-day service tends to be **mass produced and repetitive, like anywhere else**."

STUDENT AUTHOR: **Other than dinner at Rand, students are very positive about the quality of the food. Fortunately, you only need to eat there freshman year, and like most traumatic experiences, it only brings people closer together for having gone through it. However, despite the high quality and selection of what is available, the prices are ridiculously inflated, and there isn't a grocery store within walking distance.**

Student Body

African American:	9%	Male/Female:	47/53%
Asian American:	7%	Out-of-State:	83%
Hispanic:	6%	International:	3%
Native American:	<1%	Unknown:	12%
White:	63%		

Popular Faiths: The most popular faiths on campus are Protestantism and Catholicism.

Gay Pride: There is a growing gay community at Vanderbilt, and they have a very noticeable and positive presence on campus.

Economic Status: Most students come from middle- and upper-class families.

Students Speak Out
ON DORMS

Q "You **don't get to pick which building you live in**, you choose if you'd like a single or a double. Vandy/Barnard, which is nice (but small), is singles and doubles, Branscomb is all doubles, and Kissam is all singles. You don't want to end up in Kissam, so don't check the box for a single room."

Q "My freshman dorm was tiny. I lived in Branscomb and loved it. As a sophomore, I lived in North hall (all girls), and I also loved that! I don't think you can go wrong—no matter where you live, **you learn to make the best of it and have a blast**."

Q "**Freshmen, you want to live in Branscomb**. It's four dorms of freshmen, all connected, and it's the place to be. Sophomore year, the party dorm is Gillette."

STUDENT AUTHOR: **Most Vanderbilt students live on campus for their entire college careers, and it is pretty easy to see why. The University has changed the way freshmen are assigned to dorms to promote more mixing of different types of students. Odds are, you'll still end up in the sort of place you're looking for.**

> **? Did You Know?**
> 89% of undergrads live on campus.

Students Speak Out
ON GUYS & GIRLS

Q "Average guy: momma's boy who did well in high school, but wasn't exceptionally popular. Average girl: daddy's girl who was the prom/homecoming queen, head cheerleader/debutante, and the most popular girl at her high school. **Beauty and brains mix when you find valedictorians that are striking**."

Q "Both guys and girls have a **huge amount of pressure to be attractive** and stylish."

Q "The guys are very Southern. It takes some getting used to—the hair, the clothes, the shoes—but it grows on you. The **girls are pretty much debutantes**. You'll find a lot of people come from elite boarding schools or academies."

STUDENT AUTHOR: **Vanderbilt girls are beautiful and talented, the only problem being that they all tend to go for the same look, which after a while, diminishes individuality. It seems like there is a definite burden on Vandy girls to live up to this high standard. Guys are, by comparison, not quite at the level of the girls, but they are in their own right pretty impressive. Both men and women at Vanderbilt are not incredibly diverse.**

> **Traditions**
>
> **Overdress to Impress**
> This involves guys dressing up in a coat and tie and taking a date in a dress to home football games.
>
> **Running of the Pigs**
> This is when the sorority girls run to their houses the day that they find out what sorority house they've been accepted into.
>
> **Overall School Spirit**
> There is a lot of school spirit at Vandy; it's just focused on teams that are winning. The teams that succeed tend to draw big crowds.

Students Speak Out
ON ATHLETICS

Q "Varsity sports are not big on campus. It's mainly because Vanderbilt is not that good, and everyone would rather just root for their home SEC team—everyone seems to be from Kentucky, Alabama, or Georgia. IM sports are very good and very available to everyone. I really think that the **IM sports have a substantial impact on the morale of the campus**."

Q "Both **intramural and club sports are a big deal**, and they are a lot of fun. There are lots of different leagues for lots of different skill levels."

Q "**IM sports for freshman halls are pretty popular**, and a lot of times, the team will follow through until senior year."

STUDENT AUTHOR: **Vanderbilt athletics, at times, seems to be the target of ridicule within the SEC. A lot of this has to do with the size of the student body—even if every single Vanderbilt student and grad student showed up, we couldn't fill our own basketball arena. Compare this to the big state schools of the SEC, which are several times bigger and have tons of alumni within 20 minutes of their school.**

Students Speak Out
ON DRUG SCENE

Q "Drugs really aren't that big at Vanderbilt because **the drug of choice for the Vandy student is alcohol**. There is a problem with binge drinking and alcohol abuse, but drug use is hardly a speck on the radar."

Q "I think the main thing that students do is marijuana, but I don't think it's very dominant, and you **probably will never find yourself in a peer pressure situation**. I think the dominant 'drug' on campus is beer."

Q "All in all, there isn't a drug scene, unless you count **tobacco, caffeine, or alcohol**. However, it does exist, and if you want to find it, you can. Largely, students stick to the above mentioned three."

STUDENT AUTHOR: There is a small drug scene on campus, so if you really need to find drugs, I'm sure you wouldn't have too much difficulty. The poison of choice on Vanderbilt's campus, however, is alcohol. There are problems with binge drinking, but if you're smart enough to get into Vanderbilt, then you're smart enough to make your own decisions.

9:1	Student-to-Faculty Ratio
96%	Freshman Retention Rate
85%	Four-Year Graduation Rate
92%	Financial Aid Applicants Receiving Aid

Students Speak Out
SAFETY & SECURITY

Q "There are **very few incidents that affect students on the campus**. The police notify the entire community whenever an incident does occur. Relatively, it isn't that bad. The areas of Nashville that students inhabit or frequent are also very safe."

Q "We are close to downtown, but the school is in its own little bubble. I have never once felt unsafe on campus. I actually walk from my dorm to the gym at night by myself, all the while feeling safe. We also have our own police department on campus that **will answer immediately to any emergency**. They will also provide escorts if you ever feel unsafe to walk to your destination."

STUDENT AUTHOR: Truth be told, the main campus is very poorly lit; it would be a challenge for anyone to spot an emergency blue phone while standing at another one (they are too few and far between). However, Vanderbilt and its police force are very well equipped to handle any problems (and the statistics back them up).

Questions?
For more inside information and survival tips, pick up College Prowler's full-length book on this school, written by an actual student! Check it out at *www.collegeprowler.com*.

Students Speak Out
ON OVERALL EXPERIENCE

Q "I think a **lot of people come into Vanderbilt with a bit of a chip on their shoulder**. Either because they feel an Ivy League school snubbed them, or they got into an Ivy League school and couldn't afford it, but Vanderbilt gave them a scholarship. What's amazing is given all that, everyone ends up falling in love with Vandy and cannot imagine themselves anywhere else."

Q "I have **never once regretted being at Vandy—** even for a minute. I have found a lot of very good friends here, and I have had a lot of fun partying, as well. Nashville is a fun city with a lot going on. I would definitely recommend this school."

Q "Even though a few friends are like family to me now, I think I would've enjoyed my college years more if I had transferred that first year or taken a more active interest in my college search. I **needed somewhere more liberal, less preppy, and less Greek**. However, I excelled in my classes and graduated with honors, and even spent time abroad, so maybe it all worked out in the end."

STUDENT AUTHOR: Vanderbilt is big enough to accommodate almost anyone's desires and small enough to make this campus feel like home for the years you spend here. While Vanderbilt has a lot of positive qualities, it isn't the best choice for everyone. Choosing Vanderbilt means choosing to be in a situation where name-brand clothes and high-end cars have a certain amount of importance. Most students come from white upper-class families, and while they may not all fit the stereotype of wealthy snobs, money is in abundance.

Vassar College

124 Raymond Avenue; Poughkeepsie, NY 12604
(845) 437-7000; www.vassar.edu

THE BASICS:

Acceptance Rate: 29%
Setting: Suburban
F-T Undergrads: 2,406

SAT Range: 1310–1460*
Control: Private
Tuition: $39,695

Most Popular Majors: English, Psychology, Political Science, Economics, Art

*of 1600

Academics	A	Guys	B
Local Atmosphere	C+	Girls	B+
Safety & Security	B+	Athletics	C+
Computers	B+	Nightlife	D+
Facilities	B+	Greek Life	N/A
Campus Dining	C-	Drug Scene	C-
Off-Campus Dining	B-	Campus Strictness	A-
Campus Housing	A-	Parking	C
Off-Campus Housing	B-	Transportation	D-
Diversity	C+	Weather	C-

Students Speak Out
ON ACADEMICS

Q "**The teachers are definitely a strong point**. All the teachers that I have had have been extremely accessible and love to get to know the students. I can't think of a class where I didn't meet with my professor at least once outside of class if I had a problem with a paper or just wanted to talk. I find almost all of my classes very interesting. With no core curriculum, I am taking classes because I want to take them."

Q "Most professors are great, caring, and considerate, while some couldn't care less about the students and are just doing their job. **You need to make the effort** to get them to know you."

Q "This semester was interesting; I had a class that asked me to rewrite a play and another in which we folk danced as a means of introduction on the first day. I think Vassar classes have a tendency to attract teachers and **students who want to learn in non-traditional ways**, making the material really stimulating."

Q "Vassar usually has the good enough sense to **get rid of bad teachers**."

STUDENT AUTHOR: Vassar professors are approachable. They live in dorms, are with kids at lectures, and invite students to their homes. Even if Vassar professors weren't half as good as they are, the academic freedom allows students to construct their own program. They can create an independent major and are encouraged to study abroad.

Students Speak Out
ON LOCAL ATMOSPHERE

Q "**Poughkeepsie is the antithesis of a college town**. You need a car to get around off campus. Vassar is a bubble, so you don't realize that there are other universities and colleges very close by. NYC is just a quick train ride away, however, so that's a perk."

Q "Poughkeepsie is something of a ghetto. The **area immediately surrounding Vassar is charming**, though. There are a whole bunch of great restaurants and a cute, independently-run bookstore that packs a good selection into a tiny space."

Q "Poughkeepsie is easy to write-off as a dumpy town with nothing for college students to do. However, with a little effort, **lots of cultural things can be found** in the city."

Q "New Paltz, New York, home of SUNY New Paltz is a popular destination for Vassar students. A 20-minute drive away, the main street houses several cafés, restaurants, and head shops. Further down the road is the Lake Minnewaska, **which offers miles of hiking trails** and a few waterfalls."

STUDENT AUTHOR: As a student, it is easy to utilize Poughkeepsie and the surrounding area, but it is also easy not to. There are a variety of settings, from a rural countryside to a small metropolis. Though Poughkeepsie may not be New York City, it is still a city. Everything you need can be found on campus and in the surrounding areas.

Students Speak Out
ON FACILITIES

Q "**A fancy-pants athletic center was built**—very nice. The school was outfitted with new computers. Several student centers exist—the newest is really well-presented with a detailed plaster ceiling and a café."

Q "The campus is beautiful. Vassar has plenty of money to toss around to keep facilities competitive with most of the good colleges out there. Everything is at least decent, and certain **things are really, really jaw-dropping**."

Q "The facilities are very nice—constantly being updated and renovated. Some are very nice (Jewett!), while others have been around for a while. But **all are kept up**."

Q "They're great and are constantly being renovated and improved due to a seemingly bottomless donor fund. **All the facilities are sickeningly clean and new-looking**, and there are computers everywhere."

Q "The athletic facilities are huge and gorgeous, the **buildings are historic looking and well-kept**, and Building and Grounds spends a lot of time and money keeping up the arboretum and flower garden."

STUDENT AUTHOR: **While many maintain their original form, several renovations go above and beyond mere modernization. The Walker Athletic and Fitness Center is surrounded by the Vassar Golf course. For the dramatic, there are black-box theaters at the Powerhouse, Susan Stein Shiva, and the Center for Drama and Film. The student center and the ACDC provide breathtaking space to lounge or hold lectures and performances.**

Famous Alumni

Jane Fonda, Lisa Kudrow, Jackie Onassis, Meryl Streep

Students Speak Out
ON CAMPUS DINING

Q "**As a vegan, I never have a problem** finding good food on campus. The main dining hall always has vegan pizza, veggie burgers, vegetable/hummus wraps, and an entire do-it-yourself vegan stir-fry station."

Q "The food on campus is above average when compared to state schools. However, ordering in is always a pleasure. **Having only two dining places limits the choices** available but there seems to be a café open all the time. This is the place to be for coffee enthusiasts."

Q "I personally don't mind the food that much, but it totally lacks in variety. Everything tastes the same, be it fish or chicken. **I think of the dining hall as a C student** who really gets a pat on the back when he gets an A."

Q "ACDC (All Campus Dining Center) is relatively painless, as far as food consumption in the entire world goes (consider overnight camps, prisons, and homeless shelters), but you do get tired of the same old rotation of **unidentifiable food-stuffs and vegetables served with cinnamon**."

STUDENT AUTHOR: **Because Vassar is a small school, dining options are limited; students get bored of the food. However, eating is a social event at Vassar. When you stand in crowded lines waiting for food, you catch up with old acquaintances or people from class. You can walk into ACDC alone and always find someone to eat with. The meal plan is on a point system. Instead of paying on entrance, you are charged for each item you eat.**

Student Body

African American:	5%	Male/Female:	40/60%
Asian American:	10%	Out-of-State:	58%
Hispanic:	7%	International:	6%
Native American:	<1%	Unknown:	2%
White:	70%		

Popular Faiths: Religion doesn't play a large role in most students' lives, but Vassar isn't "Godless."

Gay Pride: Vassar students are extremely accepting of lesbian, gay, bisexual, and transgender people.

Economic Status: Look at any of the parking lots on campus and you'll see that Vassar has a number of wealthy students.

Students Speak Out
ON DORMS

Q "I love that **we don't have freshman dorms**. Mixing up freshmen, sophomores, and juniors is really great. The coed bathrooms contribute to the comfortable atmosphere of Vassar."

Q "After freshman year, most people (though by no means all) get singles, which is a nice perk. **Every dorm has a shared kitchen** and a TV room or two and a fancy parlor with a Steinway and a fireplace."

Q "If you like history and beautiful architecture, I would do dorm living at Vassar (as if you had any choice). **A certain myth pervades each dorm**, but they are all really nice."

STUDENT AUTHOR: **Vassar dorms are not only elegant—with their Elizabethan-style architecture—but most feel very much like homes. Also, two or more members of the faculty—complete with families and pets—live in each dorm. All students live intermingled on coed floors with coed bathrooms except for the all-female dorm, Strong. Generally, students stay in the same dorm until their senior year, when they move to Vassar-owned apartments.**

? Did You Know?
98% of undergrads live on campus.

Students Speak Out
ON GUYS & GIRLS

Q "Despite the rumors, the vast majority of Vassar men are straight. However, most lack stereotypical chauvinist macho qualities, perhaps because **Vassar students are self-secure**. Both men and women are ridiculously attractive and are more concerned with social and political issues than the average college student."

Q "There is a wide variety of guys and girls in different social groups. The girls are pretty attractive overall, and it's really not very difficult to find casual sex; **there are lots of 'sexually liberated' people** on campus."

Q "Vassar has all kinds—jocks, preps, goths, indie rockers—**you name it, Vassar has it**."

STUDENT AUTHOR: **No, Vassar isn't still a girl's school. Most guys are lanky, skinny, artsy types, and girls aren't your typical girly girls. Vassar has an open homosexual and bisexual community. Most students agree with the ideals of gender equity and gay rights that Vassar's community attempts to foster. This sexual openness is also one of the characteristics that draw students to Vassar.**

Traditions

24-hour Improv
Students set up a stage in the Retreat and perform improvisational games for 24 hours straight.

Daisy Chain
A group of sophomore women carry an elaborate chain of fresh daisies and laurel at commencement.

Overall School Spirit
Vassar students are not a bunch of cheerleaders, but they love their school. They are proud to be among a group of intelligent, independent-minded students; most are even proud of the weirder ones, too.

Students Speak Out
ON ATHLETICS

Q "Varsity sports are not that big. There are a few good teams, and they have tight groups, but they **don't really dominate the social scene**. Lots of people do IMs, and it's supposed to be fun."

Q "**We're DIII. Need I say more**? IM sports are there for those who want to get involved."

Q "So far as the sports go, it is mainly those who play varsity who support other varsity teams. The apathy for sports and **the lack of Vassar sports spirit makes it hard** for varsity teams to feel like they are really representing Vassar."

Q "A lot participate in IM sports, but it's just looked at as a way to relax and have a good time, **nothing too serious or competitive**. Varsity sport? What's that?"

STUDENT AUTHOR: **You may spot a students sporting a T-shirt with the slogan: "Vassar Football, undefeated since 1861." As Vassar doesn't actually have a football team, the T-shirt is a good indication of how most students perceive varsity sports. Intramural sports often get greater participation and draw larger crowds than varsity.**

Students Speak Out
ON DRUG SCENE

Q "I don't really know what it is like at other schools, but it seems like **you can get anything you want** pretty easily."

Q "Vassar **drug scene—it's big**. The administration knows it and lets it happen. The amount of marijuana that Vassar students go through in a typical weekend could probably cover a giant redwood. Harder drugs are readily available, but you're less likely to casually encounter them. That said, many a Vassar student eschews drug use completely and has an easy time doing so."

Q "**If you choose to avoid it, no problem**. If you choose to be a part of it, it varies from the occasional pot to hard-core drugs like cocaine. But all in good fun, of course."

STUDENT AUTHOR: **Drug use is an accepted recreation among Vassar students and regulations and policies regarding it are fairly lax. You will encounter drugs on a regular basis at Vassar. Most students have a work hard, play hard mentality. Few let drugs consume their time at Vassar.**

9:1	Student-to-Faculty Ratio
95%	Freshman Retention Rate
87%	Four-Year Graduation Rate
84%	Financial Aid Applicants Receiving Aid

Students Speak Out
SAFETY & SECURITY

Q "**You get to know the security guards** that walk around the dorms, and they'll usually just give you a warning for anything they don't want you to be doing. There have been some problems with vandalism and theft by people from off campus, but I generally feel safe."

Q "Security at Vassar is pretty good. I feel safe, but **I also keep my room locked**."

Q "Campus feels very safe. Security is often lax when enforcing no-alcohol policies but is **definitely responsive to safety issues**."

STUDENT AUTHOR: At Vassar, there is a deep sense of personal safety. Unlike most college campuses, all Vassar students can gain access to any of the dorms with their V-card, allowing students to visit other dorms easily.

> **Questions?**
> For more inside information and survival tips, pick up College Prowler's full-length book on this school, written by an actual student! Check it out at *www.collegeprowler.com*.

Students Speak Out
ON OVERALL EXPERIENCE

Q "I think you need to realize Vassar is a small place and can be overwhelming at times. But boy, can it be wonderful at times. You just **need to find your happy medium**."

Q "**I cannot picture myself anywhere else**. I have no doubt that Vassar students are more friendly, open-minded, witty, and sincere than any others."

Q "**Vassar can be pretty alienating**. It is best done with an open mind and a forgiving temperament. Don't mind the snotty people and appreciate the genuinely nice ones. I guess this is the case anywhere. Vassar is a great place to experience a liberal-arts college."

Q "I had miscalculated Vassar in the first few weeks as well; not everyone is 'artsy'—the people at Vassar are all incredibly **different and totally elusive of labeling or typing**. I also don't think of Vassar as the 'bubble' everyone says it is; people here look both inwards and outwards."

STUDENT AUTHOR: **Vassar students are spoiled with brilliant professors who spend most waking hours teaching and mentoring their students. Among breathtaking campus facilities and endless acres of greenery to play on, you'll find academic freedom and a highly-intellectual and interesting student body. The school is full of independent-minded individuals, some of whom are athletes, performers, comedians, musicians, artists, tree-hugging hippies, political and social activists, and some whom are all or none of the above.**

Villanova University

800 Lancaster Avenue; Villanova, PA 19085
(610) 519-6000; www.villanova.edu

THE BASICS:

Acceptance Rate: 39%
Setting: Suburban
F-T Undergrads: 6,673

SAT Range: 1210–1400*
Control: Private
Tuition: $31,643

Most Popular Majors: Business, Social Sciences, Engineering, Health Sciences, Communications

*of 1600

Academics	B+	Guys	A-
Local Atmosphere	B-	Girls	A
Safety & Security	A	Athletics	A-
Computers	B+	Nightlife	B
Facilities	B	Greek Life	B
Campus Dining	B+	Drug Scene	B+
Off-Campus Dining	A-	Campus Strictness	C-
Campus Housing	B	Parking	C-
Off-Campus Housing	A-	Transportation	B+
Diversity	D+	Weather	B-

Students Speak Out
ON ACADEMICS

Q "Without a doubt, **Villanova's teachers are the University's best asset**. The professors are famous for their availability through e-mail and office hours. No one fails at Villanova because the professor wasn't available to help. The core humanities seminar, required for all freshmen, is absolutely enthralling, combining aspects of history and philosophy, and every professor approaches the curriculum in different, yet engaging, ways."

Q "**Good teachers are a rarity**. They are stale, forced, and required; the bottom line is no one is that excited to be there or to do well."

Q "Most of my teachers have been relatively interesting. My **most boring classes are my lecture classes**. Overall, I have been happy with my teachers."

Q "The teachers I have had thus far are a mix. **Some are wonderful, some are horrendous**. Overall, the staff at Villanova is very intelligent. Often, what makes a teacher bad is his teaching style, not his lack of knowledge. As a student, you need to learn to be flexible with learning techniques and find what works."

STUDENT AUTHOR: If there is one thing to be said about Villanova, it is that you will walk away with a solid education. Another benefit is that there are no TAs teaching classes. Overall, Villanova does a good job providing its students with competent professors who are always willing to learn more or go beyond the books to help.

Students Speak Out
ON LOCAL ATMOSPHERE

Q "**Philadelphia, which is nearby, is brimming with possibilities**. During my first semester at Villanova, I saw four concerts, went to the Museum of Fine Arts, watched Villanova basketball at the storied Palestra, and partied at UPenn's frat row."

Q "Villanova is an **upper-middle-class town without much fear of crime**. There are many universities in the area to visit. You can always visit Philly, but there are parts of Philly you should stay away from."

Q "The Mainline is a very classy neighborhood, one that can easily give off the air of being snooty. But at the same time, **it does offer lots of nice shops, friendly cafés and restaurants**, and lots more."

Q "Villanova is set in a pretty much suburban atmosphere, but with **close proximity to the city**. There are a ton of smaller universities along the Mainline, but there is also a bunch in Philly that provide opportunities to hang out at other colleges."

STUDENT AUTHOR: Philadelphia is a good time for any college student—whether you like to party on the weekends or grab a cup of coffee and tour various art museums. In a short train ride, you can land yourself almost anywhere in the greater Philly area. If the bustle of city life is not your thing, Villanova's suburban communities also have a good deal to offer. Almost every town up and down the Mainline has a quaint small-town feel.

5 Best Things	**5 Worst Things**
1 Basketball games	1 Lack of diversity
2 Philly cheesesteaks	2 Main Campus dorms
3 Location	3 Visitation policy
4 Junior apartments	4 No Greek housing
5 The students	5 Walk between campuses

Students Speak Out
ON FACILITIES

Q "The major **facilities that are lacking are the student gyms**. There are two exercise rooms around campus. Both have machines and free weights, but neither is very impressive. The gyms are often crowded, have lines for machines, or broken ones. That is definitely one area that could stand some improvement."

Q "The facilities on campus are pretty nice, but the only problem with them is that **all of the facilities close down very early**. For example, there are no dining halls open after 10 p.m."

Q "**The student center, Connelly, is a great place to hang out**, get food, drink coffee, eat ice cream, play pool, watch movies, and attend many events. Every weekend, there are plenty of activities available for entertainment. There are always free movie showings of newly released films, and there's always a program of some sort, like a battle of the bands, a comedian, or some type of live entertainment."

Q "The facilities are outstanding at Villanova. Perhaps the athletic and student facilities are not as great as some state schools, but the facilities are **amazing for the size of the University**."

STUDENT AUTHOR: The Connelly Center is not only geographically in the middle of campus, it is also the social center, study center, and has arguably the best food on campus. It caters to the student's basic needs. One need that tends to be overlooked is the athletic facilities, but every dorm on campus is within a few minutes walk of tennis, volleyball, and basketball courts, and there is almost never a wait for a pick-up game.

Famous Alumni

Andy Allen, Maria Bello, Jim Croce, Kerry Kittles, Sonia O'Sullivan, Howie Long, Edward Pinckney, Ed Rendell, John Rowland, Brian Westbrook

Students Speak Out
ON CAMPUS DINING

Q "Villanova offers a wide range of dining services. There are three traditional dining halls, and while, like all college students, we grumble about the quality, **they are actually pretty good**. There are a number of coffee places, called 'Holy Grounds,' which offer pretty good coffee."

Q "**Campus food is good—once you get used to it**. Everyone just has to realize nothing beats home cooking. Some good spots on campus are Donahue Court (aka the Spit), and Belle Air Terrace in the Connelly Center. The dining halls are good enough. Watch out that you don't eat excessive amounts of junk food, because you will gain the Freshman 15."

Q "I have heard of worse food on other campuses. We can complain, but **it just makes food at home taste that much better**."

Q "People tend to like the Spit the best. The food is alright. **Villanova puts a lot of money into making it good**, and every month, they have some specialty night with interesting ethnic food."

STUDENT AUTHOR: College food, no matter where you go, is never even close to a home-cooked meal. That's always one of the reasons going home on breaks is that much better. That aside, Villanova has a decent selection of pretty edible food. All types of eating preferences are looked after, whether you are vegetarian, vegan, or have religious eating restrictions. Overall, Villanova has a good taste in what is served. While students like to complain, it's not all that bad.

Student Body

African American:	5%	Male/Female:	49/51%
Asian American:	6%	Out-of-State:	71%
Hispanic:	6%	International:	2%
Native American:	<1%	Unknown:	3%
White:	77%		

Popular Faiths: The most popular religion by far is Roman Catholicism.

Gay Pride: Acceptance of homosexuality is a fairly touchy subject at Villanova; most students are accepting of gay classmates, but the University follows the teachings of the Catholic Church.

Economic Status: Students sometimes attack the school as being full of rich white kids.

Students Speak Out
ON DORMS

Q "The dorms are great. The best dorms are the junior apartments. The freshman dorms are also fairly nice. Most of the sophomore dorms are older and not as nice. **Overall, they are good**. I wouldn't avoid any."

Q "The dorms are good for the sole reason that the people in them are cool. No air-conditioning is okay, but **they are large and sterile, and at times, impersonal**. I like the small ones over the large ones."

Q "Sophomore housing is the best of all four years. You can either live in apartments or off campus your junior year, and **by senior year you must live off campus**, but by that point, you are ready."

STUDENT AUTHOR: **Since Villanova requires all freshmen to live on campus, making friends is pretty easy. South Campus houses nearly all freshmen, allowing for the majority of freshmen to be familiar with people in their classes. The dorms are comfortable and friendly, giving students a mix between privacy and social environment. Living on campus is convenient and fun, and few move off before senior year.**

? Did You Know?
72% of undergrads live on campus.

Students Speak Out
ON GUYS & GIRLS

Q "**Typical prepsters!** If you are into that, you will love it—many hot preppy sorority girls, all beautiful—but if you search, you can find alternative beauty."

Q "I have found that the **girls here can be cliquey, materialistic, and very predictable**. The guys who are on varsity sports teams seem to only hang out with teammates."

Q "Going to Villanova University will make the girls you hook up with back home seem ugly. **As a guy, your standards rise at Villanova**, which leads to the common misperception that the girls are prudes; they aren't, you are just going after girls a lot better looking than you."

STUDENT AUTHOR: **Walk around for five minutes, and there will be no doubt that the overwhelming majority of students on campus are hot. With an almost perfect balance of male and female students, there is always someone out there you haven't met. Most guys and girls are intelligent, caring people. Whether you're coming to Villanova in search of a special someone, or just a hookup on the weekend, there is a roughly even balance between both.**

Traditions

Pennsylvania Special Olympics
Every year for the last 16 years, Villanova has been home to the Pennsylvania Special Olympics.

Senior Week
After everyone's packed up and gone home, the graduating seniors stay behind for a week of memories and fun.

Overall School Spirit
Students are proud to bear the name Villanova, and few will talk badly about the school in front of anyone outside the school.

Students Speak Out
ON ATHLETICS

Q "Basketball tickets are distributed on a lottery system based on your attendance at previous games, and are usually not that difficult to get if you're a loyal fan. Intramural and club sports are very big on campus, there is just about every sport offered intramurally. The **club teams are just a step below varsity** and are very competitive without the time commitment."

Q "Villanova students **live and die with the basketball team**."

Q "Football and basketball games are widely attended. **Intramural sports are fun** if you get a good group of friends to play."

Q "Sports are a **huge part of campus life**, especially basketball and football."

STUDENT AUTHOR: **One thing to be said about Villanova athletics is that the campus eats, sleeps, and breathes by the men's basketball team. Basketball games are a guaranteed fun time. Intramurals are big for those who are involved. The athletics here at Villanova are source of both entertainment and fun year round.**

Students Speak Out
ON DRUG SCENE

💬 "Pot is probably the largest drug on campus. It's cheap and easy to get. However, Villanova is a wealthy school with lots of rich kids, so harder drugs can be found. If you're looking for drugs, you'd probably be able to find them, if you're not, then **you'll probably only notice some marijuana**."

💬 "Every campus has a drug problem. Villanova's drug problem is not too bad, because **security is really tight if you are doing drugs or drinking**. Villanova is a dry campus, so watch out for public safety. Never do drugs period, because you will be caught, and may be kicked out of school."

💬 "The drug scene is **just like any other college** campus. There is drinking and use of other drugs, as well."

STUDENT AUTHOR: **Drug use on campus is hardly a visible presence. However, you can occasionally run into the softer drugs somewhere on campus. If you are looking for drugs, they are not hard to find, but it is not something prevalent on campus.**

14:1	Student-to-Faculty Ratio
94%	Freshman Retention Rate
82%	Four-Year Graduation Rate
80%	Financial Aid Applicants Receiving Aid

Students Speak Out
SAFETY & SECURITY

💬 "Villanova's campus is very safe. I have never felt nervous or uneasy about walking back to my dorm late at night after a long night at the library. **Everything is well lit**. Public Safety can be considered to be too protective, especially in the signing-in of friends."

💬 "There's a late-night shuttle service, plenty of emergency call-boxes, and Public Safety is constantly monitoring the grounds, particularly on weekends. Most **buildings have guards during the evening**, and the doors are always locked to prevent outside intruders."

💬 "The community surrounding Villanova is really the biggest reason that there is so much security on campus. It's a nice neighborhood where **everyone looks out for one another**."

STUDENT AUTHOR: **With a strong presence by Public Safety, and a safe neighborhood nestled in a quiet suburban area, there is little to worry about. While they are strict on underage drinking, they do keep a safe atmosphere around campus and allow students to be pretty much worry free walking around late at night.**

> **Questions?**
> For more inside information and survival tips, pick up College Prowler's full-length book on this school, written by an actual student! Check it out at *www.collegeprowler.com*.

Students Speak Out
ON OVERALL EXPERIENCE

💬 "I love Villanova, and I could not have asked for a better school. Some people may have a few qualms about the school, but if you go to any school, you will have that small group who does. The **class sizes are wonderful**, the spirit at basketball games is crazy, and everyone on campus is just so nice."

💬 "Villanova is not a real college deal. It is **too Catholic, too strict, and too homogenous**. I am thinking about transferring, but find cool people who are like you, and you are golden!"

💬 "I have had a decent experience so far at school. I had no idea **I had to take so many requirement classes**. My friends at other schools complain that they have four classes—well, I have six. There is not much fun on weekends, and it is surprising how many parents come visit each weekend. I have met some very cool people here, though."

💬 "My Villanova experience has been wonderful. I love the school and all it has to offer. I enjoy being **close to a city, but having a neighborhood feel**. It's a good size, so I recognize faces without getting bored."

STUDENT AUTHOR: **Going to the University gives students a unique perspective on college life. Even with a lack of diversity and a party scene that doesn't start to pick up until you are a junior, Villanova is a fun place to be. While that might not be what someone is looking for, the students that do attend end up loving the school for everything it offers, from its basketball games and rich traditions, to its Catholic heritage and the full load of academics.**

Virginia Commonwealth University

901 West Franklin Street; Richmond, VA 23284
.(804) 828-0100; www.vcu.edu

THE BASICS:

Acceptance Rate: 58%
Setting: Mid-sized city
F-T Undergrads: 18,449

SAT Range: 1450–1770*
Control: Public
Tuition: $19,724

Most Popular Majors: Visual/Performing Arts, Business, Health Professions, Psychology, Security

*of 2400

Academics	B	Guys	B+
Local Atmosphere	B+	Girls	B+
Safety & Security	B	Athletics	B+
Computers	B	Nightlife	A-
Facilities	B	Greek Life	B
Campus Dining	C+	Drug Scene	B
Off-Campus Dining	A	Campus Strictness	A
Campus Housing	B-	Parking	D+
Off-Campus Housing	C-	Transportation	B+
Diversity	A-	Weather	B

Students Speak Out
ON ACADEMICS

Q "Classes and teachers here can be really crazy and out there. If you can, **find someone who's had a class you're registering for** and get some feedback. Then it won't be so shocking when you get a teacher who is nuts."

Q "**Switching majors here can be a pain**. Don't declare until you're sure of what you want. Otherwise, you could end up losing a lot of credits and a lot of time."

Q "General requirement classes aren't nearly as good as the classes that you take specifically for your major. **It's the 'major' classes that grab your attention** and make you actually want to go to class."

Q "Graduate teachers can be cool. Usually they are **more understanding than the professors who have been around forever**. They're students, too, so they understand the pressure."

STUDENT AUTHOR: **There are common misconceptions about VCU, including that it is easy to get into, that it is only an arts school, and that it is not known outside of the Richmond area. These cannot be further from the truth. While VCU is known for having one of the largest and most comprehensive art schools in the country, there are several other departments that are continually growing and receiving national recognition. It can be overwhelming at first to attend classes at VCU since most pre-requisites are large lecture hall classes. Once a student is in their desired degree program, it is much more common to have smaller classes.**

Students Speak Out
ON LOCAL ATMOSPHERE

Q "Right around campus, I think people really cater to the VCU crowd. **There are so many schools and communities here**, though we're not singled out as VCU students, which can be nice, too."

Q "People are scared of Richmond when they come in off of I-95 because it looks bad. Yeah, there are bad areas, and it can be intimidating at first, but **if you take the time to explore you can find some really neat spots**."

Q "**Going out around the city can get to be really expensive**. If you don't have money, you have to figure out what you can do before you go out. You also really need a car if you want to really get out and explore, or you have to ride the bus."

Q "Richmond is great. There are so many different places to go and see. **It's super easy to plan a full day of activities** when your family wants to come down and visit."

STUDENT AUTHOR: **Richmond may be big and intimidating for students who didn't grow up in or around a city, but after a few weeks of exploring and meeting other students, you start to find out about the great places Richmond has to offer. The nightlife is always in full gear Downtown with its selection of bars and restaurants. The major setback some students have is figuring out how to get to the places they want to go. Richmond has a lot of great places to go and exhibits to see. It's really just a matter of how you can get there from campus.**

5 Best Things	5 Worst Things
1 Diversity	1 Parking
2 Internship opportunities	2 Housing lottery
3 Basketball	3 Crossing the streets
4 Richmond Coliseum	4 Slow Internet network
5 Lots of restaurants	5 Construction

Students Speak Out
ON FACILITIES

Q "Everywhere on campus is always busy. People are in and out. **The facilities seem to be maintained and are always clean**."

Q "Rec sports have a lot to offer. **Gym classes are free and are switched up each semester**, along with a lot of intramural sports."

Q "Cabell Library is neat and peaceful, and it's a **good way to keep out distractions when you want to study**. It has group meeting rooms, and the fourth floor is the 'silent' floor."

Q "The Siegel Center is amazing. **Group exercise classes are free**! You used to have to pay per semester, and it costs a lot for a college student. The equipment is new and maintained well by the gym staff. It's a great place to keep away the Freshman 15."

Q "Everything on campus is convenient. **The library has all it needs for researchers**, but it could use a better novel section for those of us who like to read for pleasure."

STUDENT AUTHOR: **The buildings on campus here at VCU are all unique in their own way. VCU is currently renovating Cary Street Gym, which will re-open in 2010 with a swimming pool, multiple fitness rooms, multiple basketball courts, and even a climbing wall. VCU works hard to keep facilities clean for students and renovate buildings when needed. They also take note when additions need to be made to buildings, and in the summer of 2007, they opened a convenience store on the ground level of Grace E. Harris Hall.**

Famous Alumni

Hunter "Patch" Adams, M.D., Nancy C. Everett, Stephen Furst, Brandon Inge, Saul Krugman, M.D., Sean Marshall, Debbie Matenopoulos, Cla Meredith, Dick Robertson

Students Speak Out
ON CAMPUS DINING

Q "Beware of Shafer! The food isn't horrible most days, but **it will make you feel like you want to die a few hours later**. Commons food is okay, but I still prefer off-campus places or making my own food."

Q "By the time you get to the dining hall at night, there either isn't anything left or what is left is old and **has been sitting out for hours because no one wanted to eat it**. If you go early enough when the food is fresh, though, it's delicious."

Q "I know a lot of people complain about the food on campus, but **I don't seem to have a problem eating the food from the dining hall** or the commons."

Q "Shafer food isn't the best, but **it definitely satisfies a hunger**. Subway, Quiznos, and Chick-fil-A are good."

Q "Most food is edible, but **the 'good' food from the commons isn't that great**."

STUDENT AUTHOR: **College students love to eat, but by mid-semester, most students are no longer eating at Shafer Dining Hall. Although it is buffet-style with pizza, salads, burgers, and more, the food becomes repetitive and seems to not settle well. They offer "upper meal swipes," which are just usually two swipes rather than one entry swipe. Using these swipes, students can get homemade sushi, lobster, fried rice, and sometimes a great Bananas Foster. But even these can become dull after a while.**

Student Body

African American:	20%	Male/Female:	42/58%
Asian American:	11%	Out-of-State:	7%
Hispanic:	4%	International:	3%
Native American:	1%	Unknown:	8%
White:	53%		

Popular Faiths: Christianity, Judaism, and Islam.

Gay Pride: VCU supports policies that bring equity to otherwise inequitable situations and gives open support for Lesbian, Gay, Bisexual, and Transgender (LGBT) issues.

Economic Status: Students at VCU come from various types of economic backgrounds. It is common for students to work and go to school full time in order to support themselves.

Students Speak Out
ON DORMS

Q "**Freshmen should make the decision to stay in a dorm**. They're a great way to meet other people and build a community of friends."

Q "The communal bathrooms scared me at first, but **they're only really bad on weekends** when the cleaning crew is off. Shower shoes are a must, but that's true whichever dorm you're in."

Q "**Dorms can be really hard to adjust to because you're living in a small space** with another person. If you move into the apartment-style suites after freshman year, it gets much better."

STUDENT AUTHOR: **VCU has six freshman dorms and seven apartment-style dorms for upperclassmen. There is no requirement to live on campus as a freshman. A lottery system is used to pick which students get a place on campus after their freshman year. Space is limited, especially for girls, and it is often hard to get a spot. The older freshman dorms, such as Johnson and Rhoads, are two- or three-person rooms with communal bathrooms. The newer freshman dorm, Brandt Hall, is suite-style with bathrooms shared between each set of rooms. Living in the dorms is a great way to meet people.**

> **Did You Know?**
> 22% of undergrads live on campus.

Students Speak Out
ON GUYS & GIRLS

Q "Students here range from Hollister preps to jocks to the kids who make you wonder if they got dressed in the dark. **It all depends on your personal taste**."

Q "**Tattoos and rings are common characteristics** of people here. It can be a turn on, though."

Q "Guys and girls here are nice **if you choose the right ones to hang around**."

Q "I've noticed **there are quite a lot of artsy people here**. Everyone has his or her own unique style, and I think that's pretty attractive."

STUDENT AUTHOR: **With more than 32,000 students at VCU, there has to be someone to suit your taste. Because the student body is so diverse, who's hot and who's not changes with every group of students you ask. Statistically, there are more girls than guys at VCU, but that never seems to get in the way of girls finding someone to hook up with. Students aren't always looking for someone of the opposite sex either, which seems to balance out the male-to-female ratio.**

> **Traditions**
>
> **Intercultural Festival**
> The festival is held each spring at the Monroe Park Campus, attracting more than 30 student cultural organizations and thousands of festival-goers from the entire Richmond community.
>
> **VCU Field Day**
> Compete with your fellow students in games such as the potato-sack race, the three-legged race, and the egg toss.
>
> **Overall School Spirit**
> VCU's school spirit grows as our athletic programs take top honors and we receive high honors for academic achievements. However, our school spirit pales in comparison to other universities in the state.

Students Speak Out
ON ATHLETICS

Q "I don't even know all of the teams that VCU has. I think **they focus too much on basketball**."

Q "If you want to be into the sports scene here, then you can be, but **you can also ignore it completely like I do**."

Q "Intramural sports run pretty well here, and there is a good selection to choose from. **Flag football and basketball are the most competitive** intramural sports."

Q "I played soccer all throughout high school, so when I came here, I wanted to be sure I continued with a team sport, and **I really enjoyed playing on the intramural team**. It was competitive but fun."

STUDENT AUTHOR: **The men's basketball team at VCU is the one that students immediately recognize as the favorite. There is no football team, and basketball is truly our one competitive and nationally recognized sport. If playing sports is more your thing, there are a ton of intramural opportunities for students to get involved in.**

Students Speak Out
ON DRUG SCENE

Q "If you look for drugs, you will find them, but **it's not like it's drug-city here**."

Q "Every college campus is the same. There are drugs, and **either you're into them or you're not**."

Q "I haven't really noticed it much, but I don't look for it. **I don't think many people do much more than pot**."

STUDENT AUTHOR: **Most VCU students agree that if you want to find people using drugs, you have to go looking for them. That's not to say that a drug scene doesn't exist—it just isn't highly visible on campus. Smoking pot occurs frequently at parties, but because of the strong smell, students can tell if pot is being used and make a decision to stay or leave the party. VCU states in its alcohol and drug policy that the University is committed to protecting the health, safety, and welfare of its students and the public. It offers substance abuse programs for students who think they may have a problem and counselors for students to talk to when needed.**

18:1	Student-to-Faculty Ratio
85%	Freshman Retention Rate
23%	Four-Year Graduation Rate
69%	Financial Aid Applicants Receiving Aid

Students Speak Out
SAFETY & SECURITY

Q "**Security can definitely be a hassle when coming into the dorms**. However, you do come to realize how great it actually is to have a pretty reliable security staff watching out for students."

Q "Campus safety is good. **It's obvious how hard VCU works on their security**, and you can see a cop walking on campus pretty much all day."

Q "I think most students feel safe on campus, and it's the people who don't go to school in a city that think it's scary. Yes, there are homeless people on the street, but they won't hurt you. The city campus is just something you have to get used to. **Be smart with your decisions, and you'll be fine**."

STUDENT AUTHOR: **VCU works hard to take the necessary precautions to ensure students' safety on campus and around the local area. Beginning in Fall 2007, VCU implemented new forms of communication for emergencies, including sirens and an emergency text-messaging system. Students and parents are able to register their numbers so that they will receive constant contact through their cell phones during an emergency.**

Questions?

For more inside information and survival tips, pick up College Prowler's full-length book on this school, written by an actual student! Check it out at *www.collegeprowler.com*.

Students Speak Out
ON OVERALL EXPERIENCE

Q "I'm glad I decided to come to VCU. It's not for everyone, but it's right for me. My favorite part of being here is the city. **It's livelier than a campus in a small town**, and the diversity is really great. I've made friends with people from Russia and China."

Q "VCU was not my first choice. When I came here, I wasn't sure what to think and was planning on transferring after my first year. By December, that all changed. I love the energy of the campus and how **you can always find something to do**. I'm sure a lot of people who come in feeling like I did end up leaving VCU, but it ended up being a good match for my personality."

Q "I'm learning a lot in my classes, and I enjoy the freedom that the city has given me. There is always something to do, and **it's never silent on campus**."

Q "**I met some of my best friends in the dorms**. Even though there's always going to be drama, I think VCU was a great choice for me."

STUDENT AUTHOR: **Students who attend VCU either love it or hate it. If they hate it, they most likely transfer or don't stay around campus on the weekends to find out everything the city has to offer. More and more students are enrolling at VCU, and instead of being a backup school, it's becoming the first choice for a majority of the incoming freshmen. VCU has a lot to offer, but it's up to each student to take advantage of them and make his experience here unique.**

Virginia Tech

201 Burruss Hall; Blacksburg, VA 24061
(540) 231-6252; www.vt.edu

THE BASICS:

Acceptance Rate: 67%
Setting: Rural
F-T Undergrads: 22,506

SAT Range: 1110–1300*
Control: Public
Tuition: $20,825

Most Popular Majors: Business, Engineering, Family Sciences, Biology, Social Sciences

*of 1600

Academics	B+	Guys	B
Local Atmosphere	B-	Girls	B
Safety & Security	B+	Athletics	A
Computers	A-	Nightlife	B
Facilities	B+	Greek Life	B+
Campus Dining	A	Drug Scene	B
Off-Campus Dining	B	Campus Strictness	B
Campus Housing	C	Parking	D
Off-Campus Housing	B	Transportation	B+
Diversity	C	Weather	B

Students Speak Out
ON ACADEMICS

Q "Most **teachers here are very likeable**, especially after you pick a major, and start getting to know them in your third and fourth years."

Q "For the most part, the teachers are all good. You run into your **occasional boring lecturer**, but most of the teachers I have encountered are both understanding and encouraging. Many of them are so excited about their area of expertise that their enthusiasm is catching."

Q "Teachers suck over here because they can't teach. Almost all of the professors here have some kind of research that they are doing, so **teaching is not the main focus**. The good news is that they are willing to help you in any way they can. All the professors have office hours where you can go and talk or get help."

Q "There are a wide variety of teachers. Some of them are incredibly boring, and others are the **most interesting people you have ever met**."

STUDENT AUTHOR: At the beginning of a student's time at Tech, classes are large (often 300 students or more), and are often taught by graduate students. It is easy for freshmen to feel a little lost and overwhelmed, but classes do get smaller as students get more involved in their majors. Picking a major can be a hard decision, but advisors in career services and individual departments are available to help. Registering for classes is easy; the whole process is done online.

Students Speak Out
ON LOCAL ATMOSPHERE

Q "Students make up the area. **The college town is awesome** because when you go downtown, it's filled with people your age."

Q "I love Blacksburg! Since **Blacksburg is a relatively small town**, it feels like Tech is the center. As a freshman, the campus felt like a town within the town. I was so scared because Tech is so huge, but as I learned where the buildings were, and the hangouts, and met more people, the campus became smaller."

Q "There are **so many outdoor things to do**, like go to the New River and go tubing, or hike up the Cascades, or go camping, or rock climbing."

Q "Blacksburg is a college town, so everyone is a Hokie in Blacksburg. Everyone gets along with everyone, and **it is just a great overall atmosphere**."

STUDENT AUTHOR: Living in Blacksburg combines the convenience of being able to walk everywhere with the familiarity of knowing most of the shops and restaurants in town. The town's size and location do leave some students feeling like they're in the middle of nowhere. On the plus side, there is a downtown area that caters to college student tastes. If you're a nature lover, there's plenty for you to do in and around Blacksburg. Students who are less of the outdoors type can go downtown and find restaurants, movies, and bars. By a student's fourth year of school, they might be ready to get out of Blacksburg.

5 Best Things	5 Worst Things
1 Hokie football	1 No parking
2 Engineering program	2 The wind
3 Orange and maroon	3 Large classes (300+)
4 West End	4 2 a.m. fire drills
5 University technology	5 Distance to classes

Students Speak Out
ON FACILITIES

Q "Tech has some great facilities, including two gyms, **more computer labs than you can count**, and student lounges in almost every building."

Q "The facilities vary greatly in how nice they are, because **some buildings on campus were erected in the 1800s**, and some were built just a few years back. Tech has a tendency to build new facilities, such as a gym (McComas), but keep the previously used gym in operation (Hokie Gym in War Memorial)."

Q "The athletic facilities on campus are great. We have two gyms, and one has a basketball court and swimming pool. There are plenty of outdoor tracks and tennis courts. **There's even a street hockey court**. You name the sport, and you can probably play it here."

Q "The student center is very nice. It has a lot of things to offer, but **I rarely hang out there**, other than to pick up a meal."

Q "**You get your tuition's worth** out of them, if you choose to."

STUDENT AUTHOR: Students at Tech are most impressed by the gyms, dining halls, and the newer classrooms on campus. Virginia Tech continues to improve old structures while building new ones. As for dorms, though, the majority could use some work (of the facilities on campus, the dorms are the least impressive). Tech's campus does have a neat, unified look because of the stone on the exterior of all the buildings. While the stone doesn't affect much on the inside of the buildings, it does make the campus attractive.

Famous Alumni

Frank Beamer, Kylen Hibbard, Homer Hickam, Sharyn McCrumb, Robert Richardson, Benjamin Rubin, Bruce Smith, Bruce Vorhauer

Students Speak Out
ON CAMPUS DINING

Q "You will **never go hungry** at Tech. There is a lot to eat! Try West End and D2 for some good dishes!"

Q "The food on campus is great. The dining halls offer a lot of variety, from gourmet and high class (fresh Maine lobster) to the everyday salad bar and the over-cooked, under-sized burgers. Really, Tech has **some of the best food of any campus I have been to**."

Q "The **food on campus is awesome**. It's just the way your mother used to make it, except good. We have everything from green beans and mac-n-cheese to boiled lobster."

Q "The dining halls are **nothing spectacular, at least the cafeteria-style ones**. West End, while pricey, is well worth it. Hokie Grill is good for your staple fast foods."

Q "**Food on campus is exquisite**! There isn't one place I don't like to eat."

STUDENT AUTHOR: All college students love to eat, and there seems to be something for everyone when it comes to food on Tech's campus. Many Tech students purchase meal plans and eat on campus a few times a week. Freshmen are required to get a meal plan, and can choose from three meal plan options. Eating on campus is very popular at Tech, so sometimes dining halls get very crowded during the lunch and dinner rush. With 11 dining halls to choose from, and hundreds of different dishes, it takes a while to try it all. It's easy to find healthy choices, and students can go online to find out nutritional information for all the dishes served.

Student Body

African American:	4%	Male/Female:	58/42%
Asian American:	7%	Out-of-State:	25%
Hispanic:	3%	International:	3%
Native American:	<1%	Unknown:	11%
White:	73%		

Popular Faiths: There are about 30 Christian student groups on campus, making Christianity the most represented religion at Tech.

Gay Pride: Students at Tech are generally open and accepting of their gay peers.

Economic Status: Students from many economic backgrounds go to Tech.

Students Speak Out
ON DORMS

Q "The dorms are nice and relatively large. The **sinks and mirrors in each room** are definitely a huge plus."

Q "Living in a dorm stinks, I don't care how nice or clean or big or small it is. There are too many people in one enclosed environment for it to be enjoyable. The biggest problem is that the **rooms are really small**—especially for two people. What should get you through your dormitory experience in your freshman year is knowing that you can live off campus for the next three years."

Q "The dorms are a notch below other universities I've visited. The **cinderblock walls and cold tile floors** are reminiscent of the military past of the University."

STUDENT AUTHOR: **Virginia Tech has 27 dorms and 18 Greek houses for students. Freshmen are required to live on campus their first year. Many choose to make that their one and only year in a dorm. A lottery system is used to pick who stays on campus past freshman year, and space is limited, so getting a spot can be a challenge.**

? **Did You Know?**
39% of undergrads live on campus.

Students Speak Out
ON GUYS & GIRLS

Q "Guys are generally nice, though they can be a bit fratastic. For girls, it's the same. It's a **good-looking campus**."

Q "The girls are smoking hot, and seem to be getting better and **better looking with each incoming freshman class**. Once known as a bad school to find good-looking girls, I'm determined the near future will bring descriptions of Tech as one of the best schools to meet pretty girls."

Q "The guys and girls of Tech are **very attractive**!"

Q "Well, the guys vary a lot. We are a technical school, which means **there are a lot of geeky-looking guys**."

STUDENT AUTHOR: With around 20,000 undergrads at Tech, there are bound to be at least a few hotties wandering around campus. But Tech students will tell you that there are a disproportionately large number of good-looking students at Tech, and they're distributed across academic interests. Students make sure that tests and grades don't limit them from getting out and meeting people.

Traditions

Ut Proism
This Latin phrase is Virginia Tech's motto; it means "That I May Serve."

Hokies
Virginia Tech students are Hokies, the buildings here are made of Hokie stone, and students' IDs are called their Hokie Passports.

Overall School Spirit
When you're a Hokie, you let everyone know it. Most students at Virginia Tech own a Virginia Tech T-shirt, in fact, most students own five or six.

Students Speak Out
ON ATHLETICS

Q "Both varsity sports and IM sports are popular. **Football and basketball games** are great, and the organization of IM sports is excellent."

Q "Varsity sports are huge. There is nothing like Hokie football. Everyone comes out to see the games, and it's **a wonderful experience**. The Hokies can yell like no other!"

Q "**Football is huge**. If you don't like football, don't come here."

Q "IM sports are **an excellent way to play your favorite sports**, and there are several leagues that cater to different levels of play."

STUDENT AUTHOR: Football games draw students, alumni, friends, and family to Lane stadium, leaving downtown Blacksburg silent when football games are going on. Even students who come to Tech with no interest in sports become drawn into the fierce loyalty that Tech students have for their football team. Now that Virginia Tech is in the ACC, the excitement has gone up a notch. Students also get involved with intramural sports.

Students Speak Out
ON DRUG SCENE

Q "The drug scene's going strong, but only on **more low-key drugs like pot**."

Q "What do you need drugs for? Drinking is enough. **Drugs are not a very big thing** here."

Q "There are not too many drugs beside weed that I have seen here at Tech. At least I am sure there is some other harder stuff going around, but it's kept quiet, and **not too many people know about it**."

STUDENT AUTHOR: **Students say that in order to find people using drugs at Virginia Tech, you have to go looking for them. While drug use does happen, it's not very visible around campus. If students are going to use a substance, it's usually alcohol or caffeine. The most commonly heard-about drug being used around campus is marijuana. Virginia Tech has a "zero tolerance" rule when it comes to drugs, so if you are caught using drugs it is almost guaranteed you'll be suspended—if not expelled. Alcohol, caffeine, and tobacco are the most popular substances on campus.**

16:1	Student-to-Faculty Ratio
93%	Freshman Retention Rate
51%	Four-Year Graduation Rate
39%	Financial Aid Applicants Receiving Aid

Students Speak Out
SAFETY & SECURITY

Q "Blacksburg is one of the safest places that I have ever lived. I love the fact that I can leave my car unlocked at my apartment complex and **no one will bother it**. The campus itself has security guards that walk around throughout the night."

Q "We have our petty theft—wallets, bikes, and other **small things will get stolen**."

Q "**There are always cops around**. Your security and safety should only be dependant on yourself. Tech has a very safe campus, but there are always idiots about."

Q "**Police keep a low profile** and let the little things slide, but if you need them, they get there pretty fast."

STUDENT AUTHOR: **Virginia Tech has certainly not forgotten the events of April 16, 2007. However, Virginia Tech has always had a very safe campus, and that did not change with the events of that day. If anything, it has served to make the campus an even safer place, as officials responded by heightening campus security measures to ensure students' safety.**

Questions?
For more inside information and survival tips, pick up College Prowler's full-length book on this school, written by an actual student! Check it out at *www.collegeprowler.com*.

Students Speak Out
ON OVERALL EXPERIENCE

Q "I love Virginia Tech. The students are friendly, **the town is great**, and the mountains are beautiful. I have had so many opportunities at Virginia Tech that I would not have had at a smaller school, and I have made many diverse and lasting friendships."

Q "I do indeed **wish I was in a town with something to offer everyone**, not just the freshmen trying to sneak into bars."

Q "I've **had a fabulous time** here; that's why I'm staying for grad school."

Q "Virginia Tech is **worth the cost**, and I love my department. There are countless opportunities here, and the people make it worth it. Everyone is so outgoing and nice that you feel like you have 10 thousand friends."

Q "**I enjoy Tech**, but I honestly wish I was somewhere with more diversity and parking."

STUDENT AUTHOR: **Virginia Tech students have strong school spirit, and value the education their University provides. In fact, many Tech students have such a great time as undergraduates that they stay at Tech for graduate work. Even city students can appreciate how easy it is to walk from campus to town and how safe the town is. Tech's academics have been improving each year. Students who have the best experiences at Tech find a major that they love and then get involved. Tech offers hundreds of student organizations, and more are created every year. Virginia Tech has a lot to offer its students, as long as students make the effort to take advantage of all that is available.**

Wake Forest University

1834 Wake Forest Road; Winston-Salem, NC 27106
(336) 758-5000; www.wfu.edu

THE BASICS:

Acceptance Rate: 42%
Setting: Mid-sized city
F-T Undergrads: 4,350

SAT Range: 1240–1410*
Control: Private
Tuition: $36,560

Most Popular Majors: Social Sciences, Business, Foreign Languages, Biology, Communications

*of 1600

Academics	B+	Guys	A-
Local Atmosphere	C+	Girls	A
Safety & Security	A	Athletics	A-
Computers	A	Nightlife	C+
Facilities	A	Greek Life	A+
Campus Dining	C+	Drug Scene	A-
Off-Campus Dining	B-	Campus Strictness	B-
Campus Housing	B	Parking	C-
Off-Campus Housing	B-	Transportation	D
Diversity	D	Weather	B+

Students Speak Out
ON ACADEMICS

Q "The teachers are great! They really are there to teach and not to do research. Wake gives you **an amazing education when you graduate** because of all of the liberal arts divisional requirements."

Q "While I have found a few I don't get along with, I have also encountered some of the **best I've ever had**."

Q "Grading at Wake Forest is really tough. Many professors will make up their own grading scale that's **harder than normal**, or will only give out a certain number of As. It's very challenging here, more so than you would think."

Q "The professors are truly remarkable and smart. They are also very congenial, and the class sizes are small enough to **develop relationships** with all of them."

Q "For the most part, all of my teachers were easy to talk to and simple to contact if I ever needed anything. The **workload was harsh** in every class I've taken, but nothing was impossibly difficult."

STUDENT AUTHOR: **Wake certainly has earned its reputation as "Work Forest," as the workload is demanding. However, that reputation makes success that much more valuable. Most students agree that while they're steamrolled by a landslide of work, it only makes them better equipped to face a new series of challenges. Professors are more than willing to meet with students. Wake Forest professors are regarded as brilliant, but modest.**

Students Speak Out
ON LOCAL ATMOSPHERE

Q "It's definitely a **small town with a small-town atmosphere**. I guess that keeps you out of trouble. There isn't much to do in Winston-Salem that isn't Wake Forest affiliated, but you can always go to Greensboro or Charlotte for something different."

Q "UNC-Chapel Hill and Duke are about an hour or so away in Raleigh-Durham. There is a huge social scene over there. North Carolina State isn't far away either. In Winston-Salem, there are a few small schools, but **Wake dominates**. Winston-Salem is not a bad city by any means."

Q "If you are from a small town, then you'll be happy. But, if you're from a city and are used to the party life, you may be disappointed. Basically, **there is always something to do**. You just have to find it."

Q "There are **tons of restaurants**, a few clubs, bars, movie theaters, bowling alleys, and a mall. It isn't exactly the most interesting college town, but most things occur on campus anyway, so that isn't much of a loss."

STUDENT AUTHOR: **Winston-Salem is, as many students would attest, decidedly mediocre. It doesn't quite have the resources to be considered an exciting place by any means, but it isn't a cultural wasteland either. Some fun can be found in Winston, but it may require some looking. Remember, if you're desperate for a college town, UNC isn't too far away, and most Wake students will likely end up there more than once.**

Students Speak Out
ON CAMPUS DINING

Q "On campus, the food is very satisfactory. Among the big names, we have a **Subway, a Chick-fil-A, and Pizza Hut** that offer all the things they do normally. There is also the Sundry, a mini grocery store on campus that sells almost anything and everything you can't get in the cafeterias."

Q "Wake **lacks a 24-hour food option**, as well as an all-you-can-eat buffet style. While it has its disadvantages, it does allow you to enter the food areas as often as you'd like, as you are not constrained to only a certain amount of visits, as other campus meal plans dictate."

Q "The food is **great at the beginning**, because everything's new and awesome, but after a while, it does get a little boring."

Q "I have been to other schools, and I honestly do like the food. There is **much more of a variety** at Wake than I would have expected."

Q "The food is not home-cooking, but it's probably the **best college food I've ever tasted**."

STUDENT AUTHOR: The main food court at Wake Forest isn't too bad. But, while the food's quality has actually exceeded many students' expectations, watch out for the bill. You can run your total up and over 10 dollars before you even know what hits you. The only restaurant, or anything close to one on campus, is the Magnolia Room. A buffet-style establishment featuring a daily rotating menu, it is classy enough to guilt you into wearing a clean shirt. You can eat on the balcony overlooking scenic south campus.

Students Speak Out
ON FACILITIES

Q "Facilities are **absolutely excellent**. We have everything you could possibly need, including a new student fitness center."

Q "We have a huge exercise building that offers classes and has a ton of exercise equipment. We have a **free movie theater** on campus, Starbucks, Office Depot, Wachovia, small grocery stores, and a really nice bookstore."

Q "Nearly every classroom on campus is outfitted with a **digital projector** on the ceiling, which is networked with a digital overhead, an outside cable source, a DVD player, and can be used as an external monitor for a laptop."

Q "Facilities are amazing in all aspects. **No school that I've ever been to compares** to Wake's facilities, and I visited some of the top schools in the nation such as Stanford, Duke, and USC."

Q "Facilities are all great. Wake has a ton of money and makes the **campus and buildings look immaculate**."

STUDENT AUTHOR: Z. Smith Reynolds Library houses more books and journals than you'll ever need, that is if you can pick through the cryptic directions to find what you're looking for. There are plenty of couches and padded chairs spread throughout the building to help you cram in comfort. The athletic center features an impressive variety of weight and cardio machines, as well as free weights, for a relatively small school. Reynolds Gym houses several basketball courts. Wake even has a nine-hole golf course on campus, contributing to the country club-like feel of the campus.

Students Speak Out
ON DORMS

Q "After visiting friends at other schools, I learned to appreciate just how nice the dorms at Wake are. They're **really clean, and there's a lot of room**. Having cleaning people do the bathrooms is nice. The problem for freshmen is you can't choose where you want to live, but all freshman dorms are about the same."

Q "The dorms are very nice. I got lucky and lived in the best freshman dorm, but they are all very nice, and **everything is air conditioned**."

Q "As a freshman, you can't pick your roommate. You fill out a questionnaire, and **Wake pairs you up with someone** who has similar answers."

STUDENT AUTHOR: Every room at Wake includes a microwave and mini-fridge, an added perk you won't be able to live without. Guys and girls live in opposite wings of the buildings, usually separated into A and B sides, but generally use the same common areas. Piccolo and Palmer are isolated from other dorms and both quads. Luter is regarded as the best of the bunch, being the only freshman dorm that utilizes a suite-like setup with bathrooms as a connective buffer between adjacent rooms.

> **Did You Know?**
> 69% of undergrads live on campus.

Students Speak Out
ON GUYS & GIRLS

Q "It's an expensive private school in the South, and **there are a lot of snobs**. Half the girls are daddy's little princesses. And some of the guys are like, 'Look at my nice, expensive car.'"

Q "Guys are typically the rich Abercrombie mold and girls the same. There is, I'm sorry to say, **very little variety**. This is pretty different for me given that I'm from a public, more diverse background."

Q "Everyone is gorgeous. It's kind of **intimidating**."

Q "The **guys are very hot**. I have to admit: I was surprised. I am not even going to sugarcoat it—a lot of them are gorgeous. The girls are nice, but if you are not the sorority-type girl, you might get annoyed with the sorority girls sometimes."

STUDENT AUTHOR: We could easily be featured in a J.Crew catalog. Many boast that the students are gorgeous and in shape, but some admit this can be intimidating, so it creates competition. Everyone is trendy and preppy, although there are varying levels. Not all live and die with the new Abercrombie catalog. If you're looking for variety beyond the upper-class white look and the occasional middle-class frat look, you may be disappointed.

> **Traditions**
>
> **Quad Streaking**
> Considered a way to blow off some steam during finals week, a naked run will certainly do the trick.
>
> **Rolling the Quad**
> Following any major athletic victory, students thoroughly coat every tree in the main quad in a thick layer of toilet paper.
>
> **Overall School Spirit**
> Wake Forest is bursting at the seams with school spirit. Basketball seems to drag even the most lukewarm fan out to the stadium to cheer on the Demon Deacons.

Students Speak Out
ON ATHLETICS

Q "We are Division I in all sports. The biggest is basketball. We're also very good at baseball, men and women's golf, tennis, and field hockey. **Tailgating is major before football games**."

Q "Intramural sports are also very popular, and I believe about 80 percent of the students on campus are **involved in an intramural sport**."

Q "The main sports that people on campus care about are football and men's basketball. Those are huge, and **people go crazy over them**. Other than that, sad to say, most people don't pay much attention."

Q "Varsity **sports are huge at Wake**, especially because we're a small Division I college."

STUDENT AUTHOR: If you're not familiar with the game of basketball, odds are, you will be once winter rolls around in Winston-Salem. Wake students live and die with the success of Demon Deacon basketball, and there isn't a better show in town when Wake plays UNC or Duke. Expect the campus to empty out on nights of home basketball games, when students and fans pack the Lawrence Joel Arena.

Students Speak Out
ON DRUG SCENE

Q "There are no drugs. Some people live in **substance-free housing**. People at Wake are here to learn, not to get high. There are people who go to law school or medical school. We don't fool around."

Q "**Pot is the only thing** that has a presence. If you want it, you can find it. If you don't, no one cares."

Q "Drugs are really nonexistent, other than the occasional weed smoker. **Alcohol is the norm**, and most don't stray too far away from that."

STUDENT AUTHOR: **There aren't enough drugs on campus to even consider it part of a "scene." You could argue that most students aren't even aware of a drug presence on campus. There is still, mind you, a decent amount of students that will smoke, but their impact on the campus is negligible. Harder drugs are practically unheard of at Wake. Odds are, you won't ever see them used, nor will you know anyone who uses them. Non-users feel very little pressure to indulge in drugs.**

10:1	Student-to-Faculty Ratio
94%	Freshman Retention Rate
79%	Four-Year Graduation Rate
88%	Financial Aid Applicants Receiving Aid

Students Speak Out
SAFETY & SECURITY

Q "Safety on campus is ideal—it's a gated community. I don't think any of my female friends have ever felt scared walking around campus. I **don't think you can find a safer campus**."

Q "Besides some fights and people drinking too much, I **haven't heard of anything really bad happening**."

Q "I feel very safe at Wake Forest. As long as you **use common sense**, I'm sure you'll be fine. I've never had a problem, and neither has anyone I know. Also at night, there is a campus shuttle bus called R.I.D.E., which runs from dusk to dawn. It will take you anywhere you want or need to go, so you won't ever have to walk alone."

STUDENT AUTHOR: **Considering Winston-Salem's less-than-admirable crime record, Wake Forest's campus is just about as good as it gets. The campus is essentially closed to outside traffic after 10 p.m., requiring a visitor's pass or prior permission for non-students to enter at night.**

Questions?
For more inside information and survival tips, pick up College Prowler's full-length book on this school, written by an actual student! Check it out at *www.collegeprowler.com*.

Students Speak Out
ON OVERALL EXPERIENCE

Q "You have to work hard if you come to Wake. I didn't expect it to be this much work. But everyone else works hard, too. It felt good to know that **I had earned my grades**, and I'm getting the education I'm paying for. The people are wonderful, and it is easy to get involved in anything and everything you want."

Q "I find that **everyone is very similar here**, and if you want a lot of diversity, it's not the place to be. But, if you want cultural things to do and you want to meet different people, you just have to make the effort. I've grown to like it a lot."

Q "I love Wake. I would definitely recommend it if you want a **small academic school** with a lot of teacher interaction. If you are looking for a party school, go somewhere else."

Q "The business school is providing me with a top-notch education, with which I am almost guaranteed a job, the campus is overwhelmingly beautiful, and the athletics, both club and varsity, have made Wake my **perfect college choice**. Even though its price tag is expensive, Wake is consistently rated as one of the 'best buys' of private school education."

STUDENT AUTHOR: **Most attribute their college decision to Wake Forest's reputation as an academically demanding institution that has an excellent track record of graduate school and job placement. The school's challenging curriculum provides a valuable well-rounded education that, not only prepares students for a career, but teaches them to think in a novel and resourceful manner. But, students often claim the excessive amount of work required is nearly insufferable at times.**

Warren Wilson College

701 Warren Wilson Road; Asheville, NC 28815
(800) 934-3536; www.warren-wilson.edu

THE BASICS:

Acceptance Rate: 80%
Setting: Rural
F-T Undergrads: 833

SAT Range: 1590–1920*
Control: Private
Tuition: $22,666

Most Popular Majors: Social Sciences, Natural Resources and Conservation, English, History

*of 2400

Academics	B	Guys	B
Local Atmosphere	C	Girls	B+
Safety & Security	A-	Athletics	C+
Computers	C	Nightlife	C+
Facilities	C+	Greek Life	N/A
Campus Dining	C+	Drug Scene	C+
Off-Campus Dining	A-	Campus Strictness	B+
Campus Housing	B-	Parking	B+
Off-Campus Housing	C	Transportation	B-
Diversity	D-	Weather	B+

Students Speak Out
ON ACADEMICS

Q "Many of the teachers stay in contact with their former students after they graduate. **They want students to go on and do better things**, go to graduate school, learn sustainable agriculture in Cuba, change the world."

Q "**I am surprised time after time at how far my professors will stick their neck out** to help me with something, a job reference, advice on paper topics, cookies, a walk around campus, whatever. They will do whatever is in their power to do."

Q "If classroom intimacy is what you want, then you've come to the right place. **You will never grow frustrated due to lack of attention** from the faculty."

Q "The thing about Warren Wilson is that you are always running into all your teachers—**many of them live on campus**. I think the student/teacher interaction at Warren Wilson is one of the most rewarding parts of the College."

STUDENT AUTHOR: **Warren Wilson is just a little different than most colleges and universities, and its academic courses embody its uniqueness. The small student body helps promote individual relationships between the students and their professors. Students are encouraged to develop their own project ideas and theses, rather than working straight from syllabi. Warren Wilson has a history of attempting cross-disciplinary approaches, and some classes are still taught by two or three professors from separate departments.**

Students Speak Out
ON LOCAL ATMOSPHERE

Q "Asheville has a lot of different people. Sometimes the town can get a little quiet at night, and **a lot of times there isn't much to do**. Warren Wilson students sometimes make their own campus atmosphere, and it can be really fun. Sometimes it just gets old, though."

Q "**Swannanoa is a little back-home town**. It is a small community, and there's not much available as far as local events. Asheville has a very alternative mindset, and there is a lot going on there every weekend as far as concerts and multicultural events."

Q "I love to go downtown to eat or something. **It seems like there is a lot of culture there**— plays, art, music, street performances. It's fun just to walk around and look at everything."

Q "**I wanted to strangle myself when I first got to Asheville**, but it has since grown on me. I'm more of a nature lover than I've ever been, and the people around me are very down-to-earth and friendly."

STUDENT AUTHOR: **Most Warren Wilson students spend their time more in the natural atmosphere around Swannanoa than the town aspect of Asheville. There are waterfalls, mountains, and nature trails. Downtown Asheville, located 15 minutes from campus, is a place where students can partake in a variety of cultural activities. Most students go to Asheville for the music scene, which is pretty good considering Asheville's modest size.**

Students Speak Out
ON FACILITIES

Q "Devries gym has a wide range of workout machines and weights. I am very satisfied with our gym. **Gladfelter, the cafeteria, is spacious and open**. Cowpie Café is quaint, and one can feel the sense of community there. The Fellowship Hall is a warm and inviting place, and it's a great environment for the classes (yoga, stress relief, and more) held there."

Q **"The student body at WWC has everything they need**. When you attend college in a rural environment, you can't expect to have all the amenities of an urban school (all the chain restaurants, a vibrant nightlife scene, 24-hour service, and so on)."

Q "The buildings at Warren Wilson are all kind of nice to look at, but **sometimes they get boring after a while**. I wish there was more to do on campus."

Q **"I think it's sometimes hard to meet students who don't live in your dorm** because there isn't a specific place where all the students go to hang out."

STUDENT AUTHOR: A lot of the buildings on campus are clearly well thought out, and a few of them certainly are not. Jensen is very ugly, very strange, but students just kind of get used to it. On the other hand, the science buildings Witherspoon and Morse are beautiful. There is no student union, no student bar, and no football field. But considering how small the student body is, the campus has a lot of nice facilities available, inside and out.

Famous Alumni

Jaroslava Moserova, Billy Edd Wheeler, Anne Lalley, Tony Earley, Mark Adams, Jamie Stirling, Nicole Jacobs

Students Speak Out
ON CAMPUS DINING

Q **"The food here is slightly above average** and, on top of this, much of it is actually quite healthy. It would be quite possible for someone here to go their entire freshman year without—get this—gaining the Freshman 15!"

Q **"You really have to take what you get**. At other schools, you can always say, 'I want to have spaghetti today,' or have Taco Bell or something. Unless you go off campus, you have very little ability to make decisions about what you're going to eat."

Q "I love the Cowpie Café. Sometimes, it's better than other times, but overall, **I'd say I eat much better than most people my age**."

Q "Sage Café has really good snacks and pizza, and it's a good supplement on bad cafeteria days. **Your meal plan doesn't cover Sage Café,** but it's not too expensive."

Q **"I like having an extensive salad bar**. It's something you can really count on here."

STUDENT AUTHOR: Okay, I'll be honest, the cafeteria kind of sucks. It's noisy, stressful, and there are too many lines. Warren Wilson's main eating facility is a cafeteria, called Gladfelter, and people complain about it all the time. Your room and board covers a flat rate for anything inside the cafeteria. The best advice is to bring a lot of extra Ramen noodles, brownie mix, or something, because dinner is over by 6:30 p.m., and if you stay up until 1 a.m., you're gonna get the munchies eventually.

Student Body

African American:	1%	Male/Female:	40/60%
Asian American:	1%	Out-of-State:	84%
Hispanic:	2%	International:	3%
Native American:	<1%	Unknown:	0%
White:	93%		

Popular Faiths: Most students on campus come from Christian or Jewish backgrounds.

Gay Pride: WWC is a very open community with a lot of gay and lesbian support.

Economic Status: Warren Wilson isn't cheap, and even though a lot of students qualify for financial aid, many enroll here on account of their large college funds from their parents.

Students Speak Out
ON DORMS

Q "The dorms are alright. **They're pretty laid-back, in my opinion**. After freshman year, you should be able to land something you like. If you like to party, live in Schafer. If you like to study, live in any other dorm."

Q "**The dorms here are usually very homey**. The kitchens get a good amount of use. Dorms to avoid living in: Schafer. Dorms to request: EcoDorm."

Q "As far as dorms go, **most of them are pretty cramped**. All of them are just glorified singles that they throw two students in and call doubles."

STUDENT AUTHOR: **Warren Wilson dorms are small, but for the most part, relatively nice. Most students will live with a roommate. Most buildings share a centralized kitchen, at least one common room with a TV and VCR or DVD player, and a laundry facility. The freshman dorms are considered by most to be the low point of WWC housing, but most freshmen agree that Sunderland provides a crucial social conglomeration during the first two semesters.**

Did You Know?
88% of undergrads live on campus.

Students Speak Out
ON GUYS & GIRLS

Q "The girls here are some of the most beautiful women I have ever met. I develop a new crush every day! **The guys are friendly and not football jockheads**."

Q "The students at Warren Wilson are either really hot or really funny looking. There are hardly any fat people here. **Maybe four fat people**."

Q "The girls here are wild. **They go to circus school and put nails up their nose** and do trapeze work when they're not in class. They are talented and interesting people. One girl found out about Warren Wilson when she hopped a train from Eugene and happened to get off in Asheville because she needed a break."

STUDENT AUTHOR: **A lot of guys who come to Warren Wilson are college boys who don't play competitive sports. They are nice, and some of them are quite attractive, but in a nerdy kind of way. They are the kind of guys who like strong, intelligent women to hook up with. The girls, in turn, tend to run the school. They have pretty good bodies, not because they starve themselves, but because they like to do a lot of active things.**

Traditions

Bubba Parties
Once a semester, more than half the school treks out to Dogwood Pasture for a huge kegger and bonfire.

Work Day
Warren Wilson's annual rite of spring, in which students work on various jobs around the school.

Overall School Spirit
Warren Wilson has been through a lot of changes, and the new students are well-advised to stay aware of their Warren Wilson past.

Students Speak Out
ON ATHLETICS

Q "I run cross country, and I have learned that you **don't come to Warren Wilson to play on an undefeated sports team**. You come here to play with a group of people who truly love the sport."

Q "I don't play any varsity sports, but I do play intramurals. **Intramurals are a lot of fun**, and all I know about the varsity sports is that they take up a lot of time."

Q "The sport teams are **both hilarious and entertaining at the same time**. They are a joke compared to most varsity teams at other schools."

STUDENT AUTHOR: **The major varsity sports lack the ability to impress any die-hard sports fanatic. So, if athletics are an important factor in your college decision, don't come to Warren Wilson. On the other hand, athletes who join Warren Wilson sports teams all seem to have an overwhelmingly positive experience. Intramural sports are also quite popular, and even if students aren't on an official sports team, chances are, they still do something every other day that constitutes as physical exercise.**

Students Speak Out
ON DRUG SCENE

Q "If you don't do drugs, there is a good community, and **it is not hard to still have fun**. And if you do drugs, there are a lot of people who will do drugs with you."

Q "It's not as bad as some places I've been to. I feel like there's a lot of pot on campus. **I feel like it's a huge part of the social scene**."

Q "I think the amount of drugs used on campus reflects the economic class that students come from. **They have extra money to throw away** on stuff like pot and mushrooms and acid."

STUDENT AUTHOR: **Students here have a reputation for smoking a lot of pot, since we tend to embody the pot culture—its music, its hair, its nature-loving mindset—but this isn't always related to the drug scene. And more and more, the students have been smoking less weed and drinking more cheap beer. As far as hard drugs, acid and 'shrooms play a role in the social scene, but in no way are any of these drugs a necessity to enjoy a good time at Warren Wilson.**

11:1	Student-to-Faculty Ratio
73%	Freshman Retention Rate
48%	Four-Year Graduation Rate
75%	Financial Aid Applicants Receiving Aid

Students Speak Out
SAFETY & SECURITY

Q "**I'm part of the student safety patrol**, and I can tell you that, while our task force is not as big as other larger universities, we all take our jobs of protecting the student body very seriously."

Q "We claim to be a community, which, although difficult, is what we strive for. Because of that, **security and safety rely much on students and Residence Life staff**. If there is anything of seriousness, hired security personnel are on call or on campus."

Q "I know everyone says it's really safe here, but **the campus still has its problems**. It's hard to believe it when someone's car gets smashed in, or someone tries to mug someone standing outside the gym."

STUDENT AUTHOR: **Warren Wilson students feel very safe on campus. It is not uncommon for students to leave their rooms and cars unlocked. Although some instances of assault have arisen in recent years, the general feeling from students is that they trust each other and trust the local community.**

> **Questions?**
> For more inside information and survival tips, pick up College Prowler's full-length book on this school, written by an actual student! Check it out at *www.collegeprowler.com*.

Students Speak Out
ON OVERALL EXPERIENCE

Q "I don't know if I'm glad I came here or not. I think the work program is a good idea, but **I don't think it gives you a good work ethic**. I think the only students who actually work at this school are the ones who worked jobs before they came to college."

Q "**It's a great area, and it's really fun to come to college here**. It's addicting in many ways, and it's almost hard to get away. I don't even want to leave when I graduate."

Q "I think the best part about Warren Wilson is that **the community really does care about the students**. That is visible everywhere, when you get your mail and when you buy your books."

Q "I think the College puts an image to the outer world that isn't the real picture. **In many aspects the administration is hypocritical**. Like they're sending around a survey on whether or not the College should invest in green energy, but at the same time, I don't think any of the service vehicles on campus could even pass an emissions test. RDs are expected to enforce the rules, but at the same time, once we write someone up, the administration doesn't do anything about it."

STUDENT AUTHOR: **Although many students leave Warren Wilson, they often still consider themselves Warren Wilson students, even if they transfer to other schools. The network of Warren Wilson alumni is vast, and it extends all over the globe to a wide array of jobs and service projects. Warren Wilson students like to get something done, and most of the students who leave Warren Wilson do so because they feel they have something else that needs to be completed outside of the school setting.**

Washington & Jefferson College

60 South Lincoln Street; Washington, PA 15301
(888) W-AND-JAY; www.washjeff.edu

THE BASICS:

Acceptance Rate: 34%
Setting: Suburban
F-T Undergrads: 1,517

SAT Range: 1050–1260*
Control: Private
Tuition: $31,396

Most Popular Majors: Business, Accounting, English, Psychology, History, Political Science

*of 1600

Academics	B	Guys	C+
Local Atmosphere	C-	Girls	C-
Safety & Security	A-	Athletics	B+
Computers	B-	Nightlife	C-
Facilities	B	Greek Life	A-
Campus Dining	C+	Drug Scene	B-
Off-Campus Dining	B	Campus Strictness	A
Campus Housing	B+	Parking	A-
Off-Campus Housing	C-	Transportation	C-
Diversity	D-	Weather	C+

Students Speak Out
ON ACADEMICS

Q "The workload depends on who you are and how well you want to do. If you want to carry anything above a 3.5, **you need to scratch and claw and fight for it**. This is even more true for majors like bio or chem. However, I know plenty of people who seem to float on by doing very little work but also not maintaining a high GPA."

Q "Our school has been known for its placement records into medical and law school and more recently for a growing business program. We have **seriously strong pre-health and pre-law programs**. They're not easy, but they really push to prepare you for graduate work."

Q "The workload is intense. **Every class is hard, and there are no 'blow-off' classes or majors**. When you come to W&J, you can count on being challenged in every single class. Every class will usually have a major project, a major paper, and numerous tests throughout the semester."

Q "The professors are amazing. **They know your name, give you personalized attention**, and are really understanding when extenuating circumstances prevent you from coming to class."

STUDENT AUTHOR: The academic aspect of W&J is arguably the most double-edged aspect of the college. One moment it can be viciously stressful and can readily bring even hardened veterans close to a breakdown, but the next moment it may offer world-changing ideas that make semesters worth of toil feel well worth the effort. To do well across the board requires serious dedication and focus.

Students Speak Out
ON LOCAL ATMOSPHERE

Q "Washington has a lot to offer. It has basically every restaurant you can think of, every fast-food chain, and two shopping malls, and **its close proximity to Pittsburgh is a great feature**."

Q "Washington is kind of bland and boring, really. For the most part, **there is really little to draw students into town**, except to go to one of the few restaurants, bars, or in the case of a few students, work at one of the law offices. Nothing else of note, really."

Q "**Washington is certainly not an ideal college town**. Maybe it was at one time, but there isn't a whole lot to offer students now. The bars are mostly dives, but at least they're only a few blocks from campus. The VIP on Main Street is the only real club in Washington. Most of us go to the South Side in Pittsburgh for clubs and all. It gives us a chance to get away from the stress of college and to meet new people."

Q "Washington offers a lot in addition to what the College provides. **Major shopping areas are located just a mile or two from campus**, and W&J provides transportation to and from these locations once a week."

STUDENT AUTHOR: Once you can legally hit up the bars on Main Street, then the city becomes marginally more acceptable, but that might just be the booze making your judgments for you. You'll have to explore the other towns along Route 19, venture into Pittsburgh, and get to know southwestern Pennsylvania better than you ever expected.

Students Speak Out
ON FACILITIES

Q "The Technology Center and Burnett are the two newest academic buildings, and they are by far the nicest on campus. **The library is a bit dated, but it serves its purpose well.**"

Q "The facilities are certainly functional. A lot of them have **a really nice, 'old college' sort of feel** to them. There are also a few fairly new buildings that are nice but nothing outstanding."

Q "The Henry Gymnasium has a lot to offer, even if it isn't anything flashy. The Swanson Wellness Center **houses quality exercise equipment, but it is severely undersized.** There are often long wait lines for equipment, especially when athletic teams are there."

Q "**Cameron Stadium needs some serious work.** The field is getting pitted, and the track holds water like that's its job. It had problems with flooding a few years back, and the whole thing could use some renovations."

Q "The basement of the Hub is a cool place. It **has three pool tables, a ping-pong table, an electronic dart board, arcade games,** and a student-run refreshment bar named Monticello's. The basement could use some updates, but overall, the Hub is a nice addition to the campus."

STUDENT AUTHOR: **The newer buildings like the Tech Center and Burnett are on the cutting edge (or at least just slightly behind) of academic technology. Some of the older buildings like McIlvaine and Lazear feel like antebellum relics whose last legs have long since given out. The library is perhaps the best facility available. Overall, much of the campus could use some updating.**

Students Speak Out
ON CAMPUS DINING

Q "Really, **the food services on campus are the weakest aspects of the school.** The food may seem deceptively good at first, but it really gets old fast."

Q "Parkhurst Dining Services (the same people that run the Eat 'n Park restaurant chain) runs all of the food services, and **they seem to do their best to work with suggestions and input.** They've been doing better over the years."

Q "People are always complaining about the food, but they have daily specials and **enough options, so you won't be completely bored** if you just try new things and don't always get the same items."

Q "**Our cafeteria is a great facility**, but the food is nothing to get excited about. It is always clean and the tables and chairs are not just cheap plastic junk. I might not enjoy the food all the time, but I always like eating there."

Q "Beyond the mediocre food, **they nickel-and-dime you for every little thing** and tend to run out of the good stuff quickly."

STUDENT AUTHOR: **Nothing around W&J gets more complaints than the campus food, except maybe the meal plan. That being said, the food here should be taken in stride. Sure, it isn't five-star dining, but it isn't slop either. The head chef does a good job of bringing in new dishes every so often as specials, and the cooking staff does pay some attention to the comment cards submitted by students.**

Students Speak Out
ON DORMS

Q "The dorms are really pretty nice, with the best ones being reserved for upperclassmen. The **dorms to avoid are actually some of the newer ones**, such as the new Greek housing and the Triplex. These buildings are very expensive to live in, and yet they have walls that are incredibly easy to damage."

Q "The women here can't really complain about housing. The freshman girls only ever end up living in Beau, Marshall, or Alex, all of which are **suite-style and perfectly good dorms**. The guys in Mellon and Upperclass always complain, but they really aren't terrible, just a little dingy and sub-par compared to the other dorms."

Q "**All of the dorms are pretty nice**, except for Mellon and Upperclass, the freshman male dorms. The other freshman dorms are nice because they are all suite-style."

STUDENT AUTHOR: **For many students, housing is what makes or breaks their enjoyment of W&J. For freshmen, it all boils down to luck, and even more so for freshman guys. The buildings improve as you advance through the years, and competition can be fierce to land a suite in Bica-Ross or New Res.**

 Did You Know?
92% of undergrads live on campus.

Students Speak Out
ON GUYS & GIRLS

Q "The guys are pretty cocky because **the majority of them are jocks**. If you think you're going to find your future husband here, think again."

Q "**Worst dating scene, period**. Very few girls ever stand out as being particularly interesting or unique. They try so damn hard to blend in, and then there's no reason to care to get to know them in particular."

Q "You'll find every body shape and size, every color, every way a person can look. **Just don't get your hopes up** about coming here and swimming in a sea of hotties."

Q "Over my four years here, **the girls have just kept getting hotter**. I don't know what it is, but I like it."

STUDENT AUTHOR: **At a place like W&J, your business becomes everyone else's business as quickly as it takes to fire off an IM or a text message. This isn't to say that there is no chance of a lasting relationship, but with so limited a selection, the odds are stacked pretty high against you. Complaints abound about the guys being egotistical or just plain immature. Likewise, guys levy grievances about the women being spoiled and duplicitous (if not necessarily in such proper words).**

Traditions

Anchor Splash
A national philanthropy event hosted by Delta Gamma in which each fraternity and sorority sends pledges to compete in aquatic races and events.

Street Fair
For the annual Street Fair, clubs and organizations on campus set up booths along Lincoln and Wheeling streets with games and contests.

Overall School Spirit
W&J's school spirit is more a "student spirit" because very few people seem to care about the College itself.

Students Speak Out
ON ATHLETICS

Q "It feels like a majority of the students at W&J play a varsity sport. Football, volleyball, basketball, and baseball are the main sports here. Everyone comes to the games, and they are really fun. **The football team is good year after year**, and it's something we expect here."

Q "The varsity **teams are pretty competitive**. IM sports are very popular, especially dodgeball."

Q "**Going to football games is one of the best things about fall semester**. The stadium might kind of suck, but it does its job. Our football team gets a ton of support from students."

Q "**It's all people ever seem to talk about**. I hear so much about how the teams did that I feel like I was at the games. People are way, way, way too concerned about athletics here."

STUDENT AUTHOR: **Despite its size, W&J is home to a decent variety of men's and women's sports. It isn't hard to see how W&J made *Men's Fitness* magazine's number 14 spot among America's most fit colleges. We are certainly an active campus full of students more ready to jump into a sport than to sit by and watch.**

Students Speak Out
ON DRUG SCENE

Q "It really depends on who you know. If you want to find it, you can. **If it's not your thing, you may never notice it**, aside from the occasional smell of weed in the hallways. Beyond that, marijuana is really the only super prevalent thing going on. You hear and or know about other stuff, but never to the degree of weed."

Q "W&J is a place where **the weed flows like wine**, but only if you know the right people."

Q "I think the academics here are a safety valve for drug use. If you get high all the time, there's no way you'll keep afloat. **I had a friend like that, and he flunked out within a year**. That keeps most students here under control."

STUDENT AUTHOR: **There are going to be more drugs around than you might think, but you won't notice unless you're really looking. That is, of course, except for marijuana. So many people smoke that sheer probability dictates you'll at least be around it once or twice a year. If you don't want to partake, no one is likely to hassle you about it.**

12:1	Student-to-Faculty Ratio
84%	Freshman Retention Rate
66%	Four-Year Graduation Rate
74%	Financial Aid Applicants Receiving Aid

Students Speak Out
SAFETY & SECURITY

Q "The campus police are nice and all, but **don't think that you can boss them around** or take advantage of them. No matter how lenient they can be at times, they are still the authorities around here, and they won't stand for immature or juvenile behavior."

Q "Our security guards are constantly on rounds throughout campus, so if you need one for something, it won't take you long to find one. Plus, **their office is right in the middle of campus, so it's a quick walk** no matter what."

Q "Security is typically quick to respond to calls about fights, which do occasionally break out on weekends. Unless they see you fighting or breaking school property or smell weed smoke or something, **they never bother you**."

STUDENT AUTHOR: **The campus is about as safe as you can reasonably expect from a place that isn't walled and gated. Campus security guards are constantly on patrol somewhere on campus, blue-light phones are never far off, and you're always only about five minutes from the security office anytime you're on college property.**

> **Questions?**
> For more inside information and survival tips, pick up College Prowler's full-length book on this school, written by an actual student! Check it out at *www.collegeprowler.com.*

Students Speak Out
ON OVERALL EXPERIENCE

Q "I hated my time here because of the stress and aggravation. I hated my time because of how difficult my classes were. But looking back as a senior, I'm coming to realize that **it was all that stress that made me learn to work harder**, to take classes seriously, and to learn whatever I could. It was because of all the time I spent hunched over my books and hating life that helped prepare me to take my MCATs."

Q "Who would have thought I could spend a semester in Germany then come back and learn how to brew beer then go insane learning neurochemistry? **W&J has a lot more to offer people than they realize** when they come here as little freshmen."

Q "I absolutely made the right decision coming to W&J. **The school may be hard, but we know how to have our fun**. If I could do it over again, I would definitely come here! My favorite part is being able to party however I want whenever I want. My least favorite part is the administration."

Q "**I feel that I have received a solid education**, made many life-long friends, and have had some kick-ass times. College, and life in general, is only as good as you make it out to be."

STUDENT AUTHOR: **Not many students walk out of W&J with feelings that it was "alright" or "so-so." Most shoot off to either extreme of loving it or despising its very existence. Come to think of it, many are a complicated mix of both. Regardless of where their loyalties lie at graduation, students seem to share a strikingly common belief that succeeding at W&J makes the rest of the challenges still to come comparably easier.**

Washington and Lee University

204 West Washington Street; Lexington, VA 24450
(540) 458-8400; www.wlu.edu

THE BASICS:

Acceptance Rate: 27%
Setting: Rural
F-T Undergrads: 1,774

SAT Range: 1310–1460*
Control: Private
Tuition: $37,412

Most Popular Majors: Business, Social Sciences, History, Foreign Languages, Psychology

*of 1600

Academics	A	Guys	B
Local Atmosphere	C-	Girls	B+
Safety & Security	A	Athletics	C+
Computers	A-	Nightlife	C-
Facilities	B+	Greek Life	A+
Campus Dining	C+	Drug Scene	B
Off-Campus Dining	B+	Campus Strictness	C
Campus Housing	B	Parking	C
Off-Campus Housing	A-	Transportation	C+
Diversity	D	Weather	C+

Students Speak Out
ON ACADEMICS

Q "Classes tend to be **small and discussion-based**. Freshmen can anticipate a lot of choice in their class selections, and professors and advisors who are eager to help them navigate individual classes and general education requirements."

Q "It's absolutely ridiculous for the lowest math here to be calculus—for a gen ed! I'll never use math or science again, yet I was forced to **struggle through ridiculously difficult classes**. That's not necessary. At least, there needs to be some sort of lower math and sciences for us non-techies."

Q "Freshmen can expect to be put on the spot. **Do your reading**, because you can and will be called on in class."

Q "Professors are **extremely approachable**—they love to interact with students."

Q "Because of small class sizes, it is sometimes **difficult to get into all the classes you want** without begging a professor to let you add or drop a class."

STUDENT AUTHOR: Make no mistake: academic work at Washington and Lee is intense. Professors expect a lot of effort from students. If you get an A+ here, cherish it, because it might be the only one you'll ever see. Students build personal relationships with the faculty, and can rely on them for help whenever they hit a rough spot. Students are required to take a selection of general education courses, which makes up one-third of the course load.

Students Speak Out
ON LOCAL ATMOSPHERE

Q "If you like **outdoor activities**, Lexington is the place for you. There are so many awesome national parks, hiking trails, and fly-fishing rivers. Also, the Outing Club is an unbelievable resource."

Q "The town **can be a little stifling at times**, just in terms of size, but the atmosphere is good. The college has a good relationship with the surrounding city and the Virginia Military Institute. In a town this size, you are bound to run into friends and professors everywhere you go."

Q "The Lexington area is one of the most beautiful places I've ever been. The population is rural, but the **town is charming, old, and full of intrigue**. Everything in town is basically within walking distance."

Q "**Townies aren't big fans of students**, but they sometimes have the right to be annoyed with us because we tend to forget that there is more to Lexington than W&L."

STUDENT AUTHOR: W&L is nestled in historic Lexington, deep in the heart of Virginia's Shenandoah Valley. You can catch a carriage tour and see Robert E. Lee's home. Students can hike miles of scenic trails, go tubing down the Maury River, bowl their hearts out, and work on their tan at Goshen Pass. Many students complain that, beyond the bubble of W&L, Lexington and the surrounding area offer little to keep them amused and engaged. Overall, the jury is still out on whether Lexington is an idyllic community or a boring backwater.

5 Best Things	5 Worst Things
1 Academics	1 Parking
2 Close-knit community	2 Athletic support
3 Honor Code	3 Lack of support
4 Small classes	4 Academic demands
5 Cool alumni	5 Diversity

Students Speak Out
ON FACILITIES

Q "Although some facilities are considerably older than others, **they are well kept**."

Q "The **Science Center is phenomenal**. I really like how they combine all the scientific departments into one building, which facilitates conversations across disciplines and a general prevailing attitude of teamwork and cooperation among different faculty."

Q "Many of the **classrooms are in historical sites**, so they are kept in immaculate condition—though historical furniture is not the most comfortable to sit in for long periods of time."

Q "The Elrod Commons has a theater and shows **movies recently taken off the big screen**, a month to three months after they show in theaters. The school is also trying to have comedy shows once a week, and brings bands and speakers to campus pretty often as well."

Q "I love the Fitness Center and the Commons, but Leyburn scares me. It's just **too dark and old**."

STUDENT AUTHOR: **W&L's campus sports a sparkling new exercise facility, a $30 million Student Commons, and a journalism school wired for the 21st century. Construction is under way on a state-of-the-art, 60,000 square-foot music and arts building. The school works hard at making up for what Lexington lacks in the area of entertainment. There are blights on campus, however. One is Leyburn Library—old, dark, and dreary. Studying there tends to put students to sleep. The bookstore has basic items, but students have to go off campus to find other odds and ends.**

Famous Alumni

David Brown, Meriwether Clark, Roger H. Mudd, Lewis F. Powell, Jr., Pat Robertson, John Warner, Tom Wolfe

Students Speak Out
ON CAMPUS DINING

Q "I think the **food is really good**, compared to the ones I have seen in other places."

Q "The food is pretty good. The D-Hall has been upgraded to the Marketplace, and there are **more options for students**. There is always a variety of pizza. There is also a deli bar, a different type of soup every day, a salad bar, hot dogs, burgers, and grilled chicken. The main course varies from day to day."

Q "**Nothing on campus is open 24 hours**, and something of this nature could be a big help to students studying all night."

Q "Our Café, the short-order restaurant that is open most of the day, is great for meals and snacks. Many **upperclassmen eat at fraternities** or sororities. Each house has a different cook, and there is enough variety in the food choice to make it worthwhile."

Q "It might be **more economical to cook for yourself** sometimes. So, I've reduced the number of meals in my meal plan each year."

STUDENT AUTHOR: **Students on campus have a few options when it comes time to grab some munchies or a sit-down meal. Freshmen have to purchase the full meal plan, 21 meals per week. Very few students actually eat all this food. Many feel that sleep is often more valuable than breakfast. But upperclassmen can choose from a variety of meal plans, some of them much less expensive than the freshman plan. A lot of students eat at their respective fraternity or sorority.**

Student Body

African American:	4%	Male/Female:	51/49%
Asian American:	4%	Out-of-State:	84%
Hispanic:	2%	International:	4%
Native American:	<1%	Unknown:	1%
White:	85%		

Popular Faiths: In declining order: Catholic, Episcopal, Presbyterian, and Methodist.

Gay Pride: There is not a large gay presence, but many seem accepting of others who have come out. The Gay-Straight Alliance was established and has brought a lot of attention to the issue.

Economic Status: Students here are clearly not hurting for cash. Only about 35 percent apply for aid.

Students Speak Out
ON DORMS

Q "You get the **unforgettable dorm experience** your freshman year and can roll out of bed at 8:47 and be in class at 9."

Q "Woods Creek apartments are great sophomore year because it **feels like you're living off campus**, even though technically, you aren't."

Q "Your chances of being housed on campus all four years are good if you want it, but most students live off campus as upperclassmen unless they're **living in a Greek house**."

STUDENT AUTHOR: **W&L students have to live on campus for their first two years at the University. The rooms are generally unexceptional, so whether students enjoy their accommodations depends a lot on roommates, dorm counselors, and neighbors down the hall. For incoming students, it's best to try a real freshmen dorm such as Graham-Lees. After freshman year, students tend to expand to other dorms such as Woods Creek, which offers more of an off-campus feel; they also have the option of moving into fraternity and sorority houses. Upperclassmen usually don't stay on campus, so they have last pick for housing.**

Did You Know?
43% of undergrads live on campus.

Students Speak Out
ON GUYS & GIRLS

Q "People here **aren't that promiscuous**."

Q "There aren't any set visiting hours for members of the opposite sex in the dorms. Individual freshmen halls or suites can set policies if they want to do so, but everyone tends just to operate under the general **rules of common courtesy**."

Q "There are way **more attractive girls** than attractive guys. I've seen gorgeous girls compete for guys they wouldn't look twice at if we were at a state school."

Q "**Fashion is excessively emphasized**, but many people are getting sick of the strictures and more unique dress styles are emerging."

STUDENT AUTHOR: **Men and women at Washington and Lee seem to treat each other with respect: a tradition of gentility and courtesy persists. Ladies should expect regular, if not universal, door-holding from guys here. W&L is blessed with more than its fair share of attractive ladies. Perhaps it's a "Southun thang," but most of these ladies take great pride in fixing themselves up for every special (and not-so special) occasion.**

Traditions

Fancy Dress
The Warner Center and Doremus Gym are transformed into themed dance halls for the $80,000 event.

Mock Convention
Every four years, a student-run convention is organized just like a real presidential convention.

Overall School Spirit
Even if it's not expressed in the usual ways (painted fans at games), W&L students have a lot of school spirit. Students come together for all activities.

Students Speak Out
ON ATHLETICS

Q "School spirit with regards to sports is unfortunately low. At a school based around tradition, it's **sad that more people don't go** to games and support their classmates."

Q "**Coaches are very understanding** of the heavy workload that student athletes have. This doesn't seem to take away from the competitiveness of most of the teams, as they still perform well."

Q "Intramural football and softball is very popular among the frats and law students. **Rugby is a very popular club team**, and has a sort of groupie following."

Q "**Lacrosse is the most popular sport** at our school, judging from participation by players and fans. Our football program is lacking in both players and fans, but is central to fall Saturdays, as there are tailgates and such planned."

STUDENT AUTHOR: **The University doesn't award athletic scholarships, and athletes are expected to carry their weight. This sometimes makes it tough for W&L to field successful teams. Attendance is pretty light at most games, but people turn out for Parents' Weekend and Homecoming football games.**

Students Speak Out
ON DRUG SCENE

Q "Compared to a state school, W&L's drug usage is pretty small. But **alcohol is another story**."

Q "Drug abuse seems prevalent around campus, in the sense that if you want drugs, you can probably find them. But **it isn't obvious** or being passed around the basement of a frat party."

Q "I have **never been pressured to drink** or take drugs and I have not heard of that happening to any students during the normal course of events. There is a lot of alcohol consumption on the weekends by some students at the parties, but I think the amount of alcohol consumed decreases as students get older."

STUDENT AUTHOR: Alcohol is the drug of choice at W&L, and is extremely prevalent both on and off campus. Knowing this, the University is trying to prevent drunk driving by providing free rides from parties back to campus. Students very rarely use fake IDs to get alcohol in Lexington, because the Executive Committee may consider it an honor violation. Frats hold parties four nights a week.

9:1	Student-to-Faculty Ratio
95%	Freshman Retention Rate
87%	Four-Year Graduation Rate
85%	Financial Aid Applicants Receiving Aid

Students Speak Out
SAFETY & SECURITY

Q "We have **blue-light phones**, as well as available escort service. Members of campus security are friendly and dedicated to their jobs."

Q "The cops probably spend **more time giving out noise violations** and parking tickets than actually making Lexington safer."

Q "Campus security guards are here for our protection. A couple of the officers are known for parking tickets and such, but generally, they are **looking out for your best interests**. If they see you at a party and know there is a chance of you getting arrested by walking home, they will make sure you get a Sober Ride, or will personally take you home."

STUDENT AUTHOR: Lexington is a sleepy little town at heart, an insulated cocoon with a very low rate of reported violent crime. Partly because of the one-strike Honor Code, students feel free to trust each other with their property. That trust seems to be justified nearly all of the time.

Questions?
For more inside information and survival tips, pick up College Prowler's full-length book on this school, written by an actual student! Check it out at www.collegeprowler.com.

Students Speak Out
ON OVERALL EXPERIENCE

Q "I knew that I wanted to come to W&L from the second I drove up, and it's met every single expectation that I had. The **Honor Code is everything I expected**, and the profs were more challenging—and yet more genuine—than I expected."

Q "Make sure you look into the school extensively—spend the night if you can. Know that it's almost **exclusively Greek**—you have to be a really independent person to thrive here and enjoy it if you're not going to get involved."

Q "W&L has an unfortunate **reputation as a hard-partying and hard-drinking school**."

Q "Absolutely, the **Honor Code works**. I have been affected hugely by it. I pledge everything I turn in because when I walk across the podium at graduation, I want to know that I earned that degree myself. I respect the Honor Code immensely—it's in my opinion one of the school's biggest assets, if not the biggest."

STUDENT AUTHOR: Year after year, Washington and Lee has been remarkably successful at producing happy students. Freshmen usually come in starry-eyed and leave four years later content, happy, grateful for an awesome experience, and nostalgic for all the good times gone by. The demanding expectations of faculty don't seem to put a serious damper on the general feeling of good cheer. One objective gauge of this is W&L's remarkably active and supportive alumni network, which supports the University, stays in touch to get jobs for students, and most recently chipped in cash to the tune of $240 million for massive modernization projects.

Washington University in St. Louis

1 Brookings Drive; St. Louis, MO 63130
(314) 935-5000; www.wustl.edu

THE BASICS:

Acceptance Rate: 17%
Setting: Urban
F-T Undergrads: 7,181

SAT Range: 1370–1530*
Control: Private
Tuition: $36,200

Most Popular Majors: Social Sciences, Business, Engineering, Psychology, Visual & Performing Arts

*of 1600

Academics	A-	Guys	C+
Local Atmosphere	B+	Girls	C
Safety & Security	A-	Athletics	B-
Computers	B+	Nightlife	B+
Facilities	B-	Greek Life	B+
Campus Dining	B+	Drug Scene	B-
Off-Campus Dining	B+	Campus Strictness	B+
Campus Housing	B+	Parking	B-
Off-Campus Housing	A-	Transportation	C+
Diversity	C	Weather	B-

Students Speak Out
ON ACADEMICS

Q **"The teachers are fine.** Freshmen classes are mostly lectures, but all of the professors I've had interactions with have been pretty approachable, for the most part."

Q "There are really some exceptional professors—**as opposed to just good scholars**—at Wash U. The political science department has a few great teachers, especially Prof Mertha (his courses on Chinese politics are excellent) and Prof Rehfeld. In other areas, Rich Smith teaches a terrific intro course on human evolution, virtually any course with Prof Koepnick (German film and media studies department) is interesting, and Prof Symeonoglu's intro archeology/art history course, Myths and Monuments of Antiquity, is a must."

Q "Your academic experience here depends on which teachers you have. I loved all of mine except for one. It depends on your major and who you get. When you know what classes you want to take, I absolutely recommend asking someone who's in your major who you should take. **It can make a huge difference**, even with the same class."

STUDENT AUTHOR: **Most Wash U students seem to enjoy their academic experience. There are certainly boring and exciting courses and professors in each department, so it's recommended both to ask for advice from older students and to visit multiple classes before settling on a schedule. The professors seem particularly notable for their enthusiasm in receiving visits from students during or beyond office hours.**

Students Speak Out
ON LOCAL ATMOSPHERE

Q "St. Louis is an amazing town. Wash U is located in a **relatively suburban area** just minutes away from downtown, so you have access to all the clubs and restaurants of a big city, without the traffic and pollution."

Q "The big Missouri state school, Mizzou, is in Columbia, about an hour and 45 minutes away. The good thing about that is if a band is coming through town and they missed St. Louis for some reason, sometimes they stop in Columbia. Ani Difranco is known for playing in STL, then the next night in Columbia. **That gets crazy.** Webster University (in Webster Groves) usually has a ton of cool things going on—from drag shows to plays and films."

Q "St. Louis is a really great place to live. **Stay away from East St. Louis** (it's across the river so you'd never be there anyway). The Loop is an awesome area. It's a 10-minute walk north of campus with really kick-ass restaurants, shopping, stores, and more."

Q **"St. Louis is not really a college town**, but there's a lot of fun free stuff to do in nearby Forest Park, like the zoo or art museum."

STUDENT AUTHOR: **The atmosphere in St. Louis is not one of a traditional college town. The city is big enough that kids feel they can get away and find the resources of a semi-metropolis. At the same time, the campus is in a calm suburb, where there is a laid-back Midwestern atmosphere that many students from the East Coast find appealing.**

Students Speak Out
ON FACILITIES

Q "Some departments have nicer buildings than others. The physics department building is still **stuck in the '60s**, just like the faculty. The athletic facilities also leave something to be desired."

Q "The weight room is a joke. The machines are very old and break down a lot, and the room is too small. **It's definitely not adequate** for the needs of the undergraduate and graduate students. And the other sports equipment isn't great either. If you want to borrow a badminton net, it will probably have holes in it. The basketballs are probably lopsided!"

Q "Athletic facilities are pretty good here. We have a pool, two gyms, a track, and athletic fields and stuff. **Computers here are fine**. There are zillions around and on campus. There are labs in every dorm, as well as a huge art-sci computing lab on main campus."

Q "The student center on campus is Mallinckrodt, which has the food court, an area called the Gargoyle which serves as extra seating during lunch time (and, I think, has vegetarian and Kosher food counters). At night, **the Gargoyle houses small concerts** (there's a stage), and the Roots came a few years ago!"

STUDENT AUTHOR: **The main facilities on campus are the athletic complex (the AC), Mallinckrodt Center, the computer labs, and the libraries. Less demanding students find all of these satisfactory, but many agree that the athletic complex is a bit starved for resources. Equipment and space are lacking in many areas, although it's still possible to do a wide range of sports.**

Famous Alumni

Dan Carlin, Steve Fossett, Cara Nussbaum, Jack Taylor

Students Speak Out
ON CAMPUS DINING

Q "For a college, **I think dining at Wash U is not that bad**, but I wouldn't say it's good either. I've been to other campuses, like Rice, and Wash U is definitely better, but it's nothing fantastic."

Q "On campus, the food is actually pretty good. We have the cafeteria and a deli-like place called **Bear's Den on the South 40** (where most of the on-campus housing is located). On main campus, there are tons of places: Hilltop Bakery, Holmes Lounge, and Mallinckrodt which has a bunch of options like vegetarian, sushi, pasta, soul food, and more."

Q "**Center Court is a gigantic buffet-style place** that is only open for dinner all week and offers brunch on the weekends. There's always a big variety, and you can usually find what you want."

Q "Dude, the food here rocks! I may be in the minority here, but I seriously think the food is really excellent at Wash U. **Sometimes people complain about the lack of variety** of food on campus, but I personally always feel like you can always find something to satisfy your taste buds."

STUDENT AUTHOR: **College food is notorious for being bland, unhealthy, and expensive. Wash U is guilty on the last count, but the first two are, at least, up for debate. Campus dining does offer a wide variety, including a sushi bar and tasty vegetarian counter in the Mallinckrodt Center food court, custom-made omelettes and sirloin steak in the all-you-can-eat Centre Court, ethnic food and quesadillas in Small Group Housing, and fruit smoothies and custom ice cream at Ursa's.**

Student Body

African American:	10%	Male/Female:	50/50%
Asian American:	14%	Out-of-State:	90%
Hispanic:	4%	International:	5%
Native American:	<1%	Unknown:	8%
White:	59%		

Popular Faiths: There are a lot of Jewish students on campus, but Christian groups are more numerous.

Gay Pride: The gay community isn't particularly outspoken on campus, but it has a large GLBT club called Spectrum Alliance which organizes an awareness week and other events.

Economic Status: A large majority of Wash U students are quite wealthy.

Students Speak Out
ON DORMS

Q "The dorms are all pretty nice, and the rooms are big compared to other schools. Personally, I lived in the old dorms and **I loved it**. The new dorms are really nice, too, but a different atmosphere."

Q "I'm definitely an advocate of the old dorms. In the new dorms, everyone's in their own suites with their own bathrooms. I feel like there are a lot more closed doors, and **lots less opportunities for interaction**. In the old dorms, you can see which rooms are open, which is pretty sweet, and the common bathrooms make for a more social atmosphere."

Q "As a freshman, **you have a choice between the old dorms and the new dorms**. I was in the new dorms. Basically, the old dorms are much more social and fun, but one negative is that there are communal bathrooms. In the new dorms, it feels like you're in a Comfort Inn, but it's not as social."

STUDENT AUTHOR: **Each of the dorms clustered on the infamous quad (South 40) has its own distinctive flavor and atmosphere. These particularities often produce fierce loyalties and rivalries between the students who live there—especially between the residents of the old dorms and new dorms.**

Did You Know?
73% of undergrads live on campus.

Students Speak Out
ON GUYS & GIRLS

Q "I've found it **a little tough to find hot guys** at Wash U, but they're not all nasty either. It's just a little more work than I'd like."

Q "The guys always joke that **the girls are ugly** because we're not a big state school, but guys can be like that. I found there to be a lot of really cute guys on campus. The fraternities and sororities have formals, semi-formals, and date parties all the time, which you can be invited to even if you're not in one."

Q "This isn't like Hawaii or Florida; there are **lots of smart people**."

Q "There are **a lot of different choices**—from Abercrombie guys, to sports, to artsy, to whatever—for whatever you might be into!"

STUDENT AUTHOR: **Considering the intellectual quotient of Wash U's undergrads, the kids here are surprisingly photogenic. This is partially because the highly athletic student population has a knack for staying in shape and keeping their bodies fit. Guys and girls with flat abs and big legs can regularly be seen jogging near campus, lifting weights in the AC, and playing fast-paced ultimate Frisbee in the Swamp or Mudd field.**

Traditions

WILD
It stands for Walk In Lay Down. Twice a year, the University pays for a top band/performer to play a free outdoor concert.

EnWeek
Engineering students stage all kinds of bizarre and cool events, including three-dollar pizza lunches.

Overall School Spirit
Every club/team/sorority/dorm/class/religious group has its own T-shirt, party, visor, or memorabilia of some kind, and people tend to define themselves more specifically along those lines.

Students Speak Out
ON ATHLETICS

Q "Wash U is a Division III school and **the emphasis is definitely on academics**. IM sports are really big, though, and a lot of people participate."

Q "Some varsity sports are bigger than others. I play on the soccer team, and we don't get very many fans. **Volleyball and basketball** are our two biggest varsity sports. We do have a football team, and they are pretty big, too, but volleyball and basketball get more fans because we usually win the title for those two sports."

Q "Sports are really not big at all at Wash U. That's one thing I don't like. There's not a lot of school spirit. There are, however, **lots of opportunities to play IM sports**, especially Frisbee."

Q "I didn't even know we had varsity athletics here. Truly, **sports are not big** on campus at all."

STUDENT AUTHOR: **The typical big-draw college sports struggle for any kind of following at Wash U—bleachers for these events are, at best, peppered with loyal fans and the occasional girlfriend or boyfriend. Most other sports suffer the same fate. For two sports only, turnout is never a problem women's volleyball and women's basketball.**

Students Speak Out
ON DRUG SCENE

Q "The most popular drug on campus is weed. I don't really know much about **harder drugs**, but I have heard of a few people who use them, so I know they're present."

Q "At Wash U, there's lot's of drinking, a fair amount of pot, ecstasy is becoming more prevalent, and there are a few cases of people who do coke in their rooms. I think that drinking and drugs can always be found on college campuses, and while **Wash U is certainly a fun place**, it isn't really what you'd call a 'party school.'"

Q "**Seek and you shall find**. But, in general, if you want to avoid drugs, that's also very easy. I personally never saw anyone doing drugs, but then I also tend to avoid that crowd."

STUDENT AUTHOR: **Those who have no interest in doing drugs will find it easy to build a drug-free social life at Wash U. Within certain social circles, pot is considered common currency, but unless all of your friends are potheads it shouldn't pose any social difficulties to the non-user.**

7:1	Student-to-Faculty Ratio
97%	Freshman Retention Rate
83%	Four-Year Graduation Rate
55%	Financial Aid Applicants Receiving Aid

Students Speak Out
SAFETY & SECURITY

Q "**Security on campus is great**. We have blue-light emergency phones all over campus. There are also always officers on patrol, and they have a number you can call if you want a ride."

Q "**Safety on campus is pretty good**. There are blue-light emergency phones everywhere, you need a card to get into any of the dorm buildings (so there's no way for strangers to wander in), there are proctors stationed in the lobbies of all buildings open at night, and there are constantly campus police patrolling."

Q "North of the school is a rather sketchy area, and occasionally weird people will wander from their neighborhood and onto campus. There have been a few incidents, but **as far as I am aware, nothing severe**."

STUDENT AUTHOR: **There are often detailed reports in Student Life about "green, leafy substances" being confiscated from unlucky students, stolen bottles of tequila, and other minor incidents, but overwhelmingly, there is little crime, and little reason to feel unsafe at Wash U.**

> **Questions?**
> For more inside information and survival tips, pick up College Prowler's full-length book on this school, written by an actual student! Check it out at *www.collegeprowler.com*.

Students Speak Out
ON OVERALL EXPERIENCE

Q "I wouldn't want to go anywhere else for college. So far, these two years have been awesome! I love Wash U so much and everyone I know who goes here loves it. It is a great place in a great location. **This was the best decision I could have made**. It's a great place!"

Q "What I really liked about the school was its size. **It was small, but not tiny**. I always describe it as small enough that you'll always recognize someone wherever you go, but big enough that there will always be new people to meet. The campus is really pretty. They're constantly renovating. A lot of the buildings on campus look like modern castles."

Q "Wash U has given me the opportunity to get involved, try new things, and meet a ton of people, in addition to offering me a wonderful education. **I've had to work really hard** (kind of difficult since I didn't study much in high school—but I do now). But all work and no play is definitely not the motto here!"

Q "In a word, **Wash U is incredible**! I've met the most unbelievable people and have been able to receive a fantastic education."

STUDENT AUTHOR: **Wash U is a young school, and the University is very much interested in channeling the energy and enterprises of its students into new traditions and organizations that help shape its identity. Not everybody likes Wash U from the outset (this author included). St. Louis can get dull, the academic life can become overwhelming, and the social scene will eventually feel a bit claustrophobic. But the quality of the faculty alone makes it a place where a motivated student can do anything he or she wants.**

Wellesley College

106 Central Street; Wellesley, MA 02481
(781) 283-1000; www.wellesley.edu

THE BASICS:

Acceptance Rate: 36%
Setting: Suburban
F-T Undergrads: 2,190

SAT Range: 1920–2210*
Control: Private
Tuition: $36,404

Most Popular Majors: Social Sciences, Foreign Languages, Ethnic Studies, Visual & Performing Arts

*of 2400

Academics	A	Guys	N/A
Local Atmosphere	B-	Girls	B
Safety & Security	A-	Athletics	C
Computers	B-	Nightlife	B
Facilities	B+	Greek Life	N/A
Campus Dining	B	Drug Scene	B+
Off-Campus Dining	B+	Campus Strictness	D
Campus Housing	B	Parking	C+
Off-Campus Housing	C-	Transportation	C
Diversity	A-	Weather	C-

Students Speak Out
ON ACADEMICS

Q "The professors are, on the whole, extremely smart and engaging. They're also often very **accessible and interested in the students** and seem to genuinely want to help us learn as much as possible. Most professors are engaging lecturers."

Q "The classes rock. Whatever else can be said about Wellesley, it will give you **an absolutely fabulous education**. There is the rare professor who just doesn't know how to teach, but almost all of them are incredibly dedicated, available, and every other good quality you could want in a teacher."

Q "Courses have **great titles and the information** is usually very interesting. However, never choose your classes based on the title and topic."

Q "I think that the professors at Wellesley are **really enthusiastic to be teaching** their courses, as well as teaching at Wellesley."

STUDENT AUTHOR: To facilitate the professor-choosing process, the school's e-mail system has an online conference where students can post questions about professors and get in-depth responses about professors' teaching styles. Professors invariably prove to be very dynamic in office hours, and a more extensive relationship is almost always there for the taking. Few students go through their Wellesley career without forming some kind of a close relationship with a professor. If you ask around and do your research, you can ensure some serious and exciting learning.

Students Speak Out
ON LOCAL ATMOSPHERE

Q "The Ville (as we students call the town of Wellesley) is not the most friendly of towns. Being in the midst of an upper-middle-class area, **the stores are mostly expensive boutiques** for clothing, antiques, rugs, and furniture."

Q "Simply put, the town is extremely dry and **everything closes at 9 p.m.**"

Q "We have **more socialization with MIT** and Harvard."

Q "**Boston is only a 45-minute drive** (less if you have a car), and there is plenty to do there—bars, restaurants, museums, and lots of other colleges."

Q "In Boston, you **can't spit without hitting a college**. The town of Wellesley sucks. It's rich and uptight, most of the people who live there don't like the college being in their town."

Q "Wellesley is very much **a suburban community**. There isn't much in the area, except Babson College and Olin College."

STUDENT AUTHOR: Wellesley is one of the richest communities in the country, and the shops and restaurants show it. Some feel uncomfortable in the Ville, while others feel they make townies uncomfortable. Boston is the saving grace for students—hop onto the Exchange Bus or the Commuter Rail and you're there in less than an hour. Boston, for many students, is a beacon of hope (real life! parties! men!) that breaks through the hazy, money-drenched clouds of the suburbs.

Students Speak Out
ON FACILITIES

Q "The **facilities are all top-notch**, state-of-the-art, and very clean."

Q "The athletic center **could use some more workout equipment** but is otherwise very nice. The pool is amazing, and the computer labs are great. The new student center is finished and is amazing."

Q "Facilities are, for the most part, gorgeous. I find them to be **better than most Ivy League** colleges, if not all. Our new student center is so nice considering how small and inadequate our current Schneider Center is. The athletic facilities are good, and we have new fields."

Q "It's a **gorgeous campus** and is maintained very well. The public computers are always new."

Q "The student center has the **bookstore, food, ATMs, and a café**."

STUDENT AUTHOR: The Keohane Sports Center is attractive and well maintained, with all that one would expect from a gym. The lack of exercise equipment, however, is a big complaint among students. Classrooms in Pendleton and the Science Center tend to be well laid out and high tech, though those in Founders are cramped and stuffed with Wellesley's signature big wooden straight-backed chair. The Science Center is a love-it-or-hate-it affair, with its Mondrian-esque exterior encasing the remains of the old brick building inside. The campus is indisputably gorgeous, and walking up to Tower Great Hall or the Quad can get your heart beating faster, especially when you see it for the first time.

Famous Alumni

Harriet Stratemeyer Adams (Carolyn Keene), Hillary Clinton, Nora Ephron, Jean Kilbourne, Cokie Roberts, Diane Sawyer, Lynn Scherr

Students Speak Out
ON CAMPUS DINING

Q "The **food's good compared to most schools**, though I wish we had more than just Schneider for alternatives to the dining hall food."

Q "The meal plan is excellent, because it's **unlimited and not based on a points system**. And for those wishing to spend a small amount for high-quality food, the student co-op cafè, El Table, offers healthy and delicious lunch and snack selections."

Q "Pomeroy is the vegetarian/Kosher spot, and their **salad bars are the best** and most varied on campus."

Q "Compared to other schools, Wellesley has one of the **best meal plans**. Students can have buffet-style breakfast, lunch, and dinner in any of the dining halls on campus."

Q "I'm happy that we're getting more organic foods into the dining halls. Bates has a lot of **organic and vegan foods**. I enjoy eating there and at Stone-Davis."

STUDENT AUTHOR: Everyone has their complaints, but it's possible to eat well at Wellesley. Though the meal plan is very open in some ways—we can eat as much as we like at any time during the day, and most dining halls don't keep track of guest meals—we have no options other than the dining halls and we pay for the privilege, shelling our more that $4,000 a year. There are more satisfied students who have more flexibility to the meal plan, along with more options for students dissatisfied by the dining halls.

Student Body

African American:	7%	Male/Female:	0/100%
Asian American:	28%	Out-of-State:	84%
Hispanic:	7%	International:	8%
Native American:	<1%	Unknown:	4%
White:	46%		

Popular Faiths: Wellesley has a very diverse mix of the religious, the spiritual, and the agnostic.

Gay Pride: Wellesley is extremely tolerant with many students graduating as self-proclaimed "cultural gays." National Coming Out Day is like a holiday.

Economic Status: Students run the gamut from high-society girls to first-generation college students from low socioeconomic situations.

Students Speak Out
ON DORMS

Q "I think the dorms are really nice. They're all very different, and depending on what you're looking for, you can usually **find one that's a good fit** for you. Most of the dorms have a campus personality and everyone can find a place where they're happy to live. There are certain dorms that are quieter, some are known for partying, and other ones are known for their queer community."

Q "The houses like Instead, Cervantes, and French House are really nice, **small-scale, independent** living, but they're very affinity-based."

Q "The New Dorms are psychotic and isolated. I like the Tower dorms the best because they're **social and close to everything.**"

STUDENT AUTHOR: **Wellesley was designed to promote studiousness, not sociability.** Some students also chafe at the strict supervision of residential staff. First year, you've got no choice where you live; after that, it's largely up to personal preference and your luck in the housing lottery. Even if you strike out, however, you can try for a room swap. A lake view lifts the spirits, as does a social dorm.

> **? Did You Know?**
> 98% of undergrads live on campus.

Students Speak Out
ON GUYS & GIRLS

Q "There are a **zillion 'types' of women** at Wellesley; every kind of person under the sun is represented. In general, I would call them mind-blowingly amazing, and more are hot."

Q "There are no guys at the school, obviously, and the **pickings are slim in Boston.**"

Q "No guys, but you will **make your best friends** here because the campus does foster a friendly environment."

Q "Sometimes **this place can induce complexes**—everyone seems perfect and overachieving and brilliant. But they also make good friends when they're not busy studying."

STUDENT AUTHOR: **Our dating pool tends to be guys from Boston-area** schools, and so there's a range there as well. Wellesley women date men from MIT, Harvard, BC, BU, Northeastern, Berklee (a music school), Babson, or any number of the dozens of schools in the area. The girls run the gamut from frumpy to gorgeous. Lesbians seem to be happy with the dating pool, and heterosexuals seem thrilled with the friends they've made.

> **Traditions**
>
> **Dyke Ball**
> The biggest party of the year; students dress up in Saran Wrap, show-girl costumes, or in drag.
>
> **Fifty Things to Do at Wellesley Before Graduation**
> An annual list printed by the *Wellesley News* of random things to complete before graduating.
>
> **Overall School Spirit**
> First year, the doubters and the fans are about equal in number. After four years, sentimental seniors can't say enough about the bizarre institution that has become their home.

Students Speak Out
ON ATHLETICS

Q "We have **really dedicated teams** at Wellesley, but we're not a very sports-oriented school; don't expect a massive cheering section if you play a varsity sport."

Q "Intramural sports, surprisingly, have **more fans than varsity sports,** but are not respected by varsity players. Intramural sports often have much larger teams than varsity sports, as well."

Q "I don't know much about sports on campus, except that they're **under-appreciated** and under-funded."

Q "Varsity sports aren't big on campus. Also, they are **not a priority for the school.**"

STUDENT AUTHOR: **Sports are not big at Wellesley,** but as any Division III athlete can attest, they're big for participants. Balancing intense academics with demanding athletics isn't an easy task, so Wellesley athletes are under-appreciated. Even when teams perform excellently, the college community rarely takes notice. No team is pulling in big spectators, but the crew team can count on a big campus contingent turning out for the Head of the Charles regatta in the fall.

Students Speak Out
ON DRUG SCENE

Q "Most people are at Wellesley for the academics, but if you want to unwind, **drinking and smoking aren't uncommon**."

Q "The drug scene is not big, and it can be surprising to **see people smoking**, considering so few do."

Q "**Pot, coke, and Ritalin** seem to be the biggest drugs on campus. People are pretty quiet about their drug habits, but drugs definitely do exist at Wellesley; it's just not part of the mainstream social scene."

STUDENT AUTHOR: **Depending on where they hang out and who their friends are, some students report never smelling marijuana smoke wafting down the hall, while others see classmates toke up on a daily basis. The desire to conform to—or escape—academic pressure may tempt some students to pop an Adderall while writing a paper or smoke a little to blow off steam on the weekend. Drugs that help people concentrate are both used and abused, but it's hard to tell how much.**

8:1	Student-to-Faculty Ratio
94%	Freshman Retention Rate
84%	Four-Year Graduation Rate
88%	Financial Aid Applicants Receiving Aid

Students Speak Out
SAFETY & SECURITY

Q "I'd say **the campus is very safe**. Campus police are very receptive to safety suggestions, and I never feel nervous about leaving my door unlocked or walking around at night alone."

Q "The **dorms aren't secure** at all; the alarms go off constantly, and everyone ignores them."

Q "Wellesley is known as the '**Wellesley bubble**,' and I truly feel like I live in a place that is almost impenetrable to the outside world."

Q "Campus Po spends **more time breaking up parties on weekends** and handing out parking tickets than they actually do keeping anyone out of harm's way."

STUDENT AUTHOR: **The bells system, desk workers in the dorms, is under fire from those who say it's unnecessary and those who argue that it is not strict enough. The Horizontal-Vertical rule is supposed to keep unescorted guests from roaming floor to floor. Stray men are usually rounded up quickly.**

Questions?
For more inside information and survival tips, pick up College Prowler's full-length book on this school, written by an actual student! Check it out at *www.collegeprowler.com*.

Students Speak Out
ON OVERALL EXPERIENCE

Q "I made the right decision in coming here. I have **grown intellectually and personally**, met amazing people, and my outlook on life has changed completely. I think more critically, I feel more confident, and I have developed a passion for learning that I hope I will continue to foster throughout my life."

Q "Most of the time, I'm happy to be at Wellesley. The **social scene is skewed** and makes me wonder if I'll be able to function normally after I graduate. But you work with what you're given."

Q "I really enjoy Wellesley, despite the iniquities of the weather. The **school is superb**, and Boston is a fantastic city."

Q "I would guess that most every Wellesley student has **seriously contemplated transferring**, probably a number of times. A lot of people have a real love-hate relationship with the place."

STUDENT AUTHOR: **So the nightlife stinks, it's too darn strict, and students constantly battle the fear of four years of celibacy. Hold on, why do we love this place again? Oh, right—the academics rock, it's possible to make shockingly amazing friends, the campus is gorgeous, and graduates wind up with a prestigious name on their diplomas. A community like Wellesley would be difficult to achieve in a coed environment, because living at Wellesley is like living with 2,300 sisters—you complain, you fight, and you talk about sex in ridiculously frank ways. You hate and love each other at the same time. Wellesley is intense and bizarre, both restrictive and liberating. Students learn to adapt, or they learn to overcome.**

Wesleyan University

237 High Street; Middletown, CT 06459
(860) 685-2000; www.wesleyan.edu

THE BASICS:

Acceptance Rate: 27%
Setting: Small city
F-T Undergrads: 2,796

SAT Range: 1300–1490*
Control: Private
Tuition: $38,364

Most Popular Majors: Social Sciences, Area/Ethnic Studies, Visual/Performing Arts, Psychology, English

*of 1600

Academics	A-	Guys	C
Local Atmosphere	C-	Girls	C
Safety & Security	C+	Athletics	C-
Computers	B+	Nightlife	C-
Facilities	B	Greek Life	C
Campus Dining	B	Drug Scene	C+
Off-Campus Dining	B	Campus Strictness	B
Campus Housing	B	Parking	B
Off-Campus Housing	B	Transportation	C-
Diversity	B+	Weather	C+

Students Speak Out
ON ACADEMICS

Q "I wasn't overly impressed with the professors here. There was **definitely some condescension** there. I think there's a bit of a snob thing going on at Wesleyan, and the professors feed into it. If you're not the typical Wes student, watch out!"

Q "I got to stay at Wes one summer and worked on research with a few of the professors in the biology department. That was a **wonderful experience**. The faculty is always open to working with students like that."

Q "The professors range from good to amazing. I've **had some wonderful experiences** with the Russian department (none involving Smirnov Vodka, I assure you). For the most part, professors teach their classes, not too much of that 'the TA will handle everything' kind of stuff that you get at large state universities."

Q "Most of the professors here are excellent. Occasionally, there are some professors who are better suited to do their research rather than actually teach. All are invested in what they study, but **not all are as inspiring in the classroom** as others."

STUDENT AUTHOR: While the Wesleyan work load is often tremendous (up to 150 pages of reading a day for some upper-level courses), Wesleyan allows for an unprecedented degree of academic freedom. The course load for the typical Wesleyan student is four classes per semester. However, many students take on an additional music or art course, resulting in less study time.

Students Speak Out
ON LOCAL ATMOSPHERE

Q "Middletown has what you need, and not much more. There are a couple **nice restaurants** and a movie theater, but for the most part students stay on campus or go to New York on the weekends."

Q "Middletown is **not a college town**. Period. Even if I lost a couple of fingers in a mining incident, I could still count all the bars in town on one hand. The upside, however, is that this fact is irrelevant. The campus is lively enough. There's always something going on, and it's small enough that you can pretty much make your way anywhere without much hassle."

Q "New attractions are always opening up in Middletown. There's an arts center on Green Street, and Destinta Theater is fantastic. There's not much of a nightlife, but campus offers pretty much **everything you need** as far as parties go. There's a bar or two in town, but they're seedy."

Q "Stay away from Middletown. That's all you need to know. This place is **crawling with odd people**. And not the good kind of odd, either. Most of them hate Wes students, so it's a good idea to avoid town altogether."

STUDENT AUTHOR: Middletown appears to be a quaint riverside community, not unlike a Norman Rockwell depiction. However, that whimsical, small-town ambiance exists only there. At night, crime is prevalent, especially immediately surrounding the University, and an underlying tension between the townspeople and the University can occasionally rear its ugly head.

Students Speak Out
ON FACILITIES

Q "There **isn't enough space** to hang out and eat, and what space they do have isn't utilized much."

Q "I don't play sports, but I can say that the exercise room at the gym is amazing! Really, really, amazing. The **libraries are wonderful**. They're great places to hang out, work, and do just about anything. The administration is always updating the University, and progress can be found at *www.wesleyan.edu/masterplan*."

Q "I don't know anything about the athletic facilities, other than they're **located in a castle**, which is awesome. The student centers are nice because they have pretty much everything you need: mail, money, and food."

Q "Facilities at Wesleyan aren't bad. The Center for the Arts is the best group of facilities on campus. That's where the cinema and theaters are located. The **CFA is really state-of the-art**. Wesleyan is an art-oriented school, so it makes sense that these are the best-kept facilities. Olin Library houses a collection of over one million titles, including a special collections archive with texts dating back to the 15th century."

STUDENT AUTHOR: **Sitting in a Wesleyan facility, a student will occasionally get the feeling that he or she is being catered to the utmost extreme. The art, dance, and music studios in the Center for the Arts are numerous and spacious, as are the performance spaces. However, one of the downsides to Wesleyan's constant expansion and renewal is the omnipresence of construction equipment on and around campus.**

Famous Alumni

Randall Pinkston, Paul Schiff, Sara Shandler, Beverly D. Tatum, Michael Yamashita, John Yang

Students Speak Out
ON CAMPUS DINING

Q "Food on campus isn't all that bad. It isn't great either. **The real bonus is WesShop**. It's basically a little corner store that operates in the middle of campus."

Q "As a freshman, your social life revolves around MoCon. **MoCon food is pretty good**. There are usually lots of options (salads, sandwiches, pizzas, and grilled foods). However, after a few weeks you start to realize how limited these options really are. Yes, you can always get a hamburger, but how many times can you have a hamburger in one school year before you go totally nuts?"

Q "I'm told that, compared to other schools, Wesleyan food is great. I'm not so sure, though. There are **plenty of vegan options**."

Q "Wesleyan gouges you with their meal plans. The **food is extremely overpriced** and what's more, if you're a Wesleyan student, you must have a Wesleyan meal plan. This means that even if you're living in a Program House and want to buy food for your kitchen, you more or less have to buy it from the school. It's a raw deal man—a raw deal."

STUDENT AUTHOR: **While Wesleyan's food is far from gourmet, it is very much "above-average" compared to most colleges and universities. Wesleyan is a very vegetarian- and vegan-conscious school, so non-meat and non-dairy options are always available, as are Kosher selections. Students can also choose from an entrée of the day, cold-cut sandwiches, pizza, a salad bar, ice cream, grill favorites, and even late-night eating options.**

Student Body

African American:	7%	Male/Female:	49/51%
Asian American:	11%	Out-of-State:	92%
Hispanic:	8%	International:	6%
Native American:	1%	Unknown:	6%
White:	61%		

Popular Faiths: Christianity, Judaism, Islam, and Buddhism are the most prevalent religions.

Gay Pride: While the administration has been accused of being homophobic, students are extremely open to homosexuality. Wesleyan offers a Queer Studies program and a Queer Alumi network.

Economic Status: As a private school, the majority of students are middle- or upper-middle class.

Students Speak Out
ON DORMS

Q "I think the dorms are great, mostly because there are **a lot of singles**, particularly in the Foss Hill dorms. WestCo has a wonderful sense of community."

Q "It's definitely the center of social life on Foss Hill. There was **always something going on**. Occasionally, it drove me nuts; it was impossible to get to sleep at times, with all the yelling and banging. For the most part though, it was fantastic. There's a big sense of dorm community and lots of dorm-centered activities if you're into that sort of thing."

Q "All the dorms here are decent, but I'd **recommend not living in the Butts** freshman year, just because they're a little out of the way."

Q "**WestCo is the best (Co)**. Clark is adequate for a dorm that looks like a hospital."

STUDENT AUTHOR: **For incoming freshmen, social life is centered around Foss Hill, where all students are assigned rooms during their first year. Though the social scene changes from year-to-year, there is a definite personality or, in some cases, a stigma attached to each dorm.**

> **Did You Know?**
> 99% of undergrads live on campus.

Students Speak Out
ON GUYS & GIRLS

Q "The girls at Wesleyan are amazing. Everything from **tragically hip, to gothic, to psycho cheerleader**. There are very few ditzy girls here. They're all brilliant, which can be so attractive in itself. There are also lots of flowing scarves and pseudo-hippie garb. I love it."

Q "Guys at Wes can be overly-sensitive, post-feminism types, but the girls often demand that. There seems to be a **large lesbian contingency** on campus, so I guess it's safe to say that guys don't make the grade for some girls."

Q "I get the feeling a lot of Wesleyan kids were **picked on in high school**."

Q "Guys: Long hair, beards, unwashed. Girls: **short hair, unshaven, unwashed**."

STUDENT AUTHOR: **Wesleyan is not widely recognized for the attractiveness of its students. The student body represents a wide spectrum of body and personality types. It's an extremely open place, which basically means that there is a lot of free love going on. Although there is the occasional relationship drama that happens at any university, there is also a considerable 'no fuss, no muss' mentality. This is college, after all.**

> **Traditions**
>
> **Wes Fest**
> Incoming freshmen are shown exhibits, taken tours of campus, and are lectured to by bright intellectuals.
>
> **The Douglas Cannon**
> The cannon, which appears in bizarre places, is traditionally stolen by students as a rite of passage.
>
> **Overall School Spirit**
> While traditional school spirit in the "ra-ra," banner waving sense is sparse at Wesleyan, the traditionally rebellious attitude of the student body exemplifies most enthusiasm for the school as an institution.

Students Speak Out
ON ATHLETICS

Q "**IM sports are pretty big** because a lot of people like to just round the court and play and not be competitive. Varsity sports are only big for a small crowd of students we call 'jocks.'"

Q "There's a **huge Frisbee following** at Wesleyan. I've heard of one kid who actually majored in Frisbee. There are a couple of ultimate Frisbee teams—men's, women's, and coed."

Q "You can find a good intramural team if you'd like, and take it as seriously as you want. As for varsity sports, **I never see the football team**, except on homecoming."

Q "**I wish we had some cheerleaders**."

STUDENT AUTHOR: **There is a running joke that Wesleyan harbors a secret underground legion of sports fanatics, the idea being that no one ever sees them because they hide in the weight room. Needless to say, the general consensus is that Wesleyan is not a sports-oriented school. In fact, the Wesleyan student body is composed almost entirely of kids who were picked last in gym class. Those who are athletes tend to set up their own society on the fringes of the University.**

Students Speak Out
ON DRUG SCENE

Q "Lots of drugs. **Everywhere, there are drugs**. It's a drug mentality. A lot of people smoke pot here. There's no way around that."

Q "I do drugs, and I feel like the scene at Wesleyan is **pretty tame**. There's a hardcore drug scene, but it's pretty subdued. You don't see it if you're not part of it."

Q "Most people have a 'live and let live' attitude at Wes. Not everyone does drugs, but most people aren't really opposed to them either. It's an individual choice, of course. The people who take drugs, they're **not out there pushing them** on anyone else. They want the drugs for themselves, after all."

STUDENT AUTHOR: **Let's face it—at any environmentally conscious, extremely liberal, arts-centered university, you're going to find a large amount of drugs. The drug scene at Wesleyan includes everything from excessive amounts of caffeine to heroin. Most common is illegal and excessive consumption of alcohol. However, students here feel no pressure.**

9:1	Student-to-Faculty Ratio
94%	Freshman Retention Rate
84%	Four-Year Graduation Rate
92%	Financial Aid Applicants Receiving Aid

Students Speak Out
SAFETY & SECURITY

Q "I personally feel extremely safe; you can walk around campus alone at night and **feel completely safe**. If you don't want to go somewhere alone at night, then you can just call public safety, and they will give you a ride."

Q "There have been **a few incidents of burglary**, but really not many, and most involved people who were in town at night. As long as you use common sense, there's really no danger anywhere on campus."

Q "Every year we get a mass e-mail from the administration about a 'rash of thefts' occurring around campus. The good news is that Public Safety usually turns the other cheek. The bad news is **your stuff might get stolen**. It's the price you pay for going to a laid-back school."

STUDENT AUTHOR: **Campus security is a tense issue at Wesleyan. While the campus appears clean and idyllic, there is a disturbingly high crime rate in and around Wesleyan. The majority of Middletown residents are good, friendly people, but there is a criminal element that finds its way onto campus.**

Questions?
For more inside information and survival tips, pick up College Prowler's full-length book on this school, written by an actual student! Check it out at *www.collegeprowler.com*.

Students Speak Out
ON OVERALL EXPERIENCE

Q "Wesleyan is not for everybody. It's not a 'typical college,' if there is such a thing. It's very eccentric and very artsy. It's **a place for creative people**, a place where they can grow and flourish. It's for open-minded people, people with a sense of humor. It's not for the faint of heart."

Q "I only wish the the lackluster atmosphere and sports teams at Wesleyan matched the school's academic intensity. Many times, I felt myself **longing for that 'big-school' feel**."

Q "It's an incredible school, bottom line. The degree to which you can **control your own academics** is fantastic. The school places all the power in your hands, and I really value that. The classes are amazing and so are the professors. I loved it."

Q "Wesleyan is a truly unique and wonderful place. It's so **open and accepting** of all sorts of ideas. If you're looking for new experiences in college, Wes is the place to be."

Q "I wasn't wild about Wesleyan at first. Everyone I met was so eccentric and over-the-top I thought it couldn't be real. There are **some fakers out there**, but for the most part, Wesleyan is filled with some really wonderful people."

STUDENT AUTHOR: **At Wes, one has the room to try many new things, and I'm not just talking about the drugs. I'm talking about music you've never heard before, ideas you've never considered, people so fascinating and different from one another you can't believe they all exist in the same place. Wesleyan is for students with open minds, who love to think, who love art and music, theater and film, and literature and experimentation.**

West Point Military Academy

600 Thayer Road, West Point, NY 10996
(845) 938-4041; www.usma.edu

THE BASICS:

Acceptance Rate: 16%
Setting: Suburban
F-T Undergrads: 4,553

SAT Range: 1150–1350*
Control: Public
Tuition: Free

Most Popular Majors: Economics, Political Science, Aerospace Engineering, Civil Engineering

*of 1600

Academics	B	Guys	B
Local Atmosphere	C+	Girls	C
Safety & Security	A+	Athletics	B+
Computers	A-	Nightlife	D+
Facilities	B+	Greek Life	N/A
Campus Dining	C	Drug Scene	A+
Off-Campus Dining	D+	Campus Strictness	F
Campus Housing	D	Parking	D
Off-Campus Housing	N/A	Transportation	B-
Diversity	C-	Weather	C+

Students Speak Out
ON ACADEMICS

Q "At West Point, you take a lot of classes and receive **a very broad education**, but you don't really study anything in depth. It is like they want to develop every little corner of your brain or something."

Q "After visiting the campus, **I was absolutely amazed** at how committed the entire faculty was to the success of every single cadet."

Q "Every instructor seems to think that their subject is more important than any other. It is like if you don't know astrophysics and can't make at least a C in my class, then you are not going to be a good officer. **It gets real annoying**, fast."

Q "Based on my experiences, I would say that the **civilian professors are generally better instructors** than the captains or majors who come back to the academy to teach. For the majority of officers, this is just another two to three year assignment."

STUDENT AUTHOR: **Most students at West Point feel that academics are both challenging and competitive. The professors are there to teach and not to do research. As a result, they are more than willing to go out of their way to help students, as long as the students themselves are willing to expend the necessary effort. The poise and professionalism associated with the military is definitely present in the classroom. Succeeding academically at West Point involves two major skills: working with other people and managing time.**

Students Speak Out
ON LOCAL ATMOSPHERE

Q "A lot of cadets find it strange **how much of a tourist attraction West Point actually is**. It is not uncommon to go for a jog or to just walk to class and have someone ask to have your picture taken."

Q "Definitely not like most colleges. There really is no 'college town,' and there aren't really any bars or cultural places to go to, either. Most colleges have some nice little cafés where you can socialize, but **there is absolutely nothing here**. Besides all the Army hooah stuff, there is absolutely nothing."

Q "With the exception of a museum and a pizza restaurant called Shades, there is almost nothing in Highland Falls. **West Point is very isolated**, and until you are an upperclassmen, the regimented schedule won't allow you to do much outside of what is within walking distance, so odds are that you are not going to have a lot of interaction with students from other universities."

Q "**No clubs**, plus a few bars, plus only 15 percent female cadets, equals a lot of male cadets looking at porn."

STUDENT AUTHOR: **The majority of the students at West Point are fully enamored with the Academy and are simply amazed at how beautiful campus is. However, almost no one is impressed with the town of Highland Falls; attractions and entertainment are few and far-between. Even if you did want to get out there, cadets at West Point have little time for wandering around outside of campus.**

5 Best Things	5 Worst Things
1 Unlimited opportunities	1 Missing sleep
2 Campus is beautiful	2 Drill
3 It's free	3 "Mandatory fun"
4 Guaranteed job	4 Bad weather
5 Instructors really care	5 Schedule is grueling

Students Speak Out
ON FACILITIES

Q "**Everything is gray**. If you like stone gray, then you will like it here. All of the buildings look the same on the outside, but once you step foot inside, many of them are absolutely amazing."

Q "The gym has **everything that you could possibly want**. There is a track, racquetball courts, basketball courts, squash courts, handball and volleyball courts, rooms to practice combatives, rooms with wrestling mats, weight rooms, swimming pools—everything."

Q "Eisenhower Hall is **pretty cool**. Every year they have about 60 or so major productions, which include Broadway shows, musicals, and popular rock, jazz, country western, and alternative concerts."

Q "The **classrooms are very small**. The majority of them hold maybe two dozen students, max."

Q "This place sucks! **There are very few places to hang out** and chill with friends. It is like everything that you do here has to be good for your development."

STUDENT AUTHOR: Students are more than content with the quality of the facilities at West Point. According to the majority of the cadets, West Point is trying to do everything that it can to ensure that its facilities are as up to date as possible so that they can continue to attract top athletes and students. As with any college campus, some students will complain about crowds, no matter how many facilities there are available. Whatever you're into, there's a good chance that West Point provides it.

Famous Alumni

Dwight D. Eisenhower, Ulysses S. Grant, Mike Krzyzewski, Robert E. Lee, Ryan P. Peckyno, Norman Schwarzkopf, George H. Thomas

Students Speak Out
ON CAMPUS DINING

Q "Compared to most schools, **the food sucks**. But hell, when you are in the Army you are not going to get the best food either, so you have to get used to it."

Q "You better like pasta, because that is what they feed you at the mess hall. Although eating at the mess hall allows you to save money, you will quickly find yourself **tired of eating the same meals** over and over again."

Q "Besides the mess hall, there are four places where you can eat on campus: Grant Hall, where **you can get subs** and sampler-type food; Eisenhower Hall, where you can get the same type of finger food; and the Firstie Club, where you go to eat wings and get drunk."

Q "The **food is all right**, tolerable. Every dinner buffet seems to have the same thing—rice, noodles, salad, fruit, and cake."

Q "**The setup of the mess hall is perfect**—it allows you to either sit down and eat a quick dinner, or if you are really strapped for time, take dinner back with you to your room."

STUDENT AUTHOR: Students seem to tolerate the food at West Point, and the accent is on the word tolerate. The meals at the Academy are certainly nothing to write home about. Maybe the administration is just cheap, or maybe they're trying to prepare cadets for life in the Army. Whatever the reason, cadets can be sure their meals will be filling if nothing else. There is a clear difference in quality and variety on special days.

Student Body

African American:	6%	Male/Female:	85/15%
Asian American:	7%	Out-of-State:	92%
Hispanic:	6%	International:	1%
Native American:	1%	Unknown:	0%
White:	79%		

Popular Faiths: The most popular religions are Catholic and Protestant.

Minority Clubs: There are several minority clubs on campus, like the Asian-Pacific Club and the National Society for Black Engineers.

Political Activity: Several different political beliefs are represented on campus by student groups.

Students Speak Out
ON DORMS

Q "Rooms are **pretty Spartan**. We're allowed to have a few photos, a CD player, stereo, radio, and personal computer, but no refrigerator, TV, or microwave."

Q "The rooms here are all right. Every cadet has a desk that has a computer and telephone. Each cadet has a section of the room that is his, and **each cadet is responsible for ensuring that the room is squared** away before going to class."

Q "The key about the barracks is that most of the **services are free**. For example, the Internet is free, and civilians do your laundry."

STUDENT AUTHOR: **When it comes to dorms, the majority of cadets believe that the barracks leave much to be desired. As a cadet, you have only the necessities. There are numerous rules and regulations that tell you what you can and cannot have, as well as how to arrange your room. The desired result is that everyone's room looks exactly the same. The barracks can be a very confining space. Often times, it feels like you're back home. The rooms also provide cadets with the technology they need.**

? Did You Know?
100% of undergrads live on campus.

Students Speak Out
ON GUYS & GIRLS

Q "West Point attracts **a very undesirable type of girl**. But for one reason or another, they all seem to have boyfriends. Explain that one to me."

Q "The guys here are all studs. Take me for example; I am 145 pounds of **raw steel and sex appeal**. West Point definitely has the studliest guys on the face of the planet."

Q "A large percentage of the girls here are fairly attractive, but **you are not even cognizant of the fact that they are girls** when you see them in a military environment."

Q "You see **a fair amount of female plebes** who seem to fall for some of their leadership."

STUDENT AUTHOR: **Most cadets seem to agree that there is a wide range of attractive coeds at West Point. This is in no small part due to the overall physical fitness of the campus. The Army is not quick to let you slide out of shape, for practical purposes, but this definitely factors into physical appearances of members of the opposite sex. The majority of cadets do, however, believe that the guys are, on average, better looking than the girls.**

Traditions

Minutes
Plebes have a rotating responsibility to announce ten, five, four, three, two, and one minute before formation, in a strictly formatted ritual known as "minutes."

Overall School Spirit
Through a combination of shared hardships, shared competition, and what cadets like to call "mandatory fun," the student body learns to compete and work with one another to achieve a common goal.

Students Speak Out
ON ATHLETICS

Q "Army teams compete on the NCAA Division IA intercollegiate level, both regionally and nationally, in **25 men's and women's sports**. About 30 percent of the Corps of Cadets are intercollegiate athletes."

Q "Everyone here is in really great shape. West Point is a great place to try new things. **Last year I learned how to ski** and play racquetball. This year, I want to learn how to play squash."

Q "A lot of our teams suck, but **they all play with a lot of heart**. Then again, you have to take into consideration the fact that we only have like 4,000 cadets here, while several of the colleges that we compete against have tens of thousands."

STUDENT AUTHOR: **Everyone at West Point participates in numerous varsity or intramural sports. There are several courses that are required, such as boxing, wrestling, combatives, swimming, gymnastics, as well as a lifetime sport. Intramurals and pick-up games are huge at West Point. Since so many of the cadets were athletes in high school, it is really easy to play just about any sport.**

Students Speak Out
ON DRUG SCENE

Q "The main concern is not drugs on campus, but rather drugs off campus. Cadets always try to make the most of the leave that they get— **maybe too much, sometimes**."

Q "A lot of the cadets at West Point take Creatine, as well as **other supplemental drugs**. Every now and then you will hear about a cadet who took ripped fuel or an acidic supplement and pissed hot because of the supplement."

Q "**Drugs are not a concern**, whatsoever. The closest thing to drugs is tobacco. After Buckner, you start to see some cadets start to dip."

STUDENT AUTHOR: **Drugs are not a concern at all. Because of the contained environment, the only time that cadets really even have access to drugs is when they are on leave. After every block leave, there is usually a drug test, so if a cadet does drugs while they are on leave, there is a very good chance that they will get caught. And if a cadet gets caught, he will be dismissed. It's a very simple policy at West Point—absolutely no drugs allowed.**

7:1	Student-to-Faculty Ratio
91%	Freshman Retention Rate
76%	Four-Year Graduation Rate
N/A	Financial Aid Applicants Receiving Aid

Students Speak Out
SAFETY & SECURITY

Q "There are **different levels of security taken**, depending on the current threat level. The levels of security here are generally much tighter than anywhere else."

Q "The Cadet Honor Code states that '**a cadet will not lie**, cheat, steal, or tolerate those who do.' Cadets police their own ranks."

Q "This is something that definitely makes this place special. Everyone here is completely trustworthy. **We have to trust each other**. When you leave this place, you are in charge of millions of dollars worth of equipment and, more importantly, the sons and daughters of American citizens."

STUDENT AUTHOR: **Students definitely feel safe at West Point. There are numerous checks and balances in place to ensure that the campus is safe. On top of all of the external security measures combined, every cadet considers him or herself a security officer.**

Questions?
For more inside information and survival tips, pick up College Prowler's full-length book on this school, written by an actual student! Check it out at *www.collegeprowler.com*.

Students Speak Out
ON OVERALL EXPERIENCE

Q "Life is **definitely more concentrated here**. A famous saying is that we experience more in a day than most college students experience in a week."

Q "It is important to remember that the four year West Point experience is just that—**four years, around the clock**. After the academic year is over, be ready for the summers, because there is little to no vacation time. The summers are when you get the bulk of your military training."

Q "You have to compete with everybody at everything. But competition does not override the need for teamwork. '**Cooperate and graduate**' is one of the most popular sayings at West Point, because this is a tough place to get through all on your own."

Q "I think my educational experience is far better than most of my friends at other colleges. And, I got it at a much better price! **This great education is free**. You have to work hard and be willing to serve your country."

Q "West Point crams as much as possible into the four-year experience. **You make a lot of sacrifices**, but you also get rewarded with opportunities. The first year sucks—no doubt about it. Cadet Basic Training is a little over six weeks, and it is not fun. But it is not supposed to be fun, either. You learn basic soldier skills, how to follow, and how to perform under stress. The second summer is a little better; you get to go to Fort Knox, where you are introduced to small-unit tactics and begin to gain a combined arms perspective. After the second summer, you have a lot of say as to how you spend your summers, which is a very good thing."

West Virginia University

53 Campus Drive; Morgantown, WV 26506-6201
(304) 293-0111; www.wvu.edu

THE BASICS:

Acceptance Rate: 92%
Setting: Rural
F-T Undergrads: 19,407

SAT Range: 940–1140*
Control: Public
Tuition: $13,840

Most Popular Majors: Business, Engineering, Liberal Arts, Communications

*of 1600

Academics	B-	Guys	B
Local Atmosphere	B+	Girls	B+
Safety & Security	B+	Athletics	A-
Computers	B	Nightlife	A
Facilities	A-	Greek Life	B
Campus Dining	C	Drug Scene	B
Off-Campus Dining	B+	Campus Strictness	B-
Campus Housing	B-	Parking	D
Off-Campus Housing	B	Transportation	B
Diversity	D-	Weather	C

Students Speak Out
ON ACADEMICS

Q "The teachers whom I have had experience with are all very good. Most are concerned with the success of their students and show it by having office hours for help and giving **good feedback on tests and papers**."

Q "In my experience, the **quality of teachers really ranges**. There are some really wonderful teachers who reach out and care that the students learn the material. There are others who just teach because it's a requirement of being employed at the University."

Q "Once you start taking classes in your major, it seems the teachers and classes are better. Other times, **it's hit or miss**."

Q "For the most part, the teachers are really good. Most like to see students succeed, and they **make an effort to teach the material well**."

STUDENT AUTHOR: Most students say that with the right teachers, their classes are great and worthwhile. There is not a large personal relationship between students and teachers until the students get into their major core classes. Once a student reaches those courses, the class sizes are usually smaller, which offers a more intimate setting where students can interact with their professor more easily. Some professors prefer not to give any work outside of class and just have the grade depend on a certain number of quizzes and exams. Generally, the workload is enough that students must put in enough time, or they will not make the grade.

Students Speak Out
ON LOCAL ATMOSPHERE

Q "There is almost always **a good and upbeat atmosphere around campus**, except after a football loss of course."

Q "It's a fun atmosphere in Morgantown, at least around campus, since it's **mostly college students**. Once you get out further, it becomes more like a normal town."

Q "I love the atmosphere here. **Everything you need is within a short walk away**. Plus, there is plenty to do here like nightclubs, the Rec Center, movies, and a lot of restaurants."

Q "With almost 20,000 students, it's **definitely a big college town**, and everything here is focused on the University. Downtown, there is more of a party atmosphere because of all the bars and nightclubs. The other two campuses are home to most of the professional students, and it's a whole different atmosphere."

STUDENT AUTHOR: It is absolutely evident that Morgantown is a huge college town. Even with a large part of the population being made up of students, Morgantown residents share as much school pride as students do. There is really no separation between students and residents, as they all share the same town, and they all get along together. One of the reasons for such a great atmosphere is the common love students and residents have for West Virginia football. Morgantown is also very safe throughout the day and night. The town is well lit, and there is really no unsafe area that students need to avoid.

Students Speak Out
ON CAMPUS DINING

Q "Dorm food . . . eww! **It gets pretty bland after a while**, but there is usually something worth eating."

Q "The on-campus food **could definitely use some work**."

Q "**It's best to eat at the Mountainlair** if you have time. You can use your meal plan most places. It is good food, unlike the majority of the meals at the dining hall."

Q "**Food on campus is not too bad**. Stalnaker has the best food for dining halls."

Q "**Beware of the all-you-can-eat buffets** in all the dining halls because they are the main factor in the Freshman 15!"

STUDENT AUTHOR: There are certainly a lot of options available for students to use their meal plans, but it seems that each place serves similar food. Students grow tired of the never-changing menu after eating the same meal three or four times a week. Even though the dining halls are all-you-can-eat, many students have trouble getting anything down with the lack of variety. The food served by campus dining is not exactly the healthiest option available. They will prepare vegetarian or other special requests, but they don't really go out of their way to provide a better choice for students who may be looking for healthier entrees. Freshmen, as well as anyone else living in dorms, are required to have a meal plan but can pick the smallest one if they feel it will be adequate for their needs.

Students Speak Out
ON FACILITIES

Q "There is a state-of-the-art rec center and library. There are also **many historical buildings** in which classes are held, which are also really nice. Students have it good here."

Q "The athletic facilities, like Milan Puskar Stadium and the Coliseum, are the **perfect venues** for college sporting activities."

Q "**The Rec Center is one of the best I have ever seen**. The library is also really nice. They kept the original Evansdale Library from when it was first built and added onto it in 2000."

Q "The facilities on campus are **always clean and well kept**."

Q "The **Mountainlair is a great student center** providing us with places to socialize, as well as eat and do work."

STUDENT AUTHOR: The facilities on campus truly are state-of-the-art and play a pivotal role in the lives of the students. The best facilities on campus are the Mountainlair and the Student Rec Center. The Mountainlair is truly the definition of a student union, as it has many facets that bring students together. Inside, students can find a food court, bowling alley, pool hall, video arcade, movie theater, and a radio station. There is also a large study area and a wireless hotspot for students that wish to use the building to study. There are several small convenience stores around campus that can provide students with things they need. Being that the campus is a huge part of town, there isn't really anything that either the campus or town lacks because they are joined together.

Students Speak Out
ON DORMS

Q "**Most freshmen live in Towers** because it houses many students, making it a great place to meet people during your first year. The only downfall of Towers is that it is located on Evansdale campus, which means you need to take the PRT to class everyday."

Q "**Stalnaker is awesome**, and Towers is too far away."

Q "The dorms provide a safe place to live, and freshman year, and **they are a good place to meet new friends**."

STUDENT AUTHOR: The dormitories on campus at WVU are in great shape and are excellent places for students to live. The rooms are of decent size, with new bed frames, desks, and dressers provided for the students. The carpets and walls are also in good condition and provide an all around good feel to the dorms. Every room is wired for cable TV and Internet. Dorm security of the dorms is very good, but it can sometimes be an issue of annoyance with the students. Students are required to present an ID after 9 p.m. in most dorms and can not sign in a guest after midnight on the weekends.

Did You Know?
27% of undergrads live on campus.

Students Speak Out
ON GUYS & GIRLS

Q "There are **a lot of good-looking people** here. Let's just say I'm not complaining about the scenery!"

Q "There are **many different varieties of people** here. If you know what you are looking for, I'm sure you will find it."

Q "There's a **very nice population of guys** on campus, and yes, they are hot."

Q "There are **generally good-looking girls**, and there is really a lot of different girls to choose from."

Q "There are so many different types of people here that **there is someone for everyone**."

STUDENT AUTHOR: The social scene on campus is very strong. Students at WVU are both socially and academically minded. They work hard during the day and party harder at night. One thing to remember is there are rules in the dorms about having members of the opposite sex in your room. During the day, anyone can be in the dorms, but during the evening, the rules become more strict. The ratio of males to females is almost even, so competition is minimal for the sexes.

Traditions

The Mountaineer
It is tradition for him to shoot off his musket during athletic events when a team scores, or to lead the team out onto the field.

Mountaineer Week
There are crafts, folk music players, a beard growing contest, and a contest to see how many students can fit into a PRT car.

Overall School Spirit
Students here love their school and their sports teams, and they are not afraid to show their appreciation.

Students Speak Out
ON ATHLETICS

Q "**Varsity sports are very big** at WVU. The football and basketball teams bring in the largest number of fans, but many other sports are fun to attend also."

Q "Needless to say, **WVU football is the biggest campus varsity sport**."

Q "**Sports are huge here**. Football games are the biggest thing in the state. Intramural sports are available, but they aren't overly huge."

Q "There are **a lot of intramural sports** you can sign up for at the Rec Center."

STUDENT AUTHOR: Sports garner a lot of attention and love from not only the students at WVU, but the surrounding community members, as well. There are no professional sports teams in the state of West Virginia, so the Mountaineers are the next best thing. Fan support for the University's athletic teams is extremely high, and the students take as much pride in the teams as the players do. Intramural sports are popular at WVU, but not overly anticipated. There are several sports offered in male, female, and coed leagues during all seasons of the year.

Students Speak Out
ON DRUG SCENE

💬 "Drugs are probably a problem that isn't very public because people aren't getting caught very much. **I'm sure a lot of kids do them**, though."

💬 "**Drugs are readily available**, and they can be easy to acquire if one puts effort into it."

💬 "It's **not a big thing around here**. Of course, there's a lot of drinking going on here, but that is all I hear about."

💬 "If there is a huge drug scene, **it is not very public**. I'm sure kids do drugs, but alcohol is much more apparent."

STUDENT AUTHOR: The substance that is most abused on campus is alcohol. Alcohol is easy to access, and students take advantage of it, sometimes taking it too far. There is alcohol at almost every party, and of course in the bars. There is always a chance for peer pressure, but there is enough of a non-using student body that students can feel comfortable saying no. Overall, the drug scene is not very prevalent at WVU.

22:1	Student-to-Faculty Ratio
81%	Freshman Retention Rate
25%	Four-Year Graduation Rate
85%	Financial Aid Applicants Receiving Aid

Students Speak Out
SAFETY & SECURITY

💬 "The security is good, as they are out at night watching the town, and there are **plenty of emergency call-boxes** all over campus."

💬 "The University has implemented **a system of blue towers placed around campus** with buttons on them to connect you to the police. If there is an emergency, officers are dispatched immediately. This is reassuring."

💬 "**I feel very safe here**. At any given time, there are students walking up and down the streets going to class or to eat."

💬 "**Campus police are always right around the corner if you need help**, though their main focus seems to be ticketing illegally parked cars!"

STUDENT AUTHOR: If there is any type of emergency, police are quickly dispatched and arrive in a timely manner, giving students a good sense of security. There are also many blue-light emergency phones all over campus, so students have many outlets to contact someone if they do need help.

> **Questions?**
> For more inside information and survival tips, pick up College Prowler's full-length book on this school, written by an actual student! Check it out at *www.collegeprowler.com*.

Students Speak Out
ON OVERALL EXPERIENCE

💬 "**I have enjoyed my experience at WVU** so far. I enjoy the campus and the atmosphere of a country school. I am definitely glad I go here. The great social scene doesn't hurt, either."

💬 "**I cannot complain about anything**. College is supposed to be the best years of your life, and WVU is making it happen."

💬 "I love WVU. **I wouldn't go anywhere else**."

💬 "Sometimes, it would be nice to be closer to home, but **it's worth it to be here** because I think I'm getting a great education."

STUDENT AUTHOR: Overall, students have made it pretty clear that they are really enjoying their time at WVU. It is also evident that the campus dining services are not doing a great job pleasing the students, and the parking situation on campus isn't getting any better. Considering these are two pretty important things on a college campus, the University should quickly take the right steps to move those two issues in a positive direction. The attitude at WVU seems pretty split between academics and social events. While most students attend WVU with the expectation of a great education, there are a select few who come to WVU because of the potential party scene. Either way, WVU offers something for each side. The academic programs are showing promise as more WVU grads are gaining recognition for their accomplishments. WVU is a student-oriented university, and should be considered by incoming freshmen who want to be treated to a great college education and experience.

Wheaton College (IL)

501 College Avenue; Wheaton, IL 60187-5593
(630) 752-5000; www.wheaton.edu

THE BASICS:

Acceptance Rate: 62%
Setting: Suburban
F-T Undergrads: 2,288

SAT Range: 1810–2100*
Control: Private
Tuition: $25,500

Most Popular Majors: Social Sciences, Education, Theology and Religion, English, Business

*of 2400

Academics	B+	Guys	A-
Local Atmosphere	B+	Girls	A-
Safety & Security	A	Athletics	B+
Computers	C-	Nightlife	C
Facilities	B	Greek Life	N/A
Campus Dining	C+	Drug Scene	A
Off-Campus Dining	A	Campus Strictness	B
Campus Housing	A-	Parking	B-
Off-Campus Housing	C	Transportation	B+
Diversity	D	Weather	D

Students Speak Out
ON ACADEMICS

Q "I love the teachers. **For the most part, they make the classes extremely interesting**. Of course, there is a spectrum of quality, but overall, the teachers do a wonderful job of making topics interesting."

Q "The teachers are **committed to integrating faith into their disciplines** and usually active in their fields of study. The majority is sympathetic to the personal needs and crises of their students, and the majority of my classes are interesting."

Q "I think the professors are one of the greatest aspects of Wheaton. Most of my professors see teaching at Wheaton as more than a job—it's a calling. **I have never felt like teaching was a low priority**, or that the professor was too focused on research."

Q "The profs at Wheaton are great. They are really personal and amiable towards the students. **They really care and pray for us**, which is unique. It's my theory that teachers either make or break a class, and at Wheaton, I think that most of them do a good job."

STUDENT AUTHOR: **The teachers at Wheaton are some of the finest scholars in their fields and display sincere devotion toward their students. While it has become cliché for students to constantly hear the school's catchphrase—the integration of faith and learning—the professors truly embrace it, desiring to see their students prosper in all of life's challenges, not just in academics.**

Students Speak Out
ON LOCAL ATMOSPHERE

Q "It has been a privilege to have had both the city of Wheaton and the city of Chicago as accessible points of travel during my time in Illinois. **Both are unique in their heritage**, and both offer unique perspectives into the larger created world."

Q "I love the atmosphere at Wheaton. **It's a friendly place to live**. Along with the beauty of the area also comes the fact that it's a rich community. That obviously can be seen by just driving around."

Q "Wheaton is a quiet, peaceful, family-dominated town. Unfortunately, everything closes at 9 p.m. To engage in any sort of nightlife off campus, downtown Naperville is a lively, close-by alternative. Additionally, the Metra stops on the south side of campus **allow students to be in downtown Chicago in 40 minutes**."

Q "**Wheaton has been called the'Mecca of Evangelical Christianity**,' but really, it's just an upper-middle-class suburb. It has a great library, a cute downtown area within walking distance, and nice restaurants--and it's very safe."

STUDENT AUTHOR: **Neighborhoods surrounding the school are mostly comprised of wealthy, white, church-going families (a.k.a. most of the Wheaton student body). Wheaton itself has a cozy small-town feel, with delightful parks and coffeeshops within walking distance. The cities surrounding Wheaton, namely Chicago and Naperville, are home to a much more culturally-enriching scene.**

5 Best Things	5 Worst Things
1 The students	**1** Parking tickets
2 The professors	**2** The weather
3 Spiritual atmosphere	**3** Inadequate library
4 Chicago is close by	**4** Lack of technology
5 Cafeteria food	**5** No frats or sororities

Students Speak Out
ON FACILITIES

Q "The facilities have improved dramatically over the last 10 years. **The athletic and student centers are state-of-the-art facilities**. However, the library lacks sufficient resources for all areas besides Bible and theology."

Q "Quite frankly, Wheaton is beautiful—**beautiful lawn, beautiful flowers, winding sidewalks**. It's a great layout. The Student Recreation Complex (SRC) is one of the best around, and the Beamer Student Center is phenomenal, well-equipped with air hockey, skylights, fireplaces, and really, really good grilled cheese."

Q "The athletic facility and student center are very nice, recently built, multi-million-dollar facilities. **The computers are a little outdated, but they get the job done**."

Q "Facilities are very conducive to the student body. **We have a great Sports and Recreation Complex**, with an intramural gym that has an elevated indoor track, three basketball courts, and a rock-climbing wall. Then, there's the weight room, pool, dance studio, and kick-boxing studio—really, it's physical fitness heaven."

STUDENT AUTHOR: **Wheaton's campus is very aesthetically pleasing. Everywhere you walk, there are grassy areas adorned with enchanting floral patterns. Nevertheless, the campus is not perfect. The Billy Graham Center is a complete architectural disaster inside, and everyone new to the building ends up asking for directions. All things considered, with such a small student body, the facilities are really quite impressive.**

Famous Alumni

Todd Beamer, Lisa Beamer, Dan Coats, Wes Craven, Jim Elliot, Michael Gerson, Billy Graham, Dennis Hastert, Todd Komarnicki, John Piper, John Nelson

Students Speak Out
ON CAMPUS DINING

Q "The food is great! **Almost all students have some kind of meal plan for all four years**, and the dining hall is a kind of hub to the campus. People that you might never see at any other time show up at meals—including professors."

Q "**The food is amazing**, although the other places, the Stupe and the Stupe Grill, don't have a lot of healthy options."

Q "I think it's truly remarkable how many healthy options there are at Wheaton. You definitely won't find that at many college campuses. Sure, there's tons of fantastic, artery-clogging stuff—crazy varieties of pizza, ice cream machines, burgers and fries—but there's also **two full salad bars, fruit bars, deli bars, and other stuff**."

Q "**The food on campus is nice, but overrated**. After eating there for three years, I just don't like it as much. The thing that bugs me is that all the food places are run by the same company, so there really isn't much variety, and all the food starts tasting the same."

STUDENT AUTHOR: **Wheaton has the distinct reputation of maintaining one of the best dining halls in the nation. The main dining hall, sponsored by Bon Appétit, is an all-you-can-eat buffet formally known as Anderson Commons, while students know it as SAGA. The downside of campus dining is that after the cafeteria closes, there is not much food variety. Still, you will find a significant number of students who put on their "Freshman 15" because they loved the food so much.**

Student Body

African American:	2%	Male/Female:	49/51%
Asian American:	7%	Out-of-State:	72%
Hispanic:	3%	International:	1%
Native American:	<1%	Unknown:	<1%
White:	87%		

Popular Faiths: Protestant Evangelical Christianity and Catholicism are the most popular.

Gay Pride: Although Wheaton doesn't have an official institutional stance on homosexuality, it informally stands with Church tradition, which is intolerant of all types of homosexual practice.

Economic Status: Wheaton College has students from diverse economic backgrounds.

Students Speak Out
ON DORMS

Q "Housing is good. It's tough to get off campus, but **I loved my on-campus apartment**. I think it's definitely worth it, and I'm looking forward to living on campus again my senior year."

Q "Don't miss out on the fun of dorm life. Don't worry: **there isn't any sex, drugs, or drinking**. There's just lots of fun times and typical college craziness. The RAs are superb."

Q "Both the freshman dorms are nice. All of the dorms have community bathrooms except for Fischer dorm. **People get really attached to their dorm**, and they have a lot of pride toward their dorm. So, that's kind of fun, I guess."

STUDENT AUTHOR: **All Wheaton freshmen are required to live in the dorms, and about 90 percent of the student body lives on campus. Although most college students would do anything to get off campus, housing at Wheaton is highly promoted and has profound effects on the social scene. Indeed, seniors still hang out with the people that were on their floors freshman year, and some coeds on brother-sister floors end up getting married.**

? Did You Know?
90% of undergrads live on campus.

Students Speak Out
ON GUYS & GIRLS

Q "**Most everyone at Wheaton, guys and girls alike, is very nice**. They care about your well-being and are willing to help in any way they can. As far as the dynamic between the two genders, it's like nothing I've ever seen before."

Q "**Pooling together 2,400 overachieving perfectionist Christians has some advantages**: there are lots of attractive people on campus. You can't be perfect if you aren't in shape, right?"

Q "The girls here are of a pretty good quality overall. There is definitely a large contingency that are quite good-looking, **but also many of them are very, very smart and personable** (not brainless ditzes). You'd find that most people here are pretty smart, and usually pretty driven."

STUDENT AUTHOR: **Everyone fits in at Wheaton. The student body is the friendliest you'll ever find. However, over the years, a stereotype has formed at Wheaton, making it very difficult to date around. The stereotype states, "Wheaton students only date if they're looking for a mate." Some say that a girl will not even let a guy take her out unless she can see herself marrying him.**

Traditions

Films Festival
An annual screening festival and awards ceremony for the best student-made films on campus.

Talent Show
The talent show on Parents Weekend is the most anticipated and attended event of the school year.

Overall School Spirit
Even though it has become cliché to call Wheaton the "Harvard of Evangelical Colleges," the students take pride in knowing that their school is Christian and does rank nationally in various academic categories.

Students Speak Out
ON ATHLETICS

Q "IM sports are the way to go. **Wheaton is definitely an IM sport school**. There is a big IM sports program offering two to five sports a season for all types of levels, coed and non-coed. There are always big turnouts and a lot of teams play. It is good competition. All the teams are out to win the coveted IM champion T-shirt. It's all about the T-shirt."

Q "**IM sports are bigger than the varsity sports**. Everyone participates in IM sports, and hardly anyone goes to varsity games, except for basketball."

Q "Wheaton pretty much **dominates D-III football, basketball, and soccer**. As for IMs, they are very popular—especially water polo and volleyball."

STUDENT AUTHOR: **All sports at Wheaton are often overtaken by the vast popularity of IM sports. All are beloved, but dodgeball, bowling, and water polo are some of the more obscure favorites. Everyone on a winning team of an IM sport, whether flag football or badminton, receives the coveted IM championship T-shirt, which has become incredibly popular among the students.**

Students Speak Out
ON DRUG SCENE

Q "**Drugs do happen**, but I don't hear much about it. Wheaton tries to get rid of it, but sometimes we just have to be realistic that Wheaton College is not sheltered from the world."

Q "Drugs are around. **It's pretty underground**, but if you want some, you can get some. A pretty low percentage of students actually use illegal drugs."

Q "Drugs? **I'm sure some people use them, but I've never seen any** besides seriously unhealthy amounts of caffeine."

STUDENT AUTHOR: **Most students will never even see a drug, or even a can of beer for that matter, while they attend Wheaton. In fact, to most of the student body, it seems ludicrous to have a drink or do any drugs while at school. Before you come to Wheaton, you have to sign the Community Covenant—a pledge of your integrity, giving your word that, among other things, you will not drink alcohol or abuse any kind of substance while in school.**

12:1	Student-to-Faculty Ratio
96%	Freshman Retention Rate
77%	Four-Year Graduation Rate
67%	Financial Aid Applicants Receiving Aid

Students Speak Out
SAFETY & SECURITY

Q "Let's be honest: **with Public Safety on the job, safety isn't even a factor**. They are so good, most people would be afraid to do anything wrong. You know, they have a ticket for just about everything. I've got about 17 to prove it."

Q "**Wheaton College is like the safest place on the face of this earth**. Nothing usually ever happens, nothing to worry about anyway. Yeah, campus is a safe place."

Q "No need for big fences or barricades here. **Wheaton fits in very well with the quiet residential community** surrounding the campus. It is also a very safe place to walk around, even late at night. It's not your typical 'college town' with a lot of crime or vandalism."

STUDENT AUTHOR: **Wheaton College is an exceptionally safe school. Unanimously, Wheaton students maintain a great sense of security while living on campus. Except for the occasional campus trespasser or bike theft, students rarely feel threatened.**

> **Questions?**
> For more inside information and survival tips, pick up College Prowler's full-length book on this school, written by an actual student! Check it out at www.collegeprowler.com.

Students Speak Out
ON OVERALL EXPERIENCE

Q "The best part about Wheaton is the common bonds that students share. In addition to the bond of everyone here being a Christian (students and faculty), Wheaton students are proud of their school. **We are all here because we want to be here—and it shows**. The campus attitude is energetic, upbeat, and lively. This is the perfect place for Christians to spread their wings."

Q "I love my college. **I can't imagine a better fit**, and I wouldn't trade my friendships—with students and professors—for anything."

Q "I am so glad I chose Wheaton College. Although there have been moments I've struggled, **I am grateful for the quality of the professors and peers I have met**. I have been shaped not only by my academic experience, but by my relationships as well."

Q "**The people at Wheaton have made all the difference for me**. Never have I met a group of peers that has challenged me in all aspects of my life: academically, spiritually, mentally, and relationally. I am just blown away by the quality of students here."

STUDENT AUTHOR: **The Wheaton College experience is completely unique. From a caring faculty, to impressive academics, to studying and serving abroad, to intense IM competition, to great food, to crazy dorm life—this school offers it all. However, it must be mentioned that Wheaton is not for everybody. In fact, it is a school for a very specific group of people. Wheaton is a school for those who want to grow in their Christian faith, be challenged in every area of their lives, and impact the world they live in.**

Wheaton College (MA)

26 East Main Street; Norton, MA 02766
(508) 286-8200; www.wheatoncollege.edu

THE BASICS:

Acceptance Rate: 43%   **SAT Range:** 1160–1350*
Setting: Suburban   **Control:** Private
F-T Undergrads: 1,650   **Tuition:** $38,585

Most Popular Majors: Social Sciences, Psychology, History, Visual & Performing Arts

*of 1600

Academics	B+	Guys	C+
Local Atmosphere	C-	Girls	B
Safety & Security	B	Athletics	C+
Computers	B	Nightlife	C+
Facilities	B	Greek Life	N/A
Campus Dining	A	Drug Scene	A-
Off-Campus Dining	B-	Campus Strictness	D
Campus Housing	B-	Parking	C
Off-Campus Housing	D+	Transportation	C+
Diversity	C-	Weather	C-

Students Speak Out
ON ACADEMICS

Q "**Critical thinking is very important to professors at Wheaton**, and though we may have our occasional disagreements, most of the faculty members I have personally encountered have all been extremely helpful in making sure their classes are fully understood by their students. In fact, at Wheaton, I have found that students frequently visit with their professors even after classes have ended, and new semesters have begun."

Q "The professors are one of the best things about Wheaton. They take time to get to know who you are; they **genuinely want you to develop as a student**. There are some great professors at Wheaton who make lectures interesting, and the work is challenging, but still fascinating."

Q "Many teachers are great, but it's a good idea to **ask around to find out which ones are better than others**. When you get the good ones, it's a rewarding experience."

STUDENT AUTHOR: There are some really brilliant people at Wheaton, and there are, of course, a lot of people that party a lot. Basically, you can avoid doing too much work if you want to your first couple of years. But due to the small class sizes, especially at the upper level, you have to stay on top of your work, and professors expect a lot from you. The small class sizes and the personal attention from professors are the main reasons most prospective students set their sights on Wheaton.

Students Speak Out
ON LOCAL ATMOSPHERE

Q "Norton is a town where **there isn't much to do**. Wheaton seems to be the center of this small town, and trips to CVS, Roche Brothers, Dunkin' Donuts, and Massive Video are about as exciting as Norton gets."

Q "Norton sucks. There's little to do here, but Providence and Boston are close and **public transportation is easily accessible**."

Q "Norton is a tiny town, and everything is pretty close together. The atmosphere is comfortable; it's **busy enough to feel like a city but not dangerous**. There aren't any other universities in the same town. There's nothing really exciting in Norton."

Q "I think that the people of Norton don't like to consider it a college town, because it's so small. They don't really cater much to students as in things to do and nightlife, but it's cool because the train station isn't far away, and **you can go to Boston or Providence in less than an hour**."

STUDENT AUTHOR: To be honest, Norton isn't a bustling metropolis, but if you choose Wheaton, that's probably what you're looking for anyway. Luckily, the school is so close to Boston and Providence that it isn't really an issue. At larger schools, you can feel like one amongst an uninterested crowd in which you'd be lucky to see the same face twice in the same day. But Wheaton's size, as well as the small and somewhat boring town, that it is located in makes the school feel like a real community.

5 Best Things	5 Worst Things
1 Professors	**1** High tuition
2 Class size	**2** The town of Norton
3 Research opportunities	**3** Lack of diversity
4 Spring weekend	**4** Dining hall food
5 Upper campus	**5** No dorm elevators

Students Speak Out
ON FACILITIES

Q "We **definitely could use some more cool things for students**. The student center is alright, but it only provides a place to get your mail, a small café, and a gym. The gym is okay, but the equipment was handed down from another college who was getting rid of it, so it could be better for sure."

Q "The **majority of facilities on campus are very nice**. The computer center is constantly updating its arsenal of machines and software, giving students the chance to use all the latest programs, ranging from those necessary for music making, film editing, and Web page building. The athletic department at Wheaton is also well funded and this is apparent in taking a short stroll through Haas Athletic Center."

Q "The student center is okay. There's a crappy bar called the Loft that robs you blind, a gym, game room, and a radio station. The **atmosphere here sucks, but it serves its purpose**."

STUDENT AUTHOR: In the recent years, major renovations have been undertaken at Wheaton. The one place that many students complain about, the Science Center, has undergone a multi-million dollar project in which a completely new Science Center has been built. All the buildings are modern, and those that aren't have the charm that old brick buildings covered in ivy carry with them. But even these buildings have computers and projectors in most of the classrooms, and though the exterior may seem quaint and old-fashioned, the interior is fully updated.

Famous Alumni

Adrienne Bevis Mars, Diane Farrell, Barbara Flavin Richardson, Trish Karter, Catherine Keener, Lesley Stahl, Christine Todd Whitman

Students Speak Out
ON CAMPUS DINING

Q "Well, the **pre-made food in the dining halls is not always the best**, but there are always other alternatives. We have the Lyon's Den, which is on the edge of campus. It's our own cute little coffee place. It's great, a quiet place to come and study while downing one caffeinated beverage after another."

Q "The food in the dining halls is not bad, although **by the end of the year it gets very tiresome**. The Loft is a place on campus that opens at 9 p.m. and has great popcorn chicken, but it is kind of expensive."

Q "If you're looking to seriously pack on the Freshman 15, Chase is a great place to do it—lots of grease and processed foods for you to pick from. It's **the typical college dining-hall scene**, filled with comfort foods and a dessert table at any time of the day. Generally, Chase and Emerson both offer healthier alternatives, although the salad bar does get tiring after a while."

STUDENT AUTHOR: What irks students the most is that they are required to be on the meal plan for all four years at Wheaton. The meal plan is all-you-can-eat style, but some slim girls complain that they don't eat nearly as much as the baseball players. However true this may be, students are pretty lucky to have the buffet-style meal plan, unlike at some schools where you have to ration out your meal points for each meal. One thing is for sure, you will never go hungry at Wheaton, despite the quality at times.

Student Body

African American:	5%	Male/Female:	38/62%
Asian American:	4%	Out-of-State:	67%
Hispanic:	3%	International:	3%
Native American:	<1%	Unknown:	5%
White:	79%		

Popular Faiths: Most religious activity takes place off campus, and not much is seen on or around campus.

Gay Pride: The campus is accepting of its gay students, and there are groups that organize events on campus every now and then to raise awareness.

Economic Status: Students come from all different backgrounds at Wheaton.

Students Speak Out
ON DORMS

Q "All of the dorms are pretty nice, but it depends on what you're looking for in a living environment. Besides, **the home away from home is what you make it,** and the people you live with have a big impact on whether it's a pleasant living environment or not."

Q "The rooms aren't great on lower campus, but the people are. People leaves their doors open and are friendly. There are always parties going on and everyone hangs out together. **I would recommend Meadows to freshmen** and sophomores, but upper campus is better for juniors and seniors who already have their group of friends."

STUDENT AUTHOR: For any incoming student, going straight to "ghettos," despite its reputation, will be the greatest benefit socially for anyone's freshman year. Overall, none of the dorms on campus are by any means unlivable—they are all pretty nice. But most seniors tend to live in singles, while at other schools a lot of upperclassmen are guaranteed suites or apartment-like housing. In that way, housing is a little disappointing.

 Did You Know?
91% of undergrads live on campus.

Students Speak Out
ON GUYS & GIRLS

Q "There are no guys here. I am a biology major, and in most of my classes, there have been one or maybe two guys. There are a few hot guys, but they are either players or taken by an equally cute girl. **Life is tough at Wheaton as a girl** because there are a lot of rich, pretty girls, and weird boys with only a cute boy here and there."

Q "**What guys**? Where are all the guys hiding? I want one."

Q "Wheaton looks for **well-rounded people** who will make a good addition to the environment. Most of the people I know are attractive. And I must say, I have had my share of crushes around campus, so yeah, a lot of the guys here are pretty darn hot."

STUDENT AUTHOR: The ratio of boys to girls is horribly skewed at Wheaton, perhaps as a some sort of lingering malady from the days when Wheaton was an all-girls school. The Wheaton student body is just above average. Basically, there are way too many girls looking for a relationship. There is a large handful of the well-groomed and gorgeous, but there is also a group of those that are not so concerned with their appearance.

Traditions

Boston Bash
Each fall, students grab their significant other or friends and get all fancy and go out for a night of dancing and drinks in Boston.

Chapel Doors
According to tradition, only seniors are allowed to walk through the front doors of the Cole Memorial Chapel.

Overall School Spirit
Deep down, there is a very dedicated aspect to our school spirit.

Students Speak Out
ON ATHLETICS

Q "I don't know too much about the sports programs at Wheaton aside from seeing my friends involved devoting an extremely large amount of their time to practice, games, and exercising. I have a friend on the softball team who likened being on a Wheaton sports team to joining a cult; according to her, **the devotion it takes is serious** and not for anyone not fully committed to being an excellent athlete."

Q "**Intramural sports are bigger than varsity sports**, although soccer here is a huge deal."

Q "The sports we have are **moderately big**. We have basketball, lacrosse, rugby, soccer, baseball, swimming, and others."

STUDENT AUTHOR: Wheaton allows you to be as involved or distanced from athletics as you want to be. The sports teams at Wheaton aren't an overwhelming presence. Sports teams are known to house many of the hotties on campus, as well as some dedicated party animals. Many teams get the reputation of partying heavily, but that doesn't mean that they don't put in a lot of work, too.

Students Speak Out
ON DRUG SCENE

Q "**I know many people on campus who smoke marijuana regularly**, but none who abuse it to the point of letting it interfere with their grades or extracurricular activities. I hate to keep comparing Wheaton to other schools, but at many other ones I have visited, such as the University of Massachusetts Amherst, the smell of pot is practically commonplace on campus."

Q "It is pretty chill. There **isn't all that much drug use** and people that do use drugs don't make a huge deal out of it."

Q "I don't think there are many drugs on campus. Maybe **some marijuana**, but I think that's about as far as it goes."

STUDENT AUTHOR: Wheaton students may dabble, but there aren't too many who can go all out and still get by academically—the course load at Wheaton just doesn't allow for a ton of time to be spent on drugs. Most likely, the most abused drugs are caffeine and nicotine used to help keep tired students awake for long hours of studying.

10:1	Student-to-Faculty Ratio
83%	Freshman Retention Rate
77%	Four-Year Graduation Rate
86%	Financial Aid Applicants Receiving Aid

Students Speak Out
SAFETY & SECURITY

Q "**Public safety is actually pretty lax** despite student complaints. They are not always reliable when needed, but they do offer help through programs such as their RAD rape defense course. Generally, they are pretty chill; if you have alcohol, they ask you to pour it out, unless you are being blatantly belligerent, and that's when you will get written up."

Q "I am **never afraid for my safety** on campus, even walking alone. There are warnings of things being stolen, but I leave my door unlocked, and it's never happened to me."

Q "The campus is small, so there **isn't too much to be concerned with**, but if Public Safety isn't there to walk you back to your dorm, a willing student will."

STUDENT AUTHOR: Wheaton is lacking in some of the technological aspects of campus security at other schools. For instance, we still use keys to get into our dorms rather than having the doors unlocked by swiping our ID cards. Many of the doors still do not have alarms on them, so they are left propped for days on end so anyone could walk in.

> **Questions?**
> For more inside information and survival tips, pick up College Prowler's full-length book on this school, written by an actual student! Check it out at *www.collegeprowler.com*.

Students Speak Out
ON OVERALL EXPERIENCE

Q "Wheaton, as a whole, is a wonderful place. People on campus complain all the time about the institution's idiosyncrasies, but all one has to do is visit almost any other college in the region to recognize how great ours is. The campus is absolutely beautiful, the general student mentality is one that embraces the 'work hard, play hard' approach to academics, the food is far from bad, the professors are intellectually stimulating, and **the community is one that is bonded very tightly**."

Q "Sometimes, I wish I was at a larger college so that I could have more choice in courses, but the community here is awesome, and it **feels like you are part of a family rather than just another number**."

Q "The classes and teachers are interesting, and the campus is beautiful. It **can get boring during weekends, but the weeks are busy with lots of events** (movies, vendors, fairs). Drinking and vandalism are problems, but I never feel unsafe. I'm glad I chose Wheaton."

STUDENT AUTHOR: Sometimes, students wonder what course their lives would have taken had they attended a different school—perhaps a larger one, in a city. And then the majority realize it probably couldn't have turned out any better than it has here at Wheaton. In the course of four years, Wheaton allows students to discover who they are and what they love in life, and that is far more valuable to them than being super competitive with classmates. There is an overall sense that there is more to life here than just people passing through to get a job.

Whitman College

345 Boyer Avenue; Walla Walla, WA 99362
(509) 527-5111; www.whitman.edu

THE BASICS:

Acceptance Rate: 46%
Setting: Rural
F-T Undergrads: 1,425

SAT Range: 1860–2140*
Control: Private
Tuition: $34,880

Most Popular Majors: English, Political Science, Biotechnology, History, Psychology

*of 2400

Academics	B+-	Guys	B
Local Atmosphere	C+	Girls	B+
Safety & Security	A	Athletics	C+
Computers	A-	Nightlife	C
Facilities	B-	Greek Life	B
Campus Dining	B+	Drug Scene	A-
Off-Campus Dining	B-	Campus Strictness	A-
Campus Housing	B	Parking	A
Off-Campus Housing	B+	Transportation	B-
Diversity	C	Weather	C

Students Speak Out
ON ACADEMICS

Q "Classes are often enjoyable and unexpected because they constantly **force students to look at the world in different ways** and to challenge and consider their own views."

Q "Professors at Whitman are very interested in getting to know their students, not simply on an academic level, but on a **personal level**, as well."

Q "I've found my professors to be extremely approachable and open. Several have become close personal friends, as well. Professors care about **developing a relationship**."

Q "Such a relationship allows students to achieve a more rounded education because these positive relationships foster **increased interest** in learning and analytical thinking."

Q "Classes at Whitman are demanding, be it a class of two people or of 30. Classes require **preparation and alertness**."

STUDENT AUTHOR: Experiences can depend on what classes you take, but most students find classes interesting and engaging, primarily because professors are talented in and love what they teach. Students find a comfortable environment in which to discuss all facets of academia. They generally find their professors to be animated in classes and easy to talk to both in and outside of the classroom. Whitman has loose distribution requirements—a wide range of eclectic classes—for students to not only explore their interests, but find their focus while doing so.

Students Speak Out
ON LOCAL ATMOSPHERE

Q "There's pretty much **nothing to do** in Walla Walla, unless you're bored or desperate or both. In a way, it's nice because it brings the focus of activity to Whitman, but it's always really frustrating when I want to leave Whitman for a while and experience some rich culture—and Walla Walla can't offer it."

Q "The whole area seems to be a place that **appreciates music**, which I really like. Local bands often play downtown, or local musicians will come to Whitman to see our concerts."

Q "Walla Walla has **everything I need**—a coffee shop, grocery store, thrift store, movie theater, and a couple of nice restaurants. It's good if you like the simpler life, and it's refreshing to go off campus if I'm stressed and not be bombarded with all the grittiness or busyness of a city."

Q "It is **not a cosmopolitan town**, but there are good places to go out for dinner. I grew up near a large city, so I definitely miss it, and I sometimes feel suffocated by the remoteness."

STUDENT AUTHOR: Walla Walla residents are divided when it comes to how they feel about Whitman College. Some say, "thank goodness for Whitman for bringing a more liberal perspective," while others feel that the campus creates too much difficulty and noise for the charm and quiet of Walla Walla. It does offer some lovely attractions, especially outdoors with its natural beauty. If you're someone who loves exploring the outdoors and appreciates nature, this school is very ideally located.

Students Speak Out
ON FACILITIES

Q "Facilities are **top-notch and always improving**. It seems like the school builds a new building every year and replaces the old, shotty one."

Q "I guess it all depends on when and where the money's coming from to make these improvements, but it **seems like the money could be better spent** on fixing up the academic buildings."

Q "I was **struck by how beautiful** everything looked on campus. All the buildings are well kept and beautiful, and I was pretty surprised to learn about how many more additions and improvements they're making since it didn't seem like the school really needed it. But all the same, I'm glad. It's always nicer to have newer buildings."

Q "Most buildings are very spacious and **comfortable and look beautiful**. I feel really special being able to study or have classes in really nice facilities."

Q "**Reid is my favorite** place to be—I really enjoy getting coffee and lunch with friends there."

STUDENT AUTHOR: **Many students sometimes feel spoiled with how new and pristine the facilities are, and the high quality definitely makes a difference in how pleasant it is to be in different locations. The Reid Campus Center houses the mail center, the book and gift shop, a coffeehouse, a TV and couch area, a café and ice cream bar, the RCC ballroom, a computer center, an art gallery, the Whitman radio station, offices and study rooms, the student newspaper and the student journal.**

Famous Alumni

Matt Ames, Walter Brattain, Ralph Cordiner, Ryan Crocker, William O. Douglas, John Stanton, Adam West

Students Speak Out
ON CAMPUS DINING

Q "Overall, the food is very good, and the biggest downfall of food service is that **it is very expensive**, and students are required to stay on it for their first couple of years. Students tend to sigh with relief when they move off campus."

Q "The food is better than any of the other colleges I visited as a prospie. It seems like it's **always getting better**, and the food service people send out surveys all the time to get student feedback."

Q "There is a lot of choices, and a good **vegetarian/vegan selection** in the dining halls. The best part about the dining halls is that they take peoples' comments and criticism into consideration when making the food."

Q "Bon Appetit even **buys local and organic stuff**, which is amazing. They do a great job catering to the health nuts and will listen to all requests and fill most of them. Prentiss has a great salad bar, Jewett has the best sandwiches, and Lyman is a nice getaway if you don't want a crowded dining hall for lunch."

STUDENT AUTHOR: **Like most food made in large quantities, Whitman's food service has its moments of unusual, unidentifiable culinary intrigue, though, for the most part, the food is rather delicious. Whitman offers three dining halls: Prentiss, Jewett, and Lyman. Whitman Café includes a grill, salads, a pizza oven, and ice cream. Most students purchase "Flex Dollars," which gives more variety outside of the dining halls.**

Student Body

African American:	2%	Male/Female:	45/55%
Asian American:	9%	Out-of-State:	58%
Hispanic:	3%	International:	3%
Native American:	1%	Unknown:	13%
White:	82%		

Popular Faiths: There seems to be a divide between agnostic or atheist students, and religious students are mainly Christian, Jewish, or Catholic.

Gay Pride: Most are tolerant, accepting, and open towards homosexuality, though some students still have some difficulty with these issues.

Economic Status: There's a large variety of economic status, and lower-class population is smaller.

Students Speak Out
ON DORMS

Q "Each residence hall has its own personality, but that changes from year to year with the residents. The important thing to remember is that you will have an **amazing freshman year**, even if you don't get your first choice for housing."

Q "The Interest House Community is a great place to live for a cozy home atmosphere and a chance to **mingle with people of shared interests**."

Q "Whitman seems to **place students really well**, even though students do send in their first choices of dorms. If you don't get your first choice, don't worry too much because you may end up living in a really great situation that you didn't think would fit you as well."

STUDENT AUTHOR: **The Interest House Community, a collection of 11 Whitman-owned houses, is a unique opportunity for students to live in a household setting that matches or relates to their personal interests. Whitman's residence halls are of very high quality, and they each have their quirks. Be prepared to deal with, and perhaps defend, the different reputations of each dorm and the different challenges of each.**

Did You Know?
56% of undergrads live on campus.

Students Speak Out
ON GUYS & GIRLS

Q "The **girls are quite attractive**, and most have a personality, opinions, and deeper conversational skills than your typical valley girl. There are some brain-dead, dud girls, but most of them are really smart and down to earth."

Q "Most guys at Whitman were pretty attractive, especially if you like the more **rugged-looking** guys. A lot of them are like scruffier Greek gods."

Q "I hate generalizations, but basically everyone here is very **nice and intelligent**, and typically quite attractive."

Q "It seems like it's harder for girls to meet guys than for guys to meet girls. The **ratio is skewed in the guys' favor**!"

STUDENT AUTHOR: **Many of the attractive guys end up in fraternities, and since Greek life tends to socialize internally, it's difficult for non-Greek to have a relationship with a Greek-affiliated guy. Many of the sorority girls are well primped and wear the latest fashions, but believe it or not, these girls do have personalities. Girls feel the guys are not as attractive. What they lack in attractiveness, they make up for in personality, humor, and brains.**

Traditions

Onion Fest
A huge two- to three-day ultimate Frisbee tournament with teams from the Northwest.

Whitstock
A fall musical festival at the beginning of the year with several bands, usually held outdoors.

Overall School Spirit
Though sporting events don't bring in an enormous amount of school spirit, every student is very proud to be at Whitman. Students think highly of the school, its professors, and all the resources it provides.

Students Speak Out
ON ATHLETICS

Q "Definitely play an IM or club sport! It was really nice after a long day of classes to let loose some stress and have fun with friends. Plus, people are accepting in most IM sports and recognize that students have **all kinds of athletic abilities**, despite the fact that many IM sports are pretty intense and serious."

Q "Varsity sports aren't very big, although the **basketball games get pretty good turnouts**."

Q "It is nice to participate in sports, as there is an overall **vigorousness for physical activity** and healthy lifestyle at Whitman."

Q "It seems like Whitman is not very competitive and into sports. Whitman is **more into academics**, which is not a bad thing."

STUDENT AUTHOR: **Most intramural sports are more popular than varsity sports. When a sports program is not very competitive, there is not a lot to get excited about. That void has to be filled, and IM sports are a pretty good filler. Sports are a great way to meet people outside of a living situations, but are by no means are an essential aspect of Whitman life.**

Students Speak Out
ON DRUG SCENE

Q "Alcohol seems to be the biggest form of substance abuse, and I don't think I can recall any weekend where it wasn't **readily available** at some party."

Q "For a school that hosts 'the Beer Mile,' it would seem like the obvious conclusion that **alcohol is quite integrated into the lifestyle** here. Though it can get out of control at times, most students don't drink so much that they get belligerent or pass out."

Q "I've noticed that **pot is being used more often**, and it's easier to get, which is a little worrisome. Hopefully, it won't become as popular as alcohol is on campus."

STUDENT AUTHOR: Although harder drugs do exist, they don't exist in a large enough way that they are noticed and highly problematic. Many students would rather have alcohol in abundance than any other substance. Whitman has a well-deserved reputation for being a drinking school, but this is better than being known for other drugs.

10:1	Student-to-Faculty Ratio
93%	Freshman Retention Rate
75%	Four-Year Graduation Rate
85%	Financial Aid Applicants Receiving Aid

Students Speak Out
SAFETY & SECURITY

Q "Though parts of Walla Walla have been known to have their crime, the Whitman campus overall is very safe, very good, and amazing. **I never feel threatened** walking around campus."

Q "I definitely feel comfortable leaving the door to my room unlocked. Most students do, and it's more of a pain when you need to get into your room and you have to fumble for your keys to unlock it. **The outside doors to the dorms are also locked at 9 p.m.**, so it doesn't really seem that necessary to lock individual dorm rooms."

Q "Especially with the library being open 24 hours, the whole campus is very much a **'round-the-clock' community**. Even though the school is small, I always run into someone when I'm walking around."

STUDENT AUTHOR: Since the campus is small and everything is within walking distance, it's easy for security to monitor a concentrated area, and most students never feel threatened by outside visitors or other students because the community is tightly-knit where most people know each other.

> **Questions?**
> For more inside information and survival tips, pick up College Prowler's full-length book on this school, written by an actual student! Check it out at *www.collegeprowler.com*.

Students Speak Out
ON OVERALL EXPERIENCE

Q "Whitman is a place where it's hard for people not to be themselves, which is a great quality. I think the student body is accepting of peoples' eccentricities, weird hobbies, and quirks. The place **creates an aura of comfort** for people to just be. It's great not to have to worry about this when I'm trying to do well in classes and just focus on furthering my academic education."

Q "The people are **friendly and personable**, and though there are some social hurdles to jump over, everyone finds their place and feels comfortable, eventually."

Q "My experience at Whitman **improved each successive year** I attended. I loved Whitman and wish graduation hadn't come so soon."

Q "I've always longed for the kind of close relationships I have with my professors and know they're always there to help, no matter what time of day or night. The professors genuinely love teaching, and **dedicate their lifestyles** to it— they're always welcome to give lectures at various events, and help students out with anything. I am so grateful to be in an environment that loves to learn and educate both in and out of the classroom."

STUDENT AUTHOR: Whitman also has a very strong and supportive network of alumni, which is indicative of the bond many people have with Whitman. Several feel they've grown in many positive ways by being put through the challenges of Whitman, and all-in-all, wouldn't change their experiences for the world. It's a unique and special place, unlike any environment most students have ever been in, and many think it will be difficult to leave when graduation comes.

Wilkes University

84 West South Street; Wilkes-Barre, PA 18766
(800) WILKES-U; www.wilkes.edu

THE BASICS:

Acceptance Rate: 74%
Setting: Small city
F-T Undergrads: 2,109

SAT Range: 1370–1730*
Control: Private
Tuition: $25,170

Most Popular Majors: Business, Education, Engineering, Psychology, Biology

*of 2400

Academics	B-	Guys	B
Local Atmosphere	D	Girls	B
Safety & Security	C+	Athletics	B+
Computers	B	Nightlife	B
Facilities	B	Greek Life	N/A
Campus Dining	B+	Drug Scene	C+
Off-Campus Dining	B	Campus Strictness	C+
Campus Housing	A	Parking	D
Off-Campus Housing	A	Transportation	B
Diversity	D-	Weather	C

Students Speak Out
ON ACADEMICS

Q "The majority of teachers at Wilkes are really great. **They care about their students and will be willing to help if you need it**. The negative thing about some teachers is that they do not always follow their office hours."

Q "**I think that Wilkes is slowly becoming a science college only**, and I feel that they do not advertise to and recruit students that are non-science related."

Q "The teachers are personable, and most of them try to get to know the students. **The general workload is very reasonable**; students in the pharmacy program have the greatest workload."

Q "**The teachers are fair, but only if they like you**. It's in the best interest of the student to suck up some and not cross the teachers, or you will pay come grade time. The workload is easy for communication majors."

STUDENT AUTHOR: There may be some obvious lines drawn between the science types and the arts and humanities types, but regardless of who gets a bigger budget, the programs themselves shine. Hands-on learning is something that is strived for at Wilkes, making learning at the school very fascinating. Interdisciplinary learning is another academic passion of the University. There are some weak points, however. Some people would say that classes can fill up fast, or that many top professors are still teaching 101 classes rather than the higher-level classes they may be better suited for.

Students Speak Out
ON LOCAL ATMOSPHERE

Q "The atmosphere in Wilkes-Barre is mixed. Some of the people are great and others not so much, just like any other place. **There is a heavy heterosexual, white population in the area**, which is sometimes lacking culture and diversity."

Q "Around the campus, we have everything. I think that **around campus is very college oriented**; in the summer and breaks, campus is like a ghost town."

Q "The atmosphere is college town until you get further into South Wilkes-Barre or cross South Main Street; then it's ghetto. King's is the closest college. **Stay away from the ghetto part**, and there's nothing to do except the Arena Hub."

Q "**It is a very small, condensed campus** with another college that has a small, condensed campus two to three blocks away. The feel of the city is not very collegy, but with the addition of the movie theater and the new club that is coming, the environment is changing."

STUDENT AUTHOR: Wilkes-Barre is the county seat of Luzerne County, and has a population of about 50,000 people. Aside from drinking, there is much to do when it comes to arts and entertainment. There are large and small venues, and the theater-type venues bring musicals, plays, comedians and other events aside from concerts. There are often bums, drug dealers, prostitutes, and other riff-raff that hang around the streets of downtown, however, and many would advise not going downtown alone after dark.

5 Best Things
1 Mentoring
2 Urban revitalization
3 Mansions as dorms
4 Scenic landscaping
5 Student activities

5 Worst Things
1 Limited parking
2 Local landlords
3 Crime close to campus
4 No 24-hour restaurants
5 Lots of busted parties

Students Speak Out
ON FACILITIES

Q "**The library smells like Band-Aids**, but the gym and student center are very modern and nice."

Q "Campus facilities are okay. **The library does not have a very pleasant smell**, but if you can get past that, there are a lot of valuable resources."

Q "**The facilities on campus are nice**. The library is nice and furnished. It also has a wireless network so you can bring your laptop with you. The newer classroom buildings are nice and technologically advanced. The older buildings have obviously been used more, but are still in fairly good condition. The student union is also very new looking and a nice place to be."

Q "**The student center and gym are really nice**, but the library leaves a bit to be desired. The pharmacy library is really nice."

Q "The library is nice and has neat furniture. The cafeteria and student center building is nice. **Most of the public spaces are comfortable and appealing**. For instance, the fireplace in the student union surrounded by couches is cozy."

STUDENT AUTHOR: Wilkes University boasts some pretty decent facilities. But aside from the buildings themselves, the campus is spotless, and in the nicer weather, the grass is always freshly manicured, the trees and shrubs are trimmed to perfection, the mulch is fresh, and the flowers are vibrant. This campus is kept up with, that's for sure. Many people will complain about the smell in the library (we think it is a result of the 1972 Agnes flood that devastated the whole Wyoming Valley).

Famous Alumni

Kevin Beerman, Melanie Bell, Catherine DeAngelis, Jimmy Harnen, Tom Lavan, Andy Mehalshick, Andre Miller, Dave Russo

Students Speak Out
ON CAMPUS DINING

Q "The food has actually gotten way better over the years; **I can actually identify meats from one another**. The catering service here is amazing—the meals they have prepared for special events have been tops."

Q "**The dining halls are very clean and well-maintained**. There is a brick oven in the cafeteria, which is great, and a room was added on so it is bigger, so there is more room to eat if it is busy."

Q "The food is good, but **it just seems like the variety is lacking**. We have the Rifkin Café, which is a nice spot to grab food or coffee."

Q "As a commuter, I do not have a meal plan. But for pretty cheap, **the cafeteria is all-you-can eat and a great deal**. I love the wood-fired pizza and pasta bar that is always there, and they have great selections of new foods."

Q "The dining hall isn't bad. **They are always trying to accommodate the students**."

STUDENT AUTHOR: The dining hall features spacious seating with plenty of room to dine. The cafeteria is just that: cafeteria-style in all-you-can-eat format. The features are a deli line with made-to-order sandwiches, the grill with different selections featured daily, a vegetarian bar, two hot meal lines (both are cooked in front of you), a pasta and brick-oven pizza bar, a soup and salad bar, an ice cream station, and a dessert bar with pies and cookies. That sure is a lot to choose from. There is also late-night dining, which features a limited menu.

Student Body

African American:	2%	Male/Female:	47/53%
Asian American:	2%	Out-of-State:	19%
Hispanic:	2%	International:	<1%
Native American:	<1%	Unknown:	<1%
White:	93%		

Popular Faiths: Roman Catholic is probably the most common, but students of all beliefs should feel comfortable at Wilkes.

Gay Pride: While the campus has a gay/straight alliance, some feel the Wilkes climate is not as open as they'd like.

Economic Status: Generous scholarships and aid make for a wide range of economic backgrounds.

Students Speak Out
ON DORMS

Q "The dorms are nice. **Some are coed, and some are all-female or all-male**. I wouldn't like to live in the YMCA, which are apartment-style dorms, because they are haunted, and I wouldn't want to live in the all-female dorms."

Q "**The converted mansions are the way to go**; the rooms have character and charm, especially Waller North and South."

Q "**We have mansions as dorms, and they are awesome**. We also have one traditional dorm, Evans, that is really nice. Evans is loud and you can meet a lot of people, and the mansions tend to be a little quiet."

STUDENT AUTHOR: While Wilkes has a traditional style coed dormitory, most of the residence halls are donated mansions. What makes this better than cookie-cutter residence halls is that each room is unique. Some features include stained glass windows, high ceilings, window seats, original fireplaces, beautiful trim work, and more! Some of these mansions are designated male or female, and many of them, like Rifkin, have apartment-style living.

Did You Know?
45% of undergrads live on campus.

Students Speak Out
ON GUYS & GIRLS

Q "**Most guys are hot, and girls are beautiful**. The girls I find to be most attractive because their personalities tend to be cooler, more open-minded, and more chill than the guys."

Q "There is **not a big openly LGBT population on campus**, which can be hard since I am gay, but I have many friends, faculty, and staff that support not just me but all types of students."

Q "**We are mostly a Caucasian school**. Everyone tends to be well-dressed and really friendly."

Q "Typical students at Wilkes are just like what a typical person would be like. **There are a lot of jocks in sports**, especially football, so probably big muscular type of guys. There are quite a few girls that are materialistic."

STUDENT AUTHOR: Many of the students at Wilkes are hot, smart, and if you are lucky, both. While there are many college gals who come to class in their PJs and knotty hair in a bun and baseball cap, the majority of Wilkes chicks dress to impress. Most Wilkes men would be classified as your rugged or preppy guy—the Abercrombie & Fitch type. There are also those who dress less conventionally.

Urban Legends
There are a bunch of urban legends about the buildings on campus because they are really old. In Kirby Hall, a poker game went wrong and now a ghost lives in there. In Weis, there was a fire that killed a little girl and now you can hear footsteps running up and down the steps.

Overall School Spirit
The Mayor's Cup, the annual football game between crosstown rivals Wilkes and King's College, is probably the height of yearly school spirit.

Students Speak Out
ON ATHLETICS

Q "When I first came, there weren't too many intramural sports. Now they are starting to have a lot, such as basketball, volleyball, dodgeball, table tennis, and things like that. **The varsity sports are pretty good**. I played tennis for three years, and our football team is pretty competitive."

Q "I don't play sports on campus, but **the teams are close-knit and family-like**. There are IM sports like volleyball, rugby, and basketball that are always fun."

Q "Varsity sports are a big deal, **especially football, basketball, and wrestling**."

STUDENT AUTHOR: Wilkes University has a solid reputation for a good sports program. The athletes at Wilkes are also academically some of the best students on campus. With a great coaching staff, filled with many past star Colonels, there is superb leadership. There is a great basketball rivalry with the University of Scranton, and each year, a football game against cross-town rivals King's College has both teams duking it out for the Mayor's Cup. For most of the away games, there is bus transportation provided.

Students Speak Out
ON DRUG SCENE

Q "**Alcohol is the only drug I notice that is used on campus**. I haven't seen any other drugs. However, I am sure some other types are out there."

Q "On campus, **it is not terrible**. Marijuana is pretty high in use, but if I had some stats, I bet the number of users for other drugs would be a significant drop-off from that."

Q "**There are definitely a lot of people who smoke pot**, especially (and ironically enough) the pharmacy majors."

STUDENT AUTHOR: It's very rare that a Wilkes student—on or off campus—is caught using or caught with paraphernalia. One event does come to mind— many years ago a student had a small amount of pot mailed to her in the Wilkes mailroom. Dumb move. That was probably the biggest story. However, for students who want it, whatever their "it" is, it is sure to be found off campus. But, great caution should be taken. Remember: busts galore.

15:1	Student-to-Faculty Ratio
79%	Freshman Retention Rate
44%	Four-Year Graduation Rate
89%	Financial Aid Applicants Receiving Aid

Students Speak Out
SAFETY & SECURITY

Q "On campus, **the security and safety are pretty good**. However, if you walk a block away from campus in any direction, you might want to look over your shoulder from time to time."

Q "I think Wilkes is very secure. A lot more secure than it used to be. **They just put new cameras and lighting up**. They have Public Safety patrolling the campus a lot more. There is a lot more Public Safety presence now than when I was a freshman."

Q "Security is really tight. You have to have keys to get into the dorms and swipe cards to get into the buildings. If it is late and you want to get across campus, **all you have to do is call campus security and they will walk or drive you**, depending on the weather."

STUDENT AUTHOR: Kudos must be given to Wilkes University Public Safety. It is rare that something violent happens on campus. There is a huge Public Safety presence on campus, all donning bright yellow jackets (at least in cooler weather). There is always someone in the dispatch center as well.

> **Questions?**
> For more inside information and survival tips, pick up College Prowler's full-length book on this school, written by an actual student! Check it out at *www.collegeprowler.com*.

Students Speak Out
ON OVERALL EXPERIENCE

Q "If I were to do this all over again, I would probably pick Wilkes again. I like the fact that it is close to home for me and that **it is a small, personal college**; you can really get to know your professors on a one-on-one basis."

Q "So far, this school has been great. If I could do it over again, I would definitely come back here. **They did a wonderful job choosing my roommate**. We get along great and are now the best of friends."

Q "I would not be the person I am today had I not come to Wilkes. The English department, namely professors like Dr. Culver and Dr. Fields, gave me the confidence and support I needed to follow my life as a writer. **As a result, I came back to Wilkes for my MA in creative writing**, have been doing poetry readings in Manhattan, and have my first book of poetry coming out later this year."

Q "**Yeah, I would come here again**. The people I have met and the relationships I have established with my teachers because of the small size of the University have made this an enjoyable place to go to school."

STUDENT AUTHOR: The overall experience reported by most Wilkes students is overwhelmingly positive. The outstanding mentoring environment, caring faculty, wide array of student activities, and some darn good academics overshadow the occasional blizzard and unfavorable happening on campus. Wilkes is truly a school where undergrads get the full college experience. The city of Wilkes-Barre has also improved dramatically in the past few years, presenting tons of things for students to do off campus.

Willamette University

900 State Street; Salem, OR 97301
(530) 370-6300; www.willamette.edu

THE BASICS:

Acceptance Rate: 67%
Setting: Mid-sized city
F-T Undergrads: 1,767

SAT Range: 1680–1990*
Control: Private
Tuition: $35,400

Most Popular Majors: Social Sciences, Foreign Languages, English, Biology, Historywri

*of 2400

Academics	A-	Guys	B-
Local Atmosphere	C	Girls	B
Safety & Security	A-	Athletics	C
Computers	B	Nightlife	C+
Facilities	B	Greek Life	C-
Campus Dining	A-	Drug Scene	B
Off-Campus Dining	B-	Campus Strictness	B
Campus Housing	B+	Parking	B-
Off-Campus Housing	B+	Transportation	C+
Diversity	C+	Weather	B-

Students Speak Out
ON ACADEMICS

Q "You pay for the opportunity to build one-on-one relationships with some of the most brilliant professors out there. **The school is just small enough so each student can be remembered.**"

Q "**I try to balance easy and hard classes each semester so I don't get overwhelmed.** I think anyone who enrolls in four science classes—which all come with three- to four-hour labs—in the same semester is asking for trouble."

Q "I definitely think **Willamette is in the top tier of liberal arts schools** in terms of academics. I'm constantly being challenged in my courses to think outside the box and push myself."

Q "Professors are approachable and friendly. They make you work, but **they want you to learn and enjoy learning.** Many are flexible, and if you are in a tight spot, they are willing to work with you. Some people say students are babied by our professors and by the school, but I really think they push us to be the best students we can and are a supportive community when we need them."

STUDENT AUTHOR: Academics at Willamette can be as challenging as you want them to be. The students who attend class, do their homework, and take notes have no problem getting an A or B. Yet not every student will put in the effort, and that is when it becomes difficult. Different classes and majors have varying workloads. Biology and chemistry majors may never leave the laboratory, while art history majors will be in the museum for long hours.

Students Speak Out
ON LOCAL ATMOSPHERE

Q "**The town is one of the largest in the state but feels very small.** The state capitol is across the street from campus, and the historic downtown is only a couple blocks away. There are many coffee shops and small venues for bands."

Q "Salem itself isn't great, but **it's really close to the coast and the mountains and Portland,** which is nice."

Q "You can find some cute shops and stores in downtown Salem if you take the time to look. If it's a nice day out and you don't have anything else to do, it's fun to walk downtown, grab a cup of coffee, and walk around the shops. **There are some cool galleries** where you can see work by local artists."

Q "I wish that Willamette felt more like a part of the Salem community. I've been to other schools where the people who lived in the town were so supportive of the college and the students—it really felt like a 'college town'. But there really is **no connection between Salem and Willamette,** and that's too bad."

STUDENT AUTHOR: Salem is the capital of Oregon. This prime location offers students—especially politics and history majors—opportunities for internships or the chance to participate in rallies and protests. There is also a collection of nearby boutiques, restaurants, and coffee shops. But students tend to get trapped in what is referred to as the "Willamette Bubble," and they don't venture out of the comfort of their own dorm and dining hall to discover the rich and eclectic culture of Salem.

Students Speak Out
ON FACILITIES

"The athletic center is very small, so **be prepared to wait in line to use the cardio equipment** and weights."

"**The library is great**, and it has great hours, especially during finals week. The student center is in the middle of campus and houses so many organizations, and it is easy to find your way around."

"We have a beautiful art museum on campus that I think every student should visit at least once before graduating. The University owns a sufficient collection of art, and the visiting exhibits are usually interesting. It is nice because not every university has its own art museum, so **Willamette is fortunate to have its own**."

"I used the gym a lot my freshmen year, but now I just joined my own off-campus gym. I hate that **I'm spending money on something that I can get for free on campus**, but at the same time, I want to be guaranteed a machine when I go work out."

"I love our library. There are **little study rooms at the back of each floor**, and they're perfect if you just need to go somewhere and get work done."

STUDENT AUTHOR: **Willamette offers everything a college student could need: a large student center equipped with a store that serves late-night snacks, a full laundromat, two computer labs, an on-campus coffee shop, and more than enough activities. However, Sparks Athletic Center is in less than perfect condition. The weight room is small and cramped, while the cardio space is limited.**

Students Speak Out
ON CAMPUS DINING

"Our campus makes a considerable effort to provide the students with a **wide variety of healthy meals**. I think the food is one of the best things about Willamette."

"The food at Goudy is good, but so is the dining hall itself. Compared to other schools I visited, Willamette had the best dining halls. I didn't feel like I was eating in a high school cafeteria—it had a **lively, slightly more refined atmosphere**."

"At the beginning of each year when President Pelton gives his welcoming speech to the new students, he always mentions that there are 12 different types of vegetables at the salad bar. **If the president of the school is talking about the salad bar, then you know it's a big deal.**"

"I love eating on campus because **it's the most social time of the day, especially dinner**. People usually just sit in the dining halls for an hour or two, talking and laughing. It's the best time of the day, and there is always something to choose from so you won't go hungry."

"Goudy's lunch is usually pretty tasty, but **dinner is questionable sometimes**."

STUDENT AUTHOR: **If you accept that college dining hall food isn't the same as home-cooked meals, then you will find yourself pleasantly surprised with how good it can be. Willamette makes a great effort to offer healthy choices for students. Furthermore, there is a wide variety of affordable food, and there is plenty of it! The greatest criticism would be long lines during high-traffic times.**

Students Speak Out
ON DORMS

Q "The best part about living in the dorms is the **feeling of community**. The worst part is the noise, especially if your neighbor likes to blast the Spice Girls at 2 a.m."

Q The dorms vary a lot, and **they all have very distinct identities**. Baxter Hall is substance-free and tends to attract lots of runners and folks who absolutely do not want alcohol or drugs around at all. Matthews and Belknap Halls are your standard freshman dorms."

Q "The newest and nicest on-campus housing is Kaneko Commons, but it is on the other side of the train tracks, **requiring a walk over the sky bridge to get to the main campus**."

STUDENT AUTHOR: **Dorm life at Willamette is generally how students expect dorm life to be: You will have one or two roommates, you will sleep in a twin-size bed with sheets your mother might have picked out, your closet with be approximately three feet wide, and you will be able to hear everything your neighbors say or do because the walls are so thin. But not every dorm is the same—each has its own characteristics and stereotypes.**

Did You Know?
72% of undergrads live on campus.

Students Speak Out
ON GUYS & GIRLS

Q "There's **a rumor that 70 percent of Willamette graduates marry another Willamette grad**. That's hard to believe because the students are average to unfortunate looking, with a few exceptions."

Q "The people at Willamette are just average college students. It's like if you're at the zoo and there is a cage labeled 'College Student.' Inside the cage you would see six or seven Willamette students, and **they'd all be wearing sweatshirts and talking about the importance of recycling**."

Q "I think the best situation would be to **have a girlfriend or boyfriend outside of Willamette**."

Q "**The guys and girls seem immature**. You can always find a few gems in the bunch, though."

STUDENT AUTHOR: **As unfortunate as stereotyping is, it is one of the easiest ways to describe the various types of people here. There are the Bearcat all-stars who get involved with lots of activities on campus, the "college students" who will keep your Friday nights interesting, the ultra intellects, and the miscellaneous students. All in all, anyone can fit in at Willamette because there will always be someone else who is just as excited, dedicated, active, or ready to party as you are.**

Traditions

Glee
This competition involved each class choreographing a school spirit dance number and performing for a group of judges.

Mill Streamed
It is tradition that Willamette students be thrown into Mill Stream on their birthdays.

Overall School Spirit
There is a major lack of school spirit here. Students have more pride regarding their individual activities rather than Willamette as a whole.

Students Speak Out
ON ATHLETICS

Q "**Willamette sports are kind of a joke**. No one comes to Willamette to play a sport—it's just an extracurricular activity. The people who play sports take it seriously, but the people who don't are not interested at all."

Q "Sports are definitely **second to academics** at Willamette. People who play a varsity sport are usually getting straight As in the classroom as well."

Q "**Intramurals at Willamette are incredible**! They are competitive and exciting, and the intramural supervisors running them really know their stuff."

Q "I wish Willamette had better sports teams or even just school pride. It'd be fun to go to a loud, exciting, sold-out football or basketball game, but **we're not a Division I school**, and it just won't happen."

STUDENT AUTHOR: **Willamette is a Division III school that places more emphasis on academics than athletics. This roughly means that you did not have to be first-string in high school to play a varsity sport at Willamette. In comparison to varsity sports, intramural sports are extremely competitive.**

Students Speak Out
ON DRUG SCENE

Q "The academic requirements for **maintaining scholarships make regular drug use difficult** to sustain. Marijuana is used by many students, but harder drugs are not noticeable at Willamette to most of the student body, though a few students do use harder drugs on occasion."

Q "It's annoying when **you meet a brilliant student who is also a pothead**. That seems to happen a lot at Willamette."

Q "A couple of my friends smoke pot, but other than that, I don't think I've seen any drugs on campus. **It just doesn't really seem prevalent on campus**, and it's not really something that I've spent much time thinking about."

STUDENT AUTHOR: **Drugs are not a noticeable part of life at Willamette, and there is little to no pressure to use drugs. Even smoking cigarettes—which could be considered one of the least shocking forms of drug use—is not extremely visible. The most-used drug at Willamette is marijuana, but it is not highly visible.**

10:1	Student-to-Faculty Ratio
86%	Freshman Retention Rate
60%	Four-Year Graduation Rate
86%	Financial Aid Applicants Receiving Aid

Students Speak Out
SAFETY & SECURITY

Q "Because Willamette is such a small school and everyone seems to know everyone, **there is a general sense of security** on campus. It's actually very comforting."

Q "The dorms are safe enough that people feel comfortable leaving their rooms unlocked. I've never heard of anyone's room being ransacked, so I assume it's safe."

Q "**The largest crime on campus is probably bike theft**. Aside from small incidences, safety is generally not an issue. The campus is small but not enclosed, and therefore it is good to walk with others when it is dark outside. Campus Safety is available to give rides or respond to any incidents."

STUDENT AUTHOR: Not a day goes by that you will not see a campus safety officer walk by in their crisp black uniforms or drive through campus in the maroon cars. They also travel by golf cart, which may sound strange but quickly becomes the norm. All in all, Campus Safety does their job, and students rarely feel in danger on campus.

> **Questions?**
> For more inside information and survival tips, pick up College Prowler's full-length book on this school, written by an actual student! Check it out at *www.collegeprowler.com*.

Students Speak Out
ON OVERALL EXPERIENCE

Q "Whatever you want Willamette to be, it will be. If you want a crazy party drunkfest every weekend, you can have it, but your grades will suffer. If you want to graduate magna cum laude with an acceptance letter to Harvard Law, that can happen too. **There are so many opportunities that Willamette will present**, and if you make the most of those opportunities, you will find your college career very fulfilling."

Q "Willamette has been great, but I am ready to graduate. **I feel like I've gotten all I can out of it, and I'm ready to move on**. I'm especially ready to leave Salem. I think everyone hits a wall at some point when they feel they're ready to leave Willamette."

Q "**I have met the most amazing people** and know this is the right place for me. A liberal arts education is something that I think is extremely valuable, and if I could do the college process over again, I would definitely still come here."

Q "Willamette is really small. It's nice because class sizes are small and interactions with professors are very personal. **You know everyone and thus know everyone's business**. Campus and Salem aren't super exciting, so sometimes cabin fever is an issue."

STUDENT AUTHOR: **Willamette offers a small-town location, an incredible amount of financial aid, small class sizes, and a top-rate education. Willamette students do not learn *how* to do things, they learn *about* things, which is what sets the liberal arts education apart from more technical ways of study. So students who know exactly want they want to study and have a set career path in high school should not attend Willamette.**

Williams College

988 Main Street; Williamstown, MA 01267
(413) 597-3131; www.williams.edu

THE BASICS:

Acceptance Rate: 18%
Setting: Rural
F-T Undergrads: 1,964

SAT Range: 1340–1520*
Control: Private
Tuition: $35,438

Most Popular Majors: Social Sciences, English, Art Studies, Psychology, History

*of 1600

Academics	A+	Guys	C-
Local Atmosphere	C+	Girls	C
Safety & Security	A-	Athletics	B-
Computers	C+	Nightlife	D
Facilities	A-	Greek Life	N/A
Campus Dining	B+	Drug Scene	A-
Off-Campus Dining	C+	Campus Strictness	B+
Campus Housing	B-	Parking	A-
Off-Campus Housing	C-	Transportation	C-
Diversity	B	Weather	C-

Students Speak Out
ON ACADEMICS

Q "I feel like **some of the professors were too demanding** and assigned more homework than a normal person could handle. I am pretty hardworking, but I think it is wrong to deprive yourself of sleep all the time. I know many kids develop stress-related psych disorders because of trying to cope with all of the work, and stay on top while not sleeping, eating, or socializing with friends."

Q "Upper-level classes at Williams get very intense, because that's where you begin to spend lots of time with your professors. You do have to get through some boring introductory classes first. Most **professors will be very welcoming and helpful in their office hours,** even if you are one of 50 students in the class. It gets much better in 200 and 300 levels, when class size decreases to 10 or so. You have to realize that you should be the one taking the initiative to meet your professors and do extra work."

Q "Professors at Williams are very friendly, helpful, and knowledgeable. Most are very hard graders, though, so **you will have to sweat for that A-.**"

STUDENT AUTHOR: Williams professors are accessible, articulate, and extremely erudite. While the workload does vary with separate departments, students are challenged to improve their skills and obtain new ones as well. Professors allow for each student to have his or her own style of learning, and they are supportive of everyone's individual learning process.

Students Speak Out
ON LOCAL ATMOSPHERE

Q "Williamstown is so calm and peaceful. It's beautiful during all seasons. The town is small, but **if you like the outdoors, you will really enjoy it.**"

Q "The **town is composed almost entirely of college students,** faculty, and other people related to Williams. So, while you won't meet any cool town people, you will always be surrounded by people who know how you're feeling."

Q "I don't know how to describe the local atmosphere, because there is no atmosphere. **Nothing ever happens in the town except for college-related events.** If you come from NYC, like myself, you might end up really bored. Breathing the clean air of the Berkshires is not enough sometimes, unless you spend most of your time in the library working."

Q "Williamstown might be small, but it has a lot to offer in terms of **scenery and events for the lovers of the arts.**"

STUDENT AUTHOR: Williams is not comparable to New York City in the field of diversity, but for a small town, Williamstown has a lot to offer both visitors and residents. A friendly, inviting, and intellectually stimulating atmosphere, combined with peace and the beauty of nature, makes Williamstown more than attractive. From the movie theater to the overall appearance of the town, Williamstown gives off an artsy aura. Though it is generally quiet, many students find it relaxing.

Students Speak Out
ON FACILITIES

Q "There's **any facility you might need** at Williams, from a climbing wall to a farm nearby where you can take horseback riding lessons. There is also a great lab for language learners and an office where you can borrow digital cameras, plus a lab where you could edit and improve digital photography and videos."

Q "Psych lab facilities and equipment are rarely mentioned in college catalogues, but for the sake of psych majors, I will say that **they are great**. No wonder psych is one of the most popular Williams majors."

Q "The **athletic facilities are amazing**, from the pool to the squash center to the indoor track and also the dance studio. Another strength of Williams is the labs and other science facilities that are always available to all, and they are staffed by some of the friendliest people ever."

Q "Sports facilities at Williams really couldn't be much better. Even the **outdoors fields are so well maintained that other schools can't compare**."

STUDENT AUTHOR: Want to have a special facility for basket-weaving and knot-tying? Just ask. Williams will provide the space, the equipment, and the materials at once. Luckily, most Williams facilities support activities that are much more meaningful than the ones aforementioned. The comfort of a well-designed and maintained facility helps people become better at what they do, whether it is playing the flute or kickboxing.

Famous Alumni

Sterling Brown, Steve Case, Bainbridge Colby, John Frankenheimer, James Garfield, Richard Helms, Henry Hoyt, Elia Kazan, Reza Pahlavi II

Students Speak Out
ON CAMPUS DINING

Q "I really like that the helpings are unlimited. Some think this might be why so many people gain weight, but eventually, they tend to lose it and learn to eat healthy. The dining hall staff does very nice things, like taking family recipes from students and making them. And then their **theme dinners are just awesome**. They keep everything clean and in full supply, and they have good opening hours."

Q "We have Grab 'n' Go, which is really neat, because it lets **you make your own bag lunch when you are in a rush to get to class**. Grab 'n' Go has gotten so much better these days, with the salads they offer and the brownies."

Q "The **dining hall and the Snack Bar staff are the friendliest people on campus** and anywhere else. They put so much effort into everything, and it works, from international food nights to stress busters during exam week."

Q "During exam week, the dining halls on campus do **late-night snacks**. It is just what everyone needs."

STUDENT AUTHOR: While they may not make the best veggie pizza on earth, the campus dining facilities do an adequate job of allowing vegetarians and other individuals with diverse eating habits to stay satisfied. Most of the time, the food tastes good and is fresh. Williams on-campus dining has also been very successful in creating a pleasant atmosphere for enjoying your food, and they might surprise you with new recipes and touches.

Student Body

African American:	10%	Male/Female:	50/50%
Asian American:	11%	Out-of-State:	86%
Hispanic:	9%	International:	7%
Native American:	<1%	Unknown:	0%
White:	63%		

Popular Faiths: The most popular faiths on campus are Protestantism and Catholicism.

Gay Pride: Gay pride is high, but in the past, some homophobic e-mails were sent out to the members of the Queer Student Union.

Economic Status: The majority of students are wealthy and upper-middle-class.

Students Speak Out
ON DORMS

Q "Williams College has a perverted custom called 'the housing lottery.' It's supposed to be fair, but it is not. If you are picking with upperclassmen, you could get a good number and pick whatever dorm you like, but **if you are picking with people from your class, you are screwed**."

Q "I **never had a roommate at Williams**, not even freshman year. I enjoyed the privacy very much. At the same time, I knew I could room with someone if I had wanted to, and living alone never made my social life any less fun."

Q "If you have a car, **there are some very nice dorms** you could live in. But if you don't want to walk in the cold, you might want to pick the ones that are close to buildings where classes meet."

STUDENT AUTHOR: **Although some people do get lucky, most underclassmen are crammed into small rooms and bathrooms, and even some upperclassmen end up in a room where they have to hear a drilling noise for 10 hours a day. At the same time, though, construction and renovation have had very positive impacts on some dorms, while the overall comfort, hygiene, and accessibility have always been excellent.**

Did You Know?
93% of undergrads live on campus.

Students Speak Out
ON GUYS & GIRLS

Q "If you are gay, there's going to be between **three and five hot guys on campus that are out as being gay and available**. At least two of them will not be your type of guy, and one will be too weird. The other two, hopefully, are into threesomes and will invite you to join."

Q "**Guys at Williams are very immature**. They drink too much and can be obnoxious at parties, trying to touch you. Many are good-looking, but it's not worth it."

Q "**Williams girls dress and act like guys**. I don't know how they think someone can be attracted to them. They look sloppy and don't take care of themselves."

STUDENT AUTHOR: **Guys and girls at Williams and elsewhere spend a lot of time complaining about each other, but the truth is that they are just like most college students. Most create strong friendships, and those who wish to commit do form relationships. Williams students are good-looking and athletic and like to have a lot of fun. It is said that 50 percent of Williams graduates marry another Williams student. Scary or not, this says a lot about whether we like each other.**

Traditions

Class Banners
Each class designs a banner that will represent them while at school and at reunions in the future.

Ivy Planting
At graduation, a member of the graduating class plants ivy next to a wall or a building.

Overall School Spirit
Mucho Macho Moocow Marching Band is the cheering section at football games and a big provider to school spirit.

Students Speak Out
ON ATHLETICS

Q "Athletics are great at Williams. **You really learn to be on a team and work with other people** to be successful. I think it really makes you a better person, in a way. However, it is a lot of really hard work. I don't blame people who are not on teams for holding a grudge against 'the jocks,' as they call us, because they just don't have the guts to make the sort of commitment we make every single day."

Q "I didn't like the physical education requirement at Williams. Why should **you have to take a certain number of PE classes** if it's not really your thing?"

Q "If you are not on an athletic team at Williams, your social life sucks. **Teams have their own parties**, which tend to exclude everybody else."

STUDENT AUTHOR: **Athletics at Williams is for talents and amateurs, for devoted fans and new recruits, for everyone who loves sports, and even for those who might not be that athletic at all. The wonderful facilities on campus come alive with the spirit and effort of those who learn, teach, compete, play, or just have fun.**

Students Speak Out
ON DRUG SCENE

Q "I know **people smoke weed** at Williams, but not as much as many other colleges I have visited. I like that, because nobody is pressured to do anything."

Q "People at Williams **don't really do drugs**. They play too many sports for that. We love alcohol and good cigars, though."

Q "There has to be some sort of drug scene at Williams, but **I have never seen it**, and I'm glad. If you came to college to learn and stay healthy, Williams is right for you."

Q "Despite the athletic culture of the school, people find ways to enjoy life. **Alcohol is a good thing when it's negative 40 outside**, and an occasional joint helps, too."

Q "The drug scene at Williams? **We have one?** I didn't know that."

STUDENT AUTHOR: As most students indicate, there hardly is a drug scene at Williams. Yet, there's always that voice in the corner saying that the drug scene is flourishing if you know where to look.

7:1	Student-to-Faculty Ratio
97%	Freshman Retention Rate
91%	Four-Year Graduation Rate
89%	Financial Aid Applicants Receiving Aid

Students Speak Out
SAFETY & SECURITY

Q "**Williamstown is a small town, and it's safe**. The most you can do about your personal security is make sure none of the other people in your dorm steal your shampoo in the bathroom, which they will anyway."

Q "The campus looks safe, but sometimes, things go on at parties that should never happen and that most people don't report. I think some **more female security officers would be good for this campus**."

Q "The security officers are very nice. They help people a lot, and I really like that **they offer to take you to your dorm after midnight**—not that Williamstown isn't a safe place in general."

STUDENT AUTHOR: There is no doubt that the town and college of Williams are safe. Overall, the security staff makes sure the campus is safe and that students have a reliable source for their safety needs. All-in-all, they do a good job of making one feel safe at his or her home away from home.

Questions?
For more inside information and survival tips, pick up College Prowler's full-length book on this school, written by an actual student! Check it out at www.collegeprowler.com.

Students Speak Out
ON OVERALL EXPERIENCE

Q "After four years at Williams, I don't really feel ready for the real world, just because **Williams is not the real world**. Williams is a place that shelters you from the world in many ways, and it tries to educate you in a very thorough, but not necessarily practical, way. I had a very good time attending classes, hanging out with friends, and just being myself here, because there was so little pressure to deal with the external reality of things."

Q "**Williams is great—if you are white and rich**. I realize this is true of many other places. I know, though, that the College has tried to make those of us who are not white and rich feel at home. I wish other students, too, could have this in mind, not just the institution. Socially, I was always in a group of friends from the same race as myself."

Q "Williams was the perfect place for me to keep up on my interests and passions from high school. I think I picked up a few new ones, too, and **really learned a lot in my major** because of the great faculty we have here. I like this place so much, and I am not ready to leave at all because I always feel like I am learning."

STUDENT AUTHOR: No matter what the admissions office tries to tell you, the Williams campus is not particularly diverse. Many students of color feel very alienated here, and so do white students who don't necessary fit the typical preppy profile. Besides admitting a fairly uniform and uninteresting student body, Williams has also placed them in a small and uninteresting town, where their social life is limited to keg parties with the same group of people every weekend.

Wright State University

3640 Colonel Glenn Highway; Dayton, OH 45435
(937) 775-3333; www.wright.edu

THE BASICS:

Acceptance Rate: 85%
Setting: Suburban
F-T Undergrads: 10,843

SAT Range: 870–1120
Control: Public
Tuition: $14,004

Most Popular Majors: Education, Business, Health Sciences, Engineering, Psychology

*of 1600

Academics	B-	Guys	B
Local Atmosphere	C+	Girls	B
Safety & Security	C+	Athletics	C+
Computers	A	Nightlife	C
Facilities	B	Greek Life	C-
Campus Dining	B-	Drug Scene	B
Off-Campus Dining	B	Campus Strictness	B
Campus Housing	A-	Parking	B-
Off-Campus Housing	A-	Transportation	B
Diversity	B	Weather	C+

Students Speak Out
ON ACADEMICS

Q "The teachers are well-educated and usually experienced in the field they are teaching. The **workload is sometimes overwhelming**, but it can be managed. The school is most known for its College of Computer Science and Engineering."

Q "Just like anywhere else, there are good teachers and horrible ones—more good than bad. The school is **known for its bad math department**. It's the worst department in the school."

Q "Many teachers in the engineering department are foreign. **They can be hard to understand at first**, but after a while, they are very enjoyable. As with most schools, the teachers that I have come across are hit or miss—some great, some awful, and some in between. Overall, I would say that they are good. Our school is known for being very handicap-accessible and for the amazing campus ministries of Chi Alpha."

Q For the most part, I would say **your work load is going to be moderate to heavy**, especially as you start in on your major and your junior and senior years."

STUDENT AUTHOR: The personal approach taken at Wright State is why students here succeed. Experienced and accessible, most teachers contribute to a well-rounded learning experience. Many faculty members are well-accomplished figures in their fields and in the community, so they know what they're talking about. While Wright State has outstanding business and engineering programs, all the colleges are reputable.

Students Speak Out
ON LOCAL ATMOSPHERE

Q "The atmosphere of the area surrounding WSU and the campus itself was **one of the main reasons I chose to come here**. It isn't a very busy city area, but it's not a slow country suburb either. The Fairborn/Beavercreek area is full of great shops and restaurants."

Q "I like the atmosphere of the Fairborn area alright. **I wish it were more of a typical college town**, with more houses to live in instead of primarily apartments. Sometimes it feels like campus was just dropped down kind of randomly."

Q "It's an energetic atmosphere where people are always on the go. **Be careful in certain parts of downtown after hours**. Definitely check out the Dayton Art Institute, Wright Brothers' Memorial, Air Force Museum, and the Oregon District."

Q "Wright State is right on the edge of Dayton, Ohio. I find the city rather boring. Dayton is also home to the University of Dayton and Sinclair Community College, both of which are located downtown, whereas we are much farther away. **Wright State has a suburban feel, but it is definitely not in a college town**."

STUDENT AUTHOR: Wright State is in the suburban areas of Beavercreek and Fairborn instead of downtown Dayton, which makes the area safer and less congested. At the same time, it also offers lots of shops, restaurants, and sources of entertainment. WSU's proximity to everything in the vicinity makes whatever you want just a short drive away.

5 Best Things	5 Worst Things
1 Location	1 Parking
2 Tunnels	2 Parking tickets
3 Campus recreation	3 Lack of party scene
4 Variety of majors	4 Campus food
5 Small class sizes	5 Lack of sports

Students Speak Out
ON FACILITIES

Q "The facilities, to me, are a bright spot for Wright State. **A lot of the buildings are being remodeled** or have been remodeled in the past few years, and that makes the campus look very nice."

Q "One of the best parts about Wright State is the tunnel system that connects every major building on campus. **Once you get onto campus, if you don't want to, you don't have to go outside.** Only the Fred White building is not connected, but unless you're a med student, you probably won't have to go there."

Q "The facilities on campus are generally nice. The **fitness center in the Student Union is awesome**! And I'm partial to the libraries—they're easily accessible, and the staff's always eager to help."

Q "Wright State is only 40 years old in 2007, so none of the buildings are older than that. Most of the facilities are pretty nice, and we **are constantly renovating** some part of the campus. Rike, Millett, Russ, the Joshi Center, Fred White, and the Student Union are all either recently renovated or completely new."

Q "I work at the library, and I'd say it has a lot to offer as far as **places to study, laptops to rent, and resources like you wouldn't believe**."

STUDENT AUTHOR: **Wright State's campus is as contemporary as it is innovative. Expansive, brand-new facilities provide students with most of the resources they need to learn in an environment that feels like one of the best. What Wright State doesn't have are adequate sports facilities. Instead of a track to run on, athletes run on grass.**

Famous Alumni

Ron Amos, Erik Bork, Annette Clayton, Don Brown, Kevin DeWine, Roger Kintzel, Gregory Lockhart, Ron Marshall, Gary McCullough, Adam White

Students Speak Out
ON CAMPUS DINING

Q "**You have two choices: expensive health food or cheap fast food.** Union Market has good food, but it is pricey. The Hangar is good only because it has fast food chains. They do have a nice salad bar that doesn't hurt your wallet, though."

Q "I think the food on campus is good. But **it is a little pricey**, and I don't like that freshmen in the dorms have to get such a big meal plan because you end up having to waste some of it."

Q "The food is great. I have no complaints. There is **plenty of variety between the Hangar and the Union Market**: fast food, grilled, subs, wraps, home-cooked, pastas, pizzas, Asian, etc. It's pretty expensive, but you just have to play it smart and plan accordingly."

Q "The food here is **definitely better than some campuses**."

Q "The food is too expensive, especially at the C-Store, and the hours are bad, with nothing being open late or on the weekends. **The best place is the Hangar** because of the different choices and the better prices."

STUDENT AUTHOR: **The Union Market offers several multicultural and homestyle options, and the Hangar offers mostly fast food options. There are enough choices for students to eat healthy at both locations. Each place has a salad and soup bar with a wide selection, and both have ready-made fruits and salads. However, the healthy food and the Union Market in general are more expensive than the fast food at the Hangar.**

Student Body

African American:	14%	Male/Female:	45/55%
Asian American:	3%	Out-of-State:	4%
Hispanic:	2%	International:	1%
Native American:	<1%	Unknown:	6%
White:	74%		

Popular Faiths: Christianity is the largest religious influence at Wright State.

Gay Pride: Campus groups work together to provide awareness of their supportive resources and a safe atmosphere for LGBT students in the community.

Economic Status: The student body is comprised mostly of students from middle-class families.

Students Speak Out
ON DORMS

Q "The dorms are very nice at Wright State. **If you could avoid one, it should be Hamilton Hall.** The 'Ham,' as it is called, has communal showers and bathrooms, while in all other housing you share a bathroom with three or four other people."

Q "The honors dorms are wonderful. The dorms are **suite-style with bathrooms in between every two rooms**, so you only have to share a bathroom with four people. Plus, they are only a few years old and include a weight room, tanning spa, and convenience store in the same building. However, you can find more parties in the Woods."

Q "The dorms aren't bad. They are a little small but **definitely bigger than some other ones I've seen**."

STUDENT AUTHOR: The floor plans and ages of Wright State's on-campus living facilities put them among the state's best, according to focus groups of prospective and current students. Wright State is also one of the few schools in the state to offer apartments to single students. There is no freshman housing requirement, but most freshmen choose to live on campus.

Did You Know?
22% of undergrads live on campus.

Students Speak Out
ON GUYS & GIRLS

Q "The typical female student is laid-back with a good personality and typically blonde and short. The guys are guys. **You have your jocks, punks, computer geeks, and 'unique' ones**."

Q "A typical student is 5'9" wearing a canvas shoulder bag, a pair of blue jeans, and three layered shirts, probably wears a leather bracelet, and definitely has pierced ears. Guy or girl? You decide."

Q "There are some hot guys, but **mostly they're all friendly**, and I get along with them really well."

Q "There are a lot of girls who are fun, but some of them are just **drama, drama, drama all the time**."

STUDENT AUTHOR: In general, everything in the Midwest is average. Most people at Wright State are ordinary, but they're nice people. At first glance, everyone looks the same, although there is a variety of styles, and certain people stick out more than others. Serious guys and girls mean serious relationships, and without much of a social scene, there is lack of promiscuity as well. It's hard to get into a relationship at Wright State because most students commute.

Traditions

Chalking
Every year, sidewalk squares are filled with different messages, usually about student organizations, that students draw with sidewalk chalk.

Rock Painting
Students spray paint a large rock near Lot 10. It's a good tool for students to make a point about something they feel strongly about, and it's just fun.

Overall School Spirit
School spirit is very apathetic, but it's improving.

Students Speak Out
ON ATHLETICS

Q "I think, overall, our school isn't the most popular when it comes to sports, but I think over the past few years **our school has become more notable and recognized**. I think our sports programs are just as good as the other schools within Ohio."

Q "The first thing that sticks out about varsity sports is that **WSU doesn't have a football team**. This has led to a school with a lack of school pride and school spirit."

Q "**Intramural sports are a highlight**, giving students the chance to stay active and participate. The club hockey team has competed nationally the past few years and is definitely very good."

Q "I would say the varsity sports are very well received on campus. **There seems to be a genuine interest in them**."

STUDENT AUTHOR: This is not a sports school. Wright State doesn't even have a football team. Neither is there much school spirit. Intramural sports and sports clubs are more popular than varsity sports with students who aren't varsity athletes. But even if the current scene is dismal, Wright State athletics has a future.

Students Speak Out
ON DRUG SCENE

Q "It's really hard to get drugs on campus, but it's **easier than getting a sandwich off campus**."

Q "I've seen a lot of it. It's mostly just pot, but I have seen people who were on other drugs like acid, mushrooms, or cocaine. **I've seen it all on campus**."

Q "**I don't really see a dominant drug scene** on campus, which is not to say it is nonexistent. I think alcohol consumption outweighs drug use, like marijuana and such, but I don't see it as being a problem at WSU. Most people seem to have their heads on straight."

STUDENT AUTHOR: **The drug scene at Wright State exists, but it's easily avoidable. People smoke a lot of weed, but the harder drugs are very exclusive. Drugs are easier to get off campus, and there are certain parts of Fairborn and Beavercreek where it's prevalent. At Wright State, there is no pressure to use drugs but you can find them if you want. In fact, there's more pressure not to use drugs than to use them.**

17:1	Student-to-Faculty Ratio
70%	Freshman Retention Rate
18%	Four-Year Graduation Rate
85%	Financial Aid Applicants Receiving Aid

Students Speak Out
SAFETY & SECURITY

Q "Of course, there is the occasional security issue, but overall, I think Wright State is a very safe place. I have lived on campus for three years, and I have always felt at home here. Plus, the University is **very good at making students aware of any potential threats** and ways to avoid them."

Q "Wright State campus is **very safe nowadays compared to the past couple of years**. Due to some criminal events on campus, Wright State security has become tighter and safer."

Q "Safety and security on campus is decent. **We have had some bad things happen**, such as a mugging in the parking lot, but the school responded the same night and started a nighttime dorm-to-campus shuttle."

STUDENT AUTHOR: **Wright State is safe enough that students can feel comfortable roaming campus grounds and walking to classes from their dorms at any time of day. That's not to say that crime never occurs, though. When a serious incident occurs, all students are notified of the situation and given safety advice.**

Questions?
For more inside information and survival tips, pick up College Prowler's full-length book on this school, written by an actual student! Check it out at *www.collegeprowler.com*.

Students Speak Out
ON OVERALL EXPERIENCE

Q "One of my best memories while attending Wright State was the way the other people on my floor and I **bonded and became a tight-knit circle of friends** freshman year. We were able to retain our friendships throughout the following five years and beyond."

Q "**People say 'Wright State, Wrong School.'** Two words: Don't listen. Wright State has tons of excellent programs to choose from, and there is no place I would rather be."

Q "Wright State is a great place. I would probably come here again if I had it to do all over. My favorite parts were chilling with my friends on the Quad and catching the professors and chatting with them in the Hangar. **My least favorite parts were the rising prices** and being too close to home at times."

Q "**The place has a rhythm all its own**. It's hard to explain until you've been here awhile, but there is a pacing to it, a heartbeat. The places people hang out are relatively few and close together, and so it's not really hard to find anyone. It's a pretty intimate place for a college with almost 17,000 students."

STUDENT AUTHOR: **It is easy to find good friends who share your interests and just as easy to meet many new types of people, all of whom contribute to the "outside the classroom" education that is necessary for personal growth. What many students find most valuable in their academic experience at Wright State is the relationships with their professors. As you advance in your degree, classes become smaller and the level of personal interaction with your professors becomes much greater.**

Xavier University

3800 Victory Parkway; Cincinnati, OH 45207
(513) 745-3000; www.xavier.edu

THE BASICS:

Acceptance Rate: 73%
Setting: Urban
F-T Undergrads: 3,961

SAT Range: 1050–1280*
Control: Private
Tuition: $26,250

Most Popular Majors: Business, Liberal Arts, Communications, Education, Social Sciences

*of 1600

Academics	B	Guys	C+
Local Atmosphere	C+	Girls	B-
Safety & Security	B	Athletics	A-
Computers	B+	Nightlife	C+
Facilities	B+	Greek Life	N/A
Campus Dining	C+	Drug Scene	B+
Off-Campus Dining	B+	Campus Strictness	B
Campus Housing	B+	Parking	B+
Off-Campus Housing	B-	Transportation	B-
Diversity	D+	Weather	C+

Students Speak Out
ON ACADEMICS

Q "Most teachers are **friendly and professional**. In the honors program, classes are relatively small."

Q "There have been a few classes where I thought the professor could have been a little less anal. However, overall, I have found the professors to be **very helpful and extremely interesting**. I am looking forward to getting into my major classes."

Q "I personally haven't had any trouble with any of my teachers, some of my friends have, but I think the teachers are great. I find some classes more interesting than others. The core classes are pretty boring, but once you get into the higher-level classes, **it gets more fun**."

Q "Once you get into the upper-level courses of a particular department, **the more interesting classes seem to get**. Even if the beginning classes in your major don't appeal to you as much as you'd hope, chances are you'll get what you like eventually. Also, you can check in the course catalog, and see if what's offered in the next couple of years is interesting to you."

STUDENT AUTHOR: **Xavier has been recognized nationally for many years in the area of academic excellence, and rightly so. The unique ethics/religion and society core ties many of the courses together so that all students gain a common understanding of their Jesuit education and its ethical implications.**

Students Speak Out
ON LOCAL ATMOSPHERE

Q "It's **a mix of urban ghetto and rich**, white, suburban kids. Keep off the streets at night, and go to parties with a group of people. It's the best way to stay safe."

Q "Cincinnati is mostly **a boring, conservative Midwestern city**. However, it is a particularly large city, and there are things to do."

Q "The atmosphere in this town sucks pretty bad. There isn't really a whole lot to do, unless you want to spend some serious cash. There are other universities in the area, which makes the scene a little better simply due to the availability of many, many parties. I'd say that it would be wise to stay away from certain parts of the downtown area, as they're extremely dangerous. The Playhouse in the Park, the Museum of Art, and a football game in the Pit at Elder High School are certainly things every person should **try at least once in his or her life**."

Q "Cincinnati has the characteristics common of **any middle U.S. city**. There are professional sports teams to watch, movies to go to, places to hang out, and so on."

STUDENT AUTHOR: **The atmosphere of "the Nati," as it's called by many of its locals, is culturally diverse but very conservative. There are different pockets of culture scattered throughout the area, with strong German influences in almost all of the architecture.**

5 Best Things

1 Friendly people
2 Crosstown Shootout
3 Free tutoring
4 Easy to get a job
5 You can bring your car

5 Worst Things

1 Limited nightlife
2 No football
3 Not very diverse
4 Parking on the Hill
5 Boring core classes

Students Speak Out
ON FACILITIES

Q "The student center is poorly named, because **there is little there for students**. The Cintas Center arena is great, but O'Connor is lacking."

Q "**The student center is shiny and new**, but not really good for much else than getting an overpriced sub, or the occasional cup of coffee. They change the hours that they are open all the time, so you never know when you can actually eat there."

Q "The **facilities at Xavier are beautiful**. They are the best I have ever seen."

Q "The facilities are very nice. They are all kept clean, and **we usually have all the latest equipment** available. The Gallagher Student Center is certainly among the best in the nation as far as amenities for the students, events, and things to do on a study break."

Q "The facilities at the sports center are decent at best. They could really be updated, or even rebuilt, if the necessary funds were raised for it. The computers now have flat screens in the library, so they are pretty nice. The student center is relatively new, so that is **about as nice as it comes**."

STUDENT AUTHOR: For the most part, the facilities on campus at Xavier are first class. There are many computer labs in the academic buildings and in each dorm, so students have access to computers 24 hours a day. A variety of shops and restaurants, as well as sofas and flat-screen TVs make the student center a popular place.

Famous Alumni

Ken Blackwell, Jim Bunning, Janet Smith Dickerson, John Dreyer, Dr. Charles M. Geschke, Brian Grant, Tyrone Hill, David West

Students Speak Out
ON CAMPUS DINING

Q "The dining hall and the overall quality of food are pretty decent **when compared to other schools**."

Q "Personally, I like the food at the cafeteria in the Cintas Center. A lot of my friends say they don't, but **I think it's pretty good**. If you ask me, a good turkey sandwich with some honey mustard sauce will go a long way."

Q "The food served on campus at Xavier is hit-or-miss. Sometimes, the caf will serve a really good dinner, other times, everything looks like vomit. **I've heard it's much better than other schools**, but it's certainly not your mom's home cooking."

Q "The food at the Hoff Dining Center (the Caf) is rather good, **offering healthy food along with college staples** such as pizza, hamburgers, and lunch meats."

Q "If you want to pretend you're eating at a restaurant and still be able to use your meal plan, then **go to Ryan's Pub**. The service is usually pretty slow, but the food is pretty good."

STUDENT AUTHOR: Commonly referred to as the "Caf," the Hoff Dining Hall is the money spot for a good breakfast after an all-night cram session. Overall, the food selection at Xavier is decent but can sometimes be scarce, due to there being only two dining locations. Luckily for the students, *http://xudining.com* will tell you if there's nothing exiting on the menu, from the comfort of your own dorm. If that's the case, calling in a pizza delivery is the popular choice at XU.

Student Body

African American:	9%	Male/Female:	48/52%
Asian American:	2%	Out-of-State:	47%
Hispanic:	4%	International:	1%
Native American:	1%	Unknown:	<1%
White:	82%		

Popular Faiths: Catholicism is the primary religion, since XU is a Catholic Jesuit school.

Gay Pride: Groups like the Xavier Alliance ensure that GLBT students are treated equally and have a voice in the campus community.

Economic Status: Xavier is a pricy place, so there's a major influx of upper-middle-class students.

Students Speak Out
ON DORMS

Q "Buenger, Kuhlman, the Commons, and the Village are nice. **Avoid everything else**, unless you'd like to live in Brockman for the social stuff."

Q "The dorms are all really nice. They are **much better than the average school**. For the social aspect, I would encourage all freshmen to live in Brockman. Yes, there are community bathrooms, but they are cleaned by maids, and I never experienced a line or anything."

Q "**If you like to study, then Buenger is nice**. If you like to socialize, I recommend the other three dorms. I would say Kuhlman gives you the best combination of both lives, though."

STUDENT AUTHOR: **One of the advantages of being at a smaller school is that housing is typically nicer than you would find at a major state university. At Xavier, you're usually in good shape, regardless of which of the dorms you end up in. The only all-freshman dorm is Brockman Hall, the oldest and most traditional dorm on campus. Xavier houses its upperclassmen in on-campus apartments, but getting in can be a gamble, depending on your lottery number.**

> **? Did You Know?**
> 46% of undergrads live on campus.

Students Speak Out
ON GUYS & GIRLS

Q "The guys are, for the most part, obsessed with sports, while **the girls are all Catholic** and not very hot at all."

Q "The guys and girls at Xavier are usually well dressed, and that is probably because of their general family income (upper-middle-class to upper-class). Plenty of people take part in sports and clubs, so **many of the students are in good shape**, as well."

Q "Well, I've heard from both sexes that the **choices are somewhat, um, limited**."

Q "The people here aren't exceptionally gorgeous, and **most of them honestly look the same**. The school is overwhelmingly white, and everyone dresses in preppy clothing."

STUDENT AUTHOR: **In the looks department, the females at Xavier, for the most part, don't disappoint; plus, most of them are capable of having an intelligent conversation! And plenty of the female coeds seem to find a way to look beyond negative stigmas stuck on the guys. The dating scene at X is lacking mainly because, for the most part, there are only two extremes: drunken hookups and marriage.**

> **Traditions**
>
> **The Crosstown Shootout**
> Every year, the entire town experiences a division of allegiance between XU and University of Cincinnati basketball teams.
>
> **The Pig Roast**
> This decades-old event commemorates the last week of class and is the last campus party before summer.
>
> **Overall School Spirit**
> Xavier students are definitely proud of their school, and it shows. It's hard to miss the spirit that surrounds XU.

Students Speak Out
ON ATHLETICS

Q "Basketball is the main staple of Xavier University. Unfortunately, the **other sports at the school do not get much recognition**. The intramural sports range through many popular sports and give students the chance of competing in different leagues at different levels of competition."

Q "**Basketball is life** for a lot of folks. Intramural basketball is huge, too. Come to think of it, people here are just basketball crazy."

Q "Intramural sports are **a whole lot of fun**. I play at least one each season. They're competitive enough to get a good game, but relaxed enough to have fun at the same time."

Q "The basketball team is huge. The **students get free tickets** to all the home games, and a large number of students are always present at them."

STUDENT AUTHOR: **The fact that Xavier does not have a football team hurts the athletic atmosphere on campus. However, during basketball season, there is no better place to be in the NCAA than at Xavier. Aside from varsity sports, the intramural and club programs at X are popular and well organized.**

Students Speak Out
ON DRUG SCENE

Q "As on any campus, there is the presence of drugs. From what I hear, **marijuana is the drug of choice** for the users, but some do take painkillers, and occasionally, even the harder stuff."

Q "**There isn't any pressure** to take drugs. At a liberal arts college, everyone is cool with a person's personal choices. However, if you wanted to do that stuff, I guess it is possible."

Q "Actually, if there is a drug scene, I would say it is limited, or much hidden within certain groups, because **I don't see a lot of it**. There are a number of people who spend some time with their alcohol, though."

STUDENT AUTHOR: **If you were looking for drugs, chances are, you could ask around and find someone involved in the drug scene, but its visibility is so low that you could go about your normal daily routine without being exposed to drugs, and could even go to parties where alcohol is the only drug involved.**

13:1	Student-to-Faculty Ratio
88%	Freshman Retention Rate
66%	Four-Year Graduation Rate
80%	Financial Aid Applicants Receiving Aid

Students Speak Out
SAFETY & SECURITY

Q "Security on campus is good. The surrounding area is **a bit sketchy after dark**. Just use common sense, and you'll be fine."

Q "I find on-campus security to be quite adequate. Security **officers are abundant**, and they are always available if you need some sort of help."

Q "I have never heard of any on-campus attacks upon students. There is an Xavier University police force, and **they are always on call**. There is also a shuttle which will take students to locations as far as a mile off campus. This is especially useful during late nights at school. I believe they're available for parties, as well."

STUDENT AUTHOR: **As long as you are on Xavier University property, you feel relatively safe. While neighboring streets are not quite as pristine, there seems to be a heavily enforced bubble that keeps those who live and work at Xavier safe.**

Questions?

For more inside information and survival tips, pick up College Prowler's full-length book on this school, written by an actual student! Check it out at *www.collegeprowler.com*.

Students Speak Out
ON OVERALL EXPERIENCE

Q "I really like it here, mostly because of the friends I have made, including some of my teachers. Although **I sometimes wish the school were a little bigger**, or Cincinnati was more entertaining, I enjoy it."

Q "**This school is kind of lame**. I sometimes wish I went to Ohio State or Dayton."

Q "I am enjoying Xavier very much. The friends that I have made are great, and **I am involved with many clubs** and organizations. I wish that I was a little closer to home sometimes. However, it is nice to be able to be on my own and have a little independence."

Q "I really like Xavier because of **the personal interaction in the classes** and the amount of help that professors are willing to give. With this in mind, I love being here, as I am absolutely focused on my academics and where they will take me. Most everyone here is very friendly and outgoing. But, I do think that whether or not this is the right school for someone all depends on the personality of that student."

STUDENT AUTHOR: **The combination of a small school where you can get to know everyone with a big-school atmosphere, including big-time college sports and a big city to explore, makes Xavier a fun and interesting place to be. The reason that Xavier has such a high retention rate is that people who take an honest look at Xavier normally want to go here, and rarely are they let down. It's clear when you visit here that things are laid-back, there are no gigantic parties on a weekly basis, and everything is in general serene and comfortable.**

Yale University

149 Elm Street; New Haven, CT
(203) 432-4771; www.yale.edu

THE BASICS:

Acceptance Rate: 9% **SAT Range:** 1390–1580*
Setting: Urban **Control:** Private
F-T Undergrads: 5,304 **Tuition:** $33,030

Most Popular Majors: Social Sciences, History, Interdisciplinary Studies, English, Biology

*of 1600

Academics	A	Guys	B+
Local Atmosphere	B-	Girls	C+
Safety & Security	B-	Athletics	C+
Computers	A-	Nightlife	B-
Facilities	A-	Greek Life	C-
Campus Dining	B	Drug Scene	B
Off-Campus Dining	B+	Campus Strictness	A
Campus Housing	A	Parking	C-
Off-Campus Housing	B	Transportation	C-
Diversity	B+	Weather	C+

Students Speak Out
ON ACADEMICS

Q "The professors I have met here seem pretty down to earth. Some are a bit stuck on themselves, but otherwise they're not bad. Careful, **some of these guys are in the serious market for younger women**."

Q "Most professors are excellent equally as scholars and teachers. They communicate effectively, engagingly, and with authority. It's hard to construct a schedule that isn't mostly composed of classes taught by great professors. That said, there is the occasional professor who is incoherent, either due to limited command of English or poor organizational skills. Those **professors can be identified**, and easily avoided, thanks to Yale's 'shopping period.'"

Q "Yale is known for their undergraduate focus, and **all professors are required to teach undergrads**. This is a huge advantage, since either way you are paying for their salaries; you might as well have access to them."

STUDENT AUTHOR: **Although students seem happy with their education at Yale, most realize that a successful course load depends not only on the professors and the material, but also on the careful selection of classes. If you talk to students here, some will say Yale is a breeze, and some will say it's the most challenging experience of their lives. This difference of opinion does not rely on the students' intelligence or the easiness or difficulty of their majors; it has to do with how many opportunities to learn they are willing to accept.**

Students Speak Out
ON LOCAL ATMOSPHERE

Q "New Haven tends to get a bad rap among high school students considering elite universities, but I think the city has a lot to offer. It has plenty of stores and restaurants to cater to students' needs. Beyond that, there's a **substantial amount of cultural and other resources** in the city for students to take advantage of, if they so choose. Yes, New Haven isn't as antiseptic and shiny as Princeton, NJ. But, it's a 'real' city, with real issues, and with real potential for students to get involved in the community in a meaningful way."

Q "New Haven has **started to become more of a college town**, so the parts closest to the colleges are really nice. You have to walk for a bit to get into the rougher parts, and no one really goes there because there's nothing there for us. Overall, it's fine."

Q "Even though people sometimes say that New Haven is dangerous, I haven't had any trouble. **There is an escort service available** to walk you back to your dorm when you're at the library late, have a laptop with you, or just if you feel a little nervous."

STUDENT AUTHOR: **Yale, the bastion of wealth and privilege, is surrounded by an impoverished area. However, it affords students the opportunity to interact with an urban city, a true advantage if you want to make a difference. On a different note, the area immediately around Yale is a bohemian, college town. At Yale, there is a real range of things to do, just not enough time to do it all!**

5 Best Things	5 Worst Things
1 Professors	1 Weather
2 Architecture	2 Bad neighborhoods
3 Study abroad program	3 Legacies
4 Residential system	4 No parking
5 University art gallery	5 Dating scene

Students Speak Out
ON FACILITIES

Q "**Each residential college has special features**. For example, Saybrook College has a darkroom, and Branford College has squash courts. Each college has its own buttery (small food shop), kitchen, TV room, gym, laundry room, common room, dining hall, and library."

Q "The facilities are decent. I don't have much to compare them to. The **gym is huge**. Each residential college has some special features, and some are better than others."

Q "Awesome. There's **no real student center**, but that's not a problem; there are tons of places to gather and do stuff."

Q "The library is gorgeous, and the gym is huge. There are computers everywhere—even outside the dining halls. The **facilities are definitely up to par**."

Q "The **computer clusters are up-to-date** and always available . . . I don't think we really have an official student center, though."

STUDENT AUTHOR: Most students agree that the facilities at Yale are pretty nice. The classroom buildings are often as picturesque as cathedrals, affording students the opportunity to learn amidst stained glass and Gothic stone work. There is no student center at Yale, but students agree that the lack of such a place is rarely, if ever, missed. Each residential college has a common room for meetings or just hanging out, as well as a library, dining hall, TV room, laundry room, and features such as private gyms, kitchens, darkrooms, or music rooms. Essentially, they are self-contained units.

Famous Alumni

Angela Bassett, George H.W. Bush, George W. Bush, Bill Clinton, Hillary Clinton, Jodie Foster, Ed Norton, Meryl Streep, Sigourney Weaver

Students Speak Out
ON CAMPUS DINING

Q "We have many dining halls; the food is pretty good. You will have a meal plan that allows you to eat at Commons, which is our main dining hall, and all of the 12 residential colleges has its own dining hall. There are 'Pan Geos' stations at each college that prepare things like wraps, pasta, and Asian food right in front of you. The more recently renovated colleges seem to have better food. Branford, Saybrook, and Berkeley seem to have better options. I like eating at Commons because it's open longer. Each college has a personality. You can also have **a different meal plan that gives you Flex Dollars to spend at local places** like Au Bon Pain and Yorkside Pizza."

Q "The dining hall food is mediocre at best. **The food is repetitive and fattening**. Its main downfall is self-serve, unlimited portions, so students have a tendency to consume mass quantities of food at each meal. The vegetables and fruits are usually not very fresh and a limited selection is available. For late-night snacking, each residential college has a buttery, where fried foods and other treats can be purchased for cheap prices."

STUDENT AUTHOR: The limited dining hall hours can be inconvenient for busy students whose schedules might be a bit unorthodox. Yale does not have on-campus restaurants for further options, and the dining hall plan is mandatory for those living on campus. Despite these drawbacks, dining hall food is still the most convenient option.

Student Body

African American:	8%	Male/Female:	51/49%
Asian American:	14%	Out-of-State:	92%
Hispanic:	8%	International:	8%
Native American:	1%	Unknown:	12%
White:	50%		

Popular Faiths: Almost all religions are present and supported by the Yale community.

Gay Pride: Yale is a gay-friendly campus. The sizable gay community is vocal, and is known for throwing the best parties.

Economic Status: All economic statuses are represented at Yale. There is a large proportion of wealthy students, however.

Students Speak Out
ON DORMS

Q "Yale dorms are beautiful. The fact that they are organized into residential colleges makes them more incredible, since **you become a member of the community for four years**. You cannot pick your residential college (RC), but it doesn't really matter; all of them are incredible."

Q "I consider the college housing system one of Yale's most important assets. Which college you end up in isn't really so important. My college house is usually considered one of the 'ugly' ones, but I**'ve had a wonderful experience** with the dean, master, and most importantly, the students."

Q "**All the dorms have their perks**. There are either small rooms with good location or awesome rooms off in the corners of campus. Many have been renovated."

STUDENT AUTHOR: **Most students agree that Yale's residential college system provides students a place to live and learn that surpasses any other dorm experience. By combining social activities, extracurriculars, and academics, colleges become real homes for students for the four years they are at Yale.**

> **Did You Know?**
> 86% of undergrads live on campus.

Students Speak Out
ON GUYS & GIRLS

Q "Ha ha! **Not only are they hot; they are smart**! I am partial to the people at Yale, because the impression that I got was that they were much more down to earth and relaxed than people I've been introduced to before."

Q "I'm being perfectly honest; the **common rhetoric is that the dating scene at Yale stinks**. Some people do date, and some do have boyfriends or girlfriends, but mostly people like to complain about the dating scene, saying that it's usually more random hookups."

Q "For the most part, everyone is very friendly and easy to get along with. Also, **people aren't usually too cliquey**. You know how girls can be kind of catty? The girls at Yale totally aren't at all."

STUDENT AUTHOR: **The rumor that beauty is inversely proportional to intelligence is proven wrong at Yale. Not only are many guys and girls hot, they are talented, smart, funny, and interesting, as well. Unfortunately, Yale students are also busy— often too busy to have relationships. But for those who are looking for love, there is hope. Some students do find real love; some have even been known to get married!**

> ### Traditions
>
> #### Class Day (Day Before Commencement)
> It is tradition for students to smoke a special tobacco out of a clay pipe and to wave good-bye to Yale with a white handkerchief.
>
> #### Overall School Spirit
> School spirit is strong at Yale. Students are proud of the Yale name and are willing to defend it to the death against Harvard and Princeton. This is most apparent during the Harvard-Yale weekend. Alumni flock, and practically the entire student body goes to the game to cheer the football team to victory in New Haven or Boston.

Students Speak Out
ON ATHLETICS

Q "The football game against Harvard is obviously huge. Other than that, **it's not that big**."

Q "**IM sports are huge** at Yale, since residential colleges are so important. The competition is one of the fun parts of living in a residential college."

Q "Sports **aren't ridiculously big, but they are popular**. Football, basketball, and lacrosse are all huge. My suite mates also love going to the ice hockey games, as well. IMs are popular, but it does depend on the college you're in."

Q "**It's all about what you're into**. Varsity is big if we're winning. Football is always big. Harvard-Yale games are ridiculously fun. Intramurals (IMs) are big if you're into them."

STUDENT AUTHOR: **For a school with such a strong academic reputation, Yale has a pretty strong athletic program. From IMs to varsity sports, Yale offers options for every level of enthusiast. However, some students don't even know sports exist. Sports are as important as most other extracurricular activities. There are so many interests to pursue, and they all seem to be of equal importance.**

Students Speak Out
ON DRUG SCENE

Q "The drug scene isn't huge, but **you've definitely got your groups of stoners** and druggies. I feel like few people do things beyond smoking weed. I know some people who do coke occasionally, but that's all."

Q "I know people who smoke marijuana, but I can't comment on anything harder than that. The drug scene is **not very big around here**."

Q "There's not much of a drug scene that I know of. The **drug of choice seems to be alcohol**."

STUDENT AUTHOR: The drug scene on campus is surprisingly prevalent. Many of the students have the money to support a thriving drug habit and the stress to warrant one. Furthermore, the administration is very lax about their drug policies and punishments. However, while the drug scene exists, it is easily avoided. It is generally present within certain cliques. If you don't interact with people who use them, you might never even encounter drugs on campus. Students do not have to negotiate "peer pressure."

6:1	Student-to-Faculty Ratio
99%	Freshman Retention Rate
88%	Four-Year Graduation Rate
43%	Financial Aid Applicants Receiving Aid

Students Speak Out
SAFETY & SECURITY

Q "The **campus is really safe**. You need to have an ID card and keys to get into dorms and onto the freshman part of campus after hours. Yale Police are always around, and they are very friendly. You can always call the minibus to take you back to campus if it's late and you don't feel safe. Or you can call for an escort."

Q "It's fine. **New Haven in general isn't the safest city, but campus is a very nice area**, and I've never had any sort of problem with security. You just can't go too far away from campus alone at night, which you wouldn't do anyway in any city."

Q "**Safety is a non-issue**. There is a cop sub-station right on Old Campus, plus there are lots of cop cars out at night, especially on Cross Campus. If anything, you feel overly safe here."

STUDENT AUTHOR: Although New Haven is an urban setting with its share of crime, students agree that they generally feel safe on campus and in town. Most students agree that the safety services and security are a great resource. As long as you use common sense, there is rarely a reason to feel in danger.

Questions?
For more inside information and survival tips, pick up College Prowler's full-length book on this school, written by an actual student! Check it out at www.collegeprowler.com.

Students Speak Out
ON OVERALL EXPERIENCE

Q "I've had a great experience at school, both socially and academically. I definitely couldn't imagine being anywhere else. I think there is a place for everyone at Yale, since the University offers so much and is so diverse. We're not completely cutthroat, either. It is **much more laid-back than some Ivy League schools**, but it's still competitive. There's a good balance."

Q "I find that we Yalies tend to be **more low key and more down to earth**. We don't really care if somebody's got better grades than us. It's just not that competitive—at least that's the impression I get."

Q "I enjoyed aspects of Yale. **A lot depends on which program you are interested in** and what your study interests are. Some programs are great. You will find that there is a certain level of depersonalization present at any large university. I came from a small liberal arts high school and was used to a lot of individual, personal attention—you will most likely have to fight for that."

Q "I absolutely love Yale. If you want a **good experience with just as much status**, then Yale is wonderful."

STUDENT AUTHOR: Although students often complain about their piles of work or their small dorm rooms, in the end, all these problems fade into the background of the overall picture. Instead, all they see are the gorgeous buildings, amazing classes, and brilliant faculty. At Yale, you have the opportunity to grow academically, as well as personally. Most Yalies agree that this personal development is the most important and rewarding part of their college experience.

Verbal Outtakes

In the process of creating this book, we stumbled across some student quotes that were just too special to leave out. Read on for a little more of the good, the bad, and the truly insane.

"I once saw a homeless woman gathering up and eating the stray french fries on the countertops at the Lair. It made me question the security a bit, but it wasn't like an everyday occurrence."

(Loyola Marymount University Student – Safety & Security)

"The food is what it is: mass-produced, cafeteria-style goo."

(Baylor University Student – Campus Dining)

"Guys are generally gay or have a girlfriend. Girls are left being sexually frustrated, and I think that puts a crazed look in their eyes that makes them seem hotter."

(NYU Student – Guys & Girls)

"Sometimes, I think that this school and everyone in it is completely lame. Then I see something like a couch burning in the middle of the street and think, 'Wow, somebody around here is completely nuts,' and it gives me hope."

(West Virginia University Student – Overall Experience)

"They have these T-shirts: 'University of Chicago, where the squirrels are more aggressive than the guys,' and 'University of Chicago, where the squirrels are cuter than the girls.' That pretty much sums it all up."

(University of Chicago – Guys & Girls)

"Go to Bursley [Dining Hall] and get served by 'Sexy Grandpa.' He knows everyone's name and has worked there for decades. He is a campus legend!"

(University of Michigan – Campus Dining)

"Well, now you've heard it from the horses' mouths, and contrary to aphorism, feel free to look in these horses' mouths, and even to count their teeth, because they're not selling you a load of bull. Claremont just isn't cut out to be a college town. There isn't anything to do except walk around and buy overpriced doo-dads, which (i.e., the doo-dads) your grandmother might find appealing (not to cast aspersions on your grandmother's taste) but which (i.e., the doo-dads again) will likely leave you unimpressed."

(Peter Cook, Pomona College Author)

"THE GUYS ARE JERKS AND THE GIRLS ARE HOT—AND EVERY STUCK-UP, TANNED, SKINNY INCH OF THEM TELLS YOU THAT THEY KNOW IT, TOO."

(Trinity College -- Guys & Girls)

"OVERALL, THINGS HERE ARE PRETTY SAFE. I'VE NEVER HAD A PROBLEM WALKING HOME LATE AT NIGHT. THERE IS A SERIAL RAPIST ON THE LOOSE THOUGH . . ."

(University of Virginia Student – Safety & Security)

"I generally do not party on campus. I sit at home alone drinking Natural Light and reflecting on my failed life while my dogs and my cat stare at me with disgust and shame."

(Xavier Student – Nightlife)

"The dorms aren't that special. My first year in Lothrop Hall sucks. It's old, there is no air-conditioning, and right on top is a helicopter pad. Every night, the hospital helicopter takes off and lands a ton of times; it doesn't exactly help you sleep."

(University of Pittsburgh Student – Campus Housing)

"I came pretty close to getting arrested. Where? The top of Byrd Stadium. When? Some night around my junior year. Why? Cops were on a stakeout for a few students that had been throwing objects over the top of the stadium at moving vehicles and people in front of Ellicott Hall. What was I doing on top of the stadium? Well, I was throwing just about the smoothest mack-down on a pretty little girl who will remain nameless, to prevent any further embarrassment. Oh, did I tell you I had my saxophone up there? Yeah, that was 'sealing the deal' with my young lady friend. Except for the fact that the University police, after searching me, asked me to open the case very slowly and to step back, as if I had a small arsenal of dangerous and illegal objects. The cops were also on a stakeout for people smoking pot, which prompted a body search. Ah, the memories."

(University of Maryland Student – Campus Strictness)

"The best is when the vegans found out that the fries were being cooked in animal lard. Man, were they pissed."

(Bard College Student – Campus Dining)

"There's so many different kinds of people here. You'll meet people who have never even seen marijuana, and people who've snorted enough cocaine to kill a small horse! It's just like anywhere else: if you look for it, you can find it, whatever 'it' happens to be."

(University of Michigan Student – Drug Scene)

"There are all kinds here—hot, not, geek, preppy, whatever. All intelligent, though. If you're into geeky guys who think that handmade electronic teddy bears and hand-painted war game miniatures are romantic, this is definitely a good place to start. But there are plenty of more normal guys and girls out there, and plenty are interested in playing the field if you're into that sort of thing, too."

(MIT Student – Guys & Girls)

"Drive to Earhart Road and face south, then flash your headlights three times and you will see the headlights of a ghostly motorcycle appear and disappear at the curve where the rider died. Tip—remove your keys from the ignition and set them on your dashboard before you flash your lights."

(Miami of Ohio – Urban Legends)

"All undergraduates can get 12 free condoms per quarter."

(Stanford University Student – Safety & Security)

"If you ever wanted to experience what the caste system of India might be like, this is the place for you. When you step out of the 'Baylor bubble,' you can witness the plight of homeless Americans from the safety of your BMW or other equally expensive car."

(Baylor University Student – Guys & Girls)

"Varsity sports are about as popular as heat rash. No more than a few thousand students ever attend the football games (except for the season opener, which is always packed), and more people attend the cross-dressing fashion show in the Student Union than the basketball games."

(University at Buffalo Student – Athletics)

"Security once locked me into the library after doing their check to make sure the building was closed. I was studying on a couch in a public room when the lights went out . . . Our security is inadequate at best."

(Guilford Student – Safety & Security)

"The weather is freezing, miserable, and inhospitable. You sometimes feel like God wants you to die in this freezing, hellish wasteland."

(CMU Student – Weather)

"When I lived in Salley as a freshman, we couldn't decide if it was more like living in a Mexican prison cell or with the Teenage Mutant Ninja Turtles. If you like living in a shoebox complete with roaches and moldy ceiling tiles, try Kellum Hall and Smith Hall. If you like living in a shoebox with nicer furniture try Deviney and Dorman."

(Florida State Student – Campus Housing)

"One year, I got the privilege of living in a trailer—literally, a trailer. It was because Bard over-booked and ran out of places to put freshmen. Some people had to suffer in an actual building with foundations and stairs and different floors, but I was lucky enough to score something that they use to transport horses."

(Bard College Student – Campus Dining)

"The campus is very safe—Public Safety's tactics ensure that. But watch out! They have been known to run down a student or two with their Public Safety vans—I was a victim!"

(College of the Holy Cross Student – Safety & Security)

"THE GUYS HERE ARE ALL STUDS. TAKE ME FOR EXAMPLE; I AM 145 POUNDS OF RAW STEEL AND SEX APPEAL. WEST POINT DEFINITELY HAS THE STUDLIEST GUYS ON THE FACE OF THE PLANET."

(WEST POINT STUDENT – GUYS & GIRLS)

"I don't understand how you can gain the Freshman 15 if you constantly puke and poop out the food you just ate at the Fluh. Their new slogan should be, 'Weisenfluh is not just a place to eat, it's an epidemic.'"

(Slippery Rock Student– Campus Dining)

"The dorms are a great environment. The only thing they might need to change is their 'no hamster' rule; it is an inconvenience."

(Sacramento State Student – Campus Housing)

"Flip up your collar, puff out your chest, ignore your friends when you pass them on the street, develop a virgin-whore complex, complain bitterly about any and all work you're ever assigned, and buy a North Face jacket. There, you're a student at Hamilton."

(Hamilton College Student – Guys & Girls)

"Teachers range in quality from 'stunning' to 'where the hell did you graduate from? Auburn?!'"

(University of Alabama Student – Academics)

"I remember doing the 'walk of shame' a couple of times my freshman year. Those were good times."

(University of Rhode Island Student– Guys & Girls)

"ENROLLMENT AT COLBY COLLEGE IS CONTINGENT ON BEING A SEXY BEAST."

(COLBY COLLEGE – GUYS & GIRLS)

"Profs and classes. Yes, I've heard of those. Most of the time they really interfere with my sleeping schedule, but whenever I pulled myself up out of bed and went, I was glad I did. Did you know that's where all the ladies hang out during the day?"

(Wheaton College IL Student – Academics)

"The people at Willamette are just average college students. It's like if you're at the zoo and there is a cage labeled 'College Student.' Inside the cage you would see six or seven Willamette students, and they'd all be wearing sweatshirts and talking about the importance of recycling."

(Willamette University Student -- Guys & Girls)

"Naked Potlucks happen usually on a Friday night. It's a bunch of girls sitting around naked trying to know their bodies in a non-sexual way. It was started by a bunch of girls who realized they only knew their bodies in a sexual context when they were with a guy. They figured that wasn't the only thing their bodies were capable of. Somebody usually brings wine, and someone else brings cheese. You get tipsy, you talk about girly things and exchange gossip. It's not erotic because it's not meant to be."

(New College of Florida Student – Nightlife)

"They are so strict. I think not smoking pot in the dorms is like one of the Ten Commandments or something. "

(Radford University Student – Campus Strictness)

"THE BEAN DIP AT LA HACIENDA IS AMAZING! I STOPPED GOING THERE FOR AWHILE BECAUSE MY FRIENDS GOT FOOD POISONING, BUT THE BEAN DIP BROUGHT ME BACK. IT'S JUST SO GOOD!"

(WILLAMETTE UNIVERSITY STUDENT – OFF-CAMPUS DINING)

"If I had to use three words to describe Kirksville, they would be 'lack of goodness.'"
(Truman State Student – Local Atmosphere)

Words to Know

Academic Probation – A suspension imposed on a student if he or she fails to keep up with the school's minimum academic requirements. Those unable to improve their grades after receiving this warning can face dismissal.

Beer Pong / Beirut – A drinking game involving cups of beer arranged in a pyramid shape on each side of a table. The goal is to get a ping pong ball into one of the opponent's cups by throwing the ball or hitting it with a paddle. If the ball lands in a cup, the opponent is required to drink the beer.

Bid – An invitation from a fraternity or sorority to 'pledge' (join) that specific house.

Blue-Light Phone – Brightly-colored phone posts with a blue light bulb on top. These phones exist for security purposes and are located at various outside locations around most campuses. In an emergency, a student can pick up one of these phones (free of charge) to connect with campus police or a security escort.

Campus Police – Police who are specifically assigned to a given institution. Campus police are typically not regular city officers; they are employed by the university in a full-time capacity.

Club Sports – A level of sports that falls somewhere between varsity and intramural. If a student is unable to commit to a varsity team but has a lot of passion for athletics, a club sport could be a better, less intense option. Even less demanding, intramural (IM) sports often involve no traveling and considerably less time.

Cocaine – An illegal drug. Also known as "coke" or "blow," cocaine often resembles a white crystalline or powdery substance. It is highly addictive and dangerous.

Common Application – An application with which students can apply to multiple schools.

Course Registration – The period of official class selection for the upcoming quarter or semester. Prior to registration, it is best to prepare several back-up courses in case a particular class becomes full. If a course is full, students can place themselves on the waitlist, although this still does not guarantee entry.

Division Athletics – Athletic classifications range from Division I to Division III. Division IA is the most competitive, while Division III is considered to be the least competitive.

Dorm – A dorm (or dormitory) is an on-campus housing facility. Dorms can provide a range of options from suite-style rooms to more communal options that include shared bathrooms. Most first-year students live in dorms. Some upperclassmen who wish to stay on campus also choose this option.

Early Action – An application option with which a student can apply to a school and receive an early acceptance response without a binding commitment. This system is becoming less and less available.

Early Decision – An application option that students should use only if they are certain they plan to attend the school in question. If a student applies using the early decision option and is admitted, he or she is required and bound to attend that university. Admission rates are usually higher among students who apply through early decision, as the student is clearly indicating that the school is his or her first choice.

Ecstasy – An illegal drug. Also known as "E" or "X," ecstasy looks like a pill and most resembles an aspirin. Considered a party drug, ecstasy is very dangerous and can be deadly.

Ethernet – An extremely fast Internet connection available in most university-owned residence halls. To use an Ethernet connection properly, a student will need a network card and cable for his or her computer.

Fake ID – A counterfeit identification card that contains false information. Most commonly, students get fake IDs with altered birthdates so that they appear to be older than 21 (and therefore of legal drinking age). Even though it is illegal, many college students have fake IDs in hopes of purchasing alcohol or getting into bars.

Frosh – Slang for "freshman" or "freshmen."

Hazing – Initiation rituals administered by some fraternities or sororities as part of the pledging process. Many universities have outlawed hazing due to its degrading and sometimes dangerous nature.

Intramurals (IMs) – A popular, and usually free, sport league in which students create teams and compete against one another. These sports vary in competitiveness and can include a range of activities—everything from billiards to water polo. IM sports are a great way to meet people with similar interests.

Keg – Officially called a half-barrel, a keg contains roughly 200 12-ounce servings of beer.

LSD – An illegal drug. Also known as acid, this hallucinogen most commonly resembles a tab of paper.

Marijuana – An illegal drug. Also known as weed or pot; along with alcohol, marijuana is one of the most commonly-found drugs on campuses across the country.

Major –The focal point of a student's college studies; a specific topic that is studied for a degree. Examples of majors include physics, English, history, computer science, economics, business, and music. Many students decide on a specific major before arriving on campus, while others are simply "undecided" until declaring a major. Those who are extremely interested in two areas can also choose to double major.

Meal Block – The equivalent of one meal. Students on a meal plan usually receive a fixed number of meals per week. Each meal, or "block," can be redeemed at the school's dining facilities in place of cash. Often, a student's weekly allotment of meal blocks will be forfeited if not used.

Minor – An additional focal point in a student's education. Often serving as a complement or addition to a student's main area of focus, a minor has fewer requirements and prerequisites to fulfill than a major. Minors are not required for graduation from most schools; however some students who want to explore many different interests choose to pursue both a major and a minor.

Mushrooms – An illegal drug. Also known as "'shrooms," this drug resembles regular mushrooms but is extremely hallucinogenic.

Off-Campus Housing – Housing from a particular landlord or rental group that is not affiliated with the university. Depending on the college, off-campus housing can range from extremely popular to non-existent. Students who choose to live off campus are typically given more freedom, but they also have to deal with possible subletting scenarios, furniture, bills, and other issues. In addition to these factors, rental prices and distance often affect a student's decision to move off campus.

Office Hours – Time that teachers set aside for students who have questions about coursework. Office hours are a good forum for students to go over any problems and to show interest in the subject material.

Pledging – The early phase of joining a fraternity or sorority, pledging takes place after a student has gone through rush and received a bid. Pledging usually lasts between one and two semesters. Once the pledging period is complete and a particular student has done everything that is required to become a member, that student is considered a brother or sister. If a fraternity or a sorority would decide to "haze" a group of students, this initiation would take place during the pledging period.

Private Institution – A school that does not use tax revenue to subsidize education costs. Private schools typically cost more than public schools and are usually smaller.

Prof – Slang for "professor."

Public Institution – A school that uses tax revenue to subsidize education costs. Public schools are often a good value for in-state residents and tend to be larger than most private colleges.

Quarter System (or Trimester System) – A type of academic calendar system. In this setup, students take classes for three academic periods. The first quarter usually starts in late September or early October and concludes right before Christmas. The second quarter usually starts around early to mid–January and finishes up around March or April. The last academic quarter, or "third quarter," usually starts in late March or early April and finishes up in late May or Mid-June. The fourth quarter is summer. The major difference between the quarter system and semester system is that students take more, less comprehensive courses under the quarter calendar.

RA (Resident Assistant) – A student leader who is assigned to a particular floor in a dormitory in order to help to the other students who live there. An RA's duties include ensuring student safety and providing assistance wherever possible.

Recitation – An extension of a specific course; a review session. Some classes, particularly large lectures, are supplemented with mandatory recitation sessions that provide a relatively personal class setting.

Rolling Admissions – A form of admissions. Most commonly found at public institutions, schools with this type of policy continue to accept students throughout the year until their class sizes are met. For example, some schools begin accepting students as early as December and will continue to do so until April or May.

Room and Board – This figure is typically the combined cost of a university-owned room and a meal plan.

Room Draw/Housing Lottery – A common way to pick on-campus room assignments for the following year. If a student decides to remain in university-owned housing, he is assigned a unique number that, along with seniority, is used to determine his housing for the next year.

Rush – The period in which students can meet the brothers and sisters of a particular chapter and find out if a given fraternity or sorority is right for them. Rushing a fraternity or a sorority is not a requirement at any school. The goal of rush is to give students who are serious about pledging a feel for what to expect.

Semester System – The most common type of academic calendar system at college campuses. This setup typically includes two semesters in a given school year. The fall semester starts around the end of August or early September and concludes before winter vacation. The spring semester usually starts in mid-January and ends in late April or May.

Student Center/Rec Center/Student Union – A common area on campus that often contains study areas, recreation facilities, and eateries. This building is often a good place to meet up with fellow students; depending on the school, the student center can have a huge role or a non-existent role in campus life.

Student ID – A university-issued photo ID that serves as a student's key to school-related functions. Some schools require students to show these cards in order to get into dorms, libraries, cafeterias, and other facilities. In addition to storing meal plan information, in some cases, a student ID can actually work as a debit card and allow students to purchase things from bookstores or local shops.

Suite – A type of dorm room. Unlike dorms that feature communal bathrooms shared by the entire floor, suites offer bathrooms shared only among the suite. Suite-style rooms can house anywhere from two to ten students.

TA (Teacher's Assistant) – An undergraduate or grad student who helps in some manner with a specific course. In some cases, a TA will teach a class, assist a professor, grade assignments, or conduct office hours.

Undergraduate – A student in the process of studying for his or her bachelor's degree.

About the Authors

Jill Hindenach—Albion College

Though I have already graduated from Albion College, I know that my four years at Albion will be with me forever—for better or worse. This guidebook has been a gradual effort with the help of College Prowler since I was a student. It seemed like a daunting task at first, but I'm glad I was able to take part in Albion's inaugural edition.

I hope you have as much fun reading it as I did making it.

Chagmion Antoine—Alfred University

I learned a great deal about my university while writing this review. I'm convinced now more than ever that perhaps my college experience wasn't a disaster after all. I hope readers found this book informative and entertaining. Even if you found it a little scary, I'm glad I could give you the heads up.

I am currently a recent college graduate and a wannabe journalist. I have written for publications in Connecticut, Boston, and New York, and I have had work featured on MSNBC. This is my first time writing a review, but hopefully not my last. If you have any questions, comments, suggestions, or threats, please contact me.

Thank you Mom, Sherry, Louis, Mama, Raj, Alex, the 151 girls, Robin, Dan, and everyone at College Prowler!

Carolyn Keller—Allegheny College

Writing this book has been an interesting experience. Having just received my BA in creative writing, I'm used to making stuff up. This guidebook has been an informative jaunt into the art of nonfiction. In the fall, I'll be going to NYU to pursue my MFA in fiction. Allegheny College was an overall good experience for me. I'll be glad to get into a city after spending so much time in Meadville, but it all depends on what you like. I hope the book provided you with a good unbiased view of Allegheny.

I'd like to thank everyone who helped me finish this book: Mick O'Brien, Dan Mason, Jessica Day, Jamie Nelson, Sean Holsing, Darrell Haemer, Katie Shreve, Jason McCoy, my family and everyone at College Prowler!

Katy Kujala-Korpela—Alverno College

Writing for College Prowler has given me a chance to look back on my experiences not only at Alverno but also in Milwaukee. Milwaukee is multifaceted and has so much to offer that many Alverno students, and even those who live in Milwaukee, don't know about. Sometimes I wonder how I have gotten this far, how I ended up at Alverno in the first place. Looking back, it was the best decision I have made in my life. Alverno has helped me become a strong, independent woman who thinks for herself and lives outside of what corporations try to make society consume. Alverno is about more than just taking classes to get a degree; it is about learning who you are and what kind of difference you are going to make in your community after graduation. Going away to college, I never thought I would be where I am today. Now as I approach graduation, I know what I want out of this education: I want to become a woman of influence. I have grown so much, and I would never take back any of the late night papers or the stressful weeks of presentations.

I would like to thank my parents for always saying "When you go to college" instead of "If you go to college." Without them, I wouldn't

be graduating with a double degree in history and political science. I would also like to thank my brother, who has always been my reassuring and unfaltering voice of resistance to society, as well as my boyfriend, who has supported me throughout this journey with his knowledge and emotional support. I would also like to thank all the students at Alverno who took the surveys, especially the residents in Austin Hall!

Alanna Schubach—American University

Writing this guidebook for College Prowler has been a great experience. I now know a lot more about American University and Washington, DC and can't wait to explore some new places. I'm currently a junior majoring in print journalism and Spanish, and I hope to continue writing. When at school, I write for *American Literary* and the *Eagle*, roam the clubs, hookah bars, movie theaters, and museums of the city, and act like a weirdo with my floormates. I am originally from Long Island, NY, and moving from my suburban hometown to a school in one of the most exciting and powerful cities in the world has been incredible. I hope this book has been entertaining and informative for you and that my enthusiasm for AU and DC is infectious!

Many thanks to: Mom, Dad, Julian, Nana, Omi and Opi, Erin, Lindsey, DZ, Anders, Kayley, Lini, Greg, Adrienne, Julia, MK, Josh, Shannon, Kalli, Nicole, Amanda, Aram, Megan, HC Crista, Crazy Cyrus, Ryan, The Jons, Spike, Dr. Romano, boomsauce, Andrew McCullough, and the folks at College Prowler.

Nadav Klein—Amherst College

He hails from the distant and mysterious lands of Israel, where men are still men, women are still women, and sex is still sexy. He first heard English as an infant, watching in grief as the Transformers constantly defeated his beloved Decepticons. He went to Eshel Hanassi, an all-Israeli high school with all-Israeli teachers who, after observing how eloquently he articulated his arguments and how good he looked in a suit, told him with pride, "Nadav, you're going to be a great lawyer some day, and remember where you first heard it." In addition, and without direct logical connection, he once served in the Israeli Army and dreamed of becoming a pilot. Now, he is neither a pilot nor will he become a lawyer, and the Decepticons are still getting their butts kicked in reruns.

I applied to U.S. schools while I was in the army, after having only casually inquired about the places I applied to. Now, I am living in a faraway country, trying to make sense of it all, trying to get to know who I really am, and having a ball doing it. I am humbled by the immense opportunities that Amherst has opened by admitting me, and I am, and always will be, eternally grateful to Amherst, both for having accepted an unusual person such as me, and for having supplemented the acceptance letter with enough financial aid to get me through four years. I truly believe that its people like those found in Amherst College that create and mobilize all the great things of which the human race is capable.

Hopefully I'll amount to something special in my life, and so will you. Happy trails!

Lauren Kennedy—Arizona State University

Writing this College Prowler guidebook has been a wonderful opportunity and an exciting experience! I am a senior at Arizona

State University and am eagerly finishing up my degree in business management. Although I'm majoring in business, my true heart is in writing, and I've been taking every chance to chase that dream. I'm graduating this coming spring, and I've decided to stay in the Phoenix area. That was a big decision, considering I packed up my car three years ago and drove 2,500 miles here from New York. I never thought I would want to pursue a career anywhere else than the Big Apple, but my experience here in Phoenix has brought too much good for me to turn around and leave it behind. I'm planning on working in the field of journalism when I graduate unless someone discovers me and my marvelous attempts at fiction. Either way, it feels good to be rounding the finish line and for my future to finally be in sight. My experience here at ASU has been a memorable one. If you're coming from far away, and you want that college experience that everyone talks about, this is it. I almost got stuck commuting on Long Island for four years! Moving here was the best thing I ever did for myself, and the experience of being on your own and growing into your own person is something you won't understand until you do it. I hope this book has been insightful to you, and that you at least know whether or not Arizona State is the place for you.

Love and thanks to the people for whom I am most grateful: My Family—the reason I am where I am; for being wonderful, always being there for me, loving me through, and keeping me close when I am far. My Friends (you know who you are)—for your love, help, support, laughs, advice, and nothing but good times. My Man—for loving me, reminding me of what's important, providing your support, smiles, and laughs, and for just being you.

Lindsey Nolan—Auburn University

I had a really good time writing this guidebook for you, and I sincerely hope that it has helped you out in your search for your perfect college! This is my first publication ever, but hopefully it won't be my last. I've lived in Auburn, Alabama for several years now and have grown to love the school as well as the town. Although I've lived in many places all over the country, I can honestly say that Auburn has been one of my favorites. I hope that this guidebook is helpful to you and gives you a better perspective on what Auburn University is about. I must give thanks to my parents, Hollie, Kathleen, Emily, Katie, Lee Ann, and everyone at College Prowler!

Anna Klimentievna Gatker—Babson College

I had a great time writing this book, and I would like to thank College Prowler for presenting me with such a unique opportunity! Having lived on campus for more than three years (this one being my fourth), I can honestly say that I enjoyed a well-rounded life at Babson College. By balancing social, educational, and extracurricular activities, I was able to mature in this fast-paced and exciting environment. As a result, I already know what Babson is all about and what it has to offer you throughout the years. However, being the curious person that I am, I really wanted to find out what other students thought about life here. That is the reason why the timing of this project was impeccable, making it an enjoyable piece of writing for me. First, I conducted some focus groups and surveyed the students. After reviewing everyone's responses, I found that a lot of people shared my opinions. But by approaching this project as objectively as possible, I tried to paint a picture of Babson that was both educational and fun to read for an individual like you. I also like to see people laugh, so a bit of my humor is reflected in these writings. I hope you enjoy reading about my college as much as I enjoyed writing about it!

Lastly, I would like to thank my mother, father, sister, and grandpa for helping me with this project and my success at Babson. Also, big thanks to Kate Walsh, Natalie Ruppert, and Vince Framularo for being my best friends, and for their encouragement and help with this project.

Adrian Sharp—Ball State University

When I decided to major in journalism, people told me I made the wrong decision. "Nobody reads anymore, don't you know that?" Well, I'm glad somebody still reads, and I'm glad that somebody is you. It is my sincerest hope that you found this guide informative and entertaining.

Now that you know pretty much all that's worth knowing about Ball State, I should probably tell you a little about myself. I am currently a senior working toward a Journalism Graphics major at Ball State University. I am the assistant features editor at our student newspaper, The Ball State Daily News. I am also president of the Ball State chapter of the Orthodox Christian Fellowship.

Choosing the right college or university is an important decision—some would say one of the most important you will ever make. Through quotes, statistics, and other information, I have tried my darnedest to give you, the reader, a straightforward and unbiased view of what it's like to be a student at BSU. If you have any questions or comments, feel free to contact me.

Jared Killeen—Bard College

I am a recent college graduate, an expert Bardophile, and a novice guidebook writer. I currently live in Brooklyn, NY, where I pursue such personal interests as writing, reading, and getting paid very little for a job I am only moderately enthusiastic about.

Megan Cloud—Barnard College

I still cannot believe how much there is to know about Barnard College, and how much I've learned since transferring in. Writing this book really opened my eyes to both the good and the bad of Barnard, and it has taught me some things about being aware of my surroundings.

I am a junior psychology major who isn't quite sure what her plans are after college. Hopefully, the future will include furthering my education in a graduate school somewhere closer to my home in Ft. Worth, Texas. New York has been a great experience for me so far, and I sincerely hope that you feel like you've gotten to know Barnard a little bit better. Good luck to anyone reading this in finding your future home away from home at college.

I would like to extend a very special thanks to those at College Prowler who gave me this awesome opportunity, my brother who graciously let me use the computer compulsively, Memaw and Papa for their support in all of my crazy endeavors, my mom and dad who gave me the skills and opportunity to attend college at all, and finally, to my best friend and future, Eddie.

Mikhail Sedov—Baruch College

Mikhail is an author based in New York City. A business journalism major, he served as business and features editor of The Ticker, Bernard M. Baruch College's weekly newspaper. His writing interests include creative non-fiction, feature story and fiction.

Sarah Connell—Bates College

Writing this book has been an amazing experience. Though I hope to go into publishing when I graduate, this is the first time I've ever worked on such an extensive project. Writing about Bates and seeing what other students had to say about the school also helped me get ready to return here, after having spent my junior year abroad in Cork, Ireland. I'm hoping to do my postgraduate studies at Cork next year and possibly live and work there, as well. When I graduate, I'll have degrees in English and Classics, and a Certificate in Irish Studies.

Bates was my first-choice college. It's a small, private liberal arts school with an excellent academic reputation and only about 50 miles from my home in New Hampshire. I've learned a lot while I've studied here, but probably the best part about going to Bates is the opportunity I've had to study abroad. In addition to spending a year in Ireland, I traveled to Budapest during Short Term my first year. I was able to go to 15 plays, ballets, and operas, and I also got the chance to perform in two plays myself. It was Bates's unique calendar that allowed me to go abroad in my very first year at school, and I really believe that traveling has been a vital part of my college experience.

I hope that you've gotten a more detailed picture of what living at Bates is like from reading what I, and other students, had to say about the school. If you are considering Bates, I urge you to visit the school and even spend a night here, if you can.

Kyra Mitchell—Baylor University

To this day, I can't really offer any logical explanation as to what led me to Baylor, which was why I trusted it. I've always lived a little in my imagination, and writing this book was the first step in a lifetime. I recently finished my degree with a major in English and telecommunications. It took me about a year to really find my place at Baylor, and from what I understand, that's about par for the course. This school is filled with some really amazing people, and they are the ones that get you through college. A native of Texas, my heart, along with the majority of my family, has always lain in the Northeast, but I'll never lose my roots. The opportunities Baylor, its students, and especially its faculty has presented me are unrivaled. The future is still hazy as of this writing, but one thing is for certain—I never would have made it this far if it weren't for my incredible parents, who have been my best friends for many years past, and God willing, many to come.

Coming in at a close second is my roommate for two years and heterosexual life mate, Jane. Her future burns brighter than mine, and all I can hope is to get a good tan. Additional thanks to Virginia, Jason, Allison, and Kelly, who all have a sympathetic ear for me to fill, or at least know how to fake it. Thanks to Quyen for making sure I had a roof over my head and enough food to make it to the computer every morning, and last but not least, to Bob Darden, Jill Havens, Wendy Marquart, and Amanda Moos, who have played bigger parts than they will ever know and restored my confidence in the human race. They are role models and inspirations, all in their own particular ways. A last nod is necessary for Omid at College Prowler for handling my nine million questions, responding promptly, and letting an infantile hack who calls herself a writer have a chance.

Sarah Maehl—Beloit College

After a few years at Beloit, it can get pretty hard to keep straight what you're "about." All I can tell you is that when I was 18 and a half years old, I shipped my stuff over to Beloit College, and I've just been hanging out ever since. I'm a creative writing major getting her teacher's certification, and now I am also the Beloit College expert. I never meant to become the Beloit College expert, and chances are I'll forget it all in about a year, but for now, I'm getting a kick out of watching people's eyebrows go up at parties when I blurt out the exact number of students at Beloit, or the total occupancy of the Townhouses. Those poor people are just trying to make conversation. College Prowler, you've done a number on me.

Jessica Low—Bentley College

For those of you who made it through the entire book to get to this final page, congratulations! Now is your chance to read about the person who wrote the guide that may or may not convince you that it is the school for you. As a marketing major, I held two different internships in public affairs and will soon be starting a career in public relations, hopefully with an agency in Boston. I have always enjoyed writing, for personal pleasure and as an integral part of my job function. The angle this particular College Prowler book was written from may be different than other guides because I was a second-semester senior reflecting back on my entire college life. I wanted to write this book because, as a senior, I felt I had the experience, knowledge, and resources to offer you a complete and thorough look inside campus life. It was my goal to offer an unbiased, insider's look at Bentley, and if I accomplished that, I hope to meet some of you at alumni events!

This was a tough last semester of college for me and if it wasn't for these special people, I couldn't have made it through with my sanity intact. Thank you Dad, Eric, Adam, Sandy, Gram, Loren, Amanda, Lynn, and the Barneys. I love you Mom.

Scott Kutscher—Binghamton University

I am grateful for the opportunity to write this book. After living my entire life in Queens, New York, I was fortunate enough to spend four great years at Binghamton. Putting together this book has made me realize how much I will miss the school. I will especially miss the school newspaper, *Pipe Dream*, where I worked for all four years as a writer and editor, and of course, my talented classmates and professors. After majoring in biology, I am moving on to attend the University at Buffalo School of Medicine, where I will surely go on to write bigger, more elaborate guidebooks. I hope you have enjoyed reading this book as much as I enjoyed writing it, and I hope it has been helpful for you.

Of course, I would not be where I am today without the help of many wonderful people. Thank you Mom, Dad, and Lauren for your unwavering support, Larry, Dave, Pete, Alec, Ben, Mason, Keith, Mike, Liz, the Rochstein and Kutscher clans, my fellow writers and editors at Pipe Dream, all my friends and professors in the biology department, Phi Delta Epsilon, the great people at Binghamton University, and everyone at College Prowler for giving me this opportunity.

Kelli L. Hilyer—Birmingham-Southern College

It's so exciting to finally be able to have a good answer when someone asks me "What did you do this summer?" I can proudly tell them "I wrote a book!" This experience has been both challenging and rewarding. It's allowed me to reflect on my college experience in a way that most others don't get to until it's entirely too close to graduation. When I came to Birmingham-Southern as a bright-eyed, bushy-tailed freshman from LA (lower Alabama, that is), I really didn't know what to expect. It was a big change to trade the Mobile Bay sunrises I had grown up with for the hills and valleys of Birmingham, but being in a big city has given me more opportunities than I ever imagined. As a junior at Southern, I'm writing as much as I can, and hopefully in two more years I can graduate with a degree in English and see where it takes me next.

And how could I talk about myself without thanking the people who keep me on my toes day in and day out, and those who are near and dear to my heart? I'd like to give some thanks to all my family: Dad, Katie, Mee-Maw & Pee-Paw, Jan, Kyle, Erin, and Karl; to Jennings for always being by my side; to Claire for giving me a place to stay in the 'Ham for the summer; to everyone who gave me great answers when I was in a bind; to Dr. Peter Donahue for being such a big encouragement in my journalism career; to Johnny Mac for inspiring me to be the best news reporter I can be; to Ashley Pope and Melissa Brown for editorial miracles and advice; to Cara and everyone at Over the Mountain Journal for giving me a chance to experience journalism in the real world; and of course, to College Prowler for giving me the opportunity of a lifetime!

Caren M. Walker—Boston University

I certainly hope that this information, as well as my various personal experiences, has been at least somewhat useful in your decision-making process in choosing a school. The truth is, while being prepared and advised is extremely beneficial, the best way to check out BU is to check out BU. Come visit and hang out on your own for a bit. As soon as I arrived on campus I felt comfortable and confident that I could be both happy and productive in this environment. This does not mean, however, that it will feel the same to you.

So, what am I going to do now? Right after graduation, and the completion of my thesis, I moved to LA for about eight months. I had planned to do some quality "finding myself"—but spent most of it partying and hanging out in the desert. It was around the time that I felt my brain was atrophying that I decided to return to the East Coast. I am now working as a research assistant and study coordinator in the neuroscience department at MGH (a part of Harvard Medical School).

I am planning to hit up NYC for graduate school, but I have yet to decide on a direction for study. I intend to get my PhD in something, perhaps evolutionary psychology, philosophy of mind, or cognition studies. I don't know. Remember, no matter how many friends, relatives, and complete strangers look at you and say, "So, what are you going to do?" it is okay to have no idea. I still don't. My long-term plan is to remain in an academic environment for a while. As long as my parents keep paying, I will keep going . . . indefinitely. I suggest you do the same. Do not rush into the mechanism. Feed your head.

I would like to thank the people at College Prowler for all of their help through this process, all of those at BU who offered their insight for the creation of this book, and anyone else who has provided me with little nuggets of wisdom.

Derrick S. Wong—Bowdoin College

This project has been a labor of love for me. It gave me the opportunity to learn nuances about Bowdoin, get to know my peers and administrators better, to be resourceful, and to discover my passion for journalism.

I am currently a sophomore at Bowdoin College. I serve in Student Government, write for the school newspaper (the *Orient*), and mentor local kids in Maine. I plan to major in government and history. My love for ice hockey, staying active, and coaching stems from attending a small, private high school in Vermont, my home state. I hope to one day pursue a career in journalism and business.

I'd like to thank all those who contributed to this book. Margaret Allen, Matthew O' Donnell, Lisa Randall, and James Westoff provided me support, input, and data to keep statistics and information about Bowdoin current. My mentor, John D. Moyers, gave me an unbiased perspective on life and offered his professional advice when necessary. Mary Branagan served as my partner in crime, whether as girlfriend or friend.

My guidance counselor Andrea Torello spent hours with me discussing the finer points of life and the college process. Thanks to Kevin Clark, my freshman and junior year history teacher, for helping me discover Bowdoin and for listening to my ranting in and outside of class. Doreen Marquis and Joey Solomon, my sophomore and freshman English teachers, showed me my potential and taught me to love writing.

Mary Beatty, Ann Kenney, Kelle Carmen, Judith Ring, Linda Barnes, and many more served as listening ears in high school. Jeffrey Nagle, Bernie Hershberger, Penny Martin, and others at Bowdoin College helped me adjust to the rigors of college.

My half-brother Andrew served as a reminder to do my best. My father and step-mother Annie never shied away from showing their concern and affection. I'd like to express my deepest appreciation for my step-father Bob for providing me a stable and nurturing environment

to grow up in with unconditional love. Most importantly, I would like to thank my mother for her love and support, unwavering confidence, and constructive criticism—even when I didn't want to hear it. I could not be the person I am today without her.

I hope you felt entertained by my conversational commentaries and found insights into how four years at Bowdoin College could shape your life.

Erin Wood—Bradley University

I never thought I'd be a Bradley University expert. Author, maybe. Bradley expert? Not so much. I grew up in Peoria, and Bradley was always right down the street, though I never paid it any mind. When senior year of high school rolled around, I had my heart set on a school completely different than Bradley. I went there, and I hated it. I wanted Peoria back, and for the first time in my life, I noticed Bradley. I realized I wanted a small school with personal attention, a chance to stand out, and opportunities to work in my field immediately. I didn't know during my college shopping process that that's what I was looking for because surely if that's what I wanted to begin with, I would have found Bradley, just minutes from my house.

Everyone in Peoria always talked about Bradley and "Oh, what a good school it is." I ignored them. Now, dozens of classes, lots of friends, and several amazing opportunities later, I'm the one talking about Bradley. Writing this book has been an enlightening experience. I learned things I never knew and never had any desire to discover until now. For example, U-Hall has 356 occupants. I didn't know that. Bradley produced a professional football player. I didn't know that was even possible without a football team. I'm now the proud queen of random Bradley trivia, and I love it. Test me.

Thanks to Mom, Dad, Ryan, Quinn, the FAM, and my best friends at Bradley for keeping me sane when I get stressed out.

Andrew Katz—Brandeis University

Andrew Katz was born in 1983 in New York City. He grew up in Scarsdale, New York and attended Edgemont High School. In high school he got a hand in everything from being the class president, to serving as editor of the features section of the newspaper, to starting a volunteer tutoring group. In college, this same passion for getting involved continued as Andrew served as a senator while living in the Castle Quad. He has also served as a volunteer for admissions, worked in Hillel's social action wing Mitzvah Corps, and written for the Arts section of the school newspaper, the *Justice*. His favorite activities are writing his weekly sports column for the *Justice*, his sports talk radio show, his opportunities to broadcast basketball games, and tutoring.

As part of the Brandeis Class of 2006, Andrew was undecided as to what to major in when he first came to Brandeis. He threw around American studies and politics as possible majors, and legal studies and Near Eastern and Judaic studies as possible minors. But he has finally decided on economics as a major with minors in business and journalism. He is not sure what he's going to do when he graduates Brandeis, but would like to go into a field where his love of sports can be expressed. Andrew is an avid sports fan and admits he goes to *ESPN.com* more times in a day than he visits the library in a year.

As a die-hard Yankees fan living in Red Sox country, Andrew would like to thank Aaron Boone for making his sophomore year a little more enjoyable. All joking aside, Andrew says that the real thanks go out to everyone who helped him write this book. Without their input, he would be lost. He would especially like to thank his girlfriend, Jess, who has been his biggest supporter. He would also like to thank Mom, Dad, and Gillian for putting up with him as he wrote this book—let's just say he wasn't in the mood to chit-chat most of those days.

Lastly he would like to thank the people who bought this book. Brandeis was about number four on Andrew's college list, but he admits he wouldn't go back and change his decision for anything.

He's looking forward to his last two years at Brandeis and hopes that the people who read that book can experience the same enjoyment.

Ashley Vance—Brigham Young University

I attended BYU for a little over five years, including an 18-month stint in Russia. After attempting no fewer than six other majors, I graduated in International Politics, a major the University has since discontinued, although they claim this makes my degree no less valid. I have a minor in Russian, and an interest in writing and chemistry. Writing this book has been a very enlightening experience. I have learned things that I wish I would have known while I was at BYU (we have a juggling club?), and have been able to talk about things that have become very dear to me in my five-ish years. Attending BYU was nothing like I expected it to be, and more than I hoped it would be. Having just graduated, I look forward to taking my degree out for a spin, and seeing what it can do in the "real world."

Here's where I get to thank all of the people that have put up with me taking over and even crashing their computers as I worked on this. Thanks to Mom and Dad, Megan, Jenny, Jonathan, David, Jeremy, Susie, Julia, Dan, Rebecca, and everyone at the Math Lab for putting up with me. A special thanks to College Prowler for the experience and help.

Matthew Kittay—Brown University

This book reflects a lot of time and effort, and I hope you find it as useful as I intend it to be. I picked up the project as a chance to reflect on my own experience at Brown and learn even more about the University where I spent four years of my life. I never expected to find myself writing a book.

I had a great time writing this edition of the guidebook to Brown, and I get a good deal of satisfaction knowing that people will know more about the University and what they can hope to find when they come to visit or to study at the school. Brown is a great place, and like many of the students I interviewed, there's nowhere in the world I would rather call my alma mater than Brown.

Sarah Friedman—Bryn Mawr College

Sarah Friedman came to Bryn Mawr from Sacramento California to study mathematics and economics. She spent her junior year living in London and studying at University College London. After completing her senior year at Bryn Mawr, she is interested in working for a public policy research organization before heading to grad school. Her future career plans are broad, but will hopefully incorporate much researching, writing, and traveling. She has enjoyed writing this book and hopes you find it helpful. Do send any questions or comments to sarahfriedman@collegeprowler.com The following people deserve a world of thanks for their help with this project: Mom, Dad, Sam, Evelyn, Stephanie Tyson, Lisa Mattei, Michelle Coleman, and all the Mawrters who responded to the College Prowler survey with your insightful quotes. A very special thanks to Diana Medina, Laura Silvius, Christina Alfonso, and Amanda Glendinning, all of whom contributed their time and expertise to help edit and perfect the book. Also, thank you to the folks at College Prowler for your support and patience.

Lauren Davis—Bucknell University

I've always been really interested in the college admissions process. In high school, I was one of those geeks who spent her lunchtime in the career center researching colleges. During my junior year of high school, my mother and I took two college trips to the East Coast and probably looked at 25 colleges and universities. My best advice for those of you going through the college search is to listen to your

heart. I visited many campuses where I knew from the second the rental car pulled up that the school was wrong for me. Bucknell was a campus that took my breath away from the get-go, with its gorgeous scenery and friendly people.

I am a rising junior English and French double major at Bucknell. I'm not sure yet about a career, but I'm interested in publishing and the FBI. (Yes, I'm random!) I grew up in the San Francisco Bay Area, but currently reside in Lake Tahoe, Nevada. I love the outdoors, and am often hiking, mountain biking, and lounging at the lake during the summer. At school, I have a great group of friends, and we love to party and hang out in the Caf.

Thanks, first and foremost, to my mom, who took me on all of my college visits in high school. She's almost as knowledgeable about colleges as I am. Thanks to my Dad, who helped with editing, and last but not least, thanks to my Bucknell friends and acquaintances who contributed all of the quotes and advice!

Nicole Biggers—Cal Poly

Wow. I finally finished this guidebook and now I can't think of a single thing to say about myself, which is unusual. Let's see, obviously, I'm a student at Cal Poly. I've just started my fourth and last year, which is a rare thing. Most people don't make it out for five or six years! If everything goes right, after I graduate this June I'll be heading off to China to teach conversational English for a year. After that, hopefully I'll get my credential in high school English, so I can spend the rest of my life in school and never actually have to encounter that thing known as "real life."

Thanks to my folks for putting me through college, the best experience of my life. Thanks to the profs in the English department for actually teaching me stuff, especially Dr. Cokal and Dr. Inchausti. Thanks to all the people on campus who answered my questions.

Candyce Otis—Cal Poly Pomona

When the opportunity to write this book popped up, I was stoked! I have always dreamed of writing a travel guidebook, so getting to start off by writing a college guidebook is such a blessing. Since I'm a "super senior," as we call them (fifth-year senior), I thought I knew a lot about CPP, but after writing this book I found out even more about the campus and the surrounding area. That has helped me help others on campus, and I hope it helps you out, as well!

My experience at Cal Poly has been unforgettable. I got involved in everything I possibly could: Greek life (Kappa Delta for life!), ASI, the Poly Post, and other various clubs. The best advice I could offer to you is to get involved, because your college memories are memories that will live with you forever, and the friends you make are the friends you will keep forever.

After five years at CPP, I'm set to graduate with a bachelor's degree in communications (emphasis in journalism) and a minor in marketing management. My plans for the future are still uncertain; hopefully, something will come along in the travel industry, and I will write until I can write no more!

And, of course, I have to do my special thank-yous to everyone that so graciously helped me out with writing this book and helped to support me when I thought I was going to tear my hair out: My Heavenly Father, Mom and Dad, Gram and HaHa, Aunt Cheryl, all of my sorority sisters in Kappa Delta, ASI, and of course College Prowler, whom I can't thank enough for giving me this opportunity!

Julie Ritchie—Cal State Northridge

Since I grew up in a small, rural town, I have loved every bit of living in the city. I admit that I experienced culture shock when I moved to the Valley, but I appreciate every way it has changed me. I learned so much about CSUN in writing this book that it has enriched my experience, even though I have been attending the school for four years. I am a double major in English and liberal studies. Writing this book has been one in a multiple-step process that will help me eventually become a professional writer.

Without the help and support of many people, I could not have completed this project. I would like to thank all the CSUN staff and faculty, particularly Marcelo Vazquez, Amy Matsubara, and Debbie Quinlan. Those near and dear to me also deserve my thanks: Mom, Dad, Maryanne, Angel, Neal, and Tim for always getting me out of the jam I'm in. And thanks to College Prowler for allowing college students to share their hard-earned knowledge with those who would truly benefit from it.

Mayra Sheikh—Caltech

Mayra Sheikh is currently a sophomore chemistry major. She grew up in the San Fernando Valley, which is part of the Greater Los Angeles Area. She lives (when not at school) with her parents and two younger sisters. "I really like Caltech overall, even though it is extremely difficult."

Adam Zang—Carleton College

As a junior English major at Carleton, I've been blessed with the opportunity to write this book, and have a brief respite from reading Tom Jones and numerous dense 700-page novels about female oppression in late-Victorian London. I'm from Ann Arbor, MI, and I came to Carleton because I wanted to go to a small school, get away from home, and prove that I could succeed at an academically-intense school. Carleton has provided me with opportunities to host my own radio show, spend a semester in Australia, serve as an assistant coach for Northfield High School's freshman baseball team, spend a weekend farming on a Native American reservation, meet Fay Vincent, and countless other things that I am extremely lucky to have participated in. I hope this book gives you an accurate account of what life is like at Carleton. Just remember that the quotes in this book are individual opinions. Everyone reacts differently to Carleton. I remember when I was a freshman here, living in 401 Burton, and meeting my floormates for the first time. Little did I know that I would be living in a house with four other guys from that floor my senior year. I have had a great three years here so far—except for having to read Tristram Shandy—and I hope that this book aids you in choosing a school where you'll have an excellent four years as well.

I would like to thank George Shuffleton, Ann Ness, Paul Thiboutot, Becky Zrimsek, Omid, Lauren Varacalli, Beau, Petey, Ashlea, 4th Burton, 4th and Union (Watson sucks—just wait until next year), Jose Lima, Ben Wallace, my mom, my dad, Ahja, Martin, Zangs and Kramers, the Northfield Raiders Freshman Baseball Team, Ivan Rodriguez for coming to the Tigers, the Baxters, and of course, Emily.

Daniel Liebermann—Carnegie Mellon University

I had a great time writing this book! I've been looking for a chance to express myself through my writing, and the entire experience has been very exciting. I'm hoping to publish more in the future as I continue to grow as a writer. I'm tirelessly pursuing degrees in both professional writing and business administration at Carnegie Mellon. In the future, I hope to utilize the skills I've learned in both of my majors. Pittsburgh is the first place I've lived since leaving my native Northern New Jersey. Coming to college here has been a dizzying and maturing experience to say the least. I hope this book has been insightful for you, and I hope you had a few laughs while reading it. If you have any questions or comments please contact me by e-mail. Here's where my biography takes a turn from overly narcissistic self commentary. I'd like to give many people many thanks. Thank you Mom, Dad, Amanda, Grandpa, Ragonesis, Kobuskies, Liebermann's,

Becky, CheeChee, Tom, Aaron, Drew, Jeremy, Meredith, Red Beavis, Rose, Mr. Gaul, Horatio Flatbush, Honus, Jason, Jen, Johnson, Keara, Nick, Scott, and everyone at College Prowler!

Remy Olson—Case Western Reserve University

I had a very introspective experience in writing this book. I realized what a great deal I had learned, not only about biology, but about the complicated and multifaceted institution that is Case Western Reserve University. I'm hoping to publish more in the future as I continue to grow as both a scientist and a writer. I'm now a sophomore at Case Western Reserve University pursuing the knowledge and experience necessary to make so many needed discoveries and changes in this world. Cleveland is now one of my homes along with Maui, Hawaii, where most of my nuclear family resides and where I was raised until moving to Glen Ellyn, IL, a western suburb of Chicago, where I attended high school. My experience at Case has been intense—one of study, research, and activism. The college search reaps great benefits for the shrewd and decisive, though those are very difficult approaches to maintain during such a dizzying experience that at time feels like a gamble. I hope this book has given you an edge and made it a little easier to be shrewd and decisive. If you have any questions or comments please contact me by e-mail. Special thanks to Bill, JJ, and Adam for helping expedite the process, Puiyee for the frozen provisions for late-night writing, Ann Marie for time off, and Eric for recommending Case during my ruthless and uncompromising college search.

Frankie Bustamante—Catholic University of America

took this position because I like to write and investigate, probably due to my work on our college newspaper, The Tower. And what I found, in one of those "Aha!" moments, besides the obvious information listed throughout this book, is that I really like this school. I realized that students and teachers here really have heart, are dedicated in their work, and really just enjoy their time here. I mean, let's face it, going to Catholic is a pretty penny—approximately $40,000 a year—and professors here do not make as much as many of the other D.C. schools, so it begs the question: Why do students and teachers stay? It's a legitimate feeling of community (religious and secular) and belonging that really lingers throughout your time here. The people you meet and learn from really leave a mark on you that lets you forgive any mistakes or shortcomings the University may have. I am sophomore politics major with a great group of friends and awesome teachers, and I'm glad I had the chance through College Prowler to discern just why it is I am happy here. Cheesy? Yes it is. But honest? Nothing but.

Ashley Moss—Centenary College of Louisiana

Writing this book has been a wonderful experience. My first year at Centenary I started classes with a burning desire to be a film director. After watching more films than I could ever count and getting involved in everything and anything to do with film on campus, I tweaked my career choices. I started working on screenplays, discovered that I'm a pretty good writer, and began to toy with the idea of becoming a film critic. Now I'm thinking about grad school and trying to figure out the best way to go about getting paid for watching movies. Centenary has helped me in so many ways over the years and given me opportunities I never would have thought of when I first stepped onto the campus. So bear with me as I thank all the people that helped me along the way. Sorry if this sounds like an acceptance speech given by some overbearing, teary-eyed actress; it can't be helped.

Thank you so much Mom and Dad; you've always supported me, and I am forever grateful to you. Thanks to Alysia, Frank, Will, Maryann, Kathleen, Scott, Cory, Amy, Chris, Dr. Hendricks, and all the other people that encouraged me along the way. Thanks especially to Sara, who I will always love dearly. I don't know how I'll survive grad school without you.

Alexandra R. Chase—Centre College

Writing this book has been challenging and immensely time consuming, but overall, really, really fun. I didn't realize how much I would miss my alma mater until I started writing this guidebook, and I feel envious of all the students getting ready to embark on their college careers. This book has not only consumed my last few months, but it is also in some ways the culmination of the last four years. Good luck to everyone still at Centre C!

I would like to specifically thank Nana and Papa, without you this book (or Centre) would not have been possible, my mom, Weston—I want all the weekends I spent working for you back (just kidding, I miss our coffee time already), to all the people who made Centre so much fun: Florida, Solomon (RIP), Mary, Pin, Alison, Scott, Eugenia Sophrania Number 1 Stunna' Baby Goat, Zeke, Amy, Ella, and of course, Sarah. To Miguel and Britt, I love you guys; oh yeah, and Rich, too.

Hayes Humphries—Claremont McKenna College

Well kids, all good things must come to an end, and CMC was indeed the best of things. It's been my pleasure to tell everyone how ridiculously amazing life at CMC is one last time before I graduate. I came over to the left coast four years ago not quite sure what to expect. I had been rejected from the school I had my heart set on, and I decided to take a risk and head to this CMC place, more because I wanted to be in California than because I knew anything about the school. Man, did I get lucky. It's been a great four years out here, and I'm not really willing to accept the fact that it's over. Still, I'm excited to head back east, start a new job, and settle in somewhere new. You, however, don't care what I'm doing next year; you're much more concerned with what you'll be doing next year. So, this is where I dispense a little personal advice about college as a reward to those of you who've read this far (and kudos to you for that, this is a long book).

Try not to stress about this process. It's amazing how intense and complex the college search has become, but there is shockingly little you can do at this point. Most of what colleges are evaluating you on you've already done. Sure, it helps if you get the best grades of your life first semester freshman year, and you can do a few things like interviewing with the admissions office, but mostly, your application is filled out.

Instead of worrying about whether what you've done is good enough to get you into the best tier of schools, think about this: college really is what you make of it. With a few exceptions, you can go to any school, and with the right mindset, you can get an excellent education, have a great social life, and accomplish whatever it is that you want to accomplish. College is just the where, not the how. Sure, there are some fringe benefits of going to a school like CMC: small classes, nice housing, good career services. But generally these are quality-of-life issues and you are adaptable and can live without them. So what am I trying to say? Good luck finding a school, I hope you find one you think fits you well and you get in. Should you not get in, however, keep in mind that getting into one college or another doesn't dictate anything about who you are, or what you can do.

There, it's a little touchy feely, but I've said it, and I believe it's true. I wish you a good search, come visit CMC, even if it's just to spend a fun overnight, and most of all: wish me good luck next year, as starting life in the real world can't be nearly as fun as starting college.

Eatharon Taylor—Clark Atlanta University

Writing this book has been an outstanding experience, and I really appreciate the staff at College Prowler for trusting me to complete the first Clark Atlanta University edition. Having the opportunity to write this book for prospective CAU students has been one of my proudest accomplishments. I have a great admiration for people who choose to further their education and even greater admiration for those who choose to become a part of the family! I hope this book gives you some good insight into the lifestyle of CAU Panthers, but be sure to do some additional research before you finalize your decision. Researching for this book has given me a wealth of knowledge about CAU, and I would love to answer any additional questions that you may have concerning Clark Atlanta University, or college life in general.

My past few years at Clark Atlanta University have helped me to grow tremendously as a person, and I am really thankful for all the friends, professors, and colleagues that have taught me valuable lessons that I couldn't have possibly learned anywhere else. I would like to thank God, my mom, my family, and everyone else who has contributed their time and effort to make sure I headed in the right direction. Thanks to everyone at school who gave me quotes, my god family for providing holiday meals, and my best friends from Arkansas and in Atlanta.

Thank you for considering Clark Atlanta University. Good luck on your journey to higher learning!

Mike Bertone—Clark University

I spent the beginning of my life in northern New Jersey and the rest in the Hudson Valley, New York. Coming to Clark was the best decision of my life. I met a lot of great people, learned a lot of great things, and grew up a lot in the process. I had a hard time adjusting at first, but by my sophomore year, I had fallen in love with both Worcester and Clark. The people I've met and the lessons I've learned at Clark have utterly changed my life for the better, and I am glad I attended the school.

When I received the invitation to try my hand as a writer for College Prowler, I was very enthusiastic to portray the reality of the University and discuss my time and experiences at Clark. I hope that my hand in writing this book might attract more people who would end up being dedicated Clarkies, who could come to campus with the knowledge and preparation to make them more positive and enthusiastic members of the student body. Clark isn't for everyone, but it was the perfect school for me, and for those whom it fits, it is more than just a simple four years away from home. It is the best time of your life.

I graduated from Clark with a major in philosophy. I now reside in Framingham, Massachusetts and work as a computer technician in the public sector. I would like to thank my family for their undying support, my grandparents for their love and pride, and my friends for the good times, influence, and experiences throughout the years. I would also like to thank professors Matt Malsky, Judith DeCew, Valentine Sensei, and Judge Hillman for their incredible teachings, conversations, and examples. I would have fallen far short of my goals without the help of any of these people. Thank you all very much, and thank you College Prowler for giving me the opportunity to do something positive for the school that I've loved so much.

Andrew D. Coleman—Clemson University

I had a good time writing this book. I was eager to help other students make a more informed decision in selecting a college because I know how challenging the process can be. Right now, I am a junior at Clemson University majoring in history. I have spent the fall semester of my junior year studying and doing an internship in Washington, DC. It has been an insightful and very educational experience—I would recommend a program like this to anyone. I hope this book has been useful and will help you make an informed decision when it comes time to choose a school. I give special thanks to my parents for their support and to all the folks at College Prowler, who have helped me along the way.

Allyson Rudolph—Colby College

Hi! I'm the author. While not writing college guidebooks, I actually go to college. I'm currently a sophomore at Colby. I think I am an English major, but that is subject to change on a minute-by-minute basis. I'm also a political junkie. At school I am the Arts and Entertainment editor for the *Echo*, the president of the League of Progressive Voters (like I said, political junkie), an HR, and a tour guide. I have lived in northern Virginia, the western suburbs of Chicago, and now, Maine.

Thanks to my family, especially my parents. Thanks to my friends, who I will not list by name because I would probably forget somebody or put someone last and I don't want to do that. Thanks to the College Prowler. Thanks to my teachers. Thanks to you, dear reader, for putting up with my writing.

Good luck with the college search. If you have any comments about the guidebook, or questions about Colby, the application process, the meaning of life, etc., I enjoy receiving e-mails. They make me feel loved.

Desirée Abeleda and Elisa Benson—Colgate University

Desirée—During my numerous college tours, I visited Colgate on a whim because a friend of mine was about to attend and we were in the area. I automatically fell in love with it during that first visit. The grounds and facilities were beautiful, and my tour guide obviously loved his school. I was accepted to other prestigious institutions in addition to Colgate, making my decision a bit more difficult. Then I stayed overnight during the spring of my senior year, and the love was rekindled. I knew Colgate was the right choice when I saw how much happier and enthusiastic the students at Colgate were than at any other institution I had visited, and they were not all cheerleaders. That was when I met Elisa, a spunky and energetic girl I really hoped would make the same decision as me.

Contrasting Elisa, I am pursuing a dual concentration in sociology and anthropology, with a minor concentration in writing in the social sciences. I hope to graduate and pursue graduate education in law school or journalism school. I have maintained status on the Dean's List and received the Dean's award for the past three semesters at Colgate, so hopefully those awards will help my acceptance.

Elisa—As for me, Elisa, when I'm not hanging out with Des, I'm either working at the Writing Center or Colgate's PR office, writing my weekly relationship-commentary column for the school paper, spinning punk rock tunes on 'RCU, or heading up the Colgate Activities Board Special Events committee. Oh yeah, I also find time to go to class, where I'm working toward an art and art history concentration and an interdisciplinary writing minor. Here I am, loving every minute of college life, and hoping that my input with the College Prowler guide to Colgate will help others mail the right envelope, too.

Melanie Murray—College of Charleston

Before anything else is said, I want to express how thankful I am to have been given this opportunity. This project has given me insight into a field that I know for sure I want to be doing for the rest of my life and has helped me develop a beginner's work ethic for writing that I know will only grow as time goes on. I'm a junior at the College of Charleston pursing a major in English and a double-minor in creative writing, with an emphasis in non-fiction and communications.

This is more than a first step for me, more than just an excuse to storm around the house like a weathered professional screaming, "I'm up against a deadline!" It has shown me what hard work really can accomplish. I hope you enjoyed reading this book and that it has given you a more honest and insightful glimpse into C of C.

Even though I was a crabby hermit locked in a room with a computer for months, I have many people to thank, people who have helped in more ways than one: Mom and Dad of course, Lauren, Nick, Becca, Sarah, Britt, Kathy, Jimmy, Mamie, Bo, Lauren, Leah, Liz, and everyone at College Prowler!

Matthew Hayes—College of the Holy Cross

I am a graduate of the College of the Holy Cross, where I majored in history and minored in economics. I was raised in Sea Cliff, on Long Island, and currently reside in New York City, where I work at a textbook publishing company.

Unlike many other students at Holy Cross who grew up in households steeped in Holy Cross tradition or went to Catholic high schools where Holy Cross was a well-known name, I had never heard of the school until the summer before my senior year in high school. A colleague of my father's who serves on the College's Board of Trustees told me what an excellent school it was and highly suggested that I visit. A few weeks later, I did—and as soon as I saw the campus (and met the Public Safety officer who had an Irish brogue), I was in love. Although the decision process was arduous—I was deciding between Holy Cross and a number of other top-ranked liberal arts colleges—in the end I believe I made the right choice.

In most of the ways that matter, Holy Cross prepared me well for the real world. The school's tough academic policies ensured that I left school not only four years older, but four years wiser. Unlike the traditional stereotype of Catholic education—the rote learning model that is so often lampooned—the Jesuit tradition encourages free thinking and questioning, and obtaining knowledge through understanding. This thought process is the hallmark of a Holy Cross education, and I know that it has helped me immensely in my postgraduate career.

Camille Thompson—College of William & Mary

Writing this book was an exercise in patience, as I wrote it while holding down two other jobs. It was a good experience, though, and it reminded me of how much I love W&M and can't wait to return to classes as a junior. I am pursuing a degree in English, with a minor in women's studies. I aspire to become a print journalist. To that end, I'm currently participating in an internship at the *Free Lance-Star* newspaper in Fredericksburg, Virginia, writing stories for the Life section.

When I return to W&M this fall, I will proudly serve as Assistant News Editor of the *Flat Hat*. I earned this position after writing stories for the News section nearly every week last year. I hope this book was helpful in your quest for the right college and that you enjoy wherever you end up as much as I enjoy W&M.

Thanks to: Mom and Dad for putting up with me, David for all his love, help, and encouragement, the rest of my family for loving me, David, Matt, Jon, Erin, Dillon, and Wendy for filling out my survey, the entire Flat Hat staff, especially Meghan and Stephen for putting up with me at 4 a.m., Mr. Olson, Mrs. Stovall, Glenn Barclay, Mrs. Woodcock, Mr. Stebar, Dr. Walker, Mr. L, Dr. Scholnick, Professor O'Dell, and every other teacher I've ever had, for your guidance and wisdom.

Sarah Core—College of Wooster

I am a senior at the College of Wooster, currently pursuing an English major and communication minor. I am active in many different organizations at college (mainly because I can't say no), including being a DJ for the College's own radio station, WCWS 90.9 FM. I'm also a Web master for the Babcock International Program, a member of the COW Belles, Wooster's beautiful and fabulous female a cappella group, and the cheese and hot dog girl for Circle K (a great volunteer organization). Last, but certainly not least, I like to lose sleep on Wednesday nights as the Managing Editor of the *Wooster Voice*, the College's weekly, student-run newspaper since 1883.

After college, I plan on heading to graduate school to try my hand at the journalism profession, hopefully learning a little along the way. Look for my byline to grace a publication in the near future, whether it's the *New York Times* or *Billy Bob's Quarterly Home Canning Magazine*.

A big thank you goes out to all the people who put up with me during the process of writing this guidebook, including my parents, Gordon, Lois, and Rachel Core, the entire *Voice* staff (including my News Yoda), my roommate Aubrey, who slept through my typing, Montana and his funny friends who like to distract me at 4 a.m. until I put them to work, Wooster's Career Services, Information Technology, the Longbrake Wellness Center, and Safety and Security, for bending over backward to help me get the answers I needed, and everyone at College Prowler.

Greg Lestikow and Jennifer Small—Colorado College

Thank you for picking up this book! We all learn the ins and outs of our schools as students. I had the added opportunity of seeing the college from the perspective of a resident advisor, a student mentor, a *Catalyst* copy editor and a Writing Center consultant. With all that information cluttering up my head, I leapt at the chance to pour all my accumulated knowledge into a book for incoming students and high school seniors. Actually, I'm going to use this book, even as a senior, because I finally know when Jazzman's closes, how many people fit in Mathias, and when the Irish folk singer appears at Jack Quinn's. I hope you get as much out of reading this book as I got out of writing it. After graduating with degrees in English and psychology, I hope to invade New York City and start an extraordinarily successful career in editing.

Thank you to my mom, my uncle (who first suggested CC), and especially to my grandparents for helping me find CC and helping me find myself somewhere along the way. (To everyone who isn't my mom, uncle, or grandparent, you have helped me along in your own special way. Your time in the sun will come.) Thank you to College Prowler for this great start to my aspirations of professional writing and editing!

Michelle Tompkins—Columbia University

Michelle Tompkins hails from Sacramento, California and is the youngest of four children.

Prior to attending Columbia University, she worked as a disc jockey for a Santa Rosa radio station, two Sacramento Theatre Companies and founded a talent agency in Los Angeles. When academia beckoned, she attended American River College in Sacramento and for two years was the editor-in-chief of the college newspaper, the *Current*.

At Columbia, she has served the past three years as editor-in-chief of the Observer, the literary and features magazine for Columbia School of General Studies. She will receive her BA in Film and will continue to work on creative writing projects in New York City.

Brian Sendrowski—Connecticut College

Brian Sendrowski spent incredible years at Connecticut College studying English, a subject he had earlier vowed never to major in, because English majors tend not to find jobs until after they're dead.

After graduating summa cum laude, he's pleased to report that he has discovered that they get them sooner than that. He currently resides in Ellington, Connecticut, not too far from his alma mater.

The author would like to thank everyone at College Prowler for the opportunity to write this book and all of the professors at Conn's English department with whom he had the pleasure to work. Special thanks go out to everyone at the Roth Writing Center, especially to Michael Reder for his inexhaustible enthusiasm for writing and teaching, Andrea Rossi for her service as a Faculty Adviser and constant stream of recommendation letters, and Beverly Matias for making each day at the center so much fun. And of course, never-ending thanks to Mom, Dad, Brendan, and Laura for all of your support over the years.

The author enjoys being called "the author," so if someone reading this happens to have any freelance writing jobs, feel free to e-mail him. Of course, comments and feedback are also welcome.

Oliver Striker and Maria Adelmann—Cornell University

Oliver—I recently graduated from Cornell in May from the College of Arts and Sciences. While I pursued a major in English, I was grateful for the opportunities I had to explore a wide range of different academic disciplines. Specifically, I maintained an intensive focus in business and finance, and this summer I'll be starting a job in real estate investment banking. Shortly thereafter, I expect to reminisce about my incredible college experiences at Cornell as I slave away on Wall Street for long and endless hours.

I have no doubt, thanks to the brilliant professors I've encountered, that the skills I acquired at Cornell will serve me in good stead from here on out. I intend to stay in touch with the numerous friends I made at Cornell and meet new alums here in New York City. Cornellians have an even tighter bond with their school once they graduate, and I can't wait to visit Ithaca sometime in the near future. If you have any questions or comments please feel free to e-mail me.

I would like to send special thanks to Mom and Dad, Clarissa Striker, Casey Becker, Tom Waldron, James Larocca, Matt Maxwell, Namita Khosla, and the entire team at College Prowler!

Maria—I am a sophomore in the College of Arts and Sciences, majoring in psychology and English. I have a great job in the Student Activities Office and have enjoyed learning how to peer counsel in EARS. I spend much of my free time writing and hope one day to be on the list of famous Cornellians. In the meantime, I just hope to do well on my finals.

Holly Morris—Creighton University

I came to Creighton as clueless as a honeybee on a piece of wax fruit. I was scared to make friends because I wanted to keep a perfect GPA and keep my friends from high school, all while pursuing biology—a major I knew was wrong for me. Cleaning up that mess took me a lot of work, a lot of fun, and provided me with an entirely new outlook on life as I went from hospital aid to Phonathon (University fundraiser) caller to newspaper editor, then from insecure bookworm to fun-loving sorority girl to ever-so-slightly less confused bookworm. I've been involved with service trips and organizations, the pep band, the student newspaper, literary magazine, and tutoring. I have friends who founded a Rosary Club and friends who chain smoke.

Broad experiences and amazing people helped me see Creighton from a variety of angles. I wanted to write this guide because I knew I had seen Creighton from a lot of different perspectives and would be apt neither to discourage students from coming nor to sugarcoat things like an admissions officer with a quota to fill. As a journalist, I try to tell it like it is.

I want to thank many people for their help: my college professors who have helped me grow with more than the tests, my high school and elementary teachers for the knowledge base, my parents and other family, my friends from home and here at Creighton, and everyone at College Prowler, especially my wonderful writing manager, Omid Gohari. I could never have gotten through the compilation of facts in this book without the knowledge and clarity they've all helped me to develop.

Janos Marton—Dartmouth College

I remember the college search process as an extremely exciting time, and it's great to be able to help out future generations of (hopefully Dartmouth) students. I graduated last year and received a degree in history. Born and raised in New York City, I came to Dartmouth on a whim but have loved my four years here. I'm serving my second term as student body president, am a staff writer for the *Free Press*, and a member of Chi Gamma Epsilon fraternity.

Best of luck to everyone. While I hope you find the best college for you, no matter where you end up, the next four years are going to be incredible.

Colin Eagan—Davidson College

Colin Eagan is a senior at Davidson College, where he divides his time between majoring in English and pondering life's intricacies. Colin is an editor at the college newspaper, and recently launched a new humor feature called "The Yowl." He spent his second semester of his junior year studying antiquities in Cyprus, Egypt, and Rome. If everything goes according to plan, Colin will graduate and hopefully move somewhere other than back home to Baltimore, Maryland (although secretly his mom would just love that). He dedicates this book to Lauren—who makes Davidson what it is.

Sarah Clapp—Denison University

I learned a lot from writing this book. I discovered many things about Denison University that I did not know, and that I never would have otherwise thought about, but despite the number of things that I've learned I know that there is still more for me to discover. No one book can reveal all the secrets of any campus, but it has been exciting to try. I'm an English major, and I hope to publish more as my writing skills grow.

I've lived in many places (my native Michigan, Washington DC, and Granville, Ohio). I've found Granville and the entire college journey to be an amazing learning experience. I hope your college experience, no matter which college you choose, is great, and I hope you found this book to be helpful in some way.

E. Ce Anderson—DePauw University

I'm a Third Year undergraduate at DePaul University, working on my degree in literary studies and peace, conflict and social justice studies, in my undoubtedly foolish, however well-intentioned aspirations of becoming Caesar Chavez, Eleanor Roosevelt or Hunter S. Thompson. While I ended up at DePaul rather haphazardly, after taking the forty-three-and-a-half minute drive southeast from my grassy-knolled, white-fenced suburb in the Illinois sticks, I never looked back. It hasn't always been easy, but as Jimi Hendrix would have said: I discovered the shape of my heart in Chicago. Upon graduating next year I'd like to find a career that provides an opportunity to combine law school, joining the Peace Corps, pursuing a Masters degree in creative writing, backpacking across South Africa and Israel and spending endless hours on my best friend's couch alternating between ordering Chicago-style pizza or Indian food delivery… it'll be interesting to see how that all works out.

Nella pace.

Special thanks to my cousin Andrew, who reminds me that it's okay if the setting of "One Flew Over the Cuckoo's Nest" sometimes feels homey; to my grandmother Ce, who blessed me with the genes for determination; to LeRoy Schneider, who makes the little miracles happen; and to my mother, who genuinely seems to like me and who does it all.

Kellie Lee Hasselbeck—DePauw University

I spent my entire freshman and sophomore year complaining about DePauw. Complaining because it was too small, too competitive, and in the middle of nowhere. I hated DePauw. In the past year, however, I have grown up a lot, and have come to realize that what I have at DePauw is different but special. Sure, I could have transferred to a school on the ocean where I could have surfed and laid out on the beach all day. Or I could have snowboarded my college years away at a university in the mountains of Colorado. But I didn't transfer, and I recognized why I was at college. I was there to get an education; I was there to concentrate on my academics and learn. I could never have achieved academically the way I have if I hadn't been so focused. Yeah, there isn't anything to do in Indiana, but in a bizarre and peculiar way, that's what makes DePauw such a great school.

This book represents DePauw how it is today. This may not be the DePauw tomorrow, or the DePauw three years from now . . . DePauw is changing. The bar is rising, and rising rapidly. However, that is only going to make the University stronger and more successful. I thank DePauw for all that it has shown and taught me. I'm thankful for the critical eye that DePauw has instilled in me, and I am thankful for the knowledge I have gained in and out of the classroom. I just want to take this opportunity to thank all the staff, faculty, students, friends, and family that helped me find the truth I needed to complete this book. I am thankful that I was able to write this book—I discovered a lot about DePauw, and I discovered a lot about myself.

Brooke Lewis—Dickinson College

Brooke Lewis is a double major in English and political science at Dickinson College. After graduating from Dickinson she hopes to continue her education in law school. More immediately, she is excited for the opportunity to study in Florence, Italy and hopes to travel Europe while she is there. Her hobbies include art history, reading, writing, and sports of all kinds. This is her first nationally-published work.

Ryan Murphy—Drexel University

Ryan Murphy is an English major at Drexel University. He welcomes any questions about Drexel or college in general. Please use the e-mail address below.

Margaret Campbell—Duke University

Most of this you must already know. If you're researching colleges, you've probably already come across rankings, descriptions of campuses, and admissions and financial aid statistics. This book may give you a lot more of the same, but that is not exactly its aim. You will find more information about Duke than I ever knew existed before writing this book. There are some vital questions about everyday life answered here, and more importantly, a lot of student opinions have been revealed. So it's best to take what you can find. If you're looking to spend the next four years of your life here, then you have every right to know how "real" Duke students feel about their school. This book will give you that information, and then some.

Good luck in your college hunting, and when the admissions letters come in, you should celebrate—and then feel free to thank College Prowler for making your decision that much easier.

Jonathan Doctorick—Duquesne University

I am thankful for having the opportunity to write for College Prowler. I was amazed by much of the information I unearthed. I now feel more knowledgeable about Duquesne and my hometown of Pittsburgh than I ever thought possible. I am also grateful for having this chance to see my name and work appear in a national publication.

I hope to enter into law school with my background in political science and English. I am thoroughly enjoying these two majors as well as the entire college experience at Duquesne. If all goes as planned (as I have learned sometimes does happen), College Prowler will only be the first in a long stream of publications. It never hurts to dream. Given that writing has become my true passion, I am again grateful for this opportunity to help make a prospective college student's task of choosing the right school a little less daunting. I certainly hope you have enjoyed reading this guide, had a few laughs along with me, and learned a little bit of otherwise unknown information. I wish you well on your college career, no matter where it may take you.

Enough about me and my self-absorbed commentary, however. Many people have affected my life in more ways than they may think. I now take this opportunity to thank all those who have helped me down this long, sometimes complicated road of life. Thank you Mom, Dad, Julia, Grandpa and Grandma, Jackie, Timmy, Christy, the Seton-La Salle crew, my friends at Duquesne, professors who have taught me that less than the best is not enough, everyone at College Prowler, and of course, rny dog Casper. As with everyone else, he has been there with me through it all, always willing to listen.

Anna Benfield—Earlham College

At Earlham, I am in my final semesters as a field hockey-playing, newspaper-editing, leg warmer-wearing women's studies major. I enjoy cartwheeling in the rain with my housemates and procrastinating African American lit papers with boogie club extravaganzas in front of the circulation desk. When I'm not circulating zines about radical mynstruation, I spend my time having in-depth conversations about feminist theory and finding new things to cook on our house's George Foreman grill. Whatever I'm up to, I hope you'll contact me with your thoughts or questions about Earlham.

This project wouldn't have been possible without all my fellow Earlhamites who so painstakingly (and sometimes obscenely) answered generic survey questions with their unabashed, often hilarious, honest opinions. I extend my gratitude, as well, to the Earlham faculty and staff, including Jeff Rickey, Mary Ann Stienbarger, Mary Ann Weaver, Jill Butcher, Joe Green, patient Runyan workers (including Lonnie Clark), Kathie Guyler, Tom Steffes, Pat Fessler, Karen Roeper, Jon Branstrator, Randy Kouns, and Holly Woodruff. Thanks Caitlin Rogers for your feedback on the first edition. Much gratis to Michael and everyone who let me use their computer (no thanks to the Santa Cruz library system) as I completed this book in five states on eleven different computers. Thank you, Kai for patiently allowing your Tinker to putz away on the 'puter when she should have been playing on the beach with you, showing you up with her mad skim-boarding skillz. Finally, thanks Mom, for your unconditional love and support.

Leanne E. Smith—East Carolina University

A native of Greenville, N.C., Leanne E. Smith graduated from J.H. Rose High School and studies English with a minor in French at ECU.

Early in college, Leanne learned the importance of being involved and took part in the Emerging Leaders Program, after which she worked as an orientation assistant for two years. She has been active in several student organizations, hosted shows on WZMB 91.3 FM (campus radio) for three semesters, and is a member of several

honor societies: Phi Kappa Phi , Omicron Delta Kappa National Leadership Honor Society, Sigma Tau Delta International English Honor Society, Phi Sigma Iota International Foreign Language Honor Society, Phi Eta Sigma National Honor Society, the National Society of Collegiate Scholars, Golden Key International Honor Soceity, and the Gamma Beta Phi Society. Leanne received the Gravely Foundation Award, Russell Christman Memorial Scholarship, Outstanding Senior and Outstanding Graduate Student recognitions and the John D. and Dorothy C. Ebbs Fellowship, all from the Department of English, as well as the Robert H. Wright Alumni Leadership Award from ECU's Alumni Association.

Outside of class, Leanne enjoys dancing, most often contra, salsa, and swing dancing, but she has also studied belly dancing and Highland dancing. She is a member of the Green Grass Cloggers (founded at ECU in 1971) and even did two informal clogging demos on stage with Alasdair Fraser at the Grandfather Mountain and New Hampshire Highland Games. She was also an award-winning Scottish fiddler. She is a fan of folk/ethnic music, and her camera is practically an appendage because she uses it so often. She listens to Prairie Home Companion on NPR and watches British comedy on PBS. A brazen generalist in regard to her academic journeys, she appreciates a quote uttered by one of her favorite British actresses, Patricia Routledge: "I want to do good work in good places with good people – that's all."

Leanne thanks Professor Luke Whisnant, her guide for the Directed Readings in Creative Writing for which she earned course credit for this project.

Amy Mahon—Elon University

This was a very interesting and fun opportunity for me! I am currently a freshman here at Elon, double-majoring in elementary education and theater arts, so learning more and more about my school was very interesting. It was also great that I got to meet a lot of the administrators that I will be working with in the coming years!

Aside from studies, I am also involved in the Service Learning Community here on campus for my freshman year only, and will take part in Elon Volunteers! next year (yes, with the exclamation mark). I love the opportunities for service on this campus and the encouragement from people to get involved. I am also in the Isabella Cannon Leadership Program, where we do workshops to not only learn how to be effective leaders, but how to be good listeners, followers, and workers. After all, part of being a good leader is listening to new ideas. Elon University is big on accepting new ideas and trying them out. You cannot be a leader of tomorrow if you cannot face the challenges of today with an open mind!

I strongly encourage any high school juniors or seniors to come and visit the campus, sit in on a class, talk with students and admissions counselors, and get a good feel for the school. Elon is not for everyone. Some people prefer to be on a much larger or smaller campus. Some do not want to be in a mainly conservative environment. Elon is amazing, so I challenge you to step outside the box and see for yourself whether or not you can call it home. Best of luck!

Jordan Ross—Emerson College

I decided to do this book because I wanted to gain experience working on a large writing project during my last summer of classes. It turns out that it was a lot of work, but well worth the effort. As I finish this book, I am getting ready to grab my degree and run (I've enjoyed my three years here, but am ready to leave Boston). I will miss my professors at Emerson; they have made all the difference in my experience.

Thanks for the opportunity for me to share some insight about Emerson with you. I hope this book has been useful in your college search. Your years at college should be a challenging, maturing, and fun experience. I wish you the best in finding the perfect school for you. Thanks to the professors who have encouraged and taught me so much: Jeff Seglin, Lisa Diercks, Kevin Miller, John Coffee, and Tim Weiskel. Much thanks to my parents, M.C., Leah, Taylor, Crystal, Kari, Ryan, Penny, Emily, Ethan, Shiny, Maggie, 45 Columbus, and everyone at College Prowler.

Jordan Pope-Roush—Emory University

I've had a fun time writing this guidebook and hope that it was informative and educational. Anyone who knows me knows that I have had an interesting four years at Emory, but I have always kept a positive outlook and tried to keep things fun. I am currently a senior Creative Writing major and hope to one day become President of Namibia. I am from Dayton, Ohio, and I have two last names.

Thanks to everyone who helped, to my parents for having sex that one time and thereby creating me, to my brother and sister, my dead dog Max, Pike, Avery the pit bull, Snoop Dogg, Boomer Esiason, Jesse Jackson, Thomas Jefferson, Cameron Diaz, Outkast, Barry Larkin, Jesus, all the robots, the U.S. government for always being there for me, everyone who ever looked at me, the squirrels, and Ohio for being the eighth-most populated state.

Heather M. DiRubba—Fashion Institute of Technology

I am a native New Yorker, and I had dreamed of moving to Manhattan to study at a college. I researched FIT, and it became my optimal choice—I fell in love with the programs offered and transferred here.

FIT exposed me to more career-preparing options then most students could imagine. I served on the student government as vice president of communications, traveled to conferences and seminars, studied abroad in London, and completed five internships. My years at FIT may have been extremely busy, but when I graduated I felt prepared to get out in the industry and work!

The one thing I do wish is that I had been offered the option of knowing all of the information in this book before I came here. I hope you learn about the true experience of FIT, and if you still have questions about what goes on here, feel free to e-mail me.

This is where I must take up space to recognize and thank those who have supported me throughout my years of college and in this writing process. Mom and Dad – Without your unconditional support (especially in those financially rough times), I would not be where I am right now in life. I am every grateful to you both! Gammy (my great-grandmother) – You have taught me over the years that reading and writing should be a fun and creative part of life. You are my inspiration! Anthony – You have been there for me through out my years at FIT. I can never thank you enough for listening to me on all those late nights of studying, worrying about my bills, and anything else you would allow me to vent about. You were my unofficial psychologist! Professor Roberta Elins – You taught me a great deal about public relations, FIT, and helped me in many times of need. You are a mentor to me! A final thank you goes out to my family and friends, the FIT community, College Prowler, and everyone else that has shown me their support.

Richard Bist—Florida State University

Writing this guidebook has been both fun and challenging. As a creative writing major at Florida State University, I've been challenged in most of my classes, and that in turn has helped to prepare me for writing projects such as this one. I'm looking forward to beginning my senior year this fall, and I know that when I graduate next spring, I will be ready to move on to my next challenge: graduate school. I have been lucky enough to have had this

opportunity to grow as a writer, and I hope that this is only the beginning of a fruitful writing career, both in fiction and non-fiction.

Of course, I wouldn't have made it this far if it weren't for the support, encouragement, and guidance of numerous individuals. I wish to express love and gratitude to my wife, Alecia; my parents, Paul & Joni; my in-laws, Carter & Janet; and the rest of my family. I would also like to thank Mark Winegardner, Dr. Claudia Johnson, Dr. Cadence Kidwell, Elizabeth Stuckey-French, and Dr. Russ Franklin for their guidance, both in and out of the classroom. I don't want to forget the folks at College Prowler for bestowing me with this opportunity. And last but not least, I'd like to extend a tip of the hat to the friends and well-wishers who help to keep me sane, and especially Erica, Michelle, Terri, Roosevelt, Lynette, Kristina, and Ed the Head (you know who you are!).

Emily Intravia—Fordham University

Fresh out of Fordham, I was thrilled to find a forum where I could express my experience at one of the most unique colleges in the country. I transferred to Fordham College at Lincoln Center in my sophomore year, and graduated this May with a BA in playwriting and English.

Although I missed out on the Fordham freshman experience, my three years here in New York provided me with plenty of time to take advantage of what Fordham has to offer. As a playwriting major, I watched four of my own plays produced right in the studio theaters. The quality of student theater, from the writers to the actors to the designers, is still the most impressive aspect of this university to me. Some of my other Fordham highlights include completing an internship at Comedy Central and contributing original fiction and editorials to the *Observer*. Even my work study program was an educational and rewarding experience; I was a student aide and reading tutor in a public school. I sometimes regret that I never utilized the Rose Hill campus. Perhaps it was some Manhattan snobbery, but I, like many Lincoln Center students (and likewise, Rose Hillers), considered the two campuses to be separate universities. Only after this project, which allowed me to speak with Rose Hill students and fully immerse myself in the college I ignored, did I come to appreciate the quality of life and education at the Bronx center. While I cherish my unique Lincoln Center experience, there was a part of me that was a little envious of Rose Hill's coeducational community.

As far as my future goes, I wish to continue writing in whatever capacity I can (being published is a nice bonus). I genuinely hope this guide has helped you with your college search. Choosing your college might be the biggest decision you will have to make so far, but remember, nothing is ever final. As a transfer student, I learned from my first choice (and subsequent disappointment) what I wanted out of a college experience. Enjoy your college exploration, but don't feel like this is what determines the rest of your life. Ultimately, what you do in those four years—whether it's making sculptures at Lincoln Center, conducting biological studies at Rose Hill, or taking every subject there is until you find your favorite—is your choice. Make the most of it.

Ellen Baier—Franklin & Marshall College

I am a graduate of Franklin & Marshall College, where I was honored to be the 83rd recipient of the Henry S. Williamson Medal. Right now, I live and work in Burlington, Vermont, but I originally hail from Collinsville, Illinois. I would also like to take this opportunity to thank my loving sisters Robyn, Sara, Megs, Shahed, and Marisa for their help and support with this project, as well as my friends Sarah, Obs, Amy, Kristen, Jamie, Lea, and Jess. I love you guys!

Debra A. Granberry—Furman University

I've appreciated the opportunity this book has given me to try my hand as a writer. I hope reading it has been an enlightening, and at times, perhaps entertaining experience. I'm now a senior at Furman trying to finish up degrees in both communication studies and English. I lived in Dallas, Texas my entire life, until the calling of higher education caused me to pack up my car and move a thousand miles away to Greenville. Who knows what's next?

And because I have now reached the point in my literary career where I am allowed to thank people, I would like to profusely thank several people. First, my remarkable family for always letting me go and always letting me come back. And especially my brother, a recent graduate of Furman, without whom I probably could not have finished this book. Thanks to all my friends at home, school, and elsewhere. Nicole, my roommate who put up with me while I spent all summer writing, and everyone else at Furman who helped me out with this book.

Kevan Gray—Geneva College

I guess it is time to inflate my already narcissistic ego. Currently, I am finishing my senior year at Geneva College with a double major in philosophy and writing. I am the Editor and Chief of the Cabinet, Geneva's student newspaper, and president of the Ski and Snowboard Club. Although I have been able to achieve membership in Alpha Chi, a national honors society, and met the credentials to be in the Who's Who among college students, my biggest academic achievement was receiving an A- in poli sci.

I call Greensburg, Pennsylvania, home. It was there that I began my elementary school tutelage that set the foundation for my intellectual growth and fed my curious nature. From second through tenth grade, I was home schooled. Upon attending Greensburg-Salem High School, I became active in a number of sports. However, the crowning experience of high school was being a part of the Pennsylvania Mock Trial State Champion team that went to Omaha, Nebraska to compete for a national title.

After graduation, I plan on attending law school, although I don't know where. And from there I will proceed to be a tool to fix and refine the American social and judicial systems. Although power and money will not be mine, I will hopefully sleep peacefully and have time to myself, instead of being owned by the corporate mentality that fuels the workaholic nature of most lawyers.

Now I have to fulfill my promises to all those I told that I would fit into this guidebook somehow. I thank my parents for their dedication to my education as a youngster and their support in more recent years throughout college, and my family in Nebraska who have always been loving and showed interest in my direction. I would also like to thank Dr. Robert Frazier for his intellectual guidance and friendship, Rich Grassel for his spiritual mentorship, Dr. S.S. Hanna for his persistence regarding my writing, and Dr. Lynda Szabo for introducing me to, and instilling a curiosity for, American literature and poetry.

Last, I have to squeeze my friends in here. Thanks to: Brendon for his persistent friendship since second grade, Kent for those pocket rockets you always want but rarely get, Mike for his musical expertise and self-attributed elitism, Dave M. for being so sexy, Ron for his support and concern (even if it's at three in the morning), Ben for his pretending to listen when I talk, and Eric for his tolerance. Ben and Eric, I'm proud of you, you've come a long way.

Julie Gordon—George Washington University

Julie Gordon graduated from GW with a major in journalism and a minor in English. A Livingston, New Jersey native, Julie was excited to have had the chance to write a book about something she loves so much—GW. On campus, Julie was news managing editor of the century-old GW Hatchet, the University's independent student newspaper, during her senior year. She was also University news editor her junior year, and a reporter and staff writer her sophomore year. Julie was an editorial intern at USA Today and covered the shooting at City Hall in New York, IMG founder Mark McCormack's memorial service, the New York smoking ban, and a bunch of literary and entertainment news, among other stories. Julie also interned in YM magazine's entertainment department. Julie is pursuing a career in journalism or public relations.

Julie was also involved in theater at GW. She co-founded a student-run theater company, 14th Grade Players, her sophomore year. She made her directorial debut in April 2002 with Barbara Lebow's A Shayna Maidel. Julie produced Deathtrap, by Ira Levin and served as public relations chair. Julie performed in two plays at GW—The Crucible, as Betty, and Who Made Robert DeNiro King of America?, as Samantha. She is also a member of the Screen Actors Guild.

Julie could not have written this book about GW if she had not met such wonderful people while attending school. Julia offers the following thanks: To Stefanie for being a wonderful roommate and friend for the past four years. Adina—we've had great times and have shared so much. My other friends and Hatcheteers—you're all great and have made my time at GW worthwhile. To the non-G-dubbers: Tracy, Liza, and Lauren—your friendships are so special to me. Mom and Dad—thank you for encouraging me to come to GW and pursue my writing. I love you. Emily—I wish we were in school together. I love you so much and know you'll do great in college. To those either looking at or attending GW, my time in the District has been wonderful, and I can't imagine being anywhere else."

Derek Richmond—Georgetown University

Writing this book has been an incredible experience. It turns out there was a lot more that I didn't know about Georgetown than I expected. I've learned a lot, and I hope that I have clearly and honestly presented every aspect of Georgetown to you. I am an English major in the College, and I write for the Hoya, Georgetown's finest campus newspaper. It was here that I found my penchant and propensity for writing. I was born in Ohio, but I have spent most of my life in Florida, so the DC winters have been a bit harsh on me; I am no worse for the wear, however, and I am certainly bettered by the Georgetown education.

Enough about me, though. There are a lot of people I want to thank. Thank you Mom and Dad, for the opportunities you have given me, especially all of those to which Georgetown has opened my eyes. Thank you Susie, for the art to which you have introduced me, though perhaps writing is more of a craft. Thank you Emily, for your unwavering love and support on which I depend. Thank you Mary, for the veritable compendium of trivial factoids you contributed to this project. Thank you Mitch, Bryn, Dani, Laura, and Grace for your insight into our prestigious institution, and thanks to the folks at College Prowler for offering me this incredible opportunity. And thank you. Yes, I can't forget you, because you're the one this project was all about. I hope you have enjoyed what we have put together for you. Hoya Saxa.

Jonathan Trousdale—Georgia Institute of Technology

Jonathan Trousdale is a recent graduate of Georgia Tech and currently resides in Riverdale, Georgia, near the Atlanta Airport. He spent five years at Tech studying toward a degree in public policy and economics. During much of his time at Georgia Tech, Jonathan was employed under the School of Public Policy, and gained experience assisting professors with their research in the areas of economics and public policy. He recently worked for the Office of Governor Sonny Perdue in Atlanta, assisting the governor's personal advisors, and also was heavily involved in several campus organizations. In the near future, Jonathan plans to begin work with Campus Crusade for Christ, Int'l as a campus ministry intern at the University of Sarajevo, in Bosnia.

Mike Howells—Gettysburg College

I graduated with a BA in Political Science from Gettysburg College in May of 2005—while I was deep in the throes of finishing this guidebook. I'm now currently enjoying life as a Gettysburg alum and trying not to let the fact that I don't actually have a job yet get me down. Still, I have learned a lot from writing this book, and I am sure that something will come along that will suit me just fine. I wish I had access to this kind of a book when I was looking at schools, all those years ago. I hope you find it useful.

Iain Bernhoft—Gonzaga University

Iain Bernhoft spent a happy childhood residing in the Seattle area before "flying the coop" at the tender age of 18, into the outstretched arms of Gonzaga University. He has yet to regret that decision. After cycling through many of the majors in the College of Arts and Sciences (well, the Arts ones, anyway), he settled on a double major in English and philosophy. He graduated with honors and warm wishes aplenty in May 2005, but not before spending the better part of a year studying in Florence and then at Oxford University (again thanks to the gentle ministrations of Gonzaga).

Iain has temporarily abandoned plans of graduate study in English literature to pursue a career as a bellhop. He seems to like Gonzaga so much that he can't quite move on yet, and is currently dwelling on the edge of its fair campus—a location that greatly expedited the process of writing this book. He greatly enjoys writing (particularly when combined with music, a drink, and porch sitting) and hopes to make a career of it yet.

And now, the many, many thanks: my parents and siblings, Granny, the Bros (and Trrristan!), Ted, Cory, Kristin, Liz, Mary, Claire, Franz, Liezl, Kargas, B, Lauth, Steve, the Writing Lab, Rhapsody. Some provided insight, some provided inspiration, some provided hot beverages and open ears, some provided computers, some provided sanity, a few provided the gift of life. Most of you know who you are.

Sarah Haller—Goucher College

From Havre de Grace, Maryland, Sarah Haller was a communication major at Goucher College. Actively involved on campus, Sarah participated in several student publications, served as president of her residence hall, and worked at the Julia Rogers Library. Most notably, Sarah served as managing editor of the student-run newspaper, the Quindecim, for three years. Under her watch, the staff established an online edition and added two special editions: a "Freshmen Only" edition for freshman orientation, and an "April Fool's Day" edition to put a humorous twist on campus news. She currently works full time for Homestead Publishing in both the advertising and production departments.

Lauren Standifer—Grinnell University

Despite the fact that I've only just finished my first year at Grinnell, I'm already madly in love with the place. When I was given the opportunity to write this guidebook, I was thrilled to have the chance to tell people who are trying to decide what their life is going to be like over the next four years about this little Iowan island in the sun, but I also wanted students to know about the things they should be prepared for that the college won't tell them. I hope I've managed to accomplish that in this guidebook. I apologize for any inaccuracies that I may have overlooked, or any significant details I left out, but as far as I know and have been able to find out, everything here is correct.

Right now my major is undeclared, but I think that I will soon declare a double major in physics and history. My fuzzy vision of the future after Grinnell includes graduate school, trying to save the world, and after that . . . ? First star to the right and straight on 'till morning, I suppose.

Jessica Prol—Grove City College

I hardly expected to spend so much of my summer with Grove City College. My body has stayed about five and a half hours away, but I've mentally catalogued everything from campus facilities to the people who stroll around the grounds. The research and writing experience has taught me so much about my college and myself. Initially, GCC wasn't my first-choice school, but like so many of my peers, I know that God brought me there, and I can hardly imagine other options. I am a senior English major with minors in history and philosophy. I've experienced many aspects of Grove City life—the academic rigors, campus jobs, service organizations, religious activities, and honorary recognition. What I couldn't capture in these pages is the large number of sincere, intelligent, all-around amazing friends I have made. I hope that my writing has captured even a little of GCC's character. And now, much gratitude to College Prowler for guidance, Mr. Birkett for teaching me to think and write thoroughly, the GCC administration for its efficient help, every single Grover who donated their own two cents, each unique and wonderful Sarah-friend, all the other non-Sarah Grovers or Jersey friends who joined my fan club, the Hughes's and Muscarellas's for being substitute families, Mom for always listening, Dad for aiming high, my siblings for reminding me that life is different at the ". . . lege," and Josh and Han for heroic last-minute research. Highest thanks to my Savior who gave me the time, talents, and enthusiasm for this guidebook, for my school, and for life.

Elizabeth Laird—Guilford College

I sincerely enjoyed writing this book. I still find myself rather involved with the college, so the Prowler has been fun to research. It was entertaining to catch up with students during the surveys. So many Guilford folks were excited by the opportunity to talk about the college outside of the Guilford Bubble, and without having to worry about the administration.

While at Guilford, I was involved in several different activities, all of which I loved dearly, despite the somewhat obsessive amount of time I devoted to them. I was editor of the Piper twice, as well as art editor; news director and goth/industrial music director for WQFS; religious organizations rep and ICC member for Student Senate; and a clerk and co-founder of the Pagan Mysticism Group. I deeply enjoyed my time with my various organizations throughout my years at Guilford. I also worked for Student Activities for several years, which helped me to recognize all that Guilford has to offer.

I graduated with a degree in English and philosophy with a concentration in photography. Junior year, I had a simply amazing semester abroad in London. I am currently still living in Greensboro, in part to continue to be around Guilford folk during my year off before graduate school. I plan to pursue a career in writing and attend grad school for magazine journalism. I am a fourth-generation Florida native, and some of my favorite things in the world are the Cure and cats.

Thank you to my parents and Guilford friends for your support and love. Thanks to Rebecca Saunders for giving me such a fun and wonderful job with Student Activities. My love to all the people who made my time at Guilford an important and lovely part of my life.

Jessica Adams—Gustavus Adolphus College

Jessica Adams is a 2005 graduate of Gustavus Adolphus College with a double major in English and communication studies and a minor in women's studies. She currently resides in Minneapolis where she likes to seek out offbeat record stores and ethnic restaurants that cater to her vegetarian lifestyle. Jessica loves the East Coast, the Chicago Cubs, strong black coffee, and music that the masses won't hear about until at least six months later. One day, Jessica would like to go to graduate school, but right now the idea of looking at another textbook makes her want to scream. Thus, her "big kid job" will suffice in the meantime.

She would like to thank her family, friends, everyone who has supported her, and also those that helped in the creation of this book. She would thank you all personally, but then she realized that the general public would not care about this opportunity for blazing self-importance and name-dropping. And while she can be a bit narcissistic, she realizes that she would undoubtedly forget somebody, and then she would feel really, really bad. Those who have been there for her know who they are. She thanks you for your love and support.

Katrina Lexa—Hamilton College

Writing for College Prowler has been a tremendously exciting project for me. Through the course of this adventure, I have been reminded of how much I enjoy writing. A part of me has always desired to write more, and this project has afforded me that opportunity, as I have found myself continually challenged by the task of writing a comprehensive and accurate portrait of Hamilton College. As a senior at Hamilton College, I am continuing to refine my future goals and ambitions. Attending a liberal arts college as a double concentrator in chemistry and public policy has opened up incredible opportunities, and I am constantly astounded by the personal and academic maturation that I have gained at this school, all of which has been and continues to be instrumental in my life and future. Hopefully this book has been both enjoyable and insightful for you. As with all author commentary, there are many people who deserve recognition for all the support they have given me. Thank you Mom, Dad, Colin, Josh Huling, Erin Smith, Jenny Lentz, Mollie Wright, Peter Coxeter, Stephanie Godleski, Nii Bentsie-Enchili, Justin Thompson-Tucker, Hilary King, Whitney Rothe, Ernie Digiovanni, and Heather Simmons. Also, thank you to the entire Hamilton College community, their Web site, and all the College offices, as well as everyone at College Prowler.

Stacy Hayashi—Hampshire College

I postmarked my application to Hampshire College on the day of the deadline—it was a last-minute, mostly spur-of-the-moment decision (I had just recently stumbled across the Five College Consortium), and I had the good fortune of being accepted. I didn't have any idea what I was getting into, but when I arrived on campus for the Students of Color Overnight (I hadn't ever used that term) and Accepted Students Day, the rush of activity and late-night organizing intrigued and almost overwhelmed me. Hampshire College was the only campus I visited, and I knew then and there that I didn't need to see anything else.

My academic concentration is journalism, international relations, and the intersection of the two. But Hampshire has also encouraged my forays into critical media, cultural studies, economics and social justice issues, and gender/feminist studies in my coursework. Outside the classroom, I've experienced leading campus groups, conducting independent studies, participating in internships, and studying abroad, all of which have comprised an important part of my education. These endeavors have taken me from a newsroom to a developing country to a new group meeting about fat activism and body positivity. As a staffer for the student newspaper, the Climax, I've witnessed some of the best and the worst of Hampshire, not least of which was (and is) trying to keep a struggling publication alive. It is through the Climax that I was able to speak to many people I would not have encountered otherwise. Writing for this newspaper and writing this guidebook has been something of a crash course in Hampshire history and politics, and the multiple perspectives (some included here) have informed and challenged me whether I agree with them or not.

The details of my education and experiences are microscopic in regards to the creative and inspiring projects that develop and thrive at Hampshire, and even the project of the College itself. I'm humbled and motivated by many of the projects that students, faculty, and collaborative groups produce. Hampshire, in spite of,

and perhaps because of, its flaws, is a dynamic place that brings together a variety of people with different interests. The experiences and anecdotes that result are ever evolving as Hampshire College struggles to remain an "experimenting" institution, and its trajectory depends on future classes as well as on current stakeholders. Many things have influenced me as a writer, and I'm grateful for both support and criticism, because a smile will make me comfortable, but green (or red or blue) marks push me past that comfort zone.

Candace Renee' Means—Hampton University

Candace Renee' Means was born March 31, 1983, in the Motor City, Detroit, Michigan, where she lived until she moved to her "home by the sea." While attending Cass Technical High School, Candace knew she wanted to go into the field of communications. Her freshman year of high school, after sneaking into a college day for only juniors and seniors and seeing a breathtaking presentation by Hampton University, it was then she knew she wanted to obtain a Hampton University degree.

Upon graduating from Cass Tech, Candace entered Hampton University as a broadcast journalism major. During that year, she met people from all across the world in search of the same dream as her—a Hampton degree. In her sophomore year, she would become a resident assistant; a member of the sophomore executive council, student government's women's caucus, and Hampton University's dean's list; as well as become an on-air announcer at the Hampton University radio station WHOV. This is the year her love for Hampton grew to the level of adoration it is at today. During this time, she continued to mold her writing skills and began to focus on her dream of being a journalist.

Today, Candace is a 21-year old senior at Hampton, with plans of attending graduate school. She is still an on-air announcer for WHOV. She is still undecided on the specific field she wants to pursue, but knows it will be some form of journalism.

Nicole M. Smith—Hanover College

As a junior at Hanover College, it has been my experience that the more activities you do while you are at college, the more knowledge you will take with you when you leave. I am an English major with a political science minor working toward law school, journalism, and publishing a few books. I have been involved in the Student Senate at Hanover, I am a member of Phi Mu sorority, and I work at the Writing and Speaking Center at the College.

This experience has given me knowledge that the classroom could not, and I want to thank Omid for giving me this chance and being such a mentor in writing this book. I could not have written it without the countless e-mails and exchanges between the administration at Hanover, surveys filled out by friends and acquaintances, and the community of Hanover and Madison. When I began writing this book, I decided to do it without telling the administration that I was writing a Hanover guidebook because I didn't want anything to bias the book. The administration openly and willingly answered all my e-mails and questions above and beyond the duties of their jobs. Hanover picks its employees well—thank you all.

Thank you Mom, Dad, and Sarena for your tireless support in all my endeavors. To all of my friends (who I will not name because I will mistakenly leave people out), thank you for letting me vent and question every detail of this guidebook. To my reader, I hope you have learned everything there is to know about Hanover and enjoyed reading this book.

Dominic Hood—Harvard University

Originally born in San Antonio and raised in New Orleans, my transition to the New England culture and weather of Harvard

University challenged me beyond my dreams. I'm now a junior at Harvard College and concentrating in psychology, with my own emphasis on organizational behavior. I've been excited about writing this guide because I remember the challenge of selecting a college and I wish I had found a guide like this to provide a realistic perspective on colleges, instead of relying on the admissions office propaganda. I'm not sure what I'll be doing in the future, but I'm sure writing will play a large part in my career, so this has been a great opportunity to sharpen my writing and editing skills.

Enough about me! I want to take this opportunity to especially thank my mother who has always supported my decisions and guided me in the right direction when I was uncertain of the right path. I also want to thank my father for instilling in me the sense of independence and motivation necessary to succeed in the ever-changing, fast-paced world. And finally, above all things I thank God, for without Him this book and wonderful universities like Harvard would not be possible.

Moana Evans—Harvey Mudd College

When I was a senior in high school, searching for a college, I had something like Harvard or MIT, a big ivy-lined building in the East, on my mind. I had the straight As and the SAT scores. I was set on attending a big university with a big reputation. One day, out of the blue, I received a brochure stamped "Junk Mail" on the cover. I read it cover to cover and fell in love with Mudd, this small technical school in Southern California. I wasn't sure at the time whether I would major in math or literature, but Mudd's extensive humanities program wooed me away from other liberal arts colleges. Nobody at my high school had ever heard of Harvey Mudd. And even my guidance counselor poked fun at my odd choice for a college. All of my friends were going to Princeton or Yale, as I wandered off alone to the West Coast.

Now I'm a sophomore at Mudd and more in love with my school than ever. I've been introduced to so many new things here that I never thought I would care for: swing dancing, Korean dumplings, techno music, Orson Scott Card. Every person I meet teaches me something new and interesting. I try to give some of myself to every other student here. I didn't know what to expect when I came to college, but I don't think I could have imagined a better place for me than Mudd.

As for thanking people who helped me while I was writing this book, I can only think of people at my school, the professors and students. They have been my inspiration and my friends; people to laugh with, cry with, and fail tests with. So the only other person I have to thank at the end of this book is Harvey Seeley Mudd, for founding such a college. It's a fine school, and I'll be proud to be part of it for four years of my life.

Emilie Powers—Hastings College

I honestly can't say I was over the moon about coming to Hastings College; I was pretty impartial. I didn't have a lot of time to look at colleges during my busy senior year of high school. I chose Hastings because it was at the top of my list of the few colleges I had looked at. But I don't think I could have been more pleased with my experience. I've had great classes from amazing professors and made the best friends and memories. I had such a good time my first years here that I easily got my sister to come here with me. But I have felt at home even before she got here.

I was as unsure about my majors as I was about the college, but I settled on English and Music. I've participated in Band, Color Guard, Public Relations Council, Student Senate, Alpha Phi Sigma sorority, and a few honoraries and other groups. I've held offices in most of these groups, kept up with my studies, and still had plenty of time to have some crazy small town fun that would probably shock my mother. I'm planning on going to grad school next year, probably far from this home I've known for the past few years, so writing about Hastings College has been a nice way to look back on my time here.

David Langlieb—Haverford College

Born and bred on the mean streets of Long Island, David Langlieb came to Haverford College with hopes of one day writing a guidebook about it. He is a double major in political science and growth and structure of cities, as well as an eminent Haverford gadfly. David spent two semesters as editor-in-chief of the *Bi-College News*, for which he still pens a weekly column. He also co-hosts a popular political radio show, and is a regular presence on local Democratic campaigns. He enjoys spending summers in Nevada working with compulsive gamblers, and has previously written for *Fodor's Las Vegas* and *Moon Travel Guides*. Thanks are in order for Mom, Dad, Grandma, and particularly sister Madeline, who unselfishly let David use her laptop when the desktop computer kept freezing. Love you all! To all the readers out there thinking of Haverford, e-mail me if you have any questions!

Brendan J. Fitzgerald—Hofstra University

Well, putting this book together was a lot more work than I had anticipated. In writing it, I discovered that there were still many things about Hofstra that even I wasn't aware of, and I'm in my fourth year. I'll be completing my degree this upcoming semester and will graduate in December with two academic majors. I'll have a degree in film studies and production, as well as creative writing and literature. Thus far, I've written and directed three short films and written countless short stories and personal essays that I'm hoping to put together as one collection. My true passion is writing fiction, and I continue to keep my fingers crossed that I will be a published novelist.

I'd just like to add that I have had a wonderful time at Hofstra. I've been able to develop many meaningful relationships, both with my fellow students and with many of my professors. My time here has truly been exciting. Long Island is the first place I've lived since leaving Connecticut after high school. Now, I've lived in New York year-round for the past two years, and I have had a tremendous experience. I sincerely hope this book will be helpful and insightful to at least a few people out there.

This is the customary time to reflect back on my writing experience, and to give thanks to those who have selflessly helped me on my journey. Thank you to my parents, first and foremost, for putting up with all that I've put you through; to my sisters Rose and Mary, my grandparents, my aunts, uncles and cousins, two of the best friends that money could buy (if money could buy friends) Ryan and Jared, my roommates Craig and Dave, my great friends at Hofstra Aliza, Sara, Jay, Sarah, and Philly; to a few professors that have made profound influences: Professor Paul Zimmerman, Professor Phil Katzman, and Dr. Sybil DelGaudio; and lastly, but certainly not least, to everyone at College Prowler.

Janet Lubas—Hollins University

I major in women's studies and political science. Writing this book has given me the opportunity to learn even more about my alma mater and to further appreciate all Hollins has given me these past years. It's been a rewarding and hectic process. Thanks are due to College Prowler for giving me this opportunity and all those at Hollins who offered information and support (especially Katherine Opello and Amy Eanes). Here's to the unending generosity of those professors who not only share knowledge, but joyful times as well—Profs. Downey, Stanco, Murphy, and all others who join in the fun! If you've got any questions or comments, feel free to contact me. I love feedback!

I currently work for a carpooling organization in Roanoke, VA. Thank you Erin Hofberg for being a flexible boss throughout the process of writing this book. I'm also directing and editing a documentary on the work of Charles E. Cullen; *www.charlescullen.com*. Charles, thank you for always being there for me. Your raw passion for life and art is infectious. I love you. Finally, thanks and love to my family. Long before I came to Hollins to learn feminist theories, my mother taught me the importance of pride in womanhood and of open mindedness. Thank you.

Deborah Akinyele—Howard University

I'm currently a senior—very much in the throes of Senioritis and about a million things that all seem to be pushing to get done at the same time—but still very excited to have worked on this project and gone through the process of finding out even more about my school than I had known before I started. I've always loved the art of crafting words, and now that I actually get to present my craft to the general public, I couldn't be happier.

Even though I started out as a journalism major, I quickly carved out another path for myself in the ever-growing and increasingly-popular field of speech-language pathology, and I will be eternally grateful to the wonderful people at Howard who steered me in the direction that I am following now.

A very special thank you to Omid and Adam for cutting me some much needed slack, to College Prowler for giving me the opportunity to write this book and to see my name on a dust jacket for the first time, and of course to the real HU for being my inspiration.

Proud to be a Bison for life!

Meredith Deliso—Hunter College

Meredith Deliso is a student in the CUNY Honors College at Hunter College studying media and English. She has always had an interest in journalism, which she began professionally in high school writing for the sports section in her local paper. Growing up two hours from the city in Long Island, New York, Meredith decided to come to Hunter partly for the media opportunities New York City has to offer. As a student, she has written for Hunter's the Word and has interned with several publications, ranging from business to global music, as well as a self-help book on taking risks. In her spare time, she enjoys playing the violin, tennis, and exploring the city, and in the spring of her junior year, she is looking forward to studying abroad in Ireland. She hopes you find this guide insightful. If you still have questions or comments, feel free to contact the author.

Eryn Lowe—Idaho State University

Eryn Lowe is a junior at ISU studying mass communications with an emphasis in television broadcasting. She has attended ISU for all three years of her college experience. Eryn is the only girl in a family of seven. She hopes to someday be a news anchor/reporter in a big market. Her hobbies include hanging out with her roomies, hiking, running, playing tennis, reading books, and writing for the ISU student newspaper.

Dana Almdale—Illinois State University

This book was a huge amount of fun. I was able to learn so many things that I did not know about Bloomington-Normal, Ill., and also things about Illinois State University. I am so thankful that I was given the opportunity to write this book. This experience has shown me how much I love to write. Currently, I am a senior at ISU pursuing a major in mass communications and a minor in writing. I am also a features reporter for ISU's newspaper, The Daily Vidette. Prior to that, I played on the ISU women's soccer team for my first two years and then decided to more aggressively follow my passion for writing. I hope that you enjoyed reading about ISU and were able see what an outstanding university it is.

I would not have been able to write this book if it were not for the following fabulous people. Thanks to my No. 1 fan, my dad, who

encouraged me the whole way through writing this book; to my mom, who everyday listened to me tell her exactly what I was doing with the book; to my siblings, Brooke, Brian, and Paige; to my ISU roommates who had to deal with me spending long nights at the library; to everyone at ISU who helped me obtain important information and insight; and lastly, to everyone at College Prowler!

Diego Báez—Illinois Wesleyan University

Diego Báez graduated from Illinois Wesleyan University in 2007 with a degree in English Writing. During his time at IWU, he served as editor of the campus fine arts magazine Tributaries, was a regular contributor to the school newspaper, The Argus, served as an editor for the Park Place Economist as well as the Sigma Tau Delta scholarly review, The Delta, and entertained listeners during the late hours of the evening as a DJ for the entirely student-run radio station, WESN. His poetry has appeared in the Santa Clara Review.

He plans to attend graduate school to pursue his Masters of Fine Arts in creative writing and plans to either write, teach, or work in publishing in the future, with the hope of combining all three into some conglomeration of a career. He plans to spend more time with family in South America, where he hopes to someday reside. He would like to sincerely thank the team at College Prowler for their unwavering support and assistance throughout the creation of this guidebook.

Jenny Davis—Indiana University

I've learned a ridiculous amount of information about IU through writing this book, and I'm ecstatic to have the chance to share it with prospective students. I'm currently a journalism major with a second concentration in fine art, and I work for the Indiana Daily Student as a reporter. There isn't much about IU that I don't love! I didn't even apply to any other colleges, and I haven't looked back since I got here. I'm an Indiana native hailing from the southernmost tip of the state, and I hope to eventually find a career that will allow me to travel, meet people, and above all, write. I hope this guidebook has opened up a window to IU for you, and that you picked up some useful tidbits on the way. If you have any questions or comments, feel free to e-mail me. Thanks to everyone at College Prowler for this opportunity and to my family and friends for putting up with my haranguing and never-ending questioning.

Staci Harper—Iowa State University

It has been great learning more about ISU! I hope this book has been insightful, interesting, and entertaining. I am a junior at ISU, currently majoring in English rhetorical studies with a minor in speech. I am also a leader in the Freshman Honors Program and perform with the drama workshop in Des Moines. My family lives about an hour south of Iowa State, but I stay so busy I rarely see them during the year, except holidays. I aspire to have more works of literature to my name in the future, particularly poetic in nature, so I thank College Prowler for this first step toward fame.

I'd like to thank everyone who helped me with this publication, as well as those who didn't but still deserve a pinch of gratitude. Thank you to Mike, Sean, Caleb, Jessica, Karen, Keith, Cedric, Ken, and Derek for your assistance, or at least your intention to assist. Thanks to Mom and Dad, Madeleine, JQ, Phoebe, John, Ally, and my "other parents" for your support, encouragement, and love. Thanks to Iowa State for the tremendous scholarship opportunities for high ability students, and thanks to College Prowler for this writing opportunity!

Sarah Hofius—Ithaca College

As a reporter for the college newspaper, the Ithacan, I considered myself very knowledgeable about IC before I wrote this book. Now, as I have visited practically every Ithaca Web site and every department at IC, I know more than I ever wanted to know! But seriously, I really enjoyed getting the chance to write this book, and I hope that it has helped you in your decision about IC.

My experience thus far at IC hasn't been anything short of amazing. Just a sophomore, I feel that I've accomplished so much inside and outside of the classroom, met so many interesting people, and know so much more about myself than I ever thought I would by now. As a journalism major from Erie, Pennsylvania, my love for the skill of reporting and writing has grown even stronger with my work with the Ithacan, the IC yearbook, the *Cayugan*, and this guide to IC, the first book I've written by myself.

Without these people's help and encouragement, I would never have completed this book: my family, Chris, my apartment-mates Anne, Liz, and Michelle, my wonderful Parkie friends, the staff at various offices on campus who put up with my persistence, and everyone at College Prowler. Thank you!

Theresa Carol Williams—IUPUI

Writing this book has been very educational! I attended IUPUI for over four years and had no idea about some of the information that I discovered. This goes to show that the commuter campus environment pulls away from the college experience as a whole. However, I was delighted to brag about the great tools and resources that I used while at IUPUI. I wrote and gathered information as objectively as possible, but I would like for it to be known that I am one of those students that truly valued my experience at IUPUI. It was perfect for me and my busy mind. There are so many things to fall into, and the faculty was exceptional at helping me achieve my best. I was intrigued by so many different things at IUPUI that I chose two majors (English and political science) and a minor (philosophy). My extracurricular interests ranged from raising awareness about AIDS in Africa to Juvenile Justice to writing poetry for the IUPUI literary publication, Genesis.

I would like to extend a special and endearing thank you to the professors that have inspired me most: without you I would not be writing anything: Dr. Sharon Hamilton, for helping me see how lives can be changed through literacy—I know mine has; Dr. Scott Pegg, for teaching me so much about international relations and this huge world in which we live; Dr. John McCormick, for toughening me up for grad studies; Dr. Michael Burke, for sharing your gifts in philosophy. Some of you don't even realize how much I value what you have given me. Also, thank you, David (my best-good friend).

Sylvia Florence—James Madison University

What a great opportunity to use my creativity and writing skills, while helping out wandering high school seniors and their parents, all searching for their school of choice. I am now a junior at James Madison University, relentlessly pursuing a career in print journalism, working as the assistant style/focus editor at the Breeze (our school paper), and fire fighting in the summers in Oregon. Just as I couldn't have told you my freshman year that I'd be in Virginia a couple years later, I can't tell you where in the world I will be after graduation. However, I feel confident that wherever I end up, my life has been enriched by living in Harrisonburg and attending JMU. Whether or not you decide to join the Madison ranks is your choice to make; I hope this guidebook has helped you out, answered some of your questions, and perhaps even entertained you.

With the knowledge that I haven't won an Oscar or a Pulitzer yet, I still have a list of people I would love to recognize. Thank you God, first of all, for this opportunity; thank you Mom and Dad for bugging me about this book and for always believing in and supporting me with your love, encouragement, and humor; Kyle, my favorite lil' big bro; Susan, the Machine, for being my intellectual twin and my soul

sister; all of my awesome friends at IUP and SOU for making my freshman and sophomore years unbeatable; Kelly, Natalie, Kate, Corey, Nini, and all my L-Town homies for being the amazing friends that you are; my roommates, Kim, Brook, and Chris for putting up with me and my silly questions; my roomies for next year, Carly, Kelsey, Kemper, Diana, and Katie for all their love and prayers; all my JMU friends who are too numerous too name, but too precious to leave out; and all the people at College Prowler, especially for their patience and flexibility. Thank you!

Christina Pommer—Johns Hopkins University

I hope this book has told you more about Hopkins than you've learned from all of the promotional material Hopkins has sent to you. I learned a lot about Hopkins when researching the material for this book. Much of it would have been of use during the past four years, but it's better late than never! I just graduated from Hopkins this past year with a double major in political science and writing seminars. While I had a great experience at Hopkins, it isn't the school for everyone. I hope that this book will help you decide if Hopkins is the school for you. Don't, however, rely too heavily on it. Information changes quickly, and much of the feel of the freshman class is decided by the freshmen themselves. A book can't tell you what Hopkins will be like for you, just what it has been like for other people. Make the most of your college experience.

I would like to thank many people for their help, especially Seth, Mom, Dad, College Prowler, and all of the Hopkins students who took the time to tell me about their experience at Hopkins.

Carolyn Keller—Juniata College

Hello, ¿Qué tal? I'm your author, Carolyn. I'm 23, and I'm a travel addict and writer who will hopefully be employed again by the time you receive this guidebook. I hope it was helpful. Seriously. It certainly was to me. Like I said, I'm a writer, which is slightly less employable than your usual doctor, lawyer, or chief executive. In fact, a common synonym for this position is "waitress" or "bartender," or perhaps also "journalist," which is slightly more legitimate than the first two, but only slightly, and only if you're referring to the writers at the New York Times, instead of the National Enquirer.

Yes, the time has come for me to enter the real world, and though my personal revolution shall not be televised, I'm feeling fairly ready. For that I thank Juniata and my fantastic friends and professors there, and probably Snoopy, too. They are my sanity, after all, and along with my family, my favorite and the most treasured part of my life. (Do you need a Kleenex, or Pepto Bismal after reading that? I'll see if I can get some sent up.)

Along those lines, as you can imagine, receiving this gig right out of college is threatening to give me quite the skewed perception of the road to success in my career. Regardless, I quite appreciate College Prowler for giving me a leg up amid the madness of post-grad life. Thank you kindly. And by that, I mean I'd kiss your feet if it wouldn't make both of us uncomfortable.

But you! Dear prospective student, you're in an enviable position, and accordingly should enjoy every moment of college life while it lasts. Finding the school for you is tough, but of course you will, and you'll make the most of it, and you'll find your way. And while you're wandering, try finding a way to study in another country. I went to Mexico and Spain, two amazing, beautiful countries with people I now call family and places I now call home. It's worth every moment and penny—kind of like college. And with that in mind, I wish you the best of luck with your search, and your life, too. There are many places to adventure to, after all. And after that, there's always grad school.

Dan Stahl—Kansas State University

Dan Stahl is an unprincipled charlatan whose hobbies include pretending he knows more than he does and backing his father's car into fire hydrants. He grew up in Kansas and ascribes his moral shortcomings to the fact that his parents never once offered to drive him by the world's largest ball of twine. At twelve years of age, Dan played Obsessive Compulsive Dork in a visionary take on Snow White and the Seven Dwarfs, effectively redefining the art of the home video. This is perhaps his proudest accomplishment to date.

Dan Stahl entered Kansas State University in the fall of 2003. Two years later, he hopped Manhattans, transferring to Columbia University in pursuit of a field too recondite for K-State to countenance. Dan would like to emphasize that the fact that KSU was not academically compatible with him says little to nothing about its suitability for you. Nor does his emigration bespeak either a disdain or distaste for his prior institution; on the contrary, he retains fond memories of almost everything, except being compelled to read René Descartes. He merely advises you to think your course through before embarking on it—a message which, if you're perusing this guide, is probably superfluous.

Steve Schirra—Kent State University

Steve Schirra is an undergraduate English and writing student at Kent State University. He plans to pursue a master's degree in publishing. Aside from his college guidebook writing duties, he also enjoys creative writing (check out his stuff on the Web) and journalism.

He wishes to thank his friends and family for their support, especially Lisa Clarke, who encouraged him to put down the biology textbook and write. Special thanks go to the staff of the Daily Kent Stater, Andrew Hampp, Grace Dobush, and all who offered the opinions, insights, and factoids that made this publication possible.

Jay Helmer and Zack Rosen—Kenyon College

Jay—Writing this book was a benevolent challenge for me. It required a lot of time, whish as a senior is something I have little of, and a lot of deep reflection about my school and why I love it. I have affection for Kenyon that is indescribable, and I could not imagine being happier anywhere else. I am very proud of my school and this book. A book on Kenyon essentially writes itself, but if it were not for the energy, creative talent, and wit of Zack Rosen, it would not have been possible. Thanks and much respect to Logan Winston, for his unwavering support and guidance. I give my deepest gratitude to my parents, my sister, and my teachers for getting me through Kenyon, and the history department at Kenyon for teaching me to think here. On a lighter note, I am compelled to give shout outs to those who have made my Kenyon experience—Upper Norton, LSWG, Pink Thunder, and the RA staff.

Zack—As an English major, I often question whether or not I will be able to work as a writer when I graduate college. Now that I have actually gotten myself published, I think that I am one step closer to realizing that dream. I have never before had my writing printed outside of school newspapers and YM magazine, and I am still reeling in disbelief at the fact that my name is going to be on the cover of a book. The most important decision I have made in my life was my decision to attend Kenyon, and I hope that my love for the school shows through. Happy college hunting.

P.S.—Extra thanks to my friends and my family, who I hope know what they mean to me. I owe a special debt of gratitude to Jay Helmer for giving me this incredible opportunity and turning "lanky" into a term of affection.

Amy R. Pennington—La Roche College

I was very excited to have the opportunity to write an entire book about the school that has grown so dear to me. I am a sophomore at La Roche, majoring in professional writing with a minor in French. I decided to attend La Roche because of its small environment and closeness to home (I'm a Zelienople, Pa., native). On campus, I am a member of the Theatre Group, a public relations officer for the Italian Club, a DJ for the Web radio station, and a staff writer for the student newspaper. I also work at the college bookstore and serve as a worker in the communications, media, and technology department.

Outside of La Roche, I am a committed humanitarian, and I have volunteered my time and energy to charitable organizations such as Habitat for Humanity, Meals on Wheels, Toys for Tots, and the Light of Life Homeless Shelter. I've also helped with various entertainment activities at local nursing homes. After graduation, I hope to attend the police academy and join the FBI. Later, I plan on attending law school to become an international business attorney for the FBI.

I could not have written this book if it had not been for a few wonderful people, and I would like to thank the following: Ed Stankowski, for being the best teacher I have ever had, academically and non-academically; Sophie, for being the most wonderful roommate and best friend I could ever ask for; Ann, Jarrod, Sam, Jason, and Neil, for keeping me sane during the time it took to write this (and always); Paul, for providing me with hours of entertainment, whether he knows it or not; Mom, Aunt Lisa, and Aunt Val, for supporting me in my dreams and aspirations—I love you; Jon B., for helping me manage my stress and for serving to protect our great country; Mike and Shannon, for their support and love; Jon K., you've been such an inspiration to me, and I appreciate you helping me follow my dreams and loving me no matter what; and to anyone working at or attending La Roche. I wouldn't have wanted to spend the last two years of my life anywhere else.

Pamela Roth—Lafayette College

I am working as an agent's assistant at a large talent agency specializing in film, television, commercials, and theater. I work with a Lafayette graduate, and I started at the company as an intern during my second semester of senior year; I would spend my free moments reading student surveys there that I compiled into this book. I am loving my job—it's right up my alley, and my bosses are great—and I moved into an apartment on the Upper East Side with a friend from college. At Lafayette, I was the arts and entertainment editor of the school paper for two years and news editor for one, I was also a social coordinator of my sorority, Alpha Gamma Delta, a resident advisor, and I served as the Hillel secretary for two years. What I'm always going to remember most about college are the friendships I have made (and kept) over these four and a half years. I have finally accepted that I'm never going back to Easton as a student, but I am still grateful for everything I learned there.

I guess I should thank some people for helping me achieve my own "Lafayette Experience"—to my best friends Dave and Michelle, through everything you two have been my staples, and your friendship means the absolute world to me; to Jeanette, Caroline, Amy, and Beth—my Conway girls—you have shown me what true friendship is really about, and how it can last through four long years; to all my sorority sisters, who made every formal and date party a blast; to Sarah, Mitch, Noah, and Rachael, who are officially members of my "Jew Crew" at Hillel; to Alissa and Kelley, whose true friendship I only discovered during senior year, but who have secured a place in my heart forever; and, finally, to anyone who has ever worked on the Lafayette, the single most influential activity of my collegiate career. To all the people who I couldn't mention here, I thank each and every one of you for making college the best four years of my life (so far). Last but certainly not least, I'd like to thank my family—Mom, Dad, and Elliott—who have always been my rock. And, of course, thanks to everyone at College Prowler who allowed me free reign to write such an important testimony to my college years. Good luck researching your perfect college—once you find it, you'll know.

Doris Kim—Lawrence University

Having just finished my first year at college, I completely empathize for those beginning the transition to college, but I have no pity.

The process is awful, but entirely exciting. Taking a closer look at the college I chose by putting together this book was a helpful experience for me; it confirmed everything I had hoped for in my school, thank God. I hail from California, so the change in weather and scenery was a painful sacrifice. Hopefully the knowledge I've picked up in college so far has helped display an inside perspective on college life and the inner workings of Lawrence.

I am tentatively a pre-med neuroscience major with a minor in English. I hope to become a psychiatrist or make my first million as a writer—or maybe both. Either way, College Prowler is my first foot into the world of publishing. I'd like to thank my editors for their helpfulness and patience during the process.

Larry Koestler—Lehigh University

I graduated from Lehigh, and this is the first of what I hope to be many books I will write. I majored in journalism and was a member of Delta Phi fraternity. I was a writer and editor for Lehigh's official school newspaper, the *Brown and White*, for over two years, and I had the honor and distinction of serving as editor-in-chief of the paper during my last semester at school. I also wrote two bi-monthly columns: "Senioritis," an opinion column about the trials and tribulations of being an outgoing senior, and "In Tune," a music column. All my work is archived on www.bw.lehigh.edu.

Please check out my blog, www.thisiswhatwedonow.com, as I update it daily, and if you enjoyed my writing style in this book, you'll certainly want to read what I have to say every day. I'm co-creator and a contributing writer for www.worstofnewyork.com, a hilarious satirical Web 'zine that's been steadily cultivating a rabid fan base. I was also a contributing writer for the 2005 *Shecky's Bar, Club & Lounge Guide*, so make sure to grab a copy of that as well. Feel free to e-mail. Writers love e-mail, so don't hesitate to contact me. I thoroughly enjoyed writing this guidebook, and I look forward to more freelance work in the future.

I truly had an outstanding four years at Lehigh and wouldn't trade my college experience for anything. I had a great time writing this book and I hope it was informative as well as humorous. There are a number of people who helped make this book what it is. I'd like to thank my parents, Scotty, ZW, Gold, Flax, Berbs, Lynch, Soul, Meat, Mush, my fraternity, Erica, everyone who responded to the surveys, everyone who buys this book, everyone who supports me now and in the future, and of course, the great folks over at College Prowler.

Caitlin Fackrell—Lewis & Clark College

Caitlin Fackrell was born and raised in Hawaii. Her major at Lewis & Clark College was English. She spent her first three semesters of college at the U.S. Air Force Academy. Never choose a college based on the cuteness of their uniforms.

Kim Moreau—Louisiana State University

Writing this book has taught me more about my university than I probably ever wanted to know, so if you meet me and I rattle of weird little statistical information about dorms and such, it's because of this book. But honestly, I mean that in the best way. Writing this book has been a tremendously wonderful experience and I have had such a great time. I'm going into my senior year at Louisiana State University, and it was wonderful to be able to galvanize my entire college career into a book for other would-be Tigers to read. I've lived in Baton Rouge since I can remember, and I have always loved sharing everything I know about this place with anyone who is just setting foot into our fair city. As I prepare to graduate in journalism from LSU and pursue whatever direction it takes, I know I will not stay here forever, but this town and this college have been wonderful places for me, or for that matter for anyone, to be.

I want to thank a couple of people for being so gloriously helpful to me it's ridiculous. Thanks to every LSU employee from student workers to heads of departments that helped me get everything together I needed for the guidebook. Thanks to my friends who helped me stay awake with late-night coffees, who filled out surveys, or just helped me remember the random things about LSU we loved. Thanks particularly to Jen for reading my application and giving her ever professional advice, to Kara for not trying to kill me for being awake at all hours, to Brooke for listening to me verbally tell her the entire book's contents, to Taylor for telling everyone about the book, and to everyone else for just putting up with me being crazed all the time. Thanks to Jeanne C. for your legal brain and your generosity. Thanks to DC for being the ideal LSU student. Thanks to Dad, Adrienne, and to all my other family (real or otherwise) for being so supportive.

And most of all, to my mom, you're right—someone does have to be a rock star, or at least a college guidebook writer.

Kristin Cole—Loyola Marymount University

I hope this book provided you with an insider's glance into the world of LMU and Los Angeles. I am now a sophomore at Loyola Marymount, pursing an English degree with a specialization in screenwriting. Eventually, I would like to blaze new trails as one of the few women writing edgy thrillers for the big screen. Although non-fiction is a new world for me, this book allowed me to experiment and expand my writing into a new area. More importantly, the book offered me the chance to explore LMU's past and present and reaffirm why I am here.

This book was my first foray into the publishing world, and I could not have done it without the help of so many wonderful people. First, thanks to the students, staff, and faculty of LMU who filled out surveys, answered questions, and dug up the necessary information to make this project as complete and accurate as possible. Your help was priceless. Thanks to the staff at College Prowler for providing the support and answers to string these words together. Many thanks go out to the staff of Communications and Public Affairs, especially Melissa Abraham. And, of course, much thanks and love to my mom, Ron, and Ronnie for the love and laughs. Last, but certainly not least, my dad, who has always been my biggest fan and is mentally cheering me on through everything. Thanks, Dad.

Nathan Ramin—Loyola University Chicago

Nathan Ramin was in the process of putting the finishing touches on his philosophy and classical studies degrees at Loyola when he learned about the opportunity to write for College Prowler. Although he was often uncertain what to think about his alma mater during his stay there, this book has given the author a much better perspective on things. In the end, he, like so many other students, loves Loyola, but was frustrated by the often maddening decisions made by the administration. Nate survived the school, however, and is actually surprised to admit that he is grateful to it for making him a stronger, more capable individual. He would like to continue working as a writer, and is currently looking for his next big project. Is grad school in the cards? Will Nate drop everything and move to Europe? Will the Tigers ever win the World Series again? Can our hero realize his lifelong dream to write for *National Geographic Magazine*? The author does not yet know the answer to these questions, but he can't wait to find out. Who knows, maybe you'll read about it all some day. He would, of course, be willing to answer any questions you might have for him about Loyola or the book, so feel free to e-mail him. Thanks go out to Mom, Dad, Beezer, Nick, P.J., Katie, and to all of those awesome people who filled out questionnaires but whose names are, as promised, kept confidential. Finally, thank you College Prowler!

Fred Smith—Luther College

Don't ever let anyone tell you that writing a book is easy. I feel like I've been through the ringer after researching, double-checking, and composing every fact and opinion in this book. I can honestly say I learned a lot of facts about Luther I'd never known, and I appreciate the College even more for it. Luther has definitely shaped me as a person. If I hadn't gone here, I'd be a totally different person . . . and I wouldn't have a book to show for it either! I very much appreciate the chance I got to show off my composition ability and can only hope that my puns, jokes, and other lame attempts at humor will be useful, if not just tolerated and appreciated.

I am currently in pursuit of a double major in political science and communications studies, and I am the editor-in-chief of Chips, Luther's best (and only) student-run newspaper. I'm also in pursuit of a meaningful job in a field where I can improve people's lives and not just collect a weekly paycheck. I can only hope that this book is a cornerstone in my ability for what I can do as a worker and perhaps a collector's item if I ever happen to write the next great American novel. Hey, it could happen.

I would like to dedicate this book to my family, who kept my head focused on work; my friends, who told me when I needed to get away from the keyboard and relax; Kate, for being a wonderful and amazing source of love and inspiration; and PFC Stephen Douglas Shannon, who gave his life in Iraq in my time writing this book so you and I could have a wonderful college experience and a fantastic future. Don't waste that opportunity—I know I won't.

Katherine Tylevich—Macalester College

Well, I hope that helped. I feel like a walking fact book on Macalester and the surrounding areas now, and I love it. Writing this book has been a great opportunity for me to learn many new things about the college and the Twin Cities. Nowadays, my friends turn to me when they're looking for advice on what to do on a Saturday night. I also greatly appreciate the chance I got to put my love of writing to a practical and (hopefully) helpful use through this guidebook. I am currently majoring in English with an emphasis on creative writing, and I am the features editor for the Mac Weekly. I can't tell where the future will bring me yet, but if I ever make it big, maybe this guidebook will become a collector's edition and I'll make you rich—hold on to it! Whether you liked what I had to say or not, I would love to hear from you. And, if you wish, I'd love to write back.

Cecilio Gomez—Manhattan College

Cecilio Gomez is a junior communications major at Manhattan College. He also has minors in Spanish and business at the school. He has written for the school newspaper, hosted a radio show on the campus radio station, worked in the Athletic Trainer's Room, and is currently a manager for the Manhattan College men's basketball team. His managerial work includes office work and helping with practices, and he is involved with the film exchange as part of the men's basketball team. He considers that experience to be his best and most valuable learning experience. In the spring of 2008, in addition to working with College Prowler, Cecilio obtained a job as a sports intern for ABC, which he got through the Center for Career Development at both Manhattan College and the College of Mount Saint Vincent. Cecilio has plans of being a broadcaster for a sports network (radio or television), a writer for a newspaper or book

company, or maybe a coach in basketball. Cecilio would like to give a shout out to his brothers on the men's basketball team, the coaching staff, his co-workers in the trainer's room, his family for all their support, College Prowler for the opportunity, and lastly God for all the success he has given him in 20 years. Keep the name Cecilio Gomez nearby because you will never forget it.

Amanda Minck—Manhattanville College

After being at Manhattanville for almost two years now, I feel like I have wandered into the right places. I have found the right group of friends, but I prefer to call them "family." I have chosen the right major, English education, and it fits me like a glove. Most importantly, I have come to the right college, and it is the place I call home. Manhattanville is my home. I have never felt safer and more comfortable anywhere else. It's sad for me to think that I only have two more undergrad years left. When I found Mville, it was love at first sight. I haven't fallen out of love with this school, and I don't plan on doing so, but writing this guide has made the love grow stronger. This place has got me head over heels .Rock on, College Prowler!

Seth Reeves Bowman—Marlboro College

Marlboro College is probably my favorite thing to talk about. I cherish each opportunity I'm given here. I feel as if an entire world of education up to this point is currently being celebrated and challenged simultaneously. There is no other place in which I could ever imagine myself studying for a liberal arts degree. No wonder I snapped at the chance to write this book!

I plan on continuing my studies at Marlboro, focusing on television and its impact on our global society. Luckily, I'm at a school where I can study my passion and study all of my sub-passions also (though they all connect to be one big super-passion). This book has given me a great chance to begin communicating with others about something I care for so deeply, and that is the wonderful education Marlboro College has to offer.

Jennifer Singer—Marquette University

I feel honored to have been given the chance to grow and prove myself as a writer by producing this book. I hope I have provided a great deal of useful information about Marquette University that will help you with your college decision. I am looking forward to other opportunities like this in the future, as this was truly an incredible experience. As of now, I am currently a junior at Marquette University, diligently pursuing a degree in the college of arts and sciences as an English major with a possible minor in journalism or psychology. Even though I am a native-born Milwaukee resident who has lived here for the past 20 years of her life, the so-called "college experience" at Marquette is as new and exciting as an unopened Christmas present for me.

Last, but not least, I would like to extend a special thanks and appreciation to Mom, Dad, Sarah, Matt, the Greens, the Marquette faculty and staff, all of you readers, and of course, everyone at College Prowler!

Robin Erskine-Levinson—McGill University

Whew! I cannot believe that I am finished with this book; I feel like I just lost two months of my life. And what a life it is. Before I started harassing people about filling out surveys, surfing the McGill Web site like a maniac, and researching (ahem) clubs and bars, I was a pretty normal university freshman. Majoring in sociology and English lit, I had always hoped that I would find a way to combine my love of surveys and useless data with writing, and lucky for me, College Prowler gave me a way. Building on what I am learning at McGill, I hope to continue to develop my skills and portfolio and go into publishing or a related field. In all honesty, being at McGill has been the best experience of my life. I found that once people gave me the credit to know what to do for myself, I knew what I needed to do. I hope this book has been helpful, and I hope it's helped you figure out what you need—preferably without being mind-numbingly dull, and even a little bit enjoyable. If you have any questions or comments, do not hesitate to contact me.

Clearly, I would not have had the willpower or ability to write this if it weren't for some key people. Thanks go to Relena and Lyndon, for sheltering me and letting me steal their computer. Mom and Dad for actually putting me through McGill. Flora, Joe, Annabel, Chelsea, Michaela, Meaghan, Gil, Raissa, Jane, Christina, Dave, and Joyce for doing me a favor. Leah, Simone, Martha, and Rachel for your enthusiasm. And of course, Omid and everyone at College Prowler!

Tiffany Garrett—Miami University

It's kind of funny how therapeutic complaining about your university can be, especially if you know you're helping out possible future students by doing so. But I really love Miami and I hope that you will, too—that is, if you decide it is where you would like to attend.

I recently graduated from Miami, and the four years I spent in Oxford were filled with some of the nicest people and the best experiences. Transferring to Miami from the University of Georgia was a bit of a transition, but I am happy I made the decision. Now, I am out of school with degrees in English literature and journalism and a minor in women's studies. I'm working as a copy editor in the publications industry, and I'm also planning my own Miami Merger wedding for next October.

I would like to thank everyone who helped contribute to this book: Ross, Stacey, Diana, Kimber, Tim, and my parents for allowing me to go to Miami. I wish you the best of luck in your college search, and I hope that you find a school where you will be both successful and happy.

Amy Davis—Michigan State University

Writing this book has been such an incredible experience, and I'm hoping to publish more in the future as I continue to grow as a writer. I hope to use all that I have learned through writing this book and attending MSU to create even more written works. Although East Lansing is a mere 20 minutes from my home, coming to college here has been a life changing experience. I hope this book has been insightful for you, and I also hope you do decide to attend MSU—you won't be disappointed in all of the many opportunities this university has to offer.

There are many people in my life who have helped me to become who I am today. Although written words can't convey the true extent of my appreciation, I'd like to send special thanks to my Mom, my best friend Diana, Mandy, Laurie, Brandon, Eric, Jason, Scott, and all of the wonderful people at College Prowler.

Rachelle Morvant – Middle Tennessee State University

I attended MTSU for seven years in pursuit of two separate degrees. While there, I worked as a photographer for the campus newspaper for a year and published several feature articles. I received the Siegenthaller Award for Excellence in Spring 2005, and all I had to do was work my butt off. The beauty of it is that I love what I do, and that's the primary reason for seeking higher education—to improve your skills and knowledge in the field that you love. (Or to make money—some people dig that, too.)

Over the years, I have seen many students develop into full-fledged adults. I've seen others who have become professionals while maintaining their childish curiosity for life. Throughout my experience at MTSU, I have loved and hated this University with equal intensity. Luckily, there are people here who really want to help, which offsets those who just don't care. This campus is a nice cross-section of life.

I now have a job at the local daily newspaper, and it is all because of my own hard work. However, I wouldn't have worked as hard or as long as I have without the support of friends, family, and especially the teachers, who have a passion for what they do and who try to instill that passion in their students. There just is no replacement for a committed professor.

Abbie Beane—Middlebury College

Seems I've come a long way since writing R.L. Stine knockoffs and fabricating stories about my first published novel at college interviews. Writing a book of some sort has always been a dream, or borderline fantasy, of mine, and College Prowler has given me the chance to realize it even before graduation. Most things I do or say are for the sake of irony, or in the name of a spectacular story, but writing is the exception. I genuinely love language, possibly too much, judging by my prolix style, and hope to continue using it in constructive ways while my writing grows and develops.

I suppose failing out of physics was a blessing in disguise. You see, somewhere along the "tangent line" I smartly realized that most writers end up writhing in poverty and "decided" to be a scientist—a meteorologist, in fact. Yet, by my second Newtonian physics class we had covered all my high school material, and were delving into integral calculus. Not even toting my lucky Furby to the first test could save me from the dormancy of my left-brain. Lost in endless reels of mathematical jargon, daunting deltas, and formidable forces of friction, the only thing I began to re-weigh was my career path.

So that's when I started to write again—for the student newspaper, student humor magazine, and for College Prowler. Along the way, I also inadvertently joint-majored in French and nearly starved to death in Paris during my star-studded semester abroad. In plain terms, I already have experience coping with the lifestyle of a writer.

I do wish I had a book like this one to cart around campus from the get-go at Middlebury. Instead, I wandered aimlessly for two years feigning know-how before I fumbled my way into the upper echelons of college knowledge. My hope is that readers of this guide will be vaulted into that esteemed stratosphere more quickly.

Thanks to all of those who provided quotes for this guide, made contributions to my effort, including allowing me to borrow a computer here and there, and to College Prowler for granting me this opportunity. To all those who mocked my ambitions and see no merit in becoming just another name in a sea of names at the bookstore, I'd like to send out to you a big, scary scowl with a red bow on it. Thanks again.

John Yargo—Millsaps College

At the time I write this, I am a rising junior at Millsaps College pursuing my bachelor's in English. I have been very active in student publications, currently holding the position of editor-in-chief of Stylus, as well as working with the Millsaps Players and Habitat for Humanity. Coming from a small town, like a lot of my peers, I love the opportunity to pursue my passions every day.

Susie Lee—MIT

My name is Susie Lee, and I'm a rising junior at MIT. It's funny that I wrote this because I actually didn't want to go to MIT when I was a high school senior. I never would have bought a book like this because I just didn't care about it. In fact, I only applied because I was already applying to a dozen other schools. (What was one more?) But plans change. three years later, here I am, and I am thankful everyday for my decision. My major is management and my double major and/or minor(s) change everyday. Other than that, I am active in my sorority, my research job, and the campus in general.

I am originally from Granger, Indiana, a small town near Notre Dame. Being from the Midwest, I had no idea what to expect from Boston or MIT. As I read everything that I have written, I realize that I knew almost none of the things in this book. Writing this book has caused me to re-examine my entire MIT experience at the exact time when I was starting to take everything for granted. There are so many tiny little things that no one knows unless they go here that I was more than happy to explain.

Aside from all this generic info, some of my favorite things include: good food, good books, Disney World, math, card games, Notre Dame college football, sleeping, and beautiful sunny weather.

There is a long list of people who I would like to thank. The most important people are my family. I am working as hard as I can in this life to make all the work my parents have done worthwhile. They are always proud and supportive of me in every way. Even though my picture won't end up on this page, I know my dad will buy 10 copies anyway. I also want to thank my sister, Cecile, for teaching me about the things that really matter in life and for always making me smile.

Other than that, I want to thank the following people: Dave for helping me understand who I am, Christy, Kathryn, Val, Michelle, and all the people at College Prowler for giving me this chance.

Erica Aytes—Montana State University

Writing this book has been one of the most educational experiences of my life. Not only am I now a walking dictionary of MSU facts, but I also have a better idea of which career paths I want pursue. I hope reading the book helped you make your life decisions as much as writing it helped me make mine. Right now, I'm a sophomore studying English literature and Spanish at MSU, and I love both my majors. Next year, I hope to study abroad in Spain through MSU's program in Salamanca, and after that, I'll return to Bozeman to finish up my degrees and hang out with my friends. Somewhere amidst all my traveling, I'll go back to my hometown, Pocatello, Idaho, a few times, and take advantage of some delicious home-cooked meals and family fun.

Here is the point where a lot of you will stop reading. Too bad, because I think it's one of the most important sections in the book! I would like to thank my incredibly supportive family that has encouraged me to challenge myself. Mom, Dad, and Logan, you guys are the best. As for my friends: I can't believe how amazing you all are. Whether you are living in Vermont, England, or Montana, you were all a help. A special thanks goes out to my roommates and our favorite girls up the street. Whit, thanks for being my support group leader, and Amanda, thank you for being an AdvoCat! And don't worry all you College Prowler people—I'm not forgetting you. Omid, thanks for being such a great editor and giving me the chance to do this. Just for fun, I'd also like to give a shout-out to caffeine for keeping me awake the past few weeks.

Jennifer Lewis—Mount Holyoke College

I am a lifelong native of central New Jersey, although, in the four years I spent at school, I came to love western Massachusetts. I graduated from Mount Holyoke this past May with a philosophy major and religion minor and am now contemplating the wide world beyond college. I don't know yet what I want to do, but I know it will involve writing. Currently, I am occupying myself by working at a bookstore, reading anything I can get my hands on, and teaching myself photography (I'm partial to landscapes). It was a pleasure to work on this guidebook, and even after four years, I learned a lot about my school. It's a beautiful place and I'll miss it, but I'll definitely be back for reunions. I'm proud to join the long lines of alumnae who have come before me.

Many thanks to my family and friends, and to all my fellow students who gave me valuable insights on life at MHC.

Michelle Hein—Muhlenberg College

I really enjoyed writing this book! This was a great experience that allowed me to express myself through my writing while learning a lot of interesting things about my college. I am currently a senior at Muhlenberg College where I am a Communication major and a Studio Art minor. After earning my degree, I look forward to pursuing a career that will allow me to make the most of what I have learned in both of these fields. My years at the 'Berg have been full of experiences that will make graduating and leaving very difficult. You can't fully anticipate these experiences just from reading a book, but I hope that this book has been both fun and helpful in providing you with insightful knowledge of Muhlenberg. I wish you the best of luck in your college search!

Enough about me; I'd like to turn the spotlight onto the people that gave me support, advice, helpful tidbits, and laughs while writing this book. Many thanks to my family and friends; students and faculty who responded during their busy summers; the Admissions student-workers; and College Prowler for giving me this opportunity.

Josh Rosenberg—New College of Florida

I am completing a philosophy/psychology AOC at New College of Florida. I enjoy drumming, guitar, hardcore music, and freestyle footbag. Writing this book has reacquainted me with the reasons I fell in love with New College as a prospective applicant and the reasons I continue to stay.

Whenever I speak about my school, people are interested in what a quirky, progressive place it is. I take pride in this uniqueness. I am confident the skills New College has provided me will make graduate school less strenuous. I came in as a mediocre student who was able to do well in high school with minimal effort. New College transformed me into a studious critical thinker. For a tiny liberal arts school in Sarasota, it has already emblazoned a profound mark on me.

I would like to thank all of my fellow Novo Collegians for being so eager to be interviewed. These quotes and editorials are the final product of hours of trying to determine what New College is. While I was a self-proclaimed expert on my school, my peers' opinions provided alternative perspectives, which resulted in a more comprehensive and less biased guidebook. Thanks to everyone who supported the production of this guide.

Meredith Turley—New York University

Writing this book has been a rewarding experience to say the least. New York University has such a diverse, rich background, and covering it within the confines of these pages was quite a challenge. While it's not possible to make people truly understand what it's like to live and study in New York City, hopefully this book has given you more insight. Currently, I am a senior at NYU, pursuing a major in journalism with a minor in creative writing. There's no better place to study journalism than in the heart of Manhattan, where the stories and culture flow freely from every alley, nightclub, and bar. My experience at NYU thus far has been an exciting journey full of self-examination and personal growth, and it is shaping me every day. I would like to thank the following people for all their help and support while I was writing this book. Thank you Mom, Dad, Chris, Emily, Vivo, Dan, Rebecca, Ana, Mary, John, Evan and Eleanor.

Cynthia Marvin—North Carolina State University

Writing for College Prowler has been a great experience. I wish there were a book like this when I was looking around for colleges. Sure, there are over 100 resources out there on colleges, but none of them included things the students really want to know.

As I write this, I am a junior at North Carolina State University majoring in language, writing, and rhetoric in hopes of working with a magazine or in the publishing industry. Born in Syracuse, I was primarily raised in North Carolina and lived most of my life around the Charlotte area. Attending college has allowed me to grow as an individual and truly learn about myself. This book should provide you with answers to your questions about the University and will hopefully be a fun read. Going to college is about finding the perfect mix of academics, people, and activities.

I'd like to thank many people, those who have guided me my entire life to bring me to where I am today, and those who have impacted me in college by making my experience so far the best possible. Thank you, Mom, Dad, Jennifer, Harmony, and my grandparents from Syracuse who have always pushed me hard in whatever I do. Thank you to my boyfriend Nick and roommate Carla Jo, who have become the best friends I could ask for and have always been there to support me. Lastly, thank you, Omid Gohari and College Prowler for this opportunity and all the help along the way!

Briyah A. Paley—Northeastern University

This book was a great experience for me because it brought me back to my freshman year of college when I didn't know anything about Northeastern, or where to go in Boston for a good time. I never thought I would be a published author at the age of 21! I'm a junior journalism major in the College of Arts and Sciences. I've been lucky to intern at the *New York Post*, *YM*, *Us Weekly*, and *Time Out New York*.

Coming from Manhattan, one might think I have a skewed view of other places in the country and, in part, it is true. But, living in Boston for almost three years has taught me to appreciate what each place has to offer. I'll always be a city girl at heart! Coming to college has only made me grow as a person, and I can't stress how important it is to really think about what is the best school for you. Through the ups and downs, Northeastern is the best school for me. I hope this book has helped you see what this place is all about.

I want to thank my roommate Joanna Old for answering all of my questions regarding this book. She is a great roommate and a good friend. I also want to thank my parents, Anny Dobrejcer and Michael Paley, for being supportive throughout my college search and learning with me every day. I'm grateful to my grandparents, Marjorie and Bertram Paley, for taking me out to dinner and letting me come over so much. You've helped me more than you know. I promise to do my work now! Also, a thank you goes out to Omid Gohari who had the faith that I would be able to write this guidebook.

Matt MacDonald—Northern Arizona University

Writing this has been a very rewarding experience. It's been a great chance to really raise my creative sails. I'm currently in the middle of my second year of a three-year degree program here at NAU. I'm studying journalism, theater, and electronic media. After completing my undergraduate degree, I'm hoping to study film at a prestigious graduate program so that I may one day direct the very movies I hid from my parents under the bed for so many years. Well, that or something that will set the world on fire with its ingenious forward thinking and unparalleled critical acclaim. We'll see which comes first. I'm a native of Phoenix, and my time in Flagstaff has been wonderful. I think I've really learned a lot and grown in many ways since coming to college. I hope that all the hard work and effort I've put into my time here will pay off in the future with success and happiness . . . or at least a trophy wife. You know, whatever life throws my way.

I'd really like to thank my dad, my mom, Teri, Carah, Adam, Stephanie, Mike, Judy, Dennis, Jenna, Crystal, and Rachael. I can't

forget to also include the late Dave Thomas for inventing the best spicy chicken sandwich, Sean Connery for being the best James Bond, Lindsay Lohan for being hot, and Stewie Griffin for making me giggle like a school girl. I'd also like to recognize the following for all of their help in the research of this book: Heather Tate, Krista Perkins, Linda Martin, Veronica Hipolito, Art Farmer, the wonderful city of Flagstaff, and the numerous businesses I kept bothering, as well as the many students who gave in and actually filled out this survey so that I would leave them alone and stop throwing rocks at their window at 2 a.m. Big thanks to the folks at College Prowler too—I wasn't your first choice, but no hard feelings.

And, of course, I would also like to thank you, the reader, for braving this book. I hope you found it useful and are well on your way to a successful college career. If you have any questions, comments, concerns, criticisms, date requests, checks for large sums of money, or Christmas cards, please feel free to e-mail me. I look forward to hearing from you!

Greg Feltes—Northern Illinois University

Greg Feltes graduated from Northern Illinois University with degrees in journalism and communication. He is currently finishing his education at NIU as a graduate student in the field of media studies.

Feltes has written for several media outlets and publications during his burgeoning writing career. He reported on the television show Survivor for CBS news Web sites nationwide for two years, including covering the red carpet finale of Survivor: Vanuatu in Los Angeles in December 2004. His work has also appeared in the Northern Star and on thefutoncritic.com.

Feltes dedicates this book to his mother, Lori, for making his college experience possible, and to Uday, Matt, Andrea, Genevieve, and Megan for making it exceptional.

Torea Frey—Northwestern University

I've always wanted to write my own book, and when College Prowler gave me the chance, I jumped at it. As a journalism student, I take pride in doing research and offering a fair, unbiased view of what Northwestern has to offer, and as a member of the campus community, I think I have a good deal of insight that some of those crusty old guides just can't offer. It's been quite the experience, and a little cathartic. I've learned about myself, and why I chose Northwestern, in the process of writing this guide to help you out. I hope you enjoyed the quirky humor, and that this offers you a more holistic picture of what NU is all about. There isn't much to tell about myself, just a reminder that everyone has a story, and this school is part of mine.

I can't end this without giving my props, so here goes. Thank you, thank you, thank you to the following crazies: Mommy, Shawn, Misty, Dennis Sr. and Jr., Bryan, Nathan, Alicia, Amber, Jesse, Angie, Jason, Nathan, Emma, the Rosenbaums's, the Evanston Public Library staff, Elaine, Sumeet, Tau Delta Nu, Bob, Dinah, all my professors, and everyone at College Prowler!

Sarah LeBaron von Baeyer—Oberlin College

Writing this guide about Oberlin taught me more than I ever knew about my own school. I worked on it as I traveled in the Eastern United States and Canada, stopping to write in places like Boston, Syracuse, Montreal, North Hatley, and Pictou Island, Nova Scotia. In a few months I will be a senior at Oberlin College, completing my majors in East Asian studies (Japanese) and English, with a minor in anthropology. I grew up in Quebec, and lived in Japan for a year before starting college, so Ohio was totally new ground for me. Coming to college here has, for the most part, been an enriching and exhilarating experience. I hope the information in this guide has been useful to you in the process of making a decision about where to go to college.

Without further ado, I'd like to thank all the people who took the time to share their insight and witty commentaries about Oberlin with me: Scott, Yuuki, Bess, Logan, Rachel, Kit, Emily, Oona, Tom, Natty, Becky, David, Meaghan, Mami, and Ellen. Thank you to Dad, Mom, Pierre, Scott, Anne, Craig, Chris, and Gretchen for letting me spend so much time on your computers! Finally, thank you to the Office of Admissions at Oberlin College, the Office of Health Services, ResLife, the CIT, Safety & Security, and the Office of Career Services—where I found out about College Prowler in the first place—and to everyone at College Prowler for your support.

Ethan Ambabo—Occidental College

Ethan Ambabo was born in Albuquerque, New Mexico and is currently a junior studying film and new media production, and trying his best to learn Chinese and Arabic. He hopes to combine these two skills into one major someday. No one knows why he's doing this, but it seems useful considering the world climate.

In addition to this, he is working on writing screenplays to be developed by major motion picture companies. He has had no luck so far, so if you know anyone who knows someone powerful or famous in Hollywood, send them his way. He also works as the editor of the Lookbook, so if you do end up coming to Oxy, chances are he'll see your picture and know something about you.

Friends, movies, moviemaking, writing, hockey, and dogs are his big passions in life, and you can often see him spending time on one of these things during his average day. Friends are most important to him, so he'd like to again thank all of those people who helped him out while he wrote this book. When not with them though, you may see him and his friends prowling around campus with a video camera desperately trying to make something funny for other people to see.

Other than that, Ethan is really just a talkative guy who likes to get to know as many people as he possibly can. If you happen to stop by Occidental, look him up. If anything, he can show you how immensely proud he is to be from New Mexico, and will prove to you that everyone has some connection to his wonderful state and the great food there.

Roland Becerra and Adam Jardy—Ohio State University

Roland—First and foremost, I hope you enjoyed this guidebook, and most importantly, found it somewhat useful in your current search for a college. Now, on to what you really came for—the dirt on me! I'm currently a junior majoring in English here at OSU (duh!), and though I'm leaning towards education, my real passion lies in literature, so yes, I want to be a writer. Currently I have a couple of novels on the back-burner, though I'm not sure they'll see the light of day while I'm in college. Education comes first, kiddos. I was raised in Weslaco, a small town on the southern tip of Texas, and being alone so far away from home while trying to put some much needed wrinkles on my brain has really made me appreciate all those around me. So, while I'm on that thought, I'm going to jump into the cheap family plugs and people whose constant support has helped me along the way.

Now, I wouldn't be a good son if I didn't thank the two people who decided it was a good idea to bring another person into this world—Mom, Dad, without you nothing would be possible. Thank you to Rose, Danny, Laura, Robert, Grandma, Steve, Ame, Dillon, Bob, Erin, all of my extended family, the lovely Christina for having patience with me, Luke for giving me the opportunity, and of course, everyone else at College Prowler!

Adam—Before I say anything about myself, I have to thank the people that made this possible. First, thanks to God and Jesus Christ, through whom all things are possible. An incredible amount

of thanks also goes to my family: Mom, Dad, Amy, Andy, and Rodney, who have always supported me in everything I have decided to do. I developed my love of writing in the Northwood School District, so I have to thank Mrs. Karrick, Mrs. James, and of course, Mr. Laird for all seeing some talent in me and nurturing that (until I started writing for Power of the Pen in eighth grade, I hated English!). Special shout outs to my friends, both at home in Northwood and the Bucknutty ones here at OSU. Thanks to Oasis, the Beatles, Travis, Blink-182, and Ben Folds, whose music played incessantly while I worked on this project. And of course, thanks to College Prowler for giving me this opportunity.

As for me, I am currently a senior honors student here at "the" Ohio State University (don't ever forget the "the!") majoring in journalism. I have been the sports editor and the opinions editor of the Lantern, and I am now the editor-in-chief. I am also the music editor for the Sentinel and an arena reporter for the United States College Hockey Organizations Web site (www.uscho.com). If all goes well, this will not be the last time you see my name on a book. I am a 2001 graduate of Northwood High school, and I was salutatorian of my class. Upon graduation, I hope to continue writing for a magazine of some sort (Rolling Stone, Sports Illustrated, Spin, are you listening?). I am thankful for all the good times I have had while being a Buckeye, and I look forward to all the benefits that come with it. Carmen Ohio sums it up best: "Time and change will surely show/How firm thy friendship O-HI-O!"

Jessica Cyr—Ohio University

After graduating from the Scripps School of Journalism with a bachelor's degree in magazine journalism, I am now living in Pennsylvania, and will soon begin an internship with a consumer magazine in New York City. Thanks to my education and work experience at OU, I feel completely prepared and eager to show off my skills in the professional world. I was lucky enough to be able to write for College Prowler because it has given me so much more insight and experience in publishing and writing, not to mention it was fun to write (though it did make me homesick for OU). I hope everyone enjoys this book and finds it useful, whether they decide to go to Ohio University or not. Wherever your college path leads, good luck, work hard, and don't forget to have fun!

Evan Matthew Reas—Ohio Wesleyan University

I am a junior at Ohio Wesleyan University, currently studying abroad for a year at Oxford University. I am majoring in economics with a management concentration in pursuit of my dream of becoming one of the greatest business leaders and investors in the world. I chose OWU because I truly think it can help me achieve that dream better than other colleges could due to its personal attention, top-notch faculty, and opportunities to excel in leadership positions. I have been investing in the stock market since I was 12 years old, and I know that the biggest thing that matters is results. After college, I plan to either work for a couple years or head to a top graduate school to get a master's in business administration. I have been told to do what I love, because that is what I will be best at, and I will follow that advice.

I want to sincerely thank all of my friends, including Vincent Kang of UW-Madison and Jonathan F. Lamb of William and Mary. Thanks to all the wonderful friends I have met at OWU including John Rhoades, Rachel Ryan, and my brothers of Alpha Sigma Phi, especially my big, Wesley Goodman. Dan Albert and Dale Stewart, you guys have been great friends to me, and I hope that will always be the case. Also, I want to send a thank you to all of the mentors, especially all my teachers, Dr. William Louthan, my college advisor John Boos, Boro Dropulic, and the team at Lentigen, former OWU President Tom Courtice, and the fantastic economics department.

I also want to thank all the Ohio Wesleyan alumni who have been kind enough to take time out of their schedules to talk to me. I thank everyone including Dr. Edward Miller for that.

None of my OWU experience would be possible if it weren't for alum and friend David Wetherell. I wish him the best in all his future ventures and look forward to our continued friendship. I want to say thank you to all the members of my family including my sister, Alyssa, and parents Richard and Melody. Without their support, I would not be where I am today. Finally, a special thank you goes out to God, who watches over all things in life and has given me the opportunities that I have had.

Brandon Webb—Old Dominion University

Wow. This book took a while to finish. Deadlines did get pushed back, and several weekends were spent compiling all of the necessary information—but it was fun, I'll admit. Currently, I'm a third-year student at Old Dominion University working toward a Bachelor of Fine Arts in English with an emphasis in creative writing and a minor in French. Of course, that will probably change as I finish writing this sentence—I'm massively inconsistent. Personally, I've enjoyed the times I've had at Old Dominion and may also continue to do graduate studies here. Researching the information for the book was an excellent way for me to learn more about the University and to develop my skills as a writer. Well. Enough of my self-indulgent rambling—I hope this book served its purpose and whether you (reader) plan on becoming a member of Old Dominion or enrolling in another university: Best of luck to you.

Ultra thanks to the parentals, the grandparentals, and Judith Doumas. Mucho merci to my best of friends, especially Samantha, Charlotte, and Miranda. And a delicious nod to those at College Prowler.

Steve Pinkerton—Pepperdine University

Steve Pinkerton grew up in Oregon, but eventually forsook that state's damp embrace for the sunny climes of Southern California. More recently he's taken to the hills of Boulder, Colorado, where he's toiling towards an MA in English literature. In case you're wondering, his favorite books so far are *The Sun Also Rises*, *The Brothers Karamazov*, and *Pepperdine College–Off the Record*.

He'd like to thank the following for all their enduring support of his endeavors: Mom, Dad, Shannon, Tracy, and Grandma Dot. He should also give a shout-out to Cassie, who has the most greenish-gray eyes of all time.

Lastly he'd like to thank Drs. Darrel Colson, James Thomas, David Holmes, and Lorie Goodman, without whom his appraisal of Pepperdine's academics might be significantly lower.

Joshua Gordon and Rachel Levitan—Pitzer College

Joshua—This book has been a fun and exciting project. I hope prospective students will read this guidebook and come away with a better understanding of what Pitzer is all about. I was born in San Francisco, and lived there for most of my life. For the past three years I have attended Pitzer College, which has lent a hand in shaping who I've become. I am a chemistry major, which has been a very good experience. My second semester junior year was spent happily in Beijing, China, where along with a few classmates I adventured and took classes at Beijing University. I will graduate in the spring and will leave part of my heart at Pitzer; hopefully I will survive the procedure. I have forged amazing friendships, and learned more than I imagined possible, I will miss Pitzer dearly, yet I am exited about the prospects of the future. I anticipate attending medical school. Since I am still young I hope to write another one of these someday, which may contain grand adventures.

Without certain people this guidebook would not exist. I would like to thank those people: Without Rachel Levitan I wouldn't have had time to complete it. Without my parents I wouldn't be here to write it. Without the people who filled out the survey the pages would be empty. Without the information on statistics and other knick-knacks provided by Pitzer College and more specifically Dean Marchant the numbers would be wrong. Without Erin Tyner this book would not have been as complete. Thank you all for making this as fun of an experience as possible. I almost forgot, thanks to Rachel's cats for the entertainment.

Rachel—Writing this book has been a very unique experience for me! This is the first time I have attempted such an endeavor and hope it is helpful and a bit entertaining. I am a chemistry and French major at Pitzer, just finishing my senior year. I will graduate in December, and then hopefully attend medical school next fall. After living in a small town in Northern Arizona for most of my life, I was in culture shock when I first moved to LA. It has been an exciting three-and-a-half years, full of many interesting experiences and plenty of fond memories. I am so thrilled I came to Pitzer—where else could I have double majored, studied in France, done publishable research and still graduate a semester early?

I would like to thank many people. First off, thanks Josh for giving me this opportunity to co-author this book. Thank you Mom, Dad, and Dan for, well, everything! Many thanks to Risha and Will for getting me out of a tight spot when I had way too much to do in way too little time. A special thanks to Milo and Nala for entertaining us during the long hours at the computer. Thank you to everyone at Pitzer who helped us collect facts and gave us information, and thanks to everyone at College Prowler.

Peter Cook—Pomona College

I am a recent graduate of Pomona College. No, I do not have a high-paying job yet. Yet. However, I plan to use the fame I garner from authoring this guide to jump-start my plans for world pop-cultural domination, and fame is better than money any day. It's a lofty goal, but when you wish upon a star . . . I envision myself being sort of a genetically spliced version of Donald Barthelme, Ludwig Wittgenstein, and Lou Reed. Sort of like the bastard child of higher education and pop culture. I am moving to New York where, hopefully, I will learn to "hob-nob," and then meet and wow all sorts of high-powered editors. Then I will use my new, "phat" connections to score some book rights. See? I already speak the "lingo." Currently, I'm working on a sort of modern spin-off of Don Juan. It's not like the one with Marlon Brando and Johnny Depp, where at the end Marlon Brando tries to dance with his wife, but can't because he is just too big. It's more like what I think Lord Byron would write if he were alive and kicking today. Oh, and the rhyme scheme is the same as in Don Juan, which I think is an atavistic, but just-in-the-right-sort-of-way-to-be-considered-bold kind of move.

Oh yeah, before I forget, here are my promised shout outs: Colin, Aimee, Claire, Krista, Eve, and . . . oh crud, I can't remember the rest of you. So I reneged on my promise to recognize you. What are you going to do about it? I'd like to thank my parents for putting me up while I was writing this, but I won't, because they told me to save my thanks for when I win the Pulitzer, or something else that won't "embarrass" them. Oh yeah, but I will say "hey" to Lilas. She's my girlfriend. At least, at the time of my writing this she is. Who knows what the future may hold. Gosh, that would be sort of funny if we're not together anymore when this book gets published. Wait . . . now I'm thinking I shouldn't have got that tattoo either. Oh well. Lilas, if you're reading this and we're still together, I dedicate this, my first book, to you. Oh what the heck. If we broke up, I'm still dedicating it to you. Merry Christmas. But only if I broke up with you. If you broke up with me, than this book is dedicated to my future girlfriend, whoever she may be.

Alison Fraser—Princeton University

As a native Princetonian, it has been a privilege to work on this book, and hopefully I have been able to accurately convey my enthusiasm for both town and gown. Growing up in the Princeton area has afforded me both the "townie" and student experience, which few get to have. I initially came to Princeton, like many of my peers, with the intention of going to medical school after graduation. Three semesters of college-level chemistry quickly cured me of that plan, and I graduated from Princeton with an AB in history and a certificate in American studies.

While at Princeton, I managed the Student Facebook Agency, was a member of the campus' Student Agencies—a group formed to encourage entrepreneurship on campus, and was an active member in several campus groups. I hope the shared experiences of those interviewed for this book as well as my own personal insights will help you to make the decision to come to Princeton. It is obviously not an experience for everyone, but grueling hours spent preparing thoughtful, well-researched essays for Dean's Date as well as a University-mandated senior thesis have led me to believe that Princeton provides its graduates with one of the strongest liberal arts educations in the country that effectively prepares its students for both the workplace and graduate school.

Kathryn Treadway—Providence College

When the opportunity to write this guidebook first entered my summer plans, it presented the irresistible charm that every worthwhile challenge does. I found myself drawn to it, and yet, dreading the work; so of course, I had to accept it. From that moment on, this project has directed the course of many weeks of my life—altering plans, creating stress, and if you know me, causing shaking. Through all the ups and downs, it has challenged me as a writer, forced me to scrutinize the place I call home eight months of the year, and has been a thoroughly rewarding experience, overall.

I hope this book is revealing and useful in your search for the right college. Now a junior at PC, I know, without a doubt, this is where I belong, studying English and minoring in history. I look forward to sharpening my writing skills as world news editor on the *Cowl* and wish to pursue more publishing opportunities in the future. A native of Long Island, NY, I am eager to return to PC to begin my second year as an RA.

There are so many people that I must thank for their love, support, and help during this project. My family, for putting up with my cranky, dramatic self when things get stressful. Neil, for his enthusiasm in utilizing his numerous contacts. To my girls—Karen, Monica, Siobhan, Krissy, Meg—you are the champagne bubbles in my life; gabbing, giggling, and gossiping with you make my days, weeks, months, and years. To my friend, the Yale crew-rowing, gymnast and microeconomist (wink, wink); the person who by far makes me laugh more than anyone else. To all my friends, new and old, from Kellenberg, PC, and all the places in between, you are the ones who make my daily existence extraordinary; thank you for that. To Tarra for forcing me to take a much needed two-day vacation that ended up being one of the best weekends of the summer. I cannot forget to express my gratitude to Mrs. Von and Mr. Huggard for their continual literary inspiration. And lastly, to everyone at the College Prowler for extending this opportunity to me. Thank you.

Abby Bender—Purdue University

Abigail "Abby" Bender is described by her friends as a diva, a know-it-all intellectual, and a charismatic individual who can "turn a Burger King into Broadway with her sheer presence." She graduated from Purdue with a Bachelor of Arts in public relations and French and minors in creative writing and English. While at Purdue, Abby spent a year-long stint on a study abroad program in Montpellier, France, and traveled the nation with PMO Express, Purdue's vocal jazz ensemble. Abby is a voracious bookworm with an insatiable fanaticism for Harry Potter and is currently working at a public relations firm in Saginaw, Michigan. Writing the College Prowler guidebook about Purdue, she says, has given her a chance to

jump-start her career as a published writer, as well as expound upon her pride of being a Boilermaker.

Kerith Rae—Radford University

I am a 19-year-old immigrant from South Africa, and I am the first in my family to go to college. I currently hold the status of sophomore at Radford University, and I am a double major in business management and public relations with a minor in international studies. I am very involved in campus activities at Radford, including the school newspaper, the Honors Academy, a fraternity, and a theatrical production every now and then. I am pretty much a classic over achiever with really large dreams.

I have had such an amazing time writing this book. It has been an exhilarating and frustrating experience. I must admit there were days I just wanted to give in because the task seemed so overwhelming. But I am so glad I finished, because this experience taught me so much about Radford as well as my fellow students. This opportunity has opened up my eyes to a Radford I didn't fully appreciate or understand until now.

I could not have done this without the support of my friends and family. To the cast of Trust: One Story of Pocahontas and Captain John Smith, thank you so much for putting up with me and my constant badgering to fill out the surveys—you guys were an absolute life saver. Erin Bachinsky, I cannot begin to describe how much I appreciate your helping me in fulfilling my survey obligations. Phi Sigma Kappa, thank you boys and girls for filling out my survey and always backing me up whenever I couldn't make it to an event because I was working on this book. Chris, thanks for putting up with me even when things got rough. Lastly, thanks Mom, Dad, and Tyla for telling me that I could do anything and then supporting me when I take on too much. I love you all. You're my rocks and my foundation, and I couldn't have gotten through this without you.

Ben DuPree—Reed College

Ben DuPree was born and raised in Los Angeles, California, leaving the bright lights and gigantic skyscrapers to pursue academia at Reed College. A son of two loving parents and the brother of a sometimes annoying, yet overwhelmingly fun little boy, Ben regretfully left his comfort zone behind to traverse into the unknown wilderness of Portland, Oregon. Although the journey was not without its initial hills, pits, and fierce, furry lions, Ben quickly adapted to his surroundings. Possessing nothing more than a copy of the *Iliad* and his wits, Ben fought the mighty paper monsters, traversed the social wastelands, and explored every nook and cranny that Reed offered. It is rumored that once, Ben had to use the Iliad's catalog of ships passage pages to light a life-sustaining fire, but we cannot confirm this rumor. Having survived the first year of Reed in Portland's wooded expanse, Ben buckled down and prepared to engage his second tour of duty head-on. Tempered by his experiences in the wild, Ben began taking classes in his major, English, and continued to work to improve his reading, writing, and critical thinking abilities. With his knowledge of the world expanding rapidly and feeling very secure, Ben decided that being the editor of the school newspaper, the *Reed College Quest*, would be an entrance into a land of ink and honey. With four other brave souls and two guides, Ben entered the new world of print journalism, which then proceeded to eat his liver. During the course of his sophomore year, Ben received a strange message from a new company, asking him to describe his experiences so others would not fall victim to the perils of journeying through Reed College. Knowing that fame, fortune, and possibly a diamond mine awaited him in reward for such a task, Ben readily agreed to recount his experiences, and those of others, for this company. He is still waiting for his diamond mine.

Ben hopes that you have enjoyed his colorful tale of mystery, mayhem, and wooded creatures. If any of you brave souls make it to Reed, look him up. He will love you for it, and you can bask in his greatness.

Ned McTigue—Rensselaer Polytechnic Institute

In putting this book together, I drew as much as I could from my experiences and those of my classmates to put in these pages for your consideration. As I said in the introduction, nothing can prepare you completely for a school, but I hold out hope that you have found this book in some way beneficial to helping you decide if RPI is the college that fits you. I believe that it will, and if you have any questions—about this book, anything at RPI, or just college life in general—feel free to e-mail me.

If I thanked everyone I should, the length of this book could easily double, so I'll just say thanks to Kruegdaddy, Ace, Jusczyk, Pinky, and the Captain.

Brooke Ackerley—Rhode Island School of Design

It's been a very valuable experience compiling this information about RISD. As a senior, looking back has given me perspective and a newfound appreciation for what I have gone through and what I will be taking away with me. RISD has taught me that you can support yourself doing something that you love, and although parts of our society may not feel that art is important, I have found that it touches people in ways far more profound than can be simply expressed. The students and graduates of RISD are the eyes and hands of America; we keep the rest of the country and the world seeing beauty. It is our job to observe and display that beauty in every way we can, and that job is important.

I would like to thank the textiles and English departments for supporting me and teaching me so much, the students who took time out of their busy, busy lives to tell me about themselves, and the people at College Prowler for giving prospective students a chance to better understand what they are getting themselves into.

Brooke Ackerley is a textile design major, an English concentrator (emphasis on poetry), and co-founder and editor of RISD's literary magazine *Blackletter*.

Sara Rutherford—Rhodes College

I'm currently working towards a double-major in English with a writing focus and anthropology/sociology. And, if I have enough time and brainpower in the next three years, I'd like to minor in psychology, too. I hope to utilize all of the information and skills I acquire to become a professor of English later on in life. Either that, or I want to be an independently wealthy recluse in Ireland and spend my days writing and herding sheep. Seriously. Hopefully, I'll be able to publish more in the future, and I look forward to growing as both a writer and a person in the coming years.

Rhodes was a huge change for me. I come from a very small town in rural Georgia and the size of Memphis was a little intimidating at first. I adapted quickly enough, though, and I've really grown to love the city. Rhodes academics are much more challenging than my high school ever thought of being, and I'm very happy about that, as well. I can't wait for the really tough classes to start. All in all, my college experience so far has been great, and I only plan for it to get better.

All right, I think that's quite enough of the vaingloriousness. Now it's time to thank everyone who so greatly deserves it. For all their help and support, I'd like to thank Daney Kepple and Dean Bob Johnson first and foremost; Carol Casey, Brian Hummer, and all the other Rhodes staff who were so quick to give me information; Michelle, Andrea, Rachel, Lisa, Chen-Chen, Tulisha, Diane, and Erin for helping spread the word and giving me the inside info; my mom and dad because they're the greatest; and Jacquelyn Johanna for curbing my procrastination and helping me finish up. Thank you guys so much!

Julia Schwent—Rice University

Julia Schwent, a native of the tiny mid-western town of Festus, Missouri, spent her childhood years dabbling in writing, reading, make-believing, and attending summer camps. In high school, she unleashed her inner ham through speech and theater, made beautiful music through marching and concert band, helped to run a few honors and service clubs and organizations, and stayed busily involved in general until graduating valedictorian from Herculaneum High School. She packed up her things and headed south to the Lone Star State in search of a higher education, a vocational calling, and a livelier social life than Festus had previously provided. Julia spent the next four years at Rice University, thoroughly enjoying her higher education and newfound social life, while still managing to avoid any pesky vocational callings. In college, she continued to pursue her love of fine arts through photography, drawing, and theater (directing, producing, and starring in such shows as *Cat on a Hot Tin Roof*, *Nunsense*, *Pippin*, and *Company*). Unable to let go of her childhood, she returned to Missouri to reclaim her summer camp glory days, and spent four summers as a camp counselor, sporting a whistle, a campy nickname, and a vast repertoire of kiddie campfire songs. In addition to writing this book, Julia currently works as a social research assistant for the National Center for Early Development and Learning. She hopes to work abroad in the upcoming year in order to further master the Spanish language, and afterwards plans to pursue graduate studies in the area of her vocational calling, if she should ever happen upon it.

Julia would like to thank her family and friends for their love, friendship, and unconditional support, and God for guiding her always. She would like to dedicate this book, "To Dad, Mom, Laura, and Alex, the most important people in my life, through it all."

Amy Cooper—Rochester Institute of Technology

Steph, thanks for letting me bounce ideas off of you, and for abducting me when things got too serious. Nora, Heather, and Al, I couldn't have written this book without you, because if I hadn't met you freshman year, I wouldn't have stayed. So, thank you for that. Gail, thanks for pointing out this job posting and for helping me get through this book and this year. KDR, thank you for giving me the inspiration for many things, this book included. Dr. Evans, Dr. Scanlon, and Dr. Douthwright, thank you for showing me that professors can be more than just talking heads. You taught me more than you will ever know. Joni, Ingrid, and Ruta, thank you for being the best roommates ever, and for dealing with me quizzing you, and begging you to help get surveys out—I owe you all. Chris thank you for keeping me grounded throughout the last three years and being there when I didn't know I needed you, because that's when it mattered the most. Last, but not least, Mike, thank you for being as amazing as you are, and for pushing me to follow my heart and my dreams, I never knew how much I could do until you pushed me to do it. This isn't a journey anyone takes alone—thank you to everyone who walked beside, ahead, or behind me.

Brittany Lee—Rollins College

Working on this book was a great experience. It was so nice to finally be able to write something other than term papers! I'm a sophomore at Rollins College, trying to dual-major in English and psychology with an honors degree. I grew up in Connecticut and came down to Florida, mostly to escape the snow. Now that I'm here, though, I've come to love far more about my college than the region's weather. I hope this book helps you in making the often difficult decision of where to go to college. I would additionally like to thank all those at College Prowler for giving me the opportunity to create this guidebook and for answering all the questions I had along the way.

Taryn Sauthoff—Rutgers New Bunswick

After writing this book, I don't think there's a Rutgers fact I've missed. I hope that this book gave you some information to clear your minds about the ever-confusing Rutgers University, the 10,000 colleges it seems to have, and the famous red Rutgers buses. If it's possible, come and visit Rutgers, and all of the information you have just read won't seem as confusing.

I am a third-year student double majoring in English and journalism with a minor in women's studies. I aspire to be a journalist one day because, well, writing is my life. This book definitely gave me experience in researching, and made me realize how much I absolutely love Rutgers University. This book has been a whirlwind experience, and I wholeheartedly thank everyone for helping me write it, and for not strangling me when the stress was making me crazy.

Big thank yous and hugs to the following friends, family and Rutgers administration who helped me in this College Prowler experience: Mom, Dad, Kirsten, Grandma, Grandpa, Taylor, Sandra Lanman and the Rutgers University Relations department, Mr. Roberts, Mrs. Pianko, Melissa McManus, Room 1123, Hardenberg 6, Allen 4, T-Squad, and Port Richmond friends. Also a big, tremendous thank you goes to everyone at College Prowler for your patience and understanding these past months.

Hilton Collins—Sacramento State

Working on this book educated me a lot about my school. I discovered hidden gems and secrets that had been lying right under my nose for years. Most students go to class every day without realizing everything else that's on campus beyond the classroom doors. I feel kind of sorry that I never found out about so many things until I had to write about them. Though the research involved was a huge effort for me, I'm glad I finished and got the opportunity to be published.

I'm now in my first semester as a graduate student at Sac State hoping to advance my English degree, but I've fallen in love with writing, and I might pursue that avenue more passionately than anything else, even class. I like the freedom, and besides, I'm really tired of homework! I don't know what the future holds, but when it gets here, I'll probably be sitting in front of a computer screen typing away at something. Feel free to drop me a line.

Tom Acox—Saint Joseph's University

I felt very blessed and excited about the opportunity to write this book. I'd been living in Philly for four years, and I became more involved on campus each year. I feel like I have an intimate relationship with the school and surrounding area that some students overlook or take for granted because I reported and wrote about it at the school's newspaper for close to four years.

I grew up in central New Jersey, and I was raised on a healthy diet of books, Springsteen, the beach, sports, and a curiosity about the world and the people in it. As a high school student, one of the things I liked most was the brief time I spent with the school's newspaper. After e-mailing St. Joe's to inquire about their newspaper, I was put in touch with English Chairman Dr. Gilman, who quickly convinced me to give the new English writing program he was developing a try. In that program, I spent the next four years of my life reading, writing, working for the school's weekly paper, and hosting a radio show on WSJR.

After graduation, I enrolled in the fifth-year option for English majors to pursue an MA in writing studies. For a program requirement, I interned at Philadelphia Weekly, and I found the experience so rewarding that I continued interning even after the requirement ended. One day I would love to have one of my novels published or screenplays made into a box office smash. However, bartending isn't exactly going to pay the bills for that lifestyle. So after graduation I

accepted a job at a publishing house in New York City, while continuing to write on the side.

Thanks to Mom, Dad, Didge, Maura, Grandma, Cullinane's, Sharkey's, Meehan's, Tuohy's, Condon's, Kolarsick's, Kevan G, Dirt, Tim, Dumps, Tripp, Pete, Dr. Koch, Sisters Maureen + William + Charles, Dr. Gilman, John, Steve, Birdi, Fitz's, S.P., Navdeep, Dr. Daniel T. Dombrowski, Alpha Phi, Pizza-Man, Lindsey M, all my roommates, Cona, D-Mike, Fank, Matty, Elliot, JT, Skeuse, Hill and all the Pikes, Molly, Meggers, Jackie and all the AGD girls and Drexel folks, Lauren O, Luke + Duke, Connor, Sev's Mikey, all the Quackers, all of PW, Dora, Ashley, Kate, and everyone at College Prowler!

Brian Webb—San Diego State University

Brian Webb was born and raised in Southern California where he has been roaming ever since. Currently, Brian is a junior at San Diego State University where he is pursuing a BA in journalism with a minor in English and perhaps another minor in television, film, and new media production. In the future Brian hopes to continue his writing career with fiction and nonfiction novels, as well as screenplays.

In case you're wondering, his favorite hobbies include writing, reading, golfing, traveling, swimming, going to the movies, white-water rafting, and anything else that involves the possibility of adventure, amusement, or excitement.

He'd like to thank the following people for their enduring support of his endeavors: The G.B.C., Mom, Dad, Chris, Deanna, Nana, Uncle Mike, Grandma, and all other friends, family, teachers, and mentors.

Al Schwartz—Santa Clara University

Al Schwartz is an English major at Santa Clara University. A native of Kansas, Al is an Aquarius, and was happy to do this book because it qualifies as a freelance writing assignment, and he thinks telling people he does "freelance" work sounds cool.

Justin Millan—Sarah Lawrence College

Let me tell you a little story—before I could even read, I was sure that I wanted to write novels for a living. Stephen King and Jack London were my boyhood heroes. One thing led to another, and I wound up at Sarah Lawrence College to study creative writing. Then, the unthinkable happened—I didn't get accepted into any writing classes my freshman year. I took it personally. I was crushed. Devastated! My morale hit an all-time low. I grumpily agreed to take an alternative class in visual arts. And well, well, well . . . guess who fell in love with drawing and painting? Guess who is thinking about a career in graphic design? Coming from a kid whose philosophy for 18 years was bestseller-list-or-bust, that's kind of earth-shaking. What you should know is that my story is not unique amongst SLC students. Extraordinary things do happen on this campus. Of course, there were times when I hated SLC—it certainly isn't perfect. Writing this guidebook gave me a chance to reflect on all the elements—good and bad—of this inimitable place. I hope I've cleared up a few of your questions, and perhaps helped to steer you in the right direction.

Now let me thank all the folks who went out of their way to help me with this guidebook one way or another: Bryn Pritchard, Risa Pearl, Judith Schwarzstein, Larry Hoffman, Paul Lisicki, Paula Loscocco, Kate Webber, Carter Lewis, Jora Ehrlich, Matt McMickle, Chris Flockhart, Bill Sinnott, Colleen Hennessey, Eileen Gorman, Dan Schiels, Leza Kaufman, and everyone at College Prowler.

Christine Tran—Scripps College

Born and raised in sunny Southern California, I had never heard of a place called Claremont, but nowadays I find myself never far from the bubble. Claremont is not the typical college scene or social hub, but I find that its quiet charms and peace have grown on me over the past two years. College so far has definitely been the greatest challenge that I have had to face; so many changes, so many deadlines, so many ideas, and so little time. Many say that these four years will be the best of my life, but I surely hope this is not so, not because I do not believe they will be four great years, but because Scripps has taught me that college is only the beginning, where you develop the relationships and skills to go on and pursue limitless goals. I feel that my decision to go to Scripps was the right choice, as I have found a place where I can learn and relearn to love knowledge and develop into the person I hope to be.

I am currently a junior, declared English major, biology minor on the pre-med track. When not in a lab, or cranking out a paper, I love to read, eat, and sleep. Amongst my favorite things are my friends and family, my pig-dog, music, and all things chocolate. Some of my hobbies include piano, tennis, air hockey, and riflery.

Thank you to everyone who helped me to put this guide together, all my gratitude to the Scripps student body and administration for all of their input and to College Prowler for this opportunity. I especially want to thank my family, my partner in crime for her food supply and whiz kid expertise, my chef, and everyone who endured my raising stress levels—you guys are the best.

Julia Ugarte—Seattle University

As a senior at Seattle University, it seemed like the perfect time to take advantage of an opportunity to write a book about my school. I have lived in Kent, just south of Seattle, for most of my life, and moving up to Seattle, immersing myself in college and such a unique city, has been the most dynamic change in my life thus far. As a three-year student of SU, I have played varsity soccer, been a freelance writer for the *Seattle Times*, and participated in making a difference in the surrounding community; these are only a few of the opportunities the school and the city have provided me. Researching and writing about SU has renewed my enthusiasm for the University and makes me very sorry that I have only one year left. I am an English literature major, and I hope to pursue a master's degree in teaching once I graduate. However, my secret wish has always been to be a published author before the age of 21. This project has taught me much about the writing process, and I hope it is the first of many opportunities to see my words in print. I hope this book does the University justice and is helpful to you.

As with any ambitious project, it could not have been done without the help and support of my family and friends. Thanks to everyone who put up with my pleasant neurosis and other moods characteristic of an author. And thank you especially to Mom, Dad, Mikel, Kara, Mathias, Adam, Jon, Kristin, Benji, Jack, Hobbina, Jenn, Min, Erin, Junc, Stella, anyone who received an e-mail from me, and the staff and administration at SU for allowing me to ask a million questions about the school.

Rocky Rakovic—Seton Hall University

Writing this book was a great and enjoyable experience that rivals few things that I have done since I have been in college. I am going into my fourth year at Seton Hall where I am studying communications with a concentration in journalism, and backing it up with a minor in English and a certificate in business. I have been working on the student paper, the *Setonian*, since I stepped foot into the Hall, and I greatly encourage any young writer to do the same, as well as apply to write a College Prowler book when they are an upperclassman.

I am originally from Narragansett, Rhode Island, which I do believe is the greatest piece of land on the earth. I had to regretfully leave the nest, as my big dreams of being a journalist did not have enough room in Rhode Island. So I made the logical move to the outskirts for New York City, the media capital of the world. That is why I am

attending Seton Hall as I try to find a job in the city. Because of my move out of New England and into the fast pace of New York City, I am well aware that it is hard to adjust to a new area, and I hope that I have been helpful throughout this book by sharing my experiences and tips no matter which college you choose. Sorry ladies, I'm taken.

Well, since you probably heard enough of me, here is where I roll the credits. Thank you for everything except the eyebrows, you are the most important people in my life, Bob and Pat Rakovic; thanks for not shadowing my every move, Greg, Chris, and Maggie; thank you for being my New York parents Paul and Cathleen Charron; thank you for your support and being the unofficial editor Casey Earley; thank you for helping me adjust in Jersey, Charlie and Barbara Rakovic; thank you for letting me trick you into thinking I was sick so I could have the day off and finish the book, Jimmy; thank you for your inspiration J.P. Baran; thanks for pouring me inspiration, Reggie; thank you for everything anonymous Seton Hall staff that may not want to be associated with me; thanks Jesus; a collective thank you to Jared Walters, Christian D. Tovar, Kipper Jones, Jpungles, Doates, Rich, Bobby F., Scott, Brendan, Tougas, Theo, Nahee Nahee, Ashley, Julio, Matty, Young Flanagans, Moody, Hoopy, and everyone at College Prowler!

Evan Kuhlman—Simmons College

Working on this guidebook has given me a chance to further my writing in a whole new genre. It has been exciting hearing all of the student responses. The experience has given me a better sense of the school, and what my peers value in their college experience. I left Cincinnati, Ohio for Boston, and I have never regretted my move. I have taken advantage of all the experiences Simmons has given me. My knowledge of internships and exciting classes are not just a bullet in a guidebook, I have lived them.

Having a double major in women's studies and communications with dual concentrations in public relations and journalism has exposed me to some of the most amazing professors and faculty. I am ready for the next adventure.

Thank you to all of the students, faculty and staff who answered my questions honestly and elaborately. I have learned so much from all of you.

Nicolette Stewart and Cara Jones—Skidmore College

Nicolette—Nicolette Stewart is a recent graduate of Skidmore College where she studied English and German. Born in Maryland and brought up in Upper Black Eddy, Pennsylvania, she wrote her first story at age 10 about a scary stuffed dog that came to life, and despite brief evidence of a penchant for archeology, has wanted to be a writer ever since. She is now forging into the world of custom publishing and proofreading with her sparkling new degree. She is interested in old books, records, South Africa, magical realism, yard sales, and language. When she's not writing she's biking, reading, and planning the launch of a commune in New Zealand where she will one day retire.

Thanks to College Prowler for the opportunity to actually write a book (may it be the first of many), and to put something of my own out into the world. Thanks to Mum and Pop. Thanks to the person who sends me letters and lets me send letters to him. And, last but not least, thanks to my friends, and enemies. UBE crew for life. Hasta siempre.

Cara—Cara is also a recent graduate of Skidmore with a major in English and a minor in business. Her true interests were realized after writing for the school newspaper and prying into the lives of Skidmore's athletes in her "One on One" column for sports. She interned her senior year for a local news station and has been pursuing a career in broadcast journalism. She is currently an Assistant Producer in Connecticut and a substitute teacher for special education in the public school system. She hopes to return to

Florence, Italy someday where she studied abroad and learned to appreciate fine wine and fine men.

Thanks to my Skiddie crew and the girls at home who made me a spontaneous cook, yet strangely keep my life sane and interesting. And thanks to my parents and sister, Bree, of course! My heart is with our troops, but it belongs to a sailor.

Ashley Hockenberger—Slippery Rock University

When I first learned about College Prowler, my initial reaction was that I had wished that such guides were available to me when it came time to narrow down hundreds of colleges and universities to just one. Little did I know that the college of my dreams was just an hour away from my hometown of Sewickley, PA. So, I was excited to receive the opportunity to help others in the overwhelming search. I hope to be of service to you, the reader, and offer an unbiased view of my alma mater, as substitution for Admissions Office propaganda. After this book is written, I will soon begin my search for the perfect grad school (using College Prowler tools, of course!) and try my hand, once again, at the written word—whether it be in the field of publishing, book writing, or whatever, I will be ready.

Special thanks are showered upon all of my friends and family for their continuous support and comic relief. I would like to take this opportunity to dedicate this book to my late father, who did not get to see my graduation day at SRU. Though we are apart, he has filled me with continuous inspiration and has instilled me with the many values that have made me who I am today. This book is also for my amazing sister, and especially my courageous mother, who has filled the shoes of two parents, and has offered continuous support in all of my endeavors. To each and every one of my dear friends at Slippery Rock, thank you for touching my life and making my SRU experience a memorable one.

Megan Hebard McRobert—Smith College

I've always enjoyed writing, and I love talking to people about Smith and their college decision process, so I jumped at the opportunity to write a whole book about Smith. I love it here, and I don't want to be anywhere else. At the same time, I have friends here and at other schools who are unhappy with their colleges. I think that part of that dissatisfaction comes from the fact that students are unable to see a complete picture of a school. I tried to give as a complete a picture as possible; I even learned a few things myself! I hope that this book helps you figure out what's right for you. I am currently a junior (and a proud resident of Wilder House) pursuing a major in women's studies and a minor in international relations. One of the many activities I enjoy at Smith is writing an opinion column for our weekly newspaper, the *Sophian*. Eventually, I hope to put my political and writing backgrounds to use as a journalist.

There are a million people I would like to thank who have helped throughout this process and throughout my academic and writing careers. However, I would like to dedicate this book to the memory of my grandfather, George Hebard, who passed away a few days before I got this job. He always taught me to work towards my goals and offered me unconditional support.

Stacy Seebode—Southern Methodist University

Since I was nine, I've enjoyed writing—well mainly about my overeager urge to become a doctor even though I can't stand the sight of blood. Then I took a turn down ballerina lane, reaped the benefits of injuries, and somehow managed to return to my longtime interest in writing. Currently, I am a junior journalism major and a dance minor hoping to find a job where I can utilize my creativity and partake in the freedom of expression. I'm very thankful that I have been given the opportunity to help attract the right students to SMU, as well as offer some advice to the irresolute ones. Getting away

from Georgia has been quite an eye-opener for me, and through my college experience, I have learned what the beauty of independence has to offer. I've learned how to juggle school, a job, extracurriculars, and my sanity. Yet somehow, I've managed to have the time of my life here, too. It certainly has been worthwhile for me, and hopefully this book will help you decide whether or not it can be for you, too.

Don't fret, I'm not going to write a novel about myself or anything. I would like to give some shout outs and thank yous to the people who made this book possible. Thank you to my parents, who were there for all of my frantic phone calls. My family rocks! They've all been cheering me on. Thank you to Chris for always hugging me and saying, "you can do it!" Thank you to Kristin Diver, Kristen the German, Jen, Mary B., Sam, Natasha, Prem, Skippy, T. Diddy, Dchizzle, Browns, Penmans, Shumates, Mr. Dealey, Helmuth, and my favorite Texas hotties for all your support. A warm thank you to the College Prowler team, especially Omid! You guys have been so helpful and kind. Thank you again.

Christiana Little—Southwestern University

Christiana Little, a native Austinite, is a vocal performance major here at Southwestern. She hopes to grace the great operatic stages of the world someday. Christiana is probably going to have a minor (or five) in English, communication studies, theater, psychology, or history. At Southwestern, she is very active in Chorale, Alpha Delta Pi, Sigma Phi Lambda, the Megaphone, Allies, and SU Young Democrats. When she isn't writing, singing, playing piano, or loitering at Spiderhouse Coffeeshop, Christiana can be found embroidering or playing with her chihuahua, Tipper.

Christiana would like to thank the following very important people: Mom, Dad, Grayson, Jenny, Ashley, Emily, Natalie, Tricia, Deann, Myla, Meg, Leigh, Kelsey, Kat, Braden, Aubry, Aryn, Alyssa, and all the folks who turned in surveys but forgot to leave their name. Huge thanks to Omid and everyone at College Prowler!

T. Murray—Spelman College

Ms. Tiffani "T." Murray is a graduate of Spelman College and the Georgia Institute of Technology. She is currently a project manager with Capgemini in Atlanta. Her projects have allowed her to author and direct two company-wide human resources videos and provide content for the North American internal newsletter. She has also co-authored and designed participant and facilitator guides for internal training focused on creativity, communication, and problem solving.

A published author, Ms. Murray's work has appeared in a number of print publications. She has submitted biographies to the African American National Biography, and she was also published in the 2004 anthology Delta Girls: Stories of Sisterhood. She is a staff writer for AUC Magazine and the co-founder and director of communications and special events for AUCAlumni.com. She is also the managing editor of AUCAlumni.com's online news site. T. Murray has interviewed and written feature articles on such celebrities as Sheri McGee, Kathleen McGhee Anderson, and Bryan-Michael Cox. In 2000, she was published as an anonymous writer in the Wetfeet.com insider guide to Cap, Gemini, Ernst & Young. As a contract profile writer for Match.com, she also gained a wealth of knowledge about the world of dating through her interviews with a number of subscribers. Her work with Match inspired her to write her first non-fiction book, Stuck on Stupid: A Guide for Today's Single Woman Stuck in Yesterday's Stupid Relationships. She is currently working on self-publishing SOS and her debut novel, Group Project, both to be released in 2006. A freelance writer, Ms. Murray's work has been featured on Internet sites such as MinorityProfessionalNetwork.com.

In addition to consulting for one of the original "Big 5," Ms. Murray spends her spare time planning events and was a co-chair on the planning committee for the 2005 Turner Broadcasting Systems Trumpet Awards in Atlanta. She is the daughter of Joseph and Clara

Antoinette Brown—St. John's University

I really enjoyed writing this book because it helped me to realize that people are sharing the same thoughts as me. I am going to be a junior at St. John's with a major in human services, and my future goal is to become a family lawyer. Writing is one of my biggest passions (I write and read frequently). I use writing as a mode of expressing myself, and it helps to release what is on my mind.

I tried to write about St. John's in as objective a manner as I possibly could, but unfortunately, it came across more negative than positive. I only stated the issues that others and I have had. I tried to give the whole picture—negative with the positive, and I hope this book will help the student choose if St. John's is the best for them. Don't rely solely on this book for your decision about St. John's, but investigate on your own. Research, make calls, and even speak to other students or alumni that attend or have attended St. John's University. If you have the chance, visit the campus, because the feel that you get from the campus will dramatically affect your choice.

From my own experience of struggling to pay for school, I would advise students to apply for as many scholarships as they can. Some Web sites include www.fastweb.com, www.scholarships.com, and www.finaid.com. Also, check your local library, and see what scholarships your school offers and what you have to do to get them. Start early, so you can be set before school starts and not stress about how to pay for it. It would be a shame to get into a good school but lack the resources to pay for it. Don't rely solely on financial aid. Send out your FAFSA soon after January; it will make all the difference in your financial-aid package.

I would to give a big thanks to College Prowler for making this possible. Also my mom, dad, loving grandparents, and sisters, I love you all! Thank you so much Joey and Omid from College Prowler for guiding me; you were such a big help! Also, another big thanks for all that took time to answer the survey questions. Thank you all and God bless!

Drew Ewing—St. Louis University

I am a junior in the Parks College of Engineering pursuing a degree in aerospace engineering. Outside of class, I am the arts and entertainment editor for the *University News*, vice president of the Society of Automotive Engineers Aero Design Team, and member of the Life at SLU Television Network. I spent most of my life growing up in Columbus, Ohio, though I spent this last summer in Huntsville, Alabama doing an internship, which was where a majority of this book was written. If you have any questions, concerns, comments, or propositions, don't hesitate to e-mail me.

I could not have written this alone. I relied on the help of many people in gaining information and insight into this wonderful university, and I would like to thank them now. Thank you to my parents, first and foremost, for actually letting me attend SLU, Brian O'Rourke, Sarah Smith, Michele Parrish, Pete Hale, Constance Beverly, Callie Coombs, Eric Brighton, Adam Hill, and Brooke Kreikemeier for their wealth of SLU and St. Louis information, and finally the staff of College Prowler for stroking my ever-fragile ego and asking me to write this.

Nathan Hopkins—St. Olaf College

There's this myth among high school college counselors that there is one perfect college out there for you. They make it seem like since the beginning of time fate has ordained your presence there. If all the terrestrial variables are in order, you will graduate from your predestined college or university and go on to accomplish great things. If for some reason you end up at the wrong institution of higher learning, then you will end up as a hopeless and unhappy wage-slave, flipping burgers for the rest of your miserable life.

Don't listen to people who try to sell you this crap. It's not true, and worrying about it will only plague your senior year of high school with fear and trembling. I had no clue what I was doing during my college search. I'm not really sure how I ended up at St. Olaf, and I'm sure that there are plenty of other schools I would enjoy just as much, but now that I'm here I can't see myself anywhere else. I love it here. Sure, a whole lot of that has to do with the sort of things you can read about in this book, but it mostly is because of the fantastic people I've come to know over the past years.

Anyway, good luck with your college search. I hope that you'll be as happy with your choice as I am with mine. If not, you can always transfer.

Ian Spiro—Stanford University

Ian Spiro is a senior at Stanford University, poised to receive a Bachelor's of Science in computer science in just a few months. He will take that Bachelor's of Science, put it in a paper shredder, pulp it in a paper-grinder, and recycle it into the most beautiful resume-paper the world has ever seen. Ian expects to spend the first few years out of college serving industry and "just doing the right thing." After that, he plans to marry well, and retire into a life of raising children and writing unpopular shareware programs. On the side, he may travel to Germany or create freelance Internet comics.

Ian would like to thank his dedicated bounce-back team for their service in reading over the manuscript. He would also like to thank all the people who provided quotes, as well as the College Prowler management team, for continually reminding him that his deadline had passed.

Nicholas Mrozowski—Stetson University

If you are actually reading this part of the book, well, it must be interesting, or you just want to know what sort of person wrote this thing. I will start with a little history.

Originally, I am from Antioch, Calif., where I was able to check out places like San Francisco, Monterey, and other really great spots. It was awesome being out there for a little while, but as the crime rate rose, my family decided to move around trying to dodge it. Eventually, my family succumbed to financial trouble, and we moved to Florida. We arrived in Florida on New Year's Eve and were in a Holiday Inn in Orlando when the ball dropped. We eventually made our way to Sebring, where my parents currently live. There have been many trials and tribulations that have dotted my life and shaped how I felt.

My mother came from a Protestant upbringing that was very strict. Her family was of Irish and English descent. My father was a Roman Catholic of Italian and Polish descent. This let me have my way with religion and politics. It allowed me to take on what I felt was right and explore what religion I was able to hold as my own. Beyond all of this, I have been able to see both coasts of the United States. After graduating high school, I went to the only university that accepted me—Stetson.

Stetson has held me and taught me well in the business school. I am a finance major with a business law minor. The only real trouble I have had is with the two departments that seemingly give everyone trouble, the math and economics departments. There are, however, ways to deal with it, and if you ask a few students, they will tell you which classes to take. Now here I am a junior typing away at this book. This is really brief, but it gives everyone a hint at who I am. I want to give special thanks to my father, mother, sisters, and my lovely girlfriend, Andrea, for making me who I am. Lastly, I want to thank all of my friends who have helped with quotes or have let me vent to them. Thank you!

Douglas G. Swezey—Stony Brook University

I am a native of Long Island, born and raised here. After beginning an undergraduate program in architecture at SUNY Buffalo and working at many private architecture firms, I followed my passion for the arts of architecture and poetry, finally graduating from Stony Brook University with a Bachelor of Arts in English and art history. I am proud to have had the opportunity to express the knowledge contained in this book about my home and my (now) alma mater. I hope to continue to have chances to publish my writing. I intend to pursue a Master's degree in English, and aspire to become a professor like some that I have studied under. Until that point, I will still enjoy the gift of life that God has granted me. I hope that this book helps you to realize the many opportunities available to you at Stony Brook University, and how to attain them.

My indebtedness and gratitude to the following for their help, encouragement, and support: Evelyn Prugar, Janet Swezey-Hennig, John Capela, Sr., the Prugar Family, Allison K. Swezey, and everyone at College Prowler!

I would like to dedicate this book to the loving memory of George C. Hennig (1941–2002), without whom many of the things in my life may not have been possible.

Jennifer A. Fox—Susquehanna University

Okay, so it's kind of weird writing my own brief biography. My name is Jennifer Anne Fox, and I'm a junior at Susquehanna University. I'm a double major in journalism and political science, with a minor in French. I'm the news editor of the student-run paper, The Crusader, and president of the French club. I have too many goals to list, but to make it concise, I'd like to go into the newspaper or news-magazine field and cover world politics. In my spare time (which I don't have a whole lot of), I love going running and spending time with my friends. My favorite thing about writing this book, other than getting to know more about this campus than I thought possible, is being able to tell people that I had my first book published before my 21st birthday. If that's not an ego trip, I don't know what is.

Elizabeth Collins—Swarthmore University

I've had a blast writing this book. It's been great sharing my opinions about Swarthmore with readers. Anyway, about me—I'm a junior at Swarthmore, and a sociology/anthropology major (Do you want fries with that?) and a psychology minor (What is your motivation for wanting fries with that?). I'm from Uniontown, Pennsylvania, a pseudo-suburb of Pittsburgh. Let's just say it was a big adjustment coming to Swarthmore and going back home. I'm interested in a career in journalism, and I write and edit for Swarthmore's campus newspaper, the Phoenix. I greatly appreciate the opportunity to write and publish for College Prowler. I hope my work with College Prowler will help readers to make an informative decision about Swarthmore. The college selection process is hell, but I hope this book makes it a little less painful.

I'd like to thank Mom, Dad, Annie, my family, Marci, Tim (and the 28 million kids), Ja'Dell, Elyse, Emily, Allison, Salid, Becky, Reynetta, Powen, Jaky, Adam, Melonie, friends at Swat, everyone who has helped to shape my experience at Swarthmore, and everyone at College Prowler!

Steve Krakauer—Syracuse University

Understandably, this book is not one that keeps you up late at night in dire anticipation as to what is on the next page, or a book that you sit down to read a few pages of and find yourself overwhelmed by its power. Hopefully, though, this book provides you the information you sought after and will supply you with a valuable reference tool in your years at Syracuse University. I also hope you enjoyed reading

this book as much as I enjoyed writing it. When I graduate from SU, I look forward to expanding my writing ability. As a broadcast journalism major who is also a columnist for the Daily Orange, I thoroughly relished in this opportunity to broaden my horizons and put my name on a book of my own. It was an experience I enjoyed, especially as I was able to write about Syracuse University, a place I have tremendous respect for and have a great time attending. This has also been a great learning experience for me as a writer.

I would like to thank many people who have had a major effect on both me and this project. First I want to thank my parents, whose support through this and everything else is always unwavering. Thank you for keeping your criticism constructive and your praise sincere. Hopefully, this will be the first of many times where you will see my gratitude to you on this public of a stage. I also want to thank my little sister, Alison, who I love very much. Thank you to everyone at the Westfield Leader for giving me the opportunity to have people read my writing. I learned so much during my three years with you all. Thank you to the Daily Orange for being an open outlet for my voice to be heard. Also, I want to thank Elizabeth Muller, who taught me so much during two years of the toughest English class I have ever been a part of. You truly gave me the strength to believe that someday the words "by Steve Krakauer" would be attached to a book. Thank you to Jon Adler, George Azar, Missy Burlin, Matt Chazanow, Courtney Dolloff, Rob Daurio, Bridget Fitzpatrick, Ron Levy, and Ben Kahn for their help with this project. Finally, I want to thank everyone at College Prowler for giving me this opportunity.

Tiffani Joseph—Temple University

Well, I feel good. Really. This is my first time doing something like this, and I feel good about my work. What I want most for the reader is to take one good thing and one bad thing from this book. Not something that criticizes my writing or researching techniques, I want you to take something that will help you make the best decision for your higher education.

If your parents bought this book for you, definitely take this seriously. Choosing a college to attend is a big, big, big decision. Four years (or maybe more) of your life will change for the better because of the decision you make right here. I love Temple so much that I've even thought about donating some money once I make it big. However, there are those typical problems that I've seen some Temple students run into: not having enough credits to graduate, loans not transferring, and not getting housing. All of this can be avoided if you plan ahead and talk to the administration to make sure you are on the right track.

I also had no doubt when I chose Temple. I knew what it could do for me, and more importantly, what I would take away from it. Even though the economy is rough and I know many who have graduated with no job, at Temple I was able to discover my passion in advertising and writing, and therefore not letting the job market or lack of get to me. I'm enrolled at a graduate school pursuing my goals. I hope this book will be useful.

Shout out time—thanks Mommy, Daddy, Granny, Grandpa, Jhon, Krystle, Lisa, Freeman, my peoples from Temple, my friends from Brooklyn Tech and at the Creative Circus, and College Prowler.

Raven Petty—Tennessee State University

It has been a wonderful opportunity for me to write this guidebook. I wanted to make sure that all students considering Tennessee State University knew the highlights and low points of the school. This has been a great opportunity for me to express myself and to speak to all those wonderful people who filled out surveys and did interviews. Being a minority at TSU, I was uneasy at first, but the wonderful faculty and my fellow students have always made me feel welcome and loved.

The TSU family has been amazing to me, and in most cases things went along smoothly. It is important to realize that entering college is simply the beginning of a career that will hopefully take you far in life. I am a full-time student and I work full-time at a job I have had for eight years. My experiences at TSU have only made me stronger and more reliable to those who depend on me. TSU is my second home, and I look forward to each and every day that I get closer to reaching my goal of obtaining a degree. I hope you have enjoyed reading the thoughts and opinions of the TSU student body, and we look forward to welcoming you into our family.

I'd like to really thank the people who helped me make this guidebook the masterpiece it is: Isaiah, Joey, Braxton, James, Eddie, Brian, DeShanee, Justin, Jessica, Denise, Greg, Gregory, Jonathan, Tim, John and Paul Osborne, Tahir, my wonderful grandparents, my mom, Dr. Mazzone, Professor Bradley, and Dr. Johnson. Thank you all so much for your support and patience with me through this! You all are awesome!

Ashley Marshall—Texas A&M University

I would like to thank the Academy for believing in me enough to give me this opportunity—just kidding. Writing this book has been a blast, and I hope you've had just as much fun reading it. I graduated from the fine university of Texas A&M with a journalism major. I call it a commemorative diploma. I hope to continue my passion for writing for the rest of my life. Thanks to the College Prowler staff for all their support and patience. They believe in this book so much, and it was an honor to be part of it. Thanks for buying this book and reading it! Good luck in your college endeavors. If you have any questions, e-mail me. If you have any compliments, e-mail me. If you have any complaints, e-mail Luke.

Jessica Fleming—Texas Christian University

Jessica Fleming was raised in Fort Worth and attended public school before becoming a horned frog. She is attending TCU while living at her family's home in southwest Fort Worth with her pet ferret. She enjoys a variety of movies and music, so much so that she is considering having radio-TV-film as her major. She is one of the few Fort Worth natives attending the University, and is proud to be studying alongside people ranging in origin from Austin to Budapest.

Jessica Fleming is one of around a thousand people with that name, two of whom are currently attending TCU. The specific moment she realized that TCU was the right school for her was the day that seppuku (honorable samurai suicide) was demonstrated by a student (with instruction from the professor) in her Honors History of Asian Civilizations class. Of course, there were no blades involved, and the student was applauded for his effort. This demonstration was impressive not only for the fact that the professor understood this practice, but also because it proved that the professor knew how to pass that knowledge on. Jessica feels that this hands-on approach is a vital part of the TCU learning experience.

Jessica would like to thank her family for their support, as well as Aramis, who was always more than happy to retrieve her from the library even late at night, John, the computer science major who helped find statistics when all hope seemed lost, and everyone at College Prowler for their help and understanding. She would also like to thank the many people that filled out surveys for this project, among them Sara Snyder, Natalie Trujillo, Casey, Cliff, Monique, and Xi.

Abby Stone—Texas Tech University

I did it! I graduated with a BA in journalism from the best school in the world, Texas Tech. Since I left Lubbock, I have moved to Austin and into a new life as a working girl. Although my mom assures me there is more to come, writing this book has given me a chance to look back on what I believe were the best four years of my life.

I know everyone loves his group of friends, but I am amazed at the love and closeness I feel for so many people from Tech. My girlfriends are the kind of people that just make you feel good. Together we always bring out the best in each other, and most importantly, we know exactly what it takes to have a really good time. We always had an outstanding time when it was just the girls, but all of us are boy-crazy, and Tech was full of great ones. I love all of my guy friends from Tech; not only because they are studs, but because they made parties, road trips, lunch, and even class just a little more fun. When I moved away from Lubbock, I also had to move away from these great people, but I will hold on to all of these friendships as long as they will hold on to me.

I'm so happy my mom (the biggest Tech fan who didn't attend Tech) and dad gave me such a great college opportunity. I learned a lot and loved a ton, and I am ready to take on the rest of what this world has to offer.

Rachel Clark Unkovic—Trinity College

I really enjoyed writing this book, and I hope you've enjoyed reading it, or at least that it gave you some good pointers towards what to expect from Trinity. Writing the book has helped the summer home-sickness I've been feeling for the college and my friends there. Next fall, I will be back on campus as a senior majoring in creative writing and classical civilization. After Trinity, I'll go to graduate school to pursue an MFA. in prose fiction writing. In the meantime, I plan to make the most of my last year there, because I really do believe that college is mainly what you yourself make of it. The best advice I can give you is this: decide to have fun in college, and wherever you end up, most likely you will have a blast!

Kristin Dickson—Trinity University (TX)

I wrote this book during a wonderfully busy summer and had a fabulous time doing it. I recently graduated from Trinity University Texas and am constantly looking for new projects to work on; there are never enough ways for me to learn more about writing and to try to help my style evolve. Writing for College Prowler was a great step in a process that consistently changes the way I define my life. I majored in English at Trinity, and I am ever grateful to the stacks of papers that I wrote, from the time school started until graduation, and the professors who never let me get away with turning in a sloppy first draft. I hope that this book has been helpful to you in choosing the right university, and that you tell all of your friends about it so that College Prowler can keep printing more copies.

I could never have finished this without the help and support of my friends, who will shortly be receiving one of my infamous home-cooked meals. Mum, Dad, Brian and Travis, you guys make every day meaningful to me, and remind me that there is nothing that you can't accomplish if you just keep trying. Thanks to my personal editor and best friend Agent Sugarlips who probably lost more sleep than I did. Thank you to all of the professors at Trinity who kept pushing me and asking "So, are you going to drop out of school and become a writer? Because you should really think about it," and thanks especially to College Prowler for giving me the chance to keep doing what I love.

Jessica Gasch—Truman State University

When other students would ask me what I was working on, it was great fun to nonchalantly answer, "Oh, a book." Now it's back to regular old research papers for me. As a second-year student at Truman, I spend much of my time clacking away on my laptop. Between my French and linguistics degrees, Japanese courses, Detours magazine position, and editorship with the Truman State University Index, writing—in several languages—has become second nature, and who knows where it will take me in the future. Next semester, my interests have persuaded me to study on the French

Rivera, but in the meantime, it's been a treat to talk about something a little closer to home. I hope you enjoyed the journey as much as I have. Comments and questions are appreciated.

Thank you to the College Prowler staff, especially Jennifer and Omid, for giving me this opportunity and for slaving away to turn a template into a legible book. Thanks to all of you who contributed your opinions, as well as those of you who provided desperately needed encouragement: Mom, Dad, and Jimmy, Mamas and Papas, Courtney, Diane, Annemarie, Abbey, and my favorite, Michael.

Emily Chasan—Tufts University

I had a great time writing this book! I've just returned from a semester in Madrid, and it was really exciting to be able to delve into the world of Tufts all over again. I'm hoping that this will help me progress as a writer. I'm now a senior at Tufts University pursuing degrees in both international relations and economics while serving on the executive board of the *Tufts Daily*. I hope to use everything I've learned to work in business reporting in the future. Being from Philadelphia, Boston took a little getting used to, but going to Tufts has been a wonderful experience and now I know how to say "artery" like "ahtehy." I hope this book has been insightful for you, and I hope you learned what it is really like to live on the hill.

I'd like to give many people many thanks for supporting me while I attempted to work on this book. Thank you Mom, Dad, Alex, Grandma, George, Erika, Jon, Nick, Emily, Josh, Leah, Nico, Andrea, Naushin, Rachel, and everyone at College Prowler!

Christine Huang—UC Berkeley

Christine Huang is a senior undergraduate at UC Berkeley studying sociology and psychology with an emphasis in gender studies and urbanization. She spent her formative years in sunny Irvine, Calif., where her parents still reside. After attending her last classes at Cal, she'll be heading to New York City to try her luck in the publishing world. She would like to thank her whole family (Steven, Alice, Jane, and Cheng-Chi) for their endless support and encouragement.

Tristen Chang—UC Davis

Writing this has been a wonderful experience. After finally declaring myself as an English major, I decided to plunge into the field and try my hand at freelance writing. Hopefully, this is the start of a future career in creative writing, and the start of a line of publications. I have always been fascinated by language, but what little background I have has been rooted in poetry. This book was a wonderful and challenging opportunity to expand my horizon, and I hope it offers insightful information about Davis. Currently I'm a sophomore at UCD, tirelessly working toward degrees in English and some branch of science that I haven't decided on yet—possibly microbiology or environmental science. Continuing my education here has been a dizzying and inspiring experience; I only hope that this guidebook captured some of that unquantifiable spirit. I learned a lot in the process of writing it; I hope you get something out of it, too.

I owe many people heaps of thanks for all their support during this whole experience. Thank you Mom and Dad for your faith in me, Beez for your humor, Grandma and Papa for understanding when I had to cancel plans to meet the deadlines, Aunt Deed, Uncle Keith, and the girls for the Internet connection, Adam, Donry, Laura, Gracie-Lou, Ross-Hintze's, and Adelaide for your support. Danny, Benji, Danielle, Jack, Marge, Nina, Mari-Ferrari, Matt, and everyone else who obligingly answered my questions, and all my roomies for broadening my perspective and enriching my college experience. Thank you Mr. Clark for getting this whole show on the road, and many thanks to everyone at College Prowler!

Jennifer Truong—UC Irvine

Jennifer Truong currently attends University of California, Irvine as a third year English major. She lives in southern Orange County with her family. In her spare time, she enjoys reading and creative writing. She's currently working on an independent study on family narratives, and hopes to some day earn her MFA in creative writing.

Cynthia Marie Wald—UC Riverside

Writing this book was a great experience! I'm currently a senior at the University of California, Riverside pursuing a degree in English. I'm planning to move forward with my education upon graduation, hopefully with a secondary teaching credential and a master's in education. I hope to inspire young high school minds and help them explore the English language and find excitement in literature.

I will always cherish my time as a student at UC Riverside. I have learned so much about myself through my experiences and have made what I hope to be long-lasting, close friendships. I hope this book has been insightful for you, I know I learned much about my own school in the process. Personally, I believe that, in many ways, UC Riverside, is one of the best-kept secrets in the realm of universities, as it is often overlooked.

I'd like to take a moment to thank many people from the bottom of my heart. First and foremost, I'd like to thank Mom, Dad, Jamie, and Bubby for all the love, encouragement, and support you continuously provided for me. Thank you to all my friends who took the time to help during midterms, you know who you are. Last, but definitely not least, I'd like to thank Omid, Joey, and everyone else at College Prowler for giving me such a great opportunity and unique experience!

Shelby Gunderman—UC San Diego

While writing this book I experienced a huge sense of nostalgia. I am a recent graduate and UCSD has been my home for the last four years. Working on this book reminded me of all the reasons why I have loved attending UCSD and living in San Diego. Being able to walk to the beach made all the late-night studying worth it. Writing this book has put into perspective what a unique university UCSD is. I have never once regretted my choice to come to UCSD, even during finals, and hopefully this edition of College Prowler will help you pick the best college for you. If you have any other questions about UCSD don't hesitate to e-mail me.

Kate Sandoval—UC Santa Barbara

Writing this guidebook has been such a fun way to finish off my college experience and it has been a great outlet for all of my UCSB knowledge. I also appreciate the chance to write about a subject that I truly care about. In four years, I lived in the dorms, rushed a sorority, went on a semester at sea, managed a business, learned how to sail a little, survived a year living on Del Playa Drive, had more than a few part-time jobs, took a wine class, lived downtown, and spent a year interning at *Santa Barbara Magazine* and the Alumni Association publications. Maybe most importantly, I majored in English and minored in writing and professional editing. The skills I acquired and the voice I discovered through my writing classes have prepared me for future media writing careers.

Thanks to my fam—Mom, Dad, and Laura—and to my best college friends, Michelle, Erin, Cara, Jenn, Ryan, Reid, Kari, Mark, Alyssa, Alison, and Nate. Thanks to my high school friends (also a big part of college), Melissa, Whitney, and Vickie. And, of course, thanks to College Prowler for allowing me to compose the guidebook.

Hadley Robinson—UC Santa Cruz

I am a graduating senior at UCSC, and am working to finish degrees in both history and journalism. After my experiences as a journalist at UCSC, I hope to continue writing when I graduate and would like to be a foreign correspondent in South America. I came out to sunny California from Arlington, Virginia and I have enjoyed the small-town, laid-back atmosphere that Santa Cruz has to offer. I have found my time at UCSC incredibly enhanced by good programs, good teachers, and good friends. In extracurricular activities I have written for the campus newspaper, worked for the campus radio station and I play for the women's ultimate Frisbee team.

I hope that this book has been informative, and that it can offer some valuable insight into this interesting university.

Erik Robert Flegal—UCLA

This book was a real treat to write. I finally had the opportunity to put my English major to use! I hope that this will be the first of many times to come. Running back down memory lane and rehashing the college experience makes me realize how quickly I awoke from the college dream. Now the whole experience seems like it never happened. The dream just swirls together. Take your time at UCLA, because working-life holds nothing over college-life (except a paycheck instead of a loan). Although I made my share of memories here, I'd like to think that everyone that picks up this book engages UCLA a little more deeply than I did. If I could tell prospective students to do one thing, I would say STUDY ABROAD! Regardless of the university that a student chooses to attend, the option to study abroad is golden. Don't miss it! UCLA still is an amazing university for the time that you spend in the United States. What's the one thing I would do at UCLA? Read the book and find out!

Now I send thanks and love to the following: Mommy & Daddy, Ewwwwiiiiiiinnn (now I turn on the motorbike), Grams (the one and only), Mikel (thanks for the editing help baby cakes), Shearell (you will get your woman), Jon (for being understanding with my job), Uncle Bill & Aunt Rose (I remember the phone call), Delaney (Mr. Santa Fe), Professor Little (for teaching me how to write), Train (buttermil-K, you still sleep funny), Adam (without this computer, this would not be possible), Mike (the brainstorm was a hurricane, and you still sleep real funny), CincoMomo (your help was noticed!), Steve (you never write me back), Sav (you're a little too feisty), the Andersons (just to say I love you all), Rich (for the laughs), Nancy (for the listening), UCLA departments (you know who you are) and all of the College Prowler staff for giving me this opportunity!

Aaron Edelstein—Union College

This has been a great time working to get this guidebook out to the masses. I've really enjoyed Union College, and I've really struggled through parts of it. Socially, I really believe that the Minerva system will make Union College a better place to spend four years. I'm planning on moving out to the West Coast for my own "Razor's Edge" experience, then hopefully on to medical school. I will definitely be an interesting applicant with an undergraduate degree in American ethics (organizing theme major at Union), a minor in Japanese, and a Master's in biomedical ethics. Hopefully, at the ripe age of 35, I'll start to earn a living. As a last tidbit of advice: To everyone looking for a college that will fit them perfectly—stop looking. It doesn't exist, and even if you ever find it, don't go there. Find a place that will fit you academically and make it a home for yourself. With that said, I want to thank Annette, Ally, Adam, Hugh, the Green House Croo, Tom McEvoy, and Kelly Herrington for being the best guides and teachers one could ever have.

Jessica Joseph—University at Albany

Writing this book has been exciting, fun, and a definite learning experience. This is my first publication, and hopefully will not be my last. I am a recent graduate of the University at Albany, where I majored in psychology and minored in business. Middletown, New York is where I've lived my entire life, but that is soon to change. I just recently started a job as a Professional Education Coordinator at the National Kidney Foundation in Manhattan. I hope to move into one of the five boroughs in approximately one year. The University at Albany has definitely helped me prepare for what's in store for me. I hope you found this book informative, yet fun at the same time. On another note, I'd like to thank all of the people who really helped me complete this book, Bethie, Andrew, Sara, Scarna, Kevin, Bari, Annie, Amanda, and the many people who work at the University at Albany who had to deal with my massive amounts of phone calls. And last, but definitely not least, thank you to College Prowler for giving me this tremendous opportunity!

Ben Cady—Univeristy at Buffalo

Wherever life takes me I will always be a Buffalo boy. I love this old town, and I know it like the back of my hand. If there's one thing to say about Buffalo people, it's that they're honest—there's an old T-shirt around town that says, "Buffalo: City of No Illusions." I hope you find that I brought some of that honesty to this book. I've had fun showing you around.

I came to UB after earning an International Baccalaureate diploma at Buffalo's City Honors School. After four great years, I will graduate with an Advanced Honors degree in English and a minor in political science. Currently I serve as a managing editor and columnist for the *Spectrum*, UB's student newspaper. I'm a member of Phi Beta Kappa and a varsity athlete—I run cross-country in the fall, and track and field in the spring.

When I say farewell to Buffalo, I plan to get involved in politics. I've had the good fortune of interning with the great Democratic senator Chuck Schumer in New York and the Democratic Senatorial Campaign Committee in Washington. Someday, I'd like to go to law school.

When my old track coach Dick Barry retired, he said, "Always remember two things: you never get anywhere alone, and you can never say thank you enough." In that spirit, I thank my mom and dad, my grandparents, my brother, Adam, Amanda, my girl, Mike Silverstein, Joel, Czyz, Lockett, McKenna, Strelick, and Wigton from the team, Flor, Coach Mitchell, Erin, George, Katie, Jeremy, Sam, Jen, Eric, Charity, Ben, Nick, Mike, Jim, John, Dena, Jeff, Lynn, Helene and Debbie from the paper, all of my coaches and teachers, including Mr. Anelli, Mr. Verso, Mr. Anthony, Mr. Fitz, Mr. Francescone, Mrs. Kiefer, Mr. Toy, Mr. LaChiusa, Dr. Battaglia, Dr. Hubbard, Dr. Daly, and Dr. Bono, everyone who filled out a survey, and not least of all, the good people of College Prowler for giving me this opportunity.

Merrick Wiedrich—University of Alabama

I hope as you read this book you were able to get a better understanding of the University of Alabama. After being on this campus for two years, I thought I knew all there was to know. But, even I learned so much from writing this book. I was able to see how the students as a whole feel about their school, and how this school has and is changing their lives. Now that you have read the thoughts of UA students, I hope that you, too, will come and see why so many of us have so much to say about Alabama.

I am now a junior here at the University of Alabama, studying to be a journalist. When I am not studying, I spend all of my time gaining experience for my future and living life as a UA college student to the fullest. I am currently writing for the *Crimson White*, the University's newspaper, and I am a member of Phi Mu sorority. I have learned so much from the classes I have taken, but also from the people that I have met while being here. In the future, I plan to take my brilliant education and the experiences I have had here, and continue to write and inform others about the world.

While working on this book, I have learned that college is what you make out of it. Everyone's experience is different but in the end we are all here for the same reason—Roll Tide!

Before I go, I have to thank the people that have put up with me for so long. My accomplishments and life would not be the same without the help and support from these amazing people. Thank you Mom, Dad, Roger, Guy, Aaron, Christina, Libbie, Brooke, Dejha, Megan, Adam (my biggest fan), Brian Brantley, UA's administration, Phi Mu, and College Prowler, thank you for this opportunity!

Nathan Tafoya—University of Arizona

My name is Nathan Tafoya and I like long walks on the beach and I like reading during rainstorms. Funny things always happen to me. I was raised by five mothers. All but one despised me and it is to this loving, caring woman that I dedicate my first publication. You should keep a look out for me in the future because I will one day rule the world, and it will be a nice thing for you to know that you knew me once but never again. Out.

I suppose I should thank the people at College Prowler for the opportunity to write and get paid, however miniscule the payments. Just kidding! Thank you, College Prowler people. Xoxoxo. And much love to Dave Gutierrez, UA's last edition's author.

Lily Barrish—University of Central Florida

I am starting my fifth year at UCF, and will be graduating with a degree in English/creative writing. I hope to continue writing forever, and eventually hope to land a job as an editor. I grew up in New York state with my parents and younger sister and plan on leaving Orlando after I graduate. The world is too big to stay in one place for too long.

There is no way that I could have completed this book without my very wonderful friends—Susan Baxter and Cassandra Lafser. They put in a tremendous amount of time with me and through many laughing attacks and bouts of almost crying with frustration, we ended up with a finished project. I am very proud of the work that all three of us have done, and can't wait to be a published author.

Susan graduated in the summer of 2004 with a degree in hospitality management. She grew up in New York state before moving to Jacksonville, Florida at the age of 13. Susan plans to travel around the world before settling down with a career. She hopes to be her own boss and run things her way.

Cassandra also graduated with a double-degree in advertising and public relations. Cassandra grew up in Jacksonville, Florida with her parents and younger sister. She plans to move closer to the beach and take on the world. We have lived the UCF life and loved every moment of it! Good luck!

Josh Steinman—University of Chicago

I was born and raised in Detroit, where I attended Cranbrook School for 14 years, until my matriculation at the University of Chicago a few years ago. I am studying history, international relations, and law. Around Chicago, I am a columnist for the *Maroon*, a campus tour guide, and an active member of the Alpha Epsilon Pi fraternity. I am the founder of the Chicago Historical Initiative and co-founder of the Card Club. I am on the debate team, sing in an a cappella group, and tutor middle-schoolers from the neighborhood in math. I am also an honors student. In my spare time I enjoy hiking, skiing, mountain climbing, running, and sailing. I wish to thank the following people: my mother Frances and father Kenneth, my sister Amy, my Great-Aunt

Rosalee, my grandmother Ethel and grandfather Richard. I would not be where I am today without my mentors David Dietrich, Ron Gorny, Herbert Snitz, David Watson, Jeffrey Welch, John Winter, and Jan Reelitz. Finally, I owe a debt of gratitude to the many friends who have helped me along the way, whose ranks include Maurice, Isaac, Noah, Bryan, Dan, Ben, Jacob, Manoah, John, Sam, and the rest of the Lambda Alpha chapter of AEΠ, Tara, Ben, Ira, Andrew, Ivan, Tim, Arif, Arvin, and for good measure, every person listed as my "friend" on *thefacebook.com*. Most importantly, I owe a debt of gratitude to André Phillips, Ted O'Neill, and the rest of the admissions staff for making the decision to admit me to the University of Chicago. I would finally like to thank the people at College Prowler for allowing me to dribble onto the keys of my computer, edit it, publish it, and call it the book that you are now reading.

Rachel Kellerman—University of Cincinnati

Rachel Kellerman is a fifth-year journalism student at the University of Cincinnati who is also minoring in Spanish. Aside from her studies, Rachel also works full time as the managing editor of UC's award-winning independent student newspaper, The News Record. Writing is something that is important to Rachel, in addition to letting people know the scoop on the University of Cincinnati. Therefore, this project was the perfect outlet to inform prospective students about UC while building on her writing skills… and getting published, which every journalist loves.

When Rachel gets free time (which unfortunately isn't often) she likes to get into anything and everything she can. She's a self-proclaimed "girly-tomboy" who loves rock and metal music, motorcycles, and cars but can still get her nails done and wear dresses, too. She is terrified of heights but loves skydiving and pretty much will try anything once. Or twice.

Rachel has nothing but positive experiences throughout her time at UC, which oddly enough is the last place she wanted to go to college. A native Cincinnatian, Rachel transferred to UC after just a semester away because UC was home. Since the transfer, she has had nothing but excellent classes, internships, and networking opportunities with people in her field. If she had to do it all over again, she'd definitely choose UC.

Rachel plans to begin her career in journalism once she graduates and hopes to see her byline in Rolling Stone one day. No, she didn't get the idea from the MTV reality show about being an intern with the magazine; it's been a dream of hers since she was young. Rachel is open to seeing where life takes her and likes to fly by the seat of her pants. She's hoping to land a job in a warm climate because Cincinnati's weather just isn't kosher anymore.

Jessica Amodeo—University of Colorado

After the long ceremonies and congratulations, the parties and the toasts, there was nothing left to receive. A subtle reminder was the cap and gown which sat on my dusty desk for weeks. Wondering what was to become of my life, I turned to the Internet. With an equally frustrated friend beside me, I searched countless Web sites requiring me to choose a job category to be able to classify my area of expertise. I longed for naïve attempts at understanding the world. I wanted to sit under neon lights as professors taught Hitchcock through a Marxist's perspective. But those days were behind me. I was done cramming and drinking bad coffee. The pressure of procrastinating a five-page paper had been exchanged for an assignment worth far more than a grade determined by the number of grammatical mistakes which had escaped me. Subsequent to sending out hundreds of résumés to countless companies overstating a need for employees, I assumed rejection was to be expected. Instead of dwelling in apparent failure, I ignored the limitations of a Bachelor's degree in English literature and continued to live in unacquainted bliss. By assuming the life of the college student I had been, I was able to refuse the reality that awaited me.

Yet, early one afternoon in June, I received a phone call from a company—College Prowler. They had received a résumé that I did not remember sending, but I listened anyway. I remember their questions about my credibility, but the true allure was the opportunity to be published. They asked for a sample of my writing. Days later I received a call to congratulate me on being chosen as the author of this book. So here I am, typing these words. Hopefully you will hear from me again. Regardless, without College Prowler I would have never realized such a dream, never been given an opportunity so extraordinary so early in my career.

Special thanks to my parents who granted me the privilege of a higher education, which ultimately led to the composition of this book. Thank you Adrian for introducing me to life at CU as only an older brother could. To Michael, for contributing his raw freshman wisdom and to Jenny, Kristen, Cat, Jackie, Kevin, Kasha, Dustin, Amy, Mikey, Matt, Chris, Craig, and to everyone at College Prowler—thanks again!

Colin Megill—University of Connecticut

You know, when I got here, I realized that nowhere is there a place to tell you about the bathrooms on campus. So I'm going to tell you. They're clean, depending on how anal retentive your floor and janitor are about cleaning them. The showers are really nice, but you should bring flip flops, and ones without cloth, because it gets wet and that's annoying (In a shower? Gets wet he says? No way!). The best advice I ever got in regards to college were the fateful words "bring liquid soap." I'll pass those along. Also, because I think it'd be really funny for this to be published: the locks on the bathroom stalls (at least in Northwest) are made by a company called "Hiney Hiders."

Okay, onto the serious stuff. I have to thank all of my friends who let me completely ignore them for this book and classes, yet never stopped calling me or caring how it was going. Steve Wheeler, Brad, Dan, Dan, Dan (in order of which Dan I like best), Drew, Mike, Michealla, Jordan, Beth, John, Eric, Lindsey, Mr. Harvey, Kyle, Ryan, Ryan, Matt, Crazy Asian Cheng, Crazy Russian Alina, and the faithful roomie Travis—you're the best, this book is dedicated to you, and so am I. Dedicating a book to my parents wouldn't be enough to thank them for what they've given me in life—an opportunity to truly do whatever I want, and all the tools to do it with. For working so hard so that I can have a school to write about, my life is dedicated to you both.

So you're still reading this, maybe you're actually interested in who I am. I am now officially not afraid to call myself a writer, considering I have published numerous articles for the commentary section of the *Daily Campus*, UConn's student newspaper. I swam four years varsity in high school (Hi Mr. Murin), which afforded me the nickname "Brick," because I sank when I dove my freshman and sophomore years. I play the snare drum in the marching band, which afforded me the nickname "Helmet" because they thought I looked like Rick Moranis (except for him being ugly, and me being ravishingly handsome). I hope this book has helped, and I hope to see you at the UConn football games in the future. I'll be one of the ones making a lot of noise.

Danielle Todd—University of Delaware

Writing this book was an interesting experience for me. I always tell anyone who asks that UD was not the best choice for me, but I had to attend it because I am in-state and it fits my budget. I thought I knew everything there was to know about UD, and that this book would be a piece of cake. I've lived in this town since I was eight and was sure I wouldn't even need to do any research. I was wrong. After I finished my research, I realized that there was a lot I didn't know about UD that if I had known would have made my life here so much better. I would have chosen different housing options and definitely arranged my meal plan a little better. I began to wish I had done this research before I enrolled and not when I had only one year left. The

information in this book is extremely valuable, and I wish that I had it before I became a UD student.

While completing this book, I was also surprised when it came to listing the 10 best and worst things about UD. I found my list of bests completed and in the computer long before I could come up with the 10 worst things. I had to sit and think hard to get the last couple of things. I realized that there are more good things about the University than bad. Writing this book has put a lot of things in perspective for me, including my own attitude about college.

On a more generic note, I would say I am extremely pleased that I had the opportunity to write this book. Not only did it provide me with personal growth, but it is an excellent experience for an English major. Whether I enter graduate school or search for a job, this book will show that I have the ability to be successful in whichever path I choose. I hope that this book is as helpful and informative for you to read as it has been for me to write.

Katie Niekerk—University of Denver

My passion in life is writing, which is why I was quick to jump on the opportunity to compile this book. I currently write for a small, community newspaper in Colorado, and as I continue my path in journalism, I hope to cover a wide variety of areas including business, current events, features, and yes, even politics. Attending DU has given me many memories, things to think about, and things to laugh at. Born and raised in Colorado, I'm grateful that I was able to spend my college career in such a wonderful and eclectic city. I graduated, and although I wouldn't mind staying in Colorado, I'd love to experience a different part of the world such as California, the Pacific Northwest, or London.

Thanks to all those who contributed their ideas, thoughts, and opinions for this book. Hopefully, if you're considering DU, my words have given you some insight as to whether you fit DU and vice versa. Good luck, and enjoy college—wherever you end up.

Regine Rossi—University of Florida

I finished my Bachelor's degree in English, and graduated with my Master of Education degree in English education (both from the University of Florida, of course!). I'm now teaching at the south Florida high school I attended, which is a neat, challenging, fun experience, but I loved UF and academic life so much, that it made me want to become a professor—no, really. I'm hoping to go back to graduate school to get my PhD in a few years, and maybe someday I'll get to go back to the fabulous town that has its Gator teeth firmly sunken into my soul.

I want to take a second to thank some important people: all the folks at College Prowler, naturally, for giving me the opportunity to tell everyone what a great place UF is; Carolyn Stana, John Bengston, and the whole English Proteach crew for making it that way for me; and above all else, my family and especially my terrific Ma—without whom, of course, I never even would have had a chance to try it all out. Last but not least, dear reader, I would like to thank you—yes, you!—for taking a look at this book and (I assume) considering the University of Florida.

Good luck in your search for the perfect school, and if you pick UF, maybe I'll see you around Gainesville!

Nicole Gross—University of Georgia

Working on this book was a great way for me to collect everything I want to remember from my experience and condense it down, kind of like my own little scrapbook. It has allowed me to gain writing experience and has shaped my career goals in the process. I am hoping to continue writing, in all its forms, throughout my career. I am currently a rising senior at the University of Georgia and a consumer journalism major, with an emphasis in fashion merchandising and advertising. The thing I love about writing for advertising is the search for human truths and little insights that you can convey to other people. I hope this guide has offered some kind of insight into real life at UGA, so you can get an idea of what to expect, rather than vague, meaningless descriptions from a brochure.

I guess the best way to describe my college experience so far is to call it an adventure of sorts. I have made huge mistakes, gotten arrogant, and consequently been humbled. I have learned how to meet people, give presentations to groups of 300, and make decisions like an adult. I think college is a really important time for self-discovery, and I hope wherever you choose to go, you become more of the person you want to be as an adult.

I would like to thank all my homies who gave me tips for writing this book and were continually excited for its publication. You all are the biggest reason for my many great times. Also, I would like to thank everyone at College Prowler, especially Christina and Kai who have helped me out many times. Finally, I would like to dedicate my section of this book to my mom, who will always be my biggest inspiration.

Bridget Sharkey—University of Illinois

Writing this book has taught me more about my school than living here for three years has. I cannot believe how much stuff I did not know. Hopefully, it has helped you make a more educated decision about your college choice; I only wish that I had utilized some of this information for myself a little earlier. As it is, I only have two semesters left before I graduate with a degree in English. After that, I hope to continue writing in some other form, whenever and wherever I can. I know that U of I is not the typical school one thinks of when it comes to art and literature, but I believe that it has truly helped me to become a better writer, and more importantly, a wiser observer. The teachers that I have had here have been absolutely dedicated to their students, willing and able to spend extra time with everyone. In the end, that is what has made U of I such a positive experience for me. At a big school like this, you really need teachers who will reach out to their students and build personal relationships with them, and that is exactly what we have here. It is this proximity that first attracted me to the University of Illinois. While my sister chose to live 12 hours from home at an Eastern university, I knew I needed closer ties to my hometown and family, particularly since I was only 16 years old. While most people headed off to college are generally more mature than I was, being close to home and family is important for most people. I would like to thank my writing manager, Joey Rahimi, for all the help he has given throughout this sometimes confusing experience. I would also like to thank all of my English teachers who have put up with my run-ons, my comma obsession, and my overuse of the word "consequently." Finally, I would like to thank my family for all of their help and patience. Thanks guys!

Alexander Lang—University of Iowa

"Is this Heaven?" "No, it's Iowa." The dialogue above is from the movie *Field of Dreams* and best sums up what my experience at the UI has been so far. I imagined coming to this state and seeing corn and, well, more corn. I grew up in Grosse Pointe, Michigan, which is just outside of Detroit. When I made the decision to come to the UI, I thought I might end up bored out of my mind. Instead I can't imagine myself anywhere else. I'm a sophomore and majoring in journalism and religious studies. When I'm not going to class, I often spend my time in the newsroom at the *Daily Iowan*. There is something about working in a newsroom that brings a great thrill and sense of accomplishment to my life. Writing this book allowed me to sharpen my writing skills and to have one more work published under my name. Since we all need a break from school and work, I enjoy the sports realm of the world. I love talking about and playing sports. Special thanks and dedications for this book go out first to Woman, Old Man, and Teddy (thanks for always being

there to support me), and to both Grandmas (thanks for spoiling me). Also, thanks to Jeff, the *Tower Newspaper*, Bill, and the *Daily Iowan*; you guys got me started in this business and allow me to continue to do what I love. To College Prowler, thank you for this great opportunity. Finally, thanks to my friends who have provided me with such great times and great memories.

Jonah Ballow—University of Kansas

A native of Lone Tree, Colorado I am always asked, "Why KU?" My answer to that question was easily discovered during the process of writing this book, which was a rewarding and interesting experience. I have learned about every aspect of the University of Kansas, along with several facts about the town in which I have lived for four years. With a degree in journalism, I have experienced all of the great aspects KU has to offer. My four years in college were a great learning experience. I have met some great friends, and taken part in some incredible events while at KU. My most memorable experience came during the Jayhawks Final Four run, when the students and residents of Lawrence flooded Massachusetts Street into the wee hours of the morning. When deciding on a college, read through this book, and hopefully it will help you understand KU through the student's eyes. I would like to thank many people for their ongoing support.

Thank you Mom, Dad, Jon, John, Kyle, Christine, Doll, Wes, Matt, Karo, John, Justin, Abby, Chris, Adam, Luke, and everyone else at College Prowler!

Mandy Langston—University of Kentucky

Mandy Langston didn't always enjoy every moment of her time at Kentucky, but by the end of it all was sad to leave. She worked at the *Kentucky Kernel* newspaper as a staff writer and columnist and was voted Favorite Kernel Writer. She spent much of her time reading and writing poetry at Common Grounds coffeehouse in Lexington during college.

I wish to thank my favorite "Maestro," who the University of Kentucky should be thanking as well, Buck Ryan. If you are lucky enough to have him in class, tell him I said thank you and bring a guitar—he's cool like that.

Also, I wish to thank my choir director, Dr. Lori Hetzel, for giving me a chance to make music with the most talented women on campus. You put a song in my heart and a smile on my face. Thank you to the staff of the Kentucky Kernel for reminding me that work can be as fun as you let it be. Thanks to the staff of Jimmy John's for all the late-night subs, and the Ale-8-One bottling company for all the caffeine.

Thanks Mom for all the support and rosary prayers on test days in college, and to Figgins for the late-night tailgate counseling sessions and ice cream. Amanda, Erin, Rachel, and Valarie: you girls know what loyalty means.

Thanks to the singles ministry at Victory Baptist Church for showing me Christ's love. You guys are my heart. Thank you Jesus for loving me enough to come down here to this messed up world to fight to win me. Romans 12:2.

Lindsey Coblentz—University of Louisville

When I was a senior in high school, I applied at two schools: Campbellsville University (a private school) and the University of Louisville. U of L gave me the better scholarship, so that's where I went. I used to often wonder whether or not I had made the right decision to come to U of L, but the longer I stayed there, the better it seemed. I'm a communications major who would love to go into public relations or publishing. I love writing, so naturally this was the perfect job for me. Writing for College Prowler allowed me to examine what U of L is really all about and cemented my belief that I really do fit in at this school. I may forget most of the information that I researched for this book, but I'll never forget the experience. Thanks College Prowler!

Justin M. Wozniski—University of Maine

Justin M. Wozniski is a native of Lancaster County, Pennsylvania. He attended the University of Maine as his first and only choice for higher education after spending many summers in Downeast Maine with his family. He was a journalism major at UMaine, pursued the news editorial and writing sequence, and recently earned his BA.

He has a strong interest in public affairs newspaper reporting, especially with local government and politics. His interest in this type of reporting stems from his community involvement and public service in his younger years.

Many thanks to those who have encouraged him to pursue entrepreneurial spirit in writing, as well as those who made possible the publication of his first book so quickly after his college tenure ended. Special thanks to Dad and Mom, Robert Dana, Germaine Kline, Paul Grosswiler, Angel Loredo, Gregory McManus, Meredith McIntire, Margaret Nagle, Ernest Scheyder, and Lauri Sidelko.

Jared Meyer—University of Maryland

During my sophomore year at Maryland, I decided that I wanted to be a motivational speaker and author. Fast-forward and here I am, authoring my first book, which coincidentally is about the University I attended. Given that I am now an official author, no longer promoting myself as just a former UMCP *Diamondback* columnist, I can relish in sharing with others one of the most important decisions of my young life—joining and contributing to the UMCP community.

I would like to thank a few people for investing in my character, in my ambition, and in my passion for life: to Dr. Glenn Schiraldi for introducing me to his wonderful world and perception of stress management, personal growth, and self-knowledge, to Professor Bill Nickels for teaching me the power of relationships, marketing, and self-promotion, and to my Mom and Dad for being both challenging and supportive, and for finally giving into the fact that I have and hopefully always will live my life by making passion-based decisions. This book was written based on such passion and I have them to thank for motivating me to write it.

Thanks also to my "big" brother, Seth, and sister, Samara, for being honest with me and interested in my life's adventures, to my best friends, Ben and Vito for being such great friends, to Ben and Vito's families, the Zapps's and the Mazzas's, respectively, for including me in their families and for giving me some great advice through the years, and finally to Michael, for being a friend, a mentor, and most importantly a second father to me.

Seth Pouliot—University of Massachusetts

I graduated from UMass a few months ago, and writing this book was the first job I found. I'm originally from western Massachusetts, so going to UMass seemed like the next logical step in my life after high school. I spent my entire junior year of college at the University of Alaska, Southeast in Juneau, on a domestic exchange program. Although my degree is in business management, I've been interested in a career in writing for as long as I can remember.

I hope this book has been a useful resource for you. I approached this guidebook as objectively as possible, but of course every word I wrote will reflect the fact that my experience at UMass has been uniquely personal. Many people in my life have been in some way responsible for the quality of this book, leaving myself the only one to blame for any mistakes and shortcomings, so instead of a list, I would like to say "Thank you, all."

"This isn't who it would be, if it wasn't who it is." – Phish

Shawn Wines—University of Miami

At whatever college you end up attending, you will find things you like and things you hate. The College Prowler guidebooks are a terrific example of this. There are no colleges with straight As, and none with straight Fs. If there were perfect colleges out there, everyone would flock there, and if there were totally miserable schools, they'd be empty.

The trick to enjoying college is finding a place that excels in the areas that you find important. For me, nightlife is not as important as academics. Chances are, if you narrow down what you're looking for, there will be a few schools that are right for you. Making the final decision on where to go involves a ton of factors, but you should know that there isn't just one college in the world that will make you happy. Unless you make a terrible mistake, wherever you end up going is probably going to suit your needs. You will seek out the kind of people you want to be friends with, even if you don't mean to. Your senior year of high school is a great time to have fun, but it also involves the biggest decision you've ever had to make. The best advice I can give is to do research, visit campuses, talk to students, and follow your heart. If you end up hating it, just transfer.

I'll close this out by saying thanks to the many people who've helped me complete this thing. Thanks to Julian, Sasha, Guy, Jacob, Matt, and Carey. Special thanks to Rich for driving around with me and finding out the hours of all the local restaurants who refuse to answer questions over the phone. Thanks to Rosh and Anthony for your advice and comments on all those clubs I've never been to. Thanks to Mike for your knowledge about all the bars and for being a cool enough roommate to let me sit at my computer and write this thing for four weeks, even though I know my chair blocks your view of the TV. And of course, thanks to my parents and all of my family for their never-ending love, support, advice, and friendship. Please send money.

Michael Hondorp—University of Michigan

Michael Hondorp currently resides in New York City. Among his many aspirations, he hopes to be involved in higher education administration. He is currently pursuing a role on the Broadway stage. He thanks his friends, his family, and, of course, the University of Michigan for providing him with the experience and education of a lifetime.

Amy Palmer—University of Minnesota

Phew! I am forever done with undergraduate work! This makes me feel old, wise, and full of parting wisdom—so I feel that I have to tell you everything I have learned. This tends to make me sound like a mother or older sister, sorry 'bout that! However, I am so happy to be done and have received my Bachelor of Arts in history and English, that I have nothing but good thoughts about the University of Minnesota-Twin Cities. I hope you all feel that way when you get done with your career here. I am glad to have had the opportunity to write this guidebook. It gave me a chance to learn more about the school I have been a part of for five years, and it also gave me a chance to reflect on all the great parts of going to college. I hope to be able to continue freelance writing and editing and not starve in the process.

I would like to thank my parents, sister, and brothers for all their love and support. I would also like to thank Liana Schmidt, Cindy Coelho, Jeni Skar, Jordana Mollick, Kristin Drecktrah, Nadia Hasan, Jennifer Rude, Jan Zahner, and Julie Cohen for being a great support system. Also, thanks to Elayna Carlson, Patty McPherson, and Kelly Anding for helping me think of famous people from Minnesota and Minnesotan slang—without you I would not have been able to think of as many as I did.

Ricki N. Renick—University of Mississippi

When I first got to Ole Miss, my first roommate was nuts, I had no friends to speak of, and all I could think about was going home, and how much I missed my friends. I thought I had made the biggest mistake of my entire life. The first year went by, and I found that I had a ton of friends and had begun to love Mississippi. But, since I was going into engineering, I thought that I should go somewhere that was more reputable, and I left Ole Miss and went to NC State. I got there and immediately loved the city, but the classes all had over 200 students in them. My teachers didn't know me, and when I had a question, I was too intimidated by them and their snippety ways to ask anything. I realized that engineering was not what I was meant to do. I was meant to be a writer; it was what I truly loved.

Back I went to Mississippi. None of my friends knew I was coming back, and I had decided not to go back to my Greek organization. I thought that I should find new friends outside of the Greek community. I went back and was meeting new people left and right once again. My classes were amazing, the journalism school embraced me, and I was getting involved in many facets of the student media. I was having a great time. One warm fall night, during the first semester I was back, I went out to a concert in the Grove with some friends, when all of a sudden I was tackled to the ground by an enormous hug from one of my former sorority sisters whom I hadn't seen in about a year. She was elated to see me, and begged me to come to lunch with her the next day at the sorority house. I agreed, but I was a little skeptical because I didn't want to be sucked back in. I went the next day to the house and sat down to have lunch, and a bunch of new members who had been initiated when I was gone came and sat down. They said, "Someone told us you were Ricki, and we just wanted to meet you because we have heard so many stories about you." At that moment, I knew that as long as I was at Ole Miss I would never leave it behind again.

Jason A. Rosenbaum—University of Missouri

Jason Rosenbaum was born in Chicago, IL on June 25, 1984—Jesus' half-birthday. Both of his parents went to the University of Missouri, but they somehow ended up settling in the not-so-mean streets of Chicago's northwest suburbs. During his tenure in Chicago's much-acclaimed suburban school system, he began to develop his writing abilities by scribbling out epic stories in his spare time. That led to a string of well-received Simpson's fan scripts, such as "Smile of the Last Mouth," "The Homerchurian Candidate," and possibly his most engaging piece of writing at the time, "The Progression Device." Jason also wrote a screenplay, Reason, and entered it in the Project Greenlight Internet competition—it did not make it past the first round. Currently, Jason is working on a novel that he hopes will find a home on America's bookshelves.

Jason gained subtle notoriety working for his high school and college newspapers. During his first semester at Mizzou, Jason wrote dozens of articles for the Maneater, including restaurant reviews, national, local, and feature stories, and perhaps the most exciting account of MU's Faculty Council meetings ever. During his second semester, he transformed himself into a once-weekly columnist, leading the charge against leftist piddle paddle. His work has been republished in publications as exotic as Oregon State's Daily Barometer to locales as drab as PBS's Washington Week Web site. When not writing, Jason enjoys running around Stankowski Field in his trademark Nike headband, going through the arduous grind of pledgeship for his future fraternity, Alpha Epsilon Pi, and attempting to grab his Bachelor's degree in journalism.

Shanda Aguirre—University of Montana

This May I will be a proud second-generation graduate from the University of Montana. Even though I took two brief intermissions to try other colleges on for size, I came back here to finish. I am convinced that the first time I went here they placed a magnet in my body that keeps pulling me back to Missoula.

I confess that I am probably one of the three people on this campus that does not own a Griz sweatshirt, but I plan on buying one for graduation. I am proud to be a Griz, and I will show it off.

Although I have attended UM for a total of 2 ½ years, I learned so much about the University by doing this book. I work on campus, I go to school on campus, and now I write about the campus. I have been consumed by the University of Montana. It's not so bad except for the recurring dream I've been having about the statue of the grizzly bear on campus coming alive and chasing me around campus trying to eat me. Thank the universe that it was only a dream!

Aaron Eske—University of Nebraska

It's hard to believe, but after three years and five majors I'll be entering my senior year at UNL. Today I'm an advertising major, but I have no idea what or where I'll be tomorrow. Whatever I do in the future, I hope it involves writing and a concoction of the real-life skills I picked up at the University. As for now, I'm learning how to play the guitar, managing a legislature campaign, and visiting my friends and family every chance I get.

And now for my long-winded Oscar speech. I'm very grateful to College Prowler for the opportunity to say, "I wrote the book on the University of Nebraska." I'd also like to thank my parents for cheering me on since before I could even remember, every person who ever taught me to love sentences, especially my Morrie, Gerry Shapiro, the supremely fabulous Stacy James, Lisa Lyons, who though she won't agree, is to UNL what superglue is to a model car, Annie Magnusson, Joan Kunzman, Kelley Winter, and Marsha Fortney for making it so easy to love my job, Camilo, Ian, and Adam-Cather 12 and The Omaha Mining Company forever, Erica and Caitlin for the longest, loveliest friendships of my life, Troy and Jill for consulting me on Lincoln nightlife because I'm only 20, and all my other amazing friends who are the reason I get tingles even on my ankles whenever I think about how much I've loved my time at Nebraska—Marie Joelle, Jon, Jonn, John, Jonathan B, Emily C, Emily H, Emily H2, Nick, Brittany, Joey, Jesse, Jaron, Eric, Steve, Jeannine, Catherine, Kelsey, Maggie, Sarah H, Carrie J, AJ, Melissa, Val2000, Elaination, Jill G, Katie W, Megan W, and Anna Dom. Cue the orchestra, I think I'm done.

Jeff Lewis—University of New Hampshire

My name is Jeff Lewis, and although I wish to bring peace to the world, I realize that I'm probably best off settling for just having a good time and enjoying the rest of my college career at UNH.

I was born and raised in Holderness, NH near Plymouth State College. Before you ask, I didn't go to Plymouth State College because, honestly, that is just a little too close to home. I thought UNH would be a better fit because of its size and variety of courses. I am currently pursing a major in journalism.

I particularly enjoyed writing this guidebook because I believe students should know the truth about the schools they are looking at. I believe UNH has a lot to offer to students who are not sure what direction they want to go in life. In parting, live life to the fullest and never stop exploring.

Adrianna Hopkins—University of North Carolina

It has been really fun to look over my past two years at UNC and review what I had been through and the opportunities I have yet to face. I'm a junior at UNC-Chapel Hill with a major in electronic communications (broadcast journalism) and a minor in Spanish. I'm considering another major in political science, sociology, or African American studies. I've done a lot of traveling to different universities for leadership programs, internship opportunities, and summer classes. I must say that UNC-CH is by far the most interesting, diverse, and friendly university I have visited. Of course I had to adjust to the school, just like everyone else. I've always had a room to myself, so living with a roommate was something new to me. High school academics were a breeze, but in college, I actually have to study days in advance for a test. It's weird to see TAs teaching you when they're literally only a couple of years older than you. But, UNC has such a nice and friendly atmosphere that the transition from home to college wasn't too terrible. I love UNC. And I'm so glad that I made the choice to attend this school. I hope this book gives you an inside look into and a heads-up about UNC.

I'd like thank my mom, "Moshie," and my father for supporting me in all my endeavors and for their unconditional love; my brother, "my heart," for making me laugh; my extended family for supporting me; my close friends at UNC-CH and my friends from Kansas for always having my back! Much thanks to everyone at College Prowler for giving me this opportunity. Last, but definitely not least, thanks to God.

Brook Taylor—University of North Carolina – Greensboro

As an English major and aspiring novelist, it has been a dream come true to take on a project as big as this before graduation. I want to thank Brian Crocker for inspiring me to write and Chris Lowrance for giving me my start when I was just a scared little freshman. Most importantly, the bulk of my gratitude goes to my parents for everything and my amazing partner Kat for her unwavering love and support in all aspects of my life but especially when it comes to keeping me sane. Also, I wouldn't feel right if I didn't thank Starbucks for their white chocolate mochas, which fueled the writing of this book.

Anikka M. Ayala—University of Notre Dame

Whenever I tell people that I'm studying to become a writer, their jaw drops and they give me a look of pity as though I were already a starving artist. Well, I don't know if I'm on my way to becoming a starving artist, but I do know that deciding to write is the best decision that I have ever made. I would like to sincerely thank everyone at College Prowler for giving me the opportunity to do what I love to do; it has meant the world to me. And I'd like to thank my parents, my little brother, Roli, my grandparents, all my extended family, my best friend Jeni, and last, but not least, Chuy for all their love and support.

I am currently a senior working toward an English and graphic design double major at the University of Notre Dame. If my four years have taught me anything, it is that choosing a college is one of the most important decisions a person will ever make. I have felt nothing but satisfaction with my choice, and I hope every student who pursues a higher education will feel the same way. I sincerely hope that you enjoyed reading this book and that it served as a helpful tool in your college search.

Andrea Chadderdon—University of Oklahoma

Andrea Chadderdon is an English writing major at the University of Oklahoma. When she is not reading books or traveling about the world, she is usually tuned into TLC watching one of their "personal stories." Currently, Andrea has no plans for after graduation, but assumes that she will do something with her life.

Jesse Thomas—University of Oregon

I really enjoyed the time I spent writing this book. This is the first time I have authored a text outside of my reporting experience. Through I've been reporting for more than five years, I still learned more about my writing capabilities through this experience and hope to continue to grow as a writer. I'm a senior at the University of Oregon majoring in news (editorial and electronic media), with a minor in business administration. I hope one day to be working for ESPN or working in the big time, as sports is my ultimate love. One thing is for sure—my years at the UO have been some of the best years of my life. College has taught me so much regarding how to grow as a person and mature through countless experiences. I wish you the best in all you do and your future endeavors, and I hope this book has better prepared you for your days at the UO (along with providing a little entertainment).

I must finish by giving thanks to all of those who have always been there for support, and helped me to believe there is nothing I can't accomplish. First and foremost, I'd like to thank God and give thanks to Mom, Dad, Ryan, Chris, PJ, Colin, Ty, Stephanie, Christie, Debbie Price, Danielle Wallace, Valerie Stilwell, Debbie Estes, Christie Kasubuchi, Lonnie Wells, Kylee, Janet Owens, Jay, Lauren, and everyone at College Prowler.

Jennifer Klein—University of Pennsylvania

I hope you enjoyed reading this College Prowler guidebook! Writing this book was a great way to gain valuable experience and to learn more about my school. Currently, I am a junior at Penn working towards a major in visual studies, a new interdisciplinary major that combines psychology, art history, fine arts, and other subjects to create a hodgepodge of a major which is perfect for me. Outside of class, I serve as the design editor for *34th Street*, the arts and entertainment magazine of the school newspaper, the *Daily Pennsylvanian*.

I can not say what lies ahead for me beyond my days as a student, but I know that wherever I end up, my experience at Penn will have been an integral part of getting me there. Hopefully, after reading this book, you feel that you are a step closer to entering your years as a college student. If you do, my goal has been achieved.

I would like to thank all the people who helped me create a book that reflects the opinions of students at Penn, not just my own. These very special people are none other than Kristen Ryan, Mike Lonegan, Rachel Firsch, Maggie Hennefeld, Michael Gertner, Dave Tompkins, Melanie Heckman, Scott Greenwald, Sandra Wang and Mary Boise. Thanks also to those who convinced me to try to write a book and helped make it a reality, including Mom, Dad, Nicky, Andrew, Jocelyn Nelson, Hazel Rushin, Kaitlin Chabina, and everyone at College Prowler.

Jamie Cruttenden and Tim Williams—University of Pittsburgh

Jamie—Writing this book was quite an experience! I came to College Prowler just going into my senior year and got to experience the blooming of the company almost right from the start. Now that I'm a "super senior"—aka a fifth-year senior soon to graduate—I am so blessed to have had the opportunity to write for such a great company. This book was tons of fun to write, and I hope that you enjoy reading it as much as I enjoyed writing it. If this book helps you in the least, even if you decide that Pitt isn't for you, then I have done my job as a writer in conveying information to help you make an educated decision about college. I believe that college is the best four (or five or six) years of your life, and hopefully our guidebooks help you to gather enough information to ensure that you feel the same way when your college graduation creeps up on you! I would just like to say thank you to the staff at College Prowler for giving me the opportunity to write for a company that I am proud to belong to. For all your support, encouragement, and faith in me, I cannot say thank you enough.

Tim—Though I'm originally from Penn State's backyard, I've called Pittsburgh home since my freshman year of college. For most of that time, I've been working with College Prowler in some capacity and couldn't be more thrilled to co-author the book for my own school. There's so much to do in Pittsburgh that I didn't discover until my second semester, or later, and after only my first year, I realize how important it is to have a definitive campus guide. Don't stop here, though—if you're moving to Pittsburgh, it's a great idea to check online and watch publications such as the City Paper for cultural events and community happenings. There's a lot more going on than you'd expect at first glance. When I'm not helping out with the guidebook series, I can be found at Pitt as a poetry writing major, in city parks sitting under trees, or around Squirrel Hill as a general miscreant. If you liked this book, be sure to check out the PSU guide—just don't tell anyone I recommended it!

Russell Knight—University of Puget Sound

Russell Knight came to the University of Puget Sound from Northern California. At UPS, he served as the business and advertising manager for the *Trail*, Puget Sound's student newspaper, was the student coordinator for the University's outdoor program, and gave tours to prospective students. During his junior year, Russell participated in a study abroad program in Dublin, Ireland where he worked as a research aid for the Parliament of Ireland.

Jessica Pritz—University of Rhode Island

Writing this guidebook was my first real step in becoming a writer. It was a great experience, and I had a lot of fun with it. I have had two other essays published in the past. I have always loved to write, and I hope to make a career out of it. Right now I'm in my fourth year at URI. Yes, it'll take me five years to graduate and I am in no rush to leave behind my college experience. I have decided to study journalism and I'm focusing on print and feature writing. I have no idea what lies in store for me as a journalist, just as long as I get to write and make some money doing it. I would love to find work in Rhode Island after I graduate. I would not want to have to return back to my hometown of Orange, Connecticut and move back in with my dad, (no offense dad). Anyway, I hope that you were able to learn something that you didn't otherwise know about URI.

Peter K. Hansen—University of Richmond

I had fun working on this book and look forward to publishing more in the future. I want to thank the folks at College Prowler for this opportunity and say that I feel bad because I enjoyed writing this so much that it hardly seemed like work. I graduated from UR with a major in journalism and minors in philosophy and sociology. I'm originally from Pennsylvania (go Eagles), but I currently reside in Honolulu, Hawaii, and couldn't be happier.

But, enough about me; I also want to thank several people for their help and support, especially Laz, Elo, Swilson, Jon E. Madden, Gerald Holden, VinBeth, The Paper Moon, Shadow, the BVC, the inspirational music of Jefferson Starship as well as everyone in my family—Mom & Dad, Krista, Grandmom, Steve, Ann and Chuck and everyone else I didn't mention. Mahola!

Kerri Linden—University of Rochester

When I found out about this writing opportunity from College Prowler through being on staff at UR's campus newspaper, which not to mention has opened endless doors for me, I immediately saw it as a good chance to expand my horizons and help out with a cool project. It turned into quite a project, but worth it in the end. It certainly helped me on the path to a hopeful future in writing and publishing. I'm currently a junior at the University of Rochester focusing on English and psychology and minoring in journalism, with my eye on magazine editorial for a future career. I come from about six hours southeast of Rochester, a small town in suburban Connecticut, and my years so far at UR have been rewarding and exciting to say the least. After my junior spring semester abroad in England, I hope to return to campus and fill out a last year with the remainder of my classes and some fun memories. I wrote this also in the hopes of giving some accurate views of what UR is like, and what it has to offer.

There are some people I'd like to thank, without which this book process would have been a lot more difficult. First, Emily Carpenter

at the Career Center and Helene Snihur at PR, you both were invaluable help; thanks so much. Thanks to friends who helped out with the surveys, even those who didn't know what they were getting themselves into. Thanks to people at the CT for being great—Cathy, Alissa, Colin, and everyone. Thanks to Mom and Dad for supporting me in this from the start, and thanks to College Prowler for giving me this opportunity, it's been an experience.

James Leonard—University of San Diego

San Diego has been paradise to me since I arrived here as a wide-eyed freshman many-a-moon ago. The pleasure of living in San Diego, from the environment around the beach, to the electricity of downtown, to the food (mostly the Mexican food) has hovered around me wherever I have traveled since leaving school. In Europe I missed the Carne Asada. On the East Coast I missed the Pacific. In Northern California I missed the pace and friendliness. It has been, and still is, a privilege to live in such a great town, and amidst such remarkable people, especially in this exciting period of time in the history of San Diego. If I could be born again, I'd like to be born a local. I hope this book helps you along the way to feeling the same.

I would like to thank, of course, my mother and father for funding my raucous and roller coaster college education. My wonderful girlfriend Janine Harispe who not only continues to tolerate me, but also kept me happily in burritos and board shorts while I worked on this book. All my friends who made life in San Diego what it is: Austin, Berger, the Berkeley's, Jim Black, Brandi, Brenna, Bucket, Chez Nogales, Chilton, Coach, Compton, Chuck Wood, Dixon, the Dolios, Ed, Fones, the Freeburg's, Fritz, Hurley, JB, Joe D, Juggy, Kate, Kevin, Larkin, Lerma, Leigh, the McDonough's, Moore, Nisonger, Oid, Pell, Swartz, Wu, Weasel, and the rest of the Desert, and a special thanks to my gracious third-senior-year landlords Angie, Jessica and Courtney. Also a special thanks to Elizabeth Eichelberger for all her help. I'd also like to pour some out for the Old Ox and Second Wind. You live in my heart forever. I wouldn't be the man I am today without you. Of course, there are hundreds of friends I missed, and please accept my apologies. If you know me at all you certainly helped with the book.

Sara Allshouse—University of San Francisco

I feel like I should open this section with the standard "Sara Allshouse is the author of many short stories and currently lives in San Francisco with her two cats." But I will tell you something more interesting instead, like that I write fiction for fun; I am about to graduate from USF with an English writing major and a politics minor and then go to law school. I watch *Sex and the City* and *The West Wing* religiously, and if it weren't for those shows, I wouldn't have made it through college. More importantly, I want to say I've had the best time writing this book—not only because I'll be published (though the prospect is not too shabby), but also because this opportunity, especially coming at the end of my undergraduate career, feels like a hands-on culmination of everything I've ever learned. Honestly, I've never worked so hard or so long on one thing, so seeing the results of my efforts will be absolutely exhilarating!

So please, read and re-read this book and memorize all of the facts because you're lucky to have them available to you in one place. College Prowler really does provide an insider look that is much more helpful than any book I ever read before going to college. Enjoy, and I do hope you choose USF, because it really does rock!

Jessica Foster—University of South Carolina

I'm really excited to have had the opportunity to inform people about USC. As a second-year print journalism major I take advantage of every chance to get experience writing and improve my skills, and helping to author this book has allowed me to do all of this while having fun at the same time! Born in Missouri, but raised in the Southeast, USC was a natural choice for me, considering that I live within a half-hour drive from campus. Little did I know then how many amazing people I would meet here, how many fun experiences I would have, and how much I would learn. Going to USC has been a great adventure for me thus far, and I hope that this book will help others make the college choice that is right for them, whether that college is USC or not.

I would like to give a quick thanks to some important people who have provided me with so much love and support. Thank you Mom, Dad, Lori, Michelle, Donna, Steve, Fred, Cotter's, Aunt Carmen, Luke, the many teachers who have inspired me along the way to work hard to achieve my goals, and the people at College Prowler for making this all possible.

Kerry Hacecky—University of South Dakota

You've made it to end, and if nothing else, I hope you have a better understanding of what it means to be a Coyote. At USD, I have a double-emphasis major in journalism and public relations and a minor in English. Looking back, I know I wouldn't have had half the opportunities I've been given without the education, experience, and help I've received here on campus and from a number of people around the state.

At USD, I've been active at our school newspaper, The Volante, the National Society of Collegiate Scholars, our TV station (KYOT), and in the University admissions office. Off campus, I've had fantastic work opportunities at the Sioux Falls Argus Leader, Mitchell Daily Republic, South Dakota Magazine, South Dakota Public Broadcast radio station, and Artz Photographic. Besides newspapers and magazines, this is my first, and hopefully not last, published work. In the future, I hope to utilize all the experience and education I've earned to continue my writing and contribute to eventual expertise in media relations. Being a student at USD has brought me a colorful arrangement of both maturity and education. From the laughs and lessons I've learned on Friday nights to the algebra and biology I struggled through, I'll graduate knowing I was successful in my undergraduate years. I hope this book has provided answers to the questions you've always wanted to know.

Throughout my entire life and especially since the beginning of writing this book, I've had many people behind me, supporting my efforts to succeed. In addition, I've had many in life who have been considerate enough to understand that my time, between the book, school, work, NSCS and The Volante, is scarce. Here's an overdue shout out to those that have supported all my efforts: Thank you Mom, Dad, Jess, Amanda, Dana, Barbara, Jenny, and everyone on The Volante, Meghan, Austin, Beth, Jan Hilderbrand, Jean and Les, Laura, Abby, Marissa, Adam, the Hacecky clan, Omid and everyone at College Prowler.

Whitney Meers—University of South Florida

I hope that all of the weekend nights I have sacrificed to work on this guidebook will help you in your mission to find the college that is right for you. If you decide to attend USF (and I hope that you do), you can find me riding around campus on my skateboard, working in the newsroom at the Oracle, or taking the night off to party with my friends in Ybor City. I plan to graduate from USF with BA degrees in anthropology and mass communications. After graduation, I hope to take some time to travel the world before I come back to Tampa to pursue a PhD in anthropology.

I encourage readers to remember that life isn't all about test scores and grade point averages. Have fun in college, but be responsible and don't get carried away. I'd like to give many thanks to my family, which extends far beyond those who I am related to by blood. A special thank you goes to Mom, Dad, John, Julie, and Janalise, because without you guys I would be nothing. Thanks to all of my

homies who helped me keep my sanity by religiously meeting me at the Park and Ride Ledges at 9 p.m. on weeknights to skate the box, especially Keith. Many thanks go to Todd for the summertime coastal outings and for being my best friend of eight years. Thanks to Robin Jones, Dr. Joe Callon, and Dr. Jonathan Gayles for being such outstanding role models; I hope to make you proud someday. Finally, thanks to all of my friends around the world who have helped shape me into the person I am today. Much love to all of you.

Alex Valhouli—University of Southern California

I grew up in New England, raised on the premise that the world is a classroom. My parents were both teachers; we lived a year in Barcelona and a year in New York City. When I graduated from high school, I knew that it was time for me to go west. USC was my first choice.

This would not have come together without the support of my family. Mom and Jamie, Robert and Colin, I love you all. Thank you Poppy for the Sunday afternoon talks, and Gagi for the background support. Thank you to my friends and family at USC, from the Sig's on 28th Street to my neighbors at Cardinal Gardens. More specifically, thank you Poff, Bennett, Kevin, Chase, A-Rod, McCullough, Delaney, Drew, Joey, Ian, Johnny, Rex, Blake, Wade, Harlye, Annie, Monica, Caitlin, Jen, and Bernadette for keeping me motivated. Thank you, room 207, for making it absolutely impossible for me to be productive. Thank you Julia Colyar for being my favorite teacher at USC. Thank you Dan and Robin for your guidance. Thank you Dad and Rex and Andre for everything else.

Jacob W. Williams—University of Tennessee

As a lifetime resident of East Tennessee, and a fifth-year senior at the University of Tennessee, I have spent a lifetime absorbing the culture here. I have been fortunate enough to experience other cities and colleges in small enough doses to make me realize how great I have had it in Knoxville all along. While I have given many a high school senior advice about pursuing further education, College Prowler has allowed me to reach a broader audience to share my experience and knowledge.

I currently plan to graduate with a BA in economics as well as a business minor in December. I feel that UT has started to prepare me for my ultimate career aspiration of becoming an entrepreneur. I believe that the lessons I have learned outside of the classroom are equally as valuable as textbooks and professors. Among my greatest memories are the beautiful, autumn game days I spent cheering on the Volunteers, the practical jokes I am still laughing about that I played on my fraternity brothers, and the night I spent throwing homecoming float pomps at the wonderful girl who would soon after become the love of my life.

I hope that the knowledge I have shared with you will prove advantageous as you embark on your college career. It was with purpose that I included carefully-selected excerpts of student insight. Mere statistical information and college brochures alone do not truly reflect the environment you are about to enter, and you have made a wise choice by choosing College Prowler. My goal throughout my section of this book was to answer the questions that take others a semester, or in some cases years as a student, to learn.

Erin Hall—University of Texas

Writing this book was one of the most fun things I have ever undertaken. I never thought of myself as a writer, per se, but I did know that I knew more than most people about the University of Texas. If I could make a career out of being a UT student, I definitely would, because my time here has unquestionably been the best years of my life. I grew up in the Woodlands, Texas, graduated from Woodlands High School, and I came to UT. I completed my Bachelor of Science in radio-television-film, then finished my Bachelor of Science in communication studies with an emphasis in human relations. I also completed a business foundations minor and a concentration in psychology. While at Texas, I was a member of Pi Beta Phi sorority, and I enjoyed volunteering at the Children's Hospital of Austin among other projects. I am currently still living in Austin, and I'm not in a hurry to leave.

Now that I am finished with this book, it is back to the job search, so if anyone wants to hire me, feel free to do that, as I am available. I would like to thank the people who helped me with this book: Meredith, Courtney, Mom, Kyle—thanks for always answering my questions, Rhodes, Drew, Lindsay S., Jordan, Dustin, Cameron, Alex, Focker, Tim Grahh, Tay Tay, Robert, Gavin, Michelle, Marisa, Mark, Michael Paul, Liberty, all of the Pike boys—I love y'all. Special thanks to Trey and Callaway for letting me constantly bother them, and the biggest thanks to Lindsay Hale, my personal editor, for her amazing help on this book. I couldn't have done it without you.

I would like to dedicate this book to a friend whom we lost too soon. She should have been here at UT enjoying these years with me and everyone else who loved her. This book is dedicated to Meghan Manning 2/2/80 – 5/6/97. I'm sure she's doing a "Hook 'em Horns" up in Heaven.

Jared Whitley—University of Utah

A prolific writer, Jared Whitley's written work has appeared in a variety of on-campus publications, including the *Bottom Line*, the *Century*, and *Shades*, the U's undergraduate literary magazine, which published Jared's one-act play *Parthos Bound*. Jared wrote for the *Daily Utah Chronicle*, the U's daily student-run newspaper, for three years, first as a science writer, then the news editor, and finally a feature columnist. Jared's honors thesis for his English degree was a creative non-fiction piece called, "Whitticisms: Mormon Gadfly on the Chrony Wall", which included 15 of his *Chrony* columns—six of which have won awards from the Society for Professional Journalists. To this day, Jared still gets praise, and hateful glares, for his most famous column, "Mormon Princesses and the Men Who (Try to) Love Them."

Outside of campus publications, Jared wrote for *Broker Agent Magazine* for a year, and his written work has also appeared in the Salt Lake daily newspaper, the *Deseret News*.

At the University of Utah, Jared also spent a year as press secretary for the Associated Students of the University of Utah, during which time he started the newsletter "The Crimson Times" and created a pamphlet on student services, "What does ASUU do for me?"

Jared graduated with degrees in English and German and minors in business and chemistry. His honors thesis for his German degree, "The Choice of Luthien as a Model for Medieval Christianity's Relationship with Paganism" is a research paper on J.R.R. Tolkien's *The Lord of the Rings*. Jared's career aspirations include becoming a game designer for Wizards of the Coast, a syndicated columnist, or the ambassador to Portugal.

Kevin Jonas Lenfest—University of Vermont

The University of Vermont has thus far lent me an extraordinary experience. Initially, I wanted to attend a small liberal-arts college, but after coming to UVM and settling in, I eventually found myself beyond happiness, despite its large size. For me, everything really started coming together during my sophomore year when I was more familiar with what the school and professors had to offer. I got to take more classes that I really wanted, and my real friendships were solidified. UVM rekindled my love of academics, and I am now looking forward to a possible future in the scholarly circle.

Writing this guidebook has been both a pleasure and an honor. I am currently entering my junior year at the University of Vermont,

pursuing a double major in English and religion with a focus on philosophy. As a native Vermonter, I have come to appreciate UVM for the same reasons I love Vermont: its beautiful surroundings and endless opportunities and activities for those who cannot get enough of the outdoors. Cycling throughout the green mountains and skiing during the winters have both given me unique perspectives on this picturesque state. The University of Vermont has been an invaluable transitioning step toward achieving my goal of competing in cycling, as well as a working force in opening the doors to further study in graduate school. Whatever I end up doing, I know I will be passionate about it, as passion supercedes all other priorities and, in my opinion, provides the building blocks to happiness.

If given the choice, I would not wish to go any other place. Looking back on the people I've met and the opportunities I've seized, the classes I've had, and the places I've gone, I cannot see it any other way. The more I learned, the more I grew. I have changed in many different ways since high school, all for the better, and I credit much of this to the friends I've made and my personal experience with education, experience, and life. I will never turn back.

Miriam Nicklin—University of Virginia

Having just graduated from the University of Virginia this past May with a BA in English, it has been a pleasure for me to reflect on my college experience as a whole and share that with you in this book. I know much of it, in fact most of it, is incredibly subjective, but perhaps that is the best way for you to truly get a taste of any place. So, in this book I give you my (as well as many other students') very personal experiences at UVA—by all means take them in and learn from them. And now as I close these words and the final chapters of my college career, I am sad and excited. I take with me my writing and my thriving memories of Virginia and wish that you, potential students of UVA, will come to love this place as much as I have. I thank everyone and everything that went into making this book possible.

Katie Shaw—University of Washington

Thanks to this book, I now know more than I ever wanted to know about UW, but I'm not sick of it yet. I'm a junior at UW, and I've loved every second of my college life. I dread going out into the real world, armed only with an English degree and a healthy dose of naiveté about how far it will get me. I grew up in a white-picket-fence area of Seattle with a king of comedy for a dad, an impassioned poet for a mom, and three best friends, all younger and more athletic than me, for siblings. As a senior in high school, I didn't want to go to UW, but I couldn't be happier that I got stuck here.

I hope this book helped you out a little, whether you're in the decision-making process or you're set on being a Husky. Many thanks to Madre, Padre, Lo, Mads, and Hoey, the rest of my family, all my friends at UW (especially my weirdo roommates), all my friends outside of UW, and lastly, College Prowler!

Nicole Rosario—University of Wisconsin

Writing this book was one of the best experiences I've ever had. Being able to dedicate so much time and writing into a topic I care about is really rewarding. I am currently a senior at the University of Wisconsin, majoring in creative writing and philosophy. While both areas are challenging, I feel they really tie into and complement one another. The classes for both fields are amazing, as well. I am a native Minnesotan, so Madison isn't really that far from home for me. Even so, the distance has helped me to grow and mature. I truly hope this book offers you an insight to my school.

I would like to take a moment to thank a few people who helped me with this amazing project. Thank you Mommy, Papi, Jade, Bobby, Robert, Eric, Adam, the Blanchards, and everyone at College Prowler!

Jeffrey Keenan—University of Wisconsin – Stout

From the day I moved into the dorms my freshman year at Stout I was employed by Stout Adventures. It is there where I learned about, gained experience and discovered my passion for outdoor recreation. I now am happily employed at the University of California-Riverside, managing their outdoor recreation program.

I will always treasure my time at Stout. From the day I toured campus when I was a high school student I have felt connected to the place I called home for four and half years. Stout provided me with opportunities, challenges and experiences in and out of the classroom that have shaped me into the person I am today. During my time at Stout I made several close friendships which will last a lifetime. It is people at Stout that make it an outstanding place to live and learn.

I hope this book has helped you gain a better understanding of UW-Stout. Hopefully this book will make it easier for you to make college decision. I believe Stout to be one of the best-kept-secrets in higher education. Stout is not the right fit for everyone; however it is an excellent choice for students that are career focused and who know what they want.

I would like to take a moment to recognize the many people that have helped be become the person I am today. First, and most importantly, I would like to thank my Mom & Dad for their never ending support, challenges, encouragement and love. Second, I would like to thank all the students who took time out of their day to complete my long survey. A very special thanks goes out to my dear friends Alicia, Matthew and Eric for their support and friendship throughout the years. Thanks to College Prowler for giving me this wonderful and unique opportunity.

Marek Biernacinski and Melissa Rothermel—UNLV

Marek Biernacinski and Melissa Rothermel met in their News Editing class. They share a passion for writing, with Biernacinski majoring in communications and Rothermel majoring in journalism and media studies. Both focused on print journalism with an outside area of interest in English. Both getting their start in journalism as staff writers at UNLV's student newspaper, The Rebel Yell, Biernacinski has worked as a full-time reporter in Las Vegas, and Rothermel is the managing editor of *The Rebel Yell*.

Biernacinski started his own Internet-based editing business, which has already seen much success. In addition to his experience as an editor and a journalist, he is a realtor knowledgeable on the Las Vegas market. Born in Warsaw, Poland, and bilingual, Biernacinski hopes to freelance for an English-language publication based out of Poland.

In addition to Rothermel's work at The Rebel Yell, where one of her articles was printed in the New York Times' College Online Edition, she works part-time in the public relations department of a Henderson-based marketing company and has freelanced for a local business publication. She is a founding member of UNLV's Student Chapter of the Society of Professional Journalists. A native Las Vegan, Rothermel plans to stay in Las Vegas after graduation.

Bart Brooks—Ursinus College

Writing this book has taken a lot of time out of my summer schedule, but it will most definitely be worth it when I have 500 copies of it in my room autographed and ready to go out to my faithful reader(s). All kidding aside, writing this book has been a learning experience for me. Writing travel guidebooks has been one of the more fanciful ideas of what I wanted to do with my life, and, well, writing a college guidebook is not that different. This has given me the insight of what goes into it and the rewards that come from putting so much effort into a book.

If I've learned nothing else in life, I've learned that putting more of myself into a project only means that the reward is far greater when it is finished. But I didn't do this alone, so I want to thank, first and foremost, my parents for their support over the years. A parent can be a college student's greatest resource. I'm also thankful to my family for being there for me. I would also like to thank my "home" friends Scott, Mishiloh, Jess, and Andy for their understanding while I shut myself off from the world writing this book. I would like to thank my Ursinus friends Stevie, Jeff, Jaynine, the Phi Kaps, and everyone else who has been there for me.

It would be a shame if I did not mention Sally Widman to whom I am forever indebted. She was my contact, my sanity, and my fact-checker (still, let it be known that any mistakes made are mine and no fault of hers). Lastly, I would like to thank Omid Gohari. He is the one who contacted and interviewed me for the job and provided help along the way, and without him I would not be writing this book.

See, Mom and Dad—I don't have to be a starving artist after all. I may not be able to afford your dream house in Florida just yet, but this is a nice start. Thank you for your love and patience. It means more than you'll ever realize.

Matthew Stevens—Valparaiso University

As an aspiring writer, I jumped at the chance to write this guidebook. But I wanted to write it for a reason bigger than getting experience in publishing—I had a truly awesome experience at VU, and I want to be able to share that with future students! I was an English and sociology major at VU, so everything in this book is still fresh in my mind. As a student who is now part of that "real world" they talk about so much in college, I have to say that Valpo prepared me incredibly well for life after college. I hope to continue to write, and who knows, maybe I can even make a living that way someday! I'd appreciate your comments, and am willing to field your questions.

It's only right to thank those people who've helped me on my way to writing this. Thanks to Mom, Dad, Kristin, and Marty for reading my work and standing behind me. Thanks to Amy, Kelly, and Adam for always being excited when I make small steps toward my future. Also, thanks to John Ruff, Ed Uehling, Edward Byrne, and all my awesome profs at Valpo, as well as Tim Jenkins and all the staff at Valpo who answered my every question. To all of you who responded to my surveys, especially Sage and Chad, two great friends, thank you so much. Thanks to all the folks at College Prowler for giving me this wonderful opportunity. And, saving the best for last, thank you to my wonderful wife, Kimberly, who encouraged, prodded, and provided much editorial assistance in the writing of this book. In her words, "Everyone should go to Valpo!"

Matt Woolsey—Vanderbilt University

This is my first crack at informational writing on any kind of notable scale. Hopefully, I painted an image of the school that was helpful (either in getting you to choose Vandy or in discovering this is not the college for you). A university is not simply the bricks and mortar of the buildings, but rather the life the students breathe into them. I wish that before attending, I had been able to learn from a Vandy student for a few hours—my motivation to assemble this guide.

Enough about the school! I'm originally from the San Francisco Bay Area and am really happy with my second home in Nashville. I am a double-major in literature and philosophy, with honors in arts and sciences and the department of English (both fingers crossed). For the last two years I've been on the Vanderbilt water polo team, though, after being replaced by a freshman, I'm now part of the Vanderbilt Triathlon Club. Starting in the fall, I'll be acting as the chief editor of the Lifestyles section of Vanderbilt's student newspaper, the *Vanderbilt Hustler* (named in honor of our robber baron founder).

To prevent this from becoming a resume, I'd like to thank some members of the band (so to speak): Julie Jacobs, Katie Irish, Eugene Montoya, Josh Gess, Josh Cooper, Keeley Valentino, Jennifer Montesi, Justin Elliott, Darian Duckworth, and Jeremy Sowers.

Rachel Falcone—Vassar College

You're the kind of girl who hides out in a sunny corner of the library to write her papers. The kind who will pass up almost anything for a good conversation, and who can often be found asleep on a couch with a book that's just about to fall off her lap. You're ambitious, shy, sensitive and honest. You're a varsity rower, and yes, you have some pretty impressive muscles. You're entering your third year at Vassar, a year that you will spend in London to continue to study philosophy at a university there for your junior year abroad. You're about as ready as a fish out of water to jump into the cold water of a new city. But you're also scared in the way that fear rises out of a greater, ineffable anxiety, scared of leaving the place that you just wrote an entire book about, and more notably, of leaving behind the self who lives there.

You'd like to thank several individuals. The list includes: your parents, Grace (Vassar Class of '72) and Phil, who have sacrificed the better part of their lives to raise you with so much love in a quiet suburb in New Jersey, and have never ceased to challenge you emotionally and intellectually, your brother Josh, for his wonderful humor and patience, your childhood friends, Marian and Jenny, for still being the three musketeers, your friend Sarah, for her acceptance, strength and not-to-be-matched personality; your roommates, Laura and Lila, who quite more than survived the freshman triple the three of you shared, the Vassar Crew team and coaches Mike and Kelly, for letting you know that there isn't anything more worth getting up for than playing around in boats; your 10 freshman fellowees, a most inspiring, crazy and loving group of hall mates, Liz, Annie and Eliza, for letting you laugh and cry more than you have ever known, Jason Mraz, for his music and poetry, your professors, for showing you how much you do not know, the Youth RNC "Welcoming" Committee, for organizing one of the best youth turnouts for the RNC protests and for beginning your career as a social and political activist, everyone at College Prowler, for actually publishing this, and Vassar, for giving you more than something to write about. All these people and places complete you and show you your holes. You love them in ways that you've tried to figure out for the last 20 years, and hope to continue figuring out for the next 20.

Having completed two years of your ever-inspiring liberal arts education, you have exploded into a thousand birds that you just wish would fly in formation so that you could know where they were going. You'd like to say that you'll be a writer always, but that sounds about as funny as saying that you'll always love words. What is safe to bet on is that you will always be someone, caught in a moment, trying to figure out what exactly to say.

Sean Wright—Villanova University

Writing this book has been a great time, and I have learned a lot. While it was a lot of work it was all rewarding. I hope to continue writing at some level—whether it's for a newspaper or books—well into the future. I am pursuing a double major in political science and economics, and I'm loving it here. I am a northern New Jersey native and have lived here all my life. I really hope that you enjoyed the book, and above all, found it useful in selecting a college. I remember applying to college, and hope this book eases the stress of the application process, touring, and pressure from parents. If you have any questions, comments, or want to know more about Villanova or writing, feel free to e-mail me.

Also, a book would not be a book without a section for dedications. First and foremost, I would like to thank my mom and dad, whose hard work, perseverance, and loving care helped me get to where I am today. Then, of course, there is my brother Kyle, who is the greatest sibling an older brother can ask for. I'd also like to thank Poppy, who has always been a source of guidance and tons of fun and laughs, Uncle Peter and Aunt Lisa, who are like a second set of parents who are always great to have around, and the family that is no longer with us but who have been a great source of inspiration to me. Lastly, I can't forget my friends at Villanova and home who have made my life that much more enjoyable. Without them life would be

very boring. And, of course, to all the people at College Prowler, for allowing me this unique and educational experience!

Carrie Lefler – Virginia Commonwealth University

While writing this book, I realized how great it would have been to have this guide for myself during my college search. I have learned so much about VCU that I didn't know. I had no idea how many student organizations and clubs there were or that there are more than 200 certificate and degree options in the arts, sciences, and humanities programs. Writing this guidebook has given me the opportunity to reflect on the experiences I've had and to get to know the University from all perspectives. Good, bad, or otherwise, I'm glad I chose VCU, and if I had to do it all over again, I would make the same decision.

When Dr. Judy V. Turk, director of the School of Mass Communications, told me about the opportunity to write the VCU guidebook, I immediately jumped at the chance. The idea sounded exciting, but I wasn't sure how I would fit yet another task into my crazy school and work schedule. I'm so glad I decided to write this guidebook and that Dr. Turk was confident enough in my skills to tell me about it. I will always be grateful for her confidence and guidance.

I want to take the rest of this space to thank some people who are a part of my life and my best memories at VCU. First of all, I want to thank my parents for giving me the opportunities and encouragement to succeed, even though they doubted me my first week here when I called to say classes were cancelled because of a hurricane. That's just not something a student can make up! I want to thank my professors, who I may not have always agreed with but who have only the best intentions for students. I want to thank Andrew, who is by far the best person I've ever met at the elevators on a 2 a.m. pizza run! You have kept me sane during my late nights of writing and frustrations with fact finding. To everyone I have made a memory with at VCU, yes all of you, I want to thank you. Whether we're friends, acquaintances, or we only bumped into each other, every memory made is truly special. You guys are my big 30,000-plus VCU family. Finally, thank you College Prowler for this extraordinary opportunity!

Elisabeth Grant—Virginia Tech

I have to admit that I've been very lucky to be able to have opportunities like writing for College Prowler. When I became an English major at Tech, I did so just because I enjoyed writing and reading novels. I really found a direction when I decided to have a concentration in professional writing. I took classes that caught my attention and then was able to participate in internships and organizations that allowed me to actually try out what I was studying.

I've written for Forester's Incorporated, designed and contributed work to *Happenings* (an engineering science and mechanics department publication), and participated as a staff member for two separate literary magazines at Tech (*Silhouette* and the *Brush Mountain Review*). While I've gained a strong academic foundation at Tech, I really feel that a lot of my education has come from doing work for these internships and organizations. I've challenged myself while at Tech and decided to get two degrees: a BA in English and a BS in psychology. As graduation approaches, I'm hoping to get out in the workplace and concentrate on a career in professional writing.

I hope you've enjoyed this guidebook; I had a lot of fun working on it. Let me know what you thought about the book or ask me questions about Tech.

I definitely have a few people I'd like to thank for helping me get where I am today. I'd like to thank my mom, dad, and my brother Jonathan for their constant support and encouragement. Thanks to Dr. Marie Paretti, who taught me how to find my audience and then provided me with opportunities to do so. Thanks to the English Students' Society for all the fun times. I'd also like to thank Justin, Steph, Shannon, Deanna, the lifeguards at McComas and War, and everyone else who's made my time at Tech so much fun. But most of all, thank you College Prowler for such a great opportunity!

Aaron Mass—Wake Forest University

I'm currently a junior at Wake Forest, majoring in both biology and economics, with a minor in chemistry. There's no defined goal as of yet, but I am certainly taking suggestions. Moving to Winston-Salem from New York certainly required a considerable period of adjustment; however, it was more than worthwhile and has definitely broadened my perspective. Your years at college are like no others, in terms of the excessive freedom you gain along with only limited responsibility, and that experience is priceless. I hope that this book has provided some element of insight into how Wake Forest students regard their school and everything that comes with it, and that you'll consider Wake when applying to schools.

Finally, and most importantly, I'd like to recognize everyone who helped me in any way, shape, or form. Thanks Alex, Archie, Brad, Brett, Brian, Bryan, Bubba, Chris, Coach, Donk, Gilligan, Emily, Ethan, Frenchie, Harman, Haser, Katie, Kathleen, Kenny, Kristin, Lindsay, Mojo, Morgan, Paco, Plaza, Riley, Sack, Sean, Squeaks, Tess, TJ, Tyler, Mom and Dad. I'd also like to thank my mentors, Anthony, Chris, Dan, and George for their invaluable advice, PowerBars for providing my exclusive source of sustenance and everyone at College Prowler!

Roxy Todd—Warren Wilson College

Roxy Todd, Warren Wilson graduate of 2005, is author of one rock opera and one novella. She is publisher of microfiction magazine Luxury Villa. She currently works for the Asheville Daily Planet and also as a magician's assistant with the award-winning magician Ricky D. Boone. She is working on her shorter fiction and on the publication of her novella. She also is the creator of Hamster World cartoons, which are inspired by her favorite pets, Gertude Stein and Alice B, and she is a great supporter of hamsters in need all over the world. She plans on spending the next year of her life teaching English in Germany and eventually going to graduate school to receive her MFA in writing.

Dylan Jesse—Washington & Jefferson College

As a very frustrated English and Philosophy double major, I often wonder why I have stuck with W&J for these past three years. I've had my share of problems with the school, and I have come pretty close to submitting transfer applications to go elsewhere, but for some reason I stuck with my decision to become a W&J graduate. With only one year left before I graduate (or so I'm hoping), I've been piecing together the memories I have and figuring out what it was that kept me going through those weeks of late nights in the computer labs, longer weekends wrestling with philosophy texts, and literature finals that made me doubt my very ability to comprehend the English language. I've had my share of moments shaking my fists angrily at the sky out of sheer frustration, as well as my share of incredible times with friends and professors that I will recall fondly through the remaining course of my life. At this point in my academic career, the best I can figure is that I've survived only because of a subtle love of the challenges. I like to think that I've risen enough to meet most of them.

I can say with absolute certainty that I never intended to become the resident student expert on W&J, and I wonder how it came to this. I must first and foremost extend my most sincere thanks to Dr. Kathleen McEvoy, my English advisor and head of our professional writing program. She has helped give me the skills and confidence necessary to tackle a project like this College Prowler guidebook.

Secondly, I must extend my deepest thanks to caffeine. Without you, none of this would have been possible. And to my bed: I'm sorry I haven't seen as much of you recently as I would like.

If you'll kindly permit me to offer one final piece of advice, I'd like to borrow a line from Milton's epic, Paradise Lost: "The mind is its own place, and in itself can make a Heav'n of Hell a Hell of Heav'n." Though the theological implications are drastically different, I think the line offers this insight to life here at W&J: It is however you really want to view it. You should only expect your time here to be rewarding and enjoyable if you are willing to work toward making it rewarding and enjoyable. I hope this guidebook has helped to give you a good inside perspective of this school, and I wish you the best in your college years to come, wherever it is you end up.

Jeremiah McWilliams—Washington and Lee University

You've read this far and haven't given up? I congratulate you.

Students here care deeply about what the school will look like next year, and 10 years down the road—whether it will stay true to the sense of honor, trust, and community that sets it apart. The majority of this book belongs to this student generation because without them the project would not have been possible. I hope their enthusiasm and honesty brought W&L to life for you, the reader.

Special thanks to Mom and Dad—Tim and Linda McWilliams—for pushing me to finish this project, and also to Mom for her sharp editing eye. Once an English teacher, always an English teacher. Thanks also to Jonny, Joy, and Johannah for being a lot of fun, and to Omid Gohari for being an all-around swell guy who is flexible and understanding.

So, what now? Is there life after writing a college guidebook? Let's hope so. I'm hoping to convert my politics and journalism degrees into a job as a reporter after graduation this year. I hear CBS might need an anchor, some new blood at the news desk. In the meantime, I hope to keep writing for the Trident (W&L's feistiest campus paper) and playing plenty of Halo 2.

I wish you all the best in your search to find the right college, whether that search leads you to Washington and Lee or not. Just remember, there is a place for you, and you will eventually find it. Do your homework and get lots of good advice, and things will work out. Don't hesitate to contact me to chat about W&L.

Dan Carlin—Washington University in St. Louis

Dan Carlin was born to write this guide. Raised just two blocks from Washington University, at age five he began gathering notes and conducting interviews for the College Prowler guide he was certain would one day bear his name.

A recent graduate in political science, Carlin is now a staff writer for Desert Post Weekly in Palm Springs, CA. He would like to thank his roommates, friends, cats, parents, and survey subjects for their help in putting the guide together, and he extends his eternal gratitude to the College Prowler team for hiring him.

Genevieve Brennan—Wellesley College

This is my senior year at Swells and after a leave of absence junior year to be a fruit picker in New Zealand, and a summer on a Wellesley internship in Costa Rica, I've become the sentimental senior I never thought I'd be.

I'm an English major who's bitten off more than she can chew with a creative writing senior thesis, but I'm still looking forward to long nights at Molly's and midnight swims in Lake Waban. My future is obstinately undecided, but some kind of writing seems unavoidable.

Though most students seem to toil away their time at Wellesley, I've become a bit of a hedonist. I've been in the improv comedy group Dead Serious since first year, and I manage my beloved co-op café, El Table.

Thanks to College Prowler, MaryAnn Hill, and all who contributed their opinions for this guide. Personal thanks to my family, friends from home, friends from my travels, and my Wellesley girls, who have always been there with what I needed, be it a back scratch or a beer.

John Cusick—Wesleyan University

John Cusick is a student at Wesleyan University. His articles and short stories have appeared in the *Auburn News*, the *Worcester, Massachusetts Telegram & Gazette*, and at *www.aboutteens.com*. He is a writer for the *Wesleyan Argus*, and co-hosts, co-produces and co-writes the Steve Kovacs Show on WESU 88.1 FM, Middletown. He is an occasional member in the Dead Poets Society, the Wesleyan Boogie Club, and the Atlas Thirteen Society. He is an avid fan of Steely Dan, funny hats, and drives much, much too fast.

The author would like to thank, firstly, his girlfriend Claire, whom he loves very much and who has put up with him for nearly two years now. The author also thanks his parents for their constant badgering and merciless affection, as well as his good friend Adam, without whom he would never have heard of Wesleyan University. The author also thanks, in no particular order, his very, very good friends from Wesleyan who have taught him so much and kept him in the lifestyle to which he is slowly becoming accustomed. They are: Andrea, Ashraf, Kat, Liz, Rory, and many, many more. The author would also like to thank all the people that helped bring this book together, including the extremely plucky and enthusiastic summer interns who helped him to dig up so much of the information needed to complete this guide to Wesleyan. Lastly, the author thanks Richard, Tom, Hunter, Vladimir, Truman, George, Fyodor, Jack, Bill, F. Scott, J.D., Barbara, Mary, Annie, Ernest, David, and all the rest for their wit, wisdom, and companionship.

Ryan Peckyno—West Point Military Academy

I grew up in Bradford, Pennsylvania, a small town in northwestern PA. When I was growing up, Bradford was one of those small towns where everyone knew everyone, a town where the community rallied behind its students and athletes, which created a sense of shared purpose. In high school, I participated in a number of competitive sports, and was active in a number of activities outside of school as well. Although there were times when I wished that there was more to do, I can say that I am glad that I grew up in a small town. Growing up in a small town allowed me to focus on what was important and eliminated a lot of distracters that I would have had if I grew up in a large city.

Because I did well in high school, I had the opportunity to attend the United States Military Academy. For the first two years, I was somewhat overwhelmed with all of the duties and responsibilities of a cadet. I did, however, manage to adapt, and left the Academy with one of the finest educations in the world. Besides giving me the skills to further my education and make a difference, the Academy redefined how I defined hard work. After graduating from West Point, I found that my definition of hard work had changed significantly, especially when compared to the overwhelming majority of my peers, who attended other universities.

In the military, I have had the opportunity to take the broad education that I received at West Point and aggressively build upon it. I have attacked areas, such as writing, that my transcript may say that I am weak in relative to other subjects. While in the Army, I have had the opportunity to travel quite a bit. When I was stationed at Fort Huachuca, Arizona, I took several trips with people who were at the Officer Basic Course to various parts of South America. We visited the resort areas, but we also made it a point to visit areas that

most people would have absolutely no desire to visit, such as Naco and Nogales. There were two reasons why I wanted to visit cities that were considered dangerous and were looked at by the majority of people from the area as having nothing to offer. First, I wanted to do what authors like Thomas Friedman, as well as some of our policy makers, attempt to do, and get inside the pit with people. I didn't want to just see what people want you to see; I wanted to interact with people from all socioeconomic backgrounds, including people who were considered to be the lowest of society. I wanted to see and meet people who live in abject poverty. I wanted to try to relate to people who were inherently and fundamentally different than I am. And second, I wanted to place myself outside of my comfort zone, because that is the only way that you grow.

As I lean back in my chair and reflect on all of the experiences that I have had over the past three years, I realize that, like several other people, I am at a crossroads in my career. To be quite honest, I am not sure what I want to do next. Maybe I just want to keep people guessing? I have received some great training and because I was in military intelligence (I know—it's an oxymoron), I'm quite sure that I can make up some really cool stuff, but I would rather be honest. Sure, I want to build on my broad education base and leadership training. Sure, I want to make some money so that I can become a philanthropist. And I know that it sounds cliché, but all that I really know is what I knew when I was a high school senior making a similar decision—that I want to be in a position where I can make the big time decisions that will, either indirectly or directly, affect peoples' lives.

Matthew Bretzius—West Virginia University

I'm a broadcast news major at West Virginia University. I hope to go on to graduate and get a job in the field of sports broadcasting or sports journalism. Growing up near Philadelphia, Pennsylvania, where sports tradition is great, it was not hard for me to decide what I wanted to do with my life. Writing and sports are two things I have always loved, so I figured putting them together was something that could make me very happy, as well as something I could be good at. Writing this guidebook was a chance for me to get exposure, as well as give potential students a great idea of what WVU has to offer. I hope it is found to be a fair and accurate portrayal of not only the positive, but the negative aspects of the school as well. Feel free to contact me by e-mail with questions or comments.

Steven Dziedzic—Wheaton College (IL)

I have to say that I really enjoyed writing this book! I mean, let's be honest, at times the research was a bit tedious, but it was just a fabulous experience. I hope to publish more as I continue to let the author inside me grow into a writing machine. Currently, I am a senior at Wheaton College (IL), pursuing a degree in Communications and honored with the privilege of being the senior class president. In the future, I'd love to utilize my writing ability, as well as my creativity, in my career aspirations. The Chicago-land is the only place I've lived since the move from my home in northeastern Ohio, and experiencing Wheaton College has been absolutely amazing. The school has truly touched my life, through and through, and I do pray that this book has given you an insightful look into Wheaton. I also hope that you had a cheap laugh here and there. If you have any questions or comments about anything, don't hesitate to contact me.

Well, I must give credit where credit is due, so I would like to give many people a warm thanks for this entire endeavor. Thank you Mom and Dad, Omid Gohari, George and Pat Poynor, Steve Ivester, Blaine, Leah, Lehn, Shanna, Elsie, Grant, Grim, Andrea, Johnmark, Eunice, Conni, and everyone at College Prowler! And oh, a huge thanks are in order for the one and only Maried Aybar!

Carly N. Sanders—Whitman College

Writing this book was not only a great way for me to indulge my passion for writing, but to realize what an amazing place Whitman has been for me. If it hadn't been for the Whitman Career Center forwarding me the e-mail about this opportunity, you might not be reading my words. Hopefully, this rare opportunity will help open some doors, but all I can do for now is cross my fingers and be hopeful as I finish up the last two years of my time at Whitman.

In no particular order I give the following all my sincerest, warmest, and most heartfelt thanks for contributing to me and my life, and this end product, as well, for without them, what's on these pages would not have been possible: Mom, Dad, Jamie (a.k.a. Hi-Mee), thanks for your unconditional love and support in all its forms, for that I am eternally grateful, and always proud to seek that which is unusual, humorous, unique, eccentric, and everything else beyond what's normal. Thanks to the greatest friends in the world from Bainbridge (I love you all!), Betsy, Erica, Wendy, Steve, Alice, John, Kara, Marty, Mike and family, the jump rope girls, and all of you who I may have missed, though you all know who you are—you all embody what I know to be perfect, remarkable, and extraordinary in this world and my life would not be complete without each and every one of you in it. Thank to my newfound soul mates at Whitman, Rachel (the most understanding and thoughtful human being I know—I love you more than I can say), Drew (perhaps the funniest and most talented human being I know—I love you too, of course), the Residence Life Staff—you've all seen me at my best and at my worst, yet you still love me, offer me support, and ears to listen, and for that, you have made my time at Whitman a time I'll treasure for the rest of my life. Thanks to my professors at Whitman—Hashimoto, Michelle Janning, Nanette Thrush, and Betty McCall, who never fail to inspire, humor, guide, and impassion me even in the most stressful of times, David Layton, who always taught me to seek greatness and enjoy the wonderful plainness of life, Bob McAllister, who taught me that genius lies in detail, to embrace your madness, and let all the good and the bad come out in written form, and finally, to all of the outstanding people at College Prowler, for having faith in me to write this book and for helping me take one step closer to my dreams.

Donna Talarico—Wilkes University

More than any current student on campus, Donna Talarico knows the changes Wilkes has made in the past decade because she chose Wilkes twice—first out of high school and then again for graduate studies. She was a communications studies and sociology major. She was the arts and entertainment editor of the campus newspaper, held a campus work-study job in the marketing communications office and is involved in several outreach programs with local high schools, including the annual Tom Bigler High School Journalism Conference. In March of 2005, Talarico released her first book "Kids, have you seen my backpack?" and Other Inspirational Stories of Nontraditional Students: An Adult Learner Anthology. In 2002, she also published How to Be a Professional Mascot with Intellectua. com's "Dream Jobs to Go" e-book series.

After Wilkes, Talarico plans to enter the journalism field while also pursuing a masters. She wants to find that happy medium between her interests and inspire others who are interested in the same through teaching and mentoring, all while writing and researching for articles, books and/or documentaries. She has a good start. Talarico has quite the freelancing portfolio. She has been writing for local entertainment paper The Weekender, as well as covering town meetings and writing features for local daily paper, The Times Leader. She has gone skydiving, rock climbing, and on many other adventures for the sake of a story. She also has written for GAMES magazine, the Career College Association's trade magazine The Link, and the Wilkes Universe, an alumni magazine. In addition, she has written two how-to pieces for author Jenna Glatzer's Web site absolutewrite.com. Aside from writing, Talarico also works as a freelance production crew member for a local PBS affiliate, where she floor manages Pennsylvania Polka and a ballroom dancing show and also runs camera or audio during live

fundraisers. She also ventured in front of the camera once as a contestant on the private-eye episode of a short-lived TLC reality show called Help Wanted, where she and four other hopefuls vied for a PI gig with Vinny Parco's firm. (Parco since has his own TV show called It Takes a Thief.) She placed second.

Talarico loves the outdoors, Scrabble and other word games, horror movies, Mexican food, classic & southern rock, country music, denim, inspirational books, day trips, local history, decorating, cooking and her cat. She loves the boardwalk and the shore- but she hates saltwater and sand. She also hates doing dishes and vacuuming. She is not single, but she is not married. She is cohabitating. (Read: She's waiting.)

Christine Riippi—Willamette University

Christine Noel Riippi is a prime example of the Bearcat All-Star. At some point or another during her four years at Willamette, she rowed on the varsity crew team, was a member of the National Society of Collegiate Scholars, was a founding member and player of the infamous intramural basketball team The Clamdiggers, co-wrote the Collegian's acclaimed weekly column 'Needs More Cowbell,' served as public relations director for ASWU, was the office assistant for the theatre department, served on the senior class gift committee, was a two-time Opening Days group leader, was co-president and a performer in the Willamette Improv Posse, was the two-time co-host of the annual Mr. Willamette event, hosted Relay for Life, studied abroad in Florence, Italy, and along with Maggie Shaneyfelt was selected Class Griot and honored to tell the Class of 2007 Story at Baccalaureate. She was also an active member in the Greek community, serving positions in both her sorority, Alpha Chi Omega (historian, chaplain, VP of membership development, assistant VP of education, and VP of chapter regulations and standards), as well as the Panhellenic Executive Council (VP public relations, VP of recruitment, Sigma Rho Chi). She graduated from Willamette in 2007 with a Bachelor of Arts degree, having majored in art history and minored in mathematics. Even with the abundance of activities to choose from, her favorite thing to do at Willamette was to sit by the Mill Stream with a good cup of coffee and watch the ducks.

Christine would like to thank many people for making her time at Willamette both productive and memorable. Thank you to Bill, Ellie, and Joe Riippi, Professors Hull and Hudson, Suzanne Kersh, the Unit (Laura, Gita, and Emma), all the women of Alpha Chi Omega (in particular, Shannon, Liberty, Jessica, Lauren, Anne, Grace, and Chelsea), Needs More Cowbell (Maggie and Bre), and all the many bright and shining faces that she was lucky enough to meet over the course of four years.

Alexandra Grashkina—Williams College

Alexandra Grashkina, known as Alex or Sasha, was born 06/06/1981 in Sofia, Bulgaria. She attended an American high school called ACS (American College of Sofia) and traveled to New York City as an exchange student when she was 16. Ever since, she decided that traveling was a good thing and packed her suitcase every four months or so.

Later on, she studied social sciences and languages in Williams College, Williamstown, in Fortaleza, Brazil, and in Geneva, Switzerland. Alex speaks English, Bulgarian, Russian, French, and Portuguese with very little difficulty and has intermediate knowledge of Spanish and Italian. She is now learning the Armenian alphabet.

To Williams College, Alex owes a lot, but her biggest achievement was overcoming her fear of water and learning to swim.

Currently, she works as a paralegal in civil litigation and is trying to stay out of trouble when not at work.

Chelsey J. Levingston—Wright State University

I was raised in Logan County, Ohio, but life didn't really begin until I met my best friends. Amanda Nugen, Jordan Hardman, Kari Barns, Kate Titus, Cindy Crumrn, Angie Stoodt, and Cassie Jackson have remained a huge part of my life since 7th grade. We've jammed out, hung out, and peaced out of Ben Logan High School. I now live with Amanda and Jordan. As we've watched each other grow up, it remains certain that we'll always be a part of each other's lives.

Currently a junior at Wright State, I am double majoring in journalism and accounting. I believe these majors will allow me to support and manage myself in a freelance career and give me the freedom to choose what I write about and who I work for. My friends and I hope to travel the world for the majority of our lives and retire with the satisfaction of knowing we didn't waste or regret anything.

I would like to thank the girls, the Kingdom of Saudi Arabia, Salem Alsulaiman, my grandmother "Old Lady," my brother Brian, my parents, and my peers at Wright State for their help.

David Gilmore, Jr.—Xavier University

I always knew that someday I'd want the opportunity to write a book. However, I never expected that I would be given that opportunity by the age of 20. Being able to dig deeper into Xavier University than I ever imagined has been a learning experience, to say the least.

Aside from my personal satisfaction in compiling this guide, I also hope that those who read this publication have a better sense of what life is like at Xavier. When I was a senior in high school, my main concern was that I felt like I had no idea what I was in for once I actually arrived at school. I wished I had some sort of magical book that told me things that you couldn't learn from brochures or guided tours. I hope that for the reader, this guide to Xavier becomes that magic book that helps you make what is undoubtedly one of the most important decisions a person can make at this point in their life. I am still astounded by the new and interesting things I am exposed to on a daily basis at Xavier. In the past few years, I've seen things and met people I would've never imagined existed while growing up in the sheltered paradise that is my home near Baltimore, MD. I guess you can't learn to fly unless you jump out of the nest. Looking back, I can honestly say I'm glad I took that leap.

As far as my background goes, I was born in raised in northern Baltimore County, Maryland. I graduated from Hereford High School and enrolled in Xavier that fall. My biggest writing influence and favorite author is F. Scott Fitzgerald. I was the senior sports writer at the *Xavier University Newswire*, where I covered basketball and published a column entitled "Dave Rants." In my free time I enjoy playing basketball and golf, watching movies and ESPN, and taking as many naps as humanly possible. I would also be a big moron if I didn't take this opportunity to thank some of the people who have helped me in one way or another in my infant writing career and through the composition of this guide—Mom, Dad, Dan, Holly, Robin and the rest of the family. Thanks to everyone at XU, including Nora, Jimmy, Josh, Ryan, Bob, Rabbi, Jay, Tony, Brian, T-Bag, the Way, Nick, Coccitto, Ann, Bobby Nachos, Farsad, everyone I'm forgetting, as well as all those at the Newswire, especially Steve, Jackie, Lisa, the Moskos, and Dancox. Thank you to those who have supported me back east, including Kevin Cate, Ashley Boo, Bobby, Simms, Hartman, Casner, Joe, Erin, Sarah, Liz, Carrie, DiMayo, Kyle, and about a million others. And finally, thank you to everyone at College Prowler for giving an idiot college sports writer the chance of a lifetime.

This work is dedicated in loving memory to Tobias James Harring.

Melissa Doscher—Yale University

If I had to write this guide at any other time in my life, the result would have been different and biased by my perspective at the moment. But now that I have just graduated and have had the time to reflect honestly and objectively, I can step back and see the experience for what it truly was—amazing.

As an English major, I have had the opportunity to immerse myself in what I love, to read the words of geniuses, and to participate in their legacies. But as a student at Yale, I have had the opportunity to grow as a person and to realize that I am not just a list of achievements or an academic machine—I am a human being. In my time at college, I have encountered people whose talents blow my mind and whose life experiences could make me laugh until I cry or cry until I laugh. These moments were some of the most important I experienced at Yale.

At this point, I feel prepared to enter my future, although I am completely unsure of what it holds for me—graduate school, publishing work, writing? I hope that this guide proves helpful whether it is assisting you in making a choice or informing you about your future. It is so exciting to be where you are, and I wish you the best of luck!

Off the Record

Ready for More?

Explore the School of Your Dreams—Without Setting Foot on Campus!

We currently have over 280 different insider's guides on schools across the country. Each student-written guidebook provides a comprehensive, honest, in-depth portrayal of a specific school. Every college is a unique experience, therefore each school has an entire book dedicated to it.

280+ Writers Dig for the Details You Care About

College Prowler has quotes from students about drugs on campus, Greek life, diversity, campus strictness and many other categories that don't usually pop up in traditional college guides. These quotes and categories are here to provide a helpful assessment of what's really happening on each campus. By including important, relevant facts and stats, like the average SAT score or the cost of a parking permit, you get a detailed look at the unique culture of each college.

It's like having an older friend show you around campus.

55,000 Students Share Their Opinions

To maintain objectivity, we have refused investment from colleges. Instead, we let the students tell it like it is. We fill each guide with more than 300 student responses, both positive and negative.

Students Rank 280+ Colleges

Our rankings represent student happiness, prominence, and satisfaction for each respective category. The higher the grade, the happier, the more prominent, or the more satisfied students are with the particular category.

Students Speak Out About:

- Academics
- Athletics
- Campus Dining
- Campus Housing
- Campus Strictness
- Computers
- Diversity
- Drug Scene
- Facilities
- Greek Life
- Girls
- Guys
- Local Atmosphere
- Nightlife
- Off-Campus Dining
- Off-Campus Housing
- Parking
- Safety & Security
- Transportation
- Weather

For more information about our ever-growing collection of single-school guides, visit us online at:
collegeprowler.com

Our growing collection of single-school guides . . .

Albion College
Alfred University
Allegheny College
Alverno College
American University
Amherst College
Arizona State University
Auburn University
Ball State University
Babson College
Bard College
Barnard College
Baruch College
Bates College
Baylor University
Beloit College
Bentley College
Binghamton University
Birmingham-Southern College
Boston College
Boston University
Bowdoin College
Bradley University
Brandeis University
Brigham Young University
Brown University
Bryn Mawr College
Bucknell University
Cal Poly
Cal Poly Pomona
Cal State Northridge
Caltech
Carleton College
Carnegie Mellon University
Case Western Reserve University
Catholic University of America
Centenary College of Louisiana
Centre College
Claremont McKenna College
Clark Atlanta University
Clark University (MA)
Clemson University
Colby College
Colgate University
College of Charleston
College of the Holy Cross
College of William & Mary
College of Wooster
Colorado College
Columbia University
Connecticut College
Cornell University
Creighton University
Dartmouth College
Davidson College
Denison University
DePaul University
DePauw University
Dickinson College
Drexel University
Duke University
Duquesne University
Earlham College
East Carolina University
Elon University
Emerson College
Emory University
FIT
Florida State University
Fordham University
Franklin & Marshall College
Furman University

Geneva College
George Washington University
Georgetown University
Georgia Institute of Technology
Gettysburg College
Gonzaga University
Goucher College
Grinnell College
Grove City College
Guilford College
Gustavus Adolphus College
Hamilton College
Hampshire College
Hampton University
Hanover College
Harvard University
Harvey Mudd College
Hastings College
Haverford College
Hofstra University
Hollins University
Howard University
Hunter College
Idaho State University
Illinois State University
Illinois Wesleyan University
Indiana University
Iowa State University
Ithaca College
IUPUI
James Madison University
Johns Hopkins University
Juniata College
Kansas State University
Kenyon College
Kent State University
La Roche College
Lafayette College
Lawrence University
Lehigh University
Lewis & Clark College
Louisiana State University
Loyola College in Maryland
Loyola Marymount University
Loyola University Chicago
Luther College
Macalester College
Manhattan College
Manhattanville College
Marlboro College
Marquette University
McGill University
Miami University
Michigan State University
Middle Tennessee State University
Middlebury College
Millsaps College
MIT
Montana State University
Mount Holyoke College
Muhlenberg College
New College of Florida
New York University
North Carolina State University
Northeastern University
Northern Arizona University
Northern Illinois University
Northwestern University
Oberlin College
Occidental College
Ohio State University
Ohio University

Ohio Wesleyan University
Old Dominion University
Penn State
Pepperdine University
Pitzer College
Pomona College
Princeton University
Providence College
Purdue University
Radford University
Reed College
Rensselaer Polytechnic Institute
Rhode Island School of Design
Rhodes College
Rice University
Rochester Institute of Technology
Rollins College
Rutgers New Brunswick
Sacramento State
San Diego State University
Saint Joseph's University
Santa Clara University
Sarah Lawrence College
Scripps College
Seattle University
Seton Hall University
Simmons College
Skidmore College
Slippery Rock University
Smith College
Southern Methodist University
Southwestern University
Spelman College
St. John's University
St. Louis University
St. Olaf College
Stanford University
Stetson University
Stony Brook University
Susquehanna University
Swarthmore College
Syracuse University
Temple University
Tennessee State University
Texas A&M University
Texas Christian University
Texas Tech University
Towson University
Trinity College Connecticut
Trinity University Texas
Truman State University
Tufts University
Tulane University
UC Berkeley
UC Davis
UC Irvine
UC Riverside
UC San Diego
UC Santa Barbara
UC Santa Cruz
UCLA
Union College
University at Albany
University at Buffalo
University of Alabama
University of Arizona
University of Central Florida
University of Cincinnati
University of Chicago
University of Colorado
University of Connecticut
University of Delaware

University of Denver
University of Florida
University of Georgia
University of Illinois
University of Iowa
University of Kansas
University of Kentucky
University of Louisville
University of Maine
University of Maryland
University of Massachusetts
University of Miami
University of Michigan
University of Minnesota
University of Mississippi
University of Missouri
University of Montana
University of Nebraska
University of New Hampshire
University of North Carolina
University of NC – Greensboro
University of Notre Dame
University of Oklahoma
University of Oregon
University of Pennsylvania
University of Pittsburgh
University of Puget Sound
University of Rhode Island
University of Richmond
University of Rochester
University of San Diego
University of San Francisco
University of South Carolina
University of South Dakota
University of South Florida
University of Southern California
University of Tennessee
University of Texas
University of Utah
University of Vermont
University of Virginia
University of Washington
University of Wisconsin
University of Wisconsin – Stout
UNLV
Ursinus College
Valparaiso University
Vanderbilt University
Vassar College
Villanova University
Virginia Commonwealth University
Virginia Tech
Wake Forest University
Warren Wilson College
Washington & Jefferson College
Washington & Lee University
Washington University in St. Louis
Wellesley College
Wesleyan University
West Point Military Academy
West Virginia University
Wheaton College (IL)
Wheaton College (MA)
Whitman College
Wilkes University
Willamette University
Williams College
Wright State University
Xavier University
Yale University